Europe

THE ROUGH GUIDE

There are more than one hundred and fifty Rough Guide titles
covering destinations from Amsterdam to Zimbabwe

Forthcoming titles include
Cuba • Dominican Republic • Las Vegas • Sardinia • Switzerland

Rough Guide Reference Series
Classical Music • Drum 'n' Bass • English Football • European Football
House • The Internet • Jazz • Music USA • Opera • Reggae
Rock Music • World Music

Rough Guide Phrasebooks
Czech • European • Dutch • French • German • Greek • Hindi & Urdu
Hungarian • Indonesian • Italian • Japanese • Mandarin Chinese
Mexican Spanish • Polish • Portuguese • Russian • Spanish • Swahili
Thai • Turkish • Vietnamese

Rough Guides on the Internet
www.roughguides.com

ROUGH GUIDE CREDITS

Text editors: Sophie Martin and Harriet Sharkey
Series editor: Mark Ellingham
Editorial: Martin Dunford, Jonathan Buckley, Jo Mead, Kate Berens, Amanda Tomlin, Ann-Marie Shaw, Paul Gray, Helena Smith, Judith Bamber, Kieran Falconer, Orla Duane, Olivia Eccleshall, Ruth Blackmore, Geoff Howard, Claire Saunders, Gavin Thomas, Alexander Mark Rogers, Polly Thomas, Joe Staines, Lisa Nellis, Andrew Tomičić (UK); Andrew Rosenberg, Mary Beth Maioli (US)
Production: Susanne Hillen, Andy Hilliard, Link Hall, Helen Ostick, Julia Bovis, Michelle Draycott, Anna Wray, Katie Pringle, Robert Evers

Cartography: Melissa Baker, Maxine Burke, Nichola Goodliffe, Ed Wright
Picture research: Louise Boulton
Online editors: Alan Spicer (UK); Kelly Cross (US)
Finance: John Fisher, Gary Singh, Ed Downey
Marketing & Publicity: Richard Trillo, Niki Smith, David Wearn, Jemima Broadbridge (UK); Jean-Marie Kelly, Myra Campolo, Simon Carloss (US)
Administration: Tania Hummel, Charlotte Marriott, Demelza Dallow

CONTRIBUTORS

Jon Bousfield (Bulgaria, Croatia, Slovenia, Romania); Simon Baskett (Spain); Mark Corner (Poland); Don Grisbrook (Morocco); Sharon Harris (Estonia, Latvia, Lithuania, Netherlands); Charles Hebbert (Hungary); Kate Hughes (Italy); Rob Humphreys (Austria, Czech Republic); Daniel Jacobs (Basics); Rachel Kaberry (France); Phil Lee (Norway, Belgium & Luxembourg); James McConnachie (Britain); Gordon McLachlan (Germany); Catherine Phillips (Russia); Peter Richards (Greece); Sam Stokes (Denmark, Finland, Sweden); Andrew Spooner (Turkey); Henry Stedman (Austria, Slovakia); Matthew Teller (Switzerland); Geoff Wallis (Ireland); Charles Young (Portugal).

ACKNOWLEDGEMENTS

Sophie Martin would like to thank Katie Pringle for typesetting, Maxine Burke for cartography, David Price for proofreading and Helena Smith for indexing. Many thanks, too, for the invaluable contributions from readers of the previous edition.

HELP US UPDATE

We've gone to a lot of effort to ensure that *The Rough Guide to Europe* is thoroughly up to date and accurate. However, things in Europe do change with alarming rapidity, and we'd very much appreciate any comments, corrections or additions for the next edition of the book. For the best letters, we'll send a copy of the new edition or any other Rough Guide.

Please mark letters: "Rough Guide Europe Update" and send to: Rough Guides Ltd, 62–70 Shorts Gardens, London WC2H 9AB, or Rough Guides, 375 Hudson St, 9th Floor, New York, NY 10014. Or send email to: mail@roughguides.co.uk
Online updates about this book can be found on Rough Guides' Web site at www.roughguides.com

Europe

THE ROUGH GUIDE

THE ROUGH GUIDES

TRAVEL GUIDES • PHRASEBOOKS • MUSIC AND REFERENCE GUIDES

 We set out to do something different when the first Rough Guide was published in 1982. Mark Ellingham, just out of university, was travelling in Greece. He brought along the popular guides of the day, but found they were all lacking in some way. They were either strong on ruins and museums but went on for pages without mentioning a beach or taverna. Or they were so conscious of the need to save money that they lost sight of Greece's cultural and historical significance. Also, none of the books told him anything about Greece's contemporary life – its politics, its culture, its people, and how they lived.

So with no job in prospect, Mark decided to write his own guidebook, one which aimed to provide practical information that was second to none, detailing the best beaches and the hottest clubs and restaurants, while also giving hard-hitting accounts of every sight, both famous and obscure, and providing up-to-the-minute information on contemporary culture. It was a guide that encouraged independent travellers to find the best of Greece, and was a great success, getting shortlisted for the Thomas Cook travel guide award, and encouraging Mark, along with three friends, to expand the series.

The Rough Guide list grew rapidly and the letters flooded in, indicating a much broader readership than had been anticipated, but one which uniformly appreciated the Rough Guide mix of practical detail and humour, irreverence and enthusiasm. Things haven't changed. The same four friends who began the series are still the caretakers of the Rough Guide mission today: to provide the most reliable, up-to-date and entertaining information to independent-minded travellers of all ages, on all budgets.

We now publish more than 100 titles and have offices in London and New York. The travel guides are written and researched by a dedicated team of more than 100 authors, based in Britain, Europe, the USA and Australia. We have also created a unique series of phrasebooks to accompany the travel series, along with an acclaimed series of music guides, and a best-selling pocket guide to the Internet and World Wide Web. We also publish comprehensive travel information on our Web site:

www.roughguides.com

....

PUBLISHING INFORMATION

This sixth edition published November 1999 by Rough Guides Ltd, 62–70 Shorts Gardens, London WC2H 9AB. Distributed by the Penguin Group:
Penguin Books Ltd, 27 Wrights Lane, London W8 5TZ
Penguin Books USA Inc., 375 Hudson Street, New York, NY 10014, USA
Penguin Books Australia Ltd, 487 Maroondah Highway, PO Box 257, Ringwood, Victoria 3134, Australia
Penguin Books Canada Ltd, 10 Alcorn Avenue, Toronto, Ontario, Canada M4V 1E4
Penguin Books (NZ) Ltd, 182–190 Wairau Road, Auckland 10, New Zealand
Typeset in Linotron Univers and Century Old Style to an original design by Andrew Oliver.
Printed in England by Clays Ltd, St Ives PLC
Illustrations in Part One and Part Three by Edward Briant.

Illustrations on p.1 & p.61 by Henry Iles.
© Jonathan Buckley and Martin Dunford 1999
No part of this book may be reproduced in any form without permission from the publisher except for the quotation of brief passages in reviews.
1344pp - Includes index
A catalogue record for this book is available from the British Library
ISBN 1-85825-462-7

....

CONTENTS

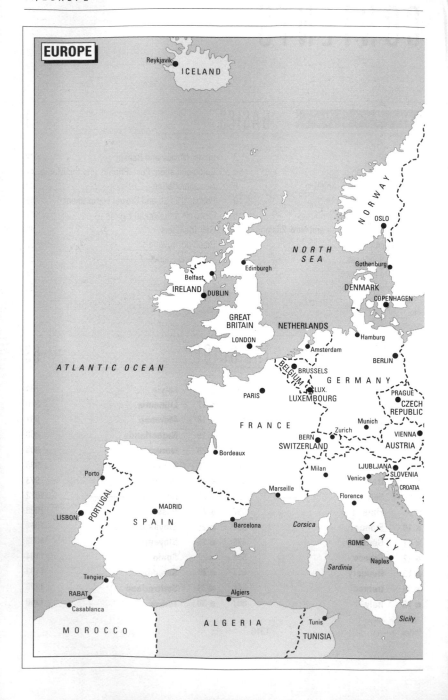

LIST OF MAPS

MAP SYMBOLS

- - -	National boundary	⊻	Viewpoint
═══	Road	♠	Museum
- - - - -	Path	■	Building
ⅅⅅⅅ	Steps	✝	Church
▬▬▬	Railway	✡	Synagogue
— —	Ferry route	⋔	Monastery
▬▬▬	River/canal	☪	Mosque
▪▪▪▪	Wall	Ⓗ	Hospital
▨	Urban area	⊠	Post office
░	Park	ⓘ	Information office
⁺⁺⁺	Christian cemetery	☜	Swimming pool
⋎⋎⋎	Muslim cemetery	Ⓜ	Metro station
⌐⌐	Jewish cemetery	Ⓢ	S-Bahn
░	Forest	Ⓤ	U-Bahn
░	Beach	⊖	London Underground Station
⌃⌃	Mountains	℗	Parking
▲	Peak	★	Bus stop
☀	Hill	⊠	Gate

Mapping for Great Britain chapter based upon Ordnance Survey mapping with the permission of The Controller of Her Majesty's Stationery Office, © Crown Copyright; Licence No: 43361U.

PART ONE

THE
BASICS

INTRODUCTION

The collapse of the division between eastern and western **Europe** at the end of the 1980s, and the ever closer ties among the fifteen countries of the European Union – increasingly a political and cultural as well as economic union – made Europe a buzzword of the early Nineties, implying shared values and, despite all the wrangling, a broad consensus of political beliefs. Some of this is inevitably a superficial analysis, but although true European unity still remains a distant dream, recent developments such as the single European currency and the opening of the Channel Tunnel have done much to bring it closer.

Conventionally, the **geographical boundaries** of Europe are the Ural Mountains in the east, the Atlantic Coast in the north and west, and the Mediterranean in the south. However, within these rough parameters Europe is massively diverse. The environment changes radically within very short distances, with bleak mountain ranges never far from broad, fertile plains, and deep, ancient forests close to scattered lake systems or river gorges. Politically and ethnically, too, it is an extraordinary patchwork: Slavic peoples are scattered through central Europe from Poland in the north to Serbia and Bulgaria in the south; the Finnish and Estonian languages bear no resemblance to the tongues of their Baltic and Scandinavian neighbours, but more to that of Hungary, over 1000km south; meanwhile Romansch, akin to ancient Latin, is spoken in the valleys of south-eastern Switzerland, while the Basques of the Western Pyrenees have a language, and even some blood groups, unrelated to any others known. These differences have become more political of late with the rise of nationalism that coincided with the fall of Communism, and borders are even now being redrawn, not always peacefully, and usually along ethnic lines defined by language, race or religion.

Where you head for obviously depends on your tastes and the kind of vacation you want: you can sample mountain air and winter sports in the Alps of France, Austria or Switzerland, lie on a beach in the swanky resorts of the south of France or Italy, or view architecture and works of art in the great cities of London, Paris, Florence or Amsterdam. Suffice to say, the lifting of restrictions on travel in eastern Europe, with only a handful of countries still requiring visas and nothing like the bureaucratic regulations there were before, means that the Continent really is there for the travelling – something manifest in the increasingly good-value rail passes (see pp.20–21 and 28–29) which cover most of the countries in this book. Although you may want to make a long hop or two by air, **rail** is indeed the way to see the Continent, highlighting the diversity of the place when you travel in a few hours from the cool temperatures of northern Europe to the rich and sultry climes of the Mediterranean. In fact, with the richness and diversity of its culture, climate, landscapes and peoples, there is no more exciting place to travel.

This book is a little eccentric in its **definition of Europe**. We have excluded countries such as Albania, Belarus, Moldova and the Ukraine, which are too far off the beaten track to be on most people's European "grand tour", while of the war-torn and strife-riven republics that have been carved out of the former Yugoslavia, only Slovenia and Croatia have been included as easily accessible and currently safe to visit.

On the other hand, we cover the British Isles and countries like Morocco and Turkey that are not strictly part of Europe, in the main because they are easy to reach on a European tour and are included by the InterRail pass. We also have chapters on Russia, Estonia, Latvia and Lithuania, though these countries are not covered by the InterRail pass.

CLIMATE AND WHEN TO GO

Europe's **climate** is as variable as everything else about the Continent. In **northwestern Europe** – Benelux, Denmark, southwestern Norway, most of France and parts of Germany, as well as the British Isles – the climate is basically a cool temperate one, with the chance of rain all year round and no great extremes of either cold or hot weather. There is no bad time to travel in most of this part of the Continent, although the winter months between November and March can be damp and miserable – especially in the upland regions – and obviously the summer period between May and September sees the most reliable and driest weather.

In **eastern Europe**, on the other hand, basically to the right of a north–south line drawn roughly through the heart of Germany and extending down as far as the western edge of Bulgaria (taking in eastern Germany, Poland, central Russia, the Baltic states, southern Sweden, the Czech and Slovak republics, Austria, Switzerland, Hungary and Romania), the climatic conditions are more extreme, with freezing winters and sometimes sweltering summers. Here the transitional spring and autumn seasons are the most pleasant time to travel; deep midwinter, especially, can be very unpleasant, although it doesn't have the dampness you associate with the northwestern European climate.

Southern Europe, principally the countries that border the Mediterranean and associated seas – southern France, Italy, Spain, Portugal, Greece and western Turkey – has the most hospitable climate in Europe, with a general pattern of warm, dry summers and mild winters. Travel is possible at any time of year here, although the peak summer months can be very hot and very busy and the deep winter ones can see some rain.

There are, too, marked regional variations, within these three broad groupings. As they're such large countries, inland Spain and France can, for example, see a **continental** type of weather as extreme as any in central Europe, and the Alpine areas of Italy, Austria and Switzerland – and other **mountain areas** like the Pyrenees, Apennines and parts of the Balkans – have a climate mainly influenced by altitude, which means extremes of cold, short summers, and long winters that always see snow. There are also, of course, the northern regions of Russia and Scandinavia, which have an **arctic climate** – again, bitterly cold, though with some surprisingly warm temperatures during the short summer when much of the region is warmed by the Gulf Stream. Winter sees the sun barely rise at all in these areas, while high summer can mean almost perpetual daylight.

There are obviously other considerations when deciding **when to go**. If you're planning to visit fairly touristed areas, especially beach resorts in the Mediterranean, avoid July and August, when the weather can be too hot and the crowds at their most congested. Bear in mind, also, that in a number of countries in Europe everyone takes their **vacation** at the same time (this is certainly true in France, Spain and Italy where everyone goes away in August). Find out the holiday month beforehand for the countries where you intend to travel, since you can expect the crush to be especially bad in the resorts; in the cities the only other people around will be fellow tourists, which can be miserable. In northern Scandinavia the climatic extremes are such that you'll find opening times severely restricted, even road and rail lines closed, outside the May–September period, making travel futile and sometimes impossible outside these months. In mountainous areas things stay open for the winter sports season, which lasts from December through to April, though outside the main resorts you'll again find many things closed. Mid-April to mid-June can be a quiet period in many mountain resorts, and you may have much of the mountains to yourselves.

TEMPERATURE CHART

	Jan	Feb	March	April	May	June	July	Aug	Sept	Oct	Nov	Dec
Amsterdam	4/40	5/42	9/49	13/56	18/64	21/70	22/72	22/71	19/67	14/57	9/48	6/42
Ankara	4/39	6/42	11/51	17/63	23/73	26/78	30/86	31/87	26/78	21/69	14/57	6/43
Athens	13/55	14/57	16/60	20/68	25/77	30/86	33/92	33/92	29/84	24/75	19/66	15/58
Berlin	2/35	3/37	8/46	13/56	19/66	22/72	24/75	23/74	20/68	13/56	7/45	3/38
Brussels	4/40	7/42	10/51	14/58	18/65	22/72	23/73	22/72	21/69	15/60	9/48	6/42
Bratislava	-1/30	0/30	5/41	10/50	13/58	12/54	20/68	19/66	16/61	10/50	4/39	0/32
Bucharest	1/34	4/38	10/50	18/64	23/74	27/81	30/86	30/85	25/78	18/65	10/49	4/39
Budapest	1/34	4/39	10/50	17/62	22/71	26/78	28/82	27/81	23/74	16/61	8/47	4/39
Copenhagen	2/36	2/36	5/41	10/51	16/61	19/67	22/71	21/70	18/64	12/54	7/45	4/40
Dublin	8/46	8/47	10/50	13/55	15/60	18/65	20/67	19/67	17/63	14/57	10/51	8/47
Helsinki	-3/26	-4/25	0/32	6/44	14/56	19/66	22/71	20/68	15/59	8/47	3/37	-1/31
Istanbul	8/46	9/47	11/51	16/60	21/69	25/77	28/82	28/82	24/76	20/68	15/59	11/51
Lisbon	14/57	15/59	17/63	20/67	21/71	25/77	27/81	28/82	26/79	22/72	17/63	15/58
London	6/43	7/44	10/50	13/56	17/62	20/69	22/71	22/71	19/65	14/58	10/50	7/45
Luxembourg	3/37	4/40	10/49	14/57	18/65	21/70	23/73	22/71	19/66	13/56	7/44	4/39
Madrid	9/47	11/52	15/59	18/65	21/70	27/80	31/87	30/85	25/77	19/65	13/55	9/48
Moscow	-9/15	-6/22	0/32	10/50	19/66	21/70	23/73	22/72	16/61	9/48	2/35	-5/24
Oslo	-2/28	-1/30	4/39	10/50	16/61	20/68	22/72	21/70	16/60	9/48	3/38	0/32
Paris	6/43	7/45	12/54	16/60	20/68	23/73	25/76	24/75	21/70	16/60	10/50	7/44
Prague	0/31	1/34	7/44	12/54	18/64	21/70	23/73	22/72	18/65	12/53	5/42	1/34
Rabat	17/63	18/65	20/68	22/71	23/74	26/78	28/82	30/83	27/81	25/77	21/70	18/65
Riga	-4/25	-3/27	2/35	10/50	16/61	21/69	22/71	21/70	17/63	11/52	4/39	-2/29
Rome	11/52	13/55	15/59	19/66	23/74	28/82	30/87	30/86	26/79	22/71	16/61	13/55
Sofia	2/35	4/39	10/50	16/60	21/69	24/76	27/81	26/79	22/70	17/63	9/48	4/38
Stockholm	-1/30	-1/30	3/37	8/47	14/58	19/67	22/71	20/68	15/60	9/49	5/40	2/35
Tallinn	-4/25	-4/25	0/32	7/45	14/57	19/66	20/68	19/66	15/59	10/50	3/38	-1/30
Vienna	1/34	3/38	8/47	15/58	19/67	23/73	25/76	24/75	20/68	14/56	7/45	3/37
Vilnius	-5/25	-3/26	1/34	12/54	18/65	21/71	23/74	22/71	17/62	11/52	4/39	-3/26
Warsaw	0/32	0/32	6/42	12/53	20/67	23/73	24/75	23/73	19/66	13/55	6/42	2/35
Zürich	2/36	5/41	10/51	15/59	19/67	23/73	25/76	24/75	20/69	14/57	7/45	3/39

Figures are average daily maximum in °C /°F

TRAVELLING FROM NORTH AMERICA

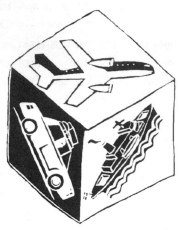

The air space between North America and Europe is one of the most heavily travelled in the world. It is served by literally dozens of airlines, both US carriers and the national airlines of almost every European country, and there is consequently a huge range of seats at a huge range of prices. It all depends on where you're travelling from, and, of course, where you want to go. There are, however, a number of "gateway" cities into which you'll find a greater – and cheaper – choice of options.

SHOPPING FOR TICKETS

Barring special offers, the cheapest of the airlines' published fares is usually an **Apex** ticket, although this will carry certain restrictions: you have to book – and pay – at least 21 days before departure, spend at least 7 days abroad (maximum stay 3 months), and you tend to get penalized if you change your schedule. There are also winter **Super Apex** tickets, sometimes known as "Eurosavers" – slightly cheaper than an ordinary Apex, but limiting your stay to between 7 and 21 days. Some airlines also issue **Special Apex** tickets to people younger than 24, often extending the maximum stay to a year. Many airlines offer youth or student fares to **under-25s**; a passport or driving licence is sufficient proof of age, though these tickets are subject to availability and can have eccentric booking conditions. It's worth remembering that most cheap return fares involve spending at least one Saturday night away and that many will only give a percentage refund if you need to cancel or alter your journey, so make sure you check the restrictions carefully before buying a ticket.

Most of the airlines maintain a fare structure which peaks between mid-June and early September and over the Christmas period, with cheaper deals available for the rest of the year, particulary during the winter months (November and March), when fewer people are travelling. You'll often find the cheapest fare by leaving from the airline's "hub" – New York, Atlanta, Dallas, Chicago, Los Angeles, San Francisco, Seattle, Vancouver, Toronto and Montréal are the main ones; hub cities also tend to have nonstop flights, with no changes at all. You do, however, need to be flexible: London, Paris, and Amsterdam are usually the cheapest "gateway cities" in Europe, simply because they are served by more flights; Milan, Rome and Frankfurt run a close second in some cases. Flying midweek rather than at the weekend is also a few dollars cheaper.

You can normally cut costs further by going through a **specialist flight agent** – either a **consolidator**, who buys up blocks of tickets from the airlines and sells them at a discount, or a **discount agent**, who in addition to dealing with discounted flights may also offer special student and youth fares and a range of other travel-related services such as travel insurance, rail passes, car rentals, tours and the like. Bear in mind, though, that penalties for changing your plans can be stiff (check the refund policy, and pay with a credit card if possible: then if you do change your mind there's a chance you can stop the payment going through). Some agents specialize in **charter flights**, which may be cheaper than anything available on a scheduled flight, but again departure dates are fixed and withdrawal penalties are high. If you travel a lot, **discount travel clubs** are another option – the annual membership fee may be worth it for benefits such as cut-price air tickets and car rental.

Remember that these companies make their money by dealing in bulk – don't expect them to answer lots of questions, and don't automatically assume that tickets from a travel specialist will be cheapest – once you get a quote, check with the airlines and you may turn up an even better deal. Be advised also that the pool of travel companies is swimming with sharks – exercise caution and never deal with a company that demands cash up front or refuses to accept payment by credit card.

A further possibility is to see if you can arrange a **courier flight**, although the hit-or-miss nature of these makes them most suitable for the single traveller who travels light and has a very flexible schedule. In return for shepherding a parcel through customs and possibly giving up your baggage allowance, you can expect to get a deeply discounted ticket. For more information on courier outfits, consult *A Simple Guide to Courier Travel* (New York: Pacific Data Sales Publishing).

If Europe is only one stop on a longer journey, you might want to consider buying a **Round-the-World (RTW) ticket**. Some travel agents can sell you an "off-the-shelf" RTW ticket that will have you touching down in about half a dozen cities (almost all include at least one in Europe); others will have to assemble a route for you, which can be more tailored to your needs but is apt to be more expensive. At the cheapest end of the scale, a low season RTW ticket with an itinerary of New York–Bangkok–Katmandu–London–New York could cost a little as $1350.

FLIGHTS FROM EASTERN AND CENTRAL USA

There are lots of options from most of the **eastern hub cities**, though most of the best deals are out of New York and Chicago to London. The official Apex 90-day-advance round-trip fare from New York to London with the major carriers (British Airways, American, etc) is, at the time of writing, $324 in low season, $599 in high season. If you don't want to book three months in advance, or be limited to a stay of just a few weeks, you should be able to find discounted fares, especially if you're a student or under-26, for around $245/$420. From Chicago, official Apex 90-day-advance fares to London are $418/$777 depending on the season, with more flexible discounted tickets at around $420/$705. To give an idea of other alternatives, discounted tickets from New York can be found for $330/$670 to Paris ($485/$815 from Chicago), $290/$680 to Frankfurt ($345/$865 from Chicago), $385/$600 to Madrid ($490/$885 from Chicago), and $630/$700 to Athens ($840/$1075 from Chicago). Some of these fares may be Special Limited promotional offers which appear from time to time, especially in the off-peak seasons. Lufthansa, for instance, have been known to offer New York–Munich round-trip tickets for $299. And, each January, Virgin Atlantic have New York–London fares, with no advance purchase necessary, for $99 each way.

FLIGHTS FROM THE WEST COAST

From the **West Coast** it's much the same story. The big airlines fly at least three times a week (sometimes daily) from Los Angeles, San Francisco and Seattle to main European cities. The major carriers have plenty of flights, with round-trip 90-day-advance Apex fares from LA starting at $468 to London. Again, you can avoid the three-month advance booking and length of stay restrictions and still find a comparatively inexpensive fare by going to a discount agent or youth travel specialist, where you can find tickets for $460/$705 (depending on the time of year) for a round trip to London, $520/$940 to Paris, $535/$900 to Frankfurt, $795/$930 to Madrid, and $505/$990 to Athens.

FLIGHTS FROM CANADA

Most of the big airlines fly to the major European hubs from **Montréal** and **Toronto** at least once daily (three times a week to the smaller airlines). From Toronto, London is your cheapest option, with the lowest round-trip fares currently at around CDN$715/CDN$960 (depending on the time of year). From Montréal to Paris you can expect to pay CDN$890/CDN$1025. Once again, a discount/student specialist such as Travel CUTS should be able to find a fare that's more flexible and, possibly, cheaper.

You have slightly less choice in the way of direct flights from **Vancouver**, but you can still make London three times daily, and other European cities several times a week. Round-trip fares to London can be had for around CDN$960/CDN$1200, depending on the season.

PACKAGES AND ORGANIZED TOURS

Although you may want to see Europe in your own time, at your own pace, you shouldn't entirely write off the idea of a **package deal**. Many agents and airlines can put together very flexible deals, sometimes amounting to no more than a flight plus car and accommodation, and they can work out a great deal cheaper than organizing things when you arrive, especially as regards car rental, which in Europe can be very expensive on the spot. They are also great for peace of mind, even if all you're doing is taking care of the first week's accommodation on a longer tour.

There are literally hundreds – perhaps thousands – of different package operators, offering everything from fly-drive deals, sun-and-sea packages and coach tours to special-interest holidays. It shouldn't be too hard, with the help of a travel agent, to find something to suit, but be sure to examine the small print of any deal (Europe's a long way from home if you end up with something you don't want), and to remember that everything in a brochure always sounds great, but doesn't always live up to the promise. Also, try only to use an operator that is a member of the United States Tour Operator Association (USTOA) or approved by the American Society of Travel Agents (ASTA).

AIRLINES IN THE USA AND CANADA

Aer Lingus ☎1-800/223 6537

Air Canada ☎1-800/776 3000

Air France US ☎1-800/237 2747; Canada, ☎1-800/667 2747

Aeroflot US ☎1-888/340 6400; Canada, call ☎1-800/555 1212 for local toll-free number.

Alitalia US ☎1-800/223 5730; Canada, ☎1-800/361 8336

American Airlines ☎1-800/433 7300

Austrian Airlines ☎1-800/843 0002

British Airways US ☎1-800/247 9297; Canada ☎1-800/668 1059

Canadian Airlines Canada ☎1-800/665 1177; US ☎1-800/426 7000

Continental Airlines ☎1-800/231 0856

Czech Airlines ☎1-800/223 2365 or 212 765 6022

Delta Airlines ☎1-800/241 4141

Finnair US ☎1-800/950 5000; Canada ☎1-800/461 8651

Iberia US ☎1-800/772 4642; Canada ☎1-800/423 7421

LOT Polish Airlines US ☎1-800/223 0593; Canada ☎1-800/361 1017

Lufthansa US ☎1-800/645 3880; Canada ☎1-800/563 5954

Malév Hungarian Airlines ☎1-800/223 6884 or 212 757 6446

Martinair Holland ☎1-800/627 8462

Northwest/KLM Airlines ☎1-800/447 4747

Olympic Airways ☎1-800/223 1226 or 212/838 3600

Royal Air Maroc ☎1-800/344 6726

Sabena ☎1-800/955 2000

SAS (Scandinavian Airlines) ☎1-800/221 2350

Swissair ☎1-800/221 4750

TAP (Air Portugal) US ☎1-800/221 7370; Canada, call ☎1-800/555 1212 for local toll-free number.

THY (Turkish Airlines) ☎1-800/874 8875 or 212/339 9650

Tower Air ☎1-800/348 6937

TWA ☎1-800/241 6522

United Airlines ☎1-800/241 6522

US Air ☎1-800/622 1015

Varig US ☎1-800/468 2744; Canada, call ☎1-800/555 1212 for local toll-free number.

Virgin Atlantic Airways ☎1-800/862 8621

DISCOUNT FLIGHT AGENTS, TRAVEL CLUBS AND CONSOLIDATORS

Air Brokers International, 150 Post St, Suite 620, San Francisco, CA 94108 (☎1-800/883 3273 or 415/397 1383; www.airbrokers.com). Consolidator and specialist in RTW and Circle-Pacific tickets.

Air Courier Association, 191 University Blvd, Suite 300, Denver, CO 80206 (☎1-800/282 1202 or 303/215 9000; www.aircourier.org). Courier flight broker.

Airhitch, 2641 Broadway, New York, NY 10025 (☎1-800/326 2009 or 212/864 2000; www.airhitch.org). Stand-by seat broker: for a set price, they guarantee to get you on a flight as close to your preferred destination as possible, within a week. Western Europe only.

Council Travel, Head Office, 205 E 42nd St, New York, NY 10017 (☎800/226-8624, 888/COUNCIL or 212/822-2700) and branches in many other US cities. Student travel organization.

Educational Travel Center, 438 N Frances St, Madison, WI 53703 (☎1-800/747 5551 or 608/256 5551; www.edtrav.com). Student/youth discount-agent.

High Adventure Travel Inc., 353 Sacramento St, Suite 600, San Francisco, CA 94111 (☎1-800/350 0637 or 415/912 5600; www.highadv.com). RTW and Circle-Pacific tickets. Web site features interactive database that lets you build and price your own RTW itinerary.

Last-Minute Travel Club, 100 Sylvan Rd, Suite 600, Woburn, MA 01801 (☎1-800/LAST-MIN). Travel club specializing in stand-by deals.

Moment's Notice, 7301 New Utrecht Ave, Brooklyn, NY 11204 (☎212/486 0500). Discount travel club.

Nouvelles Frontières USA Inc., 12 E 33rd St, New York, NY 10016 (☎1-800/366 6387 or 212/779 0600), and other branches in LA and San Francisco. French discount travel firm.

Now Voyager, 74 Varick St, Suite 307, New York, NY 10013 (☎212/431 1616). Courier flight broker.

STA Travel, 10 Downing St, New York, NY 10014 (☎1-800/777 0112), and other branches in the LA, San Francisco, Boston, Chicago, Phildelphia, etc. Worldwide specialist in independent and student travel.

TFI Tours International, 34 W 32nd St, New York, NY 10001 (☎1-800/745 8000 or 212/736-1140), and other offices in Las Vegas and Miami. Consolidator.

Travac, 989 6th Ave, New York NY 10018 (☎1-800/872 8800). Consolidator and charter broker.

Travel Avenue, 10 S Riverside, Suite 1404, Chicago, IL 60606 (☎1-800/333 3335). Discount travel agent.

Travel CUTS, 187 College St, Toronto, ON M5T 1P7 (☎1-800/667 2887 or 416/979 2406), and other branches across Canada (mostly on, or near, university campuses). Student travel specialists, with discounted fares for non-students too.

UniTravel, 11737 Administration Drive, St Louis, MO 63146 (☎1-800/325 2222 or 314/569-0900; www.unitravel.com). Consolidator.

RAIL CONTACTS IN NORTH AMERICA

BritRail Travel, 1500 Broadway, New York, NY 10036 (☎1-888/274 8724 or 1-800/677 8585; *www.britrail.com/us*). UK passes.

CIE Tours International, 100 Hanover Ave, Cedar Knolls, NJ 07927 (☎1-800/243 7687). Issues vouchers exchangeable in Ireland for Irish rail passes.

CIT Rail, 9501 W Devon Ave, Suite 502, Rosemont, IL 60018 (☎1-800/223 7987) Eurail, German and Italian passes.

DER Tours/GermanRail, 9501 W Devon Ave, Suite 400, Rosemont, IL 60018 (☎1-800/421 2929); and 904 East Mal, Etobicoke, ON M9B 6K2 (☎416/695 1209). Eurail, Europass and many individual country passes.

Orbis Polish Travel Bureau, 342 Madison Ave, Suite 1512, New York, NY 10173 (☎1-800/223 6037 or 212/867 5011). Passes for Poland.

Rail Europe, 226 Westchester Ave, White Plains, NY 10604 (☎1-800/438 7245, or 1-800/361-7245 from outside the US; *www.raileurope.com*). Official Eurail agent in North America; sells the widest range of regional and individual country passes.

ScanTours, 3439 Wade St, Los Angeles, CA 90066 (☎1-800/223 7226 or 310/636-4656). Eurail, Scandinavian and other European country passes.

US AND CANADIAN TOUR OPERATORS

Adventure Center ☎1-800/227-8747 or 510/654 1879

Adventures Abroad ☎1-800/665 3998; *www.adventures-abroad.com*

AESU Travel ☎1-800/638 7640

Altamira Tours ☎1-800/747 2869

American Express Vacations ☎1-800/241 1700

Backroads ☎1-800/462 2848 or 510/527 1555; *www.backroads.com*

BCT Scenic Walking ☎1-800/473 1210 or 760/431 7306

CIT Tours 1-800/248 8687

Contiki Tours ☎1-800/CONTIKI

Delta Vacations ☎1-800/872 7786; *www.deltavacations.com*

Eastern Europe Tours ☎1-800/641 3456, 1-800/441 1339 or 206/448 8400

EC Tours ☎1-800/388 0877

Euro-Bike/Euro-Walking Tours ☎1-800/321 6060; *www.eurobike.com*

Euro Cruises ☎1-800/688 3876 or 212/691 2099; *www.eurocruises.com*

Europe Through the Back Door Inc. ☎425/771 8303; *www.ricksteves.com*

Europe Train Tours ☎1-800/551 2085

Insight International Tours ☎1-800/582 8380

International Study Tours ☎1-800/833 2111

Jet Vacations ☎1-800/538 0999

New Frontiers ☎1-800/366 6387

Pilgrimage Tours & Travel ☎1-800/455 5514

Questers Worldwide Nature Tours ☎1-800/468 8668

Trafalgar Tours ☎1-800/854 0103

Wilderness Travel ☎1-800/368 2794; *www.wildernesstravel.com*

SPECIALISTS IN TRAVEL FOR SENIORS

Elderhostel ☎1-617/426 8056

Saga Holidays ☎1-800/343 0273

Vantage Travel ☎1-800/322 6677

TRAVELLING FROM BRITAIN

Since the opening of the Channel Tunnel, it has been possible to travel to Europe without using a plane or boat, though these will still probably be your cheapest, and often easiest, options. For destinations in northwestern Europe, train, long-distance bus and crossing the Channel by ferry tend to be best value for money, but the further you go the cheaper air travel becomes, and it's normally cheaper to fly than take the train to most parts of southern Europe, although special deals on rail passes can bring prices down considerably.

BY AIR

As ever, the best way to find the cheapest **flight** is to shop around: air travel in Europe is still highly regulated, which means that the prices quoted by the airlines can usually be undercut considerably, even on Apex fares, by going to an agent. In London, check the ads in the *Evening Standard, Time Out* or the free Australasian magazines *TNT* and *LAM* (look for them outside major tube stations). Elsewhere try local listings magazines or the classified section of the Sunday broadsheets. During the summer you can reach most of the countries of southern Europe – Portugal, Spain, Italy, Greece – on **charter flights**, block-booked by package holiday firms and usually having a few seats left over which they sell off cheap through selected **agents**, sometimes known as "bucket shops". Though they are inevitably rather restricted, with fixed return dates, a maximum validity of a month, and no chance of cancelling or changing your ticket once you've bought it, they can be very cheap – so much so in some cases that it's actually worth just using the outward portion if the return date doesn't suit. There are also flight agents who specialize in low-cost, discounted flights (charter and scheduled), some of them – like STA and Usit Campus – concentrating on deals for youths and students, though they can be a good source of bargains for everyone. In addition, there are agents specializing in offers to a specific country or group of countries on both charters and regular scheduled departures. To give a rough idea of prices booked through agents on scheduled flights in high season, reckon on paying, not including departure taxes, £80–175 to Paris, £50–95 to Brussels; £80–105 to Amsterdam; £100–210 to Scandinavia; £100–180 to the major cities of Spain or Italy; £85–200 to Athens, £140–210 to Istanbul; £150–285 to the major cities of eastern Europe. Many agents also do "open jaw" tickets, flying you into one city and out from another, not necessarily even in the same country. **One-way tickets** are normally very bad value, but some of the new "no-nonsense" airlines such as Debonair and EasyJet charge single fares each way and are often much cheaper than other airlines for return fares too. Cheap flights can also be found on Ceefax or Teletext, or on the Internet (try *www.cheapflights.co.uk*).

BY TRAIN

There are now direct **trains** for foot passengers from London to Paris (15 daily, 3hr) and Brussels (10 daily, 3hr 15min) operated by Eurostar through the Channel Tunnel. Tickets for under-26s start at £79 return to Paris, £69 to Brussels. For over-26s, the cheapest ticket is a weekend day return, which costs less than a single fare at £79 to Paris, £69 to Brussels. Through tickets for onward connections from Brussels and Paris can be booked through Rail Europe or Eurostar.

Other rail journeys from Britain involve some kind of **sea crossing**, usually by ferry or hovercraft, sometimes by catamaran. The cost of the crossing is always included in the price of the rail ticket to any foreign destination, but bear in mind that if any of your journey is by French TGV train, or any similar special express, you need to make a seat reservation in advance. You can buy an ordinary rail ticket to most parts of Europe from Wasteels, Rail Europe, and most main-line rail stations. Return tickets are valid for two months and allow for stopovers on the way, providing you stick to the prescribed route (there may be a choice, with different fares applicable).

To give some idea, return fares from London are £59 to Paris, £75 to Amsterdam (look out for Apex special offers, which may be substantially cheaper) and £65 to Brussels. Further afield, returns to Rome are £168, to Athens £378, and to Moscow £325. One-way fares are generally around two-thirds the price of a return fare. During the summer, especially if you're travelling at night or a long distance, it's best to make reservations on most legs of your journey. At night, couchettes in six-berth compartments cost around £10–15 per person, sleeper cars cost around £30–60, depending on the train, and may be 2-, 3- or 4-bed.

If you're **under 26** you are entitled to all sorts of special deals, not least **BIJ** fares, which offer cut-price rail fares to around 200 European destinations. BIJ tickets are issued by youth travel specialists such as STA and Usit Campus, as well as by Wasteels, and Rail Europe under the tag "Euro Youth". Again tickets are valid for two months and you can stop off en route. Examples of under-26 return ticket prices are: £49 to Paris, £57 to Amsterdam, £43 to Brussels, £154 to Rome, £292 to Athens and £295 to Moscow. For **rail passes** and other types of discounted rail travel, see "Travelling in Europe", pp.20–30.

BY LONG-DISTANCE BUS

A long-distance **bus**, although much less comfortable than the train, is at least a little cheaper. The main operator based in Britain is **Eurolines**, who have a network of routes spanning the Continent – north as far as Scandinavia, east to the Baltic states and Russia, and south to the major cities of Morocco and Greece. Prices can be up to a third less than the equivalent train fare, and there are marginally cheaper fares on most services for those under 26 or over 60, which undercut BIJ rail rates for the same journey. Current Eurolines fares from London's Victoria Coach Station to Paris and Amsterdam start at £28 one-way, £39 return (£31/44 without a youth or senior reduction), more in summer and at peak periods. Berlin is £52/84 (£57/91); Nice £59/99 (£66/109); Madrid £69/116 (£71/129); and Stockholm £93/138 (£103/149). Unfortunately, there are no discounted through fares from other British cities – you'll have to make your own way to London and take the bus from there. **Anglia-Lines** offer a slightly cheaper alternative to Brussels, Berlin, Hamburg and Hanover, via the Channel Tunnel. Eurolines also have Explorer tickets from London to two or more European cities and back, valid for six months: for example, London–Amsterdam–Brussels–Paris–London costs £59, London–Prague–Budapest–Vienna–London costs £119. Alternatively, you might consider Eurolines's 30- and 60-day passes, or Eurobus's flexible four-month tickets, taking in various European cities on three circular routes for set prices (see "Travelling in Europe", p.28).

BY CAR

Taking a **vehicle** to Europe, you have a choice between a sea crossing by ferry or hovercraft, or the train service through the Channel Tunnel operated by Eurotunnel.

Eurotunnel's **trains** run round-the-clock between Folkestone and Calais, carrying cars, motorcycles, coaches and their passengers, from coast-to-coast in 35–45 minutes. For daytime summer trips, advance bookings are a good idea. There are up to four departures hourly during the day (6am–10pm), and one hourly at night. One-way fares cost between £84.50 and £110 per car, including passengers, depending on the time of day, the day, and the season of travel; five-day returns cost between £109 and £175. Motorbikes cost £50–70 one-way, £70–95 for a five-day return. Bicycles are carried on two trains a day between January and October only (seats should be booked at least 24 hours in advance) for £15 one-way.

Routes across the Channel or the North Sea by **ferry**, **hovercraft** or **jetfoil** are numerous, and the fare structures confusing. Most travel agents carry brochures of the various ferry companies, giving details of fares and frequencies. Prices vary with the month, day or even hour at certain times of the year, not to mention how long you're staying and the size of your car. Basically, the more convenient or popular the time of travel, the greater the cost; obligatory sleeping accommodation on longer crossings made at night also pushes the price way above the basic rate. Although those going for a short time benefit from well-priced five-day returns and the like, price structures tend to be geared to one-way rather than round-trip travel, one benefit of which is you don't necessarily have to use the same port in both directions. On some lines students qualify for a discount.

Obviously, the crossing you decide to take depends on where you are based in Britain and where you're planning to head once across the water. The Brittany crossings are a bit out of the way for most of Europe, and are really only useful if you're planning to visit western France and perhaps drive down to Spain; Dieppe is more central, especially if you're intending to visit Paris, since it's closer than the French ports further north – Boulogne, Calais, Dunkerque. These three do, however, have the benefit of a much shorter crossing, and also leave you better placed for travelling through the heart of Europe, either through eastern France and down to Italy or into Belgium, Germany and eastern Europe. The same is true of Belgian Channel ports, though the

SEA CROSSINGS FROM BRITAIN

Route BRITAIN – EUROPE	Company	Frequency	Crossing time	Car +2 (min o/w fare incl hidden supps)	Foot passenger (min full adult o/w fare)
Dover–Calais	Sea France	15 daily	1hr 30min	£74.50–124.50	£15
Dover–Calais	P&O Stena	30–35 daily	1hr 15min	£82.50–175.50	£24
Dover–Calais (hovercraft*)	Hoverspeed	6–14 daily	35min	£80–132	£25
Dover–Ostend (catamaran)	Hoverspeed	3–5 daily	35min	£85–143	£25
Folkestone–Boulogne (catamaran)	Hoverspeed	4–5 daily	55min	£85–120	£25
Harwich–Esbjerg	Scandinavian Seaways	3–4 weekly	22hr	£163–313	£84–108
Harwich–Hamburg	Scandinavian Seaways	2–4 weekly exc mid-Jan	19hr	£115–151	£43–93
Harwich–Hook of Holland (fast ferry)	Stena	2 daily	3hr 40min	£89–135	£24–29
Hull–Rotterdam	P&O North Sea Ferries	1 daily	12hr 30min	£152–188	£37–46
Hull–Zeebrugge	P&O North Sea Ferries	1 daily	13hr 15min	£152–188	£37–46
Lerwick**–Bergen	Smyril Line	1 weekly May–Sept	12hr 30min	£107–149	£47–66
Newcastle–Amsterdam	Scandinavian Seaways	2–4 weekly exc mid-Jan	14hr	£92–188	£30–64
Newcastle–Gothenburg	Scandinavian Seaways	2 weekly	26hr	£153–315	£54–125
Newcastle–Hamburg	Scandinavian Seaways	1–2 weekly May–Sept	23hr	£115–151	£43–93
Newcastle–Haugesund, Stavanger, Bergen	Fjord Line	2–3 weekly exc mid-Jan	18hr–25hr 15min	£142–285	£41–100
Newcastle–Kristiansand	Scandinavian Seaways	2 weekly	18hr	£153–295	£54–115
Newhaven–Dieppe (catamaran)	Hoverspeed	2–3 daily	2hr 15min	£105–160	£25
Plymouth–Roscoff	Brittany Ferries	1–12 weekly	6hr–7hr 30min	£82–165	£20–35
Plymouth–Santander‡	Brittany Ferries	2 weekly March–Nov	24hr	£198–350	£56–96
Poole–Cherbourg	Brittany Ferries	1–2 daily	4hr 15min–5hr 45min	£78–162	£19–37
Portsmouth–Bilbao	P&O Portsmouth	2 weekly	35hr	£257–442	£88–134
Portsmouth–Caen	Brittany Ferries	2–3 daily	6hr–6hr 45min	£78–162	£19–37
Portsmouth–Cherbourg	P&O Portsmouth	1–7 daily	2hr 45min–7hr	£78–157	£18–32
Portsmouth–Le Havre	P&O Portsmouth	2–3 daily	5hr 30min–7hr 45min	£78–163	£18–38
Portsmouth–St Malo	Brittany Ferries	7 weekly	8hr 45min–10hr 30min	£89–179	£21–41

* sometimes catamaran Feb–Mar

** connecting service from Aberdeen – cheapest through fare for car plus two: £267–312
a few Jan–Mar sailings serve St Malo instead

‡ a few extra sailings in Feb & Mar leave from Poole, taking 31hr

crossings themselves are a little longer. The Dutch ports, principally the Hook of Holland, might be worth choosing if you're specifically travelling to the Netherlands, northern Germany or perhaps northeastern Europe or Scandinavia, but the crossings are much longer than those to France. The Hull–Rotterdam service is a useful one if you live in the north of England, but the journey from Newcastle to the Danish and Norwegian ports is long and pricey, though it may save time and be worth the money if Scandinavia is your first stop. Links to timetables for several ferry services from the UK can be found at: *www.a2btravel.com/ferry.*

HITCHING

It is possible to get a lift all the way from London to Istanbul if you happen to meet the right lorry, but in general it's a question of getting across the Channel and hitching from there. Getting across the Channel is cheap: Eurotunnel charge per car regardless of how many passengers are carried, and some ferries have flat rates for certain numbers of passengers (3–5 on Hoverspeed services, 2–8 on P&O Stena's Dover–Calais service, and 1–5 on P&O North Sea services out of Hull), so you may even be able to get over for free. Otherwise, there's usually plenty of traffic heading south from the Channel ports – note that Belgium is somewhat better for lifts than France, with Calais notoriously bad for hitching out of. See p.30 for more information on hitching.

PACKAGES AND INCLUSIVE TOURS

If you're sure of where you want to go, how long you want to spend there, and what you want to do during your time there, it's an odds-on bet there'll be a **package holiday** to suit you. Travelling this way isn't everybody's cup of tea, but it can work out cheaper, and it can also be a good idea if you're nervous of travelling alone. You can lie on a beach, take a short break in a major city, or there are any number of special-interest packages available, from hiking trips to cycling deals, although perhaps the most popular choice for young people, especially those coming from Australasia or North America for the first time, is an all-in coach tour of the major sights and cities with an operator like Top Deck or Contiki, who cater for the 18–35 age range.

DISCOUNT FLIGHT AGENTS

North South Travel, Moulsham Mill Centre, Parkway, Chelmsford, Essex CM2 7PX (☎01245/492882). Friendly, competitive travel agency, offering discounted fares worldwide – profits are used to support projects in the developing world, especially the promotion of sustainable tourism.

STA Travel, 86 Old Brompton Rd, London SW7 3LH; 117 Euston Rd, London NW1 2SX; and four more London branches (☎0171/ 361 6161); 38 North St, Brighton (☎01273/728282); 25 Queens Rd, Bristol BS8 1QE (☎0117/929 4399); 38 Sidney St, Cambridge CB2 3HX (☎01223/366966); 75 Deansgate, Manchester M3 2BW (☎0161/834 0668); 88 Vicar Lane, Leeds LS1 7JH (☎0113/244 9212); 78 Bold Street, Liverpool L1 4HR (☎0151/707 1123); 9 St Mary's Place, Newcastle-upon-Tyne NE1 7PG (☎0191/233 2111); 36 George St, Oxford OX1 2OJ (☎01865/792 800); 27 Forrest Road, Edinburgh (☎0131/226 7747); 184 Byres Rd, Glasgow G1 1JH (☎0141/338 6000); 30 Upper Kirkgate, Aberdeen (☎0122/465 8222) and branches on university campuses in London, Birmingham, Bristol,

<table>
<tr><td colspan="2" align="center">AIRLINES IN BRITAIN</td></tr>
<tr><td>Adria ☎0171/437 0143</td><td>KLM ☎08705/074074</td></tr>
<tr><td>Aer Lingus ☎0645/737747</td><td>Lauda Air ☎0171/630 5924</td></tr>
<tr><td>Aeroflot ☎0171/ 355 2233</td><td>Lithuanian Airlines ☎01293/551737</td></tr>
<tr><td>Air France ☎0845/0845 111</td><td>LOT Polish Airlines ☎0171/580 5037</td></tr>
<tr><td>Alitalia ☎0171/602 7111</td><td>Lufthansa ☎0345/737747</td></tr>
<tr><td>Austrian Airlines ☎0171/434 7300</td><td>Luxair ☎0181/745 4254</td></tr>
<tr><td>Balkan Bulgarian Airlines ☎0171/637 7637</td><td>Malév Hungarian Airlines ☎0171/439 0577</td></tr>
<tr><td>Britannia ☎01582/424155</td><td>Olympic Airways ☎0171/409 3400</td></tr>
<tr><td>British Airways ☎0345/222111</td><td>Royal Air Maroc ☎ 0171/439 4361</td></tr>
<tr><td>British Midland Airways ☎0345/554554</td><td>Ryanair ☎0541/569569</td></tr>
<tr><td>Croatia Airlines ☎0181/563 0022</td><td>Sabena ☎0345/581291</td></tr>
<tr><td>Czech Airlines ☎0171/255 1898</td><td>SAS Scandinavian Airlines ☎0845/607 2772</td></tr>
<tr><td>Debonair Airways ☎01582/634300</td><td>Swissair ☎0171/434 7300</td></tr>
<tr><td>EasyJet ☎0870/600 0000</td><td>TAP Air Portugal ☎0171/630 0900</td></tr>
<tr><td>Estonian Air ☎0171/333 0196</td><td>Tarom ☎0171/224 3693</td></tr>
<tr><td>Finnair ☎0171/408 1222</td><td>Turkish Airlines ☎0171/766 9300</td></tr>
<tr><td>Go ☎0845/605 4321</td><td>Virgin Atlantic ☎01293/747747</td></tr>
<tr><td>Iberia ☎0171/830 0011</td><td>Yugoslav Airlines ☎0171/629 2007</td></tr>
</table>

Canterbury, Cardiff, Coventry, Durham, Glasgow, Leicestershire, Leeds, Loughborough, Nottingham, Sheffield and Warwick. Worldwide specialists in low-cost flights and tours for students and under-26s, though other customers are welcome. Web site: *www.statravel.co.uk*

Trailfinders, 1 Threadneedle Street, London EC2R 8JX (all destinations ☎0171/628 7628); 215 Kensington High St, London, W8 7RG (☎0171/937 5400); 58 Deansgate, Manchester M3 2FF (☎0161/839 6969); 254–284 Sauchiehall St, Glasgow G2 3EH (☎0141/353 2224); 22–24 The Priory, Queensway, Birmingham B4 6BS (☎0121/236 1234); 48 Corn St, Bristol BS1 1HQ (☎0117/929 9000); 7–9 Ridley Place, Newcastle-upon-Tyne NE1 8JQ (☎0191/261 2345). One of the best informed and most efficient agents. Web site: *www.trailfinder.com*

The Travel Bug, 597 Cheetham Hill Rd, Manchester M8 5EJ (☎0161/721 4000); 125 Gloucester Rd, London SW7 4SF (☎0171/835 2000). Large range of discounted tickets. Web site: *www.flynow.com*

Travel Cuts, 295a Regent St, London W1R 7YA (☎0171/255 1944); 33 Princes Sq, London W2 4NG (☎0171/792 3770). British branch of Canada's main youth and student travel specialist. Web site: *www.travelcuts.co.uk*

Usit Campus, National Call Centre ☎0870/240 1010; 52 Grosvenor Gardens, London SW1W 0AG (☎0171/730 3402); 541 Bristol Rd, Selly Oak, Birmingham B29 6AU (☎0121/414 1848); 20 Fairfax St, Coventry CV1 5RY (☎01203/225777); 61 Ditchling Rd, Brighton BN1 4SD (☎01273/570226); 37–39 Queen's Rd, Clifton, Bristol BS8 1QE (☎0117/929 2494); 5 Emmanuel St, Cambridge CB1 1NE (☎01223/324283); 53 Forest Rd, Edinburgh EH1 2QP (☎0131/225 6111); 122 George St, Glasgow G1 1RF (☎0141/553 1818); 166 Deansgate, Manchester M3 3FE (☎0161/833 2046); 105–106 St Aldates, Oxford OX1 1DD (☎01865/242067); 340 Glossop Rd, Sheffield S10 2HW (☎0114/275 2552). Student/youth travel specialists, with branches also in YHA shops and on university campuses all over Britain. Web site: *www.usitcampus.co.uk*

Usit Council, 28a Poland St, London W1V 3DB (☎0171/437 7767; *www.ciee.org*). Flights and student discounts.

TOUR OPERATORS

Bike Tours, 82 Walcot St, Bath, Somerset BA1 5BD (☎01225/310859; *www.biketours.co.uk*). cycling tours of 1–2 weeks in 8 European countries.

Contiki, Wells House, 15 Elmfield Rd, Bromley, Kent BR1 1LS (☎0181/290 6422; *www.contiki.com*). Coach tours of Europe for 18–35s.

Eurocamp, Hartford Manor, Greenbank Lane, Northwich, Cheshire CW8 1HW (☎01606/787000; *www.eurocamp. co.uk*). Flexible packages for campers and caravanners, plus self-drive vacations to fixed-site tents and mobile homes.

Exodus, 9 Weir Rd, London SW12 0LT (☎0181/675 5550; *www.exodustravels.co.uk*). Walking, hiking, and touring holidays by local transport in several European countries, plus biking in France, Italy, Spain and Morocco.

Explore Worldwide, 1 Frederick St, Aldershot, Hants, GU11 1LQ (☎01252/319448; *www.explore.co.uk*). Adventure holidays in eighteen European countries.

Sunvil Holidays, Sunvil Hse, Upper Sq, Isleworth, Middx TW7 7BJ (☎0181/232 9797; *www.sunvil.co.uk*). Flexible packages and tailor-made holidays off the beaten track in Italy, Greece and Portugal.

Thomas Cook Holidays, 45 Berkeley St, London W1X 5AE, plus many high streets across London and the UK (☎0990/666222; *www.tch.thomascook.com*) Specialists in European city breaks.

Time Off, 1 Elmfield Park, Bromley, Kent (☎0345/ 336622). Flexible city breaks in various price ranges.

Top Deck Travel, 131–135 Earl's Court Rd, London SW5 9RH (☎0171/3704555; *www.dialspace.dial.pipex.com/town/close /np54/index.html*). Coach tours around Europe for young people (camping or in hotels).

Tracks, The Flots, Brookland, Romney Marsh, Kent TN29 9TG (☎0171/937 3028). Youth-orientated bus tours.

Travelscene, 11–15 St Anne's Rd, Harrow, HA1 1LQ (☎0181/427 8800). European city breaks.

FERRY OPERATORS

Brittany Ferries, Wharf Rd, Portsmouth PO2 8RU; Millbay, Plymouth PL1 3EW (☎0990/360360; *www.brittanyferries.com*). Portsmouth to Caen and St Malo; Poole to Cherbourg; Plymouth to Roscoff and Santander.

Fjord Line, Royal Quays, North Shields, Tyne and Wear NE29 6EG (☎0191/296 1313). Newcastle to Stavanger, Haugesund and Bergen.

Hoverspeed, International Hoverport, Marine Parade, Dover, Kent CT17 9TG (☎0990/240241; *www.hoverspeed.co.uk*). Dover to Calais and Ostend; Folkestone to Boulogne; Newhaven to Dieppe.

P&O Portsmouth, Peninsular House, Wharf Road, Portsmouth PO2 8TA (☎0870/242 4999; *www.poportsmouth.com*). Portsmouth to Bilbao, Cherbourg and Le Havre.

P&O North Sea Ferries, King George Dock, Hedon Rd, Hull HU9 5QA (☎01482/377177; *www.ponsf.com*). Hull to Zeebrugge and Rotterdam.

P&O Stena, Channel House, Channel View Rd, Dover, Kent CT17 9TJ (☎087/0600 0600; *www.posl.com*). Dover to Calais.

DFDS/Scandinavian Seaways, Scandinavia House, Parkeston Quay, Harwich, Essex CO12 4QG (☎0990/333000; *www.scansea.com*); 28A Queensway, London W2 3RX; Tyne Commission Quay, North Shields, NE29 6EA. Harwich to Esbjerg and Hamburg; Newcastle to Amsterdam, Gothenburg, Hamburg and Kristiansand.

SeaFrance, Eastern Docks, Dover CT16 1JA (☎0990/711711; *www.seafrance.com*). Dover to Calais.

SMS Travel and Tourism, 40 Kenway Rd, London SW5 0RA (☎0171/373 6548; *www.sms.com.mt*) Agent for Adriatica and a number of other ferry lines operating out of Italy.

Smyril Line, c/o P&O Scottish Ferries, PO Box 5, Jamieson's Quay, Aberdeen AB11 5NP (☎01224/572615; *www.smyril-line.fo*). Lerwick to Bergen, with connecting P&O Scottish service from Aberdeen.

Southern Ferries, 179 Piccadilly, London W1V 9DB (☎0171/491 4968). Agent for a number of ferries operating out of France.

Stena Line, Charter House, Park St, Ashford, Kent TN24 8EX (☎0990/707070); Parkeston Quay, Harwich, Essex CO12 4SR (☎01255/242000). Harwich to Hook of Holland.

Viamare Travel, 2 Sumatra Rd, London NW6 1PU (☎0171/431 4560; *ferries@viamare.com*). Agent for several European ferry lines.

TRAIN INFORMATION

Eurostar, 102–104 Victoria St, London SW1 5JL (☎0990/186186; *www.eurostar.com*).

Wasteels, by platform #2, Victoria Station, London SW1V 1JY (☎0171/834 7066).

Eurotunnel, Customer Service Centre, jct #12 off M20; PO Box 300, Dept 302, Folkestone, Kent CT19 4QD (☎0990/353535; *www.eurotunnel.com*).

Rail Europe (SNCF French Railways), 179 Piccadilly, London W1V 0BA (☎0990/848848).

National Rail Companies

Belgian Railways, 200a Blackfriars Foundry, Blackfriars Rd, London SE1 8EN (☎0171/593 2332; *www.b-rail.be*).

CIE Irish Bus and Rail, 185 London Rd, Croydon, Surrey CR0 2RJ (☎0181/686 0994 or 0990/143910).

German Rail, 18 Conduit St, London W1R 9TD (☎0171/317 0919; *www.bahn.de*).

Holland Rail, Chase House, Gilbert St, Ropley, Hants SO24 0BY (☎01962/773646; *www.ukconsultants.com/hollandrail*).

Most national rail companies can be contacted through their national tourist organization.

BUS INFORMATION

Anglia-Lines, Anglia House, 2a Dudley St, Luton, Beds LU2 2NT (☎0870/608 8806).

Busabout 258 Vauxhall Bridge Rd, SW1V 1BS (☎0171/950 1661; *www.busabout.com*).

Eurolines, 52 Grosvenor Gdns, London SW1W 0AU (☎0990/143219; *www.eurolines.co.uk*).

TRAVELLING FROM IRELAND

There are direct flights **from Dublin** to most major cities in mainland Europe, and connections from those or from London to practically any airport you want to fly to. There are also one or two direct flights to the Continent **from Shannon**. You may save a little money travelling by land, sea or even air to London and buying your flight there, but the small amount you'd save hardly makes it worthwhile, and if you're going to London by surface routes, you may as well go the whole hog and carry on that way into Europe.

   From Belfast, there are direct flights with KLM to Amsterdam, Sabena to Brussels, Gill Airways and Eurowings to Dusseldorf, and British Airways or British Midland to Paris. For other destinations, you'll have to change at Amsterdam, Brussels, London or Manchester.

   Although Britain is the most obvious first stop if you are **going by land and sea**, it is possible to avoid it altogether by taking a ferry direct from Cork or Rosslare to Brittany. For routes via Britain, most firms do combination "land-

FERRY CROSSINGS FROM IRELAND

Route	Company	Frequency	Crossing time	Car +2 (min o/w fare incl hidden supps)	Foot passenger (min full adult o/w fare including hidden supps)
IRELAND–BRITAIN					
Ballycastle–Campbelltown	Argyll & Antrim	2 daily June–Sept	2hr 45min	£95–120	£20–25
Belfast–Heysham (catamaran)	Seacat	1–2 daily April–Sept	4 hr	£184–204	£28–37
Belfast–Liverpool	Norse Irish Ferries	1–2 daily	8hr 30min	£85–240	£25–53
Belfast–Stranraer	Stena	2–6 daily	3hr 15min	£99–139	£20–24
Belfast– Stranraer (fast ferry)	Stena	4–5 daily	1hr 45min	£99–169	£20–27
Belfast– Stranraer (catamaran)	Seacat	1–6* daily	1hr 45min	£99–169	£15–25
Belfast–Troon	Seacat	2 daily from April	1hr 30min	£119–164	£25–28
Larne–Cairnryan	P&O European	2–3 daily	2hr 30min	£164–184	£15–25
Larne–Cairnryan (jetliner)	P&O European	5–6 daily	2hr 15min	£99–169	£15–25
Dublin–Holyhead	Irish Ferries	2 daily	1hr	£99–169	IR£20
Dublin–Holyhead (fast ferry)	Irish Ferries	3–4 daily	3hr 15min	IR£99–209	IR£35
Dublin–Holyhead	Stena	2 daily	1hr 50min	IR£119–244	not allowed
Dublin–Liverpool	Seacat	2 daily Mar–Sept	3hr 30min	IR£99–209	IR£30–39
Dun Laoghaire–Holyhead (fast ferry)	Stena	4–5 daily	3hr 45min	IR£149–259	IR£20–30
Rosslare–Fishguard	Stena	1–2 daily	1hr 40min	IR£99–209	IR£20–25
Rosslare–Fishguard (catamaran)	Stena	2–4 daily ‡	3hr 30min	IR£69–185	IR£30–41
Rosslare–Pembroke	Irish Ferries	2 daily	1hr 40min	IR£104–229	IR£20
Cork–Swansea	Swansea–Cork Ferries	3–6 weekly March–Jan	4hr	IR£69–185	IR£22–32
			10hr	IR£85–179	
IRELAND–EUROPE					
Cork–Roscoff	Brittany Ferries	1 weekly April–Oct	14hr	IR£104–295	IR£34–65
Rosslare–Cherbourg	Irish Ferries	2–4 weekly Feb–Sept	16hr	IR£119–299	IR£40–80
Rosslare–Roscoff	Irish Ferries	1–2 weekly April–Sept	15hr	IR£119–299	IR£40–80

* 1 daily after April
‡ except Jan–Mar and 7–27 Nov
Fares on sailings from the Republic are quoted in punts, from Northern Ireland in sterling, but most fares are the same in sterling or punts. For sailings from the Republic add IR£5 per person departure tax.

AIRLINES IN IRELAND

Aer Lingus Dublin ☎01/705 3333; Cork ☎021/327155; Limerick ☎061/474239; in Northern Ireland ☎0645/737747.

Aeroflot ☎01/844 6166

Air France ☎01/844 5633

Alitalia ☎01/677 5171

Austrian Airlines ☎01/608 0099

British Airways in the Republic ☎0141/222345; in Northern Ireland ☎0345/222111.

British Midland in the Republic ☎01/283 8833; in Northern Ireland ☎0345/554554.

Gill Airways in Northern Ireland ☎01232/459777; in the Republic ☎080-1232/459777.

Iberia ☎01/677 9846

KLM in the Republic ☎01/284 3823; in Northern Ireland ☎0990/074074.

Lufthansa in the Republic ☎01/844 5544; in Northern Ireland ☎0345/737747.

Olympic ☎01/608 0090

Ryanair in the Republic ☎01/609 7800; in Northern Ireland ☎0541/569569.

Sabena in the Republic ☎01/844 5454; in Northern Ireland ☎0345/581291.

SAS Scandinavian Airlines ☎01/844 5440

Swissair ☎01/677 8173

TAP Air Portugal ☎01/679 8844

bridge" fares for both ferries if you're driving (IR£160–300 for a car and up to five people to France, IR£260–395 to Spain, other fares available to the Netherlands, Germany and Scandinavia), while **direct rail tickets** generally include both boat connections anyway. These latter are available from Irish Rail in the Republic, or Northern Ireland Railways in the North, with discounted under-26 **BIJ tickets** available from these, or from USIT. International rail tickets can be booked up to two months in advance, are valid for two months, and allow stopovers en route.

RAIL PASSES AND INTERNATIONAL TRAIN TICKETS

Continental Rail Desk, Irish Rail (Euro Rail Desk), 35 Lower Abbey St, Dublin 1 (☎01/677 1871). InterRail passes and through tickets to Britain and Europe, including under-26 BIJ tickets.

Northern Ireland Railways, Great Victoria Station,28–30 Great Victoria St, Belfast BT2 7UB (☎01232/230671). InterRail passes and under-26 BIJ tickets.

TRAVEL AGENTS AND TOUR OPERATORS IN IRELAND

Budget Travel, 134 Lower Baggot St, Dublin 2 (☎01/661 1866), and other branches citywide.

Exodus, at Colette Pearson, 64 South William St, Dublin 2 (☎01/677 1029).

Explore, at Maxwells Travel, D'Olier Chambers, 1 Hawkins St, Dublin 2 (☎01/677 9479).

Express Travel Service, 18a Upper Merrion St, Dublin 2 (☎01/676 4806).

Joe Walsh Tours, 69 Upper O'Connell St, Dublin 2 (☎01/872 2555); 8–11 Lower Baggot St, Dublin 2 (☎01/676 3053); 117 Patrick St, Cork (☎021/277959). General budget fares agent.

Neenan Travel, 12 South Leinster St, Dublin 2 (☎01/676 5181; e-mail *admin@neenantrav.ie*). European city breaks.

Student & Group Travel, 1st floor, 71 Dame St, Dublin 2 (☎01-677 7834). Student specialists.

Thomas Cook, 11 Donegall Place, Belfast BT1 5AA (☎01232/550232); 118 Grafton St, Dublin 2 (☎01/677 0469). Package holiday and flight agent, with occasional discount offers.

Trailfinders, 4–5 Dawson St, Dublin 2 (☎01/677 7888). Competitive fares, plus deals on hotels, insurance, tours and car rental.

USIT, O'Connell Bridge, 19–21 Aston Quay, Dublin 2 (☎01/679 8833); Fountain Centre, College St, Belfast BT1 6ET (☎01232/324073); 10–11 Market Parade, Patrick St, Cork (☎021/270900); 33 Ferryquay St, Derry (☎01504/371888); Victoria Place, Eyre Square, Galway (☎091/565177); Central Buildings, O'Connell St, Limerick (☎061/415064); 36–37 Georges St, Waterford (☎051/872601). Ireland's main student and youth travel specialists.

FERRY OPERATORS

Argyll & Antrim Steam Packet Co, c/o Seacat, Donegall Quay, Belfast (in Northern Ireland and Britain, call ☎08705/523523; in the Republic, call ☎1800/551743). Ballycastle to Campbeltown.

Brittany Ferries, 42 Grand Parade, Cork (☎021/277801; in Northern Ireland, call ☎0990/360360). Cork to Roscoff.

Irish Ferries, 2–4 Merrion Row, Dublin 2 (☎01/661 0511; *www.irishferries.ie*); St Patrick's Bridge, Cork (☎021/551995);

Rosslare (☎053/33158); Holyhead (☎0990/329129); Liverpool (☎0990/171717). Dublin to Holyhead; Rosslare to Pembroke, Roscoff and Cherbourg.

Norse Irish Ferries, Victoria Terminal 2, West Bank Rd, Belfast BT3 9JN (☎01232/779090; *www.Norse-Irish-Ferries.co.uk*). North Brocklebank Dock, Bootle, Merseyside L20 1BY (☎0151/944 1010). Belfast to Liverpool.

P&O European Ferries, The Terminal Building, Larne Harbour, Co. Antrim BT40 1AQ (☎0990/980777; in the Republic call, ☎1800/409049; *www.poef.com*). Larne to Cairnryan.

Seacat, Seacat Terminal, Donegall Quay, Belfast BT1 3EA (☎08705/523523; in the Republic, call ☎1800/551743). Belfast to Stranraer, Dublin to Liverpool.

Stena Line, 15 Westmoreland St, Dublin 2 (☎01/204 7777); Corry Rd, Belfast BT3 9SS (☎01232/884088; *www.stenaline.co.uk*); The Harbour, Rosslare, Co Wexford (☎053/33115); Sea Terminal, Stranraer, Wigtownshire DG9 8EL (☎01776/802165); Station Approach, Holyhead, Gwynedd LL65 1DQ (☎01407/606665). Dun Laoghaire to Holyhead, Rosslare to Fishguard, Larne to Stranraer.

Swansea–Cork Ferries, 52 South Mall, Cork (☎021/271166; *scf@iol.ie*); King's Dock, Swansea, W Glamorgan SA1 8RU (☎01792/456116).

TRAVELLING FROM AUSTRALIA AND NEW ZEALAND

There are flights from Melbourne, Sydney, Brisbane and Perth to most European capitals, and there really is not a great deal of difference in the fares to the busiest destinations – a scheduled return airfare from Sydney to London, Paris, Rome, Madrid, Athens or Frankfurt should be available through travel agents for around Aus$1500 in low season, rising to Aus$1900 or more in winter (European summer), though at this time of year there are often better prices on charters to London. A one-way ticket will cost slightly more than half that, while a return flight from Auckland to Europe will cost approximately NZ$2100 in low season, rising to NZ$2600 in high season. Asian airlines often work out cheapest, and may throw in a stopover, while the extremely large Greek population of Melbourne means there are often bargain deals to be had to Athens on Olympic Airways – ring around first.

For these and other low-price tickets, the most reliable operator is STA, who also supply packages with companies such as Contiki and Top Deck and can issue rail passes. STA can also advise on visa regulations for Australian and New Zealand citizens – and for a fee will do all the paperwork for you. Bear in mind that to enter most countries your passport must be valid for at least six months after your date of arrival.

AIRLINES IN AUSTRALIA AND NEW ZEALAND

Aeroflot in Australia ☎02/9262 2233

Air New Zealand in Australia ☎13 2476; in NZ ☎09/357 3000

Britannia Airways in Australia ☎02/9251 1299

British Airways in Australia ☎02/9258 3300; in NZ ☎09/356 8690

Cathay Pacific in Australia ☎13 1747; in NZ ☎09/379 0861

Garuda in Australia ☎02/9334 9944 or 1-800/800 873; in NZ ☎09/366 1855

Gulf Air in Australia ☎02/9321 9199

Japan Airlines in Australia ☎02/9272 1111; in NZ ☎09/379 9906

KLM in Australia ☎02/9231 6333 or 1-800/505 747

Malaysia Airlines in Australia ☎13 2627; in NZ ☎09/373 2741

Olympic Airways in Australia ☎02/9251 2044

Philippine Airlines in Australia ☎02/9262 3333

Qantas in Australia ☎13 1211; in NZ ☎09/357 8900 or 0800/808 767

Singapore Airlines in Australia ☎13 1011; in NZ ☎09/379 3209 or 0-800/808 909

Thai Airways in Australia ☎13 1960; in NZ ☎09/377 3886

Virgin Atlantic in Australia ☎02/9352 6199 or 1-800/646 747

TRAVEL AGENTS IN AUSTRALIA AND NEW ZEALAND

Anywhere Travel, 345 Anzac Parade, Kingsford, Sydney (☎02/9663 0411).

Budget Travel, 16 Fort St, Auckland (☎09/366 0061 or 0800/808 040), plus branches nationwide (call ☎0800/808 040 for nearest branch).

Destinations Unlimited, 3 Milford Rd, Auckland (☎09/373 4033).

Flight Centres Australia: 82 Elizabeth St, Sydney, plus branches nationwide (call ☎13 1600 for nearest branch). New Zealand: 205 Queen St, Auckland (☎09/309 6171 or 0-800/FLIGHTS), plus branches nationwide.

Northern Gateway, 22 Cavenagh St, Darwin (☎08/8941 1394).

STA Travel, Australia: 855 George St, Sydney; 256 Flinders St, Melbourne, plus branches nationwide (call ☎13 1776 for nearest branch, ☎1300/360 960 for fastfare telesales). New Zealand: 10 High St, Auckland (☎09/309 0458, fastfare telesales ☎09/366 6673), plus branches in Wellington, Christchurch, Dunedin, Palmerston North, Hamilton and at major universities. (Web site: *www.statravelaus.com.au*; email: *traveller@statravelaus.com.au*).

Thomas Cook, Australia: 175 Pitt St, Sydney; 257 Collins St, Melbourne; plus branches nationwide (call ☎13 1771 for nearest branch, ☎1-800/063 913 for direct telesales); New Zealand: 96 Anzac Ave, Auckland (☎09/379 3920).

SPECIALIST AGENTS AND TOUR OPERATORS IN AUSTRALIA AND NEW ZEALAND

Adventure World, Australia: 73 Walker St, North Sydney (☎02/9956 7766 or 1-800/221 931), plus branches in Melbourne, Brisbane, Adelaide and Perth. New Zealand: 101 Great South Rd, Remeura, Auckland (☎09/524 5118). Agents for many adventure tour operators, including Contiki, Explore Worldwide and Top Deck.

Bentours, 11/2 Bridge St, Sydney (☎02/9241 1353). Scandinavian and Russian specialist agents, including rail passes covering these countries.

Best of Britain, 352a Military Rd, Cremorne, Sydney (☎02/9909 1055). Flights, accommodation, car rental, tours, canal boats and B&Bs throughout the British Isles.

CIT, 263 Clarence St, Sydney (☎02/9267 1255), plus offices in Melbourne, Brisbane, Adelaide and Perth. Agents specializing in all things Italian; also deal with Europe-wide rail and bus passes.

Contiki Holidays for 18–35s, 35 Spring St, Bondi Junction, Sydney (☎02/9511 2200). Frenetic tours for party animals.

European Travel Office, Australia: 122 Rosslyn St, West Melbourne (☎03/9329 8844); 368 Sussex St, Sydney (☎02/9267 7714). New Zealand: 407 Great South Rd, Auckland (☎09/525 3074). All European travel arrangements.

French Travel Connection, 2/90 Mount St, North Sydney (☎02/9956 5884). Travel and tours across France.

Grecian Tours Travel, 237a Lonsdale St, Melbourne (☎03/9663 3711). Flights and tours, including island-hopping, in Greece.

Ibertours, 84 William St, Melbourne (☎03/9670 8388 or 1-800/500 016). Spain and Morocco tour bookings.

Russian and Eastern European Travel Centre, 5/75 King St, Sydney (☎02/9262 1144), plus branches in Melbourne, Brisbane, Perth and Adelaide. Can book accommodation, cruises, train and bus travel, spa visits and tours throughout Eastern Europe and Russia.

Snow Bookings Only, 1141 Toorak Rd, Camberwell, Melbourne (☎1800/623 266). Skiing holidays in France, Switzerland & Austria.

TRAVELLING IN EUROPE

It's easy enough to travel in Europe, and a number of special deals and passes can make it fairly economical too. Air links are extensive, but also expensive, give or take the odd charter deal in season, and with the exception of Britain, where flying is the cheapest way to reach much of the Continent (see "Travelling from Britain" p.10). In any case, you really appreciate the diversity of Europe best at ground level, by way of the enormous and generally efficient web of rail, road and ferry connections that covers the Continent.

NATIONAL RAIL PASSES

Some European countries provide a **national rail pass**, which can be good value if you're doing a lot of travelling within one country, or a EuroDomino, which you buy before you leave. Main options are listed below: in general those quoted in pounds and dollars need to be bought before you leave home, either from the office of the national rail company or national tourist office, or in the case of the US, from RailEurope, the general sales agent for most European railroads. Explorer Passes for under-26s and students, put out by Usit Campus in Britain, give unlimited travel for a set period in one country or a combination of countries and can be a real bargain, but are unfortunately only available for a few countries. There is no pass as such for Russia.

Austria The VORTEILSCard rail pass gives a year's half-price travel throughout Austria for ÖS1190. A EuroDomino pass costs from £69 (£89 for over-26s) for 3 days up to £99/129 for 8 days. An Austrian Railpass gives 3 days free travel in a 15-day period for $98 plus $15 a day for up to five extra days.

Belgium A Belgian Tourrail gives 5 days' unlimited travel within a 1-month period for BF2100, and the Go Pass allows under-26s 10 single journeys of any length in 6 months for BF1420 (the over-26 version, 9+, costs BF2100 but on weekdays it is only valid after 9am). A EuroDomino pass costs from £39 (£49 for over-26s) for 3 days up to £49/69 for 8 days. Also covered by Benelux passes.

Benelux A Benelux Tourrail card gives 5 days' travel in a month on the Netherlands, Belgium and Luxembourg railways, and Luxembourg CRL buses, for £56 (£80 for over-26s, £120 for two travelling together).

Britain The BritRail pass, available from British Rail agents outside Britain, qualifies you for unlimited rail travel throughout England, Wales and Scotland for 8 days at £215 ($265 for over-26s), 15 at £280 ($400), 22 at £355 ($505), or a month at £420 ($600). It also gives a discount of around 12 percent on Eurostar Channel Tunnel services, and can be bought as a package with the discounted cross-Channel ticket. Alternatively, the BritRail Flexipass gives unlimited travel on any 4 days in two months for £185 (£235 for over-26s), 8 for £240 ($340); or 15 for £360 ($575). Other passes include the Freedom of Scotland Pass, giving 4 days' free travel in Scotland in an 8-day period at £125, 8 days in 15 at £180, 12 days in 15 at £215, and the Britail SouthEast Pass, which gives 3 days' free travel in southeast England in an 8-day period for £70, 4 days for £100, or 7 days in 15 for £135. With a BritRail pass plus Ireland, you get 5 days' travel in a month throughout Britain and Ireland (plus a round trip on Stena Sealink Irish Sea ferries) for £408, or 10 days for £570. Available in Britain, the Young Person's Railcard costs £18 and gives 33 percent reductions to full-time students and under-26s for a year.

Bulgaria A EuroDomino pass costs from £29 (£39 for over-26s) for 3 days up to £49/69 for 8 days.

Croatia A EuroDomino pass costs from £29 (£39 for over-26s) for 3 days up to £59/79 for 8 days.

Czech Republic A EuroDomino pass costs from £29 (£39 for over-26s) for 3 days up to £59/79 for 8 days. An Explorer Pass for a week's unlimited rail travel in the Czech Republic is £15; for both the Czech Republic and Slovakia, it's £23.

Denmark A EuroDomino pass costs from £49 (£59 for over-26s) for 3 days up to £79/119 for 8 days. For ScanRail passes see Scandinavia.

Finland Finnrail passes are valid for unlimited rail travel on 3, 5 or 10 days in a month and cost FM600, FM800 and FM1090 respectively. A EuroDomino pass costs from £59 (£79 for over-26s) for 3 days up to £109/149 for 8 days. For ScanRail passes see Scandinavia.

France A EuroDomino pass costs from £99 (£119 for over-26s) for 3 days up to £239/239 for 8 days. The Carte 12–25 gives 12–25 year olds 25–50 percent off all train journeys for a year for FF270, while the France Railpass costs $158 for any 3 days' travel in a month ($175 over-26, $164 each for two travelling together), with up to 6 additional rail days at $26 (over-26 $30) each.

Germany The German Rail BahnCard gives a year of unlimited half-price travel on all trains in Germany and costs £92 (under-22s, students, senior citizens and spouses of holders £46). A Ferien Ticket gives a week's unlimited rail travel within a specified area for £15 per person plus £8 each for up to 4 travelling companions. A EuroDomino pass costs from £99 (£129 for over-26s) for 3 days up to £139/189 for 8 days. A German Rail Flexipass costs $138 ($174 for over-26s, $261 for two travelling together) for any 4 days' travel in a month, rising to $210 ($306, $459) for 10 (with prices in between for 5–9 days).

Greece A EuroDomino pass costs from £39 (£49 for over-26s) for 3 days up to £49/89 for 8 days.

BY TRAIN

Though to some extent it depends on where you intend to spend most of your time, **train** is without doubt the best way to make a tour of Europe. The rail network in most countries is comprehensive, in some cases exceptionally so, and the Continent boasts some of the most scenic rail journeys you could make anywhere in the world. Train travel is relatively cheap, too, even in the richer parts of northwest Europe, where, apart from Britain (whose privatized railways are still stuck in the 1980s fad of trying to be a business rather than a public service), trains are heavily subsidized, and prices are brought down further by the multiplicity of passes and discount cards available, both Europe-wide (**InterRail** for those based in Europe or the British Isles, **Eurail** for anyone based elsewhere) and on an individual country basis. In some countries you'll find it makes more sense

Hungary An Explorer Pass gives a week's unlimited train travel for £23. A EuroDomino pass costs from £29 (£39 for over-26s) for 3 days up to £69/89 for 8 days.

Ireland Irish Rail's Rover ticket buys unlimited rail travel in the Republic and the North on any 5 days out of 15 for IR£75, with an Explorer (the same deal in the Republic only) at IR£60. Use the Emerald Card on rail and bus in the Republic and the North at IR£105 for 8 days in 15, IR£180 for 15 days in 30, or IR£90 for 8 days in 15 in the Republic only. A EuroDomino pass costs from £49 (the same for over-26s) for 3 days up to £89/99 for 8 days and is valid only in the Republic. See Britain for details of the BritIreland Pass (not available in Britain or Ireland).

Italy The Italy Railcard gives unlimited rail travel for 8 days at £128/$182, 15 at £158/$228, 21 at £186/$264, or 30 at £220/$318. A 2-month Chilometrico ticket is valid for 3,000km of travel, or 20 journeys if shorter, for up to five people within 2 months for £88 each. A EuroDomino pass costs from £79 (£99 for over-26s) for 3 days up to £109/149 for 8 days. A Flexi RailCard gives 4 days in a month for £88/$144, 8 days for £122/$202, or 12 days for £156/$259.

Luxembourg One-day rail passes are F160 each, F540 for a book of 5. A EuroDomino pass costs £19 for 8 days (6 days for over-26s, who can get 8 days for £29). A Luxembourg Card covering buses too costs F300 for one day, F500 for any 2 days in a week, and F700 for any 3 days in a week, with free entry to numerous sights as well. See also Benelux.

Morocco A EuroDomino pass costs from £29 (the same for over-26s) for 3 days up to £59/69 for 8 days.

Netherlands Rover tickets give a day's unlimited travel for £25; Multirover tickets for 2–6 people travelling together save even more on that. A Summer Tour Rover giving free travel on any 3 days in 10 during June, July and Aug costs £34 for one person, £45 for two travelling together. A HollandRail Pass gives 3 days' free travel in a month at £29 for one person, £33.50 for two travelling together (over-26s £36/54), or 5 days for £55/82.50 (£44/66) All these tickets are available in slightly pricier versions that cover buses, trams and metro services too. A EuroDomino pass costs from £29 (£39 for over-26s) for 3 days up to £79/99 for 8 days. See also Benelux.

Norway A Norway Rail Flexipass gives 3 days free travel in a month for £132, 4 days for £164, or 5 days for $185. A EuroDomino pass costs from £79 (£99 for over-26s) for 3 days up to £139/179 for 8 days. For ScanRail passes see Scandinavia.

Poland Polrail passes cost £29 (£42 for over-26s) for 8 days travel, £34/49 for 15, £39/55 for 21, and £50/71 for a month. An Explorer Pass gives you unlimited train travel over 7 days for £23, 14 days for £32, or 21 days for £45. A EuroDomino pass is rather worse value, costing from £29 (£39 for over-26s) for 3 days up to £59/69 for 8 days.

Portugal A Bilhete Turistico pass, which costs 18,000esc for a week's rail travel, 30,000esc for 2 weeks, and 42,000esc for 3, is not really worth it. A EuroDomino pass costs from £39 (£49 for over-26s) for 3 days up to £69/89 for 8 days.

Romania A EuroDomino pass costs from £29 (£39 for over-26s) for 3 days up to £69/89 for 8 days.

Scandinavia The ScanRail pass is valid on the rail networks of Denmark, Norway, Sweden and Finland and costs £99 (£132 for over-26s) for 5 days' travel in 15, £135 (£180) for 10 days in a month, and £149 (£198) for 21 days unlimited.

Slovakia A EuroDomino pass costs from £29 (the same for over-26s) for 3 days up to £49/59 for 8 days. An Explorer Pass gives a week's unlimited train travel in Slovakia and the Czech Republic for £23.

Slovenia A EuroDomino pass costs from £29 (£39 for over-26s) for 3 days up to £49/759 for 8 days.

Spain A EuroDomino pass costs from £69 (£89 for over-26s) for 3 days up to £139/189 for 8 days. A RENFE Tourist Card for 3 days' travel in 2 months is 18,358ptas, plus just under 4300ptas for each of up to 7 additional days. An Explorer Pass gives 7 days' unlimited train travel for £80, 15 days for £97, and 30 days for £126. A Spanish rail pass for 5 days unlimited travel on local services in the region of either Madrid, Barcelona or Malaga costs £9.

Sweden EuroDomino passes for Sweden cost from £99 (£119 for over-26s) for 3 days up to £159/199 for 8 days. ScanRail passes are also valid (see Scandinavia).

Switzerland The Swiss Pass, valid for unlimited travel on rail, bus and ferry routes, costs £90 for 4 days, £112 for 8, £130 for 15, and £180 for a month. Alternatives are the Swiss Flexipass (valid for any 3 days in 15 for £90) the Swiss Half-Fare Card (50 percent discount on rail travel for a month for £38), and the Swiss Card (free travel between border or airport and your main resort plus 50 percent discount on other tickets for a month at £60). A EuroDomino pass costs from £59 (£79 for over-26s) for 3 days up to £89/109 for 8 days.

Turkey A EuroDomino pass costs from £19 (£29 for over-26s) for 3 days up to £39/49 for 8 days.

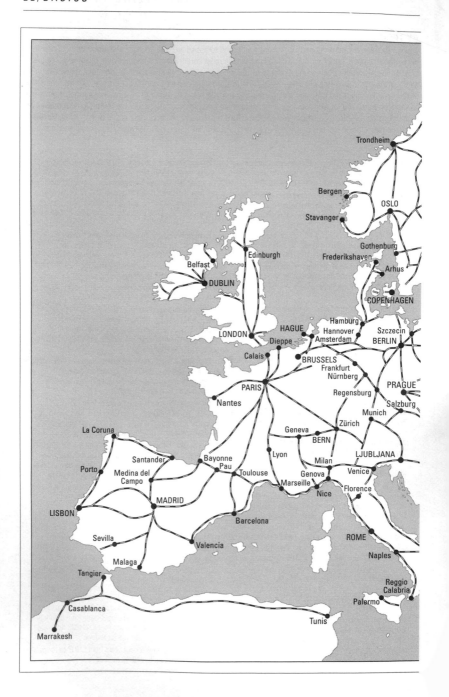

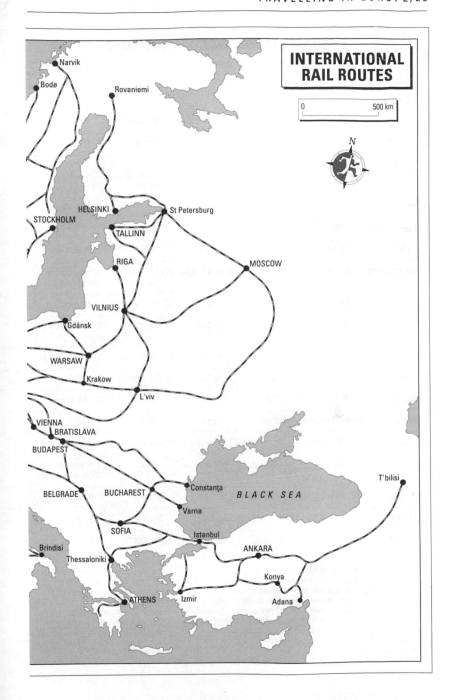

INTERNATIONAL
RAIL ROUTES

0   500 km

N

INTERNATIONAL TRAIN ROUTES

FROM \ TO	Amsterdam	Berlin	Bratislava	Brussels	Bucharest
Amsterdam	-	4 (6hr 20min)	Berlin	21 (3hr)	Vienna
Berlin	4 (6hr 10min)	-	2 (10hr)	1 (10hr 30min)	Budapest
Bratislava	Berlin	2 (10hr)	-	Vienna	1 (17hr 40min)
Brussels	21 (3hr)	1 (10hr 20min)	Vienna	-	Vienna
Bucharest	Vienna	Budapest	1 (17hr)	Vienna	-
Budapest	Vienna	3 (12hr 40min)	11 (7hr)[3]	Vienna	7 (13hr 20min)
Copenhagen	Osnabrück [1]	Malmö	Munich[2]	Cologne	Munich
Ljubljana	Munich	1 (14hr 35min)	Vienna	Munich	Budapest
Luxembourg	Brussels	Cologne	Cologne & Prague	22 (2hr 40min)	Strasbourg and Munich
Milan	Cologne	Munich	Vienna	2 (11hr 55min)	Munich[4]
Moscow	Hanover	3 weekly (28hr 35min)	6 weekly (33hr 25min)	Cologne	1 (37hr 30min)
Munich	1 (10hr 50min)	8 (9hr 10min)	Vienna	1 (10hr 45min)	1 (22hr 30min)
Paris	4 (8hr 55min)	1 (12hr 30min)	Vienna	18 (5hr 20min)	Budapest
Prague	1 (14hr 45min)	5 (4hr 50min)	6 (5hr)	Cologne	1 (22hr 55min)
Rome	Milan & Cologne	Munich	Vienna	Milan	Munich
Vienna	1 (14hr 20min)	1 (10hr)	4 (1hr 10min)[3]	1 (14hr 15min)	2 (16hr 30min)
Vilnius	Berlin	1 (20hr 30min)	Warsaw	Berlin	4 weekly (38hr 30min)
Warsaw	Berlin	4–5 (8hr 20min)	2 (7hr 50min)	Cologne	Budapest
Zagreb	Munich	1 (16hr 55min)	Budapest	Munich	Budapest
Zurich	1 (9hr)	1 (11hr 45min)	Vienna	3 (7hr 45min)	Budapest

This chart shows the number of direct daily trains between European capitals and the fastest scheduled time by ordinary services where available (those with a supplement will be faster and may be your only choice). Where there is no direct service, a suggested interchange point is given instead, but note that you may have to pick up your connecting service from a different terminal, and that you may have to wait several hours for your connection: you could take it as an opportunity to wander round town, with your bags at the baggage deposit in the meantime, or to freshen up – many major stations have washing facilities. Depending on the time of day, or day of the week, you may be able to get to your destination more quickly or conveniently with one or two extra changes of train. Note too that most trains to Russia and the Baltic states pass through Belarus or the Ukraine, and that you may therefore need a transit visa to use them (see p.31). Direct services to Athens, Istanbul and Sofia pass through Belgrade, so you may wish to check on the current political situation in Yugoslavia and the neighbouring countries before deciding to use them.

Budapest	Copenhagen	Ljubljana	Luxembourg	Milan
Vienna	Osnabrück[1]	Munich	Brussels	Cologne
3 (12hr 40min)	Malmö	1 (14hr 25min)	Cologne	Munich
11 (7hr 10min)[3]	Hamburg	Vienna	Prague & Cologne	Vienna
Vienna	Cologne	Munich	22 (2hr 40min)	2 (11hr)
7 (13hr 20min)	Munich	Budapest	Munich & Strasbourg	Munich[4]
-	Munich[2]	2 (7hr 55min)	Strasbourg	Venice
Hamburg	-	Munich	Cologne	Munich
2 (7hr 55min)	Munich	-	Zurich	1 (8hr 30min)
Strasbourg	Cologne	Zurich	-	2 (9hr 10min)
Venice	Munich	1 (8hr 05min)	2 (9hr)	-
11 weekly (33hr 20min)	Hanover	2 weekly (53hr)	Cologne	Venice [5]
3 (8hr 05min)	1 (14hr 30min)	3 (6hr 40min)	Strasbourg	3 (8hr 50 min)
1 (18hr 25 min)	Cologne	Munich	5 (3hr 45min)	3 (10hr 30min)
5 (9hr 10min)	Munich[2]	Munich	Cologne	Munich
Vienna (Mestre)[4]	Munich	Venice (Mestre)	Milan	26 (5hr 50min)
10 (3hr)[3]	Munich	2 (6hr 20min)	Strasbourg	1 (13hr 20min)
Warsaw	Malmö & Berlin	Lviv[6]	Warsaw & Cologne	Lviv & Zagreb
2 (10hr 30min)	Malmö & Berlin	Vienna	Cologne	Vienna
4 (6hr 25min)	Munich	8 (2hr 20min)	Zurich	1 (10hr 55min)
1 (14hr 40min)	Basel	1 (11hr)	3 (5hr)	9 (4hr 30min)

NOTES:

[1] Faster connection at Duisburg with a supplement.
[2] Faster via Hamburg with a supplement.
[3] There is also a hydrofoil service in summer.
[4] Slightly faster via Vienna with a supplement.
[5] Direct connection twice weekly only; on other days change also at Zagreb.
[6] On days when there is no direct train, change at Zagreb.
[7] Plus one sleeper-only train every other day.

INTERNATIONAL TRAIN ROUTES

TO / FROM	Moscow	Munich	Paris	Prague	Rome
Amsterdam	Hanover	1 (11hr 05min)	4 (8hr 05min)	1 (14hr 45min)	Cologne & Milan
Berlin	3 weekly (30hr 35min)	8 (9hr)	1 (12hr 35min)	5 (4hr 45min)	Munich
Bratislava	6 weekly (33hr 25min)	Vienna	Vienna	6 (5hr)	Vienna
Brussels	Cologne	1 (11hr 15min)	18 (4hr 40min)	Cologne	Milan
Bucharest	1 (36hr)	1 (23hr 10min)	Budapest	1 (22hr 50min)	Munich
Budapest	11 weekly (14hr 55min)	3 (8hr 25min)	1 (17hr 25min)	5 (9hr 15min)	Venice (Mestre)[4]
Copenhagen	Hanover	1 (14hr 30min)	Cologne	Munich[2]	Munich
Ljubljana	2 weekly (52hr 45min)[6]	3 (6hr 50min)	Munich	Munich	Venice (Mestre)
Luxembourg	Cologne	Strasbourg	5 (3hr 40min)	Cologne	Milan
Milan	Venice[5]	3 (8hr 10min)	3 (10hr 45min)	Munich	26 (6hr 35min)
Moscow	-	Cologne	Cologne	4 weekly (35hr)	Trieste[5]
Munich	Budapest	-	4 (9hr)	3 (9hr 30min)	2 (11hr 45min)
Paris	Cologne	4 (9hr 40min)	-	1 (14hr 55min)	1 (14hr 30min)
Prague	4 weekly (32hr)	3 (8hr 40min)	1 (15hr)	-	Munich
Rome	Trieste[5]	2 (11hr 45min)	1 (14hr 50min)	Munich	
Vienna	6 weekly (33hr 45min)	4 (6hr 35min)	2 (14hr)	3 (5hr 10min)	2 (13hr 45min)x
Vilnius	3 (15hr 10min)	Berlin	Berlin	Warsaw	Warsaw & Vienna
Warsaw	3 (19hr 45 min)	Prague	Cologne	3 (10hr 55min)	Vienna
Zagreb	1 (49hr 10min)	3 (9hr 20min)	Munich	Budapest	Venice (Mestre)
Zurich	Budapest	4 (4hr 10min)	1 (7hr 45min)	1 (10hr 40min)	1 (11hr 20min)

This chart shows the number of direct daily trains between European capitals and the fastest scheduled time by ordinary services where available (those with a supplement will be faster and may be your only choice). Where there is no direct service, a suggested interchange point is given instead, but note that you may have to pick up your connecting service from a different terminal, and that you may have to wait several hours for your connection: you could take it as an opportunity to wander round town, with your bags at the baggage deposit in the meantime, or to freshen up – many major stations have washing facilities. Depending on the time of day, or day of the week, you may be able to get to your destination more quickly or conveniently with one or two extra changes of train. Note too that most trains to Russia and the Baltic states pass through Belarus or the Ukraine, and that you may therefore need a transit visa to use them (see p.31). Direct services to Athens, Istanbul and Sofia pass through Belgrade, so you may wish to check on the current political situation in Yugoslavia and the neighbouring countries before deciding to use them

Vienna	Vilnius	Warsaw	Zagreb	Zurich
1 (14hr 20min)	Berlin	Berlin	Munich	1 (9hr)
1 (10hr)	1 (20hr 45min)	4–5 (8hr 30min)	1 (16hr 45min)	1(11hr 45min
1 (14hr 10min)	Warsaw	2 (8hr 10min)	Budapest	Vienna
1 (14hr 35min)	Berlin	Cologne	Munich	3 (8hr)
2 (15hr 50min)	4 weekly (42hr)	Budapest	Budapest	Budapest
10 (3hr)[3]	Warsaw	2 (11hr)	4 (5hr 55min)	1 (14hr 55min)
Munich	Berlin & Malmö	Berlin & Malmö	Munich	Basel
2 (6hr)	Lviv[5]	Vienna	8 (2hr 20min)	1 (11hr 35min)
Strasbourg	Cologne & Warsaw	Cologne	Zurich	3 (4hr 55min)
1 (12hr 35min)	Zagreb & Lviv	Vienna	1 (10hr 35min)	9 (4hr 30min)
6 weekly (33hr)	3 (15hr)	3 (19hr 35min)	1 (5hr)	Budapest
4 (7hr 30min)	Berlin	Prague	3 (9hr 20min)	4 (4hr 15min)
2 (15hr)	Berlin	Cologne	Munich	1 (8hr 05min)
3 (5hr 10min)	Warsaw	3 (10hr 15min)	Budapest	1 (10hr 40min)
2 (13hr 25min)	Vienna & Warsaw	Vienna	Venice (Mestre)	1 (11hr 35min)
	Warsaw	2 (11hr)	2 (7hr)	3 (9hr 05min)
Warsaw		1 (12hr 10min) [7]	Lviv	Berlin
2 (11hr 10min)	1 (12hr 20min)[7]	-	Vienna	Prague
2 (6hr 45min)	Lviv	Vienna		1 (14hr 20min)
3 (9hr 35min)	Berlin	Prague	1 (13hr 45min)	

NOTES:

[1] Faster connection at Duisburg with a supplement.
[2] Faster via Hamburg with a supplement.
[3] There is also a hydrofoil service in summer.
[4] Slightly faster via Vienna with a supplement.
[5] Direct connection twice weekly only; on other days change also at Zagreb.
[6] On days when there is no direct train, change at Zagreb.
[7] Plus one sleeper-only train every other day.

to travel by bus, but if you're travelling further afield buying a rail pass may still pay dividends. We've covered the various passes here, as well as the most important international routes and most useful addresses; full supplementary details, including frequencies and journey times of domestic services, are given throughout the guide in each country's "Travel details" section.

If you intend to do a lot of rail travel, the *Thomas Cook European Timetable* is an essential investment, detailing the main lines throughout Europe, as well as ferry connections, and is updated monthly. *Thomas Cook* also publish a rail map of Europe, which may be a good supplement to our own train map on pp.22–3.

Finally, whenever you board an international train in Europe, check the route of the car you are in, since trains frequently split, with different carriages going to different destinations.

EUROPE-WIDE RAIL PASSES

For young Europeans, probably the most popular of all the ways of travelling around the Continent is the **InterRail pass**, a ticket for unlimited travel on rail lines the length and breadth of Europe. InterRail passes are available from main stations and international rail agents (see p.15 and p.17) in Britain, Ireland and all other countries covered by the scheme. A zoning system applies for the European countries valid under the pass, as follows:

Zone A Britain and Ireland

Zone B Sweden, Norway and Finland

Zone C Denmark, Germany, Switzerland and Austria

Zone D Poland, the Czech Republic, Slovakia, Hungary and Croatia

Zone E France, Belgium, the Netherlands and Luxembourg

Zone F Spain, Portugal and Morocco

Zone G Italy, Slovenia, Greece and Turkey

Zone H Bulgaria, Romania, Yugoslavia and the Republic of Macedonia

The zones you want to travel in determine the price, which starts at £159 for under-26-year-olds (£229 over-26) for a one-zone card valid for 22 days; cards for more than one zone are valid for a month and cost £209/279 for two zones, £229/279 for three zones, and £259/349 for all the zones. To qualify, you need to have been resident in one of the participating countries for 6 months or more; you also need a valid passport.

Increasingly with both InterRail passes, you will need to pay **supplements** on most European express trains, all of them on some routes, and certainly all the most convenient ones (17 of the 18 daily trains between Paris and Brussels carry a supplement, for example, and the remaining service takes more than three times as long to cover the distance). Even where there is in theory no supplement, there is often a compulsory reservation fee, which may cost you double if you only find out about it once you're on the train.

Non-European residents aren't eligible for InterRail passes, though they can buy **BIJ tickets** (see p.11) and most agents don't in fact check residential qualifications. Better still, a **Eurail pass**, which must be bought outside Europe (but can be obtained from Usit Campus and Rail Europe in London by non-residents who were unable to get it at home), gives unlimited travel in 17 countries – Austria, Belgium, Denmark, Finland, France, Germany, Greece, Hungary, Ireland, Italy, Luxembourg, the Netherlands, Norway, Portugal, Spain, Sweden and Switzerland – fewer than InterRail, but valid for more express trains, thus saving money on supplements. The **Eurail Youthpass** (for under-26s) costs US$388/A$597 for 15 days, $499/A$777 for 21 days, $623/A$961 for one month, $882/A$1361 for two months, or $1084/A$1681; if you're 26 or over you'll have to buy a first-class pass, available in 15-day (US$554/A$854), 21-day (US$718/A$1108), one-month (US$890/A$1372), two-month (US$1260/A$1943) and three-month (US$1558/A$2400) increments. If there are two of you (three in summer), the **Eurail Saverpass** (first class only) can knock about 15 percent off the cost of the standard Eurail offerings. You stand a better chance of getting your money's worth out of a **Eurail Flexipass**, which is good for a certain number of travel days in a two-month period. This, too, comes in under-26 and first-class versions: 10 days cost US$458/A$705 for under-26s or US$654/A$1007 for first-class travel; and 15 days, US$599/A$929 or US$862/A$1327. A scaled-down version of the Flexipass, the **Europass**, allows travel in France, Germany, Italy, Spain and Switzerland for US$233/A$343 under-26, or US$348/A$518 1ˢᵗ class, for 5 days in 2 months, rising to US$513/A$804 or US$728/A$1185 for 15 days, with prices in between for 6, 8 or 10 days; there is also the option of adding adjacent "associate" countries. Eurail passes are available from the agents listed on p.9 and p.15.

BY BUS

For most people on a tour of Europe, a **bus** is something you take when there is no train. There are some countries (Greece, Turkey and Morocco are the most obvious examples) where the trains are slow or infrequent, and the bus network more widespread. But on the whole you'll find yourself using buses for the odd trip here and there, usually locally, since on long-distance journeys between major European cities it's generally slower, more uncomfortable and not particularly cheap, especially if you have a rail pass. If you have a limited itinerary, however, a **bus pass** or **circular bus ticket** can undercut a rail pass, epecially for over-26s. The **Eurolines** pass is valid for unlimited travel between twenty European cities plus London, costs £159 (£199 for over-26s) for 30 days, except between 1 June and 30 Sept when it's £199/229. For 60 days, those prices are £199/249 and £249/279. Alternatively, **Busabout** runs every two or three days on five circuits in summer, fewer in winter, taking in the major cities of thirteen European countries, with add-on connections to five more, plus a link to London and through tickets from elsewhere in Britain and Ireland. Fifteen-day tickets are £199 for youth or student card-holders, £249 for others, rising to £275/345 for 21 days, £325/425 for a month, £485/595 for two months, £595/755 for three, and £720/895 for the whole season; there are also special deals on set itineraries. Busabout passes are available at travel agents in Britain, North America or Australasia (in the US, call ☎1/416-932 9377 for further details, in Canada call any branch of Travel CUTS, in Australia ☎02/9338 1533, in New Zealand ☎09/309 5973, and in Britain ☎0171/950 1661, or check Busabout's Web site at *www.busabout.com*).

DRIVING

In order to drive in Europe you need a full and up-to-date **driver's licence**; in Italy you need to carry a translation of this, available from your national motoring organization or the state tourist office, though this does not apply to EC-approved licences such as those now issued in Britain and Ireland, which are valid throughout the EU, and in theory elsewhere in Europe too. North American and Australasian licences are also in theory valid for driving in most of Europe (in Austria and Spain you need to carry a translation of this, available from your national motoring organization), but it is better to carry an International Driving Licence, especially if you want to rent a car. These are required in some East European countries and are available from national motoring organizations for a small fee; you'll need to show your driver's licence, passport, one passport photo and proof of age (eighteen or over). You should also carry your vehicle registration document at all times (if the named owner is not present on the trip you'll need a letter from them authorizing use of the vehicle). You should also, if taking your own vehicle, be insured: your existing insurance policy may already provide third-party cover for a certain period in Europe (this is frequently the case with British policies), but for some countries you will need to take out a supplementary policy. As proof of insurance cover, it's sensible to get hold of an International Green Card from your insurers – and it's obligatory in certain countries anyway. In case of breakdown, you can take out, at extra cost, extended cover with automobile associations, although the motoring organizations of most countries operate some kind of reciprocal **breakdown** agreement with members of most foreign motoring organizations, so if you are a member it's wise to have your membership documents with you as well. Your national organization can provide a list of countries with reciprocal arrangements. A nationality plate should be displayed on the rear of your vehicle, and a warning triangle (which must be displayed if you stop on the road) and first-aid kit are either required or advised throughout Europe. A fire extinguisher is obligatory in Estonia, Lithuania, Greece and Turkey. All the countries of mainland Europe drive on the right-hand side of the road, so your headlights should be adjusted accordingly, and priority to traffic coming from the right is a common rule of the road. Pretty much every country included in this book has a decent network of main roads; only when you get onto minor roads do the differences between southern, eastern and northwestern Europe become really apparent. In most of Europe motorways are free, but in some countries tolls are levied: in Greece, Spain and Portugal these are fairly cheap; in France they cost more but the primary roads there are invariably excellent; in Italy the cost can be substantial if you're travelling long distances. Fuel prices vary from around 60¢/35p for a litre of unleaded in Poland, or 70¢/43p in Luxembourg and the Czech Republic to $1.05/64p in Denmark, or $1.12/68p in the Netherlands and Finland; petrol is also pricey in Sweden, France and Italy, while in Eastern Europe, Spain and Switzerland it is generally cheap. Leaded petrol is being withdrawn in most European countries, and is already unavailable in a few.

The alternative to taking your own car is to **rent** one on the spot. Compared to rates in North America, this can be expensive, and you may find it cheaper to arrange things in advance through one of the multinational chains, or by opting for some kind of fly-drive deal. If you do rent a car in Europe, rates for a small hatchback start at £65/$100 a week (depending on the country and the time of year) if you book in advance with a firm like Holiday Autos, usually more if you rent on the spot; we've given more precise details in the relevant sections of the guide but in general costs are higher in Scandinavia and northern Europe, lower in eastern and southern Europe. Unlimited mileage deals (as opposed to those where you pay a charge per kilometre) work

MOTORING ORGANIZATIONS

American Automobile Association (AAA), 1000 AAA Drive, Heathrow, FL 32746–5063, USA (☎407/444 7000; *www.aaa.com*).

Australian Automobile Association, 212 Northbourne Ave, Braddon, Canberra, ACT 2601 (☎02/6247 7311).

Automobile Association (AA), Fanum House, Basingstoke, Hants RG21 2EA, UK (☎0990/500600; *www.theaa.co.uk*).

Automobile Association of Ireland (AA), 23 Suffolk St, Dublin 2, Ireland (☎01/283 3555).

Canadian Automobile Association (CAA), 1145 Hunt Club Rd, Suite 200, Ottawa, ON K1V 0Y3, Canada (☎613/247 0117; *www.caa.ca*).

New Zealand Automobile Association, 17/99 Albert St, Auckland 1 (☎09/377 4660; *www.nzaa.com*).

Royal Automobile Club (RAC), PO Box 1500, Bristol BS99 2LH, UK (☎0800/550055; *www.rac.co.uk*).

CAR RENTAL RESERVATION NUMBERS

Avis US & Canada ☎1-800/331 1084; UK ☎0181/848 8733; Ireland ☎01/605 7775; Australia ☎1800/225533; New Zealand ☎0800/655111 or ☎09/526 2847. *www.avis.com*

Budget, US & Canada ☎1-800/527 0700; UK ☎0800/181181; Ireland ☎0800/973159; Australia ☎13/2727; New Zealand ☎09/375 2222. *www.budgetrentacar.com*

Dollar (Europcar/Interrent) US & Canada ☎1-800/421 6868; UK ☎0345/222525; Ireland ☎01/874 5844. *www.europcar.com*

Hertz, US ☎1-800/654 3001; Canada ☎1-800/263 0600; UK ☎0990/996699; Ireland ☎01/676 7476;

Australia ☎13/3039; New Zealand ☎09/309 0989. *www.hertz.com*

Holiday Autos, US & Canada ☎1-800/422 7737; UK ☎0990/300400; Ireland ☎01/872 9366. *www.kemwel.com*

National, US & Canada ☎1-800/CAR RENT; UK ☎0990/365365; Ireland ☎021/320755; Australia ☎03/9329 5000; New Zealand ☎0800/800115. *www.nationalcar.com*

Thrifty US & Canada ☎1-800/367 2277; UK ☎01494/442110; Ireland ☎01/679 9420; Australia ☎02/9360 4055; New Zealand ☎09/275 6666. *www.thrifty.com*

out better value and give more flexibility. To rent a car you'll need to present your driving licence, sometimes also an international driver's permit, and should be at least 21 years of age with more than one year's driving experience, though these regulations can vary; if in doubt, check in advance with the car rental company or your home motoring organization. Note also that some firms don't allow you to take their cars across country borders.

HITCHING

If you're not sticking to a definite itinerary – and, in some countries, even if you are – hitching can be as good a way to get around as any, with the added advantages of being cheaper and much more sociable. When hitching, it's important to choose a place where a car can see you in good time and preferably has a place to pull over if they decide to pick you up. Hitching on motorways is illegal pretty much throughout Europe, in which case you should try motorway service stations or slip roads – though success at these can be patchy. Travel as light as possible – enormous backpacks tend to put drivers off – and carry a decent road map. Always look clean and presentable, and always, even if you have been waiting several hours for a lift, smile. Whether you use a sign or not is up to you: opinions differ about whether it helps, but it may put off drivers who could take you part of the way. Hitching is of course always a risky business and women in particular should be wary of hitching alone. As for when to hitch, obviously you should try to avoid hitching on Sundays and public holidays if possible, when traffic will be greatly reduced, and in general it's better to make an early start during the week, when you'll pick up most long-distance traffic. Germany is by far the best country in Europe to hitch in, though the Netherlands and Belgium are good, as in general are Britain and Ireland. Southern Europe can be patchy, while Scandinavia is notoriously bad for hitching. Though it might seem like cheating, there are a few countries (France and Germany most notably) which have hitchhiking organizations, whereby you pay a fee and they put you in touch with a driver going your way who wants to share petrol costs. This may seem to take the excitement out of hitching, but if you've been waiting several days for a lift it can be a godsend.

RED TAPE AND VISAS

Since the lifting of many immigration restrictions for European Union members in January 1993, border-crossing for most EU nationals has become a much less formal procedure, with holders of most passports just having to wave their documents at border officials. Border controls between some countries, Scandinavian states in particular, are virtually nonexistent, and ten EU states (Austria, Belgium, France, Germany, Greece, Italy, Luxembourg, the Netherlands, Portugal and Spain), known as the Schengen Group, now have joint visas valid for travel in all of them, and in theory no border immigration controls between them – though this may mean more ID checks within those countries. There is talk of other EU states joining the group, though two have left and others seem to be holding back.

Citizens of the UK (but not other British passport holders), Ireland, Australia, New Zealand, Canada and the USA do not need a **visa** to enter many European countries (exceptions are listed in the next paragraph), and can usually stay for up to three months; for some countries, your passport must be valid at least six months ahead.

Everyone needs a visa to visit Russia. UK and Irish citizens need them for Romania and Turkey (the latter available at the border). Americans need visas for Turkey (available at the border); Canadians need them for Bulgaria, Latvia, Poland and Romania. Australians require visas to visit Bulgaria, the Czech Republic, Hungary, Latvia, Poland, Romania and Slovakia; New Zealanders need them for Bulgaria, Hungary, Latvia, Lithuania, Poland, Slovakia and Romania. Note that the three Baltic states (Lithuania, Latvia and Estonia) all allow entry to New Zealanders (and most other visitors) who have a visa for any one of them. Note also that you will need transit visas to cross the Ukraine and Belarus (if travelling for example from Poland, Slovakia, Hungary or Romania to Moscow), though you are exempt in the case of Belarus if travelling on a through train to Russia and in possession of a Russian visa.

When **crossing a border**, it pays to look reasonably well turned-out, and to be polite at all times, even in the face of the most overweening officialdom. On entering some countries you may be asked to show an onward ticket or sufficient funds to support yourself. Remember that governments are eager for rich tourists with lots of money to spend, but accept poor, scruffy backpackers under sufferance. Non-whites may also get the feeling that they are only accepted under sufferance by border officials in some countries, and will often be subjected to much greater scrutiny than their white fellow travellers.

Finally, don't leave it too late to get a passport before leaving home, since this can take as long as four weeks by post and be rather irksome to have to do in person.

PASSPORT OFFICES

USA Passport Office, 1111 19th St NW, Washington, DC 20005 (☎1-900/225 5674 or 202/647 0518); others in Boston, Chicago, Honolulu, Houston, Los Angeles, Miami, New Orleans, New York, Philadelphia, San Francisco, Seattle and Stamford.

Canada Passport Office, Suite 209, West Tower, Guy Farreau Complex, 200 René Lévesque Blvd West, Montreal, PQ H2Z 1X4 (☎1-800/567-6868).

UK Passport Office, 70–78 Petty France, London SW1H 9HD (☎0990/210410); others in Belfast,

Glasgow, Liverpool, Newport and Peterborough. Applications can be made at any post office.

Ireland Passport Office, Molesworth St, Dublin 2 (☎01/679 7600) and 1a South Mall, Cork (☎021/272525).

Australia There are offices in Canberra, Sydney, Newcastle, Melbourne, Brisbane, Adelaide, Perth, Hobart and Darwin; for information, call ☎13/1232.

New Zealand Passport Office, Dept of Internal Affairs, PO Box 10 526, Wellington (☎04/474 8100).

EUROPEAN EMBASSIES

AUSTRIA USA 3524 International Court, NW, Washington, DC 20008–3022 (☎202/895 6700); **Canada** 445 Wilbrod St, Ottowa, ON K1N 6M7 (☎613/789 1444); **UK** 18 Belgrave Mews West, London SW1X 8HU (☎0171/235 3731); **Ireland** 15 Ailesbury Ct, 93 Ailesbury Rd, Dublin 4 (☎01/269 4577); **Australia** 15 Talbot St, Forrest, Canberra, ACT 2603 (☎02/6295 1533).

BELGIUM USA 3330 Garfield St, NW, Washington, DC 20008 (☎202/333 6900); **Canada** 80 Elgin St, 4th floor, Ottawa, ON K1P 1B7 (☎613/236 7267); **UK** 103–105 Eaton Sq, London SW1W 9AB (☎0171/470 3700); **Ireland** 2 Shrewsbury Rd, Dublin 4 (☎01/269 2082); **Australia** 19 Arkana St, Yarralumla, Canberra, ACT 2600 (☎02/6273 2501); **New Zealand** 12th floor, Willis Corroon House, 1–3 Willeston St, PO Box 3379, Wellington (☎04/472 9558).

BRITAIN USA 3100 Massachusetts Ave, NW, Washington, DC 20008 (☎202/588 6500); **Canada** 80 Elgin St, Ottawa, ON K1P 5K7 (☎613/237 1530); **Ireland** 29 Merrion Rd, Dublin 4 (☎01/205 3700); **Australia** CBS Tower, Akuna St (cnr Bunda St), Canberra City, ACT 2601 (☎02/6257 1982); **New Zealand** 44 Hill St, PO Box 1812, Wellington (☎04/472 6049).

BULGARIA USA 1621 22nd St, NW, Washington, DC 20008 (☎202/387 7969); **Canada** 325 Stewart St, Ottawa, ON K1N 6K5 (☎613/789 3215); **UK** 186–188 Queens Gate, London SW7 5HL (☎0171/584 9400); **Ireland** 2 Burlington Rd, Dublin 2 (☎01/660 3293).

CROATIA USA 2343 Massachusetts Ave, NW, Washington, DC 20008 (☎202/588 5899); **Canada** 130 Albert St, Suite 1700, Ottowa, ON K1P 5G4 (☎613/230 7351); **UK** 21 Conway St, London W1P 5HL (☎0171/387 1790); **Australia** 14 Jindalee Cres, O'Malley, Canberra, ACT 2606 (☎02/6286 6988); **New Zealand** 131 Lincoln Rd, Henderson, Auckland (☎09/836 5581).

CZECH REPUBLIC USA 3900 Spring of Freedom St, NW, Washington, DC 20008 (☎202/274 9100); **Canada** 541 Sussex Drive, Ottawa, ON K1N 6Z6 (☎613/562 3875); **UK** 26 Kensington Palace Gdns, London W8 4QY (☎0171/243 1115); **Ireland** 57 Northumberland Rd, Ballsbridge, Dublin 4 (☎01/668 1135); **Australia** 38 Culgoa Circuit, O'Malley, Canberra, ACT 2606 (☎02/6290 1386).

DENMARK USA 3200 Whitehaven St, NW, Washington, DC 20008–3683 (☎202/234 4300); **Canada** 47 Clarence St, Suite 450, Ottawa, ON K1N 9K1 (☎613/562 1811); **UK** 55 Sloane St, London SW1X 9SR (☎0171/333 0200); **Ireland** 121–122 St Stephen's Green, Dublin 2 (☎01/475 6404); **Australia** 15 Hunter St, Yarralumla, Canberra, ACT 2600 (☎02/6273 2195); **New Zealand** Morrison Morpeth House, 105 The Terrace, PO Box 10035, Wellington (☎04/472 0020).

ESTONIA USA 2131 Massachusetts Ave, NW, Washington, DC 20008 (☎202/588 0101); **Canada** 958 Broadview Ave, Toronto, ON M4K 2R6 (☎416/461 0764); **UK** 16 Hyde Park Gate, London SW7 5DG (☎0171/589 3428); **Ireland** 24 Merlyn Park, Dublin 4 (☎01/269 1552).

FINLAND USA 3301 Massachusetts Ave, NW, Washington, DC 20008 (☎202/298 5800); **Canada** 55 Metcalfe St, Suite 850, Ottawa, ON K1P 6L5 (☎613/236 2389); **UK** 38 Chesham Pl, London SW1W 8HW (☎0171/838 6200); **Ireland** Russell House, Stokes Pl, St Stephen's Green, Dublin 2 (☎01/478 1344); **Australia** 10 Darwin Ave, Yarralumla, Canberra, ACT 2600 (☎02/6273 3800); **New Zealand** 44–52 The Terrace, PO Box 2402, Wellington (☎04/499 4599).

FRANCE USA 4101 Reservoir Rd, NW, Washington, DC 20007 (☎202/944 6000); **Canada** 42 Sussex Drive, Ottawa, ON K1M 2C9 (☎613/789 1795); **UK** 6A Cromwell Rd, London SW7 2EW (☎0171/838 2050); **Ireland** 36 Ailesbury Rd, Ballsbridge, Dublin 4 (☎01/260 1666); **Australia** 6 Perth Ave, Yarralumla, Canberra, ACT 2600 (☎02/6216 0100); **New Zealand** 13th floor, Willis Corroon Hse, 1 Willeston St, PO Box 1695, Wellington (☎04/472 0200).

GERMANY USA 4645 Reservoir Rd, NW, Washington, DC 20007–1998 (☎202/298 4000); **Canada** 1 Waverley St, 14th floor, Ottawa, ON K2P 0T8 (☎613/232 1101); **UK** 23 Belgrave Square, London SW1X 8PZ (☎0171/824 1300); **Ireland** 31 Trimleston Ave, Booterstown, Blackrock, Co Dublin (☎01/269 3011); **Australia** 119 Empire Circuit, Yarralumla, Canberra, ACT 2600 (☎02/6273 3193); **New Zealand** 90–92 Hobson St, PO Box 1687, Thorndon, Wellington (☎04/473 6063).

GREECE USA 2221 Massachusetts Ave, NW, Washington, DC 20008 (☎202/939 5800); **Canada** 76–80 MacLaren St, Ottawa, ON K2P 0K6 (☎613/238 6271); **UK** 1a Holland Park, London W11 3TP (☎0171/229 3850); **Ireland** 1 Upper Pembroke St, Dublin 2 (☎01/676 7254); **Australia** 9 Turrana St, Yarralumla, Canberra, ACT 2600 (☎02/6273 3011).

HUNGARY USA 3910 Shoemaker St, NW, Washington, DC 20008 (☎202/362 6730); **Canada** 299 Waverley St, Ottawa, ON K2P 0V9 (☎613/230 2717); **UK** 35b Eaton Pl, London SW1X 8BY (☎0171/235 5218); **Ireland** 2 Fitzwilliam Pl, Dublin 2 (☎01/661 2902); **Australia** 17 Beale Cres, Deakin, Canberra, ACT 2600 (☎02/6282 3226).

IRELAND USA 2234 Massachusetts Ave, NW, Washington, DC 20008 (☎202/462 3939); **Canada** 130 Albert St, Suite 1105, Ottawa, ON K1P 5G4 (☎613/233 6281); **UK** 17 Grosvenor Pl, London SW1X 7HR (☎0171/235 2171); **Australia** 20 Arkana St, Yarralumla, Canberra, ACT 2600 (☎02/6273 3022).

ITALY USA 1601 Fuller St, NW, Washington, DC 20009 (☎202/328 5500); **Canada** 275 Slater St, 21st floor, Ottawa, ON K1P 5H9 (☎613/232 2401); **UK** 14 Three Kings Yard, Davies St, London W1Y 2EH (☎0171/312 2200); **Ireland** 63–65 Northumberland Rd, Dublin 4 (☎01/660 1744); **Australia** 12 Grey St, Deakin, Canberra, ACT 2600 (☎02/6273 3333); **New Zealand** 34–38 Grant Rd, Thorndon, PO Box 463, Wellington (☎04/473 5339).

LATVIA USA 4325 17th St, NW, Washington, DC 20011 (☎202/726 8213); **Canada** 112 Kent St, Suite 208, Place de Ville, Tower B, Ottawa, ON K1P 5P2 (☎613/238 6868); **UK** 45 Nottingham Pl, London W1M 3FE (☎0171/312 0040).

LITHUANIA USA 2622 16th St, NW, Washington, DC 20009 (☎202/234 5860); **UK** 84 Gloucester Pl, London W1H 3HN (☎0171/486 6401).

LUXEMBOURG USA 2200 Massachusetts Ave, NW, Washington, DC 20008 (☎202/265 4171); **UK** 27 Wilton Crescent, London SW1X 8SD (☎0171/235 6961).

MOROCCO USA 1601 21st St, NW, Washington, DC 20009 (☎202/462 7979); **Canada** 38 Range Rd, Ottawa, ON K1N 8J4 (☎613/236 7391); **UK** 49 Queen's Gate Gdns, London SW7 5NE (☎0171/581 5001); **Ireland** 53 Raglan Rd, Ballsbridge, Dublin 4 (☎01/660 9449).

NETHERLANDS USA 4200 Linnean Ave, NW, Washington, DC 20008 (☎202/244 5300); **Canada** 350 Albert St, Suite 2020, Ottawa, ON K1R 1A4 (☎613/237 5030); **UK** 38 Hyde Park Gate, London SW7 5DP (☎0171/580 3200); **Ireland** 160 Merrion Rd, Dublin 4 (☎01/269 3444); **Australia** 120 Empire Circuit, Yarralumla, Canberra, ACT 2600 (☎02/6273 3111); **New Zealand** Investment Centre, 10th Floor, cnr Ballance St & Featherstone St, PO Box 840, Wellington (☎04/473 8652).

NORWAY USA 2720 34th St, NW, Washington, DC 20008–2714 (☎202/333 6000); **Canada** 90 Sparks St, Suite 532, Ottawa, ON K1P 5B4 (☎613/238 6571); **UK** 25 Belgrave Sq, London SW1X 8QD (☎0171/591 5500); **Ireland** 34 Molesworth St, Dublin 2 (☎01/662 1800); **Australia** 17 Hunter St, Yarralumla, Canberra, ACT 2600 (☎02/6273 3444); **New Zealand** 61 Molesworth St, Wellington (☎04/471 2503).

POLAND USA 2640 16th St, NW, Washington, DC 20009 (☎202/234 3800); **Canada** 443 Daly Ave, Ottawa, ON K1N 6H3 (☎613/789 0468); **UK** 47 Portland Pl, London W1N 4JH (☎0171/580 4324); **Ireland** 5 Ailesbury Rd, Dublin 4 (☎01/283 0855); **Australia** 7 Turrana St, Yarralumla, Canberra, ACT 2600 (☎02/6273 1208); **New Zealand** 17 Upland Rd, PO Box 10211, Kelburn, Wellington (☎04/471 2456).

PORTUGAL USA 2125 Kalorama Rd, NW, Washington, DC 20008 (☎202/328 8610); **Canada** 645 Island Park Drive, Ottawa, ON K1Y 0B8 (☎613/729 0883); **UK** 11 Belgrave Sq, London SW1X 8PP (☎0171/235 5331); **Ireland** Knocksinna House, Foxrock, Dublin 18 (☎01/289 4416); **Australia** 23 Culgoa Circuit, O'Malley, Canberra, ACT 2606 (☎02/6290 1733); **New Zealand** 85 Fort St, Auckland (☎09/309 1454).

ROMANIA USA 1607 23rd St, NW, Washington, DC 20008 (☎202/232 3694); **Canada** 655 Rideau St, Ottawa, ON K1N 6A3 (☎613/789 3709); **UK** 4 Palace Green, London W8 4QD (0171/937 9667); **Ireland** 47 Ailesbury Rd, Dublin 4 (☎01/269 2852); **Australia** 4 Dalman Cres, O'Malley, Canberra, ACT 2606 (☎02/6286 2343).

RUSSIA USA 2650 Wisconsin Ave, NW, Washington, DC 20007 (☎202/298 5700); **Canada** 285 Charlotte St, Ottawa ON K1N 8L5 (☎613/235 4341); **UK** 13 Kensington Palace Gdns, London W8 4QX (☎0171/229 3628); **Ireland** 186 Orwell Rd, Rathgar, Dublin 14 (☎01/492 2048); **Australia** 76 Canberra Ave, Griffith, Canberra, ACT 2603 (☎02/6295 9033);

New Zealand 57 Messines Rd, Karori, Wellington (☎04/476 6742).

SLOVAKIA USA 2201 Wisconsin Ave, Suite 250, NW, Washington, DC 20007 (☎202/965 5160); **Canada** 50 Rideau Terr, Ottawa, ON K1M 2A1 (☎613/749 4442); **UK** 25 Kensington Palace Gdns, London W8 4QY (☎0171/243 0803); **Ireland** 18 Hampton Cres, St Helen's Wood, Booterstown, Co Dublin (☎01/283 4958); **Australia** 47 Culgoa Circuit, O'Malley, Canberra, ACT 2606 (☎02/6290 1516).

SLOVENIA USA 1525 New Hampshire Ave, NW, Washington, DC 20036–1203 (☎202/667 5363); **Canada** 150 Metcalfe St, Suite 2101, Ottawa, ON K2P 1P1 (☎613/565 5781); **UK** Suite 1, Cavendish Ct, 11–15 Wigmore St, London W1H 9LA (☎0171/495 7775); **Australia** Level 6, Advance Bank Center, 60 Marcus Clarke St, Canberra City, ACT 2601 (☎02/6243 4830).

SPAIN USA 2375 Pennsylvania Ave, NW, Washington, DC 20037 (☎202/452 0100); **Canada** 74 Stanley Ave, Ottawa, ON K1M 1P4 (☎613/747 2252); **UK** 20 Draycott Place, London SW3 2SB (☎0891/600123 premium-rate charged for calls); **Ireland** 17a Merlyn Park, Dublin 4 (☎01/269 1640); **Australia** PO Box 9076, Deakin, Canberra, ACT 2600 (☎02/6273 3555).

SWEDEN USA 1501 M St, NW, Washington, DC 20005–1702 (☎202/467 2600); **Canada** 377 Dalhousie St, Ottawa, ON K1N 9N8 (☎613/241 8553); **UK** 11 Montagu Place, London W1H 2AL (☎0171/917 6400); **Ireland** Sun Alliance House, 13–17 Dawson St, Dublin 2 (☎01/671 5822); **Australia** 5 Turrana St, Yarralumla, Canberra, ACT 2600 (☎02/6270 2700); **New Zealand** 13th floor, Vogel Bldg, Aitken St, Thorndon, PO Box 12538, Wellington (☎04/499 9895).

SWITZERLAND USA 2900 Cathedral Ave, NW, Washington, DC 20008–3499 (☎202/745 7900); **Canada** 5 Marlborough Ave, Ottawa, ON K1N 8E6 (☎613/235 1837); **UK** 16–18 Montagu Place, London W1H 2BQ (☎0171/616 6000); **Ireland** 6 Ailesbury Rd, Ballsbridge, Dublin 4 (☎01/269 2515); **Australia** 7 Melbourne Ave, Forrest, Canberra, ACT 2603 (☎02/6273 3977); **New Zealand** Panama House, 22 Panama St, Wellington (☎04/472 1593).

TURKEY USA 1714 Massachusetts Ave, NW, Washington, DC 20036 (☎202/659 8200); **Canada** 197 Wurtemburg St, Ottawa, ON K1N 8L9 (☎613/789 4044); **UK** 43 Belgrave Sq, London SW1X 8PA (☎0171/393 0202); **Ireland** 11 Clyde Rd, Ballsbridge, Dublin 4 (☎01/668 5240); **Australia** 60 Mugga Way, Red Hill, Canberra, ACT 2603 (☎02/6295 0227); **New Zealand** 15–17 Murphy St, Level 8, PO Box 12–248, Wellington (☎04/472 1292).

CUSTOMS

Customs and duty-free restrictions vary throughout Europe, but are standard for EU countries at one litre of spirits, plus two litres of table wine, plus 200 cigarettes (or 250g tobacco, or fifty cigars). Since the inauguration of the Single Market, travellers between EU countries can effectively carry as much in the way of duty-paid goods as they want (so long as they are for personal use). Remember that carrying contraband such as controlled drugs, firearms or pornography is illegal, not to mention foolhardy in the extreme. If you are carrying prescribed drugs of any kind, it might be a good idea to have a copy of the prescription to flash at suspicious customs officers. If in doubt consult the relevant embassy.

HEALTH AND INSURANCE

EU citizens resident in the UK or Ireland are covered by reciprocal health agreements for free or reduced-cost emergency treatment in many of the countries in this book (main exceptions are the Baltic states, Switzerland, Slovenia, Morocco and Turkey). To claim this, you will often need only your passport, but you may also be asked for your NHS card or proof of residence. In EU countries and Norway, far from being simpler, you'll also need form E111, available from post offices, DSS offices and travel agents, which you must get before you leave. Without an E111 you won't be turned away from hospitals but you will almost certainly have to pay for any treatment or medicines. Also, in practice, some countries' doctors and hospitals charge anyway and it's up to you to claim reimbursement when you return home. **Make sure you are insured for potential medical expenses, and keep copies of receipts and prescriptions.**

There aren't many particular **health problems** you'll encounter travelling in most parts of Europe. You don't need to have any inoculations for any of the countries covered in this book, although for Morocco and Turkey typhoid jabs are advised, and for some parts of those countries, even malaria pills are advisable. When travelling, it's always a good idea to be up to date with your polio and tetanus boosters.

Tap water in most countries is drinkable, though you may prefer bottled mineral water, either for the taste (mains supply in some places can be very hard or heavily chlorinated), or to be on the safe side, though you only need to avoid tap water altogether in southern Morocco and parts of Turkey. Diarrhoea and sickness from tap water or – in southern Europe – food, are reasonably likely, if only in a mild form. The best thing to do is carry anti-diarrhoea tablets with you at all times. One of the biggest problems you may face if travelling in southern Europe is the **sun**: don't spend too much time in direct sunlight if you're not used to it, and certainly not without any kind of sun block cream; just half an hour on your first day's sunbathing is probably the limit – more than this can leave you beetroot-red and nauseated. **Mosquitoes**, too, are a problem Europe-wide, especially in the south and places where there's a lot of water around; the Netherlands, for example, harbours particularly virulent species. It's hard to know what to do about them: most people develop an immunity after a few days' exposure; until then an antihistamine cream like *phenergan* is the best antidote; Tiger Balm also works. Finally, AIDS is as much of a problem in Europe as it is in the rest of the world, and it hardly needs saying that unprotected casual sex is highly inadvisable.

For **minor health problems** it's easiest to go to the local pharmacy. You'll find these pretty much everywhere and we've detailed out-of-hours ones in the text. In **more serious cases** your nearest consulate will have a list of English-speaking doctors, as will the local tourist office, and in the larger cities we've listed the most convenient casualty departments (emergency rooms).

INSURANCE

Wherever you're travelling from, it's a very good idea to have some kind of **travel** insurance to cover you for loss of possessions and money as well as the cost of medical and dental treatment. But before buying an insurance policy, check to see what you are already covered for. This particularly applies to travellers from the USA and Canada. Internationally, **credit and charge cards** (particularly American Express) often have certain levels of medical or other insurance included, and travel insurance may also be included if you use a major credit or charge card to pay for your trip. Some package tours too may include insurance, but package operators more commonly offer an insurance deal as an extra: it might be worth checking against alternative policies, though differences in prices and cover are likely to be slight.

Always check the fine print of a policy. A 24-hour medical emergency contact number is a must, and one of the rare policies that pays your medical bills directly is better than one that reimburses you on your return home.

The per-article limit for loss or theft should cover your most valuable possession (a camcorder for example) but, conversely, don't pay for cover you don't need – such as too much baggage or a huge sum for personal liability. Make sure too that you are covered for all the things you intend to do. Activities such as skiing, climbing and scuba diving are usually specifically excluded, but can be added for a supplement, usually 20–50 percent.

For **travellers from North America**, an important thing to bear in mind is that most policies do not insure against **theft** of any kind while overseas, but apply only to items lost from, or damaged in, the custody of an identifiable, responsible third party (hotel porter, airline, baggage deposit, etc). Even in these cases you will have to contact the local police to have a complete **report** made out so that your insurer can process the claim.

Canadian provincial health plans typically provide some overseas medical coverage, although they are unlikely to pick up the full tab. Holders of official **student/teacher/youth cards** are also entitled to accident coverage and hospital in-patient benefits (annual membership is far less than the cost of comparable insurance), while university students will often find that their student health coverage extends during the vacations and for one term beyond the date of last enrolment. Finally, homeowners' or renters' insurance often covers theft or loss of documents, money and valuables while overseas, though conditions and maximum amounts vary from company to company.

If you do want a specific **travel insurance policy**, there are numerous kinds to choose from: your travel agent can usually recommend one. In the **US and Canada**, the best **premiums** are usually to be had through student/youth travel agencies; STA, for example, currently have policies available at $48–69 for 15 days (depending on the level of coverage), $80–105 for a month, $147–207 for two months, or $510–700 for a year. In the **UK**, a policy issued by a specialist travel firm like Usit Campus or STA (see pp.13–14 for addresses), or by the low-cost insurers Endsleigh Insurance and Columbus Travel Insurance should cost in the region of £28 per month for Europe and the Mediterranean (check that this includes Russia and the Baltic States if you are planning to visit them); annual cover works out a lot cheaper – around £60–110 for a year depending on the maximum length of single trips allowed within that period, which varies from one to four months. For couples or flatmates, Worldwide offer an annual multi-trip policy to any two people resident at the same address, costing £89 for trips up to 31 days, £109 for 62-day trips. In **Ireland**, Travel insurance is best obtained through a travel specialist such as USIT (see p.17). Their policies cost IR£23 for 6–10 days, IR£29 for one month. Discounts are offered to students of any age and anyone under 35. In **Australia and New Zealand**, travel insurance is put together by the airlines and travel agent groups such as Cover-More and Ready Plan in conjunction with insurance companies. Policies can be purchased from most travel agents (see p.19) or direct from insurance companies (see below). They are all similar in premium and coverage, however Ready Plan give the best value for money coverage. Adventure sports are usually covered, except mountaineering with ropes, bungee jumping and unassisted diving without an Open Water licence, so check your policy if you plan on doing any of these. A typical policy will cost A$110/NZ$130 for 2 weeks, A$180/NZ$200 for 1 month, A$280/NZ$300 for 2 months.

INSURANCE COMPANIES AND AGENTS

NORTH AMERICA

Access America, PO Box 90310, Richmond, VA 23230 (☎1-800/284 8300).

Carefree Travel Insurance, PO Box 9366, Garden City, NY 11530-9366 (☎1-800/323 3149).

Desjardins Travel Insurance 200 Ave des Commandeurs, Lévis, PQ G6V 6R2 (☎1-800/463 7830).

STA Travel, 10 Downing St, New York, NY 10014 (☎1-800/781 4040). *www.sta-travel.com*

Travel Assistance International, 1133 15th St NW, Suite 400, Washington, DC 20005 (☎1-800/821 2828).

Travel Guard, 1145 Clark St, Stevens Point, WI 54481 (☎1-800/826 1300). *www.noelgroup.com*

Travel Insurance Services, 2930 Camino Diablo, Suite 200, Walnut Creek, CA 94596 (☎1-800/937 1387).

UK

Columbus Travel Insurance, 17 Devonshire Sq, London EC2M 4SQ (☎0171/375 0011).

Endsleigh Insurance, 97–107 Southampton Row, London WC1B 4AG (☎0171/436 4451).

Marcus Hearn & Co 65–66 Shoreditch High St, London E1 6JL (☎0171/739 3444).

Worldwide, The Business Centre, 1–7 Commercial Rd, Tonbridge, Kent TN12 6YT (☎01892/833338).

AUSTRALASIA

Cover More, 9/32 Walker St, North Sydney, NSW 2060 (☎02/9202 8000 & 1800/251881).

Ready Plan, 141 Walker St, Dandenong, Vic 3175 (☎03/9791 5077 & 1800/337 462); 10/63 Albert St, Auckland (☎09/379 3208).

INFORMATION AND MAPS

Before you leave, it's worth contacting the tourist offices of the countries you're intending to visit, since most produce copious quantities of free leaflets, maps and brochures, some of which can be quite useful, both in planning your trip and when you're travelling. This is especially true for parts of central and eastern Europe, where up-to-date maps in particular are often scarcer in the country than in their tourist offices abroad. Also note that Estonia, Latvia, Lithuania and Russia do not have official tourist offices, but it may help to contact their embassies for more information. For the rest of Europe go easy, though: much of the information these places pump out can be picked up just as easily on your travels, and it can weigh a ton. Note that in Britain, far from encouraging potential visitors to call for information, national tourist boards of certain countries see this as an

opportunity to fleece the punter even before arrival with 0891 numbers and drawn-out taped messages – in fact it is usually cheaper to make an international call to their US offices.

TOURIST INFORMATION OFFICES ABROAD

AUSTRIA USA PO Box 1142, New York, NY 10108–1142 (☎212/944 6880); **UK** 14 Cork St, London W1X 1PF (☎0171/629 0461); **Australia** 36 Carrington St, 1st Floor, Sydney, NSW 2000 (☎02/9299 3621; www.austria-tourism.at).

BELGIUM USA 780 3rd Ave, Suite 1501, New York, NY 10017–7076 (☎212/758 8130); **UK** 13 Pepper St, London E14 9RW (☎0891/887799 – premium rates charged for calls; www.visitbelgium.com).

BRITAIN USA 551 5th Ave, 7th floor, New York, NY 10176 (☎1-800/GO2 BRITAIN or ☎212/986 2200); **Canada** 5915 Airport Rd, Suite 120, Mississauga, ON L4V 1T1 (☎1-888/VISIT UK or ☎905/405 1840); **Ireland** 18–19 College Green, Dublin 2 (☎01/670 8000); **Australia** Commonwealth Ave, Yarralumla, Canberra, ACT 2600 (☎0055/20273); **New Zealand** 44 Hill St, PO Box 1812, Wellington 1 (☎04/472 6049).

BULGARIA USA c/o Balkantourist, 181 E 86th St, New York, NY 10028 (☎212/722 1110).

CROATIA USA 350 5th Ave, Suite 4003, New York, NY 10118 (☎1-800/829 4416); **UK** 2 The Lanchesters, 162–164 Fulham Palace Rd, London W6 9ER (☎0181/563 7979; www.htz.hr).

CZECH REPUBLIC USA 1109 Madison Ave, New York, NY 10028 (☎212/288 0830); **Canada** 22 College St, Suite 200, Toronto, ON M5G 1Y6 (☎416/929 3700); **UK** 19 Great Portland St, London W1N 5RA (☎0171/291 9925; www.czech-tourinfo.cz).

DENMARK USA 655 3rd Ave, New York, NY 10017 (☎212/949 2326); **Canada** PO Box 115, Station N, Toronto, ON (☎416/823 9620); **UK** 55 Sloane St, London SW1X 9SY (☎0171/259 5959; www.dt.dk).

FINLAND USA PO Box 4649, Grand Central Station, New York, NY 10163–4649 (☎212/885 9700); **UK** 3rd floor, 30–35 Pall Mall, London SW1Y 5LP (☎0171/839 4048; www.mek.fi).

FRANCE USA 444 Madison Ave, 16th floor, New York, NY 10022 (☎202/331-1530); **Canada** 1981 Av McGill College, Suite 490, Montreal, PQ H3A 2W9 (☎514/288 4264); **UK** 178 Piccadilly, London W1V 0AL (☎0171/629 1272); **Ireland** 10 Suffolk St, Dublin 2 (☎01/703 4046); **Australia** 12 Castlereagh St, 12th floor, Sydney, NSW 2000 (☎02/9231 5244; www.franceguide.com).

GERMANY USA 122 E 42nd St, 52nd floor, New York, NY 10168–0072 (☎212/661 7200); **Canada** 175 Bloor St E, North Tower, Suite 604, Toronto, ON M4W 3R8 (☎416/968 1570); **UK** PO Box 2695, London W1A 3TN (☎0891/600100 – premium rates charged for calls); **Australia** c/o 143 Macquarie St, Sydney, NSW 2000 (☎02/9267 8148; www.germany-tourism.de).

GREECE USA Olympic Tower, 645 5th Ave, New York, NY 10022 (☎212/421 5777); **Canada** 1300 Bay St, Toronto, ON M5R 3K8 (☎416/968 2220); **UK** 4 Conduit St, London W1R 0DJ (☎0171/734 5997); **Australia** 51 Pitt St, Sydney, NSW 2000 (☎02/9241 1663; www.vacation.net.gr).

HUNGARY USA 150 E 58th St, 33rd Floor, New York, NY 10155 (☎212 355 0240); **UK** 41 Eaton Pl, London W1X 8AL (☎0171/823 1055; www.hungary.com).

IRELAND USA 345 Park Ave, New York, NY 10154 (☎212/418 0800); **UK** 150 New Bond St, London W1Y 0AQ (☎0171/518 0800); **Australia** 5th Level, 36 Carrington St, Sydney, NSW 2000 (☎02/9299 6177); **New Zealand** c/o Walshe's World Ltd, Dingwall Bldg, 87 Queen St, Auckland 1 (☎09/379 3708; www.ireland.travel.ie).

ITALY USA 630 5th Ave, Suite 1565, New York, NY 10111 (☎212/245 4822); **Canada** 1 pl Ville Marie, Suite 1914, Montreal, PQ H3B 3M9 (☎514/866 7667); **UK** 1 Princes St, London W1R 8AY (☎0171/408 1254; *www.enit.it*).

LUXEMBOURG USA 17 Beekman Pl, New York, NY 10022 (☎212/935 8888); **UK** 122–124 Regent St, London W1R 5FE (☎0171/434 2800; *www.luxembourg.co.uk*).

MOROCCO USA 20 E 46th St, New York, NY 10017 (☎212/557 2520); **Canada** 2001 Rue Université, Suite 1460, Montreal, PQ H3A 2A6 (☎514/842 8111); **UK** 205 Regent St, London W1R 7DE (☎0171/437 0073); **Australia** 11 West St North, Sydney, NSW 2060 (☎02/9922 4999; *www.morocco.com*).

NETHERLANDS USA 355 Lexington Ave, 21st floor, New York, NY 10017 (☎1-888/246 5526); **Canada** 25 Adelaide St E, Suite 710, Toronto, ON M5C 1YL (☎1-888/246 5526); **UK** 25–28 Buckingham Gate, London SW1E 6LD (☎0891/717777 – premium rates charged for calls; *www.visitholland.com*).

NORWAY USA 655 3rd Ave, Suite 1810, New York, NY 10017 (☎212/885 9700); **UK** Charles House, 5–11 Lower Regent St, London SW1Y 4LR (☎0171/839 6255; *www.tourist.no*).

POLAND USA 275 Madison Ave, Suite 1711, New York, NY 10016 (☎1-800/PORTUGAL);**UK** 310–312 Regent St, 1st floor, London W1R 5AJ (☎0171/580 8811; *www.poland.net/travelpage*).

PORTUGAL USA 590 5th Ave, New York, NY 10036 (☎212/354 4403); **Canada** 60 Bloor St W, Suite 1005, Toronto, ON M4W 3B8 (☎416/921 7376); **UK** 2nd floor,

22–25a Sackville St, London W1X 1DE (☎0171/494 1441); **Ireland** 54 Dawson St, Dublin 2 (☎01/670 9133; *www.portugal-insite.pt*).

ROMANIA USA 14 E 38th St, 12th floor, New York, NY 10016 (☎212/545 8484; *www.embassy.org/romania/travel/tour-off.html*).

SLOVENIA USA 345 E 12th St, New York, NY 10003 (☎212/358 9686; *www.tourist-board.si*).

SPAIN USA 666 5th Ave, New York, NY 10103 (☎212/265 8822); **Canada** 2 Bloor St W, 34th floor, Toronto, ON M4W 3E2 (☎416/961 3131);**UK** 22–23 Manchester Sq, London W1M 5AP (☎0171/486 8077).

SWEDEN USA 655 3rd Ave, 18th floor, New York, NY 10017–5617 (☎212/885 9700); **UK** 11 Montagu Pl, London W1H 2AL (☎0171/724 5868; *www.sweden.gvg.org*).

SWITZERLAND USA 608 5th Ave, New York, NY 10020 (☎212/757 5944); **Canada** 926 East Mall, Etobicoke, ON M9B 6K1 (☎416/695 2090); **UK** Swiss Centre, New Coventry St, London W1V 8EE (☎0171/734 1921); **Australia** c/o Swissair, 33 Pitt St, Sydney, NSW 2000 (☎02/9231 3744; *www.switzerland.tourism.ch*).

TURKEY USA 821 UN Plaza, New York, NY 10017 (☎212/687 2194); **Canada** 360 Albert St, Suite 801, Ottawa, ON K1R 7X7 (☎613/230 8654); **UK** 170–173 Piccadilly, London W1V 9DD (☎0171/629 7771); **Australia** Suite 101, 280 George St, Sydney, NSW 2000 (☎02/9223 3055).

If no office in your home country is listed here, apply to the embassy.

INFORMATION ON THE ROAD

Once you're travelling in Europe, you'll find on-the-spot information easy enough to pick up. Most countries have a well-equipped and widespread network of tourist offices that answer queries, dole out a range of (sometimes free) maps and brochures, and can sometimes book accommodation, or at least advise you on the best-value places if you're stuck. Tourist offices are, as you might expect, better organized in northern Europe – Scandinavia, the Netherlands, France – with branches in all but the smallest village, with mounds of information; in Greece, Turkey and eastern Europe you'll find tourist offices more infrequent and less helpful on the whole, sometimes offering no more than a couple of dog-eared brochures and a photocopied map. We've given further details, including a broad idea of opening hours, in "Practicalities" for each country.

MAPS

Whether you're doing a grand tour or confining yourself to one or two countries you will need a decent map. Though you can often buy these (or sometimes better, locally produced alternatives) on the spot, you may want to get them in advance to plan your trip – if you know what you want, Stanfords in London (perhaps the world's best map shop) and Rand McNally in the US both do maps by mail order.

Good road maps covering the whole continent include Lascelles's 1:2,600,000 map and Hallwag's 1:3,600,000 version, both of which show the road networks pretty well, though they omit most of Turkey and Morocco; of the two, only Hallwag shows railways, and not very clearly. Michelin's (1:3,000,000) is cheaper but less clear and doesn't show road numbers; nor does Kümmerley and Frey's (1:5,000,000), though it does cover Turkey and Morocco. A possible compromise is the Marco Polo map (1:4,500,000), which shows the main road routes and covers Turkey. For extensive motoring, it is better to get a large-page road atlas such as Michelin's *Tourism and Road Atlas*. If you intend to trvael mainly by rail, on the other hand, it might be worth getting the *Thomas Cook Rail Map of Europe* or Geo-Center's *Euro-Map Rail Map of Europe*. We've recommended the best maps of individual countries throughout the book. In general, though, you'll find the best series to be Bartholomew/RV, Kümmerley & Frey or Hallwag, or, in North America, those published by Rand McNally. For plans of over fifty European cities, the Falk series of detailed, indexed maps are excellent, and easy to use.

TRAVEL BOOK AND MAP OUTLETS

USA

Chicago: Rand McNally, 444 N Michigan Ave, IL 60611 (☎312/321 1751).

Maryland: Travel Books & Language Center, 4931 Cordell Ave, Bethseda, MD 20814 (☎1-800/220 2665).

New York: The Complete Traveler Bookstore, 199 Madison Ave, NY 10016 (☎212/685 9007); Rand McNally, 150 E 52nd St, NY 10022 (☎212/758 7488); Traveler's Bookstore, 22 W 52nd St, NY 10019 (☎212/664 0995).

Palo Alto: Phileas Fogg's Books & Maps, #87 Stanford Shopping Center, CA 94304 (☎1-800/533 FOGG).

San Francisco: Rand McNally, 595 Market St, CA 94105 (☎415/777 3131); Sierra Club Bookstore, 6014 College Ave, Oakland, CA 94618 (☎510/658 7470).

Santa Barbara: Map Link, 30 S La Petera Lane, Unit #5, CA 93117 (☎805/692 6777).

Vermont: Adventurous Traveler Bookstore, PO Box 1468, Williston, VT 05495 (☎1-800/282 3963; www.AdventurousTraveler.com).

Washington DC: The Map Store, 1636 1st St, DC 20006 (☎202/628 2608).

●Rand McNally have stores across the US; call ☎1-800/333 0136 (ext 2111) for the address of your nearest store, or for **direct mail** maps.

CANADA

Montreal: Ulysses Travel Bookshop, 4176 St-Denis, PQ H2W 2M5 (☎514/843 9447).

Toronto: Open Air Books and Maps, 25 Toronto St, ON M5R 2C1 (☎416/363 0719).

Vancouver: World Wide Books and Maps, 552 Seymour St, BC V6B 3J5 (☎604/687 3320).

UK AND IRELAND

London: Daunt Books, 83 Marylebone High St, W1M 3DE (☎0171/224 2295); 193 Haverstock Hill, NW3 4QL (☎0171/794 4006); National Map Centre, 22–24 Caxton St, SW1H 0QU (☎0171/222 2466; www.mapsworld.com), Stanfords, 12–14 Long Acre, WC2E 9LP (☎0171/836 1321), in the Usit Campus shop at 52 Grosvenor Gardens, SW1W 0AG (☎0171/730 1314), and in the British Airways shop at 156 Regent St, W1R 5TA (☎0171/434 4744); The Travel Bookshop, 13–15 Blenheim Crescent, W11

2EE (☎0171/229 5260; www.thetravelbookshop.co.uk).

Dublin: Eason's, 40 O'Connell St, Dublin 1 (☎01/873 3811); Waterstone's, 7 Dawson St, Dublin 2 (☎01/679 1415).

Belfast: Waterstone's, Queens Bldg, 8 Royal Ave, BT1 1DA (☎01232/247355).

Bristol: Stanfords, 29 Corn Street, BS1 1HT (☎0117/929 9966).

Cambridge: Heffers Map Shop, 3rd Floor, 19 Sidney St, CB2 3HL (☎01223/568467; www.heffers.co.uk).

Cardiff: Blackwell's, 13–17 Royal Arcade, CF1 2PR (☎01222/395036).

Glasgow: John Smith and Sons, 57–61 St Vincent St, G2 5TB (☎0141/221 7472; www.johnsmith.co.uk).

Inverness: James Thin Melven's Bookshop, 29 Union St, IV1 1QA (☎01463/233500; www.jthin.co.uk).

Leicester: The Map Shop, 30a Belvoir St, LE1 6QH (☎0116/247 1400).

Manchester: *Waterstone's*, 91 Deansgate, M3 2BW (☎0161/832 1992; www.waterstones.co.uk).

Newcastle: Newcastle Map Centre, 55 Grey St, NE1 6EF (☎0191/261 5622).

Oxford: Blackwell's Map and Travel Shop, 53 Broad St OX1 3BQ (☎01865/792792).

Worcestershire: The Map Shop, 15 High St, Upton-upon-Severn, WR8 0HJ (☎01684/593146; www.themapshop.co.uk).

●Maps by **mail or phone order** are available from Stanfords (☎0171/836 1321; sales@stanfords.co.uk) and several of the other listed suppliers.

AUSTRALIA AND NEW ZEALAND

Adelaide: The Map Shop, 16a Peel St, SA 5000 (☎08/8231 2033).

Auckland: Specialty Maps, 58 Albert St (☎09/307 2217).

Brisbane: Worldwide Maps and Guides, 187 George St, Qld 4000 (☎07/3221 4330).

Melbourne: Bowyangs, 372 Little Bourke St, Vic 3000 (☎03/9670 4383).

Perth: Perth Map Centre, 891 Hay St, WA 6000 (☎08/9322 5733).

Sydney: Travel Bookshop, Shop 3, 175 Liverpool St, NSW 2000 (☎02/9261 8200).

COSTS & MONEY

It's hard to generalize about what you're likely to spend travelling around Europe. Some countries – Finland, Switzerland and Italy – are among the priciest places to be in the world, while in others you can live like a lord on next to nothing – Turkey, for example. The collapse of the eastern European economy means that many of the countries there appear very inexpensive if you're coming from the West. However, the absorption of a number of the previously inexpensive countries of southern Europe into the EU means their costs are becoming much more in tune with the European mainstream.

Accommodation will be the largest single cost, and can really determine where you decide to travel. For example, it's hard to find a double hotel room anywhere in Scandinavia – perhaps the most expensive part of the Continent – for much under £40/$65 a night, whereas in most parts of southern Europe, and even in France, you might be paying under half that on average. Everywhere, though, even in Scandinavia, there is some form of bottom-line accommodation available, and there's always a youth hostel on hand. In general, reckon on a minimum budget of around £10/$15 a night per person in most parts of Europe.

Food and drink costs also vary wildly, although again in most parts of Europe you can assume that a restaurant meal will cost on average £5–10/$8–15 a head, with prices at the top end of the scale in Scandinavia, at the bottom end in eastern and southern Europe. **Transport** costs are something you can pin down more exactly if you have a rail pass or are renting a car. Nowhere, though, are transport costs a major burden, except perhaps in Britain where public transport is less heavily subsidized than elsewhere. Local city transport, too, is usually good, clean and efficient, and is normally fairly cheap, even in the pricier countries of northern Europe. It's hard to pinpoint an average daily budget for touring the Continent, but a bottom-line survival figure – camping, self-catering, hitching, etc – might be around £15/$25 a day per person; building in an investment for a rail pass, staying in hostels and eating out occasionally would bring this up to perhaps £20/$30 a day; while staying in private rooms or hotels and eating out once a day would mean a personal daily budget of at least £25/$40. Obviously in the more expensive countries of northern Europe you might be spending more than this, but on a wide tour this would be balanced out by spending less in southern and eastern Europe, where everything is that much cheaper.

When and where you are travelling also makes a difference. Accommodation rates tend to go up across the board in July and August, when everyone is on vacation – although paradoxically there are good deals in Scandinavia during these months. Also bear in mind that in capital cities and major resorts in the peak season everything will be a grade more expensive than anywhere else, especially if you're there when something special is going on, for example in Munich during the Beer Festival, Pamplona for the running of the bulls, Siena

THE EURO

On January 1, 1999, eleven EU countries – Austria, Belgium, Finland, France, Germany, Ireland, Italy, Luxembourg, the Netherlands, Portugal and Spain – fixed their exchange rates to a new currency, **the euro** (€), which will gradually take over as the single currency for all of them. Euro notes and coins are not scheduled to be issued until the beginning of 2002, but you can get travellers' cheques in euros, and you should not be charged commission for changing them in any of the eleven countries in the euro zone (also known as "Euroland"), nor for changing from any of their old currencies to any other (Deutschmarks to French francs, for example), though this is not always the case.

The remaining four EU countries are expected to join Euroland soon, though politicians in three of them (the UK, Denmark and Sweden) may have a hard time convincing their voters that this is a good idea (the British government has promised a referendum before joining), especially if the new currency fails to perform well against the dollar, the yen or the pound sterling. Greece will join as soon as it can get the drachma into line with the necessary financial requirements.

during the Palio. These are, in any case, times when you will be lucky to find a room at all without having booked.

As for **ways of cutting costs**, there are plenty. It makes sense, obviously, to spend less on transport by investing in some kind of rail pass, and if you're renting a car to do so for a week or more, thereby qualifying for cheaper rates. Always try to plan in advance. Although it's good to be flexible, buying one-off rail tickets and renting cars by the day can add a huge amount to your travel budget. The most obvious way to save on accommodation is to use hostels and/or camp; you can also save by planning to make some of your longer trips at night, when the cost of a couchette may undercut the cost of a night's accommodation. It's best not to be too spartan when it comes to food costs, but doing a certain amount of self-catering, especially at lunchtime when it's just as easy (and probably nicer) to have a picnic lunch rather than eat in a restaurant or café, will save money. Bear in mind, also, that if you're a student an **ISIC card** is well worth investing in. It can get you reduced (usually 50 percent, sometimes free) entry to museums and other sights – costs which can eat their way into your budget alarmingly if you're doing a lot of sightseeing – as well as qualifying you for other discounts in certain cities; it can also save you money on some transport costs, especially ferries, and especially if you are over 26. For Americans there's also a health benefit, providing up to $3000 in emergency medical coverage and $100 a day for 60 days in hospital, plus a 24-hour hotline to call in the event of a medical, legal or financial emergency. If you are not a student but under 26, the **Go-25 Card** (or FIYTO) costs the same as the ISIC and can in some countries give much the same sort of reductions. Teachers qualify for the **International Teacher Identity Card**, offering similar discounts. All these cards are available from youth travel specialists such as Council Travel, STA, USIT and Travel CUTS. Basically, it's worth flashing one or the other at every opportunity to see what you can get.

TRAVELLERS' CHEQUES AND EXCHANGE

The easiest and safest way to carry your money is in travellers' cheques, in either dollars or pounds sterling. These are available for a small commission from any bank. You should, strictly speaking, order them in advance but this isn't always necessary in larger branches, or if you get them direct from offices of the issuing companies. The usual fee for travellers' cheque sales is one or two percent, though this may be waived if you buy the cheques through a bank where you have an account. It pays to get a selection of denominations. Make sure to keep the purchase agreement and a record of cheque serial numbers safe and separate from the cheques themselves. In the event that cheques are lost or stolen, the issuing company will expect you to report the loss forthwith to their local office; most companies claim to replace lost or stolen cheques within 24 hours. The most commonly accepted travellers' cheques are American Express, with Visa a close second, and Thomas Cook trailing third. Most cheques issued by banks will be one of these three brands. You'll usually pay commission again when you cash each cheque; this varies from country to country but is normally another one percent or so, or a flat rate, in which case it makes sense to cash as many as possible at once. Keep a record of the cheques as you cash them, and you can get the value of all uncashed cheques refunded immediately if you lose them (though in practice most firms drag their feet if they can, especially when dealing with backpackers, or if fraud is suspected).

A further option if you have an account in Britain, Ireland or mainland Europe – and in some ways a more flexible one in the sense that you don't have to budget as carefully in advance – is Eurocheques, available from banks with their own cheque guarantee card. You can use your Eurocheque book in the normal way, paying for things in shops, restaurants and hotels, as well as obtaining cash in local currency from banks. For accounts in sterling or in Danish or Swedish krone, you pay around 1.5 percent commission plus a small cost for the cheque card, along with a small flat fee every time you write a cheque. For accounts in Irish pounds, no exchange commission is charged in the euro zone.

PRICES

In the guide we've quoted **prices** in local currency wherever possible, except in those countries where the weakness of the currency and the inflation rate combine to make this a meaningless exercise. In these cases – parts of eastern Europe and Turkey – we've used either US dollars, pounds sterling or Deutschmarks, depending on which hard currency is most commonly used within that country.

For accommodation prices, we've used a standard coding system throughout the guide: see p.44 for details.

APPROXIMATE EXCHANGE RATES

Current market rates (bank rates will not be as good) can be found on the London *Financial Times*'s Web site at *www.ft.com*. Alternatively, try Oanda's universal currency converter at *www.oanda.com/converter/classic*.

currency	£1	$1	E1	currency	£1	$1	E1
Austrian Schilling	20.55	12.60	13.7603*	Latvian Lat	0.95	0.58	0.64
Belgian Franc	60.25	36.90	40.3399*	Lithuanian Litas	6.55	4.00	4.40
Bulgarian Lev	2910	1780	1950	Moroccan Dirham	15.80	9.70	10.60
Croatian Kuna	11.40	7.00	7.60	Netherlands Guilder	3.30	2.00	2.20371*
Czech Koruna	56.50	34.60	37.90	Norwegian Kroner	12.70	7.80	8.50
Danish Krone	11.00	6.80	7.45	Portuguese Escudo	300	183	200.482*
Estonian Kroon	23.40	14.30	15.65	Slovakian Koruna	66.90	40.95	44.80
Euro	1.50	0.91	1	Slovenian Tolar	284	174	190
Finnish Markka	8.90	5.45	5.94573*	Spanish Peseta	248	152	166.386*
French Franc	9.80	6.00	6.55957*	Swedish Krona	13.25	8.10	8.87
German Mark	2.90	1.80	1.95583*	Swiss Franc	2.39	1.46	1.60
Greek Drachma	480	295	320	Turkish Lira	595,535	655,550	399,380
Hungarian Forint	378	232	253	UK Pound Sterling	1	0.62	0.67
Irish Pound (Punt)	1.18	0.72	0.78756*				
Italian Lira	2890	1770	1936.27*	*exact fixed rate			

You'll find that most hotels, shops and restaurants in Europe accept the major **credit cards** – Access/Mastercard, Visa, American Express and Diners Club – although they're less useful in eastern Europe, where you shouldn't depend on being able to use one. Credit cards can also come in handy as a backup source of funds, and can even save on exchange-rate commissions; just be sure someone back home is taking care of the bills if you're away for more than a month. Your card will also enable you to get cash advances from certain ATMs, mostly in western Europe, but remember that all cash advances are treated as loans, with interest accruing daily from the date of withdrawal; there may be a transaction fee on top of this, and there will invariably be a minimum amount you can draw. This varies from one country to the next, but it's usually at least the equivalent of £50–100/$80–150 in local currency. You can also apply for a PIN number and use your debit card, ATM card or cheque guarantee card to obtain money from cash dispensers in a number of European countries.

In many countries banks are the only places where you can legally change money, and they often offer the best exchange rates and lowest commission. They can also mess you around a lot, be annoyingly bureaucratic, and sting you for hidden charges, though this is improving and banks in most countries are much better in this respect than they once were. Bank opening hours are given in the text. Outside these times there are normally bureaux de change, often at train stations and airports, though rates and/or commissions may well be less favourable (always check the rate of commission first – it is sometimes as high as ten percent), and even automatic money-changing machines. Try to avoid changing money or cheques in hotels, where the rates are generally rock-bottom.

WIRING MONEY

Having **money wired** from home is never cheap, and should be considered as a last resort. Funds can be sent to most countries via MoneyGram or Western Union. Both companies' fees depend on the amount being transferred, but as an example, wiring £700/$1000 will cost around £45/$75. The funds should be available for collection (usually in local currency) from the company's local agent within minutes of being sent (you can do this in person at the company's nearest office, or over the phone using your credit card with Western Union).

If you have no money in your account, and there is no one you can persuade to send you any, then the options are inevitably limited. You can either find some casual, cash-in-hand work (see p.51), sell blood (not possible in all European countries), or, as a last resort, throw yourself on the mercy of your nearest consulate. They won't be very sympathetic or even helpful, but they may cash a cheque drawn on a home bank and supported by a cheque card. They may, if there's nothing else for it, repatriate you, though bear in mind your passport will be confiscated as soon as you set foot in your home country and you'll have to pay back all costs incurred (at top-whack rates). They rarely, if ever, lend money.

WIRING MONEY

To find the location of your nearest agent or branch call:

MONEYGRAM

Australia ☎1800/230 100
Ireland ☎1800/559372
New Zealand ☎09/379 8243 or ☎0800/262263
UK ☎00800/8971 8971
USA and Canada ☎1-800/543 4080

WESTERN UNION

Australia ☎1800/649565
Ireland ☎1800/395395
New Zealand ☎09/302 0143
UK ☎0800/833833
USA and Canada ☎1-800/325 6000

COMMUNICATIONS: POST, PHONES AND THE MEDIA

Communications throughout northwestern Europe are invariably excellent: public phones are readily available and normally work, and the postal system is reasonably efficient and easy to use. In southern Europe, services are sometimes less impressive, notably in Italy and Spain where the post is notoriously bad; and in eastern Europe the infrastructure is still very poor and services consequently unpredictable.

POST

For buying stamps and, sometimes, making telephone calls, we've listed the **central post offices** in major cities and given an idea of opening hours. Bear in mind, though, that throughout much of Europe you can avoid

the queues in post offices by buying **stamps** from newsagents and the like. If you know in advance where you're going to be and when, it is possible to receive mail through the **poste restante** (general delivery) system, whereby letters addressed "poste restante" and sent to the main post office in any town or city will be kept under your name at the relevant counter to be picked up. When collecting mail, make sure you take your passport for identification, and bear in mind, in some countries, the possibility of letters being misfiled by someone unfamiliar with your language; if there is nothing under your surname it may have been filed under your first name. If you are using American Express travellers' cheques, or have an American Express card, you can also have mail kept for you at the city centre office; again, where appropriate, we've given addresses throughout the text.

PHONES

It is often possible, especially in western Europe, to make **international calls** from a public call box; this can often be more trouble than it's worth due to the constant need to feed in change, although most countries now have phone cards, making the whole process much easier. Otherwise, you can go to a **post office**, or a **special telephone bureau**, where you can make a call from a private booth and pay afterwards. Most countries have these in one form or another, and we've listed their whereabouts in the text. Wherever possible, avoid using the telephone in your **hotel room** – it costs the earth.

To dial any country in this book from **Britain**, **Ireland** or **New Zealand**, dial ☎00, then the country code, then the city/area code, if there is one, less the initial zero (except in Russia and the Baltics, where it must be dialled; and Finland or Turkey, where you leave out the initial 9), followed by the number; from the **US** and most of **Canada**, the international access code is ☎011, from **Australia** ☎0011 – otherwise the procedure is the same. To call home from most European countries, dial ☎00, then the country code, then the city code (less the

INTERNATIONAL DIALLING CODES

Andorra ☎376	Finland ☎358	Lithuania ☎370	Russia ☎7
Australia ☎61	France ☎33	Luxembourg ☎352	Slovakia ☎421
Austria ☎43	Germany ☎49	Morocco ☎212	Slovenia ☎386
Belgium ☎32	Gibraltar ☎350	Netherlands ☎31	Spain ☎34
Bulgaria ☎359	Greece ☎30	New Zealand ☎64	Sweden ☎46
Canada ☎1	Hungary ☎36	Norway ☎47	Switzerland ☎41
Czech Republic ☎420	Ireland ☎353	Poland ☎48	Turkey ☎90
Denmark ☎45	Italy ☎39	Portugal ☎351	UK ☎44
Estonia ☎372	Latvia ☎371	Romania ☎40	USA ☎1

initial zero if there is one), then the subscriber number. Exceptions include an access code of ☎07 in Spain, ☎810 (usually) in Russia, and either ☎009, ☎007 or ☎0087 (depending on which phone company you are using) in Sweden – in Spain, Russia and Morocco, you must then wait for a new dialling tone; in Lithuania, dial ☎8, wait for a new tone, then dial ☎10; in Estonia, it's ☎8-00 – you need to wait for a new tone after the 8 only on old phones. For collect calls, Home Country Direct services are available in most of the places covered in this book. In Britain and some other countries, international calling cards available from newsagents enable you to call North America and Australasia very cheaply. Most North American, British, Irish and Australasian phone companies either allow you to call home from abroad on a credit card, or billed to your home number (call your company's customer service line before you leave to find out their toll-free access codes from the countries you will be visiting), or else issue an international calling card which can be used worldwide, and for which you will be billed on your return. If you want a calling card and do not already have one, leave yourself a few weeks to arrange it before leaving.

THE MEDIA

British **newspapers and magazines** are fairly widely available in Europe, sometimes – in the Netherlands and Belgium, for example – on the day of publication, more often the day after. They do, however, cost around three times as much as they do at home. Exceptions are the *Guardian* and *Financial Times*, which print special European editions that are cheaper and available on the day of issue. You can also find the terminally dull and self-righteous *Herald Tribune* just about everywhere, as well as the uninspiring *USA Today*; if you're lucky you may come across the odd *New York Times* or *Washington Post*, but don't count on it outside the major centres. What you will find are *Time*, *Newsweek*, and the *Economist* pretty much everywhere, as well as a host of British and American glossies.

It's cheaper to get your news by tuning a **radio** into the BBC World Service (still considered to have the most reliable news of all the media), Radio Canada, the Voice of America, or one of the many local news broadcasts in English. In northern France, the Netherlands and Belgium you can pick up BBC domestic services as well. BBC World Service **frequencies** include: 3955kHz, 6195kHz, 9410kHz, 12,095kHz on shortwave or, in western Europe, 648kHz MW, and in southeastern Europe, 1323kHz MW (programme details at *www.bbc.co.uk/world-service*). Radio Canada can be picked up at 6–6.30am GMT on 6090kHz, 9670kHz or 11,905kHz, at 2.30–3pm on 9555kHz, 11,915kHz or 15,325kHz, and at 9–10.30pm on 5995kHz, 7235kHz, 11,945kHz and 15,150kHz (programme details at *www.rcinet.ca*). VOA broadcast 4–7am and 3–10pm GMT on792kHz and 1197kHz MW, plus various frequencies in shortwave depending on the time of day – try 7170kHz, 9760kHz or 15,205kHz (programme details at *www.voa.gov*).

With the advent of cable and satellite channels, **television** has become more of a pan-European medium than radio. Sky TV, Superchannel, CNN, Eurosport and the European version of MTV are all popular across the Continent and normally available in the better hotels. In many parts of Europe there is, in any case, a reasonably wide choice of channels (by British, if not by American, standards), since a border is never far away and you can often pick up at least one other country's TV stations. This is at its most extreme in Belgium and the southern Netherlands, where as well as all the satellite and cable channels you can pick up Dutch and Belgian TV, French TV, BBC1 and BBC2, all the German stations, and even the state Italian channel.

ACCOMMODATION

Although it is obviously one of the more crucial costs to consider when planning your trip, accommodation needn't be a stumbling block to a budget-conscious tour of Europe. Indeed, even in Europe's pricier reaches the hostel system means there is always an affordable place to stay, and if you're prepared to camp you can get by on very little while staying at some excellently equipped sites. The one thing you should bear in mind is that in the more popular cities and resorts – Florence, Venice, Amsterdam, Prague, the Algarve – things can get chock-a-block during the peak summer months, and even if you've got plenty of money to throw around you should book in advance.

HOSTELS

The cheapest way for young people to travel around Europe is by using the extensive network of youth hostels that covers the Continent. Some of these are **private** places, run on a one-off basis in the major cities and resorts, but by far the majority are **official hostels**, members of Hostelling International (HI), which incorporates the national youth hostel associations of each country in the world. Youth hostelling isn't the hearty, up-at-the-crack-of-dawn and early-to-bed business it once was; indeed, hostels have been keen to shed this image of late and now appeal to a wider public, and in many countries they simply represent the best-value overnight accommodation available. Most are clean, well-run places, always offering dormitory accommodation, some – especially in Scandinavia and other parts of northern Europe – offering a range of private single and double rooms, or rooms with 4–6 beds. Many hostels also either have self-catering facilities or provide low-cost meals, and the larger ones have a range of other facilities – a swimming pool, games room, common room, etc. There is no age limit (except in Bavaria), but where there is limited space, priority is given to those under 27 years of age.

Strictly speaking, to use an HI hostel you have to be a member, although if there is room you can stay at most hostels by simply paying extra – and you can often join the HI on the spot. If you do intend to do a lot of hostelling, however, it is certainly worth joining, which you can do by becoming a member of your home country's hostelling association. Annual membership costs are low everywhere. We've detailed the hostelling situation in each country in the text, as well as giving the name and address of the relevant national hostelling organization if you want further information. The *HI Guide to Europe*, available from bookstores or national hostelling associations, is a good investment at £7.50/$10.95, detailing every official hostel in Europe and the British Isles (but not Morocco, which is covered by the *HI Guide to Africa, the Americas, Asia and the Pacific*).

ACCOMMODATION PRICE CODES

Throughout this guide, accommodation is priced on a scale of ① to ⑨, the number indicating the lowest price per night a single person could expect to pay in that establishment in high season. With hostels this is the nightly rate per person; with hotels, the price is arrived at by dividing the cost of the cheapest double room by two. The prices indicated by the codes are as follows:

① under £5/$8

② £5–10/$8–16

③ £10–15/$16–24

④ £15–20/$24–32

⑤ £20–25/$32–40

⑥ £25–30/$40–48

⑦ £30–35/$48–56

⑧ £35–40/$56–64

⑨ £40/$64 and over

YOUTH HOSTEL ASSOCIATIONS

Australia Australian Youth Hostel Association, Level 3, 10 Mallet St, Camperdown, NSW 2050 (☎02/9565 1699; *www.yha.org.au*). Annual membership adults A$44 1st year, $27 renewal, under-18s A$13.50 (free if a parent joins).

Canada Hostelling International Canada, Suite 400, 205 Catherine St, Ottawa, ON K2P 1C3 (☎613/237 7884 or 1-800/663 5777; *www.hostellingintl.ca*). Annual membership adults CDN$25, under-18s $12. Adults can also take out a two-year membership for $35.

England and Wales Youth Hostel Association (YHA), Trevelyan House, 8 St Stephen's Hill, St Alban's, Herts AL1 2DY (☎01727/845047; *www.yha/england/wales.org.uk*). London shop and information office: 14 Southampton St, London WC2E 7HY (☎0171/836 8541). Annual membership adults £11, under-18s £5.50.

Ireland An Óige, 61 Mountjoy St, Dublin 7 (☎01/830 4555; *www.irelandyha.org*). Annual membership adults IR£10, under-18s IR£4.

Northern Ireland Hostelling International Northern Ireland, 22 Donegal Rd, Belfast, BT12 5JN (☎01232/315435; *www.hini.org.uk*). Annual membership adults £8, under-18s £3.

New Zealand Youth Hostel Association of New Zealand, PO Box 436, 173 Gloucester St, Christchurch (☎03/379 9970; *www.yha.org.nz*). Annual membership adults NZ$34, under-18s NZ$12; under-15s free.

Scotland Scottish Youth Hostel Association, 7 Glebe Cres, Stirling, FK8 2JA (☎01786/891400; *www.syha.org.uk*). Annual membership adults £6, under-18s £2.50.

USA Hostelling International-American Youth Hostels (HI-AYH), 733 15th St NW, Suite 840, Washington, DC 20005 (☎202/783 6161; *www.hiayh.org*). Annual membership adults $25 and under-18s $10.

HOTELS AND PENSIONS

If you've got a bit more money to spend, you may want to upgrade from hostel accommodation to something a little more comfortable and private. With **hotels** you can really spend as much or as little as you like. Most hotels in Europe are graded on some kind of star system. One- or two-star category hotels are plain and simple on the whole, usually family-run, with a number of rooms without private facilities; sometimes breakfast won't be included. In three-star hotels all the rooms will have private facilities, prices will normally include breakfast and there may well be a phone or TV in the room; while four- and five-star places will certainly have all these, perhaps on a plusher, roomier basis, perhaps also including access to other facilities – sauna, swimming pool, etc. In the really top-level places breakfast, oddly enough, isn't always included. When it is, in the Netherlands, Britain or Germany, it's fairly sumptuous; in France it wouldn't amount to much anyway and it's no hardship to grab a croissant and coffee in the nearest café. We've only detailed one- and two-star hotels in the text, since for most people on a tour of Europe these are usually perfectly acceptable; in any case, it's not hard to find places above this level. The prices quoted in the text are for the cheapest option in peak season for one person – which usually works out as being the price of half a basic double room, generally without a private bathroom. Single rooms tend to be at least 75 percent of the price of a double, and for private facilities you can expect to pay around 25 percent extra in most countries. For information on the accommodation pricing codes we've used throughout the text, see box on previous page.

Obviously prices vary greatly, but you're rarely going to be paying less than £10/$15 for a double room even in southern Europe, while in the Netherlands the average price is around £25/$40, and in Scandinavia somewhat higher than that. In some countries **pensions** or **bed and breakfasts** (variously known as guest houses, *gasthausen* or numerous other names) – smaller, simpler affairs, usually with just a few rooms, that are sometimes part of a larger family house – are a cheaper alternative. In some countries these advertise with a sign in the window; in others they are bookable through the tourist office, which may demand a booking fee. There are various other kinds of accommodation – apartments, farmhouses, cottages, *paradors* (in Spain), *gîtes* (in France), etc – but most are geared to longer-term stays and we have only detailed them where relevant.

CAMPING

The cheapest form of accommodation is, of course, the **campsite**, either pitching your own tent or parking your caravan or camper van. Most sites make a charge per person, plus a charge per plot and another per vehicle. Obviously you'll pay less if you're travelling on foot – maybe just a couple of pounds per night between two people – but parking a car or camper van doesn't add a lot to the cost. Bear in mind also, especially in countries like

France where camping is very popular, that facilities can be excellent – though the better the facilities, the pricier the site. If you're on foot you should add in the cost and inconvenience of getting to the site, since most are on the outskirts of towns, sometimes further. Although some sites can be congested and noisy, you do, however, benefit from what can sometimes be a relatively bucolic location – often a bonus after a hard day's sightseeing. Some sites have cabins, which you can stay in for a little extra, although these are usually fairly basic affairs, only really worth considering in regions like Scandinavia where budget options are thin on the ground. In Britain, the AA issue a *Caravan and Camping Europe* guide (£8.99), which lists campsites in eleven west European countries.

If you're planning to do a lot of camping, an **international camping carnet** is a good investment, available from home motoring organizations or from the organizations listed below. It serves as useful identification, covers you for third-party insurance when camping, and is **obligatory** on sites in Portugal and some Scandinavian countries. As for **camping rough**, it's a fine idea if you can get away with it – though perhaps an entire trip of rough camping is in reality too gruelling to be truly enjoyable. In some countries it's easy – indeed in parts of Scandinavia it is a legal right, and in Greece and other southern European countries you can usually find a bit of beach to pitch down on – but in others it's almost a nonstarter and can get you into trouble with the law.

CAMPING ASSOCIATIONS

USA & Canada, Family Campers and RVers (FCRV), 4804 Transit Rd, Building 2, Depew, NY 14043 (☎1-800/245 9755; *www3.pgh.net*). Membership $25 + $10 carnet.

Britain, Camping and Caravanning Club, Greenfields House, Westwood Way, Coventry, CV4 8JH (☎01203/694995). Membership £31 + £4.50 carnet.

Ireland, Irish Camping and Caravan Club, 11 Anne Devlin Drive, Dublin 14. (☎01/495 1303). Membership IR£29 first year, IR£26 subsequent years + IR£5 carnet.

POLICE, TROUBLE AND SEXUAL HARASSMENT

Travelling around Europe should be relatively trouble-free, but, as in any part of the world, there is always the chance of petty theft. However, conditions do vary greatly from, say, Scandinavia, where you're unlikely to encounter much trouble of any kind, to poorer and potentially more troublesome regions like Morocco, Turkey or southern Italy. In order to minimize the risk of having your stuff ripped off, you should take some obvious precautions.

First and perhaps most important, you should try not to look too much like a tourist: appearing lost, even if you are, is to be avoided if you can; neither is it a good idea, especially in southern Europe, to walk around draped with cameras or expensive jewellery – the professional bag-snatchers who tour train stations can have your watch or camera off in seconds. If you're waiting for a train, keep your eyes (and hands if necessary) on your bags at all times; if you want to sleep, put everything valuable under your head as a pillow. You should be cautious when choosing a train compartment, and a woman travelling alone should avoid sharing a compartment with a lone man. If staying in a hostel, take your valuables out with you unless there's a very secure store for them on the premises; some people even make photocopies of their more crucial documentation and leave them at home; a copy of your address book, certainly, can be a good idea.

If the worst happens and you do have something stolen, inform the police immediately (we've included details of the main city police stations in the text); get a statement from them detailing exactly what has been lost, which you'll need for your insurance claim back home. Generally you'll find the police sympathetic enough, sometimes able to speak English, though unwilling to do much more than make out a report for you.

As for **offences** you might commit, it's hardly necessary to state that drugs like cocaine, amphetamines, heroin, LSD and Ecstasy are illegal all over Europe, and although use of cannabis is widespread in most countries, and legally tolerated in some (famously in the Netherlands, for example), you are never allowed to possess more than a small amount for personal use, and unlicensed sale remains illegal. Penalties for possession of hard drugs and psychedelics can be severe; in certain countries, such as Turkey, even possession of cannabis can result in a hefty prison sentence, and your consulate is unlikely to plead any kind of case for you. Other, more minor, misdemeanours you should be wary of committing include sleeping rough, which is more tolerated in some parts of Europe than others and should be undertaken everywhere with a certain amount of circumspection, and topless sunbathing, which is now fairly common throughout southern Europe but still often frowned upon, especially in parts of Greece, Turkey and Italy. As always, be sensitive, and err on the side of caution. If you're arrested for any kind of motoring offence, again don't expect your consulate to be very sympathetic; in any case, unless it's something really serious you'll probably get off with a spot-fine. The same goes for fare avoidance on public transport. It's also worth remembering that, in theory, it is illegal to be on the streets without an official ID card or passport throughout most of mainland Europe (except the Netherlands and Scandinavia). Finally, although it's much less of an issue than it once was, avoid photography around sensitive military sites or installations – you may be arrested as a spy.

One of the major irritants for women travelling through Europe is **sexual harassment**, which in Italy, Greece, Turkey, Spain and Morocco especially can be almost constant for women travelling alone or with another woman, and can put certain areas completely out of bounds. Southern European coastal areas, especially, can be a real problem, where women tourists are often regarded as being on the lookout for sex. By far the most common kind of harassment you'll come across simply consists of street whistles and cat-calls; occasionally it's more sinister and very occasionally it can be dangerous. Indifference is often the best policy, avoiding eye contact with men and at the same time appearing as confident and purposeful as possible. If this doesn't make you feel any more comfortable, shouting a few choice phrases in the local language is a good idea; don't, however, shout in English, which often seems to encourage them. You may also come across gropers on crowded buses and trains, in which case you should complain as loudly as possible – the ensuing scene should be enough to deter your assailant. The best way of avoiding more dangerous situations is to simply be as suspicious as possible: if you're hitching, don't get into a car if you've even a hint of doubt about the driver (always ask where they are going before volunteering the information yourself); indeed, don't ever get yourself into a situation where you're alone with a man you don't know. In the larger European cities we've detailed contact points and women-only bars and cafés, so if all else fails, or you just get fed up with avoiding Neanderthals, you can always seek out a completely male-free environment.

FESTIVALS AND ANNUAL EVENTS

There is always some annual event or other happening in Europe, and some of the bigger shindigs can be reason enough alone for visiting a place, some even worth planning your entire trip around. Be warned, though, that if you're intending to visit a place during its annual festival you need to plan well in advance, since accommodation can be booked up months beforehand, especially for the larger, more internationally known events.

RELIGIOUS AND TRADITIONAL FESTIVALS

Many of the festivals and annual events you'll come across were – and in many cases still are – **religion-inspired affairs**, centring on a local miracle or saint's day. **Easter**, certainly, is celebrated throughout Europe, with most verve and ceremony in Catholic and Orthodox Europe, where Easter Sunday or Monday is usually marked with some sort of procession; it's especially enthusiastically celebrated in Greece, where it is more important even than Christmas, though be aware that the Orthodox Church's Easter can in fact fall a week or two either side of the Western festival. Earlier in the year, traditionally at the beginning of **Lent** in February, **Carnival** is celebrated, most conspicuously (and perhaps most stagily) in Venice, which explodes in a riot of posing and colour to become one of the country's major tourist draws at this time of year. There are smaller, perhaps more authentic carnivals in **Viareggio**, also in Italy, and in Germany, Belgium and the Netherlands, most notably in **Cologne**, **Maastricht** and tiny **Binche** in the Ardennes, where you can view some 1500 costumed *Gilles* or dancers in the streets. Also in Belgium, in mid-Lent, catch if you can the procession of white-clad *Blanc Moussis* through the streets of Stavelot in the Ardennes – one of Europe's oddest sights. Other religious festivals you might base a trip around include the *Festa di San Gennaro* three times a year in **Naples**, when the dried blood of the city's patron saint is supposed to liquefy to prevent disaster befalling the place – it rarely fails; the *Ommegang* procession through the heart of **Brussels** city centre to commemorate a medieval miracle; the *Heilig Bloed* procession in **Bruges**, when a much-venerated relic of Christ's blood is carried shoulder-high through the town; and, in Italy, the annual procession across **Venice**'s Grand Canal to the church of the *Madonna della Salute* to recall the deliverance of the city from a seventeenth-century plague. In Morocco and Turkey, where the predominant religion is Islam, and in the Muslim areas of Bulgaria, **Ramadan**, commemorating the revelation of the Koran to Muhammad, is observed. The most important Muslim festival, it lasts a month, during which time Muslims are supposed to fast from sunrise until sunset – although otherwise, as far as is possible, life carries on as normal.

There are, of course, other, equally long-established events which have a less obvious foundation. One of the best known is the *April Feria* in **Seville**, a week's worth of flamenco music and dancing, parades and bullfights, in a frenziedly enthusiastic atmosphere. Also in Spain, for a week in early July, the *San Fermín* festival in **Pamplona** is if anything even more famous, its centrepiece – the running of the bulls along with local macho men, through the streets of the city – drawing tourists from all over the world, though there is much more to the festival than that. Also in July, at the beginning of the month (and again in mid-August), the *Palio* in **Siena** is perhaps the most spectacular annual event in Italy, a bareback horse race between representatives of the different quarters of the city around the main square, its origins dating back to medieval times. It's a brutal affair, with few rules and a great sense of deeply felt rivalry, and, although there are other Palio events in Italy, it's like no other horse race you'll ever see. At least as big a deal as the Palio and San Fermín is the **Munich** *Oktoberfest*, a huge beer festival and fair that goes on throughout the last two weeks in September. Unlike most events of its size in Europe it's less than two hundred years old, but it attracts vast numbers of people to consume gluttonous quantities of beer and food. **London**'s Notting Hill Carnival, held at the end of August, is also a recent phenomenon, a predominantly Black and Caribbean celebration that's become the world's second biggest street carnival after Rio. Other, smaller events include the great Venice *Regata Storica*, each September, a trial of skill for the city's gondoliers, and the gorgeous annual displays and processions of flowers in the **Dutch bulbfield towns** in April and May.

ARTS FESTIVALS

Festivals celebrating all or one specific aspect of the **arts** are held all over Europe throughout the year, though particularly in summer, when the weather is better suited to outdoor events. Of general international arts festivals, the **Edinburgh Arts Festival** held every August is perhaps the best known and most enjoyable, not to mention one of the most innovative, with a mass of topnotch and fringe events in every medium, from rock to cabaret to modern experimental music, dance and drama. For three weeks every year the whole city is given over to the festival and it's a wonderful time to be around if you don't mind the crowds and have booked somewhere to stay in advance. There is another major general arts festival in **Spoleto**, the *Festival dei Due Mondi*, held over two months each summer, which is Italy's leading international arts festival, though on a somewhat smaller scale than Edinburgh, while the midsummer **Avignon** festival in southern France is slanted towards drama but hosts plenty of other events besides and is again a great time to be in town. Smaller general arts festivals, though still attracting a variety of international names, include the **Holland Festival**, held in Amsterdam in June; the **Flanders Festival**, an umbrella title for all sorts of dramatic and musical events held mainly in the medieval buildings of Bruges and Ghent in July and August; and the **Dubrovnik Summer Festival**, with a host of musical events against the backdrop of the town's beautiful Renaissance centre – though the future of this is as uncertain as that of the country.

As regards more specialist gatherings, the **Montreux Jazz Festival** in July and the **North Sea Jazz Festival** in The Hague in mid-July are the Continent's premier jazz jamborees, while the same month sees the beginning of the **Salzburg Music Festival**, perhaps the foremost – if also the most conservative – serious music festival in Europe, though **London's Prom** season (July–Sept) maintains very high standards at egalitarian prices. Florence's **Maggio Musicale** is also worth catching, a festival of opera and classical music that runs from late April until early July. Less highbrow musical forms – rock, folk, etc – are celebrated, most conspicuously, at the huge **Glastonbury** festival in Britain, which will take place in 2000, though its future beyond that date is still uncertain; at the **Pink Pop Festival**, held every June in Geleen near Maastricht in the Netherlands; and the **Roskilde Festival** in Denmark. Look out also for the **Womad** get-togethers, a number of which are usually held each year at a variety of sites all over Europe, celebrating World, folk and roots music, and the excellent and still relatively small **Cambridge Folk Festival** in late July. For **films**, there is, of course, **Cannes**, though this is more of an industry affair than anything else, and the **Venice** and **Berlin** film festivals, which are more geared to the general public.

GAY TRAVELLERS

Gays and lesbians will find most of Europe a tolerant part of the world in which to travel, the west rather more so than the east. Most countries have at least in part legalized homosexual relationships, and the only part of Europe covered in this guide where homosexual acts are still against the law is Romania. Laws still in the main apply to male homosexuality; lesbianism, it would seem, doesn't officially exist, so it is in theory legal everywhere. The homosexual age of consent is, however, usually different from the heterosexual one – on average 18 years of age as opposed to 15 or 16 years. In general, the Netherlands and Scandinavia (except Finland) are the most tolerant parts of the Continent, with anti-discrimination legislation and official recognition of lesbian and gay partnerships. Reactionary laws against "outraging public decency" or "promotion" of homosexuality exist in Russia, Austria, Finland and the UK.

Most cities of any size, at least in northern Europe, have a few bars or cafés frequented by **gay men**, and it's not hard to make contact with other gay people. In the major northern capitals, certainly, the gay scene is usually fairly sophisticated, with any number of bars, bookshops, clubs and gay organizations and switchboards, though things are usually firmly slanted towards gay men. The gay capital of Europe is perhaps Amsterdam, but there is plenty of interest for gay men in London, Paris, Copenhagen, and, to a lesser extent, Madrid and Barcelona. In southern Europe, things are less developed: the main cities may have the odd gay bar, but it may not advertise itself as such, and outside of the capitals there won't be many obvious places to meet at all. **Lesbians** can likewise usually find somewhere to meet with other gay women in northern Europe, albeit on a much smaller scale than male gays, while elsewhere, in southern and eastern Europe, word-of-mouth is about the only course open. We've detailed the best of the gay scenes of the major cities in the text; for further information, contact the organizations listed below.

INTERNATIONAL GAY/LESBIAN TRAVEL CONTACTS

Damron Company, PO Box 422458, San Francisco CA 94142 (☎1-800/462 6654 or ☎415/255 0404). Publishes gay guides to Paris, London, Amsterdam, Britain, Ireland and Spain.

Ferrari Publications, PO Box 37887, Phoenix, AZ 85069 (☎1-800/962 2912 o r 602/863 2408). Publishes *Ferrari Gay Travel A to Z*, a worldwide gay and lesbian guide; *Inn Places*, a worldwide accommodation guide; the guides *Men's Travel in Your Pocket* and *Women's Travel in Your Pocket*, the quarterly *Ferrari Travel Report*; and a gay guide to Paris.

International Gay Travel Association, 4331 N Federal Hwy, Suite 304, Ft Lauderdale, FL 33308 (☎1-800/448 8550). Trade group that can provide a list of gay-owned or gay-friendly accommodation, travel agents, etc.

Pride Travel, 254 Bay St, Brighton, Melbourne, Vic 3186 (☎03/9596 3566 or 1800/061427).

Silke's Travel, 263 Oxford St, Darlinghurst, Sydney, NSW 2010 (☎02/9380 5835; www.magna.com.au/~silba).

Spartacus Gay Guide, Bruno Gmünder Verlag, Leuschnerdamm 31, 10999 Berlin, Germany (☎49-30/615 0030); at Bookazine Co, 75 Hook Rd, Bayonne, NJ 07002 (☎201/339 7777); at Prowler Press, 3 Broadbent Close, 20–22 Highgate High St, London N6 5GG (☎0181/340 7667); at Edition Habit Press, 72–80 Bourke Rd, Alexandria, NSW 2015 (☎02/9310 2098). International gay guide with information on meeting and cruising spots for gay men, but nothing much for lesbians.

TRAVELLERS WITH DISABILITIES

It's easier for disabled people to get around in northern Europe than in the south and east, which is not surprising given the fact that this part of the Continent is more developed in every other way. Wheelchair access to public buildings is, however, far from easy in many countries, as is wheelchair accessibility to public transport – indeed, the only big-city underground systems that are accessible are those in Berlin, Amsterdam, Stockholm and Helsinki, with the rest lagging far behind; buses, too, are in general out of bounds to wheelchair users, although airport facilities are improving, as are those on the cross-Channel ferries. As for rail services, these vary greatly: France, for example, has very good facilities for disabled passengers, as have Belgium, Denmark and Austria, but many other countries make little, if any, provision.

Your particular disability may govern whether you decide to see Europe on a **package tour** or **independently**. There are any number of specialist tour operators, mostly catering for physically disabled travellers, and the number of nonspecialist operators who cater for disabled clients is increasing. It's also perfectly possible to go it alone, either with your own helper or by hiring one if you require assistance while away, or by joining some kind of group tour for disabled travellers.

Pressure on space means that it is impossible for us to detail wheelchair access arrangements for everywhere we list in the guide; neither can we detail the best and worst of the operators, and for more **informa-**

CONTACTS FOR TRAVELLERS WITH DISABILITIES

NORTH AMERICA

Directions Unlimited, 720 N Bedford Rd, Bedford Hills, NY 10507 (☎914/241 1700). Travel agency specializing in custom tours for people with disabilities.

Jewish Rehabilitation Hospital, 3205 Place Alton Goldbloom, Chomedy Laval, PQ H7V 1R2 (☎514/688 9550, ext. 226). Guidebooks and travel information.

Mobility International USA, PO Box 10767, Eugene, OR 97440 (Voice and TDD: ☎541/343 1284). Information and referral services, access guides, tours and exchange programmes. Annual membership $25 (incl quarterly newsletter).

Society for the Advancement of Travel for the Handicapped (SATH), 347 5th Ave, New York, NY 10016 (☎212/447-7284; *www.sittravel.com*). Non-profit-making travel-industry referral service that passes queries on to its members as appropriate (allow plenty of time for a response).

Travel Information Service (☎215/456 9600). Telephone-only information and referral service.

Twin Peaks Press, Box 129, Vancouver, WA 98666 (☎360/694 2462 or 1-800/637 2256). Publisher of the *Directory of Travel Agencies for the Disabled* ($19.95), listing more than 370 agencies worldwide; *Travel for the Disabled* ($19.95); the *Directory of Accessible Van Rentals* ($9.95) and *Wheelchair Vagabond* ($14.95), loaded with personal tips.

BRITISH ISLES

Access Project, 39 Bradley Gdns, London W13 8HE. Publishes guides to London and Paris for disabled visitors.

Access Travel, 6 The Hillock, Astley, Lancashire M29 7GW (☎01942/888844, fax 891811). A small tour operator that can arrange flights, transfer and accommodation in France, Spain and Portugal.

Holiday Care Service, 2nd floor, Imperial Building, Victoria Rd, Horley, Surrey RH6 7PZ (☎01293/774535, Minicom ☎01293/776943). Provides free lists of accessible accommodation and information on financial help for holidays.

Tripscope, The Courtyard, Evelyn Rd, London W4 5JL (☎0181/994 9294). A national telephone information service offering free travel advice for anyone with mobility problems.

RADAR, 12 City Forum, 250 City Rd, London EC1V 8AF (☎0171/250 3222, Minicom ☎0171/250 4119). A good source of advice on holidays and travel abroad; they also publish their own guides for travellers with disabilities, including one for Europe, priced £5.

Disability Action Group, 2 Annadale Ave, Belfast BT7 3JH (☎01232/491011).

Irish Wheelchair Association, Blackheath Drive, Clontarf, Dublin 3 (☎01/833 8241; *iwa@iol.ie*). National voluntary organization for people with disabilities, including services for holidaymakers.

AUSTRALASIA

ACROD, PO Box 60, Curtin, ACT 2605 (☎02/6282 4333). Offers advice and keeps a list of travel specialists.

Disabled Persons Assembly, 173 Victoria St, Wellington (☎04/801 9100).

tion on disabled travel abroad you should get in touch with the organizations listed below. As well as their publications, look out for *The World Wheelchair Traveller* (AA Publications) by Susan Abbott and Mary Ann Tyrrell, which includes basic hints and advice, and *Access London* and *Access Paris*, with information specific to those cities, published by Access Project in the UK.

WORK AND STUDY

The opportunities for working or studying your way around Europe are almost unlimited, especially for citizens of EU nations, who benefit from the easing of restrictions on the movement of labour. You can either fix something up before you leave home and build your trip around that, or simply look out for casual labour on your travels, treating it as a way of topping up your vacation cash. Certainly the best way of discovering a country properly is to work there, learning the language if you can and discovering something about the culture. Study opportunities are also a good way of absorbing yourself in the local culture, but they invariably need to be fixed up in advance; check the newspapers for ads or contact one of the main organizations (listed overleaf) direct.

If you're just looking to supplement your spending money while you're travelling, there are any number of jobs you can pick up on the road. It's normally not hard to find **bar or restaurant work**, especially in large resort areas during the summer, and your chances will be greater if you can speak the local language – although being able to speak English may be your greatest asset in the more touristy areas; you may be asked for documentation, in which case you're better off in an EU member-state, but it's unlikely. Don't be afraid to march straight in and ask, or check the noticeboards in local bars, hostels or colleges, or the local newspapers, particularly the English-language ones. Cleaning jobs, nannying and **au pair** work are also common, if not spectacularly well paid, often just providing room and board plus pocket money, and are something you can either fix up on the spot or before you leave home. If you're staying in a place for a while, you can always place an ad or a notice yourself offering your services. The other big casual earner is farmwork, particularly **grape-picking**, which is an option in the August–October period when the vines are being harvested. The best country for this is easily France, but there's sometimes work in Germany too. Once again, you're unlikely to be asked for any kind of documentation. Also in France, along the Côte d'Azur, and in other yacht-havens like Greece and parts of southern Spain, there is sometimes **crewing** work available, though you'll obviously need some sailing experience. If this isn't up your street but you want something active to last the whole summer, tour operators are often on the lookout for **travel couriers**, though this is something better arranged from home. If you're really serious, get in touch with the companies that run bus tours for young people around Europe, who are often keen to take on new blood.

Rather better paid, and equally widespread, if only during the September to June period, is **teaching English as a foreign language** (TEFL), which is something you normally (though not exclusively) need to fix up from home. Everyone is desperate to learn English right now, all over Europe, but it is becoming harder to find English-teaching jobs without some kind of TEFL qualification. If you do organize work on the spot you may have to leave the country while your employers apply for a work permit. You'll normally be paid a liveable local salary, sometimes with somewhere to live thrown in as well, and you can often supplement your income with much more lucrative private lessons. Incidentally, North Americans and Australasians might be interested to know that the TEFL teaching season is reversed in Britain, with plenty of work available during the summer in London and on the south coast (but again, some kind of TEFL qualification is pretty well indispensable).

If you want to know more about working in Europe, a couple of **books** might come in handy: *Work your Way around the World* by Susan Griffiths (Vacation Work) and *Working Holidays*, a handbook put out by the British

Council's Central Bureau for Educational Visits and Exchanges. You could also get hold of a copy of David Woodworth's *Summer Jobs Abroad* (Vacation Work), which has details of places you could try before leaving home, while Mark Hempshell's *Working Holidays Abroad – A Practical Guide* (Kuperard) also has some good leads for short-term work. For more on TEFL possibilities, check out *Teaching English Abroad* by Sue Griffiths (Vacation Work).

Studying abroad invariably means learning a language, doing an intensive course that lasts between two weeks and three months and staying with a local family. There are plenty of places you can do this, and you should reckon on paying around £200/$300 a week including room and board – though there are lots of options; contact the Central Bureau for full details. If you know a language well, you could also apply to do a short course in another subject at a local university; once again, scan the classified sections of the newspapers back home, and keep an eye out when you're on the spot.

USEFUL ADDRESSES

AFS Intercultural Programs, 34 SW 4th Ave, Portland, OR 97204–2608 (☎1-800/AFS INFO; *www.afs.org*); 1231 Rue Ste Catherine Oueste, Suite 508, Montreal, PQ H3G 1P5; Arden Hse, Wellington St, Bingley, W Yorks BD16 2NB (☎01274/560677); c/o Interculture Ireland, 10a Lower Camden St, Dublin 2 (☎01/478 2046); Unit 12, 233 Cardigan St, Carlingford, Melbourne, Vic 4064 (☎03/9349 4722); 84–88 Dixon St, 1st floor, PO Box 11 046, Wellington (☎04/384 8066 or ☎0800/600300). Worldwide, UN-recognized organization running summer experiential programs to foster international understanding.

American Institute for Foreign Study,102 Greenwich Ave, Greenwich, CT 06830 (☎1-800/727 2437). Language study and cultural immersion for the summer or school year in Austria, Britain, the Czech Republic, France, Italy, Russia and Spain.

ASSE International, PU Box 1323, Rozelle, Sydney, NSW 2039 (☎02/9819 4777 & 1800/077509; *www.asse.com*); PO Box 340, Te Puke, New Zealand (☎07/573 5717 or 0800/488 884). International student exchanges to Scandinavia, Germany, Switzerland, the Netherlands, France, Spain, Italy and the UK; also offers summer language programmes in France, Spain and Germany.

Association for International Practical Training, 10400 Little Patuxent Pkwy, Suite 250, Columbia, MD 21044 (☎410/997 3068). Summer internships in various European countries for students who have completed at least two years of college in science, agriculture, engineering or architecture.

Australians Studying Abroad, 1st Floor, 970 High St, Armadale, Vic 3143 (☎03/9509 1955 or 1800/645755).

British Council Central Bureau for Educational Visits and Exchanges, 10 Spring Gardens, London SW1A 2BN (☎0171/389 4880; publications ☎0171/389 4880; *www.britcoun.org/cbeve*). Enables teachers to find out about development programmes abroad, or gap year students to take part in foreign language assistant programmes in France and Germany; also publishes an annual *Working Holidays* book (£9.99), available direct or from bookshops.

Council on International Educational Exchange (CIEE), 205 E 42nd St, New York, NY 10017 (☎888/COUNCIL or 212/822 2695 for volunteer projects; ☎1-800/468 5562 for work permits; *www.ciee.org*); 52 Poland St, London W1V 4JQ (☎0171/478 2000). An international organization worth contacting for advice on studying, working and volunteering in Europe. They run summer semester and one-year study programmes in Belgium, the Czech Republic, France, the Netherlands, Poland, Russia and Spain, and arrange six-month work permits in Britain, Ireland, France and Germany – they provide leads, but it's up to you to find the work. They also run volunteer projects in Belgium, the Czech Republic, Denmark, France, Germany, the Netherlands, Poland, Russia, Spain, Turkey, and the UK.

GET, PO Box 226, Garfield Drive, Paddington, Brisbane, Qld 4064 (☎07/3217 6575) Tailored educational tours worldwide.

School for International Training, Kipling Rd, PO Box 676, Brattleboro, VT 05302 (☎802/257 7751). Accredited college semesters abroad, comprising language and cultural studies, homestay and other academic work in the Czech Republic, France, Germany, Greece, the Netherlands, Ireland, Morocco, Spain, Switzerland and Russia.

Studyabroad.com (*www.studyabroad.com*). Web site with listings and links to programmes in most of the countries covered by this book.

DIRECTORY

Baggage Deposit (Left Luggage) Almost every train station of any size has facilities for left luggage, either lockers or a desk that's open long hours every day. We've given details in the major capital accounts.

Bargaining The only places where you need really do any bargaining when shopping are in Turkey – in the bazaars and carpet shops – and in the souks of Morocco. Everywhere else, even in the less developed parts of southern Italy and Greece, people would think it odd if you tried to haggle.

Children Travelling with kids is easy enough everywhere, although you'll find a marked difference in attitudes to them between northern and southern Europe. In the north you'll find people rather indifferent to children, sometimes worse – an attitude epitomized in Britain where they're regarded as something of a nuisance in public places, and barred from

entry altogether to many pubs, some restaurants, even some hotels. In the southern European nations, however – such as Italy, Spain and Turkey – children are by contrast much revered and made a fuss of in public, and, although you'll sometimes pay extra for them in hotels, they are never refused, even in restaurants or cafés. Indeed, the only problem with travelling with kids in southern Europe may be the summer heat and sun.

Contraceptives Condoms are available everywhere, and are normally reliable international brands like Durex, at least in northwestern Europe; the condoms in eastern European countries, Morocco and Turkey are of uncertain quality, however – so it's best to stock up in advance. The Pill is available everywhere, too, though often only on prescription; again, bring a sufficient supply.

Electric current The supply in Europe is 220v (240v in the British Isles), which means that anything on North American voltage normally needs a transformer. However, one or two countries (notably Spain and Morocco) still have a few places on 110v or 120v, so check before plugging in. Continental, Moroccan and Turkish sockets take two round pins, British and Irish ones take three square pins. A travel plug which adapts to all these systems is useful to carry.

Shops Opening hours vary from northern to southern Europe. Those in the north are usually open Monday–Friday all day without a break (sometimes opening late one evening midweek), opening for at least half a day on Saturday and closing on Sunday almost everywhere. In the south they tend to take a break at lunchtime, during the hottest part of the day, and open again around 4pm until perhaps 8pm. They are again generally open until at least Saturday lunchtime and closed on Sunday.

Tampons In western and southern Europe you can buy tampons in all chemists and supermarkets, although in parts of eastern Europe they can still be hard to come by. If you're travelling in the east for any length of time, best to bring a supply.

Time The places covered in this book are in four time zones. Britain, Ireland, Portugal and Morocco are in principle on GMT (or UTC), which is five hours ahead of Eastern Standard Time, eight hours ahead of Pacific Standard Time, eight hours behind western Australia, ten hours behind eastern Australia, and twelve hours behind New Zealand. Most of the Continent is an hour ahead of that, with Finland, Estonia, Latvia, Romania, Bulgaria, Greece, Turkey and the Baltic Russian enclave of Kaliningrad two hours ahead, and Moscow and St Petersburg on GMT+3. All of these countries except Morocco have daylight saving time in summer, but don't all change over at the same time (though EU countries try to) – this, plus daylight saving in North America and Australasia, can mean a further hour or two's difference.

Tipping Although it varies from one country to the next, tipping is not really the serious business it is in North America, but in many countries it is customary to leave at least something in most restaurants and cafés, if only rounding the bill up to the next major denomination. Even in swankier establishments, a ten percent tip is quite sufficient, and you shouldn't feel obliged to tip at all if the service was bad, certainly not if service has been included in the bill. In smarter hotels you should tip hall porters, etc.

CLOTHING AND SHOE SIZES

Dresses						
Continental	42	44	46	48	50	52
American	8	10	12	14	16	18
British	10	12	14	16	18	20
Men's suits						
Continental	46	48	50	52	54	56
American	36	38	40	42	44	46
British	36	38	40	42	44	46
Men's shirts						
Continental	36	38	41	43	45	
American	14	15	16	17	18	
British	14	15	16	17	18	
Women's shoes						
Continental	36	37	38	39	40	41
American	5	5.5	6.5	7	8	8.5
British	3	4	5	5.5	6.5	7
Men's shoes						
Continental	41	42	43	44	45	46
American	8	8.5	9.5	10.5	11	12
British	7	7.5	8.5	9.5	10	11

METRIC MEASURES

1 centimetre = approx 0.394 inches; 1 inch = approx 2.5cm; 1 foot = approx 30cm.

1 metre = approx 1.094 yards or 39 inches; 1 yard = approx 0.914m.

1 kilometre = approx 0.621 miles; 1 mile = approx 1.609km; 5 miles = approx 8km.

1 kilo = approx 0.551lb; 1lb = approx 454g/0.454kg; 1oz = approx 28.3g.

1 litre = approx 2.11 US pints; 1 US pint = approx 0.473 litres; 1 US quart = approx 0.946 litres.

1 litre = approx 0.264 US gallons; 1 US gallon = approx 3.785 litres.

1 litre = approx 1.76 UK pints; 1 UK pint = approx 0.568 litres; 1 UK gallon = approx 4.54litres.

1 US pint = approx 0.834 UK pint; 1 UK pint = approx 1.2 US pints; 6 US pints = approx 5 UK pints

TEMPERATURE

To convert Celsius to Farenheit, multiply by nine, divide by five and add 32.
To convert Farenheit to Celsius, take away 32, multiply by five and divide by nine.

Celsius	0	10	20	30	40
Farenheit	32	50	68	86	104

LANGUAGE

If you're making a general tour of Europe you can't hope always to speak the language of the country you're travelling in, and in any case in Germany, Scandinavia, and especially the Netherlands and Switzerland, many people, particularly the young, speak reasonable English. That said, it is polite to know at least a few very basic words and phrases wherever you happen to be, which is why we've included the chart on the following pages, and a smattering of French, German or Russian is handy everywhere as a common language if English fails.

Rough Guides phrasebooks are now available for Czech, French, German, Greek, Hungarian, Italian, Polish, Portuguese, Russian, Spanish and Turkish. Pocket **dictionaries** can easily be bought for most European languages in the countries where they are spoken, and usually at home too. If you want to get to grips further with any of the languages, Routledge's "Colloquial" series is the best place you could start.

BULGARIAN, CZECH AND DANISH

	Bulgarian	Czech	Danish
Yes	Da	Ano	Ja
No	Ne	Ne	Nej
Please	Molya	Prosím	Vaerså venlig
Thank you	Blagodarya	Dikuju	Tak
Hello/Good day	Dobâr den	Dobry den/ahoj	Goddag
Goodbye	Dovizhdane	Na shledanou	Farvel
Excuse me	Izvinyavaïte	Promiqte	Undskyld
Where	Kude	Kde	Hvor
When	Koga	Kdy	Hvornår
How	Kak	Jak	Hvordan
Left	Lyavo	Vlevo	Venstre
Right	Dyasno	Vpravo	Højre
Large	Golyama	Velk	Stor
Small	Malko	Maly	Lille
Good	Dobro	Dobry	God
Bad	Plosho	Spatny	Dårlig
Near	Blizo	Blízko	Naer
Far	Daleche	Daleko	Fjern
Cheap	Eftino	Levn,	Billig
Expensive	Skupo	Drah,	Dyr
Open	Otvoreno	Otevueno	Åben
Closed	Zatvoreno	Zavueno	Lukket
Today	Dnes	Dnes	I dag
Yesterday	Vechera	Vaera	I går
Tomorrow	Utre	Zítra	I morgen
Day	Den	Den	Dag
Week	Sedmitza	Tyden	Uge
Month	Mesetz	Mesíc	Måned
Year	Godina	Rok	År
How much is....?	Kolko...?	Kolík stojí...?	Hvor koster er...?
What time is it?	Kolko e chasut?	Kolík je hodin?	Hvad er klokken?
Where is...?	Kude e	Kde je...?	Hvor er...?
I don't understand	Ne vi razbiram	Nerozumím	Jeg forstår ikke
Do you speak English?	Govorite li Angliski?	Miuvíte Anglicky?	Taler de Engelsk?
Please write it down	Molya napishete go	Prosím, napiyte to	Vaer venlig at skrive det
One	Edin	Jeden	En
Two	Dve	Dva	To
Three	Tri	Tri	Tre
Four	Chetiri	Ctyri	Fire
Five	Pet	Pet	Fem
Six	Shest	Sest	Seks
Seven	Sedem	Sedm	Syv
Eight	Osem	Osum	Otte
Nine	Devet	Devet	Ni
Ten	Deset	Deset	Ti

DUTCH, ESTONIAN AND FINNISH

	Dutch	Estonian	Finnish
Yes	Ja	Jaa	Kyllä
No	Nee	Ei	Ei
Please	Alstublieft	Palun	Olkaa hyvä
Thank you	Dank u/Bedankt	Tänan	Kiitos
Hello/Good day	Dag	Tere	Hyvää
Goodbye	Tot ziens	Head aega	Hyvästi
Excuse me	Pardon	Vabandage	Anteeksi
Where	Waar	Kus	Missä
When	Wanneer	Millal	Milloin
How	Hoe	Kuidas	Kuinka
Left	Links	Vasak	Vasen
Right	Rechts	Parem	Oikea
Large	Groot	Suur	Suuri
Small	Klein	Väike	Pieni
Good	Goed	Hea	Hyvä
Bad	Slecht	Halb	Paha
Near	Dichtbij	Lähedal	Lähellä
Far	Ver	Kaugel	Kaukana
Cheap	Goedkoop	Odav	Halpa
Expensive	Duur	Kallis	Kallis
Open	Open	Avatud	Avoin
Closed	Dicht	Suletud	Suljettu
Today	Vandaag	Täna	Tänään
Yesterday	Gisteren	Eile	Eilen
Tomorrow	Morgen	Homme	Huomenna
Day	Dag	Päev	Päivä
Week	Week	Nädal	Viikko
Month	Maand	Kuu	Kuukausi
Year	Jaar	Aasta	Vuosi
How much is....?	Wat kost....?	Kui palju maksab ...?	Kuinka paljon on ...?
What time is it?	Hoe laat is het?	Mis kell praegu on?	Paljonko kello on?
Where is...?	Waar is...?	Kus on ...?	Missä on...?
I don't understand	Ik begrijp het niet	Ma ei saa aru	En ymmärrä
Do you speak English?	Spreekt u Engels?	Kas te räägite inglise keelt?	Puhutteko Englantia?
Please write it down	Wilt u het opschrijven, alstublieft	Palun kirjutage see üles.	Olkaa hyvä ja kiarjoit-takaa se
One	Een	Üks	Yksi
Two	Twee	Tkaks	Kaksi
Three	Drie	Kolm	Kolme
Four	Vier	Neli	Neljä
Five	Vijf	Viis	Viisi
Six	Zes	Kuus	Kuusi
Seven	Zeven	Seitse	Seitsemän
Eight	Acht	Kaheksa	Kahdeksan
Nine	Negen	Üheksa	Yhdeksän
Ten	Tien	Kümme	Kymmenen

FRENCH, GERMAN AND GREEK

	French	German	Greek
Yes	Oui	Ja	Néh
No	Non	Nein	Óhi
Please	S'il vous plaît	Bitte	Parakaló
Thank you	Merci	Danke	Efharistó
Hello/Good day	Bonjour	Güten Tag	Adío
Goodbye	Au revoir	Auf Wiedersehen	Hérete
Excuse me	Pardon	Entschuldigen Sie, bitte	Signómi
Where	Où	Wo	Pou
When	Quand	Wann	Póte
How	Comment	Wie	Pos
Left	Gauche	Links	Aristerá
Right	Droite	Rechts	Dheksiá
Large	Grand	Gross	Megálo
Small	Petit	Klein	Mikró
Good	Bon	Gut	Kaló
Bad	Mauvais	Schlecht	Kakó
Near	Près	Nah	Kondá
Far	Loin	Weit	Makriá
Cheap	Bon marché	Billig	Fthinós
Expensive	Cher	Teuer	Akrivós
Open	Ouvert	Offen	Aniktós
Closed	Fermé	Geschlossen	Klistós
Today	Aujourd'hui	Heute	Símera
Yesterday	Hier	Gestern	Khthés
Tomorrow	Demain	Morgen	Ávrio
Day	Jour	Tag	Méra
Week	Semaine	Woche	Iméra
Month	Mois	Monat	Evdomáda
Year	Année	Jahr	Chrónos
How much is....?	Combien est...?	Wieviel kostet....?	Póso káni...?
What time is it?	Quelle heure est-il?	Wieviel Uhr ist es?	Ti óra inai...?
Where is...?	Où est...?	Wo ist...?	Pou íne...?
I don't understand	Je ne comprends pas	Ich verstehe nicht	Dhen katalavéno
Do you speak English?	Parlez-vous anglais?	Sprechen Sie Englisch?	Ksérite Angliká?
Please write it down	Veuillez me l'écrire	Bitte schreiben Sie es	Parakaló grápiste to
One	Un	Eins	Éna
Two	Deux	Zwei	Dhío
Three	Trois	Drei	Tría
Four	Quatre	Vier	Téseres
Five	Cinq	Fünf	Pénde
Six	Six	Sechs	Éksi
Seven	Sept	Sieben	Eftá
Eight	Huit	Acht	Októ
Nine	Neuf	Neun	Enyá
Ten	Dix	Zehn	Dhéka

HUNGARIAN, ITALIAN AND LATVIAN

	Hungarian	Italian	Latvian
Yes	Igen	Si	Jā
No	Nem	No	Nē
Please	Kérem	Per favore	Lūdzu
Thank you	Köszönöm	Grazie	Paldies
Hello/Good day	Jó napot	Ciao/buon giorno	Labdien
Goodbye	Viszontlá-tásta	Ciao/arriverderci	Uz redzēšyanos
Excuse me	Bocsánat	Mi scusi/prego	Atvainojiet
Where	Hol	Dove	Kur
When	Mikor	Quando	Kad
How	Hogyan	Come	Cik
Left	Balra	Sinistra	Kreisi
Right	Jobbra	Destra	Labi
Large	Nagy	Grande	Liels
Small	Kicsi	Piccolo	Mazs
Good	Jó	Buono	Labs
Bad	Rossz	Cattivo	Slikts
Near	Közel	Vicino	Tuvs
Far	Távol	Lontano	Tās
Cheap	Olcsó	Buon mercato	Lēts
Expensive	Drága	Caro	Dārgs
Open	Nyitva	Aperto	Atvērts
Closed	Zárva	Chiuso	Slēgts
Today	Ma	Oggi	Yodien
Yesterday	Tegnap	Ieri	Vakar
Tomorrow	Holnap	Domani	Rīt
Day	Nap	Giorno	Diena
Week	Hét	Settimana	Bedeka
Month	Hónap	Mese	Menesis
Year	Ev	Anno	Gads
How much is....?	Mennyibe Kerül...?	Quanto è...?	Cik tas maksā ...?
What time is it?	Hány óra?	Che ore sono?	Cik ir pulkstenis?
Where is...?	Hol van?	Dov'è...?	Kur ir ...?
I don't understand	Nem értem	Non ho capito	Es nesaprotu
Do you speak English?	Beszél Angolul?	Parla Inglese?	Vai jūs runājat Angliski?
Please write it down	Legyen szives, irja le	Lo scriva, per favore	Lūdzu uzrakstiet
One	Egy	Uno	Viens
Two	Kettö	Due	Divi
Three	Három	Tre	Trīs
Four	Négy	Quattro	CÜetri
Five	Ot	Cinque	Pieci
Six	Hayt	Sei	Seyi
Seven	Hét	Sette	Septiņi
Eight	Nyolc	Otto	Astoņi
Nine	Kilenc	Nove	Deviņi
Ten	Tíz	Dieci	Desmit

LITHUANIAN, NORWEGIAN AND POLISH

	Lithuanian	Norwegian	Polish
Yes	Taip	Ja	Tak
No	Ne	Nei	Nie
Please	Prayau	Vaer så god	Prosze
Thank you	Aaiu	Takk	Dziekuje
Hello/Good day	Labas	God dag	Dzien dobry
Goodbye	Viso gero	Adjø	Do widzenia
Excuse me	Atsiprayau	Unnskyld	Przepraszam
Where	Kur	Hvor	Gdzie
When	Kada	Når	Kiedy
How	Kaip	Hvordan	Jak
Left	Kairė	Venstre	Na lewo
Right	Deyinė	Høyre	Na prawo
Large	Didelis	Stor	Wielki
Small	Mažas	Liten	Maly
Good	Geras	God	Dobry
Bad	Blogas	Dårlig	Zly
Near	Artimas	I naerheten	Blisko
Far	Tolimas	Langt Borte	Daleko
Cheap	Pigus	Billig	Tani
Expensive	Brangus	Dyr	Drogi
Open	Atidarytas	Åpen	Otwarty
Closed	Uždarytas	Lukket	Zamknięty
Today	Yiandien	I dag	Dzisiaj
Yesterday	Vakar	I går	Wczoraj
Tomorrow	Rytdiena	I morgen	Jutro
Day	Diena	Dag	Dzie0
Week	Savaitė	Uke	Tydzień
Month	Mėnuo	Måned	Miesiąc
Year	Metai	År	Rok
How much is....?	Kiek kainuoja ...?	Hvor mye er...?	Lle Losztuje...?
What time is it?	Kiek valand-?	Hvor mange er klokken?	Która godzina?
Where is...?	Kur yra ...?	Hvor er...?	Gdzie jest . . . ?
I don't understand	Nesuprantu	Jeg forstår ikke	Nie rozemiem
Do you speak English?	Ar j-s kalbate angliykai?	Snakker de Englesk?	Pani mówi po Angielsku?
Please write it down	Prayau užrayyti	Vennligst skriv det ned	Proszę to napisać
One	Vienas	En	Jeden
Two	Du/dvi	To	Dwa
Three	Trys	Tre	Trzy
Four	Keturi	Fire	Cztery
Five	Penki	Fem	Piec
Six	Yeyi	Seks	Szesc
Seven	Septyni	Sju	Siedem
Eight	Aytuoni	Åtte	Osiem
Nine	Devyni	Ni	Dziewiec
Ten	Deyimt	Ti	Dziesiec

PORTUGESE, ROMANIAN AND RUSSIAN

	Portuguese	Romanian	Russian
Yes	Sim	Da	Da
No	Não	Nu	Net
Please	Por favor	Vd rog	Pozháluysta
Thank you	Obrigado	Mulmumesc	Spasíbo
Hello/Good day	Olá	Salut/Buna ziua	zdrávstvuyte
Goodbye	Adeus	La revedere	Do svidániya
Excuse me	Desculpe	Permitemi-mi	Izvinite
Where	Onde	Unde	Gde
When	Quando	Cînd	Kogdá
How	Como	Cum	Kak
Left	Esquerda	Stînga	Nalévo
Right	Direita	Dreapta	Naprávo
Large	Grande	Mare	Bolshóy
Small	Pequeno	Mic	Málenkiy
Good	Bom	Bun/Bîne	Khoróshiy
Bad	Mau	Rdu	Plokhóy
Near	Perto	Apropriat	Bleezkiy
Far	Longe	Departe	Da-lyiko
Cheap	Barato	Ieftin	Dyi-shovee
Expensive	Caro	Scump	Daragoy
Open	Aberto	Închis	Otkryto
Closed	Fechado	Deschis	Zakryto
Today	Hoje	Azi	Syivo-dnya
Yesterday	Ontem	Ieri	Vcherá
Tomorrow	Amanhã	Mîine	Závtra
Day	Dia	Zi	Dyin
Week	Semana	Sdptdmînd	Nyi-dyel-ya
Month	Mês	Lund	Mye-syats
Year	Ano	An	Got
How much is....?	Quanto e... ?	Cît costa...?	Skólko stóit?
What time is it?	Que horas sao?	Ce ora este?	Katoree chass?
Where is...?	Onde é...?	Unde este...?	Gde.....?
I don't understand	Não comprendo	Nu înteleg	Ya ne ponimáyu
Do you speak English?	Fala Inglés?	Vorbimi Englezeste?	Vy govoríte po-anglíyski?
Please write it down	Escreva-mo, por favor	Vd rog scriemi	Zapishíte éto pozháluysta (means could you write it down?)
One	Um	Unu	Odín
Two	Dois	Doi	Dva
Three	Três	Trei	Tri
Four	Quatro	Patru	Chetyre
Five	Cinco	Cinci	Pyat
Six	Seis	Sase	Shest
Seven	Sete	Sapte	Sem
Eight	Oito	Opt	Vósem
Nine	Nove	Noua	Dévyat
Ten	Dez	Zece	Désyat

SERBO-CROAT, SLOVENE AND SPANISH

	Serbo-Croat	Slovene	Spanish
Yes	Da	Ja	Si
No	Ne	Ne	No
Please	Molim	Prosim	Por favor
Thank you	Hvala	Hvala	Gracias
Hello/Good day	Bog/Dobar dan	ivjo/Dober dan	Hola
Goodbye	Bog/Do vidjenja	Nasvidenje	Adios
Excuse me	Izvinite	Oprostite	Con permiso
Where	Gdje	Kje	¿Dónde?
When	Kada	Kdaj	¿Cuándo?
How	Kako	Kako	¿Cómo?
Left	Lijevo	Levo	Izquierda
Right	Desno	Desno	Derecha
Large	Veliko	Veliko	Gran
Small	Malo	Majhno	Pequeño
Good	Dobro	Dobro	Buen
Bad	Loče	Slabo	Mal
Near	Blizu	Blizu	Próximo
Far	Daleko	Daleč	Lejos
Cheap	Jeftino	Poceni	Barato
Expensive	Skupo	Drago	Caro
Open	Otvoreno	Odprto	Abierto
Closed	Zatvoreno	Zaprto	Cerrado
Today	Danas	Danes	Hoy
Yesterday	Juče	Včeraj	Ayer
Tomorrow	Sutra	Jutri	Mañana
Day	Dan	Dan	Día
Week	Tjedan	Teden	Semana
Month	Mjesec	Mesec	Mes
Year	Godina	Leto	Año
How much is....?	Koliko stoji..?	Koliko stane?	¿Cuánto cuesta...?
What time is it?	Koliko je sati?	Koliko je ura?	¿Tiene la hora?
Where is...?	Gdje je..?	Kje je	¿Dónde está...?
I don't understand	Ne razumijem	Ne razumem	No entiendo
Do you speak English?	Govorite li engleski?	Govorite angleško?	¿Habla Inglés?
Please write it down	Napišite ga molim.	Prosim, če mi napišete	Escríbamelo, por favor
One	jedan	ena	Un/Una
Two	dva	dve	Dos
Three	tri	tri	Tres
Four	četiri	štiri	Cuatro
Five	pet	pet	Cinco
Six	šest	šest	Seis
Seven	sedam	sedem	Siete
Eight	osam	osem	Ocho
Nine	devet	devet	Nueve
Ten	deset	deset	Diez

SWEDISH AND TURKISH

	Swedish	Turkish
Yes	Ja	Evet
No	Nej	Yok
Please	Var så god	Lütfen
Thank you	Tack	Tesekkür ederim
Hello/Good day	Hej	Merhaba
Goodbye	Adjö	Allahaismarladik
Excuse me	Ursäkta mig	Pardon
Where	Var	. . . nerede
When	När	Ne zaman
How	Hur	Nasfl
Left	Vänster	Sol
Right	Höger	Sag
Large	Stor	Büyuk
Small	Liten	Kücük
Good	Bra	Iyi
Bad	Dalig	Kötü
Near	Nära	Yakin
Far	Avlägsen	Uzak
Cheap	Billig	Ucuz
Expensive	Dyr	Pahalf
Open	Öppen	Açfk
Closed	Stängd	Kapalf
Today	I dag	Bugün
Yesterday	I går	Dün
Tomorrow	I morgon	Yarin
Day	Dag	Gün
Week	Vecka	Hafta
Month	Månad	Ay
Year	Är	Sene
How much is....?	Vad kostar det...?	Ne kadar...?
What time is it?	Hur mycket är klockan?	Saatiniz var mi?
Where is...?	Var är...?	Nerede...?
I don't understand	Jag förstår int	Anlamadim Ingilizce
Do you speak English?	Talar ni Engelska?	Biliyormusunuz?
Please write it down	Skulle ni kunna skriva det?	Onu yazarmfsfnfz
One	Ett	Bir
Two	Två	Iki
Three	Tre	Uç
Four	Fyra	Dört
Five	Fem	Bes
Six	Sex	Alti
Seven	Sju	Yedi
Eight	Ätta	Sekiz
Nine	Nio	Dokuz
Ten	Tio	On

PART TWO

THE
GUIDE

CHAPTER 1

AUSTRIA

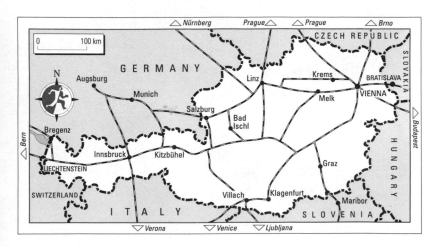

Introduction

For centuries the heart of an empire which played a pivotal role in the political and cultural destiny of Europe, **Austria** underwent several decades of change and uncertainty in the twentieth century. The interwar state, shorn of its empire and racked by economic problems and political strife, fell prey to the promise of a greater Germany. But postwar stability has seen the growth of a genuine patriotism, while the end of the Cold War has put the country, and its capital, **Vienna**, back at the heart of Europe.

The ethos of Austrian society is solidly bourgeois, although the Socialist party has been the strongest influence in government over past decades; and despite endless scandals, and the deep divisions created by the Waldheim controversy, an almost Scandinavian emphasis on social policy continues to be the guiding principle of national life.

Austria is primarily known for two contrasting attractions – the fading Imperial glories of Vienna, and the variety of its Alpine hinterland. **Vienna** is the gateway to much of central Europe and a good place to soak up the culture of *Mitteleuropa* before heading towards the Magyar and Slav lands over which the city once held sway. Less renowned provincial capitals like **Graz** and **Linz** provide a similar level of culture and vitality. The most dramatic of Austria's Alpine scenery is west of here, in and around the **Tirol**, whose capital, **Innsbruck**, provides the best base for exploration. **Salzburg**, however, between Innsbruck and Vienna, represents urban Austria at its most picturesque, an intoxicating Baroque city within easy striking distance of the mountains and lakes of the **Salzkammergut** to the east.

Information and maps

Tourist offices are plentiful and come under an assortment of names, often just Information, or Verkehrsamt, Fremdenverkehrsverein or other variants. All are helpful and well organized, often hand out free maps and almost always book accommodation, sometimes for a small fee, a deposit, or both. They are open all day, every day, in the larger cities during the summer; outside this period, and in smaller towns and remote areas, times may be restricted to a few hours on weekday mornings.

There are plenty of good general **maps** of Austria, one of the best is the 1:500,000 Freytag & Berndt. The 1:200,000 *Generalkarte* series of regional maps are useful for lengthier touring, as are the more detailed 1:50,000 Freytag & Berndt *Wanderkarten* and rival Kompas *Wanderkarten*, both covering all the Alpine districts and many rural eastern areas as well.

Money and banks

Austria's unit of **currency** is the Schilling, which is divided into 100 Groschen. There are coins for 5, 10 and 50 Groschen, 1, 5, 10 and 20 Schilling; notes for 20, 50, 100, 500, 1000 and 5000 Schilling. Prices are usually preceded by the initials öS. The rate of exchange currently hovers around öS20 to £1.

Banking hours tend to be Mon–Fri 8am–12.30pm and 1.30–3pm; in Vienna they're Mon–Wed and Fri 8am–3pm, Thurs 8am–5.30pm (smaller Viennese branches take an hour for lunch). Post offices charge slightly less commission on exchange transactions than banks do, and in larger cities they are open longer hours.

Communications

Most **post offices** are open Mon–Fri 8am–noon and 2–6pm; in larger cities they do without the lunch break and open Sat 8–10am as well; some are open 24 hours. You can also buy stamps at tobacconists (Tabak-Trafik).

The smallest coin accepted in public call boxes is öS1 and a couple of these should suffice for a local call; insert öS10 and upwards if calling long distance, or buy a phone card (*Telefonkarte*), available from tobacconists, and seek out a card phone. You can make **international calls** from all public telephones, but it's easier from larger post offices, which have booths. The operator number is ☎1611 for domestic calls, ☎1616 for international.

Getting around

Traversing Austria by public transport is easy, and usually very scenic. Trains cover the country fairly comprehensively, supplemented in remoter regions by buses.

■ Trains and buses

Austrian Federal Railways (Österreichische Bundesbahnen or ÖBB) run a punctual, clean and comfortable network, which includes most towns of any size. **Trains** marked EC (international expresses), SC or IC (inter-city), or D (express) are the fastest. Those designated E (*Eilzug*) are "semi-fast trains", stopping at most intermediate points; the slowest, local services are designated by number only. Fares are calculated according to distance, with the first 100km costing öS156. If you don't have an InterRail/Eurail pass, Austrian **passes** worth considering include the Puzzle ticket (öS1090, under-26s öS660), which allows 4 days' free travel over a 10-day period in one of four zones – west (Vorarlberg, Tyrol, Land Salzburg), south (Salzburg, Carinthia, Styria), north (Upper Austria, Lower Austria, Vienna, Burgenland) and east (Lower Austria, Vienna, Burgenland, Styria); and the month-long Bundesnetzkarte, which gives unlimited travel on the entire network and costs öS4300. The **national timetable** (*Österreichische Kursbuch*), detailing the whole network, complete with lake and Danube transport, costs öS100; timetable leaflets covering major routes are free at stations.

Austria's **Bahn- and Postbus** system fills the gaps in the network, serving the remoter villages and otherwise inaccessible Alpine valleys. Where there is a choice, you will find trains easier and quicker, and bus fares are only slightly cheaper at öS130 per 100km. As a general rule, Bahnbus services, operated by ÖBB, depart from outside train stations; the Postbus tends to stop outside the post office. Twenty-four-hour or seven-day regional **travelcards** (*Netzkarte*), covering both trains and buses, are available in many regions of Austria, but prices – and areas of coverage – vary widely from place to place.

■ Driving, hitching and cycling

Given the deals available on Austria's trains, **driving** is not a budget option. National speed limits are 50kph in built-up areas, 100kph on normal roads, and 130kph on motorways. All Austria's Autobahns are subject to a single **toll**, which basically involves buying a windscreen sticker (*Vignette*) from the petrol stations or shops found at border posts when entering the country. You can also buy them from post offices and tobacconists once inside the country. A 10-day pass costs öS70 (and you'll need to buy a 10-day one even if you're merely passing straight through the country); 2-months öS140; and 12-months öS550 (motorbikers get a 50 percent reduction on the 12-month pass, but none on the others). You don't need a *Vignette* at all if you intend to stick to normal main roads; however those caught driving on Austria's Autobahns without displaying one will be subject to an öS1100 fine.

If you break down, the **Österreichischer Automobile, Motorrad und Touring Club** has a 24-hour breakdown service (☎120). **Car rental** charges are around öS850 per day with unlimited mileage with the multinationals, although you may land something cheaper with smaller local firms. You need to be over 21 to rent a car.

Hitching can be difficult away from the main east–west routes, and many locals make use of the Mitfahrzentrale (3, Invalidenstrasse 15, Vienna; ☎0222/715 00 66), an agency that puts potential hitchers in touch with drivers willing to take passengers for a fee – usually significantly cheaper than public transport.

Austria is very **bicycle**-friendly, with cycle lanes in all major towns. All except the smallest train stations rent out bikes for öS90 per day, öS65 if you have a valid train ticket. You can return them to any station.

Accommodation

Despite profiteering in tourist centres like Vienna and Salzburg, accommodation need not be expensive, and, although it can be a scramble in July and August, finding a room doesn't present too many problems. Most tourist offices book accommodation with little fuss, usually for a fee (around öS35) and deposit.

■ Hotels, pensions and private rooms

A high standard of cleanliness and comfort can usually be taken for granted in Austrian **hotels**, although in resorts and larger towns prices can be high. Expect to pay öS700–800 for a double with bathroom, slightly less for rooms without private facilities. Good-value **bed and breakfast** accommodation is usually available in the many small family-run hotels known as *Gasthöfe* and *Gasthäuser*, with prices starting at öS500–600 for a double. In the larger towns and cities **pensions** situated in large apartment blocks offer similar prices. Most (though not all) tourist offices also have a stock of **private rooms**, although in well-travelled rural areas where the locals depend a great deal on tourism, roadside signs offering *Zimmer Frei* are fairly ubiquitous anyway. Prices hover around the öS400–600 mark for double rooms.

■ Hostels and student accommodation

Youth hostels (*Jugendherberge* or *Jugendgästehaus*) are fairly widespread in Austria, with around 100 in all. Standards vary from the hearty, basic rural variety to the well-appointed (but crowded) hostels of the larger cities. Rates are öS140–220, normally including a nominal breakfast. Sheet sleeping bags are obligatory, although the cost of renting one is often included in the charge. Many hostels serve other meals besides breakfast for öS50–75. Austria's hostels are administered by two separate organizations (both HI-affiliated) and for full lists and addresses you'll have to write to both of them: Österreichisches Jugendherbergswerk, at Helferstorferstrasse 4, 1010 Wien (☎0222/533 18 33); and Österreichischer Jugendherbergsverband, Schottenring 28, 1010 Wien (☎0222/533 53 53).

ACCOMMODATION PRICE CODES

Throughout this guide, accommodation is priced on a scale of ① to ⑨, the number indicating the lowest price per night a single person could expect to pay in that establishment in high season. With hostels this is the nightly rate per person; with hotels, the price is arrived at by dividing the cost of the cheapest double room by two. The prices indicated by the codes are as follows:

① under £5 / $8	④ £15–20 / $24–32	⑦ £30–35 / $48–56
② £5–10 / $8–16	⑤ £20–25 / $32–40	⑧ £35–40 / $56–64
③ £10–15 / $16–24	⑥ £25–30 / $40–48	⑨ £40 / $64 and over

■ Camping

Austria's high standards of accommodation are reflected in the country's **campsites**, the vast majority of which have laundry facilities, shops and snack bars, as well as the standard necessities. Most are open May–Sept, although in the winter-sports resorts of western Austria many never close. Expect to pay about öS60–80 per person, öS40–70 per pitch, plus öS20–50 for a vehicle.

Food and drink

Foodstuffs in Austria are expensive, which makes eating out marginally cheaper than self-catering. Drinking, while never cheap, is affordable, and the country's bars and cafés are among its real joys.

■ Food

For ready-made snacks, try a *Konditorei* or confectioner's, which sell sweet pastries and cakes, as well as sandwiches. **Street food** centres around the ubiquitous *Würstelstand*, which sells hot dogs, *Bratwurst* (grilled sausage), *Käsekrainer* (spicy sausage with cheese), *Bosna* (spicy, thin Balkan sausage) or *Currywurst*, usually chopped up and served with a *Semmel* or bread roll, along with a dollop of *Senf* (mustard) and *Dose* (can) of beer. *Schnell-Imbiss* or *Bufet* establishments serve similar fare, augmented by hamburgers and simple grills.

It's difficult to make hard distinctions between places to eat and places to drink – most establishments offer **snacks and meals** of some kind. Similarly, it's possible just to have a drink in most restaurants. Town-centre *Kaffeehäuser* or cafés tend to be the most expensive places to eat, while food served in bars can be great value. Light meals and snacks include pizzas from about öS70; all restaurant and café menus have filling central European standbys such as spicy *Serbische Bohnensuppe* (Serbian bean soup) and *Gulaschsuppe* (goulash soup) for around öS50. Main dishes (*Hauptspeisen*) are dominated by veal – *Schnitzel* – often accompanied by potatoes and a vegetable or salad: *Wienerschnitzel*

is fried in breadcrumbs, *Pariser* in batter, *Natur* served on its own or with a creamy sauce. In general you can expect to pay öS80–140 for a standard main course, though set lunchtime menus (*Mittagsmenü*), even in more costly establishments, always offer a wide range of cheaper dishes. Desserts (*Mehlspeisen*) include a wide range of sweets and pastries: various types of Torte (including the famous rich chocolate *Sachertorte*); strudel, cheesecake; and *Palatschinken* (or pancake, with various nut or jam fillings) are all common.

■ Drink

For urban Austrians, daytime drinking traditionally centres around the *Kaffeehaus* or **café** – relaxed places furnished with a stock of the day's newspapers. They serve alcoholic and soft drinks, snacks and cakes, alongside a wide range of different coffees: a *Schwarzer* is small and black, a *Brauner* comes with a little milk, while a *Melange* is half-coffee and half-milk; a *Kurzer* is a small espresso; an *Einspänner* is a glass of black coffee topped with *Schlag*, the ubiquitous whipped cream that is offered with most pastries and cakes. A cup of coffee in one of these places is, however, pricey at öS25–35, and numerous stand-up **coffee bars** (many part of the Julius Meinl or Eduscho chains) are a much cheaper alternative at öS15 a cup.

Night-time drinking centres around a growing number of youthful **bars** and *Musikcafés*, although more traditional *Bierstuben* and *Weinstuben* are still thick on the ground, especially in rural areas. Austrian **beers**, while of a high standard, don't come in the infinite variety found in Germany. Most establishments serve the local brew on tap, either by the *Krügerl* (half-litre, for around öS35), *Seidel* (third-litre, öS25–30) or *Pfiff* (fifth of a litre, öS12–18), while also keeping a few international speciality beers in bottles. Wine, usually sold by the quarter-litre (*Viertel*), is often cheaper than other alcoholic drinks and is widely consumed. The *Weinkeller* is a regular sight in Austrian towns and cities; around Vienna wine is consumed in a *Heuriger*, a traditional tavern in the vine-producing suburbs, customarily serving cold food as well. In autumn a lot of establishments serve *Sturm*, a misty, part-fermented concoction made from newly harvested grapes.

Opening hours and holidays

Most **shops** open Mon–Sat 9am–6pm. Beware of a two-hour lunch break outside major cities, and remember that not all shops have yet begun to take advantage of Saturday afternoon opening hours. There are few opportunities for late-night shopping, save for basic provision stores in the larger train stations. All shops and banks will be closed, and most museums will at least have reduced hours, on the following **public holidays**: Jan 1; Jan 6; Easter Monday; May 1; Ascension Day; Whit Monday; Corpus Christi; Aug 15; Oct 26; Nov 1; Dec 8; Dec 25 and 26.

Emergencies

Although the traditionally laid-back Austrians lack the German and Swiss reverence for rules and regu-

EMERGENCY NUMBERS

Police ☎133; ambulance ☎144; fire ☎122.

lations, the country is still extremely law-abiding, and is a reasonably safe place to travel. This doesn't prevent the tabloids from complaining about the increase in urban **crime**, which the political right attributes to East Europeans. Austrian **police** have a leisurely but efficient attitude to complaints, and all but the most harassed inner-city cop can be relied upon to be courteous to strangers. There are few places where female travellers will feel ill at ease, except for some outer districts of Vienna and Graz. Hitting children is illegal in Austria, though the law is practically unenforceable.

As for **health**, city hospital casualty departments will treat you and ask questions later. For prescriptions, pharmacies or *Apotheke* tend to follow normal shopping hours. A rota system covers night-time and weekend opening; each pharmacy has details of those open posted up in the window.

VIENNA

Most newcomers to **VIENNA** arrive with a firm image in their minds: a romantic place full of Habsburg nostalgia and musical resonances. Visually it's unlikely to disappoint: an eclectic feast of architectural styles, from eighteenth-century High Baroque through monumental nineteenth-century imperial projects to modernist experiments and enlightened municipal planning. However, the capital often seems aloof from the rest of the country; Alpine Austrians look on it as an alien eastern metropolis with an impenetrable dialect, staffed by an army of fund-draining bureaucrats. The former imperial city has had a tough time of it in the twentieth century, deprived of its hinterland by World War I, then washed up on the edge of western Europe by the Cold War. Its population has dropped by a quarter since 1910, and its image is one of melancholy and decay, though the latter is perhaps more a romantic affectation than a realistic portrait of the city today.

The first settlement of any substance here, Roman Vindobona, was never much more than a garrison town, and it was only with the rise of the Babenberg clan in the tenth century that Vienna became an important centre. In 1278 the city fell to Rudolf of Habsburg, but had to compete for centuries with Prague, Linz and Graz as the imperial residence on account of its vulnerability to attack from the Turks, who first laid siege to it in 1529. It was only with the removal of the Turkish threat in 1683 that the court based itself here permanently. The great aristocratic families, grown fat on the profits of the Turkish wars, flooded in to build palaces and summer residences in a frenzy of construction that gave Vienna its Baroque character.

Imperial Vienna was never a wholly German city; as the capital of a cosmopolitan empire, it attracted great minds from all over central Europe. By the end of the Habsburg era it had become a breeding ground for the ideological movements of the age: nationalism, socialism, Zionism and anti-Semitism all flourished here. This turbulence was reflected in the cultural sphere, and the ghosts of Freud, Klimt, Schiele, Mahler and Schönberg are nowadays bigger tourist draws than old stand-bys like the Lipizzaner horses and the Vienna Boys' Choir. There is more to Vienna than *fin-de-siècle* decadence, however; a strong, home-grown, youthful culture, coupled with new influences from former Eastern Bloc neighbours, has placed the city at the heart of European cultural life once again.

Arrival and information

Trains from the west and from Hungary terminate at the **Westbahnhof**, situated on the outer ring road or Gürtel 2km west of the centre close to Mariahilferstrasse, Vienna's brashest shopping street; from here the U-Bahn metro line (U3) leads directly into the city centre. Trains from eastern Europe, Italy and the Balkans arrive at the **Südbahnhof**, 2km south of the centre; from here tram #D goes down Prinz-Eugen-Strasse to Schwarzenbergplatz and the Ring. Some trains arrive at **Wien-Nord**, 2km northeast of the city centre (U-Bahn Praterstern), or at **Franz-Josefs-Bahnhof**, 2km to the north, connected to the Ring by tram #D.

Most international buses arrive at Vienna's **main bus terminal** beside Wien-Mitte, on the eastern edge of the city centre (U-Bahn Landstrasse). If you arrive on one of the **DDSG boat** services from further up the Danube, or from Bratislava or Budapest, you'll find yourself disembarking at the Reichsbrücke, some way northeast of the city centre; the nearest station (U-Bahn Vorgartenstrasse) is five minutes' walk away, one block west of Mexicoplatz.

The city's **airport** is Flughafen Wien-Schwechat, 20km southeast of the centre. The airport is connected to the city centre by the S-Bahn line S7 (öS38), which runs underneath the airport; trains leave every thirty minutes, taking half an hour to reach Wien-Mitte, near the Ring. In addition, there's a regular bus (every 20min; öS70) to the City Air Terminal, next door to Wien-Mitte. Other buses run from the airport to both main train stations. Taxis cost around öS400.

All points of arrival have **tourist kiosks** with accommodation booking facilities. In the city centre, the main **tourist office** is at Kärntnerstrasse 38 (daily 9am–7pm; ☎0222/513 88 92) and has maps, brochures and a room booking service (öS40). There's also an **information**

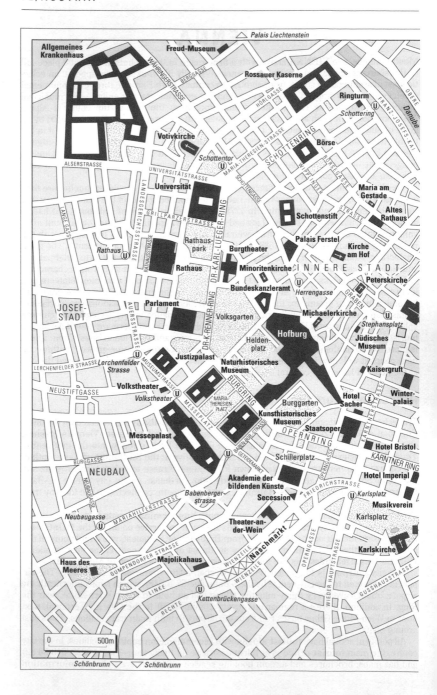

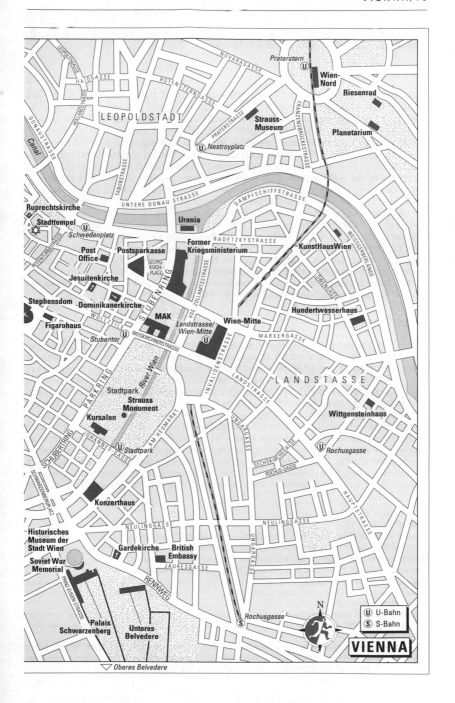

VIENNA

centre for young people at Bellariapassage (Mon–Sat noon–7pm; ☎0222/17 79), below Dr.-Karl-Renner-Ring, which also sells tickets for gigs.

City transport

Vienna is divided into numbered **districts** (*Bezirke*). District 1 is the Innere Stadt, the area enclosed by the Ringstrasse; districts 2–9 are arranged clockwise around it; beyond here, districts 10–23 are a fair way out from the city centre. All Viennese **addresses** begin with the number of the district, followed by the name of the street, and then the number of the house or building. So many of Vienna's attractions are within the Innere Stadt that you can do and see a great deal on foot. Otherwise **public transport** consists of a combination of **trams** (*Strassenbahn*, colloquially known as *Bim*) **buses**; and the ultra-clean **U-Bahn** or metro, which has five lines; complemented by the **S-Bahn** (*Schnellbahn*) network of fast commuter trains. You're expected to buy your ticket in advance from the ticket booths or machines at U-Bahn stations and from tobacconists, and punch it on board buses and trams or before entering the U- or S-Bahn. Fares are calculated on a zonal basis: tickets for the central zone (covering most of Vienna) cost öS19 and allow any number of changes, on any mode of transport. If you're going to be using public transport a fair bit, invest in a **travel pass** (*Netzkarte*), valid for 24 hours (öS60) or 72 hours (öS150); they must be punched once, at the beginning of the first journey. Be warned that the penalty for fare-dodging is öS500, plus the fare. Public transport runs between 5am and midnight; at other times half-hourly **night buses** radiate out from Schwedenplatz – there's a flat fare of öS25 and travel passes are not valid. **Taxis** are notoriously difficult to hail; try the ranks outside the big hotels or main stations, or phone ☎313 00 or ☎601 60.

Accommodation

There's an abundance of **accommodation** in Vienna for those prepared to splash out. However, extreme pressure on the cheaper end of the market means that booking ahead is essential in summer, and advisable during the rest of the year. It's hard to find anything very affordable in the central area, and the cheapest double rooms within reach of it will set you back at least öS350 a head. The likeliest hunting grounds are in the western districts between the Ring and the Gürtel (districts 5–9); places here are often located on the upper floors of nineteenth-century apartment buildings, and have undeniable character. Vienna's youth hostels are clean and efficient, but often full – the official HI hostels all have lock-outs from 9am.

The tourist offices can book **private rooms** for around öS350 per person (with a minimum stay of three nights), but these go quickly and are often in distant suburbs. You could also try the Mitwohnzentrale, 8, Laudongasse 7 (Mon–Fri 10am–2pm & 3–6pm; ☎0222/402 60 61), which tends to be a little cheaper and also offers weekly rates; or the nearby youth travel specialists ÖKISTA, at 9, Türkenstrasse 8 (Mon–Wed & Fri 9.30am–4pm, Thurs 9.30am–5.30pm; ☎0222/401 48).

Hostels

Hostel Ruthensteiner, 15, Robert-Hamerling-Gasse 24 (☎0222/893 42 02). Conveniently located within easy walking distance of the Westbahnhof. Breakfast is extra. No curfew. U-Bahn Westbahnhof. ②.

Hostel Zöhrer, 8, Skodagasse 26 (☎0222/406 07 30). A small private hostel in a nice bit of town between the Ring and Gürtel. No curfew. Tram #5 or #33 or U-Bahn Josefstädter Strasse. ③.

Jugendgästehaus Brigittenau, 20, Friedrich-Engels-Platz 24 (☎0222/332 82 94). Big HI hostel in a dour suburb, but the most likely one to have beds available. 1am curfew. Tram #N from U-Bahn Schwedenplatz or Dresdner Strasse. ②.

Jugendgästehaus Hütteldorf-Hacking, 13, Schlossberggasse 8 (☎0222/877 15 01). HI hostel that's a bit far out, but pleasantly situated on the edge of Lainzer Tiergarten. 11.45pm curfew, though you can buy a late-entry pass. U-Bahn Hütteldorf. ②.

Jugendherberge Myrthengasse/Neustiftgasse, 7, Myrthengasse 7/Neustiftgasse 85 (☎0222/523 63 16). The best of the HI bunch, centrally located, with small dorms and friendly management. 1am curfew. Book in advance. A short walk up Neustiftgasse from U-Bahn Volkstheater. ②.

Porzellaneum, 9, Porzellangasse 30 (☎0222/317 72 82). Centrally located student rooms, with free showers and a nice courtyard out back. Open July–Sept only. Tram #D from the Ring. ③.

Hotels and pensions

Pension Bosch, 3, Keilgasse 13 (☎0222/798 61 79). Near the Südbahnhof, in a quiet backstreet behind the Belvedere palace and gardens. ⑤.

Pension Dr. Geissler, 1, Postgasse 14 (☎0222/533 28 03). Modern pension, ideally placed in the centre. U-Bahn Schwedenplatz. ⑤.

Pension Esterházy, 6, Nelkengasse 3 (☎0222/587 51 59). Fairly basic but acceptable breakfastless pension; no advance booking possible. U-Bahn Neubaugasse. ③.

Pension Falstaff, 9, Müllnergasse 5 (☎0222/317 91 27). Highly regarded, comfortable place. Tram #D from Ring. ④.

Hotel Kugel, 7, Siebensterngasse 43 (☎0222/523 33 55). Jovial owners and good location just beyond the Ring. U-Bahn Neubaugasse. ⑤.

Pension Lindenhof, 7, Lindengasse 4 (☎0222/523 04 98). Appealing rooms with creaky parquet flooring. U-Bahn Neubaugasse. ⑤.

Pension Mozart, 6, Theobaldgasse 15 (☎0222/587 85 05). No frills pension just beyond the Ring. U-Bahn Neubaugasse/Babenbergerstrasse. ④.

Hotel Orient, 1, Tiefer Graben 30 (☎0222/533 73 07). Mind-bogglingly exotic decor and a wide range of prices. ⑤–⑨.

Hotel Post, 1, Fleischmarkt 24 (☎0222/515 83). A civilized, central hotel with big old rooms. U-Bahn Schwedenplatz. ⑤.

Hotel Praterstern, 2, Mayergasse 6 (☎0222/214 01 23). Turn-of-the century hotel close to the Prater. U-Bahn Nestroyplatz. ④.

Pension Quisisana, 6, Windmühlgasse 6 (☎0222/587 33 41). Small rooms in a pension run by friendly couple near Mariahilferstrasse. U-Bahn Neubaugasse. ③.

Pension Riedl, 1, Georg-Coch-Platz 3 (☎0222/512 79 19). Bright, cheerful pension just by the Ring; small rooms with shower and toilet. U-Bahn Schwedenplatz/Wien-Mitte. ⑥.

Pension Wild, 8, Langegasse 10 (☎0222/406 51 74). A favourite choice among backpackers, a short walk from the Ring in a student district behind the university. Booking essential. U-Bahn Lerchenfelder Strasse. ④.

Campsites

Camping Klosterneuburg, Donaupark (☎02243/527 27). Busy, but friendly site just outside the city limits, with very fast train connections to Vienna. S-Bahn Klosterneuburg-Kierling. Open Feb–Nov.

Camping Rodaun, 23, An der Au 2 (☎0222/888 41 54). Nice location by a stream in the very southwestern outskirts. Tram #60 from U-Bahn Hietzing. Open mid-March to mid-Nov.

Wien-West, 14, Hüttelbergstrasse 80 (☎0222/914 23 14). In the far western suburbs, close to the Wienerwald. It also has huts that sleep four (closed Feb; öS400).

The City

Vienna has a compact **historical centre**, bound to the northeast by the Danube canal and surrounded on all other sides by the majestic sweep of the Ringstrasse. From here, the main arteries of communication radiate outwards before reaching another ring road, the Gürtel (literally "belt"), further west. Most of the important sights are concentrated in this tourist-clogged district and along the Ring, but a lot of the essential Vienna lies beyond it, in the initially forbidding grid of barracks-like nineteenth-century apartment blocks; and there are outlying sights such as the imperial palace at **Schönbrunn**, or the funfair and parklands of the **Prater**. With judicious use of public transport, you can see a great deal in a couple of days.

Stephansplatz

The obvious place to begin is the central **Stephansplatz**, a lively pedestrianized square overlooked by the Gothic bulk of the **Stephansdom** (Mon–Sat 9am–noon & 1–5pm, Sun 12.30–5pm; free), whose spire, nicknamed *Steffl* (Little Stephen) by the locals, together with the brightly coloured chevrons of its tiled roof, still dominates the Vienna skyline. Inside, the high vaulted interior is studded with Baroque detail. The highlight is an early sixteenth-century carved stone pulpit with portraits of the four fathers of the Christian church, naturalistically sculpted by Anton Pilgram, who "signed" his work by showing himself peering from a window below the pulpit stairs. The area beyond the transepts is roped off, so to get a good look at the Wiener Neustädter Altar, a masterpiece of late Gothic art, and, to its right, the tomb of the Holy Roman Emperor Friedrich III, you must sign up for a guided tour (Mon–Sat 10.30am & 3pm, Sun 3pm; June–Sept also Sat 7pm; öS40).

Other features of interest include the **catacombs** (guided tours every 30min–1hr; Mon–Sat 10–11.30am & 2–4.30pm, Sun 2–4.30pm; öS40), where, among other macabre remains, the entrails of illustrious Habsburgs are housed in bronze caskets; and the smaller of the cathedral's two towers, which can be ascended by lift (daily 8.30am–5pm; öS40) for a look at the *Pummerin*, or great bell – though the 137-metre-high *Steffl* (daily 9am–5.30pm; öS30), a blind scramble up intestinal stairways, has better views. Finally, the seventeenth-century Archbishop's Palace, on the north side of the cathedal at Stephansplatz 6, contains the **Dom-** and **Diözesanmuseum** (Tues, Wed, Fri & Sat 10am–4pm, Thurs 10am–6pm, Sun 10am–1pm; öS40), in which the church silver is outshone by a collection of marvellous fifteenth-century devotional paintings.

East of Stephansplatz

The warren of alleyways east of the cathedral preserves something of the medieval character of the city, although the architecture reflects centuries of continuous rebuilding. The medieval house on Raubensteingasse 8 where **Mozart** died while at work on his *Requiem* has long since disappeared, but is commemorated by a small memorial on the top floor of the Steffl department store that now occupies the site. The only one of the composer's numerous residences to survive is the so-called **Figarohaus**, immediately east of the cathedral at Domgasse 5 (Tues–Sun 9am–6pm; öS25), though there's little to see inside. A much more intriguing find is the **Treasury of the Order of Teutonic Knights** (Schatzkammer des Deutschen Ordens), around the corner at Singerstrasse 7 (May–Oct Mon, Thurs & Sun 10am–noon, Wed 3–5pm, Fri & Sat 10am–noon & 3–5pm; Nov–April closed Fri morning & Sun; öS50), where you can view ceremonial regalia and domestic trinkets assembled by seven centuries of Grand Masters. The almost pastorally peaceful courtyard to the rear contains another of apartment-hopping Mozart's fleeting addresses.

A little further eastward, the seventeenth-century **Jesuitenkirche** on Dr.-Ignaz-Seipel-Platz is a valuable piece of early Baroque architecture, much of the sumptuous interior the work of Andrea Pozzo, invited to Vienna by Leopold I in 1702 to spearhead the city's artistic revival with an injection of Italian Jesuit style. Further in this direction is the early modernist **Postsparkasse** (Postal Savings Bank) on Georg-Coch-Platz (Mon–Wed & Fri 8am–3pm, Thurs 8am–5.30pm; free), completed in 1912 by the doyen of Vienna's turn-of-the-century architects, Otto Wagner.

Not far away, on the other side of Stubenring is perhaps Vienna's most enjoyable museum, known simply as the **MAK** (Tues–Sun 10am–6pm, Thurs 10am–9pm; öS90). The highlights of its superlative, highly eclectic collection, stretching from the Romanesque period to the twentieth century, are Klimt's *Stoclet Frieze* and the unrivalled collection of Wiener Werkstätte products. But what really sets it apart is the museum's provocative makeover, completed in 1993, which gave some of Austria's leading designers free rein to create a unique series of rooms, each one individually designed.

Kärntnerstrasse, Graben and Kohlmarkt

From Stephansplatz, **Kärntnerstrasse** leads off southwest, a continuous pedestrianized ribbon lined with street entertainers and elegant shops that ends at the city's illustrious **Staatsoper**, opened in 1869 as the first phase of the development of the Ringstrasse. Halfway along Kärntnerstrasse and one block to the west lies **Neuer Markt**, centred on the writhing figures of the Donnerbrunnen, a copy of an eighteenth-century fountain in which animated nudes symbolize four of the rivers feeding into the Danube. At the southwest exit of the square, a Capuchin church houses the **Kaisergruft** (daily 9.30am–4pm; öS40), where

Habsburg family members were interred from 1633. Maria Theresa reputedly came here on the eighteenth of every month to commune with the remains of her late husband Franz Stephan, and was eventually placed beside him in a riotously ornamented sarcophagus of stunning proportions – a stark contrast to the humble, unadorned coffin of her enlightened successor, Josef II.

The prime shopping streets of **Graben** and **Kohlmarkt**, which lead northwest off Stephansplatz, retain an air of exclusivity that Kärntnerstrasse has lost. Just off Graben, at Dorotheergasse 11, is the city's intriguing, state-of-the-art **Jüdisches Museum** (daily except Sat 10am–6pm, Thurs 10am–9pm; öS70). On the whole, the curators have rejected the usual static display cabinets and newsreel photos of past atrocities. Instead, the emphasis of the museum's excellent temporary exhibitions on the first floor is on contemporary Jewish life, while on the second floor, visitors are confronted with a series of free-standing glass panels imprinted with holograms, ghostly images of the city's once vast Jewish population.

At the far end of Kohlmarkt is Michaelerplatz, site of the **Looshaus**. Built as a department store in 1911 by pioneering modernist Adolf Loos, it marked a total break with the *Jugendstil* (literally "youth style") confections of Otto Wagner. Its initial unpopularity was largely due to the fact that it was constructed directly opposite the statue-laden nineteenth-century Michaelertor, entrance to the Habsburgs' city residence, the Hofburg.

The Hofburg

The rambling complex of the **Hofburg** has been much messed around since Rudolf I took possession of an earlier Bohemian fortress on the site in 1278. It now contains a range of museums with imperial connections, beginning with the rather dull parade of **Kaiserappartements** (daily 9am–4.30pm; öS80) on the north side of the main courtyard. To the southeast is the brightly painted entrance to the Schweizerhof, a smaller courtyard where you'll find the much more impressive **Schatzkammer** or Imperial Treasury (daily except Tues 10am–6pm; öS80), which holds the tenth-century crown of the Holy Roman Emperor, and the Holy Lance with which Jesus's flank was supposedly pierced (actually of ninth-century origin). Steps beside the Schatzkammer lead up to the **Burgkapelle** (Palace Chapel), primarily known as the venue for Mass in the company of the Vienna Boys' Choir (Wiener Sängerknaben; mid-Sept to June Sun 9.15am), for which you can obtain free standing-room only tickets from 8.15am.

Another monument to the Habsburgs' hoarding instincts is the ornate Baroque **Prunksaal** (Great Hall; mid-May to Oct Mon–Sat 10am–4pm, Sun 10am–1pm; Nov to mid-May Mon–Sat 10am–noon; öS60), overlooking Josefsplatz, worth a glimpse for its frescoes, globes and gold-bound volumes. On the other side of Josefsplatz, a door leads to the Stallburg imperial stables, home to the performing white horses of the **Spanish Riding School** (Spanische Reitschule). Tickets for performances (March–June & Sept–Dec) are expensive (öS250–900) and difficult to obtain; check with the Austrian tourist office at home first if you're seriously interested. Training sessions are open to the public (mid-Jan to June & late August to mid-Dec Tues–Sat 10am–noon; öS100). Failing this, you can peek at the dozing beasts and watch **videos** of their manoeuvres at the **Lipizzaner Museum** in the Stallburg (daily 9am–6pm; öS50).

To the west of the Hofburg is Heldenplatz, an enormous open space partially enclosed by the great curve of the palace's **Neue Burg**, a bombastic neo-Renaissance edifice completed only in 1913. Steps lead up to a series of museums (daily except Tues 10am–6pm; öS30), all of which are covered by one ticket. The exhibits include early musical instruments, arms and armour, and finds of Austrian archeologists from Ephesus in Asia Minor. A separate entrance leads to the **Museum für Volkerkünde** (daily except Tues: Jan–March 10am–6pm; April–Dec 10am–4pm; öS80); which features the collections of Captain Cook, Aztec treasures and other ethnographical exhibits.

The Kunsthistorisches and Naturhistorisches Museum

Across the Ring from Heldenplatz, Maria-Theresien-Platz is framed by two late nineteenth-century museums designed to accommodate the vast imperial collections. On the left is one of the richest fine arts museums in the world, the **Kunsthistorisches Museum** (Tues–Sun 10am–6pm; öS100). Its ground floor is largely given over to decorative arts and the ancient world, with impressive Egyptian, Greek and Roman collections, while the fine arts section (also open Thurs 6–9pm) upstairs is a good place to gain a perspective on the German Renaissance – the Gothic-infused canvases of Danubian painters like Altdorfer and the two Cranachs providing a link between the medieval world and the perfection of Dürer. Rubens, Caravaggio and Velázquez are well represented, along with two fine Rembrandt self-portraits and a portrait of the artist's mother. However, it's the unparalleled collection of Pieter Brueghel the Elder that attracts most visitors, pictures such as *The Meeting of Lent and Carnival* and the famous winter scenery of the *Return of the Hunters* portraying the seasons and peasant festivities of the sixteenth-century Netherlands (then Habsburg dominions).

Immediately opposite is the architecturally identical **Naturhistorisches Museum** (daily except Tues 9am–6pm; öS30), which has changed little since it was opened by Franz-Josef over a hundred years ago. It's basically a depository for rocks and stuffed fauna, though it also boasts seventh-century-BC Celtic grave finds from the Salzkammergut village of Hallstatt, plus a copy of the *Venus of Willendorf*, a small stone figure carved by paleolithic inhabitants of the Danube valley some 25,000 years ago.

Rathausplatz

This is a good place at which to begin an exploration of the **Ringstrasse**, built to fill the gap created when the last of the city's fortifications were demolished in 1857 and subsequently lined with monumental civic buildings – "Ringstrasse Historicism" became a byword for the bombastic taste of the late Habsburg bourgeoisie. The broad sweep of the Ring wasn't just a symbol of imperial and municipal prestige: it was designed to facilitate the mobility of cannons in the event of any rebellious incursions from the proletarian districts beyond.

Rathausplatz is the Ringstrasse's showpiece square, framed by no fewer than four monumental public buildings – the Rathaus, the Burgtheater, Parliament and the University – all completed in the 1880s. The most imposing building of the four is the cathedralesque **Rathaus**, parts of which are accessible on guided tours (Mon, Wed & Fri 1pm; free). Directly opposite the Rathaus stands the **Burgtheater**, flanked by two grandiose staircases decorated with frescoes by, among others, Gustav Klimt. The **Parliament building** is an imposing pastiche of Greco-Roman styles fronted by a monumental statue of Pallas Athene.

Karlsplatz

Karlsplatz, a modern, landscaped square just beyond the Ring from the Staatsoper, is an important transport interchange, where westward explorations of the city, making use of the U4 metro line, can begin. Immediately above the station, Otto Wagner's elegant *Jugendstil* station pavilions are now used as a café and exhibition space (April–Oct Tues–Sun 9am–12.15pm & 1–4.30pm; öS25). The square is dominated by the **Karlskirche** (Mon–Sat 9–11.30am & 1–5pm, Sun 1–5pm; free), the crowning achievement of Austria's foremost Baroque architect, Fischer von Erlach. Built by order of Emperor Karl IV in thanks for deliverance from the plague of 1713, it's an eclectic jumble, with an oval dome perched atop a Classical colonnade, flanked by replicas of Trajan's column in Rome. The **Museum der Stadt Wien** (Tues–Sun 9am–4.30pm; öS50) next door includes three floors of medieval sculpture and painting, arms and armour recalling the city's struggles against the Turks, a reconstruction of Adolf Loos's ascetic living quarters, several works by Klimt and Schiele, and a model of the city as it was before the Ring was built.

Over on the west side of Karlsplatz, stands the **Secession** (Tues–Fri 10am–6pm, Sat & Sun 10am–4pm; öS40) building, built in 1897 as the headquarters of Vienna's Art Nouveau movement. Led by Gustav Klimt, this younger generation rebelled against academic historicism in favour of something more modern, although the *Jugendstil* (literally "youth style") they initiated was in many ways equally nostalgic. The building itself is a case in point, though the "gilded cabbage" that crowns it is in a league of its own. One of Klimt's most characteristic works, the *Beethoven Frieze*, created for an exhibition of 1902, dominates the basement.

while the rest of the building is used for contemporary exhibitions (öS60). Immediately behind the Secession, on Schillerplatz, is the **Akademie der bildenden Künste** (Tues–Sun 10am–4pm; öS50), which has an often overlooked collection, strong in Flemish works, including Bosch's triptych, *The Last Judgement*.

South of the Ring

Immediately south of the Ring, beyond Schwarzenbergplatz (one stop on tram #71 or walk up Rennweg) lies the **Belvedere**, built by Lukas von Hildebrandt for Prince Eugene of Savoy between 1714 and 1723. It's in two parts, the more modest Unteres Belvedere, and the Oberes Belvedere, separated by 500m of landscaped gardens. The whole is now home to the **Österreichisches Galerie** (Tues–Sun 10am–5pm; öS60), a good introduction to the nation's art history, starting with the Gothic and Baroque collections in the Unteres Belvedere, which retains much of its original, lavish decor. Most people, though, head for the Oberes Belvedere, where Klimt, Schiele and Kokoschka each have a room to themselves, along with plenty of examples of the sentimental bourgeois tastes of the time against which they rebelled.

Beyond the Belvedere, the area around the Südbahnhof has a distinctly Balkan feel, with scattered ethnic bars and restaurants providing a meeting place for emigrants from the former Yugoslavia and Turkey. Heading southeast from the Südbahnhof through the Schweizer Garten brings you to two more traditional tourist sights: the **Museum des 20 Jahrhunderts** (Tues–Sun 10am–6pm; öS45), which mounts exhibitions of contemporary art and, slightly further on, the **Heeresgeschichtliches Museum** (daily except Fri 10am–4pm; öS40), which recounts the glories of the Austrian military with weaponry, uniforms and a lot of exquisite sixteenth- and seventeenth-century engravings. One of the highlights is the Gräf & Stift open-top car in which Archduke Ferdinand and his wife Sophie Chotek were assassinated in Sarajevo in June 1914; his bloodstained uniform lies nearby.

Ten minutes' walk from here (or tram #71 from Schwarzenbergplatz) is the **St Marxer Friedhof**, on Leberstrasse (daily 7am–dusk), formerly Vienna's principal cemetery. Among the shaded rows of fine early nineteenth-century tombstones lies Wolfgang Amadeus Mozart, although his precise location remains a mystery, due to Josef II's late eighteenth-century ban on opulent funerals. The monument marking the area in which the composer was interred – a broken column accompanied by a cherub – was erected in the 1890s, the original one, raised in 1859, having been moved to Vienna's greatest necropolis, the **Zentralfriedhof** (Central Cemetery) on Simmeringer Hauptstrasse, further down the #71 tram line (daily: March–Oct 7am–6/7pm; Nov–Feb 8am–5pm; free), in which graves of eminent Viennese are grouped by profession. The musicians, principally Beethoven, Schubert, Brahms and the Strauss family lie a short way beyond Gate 2, to the left of the central avenue. Schönberg's uncompromisingly modern, cuboid gravestone is set apart from the rest, next to former Austrian chancellor Bruno Kreisky.

East of the Ring

One of Vienna's most popular tourist attractions, the brightly-coloured kitsch **Hundertwasserhaus** (tram #N to Hetzgasse from Schwedenplatz U-Bahn), lies in the unassuming residential area of Landstrasse, east of the Ring. Following his philosophy that "the straight line is godless", the Austrian artist Friedensreich Hundertwasser transformed some dour council housing on the corner of Löwengasse and Kegelgasse into a higgledy-piggledy, childlike ensemble that caught the popular imagination. Understandably, the residents were none too happy when hordes of pilgrims began ringing on their doorbells, asking to be shown round, so Hundertwasser obliged with a shopping arcade opposite, called **Kalke Village**, where you can get the full Hundertwasser experience, the most disconcerting aspect of which is his penchant for uneven floors. There's another of Hundertwasser's Gaudi-esque conversions, **KunstHausWien** (daily 10am–7pm; öS90, half price Mon), three blocks north up Untere Weissgerberstrasse, featuring a gallery devoted to Hundertwasser's own paintings and inventions, and temporary exhibitions (another öS90; combined ticket öS140) by other headline-grabbing contemporary artists.

On the other side of the Danube canal, which runs east of the centre, is **Leopoldstadt**, home to a thriving Jewish community until the Nazi Holocaust. The district's main attraction is the **Prater** (U-Bahn Praterstern), a large expanse of parkland that stretches for miles between the Danube canal and the river itself. Formerly the royal hunting grounds, the public were allowed access to the Prater by Josef II, who often walked here himself, quixotically ordering passing members of the public not to salute him. The funfair at the northern end is renowned for the **Riesenrad** (April daily 10am–11pm; May–Sept daily 9am–midnight; Oct daily 10am–10pm; Nov & Christmas–Epiphany daily 10am–6pm; rest of Dec Sat & Sun 10am–6pm; öS50), the giant Ferris wheel featured in Carol Reed's film *The Third Man*. In summer, you can take U1 east from Praterstern to the **Donauinsel**, an island in the middle of the Danube crisscrossed with cycle paths, which becomes the city's most popular bathing area throughout the summer.

North of the Ring

Sigmund Freud moved to the second floor of Berggasse 19, six blocks north of the Ring, in 1891 and stayed here until June 4, 1938, when he and his family fled to London. His apartment, now the **Freud Museum** (July–Sept daily 9am–6pm; Oct–June 9am–4pm; öS60), is a place of pilgrimage, even though Freud took almost all his possessions with him into exile. His hat, coat and walking stick are still here, however, and there's home-movie footage from the 1930s, but the only room with any original decor is the waiting room.

Hidden away down the backstreet of Fürstengasse, three blocks north of the Freud Museum, the Baroque **Palais Liechtenstein** (Tues–Sun 10am–6pm; öS45), provides an incongruous setting for Vienna's **Museum Moderner Kunst** (Museum of Modern Art), which houses a large permanent collection ranging from paintings by Picasso, Kokoschka and Kupka to Pop Art, and works by the leading figures of Wiener Aktionismus, Vienna's very own, extremely violent, version of 1960s performance art.

Schönbrunn and the west

The biggest attraction in the west of the city is the imperial summer palace of **Schönbrunn** (daily: April–Oct 8.30am–5pm; Nov–March until 4.30pm; öS90–140), reachable by U4 to Schönbrunn or Hietzing. This was originally a royal hunting lodge until Leopold I commissioned Fischer von Erlach to draw up plans for a palace on the model of residences like Versailles. The plans proved too expensive, however, and what was eventually completed during the reign of Maria Theresa, was, for all its size and elegance, far more modest. There are three types of tour around the palace rooms: self-guided (with audiophone commentary in English); the "Imperial Tour" (öS90) of 22 state rooms; or the "Grand Tour" (öS120) of all 40 rooms. There's little point in opting for the shorter tour in order to save money, since it misses out the best rooms – such as the Millions Room, a rosewood-panelled room covered from floor to ceiling with wildly irregular Rococo cartouches, each holding a Persian miniature watercolour. There's a **Coach and Carriage Museum** (Wagenburg; April–Oct daily 9am–6pm; Nov–March Tues–Sun 10am–4pm; öS30) in the palace's right wing, but you'd do better to concentrate on strolling through the formal gardens, overlooked by the frolicking statuary of the Neptune Fountain, and the more distant Gloriette, a hilltop colonnaded monument, now a café, from which you can enjoy splendid views back towards the city. The palace grounds and gardens (daily 6am–dusk; free) also hold Vienna's Tiergarten or **Zoo** (daily 9am–dusk; öS90) and **Palmenhaus** (daily: May–Sept 9.30am–6pm; Oct–April 9.30am–5pm; öS45), a glasshouse full of tropical ferns.

On the western fringes of the city, **Lainzer Tiergarten** (Easter–Oct Wed–Sun 8am–dusk) is a vast game preserve. Wilder parts of the park can be reached from U4 Hütteldorf, but a more interesting point of access is the **Lainzertor**, reached via U4 to Hietzing, then tram #60 or #61 to Hofwiesengasse, followed by either bus #60B or a twenty-minute walk. Once inside, paths lead to the **Hermesvilla** (Wed–Sun 9am–4.30pm; öS50), built for Franz-Jozef's wife Elisabeth in the 1880s and stuffed with the furnishings of the period.

Eating and drinking

As in the rest of Austria, the boundaries separating eating from drinking places can be pretty blurred, and recommendations inevitably overlap. The traditional venue for **eating out** in Vienna is the *Beisl*, an intimate neighbourhood place, somewhere between restaurant and pub, providing good home cooking and a cosy refuge for local beer drinkers. There are plenty of these both within and beyond the Ring, the best places to look being districts 6, 7 and 8. Vienna is also the true home of the traditional *Kaffeehaus* or café – largely a venue for good-value lunchtime food, afternoon coffee and cakes, and late-night drinking. Those within the Ring tend to be touristy and overpriced, but many are dripping with atmosphere and continue to be patronized by the Viennese themselves.

For **food on the move**, the *Würstelstand* is as big an institution in Vienna as anywhere else in Austria, although beware that your *Würst* tends to be priced according to weight; look out for *Leberkäse*, a slice of spicy meat sandwiched between two halves of a *Semmel*. There are plenty of lunchtime stand-up snack bars and places selling bite-size open-topped sandwiches, *Brötchen*, in the city centre, one of the most famous being *Trzesniewski*, Dorotheergasse 1, off Graben. *Zum schwarzen Kameel*, Bognergasse 5, has sandwiches and a good delicatessen, while if you want to sit down, the *Naschmarkt* chain of **self-service restaurants** has branches at Schottengasse 1 and Mariahilferstrasse 85. The **Naschmarkt** itself – the city's main fruit and veg market off Karlsplatz – is a great place to assemble a picnic or grab a tasty take-away, and also home to numerous cheap cafés attached to the various stalls. Finally, another budget option are the student **mensas**, which serve subsidized three-course lunches. You don't actually have to be a student, and some, like the Technical University mensa on Resselgasse, behind Karlsplatz, are even open in the vacations.

Cafés

Alt Wien, 1, Bäckerstrasse 9. Bohemian *Kaffeehaus* atmosphere, open until 2am. Good food if you can find a table.

Benno, 8, Alserstrasse 67. Café with a collection of puzzles and board games. Good snacks too. Open until 2am.

Berg, 9, Berggasse 8. Trendy modern café, with good food and relaxed, mostly gay, clientele. Open until 1am.

Central, 1, Herrengasse 14. Traditional meeting place of Vienna's intelligentsia, and Trotsky's favourite café, this is probably the most ornate of Vienna's cafés. Closed Sun.

Demel, 1, Kohlmarkt 14. Vienna's most prestigious patisserie, with a café attached, and seafood offshoot opposite.

Drechsler, 6, Linke Wienzeile 22. Opens at 4am for the stallholders of the Naschmarkt. A good place for breakfast after the bars and clubs have closed. Closed Sun.

Europa, 7, Zollergasse 8. Lively, spacious café with great food, just off the Mariahilferstrasse. Open until 4am.

Hawelka, 1, Dorotheegasse 6. Famed for its smoky, Bohemian atmosphere, this is a popular night-time drinking venue, open until 2am. Closed Tues & Sat.

Landtmann, 1, Dr.-Karl-Lueger-Ring 4. Traditional haunt of politicians and civil servants, preserving a refined, old-world ambience despite its position on the well-trodden tourist trail – Freud used to drink here.

Museum, 1, Friedrichstrasse 6. Century-old arty café, within range of both the Academy and Secession. The original sparse interior, designed by Adolf Loos, is no more, however.

Palmenhaus, 1, Burggarten. Stylish café set amidst the palms of the greenhouse in the Burggarten. Open until 2am.

Prückel, 1, Stubenring 24. Favourite refuge of elderly Viennese matrons and younger art students in between bouts of shopping.

Schwarzenberg, 1, Kärntner Ring 17. Opulent café overlooking Schwarzenbergplatz, with huge mirrors and a great cake cabinet.

Sperl, 6, Gumpendorferstrasse 11. The recently renovated turn-of-the-century interior is one of the set pieces of the Vienna coffee-house scene.

Stein, 9, Währingerstrasse 6. Big, trendy, designer café, with funky music, on-line facilities and decent food. Open until 1am.

Restaurants

Bizi, 1, Rotenturmstrasse. Big sit-down, self-service pizzeria. Cheap, central and quite pleasant.

Figlmüller, 1, Wollzeile 5. The place to eat Wienerschnitzel – at around öS150 a go.

Fischer Bräu, 19, Billrothstrasse 17. Very civilized micro-brewery pub near the Gürtel, producing a great, lemony, misty beer. Lots of tasty snacks and more substantial pub fare to be consumed.

Glacisbeisl, 7, Messeplatz. Hidden away in the entrails of the Messepalast on the Ring, this is a popular venue in summer. Good vegetarian selections.

Hunger-Künstler, 6, Gumpendorferstrasse 48. Candle-lit restaurant serving Vorarlberg specialities and plenty of veggie options.

Oswald und Kalb, 1, Bäckerstrasse 14. Traditional, dimly-lit Gasthaus specializing in Styrian dishes. Evenings only, until 2am.

Pontoni, 7, Burggasse/Halbgasse. A modish crowd frequent this stripped-down Beisl; the food is traditional but imaginatively presented and freshly prepared.

Schnitzelwirt, 7, Neubaugasse 52. Another great place to eat Wienerschnitzel – and they're cheaper than those at Figlmüller.

Schweizerhaus, 2, Strasse des 1 Mai 116, in the Prater. Known for its draught Czech beer and roast pork specialities.

Siebenstern Bräu, 7, Siebensterngasse 19. Popular modern Bierkeller, which brews its own beer and serves solid Viennese food.

Spatzennest, 7, Ullrichsplatz 1. Traditional, inexpensive food, beer and ambience, near the Spittelberg area. Closed Fri & Sat.

Spittelberg, 7, Spittelberggasse 12. Chic evening-only brasserie with some veggie options, and delicious (sweet and savoury) crepes.

Witwe Bolte, 7, Gutenberggasse 13. In the charming backstreets of Spittelberg, serving good cheap Viennese fare.

Wratschko & Schmid, 7, Neustiftgasse 51. Relaxed, evening-only Beisl that's a real favourite with the locals, just down the street from the city's central youth hostel. Closed Sun.

Wrenkh, 1, Bauernmarkt 10. Fashionable vegetarian restaurant just north of Stephansplatz. Closed Sun.

Zu den drei Hacken, 1, Singerstrasse 28. Unpretentious place serving decent, simple Gulasch – quite a boon in this part of the city. Closed Sun.

Nightlife

For night-time **drinking**, the best place to head for in the centre is the so-called Bermuda Triangle, a network of alleyways centred on Rabensteig, off Rotenturmstrasse near the Danube canal; you could also try the narrow lanes around Sonnenfelsgasse and Bäckerstrasse, on the other side of Rotenturmstrasse. Beyond the Ring, the *Musikcafés* and bars of districts 6, 7 and 8 are well worth exploring: lively places with a youthful clientele, usually with some kind of music. At some clubs, you may have to pay an entrance fee (anything up to öS100). For details of what's on, the local listings magazine, *Falter*, has comprehensive details of the week's cultural programme, and is pretty easy to decipher even if you have scant German.

Musikcafés, live venues and clubs

American Bar, 1, Kärntnerstrasse 59. Small, dark late-night bar with surprisingly rich interior by Adolf Loos. Shame about the strip club next door. Open until 2am.

B72, 8, Stadtbahnbögen 72, Hernalser Gürtel. Dark, designer dance club underneath the U-Bahn arches. Open until 4am.

Blue Box, 7, Richtergasse 8. *Musikcafé* with resident DJs and a good snack menu.

Chelsea, 8, U-Bahnbögen 29–31, Lerchenfelder Gürtel. Punky anglophile haunt with regular live music downstairs.

Donau, 7, Karl Schweighofergasse 10. Lugubrious *Musikcafé*, with resident DJs and weird projections on the walls.

Jazzland, 1, Franz-Josefs-Kai 29. Vienna's main trad-jazz venue.

Krah Krah, 1, Rabensteig 8. Crowded, youthful bar known for its staggering selection of bottled beers; occasional jazz music.

Nachtasyl, 6, Stumpergasse 53. Managed by an expatriate Czech. Bohemian beer-hall atmosphere and occasional live music. Near Westbahnhof.

P1, 1, Rotgasse 9. Big city-centre disco playing commercial dance music to a youngish crowd.

Rhiz, 8, Stadtbahnbögen 37–38, Lerchenfelder Gürtel. A cross between a bar, a *Musikcafé* and a club, with DJs spinning everything from dance to trance. Open until 4am.

Rosa-Lila-Villa, 6, Linke Wienzeile 102. Gay and lesbian centre with late-night café. Open until 2am. U4 Pilgramgasse.

Szene Wien, 11, Hauffgasse 26. Live music venue run by a radical bunch of rockers from Simmering. Tram #71 from Schwarzenbergplatz.

Tunnel, 8, Florianigasse 39. Large, studenty establishment with frequent live bands in cellar, and deservedly popular food.

U4, 12, Schönbrunnerstrasse 222. Dark, cavernous disco, mostly rock/indie, with frequent gigs; a mecca of the alternative crowd. Gay and lesbian night Thurs. U4 Meidling-Hauptstrasse.

Volksgarten, 1, Burgring 1. Situated in the park of the same name, Vienna's trendiest house and techno nightclub. A firm favourite with the dance crowd.

w.u.k., 9, Währingerstrasse 59. Old school now an arts venue run by a sprinkling of anarchists and others. Café, live music and much more.

Opera, ballet and classical music

You can catch high-class international **opera** and **ballet** at the Staatsoper, 1, Opernring 2, and opera and operetta at the Volksoper, 9, Währingerstrasse 78. There's a huge number of **classical music** venues, of which the principal ones are the Musikverein, 1, Karlsplatz 6, home of the Vienna Philharmonic, and the Konzerthaus, 3, Lothringerstrasse 50. Bookings can be made for the above venues at Bundestheaterkassen, 1, Hanuschgasse 3, though you can get cheap standing-room tickets (*Stehplätze*) at the above venues by queuing up an hour before the performance.

Listings

Airlines Austrian Airlines 1, Kärntner Ring 18 (☎0222/505 57 57-1789); British Airways 1, Kärntner Ring 10 (☎0222/505 76 91).

Bicycle rental The cheapest place to rent bicycles is at one of the mainline stations: Westbahnhof, Südbahnhof and Wien-Nord. The charges are reduced on production of a valid train ticket.

Books and newspapers Shakespeare & Co, 1, Sterngasse 2, for English-language books; Morawa, 1, Wollzeile 11, for international newspapers and magazines.

Car rental Avis, 1, Opernring 1 (☎0222/587 35 95); Hertz, 1, Kärntnerring 17 (☎0222/512 86 77).

Cinema Full listings appear in *Falter*. "OF" or "OmU" after the title means that the film is not dubbed; "Omengu" means it's got English subtitles. Burg, 1, Opernring 19, and Top, 6, Rahlgasse 1, both have regular showings of original-language films.

Embassies Australia, 4, Mattiellistrasse 2–4 (☎0222/512 85 80); Canada, 1. Laurenzerberg 2 (☎0222/531 38-3000); Great Britain, 3, Jauresgasse 12 (☎0222/716 13); Ireland, 3, *Hotel Hilton*, Landstrasse Hauptstrasse 2 (☎0222/715 42 46); USA, 9, Boltzmanngasse 16 (☎0222/313 39).

Exchange Outside banking hours, try the offices at the Westbahnhof (daily 7am–10pm), or the Südbahnhof (daily 6.30am–9pm) train stations.

Hospital Allegemeines Krankenhaus, 9, Währinger Gürtel 18–20; U6 Michelbeuern-AKH.

Laundry 7, Urban-Loritz-Platz (U-Bahn Burggasse-Stadthalle).

Post office and telephones at 1, Fleischmarkt 19 (24hr).

Travel agent ÖKISTA, 9, Türkenstrasse 8, is best for discount flights and train tickets.

THE DANUBE VALLEY AND LINZ

Heading west from Vienna, there are two alternative routes for onward travel: to Salzburg, around three hours away, and then on to Munich or Innsbruck; or a more leisurely route following the Danube through the **Wachau**, a tortuously winding stretch of water where vine-bearing, ruin-encrusted hills roll down to the river from the north. Wachau is an Austria decidedly different from either cosmopolitan Vienna or the Alpine southwest, and accommodation here is generally cheaper than in either place. At the eastern entrance to the region, within easy reach of Vienna by train, is the historic town of **Krems**, with its older, medieval suburb of Stein; further on lies **Melk**, with its fine Benedictine monastery overlooking the river. Transport to Salzburg from Melk is pretty straightforward, although the industrialized, but culturally vibrant, northern city of **Linz** has enough of interest to make a further stopoff worthwhile. Note that trains to Krems leave from Vienna's Franz-Josefs-Bahnhof (FJB), while Melk is reached on the main line from Westbahnhof (with a possible change at St Pölten).

The most stylish way to travel is by **boat**. The DDSG line operates weekend services between Vienna, Linz and Passau during the summer and year-round services (4 daily in summer) between Krems and Melk, the most scenic stretch. The journey takes about three hours upstream, two in the opposite direction, and costs about öS250 each way; making your way along the river by shorter hops will work out more expensive, although Eurail holders can travel free and those with an InterRail get a fifty percent reduction.

Krems

KREMS, which clings to the hilly north bank of the Danube, is actually made up of three previously separate settlements: Krems, Und and Stein. The main thoroughfare, **Landstrasse**, is a couple of blocks north of the train station, a pedestrianized shopping-street studded with old buildings, including a sixteenth-century **Rathaus**. Above, a series of small squares preserves the late medieval character of this provincial wine-growing town. One of these, Pfarrplatz, is dominated by the **Pfarrkirche**, with an interior rich in High Baroque furnishings. A covered stairway behind it leads up to the imposing Gothic **Piaristenkirche**, with several altarpieces by Baroque artist Johann Martin Schmidt, who is also celebrated in the town's **Wienstadt Museum** in Körnermarkt, west of Pfarrplatz (Tues 9am–6pm, Wed–Sun 1–6pm; öS40), atmospherically located in a dour thirteenth-century Dominican church. There's something dark and tortured about Schmidt's work that makes it compulsive viewing. Born in nearby Grafenwörth in 1718, he trained under local artisans and set up his own workshop in Krems, eschewing the cosmopolitan art scene of the capital, and it's this attachment to provincial roots that sets his work apart from the more academic painters of the Austrian Baroque. The rest of the museum amounts to a mildly diverting trot through the history of viniculture in the region.

At the western end of Landstrasse, the **Steinertor**, a monstrously belfried fifteenth-century town gate, confusingly marks the end of Krems' old town, while Kremsor Tor (a ten-minute walk away along Kasernstrasse) signals the beginning of **Stein** – a sequence of Renaissance town houses and crumbling old facades, opening out every hundred metres or so into small cobbled squares. Just before you pass under Stein's Kremsor Tor, check out the **Kunst-Halle-Krems** (Tues–Sun 10am–6pm; öS80), the town's new arts venue, which hosts major modern art exhibitions, both here and in the impressive shell of the thirteenth-century **Minoritenkirche**, halfway along Steinerlandstrasse. Further along, steps climb up to the fourteenth-century **Frauenbergkirche**, now a chapel commemorating Austrian war dead. Traces of faded medieval frescoes can still be made out on the walls.

Practicalities

The local **tourist office** is situated in the former Und monastery, halfway between Krems and Stein at Undstrasse 6 (May–Oct Mon–Fri 9am–6pm, Sat & Sun 10am–noon & 1–6pm;

Nov–April Mon–Fri 8.30am–noon & 1.30–5pm). If you're planning on staying in town, there's a fairly serviceable **youth hostel** one block south of the tourist office at Ringstrasse 77 (April–Sept; ☎02732/834 52), while the nearest **campsite** (mid-April to Oct; ☎02732/844 55) is just a few minutes' walk south of town over the railway lines by the river bank. Both *Gästehaus Einzinger*, Steiner Landstrasse 82 (☎02732/82316; ⑤), in Stein, and *Hotel Alte Post*, Obere Landstrasse 32 (☎02732/822 76; ⑤), in Krems, have doubles overlooking arcaded courtyards. A convenient place to **eat** is *Gozzoburg*, at the bottom of Hoher Markt (closed Tues), which serves no-nonsense traditional dishes; *Halil*, Pfarrplatz 8, serves decent pasta and pizza. For **entertainment**, the varied programme of events at the Kunst-Halle-Krems is probably your best bet.

Dürnstein and Melk

Following the north bank of the Danube from Krems to Melk takes you first to **DÜRNSTEIN**, which sits below a rocky promontory commanding a bend in the river. The village is known primarily for the meagre **ruined castle** where Richard the Lionheart was locked up in the winter of 1192–93 after being kidnapped by Duke Leopold V of Austria. Below it stands a monastery **church**, with an unmissable ice-blue and white tower; the interior is less richly decorated, though the stucco reliefs on the ceiling are exceptional.

For real High Baroque excess, head for the Benedictine monastery at **MELK** – a pilgrimage centre associated with the Irish missionary Saint Coloman – designed by the local architect Jakob Prandtauer in the first half of the eighteenth century. The monumental coffee-cake monastery, perched on a bluff over the river, dominates the town. Highlights of the interior (daily: Palm Sunday to early Nov 9am–5/6pm; early Nov to Palm Sunday guided tours only at 11am & 2pm; öS50–65) are the exquisite library, with a cherub-infested ceiling by Troger, and the monastery church, with similarly impressive work by Rottmayr.

Melk's **river station** is situated about ten minutes' walk east of town. The **train station** is to be found at the head of Bahnhofstrasse, which leads directly into the old town. The **tourist office**, on Abbe-Stadler-Gasse (April–Oct Mon–Sat 9am–7pm, Sun 10am–2pm; Nov–March Mon–Fri 9am–noon & 1–4pm), has a substantial stock of **private rooms**, though most are out of the centre. Melk's **youth hostel** is at Abt-Karl-Strasse 42 (☎02752/26 81; March–Oct), roughly five minutes on foot from the train station; the **campsite** (☎02752/3291; March–Nov) occupies a pleasant riverside site near the river station.

Linz and around

Away from its heavy industrial suburbs, the Upper Austrian capital of **LINZ** is a pleasant Baroque city straddling the Danube. However, the city's greatest claim to fame is as the childhood home of Adolf Hitler, something about which the local tourist board is understandably coy. Inspired by nostalgic memories of schooldays spent here, Hitler spent his last days in his Berlin bunker poring over a model of the city planning its lavish reconstruction.

The City

A tour of the city should perhaps start at the rectangular expanse of the **Hauptplatz** or main square, with its tall, pastel-coloured facades, and central Trinity Column, crowned by a gilded sunburst. The pea-green **Alter Dom** (daily 7am–noon & 3–7pm) to the southeast of the square is an unusually stern piece of seventeenth-century architecture. In the **Pfarrkirche** round the corner to the north, a gargantuan marble slab contains Emperor Friedrich III's heart (the rest of him is in Vienna's Stephansdom). To the west of Hauptplatz lies a pedestrianized quarter rich in Baroque houses leading up to the fifteenth-century **Schloss** (Tues–Fri 9am–5pm, Sat & Sun 10am–4pm; öS50), two blocks west of Hauptplatz, the former residence of Emperor Friedrich III, who made Linz the imperial capital for four years from 1489. Inside, there's little dramatic to see save for a good view across the Danube. The castle's museum is particularly strong on medieval weaponry, musical instruments and folk art – it also contains a large but uneven art collection with a smattering of works by Klimt,

Schiele and Kokoschka plus a wonderful room of exquisite *fin-de-siècle* glassware and accessories.

The streets east of Hauptplatz contain a couple more museums: the **Stadtmuseum Nordico**, Bethlehemstrasse 7 (Mon–Fri 9am–6pm, Sat & Sun 3–5pm; free), which hosts modern art exhibitions and contains a model of the town from 1740; and the **Landesmuseum**, Museumstrasse 14 (Tues–Fri 9am–6pm, Sat & Sun 10am–6pm; öS50), which likewise plays host to temporary shows – usually prestigious selections from Austrian art history as well as natural history exhibitions.

However, you're better off strolling across to the suburb of **Urfahr**, on the north bank of the river, where you'll find Linz's most recent attraction, the **Ars Electronica Center** (Wed–Sun 11am–7pm; öS80), a museum dedicated to new technology, immediately on your right after you've crossed the bridge. Even if you're barely computer-literate, this place is fun, and though most of the instructions are in German, the helpful staff speak English. You can play around with various pieces of state-of-the-art computer equipment, but the highlight is a visit to the "CAVE", a virtual reality room with 3D projections on three walls and the floor – you need to get here early to book a ticket for this (no extra charge).

Also in Urfahr, on the first floor of the supremely unattractive Lentia 2000 shopping centre on Blütenstrasse, is the **Neue Galerie** (Mon–Wed & Fri 10am–6pm, Thurs until 10pm, Sat 10am–1pm; öS60), which has a small, permanent collection of modern art, including a few works by Klimt, Kokoschka, Schiele and their lesser-known contemporaries. The only other reason to visit Urfahr is to take a ride on the **Pöstlingbergbahn**, a narrow-gauge railway which climbs to the eighteenth-century pilgrimage church of **Pöstlingberg** – a good vantage point for sweeping views of the valley; trains leave from a twee station at the end of the #3 tram line every twenty minutes (Mon–Sat 5.20am–8pm, Sun 7.15am–8pm; öS40)

Practicalities

Linz's **train station** is 2km south of the centre, on the other side of the city's main artery, Landstrasse, and connected with the central Hauptplatz by tram #3. To get into the centre, you can buy a single tram ticket (Midi; öS18), or a day ticket (Maxi; öS35). There's a **tourist office** in the Altes Rathaus on Hauptplatz (May–Oct Mon–Fri 7am–7pm, Sat 9am–7pm, Sun 10am–7pm; Nov–April Mon–Fri 8am–7pm, Sat 9am–6pm, Sun 10am–6pm). Affordable central **accommodation** is thin on the ground, the only feasible options are the *Wilder Mann*, ten minutes' walk from the station off Goethestrasse 14 (☎0732/65 60 78; ⑤); the *Goldenes Dachl*, Hafnerstrasse 27 (☎0732/67 54 80; ④), one block south of the neo-Gothic city cathedral, west of Landstrasse; or the *Goldener Anker*, Hofgasse 5 (☎0732/77 10 88; ⑤), just off the main square. There's a small but pleasant **youth hostel** at Kapuzinerstrasse 14 (☎0732/78 27 20; no curfew; March to mid-Nov), ten minutes west of Hauptplatz; and two bigger **hostels** at Stanglhofweg 3 (☎0732/66 44 34; mid-Jan to mid-Dec), off Roseggerstrasse, near the botanical gardens (bus #27 from the train station), and at Blütenstrasse 23 (☎0732/23 70 78) in the Lentia 2000 shopping centre across the river in Urfahr. The city's main **campsite** is 5km southeast of the centre on the Pichlinger See (☎0732/30 53 14; March–Nov), reached by hourly bus or local train from the Hauptbahnhof, but it's too close to the autobahn for comfort. For a more peaceful site (tents only) head to the Pleschinger See (☎0732/24 78 70; May–Sept), 3km northeast of the centre, on the north bank of the Danube; take bus #33 or #33a from Reindlstrasse in Urfahr.

There are plenty of **bars and restaurants** around the Hauptplatz and in the largely pedestrianized streets immediately to the west. *Mangolds*, Hauptplatz 6, is a self-service vegetarian café with cheap but tasty food and a great salad bar; while *Klosterhof*, Landstrasse 30, serves solid Austrian food in the labyrinthine rooms of a former monastery – it also boasts the city's largest beer garden. *Gelbes Krokodil* (closed Sat & Sun lunch), Dametzstrasse 30, is a superb, stylish café inside the city's Moviemento arts cinema, with an excellent selection of Med-influenced food. *Traxlmayr*, Promenade 16, southwest of Hauptplatz, a traditional coffee house and local institution, is a good place to treat yourself to a slice of *Linzer Torte*, the local chocolate cake. *Alte Welt*, Hauptplatz 4 (closed Sun), is a trendy **wine bar** that features reg ular live jazz, folk- and world-music bands; alternatively try one of the *Weinkellers* along the river front in Urfahr, all good places to sample the white wines of the Mühlviertel, the vine-covered hills north of the city. For late-night drinking, try *Kistl*, Altstadt 17, a lively bar with tasty snacks.

Around Linz

Of a couple of worthwhile excursions from Linz, one of the most popular is to the Augustinian **Monastery of St Florian**, 7km southeast and accessible by the occasional bus (#2040 or #2042). Local-born composer Anton Bruckner was a choirboy here in the 1830s, and returned in later life to become the monastery's organist. The complex was rebuilt by Prandtauer, fresh from supervising similar work at Melk. For much of the year access is restricted to the abbey church, in whose crypt Bruckner is buried directly underneath the organ. From April to October you can take a guided tour of the interior (daily 10am, 11am, 1pm, 2pm & 3pm; öS60); highlights include Prince Eugene's four-poster bed, an over-the-top half-Turkish, half-Rococo confection. There's also an excellent collection of paintings by Albrecht Altdorfer, a prolific early sixteenth-century master whose work blends the German Gothic and Italian Renaissance styles.

The former granite quarry at **Mauthausen** (daily: Feb, March & Oct to mid-Dec 8am–4pm; April–Sept 8am–6pm; öS25), 20km east of Linz, was used by the Nazis as a concentration camp from 1938. Personal memorials to loved ones are interspersed throughout the huge granite fortress, along with numerous official national war memorials. Getting to the camp by public transport is not easy: take the train towards Vienna and change to the local line at St Valentin. Mauthausen train station is a good 5km from the camp itself, so your best option is to rent a bike from the station.

SOUTHEAST AUSTRIA

The **southeastern** corner of Austria, despite the subalpine terrain of the central province of Styria and the sun-baked plains of the Burgenland, is bypassed by most visitors. The area contains a wealth of diffuse attractions, though these demand leisurely exploration, and the only obvious focus of concentrated interest is the Styrian provincial capital of **Graz**.

Graz

Austria's second city, **GRAZ** owes its importance to the defence of central Europe against the Turks. From the fifteenth century, Graz was constantly under arms, rendering it far more secure than Vienna. This led to a modest seventeenth-century flowering of the arts; the Baroque style appeared in Graz before its adoption elsewhere in Austria. During the last years of the empire, the city's mild climate made it a popular retirement choice for ageing officers and civil servants, and its reputation as a conservative town swarming with pensioners has proved hard to shake off. Nowadays, however, it is a rich and culturally varied city, with plentiful night-time diversions, partly due to its 30,000-strong student population.

Arrival and accommodation

Graz's **train station** is on the western edge of town, a fifteen-minute walk or short tram ride (#1, #3 #6 or #7) from the central Hauptplatz. There's a **tourist office** at the station (Mon–Fri 9am–6pm, Sat 9am–3pm) and a bigger one a couple of hundred metres from Hauptplatz at Herrengasse 16 (same hours plus Sun 10am–3pm), which can book private rooms from around öS250 per person, although these are almost all a lengthy bus ride from the centre. The town's **youth hostel** is four blocks south of the station at Idlhofgasse 74 (☎0316/91 48 76; ③). The nearby *Hotel Strasser*, Eggenburger Gürtel 11 (☎0316/91 39 77; ④), fills quickly. More convenient for the centre is *Pension Iris*, Bergmanngasse 10 (☎0316/32 20 81; ⑤), north of the Stadtpark.

The City

Graz is compact and easy to explore, most sights being within striking distance of **Hauptplatz**, a broad market square in the centre of which is a statue of the Habsburg Archduke Johann, a popular nineteenth-century benefactor. Herrengasse leads off to the south towards the **Landhaus**, a sixteenth-century town hall with Italianate arcading in the courtyard. Next door **Zeughaus**, Herrengasse 16 (April–Oct Mon–Fri 9am–5pm, Sat & Sun 9am–1pm; öS30) is an armoury whose galleries bristle with weaponry used to keep the Turks at bay. The main attraction west of Herrengasse is the **Landesmuseum Johanneum**, founded by Archduke Johann, a vast collection housed in different locations; entrance to the natural history section (Mon–Fri 9am–6pm, Sat & Sun 9am–noon; öS30) is at Raubergasse 10, while the more interesting **Alte Galerie** (Tues–Fri 10am–5pm, Sat & Sun 10am–1pm; öS55) at Neutorgasse 45, houses a collection rich in Gothic devotional paintings. A fifteenth-century altarpiece by the illustrious Tyrolean Michael Pacher depicts the martyrdom of Thomas à Becket, and, among other Flemish paintings, there's a grippingly macabre *Triumph of Death* by Bruegel.

On the other side of Herrengasse, Stempfergasse leads into a neighbourhood of narrow alleyways that dog-leg their way up the hill towards the **Mausoleum of Ferdinand II** (Mon–Thurs & Sat 11am–noon & 2–3pm; öS20). It's a fine example of the early Baroque style, begun in 1614 when its intended incumbent was a healthy 36-year-old. Next door is the **Domkirche**, immediately north of which is the **Burg**, an erstwhile imperial residence now given over to local government offices; peer through the archway at the end of the first courtyard to view the unique double spiral of a fifteenth-century Gothic staircase. From here Hofgasse descends to the bustling shopping street of **Sporgasse**, where the Saurau palace at no. 25 features a Turkish figure throwing himself from a small window.

A short way north of Hauptplatz, down Sackstrasse, the **Neue Galerie** (Tues–Sat 10am–6pm, Sun 10am–1pm; öS40), housed in the seventeenth-century Herberstein Palace, displays nineteenth- and twentieth-century works including a sprinkling of Klimts and Schieles. From Schlossbergplatz a balustraded stone staircase zigzags up to the **Schlossberg**, a wooded hill overlooking the town; the Schlossbergbahn funicular, a little further along Sackstrasse, makes the same trip (every 15min 9am–10pm). The Schloss from which its name derives was destroyed by Napoleon in 1809; only two prominent features survive – the sixteenth-century **Uhrturm** or clock tower, whose steep overhanging roof figures prominently in the town's tourist literature, and the more distant **Glockenturm** or bell tower of the same period. Paths descend south from the Schlossberg to the elegant sweep of the **Stadtpark**, a leafy barrier between the city and the residential suburbs beyond.

Some 4km west of the town centre, at the end of tram line #1, are the luxurious state rooms of **Schloss Eggenburg**, Eggenberger Allee 90 (daily 9am–noon & 1–5pm; öS80), built in 1625 for Hans Ulrich of Eggenburg, Ferdinand II's First Minister. Tickets include a guided tour of the state rooms as well as the Schloss's museums. The archeological collection is strong on prehistory, its most valued exhibit being the Strettweg chariot – a remarkable eighth-century-BC wheeled platform peopled by small, weapon-wielding figures.

Eating, drinking and nightlife

Graz is foremost among Austria's provincial cities in preserving the culture of the *Kaffeehaus*. *Hofcafé Edegger Tax*, Hofgasse 8, is the sumptuous refuge of the city's more sedate citizens; the more modern *Operncafé*, Opernring 22, attracts a more youthful crowd and is equally popular in the evening; whilst *Café Promenade*, Erzherzog-Johann-Allee, is an attractive pavilion in the middle of the Stadtpark.

For something more substantial than munching a *Wurst* on Hauptplatz or visiting the fishy *Nordsee* outlet on Herrenstrasse, try *Gambrinuskeller*, Farbergasse 6–8 (closed Sun & Mon), which has a wide choice of reasonably priced **food**, including kebabs, stuffed peppers and other Balkan dishes; or *Glockenspielkeller*, Mehlplatz 3, with more standard Austrian fare and pleasant outdoor seating. *Pizzeria Catharina*, Sporgasse 32, has a wide range of inexpensive pizzas; and *Mangolds*, Griesgasse 11 (closed Sun) across the river, offers self-service health food in antiseptic surroundings – though it closes at 8pm. Many of the best places to **drink** are in the alleys just east of the Hauptplatz – *MI*, Färberplatz, and *Tom's Bierklinik*, Färbergasse 1, are among the most characterful. It's also worth venturing out to the cafés and bars which cluster in the streets around the university, east of the Stadtpark: *Café Harrach*, Harrachgasse 26, and *Bier Baron*, Heinrichstrasse 56, are both student favourites, serving inexpensive food; while *Jedermann*, Leonhardgasse 3; and *Park House*, a pavilion in the Stadtpark, are both late bars with resident DJs.

SALZBURG AND THE SALZKAMMERGUT

Salzburg, straddling the border with Germany, is Austria's most heavily touristed city after Vienna – a magnet for those seeking the best of Austria's Baroque heritage and a taste of sub-alpine scenery. The most accessible and popular of these mountain areas is the **Salzkammergut**, a region of glacier-carved lakes and craggy peaks a couple of hours to the east by bus or train.

Salzburg

The Austrian writer Thomas Bernhard, an acerbic critic of the postwar state who spent his formative years in **SALZBURG**, called his home town "a fatal illness", whose Catholicism, conservatism and sheer snobbery drove its citizens to a miserable end. Yet for many visitors Salzburg represents the quintessential Austria, offering the best of the country's Baroque architecture, subalpine air, and a musical heritage largely provided by the city's most famous son, Wolfgang Amadeus Mozart, whose bright-eyed visage peers from every box of the city's ubiquitous chocolate delicacy, the *Mozartkügel*.

Despite this, for much of its history Salzburg either belonged to the Bavarian sphere or was an independent city-state, only becoming part of the Habsburg domain in 1816. In the Middle Ages the city looked west, its powerful archbishops serving a see which extended over much of southern Germany, prosperous on the proceeds of the Salzkammergut salt trade. The city's High Baroque appearance is largely due to the ambition of sixteenth- and seventeenth-century Prince-Archbishops Wolf Dietrich and Paris Lodron, who hired artists and craftsmen from south of the Alps to recast Salzburg on the model of Rome.

Arrival and accommodation

Salzburg's **airport** is 5km west of town on the Innsbrucker Bundesstrasse and is linked to the city's train station by bus #77. It's over a kilometre into town from the train station, but there are regular buses covering the distance (#1, #2, #5, #6, #51 and #55 all go to Makartplatz on the east bank); a 24-hour pass (*Netzkarte*) costs öS38. There's a **tourist kiosk** at the train station (platform 2a; daily 8.30am–9pm), which sells maps, has accommodation details and books rooms for an öS35 fee; but the main **tourist office** is at Mozartplatz 5 in the old town centre (May–Oct daily 9am–8pm; Nov–April Mon–Sat 9am–6pm). Of the **hostels**, most conveniently placed are the *YO-HO International Youth Hotel Obermair*, Paracelsusstrasse 9 (☎662/87 96 46; ②), a lively place nicely poised between the train station and main sights; and the *Haunspergstrasse* hostel, three blocks west of the train station at Haunspergstrasse 27 (☎0662/87 50 30; ②; midnight curfew; July & Aug). As for **hotels**, rooms fill quickly in summer and can be pricey. The *Schwarzes Rössl*, Priesterhausgasse 6 (☎0662/87 44 26; ④; July–Sept), is a marvellous, creaky old building in a good location; or try the *Hinterbrühl*, Schanzlgasse 12 (☎0662/84 67 98; ③). *Bergland*, Rupertgasse 15 (☎0662/87 23 18; ④), is a friendly place on the right bank, 1km northeast of the centre – handy for both sightseeing and the train station. *Camping Gnigl*, Parscher Strasse 4, is the most convenient campsite, bus #29 from Makartplatz (mid-May to mid-Sept).

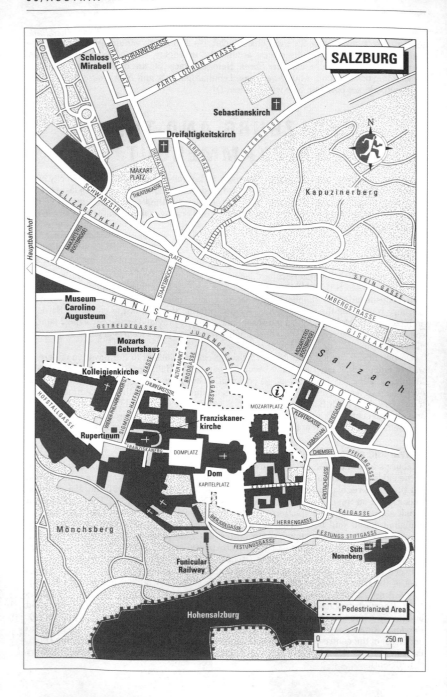

SALZBURG

Schloss Mirabell
Sebastianskirch
Dreifaltigkeitskirch
MAKART PLATZ
Kapuzinerberg
Museum Carolino Augusteum
Mozarts Geburtshaus
Kolleigienkirche
Rupertinum
Franziskaner-kirche
Dom
Mönchsberg
Funicular Railway
Stift Nonnberg
Hohensalzburg
Pedestrianized Area

0   250 m

The City

Salzburg has a compact centre and an easily walkable concentration of sights. The ensemble of archiepiscopal buildings in the centre, on the **west bank** of the river, forms a tight-knit network of alleys and squares, overlooked by the brooding presence of the medieval Hohensalzburg castle. From here it's a short hop over the River Salzach to a narrow ribbon of essential sights on the **east bank**.

THE WEST BANK

From the Staatsbrücke, the main bridge across the River Salzach, **Judengasse** funnels tourists up into **Mozartplatz**, home to a statue of the composer and overlooked by the **Glockenspiel**, a seventeenth-century musical clock whose chimes attract crowds at 7am, 11am and 6pm. The complex of Baroque buildings on the right exudes the ecclesiastical and temporal power wielded by Salzburg's archbishops, whose erstwhile living quarters – the **Residenz** – dominate the west side of the adjacent **Residenzplatz**. Guided tours of the building (July & Aug every 30min 10am–4.30pm; Sept–June hourly 10am–noon & 2–3pm; öS50) take you through a sequence of state rooms while, one floor above, the **Residenzgalerie** (April–Sept daily 10am–5pm; Oct–March Mon, Tues & Thurs–Sun 10am–5pm; öS50) offers a fine display of archiepiscopal acquisitions, including works by Rembrandt and Caravaggio, and a fairly comprehensive collection of Flemish works. From here arches lead through to **Domplatz**, dominated by the pale marble facade of the **Dom** – an impressively cavernous but otherwise undistinguished Renaissance structure put up by Archbishop Wolf Dietrich in 1628. The cathedral **museum** (mid-May to mid-Oct daily 10am–5pm; öS50) holds the collection of artworks and curiosities assembled by seventeenth-century Archbishop Guidobaldo Thun.

At the opposite end of the Domplatz an archway leads through to the Gothic **Franziskanerkirche**, a thirteenth-century reconstruction of an eighth-century edifice that houses a fine Baroque altar by Fischer von Erlach around an earlier, Gothic Madonna and Child sculpted by the Tyrolean master Michael Pacher. The altar is enclosed by an arc of nine chapels, adorned by a frenzy of stucco ornamentation. Look, also, for the twelfth-century marble lion which guards the stairway to the pulpit. Around the corner is the **Rupertinum**, Wiener-Philharmonikergasse 9 (mid-July to Sept Mon & Thurs–Sun 9am–5pm, Wed until 9pm; Oct to mid-July Tues & Thurs–Sun 10am–5pm, Wed 10am–9pm; öS40), a picture gallery devoted to twentieth-century work and touring exhibitions, with a nice secluded café. Art exhibitions often grace the cavernous interior of Fischer von Erlach's sizeable if graceless **Kollegienkirche** or University Church, on the adjacent Universitätsplatz. Around the back of the church, Hofstallgasse is dominated by the modern **Festspielhaus**, a principal venue for the Salzburg festival. Northeast of here, the **Museum Carolino-Augusteum**, Museumplatz 1 (Tues 9am–8pm, Wed–Sun 9am–5pm; öS40), contains Roman finds from the town centre, including a reconstructed mosaic retrieved from beneath Mozartplatz, more Gothic religious art, and a room devoted to moralistic works by the late-nineteenth-century local painter Hans Makar. Getreidegasse leads east back towards the centre, lined with opulent boutiques, painted facades and wrought-iron shop signs. At no. 9 is **Mozart's Geburtshaus** or birthplace (daily: July & Aug 9am–7pm; Sept–June 9am–6pm; öS65; combined ticket with Gewohnhaus öS100). Born in 1756, the musical prodigy spent his first seventeen years in this house. Now a rather overcrowded place of pilgrimage, it harbours some fascinating period instruments, including a baby-sized violin used by the composer as a child.

You can get up to the **Höhensalzburg**, which commands excellent views across town from Mönchberg, by funicular from Kapitelplatz behind the cathedral, although the journey on foot isn't as hard or as time-consuming as it looks. Begun around 1070 to provide the archbishops with a refuge from belligerent German princes, the fortress (daily: July–Sept 8am–7pm; April–June & Oct 9am–6pm; Nov–March 9am–5pm; öS35) was gradually transformed into a more salubrious courtly seat. State rooms can be visited by guided tour (öS30), although a roam around the ramparts and passageways of the castle is enough to gain a feel for the place. Paths lead east from the fortress to another piece of pre-Baroque Salzburg, the **Stift Nonnberg**, whose church is a largely fifteenth-century Gothic rebuilding of an earlier Romanesque structure.

THE EAST BANK

Streets on the eastern bank of the river radiate out from **Platzl**, a small square at the foot of the Kapuzinerberg, named after a Capuchin monastery at the summit. Neither the monastery church nor the view really warrant the stiff climb, and a more interesting walk takes you from Platzl up Linzergasse to the **Sebastianskirche** and its fascinating graveyard, last resting place of the Renaissance humanist and alchemist Paracelsus and home to the mausoleum of Wolf Dietrich, tiled with an almost Islamic delicacy. Two blocks northwest of Platzl is Makartplatz, where **Mozart's Gewohnhaus** or family home (1773–1787) is located (daily: July & Aug 9am–6pm; Sept–June 10am–6pm; öS65; combined ticket with Geburtshaus öS100), containing an engrossing multimedia history of the composer and his times. Fischer von Erlach's **Dreifaltigkeitskirche** or Church of the Holy Trinity stands nearby, notable for the elegant curve of its exterior and murky frescoes by Rottmayr inside. Dreifaltigkeitsgasse brings you shortly to the **Schloss Mirabell**, on the site of a previous palace built by Wolf Dietrich for his mistress Salome, with whom the energetic prelate was rumoured to have sired a dozen children. Completely rebuilt by Lukas von Hildebrandt in the early eighteenth century, and further reconstructed after a fire in the nineteenth, it's now a prestigious venue for classical concerts. Its most outstanding features are the cherub-lined staircase by Baroque master George Raphael Donner and the ornate gardens, the rose-filled high ground of the adjoining Kurgarten which offers a much-photographed view back across the city towards the Höhensalzburg.

Eating and drinking

If you're just after a **snack**, there are plenty of outlets around Judengasse and Alter Markt offering sandwiches and suchlike. Salzburg is full of elegant cafés; the most renowned are *Tomasselli*, Alte Markt 9, and – if you can stand the snooty waiters – *Bazar*, Schwarzstrasse 3, on the east bank with a nice terrace overlooking the Salzach. *Kaffehäferl*, Universitätsplatz 6, is more intimate and has a good range of lunchtime snacks. For more substantial eating, *Resch & Lieblich*, next to the Festspielhaus at Toscaninihof 1, offers good-value Austrian cuisine in dining rooms carved out of the cliff of the Hohensalzburg hill. *Gablerbräu*, Linzergasse 9, serves good Austrian grub and has several vegetarian options, as does *Stieglkeller*, Festungsgasse 10 (May–Sept only), which provides pleasant outdoor seating on the way up to the Burg – it's also a good place for drinking beer on warm evenings. *Sternbrau* is a massive beer garden and restaurant complex occupying two courtyards between Griesgasse and Getriedegasse. *Zur Glocke*, Schanzlgasse 2, is a smaller establishment just east of the old town with homely Austrian cooking; and *Andreas Hofer*, on the right bank of the Salzach at Steingasse 65, serves up Tirolean specialities in atmospheric candle-lit rooms. There are numerous night-time **drinking** venues along Rudolfskai on the left bank and Giselakai opposite on the right bank. Further afield, *Augustiner Bräu*, Augustinerstrasse 4–6, is a vast open-air courtyard fifteen minutes northeast of the centre serving vast mugs of locally brewed beer; *Zum fidelen Affen*, Priesterhausgasse 8, is a smaller pub-like place with excellent beer on tap; whilst *Almrausch*, Imbergstrasse 22, has traditional alpine music on tape and a folk-fixated clientele.

The Salzburg Festival

The **Salzburg Festival** has been running since 1920 and is one of Europe's premier festivals of classical music, opera and theatre – running from the last week of July and continuing throughout August. Tickets are hard to come by: write to Salzburger Festspiele, Postfach 40, 5010 Salzburg, for programme and booking details. Some standing places for the outdoor performances are available on a stand-by basis; check with the box office on Hofstallgasse (☎0662/84 25 41).

Listings

Airlines Austrian Airlines, at the airport (☎0662/88 45 11); British Airways, Griesgasse 29 (☎0662/84 21 08); Lauda Air, at the airport (☎0662/85 45 33).

Car rental Avis, F-Porsche-Strasse 7 (☎0662/87 72 78); Budget, Rainerstrasse 17 (☎0662/87 34 52).

Consulates Great Britain, Alter Markt 4 (☎0662/84 81 33); US, Herbert-von-Karajan-Platz 1 (☎0662/84 87 76).
Exchange Outside banking hours in the train station (daily 7am–9pm).
Hospital Müllner Hauptstrasse 48 (☎0662/4482).
Post office The main office is at Residenzplatz 9 (Mon–Fri 7am–7pm, Sat 8am–10am); also the best place to find phone booths.
Taxis ☎81 11; ☎66 10 66.
Travel agents Landesreisebüro, Getreidegasse 24 (☎0662/84 68 46); ÖKISTA, Wolf-Dietrich-Strasse 31 (☎0662/88 32 52).

The Salzkammergut

Straddling the border between Land Salzburg and Upper Austria, the peaks of the **Salzkammergut** may not be as lofty as those further south, but the glacier-carved troughs that separate them make for some spectacular scenery. Most of the towns and villages in the area are modest places, quiet throughout much of the year until the annual summer influx of visitors. It's a good area for making use of plentiful private rooms and *Gasthöfe*. The natural transport and commercial hub of the region is the nineteenth-century spa town of **Bad Ischl**, 60km east of Salzburg, close by two of the most scenic Salzkammergut lakes – the **Wolfgangersee** and **Hallstättersee**. You can reach Bad Ischl by train by way of a branch line off the main Salzburg–Vienna route from Attnang-Puchheim – or from Stainach-Irdning on the Graz–Salzburg route to the south. From Salzburg, a bus is the most direct route.

St Wolfgang

Hourly buses from Salzburg to Bad-Ischl run east along the southern shores of the Wolfgangersee, though they bypass the lake's main attraction, the village of **ST WOLF-GANG**, on the opposite shore. Get off the bus at the village of **Strobl**, at the lake's eastern end, and pick up a connecting bus to the village from there. A traditional stomping ground of lakes-and-mountains package-tourists, St Wolfgang can be crowded in summer, but you should make a point of stopping off, if only to visit the **Pilgrimage Church** (Mon–Sat 9am–4/5.30pm, Sun 11.30am–4/5pm), just above the lake shore, which contains a high altar by Michael Pacher. An extravagantly pinnacled structure some twelve metres in height, the altar was a joint venture with Michael's pupil Friedrich Pacher (no relation), and was completed some time in 1481. Normally only the outer panels are on display, depicting scenes from the life of St Wolfgang, who lived as a hermit on the shores of the lake, but on Sundays the wings are opened to allow a glimpse of scenes from the life of Christ. The brightly gilded, sculpted scenes of the coronation of the Virgin, which form the altar's centrepiece, are only revealed on religious holidays and festivals. Ascents of the local peak, the **Schafberg**, by mountain railway (May–Sept; InterRail/Eurail concessions), are possible from a station on the western edge of town. The **tourist office**, Pilgerstrasse 28 (Mon–Fri 8am–6pm, Sat 8am–noon) will fix you up with a private room if you want to stay.

Bad Ischl

The elegant town houses, fountains and gardens of **BAD ISCHL** have an air of bourgeois repose. The soothing properties of the waters here prompted the penultimate Habsburg emperor, Franz Josef, to spend each summer here in the **Kaiservilla** (May to mid-Oct daily 9–11.45am & 1–4.45pm; öS100), across the River Ischl from the centre. Beyond the villa (which is crammed with victims of the emperor's hunting expeditions) stretches a park containing the **Marmorschlössel** (April–Oct daily 9.30am–5pm; öS15), an exquisite neo-Gothic garden retreat built for the Empress Elizabeth; it now houses a small museum of photography. The **tourist office** near the station at Bahnhofstrasse 6 (June–Sept Mon–Fri 8am–6pm, Sat 8am–4pm, Sun 10am–noon; Oct–May Mon–Fri 9am–noon & 1–5.30pm) will direct you to the town's numerous **private rooms**. There's a **youth hostel** at Am Rechensteg 5 (☎06132/26577; ②); and a clean and comfy **pension**, *Haus Eglmoos* at Eglmoosgasse 14 (☎06132/23154; ③).

Hallstatt

The real jewel of the Salzkammergut is **HALLSTATT**, occupying a dramatic position 20km south of Bad Ischl on the western shores of Hallstättersee, jutting out into the lake at the base of a precipitous cliff. Before the building of the road along the western side of the lake, local transport was provided by a sharp-prowed boat known as a *Fuhr*, propelled by a single paddle at the stern, rather like a punt; a few still ply the lake, emerging from the characteristic wooden boathouses that line the shore.

Hallstatt gave its name to a distinct period of Iron-Age culture after Celtic remains were discovered in the salt mines above the town. Many of the finds which made the town famous, date back to the ninth century BC, and can now be seen in the **Prehistoric Museum** (daily: May–Sept 10am–6pm; Nov–April 1–5pm; öS30) – they include wooden mining implements, pit props and hide rucksacks used by Iron-Age miners, alongside more ornamental objects such as jewellery and ornate dagger handles. The same ticket is valid for the nearby **Heimat Museum** (same hours), full of the natural historical and anthropological collections of Friedrich Morton, the archeologist who worked on the sites in the 1930s. Tableaux on the history of salt mining illustrate working conditions through the centuries.

Hallstatt's **Pfarrkirche**, uphill from the water's edge, has a south portal adorned with Calvary scenes painted around 1500. Inside, a late medieval altar contains scenes from the life of Mary and the early life of Jesus, and in an adjoining chapel is the central panel of an earlier, mid-fifteenth-century altar, with another Crucifixion scene – the wing panels were carried off by thieves in 1987. In the graveyard outside stands a small stone structure known as the **Beinhaus**, traditionally the repository for the skulls of villagers, with their bones neatly stacked below like firewood. The skulls, some of them quite recent, are inscribed with the names of the deceased and date of their death, and are often decorated with finely painted floral patterns. Steep paths behind the graveyard lead up to a highland valley, the Salzachtal, where the **salt mines** that provided the area's prosperity are viewable on regular guided tours (May to mid-Oct daily 9.30am–3.30/4.30pm; öS140). Between May and October you can also take the **funicular** (öS110 return) up here from the nearby suburb of Lahn.

Hallstatt's **train station** is on the opposite side of the lake to the town, a local ferry meeting all incoming trains. However, after about 6pm trains don't stop here and instead continue on to the village of Obertraun, a five-kilometre walk away along the shores of the lake. Hallstatt's **tourist office** is centrally located at Seestrasse 169 (July & Aug Mon–Fri 8am–6pm, Sat 10am–6pm, Sun 10am–2pm; Sept–June Mon–Fri 9am–noon & 1–5pm), and can arrange **accommodation** in private rooms or guesthouses, of which *Frühstuckspension Sarstein*, 200m north of the landing stage at Gosaumühlestrasse 83 (☎06134/8271; ③) is one of the nicest. *Gasthaus Zur Mühle*, set back from the landing stage at Kirchenweg 36 (☎06134/8318; ②) offers hostel-style accommodation in dorms. *Bräugasthof Lobisser*, Seestrasse 120, purveys solid Austrian **food** and good **beer**.

WESTERN AUSTRIA

West of Salzburg towards the mountain province of the **Tirol**, the grandiose scenery of Austria's Alpine heartland begins to unfold in earnest. Most of the trains from Vienna and Salzburg travel through a corner of Bavaria before joining the Inn valley and climbing back into Austria to the Tirolean capital, **Innsbruck**. A less direct but more scenic route (and one you will be more likely to follow if coming from Graz and the southeast) cuts between the Kitzbühler Alpen and the majestic **Hoher Tauern** (site of Austria's highest peak, the Grossglockner), before joining the River Inn at Wörgl. Settlements such as the exclusive resort-town of **Kitzbühel** provide potential stopoffs on the way, although it's Innsbruck which offers the most convenient mix of urban sights and Alpine splendour. Further west towards Switzerland, the **Vorarlberg** is a distant, isolated extremity of Austria, though its capital, **Bregenz**, on the shores of Lake Constance (or *Bodensee* in German), makes for a tranquil stop before pressing on.

Kitzbühel

KITZBÜHEL began life as a sixteenth-century copper- and silver-mining town, and preserves an exceedingly pretty medieval centre, despite the suburbs that clutter the valley below. From the train station, head down Bahnhofstrasse and turn left at the end; the town centre is a dull fifteen-minute stroll from here. Downtown Kitzbühel revolves around two squares, **Vorderstadt** and **Hinterstadt**. A twelfth-century pile at the southern end of Hinterstadt contains a small **museum** of local history (Mon–Sat 9am–noon; öS30), offering a jumble of folk crafts and mining implements which reveal some of the industrial grit behind the tinseltown that Kitzbühel has since become. Some of the mining wealth no doubt went into the brightly coloured facades of the town houses lining Vorderstadt, now the backdrop to a promenade of pensioners ambling endlessly up and down. Perched above are two worthwhile churches, the fifteenth-century Gothic **Pfarrkirche**, whose overhanging roof covers some medieval frescoes in the choir, and, immediately above it, the **Liebfrauenkirche**, with a monumental tower and more frescoes in the graveyard chapel.

The **tourist office** is at Hinterstadt 18 (July–Sept & mid-Dec to mid-April Mon–Fri 8am–6pm, Sat 8am–noon & 4–6pm; mid-April to June & Oct to mid-Dec Mon–Fri 8am–noon & 2–6pm), and can arrange **accommodation** either in private homes or in any number of inexpensive pensions. *Hörl*, Josef-Pirchler-Strasse 60 (☎05356/3144; ③), is a cosy pension between the train station and the centre. For **food**, *Huberbräu Stüberl*, Vorderstadt 18, is a cosy central place offering solid Austrian fare; and *Chizzo*, Josef-Herold-Strasse 2, has an affordable range of Tirolean specialities. For **drinking**, try the numerous bars around Vorderstadt and Hinterstadt. If you want to escape into the beautiful highland scenery close by, take the **Hahnehkamm** chairlift (*gondola*) at the end of Heroldstrasse, ten minutes west of Hinterstadt; or the **Kitzsteinhorn** chairlift over on the eastern side of town. Both destinations offer a network of high-altitude hiking trails, and sumptuous views back into the valley.

Innsbruck

Located high in the Alps, with ski resorts within easy reach, **INNSBRUCK** is primarily known as a winter-vacation centre. However, the city is rich in history, too: Maximilian I based the imperial court here in the 1490s, suddenly placing this provincial Alpine town at the heart of European politics and culture. It remained an imperial residence for a century and a half, so it's perhaps not surprising that its incorporation into Bavaria (a move precipitated by the Napoleonic carve-up of Europe) produced an insurrectionary movement under the local hero after whom so many streets and squares are named – Andreas Hofer.

Arrival and accommodation

The **tourist kiosk** in Innsbruck's **train station** (daily 9am–10pm) offers a speedy room-booking service for a small fee and a refundable deposit. The main **tourist office** is centrally located at Burggraben 3 (daily 8am–7pm). Best placed of the **hostels** is the *MK Jugendzentrum*, Sillgasse 8a (☎0512/57 13 11; ②), midway between the train station and the old town. Other options include: *Paula*, Weiherburggasse 15 (☎0512/29 22 62; ③), a friendly **pension** with fine views across the city from a hillside spot north of the Inn; the *Innrain*, Innrain 38 (☎0512/58 89 81; ③), a small *Gasthof* on the south bank of the river; and *Hotel-Pension Binder*, Dr-Glatz-Strasse 20 (☎0512/33 43 6; ④), clean and friendly, in a suburban street twenty minutes south of the centre. The only **campsite** is *Camping Innsbruck Kranebitten*, 5km west of the city centre; take bus #LK from Boznerplatz, a block west of the station.

The City

Most of what you will want to see in Innsbruck is confined to the central precincts of the **Altstadt**, a small area bounded by the river and the Graben, following the course of the moat which used to surround the medieval town. Leading up to this, Innsbruck's main artery is

Maria-Theresien-Strasse, famed for the view north towards the great rock wall of the Nordkette, the mountain which dominates the city. At its southern end, three blocks west of the train station down Salurnerstrasse, the triumphal arch, **Triumphpforte**, was built in advance of celebrations marking the marriage of Maria Theresa's son Leopold in 1756. Halfway along, the **Annasäule**, a column supporting a statue of the Virgin, but named after St Anne, who appears at the base, was erected to commemorate the retreat of the Bavarians, who had been menacing the Tirol, on St Anne's day (July 26), 1703.

North of here, Herzog-Friedrich-Strasse leads into the centre, opening out into a plaza overlooked by the **Goldenes Dachl**, or golden roof – though the tiles which give the roof its name are actually copper, added in the 1490s to cover a window from which the imperial court could observe the square below. Inside is the **Maximilianeum** (daily 10am–6pm, öS70), a flashy and insubstantial museum of Kaiser Maximilian's life and times, illustrated by a few exhibits and a short video show. An alley to the right leads down to Domplatz and the **Domkirche St Jakob**, home to a valuable *Madonna and Child* by German master Lucas Cranach the Elder, although it is buried in the fussy Baroque detail of the altar. The adjacent **Hofburg**, entered from Rennweg, at the end of Hofgasse around the corner, has late medieval roots but was remodelled in the eighteenth century; its Rococo state apartments are unremarkable save for the cavernous ballroom (mid-May to mid-Oct daily 9am–5pm; mid-Oct to mid-May Mon–Sat 9am–4pm; öS35).

At the head of the Rennweg is the **Hofkirche**, an outwardly unassuming building which nevertheless contains the most impressive of Innsbruck's imperial monuments, the **Cenotaph of Emperor Maximilian** (June–Sept daily 9am–5/5.30pm; öS40, combined ticket with the Tiroler Volkskunstmuseum). This extraordinary project was originally envisaged as a series of 40 larger-than-life statues, 100 statuettes and 32 busts of Roman emperors, representing both the real and the spiritual ancestors of Maximilian, but in the end only 32 of the statuettes and 20 of the busts were completed. The resulting ensemble is still impressive, though the effect is dulled slightly by the knowledge that the emperor is actually buried at the other end of Austria in Wiener Neustadt. Upstairs is the *Silberkapelle* or silver chapel, named after the silver Madonna that adorns the far wall. She is faced by Archduke Ferdinand II's suit of armour, suspended in a kneeling position halfway up the wall. The bones of the man himself are housed directly below.

Entrance to the Hofkirche is through the same door as the **Tiroler Volkskunstmuseum** (Mon–Sat 9am–5pm, Sun 9am–noon; öS40), which has an endless series of wood-panelled Tirolean peasant interiors, and models of Tirolean village architecture. The **Tiroler Landesmuseum Ferdinandeum**, a short walk south at Museumstrasse 15 (Mon–Wed & Fri–Sun 10am–5pm, Thurs also 7am–9pm; öS40), is more engaging, with its large collection of Gothic paintings. Most originate from the churches of the South Tirol (now in Italy), although some are by the "Pustertal painters" based around Bruneck (now Brunico in Italy) in the East Tirol, pre-eminent among whom were Michael and Friedrich Pacher, who imported Italian Renaissance techniques into German painting and sculpture.

Also worth a visit is **Schloss Ambras** (April–Oct Mon & Wed–Sun 10am–5pm; öS60), 2km southeast of the centre and accessible by tram #6. It was the home of sixteenth-century **Archduke Ferdinand** of Tirol, and still houses his cabinet of curiosities, a strange collection of artworks and objects from around the globe.

The quickest route to higher altitudes is the **Hungerburgbahn**, which leaves from a station at the end of Rennweg (end of tram lines #1 and #6), calling at an intermediate station for the **Alpenzoo** (daily 9am–6pm; öS50) – a collection of animals indigenous to mountain regions – before reaching the Hungerburg plateau itself, a good base for hikes. A three-stage sequence of cable cars continues from here to just below the summit of the **Nordkette** itself.

Eating, drinking and nightlife

The streets around the Goldenes Dachl are a good source of **places to eat**, packed with old coaching inns transformed into restaurants. The inexpensive *Ottoburg*, Herzog-Friedrich-Strasse 1, is one of the most atmospheric and has at least one **vegetarian** main dish; but for better veggie options try *Philippine*, ten minutes south of the centre at Müllerstrasse 9, an eccentrically decorated restaurant with a wide choice of vegetarian dishes. Other options include: the *Weisses Rössl*, Kiebachgasse 8, a wood-panelled restaurant on the first floor serving Tirolean specialities; *Stiftskeller*, Stiftgasse 1, offering a good choice of fresh fish; and *La Cucina*, Museumstrasse 26, with a wide range of reasonably priced pizza and pasta dishes. There are plenty of convivial **drinking venues** in Innsbruck's old town: *Prometheus*, Hofgasse 2, is one of the best, with an intimate bar upsairs and a disco in the cellar. A string of bars lurk beneath the railway arches (*Viaduktbogen*) east of the centre; *Weli*, at no. 26, is an informal café/bar with good food; *Klappe*, at no. 21, and *Plateau*, at no. 51, have louder music and are more club-like in style. *Innkeller*, on the other side of the river at Innstrasse 1, is another popular late-night haunt. *Treibhaus*, Angerzellgasse 8, is the place to look for live jazz, folk and alternative theatre.

Listings

Car rental Avis, Salurnerstrasse 15 (☎05222/57 17 54); Hertz, Südtirolerplatz 1 (☎05222/58 09 01).

Consulates Great Britain, Matthias-Schmid-Strasse 12 (☎05222/58 83 20).

Exchange Out of banking hours try the main tourist office or the train station.

Hiking tours Hiking tours depart daily at 8.30am (June–Sept) from Innsbruck Congress Centre, and are free to those staying in town for three nights or more; check with the tourist office for details.

Hospital Universitätklinik, Anichstrasse 35 (☎05222/50 40).

Post office The office at Maximilianstrasse 2 is open 24hr.

Telephones At the post office.

Travel agents ÖKISTA, Josef-Hirn-Strasse 7 (☎05222/58 89 97); Tiroler Landesreisebüro, Wilhelm-Griel-Strasse (☎05222/59885).

Bregenz

Stretched along the southern shores of Lake Constance, **BREGENZ** is an obvious staging post on journeys into neighbouring Bavaria to the north, or Switzerland to the west. The Vorarlbergers who live here speak a dialect close to Swiss German, and have always considered themselves separate from the rest of Austria. In November 1918 they declared independence and requested union with Switzerland, but this was denied by the Great Powers.

The Town

At first sight Bregenz is a curiously disjointed town, the tranquil lakeside parks cut off from the main body of the town by the main road and rail links along the shore of Lake Constance. Most of the interest sights are located in the old town, up the hill from the lake, around St **Martinsturm**, an early seventeenth-century tower crowned by a bulbous wooden dome. There's a small **museum** inside (May–Sept Tues–Sun 9am–6pm; öS30) containing arms and armour, and views down towards the lake. Up the street from here is the seventeenth-century **town hall**, an immense half-timbered construction with a steeply inclined roof. Down in the modern town nearest the lake, the **Kunsthaus Bregenz** (daily 10am–5pm; öS40) on Kornmarkt has a collection of modern Austrian art. The **Vorarlberger Landesmuseum**, Kornmarkt 1 (Tues–Sun 9am–noon & 2–5pm; öS40), has some outstanding paintings by sixteenth-century artists like Wolf Huber and Jörg Frosch, who had workshops in the nearby town of Feldkirch, and a selection of portraits and Classical scenes by Angelika Kauffmann, the Vorarlberg painter who achieved success in late eighteenth-century London. Beyond here, leafy **parklands** line the lake, at the western end of which stands the **Festspielhaus**, a modern concert hall built to accommodate the operatic and orchestral concerts of the Bregenz Festival, which usually runs from the last week in July to mid-August. The most popular excursion from Bregenz, however, is by cable car from a station at the eastern end of town to the **Pfänder** (July–Sept daily 9am–10.30pm; shorter hours rest of year), a wooded hill commanding an excellent panorama of the lake.

Practicalities

The **tourist office**, Anton Schneider-Strasse 4a (July–Sept Mon–Sat 9am–7pm; Oct–June Mon–Fri 9am–noon & 2–6pm, Sat 9am–noon), can book **rooms** for öS250 a head plus a öS20 fee. *Gästehaus Tannenbach*, im Gehren 1 (☎05574/44174; ③), is the best of the smaller pensions, in a quiet street east of the centre; *Gasthof Adler*, Vorklostergasse 66 (☎05574/31788; ③) is a good and inexpensive **hotel**. The **youth hostel** is at Belrupstrasse 16a (☎05574/42867; ②). *Seecamping*, Bodengasse 7, is a large **campsite** by the lake, 2km west of town. *Günz*, Anton-Schneider-Strasse 38, is an inexpensive source of traditional Austrian **food** in town; *Goldener Hirschen*, Kirchstrasse 8, is a more atmospheric, pub-like venue with slightly more expensive eats. Best of the central **bars** are *Erste Akt*, Kornmarktstrasse 24; and *Viva*, Seestrasse 7, which has a Mexican restaurant attached.

travel details

Trains

Vienna (Franz-Josefs Bahnhof) to: Krems (hourly; 1hr–1hr 15min).

Vienna (Südbahnhof) to: Graz (every 2hr; 2hr 40min).

Vienna (Westbahnhof) to: Attnang-Pucheim (hourly; 2hr 30min); Bregenz (8 daily; 10hr); Innsbruck (every 2hr; 5hr 20min); Linz (1–2 hourly; 2hr); Melk (every 1–2hr; 1hr); Salzburg (1–2 hourly; 3hr–3hr 20min).

Attnang-Pucheim to: Bad Ischl (hourly; 1hr); Gmunden (hourly; 20min); Hallstadt (hourly; 1hr 30 min).

Bad Ischl to: St Wolfgang (hourly; 40min).

Graz to: Innsbruck (7 daily; 6hr); Linz (every 2hr; 3hr 30min); Salzburg (8 daily; 4hr 30min).

Innsbruck to: Bregenz (10 daily; 2hr).

Salzburg to: Attnang-Pucheim (hourly; 45min); Innsbruck (8 daily; 2hr 30min); Kitzbühel (hourly; 1hr 45min); Linz (hourly; 1hr 20min).

Buses

Krems to: Melk (4 daily; 1hr).

Linz to St Florian (Mon–Fri every 2hr; 35min).

Salzburg to: Bad Ischl (hourly; 1hr 30min); Ströbl (hourly; 1hr).

CHAPTER 2

BELGIUM AND LUXEMBOURG

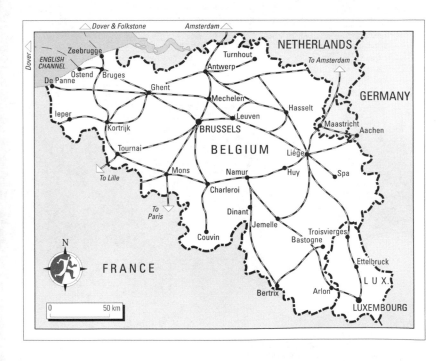

Introduction

A federal country, with three official languages and an intense regional rivalry, Belgium has a cultural diversity that belies its rather dull reputation among travellers. Its population of around ten million is divided between Flemish-speakers (about sixty percent) and French-speaking Walloons (forty percent), with a few pockets of German-speakers in the east. Prosperity has shifted back and forth between the two communities over the centuries, and relations remain acrimonious. The constitution was redrawn in 1980 on a federal basis, with three separate entities: the Flemish North, Walloon South, and Brussels, which is officially bilingual (although its population is eighty percent French-speaking).

The north and south of **Belgium** are visually very different. Marking the meeting of the two, **Brussels**, the capital, is a culturally varied city at the heart of the European Union. The **north**, made up of the provinces of West and East Flanders, Antwerp, Limburg and much of Brabant, is mainly flat, with a landscape and architecture not unlike Holland. **Antwerp** is the largest city, a bustling old port with doses of high art, redolent of its sixteenth-century golden age. Further south and west are the great historic cities, **Bruges** and **Ghent**, with a stunning concentration of Flemish art and architecture. Another enjoyable, inland Flanders town is the cathedral city of **Mechelen**, halfway between Brussels and Antwerp. The southern reaches of **Brabant** are French-speaking, and merge into the Walloon province of **Hainaut** – rich agricultural country, scarred by pockets of industry and boasting the historic city of **Tournai**. East of here lies Belgium's most scenically rewarding region, the **Ardennes**, an area of deep, wooded valleys, high elevations and dark caverns.

The Ardennes reach across the border into the northern part of the **Grand Duchy of Luxembourg**, a verdant landscape of rushing rivers and high hills topped with crumbling castles. **Diekirch**, **Vianden** and **Echternach** are perhaps the three best centres for touring the countryside, and **Luxembourg City** itself is at least worth a stop, although its population of around 75,000 is tiny by capital-city standards.

Information and maps

In both Belgium and Luxembourg there are **tourist offices** in all but the smallest villages. They usually provide free maps, and in the larger towns offer an accommodation service. As for **maps**, the Belgian Tourist Office gives out a decent free map of the country that indicates the most important highways as well as provincial and international boundaries. Otherwise, the best-value general road map is the clear and easy-to-use Baedeker & AA Belgium and Luxembourg (1:250,000) map.

Money and banks

Pending its replacement by the Euro, the **currency** in both Belgium and Luxembourg is the franc (abbreviated as F, or BEF and LUF). The Belgian and Luxembourg francs are interchangeable, though, while Belgian francs can be used without difficulty in Luxembourg, the reverse is not always the case. Both currencies divide into 100 centimes, and come in coins worth 1, 5, 20 and 50 francs, and notes worth 100, 500, 1000, 2000 and 10,000 francs. **Banks** are the best places to change money. In Belgium they are open Mon–Fri 9am–4pm, in Luxembourg 9am–4.30pm, often with a one-hour lunch break between noon and 2pm; some city banks also open on Saturday mornings. You can also change money in larger cities at train stations, some hotels, and **bureaux de change**, though the rates are less favourable; you can obtain cash through ATMs in Brussels and elsewhere if you have the appropriate card with a PIN number – ask your bank for further details.

Communications

In Belgium **post offices** are open Mon–Fri 9am–noon & 2–4pm, and in Luxembourg Mon–Fri 9am–noon & 1.30–5pm. Some open Saturday mornings, too. Public **phones** take F5, F20 and sometimes F50 coins, though in Belgium and Luxembourg many take cards only; these are available from newsagents and post offices for F200 or F1000 (Belgium), F250 and F550 (Luxembourg). There are no area phone codes in Luxembourg. The international operator numbers are ☎1324 in Belgium, ☎0010 in Luxembourg, and they handle collect calls.

Getting around

Travelling around Belgium is rarely a problem. Distances are short, and an efficient, reasonably priced train service links the major centres. Luxembourg, on the other hand, can be problematic: the train network is not extensive, and bus timetables demand careful study.

■ Trains and buses

Run by the Societé National Chemin de Fer de Belgique/Belgische Spoorwegen (Belgian Railways),

Belgium's rail system is comprehensive and efficient, and fares are comparatively low. InterRail and Eurail passes are valid throughout the network, as is the **Belgian Tourrail pass**, which gives entitlement to five days' unlimited rail travel within a month for F2100. There is also the so-called **Fixed-price reduction card** (*Carte de réduction à prix fixé/Reduktiekaart*), which costs F600 and allows you to purchase tickets at half-price during a specified monthly period, or the under−26 **Go Pass**, valid for ten second-class, single journeys within six months (F1420). Consider also the **Benelux Tourrail Card**, which gives five days' train travel in a month for F3100 (over-26s F4400) throughout Belgium, Luxembourg and the Netherlands. Belgian Railways publish **information** on their various offers and services, and all are detailed in their comprehensive national and international timetable book, *Indicateur/ Spoorboekje*, which has an English-language section and is available for F150 from major train stations. As so much of Belgium is covered by the rail network, **buses** are only really used for travelling short distances, or in parts of the Ardennes where there are fewer rail lines.

In **Luxembourg** trains are run by Chemins de Fer Luxembourgeois (CFL). There's one main north–south route down the middle of the country to Luxembourg City, but apart from that only a few lines branch out from the capital, and the system is mainly supplemented by **buses**. Fares are comparable with those in Belgium, and there are a number of passes available, giving unlimited train and bus travel for periods lasting from one day to one month: the price for a **one-day pass** is F160, F640 for a pack of five.

■ Driving

Both countries are well covered by networks of main **roads** and (toll-free) **motorways**, and congestion is normally tolerable outside the major cities. The speed limit in built-up areas is 50kph, on main roads 90kph and on motorways 120kph. Seat belts are compulsory in both countries, and penalties for drunken driving stiff. Spot fines are common for some offences, and in Luxembourg it's obligatory to always carry at least F600 on you for payment of fines – although fines can range between F500 and F3000. The leading national motoring organization in Belgium is the Touring Club de Belgique (TCB), rue Joseph II, 25, Brussels 1040 (☎02/223 2211). In Luxembourg there's the Automobile Club of Luxembourg (ACL), route de Longwy 54, L-8007 Bertrange (☎45 00 45; *www.acl.lu/*). Both organizations can be called upon in case of breakdown – and most major roads are dotted with phones – but only if your insurance grants you affiliated membership; check this out before

departure. For emergency telephone numbers, see the box on p.104. **Car rental** in both countries is quite pricey, about F15,000 a week with unlimited mileage, though there are cheaper weekend rates.

■ Cycling

Cycling is something of a national sport in **Belgium**, and the distances and flat terrain make it a fairly effortless way of getting around. You have to be selective, however; cycling in most big cities and on the majority of trunk roads – where cycle lanes are unusual – is precarious. Once you've reached the countryside, though, there are dozens of clearly signposted cycle routes to follow. Fortunately, you can rent a bike from around 35 train stations. Rates are economical: reckon on F335 a day, though note that some train excursion tickets include the cost of bike rental. Non-Belgians have to stump up a refundable deposit of F500. For a list of train stations offering this service, get a copy of Belgian Railways' *Train & Vélo (Trein & Fiets)* leaflet. It is possible to take your bike on the train for about F150 per journey.

In **Luxembourg** you can rent bikes throughout the country for around F450 a day, and you can take your bike on trains for F40 per journey. The Luxembourg Tourist Office issues a booklet showing cycle routes.

Accommodation

Inevitably, hotel **accommodation** is one of the major expenses you will incur on a trip to Belgium and Luxembourg – indeed, if you're after a degree of comfort, it's going to be the costliest item by far. There are, however, budget alternatives, principally the no-frills end of the hotel market, private rooms arranged via the local tourist office and unofficial and HI-registered youth hostels, though these are largely confined to the larger, tourist-orientated cities.

■ Hotels and private rooms

In both countries prices range from F1500–2000 for a double room in the cheapest one-star **hotel** to F4000 in big city hotels – more if you go for somewhere really luxurious; in cheaper establishments breakfast isn't always included. During the summer you'd be well advised to book ahead, by either phoning the hotel direct or by contacting the local tourist office at least two weeks in advance. Hotel **reservations** can be made through most tourist offices for free, though they'll often require a deposit. The Belgian Tourist Office produces two comprehensive accommodation guides, one for the north and one for the south – the latter including Brussels. The Luxembourg Tourist Office also produces a booklet of approved hotels.

ACCOMMODATION PRICE CODES

Throughout this guide, accommodation is priced on a scale of ① to ⑨, the number indicating the lowest price per night a single person could expect to pay in that establishment in high season. With hostels this is the nightly rate per person; with hotels, the price is arrived at by dividing the cost of the cheapest double room by two. The prices indicated by the codes are as follows:

① under £5 / $8	④ £15–20 / $24–32	⑦ £30–35 / $48–56
② £5–10 / $8–16	⑤ £20–25 / $32–40	⑧ £35–40 / $56–64
③ £10–15 / $16–24	⑥ £25–30 / $40–48	⑨ £40 / $64 and over

Private rooms, bookable through local tourist offices, again at no charge, are slightly cheaper (around F1000–F1500 a night for a double) but they are often inconveniently situated.

■ Hostels and student rooms

Belgium has more than 30 HI **youth hostels**, run by two separate organizations, one for Flanders – Vlaamse Jeugdherbergcentrale, Van Stralenstraat 40, B-2060 Antwerp (☎03/232 72 18) – another for Wallonia – Les Auberges de Jeunesse de Wallonie, rue Van Oost 52, B-1030 Brussels (☎02/215 31 00). Most Belgian **hostels** charge a flat rate per person of around F380 for members, though in major centres such as Ghent you can expect to pay F500–650; breakfast is included. Many hostels also offer meals for F150–300. During the summer you should book in advance wherever possible.

Some of the larger cities – Antwerp and Brussels, for example – have a number of **unofficial youth hostels**. These normally charge about F500 for a dormitory bed and are often just as comfortable. You'll also find some universities offering **student rooms** for rent during the summer vacation, Ghent being a good example. Rooms are frugal and rates are reasonable – reckon on about F500 per person per night.

There are 14 youth hostels in **Luxembourg**, all of which are members of the Auberges de Jeunesse Luxembourgeoises (AJL), rue du Fort Olisy 2, L-2261 Luxembourg (☎22 55 88). Rates for HI members are F350–750 per person, with the Luxembourg City hostel at the top end of the price range. Breakfast is always included; lunch or dinner is F200–300. Sheets can also be rented for an extra F125.

■ Camping

Camping is a popular pastime in both Belgium and Luxembourg, but many sites are located with the motorist in mind. There are around 500 sites in **Belgium**, most of them well-equipped and listed in the Belgian Tourist Office's *Camping* leaflet, broadly classified on a one- to five-star basis. The vast majority are one-star establishments, for which a family of

two adults, two children, a car and a tent can expect to pay between F500–700 per night; **Luxembourg** has a little over one hundred campsites, all detailed in the free booklet available from the national tourist board. They are classified into three broad bands with each category having minimum standards. The majority are in Category 1, the best-equipped and most expensive classification. Prices vary considerably even within each category, but are usually between F70 and F140 per person, plus F100–150 for a site.

Food and drink

Belgian cuisine is held in high regard, second only – if not equal – to French, and the country also offers a wide range of ethnic food. Luxembourg's food is less varied, more Germanic – but you can still eat out extremely well. As for drink, beer is one of the real delights of Belgium, and Luxembourg produces some very drinkable white wines along its side of the Moselle.

■ Food

Southern Belgian cuisine is not unlike traditional French, retaining the fondness for rich sauces and ingredients that the latter has to some extent lost of late. In Flanders the food is more akin to that of Holland, with many interesting traditional dishes. Pork, beef, game, fish and seafood, especially mussels, are staple items, often cooked with butter, cream and herbs, or sometimes beer. Soups, too, are common: hearty affairs, especially in the south and the **Ardennes**, a region also renowned for its smoked ham and pâté.

In most parts of Belgium and Luxembourg you'll **start the day** in routine Continental fashion with a cup of coffee and a roll or croissant. Later in the day, the most obvious **snack** is a portion of *frites* – served everywhere in Belgium from *friture* stalls, with just salt or mayonnaise, or, as in Holland, with more exotic dressings. Other street stalls, especially in the north, sell various sausages, and everywhere there are stands selling waffles (*gaufres*), piping hot with jam and honey. There are also the usual burger joints, including the *Belgian Quick* chain.

Many **bars** do meals, at least at lunchtimes, and a host of **cafés** serve basic dishes – omelettes, steak or mussels with chips (virtually the Belgian national dish). The distinction between the two is, however, becoming increasingly blurred with **café/bars** often the most fashionable place to be, especially in the city. You can expect to pay about F200 for an omelette; anything more substantial will cost F350–500, though most places have a dish of the day for F400–500. Though they serve very similar food, **restaurants** are more expensive, and sometimes only open in the evening. A main course will rarely cost under F350, with F500 being a more usual price, particularly in Luxembourg.

Belgium is also renowned for its **chocolate**. The big Belgian *chocolatiers*, Godiva and Leonidas, have shops in all the main towns and cities, and their pralines and truffles are almost worth the trip alone. Of the two, Leonidas is the cheaper; reckon on spending F300 or so for 500g of their chocolates.

■ Drink

The price of food in Belgium and Luxembourg is compensated for by the low cost of **drinking**, especially if you like **beer**, which is always good and comes in numerous varieties. Ask for a *bière* in a **bar** and you'll be served a half-litre glass of whatever the bar has on tap. The most common Belgian brands are Stella Artois, Jupiler and Maes. In Luxembourg the most widespread brands are Diekirch, Mousel and Bofferding. There are also any number of **speciality beers**, usually served by the bottle but occasionally on draught. The most famous is perhaps *lambic*, the generic title for beer brewed in the Brussels area which is fermented by contact with the yeast in the air. A blend of old and young *lambic* beers is known as *gueuze*, a cidery concoction sold in all Brussels bars. There's also *kriek* – *lambic* with cherries added – and *faro*, given a distinctive and refreshing flavour by adding candy sugar. Try also some of the strong ales brewed by the country's five Trappist monasteries; the most widely available being Chimay, brewed in Hainaut. **Bar prices** don't vary greatly: in Belgium you'll pay around F60 for a glass of beer, while in Luxembourg, F55 is the usual price. In the swankiest places, you'll pay around F150 for beers like Duvel and Chimay.

French **wines** are the most commonly drunk, although **Luxembourg** is a wine producer, and its white and sparkling wines, produced along the north bank of the Moselle, are very drinkable: in the shops they go for around F250–350 a bottle of sparkling stuff, F250 for ordinary white wine. In restaurants they'll cost two or three times as much.

There's no national Belgian **spirit**, but all the usual kinds are widely available, at about F60 a glass in a bar. You will also find Dutch-style *jenever* in most bars in the north. In Luxembourg spirits are cheaper than elsewhere in Europe. You'll also come across home-produced *eau de vie*, distilled from various fruits and around fifty percent alcohol by volume.

Opening hours and holidays

In both Belgium and Luxembourg, the weekend fades painlessly into the week with some shops staying closed till late on Monday morning, even in major cities. Nonetheless, normal **shopping hours** are Monday through Saturday 10am to 6pm or 7pm, with most supermarkets staying open on Fridays till 8pm or 9pm and many smaller places shutting down a little earlier on Saturday. In the big cities, a smattering of convenience stores (*magasins de nuit*/*avondwinkels*) stay open either all night or until around 1 or 2am every day including Sundays, and some souvenir shops open late or on Sunday. Most museums are open Tues–Sat 9am–4/5pm, and often on Sunday. Outside the April–Sept period, many sightseeing places close unless they're of prime touristic importance.

Shops, banks and many museums are closed on the following **public holidays**: 1 Jan; Easter Monday; May 1; Ascension (around mid-May); Whit Monday; Assumption (mid-Aug); Nov 1; Nov 11 (Belgium only); 25 Dec. In addition, the Luxembourg national day is June 23, Belgium's is July 21.

Emergencies

The Belgian **police force** is not quite the friendly bunch you find in the Netherlands, but the country is relatively free of street crime and you shouldn't have much cause to come into contact with them. As far as **personal safety** goes, it's fairly safe to walk anywhere in the centres of the larger cities at any time of day, though you should obviously be wary of badly lit or empty streets; parts of Brussels and Antwerp especially can be intimidating and are best avoided after dark. If you are unlucky enough to have **something stolen**, report it immediately to the nearest police station. Get a police report number, or better still a copy of the statement itself, for your insurance claim when you get home.

EMERGENCY NUMBERS

Belgium
Ambulance & Fire ☎100; Police ☎101.

Luxembourg
Police ☎113; all other services, including late-opening chemists, doctors and dentists ☎112.

BRUSSELS

Wherever else you go in Belgium, it's likely that at some point you'll wind up in **BRUSSELS**. The city is the major air gateway for the country; it's on the main routes heading inland from the Channel ports via the Flemish art towns; trains arrive here direct from London via the Channel Tunnel; and, in addition, it's a convenient stopover on the train between France and the Netherlands.

Brussels takes its name from Broekzele, or "village of the marsh", which grew up in the sixth century on the trade route between Cologne and the towns of Bruges and Ghent. Under the Habsburgs, the town flourished, eventually becoming capital of the Spanish Netherlands; later Brussels took turns with The Hague as capital of the new United Kingdom of the Netherlands. In the nineteenth century it became the capital of newly-independent Belgium, and was kitted out with all the attributes of a modern European capital. Since World War II, the city's appointment as headquarters of both NATO and the EU has instigated many major development projects, not least a rudimentary metro system.

It's true that the city has a reputation as a dull centre of commerce and bureaucracy, but this is thoroughly unfair. Brussels has architecture and museums to rank with the best of Europe, a well-preserved medieval centre, and an energetic street- and nightlife. It's also very much an international city with European civil servants and business people, together with immigrants from Africa, Turkey and the Mediterranean, constituting a quarter of the population.

Arrival and information

Brussels has three main **train stations** – Bruxelles-Nord, Bruxelles-Centrale and Bruxelles-Midi, each a few minutes apart; almost all **domestic** trains stop at all three. The majority of **international** services only stop at Bruxelles-Midi, including Eurostar trains from London via the Channel Tunnel and Thalys express trains from Amsterdam, Paris Cologne and Aachen.

Bruxelles-Centrale is, as its name suggests, the most central of the city's three main stations, a five-minute walk from the Grand-Place; **Bruxelles-Nord** lies amongst the bristling tower blocks of the business area just north of the main ring road; and **Bruxelles-Midi** is located in a depressed immigrant area to the south of the city centre. Note that on bus timetables and the city transit system, Bruxelles-Nord appears as *Gare du Nord*; Bruxelles-Centrale as *Gare Centrale*; and Bruxelles-Midi as *Gare du Midi*. The former is the name of the main-line train station, while the latter signifies the métro stop. You can travel between the three by both rail and métro. Eurolines **buses** drop off (and pick up) from the Gare du Nord complex. The **airport** is in Zaventem – 13km northeast of the city centre – and from here there are three trains an hour to the city's three main train stations (25min; F90). Trains run from 5.30am until around midnight; after that you'll need to take a **taxi**: reckon on paying around F1400 to the centre.

There's a **tourist information desk** at the airport: it has a reasonable range of information on Belgium as a whole, though it's much better equipped to deal with enquiries about

---

LANGUAGE

In Brussels, the **languages** of the French- and Flemish-speaking communities have parity. This means that every instance of the written word, from road signs to the yellow pages, has to appear in both languages. Visitors soon adjust, but on arrival this can be very confusing, especially in the names of the city's three main **train stations**: Bruxelles-Nord (in Flemish it's Brussel-Noord), Bruxelles-Centrale (Brussel-Centraal), and, most bewildering of the lot, Bruxelles-Midi (Brussel-Zuid). Note that for simplicity we've used the French version of street names, sights, etc.

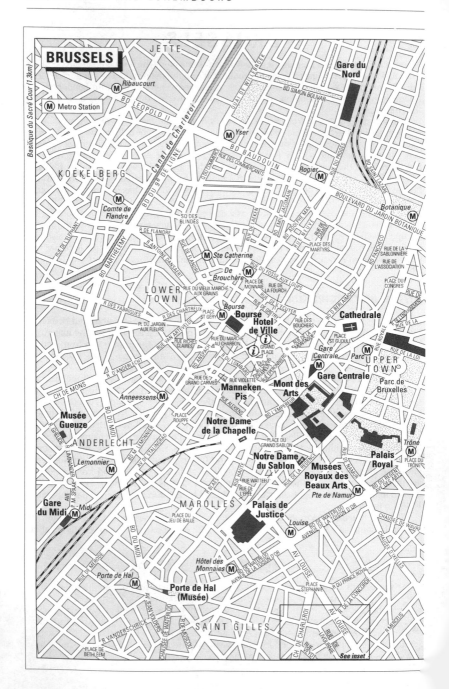

Basilique du Sacré Cœur (1.3km)

BRUSSELS

JETTE

Gare du Nord

Ⓜ Ribaucourt

BD LEOPOLD II

Ⓜ Metro Station

BD SIMON BOLIVAR

QUAI DE WILLEBROEK

Canal de Charleroi

Ⓜ Yser

BD BAUDOUIN

RUE DES COMMERCANTS

BD DU 9e DE LIGNE

Rogier Ⓜ

BOULEVARD DU JARDIN BOTANIQUE

Botanique Ⓜ

KOEKELBERG

Ⓜ Comte de Flandre

SQ DES BLINDES

PLACE DES MARTYRS

RUE DE LA SABLONNIERE

RUE DE L'ASSOCIATION

R DE FLANDRE

Ⓜ Ste Catherine

De Brouchère

PLACE DE LA MONNAIE

RUE DU FOSSE AUX LOUPS

RUE DE LA FOURCH

PLACE DU CONGRES

LOWER TOWN

RUE DU VIEUX MARCHE AUX GRAINS

RUE DE L'ECUYER

R DES FABRIQUES

Bourse

PLACE ST GERY

Bourse

Hotel de Ville

Cathedrale

PL DU JARDIN AUX FLEURS

RUE DES BOUCHERS

PLACE STE GUDULE

Gare Centrale

Ⓜ

UPPER TOWN

ⓘ GRAND PLACE

Parc

Anneessens Ⓜ

Manneken Pis

Gare Centrale

Parc de Bruxelles

Mont des Arts

Musée Gueuze

Ⓜ

Notre Dame de la Chapelle

PLACE DU GRAND SABLON

Trône Ⓜ

Lemonnier Ⓜ

Notre Dame du Sablon

Musées Royaux des Beaux Arts

Palais Royal

PLACE DU TRÔNE

ANDERLECHT

Pte de Namur

MAROLLES

Palais de Justice

Louise

Gare du Midi Ⓜ Midi

PLACE DU JEU DE BALLE

Hôtel des Monnaies Ⓜ

Porte de Hal Ⓜ

Porte de Hal (Musée)

PLACE STEPHANIE

AV LOUISE

SAINT GILLES

CH DE CHARLEROI

See inset

PLACE DE BETHLEEM

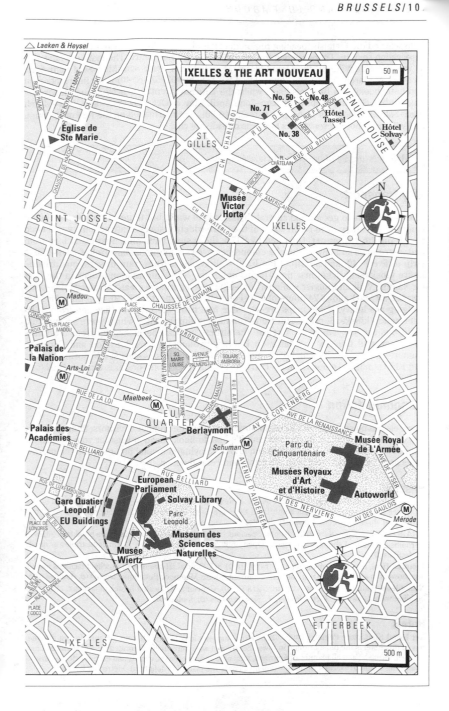

△ Laeken & Heysel

IXELLES & THE ART NOUVEAU

0   50 m

No. 50   No. 48
No. 71   Hôtel
ST   Tassel   Hôtel
GILLES   No. 38   Solvay

CH CHARLEROI
RUE DE FACQZ
RUE FAIDER
RUE P JANSON
RUE DU BAILLI

PL.
CHÂTELAIN
RUE AFRICAINE
RUE AMÉRICAINE

CH DE WATERLOO

Musée
Victor
Horta

IXELLES

N

Église de
Ste Marie

RUE ROYALE STE MARIE
CH DE HAECHT
RUE DE PALAIS
CHAUSSÉE DE HAECHT

SAINT JOSSE

Madou Ⓜ
PLACE
ST JOSSE   CHAUSSÉE DE LOUVAIN
CONGRES
CROIX DE FER   PLACE
MADOU   RUE DES EBURONS
BD BISCHOFFSHEIM

Palais de
la Nation
Arts-Loi Ⓜ   SQ
MARIE   AVENUE
LOUISE   PALMERSTON   SQUARE
AMBIORIX

AVE LIVINGSTONE

RUE DE LA LOI
Maelbeek Ⓜ
RUE DU TACITURNE
RUE ARCHIMÈDE
RUE DU CORTENBERG

Palais des
Académies   E U
QUARTER
Berlaymont   AVE DE LA RENAISSANCE

RUE BELLIARD

Schuman Ⓜ   Parc du   Musée Royal
Cinquantenaire   de L'Armée

European   Musées Royaux
Parliament   d'Art
Gare Quatier   Solvay Library   et d'Histoire   Autoworld
Leopold   AVENUE D'AUDERGEM
EU Buildings   Parc   AV DES NERVIENS
Leopold
PLACE DE
LONDRES   Museum des   AV DES GAULOIS
Musée   Sciences   Mérode Ⓜ
Wiertz   Naturelles

RUE DE LUXEMBOURG
RUE DU TRÔNE

PLACE
F COCO

IXELLES   N

ETTERBEEK

0   500 m

Brussels and the Flemish-speaking region than it is about Wallonia. It also offers a free hotel reservation service. There are two **tourist offices** in the city centre. The main one, the **TIB** in the Hôtel de Ville on the Grand-Place (Mon–Sat 9am–6pm; Sun: May–Sept 9am–6pm, Oct–Dec & March–April 10am–2pm, closed Jan & Feb; ☎02/513 89 40) is for information on and hotel booking in Brussels itself; whilst the **Tourism Centre**, nearby at rue du Marché aux Herbes 63 (June–Sept daily 9am–7pm; April, May & Oct daily 9am–6pm, Nov–March Mon–Sat 9am–6pm, Sun 1pm–5pm; ☎02/504 03 90), has information on the rest of Belgium, and will make hotel reservations for areas outside the city.

Brussels' tourist office Web site is *www.tib.be*

City transport

The easiest way to get around central Brussels is to **walk**, but to get from one side of the centre to the other, or to reach some of the more widely dispersed attractions, you'll need to use **public transport**. Operated by STIB, the system runs on a mixture of bus, tram and metro lines and covers the city comprehensively. A single flat-fare **ticket** costs F50, a strip of five F240, and a strip of ten F330 – all available from tram drivers, bus drivers, metro kiosks and ticket machines (coins only), the STIB information offices in the Port de Namur, Midi and Rogier stations, and some newsagents. A go-as-you-please **day-pass** (*carte d'un jour*) allows 24 hours of travel on public transport for F130. Spot fines for fare-dodging are heavy. Route maps are available free from the tourist office and from STIB information kiosks. Services run from 6am until midnight, after which there's a sporadic night bus service. **Taxis** don't cruise the streets but can be picked up from the ranks spread around the city – notably on Bourse, Brouckère, Grand Sablon and Porte de Namur – and outside leading hotels and at train stations. Prices start at F95 during the day and F170 at night. To book, phone Taxis Verts (☎02/349 49 49) or Taxis Orange (☎02/513 62 00).

Accommodation

Brussels has no shortage of **places to stay**, but given the number of visitors, finding a room can be hard, particularly in summer, and it's best to book ahead at least for your first night. Tourist offices can book hotel rooms on arrival. Staying in a hotel on or around the narrow lanes near the Grand-Place is an attractive and central option.

Hostels

Bruegel, rue du Saint Esprit 2 (☎02/511 04 36). Housed in a modern building, this official HI hostel is centrally located – a ten-minute walk south from the Gare Centrale. Some doubles, but mostly 4- to 12-bed dorms with shared showers. Dorms ②, doubles ③.

CHAB, rue Traversière 8 (☎02/217 01 58). Spacious independent hostel. Price includes breakfast. Sinks in all rooms, but shared showers and toilets. Open until 2am. Métro Botanique. Dorm beds, triples or quads ②, doubles ③.

Jacques Brel, rue de la Sablonnière 30 (☎02/218 01 87). Official HI hostel with excellent facilities including showers in every room. Own bar and restaurant. Métro Madou or Botanique. Dorms ②, doubles ③.

New Sleep Well, rue du Damier 23 (☎02/218 50 50). Conveniently located hostel, in a smart, clean new building with its own bar. Métro Rogier. Triples or quads ②; doubles ③.

Hotels

Art Hotel Siru, place Rogier 1 (☎02/203 35 80). It may not look like much from the outside, but the interior of this hotel is the most original in town. Each room was individually decorated by an art student in a modernistic style, and all manner of figurines, mini-polysterene effigies, murals and cartoon strips – everything from Tintin to Marilyn Monroe – pop up all over the place. It's delightful. Métro Rogier. ⑥.

Astrid, place du Samedi 11 (☎02/219 31 19). Crisp, modern hotel with smart, comfortable rooms in the fashionable Ste Catherine area. Substantial weekend discounts. Métro Ste Catherine ⑦.

Du Congrès, rue du Congrès 42 (☎02/217 18 90). Three-star hotel in a good-looking, turn-of-the-century mansion about five minutes' walk from the cathedral. A popular hotel with pleasant rooms, so advance booking is advised. F1000 discounts at the weekend. Métro Madou. ⑦.

Eperonniers, rue des Eperonniers 1 (☎02/513 53 66). No frills, but excellent position near Grand-Place. Métro Gare Centrale. ④.

Georges V, rue 't Kint 23 (☎02/513 50 93). Ramshackle period hotel in a quiet neighbourhood of big, old, balconied and grilled town houses. Breakfast included. Métro Bourse. ⑤.

La Légende, rue du Lombard 35 (☎02/512 82 90). Pleasant if frugal accommodation in an old building set around a courtyard in the heart of the city, just metres from the Grand-Place. Half the rooms have sinks but not showers – en-suite rooms cost about F1000 extra. Métro Bourse. ③.

Sabina, rue du Nord 78 (02/218 26 37). Spruce, pretty rooms in a turn-of-the-century house in a quiet residential area that was once a favourite haunt of the city's nineteenth-century bourgeoisie, with a beamed and panelled breakfast room. Good value. Métro Madou. ④.

Windsor, place Rouppe 13 (☎02/511 20 14). Clean, simple and cheerful rooms with breakfast included. Métro Anneessens. ⑤.

The City

The centre of Brussels is enclosed within a rough pentagon of boulevards following the former course of the medieval city walls. It is divided between the Upper and Lower Towns, the neighbourhoods generally becoming more bourgeois the higher you go. The greater part of the centre is occupied by the **Lower Town**, of which the Grand-Place – perhaps the best-preserved city square in Europe – is the unquestionable focus. South of here, the busy centre fades into the old working-class streets of the Marolles district and Gare du Midi, now a depressed, predominantly immigrant area; north, the shopping street of rue Neuve leads up to place Rogier and the office blocks which surround the Gare du Nord. The **Upper Town** is quite different in feel from the rest of the centre, with statuesque buildings lining wide, classical boulevards and squares. Appropriately, it's the home of the Belgian parliament and government departments, some of the major museums and the swishest shops.

The Lower Town

The obvious place to begin any tour of the **Lower Town** is the **Grand-Place**, the commercial hub of the city since the Middle Ages – though only the Hôtel de Ville and one guildhouse survived a 36-hour bombardment by the French in 1695. The **Hôtel de Ville** (tours in English April–Sept Tues 11.30am & 3.15pm, Wed 3.15pm, Sun 12.15pm; Oct–March Tues only; F75) still dominates, and inside you can view various official rooms; most dazzling is the sixteenth-century council chamber, decorated with gilt moulding, faded tapestries and an oak floor inlaid with ebony. But the real glory of the Grand-Place lies in the **guildhouses**, rebuilt in the early eighteenth century, their slender facades swirling with exuberant carving and sculpture. The western side of the square is perhaps the most impressive. At no. 1, the **Roi d'Espagne** was once the headquarters of the guild of bakers and is named after its bust of Charles II, the last of the Spanish Habsburgs, which is flanked by Moorish and Native American prisoners to symbolize his mastery of a vast empire. At no. 4 comes the **Maison de Sac**, the headquarters of the carpenters and coopers – the upper storeys were appropriately designed by a cabinet-maker, and feature pilasters and caryatids which resemble the ornate legs of Baroque furniture. Next door, the **Maison de la Louve**, at no. 5, is the only guildhouse to have survived the French bombardment intact, its elegant pilastered facade fronting the former home of the archers' guild, studded with pious representations of concepts like Peace and Discord, together with a pediment relief of Apollo firing at a python. Adjoining it, at no. 6, the **Maison du Cornet**, was the headquarters of the boatsmen's guild, a fanciful creation of 1697 whose top storey resembles the stern of a ship. The adjacent **Maison du Renard** was the house of the haberdashers' guild: on the ground floor animated cherubs in bas-relief play at haberdashery, while a scrawny, gilded fox – after which the house is named – squats above the door.

Most of the northern side of the square is taken up by the sturdy neo-Gothic **Maison du Roi**, a reconstruction of a sixteenth-century building that now houses the **Musée de la Ville de Bruxelles** (Mon–Fri 10am–12.30pm & 1.30–5pm, Sat & Sun 10am–1pm; F80), where you'll find an eclectic collection of locally manufactured tapestries, ceramics, pewterware and porcelain. To the south, rue de l'Etuve leads down to the **Manneken Pis**, a diminutive statue of a little boy pissing that's supposed to embody the "irreverent spirit" of the city and is today one of Brussels' biggest tourist draws. Jerome Duquesnoy cast the original statue in the 1600s, but it was stolen several times and the current one is a copy.

Northwest of the Grand-Place

To the northwest of the Grand-Place, at the end of rue au Beurre, the **Bourse** (or Stock Exchange), a Neoclassical structure of 1873, caked with fruit, fronds, languishing nudes and frolicking *putti*, hides the view of busy boulevard Anspach beyond. Right up the boulevard is **place de Brouckère**, Brussels' modern centre, a busy traffic-choked junction surrounded by advertising hoardings, and, close by, **place de la Monnaie** – an uninteresting modern square that's home to the **Théâtre de la Monnaie**, the city opera house. From here, **rue Neuve** forges north, a mundane pedestrianized shopping street meeting the inner ring at the junction of **place Rogier**, beyond which lies the Gare du Nord and ultimately the seedy red-light area. About a third of the way up rue Neuve, **place des Martyrs** is a cool, rational square imposed on the city by the Habsburgs that is nowadays one of its most haunting sights, a forlorn, abandoned open space, with many of the buildings around it being redeveloped into apartments. Beyond the square, at 20 rue des Sables, the **Grand Magasin Waucquez**, one-time department store designed at the turn of the century by Victor Horta, now houses the **Centre Belge de la Bande Dessinée** (Tues–Sun 10am–6pm; F200), whose various displays are devoted to the history of the Belgian comic strip, focusing on a wide range of cartoonists, with specific sections on animation and, of course, Hergé's Tintin.

The Quartier Marolles

In the opposite direction from the Grand-Place, **Notre Dame de la Chapelle**, a sprawling Gothic structure, is the city's oldest church, founded in 1134. Its main claim to fame is the memorial plaque over the tomb of Pieter Bruegel the Elder in the third chapel of the south aisle – Bruegel is supposed to have lived and died down the street at rue Haute 132. With parallel rue Blaes, rue Haute forms the spine of the **Quartier Marolles** – an earthy neighbourhood of cheap restaurants, shops and bars that grew up in the seventeenth century as a centre for artisans working on the nearby mansions of Sablon. Today, gentrification is creeping into the district, but it's got some way to go, and **place du Jeu de Balle**, the heart of Marolles, is still the scene of the city's best **flea market** (daily from 7am), which is at its busiest on Sundays. Beyond, the area around the **Gare du Midi** is home to the city's many North African immigrants, a depressed quarter with an uneasy undertow by day and sometimes overtly threatening at night. However, it's well worth venturing down here on a Sunday morning, when a vibrant souk-like **market** is held under the arches of the station.

The Upper Town

The steep slope that marks the start of the **Upper Town** rises just a couple of minutes' walk from the Grand-Place at the east end of rue d'Arenberg. Here you'll find the city's **Cathedral** (daily 8am–6pm; free), a Brabantine-Gothic building begun in 1220 and dedicated jointly to St Michael and Ste Gudule, the patrons of Brussels. The cathedral sports a striking twin-towered, whitestone facade, with the central doorway trimmed by fanciful tracery and statues of the Three Wise Men and the Apostles. However, the intensity of the decoration fades away inside, where the triple-aisled nave is an airy affair supported by plain, heavy-duty columns topped with capitals carved with curled leaves – or crockets. The interior is also short on furnishings and fittings, reflecting the combined efforts of the Protestants, who ransacked the church (and stole the shrine of Ste Gudule) in the seventeenth century, and the French Republican army, who wrecked the place one hundred or so years later. Two survivors are the massive oak pulpit, an extravagant chunk of frippery by the Antwerp sculptor Hendrik

Verbruggen, and the superb sixteenth-century **stained glass** windows in the transepts and above the main doors.

Five minutes' walk south of the cathedral, the so-called **Mont des Arts** also occupies the slopes of the Upper Town, its collection of severe geometric buildings given over to a variety of government- and arts-related activities. In the middle, a wide stairway climbs up towards **place Royale** and **rue Royale**, the grandiose backbone of the Upper Town. Around the corner, the **Palais du Roi** (July to mid-Sept Tues–Sun 10.30am-4.30pm; free) is something of an anticlimax, a sombre conversion of some eighteenth-century town houses that isn't actually lived in by the Belgian royals; sumptuous rooms, especially the Throne Room, and tapestries designed by Goya, are the highlights of a visit. Opposite is the **Parc de Bruxelles**, the most central of the city's parks.

Musées Royaux des Beaux Arts

Just off place Royale, the **Musées Royaux des Beaux Arts**, rue de la Régence 3, comprises Belgium's most satisfying collection of fine art, with the outstanding permanent collection featuring examples of the work of every major Belgian artist, supplemented by internationally acclaimed exhibitions. Though they share the same entrance, there are actually two museums here – the **Musée d'Art Ancien** (Tues–Sun 10am–noon & 1–5pm) and the adjacent **Musée d'Art Moderne** (Tues–Sun 10am–1pm & 2–5pm), the former displaying older works up to the late eighteenth century, the latter more modern works through to contemporary art. The admission fee of F150 covers both museums, but not necessarily the temporary exhibitions. The permanent collection is much too big to absorb in one go – and it's best to see the two museums on separate visits. The paintings are made readily comprehensible by a system of colour-coded areas.

In the **Musée d'Art Ancien**, the **blue area** takes in paintings of the fifteenth and sixteenth centuries, including the sharply observed nudes of *Adam and Eve* by Lucas Cranach; a marvellous *Triptych of the Holy Kindred* by Quentin Matsys; several delicately realistic paintings by Rogier van der Weyden, including an exquisite *Lamentation;* Jan Mostaert's wonderfully busy *Passion*; and Pieter Bruegel the Elder's most haunting work, *The Fall of Icarus*. The **brown area** concentrates on work of the seventeenth and eighteenth centuries, notably some glorious canvases by Rubens and his contemporaries Jacob Jordaen and Antony van Dyck. Moving on into the **Musée d'Art Moderne**, the **yellow area** begins with the Neoclassicism of Jacques Louis David, whose famous *Death of Marat* is here, and continues with the dramatic Romantic canvases of Géricault and Delacroix. Then comes the Realism of Courbet, Charles de Groux and Constantin Meunier, plus a sample of Symbolist paintings, including those of Fernand Khnopff. French painters are represented by the likes of Bonnard, Gauguin and Monet, though the highlight of the late nineteenth century works on display are the disconcerting canvases of the Belgian James Ensor. The **green area** boasts an extremely varied collection of modern art and sculpture, laid out on six subterranean levels. There are fine examples of Fauvism, Cubism, Futurism, Expressionism, and, above all, Surrealism, with the oddly erotic works of Paul Delvaux; a small show of paintings by Magritte; a fine Dali, *The Temptation of St Anthony;* and an eerie Francis Bacon, *The Pope with the Owls*.

The Sablon Neighbourhood

From the Beaux Arts it's a short walk south to the **place du Petit Sablon**, a small rectangular area off to the left of rue de la Régence that's decorated with 48 statues representing the medieval guilds, and a fountain surmounted by the Counts Egmont and Hoorn, beheaded on the Grand-Place for their opposition to Spanish tyranny in the 1500s. On the corner of rue de la Regence, the **Musée Instrumental** (Tues–Fri 9.30am–4.45pm, Sat 10am–4.45pm; F80) has a dusty collection of old musical instruments that's enlivened by a display devoted to Adolphe Sax, the Belgian-born inventor of the saxophone. On the other side of the street, the fifteenth-century church of **Notre Dame du Sablon** began life as a chapel for the medieval guild of archers; the present church was built after a statue of Mary with powers of healing was brought by boat from Antwerp, an event still celebrated each July by the

Ommegang procession. Behind the church, the sloping wedge of **place du Grand Sablon** is the centre of one of the city's wealthiest districts and scene of a lively weekend antiques market. At the southern end of rue de la Regence is the immense **Palais de Justice**. Built in 1883, it is actually larger than St Peter's in Rome.

Outside the petit ring: the parks and outer boroughs

Brussels by no means ends with the *petit ring*. East of this inner ring road, the **Quartier Leopold** takes its name from the late nineteenth-century king of Belgium, who laid out much of the area with wide boulevards, monuments and statues. More recently, the district has been colonized by the huge concrete and glass high-rises of the EU, notably the winged **Berlaymont** building (Métro Schuman), whose main claim to fame is the money and time it's taken to remove the asbestos put in during its construction in the 1960s. The latest addition to the sprawling EU complex is the lavish **Hémicycle européen**, an imposing series of structures culminating with the spectacular curved glass roof of the brand new EU Parliament building. If you want to take a look, the parliament building is a couple of minutes' walk from place du Luxembourg, behind the Gare Quartier Leopold train station.

Just south of the ring road is **St Gilles**, a gritty multiracial borough that stretches from the refinement of ave Louise in the east to the solidly immigrant quarters around the Gare du Midi. The main reason to trek out here is the **Musée Victor Horta**, the former home of the Belgian Art Nouveau architect at rue Américaine 25 (Tues–Sun 2–5.30pm; F150, F200 at weekends), accessible by tram #92 from place Louise. The exterior is modest, but inside are all the architect's trademarks: crisp, bright rooms spiralling around a superbly worked staircase, stained glass, sculpture, and ornate furniture and panelling.

West of the city centre, **Anderlecht** is a dull, grimy quarter most famous for its football team. That said, it's worth making the effort to see the mustily evocative **Musée Bruxellois de la Gueze**, in the Cantillon Brewery, at rue Gheude 56 (Mon–Fri 8.30am–5pm, Sat & Sun 10am–5pm; F100), ten minutes' walk from Midi station. This friendly, family-run brewery is the last in Brussels still brewing *gueuze* beer according to traditional methods. The self-guided tour (using an excellent English-language leaflet) shows how the beer is allowed to ferment naturally, reacting with yeasts peculiar to the Brussels air. The result is unique, as you can find out at the tasting at the end.

North of the ring road, **Laeken** is the royal suburb of Brussels. Its large public **park** is best known for the **Atomium** (daily: April–Aug 9am–8pm; Sept–March 10am–6pm; F200), a hugely magnified model of a molecule built for the 1958 World Fair (Métro Heysel). Something of a symbol of the city, it contains an unremarkable science museum, but the main sensation is the disorientating feeling of travelling from sphere to sphere by escalator.

Eating and drinking

Brussels has an international reputation for the quality of its cuisine, which is richly deserved. Even at the dowdiest snack bar, you'll almost always find that the food is well-prepared and generously seasoned – and then there are the city's **restaurants**, many of which equal anywhere in Paris. Traditional Bruxellois dishes feature on many restaurant menus, canny amalgamations of Walloon and Flemish ingredients and cooking styles – whether it be rabbit cooked in *gueuze* beer or steamed pigs' feet. The city is also among Europe's best for sampling a wide range of different cuisines – from the ubiquitous Italian places and the Turkish restaurants of St Josse through to Spanish, Vietnamese, Japanese, and even Buddhist vegetarian restaurants. You can also eat magnificent fish and seafood, especially in and around the fashionable district of Ste Catherine.

For the most part, eating out is rarely inexpensive, but the **prices** are almost universally justified by the quality. As a general rule the less formal the restaurant, the less expensive the meal – and indeed it's hard to distinguish between the less expensive restaurants and the city's **cafés**, some of which provide some of the tastiest food in town. In addition, many **bars** serve food, often just spaghetti, sandwiches and *croque monsieurs*, but many have wider ranging menus, taking in traditional Brussels cuisine.

For **fast food**, aside from the multinational burger and pizza chains, there are plenty of *frites* stands and kebab places around the Grand-Place, notably on rue du Marché aux Fromages and near the beginning of rue des Bouchers. Pitta is also popular, stuffed with a wide range of fillings – though vegetarian ones are rare – along with the more substantial thin Turkish pizzas, or *pide*, topped with combinations of cheese, ground meat or even a fried egg, sold at any number of cafés along the chausée de Haecht and rue du Méridien in St Josse.

For straight **drinking**, the enormous variety of bars and cafés is one of the city's real joys – sumptuous Art Nouveau cafés, traditional bars with ceilings stained brown by a century's smoke, speciality-beer bars with literally hundreds of different varieties of ale, and, of course, more modern hangouts. Many of the centrally located bars are much frequented by tourists and expats, but outside the centre, and even tucked away off the Grand-Place, there are places which remain refreshingly local. Bars also stay open late – most until 2 or 3am, some until dawn.

Restaurants

Bij den Boer, quai aux Briques 60. There's nothing pretentious here in this excellent neighbourhood café/bar with its tiled floor and bygones on the wall. A great place for a drink or a meal in the traditional Belgian manner.

Brasserie Horta, rue des Sables 20. The café of the Centre Belge de la Bande Dessinée, serving imaginative snacks and light meals in a delightful Horta-designed Art Nouveau setting. Popular drinking spot with a young crowd. Light meals from F300.

Chez Léon, rue des Bouchers 18. Touristy but good-value restaurant near the Grand-Place serving traditional Belgian fare. Most famous for its mussel dishes.

La Grande Porte, rue Notre–Seigneur 9. Cosy and crowded place serving good traditional food. Main meals cost around F525. Closed Sun.

't Kelderke, Grand-Place 15. Boisterous, excellent-value cellar restaurant on the Grand-Place. No reservations, so you might have to queue. The new *'t Kelderke estaminet* next door has regular live music.

Le Pré Salé, rue de Flandre 16. Friendly, old-fashioned neighbourhood restaurant just off place Ste-Catherine, and a nice alternative to the swankier eateries of the district. Great mussels and other Belgian specialities. Menu about F1000, main courses around F425. Closed Mon.

Sahbaz, chaussée de Haecht 102. Reckoned to be the city's best Turkish restaurant; friendly atmosphere and cheap too.

In't Spinnekopke, place du Jardin–aux-Fleurs 1. Ancient restaurant and bar near the Bourse that serves many traditional Bruxellois dishes cooked in beer as well as lots of fish and mussels. Not especially cheap – dish of the day from about F500. Closed Sun.

Au Stekerlapatte, rue des Prêtres 6. On the far side of the Palais de Justice, a wonderful old brasserie, usually packed with a youngish crowd, serving main meals for around F500.

Totem, rue des Grands Carmes 6. Though hidden away behind the Grand-Place, this small but fashionable ground floor restaurant is a hit with Brussels-based veggies, who come for the friendly atmosphere and wholesome food – organic soups, fresh salads, tofu, and a delicious selection of cakes and pastries. It's quite cheap too, a main course costing less than F350, and there's a good choice of organic wines. Open Wed–Sun 2–11pm. Métro Bourse.

Bars and cafés

À la Bécasse, rue Tabora 11. Spartan, old-fashioned bar right near the Bourse that is one of the few remaining venues for sampling *lambic* – which can be bought by the jug and shared – along with simple bar snacks.

Le Cirio, rue de la Bourse 18. One of Brussels' oldest café/bars, sumptuously decorated in *fin-de-siècle* style.

Le Falstaff, rue Henri Maus 17–23. Art Nouveau café/brasserie next to the Bourse. Full of atmosphere and usually packed, though fairly impersonal. Also serves snacks and full meals.

La Fleur en Papier Doré, rue des Alexiens 55. Cluttered, cosy locals' bar, with walls covered with doodles and poems and a couple of cats prowling around the place. Once a watering-hole of René Magritte.

Le Greenwich, rue des Chartreux 7. Brussels' traditional chess café with a lovely old wood-panelled and mirrored interior. Laid-back atmosphere. Close to place St Géry.

À l'Image de Notre-Dame, rue du Marché aux Herbes 6. A welcoming if extremely quiet bar at the end of a long alley, decorated like an old Dutch kitchen. Good range of speciality bers. Near the Grand-Place.

À la Mort Subite, rue Montagne-aux-Herbes-Potagères 7. Popular bar with a wonderful 1920s interior. Snacks served, or just order a plate of nibbles – cheese cubes, salami, chips – to accompany your Mort Subite beer.

Rick's, ave Louise 344. A gathering place of resident English-speakers for close on thirty years. Full menu available, though it's most famous for its ribs.

Au Soleil, rue Marché au Charbon 86. Popular bar with a wide choice of beer, crowded until late every night with a young and trendy crowd.

Toone, down an alley off petite rue des Bouchers 21. Cosy, largely undiscovered bar belonging to the Toone puppet theatre. One of the centre's most congenial watering-holes.

L'Ultime Atome, rue Saint Boniface 14, Ixelles. Affable café serving a range of 75 beers and an excellent and varied menu to a youngish clientele. Out in the suburb of Ixelles.

Wittamer, place du Grand Sablon 12–13. Brussels' most famous patisserie, established in 1910 and still run by the Wittamer family. Gorgeous, if pricey, pastries and cakes. Tables outside are for coffee and drinks only.

Nightlife

As far as **nightlife** goes, you may be perfectly happy to while away the evenings in one of the city's restaurants or bars, but Brussels is also a reasonably good place to catch **live bands** with nightspots scattered across the city centre and the suburbs. **Clubs** are less impressive, but entry **prices** are low: you rarely have to pay more than F400 and many of the smaller clubs have no cover at all, though you do have to tip the bouncer a nominal fee (F20) on the way in. As a general rule, clubs **open** Thursday to Saturday from 11pm to 5/6am. The best English-language source of **listings** is the weekly magazine *The Bulletin* (out on Wednesdays; F90); the Wednesday pull-out in the newspaper *Le Soir* is also useful. **Tickets** for most things are available from FNAC in City 2, a shopping centre on rue Neuve, or from the tourist office on the Grand-Place.

Concert halls

Forest National, ave du Globe 36 (☎02/340 22 11). Brussels' main venue for big-name international concerts, holding around 11,000 people.

Palais des Beaux Arts, rue Ravenstein 23 (☎02/507 82 00). With a concert hall holding around 2000, the Palais is used for anything from contemporary dance to Tom Jones, though the main slant is on classical music.

Live music bars

L'Archiduc, rue Antoine Dansaert 6. Small and tasteful bar with regular live jazz on the weekend. Near place St Géry.

Le Cercle, rue Sainte-Anne 20-22, just off place du Grand Sablon. Live music three or four times a week – everything from jazz and Latino through to *Chanson Française*. A relaxed and easy atmosphere and the bands are usually very good.

Magasin 4, rue du Magasin 4 (☎02/223 34 74). This small converted warehouse is a great place for catching up-and-coming rock and indie bands. Only open when there's a gig, so check listings – or phone – before you set out. Entrance around F300. Métro Yser.

Sounds, rue de la Tulipe 28. Earthy bar in the suburb of Ixelles serving up Latin jazz and R&B.

Travers, rue Traversière 11. Informal jazz club with a reputation for showcasing up-and-coming Belgian musicians.

Clubs

Le Bazaar, rue des Capucins 63. In the Marolles, off rue Haute. Split-level club with a dimly lit restaurant upstairs and a dance floor below playing funk, soul, rock and indie.

Cartagena, rue du Marché au Charbon 70. Enjoyable downtown club offering arguably the best and certainly the widest range of South American and Latin sounds in town. Attracts a late-twenties age group, and gets going around midnight. Open Friday and Saturday nights only.

The Fuse, rue Blaes 208. Large, young, and vibrant techno, jungle and house club in the Marolles district. Big-name, international DJs are a regular feature. Chill-out rooms and visuals. Saturday nights only.

Pitt's Bar, rue des Minimes 53. Near the Palais de Justice, the music here is techno, garage, bhangra and house. Popular with students. Open Tues to Sun.

Who's Who Land, rue du Poinçon 17. In the Marolles, this trendy house club (with occasional foam parties) often sees enormous teenage crowds, even from abroad. Open Thurs–Sat (Thurs is rap and ragga night).

Listings

Airlines Aer Lingus, rue du Trône 98 (☎02/548 9848); British Airways, rue du Trône 98 (☎02/725 6000); British Midland, avenue des Pléiades (☎02/772 9400); KLM, at the airport (☎02/507 7070); Sabena, at the airport (☎02/723 3111).

Airport information 24hr information line ☎02/723 23 45.

American Express place Louise 2 (Mon–Fri 9am–5.30pm; ☎02/676 27 27).

Books Waterstones, bd Adolphe Max 71–75, is the best central source of English-language books and magazines.

Car rental Avis, rue Américaine 145 (☎02/537 1280) and at the airport (☎02/720 0944); Budget, at the airport (☎02/753 2170); Europcar-Interrent, avenue Louise 235 (☎02/640 9400) and at the airport (☎02/721 0592); Hertz, at the airport (☎02/720 6044).

Embassies Australia, rue Guimard 6 (☎02/286 05 00); Canada, ave de Tervueren 2 (☎02/741 06 11); Ireland, rue Froissart 89 (☎02/230 53 37); New Zealand, bd de Régent 47 (☎02/512 10 40); UK, rue d'Arlon 85 (☎02/287 62 11); USA, bd de Régent 27 (☎02/508 21 11).

Exchange Outside bank hours you can change money and travellers' cheques at bureaux de change in the Gare du Nord (daily 7am–10pm), Gare du Midi (daily 7am–10pm), and the Gare Centrale (daily 7am–9pm), though none of these places give cash advances on credit cards. Otherwise there's GWK Change, rue du Marché aux Herbes 88 (daily 9am–6pm), and Best Change, rue de la Colline 2 (daily 9am–7pm). There are also bureaux de change at the airport. There are ATMs dotted right across the city centre – check with your home bank for accessibility and access codes in regard to your own bank cashcard.

Gay and lesbian scene For the most up-to-date information on the Brussels gay scene, contact Tels Quels, rue du Marché au Charbon 81 (daily 5pm–2am; ☎02/512 4587) – something of a city institution, a social centre with a political slant that welcomes both lesbians and gay men.

Hospital Medical emergencies and ambulances on ☎100.

Laundry Quick Wash, rue de Flandre 129.

Left luggage All the main train stations have left-luggage facilities, as well as coin-operated lockers.

Post office The main central post office is on the first floor of the Centre Monnaie, place de la Monnaie (Mon–Fri 8am–7pm, Sat 9.30am–3pm).

Train enquiries Belgian Rail ☎555 2525; British Rail International, rue de la Montagne 50 (☎02/548 0040); Le Shuttle, boulevard de L'Impératrice 56 (☎02/512 7999); Eurostar, Gare du Midi (☎02/224 8856).

Women's contacts Artemys, Galerie Bortier 8–10, off rue St Jean, is Brussels' largest feminist bookstore with English-speaking staff and a noticeboard upstairs. Amazone, rue du Méridien 10 (☎02/229 3800), brings together under one roof many different women's organizations, and has a café too.

NORTHERN BELGIUM

North of Brussels, Belgium is entirely Flemish-speaking. The provinces of East and West Flanders, Antwerp, Limburg and North Brabant represent one-third of the Belgian federation, and their people have maintained a distinctive cultural and linguistic identity. It's dull countryside on the whole, but a string of fine historic cities more than compensates. **Antwerp**, a large old port with many reminders of its sixteenth-century golden age, is due north of Brussels. Between the two is the ecclesiastical capital of the country, **Mechelen**, which merits a brief stop, while to the west is the heartland of Flemish-speaking Belgium, a stupendously prosperous region in the Middle Ages and home to much of the country's industrial base. There are many reminders of the area's medieval greatness, but the most vivid lie to the west in the ancient cloth cities of **Ghent** and **Bruges**, whose well-preserved old centres hold marvellous collections of early Flemish art.

Mechelen

Home of the Primate of Belgium, **MECHELEN** was one of the more powerful cities of medieval Flanders, even overshadowing Brussels when the Burgundian prince Charles the Bold decided to base his administration here in 1473. Nowadays, Mechelen has a surprisingly provincial atmosphere, a likeably low-key contrast to Antwerp and Brussels.

The centre of town, **Grote Markt**, is flanked on the eastern side by the **Stadhuis**, whose incoherent appearance is the result of a half-finished sixteenth-century rebuilding: the plan was to replace the dour medieval original with a delicately fluted Renaissance edifice, but the money ran out halfway through. In front of the Stadhuis, just outside the tourist office, is a modern sculpture showing the town's grotesque mascot, **Op Signoorke**, being tossed in a blanket. A little way west, the **Cathedral of St Rombout** (Mon–Sat 8.30am–5.30pm, Sun 2–5.30pm; free), a gigantic church completed in 1546, dominates the centre of town. The thirteenth-century nave has all the cloistered elegance of the Brabantine Gothic style, and in the south transept hangs Van Dyck's muscular *Crucifixion*, while the elaborate doors at the rear of the high altar hide the remains of St Rombout himself. The tower contains Belgium's finest carillon, a fifteenth-century affair of 49 bells, which resounds over the town on high days and holidays. There are also regular, hour-long performances on Saturdays (11.30am), Sundays (3pm), and from June through to mid-September on Monday evenings (8.30pm).

A short walk north at the end of St Jansstraat, the **Museum Hof van Busleyden** (Tues–Fri 10am–noon & 2–5pm, Sat & Sun 2–6pm; F75) is housed in a splendid sixteenth-century mansion and includes a display of miscellaneous bells, a room devoted to Mechelen's guilds, a range of Gallo-Roman artefacts, and an unusual assortment of unattributed paintings. Biest leads southeast from here to Veemarkt where the church of **St Pieter en St Paulus** (May–Sept Mon–Fri 9am–noon & 2.30–7pm, Sat & Sun 9am–noon & 2.30–5pm; Oct–April daily 9am–noon) was built for the Jesuits in the seventeenth century. The interior has an oak pulpit that pays tribute to the order's missionary work, carved in 1701 by Hendrik Verbruggen, with a globe near its base attached to representations of the four continents known at the time.

Practicalities

From Mechelen's **train station** it's about fifteen minutes' walk north to the centre, straight down Hendrik Consciencestraat. The **tourist office**, in the Stadhuis on the east side of the Grote Markt (March–Oct Mon–Fri 8am–6pm, Nov–Feb Mon–Fri 8am–5pm; March–Sept also Sat & Sun 8.30am–12.30pm & 1.30–5pm, Oct–Feb Sat & Sun 10am–noon & 2–4.30pm; ☎015/29 76 55), can arrange **accommodation** in one of the few private rooms (F1500–F2000 per double). The town has just one recommendable, central hotel, the four-star *Alfa Alba*, Korenmarkt 22 (☎015/42 03 03; ⑥). There are plenty of places to **eat** on and around Grote Markt, but the best places are down by the river Dijle – try the seafood delicacies of *De Gulden Rabat* at Vismarkt 18 or the good-value Spanish food at *Madrid*, off Ijzerenleen at Lange Schipstraat 4 (closed Tues). **Bars** worth trying include the lively *Lord Nelson* and the *Arms of York*, on Wollemarkt, or the fashionable *De Cirque* on Nauwstraat, a narrow side-street off Ijzerenleen.

Antwerp

Belgium's second city, **ANTWERP**, fans out from the east bank of the Scheldt about 50km north of Brussels. Many people prefer it to the capital: though not an immediately likeable place, it has a denser concentration of things to see, not least some fine churches and distinguished museums – reminders of its auspicious past as centre of a wide trading empire. It also has a more focused character: in recent years, the city has become the effective capital of Flemish Belgium, a lively cultural centre with a spirited nightlife. On the surface it's not a wealthy city – the area around the docks especially is run-down and seedy – but its diamond industry (centred behind the dusty facades around Centraal Station) is the world's largest. On a less contemporary note, there is also the enormous legacy of Rubens, some of whose finest works adorn Antwerp's galleries and churches.

Arrival and accommodation

Most trains stop at Centraal Station, about 2km east of Grote Markt and connected with the centre by tram #2 or #15 to Groenplaats (direction Linkeroever) from the Diamant underground station. A useful tram and bus system serves the city and its suburbs from a number of points around Centraal Station, principally Pelikaanstraat and Koningin Astridplein. The city transport information office in Diamant underground station (Mon–Fri 8am–12.30pm & 1.30–4pm) sells tickets and has free maps of the transport system. A standard single fare costs F40, a ten-strip *Rittenkaart* F290, a 24-hour unlimited travel tourist card F110. Tickets (but not the 24-hour pass) are also available from bus and tram drivers.

Antwerp's tourist office is at Grote Markt 15 (Mon–Sat 9am–6pm, Sun 9am–5pm); it has detailed city maps, and can make accommodation reservations. Two of the cheapest hostels are the *New International Youth Hotel*, Provinciestraat 256 (☎03/230 05 22; ①), just a ten-minute walk south from Centraal Station; and the nearby *Scoutel Jeugdverblifcentrum*, Stoomstraat 3–7 (☎03/226 46 06; ③). Another possibility is the *International Zeemanshuis* (Seamen's House), a ten-minute walk north of the Grote Markt at Falconrui 21 (☎03/227 54 33; ③). The HI youth hostel (closed 10am–4pm) is 5km south of the centre at Eric Sasselaan 2 (☎03/238 02 73; ①) – take tram #2 from Centraal Station (direction Hoboken). Among moderately priced and reasonably central hotels, the options include: *Eden*, Lange Herentalsestraat 25 (☎03/233 06 08; ⑥), a modern, medium-sized hotel in the diamond district near the station; *Ibis Antwerpen Centrum*, Meistraat 39 (☎03/231 88 30; ⑤), a standard chain-hotel in a decent location close to the Rubenshuis; *Prinse*, Keizerstraat 63 (☎03/226 40 50; ⑦), a smart if slightly characterless hotel whose modern furnishings and fittings occupy a big old house in a good, quiet location just five minutes' walk north of the Rubenshuis; and *Cammerpoorte* Nationalestraat 38 (☎231 97 36; ⑤), a frugal one-star hotel with reasonable prices and a handy location, just five minutes' walk south of Groenplaaats.

The City

The centre of Antwerp is Grote Markt, at the heart of which stands the Brabo Fountain, a haphazard pile of rocks surmounted by a bronze of Silvius Brabo, depicted flinging the hand of the giant Antigonus – who terrorized passing ships – into the Scheldt. The north side of Grote Markt is lined with daintily restored sixteenth-century guildhouses, though they are overshadowed by the Stadhuis, completed in 1566 to a design by Cornelis Floris (tours Mon, Tues, Wed & Fri 11am, 2pm, 3pm, Sat 2pm, 3pm; F30) and one of the most important buildings of the Northern Renaissance. Among rooms you can visit are the Leys Room, named after Baron Hendrik Leys, who painted the frescoes in the 1860s, and the Wedding Room, which has a chimneypiece decorated with two caryatids by Floris.

Southeast of Grote Markt, the Onze Lieve Vrouwe Cathedral (Mon–Fri 10am–5pm, Sat 10am–3pm, Sun 1–4pm; F70) is one of the finest Gothic churches in Belgium, mostly the work of Jan and Pieter Appelmans in the middle of the fifteenth century. The broad nave is notable primarily for its paintings by Rubens, of which the *Descent from the Cross*, to the right of the central crossing, is the most beautiful. In the ambulatory – the second chapel down the right hand side – is a *Resurrection* triptych by Rubens, painted for the tomb of his friend Jan Moretus in 1612. Moretus is also remembered by the Plantin-Moretus Museum on Vrijdagmarkt, south of Grote Markt (Tues–Sun 10am–4.45pm; F100), housed in the mansion of his father-in-law, the printer Christopher Plantin. One of Antwerp's most interesting museums, it provides a marvellous insight into how Plantin and his family conducted their business. Highlights include a delightful seventeenth-century bookshop, the old print room, and examples of Plantin's work. There are also sketches by Rubens, who occasionally worked for the family as an illustrator.

Fifteen minutes' walk south (or tram #8 from Groenplaats), the Museum voor Schone Kunsten (Tues–Sun 10am–5pm; F150) has one of the country's finest art collections. Its early Flemish section includes two charming works by Jan van Eyck – a tiny *Madonna at the Fountain* and a *St Barbara* – along with works by Memling, Rogier van der Weyden and Quentin Matsys, whose triptych of the *Lamentation* was commissioned for Antwerp Cathedral in 1511. Rubens has two large rooms to himself, in which one very large canvas

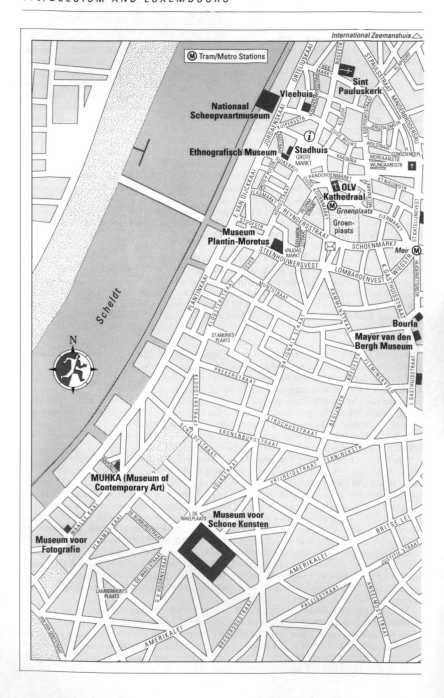

International Zeemanshuis

Tram/Metro Stations

Sint
Pauluskerk

Vleehuis

Nationaal
Scheepvaartmuseum

Ethnografisch Museum

Stadhuis
GROTE
MARKT

OLV
Kathedraal

Groenplaats

Groen-
plaats

Meir

Museum
Plantin-Moretus

Bourla

Mayer van den
Bergh Museum

MUHKA (Museum of
Contemporary Art)

Museum voor
Schone Kunsten

Museum voor
Fotografie

Scheldt

N

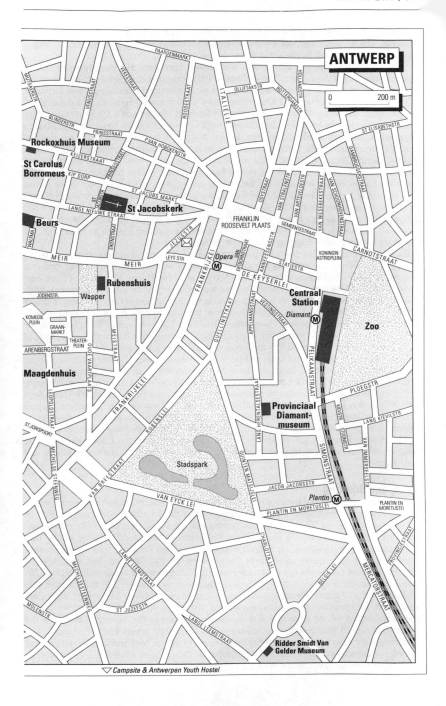

ANTWERP

0   200 m

Rockoxhuis Museum

St Carolus
Borromeus

St Jacobskerk

Beurs

FRANKLIN
ROOSEVELT PLAATS

Opera

MEIR

Rubenshuis

Wapper

Centraal
Station

Diamant

Zoo

KONINGIN
ASTRIDPLEIN

Komedie
Plein

Graan-
markt

Theater-
plein

Arenbergstraat

Maagdenhuis

Provinciaal
Diamant-
museum

Stadspark

Plantin

PLANTIN EN
MORETUSEI

Ridder Smidt Van
Gelder Museum

▽ *Campsite & Antwerpen Youth Hostel*

stands out: the *Adoration of the Magi*, a beautifully human work apparently completed in a fortnight. The museum also has a comprehensive collection of modern Belgian art, including the paintings of Paul Delvaux and James Ensor.

North, back towards the city centre, the **Mayer van den Bergh Museum**, Lange Gasthuisstraat 19 (Tues–Sun 10am–4.45pm; F100), contains delightful examples of the applied arts, from tapestries to ceramics, silverware, illuminated manuscripts and furniture, in a crowded reconstruction of a sixteenth-century town house. There are also some excellent paintings, including a *Crucifixion* triptych by Quentin Matsys and a *St Christopher* by Jan Mostaert – though the museum's best-known work is Bruegel's *Dulle Griet* or "Mad Meg", a misogynistic allegory in which a woman, loaded down with possessions, stalks the gates of Hell. It's a ten-minute walk northeast from here to the **Rubenshuis** at Wapper 9 (Tues–Sun 10am–4.45pm; F100), the former home and studio of the artist, now restored as a museum. Unfortunately, there are only one or two of his less distinguished paintings here, but the restoration of the rooms is convincing; behind the house, the garden is laid out in the formal style of his day. Rubens died in 1640 and was buried in the **St Jacobskerk**, just north of here on Lange Nieuwstraat (April–Oct Mon–Sat 2–5pm; Nov–March Mon–Sat 9am–noon; F50). Rubens and his immediate family are buried in the chapel behind the high altar, where, in one of his last works, *Our Lady Surrounded by Saints*, he painted himself as St George, his two wives as Martha and Mary, and his father as St Jerome.

Back in the centre of the town, on the waterfront at the far end of Suikerrui from Grote Markt, is the **Steen**, the remaining gatehouse of what was once an impressive medieval fortress. Today the Steen houses the **National Maritime Museum** (Tues–Sun 10am–4.45pm; F100), whose cramped rooms feature exhibits on inland navigation, shipbuilding and waterfront life. The open-air section has a long line of tugs and barges under a rickety corrugated roof. Crossing Jordaenskaai from here, it's a couple of minutes' walk east to the impressively gabled **Vleeshuis** (Tues–Sun 10am–4.45pm; F100), built for the guild of butchers in 1503 and today used to display a large but incoherent collection of applied arts – there are several fine medieval woodcarvings and a good set of antique musical instruments on the ground floor and period rooms up above. The streets around here, badly damaged by wartime bombing, have been redeveloped in a cosy pastiche of what went before, forming a stark contrast to the dilapidated **red-light area** beyond. A couple of minutes' walk along Vleeshouwersstraat on Veemarkt, the **St Pauluskerk** (May–Sept daily 2–5pm; free) is a dignified late-Gothic church of 1517 whose most prominent feature is the extraordinary mid-seventeenth-century carving of the confessionals and choir stalls. Rubens' *Scourging at the Pillar* is among a set of fifteen canvases hung on the north aisle wall in 1617 to illustrate the Mysteries of the Rosary. Outside, the **Calvaryberg** grotto clings to the buttresses of the south transept, eerily adorned with statues of Christ and other figures.

Eating and drinking

Antwerp is an enjoyable and inexpensive place to **eat**, full of informal café/restaurants, which excel at combining traditional Flemish techniques and dishes with Mediterranean, French and vegetarian cuisines. There are places serving delicious food all over the city centre, and you don't even pay much of a premium on or around Grote Markt. Several of the best café/restaurants are clustered on Suikerrui and Grote Pieter Potstraat, and there's another concentration in the vicinity of Hendrik Conscienceplein. For **food on the run**, try the kebab and falafel takeaways on Oude Koornmark. Recommended restaurants include *Het Elfde Gebod*, on the north side of the cathedral, which serves light meals in an eccentric, statue-filled interior; *Facade*, Hendrik Conscienceplein 18, a laid-back, funky café with good music and inexpensive vegetarian, meat and fish dishes; and *Het Dagelijks Brood*, Steenhouwersvest 48, an enjoyable and distinctive café where the variety of breads is the main event, served with delicious, wholesome soups and light meals (daily 7am–7pm). For something a tad more expensive, try either *Hoorn des Overloed*, Melkmarkt 1, an outstanding seafood restaurant near the cathedral, or *Metalurgie*, Grote Pieter Potstraat 1, off Suikerrui, a popular, groovy café/restaurant with a good line in traditional Flemish food.

Antwerp is also a fine place to **drink**. There are loads of bars in the city centre, notably those on Groenplaats, whose terraces make a nice place to watch the world go by. More specifically, *Den Engel*, on the northwest corner of the Grote Markt, is an agreeable place, as is *Den Billekletser*, across Grote Markt at Hoogstraat 22. Just south, you could try *De Volle Maan*, Oude Koornmarkt 7, or the more staid *De Cluyse*, across the street at Oude Koornmarkt 26, in an atmospheric thirteenth-century cellar. Failing that, there's the wild and wonderful *Café Pelikaan*, on the north side of the cathedral. One of the hippest bars in Antwerp is *De Muze* at Melkmarkt 15, with a young and trendy crowd and frequent live jazz. The long-established *Kulminator*, five minutes' walk south of the centre at Vleminckveld 32–34, claims to stock 500 speciality beers; alternatively head for the *jenever* (gin) specialists, *De Vagrant*, Reyndersstraat 21.The favourite local tipple, incidentally, is *De Koninck*, drunk by the *bolleke*, or small, stemmed glass.

Ghent

The seat of the Counts of Flanders and the largest town in western Europe during the thirteenth and fourteenth centuries, **GHENT** was at the heart of the Flemish cloth trade. By 1350, the city boasted a population of 50,000, of whom no less than 5000 were directly involved in the industry. However, the cloth trade began to decline in the early sixteenth century and although many of the city's merchants switched to exporting surplus grain from France, Ghent slowly declined. Better times returned in the nineteenth century when Ghent industrialized and it's now the third largest city in Belgium. Ghent is a less immediately picturesque place than Bruges, but this is much to its advantage in so far as it's never overrun by tourists.

Arrival and accommodation

Of Ghent's three **train stations**, the most useful is **St Pieters**, 2km south of the centre and connected by **trams** #1, #10, #11, #12 and #13. The **tourist office** is in the crypt of the old belfry, the Belfort, right in the centre on the Botermarkt (daily: April–Oct 9.30am–6.30pm; Nov–March 9.30am–12.30pm & 1.15–4.30pm). The plush, modern *De Draecke* **youth hostel** is a few minutes' walk from the castle at Sint-Widostraat 11, just off Braderijstraat (☎09/233 70 50; ②). Between mid-July and the end of September, **student rooms** are let for F500 per person including breakfast; ask at the tourist office for further details. Among several reasonably priced, central **hotels** there's *Ibis Gent Centrum Kathedraal*, Limburgstraat 2 (☎09/233 00 00; ⑤), a handily situated hotel with comfortable modern rooms opposite the cathedral; *Ibis Gent Centrum Opera*, Nederkouter 24–26 (☎09/225 07 07; ⑤), a spick-and-span, five-storey block five-minutes' walk south of the Korenmarkt; and *Erasmus*, Poel 25 (☎09/224 21 95; ⑤), a charming, family-run hotel located in an old and commodious town house just off the Korenlei. The best **campsite** is *Camping Blaarmeersen* at Zuiderlaan 12, west of the centre (March to mid-Oct) – take bus #38 from Korenmarkt.

The best way of seeing the sights is on foot, but Ghent is a large city and you may find you have to use a **tram** or **bus** at some point. Standard single fares cost F40, and a ten-journey *Rittenkaart* F290. Single tickets can be bought direct from the driver; *Rittenkaarts* are sold at shops and kiosks all over town.

The City

The best place to start exploring is at the mainly Gothic **St Baaf's Cathedral**, squeezed into the corner of St Baafsplein (daily 8.30–6pm; free). Inside, a small chapel (April–Oct Mon–Sat 9.30am–noon & 2–6pm, Sun 1–6pm; Nov–March Mon–Sat 10.30am–noon & 2.30–4pm, Sun 2–5pm; F60 includes crypt) holds Ghent's greatest treasure, the altarpiece of the *Adoration of the Mystic Lamb*, an early fifteenth-century work believed to be by Jan van Eyck. The cover screens display an Annunciation scene with the archangel Gabriel's wings reaching up to the timbered ceiling of a Flemish house; on the inside – only revealed when the shutters were opened on Sundays and feast days – the upper level shows God the Father, the Virgin and John the Baptist, while in the lower panel is the Lamb, approached by various figures in par-

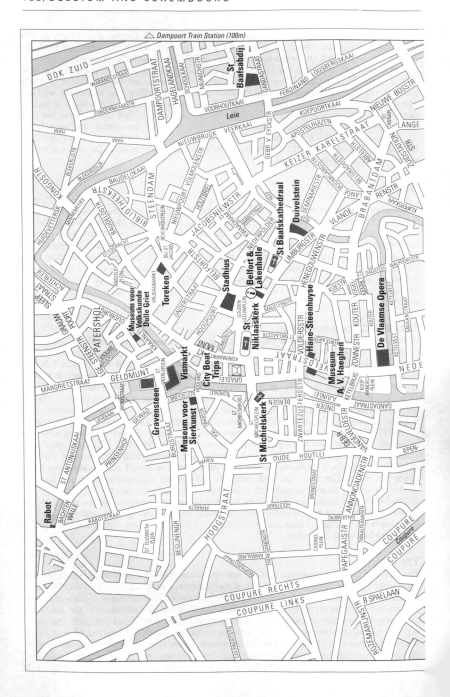

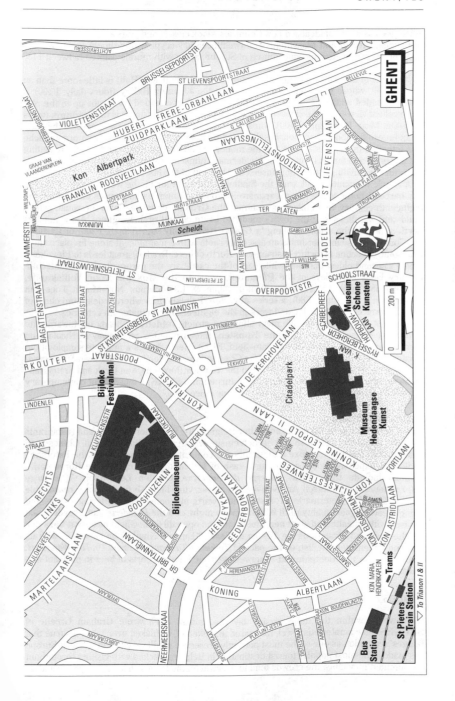

adise, seen as a sort of idealized Low Countries – look closely and you can see the cathedrals of Bruges, Utrecht and Maastricht. The twelfth-century crypt (same times) preserves features of the earlier Romanesque church of St John, along with murals painted between 1480 and 1540.

Just west of St Baaf's, the fifteenth-century **Lakenhalle** (Cloth Hall) is little more than an empty shell, whose first-floor entrance leads to the adjoining **Belfry** (tours daily; F100), a much-amended edifice from the fourteenth century. A glass-sided lift climbs up to the roof for excellent views over the city centre. A few strides away to the north is the **Stadhuis** (tours May–Oct Mon–Thurs 2pm; F100), whose long facade was erected in two phases – the earlier and more flamboyant section was designed by Rombout Keldermans. Each ornate niche was intended to hold a statuette, but the money ran out; the present carvings, representing the powerful and famous – including Keldermans himself rubbing his chin and studying his plans for the building – were only inserted at the end of the last century.

A couple of minutes' walk from the Stadhuis, **Korenlei** forms the western side of the old city harbour, home to a series of expansive, high-gabled merchants' houses dating from the eighteenth century. In architectural contrast, the **Graslei**, opposite, holds the squat, gabled guild- and warehouses of the town's medieval boatmen and grain-weighers. A few minutes north of here is the sinister-looking **'s Gravensteen** (daily 9am–5/6pm; F200) or Castle of the Counts, whose interior holds an assembly room with a magnificent stone fireplace and a gruesome collection of torture instruments. North of here, Braderijstraat leads to **Lievekaai**, Ghent's second oldest harbour, while east of the castle are the part-gentrified, seventeenth-century lanes and alleys of the **Patershol**, home to the **Museum voor Volkskunde**, Kraanlei 65 (April–Oct Tues–Sun 9am–12.30pm & 1.30–5.30pm; Nov–March Tues–Sun 10am–noon & 1.30–5pm; F80), a series of restored almshouses where a delightful chain of period rooms depicts local life and work in the eighteenth and nineteenth centuries.

South of the centre, Ghent's main shopping street, **Veldstraat**, heads off towards the impressive **Museum voor Schone Kunsten**, fifteen minutes' walk away at Nicolaas de Liemaeckereplein 3 (Tues–Sun 9.30am–5pm; F100). Here, there's a first-rate sample of old masters including Bosch's *Carrying of the Cross* and the smaller, less well-known *St Jerome at Prayer*, along with work by Pieter Bruegel the Younger, Jordaens, Van Dyck and Frans Hals. Opposite, the old casino has recently been turned into **SMAK**, a museum of contemporary art, which illustrates every major artistic theme since 1945.

Eating and drinking

Ghent is as fine a place to **eat** as any other Belgian city: its numerous cafés and restaurants offer the very best of Flemish and French cuisines, with a sprinkling of Italian, Chinese and Arab places. The more deluxe restaurants are concentrated in and around the Patershol, while less expensive spots, including a rash of fast food joints, cluster the Korenmarkt. Options include the central *Auberge de Fonteyne*, Gouden Leeuwplein 7, a large café/restaurant with kitsch Art Nouveau decor serving Flemish food at very reasonable prices; *Pascalino*, Botermarkt 11, a straightforward, inexpensive café offering snacks and filling meals of good quality until 9.30pm every night; and the *Brooderie*, Jan Breydelstraat 8, a café with a healthfood slant near the castle and open till 6pm. Ghent has great **bars** too: try the dark and mysterious *De Tap en de Tepel* ("Tap and Nipple") on Gewad 7, with its vast and expensive wine list; or the packed *Tolhuisje Tavern* on Graslei 10. *Het Waterhuis*, near the castle at Groentenmarkt 9, serves over one hundred sorts of beer in pleasant surroundings.

Bruges

"Somewhere within the dingy casing lay the ancient city", wrote Graham Greene of **BRUGES**, "like a notorious jewel, too stared at, talked of, trafficked over." And it's true that Bruges' reputation as one of the most perfectly preserved medieval cities in western Europe has made it the most popular tourist destination in Belgium, packed with visitors throughout the summer. Inevitably, the crowds tend to overwhelm the town's charms, but you would be mad to come to Flanders and miss the place: its museums, to name just one attraction, hold some of the country's finest collections of Flemish art; and its intimate, winding streets, woven around a pattern of narrow canals and lined with gorgeous ancient buildings, live up to even the most inflated hype.

By the fourteenth century Bruges shared effective control of the cloth trade with its two great rivals, Ghent and Ypres, turning high-quality English wool into thousands of items of clothing that were exported all over the known world. It was an immensely profitable business, and made the city a centre of international trade: at its height, the town was a key member of the Hanseatic League, the most powerful economic alliance in medieval Europe. By the end of the fifteenth century, though, Bruges was in decline, partly because of a recession in the cloth trade, but principally because the Zwin river – the city's vital link to the North Sea – was silting up. By the 1530s the town's sea trade had collapsed completely, and Bruges simply withered away. Frozen in time, Bruges escaped damage in both world wars to emerge the perfect tourist attraction.

Arrival and accommodation

Bruges' **train station** is twenty minutes' walk or a short bus ride southwest of the town centre. The station has a **hotel booking** service (April–Sept Mon–Sat 9.30am–6pm; Oct–March Mon–Sat 9am–1.15pm & 1.45–5.30pm), as has the **tourist office** in the city centre at Burg 11 (April–Sept Mon–Fri 9.30am–6.30pm, Sat & Sun 10am–noon & 2–6.30pm; Oct–March Mon–Fri 9.30am–5pm, Sat & Sun 9.30am–1pm & 2–5.30pm), where there's also a bureau de change, useful free maps and bus timetables. There are several **unofficial youth hostels** with dormitory beds and limited supplies of smaller rooms, including the *Bauhaus International Youth Hotel*, fifteen minutes' walk east of Burg at Langestraat 135–137 (☎050/34 10 93; ②), and the first-rate *Passage*, Dweersstraat 24 (☎050/34 02 32; b). There's an official **youth hostel**, *Europa*, 2km south of the centre at Baron Ruzettelaan 143 (☎050/35 26 79; ②; take bus #2 from the train station) and a cluster of routine but reasonably priced **hotels** west of Markt around 't Zand: try the *Speelmanshuys*, 't Zand 3 (☎050/33 95 52; ③). Alternatively, try the cosy *Cordoeanier*, Cordoeaniersstraat 18 (☎050/33 90 51; ④), or the tiny *Pension Geestelijk Hof*, just west of the Burg at Heilige Geeststraat 2 (☎050/34 25 94; ③). There's an all-year **campsite**, *St Michiel*, 3km southwest of the train station at Tillegemstraat 55; take bus #7 from the train station and get off at the junction of St Michielslaan and Rijselstraat.

The City

The older sections of Bruges fan out from two central squares, Markt and Burg. **Markt**, edged on three sides by nineteenth-century gabled buildings, is the larger of the two, an impressive open space, on the south side of which the octagonal **Belfry** (daily April–Sept 9.30am–5pm; Oct–March 9.30am–12.30pm & 1.30–5pm; F100) was built in the thirteenth century when the town was at its richest and most extravagant. Inside, the staircase passes the room where the town charters were locked for safekeeping, and an eighteenth-century carillon, before emerging onto the roof. At the foot of the belfry, the rectangular **Hallen** is a much-restored edifice dating from the thirteenth century, its style and structure modelled on the cloth hall at Ieper (Ypres). From the Markt, Breidelstraat leads through to **Burg**, whose southern half is fringed by the city's finest group of buildings. One of the best is the **Heilig Bloed Basiliek** (Basilica of the Holy Blood; April–Sept daily 9.30am–noon & 2–6pm; Oct–March 10am–noon & 2–4pm, closed Wed pm; free), named after a phial of the blood of Christ that dried out soon after it was brought here in 1150 and then miraculously liquefied every Friday at 6pm until 1325. The twelfth-century basilica divides into a shadowy Lower Chapel, built to house a relic of St Basil, and an Upper Chapel where the rock-crystal phial is stored in a grandiose silver tabernacle given by Albert and Isabella of Spain in 1611. The Holy Blood is still venerated here on Fridays at 6pm, and on Ascension Day (mid-May) it is carried through the town in a colourful but solemn procession, the *Helig-Bloedprocessie*. In the tiny **Treasury** (F40) you'll find the jewel-encrusted reliquary that holds the Holy Blood during the procession.

To the left of the basilica, the **Stadhuis** has a beautiful, turreted sandstone facade, a much-copied exterior that dates from 1376, though its statues of the counts and countesses of

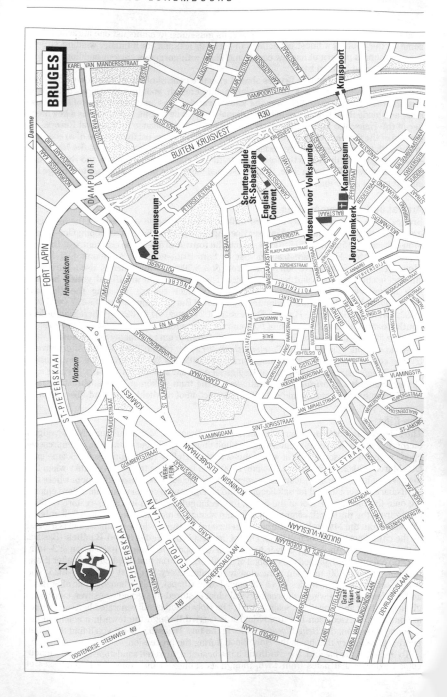

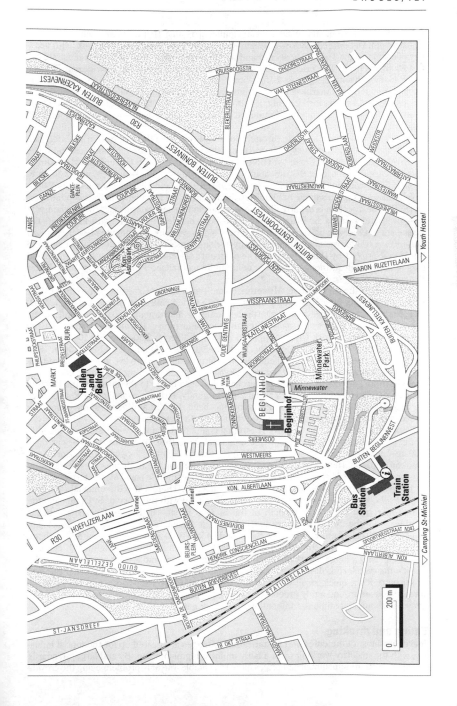

Flanders are replacements. Inside, the magnificent Gothic Hall of 1400 (daily: April–Sept 9.30am–5pm; Oct–March 9.30am–12.30pm & 2–5pm; F100) is well worth a look, with vault-keys depicting New Testament scenes and paintings commissioned in 1895 to illustrate the history of the town. The price of admission covers entry to the **Renaissancezaal Brugse Vrije** (daily 9.30am–12.30pm & 1.15/2–5pm), also on the square, where there's just one exhibit, an enormous marble-and-oak chimneypiece located in the old Magistrates' Hall. A fine example of Renaissance carving, it was completed in 1531 to celebrate the defeat of the French at Pavia in 1525, and is dominated by figures of the Emperor Charles V and his Austrian and Spanish relatives.

Heading south from the Burg, through the archway next to the Stadhuis, it's a brief walk to both the eighteenth-century **Vismarkt**, and the huddle of picturesque houses that make up **Huidenvettersplein**. Close by, **Dijver** follows the canal to the **Groeninge Museum** at Dijver 12 (April–Sept daily 9.30am–5pm; Oct–March Mon & Wed–Sun 9.30am–12.30pm & 2–5pm; F200, combined ticket with Memling, Arentshuis and Gruuthuse museums F400), which houses a superb sample of Flemish paintings from the fourteenth to the twentieth centuries. The best section is of early Flemish work, including several canvases by Jan van Eyck, who lived and worked in Bruges from 1430 until his death eleven years later, and the *Judgement of Cambyses* by Gerard David. There's also work by Hieronymus Bosch, his *Last Judgement* a trio of panels crammed with mysterious beasts and scenes of awful cruelty, and the *Moreel Triptych* by Hans Memling. The museum's selection of seventeenth-century paintings is more modest, though there's a delightfully naturalistic *Peasant Lawyer* after Pieter Bruegel the Younger.

At Dijver 17 the **Gruuthuse Museum** (same times as the Groeninge Museum; F130), sited in a rambling fifteenth-century mansion, has a varied collection of fine and applied art, including fine intricately carved altarpieces, musical instruments, sixteenth- and seventeenth-century tapestries and many different types of furniture. Beyond the Gruuthuse, the **Onze Lieve Vrouwekerk** (April–Sept Mon–Fri 10–11.30am & 2.30–5pm, Sat 10–11.30am & 2.30–4pm, Sun 2.30–5pm; Oct–March Mon–Sat 10–11.30am & 2.30–4.30pm, Sun 2.30–4.30pm; free) is a massive shambles of different dates and styles, among whose treasures is a delicate marble *Madonna and Child* by Michelangelo, an influential early work brought from Tuscany by a Flemish merchant. It is also home to the mausoleums (F60) of Charles the Bold and his daughter Mary of Burgundy, striking examples of Renaissance carving. The earth beneath the mausoleums has been dug out and mirrors now reveal the frescoes painted on the tomb walls at the start of the sixteenth century.

Opposite the church, the **St Jans Hospitaal** complex contains a well-preserved fifteenth-century dispensary and the small but important **Memling Museum** (April–Sept daily 9.30am–5pm; Oct–March daily except Wed 9.30am–12.30pm & 2–5pm; F160). Born near Frankfurt in 1433, Hans Memling spent most of his working life in Bruges. Of the six paintings on display, the *Mystical Marriage of St Catherine*, the middle panel of an altarpiece painted between 1475 and 1479, is perhaps the most notable. There's also the unusual *Reliquary of St Ursula*, a miniature wooden Gothic church painted with the story of St Ursula and the 11,000 martyred virgins. Just north of the St Jans Hospitaal, Heilige Geeststraat heads northwest to the **Sint Salvators-kathedraal** (St Saviour's Cathedral; Mon 2–5.45pm, Tues–Fri 8.30–11.45am & 2–5.45pm, Sat 8.30–11.45am & 2–5pm, Sun 9–noon & 3–5.45pm; free), a replacement for the cathedral destroyed by the French in the eighteenth century. Emerging from a long-term restoration, the soaring columns and arches are quite splendid, but it's the wonderful, flowing tapestries hanging in the choir which really catch the eye. From here, it's a quick stroll down to the **Begijnhof** (daily 9am–6pm), a circle of white-washed houses around a tidy green. Nearby, the picturesque **Minnewater** was once used as a town harbour, and still has a fifteenth-century lock gate.

Eating and drinking

Inevitably, most of the **cafés** and **restaurants** in Bruges are geared up for the tourist industry, with the majority working from a fairly uniform Flemish menu. By and large, standards are high, portions substantial and prices quite reasonable, the only problem being the crowds that make many city-centre places unbearable in the peak season. Several of the youth hostels offer **inexpensive meals**, the best of which are those served up by the *Passage*, Dweersstraat 26, and the *Bauhaus*, Langestraat 135. For fresh **seafood** snacks, the fish shops along the Vismarkt are a good bet, with delicious prepared specialities for around F300.

Among Bruges's many **eateries**, try *Taverne Curiosa*, Vlamingstraat 22, a lively bar/restaurant in an old vaulted cellar a couple of minutes' walk north of the Markt; *Het Dagelijks Brood*, Philipstockstraat 21, an excellent bread shop which doubles as a wholefood café with one, long wooden table; *La Dentellière*, Wijngaardstraat 33, the most agreeable of the somewhat overpriced restaurants around the Minnewater; *Den Dyver*, Dijver 5, a first-rate restaurant specializing in Flemish dishes cooked in beer – the quail and rabbit are magnificent; *Erasmus*, Wollestraat 35, a straightforward, brightly-lit café with reasonably priced, mostly Flemish dishes; or *Beethoven*, St Amandsstraat 6, a cosy family-run restaurant serving top-notch Belgian dishes at expensive prices. As for **bars**, *'t Brugs Beertje*, Kemelstraat 5, is a small and friendly speciality beer bar that claims a stock of two hundred ales; *'t Dreupelhuisje*, Kemelstraat 9, is a tiny bar specializing in *jenevers* and advocaats, of which it has an excellent range; and the *Oude Vlissinghe*, Blekerstraat 2, is – with its wood panelling, old paintings and long wooden tables – one of the oldest and most distinctive bars in town. The *Cactusclub*, in the city centre at St Jakobsstraat 33 (☎34 86 43), hosts quality bands – everything from rock and R&B through to jazz and touring DJs.

SOUTHERN BELGIUM

South of Brussels, the western reaches of Wallonia are given over mainly to the French-speaking province of Hainaut, whose rolling farmland is marked by pockets of industrialization, which coalesce between Mons and Charleroi. The highlight of the province is **Tournai**, a vibrant, unpretentious city with a number of decent museums and the finest Romanesque-Gothic cathedral in the country. East of Charleroi lie the high wooded hills of the **Ardennes**, covered by the three provinces of Namur in the west, Luxembourg in the south and Liège in the east. The best gateway towns for the Ardennes, which are well worth exploring on the way south into Luxembourg and Germany, are the lively provincial centre of **Namur**, an hour from Brussels by train, and **Dinant** – a small but much visited town beside the Meuse a further thirty-minute train journey south.

Tournai

TOURNAI is the nearest southern Belgium has to the Flemish "art towns" of Flanders and the north, and is a pleasant spot to spend a couple of nights. The town was badly damaged by Allied bombing during World War II, but the cathedral, arguably the finest in the country, survived pretty much unscathed, as did the narrow lanes and alleys of the medieval street plan during the subsequent rebuilding.

Most things of interest are on the southern side of the river, grouped around or within easy walking distance of the sprawling **Grand-Place**. Dominating the skyline with its distinctive five towers is Tournai's Romanesque **Cathédrale Notre-Dame** (daily 9am–noon & 2–4/6pm; free), built out of the local slate-coloured marble. The most unusual feature of the exterior is the fascinating Porte Mantile, a Romanesque doorway on its north side, adorned with forceful, almost pagan carvings of the virtues and vices. Inside, the nave was erected in 1171, its intricately carved capitals leading down to a choir that was the first manifestation of the Gothic style in Belgium. Be sure to visit the treasury (F30), which houses two important thirteenth-century gilt reliquaries – the Romanesque-Gothic *châsse de Notre-Dame* (1205) by Nicolas de Verdun, and the *châsse de Saint Eleuthère* (1247) – as well as a stunning *Ecco Homo* by Quentin Matsys.

Close to the cathedral, virtually on the corner of the Grand-Place, the **Belfry** is the oldest in Belgium, its lower portion dating from 1200. Close by, on place Reine Astrid, is the **Musée de la Tapisserie** (daily except Tues 10am–noon & 2–5.30pm; F80), which features old tapestries on the ground floor and modern works above – Tournai was among the most important pictorial tapestry centres in Belgium in the fifteenth and sixteenth centuries. Just along the street, cut up through the gardens to the **Hôtel de Ville**, the grandest of several municipal buildings that share the same compound. Behind here, the **Musée des Beaux Arts** (daily except Tues 10am–noon & 2–5.30pm; F120), housed in an elegant late-1920s building by Victor Horta, has a well-displayed collection of mainly Belgian painting from the Flemish primitives to the twentieth century.

Practicalities

Tournai's **train station** is on the northern edge of the town about 600m from the river. The **tourist office** at rue du Vieux Marché-aux-Poteries 14, opposite the Belfry (Mon–Fri 9am–7pm, Sat & Sun 10am–noon & 2–6pm), has a list of **hotels**. The cheapest are on or around the Grand-Place: the *De la Tour St-Georges*, Place de Nédonchel 2 (☎069/22 50 35; ③) has dowdy but perfectly adequate rooms and is located just behind the Halle aux Draps. Much better – and much more expensive – is the *Hotel d'Alcantara*, rue des Bouchers St-Jacques 2 (☎069/21 26 48; ⑥), a delightful and chic modern hotel slotted in behind an old facade about 400m northwest of the Grand-Place. There's also a first-rate **youth hostel**, centrally placed, about five minutes' walk from the Belfry at rue St-Martin 64 (☎069/21 61 36; ②; Feb–Dec).

As for **food**, the *Bistro de la Cathédrale*, next door to the tourist office at rue Vieux Marché-aux-Poteries 15, serves a number of excellent daily specials and is a good spot to try the local speciality, *lapin à la Tournaissienne* (rabbit cooked in beer); *Chez Pietro*, rue del'Hôpital Notre-Dame 15, is an extremely popular Italian place serving an inexpensive range of tasty pizzas and pastas; and *Petit Bedon*, rue des Maux 6, is an affordable restaurant on the west side of the Grand-Place, with a good line in horsemeat (closed Wed). The best **bars** are strung out along the river on quais Notre Dame and Marché Poisson.

Namur

Known as the "Gateway to the Ardennes", **NAMUR** is a logical first stop if you're heading into the region from the north or west, though without a car the dark forests and hills are still a long way off. That said, the town feels refreshingly free of the industrial belt of Hainaut, and its elegant, mansion-filled centre is the backdrop of a night scene lent vigour by the university.

Cutting through the centre of town, **rue de l'Ange** is Namur's main shopping street, running north into the rue de Fer, where the **Musée des Arts Anciens du Namurois** (Tues–Sun 10am–5/6pm; F50) has displays of the work of Mosan goldsmiths and silversmiths of the eleventh to thirteenth centuries. Leaving the museum, it's a short stroll southwest to the finest of Namur's churches, the **Église Saint Loup**, a Baroque extravagance that overshadows a narrow pedestrianized street, rue du Collège. Built for the Jesuits between 1621 and 1645, the church boasts a breezy, flowing facade and a sumptuous interior of marble walls and sandstone vaulting. At the west end of rue du Collège, on place St-Aubain, the **Cathédrale St-Aubain** might well be the ugliest church in Belgium, a monstrous Neoclassical pile remarkably devoid of any charm. The interior isn't much better, acres of creamy white paint and a choir decorated with melodramatic paintings by Jacques Nicolai, one of Rubens' less talented pupils.

Heading south from the cathedral towards the river, turn left along rue des Brasseurs and then first left for the **Musée Felicien Rops**, rue Fumal 12 (daily 10am–5pm, closed Mon except during July & Aug; F100), devoted to the life and work of the eponymous painter, graphic artist and illustrator, who is best known for his erotic drawings, which reveal an obsession with the macabre and perverse – characteristically skeletons, nuns and priests depicted in oddly compromising poses. The museum possesses a large collection of his works and is currently being extended to provide enough space to display it all. East of here, the **Trésor d'Oignies**, rue Julie Billiart 17 (Tues–Sat 10am–noon & 2–5pm, Sun 2–5pm; ring for entry; F50), is Namur's best museum, located in a nunnery and holding a unique collection of the beautiful gold and silver reliquaries and devotional pieces created by local crafts-man Hugo d'Oignies in the first half of the thirteenth century; the nuns give the guided tour. Across the Sambre River Bridge, Namur's **Citadel** (June–Sept & Easter daily 11am–5pm; April–May, except Easter, Sat & Sun only 11am–5pm; F210) is inevitably the city's major attraction, and deservedly so. Originally constructed in medieval times to defend Namur's strategic position at the junction of the Sambre and Meuse rivers, it was later turned into one of the most impregnable fortresses in Europe by Vauban and the Dutchman Coheoorn. It's a huge, sprawling place, accessible by cable car (April–Sept daily 10am–7pm, rest of the year Sat & Sun 10am–6pm; F190 round-trip, F160 one-way) from near the car park on the south side of the Pont du Musée. The entrance fee includes an audiovisual display, a miniature train ride around the grounds, and a guided tour of the deepest underground passages, as well as access to the fortress's wildlife and armaments museums.

Practicalities

Namur's **train station** is on the northern edge of the city centre, on place de la Station, close to the **tourist office** on square Léopold (daily April–Sept 9.30am–6pm; Oct–Mar 9.30am–12.30pm & 1–4pm). From here, it's a ten-minute walk along rue de Fer to the town centre, situated on the north bank of the Sambre River near its confluence with the Meuse. Both the tourist office and the seasonal **information chalet** (April–Sept daily 9.30am–6pm), over the bridge on the south bank of the Sambre, sell combined tickets for town sights, including the citadel and major museums. Namur's cheapest recommendable **hotel** is *L'Excelsior*, avenue de la Gare 4 (☎081/23 18 13; ③), a mundane budget place a few metres from the train station. Down by the Meuse, the *Beauregard*, avenue Baron Moreau 1 (☎081/23 00 28; ⑦), is much more enticing, a swish hotel adjoining the casino and with attractive, large and modern rooms. Alternatively there's a **youth hostel** on the far edge of town beyond the casino, twenty minutes' walk from the centre, at ave Felicien Rops 8 (☎081/22 36 88; ①) – take bus #3 or #4 from the station.

Namur is a great place to **eat and drink**, and there are lots of places to do both in the nar-row streets around rue de l'Ange. Down near the river, at rue des Brasseurs 61, is *Aux Petits Brasseurs*, a smart little bistro serving excellent Franco-Belgian cuisine with prices to match, or you could try *La Fondue*, rue St Jean 19, a medium-sized restaurant serving excellent fondues and steaks for around F600 a head; it's just off place Marché-aux-Legumes. Not far away is *L'Ecailler des Halles*, rue de la Halle 5, an upmarket deli with a small restaurant serving excel-lent seafood. For dinner it's hard to beat *La Petite Fugue*, on place Chanoine Descamps – an out-standing restaurant with mouth-watering Franco-Belgian dishes at around F1200 for a three-course feast. *Henry's Bar*, by the cathedral at place St-Aubain 3, is a bustling brasserie with a simple French menu and plenty of good Belgian beer; close by, behind the cathedral at rue du Séminaire 4, is *Le Chapitre*, with an excellent selection of domestic beers. The *Piano Bar*, on place Marché-aux-Légumes, is one of the town's trendiest bars with live jazz on the weekend.

Dinant

At the centre of the Meuse Valley tourist industry, **DINANT** is a pretty little town slung along the river beneath craggy green cliffs about 30km south of Namur. A handy base for ventur-ing into the surrounding countryside either by boat or on foot, its only drawback is its popu-larity – on summer weekends the place literally heaves with visitors. The town also has a cou-ple of minor attractions of its own, the Gothic church of **Notre-Dame** (daily 10.30–6pm; free), topped with the bulbous spire that features on all the brochures, and the mainly nine-teenth-century **citadel** (daily 10am–4/6pm; Nov, Dec, Feb & March closed Fri; closed all Jan), right behind the church and reached either by cable car (F195) or by a long flight of steps (F135); the fortress is, however, a bit dull if you've already been to the one in Namur.

Practicalities

Dinant's **train station** is on the opposite side of the river and five minutes' walk from the town centre: head right then turn left across the central bridge. The **tourist office**

(June–Aug daily 9am–8pm, rest of the year daily 8.30am–noon & 2–5pm) is a brief stroll from the main square, place Reine Astrid, and one block up from the river at rue Grande 37. There's surprisingly little choice when it comes to **accommodation**, but the*Taverne Le Rouge et Noir* (☎082/22 69 44; ③), at rue Grande 26, has a few frugal rooms above its bar-restaurant, whilst the *Hôtel de la Couronne*, in the middle of town by the church at rue Adolphe Sax 1 (☎082/22 24 41; ④), has comfortable rooms with routine modern fittings. There's no hostel, but there are plenty of **campsites**, the closest being *Camping de Bouvignes* (☎082/22 40 02; March–Oct), a kilometre or so out of town.

For **food**, most of the town's cafés and restaurants are geared up for the day-trippers, but there are still several good spots including the water's edge *Villa Casanova*, ave Churchill 9, which has tasty pasta and pizza dishes from around F300, and the *Duc de Bourgogne*, place Reine-Astrid, where the mussels are superb. *Le Sax*, place Reine Astrid 13, is an unpretentious **bar** with a good beer selection – sit outside and watch the floodlit citadel.

As for **hiking** and **biking**, the Dinant tourist office sells the *Dinant et ses anciennes communes map*, which shows fifteen circular walks, five mountain-bike routes and one cycling circuit in the area. Each of the walks has a designated starting point in or near town. The bike routes range from five to forty kilometres, though to see the most attractive scenery you need to get out on the longer trails. You can normally **rent mountain bikes** from the canoe operators in nearby Anseremme, try Kayaks Ansiaux (☎082/22 23 25), or ask at the Dinant tourist office for the best local deals.

LUXEMBOURG

Across the border from the Belgian province of Luxembourg, the **Grand Duchy of Luxembourg** is one of Europe's smallest sovereign states, a tiny independent principality with a population of around 400,000. As a country, it's relatively neglected by travellers, most people tending to write it off as a dull and expensive financial centre, but this is a mistake. Compared to much of Europe, its attractions are indeed fairly low-key, and it is pricey, but it has marvellous scenery in abundance: the green hills of the Ardennes spreading over the border to form a glorious heartland of deep wooded valleys spiked with sharp craggy hilltops crowned with castles.

The capital, dramatically-sited **Luxembourg City**, is almost impossible to avoid if you're not travelling by car. Home to something like a fifth of the population, it is the country's only genuinely urban environment, and well worth one or two nights' stay. The **central** part of Luxembourg is, however, even more spectacular, rucking up into rich green hills and valleys that reach their climax in the narrowing **north** of the country around **Echternach**, a tiny town dominated by its ancient abbey, and **Vianden**, with its magnificent castle.

Once part of the Spanish and later Austrian Netherlands, Luxembourg today is an independent constitutional monarchy. Although everyone speaks the indigenous language, Letzebuergesch – a dialect of German that sounds a bit like Dutch – most also speak French and German and many speak English too. Indeed, multilingualism is one of Luxembourg's most admirable features and different languages are favoured for different purposes – French is the official language of the government and judiciary, the one you'll see on street signs and suchlike, whilst German is the language most used by the press.

Luxembourg City

The city of **LUXEMBOURG** is one of the most spectacularly sited capitals in Europe, the deep canyons of its two rivers, the Alzette and Pétrusse, lending it an almost perfect strategic location. It's a tiny place by capital city standards, and broadly divides into three distinct sections. The **old town**, on the northern side of the Pétrusse valley, is not noticeably very ancient, but its tight grid of streets, home to most of the city's sights, makes for a pleasant, lively area by day. On the opposite side of the Pétrusse, connected by two bridges, the Pont Adolphe and Pasarelle, lies the **modern city** – less attractive and of no real interest beyond being the loca-

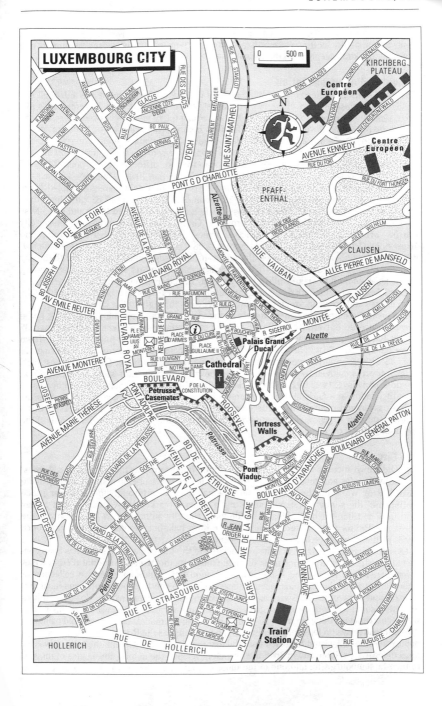

tion of the city's train station and cheap hotels. The **valleys** themselves, far below and most easily accessible by lift from place St-Esprit, are a curious mixture of houses, allotments and parkland, banking steeply up to the massive bastions that secure the old centre.

Arrival and accommodation

The **train station**, a fifteen-minute walk south of the city centre proper, is the hub of all city bus lines and close to many of the city's cheapest (and dreariest) hotels. Luxembourg's **airport**, Findel, is 6km east of the city; bus #9 runs every thirty minutes between here and the bus stops in the old town on place E. Hamilius before proceeding on to the train station (25min; F40). There are also faster but less regular Luxair buses, connecting with major flights (F120). You'll pay about F600 for a **taxi** from the airport to the station, F700 into the city centre. There are branches of the national **tourist office** at the airport (Mon–Fri 10am–2.30pm & 4–7pm, Sat 10am–1.45pm, plus April–Oct Sun 10am–2.30pm & 3.30–6.30pm 10am–6.30pm; ☎42 82 82 21) and at the station (late Sept to June daily 9am–noon & 2–6.30pm, July to mid-Sept Mon–Sat 9am–7pm, Sun 9am–noon & 2–6.30pm; ☎42 82 82 20). These have city maps, transit maps, all manner of glossy leaflets, details of guided tours and can advise on – and book – accommodation right across the Grand Duchy. There's also the busier city **tourist office**, in the centre on place d'Armes (April–Sept Mon–Sat 9am–7pm, Sun 10am–6pm; Oct–March Mon–Sat 9am–6pm; ☎22 28 09;*www.luxembourg-city.lu/touristinfo/)*, which offers much the same facilities, though, as its name suggests, it deals only with the city – not the rest of the Grand Duchy. There is a reasonable urban **bus** system, but Luxembourg City is small enough to make **walking** the best way of getting around. If you do have to take a bus, tickets cost a flat F40; day tickets are available for F160, or in a block of five for F640, from drivers and are valid for all train and bus services throughout the country.

Amongst the bargain-basement **hotels** in the vicinity of the train station, the pick is the *Empire*, place de la Gare 34 (☎48 52 52; ⑤), a straightforward modern hotel with just 35 rooms. Rather more appealing, however, are the *Schintgen*, a pleasant hotel in the Old Town at rue Notre Dame 6 (☎22 28 44; ⑥), and the smart and spotless *Francais*, place d'Armes 14 (☎47 45 34; ⑥), an attractive three-star overlooking the main square. One of the best locations in town is enjoyed by the **youth hostel**, down in the valley off Montée de Clausen at rue du Fort Olisy 2 (☎22 68 89; ②); it's close to the Mousel brewery and reached by bus #9 from the station or a fairly strenuous twenty-minute walk. There are a couple of **campsites** within easy reach of the centre; the nearest is *Camping Bon Accueil*, rue du Camping 2 (April–Sept; ☎36 70 69), a small campground located by the riverside just 5km south of the city in the village of Alzingen.

The City

The Old Town focuses on two squares, the most important of which is **place d'Armes**, fringed with cafés and restaurants. To the north lie the city's principal shops, mainly along **Grand Rue**, while on the southern side a small alley cuts through to the larger **place Guillaume**, the venue of Luxembourg's main general market on Wednesday and Friday mornings and flanked by the bland buildings of the city authorities. A block away is the Ruritanian **Palais Grand-Ducal**, originally the town hall, but adopted by the Luxembourg royals as their residence in the nineteenth century.

Close by, a group of patrician mansions bordering the Marché aux Poissons has been converted into the city's largest and most diverting museum, the **Musée National d'Histoire et d'Art** (Tues–Sun 10am–5pm; F100), whose ground floor holds an extensive collection of Gallo-Roman archeological finds, mainly unearthed in the south of the country and including bronzes and terracottas, glassware and a magnificent mosaic from Vichten. Up above, things get rather confused, with a winding stairway leading to a veritable rabbit warren of tiny rooms which contain everything from military knick-knacks and a modest collection of old paintings through to displays on local folklore. East of the museum lies the **Rocher du Bock**, a strongpoint where, in 963, Count Siegfried built the fort that was to develop into the town. It was an ideal defensive position, and in 1648 the French developed the natural advantages of the site to turn Luxembourg City into one of the most strongly defended fortresses in Europe. The streets here cling to the edge of the plateau, overlooking the sharp drop below, at the bottom of which nestle the slate-roofed houses of **Grund** – accessible by lift from place St-Esprit (see below). The most substantial and accessible fortifications are the **Bock casemates** (daily March–Oct 10am–5pm; F70). Used as bomb shelters during World War II, their galleries honeycomb the long protrusion of the Bock. There's nothing much to see beyond a few rusty old cannons, but there are fine views over the city's spires and aqueducts. From the Rocher du Bock you can follow the dramatic **chemin de la Corniche** to place St-Esprit, where the top of the gigantic **Citadelle du St-Esprit** bastion, built in 1685 by Vauban, has been levelled off and is now a grassy park. There are more casemates close by, the **Casemates de la Pétrusse** (Easter & July–Sept guided tours 11am–4pm; F70), hollowed out by the Spanish in 1674 and accessible by way of some steps on place de la Constitution. The nearby **Cathédrale Notre-Dame**, whose slender black spire dominates the city's puckered skyline, dates from 1613, but it has been remodelled on several occasions, creating the architectural jumble that exists today: the transepts and choir are in a clumping Art Deco style, whereas the (much more appealing) seventeenth-century nave is Renaissance. Inside, items of interest are few and far between, but there is a plaque in the nave honouring those priests killed in World War II and the Baroque gallery at the back of the nave is a likeable affair graced by alabaster angels and garlands of flowers. In the apse is the country's most venerated icon, *The Comforter of the Afflicted*, a medieval lime-wood effigy of the Madonna and child which is frequently dressed up in all manner of lavish gear with crowns and spectres, lace frills and gold brocade.

Eating, drinking and nightlife

Luxembourg City's Old Town is crowded with **cafés** and **restaurants** from inexpensive places where a filling *plat du jour* will cost you a reasonable F350 through to lavish establishments with main courses costing twice as much – occasionally more. French cuisine is popular here and traditional Luxembourgish dishes are found on many menus too, mostly meaty affairs such as neck of pork with broad beans (*judd mat gaardebounen*), black sausage (*blutwurst*) and chicken in Riesling (*hahnchen im Riesling*). Keep an eye out also for *Gromperenkichelchen* – potato cakes usually served with apple sauce – and in winter, stalls and cafés selling *Glühwein*, hot wine mulled with cloves. One of the great Luxembourg traditions is **coffee and cakes** in a salon or one of the city's numerous patisseries – *Oberweis*, at Grand Rue 19, is as good as any – and here, as in Belgium, pavement cafés are thronged in the summertime, with place d'Armes being the place to head for. Multilingual menus are the norm. Recommended **restaurants** include the *Brasserie Chimay*, rue Chimay 15, a small, pleasantly old-fashioned café/restaurant off place d'Armes offering traditional, straightforward dishes at inexpensive prices; and the pavement café of the *Hôtel Francais*, which serves tasty salads and a wide-ranging menu including several Luxembourgish favourites. Otherwise, *Giorgio's Pizzeria*, rue du Nord 11 (closed Sun), is a sociable and eminently fashionable place that serves delicious pizzas from F350; the *Maison des Brasseurs*, Grande Rue 48 (closed Sun) is a long-established, reasonably priced restaurant providing delicious Luxembourgish dishes, with sauerkraut the house speciality; and *Restaurant Club 5*, rue Chimay 5, has long been one of the city centre's trendier hangouts, with an excellent restaurant upstairs and a café/bar down below. At both, the speciality is *carpaccio* – thin slices of air-dried beef served with fries and salad.

Most visitors are content to drink where they eat, but there is a lively **bar** and **club** scene spread around the various parts of town, with bars in the Old Town, Grund and Clausen, and clubs mostly west of the train station in Hollerich. Opening hours are fairly elastic, but bars usually stay open till around 1am, clubs till 3am. While you're out on the tiles, try one of the local pilsener ales such as Mousel or the tasty *Bofferding* brews, which are the most widely available. Good **bars** to try include the funky *Chiggeri*, rue du Nord 11, which attracts a lively, youthful crowd to its groovy Old Town premises and – catering for a slightly older crowd – the *Café des Artistes*, Montée du Grund 2, a charming café/bar close to the bridge in Grund with piano accompaniment and Luxembourg singalongs. For clubs, there's Didjeridoo, rue Bouillon 31, Hollerich, a boisterous club west of the train station offering a wide range of sounds (Wed, Fri & Sat) and *Melusina*, rue de la Tour Jacob 145, Clausen, with varied sounds plus live jazz and folk music nights.

Listings

Airlines British Airways, at the airport (☎0800 2000); Lunar, at the airport (☎47 98 42 42); Sabena, at the airport (☎47 98 25 88). Icelandair, the only airline to fly direct from the US to Luxembourg, is at rue Glesener 59 (☎40 27 27 27).

Airport enquiries ☎47 96 29 75.

American Express ave de la Porte-Neuve 34 (☎22 85 55).

Bike rental rue Bisserwe 8, Grund (Mon–Fri 1–8pm, Sat & Sun 9am–noon & 1–8pm; ☎47 96 23 83); F100 an hour, F250 for a half-day, F400 a day, and F2000 for a week. Discounts of 20 percent available for groups and under-26s. Advance booking is advised, and a repair service is also available. A cycle trail encircles the city – details here or at the tourist office.

Car rental Avis, place de la Gare 2 (☎48 95 95), and at the airport (☎43 51 71); Europcar, route de Thionville 84 (☎40 42 28), and at the airport (☎43 45 88); Hertz, at the airport (☎43 46 45); Thrifty, blvd Prince Henri (☎22 11 81) and at the airport (☎43 52 43).

Festivals The city's main knees-up is the *Schueberfouer*, three weeks of jollity beginning in late August and with one of the biggest funfairs in Europe.

Doctor Dial ☎112 for medical assistance.

Embassies Belgium, rue des Girondins 4 (☎44 27 46); Ireland, route d'Arlon 28 (☎45 06 10); Netherlands, rue C M Spoo 5 (☎22 75 70); UK, Boulevard Roosevelt 14 (☎22 98 64); USA, Boulevard E Servais 22 (☎46 01 23).

Emergencies Fire and Ambulance ☎112. Police ☎113.

Laundry Quick-Wash, rue de Strasbourg 31; several dry cleaners around the city – look out for branches of 5 à sec.

Left luggage There are coin-operated lockers and a luggage office at the train station.

Newspapers English-language newspapers are available from most newsagents from about 11am on the day of publication.

Pharmacies Molitor, place d'Armes 5 and Mortier, avenue de la Gare 11. Duty rotas are displayed in pharmacy windows.

Police Main station: rue Glesener 58–60. Emergencies: ☎113.

Post office The main post office is on place Emile Hamilius (Mon–Fri 7am–7pm, Sat 7am–5pm). There's also an office opposite the train station (Mon–Fri 9am–noon & 1-5pm, Sat 9am–noon).

Train enquiries The CFL office in the station is open daily 7am–8pm (☎49 90 49 90).

Walking tours The city tourist office in place d'Armes co-ordinates a first-rate programme of guided walking tours. Options include a City Promenade (Easter–Oct 1 daily, Nov–Easter 3 weekly; 2hr; F240); the Vauban Walk (May–Oct 1 weekly; 2hr; F240); and the Wenzel Walk (May–Oct 1 weekly; 2hr; F280) – touted as 1000 years in 100 minutes – which starts from the Bock casemates, and takes you right around the fortifications on the east side of the Old Town.

The Grand Duchy

Having explored Luxembourg City, you may want to get out to see something of the rest of the **Grand Duchy**, about two-thirds of which is feasibly visited on day-trips, especially with a car. To the north, the first major rail junction is **Ettelbruck**, within easy striking distance by bus of some of the country's finest scenery. Here, confined by the Sûre River, which forms the border between Luxembourg and Germany, is an area of thickly wooded hills and rocky valleys known optimistically as **Petit Suisse** or "Little Switzerland". **Echternach** has long been the main centre of this region and, along with picturesque **Vianden** further north, is the best base for nosing round the Luxembourg Ardennes.

Echternach

Now a town of some 4000 people, **ECHTERNACH** grew up around an abbey founded here in 698 by the English missionary St Willibrord. The centre is the wedge-shaped **place du Marché**, an elegant conglomeration of ancient buildings, notably the fifteenth-century turreted **Town Hall**, with its Gothic loggia of 1520. The town's real attraction is, however, the **abbey** itself, just north of place du Marché, signalled by the spires of its enormous **church**, rebuilt to a former eleventh-century plan after heavy bomb damage in 1944. The most diverting part of the interior is the crypt dating from around 900, its walls bearing some antique frescoes and the primitive coffin of the saint himself, covered by an ornate, modern canopy. The huge abbey complex spreads out beyond the church to a set of formal gardens by the river, its mainly eighteenth-cen tury buildings now given over to secular activities. One houses the **Musée de l'Abbaye** (April–Oct daily 10am–noon & 2–6pm; Nov–March Sat & Sun 2–5pm; F50), with stone fragments from St Willibrord's original foundation and the eleventh-century *Codex Aureus* of Echternach, whose superb jewelled cover, from 990, was the work of a Trier craftsman.

The **bus station** is five minutes from the centre, at the end of rue de la Gare. The **tourist office**, opposite the abbey church (Mon–Fri 9am–noon & 2–5pm, also June-Aug Sat & Sun 9am–noon & 2–5pm; ☎72 02 30), has maps and information on **accommodation**. There are plenty of **hotels** along rue de la Gare: try the *Regine* at no. 53 (☎72 74 52; ④); the *Pavillon* at no. 2 (☎72 98 09; ④); or the *Petite Poète*, very central on place du Marché 13 (☎72 00 72; ③). There's a **campsite** 300m beyond the bus station following the river out of town, and a **youth hostel** at rue André Duchscher 9 (☎72 01 58; ②; mid-Feb to mid-Nov), south from the corner of place du Marché and rue de la Gare. The *Benelux* **restaurant**, on the same corner, offers good quality and reasonably priced meals.

Vianden

Probably the most strikingly sited of all Luxembourg's provincial towns, **VIANDEN** is still surrounded by ramparts and dominated by its hilltop **castle** (daily 10am–4/6pm; F120), a mostly eleventh-century edifice garnished with everything from Romanesque to Renaissance features. Inside, some rooms have been partly furnished in period style – the Banqueting Hall and the huge Counts' Hall decorated with seventeenth-century tapestries – but much has been left empty, notably the long Byzantine Room and the octagonal upper chapel, surrounded by a narrow defensive walkway. For more authentic mustiness, peek down the well just off the old kitchen, and leave through the Gothic dungeon. You can survey the castle from the hill above by taking the cable car to its 450-metre-high summit (daily: summer 9.30am–6.30pm; winter 10am–6pm; F160 return) from rue du Sanatorium, just off rue Victor Hugo. At the top there's a restaurant with a terrace, and you can walk down to the castle by way of a footpath.

Buses to Vianden stop on the far eastern edge of town on the route de la Frontière, about five minutes' walk from the **tourist office** (June–Aug daily 9.30am–noon & 1–6pm, Sept–May Mon–Fri 9am–noon & 2–6pm), on the main street, rue de Vieux Marché, by the bridge. For somewhere to stay, try the **hotel**-lined Grand Rue where the best of the budget options include the *Hôtel Collette*, at no. 68–70 (April-Nov; ☎84 004; ④), and the *Hôtel Heintz*, no. 55 (☎83 41 55; ④), a comfortable, friendly place with a first-rate restaurant. On the other side of the river is the equally pleasant *Auberge de l'Our*, rue de la Gare 35 (☎83 46 75; ④). There's also a **youth hostel** at the top of Grand Rue at Montée du Château 3, a strenuous twenty-minute walk uphill from the bus station (☎83 41 77; ②; mid-March to mid-Nov). The nearest **campsite** is *Op dem Deich*, by the river near the bus station. For **food**, the restaurant of the *Auberge de l'Our*, serves a good range of local specialities, though its riverside terrace means it gets very busy; alternatively head for the *Café de la Poste* on Grand Rue.

travel details

Trains

Antwerp to: Bruges (hourly; 1hr 20min); Ghent (hourly; 1hr 20min).

Bruges to: Ostend (every 20min; 15min); Zeebrugge (hourly; 15min).

Brussels to: Antwerp (every 30min; 40min); Bruges (every 30min; 1hr); Ghent (every 30min; 40min); Luxembourg (every 2hr; 2hr 30min); Mechelen (every 30min; 20min); Namur (hourly; 50min); Ostend (hourly; 1hr 20min); Tournai (hourly; 1hr).

Luxembourg to: Brussels (every 2hr; 2hr 30min); Ettelbruck (hourly; 1hr); Liège for Maastricht (7 daily; 2hr 30min); Namur (hourly; 1hr 50min).

Namur to: Dinant (2 hourly; 30min); Luxembourg (hourly; 1hr 50min).

Buses

Diekirch to: Echternach (10 daily; 35min); Vianden (hourly; 20min).

Ettelbruck to: Echternach (10 daily; 45min); Vianden (12 daily; 30min).

Luxembourg to: Echternach (10 daily; 1hr 10min); Vianden (2 daily; 55min).

CHAPTER 3

BRITAIN

© Crown copyright

Introduction

Though detached from the continent of Europe by just a few miles of water, **Britain** is permeated by a strong sense of its cultural separateness. From the extravagant ceremonials of state to such humble institutions as the village pub, life in Britain retains a continuity with a past that has little in common with its economic partners across the Channel. Although the new Labour Government elected in May 1997 – after eighteen years of Conservative power in Britain – has moved much closer towards acceptance of European unity, many citizens still have problems with the concept of the United Kingdom itself. Northern Ireland – covered in our chapter on the island as a whole – is but the most intractable aspect of national identity. Wales and Scotland, with long traditions of independent nationhood, have their own, vividly autonomous cultures. Some belated recognition of this has resulted in the establishment of political Assemblies for each country, albeit with limited and differing powers for each. Even within England itself, regional differences are more pronounced than one might expect in a country of this size.

Yet the complexity of Britain is not always obvious. The high streets of its cities and towns are beginning to resemble each other more than ever before, with nationwide shops and businesses – many of them multinationals – driving out locally based firms. The tourist infrastructure is very well developed but the growth of a nostalgia-obsessed heritage industry has produced a plethora of museums and theme parks that conjure a rose-tinted simulation of the nation's past. However, the process of discovering the variety of Britain is an immensely satisfying experience. The country is rich in monuments that attest to its intricate history, from ancient hill forts and Roman villas, through a host of medieval cathedrals, to the ambitious civic projects of the Industrial Revolution. In addition, many of the national museums and art galleries are the equal of any in Europe.

For cultural sightseeing as for nightlife, **London** is a ceaselessly entertaining city, and inevitably it's the one place that features on everyone's itinerary. Within the heavily built-up southeast, **Brighton** and **Canterbury** offer contrasting diversions – the former an irresistibly seedy resort, the latter one of Britain's finest medieval cities. The southwest of England, with the rugged moorlands of **Devon** and the rocky coastline of **Cornwall**, is an altogether wilder region, albeit one that pulls in droves of visitors in the height of summer. In the centre of the country, the chief attractions are the university cities of **Oxford** and **Cambridge**, and Shakespeare's town, **Stratford-upon-Avon**, though the often bypassed city of **Norwich**, over in the picturesque flatlands of East Anglia, can be equally rewarding. In the north of England, the industrial cities of **Liverpool**, **Newcastle** and **Manchester** are gritty and lively places, and **York** and **Durham** have splendid historical treasures, but the landscape is again the real magnet, especially the uplands of the **Lake District** and the dales of **Yorkshire**. For true wilderness, however, you're better off heading to the mountains of **Wales** or the Scottish **Highlands**. The finest of Scotland's lochs, glens and peaks, and the magnificent scenery of the west coast **islands**, can be reached easily from the contrasting cities of **Glasgow** and **Edinburgh** – the latter perhaps the most attractive urban landscape in Britain.

Information and maps

Tourist offices (usually called Tourist Information Centres) exist in virtually every British town. In high season, the average opening hours are much the same as standard shop hours, with the difference that they'll be open on a Sunday; in winter, it's usual for a tourist office to close a couple of hours earlier each day, with some rural offices closing altogether. All offer a basic range of information on accommodation, local public transport, and maps. In many cases this is free, but a growing number of offices make a small charge for an accommodation list or a town guide with an accompanying street plan. Areas designated as National Parks (such as the Lake District, Exmoor and Dartmoor) also have a fair sprinkling of National Park Information Centres, which are generally more expert in giving guidance on local walks and outdoor pursuits.

The most comprehensive series of **maps** is produced by the Ordnance Survey. The 204 maps in their 1:50,000 Landranger series cover the whole country and are just about detailed enough to serve as a walking and hiking aid. The more detailed 1:25,000 Explorer series is invaluable for serious walking, while the Outdoor Leisure series (also 1:25,000) is devoted to Britain's National Parks and Areas of Outstanding National Beauty. The best **road maps** are the Collins and Ordnance Survey road atlases.

Money and banks

The British **pound** is divided into 100 pence; coins come in denominations of 1p, 2p, 5p, 10p, 20p, 50p, £1 and £2; notes in £5, £10, £20 and £50. A note for £1 still exists in Scotland (as do £100 notes), whose banks still issue their own banknotes. Scottish currency is legal tender throughout Britain, although some traders south of the border may be unwilling to accept it.

Normal **banking hours** are Mon–Fri 9.30am–4.30pm. Some branches also stay open for a few hours on Saturday mornings, but there are few hard and fast rules. Almost all banks have Automatic Teller Machines which accept a wide range of debit and credit cards.

Communications

Post offices are usually open Mon–Fri 9am–5.30pm, Sat 9am–12.30/1pm, though some town centre offices may have extended hours. Stamps can be bought at post offices, from vending machines outside, or from an increasing number of newsagents, although they usually only sell books of four or ten stamps.

Most public **payphones** are operated by British Telecom, though you'll also see other companies' phone boxes in a variety of colours, especially in London. Most Telecom phones now take all coins from 10p upwards as well as **phonecards**, available from post offices and most newsagents in denominations of £2, £5 and £10; an increasing number even accept credit cards. Inland calls are cheapest between 6pm and 8am and at weekends. The operator number is ☎100, directory enquiries is ☎192, and international directory enquiries is ☎155.

For **email** and Internet access, cyber-cafés are common in the major cities, and you'll even find some hostels provide access.

Getting around

Most significant places in the country are accessible by train or by bus, usually by both. **Public transport** in Britain has been shaken up by large-scale privatization but promised price cuts have failed to materialize, leaving costs still among the highest in Europe. In some cases it can actually be cheaper to fly than to take the train (see London listings for budget airlines), although bus travel is better value.

■ Trains

The **rail** network covers most of the country, but it's a London-centric system; travelling out from London is usually extremely quick, but traversing the country from east to west can be less easy. The network has been privatized in recent years. the trains on each part being run by a different operating company; the stations and lines themselves are owned by Railtrack.

The system's main drawback is that standard fares are extremely high, and the pricing system can be bafflingly complicated. **Saver and Supersaver returns** are the cheapest standard tickets, sometimes less expensive than a single; on certain major intercity routes you also get massively reduced **Apex** and **Superapex** tickets, which have to be booked respectively a week and two weeks in advance; book as early as you can, as there's only a limited number of these tickets available on each service. The price of an ordinary return depends on the day of travel, Fridays being more expensive than the rest of the week, and weekends in general being pricier than weekdays. On several mainline routes the cost of your trip depends on the time of day you travel. If travelling on routes between London and other major cities during public holidays or around Christmas it's advisable to **book a seat** a couple of days in advance. Seat reservations are usually free if made at the same time as purchasing a ticket, although on some routes an extra £1 can be charged for advance bookings.

The only feasible way to get around by train in Britain is to buy a special pass. In addition to InterRail (which gives only thirty-percent discounts) there's a series of **Britrail** passes only available outside the country. Prices vary according to the country of purchase; contact a Rail Europe office within Europe, a BritRail office in Canada or the States, or a travel agent for details. A Consecutive Day Pass allows you continuous travel over a period of 4, 8, 15 or 22 days, while a Flexipass can be used on any 4, 8 or 15 days within a period of two months; they also give a discount of around 12 percent on Eurostar Channel Tunnel services. Inside the UK, a **Young Person's Railcard**, from all station ticket offices for £18, allows thirty-percent reductions on travel for those under 26 or in full-time study, with discounts on ferries to Ireland. There are also regional passes, like the seven-day Freedom of Wales and the Highlands and Islands passes, but these are only attractive if you're exploring these particular areas very intensively. Eurail passes are not valid in Britain.

■ Buses

The long-distance **coach** (bus) services run by **National Express** duplicate many intercity rail routes, very often at half the price or less. The frequency of service is often comparable to rail, and in some instances the difference in journey time isn't great enough to be a deciding factor. Coaches are comfortable, and longer journeys – designated Rapide services – often have drinks and sandwiches available on board. National Express's equivalent company in Scotland is Scottish Citylink, which operates services between Scotland and England and within Scotland itself. Students and young people under 26 can buy a **Discount Card**, giving a third off standard fares. Non-UK residents are entitled to a **Tourist Trail Pass**, which offers unlimited travel on the National Express network for 2 days within 3 consecutive days (£49/£39 under 25s), 5 days within 10 (£85/£69), 7 days within 21 (£120/£94) or 14 days within 30 (£187/£143).

Local bus services are run by a bewildering array of companies, some private, some not; in most cases, however, timetables and routes are well integrated. As a rule, the further away from urban areas you get, the less frequent and more expensive bus services become, but there are very few rural areas which aren't served by at least the occasional privately owned minibus.

■ Driving and hitching

Unlike continental Europe, Britain drives on the left, a situation which makes the roads around the Channel ports particularly hazardous. **Speed limits** are 30 or 40mph in built-up areas, 70mph on motorways and dual carriageways, 60mph on most other roads. **Car rental** costs from around £130 per week with unlimited mileage; many towns will have small companies whose rates undercut the big names, but you'll have to return the car to the place from which you rented it. The Automobile Association and the Royal Automobile Club both operate 24-hour emergency breakdown services. On motorways they can be called from roadside booths; elsewhere ring ☎0800/887766 (AA) or ☎0800/828282 (RAC); both numbers are free.

The extensive motorway network and the density of traffic makes long-distance **hitching** relatively easy, though in rural areas you might be hanging around a long time. As in the rest of Europe, it's not advisable to hitch alone.

Accommodation

The prevalence of bed and breakfasts and youth hostels ensures that budget **accommodation** isn't hard to come by in the UK. Many tourist offices will book local rooms for you, but you should expect to pay at least a ten-percent deposit. Most also operate a "Book a Bed Ahead" service for accommodation in other towns, which usually costs £3.

■ Hotels and bed and breakfast

Hotel accommodation in Britain is generally of a high quality but it's also expensive – in tourist cities it's difficult to find a double for less than £50, although more expensive places sometimes offer cheap rates at weekends. Fortunately, there's a wide range of budget accommodation in the form of guesthouses or **bed and breakfasts** – often a comfortable room in a family home, followed by a substantial breakfast, from around £15 a head – a few pounds more in the affluent south, and a lot more in London. Many B&Bs have a small number of rooms so several days' advance booking is advisable in summer and holiday periods.

■ Hostels and camping

Britain has an extensive network of **HI hostels**, operated by the autonomous associations for Scotland and for England and Wales. In Scotland a bed for the night can cost as little as £4, except in the cities, where you can pay more than twice that. In England and Wales the charge for under-18s is generally nearer the £10 mark, and considerably higher in London; over-18s pay around fifty percent more. Catering varies with the size of the hostel, from a set meal at a set time in the smaller ones to a cafeteria system in the bigger ones. Some of the more basic hostels – and all rural ones in Scotland – still retain a duty roster where you may be set a few cleaning chores, but generally hostels are shedding this old-fashioned image in an attempt to attract a wider public. The YHA for England and Wales is at Trevelyan House, 8 St Stephen's Hill, St Albans, Herts AL1 2DY (☎01727/855215); the Scottish YHA is at 76 Glebe Crescent, Stirling FK8 2JA (☎01786/891400).

ACCOMMODATION PRICE CODES

Throughout this guide, accommodation is priced on a scale of ① to ⑨, the number indicating the lowest price per night a single person could expect to pay in that establishment in high season. With hostels this is the nightly rate per person; with hotels, the price is arrived at by dividing the cost of the cheapest double room by two. The prices indicated by the codes are as follows:

① under £5 / $8	④ £15–20 / $24–32	⑦ £30–35 / $48–56
② £5–10 / $8–16	⑤ £20–25 / $32–40	⑧ £35–40 / $56–64
③ £10–15 / $16–24	⑥ £25–30 / $40–48	⑨ £40 / $64 and over

There are more than 750 official **campsites** in Britain, charging from £5 per tent per night. In the countryside farmers will let you camp in a field if you ask, sometimes charging a couple of pounds for the privilege. Camping rough is illegal in designated parkland and nature reserves.

Food and drink

British **cuisine** has long had a poor reputation, but it's possible to eat well and cheaply, thanks chiefly to the influence of immigrant communities. Social life has always focused more on drinking than eating, however, and the British pub is often the best introduction to a town.

■ Food

In many B&Bs you'll be offered an **"English breakfast"** – basically sausage, bacon and eggs. These days, however, the British are a nation of cereal eaters, and most places will give you this option as well. Though every major town will have its upmarket restaurant specializing in classic meat-based British food, for most people the quintessential British meal is **fish and chips**, a dish that can vary from the succulently fresh to the indigestibly greasy. Recently, however, the ubiquitous fish-and-chip shops ("chippies") have begun to be outnumbered by pizza, kebab and burger outlets on Britain's high streets. Another standard feature is the so-called "greasy spoon" **café**, where the average menu will include bacon sandwiches and cholesterol-rich variations on sausage, bacon, beans, fried egg and chips.

Most mid-range menus consist of meat-and-vegetable dishes such as steak and kidney pie, shepherd's pie, chops and steaks, accompanied by boiled potatoes and plain veg. However, there's an increasing number of **vegetarian** restaurants, especially in the larger towns, and most restaurants make some attempt to cater for vegetarians.

Many **pubs** serve food of one sort or another, usually at lunchtime only, and though this often consists of microwaved pies and chips, the range and quality is improving. For sit-down eating, though, the innumerable types of **ethnic restaurant** offer the best-value good-quality meals. In every town of any size you'll find Chinese, Indian, Italian or other specialities, with the widest choice in London and the industrial cities of the north. Indian "curry houses" in particular are beginning to be regarded as something of a national institution.

■ Drink

Drinking traditionally takes place in a public house, or **pub**, where a standard range of draught beers and lagers – sold by the pint or half-pint – generates most of the business. Each region has its own specialist brewers that maintain the traditional flavours of English beer, though imported bottled beers are also fashionable. A growing number of pubs now serve tea and coffee during the day. In England, pubs are generally open daily 11am–11pm (some close between about 3pm and 5.30pm). Hours are often longer in Scotland, while Sunday closing is common in Wales. In bigger towns there's an increasing number of wine bars, European-style cafés and brasseries, which also serve food.

In Scotland, the national drink is of course **whisky**, a spirit of far greater subtlety than the bland mass-marketed whiskies might lead you to believe. The best are the single malts, produced by a single distillery from local spring water which gives each label its special taste. Outside of Scotland you're unlikely to find a decent choice of whiskies in a pub.

Opening hours, holidays and sites

General **shop hours** are Mon–Sat 9am–5.30/6pm, although there's an increasing amount of Sunday and late-night shopping in big towns, and in Scotland you'll find more places open on a Sunday than in England. Many small towns still retain an "early closing day" when shops close at 1pm – Wednesday is the favourite.

Public holidays in England and Wales are: Jan 1; Good Friday; Easter Monday; first Mon after May 1; last Mon in May; last Mon in August; Dec 25 & 26. In Scotland Jan 1, Jan 2 and Dec 25 are the only fixed public holidays – otherwise towns are left to pick their own holidays.

Many of Britain's great national museums are free, but many stately homes and monuments are administered by the state-run **English Heritage** or **Historic Scotland**, whose entry fees can be high. Annual membership of each organization can be obtained at any of their sites and is probably worth it if you're visiting more than half a dozen. EH membership costs £27 (£14 for under-26), HS membership £24 (£17); each allows half-price entry to the other's properties. Wales is famous for its dramatic ruined castles and churches, many of them cared for by **CADW**, Welsh Historic Monuments; annual membership (£22, £15 for under-20s) is available at any CADW property, or you can buy 3- or 7-day Explorer passes (£9/£15). The private **National Trust** or **National Trust for Scotland** also run a large number of gardens and stately homes, but annual membership is expensive. The **Great British Heritage**

Pass, which covers entry to properties administered by all the organizations above and many others too, is worth considering; it's available from the British Travel Centre and Tourist Information Centres (7 days £30, 15 days £42, 1 month £56). All but the biggest churches and cathedrals are free, although most charge for access to towers, museums, cloisters and the like, and nearly all request donations.

Emergencies

Although the traditional image of the friendly British bobby has become increasingly tarnished, **police** remain approachable and helpful. Tourists aren't a particular target for criminals except perhaps in the crowds of central London, where you should be on your guard against pickpockets. Britain's bigger conurbations all contain inner-city areas where you may feel uneasy after dark, but these are usually away from tourist sights.

Pharmacists can dispense only a limited range of drugs without a doctor's prescription. Most pharmacies are open standard shop hours, though in large towns some may stay open as late as 10pm. Local newspapers carry lists of late-opening pharmacies. Doctors' surgeries tend to be open from about 9am to noon and then for a couple of hours in the evenings; outside surgery hours, you can turn up at the casualty department of the local hospital for complaints that require immediate attention – unless it's an emergency, in which case ring for an ambulance.

EMERGENCY NUMBERS

Fire, Police & Ambulance ☎999.

LONDON

With a population of over seven million, **LONDON** is by far Europe's biggest city, spreading over an area of more than 1500 square kilometres from its core on the River Thames. This is where the country's news and money are made, and if Londoners' sense of superiority causes some resentment in the regions, it's undeniable that the city has a unique aura of excitement and success. During 1999, London worked hard to prepare for the millennium, spending vast sums of money and, for visitors, 2000 will be a bonanza year. The main focus of celebration will be the long-neglected River Thames, along which river trips will run from the new Millennium Dome in the east to Westminster in the west, linking a wealth of historic buildings, theatres, galleries and bridges – including the new pedestrian Millenium Bridge connecting St Paul's with the monumental power station on the south bank which will house the new Tate gallery.

London is both a thrilling and a contrasting city, where ostentatious private affluence lives uncomfortably close to poverty and public neglect. Its central thoroughfares, buzzing far into the night, are interspersed with quiet squares and explorable alleyways. It's a very green city too, with sizeable parks right in the centre – Hyde Park, Green Park and St James's – and the vast open spaces of Hampstead Heath, Greenwich, Richmond and Kew on the periphery. Its museums and galleries are as rich and varied as you'll find anywhere, and many are still free. And, of course, the city is replete with monuments of the capital's past, from its Roman origins to its role at the centre of the British Empire.

The **Romans** founded the town of Londinium on the north bank of the Thames soon after invading Britain in 43 AD, but the city's expansion didn't really begin until the eleventh century, when the last successful invader of Britain, **William of Normandy**, became the first king of England to be crowned in Westminster Abbey. Subsequent monarchs left their imprint, but many of the city's finest structures were destroyed in a few hours in 1666, when the **Great Fire of London** eradicated over 13,000 houses and nearly 90 churches. Sir Christopher Wren was commissioned to replace much of the lost architecture, and rose to the challenge by designing such masterpieces as St Paul's Cathedral. Unfortunately, only a portion of the post-Fire splendours has survived, due partly to the German bombing raids of the **Blitz** of 1940–41 and partly to some unimaginative modern development, which has lumbered London with the sort of concrete-and-glass mediocrity that has given modern architects a bad name. However, London's special atmosphere comes not from the appearance of its streets but from its people. This has been a multicultural city since at least the seventeenth century, when it was a haven for Huguenot (French Protestant) refugees. This century has seen the arrival of thousands from the Caribbean, the Indian subcontinent, West Africa, the Mediterranean and the Far East, playing a large part in defining the character of a metropolis that is not so much a single organism as a patchwork of sub-cities.

Arrival

Flying into London, you'll arrive at one of the capital's four international airports – Heathrow, Gatwick, Stansted or Luton – each of which is less than an hour from the city centre. From **Heathrow**, twelve miles west of the city, the journey couldn't be easier. The **Piccadilly underground line** connects the airport to central London in under an hour (£3.40), with one station serving terminals 1, 2 and 3, another serving terminal 4. Alternatively there's the smart, fast and expensive Heathrow Express **rail** link, which connects the airport to Paddington Station (every 15min; £10); or two **Airbus** services, which run during the day from outside all Heathrow terminals. The #A1 runs south of Hyde Park to Victoria station, while the #A2 follows a more northern line to terminate at King's Cross Station; both stop at numerous central destinations along the way (every 30min; journey time one hour; £6). After midnight, **night bus** #N97 runs every thirty minutes from Heathrow to Trafalgar Square. **Taxis** are plentiful, but will set you back around £35.

Gatwick Airport is thirty miles south of the city, and the nonstop Gatwick Express **rail** service runs from both airport terminals into Victoria Train Station (every 15min, journey time 30min; £9.50). Connex run cheaper services along the same route (every 15min, journey time

35min; £8.20) and Thameslink run services to London Bridge and King's Cross (every 15min, journey time 30–45min; £9.20/£9.50). Flightline **buses** depart for Victoria Coach Station from Gatwick's North and South terminals (hourly 5am–8pm, journey time 90min; £7.50).

The smaller **Stansted Airport** lies 34 miles northeast of the capital and is served by Skytrain **trains** to Liverpool St and Tottenham Hale (every 30min 5am–11pm, journey time 40min; £10.40), where you can connect with London's **underground** services. Flightline **coaches** also run a daily service (hourly; 8am–10pm, journey time 1hr 40min; £9).

Luton is the smallest airport and the furthest away at 37 miles north of the capital. Minibuses link the airport and Luton Parkway station, from where **trains** run to King's Cross Thameslink (every 10min, journey time 30–50min; £10.80) or bus #757 runs directly to Marble Arch and Victoria (every 30min, journey time 1hr 25min; £7.20).

Travelling from abroad by **bus or train**, you'll arrive at Victoria's train station, which serves the English Channel ports, or its coach station, a couple of hundred yards south down Buckingham Palace Rd – or at Waterloo, whose new international rail terminal serves Eurostar trains using the Channel Tunnel. Arriving by train from elsewhere in Britain, you'll come into one of London's numerous mainline stations, all of which have adjacent underground stations that link into the city centre's underground network. For details of train connections between other parts of Britain and the mainline stations, see travel details on p.228.

Information

London Tourist Board (LTB) has a desk at Heathrow Airport in the underground station concourse for terminals 1, 2 and 3 (daily 8am–6pm), but the overcrowded and understaffed **main office** is in the forecourt of **Victoria train station** (April–Oct daily 8am–7pm; Nov–March Mon–Sat 8am–6pm, Sun 8.30am–4pm). The best of the other central offices is near Piccadilly Circus in the British Travel Centre, 12 Lower Regent St (Mon–Fri 9am–6.30pm, Sat & Sun 10am–4/5pm). Others can be found at Liverpool St underground station (Mon–Fri 8am–6pm, Sat & Sun 8.45am–5.30pm) and in the arrivals hall at Waterloo Station International Terminal (daily 8.30am–10.30pm). None of these offices will accept telephone queries – the best the LTB can manage is a long-winded and dull pre-recorded message service; the **British Travel Authority** has a telephone information service (☎0181/846 9000) for specific tourist enquiries.

Serious museum addicts should consider buying the **London White Card**, which gives you entry into a selection of museums, including the London Transport Museum, MOMI, National Maritime Museum, Natural History Museum, Science Museum, the V&A and others. The three-day card costs £16 and the seven-day £26; they are available from any of the above museums and from some tourist offices.

City transport

The fastest way of moving around the city is by **underground**, or **tube**, as it's known to all Londoners. Operating from around 5.30am until around 12.30am, the thirteen different lines cross much of the metropolis, although south London is not well covered. Tickets are bought from machines or from a ticket booth in the station entrance hall – or from an increasing number of newsagents; the minimum for a single journey in central London (zone 1) is £1.40, or you can buy a carnet of ten tickets for £10. A **travelcard**, on sale from machines and ticket booths at all tube stations, is also valid for the bus and suburban rail networks, and will quickly save a lot of money. One-day travelcards, valid on weekdays from 9.30am and all day at weekends, cost £3.80 for zones 1 and 2, which should cover virtually everything you'll want to see, rising to £4.50 for all six zones (which includes Heathrow). Weekend travelcards, valid for travel all day Saturday and Sunday, cost £5.70 for zones 1 and 2, rising to £6.70 for all zones. Adults accompanied by children can buy one-day family travelcards for £3 and £3.60 respectively (plus 60p for each child). If you're travelling before 9.30am, you can buy an LT card instead, valid on buses and tubes only and costing £4.80 for zones 1 and 2, rising to £7.50 for all zones. Weekly travelcards are even more economical, beginning at £14.30 for zone 1

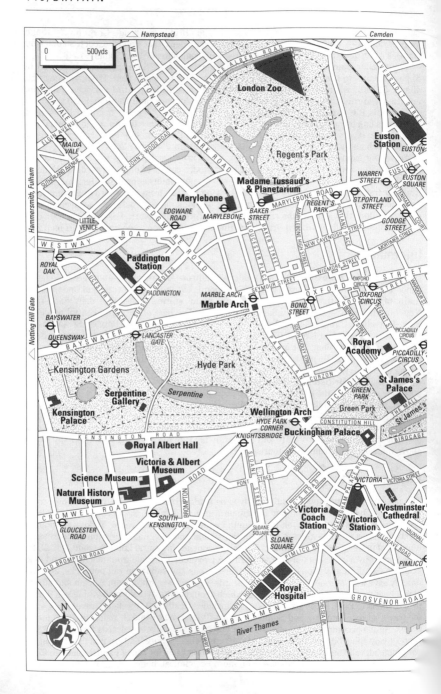

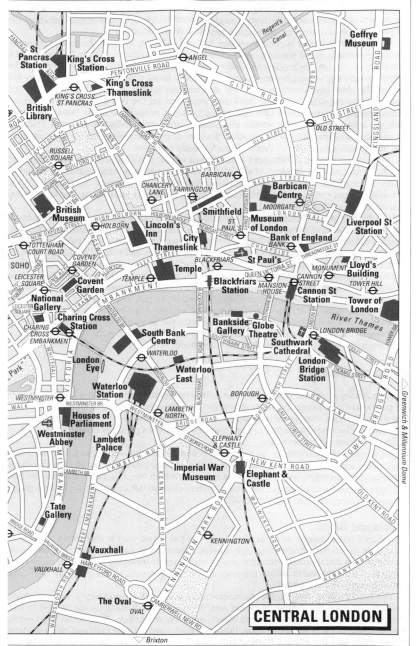

St Pancras Station

King's Cross Station

King's Cross Thameslink

British Library

KING'S CROSS ST PANCRAS

RUSSELL SQUARE

GUILFORD STREET

ANGEL

PENTONVILLE ROAD

ST JOHN STREET

CITY ROAD

OLD STREET

OLD STREET

KINGSLAND ROAD

Geffrye Museum

Regent's Canal

NEW NORTH ROAD

British Museum

HOLBORN

HIGH HOLBORN

CHANCERY LANE

FARRINGDON

BARBICAN

CLERKENWELL ROAD

BEECH STREET

MOORGATE

LONDON WALL

Barbican Centre

Museum of London

Liverpool St Station

TOTTENHAM COURT ROAD

COVENT GARDEN

LEICESTER SQUARE

SOHO

Lincoln's Inn

City Thameslink

Smithfield

ST PAUL'S

NEWGATE STREET

St Paul's

Bank of England

CHEAPSIDE

BANK

THREADNEEDLE ST

Lloyd's Building

MONUMENT

National Gallery

Covent Garden

Temple

TEMPLE

Blackfriars Station

BLACKFRIARS

QUEEN VICTORIA ST

MANSION HOUSE

Cannon St Station

CANNON STREET

TOWER HILL

Tower of London

Charing Cross Station

CHARING CROSS

EMBANKMENT

STRAND

EMBANKMENT

BLACKFRIARS BR.

Bankside Gallery

Globe Theatre

SOUTHWARK STREET

Southwark Cathedral

LONDON BRIDGE

River Thames

TOOLEY STREET

South Bank Centre

WATERLOO

London Eye

Waterloo Station

WESTMINSTER

WESTMINSTER BR.

Waterloo East

WATERLOO ROAD

BLACKFRIARS ROAD

LAMBETH NORTH

BOROUGH

London Bridge Station

ST THOMAS STREET

BOROUGH HIGH STREET

GREAT DOVER STREET

LONG LANE

BRIDGE ROAD

Greenwich & Millennium Dome

Houses of Parliament

Westminster Abbey

Lambeth Palace

WESTMINSTER BRIDGE ROAD

LAMBETH BR.

LAMBETH ROAD

Imperial War Museum

ELEPHANT & CASTLE

ST GEORGE'S ROAD

Elephant & Castle

NEW KENT ROAD

WALWORTH ROAD

OLD KENT ROAD

TOWER BRIDGE ROAD

Tate Gallery

MILLBANK

KENNINGTON ROAD

KENNINGTON PARK ROAD

Vauxhall

VAUXHALL BRIDGE

ALBERT EMBANKMENT

HARLEYFORD ROAD

KENNINGTON

ALBANY ROAD

WANDSWORTH ROAD

The Oval

OVAL

CAMBERWELL NEW RD.

BRIXTON

CENTRAL LONDON

© Crown copyright

only or £17.60 for zones 1 & 2; these and season tickets for longer periods can only be bought by carriers of a **photocard**, which you can get, free of charge, from tube station ticket booths on presentation of a passport photo and a passport or identity card.

The network of **buses** is comprehensive, but you will soon find that the tube is generally quicker, especially in the summer, when central London becomes a logjam. Journeys cost a minimum of 70p, but the average trip in the centre will cost around £1; normally you pay the driver on entering, although some routes – especially those which traverse the centre – are covered by older buses with an open rear platform and staffed by a conductor. A lot of bus stops are request stops, so if you don't stick your arm out the bus will drive past. Regular buses operate between about 6am and midnight, and a network of **night buses** (prefixed with the letter "N") operates outside this period, with routes radiating out from Trafalgar Square at approximately hourly intervals. Fares are more expensive on night buses and one-day travelcards aren't valid on them – though weekly ones are.

The principal **London Transport information office**, providing excellent free maps and details of bus and tube services, is at Victoria station (daily 9am–6pm), and there are other desks at Heathrow Airport, and at Euston, King's Cross, Liverpool St, Oxford Circus, Piccadilly Circus and St James' Park stations. There's also a 24-hour phone line for information on all bus and tube services (☎0171/222 1234).

If you're in a group of three or more, London's metered **black cabs** can be an economical way of getting around the centre of town – a ride across the centre, from Euston to Victoria, should cost around £8. A yellow light over the windscreen tells you if the cab is available – just stick your arm out to hail it – or to book one in advance, call ☎0171/272 0272. London's cabbies are the best trained in Europe – every one of them knows the shortest route between any two points in the capital, and won't rip you off by taking another route. **Minicabs** are less reliable than black cabs, as their drivers are private individuals rather than trained professionals; however, they are often considerably cheaper, so you might want to take one back from your late-night club. There are hundreds of minicab firms in the phone book, but the best way to pick one is to take the advice of the place you're at, unless you want to be certain of a woman driver, in which case call Ladycabs (☎0171/254 3501). Although nearly all minicabs are metered, it's best to ask the fare beforehand.

Accommodation

London is a very expensive city, and lower-cost **accommodation** in central London tends to be poor quality. However, the sheer size of the place means that there is little chance of failing to find a room, even in midsummer, and the underground network makes accommodation outside the centre a feasible option. The capital also has plenty of **hostel** space, both in YHA properties and student halls.

We've given phone numbers for all our listed accommodation, but if you fail to find something you could always pay someone else to do the phoning round for you: all the LTB offices listed on p.147 operate a **room booking service**, for which they charge £5, and take the first day of the room fee in advance. Credit card holders can also book through the LTB by phone (Mon–Fri 9.30am–5.30pm ☎0171/932 2020).

Hotels and B&Bs

You should phone **hotels** as far in advance as you can if you want to stay within a couple of tube stops of the West End during high season; expect to pay not much less than £40 for an unexceptional double room without a private bathroom. If travelling with two or more companions, it's always worth asking the price of the family rooms, which generally sleep four and can save you a few pounds.

The best value of the central accommodation areas is **Bloomsbury** – an area which radiates out from the British Museum and the nearby B&B-filled Gower St, and is less than ten minutes' walk from Oxford Street and Covent Garden. West of the city centre, **Paddington** is a less attractive zone, though it does border Hyde Park and, at its western edges, runs into the vibrant Notting Hill area. For cheap places in this area, check out

Norfolk Square and Sussex Gardens. Slightly further from the city's main sights, but the area most favoured by budget travellers, is the network of streets around **Earl's Court** tube, which are packed with cheap, backpacker-orientated establishments – around here, head first for Penywern and Trebovir roads. The streets around **Victoria Station** also harbour dozens of inexpensive B&Bs – notably along Belgrave Rd and Ebury St – though the area itself lacks the liveliness of Earl's Court and tends to go dead after the offices shut for the night.

BLOOMSBURY

Arran House Hotel, 77–79 Gower St, WC1 (☎0171/636 2186). Bright, well-kept B&B with TV lounge, library, laundry and garden. Goodge St tube. ⑥.

Avalon Hotel, 46 Cartwright Gardens, WC1 (☎0171/387 2366). Situated in a pleasant Georgian crescent – all rooms have TV, some en suite. Euston or Russell Square tube. ⑥.

Hotel Cavendish, 73 Gower St, WC1 (☎0171/636 9079). Clean, tastefully decorated guest house, one of the best on Gower St. Goodge St tube. ⑤.

Cosmo-Bedford House Hotel, 27 Bloomsbury Square, WC1 (☎0171/636 4661). Centrally located budget-conscious hotel, close to the British Museum. Holborn tube. ⑥.

Garth Hotel, 69 Gower St, WC1 (☎0171/636 5761). Good-value, very friendly establishment. Japanese breakfast an option. Tottenham Court Rd or Goodge St tube. ⑤.

Jesmond Dene Hotel, 27 Argyle St, WC1 (☎0171/837 4654). Cheap, hospitable B&B in an otherwise seedy area, where most hotels cater for those on welfare. King's Cross tube. ⑤.

Ridgemount Hotel, 65–67 Gower St, WC1 (☎0171/636 1141). Another good budget B&B, with garden and free hot drinks machine. Goodge St tube. ⑤.

Museum Inn, 27 Montague St, WC1 (☎0171/580 5360). Small backpacker hostel right opposite the British Museum with the usual friendly young crowd. Russell Square or Holborn tube. ③.

PADDINGTON

Garden Court Hotel, 30–31 Kensington Garden Square, W2 (☎0171/229 2553). Presentable, family-run hotel close to Portobello Market. Paddington tube. ⑥.

Hyde Park House, 48 St Petersburgh Place, W2 (☎0171/229 9652). Small, popular B&B in a pleasant street. Shared facilities. Queensway tube. ⑤.

Leinster Inn, 7–12 Leinster Square, W2 (☎0171/229 9641). Huge, noisy backpacker hostel close to the lively Notting Hill area, with a variety of rooms from singles to shared eight-bed dorms and various facilities including a canteen, all-night bar and Internet access. Notting Hill Gate or Bayswater tube. ③.

Quest Hotel, 45 Queensborough Terrace, W2 (☎0171/229 7782). Small, friendly backpacker place just north of Hyde Park, with the standard wacky paintwork and loud music. Bayswater or Queensway tube. ③.

The Porchester Hotel, 33 Princes Square, W2 (☎0171/221 2101). Friendly but aseptic budget hotel on a quiet square just off lively Queensway, with an excellent-value restaurant and bar. Bayswater or Queensway tube. Dorms ④, doubles ⑥.

St David's Hotel, 16 Norfolk Square, W2 (☎0171/723 3856). Pleasant, well-appointed B&B in a quiet, attractive square. Serves big breakfasts. Paddington tube. ⑥.

Sass House, 10–11 Craven Terrace, W2 (☎0171/262 2325). Location near Hyde Park in a nice street – all rooms are en suite with breakfast. Lancaster Gate or Paddington tube. ⑤.

EARL'S COURT

Boka Hotel, 33–35 Eardley Crescent, SW5 (☎0171/373 2844). B&B popular with Aussies and South Africans. Earl's Court tube. ④.

Manor Hotel, 23 Nevern Place, SW5 (☎0171/370 6018). Reasonably priced rooms just off Earl's Court Rd. Earl's Court tube. ⑤.

Merlyn Court Hotel, 2 Barkston Gardens, SW5 (☎0171/370 1640). Plain but serviceable, mostly en-suite rooms in quiet square off Earl's Court Rd. Earl's Court tube. ⑤.

Philbeach Hotel, 30–31 Philbeach Gardens, SW5 (☎0171/373 1244). Friendly gay hotel, with nice restaurant. Earl's Court tube. ⑥.

Windsor House, 12 Penywern Rd, SW5 (☎0171/373 9087). Simple rooms in a large old Victorian terrace; use of garden and kitchen facilities. Earl's Court tube. ④.

York House Hotel, 28 Philbeach Gardens, SW5 (☎0171/373 7519). Roomy B&B that does large discounts for weekly stays. Earl's Court tube. ⑤.

VICTORIA

Brindle House Hotel, 1 Warwick Place North, SW1 (☎0171/828 0057). Small, quiet B&B off Warwick Way; all rooms have a TV. Victoria tube. ⑤.

Cherry Court Hotel, 23 Hugh St, SW1 (☎0171/828 2840). Run-down, small but cheap rooms with TVs. Victoria tube. ④.

Easton Hotel, 36–40 Belgrave Rd, SW1 (☎0171/834 5938). Past its prime, but one of the biggest B&Bs in the Victoria area, so worth trying in peak season. Victoria tube. ④.

Leicester Hotel, 18–24 Belgrave Rd, SW1 (☎0171/233 6636). Good B&B between the coach and train stations, popular with young travellers. Victoria tube. ④.

Luna & Simone Hotel, 47 Belgrave Rd, SW1 (☎0171/834 5897). Inexpensive B&B that needs to be booked at least one month ahead in summer. Victoria tube. ⑤.

Oxford House Hotel, 92–94 Cambridge St, SW1 (☎0171/834 6467). Very friendly B&B with marvellous food, so booking essential. Victoria tube. ⑤.

Stanley House, 19–21 Belgrave Rd, SW1 (☎0171/834 5042). Large, friendly and well-appointed B&B offering a ten-percent discount for weekly stays; all rooms have TV. Victoria tube. ⑥.

Hostels and camping

Most YHA **hostels** in London are a touch less basic and significantly more expensive than those in the provinces, but in summer you'll have to arrive as early as possible to stand a chance of getting a room, and you're usually limited to a maximum stay of four consecutive nights. Calling the YHA's Central Bookings line (☎0171/373 3400) can save time and shoe leather. Some accommodation in **student halls of residence** is available outside term time, although much of it is hardly cheaper than B&Bs. Colleges with cheaper alternatives include the London School of Economics (☎0171/955 7531), which has centrally located singles from around £18, and King's College (☎0171/928 3777), which has single rooms for £25 in Westminster and from £13 in outlying, but pleasant Hampstead. London's **campsites** are all out on the perimeters of the city, offering pitches for around £4, plus a fee of around £3 per person per night (reductions for children and for low season).

YHA HOSTELS

City of London, 36 Carter Lane, EC4 (☎0171/236 4965). In the City – a desolate area at night – and with crowded dorms or private rooms. St Paul's or Blackfriars tube. ⑤.

Earl's Court, 38 Bolton Gardens, SW5 (☎0171/373 7083). Comfortable and fairly capacious. Earl's Court tube. ④.

Hampstead Heath, 4 Wellgarth Rd, NW11 (☎0181/458 9054). One of the biggest and best appointed, near the wilds of Hampstead Heath. Golders Green tube. ④.

Holland House, Holland Walk, W8 (☎0171/937 0748). Nicely situated and fairly convenient for the centre, with large dorms. Holland Park or High St Kensington tube. ④.

Oxford St, 14 Noel St, W1 (☎0171/734 1618). In the heart of the West End, but with only 75 beds, it fills up very fast. Oxford Circus or Tottenham Court Rd tube. ④.

Rotherhithe, Island Yard, Salter Rd, SE16 (☎0171/232 2114). Inconveniently sited on the East London tube line, but a viable option in peak season, with 320 beds available. Rotherhithe tube or bus #P11 from Waterloo. ⑤.

St Pancras International, 79 Euston Road, NW1 (☎0171/388 9998). Sparkling new hostel in a good situation opposite St Pancras and within walking distance of lively Camden, with small dorms and twins. King's Cross tube. ⑤.

CAMPSITES

Crystal Palace, Crystal Palace Parade, SE19 (☎0181/778 7155). All-year site, maximum one-week stay in summer, two weeks in winter. Mainline train from London Bridge to Crystal Palace.

Hackney Camping, Millfields Rd, Hackney Marshes, E5 (☎0181/985 7656). Big, cheap site by a canal, but very inconvenient, way over in the east of the city. Bus #38 from Victoria to Hackney Central, then walk down Millfields Rd. Open June–Aug.

Tent City Summer Tourist Hostel, Old Oak Common Lane, East Acton, W3 (☎0181/743 5708). The cheapest beds in London: dorm accommodation in fourteen large tents (single sex and mixed) for £6 per night, or you can pitch your own tent for the same price. Open June to mid-Sept. East Acton tube.

The City

London is not a city with a single centre. The money markets are over in the eastern part of the inner core, in the district known, confusingly for first-time visitors, as the City of London. The heaviest consumer spending is done around Oxford Street away to the west, while the hubs of political and royal London – Parliament and Buckingham Palace – are close to neither. But the area that feels like the fulcrum is the **West End**, lying between these points and defined roughly by the neighbouring spaces of Piccadilly Circus, Leicester Square and Trafalgar Square. **Leicester Square** is liveliest at night, with people on their way to its big-screen cinemas or to the clubs and restaurants of multi-ethnic Soho immediately to the north. **Piccadilly Circus** is hectic throughout the day, its tarmac choked with cars and buses, its facades lurid with colossal neon advertisements. There's always a gang of wide-eyed sight-seers and more desperate cases around the statue popularly referred to as Eros, although it began life as an Angel of Christian Charity, built in honour of Victorian philanthropist Lord Shaftesbury. The street named after him curves away to the east, while to the north runs the elegant curve of Regent Street.

Trafalgar Square and the National Gallery

The huge traffic island of **Trafalgar Square** is dominated by Nelson's Column, a vast pillar surmounted by a statue of Admiral Horatio Nelson, who died in the defeat of the French navy at the Battle of Trafalgar in 1805. Four lions designed by Victorian painter Edwin Landseer guard the column's base, and two adjacent fountains provide a magnet for overheating sight-seers during the summer. At the south of the square, a small statue of Charles I marks the original site of **Charing Cross**, from which all distances from the capital are measured. The place derives its name from the last of twelve crosses erected by Edward I to mark the funeral procession of his wife Eleanor; a nineteenth-century replica now stands in the forecourt of Charing Cross train station, just up the Strand to the east.

The bulk of the **National Gallery** (Mon–Sat 10am–6pm, Wed until 8pm, Sun noon–6pm; free except for special exhibitions), one of the world's great art collections, extends across the north side of the square. A quick tally of the National's Italian masterpieces includes works by Piero della Francesca, Raphael, Botticelli, Uccello, Michelangelo, Caravaggio, Titian, Veronese and Mantegna. From Spain there are dazzling pieces by Velázquez (including the *Rokeby Venus*), El Greco and Goya. From the Low Countries there's Memlinck, van Eyck (the *Arnolfini Marriage*), van der Weyden and Rubens, and some of Rembrandt's most searching portraits. Poussin, Lorrain, Watteau and the only David paintings in the country are the earlier highlights of a French contingent that comes right to the present century with Seurat, Cézanne and Monet.

If you want to take the art chronologically, you should start in the new Sainsbury Wing, a timidly postmodern building opened in 1991. The compactness of the rooms makes it impossible to get a clear view of many of the pictures at peak times (Sunday afternoon is often hellish), and there's nearly always a snarl-up created by people queuing to pay reverence to the Leonardo cartoon, installed in a bullet-proof chapel behind his *Virgin of the Rocks*. High Renaissance and later works are displayed in the main building – don't overlook the basement galleries, which are stacked with excellent pictures.

The western side of Trafalgar Square is occupied by St Martin-in-the-Fields, James Gibbs' stately early eighteenth-century church, which combines classical columns and pediment with a distinctly un-classical spire. Opposite here, around the side of the National Gallery in St Martin's Place, is the **National Portrait Gallery** (Mon–Sat 10am–6pm, Sun noon–6pm; free), founded in 1856 to house uplifting depictions of the good and the great. Despite some fine pieces such as Hans Holbein's larger-than-life drawing of Henry VIII, many of the portraits are of less intrinsic interest than their subjects. The collection is arranged with the Tudors on the top floor, eminent Victorians grouped by profession in the middle, and twentieth-century pop stars, sports personalities, politicians and royalty at the bottom. From time to time a part of the building is given over to a special exhibition – the photography shows are often excellent.

From Whitehall to Westminster Abbey

Trafalgar Square is joined to Parliament Square by the broad sweep of **Whitehall**, the site of the main concentration of government buildings and civil service offices. The original Whitehall was a palace built for King Henry VIII and subsequently extended, but little survived a fire of 1698. The only remnant is the supremely elegant **Banqueting House** (Mon–Sat 10am–5pm, sometimes closed for functions; £3.50), built by Inigo Jones for James I in the Palladian style and decorated with vast ceiling paintings by Rubens, glorifying the Stuart dynasty. They were commissioned by James' son Charles I – who in 1649 stepped onto the executioner's scaffold from one of the building's front windows.

Current monarchical tradition is displayed at the **Horse Guards** building on the opposite side of the road. Mounted sentries of the Queen's Life Guard, in ceremonial uniform, are posted daily here from 10am to 4pm, after which they are replaced by horseless colleagues. Try to time your visit to coincide with the changing of the guard (Mon–Sat 11am, Sun 10am), when a squad of mounted troops in full livery arrives from the Parade Ground to the rear.

Further down this west side of Whitehall is the most famous street in the city, **Downing Street**. Number 10 has been the residence of the Prime Minister since the house was presented to Sir Robert Walpole by King George II in 1732. Nowadays you can only gaze at the doorway from afar, as public access has been denied since Margaret Thatcher ordered a pair of wrought-iron gates to be installed at the junction with Whitehall. During the Blitz the government was forced to vacate Downing Street in favour of a bunker in King Charles Street, which separates the Home Office from the Foreign Office. The restored **Cabinet War Rooms** (daily 10am–6pm; £4.60) now provide a glimpse of the claustrophobic suites from which Churchill directed wartime operations.

THE HOUSES OF PARLIAMENT

The **Houses of Parliament** (or Palace of Westminster, to give it its proper title) stand on the site of the palace that was the seat of the English kings for five centuries before Henry VIII moved the court to Whitehall. Following Henry's death, the House of Commons, previously ensconced in the chapterhouse of Westminster Abbey, moved into the Palace – a jumble of buildings which burned down in 1834. Save for a few pieces of the original structure buried deep inside the current edifice, what one sees today is entirely nineteenth-century. The architect Charles Barry was told to construct something which expressed national greatness through the use of Gothic or Elizabethan styles. The resulting orgy of pinnacles and tracery is restrained by the building's blocky symmetry. Although the angular Victoria Tower at the south end is higher, the more ornate clock tower to the north is more famous; "Big Ben", the name applied to this tower, is in fact the name of its main bell.

The Victorian love of pseudo-Gothic detail shines through in the warren of committee rooms and offices, which were largely the responsibility of Barry's assistant on the project, Augustus Pugin, who was to become the leading ideologue of the Gothic revival. Both the House of Commons and the House of Lords have public galleries, the public being let in from about 2.30pm Monday to Thursday and 9.30am on Wednesdays and Fridays. Queues are long, numbers restricted and security procedures lengthy. To avoid the crush, simply turn up after 6pm, when most tourists have gone home (parliament sits until 10pm). However, to join a guided tour or get to see Prime Minister's Question Time (Weds only 3–3.30pm) in the Commons – the livelier house – you must obtain tickets from your local MP or embassy in London several weeks in advance. Note that recesses occur at Christmas, Easter, and from August to mid-October. The public entrance leads into one of the few remaining parts of the original Palace of Westminster, the eleventh-century **Westminster Hall**, a cavernous space with a magnificent fourteenth-century oak-beamed roof.

WESTMINSTER ABBEY

Westminster Abbey (Mon–Fri 9am–4.45pm, Sat 9am–2.45pm, last admission one hour before closing; Royal chapels £5; Chapter House, daily 10am–5.30pm, Undercroft Museum & Pyx Chamber daily 10.30am–4pm; combined ticket £2.50), on the western side of Parliament Square, was founded in the eighth century, then rebuilt by the eleventh-century monarch

Edward the Confessor and by Henry III in the thirteenth. From William the Conqueror onwards, the Abbey has been the venue for all but two coronations and the site of all royal burials for the half-millennium between Henry III and George II – and, famously, the location of the memorial service for Diana, Princess of Wales, following her death in Paris in the summer of 1997. Many of the nation's most famous citizens are honoured here, too, and the interior is crowded with monuments, reliefs and statuary. The north transept, traditionally reserved for statesmen, includes monuments to the nineteenth-century prime ministers Peel, Palmerston and Gladstone; Poet's Corner, in the south transept, contains the graves or memorials of Geoffrey Chaucer, Lord Tennyson, T.S. Eliot and many others. Behind the high altar is the chapel of Edward the Confessor, canonized in the twelfth century and still adored by pilgrims for his powers of healing. In front of Edward's tomb is the Coronation Chair, an oak monstrosity dating from around 1300. The latter used to squat above the Stone of Scone – the Scottish coronation stone pilfered by Edward I in 1297, but returned to the Scots by John Major in 1996. Many of the nearby royal tombs are surmounted by superb effigies; one of the finest is the black marble sarcophagus of Henry VII and his spouse, housed at the rear of the abbey below an elaborate fan-vaulted ceiling of Henry VII's chapel. The ambulatory is the dual resting place of his granddaughters, Queen Elizabeth I and Queen Mary.

Doors on the south side of the nave lead to the **Great Cloister** (10am–6pm; free), at the eastern end of which are entrances to the chapterhouse, retaining its thirteenth-century paving stones; the chamber of the pyx – the sacristy of Edward the Confessor's church and subsequently the royal treasury; and the Norman undercroft, now housing the Abbey museum, in which several generations of royal death masks are displayed.

The Tate Gallery

From Parliament Square the unattractive Millbank runs south along the river towards the **Tate Gallery** (daily 10am–5.50pm; free, except for temporary exhibitions), with both the national collection of British art from the sixteenth century onwards and an international display of modern art. With the exception of the roomful of glutinous Pre-Raphaelites, the quintessentially English landscapes of John Constable, and the Turner paintings crammed into the adjoining postmodern Clore Gallery, the native art is not what draws the crowds. Though underfunded by the standards of the world's top galleries, the Tate has a massive stock of twentieth-century pieces, and the modern collection is rehung every nine months to ensure a decent airing for the whole range. Thus it's difficult to predict what will be on display, but certain names survive every rearrangement: Picasso, Matisse, Degas, and Pollock, to select just a few. Comprehensive assemblies of Constructivism, Surrealism, Minimal Art, Pop Art, Dada and Expressionism (both Abstract and Germanic) are regular attractions, and there's nearly always a temporary exhibition in progress – ranging from modest one-artist shows to surveys of entire movements. As with the National Gallery, weekends can be a real crush, especially Sunday afternoon, a favourite slot with the coach parties.

In May 2000, this will become the Tate Gallery of British Art, with British art from 1500 onwards. There will be new gallery space for major artists such as Hogarth, Blake, Constable and Spencer, more contemporary art, and a vigorous programme of thematic displays and important temporary exhibitions. The Tate Gallery of Modern Art will open in May 2000 at Bankside Power Station on the South Bank, (see p.159).

The Mall

The southwestern exit of Trafalgar Square is marked by the imposing Admiralty Arch, built in 1910 as the eastern half of a memorial to Queen Victoria; the rest is half a mile away down the tree-lined avenue of **The Mall** in the shape of the statue of Victory in front of Buckingham Palace. Just beyond Admiralty Arch, ranged above the Mall, is Carlton House Terrace, a stretch of imposing Regency town houses built by John Nash. Part of Nash's building is now inhabited by the Institute of Contemporary Arts, or **ICA** (Mon noon–11pm, Tues–Sat noon–1am, Sun noon–10.30pm; galleries only daily noon–7.30pm, Fri until 9pm; day pass Mon–Fri £1.50, Sat & Sun £2.50), the city's main forum for the avant-garde, with frequently changing exhibitions, films and performances.

Nash was also responsible for landscaping **St James's Park**, which stretches south of the Mall, its lake providing an inner-city reserve for wildfowl and a recreation area for the employees of Whitehall. Continuing towards Buckingham Palace, the Mall passes the back of St James's Palace, a hospital until bon viveur Henry VIII acquired it and began the construction of yet another palace. Ambassadors to the UK are still officially known as Ambassador to the Court of St James, although the court itself has since moved down the road. The palace – now Prince Charles' residence – is closed to visitors, as is Clarence House – residence of the Queen Mother – at the end of the Mall.

Buckingham Palace has served as the monarch's permanent residence since the accession of Queen Victoria, and the building's exterior, remodelled in 1913, is as bland as it's possible to be. The palace has, however, been open to the public since 1993 for two months of the year (daily Aug & Sept 9.30am–4pm; £9.50); at other times there's not much to do save to await the **Changing of the Guard**, when mounted troops ride down the Mall from St James' Palace (April–July daily 11.30am; alternate days Aug–March; no band if it rains). Around the south side on Buckingham Gate is the **Queen's Picture Gallery** (daily 9.30am–4pm; £4), a rotating selection of paintings taken from the rich royal collections, which include Reynolds, Gainsborough, Rubens, Rembrandt and masses of Canaletto.

Hyde Park and beyond

Following Constitution Hill along the north side of Buckingham Palace brings you to **Hyde Park Corner**, where a Triumphal Arch celebrates Wellington's victory at Waterloo in 1815. Wellington, mounted on his favourite horse, stands below, facing his former residence, Apsley House, on the northern corner of Piccadilly. Known during the Iron Duke's lifetime as "Number One, London", the house is now a **Wellington Museum** (Tues–Sun 11am–5pm; £4.50), which, as well as Wellington's effects, features a curious nude statue of the vanquished Napoleon, sculpted by Italian Neoclassicist Canova. At the northeastern extremity of the park is **Marble Arch**, built by Nash in imitation of the arch of Constantine in Rome, and shifted here from in front of Buckingham Palace in 1851. This corner of the park is dominated by **Speaker's Corner**, a Sunday forum for soap-box orators since 1866, when riots persuaded the government to create this island of unfettered speech. Nowadays it's a place to go and enjoy a little theatre, both from the cranks who expound their views and from the often more inventive hecklers. In the middle of the park is the **Serpentine** lake, with a popular lido towards its centre; the nearby **Serpentine Gallery** (daily 10am–6pm; free) hosts contemporary art exhibitions. To the west the park merges into Kensington Gardens, leading up to **Kensington Palace** (April–Sept daily 10am–5pm, Oct–March Wed–Sun 10am–4pm; £8.50), Diana's London residence following her separation from Prince Charles; the gardens to the fore of the Palace were buried under truck-loads of flowers in September 1997, sent by mourners after the Princess's death. The rooms you are permitted to see (by guided tour only) are a series of late eighteenth- and early nineteenth-century state apartments, with a display of court costume.

A short walk north from Kensington Palace takes you into the Notting Hill district, worth visiting on August Bank Holiday weekend for the riotous **Notting Hill Carnival**, and on any Saturday of the year for the **Portobello Road market**, where hundreds of dealers sell lorryloads of antiques and junk.

The Kensington museums

At the southern end of Kensington Gardens is the **Albert Memorial**, an over-decorated Gothic canopy covering a statue of Queen Victoria's much-mourned consort, who died in 1861, which has recently been stunningly regilded after being painted black during the Blitz; he's also the dedicatee of the Royal Albert Hall, home of the famous "Proms", across the road, which was completed in 1871 on the model of the Pantheon in Rome. To the east of the Albert Hall, Exhibition Road heads south to South Kensington and London's richest concentration of museums. The biggest museum is the **Victoria and Albert** (Mon noon–5.45pm, Tues–Sun 10am–5.45pm; £5), containing the world's finest collection of decorative arts. All historic periods and civilizations are represented in the V&A's eleven-kilometre maze of halls and corridors, with especially strong collections of Byzantine and medieval reliquaries, religious sculpture and other devotional items. The Raphael cartoons, a series of designs for tapestries now in the Vatican, are another highlight, while the Nehru Gallery holds one of the world's biggest assemblies of Indian sculpture. The museum's Cast Rooms are worth an afternoon in themselves, with their full-scale replicas of Michelangelo's *David*, Trajan's Column and scores of other sculptural masterpieces. In addition, the V&A's temporary shows are among the best to be seen in Britain.

The **Natural History Museum**, across the way on Cromwell Rd (Mon–Sat 10am–5.50pm, Sun 11am–5.50pm; £6, free after 4.30pm Mon–Fri, after 5pm Sat & Sun), usually enthrals the kids, with its massive-jawed skeletons and models of Tyrannosaurus Rex and even an animated tableau of the more grisly of its prehistoric colleagues. Inventive displays on human biology and ecology are pitched at a different audience, though there are plenty of buttons to press when the concentration flags. The same ticket gets you into the neighbouring Earth Galleries, partially refurbished with a Kobe earthquake simulator and other spectacular new galleries explaining volcanic eruptions, tectonic plates and other acts of God. Understandably, the **Science Museum** in Exhibition Rd (daily 10am–6pm; £6.50, free after 4.30pm) gives a lot of space to British innovation in the era of the Industrial Revolution, featuring eighteenth-century steam engines, George Stephenson's 1813 *Puffing Billy*, and the achievements of the likes of Humphrey Davy, Michael Faraday and Isambard Kingdom Brunel. It's far from being a chauvinistic show, however, and the museum offers some of the most stimulating interactive displays in London, as it roams through every conceivable area of experimental science, including information technology, space travel and medicine.

Covent Garden and the British Museum

To the northeast of Trafalgar Square lies the area of **Covent Garden**, whose centrepiece is the splendid nineteenth-century market hall which housed London's principal fruit and vegetable market until the 1970s. The structure now shelters a gaggle of tasteful shops and arty stalls – a microcosm of this swish district as a whole. The surrounding piazza, laid out by Inigo Jones in the seventeenth century and dominated on the western side by Jones' classical St Paul's Church, is a semi-institutionalized venue for buskers and more ambitious street performers.

From here it's a short walk northwards up fashionable Neal Street to the district of Bloomsbury, home to the **British Museum** on Great Russell St (Mon–Sat 10am–5pm, Sun noon–6pm; free). As with the V&A, the British Museum is too big to be seen in one go – the best advice is to check the floor plans as you go in, and make for the two or three displays that interest you most. Whichever sections you pick, the exhibits will include some breathtaking items. Archeological treasures of the ancient world dominate the ground floor, where the heaviest flow of visitors winds towards the Elgin Marbles from the Parthenon. A whole room is devoted to these glorious sculptures, the main series of which probably depicts scenes from a procession in honour of the goddess Athena.

A wander through the surrounding areas will take you past Roman mosaics and the exquisite Portland Vase; amazing Assyrian finds, including huge winged beasts with human heads from a royal palace near Nineveh; and a hoard of Egyptian antiquities that features the Rosetta Stone, whose trilingual inscription enabled scholars to decode hieroglyphs for the first time. A huge Egyptian mummy collection is located on the first floor, where a couple of preserved corpses come in for some ghoulish scrutiny – a sand-desiccated Egyptian and the 2000-year-old Lindow Man, preserved in Cheshire bog after his sacrificial death. On the same floor, various treasure troves display some extraordinary craftwork; two of the most remarkable were found in East Anglia – Saxon pieces from Sutton Hoo, and the Roman silverwork known as the Mildenhall Treasure.

The building once housed the **British Library**, centred around the famous circular **Reading Room**, where Karl Marx once sat and studied. In September 2000, the long-hidden central courtyard housing the ethnographic collection, the African galleries and virtual reality displays, will be reopened under a giant glass roof. The library has now been transferred to an acclaimed new building situated next to St Pancras Station on Euston Rd.

North of the centre

The grid of streets separating Oxford Street from Regent's Park to the north holds little of interest, save for a cluster of sights along the Marylebone Road, near Baker St tube station.

Madame Tussauds (daily 9.30am–5.30pm; £9.75, joint ticket with Planetarium £12) has been renowned for its wax approximations of the rich and famous ever since the good lady arrived in London in 1802, bearing sculpted heads of the guillotined from revolutionary France. The choice of celebrities on display fluctuates according to fashion, but permanent exhibits include the Chamber of Horrors, which panders to a fascination with mass murderers. The next-door **London Planetarium** (same times as Madame Tussauds; shows every 40min; £5.85) features illuminated displays of the heavens, projected onto the inner surface of a vast dome.

The ring around **Regent's Park** is flanked by Nash's Regency terraces, some of the most elegant residential buildings in London. At the northern end of the park is **London Zoo** (daily 10am–4/5.30pm; £8.50), which, despite holding one of the world's longest-established and most varied collections of animals, continues to struggle to make ends meet.

Just five minutes' walk from the north side of the park lies trendy **Camden Town**, whose vast **weekend market** – centred on Camden Lock, beside the canal – is now less of a genuine street mart than a tourist-angled performance. The number of stalls multiplies with each month, even if the range of stuff on offer doesn't – it's mostly throwaway clothes and jewellery, and ranks of bootleg tapes.

Beyond here, several pleasant residential neighbourhoods deserve exploration. The affluent suburb of **Hampstead** retains a small-town atmosphere and excellent walking opportunities on Hampstead Heath, one of the few wild areas left within reach of central London. One major attraction east of Hampstead is **Highgate Cemetery**, ranged on both sides of Swains Lane (Highgate or Archway tube, or bus #C2 to Parliament Hill Fields). Opened in 1838 as a private venture, Highgate was the preferred resting place of wealthy Victorian families and the cemetery is full of monuments to their vanity; the older, more atmospheric western cemetery can only be seen on a guided tour (March–Nov Mon–Fri noon, 2pm & 3/4pm, Sat & Sun hourly 11am–3/4pm; Dec–Feb Sat & Sun only 11am–3pm; £3), whilst the eastern side, whose most famous denizen is Karl Marx, is open for a general wander (Mon–Fri 10am–4/5pm, Sat & Sun 11am–4/5pm).

The City of London

Once the fortified heart of the capital, the **City of London** is now its financial district. Few people actually live here, making it a desolate place after nightfall. The area also suffered more in the Blitz than anywhere bar the East End, and soulless postwar buildings further detract from its appeal. An earlier conflagration, the 1666 Great Fire of London, led to an era of much more dignified rebuilding and produced the area's finest structure, **St Paul's Cathedral** (Mon–Sat 8.30am–4pm; £4; galleries 9.30am–4pm; £3.50, combined ticket £6) – just one of over fifty church commissions Sir Christopher Wren received in the wake of the blaze. His Baroque design is fronted by a double-storey colonnaded portico flanked by towers, but the most distinctive feature is the dome, second in size only to St Peter's in Rome, and still a dominating presence on the London skyline. In fact it's a triple dome, its interior cupola separated from the wooden, lead-covered outer skin by a funnel-shaped brick structure. The interior of the church is filled with funerary monuments, predominantly military figures and obscure statesmen – the only memorial to have survived from the original cathedral is an effigy of the poet John Donne, once Dean of St Paul's, in the south aisle of the choir.

A staircase in the south transept leads up to a series of galleries in the dome. The internal **Whispering Gallery** is the first, so called because of its acoustic properties – words whispered to the wall on one side of the gallery are distinctly audible on the other. The broad exterior Stone Gallery and the uppermost Golden Gallery both offer good panoramas of the city. Close to the entrance to the galleries is the staircase to the **Crypt**, the resting place of Wren himself; his son composed the inscription that graces his tomb – *lector, si monumentum requiris, circumspice* (reader, if you seek his monument, look around). The architect is joined by Turner, Reynolds and other artists, but the most imposing sarcophagi are the twin black monstrosities occupied by the Duke of Wellington and Lord Nelson.

A few minutes north of St Paul's is the **Barbican**, a topnotch residential complex that incorporates an arts centre that was planned as London's answer to the Pompidou Centre, but remains largely unloved. However, it does house a cinema as well as a theatre, and holds various jazz and classical concerts on its many levels. The **Museum of London** (Tues–Sat 10am–5.50pm, Sun noon–5.50pm; £5, free after 4.30pm) occupies its southwestern corner, displaying a wealth of artefacts from Roman London and offering an educative trot through subsequent epochs; the models of London in previous centuries are particularly interesting.

The **Tower of London** (Mon–Sat 9am–6pm, Sun 10am–6pm, last admission 5pm; £9.50) marks the eastern extent of the old city. It's usually thought of as a place of imprisonment and death, but has variously been used as an armoury, royal residence and repository of the Crown's treasure. The Tower's oldest feature is the central **White Tower**, built by William the Conqueror, although the ubiquitous Christopher Wren adorned each corner with cupolas. The inner wall, with its numerous towers, was built in the time of Henry III, and a further line of fortifications was added by Edward I, so much of what's visible today was already in place by the end of the thirteenth century. Once inside, you can explore the complex on your own, although free tours of the Tower are given by Yeomen of the Guard – better known as "Beefeaters", ex-servicemen in Tudor costume – every half-hour. The White Tower itself holds part of the **Royal Armouries** collection (the rest resides in Leeds), and, on the second floor, the Norman Chapel of St John, London's oldest church. Surrounding the White Tower is the Tower Green, where the executions took place of those traitors lucky enough to be spared the public executions on nearby Tower Hill. A stone marks the spot where Lady Jane Grey, Anne Boleyn, Catherine Howard and four others met their end. The Waterloo Barracks contain the **Crown Jewels**, the majority of which postdate the period of the Commonwealth (1649–60), when most were melted down. The three largest cut diamonds in the world are on display here; the most famous of them, the Koh-i-noor, is set into a crown made for the Queen Mother in 1937. On the south side of the complex, the **Bloody Tower** contains the room thought to have seen the murder of the "Princes in the Tower", Edward V and his brother, as well as the quarters where Walter Raleigh spent thirteen years of captivity writing his *History of the World*. Below lies **Traitor's Gate**, through which prisoners were delivered after being ferried down the Thames from the courts of justice at Westminster.

Views from the Tower are dominated by the twin towers of **Tower Bridge**, built in the 1880s and characterized by a roadway which is raised to allow ships access to the upper reaches of the Thames. The main attraction of the guided tour is a wander across the walkways linking the summits of the towers (April–Oct daily 10am–6.30pm; Nov–March 9.30am–6pm; £5.95). Intended for public use when the bridge was first built, the walkways were closed in 1909 due to their popularity with the suicidal and prostitutes.

South of the river: Waterloo to Greenwich

South London is alien territory to many who live and work north of the Thames. However, the south bank of the river has recently been transformed into a delightful walkway beginning at the **London Eye**, a giant (135m) ferris wheel on Jubilee Gardens. The 25-minute ride should provide an unrivalled – if heart-stopping – view over London. On the other side of Hungerford Bridge, with its brand new pedestrian walkways, is the more established **South Bank Centre**. This modern arts complex embraces the Royal National Theatre, the National Film Theatre, Hayward Gallery and a trio of concert halls, the largest of which is the Royal Festival Hall. The Museum of the Moving Image, or **MOMI** (daily 10am–6pm, last admission 5pm; £6.25), provides a history of cinema and television with various interactive displays – an extremely adroit use of a cramped site under Waterloo Bridge. The **Hayward Gallery** (Thurs–Mon 10am–6pm, Tues & Wed 10am–8pm; variable price) hosts prestigious, often contemporary, exhibitions.

The riverfront stretching eastward from the South Bank Centre to **London Bridge** is defined by Bankside power station, an imposing brick building designed by Sir Giles Gilbert Scott, which is currently being transformed into a fourth branch of the **Tate Gallery of Modern Art**. Due to open in May 2000 (times and prices to be announced), the state-of-the-art gallery within the power station's facade should be an ideal showcase for the Tate's marvellous collection. From spring 2000, the pedestrian **Millennium Bridge** will link the gallery with St Paul's Steps in the City.

The Bankside area was once the pleasure quarter of Tudor and Stuart London, beyond the jurisdiction of the city authorities and thus a place in which brothels and other disreputable institutions (notably **theatres** associated with Shakespeare and his contemporaries, such as the Rose, the Swan and the Globe) could flourish. The **Globe** has recently been rebuilt in its original form beside the power station with an accompanying exhibition on Shakespeare and the history of the locality. You can take a guided tour of the theatre (May–Sept Tues–Sun 9am–noon, Mon 9am–5pm; Oct–April daily 10am–5pm; £6) or better still, go to a live performance (summer only; ☎0171/401 9919) in the timber-built thatched arena. Further east, you come to Clink St, home of the **Clink** (daily 10am–6pm; £4), a small museum on the site of a former prison of the same name, detailing the riverside lowlife who often ended up incarcerated there. **Southwark Cathedral** – the finest Gothic church in the capital after Westminster Abbey – stands at the southern end of London Bridge. Inside, the most conspicuous feature is the brightly painted tomb of poet John Gower, a contemporary of Chaucer.

One other national institution located south of the Thames is the **Imperial War Museum** on Lambeth Rd (daily 10am–6pm; £5, free after 4.30pm). Though it does feature galleries of uniforms and weaponry, this is not the celebration of imperialistic bloodletting its name might suggest. The museum houses some incisive examples of war art, and uses a good deal of stagecraft to convey the miseries of combat, with re-creations of World War I trenches and a simulation of bomb-ravaged wartime London.

Greenwich and the Millennium Dome

Eight miles east of central London, **GREENWICH** is steeped in naval history; it is also the site of the Greenwich meridian and the new Millennium Dome. The quickest way to get here is by rail from Charing Cross, or on the Docklands Light Railway from Tower Hill to Cutty Sark, where a pedestrian tunnel leads under the Thames to Greenwich on the other side. Standing in a dry dock next to Greenwich pier is the **Cutty Sark** (Mon–Sat 10am–5/6pm, Sun noon–5/6pm; £3.50), one of the last of the clippers: sail-powered cargo vessels built for speed and used on long-distance routes bringing wool, tea and other produce to London from the far-flung corners of the Empire – until rendered obsolete by the arrival of steam. Next to it is *Gypsy Moth IV*, the vessel used in Sir Francis Chichester's 1965–66 solo circumnavigation of the earth (April–Oct Mon–Fri 10am–1pm & 2–5/6pm, Sat 10am–5/6pm, Sun noon–5/6pm; 50p). Hugging the riverfront to the east is the extraordinary Baroque facade of the **Royal Naval College** (daily 2.30–4.45pm; free), probably Wren's finest work after St Paul's. Across the road is the **National Maritime Museum** (daily 10am–5pm; combined ticket with the Queen's House and the Old Royal Observatory £5), exhibiting model ships, charts and globes, and recently rejuvenated with some inventive new galleries under an enormous glazed roof. The next-door **Queen's House** (same hours as above) is an impressively simple classical box built for Henrietta Maria by Inigo Jones, the first example of domestic Palladian architecture in Britain. From here Greenwich Park stretches up the hill, crowned by the **Old Royal Observatory** (same hours as above), another largely Wren-inspired structure, through which the Greenwich meridian runs. The museum houses a brain-stretching display of timepieces, telescopes and navigational equipment and, if you've lost track of the time, you can always check the Millennium Countdown Clock, positioned on the Meridian Line.

Squatting on reclaimed wasteland two miles further downstream, the **Millennium Dome** is huge in size, price and controversy, and hardly stands large in British affections. It opens on New Year's Day 2000, and will be divided into fourteen themed zones around a central performance area, celebrating and explaining various areas of human experience such as work, play, environment, communication, the body and the mind, through hi-tech displays and effects. Tickets will have to be pre-booked through travel agents and are expected to cost more than £20. Alongside is the so-called Baby Dome, a large-capacity theatre with film and concert facilities. The Dome is best accessed by tube from Waterloo or Charing Cross on the Jubilee line. Scenic, but expensive, boat trips will also link the site to a number of riverside piers including Greenwich, the Tower of London, Charing Cross and the London Eye, and there will be a bus link between the Dome and Greenwich proper.

The western outskirts: Kew to Windsor

Another possible boat trip is upstream to Kew, disembarking for the wonderful **Royal Botanical Gardens** (daily 9.30am–dusk; £5), where over 50,000 species are grown in the plantations and glasshouses of a 300-acre site.

Further upstream, thirteen miles southwest of the centre, you'll find the finest of Tudor palaces, **Hampton Court Palace** (Mon 10.15am–4.30/6pm, Tues–Sun 9.30am–4.30/6pm; £9.25 including maze; mainline trains from Waterloo to Hampton Court). Cardinal Wolsey commissioned this immense house in 1516, then handed it to Henry VIII in a vain attempt to win back his favour. Henry enlarged and improved the palace, but it was William III who made the most radical alterations, hiring Sir Christopher Wren to remodel the buildings. **William and Mary's Apartments** are chock-full of treasures, while the highlight of **Henry VIII's State Apartments** is the **Great Hall** with its astonishing hammerbeam roof. There is plenty more to see in the sixty-acre **grounds** (7am–dusk; free): the Great Vine, grown from a cutting in 1768 and now averaging about seven hundred pounds of black grapes per year; William III's Banqueting House (April–Sept); and the Lower Orangery, a gallery for Mantegna's heroic canvases, *The Triumphs of Caesar*. The famous **maze**, laid out in 1714, lies north of the palace.

Windsor, 21 miles west of central London, is dominated by **Windsor Castle** (daily 10am–4/5.30pm; £10), which began its days as a wooden fortress built by William the Conqueror, with numerous later monarchs having had a hand in its evolution. Some of their work was undone by a huge fire in November 1992, but the magnificent **State Apartments** have reopened after meticulous restoration. Highlights include Van Dyck's triptych of Charles I in the King's Drawing Room; the Queen's Ballroom, dominated by an enormous silver mirror and table, and more Van Dyck paintings; and the vast array of crested helmets and sixteenth-century armour in the Queen's Guard Chamber, which includes an etched gold suit made for Prince Hal. A separate gallery to the left of the main entrance holds exhibitions of the royal art collection – Windsor possesses the world's finest collection of drawings and notebooks by Leonardo da Vinci. A visit to the castle should take in **St George's Chapel** (closed Sun); a glorious fan-vaulted perpendicular structure, ranking with King's College Chapel in Cambridge, it contains the tombs of numerous kings and queens.

Crossing the footbridge at the end of Thames Avenue in Windsor village brings you to **Eton**, where the *raison d'être* is of course **Eton College** (April, July & Aug daily 10.30am–4.30pm; May, June & Sept daily 2–4.30pm; £2.60; guided tours 2.15pm & 3.15pm; £3.80; ring ☎01753/871000 for exact dates), the ultra-exclusive and inexcusably powerful school founded by Henry VI in 1440.

Eating

London is renowned as one of the best cities in the world for **eating**, with new restaurants opening almost daily. Its cosmopolitan population means you can find a restaurant representing almost any nationality or culture you can think of and, despite the city's expensive reputation, there are cheap places to be found, especially around the main tourist drags of **Soho** and **Covent Garden**. Soho has long been one of the city's restaurant focuses, while **Chinatown**, on the other side of Shaftesbury Avenue, offers value-for-money eating right in the centre of town. But to sample the full range of possibilities you need to get out of the West End – to the Indian restaurants of Brick Lane in the East End and Drummond St near Euston, or to the eateries of the trendy neighbourhoods of Camden Town and Islington – a short tube ride away to the north. There are also plenty of spots to pick up a street **snack** or cheap **lunch** – and some of these quick-stop places are good stand-bys for an evening filler. The usual burger and pizza chains are on every corner, and there are any number of sandwich shops, which – if they have seating – may well serve hot meals too, from omelettes and fry-ups to meat-and-two-veg daily specials, normally for around £3.

Snacks and quick meals

Bar Italia, 22 Frith St, W1. A tiny 24hr café that's a Soho institution, serving coffee, sandwiches, pizza, etc until around 4am. Popular with late-night clubbers and those here to watch the Italian league football on the giant screen. Leicester Square tube.

Café in the Crypt, St Martin-in-the-Fields church, Duncannon St, WC2. Good-quality buffet food makes this an ideal spot to fill up at before hitting the West End for the evening, or after a tour of the National Gallery. Charing Cross tube.

Carrie Awaze II, 27 Endell St, W1. Experience a range of weird-and-wonderful sandwiches, curries and salads while the charismatic owner serenades customers on the sitar. Covent Garden tube.

Centrale, 16 Moor St, W1. Tiny Italian greasy spoon that serves up large plates of pasta and omelettes. You may have to wait for – or share – a table. Unlicensed. Leicester Square tube.

Ed's Easy Diner, 12 Moor St, W1. Sit at the counter and consume the best burgers and chips in London in this licensed fifties-theme bar. Leicester Square tube.

Food For Thought, 31 Neal St, WC2. Very small vegetarian restaurant – the food is great and inexpensive, but don't expect to linger. Unlicensed. Covent Garden tube.

Lisboa Patisserie, 57 Goldbourne Rd, W10. Portuguese *pasteleria* just beyond Portobello market; perfect for a coffee after a Saturday spent browsing.

Mildred's, 58 Greek St, W1. Spartan wholefood café with organic drinks and a young, down-to-earth Soho crowd. Tottenham Court Rd tube.

Paprike, 1 Neal's Yard, WC2. Simplest and cheapest of the excellent cafés on atmospheric Neal's Yard, a former hippy hangout in the centre of Covent Garden. Good lunchtime specials and outdoor seating. Covent Garden tube.

Pollo, 20 Old Compton St, W1. The best-value Italian food in town. Always packed, though the queues move quickly. Leicester Square tube.

Stockpot, 18 Old Compton St, W1 (Leicester Square tube); 40 Panton St, SW1 (Piccadilly Circus) and 6 Basil St, SW3 (Knightsbridge). Filling bistro-style grub at rock-bottom prices.

Restaurants

Belgo Centraal, 50 Earlham St, WC2. Hugely popular basement restaurant serving heaps of mussels, fries and beer – the various lunchtime deals are hard to beat. Covent Garden tube.

Café Delancey, 3 Delancey St, NW1. Comfortable Camden brasserie that's good for both a quick coffee and a snack, and reasonably priced full lunches and dinners. Camden Town tube.

Café Pacifico, 5 Langley St, WC2. Rated as the best Mexican restaurant in central London, though that isn't saying much. Fairly quiet during the day, unbelievably noisy in the evening. Good bar. Covent Garden or Leicester Square tube.

Daquise, 20 Thurloe St, SW7. Something of a cult, with its gloomy Eastern Bloc decor, long-suffering staff and heartily utilitarian Polish food. Good place for a quick bite and a shot of vodka after the South Kensington museums. South Kensington tube.

Diwana Bhel Poori House, 121 Drummond St, NW1. Unlicensed, cheap and very tasty south Indian restaurant. Euston tube.

Efes, 80 Great Titchfield St, W1. Vast Turkish kebab restaurant. Reliable, tasty hunks of meat and friendly service. Oxford Circus or Great Portland St tube.

Hong Kong, 6–7 Lisle St, WC2. Has probably the best vegetarian menu in Chinatown, and does excellent *dim sum*. Leicester Square tube.

India Club, 143 Strand, WC2. Faded canteen-style restaurant above the *Strand Continental Hotel* serving homely Indian food that's authentic enough for the discerning staff of the Indian Embassy opposite. Holborn tube.

Jimmy's, 23 Frith St, W1. Basement Greek-Cypriot restaurant that's long been part of the Soho cheap-eating scene. Leicester Square tube.

Joe Allen, 13 Exeter St, WC2. London branch of the well-known American restaurant group, with the familiar chequered tablecloths and bar-room atmosphere. The burgers are excellent, but you have to ask for them – they are not on the menu. Not especially cheap, though, and always very busy. Charing Cross or Covent Garden tube.

Kettner's, 29 Romilly St, W1. Grand old place with high ceilings and a pianist, though actually part of the Pizza Express chain and consequently cheaper than you'd expect from the ambience. Leicester Square tube.

Lorelei, 21 Bateman St, W1. Tiny unlicensed pizza and pasta restaurant offering Soho's cheapest route to a full stomach. Tottenham Court Rd tube.

Nazrul, 130 Brick Lane, El. This is the cheapest and one of the best of the Brick Lane cafés, drawing a student crowd. Unlicensed. Aldgate East tube.

New World, 1 Gerrard Place, W1. Though this vast Chinese restaurant is open in the evenings too, its strength is the lunchtime *dim sum*. Leicester Square tube.

Nontas, 14–16 Camden High St, NW1. Archetypal boisterous Greek taverna, doing all the basics well. Camden Town tube.

Palms, 39 King St, WC2. Covent Garden pasta joint popular with the after-office crowd. Big portions, nononsense service, decent prices. Covent Garden tube.

Pizza Express, 10 Dean St, W1; 30 Coptic St, WC1 (both Tottenham Court Rd tube); and numerous other branches all over London. Easily the best of the pizza chains, doing a good line in thin-crust pizzas at reasonable prices. The Dean St branch houses one of London's leading jazz venues in the basement; the one in Coptic St is located in a former dairy.

Pizzeria Condotti, 4 Mill St, W1. Some of the capital's best pizzas in upscale surroundings – book at lunchtime. Oxford Circus tube.

Poons, 4 Leicester St and 27 Lisle St, both WC2 (both Leicester Square tube). The Lisle St branch, the original, is a tatty café quite unlike its smarter Leicester St offspring, but many think it serves better Chinese food. There are other branches in the Whiteley's complex on Queensway, W2 and at 50 Woburn Place, WC1.

La Quercia d'Oro, 16a Endell St, WC2. Shabby, cheerful, basic Italian eatery, with big rustic portions. Covent Garden tube.

Ravi Shankar, 133 Drummond St, NW1. One of the best of several cheap south Indian restaurants on this street. Euston tube.

Spaghetti House, 30 St Martin's Lane, WC2. Central branch of a London-wide chain that serves excellent pasta meals and more substantial dishes for reasonable prices. Charing Cross tube.

Le Taj, 134 Brick Lane, E1. One of the classiest of the Brick Lane restaurants, with good Bangladeshi specialities. Aldgate East tube.

Tokyo Diner, 2 Newport Place, WC2. Brilliant Japanese diner, serving authentic food at a fraction of the cost of its rivals. Perfect service. Leicester Square tube.

Wagamama, 4 Streatham St, WC1. Vastly popular place with a hi-tech interior, communal bench seating and waiters who take orders on hand-held computers. Filling but questionably authentic meals. Expect to queue. Tottenham Court Rd tube. Branches at 10a Lexington St and 10a Wigmore St.

Yung's, 23 Wardour St, W1. Three-storey Cantonese serving excellent food. Open 5pm–4.30am. Leicester Square tube.

Drinking

Central London is full of **pubs**, and, although you'll find much pleasanter places in the neighbourhoods further out, there are one or two watering holes that retain an element of character. Expect prices to be well above what you might have been used to paying anywhere else in Britain but, on the plus side, pub food in London is often more adventurous than outside the capital.

Albert, 52 Victoria St, SW1. Handily situated pub serving good food, including hearty breakfasts in the upstairs restaurant. St James's Park tube.

Alphabet Bar, 61 Beak St, W1. One of the latest ultra-trendy cocktail bars serving the infamous absinthe. Piccadilly Circus tube.

Argyll Arms, 18 Argyll St, W1. One of the pleasanter places in the immediate orbit of Oxford St, with original glass and wood fittings. Oxford Circus tube.

Blackfriar, 174 Queen Victoria St, EC4. Art Nouveau landmark, handy for the City sights. Closed Sat & Sun. Blackfriars tube.

Camden Head, 2 Camden Walk, N1. A popular Islington local, handy for the Camden Passage antiques trade. Reasonable lunchtime food too. Angel tube.

Cittie of York, 22 High Holborn, WC1. Passable food is served upstairs, but the cellar bar is a more atmospheric place to savour the Sam Smith's beer. Holborn tube.

Coach & Horses, 29 Greek St, W1. Long-standing – and, for once, little-changed – haunt of the ghosts of old Soho, popular with nightclubbers and art students from nearby St Martin's College. Leicester Square tube.

Cutty Sark, Ballast Quay off Lassell St, Greenwich. Ancient riverside pub with a nautical theme, outside tables and fine views of Docklands and the Dome. DLR (tube) to Cutty Sark, then walk downstream.

Dog & Duck, 18 Bateman St, W1. Tiny Soho pub that retains much of its old character and has a loyal clientele. Leicester Square tube.

Flask, 14 Flask Walk, NW3. Convivial Hampstead local, close to the tube station and serving good food and real ale. Hampstead tube.

French House, 49 Dean St W1. Half pints only are served at this tiny, characterful pub, home to the French Resistance during the war and to arty Soho types today. Leicester Square tube.

Fusilier & Firkin, 7–8 Chalk Farm Rd, NW1. Fine Firkin pub opposite Camden Lock market, heaving at weekends. Camden Town tube.

George Inn, 77 Borough High St, SE1. Magnificent seventeenth-century coaching inn, now owned by the National Trust. Borough tube.

Gordon's, Villiers St, WC2. Cellar wine bar that looks like it hasn't seen a lick of paint since World War II. Excellent, varied wine list, decent buffet food and genial atmosphere – a favourite with the neighbourhood's office workers. Open Mon–Fri. Charing Cross or Embankment tube.

Hamilton Hall, Liverpool St Station, EC2. Cavernous, gilded former ballroom of the *Great Eastern Hotel*, packed out with City commuters but a great place nonetheless. Liverpool St tube.

King's Head, 115 Upper St, N1. Busy pub in the heart of Islington that has regular live music and a fringe theatre. For some reason the bar staff quote prices in "old money". Angel tube.

Lamb, 94 Lambs Conduit St, WC1. Pleasant pub with a marvellously well-preserved Victorian interior of mirrors, old wood and "snob" screens. Russell Square tube.

Lamb & Flag, 33 Rose St, WC2. Busy and pleasantly unchanged pub tucked away down a Covent Garden alley, between Garrick St and Floral St. Decent food. Leicester Square tube.

Moon Under Water, 105 Charing Cross Rd, W1. Part of the Weatherspoon's chain and therefore very cheap; housed in a cavernous ex-concert hall. Tottenham Court Rd tube.

Museum Tavern, 49 Great Russell St, WC1. Large and characterful old pub, right opposite the main entrance to the British Museum. Tottenham Court Rd or Russell Square tube.

Old Queen's Head, 44 Essex Rd, N1. Cool minimalist decor and an original Elizabethan fireplace – go early, it gets packed. Angel tube.

Paviour's Arms, Page St, SW1. Untouched Art Deco pub, close to the Tate Gallery. Pimlico tube.

Princess Louise, 208 High Holborn, WC1. Old-fashioned place, with high ceilings, lots of glass and a good range of real ales. Holborn or Chancery Lane tube.

Salisbury, 90 St Martin's Lane, WC2. One of the most beautifully preserved Victorian pubs in the capital. Leicester Square tube.

Star, 6 Belgrave Mews West, SW1. Two-storey pub in one of London's most expensive residential areas. Fine beer and very classy food. Knightsbridge tube.

Warrington, 93 Warrington Crescent, W9. Yet another architectural gem – flamboyant Art Nouveau – in an area replete with them. Excellent Thai food upstairs. Warwick Ave tube.

Ye Olde Mitre, 1 Ely Court, Ely Place, EC1. Ancient two-bar pub, popular with City wage-slaves. Chancery Lane tube.

Nightlife

No matter what your taste, you'll find what you're looking for in London, a city that in many ways becomes a more appealing place after dark. The capital's rich ethnic mix and concentration of creative talent gives it a diversity and energy that no other town in England comes close to matching – Birmingham might have a better concert hall, Manchester might have a couple of hot clubs, but nowhere can match the capital's consistent quality and choice. The weekly calendar of gigs, movies, plays and other events is charted most completely in *Time Out*, the main **listings magazine**.

As for **clubs**, London continues to maintain its status as dance-music capital of Europe and favourite destination of visiting DJs from all over the world. Late-night licences allow many venues to keep serving alcohol until 6am or even later, although the club scene is still most heavily fuelled by ever-popular proscribed chemicals including Ecstasy, speed and cocaine. At weekends you'll find most of the major venues play the latest dance sounds – house, garage and drum'n'bass – while "alternative" nights, playing funk, seventies, indie or R&B, tend to feature on weekdays; check *Time Out* or dance magazines such as *DJ, Eternity* or *Mixmag*. Prices vary enormously, with small midweek nights starting at under £5 and large weekend events charging as much as £25 – around £10 would be the average for a Saturday night, but bear in mind that the mark-up on drinks is phenomenal. Most clubs open their doors between 10pm and midnight and host a different club on each night of the week.

The **live music** scene is amazingly diverse, encompassing all variations of rock music, from big names on tour at the city's main venues, through to a network of indie and pub bands in more intimate surroundings. There's a fair slice of World Music too, especially African, Latin and Caribbean bands, and a smattering of clubs and pubs devoted to Irish music and English roots. Entry prices for gigs run much the same as clubs, though bar prices tend to be lower; for pub gigs, admission is often free.

Though a stroll through the West End can create the impression that Lloyd-Webber musicals and revivals of clapped-out plays have a stranglehold on London's **theatres**, the theatre scene is less staid than it might appear. Apart from the classic productions of the major repertory companies, there's a large fringe circuit, staging often provocative pieces in venues that range from proper independent auditoriums to back rooms in pubs. **Cinema** is not as adventurous as it is in some European capitals, with the number of repertory houses diminishing steadily, but there's a decent spread of screenings of general-release and rerun films each night of the week. With two opera houses and several well-equipped concert halls, London's programme of **classical music** is excellent, and the annual Proms season represents Europe's most accessible festival of highbrow music. For most plays and concerts you should be able to get a seat for less than £15 in the West End, or less at venues off the main circuit.

Clubs and discos

Bagley's, King's Cross Goods Yard, off York Way, N1. Vast warehouse-style venue, with a different DJ or ambience in each room. King's Cross tube.

Bar Rumba, 36 Shaftesbury Ave, W1. Still maintains a Latin flavour with pre-club dance classes, but you'll find anything from drum'n'bass to R&B at this friendly club. Live shows too. Piccadilly Circus tube.

The End, 16a West Central St, WC1. Big beat house meets techno. Tottenham Court Rd tube.

The Fridge, Town Hall Parade, Brixton, SW2. South London's glam night out, specializing in techno and house and featuring one of London's biggest gay nights on Tuesdays. Brixton tube.

Gardening Club, 4 Covent Garden Piazza, WC2. Small, trendy and nearly always reliable for a good night's clubbing. Covent Garden tube.

Gossips, 69 Dean St, W1. Dingy basement that seems to have been running forever, with an alternative flavour. Tottenham Court Rd or Leicester Square tube.

Heaven, Villiers St, WC2. Smiley, dressy club with two large floors and a big gay presence, although the music and atmosphere also attracts a mixed crowd.

Hippodrome, Charing Cross Rd, WC2. London's leading neon palace and a byword for tackiness. Leicester Square tube.

Limelight, 136 Shaftesbury Ave, W1. Super trendy when it opened a few years back, now overpriced – though it has the occasional good night. Leicester Square tube.

Mass, St Matthew's Church, Brixton, SW2. Up-and-coming new club for serious techno and cutting-edge sounds. Brixton tube.

Ministry of Sound, 103 Gaunt St, SE1. Large, long-running club on three floors that is practically an institution; has one of the best sound systems around. Elephant & Castle tube.

Subterania, 12 Acklam Rd, W10. Worth a visit for its diverse (but dressy) club nights on Fridays and Saturdays – if you can get in. Ladbroke Grove tube.

Turnmills, 63 Clerkenwell Rd, EC1. Home to Trade and other gay – though not exclusively so – nights.

Velvet Room, 143 Charing Cross Rd, WC2. Very cool; velvet-dripping interior; happy-house tunes. Tottenham Court Rd tube.

Wag, 35 Wardour St, W1. A hot spot in the mid-1980s, now hugely popular for its Eighties retro night on Saturday, and still going strong through the week. Piccadilly Circus tube.

WKD Café, 18 KentishTown Rd. Small bar-cum-club with an intimate, relaxed feel and a friendly, mixed crowd. Camden Town tube.

Live venues

12-Bar Club, 23 Denmark Place, WC2. Atmospheric small club in an old forge up an alley behind Andy's Guitar Workshop. Blues, new songwriters, acoustic bands. Tottenham Court Rd tube.

100 Club, 100 Oxford St, W1. Unpretentious and inexpensive jazz venue that moonlights as a venue for fairly big rock and mainstream acts. Tottenham Court Rd tube.

606 Club, 90 Lots Rd, SW10. London's newest all-jazz venue, located off the untrendy part of the King's Rd. Fulham Broadway tube.

Africa Centre, 38 King St, WC2. African-flavoured music which draws heavily on a London-based African audience. Covent Garden tube.

Astoria, 157 Charing Cross Rd, W1. One of London's best-used venues – a large balconied theatre that has live bands and clubs. Tottenham Court Rd tube.

Borderline, Orange Yard, Manette St, W1. Intimate venue with diverse musical policy, often focused on up-and-coming American acts. Tottenham Court Rd tube.

Brixton Academy, 211 Stockwell Rd, SW9. Massive Victorian hall used for concerts and club nights. Brixton tube.

Falcon, 234 Royal College St, NW1. Medium-sized venue attracting up-and-coming rock and indie acts. Camden Town tube.

The Forum, 9–17 Highgate Rd, NW5. Perhaps the capital's best medium-sized venue – large enough to attract established bands, but also a prime spot for newer talent. Kentish Town tube.

The Garage, 20 Highbury Corner, N5. Eclectic indie-based mix with a more acoustic focus upstairs. Highbury and Islington tube.

Jazz Café, 5 Parkway, NW1. Slick, modern jazz venue with an adventurous booking policy. Camden Town tube.

Mean Fiddler, 28a Harlesden High St, NW10. Small venue with eclectic policy ranging from folk to rock. Willesden Junction tube.

The Rock Garden, 6–7 Covent Garden Piazza, WC2. Mostly a stage for exceptionally obscure bands, with the odd club night. Covent Garden tube.

Ronnie Scott's, 47 Frith St, W1. The most famous jazz club in London: small, smoky and rather precious. Nonetheless, it's still the place for top-line names. Leicester Square tube.

Salsa Club, 96 Charing Cross Rd, WC2. One of the best of the Latino venues catering for the ongoing craze, with bands and club nights. Tottenham Court Rd tube.

Shepherds Bush Empire, Shepherds Bush Green, W12. Rising star of the medium-sized venue circuit with an imaginative booking policy. Shepherds Bush tube.

Underworld, 174 Camden High St, NW1. Good for new bands, with sporadic club nights. Camden Town tube.

ULU, Manning Hall, Malet St, W1. The best of London's university venues, with an exceptionally cheap bar. Russell Square tube.

Wembley Arena, Empire Way. Main venue for megabands. Wembley Park tube.

The gay and lesbian scenes

The gay and lesbian scenes in London are livelier than almost anywhere else in Europe, with a vast range of venues from quiet bars to cruisy clubs and frenetic discos – Soho is the rising "gay village", focused on Old Compton St. Apart from *Time Out*, you should check the up-to-the-minute listings in *Capital Gay* and *The Pink Paper*, two free weekly newspapers available in all the places listed below. An excellent source of information on all aspects of gay London is the London Lesbian and Gay Switchboard (☎0171/837 7324), which operates around the clock.

BARS AND CLUBS

Angel, 65 Graham St, N1. Relaxed gay café/bar attracting a youngish crowd. Angel tube.

The Black Cap, 171 Camden High St, NW1. North London gay institution – a big cabaret venue on the drag scene. Camden Town tube.

Brompton's, 294 Old Brompton Rd, SW5. Long-established gay bar, pulling a mixture of tourists, local yuppies and clones. Earl's Court tube.

Compton's of Soho, 53 Old Compton St, W1. Welcoming, long-standing loud gay pub that has seen a dozen or so new gay cafés, bars and shops grow up around it. Leicester Square tube.

Duke of Clarence, 140 Rotherfield St, N1. Down-to-earth lesbian bar with pool tables and a beer garden. Angel or Highbury & Islington tube.

Freedom, 60–66 Wardour St, W1. Trendy café-bar with three rooms attracting a mixed crowd, although the top floor has a more cruisy feel. Leicester Square tube.

Fridge Bar/Café, Town Hall Parade, Brixton, SW2. The regular Tuesday-night "Daisy Chain" is one of London's wildest gay and lesbian raves. Brixton tube.

King William IV, 75 Hampstead High St, NW3. Long-established, relaxed north London gay pub. Hampstead tube.

Market Tavern, Market Towers, 1 Nine Elms Lane, SW8. Most people's choice as the best gay pub in south London, with a large dance floor out front and a quiet bar in the back. Vauxhall tube.

Ted's Place, 305a North End Rd, W14. Mixed, bisexual and TS/TV nights, lesbian "Blind Date" and assorted outbreaks of frivolity. West Kensington tube.

The Village Soho, 81 Wardour St, W1. Chic, continental-style café/bar in London's "gay village". Leicester Square tube.

Theatre and cinema

London's big two **theatre** companies are the **National Theatre**, performing in three theatres on the South Bank (☎0171/452 3333), and the **Royal Shakespeare Company**, whose productions transfer to the two houses in the Barbican after their run in Stratford (☎0171/638 8891). For a show that's had good reviews, tickets under £10 are difficult to come by at either, but it's always worth ringing their box offices for details of stand-by deals, which can get you the best seat in the house for as little as £5 if you're a student, otherwise £10. Similar deals are offered by many of London's scores of theatres. During the summer months you can also see Shakespeare performed in the authentic setting of the reconstructed **Globe Theatre** (☎0171/401 9919). Venues with a reputation for challenging productions include the Almeida, Donmar Warehouse, Young Vic, Tricycle and the ICA, not to mention the Royal Court in Sloane Square.

A booth in Leicester Square sells **half-price theatre tickets** for that day's performances at all the West End theatres, but they specialize in the top end of the price range; the Charing Cross Rd and Leicester Square areas also have offices that can get tickets for virtually all shows, but the mark-up can be as high as two hundred percent. Don't buy tickets from touts – their mark-ups are outrageous, and there's no guarantee that the tickets are genuine.

Leicester Square and environs (Piccadilly, Haymarket, Lower Regent St) have the main concentration of big-screen **cinemas** showing new releases; seats tend to cost upwards of £7. The main repertory cinemas in the centre are the **National Film Theatre** on the South Bank and the **ICA**, both of which charge for day-membership on top of the ticket price. After a spate of closures, London has very few other repertory cinemas: the Everyman in Hampstead has perhaps the most interesting programmes. There are, however, several excellent independent cinemas for new art-house releases – it's always worth checking what's on at the Renoir (Russell Square), the Gate (Notting Hill) and the Metro (Rupert St, near Leicester Square).

Classical music, opera and dance

For **classical concerts** the principal venue is the **South Bank Centre**, where the biggest names appear at the Festival Hall, with more specialized programmes being staged in the Queen Elizabeth Hall and Purcell Room (all three halls ☎0171/960 4242). Programmes in the concert hall of the **Barbican Centre** on Silk St (☎0171/638 8891), are too often pitched at the corporate audience, though it has the occasional classy recital; for chamber music and Lieder recitals, the **Wigmore Hall**, 36 Wigmore St (☎0171/935 2141), is many people's favourite. Tickets for all these venues begin at about £5, with cheap stand-bys sometimes available to students on the evening of the performance.

From July to September each year the **Proms** at the **Royal Albert Hall** (☎0171/589 8212) feature at least one concert daily, with hundreds of standing tickets sold for just a couple of pounds on the night. The acoustics aren't the world's best, but the calibre of the performers is unbeatable, and the programme is a fascinating mix of standards and new or obscure works. The hall is so vast that only megastars like Jessye Norman can pack it out, so if you turn up half an hour before the show starts there should be little risk of being turned away.

The traditional **Royal Opera House** in Covent Garden has now reopened after major restoration work. It also houses the **Royal Ballet Company**, whose glamorous stars include Darcey Bussell and Sylvie Guillem. The **English National Opera** at the Coliseum, St

Martin's Lane (☎0171/632 8300), is a more democratic institution with more radical productions and a policy of performing all works in English. Tickets begin at £7 and any unsold seats are released on the day of the performance at greatly reduced prices. In addition to the big two opera houses, smaller halls often stage more innovative productions by touring companies such as Opera North – the Queen Elizabeth Hall is a regular venue.Visiting classical companies also appear regularly at the Coliseum, and less frequently at the Royal Albert Hall, while Sadler's Wells, Rosebery Ave, EC1 (☎0171/863 8198) is the main venue for ballet and classical dance. London's **contemporary dance** scene is no less exciting – adventurous programmes are staged at the South Bank and at the ICA, as well as at numerous, more ad hoc venues.

Listings

Airlines American Airlines, 15 Berkeley St, W1 (☎0345/789789); British Airways, 156 Regent St, W1 (☎0345/222111); Lufthansa, 10 Old Bond St, W1 (☎0345/737747); Virgin Atlantic, Virgin Megastore, 14 Oxford St, W1 (☎01293/747747). Budget airlines: Debonair (☎0541/500300); Easyjet (☎0990/292929); Go (☎08456/054321); Ryanair (☎0541/569569).

Airports Gatwick (☎01293/535353); Heathrow (☎0181/759 4321); Luton (☎01582/405100); Stansted (☎01279/680500).

American Express 6 Haymarket, SW1 (☎0171/930 4411).

Bicycle rental Bike Fix, 48 Lambs Conduit St, WC1 (☎0171/405 1218).

Books Foyles, 119 Charing Cross Rd, WC2, is the best-known London general bookshop but is badly stocked and chaotically organized. Neighbouring Waterstone's is preferable, as are Books Etc and Blackwells, opposite, and Dillons, 82 Gower St, WC1 – the university bookshop. For more radical publications, call in at Compendium, 234 Camden High St, NW1 (Camden Town tube). Two of London's best art bookshops are Shipley, 70 Charing Cross Rd, WC2, and nearby Zwemmer's. For maps and travel books, go to Stanford's, 12 Long Acre, WC2.

Bus station Long-distance coach services depart from Victoria Coach Station, Buckingham Palace Rd (Victoria tube). National Express ticket offices (timetable info ☎0990/808080) can be found here and at Eurolines, 52 Grosvenor Gdns, SW1 (☎0171/730 8235), which also operates European services.

Car rental Holiday Autos (☎0990/300453) offer the best rates, but the big firms all have outlets across London – ring their central offices to find the nearest one: Avis (☎0990/900500); Hertz (☎0990/996699); Europcar (☎0870/6075000); National (☎0171/8200202.

Dentist For emergency dental service phone ☎0171/955 2185 (Mon–Fri) or ☎0171/380 9857 (Sat & Sun).

Embassies Australia, Australia House, The Strand, WC2 (☎0171/379 4334); Canada, 1 Grosvenor Square, W1 (☎0171/258 6600); Ireland, 17 Grosvenor Place, SW1 (☎0171/235 2171); Netherlands, 38 Hyde Park Gate, SW7 (☎0171/590 3200); New Zealand, New Zealand House, 80 Haymarket, SW1 (☎0171/930 8422); USA, 24 Grosvenor Sq, W1 (☎0171/499 9000).

Exchange Shopping areas such as Oxford St and Covent Garden are littered with private exchange offices, and there are 24hr booths at the biggest central tube stations, but their rates are always worse than the banks. You'll find major branches of all the banks around Oxford St, Regent St and Piccadilly.

Hospitals The most central hospitals with 24hr emergency units are: Guy's, St Thomas St, SE1 (☎0171/955 5000); St Thomas's, Lambeth Palace Rd, SE1 (☎0171/928 9292); University College, Gower St, W1 (☎0171/387 9300).

Internet Access Café Internet, 22–24 Buckingham Palace Rd, SW1; Cyberia, 39 Whitfield St, W1; Cyberspy, 15 Golden Square, W1; Miajack, 4 King's Cross Bridge, N1; Shoot N Surf, Commonwealth House, 1–19 New Oxford St, WC1.

Left luggage Services at the following train stations: Euston (24hr daily); Paddington (24hr daily); Victoria (daily 7am–10.15pm); Waterloo (daily 8am–10pm).

London Transport enquiries ☎0171/222 1234.

Pharmacies Every police station keeps a list of emergency pharmacies in its area; otherwise try Bliss, 5 Marble Arch, W1 (daily 9am–midnight), also at 50–56 Willesden Lane, NW6 (daily 9am–2am).

Police HQ is New Scotland Yard, 1 Drummond Gate, SW1 (☎0171/230 1212), but 27 Savile Row, W1 (☎0171/437 1212) is the most convenient West End station.

Post offices The Trafalgar Square post office, 24–28 William IV St, WC2, has the longest opening hours: Mon–Sat 8am–8pm. Poste restante mail should be sent to this branch.

Train stations and information As a broad guide, Euston handles services to the Northwest, north Wales and Glasgow; King's Cross the Northeast and Edinburgh; Liverpool St eastern England; Paddington west ern England and south Wales; Victoria, Charing Cross and Waterloo southeast England. For all enquiries, call ☎0345/484950.

Travel agents Campus Travel, 52 Grosvenor Gdns, SW1 (☎0171/730 3402); Council Travel, 28a Poland St, W1 (☎0171/437 7767); STA Travel, 86 Old Brompton Rd, SW7 (☎0171/361 6161); Trailfinders, 215 Kensington High St, W8 (☎0171/937 5400); Travel Cuts, 295a Regent St, W1 (☎0171/255 1944).

SOUTHEAST ENGLAND

Nestling in self-satisfied prosperity, **southeast England** is the richest part of the country, due to its agricultural wealth and proximity to the capital. Swift, frequent rail and bus services make it ideal for day-trips from London. Medieval ecclesiastical power bases like **Canterbury** and **Winchester** offer an introduction to the nation's history, while on the coast you can choose between the upbeat hedonism of **Brighton**, London's playground by the sea, and the quieter, more traditional pleasures of the **Dover** area – also a pleasant stopover for those entering or leaving the country by ferry.

Canterbury

CANTERBURY, one of the oldest centres of Christianity in England, was home to the country's most famous martyr, archbishop Thomas à Becket, who fell victim to Church–State rivalry in 1170. It became one of northern Europe's great pilgrimage sites, as Chaucer's *Canterbury Tales* attest, until Henry VIII had the martyr's shrine demolished in 1538. The cathedral remains the focal point of a compact town centre, which is enclosed on three sides by medieval walls. Today it's thronged with visitors, particularly in summer, but is not over-commercialized.

Built in stages from the eleventh century onwards, the **Cathedral** (Mon–Fri 9am–5.30pm, Sat 9am–2.30pm, Sun 12.30–2.30pm & 4.30–5.30pm; £3) derives its distinctive presence from the perpendicular thrust of the late Gothic towers, dominated by the central, fifteenth-century Bell Harry tower. Notable features of the high vaulted interior are the tombs of Henry IV and his wife, and the gilded effigy of the Black Prince, both in the Trinity chapel behind the main altar. The spot where Becket was killed in the northwest transept is marked by a modern shrine, with a crude sculpture of the murder weapons suspended above. Steps descend from here to the heavy Romanesque arches of the **crypt**, one of the few remaining visible relics of the Norman cathedral.

East of the cathedral, opposite the coach park, are the evocative ruins of **St Augustine's Abbey** (daily 10am–4/5/6pm; £2.50), on the site of a church built by St Augustine, who began the conversion of the English in 597. Most of the town's other sights are located on or near the High St. The **Eastbridge Hospital** (Mon–Sat 10am–4.45pm; £1), on the other side of the street from the library, was founded in the twelfth century to provide poor pilgrims with shelter, and a thirteenth-century wall painting of Jesus is still faintly visible in the refectory upstairs. The **West Gate**, at the far end of St Peter's St (a continuation of High St), is the only one of the town's medieval gates to survive; it houses a small museum (Mon–Sat 11am–12.30pm & 1.30–3.30pm; 90p) containing weaponry used by the medieval city guard. The **Canterbury Tales** on St Margaret St (March–Oct daily 9/9.30am–5.30pm; Nov–Feb Sun–Fri 10am–4.30pm, Sat 9.30am–5.30pm; £5.25), presents the city's heritage with the recorded voices of Chaucerian characters guiding you around a series of waxwork tableaux.

Practicalities

Most **trains** on the main line between London Victoria and Dover arrive at Canterbury East, from where it's a short walk north into the walled town; less frequent trains from Charing Cross and some from Victoria arrive at Canterbury West, just outside the West Gate, also just ten minutes from the centre. The **bus station** is on St George's Lane; a left turn at the bottom of the forecourt brings you directly onto the High St. The **tourist office** is located just off the High St at 34 St Margaret's St (daily 9.30am–5/5.30pm; ☎01227/766567), and will find you a B&B for a £1 fee, although you shouldn't have too much difficulty finding somewhere yourself. Among the cheaper places **to stay** are: *The White House*, 6 St Peter's Lane (☎01227/761836; ⑤); *Wincheap Guest House*, 94 Wincheap (☎01227/762309; ④); and *Yorke Lodge*, 50 London Rd (☎01227/451243; ⑤). There's also a YHA **hostel** about half a mile out of town towards Dover at 54 New Dover Rd (☎01227/462911; ③; bus #54 or a 15min walk) and an independent hostel called *Kipps* at 40 Nunnery Fields, a short walk south of the centre (☎01227/786121; ②).

There are plenty of places to **eat and drink** in the town centre, including the *Tapas en Las Trece* at 13 Palace St and the nearby *Bell and Crown*, a friendly local pub with excellent home-cooked food. *Marlowe's*, on St Peter's St, serves standard Tex-Mex fare in huge, affordable portions, or you can pay the extra for Italian-influenced food at *Il Pozzo* on Guildhall Street. For a **drink**, try the *Miller's Arms*, next to the river on Mill Lane – a picturesque place for a pint in summer, it also has an excellent restaurant – or *Alberry's*, a lively late bar on St Margaret Street.

Dover

DOVER, the port through which the majority of cross-Channel traffic is funnelled, is more a ferry port than a seaside resort, but it does have several historic attractions and provides a good base for explorations of the Kent coast. Furthermore, as night-time transport to London is poor (the last bus leaves at 8.30pm; last train at 10pm), you may be forced to stay here anyway.

Dover's main **ferry terminal** is located less than a mile east of town at the Eastern Docks (London buses pick up and put down here); **hovercraft** depart from the more central Western Docks. **Trains** arrive at Priory Station, a ten-minute walk northwest of the centre, while the **bus station** is in the heart of town on Pencester St. The **tourist office** is parallel to the drab seafront on Townwall St (daily: Sept–June 10am–6pm; July–Aug 8am–7.30pm; ☎01304/205108), and staff will direct you to the numerous **B&Bs** along the Folkestone Rd: *Linden* at no. 231 is recommended (☎01304/205449; ④). There's a crowded **youth hostel** at Charlton House, 306 London Rd (☎01304/201314; ③); overspill dorms are opened at 14 Goodwyne Rd in summer. The YMCA (☎01304/206138; ②) is the cheapest option, but very basic, although a smarter new building is due to open on Princes St. Eating and drinking centres around the Market Square: for cheap **eats** try *Munchies* at 3 Bench St or the basic Italian food at *Piazza* on King St; the better **pubs** include *Jay's* on King St and the *Eight Bells* on Bannon St.

Views of Dover's famous White Cliffs are best enjoyed from a boat several miles out, although you can amble around on the grassy summit, where on a clear day you can make out the eerie sight of Calais' equivalent cliffs, just twenty miles away. **Dover Castle** (daily: April–Oct 10am–4/6pm; £6.60), a rambling assemblage of medieval fortifications dominated by a Norman keep, stands on a bluff between the Eastern Docks and the town. Inside the castle complex are a Roman lighthouse dating from the first century AD, and Hellfire Corner, the warren of tunnels used as a command post by the British navy during World War II. The tourist itinerary in town is dominated by the recently refurbished **White Cliffs Experience** (daily 10am–3/5pm; £5.50), an extravagant stage-set of a museum which includes tableaux representing the Roman invasion (Julius Caesar landed up the coast near Deal in 55 BC), and a Dover street scene from 1944.

Brighton

BRIGHTON is a place in which to enjoy the atmosphere of a quintessential pleasure resort rather than view historical sights or relax by the sea. The town has been a prime target for day-tripping Londoners since the late eighteenth century, and its status as the nearest convenient venue for a libidinous weekend gave it a racy reputation which still lingers. The wide range of nightlife owes a lot to the student population of two universities – Brighton and

Sussex – and an art college, while in summer the music and arts festival – running for three weeks in May – and the scores of English-language schools give an international edge to the town's youthful feel.

From Brighton's **train station** it's a ten-minute straight stroll down to the seafront, four miles of shelving pebbles bordered by a balustraded promenade. If you arrive on the **coach**, you'll be put down in Pool Valley, which opens out onto the front. The **Palace Pier**, an obligatory call, is basically a half-mile amusement arcade lined with booths selling fish and chips, candyfloss and junky souvenirs. From here the antiquated locomotives of Volk's train (April–Sept daily 11am–5pm; £1), the first electric train in the country, run eastward towards the Marina and the nudist beach. On the west side you can see – but not enter – the brooding **West Pier**, severed from the mainland following gale damage in 1987, and decaying further each year despite various rescue plans.

A block back from the promenade are **The Lanes**, a shopping area of narrow alleys preserving the layout, but little of the ambience, of the fishing port Brighton used to be before seaside tourism took off. Inland from here, overlooking the main traffic confluence of the Old Steine, are the distinctive domes of the **Royal Pavilion** (daily 10am–5/6pm; £4.50), an unmissable Oriental pastiche built in 1817 for the future George IV. Brighton's **Museum and Art Gallery** (Mon–Sat 10am–5.45pm, Sun 2–5pm, closed Wed; free) is just around the corner on Church St. Nondescript paintings are followed by a display of furniture and ceramics through the ages, which includes some valuable Art Nouveau and Art Deco items (Dali's famous "lip sofa" is a surreal novelty) and a selection of local ephemera; many galleries have been refitted for the millennium. Temporary exhibitions add to the interest and can absorb a couple of hours. North of Church St is the arty/bohemian quarter of **North Laine**, with plenty of secondhand clothes, record and junk shops interspersed with trendier boutiques and coffee shops.

Practicalities

The **tourist office**, at 10 Bartholomew Square in the Lanes (March–Oct Mon–Fri 9am–5/6pm, Sat 10am–5/6pm, Sun 10am–4/5pm; Nov–Feb closed Sun; ☎01273/292599), will book rooms in town for a £1 commission. **B&Bs** are scattered around, with a concentration at the eastern end of town behind Marine Parade. If booking ahead, try *Calvaire Guest House*, 34 Upper Rock Gdns (☎01273/696899; ⑤), just above Marine Parade; or the *Queensbury Hotel*, 58 Regency Square (☎01273/325558; ⑤), close to the beach. Brighton's **youth hostel** at Patcham Place (☎01273/556196; ③), four miles north on the A23 to London, is not very convenient; buses #5, #5a, #56, #107, #770 and #772 pass nearby. *Brighton Backpackers*, just off the seafront at 75 Middle St (☎01273/777717; ②), is a much livelier alternative, with a quieter annexe around the corner. In between the two is the more spacious *Baggie's Backpackers*, at 33 Oriental Place (☎01273/733740; ②; sometimes closed in winter).

The Lanes and the surrounding streets have a good selection of **restaurants and cafés**, ranging from the budget Indian buffet at *Bombay Aloo*, at 39 Ship Street, to *Wheeler's* decadent oyster-bar. Especially popular are *Food for Friends*, 17 Prince Albert St, an inexpensive but classy vegetarian restaurant, and *Al Forno*, a cosy pizzeria tucked into a corner by the East St entrance to the Lanes. For drinking, the **pubs** of the Lanes are very popular, or you could try the classy *Prodigal*, on the seafront just west of the bus station, but you'll find the atmosphere less pushy at the *George* on Trafalgar St, near the station, which also does vegetarian food, or the lively *Mash Tun* on New Road by the pavilion. Brighton's prominent **gay scene** centres in the area around St James St; check out *Dr Brighton's* on the seafront near the *Queen's Hotel*.

Nightlife is hectic throughout the year, and there's probably more live music here than anywhere else outside London. For listings, pick up a copy of two listings magazines – *The Brighton Scene* or *The Latest*. Foremost among the **clubs** are the *Honey Club* and the *Zap Club* on Old Ship Beach in the seafront arcades, the *Escape Club*, 10 Marine Parade, and the predominantly gay *Revenge* on Old Steine.

Winchester

WINCHESTER's rural tranquillity betrays little of its former importance as the political and ecclesiastical power base of southern England. A town of Roman foundation, Winchester rose to prominence in the ninth century as King Alfred the Great's capital, and remained an important locus of power well into the Middle Ages. The shrine of Saint Swithin, Alfred's tutor and bishop of Winchester, made the town an important destination for pilgrims, and the flow of European merchants to the annual Saint Giles' fair kept the civic coffers full.

Alfred's statue stands at the eastern end of the Broadway, the town's main thoroughfare, becoming High St as it progresses west. Much of the exterior of the **Cathedral** (daily 7.15am–6.30pm; £2.50 donation requested), to the south, is twelfth century, although bits of earlier masonry show through here and there, in particular the Norman stonework of the south transept. The vault is currently undergoing restoration, but the scaffolding will be removed by early 2000. Raised above a screen surrounding the high altar are mortuary chests holding the remains of the pre-Conquest kings of England. The Angel chapel contains sixteenth-century wall paintings of the miracles of the Virgin Mary, although a modern replica now covers the originals in order to protect them. Jane Austen is buried on the south side of the nave; the inscription on the floor slab remembers her merely as the daughter of a local clergyman, making no mention of her renown as a novelist.

Immediately outside are traces of the original Saxon cathedral, built by Cenwalh, king of Wessex, in the mid-seventh century. The true grandeur of this structure is shown by a model in the **City Museum** (April–Sept Tues–Sat 10am–5pm, Sun & Mon 2–5pm; Oct–March closed Mon; free) on the western side of the cathedral close; other exhibits include mosaics and pottery from Roman Winchester. On the other side of the cathedral close is the fourteenth-century Pilgrims Hall, from where a signposted route leads through a medieval quarter to **Winchester College**, the oldest of Britain's public schools. The school's quadrangles and chapel are open to visitors (Mon–Sat 10am–1pm & 2–5pm, Sun 2–5pm; £2.50). It's then a 25-minute walk across the Water Meadow to the medieval almshouse of **St Cross** (April–Oct Mon–Sat 9.30am–5pm; Nov–March Mon–Sat 10.30am–3.30pm; £2), with fifteenth-century courtyards and a church containing a triptych by the Flemish painter Mabuse.

At the western end of High St, the **West Gate** (Feb–Oct Mon–Fri 10am–5pm, Sat 10am–1pm & 2–5pm, Sun 2–5pm; Feb, Mar & Oct closed Mon; 30p) contains artefacts relating to its seventeenth-century role as a debtors' prison. Beyond it, behind modern council offices, is the thirteenth-century **Great Hall** (summer daily 10am–5pm; winter Sat & Sun 10am–4pm; free), a banqueting chamber used by successive kings of England and renowned for the fourteenth-century Round Table which now hangs from the wall. Some two centuries after its construction the table was inscribed with the names of King Arthur's knights, probably for the visit of Emperor Charles V, who was entertained here by Henry VIII in 1522.

Practicalities

Winchester **train station** is five minutes north of the West Gate. The **bus terminal** is on High St; just opposite is the Guildhall, in which the **tourist office** is installed (June to mid-Sept Mon–Sat 10am–6pm, Sun 11am–2pm; mid-Sept to May Mon–Sat 10am–5pm; ☎01962/840500). Winchester's affluence is reflected in both the style and prices of its **B&Bs**, most of which cluster in the streets between St Cross Rd and Christchurch Rd, south of town. *The Farells*, at 5 Ranelagh Rd (☎01962/869555; ④), is a cosy option, with some en-suite bathrooms, or try the central and cheap *Sullivans*, at 29 Stockbridge Road beside the railway station (☎01962/862027; ③). There's an atmospheric **youth hostel** in the City Mill, just past Alfred's statue (☎01962/853723; ③; April–Sept). For **food**, the *Wykeham Arms*, 75 Kingsgate St, offers imaginative meals, served in a labyrinthine interior with intimate spaces, while the *India Arms*, opposite the tourist office, dishes up economically priced lunches.

THE WEST COUNTRY

The **West Country** has never been a precise geographical term, and there will always be a certain amount of argument as to where it actually starts. But as a broad generalization, the cosmopolitan feel of the southeast begins to fade into a slower, rural pace of life from **Salisbury** onwards, becoming more pronounced the further west you travel. In Neolithic times a rich and powerful culture evolved here, as shown by monuments such as **Stonehenge** and **Avebury**, and the isolated moorland sites of inland **Cornwall**. The main urban attractions of western England are **Bristol**, Exeter, Plymouth and the well-preserved Regency spa town of **Bath**, while those in search of rural peace and quiet should head for wilder areas such as **Exmoor** or the more compelling bleakness of **Dartmoor**. The western extremities of Britain include some of the most beautiful stretches of coastline, its rugged, rocky shores battered by the Atlantic, although the excellent sandy beaches make it one of the country's busiest corners over the summer. All of the region's major centres can be reached fairly easily by rail or coach direct from London. Local bus services cover most areas, although in the rural depths of Exmoor and Dartmoor they can be very sparse indeed.

Salisbury and Salisbury Plain

SALISBURY's central feature is the elegant spire of its **Cathedral** (daily 7am–6.15/8.15pm; £2.50 donation requested), the tallest in the country, rising over four hundred feet above the lawns of the cathedral close. With the exception of the spire, the cathedral was almost entirely completed in the thirteenth century, and is one of the few great English churches that is not a hotchpotch of different styles. Prominent among the features of the interior are the fourteenth-century clock just inside the north porch, one of the oldest working timepieces in the country, and an exceptional Tudor memorial to the Earl of Hertford, Lady Jane Grey's brother-in-law, in the Lady Chapel at the eastern end of the church. An octagonal **chapterhouse**, approached via the extensive cloisters (Mon–Sat 9.30am–5.30/7.45pm; free), holds a collection of precious manuscripts, among which is one of the four original copies of the Magna Carta. For the postcard view of the cathedral immortalized by Constable, wander across the meadows and over the River Avon to **Harnham**, where you can have lunch or a drink at the *Old Mill* pub.

Most of Salisbury's remaining sights are grouped in a sequence of historic houses around the close, the old walled inner town around the cathedral. The **Salisbury and South Wiltshire Museum** (Mon–Sat 10am–5pm; July & Aug also Sun 2–5pm; £3), opposite the main portal of the cathedral on West Walk, is a good place to bone up on the Neolithic history of Wessex before heading out to Stonehenge and Avebury. The **Mompesson House** on the close's North Walk (April–Oct Mon–Wed, Sat & Sun noon–5.30pm; £3.40) is a fine eighteenth-century house complete with Georgian furniture and fittings.

A ten-minute hop on any of the Andover- or Amesbury-bound buses (every 15min) takes you to the ruins of **Old Sarum** (daily 10am–4/5/6pm; £2), abandoned in the fourteenth century when the bishopric moved to Salisbury. Traces of the medieval town are visible in the outlines of its Norman cathedral and castle mound, but the ditch-encircled site is far older, populated in Iron Age, Roman and Saxon times.

Practicalities

Salisbury's **train station** is across the River Avon on South Western Rd, a short walk northwest of town. **Buses** (poor London connections) terminate behind Endless St, a block north of which is the **tourist office** in Fish Row, just off the Market Place (Mon–Sat 9.30am–5/6/7pm, Sun 10.30am–4.30/5pm; ☎01722/334956). There's an excellent YHA **hostel** at Milford Hill House, Milford Hill, five minutes east of the city centre (☎01722/327572; ②), and a smaller, independent hostel, *Matt & Tiggy's*, in Salt Lane (☎01722/327443; ②) near the bus station. Most **B&Bs** inhabit an arc north of town beyond the train station; if booking ahead, try the *Clovelley Hotel* at 17–19 Mill Rd (☎01722/322055; ⑤), *Farthings Guest House* at 9 Swaynes Close (☎01722/330749; ④), or the sixteenth-century *Old Bakery*, a B&B at 35 Bedwin St (☎01722/320100; ④). Salisbury has a poor choice of cheap places to **eat**, but you can try the *Coach and Horses* on Winchester St for an imaginative menu or the ancient *Haunch of Venison* for more traditional cuisine; the *Café Parisien* on the market square does snacks and has outdoor tables. For **pubs** look for *The Oddfellows Arms* on Milford St, or the charmingly wonky fifteenth-century *New Inn* on New Street, which is no-smoking.

Stonehenge

The uplands northwest of Salisbury were a thriving centre of Neolithic civilization, the greatest legacy of which is **Stonehenge** (daily: June–Aug 9am–7pm; rest of year 9.30am–5/6pm; £4). It is served by five daily buses from Salisbury, three on Sundays, and eight during June, July and August. You can also take a tour – ask at the bus station for details – or get an Explorer pass, which costs £4 and is valid all day including travel to Avebury and Bath.

The monument's age is being constantly revised as research progresses, but it's known that it was built in several distinct stages and adapted to the needs of successive cultures. The first Stonehenge probably consisted of a circular ditch dug somewhere between 2600 and 2200 BC. This was followed by the construction within the ditch of two concentric circles of sixty bluestones, thought to have originated in the Presili Mountains of southern Wales. At least two more centuries elapsed before the outer circle and inner horseshoe were put in place, made up of local Wiltshire sarsen stones, the twenty-foot uprights topped by horizontal slabs. The way in which the sun's rays penetrate the central enclosure at dawn on midsummer's day has led to speculation about Stonehenge's role as either an astronomical observatory or a place of sun worship, but knowledge of the cultures responsible for building it is too scanty to reach any firm conclusions. Overlooking the point where the A303 and A344 meet, the stones themselves are controversially fenced off to prevent the erosion caused by thousands of summer day-trippers, although you can now enter as far as a rope barrier. The only way to enter the circle itself is to take a guided tour at sunrise or sunset costing £25 a head – ask at the tourist office in Salisbury.

Avebury

Salisbury also serves as a base for visiting the equally important – and much more atmospheric – Neolithic site at **AVEBURY**. The #5 Salisbury–Swindon bus (two/three daily) passes through Avebury village, and catching the 9.20am bus from Salisbury and returning from Avebury at 3pm makes a day-trip feasible.

The Avebury monoliths were erected some time between 2600 and 2100 BC, and their main circle – with a diameter of some 400yd – forms a monument bigger in scale than Stonehenge, albeit not as impressive in its architectural sophistication. Further lines of standing stones form the West Kennet Avenue, thought to be a processional way, running two miles south to the so-called Sanctuary, possibly a gathering place of religious significance, where a small circle of stones surrounds the site of a wooden hut constructed around 3000 BC. All this is best considered with a pint or two from the *Red Lion* village pub, set right beside the main stone circle.

To walk off the beer, follow a section of the **Ridgeway**, a 4000-year-old prehistoric highway, which loops northeast from Overton Hill, just south of the village; it once ran the breadth of Britain and can still be walked or cycled (it is signposted as a National Trust trail) as far as Ivinghoe Beacon in Hertfordshire. Avebury's little **Archeological Museum** (daily 10am–4/6pm; £1.50) has a display on it as well as the monoliths and other ancient sites in the vicinity. Among the most interesting and accessible are **Silbury Hill**, an enormous conical mound constructed around 2800 BC, two miles southeast of the village, and **West Kennet Long Barrow** just beyond, an impressive stone passage grave in use for over 1500 years from about 3700 BC.

Bath

The last main stop on the rail line to Bristol is the handsome town of **BATH**, an ancient Roman spa town revived by eighteenth-century high society. It's the extensive reconstruction put into effect by Neoclassicist architects John Wood and his son, John Wood the Younger, that gives the town its distinctive appearance, with endless terraces of weathered sandstone fringed by spindly black railings.

In the Roman era, a hot spring sacred to the Celtic goddess of the waters, Sulis, provided the centrepiece of an extensive bath complex, now restored as the **Roman Baths and Museum** (April–Sept daily 9am–6pm, Aug late opening daily 8–10pm; Oct–March Mon–Sat 9.30am–5pm; £6.30; combined ticket with Costume Museum £8.40). The pools, pipes and underfloor heating are remarkable demonstrations of the ingenuity of Roman engineering. The Pump Room, built above the Roman site in the eighteenth century, is the place to sample the waters while listening to genteel tunes from the resident chamber ensemble, and from 2001 you'll be able to move next door to bathe or receive any number of health treatments in the modern **Bath Millennium Spa** (daily 7am–10pm). The neighbouring **Abbey** (Mon–Sat 9am–4.30pm, Sun closed during services) is renowned for the lofty fifteenth-century vault of its choir and the dense carpet of gravestones and memorials which cover the floor. The Abbey's **Heritage Vaults** (Mon–Sat 10am–4pm; £2) house Saxon and Norman sculpture and a reconstruction of the original building.

The best of Bath's eighteenth-century architecture is on the high ground to the north of the town centre, where the well-proportioned urban planning of the Woods is best showcased by the elegant Circus and the adjacent **Royal Crescent**. The house at no. 1 Royal Crescent is now a museum (mid-Feb to Nov Tues–Sun 10.30am–4/5pm; £3.80), showing how the Crescent's houses would have looked in the Regency period. The social calendar of Bath's elite centred on John Wood the Younger's **Assembly Rooms** (daily 10am–4.30pm; free), just east of the Circus; recently renovated, it includes a **Museum of Costume** (same times; £3.80) in the basement. The nearby Octagon, just off Milsom St, now houses the **Royal Photographic Society** (daily 9.30am–5.30pm; £2.50), an impressive survey of the development of photographic technology.

The triple arches of Pulteney Bridge lead from the town centre across the River Avon, and up Great Pulteney St to the **Holburne Art Museum** (mid-Feb to mid-Dec Tues–Sat 11am–5pm, Sun 2.30–5.30pm; April–Oct also open Mon; £3.50), which contains silver, porcelain and furniture from the Regency period. Just south of the town centre at 19 New King St is the **Herschel House** (March–Oct daily 2–5pm; Nov–Feb Sat & Sun only; £2.50), another eighteenth-century interior, housing the home-made telescope with which astronomer William Herschel first spotted Uranus in 1781.

Practicalities

Train and **bus stations** are both situated at the top of Manvers St, five minutes south of the centre. The **tourist office** is just off the Abbey churchyard (Mon–Sat 9.30am–5/6pm, Sun 10am–4pm; ☎01225/477101). Bath's **youth hostel** is halfway up Bathwick Hill (☎01225/465674; ②), one and a half miles east of town (bus #18). There's also the more relaxed and central *Backpackers' Hostel* (☎01225/446787; ②) at 13 Pierrepont St, five minutes' walk north from the train and bus stations, or the central YMCA (☎01225/460471; ③) on Broad Street Place, with rooms and dorms. Economically priced **B&Bs** include the Henry Guest House, 6 Henry St, near the Abbey (☎01225/424052; ④), and *the Albany Guest House*, at 24 Crescent Gdns (☎01225/313339; ④). The main tourist thoroughfares and neighbouring backstreets provide a huge number of tearooms. For less delicate fare, head for *Evan's*, next to Marks and Spencer in the main shopping area, which is renowned as one of the West Country's best fish-and-chip shops. *Scoff's*, in the square below the Theatre Royal is a wonderful wholefood café with tables inside and on the street, while *Demuth's* vegetarian restaurant on North Parade Passage off Abbey Green is more upmarket but still good value. On nearby Monmouth St, immediately behind the theatre, stands one of the city's newest and trendiest café-bars, the *Raincheck Bar*. The best pubs include *The Bell* on Walcot St, with live music three nights each week, *The Porter* on George St, with cheap lunches and DJs in the evenings, and the *Pig and Fiddle*, opposite the Hilton on Saracen St, a local-brewery pub with a good mixed atmosphere.

Bristol

Situated on a succession of lumpy hills just inland from the mouth of the Avon, the thriving city of **BRISTOL** grew rich on transatlantic trade – slaving, in particular – to become England's second city in the early part of the nineteenth century. It's slipped down the table since, but remains a wealthy, commercial centre, home to tobacco and aviation industries and a major university. The current millennial redevelopment of the docks area and parts of the centre aims to provide a more attractive focus for Bristol's vibrant, but still rather scattered, arts and nightlife scene.

The city "centre" – in so much as there is one – is an elongated oval traffic interchange, the Hippodrome, soon to be redeveloped and partially pedestrianized. To the east, the more intimate Old City is gradually seeing an influx of bars and restaurants, while on its south side is the **Floating Harbour**, an area of waterways which formed the commercial hub of the nineteenth-century town, now the scene of a good deal of renovation. A couple of important cultural institutions are to be found in converted warehouses here: the **Arnolfini Gallery** on Narrow Quay (Mon–Sat 10am–7pm, Sun noon–6pm; free), one of Britain's best contemporary arts venues, and the **Watershed Arts Centre**, directly opposite. Both have pleasant, reasonably priced cafés that stay open until late. Directly across from here is the **Harbourside** area, focus of the millennium project, "at-Bristol", where two interactive centres, Explore-at-Bristol (a science museum and technology park) and Wildscreen-at-Bristol (a wildlife museum and botanical park) are due to open in spring 2000.

Across a swing bridge from the Arnolfini, on Prince's Wharf, is the new and imaginative **Bristol Industrial Museum** (April–Oct Sat–Wed 10am–5pm; Nov–March Sat & Sun only; free). Just east of here, at the end of Redcliffe Parade, rises the Gothic church of **St Mary Redcliffe** (daily 8am–5/8pm), described by Queen Elizabeth I as the "godliest, fairest, and most famous parish church in England". To the west of the Industrial Museum, ten minutes' walk along the quayside (or bus #511) and a right turn onto Gas Ferry Rd brings you to the **Maritime Heritage Centre** (daily 10am–4.30/5.30pm; free), celebrating Bristol's shipbuilding past and providing access to a replica of the fifteenth-century *Matthew* and Brunel's **SS Great Britain** (ticket for both ships £6), the first iron, propellor-driven ship, which was launched from the dock in 1843. These are due to be linked to the Harbourside area opposite by a new ferry.

Returning to the "centre", and heading uphill, past College Green – flanked by the city's **Cathedral** (not a patch on St Mary's) – you can follow Park St to the university's Wills Memorial Building, a Victorian neo-Gothic monster, endowed by the local tobacco dynasty along with the adjacent **Bristol City Museum and Art Gallery** (daily 10am–5pm; free), which, beyond its offerings of Egyptology, dinosaurs and giant elks, has a half-decent art collection, predictably strongest on the Victorian Pre-Raphaelites. If this leaves you in need of some fresh air, take the street opposite the museum to **Brandon Hill**, topped by a splendid folly, **Cabot Tower** (free), from which vantage point you can cast an eye over much of the city, with the old docks spread out below you to the south, the suburb of Clifton and its suspension bridge to the west.

The rest of your time is best spent wandering around **CLIFTON**, whose airy terraces, crescents and circuses are reminiscent of the Georgian splendours of nearby Bath. It's a somewhat genteel quarter, but full of enticing pubs and with a spectacular focus in the **Clifton Suspension Bridge**, a glorious creation by the indefatigable engineer and railway builder Isambard Kingdom Brunel, spanning the limestone abyss of the Avon Gorge. On a low ridge above the bridge is the **Observatory** (daily: summer 11am–6pm; winter noon–3pm; closed when cloudy; £1), another Victorian job, in whose dome is a camera obscura, encompassing views of the gorge and bridge.

Practicalities

Bristol's Temple Meads **train station** is a five-minute bus ride southeast of the centre, although it is due to be linked to the centre via a pedestrian walkway. The **bus station** is just north of the centre on Marlborough St. There's a **tourist office** in St Nicholas's Church beside Bristol Bridge (Mon–Sat 9.30am–5.30pm, Sun 11am–4pm; ☎0117/926 0767). The **youth hostel**, at 14 Narrow Quay (☎0117/922 1659; ③), is splendidly situated in an old wharfside building next to the Arnolfini Gallery; another independent hostel may be opening by summer 2000 – check at the tourist office. For **B&Bs**, Clifton is the most pleasant location: two possibilites in this area are the *Oakfield Hotel*, 52 Oakfield Rd (☎0117/973 5556; ④) just off Whiteladies Rd, and *K Linton Homes*, 3 Lansdown Rd (☎0117/973 7326; ④) near Clifton Village.

For **food and drink**, the stretch between Clifton and the city centre – from Park St up Queen's Rd to Whiteladies Rd – offers a vast choice of ethnic eats and late bars. In Clifton itself don't miss the *Coronation Tap* (on an obscure alley – ask for it by name), a classic scrumpy (cider) bar whose regulars show the effects. In the city centre most of the action is in the Old City and down to the waterfront around Queen's Square, close to the massive Harbourside redevelopment. Two pubs of note are on King St, opposite the Old Vic: the ancient *Llandoger Trow* and *The Old Duke* – the latter with live jazz. Nearby, on the Grove, in an old police building over the water, the *Riverstation* has an upmarket restaurant and good-value deli-bar while, further along, the *Mud Dock Café* is a pricey and very trendy café-bar.

The Bristol-based listings magazine *Venue* is a vital source for details of **cultural activities and nightlife**. There's usually a lot on, with art cinemas at both the Arnolfini and Watershed, and a renowned repertory company at the Bristol Old Vic on King St. Bristol's vibrant music scene has risen to prominence in recent years and produced a host of influential names (Tricky, Massive Attack, Portishead). Top clubs include *Thekla* on The Grove, the massive new *Evolution* next to the Watershed and *Café Blue* in the Old Fire Station on Silver St. The *Bristol Bierkeller* on All Saints St is good for gigs as well as club nights; you'll also catch indie bands at the *Anson Rooms* in the Student Union on Queens Rd.

Wells and Glastonbury

A small town dwarfed by its extraordinary cathedral, **WELLS** is served by shoals of buses from nearby Bath and Bristol, all arriving at Princes Rd bus station, five minutes from the centre. Follow Cuthbert St eastwards from here to the picturesque inn-lined Market Place, and the **tourist office** in the Town Hall (daily: April–Oct 9.30am–5.30pm; Nov–March 10am–4pm; ☎01749/672552). From here a gateway leads through to the cathedral close, bringing you face to face with an intoxicating array of Gothic statuary, mostly from the 1230s and 1240s. Inside, the great interlacing "scissor-arches" at the crossing were devised to support the unstable tower, while in the north transept a fourteenth-century clock strikes the quarter hours. South of the cathedral, a drawbridge leads across a swan-filled moat to the **Bishop's Palace** (Easter–Oct Tues–Fri 10.30am–6pm, Sun 2–6pm; Aug daily 10.30am–6pm; £3), where opulently furnished rooms are watched over by portraits of former bishops. On the other side of the cathedral close are the town **Museum** (Easter–June, Sept & Oct daily 10am–5.30pm; July & Aug daily 10am–8pm; Nov–Easter Wed–Sun 11am–4pm; £2) and the **Vicar's Close**, a row of fourteenth-century terraced houses. The tourist office has a list of B&Bs, but the nearest **youth hostel** is six miles northwest in the village of Cheddar (☎01934/742494; ③), reached on buses #126 or #826. The dramatic **Cheddar Gorge**, formed by the collapse of a cave system, is walkable from here.

Buses #163, #376 and #676 head southeast from Wells to **GLASTONBURY**, a small rural town whose associations with the Holy Grail and King Arthur – the **Tor**, a natural mound overlooking the town, is identified with the Isle of Avalon – have made it a magnet for those with a taste for the mystical. The town itself is not much more than a High Street, the lower end of which, around the Market Cross, is overrun by New Age book- and crystal shops. There's an intriguing **Lake Village Museum** (daily 10am–4/5.30pm; £2.50) housed in the Tribunal, a fifteenth-century courthouse, which contains relics from a Celtic lake village excavated to the east of the town, including excellent examples of pottery and a wooden canoe from the period. The impressive ruins of the **Abbey** are approached around the corner from Magdalene St (Sept–May daily 10am–dusk; June–Aug 9am–6pm; £1.50); this was the oldest Christian establishment in continuous use in England until Henry VIII put an end to it. A mile to the east is the Tor, at the base of which stands the natural spring known as **Chalice Well** (daily 10am–4/5.30pm; £1). The ferrous waters which flow from the hillside here were popularly thought to have gained their colour from the blood of Christ, supposedly flowing from the Holy Grail, buried here by Joseph. On top of the Tor stands a tower, all that remains of a fourteenth-century church; the views from here are spectacular, and the Tor is a popular place from which to observe the sunrise on the summer solstice.

By nightfall Glastonbury reverts to sleepy rural stillness – except over the summer solstice and during the Glastonbury Festival, which is held in June most years and draws around 80,000 people to its three-day binge of music and miscellaneous events. At other times, if you're looking for excitement it's best to press on. If you choose not to, the **tourist office**, housed in the Tribunal on High St (same hours as Lake Village Museum; ☎01458/832954), will find a room, or you can find a basic dorm bed and a friendly crowd at the *Glastonbury Backpackers* (☎01458/833353; ②) on Market Place. Glastonbury has a convenient **campsite**, the *Old Oaks Touring Park*, at Wick Farm on the far side of the Tor (☎01458/831437; March–Oct). For **food and drink**, the *Backpackers* has cheap, filling meals and a lively bar with events, or you'll find well-priced veggie food at the *Global Café* on the High St.

Dartmoor

Dartmoor is one of England's most beautiful wilderness areas, an expanse of wild uplands that's home to an indigenous species of wild pony and dotted with **tors**, characteristic wind-eroded pillars of granite. The main focus for visitors in the middle of the park is **POST-BRIDGE**, easily reached by local bus from Plymouth. Famous for its medieval bridge over the East Dart river, this is a good starting point for walks in the woodlands surrounding Bellever Tor to the south. Postbridge's **tourist office**, on the main road through the village (April–Oct daily 10am–5pm; Nov–March Mon–Sat 10am–4pm; ☎01822/880272), will supply information on the national park. The nearest **youth hostel** is at Bellever, one mile south (☎01822/880227; ②; April–Oct).

The most untamed parts of the moor, around its highest points of High Willhays and Yes Tor, are above the market town of **OKEHAMPTON** – served by the four-times-daily #86 bus from Plymouth or the daily #83 or #84 to Tavistock (from where there are regular buses), or the more frequent #628, #51, #X9 and #X10 services from Exeter. Despite the stark beauty of the terrain, this part of the moor is used by the Ministry of Defence as a firing range: details of times when it's safe to walk the moor are available from the **tourist office** on West St (April, May & Oct Mon–Sat 10am–5pm; June–Sept daily 10am–5pm; Nov–March Mon–Sat 10am–5pm; ☎01837/53020), which also operates a room-booking service. Okehampton has a couple of attractions in its own right. The **Museum of Dartmoor Life** next to the tourist office (Mon–Sat 10am–4/5pm; June–Sept daily 10am–5pm; £1.60) offers interesting anthropological insights, including a look at life in one of the Dartmoor longhouses, the stone and turf huts in which the moorland natives used to live. Surrounded by woods one mile southwest of town is the now crumbling Norman keep of **Okehampton Castle** (April–Oct daily 10am–6pm; £2.30).

Cornwall

England's westernmost county, **Cornwall** includes some of the country's most scenic stretches of coastline. Largely a rocky, rugged area, the Cornish coast also features some extensive sandy beaches, making it England's busiest seaside destination; beware of the summer crush in principal resorts like St Ives and Newquay. The Lizard Peninsula and Land's End are the obvious places to gain access to the more dramatic stretches of the coast:

Falmouth and Penzance respectively provide convenient bases from which to explore them. Penzance can be reached direct from London by train – Falmouth, St Ives and Newquay each require at least one change.

Penzance

The busy port of **PENZANCE** forms the natural gateway to England's westernmost extremity, the Penwith Peninsula, and all the major sights of the region can be reached by day-trips from here. From the **train station** located at the northern end of town, Market Jew St threads its way through the town centre, culminating in the Neoclassical facade of Market House, fronted by a statue of local-born chemist and inventor Sir Humphrey Davy. A left turn into Chapel St brings you to the **Maritime Museum** (Easter–Oct Mon–Sat 10am–4pm; £2), which re-creates the interior of an eighteenth-century man-of-war. West of here, a series of parks and gardens punctuate the quiet residential streets overlooking the promenade. The **Penzance and District Museum**, off Morrab Rd (Mon–Sat 10.30am–4.30pm; Mon–Fri £1, Sat free), features works by members of the Newlyn school, late nineteenth-century painters of local seascapes.

Modern paintings are showcased at the **Newlyn Art Gallery** (Mon–Sat 10am–5pm), an eminently walkable mile and a half west along the coast road in Newlyn itself. A working fishing village, Newlyn is a little more authentic than its southerly neighbour, the much-visited **Mousehole**, a jumble of harbourside cottages easily reached by local bus (#5B or #6A) from Penzance.

The view east across the bay from Penzance is dominated by **St Michael's Mount**, site of a fortified medieval monastery perched on an offshore pinnacle of rock. At low tide, the Mount is joined by a cobbled causeway to the mainland village of Marazion (buses every 20min from Penzance); at other times a regular boat shuttle links the Mount with the village. You can amble around part of the Mount's shoreline, but most of the rock lies within the grounds of the abbey and castle (April–Oct Mon–Fri 10.30am–4.45pm; Nov–March by guided tour in good weather only Mon, Wed & Fri 11am, noon, 2pm & 3pm; £3.90, ferry £1), now a stately home belonging to Lord St Levan.

Penzance's **train** and **bus stations** are at the northeastern end of town, a step away from Market Jew St. The **tourist office** (Mon–Fri 9am–5pm, Sat 10am–1pm; ☎01736/362207) is in the bus station and will fix up B&B **accommodation**, most of which congregates at the western end of town around Morrab Rd. The comfortable **youth hostel**, Castle Horneck, Alverton (☎01736/362666; ②), is a short walk along the Land's End road, or there's an independent hostel, *Penzance Backpackers*, on Alexandra Rd (☎01736/363836; ②). For unwinding in the evening, head for town-centre **pubs** like the *Star* on Market Jew St, or the more touristy *Admiral Benbow* on Chapel St, a seventeenth-century house with maritime fittings with a bar upstairs and a pricey restaurant downstairs. Over the summer, look out for live folk music at the *Acorn*, Parade St.

Land's End

Land's End exerts a hold over the popular imagination that the site itself can't always live up to – especially now that a small **theme park** has been built here (daily 10am–5/6pm; site admission free, various charges for attractions). The coastal path, however, remains a public right of way, and, despite commercialization, a visit is really worthwhile, with beautiful clifftop walks overlooking some spectacular wave-carved rocks. One and a half miles north is the secluded village of Sennen Cove, overlooking the extensive sandy beaches of Whitesand Bay, where you'll find the *Land's End Backpacker's Hostel* at Whitesands Lodge (☎01736/871776; ②). Head a similar distance south for the more rugged beauty of Mill Bay.

Four miles north of Land's End is an equally spectacular stretch of coast around **Cape Cornwall**, less crowded than its more famous neighbour, although a popular venue for observing dramatic sunsets. The cape itself is a mile west of the former tin-mining village of St Just; the walk here from Land's End is recommended, although it's also easily reached by bus from Penzance. St Just is also the site of the nearest **youth hostel** to Land's End at Letcha Vean, half a mile south of town (☎01736/788437; ②; March–Oct).

St Ives

Lying across the peninsula from Penzance on Cornwall's north coast, the fishing village of **ST IVES** is the quintessential Cornish resort, featuring a maze of narrow streets lined with whitewashed cottages, good sandy beaches and lush subtropical flora. The village's erstwhile tranquillity attracted several major artists earlier this century – Ben Nicholson, Barbara Hepworth and Naum Gabo among them. Insipid sunsets and other tourist fodder now fill the small galleries which cram the streets, but there's some more challenging work on show in the **Tate Gallery** (April–Sept Mon–Sat 11am–7pm, Sun 11am–5pm; Oct–March Tues–Sun 10.30am–5.30pm; £3.90) on Porthmeor Beach, featuring the work of the various St Ives schools. A combined ticket (£6) admits you to the **Barbara Hepworth Museum** (same hours as Tate; separate ticket £3), which preserves the studio of the modernist sculptor. Her photos of Cornwall quoits and landscapes provide clues to the inspiration behind her sleek monoliths, many splendid examples of which are displayed in the garden. Of the town's three beaches, the north-facing Porthmeor occasionally has good surf, and boards can be rented at the beach. The **tourist office** in the Guildhall, Street An Pol (June–Aug Mon–Sat 9.30am–6pm, Sun 10am–1pm; Sept–May Mon–Fri 9am–5/5.30pm, Sat 10am–1pm; ☎01736/797600), has a room-booking service.

CENTRAL AND EASTERN ENGLAND

Central England was the powerhouse of the Industrial Revolution, and although vast areas of the Midlands are greener than most people realize, it is still predominantly a region of unattractive manufacturing towns. The regional centre is **Birmingham**, hub of an industrial sprawl which encompasses some three million people – making it Britain's second largest city. Though Birmingham has one of the best concert halls and orchestras in the country, the conurbation is unlikely to feature on a hurried tour of Britain. Still, two of England's essential sights are to the south of the Midlands core, and within easy reach of London: **Stratford-upon-Avon**, home of William Shakespeare, and the university town of **Oxford**.

Eastern England is primarily known for the endless flat expanses of East Anglia, long isolated by the Fens, areas of wetland which were substantially drained only in recent centuries. Of the many historical towns that dot the landscape, the university town of **Cambridge** is the obvious draw, although, further east, the more workaday town of **Norwich** preserves a surprising amount of its medieval and Tudor heritage.

Oxford

Preconceptions about the aristocratic atmosphere of **OXFORD** are now slightly wide of the mark, for the city's university has lost much of its social exclusivity. Yet the privileges of Oxford, embodied in its fine architecture, are what make the place an unmissable stop, and it couldn't be easier to visit – it's only ninety minutes from London's Paddington station by rail, and various bus companies make the trip from Victoria – either from Grosvenor Gardens outside the train station or from the coach station itself – ensuring departures every ten to fifteen minutes for as little as £6 day return.

Students were originally attracted here by the scholars attached to the Oxford monasteries, before their ranks were swelled by the expulsion of English students from Paris in 1167. By the sixteenth century the collegiate system began to take shape, with students and tutors living, working and taking their meals together in the same complex of buildings – usually a couple of courtyards (quads) with a chapel, library and dining hall. Most Oxford colleges follow this basic pattern, forming a dense maze of historic buildings in the heart of the city. Access to many of the colleges may be restricted during term time, and they often close to visitors entirely in May and June, when exams are approaching.

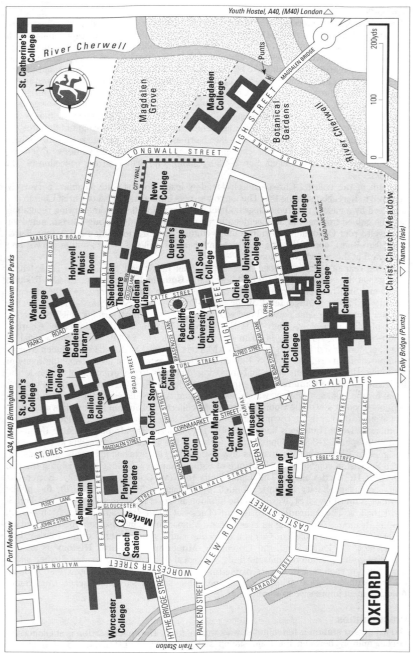

Youth Hostel, A40, (M40) London △

River Cherwell

St. Catherine's College

N

Magdalen Grove

Magdalen College

Punts

MAGDALEN BRIDGE

HIGH STREET

ROSE LANE

Botanical Gardens

River Cherwell

200yds

100

0

LONGWALL STREET

△ University Museum and Parks

JOWETT WALK

CITY WALL

New College

QUEEN'S LANE

Merton College

DEAD MAN'S WALK

Christ Church Meadow

MANSFIELD ROAD

SAVILE ROAD

Holywell Music Room

HOLYWELL STREET

Queen's College

All Soul's College

University College

Oriel College

MERTON STREET

Corpus Christi College

▷ Thames (Isis)

△ A34, (M40) Birmingham

Wadham College

Sheldonian Theatre

NEW COLLEGE LANE

Bodleian Library

CATTE STREET

Radcliffe Camera

University Church

HIGH STREET

ORIEL SQUARE

Cathedral

New Bodleian Library

PARKS ROAD

BRASENOSE LANE

BEAR LANE

Christ Church College

▷ Folly Bridge (Punts)

St. John's College

Trinity College

Balliol College

BROAD STREET

Exeter College

SHIP STREET

TURL STREET

MARKET STREET

ALFRED STREET

BLUE BOAR STREET

ST. ALDATES

△ Port Meadow

ST. GILES

The Oxford Story

MAGDALEN STREET

CORNMARKET STREET

CARFAX

QUEEN ST.

Covered Market

Carfax Tower

St. Museum of Oxford

PEMBROKE STREET

BREWER STREET

ROSE PLACE

Ashmolean Museum

BEAUMONT STREET

Playhouse Theatre

ST. MICHAEL'S STREET

NEW INN HALL STREET

GEORGE STREET

Oxford Union

Museum of Modern Art

ST. EBBE'S STREET

PUSEY LANE

ST. JOHN'S STREET

GLOUCESTER STREET

Market i

Coach Station

WALTON STREET

NEW ROAD

CASTLE STREET

WORCESTER STREET

HYTHE BRIDGE STREET

PARK END STREET

PARADISE STREET

△ Train Station

Worcester College

OXFORD

© Crown copyright

The City

The main point of reference is **Carfax**, a central crossroads overlooked by the fourteenth-century **Carfax Tower** (April–Oct daily 10am–5.30pm; £1.20), last surviving remnant of a church of the same name and the first of many opportunities to enjoy a panorama of the Oxford skyline. Avoid the bus- and shopper-choked Cornmarket and head south down St Aldate's, which leads past Pembroke St – home to Oxford's world-class Museum of Modern Art, or **MOMA** (Tues, Wed & Fri–Sun 11am–6pm, Thurs 11am–9pm; £2.50) – down to the biggest of Oxford's colleges, **Christ Church** (Mon–Sat 9.30am–5.30pm, Sun 11.30am–5.30pm; £3). The main entrance passes underneath the dome of Tom Tower, built in 1681 by Christopher Wren, before opening onto the vast expanse of Tom Quad, mostly dating from the college's foundation in the sixteenth century. It is an indication of the prestige and wealth of the college that the city's late Norman cathedral also serves as the college chapel. From Oriel Square you can enter the college's **Picture Gallery** (Mon–Sat 10.30am–1pm & 2–4.30/5.30pm, Sun 2–4.30/5.30pm; £1), with a strong collection of Old Masters.

South of the college, Christ Church Meadow leads down to the Thames, perversely referred to hereabouts as the Isis. The narrow streets immediately east of Christ Church are occupied by a cluster of three colleges: **Oriel**, renowned for its fearsome rowing reputation and the gabled frontages of its seventeenth-century Front Quad; **Corpus Christi**, noted for its paved Front Quad and sixteenth-century sundial; and **Merton** (Mon–Fri 2–4pm, Sat & Sun 10am–4pm), one of the original thirteenth-century colleges, which still preserves one courtyard of the period, Mob Quad.

At the rear of Merton College, Deadman's Walk heads east to join Rose Lane, which emerges at the eastern end of High St beside the **Botanical Gardens** (9am–4.30/5.30pm; £2.50) and the Cherwell river where you can hire punts in summer. Opposite is the fifteenth-century bell tower of **Magdalen College** (Mon–Fri noon–6pm; Sat & Sun 2–6pm; £1.50); the Cloister Quad of the same period, lined with gargoyles, is the most striking of its courtyards. West of Magdalen along High St is **St Mary's Church**, aka the "University Church" (Mon–Sat 9am–5/7pm, Sun 11.30am–5.30pm/dusk; tower £1.40), scene of the trial of Cranmer, Ridley and Latimer, the "Oxford Martyrs" burned at the stake by Queen Mary's counter-reforming regime in 1555. Behind the church extends an area containing many of the university's most important and imposing buildings, most dramatic of which is the Italianate **Radcliffe Camera**. Built in the 1730s by James Gibbs, it is now used as a reading room for the Bodleian Library, whose main building is immediately to the north in the Old Schools Quad. A few of the Bodleian's immense collection of ancient manuscripts are selected for public display in the Divinity School (Mon–Fri 9am–5pm, Sat 9am–12.30pm; free, guided tours of Duke Humfrey's library, £3.50). The adjacent **Sheldonian Theatre** (Mon–Sat 10am–12.30pm & 2–3.30/4.30pm; £1.50), a copy of the Theatre of Marcellus in Rome, was designed by Christopher Wren and is now a venue for concerts and university functions.

To the east, a copy of Venice's Bridge of Sighs spans New College Lane, joining the two halves of Hertford College. The Lane winds to **New College** itself (daily: Easter–Oct 11am–5pm; Nov–Easter 2–4pm), founded by William of Wykeham in 1379; the public entrance is on Holywell St. West from the Sheldonian, several colleges cluster around Turl St and Broad St. The **Ashmolean Museum** (Tues–Sat 10am–4pm, Sun 2–4pm, Mon 2–5pm; free) in Beaumont St is strong on classical and Minoan finds, and also has a broad-based art gallery featuring an excellent Oriental collection and a good selection of the English Pre-Raphaelites. On Parks Road, the **University Museum of Natural History** is an odd Victorian-gothic pile full of dinosaur finds, zoological displays and rocks, but further inside you'll find the esoteric **Pitt Rivers Museum**, housing case after case of bizarre archeological and anthropological artefacts, including some famous shrunken heads from South America, in an impressive iron-vaulted gallery.

Practicalities

Oxford's **train station** is ten minutes' walk west of town. The **coach station** is at Gloucester Green, midway between the train station and the centre. The **tourist office** is also in

Belvedere Palace, Vienna, Austria

Salzburger Land mountainscape, Austria

Dubrovnik, Croatia

Rila Monastery, Bulgaria

Bridges over the Vltava, Prague, Czech Republic

Alexandâr Nevski Church, Sofia, Bulgaria

The Vismarkt, Bruges, Belgium

Roskilde Cathedral, Denmark

Landscape in Finland

PETER WILSON

Flower shop, Ile St-Louis, Paris, France

MICHAEL JENNER

Louvre pyramid, Paris, France

Gloucester Green, in the Old School (winter Mon–Sat 9.30am–5pm; summer also Sun 10am–3.30pm; ☎01865/726871); they will book rooms for a £2.50 fee.

There's an overloaded YHA **youth hostel** in the suburb of Headington, half an hour east of central Oxford at Jack Straws Lane (☎01865/762997; ②), and the much more central *Backpackers' Hostel* at 9a Hythe Bridge St (☎01865/721761; ③). Double rooms in **B&Bs** tend to hover between £35 and £45 in high season, and booking ahead is strongly advised. Recommended places are *Tara House*, 10 Holywell St, opposite New College (deaf messaging service ☎0800 515152, quote ☎01865 202953; ④), *Walton Guest House*, 169 Walton St (☎01865/552137; ④) and the genteel and more upmarket *Norham Guest House*, 16 Norham Rd (☎01865/515352; ⑤). The nearest **campsite** is *Oxford Camping International*, 426 Abingdon Rd (☎01865/246551), a mile and a half south of the centre.

For **meals**, the Covered Market between High St and Market St has a plethora of sandwich and snack bars, including the quirky *Georgina's*, or try the *King's Arms*, the quintessential university pub, for bar meals. More upmarket are *Browns*, on Woodstock Rd, a smart Oxford classic, *Gee's*, on Banbury Rd – smarter still – and a handful of French café-restaurants on Little Clarendon St. You'll also find the popular *George & Davis* ice cream parlour on the same street and a number of ethnic restaurants just beyond on Walton St; the best of these is *Jamal's*. Among the many distinctive **pubs** are the tiny, ramshackle *Bear* on Alfred St; *The Old Tom* on St Aldates; *The Eagle and Child* on St Giles, a favourite of J.R.R. Tolkien and C.S. Lewis; and *The Turf Tavern*, hidden under the old city wall on Bath Place off Holywell St.

The monthly publication *This Month in Oxford* and the weekly broadsheet *Daily Information* (pinned to walls in colleges and pubs) provide details of **concerts**. There is a fairly good arts cinema, *The Phoenix*, on Walton St, and in summer look out for open-air theatre, often Shakespeare, in the college gardens. For live music, try *The Firkin and Philanderer* on Walton St and *The Old Fire Station* on Gloucester Green which also has theatre and club nights; larger visiting acts play at the *Apollo Theatre* on George St. Of the clubs, *Park End* on Park End St and *Club Latino* on the Plain are among the more popular.

Blenheim Palace

Half-hourly buses depart from the bus station or Cornmarket towards the village of Woodstock, eight miles north and site of **Blenheim Palace** (mid-March to Oct daily 10.30am–5.30pm; £7.80; park open all year 9am–4.45pm; £5 with car, £1 on foot). The palace was built by John Vanbrugh for John Churchill, the first Duke of Marlborough, whom the king wished to reward for defeating the army of Louis XIV at Blenheim in 1704. The stern exterior is an unambiguous expression of power; inside, things are marginally more homely, with opulently furnished period state rooms and a Churchill Exhibition, which includes a few of Winston's attempts at painting and a re-creation of the room in which he was born. Italianate gardens are laid out to the rear of the palace, a contrast with the open spaces of Capability Brown's landscaped parkland, unlikely setting for a Butterfly House (March–Oct daily 10am–6pm).

Stratford-upon-Avon

Blessed with a higher than average sprinkling of Tudor and Jacobean half-timbered houses, **STRATFORD-UPON-AVON** has put itself firmly on the tourist map by making the most of the five sights associated with William Shakespeare, who was born here on April 23, 1564. There are three restored properties linked with the Bard or members of his family in the town proper and two within easy reach of it. If you've time to visit them all, combined tickets (£7.50 for the three town properties, £11 for all five) may be worth considering.

Shakespeare's Birthplace (April–Oct Mon–Sat 9am–5pm, Sun 9.30am–5pm; Nov–March Mon–Sat 9.30am–4pm, Sun 10am–4pm; £4.90), a pale-ochre, half-timbered structure on Henley St, is entered from the informative Shakespeare Centre just up the road, which has its own exhibition on Elizabethan life. Although a bit of a crush over summer, the house provides an evocative re-creation of Elizabethan life. John Shakespeare, William's father, was a glove-maker and wool dealer who served on the town council, and the rooms, although sparsely furnished, point to a life of relative comfort.

Prominent among the Elizabethan facades of High St is that of the **Harvard House** (May–Oct Tues–Sat 10am–4.30pm, Sun 10.30am–4.30pm; free); inside is a further taste of the living quarters of the Tudor era and the Neish Collection of pewter, but the house's real attraction lies in the intricately carved timbers of the exterior. Heading southwest, High St becomes Chapel St and leads to **New Place**, site of the home where Shakespeare died in 1616. Sadly, the house no longer stands, demolished by a subsequent owner in·1759, who was apparently tired of visitors. The Elizabethan Garden, however, has been re-created and is entered via the next-door **Nash's House** (same hours as Shakespeare's Birthplace; £3.30), home of Thomas Nash, husband of Shakespeare's granddaughter Elizabeth Hall. The half-timbered frontage is a 1911 replica, with the Tudor interior re-creating the atmosphere of a middle-class seventeenth-century home, while upstairs is a small museum devoted to the town's history, with mementoes of the 1769 Shakespeare Jubilee mounted by the actor David Garrick, who did much to promote the town as a place of literary pilgrimage.

Across the road on the corner of Chapel Lane and Church St is the medieval **Guild Chapel**, with some frescoes from around 1500. Behind the chapel is the half-timbered frontage of the King Edward VI Grammar School, supposedly attended by the Bard. Continuing along Church St, a left turn leads into Old Town and **Hall's Croft** (same ticket as Nash House), home of Shakespeare's son-in-law Dr John Hall. The interior is furnished in period style, with a selection of antique medicines and herbal remedies from the doctor's dispensary. From here it's a five-minute walk to Shakespeare's last resting place, the **Holy Trinity Church** on the banks of the Avon. About a mile and a half east of Stratford is the village of Shottery, site of **Anne Hathaway's Cottage** (same hours as the Birthplace; £3.90), home of Shakespeare's wife.

Practicalities

Stratford's **train station** is half a mile west of town. Buses terminate right in the middle of things at the bottom of Bridgeway, two minutes away from the **tourist office** at Bridgefoot (Mon–Sat 9am–5/6pm; April–Oct also Sun 11am–5pm; ☎01789/293127). There's a **youth hostel** in Hemmingford House, Alveston (☎01789/297093; ③), two miles east (#18 or #X18 buses) and you'll find dorms and cheap meals at the excellent *Backpackers' Hotel* (☎01789/263838; ③) on Greenhill St between town and the train station. The town has a wealth of **B&B** accommodation, much of it located in the southwest corner of town around Evesham Place, but rooms fill up speedily during the tourist season. First choices are *Bronhill House*, 260 Alcester Rd (☎01789/299169; ④) and the *Naini-Tal*, 63A Evesham Rd (☎01789/204956; ④), though both roads have a number of inexpensive alternatives.

Stratford is an expensive place to eat, but the *Kingfisher Fish Bar*, Ely St, is a traditional and inexpensive fish-and-chip shop in the town centre. Sheep St is lined with more cosmopolitan restaurants, including the popular *Opposition*. Amongst Stratford's plentiful **pubs**, the most famous is the *Black Swan* (better know as the *Dirty Duck*) on Waterside. Finally, tickets for the **Royal Shakespeare Company**, which performs in three theatres on the banks of the Avon – the main house, the smaller Swan and the experimental Other Place – begin at around £6, with stand-bys sometimes available. Sell-outs are very common, so book your seat as far in advance as possible (☎01789/295623).

Cambridge

Tradition has it that the University of **CAMBRIDGE** was founded by refugees from Oxford, who fled the town after one of their number was lynched by hostile townsfolk; rivalry has existed between the two institutions ever since. On the whole, Cambridge is a quieter, more secluded place, but viewed from the famed Backs – the green swathe of land straddling the River Cam – the collegiate architecture has a dramatic presence.

A logical place to begin a tour is the **Fitzwilliam Museum**, at the southern end of the centre on Trumpington St (Tues–Sat 10am–5pm, Sun 2.15–5pm; free). The archeological collections on the ground floor contain an imposing relief of Assyrian King Ashurnasirpal II alongside strong Egyptian and Greek sections; upstairs, the art collection includes a couple of Titians, a Veronese, a Tintoretto, a good selection of Pre-Raphaelites and Impressionists, and a fine Odalisque by Delacroix, not to mention an eclectic selection of twentieth-century works.

Founded in 1284, neighbouring **Peterhouse** is Cambridge's oldest college, but little of the original architecture survives. The college's most interesting feature is the seventeenth-century chapel, a hybrid structure flanked by classical colonnades and sporting light-hearted Baroque gables. The Cloister Court of **Queens' College** (April–Oct 10am–12.45pm & 1.45–4.30pm; £1) halfway down Silver St is original Tudor, but its timber-roofed Hall is a nineteenth-century medievalist construction, decorated by William Morris. The contemporaneous neo-Gothic gatehouse of King's College, hogging the limelight on King's Parade, leads through to **King's College Chapel** (Mon–Sat 9.30am–4.30pm, Sun 10am–4.30/5pm; £3), one of the best examples of late Perpendicular architecture in Britain. Begun by the college founder Henry VI in the 1450s, it boasts an extravagantly fan-vaulted ceiling, supported by a wall of stained glass on each side, an intricately carved choir screen, added in the 1530s and probably Florentine work, and Rubens's *Adoration of the Magi* over the main altar.

Next door to King's is the **Senate House**, an exercise in Palladian classicism by James Gibbs, and the scene of graduation ceremonies in June. The nineteenth-century turreted monstrosity next door marks the southern entrance to **Gonville and Caius** (pronounced "keys") **College**, hiding a fascinating series of sixteenth-century courtyards. Caius Court bears much of the personality of the college's co-founder John Keys, a widely travelled philosopher and physician who Latinized his surname, as was the custom with men of learning. He placed a gate on each side of two courts – the Gates of Wisdom, Humility, Virtue and Honour – each representing a different stage on the path to academic enlightenment; the Gate of Honour on the south side of the court, capped with sundials, is the most ornate.

The Great Court of **Trinity College** (March–Nov daily 10am–5pm; £1.75), the largest of Cambridge's colleges, is the finest ensemble of Tudor-period buildings in the city. Another Tudor gatehouse marks the entrance to **St John's** (March–Oct Mon–Fri 10am–5pm, Sat & Sun 9.30am–5pm; £1.75) and more fine sixteenth-century courts. Standing on the corner where St John St meets Bridge St is the **Round Church**, built in the twelfth century on the model of the Church of the Holy Sepulchre in Jerusalem; the spire is a nineteenth-century addition, but Norman pillars remain inside. Just beyond here, Magdalene Bridge is a good place to rent boats for a leisurely punt down the river. Across the bridge, **Magdalene College** (pronounced "Maudlin"), straddles both sides of the street, the oldest parts of which are to the east. A couple of sixteenth-century courts lead through to the Pepys Library, named after the Magdalene old boy whose collection of books has been on display here since 1742. His diary is on permanent view. **Jesus College**, reached from Jesus Lane by a narrow alleyway known as the Chimney, holds a chapel which contains original medieval elements, but many of the Victorian architects engaged in the Gothic revival were involved in the chapel's reconstruction, making for an interesting hybrid. Ceiling paintings were provided by William Morris, who – together with Burne-Jones and Ford Madox Brown – also provided designs for the windows. **Christ's College**, south of Jesus on St Andrew's St, has one of Cambridge's finest Tudor gate towers, adorned with coats of arms of the Beaufort family and mythical, antelope-like beasts. The fifteenth-century stained glass in the college chapel depicts, among others, Henry VI and Henry VII.

Practicalities

Cambridge's **train station** is a dull, twenty-minute trudge south of the centre; alternatively, take shuttle buses #1, #2 or #3 from Emmanuel St (every 10min 8am–6pm, skeleton service until 11pm). The **bus station** is on Drummer St, a couple of blocks east of the **tourist office** on Wheeler St, behind the town hall (Mon–Fri 9/10am–5.30/6pm, Sat 9/10am–5pm; Easter–Oct also Sun 10.30am–3.30pm; ☎01223/322640). The busy **youth hostel** is at 97 Tenison Rd (☎01223/354601; ③), not far from the train station. **B&Bs** are grouped near the station and around Chesterton Rd to the north. Amongst the best are the *Six Steps*

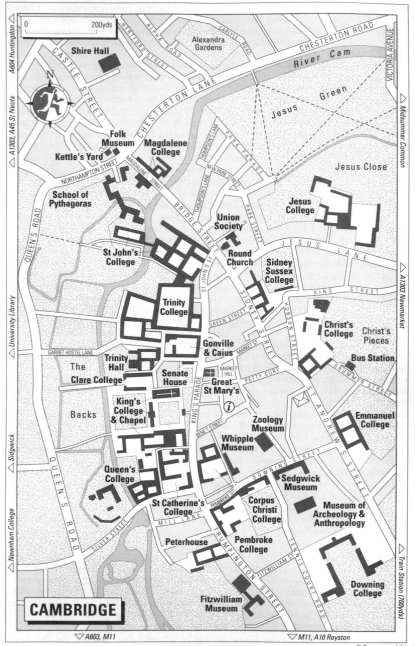

CAMBRIDGE

© Crown copyright

Guesthouse, 93 Tenison Rd (☎01223/353968; ④); *Dresden Villa Guest House*, 34 Cherry Hinton Rd (☎01223/247539; ④); *Netley Lodge*, 112 Chesterton Rd (☎01223/363845; ④); and *Lyngamore House*, 35–37 Chesterton Rd (☎01233/312369; ③). The nearest **campsite** is *Highfield Farm*, Long Rd, Comberton (☎01223/262308; bus #118 or #119).

For **food**, *Brown's*, opposite the Fitzwilliam Museum, is a vast and bustling brasserie good for both full meals and just a snack and a coffee. *Effe's*, at 78 King St, is a deservedly popular and inexpensive Turkish restaurant specializing in chargrilled meats, and *Rainbow*, 9a Kings Parade, is the only vegetarian restaurant in town. As for **pubs**, the *Boathouse*, 14 Chesterton Rd, and the well-loved *Anchor*, Mill Pond, both overlook the Cam and are good places for a bar lunch or beery evening, perfect for a drink by the river. Others to check out are the *Eagle*, a historic inn with an old cobbled courtyard, and the *Free Press*, popular with the rowing fraternity. The *Fez Club*, 15 Market Passage, is the nearest thing to a decent club, whilst The Corn Exchange in Wheeler St is the major venue for big bands. *What's On in Cambridge*, a freesheet distributed by the tourist office, has details, as does the student weekly, *Varsity*.

Norwich

NORWICH was England's second city in Tudor times, serving a vast hinterland of cloth producers in the eastern counties, whose work was exported from here to the Continent. Due to its isolated position beyond the Fens, the city often had closer cultural and trading links with the Low Countries than with London; the overland journey to the capital took far longer than crossing the Channel.

The twelfth-century **Castle Keep** (Mon–Sat 10am–5pm, Sun 2–5pm; July–Sept £3.10, Oct–June £2.30, battlements and dungeons tour additional £1.50), replete with blind arcading, a rare piece of ornamentation on a military structure, stands in the centre of town. The **Museum and Art Gallery** inside (same hours, £2.30), contains a representative selection of landscapes by painters of the nineteenth-century Norwich School, whose outstanding figures were John Sell Cotman and John Crome. West of the castle stretches the largely pedestrianized city centre, where you'll find the twelfth-century **Guildhall**, built from the Norfolk flint that gives a glass-like quality to many of the city's older buildings. Two blocks north of the castle, the **Bridewell Museum** (Easter–Sept Tues–Sat 10am–5pm; £1.20) has artefacts illustrating the town's trades and professions, including a steam-powered fire engine, while the fifteenth-century church of **St Peter Hungate** (April–Sept Mon–Sat 10am–5pm), two minutes' walk northeast, has been converted into a museum exhibiting medieval illustrated manuscripts and church brasses. Nearby, the descending cobbled lane of Elm Hill evokes something of the atmosphere of Tudor Norwich with a few half-timbered buildings. Immediately east of here is the **Cathedral** (daily 7.30am–6/7pm; donation encouraged), whose twelfth-century nave retains a couple of heavily ornamented Norman piers. Look out also for some fine examples of medieval art: the fourteenth-century *Dispenser Reredos* in St Luke's chapel and medieval frescoes in the treasury on the north side of the altar. Beyond the cathedral to the east are the best of Norwich's riverside walks, following the Wensum past the ruined Cow Tower.

The University of East Anglia on the western outskirts of the city holds a fabulous collection of sculpture and painting from all over the world in the hi-tech **Sainsbury Centre for Visual Arts** (Tues–Sun 11am–5pm; £2), where Picasso and Modigliani rub shoulders with Egyptian antiquities. To get to UEA, take bus #4, #5, #26, #27 or #35 from Castle Meadow.

Practicalities

Norwich's **train station** is ten minutes downhill from the Castle Keep across the River Wensum to the east. **Buses** terminate on Surrey St, five minutes to the south of the Castle. The **tourist office** is in the Guildhall (Mon–Sat 9.30am–4.30/5pm; ☎01603/666071). There's a YHA **hostel** at 112 Turner Rd (☎01603/627647; ②; March–Oct); a YMCA at 48 St Giles St (☎01603/620269; ②); and a YWCA at 61 Bethel St (☎01603/625982; ②). **B&B** accommodation worth trying includes the *Abbey Hotel*, 16 Stracey Rd (☎01603/612915; ④); *Arrow Hotel*, 2 Britannia Rd (☎01603/628051; ④); *Bristol House*, 80 Unthank Rd (☎01603/625729; ④); and

Chiltern House, 2 Trafford Rd (☎01603/663033; ④). The nearest **campsite** is *Lakenham* (☎01603/620060; April–Sept), a mile or so south on Martineau Lane, off King St. Centrally located places to **eat** are *Pizza One* on Tombland next to the cathedral close, and *Hector's House* on Bedford St; a livelier place veggies should home in on is *Tree House*, above the *Rainbow* healthfood shop on Dove St. On St Benedicts St is the *Plough* and on George St the *Red Lion*, both good pubs popular with students. By way of a contrast, you could try the *Gardeners/Murderers*, a loud maze of a pub on Timber Hill, or the *Waterfront*, 139–141 King St, Norwich's principal club and alternative music venue.

NORTHERN ENGLAND

The main tourist draw of **northern England** is the **Lake District**, but the windswept grandeur of the Pennines, especially the upland valleys of the **Yorkshire Dales National Park**, is equally worthy of exploration. However, to restrict yourself purely to the northern outdoors would be to do a great disservice to regional cities such as **Liverpool**, **Manchester** and **Newcastle**. These were little more than villages until the Industrial Revolution, and their centres are alive with the ostentatious civic architecture of nineteenth-century capitalism. An entirely different angle on northern history is provided by the great medieval ecclesiastical centres of **Durham** and **York**, where famous cathedrals provide a focus for extensive medieval remains.

Liverpool

It's ironic that the city known the world over for its supreme contributions to British culture, chiefly in popular music and on the football field, should also appear the most run-down. **LIVERPOOL**, more than anywhere else, suffered from the economic pressures of the 1980s, leaving the docks largely defunct and the city with record numbers of unemployed. The later eighties, however, brought an ambitious urban renewal plan, with the docks as cultural centre, tourist attraction and trendy nightlife spot. The success of this, and the pride and aggressive wit of Liverpudlians, make the city a warm and invigorating place to visit. If you plan to visit several museums, it might be worth buying an NMGM (National Museums and Galleries of Merseyside) pass, which costs £3 and gives entry to eight museums and galleries for a year.

Liverpool's central layout is easy to assimilate: a grid of downtown streets separates Lime St train station in the east from the Mersey to the west. Behind the station, Mount Pleasant heads uphill towards the university and a lively student quarter. **Lime Street** itself is the scene of a fine ensemble of public buildings: immediately opposite the station, **St George's Hall** (Aug Mon–Sat 11am–4pm; £1.50) exemplifies the municipal classicism which spread throughout industrial Britain early last century. Just north of the hall is the **Walker Art Gallery** (Mon–Sat 10am–5pm, Sun noon–5pm; NMGM), one of the richest collections outside London. The odd Rubens and Rembrandt counterpoint a fairly representative jaunt through British art history, with Turner, Gainsborough, Joseph Wright of Derby, and Stubbs all being well represented – as, inevitably, are the Pre-Raphaelites. Going down the hill from the Walker you'll pass the **Liverpool Museum and Planetarium** (same hours; museum NMGM, planetarium £1.20), five floors of varied exhibits featuring anthropology, stuffed beasts, Amazonian rain forests, a basement aquarium and, of course, a planetarium.

From here it's an uneventful walk westwards to the **Pier Head** and Liverpool's waterfront, from where it's worth taking one of the regular ferries to Birkenhead for the views back towards the city. To the south are the great dock basins, many still undergoing renovation, with **Albert Dock** as the completed showpiece. The main focus here is the newly refurbished **Tate Gallery** (Tues–Sun 10am–6pm; free), one of two provincial arms of London's Tate (the other is in St Ives, Cornwall), borrowing part of the capital's collection for a few months at a time. Occupying the other side of the dock is the **Maritime Museum** (daily 10am–5pm; NMGM), including models of the vessels that used to ply the Mersey and a recreation of conditions on board an emigrant ship bound for America. In the basement an exhibition entitled "Transatlantic Slavery: Against Human Dignity" displays an honest and shocking account of the conditions forced upon African slaves who were the source of Liverpool's wealth in the eighteenth and nineteenth centuries. The Albert Dock is also home to **The Beatles Story** (daily 10am–4/5pm; £6.45), a concentrated multimedia attempt to capture the essence of the Fab Four's rise from Hamburg rags to Abbey Road riches. Back in the town centre, the area around Mathew Street has been designated the "Cavern Quarter". The current Cavern Club is only a rebuilt version of the original, but its history and numerous souvenirs are exhibited in the pub of the same name opposite. You can take a guided tour of all the other sites associated with the band, such as Penny Lane and Strawberry Fields, or even attend the annual International Beatles Festival held at the end of August (details of both from Cavern City Tours ☎0151/236 9091).

The major attractions to the east and south of Lime Street are the city's two cathedrals; both are twentieth-century but they could hardly differ more in style. The Roman Catholic **Metropolitan Cathedral of Christ the King** (daily 8am–6pm; free), ten minutes' walk up Mount Pleasant, is a vast, inverted-funnel-shaped building, whose fading modern architecture belies the beauty of its interior – the profusion of stained-glass windows bathing it in a surreal blue light. Hope Street, opposite, links the Metropolitan with the Anglican **Liverpool Cathedral** (daily 8am–6pm; free, entrance to tower £2), the largest in the country. Designed by Giles Gilbert Scott in 1903 while still in his early twenties, this traditionalist mass of pale-red stone wasn't completely finished until 1978. Immediately below, in the deep trench of a former quarry, tunnelled walkways provide an interesting excursion through the cathedral graveyard.

Practicalities

Trains arrive at Lime St station on the eastern fringe of the town centre; **buses** stop at the smart new station on Norton St, northeast of Lime St station. A short walk across Lime St and down Elliott St brings you to the **Merseyside Welcome Centre** in the Clayton Square shopping mall (Mon–Sat 9.30am–5.30pm; ☎0151/709 3631). There's another **tourist office** in the Albert Dock (daily 10am–5.30pm; ☎0151/708 8854); both book accommodation without charge. Hostel **accommodation** centres around the noisy but friendly YMCA, 56–60 Mount Pleasant (☎0151/709 9516; ③); the YWCA, 1 Rodney St (☎0151/709 7791; ③); and the *Embassie Youth Hostel*, 1 Falkner Square, near the junction of Grove St and Upper Parliament St (☎0151/707 1089; ③). Liverpool John Moore's University offers the best university accommodation (☎0151/709 3197; ②; mid-June to early Sept). The *Feathers Hotel*, 117–125 Mount Pleasant (☎0151/709 9655; ⑤) is the best of the many hotels on that street.

There's a wide range of inexpensive ethnic **food** around Mount Pleasant, Hardman St and the grid of streets in between. Otherwise, *Harry Ramsden's* on Brunswick Way cooks up excellent fish and chips, the *Liverpool Cathedral Refectory* has good value lunches and the solar-powered *Hub Café*, 9 Berry St, serves vegetarian cuisine. The *Philharmonic Dining Rooms*, Hope St, is Liverpool's most characteristic **pub**, with a carefully re-created Victorian interior. Currently more trendy are several late-night café-bars: *Baa Bar*, 43–45 Fleet St, is the most stylish of these, while *The Hub*, 9 Berry St, is hugely popular for its alternative variety acts. For **nightlife**, *Cream*, off Hanover St and the *Cavern Club* on Matthew St are both popular clubs, while *Escape*, Paradise St, is a leading gay club. The *Picket*, 24 Hardman St and the *Hanover*, 62 Hanover St have the best selection of bands, but *Zanzibar* and *Heebieejeebies*, both on Seel St, have a more varied programme, ranging from indie to jazz. The *Royal Court* (closed for refurbishment at time of writing) is the main venue for touring bands.

Manchester

MANCHESTER has a similarly hard-bitten edge to its neighbour and, like Liverpool, its attractions have much to do with music and football – with the crucial difference that the Manchester music and club scene, though diminished from the heady "Madchester" days, is perhaps more vibrant than its rival's, and the city's premier team, Manchester United, has triumphed consistently over Liverpool over the past few years. The redesign and rebuilding of the city centre, after much of it was devastated by an IRA bomb in 1996, has been quick and impressive and has brought with it a welter of new shops, bars and restaurants in what has come to be known as "the post-bomb boom". The £500,000,000 programme is due to be completed by 2001, although many projects will be finished a year earlier, including a new square and park area around the cathedral and a vast entertainment centre in the old Printworks off Corporation St.

Piccadilly Gardens, an untidy square with a bus station in the middle, passes for a central focus. The main shopping thoroughfare of Market Street runs west from here, traversing the city's heart. It throws up possibly one of Manchester's ugliest buildings, the huge Arndale shopping centre – which took the brunt of the 1996 bomb and is thankfully being completely overhauled – and leads eventually to **St Anns Square**, a sociably pedestrianized shopping, eating and entertainment area. The square is home to the **Royal Exchange** building, now restored as a theatre and fashionable shopping centre following serious bomb damage. Turning right onto Victoria Street at Market Street's western end, it's strange to come upon the demure fifteenth-century **Cathedral**, a fine Perpendicular structure renowned for the wood carving of its choir stalls and, just to the left of the choir, a small stone bearing an eighth-century carving of an angel. From here, drab Deansgate leads south to the **John Rylands Library** at no. 150 (Mon–Fri 10am–5.30pm, Sat 10am–1pm; free), which exhibits a small and constantly changing selection of rare and ancient items, ranging from Egyptian papyri to early examples of European printing. A left turn into Brazenose Street brings you to Albert Square and the **Town Hall** (daily 9am–5pm), an overbearing example of the Victorian Gothic revival. Southeast of it on Peter St is the Neo-Renaissance **Free Trade Hall**, a good venue for classical music and jazz and the original home of northern England's best orchestra, the Hallé, now housed in the new 2400-seater Bridgwater Hall by the G-Mex centre.

A block east of the town hall on Mosley St is the City Art Gallery, closed for restoration until summer 2001. For a celebration of the triumphs of industrialization, head for the **Museum of Science and Industry** on Liverpool Rd, at the southern end of Deansgate (daily 10am–5pm; £5), where exhibits include steam engines, textile machinery and a glimpse of the Manchester sewer system. The nearby **Granada TV Studios**, Water St (Mon–Fri 9.45am–3pm; Sat & Sun 9.45am–4pm; reduced hours in winter; £14.99; ☎0161/832 0880), offers various virtual reality rides and film-set tours, including along Coronation Street, the eponymous home of one of Britain's most popular soaps.

Heading southeast from the town hall along Oxford Rd brings you to the **Manchester Museum** (Mon–Sat 10am–5pm; free), housed in university buildings, with an extensive Egyptology collection. Further on, the **Whitworth Art Gallery** (Mon–Sat 10am–5pm, Sun 2–5pm; free) specializes in textiles; English Tudor embroideries and elegant Indian and Far Eastern silks provide the interest.

One of the latest and probably the most popular attractions is the **Manchester United Football Club Museum** (daily 9.30am–5pm; £4.50, with ground tour £7.50), housed in the North Stand of the club's Old Trafford Ground, easily accessible by the Metrolink tram to the station of the same name, or by bus #256 or #257. The museum houses displays of kits and trophies and you can wallow in the team's past and present glories or access the career details of even the most obscure player.

Practicalities

Most **trains** arrive at Piccadilly station; most services for the north terminate at Victoria, a little way northwest and linked to Piccadilly by the Metrolink tram system. **Buses** stop at Chorlton St, close to Piccadilly. The **tourist office** is in the town hall extension, on Lloyd St (Mon–Sat 10am–5.30pm, Sun 11am–4pm; ☎0161/234 3157). For **accommodation**, try the new, large youth hostel on Potato Wharf (☎0161/839 9960; ③); or one of two backpackers' places two miles out in Stretford – *Peppers* at 17 Great Stone Rd (☎0161/848 9770; ②) or *Joan's Place* at 10 Hornby Rd (☎0161/872 3499; ③), both five minutes' walk from Old Trafford Metrolink. More central is *Monroe's Hotel*, 38 London Rd, opposite Piccadilly station

(☎0161/236 0564; ④). In summer you should also be able to find rooms in student halls of residence (☎0161/275 2156; ④).

For budget **eating**, head a couple of blocks east of the town hall to Faulkner St, the hub of Manchester's Chinatown. Alternatively, try the excellent vegetarian café, the *Fallen Angel*, at 263 Upper Brook St, or the *Punjab Sweethouse*, 177 Wilmslow Rd, which does superb South Indian food. Wilmslow Road, which runs through the student quarter, is lined with cheap ethnic restaurants; try *60/40* at no. 448 for good vegetarian food. The trendiest places to drink are in the up-and-coming Castlefield area, Oldham St in the northern quarter, or the "gay village" on the Rochdale Canal, although café-bars have sprung up all over the city. Favourites are *Metz*, 3 Brazil St, in the gay village, and, on the opposite side of the canal, *Manto*, 46 Canal St.

For details of the city's **nightlife**, pick up a copy of the fortnightly *City Life*. Manchester's lively club scene has gone through a lot of changes as a result of police and gangland pressure, or perhaps just because of a trend towards smaller clubs, finally forcing the most famous venue, the *Haçienda*, to close permanently in 1997. *Cyberia*, Oxford St (with Internet access), and *The Boardwalk*, Little Peter St, are long-standing favourites. *Velvet Underground*, 111 Deansgate, and *Paradise Factory*, 112–116 Princess St, are two of the liveliest crop of house and dance clubs, with regular gay and lesbian nights. More alternative is the *Band on the Wall*, Swan St, mixing jazz, roots and funk with straight-up club nights. Catch up-and-coming bands at *The Roadhouse*, Newton St – bigger acts play at the *Academy*, Oxford Rd; the Manchester University Students' Union next door; the G-Mex centre on the corner of Windmill St and Mosley St; or the MEN Arena (still often known and signposted as the NYNEX arena) behind Victoria station.

The Lake District

The site of England's highest peaks and its biggest concentration of lakes, the glacier-carved **Lake District** is the nation's most popular walking and hiking area. The weather changes quickly here, but the sudden shifts of light on the bracken and moorland grasses, and on the slate of the local buildings, are part of the area's appeal. The most direct way of reaching the Lake District is via the London–Glasgow main line, disembarking at Lancaster, from where bus #555 (Mon–Sat hourly, Sun every 2hr) runs right through the Lake District, calling at Windermere, Ambleside, Grasmere and Keswick. Alternatively, you could get off at Oxenholme, connecting with a branch line to Windermere; or Penrith, where buses #105 and #X5 run to Keswick. Public transport in the area is dramatically reduced on Sundays.

Windermere and around

Largest and southernmost of the lakes, **Windermere** is also the most accessible and therefore one of the most crowded areas in summer. The town of Windermere itself is set back from the lake, and there's little to do here save stroll down to the sister town of Bowness a mile to the south on the waterfront. Windermere's **tourist office** is just outside the train station (daily 9am–6pm; ☎015394/46499), while the nearest **hostel** is a couple of miles north, just off Ullswater Rd (☎015394/43543; ②). From Bowness (where there's another information office), there's a choice of **ferries**. The first crosses the lake from half a mile south of the centre, from where it's a steep two-mile walk to the village of Near Sawrey and **Hill Top Farm** (April–Oct daily 11am–4.30pm; £3.20), home of Beatrix Potter and still crammed with her effects. The other, originating from Lakeside at the southern tip of the lake, calls at Bowness Pier right in Bowness, continuing to **AMBLESIDE** at the northern end – also served by bus #555 from Windermere and Bowness. Thronged with visitors throughout the year, the pubs here are busier and the range of food wider than down the lake. Ambleside's most unlikely resident was German Dadaist Kurt Schwitters, who settled here in 1945; his gravestone can be seen in Ambleside cemetery. The **tourist office** is in the central buildings by the Market Cross, off Church St (Easter–Oct daily 9am–5pm; Nov–Easter Tues–Sat 9am–1pm & 2–5pm; ☎015394/32582). Ambleside's **youth hostel** is at Waterhead, fifteen minutes south of town on the shore (☎015394/32304; ③).

Hawkshead and Coniston

Buses #505 and #506 run from Ambleside to Hawkshead and Coniston (Mon–Sat 8 daily, Sun 3 daily), both refreshingly peaceful places after the hurly-burly of Windermere. Six miles southwest of Ambleside, the whitewashed cottages of **HAWKSHEAD** harbour some marvellous village pubs and the school where Wordsworth was a pupil. The **Hawkshead Grammar School** (Easter–Oct Mon–Sat 10am–12.30pm & 1.30–5pm, Sun 1–5pm; £2) contains a desk carved with the young delinquent's name, and more ancient mementoes of the school's long history. The nearby **Beatrix Potter Gallery** (late-March to Oct Sun–Thurs 10.30am–4.30pm; £2.70) contains objects relating to the author's characters. A small **tourist office** (Easter–Nov daily 9.30am–5.30/6pm; Dec–Easter Sat & Sun 10am–3.30pm) next to the bus stop handles a range of B&B and farmhouse accommodation; the plush, family-orientated **hostel** at Esthwaite Lodge (☎015394/36293; ③), a mile south of town, is one of the best in the country.

Four miles southwest of Hawkshead lies **Grizedale Forest**, an industrial plantation littered with intriguing wood sculptures. Straddling the only road into the forest, the Grizedale Forest Centre (daily 10am–5pm) sells trail maps for walkers and cyclists: bikes can be hired from a booth across the road for £14 a day. Walking through the forest from Hawkshead and descending towards **Lake Coniston** is a good way of reaching the village of the same name, another elegant cluster of whitewashed houses nestling beneath the target for local hikers, Coniston Old Man. There's a **hostel** north of the village at Holly How, Far End (☎015394/41323; ②), and another above Coniston on the slopes of Old Man, at Coppermines House (☎015394/41261; ②). The most popular walk from Coniston – and one which can also be approached from Hawkshead – is to **Tarn Hows**, three miles northeast, a lake surrounded by wooded high ground, with several vantage points across the hills.

The *Steam Yacht Gondola* crisscrosses the lake (April–Nov 4–5 daily; £4.50 round-trip), providing the best means of getting to the elegant lakeside villa, **Brantwood** (mid-March to mid-Nov daily 11am–5.30pm; rest of year Wed–Sun 11am–4pm; £3.70), once inhabited by the art historian John Ruskin. The *Coniston Launch* runs all year (return ticket with entrance to Brantwood £6.90). Distressed by the effects of the Industrial Revolution, Ruskin looked back on the medieval era as a golden age of pre-capitalist harmony, providing the theoretical substance for the work of the Pre-Raphaelites. The house is full of Ruskin's own drawings and sketches, as well as items relating to the painters he inspired.

Rydal and Grasmere

The trusty #555 bus connects Ambleside with the heart of Wordsworth country, but it's an expedition which you could easily accomplish on foot. The tiny village of **RYDAL** was where Wordsworth made his home from 1813 until his death in 1850; his actual house, **Rydal Mount** (March–Oct daily 9.30am–5pm; Nov–Feb Wed–Mon 10am–4pm; £3.50), is famous largely for the gardens laid out by Wordsworth himself. Paths on either side of Rydal Water cover the two miles to **GRASMERE**, site of Wordsworth's more famous abode, **Dove Cottage**. The cottage (Feb–Dec daily 9.30am–5pm; £4.40) is an ascetic, cramped farmhouse, and you may have to queue before being admitted. The adjoining museum has portraits and manuscripts relating to Wordsworth, Coleridge – who regularly hiked over from Keswick to visit him here – and de Quincey, biographer of the Lake poets, who took over Dove Cottage after Wordsworth's move to Rydal. Wordsworth and his sister Dorothy lie in simple graves in the churchyard of St Oswald's, in the heart of the village. Grasmere's **tourist office** is on Redbank Rd just before the church (April–Oct daily 9.30am–5.30pm; rest of year Sat & Sun only 10am–3.30pm; ☎015394/35245). A host of tearooms and cafés cater for the endless procession of tourists. There are two **hostels**: the nearer is at Butterslip How (☎015394/35316; ②), ten minutes north of the village; the more basic *Thorney How* (☎015394/35591; ②) is one mile out on Easedale Rd.

Keswick

Principal centre for the northern lakes, **KESWICK** lies on the northern fringes of **Derwentwater**, one of the few stretches of water in the area which can be walked all the way around. The main hiking attraction is **Skiddaw** to the north; inhospitable **Blencathra**, or Saddleback, five miles east, makes a more challenging day's climb. The town itself doesn't have a great many attractions: beyond a visit to the **Cumberland Pencil Museum** (daily 9.30am–4pm; £2), the best thing to do in Keswick is to hike a mile and a half eastwards to **Castlerigg Stone Circle**, a Neolithic monument which commands a spectacular view of the amphitheatre of mountains surrounding Thirlmere. The **tourist office** is in the Moot Hall, Market Square (daily 9.30am–4.30/5/6pm; ☎017687/72645). The nearest **youth hostel** (☎017687/72484; ③) is on Station Rd by the river, the other is on the eastern shores of Derwentwater, two miles south, in Barrow House (☎017687/77246; ③).

York

It's the medieval Minster, alleyways and ancient stone walls that draw tourists to **YORK**, but the city's character-forming experiences go back a lot further than that. It was adopted by the Romans as a base for their operations against the Brigantes, a fearsome tribe holding sway over the north from around the Humber estuary. It became the principal northern head-quarters of the conquerors, and when the Emperor Severus, over here on a Scot-bashing expedition in 208, decided to split the administration of Britain into two halves, he made York one of the capitals. York's position as the north's spiritual capital dates from 627, when Edwin of Northumbria adopted Christianity – the faith of his Kentish wife. Northumbrian power crumbled in the face of a Danish invasion, the Danes sacking York in 866 and destroying one of the best libraries in western Europe in the process. By 876, one of the Danish leaders, Halfdan, had settled here with half the Viking army, beginning a century of Scandinavian rule in York and adding another layer to a tradition of northern independence.

Without doubt, one of the best introductions to York is a stroll along the city walls (open till dusk), a three-mile circuit that takes in the medieval Bars, or gates. **Bootham Bar**, adjacent to the tourist office, is as good a place as any to start, and progressing northeastwards from here will give you good views overlooking the Minster. Immediately opposite the tourist office, the **City Art Gallery** (Mon–Sat 9.30am–4.30pm, Sun 2.30–4.30pm; free) includes portraits of local Tudor worthies and a room devoted to the sentimental, moralizing work of local-born nineteenth-century artist William Etty, plus displays devoted to other local art and artists. The next-door Museum Gardens lead to the ruins of the Benedictine abbey of St Mary and the **Yorkshire Museum** (April–Oct daily 10am–5pm; Nov–March Mon–Sat 10am–5pm, Sun 1–5pm; £3.50), which contains much of the abbey's medieval sculpture, a Roman mosaic and a good selection of Saxon and Viking finds. In the same park are the remains of a tower built by Constantius at the end of the third century.

Ever since Edwin built a wooden chapel on the site in preparation for his baptism into the faith, **York Minster** (daily 7am–dusk) has been the centre of spiritual authority for the north of England. Most of what's visible now was built in stages between the 1220s and the 1470s, gradually blotting out an earlier Norman edifice. The straight lines of the Minster are a good example of English architecture's transition from the Gothic style of medieval Europe to the home-grown Perpendicular. Inside, the apocalyptic scenes of the East Window, completed in 1405, and the abstract thirteenth-century *Five Sisters* window present the finest collection of stained glass in the country. The octagonal **Chapterhouse** (May–Sept Mon–Sat 10am–6.30pm, Sun 12.30–6pm; Oct–April Mon–Sat 10am–4.30pm, Sun 12.30–4pm; 70p) usually contains a few medieval manuscripts from the Minster's rich collection. You can also descend to the foundations (same hours; £2), where you can see remnants and artefacts from the previous Roman and Norman buildings, set against the extraordinary steel and concrete engineering works which saved the tower from collapsing in the1960s. It's now safe to ascend the central lantern tower (same hours; £2.50), for views down on the medieval pattern of narrow streets just south of the minster, known as the **Shambles**, and out northwards to the Yorkshire Moors.

A taste of the Viking period in the history of York is provided by the **Jorvik Viking Centre** located on Coppergate Walk (daily 9am–3.30/5.30pm; £4.99). A remote-control dodgem car propels you through a re-creation of Jorvik's streets, complete with appropriate smells and

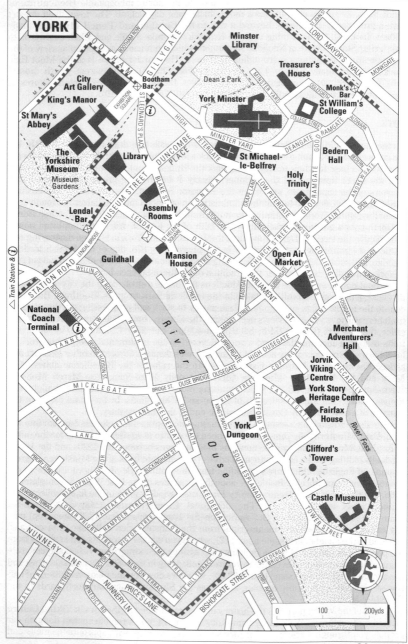

© Crown copyright

recorded sounds, while an informative commentary booms authoritatively from a loud-speaker built in behind the seat. With an eye to archeological integrity, however, the journey continues past the site of the excavations themselves, blackened shapes in the earth show-ing the foundations of the wattle-and-daub huts, and the faces of the wax dummies are care-ful reconstructions made from skulls found in the digs.

The **Merchant Adventurers' Hall** on Fossgate (daily 8.30am–3.30/5pm, closed Sun mid-Nov to mid-March; £1.90) is a well-preserved structure dating from the fourteenth century. Despite the romantic connotations of the title, this was the guild headquarters of the solid, middle-class businessmen who controlled the local wool export trade and whose portraits adorn the wood-panelled rooms.

Originally the keep of York castle, **Clifford's Tower** (daily: April–June, Sept & Oct 10am–6pm; July & Aug 9.30am–7pm; Nov–March 10am–4pm/dusk; £1.70) was the site of one of the most bizarre episodes of medieval anti-Semitism. Following a city fire, for which the Jewish community was blamed by the mob, the Jews took refuge here, then committed mass suicide in order to avoid being massacred. There's little to see in the tower itself, save for a commanding view from the top. The **Castle Museum** (Mon–Sat 9.30am–4/5.30pm, Sun 10am–4/5.30pm; £4.50) was one of the first British museums to indulge in full-scale re-cre-ations of life in bygone times, and it's still one of the best of the genre; "Kirkgate" and "Half Moon Court" – reconstructed street scenes of the Victorian and Edwardian periods – are masterpieces of evocative detail. One last museum is worth a call: the **National Railway Museum**, just beyond the station on Leeman Rd (daily 10am–6pm; £4.80), contains the nation's finest collection of steam locomotives.

Practicalities

York's magnificent **train station** is east of the centre, just outside the city walls; the **bus sta-tion** is at Rougier St, slightly nearer town in the same direction. There's a **tourist office** in the train station (April–Sept Mon–Sat 9am–8pm, Sun 10am–5pm; Oct–March Mon–Sat 9.30am–5.30pm, Sun 10am–4/5pm; ☎01904/621756) and at Exhibition Square and at 20 George Hudson St; each offers a room-booking service for £3. Backpacker **hostels** are good, including the top-of-the-range YHA, twenty minutes from the centre at Water End, Clifton (☎01904/653147; ③). Near the bus station are the excellent *York Backpackers Hostel*, 88 Micklegate (☎01904/627720; ②–③) in a converted Georgian mansion, and the more insti-tutional *York Youth Hotel*, 11–13 Bishophill Senior (☎01904/625904; ②–③), both offering rooms and dormitories. Good **B&Bs** are concentrated in the Bootham area, to the west of the Minster: try *Abbeyfields*, 19 Bootham Terrace (☎01904/636471; ⑤) or *Holme Lea Manor*, 18 St Peter's Grove (☎01904/623529; ⑤). Among York's numerous **tearooms**, *Betty's*, St Helen's Square, is the most elegant. Good places for **pub** food are the *Golden Slipper*, Goodramgate, the *Hole in the Wall*, at High Petergate, and the *Mason's Arms* near the Castle Museum on Fishergate.

Durham

Seen from the train, **DURHAM** presents a magnificent sight, with cathedral and castle perched atop a bluff enclosed by a loop of the River Wear, and linked to the suburbs by a series of sturdy bridges. Nowadays a quiet provincial town with a strong student presence, Durham was once one of northern England's power bases: the bishops of Durham were vir-tual royal agents in the north for much of the medieval era, responsible for defending a cru-cial border province frequently menaced by the Scots.

The town initially owed its reputation to the possession of the remains of Saint Cuthbert, an early prior of Lindisfarne, which were evacuated to Durham in the ninth century because of Viking raids. His shrine has dominated the eastern end of the **Cathedral** (daily 7.15am–6/8pm; donation requested) ever since. The cathedral itself is the finest example of Norman architecture in England, even though the exterior has suffered a great deal from the erosion of time and the muddle-headed efforts of an eighteenth-century renovator, who began chiselling away at the stone to improve the finish. A series of intricately carved pillars, decorated with chevrons and other geometric designs, lines the nave, and medieval frescoes depicting St Cuthbert are just visible in the Galilee Chapel, which contains the remains of the Venerable Bede, brought here from Jarrow in 1020. The original carved coffin of St Cuthbert and other antiquities can be seen in the **Treasuries of St Cuthbert** (Mon–Sat 10am–4.30pm, Sun 2–4.30pm; £2), adjacent to the cloisters.

On the opposite side of Palace Green is the Norman **Castle** (April–Sept Mon–Sat 10am–12.30pm & 2–4pm, Sun 2–4pm; Sept–Mar Mon, Wed, Sat & Sun 2–4pm; £3), now halls of residence for a few of Durham's luckier students, but preserving a solid twelfth-century chapel thought to have once served as a strongroom; look out for the naive carvings adorning the capitals of the pillars. Both the cathedral and castle are surrounded by North and South Bailey, a continuous street that curves around the hillside, lined with eighteenth- and nineteenth-century buildings that are now largely the preserve of the university. Pathways along the river bank below pass the **Museum of Archeology** in the old fulling mill (April–Oct daily 11am–4pm; Nov–March Mon, Thurs & Fri 12.30–3pm, Sat & Sun 11.30am–3.30pm; £1), which houses a very modest selection of prehistoric, Roman and Saxon finds.

Practicalities

The **train station** is ten minutes' walk from the centre, either via Millburngate Bridge or via North Rd – the site of the **bus station** – and the pedestrianized Framwellgate Bridge. **Minibuses** link the cathedral with the bus station. The **tourist office**, in Market Place (July & Aug Mon–Sat 10am–6pm, Sun 2–5pm; rest of year Mon–Sat 10am–5pm; ☎0191/384 3720), will book accommodation for a ten percent deposit.

Guest houses and B&Bs are concentrated on Gilesgate, northeast of Market Place, and around Crossgate, south of the bus station. Convenient choices include *Green Grove Guest House*, 99 Gilesgate (☎0191/384 4361; ④), and *Colebrick*, 21 Cross Gate (☎0191/384 9585; ⑤). During student vacations the colleges of Durham University provide dormitory-style private rooms (④) – ask for details at the tourist office. The nearest **campsite**, the *Grange Camping and Caravan Site* (☎0191/384 4778; ②), is three miles northeast of the city on Meadow Lane, Carrville; take bus #220 or #222 for Sunderland and get off at the Grange Garage. For good value **food**, *Vennel's Café*, Saddler's Yard (daily 9.30am–5pm), serves great snacks in a lovely little hidden courtyard, while on Elvet Bridge you'll find *Oscars Café*, a popular student place, and the cheap *Pizzeria Romeo* further down. For **drinking**, try the *Market Tavern* on the marketplace for a traditional pub, or *Saints*, directly underneath the indoor market, a trendy bar overlooking the river with cheap meals, Internet access and DJ nights.

Newcastle upon Tyne and Hadrian's Wall

A grim, industrial city with a proud shipbuilding heritage – an industry now in severe decline – **NEWCASTLE** has an undeniable raw vigour and serves as a good base for explorations of **Hadrian's Wall**, a second-century barricade that stretches from the east to west coast. Your first taste of the city if arriving by rail will be the three bridges joining the city with the suburb of Gateshead, the River Tyne and the newly redeveloped quaysides lying far below. The single steel arch of the Tyne Bridge, built in 1928, is very much the city's trademark.

The centre owes much of its character to John Dobson, who remodelled Newcastle along Neoclassical lines in the early nineteenth century. His most imposing legacy is the sweep of Grey Street, leading south from the lofty Grecian column of Grey's Monument, the city's central landmark. Newcastle's status as a border stronghold is remembered in the **castle**, with its Norman keep (Tues–Sun 9.30am–4.30/5.30pm; £1.50), which offers good rooftop views and a succession of draughty rooms, including a Norman chapel in the basement. The city's main art collection is housed in the **Laing Art Gallery** on Higham Place (Mon–Sat 10am–5pm, Sun 2–5pm; free). A venue for prestigious contemporary exhibitions, it also houses an excellent selection of Victorian painting, including the manic biblical works of local artist John Martin.

The university campus on Haymarket, on the northern fringes of the city centre, contains a trio of worthwhile museums. **The Museum of Antiquities** (Mon–Sat 10am–5pm; free) is a good introduction to the frontier culture of Hadrian's Wall, including a reconstruction of a *Mithraeum* – a temple to the Middle Eastern deity Mithras, imported to the region by Roman soldiers serving on the Wall – which once stood in the nearby town of Carrawburgh. The **Hatton Gallery** (Mon–Fri 10am–5.30pm, Sat in term time 10am–4.30pm; free) attracts touring exhibitions of contemporary art and has a small permanent collection that includes the one surviving wall of Kurt Schwitters' barn studio in Ambleside and a wealth of African sculpture.

Practicalities

Newcastle's **Central Station** is ten minutes' walk south of the centre; the **bus station**, on Gallowgate, is a couple of minutes west. The **tourist office** in Central Station (June–Sept Mon–Fri 10am–8pm, Sat 9am–5pm, Sun 10am–4pm; Oct–May Mon–Sat 10am–5pm; ☎0191/230 0030) can book **accommodation**. There's a hostel at 107 Jesmond Rd (☎0191/281 2570; ③). Jesmond is also the main location for **B&B** accommodation, which is mainly clustered around Osborne Rd; try the *George Hotel* at no. 88 (☎0191/281 4442; ⑤), or the *Westland Hotel* round the corner at 27 Osborne Av (☎0191/281 0412; ⑤). City-centre pubs and bars are clustered around Bigg Market, a block east of Grey St, although there are trendier (and pricier) options down on the quayside. Be sure to check out the *Crown Posada*, 31 The Side, and the nearby *Cooperage*, 32 The Close, both cosy quayside **pubs** with a good range of beers. The best-value **eating** in town is at *Breadcrumbs*, 5 St Mary's Place and *Mathers*, 4 Old Eldon Square. More upmarket meals are available at the trendy *Café Procope*, 35 The Side, next to the *Crown Posada* pub. The city's foremost **live music** and **club** venue is the *Riverside*, 57–59 Melbourne St (☎0191/261 4386); look out for other acts performing at Newcastle University Students' Union, Haymarket.

The Wall

Preserving the *Pax Romana* over the troublesome tribes of Britain's extremities was always a difficult task when there were more important frontiers in Europe and Asia to defend, and the Emperor Hadrian opted for containment rather than outright conquest. The turf and stone wall which bears the emperor's name was the result, punctuated by **mile castles**, strong points spaced at one-mile intervals, and by sixteen more substantially garrisoned forts. Regular trains and hourly buses (#685) on the Newcastle–Carlisle route pass by many of the sites: you should be able to see a little of the Wall and return to Newcastle before nightfall. The best base is the market town of **HEXHAM**, 30–45 minutes west of Newcastle by regular train or bus, which has plenty of **accommodation** and a basic **youth hostel** in nearby Acomb (☎01434/602864; ②). A summer bus service (#880) links the town with all the main sites along Hadrian's Wall, and in summer it sometimes links through to Newcastle on Sundays, but check at the **bus station**. There's also an independent hostel (☎01434/688 688; ②) just west at Haydon Bridge.

WALES

The relationship between England and **Wales** has never been entirely easy. Impatient with constant demarcation disputes, the eighth-century Saxon king Offa constructed a dyke to separate the two countries; today, a long-distance footpath running from near Chepstow in the south to Prestatyn in the north follows its route. During Edward I's reign the last of the Welsh native princes, Llewelyn ap Gruffyd, was killed, and Wales passed uneasily under English rule. Trouble flared again with the rebellion of Owain Glyndûr in the fifteenth century, but finally, when the Welsh prince Henry Tudor defeated Richard III at the Battle of Bosworth to become king of England, he paved the way for the 1536 Act of Union, which joined the English and Welsh in restless but perpetual partnership.

Contact with England has watered down the indigenous Welsh culture; bricked-up, decaying chapels stand as reminders of the days when Sunday services and chapel choirs were central to community life. The **Eisteddfod** festivals of Welsh music, poetry and dance still take place throughout the country in summer – the International Music Eisteddfod in

Llangollen being the best known, if corrupted, example – but harp-playing and the carving of lovespoons survive more or less courtesy of the tourism industry. Nevertheless, the Welsh language is undergoing a revival and you'll see it on bilingual road signs all over the country – but are most likely to hear it spoken in north and mid-Wales. Some Welsh place names have never been Anglicized, but where alternative names do exist, we've given them in the text.

Much of the country, particularly the **Brecon Beacons** and **Black Mountains** in the south and **Snowdonia** in the north, is relentlessly mountainous and offers wonderful walking and climbing terrain. **Pembrokeshire** to the west also boasts a spectacular rugged coastline, dotted with offshore island nature reserves. The biggest towns, including **Cardiff, Swansea, Aberystwyth** and **Caernarfon**, cling to the coastal lowlands, but even there the mountains are no more than a bus ride away.

South Wales

Following the completion in 1996 of a second suspension bridge across the River Severn, most traffic approaches South Wales via the flat and featureless no-man's-land east of Newport, along the new M4 motorway. But if you want to take in the area's most spectacular historic monument en route, you'll have to cross the estuary on the old bridge via the M48, four miles north, which will bring you out at the old market town of **CHEPSTOW** (Cas-Gwent), encircled on three sides by thirteenth-century walls and on the fourth by the River Wye. The bridge across the Wye gives stunning views of cliff-faces soaring above the river and of the first stone **castle** the Normans built in Wales (April–Oct daily 9.30am–6.30pm; Nov–March Mon–Sat 9.30am–4pm, Sun 11am–5pm; £3.30). Opposite the castle is Gwy House, an eighteenth-century town house now home to **Chepstow Museum** (Mon–Sat 11am–1pm & 2–5pm, Sun 2–5pm; £1). Nothing in Chepstow itself can match the five-mile stroll along the Wye to the impossibly romantic ruins of **Tintern Abbey** (same hours as Chepstow castle; £2.20), built by the Cistercians in the twelfth century. The nave walls rise to such a height that, from a distance, you might think the church still stood intact beneath the overhang of the wooded cliff – only when you get close do you find the roof is long gone. If you don't fancy walking, catch Red and White bus #69, which runs from Chepstow to Tintern and on to Monmouth, eight miles north, every one to two hours. You can top up for the return journey in the fourteenth-century *Moon and Sixpence* – almost a mile north of the Abbey by the river – which does excellent **bar meals**. In town, the *Coach and Horses Inn* on Welsh St offers B&B **accommodation** (π01291/622626; ④) and for a characterful, inexpensive place to stay, head one mile east across the Wye to *Upper Sedbury House* (π01291/627173; ④); alternatively, try the YHA hostel (π01594/530272; ③) at St Briavels, seven miles north over the river in England and two miles off the #69 bus route, housed in a converted castle.

Arriving by train from London, you'll glimpse Chepstow Castle from the window, but **NEWPORT** (Casnewydd) will be the first stop; Red and White buses #64 and #X73 run here from Chepstow. An unexciting city to linger in, Newport is nevertheless a useful base for exploring the nearby Roman remains – and for getting into the Brecon Beacons. **CAERLEON**, a small, traffic-bedevilled town three miles to the northeast, but almost swallowed up by Newport, preserves the extensive remains of Roman baths, while its state-of-the-art **Legionary Museum**, High St (Mon–Sat 10am–4.30/6pm, Sun 2–4.30/6pm; £2.10, £3.30 combined ticket with baths), contains finds from all the adjacent sites. The museum stands opposite the road leading to the less dramatic remains of the barracks and amphitheatre, and sells an inclusive entrance ticket for all sites. Further down High St there's a small **tourist office** (daily 10am–1pm & 2–4.30/6pm; π01633/422656) and the **Fortress Baths**, an extension of the museum built on the site of a 75 AD bath house (same hours as museum; £1.70, £3.30 combined ticket with Legionary Museum). The best place to stay is out in Caerleon at the wonderful *Clawdd Fann* (π01633/423250; ③) on Bullmoor Rd.

The Brecon Beacons

About fifteen miles north of Newport, and served by hourly trains from there, the market town of **ABERGAVENNY** (Y Fenni) sits in the fold between seven green hills and is the main base for exploring the eastern Brecon Beacons National Park. Before setting out for the mountains, pick up maps from the combined **tourist office** and **national park information office** (March–Oct daily 10am–6pm; ☎01873/857588) at Swan Meadow, Monmouth St, a stone's throw from the bus station – and check what sort of weather you can expect, as sudden mists can play havoc. The most accessible walking areas are the **Sugar Loaf** (1955ft), four miles to the northwest, and **Skirrid Fawr** (1595ft), three miles to the north. The railway station is five minutes' walk away on Station Rd off the Monmouth Rd. For **B&B** try the excellent *Pentre House* (☎01873/853435; ④), a mile out on the road to Brecon.

CRICKHOWELL, a friendly village with a fine medieval bridge five miles west of Abergavenny, is a more picturesque kicking-off point for explorations. Red and White bus #21 runs a two-hourly (not Sun) service from Abergavenny and Newport through Crickhowell to Brecon. A six-mile hike into the Black Mountains from Crickhowell takes you through remote and occasionally bleak countryside to tiny **Partrishow Church**; inside, you'll find a rare rood screen complete with carved wooden loft and a mural of Father Time. To **stay** in Crickhowell try the *Dragon Hotel*, High St (☎01873/810362; ⑥). The **tourist office**, Beaufort St (April–Oct Mon–Sat 10am–6pm; ☎01873/812105), can help find alternatives.

Eight miles west, the largest central Brecon Beacons are accessible from **BRECON** (Aberhonddu), a sleepy little town springing to life on Tuesdays and Fridays for livestock and indoor markets and once a year for the huge Brecon Jazz Festival in mid-August. It's served by bus #21 from Crickhowell. For details of the numerous trekking routes into the Beacons and an extensive programme of guided walks, call at the national park **information office** (daily: April–Oct 10am–6pm, Nov–March 9am–4.45pm; ☎01874/622485) which shares the same building as the tourist office in the cattle market car park. B&B **accommodation** can be had at *Beacons Guest House*, 16 Bridge St (☎01874/623339; ④), and *Tir Bach Guest House*, 13 Alexandra Rd (☎01874/624551; ④). The Ty'n-y-Caeau **youth hostel** is two miles east of Brecon at Groesffordd (☎01874/665270; ②), a mile off the #21 bus route. There's also an independent hostel in the area, the *Held Bunkhouse*, at Cantref (☎01874/624646; ③), one mile southeast.

Cardiff and around

CARDIFF (Caerdydd), the Welsh capital, is rapidly picking itself up again after the collapse of the coal-mining industry – particularly since the recent devolution of Wales – and its narrow Victorian shopping arcades are interspersed with spanking new shopping centres and wide pedestrian precincts which seem to have sprung up at random. You are most likely to arrive at **Cardiff Central Station** or the adjacent **bus terminal**, south of the city centre off Penarth Rd, although some local rail services leave from Queen St station to the west. You can pick up free maps and information at the **tourist office** at Central Station (Mon–Sat 9/10am–5.30/6.30pm, Sun 10am–4pm; ☎01222/227281).

Cardiff Castle (daily 10am–4.30/6pm; £5) is a good place to start your city tour. Standing on a Roman site developed by the Normans, it was embellished by William Burges in the 1860s, and each room is now a wonderful example of Victorian "medieval" decoration; best of all are the Chaucer Room, the Banqueting Hall, the Arab Room and the Fairy-tale Nursery. Five minutes' walk away, the **National Museum and Gallery of Wales** in Cathays Park (Tues–Sun 10am–5pm; £4) houses a version of Rodin's *The Kiss*, a fine collection of Impressionist paintings, and natural history and archeological exhibits.

The **Cardiff Bay** area – reached by bus #8 from Central Station – has seen massive redevelopment in preparation for the long-awaited opening of the Welsh Assembly, with waterfront walks, hotels and restaurants. You can also visit **Techniquest**, a hands-on science exhibition (Mon–Fri 9.30am–4.30pm, Sat & Sun 10.30am–5pm; £4.75).

The **Museum of Welsh Life** at St Fagans, four miles from the centre (bus #32 or the more frequent #56 from opposite the castle), is a 100-acre open-air museum packed with reconstructed rural buildings from all over Wales (daily 10am–5pm; £5.25); a good time to visit is May Day, when a huge fair is held here. Finally, for a revealing glimpse of coal-mining life in the valleys, catch the hourly bus #23 to visit the **Blaenafon Big Pit Mining Museum** (March–Nov daily 9.30am–5pm; Feb Tues–Thurs only; £5.50), housed in a mine which ceased production only in 1980; the former miners now find employment as tour guides. You descend 294 feet in a miners' cage to inspect coalfaces, underground roadways and haulage engines dating back almost 200 years.

Fans of William Burges' exquisite and elaborate style of decor shouldn't miss **Castell Coch** ("Red Castle") off the A470 at Tongwynlais (April–Oct daily 9.30am–6.30pm; Nov–March Mon–Sat 9.30am–4pm, Sun 11am–4pm; £2.50). Built on the site of a thirteenth-century castle and perched dramatically on a steep, forested hillside, Burges' lavish Victorian showpiece was commissioned by the third Lord Bute as a country retreat. While the outside is functional, with a fully operational portcullis and drawbridge, inside there are fantastically vaulted ceilings and astonishing decorations and furnishings.

Cardiff's **youth hostel** is a couple of miles from the centre at 2 Wedal Rd (☎01222/462303; ③) or you can try the independent *Cardiff International Backpackers*, 96 Neville St (☎01222/345577; ③). For **B&B**, try *Rosanna*, at 175 Cathedral Rd (☎01222/229780; ③), fifteen minutes' walk west of the train station, across the River Taff, or *Ferriers*, at 130 Cathedral Rd (☎01222/383413; ④). To sample laverbread and other Welsh delicacies, head for *Celtic Cauldron* in the shopping arcade opposite the castle. Bistro-style **meals** can be had in *Henry's Bar* in Park Place. Real-ale lovers can sample Cardiff's own Brains brew surrounded by rugby memorabilia in the *Old Arcade*, Church St.

Pembroke and the Pembrokeshire Coast National Park

PEMBROKE (Penfro), birthplace of Henry VII, is a sleepy town lying at the heart of the Pembrokeshire Coast National Park, and easily accessible by train from Cardiff. Centrepiece of the town itself is the magnificent water-surrounded **Castle** (April–Sept daily 9.30am–6pm; rest of year 10am–4/5pm; £3), whose circular keep, dating from 1200, offers fine views of the countryside. The castle overshadows the high street where shops are shoehorned into an assortment of Tudor and Georgian buildings, one of them housing the **Museum of the Home**, an eclectic collection of exhibits ranging from toys and games to fashion accessories (May–Sept Mon–Thurs 11am–5pm; £1.20).

The nearest **hostels** to Pembroke are at Broad Haven, Haverfordwest (☎01437/781688; ②), and Pentlepoir, Saundersfoot (☎01834/812333; ②), both a short bus hop away. In Pembroke, inexpensive **B&B** can be had at the *Connaught Guest House,* 123 Main St (☎01646/684655; ③). Twice-daily **ferries** to Rosslare, Ireland, leave from Pembroke Dock, two miles to the north, taking four hours for the crossing.

The **Pembrokeshire Coast National Park** sweeps from Pendine Sands near Llansteffan to Poppit Sands near Cardigan, and the coastal path includes some of Wales' most stunning and remote scenery, offering sheer cliff-faces, panoramic sea views and excellent seabird-watching. Tricky though it may be without a car, it's worth trying to get to Saint Govan's Head – directly south of Pembroke near Broad Haven – where a chapel clings, barely credibly, to the rock face.

From Pembroke, bus #359 takes you to Haverfordwest where you can catch #411 for the sixteen-mile journey west to **SAINT DAVID'S** (Tyddewi), where a breathtakingly beautiful **Cathedral**, delicately tinted purple, green and yellow by a combination of lichen and geology, hides in a dip below the high street. Constructed between 1180 and 1522, but heavily restored in the last century, the cathedral hosts a prestigious classical music festival each May. Across a thin trickle of river thousands of jackdaws congregate around the extensive remains of the fourteenth-century **Bishop's Palace** (Easter–Oct daily 9.30am–6.30pm; Nov–Easter Mon–Sat 9.30am–4pm, Sun 2–4pm; £1.70), adding to the beauty of the setting. There's a **youth hostel** at Llaethdy, two miles west (☎01437/720345; ②), and several **B&Bs** in St David's: try *Pen Albro*, 18 Goat St (☎01437/721865; ④), or *Alandale*, 43 Nun St (☎01437/720404; ④). The **tourist office** is in the Grove, High St (April–Oct daily 9.30am–5.30pm, rest of year Mon–Sat 10am–4pm; ☎01437/720392).

Seventeen miles further north along the route of the #411 is **FISHGUARD** (Abergwaun), an attractive fishing port and the other ferry embarkation point for Rosslare, with two ferry sailings daily (3hr 30min) and four fast catamaran crossings (1hr 40min). *The Hamilton Backpacker Lodge*, an independent **hostel**, 21–23 Hamilton St (☎01348/874797; dorms ②, twins ③), and the *Fishguard Bay Hotel*, Quay St (☎01348/873571; ④), are used to people arriving late or departing early.

Mid-Wales

Mid-Wales, an area of wild mountain roads, hidden valleys and genteel ex-spa towns, is the least visited part of the country, perhaps because access is a little trickier. Nevertheless, it's worth making the effort, because it's here more than anywhere else that you'll discover the traditional rural Wales, in quiet towns where the pub conversation takes place in Welsh rather than English. But this is also "alternative" Wales at its most hippyish – look out for health-food shops and trendy bookshops, their English-speaking owners often escapees from the Midlands.

To get to mid-Wales, there's a handy **train** service from Shrewsbury which passes through **WELSHPOOL** (Trallwng) and continues to Aberystwyth (every 2–3hr). Welshpool is a market town full of the distinctive black-and-white half-timbered houses typical of the Welsh–English borders. It's worth a stop simply to visit thirteenth-century **Powis Castle** (April–June, Sept & Oct Wed–Sun 1–5pm; July & Aug Tues–Sun 1–5pm; gardens same dates 11am–6pm; £7.50 including Clive Museum). A gorgeous honey-coloured building that's been continuously inhabited for 500 years, the castle houses Wales' best collection of furniture, tapestries and pictures, as well as the Clive of India collection of Indian treasures. Capability Brown designed the terraced gardens. If you decide to stay, **B&B** is available at *Montgomery House*, Salop Rd (☎01938/552693; ③).

Aberystwyth and around

ABERYSTWYTH is a lively seaside resort of neat Victorian terraces and a thriving student culture. Best place to start exploring is the **tourist office**, Terrace Rd, just off Marine Parade (Easter–Oct daily 10am–5/6pm; Nov–Easter Mon–Sat 10am–5pm; ☎01970/612125); upstairs, the Ceredigion Museum contains coracles once used by local fishermen and a reconstructed cottage interior. Most of the action centres on the seafront, where one of Edward I's castles bestrides a windy headland to the south. There's also a Victorian camera obscura which can be reached via an electric cliff train to the north (Easter–Oct daily 10am–6pm; £2 return). For a more extended rail trip, you could take the **Vale of Rheidol** steam train service to **Devil's Bridge** (3hr return trip, 1hr to Devil's Bridge; £10.50), a canyon where three bridges of assorted ages and in assorted conditions span a dramatic waterfall; the service can get very busy in the middle of the day.

Aberystwyth seafront is lined with Victorian **guesthouses**, all much of a muchness; try *Brendan*, 19 Marine Terrace (☎01970/612252; ④) or *Helmsman* further along at no. 43 (☎01970/624132; ⑤). Check out the University Arts Centre on Penglais Hill for films, plays, exhibitions and other events (closed mid-May to mid-June). *Y-Graig*, 34 Pier St, is a great place to eat vegetarian **food**, and the owner is a mine of information on what's going on locally.

North of Aberystwyth the train passes through a succession of seaside resorts, some small and discreet, others large and upfront, before reaching **ABERDOVEY** (Aberdyfi), a quiet village beautifully situated at the mouth of the River Dovey. Its seafront is lined with **B&Bs** which do a roaring trade in summer: try *Brodawel*, Tywyn Rd (☎01654/767347; ⑥), or *Cantref*, in Penrhos (☎01654/767273; ③) near Aberdovey train station.

Mainline trains follow the coast north to down-at-heel Barmouth, where you can catch bus #94 (Mon–Sat 7 daily; Sun 3 daily) inland to **DOLGELLAU**, a base for exploring **Cadair Idris**. The mountain looms over the southern side of town, its summit accessible via a tough six-mile trek along the Pony Path starting three miles south of Dolgellau. The **tourist office** is on Eldon Square (Easter–Oct daily 10am–6pm; Nov–Easter Thurs–Mon 10am–5pm; ☎01341/422888). If you fancy staying, try *Aben Café*, Smithfield St (☎01341/422460; ④), centrally placed above a greasy caff, or *Ivy House* on Finsbury Square (☎01341/422535; ④).

If you prefer to stick to the coast, trains from Barmouth head north to **HARLECH**, where one of the best of Edward I's great castles, later Glyndûr's residence, towers above everything else on a rocky crag overlooking the sea (April–Oct daily 9.30am–6.30pm; Nov–March Mon–Sat 9.30am–4pm, Sun 11–4pm; £3); the ramparts offer panoramic views over Snowdonia on one side and Tremadog Bay on the other. The town itself huddles apologetically behind the castle with little to say for itself, but if you want **to stay**, try the *Aris Guest House*, 4 Pen-y-Bryn (☎01766/780409; ④) or *Byrdir*, High St (☎01766/780316; ④), fifty yards from the **tourist office** (Easter–Oct daily 10am–6pm; ☎01766/780658).

North Wales

Snowdonia is the glory of **North Wales**, with some of the most dramatic mountain scenery Britain has to offer, with jagged peaks, towering waterfalls and stunning glacial lakes. Not surprisingly, walkers congregate here in strength, and the villages around the area's highest peak, Snowdon, see steady tourist traffic even in the coldest, bleakest months of the year. Whatever season you're here, make sure you go equipped with suitable shoes, warm clothing, and food and drink to see you through any unexpected hitches. There are two main **rail routes** into North Wales: up the west coast from mid-Wales, or along the northern littoral from Chester to Bangor and Holyhead with a branch to Betws-y-Coed and Blaenau Ffestiniog. The main A5 road cuts through Llangollen to the heart of Snowdonia.

Blaenau Ffestiniog and Betws-y-Coed

The private train (April–Oct 11 daily; Nov–March 2 daily, weekends only; 01766/512340) runs inland from Porthmadog, a few miles north of Harlech, as far as the slate-quarrying town of **BLAENAU FFESTINIOG**, a fourteen-mile journey through the Snowdonia National Park. On a grey day, Blaenau Ffestiniog can look particularly desolate, but it's worth a call for the **Llechwedd Slate Caverns** a mile north, reached by "Clipper" bus. A train takes visitors into the side of the mountain, past an underground lake and spectacular caverns to the very bottom of the mine, on Britain's steepest train incline (daily 10am–4.15/5.15pm; £6.75). Should the brooding scenery have cast its spell over you, **B&B** can be had at *Afallon*, Manod Rd (01766/830468; ③).

You'll probably want to push on to **BETWS-Y-COED**, ten miles northeast by mainline train. A popular base for Snowdonia National Park – though no serious walks start here – the town has one of the prettiest settings in Wales but is overrun with visitors in summer, many coming here just to see the **Swallow Falls** in the wooded Llugwy Valley, two miles west of town. If you want to stay to appreciate the wood-and-water setting after the day-trippers have moved on, try the **B&B** above the *Riverside Restaurant*, Holyhead Rd (☎01690/710650; ③), though keen walkers would be better catered for at the **youth hostel** (☎01690/720225; ②) at Capel Curig six miles west (bus #19). In Betws-y-Coed the *Glan Aber* pub and *Pont-y-Pair*, both on Holyhead Rd, do reasonable bar meals and are the liveliest places for a drink. There's a **tourist office** (daily: Easter–Oct 10am–6pm; Nov–Easter 9.30am–12.30 & 1.30–4.30pm; ☎01690/710426). From Betws-y-Coed there are trains and buses to Llandudno Junction, for train connections to the main line from Chester.

Conwy and Caernarfon

Following the North Wales coast west, twice-hourly trains from Chester pass through a string of unappealing resorts before coming to **CONWY**, where Edward I's **Castle** (April to mid-Oct daily 9.30am–6.30pm; mid-Oct to March Mon–Sat 9.30am–4pm, Sun 11am–4pm; £3) and the town walls have been listed by UNESCO as a World Heritage Site. The ramparts offer fine views of Telford's recently restored 1826 **suspension bridge** (July & Aug daily 10am–5pm; April–June, Sept & Oct Wed–Mon 10am–5pm; £1) over the River Conwy. For **B&B** try *Pen-y-Bryn*, Lancaster Square (☎01492/596445; ④), or *Gwynedd Guesthouse*, 10 Upper Gate St (☎01492/596537; ④). The castle also houses the **tourist office** (same hours as castle; ☎01492/592248).

North-coast trains converge on Bangor before heading north for Anglesey. To get to **CAERNARFON** – the springboard for trips into Snowdonia from the north – you'll need bus #5 or #5B from the bus station off Bangor High St. Since 1301 all Princes of Wales have been invested in **Caernarfon Castle** (April–Oct daily 9.30am–6.30pm; Nov–March Mon–Sat 9.30am–4pm, Sun 11am–4pm; £4.20), built in 1283 and arguably the most splendid castle in Britain. The walls completely dominate the town, but form just a shell enclosing a three-acre space. As for Caernarfon itself, time hasn't been particularly kind to it, and suburbs full of high-rise flats provide a disappointing setting for such splendour.

Tourist information is available at Oriel Pendeitsh, Castle St (April–Oct daily 10am–6pm; Nov–March Mon–Fri 9.30am–4.30pm, Sat & Sun 9am–4.30pm; ☎01286/672232). In town, the cheapest place **to stay** is *Trotters*, an independent hostel at 2 High St (☎01286/672963; ①). For more plush surroundings, try the *Wallasea Guesthouse* (☎01286/673564; ③), overlooking the river at 21 Segontium Terrace, or some of the hotels along North Rd.

Llanberis and Snowdon

Half-hourly #88 and the less frequent #11 buses run the seven miles from Caernarfon to **LLAN-BERIS**, a lakeside village bursting to grow into a town in the shadow of **Snowdon** (Yr Wyddfa), at 3560ft the highest mountain in England and Wales. With the biggest concentration of guest-houses, hostels and restaurants in Snowdonia, it offers the perfect base for mountain exploration, however tentative. The longest but easiest ascent of the mountain is the Llanbens Path, a signposted five-mile hike, manageable by anyone reasonably fit, although the final stretch involves a bit of a scramble. Alternatively, you can cop out and take the normally steam-hauled **Snowdon Mountain Railway**, which operates from Llanberis to the summit café, pub and post office, weather permitting, daily from mid-March to October; at the season's start and end trains may terminate at Clogwyn, three-quarters of the way up the mountain. Return tickets (£14.50) permit half an hour's viewing from the summit. The slate quarries which sear Llanberis' surroundings now lie idle, the **Welsh Slate Museum** (Easter–Sept daily 9.30am–5.30pm; Oct–Easter Mon–Fri 10am–4.30pm; £3) remaining as a memorial to the workers' tough lives. Nearby the Dinorwig Pumped Storage Hydro Station is carved out of the mountain and can be visited on underground tours starting at the **Electric Mountain Museum** (Easter–Sept daily 9.30am–5.30pm; Oct–Dec daily 10.30am–4.30pm; Feb–Easter Thurs–Sun 10.30am–4.30pm; £5), whose displays take a Disney approach to the complexities of Welsh history.

Walkers have a choice of several different **youth hostels**, all served by Gwynedd bus #11 from Llanberis, and each at the base of a footpath up Snowdon: *Llanberis*, Llwyn Celyn (☎01286/870280; ②); *Snowdon Ranger*, Rhyd Ddu (☎01286/650391; ②); *Bryn Gwynant*, Nant Gwynant (☎01766/890251; ②); and *Pen-y-Pass*, Nant Gwynant (☎01286/870428; ②). High St is lined with small **hotels**: try *The Heights* at no. 74 (☎01286/871179; ⑤), which also has cheap eight-bed dorms (②), or *Plas Coch*, a pleasant low-cost B&B (☎01286/872122; ③), which offers great mountain views and traditional food. Tourist **information** is available at 41 High St (Easter–Oct daily 10am–4pm; Nov–Easter closed Mon & Tues; ☎01286/870765).

Anglesey and Holyhead

The Menai Bridge was built by Thomas Telford in 1826 to connect North Wales with the island of **ANGLESEY** (Ynus Môn) across the Menai Straits, but is now little used as most road and rail traffic flows past across the new bridge. The bridge itself is one of the two chief sights on Anglesey, the other being **Beaumaris Castle** (April to mid-Oct daily 9.30am–6.30pm; mid-Oct to March Mon–Sat 9.30am–4pm, Sun 11am–4pm; £2.20), reached by bus #53, #57 or #58 from Bangor or Menai Bridge station. The last of Edward I's master-pieces, it was built in 1295 to guard the Menai Straits and has a fairy-tale moat enclosing its twelve towers.

Most tourist traffic in this direction is heading for **HOLYHEAD** (Caergybi), the busiest ferry port for Ireland, with at least five daily ferry and fast catamaran sailings to Dublin and bargain day-trips, sometimes for under £10. If you need somewhere **to stay** before your boat sails, the following B&Bs are all within a few minute's walk of the terminal: *Wavecrest*, 93 Newry St(☎01407/763637; ④); *Orotavia*, 66 Walthew Ave (☎01407/760259; ③); and the very good *Yr Hendre*, Porth-y-Felin Rd (☎01407/762929; ⑤). The **tourist office** (Easter–Oct daily 10am–6pm; Nov–Easter Mon–Sat 10am–4.30pm; ☎01407/762622) on Penrhos Beach Rd, posts a list on its door out of office hours of the **B&Bs** that accept late arrivals.

SCOTLAND

Scotland presents a model example of how a small nation can retain its identity within the confines of a larger one. Unlike the Welsh, the Scots successfully repulsed the expansionist designs of England, and when the old enemies first formed a union in 1603, it was because King James VI of Scotland inherited the English throne, though the parliaments were not united for another hundred years. Even then, Scotland retained many of its own institutions, notably distinctive legal and educational systems, and in 1997 the Scots voted to re-establish a parliament with limited tax-raising powers; it is yet to be seen whether this will lead towards full independence.

Most of the population clusters in the narrow central belt between the two principal cities: stately **Edinburgh**, the national capital, with its magnificent architecture and imperious natural setting, and earthy **Glasgow**, a powerhouse of the Industrial Revolution and still a hard-working, hard-playing place. The third city, **Aberdeen**, set in one of the rare strips of lowland in the north, is now fabulously wealthy from the proceeds of offshore oil, and its pristine granite buildings and abundant parks and gardens look even more immaculate than ever.

Yet it's the **Highlands**, severely depopulated but comprising over two-thirds of the total area, which provide most peoples' enduring image of Scotland. The dramatic landscapes are further enhanced by the volatile climate, producing an extraordinary variety of moods and colours. Here you'll find some of the last wildernesses in Europe, though even the highest mountain, **Ben Nevis**, is an uncomplicated ascent for the average walker, while much of the finest scenery – such as the famous **lochs**, Lomond and Ness, and the islands of the **Hebrides** – can be enjoyed without too much effort.

Edinburgh

EDINBURGH is the showcase capital of Scotland, a well-heeled, cosmopolitan and cultured place which regularly tops the polls as Britain's best place to live. Its natural contours, stone-built houses and monuments make it visually stunning: the fairy-tale castle, perched on the summit of an extinct volcano, looks over the rooftops towards the 823-foot hill of Arthur's Seat, from where there are breathtaking vistas of hills and water. Inevitably, the city is suffering from the increasingly intrusive trappings of the tourist trade. The 430,000 population swells massively in high season, peaking during Festival time, when an estimated one million visitors come to town for the biggest arts event in Europe. Yet despite this annual invasion, and despite its proximity to the border, Edinburgh is emphatically Scottish – and is now building a parliament to prove it.

The centre has two distinct parts. The castle rock is the core of the ancient capital, where nobles and servants lived side by side for centuries within the tight defensive walls. Edinburgh earned the nickname "Auld Reekie" for the smog and smell generated by the cramped inhabitants of this **Old Town**, where the streets ran with sewage tipped out of tenement windows and disease was rife. The riddle of medieval streets and alleyways remained a run-down slum well into this century. The **New Town** was begun in the late 1700s with the announcement of a plan to develop farmland lying to the north of the castle rock. Edinburgh's wealthier worthies speculated profitably on tracts of this land and engaged the services of eminent architects in their development. The result of their labours was an outstanding example of Georgian town planning, still largely intact.

Arrival and information

Edinburgh **airport** is eight miles west of the centre; regular bus connections operate around the clock. Waverley Station, the main **rail** terminal, is situated right in the centre: emerging from the station, a right turn will take you into the New Town and Princes Street, while to the left is the Old Town and the castle. The **bus** terminal for local and intercity services is on St Andrew Square, across Princes St from Waverley; information on routes and times is available from the Lothian Region Transport Office, a hundred yards to the left of the Waverley's

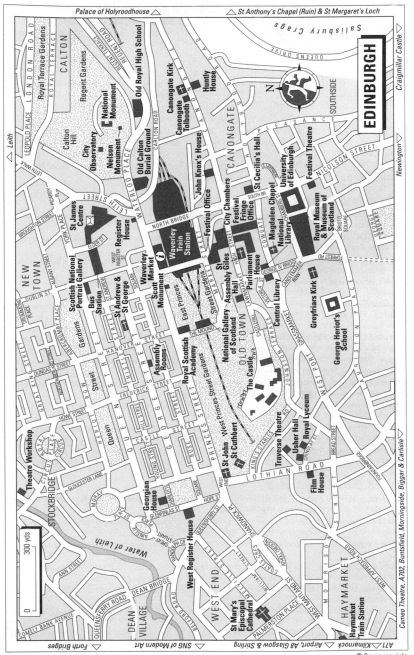

EDINBURGH

© Crown copyright

main entrance, at the junction of Waverley Bridge and Market St. The main **tourist office** is at 3 Princes St, above the station on the top level of Waverley Market (Mon–Sat 9am–6/8pm, Sun 10am–6/8pm; ☎0131/473 3800). When the office is closed there is a 24-hour computerized information service at the door.

Accommodation

The tourist office has details of all grades of **accommodation**, from five-star hotels to youth hostels, and can supply copies of the *Edinburgh Accommodation Guide* (£1), which lists over 500 places. The office will book rooms for £3 plus a ten-percent deposit. Hotel rooms and hostel accommodation in the city centre may prove hard to come by in peak season, but **B&B** is offered in hundreds of houses around the city, with prices as low as £15 per person, though the average is considerably higher. In addition, the universities and colleges let out student rooms, mostly during the summer, while campers are served by three sites on the fringes of the city. Bear in mind that during the Festival (mid-Aug to early Sept) there is little chance of getting cheap accommodation unless you've booked ahead.

HOSTELS AND CAMPUS ACCOMMODATION

Belford Hostel, 6–8 Douglas Gardens (☎0131/225 6209). Housed in a redundant Arts and Crafts church near the West End of the city centre. Dorm beds ③; doubles ④.

Brodies Backpacker Hostel, 12 High St (☎0131/556 6770). Small, homely and well situated towards the foot of the Royal Mile. ③.

Edinburgh Backpackers Hostel, 65 Cockburn St (☎0131/220 1717). Superior, well-thought-out hostel – right down to the tartan bedspreads. Dorm beds ③; doubles ④.

Hostel Bruntsfield, 7 Bruntsfield Crescent (☎0131/447 2994). Strictly run HI hostel one mile south of Princes St – take bus #11, #15, #16 or #17. Open 7am–2am. ②.

Hostel Eglinton, 18 Eglinton Crescent (☎0131/337 1120). To the west of the centre, near Haymarket train station, the last stop before Waverley. More easy-going HI than the Bruntsfield place. Curfew 2am. Closed Dec. ③.

Kinnaird Christian Hostel, 14 Coates Crescent (☎0131/225 3608). Women, married couples and families only. Single rooms ⑤; beds in shared room ③.

Napier University, 219 Colinton Rd (☎0131/444 2266 ext 4621). Double, single and twin rooms during Easter vacation & July–Sept. Rates include breakfast. ⑤.

Pollock Halls of Residence, 18 Holyrood Park Rd (☎0131/667 0662). Single and double rooms during Easter vacation & late June to late Sept. Rates include breakfast. ⑥.

Playfair House Hostel, 8 Blenheim Place, Royal Terrace (☎0131/478 0007). Luxurious hostel in superb location behind Calton Hill. Dorm beds ③; doubles ④.

Princes Street West Backpackers, 3 Queensferry St (☎0131/226 2939). A cosmopolitan hostel in a historic court building at the east end of Princes St, but rooms are shabby. Dorm beds ②; doubles ③.

Royal Mile Backpackers, 105 High St (☎0131/557 6120). Popular, well-kept hostel with a larger branch opposite at 8 Blackfriars St and a very smart building at 15 Johnston Terrace below the Castle. ③

HOTELS AND GUESTHOUSES

Ailsa Craig, 24 Royal Terrace (☎0131/556 1022). Well-furnished and friendly family hotel, superbly located behind Calton Hill with views across the Firth. ⑦.

Arrandale House, 28 Mayfield Gardens (☎0131/667 6029). Friendly establishment on the south side, within easy reach of the centre by bus #50. Open April–Oct. ⑥.

Clifton Private Hotel, 1 Clifton Terrace (☎0131/337 1002). Family-run hotel opposite Haymarket station. ⑤.

Brodie's Guest House, 22 East Claremont St (☎0131/556 4032). Friendly B&B in a Victorian town house, ideally located on the eastern edge of the New Town. Rates include a good breakfast. ⑤.

International Guest House, 37 Mayfield Gdns (☎0131/667 2511). Good reputation for comfortable and clean accommodation. ⑥.

Marrakech Hotel, 30 London St (☎0131/556 4444). Another family-run place, with an excellent Moroccan restaurant in the basement. ⑦.

St Bernard's, 22 St Bernard's Crescent (☎0131/332 2339). In the elegant surroundings of Georgian Stockbridge. ⑥.

Teviotdale House, 53 Grange Loan (☎0131/667 4376). Probably the best B&B in the city – all rooms have private facilities and the food is glorious. ⑥.

Thrums Hotel, 14–15 Minto St (☎0131/667 5545). Excellent hotel with equally classy restaurant attached. ⑧.

CAMPSITES

Little France, 219 Old Dalkeith Rd (☎0131/666 2326). Three miles south of the centre, reached by bus #33, #82 or #89 from Princes St. Open April–Sept; £7 per night, £8 in July & Aug.

Mortonhall Park, 38 Mortonhall Gate, Frogston Rd East (☎0131/664 1533). Five miles out, near the Braid Hills – bus #11 from Princes St. Open mid-March to Oct; £8–12.75 per night.

Edinburgh Caravan Club Site, Marine Drive, Silverknowes (☎0131/312 6874). Pleasant site close to the shore; a twenty-minute ride on bus #14 from North Bridge. Open April–Sept; £7.50 per night.

The City

The cobbled **Royal Mile** – composed of Castlehill, Lawnmarket, High St and Canongate – is the busiest stretch of the tourist itinerary and the central thoroughfare of the Old Town, connecting the Palace of **Holyroodhouse** to the **Castle** (daily 9.30am–5/6pm; £6). For centuries the seat of kings, the castle is thought to have evolved from an Iron Age fort, the sheer volcanic rock on which it stands providing formidable defence on three sides. Within its precincts is St Margaret's Chapel, a Norman church that's probably the oldest building in the city. Also open to the public are the state apartments, including the room in which James VI of Scotland was born, the Great Hall with its magnificent hammerbeam roof, the ancient crown jewels of Scotland and the even older Stone of Destiny, the coronation stone of the kings of Scotland. There's a large military museum here, too, and the castle esplanade provides a dramatic setting for the world-famous Military Tattoo, staged every year during the Festival.

Descending the Lawnmarket from the castle, you'll pass **Gladstone's Land**, named after the merchant who set up shop there in 1617; inside, the National Trust for Scotland has restored the painted ceilings and furnished the upper floors as they would have been during his day (April–Oct Mon–Sat 10am–5pm, Sun 2–5pm; £3). **The Writers' Museum** (or **Lady Stair's House**), behind Gladstone's Land, is dedicated to Sir Walter Scott, Robert Burns and Robert Louis Stevenson, with memorabilia of the trio housed on three floors of the seventeenth-century building (Mon–Sat 10am–5pm; also Sun 2am–5pm during Festival; free).

The High St section starts at **St Giles' Cathedral** (Mon–Sat 9am–5pm, Sun 1–5pm), whose beautiful crown-shaped spire is an Edinburgh landmark. In all likelihood there's been a church here since the eighth century, but the existing building is chiefly late fourteenth and early fifteenth century, with large-scale alterations carried out in the nineteenth. At the east end of the simple and impressive interior, the Thistle Chapel, designed in 1911, is an amazing display of mock-Gothic woodcarving. The heart-shaped cobble pattern set outside the west door is known as the Heart of Midlothian – passers-by traditionally spit on it for luck. To the rear are the Neoclassical law courts, which incorporate the seventeenth-century **Parliament House**, under whose spectacular hammerbeam roof the Scottish parliament met until the 1707 Union with England. Heading south across George IV Bridge, you come to Chambers St, home of the stunning new **Museum of Scotland** building, which dominates the street, and the old **Royal Museum** (both Mon–Sat 10am–5pm, Sun noon–5pm; also Tues until 8pm; £3), which houses a typically rich collection of colonial acquisitions. The skilfully designed new museum is more interesting, telling the history of Scotland through its artefacts, perhaps the most fascinating of which are the Lewis chessmen, exquisitely idiosyncratic twelfth-century pieces carved from walrus ivory.

Canongate starts at the junction of St Mary's and Jeffrey streets, the original city boundary. Jeffrey St descends towards the station and Market St, site of the **City Art Centre** (Mon–Sat 10am–5pm; also Sun 2–5pm during Festival; free, except for special exhibitions). Much refurbished, the Art Centre houses the city's collection of paintings, prints, drawings and sculpture and runs a busy programme of temporary exhibitions, from international blockbusters to community-based displays. Across the street, the **Fruitmarket Gallery** (Tues–Sat 10am–6pm, Sun noon–5pm) has an international reputation for its modern-art exhibitions.

Before the New Town was built, Canongate was the chic end of the Royal Mile, where nobles and merchants established their homes. Moray House, with its balcony jutting out over the pavement, is a rare survivor, as is sixteenth-century **Huntly House** (Mon–Sat 10am–5pm; also Sun 2–5pm during Festival; free), now a museum focusing on the history of the city. Across the road is **Canongate Tolbooth** (same hours; free), once a prison, now a museum dedicated to Edinburgh's social history; it features reconstructed interiors such as a wartime kitchen and a washhouse. Nearby **Canongate Kirk**, set back from the street, was built in the late 1600s after the parish church in Holyrood Abbey was converted into a Catholic chapel. The simple church is used by the royal family whenever they are at Holyrood, as the coat of arms on one of the pews indicates.

Just south of Canongate is the site of the new Scottish **Parliament**, unfinished at the time of writing, but sure to be a major draw. South again, backing onto Holyrood Park, is the futuristic tented structure of **Our Dynamic Earth** (April–Oct daily 10am–6pm; Nov–March Wed–Sat 10am–5pm; £5.95), a hi-tech exhibition on the earth and the environment using audio-visual tactile displays.

The **Palace of Holyroodhouse** (tours daily 9.30am–3.45/5.15pm; £5.30), the Royal Family's official residence in Scotland, looks out over the Queen's Park, 650 acres of wilderness in the heart of the city. Except when the dignitaries are in residence or when there are garden parties, the public are admitted to the sumptuous state rooms and historic apartments, which include the chamber where Mary Queen of Scots, pregnant with her son James VI, witnessed the murder of her courtier David Rizzio by associates of her husband. The gaunt, roofless ruins of Holyrood Abbey stand within the palace grounds; dating mainly from the turn of the thirteenth century, they were the inspiration for Mendelssohn's *Scottish Symphony*. From the palace, fine walks lead across parkland up to the arc of the **Salisbury Crags** and **Arthur's Seat** beyond, where a fairly stiff climb is rewarded with magnificent views of the city and over the Firth of Forth towards Fife.

THE NEW TOWN

The most pleasant route from the Old Town to the Georgian grid of the New Town is to descend the Mound to the **National Gallery of Scotland** (Mon–Sat 10am–5pm, Sun 2–5pm; free), one of the best small collections in Europe. Arranged chronologically, it includes representative or important works from a large number of major European artists, including Raphael, Titian, Rembrandt, Rubens and El Greco, and of course an unrivalled show of Scottish works, including David Wilkie's *Pitlessie Fair*, Henry Raeburn's *The Reverend Robert Walker Skating* – a postcard favourite – and Allan Ramsay's *Portrait of Rousseau*. Opposite, the **Royal Scottish Academy** is the grandest exhibition space in the city, usually hosting a major international show during the Festival.

The Academy looks onto the broad avenue of **Princes Street**, the main shopping area, with homogenized chain stores crammed in cheek by jowl. A hundred yards to the east is the spire of the **Scott Monument**, decorated with figures from Sir Walter's novels and now oddly piebald following restoration work. Equally conspicuous is the **National Monument** atop Calton Hill, at the far eastern end of Princes St; it would have been a copy of the Parthenon had money not run out in 1829.

Built along a ridge parallel to Princes St, **George Street** capitalizes on the views to the north: standing at its junction with Hanover Street you look down across the New Town, out towards the Firth of Forth and over to the hills of Fife. The **Assembly Rooms**, 54 George St, are a glorious confection of ornate plasterwork and extravagant chandeliers; one of the most exciting theatre venues during the Festival, at other times they're used for a variety of purposes, from tea dances to craft fairs. At its western end George Street runs into the most elegant square in the New Town – Robert Adam's suave **Charlotte Square**. The National Trust for Scotland has restored no. 7 – the **Georgian House** (April–Oct Mon–Sat 10am–4.30pm, Sun 2–4.30pm; £4.20) – to a state of pristine perfection, stocking it with magnificent specimens from the workshops of Hepplewhite, Sheraton and Chippendale, the great names of eighteenth-century furniture.

North of George Street is the broad avenue of Queen St, at whose eastern end stands the **Scottish National Portrait Gallery** (Mon–Sat 10am–5pm, Sun 2–5pm; free). As well as a collection of portraits of prominent Scots – many of them outstanding examples of the genre – it contains a collection of photographic works from the beginnings of the art to the present day.

STOCKBRIDGE

In the northwest corner of the New Town, beyond Queen St Gardens, lies **Stockbridge**, a smart residential suburb with bohemian pretensions – especially noticeable around the atmospheric huddle of old mill buildings known as Dean Village. From here Belford Rd leads up to the **Scottish National Gallery of Modern Art** (Mon–Sat 10am–5pm, Sun 2–5pm; free), where the likes of Matisse, Picasso, Giacometti and Mondrian share space with modern Scottish artists such as Paolozzi and Ian Hamilton Finlay. Although the gallery doesn't quite match the comprehensiveness of London's Tate, it nonetheless has examples from most of the significant groupings of the twentieth century, from Fauvism, Cubism and Expressionism right down to Pop Art and Minimalism, while the wooded grounds make a fine setting for the sculptures of Moore, Epstein and many others.

Another luscious retreat from the city is offered by the **Royal Botanic Garden** (daily 9.30am–dusk; free) on the north side of Stockbridge, entered from either Arboretum Place or Inverleith Row; it's served by buses #7a, #8, #23 and #37 from the city centre. Covering seventy acres, the gardens support a vast array of rare plants from around the world in their landscaped grounds and magnificent hothouses.

Eating and drinking

Edinburgh is well served with **restaurants** to suit most tastes, but – as with accommodation – there's a lot of pressure on space in the better places. Whatever you plump for, be sure to book in advance at the ones for which we've given phone numbers. Unless specified otherwise, you can eat well at all our recommendations for under £10. Edinburgh's **cafés** are among the most enjoyable spots in the city – serving coffee, food and most often alcohol too, and sometimes doubling as exhibition and performance spaces during the Festival. The city's multitudinous **bars** are among the most congenial in the country, with live music a frequent bonus.

RESTAURANTS

Bar Roma, 39a Queensferry Road (☎0131/226 2977). Above average Italian with fairly moderate prices, great atmosphere and late-hours – packed most nights.

Café 9, 9a Castle St. Self-service basement café with more healthy food than the usual; one of the few cheap places anywhere near Princes St.

Good Year, 21 Argyle Place (☎0131/229 4404). Cantonese and Peking style. Good family atmosphere and inexpensive food (average dish £3). Unlicensed, so bring your own bottle.

Kalpna, 2–3 St Patrick Square (☎0131/667 9890) Prize-winning and inexpensive vegetarian Indian; delicious, if small, portions.

Khushi's, 16 Drummond St. Basic, but popular and very cheap curries in the former university canteen; unlicensed.

Henderson's, 94 Hanover St. Well-known self-service restaurant with a lively atmosphere, good-value vegetarian food and occasional live music.

Martin's, 70 Rose St, North Lane (☎0131/225 3106). One of the best restaurants in Edinburgh specializing in wild and organic Scottish foods; lunch from £10, dinner from £30.

Loon Fung, 2 Warriston Place, Canonmills (☎0131/556 1781) and 32 Grindlay St (☎0131/229 5757). Cantonese-style, seafood a speciality. No-nonsense staff. Meals from around £12.

Pierre Victoire, 10 Victoria St (☎0131/225 1721), 38 Grassmarket (☎0131/226 2442), 8 Union St (☎0131/557 8451) and 5 Dock Place, Leith (☎0131/555 6178). Excellent bargain menus presented with Gallic dash.

Queen Street Oyster Bar, 16a Queen St (☎0131/226 2530). Frequented by BBC staff; serves tasty dishes prepared in a postage-stamp kitchen. Stocks Belgian Trappist beers.

St James' Oyster Bar, 1 Calton Rd. Busy city-centre musicians' hangout. Occasional live music.

Le Sept, 7 Old Fishmarket Close (☎0131/225 5428). Upstairs gets busy early, serving filling crepes and a good vegetarian selection at reasonable prices. Downstairs is posher and pricier.

The Shore, 3–4 The Shore, Leith (☎0131/553 5080). Popular haunt with a menu centred on seafood; live music every evening except Sundays.

Skipper's, 1a Dock Pl, Leith (☎0131/554 1018). Fresh seafood. Three-course fixed-price dinner menu £20, main course lunch dishes from £7.50.

Tinelli, 139 Easter Rd (☎0131/652 1932). A well-kept secret: small and efficient dining room serving the real North Italian thing.

Viva Mexico, 41 Cockburn St (☎0131/226 5145) and 50 East Fountainbridge (☎0131/228 4005). Run by Mexican–Scot husband and wife team. Lavish portions and great margaritas.

BARS AND CAFÉS

Bannerman's Bar, 55 Niddry St. The best pub in the street, with an old-world atmosphere and a good range of real ales and food.

Blue Moon Café, 36 Broughton St. Coffee and snacks at this friendly lesbian/gay institution; straights welcome too.

Café Royal, 17a West Register St, off Princes St. Beautiful horseshoe-shaped bar, original Victorian decor, frequented after office hours by city professionals. Open Thurs–Sat.

Cyberia Internet Café, 88 Hanover St. A relaxing place to wind down and log on.

Fiddlers Arms, 9 Grassmarket. Monday night is folk night, when the impromptu music sessions start up.

Hebrides Bar, 17 Market St. Tiny old-fashioned bar near the station where Highlanders gather. Good crack, friendly service and occasional song.

Malt Shovel, 13 Cockburn St. Good beer, plenty of local colour and a wide choice of single malt whiskies; live jazz some evenings.

Mathers, 25 Broughton St. Old-fashioned and amiable bar for serious stout aficionados.

Nightlife

Edinburgh's nightlife is as lively as that of any city in Britain, and venues change name and location with such speed that the only way to keep up with what's going on is to get hold of *The List* magazine, a comprehensive source of information published fortnightly. The Playhouse theatre generally has long-running musicals, with occasional rock bands. The *Attic* in the Cowgate, and the *Canon's Gait* on Canongate have local indie and rock bands, while the *Tron* on Hunter Square has a variety of folk, jazz and comedy nights. Visiting bands play the *Venue*, Calton Rd, and *La Belle Angèle*, Cowgate. There is a lively **club** scene: currently most popular are *The Vaults*, Niddry St, the *Potterow*, Bristo Square, the *Cavendish* at West Tollcross with a long-running Afro-Latino night on Saturdays, and *The Liquid Room* on Victoria St. There are a number of mainstream discos on Lothian Rd, the largest being *Revolution*. Gay nightlife is centred round the top of Leith Walk, notably at *CCBloom's* next to the Playhouse on Greenside Place.

The Festival

The **Edinburgh Festival**, billed as the world's largest arts jamboree, was founded in 1947, and now attracts artists of all descriptions for three weeks in August and September. The show is, in fact, a multiplicity of festivals, with the official programme traditionally presenting uncontroversial highbrow fare, while the frenetic Fringe offers a melange of just about everything else in the field of the performing and visual arts. In addition, there's a Film Festival focusing on the latest movies, a Jazz Festival, and a Book Festival. A Folk Festival takes place in early April. Tickets are available at the venues and from the International Festival Office at 21 Market St (☎0131/473 2000 or 473 2001) and the Fringe Office at 180 High St (☎0131/226 5257).

Listings

Airport enquiries ☎0131/333 1000.

Bicycle rental Central Cycles, 13 Lochrin Place (☎0131/228 6333); Sandy Gilchrist Cycles, 1 Cadzow Place (☎0131/652 1760).

Bus enquiries National Express ☎0990/808080; Scottish Citylink ☎0990/505050; local services ☎0131/554 4494.

Car rental Arnold Clark, Lochrin Place, Tollcross (☎0131/228 4747); Avis, 100 Dalvy Rd (☎0131/337 6363); Budget, 111 Glasgow Rd (☎0131/334 7740); Turner Hire Drive, 47 Annandale St (☎0131/557 0304).

Consulates Australia, Strand (☎0131/555 4500); Canada, 30 Lothian Rd (☎0131/220 4333); US, 3 Regent Terrace (☎0131/556 8315).

Hospital Royal Infirmary, Lauriston Place (☎0131/536 1000).
Pharmacy Boots, 48 Shandwick Place, is open Mon–Sat 9am–9pm, Sun 11am–4.30pm.
Police Fettes Ave (☎0131/311 3131).
Post office The central post office is in St James' Shopping Centre, off Leith St near the bus station; Mon 9am–5.30pm, Tues–Fri 8.30am–5.30pm, Sat 8.30am–6pm.
Taxis Capital Castle Cabs ☎0131/228 2555; Central Taxis ☎0131/229 2468; City Cabs ☎0131/228 1211.
Train enquiries ☎0345/484950.

Glasgow

The largest city in Scotland, home to three-quarters of a million people, **GLASGOW** was once even more prominent than it is today. Known as the "second city of the Empire", it thrived on the tobacco trade with the American colonies, on cotton production and, most famously, on the shipbuilding on the River Clyde. The civic architecture of Victorian Glasgow was as grand as any in Britain, and the West End suburbs were regarded as among the best designed in the country. Since this heyday, however, it has not enjoyed the best of reputations. The Gorbals area became notorious as one of the worst slums in Europe, and the city's association with violence and heavy drinking stuck to it like a curse.

Like so many dockland cities, Glasgow is undergoing another change of image nowadays – a change symbolized by its selection as the European City of Culture in 1990 and City of Architecture and Design in 1999, and by the urban renewal programmes around Glasgow Green and the Merchant City. The city is a vital mix of old and new, with a generosity of spirit that is impossible to ignore and a sense of humour that can be a tonic after the primness of Edinburgh.

Arrival and accommodation

Glasgow **airport** is eight miles west of the city, served by buses every fifteen minutes (£2.50) to the central Buchanan St **bus station** – **Prestwick** airport in Ayrshire handles a smaller number of flights; half-hourly trains link it with Glasgow Central station. Glasgow has two central **train stations**, Queen St and Central, the former handling traffic to Edinburgh and the north, the latter serving destinations to the south. Glasgow is easy to explore on foot – you can walk from the city centre to the West End in about half an hour. Should you tire of the pavements, the **Underground** is one of the cheapest and easiest ways to get around the centre, operating on a circular chain of fifteen stations with a flat fare of 65p, or £3.40 for a day pass. You could also try the "Discovering Glasgow" bus tour (£6.50), which you can hop on and off; tickets can be purchased from stations, bus travel information centres and the tourist office.

The very helpful polyglot **tourist information centre** is on the south side of George Square, near the top of Queen St (April–Sept Mon–Sat 9am–7/8pm, Sun 10am–6pm; Oct–March Mon–Sat 9am–6pm; ☎0141/204 4400). It issues the usual glut of leaflets and maps and can book accommodation. There's also an information centre at Glasgow airport (Mon–Sat 7.30am–5pm; Sun 7.30am–3.30pm).

The HI **youth hostel** is in the West End at 7–8 Park Terrace (☎0141/332 3004; ③). Nearby is the independent *Glasgow Backpackers' Hostel*, 17 Park Terrace (☎0141/332 9099; ③; July–Sept) and a number of reasonably priced **B&Bs**. The West End has the small *Alamo Guest House*, 46 Gray St (☎0141/339 2395; ④) and the busy *Sandyford Hotel*, 904 Sauchiehall St (☎0141/334 0000; ⑤). More central are a number of options on the west end of Renfrew St, including the cheap, popular *Hazelcourt Hotel*, (☎0141/332 7737; ③) and the swish *Old School*, 194 Renfrew St (☎0141/332 7600; ⑤). In the heart of the Merchant City is the very Scottish *Babbity Bowster*, 16–18 Blackfriars St (☎0141/552 5055; ⑤) with an award-winning restaurant and stylish pub attached.

During the Easter and summer holidays, both Glasgow (☎0141/330 5385) and Strathclyde (☎0141/553 4148) universities let rooms for B&B accommodation. The YMCA at 33 Petershill Drive has similar accommodation (☎0141/558 6166; ③) and a number of self-catering flats which sleep between four and six people and can be rented for one night or more.

The City

Glasgow's centre lies on the north bank of the Clyde, specifically around the grandiose and frenetic **George Square**. Just south of the square, down Queen St, is the **Gallery of Modern Art** (Oct–March Mon–Sat 9.30am–1pm & 2–4pm, Sun 2–4pm; April–Sept Mon–Sat 9.30am–6pm, Sun 2–5pm; free). Formerly a "temple of commerce" built by one of the eighteenth-century "tobacco lords", it now houses an exciting collection of contemporary Scottish art, notably works by Ken Currie and John Bellany. East of George Square on Castle St is the **Cathedral**. Built in 1136, destroyed in 1192 and rebuilt soon after, it's the only Scottish mainland cathedral to have escaped the hands of the country's religious reformers in the sixteenth century, whose hatred of anything that smacked of idolatry wrecked many of Scotland's ancient churches. This one survived chiefly thanks to the intervention of the city guilds. The magnificent vaulted crypt – the Laigh Kirk – is the principal remnant of the twelfth century, and contains the tomb of Saint Mungo, the city's patron. Compared to many English cathedrals, it's a modest-sized building, dominated by the adjacent **Necropolis**, resting place of the magnates who made Glasgow rich. Opened in 1832, and including a colossal figure of arch-reformer John Knox, the Necropolis is a compendium of jumbled pastiche architecture, its vaults mimicking every style from Byzantine to Gothic and Ottoman. On the other side of the cathedral is the **Provand's Lordship** (Mon–Sat 10am–5pm, Sun 11am–5pm; free), the oldest house in Glasgow. Built late in the fifteenth century as a priest's dwelling, it's now furnished with items mostly dating from later centuries, complete with waxwork occupants.

If you follow Cathedral St west to Buchanan St and then turn right, you'll swing into Glasgow's most famous thoroughfare – the much-smartened and now pedestrianized **Sauchiehall Street**. About halfway along, one block to the north, is the **Glasgow School of Art**, 167 Renfrew St, three of whose recent graduates – Steven Campbell, Ken Currie and Peter Howson – are among the most fashionable names in British art. The school itself is as remarkable as anything to have emerged from it: built by Charles Rennie Mackintosh – whose distinctively streamlined Art Nouveau designs appear in jewellers, furniture outlets and various other shops in Glasgow – it's a remarkable fusion of Scottish manor house solidity and modernist refinement. The interior, making maximum use of natural light, was furnished and fitted entirely by Mackintosh, and can be seen on a guided tour (Mon–Fri 11am & 2pm, Sat 10.30am; £3.50; booking advised ☎0141/332 9797).

An entirely different kind of interior is on view a short distance north of here, in the **Tenement House**, 145 Buccleuch St (March–Oct daily 2–5pm; £3). For half a century its rooms were occupied by one Agnes Toward, who seems to have been incapable of throwing anything away. Now run by the National Trust for Scotland, her home is full of nineteenth-century furniture and bric-a-brac, from box beds and gas lamps to bars of soap – an intriguing if sanitized vision of working-class life.

Immediately west, past the salubrious crescents of the West End, **Kelvingrove Park** is home to the **Glasgow Art Gallery and Museum** (Mon–Sat 10am–5pm, Sun 11am–5pm; free), a first-rate collection founded on donations from various captains of industry. Its particular strengths are pictures from Italy, the Low Countries and nineteenth-century France: Rembrandt's *Man in Armour* is perhaps the single most arresting painting, and there are notable pieces from Jordaens, Millet, van Gogh and Monet. Across the road in the Kelvin Hall, Argyle St, the **Transport Museum** (Mon–Sat 10am–5pm, Sun 11am–5pm; free) boasts fleets of trams, cars and motorbikes, with models and photos celebrating the Clyde shipyards and a reconstruction of a Glasgow street of 1938. On the northern edge of the park the campus of Glasgow University houses the **Hunterian Museum** (Mon–Sat 9.30am–5pm; free), a miscellany of things zoological and archeological, centred on one of the world's finest coin collections. It also proudly displays Scotland's solitary dinosaur. The nearby **Hunterian Art Gallery** (same hours) has works by Chardin, Stubbs and Rembrandt, plus a display of nineteenth- and twentieth-century Scottish art, but the highlights are a comprehensive survey of the output of James Abbott McNeill Whistler (only Washington has a larger collection), and the reconstructed interior of Charles Rennie Mackintosh's house – an astonishingly fresh creation, even half a century after his death. The Hunterian also has Scotland's best print collection, extracts from which form the exhibits in the ever-changing shows in the special print gallery.

Glasgow Green, down by the river to the east of George Square, is the site of major redevelopment centred around "Homes for the Future" – innovative new housing designs continuing Glasgow's tradition of radical modern architecture. On the Green stands the recently refurbished **People's Palace** (Mon–Sat 10am–5pm, Sun 11am–5pm; free), opened as a cultural centre for the East End in 1898. It now records the social history of the city, giving most of its space to memorabilia of Victorian Glasgow. No visit to Glasgow would be complete without a trip to the **Barras**, a huge market selling bric-a-brac, clothes, furniture, food and plants. Held every Saturday and Sunday, just off Gallowgate to the north of Glasgow Green, it starts mid-morning and runs all day, invariably drawing an enormous crowd.

Glasgow's highest-profile sight, though, is just under four miles south of the centre, in **Pollok Country Park** (bus #45, #48 or #57 from Union St). Housed in a custom-built gallery, the **Burrell Collection** (Mon–Sat 10am–5pm, Sun 11am–5pm; free) was accumulated by just one man, Sir William Burrell, who began collecting at the age of 15 and kept going until his death at 96, buying an average of two pieces a week. Works by Memling, Cézanne, Degas, Bellini and Géricault feature among the paintings, while in adjoining galleries there are pieces from ancient Rome and Greece, medieval European arts and crafts, and a massive selection of Chinese artefacts, with outstanding ceramics, jades and bronzes. Somewhat overshadowed by the Burrell, the nearby **Pollok House** (daily 10/11am–4/5pm; free) is a lovely eighteenth-century mansion containing Spanish paintings by such luminaries as El Greco, Goya and Murillo, in addition to works by William Blake and some fine furniture.

Eating, drinking and nightlife

For **breakfast and snacks**, one of the best and cheapest places is the *Grosvenor Café*, Ashton Lane, just off Byres Rd in the West End. On the same street, *Ashoka* does excellent-value *thalis* (Indian meals), while on Byres Rd itself the *University Café* is a cheap treat, with filling chip-based meals and great ice creams. The most elegant place for a light meal is the Mackintosh-designed *Willow Tea Rooms*, at 217 Sauchiehall St. In the Merchant City, hip *Café Gandolfi*, Albion St, is good for medium-priced snacks, meals and drinks, the *Tron Bar*, Trongate, carries a good and varied menu and has a more upmarket restaurant behind, and the *Fire Station*, Ingram St, does half-price pasta dishes daily between 5pm and 7pm. For innovative vegetarian food, try the *Vegville Diner*, St George's Rd or, for the best of Scottish cooking at moderate prices, join the academics and arty set at the *Ubiquitous Chip*, 12 Ashton Lane.

Glasgow has a bewildering number of **pubs**, from watering holes which have been quenching the city's thirst for years, to new and trendy bars which spring up and often disappear swiftly. *The Horseshoe Bar*, Drury St, is one of the old school, with plenty of atmosphere. If you want a Scottish theme, make for the *Uisge Beatha* on Woodlands Rd. Also recommended are the *Halt Bar*, Woodlands Rd (often with live music), *Bargo*, Albion Rd (trendy pre-club crowd with DJs), and the *Scotia Bar*, Stockwell St (live folk music).

The **Mayfest**, a carnival of formal and informal music and theatre is cancelled for May 1999, but may run in 2000. For details check the *Evening Times* newspaper, or the fortnightly magazine *The List* – also the best source for nightlife information. Currently trendy clubs include the *Sub Club*, 22 Jamaica St, *The Arches*, on adjoining Midland St, and *The Tunnel*, 84 Mitchell St. For theatre, the Tron in Trongate and the Citizens, Gorbals St, are among the most stimulating in Britain, while the **Centre for Contemporary Arts**, 346–354 Sauchiehall St, has a reputation for controversial exhibitions and performances. Finally, the wonderful Glasgow Film Theatre, Rose St, shows art films and old favourites.

The Borders

Scotland's **Border Country**, an upland region of rich farmland, secluded valleys, quiet villages and bustling little market towns, was for centuries the frontline between Scotland and England, and its history became an inspiration for its most famous resident, Sir Walter Scott, whose writings were to create the enduring romanticized image of Scotland. During the twelfth-century reign of King David I, four magnificent abbeys were built in the region as showpieces of the independent Scottish state, and these now rank among the most evocative ruins in Europe. The defensive towers which were their secular counterparts were often replaced in more peaceful times by magnificent **stately homes**, including several of Scotland's finest. No longer served by rail, the Border towns are connected to each other and to Edinburgh by plentiful **bus services**. Free timetables are available from local tourist offices, who will book **accommodation** anywhere in the region without charge – though the main places of interest can easily be visited on day-trips from Edinburgh.

Melrose and around

If you've only time to visit one Border town, **MELROSE**, 37 miles south of Edinburgh, makes the obvious choice. The town is very pretty and superbly set between the triple-peaked Eildon Hills and the supremely beautiful **Abbey** (April–Sept daily 9.30am–6.30pm; Oct–March Mon–Sat 9.30am–4.30pm, Sun 2–4.30pm; £2.80). It's best seen on a bright morning, with the sun streaming through the tracery of the exquisite east and south windows and illuminating the richly sculpted capitals and cornices of the nave.

Scott's custom-built home, **Abbotsford House** (June–Sept daily 10am–5pm; mid-March to May & Oct Mon–Sat 10am–5pm, Sun 2–5pm; £3.50), lies a couple of miles west of Melrose, just off the road to Galashiels. Self-consciously over-the-top, it attempts to give a physical presence to the mythical world of his novels. Details from Scotland's great ruined or unfinished buildings are aped in the architecture, while the rooms overflow with souvenirs of the military heroes of the nation's past. More aesthetically pleasing is Scott's burial place, **Dryburgh Abbey** (April–Sept daily 9.30am–6.30pm; Oct–March Mon–Sat 9.30am–4.30pm & Sun 2–4.30pm; £2.30), near the village of St Boswells, five miles southeast of Melrose. The early Gothic transept housing the writer's grave – and that of Field Marshal Haig, of World War I notoriety – is the only part of the church to have survived, but the monastic buildings are partly intact. Best of all is the wonderfully secluded setting by the Tweed, all gentle hills and ancient woodland.

The Melrose **tourist office** (July & Aug Mon–Sat 10am–6.30pm, Sun 10am–6pm; March–June & Sept Mon–Sat 10am–5pm, Sun 10am–2pm; Oct Mon–Sat 10am–1pm; ☎01896/822555) is directly opposite the abbey. The **youth hostel** (☎01896/822521; ②) is in an old Victorian villa, again overlooking the abbey. There's a plentiful supply of **B&Bs**, including one on High St and a couple each on Buccleuch and Abbey streets. The old coaching inns in and around the central Market Place are a pricey accommodation option, but rather more affordable for **eating** and **drinking**: *Burt's* is excellent, but *The Ship* nearby on the square is even better.

Kelso and around

KELSO, twelve miles east of Melrose, lies at the point where the Tweed is joined by its main tributary, the Teviot. Here the **Abbey** (Mon–Sat 9.30am–4/6pm, Sun 2–4/6pm; free) was the grandest in the Borders but is now the most ruined by far: the magnificent fragment represents only the western transept and tower. Across the park to the northwest of the abbey is the eccentric octagonal **Old Parish Church**; further west is the spacious Georgian **Market Square**, the largest in Scotland, dominated by the town hall and the *Cross Keys Hotel*, once the most celebrated of several coaching inns in Kelso.

At the northern edge of town is **Floors Castle** (Easter–Oct daily 10am–4.30pm; £5), the largest inhabited house in Scotland. William Adam's original construction was given its overloaded Romantic look by William Playfair in the 1840s, and the interior is no less rich, containing a superb set of Gobelin tapestries. An even more impressive stately home, **Mellerstain House** (May–Sept Sun–Fri 12.30–5pm; £4.50), lies six miles northwest of Kelso. Here Robert Adam created a stunning sequence of luxuriant interiors, including some dazzling plasterwork ceilings – the library's is outstanding.

Kelso's **tourist office** is on the Market Square (summer Mon–Sat 9.30am–6.30pm, Sun 10am–6pm; shorter hours rest of year; ☎01573/223464). B&B **accommodation** is scattered all over town, with a couple of places on Roxburgh St, just off Market Square.

St Andrews

Notwithstanding a population which barely reaches five figures, **ST ANDREWS**, situated on the Fife coast 56 miles northeast of Edinburgh, has the air of a place of importance. Retaining memories of its days as medieval Scotland's academic and religious metropolis, it is still the Scottish answer to Oxford or Cambridge, with only slightly less snob appeal – you'll hear upper-class English and American accents in term time. St Andrews can be reached by bus from Edinburgh in just under two hours, and is a feasible day excursion. There are no direct rail services, though frequent **buses** connect with the **train** station five miles away in Leuchars, where the parish church incorporates the most beautiful and intact piece of Norman architecture in Scotland.

The town has an exalted place in Scottish sporting history too. Entering St Andrews from the Edinburgh road, you pass no fewer than four golf links, the last of which is the **Old Course**, the most famous and – in the opinion of Jack Nicklaus – the best in the world. At the southern end of the Old Course, down towards the waterfront, is the award-winning **British Golf Museum** (mid-April to mid-Oct daily 9.30am–5.30pm; mid-Oct to mid-April Thurs–Mon 11am–3pm; £3.75), where the excellent exhibition details everything you wanted to know – and more – about 500 years of golf. Immediately south of the Old Course begins North Street, one of St Andrews' two main arteries. Much of it is taken up by university buildings, with the tower of **St Salvator's College** rising proudly above all else. Together with the adjoining chapel, this dates from 1450 and is the earliest surviving part of the university. Tours of the academic buildings have been suspended, but may resume in the future – ask here or at the tourist office.

Further east, the ruined St Andrew's **Castle** (daily 9.30am–4.30/6.30pm; £2.50, or £3.50 with cathedral visitor centre) can be reached down North Castle St. Commanding a prominent headland, it began as a fortress, but was partly transformed by the local archbishops into a Renaissance palace, of which little more than the facade survives. A short distance further along the coast is the equally ruined Gothic **Cathedral** (same times; free), the mother church of medieval Scotland and the largest and grandest ever built in the country. Even though little more then the cemetery survives, the intact east wall and the exposed foundations give an idea of the vast scale of what has been lost. The **visitor centre** (same times as castle; £1.80) contains the *St Andrews Sarcophagus*, probably ninth-century, one of the most refined products of the so-called Dark Ages. With the entrance ticket you can get a token to ascend the austere Romanesque **St Rule's Tower** – part of the priory that the cathedral replaced – for superb views over the sea and town.

Outside the cathedral enclosure and now forming an entrance to the coastal road southwards are **the Pends**, huge fourteenth-century arches which served as the main gateway to the priory. Running westwards from the Pends is South Street, site of more historic university buildings and of **Holy Trinity** parish church (summer daily 10am–noon & 2–4pm), partly fifteenth-century but much altered. Incongruously for a bastion of Presbyterianism, it contains a spectacular marble monument to Archbishop Sharp, whose attempts to change the administration of the church in Scotland led to his murder by the Presbyterian party. Further along are the elegant ruins of Blackfriars monastery, while the street terminates at the **West Port**, a well-preserved, late sixteenth-century gateway that now creates a traffic bottleneck.

Practicalities

The **tourist office**, 70 Market St (summer Mon–Sat 9.30am–8pm, Sun 11am–6pm; shorter hours rest of year; ☎01334/472021) will book **rooms** for a £1.50 charge – worth paying in the summer and during big golf tournaments when accommodation is in short supply. A particularly dense concentration of guesthouses can be found on Murray Place and Murray Park, off North St and close to the Old Course; the price and quality is consistently quite high. Often more expensive, **student residences** can be used as a summer fall-back (☎01335/462000; ③). There are also a number of good, but more pricey hotels on The Scores, the road leading from the Old Course to the castle, with good sea views. The *Golf*

Hotel, 40 The Scores (☎01334/472611; ⑨), offer mod-sized rooms with comfy beds and sofas. It also has a superb restaurant.

For **eating**, student favourites are *Brambles*, College St, *Ma Bell's* on The Scores, and *Ziggy's* grill-house on Murray Place. The best **pubs** are around the Old Course and along The Scores, although a particularly popular student place is the *Victoria Café*, 1 St Mary's Place, at the west end of Market St. Superb ice cream is served at *Jannetta's*, 31 South St, and sumptuous cakes and handmade chocolates are sold at *Fisher & Donaldson*, Church St.

Stirling

Occupying a key strategic position between the Highlands and Lowlands at the easiest crossing of the River Forth, **STIRLING** has played a major role throughout Scottish history. Imperiously set on a rocky crag, its **Castle** (daily 9.30am–5/6.30pm; £4.50) combined the functions of a fortress with those of a royal palace. The highlights of the extremely diverse buildings within the complex are the **Royal Palace**, dating from the late Renaissance, and the earlier **Great Hall**, where recent restoration, including a complete rebuilding of the vast hammerbeam roof, has revealed the original form and scale.

The oldest part of Stirling is grouped around the streets leading up to the castle. Just downhill, on Castle Wynd, stands a richly decorated facade, all that remains of **Mar's Wark**, one of two imposing Renaissance town houses. The other, **Argyll's Lodging** (9.30am–4.15/5.15pm; £2.80 or £5 joint ticket with castle), is intact, with some rooms furnished in period style. Beyond stands the Gothic **Church of the Holy Rude** (May–Sept Mon–Fri 10am–5pm), which boasts a fine timber roof. Here the infant James VI – later the first monarch of the United Kingdom – was crowned King of Scotland in 1567. To the side of the church is the E-shaped seventeenth-century building known as the **Guildhall**, which began life as a grand almshouse.

From here, Broad St slopes down to the lower town. Proceeding north along Upper Bridge St then Union St, you come to the fifteenth-century **Old Bridge**, a replacement for the wooden construction that was the scene of Sir William Wallace's victory over the English in 1297, a crucial episode in the Wars of Independence. The Scottish hero was commemorated in Victorian times by the construction of the **Wallace Monument** (daily; Nov–Feb 10am–4pm; March–May & Oct 10am–5pm; June & Sept 10am–6pm; July & Aug 9.30am–6.30pm; £3), about a mile further north. Though the recently refurbished building seems ugly close up, compensation comes in the quite stupendous views – finer even than those from the castle. In the foreground can be seen **Stirling University**, the youngest in Scotland and sometimes claimed as the most beautiful campus in the world.

The Stirling **tourist office** is at 41 Dumbarton Rd in the lower part of town (Oct–Mar Mon–Fri 10am–5pm, Sat 10am–4pm; April & May Mon–Sat 9am–5pm; June–Sept Mon–Sat 9am–6/7pm, Sun 10am–4/5pm; ☎01786/475019). Many of the numerous **guesthouses** are clustered in the King's Park area to the south of town and along the A91 towards the Wallace Monument. Between June and September, it's possible to stay in the university **residences** (☎01786/467141; ②), reached by regular buses (#51, #52, #53 and #81) from the bus station. The new grade-one **youth hostel** is on St John St (☎01786/473730; ②) at the top of town. It occupies a converted church, and all rooms have en-suite showers and toilets. The picturesque *Witches Craig* **campsite** is three miles east of town, off the A91 road to St Andrews, and served by frequent Hillfoot-bound buses (☎01786/474947; ②; April–Oct). For **eating** and **drinking**, try the lively *Barnton Bar and Bistro*, Barnton St, or the traditional *Porter's*, on Port St, for a cheap lunch.

Loch Lomond

The name of **Loch Lomond** – the largest stretch of fresh water in Britain – is almost as famous as Loch Ness, thanks to the ballad about its "bonnie, bonnie banks", said to be written by a Jacobite prisoner. The easiest way to get to the loch is to take one of the frequent buses from Glasgow to **BALLOCH** at its southern tip, from where you can take a cruise around the 33 islands nearby. Above the marina is Loch Lomond's main **tourist office** (July & Aug daily 9.30am–7.30pm; April–June, Sept & Oct daily 10am–5.30pm; ☎01389/753533); they'll find you a **B&B** – of which there's a plentiful supply in the area – without charge. A couple of miles up the west side of the loch is Scotland's plushest **youth hostel** (☎01389/850226; ②); there is another beautifully sited hostel at Rowardennan (☎01360/870259; ②). There are **campsites** in all the villages mentioned below.

Only the **western shore** is developed, with the A82 seldom straying far from its banks. The West Highland train – the line from Glasgow to Mallaig, with a branch line to Oban – joins the loch seventeen miles north of Balloch at Tarbet, and has one other station eight miles further on at Ardlui, at the mountain-framed head of the loch. There are, however, plenty of buses down this shore from Balloch.

No buses run on the **eastern shore**, much of which can only be traversed by the footpath which forms part of the West Highland Way. The easiest access to the graceful peak of **Ben Lomond** (3192ft) is by ferry from Inverbeg (south of Tarbet) to Rowardennan. From the latter it's a three-hour hike to the top of the most popular of Scotland's great "Munros" (mountains over 3000ft).

Oban and the southern Hebrides

The southernmost of the Hebrides – notably the large island of **Mull**, the tiny sacred isle of **Iona** and the spectacular rock of **Staffa** – are among the most compelling of the entire archipelago and the easiest to reach from central Scotland. Their main point of access is **Oban**, fifty miles south of Fort William. A scenic **bus** running along Loch Linnhe provides the quicker and cheaper approach from Fort William; if you're visiting Glencoe, this can be picked up at Ballachulish, not much more than a mile west of Glencoe Village. Approaching Oban **from the south** by train, you take the West Highland line to the hill-walking resort of Crianlarich, where the train divides, one part continuing north through Fort William, the other branching west to Oban.

Oban

Solidly Victorian in appearance, **OBAN** is an attractive enough place, if uncomfortably crowded for at least five months of the year. It has a superb setting, the island of Kerrera providing its bay with a natural shelter, and a further distinctive note is struck by the huge circular **McCaig's Tower** on a hilltop above the town. Imitating the Colosseum in Rome, it was the brainchild of a local banker a century ago, who had the twin aims of alleviating local unemployment and creating a family mausoleum. Work never progressed further than the exterior walls, but the folly provides a wonderful seaward panorama, particularly at sunset. Equally beautiful evening views can be had by walking along the northern shore of the bay, either from or below the medieval ruins of **Dunollie Castle**. Another attraction is the **Oban Distillery** on Stafford St in the town centre (guided tours: Easter–June & Oct Mon–Fri 9.30am–5pm, Sat 9.30–5pm; July–Sept Mon–Sat 9.30am–8.30pm; last tour 1hr before closing; £3).

Caledonian MacBrayne's **ferry terminal** for services to the Hebrides is just a stone's throw from the **train station**, which has the **bus terminus** on its other side. A host of private **boat operators** can be found in the harbour area, particularly along its northern side: their excursions – to the castles of Mull, to the seal colonies, or to Staffa – are worth considering, particularly if you're pushed for time. One thing to bear in mind if you're arriving early in the morning on an overnight ferry is that there's nowhere to grab a bite to eat until at least 8am.

The **tourist office** (Mon–Fri 9am–5.30pm, Sat & Sun noon–4pm; extended hours in high season; ☎01631/563122) is tucked away on Argyll Square just to the east of the bus terminus; a small fee is charged for finding **accommodation**. Should you wish to look yourself, there are dozens of B&Bs in town, particularly on the elevated Ardconnell and Dalrach roads and the southerly Soroba Rd. The largest concentration of **hotels** is on the Esplanade, where you'll find the official **youth hostel** (☎01631/562025; ②) just beyond the cathedral. There are two other hostelling possibilities: Jeremy Inglis' place at 21 Airds Crescent (☎01631/565065;

②) and the *Backpacker's Lodge*, Breadalbane St (☎01631/566624; ②). The nearest campsite is about two miles north at Ganavan Sands (☎01631/562179; ②). **Eating** possibilities tend to be dominated by standard pub fare, but Oban's fish-and-chip shops are much better than average, especially *Onorio's* on George St.

Mull

The chief appeal of **Mull** is its remarkably undulating coastline – three hundred miles of it in total. Despite its proximity to the mainland, the slower pace of life is clearly apparent: most roads are single track, with only a handful of (very cheap) buses linking the main settlements. **CRAIGNURE** is the main entry point, linked to Oban by eight car ferries daily, with a journey time of forty minutes. The village itself is fairly nondescript, but it offers a few guesthouses, a **campsite**, bike hire and a tourist office.

Both of Mull's most important historic monuments lie in the immediate vicinity. **Torosay Castle** (mid-April to mid-Oct daily 10.30am–5.30pm; £4.50) is in the full-blown Victorian Baronial style, set in a magnificent garden complete with a path lined with life-sized eighteenth-century statues. The mile and a half between Craignure and the castle can be covered by **Mull Rail** (April–Oct daily 11am–5pm; £3.30 return), the smallest line in Britain. A further mile and a half along the bay is **Duart Castle** (May to mid-Oct daily 10.30am–6pm; £3.50), the thirteenth-century stronghold of the MacLean clan. You can peek in the dungeons and ascend to the rooftops, but the castle is seen to best advantage from the ferry.

TOBERMORY, Mull's picturesque pint-sized "capital", is 22 miles northwest of Craignure and served by up to five buses a day. The **tourist office** (April–Oct Mon–Sat 9am–5/6pm, Sun 10am–4pm; ☎01648/302182) is in the Cal-Mac ticket office at the far northern end of the harbour. The island's sole bank and youth hostel (☎01688/302481; ②) are both on Main St. Guesthouses are in ample supply, but the best is *Fa'lte*, also on Main St (☎01688/302495; ④).

Mull's longest road (three buses each way Mon–Sat) is that covering the 35 miles between Craignure and Fionnphort, the port for Iona. This cuts through Glen More, past the island's highest peak, the mighty – and extinct – volcano of **Ben More** (3169ft), then follows the shore of the long sea loch, Loch Scridain. Both Fionnphort and Bunessan, five miles to the east, have several B&B options: either is worth considering for an overnight stop, given the accommodation shortage on Iona and the beauty of the coastline to the south.

Iona and Staffa

Just three miles long and no more than a mile wide, **Iona** nevertheless manages to encapsulate all the enchantment and mystique of the Hebrides. Its chief claim to fame is as one of the cradles of British Christianity: Saint Columba arrived here from Ireland in 563 and established a monastery which was responsible for the conversion of more or less all of Scotland and northern England. Reached in a few minutes by regular ferry from Fionnphort, Iona is a feasible day excursion by public transport from Oban in summer, and in high season the island is often overrun by organized tours from the mainland. To appreciate its special atmosphere and to have time to see the whole island, including the usually overlooked west coast, it's necessary to spend at least one night either here or in Fionnphort. The two hotels are fairly expensive, but bed and breakfast **accommodation** is available in a few houses in the harbour area.

No buildings remain from Columba's time: the present **Abbey**, which dominates all views of the island, dates from a re-establishment of monasticism here by the Benedictines in around 1200. Extensively rebuilt in the fifteenth and sixteenth centuries, it fell into decay after the Reformation and was only restored in the present century, with the latest revival of religious life: the now-flourishing multidenominational Iona Community. Adjoining the facade is a small chamber, traditionally assumed to be Saint Columba's grave. In front stand three delicately carved **crosses** from the eighth and ninth centuries, among the masterpieces of European sculpture of the Dark Ages. The finest of these is now represented by a copy, the original having been moved to the Abbey **Museum** housed in the monastic infirmary behind the abbey.

South of the church is the oldest building on the island, **St Oran's Chapel**, with a Norman door dating from the eleventh century. It stands at the centre of the sacred burial ground,

Reilig Odhrain, which is said to contain the graves of sixty kings of Norway, Ireland and Scotland, including the two immortalized by Shakespeare – Duncan and Macbeth. Walking back to the harbour, you pass MacLean's Cross, a fifteenth-century interpretation of those in the abbey grounds, and the ruins of a **nunnery** founded around the same time as the Benedictine abbey.

A basaltic mass rising direct from the sea, **Staffa** is the most romantic and dramatic of Scotland's plethora of uninhabited islands. On one side, its perpendicular rockface has been cut into caverns of cathedral-like dimensions, notably **Fingal's Cave**, whose haunting noises inspired Mendelssohn's *Hebrides Overture*. Storms and rough seas do lead to cancellations of scheduled voyages, but ultramodern sailing craft can get to the island in conditions that used to be too difficult. The two main **operators**, both based at Iona harbour and charging around £12.50, are Gordon Grant (☎01681/700338) and David Kirkpatrick (☎01681/700358). The return trip, calling at Fionnphort, lasts about two and a half hours, with an hour ashore and a foray into Fingal's Cave if weather permits.

Lochaber

As the **Lochaber** district contains **Ben Nevis**, Britain's highest mountain, and **Glencoe**, its most famous glen, it's small wonder that it has become one of the most popular parts of the Highlands. The hub of the area is **Fort William**, which is served by buses from Glasgow and Inverness but is better approached on the **West Highland railway**, Scotland's most scenic and most brilliantly engineered rail route, crossing countryside which can otherwise only be seen from long-distance footpaths. From the junction at Crianlarich, the line climbs around Beinn Odhar on a unique horseshoe-shaped loop of viaducts, then crosses the desolate peat bogs of Rannoch Moor, where the track had to be laid on a mattress of tree roots, brushwood and thousands of tons of earth and ashes. Skirting Loch Ossian, the train descends steeply along the entire length of Loch Treig, then circumnavigates Ben Nevis to approach Fort William from the northeast, through the dramatic Monessie Gorge, Roy Bridge and the southernmost reach of the Great Glen.

Fort William and Glen Nevis

Having just celebrated its three-hundredth birthday, **FORT WILLIAM** is a mere stripling by Scottish standards. Nothing remains of the fort which preceded the town and gave it its name, nor is there anything much in the way of conventional sights – it's chiefly of use as a base for the countryside and for having the only decent shops within a radius of fifty miles. Its setting, just beyond the point where Loch Eil merges with the huge Loch Linnhe, is its strongest feature, though in the town itself you're hardly aware of the presence of the great mountain in whose lee it lies.

The **tourist office** (Mon–Fri 9am–5pm, Sat 9am–4pm; ☎01397/703781) is on Cameron Square, about halfway down High St. There are dozens of **accommodation** possibilities, with the largest concentration of **B&Bs** lying in and around Fassifern Rd, slightly uphill from the train station. The most convenient bases for seeing the best of the scenery, however, are the **campsite** (☎01397/702191; ②; mid-March to mid-Oct) and the **youth hostel** (☎01397/702336; ③), both located just under three miles down **Glen Nevis**. Occasional buses, terminating at the hostel, run this lovely route, departing from Middle St, between High St and the loch. The easiest **walk** in the area is to continue up the glen on the road or accompanying footpath; there are wonderful and constantly changing views of Ben Nevis on one side and the peaks of Mamore Forest on the other, with the additional bonus of several waterfalls and cascades.

Top attraction, however, is the ascent of **Ben Nevis** (4406ft) itself. Although it gives the impression of being a brute of a mountain – particularly when seen from its precipitous northern side – it's actually rather a gentle climb, with a well-defined path carved out of the whaleback south side from the bridge opposite the youth hostel. Reckon on about four hours for the ascent, two for the descent and plenty of time for the vast plateau-like summit; you may have to do a fair amount of trudging through snow towards the end. The **views** are all you'd expect, though they might be better from halfway up, as the top is often shrouded in mist.

Glencoe

Easily reached by buses on the Glasgow–Fort-William route, **Glencoe** stretches southeast from the shore of Loch Leven, some fifteen miles south of Fort William. Its name translates as "the Vale of Weeping", a doubly appropriate title: not only was it the site of the infamous massacre in 1692 of the MacDonalds by the Campbells, it can be drenched by rain at all seasons of the year, making its untamed scenery look all the more dramatic and menacing. The massacre, ordered by King William III as punishment for the failure of the MacDonald chief to take his oath of loyalty, took place in the vicinity of **GLENCOE VILLAGE**, which is set back from Loch Leven and in the shadow of the Pap of Glencoe, with its distinctively head-shaped summit. Here you'll find several B&Bs; most of the cheaper accommodation options – the **youth hostel** (☎01855/811219; ②), and the Leacantuim Farm **bunkhouse** and **campsite** (both ☎01855/811256; ②) – are down the old road southeast along the banks of the River Coe.

At the point where the old road rejoins the main A82 is the National Trust for Scotland's **visitor centre** (April–Oct 10am–5pm; 50p), which owns most of Glencoe. Ask here for detailed **hiking** information: the ridges to the east are among the finest on mainland Britain, but are for experienced hill-walkers and climbers only.

From Fort William to Mallaig

For the 47-mile journey from Fort William to the Skye ferry port at Mallaig, the **train** just has the edge on the bus, in summer a steam service operates on certain days. At Banavie, just a couple of miles after Fort William, the line crosses the Caledonian Canal and passes the spectacular flight of locks known as Neptune's Staircase. Wonderful views back towards the crushing mass of Ben Nevis come before the line reaches the northern shore of Loch Sheil, after which it passes over a mighty curved viaduct, the first concrete construction of its kind in Britain. Approaching Mallaig, the train proceeds past the rock-strewn Sound of Arisaig and along the length of Loch Eilt before passing between Loch Morar – the deepest in the country at over 1000ft – and the silver sands.

The little fishing port of **MALLAIG** is linked by ferry to Armadale in Skye. Caledonian MacBrayne also have two or three sailings a week to the "Small Isles" – Muck, Eigg, Rhum and Canna. The village makes a pleasant base for exploring the area, boasting a better than average independent hostel, *Sheena's Bunkhouse*, just above the harbour (☎01687/462764; ②), as well as plenty of inexpensive guesthouses; if necessary, the **tourist office** by the harbour (summer Mon–Sat 9am–8pm, Sun 10am–5pm; shorter hours at other times; ☎01687/462170) will find a room.

Skye

The closest Hebridean island to the mainland, **Skye** is also the most beguiling, its richly varied scenery including Britain's most daunting mountain range, lush stretches of greenery and a coastline indented with majestic sea lochs. The tranquil present is the mirror opposite of the island's turbulent past. Throughout the Middle Ages, it was fiercely disputed by the rival MacLeods and MacDonalds, and the later conversion of the chiefs to landlords led to impoverishment for the majority of the population, provoking an armed uprising – the last in British history – in 1881.

For all its beauties, some words of warning are in order for visitors to Skye. Not for nothing is it nicknamed the "Misty Isle": the scenery is often covered from sight for days on end, even in summer – though the atmospheric light is part of Skye's charm, and the island is at its most magical when a spell of bad weather suddenly clears. Secondly, Skye isn't a place which can be seen in a hurry: many of the most beautiful spots are only accessible on foot, and are often far from the villages. Thirdly, bus services, other than on the main north–south route, are sparse as well as being the most expensive in Scotland.

Southern Skye

Two ferries make the crossing to Skye from the mainland. The first is from Mallaig to **ARMADALE** (mid-Oct to March Mon–Sat 3 daily; April to mid-Oct Mon–Sat 7 daily, Sun 1 daily; £2.60), where there's a **youth hostel** (☎01471/844260; ②; mid-March to Sept) along the shore from the harbour and a few guesthouses in the adjacent village of Ardvasar. The shorter crossing is the more picturesque trip from Glenelg to Kylerhea (as required; Easter–Oct Mon–Sat, mid-May to Aug additional Sun service). Buses and trains make the crossing from Kyle of Lochalsh to Kyleakin over the controversial Skye Bridge, a blot on the landscape and the most expensive toll bridge in Europe. **KYLEAKIN** has a picturesque harbour, dominated by the ruined Castle Moil. The island's official **youth hostel** is a few minutes walk from the ferry dock (☎01599/534585; ②) and another, privately run one, *Skye Backpacker's* is nearby (☎01599/534510, ②); there are also plenty of genuine guesthouses including the one run by *Mrs MacLennan* at 16 Kyleside (☎01599/534468; ④).

That said, there's little reason to stay and **BROADFORD**, eight miles north at the island's crossroads, makes a much better base for touring the island and has a small **tourist office** (summer Mon–Sat 8.30am–5.30pm; ☎01471/822361). It offers a wider choice of accommodation, including another **youth hostel** (☎01471/822442; ②; Feb–Dec) on the west shore of the bay, which rents **bikes**, or the much more beautiful and simple *Fossil Bothy* (☎01471/822297; ②), an independent hostel on the east side of the bay.

The Cuillins

The **Cuillins** in western Skye are among the great natural wonders of Europe, and although some of the peaks do require climbing skills, there are other summits well within the capability of normal walkers, while wonderful views of the range can be had without expending any energy at all. One of the classic views is across the dark waters of Loch Scavaig from the beach of Elgol, fourteen miles west of Broadford via the most beautiful road in Skye; the return trip can be made by post bus on working days and there are **boat trips** from Elgol to Loch Coruisk, run by Bella Jane (☎0800/7313089).

The northern starting point for exploration of the Black Cuillins is **SLIGACHAN**, sixteen miles from Broadford along the main A850 coastal road; there's little more to this hamlet than the expensive *Sligachan* hotel (☎01478/650204; ⑧), and a **campsite** (April–Oct). The most rewarding hike is down Glen Sligachan by the path to Loch Coruisk: the full return trip is a very long day's walk, though there's no need to proceed further than the Druim Hain ridge, five miles away, from which the whole of the Cuillins can be seen.

Really serious hill-walkers head for **GLEN BRITTLE**, fifteen miles southwest of Sligachan by road (daily bus each way), or eight miles by footpath. The **youth hostel** (☎01478/640278; ②; mid-March to Oct) here is a climbing centre, and guided hikes into the Cuillins are on offer. There's also a **campsite** not too far away by the beach (☎01478/640404; ②; April–Sept), but other accommodation is limited to a single B&B and holiday cottages that can only be rented by the week.

Trotternish

Skye's largest peninsula is **Trotternish**, which forms the northeastern part of the island. The gateway to this is the "capital" of **PORTREE**, which, from a visitor's point of view, is chiefly of note for having the shops and banks which are otherwise a rare commodity in Skye. Here also is the main **tourist office** on Bayfield Rd (April–June & Sept Mon–Sat 9am–5.30pm; July & Aug Mon–Sat 9am–8pm, Sun 10am–4pm; Oct–March Mon–Fri 9am–5pm; ☎01478/612137). The town brims over with the island's largest choice of **B&Bs**, and there are a couple of independent hostels, including the *Portree Independent Hostel* (☎01478/613737; ②), but there are many more congenial bases.

The most imposing scenery is to be found on the east coast of the peninsula, north of Portree – most of the buses linking Glasgow and Portree go around the island to Uig, seventeen miles away on the west coast, duplicating the route of some local buses. Some nine miles from Portree, at the edge of the Storr ridge, is a 165-foot obelisk known as **the Old Man of Storr**, while a further ten miles north, rising above Staffin Bay, are the **Quiraing** –

a forest of mighty pinnacles including the Needle, the Prison and the Table, where Victorian ramblers used to picnic and play cricket. The straggling village of **UIG** is the ferry port for departures to the islands of the Outer Hebrides, with sailings to Tarbert in Harris and Lochmaddy in North Uist. As well as several guesthouses, there is a **youth hostel** (☎01470/542211; ②; mid-March to Oct) and a **campsite**, both off the Portree road at the southern end.

Northwestern Skye

DUNVEGAN, set on a sea loch between the peninsulas of Vaternish and Duirnish, some 22 miles from Portree, is the main centre of the secluded northwestern corner of Skye. Just north of the village is the **Castle** (April–Oct daily 10am–5pm, Nov–March 11am–4pm; £5.20), the stronghold of the MacLeods and by far the most notable monument on Skye. Although prettified last century, the outlines of the medieval fortress are still apparent. Inside, you can see the now rather tatty Fairy Flag, a Byzantine cloth allegedly given to a chief by his fairy wife and possessing the magic to save the clan on three occasions, two of which have already been used up. Also on show is the Dunvegan Horn, which each heir-apparent must, at the time of coming of age, fill with claret and drain in one gulp. There's the added bonus of well-tended gardens, while, between May and October, excursion boats sail from the harbour to the nearby seal colonies.

Of the **guesthouses**, the best budget option is the beautifully situated *Silverdale* (☎01470/521251; ⑤), out towards Cobust; alternatively, there's a **campsite** (☎01470/220206; ②; April–Sept) just off the road to Portree.

Inverness and around

The capital and only large town of the Highlands, **INVERNESS** lies 160 miles north of Edinburgh, the rail line between the two traversing the gentle southern Highland country-side of Perthshire, before skirting the western fringe of the stark Cairngorms. Approaching it from the west, there's the magnificent eighty-mile train journey from Kyle of Lochalsh, a route that runs through **Wester Ross**, one of the grandest and most varied landscapes in Britain. If you're using this approach, try to travel on *The Clansman* (mid-June to Aug departs Kyle 3.10pm), a train whose tourist provisions include an observation car.

The Town

The one asset Inverness itself has is its setting astride the River Ness at the head of the Beauly Firth. Despite having been a place of importance for a millennium – it was probably the capital of the Pictish kingdom and the site of Macbeth's castle – there's nothing remarkable to see, nor any particularly strong sense of character. The only attractions of historical interest are situated some six miles east of town, and can be reached by regular buses. **Culloden Moor** was the scene in 1746 of the last pitched battle on British soil, when the troops of "Butcher" Cumberland crushed Bonnie Prince Charlie's army of volunteers in just forty minutes. This ended forever Stuart ambitions of maintaining the monarchy, and marked the beginning of the break-up of the clan system which had ruled Highland society for cen-turies. A **visitor centre** (April–Oct daily 9am–6pm; Feb–March, Nov & Dec daily 10am–4pm; £3.20) has displays describing the action. About a mile below the battlefield are the **Clava Cairns**, a late-Neolithic burial site comprising three stone cairns.

In Inverness itself, the one outstanding attraction is **Balnain House** (daily 10am–5/8pm; £1.75), a recently founded museum which, with the help of listening posts and an interactive exhibition, traces the development of Highland music from its prehistoric roots to modern electric folk-rock bands. It also has a congenial café downstairs where ceilidhs, sessions and recitals take place throughout the summer.

Twelve miles east of Inverness lies **Cawdor Castle** (May to mid-Oct 10am–5pm; £5.40), set in lovely gardens and parkland. The original fourteenth-century keep has grown towers, turrets and battlements over the years, and, approached over its drawbridge, it's real fairy-tale stuff.

As well as the only big choice of shops, restaurants and nightlife in the Highlands, you'll find **B&Bs** by the score in Inverness. These tend to fill up in summer, but the **tourist office** on Castle Wynd (Mon–Fri 9am–5pm, Sat & Sun 9.30am–5pm; ☎01463/234353) will find a room (and charge you £3 for the service). The **youth hostel** (☎01463/231771; ③) is on Victoria Drive, off Milburn Rd; there's also a plethora of independent hostels, including the *Inverness Student Hotel*, 8 Culduthel Rd (☎01463/236556; ②). **Campsites** can be found at Culloden (②; March–Oct) and on the road to Loch Ness, and there's a big site at Bught Parl west of the river, in Inverness itself (①).

Loch Ness

Loch Ness forms part of the natural fault line known as the Great Glen, which slices across the Highlands between Inverness and Fort William. Early last century, Thomas Telford linked the glen's lochs by means of the **Caledonian Canal**, which enabled ships to pass between the North Sea and the Atlantic without having to navigate Scotland's treacherous northern coast. The Pleasure craft now ply the canal and its lochs, the link having long lost its commercial significance. Summer **cruises** from Inverness (Easter–Oct; book at the tourist office) provide the most straightforward way of seeing the terrain; they depart from Tomnahurich Bridge, just over a mile south of the centre. The most popular trip is to Urquhart Castle, costing around £11 return. Alternatively, try Forbes' minibus tour of the loch (also bookable at the tourist office), pitched mainly at young backpackers and a sociable way to take in the area's most impressive landscape.

That said, most visitors are hardly bothered by the scenery, hoping instead to catch a glimpse of the elusive **"Nessie"**. Tales of the monster date back at least as far as the seventh century, when it came out second best in an altercation with Saint Columba. However, the possibility that a mysterious prehistoric creature might be living in the loch only attracted worldwide attention in the 1930s, when sightings were reported during the construction of the road along its western shore. Numerous appearances have been reported since, but even the most hi-tech surveys of the loch have failed to come up with conclusive evidence.

To find out the whole story, take a bus to **DRUMNADROCHIT**, fourteen miles from Inverness, where you can visit the **Official Loch Ness Monster Exhibition Centre** (daily: Easter–May 9.30am–5.30pm, June & Sept until 6.30pm, July & Aug until 8.30pm, Oct until 6pm, Nov–May 10am–4pm; £4.30). There are also cruises from here, predictably focusing on "Nessie" lore. Most photographs allegedly showing the monster have been taken a couple of miles further south, around the ruined **Urquhart Castle** (Oct–March daily 9.30am–4.30pm; April–Sept daily 9.30–6.30pm; £3.80), once one of Scotland's largest as well as most beautifully sited fortresses.

Aberdeen

Set on the North Sea coast between the Don and Dee rivers some 120 miles north of Edinburgh, **ABERDEEN** is the third city of Scotland and Europe's boom town of the last two decades. Solid and hard-wearing like the distinctively coloured granite that so many of the city's buildings are made of, it has been nicknamed the "Silver City", although its wealth is built on oil and "grey" would more accurately describe the colour of the stone.

Until a hundred years ago, Aberdeen was two separate towns a couple of miles apart. While Old Aberdeen slumbered in academic and ecclesiastical tranquillity, the newer town became a major port and commercial centre, and was subject to grandiose planning schemes. The most ambitious of these, in the early nineteenth century, included the layout of spacious **Union Street**, which runs for more than a mile westwards from Castlegate, the square which fronted the long-vanished castle. Here you can see the richly carved seventeenth-century **Mercat Cross**, the finest example of this essential adornment of a Scottish burgh. Opposite stands the vast bulk of the nineteenth-century Town House, which houses the entertaining **Tolbooth Museum** (April–Sept Tues–Sat 10am–5pm, Sun 2–5pm; £2.50), while a short way down King St is **St Andrew's Cathedral** (May–Sept Mon–Sat 10am–4pm). This is the mother-church of the American Episcopal Church, the first American bishop having been consecrated in Aberdeen in 1784.

Proceeding along Union Street, then left down Shiprow, brings you to **Provost Ross's House**, a sixteenth-century mansion now containing the award-winning **Maritime Museum** (Mon–Sat 10am–5pm, Sun 11am–5pm; £1), which describes Aberdeen's relationship with the sea through imaginative displays, films and models, including a thirty-foot oil rig. A further short walk downhill is the bustling **harbour** area, seen at its best before 8am, when the daily fish market winds up business.

Across Union Street from Shiprow is Broad Street, dominated by **Marischal College**, the younger half of Aberdeen University. Its facade, a historicist extravaganza from the beginning of the present century, is probably the most spectacular piece of granite architecture in existence. Nestling in stranded isolation behind the hideous municipal offices opposite is the oldest surviving residential building in the city, **Provost Skene's House** (Mon–Sat 10am–5pm; free). Highlight of the interior is the sixteenth-century Painted Gallery, whose wooden ceiling is covered with depictions of religious scenes. Just west of here, on the north side of Union Street, is the weird "**Mither Kirk**" of St Nicholas (May–Sept Mon–Fri noon–4pm, Sat 1–3pm; Oct–April 10am–1pm), so-called for being the main pre-Reformation church in Aberdeen. Tellingly, four separate churches now nestle in the shell of the original.

Ten minutes from the centre by bus #20, **Old Aberdeen** preserves the atmosphere of a cloistered academic community. Dominating High St is **King's College**, the university's older half. The chapel (Mon–Sat 9am–4.30pm), founded just a few years after the college at the end of the fifteenth century, boasts an outstanding crown spire; inside is a remarkably complete set of flamboyant late medieval furnishings. Closing the top end of the street is the Georgian **Old Town House**, now a public library. Over St Machar Drive lie the **Chanonry**, formerly a walled precinct and still with many fine houses, and **Botanical Gardens** (Oct–April Mon–Fri 9am–4.30pm; May–Sept also Sat & Sun 2–5pm; free). At the end of the Chanonry is the former cathedral, **St Machar's** (daily 9am–5pm), Aberdeen's first great granite construction. Its early fifteenth-century facade is a highly original, fortress-like design; equally impressive is the huge sixteenth-century heraldic ceiling covering the nave, which bears the coats of arms of the royal houses of Europe and the bishops and nobles of Scotland. A walk of about a mile through Seaton Park leads to Bridgend of Balgownie, a cluster of restored houses, beyond which is the **Brig o' Balgownie**, a graceful, single-arched, fourteenth-century bridge. Duthie Park, three miles south of the centre (bus #6, #16 and #17 from Union St) houses the **Winter Gardens**, a large tropical glasshouse stocked with fish, birds and the usual tropical plants. Local tradition claims that Aberdonians go there to save on the heating bills; on a cold day you may feel tempted to join them.

Practicalities

Both **bus** and **train** stations are on Guild St, a couple of minutes' downhill walk from Union St. The **tourist office** (June–Sept Mon–Sat 9am–5pm, Sun 10am–2pm; Oct–May Mon–Fri 9am–5pm, Sat 10am–2pm, closed Sun; ☎01244/632727) is on Broad St, just off the eastern end of Union St. The main concentrations of **guesthouses** are on Bon Accord St (south from Union St) and on the Great Western Rd. The **youth hostel** is at 8 Queen's Rd (☎01224/646988; ②), west of the centre on the route of bus #15, while the **campsite** (☎01224/321268; April–Sept) is in the suburban Hazlehead Park: take bus #4 or #14.

Top of the list for eating is *Ashvale Fish Restaurant*, 44–48 Great Western Rd, long rated as the best **fish-and-chip** shop in Britain. Decent pub grub is available in most of the city's hostelries, among which the *Blue Lamp* on Gallowgate and the *Howff* on Union St are recommended. Belmont Street, running from the centre of Union St also has a number of possibilities, including the busy *Wild Boar*, which transforms into a club-bar at night, with DJs and live music. For **drinking**, just down Belmont St the *Wodka Bar* serves a range of bizarre home-made flavoured vodkas, while round the corner in Little Belmont St *Ma Cameron's* is an Aberdeen institution. In Old Aberdeen, the *St Machar Bar* is a popular student hang-out.

travel details

Trains

London to: Aberdeen (10 daily; 7hr 30min); Aberystwyth (change at Birmingham; 7 daily; 5hr); Bath (every 30min; 1hr 20min); Brighton (every 15min; 1hr 10min); Bristol (every 30min; 1hr 30min); Canterbury (every 30min; 1hr 20min-2hr 10min); Cardiff (hourly; 2hr-2hr 20min); Dover (every 30min; 1hr 45min); Durham (hourly; 2hr 45min); Edinburgh (every 30min; 4hr-4hr 30min); Glasgow (15 daily; 5hr 30min-6hr); Liverpool (hourly; 2hr 45min); Manchester (20 daily; 2hr 40min); Newport (hourly; 1hr 45min); Norwich (every 30min; 1hr 50min); Oxford (every 20-30min; 1hr); Penzance (8 daily; 5hr 30min-6hr); Stratford (5 daily; 2hr 15min); Winchester (every 15min; 1hr); York (every 30min; 2hr).

Bristol to: Bath (24 daily; 15min); Cardiff (every 30min; 40min-1hr); Manchester (5 daily; 3hr 30min); Oxford (11 daily; 1hr 20min); Salisbury (hourly; 1hr 10min); York (6 daily; 4hr).

Edinburgh to: Aberdeen (hourly; 2hr 40min); Durham (hourly; 1hr 45min); Glasgow (every 30min; 50min); Inverness (6 daily; 3hr 30min); Newcastle (every 30min; 1hr 30min); Leuchars for St Andrews (hourly; 1hr); Stirling (every 30min; 50min); York (hourly; 2hr 30min).

Glasgow to: Aberdeen (hourly; 2hr 40min); Fort William (5 daily; 3hr 45min); Inverness (some change at Perth; 8 daily; 4hr); Mallaig (5 daily; 5hr 20min); Preston for Liverpool and Manchester (13 daily; 1hr 30min); Newcastle (every 2hr; 2hr 30min); Oban (8 daily; 3hr); Stirling (every 30min; 30min).

Inverness to: Aberdeen (10 daily; 2hr 15min); Stirling (some change at Perth; 8 daily; 3hr).

Liverpool to: Cardiff (some change at Crewe; 13 daily; 4hr); Manchester (every 20min; 1hr); Preston for Glasgow and Edinburgh (hourly; 1hr); York (hourly; 2hr 20min).

Manchester to: Newcastle (12 daily; 2hr 50min); York (every 30min; 1hr 40min); Preston for Glasgow (every 20min; 1hr); Windermere (5 daily; 2hr 10min).

Buses

London to: Aberdeen (3 daily; 11hr 30min-12hr); Aberystwyth (1 daily; 7hr 20min); Bangor (for Holyhead; 2 daily; 7hr 35min); Bath (11 daily; 3hr-3hr 30min); Brighton (18 daily; 1hr 50min); Bristol (9 daily; 3hr); Cambridge (19 daily; 1hr 50min); Canterbury (18 daily; 1hr 50min); Cardiff (6 daily; 3hr 10min); Dover (23 daily; 2hr 15min-2hr

45min); Durham (5 daily; 5hr 30min); Edinburgh (2 daily; 8hr 30min-9hr 10min); Fort William (2 daily; 13hr); Glasgow (4 daily; 7hr 45min-8hr 50 min); Inverness (3 daily; 12hr 20min-13hr 10min); Lancaster (4 daily; 5hr 50min-7hr 30min); Liverpool (5 daily; 4hr 45min); Manchester (7 daily; 4hr 35min); Newcastle (5-8 daily; 6hr); Newport (6 daily; 2hr 45min); Norwich (6 daily; 2hr 45min-3hr); Oxford (every 12min; 1hr 30min-2hr); Penzance (5 daily; 7hr 45min-9hr 15min); Salisbury (2-3 daily; 2hr 45min); Stirling (4 daily; 8hr 55min-9hr 40min); Stratford (3 daily; 2hr 45min-3hr 15min); Winchester (7 daily; 2hr); York (3 daily; 4hr 30min).

Bristol to: Bath (every 15min; 50min); Cardiff (hourly; 1hr 10min); Manchester (2 daily; 5hr); Oxford (2 daily; 2hr 30min); Salisbury (1 daily; 3hr); Wells (1 daily; 1hr 20min).

Edinburgh to: Aberdeen (change at Perth or Dundee; hourly; 4hr); Durham (1 daily; 4hr 30min); Fort William (1 daily; 3hr 50min); Glasgow (every 20min; 1hr 10min); Inverness (hourly; 4hr); Kyle of Lochalsh for Skye (1 daily 2hr 15min); Manchester (3 daily; 6hr 30min); Melrose (every 30min; 2hr 15min); Newcastle (3 daily; 3hr); St Andrews (every 30min; 2hr-3hr); Stirling (every 30min; 1hr-1hr 50min).

Glasgow to: Aberdeen (hourly; 3hr 10min-4hr 15min); Fort William (3 daily; 3hr 45min); Glencoe (4 daily; 2hr 30min); Inverness (7 daily; 4hr); Kyle of Lochalsh for Skye (3 daily; 5hr-5hr 50min); Lancaster (2 daily; 3hr 15min); Liverpool (2 daily; 4hr 40min-5hr 15min); Manchester (3 daily; 4hr 30min-5hr); Newcastle (2 daily; 2hr 30min); Oban (3 daily; 3hr); Portree (3 daily; 6hr 15min-7hr); St Andrews (12 daily; 2hr 20min); Stirling (hourly; 45min).

Fort William to: Inverness (7 daily; 1hr 50min); Mallaig (4 daily; 1hr 30min); Oban (4 daily; 1hr 45min); Portree (3 daily; 3hr); Stirling (4 daily; 3hr 20min).

Inverness to: Aberdeen (13 daily; 3hr 25min); Portree (2 daily; 3hr 10min); Stirling (4 daily; 3hr 20min).

Liverpool to: Cardiff (4 daily; 5hr 40min-6hr 40min); Manchester (23 daily; 50min); Newcastle (5 daily; 4hr 30min-7hr 30min); Oxford (4 daily; 4hr 45min-5hr 25min); Stratford (2 daily; 4hr 35min); Windermere (2 daily; 4hr 30min-5hr 45min); York (3 daily; 3hr 40min-4hr 45min).

Manchester to: Durham (3 daily; 4hr 15min-4hr 45min); Glasgow (3 daily; 4hr 30min-5hr); Leeds (17 daily; 1hr-1hr 25min); Newcastle (5 daily; 4hr 50min-5hr 45min); Windermere (2 daily; 2hr 45min-4hr); York (3 daily; 2hr 30min-3hr).

CHAPTER 4

BULGARIA

Introduction

If Westerners have an image of **Bulgaria**, it tends to be coloured by the murky intrigues of Balkan politics, exemplified by the infamous tales of poisoned umbrellas and plots to kill the pope. From the Bulgarians' standpoint, though, the nation has come a long way since it threw off the 500-year-old yoke of the Ottoman Empire in the 1870s, and is now struggling to cope with the aftermath of Communist misrule. Renaming themselves the Bulgarian Socialist Party, the Communists long remained the dominant force in national politics after 1989, and progress towards free-market reforms was lethargic, to say the least. The election of a right-of-centre government in April 1997 gave ground for new hope, although low wages and high unemployment remain ever-present features of Bulgarian life.

Independent travel here is not common, but there are relatively few restrictions, the costs are low, and for the committed there is much to take in. The main attractions are the mountainous scenery, and the web of towns and villages with a crafts tradition, where you'll find the wonderfully romantic architecture of the National Revival era. Foremost among these are **Koprivshtitsa** in the Sredna Gora range; **Bansko** in the Pirin mountains; **Plovdiv**, the second largest city; and **Veliko Târnovo**, the medieval capital. The monasteries can be startling, too – the finest, **Rila**, is on every tourist's itinerary. For urban thrills, the capital **Sofia** and the animated coastal resort of **Varna** are the places to aim for.

Information and maps

The idea of publicly funded **tourist information offices** is new to Bulgaria, and most towns have yet to establish one. Nearly all main towns have accommodation agencies responsible for handling private rooms; they might also book other forms of accommodation and provide local maps, although they're usually pretty hopeless at giving other information. Though staff in Sofia and the main resorts generally speak English, knowledge of foreign languages elsewhere in the country is patchy.

The best **map** currently available is Freytag and Berndt's map of Romania and Bulgaria. Once in the country, you're limited to much less detailed and often out-of-date maps. Street plans of Sofia, Plovdiv and Varna are widely available, but plans for other cities are often out of print.

Money and banks

Bulgaria's national currency – the **lev** – is one of the weakest in Europe, which has made Bulgaria an extremely cheap place to travel, inflation notwithstanding. The **exchange rate** offered at banks is realistic enough to destroy the appeal of the black market, and new private exchange offices often have even better rates. It's best to bring a good supply of foreign currency with you, as many smaller banks and offices won't accept travellers' cheques, and credit cards are virtually useless outside top hotels and elite restaurants.

Bulgarian currency comes in 100, 200, 500, 1000, 2000, 10,000, 20,000 and 50,000 leva notes, as well as relatively worthless coins of 1, 2, 5, 10, 50 and 100 leva. Government plans to **reform the currency** by knocking three noughts off current values (thus making the 50,000 leva note equal to 50 new leva) may have been enacted by the time you arrive. You can change surplus leva back into hard currency in banks and exchange bureaux before leaving (you may be asked to produce your original exchange receipts), but often at a highly disadvantageous rate.

Communications

Street kiosks sell envelopes (*plika*) and sometimes stamps (*marki*), although the latter are often only sold at **post offices**, usually open Mon–Sat 8.30am–7.30pm. The main *Poshta* will have a **poste restante**, but postal officers tend to return mail to sender if not claimed immediately.

Coin-operated public telephones (which accept the increasingly hard-to-find 2-leva coins) rarely work, and it's usually better to use one of the card phones operated by Betkom or Bulfon – Betkom are marginally more reliable. **Phonecards** (*fonkarta*) for both systems are available from post offices and some shops. For international calls, it's easier to go to a post office. The **operator number** for domestic calls is ☎121, for international calls ☎0123.

■ Body language

Bulgarians shake their heads when they mean "yes" and nod when they mean "no". Sometimes they reverse these gestures if they know they're speaking to foreigners, thereby complicating the issue further. Emphatic use of the words *da* (yes) and *ne* (no) should be enough to avoid misunderstandings.

Getting around

Public transport in Bulgaria is inexpensive, although vehicles and carriages tend to be outmoded and dirty. Bear in mind that bus and train journeys are notoriously slow – a product of mountainous terrain and badly maintained routes.

■ Trains

Bulgarian State Railways (BDZh) can get you to most towns; trains are punctual if slow, and fares low – to the coast from Sofia for as little as £5/$8 first class. Express services (*Ekspresen*) are restricted to trunk routes, but on all except the humblest branch lines you'll find so-called Rapid (*bârz vlak*) trains. Use these rather than the snail-like *pâtnicheski* services unless you're planning to alight at some particularly minor halt. Long-distance/overnight trains have reasonably priced couchettes (*kushet*) and/or sleepers (*spalen vagon*). For these, on all expresses and many rapids, you need seat **reservations** (*zapazeni mesta*) as well as **tickets** (*bileti*). In large towns, it's usually easier to obtain tickets and reservations from **railway booking offices** (BDZh) or **transport service bureaux** (*kompleksni transportni uslugi*) rather than the station, and wise to book a day in advance. Advance bookings are required for **international tickets**, handled by a separate organization, the *Rila Agency*. Most stations have **left-luggage offices** (*garderob*). InterRail passes are valid in Bulgaria, Eurail are not.

■ Buses

Practically everywhere is accessible by **bus** (*avtobus*), though in remoter areas there may only be two or three services a day. Generally, you can buy a ticket at least an hour in advance when travelling between towns, but on some routes they're only sold when the bus arrives. On rural routes, tickets are often sold by the driver rather than at the terminal.

■ Driving and hitching

To drive in Bulgaria you'll need a current **driving licence**, third-party insurance plus a Green Card – which can be bought at the border. Entering Bulgaria, your vehicle will be registered with a special "visa tag" which must be presented on leaving the country – a rule intended to prevent foreigners from selling their cars here. Speed limits are 50–60kph in towns, 120kph on express roads, and 80kph on all other roads. **Car rental** is arranged by major travel agents in the bigger towns, who reckon payment in US dollars – expect to pay $350 per week with unlimited mileage.

You'll find filling stations spaced every 30–40km apart along the highways, but queues are common. **Breakdown assistance** is available only on the principal highways – the emergency number is ☎146.

Hitching is possible in parts of Bulgaria where public transport is sparse; otherwise, people expect you to catch the bus. Hitching alone is not advised.

Accommodation

Although foreigners are required to pay five to ten times the rate charged to Bulgarians, **accommodation** in Bulgaria is still very cheap by Western standards. Though prices are sometimes quoted in dollars, you can pay in local currency, and only rarely are you required to produce exchange receipts to prove that you've obtained your leva legally – but it's best to keep a few just in case.

■ Hotels

Most one- or two-star **hotels** (for the most part uninspiring high-rise blocks) rent doubles for £10–15/$16–24 a head, a little more in Sofia and Plovdiv. Cosier family-run hotels are beginning to appear on the coast and in village resorts like Koprivshtitsa, Bansko and Melnik, offering a higher level of service often for a much lower price.

ACCOMMODATION PRICE CODES

Throughout this guide, accommodation is priced on a scale of ① to ⑨, the number indicating the lowest price per night a single person could expect to pay in that establishment in high season. With hostels this is the nightly rate per person; with hotels, the price is arrived at by dividing the cost of the cheapest double room by two. The prices indicated by the codes are as follows:

① under £5 / $8	④ £15–20 / $24–32	⑦ £30–35 / $48–56
② £5–10 / $8–16	⑤ £20–25 / $32–40	⑧ £35–40 / $56–64
③ £10–15 / $16–24	⑥ £25–30 / $40–48	⑨ £40 / $64 and over

■ Private rooms

Private rooms (*chastni kvartiri*) are available in most large towns, and are usually administered by accommodation agencies, although in the smaller resorts you can usually find a room by asking around – expect to pay around £5–10/$10–15 for a double, more in Sofia and Plovdiv. Single travellers usually get a small reduction on the price of a double. The quality varies enormously (it's rarely possible to inspect the place first), but as a rule, private rooms in big cities will be in large residential blocks, while those in village resorts can often be in atmospheric, traditional-style houses.

■ Campsites and hostels

Some towns of interest have a **campsite** (*Kamping*) on the outskirts, although these can be unkempt affairs with bad connections to the town centre. The majority have two-person chalets (£5–10/$10–15 per night). **Camping rough** is illegal and punishable with a fine. **Hostels** (*Turisticheska spalnya*) are thin on the ground, although those that exist (in Plovdiv or at Rila monastery for example) are well run and accustomed to foreigners.

Food and drink

Fresh fruit and vegetables have long formed the basis of Bulgarian cuisine, a tradition rarely reflected in restaurants, where menus have become pretty standardized and uninspiring. Grilled meats are the backbone of most Bulgarian restaurant meals, although you'll sometimes find more traditional roasted or stewed dishes.

■ Food

Sit-down food is eaten in either a **restorant** (restaurant) or a **mehana** (taverna). There's little difference between the two, save for the fact that a *mehana* is likely to offer folksy decor and a wider range of traditional Bulgarian dishes – wherever you go, you're unlikely to spend more than £5/$8 for a main course, salad and drink.

Foremost among **snacks** are *kebapcheta*, grilled mincemeat served with a chunk of bread, or variations on the theme like *shishche* (shish kebab) or *kebap*. Another favourite is the *banitsa*, a flaky-pastry envelope with a filling – usually cheese; it's sold by street vendors in the morning and evening, to people going to and from work. Elsewhere, *hamburgeri* (basically anything placed between two halves of a bun), *sandvichi* (sandwiches) and *pitsi* (pizzas) dominate the fast-food repertoire. Bulgarians consider

their **yoghurt** (*kiselo mlyako*) the world's finest, and hardly miss a day without consuming a glass.

Mainstay of any Bulgarian restaurant menu are the **grilled meats**, of which *kebapcheta* and *kyofte* (meatballs) are the most common. More substantial are chops (*pârzhola* or *kotlet*) or fillets (*file*), invariably *teleshko* (veal) or *svinsko* (pork). In the grander restaurants the main course will be accompanied by potatoes (*kartofi*) and a couple of vegetables, as well as bread: sometimes a *pitka* or small bread bun. Lower down the scale, you may just get chips (*pârzheni kartofi*) and a couple of slices of a stale loaf.

The most characteristic **traditional Bulgarian dishes** are those baked and served in earthenware pots. The best known dish is *gyuvech* (which literally means "earthenware dish"), a rich stew comprising peppers, aubergines and beans, to which are added either meat or meat stock. *Kavarma*, a spicy meat stew (often pork), is prepared in a similar fashion.

Finally, along the coast and around the highland lakes and reservoirs, there's **fish** (*riba*) – most often fried or grilled, but sometimes in a soup or stew.

Vegetarian meals (*yastia bez meso*) are hard to obtain, although *gyuveche* (a variety of *gyuvech* featuring baked vegetables) and *kachkaval pane* (cheese fried in breadcrumbs) are worth trying if they're offered.

Pancakes – sweet or savoury – are sold in **patisseries** or *Sladkarnitsa*, alongside various cakes (*torta*) and the occasional gooey oriental treat, such as *baklava*.

■ Drink

From having an insular **wine** industry before World War II, Bulgaria has muscled its way into the forefront of the world's export market. Among the **reds** are full-bodied Cabernet, heavier, mellower Melnik and Gâmza, rich, dark Mavrud, and the smooth, strawberry-flavoured Haskovski Merlot. The sweeter **whites** are preferable to Dimyat unless you like your wine very dry; Karlovski Misket (Muscatel) and Tamyanka are widely available, the golden-coloured Euxinovgrad much harder to find.

Cheap native **spirits** are highly potent, drunk diluted with water in the case of *mastika* (like ouzo in Greece) or downed in one, Balkan-style, in the case of *rakiya* – brandy made from either plums (*slivova*) or grapes (*grozdova*). Bulgarian **beer** has improved immeasurably in recent years, and brands such as Zagorka and Astika are infinitely preferable to pricey imported alternatives.

Coke and Pepsi are sold everywhere, and the Bulgarians have their own millet-based beverage, Boza, which tastes like liquidized shredded wheat. Patisseries serve **coffee** (*kafe*), which if you don't specify will probably come *espresso*, though you will sometimes encounter *kapuchino* or *kafe sâs smetana* (coffee with cream). **Tea** (*chai*) is nearly always herbal – ask for *cheren chai* (literally "black tea") if you want the real stuff.

Opening hours and holidays

Big-city shops and supermarkets are generally **open** Mon–Sat 8.30am–6pm or later. In rural areas and small towns, a kind of unofficial siesta may prevail between noon and 3pm. All shops, offices and banks, and many museums, are closed on the following days: Jan 1; March 3; Easter Sunday; Easter Monday; May 1; May 24; Dec 25 and 26. Museum entry charges are usually higher for foreigners than for the locals, although producing a student card will secure a discount.

Emergencies

Petty theft is a danger on the coast, and the Bulgarian **police** can be slow in filling out insurance reports unless you're insistent. If you're driving on roads near the Turkish (or Serbian) border, watch out for traffic cops charging foreign drivers spot fines for spurious offences. **Consulates** may be helpful in some respects, but they never lend cash to nationals who've run out or been robbed. **Women** travelling alone can expect to encounter stares, comments and sometimes worse from macho types, and discos on the coast are pretty much seen as cattle-markets, but a firm response should be enough to cope with most situations.

If you need a **doctor** (*lekar*) or dentist (*zâbolekar*), go to the nearest *Poliklinika* (health centre), whose staff might well speak English or German. Emergency treatment is free of charge although you must pay for **medicines** – larger towns will have at least one 24-hour pharmacy.

EMERGENCY NUMBERS

Police ☎166; Ambulance ☎150; Fire ☎160.

SOFIA

Gone are the days when **SOFIA** resembled a kind of communist Geneva, with fresh wreaths stacked against its monuments and a police force that one could imagine clubbing litterbugs and jaywalkers. The downtown streets and parks are still fairly spruce, but the emergence of free enterprise, with traders hawking goods from pavement stalls and privately owned cafés crammed into alleyways, has given the capital a new vigour. The mixture of chaos and decay which characterizes most of Sofia's points of arrival makes it an unwelcoming city for first-time visitors, but once you've settled in and begun to explore, you'll find it surprisingly laid-back for a capital city. Though it's hardly a great European metropolis brimming with fine sights, the place comes into its own on fine spring and summer days, when the downtown streets and their pavement cafés begin to buzz with life. Urban pursuits can be combined with the outdoor recreational possibilities offered by verdant **Mount Vitosha**, an easily-accessible 12km to the south. Despite occasional concerts and a few discos, entertainment still revolves around the evening promenade or *korso*, followed by a drink in one of the cafés, bars or beer halls.

The city was founded by a Thracian tribe some 3000 years ago, and various **Byzantine ruins** attest to its zenith under Constantine (306–337). The Bulgars didn't arrive on the scene until the ninth century, and with the notable exception of the thirteenth-century Boyana Church, their cultural monuments largely disappeared during the Turkish occupation (1381–1878), of which the sole visible legacy is a couple of stately **mosques**. Sofia's finest architecture postdates Bulgaria's liberation: handsome public buildings and parks, and the magnificent Aleksandâr Nevski Cathedral.

Arrival and information

Trains arrive at **Central Station** (*Tsentralna Gara*), a concrete hive harbouring a couple of exchange bureaux, but little else to welcome the visitor. Five minutes' ride along bul Knyaginya Mariya Luiza (tram #1 or #7) is Sveta Nedelya Square, within walking distance of several hotels and the main accommodation bureaux (see below). Most national **buses** arrive in the various bus parks situated around the *Hotel Princess* (still known to locals by its former name, *Novotel Europa*), just opposite the train station, although some Bansko services and Blagoevgrad buses (for connections to Rila monastery) use the Ovcha Kupel terminal, 5km southwest of the centre along bul Tsar Boris III (tram #5 from behind the National History Museum). International buses (daily connections with Istanbul, Salonika, Athens and Skopje) arrive either near the *Hotel Princess* or at a small terminal at Damian Gruev 38, ten minutes' walk west of the centre. Bus #84, running every ten to twenty minutes, connects **Sofia Airport** with the Orlov Most, from where you can walk into the city centre; the last bus leaves the airport at around 11.30pm.

City transport

The **public transport** network – consisting of buses (*avtobus*), trolleybuses (*troleibus*) and, slowest of all, trams (*tramvai*) – runs between 5am and midnight and is ridiculously cheap and reasonably efficient. There's a **flat fare** of around 15c on all urban routes; tickets (*bileti*) are sold from street kiosks and must be punched on board the vehicle (inspections are frequent and there are spot fines for fare-dodgers). Kiosks at the more important tram-stops sell one-day tickets (*karta za edin den*; 60c) and five-day tickets (*karta za pet dena*; $1.50). **Taxis** charge about 25c per kilometre until nightfall, after which rates tend to double.

Accommodation

The budget **hotels** you'll pass if walking into town from the train station are the kind of flop houses it's prudent to avoid, and most of central Sofia's older hotels are overpriced considering the level of comfort they are able to offer. The smaller family-run hotels are the best

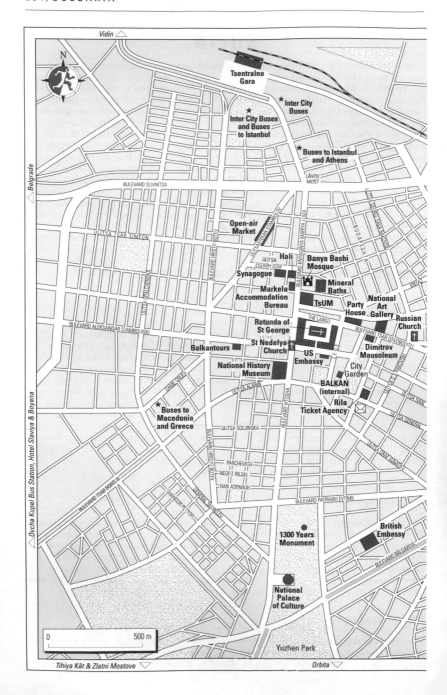

Vidin △

N

Tsentralna
Gara

★ Inter City
Buses

★ Inter City Buses
and Buses
to Istanbul

★ Buses to Istanbul
and Athens

LAVOV
MOST

△ Belgrade

BULEVARD SLIVNITSA

ULITSA TSAR SIMEON

Open-air
Market

Hali

Banya Bashi
Mosque

Synagogue

ULITSA
EXZARH IOSIF

Markela
Accommodation
Bureau

Mineral
Baths

TsUM

Party
House

National
Art
Gallery

Russian
Church

BULEVARD ALEKSANDAR STAMBOLIISKI

THE LARGO

BULEVARD TSAR OSVOBODITEL

Rotunda of
St George

Balkantours

St Nedelya
Church

US
Embassy

Dimitrov
Mausoleum

National History
Museum

City
Garden

BALKAN
(internal)

★ Buses to
Macedonia
and Greece

Rila
Ticket Agency

ULITSA SOLUNSKA

PARCHEVICH

NEOFIT RILSKI

HAN ASPARUH

BULEVARD PATRIARH EVTIMII

△ Ovcha Kupel Bus Station, Hotel Slaviya & Boyana

1300 Years
Monument

British
Embassy

BULEVARD BALGARIYA

National
Palace
of Culture

0   500 m

Tihiya Kât & Zlatni Mostove ▽

Yuzhen Park

Orbita ▽

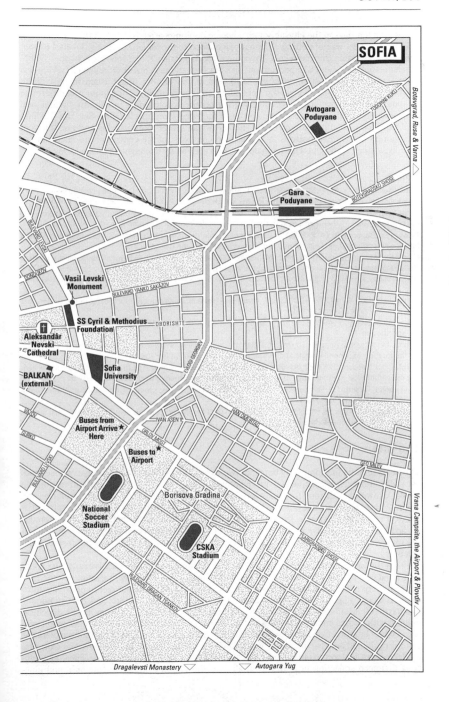

Avtogara
Poduyane

Gara
Poduyane

Botevgrad, Ruse & Varna ▷

TODORINI KUKLI

BOTEVGRADSKO SHOSE

Vasil Levski
Monument

BULEVARD EVLOGI

MONDUKOV

BULEVARD YANKO SAKAZOV

SS Cyril & Methodius
Foundation

OBORISHTE

Aleksandâr
Nevski
Cathedral

EVLOGI GEORGIEV

Sofia
University

BALKAN
(external)

VAZOV

GURKO

BULEVARD LEVSKI

Buses from
Airport Arrive ★
Here

IVAN ASEN II

HAN OMURTAG

ORLOV MOST

Buses to ★
Airport

GEO MILEV

National
Soccer
Stadium

Borisova Gradina

Vrana Campsite, the Airport & Plovdiv ▷

CSKA
Stadium

SARBRADSKO SHOSE

BULEVARD DRAGAN TSANKOV

Dragalevsti Monastery ▽   ▽ Avtogara Yug

bases for a few days in the city, although advance bookings are advisable. A **private room** is still the cheapest way of getting a decent place close to the action. Centrally located private rooms are available from Markela, Knyaginya Mariya Luiza 23A (Mon–Fri 8.30am–7.30pm, Sat 9am–4pm) for about $10 per person; or from Balkantours, bul Stamboliiski 27 (Mon–Fri 10am–7pm, Sat 10am–2pm; ☎02/987-7233) and at the airport (daily 10am till last flight; ☎02/796-293), for $7–10 per person depending on length of stay. There's no real difference in room quality between the two, although Markela's rooms may be slightly further out. Odysseia-IN, Stamboliiski 20 (entrance round the corner on Lavele; Mon–Sat 9am–7.30pm; ☎02/989-0538), can book rooms in the smaller private hotels both in Sofia and elsewhere in the country. Sofia's **campsite** is at Vrana, 8km southeast of the centre on the main road to Plovdiv, a quiet, leafy spot with bungalows (③), reached by trolleybus #4 from Orlov Most.

Hotels

Baldzhieva, ul Tsar Asen 23 (☎02/981-1257). Small, privately owned hotel in a nicely refurbished town house just one block west of bul Vitosha. Rooms are clean and cosy, all with phone, fridge, TV and WC. ④.

Deva-Spartak, bul Arsenalski (☎02/661-261). Small, modern place with tidy en-suite rooms, 2km south of the centre beyond Yuzhen Park, next to the Spartak swimming pool. Tram #6 from the station. ⑤.

Enny, Pop Bogomil 46 (☎02/834-395). Small and simple downtown hotel just off bul Knyaginya Mariya Luiza, with cramped but clean rooms, and shared facilities in the hallway. ③.

Ganesha, Al von Humboldt 26 (☎02/707-936 or 718-798). A converted apartment block on a suburban street, midway between the city centre and the airport. Neat rooms have en-suite shower, satellite TV and small balcony. Bus #213 or #313 from the train station, or bus #84 from the airport to the *Hotel Pliska* stop. ③

Maya, Trapezitsa 4 (☎02/894-611). Small, family-run place in an apartment block bang in the centre, just opposite the Largo. Rooms have TV. ③.

Niky, Neofit Rilski 16 (☎02/511-915). Small hotel just off the main bul Vitosha. Tiny rooms, but most have TV and shower. ③.

Orbita, bul Dzheimz Bauchâr 76 (☎02/639-3444). Characterless postwar block with plain en-suites, handy for the foothills of Mount Vitosha and Yuzhen Park. Tram #9 from the station. ④.

Shipka, bul Totleben 34A (☎02/91960). Former army-owned hotel on the southwestern fringes of the centre, but within easy walking range of the sights. Clean en-suite rooms. Breakfast included. ⑤.

Slavyanska Beseda, ul Slavyanska 3 (☎02/880-441). Characterless, gloomy Communist-era hotel, but a fairly central and affordable mid-range choice. ⑤.

Tsar Asen, Tsar Asen 68 (☎02/547-801). Another small family-run pension nestling in residential streets just west of the National Palace of Culture. ③.

The City

The heart of Sofia fits compactly between two rivers, the Perlovets and Vladaya, whose modest width didn't deter architects from designing a fancy bridge for both of them during the 1890s. Crowned with four ferocious-looking statues and set amidst weeping willows, the **Orlov Most** (Eagle Bridge), to the east of the centre, marks the spot where liberated prisoners of war were greeted by their victorious Russian allies and compatriots in 1878. Popular regard for the "Slav elder brother" stems from Russian support for Bulgarian liberation in the nineteenth century, and has little or no parallel in most other parts of the former eastern bloc.

From the bridge it's a brief stroll up bul Tsar Osvoboditel to **Sofia University**, the country's most prestigious seat of learning. In the distance, across the park, a glint of gold betrays the proximity of the **Aleksandâr Nevski** Cathedral, one of the finest pieces of architecture in the Balkans. Financed by public subscription and built between 1882 and 1924 to honour the 200,000 Russian casualties of the 1877–78 War of Liberation, it's a magnificent structure, bulging with domes and semi-domes and glittering with gold leaf. Within the cavernous interior, a white-bearded God glowers down from the main cupola, an angelic sunburst covers the central vault, and as a parting shot, Vasnetsov's *Day of Judgement* looms above the exit. The modern crypt, entered from outside (10.30am–12.30pm & 2–5.30pm, closed Tues; $2), contains a superb collection of **icons** from all over the country, mostly eighteenth- and nineteenth-century pieces – though look out for some medieval gems from the coastal towns of Nesebâr and Sozopol.

An imposing gallery on the northeastern edge of the cathedral square houses the **SS Cyril and Methodius Foundation** (Wed–Mon 11am–6pm; $1.50), an international art collection which devotes a lot of space to second-division French artists, though there are a couple of Delacroix sketches and a small Picasso etching.

Heading west across the square, you'll pass two recumbent lions flanking the Tomb of the Unknown Soldier, set beside the wall of the brown-brick **Church of Sveta Sofia**. Raised during the sixth-century reign of Justinian, it follows the classic Byzantine plan of a regular cross with a dome at the intersection.

The best route from here is to cut down past the building housing the National Assembly on to **Bulevard Tsar Osvoboditel**, an attractive thoroughfare surfaced with yellow stone and partly lined with chestnut trees. West along the boulevard is the **Russian Church**, a zany firecracker of a building with an exuberant bright-yellow tiled exterior, five gilded domes and an emerald spire, concealing a dark, candlewax-scented interior. Close by is the **Natural Science Museum** (daily 10am–5pm; 50c), which presents a thorough visual catalogue of Bulgarian wildlife and a gripping selection of snakes and lizards.

At its western end bul Tsar Osvoboditel opens into **ploshtad Alexander Battenberg**, named after the German aristocrat chosen to be the newly independent country's first monarch in 1878. The square was once the scene of Communist rallies and parades, and is still dominated by the (now empty) mausoleum of Georgi Dimitrov, first leader of the People's Republic of Bulgaria. Opposite, in the former royal palace, are the uninspiring **National Art Gallery** (Tues–Sun 10.30am–6pm; $1) and the more interesting **Ethnographic Museum** (Tues–Sun 11am–4pm; $1), where costumes and craft objects provide a thorough introduction to Bulgarian folklore.

Since World War II the seat of power has shifted westwards to the **Largo**. Flanked on three sides by severe monumental buildings, this elongated plaza was built on the ruins of central Sofia, pulverized by British and American bombers in the autumn of 1944. Of the complex, the white, colonnaded supertanker of the former **Party House**, originally the home of the Communist hierarchy, is the most arresting structure. Protesters set fire to it in the summer of 1990 (smoke-blackened walls bear testimony to their discontent), but the Party wasn't ejected from the building until early 1992. In front of the Party House, a pedestrian subway provides glimpses of the Roman era fortress walls built to protect the eastern entrance to the city. Just south of the Party House, a fifteenth-century mosque now holds the **Archeological Museum** (Tues–Sun 10am–4.30pm; $1), with a modest collection of Thracian and Greek finds, and medieval frescoes plucked from crumbling church walls throughout Bulgaria.

Immediately west of here, the *Sheraton Hotel*'s sombre wings run round a courtyard containing Sofia's oldest church, the fourth-century **Rotunda of St George**. It contains frescoes from the eighth century onwards, although most eyes are drawn to the fourteenth-century Christ the Pantokrator, surrounded by a frieze of 22 prophets, in the dome. On the northern side of the Largo, an equally large structure houses the Council of Ministers (Bulgaria's cabinet), and Sofia's main department store, the **TsUM**. Another underpass gives access to a sunken plaza laid out with café tables, whose bright awnings contrast with the weathered brick and stone **Church of Sveta Petka Samardzhiiska**, containing fragmentary and much-restored frescoes. It's barely recognizable as a church, and was built this way so as not to irritate the Turkish conquerors.

The square elongates northwards to join **Bulevard Knyaginya Mariya Luiza**, lined with greyish turn-of-the-century buildings. Here the **Banya Bashi Mosque** catches the eye, built in 1576 by Hadzhi Mimar Sonah, who also designed the great mosque at Edirne in Turkey. Behind stand Sofia's **mineral baths**, housed in a candy-striped turn-of-the-century building which has recently been restored and hosts occasional historical exhibitions. The **Church of St Nedelya**, marking the southern boundary of pl Sveta Nedelya, was constructed after the liberation as the successor to a number of churches that have stood here since medieval times. South of St Nedelya, the silhouette of Mount Vitosha surmounts the rooftops of **Vitosha Bulevard**, Sofia's main shopping street.

The **National History Museum** occupies the former Palace of Justice on the western side of the boulevard (Tues–Thurs, Sat & Sun 10.30am–5.30pm, Fri 2–5.30pm; $4). On the ground floor, pride of place is given to the magnificent gold treasures of Vâlchitrân and Panagyurishte and the fourth-century BC silver treasure of Rogozen, all of which demonstrate the achievements of Thracian civilization. Bas-reliefs, ceramics, silverware and frescoes give some idea of the artistic heights attained during the medieval era, when Pliska, Preslav and Veliko Târnovo enjoyed their heyday as capitals – although these pale before the collection of ecclesiastical art displayed upstairs. The upper floor also exhibits a wonderful collection of nineteenth-century folk costumes and carpets.

Heading east from bul Vitosha, the shop-flanked **Graf** meanders to the **Friendship Bridge** (Most na Druzhba), one of the approaches to **Borisova Gradina** ("Boris's Garden", after Bulgaria's inter-war monarch, Tsar Boris III). The park itself is the oldest and largest in Sofia, with a rich variety of flowers and trees and two huge football stadiums. As an evening parade ground for the city's burgeoning youth culture, Borisova Gradina is outshone by **Yuzhen Park**, at the southern end of bul Vitosha. It's dominated by the **National Palace of Culture** (NDK), an ultramodern concert and congress centre, built in honour of Todor Zhivkov's daughter Lyudmila.

Mount Vitosha

A wooded mass of granite 20km long and 16km wide, **Mount Vitosha** is where Sofians come for picnics, views or skiing, and the ascent of its highest peak, the 2290m **Cherni Vrâh**, has become a traditional test of stamina. Public transport to the mountain is straightforward, although there are fewer buses on weekdays than at weekends.

One approach is to take tram #5 from behind the National History Museum to Ovcha Kupel bus station, then change to bus #61, which climbs through the forests towards **ZLAT-NI MOSTOVE**, a beauty spot on the western shoulder of Mount Vitosha beside the so-called **Stone River**. Beneath the large boulders running down the mountainside is a rivulet which once attracted gold-panners. Trails lead up beside the rivulet towards the mountain's upper reaches: Cherni Vrâh is about two to three hours' walk from here.

Another route up Vitosha is on tram #12 from Graf Ignatiev to the Hladilnika terminus on bul Cherni Vrâh, and then bus #66 to the resort centre of **ALEKO**. Aleko can also be reached by taking bus #64 or #93 from Hladilnika to the suburb of **Dragalevtsi**, where there's a **chairlift** (*lifta*; daily in winter season; rest of year weekends only); or taking bus #122 from Hladilnika to **Simeonovo**, starting point for the Aleko-bound **gondola** (daily in winter season; rest of year weekends only). However you get there, Aleko is well-served with snack bars, restaurants and innumerable walking trails. The peak of Cherni Vrâh is an easy forty-metre walk from here. From November to late spring Aleko is a thriving winter sports centre, with a range of pistes to suit all grades of skiers and a couple of ski schools that rent out gear.

Eating, drinking and entertainment

Market economics and creeping Westernization have made big changes in the range of food, drink and nightlife, ensuring that the Bulgarian capital is no longer the stern and joyless place it was before 1989. Indigenous grilled **snack foods** have been largely replaced by hamburgers, sandwiches and pizzas, served at kiosks and fast-food joints throughout the city. *Kenar*, with branches at bul Vitosha 19 and bul Stamboliiski 55, offer take-away sandwiches and salads made from traditional Bulgarian ingredients. Sofia's **restaurants** have undergone a facelift, with many dingy, unprofitable places closing down to be replaced by rather more garish, cosmopolitan haunts, most of which feature live musical entertainment. Menus continue to be rather one-dimensional, but if you tire of the standard Bulgarian meal of grilled meat plus salad, various restaurants offering foreign cuisine present alternatives.

Daytime **drinking** takes place in the cafés around bul Vitosha or around the numerous kiosks which dot the city's open spaces. **Bars** are on the increase, although many of them are hastily built affairs stationed in the owner's basement or garage. If you're renting a room in suburban Sofia, you'll probably find a couple of these small and intimate drinking venues on your block: otherwise, the streets either side of bul Vitosha are the best places to look in the city centre.

Restaurants

Baalbek, Vasil Levski 4. Highly-regarded Lebanese establishment, with sit-down restaurant upstairs and fast food counter (offering kebabs, shawarma and falafel) on the ground floor.

Chen, Rakovski 86. Popular Chinese restaurant with authentic food, just opposite the opera house.

Eddy's Tex Mex Diner, bul Vitosha 4. Tacos, tortillas and steaks in a raucous atmosphere. With live music at weekends, it's a good place to drink too.

Europa,ul Alabin 34. Good chicken dishes at moderate prices, in a basement next to the cinema of the same name.

King's Club, Vitosha 108. Indonesian restaurant with lots of satay and fried rice dishes.

Otvåd aleyata, zad shkafa ("Beyond the alley, behind the cupboard"), Budapeshta 31 (☎02/835-581). Restaurant three blocks east of TsUM department store, popular with the expat community and offering an inventive blend of international and Bulgarian cuisine. Reserve in advance.

Ramayana, Hristo Belchev 32. Pretty authentic Indian restaurant one block east of bul Vitosha, with a range of vegetarian options.

Retrokristal, pl Kristal. Upmarket venue above the *Kristal Café*, with antique-shop decor and attentive service. The menu offers an imaginative spin on traditional Bulgarian favourites with some excellent salads and a good range of vegetarian courses.

Trops-kåshta, Alabin 24. Excellent value self-service restaurant offering tasty Bulgarian standards. Open until 9pm only. There's another branch just east of pl Sveta Nedelya on ul Sâborna.

Ugo II, Neofit Rilski. Stylish and dependable pizzeria in the side streets just off bul Vitosha.

Cafés, bars and discos

Biblioteka, Oborishte. Busy, youthful, rock and pop-orientated disco beneath the National Library building, one block north of Sofia university. Cover charge $1.

Club 703, Tsar Shishman 24. A popular, pub-like after-work venue, just south of the National Assembly.

Chervilo, Tsar Osvoboditel. Bar and disco with a different style of music every night.

Funky's, Shandor Petyofi 26. Basement bar with imported beers and nightly live music. Cover charge of $1.

Indigo, Yuzhen Park. Large club venue behind the national soccer stadium. Events range from commercial disco to rave.

Jimmy's Sladoledena kåshta, General Parensov 25. Mecca for ice cream (both eat-in and take-out), as well as the usual coffee-and-cake café fare.

Markrit, Patriarh Evtimii 61. Wicker furniture and potted plants make this the best place in central Sofia for a relaxed, intimate drink.

J.J. Murphy's, Kârnigradska. Friendly Irish pub catering for a mixture of Bulgarians and expats. Western prices.

Pri Kmeta, Parizhka. Roomy basement beer hall near the Aleksandâr Nevsky church. Good food, and occasional noisy disco.

Schweik, Vitosha 1A. International beers (including excellent Czech ones) and sausagey snacks in a basement just off Vitosha.

Swingin' Hall, Dragan Tsankov 8. Modern suburban bar serving imported drinks at Western prices. Live music (usually pop/rock or jazz) on two stages. Open well after midnight. Cover charge.

Tequila, Levski Pametnik. Classy but regularly heaving late-night drinking joint above the *Hotel Serdika*. Cover charge.

Vienska sladkarnitsa/Wiener Konditorei, Orlov Most. Excellent coffee and sumptuous cakes in stylish surroundings.

Listings

Airlines Aeroflot, Oborishte 23 (☎02/943-4489); Air France, ul Sâborna 2 (☎02/981-7830); Austrian Airlines, bul Vitosha 41 (☎02/980-2323); British Airways, Alabin 56 (☎02/981-7000); Lufthansa, ul Sâborna 9 (☎02/980-4101); Swissair, Angel Kânchev 1 (☎02/980-4459); Balkan, pl Narodno Sâbranie 12 (☎02/880-663). **Airport information** Domestic flights ☎02/722-414; international flights ☎02/798-035.

Car rental Avis, *Hotel Sheraton* (☎02/988-8176), and at the airport (☎02/738-023); Hertz at the airport (☎02/791-447).

Embassies and consulates Britain, bul Levski 38 (☎02/980-1220); USA, ul Sâborna 1 (☎02/980-5241).

Libraries American Center, Kârnigradska 18 (daily 1–5pm); British Council, Tulovo 7 (Mon–Fri 9am–noon & 2–5pm).

Medical emergencies The main accident and emergency department is at the Pirogov hospital, bul Totleben 21 (☎51531).

Pharmacies 24hr service at pl Sveta Nedelya 5.

Post office ul General Gurko (daily 7am–9pm).

Telephones On ul Stefan Karadzha, behind the post office; open 24 hrs.

Taxis Okay Supertrans ☎2121; Inex ☎91919.

Train tickets International tickets can be bought at the station (Tsentrala Gara) or from the Rila Bureau, General Gurko 5 (Mon–Fri 8am–7pm, Sat 9am–2pm).

Travel agents Odysseia-in, Stamboliiski 20 (☎02/989-0538), can pre-book accommodation in small hotels throughout Bulgaria or find you a place on one of their hiking tours; USIT Colours (Travel Byte), bul Levski 35 (☎02/981-1900), handle discount international air tickets.

SOUTHERN BULGARIA

Trains heading from Bulgaria to Greece follow the Struma Valley south from Sofia, skirting some of the country's most grandiose mountains on the way. Formerly noted for their bandits and hermits, the Rila and Pirin Mountains contain Bulgaria's highest, stormiest peaks, swathed in forests and dotted with alpine lakes awaiting anyone prepared to hike or risk their car's suspension on the backroads. If time is short, the two spots to select are the most revered of Bulgarian monasteries, **Rila**, lying some 30km east of the main southbound route, and the village of **Melnik**, known both for its wine and its vernacular architecture. More traditional architecture is to be found in the village of **Bansko** on the eastern side of the Pirin range, a small detour from the main north–south route.

Another much-travelled route heads southeast from Sofia towards Istanbul, through the Plain of Thrace, a fertile region that was the heartland of the ancient Thracians, whose culture began to emerge during the third millennium BC. The main road and rail lines now linking Istanbul and Sofia essentially follow the course of the Roman Serdica–Constantinople road, past towns ruled by the Ottomans for so long that foreigners used to call this "European Turkey". Of these, the most important is **Plovdiv**, Bulgaria's second city, whose old quarter is a wonderful melange of Renaissance mansions, mosques and classical remains, spread over three hills. Thirty kilometres east of Plovdiv is the **Bachkovo Monastery**, whose churches and courtyards contain some of Bulgaria's most vivid frescoes.

The Rila Monastery

The best-known of Bulgaria's monasteries, famed for its architecture and mountainous setting, **Rila** receives a steady stream of visitors, many of whom come on excursions from Sofia. You can treat Rila as a day-trip from the capital if you book a coach tour with a travel agent in Sofia (such as Balkantours, bul Stamboliiski 27; around $40), or travel with the (summeronly) daily bus service which leaves Sofia's Ovcha Kupel terminal at 6.30am. Otherwise, public transport is so meagre that you'll have to stay the night: catch a bus or train from Sofia to Blagoevgrad in the Struma Valley, where you can catch local buses to Rila village, 27km short of Rila Monastery. Here, you can change to one of three daily buses to the monastery itself.

The single road to the **Rila Monastery** runs above the foaming River Rilska, fed by innumerable springs from the surrounding mountains, which are covered with pine and beech trees beneath peaks flecked with snow. Even today there's a palpable sense of isolation, and it's easy to see why Ivan Rilski – or **John of Rila** – chose this valley to escape the savagery of feudal life and the laxity of the established monasteries at the end of the ninth century. The current foundation, 4km from John's original hermitage, was plundered during the eighteenth century and repairs had hardly begun when the whole structure burned down in 1833.

Its resurrection was presented as a religious and patriotic duty: public donations poured in throughout the last century, and the east wing was built as recently as 1961 to display the treasury.

Ringed by mighty walls, the monastery has the outward appearance of a fortress, but past the west gate this impression is negated by the beauty of the interior, which even the crowds can't mar. Graceful arches above the flagstoned courtyard support tiers of monastic cells, and stairways ascend to top-floor balconies which – viewed from below – resemble outstretched flower petals. Bold red stripes and black-and-white check patterns enliven the facade, contrasting with the sombre mountains behind and creating a harmony between the cloisters and the **Church** within. Richly coloured frescoes shelter beneath the porch of the monastery church and cover much of its interior. The iconostasis is particularly splendid, almost 10m wide and covered by a mass of intricate carvings and gold leaf.

Beside the church is **Hrelyo's Tower**, the sole remaining building from the fourteenth century. Cauldrons, which were once used to prepare food for pilgrims, occupy the kitchen on the ground floor of the north wing, where the soot-encrusted ceiling has the shape and texture of a huge termite's nest. Things are more salubrious on the floors above, where the spartan refectory and some of the panelled guest rooms are open for inspection. The **ethnographic collection** (daily 8am–5pm) is notable for its carpets and silverware, while beneath the east wing there's a wealth of objects in the **treasury** (same hours). These include icons and medieval Gospels, Rila's charter from Tsar Ivan Shishman, written on leather and sealed with gold in 1378, and a miniature cross made by the monk Raphael during the 1970s. Containing more than 1500 human figures, each the size of a grain of rice, the cross took Raphael twelve years to carve with a needle, and cost him his eyesight.

It's possible to **stay** in the monastery cells for about $16 a night if you don't mind the lack of hot water and the curfew (10pm or earlier; check before going out for the evening). Otherwise, try the *Turisticheska spalnya* (②) just outside the monastery's eastern gate, the three-star *Hotel Tsarev Vrah* (☎07054/2280; ④), about 200m further on, or the older but still agreeable *Hotel Rilets* (☎07054/2106; ④), 2km further east. Near the *Rilets* the primitive *Bor* **camping** occupies an attractive riverside site. The more comfortable *Camping Zodiac* (☎07054/2291), another 200m east, rents out four-person chalets (②).

For **snacks**, delicious bread can be obtained at the bakery (which is run by monks), just outside the monastery's east gate. For more substantial meals, the **restaurants** at the hotels *Tsarev Vrah* and *Rilets* are preferable to the outlets near the monastery gates, which sometimes overcharge stray foreigners. **Nightlife** is limited to the plush bar of the *Rilets*, where there's sometimes a disco.

Melnik and around

Approaching the village of **MELNIK** on the bus from Sandanski, the nearest major town, you catch glimpses of the wall of mountains which allowed the townsfolk to thumb their noses at Byzantium during the eleventh century. The village hides until the last moment, encircled by hard-edged crags, scree slopes and rounded sandstone cones. With its whitewashed stone houses on timber props festooned with flowers, its cobbled alleys and its narrow courtyards, Melnik is stunning – but socially and economically it's fast becoming a fossil. In 1880 the village had 20,000 inhabitants, 75 churches and a thriving market on the Charshiya, the main street. The economy waned towards the end of the last century, and the Balkan War of 1913 saw Melnik burned to the ground and its trade routes sundered. Nowadays there are only 570 inhabitants and the village survives on **wine-making** – the traditional stand-by – and tourism.

Melnik's backstreets invite aimless wandering and guarantee a succession of eye-catching details. It's oldest ruin – known as the Byzantine or **Bolyar House** – is sited on the high ground immediately east of the centre, and was clearly built with defence in mind. It was probably the residence of Melnik's thirteenth-century overlord, Alexei Slav, who invited rich Greeks to settle here. Southeast of the Bolyar House you'll see the balustraded tower of the **Church of Sveti Nikolai**. Inside, a wooden bishop's throne decorated with light-blue floral patterns offsets a fine iconostasis, on which white-bearded St Nicholas himself is prominently featured.

The houses that belonged to the village's Greek entrepreneurs, rebuilt during the National Revival, are now Melnik's most impressive buildings, and none more so than the old **Kordopulov Mansion** (Tues–Sun 8am–noon & 1.30–6pm) situated on the eastern outskirts. The stone-walled house protrudes from the hillside, its windows surveying every approach. The spacious rooms are intimate, the reception room a superb fusion of Greek and Bulgarian crafts, with an intricate lattice-work ceiling and a multitude of stained-glass windows.

Several steep and slippery tracks lead up the hillside immediately south of the Kordopulov house onto the **Nikolova Gora**, a wooded plateau bearing the ruins of a couple of monasteries and, at its western end, a medieval fortress. The view from the latter – with pyramidal sandstone formations rearing to the left and right – is spectacular.

A more strenuous walk heads northeast towards **Rozhen monastery**. You can either take the asphalt road to Rozhen from the west end of Melnik village (1hr 30min), or the more direct path over the mountains (1hr). For the latter, follow the gulley at the eastern end of Melnik village, take the right-hand fork after a kilometre and a half, and look for a steep path which ascends the hillside to your left. Views of rippling mountains reward the effort, although the subsequent descent to the monastery has been narrowed by soil erosion, and can be unsuitable for those who don't have a head for heights. The monastery itself has a beautiful, balconied courtyard, and the village of Rozhen below is just as pretty as Melnik, although less developed.

Practicalities

There's one **bus** a day from Sofia to Melnik (currently leaving at 2pm from behind the *Hotel Princess*) – otherwise take one of the more frequent buses from Sofia to Sandanski, 15km short of Melnik, and change to one of the local minibuses (5 daily). Try and avoid travelling to Sandanski by rail – the train station is miles away from the town centre. The **Visitor's Centre** in Sandanski, in the main square, just down from the bus stop (Mon–Fri 9am–5pm; ☎0746/2403; *bicc@omega.bg*) can arrange **rooms** for you in Melnik – otherwise just head for the village and ask around. There are plenty of small bed-and-breakfast hotels in the village: Milushevata Kâshta (☎07437/326; ②) is a cosy place up some steps on the south side of the main street; while Uzunovata Kâshta (☎07437/270; ③) is a traditional-style house at the eastern end of the village. Of the half-dozen **places to eat**, the best are Loznitsite on the main street, offering traditional meat-based dishes in a stone-built house; and Menchevata Kashta further east, which offers a broad range of Bulgarian food and a few vegetarian options – try *gyuveche po makedonski*, local vegetables baked in a pot.

Bansko and around

Lying some 40km east of the main Struma valley route, **BANSKO** is the main centre for walking and skiing on the eastern slopes of the Pirin mountains. It's a traditional agricultural centre and a growing tourist resort, boasting a wealth of stone-built nineteenth-century farmhouses and a growing number of small, B&B-style hotels. Though connected to Sofia and other towns by bus (see below), Bansko can also be reached by a narrow-gauge railway which leaves the main Sofia–Plovdiv line at **Septemvri** and forges its way across the highlands. It's one of the most scenic trips in the Balkans, but also one of the slowest, taking five hours to cover a distance of just over 100km.

Bansko centres around the modern pedestrianized pl Nikola Vaptsarov, where the **Nikola Vaptsarov Museum** (Mon–Fri 8am–6pm, Sat & Sun 8am–noon & 2–6pm) contains a display relating to the local-born poet and socialist martyr, as well as housing a crafts exhibition where you can purchase distinctive local rugs. Immediately north of here, pl Vâzrazhdane is watched over by the solid stone tower of the **Church of Sveta Troitsa**, whose interior contains exquisite nineteenth-century frescos and icons. On the opposite side of the square, the **Rilski Convent** contains an **Icon Museum** (Mon–Fri 9am–noon & 2–5pm) devoted to the achievements of Bansko's nineteenth-century icon painters – a school largely centred around the Vienna-educated Toma Vishanov, who with pupils Dimitâr and Simeon Molerov, travelled from village to village decorating local churches.

The easiest way of getting into the **Pirin mountains** from Bansko is to walk (or take a taxi) west to the Vihren hut (where dorm accommodation is available; ②), a steep 14km uphill. This is the main trail-head for hikes towards the 2914m summit of **Mt Vihren** (Bulgaria's second-highest peak), or gentler rambles around the meadows and lakes nearby.

Practicalities

There are five buses a day to Bansko from Sofia, although if you're approaching the area from Rila or Melnik, it's far easier to head for Blagoevgrad in the Struma valley and change buses there. Bansko's **bus and train stations** are on the northern fringes of town, ten minutes' walk from the central pl Vaptsarov, where a **tourist information centre** (Mon–Fri 9am–1pm & 3–7pm; ☎07443/5048) lurks in an arcade below the palace of culture. The staff will advise on hiking in the region and accommodation in town. Best of the family-run **hotels** are *Albert*, ul. Byalo More 12 (☎07443/4264; ④), a cosy place with en-suite rooms just off pl Vâzrazhdane; *Dzhangal*, Gotse Delchev 24 (☎07443/2661; ③), in a quiet area ten minutes' walk from the centre and featuring a garden, barbecue and sauna; *Dvata Smârcha*, Velyan Ognev 2 (☎07443/2637; ③), a friendly place off pl Vâzrazhdane whose owners serve delicious food; and the nearby *Matsureva Kâshta*, Velyan Ognev 7 (☎07443/2714; ③), with rooms furnished in traditional rural style. For **eating**, there are over forty tavernas offering traditional specialities: *Sirleshtova Kâshta*, *Bayrakovata Mehana* and *Dyado Pene*, all grouped around the centre, are among the most atmospheric.

Plovdiv

The country's second largest city, **PLOVDIV** is one of its most attractive and vibrant centres, and arguably has more to recommend it than Sofia. The old town embodies Plovdiv's long history – Thracian fortifications subsumed by Macedonian masonry, overlaid with Byzantine walls and by great timber-framed mansions erected during the Bulgarian renaissance, symbolically looking down upon the derelict Ottoman mosques and artisans' dwellings of the lower town. But Plovdiv isn't merely a parade of antiquities: the city's arts festivals and trade fairs rival Sofia's, and its restaurants and promenade are equal to those of the capital.

Arrival and accommodation

Trains arrive at Tsentrala Gara on the southern fringe of the centre, and the two **bus terminals** are nearby. Rodopi, serving the mountain resorts to the south, is just on the other side of the tracks, while Autogara Yug, serving the southeast, is one block east. Private **rooms** are available from Esperansa, Ivan Vazov 14 (on leaving the station, go anticlockwise round the square and it's the second street on the right; daily 11am–5pm; ☎032/260653), which has centrally located rooms for $8–10. Try also Pâldin Tours, bul Bâlgariya 106 (daily 9am–5.30pm; ☎032/555120; take bus #2 or #102 from the station and alight once you've crossed the river). Basic **hostel** accommodation is available in the atmospheric but over-subscribed *Turisticheski Dom* (☎032/633211; ②) in the old town at ul Slaveikov 5; or *Ucheben Tsentar*, Konstantin Nunkov 13a (☎032/772847; ②), is a tower-block postgrad hostel in a residential district south of the train station – take the underpass to the far side of the tracks, pass through the Rodopi bus station, continue past the Spartak football stadium and take the fourth right. The *Bâlgariya* **hotel**, Patriarh Evtimii 13, just off the main ul Knyaz Aleksandâr (☎032/626064, ⑤), has shabby but acceptable en-suites; while *Noviz*, a fifteen-minute walk north of the station at bul Ruski 55 (☎032/631281; ⑤) is newer and far more stylish, with TV and minibar in all rooms.

Central Plovdiv

Central Plovdiv revolves around the large **Tsentralen** square, dominated by the ponderously Stalinist *Hotel Trimontsium*. Heading north from here, the pedestrianized Knyaz Aleksandâr is lined with shops, cinemas and bars, with terraces from which people watch life going by. Off to the right, Gavril Genov and Stanislav Dospevski streets lead up past the lovely church of **Sveta Marina**, which has boldly coloured murals beneath its porch and beguiling creatures peeping out from the wooden foliage of its iconostasis.

Further north, Knyaz Aleksandâr gives onto the arresting **ploshtad Dzhumaya**, surrounded by small cafés packed with students, whiskery elders and corpulent *bons viveurs*. The ruins of a **Roman Stadium**, visible in a pit beneath the square, are just a fragment of the arena where up to 30,000 spectators watched chariot races, wrestling, athletics and other events. Among the variously styled buildings around here, the **Dzhumaya Mosque** (open for noon prayers on Friday), with its diamond-patterned minaret and lead-sheathed domes, steals the show. It's believed that the mosque dates back to the reign of Sultan Murad II (1359–85), and its thick walls and the configuration of the prayer hall – divided by four columns into nine squares – are typical of mosques of that period. From the square, ul Raiko Daskalov continues north to meet bul Hristo Danov and two further relics of Turkish rule: the leaden domes and sturdy masonry identify the *Chifte Hamam* as an original **Turkish bath**, while the zigzag brickwork on the minaret of the **Imaret Mosque** livens up the ponderous bulk of the building.

With its cobbled streets and orieled mansions covering one of Plovdiv's three hills, Plovdiv's **Old Quarter** is a painter's dream and a cartographer's nightmare. As good a route as any is to start from pl Dzhumaya, and head east up ul Sâborna. Blackened **fortress walls** dating from Byzantine times can be seen around streets such as Knyaz Tsertelov and Sâborna, sometimes incorporated into the dozens of **National Revival-style houses** that are Plovdiv's speciality. Typically, these rest upon an incline and expand with each storey by means of timber-framed oriels – cleverly resolving the problem posed by the scarcity of groundspace. Outside and inside, the walls are frequently decorated with niches, floral motifs or false columns painted in the style known as *alafranga*, executed by itinerant artists. At the top of Sâborna, the **Church of SS Constantine and Elena** contains a fine gilt iconostasis by Ivan Pashkula, partly decorated by the prolific nineteenth-century artist Zahari Zograf, whose work also appears in the adjacent **Museum of Icons** (Tues–Sun 9.30am–12.30pm & 2–6pm). A little further uphill is the **Hisar Gate**, just north of which stands Plovdiv's most photographed building – the **Kuyumdzhioglu House**. Named for the Greek who commissioned it in 1847, the house graces a garden which you enter from ul Dr Chomakov, and combines Baroque and native folk motifs in its richly decorated facade, with its undulating pediment echoing the line of the carrying-yoke. The **Ethnographic Museum** (Tues–Sun 9am–noon & 2–5pm; $1.50) in the mansion's lower rooms is mundane, but upstairs the elegant rooms opening off the grand reception hall are furnished with objects reflecting the owner's taste for Viennese and French Baroque, and filled with showcases of sumptuous jewellery and traditional peasant costumes. Heading west from the Hisar Gate, a road leads downhill to ul Artin Gidikov, where the **Hindlian House** at no. 4 (daily: summer 9am–5.15pm; winter 9am–noon; $1), former home of an Armenian merchant, harbours some of Plovdiv's most sumptuous nineteenth-century interiors.

Eating and drinking

Several **restaurants** in the old town serve good Bulgarian food in elegant surroundings. The *Alafrangite*, ul Nektariev 15, and the *Trakiiski Stan*, ul Pâldin 7, occupy the nicest nineteenth-century buildings, but food and service can sometimes be pretty average. The *Pâldin*, ul Knyaz Tsertelev 3, is a step up in quality, although an excellent meal will still only cost $15–20. In the new town, *Gremi*, just off Tsentralen on bul Vâzrazhdane, has a palm-filled garden and good grills and fish, while *Rimska Pizzeria*, pl Dzhumaya, has reasonably authentic good-value pizzas. *Knyaz Aleksandâr* – awash with hamburger, doner kebab and pizza outlet – is the place to look for cheaper **snack** fare.

Drinking takes place in the pavement cafés of ul Knyaz Aleksandâr and pl Stamboliiski. If the weather's not good enough for sitting outside, *Iguana* on Sasho Dimitrov is cosy and intimate; while *Flying High*, a block west of Kynaz Aleksandâr on ul Naiden Gerov, has a lively bar upstairs and a disco (*Underground*) downstairs. *Florida* on ul Vaptsarov, west of Tsentralen beyond the park, is a techno-orientated disco that gets going after 11pm.

Bachkovo Monastery

The most attractive destination to the south of Plovdiv is **Bachkovo Monastery**, an easy daytrip from the city (5 daily buses from Plovdiv's Rodopi station, destination Smolyan). Alternatively, take a bus from Plovdiv-Yug to the town of Asenovgrad (every 30min), and pick up a local bus from there. The fortress-like stone houses of **BACHKOVO** village, overgrown with flowers, give no indication of the exuberance of the monastery, a kilometre or so further up the road. Founded in 1038 by two Georgians in the service of the Byzantine Empire, this is Bulgaria's second largest monastery and, like Rila, has been declared a UNESCO World Heritage Site.

A great iron-studded door admits visitors to the cobblestoned courtyard, surrounded by vine-wreathed wooden galleries and kept free of grass by sheep. Along one wall of the courtyard, frescoes provide a pictorial narrative of the monastery's history, showing Bachkovo roughly as it appears today, but watched over by God's eye and a celestial Madonna and Child. Beneath the vaulted porch of Bachkovo's principal church, **Sveta Bogoroditsa**, are frescoes depicting the horrors in store for sinners, but the entrance itself is more cheerful, overseen by the Holy Trinity. Floral motifs in a naive style decorate the beams of the interior, where the iconostasis bears a fourteenth-century Georgian icon of the Virgin.

The church of **St Nicholas**, originally founded during the nineteenth century and recently restored, features a fine *Last Judgement* covering the porch exterior, which includes portraits of the artist, Zahari Zograf, and of two of his colleagues in the upper left-hand corner. In the old refectory you can see *The Procession of the Miraculous Icon,* executed by Zograf's pupils, which repeats the pilgrimage scene portrayed on the wall of the courtyard. Finally, **Sveta Troitsa**, standing 300m from the main gate, contains a number of early medieval frescoes and life-sized portraits of Tsar Ivan Aleksandâr and the royal family, who lavishly endowed the monastery in the fourteenth century.

You can **stay** in the monastery for $6 a night, although there's no hot water. There are three **restaurants** outside the monastery – *Vodopad* is the best.

Travelling on from Plovdiv

There's a daily **train** to Istanbul (the overnight *Balkan Express*, which currently leaves Plovdiv at 11pm); Turkish visas can be purchased for £10 sterling at the Kapikule frontier – have the exact sum ready in cash (and it must be in sterling), as they don't always have change and won't let you in without it. There's a wider choice of **international buses**, which leave from Tsentralen Square in front of the *Hotel Trimontsium*. There are three daily buses to Thessaloniki, one to Istanbul and one to Athens. Tickets are available from Matpu, in the pedestrian underpass beneath Tsentralen Square, or from the Plovdiv City Transport Office in the building of the State Philarmonic Orchestra, next door to the *Hotel Trimontsium*.

NORTHERN BULGARIA

Routes from Sofia to the Black Sea coast take you through the mountainous terrain of central and northern Bulgaria – a gruelling eight- or nine-hour ride that's worth interrupting to savour something of the country's heartland. For over a thousand years, the "Old Mountain" (Stara Planina) – known to foreigners as the **Balkan range** – has been the cradle of the Bulgarian nation. It was here that the Khans established and ruled over the feudal realm known as the "First Kingdom". Here, too, after a period of Byzantine control, the Boyars proclaimed the "Second Kingdom" and created a magnificent capital at **Veliko Târnovo** – which remains one of Bulgaria's most impressive cities. Closer to the capital, the **Sredna Gora**

(Central Range) was inhabited as early as the fifth millennium BC, but for Bulgarians this forested region is best known as the "land of the April Rising", the nineteenth-century rebellion for which the highly picturesque **Koprivshtitsa** will always be remembered.

Although they lie some way off the main rail lines from Sofia, neither Veliko Târnovo nor Koprivshtitsa is difficult to reach. The former lies just south of Gorna Oryahovitsa, a major rail junction midway between Varna and Sofia, from where you can pick up a local train or bus; the latter is served by a stop on the Sofia–Burgas line, whose three daily trains in each direction are met by local buses to ferry you the 12km to the village itself.

Koprivshtitsa

Seen from a distance, **KOPRIVSHTITSA** looks almost too lovely to be real, its half-timbered houses lying in a valley amid wooded hills. It would be an oasis of rural calm if not for the tourists drawn by the superb architecture and Bulgarians paying homage to a landmark in their nation's history. From the Place of the Scimitar Charge to the Street of the Counter Attack, there's hardly a part of Koprivshtitsa that isn't named for an episode or participant in the **April Rising of 1876**. As neighbouring towns were burned by the Bashibazouks – the irregular troops recruited by the Turks to put the rebels in their place – refugees flooded into Koprivshtitsa, spreading panic. The rebels eventually took to the hills while local traders bribed the Bashibazouks to spare the village – and so Koprivshtitsa survived unscathed to be admired by subsequent generations as a symbol of heroism.

You arrive at a small bus station 100m south of the main square, where a street running off to the west leads down to the **Oslekov House** (Tues–Sun 8am–noon & 1.30–5.30pm), the finest in Koprivshtitsa, with pillars of cypress wood imported from Lebanon supporting the facade. Its Red Room is particularly impressive, with a vast wooden ceiling carved with geometric motifs. One of the medallions painted on the wall shows the original, symmetrical plan of the house, never realized as Oslekov's neighbours refused to sell him the necessary land. Further along, the street joins ul Debelyanov, which straddles a hill between two bridges and boasts some more lovely buildings. Near the Surlya Bridge is the birthplace of the poet **Dimcho Debelyanov** (no. 6), who is buried in the yard of the hilltop **Church of the Holy Virgin**. Built in 1817 and partly sunk into the ground to comply with Ottoman restrictions, the church contains icons by nineteenth-century artist Zahari Zograf.

A gate at the rear of the churchyard leads to the birthplace of **Todor Kableshkov** (same times), leader of the local rebels. Kableshkov's house now displays the insurgents' silk banner embroidered with the Bulgarian Lion and "Liberty or Death!", and one of the twenty **cherry-tree cannons** secretly manufactured by the rebels. Although one bore the engraved slogan "End of the Turkish Empire, 1876", the cannons soon became a liability, as they tended to blow up.

On the opposite side of the river at the southern end of the village, steps lead up to the birthplace of another major figure in the uprising, **George Benkovski** (Mon & Wed–Sun 8am–noon & 1.30–5.30pm). A tailor by profession, he made the insurgents' banner and uniforms and commanded a rebel band on Mount Eledzhik, which fought its way north until it was wiped out near Teteven.

Practicalities

A **tourist office** on the main square books private **rooms** in charming village houses for around $10, and there are plenty of small bed-and-breakfast places scattered around the village if you ask around. The *Byaloto Konche* (☎997184/2250; ②), across the road from the Oslekov House, has delightful rooms in the National Revival style; while the *Panorama*, at the south end of the village near the Benkovski House (☎02/546-747; ②), has neat modern rooms with en-suite facilities. For **eating and drinking**, the best places to sample traditional food are the *Dyado Liben Inn*, in a fine nineteenth-century mansion opposite the main square; and *Lomeva Kashta*, a folk-style restaurant just north of the square.

Veliko Târnovo

Even the dour Prussian Field-Marshal, Von Moltke was moved to remark that he had "never seen a town of more romantic location" than **VELIKO TÂRNOVO**, which seems poised to leap into the chasms that divide the city. Medieval fortifications add melodrama to the scene, and the huddles of antique houses seem bound to the rocks by wild lilac and vines. But for Bulgarians the city has a deeper significance. When the National Assembly met here to draft Bulgaria's first constitution in 1879, it did so in the former capital of the Second Kingdom (1185–1396), whose civilization was snuffed out by the Turks.

The Town

Modern Târnovo revolves around the **Mother Bulgaria** (Mayka Bâlgariya) **monument**: from here bul Nezavisimost (which becomes ul Stefan Stambolov after a few hundred metres) heads northeast into the network of narrow streets which curve around the heights above the River Yantra and mark out the old town, with its photogenic houses teetering over limited ground space. From the old bazaar at the junction of ul Rakovski and pl Georgi Kirkov, alleyways climb from Stefan Stambolov to the peaceful old **Varosh Quarter**, where a couple of nineteenth-century churches are verging on decrepitude.

Continuing along Stefan Stambolov, you'll notice steps leading off downhill to **ulitsa General Gurko**, a street lined with picturesque nineteenth-century houses perched along the curve of the ravine. Don't miss the **Sarafina House** at no. 88 (Tues–Sun 9am–noon & 1–6pm), which is so contrived that only two floors are visible from General Gurko but a further three overhang the river. The interior is notable for the splendid octagonal vestibule with wrought-iron fixtures and a panelled rosette-ceiling. Rejoining Stefan Stambolov and continuing downhill, you can't miss the spacious blue and white edifice where the first Bulgarian parliament assembled in 1878. It's now occupied by a **Museum of the National Revival** and the Constituent Assembly (8am–noon & 1–6pm, closed Tues; $2), which has an excellent display of icons in the basement.

From here, Ivan Vazov leads directly to the medieval fortress, **Tsarevets** (daily 8am–dusk; $2). Approaching it along the stone causeway, you appreciate how the boyars Petâr and Asen were emboldened by possession of this citadel to lead a rebellion against Byzantium in 1185. Byzantine attempts to retake Târnovo were succesfully beaten off, and Tsarevets remained the centre of Bulgarian power until 1393, when the Ottoman Turks plundered it after a three-month siege. The partially restored fortress is entered via the **Asenova Gate** halfway along the western ramparts; to the right, paths lead round to a bastion known as **Baldwin's Tower**, where the Latin Emperor of the East, Baldwin of Flanders, was incarcerated by Asen's successor Kaloyan. Above lie the scrappy ruins of the royal palace and a replica of the thirteenth-century **Church of the Blessed Saviour**, ribbed with red brick and inset with green and orange ceramics.

Downhill to the west of Tsarevets lies the **Asenova Quarter**, where chickens strut and children fish beside the river. The only one of its medieval churches currently open is the **Church of SS Peter and Paul** (Easter–Sept only), which contains several capitals carved with vine leaves and some well-preserved frescoes of which the oldest – dating back to the fourteenth century – is the Pietà opposite the altar.

Practicalities

All **trains** between Sofia and Varna stop at Gorna Oryahovitsa, from where local trains (8 daily) cover the remaining 12km to Veliko Târnovo **train station**, which stands 2km south of the city's centre – buses #4 and #13 run to the Mother Bulgaria monument.

The *Hotel Etâr*, just downhill from here at ul Ivailo 2 (☎062/626851; ③) is an unkempt high-rise with good views of the old town. The nearby *Orbita*, Hristo Botev 15 (☎062/622041; ②) with hostel-type **accommodation** in four-person dorms, and the *Turistichni Dom Trapezitsa*, Stefan Stambolov 79 (☎062/22061; ②), are cheaper options. If you want to stay in the old town try the family-run *Deyan*, in the Varosh quarter at Yanaki Donchev 22 (☎062/30532; ③).

The terrace of the *Voennen Klub* (Officers' Club) opposite the Mother Bulgaria monument is popular for its simple grilled **food**. Otherwise, best of the restaurants are the small family-run places just off Stefan Stambolov – follow signs pointing down the steps to find *Mehana Belite Brezi* and the nearby *Starata Mehana*, both serving good home-cooked meals. Further towards Tsarevets, *Lâv*, Chitalishtna 3, serves the best trad Bulgarian fare in town. For **drinking**, there are numerous cafés along the main drag, with little to distinguish between them.

THE COAST

It was the Soviet leader Khrushchev who first suggested that the Black Sea coastline be developed for tourism, and since then the **resorts** have mushroomed, growing increasingly sophisticated as the prototype mega-complexes have been followed by "holiday villages". With fine weather and safe bathing practically guaranteed, the selling of the coast has been a success in economic terms, but with the exception of ancient **Sozopol** and touristy **Nesebâr**, there's little to please the eye. Of the coast's two main towns – **Varna** and **Burgas** – the former is by far preferable as a base for getting to the less-developed spots.

Varna

VARNA's origins go back almost five millennia, but it wasn't until seafaring Greeks founded a colony here in 585 BC that the town became a port. The modern city is both a shipyard and port for commercial freighters and the navy, and a riviera town visited by tourists of every nationality. It's a cosmopolitan place and a nice one to stroll through: Baroque, turn-of-the-century and contemporary architecture pleasantly blended with shady promenades and a handsome seaside garden.

Social life revolves around the **ploshtad Nezavisimost**, where the opera house and theatre provide a backdrop for an ensemble of restaurants and cafés. The square is the starting point of Varna's evening promenade, which flows eastward from here along bul Knyaz Boris I towards bul Slivnitsa and the seaside gardens. Beyond the opera house, Varna's main lateral boulevard cuts through pl Mitropolit Simeon, to the domed **Cathedral of the Assumption**. Constructed in 1886 along the lines of St Petersburg's cathedral, it contains a splendid iconostasis and carved bishop's throne, and murals painted after the last war.

Exhibits in the **Archeology Museum** on the corner of Mariya Luiza and Slivnitsa (Tues–Sun 10am–5pm; $1) fill forty halls, three of them devoted to skeletons and artefacts from a necropolis where a hoard of 4500-year-old gold objects was discovered in 1972. Other halls display Greek and Roman antiquities, medieval weaponry and ecclesiastical art, while upstairs there's an excellent icon gallery.

South of the centre, on ul Han Krum, you'll stumble upon the impressive second-century **Roman baths** (Tues–Sun 10am–5pm; $2). The **Ethnographic Museum** (Tues–Sun 10am–5pm; $1.50), occupying an old house ten minutes' west of here on ul Panagyurishte, contains a fine display of costumes and jewellery, and a variety of "ritual loaves" – among them the foot-shaped *Proshtupalnik*, which was baked to celebrate a child's first steps.

The boat responsible for the Navy's only victory – the *Drâzhki* (*Intrepid*) – is honourably embedded on the waterfront outside the **Navy Museum** (daily 9am–noon & 1.30–5pm; $1.25); it sank the Turkish cruiser *Hamidie* off Cape Kaliakra in 1912. The museum traces sea power and commerce on the Black Sea and the lower Danube back to its earliest days.

Practicalities

Each of the main points of arrival has good bus connections with the centre. You'll approach the centre from the northwest if you come in from the **bus terminal** (bus #1, #22 or #41) on bul Vladislav Varnenchik or Varna **airport** (#409), whereas travellers coming in at the **train station** can walk up ul Tsar Simeon into the centre in ten minutes.

Private rooms in central Varna (②) can be obtained from the Isak bureau (variable hours) inside the train station, M92 George (variable hours) across the road at Tsar Simeon 36b, or Balkantourist/Varnenski Bryag ten minutes' further uphill at ul Musala 3 (Mon–Fri 8.30am–12.30pm & 1–6pm). Best of the cheap **hotels** are the ageing but comfy *Voennomorski Klub*, opposite the cathedral at bul Varnenchik 2 (☎052/238312; ③), and the friendly, motel-style *Akropolis*, 500m east of the train station at Tsar Ivan Shishman 3 (☎052/603108; ④). *Santa Marina*, just behind bul Slivnitsa at ul Baba Rada 28 (☎052/603826; ⑤), is a lovely downtown pension.

Most of Varna's **eating and drinking** venues are to be found along bul Knyaz Boris I and bul Slivnitsa – the latter a seemingly unbroken strip of touristy cafés, bars and restaurants, although venues change from one season to the next. For the best food and service, stick to the backstreets: *Staviko*, round the corner from the Roman baths at ul osmi Noemvri 11, has good quality Bulgarian standards; *Paraklisa*, near the Navy Museum on bul Primorski, offers the most imaginative spin on traditional Balkan dishes; and *Titanic*, in the grid of streets north of Knyaz Boris I at Ivan Vazov 39, is an elegant café-bar with intimate restaurant upstairs. The municipal **beach**, reached by pathways descending from the seaside gardens, is lined with open-air bars and **discos** although few of these have regular names.

The southern coast

BURGAS, the south coast's prime urban centre, can be reached by train from Sofia and Plovdiv, or by bus from Varna. The town provides easy access to the museum town of Nesebâr to the north or the attractive fishing village of Sozopol to the south. There are regular buses from the airport into town, and other points of arrival are clustered near the port. If it's necessary to stay, private **accommodation** can be arranged by Diamat, Tsar Simeon 15, with rooms from $8.

Nesebâr

Founded by the Greeks, **NESEBÂR** – 35km northeast of Burgas and served by buses every 45 minutes – was later used by the Byzantines as a base from which to assail the Bulgarian First Kingdom, provoking Khan Krum to seize it in 812. Thereafter ownership alternated between Bulgaria and Byzantium until the Ottomans captured it in 1453. The town's decline to a humble fishing port under Turkish rule left Nesebâr's **Byzantine churches** reasonably intact, and nowadays the town depends on them for its tourist appeal, a constant stream of visitors crossing the slender isthmus connecting the old town with the mainland.

Buses arrive at the harbour at the western end of town, above which lies an **Archeological Museum** (Mon–Fri 9am–7pm, Sat & Sun 9am–1.30pm & 2–7pm; $1.30) containing ancient Greek tombstones and a feast of medieval icons. Immediately beyond this is the first of Nesebâr's churches, the **Church of Christ the Pantokrator**. Completed during the fourteenth-century reign of Tsar Aleksandâr, its blind niches, turquoise ceramic inlays and red-brick motifs are characteristic of latter-day Byzantine architecture, although the frieze of swastikas – a symbol of the sun and continual change – is unusual. Slightly downhill on ul Mitropolitska, **St John the Baptist** (now an art gallery) also has a cruciform plan, but its undressed stone exterior dates it as a tenth- or eleventh-century building.

Overhung by half-timbered houses carved with sun-signs, fish and other symbols, ul Aheloi branches off from ul Mitropolitska towards the **Church of Sveti Spas** (Mon–Fri 9am–1.30pm & 2–5.30pm, Sat & Sun 9.30am–1.30pm; $1), outwardly unremarkable but filled with seventeenth-century frescoes. Diagonally opposite is the now ruined **Church of the Archangels Michael and Gabriel**, patterned not unlike the Pantokrator. A few steps to the east lies the ruined **Old Metropolitan Church**, dominating a plaza filled with pavement cafés, street traders and hawkers. The church itself dates back to the fifth or sixth century, and it was here that bishops officiated during the city's heyday. South of the town's main street, down ul Ribarska, lies the **New Metropolitan Church** (also known as *Sveti Stefan*; daily 9am–1pm & 2–6pm; $1), whose interior fresco of the *Forty Martyrs*, on the west wall, gives pride of place to the patron who financed the church's enlargement during the fifteenth century. Just downhill from here there's the ruined **Church of St John Aliturgetos**, standing in splendid isolation beside the shore and representing the zenith of Byzantine architecture in Bulgaria. Its exterior decoration is strikingly varied, employing limestone, red bricks, crosses, mussel shells and ceramic plaques, with a representation of a human figure composed of limestone blocks incorporated into the north wall.

Private rooms (②–③), many in fine old houses, are available from several agencies; you'll see signs along the main street directing you towards three of the longest established: Mesambria-93, Gama Tours and Stoyanovi-94. The *Morska Perla*, behind the post office (☎0554/45606; ④), is a family-run **hotel** with clean en-suites. There are plenty of places to get **food**. Around the harbour are kiosks serving fresh mackerel and chips. The old town is crammed with restaurants; the sea-facing *Neptun*, towards the far end of town, is reasonably reliable, while the *Plakamo*, just downhill from the New Metropolitan Church at Ivan Aleksandâr 8, is family-run and relatively sheltered. *Bar Burgas*, Mena 10, is one of the better places to enjoy an evening **drink**.

Sozopol

SOZOPOL, the oldest settlement on the coast, was founded in the seventh century BC by Ionian colonists from Miletus, who called the town Apollonia and prospered by trading Greek textiles and wine for honey and corn. Today it's a busy fishing port and the favoured resort of Bulgaria's literary and artistic set. The **Church of the Holy Virgin** (for opening times enquire at the Archeological Museum, see below), built in the nineteenth century, features a finely carved iconostasis and bishop's throne, but it's the old houses that give Sozopol its charm. With space at a premium, their upper storeys project so far out that houses on opposite sides of the narrow, cobbled streets almost meet. Sozopol's **Archeological Museum** (Mon–Fri 8am–4.30pm, Sat & Sun 10am–2pm), hidden behind the library, should not be missed, for its collection of amphoras dredged from the surrounding waters and its display of exquisitely decorated Greek vases called *kraters*.

The hourly **buses** from Burgas arrive at the southern edge of the old town opposite the main beach. Head southeast from here along ul Republikanska to reach the Lotos and Alma **accommodation** bureaux on ul Ropotamo 1; atmospheric old rooms in the old town or more roomy apartments in the new town go for about $10. Otherwise, just ask around – everyone in Sozopol rents out rooms over the summer. The *Mehana Sozopol*, ul Apoloniya, and the *Vyatarna Melnitsa*, ul Morski Skali, are a couple of good, if touristy, **restaurants** – both featuring occasional live music. The Italian-influenced food at *Cazanova*, on the cliffside path on the east side of the old town, attracts a trendier crowd.

travel details

Trains

Sofia to: Blagoevgrad (8 daily; 2hr 30min–3hr 30min); Burgas (4 daily; 6–8hr); Gorna Oryahovitsa (hourly; 4hr 15min); Koprivshtitsa (5 daily; 1hr 40min–2hr 20min); Plovdiv (10 daily; 2hr 30min–3hr); Sandanski (5 daily; 3hr 30min–4hr 30min); Varna (5 daily; 9hr).

Gorna Oryahovitsa to: Veliko Târnovo (8 daily; 30min).

Plovdiv to: Burgas (4 daily; 5hr); Sofia (10 daily; 2hr 30min–3hr); Veliko Târnovo (1 daily; 5hr).

Buses

Sofia to: Bansko (5 daily; 3hr); Koprivshtitsa (1 daily; 2hr); Plovdiv (5 daily; 2hr); Rila monastery (summer only: 1 daily; 3hr); Sandanski (5 daily; 3hr); Veliko Târnovo (2 daily; 4hr).

Blagoevgrad to: Bansko (8 daily; 1hr); Rila village (hourly; 35min).

Burgas to: Nesebâr (every 45min; 50min); Sozopol (hourly; 40min); Varna (4 daily; 3hr).

Dupnitsa to: Rila monastery (2 daily; 1hr); Rila village (4 daily; 30min).

Gorna Oryahovitsa to: Veliko Târnovo (every 30min; 30min).

Plovdiv to: Bachkovo (6 daily; 40min).

Rila village to: Rila monastery (3 daily; 30min).

Sandanski to: Melnik (3 daily; 40min).

CHAPTER 5

CROATIA

Introduction

Croatia (Hrvatska) has come a long way since the summer of 1991, when foreign tourists fled from a region standing on the verge of war. Now that stability has returned, visitors are steadily returning to a country which boasts one of the most outstanding stretches of coastline that Europe has to offer. This return to normality has been keenly awaited by Croats, but patriotism – and a sense of the nation's place in history – remains a serious business here. Croatia was an independent kingdom in the tenth century, fell under the rule of Hungary in the eleventh, and was subsequently absorbed by the Austro-Hungarian Empire before becoming part of the new state of Yugoslavia in 1918. Croatian aspirations were frustrated by a Yugoslav state which was initially dominated by Serbs, and then (after 1945) ruled by Communists. Croatia's declaration of independence on 25 June 1991 was fiercely contested by a Serb-dominated Yugoslav army eager to preserve their control over portions of Croatia in which groups of ethnic Serbs lived. The period of war – and fragile, UN-supervised ceasefire that followed – was finally brought to a close by the victorious Croatian offensives of spring 1995.

Croatia's capital, **Zagreb**, is a typical central-European metropolis, combining elegant nineteenth-century architecture with plenty of cultural diversions and a vibrant café life. At the northern end of the Adriatic coast, the peninsula of **Istria** contains many of the country's most developed resorts, with old Venetian towns like **Poreč** and **Rovinj** rubbing shoulders with the raffish port of **Pula** and elegant, turn-of-the-century **Opatija**. Further south lies **Dalmatia**, a dramatic, mountain-fringed stretch of coastline studded with islands. Dalmatia's main town is **Split**, an ancient Roman settlement and modern port which provides a jumping-off point to the most enchanting of Croatia's islands, **Brač**, **Hvar** and **Korčula**, where you'll find lively fishing villages and the best of the beaches. South of Split lies the walled medieval city of **Dubrovnik**, site of an important festival in the summer and a magical place to be whatever the season.

Information and maps

Most towns of any size have a **tourist office** (*turistički ured*) run by the local authority, who will happily give out brochures and local maps if they have any available; English is widely spoken in these places. Many offices will also book private rooms, or at least direct you to an agency that does. Freytag & Berndt produce a good 1:600,000 **map** of Croatia, Slovenia and Bosnia-Hercegovina; as well as a

1:100,000 map of Istria. Generalkarte produce a 1:200,000 map of the Adriatic coast.

Money and banks

Croatia's unit of currency is the **kuna** (kn), which is divided into 100 lipa. Coins come in denominations of 1, 5, 10, 20 and 50 lipa, and 1, 2, and 5 kuna; and there are notes of 5, 10, 20, 50, 100, 500 and 1000 kuna. The exchange rate is 10kn to £1, 6.50kn to $1. Although accommodation and ferry prices are often quoted in dollars or Deutschmarks, you pay in kuna.

Banks (*banka*) are generally open Monday to Friday 7.30am–7pm (sometimes with a break for lunch), and Saturday 7.30–11.30am. Money can also be changed in post offices, travel agencies and exchange bureaux (*mjenjačnica*), which have more flexible hours. Credit cards are only accepted in the bigger hotels and more expensive restaurants, although you can use them to get cash from ATMs and the bigger banks.

Communications

Most **post offices** (*pošta* or HPT) are open Monday to Friday 7.30am–7pm & Saturday 8am–1pm. In big towns and resorts, some offices are open daily, sometimes until 10pm. Stamps (*marke*) can also be bought at newsstands.

Public **telephones** use magnetic cards (*telekarta*), which you can pick up from post offices or newspaper kiosks. When making long-distance and international calls, it's usually easier to go to the post office, where you're assigned a cabin and given the bill afterwards.

Getting around

Trains are of limited value in a country with such a small rail network, although they do connect Zagreb with the coastal towns of Rijeka and Split. Elsewhere, Croatia is well served by an extensive and reliable bus network. Ferries offer a leisurely way of getting up and down the coast, and provide the only transport to Croatia's many Adriatic islands.

■ Trains and buses

Croatian railways (Hrvatske eljeznice) run a smooth and efficient service. **Trains** (*vlak*, plural *vlakovi*) are divided into *putnički* (slow ones which stop at every halt) and *IC* (inter-city trains which are faster and more expensive). There's an overnight service from Zagreb to Split, for which places in couchettes (*kušet*) and sleeping cars (spalnica) are best made in advance. Timetables (vozni red) are usually displayed on boards in stations – odlazak means departure, dolazak means arrival.

Croatia's **bus network** is run by a confusing array of small local companies, but services are well integrated and bus stations tend to be well-organized affairs with clearly listed departure times and efficient booking facilities. If you're at a big city bus station, tickets (karta) must be obtained from ticket windows before boarding the bus. Elsewhere, they can be bought from the driver. It's a good idea to buy tickets well in advance in summer if you can, especially for any services running to, or along, the coast. You'll be charged extra for cumbersome items of baggage, which must be stored in the hold.

■ Driving and hitching

The **road system** is comprehensive, but not always of good quality once you get beyond the main highways. Stretches of the Zagreb–Rijeka and Zagreb–Split routes are classified as motorway (autoput) and are subject to a modest toll, although elsewhere the main routes (especially the main road down the Adriatic coast) are single-lane roads, often clogged by traffic – especially in summer, when movement up and down the coast can be time-consuming. Off the beaten track, roads can be badly maintained. **Speed limits** in Croatia are 60kph in built-up areas, 80kph on normal roads, 100kph on highways and 120kph on motorways. If you break down, the Croatian automobile club (HAK) has a 24-hour emergency service (☎987). **Car rental** charges are expensive at around £75/$120 a day for a reliable car with unlimited mileage.

Hitching on the main routes between Zagreb and the coast is fairly common – but be prepared to wait a long time for a lift. Anywhere else in the country, prospects for hitching are fairly bad.

■ Ferries

Jadrolinija operate **ferry services** down the coast on the Rijeka–Zadar–Split–Korčula–Dubrovnik route at least once a day in both directions between June and August, and four or five times weekly for the rest of the year. Rijeka to Dubrovnik is a 22-hour journey, involving one night on the boat. In addition, ferries link Split with the islands of Brač, Hvar and Korčula; there is also a Dobrovnik–Korčula service. Ferries are also a good way of moving on from Croatia, with connections to Italy (Split to Ancona and Dubrovnik to Bari) and Greece (Dubrovnik to Igoumenitsa).

Prices (always quoted in dollars, but payable in kuna) are reasonable for short trips: for example, Split to Hvar costs around $4. For longer journeys, prices vary greatly according to the level of comfort you require. The cheapest Rijeka–Dubrovnik fare is $20, while you'll pay double that for a couchette-style bunk bed, and three times more for a bed in a well-appointed cabin; taking a car on the same journey costs an extra $75, $25 for a motorbike, but bicycles travel free of charge. Book in advance for longer journeys wherever possible; addresses and phone numbers are provided in the text where relevant.

Accommodation

Private rooms have long been the mainstay of Croatian tourism, especially on the coast, and represent an inexpensive way of finding a bed for the night. There are well-appointed campsites all along the Adriatic coast, although Croatian hotels tend to be bland and overpriced. Wherever you stay in Croatia, you're obliged to register with the local police on arrival. If you're staying in a hotel, hostel, campsite, or a private room arranged by an agency, this will be done for you. If you're staying with a friend, or in a room offered to you by a private individual, you'll have to undertake the job of registration yourself.

■ Hotels and private rooms

Croatian **hotels** tend to be modern multi-storey affairs providing modern comforts but little atmosphere. They are classified by letter: generally speaking, C-class hotels have rooms with shared WC and

---

ACCOMMODATION PRICE CODES

Throughout this guide, accommodation is priced on a scale of ① to ⑨, the number indicating the lowest price per night a single person could expect to pay in that establishment in high season. With hostels this is the nightly rate per person; with hotels, the price is arrived at by dividing the cost of the cheapest double room by two. The prices indicated by the codes are as follows:

① under £5 / $8	④ £15–20 / $24–32	⑦ £30–35 / $48–56
② £5–10 / $8–16	⑤ £20–25 / $32–40	⑧ £35–40 / $56–64
③ £10–15 / $16–24	⑥ £25–30 / $40–48	⑨ £40 / $64 and over

bathroom; B-class have rooms with en-suite facilities; A–class is business class; and L–class are in the international luxury bracket. A double room in a C-class establishment will cost around £30/$45, although these tend to be in short supply, and in many towns you'll be dependent on B-class places, where you should expect to pay £40/$60 a double.

Private rooms (*privatne sobe*) are available just about everywhere in Croatia. Bookings are administered either by the local tourist office or by private travel agencies. Agencies are usually open daily 8am–8pm in summer, although they may take a long break on Sunday afternoons. You may also be offered rooms by people waiting outside train, bus and ferry stations. Don't be afraid to take a room offered in this manner, but be sure to establish the location of the room and agree a price before setting off – and if anything makes you feel uncomfortable about the situation, don't go. However you find a room, you can usually examine it before committing yourself to paying for it. Prices hover around £6/$9 per person for a simple double sharing your host's WC and bathroom, rising to around £8/$13 per person for a double with en-suite facilities; stays of less than three nights are subject to a surcharge of 30 percent or over. Places fill up quickly in July and August, when it's a good idea to arrive in town early in order to begin your search. Single travellers sometimes find it difficult to get a room in high season unless they're prepared to pay the price of a double.

■ Hostels and campsites

HI-affiliated **youth hostels** are thin on the ground, although those that exist – mostly in the big cities – are on the whole clean and well run. You can get details from Hrvatski Ferijalni I Hotelski Savez, De manova 9, Zagreb (☎01/435-781). In addition, **student halls of residence** are often let out cheap to travellers during the summer vacation – usually mid-July to the end of August. For both, expect to pay £10–15/$15–$22 for a bed.

Campsites abound on the Adriatic coast, and tend to be large-scale, well-appointed affairs with plentiful facilities, restaurants and shops. Most of them are open from May to September. Two people travelling with a tent can expect to pay around £8/$12 per night; add about £2/$3 for a vehicle.

Food and drink

There's a varied and distinctive range of cuisine on offer in Croatia, largely because the country straddles two culinary cultures: the fish-and-seafood-dominated cuisine of the Mediterranean, and the hearty meat-orientated fare of central Europe.

■ Food

Basic **self-catering** and picnic ingredients like cheese (*sir*), vegetables (*povrc'e*) and fruit (*voc'e*) can be bought at a supermarket (*samoposluga*) or open-air market (*tržnica*). Bread (*kruh*) is bought from either a supermarket or a *pekara* (bakery). For breakfasts and fast food, look out for street stalls or snack-food outlets selling *burek*, a flaky pastry filled with cheese; or grilled meats such as *c'evapčić'i* (rissoles of minced beef, pork or lamb), and *pljeskavica* (a hamburger-like mixture of the same meats).

For more relaxed, sit-down eating, a **restaurant** menu (*jelovnik*) will usually include Croatian speciality starters like *pršut* (home-cured ham), as well as a range of soups (*juha*). Typical main courses include *punjene paprike* (peppers stuffed with rice and meat), *gulaš* (goulasch), or some kind of *odrezak* (fillet of meat, often pan-fried), usually either *svinjski* (pork) or *teleš ki* (veal). *Mješ ano meso* (mixed grill) is a mixture of the above meats, plus *jetra* (liver). Lamb, often roasted, is *jagnjetina*. Traditional dishes from the area around Zagreb include *purica z mlincima* (turkey with pasta noodles), and *strukli* (ravioli-like blobs of pasta dough with a cheese filling). Another typically Croatian main course is *pasticada* (beef and bacon cooked in vinegar and wine). On the coast, you'll be regaled with every kind of seafood. *Riba* (fish) can come either *na žaru* (grilled) or *u pečnici* (baked). *Brodet* is a hot peppery fish soup. Otherwise, the main menu items to look out for on the coast are *lignje* (squid), *škampa* (scampi), *rakovica* (crab), *oštrige* (oysters), *kalamari* (squid), *školjke* (mussels) and *jastog* (lobster); *crni rizoto* is risotto with squid. No Croatian town is without at least one pizzeria, often the cheapest place to eat and the easiest, if not the most imaginative, source of a **vegetarian** meal.

Typical **desserts** include *palačinke* (pancakes), *voc'na salata* (fruit salad) and *sladoled* (ice cream).

■ Drink

Daytime drinking takes place in a *kavana* (café) or a *slasticarnica* (patisserie). **Coffee** (*kava*) is usually served black unless specified otherwise – ask for *mlijeko* (milk) or *šlag* (cream). Tea (*čaj*) is widely available, but is drunk without milk.

Night-time drinking takes place in a growing number of small café/bars. Croatian **beer** (*pivo*) is of the light lager variety; *Karlovačko* and *Ožujsko* are two good local brands to look out for. The local wine (*vino*) is consistently good and reasonably cheap. In Dalmatia there are some pleasant whites, crisp dry wines like *Kastelet*, *Grk* and *Posip*, as well as reds like the dark heady *Dingač* and *Babić*. In Istria, *Semion* is a bone-dry white, and *Teran* a light fresh red. Local spirits include *loza*, a clear grape-based spirit; *travar-*

ica, herbal brandy; *vinjak*, locally produced cognac, and *Maraskino*, a cherry liqueur from Dalmatia.

Opening hours and holidays

Most **shops** open Monday to Friday 9am–6pm and Saturday 9am–1pm, although many food shops, supermarkets and outdoor markets are open daily 7am–7pm. **Museum and gallery** times vary from one place to another, although most are closed on Monday.

All shops and banks will be closed on the following **public holidays**: January 1; January 6; Easter Monday; May 1 (Labour Day); May 30 (Day of Croatian Statehood); June 22 (Day of the 1941 Anti-Fascist Uprising); August 5 (National Thanksgiving Day); August 15 (Assumption); November 1 (All Saints' Day); and December 25 and 26.

Emergencies

The crime rate in Croatia is low by European standards. Croatian **police** (*policija*) are generally helpful when dealing with holidaymakers, although can be slow when filling out reports. Police often make routine checks on identity cards and other documents; always carry your **passport**.

Hospital treatment is free to EU citizens. **Pharmacies** (*ljekarna*) tend to follow normal shopping hours, and a rota system covers night-time and weekend opening; details are posted in the window of each pharmacy.

You're unlikely to see too many reminders of the **recent war** during your travels round Croatia. Apart from Dubrovnik, which was heavily shelled by Serb and Montenegrin troops in 1991 and 1992, none of the places featured in this chapter were part of a war zone. Most of the fighting took place in areas well away from the tourist spots – and it's currently safe to travel anywhere in the country.

EMERGENCY NUMBERS

Police ☎92; Ambulance ☎94; Fire ☎93.

ZAGREB

Capital of an independent state since 1991, **ZAGREB** has served as the cultural and political focus of the nation for over two hundred years – the previous administrative centre, Varaždin, having been destroyed by fire in 1776. The city grew out of two medieval communities, **Kaptol**, to the east, and **Gradec**, to the west, each sited on a hill and divided by a river long since dried up but nowadays marked by a street known as Tkalčićeva. Kaptol (meaning "Cathedral Chapter") was a religious centre and the seat of an archbishop; Gradec was ruled by a group of Croatian nobles. The two communities became bitter rivals, and remained so until the sixteenth century, when the threat of Turkish invasion caused them to unite against the common enemy; they took the name Zagreb, which means, literally, "behind the hill". Zagreb grew rapidly in the nineteenth century, and the majority of its buildings are relatively well-preserved, grand, peach-coloured monuments to the self-esteem of the Austro-Hungarian Empire. Nowadays, with a population topping one million, Zagreb is the vibrant and boisterous capital of a newly self-confident nation. A handful of good museums and a vibrant nightlife ensure that a few days here will be well spent.

Arrival, information and city transport

Zagreb's central **train station**, or Glavni Kolodvor, is on Tomislavov Trg, on the southern edge of the city centre, a ten-minute walk from Trg bana Jelačiča, the main square. The main **bus station** is a fifteen-minute walk east of the railway station, at the junction of Branimirova and Držićeva – trams #2, #3 and #6 run to the railway station from here; get off at the second stop. Zagreb's **airport** is about 10km southeast of the city, connected with the main bus station by a half-hourly Croatia Airways bus (7.30am–8pm, at other times services run to connect with flights; 25kn).

There are two **tourist offices** in central Zagreb, one at Trg N. Zrinskog 14 (summer: Mon–Fri 8am–8pm, Sat & Sun 9am–6pm; winter: Mon–Fri 9am–5pm, ☎01/45-52-867) and another at Trg bana Jelačiča 11 (summer: same times; winter: Mon–Fri 8.30am–8pm, Sat 10am–6pm, Sun 10am–2pm; ☎01/48-14-051). Both have maps, up-to-date leaflets on events, and can help out with general queries, though neither can arrange accommodation.

Zagreb has an efficient and comprehensive **public transport** network of trams and, to a lesser extent, buses, though much of the city centre can easily be seen on foot. For both buses and trams, there's a flat fare per journey of 4.50kn; **tickets** (*karte*) are valid for ninety minutes in one direction and are sold from newspaper kiosks. Validate your ticket by punching it in the machines on board the trams. The train station and Trg bana Jelačiča are the two main hubs of the city transport system.

Accommodation

It's difficult to find cheap **accommodation** in Zagreb, especially during the summer. **Hotels** are relatively expensive and **hostel beds** are often reserved way in advance. The **private-room** market has all but disappeared, and none of the central travel agencies are currently offering any help.

There's a **youth hostel** conveniently placed at Petrinjska 77 (☎01/434-964; ② dorm bed, ③ room), five minutes' walk from the railway station. The nearest **campsite** is 10km southeast of town at the *Plitvice Motel* beside the main Zagreb–Ljubljana motorway – there's no public transport.

Hotels

Astoria, Petrinjska 71 (☎01/48-41-222). Slightly dingy though clean en-suites with TV. Convenient for the train and bus stations. ⑤.

Central, Branimirova 3 (☎01/48-41-122). Small rooms with en-suite facilities and TV opposite the railway station. ⑥.

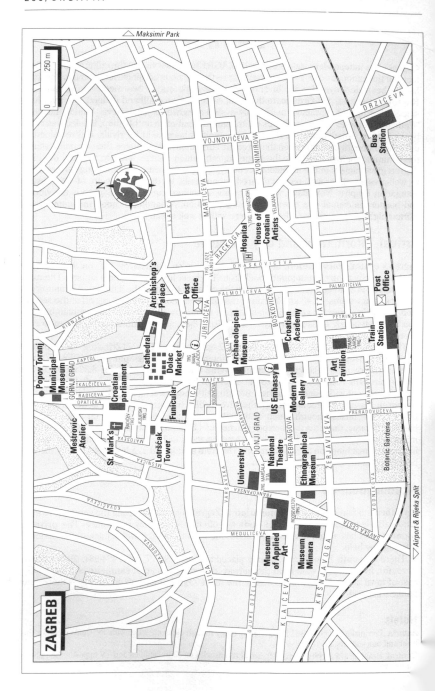

ZAGREB

Maksimir Park

250 m

N

Popov Toranj
Municipal Museum
Meštrović Atelier
St. Mark's
Croatian parliament
Lotrščak Tower
Funicular
Cathedral
Dolac Market
Archbishop's Palace
Post Office
Archaeological Museum
Croatian Academy
Hospital
House of Croatian Artists
Post Office
Train Station
Art Pavilion
US Embassy
Modern Art Gallery
University
National Theatre
Ethnographical Museum
Museum of Applied Art
Museum Mimara
Botanic Gardens
Bus Station

VOJNOVIĆEVA
MARTIĆEVA
VLAŠKA
ZVONIMIROVA
DRŽIĆEVA
TRG BANA HRVATSKIH VELIKANA
RAČKOGA
TRG JOZE VLANOVIĆA
DRAŠKOVIĆEVA
PALMOTIĆEVA
BOŠKOVIĆEVA
HATZOVA
BRANIMIROVA
PALMOTIĆEVA
PETRINJSKA
TOMIŠ LAVOV TRG
JURIŠIĆEVA
TESLINA
PRAŠKA
GAJEVA
MIHANOVIĆEVA
PRERADOVIĆEVA
HEBRANGOVA
ŽERJAVIĆEVA
VODNIKOVA
SAVSKA CESTA
GORNJI GRAD
KAPTOL
RADIĆEVA
OPATIČKA
TKALČIĆEVA
RIBNJAK
ILICA
JEZUITSKI TRG
MATOŠEVA
BAŠIĆEVA TRG
MESNIČKA
KOVAČIĆEVA
NAZOROVA
GUNDULIĆA
MAŽURANIĆEVA
BOGOVIĆEVA
DONJI GRAD
TRG MARŠALA TITA
VARŠAVSKA
FRANKOPANSKA
ROOSEVELTOV TRG
MEDULIĆEVA
ILICA
KLAIĆEVA
KRŠNJAVOGA
G. JURE DEŽELIĆA

Airport & Rijeka Split

Dubrovnik, Gajeva 1 (☎01/48-73-555). Modern glass-and-steel palace just off the central square. Recently refurbished to international business standard, and prices are creeping up. ⑧.

Ilica, Ilica 102 (☎01/37-77-522). Modern, smart and friendly B&B with ensuite rooms 1.5km west of the main square. Only twelve rooms, so ring in advance. ⑨.

Jadran, Vlaska 50 (☎01/45-53-777). Cheapest of the downtown hotels offering en-suite rooms. Just east of the city centre and fifteen minutes' walk from the train station at the top end of Draskovićeva. ④.

Lido, Jarun (☎01/38-32-839). Small hotel at the eastern end of Lake Jarun, 4km southwest of the centre. Attractive loft rooms with en-suite facilities. Tram #17 from Trg bana Jelačića. ⑦.

Pension Jägerhorn, Ilica 14 (☎01/48-30-161). In a courtyard just off the main shopping street. Comfortable, central and soon fills up. ⑦.

The City

Modern Zagreb splits neatly into three parts. **Donji Grad** or "Lower Town", which extends north from the train station to the main square (Trg bana Jelačića), is the bustling centre of the modern city. Uphill from here, to the northeast and the northwest, are the older quarters of **Kaptol** (the "Cathedral Chapter") and **Gradec** (the "Upper Town"), both peaceful districts of ancient mansions, quiet squares and leafy parks.

Donji Grad

The **railway station** is as good a place as any to start an exploration of the city. **Tomislavov Trg**, opposite the station, is the first in a series of three shady, green squares which form the backbone of the lower town. Taking its name from the tenth-century Croatian king – there's a horseback-statue of him in the centre of the square – Tomislavov Trg's main attraction is the **Art Pavilion** (Umjetnički Paviljon; Mon–Sat 11am–7pm, Sun 10am–1pm; 10kn), built in 1898 and now hosting art exhibitions in its gilded stucco and mock-marble interior. Behind the pavilion lies the second of the three squares, **Strossmayerov Trg**, at the end of which stands another palatial nineteenth-century building, the brick-built **Croatian Academy of Science and Arts**, founded as the Yugoslavian Academy of Science and Arts by the nineteenth-century Bishop Strossmayer, a Croatian patriot and keen supporter of the Yugoslav ideal. His statue, the work of Croatia's greatest sculptor, Ivan Meštrović (1883–1962), sits among the trees in front of the building. The **Archeological Museum** (Arheoloski muzej; Tues–Fri 10am–5pm, Sat & Sun 10am–1pm; 15kn) lies to the north of here, in the last of the three squares, **Trg N. Zrinjskog** (marked on some maps as "Zrinjevac"); the museum has pieces from prehistoric times to the Middle Ages, including fragments from the so-called "Krapina Man" (*Homo Krapinensis*, a Neanderthal skeleton found 55km north of Zagreb), ancient Roman and Greek artefacts, and a selection of Egyptian antiquities.

Walk up from here and you're on Zagreb's main square, **Trg bana Jelačića**, flanked by cafés, hotels and department stores, and hectic with the whizz of trams and hurrying pedestrians. The statue in the centre of the square is of the nineteenth-century governer of Croatia, ban Jelačić; the tall clock to the east is where half the city seems to agree to meet in the evenings. From here, Jurišićeva runs east towards Trg hrvatskih velikana and the **House of Croatian Artists** (Dom Hrvatskih Likovnih Umjetnika; Mon 2–7pm, Tues–Sun 11am–7pm), housed in a pavilion designed by Meštrović in the 1930s and containing displays of contemporary painting and sculpture. There's not much else to tempt you further east from here except for the **Maksimir Park**, which is Zagreb's largest open space, reachable by tram #4, #7, #11 or #12. The park was founded in 1794, and is a carefully landscaped enclosure containing a belvedere, an eighteenth-century mock Swiss-chalet (now a café), and five lakes – the city's **zoo** (daily 9am–6pm; 20kn) stands on an islet in one of them.

Heading west from Trg bana Jelačića, **Ilica** is the city's main shopping street, running just below the hill of Gradec. A little way down and off to the right, you can take a **funicular** (*uspinjača*; daily 6.30am–9pm every 10 minutes; 2kn) up to Strossmayerovo Setaliste at the top, or cut down via **Preradovićev Trg**, a small lively square where there's a flower market, to **Trg Maršala Tita**. This is a grandiose open space, centring on the late-nineteenth-century **Croatian National Theatre** (Hrvatsko narodno kazalište), a solid ochre-coloured pile behind yet another work by Ivan Meštrović, the strangely erotic *Well of Life*. Across the square, the **Museum of Arts and Crafts** (Muzej za Umjetnost i Obrt; Tues–Fri 10am–6pm, Sat & Sun 10am–1pm; 20kn) boasts an impressive display of furniture, ceramics, clothes and textiles from the Renaissance to the present day. On the southern side of the square, on Trg Ivana Mažuranića, the **Ethnographic Museum** (Etnografski muzej; Tues, Wed & Thurs 10am–6pm, Fri, Sat & Sun 10am–1pm; 20kn) has a collection of costumes from every corner of the country, as well as an engaging heap of artefacts brought back from the South Pacific, Asia and Africa by intrepid Croatian explorers.

A couple of minutes west, on Rooseveltov Trg, lies Zagreb's most prestigious art collection, the **Mimara Museum** (Tues–Sat 10am–5pm, Sun 10am–2pm; 25kn), housing the art and archeological collection of one Ante Topić Mimara, a native of Zagreb who spent much of his life in Austria. On the ground floor there are exhibits of ancient glass from Egypt, Greece, Syria and the Roman Empire, seventeenth- and nineteenth-century oriental carpets, and Chinese art from the Shang through to the Song dynasty. Upstairs, there's a collection of European paintings. Most periods of art are covered, although a degree of controversy surrounds the attributions: most works are labelled "school of..." or "workshop of..." in order to keep the art experts happy.

Kaptol and Gradec

Behind Trg bana Jelačića, the filigree spires of Zagreb's **Cathedral** mark the edge of the district (and street) known as **Kaptol**, ringed by the ivy-cloaked turrets of the eighteenth-century **Archbishop's Palace** – "a sumptuous Kremlin" fancied the archeologist Arthur Evans before its decimation by an earthquake in 1880. After the disaster, the cathedral was rebuilt in an enthusiastic neo-Gothic style, a high, bare structure inside, with very little left from the years before the earthquake – only four Renaissance benches from the early sixteenth century and a painting of the *Passion* from about 1500, part of which has been ascribed to Dürer, remain. But the church is the symbolic centre of Croatian Catholicism – and, as such, of Croatian patriotism. Behind the altar lies the final resting place of Archbishop Stepinac, head of the Croat church in the Forties and imprisoned by the Communists after World War II.

Immediately west from Kaptol, **Gradec** is the most ancient and atmospheric part of Zagreb, a leafy, tranquil backwater of tiny streets, small squares and Baroque palaces, whose mottled brown roofs peek out from the hill to the west. Make your way to the **Dolac market**, which occupies several tiers immediately behind Trg bana Jelačića; this is the city's main food-market, a feast of fruit, vegetables, meat and fish held every morning. From the far side of Dolac market, **Tkalčićeva** spears north, following the course of the river which once formed the boundary between Kaptol and Gradec. Entry to Gradec proper from here is by way of the so-called **Krvavi Most** or "Bloody Bridge", which connects the street with Radićeva. On the far side of Radićeva, the **Kamenita Vrata** – literally the "stone gate" – is a gloomy tunnel with a small shrine that formed part of Gradec's original fortifications. Beyond the gate, Habdelićeva leads south to **Katarinin Trg**, home to the **Gallery of Modern Art** (Muzej suvremene umjetnosti; Tues–Sat 11am–7pm, Sun 10am–1pm) which mounts imaginative temporary shows from home and abroad. Close by, the fourteenth-century **Kula Lotrščak** or "Burglars' Tower" (Mon–Sat 10am–6pm, Sun 10am–1pm; 10kn), marks the top station of the funicular railway down to Ilica in the lower town. The views from the top, over the rest of the city and the plains beyond, are terrific. North of the tower, the **Gallery of Naïve Art**, Ćirilometodska 3 (Galerija naivne umjetnosti; Tues–Fri 10am–6pm, Sat & Sun 10am–1pm; 20kn), is an impressive collection of the naïve, peasant artists of rural Croatia. At the northern end of Ćirilometodska, Markov Trg is the core of Gradec – fringed by government offices, the square's focus is the squat church of **Sv Marko**, a much renovated structure whose coloured tiled roof displays the coats-of-arms of the constituent parts of Croatia. It was in this square that Croatian hero Matija Gubec, leader of the sixteenth-century peasants' revolt, was mockingly seated in a throne by the Hungarian authorities and crowned with a band of white-hot steel.

Just north of Markov Trg, at Mletačka 8 is the **Meštrović Atelier** (Mon–Fri 9am–2pm 20kn), an exhibition dedicated to the local sculptor – Croatia's most famous twentieth-cer tury artist – in his former home and studio. On display are sketches, photographs, memorabilia from exhibitions worldwide, and small-scale studies of his more familiar public creations. Left off Markov Trg, the **Historical Museum of Croatia**, at Matoševa 9 (Hrvatski povijesni muzej; Mon–Fri 10am–5pm, Sat & Sun 10am–1pm; 10kn), is the venue for prestigious temporary exhibitions. To the north of here, the **Natural History Museum** (Hrvatski prirodoslovni muzej; Tues–Fri 10am–5pm, Sat & Sun 10am–1pm; 10kn) offers displays on the animal life of Croatia and collections of fossils and minerals. The **Museum of Zagreb**, at Opatička 20 (Muzej grada Zagreba; Tues–Fri 10am–6pm, Sat & Sun 10am–1pm; 20kn), close to the thirteenth-century Popov Toranj or "Priest's Tower", is better, telling the tale of Zagreb's development from medieval times to the early twentieth century with the help of paintings and lumber from the city's wealthier households, and the original seventeenth-century statues which once adorned the portals of the city's cathedral.

Eating, drinking and nightlife

Whatever your budget, there's no shortage of places to **eat** in Zagreb. There's a wide range of Croatian cuisine, and any number of pizzerias, especially along Tkalčićeva. For **snack food**, the best place to find *burek* or cheap grills is the area around Dolac market, just above Trg bana Jelačića. *Pingvin*, inside the courtyard at Teslina 7, is a good sandwich bar open until 2am. There's a 24-hour bakery, *Pekarna Dora*, between the train station and the centre at Strossmayerov Trg 7. **Picnic supplies** can be purchased from the stalls of Dolac or from the Jabuka supermarket (daily 7am–midnight) in the subterranean Importanne shopping centre in front of the train station. For restaurants, you can expect to pay 80–120kn for a decent meal and most places that we've listed are within that price range. If it's necessary to book a table in advance, we've included a telephone number.

There's a wealth of **cafés and bars** offering outdoor seating in the pedestrian area around Gajeva and Bogovićeva, and along Tkalčićeva, just north of Trg bana Jelačića: it's really a question of finding a free table to watch the world go by.

Restaurants

Boban, Gajeva 9. Popular and central pasta venue in the vaulted basement of the café of the same name. Owned by soccer star Zvonimir Boban.

Cantinetta, Teslina 14. Good-quality Croatian and Italian food just south of the main square. Chic, but not too expensive.

Klub A. G. Matoš, Gajeva 2 (☎01/429-544). Smart, top-quality Croatian/international restaurant above the Znanje bookshop on the main square. Entrance from the arcade round the back.

Korčula, Nikola Tesle 17. Well-regarded fish restaurant which serves excellent squid. Open till midnight.

Lopud, Kaptol 10 (☎01/48-14-594). Well-respected seafood restaurant just north of the cathedral, offering fresh fish flown in every morning from Dubrovnik. Book in advance.

Marco Polo, Dolac market. Cheap, enormous and reasonably authentic pizzas – some pasta dishes too.

Pivnica Medvedgrad, Savska 56. In an unfashionable part of town, 1.5km southwest of the centre, but the traditional Croatian meat dishes are served in large, cheap portions and the beer is excellent.

Pod Grčkim Topom, Zakmardijeve stube 5 (☎01/430-690). Good Croatian food in a small restaurant on the steps leading down from Strossmayerovo Setaliste to Trg bana Jelacica, with a terrace overlooking the lower town. Open till midnight.

Rubelj, Dolac market. Cheapest place in the centre for simple but tasty grilled-meat standards.

Stari Fijaker, Mesnička 6. A dimly lit, intimate restaurant serving local cuisine.

Cafés and bars

Atrij, Teslina 7. One of several café/bars in a courtyard just south of the main square, heaving with bright young things at weekends.

Bulldog Pub, Bogovićeva. A typically elegant Zagreb bar and pavement café, this is one of the most popular meeting places in the town centre.

Dobar Zvuk, Gajeva 18. Popular, pub-style café-bar with moderately bohemian clientele.

Tolkein, Vranicanijeva. Relaxed Gradec bar, with a pleasant leafy courtyard.

Žabica, Opatička 5. Old-style, low-ceilinged coffee house in Gradec offering excellent cakes.

Music, theatre and festivals

Zagreb offers a rich and varied diet of high culture, with the Croatian National Theatre at Trg maršala Tita 15 (Hrvatsko Narodno Kazalište; ticket office Mon–Fri 10am–1pm & 5–7.30pm, Sat 10am–1pm & 90min before each performance; Sun 30min before each performance; ☎01/48-28-532), providing the focus for serious, Croatian-language **drama**, as well as **opera** and **ballet**. The city's main **orchestral-music** venue is the Lisinski Concert Hall south of the train station at Trg Stjepana Radica 4 (Dvorana Vatroslav Lisinski; ticket office Mon–Fri 9am–8pm, Sat 9am–2pm; ☎01/6121-166). Intimate **chamber-music** concerts take place at the Croatian Musical Institute (Hrvatski glazbeni zavod), Gundulićeva 6 (☎01/424-533). The free monthly English-language pamphlet *Events and Performances*, available from the Zagreb tourist office, contains **listings** of all forthcoming events.

Zagreb's annual **folklore festival**, held at the end of July, is one of the city's biggest events, with performances of ethnic music and dance from all over the world. Venues include the Lisinski Concert Hall and outdoor stages all over town. Advance information is available from the tourist office.

Discos and clubs

Nightlife centres around a moderate selection of discos and clubs, many of which present the best opportunities for catching live rock and jazz.

Aquarius, Jarun. Popular venue at the eastern end of Lake Jarun, 4km southwest of the centre, specializing in techno and drum 'n' bass. Occasional host to live bands.

BP Club, Teslina 7. Jazz club and relaxed late-night drinking haunt, although it can be difficult to get in when live bands are playing.

Gjuro II, Medvešćak 58. Varied programme of dance music and alternative rock, with regular live music.

Kulušić, Hrvojeva 6. Mainstream commercial disco, with occasional live rock.

Lapidarij, Habdelićeva 1. Long-established club with themed nights ranging from mainstream dance music to indie rock.

Listings

Airlines British Airways, *Sheraton Hotel*, Kneza Borne 2 (☎01/45-53-336); Croatia Airlines, Trg N. Zrinskog 17 (☎01/45-51-244).

Airport enquiries ☎01/65-25-222.

American Express Lastovska 23 (☎01/61-24-422).

British Council Ilica 12 (Mon–Fri 7.30am–2.30pm; ☎01/424-733). Library, newspapers, reading room.

Bus enquiries ☎060/313-333.

Car rental Budget, *Sheraton Hotel*, Kneza Borne 2 (☎01/45-54-936); Hertz, Kačićeva 9a (☎01/48-47-222); Unis, Gajeva 29a (☎01/424-849) and at the airport (☎01/525-006).

Embassies Australia, *Hotel Esplanade*, Mihanovićeva 1 (☎01/457-7433); Britain, Vlaška 121 (☎01/45-55-310); Canada, *Hotel Esplanade*, Mihanovićeva 1 (☎01/45-77-905); US, Hebrangova 2 (☎01/45-55-500).

Ferry tickets Jadrolinija, Zrinjevac 20 (☎01/421-777).

Hospital The main casualty department is at Draskovićeva 19.

Left luggage At the railway station.

Pharmacy 24-hour pharmacy at Trg bana Jelačića 3.

Post offices Jurišićeva 13 and Branimirova 4 (both Mon–Fri 7am–8pm, Sat 7am–7pm).

Taxis Ranks outside the train station. To book, call ☎01/682-505, 682-558.

Train station Information on ☎9830 (domestic services), ☎01/45-73-238 (international).

Telephones International telephone calls can be made at either of the main post offices listed above.

Travel agents. Croatia Express, Teslina 4 (☎01/48-11-842); Dalmacijaturist, Zrinjevac 16 (☎01/427-611); Generaltourist, Praška 5 (☎01/48-11-033); Kvarner Express, Praška 4 (☎01/48-10-522).

ISTRIA

A large peninsula jutting into the northern Adriatic, **Istria** (*Istra*) is Croatian tourism at its most developed. Many of the towns here were tourist resorts back in the last century, and in recent years their proximity to northern Europe has ensured an annual influx of sun-seekers from Germany, Austria and the Netherlands. Yet the growth of modern hotel complexes, sprawling campsites and (mainly concrete) beaches has done little to detract from the essential charm of the region. This stretch of the coast was under Venetian rule for 400 years and there's still a fair-sized Italian community, with Italian very much the second language of the region. Regular trains and buses from Zagreb (and the Slovene capital Ljubljana, another good gateway to the region) arrive at Istria's largest centre, the port city of **Pula**. With its Roman amphitheatre and other relics of Roman occupation, it's a rewarding place to spend a couple of days – rooms are relatively easy to come by and most of Istria's interesting spots are only a bus ride away. On the western side of the Istrian peninsula, resort towns like **Poreč** and **Rovinj**, with their cobbled piazzas and shuttered houses, are almost overwhelmingly pretty. **Opatija** to the southeast couldn't be more different – a former Austro-Hungarian society resort which still sports the refined air of *Mitteleuropa*.

Pula

Once the chief port of the Austro-Hungarian Empire, **PULA** is an engaging combination of working port, naval base and brash riviera town. The Romans put the city squarely on the map when they arrived in 177 BC, transforming it into an important commercial centre. Most obvious relic of their rule is the first century BC **Amphitheatre** (amfiteatar; daily 8am–8pm; 30kn) just north of the centre, a great grey elliptical skein of connecting arches, silhouetted against the skyline from wherever you stand in the city. It's the sixth largest in the world, and once had space for over 23,000 spectators. The outer shell is fairly complete, as is one of the towers, up which a slightly hair-raising climb gives a good sense of the enormity of the structure and a view of Pula's industrious harbour. You can also explore some of the cavernous rooms underneath, which would have been used for keeping wild animals and Christians before they met their death. They're now given over to piles of crusty amphora, and reconstructed olive presses.

South of the amphitheatre, central Pula circles a pyramidal hill, scaled by secluded streets and topped with a star-shaped Venetian fortress. On the eastern side of the hill, Istarska (which subsequently becomes Giardini) leads down to the first-century BC **Triumphal Arch of the Sergians** (Slavoluk obitelja Sergijevaca), through which ul Sergijevaca, a lively pedestrianized thoroughfare, leads in turn to a square known as **Forum** – site of the ancient Roman forum and these days the centre of Pula's old quarter. On the far side of here, the slim form of the **Temple of Augustus** was built between 2 BC and 14 AD to celebrate the cult of the emperor; the high Corinthian columns of its frontage intact and imposing, this is one of the best examples of a Roman temple outside Italy.

Heading north from Forum along Kandlerova leads to Pula's **Cathedral** (daily 7am–noon & 4–6pm), a broad, simple and very spacious structure that is another mixture of periods and styles: a fifteenth-century renovation of a Romanesque basilica built on the foundations of a Roman temple. Inside, the high altar consists of a third-century marble Roman sarcophagus, said to have once contained the remains of the eleventh-century Hungarian King Solomon. From the cathedral, you can follow streets up to the top of the hill, the site of the original Roman Capitol and now the home of a mossy seventeenth-century **fortress**, built by the Venetians and now housing the pretty inessential **Historical Museum of Istria** (daily 8am–5pm; 7kn). You're better off following tracks to the far side of the fortress where there are the remains of a small **Roman Theatre**, and the **Archeological Museum** (Arheoloski muzej; May–Sept Mon–Sat 9am–6pm, Sun 9am–3pm; Oct–April Mon–Fri 9am–2pm; 20kn), which hides in the trees next to the second-century AD Porta Gemina. Inside the museum are pillars and toga-clad statues mingling haphazardly with ceramics, jewellery and trinkets from all over Istria, some dating back to prehistoric times.

Practicalities

Pula's **train station** is a ten-minute walk north of the town centre, at the far end of Kolodvorska; the **bus station** is along Istarska, just south of the amphitheatre. The **tourist office**, between the bus station and the amphitheatre at Istarska 11 (daily 9am–1pm; ☎052/33557), can provide information and useful maps, but does not offer a private room booking service. For this, you need to go down Istarska in the opposite direction to Arenatours at Giardini 4 (daily 7am–9pm; ☎052/34-355), or head for Kvarner Express on the seafront at Riva 14 (Mon–Sat 9am–7pm; ☎052/2259). **Hotels** are thin on the ground in central Pula, although the *Riviera*, a peeling, turn-of-the-century edifice between the train station and the centre at Splitska 1 (☎052/211-166; ④), is reasonable. There's also a **youth hostel**, at Valsaline bay, 4km south of the centre (☎052/210-002; dorm beds ②); take bus #2 or #7 from Giardini to Vila Idola and then bear right towards the bay. The nearest **campsite** is *Stoja*, on a rocky wooded peninsula 3km southeast of town (☎052/24144); take bus #1 from Giardini.

Most **eating and drinking** venues are concentrated around the arena, Forum and Kandlerova. *Delfin*, opposite the cathedral at Kandlerova 17, offers inexpensive fish dishes; *Jupiter*, below the fortress at Castropola 38, is the best of the pizzerias; while *Vespasian*, below the amphitheatre at Amfiteatarska 11 is the place to go for mid-priced Croatian standards. Best of the drinking haunts are *Ulix*, an elegant bar next to the triumphal arch; and *Bounty Pub*, an animated place with plenty of outdoor seating two blocks east of the arch at Veronska 8. In the summer, the amphitheatre is used to stage pop events and world-class opera; details can be obtained from the tourist office.

Rovinj and around

There are few more pleasant towns in Istria than **ROVINJ**, which lies forty kilometres north of Pula. Its harbour is a likeable mix of fishing boats and swanky yachts, its quaysides a blend of sunshaded café-tables and the thick orange of fishermen's nets. Rovinj is the most Italian town on this coast: there's an Italian high school, street-names are in Italian, and the language is widely spoken in the town. From the main square, **Trg Maršala Tita**, the Baroque **Vrata Sv Križa** leads up to Grisia Ulica, which is lined with ateliers and galleries selling local art. It climbs steeply through the heart of the old town to the **Crkva Sv Eufemije** (daily 10am–noon & 4–7pm), dominating Rovinj from the top of its stumpy peninsula. This eighteenth-century church, Baroque in style, has the sixth-century sarcophagus of the saint inside, and offers the chance to climb its 58-metre-high tower (same times; 10kn). Back on Maršala Tita, the **Town Museum** (Zavičajni muzej Rovinj; Tues–Sat 10.30am–2pm & 6–8pm, Sun 7–10pm; 10kn) has the usual collection of archeological oddments, antique furniture and exhibitions of Croatian art. North of here is **Trg Valdibora**, home to a small fruit and vegetable market, from where Obala Palih Boraca leads along the waterfront to the Marine Biological Institute at Obala Giordano Paliaga 5; the institute's **aquarium** (Easter–Oct daily 9am–9pm; 10kn) has tanks of Adriatic flora and marine life.

Paths on the south side of Rovinj's busy harbour lead beyond the *Hotel Park* towards **Zlatni Rt**, a densely-forested cape, crisscrossed by numerous tracks and fringed by rocky **beaches**. Other spots for bathing can be found on the two islands just offshore from Rovinj – **Sveta Katerina**, the nearer of the two, and **Crveni Otok**, just outside Rovinj's bay; both are linked every thirty minutes by boats from the harbour and are home to a couple of hotels, a handful of pebbly beaches and some reasonable places to swim.

Practicalities

Rovinj's **bus station** is five minutes' walk southeast of the town centre, just off Trg Na Lokvi, at the junction of Carrera and Carducci. **Private rooms** can be obtained from Lokva, opposite the bus station at Carducci 4 (☎052/813-365); and Kompas Istra, by the waterfront o

Trg Marsala Tita (☎052/813-211). Of the **hotels**, the *Adriatic*, Trg M. Tita (☎052/815-088; ⑤) is a venerable establishment by the port; while the *Katarina* on the island of Sveta Katarina (☎052/811-233; ④) is a comfortable off-shore alternative. The nearest **campsite** is the *Polari* (☎052/813-441), 3km south and reached by regular bus. For **eating**, there are lots of fish restaurants around town try: the *Sidro*, by the water on Obala Alda Rismonda; or the nearby *Amfora*, A. Rismonda 23, renowned for its shellfish.

Poreč and around

Regular buses head north from Rovinj towards **POREČ**, Istria's largest and busiest resort. Another peninsula town with an ordered mesh of streets that dates from its days as a Roman encampment, Poreč's star historic turn is the **Basilica of Euphrasius** (Eufrazijeva basilika; daily 8am–noon & 3–6pm; free), a sixth-century Byzantine structure harbouring mosaics claimed by some experts to be comparable with those at Ravenna. Situated just off Ljubljanska, in the centre of Poreč, the basilica is at the heart of a religious complex, established by Bishop Euphrasius in 543, which includes a bishop's palace, atrium, baptistery, and campanile. Entry is through the **Atrium**, an arcaded courtyard that was heavily restored in the last century but still has ancient bits of masonry incorporated in its walls. Beyond lies the **Bishop's Palace** (10kn), a seventeenth-century building harbouring a display of mosaic fragments which once adorned the basilica floor. To the left of here is the octagonal Baptistery. The basilica itself is a rather bare structure, save for the wall **mosaics** above the altar which are studded with semi-precious gems, encrusted with mother-of-pearl and emblazoned everywhere with Euphrasius's personal monogram: he was, it's said, a notoriously arrogant man. The central part of the composition shows the Virgin enthroned with Child, flanked by a worldly Euphrasius holding a model of his church. Underneath are scenes of the *Annunciation* and *Visitation*, the latter surprisingly realistic, with the imaginative invention of a doltish eavesdropping servant.

Due east of the basilica is ul Dekumanska, which follows the line of the ancient Roman *decumanus* (main street) and opens out into a square busy with street artists and tourist traffic. The **Poreč Museum** at ul Dekumanska 9 (daily 9am–noon & 5–8pm; 10kn), housed in the Baroque Sinčić Palace, displays Greek and Roman finds from the surrounding area. Heading south, towards the end of the peninsula, you'll find the distinctive thirteenth-century **Romanesque House**, with an unusual projecting wooden balcony – a venue for art shows. Further on is **Trg Marafor**, with its remains of Roman temples to Mars and Neptune. Little is known about these and they're not much more than heaps of rubble really, the interesting parts having found their way into the town museum.

The **beaches** around the old town can get crowded. As an alternative, take a boat from the Riviera jetty (7am–11pm every 30min; 12kn) to the island of **Sv Nikola** across the water, or walk south beyond the marina where pathways head along a rocky coastline shaded by gnarled pines.

Practicalities

Poreč's **bus station** is just outside the town centre, behind the marina. From here, it's a five-minute walk to the **tourist office** at Zagrebačka 11 (daily 8am–10pm; ☎052/451-458), which provides information and will point you in the direction of agencies offering **rooms**: Adriatic, just down the road from the tourist office at Trg Slobode 2a (☎052/452-220); or Atlas, on the waterfront at Obala Marsala Tita 21 (☎052/432-184), are probably the easiest to find. For **hotels**, try the friendly and central *Poreč*, just behind the bus station on Rade Končara 1 (☎052/451-811; ④). The closest **campsites** are at the Zelena Laguna complex, a few kilometres south – *Zelena Laguna* and, further south, *Bijela Uvala* – reachable by hourly bus from the bus station.

As for **food**, there's a good sprinkling of places in the old town. *Amicus*, just off Dekumanska at Eufrazijeva 45, offers good quality and good value pizza, grilled meat and seafood; the *Sarajevo Grill*, on Dekumanska, has a good array of meat dishes; while *Sofora*, Obala Maršala Tita 13, is one of the best places to eat fish. Central Poreč is full of cafés and bars with outdoor seating; it's really a question of deciding which brand of blaring music you're happy to tolerate.

Opatija and around

The major resort on Istria's eastern shore is **OPATIJA**, a nineteenth-century spa resort nestling beneath the peninsula's coastal mountains. Despite a scattering of elegant, turn-of-the-century mansions, the town's real attraction is the **Šetalište Franza Josefa** promenade, which runs along the rocky seafront to the sleepy fishing village of Volosko (2km to the north) and the sedate resort of Lovran (6km south). Opatija was originally a favourite with aristocratic Habsburgs and remains popular with the local elite, so it's a good place simply to hang out and observe Croatia's smart set at play. As for **beaches**, Opatija's is concrete and crowded; the most attractive shingle beach in the area is at Medveja, 3km southwest of Lovran. Bus #32 (destination Mošćeniaka Draga or Brsec) runs hourly to Medveja, and all #32 services make the journey to Volosko and Lovran (every 15min).

Accommodation in Opatija is expensive unless you opt for a **private room**: the **tourist office** at Maršala Tita 101 (daily 8am–7pm; ☎051/271-710), will put you on to the local agencies, of which Kompas, just up the road at Maršala Tita 110, is the nearest at hand. The *Palace-Bellevue* **hotel** right next to the bus station at Maršala Tita 200 (☎051/271-811; ④) is a fine old Habsburg edifice bang in the heart of things. Of the numerous bland hotels further along Maršala Tita catering for the package trade, the *Jadran* (☎051/271-100; ⑤) is the most reasonable. The *Villa Liana*, 1km south of Lovran along the coast road (☎051/712-742; ④), offers bed-and-breakfast accommodation in large, old-fashioned rooms. Best of the local **campsites** is at Medveja, attractively placed in a steep-sided valley with direct access to the beach (☎051/291-191). For **eating**, *Madonnina*, signed off the main road downhill from Opatija's tourist office, serves cheap and reliable pizzas; *Gusto*, at Maršala Tita 266 in the southwestern end of town, offers big grills at a reasonable price; and *Grill Kvarner*, overlooking the harbour in Lovran, is a good place for fresh seafood. Best of the **bars** are *Vološćica* on the waterfront at Volosko, and *Galija* in Opatija harbour.

Moving on from Istria: Rijeka

Travelling on from Istria towards Zagreb or Dalmatia, most routes lead through the brusque port city of **RIJEKA** (bus #32 from Opatija; 20kn), hardly worth a stopoff in its own right but an important transport hub for onward travel. Regular buses run from Rijeka to Zagreb, Split and Dubrovnik; and it's also the starting point for the once-daily Jadrolinija coastal ferry, which calls in at Split and Dubrovnik on its way south. Rijeka is easy to get in and out of. Train and bus stations are about 400m apart; the former at the western end of Borisa Kidriča, the latter at the eastern end of the same street on Trg Žabica. The **Jadrolinija ferry office** (daily 7am–6pm, Wed & Sun 7am–8pm; ☎051/22356) is just along the waterfront from the bus station at Riva 16.

DALMATIA

Stretching from Zadar in the north to the Montenegrin border in the south, the region of **Dalmatia** (Dalmacija) possesses one of Europe's most dramatic shorelines, the sheer wall of Croatia's mountain ranges sweeping down to the sea from stark, grey heights, scattering islands in their path. For centuries, the region was ruled by Venice, spawning towns, churches and an architecture that wouldn't look out of place on the other side of the water. All along, well-preserved medieval towns sit on tiny islands or just above the sea on slim peninsulas, beneath a grizzled karst landscape that drops precipitously into some of the clearest – and cleanest – water anywhere. The main centres to aim for are in southern Dalmatia: the provincial capital **Split** is served by buses and trains from Zagreb and provides onward bus connections with the walled city of **Dubrovnik**. Ferry connections with the best of the islands – **Brač**, **Hvar**, and **Korčula** – are also made from Split.

Split

By far the largest city in Dalmatia, and its major transit point, **SPLIT** is one of the most enticing spots on the Dalmatian coast; a hectic city, full of shouting stall-owners and travellers on the move. At the heart of all this, hemmed in by the sprawling estates and a modern harbour, lies a crumbling old town built within the precincts of Diocletian's Palace, one of the most outstanding classical remains in Europe. The palace was built as a retirement home by Dalmatian-born Roman Emperor Diocletian in AD 305, and although it fell into disrepair soon after his death, the palace's shell was used as a refuge by those fleeing the Byzantine city of Salona (6km inland), sacked by the Avars in 614. Modified and built-onto over the centuries, Diocletian's Palace has remained the core of Split ever since.

Arrival, information and accommodation

The main **bus and railway stations** are next door to each other on Obala Kneza Domagoja, five minutes' walk from the centre, just around the harbour; the **ferry terminal** for both domestic and international ferries, together with the Jadrolinija booking office, is a few hundred metres south of here. Split's **airport** is some 16km west of town. Croatia Airlines buses (20kn) connect with scheduled flights and run into central Split, dropping you right on the waterfront; alternatively, a taxi will set you back about 160kn.

Split's tourist office doesn't have an office open to public as yet, so you'll have to make do with the more commercially-oriented Turist Biro, on the waterfront at Obala narodnog preporoda 12 (☎021/342-142), which has maps for sale and arranges accommodation in **private rooms**. Most reasonable of the **hotels** are the *Slavija*, which has basic rooms (some with shower, some without) in the old town at Buvinova 3 (☎021/47-053; ③); the more comfortable *Bellevue* on the western fringes of the old town at bana Jelačića 2 (☎021/585-701; ④); and the *Marjan*, (☎021/342-866; ⑤), a more business-oriented place five minutes' further west at Obala kneza Branimira 8.

The City

Most of Split's attractions are concentrated in the compact **old centre** behind the waterfront, largely made up of the remains of Diocletian's Palace. The palace was begun in AD 295 and finished ten years later, when the emperor came back to his native Dalmatia to escape the cares of the empire, cure his rheumatism and grow cabbages. However Diocletian continued to maintain an elaborate court here, in a building that mixed luxurious palatial apartments with the infrastructure of a Roman garrison. The best place to start a tour of the palace area is on the seaward side, through the **Bronze Gate** (Mjedena Vrata), a functional gateway giving access to the sea that once came right up to the palace itself. Inside, you find yourself in a vaulted hall, from which imposing steps lead through the now domeless vestibule to the Peristil. Little remains of the imperial apartments to the left, but you can get some idea of their grandeur and floor-plan by visiting the **subterranean halls** (summer daily 8am–8pm; rest of the year 8am–noon & 4–7pm) beneath the houses which now stand on the site; the entrance is to the left of the Mjedena Vrata. Through the vaulted hall, which is usually full of stalls selling arts and crafts, and up the steps, is the **Peristil**, once the central courtyard of the palace complex. These days it serves as the main town square, crowded with cafés and surrounded by remnants of the stately arches that framed the square. At the southern end, steps lead up to the **vestibule**, a round, formerly domed building that is the only part of the imperial apartment area of the palace that's anything like complete. It was here that subjects would wait in apprehension before being admitted to Diocletian himself.

On the east side of the Peristil stands one of two black granite Egyptian sphinxes, dating from around 15 BC, which originally flanked the entrance to Diocletian's mausoleum, an octagonal building surrounded by an arcade of Corinthian columns that's since been converted into Split's **Cathedral** (Mon–Sat 7am–noon & 4–7pm). Diocletian's body is known to have rested here for 170 years until one day it disappeared – no one knows why or where. On the right of the entrance is the **campanile**, a Romanesque structure much restored in the late nineteenth century. The haul up is worth the effort for the panoramic view over the city and beyond. As for the cathedral itself, its most immediate feature is the walnut and oak main **doorway**, carved with an inspired comic strip showing *Scenes from the Life of Christ* -- the work of local artist Andrija Buvina in 1214. Inside the cathedral is an odd hotchpotch of styles, the dome ringed by two series of decorative Corinthian columns and a frieze which contains portraits of Diocletian and his wife. The **pulpit** is a beautifully proportioned example of Romanesque art, sitting on capitals tangled with snakes, strange beasts and foliage. But the church's finest feature is the Altar of St Anastasius, on which a cruelly realistic *Flagellation of Christ* – completed by local artist Juraj Dalmatinac in 1448 – shows Jesus pawed and brutalized by some peculiarly oafish persecutors.

Opposite the cathedral, a narrow alley runs from a gap in the arched arcade down to the **Baptistery** (opening times vary, check at the cathedral). Another pre-Christian edifice, variously attributed to the cults of Janus and Jupiter, this is an attractive building with a richly coffered ceiling and well-preserved relief of Apollo on the eastern portal. Later Christian additions include a skinny *John the Baptist* by Meštrović (a late work of 1954), and, more famously, an eleventh-century baptismal font with a relief popularly believed to be a grovelling subject paying homage to a Croatian king.

A block north of the cathedral on Papalićeva, the flowery Gothic Papalić Palace now houses the **City Museum** (Tues–Fri 9am–noon & 5–8pm, Sat & Sun 10am–noon; 10kn), which displays city documents, weaponry and fragments of sculpture. Just north of here, reached by following Dioklecijanova, is the grandest and best preserved of the palace gates, the **Golden Gate** or Zlatna Vrata. Just outside there's another Mestrović, a gigantic statue of the fourth-century Bishop **Grgur Ninski**. Ninski is an important historical character for the Croats since he fought Rome for the right of his people to use their own language in the liturgy.

Fifteen minutes' walk northwest of here, the **Archeological Museum** at Zrinsko Frankopanska 25 (Arheoloski muzej; Tues–Sat 9am–1pm & 5–8pm, Sun 10am–noon; 20kn) contains comprehensive, if poorly labelled, displays of Illyrian, Greek, medieval and Roman artefacts that conjure up a picture of life for the average noble of the time. Exhibits include delicate votive figurines, amulets, and jewellery embellished with tiny peep-shows of lewd love-making. Outside, the arcaded courtyard is crammed with a wonderful array of Greek, Roman and early Christian gravestones, sarcophagi and decorative sculpture.

Crisscrossed by footpaths and minor roads, the woods of the **Marjan peninsula** west of the old town are the best place to head for if you want to exchange central Split's turmoil for some peace and quiet. On foot, the peninsula is accessible from Obala hrvatskog narodnog preporoda via Sperun and then Senjska, which cuts up through the slopes of the **Varoš** district. Most of Marjan's visitors stick to the road around the edge of the promontory with its infrequent, tiny rocky **beaches**; the Bene beach, on the far northern side, is especially popular. From the road, tracks lead up into the heart of the Marjan Park, which is thickly wooded with pines, rising to its peak at 175m. The main historical attractions of Marjan are on the lower, southern edge, along Šetalište Ivana Meštrovića. First of these is the **Museum of Croatian Archeological Monuments** (Muzej Hrvatskih arheoloskih spomenika; Tues–Sat 9am–4pm, Sun 9am–noon; 20kn), fifteen minutes' walk west of the centre or bus #2 from the seafront, an oversized modern pavilion housing a disappointing collection of jewellery, weapons and fragmentary reconstructions of chancel screens and ciboria from ninth- and tenth-century Croat churches. A couple of minutes' walk away, the **Meštrović Gallery**, Ivana Meštrovića 39 (Galerija Ivana Meštrovića; Tues–Sun 11am–6pm; 20kn), is another Croatian shrine, housed in the ostentatious Neoclassical building that was built – and lived in – by Croatia's most famous twentieth-century artist, Ivan Meštrović (1883–1962). The gallery displays many of his smaller statues – boldly fashioned bodies curled into elegant poses and greatly influenced by Croatian folk art. Mestrović's former workshop, **Kaštelet**, (check at the Meštrović Gallery first) is 300m up the same road, and contains a chapel decorated with one of the sculptor's most important set-piece works, a series of wood-carved reliefs showing scenes from the *Stations of the Cross*.

Beaches

The main city beach is **Bačvice**, a few minutes' walk south past the railway station, though it's small, crowded and a little too close to Split's polluted harbour for comfort. Rather better, though still crowded, are the beaches that dent the far edges of the Marjan peninsula – **Bene** on the northern side, and **Kašjuni** on the southern side – though inevitably these involve more walking.

Eating and drinking

For **eating**, the daily market at the eastern edge of the old town is an excellent place to shop for fruit, veg and local cheeses, while the 24-hour bakery directly opposite the market on Zagrebačka is something of a late-night Split institution. There are few restaurants in the old town, although *Sarajevo*, Domaldova 6, has a good range of Croatian meat and fish dishes. Further afield, *Galija* at Matošića 2 on the western fringes of the old town, is the best of the pizzerias; while *Konoba kod Jože* at Sredmanuška 4, ten minutes' northeast of the old town, is an atmospheric place specializing in seafood. *Konoba Varoš*, up behind the *Bellevue Hotel* at ban Mladenova 7, is another traditional Dalmatian restaurant.

There are plenty of pavement cafés along the seafront for daytime and evening **drinking**, though they are usually packed. The best of the rest are the bars within the old town: try *Planet Jazz*, a bohemian hangout on Grgura Ninskog; the similar *Jazz III* on Vukičovićeva; or the *Star Rock Café*, just off Marmontova, a roomy bar decked out in rock memorabilia. *Music Club Kada*, in an alleyway off Zagrebačka just opposite the market, has regular live rock or jazz music. *Obojena Svjetlost*, on the beach beneath the Meštrović gallery, is an animated open-air disco/bar that stays open until the early hours.

Brač

The third largest island on the Adriatic coast, **Brač** is famous for its milk-white marble, which has been used in places as diverse as Berlin's Reichstag, the high altar of Liverpool's Metropolitan Cathedral, the White House in Washington – and, of course, Diocletian's Palace. In addition to the marble, a great many islanders were once dependent on the grape harvest, though the phylloxera (vine lice) epidemics of the late nineteenth century and early twentieth century forced many of them to emigrate. Even today, as you cross Brač's interior, the signs of this depopulation are all around in the tumbledown walls and overgrown fields.

The easiest way to reach Brač is by **ferry** from Split to **Supetar**, an engagingly laid-back fishing port on the north side of the island, from where it's a straightforward bus journey to **Bol**, a major windsurfing centre on the island's south coast and site of one of the Adriatic's most famous beaches.

Supetar

Though the largest town on the island, **SUPETAR** is a rather sleepy village onto which package tourism has been painlessly grafted. There's little of specific interest, save for several attractive shingle **beaches** which stretch away westwards from the town's harbour, and the **Petrinović Mausoleum**, a neo-Byzantine confection on a wooded promontory 1km west of town, built by sculptor Toma Rosandić to honour a local businessman.

Supetar's **tourist office** beside the ferry dock at Porat 1 (daily 9am–9pm; ☎021/630-551) will arrange **private rooms** for you. There's also the *Palute* at Put pasika 16 (☎021/631-541; ③), a friendly and agreeable pension offering bed-and-breakfast accommodation just west of the centre. The **Hotel** *Britanida*, 200m east of the ferry dock at Hrvatskih velikana 26 (☎021/630-017; ④), is a step up in comfort; but avoid the line of overpriced package hotels behind the beaches. Best of the places to **eat** on the harbourfront is *Palute* at Porat 4, which serves good grilled fish. *Vinotoka*, just inland from the harbour at Dobova 6, has a wide range of traditional Croatian food and an extensive choice of local wines. The clear waters around

Supetar are perfect for **scuba diving**; the Dive Center Kaktus in the *Kaktus Hotel* complex (☎021/630-421) rents out gear and arranges scuba and snorkelling crash courses from around 200kn.

Bol

Stranded on the far side of the Vidova Gora mountains, there's no denying the beauty of **BOL**'s setting, or the charm of its old stone houses. The main attraction of the village is its beach, **Zlatni Rat** (Golden Cape), which lies to the west of the centre along the wooded shoreline. Unusually sandy and unusually beautiful, the cape juts into the sea in the form of a giant "Y", changing shape slightly from day to day as the wind plays across it. It does, however, get very crowded during summer. When you're through with the beach, look in at the late-fifteenth-century **Dominican Monastery** (daily 5–7pm; 10kn), perched high on the clifftop just east of Bol's centre. Its location is dramatic, and the monastery museum holds among its small collection a *Madonna with Child* by Tintoretto.

Buses from Supetar stop just west of Bol's harbour, at the far end of which stands the **tourist office** (June–Aug daily 8am–10pm; Sept–May Mon–Fri 8.30am–3pm; ☎021/635-122), which has free leaflets and maps. **Private rooms** can be obtained from Boltours, 100m west of the bus stop at Vladimira Nazora 18 (daily 9am–2pm & 5–8pm; ☎021/635-693). For **eating**, there are numerous places along the waterfront, although *Gust*, above the tourist office at F. Radića 14, has the widest range of traditional food. There are a couple of **windsurfing** centres on the shoreline west of town, on the way to Zlatni Rat, which offer board rental and a range of courses for beginners. Big Blue (☎021/635-614), with offices next to the tourist office and in front of the *Hotel Borak*, is one of the most reliable. These centres also rent out **mountain bikes** (£7 a day) – useful if you want to get to Blaca.

Blaca

One way to escape Bol's crowds is to make for the hermitage of **Blaca**, tucked away at the head of a valley well to the west of the town. You can walk there by following the road, subsequently a track, which heads west from Bol, before heading inland at Blaca bay – the route is well signposted, but the trip takes three hours each way. If you have your own transport on the other hand, follow the signposted track (just about passable for cars, but rough on the suspension) which leaves the main road from Bol to Supetar. At the track's end, head on foot along the path downhill, which leads to the monastery in about forty minutes. The **hermitage** (Tues–Sun 8am–5pm, but check in the tourist office at Bol or Supetar as times can vary; 20kn) was founded in 1588 by monks fleeing the Turks; the last resident was an enthusiastic astronomer who left all sorts of bits and bobs, including an assortment of old clocks and a stock of lithographs by Poussin. But the principal attraction is the hermitage's setting, hugging the sides of a narrow, scrub-covered ravine.

Hvar

One of the most hyped of all the Croatian islands, **HVAR** is undeniably beautiful – a slim, green slice of land punctured by jagged inlets and cloaked with hills of spongy lavender. Tourist development hasn't been too crass, and the island's main centre, **Hvar town**, retains much of its old Venetian fishing-port charm. **Ferries** run between here and Split once daily, and to **Starigrad**, farther east, roughly four times daily. The Dubrovnik–Rijeka coastal ferry stops at Hvar town once a day in summer, less frequently through the rest of the year.

Hvar town

The best view of **HVAR TOWN** is from the sea, the tiny town centre contoured around the bay, grainy-white and brown with green splashes of palms and pines bursting from every crack and cranny. At the centre, the creamy brown triangular main square cuts its way in, flanked by the arcaded bulk of the Venetian arsenal. The upper storey of the arsenal was added in 1612 to house the city **theatre**, the oldest in Croatia and one of the first in Europe

It's since been converted to a cinema, but the painted Baroque interior has survived pretty much intact (daily: summer 9am–1pm & 8–10pm; winter daily 11am–noon; 10kn). The piazza culminates in the skeletal campanile of Hvar's **Cathedral** (no fixed opening times, but usually open mornings), a sixteenth-century construction with an eighteenth-century facade that's a characteristic mixture of Gothic and Renaissance styles. Inside is routine enough, but the **Bishop's Treasury** (daily: summer 9am–noon & 5–7pm; winter 10am–noon; 20kn) is worth the entry fee for its small but fine selection of chalices, reliquaries and embroidery. Look out for a nicely worked sixteenth-century crozier, carved into a serpent, encrusted with saints and embossed with a figure of the Virgin attended by Moses and an Archangel.

The rest of the old town backs away from the piazza in an elegant confusion of twisting lanes and alleys. Up above, the **Fortress** (June–Sept daily 9am–7pm; 5kn) is a good example of sixteenth-century military architecture. The views over Hvar and the islands beyond are well worth the trek to the top. From the fort you can pick out the fifteenth-century **Franciscan Monastery** (Mon–Fri 9am–noon & 4–6pm; 10km), to the left of the harbour, a sliver of white against the blue of the sea. The monastery has a small collection of paintings, mostly obscure Venetian, which includes a tender, dark and modernistic *Ecce Homo* by Leandro Bassano and a melodramatic, almost life-size *Last Supper* attributed to Matteo Ingoli. Stretched right across the wall, Ingoli's figures seem oddly frozen – a clash between a highly stylized, medieval religious art and the pre-Renaissance realism of some of the body postures. Next door, the monastic **church** is pleasingly simple, with beautifully carved choir stalls and a fanciful partition dating from 1583; look out for the extravagant dragon candleholders that push out above the panel detail below.

The **beaches** nearest to Hvar town are rocky and crowded, and it's best to make your way towards the **Pakleni Otoci** (the Islands of Hell), just to the west of Hvar. Easily reached by water taxi from the harbour (about 15kn each way), the Pakleni Otoci is a chain of eleven wooded islands, only three of which have any facilities (simple bars and restaurants): Jerolim island, the nearest, offers nudist bathing (FKK); next is Marinkovac – partly nudist, but with a main beach, U Stipanska; then Sv Klement, the largest of the islands – here, most people head for Palmižana, one of its most attractive coves with a fine shingle beach. Water taxis will take you to any of the other islands, but you'll need to take your own food and drink. **Camping** is forbidden throughout Pakleni.

PRACTICALITIES

Hvar town's **tourist office** (July & Aug daily 7am–10pm; rest of year Mon–Sat 8am–noon, Sun 9am–1pm) is on the waterfront below the theatre; for assistance in booking **private rooms**, however, you should head for the Mengola agency, also on the harbour (☎021/742-099). The local **hotels** are not cheap, and are often full in July and August. The characterless but acceptable *Dalmacija*, on the eastern side of the harbour (☎021/741-120; ⑤), and the *Delfin*, over on the western side (☎021/741-168; ⑤), are as reasonable as you'll get.

There are dozens of **restaurants** in Hvar town, so eating out is not a problem. *Leonardo* on the harbour is the most consistent of the pizzerias; while *Macondo*, signposted in a backstreet uphill from the harbour, and *Ugo*, nearby on Petra Hektorovića, are the best places for meat and fish. For **drinking**, there are several cafés and bars around the harbour. *Sidro* and *Atelier* are two of the best bars for evening drinking.

The **Jadrolinija ferry** office (☎021/741-132) is along the quay towards the Franciscan Monastery.

Starigrad

Some 20km east across the mountains from Hvar town, **STARIGRAD** is Hvar's second fiddle, a popular and busy resort straggling along the sides of a deep bay. The old part of Starigrad has been pleasantly renovated, and backs onto the main street as it twists its way along the waterside. The only real sight is the **Tvrdalj** (June–Sept daily 10am–noon & 5–7pm; 10kn), the summer house and garden of sixteenth-century poet Petar Hektorović. There's not much to see save for a cloister surrounding a mullet-packed fishpond, although it's a restful place in which to spend some time.

Buses from the ferry dock (4km west of town) and from Hvar town drop you right on the harbour; walk along the eastern side to reach the **tourist office** (July–Aug daily 8am–10pm; rest of year Mon–Fri 8am–2pm, Sat 10am–noon; ☎021/765-763). The Mistral agency, next to the bus stop (☎021/765-281), will arrange **accommodation** in private rooms.

Jelsa

Five kilometres east of Starigrad, the tiny port and fishing village of **JELSA** sits prettily by a wooded bay. Tucked away behind a nineteenth-century waterfront, the old town rises up the hill, a warren of ancient alleys and lanes. Just off the quayside, the charming sixteenth-century chapel of **Sv Ivan** is crammed into one of the old squares, overhung by the balconies of the surrounding Renaissance buildings. Up from here, the town's main **church** is similarly fortified, and even managed to resist the Turkish attack of 1571, though it's hard to make out the original design as the facade and bell tower were added in the nineteenth century.

Buses stop about 300m inland from the harbour, where you'll find a **tourist office** on the western side (June–Sept daily 9am–7pm; rest of year 9am–noon; ☎021/761-017). Next door is the Atlas agency (☎021/761-231), which can arrange accommodation in **private rooms**. There's also a **campsite**, the *Mina*, on a promontory overlooking the sea at the eastern end of town.

Korčula

Like so many islands along this coast, **KORČULA** was first settled by the Greeks, who gave it the name Korkyra Melaina or "Black Corfu" for its dark and densely wooded appearance. Even now, it's one of the greenest of the Adriatic islands, and one of the most popular. The island's main settlement is Korčula town, and the rest of the island, although beautifully wild and untouched, lacks any real centres. The main coastal **ferry** drops you right in the harbour of Korčula town. In addition, local ferries travel daily between Split and Vela Luka at the western end of Korčula island, from where there's a connecting bus service to Korčula town. There's also a **direct bus service** (1 daily) from Dubrovnik, which crosses the narrow stretch of water dividing the island from the mainland via car ferry from Orebić.

Korčula town

KORČULA TOWN sits on a beetle-shaped hump of land, a medieval walled city ribbed with a series of narrow streets that branch off the spine of the main street like the veins of a leaf. The Venetians first arrived here in the eleventh century, and stayed, on and off, for nearly eight centuries. Their influence is particularly in evidence in Korčula's old town, which huddles around the **Cathedral of Sv Marko**, squeezed into a space between the buildings that roughly passes for a main square. The cathedral facade is decorated with a gorgeous fluted rose window and a bizarre cornice frilled with strange beasts. The interior, reached through a door framed by statues of Adam and Eve, is one of the loveliest in the region – a curious mixture of styles which range from the Gothic forms of the nave to the Renaissance northern aisle, tacked on some time in the sixteenth century, the whole appealingly squashed into a space quite obviously too small for it. The clutter of artefacts ranges from pikes used against sixteenth-century Algerian corsair Uliz Ali, to paintings that include an altarpiece by Leandro Bassano, in the south aisle, and an early Tintoretto, behind the high altar and difficult to make out. However, the best of the church's treasures have been removed to the **Bishop's Treasury** (daily: summer 9am–1pm & 4–7pm; winter 9am–1pm; 10kn), a couple of doors down. This is one of the best small collections of fine and sacral art in the country, with an exquisite set of paintings, including a striking *Portrait of a Man* by Carpaccio, a perceptive *Virgin and Child* by Bassano, some Tiepolo studies of hands and some Raphael drawings, and a tiny *Madonna* by a local Renaissance artist, Blaž Jurjev of Trogir. There is also a Leonardo da Vinci sketch of a soldier wearing a costume that bears a striking resemblance to that of the Moreška dancers (see opposite). Oddities include an ivory statuette of Mary Queen of Scots, whose skirts open to reveal kneeling figures in doublet and hose. How this got here, no one knows.

Opposite the treasury, a former Venetian palace holds the **Town Museum** (Gradski muzej; Mon–Sat 9am–noon & 5–7pm), whose more modest display contains a plaster cast of a fourth-century BC Greek tablet from Lumbarda – the earliest evidence of civilization on Korčula – and some faded photos featuring Fitzroy Maclean (skinny, cropped, with a beret). Brigadier Maclean was head of an itinerant Allied mission to occupied Yugoslavia. His job, according to Winston Churchill, was to "find out who is killing most Germans and suggest means by which we could help them kill more". Maclean's report supported Tito and the Communists, rather than the reactionary Serbian Četniks, and was instrumental in changing British government policy in their favour. Tito was duly grateful, and after the war exempted Maclean from the usual rules on house purchase by foreigners to allow him to buy a retirement home here on Korčula.

Close by the main square, down a turning to the right, is another remnant from Venetian times, the so-called **House of Marco Polo** (daily 9am–1pm; 10kn). Korčula claims to be the birthplace of Marco Polo – a claim not as extravagant as it might first appear. The Venetians recruited many of their sea captains from their colonies, and Polo was indeed captured by the Genoese off the island in 1298, after which he used his time in prison to write his *Travels*. Whatever the truth of the matter, it seems unlikely that he had any connection with this seventeenth-century house, which is these days little more than an empty shell with some terrible twentieth-century prints on the walls.

Back down the main street, follow the signs to the **Icon Gallery** (Mon–Sat 9am–noon & 4–7pm), where there's a permanent display of icons in the rooms of the All Saints' Brotherhood. Most of the exhibits were looted from the Cretans in the seventeenth century, and the best is the fifteenth-century triptych of *The Passion*.

The nearest **beaches** to the old town are on the headland southeast of town around the *Hotel Marko Polo*, though they're crowded, rocky and uncomfortable. A better bet is to head off by **water taxi** from the old harbour to one of the **Skoji** islands just offshore. The largest and nearest of these is **Badija**, where the track from the quay leads to the shabby *Badija Hotel* and sports complex, incongruously sited in a renovated fifteenth-century Franciscan monastery – to the right of here are some secluded beaches and a couple of basic snack bars. The waters on this side are crystal clear and a favourite pastime is making your own Lilo from the mass of drying seaweed. Water taxis also make regular trips to the islet of **Stupe**, where nudist bathing is possible; the islet also has a restaurant and a couple of bars. If you want to visit the other, more obscure, islets you'll have to negotiate your own price with the boatman and take your own food and water. Camping is forbidden.

PRACTICALITIES

Korčula's **bus station** is 400m southeast of the old town. Work your way round to the northwestern side of the peninsula to find the **tourist office** (June–Sept daily 7am–8pm; rest of year Mon–Sat 8am–noon & 5–8pm, Sun 8am–noon; ☎021/715-701), although rooms are handled by Marco Polo (☎021/715-400) between the bus station and the entrance to the old town. Cheapest of the **hotels** is the *Park*, a package-tour-orientated place in a bay southeast of the centre (☎020/726-004; ⑤); while the *Korčula* (☎050/711-078; ⑦) is a slightly grander affair on the harbourfront on the western side of the old town. The nearest **campsite** is *Autocamp Kalac* (☎020/711-336), about 2km southeast of town and reached by hourly buses for Lumbarda.

Not surprisingly, most **restaurants** in the old town tend to be expensive. One exception is the excellent *Adio Mare*, near Marco Polo's House, one of the best restaurants on the coast and justifiably popular; arrive early to make sure of a table. A good second choice is the restaurant *Planjak*, a couple of minutes from the main gate into the old city, down towards the harbour. If they're both full, try the pizza restaurant at the top of the stairway by the *Hotel Korčula*. Wherever you eat, do try some of the **local wines**, some of which are excellent: look out for the delicious dry white Grk from Lumbarda, Posip from Smokvica, or the headache-inducing red Dingač from Postup on Peljesac.

Performances of Korčula's famous **folk dance**, the **Moreška**, take place outside the *Park Hotel* every Thursday evening (9pm) during the summer. The dance is the story of a conflict between the Turks (in red) and the Moors (in black): the heroine, Bula (literally "veiled woman"), is kidnapped by the evil foreign king and his army, and her betrothed tries to win her back in a ritualized sword fight which takes place within a shifting circle of dancers. The dance gets gradually more and more frantic, the swords clashing furiously, rising to a climax in which the evil king is forced to surrender while his adversary unchains Bula and carries her off, triumphant.

Dubrovnik

DUBROVNIK is a beautifully preserved fortified town pressed against the sea within magnificent medieval walls. Considered the jewel in the crown of Croatian tourism, Dubrovnik was the subject of a largely spiteful attack by Yugoslav forces in autumn 1991. Bombarding the town from the rocky heights above, and aided by a blockade by the Yugoslav navy, they subjected Dubrovnik to an eight-month siege that was only broken by the UN-mediated ceasefire of May 1992. Now almost totally rebuilt and restored, the town is back on the tourist map with a vengeance.

Dubrovnik was first settled by Roman refugees in the early seventh century, when the nearby city of Epidaurus (now Cavtat) was sacked by the Slavs. They took up residence on the southern part of what is now the old town, then an island, and gave their settlement the name Ragusa. The Slavs, meanwhile, settled on the wooded mainland opposite, from which the name Dubrovnik (from *dubrava*, meaning a "glade") came. Before long the slim channel between the two was filled in and the two sides merged, producing a Latin-Slav culture unique to the region. Sandwiched between Muslim and Christian powers, Ragusa exploited its favourable position on the Adriatic with a maritime and commercial genius unmatched anywhere else in Europe at the time, and by the mid-fourteenth century, having shaken off the yoke of first the Byzantines and then the Venetians, had become a successful and self-con-

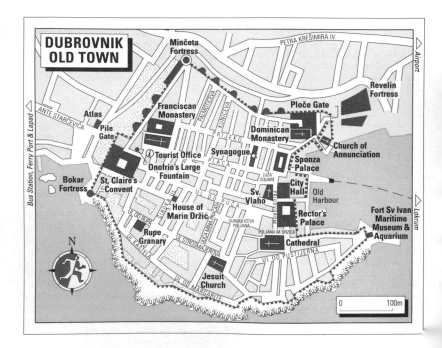

tained city state, its merchants trading far and wide. Dubrovnik fended off the attentions of the Ottoman Empire with cunning and pragmatic obsequiousness – and regular payment of enormous tributes. It continued to prosper until 1667, when an earthquake killed around 5000 people and destroyed many of the city's buildings. Though the city-state survived, it fell into decline and, in 1808, it was formally dissolved by Napoleon.

Arrival, information and accommodation

Both **ferry and bus terminals** are located in the port suburb of Gruž, 3km west of the old town. The main western entrance to the old town, the Pile Gate, is a thirty-minute slog along ul Ante Starčevića and you'd be better off catching a bus – #1a and #3 from the ferry terminal, #1a, #3 or #6 from behind the bus station. Flat-fare tickets for local buses are bought from the driver (exact change only; 6kn) or from newspaper kiosks (5kn). Dubrovnik's **airport** is situated some 20km south of the city, close to the resort town of Cavtat; Croatia Airways buses meet all arrivals and run to the town bus station, returning from there ninety minutes before each departure.

The **tourist office** in the old town just inside the Pile Gate (Mon–Sat 8am–7.30pm; ☎020/426-354), is a private venture rather than a tourist association-sponsored affair, and sells city maps and can book **private rooms**. There are numerous other accommodation agencies, too: Gulliver, Obala S. Radića 31 (☎020/411-088) is conveniently located opposite the ferry terminal; and Atlas has an office outside the Pile Gate at Starčevića 1 (☎020/422-222), and another at the eastern entrance to the old town at F. Suplia 2 (☎020/432-093). You'll probably be approached by landladies offering rooms at both the bus station and the ferry terminal – they're worth considering if you arrive late at night, and will probably work out cheaper than those obtained through agencies. There's a basic **youth hostel** at bana Jelačića 15/17 (☎020/23241; ②) – head up Ante Starčevića from the bus station and turn uphill to the right after five minutes. There's a dearth of affordable **hotels** near the old town, and you're restricted to staying a walk or bus ride away. *Lero*, 1.5km west of Pile Gate at Iva Vojnovića 14 (☎020/411-455; ④) has modern en-suites with TV; while *Petka*, Obala Stjepan Radića 38 (020/418-008; ④) has smaller rooms but has the advantage of being opposite the ferry terminal. Most of the big package hotels are on the Lapad peninsula 5km west of the Pile Gate (bus #6). *Zagreb*, Šetalište Kralja Zvonimira 27 (summer only; ☎020/431-011; ④), is a pleasant, turn-of-the-century building near Lapad beach; the nearby *Sumratin*, Šetalište Kralja Zvonimira 31 (☎020/416-950; ④) is plainer but reasonably comfortable.

The City

The main entrance to Dubrovnik's old town (stari grad) is the **Pile Gate**, a fifteenth-century construction decorated with a statue of St Blaise (Sv Vlaho), the city's protector, set in a niche above the arch. Inside, and accessible from the Pile Gate, the best way to get your bearings is by making a tour of the **city walls** (gradske zidine; daily: summer 9am–7.30pm, winter 10am–3pm; 10kn), 25m high and with all its towers intact. Some parts date back to the tenth century, but most of the original construction was undertaken in the twelfth and thirteenth centuries, with subsequent rebuildings (and reinforcements) being carried out over the years. Of the various towers and bastions that punctuate the walls, the **Minčeta fortress**, which marks the northeastern side, is perhaps the most impressive, built in 1455 to plans drawn up by Dalmatian architect Juraj Dalmatinac and the Italian Michelozzi.

Within the walls, Dubrovnik is a sea of roofs faded into a pastel patchwork, punctured now and then by a sculpted dome or tower. At ground level, just inside the Pile Gate, **Onofrio's Large Fountain**, built in 1444, is a bulbous-domed affair at which visitors to this hygiene-conscious city had to wash themselves before they were admitted any further. Across the street is the fourteenth-century **Franciscan Monastery** complex (Franjevački samostan; free access); its treasury (daily 9am–5pm; 5kn) holds some fine Gothic reliquaries and manuscripts tracing the development of musical scoring, together with relics from the apothecary's shop, dating from 1317, which claims to be the oldest in Europe.

From outside the monastery church, **Stradun** (also known as Placa), the city's main street, runs dead straight across the old town, its limestone surface polished to a slippery shine by the tramping of thousands of feet. Its far end broadens into the pigeon-choked **Luža Square**, the centre of the medieval town and even today hub of much of its activity. On the left, the **Sponza Palace** was once the customs house and mint, a building which grew in storeys as Dubrovnik grew in wealth, with a facade that's an elegant weld of florid Venetian Gothic and quieter Renaissance forms; dating from 1522, its majestic courtyard is given over to contemporary art exhibitions (opening times and prices variable). Across the square, the Baroque-style **Crkva Sv Vlaha**, built in 1714 to replace an earlier church, serves as a graceful counterpoint to the palace. Outside the church stands the carved figure of an armoured knight, usually referred to as **Orlando's Column**. Surprisingly for such an insignificant-looking object, this was the focal point of the city-state: erected in 1428 as a morale-boosting monument to freedom, it was here that government ordinances were promulgated and punishments executed. Orlando's right arm was also the standard measurement of length (the Ragusan cubit); at the base of the column you can still see a line of the same length cut in the stone. On the eastern side of the square a Gothic arch leads through to an alley which winds past the **Dominican monastery**. Here, an arcaded courtyard filled with palms and orange trees leads to a small **museum** (daily 9am–5pm; 5kn), displaying outstanding examples of local sixteenth-century religious art.

Back on Luža, a street leads round the back of Sv Vlaho towards the fifteenth-century **Rector's Palace** (Knežev dvor), the seat of the Ragusan government, in which the incumbent Rector sat out his month's term of office. The building was, effectively, a prison: the Rector had no real power and could only leave with the say-so of the nobles who elected him. From the palace atrium an imposing staircase leads up to the balcony; the former state rooms lead off here, including the rooms of the city council, the Rector's study and the quarters of the palace guard. Today these are given over to the **City Museum** (Gradski muzej; Mon–Sat 9am–1pm; 10kn), though for the most part it's a rather paltry collection, with mediocre sixteenth-century paintings and dull furniture. The highlight is the work of the fifteenth-century Dalmatian artist, Blaž Jurjev, notably a polyptych of *Our Lady*.

Across the square from the palace, Dubrovnik's seventeenth-century **Cathedral** is a rather plain building, although there's an impressive Titian polyptych of *The Assumption* inside. The **Treasury** (daily 9am–noon & 3–6pm; 5kn) boasts a twelfth-century skull reliquary of St Blaise, an exquisite piece in the shape of a Byzantine crown, stuck with portraits of saints and frosted with delicate gold and enamel filigree work. Even more eye-catching is a bizarre fifteenth-century *Allegory of the Flora and Fauna of Dubrovnik* in the form of a jug and basin festooned with snakes, fish and lizards clambering over thick clumps of seaweed.

From the cathedral, it's a short walk through to the small town harbour, dominated by the monolithic hulk of the **Fort of Sv Ivan**. The fort has been refurbished to house a downstairs **aquarium** (Akvarium; daily 10am–6pm; 15kn), full of local marine life; upstairs is the **maritime museum** (Pomorski muzej; Tues–Sun 9am–1pm; 10kn), which traces the history of Ragusan sea power through a display of naval artefacts and model boats.

Walking back east from here, you skirt one of the city's oldest quarters, **Pustijerna**, much of which predates the seventeenth-century earthquake. On the far side, the church of **Sv Ignacija**, Dubrovnik's largest, is a Jesuit confection, modelled, like most Jesuit places of worship, on the enormous church of Gesù in Rome. The steps that lead down from here also had a Roman model – the Spanish Steps – and they sweep down to **Gundulićeva Poljana**, the square behind the cathedral which is the site of the city's morning fruit and vegetable market. The statue in the middle is of Ivan Gundulić, the early seventeenth-century poet and native of Dubrovnik who wrote a long poem, *Osman*, on the battles between the Turks and Christian Slavs, and after whom the square is named. From here, Od Puča leads west through the maze of streets that make up the city centre, stepped alleys branching right to meet the southern sea-walls. One of these, Široka Ulica, leads to the **house of Marin Držić** at no. 7 (Mon–Fri 9am–1pm, Sat 10am–noon; 10kn). Dubrovnik's greatest sixteenth-century playwright is remembered here in an imaginative display (featuring English headphone commentary and a short video), which manages to conjure up something of the city's Renaissance past. The main city **beach** is a short walk east of the old town – noisy and crowded with radios and flirting adolescents. There's an equally crowded, but somewhat cleaner, beach on the Lapad peninsula 5km to the west. The best bet is to catch one of the **boats** from the old city jetty (May–Oct 9am–6pm, every 30min, journey time 10min; 15kn return) to the wooded island of **Lokrum**. Reputedly the island where Richard the Lionheart was shipwrecked, Lokrum is crisscrossed by shady paths overhung by pines. Extensive rocky beaches run along the eastern end of the island, and there's a nudist section (FKK) at the far eastern tip.

Eating and drinking

For self-catering, there are regular fruit and vegetable **markets** (Mon–Sat mornings) on Gundulićeva Poljana and on the waterfront at Gruž you can also buy fresh fish as soon as the boats come in. For **snacks**, try the sandwich bars lining the alleys running uphill from Stradun, notably *Kaktus* on Vetranovićeva. There's no shortage of **restaurants** in the old town. Prijeko, the street running parallel to Stradun to the north, is especially stacked with eateries. *Moby Dick*, half way along Prijeko, is a dependable place for grilled meat and fish dishes; while *Rozarij*, tucked away on the corner of Prijeko and Zlatarska, is cosy, intimate and good for fresh fish. *Jadran*, behind Onofrio's fountain, offers a wide range of Croatian standards and has outdoor seating in the cloister of a former nunnery; while *Dubrovnik*, south of Stradun at M. Kaboge 5, has a pleasant rooftop terrace.

The pavement cafés at the eastern end of Stradun are the places for daytime and evening **drinking**, although none of them have much atmosphere if the weather's not suitable for sitting outside. On such occasions it's best to head for the smaller café/bars in the backstreets: *Mirage*, Bunićeva Poljana, is a popular meeting point for Dubrovnik youth; while *Hard Jazz Café Troubadur* on the same square caters for a slightly older crowd. *Otok*, Pobijana 8, is an alternative cultural centre whose café/bar attracts bohemian types. Outside the centre, ulica bana Jelačića, just above the bus station, is lined with bars buzzing until late on summer evenings – although none stand out individually. For clubbing, *Arsenal*, outside the Pile Gate, stages all-night rave and techno events on summer weekends – posters plastered around the entrance will provide some idea of what's on.

The Dubrovnik Festival

Dubrovnik's **Summer Festival** (early July to late Aug) is a good, if crowded, time to be in town, with classical concerts and theatre performances in most of Dubrovnik's courtyards, squares and bastions – sometimes the only chance to see the inside of them. Seats can be pricey and are often booked well in advance. For further details contact Dubrovački ljetni festival, Poljana Paska Miličevića 1 (☎020/412-288).

Listings

Airlines Croatia Airlines, Brsalje 9 (☎020/413-777; Mon–Fri 8am–4pm, Sat 9am–noon).

Bus station put Republike 38 (☎020/23088).

Car rental Budget, Obala S. Radića 20 (☎020/411-649); Gulliver, Obala S. Radića 31 (☎020/411-088)

Exchange Dubrovačka Banka, Stradun (Mon–Fri 7.30am–1pm & 2–7pm, Sat 7.30am–1pm); Gospodarsko-Kreditna Banka, Pile Gate (daily 8am–8pm).

Ferries Tickets from Jadrolinija, Obala S. Radića 40 (☎020/418-000); and Globetour, Stradun (☎020/428-992).

Left luggage At the bus station (daily 4.50am–9.30pm).

Post office/telephone Ante Starčevića 2 (Mon–Fri 7am–8pm, Sat 7am–7pm, Sun 8am–2pm).

Taxis Ranks outside the bus station and the Pile Gate. To book, call ☎24343.

Travel agents Atlas, Ante Starčevića 1 (☎020/442-222).

travel details

Trains
Zagreb to: Pula (2 daily; 6hr 40min); Rijeka (6 daily; 4hr); Split (3 daily; 9hr–10hr 30min).
Pula to: Zagreb (2 daily; 6hr 40min).

Buses
Zagreb to: Dubrovnik (8 daily; 11hr); Opatija (4 daily; 4hr 30min); Poreč (6 daily; 5hr); Pula (10 daily; 6hr); Rijeka (hourly; 4hr); Rovinj (1 daily; 9hr); Split (hourly; 7-9hr).
Dubrovnik to: Korčula (1 daily; 3hr 30min); Split (12 daily; 4hr 30min); Zagreb (8 daily; 11hr).
Hvar town to: Jelsa (13 daily; 55min); Starigrad (7 daily; 35min).
Poreč to: Opatija (8 daily; 4hr); Rijeka (8 daily; 4hr 30min); Pula (10 daily; 2hr); Zagreb (6 daily; 7hr).
Pula to: Opatija (hourly; 2hr); Poreč (10 daily; 2hr); Rijeka (hourly; 2hr 30min); Rovinj (hourly; 1hr); Split (4 daily; 10hr); Zagreb (10 daily; 6hr).
Rijeka to: Dubrovnik (3 daily; 13hr); Pula (hourly; 2hr 30min); Split (3 daily; 8hr); Zagreb (hourly; 4hr).

Rovinj to: Poreč (6 daily; 50min); Pula (hourly; 1hr); Rijeka (7 daily; 5hr).
Split to: Dubrovnik (12 daily; 4hr 30min); Pula (3 daily; 10hr); Rijeka (3 daily; 8hr); Zagreb (hourly; 7-9hr).
Supetar to: Bol (5 daily; 1hr).

Ferries
Dubrovnik to: Stari Grad, Hvar (1 daily in summer; 3–4 times weekly in winter; 7hr); Korčula (1 daily in summer; 3–4 times weekly in winter; 4hr); Rijeka (1 daily in summer; 3–4 times weekly in winter; 21hr); Split (1 daily in summer; 3–4 times weekly in winter; 8hr).
Rijeka to: Dubrovnik (1 daily in summer; 3–4 times weekly in winter; 20hr); Korčula (1 daily in summer; 3–4 times weekly in winter; 18hr); Split (1 daily in summer; 3–4 times weekly in winter; 12hr); Hvar (1 daily in summer; 3–4 times weekly in winter; 14hr).
Split to: Dubrovnik (1 daily; 8hr); Hvar (1 daily; 2hr); Korčula (2 daily; 4hr); Rijeka (1 daily; 12hr); Stari Grad, Hvar (4 daily; 2hr); Supetar, Brač (7 daily; 1hr).

CHAPTER 6

CZECH REPUBLIC

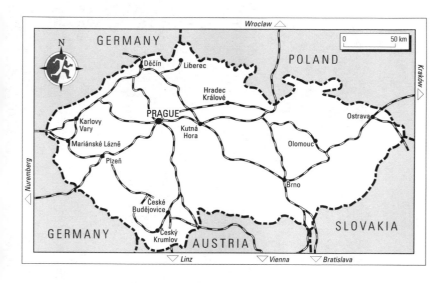

Introduction

Czechoslovakia's "Velvet Revolution" in November 1989 was probably the most unequivocably positive of eastern Europe's anti-Communist upheavals, as the Czechs and Slovaks shrugged off 41 years of Communist rule without a shot being fired. But the euphoria and unity of those first few months evaporated more quickly than anyone could have imagined. Just three years on, the country split into two separate states: the **Czech Republic** and Slovakia. The Czechs – always the most urbane, agnostic and liberal of the Slav nations – have fared well, enjoying much longer periods of political and economic stability, and attracting more Western investment than their former eastern bloc rivals.

Almost untouched by this century's wars, the capital, **Prague**, is justifiably one of the most popular destinations in Europe. An incredibly beautiful city with a wealth of architecture from Gothic cathedrals and Baroque palaces to Art Nouveau cafés and Cubist villas, it's also a lively meeting place for young people from all over Europe. The lush, surrounding countryside of **Bohemia** is studded with well-preserved medieval towns, especially in the south around **České Budějovice**. In the west, you'll find the old watering-holes of the European aristocracy, the spa towns of **Karlovy Vary** and **Mariánské Lázně**. The country's eastern province, **Moravia**, is every bit as beautiful, only less touristed. **Olomouc** is the most attractive town here, but **Brno**, the regional capital, has its own peculiar pleasures.

Information and maps

Prague has an excellent chain of **tourist offices** specifically set up to give information to foreign visitors (look for the "PIS" sign). Most other cities and towns have their own tourist offices (*informační centrum*); they are generally open Mon–Fri 9am–noon & 1–5pm, plus Sat (and even occasionally Sun) mornings in high season. A comprehensive range of **maps** is available in the country. You can buy them, often very cheaply, from bookshops and some hotels – ask for a *plán města* (town plan) or *mapa okoli* (regional map). For road maps, the 1:100,000 *Euroatlas* produced by Kartografie Praha is the best, marking all campsites and petrol stations. For **hiking**, the 1:100,000 *turistická mapa* series details the country's complex network of footpaths.

Money and banks

The **currency** in the Czech Republic is the Czech crown, or *koruna česká* (kč), which is divided into one hundred heller or *halér* (h). Coins come in 10h, 20h, 50h, 1kč, 2kč, 5kč, 10kč, 20kč and 50kč; notes as 20kč, 50kč, 100kč, 200kč, 500kč, 1000kč, 2000kč and 5000kč. The crown is now fully convertible, though you may find problems getting hold of any in foreign banks.

Banks are the best places to change money; they are open Mon–Fri 8am–5pm, often with a break at lunchtime. **Travellers' cheques** in US dollars or Deutschmarks are undoubtedly the safest way of carrying money, though it's a good idea to keep some hard currency in **cash** for emergencies. **Credit cards** are accepted in most hotels, upmarket restaurants and some shops; you can also use them to get cash from certain ATMs.

Communications

Most **post offices** (*pošta*) are open Mon–Fri 7am–5pm, Sat 7am–noon. Look out for the right sign to avoid queuing unnecessarily: *známky* (stamps), *dopisy* (letters) or *balky* (parcels). You can also buy stamps from tobacconists and kiosks, though often only for domestic mail. **Poste restante** services are available in major towns, but remember to write *Pošta 1* (the main office), followed by the name of the town.

The majority of **public phones** only take phone cards (*telefonní karty*), available in 50, 100 or 150 units from post offices, tobacconists and some shops. You can make local or international calls from all card phones, all of which have instructions in English. **International calls** are charged at a rate of about $1 a minute to the UK, and $2 a minute to the US, Canada and Australia.

Getting around

The most pleasant way of travelling around the Czech Republic is by train – it's scenic, safe and inexpensive. If you're in a hurry, however, buses are nearly always quicker and more frequent.

■ Trains

The Czech Republic has one of the most comprehensive rail networks in Europe. Czech Railways (České dráhy or ČD), run two main types of **trains**: *rychlík* trains are faster, stopping only at major towns, while *osobní* trains stop at just about every station and can travel as slowly as 30kph. In addition, there are fast InterCity (IC), and EuroCity (EC) expresses, for which you must pay a supplement. **Tickets** (*jízdenky*) for domestic journeys can be bought at the station (*nádraží*) before or on the day of departure. Fares are still cheap – a second-class single from Prague to

Brno costs around £5/$8 – but rising. AD runs reasonably priced **sleepers** to and from a number of cities in neighbouring countries. You must, however, book as far in advance as possible and in any case no later than six hours before departure. InterRail passes are valid; Eurail passes are not.

■ Buses

Regional **buses** (*autobus*) – mostly run by the state bus company, Česká státní automobilová doprava (ČSAD) – travel to most destinations, with private companies like ČEBUS providing an alternative on popular inter-city routes. Bus stations are usually next to the train station, and if there's no separate terminal you'll have to buy your ticket from the driver. It's essential to book your ticket in advance if you're travelling at the weekend or early in the morning on one of the main routes.

■ Driving and motorcycling

With vehicle ownership still out of reach of most of the population, travelling by **car** remains a relaxing way to tour the Czech Republic. **Speed limits** are 130kph on motorways, 90kph on other roads, and 50kph in all cities, towns and villages. Seat belts are compulsory at all times, and you are not allowed to drink any alcohol if you're driving. If you want to travel on any motorway within the Czech Republic, you'll need a **motorway tax disc** (*dálniční známka*), which currently costs around 800kč a year and is available from all border crossings and most post offices and petrol stations. **Fuel** is fairly cheap by European standards; *natural* is the word used for lead-free petrol. If you **break down**, dial ☎154. The major **car rental** firms currently charge around £250/$400 per week for a small car with unlimited mileage, though local firms offer much more reasonable rates.

Accommodation

Accommodation remains the most expensive aspect of travelling in the Czech Republic. There is no organized youth hostel system, as such, though some places are now affiliated with Hostelling International. Private rooms are available all over the country, and more often than not the local tourist office will help to book a room.

■ Hotels and private rooms

Hotels are still occasionally priced up for foreigners and are in any case fairly expensive, especially in Prague. The old state hotels are slowly being refurbished by their new owners, and many new hotels and pensions have opened, particularly in the more heavily touristed areas. In the newer places, continental breakfast is normally included.

Private rooms are available in Prague, Brno and several other towns on the tourist trail, and are often the best bet. Elsewhere, just keep your eyes peeled for signs saying *Zimmer Frei*. Prices start at around 400kč per person per night, but expect to pay more in Prague.

■ Hostels and campsites

Prague now has a number of **youth hostels** which offer varying degrees of discomfort; otherwise hostels (*turistická ubytovna*) are mostly occupied by migrant workers or sports groups. The student travel organization CKM can arrange cheap **student accommodation** in the big university towns during July and August and usually charge 200kč per person for dorm beds.

Campsites, known as *autokemp*, are plentiful all over the Czech Republic; the facilities are often basic and the ones known as *tábořiště* are even more rudimentary. Most have **bungalows** (*chata*) for anything upwards of 500kč for two people. Very few sites remain open all year, and most don't open until May, closing mid- to late September. Even though prices are still inflated for foreigners, camping charges are minimal.

Food and drink

Forty years of culinary isolation under the Communists introduced few innovations to the Germanic-influenced **Czech cuisine**, with its predilection for big slabs of meat served with lashings of gravy, dumplings and sauerkraut.

ACCOMMODATION PRICE CODES

Throughout this guide, accommodation is priced on a scale of ① to ⑨, the number indicating the lowest price per night a single person could expect to pay in that establishment in high season. With hostels this is the nightly rate per person; with hotels, the price is arrived at by dividing the cost of the cheapest double room by two. The prices indicated by the codes are as follows:

① under £5 / $8	④ £15–20 / $24–32	⑦ £30–35 / $48–56
② £5–10 / $8–16	⑤ £20–25 / $32–40	⑧ £35–40 / $56–64
③ £10–15 / $16–24	⑥ £25–30 / $40–48	⑨ £40 / $64 and over

■ Food

Most Czechs get up around 5am or 6am, so they seldom start the day with anything other than a quick cup of coffee. The usual mid-morning **snack** at the **bufet** (stand-up canteen) is the ubiquitous *párek*, a frankfurter dipped in mustard and served with a white roll (*v rohlíku*). Other popular snacks include *bramborák*, a potato patty with flecks of bacon, and *smažený sýr* – a slab of melted cheese fried in breadcrumbs and served with a roll (*v housce*).

Like the Austrians who once ruled them, the Czechs have a sweet tooth, and coffee and cake is part of the daily ritual. **Coffee** (*káva*) is drunk black and described rather hopefully as "Turkish" or *turecká*. The **cake shop** (*cukrárna*) is an important part of the country's social life, particularly on Sunday mornings when it's often the only place that's open. Whatever the season, Czechs have to have their daily fix of **ice cream** (*zmrzlina*), dispensed from window kiosks in the sides of buildings.

Outside of Prague, eating out is inexpensive; **restaurants** (*restaurace*) nearly always display their menus and prices outside. They serve hot meals nonstop from about 11am until 11pm (more like 10pm outside Prague), though the choice of food is often widest at lunch (noon–2pm), traditionally the main meal of the day. Most **pubs** (*pivnice*) also serve a few simple hot dishes, as do **wine cellars** (*vinárna*).

Most lunchtime menus start with **soup** (*polévka*), one of the country's culinary strong points. **Main courses** are overwhelmingly based on pork or beef, but one treat is carp (*kapr*), traditional at Christmas and cheaply and widely offered just about everywhere, along with trout (*pstruh*). Main courses are served with **dumplings** (*knedlíky*) or **vegetables**, most commonly potatoes and sauerkraut. With the exception of *palačinky* (pancakes) filled with chocolate or fruit and cream, **desserts**, where they exist at all, can be pretty uninspiring.

■ Drink

Even the most simple *bufet* in the Czech Lands almost invariably has draught **beer** (*pivo*). The *pivnice* (which close around 10 or 11pm) is a predominantly male affair, where much heavy drinking goes on. Women tend to head for the more mixed atmosphere of the **wine bars** (*vinárna*), which have slightly later opening hours and often double as upmarket restaurants or nightclubs.

The Czech Republic tops the world league table of **beer** consumption, even beating the Germans – hardly surprising since its beer ranks among the best in the world. The most natural starting point for any beer tour is the Bohemian city of **Plzeň** (Pilsen),

whose bottom-fermented local beer is the original Pils. The other big brewing town is **České Budějovice** (Budweis), home to Budvar, a mild beer by Bohemian standards but still leagues ahead of the American Budweiser.

The republic also produces a modest selection of medium-quality **wines**, the largest wine-producing region is southern Moravia. The home-production of **brandies** is a national pastime, resulting in some almost terminally strong brews. The most famous – and peculiar – Czech spirit is *becherovka*, a medicinal-tasting herbal tipple from Karlovy Vary.

Opening hours and holidays

Shops in the Czech Republic are open Mon–Fri 9am–5pm, with some shops and most supermarkets staying open till 6pm or later. Smaller shops close for lunch for an hour or so sometime between noon and 2pm, while others stay open late on Thursdays. Shops that open on Saturday tend to close for the day at noon or 1pm. Count on most shops being closed on Sunday.

The basic opening hours for **castles and monasteries** are Tues–Sun 9am–noon, & 2–5pm; opening is often restricted to weekends and holidays in April and October; and most close for the rest of the year. In Prague the main museums open Tues–Sun 10am–6pm, though there are exceptions. Whatever the time of year, if you want to see the interior of a building, nine times out of ten you'll be forced to go on a **guided tour** (nearly always in Czech only, occasionally German) that will last at least 45 minutes. Ask for an *anglický text*, an often unintentionally hilarious English resumé. Entrance tickets rarely cost more than 50–100kč, so prices are not quoted in the text except where the entrance fee is prohibitive; the last tour usually leaves an hour before the advertised closing time.

Public holidays include Jan 1; Easter Monday; May 1; May 8; July 5 (the day saints Cyril and Methodius introduced Christianity into the Czech Lands); July 6 (the anniversary of the death of Jan Hus); Oct 28 (the anniversary of the Foundation of the Republic); Dec 24–26.

Emergencies

Since the revolution, public confidence in the **police** (*policie*) has declined as the crime level has risen. For tourists, theft from cars and hotel rooms is the biggest worry. The best way to protect against such disasters is to take out travel insurance; report any thefts to the nearest police station immediately in order to get a statement detailing what you've lost for your insurance claim. Everyone is obliged to carry some form of ID and you should carry your **passport** with you at all times, though you're unlikely to get stopped unless you're driving.

Minor ailments can be easily dealt with by the **chemist** (*lékárna*), but language is likely to be a problem outside the capital. If it's a repeat prescription you want, take any empty bottles or remaining pills along with you. If the chemist can't help, they'll be able to direct you to a **hospital** (*nemocnice*). If you do have to pay for any medication, keep the receipts for claiming on your insurance once you're home.

EMERGENCY NUMBERS

Police ☎150; Ambulance ☎155; Fire ☎158.

PRAGUE

Prague (Praha) is one of the least "eastern" European cities you could imagine. Architecturally it is a revelation: few other cities anywhere in Europe look so good – and no other European capital can present six hundred years of architecture so completely untouched by natural disaster or war. Hardly surprising, then, that a staggering ninety percent of Western visitors spend all their time in and around the capital and that Praguers exude an air of confidence about their city.

Prague rose to prominence in the ninth century under Prince Bořivoj, its first Christian ruler and founder of the Přemyslid dynasty. His grandson, Prince Václav, became the Good "King" Wenceslas of the Christmas carol and the country's patron saint. The city prospered from its position on the central European trade routes, but it was after the dynasty died out in 1306 that Prague enjoyed its **golden age**. In just thirty years Charles IV of Luxembourg transformed it into one of the most important cities in fourteenth-century Europe, founding an entire new town, Nové Město, to accommodate the influx of students. Following the execution of the reformist preacher Jan Hus in 1415, the country became engulfed in **religious wars**, and trouble broke out again between the Protestant nobles and the Catholic Habsburgs in 1618. The full force of the Counter-Reformation was brought to bear on the city's people, though the spurt of Baroque rebuilding that went with it gave Prague its most striking architectural aspect.

After two centuries as little more than a provincial town in the Habsburg Empire, Prague was dragged out of the doldrums by the **Industrial Revolution** and the **národní obrození**, the Czech national revival that led to the foundation of the **First Republic** in 1918. After World War II, which it survived substantially unscathed, Prague disappeared completely behind the Iron Curtain. The city briefly re-emerged onto the world stage during the cultural blossoming of the **Prague Spring** in 1968, but the decisive break came in November 1989, when a peaceful student demonstration, brutally broken up by the police, triggered off the **Velvet Revolution** which eventually toppled the Communist government. The exhilarating popular unity of that period is now history, but there is still a great sense of new-found potential in the capital.

Arrival and information

Prague's **airport**, Ruzyně, is 10km northwest of the city. The cheapest way of getting into town is by bus #119 (every 10–15min), a thirty-minute ride to the Dejvická metro station at the end of metro line A. Alternatively, there's the **express minibus** (every 30min), which stops first at Dejvická metro station, and ends up at náměstí Republiky (90kč). The express minibuses will also take you straight to your hotel if you wish for around 350kč per drop-off – a bargain if there's a few of you. Arriving by **train** from the west, you're most likely to end up at the **Praha hlavní nádraží**, on the edge of Nové Město and Vinohrady. It's only a short walk to Wenceslas Square from here, and there's also a metro station inside the station. International expresses, passing through Prague, often stop only at **Praha-Holešovice**, north of the city centre at the end of metro line C. Some trains from Moravia and Slovakia wind up at the central **Masarykovo nádraží**, near náměstí Republiky; and provincial trains from the south usually get no further than **Praha-Smíchov**, connected to the centre by metro line B. There are lockers and **left-luggage** offices (open 24hr) at all these stations. The main **bus station** is Praha-Florenc, on the eastern edge of Nové Město, on metro line B.

The best place to go for information is the **Prague Information Service**, or PIS (Pražská informační služba), whose main branch is at Na příkopě 20 (Mon–Fri 8.30am–7pm, Sat & Sun 9am–5pm). The staff speak English and will be able to answer most inquiries, arrange private accommodation, sell maps and guides and act as a ticket agency. As for listings, it's worth getting hold of the free English-language monthly *Culture in Prague*, or the fortnightly *Do města/Downtown*. The English-language newspaper *Prague Post*, which comes out every Wednesday, also has a good selective listings section. There are additional PIS offices in the main train station, and underneath the astronomical clock on Staroměstské náměstí.

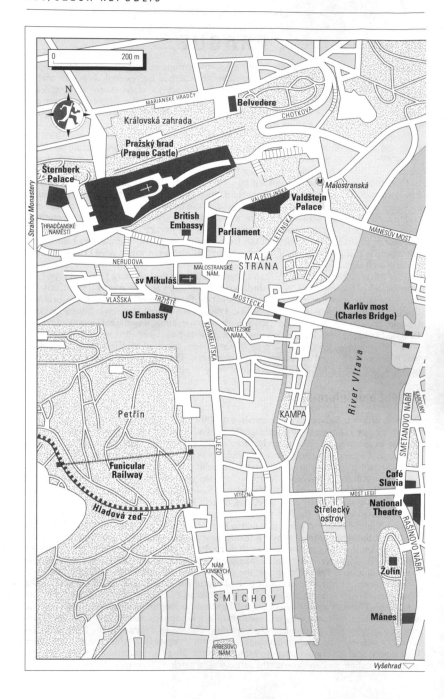

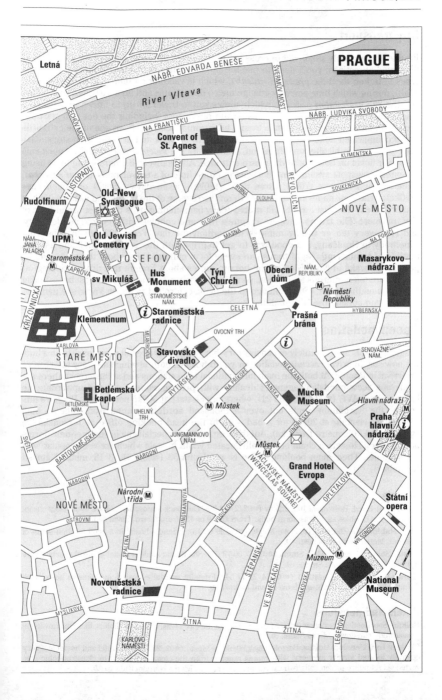

City transport

Prague is reasonably small, but to cross the city quickly, or reach some of the more widely dispersed attractions, you'll need to use the public transport system. There are two main types of **ticket**: the 12kč *přestupní jízdenka*, which is valid for an hour (ninety minutes off-peak), during which time you may change metro lines, trams and buses as often as you like, and the 8kč *nepřestupní jízdenka*, which allows you to travel for up to fifteen minutes on a single tram or bus, or up to four stops on the metro (not including the one you start at). Tickets must be bought in advance from a tobacconist, kiosk or from one of the extraordinarily complicated ticket machines inside all metro stations and at some tram stops; basically, you want to hit the top left button, followed by the *výdej/enter* button. You must validate your ticket on board or at the metro entrance. Alternatively, if you're going to be using the public transport system a lot, it's worth getting hold of a **travel pass** (*denní jízdenka*), available for 24 hours (70kč), three days (180kč), seven days (250kč) or fifteen days (280kč); write your name and date of birth on the reverse of the ticket, and validate it when you first use it. The fast Soviet-built **metro** (daily 5am–midnight) is the most useful form of city transport. The **trams** navigate Prague's hills and cobbles with remarkable dexterity, and run every ten or twenty minutes throughout the day. Tram #22, which runs from Vinohrady to Hradčany, is a good way to get to grips with the lie of the land, and a cheap method of sightseeing. Night trams run every forty minutes throughout the night, and all pass by Lazarská in Nové Město. The horror stories about Prague **taxi** drivers ripping off tourists are too numerous to mention, so if you do wish to take a cab, your best bet is to flag one down on the street, rather than go to the mafia-controlled ranks on Václavské náměstí, Národní and outside the Obecní dům.

Accommodation

Prague's **hotels** are extremely expensive for what you get. As a result most tourists on a budget now stay in private accommodation or youth hostels, both of which are easy to organize on arrival in Prague. At both the main international train stations and at the airport, there are numerous accommodation agencies dealing with **private rooms** (② and upwards): the largest one is AVE (☎02/24 22 35 21), where prices start at 500kč per person. Prague's university, the Karolinum, rents out over a thousand **student rooms** from June to mid-September, starting at 200kč for a bed – go to the head booking office at Terronská 28, (☎02/24 31 11 05; metro Dejvická). Another organization specializing in summer-only dorms is Traveller's Hostels, a chain of centrally located youth hostels which are very popular with US students. Their main booking office is at Dlouhá 33 (☎02/231 13 18; metro Náměstí Republiky).

Hostels

Clown and Bard, Bořivojova 102, Žižkov (☎02/27 24 36). Laid-back atmosphere, clean, undeniably cheap, and rents out doubles as well as dorm beds. Tram #5, #9 or #26 from metro Hlavní nádraží. ②.

Club Habitat, Na Zbořenci 10, Nové Město (☎02/29 03 15). Friendly hostel in a good location south of Národní. Metro Karlovo náměstí. ②.

Hostel Sokol, Újezd 40, Malá Strana (☎02/57 00 73 97). Shambolic student hostel in Sokol sports centre right in the heart of Malá Strana. ①.

Libra Q, Senovážné náměstí 21 (☎02/24 23 17 54). Friendly, centrally located, inexpensive hostel with dorm beds and cheap doubles. Metro Hlavní nádraží. ②.

Hotels and pensions

Balkán, Svornosti 28, Smíchov (☎02/54 07 77). One of the city's least expensive hotels; like Smíchov itself, reassuringly run-down. Metro Anděl. ③.

Cloister Inn/Pension Unitas, Bartolomějská 9, Staré Město (☎02/232 77 00). Hotel and hostel in a very centrally located former nunnery, with rooms ranging from the clean and bright to claustrophobic converted secret-police prison cells (where Havel once stayed). Metro Národní třída. ⑤–⑦.

Dum U velké boty, Vlašská 30, Malá Strana (☎02/57 31 11 07). The most delightful, tastefully decorated pension, run by a very welcoming couple. ⑤.

Grand Hotel Evropa, Václavské náměstí 25, Nové Město (☎02/24 22 81 17). Beautiful Art Nouveau hotel – go now before the prices are modernized along with the rooms. Metro Muzeum. ⑨.

Hlávkova kolej, Jenštynská 1, Nové Město (☎02/29 00 98). Former student hostel with spartan but clean en-suite doubles. Metro Karlovo náměstí. ④.

Legie, Sokolská 33, Nové Město (☎02/24 92 02 54). A short stroll from Wenceslas Square. It looks bad from the outside, but the rooms are fine inside and all en-suite. Metro I. P. Pavlova. ⑨.

U krále Jiřího, Liliová 10, Staré Město (☎02/24 22 20 13). Eight cosy attic rooms above an "Irish" pub, deep in the heart of the old town. Metro Staroměstská. ⑥.

U medvídků, Na Perštýně 7, Staré Město (☎02/24 21 19 16). Eight plain rooms over a pub in the centre of the old town; booking ahead essential. Metro Národní třída. ④.

Campsites

Džbán, Nad lávkou 3, Vokovice. Tram #20 or #26 from metro Dejvická; the site is 4km west of the centre, down Benešova. Open all year.

Intercamp Kotva, U ledáren 55, Braník. Tram #3 or #17 from metro Karlovo náměstí. The oldest, and nicest, site, with a riverside location 6km south of the city. Open April–Oct.

Trojská, Trojská 375, Troja. One of a whole host of back garden sites, 3km north of the centre, on the road to the Troja château. Bus #112 from metro Nádraží Holešovice. Open all year.

The City

The **River Vltava** (Moldau in German) divides the capital into two unequal halves: the steeply inclined left bank, which accommodates the quarters of Hradčany and Malá Strana, and the more gentle, sprawling right bank, which includes Staré Město, Josefov and Nové Město. **Hradčany**, on the hill, contains the most obvious sights – the castle itself, the cathedral and the former palaces of the aristocracy. Below Hradčany, **Malá Strana** (Little Quarter), with its narrow eighteenth-century streets, is the city's ministerial and diplomatic quarter, though its Baroque gardens are there for all to enjoy. Over the river, on the right bank, **Staré Město** (Old Town) is a web of alleys and passageways centred on the city's most beautiful square, Staroměstské náměsti. Enclosed within the boundaries of Staré Město is **Josefov**, the old Jewish quarter, now down to a handful of synagogues and a cemetery. **Nové Město** (New Town), the focus of the modern city, covers the largest area, laid out in long wide boulevards – most famously Wenceslas Square – stretching south and east of the old town.

Hradčany

Hradčany's *raison d'être* is its **Castle**, or *Hrad*, built on the site of one of the original hill settlements of the Slav tribes who migrated here in the seventh or eighth century. Viewed from the Charles Bridge (Karlův most), Prague Castle stands aloof from the rest of the city, protected by a sheer wall that's breached only by the great mass of **St Vitus Cathedral** (daily 9am–4/5pm). Building started under Charles IV, who summoned the precocious 23-year-old German mason **Peter Parler** to work on the church. But only the choir and the south transept were finished when Charles died in 1399, and building did not begin again in earnest until the nineteenth century. The sooty Prague air has made it hard now to differentiate between the two building periods, but the eastern section recalls the building's authentic Gothic roots and the south door, or **Golden Gate** (Zlatá brána), is also pure Parler in style.

The Cathedral is the country's largest church, and, once inside, it's difficult not to be impressed by its sheer height. The grand chapel of **sv Václav**, by the south door, is easily the main attraction. Built by Parler, its rich decoration resembles the inside of a jewel casket: the gilded chapel walls are inlaid with over 1300 semiprecious stones, set around ethereal fourteenth-century Biblical frescoes, while above, the tragedy of Wenceslas unfolds in later paintings. A door in the south wall gives access to a staircase leading to the coronation chamber which houses the Bohemian crown jewels, including the gold crown of Saint Wenceslas. At the centre of the choir, within a fine Renaissance grill, cherubs lark about on the sixteenth-century marble **Imperial Mausoleum**, commissioned by Rudolf II for his grandfather, Ferdinand I, and father, Maximilian II.

If you want to see the choir or the ambulatory, you'll need to buy a ticket (currently 100kč), valid for three days, which also gives you entry into a handful of other sights in the castle, including the **Old Royal Palace** (Starý královský palác), just across the courtyard from the south door of the cathedral, and home to the princes and kings of Bohemia from the eleventh to the seventeenth centuries. It's a sandwich of royal apartments, built one on top of the other by successive generations – these days you enter at the third and top floor, built at the end of the fifteenth century. The massive Vladislav Hall (Vladislavský sál) is where the early Bohemian kings were elected, and where every president since Masaryk has been sworn into office – including Havel on December 29, 1989.

Don't be fooled by the uninspiring red facade of the **Basilica of sv Jiří** – this is Prague's most beautiful Romanesque monument, its inside meticulously restored to re-create the crumble-coloured basilica which replaced the original tenth-century church in 1173. Next door, the **Convent of sv Jiří** (Jiřský klášter), founded in 973, now houses the National Gallery's **Old Bohemian art collection** (Tues–Sun 10am–6pm), incorporating a remarkable collection of Gothic art – including the original of the bronze equestrian figure of Saint George that stands in the central courtyard. Round the corner from the convent is the **Golden Lane** (Zlatá ulička), a blind alley of miniature seventeenth-century cottages in dolly-mixture colours. A plaque at no. 22 commemorates Franz Kafka's brief sojourn here during World War I.

North of the castle walls, across the Powder Bridge (Prasný most), is the entrance to the **Královská zahrada** (May–Oct Tues–Sun 10am–5.45pm), founded by Ferdinand I and still the best-kept gardens in the country, with functioning fountains and immaculately cropped lawns. At the end of the gardens is Prague's most celebrated Renaissance legacy, the **Belvedér** (Tues–Sun 10am–6pm), a delicately arcaded summer house, now an art gallery.

TO THE STRAHOV MONASTERY

Hradčanské náměstí (Castle Square) fans out from the castle's main gates, surrounded by the oversized palaces of the old nobility. A passage down the side of the Archbishop's Palace leads to the early eighteenth-century **Šternberk Palace** (Tues–Sun 10am–6pm), housing the National Gallery's relatively modest **Old European art collection** (ie non-Czech), which primarily consists of works from the fifteenth to the eighteenth centuries, the most significant of which is the *Festival of the Rosary* by Dürer.

Nestling in a shallow dip to the northwest, **Nový Svět** is all that is left of the medieval slums, painted up and sanitized in the nineteenth century. Uphill from Nový Svět, Loretánské náměstí is dominated by the brutal 150-metre-long facade of the **Černín Palace**. The facade of the **Loreta** (Tues–Sun 9am–12.15pm & 1–4.30pm), immediately opposite, is a perfect antidote, all hot flourishes and twirls, topped by a tower which lights up like a Chinese lantern at night – and which by day clanks out a tuneless version of the hymn *We Greet Thee a Thousand Times* on its 27 Dutch bells. However, the two-storey cloisters and chapels are just the outer casing for the main focus of the complex, the Santa Casa, a shrine that was built a century earlier. You can get some idea of the shrine's popularity with the Bohemian nobility in the **treasury**, much ransacked over the years but still stuffed full of gold. The padded ceilings and low lighting create a kind of giant jewellery box for the master exhibit, a ghastly Viennese silver monstrance studded with diamonds and standing over three feet high.

A short way west up Pohořelec from Loretánské náměstí, the chunky remnants of the eighteenth-century fortifications mark the edge of the old city. Close by sits the **Strahov Monastery** (Strahovský klášter), which managed to escape the 1783 dissolution of the monasteries and continued to function until the Communists closed down all religious orders in 1948. Through the cobbled courtyard, past a small church and chapel, is the monastery proper, famous for its rich collection of manuscripts and its ornate **libraries** (daily 9am–noon & 1–5pm). Leaving through a narrow doorway in the eastern wall, you enter the gardens and orchards of the **Strahovská zahrada**, from where you can see the whole city in perspective.

Malá Strana

More than anywhere else, **Malá Strana**, the "Little Quarter", conforms to the image of Prague as the quintessential Baroque city. Its focus is the sloping, cobbled **Malostranské náměstí**, a busy square split in two by the former Jesuit seminary and church of **sv Mikuláš** (daily 9am–4pm), the most magnificent Baroque building in the city. Nothing of the plain west facade prepares you for the overwhelming High Baroque interior – the fresco in the nave alone covers over 1500 square metres, and portrays some of the more fanciful feats of St Nicholas.

Follow Tomášská north from the square and you'll arrive at the **Valdštejn Palace**. The largest palace complex in the city after the castle, it was built by Albrecht von Waldstein, who demolished 21 houses to make space for a palace befitting the most powerful man in central Europe. The only part accessible to the public is the south wing, which contains a small exhibition on the history of Czech education; as for the rest, you'll have to make do with the view from the formal gardens (daily: mid-March to April & Oct 10am–6pm; May–Sept 9am–7pm), access to which is from a concealed entrance off Letenská.

South of the main square, a continuation of Karmelitská brings you to the funicular railway up **Petřín** hill, a bigger and better green space than most in Prague. It's good for a picnic, and topped by a scaled-down version of the Eiffel Tower, one of a number of sights set up in the park for the 1891 Prague Exhibition.

Staré Město

Staré Město, the "Old Town", founded in the early thirteenth century, is where most of the capital's markets, shops, restaurants and pubs are located. It is linked to Malá Strana by the city's most familiar monument, the **Charles Bridge** (Karlův most), begun in 1357. The statues that line it – brilliant pieces of Jesuit propaganda added during the Counter-Reformation – have made it renowned throughout Europe. Cross to Staré Město and you're in busy **Křížovnické náměstí**, from where the narrow, crowded **Karlova** winds past the massive **Klementinum**, the former Jesuit College, completed just before the order were turfed out of the country in 1773. It now serves as the university library, though the first floor has temporary exhibitions of some of the library's prize possessions, and there are regular concerts in the **Mirrored Chapel** (Zrcadlová kaple).

At the end of the street is **Staroměstské náměstí**, the most spectacular square in Prague. From the eleventh century, it was Prague's main marketplace. At its centre is the dramatic Art Nouveau **Jan Hus Monument**. When John of Luxembourg gave Prague the right to have a town hall in 1338, the community bought a corner house on the square, gradually incorporating neighbouring buildings to form the **Old Town Hall** (Staroměstská radnice). Over the next century, the east wing was added, but only its graceful Gothic oriel and wedge-tower survived the arson of retreating Nazis. On the south facade, the central powder-red building now forms the entrance to the whole complex (Mon 10am–5pm, Tues–Sun 9am–6pm). You can also climb the tower – one of the few with access for the disabled – and get a close-up view of the figures of of Christ and the Apostles which take part in a mechanical performance on the town hall's **Astronomical Clock** every hour (daily 8am–8pm).

The Staré Město's most impressive Gothic structure is the mighty **Týn Church**, whose twin towers rise like giant antennae above the two arcaded houses which otherwise obscure its facade. It was completed during the reign of George of Podgbrady (1436–1471), the one and only Hussite King of Bohemia, but little of the interior survived its ferocious Catholicization. One exception is the fine north portal and canopy which bear the hallmark of Peter Parler's workshop; the fifteenth-century pulpit, its panels enhanced by some sensitive nineteenth-century icons, also stands out from the morass of black and gold Baroque altarpieces. The pillar on the right of the chancel steps contains the marble tomb of the Danish astronomer Tycho Brahe, who died of a burst bladder at one of Rudolf II's notorious binges in 1601.

JOSEFOV

Within the Staré Město lies **Josefov**, the Jewish quarter of the city until the end of the nineteenth century, when the Jews, gypsies and prostitutes were cleared out of this ghetto area in order to create a beautiful bourgeois city on Parisian lines. Kafka spent most of his life in and around Josefov, and the destruction of the Jewish quarter, which continued throughout his childhood, had a profound effect on his psyche.

All the "sights" of Josefov, bar the Old-New Synagogue, are covered by one 250kč ticket available from any of the quarter's box offices (daily except Sat 9am–4.30/6pm). The best place to begin is the **Pinkas Synagogue** on Široká, which contains a chilling memorial to the 77,297 Czechoslovak Jews who were killed during the Holocaust – the names of all the victims cover the walls, while children's drawings from the Theresienstadt (Terezín) ghetto are displayed in the women's gallery. From here, you enter the **Old Jewish Cemetery** (Starý Židovský hřbitov), which was established in the fifteenth century and was in use until 1787, by which time there were some 100,000 graves here piled on top of one another. Get there before the crowds, and it can be a poignant reminder of the ghetto, its inhabitants subjected to inhuman overcrowding even in death.

Pařížská, the ultimate bourgeois avenue now runs through the heart of the old ghetto in a riot of turn-of-the-century sculpturing, spikes and turrets. Halfway down here, on the left, is the steep brick gable of the **Old-New Synagogue** (Staronová synagóga; 200kč), completed in the fourteenth century and still the religious centre of Prague's 2000-strong Jewish community. Originally it was known simply as the New Synagogue, but after several fires gutted the ghetto it became the oldest synagogue building in the quarter – hence its strange name.

Opposite the synagogue is the **Jewish Town Hall** (Židovská radnice), founded in the sixteenth century and later turned into a creamy-pink Baroque house crowned by a wooden clocktower. In addition to the four main clocks, there's a Hebrew one stuck on the north gable, which (like the Hebrew script) goes "backwards". The nearby seventeenth-century **Klausen Synagogue** and the neo-Gothic **Maisl Synagogue** display some beautiful religious objects and attempt to explain the basics of the Jewish religion, while the newly restored and highly ornate neo-Byzantine **Spanish Synagogue**, down Široká, on the other side of Pařížská, contains an exhibition on the history of the city's Jewish community.

Nové Město

Nové Město, the "New Town", now a sprawling late nineteenth-century bourgeois quarter, was actually founded in 1348 by Charles IV. The borderline between Staré and Nové Město is made up by the continuous boulevards of **Národní** and **Na příkopě**, a boomerang curve which follows the course of the old moat. The city's most flamboyant Art Nouveau buildings are ranged along much of the avenue – Prague's busiest shopping street and the most expensive slice of real estate in the country. This was also the unlikely setting for the November 17 demonstration that sparked off the Velvet Revolution.

At the river end of Národní is the gold-crested **National Theatre** (Národní divadlo), a proud symbol of the Czech nation. Refused money by the Austrian state, Czechs of all classes dug deep into their pockets to raise funds for the venture themselves. Halfway along Na příkopě you can visit the new **Mucha Museum**, at Panská 7 (daily 10am–6pm; 120kč), dedicated to the country's best-known artist, Alfons Mucha, whose Art Nouveau posters can be seen on sale all over the city.

At the far end of Na příkopě, on náměstí Republiky, stands the **Municipal House** (Obecní dům). Begun in 1903, it was decorated inside and out with the help of almost every artist connected with the Czech Secession. The easiest way of soaking up the hall-like interior, peppered with Art Nouveau mosaics and pendulous brass chandeliers, is to have a meal in the restaurant, or a coffee in the equally cavernous café. If you're keen to see more of the interior, you can visit the excellent temporary exhibitions held on the second floor, or sign up for a guided tour.

Cross the boulevard at its central point and you're into the pivot of modern Prague and the political focus of the events of November 1989 – the wide, gently sloping **Wenceslas Square** (Václavské náměstí). The square's history of protest goes back to the Prague Spring of 1968: towards the top end, there's a small memorial to the victims of Communism, the most famous of whom, the 21-year-old student Jan Palach, set himself alight on this very spot in

January 1969 in protest against the Soviet occupation. A six-lane freeway effectively cuts off the square from the **National Museum** (daily: May–Sept 10am–6pm; Oct–April 9am–5pm), one of the great symbols of the nineteenth-century Czech national revival, with its monumental glass cupola, sculptural decoration and frescoes from Czech history. However, unless you're a geologist or a zoologist you're likely to be unmoved by the exhibits.

Trade Fair Palace: Museum of Modern Art

There's just one compelling reason to venture into Prague's suburbs, and that is to visit the city's long-awaited, new modern-art museum, housed in a vast functionalist 1920s building, known as the **Trade Fair Palace** (Veletržní palác; Tues–Sun 10am–6pm, Thurs until 9pm), on Dukelských hrdiny (tram #5 from náměstí Republiky). The museum's *raison d'être* is its unrivalled permanent collection of twentieth-century Czech art, but it also houses the National Gallery's modest collection of nineteenth- and twentieth-century European art, including works by Klimt, Schiele, Picasso and the French Impressionists.

Eating

There are three main types of establishment in Prague and elsewhere in the country where you can get something to eat: a **restaurant** (*restaurace*), where eating is ostensibly the main activity; a **wine bar** (*vinárna*), which tends to think of itself as a touch more exclusive; and, that most typical of Czech institutions, the **pub** (*pivnice*), though these are largely concerned with serious drinking – and are covered in the next section. In practice, these definitions are blurred, with some places having *restaurace* and *pivnice* sections under the same roof, some *vinárna* offering food, some only wine, and so on.

Bar Bar, Všehrdova 17, Malá Strana. Arty crêperie with big, cheap salads and sweet and savoury pancakes. Metro Malostranská.

Bazaar Mediterranée, Nerudova 40, Malá Strana. Sprawling wine cellar with a great terrace that hits the spot with the food, and is understandably popular with folk heading up to or down from the castle. Metro Malostranská.

Country Life, Melantrichova 15, Staré Město. Popular, sit-down veggie place with a health food shop attached. Closed Sat. Metro Můstek.

U Góvindy, Soukenická 27, Nové Město. Self-service veggie slop from the local Hare Krishna posse. Closed Sun. Metro náměstí Republiky.

Hogo Fogo, Salvátorská 4, Staré Město. Monochrome decor and cheap, filling Czech food at this popular student hangout. Metro Staroměstská.

Lotos, Platnépská 13, Staré Město. Veggie versions of classic Czech dishes in non-smoking environment. Metro Staroměstská.

Massada, Michalská 16, Staré Město. Overpriced beer, but the kosher food is fine. Metro Můstek.

Pizzeria Kmotra, V jirchářích 12, Nové Město. Sweaty and very popular basement pizza place in the back-streets behind Národní. Metro Národní třída.

Radost FX Café, Bělehradská 120, Vinohrady. Best veggie food in town attracts a largely expat posse; open till very late. Metro I.P. Pavlova.

Café Colonial, Široká 6, Staré Město. Pricey French brasserie style food, located right by Josefov, and therefore very popular with tourists. Metro Staroměstská.

Reykjavík, Karlova 20, Staré Město. The owners (and the fish) really are Icelandic, though the cuisine is pretty international. Very satisfying though fairly pricey. Metro Staroměstská.

Drinking

Prague **cafés** are starting to blossom again, and the choice is pretty varied – from Art Nouveau relics and swish espresso bars (both of which are called *kavárna* and are licensed), to simple sugar and caffeine joints (*cukrárna*). For no-nonsense boozing you need to head for a **pub** (*pivnice*), which invariably serves excellent beer by the half-litre, but many of which close around 11pm. For late-night drinking, head for one of the clubs or all-night bars.

Café Slavia, Národní 1, Nové Město. Famous Prague café, situated opposite the Národní divadlo. Metro Národní třída.

Dobrá čajovna, Boršov 6, Staré Město. Buddhist tea house off Karoliny Světlé; no smoking, no alcohol, just chilling out. Metro Staroměstská.

Grand Hotel Evropa, Václavské náměstí 25, Nové Město. The place to be seen on Wenceslas Square is on the *Evropa*'s summer terrace, but the Art Nouveau decor is at its best inside. Daily 7am–midnight. Metro Muzeum.

Gulu Gulu, Betlémské náměstí 8, Staré Město. Miro scribblings on the wall of this very popular café in the heart of the old town. Metro Národní třída.

Jo's Bar, Malostranské náměstí 7, Malá Strana. Narrow bar serving hot Tex-Mex food – something of an expat and backpacker institution. Metro Malostranská.

Louvre, Národní 20. High ceiling, mirrors, daily papers and a billiard hall, this first-floor café is a fair approximation of a typical Viennese *Kaffeehaus*. Metro Národní třída.

Marquis de Sade, Templová 8, Staré Město. High ceilings, comfy sofas, dubious live music and crap beer, but a great atmosphere till early in the morning. Metro náměstí Republiky.

Molly Malone's, U obecního dvora 4, Staré Město. Best of Prague's Irish pubs with open fire and draught Guinness. Metro Staroměstská.

Novoměstský pivovar, Vodičkova 20, Nové Město. New micro-brewery, which serves up its own misty brew along with solid Czech food. Metro Můstek.

Obecní dům, náměstí Republiky 5, Nové Město. Glorious Art Nouveau décor, and impeccable service, good cake trolley and even a few Internet terminals. Metro náměstí Republiky.

Terminal Bar, Soukenická 6, Nové Město. Prague's trendiest Internet café is also a great place to chill out, especially in the downstairs retro bar. Metro náměstí Republiky.

U černého vola, Loretánské náměstí 1, Hradčany. Does a brisk business providing the popular light beer Velkopopovický kozel 12° in huge quantities to locals. Tram #22 from metro Malostranská.

U staleté baby, Na Kampě 15, Malá Strana. A nice pub on the island below the Charles Bridge, tucked away round the corner and therefore avoiding the worst of the crowds. Metro Malostranská.

Velryba, Opatovická 24, Nové Město. Smoky café, with cheap Czech food and a stunning array of malt whiskies. Metro Národní třída.

Nightlife

As far as **live music** is concerned, the classical scene still has the edge in Prague, though a couple of new jazz clubs have livened up the scene. **Discos and nightclubs** continue to boom around Wenceslas Square, but they serve more as indoor red-light districts. Predictably enough, with a playwright as president, **theatre** in Prague is thriving; without knowing the language, however, your scope is limited, though there's a tradition of innovative mime, puppetry and "black light" theatre in the city. **Tickets** are cheap and available from any Ticketpro outlet (there's one in the PIS), as well as from the venues themselves. **Listings** are best found in the English-language weekly *Prague Post*, the bi-lingual fortnightly *Do města/Downtown*, or the Czech monthly *Přehled*.

Classical music and opera

Classical concerts take place throughout the year in concert halls and churches, the biggest event being the Prague Spring (*Pražské jaro*) **international music festival**, which traditionally begins on May 12, the day of Smetana's death, with a performance of *Má vlast*, and finishes on June 2 with a rendition of Beethoven's Ninth. As well as the main venues, watch out for concerts in the churches and palaces, especially in summer.

Rudolfinum, Alsovo nábřeží, Národní 2, Staré Město. Stunning Neo-Renaissance concert hall and home to the Czech Philharmonic. Metro Staroměstská.

Státní opera Praha, Wilsonova 4, Nové Město. The former German opera house, and the city's second-choice venue for opera and ballet. Metro Muzeum.

Stavovské divadlo, Ovocný trh 1, Staré Město. Prague's main opera house, which witnessed the première of Mozart's *Don Giovanni*. Metro Můstek.

Jazz and rock

Akropolis, Kubelíkova 27, Žižkov. Decent live arts/gig venue in the backstreets of seedy Žižkov. Doors open 7.30am. Tram #5, #9 or #26.

AghaRTA, Jazz Centrum, Krakovská 5, Nové Město. Prague's best jazz club with a good mix of foreigners and locals. Open until 1am. Metro Muzeum.

Lucerna Music Bar, Vodičkova 36, Nové Město. Central, small dance space, live music, occasionally jazz. Metro Můstek/Muzeum.

Radost FX, Bělehradská 120, Vinohrady. By far the best dance club in Prague, with a great veggie café attached. Open until 6am. Metro I.P. Pavlova.

Reduta, Národní 20, Nové Město. Prague's oldest-established jazz club, serving up anything from trad to modern. Open Mon–Fri until 2am, though the music stops at midnight.

Roxy, Dlouhá 33, Staré Město. Good mix of trendy café and clubby venue – worth checking out. Metro náměstí Republiky.

Listings

Airlines British Airways, Staroměstské náměstí 10, Staré Město (☎02/24 81 37 28); ČSA, V celnici 5, Nové Město (☎02/20 10 41 11).

American Express, Václavské náměstí 56, Nové Město (daily 9am–7pm).

Books The Globe, Janovského 14, Holešovice; metro Vltavská. The expat hangout with a café attached. Open daily 10am–midnight.

Car rental Avis, Klimentská 46, Nové Město (☎02/21 85 12 25); Budget, Čistovická 100, Dejvice (☎02/302 57 13).

Embassies Australia, Na Ořechovce, Střešovice (☎02/24 31 00 71); Canada, Mickiewiczova 6, Hradčany (☎02/24 31 11 08); Great Britain, Thunovská 14, Malá Strana (☎02/24 51 04 39); Ireland, Tržiště 15, Malá Strana (☎02/53 09 02); USA, Tržiště 15, Malá Strana (☎02/24 51 08 47). Nationals of New Zealand should contact the Australian Embassy.

Exchange There's a very reasonable 24-hour exchange service at the airport and at 28 října 13, Nové Město.

Gay Prague For up-to-date information on the Prague gay scene, try the Gay Information Centre (☎02/26 44 08).

Laundry Laundry Kings, Dejvická 16, Dejvice; metro Hradčanská (Mon–Fri 6am–10pm, Sat & Sun 8am–10pm).

Pharmacy 24-hour service at Belgická 37, Vinohrady; metro náměstí Míru.

Post office The main post office is at Jindřisská 14, Nové Město; there's a 24-hour service for parcels, telegrams and telephones.

BOHEMIA

Prague is the natural centre and capital of Bohemia; the rest divides easily into four geographical districts. **South Bohemia,** bordered by the Šumava Mountains, is the least spoilt; its largest town by far is the brewing centre of **České Budějovice,** and its chief attraction, aside from the thickly forested hills, is a series of well-preserved medieval towns, whose undisputed gem is **Český Krumlov.** Neighbouring **West Bohemia** has a similar mix of rolling woods and hills, despite the industrial nature of its capital **Plzeň,** home of Pilsen beer and the Škoda empire. Beyond here, as you approach the German border, Bohemia's famous **Spa Region** unfolds, with magnificent resorts such as **Mariánské Lázně** and **Karlovy Vary** enjoying sparkling reputations. **North Bohemia** has real problems: devastated by industrialization, many parts are virtually uninhabitable. **East Bohemia** has suffered indirectly from the polluting industries of its neighbour, but remains relatively blight-free. There's some great walking and climbing country here, but the only essential stop on a quick tour is the silver-mining centre of **Kutná Hora.**

České Budějovice

Since its foundation in 1265, **ČESKÉ BUDĚJOVICE** (Budweis) – just two hours by train from Prague – has been a self-assured place, convinced of its own importance. Its wealth, based on medieval silver mines and its position on the salt route from Linz to Prague, was wiped out in the seventeenth century by war and fire, but the Habsburgs lavishly reconstructed most of České Budějovice in the eighteenth century. Its real renown, however, is for its local brew Budvar, better known abroad under its original German name, Budweiser.

České Budějovice has a compact old town that's only a five-minute walk from the **train** and **bus stations**, both situated to the east of the city centre, along the pedestrianized Lannova třída. The medieval grid plan leads inevitably to the magnificent central **náměstí Přemysla Otakara II**, one of Europe's largest market squares. Its buildings are elegant enough, but it's the arcades and the octagonal **Samson's Fountain** – once the only tap in town – that make the greatest impression. The 72-metre status symbol, the **Black Tower** (Černá věž), one of the few survivors of the 1641 fire, leans gently to one side of the square; its roof gallery (daily: March–June 10am–6pm; July & Aug 10am–7pm; Sept–Nov 9am–5pm) provides superb views.

When the weather's fine, people tend to promenade by the banks of the Malše, where parts of the original town walls have survived along with some of České Budějovice's oldest buildings. All that is left of the bishop's palace is the serene **garden** (May–Sept daily 8am–6pm), accessible through a small gateway in the walls. Round the corner, on Piaristické náměstí, stands the thoroughly medieval **zbrojnice** (one-time arsenal), once the centre of the town's all-important salt trade. The Budvar **brewery** is out on the road to Prague (bus #2 or #4), and has recently opened its gates to the public (Mon–Fri 9am–3pm; ☎038/770 53 41); there's also an inexpensive *pivnice* inside the brewery.

České Budějovice's popularity with neighbouring Austrians and Germans means that **hotels** tend to charge over the odds. The best-value options, are *Penzion Centrum* (☎038/635 20 30; ③), off Kanovnická at Na mlýnské stoce 6; or *Malý pivovar*, Karla IV 100 (☎038/731 32 85; ⑤). There's a **tourist office** (May–Sept daily 8.30am–6pm; Oct-March Mon–Fri 9am–5.30pm, Sat 9am–noon) at no. 2 on the main square, too, where you can book private rooms. From July to September rooms are available in **student hostels** – go to CKM, Lannova 63, to get the addresses of current hostels. There's also a good **campsite** at Dlouhá louka (bus #16 from station; May–Sept). The most famous hostelry in town is *Masné krámy* at Krajinská 29, which serves huge quantities of Budvar and Czech **food**, all day. Another good *pivnice* is *U tří korun*, Radniční 9, which serves Pilsner Urquell and inexpensive pub food, while at the *U zlatého soudku* you can drink the town's other, equally excellent beer, Samson.

Český Krumlov

Squeezed into a tight S-bend of the River Vltava, **ČESKÝ KRUMLOV** (Krumau) is undoubtedly one of the most picturesque towns in the country, having hardly changed in the last three hundred years. This, however, is no secret, and the crowds can get pretty thick in the height of summer.

The **train station** is twenty minutes' walk north of the old town, up a precipitous set of steps, while the **bus station** is closer to the heart of town, on the right bank. The twisting River Vltava divides the town into two segments: the circular staré město (old town) on the right bank and the Latrán quarter on the hillier left bank. For centuries, the focal point has been the town's **castle**, the Krumlovský zámek (April–Oct Tues–Sun 9am–noon & 1–3/4/5pm; 110kč) in the Latrán quarter, as good a place as any to begin a roam; there's a choice of two guided tours: one concentrating on feudal opulence, the other peaking at the castle's eighteenth-century Rococo ballroom. Another covered walkway puts you high above the town in the unexpectedly expansive **terraced gardens** (open all year).

The shabby houses leaning in on Latrán lead to a wooden ramp-like bridge which connects with the staré město. Head straight up the soft incline of Radniani to the main square, where a long, white Renaissance entablature connects two-and-a-half Gothic houses to create the **town hall** (radnice). On the other side, the high lancet windows of the church of St **Vitus** rise above the ramshackle rooftops. Continuing east off the square, down Horní, the beautiful sixteenth-century Jesuit college now provides space for the *Hotel Růže*. Opposite, the local **Museum** (Tues–Fri 9am–noon & 12.30pm–5pm, Sat & Sun 1–4pm) includes a reconstructed seventeenth-century shop interior among its exhibits. While you're there ask for directions to the new **Shiele Centrum** (daily 10am–6pm; 120kč), on Široká, a whole series of galleries and exhibition halls housed in a fifteenth-century former brewery in the staré město. The centre is devoted to the Austrian painter Egon Schiele, who moved here briefly in 1911, and contains many of his drawings and paintings, as well as featuring contemporary artists.

There's a **tourist office** (Mon–Fri 9am–6pm, Sat & Sun 10am–4pm) on the main square in the staré město, which can organize private rooms for you. *Hotel Růže* (☎0337/71 11 41; ⑤) is the town's most beautiful old hotel; the *Krumlov* on the main square (☎0337/71 15 65; ④) is much plainer inside; a better bet is the new pub/pension, *Na louži*, Kájovská 66 (☎0337/71 12 80; ②), opposite the Shiele Centrum. An even cheaper option is *U vodníka* hostel (☎0337/71 18 01; ①); to get there follow Horní out of the old town and turn right into Rooseveltova. There's also a primitive **campsite** (May–Sept), 2km south on road 160 to Nové Spolí. As far as **eating** goes, the choice has improved considerably: the restaurant in *Hotel Konvice*, Horní 144, is good, as is the fish restaurant *Rybařská bašta*, off Široká. A cheaper option still is to head for the stand-up *Krumlovská fontána*, on náměstí Svornosti. **Drinking** is best done at the *Krumovské pivnice*, off Latrán next to the brewery, or at the aforementioned *Na louži*.

Plzeň

PLZEŇ (Pilsen) is Bohemia's second city, with a population of 175,000. The skyline is a symphony of smoke and steam, yet despite its industrial character, there are compensations – a large number of students, eclectic architecture and an unending supply of (probably) the best **beer** in the world, all of which make Plzeň a popular stopoff on the main rail line between Prague and the west. Plzeň's **train stations** are works of art in themselves: there are numerous minor ones within the city boundaries, but without doubt your likeliest point of arrival is the Hlavní nádraží, east of the city centre. The **bus terminal** is on the west side of town. From both stations, the city centre is only a short walk away, or a few stops on tram #2 (and #1 from the train station).

The main square, **náměstí Republiky**, presents a full range of architectural styles, starting with the exalted heights of the Gothic church of **sv Bartoloměj**, its bile-green spire (daily 10am–6pm) reaching up more than one hundred metres. Over the way rises the Italianate **Old Town Hall** (Stará radnice), self-importantly one storey higher than the rest of the square. Here and there other old buildings survive, but the vast majority of Plzeň's buildings hail from the city's heyday during the industrial expansion around the turn of the century. In the old town, this produced some wonderful variations on neohistorical themes and Art Nouveau motifs, particularly to the north and west of the main square.

But the reason most people come to Plzeň is to sample its famous 12° Plzeňský Prazdroj, or **Pilsner Urquell** (its Germanized export name). Beer has been brewed in the town since it was founded in 1295, but it wasn't until 1842 that the famous Bürgerliches Brauhaus was built, after a near-riot by the townsfolk over the declining quality of their brew. For a **guided tour** of the **brewery**, you'll need to ring in advance (Mon–Fri ☎019/706 28 88). There are a range of tours lasting up to two hours, but you have to pay extra for a tasting, after which you get to keep the glass. You could, of course, just settle for a glass of the real thing at the vast *Na stilce* pub (daily from 11am), beyond the brewery's triumphal arch. The truly dedicated can then head for the **Brewery Museum** (Pivovarské muzeum; June to mid-Oct daily 10am–6pm; mid-Oct to May Tues–Sun 9am–5pm) at the end of Veleslavínova.

Finding a vacancy in one of Plzeň's **hotels** presents few problems, though rooms don't come cheap. There are some reasonable rooms at the faded *Slovan*, Smetanovy sady 1 (☎019/722 72 56; ②–④), and better ones at the *Continental*, Zbrojnická 8 (☎019/723 64 79; ②), and a decent pension at Solní 8 (☎019/723 6652; ②). **Private rooms** are available from the **tourist office** (daily 9am–5pm), on the main square next door to the town hall. Alternatively, you can stay at the **student hostel** at Bolevecká 30 (①) tram #4 north along Karlovarská. Bus #20 from the train station will drop you at the *Bílá hora* **campsite** (April–Sept), in the northern suburb of the same name.

All the hotels have **restaurants** attached but for cheap meals you might as well combine your **eating** with your **drinking**. Apart from *Na stílce*, you can get Pilsner Urquell (and cheap grub) at the wood-panelled *U Salzmannů* on Pražská. Gambrinus, Plzeň's other main beer, is best at *U Žumbery* on Bezručova.

The Spa Region

The big West Bohemian spas – especially **Mariánské Lázně** and **Karlovy Vary** – were the Côte d'Azur of Habsburg Europe in the nineteenth century, attracting the great names of *Mitteleuropa*. What was the prerogative of the mega-wealthy became the right of the toiling masses after the postwar nationalization of the entire spa industry enabled every factory worker and trade union member to receive three weeks' annual holiday at a spa pension. Nowadays, the wealthy Germans are back, joined by increasing numbers of Russians, though the area has still a long way to go before it catches up with the likes of Baden-Baden.

Mariánské Lázně

Once one of the most fashionable European spas, **MARIÁNSKÉ LÁZNĚ** (Marienbad) is much less exclusive today. The riotous, turn-of-the-century architecture is gradually being restored and the old state spa buildings are beginning to open up their doors to the public once again. Buses and trains stop 3km from the spa, from where trolley bus #5 (pay the driver) runs the remaining distance, up Hlavní třída to the *Hotel Excelsior*. As far as the eye can see, sumptuous, regal spa buildings, most dating from the second half of the nineteenth century, rise up from the pine-clad surrounds.

The focal point of the spa, overlooking the town, is the **Kolonáda**. Easily the most beautiful wrought-iron colonnade in Bohemia, it gently curves like a whale-ribbed railway station, the atmosphere relentlessly genteel and sober. In summer, Bohemian bands and orchestras give daily concerts here, while German tourists buy up the Bohemian crystal in the upstairs gallery. Access to the colonnade's life-giving faucets is restricted (daily 6am–noon & 4–6pm), though the spa's first and foremost **spring**, Kpížový pramen, is accessible all day and night. Mariánské Lázně's altitude lends an almost subalpine freshness to the air, even at the height of summer, and **walking** is as important to "the cure" as the various specialized treatments. At the end of the Kolonáda, by the new "singing fountain", there's a map showing the various marked walks around the spa.

If you want to **stay**, rooms are cheap at the faded *Hotel Krakonoš* (☎0165/62 26 24; ①) in the hills to the east and accessible by cable car from Dusíkova or by bus #12; it also serves as an HI hostel. The *Kossuth*, Ruská 77 (☎0165/62 28 61; ②) is similarly rundown, but the *Bohemia,* Hlavní třída 100 (☎0165/62 32 51; ③), is central and classy. **Private rooms** are available from the **tourist office** at Hlavní 47 (Mon–Fri 9am–6pm, Sat & Sun 9am–5pm). Otherwise there's a small **campsite** with cheap bungalows at *Motel Start* on Plzeňská (☎0165/62 20 62). Hlavní třída is punctuated with **cafés**, shops and **restaurants**, some hinting at bygone opulence; *Café Polonia*, Hlavní třída 50, offers cakes as rich as its stucco decoration. The *Classic*, further down at Hlavní 50 is a good choice, as is *U zlaté koule*, Nerova 26. *Pizzeria U Mülleru*, Na průhonu 24, does decent pizzas and pasta.

Karlovy Vary

KARLOVY VARY (Karlsbad), king of the Bohemian spas, is one of the most cosmopolitan Czech towns. Its international clientele annually doubles the local population, which is further supplemented by thousands of able-bodied tourists in summer, when the narrow valley resounds with German and the multifarious languages of central Europe.

The **bus station** and the main **train station** are on opposing sides of the River Ohře (Eger), both in the modern part of town. Half a kilometre south, the pedestrianized **spa quarter** stretches along the winding Teplá Valley. Unfortunately, many visitors' first impressions are marred by the inexcusable concrete scab of *Hotel Thermal*, for whose sake a large slice of the old town bit the dust. Behind it is the open-air spring-water **swimming pool**, high above the river. As the valley narrows, the river disappears under a wide terrace in front of the graceful **Mlýnská kolonáda**, each of whose four springs is more scalding than the last. Most powerful of the town's twelve springs is the **Sprudel** (*Vřídlo* to the Czechs), which belches out over 2500 gallons every hour. The smooth marble floor of the modern **Vřídelní kolonáda** (the old one was melted down for armaments by the Nazis) allows patients to shuffle up and down contentedly, while inside the glass rotunda the geyser shoots hot water forty feet upwards. Clouds of steam obscure a view of Dientzenhofer's Baroque masterpiece, the **church of sv Maria Magdalána**, pitched nearby on a precipitous site. South of the Sprudel is Karlovy Vary's most famous shopping street, the **Stará louka** (Alte Wiese). Its shops exude little of the snobbery of former days, and the tea and cakes served on marble tables at the *Elefant Café* are among the few reminders of the halcyon era. At the end of Stará louka is the **Grand Hotel Pupp**, founded in 1701 as the greatest hotel in the world. Despite its lacklustre modernization, it can't fail to impress, and the cakes are still made to Mr Pupp's recipes.

It's best to start looking for accommodation early in the day. ČEDOK, on the corner of Moskevská and dr. Bechera can organize **private rooms**, as can W Privat on náměstí Republiky (Mon–Fri 8.30am–5pm, Sat & Sun 9.30am–1pm) near the bus station. Moderately priced **hotels** include the *Adria*, Západní 1 (☎017/322 37 65; ③); the *Kavalerie*, T.G. Masaryka 43 (☎017/322 96 13; ③), the best value in this range; and the modern *Pension Holiday*, Ondřičkova 26 (☎017/322 06 49; ③). Karlovy Vary's **campsite** (May–Sept; bus #7) is up the Teplá Valley at *Motel Březová*; it also has bungalows for rent. The main restaurant at the *Grand Hotel Pupp* is the place **to eat**, but it's not cheap and you must reserve a table. Otherwise, you're best off sticking to the hotel restaurants; a cheaper alternative is the vegetarian restaurant at I.P. Pavlova 25, near the *Hotel Thermal*.

Kutná Hora

Undisputed gem of the region east of Prague is **KUTNÁ HORA** (Kuttenberg), 60km from the capital and once one of the most important towns in the country. In 1308 Václav II founded the royal mint here, and the town's sudden wealth allowed it to underwrite the construction of one of the most magnificent churches in central Europe, plus a number of other prestigious monuments. By the late Middle Ages its population was equal to that of London, its shantytown suburbs straggling across what are now green fields. When the silver mines dried up at the end of the sixteenth century, Kutná Hora's importance came to an abrupt end.

The easiest way to get here from Prague is by bus, as the main train station is several kilometres from the centre, whereas the buses stop just across the ring road. The small houses which line the town's medieval lanes give little idea of its former glories, and the same goes for **Palackého náměstí**, nominally the main square though it's no showpiece. A narrow alleyway on the south side of the square leads to the leafy Havličkovo náměstí, off of which is the **Italian Court** (Vlašský dvůr), where Florentine workers produced Prague's silver *Groschen*, a coin used throughout central Europe until the nineteenth century. The building itself has been mucked about over the centuries, though the short guided tour (daily 9/10am–4/5/6pm) is interesting enough. Better still, head for the **Mining Museum** (April–Oct Tues–Sun 9am–5/6pm), the other side of sv Jakub, the town's oldest church. Here, you can pick up a white coat, miner's helmet and torch, and visit some of the medieval mines that were discovered beneath an old fort in the 1960s.

The Jesuits arrived too late to exploit the town's silver stocks, but with their own funds they built a **Jesuit College** on the ridge to the southwest of town. With its gallery of saints and holy men, it was a crude attempt to eclipse the astounding achievement of the neighbouring **Cathedral of sv Barbora** (Tues–Sun: May–Sept 9am–5.30pm; Oct–April 9am–11.30am & 1/2–3.30pm). Not to be outdone by the St Vitus Cathedral in Prague, the miners of Kutná Hora financed the construction of a great cathedral of their own, dedicated to Barbara, the patron saint of miners and gunners. The foundations were probably laid by Peter Parler himself in the 1380s, but work was interrupted by the Hussite wars, and the church remained unfinished until the late nineteenth century. From the outside it's an incredible sight, bristling with pinnacles, finials and flying buttresses supporting a roof of three tent-like towers and unequal needle-sharp spires. Inside, cold light streams through the plain glass, lighting up a vaulted nave whose ribs form branches and petals stamped with coats of arms belonging to Václav II and the miners' guilds.

While you're in Kutná Hora, don't miss the weird subterranean *kostnice* or **ossuary** (daily: 8/9am–noon & 1–4/5pm), overflowing with 40,000 complete sets of bones, moulded into sculptures and decorations. To get there, take bus #1 or #4 to the giant tobacco factory; you'll find the ossuary behind a Baroque church.

The **tourist office** at Palackeho náměstí 5 (Mon–Fri 9am–6.30pm; April–Oct also Sat & Sun 9am–5pm) can arrange **accommodation** in private rooms. Follow signs to the *turistická ubytovna* or **hostel** (☎0327/34 63; ①) for the cheapest **accommodation** in town; reception is open only 5–6pm. There are two good pensions to choose from: *U hrnčíře*, Barborská 24 (☎0327/21 13; ②), and the comfortable *U vlašského dvora*, just off Palackého náměstí on 28 října (☎0327/46 18; ③). The nearest **campsite** is the unlikely sounding *Santa Barbara* on Česká (April–Oct).

MORAVIA

Wedged between Bohemia and Slovakia, **Moravia** (Morava) is the smallest of the three provinces which once made up Czechoslovakia, and shares characteristics with both its big brothers. Like Bohemia, much of Moravia is heavily industrialized, while the region's folk roots, traditions and even religion are as strongly felt here as in parts of Slovakia. The Moravian capital, **Brno**, a once-grand nineteenth-century city, is within easy striking distance of Moravia's **karst region**. In the northern half of the province, the Baroque riches of the Moravian prince-bishopric have left their mark on the old capital, **Olomouc**, now a thriving university town and the region's main attraction. The rest of the North Moravian corridor, forming the gateway to Poland, is a virtual rerun of North Bohemia, a black hole into which few venture voluntarily.

Brno

BRNO (Brünn) "welcomes the visitor with new constructions", as the Communist-era travel brochures used to euphemistically put it. In fact, the high-rise tenements that surround the city play a major part in discouraging travellers from stopping here. But as the second largest city in the Czech Republic, with a couple of really good museums and galleries plus a handful of other sights and a fair bit of nightlife, it's worth a day or two of anyone's time.

Brno was a late developer, the first cloth factory being founded in 1766, but by the end of the nineteenth century this was easily the largest city in Moravia. Between the wars Brno enjoyed a cultural boom, heralded by the 1928 Exhibition of Contemporary Culture which provided an impetus for much of the city's modernist architecture. After the war, Brno's German-speakers (one quarter of the population) were sent packing on foot to Vienna. Capital fled with the capitalists and centralized state funds were diverted to Prague and Bratislava, pushing Brno firmly into third (now second) place.

Arrival and accommodation

The splendour of Brno's main **train station** is a great introduction to the city; not so the main **bus station**, connected to the train station by an overhead walkway. Both stations have lockers and there's a 24-hour left-luggage office at the train station. Most of Brno's sights are within easy walking distance of the train station, although **trams** will take you almost anywhere in the city within minutes. Brno has, unfortunately, adopted Prague's complex system of ticketing: you need to buy either a 5kč ticket for 2 zones (*pásma*), which will last you fifteen minutes without changing trams or buses, or an 8kč ticket, again for 2 zones, which is valid for an hour and allows changes between trams or buses. Tickets must be bought beforehand from kiosks, hotel lobbies or yellow ticket machines, and validated on board.

The main **tourist office** is in the Old Town Hall (Stará radnice) on Radnická (Mon–Fri 8am–6pm, Sat & Sun 9am–5pm) and there's also a smaller bureau in the train station. They will book you a private room or a hotel room and can sell you a map and various guides. Hostel accommodation is available all year round, but it's not conveniently located: *Interservis*, Sladkého 13 (☎05/45 23 42 32), is a short walk from the southern terminus for tram #9 and #12. The cheapest hotel in the centre is *Avion*, Česká 20 (☎05/42 21 50 16; ②), *Pegas*, Jakubská 4 (☎05/42 21 12 32; ④), just off Česká, or *U Jakuba*, on Jakubské náměstí (☎05/42 21 07 95; ③). Best of Brno's **campsites** is the *Radka* site (June–Aug), 10km north-west of the city on the shores of the Brno dam (tram #1, #3 or #11).

The City

From the station a steady stream of people plough up and down **Masarykova**, a hazardous cocktail of cobbles, steaming sewer covers and tram lines. Don't let that stop you from looking up at the five-storey mansions, some laden with a fantastic mantle of decoration. To the left as you head up Masarykova is **Zelný trh**, a low-key vegetable market on a sloping cobbled square, with a huge fountain by Fischer von Erlach in its centre. At the top of the square, the plain mass of the Dietrichstein Palace contains the **Moravian Museum** (Moravské zemské muzeum; Tues–Sat 9am–6pm), a worthy collection of ancient and medieval artefacts. Much more interesting, if only for their macabre value, is the **Capuchin Crypt** (Kapucinská hrobka; Tues–Sat 9am–noon & 2–4.30pm, Sun 11–11.45am & 2–4.30pm) to the far south of the square, a gruesome collection of dead monks and top nobs mummified in the crypt of the Capuchin church.

Clearly visible from Zelný trh is the **Old Town Hall** (Stará radnice; daily 7am–8pm). Anton Pilgram's Gothic doorway is its best feature, the thistly pinnacle above the statue of Justice symbolically twisted – Pilgram's revenge on the town aldermen who short-changed him for his work. Inside, the courtyards and passageways are jam-packed with tour groups, most of them here to see the so-called Brno dragon (actually a stuffed crocodile) and the Brno Wheel, made in 1636 by a cartwright from Lednice, who bet a friend that he could fell a tree, make a wheel and roll it 50km to Brno all before sunset. He won the bet, but people began to suspect that he must have been in league with the devil – his business fell off and he died in poverty. If you're still hazy on the geography of the town, the tower is worth a climb for the panorama across the red-tiled rooftops.

Southwest of the square, the Petrov hill – on which the **Cathedral of St Peter and Paul** stands – is one of the best places in which to make a quick escape from the choked streets below. The cathedral's needle-sharp Gothic spires dominate the skyline for miles around, but close up, the crude nineteenth-century rebuilding has made it a lukewarm affair.

Back down on Masarykova, follow the flow north and you'll end up at **náměstí Svobody** – far short of magnificent but nonetheless the place where most of Brno come to do their shopping. On the northeast corner of the square, the **Ethnographical Museum** (Tues–Sun 9am–5pm) houses a large collection of Moravian stuff, as well as occasionally hosting exhibitions on other countries.

One of Brno's finest late nineteenth-century buildings is the **Mahen Theatre**, to the east of the square down Kobližná. This confident building was the first theatre in the Austro-Hungarian Empire to be fitted with electric lightbulbs. The squat **Dům umění** is an ugly companion, but it contains one of Brno's most innovative art galleries and performance venues. A little further up Rooseveltova, the grey and unappealing **Janáček Theatre** was built in the 1960s as the country's largest opera house. Across the park and a short way up Kounicova on the corner with Smetanova, there's a modest **museum** (Mon–Fri 8am–noon & 1–4pm) celebrating the life and music of **Leoš Janáček**, where you can sit back and relax to his compositions. He moved to Brno at the age of eleven and spent most of his life here, founding the Brno Conservatoire in 1882.

On the western edge of the city centre, the **UPM** on Husova (Tues–Sun 10am–6pm) contains the country's best collection of modern applied art, displaying everything from avant-garde photomontages to swirling Art Nouveau vases; it also has excellent temporary shows. At the **Pražák Palace** (Tues–Sun 10am–6pm), a little further down the road, there's an excellent cross-section of twentieth-century Czech art on permanent display. Skulking in the woods above the gallery is the barely visible **Špilberk Castle**, one of the worst prisons in the Habsburg Empire, and later a notorious Nazi jail; the newly renovated **dungeons** (Tues–Sun 9am–5pm) are now open to the public.

Further west still, where the River Svratka opens onto the plain (tram #1 or #18 from the station), is the **Výstaviště exhibition grounds**. The main buildings were laid out in 1928 for the Exhibition of Contemporary Culture; most of the leading Czech architects of the day were involved. On the opposite side of town, modernist guru Mies van der Rohe built the **Vila Tugendhat** (Wed–Sun 10am–6pm) in the same functionalist style as the above-mentioned Výstaviště; the house is at Černopolní 45, off Merhautova, itself a continuation of M. Horákové; take tram #5, #9, #17 or #21 three stops east from Joštova, and then walk north three blocks up Černopolní.

Eating and drinking

The **eating and drinking** scene has improved enormously over the last few years. The most popular café around is the Yugoslav-run *Adria*, on Masarykova, which serves great ice cream and pizzas, but if you want to sit outside and sup beer Czech-style, try *Špalíček*, at the top of Zelný trh, which has tables outside in summer and lashings of Gambrinus beer from Plzeň, or you could try out the replica functionalist café, *Zemanova kavárna*, near the Janáček Theatre. The brand-new brewery tap (and pension), *Pegas*, on Jakubská, is deservedly popular. *Skleněna louka*, Kounicova 23 is a late-night pub-venue worth checking out, as is the regular nightclub *Mersey*, Minská 15 (take any tram heading up Veveří).

Olomouc

Occupying the crucial Morava crossing-point on the road to Kraków, **OLOMOUC** (pronounced "Olla-moats") was the capital of Moravia from the Middle Ages to the mid-seventeenth century and the seat of the bishopric for even longer. All this attracted the destructive attention of Swedish troops in the Thirty Years' War, though the wealth of the Church and its strategic trading position kept the place going. And with a well-preserved old town, sloping cobbled squares and a plethora of Baroque fountains, not to mention a healthy quota of university students, Olomouc has a great deal going for it.

The **staré město** is a strange contorted shape, squeezed in the middle by an arm of the Morava. Train and bus terminals are a kilometre or so east, so on arrival take any tram heading west up Masarykova and get off after three or four stops. In the western half of the old town, all roads lead to the city's two central cobbled main squares, which are hinged to one another at right angles. At the centre of the upper square, the irregular **Horní náměstí**, stands the amalgamation of buildings that collectively make up the **town hall** or radnice. From its creamy rendering the occasional late Gothic or Renaissance gesture emerges – notably the handsome lanterned tower soaring to its conclusion of baubles and pinnacles. On the north side, next to the arcade of shops, is an astronomical clock which was destroyed in the war. The remake chimes all right, but the hourly mechanical show is disappointing.

Big enough to be a chapel, the **Holy Trinity Column** to the west of the town hall is the country's largest plague column; many such monuments were erected as thanksgiving for deliverance from the forces of Protestantism, but few are left standing. Set into the west facade of the square is the **Moravian Theatre**, where Mahler arrived as the newly appointed *Kapellmeister* in 1883; the local press took an instant dislike to him, and he lasted just three months. Olomouc makes a big fuss of its sculpture, like that adorning the Edelmann Palace (no. 28), and even more of the **fountains** that grace each of Olomouc's six ancient market squares. Horní náměstí boasts two: Hercules, looking unusually athletic for his years, and a vigorous depiction of Julius Caesar – the fabled founder of the city – bucking on a steed which coughs water from its mouth.

Two of the city's best-looking backstreets, Skolní and Michalská, lead southeast from Horní náměstí, up to the **church of sv Michal**, plain on the outside but inside clad in a masterly excess of Baroque. Firmly wedged between the two sections of the old town is the obligatory **Jesuit church of Panna Maria Sněžná**, deemed particularly necessary in a city where Protestantism had spread like wildfire in the sixteenth century. Jutting out into the road, it signals the gateway to the less hectic part of town. The great mass of the former Jesuit College, now the **Palacký University**, dominates the first square, náměstí Republiky, opposite which is the dull town museum and, next door, the vastly superior **art museum** (muzeum umění; Tues–Sun 10am–6pm); the top floor houses a fascinating selection of twentieth-century works by local-born artists and features a viewing tower.

Three blocks east of náměstí Republiky, the **Cathedral**, or Dóm, of sv Václav comes into view. Though it started life as a Romanesque basilica, the current structure is mostly nineteenth-century neo-Gothic. However, the walls and pillars of the nave are prettily painted in Romanesque style, and the crypt (Mon–Thurs & Sat 9am–5pm, Fri 1–5pm, Sun 11am–5pm) has a wonderful display of gory reliquaries and priestly sartorial wealth.

Practicalities

The **tourist office** (Mon–Fri 8.30am–5pm) in the town hall will book **private rooms** for you. Cheap rooms are hard to come by in Olomouc – the only bargain is the *Sigma* (☎068/26941; ③), opposite the train station, or the centrally located pension *U dómu*, Dómská 4 (☎068/522 05 01; ③), near the cathedral. Rooms can be even harder to come by in May when the Spring Music Festival follows the Flower Festival.

For **restaurants**, the *U červeného volka* on Dolní náměstí is a cheap place with a wide range of veggie dishes, but *Caesar Pizzeria* in the cobbled vaults under the town hall is by far the most popular joint in town. A good range of cakes can be found in the *Maruska cukrárna* on 28 října. In the evenings head for the *Café Mahler*, on the east side of the town hall, or a backstreet pub like *U bakláre*, Žerotinovo náměstí. The *Depo no. 8* at náměstí Republiky 1, has occasional DJs and bands, as does the *U-Klub* at the Studentcentrum at the far end of Křížovského.

travel details

Trains

Prague to: Brno (hourly; 3hr–4hr 30min); České Budějovice (9 daily; 2hr 30min–4hr 20min); Karlovy Vary (6 daily; 3hr 20min–4hr); Mariánské Lázně (8 daily; 2hr); Olomouc (every 1–2hr; 3hr–3hr 30min); Plzeň (12 daily; 1hr 35min).

Brno to: Olomouc (4–6 daily; 2hr).

České Budějovice to: Brno (3–5 daily; 4hr 10min–4hr 30min); Český Krumlov (up to 9 daily; 50min–1hr); Plzeň (up to 8 daily; 1hr 50min–3hr 20min).

Mariánské Lázně to: Karlovy Vary (6–8 daily; 1hr 30min).

Buses

Prague to: Brno (hourly; 2hr); Český Krumlov (up to 3 daily; 3hr 20min); České Budějovice (up to 12 daily; 2hr 25min–3hr 20min); Karlovy Vary (10 daily; 2hr 30min); Kutná Hora (8 daily; 1hr 15min–1hr 30min).

CHAPTER 7

DENMARK

Kristiansand △ Oslo △ Larvik △ △ Oslo

0   50 km

△ Tórshavn

Skagen
Gothenburg
Hirtshals
S k a g e r r a k
Frederikshaven
SWEDEN
Hanstholm
N
Thisted
Aalborg
K a t t e g a t
Varberg
Lemvig
Viborg
Randers
Grenå
Silkeborg
Ebeltoft
Helsingborg
Århus
Helsingør
Hillerød
JUTLAND
COPENHAGEN
Vejle
Kalundborg
Malmø
Fredericia
Roskilde
Esbjerg
Odense
Kerteminde
Ringsted
ZEALAND
Ribe
FUNEN
Næstved
Tønder
Fåborg
Svendborg

Harwich & Newcastle △
△ Tórshavn

Flensburg
Gelting
Bagenkop
Rødby
Nykøbing
GERMANY
Gedser
Kiel ▽
▽ Rostock & Puttgarden

Introduction

Delicately balanced between Scandinavia proper and mainland Europe, **Denmark** is a difficult country to pin down. In many ways it shares the characteristics of both regions: it's an EU member, and has prices and drinking laws that are broadly in line with those in the rest of Europe. But Danish social policies and the style of government in the country are distinctly Scandinavian: social benefits and the standard of living are high, and its politics are very much that of consensus.

Denmark is the easiest Scandinavian country in which to travel, both in terms of cost and distance, but the landscape itself is the region's least dramatic: very green and flat, largely farmland interrupted by innumerable pretty villages. Apart from a scattering of small islands, three main land masses make up the country – the islands of Zealand and Funen and the peninsula of Jutland, which extends northwards from Germany.

The vast majority of visitors make for **Zealand** (Sjælland), and, more specifically, **Copenhagen**, the country's one large city and an exciting focal point, with a beautiful old centre, a good array of museums and a boisterous nightlife. Zealand's smaller neighbour, **Funen** (Fyn), has only one positive urban draw in **Odense**, and otherwise is a sedate place, renowned for its cute villages and the sandy beaches of its fragmented southern coast. Only **Jutland** (Jylland) is far enough away from Copenhagen to enjoy a truly individual flavour, as well as Denmark's most varied scenery, ranging from soft green hills to desolate heathlands. **Århus** and **Aalborg** are two of the liveliest cities outside the capital.

Information and maps

All towns and some villages will have a **tourist office**, giving out free maps and sometimes able to book accommodation and change money. Most railway and motorway service stations also offer a hotel booking service. In large cities tourist offices sell useful **discount cards** giving reductions on public transport, museum entry and the like. They're open long hours every day in the most popular places, but have much reduced times outside the April to September period. The best general **map** of Denmark is the Hallwag one.

Money and banks

Coming from any of the other Scandinavian countries, Denmark seems remarkably cheap, with prices roughly only 10–20 percent higher than other western European countries. **Danish currency** is the krone (plural kroner), made up of 100øre, and it comes in notes of 50kr, 100kr, 200kr, 500kr, 1000kr, and coins of 25øre, 50øre, 1kr, 2kr, 5kr, 10kr, 20kr. **Banks** are the best places to change travellers' cheques and foreign cash; there's a uniform commission of 25kr per transaction, so change as much as possible in one go. Banking hours are Mon–Fri 9.30am–4pm, Thurs until 6pm. Most airports and ferry terminals have late-opening exchange facilities, and automatic cash machines are everywhere.

Communications

Most **post offices** are open Mon–Fri 9am–5pm, Sat 9am–1pm, with reduced hours in smaller communities. You can buy stamps either there or from most newsagents; mail to other parts of Europe under 20g costs 4kr and 5.25kr for the rest of the world. Danish **public telephones** come in two forms. Coin-operated ones are red and require a minimum of 2 x 1kr for a local call (the machines irritatingly swallow one of the coins if the number is engaged), and 5kr to go international; plastic for the blue card phones comes in denominations of 30kr, 50kr and 100kr and works out a little cheaper. One thing to remember when dialling Danish numbers is to always use the area code. The international access code is ☎00; Danish directory enquiries (20kr) are on ☎118, international (also 20kr) on ☎113, with almost all operators speaking English.

Getting around

Despite being an island country, Denmark is a swift and easy place to travel. All types of public transport – trains, buses and ferries – are punctual and efficient, and the timetables are well integrated.

■ Trains, buses and ferries

Trains are easily the best way to get about. Danske Statsbaner (DSB) – Danish State Railways – run an exhaustive and reliable network. Train types range from the large intercity expresses (ICs) to smaller local trains (*persontog*). **Tickets** should be bought in advance from the station, one-way tickets allowing you to break your journey once, although travel must be completed in one day. Fares are calculated on a zonal system: Copenhagen to Århus – probably the longest single trip you'll make – costs 240kr including seat reservation, and your train ticket will get you around on the local buses in the departure and arrival town of your journey. Buying a return offers no savings over two singles. Seat reservations are necessary on all IC trains (20kr) – InterRail and Eurail passes are valid, as is the **ScanRail pass**, which costs £126/$202 (or £94/$150 if you are under 25) for 5 days' travel in 15, £171/$274 (or £128/$205) for 10 days' travel in a month, £198/$317 for 21 consecutive days (£149/$238). This gives you unlimited travel in the four main Scandinavian countries, plus large discounts on many ferry crossings and bus journeys. The new **Øresund Link**, due to open in May 2000, means train travel between Denmark and Sweden is now a possibility.

DSB's *Køreplan* (free) details all train, bus and ferry services, including the local Copenhagen S-train system and all private services; smaller timetables detailing specific routes are available free at tourist offices and station booking counters.

There are a few out-of-the-way regions trains fail to penetrate, and these can easily be crossed by **buses**, which often run in conjunction with the trains, some operated privately, some by DSB – on which railcards are valid. Much of Funen and the northeast of Jutland is barely touched by trains, and you can save several hours by taking the bus. Abildskous Rutebiler (☎86.78.48.88) run from Århus to Copenhagen (150kr per person one way, 280kr return) and Århus to Ålborg (98kr per person). Fjerritslev-København (☎98.21.12.75) link towns in Jutland with Copenhagen stopping at Ålborg, Løgstør, Aars, Hobro, Hadsund, Randers, Grenå, Århus and Ebeltoft – the fare from Fjerritslev to Copenhagen is 200kr per person. Thinggaard Rutebiler (☎98.11.66.00) provide a service from Ålborg to Copenhagen (180kr) and Frederikshavn to Esbjerg (190kr one way). The quickest and most convenient way to travel by bus around Jutland is to take one of the X-busser. You can get information about routes and destinations by calling their office (☎98.90.09.00) – ask for a timetable (*køreplan*), which the staff will be happy to send you free of charge.

Ferries link all the Danish islands, and where applicable train and bus fares include the cost of crossings (although you can also pay at the terminal and walk on); the smaller ferry crossings normally cost 10–40kr for foot passengers.

■ Driving and hitching

Given the excellence of the Danish public transport system, the size of the country and the comparatively high price of petrol, **driving** isn't really economical unless you're travelling in a group. Danes drive on the right, and there's a speed limit in towns of 50kph, 80kph in open country and 110kph on motorways – speed traps lead to hefty fines. Like the other Scandinavian countries, dipped headlights have to be used during daylight hours. There are random breath

tests, and the penalties for drunk driving are severe. When parking unmetered in a town, a parking-time disc must be displayed; you'll be able to get one from a tourist office, police station or bank. The national motoring organization, Forenede Danske Motorejere, operates a breakdown service Mon–Fri 9am–5pm, Sat 10am–1pm (☎45.93.08.00); if you find yourself stranded outside those hours, motorway assistance can be summoned from call boxes by the road – although a standard call-out fee will be charged. **Car rental** in Denmark starts at around 2000kr a week for a small hatchback with unlimited mileage (you'll need your driving licence). **Hitching** is illegal on motorways but fairly easy elsewhere.

■ Cycling

Cycling is the best way to appreciate Denmark's mostly flat landscape. Most country roads have sparse vehicle traffic and all large towns have cycle tracks. Bikes can be **rented** at nearly all youth hostels, bike shops and tourist offices and some train stations from 35kr per day, 75–185kr per week, although there's often a 200kr deposit. IC and certain regional trains (marked on timetables) won't accept bikes. On those that do, you'll have to pay 25kr, or 50kr if the trip includes a ferry crossing.

Accommodation

While much less costly than it can be in other Scandinavian countries, **accommodation** is still going to be your major daily expense in Denmark. Hotels, however, are by no means off-limits if you are prepared to seek out the better offers, and both the youth hostels and campsites that you'll come across are plentiful and of a uniformly high standard.

■ Hotels and private rooms

Most Danish **hotel** rooms include phone, TV and bathroom, for which you'll pay around 500kr for a double, although in most large towns you'll also find hotels offering rooms without bathrooms for as little as 350kr for a double. One advantage of staying in a hotel is the inclusive all-you-can-eat breakfast – so large you won't need to buy lunch. Only in peak season will you need to book in advance. Danish tourist offices overseas can provide a free list of hotels throughout the country, though much more accurate and extensive information can be found at local tourist offices. Tourist offices can also supply details of **private rooms** in someone's home, for which you should reckon on paying 200–350kr a double. Alternatively, staying on farms (*Bondegårdsferie*) is becoming increasingly popular in Denmark, with

ACCOMMODATION PRICE CODES

Throughout this guide, accommodation is priced on a scale of ① to ⑨, the number indicating the lowest price per night a single person could expect to pay in that establishment in high season. With hostels this is the nightly rate per person; with hotels, the price is arrived at by dividing the cost of the cheapest double room by two. The prices indicated by the codes are as follows:

① under £5 / $8	④ £15–20 / $24–32	⑦ £30–35 / $48–56
② £5–10 / $8–16	⑤ £20–25 / $32–40	⑧ £35–40 / $56–64
③ £10–15 / $16–24	⑥ £25–30 / $40–48	⑨ £40 / $64 and over

many of them offering accommodation and the chance to watch a farm at work. Information and catalogues can be obtained from Ferie på Landet, Søndergade 26, 8700 Horsens (☎70.10.41.90)

■ Hostels and sleep-ins

Youth **hostels** are the cheapest option under a roof. Every town has one, they're much less pricey than hotels and they have a high degree of comfort, most offering a choice of private rooms, often with toilets and showers, or dorm accommodation; nearly all have cooking facilities. Rates are around 75kr per person for a dorm bed; non-HI members pay an extra 25kr a night. An **IYHF card** will cost you 50kr. It's rare for hostels other than those in major towns or ferry ports to be full, but during the summer it's still wise to phone ahead. As with all Scandinavian hostels, sleeping bags are not allowed, so you have to carry a sheet bag or hire hostel linen. If you're doing a lot of hostelling, it's worth contacting Danmarks Vandrerhjem, Vesterbrogade 39, DK-1620, Copenhagen V. (☎31.31.36.12), for their hostel guide (25kr).

Sometimes cheaper still, and occasionally free, are sleep-ins, usually open in the main towns for a two-week period during the summer (late June/early July). You need your own sleeping bag, sometimes only one night's stay is permitted and there may be an age restriction. Sleep-ins come and go, however; check the current situation at a tourist office.

■ Campsites and cabins

If you don't have an International Camping Card from a camping organization at home, you'll need a Visitor's Pass to **camp** in Denmark, which costs 24kr per person (48kr for a family) from any campsite and is valid on all official sites until the year's end. Campsites are virtually everywhere. All sites open through the three summer months, many from April to September, while a few stay open all year. There's a rigid grading system: one-star sites have drinking water and toilets; two-stars have, in addition, showers, laundry and a food shop within a kilometre; three-stars, by far the majority, have all the above plus a TV-room, shop, cafeteria, etc. Prices vary only slightly, three-stars charging 32–42kr per person, others a few kroner less.

Many sites also have **cabin accommodation**, usually with cooking facilities, for upwards of 900kr for a six-berth affair, although these are often booked up throughout the summer. Any tourist office will give you a free leaflet listing all the sites. **Camping rough** without permission is illegal, and an on-the-spot fine may be imposed.

Food and drink

There are plenty of ways to eat affordably and healthily in Denmark, and with plenty of variety, too. Much the same applies to drink: the only Scandinavian country free of social drinking taboos, Denmark is an imbiber's delight – both for its choice of tipples and the number of places they can be sampled.

■ Food

Traditional Danish **food** centres on meat and fish, served with potatoes and another, usually boiled, vegetable. **Breakfast** (*morgenmad*) can be the tastiest Danish meal, and almost all hotels offer a sumptuous breakfast as a matter of course, as do youth hostels: a table laden with cereals, bread, cheese, boiled eggs, fruit juice, milk and tea for around 40kr. Breakfast elsewhere is less substantial: many cafés offer a basic one for 15–40kr. Later in the day, a tight budget may leave you dependent on self-catering. As for **snacks**, you can buy *smørrebrød* – open sandwiches heaped with meat, fish or cheese, and assorted trimmings – for 10–20kr from special shops, at least one of which will be open until 10pm. There are also fast-food stands (*pølsevogn*) in all main streets and at train stations, serving various hot sausages (*pølser*), toasted sandwiches (*parisertoast*) and chips (*pommes frites*). The size refers to the actual chips and not the portion. If you just want a cup of coffee or tea, cafés serve both; help it down with a Danish pastry (*wienerbrød*), tastier and much less sweet than the imitations sold under the name elsewhere.

You can find an excellent-value **lunch** (*frokost*) simply by walking around at lunchtime and reading the signs chalked up outside a café, restaurant or bodega (a bar which sells no-frills food). You'll often see the word *tilbud*, which refers to the "special" priced dish, or *dagens ret*, "dish of the day" – a plate of chilli con carne or lasagne for around 45kr, or a two-course set lunch for about 60kr. Some restaurants offer the Dan Menu, designed to make ordering and eating Danish food easy for tourists and comprising a two-course meal for 75kr, while many more carry a fixed-price (75–90kr) three-course lunch. You can also usually get a choice of three or four *smørrebrød* for about 75kr. Elsewhere, the American burger franchises are commonplace, as are pizzerias, many of which offer special deals such as all-you-can-eat-salad with a basic pizza for 45kr. You can also get a very ordinary self-service meat, fish or omelette lunch in a supermarket cafeteria for 40–75kr.

Dinner (*aftensmad*) presents as much choice as does lunch, but the cost is likely to be much higher, although many youth hostels serve filling evening meals for 45–50kr. For 60–80kr you can fill up in an **ethnic restaurant**, most commonly Chinese and Middle Eastern, many of which, besides à la carte dishes, have a help-yourself table. Sadly, the same **Danish restaurants** that are promising for lunch turn into expense-account affairs at night, although a few serve the 75kr Dan Menu into the evening. If you plan to save money by eating in, head for Netto supermarkets, where the food and drink are cheap and of excellent quality. A bottle of beer can cost as little as 3kr, as long as you return the glass bottle – in turn you'll get your tax reimbursed.

■ Drink

Although you can buy booze much more cheaply from supermarkets, the most sociable places to drink are pubs and cafés, where the emphasis is on beer. There are also bars and bodegas, in which, as a very general rule, the mood tends to favour wines and spirits and the customers are a bit older. The cheapest beer is draught beer (*Fadøl*), half a litre of which costs 25–30kr. Draught is a touch weaker than bottled beer, which costs 20–25kr for a third of a litre, and is a great deal less potent than the export beers (*Guldøl* or *Eksport-Øl*) costing 25–30kr a bottle. The most common brands are Carlsberg and Tuborg; Lys Pilsner is a very low alcohol lager, more like a soft drink. Most international wines and spirits are widely available, a shot of the hard stuff costing 15–20kr in a bar, a glass of wine upwards of 15kr. You should also investigate the many varieties of the schnapps-like Akvavit, which Danes consume as eagerly as beer; a tasty relative is the hot and strong Gammel Dansk Bitter Dram – Akvavit-based but made with bitters and drunk occasionally at breakfast time.

Opening hours and holidays

Standard shopping hours are Mon–Fri 9.30/10am–5.30/7pm, Sat 9am–4pm. All shops and banks are closed, and public transport and many museums run to Sunday schedules on the following days: Jan 1; Maundy Thursday; Good Friday; Easter Day; Easter Monday; Prayer Day (fourth Friday after Easter); Ascension (around mid-May); Whit Sunday; Whit Monday; Constitution Day (June 5); Dec 24 (afternoon only); Dec 25 and Dec 26. On International Workers' Day, which falls on May 1, many offices and shops close at noon.

Emergencies

You're likely to have little cause to trouble the Danish **police**, as street crime and hassle is minimal in Denmark – but if you do, you'll find them helpful and almost certainly able to speak English. For prescriptions, **doctors'** consultations and dental work – but not hospital visits – you have to pay on the spot, but to get a full refund, take your receipt, E111 and passport to the local health office.

EMERGENCY NUMBERS

All emergencies ☎112.

COPENHAGEN AND AROUND

COPENHAGEN, as any Dane will tell you, is no introduction to Denmark; indeed, a greater contrast with the sleepy provincialism of the rest of the country would be hard to find. Despite that, the city completely dominates Denmark: it is the seat of all the nation's institutions – politics, finance and the arts. Copenhagen is also easily Scandinavia's most affordable capital, and one of Europe's most user-friendly cities, welcoming and fairly small, with a compact, strollable centre largely given over to pedestrians. In summer, there's a varied range of lively street entertainment, while at night there's a plethora of cosy bars and an intimate club and live-music network that can hardly be bettered. For daytime sights, the city has first-rate galleries housing collections of Danish and international art, as well as a worthy batch of smaller museums.

There was no more than a tiny fishing settlement here until the twelfth century, when Bishop Absalon oversaw the building of a castle on the site of the present Christiansborg. The settlement's prosperity grew after Erik of Pomerania granted special privileges and imposed the Sound Toll on vessels passing through the Øresund, then under Danish control, which gave the expanding city tidy profits and enabled a self-confident trading centre to flourish. Following the demise of the Hanseatic ports, the city became the Baltic's principal harbour, earning the name København ("merchant's port"), and in 1443 it was made the Danish capital. A century later, Christian IV began the building programme that was the basis of the modern city: up went Rosenborg Slot, Børsen, Rundetårnet, and the districts of Nyboder and Christianshavn; and, in 1669, Frederik III graced the city with its first royal palace, Amalienborg, for his queen, Sophie Amalie.

Arrival and information

However you get to Copenhagen you'll find yourself within easy reach of the centre. Trains pull into the **Central Station**, near Vesterbrogade, where there's an InterRail Centre (daily mid-June to late Sept 6.30am–midnight) downstairs with left-luggage lockers, showers (10kr), cooking facilities and a message board for rail-pass holders. **Long-distance buses** from other parts of Denmark each stop a short bus or S-train ride from the centre: buses from Århus stop at Valby; from Aalborg at Ryparken Station on S-train line H; and those from Hanstholm on Hans Knudsest Plads. **Ferries** and catamarans from Norway and Sweden dock close to Nyhavn, a few minutes' walk from the inner city. **Planes** use Kastrup Airport, 8km from the city, which is connected with the Central Station in Copenhagen by the new Øresund Link train (every 20min 4.55am–12.15am; journey time 12min; 16.50kr) and by Express Bus (every 15min 6.30am–11.10pm; journey time 30min; 35kr).

For maps, general information and accommodation in hotels and hostels (booking fee 15kr), head for the **tourist office**, Bernstorffsgade 1 (May to mid-Sept daily 9am–8pm; rest of year Mon–Fri 9am–4.30pm, Sat 9am–1.30pm; ☎33.11.13.25), across the road from the train station. You can buy a **Copenhagen Card** here, valid for the entire metropolitan transport system (which includes much of eastern Zealand) and giving entry to virtually every museum in the area. A 24-hour card costs 155kr, those for 48 hours and 72 hours cost 255kr and 320kr respectively. Cards are also sold in other tourist offices, hotels and travel agents and at the train station.

Far better for youth and budget-orientated help is **Use-It**, centrally placed in the Huset complex at Rådhusstræde 13 (mid-June to mid-Sept daily 9am–7pm; rest of year Mon–Wed 11am–4pm, Thurs 11am–6pm, Fri 11am–2pm; ☎33.73.06.20;). It provides a wide range of help for travellers, including poste restante and email services, accommodation and entertainment information, luggage storage facilities and a very useful free magazine called *Playtime*. The staff fall over themselves to help you find a room in the busy summer period and if you are willing to queue, use of the Internet is free. **Wonderful Copenhagen**, near the Planetarium at Gammel Kongevejl 1 (☎33.25.74.00; *www.woco.dk*), is less personable, but its web site is good for information on forthcoming events.

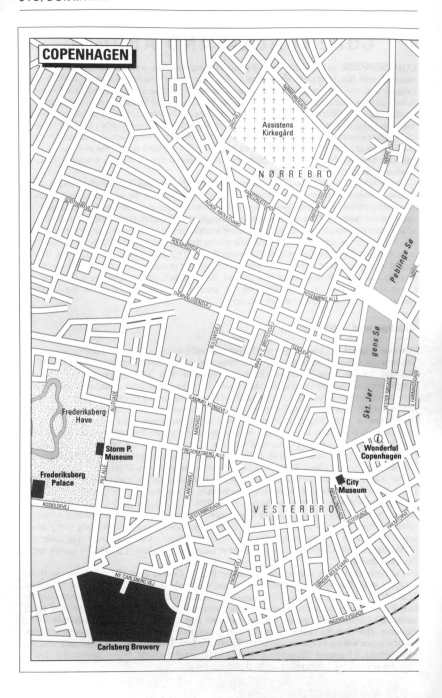

COPENHAGEN

NØRREBROGADE

JAGTVEJ

Assistens
Kirkegård

NØRRE ALLÉ

N Ø R R E B R O

GODTHÅBSVEJ

PANTZAURSSGADE

AGADE ÅBOULEVARD

GRIFFENFELDSGADE

ROLIGHEDSVEJ

Peblinge Sø

NØRRE

THORVALDSENSVEJ

ROSENØRNS ALLÉ

BÜLOWSVEJ

BRAM. H. C. ØRSTEDSVEJ

DANASVEJ

gens Sø

Skt. Jør

VESTER SØGADE

V. FARIMAGSGADE

ALLÉGADE

GAMMEL KONGEVEJ

MADVIGS

Frederiksberg
Have

Storm P.
Museum

Wonderful
Copenhagen

PILE ALLÉ

P. ANTANVEJ

FREDERIKSBERG ALLÉ

City
Museum

ABSALONSGADE

Frederiksberg
Palace

ROSKILDEVEJ

VESTERBROGADE

V E S T E R B R O

ISTEDGADE

HALMTORVET

NY CARLSBERG VEJ

ENGHAVEJ

SØNDER BOULEVARD

Carlsberg Brewery

INGERSLEVSGADE

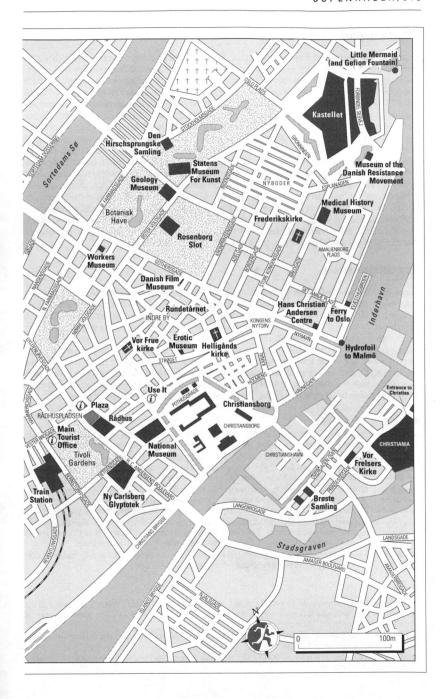

Little Mermaid
(and Gefion Fountain)

Kastellet

Museum of the
Danish Resistance
Movement

Den
Hirschsprungske
Samling

Statens
Museum
For Kunst

NYBODER

Geology
Museum

Medical History
Museum

Botanisk
Have

Frederikskirke

Rosenborg
Slot

AMALIENBORG
PLADS

Workers
Museum

Danish Film
Museum

SKT ANNÆ PLADS

Rundetårnet

Hans Christian
Andersen
Centre

Ferry
to Oslo

INDRE BY

KONGENS
NYTORV

Vor Frue
kirke

Erotic
Museum

Helligånds
kirke

NYHAVN

STRØGET

Hydrofoil
to Malmö

HOLMENS

Use It

Entrance to
Christies

Plaza

POTHUSGADE

Christiansborg

RÅDHUSPLADSEN

Rådhus

CHRISTIANSBORG

Main
Tourist
Office

National
Museum

CHRISTIANIA

Tivoli
Gardens

CHRISTIANSHAVN

Vor
Frelsers
Kirke

Train
Station

Ny Carlsberg
Glyptotek

Brøste
Samling

LANGEBROGADE

LANDSGADE

Stadsgraven

AMAGER BOULEVARD

0   100m

City transport

An integrated network of **buses** and electric **S-trains** (S-tog) covers a zonal system over the whole of Copenhagen and the surrounding areas between 5am and 12.30am, after which a night bus (Natbusserne) system comes into operation. You can use InterRail or Eurail cards on the S-trains, but otherwise the best option after a Copenhagen Card (see above) or the 24-hour *Timer* ticket (70kr) – which covers the same transportation area but without admission to museums – is either a two-zone (70kr) *Klippekort* or a three-zone (85kr) *Rabatkort*, which has ten stamps you cancel individually; one stamp on a two-zone card gives unlimited transfers within one hour in two zones; one stamp on a three-zone card lasts an hour and a half. Double stamping allows even longer journeys. For a single journey of less than an hour, use a *Grundbillet* (11kr), valid for unlimited transfers within two zones in that time. Tickets can be bought on board buses or at train stations and should be stamped when boarding the bus or in the machines on station platforms. A passenger without a valid ticket faces an instant fine of 500kr. Route maps cost 10kr from stations, but most free maps of the city include bus lines and a diagram of the S-train network. The basic **taxi** fare is 22kr plus 7.70kr per kilometre (9.60kr after 6pm and at weekends) – only worthwhile if several people are sharing. A new innovation is the **City Bike scheme**, whereby bikes can be borrowed from racks spread throughout the city for a 20kr deposit, which is returned when the bike is locked back into any other city rack after use.

Accommodation

Accommodation of all kinds is easy to come by in Copenhagen, and almost all of it is central. Only if you're going to be arriving late, or during July and August, is it necessary to book in advance. Most of the cheaper **hotels** are just outside the main centre, around Istedgade, a slightly seedy area on the far side of the train station, while there is also a good range of mid-priced hotels around Nyhavn, on the opposite side of the Indre By. Enquire at the tourist office early in the day and you may get a double room for as little as 300kr; **private rooms**, most of which are in the inner suburbs, are also mainly within this price range. Copenhagen has a great, though less central, selection of **hostel accommodation**, and space is only likely to be a problem in the peak summer months, when you should phone ahead or turn up as early as possible to be sure of a place. Breakfast is not included in the prices given.

Hostels

Bellahøj, Herbergsvejen 8 (☎38.28.97.15). Official hostel with large dorms, but more cosy than its rivals, and just fifteen minutes from the city centre on buses #2 and #11. No curfew. Open all year. ②.

City Public Hostel, Absalonsgade 8 (☎32.31.20.70). Handily placed ten minutes' walk from the train station between Vesterbrogade and Istedgade, with a noisy 60-bed dormitory on the lower floor, and less crowded conditions on other levels. Buses #6 and #16 stop close by. No curfew. Open May–Aug. ②.

Copenhagen Hostel, Vejlands allæ 200, Amager (☎32.52.29.08). Official hostel with fairly frugal and sometimes noisy 2- and 5-bed rooms. Get to it on bus #46 (daytime only), or take the C line S-train to Valby or Sjælør, then a #37 bus towards Holmens Bro, a thirty-minute journey. No curfew. Open all year. ②.

Sleep-In, Blegdamsvej 132 (☎35.26.50.59). A vast hall divided into 4-bed compartments. Nice atmosphere, with a young staff and sporadic live gigs. Ten minutes from the centre on S-train A, B or C, or by bus #1 towards Hellerup or #6 towards Ryvang. No curfew. Open July–Aug. ②, including breakfast.

YWCA/Interpoint, Valdemarsgade 15 (☎33.31.15.74). Fifteen minutes' walk from Central Station or take bus #3, #6 or #16. Open July to mid-Aug 8am–noon & 3.30pm–12.30am. ②.

Hotels

Jørgensens Hotel, Rømersgade 11 (☎33.13.81.86). North of Istedgade on Isreals Plads, this is one of the cheapest hotels in town and is popular with gay travellers. It also offers summer dorm accommodation at even cheaper prices. ⑤.

Ibsens Hotel, Vendersgade 23 (☎33.13.19.13). Relaxed and friendly. Popular with businessmen from Jutland because the owner is Jute. ⑥.

Missionhotellet Nebo, Istedgade 6 (☎31.21.12.17). Small, friendly, and one of the best deals in the tame red light area of the city. ⑤.

Saga Hotel, Colbjørnsensgade 18-20 (☎31.24.49.44). Cheap for a central hotel and a stone's throw from Central Station (head out the back exit of the station). On the edge of the red light district. ⑤.

Sophie Amalie, Skt. Annæ Plads 21 (☎33.13.34.00). Large luxurious rooms right by the harbour. Good if you want to pamper yourself. ⑨.

Campsites

Absalon, 132 Korsdalsvej, Rødovre (☎36.41.06.00). Reasonable site about 9km southwest of the city and open all year. S-train line B to Brøndby-Øster, then a fifteen-minute walk or bus #550 S.

Bellahøj, on Hvidkildevej (☎31.10.11.50), near the Bellahøj hostel. Central but grim, with long queues for the showers. Reached by bus #2. Open June–Aug.

Charlottenlund Strandpark, Strandvejen 144B, Charlottenlund (☎39.62.36.88). Beautifully situated at Charlottenlund Beach. Reached by bus #6. Open May–Aug.

Nærum, on Ravnebakken (☎45.80.19.57). A long way out from the centre but very pleasant. Take a train to Jægersborg, then private train (InterRail and Eurail not valid; Copenhagen Card valid) to Nærum. Open mid-April to mid-Sept.

The City

Seeing Copenhagen is a doddle. Most of what you're likely to want to see can be found in the city's relatively small centre, between the long scythe of the harbour and a semicircular series of lakes. **Indre By** forms the city's inner core, an intricate maze of streets, squares and alleys. The main way into Indre By is from the buzzing open space of Rådhuspladsen, where the **Rådhus** (Mon–Fri 10am–3pm, guided tours at 3pm; 20kr) has an elegant main hall that retains many of its original turn-of-the-century features and a **bell tower** (tours June–Sept Mon–Fri 10am, noon & 2pm, Sat noon; Oct–May Mon–Sat noon; 10kr) that gives views over the city. Jens **Olsen's World Clock** (Mon–Fri 10am–4pm, Sat 10am–1pm; 10kr), in a room close to the entrance, took 27 years to perfect and contains a 570,000-year calendar plotting moon and sun eclipses, solar time, local time and various planetary orbits – all with astounding accuracy.

Beyond here, **Strøget** leads into the heart of the city, a pedestrianized street lined by pricey stores and fast-food dives, whose appeal is in the walkers, roller-skaters and street entertainers who parade along it. The liveliest part is around Gammeltorv and Nytorv, two squares ("old" and "new") on either side of Strøget, where there's a morning fruit and vegetable market and jewellery and bric-a-brac stalls. A few minutes further on, the **Helligånds Kirke** (daily noon–4pm) is one of the oldest churches in the city, founded in the fourteenth century and largely rebuilt from 1728 onwards. Its summer café and the art shows and exhibitions held inside provide a good excuse for a peek at the church's vaulted ceiling and slender granite columns. At the end of Strøget, **Kongens Nytorv** is the city's largest square, with an equestrian statue of its creator, Christian V, in its centre and a couple of grandly ageing structures around two of its shallow angles, most notably **Charlottenborg** – finished in 1683, at the same time as the square itself, for a son of Frederik III. Since 1754 it has been the home of the Royal Academy of Art, which uses some of the spacious rooms for decidedly eclectic art exhibitions.

There's more to see among the tangle of buildings and streets **west of Strøget**, not least the old university area, sometimes called the Latin Quarter, where the **Vor Frue Kirke** (Mon–Sat 9am–5pm, Sun noon–4pm), Copenhagen's cathedral, dates from 1829. The weighty figure of Christ behind the altar and the solemn statues of the Apostles, some crafted by Bertel Thorvaldsen, others by his pupils, merit a quick call. Northeast, the **Rundetårnet** (summer Mon–Sat 10am–8pm and until 10pm on Tues & Wed, Sun noon–8pm; winter Mon–Sat 10am–5pm, Sun noon–5pm; 15kr), whose summit is reached by a spiral ramp, was built by Christian IV as an observatory. Close by, the **Musical History Museum**, just off Kultorvet at Åbenrå 30 (May–Sept Mon–Wed & Fri 1–4pm; Oct–April Mon, Wed, Sat & Sun 1–4pm; 20kr) holds an impressive quantity of musical instruments and sound-making devices, spanning the globe and the last thousand years. Many musical recordings can be listened to through headphones, and guided tours take place every Wednesday at 11am. The **Erotic Museum** at Købmagergarde 24 (May–Sept daily 10am–11pm; Oct–April Mon–Fri & Sun 11am–8pm, Sat 10am–9pm; 59kr) was moved recently from its former home in the red-light district and exhibits a mixture of titillating historical photos, sex toys and waxworks.

Over Nørre Voldgade, the **Workers Museum** at Rømersgade 22 (July–Oct daily 10am–4pm; rest of year Tues–Sun 10am–4pm; 30kr) is an engrossing guide to working-class life in Copenhagen from the Thirties to the Fifties using reconstructions and authentic period materials.

Nørrebro, northwest of the train station, has shed its crime-related reputation and is now a lively, young area that buzzes right through the night. Directly behind the station is Vesterbro, the city's slightly seedy though unthreatening red light district.

North of Gothersgade

Gothersgade, the road marking the northern perimeter of Indre by, is home to the **Danish Film Museum** (Mon, Tues, Thurs & Fri noon–4pm; free), which displays cameras, props and other remnants of an early film industry that before Hollywood and the talkies was among the world's best. There's a profound change of mood once you cross Gothersgade: the congenial alleys of the old city give way to long, broad streets and proud, aristocratic structures. Running from Kongens Nytorv, a slender canal divides the two sides of **Nyhavn**, picturesquely lined by eighteenth-century houses – now bars and cafés – that was until recently frequented by docked sailors; they earned the area a racy reputation, but it's now in the advanced stages of gentrification and is *the* place to be seen enjoying a beer in the summer season. Just north, the cobbled Amalienborg Plads focuses on a statue of Frederik V flanked by four identical Rococo palaces. Two serve as royal residences, and there's a changing of the guard each day at noon when the monarch is at home. Between the square and the harbour are the lavish gardens of Amaliehaven, while in the opposite direction the great marble dome of **Frederikskirke**, also known as "Marmorkirken," meaning marble church (Mon–Fri 10.30am–4.30pm, Wed until 6pm, Sat & Sun noon–4.30pm; free guided tours daily at 1pm & 1–3pm in summer), was modelled on St Peter's in Rome. It was begun in 1749 but because of its enormous cost remained unfinished until a century and a half later. The reward of joining a guided tour is the chance to climb to the whispering gallery and step out onto the rim of the dome itself. Further along Bredgade, a German armoured car commandeered by Danes to bring news of the Nazi surrender marks the entrance to the **Museum of the Danish Resistance Movement** (Frihedsmuseeti; May to mid-Sept Tues–Sat 10am–4pm, Sun 10am–5pm; rest of year Tues–Sat 11am–3pm, Sun 11am–4pm; free).

The road behind the museum crosses into the grounds of the **Kastellet** (daily 6am–sunset; free), a fortress built by Christian IV and expanded by his successors through the seventeenth century. It's now occupied by the Danish army and closed to the public, but on a nearby corner the **Little Mermaid** has, since its unveiling in 1913, been one of the city's most massive tourist targets, a bronze statue of a Hans Christian Andersen character, sculpted by Edvard Erichsen and paid for by the boss of the Carlsberg brewery. It's worth enduring the crowds for the more spectacular Gefion Fountain, a short walk to the south, which shows the goddess Gefion with her four sons, whom she's turned into oxen having been promised, in return, as much land as she can plough in a single night.

Still north of Gothersgade, but away from the harbour across Store Kongensgade, lies **Nyboder**, a curious area of narrow streets lined with rows of compact yellow dwellings, originally built by Christian IV to encourage his sailors to live in the city. The area declined into a slum, but a recent overhaul has made it increasingly sought after. The oldest (and cutest) houses can be found along Skt. Pauls Gade; Baron Bolton's Court, tucked behind the corner of Gothersgade and Store Kongensgade, is a revamped precinct of eighteenth-century town houses holding shops and restaurants and hosting live jazz in summer. Across Sølvgade from Nyboder is the main entrance to **Rosenborg Slot**. This Dutch Renaissance-style palace served as the main residence of Christian IV and, until the end of the nineteenth century, of the monarchs who succeeded him. The main building displays the rooms and furnishings used by the regal occupants, although the highlight is the downstairs treasury (separate entrance; hours as Kastellet), which displays the rich accessories worn by Christian IV. Adjacent to Rosenborg Slot is **Kongens Have**, the city's oldest public park and a popular place for picnics while on the west side is the **Botanical Garden** (Botanisk Have; daily 8.30am–4/6pm; free).

The neighbouring **Statens Museum for Kunst** (Tues & Thurs–Sun 10am–5pm, Wed 10am–8pm; 40kr, free on Wed), was recently extended with a modern flavour which complements the grand old building and increases its capacity by fifty percent. The mammoth collection of art (*kunst*) embraces some minor Picassos and more major works by Matisse and Braque, Cranach, El Greco, Titian, Rubens, Poussin and Claude Lorrain – although it's Emil Nolde, with his gross pieces showing bloated ravens, hunched figures and manic children, who manages to steal the show. The new section mostly houses contemporary Danish art. The Skagen artists (see p.334), known for their interesting use of light, are amongst a nearby collection of twentieth-century Danish art across the park, behind the museum, at **Den Hirschsprungske Samling** on Stockholmsgade (Mon & Thurs–Sun 11am–4pm, Wed 11am–9pm; 25kr).

Christiansborg

Christiansborg sits on the island of Slotsholmen, tenuously connected to Indre by several short bridges. It was here, in the twelfth century, that Bishop Absalon built the castle that instigated the city. The drab royal palace completed in 1916 that now occupies the site is today primarily given over to government offices and the state parliament or **Folketinget** (guided tours on the hour June–Aug Mon–Fri & Sun 10am–4pm; rest of year Sun 10am, 11am & 1–4pm; free). Close to the bus stop on Christiansborg Slotsplads is the doorway to the **Ruins under Christiansborg** (May–Sept daily 9.30am–3.30pm; Oct–April Tues, Thurs, Sat & Sun 9.30am–3.30pm; 15kr), where a staircase leads down to the remains of Absalon's original building – surprisingly absorbing, the mood enhanced by the semidarkness and lack of external noise. In and around Christiansborg's courtyard there are a number of other, less captivating museums, including the **Royal Stables** (May–Sept Fri–Sun 2–4pm; Oct–April Sat & Sun 2–4pm; 10kr); a **Theatre Museum** (Wed 2–4pm, Sun noon–4pm; 20kr), housed in what was the eighteenth-century Court Theatre; and an **Armoury Museum** (Tues–Sun 10am–4pm; 20kr).

On the far side of Slotsholmen, the **Thorvaldsens Museum** (Tues–Sun 10am–5pm; free) is the home of an enormous collection of work and memorabilia (and the body) of Denmark's most famous sculptor, who lived from 1770 to 1844. The labels of the great, hulking statues read like a roll call of the famous and infamous: Vulcan, Adonis, Gutenberg, Pius VII and Maximilian; and the Christ Hall contains the huge casts of the Christ and Apostles statues that can be seen in Vor Frue Kirke. There's another major collection a short walk away over the Slotsholmen moat, in the **National Museum** (Tues–Sun 10am–5pm; 30kr), which has excellent displays on Danish prehistory and Viking days – jewellery, sacrificial gifts, bones and even bodies, all remarkably well preserved by Danish peat bogs.

Christianshavn and Christiania

From Christiansborg, a bridge crosses to **Christianshavn**, built by Christian IV as an autonomous new town in the early sixteenth century as housing for shipbuilding workers. It was given features more common to Dutch ports of the time, even down to a small canal, and in parts is more redolent of Amsterdam than Copenhagen. Reaching skywards on the other side of Torvegade is the blue-and-gold spire of **Vor Frelsers Kirke** (mid-March–Oct Mon–Sat 9am–3.30pm, Sun noon–3.30pm; rest of year Mon–Sat 10am–1.30pm, Sun noon–1.30pm; 10kr), which, with its helter-skelter-like outside staircase, was added to the otherwise plain church in the mid-eighteenth century, instantly becoming one of the more recognizable features on the city's horizon.

A few streets from Vor Frelsers Kirke, **Christiania** is a former barracks area that was colonized by hippies after declaring itself a "free city" in 1971, and hopes soon to get its own currency. A pseudo-Statue of Liberty greets visitors as they pass under the little arched entrance and head for the open hash market, where smoking is tolerated by the government. Bob Marley and John Lennon blare out from the bars and the area is awash with psychedelic painting. Christiania's population is currently around a thousand, but it swells in summer when curious tourists flood in to take in the scene, browse the market and perhaps rent a pony to ride around the beautiful lake. Residents ask visitors not to camp or point cameras directly at them. The craft shops and restaurants are fairly cheap, and nearly all are good, with a couple of innovative music and performance art venues. If you are hungry, head for *Morrgenstedet*, a clean and friendly restaurant close to the market, with the option of outside seats (12pm–9pm; closed Tues). For information, call in to Galopperiet (Tues–Sun noon–5pm), to the right of the main entrance on Prinsessegade, which also has an interesting gallery. For the really keen, there are guided tours of the area during the summer which take in Pusherstreet (unofficially named after the open dealing and smoking of hashish that goes on there), but you have to book at least one day in advance (☎31.57.96.70; 20kr per person, minimum 6 people per tour; 2hr).

Along Vesterbrogade

Hectic **Vesterbrogade** begins on the far side of Rådhuspladsen, and its first attraction is perhaps Copenhagen's most famous, the **Tivoli Gardens** (daily late April to mid-Sept 11am–midnight; 39kr; 45kr if you take advantage of late opening until 1am June–Aug, Fri & Sat), whose opening each year on or around May 1 marks the beginning of summer. Throughout the season, the gardens feature fairground rides, fireworks, fountains, and a variety of nightly entertainment in the central arena which can include everything from acrobats and jugglers to the mid-Atlantic tones of various fixed-grin crooners. It's rather overrated and expensive, but you can still have an enjoyable evening wandering among the revellers of all ages. On the other side of Tietgensgade, the **Ny Carlsberg Glyptotek** (Tues–Sun 10am–4pm; 15kr, free on Wed & Sun), is Copenhagen's finest gallery, with a stirring array of Greek, Roman and Egyptian art and artefacts, as well as what is reckoned to be the biggest and best collection of Etruscan art outside Italy. There are, too, excellent examples of modern European art, including a complete collection of Degas casts, Manet's *Absinthe Drinker* and an antechamber with early work by Man Ray, some Chagall sketches and a Picasso plate.

In the narrow streets between Vesterbrogade and Istedgade, a few pornography shops remain as evidence of this increasingly respectable area's former role as Copenhagen's red light district. At Vesterbrogade 59, the **City Museum** (May–Sept Tues–Sun 10am–4pm; Oct–April Tues–Sun 1–4pm; free) has reconstructed ramshackle house exteriors and tradesmen's signs from early Copenhagen, a large room recording the form Christian IV gave the city, and a collection of memorabilia concerning the nineteenth-century Danish philosopher Søren Kierkegaard. Further along Vesterbrogade, down Enghavevej and along Ny Carlsberg Vej (bus #6), the tours of the **Carlsberg Brewery** (Mon–Fri 11am & 2pm; free) are well worth joining if only for the free booze provided at the end.

Eating and drinking

Whatever you feel like **eating** you'll find a wider choice and lower prices in Copenhagen than in any other Scandinavian capital. In the city centre, the areas around Kultorvet and along Studiestræde are loaded with great places to eat. Farther afield, Nørrebro across Peblinge Sø draws the trendy set, and Vesterbrogade turns up a number of lower key places, better the further you venture. An almost unchartable network of **cafés** and bars serving drinks and snacks covers Copenhagen. The best are in or close to Indre By, and it's no hardship to sample several on the same night, though bear in mind that on Fridays and Saturdays you'll probably need to queue.

If you're **self-catering**, there are numerous *smørrebrød* outlets – Smørrebrødskunsten, on the corner of Magstræde at Rådhusstræde, and Centrum Smørrebrød, Vesterbrogade 6c, are two of the most central. For more general food shopping, Brugsen, Axeltorv 2, and Irma, Vesterbrogade 1 and Borgergade 28, are cheaper than their counterparts on Strøget.

Snacks and pizzerias

Bar Bar Bar, Vesterbrogade 51. A stylish and relaxed place for a coffee, drink or light snack. A popular meeting place.

Café au Lait, Nørre Voldgade 27. Opposite the Nørreport S-train station, a pleasantly unflustered place for a coffee or snack. Also branches at Gothersgade 11, Vesterbrogade 16 and Værnedamsvej 16.

Café Post Salut, Rådhusstræde 13. Located in the Huset complex, this is a popular spot for breakfast from 20kr.

Italiano, Fiolstræde 2. Centrally placed and basic, selling pizzas from around 60kr.

Shawarma, Stroget. Excellent shawarmas and pitta-bread with falafels and kebabs. Prices start at 22kr.

Vagabondo's Cantina, Vesterbrogade 70. The most central of several branches of this dependable pizza chain, where hunger can be sated for less than 50kr.

Restaurants

Al Mercante, midway along Bredgade. If you want to splash out, this is the finest Italian in town. At 11pm, the mood changes as the disco swings into action and everyone starts dancing on the tables.

Bali, Lille Kongen Nytorv 19. Indonesian restaurant that does a good rice tafel for around 168kr.

Bananrepublikken A/S, Nørrebrogade 13. Ethnic foods with a modern Danish edge include the best tapas in Denmark. Brunch from 38kr, other meals from around 100kr. Also has live music.

Den Grønne Kælder, Klarebodene 10. A simple tiled-floor vegetarian eatery with a very filling grøn platte for 49kr. Mon–Sat until 9pm.

Hackenbusch, Vesterbrogade 124. Inexpensive and colourful café/bar with an inventive if short blackboard menu. Dishes (always one vegetarian) from 70kr.

Koh I Noor, Vesterbrogade 33. A mix of Indian, Pakistani and Halal vegetarian dishes. Open until 2am.

Los Flamencos, Admiralsgade 1, near the Parliament building. Authentically Spanish restaurant in the basement, serving excellent tapas.

Mongolian Barbecue, Stormgarde 35. Offers a rare opportunity to sample traditional Mongol fare. Evenings only.

Morgernsredet, Langgade in Christiania. Generous, inexpensive portions. Vegetarian options. Smoking and alcohol prohibited. Closed Tues.

Nyhavns Færgekro, Nyhavn 5. Unpretentious and thoroughly tasty traditional food, available either from the lunchtime fish-laden open table or the à la carte restaurant upstairs.

Pasta Basta, Valkensdorfsgade 22. Help yourself from the nine cold pasta bowls for 69kr. Open until 5am.

Peder Oxe, Gråbrødretorv 11. Three hunks of smørrebrød for 78kr, at lunchtimes only. Excellent value.

Rust, Guldbergsgade 8. Fashionable bar-cum-rock-venue which also houses a good-value restaurant. Two courses for 100kr. See also "Nightlife".

Sala Thai, Vesterbrogade 107. Thai food cooked in the authentic manner.

Shezan, Viktoriagarde 22. Serves Pakistani food.

Spisehuset, Rådhusstræde 13. In the Huset building, with a varied and wholesome menu, including daily specials for 68–72kr.

Spiseloppen, Christiania. Award-winning restaurant with reasonable prices. Meals from 65kr.

Bars

Barcelona, Fælledvej 21. Chic and very much the place to be seen, though you pay for the privilege. Live bands on Tues & Fri.

Café Sommersko, Kronprinsensgade 6. Sizeable bar, crowded most nights. Free live music on Sun afternoons.

Cellars, Vestergade 3. Head here for the cheapest beer in town and a friendly, relaxed atmosphere.

Dan Turell, Store Regnegade 3. Something of an institution with the artier student crowd and a fine place for a sociable tipple. Open 11–2am.

Floss, Larsbjørnsstræde 10. Intimate venue with a wide selection of spirits and an eclectic clientele.

Krasnapolsky, Vestergade 10. The Danish avant-garde art hanging on the wall reflects the trend-setting reputation of this ultramodern watering hole. Tasty food too.

Peder Hvitfeldt, P. Hvitfeldtsstræde 15. Spit-and-sawdust place which is immensely popular. Come early if you want to sit down.

Sabine's Cafeteria, Teglgårdstræde 4. Frequented by the young and beautiful as the first stop of the evening.

Stereo Bar, Linnægade 16A. This once trendy bar has mellowed with age, becoming a sociable hangout. It has a small dance floor in the basement and is open till 3am.

Universitetscaféen, Fiolstræde 2. A prime central location and long hours (until 5am).

Nightlife

The city is a pretty good place for **live music**. Major international names visit regularly, and there are always plenty of minor gigs in cafés and bars, often free early in the week. You can get the latest on who's playing where by reading *Neon Guiden*, or *Gaffa* (free from music and record shops), or the monthly *Use It News*, available from the Huset building at Rådhusstræde 13. If you get a craving for the dance floor, you'll find discos much like those in any major city, busy between midnight and 5am. Dress codes are fairly easy-going; drink prices are seldom hiked-up and admission is fairly cheap at 30–50kr.

Live music

Bananrepublikken A/S, Nørrebrogade 13. One of the best places to hear world music. See also "Restaurants".

Copenhagen Jazz House, Niels Memmingsensgade 10. Laid-back jazz concerts, followed by a jazz, funk and mainstream disco. Entrance 50kr.

Femøren, Amager. Venue for open-air rock concerts from June to Aug. Get there by bus #12 or #13.

La Fontaine, Kompagnistræde 11. Jazz club open from 8pm–6am.

Loppen, Bådsmandsstræde 43, Christiania. Regular rock, jazz and performance artists.

Musikcaféen, Rådhusstræde 13. The mainstream rock part of Huset, with regular live bands.

Pavillonen, Fælledparken, near Borgmester Jensens Allæ. Open-air venue for free Latin/jazz/rock concerts and sometimes movies. Barbecued food too.

Pumpehuset, Studiestræde 52. A broad sweep of middle-strata rock, hip-hop and funk from Denmark and around the world about three times a month.

Rust, Guldbergsgade 8, Nørrebro. Usually rock bands on Thurs and at weekends.

Discos

Annabell's, Lille Kongensgade 16. Comparatively upmarket. Younger, brasher crowd Fri & Sat.

Distotek In, Nørregade 1. Cavernous disco playing mainstream hits.

Lille Vega, Enghavevej 40. Trendy place playing soul and funk Thurs & Fri, and hardcore techno on Sat.

Gay Copenhagen

Denmark has a very liberal attitude to gay men and lesbians. The age of consent is fifteen and for over a decade homosexuals have enjoyed the same inheritance rights as heterosexuals and can marry at registry offices, as long as one of the partners is Danish. Copenhagen itself has a lively **gay scene**, which includes a couple of hotels at which gays are especially welcome – *Jørgensens Rømersgade* 11 (☎33.13.97.43), and the *Hotel Windsor*, Frederiksborggade 30 (☎33.11.08.30), which is exclusively gay. For **information**, contact the National Organization for Gay Men and Women, Teglgårdstræde 13 (☎33.13.19.48) – which also has a bookshop, disco and café – or the gay switchboard (☎33.13.01.12), or get hold of a copy of *Hotside* magazine. As for gay bars, the *Amigo Bar*, Schønbergsgade 4, is frequented by gay men of all ages, while *Sebastian*, Hyskenstræde 10, draws a predominantly young trendy crowd. *Pan Club*, Knabrostræde 3, part of the largest gay centre in the country, has a great disco. *After Dark*, Studiestræde 31, has a great bar and disco often featuring drag shows. About the only primarily lesbian place is the café/bar *Babooshka* at Turesensgade 6.

Listings

Airlines British Airways Rådhuspladsen 16 (☎33.14.60.00); SAS, SAS Building, Hammerischgade 1–5 (☎32.54.17.01).

American Express Amagertorv 18 (☎33.12.23.01).

Books The Book Trader, Skindergade 23, has old and new books in English.

Car rental Avis, Kampmannsgade 1 (☎33.15.22.99); Hertz, Ved Vesterport 3 (☎33.12.77.00); InterRent/Europcar, GI. Kongevej (☎33.55.99.00).

Embassies Australia, Kristianiasgade 21 (☎35.26.22.44); Britain, Kastelsvej 40 (☎33.44.52.00); Canada, Kristen Bernikowsgade 1 (☎33.12.22.99); Ireland, Østbanegade 21 (☎31.42.32.33); Netherlands, Toldbodgade 33 (☎33.15.62.93); New Zealand, use the British Embassy; USA, Dag Hammerskjölds Allé 24 (☎31.42.31.44).

Doctor ☎33.93.63.00 (9am–4pm). Emergencies ☎112.

Exchange The Bank of Tivoli, Vesterbrogade 3, is open noon–11pm during the summer. Otherwise change money at Central Station (daily 6.45am–10pm).

Hospital Rigshospitalet, Blegdamsvej 9 (☎35.45.35.45).

Laundry Vascomat, Borgergade 2; Møntvask, Nansengade 39.

Left luggage Lockers at Central Station (5.30–1am; 20kr); larger ones at Use-It, Rådhusstræde 13.

Pharmacies Steno Apotek, Vesterbrogade 6, and Sønderbro Apotek, Amagerbrogade 158, are both open 24hr.

Police ☎38.74.88.22. Emergencies ☎112.

Post office Main office at Tietgensgade 36-37 (Mon–Fri 10am–6pm, Sat 9am–1pm). Also at Central Station (Mon–Fri 8am–10pm, Sat 9am–4pm, Sun 10am–5pm). For poste restante, go to Use-it in the Huset complex at Rådhusstræde 13 (mid-June to mid-Sept daily 9am–7pm; rest of year Mon–Wed 11am–4pm, Thurs 11am–6pm, Fri 11am–2pm; ☎33.73.06.20).

Travel agents DIS, Skindergade 28 (☎33.11.00.44); Kilroy Travels, Skindergade 28 (☎33.11.00.44).

Women Copenhagen's main women's centre is Dannerhuset, Nansensgade 1 (☎33.14.16.76), with a café (Mon–Wed 5–8pm) and bookshop (Mon–Fri 5–10.30pm).

Day-trips from Copenhagen

If the weather's good, take a trip to the Amager **beaches** on bus #12 along Øresundsvej. On the other side of the airport from the beaches lies **DRAGØR**, an atmospheric cobbled fishing village which has good local history collections in the **Dragør Museum** (May–Sept Tues–Fri 2–5pm, Sat & Sun noon–6pm; 10kr), by the harbour, and the **Amager Museum** (June–Aug Wed–Sun noon–4pm; Sept–May Wed & Sun noon–4pm; 10kr), just off the Copenhagen road at the extreme western edge of the village. From the city, take buses #30 or #33. Failing that, if you're in the mood for an amusement park but can't afford Tivoli, venture out to **BAKKEN** (end March to Aug daily noon–midnight; free), close to the Klampenborg stop at the end of line C on the S-train network, which has been an amusement park since the sixteenth century. Besides swings and rollercoasters, it offers pleasant walks through woods of oak and beech, which were once royal hunting grounds.

The most noteworthy attractions are a little further away from Copenhagen. A fifteen-minute walk from Runsted Kyst train station, the **Karen Blixen Museum** (May–Sept daily 10am–5pm; Oct–April Wed–Fri 1–4pm, Sat & Sun 11am–4pm; 30kr) is housed in what used to be the home of the author of *Out of Africa*, who wrote under the name of Isak Dinesen. In **HUMLEBÆK**, 10km further north and a short walk from the train station, you'll find **Louisiana**, a modern art gallery on the northern edge of the village at Gammel Strandvej 13 (daily 10am–5pm, Wed until 10pm; 53kr). The museum's setting alone is worth the journey, as it harmoniously combines art, architecture and the natural landscape. The museum's American section, sited in the south corridor, stands out, with its collection of pieces by Edward Kienholz and Malcolm Morley's scintillatingly gross *Pacific Telephone Los Angeles Yellow Pages*. In addition you'll find some of Giacometti's strange gangly figures haunting a room of their own off the north corridor, and an equally affecting handful of sculptures by Max Ernst, squatting outside the windows, leering in.

Also feasible as a day-trip is the short hop to **Sweden** on the new Øresund Link train, a part-tunnel part-bridge that is due to open in May 2000. Both the Danish and Swedish governments have invested heavily in the project, which carries a railway and road from Copenhagen to Malmö.

THE REST OF ZEALAND

You will discover how different the rest of Denmark is when you venture outside Copenhagen – worthwhile even if you're just passing through. As home to the capital, **Zealand** is Denmark's most important and most visited region, and, with a swift metropolitan transport network covering almost half of the island, you can always make it back to the capital in time for an evening drink. North of Copenhagen, **Helsingør**, the departure point for ferries to Sweden, is the site of the renowned fortification Kronborg Slot – though Frederiksborg Slot, at nearby **Hillerød**, is if anything more impressive. West of Copenhagen, and on the main route to Funen, is **Roskilde**, a former capital with an extravagant cathedral that's still the last resting place for Danish monarchs, and with a gorgeous location on the Roskilde fjord – from where five Viking boats were salvaged and are now restored and displayed in a specially built museum.

Hillerød

Last stop on lines A and E of the S-train network from Copenhagen, **HILLERØD** has a castle which pushes the more famous Kronborg into second place: **Frederiksborg Slot** (Mon–Sat 10am–5pm; 40kr) lies decorously across three small islands on an artificial lake. The Frederiksborg ferry crosses the castle lake daily from May to September (on the hour; 15kr). Buses #701, #702 and #703 run from the train station to the castle but walking only takes about twenty minutes, following the signs through town.

The castle was the home of Frederik II and birthplace of his son Christian IV. At the turn of the seventeenth century, under the auspices of Christian, rebuilding began in an unorthodox Dutch Renaissance style. It's the unusual aspects of the monarch's design – prolific use of towers and spires, pointed Gothic arches and flowery window ornamentation – which still stand out, despite the changes wrought by fire and restoration. Inside there's a museum of Danish history, largely funded by the Carlsberg brewery magnate Carl Jacobsen. The illustrated guide to the museum costs 25kr, but most rooms have detailed descriptions in English pasted up on the walls. Two rooms deserve special mention: the exquisite chapel, where monarchs were anointed between 1671 and 1840, and the Great Hall above, a reconstruction but still beautiful, bare but for the staggering wall and ceiling decorations – tapestries, wall-reliefs, portraits and a glistening black marble fireplace.

The **tourist office** at Slangenrupsgade 2 (June–Aug Mon–Fri 10am–6pm, Sat 10am–5pm; rest of year Mon–Fri 10am–5pm, Sat 10am–1pm) offers **private rooms** for around 100–125kr per person (25kr booking fee). Few of Hillerød's **hotels** can match the prices you might find in Copenhagen but you could try *Hotel Hillerød*, Milnersvej 41 (☎48.24.08.00; ⑨). The only budget accommodation is the **campsite** (Easter to mid-Sept), at Dyrskuepladsen, 1km from the centre.

Helsingør

First impressions of **HELSINGØR**, 30min north of Hillerød, are none too enticing, but away from the hustle of its terminals it is a quiet and likeable town. Its position on the four-kilometre strip of water linking the North Sea and the Baltic brought the town prosperity when, in 1429, the Sound Toll was imposed on passing vessels – an upturn only matched in magnitude by the severe decline following the abolition of the toll in the nineteenth century. Shipbuilding brought back some of the town's self-assurance, but today it's once again the whisker of water between Denmark and Sweden, and the ferries across it to Helsingborg, which account for most of Helsingør's through traffic.

The town's other great tourist draw is **Kronborg Slot** (May–Sept daily 10.30am–5pm; rest of year Tues–Sun 11am–3/4pm; 30kr, Copenhagen Card not valid), principally because of its literary associations as Elsinore Castle, whose ramparts Shakespeare's Prince Hamlet supposedly strode. Actually, the playwright never visited Helsingør, and the tenth-century cha acter Amleth on whom his hero was based long predates the castle. Nevertheless, there is a thriving Hamlet souvenir business, and during the summer the numbers visiting the place make guided tours impossible. The present castle dates from the sixteenth century; Frederik II commissioned the Dutch architects van Opbergen and van Paaschen to construct it on the site of an earlier fortress. Various bits have been destroyed and rebuilt since, but it remains a grand affair, enhanced immeasurably by its setting; and the interior, particularly the royal chapel, is spectacularly ornate. The castle also houses the national **Maritime Museum** (25kr, 15kr with a ticket for the castle itself, Copenhagen Card not valid), an uninteresting collection of model ships and nautical knick-knacks.

Moving away from Kronborg and the harbour area, Helsingør has a well-preserved medieval quarter, worth a stroll through. **Stengade** is the main pedestrianized street, linked by a number of narrow alleyways to Axeltorv, the town's small market square and usually a good spot to linger over a beer. Near the corner of Stengade and Skt. Annagade, the spired **Skt. Olai's Kirke** is now Helsingør's cathedral. Just beyond is the **Karmeliterklostret**, the best-preserved medieval monastic complex in Scandinavia (daily noon–4pm; guided tours 15kr). Its former hospital contains the **Town Museum** (daily noon–4pm; 10kr), which prided itself on brain operations – the unnerving tools of which are still here, together with diagrams of the corrective insertions made into patients' heads.

Practicalities

Buses stop outside the noisy combined **train station** and **ferry terminal**. You can pick up a free map from the **tourist office** (mid-June to Aug Mon–Fri 9.30am–7pm, Sat 10am–6pm; Sept to mid-June Mon–Fri 9.30am–5pm, Sat 10am–1pm) across Strandgade from the train station, and you can also book **private rooms** for 250–300kr a double (25kr booking fee). The closest thing to a cheap **hotel** is *Hotel Skandia*, Bramstræde 1 (☎49.21.09.02; ⑤). More affordably, there is a **youth hostel** (☎49.21.16.40; ②) on the beach, a twenty-minute walk to the north along the coastal road (Ndr. Strandvej), or accessible on bus #340 from the station. The **campsite**, at Campingvej 1, is closer to town and also by a beach, between the main road, Lappen, and the sea; take the private train (Copenhagen Card valid, rail passes not) to Marienlyst or bus #340. For **food**, *Kloster Caféen*, Skt. Annagade 35, is a prime lunchtime spot for its set menu and sizeable sandwiches; the well-named *Salat Cafeen*, Stengade 48, dishes up large plates for 45kr with fruit tarts to follow; or try the varied delights of *Færgegården*, Stengade 81b.

Two **ferry lines** make the twenty-minute crossing from Helsingør to Helsingborg in Sweden. The main one, and probably the best option, is the Scandlines boat leaving every 10–30 minutes around the clock from the main terminal by the train station and costing 28kr return, 20kr one way. The alternative crossing, costing 28kr for a return and 18kr one way, is with Sundbusserne, who operate small craft, often heavily buffeted by the choppy waters, every 20–30 minutes between 6am and 8.30pm. For both companies rail passes are valid and a Copenhagen Card gives a fifty percent discount.

Roskilde

There's very little between Copenhagen and the west Zealand coast in the way of things to explore, except for the ancient former Danish capital of **ROSKILDE**, less than half an hour by train from the capital. The arrival of Bishop Absalon in the twelfth century made the place the base of the Danish Church, and as a consequence the national capital. Importance waned after the Reformation, and Roskilde came to function mainly as a market for the neighbouring rural communities – which it still is, as well as being dormitory territory for Copenhagen commuters. Its ancient centre is one of Denmark's most appealing – well worth a look on your way west to Odense.

The major pointer to the town's former status is the fabulous **Roskilde Domkirke** (mid-June to Sept Mon–Fri 9am–4.45pm, Sat 9am–noon, Sun 12.30–3.45pm; rest of year closed Mon; reduced hours in winter; 12kr), founded in 1170 and finished during the fourteenth century, although portions have been added since. Four royal chapels house a claustrophobic collection of coffins containing the regal remains of twenty kings and seventeen queens. The most richly endowed chapel is that of Christian IV, a previously austere resting place jazzed up in the early nineteenth century with bronze statues, wall-length frescoes and vast paintings of scenes from his reign. From one end of the cathedral, a roofed passageway, the **Arch of Absalon**, feeds into the **Bishop's Palace**, housing the **Palace Collections** (summer daily 11am–4pm; winter Sat & Sun 1–3pm; 5kr), made up of paintings, furniture and other artefacts belonging to the wealthiest Roskilde families of the eighteenth and nineteenth centuries. In the same building is the **Museum of Contemporary Art** (Tues–Fri 11am–5pm, Sat & Sun noon–4pm; 10kr), hosting high-standard temporary exhibitions and a charming small sculpture garden.

The history of the town recorded in the **Roskilde Museum** at Skt. Ols Gade 15 & 18 (daily 11am–4pm; 20kr) is a little more enticing, with strong sections on medieval pottery and toys, although time is really better spent at the absorbing **Viking Ship Museum** (daily 9/10am–4/5pm; 40kr), in Strandengen on the banks of the fjord. Inside, five excellent specimens of Viking shipbuilding are proudly displayed: there's a deep-sea trader, a merchant ship, a warship, a ferry and a longship, each one retrieved from the fjord where they had been sunk to block invading forces. The Museum also includes the newly built Museum Island where you can watch new Viking ships being built.

The **tourist office** (April–June Mon–Fri 9am–5pm, Sat 10am–1pm; July–Aug Mon–Fri 9am–6pm, Sat 9am–3pm, Sun 10am–2pm; Sept–April Mon–Thurs 9am–5pm, Fri 9am–4pm, Sat 10am–1pm) is at Gullandsstræde 15, a short walk from the main square. If you decide to stay, there's a **campsite** (☎46.75.79.96) on the wooded edge of the fjord 4km away – an appealing setting which makes it very crowded at peak times; it's open from April to September, and linked to the town centre by bus #602, Veddelev direction. The **youth hostel** is at Havnevej near the harbour; ask at the tourist office for details. Neither the hostel nor the campsite are worth bothering with if you're here for the **Roskilde Festival**, one of the largest open-air rock events in Europe, attracting around ninety thousand people annually. The festival takes place late June/early July and there's a special, free camping ground beside the festival site, to which shuttle buses run from the train station every ten minutes – ask at the tourist office for further information. For **lunch**, coffee or a game of backgammon, head for *Café Satchmo*, signposted off Algade; for a beer try the informal *Café Grunk* on Store Gråborstræde.

FUNEN

Known as "the Garden of Denmark", partly for the lawn-like neatness of its fields, partly for the immense amounts of fruit and veg which come from them, **Funen** is the smaller of the two main Danish islands. The pastoral outlook of the place and the coastline draw many visitors, but its attractions are mainly low-profile cultural things, such as the various collections of the "Funen painters" and the birthplaces of writer Hans Christian Andersen and composer Carl Nielsen. **Odense**, Denmark's third city, is easily the island's main attraction. Close to this, the former fishing town of **Kerteminde** retains some faded charm, and is near the Ladby Boat, an important Viking relic.

Odense

ODENSE is proud to be the birthplace of Denmark's best-loved writer, Hans Christian Andersen, as well as the childhood home of composer Carl Neilsen. Named after Odin, chief of the pagan gods, Odense is one of the oldest settlements in the country and was even home to King Knud II, canonized after his murder here in 1086. Much of the pleasantly sleepy city is pedestrianized making it a perfect place to saunter about. You can also cycle along the old rail tracks, which have been converted into bicycle paths, or along the canal's edge past the elegant Danish mansions painted in mustard, terracotta and sky blue. The city has a range of good museums and a nightlife that's surprisingly lively, with the focus on live music and jazz

Arrival and accommodation

Long-distance buses and trains both terminate at the **train station**, a ten-minute walk from the city centre, where you'll find the **tourist office** (mid-June to Aug Mon–Sat 9am–7pm, Sun 11am–7pm; rest of year Mon–Fri 9am–4.30pm, Sat 10am–1pm) next to the bus station on the Vestergade side of the Rådhus. They sell the useful **Adventure Pass** (50–90kr), which gets you discounts on entrance to all of Odense's museums and gives unlimited travel on local buses for one and two days respectively. The only cheap options among Odense's **hotels** are *Det Lille Hotel*, Dronningensgade 5 (☎66.12.28.21; ④), and the *Ydes Hotel*, Hans Tausens Gade 11 (☎66.12.11.31; ④). There's a youth hostel at Kragsbjergvej 121 (☎66.13.04.25; ②; mid-Feb to Nov) – take bus #61, #62, #63 or #64 south to Tornbjerg or Fraugade and get out along Munkebjergvej at the junction with Vissenbjergvej. The closest **campsite** (☎66.11.47.02) is at Odensevej 102, near the Funen Village; take bus #42 from the Rådhus or station to Skt. Klemens. For **Internet** use, head for *Game Play*, Kongensgade 70 (daily 2pm–12am; 30kr per hour); *Vortex*, Vestergade 63 (daily 12pm–12am; 25kr per hour; entrance on Dronningensgade); *Net Cafe 5000*, Vindegade 43 (daily until midnight; 25kr per hour); or the large local library in the train station.

The Town

Save for an outlying museum, Odense is easily seen on foot, and you may as well start with the city's major collection: the **Hans Christian Andersen Museum** at Hans Jensen Stræde 37–45 (daily: June–Aug 9.30am–7pm; Sept–May 10am–4pm; 25kr), in the house where the writer was born in 1805. The son of a hard-up cobbler, Andersen was only really accepted in his own country towards the end of his life, which was perhaps why he travelled widely and often, and left Odense at the first opportunity. The museum is stuffed with intriguing items – bits of school reports, early notes and manuscripts of his books, illustrations from the tales, an invitation from Charles Dickens to stay in England, and paraphernalia from his travels. A separate gallery has headphones for listening to some of Andersen's best-known tales and screens a sloppy slide-show, though plans for renovating the museum and making more of Andersen's fabulous imagination are under way.

The area around the museum, despite being all half-timbered houses and clean, car-free cobbled streets, lacks character; indeed, if Andersen were around he'd hardly recognize the neighbourhood, which is now one of Odense's most expensive. For far more realistic local history, head to **Møntergården**, a few streets away at Overgade 48–50 (daily 10am–4pm; 15kr), where there's an engrossing assemblage of artefacts dating from the city's earliest settlements to the Nazi occupation, plus an immense coin collection. There's more about Andersen at Munkemøllestræde 3–5, between Skt. Knud Plads and Klosterbakken, in the tiny **Hans Christian Andersen's Childhood Home** (June–Aug daily 10am–4pm; rest of year Tues–Sun 11am–3pm; 5kr), where Andersen lived from 1807 to 1819. More interesting, though, is the nearby **Skt. Knud's Kirke** (mid-May to mid-Sept Mon–Sat 10am–5pm; June–Aug also Sun 11.30am–3.30pm; rest of year Mon–Fri 10am–4pm, Sat 10am–2pm; free), whose crypt holds one of the most unusual and ancient finds Denmark has to offer – the skeletons of King Knud II and his brother Benedikt, both slain in 1086 by Jutish farmers angry at the taxes Knud imposed on them – Knud was canonized soon after. The cathedral is the only example of pure Gothic church architecture in the country; its finely detailed sixteenth-century wooden altarpiece, saturated with gold leaf, is one of the greatest works of the Lübeck master, Claus Berg.

The **Art Museum of Funen** situated at Jernbanegade 13 (daily 10am–4pm; 15kr), just a few minutes' walk away, will give you a good idea of the region's importance to the Danish art world during the late nineteenth century, when a number of Funen-based painters abandoned portraiture for impressionistic landscapes and studies recording the lives of the peasantry. The collection contains some stirring works by Vilhelm Hammershøi, P.S. Krøyer, Michael and Anne Ancher, and H.A. Benedekilke's enormously emotive *The Cry*. A short walk to the east, at Claus Bergs Gade 11, the **Carl Nielsen Museum** is Odense's newest museum (Tues–Sun 10am–4pm; 15kr). Born in a village just outside Odense, Nielsen is best remembered in Denmark for his popular songs, though it was his operas, choral pieces and symphonies that established him as a major international composer. The exhibits, detailing Nielsen's life and achievements, are enlivened by the accomplished sculptures of his wife, Anne Marie, and you can listen to some of his work on headphones.

South of the Odense centre at Sejerskovvej 20 is **Funen Village** (June–Aug daily 9.30am–7pm; April, May & Sept Tues–Sun 10am–5pm; Nov–March Sun 11am–3pm; 25kr), an open-air museum made up of a reconstructed nineteenth-century country village of original buildings taken from all over Funen, painstakingly reassembled and refurnished. In summer, some of the old trades are revived in the former workshops and crafthouses, and free shows are regularly staged at the open-air theatre. Though often crowded, it's well worth a call, and you should watch out for the village-brewed beer – handed out free on special occasions. Bus #42 runs to the village from the city centre (get off at the sign Den Fynske Landsby), or you can do what the locals do and take the Odense Åfart boat from Munke Mose (mid-April to Mid-Oct; six times daily; ☎65.95.79.96), stopping on the way at **Odense Zoo** (daily: 9am–4/6pm; 55kr).

Eating, drinking and nightlife

There are plenty of **restaurants** and **snack bars** in the city centre, and some good bargains to be had. *Eventyr*, Overgade 18, is a reliable spot for sandwiches, while for more substantial eating, the best and oldest of the many pizzerias is *Pizzeria Ristorante Italiano*, Vesterbrogade 9. You might also try the Thai food of the *Asia House*, Østre Stationsvej 40, Mexican dishes at *Birdy's Café*, Nørregade 21, or the vegetarian specialities of *Det Grønne Café*, Vintappestræde 13. If you'd prefer a steak, head for *Jensens Bøfhus*, Kongensgade 10. For evening **drinking**, try *Carlsen's Kvarter* an inexpensive, Irish pub on Læssøgade which serves fine beers; otherwise drop into the fashionable *Café Biografen*, one of many eating and drinking spots in Brandts Passage, which has a little three-screen cinema, that tends to show more arty films than the seven-screen complex in the train station. At the passage entrance, *Cuckoo's Nest* is a favourite for drinks or a light snack before moving around the corner to the *Cotton Club*, Pantheonsgade 5c, for swing to fusion **jazz** until early morning. The *Badstuen* art centre, Østre Stationsvej 26, has a café that occasionally hosts raucous live **bands**, as does *Rytmeposten* across the road at Østre Stationsvej 27a. There's bluesier fare to be found in the likeably scruffy *Musikkælderen*, Dronningsgengade 2B, and easier rock at *Kong Græs*, Asylgade 7.

Kerteminde and around

A thirty-minute bus ride (#890) northeast from Odense takes you to **KERTEMINDE**, a sailing and holiday centre that has a prettily preserved nucleus of shops and houses around its fifteenth-century Skt. Laurentius Kirke. On Strandgade, the **Town Museum** (March–Oct daily 10am–4pm; 15kr) has five reconstructed craft workshops and a collection of local fishing equipment. Kerteminde was home to the "birdman of Funen", the late-nineteenth-century ornithological painter Johannes Larsen. A fairly lengthy stroll around the marina and along Møllebakken brings you to the **Johannes Larsen Museum** (June–Aug daily 10am–5pm; Sept, Oct & March–May Tues–Sun 10am–4pm; 30kr) – the painter's house, kept as it was when he lived there, with his furnishings, knick-knacks, canvases and, in the dining room, his astonishing wall-paintings.

Kerteminde's **tourist office** is opposite the Skt. Laurentius Kirke, across a small alleyway (mid-June to Aug Mon–Sat 9am–5pm; rest of year Mon–Fri 9am–4pm, Sat 9.30am–12.30pm). The only low-cost accommodation option is the **youth hostel** at Skovvej 46 (☎65.32.39.29; ②), a twenty-minute walk from the centre (cross the Kerteminde Fjord by the road bridge and take the first major road left and immediately right). There's also a **campsite** (☎65.32.19.71; mid-April to mid-Sept) with cabins, at Hindsholmvej 80, not far from the Larsen Museum, on the main road along the seafront – a thirty-minute walk from the centre.

About 4km from Kerteminde, along the banks of the fjord at Vikingvej 123, is the **Ladby Boat** (May–Oct daily 10am–4/6pm; Nov–April Tues–Sun 11am–3pm; 20kr), a vessel dredged up from the fjord and found to be the burial place of a Viking chieftain. The craft, along with the weapons, hunting dogs and horses which accompanied the deceased on his journey to Valhalla, is kept in a small purpose-built museum, and is well worth the trip out. The infrequent bus #482 stops here and motorboats make the run out in summer, although it's a pleasant enough walk or cycle.

JUTLAND

Long ago, the people of **Jutland**, the Jutes, were a separate tribe from the more warlike Danes who occupied the eastern islands. In pagan times, the peninsula had its own rulers and much power, and it was here that the legendary ninth-century monarch Harald Bluetooth began the process that turned the two tribes into a unified Christian nation. By the dawn of the Viking era, however, the battling Danes had spread west, absorbing the Jutes, and real power gradually shifted towards Zealand. This is where it has largely stayed, making unhurried lifestyles and rural calm the overriding impression of Jutland for most visitors; indeed, its distance from Copenhagen makes it perhaps the most distinct and interesting area in the country. In the south, Schleswig is a territory long battled over by Denmark and Germany, though beyond the immaculately restored town of **Ribe** it holds little of abiding interest. **Esbjerg**, further north, is dull too, but as a major ferry port you might well pass through. The old military stronghold of **Fredericia** is worth a brief stop before reaching Århus halfway up the eastern coast, Jutland's main urban centre and Denmark's second city. Further inland, the landscape is the country's most dramatic – stark heather-clad moors, dense forests and swooping gorges. Ancient **Viborg** is the best base for this, from where you can head north to vibrant **Aalborg**, on the southern bank of the Limfjord, which cuts deep into Jutland this far north – across which the landscape reaches a crescendo of storm-lashed savagery around **Skagen**, on the very tip of the peninsula. **Frederikshavn**, on the way, is the port for boats to Norway and Sweden.

Fredericia

FREDERICIA – junction of all the rail routes in east Jutland and those connecting the peninsula with Funen – has one of the oddest histories (and layouts) in Denmark. It was founded in 1650 by Frederik III, who envisaged a strategically placed reserve capital and a base from which to defend Jutland. Three nearby villages were demolished and their inhabitants forced to assist in the building of the new town. Military criteria resulted in wide streets that followed a strict grid system and low buildings enclosed by high earthen ramparts, making the town invisible to approaching armies. The train age made Fredericia a transport centre and its harbour expanded as a consequence. But it still retains a soldiering air, full of memorials to heroes and victories, and is the venue of the only military tattoo in Denmark.

The twenty-minute walk from the **train station** along Vesterbrogade toward the town centre takes you past the most impressive section of the old ramparts. They stretch for 4km and rise 15m above the streets, and walking along the top gives a good view of the layout of the town. But it's the **Landsoldaten** statue, opposite Princes Port, which best exemplifies the local spirit. The bronze figure holds a rifle in its left hand, a sprig of leaves in the right, and its left foot rests on a captured cannon. The inscription on the statue reads "6 Juli 1849", the day the town's battalion made a momentous sortie against German troops in the first Schleswig war – an anniversary celebrated as Fredericia Day. The downside of the battle was the 500 Danes who were killed and lie in a mass grave in the grounds of Trinitatis Kirke in Kongensgade. Predictably, 300 years of armed conflict also form the core of the displays at the **Fredericia Museum**, Jernbanegade 10 (mid-June to mid-Aug daily 11am–5pm; rest of year Tues–Sun noon–4pm; 20kr), along with local house interiors from the seventeenth and eighteenth centuries and a dreary selection of archeological finds.

Fredericia's **tourist office** (mid-June to Aug Mon–Fri 9am–6pm, Sat 9am–3pm; rest of year Mon–Fri 9.30am–5pm, Sat 10am–1pm) is on the corner of Danmarksgade and Norgesgade. Unless you want to laze on Fredericia's fine **beaches**, which begin at the eastern end of the ramparts, there's little reason to hang around very long. If you do want to stay, however, try the **youth hostel** at Vester Ringvej 98 (☎75.92.12.87; ②), a short bus ride from the train station, or the **campsite**, (☎75.95.71.83; April–Oct), on the Vejle fjord, adjacent to a public beach.

Esbjerg

The only large city in southern Jutland is **ESBJERG**, which was purpose-built as a deepwater harbour during the nineteenth century and has generally been thought of as being gloomy and run-down. However, it is in the process of massive redevelopment and it's environment and cultural life are being dramatically improved.

The best way to get a sense of the city's newness is by dropping into the **Esbjerg Museum** (Tues–Sun 10am–4pm; 20kr) at Torvegade 45, with its new gallery devoted to amber along with a display recalling the so-called "American period" from the 1890s, when Esbjerg's rapid growth matched that of the US gold-rush towns. Also within easy reach of the centre is the **Museum of Art** (daily 10am–4pm; 20kr), although its modern Danish art works are fairly limp affairs, and you'd do better to visit art displays in the recently refurbished Watertower next door (same hours; 10kr), or the **Museum of Printing** (June–Dec daily noon–4pm; Jan–May Tues–Fri 1–4pm; 15kr), at Borgergade 6, which has an entertaining assortment of hand-, foot- and steam-operated presses as well as more recent printing machines. With more time to spare, take a bus (#1, #2, #6 or #8 from Skolegade) to the large **Fisheries and Maritime Museum and Sealarium** on Tarphagevej (daily 10am–5/6pm; 40kr), where you can cast an eye over the vestiges of the early Esbjerg fishing fleet and clamber around inside a spooky wartime bunker built by the Germans. The Sealarium is part of a seal research centre, which often rescues pups marooned on sandbanks, then feeds them for the public's entertainment at 11am & 2.30pm daily. Opposite is Svend Wiig Hansen's nine-metre-high *Man meets the Sea*, an austere, blandly modernist sculpture of four white, seated figures.

Esbjerg's **tourist office** is at Skolegade 33 (Mon–Fri 10am–5pm, Sat 10am–1/3.30pm), on a corner of the main square; an **Esbjerg Pass** (90kr), available from the tourist office, covers entry to all the town's museums and a round trip of the harbour. The passenger harbour is a twenty-minute well-signposted walk from the city centre, and **trains** to and from Copenhagen connect directly with the **ferries**, using the harbour station. The main **train station** is at the end of Skolegade. The cheapest central **hotels** are *Palads Hotel*, Skoklegade 14 (☎75.18.16.24; ⑤) and the *Park Hotel* at Torvegade 31 (☎75.12.08.68; ⑤). A little more upmarket is the *Hotel Ansgar*, Skolegade 36 (☎75.12.82.44; ⑦). The **youth hostel** is at Gammel Vardevej 80 (☎75.12.42.58; ②), 25 minutes' walk, or buses #1, #4, #12, #40 or #41 from Skolegade. There is also an excellent **campsite** with cabins at Gudenåvej 20 (☎75.15.88.22; mid-May to mid-Oct), reached by buses #1 and #7. The Esbjerg **eating** options are fairly limited if you're on a tight budget, although you can get a decent two-course lunch for around 70kr at the *Park Hotel*, while inexpensive, but mainly meat, dishes can be found at *Jensens Bøfhus*, Kongensgade 9. If filling your stomach is the primary concern, then *Made in Italy* is the best among the many restaurants on Kongensgade, which all offer 39kr lunchtime pizza and salad-bar deals. A good place to **drink** is *Café Christian IX*, overlooking Torvet, which occasionally has live music.

Ribe

Just under an hour south by train from Esbjerg, the exquisitely preserved town of **RIBE** was once a major stopover point for pilgrims on their way to Rome, as well as a significant port, until thwarted by the Reformation and the sanding-up of the harbour. Since then, not much appears to have changed. The surrounding marshlands, which have prevented the development of any large-scale industry, and a long-standing preservation programme, have enabled Ribe to keep the appearance and size of medieval times, making it a delight to wander in.

From Ribe's train station, Dagmarsgade leads to Torvet and the towering **Domkirke** (summer Mon–Sat 10am–5/6pm, Sun noon–5/6pm; winter Mon–Sat 11am–3/4pm, Sun noon–3/4pm; 7kr; tours in summer at 11.30am & 1pm; 35kr), begun around 1150. Only the "Cat's Head Door" on the south side remains from the original construction and the church's interior is not as spectacular as either its size or long history might suggest – though you can normally climb the red-brick tower and peer out over the town. Behind the cathedral, the **Weis' Stue** is a tiny inn built around 1600, from which the Nightwatchman of Ribe makes his rounds (June–Aug 8pm & 10pm; May–Sept 10pm) – a throwback to the days when Danish towns were patrolled by guards looking for unattended candles, though these days he stops at points of interest to explain the town's history to tourists. It's free and can be fun. The **Viking Museum** (summer daily 10am–4/5pm; winter closed Mon; 30kr), nearby on Odins Plads, offers an informative display on Ribe's past, including archeological finds and interactive computer exhibits. If you haven't had enough of Vikings, you can watch their daily life in action at the **Ribe Vikingecenter** (Tues–Fri 11am–4pm; 30kr), 3km south of the town centre at Lustrupvej, where staff in Viking dress give pottery demonstrations and cook over open fires.

The **tourist office** (mid-June to Aug Mon–Fri 9.30am–5.30pm, Sat 9am–5pm, Sun 10am–2pm; rest of year Mon–Fri 9.30am–4.30pm, Sat 10am–1pm) is behind the cathedral, opposite the Weis' Stue; it has a full list of **private homes**. There's also a **youth hostel** (☎75.42.06.20; ②; Feb–Nov), on the opposite side of the river from Skibbroen: cross the river bridge and turn left into Sct. Peders Gade. Failing that, there are several moderately priced places such as the *Weis' Stue* (☎75.42.07.00; ④), which is opposite the atmospheric but expensive *Hotel Dagmar* (☎75.42.00.33; ⑨), the oldest hotel in Denmark. For an evening **drink** try *Stenborhus* on Stenbogade, which attracts artists, students and musicians and has live blues, folk or rock bands at least once a week. A daytime and evening alternative with **food** and excellent coffee is *Valdemar Sejr* next to the art gallery on Sct. Nicolaj Gade. The nearest **campsite**, which also has cabins, is 2km from Ribe, along Farupvej (☎75.41.07.77; bus #771).

Århus

Geographically at the heart of the country and often regarded as Denmark's cultural capital, ÅRHUS typifies all that's good about Danish cities: it's small enough to get to know in a few hours, yet big and lively enough to fill both days and nights. Despite Viking-era origins, the city's present-day prosperity is due to its long, sheltered bay, on which the first harbour was constructed during the fifteenth century, and the more recent advent of railways, which made Århus a nationally important trade and transport centre. Easily reached by train from all the country's bigger towns, and by ferry from Zealand, Århus also receives nonstop flights from London. There's certainly no better place for a first taste of Denmark.

Arrival and accommodation

Trains, **buses** and **ferries** all stop on the southern edge of the city centre, a short walk from the **tourist office** in Park Allé (summer Mon–Fri 9.30am–6pm, Sat 10am–1pm, Sun 9.30am–1pm; winter Mon–Fri 9.30am–4.30pm, Sat 10am–1pm), on the first floor of the city's Rådhus. **Airport** buses from Tirstrup connect regularly with the train station (50min; 50kr). Buses form the city's public transport system, which is divided into four zones: one and two cover the centre; three and four reach into the country; a basic ticket costs 13kr from machines on board and is valid for any number of journeys during the time stamped on it (usually two hours). However, getting around is best done on foot: Århus has a compact centre and you'll seldom need to use the buses unless you're venturing out to the beaches or woods on the outskirts. An **Århus Pass**, (110kr for a 48-hour pass, 155kr for a week), covers free bus travel and entrance to most museums and sightseeing tours (though you must book these at the tourist office first).

The **tourist office** (☎89.40.67.00) can arrange accommodation in **private rooms** for 150kr a night plus a 25kr booking fee. The Århus **youth hostel**, 4km from the centre at Marienlundsvej 10 (☎86.16.72.98; ②; bus #1, #6, #9 or #16), is beautifully situated in the middle of Risskov wood and close to Den Permanente beach, to which locals flock in summer. The new *Århus City Sleep-In*, Havnegade 20 (☎86.19.20.55; ②) is more central and has an

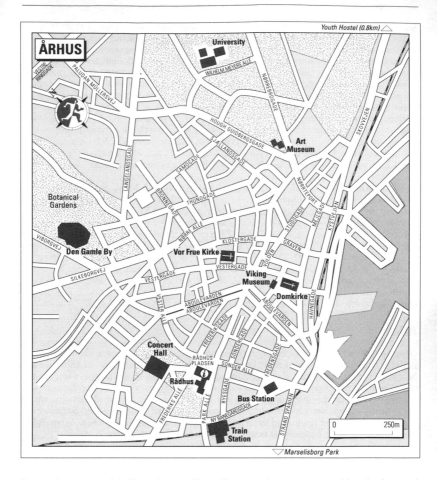

Marselisborg Park

impressive range of facilities for travellers. There are just two reasonably priced central **hotels**: *Eriksens* at Banegårdsgade 6 (☎86.13.62.96; ④) and *Pøtmølle*, Pøtmøllevej 80 (☎86.96.51.00; ④). Of a number of **campsites**, the two most useful are *Blommehaven* (April to early Sept; bus #6 or #19), overlooking the bay 3km south of the city centre, and *Århus Nord*, 9km north, which has cabins and is open year round – take bus #117 or #118 from the bus station.

The City

Århus divides into two clearly defined parts: the old section, close to the cathedral, a tight cluster of medieval streets, and, surrounding this, a less characterful modern sector. **Søndergade** is the city's main street, a pedestrianized strip that leads down into Bispetorvet and the old centre, the streets of which form a web around the **Domkirke** (May–Sept Mon–Sat 9.30am–4pm; Oct–April Mon–Sat 10am–3pm), a massive if plain Gothic church, most of which dates from the fifteenth century, the original twelfth-century structure having been destroyed by fire. At the eastern end, the altarpiece is a grand triptych by the noted Bernt Notkes. Look also at the painted glass window behind the altar, the work of the

Norwegian Emmanuel Vigeland (brother of Gustav). The area around the cathedral is a leisurely district of browsable shops and enticing cafés. On Clements Torv, across the road from the cathedral inside Unibank, the **Viking Museum** (Mon–Wed & Fri 9.30am–4pm, Thurs 9.30am–6pm; free) displays Viking finds, including sections of the original ramparts and some Viking craftsmen's tools, alongside some informative accounts of early Århus. Close by, at Domkirkeplads 5, the **Women's Museum** (Tues–Sun 10am–4/5pm; 20kr) stages temporary exhibitions on many aspects of women's lives and lifestyles past and present. West along Vestergade, the thirteenth-century **Vor Frue Kirke** (May–Aug Mon–Fri 10am–4pm, Sat 10am–2pm; Sept–April Mon–Fri 10am–2pm, Sat 10am–noon) is actually the site of three churches, most notable of which is the atmospheric eleventh-century crypt church, discovered beneath several centuries-worth of rubbish during restoration work on the main church in the 1950s. Look in, also, at the main church, for Claus Berg's detailed altarpiece, and, through the cloister remaining from the pre-Reformation monastery, now an old folks' home, for the medieval frescoes inside the third church, which depict local working people rather than biblical scenes.

If you've visited the tourist office, you've already been inside the least interesting section of one of the modern city's major sights, the **Århus Rådhus**, a controversial structure built in the 1940s. You're free to walk in and look for yourself, but it's best to take a guided tour (10kr) conducted in English at 11am on weekdays during the summer. Above the entrance hangs Hagedorn Olsen's huge mural, *A Human Society*, symbolically depicting the city emerging from World War II. Perhaps most interesting are the walls of the small civic room; Albert Naur, who designed them during the Nazi occupation, concealed various Allied insignia in their intricate floral patterns. Finally, a lift (late June to early Sept noon & 2pm; 5kr, included in the tour) climbs to the bell tower and a view over the city and across the bay.

It's a short walk from here to the city's best-known attraction, **Den Gamle By**, on Viborgvej (daily: May–Sept 9am–5/6pm; rest of year 10/11am–3/4pm; 50kr), an open-air museum of traditional Danish life, with sixty-odd half-timbered houses from all over the country, dismantled and moved here piece by piece. Many of the craftsmen's buildings are used for their original purpose, the overall aim of the place being to give an impression of an old Danish market town, something it does very effectively. Fans of Danish art may well prefer to visit the **Århus Art Museum** (Tues–Sun 10am–5pm; 30kr) in Vennelystparken, a little way north, with works from the late eighteenth century to the modern day, including the radiant canvases of Asger Jorn and Richard Mortensen, and Bjørn Nørgaard's sculptured version of Christian IV's tomb: the original, in Roskilde Cathedral (see p.323), is stacked with riches; this one features a coffee cup, an egg and a ballpoint pen.

The Outskirts

On Sundays Århus resembles a ghost town, with most locals spending the day in the parks or beaches on the city's outskirts. The closest beaches are just north of the city at Riis Skov, easily reached with buses #6, #9 or #16. Otherwise, the Marselisborg Skov is the city's largest park, home to the Marselisborg Slot, summer residence of the Danish royals, the landscaped grounds of which can be visited when the monarch isn't staying. Further east paths run down to rarely crowded pebbly beaches, and, near the junction of Ørnerdevej and Thormsøllervej, to the Dyrehaven or Deer Park. A few kilometres further on, the **Moesgård Prehistoric Museum** (Feb–Sept daily 10am–5pm; Oct–Jan Tues–Sun 10am–4pm; 45kr), reached direct on bus #6, details Danish civilizations from the Stone Age onwards with copious finds and easy-to-follow illustrations. Its most notable exhibit is the "Grauballe Man", a body dated 80 BC discovered to the west of Århus in a peat bog and thus amazingly well preserved. From the museum, a "prehistoric tramway" runs 3km to the sea, past a scattering of reassembled prehistoric dwellings, monuments and burial places. If you don't have the energy for any more walking, you can take a #19 bus back to the city from here; the stop is a hundred metres to the north. If you do, the Queen's Summer Residence is nearby in Marselisborg.

Eating, drinking and nightlife

If cash is tight, or you're stocking up for a picnic, use the Special Smørrebrød outlet at Sønder Allé 2, or the late-opening supermarket (8am–midnight) at the train station. Cruising the old-town **cafés** and **restaurants** will turn up plenty of lunchtime specials for around 55kr; for instance *Mackie's Pizza*, 9 Skt. Clemens Torv, and around the corner the theatrical *Pind's Café* at Skolegade 11, which often looks shut but does excellent *smørrebrød*. For something quick and inexpensive head for the Vietnamese-run *Kowloon Kinesisk Grill*, on Banegærdsgade. If you have a bit more money, try the wok buffet at the *China Wok House*, Sødderallé 9, where for 98kr you can choose your ingredients and have them stir fried in front of you. *Italia*, at Åboulevarden 9, is good value, as are *Kif Kif* Gallorant, Mejlgade 41, and the highly rated **vegetarian** meals at *Kulturgyngen*, Fronthuset Mejlgade 53. If you can afford a bit more, try visiting the beautiful Marselisborg Havn harbour, which has a number of restaurants including the superb *Seafood*.

Århus, and Aalborg, further north, are the only places in Denmark with a **nightlife** to match that of Copenhagen. The city has particularly wonderful **bars**, many situated in the streets close to the cathedral, including the movie-themed *Casablanca* at Rosensgade 12, the pricey *Carlton* nearby at no. 23, and *Englen* and *Kindrødt* on Studsgade. The cream of Danish and international rock acts can be found at *Huset*, Vester Allé 15, with its restaurant and cinema; *Fatter Eskil*, Skolegade 25, and *Kulturgyngen*, Fronthuset, Mejlgade 53, have more run-of-the-mill blues bands. *Blitz*, Klostergade 34, currently hosts the hottest **club scene**, while the leading **jazz** venue is the smoky, atmospheric *Bent J*, at Nørre Allé 66.

Listings

Airlines SAS ☎70.10.20.00; for domestic ☎70.10.30.00.

Car rental Avis, Jens Baggesens Vej 88c (☎86.16.10.99); InterRent/Europcar, Sønder Allé 35 (☎86.12.35.00).

Hospitals Århus Kommunehospital, on Nørrebrogade. For a doctor, call ☎86.20.10.22 (4pm–8am).

Pharmacy Løve Apoteket, Store Torv 5 (☎86.12.00.22) is open 24hr.

Police Århus Politization, Ridderstræde (☎86.13.30.00).

Post office On Banegærdpladsen, by the station (Mon–Fri 9am–6pm, Sat 10am–1pm).

Viborg

For a long time the junction of the major roads across Jutland, **VIBORG** was once one of the most important communities in the country. From Knud in 1027 to Christian V in 1655, all Danish kings were crowned here, and until the early nineteenth century the town was the seat of a provincial assembly. As the national administrative axis shifted towards Zealand, however, Viborg's importance waned, and although it still has the high court of West Denmark, it's now primarily a market town for the local farming community.

The twin towers of the **Domkirke** (June–Aug Mon–Sat 10am–5pm, Sun noon–5pm; Oct–April Mon–Sat 11am–3pm, Sun noon–3pm) are the most visible features of the compact town centre, and the most compelling reminder of Viborg's former glories. The interior is dominated by the brilliant frescoes of Joakim Skovgaard, whose work can also be seen in the **Skovgaard Museum** (daily: June–Aug 10am–12.30pm & 1.30–5pm; Sept–May 1.30–5pm; free), inside the former Rådhus across Gammel Torv. For a broader perspective of Viborg's past, keep an hour spare for exploring the **District Museum** on the northern side of Hjultorvet between Vestergade and Skt. Mathias Gade (June–Aug daily 11am–5pm; Sept–May Tues–Fri 2–5pm, Sat & Sun 11am–5pm; 10kr), which has everything from prehistoric artefacts to clothes, furniture and household appliances.

The **tourist office** on Nytorv (summer Mon–Sat 9am–5pm; winter Mon–Fri 9am–4pm, Sat 9.30am–12.30pm) can supply a handy map for exploring old Viborg and advise on **accommodation**. In town, *Palads Hotel*, 5 Sct. Mathias Gade (☎86.62.37.00; ⑨), often has reduced rates. The more affordable **youth hostel** (☎86.67.17.81; ③) and **campsite** (with cabins), are both 2km across the lake from the town centre, along Vinkelvej (bus #707).

Aalborg

The main city of north Jutland and the fourth largest in Denmark, **AALBORG** hugs the southern bank of the Limfjord and boasts a nightlife and music scene to rival Copenhagen's. The most obvious place to spend a night or two before venturing into the wilder countryside beyond, Aalborg is the main transport terminus for the region, and boasts a well-preserved old centre dating from its seventeenth-century trading heyday. The era is perhaps best exemplified by the Jens Bangs Stenhus opposite the tourist office, a grandiose five storeys in the Dutch Renaissance style, which has functioned as a pharmacy since it was built. The commercial roots of the city are further evidenced by the collection of portraits of the town's merchants that hang inside the **Budolfi Domkirke** (Mon–Fri 9am–4pm, Sat 9am–noon/3pm), behind: a small but elegant specimen of sixteenth-century Gothic, built on the site of an eleventh-century wooden church, from which a few tombs remain, embedded in the walls close to the altar. Outside, across the square, the **Aalborg Historical Museum** at Algade 48 (Tues–Sun 10am–5pm; 10kr) has fairly routine displays, apart from an impressive glasswork collection. Behind here, just off Gammel Torv, the fifteenth-century **Monastery of the Holy Ghost** can be viewed by way of guided tours (late June to late Aug Tues & Thurs at 1.30pm; 25kr), which take in the monks' refectory, kept largely unchanged since the last monk left, and the small Friar's room, the only part of the monastery in which nuns (from the adjoining nunnery) were permitted. Most interesting, however, are the frescoes which cover the entire ceiling of the chapel.

On the other side of Østerågade, the sixteenth-century **Aalborghus** is worth visiting for a trip round its severely gloomy **dungeon** (May–Oct Mon–Fri 8am–5pm; free). Outside the centre of town, the **North Jutland Art Museum** located on Kong Christians Allé (July & Aug daily 10am–5pm; rest of year closed Mon; 30kr), close to the junction with Vesterbro (buses #8, #10 & #11 or a fifteen-minute walk), and housed in a building designed by the Finnish architect Alvar Aalto, is one of the country's better modern art collections, featuring, alongside numerous Danish contributions, works by Max Ernst, Andy Warhol, Le Corbusier and Claes Oldenburg. After leaving the museum, you can get a grand view over the city and the Limfjord by ascending the **Aalborg Tower** (mid-May to mid-Oct daily 11am–5/7pm; 20kr), on the hill just behind.The **Aalborg Maritime Museum**, 2km west of the centre at Vestrefjordvej 81 (daily mid-April to mid-Oct 11am–5/7pm; 40kr) recalls the city's time as an important shipbuilding port. The highlight is inspecting the tight working and living conditions in "Springeren", the 54-metre-long submarine which now forms the museum's centrepiece.

Practicalities

The **tourist office** is centrally placed at Østerågade 8 (mid-June to mid-Aug Mon–Fri 9am–6pm, Sat 9am–5pm; rest of year Mon–Fri 9am–4.30pm, Sat 10am–1pm). The cheapest **hotels** are the *Aalborg Sømandshjem*, Østerbro 27 (☎98.12.19.99; ⑤) and the *Missionshotellet Krogen*, Skibstedsvej 4 (☎98.12.17.05; ⑤). There's a large **youth hostel** (☎98.11.60.44; ②; reservations necessary Sept–May), 3km west of the town on the Limfjord bank beside the marina – take bus #8 from the centre to the end of its route – and, about 300m away, a **campsite**, *Strandparken* (May–Sept). For a little more adventure, catch the half-hourly **ferry** (8am–11pm; 12kr) from near the campsite to Egholm, an island in Limfjord with free camping under open-sided shelters. In pursuit of **food and drink**, almost everybody heads for Jomfru Ane Gade, a small street close to the harbour between Bispensgade and Borgergade, on which a number of restaurants/bars advertise daily specials: the most reliable are *Fyrtøjet* at no. 7, and *Dirch's Regensen* at no. 16, both of which generally have lunches for 50–60kr. Aalborg Kongres & Kultur Center at Europa Pads 4 (☎99.35.55.66) always has a new music event.

Frederikshavn

FREDERIKSHAVN is neither pretty nor particularly interesting, and as a ferry port it's usually full of Swedes and Norwegians taking advantage of Denmark's liberal boozing laws. But the town is virtually unavoidable if you're heading north, being at the end of the rail route from Aalborg. If you've an international ferry to meet at Hirtshals, change to the private train (InterRail fifty-percent reduction, Eurail not valid) at Hjørring.

If you have half an hour to spare, visit the squat white tower, **Krudttårnet** (daily June to mid-Sept 10.30am–5pm; 10kr), near the station, which has maps detailing the harbour's seventeenth-century fortifications and a collection of military paraphernalia from the seventeenth to the nineteenth centuries. With more time, take bus #1 or #2 to Møllehuset and walk on through Bangsboparken to the **Bangsbo-Museet** (summer daily 10am–5pm; winter closed Mon; 20kr), where displays chart the development of Frederikshavn from the 1600s, alongside the grotesque but engrossing "Collection of Human Hairwork" and an assortment of maritime exhibits, distinguished only by the twelfth-century Ellingå Ship and an exhibition covering the German occupation during World War II and the Danish resistance movement.

Buses and trains into Frederikshavn both stop at the **train station**, a short walk along Skippergade and Denmarksgade from the town centre. Some continue to the **ferry terminal** near Havnepladsen, also close to the centre where Stena Line ferries leave for Oslo, and boats (InterRail fifty-percent reduction) and the cheaper and much quicker sea catamarans make for Gothenburg. The **tourist office** is close by at Brotorvet 1, on the corner of Rådhus Allé and Havnepladsen (mid-June to mid-Aug Mon–Sat 8.30am–8.30pm, Sun 11am–2pm; rest of year Mon–Fri 8.30/9am–4/5pm, Sat 11am–2pm). The cheapest **hotels** are both central: *Discount Logi Teglgården*, Teglgårdsvej 3 (☎98.42.04.44; ③), and *Fr. Havn Sømandshjem og* at Tordenskjoldsgade 15b (☎98.42.09.77; ⑤). There's a **youth hostel** at Buhlsvej 6 (☎98.42.14.75; ②), 1500m from the train station, and a cabin-equipped campsite, Nordstrand, at Apholmenvej 40 (☎98.42.93.50; April–Sept; bus #4), 3km north of the centre off Nordre Strandvej.

Skagen

If you have the option, skip Frederikshavn altogether in favour of **SKAGEN**, 40km north, which perches almost at the very top of Jutland amid a desolate landscape of heather-topped sand dunes. It can be reached by private bus or train (Eurail not valid, Scanrail and InterRail fifty-percent reduction on both) roughly once an hour. The bus is the best choice if you're planning to stay at the Skagen youth hostel, as it stops outside.

Sunlight seems to gain extra brightness as it bounces off the two seas which collide off Skagen's coast, something which attracted the **Skagen artists** in the late nineteenth century, who arrived in the small fishing community during 1873 and 1874 and often met in the bar of *Brøndum's Hotel*, off Brøndumsvej, the grounds of which now house the **Skagen Museum** (May–Sept daily 10am–5/6pm; April & Oct Tues–Sun 11am–4pm; Nov–March Wed–Fri 1–4pm, Sat 11am–4pm, Sun 11am–3pm; 40kr). Many of the canvases depict local scenes, using the town's strong natural light to capture subtleties of colour. The hotel owner's stepsister, Anna, herself a skilful painter, married one of the group's leading lights, Michael Ancher. Nearby, at Markvej 2, is **Michael and Anna Anchers' Hus** (May–Sept daily 10am–5/6pm; Oct daily 11am–3pm; Nov–April Sat & Sun 11am–3pm; 25kr), evoking the atmosphere of the time through an assortment of squeezed tubes of paint, sketches, paintings, piles of canvases, books and ornaments.

The artists made Skagen fashionable, and the town continues to be a popular holiday destination. But it still bears many marks of its tough past as a fishing community, the history of which is excellently documented in **Skagen Fortidsminder** on P.K. Nielsensvej, a fifteen-minute walk south along Skt. Laurentii Vej from the centre (March–Nov daily 10am–4/5pm; 25kr). Amid the dunes south of town, a further twenty minutes' walk along Skt. Laurentii Vej, Damstedvej and Gammel Kirkesti, is **Den Tilsandede Kirke**, "The Buried Church" (June–Aug 11am–5pm; 8kr). This fourteenth-century church was swallowed by sandstorms during the eighteenth century. Part of the tower is open to the public, while the floor and cemetery lie beneath the sands. The forces of nature can be further appreciated at Grenen, a lighthouse and restaurant 4km north of Skagen (hourly bus #79), along Skt. Laurentii Vej, Fyrvej and the beach, where two seas – the Kattegat and Skagerrak – meet with a powerful clashing of waves. You can also get there by a tractor-drawn bus (April–Oct; 15kr return) – aptly named the *Sandormen* (lugworm) – although it's an enjoyable walk as the scenery is beautiful.

Practicalities

The combined **bus and train station** is on Skt. Laurentii Vej, and plays host to the **tourist office** (mid-June to early-Aug daily 9am–7pm; rest of year reduced hours; ☎98.44.13.77); check here for details of the summer sleep-in, whose location is liable to change. Otherwise, for its artistic associations, *Brøndum's Hotel*, Anchervej 3 (☎98.44.15.55; ⑦), is by far the most atmospheric spot to stay – book well ahead in summer. A little cheaper is *Sømandshjem*, Østre Strandvej 2 (☎98.44.21.10; ⑤), which also serves up bargain meals. Or try *Hotel Plesner*, Holstvej 8 (☎98.44.68.44; ⑤); or *Clausens Hotel*, Skt. Laurentii Vej 35 (☎98.45.01.66; ⑤). There are two **youth hostels**: one at Rolighedsvej 2 (☎98.44.22.00; ②) and one at Højensvej 32 in Gammel Skagen (☎98.44.13.56; ②; late June to early Aug; bus #78 to Frederikshaven), 3km west of Skagen. Of a number of **campsites**, the most accessible are *Grenen* (☎98.44.25.46; mid-June to mid-Aug), to the north along Fyrvej, which has cabins, and *Poul Eeg's* (☎98.44.14.70; late June & July), on Batterivej, left off Oddenvej just before the town centre.

travel details

Trains

Copenhagen to: Aalborg (every 2hr; 4hr 40min); Århus (12 daily; 3hr 10min); Esbjerg (9 daily; 2hr 40min); Helsingør (30 daily; 50min); Odense (25 daily; 1hr 30min); Ringsted (20 daily; 37min); Roskilde (25 daily; 20min).

Århus to: Aalborg (hourly; 1hr 15min–1hr 40min); Frederikshavn (every 2hr; 3hr); Viborg (every 30min; 1hr).

Esbjerg to: Århus (hourly, change at Fredericia; 3hr 15min); Fredericia (25 daily; 1hr); Ribe (hourly; 36min).

Fredericia to: Århus (25 daily; 1hr 20min).

Frederikshavn to: Aalborg (23 daily; 1hr 15min); Skagen (12 daily; 50min).

Helsingør to: Hillerød (hourly; 30min).

Odense to: Århus (30 daily; 2hr); Esbjerg (30 daily; 2hr); Nyborg (32 daily, linking with the DSB ferry to Korsør; 20min).

Roskilde to: Kalundborg (hourly 1hr 15min); Korsør (25 daily, connects with ferry to Funen; 1hr).

Buses

Copenhagen to: Aalborg (2–3 daily; 6hr); Århus (3–4 daily; 4hr 30min); Hanstholm (1 daily; 8hr 45min); Helsingør (30 daily; 1hr).

Århus to: Copenhagen (3–4 daily; 4hr 30min).

Frederikshavn to: Skagen (8 daily; 1hr).

Kerteminde to: Nyborg (17 daily; 30min).

Odense to: Kerteminde (42 daily; 30min); Nyborg (14 daily; 1hr).

Ferries

Kalundborg to: Århus (ferry 2–8 daily; 3hr; catamaran 3–5 daily; 1hr 40min).

Korsør to: Nyborg (19–30 daily; 1hr).

CHAPTER 8

ESTONIA

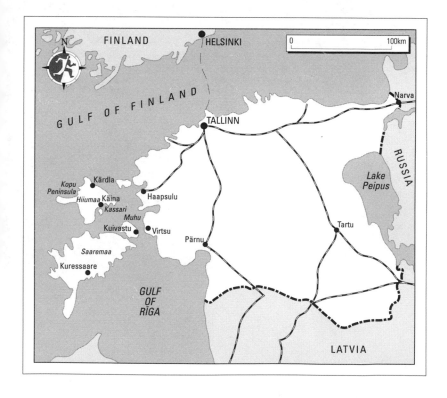

Introduction

It's a tribute to the resilience of the **Estonians** that during the short years since the Declaration of Independence in August 1991 they've transformed their country from a dour outpost of the former Soviet Union into a viable nation with the most stable economy in the Baltic region. This is even more impressive in the light of the fact that Estonians have ruled their own country for barely thirty years out of the past eight hundred. A Finno-Ugric people related to the Finns, the Estonians have had the misfortune to be surrounded by powerful, warlike neighbours. The first to conquer Estonia were the Danes, who arrived at the start of the thirteenth century; they were succeeded in turn by German crusading knights, Swedes and then Russians. Following a mid-nineteenth-century cultural and linguistic revival known as the National Awakening, the collapse of Germany and Tsarist Russia allowed the Estonians to snatch their independence in 1918. Their brief freedom between the two world wars was extinguished by the Soviets in 1940 and Estonia disappeared from view again. When the country re-emerged from the Soviet shadow in 1991, some forty percent of its population were Russians who had been encouraged to settle there during the Soviet era.

The capital **Tallinn** is an atmospheric city with a magnificent medieval centre and lively nightlife. Two other major cities, **Tartu**, a historic university town, and **Pärnu**, a major seaside resort, are worth a day or so each. Estonia's low population means that the countryside – around forty percent of which is covered by forest and much of the rest by lakes – is generally empty and unspoilt. To get a feel for it at its best, head for the Baltic islands of **Saaremaa** and **Hiiumaa**. **Kuressaare**, capital of the former, is home to one of the finest castles in the Baltics.

Information and maps

There are **tourist offices** in all the places covered in this chapter, which can be useful for booking bed & breakfast accommodation and hotel rooms. Most will also have a few **maps**, brochures and limited information on specific sights. The useful Kümmerly & Frey 1:1,000,000 map of the Baltic States covers Estonia and includes a rudimentary street plan of central Tallinn. Jāņa Sēta maps, which are produced in Latvia, are excellent. If you're planning to travel extensively in Estonia it could be worth investing in the Euromap 1:300 000 map of the country. The best detailed street map of Tallinn is the Falk Plan which includes enlarged Inner and Old Town sections and also covers public transport routes. For other destinations, local tourist offices and bookshops will usually have reasonably priced maps and plans. It's worth mentioning that in Estonia (as in the other two Baltic States, Latvia and Lithuania) you can usually get into museums at a reduced price, without having to show ID, if you look suitably student-like.

The following terms or their abbreviations are commonly encountered in Estonian **addresses**: *mantee* (mnt.) – road; *puistee* (pst.) – avenue; *tänav* (tn.) – street. Normally when giving an address or naming a street in Estonia *tänav* is not actually used – the street's name alone is enough.

Money and banks

The unit of currency is the **kroon**, normally abbreviated to EEK (Eesti kroon – Estonian Crown), and is divided into 100 sents. Notes come in 1, 2, 5, 10, 25, 50, 100 and 500EEK denominations and coins in 0.05, 0.10, 0.20, 0.50, 1 and 5 EEK denominations. The kroon's value is determined by the value of the German Mark and the current exchange rate is approximately 22EEK to £1 and 13EEK to $1.

Bank (*pank*) **opening hours** in large towns are usually Monday to Friday 9am–4pm, many staying open until 6pm, and most major banks also opening Saturday 9am–4pm. As well as exchanging cash, major banks such as the Tallinna Pank and Hansapank will also cash traveller's cheques (Thomas Cook and American Express preferred) and give you an advance on your Visa card for a commission of around three percent. All banks charge commission. Outside banking hours cash can be exchanged in **exchange offices** (Valuutavahetus), and in Tallinn some of the big hotels accept traveller's cheques. Visa card holders can get cash from the ATM machine in the foyer of the *Viru Hotel* in Tallinn and from some of the ATMs around the country. **Credit cards** can be used in some of the more expensive hotels, restaurants and stores, and in some petrol stations in Tallinn, and although you will find places that accept cards outside Tallinn, don't rely on being able to use them.

Communications

Most **post offices** (*postkontor*) are open Monday to Friday 9am–7pm and Saturday 9am–3pm. You can buy stamps here and at some shops, hotels, and kiosks. You can use **public telephones**, most of which now operate on magnetic cards (available in denominations of 30, 50 and 100EEK), for both local and long-distance calls. You can also phone long-distance from a post office or telephone centre where you'll be assigned a phone and asked to pay up front for the number of minutes you expect to talk – don't underestimate because they cut you off automatically. When calling an old analogue phone (recognizable by their six-digit numbers) dial a 2 before the number. For long-distance calls dial 8, wait for a new dial tone, then dial the area code and number. For international calls dial 8, wait for the new tone then dial 00 followed by the country code, area code and number.

Getting around

The destinations covered in this chapter are all easily reached by bus and/or rail. Travelling by bus is generally slightly quicker but also slightly more expensive than travelling by train.

■ Trains and buses

It's best to buy long-distance **bus** tickets in advance. Opt for an express (*ekspress*) bus if possible to avoid frequent stops. Make sure that your ticket entitles you to a seat, or you may have to stand in the aisle for the whole journey. Normally **luggage** is taken on board – if you have a large bag you may have to pay extra to have it stowed in the luggage compartment. Buses are also useful for travelling to the other Baltic countries with services linking Tallinn, Vilnius and Rīga.

Train tickets should also be bought in advance – stations have separate windows for long-distance (*rahvusvaheline*) and suburban (*linnalähedane*) trains. Long-distance services are divided into the following categories: *reisirong* (passenger) and *kiir* (fast). Both are slow but the latter, usually requiring a reservation, won't stop at every second village. Train information is available from station timetable boards – the Estonian for departure is *väljub*, and arrival is *saabub*. A Baltic Explorer **rail pass** gives you unlimited travel throughout Estonia and other Baltic Republics; it's available to ISIC-card holders, under-26s, and ITIC-card holders and their accompanying spouses. For further information on the latest

conditions of use and prices contact the International Rail Centre or USIT Campus, both in London.

■ Driving, hitching and cycling

Driving in Estonia is not too nerve-wracking, with main roads in reasonable condition and traffic fairly light outside the towns. Reckless driving is the exception rather than the rule, but watch out for people showing off in BMWs and four-wheel drives. There's no motorway to speak of – just a few stretches of two-lane highway either side of Tallinn and another near Pärnu. **Petrol stations** can be a little thin on the ground in rural areas, so carry a spare can. Speed limits are 50kph in built-up areas and 70 to 100kph on the open road. In towns it's forbidden to overtake stationary trams so that passengers can alight in safety, and it's against the law to drive after drinking any alcohol. **Car rental** costs around $60 per day from one of the big companies, as little as half that from some local firms – though their contracts can be dubious, insurance coverage sketchy and cars not necessarily maintained properly. If you are not the car's owner a valid photo ID licence is required along with proof of insurance, the car's registration, and a letter of authorization. **Hitching** is fairly common between major centres and holiday destinations, and you'll be expected to make a contribution towards petrol. Estonia, being predominantly flat, is reasonable for **cycling** but there aren't any cycle lanes and you can't expect much consideration from other road users.

Accommodation

Though cheaper than in western Europe, **accommodation** in Estonia is still going to take a large chunk out of most budgets. However, it is possible to keep costs down by staying in private rooms, and most towns have one or two reasonable budget hotels. If money isn't an issue you'll have few problems finding a decent place to stay.

■ Private rooms and hotels

For budget travellers **private room** accommodation is often the best option, usually costing between 200 and 600EEK per person. This can be arranged through local tourist offices or private agencies. You should be able to find plain but clean **hotel** rooms for between 200 and 400EEK per person, often in converted student hostels or apartment buildings, and better value for money than the purpose-built Soviet-era places. There's still a shortage of small, mid-range pension-type establishments though these are gradually starting to appear in the more popular destinations – expect to pay between 200 and 350EEK per night. Prices for mid-range and expensive places usually include breakfast, and many places accept credit cards. In all but the very cheapest hotels there will usually be at least one English-speaking member of staff.

■ Hostels and campsites

Estonia has a network of **youth hostels**, though these are often merely student dorms converted for the summer months. Contact the Estonian Youth Hostel Association (EYHA), Tartari 39, room 310 Tallinn (daily 9.30am–7pm; ☎2/6461 457) for the latest details. Hostel accommodation, where available, costs around 100 to 200EEK per person. An ex-Soviet phenomenon is the **cabin campsite** (*kämping*), usually offering accommodation in three- to four-bed cabins (shared facilities) for around 180 to 260EEK per person. Many of these places will also let you pitch a tent, an option which works out slightly cheaper than sleeping under a roof.

Food and drink

Elderly expats aside, not too many people come to Estonia for the food. The national cuisine consists mainly of pig by-products teamed with potatoes and other home vegetable-patch produce. Note that you're very likely to encounter indigenous recipes in Estonian restaurants where, in true post-Soviet style, stodgy meat and two veg dishes dominate most menus.

■ Food

Soup (*supp*), dark bread (*leib*), sour cream (*hapukoor*) and herring (*heeringas*) figure prominently in the Estonian diet, a culinary legacy of the country's largely peasant past, and if you like your food without frills you can eat very well here. A typical **national dish** is *verevorst and mulgikapsad* (blood sausage and sauerkraut), and you're also likely to encounter various kinds of smoked fish, particularly eel (*angerjas*), perch (*ahven*) and pike (*haug*).

You'll really have to be invited into a local home to enjoy Estonian food at its best as, unfortunately, the average **restaurant** (*restoran*) tends to serve up uninspired dishes like *karbonaad*, a fatty slab of meat fried in batter with potatoes. You might occasionally encounter game, and several ethnic restaurants break the culinary monotony in Tallinn. **Vegetarianism** is not a widely understood concept. When eating out you're often better off heading for bars and cafés, many of which serve snack dishes and even full meals, and where the bill is likely to be less than in a restaurant. By and large you should be able to have a decent meal (two courses and a drink) for less than 90EEK and you'd have to really push the boat out for the bill to come to more than 200EEK.

If you really want to keep costs down there are various **fast-food** options. Rock bottom is the increasingly rare Soviet-era canteen (*söökla*) dishing up basic workers' stodge at less than 20EEK for a main course. A step up from these relics are the various Western-style places where a good rule of thumb is to steer clear of the burgers and hot dogs and go for chicken or pizza. For **self-catering**, food shopping poses no major problems with staples like bread, cheese, smoked meat and tinned fish all available in supermarkets, and fresh fruit and vegetables available in markets.

■ Drink

Estonians are enthusiastic drinkers with **beer** (*õlu*) being the most popular tipple. The ubiquitous local brand is *Saku* which comes in three main forms, *Originaal*, an insipid lager, *Rock*, which is slightly stronger but still fairly forgettable, and *Tume*, a dark ale that's about the best of a bad lot. The strongest brews are found on the islands – *Saaremaa õlu* is the best known. In bars a lot of people favour **vodka** (*viin*) with mixers which, thanks to generous measures, is a more cost-effective route to oblivion. **Local alcoholic specialities** include *hõõgvein* (mulled wine) and *Vana Tallinn*, a pungent dark liqueur which some suicidal souls mix with vodka.

The commonest drinking haunt is the lugubrious, male-dominated *keldribaar*, though some bigger towns have more lively places, and Tallinn boasts a couple of hip hangouts that could hold their own in any European capital. If you're not boozing, head for a *kohvik* (café), where, although alcohol is usually served, getting drunk is not a priority. In Estonia **coffee** (*kohv*) is often served Turkish style, and **tea** (*tee*) is served without milk.

Opening hours and holidays

Most **shops** are open Monday to Friday 9/10am–6/7pm and Saturday 10am–2/3pm. Some food shops stay open until 10pm or later and are also open on Sundays. **Public holidays** when most shops and all banks will be closed are as follows: Jan 1; Feb 24 (Independence Day); Good Friday; Easter Monday; May 1; June 23 (Victory Day); June 24 (St John's Day); Dec 25 & 26.

Emergencies

Estonians claim that their country is a hotbed of crime and that visitors run a routine risk of being robbed and murdered, particularly in Tallinn. The truth is that while there are problems with theft and street crime they're probably no worse than anywhere else, and if you keep your wits about you and avoid staggering around the backstreets drunk after dark you should come to no harm. The Estonian **police** (*politsei*) are mostly very young and some may speak a little English, but don't bank on it. As far as **health** goes, though emergency health care is free in Estonia, the country's hospitals are under-equipped and if you fall seriously ill it's best to head for home if possible. No immunizations are required for Estonia.

EMERGENCY NUMBERS

Police ☎002; Ambulance ☎003; Fire ☎001.

TALLINN

The port city of **TALLINN**, Estonia's compact, human-scale capital, has been shaped by nearly a millennium of outside influence. Its name, derived from *taani linnus*, meaning "Danish Fort", is a reminder of the fact that the city was founded by the Danes at the beginning of the thirteenth century, and since that time political control has nearly always been in the hands of foreigners – Germans, Swedes and Russians. The Germans have undoubtedly had the most lasting influence on the city; Tallinn was one of the leading cities of the Hanseatic League, the German-dominated association of Baltic trading cities, and for centuries it was known to the outside world by its German name, Reval. Even when Estonia was ruled by the kings of Sweden or the tsars of Russia, the city's public life was controlled by the German nobility, and its commerce run by German merchants. Today reminders of foreign rule abound in the streets of Tallinn, where each of the city's one-time rulers have left their mark. Everything about Tallinn, from the fortress of the Germanic knights above the Old Town to the grimmest Soviet-era satellite suburb reveals something of its past, making it a fascinating place to explore.

Arrival, information and city transport

Tallinn's international **train station** is the Balti jaam at Toompuiestee 35, just northwest of the Old Town, while the city's **bus terminal** (*Autobussijaam*) is at Lastekodu 46, a couple of kilometres southeast of the centre – trams #2 and #4 run from nearby Tartu mnt. to Viru väljak. For those coming in by **sea** the passenger port (*Reisisadam*) is just northeast of the centre on Sadama 29. The **airport** (*Lennujaam*) is 3km southeast of the city centre and linked to Vabaduse väljak by bus #2 (every 20–30min, journey time 10min; 7EEK). Tallinn's **tourist office** at Raekoja Plats 10 (March–Nov Mon–Fri 9am–6pm, Sat & Sun 10am–4pm; Dec–Feb Mon–Fri 9am–5pm, Sat & Sun 10am–4pm; ☎2/631 3940) sells various maps and city guides and has limited information about other destinations in Estonia. You can also buy a **Tallinn Card** here, which entitles you to free use of public transport, free entrance to museums, a free tour of the city, discounts on car hire and savings in some shops and cafes. A 24-hour card costs 195EEK, a 48-hour one 270EEK, and a 72-hour one 325EEK – it's worth doing a few sums to work out if a card will actually give any savings on your planned itinerary. Good sources of up-to-the-minute listings and what's on in the city are *Tallinn This Week* (free) and the very good Tallinn-based *City Paper* which also contains information about Tartu, Pärnu, Rīga and Vilnius. The excellent *Tallinn In Your Pocket* city guide (14EEK) is available from shops and hotels.

Though most of Tallinn's sights can be covered on foot, the city has an extensive **tram**, **bus** and **trolleybus** network should you need to travel further afield. Services are frequent and cheap, though usually crowded, with tickets (*talungid*) common to all three systems available from kiosks near stops for 5EEK or from the driver for 7EEK. Tickets should be validated using the on-board punches. **Taxis** are reasonably cheap (around 6EEK per km, slightly more after 10pm) though as a foreigner you may occasionally find your meter running faster than it should. Try to ensure that you're not charged the evening rate during the day. Most companies have a minimum charge of 25EEK, but a taxi from one point in the city centre to another should never exceed 30EEK.

Accommodation

There's a shortage of cheap and mid-range hotels in central Tallinn, making **private rooms** the best value for money if you want to be close to the heart of things. Bed & Breakfast, Rasastra (☎2/6412 291), offer central doubles with prices beginning at 200EEK, though rooms in the suburbs tend to be cheaper. There's also a central **youth hostel**, *The Barn*, Väike-Karja 1 (☎2/631 3252), with beds in dorm rooms from 195EEK (ten-percent discount for HI and Peace Corp members) – there's no sign so look for the *Erootika Baar*. For infor-

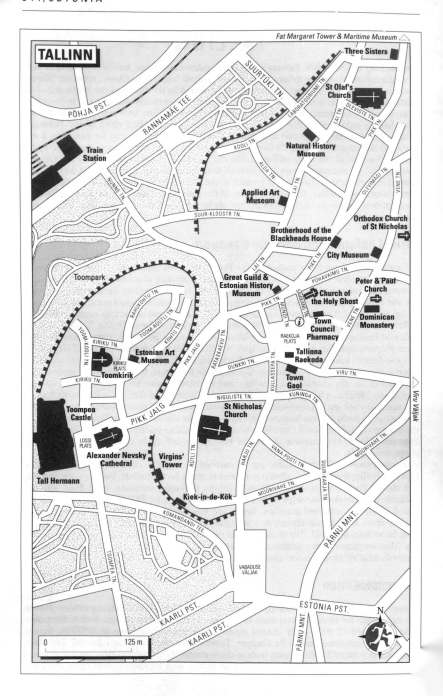

Fat Margaret Tower & Maritime Museum

TALLINN

Three Sisters

St Olaf's Church

PÕHJA PST.

RANNAMÄE TEE

SUURTÜKI TN.

LABORATOORIUMI TN.

OLEVISTE TN.

LAI TN.

PIKK TN.

OLEVIMÄGI TN.

VENE TN.

Train Station

KOOLI TN.

Natural History Museum

ALDA TN.

NUNNE TN.

Applied Art Museum

SUUR-KLOOSTR TN.

Orthodox Church of St Nicholas

Toompark

Brotherhood of the Blackheads House

City Museum

RAHUKOHTU TN.

TOOM-RÜÜTLI TN.

KOHTU TN.

Great Guild & Estonian History Museum

PÜHAVAIMU TN.

Peter & Paul Church

PIKK TN.

Church of the Holy Ghost

SAIAKANG TN.

TOOM-KOOLI TN.

KIRIKU TN.

MÜNDI TN.

Dominican Monastery

VENE TN.

Estonian Art Museum

KIRIKU PLATS

PIKK JALG

RATASKAEVU TN.

RAEKOJA PLATS

Town Council Pharmacy

Toomkirik

KIRIKU TN.

DUNKRI TN.

Tallinna Raekoda

KULLASSEPA TN.

VIRU TN.

Toompea Castle

PIKK JALG

NIGULISTE TN.

Town Gaol

KUNINGA TN.

LOSSI PLATS

St Nicholas Church

Alexander Nevsky Cathedral

Virgins' Tower

RÜTLI TN.

HARJU TN.

VANA-POSTI TN.

MÜÜRIVAHE TN.

Tall Hermann

Kiek-in-de-Kök

MÜÜRIVAHE TN.

SUUR-KARJA TN.

KOMANDANDI TEE

TOOMPEA TN.

VABADUSE VÄLJAK

PÄRNU MNT.

Viru Väljak

ESTONIA PST.

KAARLI PST.

PÄRNU MNT.

KAARLI PST.

N

0   125 m

mation on other hostel accommodation in the city contact the Estonian Youth Hostel Association, Tartari 39, room 310 (daily 9.30am–7pm; ☎2/6461 457) who have a large hostel at Vikerlase 15, with beds from 100EEK per person with ten-percent HI discount (bus #67 from Viru väljak). You can also stay in dorm rooms at the bus station (120EEK per person). The most accessible **campsite** is *Kalev Camping*, Kloostrimetsa tee 56a, with cabin accommodation at 180EEK for two people and space for tents (85EEK per tent).

Hotels

Central, Narva mnt. 7 (☎2/633 9800). Newly renovated hotel. Friendly, English-speaking staff and extensive facilities. ⑥.

Dorell, Karu 39 (☎2/626 1200). Entrance is through a passage on Narva mnt. A 10min walk from the Old Town, this place is pretty good value. Shared facilities or rooms to yourself. Parking available. ③.

Eeslitall, Dunkri 4/6 (☎2/631 3755). A small, basic and central pension. Facilities on corridor. ③.

Kelluka, Kelluka tee 11 (☎2/238 811). Quiet, pension-type place on the northeastern edge of town. Facilities include a sauna and pool – recommended if your funds stretch that far. Bus #5 from the centre to the Helmiku stop. ④.

Kristine, Luha 16 (☎2/646 4600). Quiet, friendly place with hostel atmosphere, around 15 minutes' walk from the centre. The rooms are plain but have en-suite facilities. Bus #5, #18, #36 or tram #3, #4 from the centre. ③.

Mihkli, Endla 23 (☎2/453 704). Only 10min from the centre on foot, this is a clean, peaceful hotel with modern, comfortable rooms. ⑤.

Pirita, Regati pst. 1 (☎2/639 8600). Just 6km northeast of the city centre in Pirita, the hotel was built for the 1980 Olympics. Despite the spartan rooms, the hotel has good facilities including money exchange, bar, pool and free morning sauna. Bus #1 from Viru väljak. ⑤.

TKTK Üliopilashotell, Nomme tee 47 (☎2/655 2679). Advertised as a "students hotel", this has decent rooms at good rates. Take trolleybus #2 or #3 from the town centre, or #4 from the train station to Tedre. ②.

Viru, Viru väljak (☎2/630 1390). All the big hotel comforts and conveniences make this 22-storey Finnish-owned place on the edge of the Old Town very popular with tour groups. Noisy in the morning. ⑧.

The City

The heart of Tallinn and location of most of its sights is the Old Town (Vanalinn), once enclosed by the city's medieval walls. At its centre is the **Town Hall Square**, the medieval marketplace, above which looms **Toompea**, the hilltop stronghold of the German Knights who controlled the city during the Middle Ages. There's little to do or see in the streets outside the Old Town, and Tallinn's remaining attractions are located in outlying districts.

Around Town Hall Square

Town Hall Square (Raekoja plats), the cobbled and gently sloping market square at the heart of the Old Town, is as old as the city itself. On its southern side stands an austere reminder of the Hanseatic past: the **Town Hall** (Tallinna Raekoda), a plain limestone building completed in 1404. The only hint of frivolity is the presence of a couple of water-spouts in the shape of green-painted dragons just below roof level. Near the summit of the slender steeple you'll spy Vana Toomas (Old Thomas), a sixteenth-century weather vane depicting a medieval mercenary, which has become Tallinn's city emblem. Inside, the two main chambers – the Citizens' Hall and the Council Hall – are almost devoid of ornamentation, except for the latter's elaborately carved benches, the oldest surviving woodcarvings in the country.

Of the other old buildings which line the square, the most venerable is the **Town Council Pharmacy** (Raeapteek) in the northeastern corner, whose dull grey facade dates from the seventeenth century, though the building is known to have existed in 1422 and may be much older. If the Raeapteek leaves you underwhelmed, head for the former Town Jail (Raevangla) behind the town hall at Raekoja 4/6, which now houses the **Town Hall Museum** or Raemuuseum (Thurs–Mon 10.30am–5.30pm; 10EEK), an entertaining little photographic collection with views of Tallinn from the days when it was still known as Reval, and portraits of Estonians in traditional costume (captions in English).

Close to Raekoja plats are a couple of churches that neatly underline the social divisions of medieval Tallinn. The fourteenth-century **Church of the Holy Ghost** (Pühavaimu kirik) tucked away on Pühavaimu – reached via a small passage called Saiakang tänav next to the Raeapteek – is the city's most appealing church, a small Gothic building with stuccoed lime-stone walls, stepped gables and a tall, verdigris-coated spire. Originally the Town Hall chapel, this later became the place where the native Estonian population worshipped, and in 1535 priests from here compiled an Estonian-language Lutheran catechism, an important affirma-tion of identity at a time when most Estonians had been reduced to serf status. The ornate clock set into the wall above the entrance dates from 1680 and is the oldest public timepiece in Tallinn. The interior of the church – all dark-veneered wood and cream-painted walls – has an intimate beauty, and contains one of the city's most significant pieces of religious art, an extraordinary triptych altar depicting the *Descent of the Holy Ghost* (1483) by the Lübeck mas-ter Bernt Notke.

Contrasting sharply is **St Nicholas Church** (Niguliste kirik), sitting on raised open ground just southwest of Raekoja plats. This late-Gothic edifice with its huge limestone basil-ica and vast white tower was originally built by German merchants. Most of what can be seen today dates from the fifteenth century, and has been extensively restored following Soviet bombing raids at the end of World War II. These days the church is a **museum** (Oct–March Wed–Sun 11am–6pm; April–Sept Thurs–Sun 11am–6pm; 7EEK; English-language pamphlets available) of religious art, its dominating exhibit a spectacular double-winged altar by Herman Rode of Lübeck from 1481, and a largish fragment from a fifteenth-century *danse macabre* frieze by Bernt Notke.

Toompea

From the environs of Town Hall Square the most obvious goal is **Toompea** (from the German, *Domberg*, meaning "Cathedral Hill"), the hill where the Danes built their fortress after conquering what is now Tallinn in 1219. According to legend Toompea is also the grave of Kalev, the mythical ancestor of the Estonians. The most atmospheric approach is through the sturdy gate tower – built by the Teutonic Knights to contain the Old Town's inhabitants in times of unrest – at the foot of Pikk jalg (Long Leg). This is the cobbled continuation of Pikk, the Old Town's main street, and climbs up to Lossi plats (Castle Square), dominated by the incongruous-looking **Alexander Nevsky Cathedral** (Aleksander Nevski Katedraal). This gaudy, onion-domed concoction, complete with tacky souvenir shop, built at the turn of the century for the city's Orthodox population, is an enduring reminder of the two centuries Tallinn spent under the rule of the Russian tsars.

At the head of Lossi plats is **Toompea Castle** (Toompea Loss), on the site of the original Danish fortification. Today's castle is the descendant of a stone fortress built by the Knights of the Sword, the Germanic crusaders who kicked out the Danes in 1227 and controlled the city until 1238 (when the Danes returned). The castle has been altered by every conqueror who raised their flag above it since then; these days it wears a shocking-pink Baroque facade, the result of an eighteenth-century rebuild under Catherine the Great. The northern and western walls are the most original part of the castle, and include three defensive towers, the most impressive of which is the fifty-metre **Tall Hermann** (Pikk Hermann) from 1371 at the southwestern corner.

Toompea Castle is now home to the Riigikogu, Estonia's parliament, and is therefore out of bounds to the public, but nearby a couple of towers that formed part of the Old Town for-tifications are accessible. A narrow archway in the medieval walls just south of the Alexander Nevsky Cathedral leads to the ironically named **Virgins' Tower** (Neitsitorn) which was once a prison for prostitutes and is now home to a café/bar. A little south of here on Komandandi tee is the impregnable-looking **Kiek-in-de-Kök tower** dating from 1475, whose name means "look in the kitchen" in Low German. Kiek-in-de-Kök now contains a **museum** (Tues–Fri 10.30am–5.30pm, Sat & Sun 11am–4.30pm; 7EEK) devoted to the history of Tallinn fortifica-tions, with all exhibits labelled in English.

From Lossi plats Toom Kooli leads north to the **Toomkirik/St Mary's Church** (Dome Church; Tues–Sun 9am–3.30pm; English-language leaflet 3EEK), the city's understated

Lutheran cathedral, originally a wooden church built here by the Danes soon after their arrival in Tallinn. This was replaced by a stone building and named a cathedral in 1240, though the church's present appearance is the result of a 1686 rebuild. Consequently, the cathedral's exterior is hard to pin down stylistically, the Gothic lines of the nave and tower softened by the addition of Baroque side chapels and a spire. The interior is worth dropping in on to admire the fine tombs and the ornate seventeenth-century pulpit by Christian Ackerman, who also carved many of the 107 coats of arms of noble families which adorn the white walls of the vaulted nave and choir. The interior also offers an interesting insight into the social divisions of the church's original congregation; while normal people sat in the pale green pews, local notables had glass-enclosed family boxes to enable them to keep their distance from the hoi polloi.

A stone's throw from the Toomkirik, in a peppermint green neo-Renaissance palace, is the **Estonian Art Museum**, Kiriku plats 1 (Eesti Kunstimuuseum; Wed–Sun 11am–6pm; 10EEK), housed here temporarily pending its return to Kadriorg Palace. This small museum, tracing the development of art in Estonia, displays a range of works from conventional nineteenth-century studies of Tallinn and portraits of peasants in traditional costume to twentieth-century paintings heavily influenced by European artistic trends like Expressionism.

Elsewhere in the Old Town

The remainder of the Old Town contains the commercial streets of medieval Tallinn, lined by merchants' residences and warehouses. Pikk tänav (Long Street), running northeast from Pikk jalg gate and linking Toompea with the port area, has some of the city's most important secular buildings from the Hanseatic period, kicking off with the **Great Guild** (Suur Gild) at Pikk 17. Completed in 1430 this was the city's main guild, meeting place of the German merchants who controlled the city's wealth. Its gloomy Gothic facade now fronts the **Estonian History Museum** (Ajaloomuuseum; 11am–6pm; closed Wed; 5EEK) where a predictable array of weapons, domestic objects and jewellery offers an uninspiring history of Estonia from the Stone Age to the eighteenth century. A side room has more interesting displays of traditional costumes. Exhibits are labelled in Estonian and Russian but there are also English summaries.

If the appearance of their headquarters is anything to go by, the guild who occupied the **House of the Brotherhood of the Blackheads** (Mustpeade Maja), Pikk 26, were a more exuberant bunch than the merchants of the Great Guild. The Renaissance facade of their building, inset with an elaborate stone portal and richly decorated door, cuts a bit of dash amid the stolidity of Pikk. According to legend the guild was founded to defend Tallinn during the Estonian uprising of St George's Day in 1343, though in later years it seems to have degenerated into a drinking club for bachelor merchants. The Brotherhood moved here in 1531 and remained until the guild was abolished by the Soviets in 1940. These days their building houses a concert hall – you can look inside for 10EEK.

Continuing along Pikk brings you to the **St Olaf's Church** (Oleviste kirik), first mentioned in 1267 and named in honour of King Olaf II of Norway, who was canonized for battling against pagans in Scandinavia. Were it not for its size this slab-towered Gothic structure would not be particularly eye-catching, and extensive renovation between 1829 and 1840 has left it with an unexceptional nineteenth-century interior. The church is chiefly famous for the height of its spire which reaches 124 metres today and was even taller in the past. According to local legend the citizens of Tallinn wanted the church to have the highest spire in the world in order to attract passing ships and bring trade into the city. Whether Tallinn's prosperity during the Middle Ages had anything to do with the visibility of the church spire is not known, but between 1625 and 1820 the church burned down eight times as a result of lightning striking the tower.

Bearing witness to the city's medieval wealth are the Old Town's merchants' houses. The best example are the **Three Sisters** (Kolm Õde), a gabled group at Pikk 71. Supremely functional with loading hatches and winch-arms set into their facades, these would have served as combined dwelling places, warehouses and offices, and are among the city's best-preserved Hanseatic buildings. At its far end Pikk is straddled by the **Great Coast Gate** (Suur

Rannavärav), a sixteenth-century city gate flanked by two towers. The larger of these, the aptly named "Fat Margaret Tower" (Paks Margareeta) has walls four metres thick and now houses the **Estonian Maritime Museum** (Mere Museum), a surprisingly diverting collection of model boats and nautical ephemera spread out over several floors (Wed–Sun 10am–5.30pm; 10EEK; Estonian, Russian and some English captions).

West of Lai is one of the longest-surviving sections of Tallinn's medieval city wall, complete with nine towers – to reach it, head down Suur-Kloostri. The walls that surrounded the Old Town were largely constructed during the fourteenth century, but they were added to and enhanced over succeeding centuries until improvements in artillery rendered them obsolete during the eighteenth century. Today just under two kilometres of city wall survive, along with eighteen towers.

The eastern outskirts

Kadriorg Park, a large, heavily wooded park a couple of kilometres east from the Old Town, is closely associated with the Russian Tsar Peter the Great, who first visited Tallinn in 1711, the year after Russia conquered Livonia and Estonia from Sweden. The main entrance to the park is at the junction of Weizenbergi tänav and Leineri tänav (tram #1 or #3 from Viru väljak). Weizenbergi cuts through the park, running straight past **Kadriorg Palace** (Kadrioru Loss), a Baroque residence designed by the Italian architect Niccolò Michetti, which Peter had built for his wife Catherine (Kadriorg is Estonian for "Catherine's Valley"). These days the palace is the official home of the Estonian Art Museum, though at the moment it's being refurbished and the collection is housed in temporary accommodation on Toompea. The smaller palace behind it is now home to Estonia's president. While waiting for the palace to be completed Peter lived in a small cottage in the grounds of the park. Today this simple building at the junction of Weizenbergi and Mäekalda houses the **Peter the Great House Museum** (Peeter Esimese Majamuuseum; May–Sept Wed–Sun 11.30am–4.30pm; 4EEK) with furniture from the time Peter lived there, along with a few objects from the palace.

Walking down Mäekalda from Peter's cottage leads, after around fifteen minutes, to Narva mnt. On the other side of this busy road is the **Song Bowl** (Lauluväljak), a vast amphitheatre that's the venue for Estonia's Song Festivals. These gatherings, featuring massed choirs thousands strong, have been an important form of national expression in Estonia since the first all-Estonia Song Festival was held in Tartu in 1869, and are held every two years. The present structure, which can accommodate 15,000 singers (with room for a further 30,000 or so on the platform in front of the stage), went up in 1960. The Song Bowl grounds were filled to capacity for the September 1988 festival which was a significant public expression of longing for independence from Soviet rule, and gave rise to the epithet "Singing Revolution".

A few hundred metres past the amphitheatre is **Maarjamäe Palace** (Maarjamae Loss), a neo-Gothic residence built for a Russian count in the 1870s, which looks out over Tallinn Bay at Pirita tee. The building now houses a branch of the **History Museum** (Ajaloomuuseum; Wed–Sun 11am–6pm; 5EEK), covering the mid-nineteenth century onwards, and is far more interesting and imaginative than its city-centre counterpart. The display starts with a section on urban and rural life in nineteenth-century Estonia which includes a few re-created domestic interiors, before moving on to the political and social upheavals of the early twentieth century. Later sections have information on the Molotov-Ribbentrop "secret protocols" which effectively handed the Baltic Republics to Stalin, leading into material about the fate of Estonia during World War II, and the activities of the "Forest Brothers", Estonian partisans who carried on the battle against Soviet occupation into the 1950s. Most exhibits have English captions but the earlier sections are in Estonian and Russian only.

The western outskirts

At the other end of Tallinn on the western outskirts of the town is the **Open-Air Museum** (Vabaõhumuuseum; daily: May–Aug 10am–8pm; Sept 10am–6pm; Oct 10am–5pm; Nov–April 10am–4pm; 10EEK), a collection of eighteenth- and nineteenth-century village buildings gathered here from different parts of the country. The exhibits illustrate how Estonian farms developed, from all-timber structures with humans and animals living cheek by jowl, to mor sophisticated stone buildings. The museum also includes an appealing wooden church and a windmill, though for many visitors the biggest attraction is the Kolu Kõrts café which serves up traditional bean soup and beer. The museum site slopes down to the sea and is known by the Italian name Rocca al Mare (Rock by the Sea), having been thus christened by a merchant who built himself a mansion here during the late nineteenth century. Get there by bus #21 from the train station or bus #6 from Vabaduse väljak.

Eating, drinking and nightlife

Meat and potatoes figure heavily on most **restaurant** menus in Tallinn, with alternatives available in a handful of ethnic places. Vegetarians are not well catered for, though a few places make a token effort. Many **cafés** and **bars** do **snacks** or even full meals, an option which will usually work out cheaper than eating in a restaurant.

Bars and cafés are your best bet for a good time, with many featuring live music and/or dancing. Things can get pretty wild, though, with occasional fights, particularly at weekends when boatloads of Finnish tourists hit town, intent on drinking themselves to a standstill. Most of Tallinn's discos aren't particularly recommendable and often attract mafia types. More underground, dance-music-orientated events tend to change location frequently and are advertised by flyposters – if you can't spot any try asking around in the city's hipper bars.

Cafés and snacks

Buon Giorno, Muurivahe 17. Good place for soups and breakfast. Mon–Fri 8am–10pm, Sat & Sun 9am–10pm.

Gnoom, Viru 2. Old-fashioned café with a genteel atmosphere, and cakes and snack dishes on the menu. Sun–Thurs 11am–11pm, Fri & Sat until 2am.

Kompass, Narva 7c (in the Central Hotel). Buffet/salad bar with wrapped sandwiches to take away. Open Sun–Thurs noon–11pm, Fri & Sat until 3am.

Lemmik, Viru 18. Popular place with good, inexpensive meals, which include soups and salads. Open 24hr.

McDonald's, Viru 24. Pricey by local standards but always busy. Daily 8am–midnight.

Maiasmokk, Pikk 16. Tallinn's most venerable café – founded in 1864 – with a beautiful wood-panelled interior. You may have to queue for a seat as it's hugely popular with elderly ladies taking a coffee-and-pastries break from shopping. Mon–Sat 10am–6pm, Sun 8am–7pm.

Pappa Pizza, Dunkri 6. Comfortable pizzeria with good thin-crust pizzas. Open daily 11am–11pm.

Pizza Americana/Grill Mexicana, Pikk 1–3. A combined pizzeria/bar-grill with the "best pizza in town" (deep dish) and Mexican favourites. Mon–Thurs noon–10pm, Fri & Sat noon–11pm, Sun noon–9pm.

Restaurants

Astoria, Vabaduse väljak 4 (☎2/448 462). A pricey luxury restaurant with an over-the-top floor show and a menu drawn from the international meat and potatoes lexicon. Popular with Tallinn's nouveau riche. Booking essential. Daily noon–7pm & 8pm–2am.

Controvento, Vene 12 (☎2/644 0470). Tasteful and authentic Italian restaurant in a fourteenth-century granary. Good selection of pizza and pasta dishes and a decent wine list. Main courses from around 80EEK. Reservations recommended. Daily 12.30pm–11pm. Café open Sun–Thurs 11am–midnight, Fri & Sat 11am–1am.

Damodara, Lauteri 1. Hare Krishna-run veggie place with cheap food and lectures (in Estonian) in the evenings. Open 11am–6pm.

Eeslitall Restoran, Dunkri 4/6. Probably Tallinn's most famous restaurant. Pasta and chicken dishes augment the basic pork and potatoes selection, but avoid the salad bar. Sun–Thurs 10am–midnight, Fri & Sat 10am–1am.

Egeri Kelder, Roosikrantsi 6. Hungarian, spicy meals. Closed Sun.

Golden Dragon, Pikk 37. Highly recommended Chinese place with a large variety of fish and vegetarian options. Daily noon–11pm.

Maharaja Restaurant, Raekoja plats 13. Authentic, but expensive, Indian cuisine with main courses at 140-400EEK. Daily noon–11pm.

Mõõkkala, Rüütli 16/18. Excellent, if a little pricey, seafood place in the cellar of what used to be the Tallinn executioner's house. Daily noon–midnight.

Roosikrantsi, Vabaduse väljak. Smart and expensive place dishing up credible French and Belgian cuisine. Mon–Fri 8am–midnight, Sat & Sun noon–midnight.

'Sub Monte, Rüütli 4. Pricey and slightly starchy cellar place where game dishes occasionally appear on the menu. Daily noon–11pm

Tiina, Nunne 18. The place for traditional Estonian dishes. The food isn't bad but the ersatz folksy atmosphere may give you indigestion. Moderately priced. Daily noon–11pm.

Toomkooli, Toom Kooli 13. Airy restaurant with outdoor seating, perched on the western side of Toompea, and offering a mix of local and international dishes. Main courses from around 90EEK. Daily noon–11pm.

Vanaema Juures, Rataskaevn 12 (☎2/631 3928). Cosy, elegant cellar restaurant with a country theme and local dishes such as pork, trout and wild boar with wine sauce. Meals average 150EEK. Reservations necessary. Mon–Sat noon–10pm, Sun noon–6pm.

Bars

Baieri Kelder, Roosikrantsi 2a. Bavarian-style cellar serving drinks and meals. Can get a little stuffy at times. Daily noon–11pm.

Diesel Boots, Lai 25. "Genuine American Bar" packed with ephemera that draws a *Saku*-swilling local crowd. Daily noon–2am.

George Browne's, Harju 6. A busy "Irish pub" popular with expats and locals alike. A pint of Guinness will set you back 38EEK - local beer is cheaper. Fill up on spaghetti, burgers and fries if you get hungry. Live music some nights. Daily noon–midnight.

Guitar Safari, Muurivahe 22. Popular venue for live bands and dancing, open until 3am.

Hell Hunt, Pikk 39. The name means "Gentle Wolf" and this is the most popular, most congenial and perhaps most authentic of Tallinn's Irish bars, usually packed with young people. A basement and outside seating to the rear. Vaguely Irish food available. Sun & Mon 11am–1am, Tues–Thurs 11am–2am, Fri & Sat 11am–3am.

Kloostri Ait, Vene 14. With its enormous open fire and intellectual-ish crowd this is quieter than most beer-swilling places. Also serves coffee and snacks. Sun–Thurs noon–midnight, Fri & Sat noon–2am.

Neitsitorn, Lühike jalg 9a. Several bars spread over four floors in a tower that forms part of the Old Town walls. A little bit pricey though the basement bar is a good place to sample *hõõgvein*. Snacks available. Daily 11am–10pm.

Nimega Baar/The Bar With A Name, Suur-Karja 13. Scottish-owned bar serving British food. Slightly older clientele than its sibling bar at number 4/6, where international boy is inclined to meet international girl, and live soccer matches are often screened. Both open Sun–Thurs 11am–2am, Fri & Sat 11am–4am or later.

Ruby Tuesday, Pikk 11. The place to go for cocktails, with a dance floor, dartboard, pool table and friendly staff. Food available too. Themed nights some evenings. Sun–Thurs 10am–2am, Fri & Sat 10am–4am.

Von Krahli Theatre Bar, Rataskaevu 10/12. Hip hangout that's always packed with bright young things. The atmosphere is friendly and there's frequent live music and dancing. Beer costs 25EEK, though locals favour vodka with orange juice. Sun–Thurs noon–1am, Fri & Sat noon–3am.

Live music and discos

Bonnie & Clyde, in the *Olümpia Hotel*, Liivalaia 33. Live bands usually on Saturdays and a dance floor occupied by the young and beautiful. Open Sun 1pm–4am, Tues–Thurs 9pm–3am, Fri & Sat 9pm–4am. 70EEK.

Café Amigo, in the *Viru Hotel*, Viru väljak 4. Heaving but likeable disco playing mainstream dance music for locals and tourists into the early hours. Open Sun–Thurs 9pm–4am, Fri & Sat until 5am. 50EEK.

Dekoltee, Ahtri 10. In a converted warehouse near the port, this disco/bar/casino boasts a big laser light show and claims to be the largest nightclub in the Baltics. Classy and expensive. Wed & Thurs 10pm–4am, Fri & Sat 10pm–5am. 70EEK.

Hollywood Club, Vana-Posti 8. Popular Old Town dance club.Trendy and busy. No trainers. 35–60EEK.

Manhattan Underground, Pikk 11. Dance club in the basement of *Ruby Tuesday*. Wed & Thurs 4pm–2am, Fri & Sat until 3am. 10–15EEK.

Von Krahli, Rataskaevu 10. Live music and London DJs hosting "Mutant Discos" once a month. Sun–Thurs noon–1am, Fri & Sat noon–3am. 70–100EEK.

Classical music, opera and ballet

The Estonia Theatre and the Estonia Concert Hall, both at Estonia pst. 4 (☎2/6449 3198; box office Mon–Fri noon–7pm, Sat noon–5pm) are reliable venues, the former for ballet, oper and musicals, the latter for classical music and choral works including performances by the Estonian National Symphony Orchestra. Other venues for concerts include the Niguliste Church, the Town Hall, the House of the Brotherhood of Blackheads and the Dominican Monastery on Vene.

Listings

Airlines Estonian Air, Vabaduse valjak 10 (☎2/631 3302); Finnair, Roosikrantsi 2 (☎2/611 0950); Lufthansa, Parnu 10 (☎2/631 4444); SAS, Rävala 2 (☎2/631 2240).

Airport information (☎2/638 8888).

Books Kupar, Harju 1, sells maps and locally produced English guides. Mon–Fri 10am–7pm, Sat 11am–5pm.

Car Rental Avis, Liivalaia 33 (☎2/631 5931) and at the airport; Europcar, Airport (☎2/638 8031); Budget, Airport, (☎2/638 8600); Hertz, Estonia 7 (☎2/631 2337) and at the airport.

Embassies United Kingdom, Kentmanni 20 (☎2/631 3461); USA, Kentmanni 20 (☎2/631 2021).

Exchange Outside banking hours, try *Palace Hotel*, Viru väljak.

Hospital Mustamäe, Sütiste 19 (☎2/525 652). Open 24 hours daily.

Internet Access Library Internetisaal, Estonian National Library, Tonismagi 2, 7th floor (Mon, Tues & Fri noon–6pm, Wed & Thurs noon–4pm; 40EEK per hour, plus 5EEK to obtain a day-pass for entry to the library). Reservations essential.

Laundry Vendlus, Parnu 48. Self and full-service available. Mon–Sat 8am–8pm, Sun 8am–5pm.

Left luggage Try the main train station at Toompuiestee 35 (5am–midnight; 10EEK), the bus station at Lastekodu 46 (4–10EEK), or *Viru Hotel* (8am–10pm; 20EEK).

Pharmacies Tonismae Apteek, Tõnismägi 5; Tallinna Linna Apteek, Pärnu mnt. 10.

Police On Pärnu mnt. 11, (☎2/6123 523).

Post office Narva mnt. 1, opposite the Viru Hotel (Mon–Fri 8am–7pm, Sat 9am–5pm).

Taxis Tulika (☎2/655 2552); Linnatakso (☎2/644 2442).

Telephones Next to the post office on Narva mnt. 1 (Mon–Fri 8am–7pm, Sat 9am–4pm).

THE REST OF ESTONIA

The islands of **Saaremaa** and **Hiiumaa**, off the west coast of Estonia, are both easily reached from Tallinn and immensely popular as holiday and weekend home destinations. Saaremaa, at 2922 square kilometres, the largest of Estonia's 1500 islands, is the more developed of the two, with tourist facilities already well established. Hiiumaa, smaller at 1024 square kilometres, remains remarkably unspoilt, its forests and coastline ripe for exploration. Elsewhere on the mainland, **Tartu**, the former Hansa city of Dorpat 190km southeast of Tallinn, is regarded by many Estonians as the spiritual capital of Estonia, thanks to its role in the nineteenth-century National Awakening. These days it's a laid-back university town with a population of 95,500 and a small and easily walkable Old Town. **Pärnu**, west of Tartu, is Estonia's fifth largest city with a population of 55,000, and has grown up around the nucleus of a castle built by the Livonian Order in the thirteenth century. There are a handful of sights in the Old Town but Pärnu's main claim to fame is as Estonia's major mainland resort, and its sandy beach still draws thousands of visitors every summer – particularly during the jazz festival in July.

Saaremaa

Cloaked with pine trees and juniper bushes, and littered with glacial boulders, the island of **SAAREMAA** is a tranquil place with Kuressaare as its major town. It was the last part of Estonia to come under foreign control (when the Knights of the Sword captured it in 1227) and the locals have always maintained a strong-minded indifference to the influence of foreign occupiers, leading many to claim that the island is one of the most authentically Estonian parts of the country.

To get to Saaremaa take the ferry from Virtsu on the mainland to Kuivastu on Muhu island. If you're travelling by car try and book a ferry ticket in advance, otherwise you may end up queuing for hours. A causeway links Muhu with Saaremaa.

Kuressaare

Approaching **KURESSAARE**, Saaremaa's main town, don't be put off by the ugly Soviet-era industrial zone that surrounds it – the centre remains much as it was before World War II and is home to one of the finest castles in the Baltic region. At the heart of the town is its central **Square** (Kesk väljak) – if you've arrived by bus turn left into Tallinna from Pihtla, where the bus station is located, to reach it.

On the square you'll find Kuressaare's oldest building (after the castle), the yellow-painted **Town Hall** (Raekoda) dating from 1670, its door guarded by stone lions, and, facing it, the **Weigh House** (Vaekoda), another yellow building with a stepped gable. From the square Lossi runs south past a monument to the dead of the 1918–20 War of Independence, when the Estonians beat off Soviet and German forces, recently restored to pride of place after a lengthy Soviet-era absence. Continuing, the street runs past the eighteenth-century **Nikolai kirik**, a white Orthodox church with green onion domes. The church has an Estonian rather than Russian congregation, a reminder of the fact that an estimated twenty percent of Estonia's population joined the Orthodox Church when the country belonged to the Russian Empire. The interior, with icons set in white-painted frames, is noticeably plainer than in Orthodox churches with predominantly Russian congregations.

Lossi leads to the magnificent **Kuressaare Castle** (Kuressaare Kindlus), a vast fortress built from locally quarried dolomite. Set on an artificial island surrounded by a moat, the castle was founded during the 1260s as a stronghold for the bishop of Ösel-Wiek who controlled western Estonia from his base on mainland Haapsalu. The castle as it stands today dates largely from the fourteenth century and is a formidable structure, protected by huge seventeenth-century ramparts. The labyrinthine keep houses the **Saaremaa Regional Museum** (Saaremaa Koduloomuuseum; Wed–Sun 11am–7pm; 30EEK), an interesting but confusingly laid out collection that covers the history and culture of the island from prehistoric times to date. The various sections are summarized in English but detailed labelling is in Estonian and Russian only. It's also possible to view the spartan living quarters of the bishops on the ground floor and climb the watchtowers. **Pikk Hermann**, the eastern (and thinner) corner tower is linked to the rest of the keep only by a wooden drawbridge. In the park surrounding the castle moat you'll find the wooden Kuursaal building from 1889, which makes a decent place for a drink or meal.

The **tourist office** (mid-May to mid-Sept Mon–Fri 9am–5pm; rest of year daily 9am–7pm; ☎245/33120) is in the **town hall** on Kesk valjak, and can book private rooms in Kuressaare and across the island for around 150EEK per person. About the cheapest hotel in town is the *Hotel Mardi*, Vallimaa 5a (☎245/33285; ②), which is actually part-hotel and part-hostel – it has a cheap but excellent restaurant too; hostel beds are only available May to August. For a bit more comfort head for *Repo*, Vallimaa 1a (☎245/55111; ③), a friendly, pension-type establishment that's about the best in town, though it's often fully booked. There are two **campsites** of note: *Mandjala camping site* (☎245/75193), near Nasva, has places in cottages (150EEK per person, including breakfast) or you can camp for 15–20EEK per person; and *Karujarve* camping at the lake of Karujarve (☎245/42181) has cabins for two people at 250EEK or tent spaces for 30EEK.

The smartest **restaurant** in town is the *Vannallin*, Kauba 8, while the *Veski*, Pärna 19, dishes up pork and potato variations in an old windmill. Another atmospheric venue is the *Kohvik Kuursaal* in the Kuursaal building in the castle park, offering soup, sandwiches and fish dishes – open daily until 10pm with terrace seating. *Lonkav Konu*, Kauba 6, is a pseudo-Irish pub with lots of beers on tap, a pool table and pub grub Estonian-style. The gloomy *Raekelder* in the basement of the town hall building serves **drinks** and grilled chicken and closes at midnight. While in town don't forget to try Saaremaa-brewed beer, which packs a bit more of a punch than *Saku*.

Elsewhere on Saaremaa

Exploring the rest of Saaremaa is one way of getting acquainted with the unspoilt Estonian countryside. The places described below are all within easy reach of Kuressaare – if you want to explore further afield the island **tourist office** has information about more far-flung attractions and on how best to get around Saaremaa by public transport. Thanks to its largely flat terrain, though, exploring the island by bike is also a viable option.

KAARMA, just over 10km north of Kuressaare, is a small village that's the centre of the local dolomite-mining industry. More interestingly, it's also the location of the thirteenth-century **Kaarma kirik**, a large, red-roofed church containing a christening stone from the same period, and a pulpit supported by a wooden Joseph figure from 1450. The church's graveyard is littered with ancient stone crosses – the oldest are the so-called "sun crosses" – crosses set within a circle carved in stone. In woods at the edge of the village of **KAALI**, 10km northeast of Kaarma, is a murky green pool about 100m in diameter, created by the impact of a meteorite during the eighth century BC. Though not particularly spectacular, it is one of the world's few easily accessible meteorite craters, and the locals are very proud of it. Around 15km north of Kaali is **ANGLA**, with five much-photographed wooden windmills by the roadside. A right turn just past the windmills leads to the thirteenth-century **Karja kirik**, a plain white village church with an unusual crucifixion carving above its side door. Inside the church are more stone carvings, depicting religious figures and scenes from village life.

Hiiumaa

Most of **HIIUMAA** island is forested (elk, wild boar and lynx are among the local fauna) with swathes of peat moor and swamp at its heart. The sandy, rocky soil is of little agricultural use and supports a permanent population of just 12,000 but, like Saaremaa, Hiiumaa is a very popular holiday destination and weekend/summer-house location. Places to head for are the smaller island of **Kassari**, linked to southern Hiiumaa by a causeway, and the **Kõpu peninsula** at the western end of the island. Mainland ferries arrive in Hiiumaa at Heltermaa from Rohuküla near Haapsalu and there's also a ferry service (summer only) to Hiiumaa from Triigi on Saaremaa.

Hiiumaa's capital is **KÄRDLA**, an uneventful little town that's a centre for local services but has nothing else to detain you. The centre of the town is **Kesk väljak** just south of the bus station. Here you'll find a few shops and a bank. The **tourist office**, Hiiu 1, Central Square (mid-April to mid-May Mon–Fri 9am–5pm, Sat 10am–2pm; mid-May to mid-Sept Mon–Fri 9am–6pm, Sat & Sun 10am–2pm; mid–Sept to mid-April Mon–Fri 10am–4pm; ☎246/330331), can arrange both private room and hotel **accommodation**. They also have maps and a detailed English-language island guide called *The Lighthouse Tour*. The cheapest hotel in town is *Kärdla Võõrastemaja*, Vabaduse 13 (☎246/96581; ①). Other possibilities include *Sõnajala*, Leigri väljak (☎246/31220; ②), with apartment-style accommodation; *Padu*, Heltermaa mnt. 22 (☎246/98034; ③); and the *Nuutri*, Nuutri 4 (☎246/98023; ③), a pleasant bed and breakfast. The only place to **eat** is the *Restoran-Baar Priiankru*, Sadama 4, with slow service and fairly unpleasant food.

The small island of **KASSARI**, traversed by a single main road, is a peaceful place of forests and fields. In its northeastern corner is **Kassari Kabel**, the only reed-roofed church in the country. To get there take a right turn off the main road just east of the museum, then take a left and keep going past a windmill until you find the chapel sheltering under the trees, its graveyard filled with iron memorial crosses. **Sääre Tirp** is a promontory jutting out into the sea at the southern end of the island. Follow the signpost from the main road down a track that terminates in a car park after a couple of kilometres. From here a path flanked by juniper bushes leads to the foot of Sääre Tirp, ending in a shingle spit that peters out into the sea after a couple of hundred metres.

All of Kassari can be covered on foot if you make a day of it, and it also makes a good place to explore by bike. If you want to stay overnight head for the well-appointed **hotel**, *Liilia*, Hiiu mnt. 22 (☎246/92146; ④) which also has a reasonable **restaurant**. *Puulaid Camping*, between Käina Bay and Jausa Bay on the road to Kassari, has cabin accommodation (①). There's also a campsite with no facilities near the Sääre Tirp car park where you can camp for free. If you want a little more comfort contact the Kärdla **tourist office** for information about private rooms in the area.

Forty kilometres or so west of Kärdla the **Kõpu peninsula** juts out into the sea. The main sight here is the **Kõpu Lighthouse** (Kõpu Tuletorn), one of the oldest continuously operating lighthouses in the world. The heavily buttressed lower part dates back to 1531 and was built at the request of the Hanseatic League to warn ships away from the Hiiu Madal sandbank and the pirate-infested coastline. Initially a pyre was burned at the top, but in 1845 a properly enclosed light was built. You can climb to the top for a view of trees and sea (admission 5EEK). At the western end of the peninsula along 12km of rough road in Ristna is another lighthouse, a maroon-coloured steel structure built in France in 1874. Local legend has it that there was a third lighthouse in the forest, whose purpose was to lure ships onto the rocks where they could be plundered.

Tartu

TARTU's main sights lie between **Cathedral Hill** (Toomemägi), right in the centre of Tartu, and the Emajõgi river. The train station is about 500m southwest of the city centre at Vaksali 6, and the bus station is just east of the centre at Turu 2.

Tartu's focal point is its cobbled **Town Hall Square** (Raekoja plats) lined by prim Neoclassical buildings, the most eye-catching of which is the **Town Hall** (Raekoda), a toy-town edifice at the head of the square, painted lilac and purple and topped by a spire. The Neoclassical architectural theme continues in the yellow and white stucco facade of the main **Tartu University** (Tartu Ülikooli) building at Ülikooli 18, a couple of hundred metres north of Raekoja plats. The university was founded by the Swedish king Gustaf Adolphus in 1632 but closed by the Russians and not reopened again until the start of the nineteenth century (the present building dates from then). It wasn't until the country achieved independence after World War I, however, that Estonians finally supplanted Germans in the lecture hall.

A hundred metres or so beyond the university is the red-brick shell of the Gothic **St John's Church** (Jaani kirik), founded in 1330, bombed out in 1944 and now undergoing extensive restoration. The building is inaccessible, but from the street you can admire the unusual terracotta sculptures in niches that surround the main entrance. From behind the Town Hall, Lossi climbs **Cathedral Hill** (Toomemägi), now a pleasant park with a few historic buildings dotted among its trees. On the way up, the street passes beneath **Angel's Bridge** (Inglisild), a brightly painted wooden bridge dating from the nineteenth century. At the top of the hill you'll find the remains of the red-brick **Cathedral** (Toomkirik), built by the Knights of the Sword during the thirteenth century. The cathedral was ruined during the Reformation and subsequently used as a barn.

Within a few minutes' walk of Toomemägi are Tartu's two main museums. The **Town Museum** (Tartu Linnamuuseum), Oru 2 (Wed–Sun 11am–6pm; 2EEK; English-language hand-out) has local archeological finds, material on the National Awakening, and exhibits about life in Tartu during the eighteenth and nineteenth centuries. It's worth a quick visit but if you're pressed for time the **Estonian National Museum**, J. Kuperjanovi 9 (Eesti Rahva Muuseum; Wed–Sun 11am–6pm; 5EEK, free on Fri), is a better bet. Devoted to peasant life and the development of agriculture in Estonia, it includes some imaginatively re-created farmhouse interiors (including a depiction of a wedding party). Most exhibits have English labels.

Practicalities

Tartu's **tourist office** is at Raekoja plats 14 (Mon–Fri 10am–6pm, Sat 10am–3pm; ☎27/432 141) and can provide you with town plans. Private room **accommodation** can be arranged with E-Turist Reisiburoo OU at Jaan 4 (☎27/441 681); rooms in and around the town centre start from 200EEK per person. Of Tartu's hotels the pleasant *Park Hotel*, Vallikravi 23 (☎27/433 663; ②), is centrally located in the leafy shadow of Toomemägi. Another possibility is *Tarim*, Rahu 8 (☎234/475 433; ②), offering self-catering apartments some way south of the centre (bus #4 from the station). The *Tartu*, Soola 3 (☎27/432 091; ④), the long yellow building behind the bus station, is overpriced but offers discounts to HI card-holders.

For fast **food** try the *Rüütli Bistro*, Ruutli 2. More upmarket restaurants include the reasonably priced *Püssirohukelder*, Lossi 28 – worth visiting for its gunpowder cellar location alone – and the *Restaurant Taverna*, Raekoja plats 20, a smart but reasonable Italian place that also does some local dishes. For **drinking** the best place is *Illegaard*, Ülikooli 5, an arty cellar bar/club – it's a members-only place after 5pm, but if you're nice to the doorman he may let you in (entrance via an unmarked door in courtyard). Open to all is the *Central*, Raekoja plats 3/Küüni 1, with outdoor seating in the courtyard, and *Rotund*, a pavilion with outdoor seating next to the cathedral on Toomemägi.

Pärnu

PÄRNU's sights are mostly clustered in the **Old Town**, on and around Rüütli and Kuninga. The town's **bus station** is on Pikk at the northeastern edge of the Old Town (information & ticket office is across the street at Ringi 3), and the **train station** is about 5km east of the centre at Riia mnt. 116.

Rüütli, lined with two-storey wooden houses, is the Old Town's main thoroughfare, cutting east–west through the centre. Near the junction with Aia is the **Parnu Museum** (Linnamuuseum), Rüütli 53 (Wed–Sun 11am–5pm; 7EEK), devoted to local history, and housing some of Estonia's oldest archeological finds – dating back to 8000 BC – and examples of local traditional costume. The oldest building in town is the **Red Tower** (Punane Torn), a fifteenth-century remnant of the medieval city walls on Hommiku, running north from Rüütli a few blocks west of the museum. Despite its name the tower is actually white – only the roof and window frames are red – and it now houses an antique shop.

Pühavaimu, a few blocks to the west, has a pair of respectable-looking seventeenth-century houses near the junction with Malmö, one in lemon yellow, the other in washed-out green with a large gabled vestibule. Moving west from Pühavaimu along Uus leads to Pärnu's prim Neoclassical ochre-coloured **Town Hall** (Raekoda) from 1788. Facing it is a grey *Jugendstil* municipal building from the early part of this century, part of which now houses the city **tourist office** (see below). Nearby, on the corner of Uus and Vee is the **Catherine Church** (Jekateriina kirik) a green-domed and multispired Orthodox church from 1760 named after the Russian empress Catherine the Great. The interior is abundantly furnished with icons but is open for services only.

From the Catherine Church, Vee runs down to **Kuninga**, the Old Town's other major street. At the western end of Kuninga is the seventeenth-century **Tallinn Gate** (Tallinna värav), a rather elegant relic of the Swedish occupation, set into the remains of the city ramparts and now home to a bar (*Baar Tallinna Värav*, see below). To see the gate at its best head into the park on its outer side from where, with its massive gable and decorative pillars, it looks more like a Baroque chapel. Heading east along Kuninga leads to the Lutheran **Elizabeth Church** (Elisabethi kirik; Mon–Fri 10am–2pm) dating from 1747, with a maroon and ochre Baroque exterior and plain, wood-panelled interior. Continuing along Kuninga takes you past some wooden houses to the **Koidula Park** with a statue of poet Lydia Koidula (1843–86), whose collection of verses the *Nightingale of Emajõgi* is one of the major works of the National Awakening.

From Koidula Park, Pühavaimu and then Supeluse run down to the city's **resort area**, passing beneath the trees of the Rannapark, a shady park separating the town from the beach. At the southern end of Supeluse are the grand, colonnaded Neoclassical **Pärnu Mud-Baths** (Pärnu Mudaravila), built in 1926, and painted in the familiar ochre. Nearby is Pärnu's sandy, white beach, immensely busy at weekends and on public holidays. To escape the crowds make for the dunes east of the Mud Baths, but if you want to mingle with the masses head in the opposite direction towards the stretch of open sand backed by the upmarket *Sunset Club*, a smart club/bar with a terrace. Beyond this is a 100m concrete terrace backed by lower rent kiosks, bars, cafés and ice-cream places.

Practicalities

Pärnu **tourist office** is at Munga 2 (June–Aug Mon–Fri 9am–6pm Sat & Sun 10am–3pm; Sept–May Mon–Fri 9am–5pm; ☎244/40639). English-speaking staff have maps and can give details about hotels and private room **accommodation**. Best of the cheaper **hotels** is the *Seedri*, Seedri 4 (☎244/43350; ②), with plain but clean doubles (shared facilities), between the Old Town and the beach. *Kajakas*, Seedri 2 (☎244/43098; ②), is similar but slightly more expensive. The best mid-range place is the *Vesiroos*, Esplanaadi 42a (☎244/43534; ③), a Deco building just south of the Old Town. Cheaper accommodation options are limited to out-of-town **camping** places such as *Kämping Valgerand* (with cabins, ①), 10km west of town.

Pärnu has over a hundred bars, cafés and restaurants but unfortunately very few of them are noteworthy. For **food**, the *Jahisaal*, Hospidali 6, is a moderately priced but gloomy cellar restaurant where perch, elk and boar feature on the menu; while *Trahter Postipoiss*, Vee 12, flies the meat and potatoes flag in a nineteenth-century post house. The *Victoria*, Kuninga 25, has a slightly more eclectic menu and, though expensive by local standards, isn't out of reach (main dishes from 100EEK). Alternatively, *Pappa Pizza*, Kuninga 34, has good cheap pizzas and a salad bar. On the **drinking** front the *Baar Tallinna Värav*, Kuninga 1, in the town's only surviving city gate, has an outside terrace and is a good spot for a beer (also serves food).

travel details

Trains

Tallinn to: Pärnu (2 daily; 3hr); St Petersburg (1 daily; 11hr).
Pärnu to: Tallinn (2 daily; 3hr).
Tartu to: Tallinn (4 daily; 3hr).

Buses

Tallinn to: Haapsalu (7 daily; 2hr); Kuressaare (Saaremaa; 6 daily; 4hr 30min); Pärnu (10 daily; 2hr 30min); Rīga (4 daily; 6hr); St Petersburg (2 daily; 9hr); Tartu (20 daily; 2hr 30min); Vilnius (7 daily; 12hr).

Kuressaare to: Tallinn (up to 11 daily; 4hr 30min).
Pärnu to: Tallinn (up to 10 daily; 2hr).
Tartu to: Tallinn (25 daily; 2hr 30min)

Ferries

Tallinn to: Helsinki (around 7 daily; 1hr 30min–3hr).
Rohuküla to: Helternaa (12 daily; 1hr 30min).
Triigi to: Orjaku (5 daily in summer; 1hr 30min).
Virtsu to: Kuivastu for Saaremaa (12-20 daily; 30min).

CHAPTER 9

FINLAND

Introduction

Mainland Scandinavia's most culturally isolated and least understood country, **Finland** has been independent only since 1917, having been ruled for hundreds of years by imperial powers: first the Swedes and then the tsarist Russians. Much of its history involves a struggle for recognition and survival, and it's not surprising that modern-day Finns have a well-developed sense of their own culture, manifest in the widely popular Golden Age paintings of Gallen-Kallela and others, the music of Sibelius, the National Romantic style of architecture, and the deeply ingrained values of rural life. These qualities are traditionally best exemplified by the small but significant proportion of Finns who come from **Karelia**, a large tract of land now scythed in two by the Finnish–Russian border.

Finland is mostly flat and punctuated by huge forests and lakes; you'll need to travel around a lot to appreciate its wide regional variations. **The South** contains the least dramatic scenery, but the capital, **Helsinki**, more than compensates, with its brilliant architecture and superb collections of national history and art. Stretching from the Russian border in the east to the industrial city of **Tampere**, the vast waters of the **Lake Region** provide a natural means of transport for the timber industry – indeed, water here is a more common sight than land. Towns lie on narrow ridges between lakes, giving even major manufacturing centres green and easily accessible surrounds. North of here, Finland ranges from the flat western coast of **Ostrobothnia** to the thickly forested heartland of **Kainuu** and gradually rising fells of **Lappland**, home to Finland's most alluring terrain – and the *Sámi*, the seminomadic reindeer herders found all over northern Scandinavia. Furthermore, with the freeing-up of travel restrictions to Russia and especially Estonia, Helsinki has become a base for trips to Tallinn, St Petersburg and the former Finnish town of Viborg, now just inside Russia.

Information and maps

Most towns have some sort of **tourist office**, with free maps and information, and which sometimes book accommodation. In summer they open every day, usually for long hours in more popular centres; in winter, opening hours will be much reduced, if they open at all. The best general **map** of Finland is the *Daily Telegraph* one; there is also an excellent map in the *Finland: Budget Accommodation* booklet, available from tourist offices.

Money and banks

Finland comes with a reputation for high expense. This is still deserved, though with reasonably careful budgeting the country costs no more than any European capital, and public transport can be noticeably cheaper. Finnish currency is the **markka**, which divides into 100 *penniä*. Coins are 10 and 50p, 1, 5 and 10mk. Notes are 20, 50, 100, 500 and 1000mk. Travellers' cheques and currency can be changed at most **banks** (Mon–Fri 9.15am–4.15pm); the charge is usually 15mk, though several people changing money together need only pay the commission charge once. You can also change money at hotels, but normally at a worse rate. Some banks have exchange desks at transport terminals which open to meet international arrivals. **Credit card** cash advances – up to 1000mk a time – can be made from Solo cash machines.

Communications

In general, communications in Finland are dependable and quick, although in the far north and parts of the east minor delays arise due to geographical remoteness. You can buy stamps from a **post office** (normally open Mon–Fri 9am–5pm), from the street stands (*R-kioski*), and at some hotels: 3.20mk priority class, 2.60mk economy to Europe; 3.40mk priority or 2.40mk economy to the rest of the world.

An out-of-order **public phone** is virtually unheard of in Finland, although many of them, widely found on streets and at transport centres, have a dilapidated look. The minimum cost of a **local call** is 2mk. Phones take 1mk, 5mk and 10mk coins, which run out rapidly, so have a supply of small change to hand. However, payphones are being phased out and *Nonstop* card phones can be found taking 30, 50, 70 and 100mk. Cards (*kortti*) are available at sites listed on the phone, usually nearby ticket offices, the post office or R-kiosks (minimum call charge 5mk). Some card phones accept major credit cards. **International calls** are cheapest between 10pm and 8am but calls from hotels can be frighteningly expensive. The operator numbers are ☎118 for domestic calls and ☎92020 for international calls. The international access code is 990.

Getting around

You'll have few headaches getting around the more populated parts of Finland. The chief forms of public transport are trains, backed up, particularly on east–west journeys, by long-distance buses. For the most part trains and buses integrate well, and you'll only need to plan with care when travelling through the remoter areas of the far north and east.

■ Trains and buses

The swiftest land link between Finland's major cities is invariably **trains**, operated by the national company, **VR**. Large, comfortable express trains (and a growing number of super-smooth *Inter-city* and *EP* or special express trains) serve the principal **north–south** routes several times a day. Elsewhere, especially on east–west hauls through sparsely populated regions, rail services tend to be skeletal and trains are often tiny or replaced by buses though rail passes are still valid. The Arctic north is not served by trains at all. For the Finnish State Railways call ☎0100121 (from Finland) or ☎00 358-97075706 (from outside Finland).

InterRail and ScanRail passes (see "Getting around" in Sweden chapter) are valid on all trains. If you don't have one of these and are planning a lot of travelling, get a **Finnrail Pass** before arriving in Finland, from either the Finnish Tourist Board or a travel agent. This costs £67/$109 for 3 days' travel in a month, £90/$146 for 5 days and £122/$198 for 10 days. The pass is valid for travel on the entire rail network. Ordinary fares are surprisingly reasonable. One-way tickets are valid for 8 days, returns for a month and you can break your journey once in each direction, provided the ticket is stamped at the station where you stop and the total distance covered is over 80km. If there are three or more of you travelling together, group tickets, available from a train station or travel agent, can cut fares by at least 20 percent. **Seat reservations**, costing 20mk, are a good idea at weekends and holidays; on *EP* and *IC* trains a supplement of between 20 and 80mk must be paid, which includes (compulsory) seat reservation. **Sleeping berths** are also available on a number of routes, for 60mk sharing a three-berth, 120mk sharing a twin. The complete **timetable** (*Suomen Kulkuneuvot*) of Finnish rail, bus, ferry and air routes costs 95mk from bookshops and kiosks, though the *Taskuaikataulu* booklet (5mk) from any tourist office or station covers the major connections.

Buses – run by local private companies but with a common ticket system – cover the whole country, and are often quicker and more frequent than trains over the shorter east–west hops. **Fares** are approximately 85mk for 100km, 215mk for a 400km journey; seat reservations cost 12mk. All types of ticket can be purchased at a bus station or at most travel agents; only ordinary one-way tickets can be bought when boarding the bus. Of the **discount tickets** available, return fares are 10 percent less than two one-ways, three or more people travelling 80km or more qualify for a

group reduction of 20 percent; holders of YIEE/FIYTO and GO-25 (60mk for those under 26) cards get a 30 percent reduction on trips of similar length. A 10mk supplement is charged on express buses. **Students** can also buy a bus travel discount card for 50mk (certificate from school or college and photo required), giving 35–50 percent reductions on journeys of 80km or more. If you're going to travel a lot by bus, get a **Coach Holiday Ticket**, which gives 1000km of travel over any two-week period for 350mk, from any long-distance bus station. The **timetable** (*Pikavuoroaikataulut*), available at all main bus stations, lists all the routes in the country.

For further information on **youth and student travel**, contact Kilroy Travel in Helsinki (☎09/6807811), where you can get a *Discounts for Youth Travel* brochure.

■ Driving, hitching and cycling

If you **bring your own car** to Finland, it's advisable (though not compulsory) to have a Green Card as proof of insurance. If you are involved in an **accident**, report it at once to the Finnish Motor Insurers' Bureau, Bulevardi 28, 00120 Helsinki (☎09/680401), or the Finnish Automobile Association (☎09/6940022). Though **roads** are generally good, there can be problems with melting snows, usually during April and May in the south and during June in the far north. The speed limit is 40–60 kph in built-up areas, 100kph on major roads, 120kph on motorways. If not signposted, the basic limit is 80kph. Other rules of the road include using headlights when driving outside built-up areas and the compulsory wearing of seatbelts by drivers and all passengers; as elsewhere in Scandinavia, there are severe penalties for drunk driving. **Car rental** is expensive, at 200–600mk per day, plus up to 5mk per kilometre. You need a valid driving licence, at least a year's driving experience, and to be aged at least between 19 and 25, depending on the company; some agencies require a credit card to pay the deposit.

Hitching is generally easy, and sometimes the quickest means of transport between two spots. Finland's large student population has helped accustom drivers to the practice, and you shouldn't have to wait too long for a ride. For information about **cycling**, contact Mountain Bike Club Finland (☎09/611052) or ask for the special booklet at the tourist office.

Accommodation

You'll always be able to find some kind of **accommodation** in Finland to suit you. Prices can be high, and only by being aware of special offers will you be

ACCOMMODATION PRICE CODES

Throughout this guide, accommodation is priced on a scale of ① to ⑨, the number indicating the lowest price per night a single person could expect to pay in that establishment in high season. With hostels this is the nightly rate per person; with hotels, the price is arrived at by dividing the cost of the cheapest double room by two. The prices indicated by the codes are as follows:

① under £5 / $8
② £5–10 / $8–16
③ £10–15 / $16–24
④ £15–20 / $24–32
⑤ £20–25 / $32–40
⑥ £25–30 / $40–48
⑦ £30–35 / $48–56
⑧ £35–40 / $56–64
⑨ £40 / $64 and over

able to sleep well on a budget. **Bookings** all over Finland can be made through Hotel Booking Centre (☎09/22881400), situated inside the City Tourist Office in Helsinki. The free *Finland: Budget Accommodation* booklet, available from any tourist office, contains a comprehensive list of hostels and campsites, and an excellent map of the country.

■ Hotels

Finnish **hotels** normally come with all the facilities: TV, phone and private bathroom are standard fixtures and breakfast is invariably included in the price. Costs can be formidable – sometimes in excess of 500mk – but planning ahead and taking advantage of various discount schemes and summer reductions can cut prices to around 300mk per person. Expense can also be trimmed under the **Finncheque** system, available outside Finland from the Finnish Tourist Board or a specialist travel agent, which offers an unlimited number of vouchers, costing 200mk each per person per night, entitling the holder to a room in hotels in participating chains between June and mid-September – there's often a surcharge of 80mk in more expensive hotels, though in cheaper places lunch is thrown in. The downmarket Scanhotel chain offers a 50 percent discount to holders of ISIC cards (daily end June to mid-Aug, weekends rest of the year), lowering their prices to 450mk for a double room including breakfast for two; but note that the chain's ten hotels don't cover much of the country, and beware of "quality surcharges". In many towns you'll also find **tourist hotels** (*matkustajakoti*), a more basic type of hotel usually charging 200–300mk per person, although they are often full during summer. **Summer hotels** (*kesähotelli*) are another possibility, basically accommodation in student blocks, from June to the end of August. Bookable in Finland through travel agents, they cost around 225mk per person.

■ Youth hostels

The cheapest option, and always spotlessly clean, are **youth hostels** (*retkeilymaja*). There are around

150 throughout the country and each city has at least one. It's always advisable to book ahead, especially between June and August. Many hostels close altogether after mid-August until the following June. Hostels cost between 60mk and 150mk per person, and range from the basic dormitory type to those with two-bedded rooms and a bathroom between three. Bedlinen, if not included, costs an extra 20–30mk; Finnish health regulations prohibit the use of sleeping bags in hostels. Hostelling International cards, while not obligatory, reduce an overnight stay by 15mk. Alternatively, you can get a similar reduction by buying an International Guest card for 90mk at the Finnish Hostel Association at Yrjönkatu 38B, 00100 Helsinki (☎09/6940377).

■ Campsites and camping cottages

Official **campsites** (*leirintäalue*) are plentiful in Finland. Most open from May or June until August or September, although some stay open longer and a few all year. Sites are **graded** on a star system: one-star sites are in rural areas and are fairly basic; two-star sites have running water, toilets and showers; three-star sites, often on the outskirts of major towns, have hot water and full cooking and laundry facilities. The cost for two people sharing is 30–90mk depending on the rating. Many three-star sites also have **camping cottages**, from simple sleeping accommodation for two to six people, to luxury places equipped with TV, sauna and kitchen. The cabins cost 600–3000mk per week; it's advisable to book as far ahead as possible during July or August. Without an International Camping Card you'll need a National Camping Card, available at every site for 20mk and valid for a year. **Camping rough** is illegal without the landowner's permission.

Food and drink

Finnish food can be pricey, but you can keep a grip on the expense by self-catering. Though tempered by many regulations, alcohol is more widely available than in much of the rest of Scandinavia.

■ Food

Though it may at first seem a stodgy, unsophisticated cuisine, **Finnish food** is an interesting mix of western and eastern influences, with Scandinavian-style fish specialities and exotic meats like reindeer and elk alongside dishes that bear a Russian stamp – pastries, and casseroles strong on cabbage and pork. If you're staying in a hotel, **breakfast** (*aamiainen*) is a sumptuous affair, a buffet of herring, eggs, cereals, cheese, salami and bread. Later in the day you can lunch on the economical **snacks** sold in ubiquitous market halls (*kauppahalli*) or in their adjoining cafeterias, where you are charged by the weight of food on your plate. Most train stations and some bus stations and supermarkets also have cafeterias proffering a selection of snacks and light meals, and the Grilli and Nakkikioski street stands turn out burgers and hot dogs for 14–20mk. Otherwise, campus cafeterias or **mensas** are the cheapest places to get a hot dish, with a choice of three menus, with bread and coffee, for 12–20mk. Theoretically you have to be a student but you are unlikely to be asked for ID, though if you can prove you're a student, a discount is in order. In a regular restaurant, or *ravintola*, **lunch** (*lounas*) is the cheapest time to eat. Many places offering a lunchtime buffet table (*voileipäpöytä* or *seisova pöytä*) stacked with a choice of traditional goodies for a set price of around 50–75mk. A *baari*, an unlicensed restaurant with a range of Finnish dishes and snacks, is another low-cost option, although most close early – at 5 or 6pm. On Thursdays every *baari* in the country dishes up *hernekeitto ja pannukakut*, thick pea soup with black rye bread, followed by pancakes with strawberry jam, for around 35mk. You'll get much the same fare in a *kahvila*, though these can be a little pricier, especially in larger cities. Pizzerias, too, are widespread, serving "lunch specials" for 35–50mk.

■ Drink

Finland's **alcohol laws** are as bizarre as those of Norway and Sweden but, unlike in those countries, boozing has always been tackled enthusiastically and the Finnish are now keen to fall in line with the comparably pro-booze attitude of the rest of the EU. For the time being, though, the government-run **ALKO** shops (Mon–Thurs 10am–5pm, Fri 10am–6pm, Sat 9am–2pm; closed Sat May–Sept) are the only places with a licence for selling stronger alcohol.

Beer (*olut*) falls into three categories: "light beer" (I-Olut), like a soft drink; "medium strength beer" (*Keskiolut*, III-Olut), perceptibly alcoholic, sold in shops and cafés; and "strong beer" (A-Olut or IV-Olut), on a par with the stronger European beers, and only available at fully licensed restaurants, clubs and ALKO shops. Even the smallest town will have one, and prices don't vary. Strong beers, like Lapin Kulta Export, Karjala, Lahden A, Olvi Export and Koff porter, cost 7.90mk for a 300ml bottle. Imported beers go for 9.90–10.20mk a bottle. As for **spirits**, Finlandia vodka is 150mk per litre; there's also a popular rough form of vodka called Koskenkorva at 140mk.

Most restaurants have a full licence, and some are actually frequented more for drinking than eating. To add to the confusion, some so-called "pubs" are not licensed. There are also **dance restaurants** (*tanssiravintola*), which serve food as well as drink, and are popular with the over-40s and charge 14–35mk admission – expect to queue for entry into the most popular bars. There's always either a doorman (*portsari*) – whom some tip (usually 5–7mk) on leaving – or an obligatory cloakroom (again usually 5–7mk). Bars are usually open until midnight or 1am and service stops half an hour before closing. A common order is a *tuoppi* – a half-litre glass of draught beer. Wherever you seek alcohol, you have to be 18 to buy beer and wine, and 20 for spirits.

Opening hours and holidays

Shops are usually open Mon–Fri 9am–6pm, Sat 9am–4pm. Shops and banks will be closed on the following **public holidays**, when most public transport and museums operate to a Sunday schedule: Jan 1; Jan 6 (Epiphany); Good Friday and Easter weekend; May 1; Midsummer's Eve and Day; All Saint's Day (the Sat between Oct 31 and Nov 6); Dec 6; Dec 24, 25 and 26.

Emergencies

As in other Scandinavian countries, you probably won't have much cause to come into contact with the Finnish **police**, though if you do they are likely to speak English. As for **health problems**, if you're insured, you'll save time by seeing a doctor at a private health centre (*Lääkäriasema*) rather than queuing at a national health centre (*Terveyskeskus*). Medicines must be paid for at a **pharmacy** (*apteekki*) although, provided you have your passport, you won't be charged more than a Finn.

EMERGENCY NUMBERS
All emergencies ☎112.

HELSINKI

The southern coast of Finland is the most populated, industrialized and richest part of the country, with the densest concentration, not surprisingly, around the capital, **HELSINKI**. A city of half a million people, Helsinki is quite different from the other Scandinavian capitals, closer both in mood and looks to the major cities of eastern Europe. For years an outpost of the Russian Empire, its very shape and form is derived from its powerful neighbour. Yet through the twentieth century the city has become a showcase of independent Finland, much of its impressive architecture drawing inspiration from the dawning of Finnish nationalism and the rise of the republic. The streets have a youthful buzz, the short summer acknowledged by crowds strolling the boulevards and socializing in the outdoor cafés and restaurants. At night the pace picks up, with a great selection of pubs and clubs, free rock concerts in the numerous parks, and an impressive quota of fringe events.

Arrival and information

However you travel you arrive close to the city centre. The **ferry** lines Viking and Silja, and the Tallink hydrofoils, have terminals on the South Harbour, from where it's less than 1km to the centre. Other ferry lines, to Tallinn, Tallink and Eestin Linjat, use the terminal at the West Harbour. The **train station** is in the heart of the centre, next to one of the two bus terminals. Across Mannerheimintie and a short way up Simonkatu is the other bus terminal and the **long-distance bus station**. Helsinki's **airport**, Vantaa, is 20km to the north, connected by buses to the Finnair terminal under the *Inter-Continental Hotel*, halfway between the city centre and the Olympic Stadium, and to the train station (every 15–30min; 22mk).

The **City Tourist Office** at Pohjoisesplanadi 19 (May–Sept Mon–Fri 9am–7pm, Sat & Sun 9am–3pm; Oct–April Mon–Fri 9am–5pm, Sat 9am–3pm; ☎09/1693757) has free street and transport maps and useful free tourist magazines, including *Helsinki This Week*, *City* and *Helsinki Happens*. There is also a Hotel Booking Centre desk (☎09/22881400). If staying for a while, consider purchasing a **Helsinki Card**, giving unlimited travel on public transport and free entry to more than forty museums. The three-day card (180mk) is the best value, although there are also two-day (150mk) and one-day (120mk) versions. For information on the rest of the country, use the **Finnish Tourist Board** across the road at Eteläesplanadi 4 (June–Aug Mon–Fri 8.30am–5pm, Wed until 6pm, Sat 10am–2pm; rest of year Mon–Fri 8.30am–4pm, Wed until 5pm; ☎09/41769300).

City transport

Most of the things you might want to see are within walking distance of one another. However, quick hops across the centre are easily done by way of an efficient and integrated tram, bus and small metro system. A one-way journey costs 10mk and unlimited transfers are allowed within one hour (on the trams, a one-way ticket is also available for 7mk, which does not allow any transfers). A **multitrip** ticket gives ten rides for 75mk. A **tourist ticket** lasts one (25mk), three (50mk) or five days (75mk), and permits travel on buses and trams displaying double arrows (effectively all of them). One-way tickets are bought on board, others from the bus station, tourist office or kiosks around the centre, and **metro** tickets can be bought from the machines in the stations. Of **tram** routes, #3T, which follows a figure-of-eight route around the centre, is the most useful. **Taxis** have a basic charge of 20mk in the day, 30mk at night, with a charge per kilometre, plus a surcharge after 6pm and on weekends, and even more after 10pm. **Bicycles** can be rented at the Olympic Stadium, P. Stadionintie 3B (☎09/496071) or at Greenbike, Mennerheimintie 13, opposite Parliament House (☎09/85022850).

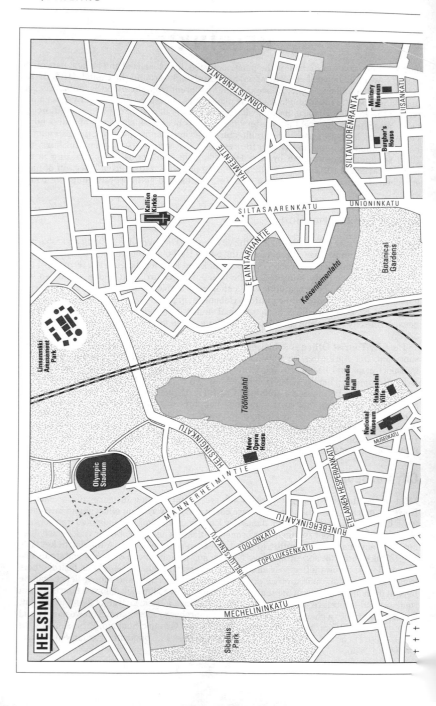

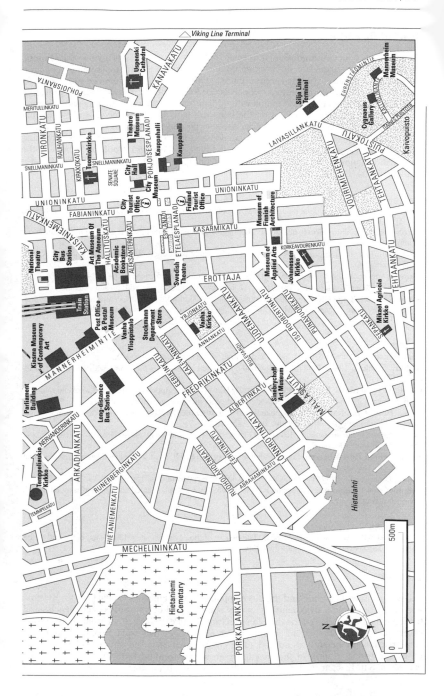

Accommodation

There's plenty of **accommodation** in Helsinki, but by far the bulk of it is in mid-range **hotels**, which go for 400–700mk for the average double – although several top-notch places drop their prices dramatically in the summer tourist season, and all have reduced rates at weekends. Otherwise there are a number of cheaper, if less luxurious, **tourist hotels**, providing basic accommodation in private rooms without bathrooms, and a few **hostels** with dormitories, though there may be a limit on the length of stay during the peak summer period. Wherever you stay, you should book as far ahead as possible: the various cut-price hotel deals get snapped up quickly, and hostel space can be tight in summer. If you don't have anything reserved, you can book hotel rooms and hostel beds at the **Hotel Booking Centre** at the train station (summer Mon–Fri 9am–9pm, Sat till 7pm, Sun 10am–6pm; winter Mon–Fri 9am–6pm; ☎09/171133).

Hostels

Hostel Academica, Hietaniemenkatu 14 (☎09/13114334). Well placed with double rooms. Open June to Aug. HI and student card discounts. ④.
Eurohostel, Linnankutu 9 (☎09/622 0470). The biggest in Finland, this hostel is close to the Viking ferry terminal and has a free sauna. ④.
Erottajanpuisto, Uudenmaankatu 9 (☎09/642169). Usefully positioned, and especially good for several people sharing. ④.
Lönnrot, Lönnrotinkatu 16 (☎09/6932590). Basic, but centrally placed, close to the Old Church. ④.
Omapohja, Itäinen Teatterikuja 3 (☎09/666211). Dorms and rooms, some with en-suite facilities. ③.
Stadion Hostel, in the Olympic Stadium (☎09/496071). A 3km hike from the centre and often crowded, but cheap and open all year. Trams #3T, #7A, #7B and #10 stop outside stadium; follow the signs from there. ②.

Hotels

Anna, Annankatu 1 (☎09/616621). Small and central, with a cosy atmosphere. ⑨.
Arthur, Vuorikatu 19B (☎09/17344215). Good-quality hotel, discounts for rooms without en-suite facilities. ⑨.
Cumulus Kaisaniemi, Katajanokanlaituri 7 (☎09/172881). Well-equipped rooms, good weekend rates. ⑨.
Finn, Kalevankatu 3b (☎09/640904). A modern and peaceful place, virtually in the city centre. ⑧.
Artica Hotel Grand Marina, Katajanokanlaitun 23 (☎09/16661). Vast converted 1930s customs house, close to Viking Lineboats. Very elegant. ⑨.
Kongressikoti, Snellmaninkatu 15a (☎09/1356839). Clean and cosy place close to Senate square. Discounts for longer stays. ⑥.
Seaside Hotel Best Western, Ruoholahdenranta 3 (☎09/69360). Next to the new Länsisatama Terminal for ferries to Tallinn. ⑤.
Skatta, Linnankatu 3 (☎09/659233). Close to the Viking ferry terminal. Trams #2, #4. ⑧.
Summer Hotel Satakunta, Lapinrinne 1 (☎09/69585231). Centrally located and doubles as an HI hostel. Open June–Aug. ③.

Campsites

Rastila, Itäkeskus Vuosaari (☎09/316551). The nearer of the city's two sites, 13km east, at the end of the metro line and served by buses #90, #90A, #96.

The City

Following a devastating fire and the city's appointment as Finland's capital in 1812, Helsinki was totally rebuilt in a style befitting its new status: a grid of wide streets and Neoclassical brick buildings modelled on the then Russian capital, St Petersburg. It's a tribute to the vision of planner Johan Ehrenström and architect Carl Engel that from **Senate Square** to **Esplanadi** the grandeur has endured, often quite dramatically. The square itself is dominated by the exquisite form of the recently renovated **Tuomiokirkko** (June–Aug Mon–Sat 9am–6pm, Sun 12–6pm; winter Mon–Sat 10am–4pm, Sun noon–4pm), designed, like most of the other buildings on the square, by Engel, and completed after his death in 1852. After the elegance of the exterior, the spartan Lutheran interior comes as a disappointment; better is the gloomily atmospheric **crypt** (open by arrangement; entrance on Kirkkokatu; ☎09/62208623), now often used for exhibitions. Walking east, the square at the end of Aleksanterinkatu is overlooked by the onion domes of the Russian Orthodox **Uspenski Cathedral** (Tues–Fri 9.30am–4pm, Sat 9.30am–2pm, Sun noon–3pm). Inside, a rich display of icons glitters while incense mingles with the sound of Slavonic choirs. Beyond it is Katajanokka, a wedge of land extending between the harbours, where a dockland development programme is converting the old warehouses into pricey new restaurants and apartments for Helsinki's yuppies. Just a block south of Senate Square, the new **City Museum** at Sofiankatu 4 (Mon–Fri 9am–5pm, Sat & Sun 11am–5pm; 20mk) offers a hi-tech record of Helsinki life in an impressive permanent exhibition called "Time".

Across a mishmash of tramlines from South Harbour is **Esplanadi**. At the height of the mid-nineteenth-century language conflict, Finns would walk on the south side and Swedes on the north of this neat boulevard. Nowadays it's dominated at lunchtime by office workers, later in the afternoon by buskers, and at night by couples strolling hand-in-hand along the central pathway to free musical accompaniment from the hut in the middle. Close by, on the corner of Aleksanterinkatu and Mannerheimintie, is the Constructivist brick exterior of the **Stockmann Department Store**. Europe's largest, it sells everything from bubble gum to Persian rugs. Opposite, the **Vanha Ylioppistalo** – the old Students' House – is the home of the Finnish Students' Union and holds the **Vanhan Galleria**, a small gallery with frequent modern art events and various arty cafés. A few strides further along Mannerheimintie, steps head down to **Tunneli**, an underground complex of shops that leads to one of the city's most enjoyable structures, **Helsinki train station**. This solid yet graceful 1914 building is often thought of as architect Eliel Saarinen's finest work. Beside the station is the imposing granite **National Theatre**, home of Finnish drama since 1872. Inside, Wäinö Aaltonen's bronze sculpture remembers Aleksis Kivi, who died insane and impoverished before being acknowledged as Finland's greatest playwright. Since no one knew what Kivi actually looked like, this imaginary likeness came to be regarded as the true one. Directly opposite the bus station is the **Art Museum of the Ateneum** (Tues & Fri 9am–6pm, Wed & Thurs 9am–8pm, Sat & Sun 11am–5pm; 15mk, 45mk for special exhibitions). Its stirring selection of late-nineteenth-century works – including Akseli Gallén-Kallela and Albert Edelfelt's scenes from the Finnish epic, the *Kalevala*, and Juho Rissanen's moody studies of peasant life – recalls a time when the spirit of nationalism was surging through the country.

Along Mannerheimintie

Mannerheimintie – named after the Finnish soldier and statesman C.G.E. Mannerheim – spears north from the city centre. On the left, the **Parliament Building** (guided tours Sat 11am & noon, 1pm by arrangement; Sun noon & 1pm; July & Aug also Mon–Fri 2pm; free), with its pompous columns and choking air of solemnity, was the work of J.S. Sirén, completed in 1931. Further along, **Kiasma**, the museum of contemporary international art, is new and well worth a visit (Tues 9am–5pm, Wed–Sun 10am–10pm; 25mk). The collection includes installations in which sound, moving images and smell add a sensory dimension to the experience. North of here, the **National Museum** (Tues 11am–8pm, Wed–Sun 11am–4pm; 15mk) is a joint effort of the three giants of Finnish architecture, Armas Lindgren, Herman Gesellius and Eliel Saarinen. Its design is steeped in Finnish history, drawing on the country's medieval churches and granite castles, while Gallén-Kallela's interior decorations illustrate scenes from the *Kalevala*. The exhibits, from prehistory to the present, are exhaustive; it's best to concentrate on a few specific sections, such as the marvellously restored seventeenth-century manor house interior and the ethnographic displays from the nation's varied regions.

Directly opposite, **Finlandia Hall** (guided tours by appointment, call ☎09/40241; 20mk) was designed in the 1970s by the country's premier architect, Alvar Aalto. It was envisaged as part of a grand plan, begun by Eliel Saarinen and still under discussion, to rearrange the city centre. Inside, Aalto's characteristic asymmetry and hallmark wave pattern (the architect's surname means "wave") are everywhere, from the walls and ceilings through to the lamps and vases. The 1840s Neoclassical **Hakasalmi Villa** (Wed–Sun 11am–5pm; 15mk) next door houses one of four satellite museums belonging to the new City Museum (see above). Exhibitions are all temporary, but usually striking. Finland's new **Opera House** (Mon–Fri 9am–6pm, Sat 3–6pm) is a little further up Mannerheimintie. Like so much contemporary Finnish architecture, it's a white, Lego-like expanse, but the interior is enlivened by displays of colourful costume. A little way north, the **Olympic Stadium** is clearly visible. Originally intended for the 1940 Olympics, it hosted the first postwar games in 1952. Its **tower** (Mon–Fri 9am–8pm, Sat & Sun 9am–6pm; 10mk) gives an unsurpassed view over the city and a chunk of the southern coast. Back towards the city centre, the **Hietaniemi Cemetery** houses the graves of some of the big names of Finnish history – Mannerheim, Engel and Alvar Aalto, whose witty little tombstone, with its chopped Neoclassical column, stands beside the main entrance; next to it is the larger marker of Gallén-Kallela, his initials woven around a painter's palette. East of here, at Lutherinkatu 3, is the late-1960s **Temppeliaukio kirkko** (Rock Church; Mon–Fri 10am–8pm, Sat 10am–6pm, Sun noon–1.45pm & 3.15–5.45pm). Blasted from a single lump of granite beneath a domed copper roof, it's a thrill to be inside.

South of Esplanadi

South of Esplanadi on Korkeavourenkatu, the excellent **Museum of Art & Design** (Mon–Fri 12–7pm, Sat & Sun 12–6pm; 50mk) traces the relationship between art and industry in Finnish history, with explanatory texts and period exhibits. Northwest of here is the **Vanha kirkko** (Old Church). Engel's humble wooden structure was the first Lutheran church to be erected after Helsinki became the capital. A short walk south, the **Sinebrychoff Art Museum** at Bulevardi 40 (Mon, Thurs & Fri 9am–6pm, Wed 9am–8pm, Sat & Sun 11am–5pm; closed Jan & Feb; 10mk, 35mk for special exhibitions) houses mostly seventeenth-century Flemish and Dutch paintings, including some excellent miniatures. A few blocks from the end of Kasarminkatu is the large and rocky **Kaivopuisto** park, where nobility from St Petersburg came to sample the waters at its 1830s spa house. The park also contains the **Mannerheim Museum** (Fri–Sun 11am–4pm; 40mk), the house where the famous Finnish commander spent his later years. Mannerheim led the Whites during the Civil War of 1918, and two decades later the Finnish campaigns in the Winter and Continuation Wars. His political influence was considerable, including a brief spell as president. The interior – cluttered with the plunder of his travels – is much as it was when he died in 1951. Close by is the yellow-turreted house of another famous Finn, Frederik Cygnaeus. Inside, the beautifully laid-out **Cygnaeus Gallery** (Wed 11am–7pm, Thurs–Sun 11am–4pm; 15mk), displays his collection of bird and nature studies by the von Wright brothers.

Suomenlinna and Seurasaari

Built by the Swedes in 1748 to protect Helsinki from seaborne attack, the fortress of **Suomenlinna** stands on five interconnected islands and is the biggest sea fortress in the world. Reachable by ferry every thirty minutes from the South Harbour, it makes a rewarding break from the city. You can visit independently, or take one of the hour-long summer **guided walking tours**, beginning close to the ferry stage and conducted in English (June–Aug daily 10.30am, 1pm & 3pm; 20mk). Suomenlinna has a few museums, though none is particularly riveting. The **Nordic Arts Centre** (Tues–Sun 11am–5.45pm; closed August; free) has small displays of contemporary arts from the Nordic countries. The **Ehrensvärd Museum** (summer daily 10am–5pm; Sept daily 10am–4pm; closed rest of year; 10mk) is the residence used by the first commander of the fortress, Augustin Ehrensvärd, who oversaw the building of Suomenlinna and now lies in an elaborate tomb in the grounds; his personal effects remain inside the house alongside displays on the fort's construction. The **Armfelt Museum** (mid-May to Aug daily 11am–5pm; 6mk) contains the eighteenth- and nineteenth-century family heirlooms of the Armfelt clan who lived in the Joensuu Manor at Halikko. Finally, the **Coastal Artillery Museum** (May–Sept daily 10am–4.45pm; Oct to mid-May Sat & Sun 11am–3pm; 10mk) records Suomenlinna's defensive actions and, for another 5mk, lets visitors clamber around the claustrophobic World War II submarine *Vesikko*.

There are more museums close by the small wooded island of **Seurasaari**, a fifteen-minute tram (#4) or bus (#24) ride from the city centre. The tram stops a few hundred metres north, at the junction of Tamminiementie and Meilahdentie, conveniently close to the **Helsinki City Art Museum** (Wed–Sun 11am–6.30pm; 15-45mk), one of the best, if most disorganized, collections of modern Finnish art. A few minutes' walk away, towards the Seurasaari bridge, is the long driveway leading to the **Urho Kekkonen Museum** (mid-May to mid-Aug daily 11am–5pm; rest of year closed Mon; 20mk), the villa where the former president lived from 1956 until his death in 1986, and the former official home of all Finnish presidents. Kekkonen played a vital role in the establishment of Finnish neutrality, gaining the favour of Soviet leaders, legend has it, by taking them to a sauna. The place feels far from institutional, with its birch-wood furniture and large windows giving peaceful views of surrounding trees, water and wildlife. Close by, on Seurasaari itself, is the **Seurasaari Open Air Museum** (June–Aug daily 11am–5pm, Wed until 7pm; Sept–May Mon–Fri 9am–3pm, Sat & Sun 11am–5pm; 15mk), a collection of vernacular buildings from all over Finland.

Eating and drinking

Eating in Helsinki, as in the rest of Finland, isn't cheap, but there is a lot of choice, and, with planning, a number of ways to stretch funds – many places offer good-value lunchtime deals, and there are plenty of affordable ethnic restaurants. The stalls of the modest-sized **Market Square** (Kauppatori; Mon–Fri 7am–2pm, Sat 7am–3pm; summer also Mon–Fri 3.30–8pm) are laden with fresh fruit and veg; the **Old Market Hall** (Kauppahalli; Mon–Fri 8am–5pm, Sat 8am–3pm), further along, is good for snacks and reindeer kebabs. For fast food, *Jaskan Grilli*, on Töölönkatu behind the National Museum, is said to be the best of its kind in Finland; the grill on the corner of Fredrikinkatu and Arkadiankatu is also good, and makes its own burgers. Helsinki has several **student mensas**, two of which are centrally located at Aleksanterinkatu 5 and Yliopistonkatu 3. One or the other will be open in summer; both will be open during term time.

Drinking can be enjoyed in the city's many pub-like restaurants; on Fridays and Saturdays it's best to arrive as early as possible to get a seat without having to queue. Most drinking dives also serve food, although the grub is seldom at its best in the evening. If you want a drink but are feeling antisocial, or just hard-up, self-service ALKO shops are located at Fabianinkatu 9–11 and Kaivokatu 10.

Cafés and snacks
Café Ekberg, Bulevardi 9. Nineteenth-century fixtures and a deliberately *fin-de-siècle* atmosphere, with starched waitresses bringing open sandwiches and pastries to marble tables.

Café Eliel, Helsinki train station. Airy Art Nouveau interior with a good-value self-service breakfast.

Café Esplanadi, corner of Mikonkatu and Esplanadi. One of the trendiest cafés for people-watching, sipping a cappuccino at outdoor tables.

Café Fazer, Kluuvikatu 3. Helsinki's best-known bakery, justly celebrated for its pastries. Stays open late for the movie crowd.

Café Strindberg, Pohjoisesplanadi. The place to see and be seen.

Café Tamminiementie, Tamminiementie 8. Perhaps the city centre's nicest café, with excellent home-made cakes and countless varieties of tea.

Café Ursula, Kaivopuisto. On the beach at the edge of the Kaivopuisto park, with a wonderful view from the outdoor terrace. There's a new Ursula at Pohjoisesplanadi 21, which is good for cakes too.

Kappeli, Esplanadi Park. An elegant glasshouse, often crowded but with a relaxed atmosphere. The cellar is also a great spot for an evening drink.

Restaurants
Cantina West, Kasarminkatu 23. Outrageously popular Tex-Mex eatery.

Kasakka, Meritullinkatu 13. Great atmosphere and food in this old-style Russian restaurant.

Kasvisravintola, Korkeavuorenkatu 4. One of the best veggie restaurants in the city.

Planet Hollywood Mikonkatu 9. Much hyped American diner, crammed with movie memorabilia.

Mama Rosa Runeberginkatu 55. A classic pizzeria also serving fish steaks and pasta. One of the city's best mid-priced restaurants (daily 11am–midnight).

Namaskar, Mannerheimintie 100. Popular evening buffet (95mk) and plenty of vegetarian options.

Sipoli Kanavarantu 3. Taste-bud thrilling, formal and glamorous, with prices to match – a perfect splash-out.

Saslik, Neitystpolku 12. Pricey but delicious authentic Russian grub which you can eat to the sound of traditional troubadours in the evening.

La Vista, Eterlaranta 10. One of the oldest Italian restaurants in town, with a good view down onto the Market Hall. No pizza.

Wienerwald, Kaivakatu, opposite the train station. A sort of Austrian Pizza Hut with good-value Austrian meat and fish dishes.

Zetor, Mannerheimintie 3-5. Typically Finnish grub, home-made ale and interiors designed by the Leningrad Cowboys.

Bars

Angleterre, Fredrikinkatu 47. Utterly Finnish despite the Dickensian fixtures.

Ateljee Bar, on the roof of *Hotel Torni*, Yrjönkatu 26. Offers the best views of Helsinki in a genteel atmosphere.

Bar Nº9, Uuudenmaankatu 9. A popular hangout for professionals at lunchtime and bohemians in the evening, it has a beer list and menu as cosmopolitan as its staff. Food is reasonably cheap and filling and there is always a vegetarian option.

Bulevardia, Bulevardi 34. Art Deco fittings by 1930s architect Pauli Blomstedt; special lunch deals for 40mk.

Elite, Eteläinen Hesperiankatu 22. Once the haunt of the city's artists, many of whom would settle the bill with paintings – a selection of which line the walls. Especially good in summer, when you can drink on the terrace.

No Name Irish Bar, Töölönkatu 2. Looks like an American cocktail bar and pulls an intriguing mix of locals.

O'Malley's, *Hotel Torni*, Yrjönkatu. Guinness on tap and live music.

Richard O'Donaghue's, Rikhardinkatu 4. Close to the editorial offices of the major Helsinki newspapers. Usually contains a few hacks crying over lost scoops – good food, too.

St Urho's Pub, Museokatu 10. One of the most popular student pubs. Guitars, a piano, etc, available for spontaneous jam sessions.

Vanhan Kahvila, Mannerheimintie 3. A self-service and comparatively cheap bar. Arrive early for a seat on the balcony overlooking the bustle of the streets below.

Vanhan Kellari, Mannerheimintie 3. Downstairs from the *Vanhan Kahvila*, its underground setting and bench-style seating help promote a cosy and smoky, if drunken, atmosphere.

Nightlife

Helsinki has a vibrant night scene, notably several venues putting on a steady diet of **live music** (35–50mk) and free gigs almost every summer Sunday in Kaivopuisto park. There is also a wide range of **clubs and discos**, for which admission is usually around 35mk, half that Monday to Thursday and often free before 10pm. For details of **what's on**, read the entertainments page of *Helsingin Sanomat*, or the free fortnightly paper, *City*, found in record shops, bookshops, department stores and tourist offices. **Tickets** for most events can be bought at Lippupalvelu, Mannerheimintie 5 (Mon–Fri 9.30am–4.30pm, Sat 10am–2pm; ☎09/179 568), and Tiketti, on the second floor of the Forum shopping centre, off Mannerheimintie (Mon–Fri 9am–5pm; ☎09/693 2255).

Clubs and venues

Bar Fat Mama, Kaisaniemenkatu 6. Eclectic, marginal live music (daily from 10.30pm).

Botta, Museokatu 10. Vibrant dance music of various hues most nights.

DTM (Don't Tell Mama), Annankatu 32. Helsinki's legendary gay night club which occasionally hosts classy drag shows.

Kerma, Erottaja 7. One of the top clubs in Helsinki. Big dance floor. Jazz on Thurs, Salsa on Fri, House on Sat with international DJs and everyone in their best club dress. Open till 4am at weekends. Entrance 30–40mk.

KY-Exit, Pohjoinen Rautatiekatu 21. Sometimes has foreign bands; more often lively disco nights.

Storyville, Museokatu 8. Popular venue for nightly live jazz. Good food, too.

Tavastia, Urho Kekkosenkatu 4–6. Major showcase for Finnish and Swedish bands.

Vanha Maestro, Fredrikinkatu 51–53. The place for traditional dancing. A legend among enthusiasts of *humppa*, a Finnish dance related to the waltz and tango. Admission 10–30mk.

Vanha Ylioppilastalo, Mannerheimintie 3. Main venue for international indie bands.

Listings

Airlines British Airways, Aleksanterinkatu 21a (☎0800/178378) opposite the Stockman Department Store; Finnair, Mannerheimintie 102 (☎09/81881); SAS, Pohjoisesplanadi (☎09/177433).

Books Academic Bookstore, Pohjoisesplanadi 39, has a good stock of English paperbacks.

Car rental Avis, Fredrikinkatu 67 (☎09/441114); Budget, Toinen Linja 29 (☎09/735964); Europcar/InterRent, Hitsaajank 7c (☎09/75155300); Hertz, Mannerheimintie 44 (☎09/16671200).

Embassies Britain, Itäinen Puistotie 17 (☎09/22865100); Canada, Pohjoisesplanadi 25B (☎09/171141); Ireland, Erottajankatu 7A (☎09/646006); USA, Itäinen Puistotie 14A (☎09/171931).

Exchange Best done at banks, otherwise try the airport (6.30am–11pm); Katajanokka harbour, where Viking and Finnjet dock (daily 9–11.30am & 3.45–6pm); or Forex at the train station (daily 8am–9pm).

Gay Helsinki See *Z* magazine, widely available in larger newsagents or drop into *Lost and Found*, Annankatu 6, a relaxed café/bar-cum-restaurant-and-disco whose staff are friendly, helpful and speak excellent English. SETA, Heitalahdenkatu 2B 16, is the state-supported gay organization (☎09/6123233; *www.seta.fi*).

Hospital Töölö Hospital, Töölönkatu 40; University Central Hopsital, Haartmaninkatu 4. (Both ☎09/4711)

Laundry Punavuorenkatu 3 and Runeberginkatu 47.

Left luggage Long-distance bus station (Mon–Fri 9am–8pm, Sat 7am–6pm, Sun 9am-6pm); lockers at train station (daily 6.30am–10pm).

Pharmacies Yliopiston Apteekki, Mannerheimintie 96 (24hr); Mannerheimintie 5 (daily 7am–midnight).

Police Pieni Roobertinkatu 1-3 (☎1891).

Post office The main office, with poste restante services, is at Mannerheimaukio 1A (Mon–Fri 9am–5pm).

Around Helsinki

There's little in Helsinki's outlying area that's worth venturing out for. But a couple of places, both an easy day-trip from the city, merit a visit – the home of the composer Sibelius at **Järvenpää**, and the evocative old town of **Porvoo**.

Järvenpää

Around 40km north of Helsinki, and easy to get to by bus or train, **JÄRVENPÄÄ** is the site of **Ainola** (June–Aug Tues–Sun 11am–5pm; May & Sept Wed–Sun 11am–5pm; 20mk) – the house where Jean Sibelius lived from 1904 with his wife, Aino, after whom the place is named. Long seen as the authentic voice of Finnish national identity, Sibelius is now also considered one of the world's great composers. His early pieces, inspired by the Finnish folk epic, the *Kalevala*, and the nationalist mood of the times, incurred the wrath of the country's Russian rulers. In 1899 they banned performances of his rousing *Finlandia* under any name which suggested its patriotic sentiment, and the piece was published as "Opus 26, No. 7". He is still revered in Finland, despite his notorious bouts of heavy drinking and angst-ridden last years that became known as "the silence from Järvenpää". This tranquil place, close to lakes and forests, is an object of pilgrimage for devotees, although there is little to see other than books, furnishings and a few paintings. The composer's simple grave is in the grounds.

Porvoo

One of the oldest towns on the south coast, **PORVOO**, 50km east of Helsinki, with its narrow cobbled streets lined by small wooden buildings, gives a sense of the Finnish life which predated the capital's bold squares and Neoclassical geometry – although its elegant riverside setting and unhurried mood mean it's inevitably popular with tourists.

Close to the station, visit the preserved **Johan Ludwig Runeberg House**, Aleksanterinkatu 3 (May–Aug Mon–Sat 10am–4pm, Sun 11am–5pm; Sept–April closed Mon & Tues; 10mk), where the famed Finnish poet lived from 1852 while a teacher at the town school. Despite writing in Swedish, he greatly aided the nation's sense of self-esteem, and one of his poems provided the lyrics for the Finnish national anthem. Across the road, the **Walter Runeberg Gallery** (same hours and ticket price) has a collection of sculpture by Johan Runeberg's third son, one of Finland's more celebrated sculptors. The old town is built around the hill on the other side of Mannerheimkatu, crowned by the fifteenth-century **Tuomiokirkko** (May–Sept Mon–Fri 10am–6pm, Sat 10am–2pm, Sun 2–5pm; Oct–April Tues–Sat 10am–2pm, Sun 2–4pm), where Alexander I proclaimed Finland a Russian Grand Duchy and convened the first Finnish Diet. This, and other aspects of the town's past, can be explored in the **Porvoo Museum** (May–Aug daily 11am–4pm; Sept–April Wed–Sun noon–4pm; 15mk) at the foot of the hill in the main square, by way of a selection of furnishings, musical instruments and oddities largely dating from the days of Russian rule.

Buses run all day from Helsinki to Porvoo, and a one-way trip costs around 40mk. There's also a **boat**, the *J. L. Runeberg*, which sails through the summer (1–3 times weekly) from Helsinki's South Harbour, arriving in Porvoo at 1.15pm and leaving at 4pm; a return fare is 150mk. The **tourist office** is opposite the **bus station**, at Rauhankatu 4 (late June to Aug Mon–Fri 10am–6pm, Sat & Sun 10am–4pm; rest of year Mon–Fri 10am–4.30pm, Sat 10am–2pm; ☎019/580145), and has free maps of the town. **Spending a night** in Porvoo leaves you well-placed to continue into Finland's southeastern corner, though rates are steep. There is, however, a **youth hostel**, open all year, at Linnankoskenkatu 1–3 (☎019/5230012; ②), and a **campsite** (☎019/581967; June to mid-Aug), 2km from the town centre.

THE SOUTHWEST

The area immediately west of Helsinki is probably the blandest section of the country, endless forests interrupted only by modest-sized patches of water and virtually identical villages and small towns. The far southwestern corner, however, is more interesting, with islands and inlets around a jagged shoreline and some of the country's distinctive Finnish-Swedish coastal communities. The country's former capital, **Turku**, is the main target, historically and visually one of Finland's most enticing cities.

Turku

TURKU was once the national capital but lost its status in 1812 and most of its buildings in a ferocious fire in 1827. These days it's a small and highly sociable city, bristling with history and culture and with a sparkling nightlife, thanks to the boom years under Swedish rule and the students from its two universities. Many of its Swedish-speaking contingent still consider Åbo – the Swedish name for Turku – the real capital and Helsinki just an upstart.

Arrival and accommodation

The river Aura splits the city, its tree-lined banks forming a natural promenade as well as a useful landmark. On the northern side of the river is Turku's central grid, where you'll find the **tourist office** at Aurakatu 4 (Mon–Fri 8.30am–6pm, Sat & Sun 10am–4pm; ☎02/2627444). Both the **train** and **bus station** are within easy walking distance of the river, just north of the centre. If you are making for the Stockholm ferry, you can stay on the train to the terminal 2km west or catch bus #1 on Linnankatu. The **InterRail Centre** is currently at Läntinen Rantakatu 47 (July to mid-Aug Mon–Sat 8am–10pm), right by the river, where you can shower, leave luggage, rent bicycles and eat cheaply. For Interail information outside the summer months, go to Matkailutoimisto, Aurakatu 4, (Mon–Sat 8.30am–6pm; ☎02/262744) **Bikes** can also be rented from T. Saario, Tuureporinkatu 19 (☎02/316356).

There are some good deals to be had at Turku's mid-range **hotels**, especially if you have an early reservation and pick a weekend. Try *Hotel Julia*, Eerikenkatu 4 (☎02/336311; ⑧), *Ramada Hotel*, Eerikenkatu 28 (☎02/338211; ⑦), or *Seurahuone*, Eerikenkatu 23 (☎02/337301; ⑥). For tighter budgets, try the more basic **tourist hotels**, *Astro Hotel*, Humalistonkatu 18 (☎02/2517838; ④), *Good Morning Hotel Turku*, Yliopistonkatu 29A (☎02/2320921; ⑤) or *Nukkumatti Hotel*, Salakunnant 177 (☎02/2110112; ⑤). There's an excellent **youth hostel**, *Hostel Turku* by the river at Linnankatu 39 (☎02/2316578; ②); take bus # 30 from the train station. The nearest **campsite** (☎02/2589100; June to mid-Aug; bus #8) is on the island of Ruissalo, which has two sandy beaches and overlooks Turku harbour.

The City

Though it's not much of a taster for the actual city, **Turku Art Museum** (Tues, Fri & Sat 10am–4pm, Wed & Thurs 10am–7pm, Sun 11am–6pm; 30mk), occupying a granite Art Nouveau structure close to the train station, is one of the better collections of Finnish art, with works by all the great names of the country's golden age plus a commendable stock of moderns. To get to grips with Turku itself, and its pivotal place in Finnish history, cut through the centre to the river, and the tree-framed space which before the great fire of 1827 was the bustling heart of the community, overlooked by the **Tuomiokirkko** (daily: winter 9am–7pm; summer 9am–8pm). Turku's cathedral, it was erected in the thirteenth century, and is still the centre of the Finnish Church. Despite repeated fires, a number of features survive, notably the deliriously ornate seventeenth-century tomb of Torsten Stålhandske, commander of the Finnish cavalry during the Thirty Years' War. A little further along lies Catherina Månsdotter, the wife of the Swedish King Erik XIV with whom, in the mid-sixteenth century, she was imprisoned in Turku Castle. The window behind it carries her stained-glass image and if you crane your neck to the left, you'll see a wall plaque bearing her only known likeness. For 10mk, the **museum** upstairs gives a stronger insight into the cathedral's past, with an assortment of ancient jugs, goblets and textiles. Steps away on the bank of the Aurajoki river is Turku's newest and most splendid museum, the combined **Aboa Vetus and Ars Nova** (May to Aug daily 10am–7pm; rest of year Tues–Sun 11am–7pm; 35mk each, 50mk combined ticket). The name translates as "Old Turku, New Art"; digging the foundations of the modern art gallery revealed a warren of medieval lanes which are now on view beneath the glass floor of the building. The modern art gallery comprises 350 striking works plus temporary exhibitions, and there's a great café too.

Just north of the cathedral is the sleek low form of the **Sibelius Museum** (Tues–Sun 11am–3pm, Wed also 6–8pm; 15mk), which – although Sibelius had no direct connection with Turku – displays family photo albums and original manuscripts, the great man's hat, walking stick and even his final half-smoked cigar, alongside exhibits covering the musical history of the country. There is also a concert hall where you can listen to recorded requests. South of here, the engrossing **Luostarinmäki Handicrafts Museum** on Vartiovuorenkatu (summer daily 10am–6pm; winter Tues–Sun 10am–3pm; 20mk; guided tours in English, with demonstrations, from June to Aug) is one of the best and most authentic open-air museums in Finland, and as true a record of old Turku as exists. Following a severe fire in 1775 rigorous restrictions were imposed on new buildings but, due to a legal technicality, they didn't apply in this district. The wooden houses here were built by local working people in traditional style and they became a museum as descendants of the original owners died and the town bought them up. The chief inhabitants now are the museum volunteers who dress up in period attire and demonstrate the old handicrafts.

A short walk away, on the southern bank of the river, is another worthwhile indoor collection: the **Wäinö Aaltonen Museum** (Tues–Sun 11am–7pm; 15mk, 30mk for special exhibitions), devoted to the best-known modern Finnish sculptor, who grew up close to Turku and studied at the local art school. Aaltonen dominated his field throughout the 1920s and 1930s, and his influence is still felt today; his imaginative and sensitive work turns up in every major Finnish town.

Back in the direction of the cathedral, a wooden staircase runs up to the front door of the **Museum of Pharmacy and Quensel House** (daily: winter 10am–3pm; summer 10am–6pm; 15mk), home to a seventeenth-century judge and, later, one Professor Josef Gustaf Pipping – the "father of Finnish medicine" – and decorated with period furnishings and chemists' implements from around the country. Along Linnankatu from here, towards the mouth of the river, is **Turku Castle** (summer daily 10am–6pm; winter Tues–Sun 10am–3pm & Mon 2–7pm; 30mk). The featureless exterior conceals a maze of cobbled courtyards, corridors and staircases, with a bewildering array of finds and displays. The castle probably went up around 1280; the seat of government for centuries, its gradual expansion accounts for the patchwork architecture.

Eating and drinking

If money's very tight, *Gadolinia*, a **student mensa**, part of Åbo Akademi on Henrikenkatu, offers Turku's cheapest **food**. The *Italia*, Linnankatu 3, produces sizeable and affordably-priced pizzas. For excellent food at sensible prices, it's worth trekking out to *Turun Hotelli Ravintola Oppilaitos* in the Data Centre, close to Turku hospital (take the train one stop to Kupittaa). It's run by the catering college – the food is really good and service almost too attentive. The **Market Square** (Kauppatori) and the effervescent **Market Hall** (Kauppahalli; Mon–Fri 8am–5pm, Sat 8am–2pm) are both near the tourist office. For **eating**, there are two riverside restaurants, *Pinella*, in Porthaninkatupuisto, or *Herman*, Läntinen Rantakatu 37 (☎02/2303333), set in a bright, airy storehouse dating from 1849, with main courses costing around 50–100mk. Floating restaurants change each summer, but look out for *Papa Joe*, *Svarte Rudolph* and *Lulu*. Popular **drinking** venues are *Uusi Apteekki*, Kaskenkatu 1, which, true to its name, is an old pharmacy complete with ancient fittings; and the atmospheric *Koulu Brewery Restaurant*, Eerikinkatu 18, where they brew their own beer and serve reasonably priced Finnish lunches in an old schoolhouse. Consider also the "English-style" pub the *Hunter's Inn*, west of *Hotel Julia* at Brahenkatu 3.

THE LAKE REGION

About a third of Finland is consumed by the **Lake Region**, a huge area of bays, inlets and islands, interspersed with dense forests. Despite holding much of Finland's industry, it's a tranquil, verdant region, and even **Tampere**, Finland's major industrial city, enjoys a peaceful lakeside setting, as well as being easily accessible from Helsinki by train. The eastern part of the Lake Region is the most atmospheric, slender ridges furred with conifers linking the few sizeable landmasses, reached from Tampere via **Jyväskylä**, whose wealth of buildings by Alvar Aalto make it a worthwhile break. Direct from Helsinki, the route goes via dull Lahti to the lakes' regional centre, **Savonlinna**, which stretches delectably across several islands and boasts a superb medieval castle. Further north, **Kuopio**, where many displaced Karelians settled after World War II, makes a decent break on the way up to Kajaani.

Tampere

TAMPERE, a leafy place of parks and lakes, is Finland's biggest manufacturing centre and Scandinavia's largest inland city. Its rapid growth began just over a century ago, when Tsar Alexander I abolished taxes on local trade, encouraging the Scotsman James Finlayson to open a textile factory, drawing labour from rural areas where traditional crafts were in decline. Metalwork and shoe factories soon followed, their owners paternally supplying culture to the workforce by promoting a vigorous local arts scene. Free outdoor rock and jazz concerts, lavish theatrical productions and one of the best modern art collections in Finland maintain such traditions to this day.

The City

Almost everything of consequence is within the central section, bordered on two sides by lakes Näsijärvi and Pyhäjärvi. The main streets run off either side of Hämeenkatu, which leads directly from the train station across Hämeensilta. Left off Hämeenkatu, up slender Hämeenpuisto, the Tampere Workers' Theatre and **Lenin Museum** (Mon–Fri 9am–6pm, Sat & Sun 11am–4pm; 15mk) remembers the time when, after the abortive 1905 revolution in Russia, Lenin lived in Finland and attended the Tampere conferences, held in what is now the museum. It was here that he first met Stalin, although this is barely mentioned, the two displays concentrating instead on Lenin himself and his relationship with Finland. Northwest of here there's more labour history, where some thirty homes have been preserved as the **Workers' Museum of Amuri** at Makasiininkatu 12 (early May to mid-Sept Tues–Fri 9am–5pm, Sat & Sun 11am–5pm; 20mk), a simple but affecting place which records the family life of working people over a hundred-year period. In each home there's a description of the inhabitants and their jobs, and authentic articles from relevant periods – from tables to family photos, newspapers and biscuit packets. Around the corner at Puutarhakatu 34, the **Art Museum of Tampere** (Tues–Sun 10am–6pm; 20mk–40mk) holds powerful if staid temporary exhibitions. If you're looking for Finnish art you might be better off visiting the **Hiekka Art Gallery**, a few minutes' walk away at Pirkankatu 6 (Wed & Thurs 3–6pm, Sun noon–3pm; 20mk), which has sketches by Gallén-Kallela and Helene Schjerfbeck, and superb silver and other metalwork donated by one Kustaa Hiekka. Better still is the tremendous **Sara Hildén Art Museum** (daily 11am–6pm; 20mk), built on the shores of Näsijärvi (bus #16 from the bus station or the central square), a quirky collection of Finnish and foreign modern works. Occupying the same waterside strip as the Hildén collection is **Särkänniemi**, a tourist complex with dolphinarium, aquarium, planetarium and observation tower, though it might be more profitable to cross instead to the other side of the town centre to the city's cathedral, the **Tuomikirkko**, Tuomiokirkonkatu 3 (daily May–Aug 8am–6pm; rest of year 11am–3pm; free), decorated with gorily symbolic frescoes by Hugo Simberg including the *Garden of Death*, where skeletons happily water plants.

Practicalities

The city's **tourist office** is by the river, 500m from the **train station** at Verkatehtaankatu 2 (June–Aug Mon–Fri 8.30am–8pm, Sat 8.30am–6pm, Sun 11.30am–6pm; Sept–May Mon–Fri 8.30am–5pm; ☎03/31466800), and a similar distance along Hatanpään from the **bus station**. **Bicycles** can be rented from Nippeli, Juvankatu 1 (☎03/632900), and K. Saarinen, Lapintie 6 (☎03/2124074). Handily located, moderately priced **hotels** include the *Victoria*, Itsenäsyydenkatu 1 (☎03/2425111; ⑤), and *Sokos' Hotel Villa*, Sumeliaksenkatu 14 (☎03/2626267; ⑤). There are dorm beds at the impersonal summer **hostel**, *Domus*, Pellervonkatu 9 (☎03/2550000; ③), 1km east of the train station, though the best cheap accommodation is at *Uimahallin maja*, centrally located at Pirkankatu 10–12 (☎03/2229460; ③) and at the *NNKY* opposite the cathedral at Tuomiokirkonkatu 12a (☎03/2524020; ②; June–Aug). The nearest **campsite** is *Härmälä*, 5km south (☎03/2651355; mid-May to late Aug; bus #1).

Eating and drinking

The cheapest places to eat are the **student mensas** at the university at the end of Yliopistonkatu. Still cheap are the usual pizza joints such as *Rosso* on the second floor of the *Hostel Uimahallion Maja*, Pirkankatu 10–12 (nightly till 11.45pm). For relaxed posing, *Brasserie Arcia*, Hämeenkatu 14 (daily 7am–2am), serves fine filled baguettes as well as full meals. For a Tampere speciality, try *mustamakkara*, the local black sausage, at the *Laukontori* open-air **market** by the rapids. For **pubs**, try the popular *Plevna*, a German-style beer hall in a converted factory on Kuninkaankatu, which is especially busy at weekends; for live music, head for *Tullikamari*, a **nightclub** in an old customs house on Itsenäsyydenkatu behind the train station.

Savonlinna and around

Leisurely draped across islands, **SAVONLINNA** is one of the most relaxed towns in Finland, a woodworking centre that also makes a decent living from tourism and its annual **opera festival** in July. It's packed throughout summer and if you haven't booked well ahead don't expect to find somewhere to stay. However, out of peak season its streets and beaches are uncluttered, and the town's easy-going mood – enhanced by the slow glide of pleasure crafts from its harbour – makes it a pleasant place to linger.

The best locations for soaking up the atmosphere are the **harbour** and **market square** (kauppatori) at the end of Olavinkatu, where you can cast an eye over the grand *Seurahuone Hotel* facing the **market hall** (kauppahalli). Erected in 1901, it became a notorious speakeasy, selling "hard tea" laced with brandy and home-brewed *pirttu*. The hotel burned down in 1947, but though the forbidden pleasures are long gone and their current equivalents at the bar are forbiddingly expensive, you can still admire the reconstructed 1940s decor with its Art Nouveau fripperies. Follow the harbour around Linnankatu, or better still around the sandy edge of Pihlajavesi, which brings you to atmospheric **Olavinlinna Castle** (daily 10am–3/5pm; 25mk), perched on a small island. Catch one of the hourly guided tours, in English during the summer, as the castle's excellent state of repair is matched by an intriguing history. Founded in 1475, it witnessed a series of bloody conflicts until the Russians claimed permanent possession in 1743. When Finland became a tsarist Grand Duchy the fort was relegated to being the town jail, and the Russians added the brick extensions to the towers. The brick cubicles which jut out from the main living rooms are possibly the first WCs in Finland; there's a drop through the pan to the river several dozen metres below. You can spend half a day here exploring two small museums. The **Orthodox Museum** has a dozen fine relics rescued from Valamo and Viipuri (both now in Russia) and the lunches in the café are excellent. The **Provincial Museum** (July daily 10am–8pm; rest of year Tues–Sun 11am–5pm; 25mk) occupies an old granary and displays an intriguing account of the evolution of local life, with rock paintings and a 4000-year-old piece of amber with a carving of a human on it found nearby. At the end of the jetty, there are a couple of turn-of-the-century **Museum ships** (June–Aug), which earned their keep plying the Saimaa waterways, sometimes travelling as far as St Petersburg and Lübeck.

Practicalities

Of the two **train stations**, be sure to get off at Savonlinna-Kauppatori, just across the main bridge from the **tourist office** at Puistokatu 1 (June daily 8am–6pm; July daily 8am–10pm; Aug–Sept Mon–Fri 9am–4pm; ☎015/273492). The **bus station** is off the main island but within easy walking distance of the town centre. **Bikes** can be rented at several places on Olavinkatu, including Koponen at no. 42 (☎015/533977).

The most central **accommodation** is the private hostel *Hospits*, Linnankatu 20 (☎015/515661; ③). There is an official **youth hostel**, *Malakias*, Pihlajavedenkuja 6 (☎015/7395430; ③; July to early Aug), 2km west of the centre along Tulliportinkatu and then Savontie, and a summer hotel, the *Vuorilinna*, on Kasinonsaari (☎015/73950; ③), five minutes over the bridge from the marketplace. Alternatively, there's a Christian youth hostel, *Savolinna Kristillinen Opisto*, 6km out of town (☎015/537007; ③); take bus #9 to Parnalante and it's a 100m walk. The nearest **campsite** is 7km from the centre at Vuohimäki (☎015/537353; June–Aug). Anything sold around the harbour is liable to be overpriced; you can find cheaper, better **food** in the pizza joints along Olavinkatu and Tulliportinkatu. *Majakka*, Satamakatu 11, offers good Finnish nosh at lunchtime, though the most adventurous place to try is *Paviljonki*, Rajalatiendenkatu 4, where Finland's top trainee chefs serve their latest creations. Both the food and service are excellent, with lunch costing around 45–55mk. In the evening most people head for the extensive *Tres Hombres*, for **drinking**, **dancing** and excellent Tex-Mex food.

Around Savonlinna

Deep in the heart of the Lake Region, Savonlinna boasts beautiful scenery all around, as well as being a jumping-off point for several striking places a little way beyond. Closest is the **Punkaharju Ridge**, a narrow strip of land between the Puruvesi and Pihlajavesi lakes, 28km from town. Locals say it has the healthiest air in the world, super-oxygenated by abundant conifers. With the water never more than a few metres away on either side, this is the Lake Region at its most breathtakingly beautiful. The ridge is traversable by road and rail, both running into the town of Punkaharju and passing the incredible **Retretti Arts Cent** (10am–6pm/7pm; 65mk), situated in man-made caves gouged into three-billion-year-old rock, and with a large sculpture park outside, in which fibreglass human figures by Olavi Lanu are cunningly entwined with natural forms. Trains between Savonlinna and Parikkala (on the Helsinki–Joensuu line) call at Retretti train station, but are few and far between. Buses are more reliable, but it's best to check times with the tourist office first. A more expensive, but very pleasant, option is to travel by **boat** from Savonlinna harbour (summer 1 daily; 130mk return).

Kuopio

Superficially cosmopolitan, with smart broad streets and modern buildings, **KUOPIO** is the only city in a vast expanse of countryside, and its earthy peasant heritage is always felt: traditional dress is common, sophistication is rare – and everything takes a back seat to unbridled revelry when the night comes.

All the sights are within the immediate central area, with one exception: the wonderful **Orthodox Church Museum** (May–Aug Tues–Sun 10am–4pm; Sept–April Mon–Fri noon–3pm, Sat & Sun noon–5pm; 20mk) on the brow of the hill, the road to which begins at the junction of Asemakatu and Puistokatu. The museum houses many objects from the nearby Valamo Monastery, and it's easy to spend several hours wandering around elaborate icons, gold-embossed Bibles, gowns, prayer books and other extravagant items. Back in the centre, the block formed by Kirkkokatu and Kuninkaankatu holds the **Kuopio Open-Air Museum** (mid-May to mid-Sept daily 10am–5pm, Wed until 7pm; mid-Sept to mid-May Tues–Sun 10am–3pm; 15mk), whose buildings, still in their original locations, have interiors decked out to show housing conditions of ordinary townspeople from the late eighteenth century to the 1930s. A few streets away is another old house, **J.V. Snellman's Home**, by the corner of Snellmaninkatu and Minna Canthinkatu (mid-May to mid-Sept daily 10am–5pm, Wed till 7pm; rest of year by appointment, call ☎017/182624; 10mk). Snellman lived here after the Swedish-speaking ruling class expelled him from his university post in 1843, and he became head of the local school and continued his struggle to have Finnish granted the status of official language. Perhaps the best course in Kuopio, though, is to simply hang around the passenger **harbour** at the end of Kauppakatu, from where boats make the 11hr trip to Savonlinna (250mk) among other destinations, while a day-long cruise (mid-June to mid-Aug 9.30am; 240mk) gives the easiest access to **Valamo Monastery**. The spiritual headquarters of Orthodox Karelia since the thirteenth century, it was resited here during World War II.

Practicalities

The **bus station** is at one end of Puijonkatu, which leads past the **train station** into **Market Square** (kauppatori). The **Market Hall** (kauppahalli; Mon–Fri 8am–5pm, Sat 8am–2pm) forms a colourful contrast with the glass fronts of the encircling department stores. Opposite stands the nineteenth-century City Hall and, around its side, the **tourist office** at Haapaniemenkatu 17 (June–Aug Mon–Fri 9am–6pm, Sat 9am–4pm; rest of year Mon–Fri 9am–5pm; ☎017/182584). **Bikes** can be rented at Puijon Pyöräpiste, Kauppakatu 26 (☎071/2633273).

The **youth hostel** *Rauhalahti* is at Katiskaniementie 8 (☎017/473473; ②), a thirty-minute walk or short bus-ride from the tourist office. There is also a more central, **private hostel** – *Puijo-hovi*, Vuorikatu 35 (☎017/2614943; ③), straight ahead from the station. The **campsite** (☎017/361244; late May to Aug) is 5km to the south, though it's served by frequent buses. For more luxurious accommodation, *Puijonsarvi*, Minna Canthin katu 16 (☎017/170111; ⑦) boasts a nightclub, private saunas and lake views. Close to Kauppakatu is a small **market** which continues into the evening from June to August, and is the best place to sample the local speciality, *kalakukko*, a kind of bread pie of fish and pork. Away from the harbour-side market, **food** is less exotic: *Henry's Pub*, Kauppakatu 18, does cheapish lunches. During the summer you might also try the vibrant *Wanha Satma*, a mid-priced, outdoor place ideal for soaking up the bustling harbour atmosphere.

NORTHERN FINLAND

The three northern regions of Ostrobothnia, Kainuu and Lappland take up by far the largest portion of Finland. Unlike the populous south or more industrialized sections of the Lake Region, they're predominantly rural, their small communities separated by long distances. The coast of **Ostrobothnia**, home to most of the country's Swedish-speakers, is fairly affluent due to the flat and fertile farmlands, though you're unlikely to visit it except to take a ferry to Sweden from either **Vaasa** or **Kokkola**. Busy and expanding **Oulu**, the region's major city, is a pleasing town, while the border town of **Tornio** to the north is mainly visited by Swedes drinking their sorrows away. **Kainuu** – the thickly forested, thinly populated heart of Finland – has traditionally been a poor peasant land, though this is being alleviated by the marketing of the area's strong natural appeal – woods, rivers, hills and wide stretches of barely inhabited country, as well as a pleasant main centre in **Kajaani**. **Lappland**, too, is poor, remote territory, excitingly unexplored, although the bland town of **Rovaniemi**, the main gateway, shows little sign of any of this. However, it is the junction for the two major road routes into the **Arctic North**, whose wide open spaces are home to several thousand *Sámi*, who have lived in harmony with this special, harsh environment for millennia.

Kajaani

KAJAANI, 178km southeast of Oulu, could hardly be more of a contrast to the communities of the Bothnian coast. Though small and pastoral, the town is by far the biggest settlement in this very rural part of Finland and offers some insight into Finnish life away from the more prosperous regions. Fittingly, it was in Kajaani that Elias Lönnrot wrote the final parts of the *Kalevala*, the nineteenth-century collection of Finnish folk tales which extolled the virtues of traditional peasant life.

From the **train station**, Kauppakatu leads directly into Kajaani's minuscule centre. The decorative exterior of the **Kainuu Museum** at Asemakatu 4 (Mon–Fri noon–3pm, Wed till 8pm, Sun noon–5pm; 10mk) holds an engrossingly ramshackle collection of local art and history that says a lot about the down-to-earth qualities of the area, as does the dramatic **Kajaani kirkko** (June to mid-Aug daily 10am–8pm; rest of year Mon–Sat 5–7pm), whose wooden frame, weird turrets and angular arches, heralded as the epitome of neo-Gothic style when the church was completed in 1896, resemble a leftover from a *Munsters* set. More historically significant, the ruined **Kajaani Castle** was built in the seventeenth century to forestall a Russian attack, and later served as a prison where troublesome Swede Johannes Messenius was incarcerated. Although schemes to rebuild it are constantly bandied about, the castle was ruined so long ago that nobody's sure what it actually looked like.

The **tourist office** is at Pohjolankatu 16 (June–Aug Mon–Fri 9am–6pm, Sat 9am–1pm; rest of year Mon–Fri 9am–5pm; ☎08/6155555). The official **youth hostel** is the central *Huone ja aamiainen* at Pohjolankatu 4 (☎08/622254; ③); the **campsite** (☎08/622703; June–Aug) is by the river.

Oulu

OULU, 178km northwest of Kajaani, is currently the national leader in the computing and microchip industries. During the last century it was the centre of the world's tar industry and the city's affluence and vibrant cultural scene date from that time, though the old buildings clustered around the river bank are now somewhat overshadowed by the faceless office blocks of the past twenty years. In the centre of town on Kirkkokatu, the **City Hall** retains some of the grandeur of the late nineteenth century, when it was built as a luxury hotel, and you can peek in at the wall paintings and enclosed gardens that remain from the old days. Further along Kirkkokatu, the copper-domed and stuccoed **Tuomiokirkko**, or cathedral (daily summer 10am–7pm; rest of year noon–1pm), seems anachronistic amid the bulky blocks of modern Oulu. Inside the vestry, open on request, is a portrait of Johannes Messenius, the Swedish historian, supposedly painted by Cornelius Arenditz in 1611 and believed to be the oldest surviving oil portrait in Finland. Across the small canal just north of the cathedral, the **North Ostrobothnia Museum** (Mon, Tues & Thurs 10am–6pm, Wed 10am–8pm, Sat & Sun 11am–5pm; 10mk), packed with tar-stained remnants from Oulu's past, is a large regional collection with a good *Sámi* section. If something more up-to-the-minute appeals, make for **Tietomaa,** a few steps away at Nakatehtaankatu 6 (May–Aug daily 10am–6/8pm; Sept–April Mon–Fri 10am–4pm, Sat & Sun 10am–6pm; 50mk), where experiencing virtual reality to the strains of *Tubular Bells* is the main draw among all the pseudo-educational computer- and physics-related gear.

The connected **train station** and **bus station** are linked to the city centre by several parallel streets feeding to the kauppatori and kauppahalli (**markets**) by the water beyond. The **tourist office** is at Torikatu 10 (July Mon–Sat 9am–6pm, Sun 10am–4pm; rest of year Mon–Fri 9am–4pm; ☎08/3141295). **Bikes** can be rented from Jussin Pyöräpiste, Albertinkatu 11 (☎08/3114983). Low-cost **accommodation** in the centre is available at the *Hotel Turisti,* opposite the train station at Rautatienkatu 9 (☎08/375233; ④), which provides hostel-type accommodation during summer, when it takes the overspill from the official **youth hostel** at Kajaanintie 36 (☎08/3136311; ②; June–Aug), a fifteen-minute walk from the train station. There's a **campsite** (☎08/5541541) with cabins at Mustassaari on Hietasaari Island, 4km from town; take bus #5 from outside the tourist office. Oulu boasts some charming **cafés** including *Sokeri Jussi* in an old salt warehouse on Pikisaanie just over the bridge from the mainland, while *Katri Antell* on Rotuaari (Mon–Fri 8.30am–5pm, Sat 9am–2.30pm) is justly famed for its luscious, but expensive, cakes. Cheapest **meals** are at the numerous pizzerias – *Fantasia* serves the best and also has a selection of Finnish dishes if you are sick of pizza – while *The Royal Garden* opposite the train station has a tasty Chinese lunchtime buffet on weekdays for only 38mk. For extravagant waterside dining, try *Neptunus* for fish and meat in a boat moored by the market square, and for sheer style, the ultra swish *Franzen Café* in a charismatic old building opposite the cathedral at Kirkkokatu 2; the cellar bar is known for its German beers and sausages. For **nightlife** try the disco *45 Special,* which has three different dance floors and a mixed clientele (entrance 20mk).

Rovaniemi and around

Relatively easy to reach by rail from Ostrobothnia or Kainuu, **ROVANIEMI** is touted as the capital of Lappland, though it's more an administrative than cultural capital, and the tourists who arrive on day-trips from Helsinki expecting sleighs and tents are normally disappointed. The wooden huts of old Rovaniemi were razed by departing Germans at the close of World War II and the town was completely rebuilt during the late 1940s. Alvar Aalto's bold but impractical design has the roads forming the shape of reindeer antlers – fine if you're travelling by helicopter but it makes journeys on foot far longer than they need be. Rovaniemi is a likeable enough town, though most visitors only use it as a short-term stopover, or to study *Sámi* culture.

Aside from eating reindeer in the local restaurants, the best way to prepare yourself for what lies further north is to visit the 172m-long glass tunnel of **Arktikum,** Pohjoisranta 4 (May–Aug daily 10am–6pm; Sept–June closed Mon; 50mk), symbolically pointing north across Ounasjoki from its surrounding landscape of arctic flora. Subterranean galleries along one side house the **Provincial Museum of Lappland,** a thoughtful museum placing genuine *Sámi* crafts and costumes alongside the imitations sold in souvenir shops to emphasize the romanticization of their culture. It also demonstrates the changes in the use of tools and clothing – anoraks and Wellington boots have replaced traditional apparel, which has caused a young generation of *Sámi* to be plagued by rheumatism and foot trouble. If you don't speak fluent Finnish or *Sámi,* you'll have to rely on an adequate synopsis in English borrowed from the reception area. Across the corridor is the **Arctic Centre,** which gives a thorough treatment of all things circumpolar, from Inuit and Aleut languages to mineral exploration and hunting from kayaks decked out in rather dashing walrus-gut waterproofs.

The remaining sights are on the south side of town near the **bus** and **train stations,** where three pristine Aalto-designed civic buildings line Hallituskatu. **Lappia House** (guided tours mid-June to mid-Aug Mon–Fri 10am–2pm; 10mk) has a theatre and concert hall, and next door, the **library** (Mon–Fri 11am–7/8pm, Sat 10am–3/4pm) has a **Lappland Department** (also open Sun noon–4pm), with a staggering hoard of books in many languages covering every *Sámi*-related subject – a growing collection and the largest of its kind. Other attractions are few. At Kirkkotie 1, **Rovaniemi Seurakunta** church (June–Aug daily 9am–9pm) repays a peek with its huge altar fresco, *Fountain of Life*, by Lennart Segerstråle, an odd work pitching the struggle between good and evil into a Lappish setting. But most other things of interest are outside town, not least the **Arctic Circle**, 8km north and connected roughly hourly to the centre by bus #8 or #10 – though there's not much to see on arrival. Near the circle and served by the same buses, is **Santa Claus Village** (June to mid-Aug daily 8am–8pm; Christmas period daily 9am–8pm; rest of year Mon–Fri 11am–7pm, Sat 10am–4pm; free), a large log cabin where you can meet Father Christmas all year round, contemplate reindeer grazing in the adjoining farm and leave your name for a Christmas card from Santa himself. If you've time to kill and the weather isn't too cold (Rovaniemi's prone to chilly snaps even in summer), two outdoor museums lie near each other just beyond town, accessible by buses #3, #6, or a four-kilometre walk. The **Ethnographical Museum Pöykkölä** (June–Aug Tues–Sun noon–6pm; 10mk) is a collection of farm buildings which belonged to the Pöykkölä family from 1640 to 1910, and forms part of a pot-pourri of things pertaining to reindeer husbandry, salmon fishing and rural life in general. Five hundred metres up the road, the **Lappish Forestry Museum** (June–Aug Tues–Sun noon–6pm; 10mk) reconstructs the unglamorous reality of life in a lumber camp. South of the Arctic Circle, the **Midnight Sun** is visible from town for a couple of weeks either side of midsummer. The best spots are the striking "Lumberjack's Candlestick" bridge or thirty minutes' walk on the far side atop the conifer and mosquito-clad hill, Ounasvaara.

Practicalities

The main **tourist office** is at Koskikatu 1 (June–Aug Mon–Fri 8am–6pm, Sat & Sun 11.30am–4pm; rest of year Mon–Fri 8am–4pm; ☎016/346270). The **youth hostel**, *Tervashonka* at Hallituskatu 16 (☎016/344644; ②), is always crowded in summer – try to book in advance. Otherwise you can fall back on the **guesthouses**, all within five minutes' walk of the train station: *Matka Borealis*, Asemieskatu 1 (☎016/3420130; ③); *Outa*, Ukkoherrantie 16 (☎016/312474; ②); and *Ammattioppilaitoksen*, Kairatie 75 (☎016/3313740; ②; mid-June to early Aug). The only other budget accommodation is the **campsite** (☎016/345304; June–Aug) on the far bank of Ounasjoki, facing town, a thirty-minute walk from the station. For filling **food** at very reasonable prices try *Café Kisälli*, Korkalonkatu 35 (Mon–Fri 8.30am–5pm) or the neighbouring *Oppipoika* restaurant, which belongs to the catering school and serves good evening meals.

travel details

Trains

Helsinki to: Jyväskylä (12 daily; 3hr 30mins); Kajaani (7 daily; 7hr); Kuopio (5 daily; 5hr); Oulu (8 daily; 7hr); Rovaniemi (13 daily; 9hr 45min); Tampere (22 daily; 2hr); Turku (12 daily; 2hr).

Jyväskylä to: Tampere (9 daily; 2hr).

Kokkola to: Helsinki (9 daily; 5hr); Oulu (6 daily; 2hr 30min); Tampere (9 daily; 3hr).

Kuopio to: Jyväskylä (5 daily; 1hr 50min); Kajaani (4 daily; 2hr 15min).

Oulu to: Kajaani (3 daily; 2hr 20min); Rovaniemi (7 daily; 3hr); Tornio (4 daily; 2hr 15min).

Pori to: Tampere (7 daily; 1hr 30min).

Tampere to: Helsinki (12 daily; 2hr 15min); Oulu (7 daily; 5hr); Pori (7 daily; 1hr 30min); Savonlinna (2 daily; 4hr); Turku (7 daily; 2hr 15min).

Turku to: Tampere (8 daily; 1hr 50min).

Vaasa to: Helsinki (7 daily; 4hr 30min); Jyväskylä (3 daily; 5hr 30min); Oulu (3 daily; 5hr 30min); Tampere (4 daily; 2hr 30min).

Buses

Helsinki to: Jyväskylä (8 daily; 5hr); Kotka (10 daily; 2hr 10min); Lahti (26 daily; 1hr 30min); Mikkeli (8 daily; 4hr); Porvoo (18 daily; 1hr); Savonlinna (3 daily; 5hr 30min); Tampere (20 daily; 2hr 30min); Turku (21 daily; 2hr 30min).

Kuopio to: Jyväskylä (3 daily; 2hr 15min).

Savonlinna to: Kuopio (4 daily; 3hr 40min).

Tampere to: Helsinki (12 daily; 2hr 15min–3hr); Turku (5 daily; 2hr 30min).

Turku to: Pori (7 daily; 2hr).

CHAPTER 10

FRANCE

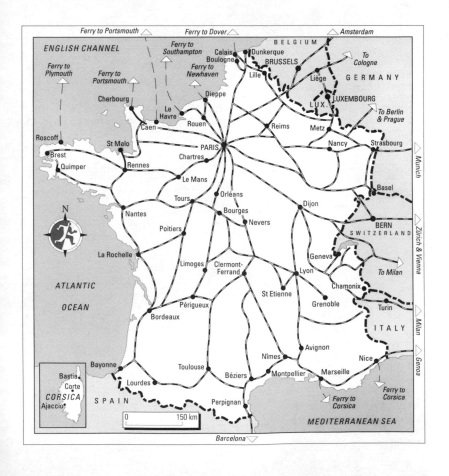

Introduction

Straddling the continent between the Iberian peninsula and the nations of central Europe, **France** is a core country on any European tour. It would be hard to exhaust its diversity in a lifetime of visits. Each area looks different, feels different, has its own style of architecture and food and often its own patois or dialect. There is an astonishing variety of things to see, whether it's the Gothic cathedrals of the north, the châteaux of the Loire or the Roman monuments of the south. The countryside, too, has its own appeal, seemingly little changed for hundreds of years.

Travelling in France is easy. Budget restaurants and hotels proliferate; the rail and road networks are efficient; and the tourist information service is highly organized. As for where to go, it's hard to know where to begin. If you arrive in the north, you may pass through the Channel ports of **Flanders**, **Artois** and **Normandy** to **Paris**, one of Europe's most elegant and compelling capitals. To the west lie the rocky coasts of **Brittany** and, further south, the châteaux of the **Loire**, although most people push on south to the limestone hills of **Provence**, the canyons of the **Pyrenees** and the glorious Mediterranean coastline of the **Côte d'Azur**. There are good reasons, however, for taking things more slowly, not least the Germanic towns of **Alsace** in the east, the gorgeous hills and valleys of the **Lot** and the **Dordogne**, and, more adventurously, the **Massif Central** – France's high and rugged heartland.

Information and maps

You'll find a Syndicat d'Initiative (SI) in practically every town and many villages, giving local **information**, listings of things to see, free maps and occasionally bike rental. Some can book accommodation anywhere in France. In larger cities and tourist resorts these will be open every day during the high season, often without a break, although times are greatly cut back in most places in the winter months.

The best **road map** of France is the Michelin 1:1,000,000 scale one. A useful free map for car drivers, obtainable from filling stations and traffic information kiosks in France, is the *Bison Futé*, showing alternative back routes. For more **regional detail**, the Michelin yellow series (scale 1:200,000) is best for the motorist. If you're planning to **walk or cycle**, check the IGN green (1:100,000 and 1:50,000) and blue (1:25,000) maps.

Money and banks

French currency is the **franc**, which is divided into 100 centimes and comes in notes of F20, 50, 100 and 500, and coins of F1, 2, 5 and 10, and 5, 10, 20, 50c. The best place to change money is a bank: standard **banking hours** are Mon–Fri 9am–noon & 2–4pm, some are also open on Saturdays. Rates of exchange and commissions vary greatly; the Banque Nationale de Paris often offer the best rate for the least commission. Outside of banking hours, there are **exchange counters** at the train stations of all big cities, and usually one or two in the town centre as well, though normally they offer a much worse deal.

Communications

Post offices (la Poste) are generally open Mon–Fri 8am–noon & 2–5pm, Sat 8am–noon, although you can buy **stamps** (*timbres*) with less queuing from *tabacs*.

You can make international **phone calls** from any box (*cabine*), and many post offices have metered booths from which you can make calls and pay afterwards. Some phones take 50c, F1, 5 and 10 coins, but most now only take **phone cards**, available for F49 and F97 from post offices and *tabacs*. For calls within France – local or long distance – dial all 10 digits of the number. To call Monaco from France, prefix the 8-digit number with 00377. The operator number is ☎13.

Getting around

With the most extensive railway network in western Europe, run by the SNCF, France is a country best travelled by rail. The only areas not well served are the mountains, but there rail routes are replaced by SNCF buses. The private bus services are confusing and unco-ordinated.

■ Trains and buses

SNCF **trains** are by and large clean, fast and frequent. **Fares** are reasonable, with a 300km journey costing 180F and a 600km journey at 305F off-peak. The ultrafast and ever more numerous TGVs (Trains à Grande Vitesse) require a supplement at peak times and compulsory reservation, costing around F20. The slowest trains are those marked *Autotrain* in the timetable, stopping at all stations.

The under-26 InterRail and all Eurail **passes** are valid throughout the country, as is the EuroDomino pass, though you have to buy it before you enter the country. SNCF also offer a whole range of **discount fares**, depending on colour-coded time periods: blue and white; *période bleue* covers most of the year and gives the largest discounts (50 percent). All tickets (not passes) must be stamped in the orange machines on station platforms. Rail journeys may be broken any time, anywhere, for up to 24 hours. On night trains, an extra F100 or so will buy you a **couchette**.

Regional **rail maps** and **timetables** are on sale at tobacconists; leaflet timetables are available free at train stations (*gares SNCF*). All but the smallest stations have an information desk and most have *consignes automatiques* – coin-operated left-luggage lockers. Many also rent out bicycles (see below).

Autocar at the top of a timetable column means it's an **SNCF bus service**, on which rail tickets and passes are valid. With the exception of these, the only time you'll need to take a **bus** is in cities – indeed the most frustrating thing about buses is that they rarely serve regions outside the SNCF network – precisely where you need them. In larger towns the bus station (*gare routière*) is normally next to the train station.

■ Driving, hitching and cycling

Taking a **car** gives you enormous advantages of access to remote areas, especially if you're camping. Overseas drivers' licences are valid in France; you should also carry your vehicle registration document and insurance papers. Motorways (*autoroutes*) are fairly extensive and fast, but the tolls are expensive; you might prefer to use the older "N" roads, which are fast enough, or "D" roads, the next grade down. An antiquated **rule of the road** which is still operative in some areas is that you must give way to traffic on your right (*priorité à droite*), even from an incoming minor road – though on main roads there are nearly always signs to the contrary, usually a yellow diamond road sign. The same sign with a black diagonal slash, or a red edged inverted triangle containing a sideways black cross means that you must give way to traffic coming from the right. (The triangle sign usually appears only before individual junctions.) **Speed limits** are 130kph on motorways, 110kph on major roads, 90kph on other roads and 50kph in towns. Fines are exacted on the spot and only cash is accepted: the minimum for speeding is F1300 and for exceeding the drink-driving level F2500–5000. For **information** on traffic and weather conditions on the motorways call Service d'Information des Autoroutes on ☎08.36.68.10.77 (24hr). In case of **breakdown**, there are emergency phones every 2km on the motorways. **Car rental** is about F2000–2500 a week for a small hatchback, with unlimited mileage.

Hitching, you'll have to rely almost exclusively on car drivers, and the French aren't renowned for their sympathy to hitchhikers. On motorways the toll-booths at each major junction are the best bet for picking up long lifts. You might be better off contacting Allostop Provoya, a national organization with offices in Paris (8 rue Rochambeau, on square Montholon; ☎01.53.20.42.42), and a few other major towns. In return for a registration fee, they'll match you up with a driver who is going your way and wants to share petrol costs.

Keen **cyclists** are much admired in France. Traffic keeps a respectful distance (save in the big cities) and restaurants and hotels go out of their way to find a safe place for your bike. Bikes go free on some SNCF trains, though on others you have to pay F195 to send it to your destination – for details, consult the free leaflet *Train et Vélo*, available from most stations. Some SNCF stations also **rent bikes** for around F45 per day plus F1000–1500 deposit (or a credit card number). You can return the bike to any other specified station.

Accommodation

For most of the year it's possible to turn up in any French town and find a room, or a place on a campsite. Booking a couple of nights in advance can, however, be reassuring, and is essential from mid-July to mid-Aug, when the French take their vacations. The first weekend of August is the busiest time of all, though campsites are still usually okay unless you're travelling with a caravan.

■ Hotels

All French **hotels** are officially graded, and prices are relatively uniform. Ungraded and single-star hotels go for F100–200 per double, and are often very good; for a private bath, reckon on paying around F30–50 more, plus sometimes F20–35 for breakfast – although there is no obligation to take this and you will nearly always do better at a café. For a room in a two-star place, which will normally always include a private bath, reckon on F150–250 on average. It is illegal for hotels to insist on your taking meals, but they often do, and in busy resorts you may not find a room unless you agree.

In country areas you will come across **chambres d'hôte** – bed & breakfast accommodation in someone's house or farm. These vary in standard but are rarely especially cheap, usually costing the equivalent of a two-star hotel. Full **accommodation lists** for each province are available from any French Government Tourist Office or from local SIs. In peak season it is worth getting hold of these, together with a handbook for the Logis de France – independent hotels, promoted for their consistently good

---

ACCOMMODATION PRICE CODES

Throughout this guide, accommodation is priced on a scale of ① to ⑨, the number indicating the lowest price per night a single person could expect to pay in that establishment in high season. With hostels this is the nightly rate per person; with hotels, the price is arrived at by dividing the cost of the cheapest double room by two. The prices indicated by the codes are as follows:

① under £5 / $8
② £5–10 / $8–16
③ £10–15 / $16–24

④ £15–20 / $24–32
⑤ £20–25 / $32–40
⑥ £25–30 / $40–48

⑦ £30–35 / $48–56
⑧ £35–40 / $56–64
⑨ £40 / $64 and over

---

food and reasonably priced rooms; they're recognizable by a green and yellow logo.

■ Hostels and foyers

France boasts a wide network of official **youth hostels** or *auberges de jeunesse*, and most are of a high standard. However, while cheap – F40–90 for a dormitory bed (more in Paris) – they are sometimes no less expensive than the cheapest hotel room for a couple – particularly if you take into account fares to their sometimes inaccessible locations. You can sometimes cut costs, however, by preparing your own food in their kitchens, or eating in their cheap canteens. There are two rival youth hostel associations: the Fédération Unie des Auberges de Jeunesse, 27 rue Pajol, 75018 Paris (☎01.44.89.87.27), and the Ligue Française pour les Auberges de Jeunesse, 38 bd Raspail, 75007 Paris (☎01.44.16.78.78). HI membership covers both organizations, although only the former's hostels are detailed in their handbook.

A few large towns provide a more luxurious standard of hostel accommodation in **Foyers des Jeunes Travailleurs/euses**, residential hostels for young workers and students, charging around F60 for an individual room. They also normally have a good canteen. In rural areas, **gîtes d'étape** – less formal than the youth hostels, often run by the local village or municipality – provide bunk beds and primitive kitchen facilities. French Government tourist offices can provide regional listings and will recommend independent guides to *gîtes* and *chambres d'hôte*.

■ Campsites

Practically every village and town in the country has at least one **campsite** to cater for the thousands of French people who spend their holiday under canvas. The cheapest – starting at F26 per person per night – is usually the *Camping Municipal*, normally clean, well-equipped and in a prime location. On the coast especially, there are superior campsites where you'll pay similar amounts to a hotel room for what can be extensive facilities. Inland, camping on somebody's farm is another possibility. Lists of sites are available

from the Tourist Board. Never **camp rough** (*camping sauvage*) on anyone's land without asking permission – farmers have been known to shoot before asking questions.

Food and drink

French food is as good a reason as any for a visit to France. Cooking has art status, the top chefs are stars, and dining out is a national pastime, whether it's at the local brasserie or a famed house of *haute cuisine*. It also doesn't have to cost much as long as you avoid tourist hot spots.

■ Food

Generally the best place to eat **breakfast** is in a bar or café. Most serve buttered baguettes (French bread) and have a basket of croissants or hard-boiled eggs on the counter, to which you can help yourself; the waiter will keep an eye on how much you've eaten and bill you accordingly. Coffee is invariably espresso and strong. *Un café* or *un express* is black; *un crème* is with milk; *un grand café* is a large cup. In the morning, ask for *café au lait* – espresso in a large cup or bowl with hot milk. Ordinary tea (*thé*) is not often drunk; to have milk with it, ask for *un peu de lait frais*. *Chocolat chaud* – hot chocolate – can be had in any café. Every bar or café displays a full price list for drinks at the bar (*au comptoir*), sitting down (*la salle*), or on the terrace (*la terrasse*) – each progressively more expensive.

Cafés are often the best option for **lunch** as well, serving omelettes, fried eggs and sandwiches (generally half-baguettes filled with cheese or meat), and *croque-monsieurs* and *-madames* (variations on the grilled-cheese sandwich). On street stalls you'll also find *frites*, *crêpes*, *galettes* (wholewheat pancakes), *gaufres* (waffles) and Tunisian snacks like *brik à l'oeuf* (fried pastry with egg) and *merguez* (spicy sausage). For **picnic and takeaway food**, there's nothing to beat the *charcuterie* (delicatessen) ready-made dishes – salads, meats and fully prepared main courses – also available at supermarket *charcuterie* counters.

You buy by weight, or you can ask for *une tranche* (a slice), *une barquette* (a carton) or *une part* (a portion).

You can also eat lunch at a **brasserie** – like a restaurant, only open all day and geared more to quicker meals; **restaurants** tend to stick to the traditional meal times of noon–2pm & 7–9.30/10.30pm. In major cities, town centre brasseries often serve until 11pm or midnight. Prices at both are posted outside. Normally there is a choice between one or more *menus fixes*, and *à la carte* or choosing from the menu, which is more expensive (but often the only option available after 9pm). Look out, at both lunch and dinnertime, for the **plat du jour** (daily special), which for F40–80 in a cheap restaurant will often be the most interesting and best-value thing on the menu. *Service compris* means the service charge is included; if not, you need to add 15 percent. Wine (*vin*) or a drink (*boisson*) may be included in a *menu fixe*; when ordering your own wine, ask for *un quart*, *un demi-litre* or *une carafe* (a litre). You'll normally be given the house wine unless you specify otherwise.

■ Drink

Where you can eat you can invariably drink, and vice versa. **Drinking** is done at a leisurely pace whether it's a prelude to food (*apéritif*), a sequel (*digestif*) or the accompaniment, and **cafés** are the standard places to do it. **Wine** (*vin*) is drunk at just about every meal or social occasion. *Vin de table* or *vin ordinaire* (table wine) is generally drinkable and always cheap. In wine-producing areas the local table wine can be very good indeed. *AOC* (*Appellation d'Origine Contrôlée*) wines are another matter. They can be excellent value at the lower end of the scale – favourable French taxes keep prices down to £1 ($1.30) or so a bottle, but serious wines command serious prices. In a café, a **glass of wine** is simply *un rouge* or *un blanc*. If it is an *AOC* wine you may have the choice of *un ballon* (round glass) or a smaller glass (*un verre*).

The familiar Belgian and German brands account for most of the **beer** you'll find, plus home-grown brands from Alsace. Draught (*à la pression*) is the cheapest alcoholic drink you can have next to wine – ask for *un demi* (330ml). Stronger alcohol is drunk from 5am as a pre-work fortifier, right through the day: **cognac** or **armagnac** brandies, dozens of *eaux de vie* (distilled from fruit) and **liqueurs**. Measures are generous, but don't come cheap. *Pastis*, aniseed drinks such as Pernod or Ricard, are popular, diluted with water and ice (*glaçons*) – very refreshing and not expensive.

On the **soft drink** front, bottled fruit juices include apricot (*jus d'abricot*), blackcurrant (*cassis*) and so on. You can also get fresh orange and lemon juice (*orange/citron pressé*). Bottles of **spring water** (*eau*

minérale) – either sparkling (*eau pétillante*) or still (*eau plate*) – abound.

Opening hours and holidays

The basic **working hours** in France are 8am–noon & 2–6.30pm. Food shops often don't reopen till halfway through the afternoon, closing at around 7.30/8pm. Sunday and Monday are the standard **closing days**, though you'll always find at least one *boulangerie* (baker) open. **Museums** open at around 10am and close between 5 and 6pm, with reduced hours outside mid-May to mid-September, sometimes even outside July and August. They also usually close on Monday or Tuesday, usually the latter. Admission charges can be off-putting, though most state-owned museums give reductions to students, so always carry your ISIC card. All shops, museums and offices are closed on the following **national holidays**: Jan 1; Easter Sunday; Easter Monday; Ascension Day; Whitsun (seventh Sunday after Easter, plus the Monday); May 1; May 8; July 14; Aug 15; Nov 1; Nov 11; Dec 25.

Emergencies

There are two main types of French police – the **Police Nationale** and the **Gendarmerie Nationale**. For all practical purposes, they are indistinguishable; if you need to report a theft, or other incident, you can go to either. You can be stopped anywhere in France and asked to produce ID, so always carry your passport and bear in mind it's not worth being difficult or facetious.

Under the French social security system every **hospital** visit, doctor's consultation and prescribed medicine is charged, though in an emergency not upfront. Although all employed French people are entitled to a refund of 70–75 percent of their medical expenses, this can still leave a hefty shortfall, especially after a stay in hospital. In **emergencies** you will always be admitted to the **local hospital** (*hôpital*) whether under your own power or by ambulance. To find a **doctor**, stop at any *pharmacie* and ask for an address. Consultation fees for a visit should be F100–150 and in any case you'll be given a *Feuille de Soins* (Statement of Treatment) for later documentation of insurance claims. Prescriptions should be taken to a *pharmacie*, which is also equipped – and obliged – to give first aid (for a fee). For minor illnesses pharmacists will dispense free advice and a wide range of medication.

EMERGENCY NUMBERS

Police ☎17; Ambulance ☎15; Fire ☎18.

PARIS

PARIS is the paragon of style – perhaps the most captivating city in Europe. Yet it is also deeply traditional, a village-like and, in parts, dilapidated metropolis. Famous names and events are invested with a glamour that elevates the city and its people to a legendary realm, and it still clings to its status as an artistic, intellectual and literary pacesetter.

The city's history has conspired to create this sense of being apart. From a shaky start the kings of France, whose seat was Paris, gradually extended their control over their feudal rivals, centralizing administrative, legal, financial and political power as they did so. The supremely autocratic Louis XIV made Paris into a glorious symbol of the pre-eminence of the State, a tradition his successors have been happy to follow. Napoleon I added to the Louvre and built the Arc de Triomphe, the Madeleine and the Arc du Carrousel. Napoleon III had Baron Haussmann redraw the city centre, while recent presidents have initiated the skyscrapers at La Défense, the Tour Montparnasse, Beaubourg and Les Halles shopping precinct, the space-age Parc de la Villette complex, the glass pyramid entrance to the Louvre, the Musée d'Orsay, the Bastille opera house, and the new National Library.

Nowadays the most tangible and immediate pleasures of Paris are to be found in its **street life** and along the lively banks of the river Seine. Few cities can compete with the cafés, bars and restaurants – modern and trendy, local and traditional, humble and pretentious – that line every street and boulevard. And the city's compactness makes it possible to experience the individual feel of the different *quartiers*. You can move easily, even on foot, from the calm, almost small-town atmosphere of **Montmartre** and parts of the Latin Quarter to the busy commercial centres of the **Bourse** and **Opéra** or to the aristocratic mansions of the **Marais**. An imposing backdrop is provided by the monumental architecture of the **Arc de Triomphe**, the **Louvre**, the **Eiffel Tower**, the **Hôtel de Ville**, the bridges and the institutions of the state. As for entertainment, the city's strong points are in film and music. Paris is a real cinema capital, and the best Parisian music encompasses jazz, avant-garde, salsa and, currently, Europe's most vibrant African music scene.

Arrival and information

The two main Paris **airports** are Roissy-Charles de Gaulle and Orly. **Charles de Gaulle**, northeast of the city, is connected to the Gare du Nord by Roissyrail, a combination of free shuttle bus and RER train (every 15min 5am–midnight; journey time 35min; F48). There's also the Roissybus, which terminates at Opéra (every 15–20min 6am–11pm; journey time 45min; F45), or the more expensive Air France **bus**, which departs from both terminals ending up at the Porte Maillot metro on av MacManon, 100m from the Arc de Triomphe (every 15–20min 6am–11pm; F60) or at Montparnasse in front of the *Hotel Meridien* (every 30min 7am–9.30pm; F70). **Taxis** into central Paris cost F205–250 (plus F6–8 for each piece of luggage), and take 45 to 60 minutes. **Orly**, south of Paris, has two bus/rail links, Orly-Rail (every 15min 6am–11pm; F45), to the Gare d'Austerlitz and other Left Bank stops, and Orlyval, a fast train shuttle link to RER line B station Antony, thence metro connection to Denfert-Rochereau, St-Michel and Châtelet (every 5–7min 6am–7pm; F57). Alternatively, there are Air France buses to the Gare des Invalides via Montparnasse (every 12min 6am–11pm; F45), or Orlybus to the Denfert-Rochereau metro (every 15–20min 5.30am–11pm; journey time 30min; F30). A **taxi** will cost between F140 and F170.

Paris has six main-line **train** stations, all on the metro system. Services from Boulogne, Calais, Belgium, Holland and Scandinavia arrive at the **Gare du Nord**, as does Eurostar's Channel Tunnel service from Britain; Eurostar have their own booking offices and departure lounge on a raised tier at one side of the station. The **Gare de l'Est** serves eastern France, Germany, Switzerland and Austria; **Gare St-Lazare** serves Dieppe and the Normandy coast; **Gare de Lyon** is the arrival point of trains from the Alps, the south, Italy and Greece; **Gare Montparnasse** is the terminus for Versailles, Chartres, Brittany and the Atlantic coast; **Gare d'Austerlitz** is the station for trains from the southwest and southern Atlantic coast. National and international train tickets can be purchased at any SNCF main-line station. All long-dis-

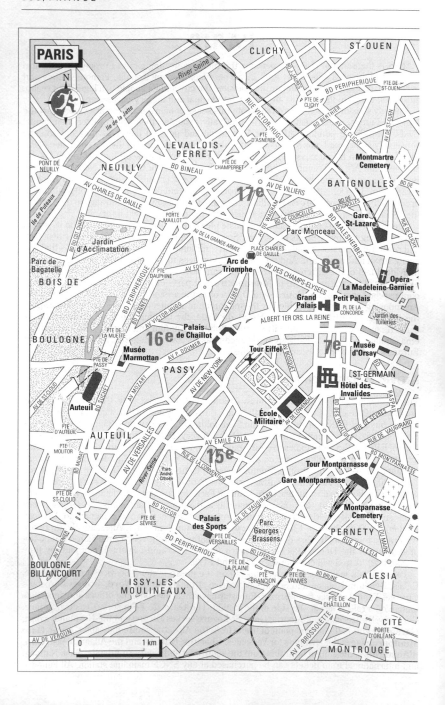

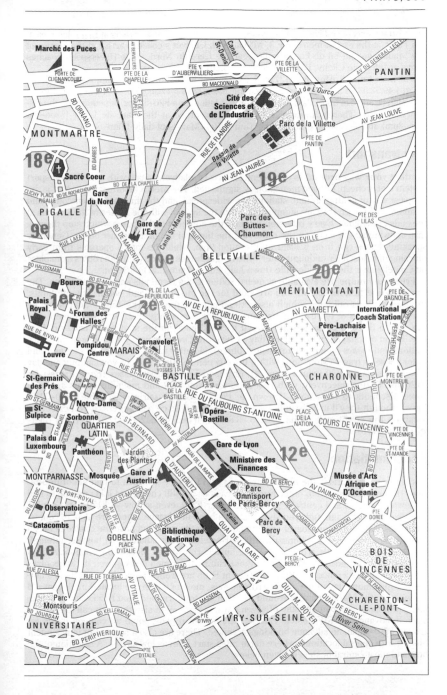

tance **buses** except Gulliver's and Hoverspeed use the main *gare routière* at Bagnolet in eastern Paris, at the end of métro line 3, M° Gallieni; Gulliver's coaches arrive at the corner of rue Maubeuge and bd de La Chapelle near the Gare du Nord, while Hoverspeed coaches arrive at 165 av de Clichy, 17e (M° Porte du Clichy or M° Brochant).

The main **tourist office** is at 127 av des Champs-Élysées (daily 9am–8pm; ☎01.49.52.53.54 or ☎01.49.52.53.56 for recorded information; *www.paris-touristoffice.com*). They have maps and leaflets, and can book last-minute accommodation for a F20–55 fee, depending on the category of hotel. There's an annexe of the tourist office at the Gare de Lyon (Mon–Sat 8am–8pm) and a seasonal office by the Tour Eiffel (May–Sept daily 11am–6pm).

City transport

Finding your way around is easy: central Paris is relatively small, with a public transport system that is cheap, fast and meticulously signposted. The **metro** (abbreviated as M°) is the simplest way of getting around: stations are widespread, and the lines are colour-coded and numbered, although they are signposted within the system with the names of the stations at the ends of the lines. Every **bus** stop displays the numbers of the buses which stop there, a map showing all the stops on the route and the times of the first and last buses. Generally speaking, buses run from 6.30am until around 9pm, while the métro operates from early morning until just after midnight, after which **night buses** run on eighteen routes from place du Châtelet near the Hôtel de Ville (town hall) hourly from 1.30 to 5.30am.

Free route **maps** are available at metro stations, bus terminals and tourist offices. The same flat-fare **tickets** cost F8 and are valid for the bus, metro and, within the city limits, the RER express rail lines, which also extend out into the suburbs. Single tickets can be bought in *carnets* of ten from any station or *tabac* – currently F52. Be sure to keep your ticket until the end of the journey; you'll be fined F300 on the spot if you can't produce one. If you are staying more than a day or two, the *Carte Orange*, obtainable at all metro stations and *tabacs* (you need a passport photo), is better value, costing F80 (zones 1 and 2) for a week's travel (Mon–Sun) within the city centre. Alternatively, you can buy one-day *Mobilis* passes for F30 (zones 1 and 2), or 3- and 5-day tourist passes (*Paris Visites*) for F120 and F170 respectively, with first-class travel on RER and main-line trains and with some discounts to attractions thrown in. Paris **taxis** are fairly reasonable (F40–70 in Paris), though they'll usually only take a maximum of three passengers. If you can't find a cab on the street, call Alpha ☎01.45.85.85.85, Artaxi ☎01.42.41.50.50, or Taxis Bleus ☎01.49.36.10.10.

Accommodation

Not surprisingly, Paris is the most expensive part of France in which to find **accommodation**. However, compared to other European capitals it's still cheap, and it is possible to find somewhere decent and centrally placed for under F250, even as low as F170, for a double room without bath, although you should always book in advance. There are also, of course, numerous places offering **hostel** accommodation. In the main you have the choice between the hostels of three organizations: the official Hostelling International (HI) hostels, although only two of their hostels are at all central; hostels run by the Maison Internationale de la Jeunesse et des Étudiants (MIJE); and those run by the Union des Centres de Rencontres Internationaux de France (UCRIF). HI rates in Paris are from F115 a night and there's normally a maximum stay of five days. MIJE hostels, most of which are located in elegant old mansions in the Marais, charge around F125 a night for dorm beds and F158 each for a double, and impose a maximum stay of seven days; bear in mind also that you can't reserve a place in advance. UCRIF hostels charge F120 for dorm beds; some do canteen meals for around F50 – again no advance bookings accepted. There are also a number of independent hostels with central locations, where dorm rates start from as low as F80. A selection of the best and most central hostels is given below.

Hostels

Aloha, 1 rue Borromé, 15e (☎01.42.73.03.03). Independent hostel, and one of the cheapest places to stay. Own bar serving some of the cheapest beer in town. Young and noisy atmosphere. Book before 9am. Mº Volontaires. ②.

Auberge Internationale des Jeunes, 10 rue Trousseau, 11e (☎01.47.00.62.00). Despite the official-sounding name, a laid-back independent (but very noisy) hostel in a great location 5min walk from the Bastille. Clean and professionally run with 24hr reception, generous breakfast and free luggage storage. Mº Ledru-Rollin. ②.

BVJ Centre, 20 rue Jean-Jacques-Rousseau, 1er (☎01.53.00.90.90; ②); 11 rue Thérèse, 1er (☎01.42.60.77.23; ②); and 44 rue des Bernardins, 5e (☎01.43.29.34.80; ②). Three central UCRIF hostels, with little to distinguish between them.

3 Canards (Three Ducks), 6 place Étienne-Pernet, 15e (☎01.48.42.04.05). Another independent party hostel with bar, beer and use of kitchen facilities. Book ahead May–Oct. Mº Félix Faure. ②.

D'Artagnan, 80 rue Vitruve, 20e (☎01.40.32.34.56). Enormous HI hostel, with lots of facilities, but a fair way out on the eastern fringes of the city. Mº Porte de Bagnolet. ②.

Jules Ferry, 8 bd Jules-Ferry, 11e (☎01.43.57.55.60). In the lively area at the foot of the Belleville hill, smaller and more central than *D'Artagnan*, the other official HI hostel. Very difficult to get a bed. Mº République. ②.

Le Fauconnier, 11 rue du Fauconnier, 4e (☎01.42.74.23.45). MIJE hostel in a superbly renovated seventeenth-century mansion with a courtyard. Breakfast included. Mº St-Paul/Pont-Marie. Dorms (sleep 4–8) ②; rooms (with shower) ③.

Le Fourcy, 6 rue de Fourcy, 4e (☎01.42.74.23.45). MIJE place in a beautiful mansion with a small garden and restaurant with menus from F50. Dorms only (sleep 4–8). Mº St-Paul. ②.

Maubuisson, 12 rue des Barres, 4e (☎01.42.74.23.45). MIJE hostel in a magnificent medieval building in a quiet street. Restaurant meals from F42. Singles and doubles available. Breakfast included. Mº Pont-Marie/Hôtel-de-Ville. ②.

Résidence Bastille, 151 av Ledru-Rollin, 11e (☎01.43.79.53.86). MIJE hostel. Mº Ledru-Rollin/Bastille/Voltaire. ②.

Hotels

Hôtel des Alliés, 20 rue Berthollet, 5e (☎01.43.31.47.52). Simple and clean. Bargain prices. Mº Censier-Daubenton. ④.

Avenir-Jonquière, 23 rue de la Jonquière, 17e (☎01.46.27.83.41). Clean and friendly. Mº Guy-Môquet. ③.

Hôtel des Carmes, 5 rue des Carmes, 5e (☎01.43.29.42.93). Well established and reasonable. Mº Maubert-Mutualité. ⑤.

Castex, 5 rue Castex, 4e (☎01.42.72.31.52). Friendly, family-run hotel in a quiet street on the edge of the Marais. Spacious rooms with bath/shower and many also have toilets. Mº Bastille. ④.

Le Central, 6 rue Descartes, 5e (☎01.46.33.57.93). Clean and decent accommodation on top of the Montagne Ste-Geneviève. Mº Maubert Mutualité. ③.

Grand Hôtel du Loiret, 8 rue des Mauvais-Garçons, 4e (☎01.48.87.77.00). Simple place but good value. Mº Hotel-de-Ville. ③.

Hôtel du Dragon, 36 rue du Dragon, 6e (☎01.45.48.51.05). Great location and nice people – good value. Mº St-Germain-des-Prés. ⑤.

Henri IV, 25 place Dauphine, 1er (☎01.43.54.44.53). Well-known cheapie in the beautiful place Dauphine on the Île de la Cité. Breakfast included. Booking essential. Mº Pont-Neuf. ③.

Idéal, 3 rue des Trois-Frères, 18e (☎01.46.06.63.63). Marvellous location on the slopes of Montmartre. A real bargain. Mº Abbesses. ④.

Jeanne d'Arc, 3 rue de Jarente, 4e (☎01.48.87.62.11). Clean, quiet and attractive. The Marais location – just by the lively place du Marché Ste-Catherine – means you have to reserve. Mº St-Paul. ⑦.

Lévêque, 29 rue Cler, 7e (☎01.47.05.49.15). Clean and decent; nice people who speak some English. Book one month ahead. Mº École-Militaire. ⑤.

Marignan, 13 rue du Sommerard, 5e (☎01.43.54.63.81). One of the best bargains in town. You'll need to book a month ahead in summer. Mº Maubert-Mutualité. ③.

Nouvelle France, 31 rue Keller, 11e (☎01.47.00.40.74). Cheap and ideally located in an arty street with a gay focus near the Bastille nightlife of rue de Lappe and rue de la Roquette. Mº Bastille. ②.

Pratic, 20 rue de l'Ingénieur-Robert-Keller, 15e (☎01.45.77.70.58). Clean and friendly. Close to the Eiffel Tower. Mº Charles-Michels. ④.

Tiquetonne, 6 rue Tiquetonne, 2e (☎01.42.36.94.58). Good value in an attractive small street. Closed Aug. Mº Étienne-Marcel. ④.

Campsite

The closest **campsite** to the centre of Paris is by the Seine in the Bois de Boulogne on the allée du Bord-de-l'Eau, 16e (open all year; ☎01.45.24.30.00). The ground is pebbly, but the site is well equipped and has a useful information office. It's usually booked out in summer. Take the metro to Porte-Maillot then bus #244 to Route des Moulins.

The City

Paris is split into two halves by the Seine. On the north of the river, the **Right Bank** (*rive droite*) is home to the grand boulevards and most monumental buildings, many dating from Haussmann's nineteenth-century redevelopment, and is where you'll spend most time, during the day at least. The top museums are here – the Louvre and Beaubourg, to name just two – as well as the city's widest range of shops around rue de Rivoli and Les Halles; and there are also peaceful quarters like the Marais for idle strolling. The **Left Bank** (*rive gauche*) has a noticeably different feel, its very name conjuring Bohemian, dissident, intellectual connotations, and something of this atmosphere survives in Paris' best range of bars and restaurants, and its most wanderable streets. The areas around St-Germain and St-Michel are full of nooks and crannies to explore.

Parts of Paris, of course, don't sit easily in either category. **Montmartre**, rising up to the north of the centre, has managed to retain a village-like, almost rural atmosphere with its colourful mixture of locals and artists despite the daily influx of tourists. Undisturbed by tourism, the dilapidated working-class quarters of **eastern Paris** offer a rich ethnic slice of Parisian street life and in direct contrast, technological wonder is paraded at the ground-breaking science museum constructed in the recently renovated **Parc de La Villette**. If you're planning to visit any museums, it's worth knowing that many have reduced fees for under-25s, are often free for children and reduce their fees by up to half on Sunday. They are often closed on Mondays or Tuesdays and, if you plan to see more than a few during your stay, it's a good idea to invest in a **museum pass** (one day F80, three consecutive days F160, five consecutive days F240). You can get them from participating museums, some tourist offices, the larger metro stations and FNAC ticket offices (there's one in Les Halles) and they'll certainly encourage you to be more adventurous with the vast choice of museums and monuments in Paris.

The Voie Triomphale

As good a place as any to start exploring is along the **Voie Triomphale** (Triumphal Way), which stretches in a straight line from the Louvre to the corporate skyscrapers at La Défense, 9km away, and has some of the city's most famous landmarks. The best view is from the top of the **Arc de Triomphe**, Napoleon's homage to the armies of France and himself (Tues–Sat 9.30/10am–10.30/11pm, Sun & Mon 9.30am–6/6.30pm; F35), at the centre of **place Charles-de-Gaulle** (still better known as place de l'Étoile) where traffic from the twelve avenues leading into it meets in a heart-stopping display of horn blaring and near misses (metro Charles-de-Gaulle-Étoile). From here the **Champs-Élysées** descends gracefully to the equally traffic-bound **place de la Concorde**, whose centrepiece, an obelisk from the temple of Luxor, was offered as a favour-currying gesture by the viceroy of Egypt in 1829. The symmetry continues beyond the square in the formal layout of the **Jardin des Tuileries** which stretch down to the Louvre. Towards the river, the **Orangerie** (currently undergoing renovation, due to open in Autumn 2001) displays Monet's largest water-lily paintings, as well as Cézanne's southern landscapes and portraits by van Dongen, Utrillo and Modigliani.

The Louvre

On the far side of the Jardin des Tuileries, the **Louvre** (Mon & Wed–Sun 9am–6pm; Richelieu Wing open Mon until 9.45pm; whole museum open Wed until 9.45pm; F45, F26 Sun

& after 3pm, free first Sun of month; metro Palais Royal-Musée du Louvre/Louvre-Rivoli) was first opened to the public in 1793, during the Revolution, and within a decade Napoleon had made it the largest art collection on earth with the takings from his empire. It's still a vast collection, and it is estimated that you would need at least two months to cover everything exhibited in any detail, but although it is at first overwhelming and seemingly nonsensical, the layout of the museum is a delight to discover. I.M. Pei's stunning glass pyramid is the main entrance to the Louvre, although alternative access directly from the metro or from rue de Rivoli via passage Richelieu avoids the queues for the pyramid. Beneath the pyramid, a subterranean concourse gives onto the newly arranged sections of the museum: Sully (around the Cour Carrée), Denon (the south wing) and Richelieu (the north wing).

The **seven basic categories** of the museum's collections are Oriental antiquities; Egyptian antiquities; Greek, Etruscan and Roman antiquities; sculpture; decorative arts; painting; and graphic arts. Each category spreads out over more than one wing and several floors. Recent building work has also provided an opportunity to excavate the remains of the **medieval Louvre** – Philippe-Auguste's twelfth-century fortress and Charles V's fourteenth-century palace conversion – under the Cour Carrée. The foundations and archeological findings are now on show along with a permanent exhibition on the history of the Louvre on the *entresol* floor in the Sully wing. **Oriental Antiquities** – including the newly presented Islamic Art collection – covers the Sumerian, Babylonian, Assyrian and Phoenician civilizations, plus the art of ancient Persia. **Egyptian Antiquities** contains jewellery, domestic objects, sandals, sarcophagi and dozens of examples of the delicate naturalism of Egyptian decorative technique, and statues like the pink granite *Mastaba Sphinx*. **Greek and Roman Antiquities**, divided between the Denon and Sully wings, include the *Winged Victory of Samothrace* and *Venus de Milo*. The **Applied Arts** collection is heavily weighted on the side of vulgar imperial opulence, but also includes a great deal of impressive tapestry as well as smaller, less public items, such as the carved Parisian ivories of the thirteenth century and the Limoges enamels. **Sculpture** covers the entire development of the art in France from Romanesque to Rodin, all in the new Richelieu wing, and Italian and northern European sculpture in Denon, including Michelangelo's *Slaves*, designed for the tomb of Pope Julius II. The largest section by far is **paintings**: French from the year dot to mid-nineteenth century, along with Italian, Dutch, German, Flemish and Spanish. The *Mona Lisa* in Denon is the painting most people head for, and is normally swamped with onlookers, no one paying the slightest attention to the other Leonardos nearby, such as the *Virgin of the Rocks*. There is a good selection of other Italian paintings, including works by Giotto, Botticelli, Titian, Tintoretto and Mantegna (a *Crucifixion*), one of Uccello's *Battle of San Romano* series and, most strikingly, Paolo Veronese's huge *Marriage at Cana*, painted in 1563.

Among the Flemish and Dutch paintings in the Richelieu Wing are Quentin Matsys' moralistic *Moneychanger and his Wife*, Memling's *Mystic Marriage of St Catherine*, Rembrandt's masterful *Supper at Emmaus*, and several works by Rubens. The works of Caravaggio are also richly represented, and the two exquisite Vermeers in the last part of the Richelieu are certainly worth the wait. There are French paintings of all periods, notably works by Poussin and later canvases by the great nineteenth-century artists David, Ingres, Delacroix and Géricault – whose harrowing *Raft of the Medusa* made his name as an artist. Look out, too, for Courbet's later *Funeral at Ornans*, perhaps the best-known Realist painting of all, its events rendered with dour, impassive precision.

The **north wing** of the Louvre, entered from rue de Rivoli, is given over to three related museums. The **Musée des Arts Décoratifs** (Tues, Thurs & Fri 11am–6pm, Wed 11am–9pm, Sat & Sun 10am–6pm; F30; metro Palais Royal-Musée du Louvre) is devoted to interior design, with furnishings and fittings from the Middle Ages to the 1990s. The contemporary section is fairly meagre, but the rest of the twentieth century is fascinating, and includes a bedroom by Guimard, Jeanne Lanvin's Art Deco apartments and a salon created by Georges Hoentschel for the 1900 Expo. However, if you plan to visit note that it is currently undergoing renovation and is only partly open with a complete reopening planned for mid-2001. The smaller museum, the **Musée de la Mode et du Textile** (same hours and ticket as above) pays homage to Paris fashion with a collection of haute couture from the seventeenth century to the present day. The Musée de la Publicité is due to open in the year 2000 and deals with the art of advertising from nineteenth-century poster art to contemporary electronic publicity.

The Opéra, Les Halles and the Pompidou Centre

A short walk north of the Louvre is the **Opéra-Garnier**, on place de l'Opéra, a preposterously ornate building designed by Charles Garnier and built in 1875 as the venue for opera in Paris. Since the completion of the Bastille opera house it has been used chiefly for ballet. You can visit the splendid interior (daily 10am–5pm; F30; metro Opéra), including the auditorium, where the domed ceiling is the work of Chagall, and the entrance fee includes admission to the small museum. A short walk east brings you to the area around the former **Les Halles** (a covered market) which was redeveloped in the 1970s amid widespread opposition and is now promoted as the heart of trendy Paris. In truth, the multi-layered shopping precinct at its core – the **Forum des Halles** – is a tacky affair, and it can be unsafe, too, especially at night – hence the high-profile police presence. During the day the main flow of feet is from here to the **Pompidou Centre** (Beaubourg), a little way east. This seminal design by Renzo Piano and Richard Rogers was the first public structure to manifest the hi-tech notion of wearing its innards – colourful tubing – on the outside, and has an average of 25,000 visitors a day. Much-needed renovation work was under way at the time of writing, but it is due to reopen on December 31, 1999, when more space will be given to the highly popular multimedia library and its ever-growing modern art collection, the **Musée National d'Art Moderne** (prices and times to be announced; metro Rambuteau). This is a permanent exhibition of twentieth-century art from the late Impressionists to late 1980s. Early paintings include canvases by Henri Rousseau – *La Charmeuse de Serpent* – and Picasso, whose *Femme Assise* of 1909 introduces Cubism, represented in its fuller development by Braque's *L'Homme à la Guitare* and Léger's *Les Acrobates en Gris*. Among abstracts, there's the sensuous rhythm of colour in Sonia Delaunay's *Prismes Électriques* and a good showing of Kandinsky at his most playful. Dalí disturbs, amuses or infuriates with *Six Apparitions de Lénine sur un Piano* and there are further Surrealist images by Magritte and de Chirico. One of the most compulsive German pictures is the portrait of the journalist *Sylvia von Harden* by Otto Dix. Among the more recent canvases, Francis Bacon's work figures prominently, as do the provocative images of the Pop Art movement – not least Warhol's *Electric Chair*.

The Marais, the Bastille and Île St-Louis

Just east of Beaubourg, the **Marais** is a formerly fashionable aristocratic district that until twenty years ago was one of the city centre's poorer quarters. Since then, regentrification has turned the renovated mansions into museums, offices and chic apartments flanked by designer clothes shops. A little way down the neighbourhood's main drag, rue des Francs-Bourgeois, one of the grandest Marais mansions houses the **Musée Carnavalet** (entrance at 23 rue de Sévigné around the corner; Tues–Sun 10am–5.40pm; F27; metro St-Paul), which presents the history of Paris from the reign of François I to the early twentieth century, with models, maps and plans, reconstructions of interiors and mementoes of the 1789 Revolution. Slightly further north, at 71 rue du Temple, the **Musée d'Art et d'Histoire du Judaïsme** (Mon–Fri 11am–6pm, Sun 10am–6pm; F40 including audioguide; metro Rambuteau) has a fascinating display of Jewish artefacts and historical documents as well as some fine modern paintings by the likes of Chagall and Soutine.

A short walk east, another mansion, the grandiloquent seventeenth-century Hôtel Juigné Salé at 5 rue de Thorigny, is home to the **Musée Picasso** (Mon & Wed–Sun 9.30am–5.30/6pm; F30; metro Chemin Vert/St-Paul), the largest collection of Picassos anywhere. A large proportion of the pictures were the personal property of the artist at the time of his death, and are displayed alongside paintings he bought or was given, his African masks and sculptures, photographs, letters and other personal memorabilia. The paintings of his wives, lovers and family are some of the most endearing, and there are references to his political commitments, too, in his delegate credentials for the 1948 World Congress of Peace, and the *Massacre en Corée* from 1951.

At the far end of rue des Francs-Bourgeois, off to the right, **place des Vosges** (originally known as Place Royale) is a masterpiece of aristocratic urban planning, a vast square of stone and brick symmetry built for Henri IV and Louis XIII. It is one of the city's most charming squares and, unusually for Paris, the grass is fit for sprawling on, making the relaxing park a great spot for a picnic. You can check out the surrounding mansions in the form of the **Maison Victor Hugo** (Tues–Sun 10am–5.40pm; F27; metro Bastille), once home to the writer of the oft-adapted *Les Miserables*; not surprisingly, a whole room is devoted to posters of its various stage productions.

A short walk southeast, heading for the landmark column with the gilded "Spirit of Liberty" is **place de la Bastille**, the site of the storming of the Bastille in 1789. The column was erected not to commemorate the surrender in 1789 of the prison, which was subsequently demolished, but the July Revolution of 1830 – although it is the 1789 Bastille Day that France celebrates on July 14. The Bicentennial in 1989 was marked by the inauguration of the **Opéra-Bastille**, on the far side of the square, a bloated building that caused great controversy when it went up – a "hippopotamus in a bathtub", one critic called it.

Just south from here, across Henri IV bridge, the **Île St-Louis** is one of the centre's swankier quarters, with no monuments or museums, just high houses on single-lane streets. It's a peaceful and atmospheric route through to the Île de la Cité, either strolling down the centre along the shop-filled rue Île-St-Louis, a real weekend promenade with pedestrians taking over the street – many intent on queuing for an ice-cream at the famous *Berthillon* – or along the tree-lined quais down by the Seine. It is particularly atmospheric at night as the lights from the *Bateaux Mouches* cast shadows of the trees over the buildings, whose lit-up windows offer a glimpse of their elegant interiors.

Île de la Cité

Île de la Cité is where Paris began, the original site of the Roman garrison and later of the palace of the Merovingian kings and the counts of Paris, who in 987 became kings of France. Nowadays the main lure, however, is the stupendous **Cathédrale de Notre-Dame** (Mon–Fri & Sun 8am–7pm, Sat 8am–12.30 & 2–7pm; free; metro Cité), begun in 1160 under the auspices of Bishop de Sully and completed around 1245. In the nineteenth century, Viollet-le-Duc carried out extensive renovation work, remaking most of the statuary and adding the steeple and baleful-looking gargoyles, which you can see close up if you brave the 387-step ascent of the towers (daily 9.30/10am–5/7.30pm; F32, or F50 combined ticket with the crypt). The sculpture of the west front portals is amazingly detailed, dating mainly from the twelfth and thirteenth centuries while, inside, the immediately striking feature is the dramatic contrast between the darkness of the nave and the light falling on the first great clustered pillars of the choir. It is the end walls of the transepts which admit all this light, nearly two-thirds glass, including two magnificent rose windows in imperial purple – additions made in 1267. In front of the cathedral, the **crypte archéologique** (daily 10am–4.30/6pm; F32, F50 with towers) holds the remains of the original cathedral, as well as streets and houses of the Cité back as far as the Roman era. At weekends and during summer getting in to see the cathedral may involve queuing for a while, as this is the real tourist heart of Paris and things can get crowded.

At the other end of the island, the dull mass of the **Palais de Justice** swallowed up the palace that was home to the French kings until the bloody revolt of 1358 frightened them into the greater security of the Louvre. The only part of the older complex that remains in its entirety is Louis IX's **Ste-Chapelle** at 4 bd du Palais (daily: April–Sept 9.30am–6.30pm; Oct–March 10am–5pm; F32, or F50 combined with the Conciergerie; metro Cité), built to house a collection of holy relics and one of the finest achievements of French Gothic style, lent a fragility by its height and huge expanses of glorious stained glass, most of which is original. You should also visit the **Conciergerie**, whose entrance is around the corner facing the river on quai de l'Horloge (daily: April–Sept 9.30am–6.30pm; Oct–March 10am–5pm; F32, or F50 combined with the Ste-Chapelle), Paris' oldest prison, where Marie-Antoinette and, in their turn, the leading figures of the Revolution, were incarcerated before execution. Its chief interest is the enormous late Gothic *Salle des Gens d'Arme*, canteen and recreation room of the royal household staff, as well as Marie-Antoinette's cell and various macabre mementoes of the guillotine's victims. Outside the Conciergerie is the Tour de l'Horloge built in 1370, Paris' first public clock.

The Beaux-Quartiers, Bois de Boulogne and La Défense

South and west of the Arc de Triomphe lie the so-called **Beaux Quartiers**, the 16e and 17e *arrondissements*, in turns aristocratic and rich, bourgeois and staid districts, mainly residential, that hold little of interest save the wonderful **Musée Marmottan**, 2 rue Louis-Boilly (Tues–Sun 10am–5pm; F40; metro Muette), whose Monet paintings were bequeathed by the artist's son. Among them is the canvas entitled *Impression, Soleil Levant*, an 1872 rendering of a misty sunrise over Le Havre, whose title unwittingly gave the Impressionist movement its name. There's also a dazzling collection of almost abstract canvases from Monet's last years at Giverny. Beyond the museum, the **Bois de Boulogne** (open daily), running all down the west side of the 16e, is the city centre's largest open space, supposedly modelled on Hyde Park, and offering all sorts of facilities – various museums, a children's amusement-park-cum-zoo, a formal garden with beautiful displays of flowers in the spring, a riding school, boating on the Lac Inférieur, wild walks in its southeast corner, and, of course, the racecourses of Longchamp and Auteuil – although it's long been known for its prodigious sexual pick-up activity after dark.

La **Défense** is nowadays high on the list of places to which visitors to Paris must pay homage. The best way to approach Paris' prestige business district is to take the metro to Esplanade de la Défense and walk the long pedestrianized stretch lined with cinemas, restaurants, large shops and company headquarters. The district is complete with waterfalls and scattered art works by Miró and Alexander Calder and the impressive sight of **La Grande Arche** looming on the horizon. Transparent lifts (daily 10am–7pm; F40; metro Grande Arche de la Défense) can take you on a thrilling ride up open shafts to the top of this 112-metre tall hollow cube, built in 1989 and clad in white marble. However, the lift is pricey and the views – right down the Voie Triumphale to the Arc de Triomphe – are no more impressive than those gained from the series of steps which lead up to the Arch and provide a popular point for viewing or just sitting about.

The Eiffel Tower, Les Invalides and the Musée d'Orsay

A short walk south of place de l'Étoile, the **Musée d'Art Moderne de la Ville de Paris** in the Palais de Tokyo, no. 11, av du Président-Wilson (Tues–Fri 10am–5.30pm, Sat & Sun 10am–6.45pm; F30; metro Trocadéro) displays examples of the schools and trends of twentieth-century art, as well as sculpture and painting by contemporary artists. Among the most spectacular works on show are Robert and Sonia Delaunay's huge whirling wheels and cogs of rainbow colour, the leaping figures of Matisse's *La Danse* and Dufy's enormous mural, *La Fée Électricité* (done for the electricity board), illustrating the story of electricity from Aristotle to the modern power station, in 250 colourful panels. A short walk down the river, at Trocadéro, the terrace of the **Palais de Chaillot** – home to several uninteresting museums – gives splendid vistas across the river to the **Tour Eiffel**, especially at night. Though no conventional beauty, this is nonetheless an amazing structure, at 300m the tallest building in the world when it was completed in 1889, by Gustave Eiffel. Reactions to it were violent, but it stole the show at the 1889 Exposition, for which it had been constructed. It's possible to go right to the top (July & Aug daily 9am–midnight; rest of year 9.30am–11pm; by lift it's F20 to the first floor, F42 to the second and F59 to the third; to walk its F14, but you can only go as far as the second floor; metro Bir Hakeim/RER Champ de Mars). Although the queues for the final stage can be massive during high season it is only really worth it on an absolutely clear day. The queues are much smaller at night when the view is even more impressive.

To the east, the **Esplanade des Invalides** strikes south from the river to the wide facade of the **Hôtel des Invalides**, built as a home for invalided soldiers on the orders of Louis XIV and topped by a distinctive gilded dome which is a real Paris landmark. One of its two churches was intended as a mausoleum for the king but now contains the mortal remains of Napoleon, enclosed within a gallery decorated with friezes of execrable taste and captioned with quotations of awesome conceit from the great man, while the main part of the building houses the vast **Musée de l'Armée** (daily 10am–5/5.45pm; F37; metro La Tour Maubourg/Varenne). Immediately east, the **Musée Rodin**, at no. 77 on the corner of rue de Varenne, housed in a beautiful eighteenth-century mansion which the sculptor leased from the State in return for the gift of all his work at his death (April–Sept Tues–Sun 9.30am–5.45pm, garden until 6.45pm; rest of year museum & garden 9.30am–4.45pm; F28, garden only F5; metro Varenne), represents the whole of Rodin's work. Larger projects like *The Burghers of Calais* and *The Thinker* are exhibited in the garden, while indoors are works in marble like *The Kiss, The Hand of God* and *The Cathedral*.

A little way northeast along the river, on the quai d'Orsay, the **Musée d'Orsay** (Tues, Wed and Fri–Sat 9/10am–6pm, Thurs 9/10am–9.45pm, Sun 9am–6pm; F40; RER Musée d'Orsay/metro Solférino) is the newest of the city's big museums and rated one of the most enjoyable by visitors. It was converted from the disused Gare d'Orsay in the mid-1980s and now houses the painting and sculpture of the pre-modern period, 1848–1914 – bridging the gap between the Louvre and the Beaubourg. On the ground floor, there are a few canvases by Ingres and Delacroix, whose work serves to illustrate the transition from the early nineteenth century. The Symbolists and early Degas follow, while in the galleries to the left Daumier, Corot, Millet and the Realist school lead on to Manet's *Olympia* – controversial for its colour contrasts and sensual surfaces, as well as for its portrayal of Olympia as nothing more than a high-class whore. On the top level there are the first Impressionist works with landscapes and outdoor scenes by Renoir, Sisley, Pissarro and Monet – including his water lilies, along with five of his Rouen cathedral series. Cézanne is also wonderfully represented, while the rest of this level is given over to Gauguin post- and pre-Tahiti, a number of *pointilliste* works by Seurat and the blinding colours of Van Gogh, as well as some superb Bonnards and Vuillards and lots of Toulouse-Lautrec at his brothelling best.

The Latin Quarter, St-Germain and Montparnasse

The warren of medieval lanes around the boulevards St-Michel and St-Germain is known as the **Quartier Latin** because that was the language of the university sited there right up until 1789. The pivotal point of the area is **place St-Michel**, where the tree-lined **boulevard St-Michel** begins, its cafés and shops jammed with people, mainly young and, in summer, largely foreign. **Rue de la Huchette**, the Mecca of beats and bums in the post-World War II years, is now a tourist trap given over to Greek restaurants of indifferent quality and inflated prices, as is the adjoining rue Xavier-Privas, with the odd couscous joint thrown in. Close by the St-Michel/St-Germain junction, the walls of the third-century Roman baths are visible in the garden of the Hôtel de Cluny on place Paul-Poinlevé. The hotel is a sixteenth-century mansion built by the abbots of the powerful Cluny monastery as their Paris pied-à-terre and now houses the **Musée National du Moyen Age – Thermes de Cluny** (Mon & Wed–Sun 9.15am–5.45pm; F30, F20 on Sun; metro Cluny-La Sorbonne), a treasure-house of medieval art that includes some wonderful, finely detailed tapestries. The real masterpiece is the late fifteenth-century *La Dame à la Licorne* – six highly symbolic medieval scenes featuring a beautiful woman flanked by a lion and a unicorn, probably made in Brussels.

Immediately south of here, the **Montagne Ste-Geneviève** slopes up to the domed **Panthéon**, Louis XIV's thankyou to Ste Geneviève, patron saint of Paris, for curing him of illness, which was transformed during the Revolution into a mausoleum for the great: its incumbents include Voltaire, Rousseau, Zola and Hugo (daily: April–Sept 9.30am–6.30pm; Oct–March 10am–5.30pm; F32; metro Cardinal Lemoine/RER Luxembourg). Down rue Soufflot from here, across bd St-Michel, you might prefer to while away a few hours in the elegant surrounds of the **Jardin du Luxembourg**, laid out by Marie de Médici, Henri IV's widow, to remind her of the Palazzo Pitti and Giardino di Bóboli of her native Florence. They are the chief recreation ground of the Left Bank, with tennis courts, a *boules* pitch, toy yachts to rent on the pond and, in the southeast corner, a miniature orchard of elaborately espaliered pear trees.

Beyond the Luxembourg gardens, the northern half of the 6e *arrondissement* is one of the most attractive parts of the city, full of bookshops, art galleries, antique shops, cafés and restaurants. It is also, perhaps, its most culturally historic: Picasso painted *Guernica* in rue des Grands-Augustins; in rue Visconti, Delacroix painted and Balzac's printing business went bust; and in the parallel rue des Beaux-Arts, Oscar Wilde died and the crazy poet Gérard de Nerval went walking with a lobster on a blue ribbon. **Place St-Germain-des-Prés**, the hub of the *quartier*, is the site of the *Deux Magots* café, renowned for the number of politico-literary backsides that have shined its seats. On the other side of the Luxembourg gardens, **Montparnasse** also trades on its association with the colourful characters of the interwar artistic and literary boom, many of whom were habitués of the cafés *Select, Coupole, Dôme* and *Rotonde* on **bd du Montparnasse**. Close by, the colossal 59-storey skyscraper **Tour Montparnasse** on av du Maine has become one of the city's principal landmarks since its construction in 1973; it can be climbed for less than the Eiffel Tower, but it is more than one hundred metres shorter (daily 9.30am–10.30/11.30pm; F32 to 56th floor including a film on Paris, F42 to 59th floor; metro Montparnasse-Bienvenüe). A short walk down bd Edgar-Quinet, the **Montparnasse cemetery** (April–Oct Mon–Fri 8am–6pm, Sat 8.30am–6pm, Sun 9am–6pm; Nov–March closes at 5.30pm; free; metro Edgar-Quinet) has plenty of illustrious names, from Baudelaire to Sartre and André Citroën to Serge Gainsbourg. Not far from the southeastern edge of the cemetery, on place Denfert Rochereau, are the much spookier **catacombs** (Tues–Fri 2–4pm, Sat & Sun 9–11am; F27; metro Denfert-Rochereau); a series of damp underground tunnels dating from the Roman occupation, containing the skulls and bones from overflowing eighteenth-century churchyards.

Montmartre and eastern Paris

Montmartre lies in the middle of the largely petit bourgeois and working-class 18e *arrondissement*, a mixture of depressing slums towards the Gare du Nord and Gare de l'Est, and respectable, almost countrified pockets around its main focus on the hill, the **Butte Montmartre**. You can get up here by **funicular** from place Suzanne-Valadon or, for a quieter and prettier approach – though not for the unfit – climb up via place des Abbesses. The **place du Tertre** is the heart of touristic Montmartre, photogenic but totally bogus, jammed with tourists, overpriced restaurants and "artists" doing quick portraits while you wait. Close by, the nineteenth-century church of **Sacré-Coeur** (daily 7.30am–11pm; free; metro Anvers/Abbesses) is, with the Eiffel Tower, one of the classics of the Paris skyline, although the best thing about it is the view from the top (dome and crypt daily 9am–6/7pm; F15 each).

North of place du Tertre, the house that holds the **Musée de Montmartre** at 12 rue Cortot (Tues–Sun 11am–6pm; F25; metro Lamarck-Caulaincourt) was rented at various times by Renoir, Dufy, Suzanne Valadon and her alcoholic son Utrillo, but its exhibits are disappointing. Close by, off rue Lepic, the **Moulin de la Galette** is the only survivor of Montmartre's forty-odd windmills, immortalized by Renoir. Down the hill from here the artistic associations continue in the **Moulin Rouge** on bd de Clichy – although these days it's a mere shadow of its former self. This stretch – known as **Pigalle** – has always been a sleazy neighbourhood, the centre of the boulevard occupied by funfair sideshows while the pavements are dotted with transvestite prostitutes on the lookout. At the western end, a little way up rue Caulaincourt, the **Montmartre cemetery** (Mon–Fri 8am–5.30pm, Sat 8am–8.30pm, Sun 8am–9pm; metro Blanche) holds the graves of Zola, Stendhal, Berlioz, Degas, Offenbach and François Truffaut among others. Way north, on the other side of the bd Périphérique from the porte de Clignancourt, the **puces de St-Ouen** (Sat, Sun & Mon 7.30am–7pm; metro Porte de Clignancourt) claims to be the largest flea market in the world. Although the core of the market still deals with expensive antiques and bric-a-brac, you can find just about everything here, along the further reaches of rue Fabre and rue Lécuyer, including second-hand clothes, records, ethnic accessories and army surplus.

East of Montmartre, the **Bassin de La Villette** and the **canals** at the northeastern gate of the city were for generations the centre of a densely populated working-class district but they have recently become the subject of yet another big Paris redevelopment, whose major extravagance is the **Cité des Sciences et de l'Industrie** in the **Parc de La Villette**, built into the concrete hulk of the abandoned abattoirs on the north side of the canal de l'Ourcq (Tues–Sat 10am–6pm, Sun 10am–7pm; planetarium from 11am; F50; metro Porte de

Pantin). Three times the size of Beaubourg, this is the most astounding monument to be added to the capital in the last decade, and is worth visiting for the interior alone – all glass and stainless steel, cantilevered platforms and suspended walkways, the different levels linked by lifts and escalators around a huge central space. Its permanent exhibition, Explora, on the top two floors, is the science museum to end all science museums, covering subjects such as microbes, maths, sounds, robots, flying, energy, space, information and language. You can intervene in stories acted out on videos, changing the behaviour of the characters to engineer a different outcome; steer robots through mazes; and make music by your own movements.

South of La Villette, Paris' **eastern** districts – Belleville, Ménilmontant – are among the poorest of the city and not on most visitors' itineraries. However, the **Père-Lachaise cemetery** draws a fair number of tourists (daily 7.30am–6pm; metro Père-Lachaise), most of them heading for Jim Morrison's small, guarded grave in the east of the cemetery, and Oscar Wilde's more extravagant tomb. There are countless famous others buried here – Edith Piaf, Modigliani, Abélard and Heloïse, Sarah Bernhardt, Ingres and Corot, Delacroix and Balzac, to name only a few.

South of Père-Lachaise, the **Bois de Vincennes** is the city's other big open space, where you can spend an afternoon boating on Lac Daumesnil or feeding the ducks on Lac des Minimes on the other side of the wood (bus #112 from metro Vincennes). On the western edge, the **Musée des Arts d'Afrique et d'Océanie**, 293 av Daumesnil (Mon & Wed–Fri 10am–5.30pm, Sat & Sun 10am–6pm; F30; metro Porte-Dorée) is a rewarding museum, one of the least crowded in the city, with a gathering of pieces from the old French colonies – masks and statues, furniture, adornments and tools.

Eating

Contrary to what you might expect, **eating out** in Paris need not be an enormous extravagance. There are numerous fixed-price menus under F80 providing simple but well-cooked fare; paying a little more than this gives you the chance to try out a greater range of dishes, and once over F150 you should be getting some gourmet satisfaction. There is a wide range of ethnic restaurants, too – North and West African, Chinese, Japanese, Vietnamese, Greek and lots more, though they are not necessarily any cheaper. The number of vegetarian restaurants is on the increase, so although there's not exactly one in every street, being a veggie in Paris is now much easier than it used to be. Indian, Jewish and Italian restaurants are also a good bet for non-meat dishes. In general, the latest you can walk into a restaurant and order is about 10pm. Anyone in possession of an ISIC card is eligible to apply for tickets for the **university restaurants** run by CROUS, 39 av Georges-Bernanos, 5e. CROUS will provide a list of addresses, but tickets must be purchased from the restaurants themselves. Students at French universities can eat for F13.70, ISIC holders F23, otherwise F28.20.

Snacks, sandwiches, cakes and ice cream

Angélina, 226 rue de Rivoli, 1er. A long-established gilded cage for the well-coiffed to sip the best hot chocolate in town, plus high-quality pastries and desserts. Open 9am–7pm; closed Tues in July and Aug.

Berthillon, 31 rue St-Louis-en-l'Île, 4e. Long queues for the best ice creams and sorbets in town. Open Wed–Sun 10am–8pm.

Café de la Mosquée, 39 rue Geoffroy St Hilaire, 5e. Drink sweet mint tea and eat even sweeter cakes in this oasis of calm, popular with women. The less shrouded and very boisterous restaurant next door serves some of Paris' best couscous. Open daily 10am–10.30pm.

Café Martini, 11 rue du Pas-de-la-Mule, 4e. Italian café just down from place des Vosges; a relaxing place for a cappuccino or a generous warm Italian sandwich while listening to jazz. You can opt for takeaway and picnic on the grass of the place des Vosges.

Drugstore Élysées, 133 av des Champs-Élysées, 8e. All-day food, along with books, newspapers, tobacco, etc. Prices are reasonable and the food much better than the decor suggests. Another branch at 1 av Matignon, 8e.

Fauchon, 26 place de la Madeleine, 8e. Narrow counters at which to gobble wonderful *pâtisseries, plats du jour* and sandwiches – at a price.

Fleur de Lotus, 2 rue du Roi-de-Sicile, 4e. Cheap Vietnamese dishes, heated up while you wait – to take away or eat on the premises.

Lina's Sandwiches, 50 rue Étienne-Marcel, 2e. A spacious, stylish place for your designer-shopping break.

Le Loir dans la Théière (The Dormouse in the Teapot), 3 rue des Rosiers, 4e. This peaceful retreat has a laid-back, quirky atmosphere with leather armchairs, big tables and naive paintings on the walls. Sunday brunch, superb midday *tartes* (from F48) and omelettes, fruit teas of every description and cakes served all day.

Sacha Finkelsztajn, 27 rue des Rosiers, 4e. Gorgeous East European breads, cakes, gefilte fish, blinis and borscht to take away. Closed Mon, Tues & all of August.

La Samaritaine, 19 rue de la Monnaie, 1e. Wonderful views over Paris – the Pont Neuf, la Monnaie and the Conciergerie – from the inexpensive self-service rooftop café of this Art Deco department store.

La Tartine, 24 rue de Rivoli, 4e. A good selection of affordable wines, plus excellent cheese and snacks. Closed Tues & Aug.

Restaurants and brasseries

Al-Mina, 9 rue du Nil, 2e. Tasty Middle Eastern fare from this excellent Lebanese restaurant. Menus from F60.

Le Baptiste, 11 rue des Boulangers, 5e. Noisy, friendly and full of students in a cosy stone and wood interior. Tucked away in a narrow street rising up from M° Jussieu. Bistro menu from F71, restaurant menu from F128. Closed Sat lunch & Sun.

Bistro de la Sorbonne, 4 rue Toullier, 5e. Help-yourself starters and salads, good ices and *crêpes flambées*. Couscous is a speciality. Menus range from F69–140. Large portions. Closed Sun.

Café Mouffetard, 116 rue Mouffetard, 5e. Traditional faded Parisian café/brasserie. Popular with locals for its good, cheap fare and divine desserts, large tables, nostalgic feel and views of the lively local market.

Chardenoux, 1 rue Jules-Vallès, 11e. An authentic oldie, with engraved mirrors dating back to 1900, that still serves solid meaty fare at moderate prices.

Chartier, 7 rue du Faubourg-Montmartre, 9e. Good cheap food served at a run in an original and quite splendid turn-of-the-century soup kitchen. Closes 10pm. Menus under F100, but expect to queue.

La Chaumière, 46 av Secrétan, 19e. A superb gourmet restaurant at out-of-town prices. If you're visiting Parc Buttes Chaumont and have the urge to splurge, this is the place to head for.

Chez Justine, 96 rue Oberkampf, 11e. Well recommended for traditional cooking at very reasonable prices. F60 for a main course. Closed Aug.

Le Commerce, 51 rue du Commerce, 15e. Long-established, serving nourishing, cheap food. Menus from F85.

Drouot, 103 rue de Richelieu, 2e. Good, cheap food, served at a frantic pace, in an Art Nouveau setting.

Flo, 7 cours des Petites-Écuries, 10e. Handsome old-time brasserie, where you eat elbow-to-elbow at long tables. Excellent food and thoroughly enjoyable atmosphere. Menus F120–190.

Le Fouta Djalon, 27 bd Saint Martin, 3e. A crowded, family-run African restaurant near République and Strasbourg St Denis metros. There's often a hefty delay between ordering and eating but the massive, spicy African specialities are well worth the wait.

Goldenburg's, 7 rue des Rosiers, 4e. The best-known Jewish restaurant in the capital; its borscht, blinis, strudels and other central European dishes are a treat. *Plat du jour* F80.

Lao Thai, 128 rue de Tolbiac, 13e. Spacious, glass-fronted restaurant on a busy corner. Serves spicy Thai and Laotian food at moderate prices.

L'Incroyable, 26 rue de Richelieu, 1er. Hidden in a tiny passage, this diminutive restaurant serves decent and cheap meals.

L'Oustal Dellac, 80 bd Richard-Lenoir, 11e. A leftover from the pre-Opéra days when this was a *quartier populaire*. Simple and satisfying fare, though it closes at 9pm. Menus from F64.

Orestias, 4 rue Grégoire-de-Tours, 6e. A mixture of Greek and French cuisine. Good helpings, very cheap but can get very crowded as a result.

Perraudin, 157 rue St-Jacques, 5e. Well-known, traditional bistro with menus from about F60 at lunchtime, and F150 in the evening.

Le Petit Mabillon, 6 rue Mabillon, 6e. Small Italian restaurant, popular for good food at reasonable prices. Menu from F77.

Le Petit Prince, 12 rue Lanneau, 5e. Good food in a restaurant full of Latin Quarter charm in one of the *quartier's* oldest lanes. Menus start at around F130.

Le Petit Saint-Benoît, 4 rue St-Benoît, 6e. A simple, genuine and very appealing local for the neighbourhood's chattering classes. Solid traditional fare.

La Petite Légume, 36 rue des Boulangers, 5e. Tiny homely vegetarian café with a mezzanine level. Downstairs it feels like you're in someone's kitchen. Serious macrobiotic and organic-only approach, though a bit of fish is served. Main dishes for around F58. Closed Sun.

Port de Pidjiguiti, 28 rue Etex, 18e. Pleasant atmosphere and excellent food. Run by a village in Guinea-Bissau, whose inhabitants take turns in staffing the restaurant; the proceeds go to the village. Menus from F100.

Au Rendez-vous des Camioneurs, 34 rue des Plantes, 14e. No lorry drivers any more, but good food. Small and popular, menu at F72 with a quart of wine for under F15. Closed at weekends & during Aug.

Restaurant des Beaux-Arts, 11 rue Bonaparte, 6e. The traditional hangout of the art students from across the way. The choice is wide, portions generous and the queues long. Menu at F79.

Les Temp des Cérises, 18–20 rue de la Butte-aux-Cailles, 13e. A well-established workers' co-op with elbow-to-elbow seating and menus under F120.

Thoumieux, 79 rue St-Dominique, 7e. Large and popular establishment in this rather smart district, with menus starting at F82.

La Vallée de Bambou, 35 rue Gay-Lussac, 5e. You usually have to wait in line for this popular Chinese restaurant. The cheapest menu is excellent value.

Le Vaudeville, 29 rue Vivienne, 2e. A lively late-night brasserie – where it's often necessary to queue – with good food and an attractive marble-and-mosaic interior. Menu at F132.

Drinking

Most of Paris' main squares and boulevards have **cafés** spreading out onto the pavements and, although these are usually the priciest places to drink, it can be worth paying the earth for a coffee for the chance to observe the street life. Using the terrace or seating inside the café means you will pay around double the price you would pay at the bar. If you find a bar with stools, you can get the best of both worlds. The Left Bank harbours some of the city's best-known and longest-established cafés on boulevards Montparnasse and St-Germain, while the presence of the university means there are plenty of places to drink around place de la Sorbonne and rue Soufflot. The Bastille is now livelier than ever as the new Opéra and rocketing property values bring headlong development, as is Les Halles – though the latter's trade is principally among out-of-towners up for the bright lights. The Marais offers small crowded watering holes, and many gay bars; and there are many bars in Montmartre, while Memilmontant and Belleville are less obvious but popular drinking haunts. Revitalized, ironically, by the English, you'll also find **wine bars**, the best of which are long-established places serving food as well as decent wine by the glass – as well as establishments more geared to **beer**, most inspired by Belgian or British watering holes.

Académie de la Bière, 88 bd Port-Royal, 5e. Large selection of beers from around the world, with a focus on Belgian varieties. Also food – good mussels and fries, Belgian cheeses and charcuterie.

Bar La Fontaine, 1 rue de Charonne, 11e. Perfect corner spot for watching a slice of life from the pavement tables. An easygoing place where the clientele ranges from old blokes in berets to a casual but hip twenty-something crowd, with a soundtrack of funk and soul. Open until 2am Fri & Sat, rest of week until 1am or later.

Le Baron Rouge, 1 rue Théophile-Roussel, 12e. A crowded and popular bar, serving cheese, *charcuterie* and wines to taste at reasonable prices.

Café Oz, 184 rue St-Jacques, 5e. Australian-run bar, complete with convincing Aboriginal cave paintings and more kitsch souvenirs from down-under. It's considered a fun night out by Parisians, not just tourists. Staff keep the jokes running and there's even Aussie meat pies to tuck in to, plus a big range of Australian beers and wines. Daily 4pm–2am.

Le Depanneur, 27 rue Fontaine, 9e. Popular all-night bar on a busy corner just down from Place Blanche and the Moulin Rouge.

Les Deux Magots, 170 bd St-Germain, 6e. Former haunt of Sartre and numerous famous others from the postwar years. Touristy now, with a terrace often besieged by buskers. Open until 2am, closed one week in Jan.

Au Général Lafayette, 52 rue Lafayette, 9e. Beer-drinking hangout with a dozen draughts, including Guinness, and many more bottled. Mixed clientele and a pleasant, quiet feel.

La Gueuze, 19 rue Soufflot, 5e. Comfy surroundings, decent food and numerous Belgian bottles and several draughts, including cherry *kriek*.

Café de l'Industrie, corner of rue Sedaine and rue St-Sabin, 11e. Rugs on the floor around solid old wooden tables, paintings and miscellaneous objects on the walls, and a young, unpretentious crowd. Closed Sat.

Café de la Mairie, 8 place St Sulpice, 6e. Famous yet unpretentious café which holds an enviable position overlooking St Sulpice.

La Fresque, 100 rue Rambuteau, 1er. Nicely dingy place, formerly a snail merchant's hall, and still retaining the original decor. Closed Sun lunch.

L'Oiseau Bariolé, 16 rue Ste-Croix-de-la-Bretonnerie, 4e. Small and friendly, surreal paintings on glass, and full of Americans. *Plats du jour*, omelettes and Breton cider. The place where the Marais drinkers inevitably end up as it's open until dawn.

Le Piano Vache, 8 rue Laplace off rue de la Montagne-Ste-Geneviève, 5e. Long-established student bar with canned music and relaxed atmosphere.

Polly Magoo, 11 rue St-Jacques, 5e. A scruffy all-night bar frequented by chess addicts.

Pub Saint-Germain des Prés, 17 rue de l'Ancienne-Comédie, 6e. Hundreds of bottled beers and 26 on draught. Spread over 5 floors, it's huge – and crowded. Hot food at mealtimes, otherwise cold snacks. Open 24hr.

Le Rubis, 10 rue du Marché-St-Honoré, 1er. One of the oldest wine bars in Paris, with a reputation for having among the best wines, plus excellent snacks and *plats du jour.*

Le Sancerre, 35 rue des Abbesses, 18e. The self-conscious hub of the butte Montmartre. Black leather jacket optional. Playing a high-volume rock soundtrack, this place is packed, pulsating and great for people-watching.

Le Select, 99 bd du Montparnasse, 6e. The least spoilt of the swanky Montparnasse cafés, still thriving since its 1920s heyday.

Tigh Johnny's, 55 rue Montmartre, 2e. A mostly Irish clientele at this bar that serves a reasonably priced Guinness. Has monthly poetry readings and sometimes Celtic bands make an appearance.

Le Violon Dingue, 46 rue de la Montagne-Ste-Geneviève, 5e. A long, dark student pub, noisy and friendly. Happy hour 8pm–10pm; closed Sun & Mon.

Web Bar, 32 rue de Picardie, 3e. Paris' Internet café is very Marais-chic, and is more a multimedia centre with films and videos also on the menu, as well as less hi-tech storytelling and chess. Mon–Sat 8.30am–2am, Sun noon–midnight.

Nightlife

Nightlife in Paris is as lively and diverse as you would expect. Its reputation for **live music** has recovered over the last decade with the growth in popularity of world music – for which Paris is a centre second to none – and there is excellent jazz in numerous St-Germain and Les Halles clubs. The tradition of *chansons* – epitomized by Edith Piaf and developed to its greatest heights by Leo Ferré, Georges Brassens and Jacques Brel – endures too, and classical music and opera takes up twice the space of "jazz-pop-folk-rock" in the listings magazines. If you're just looking for a place to dance, **clubs** come and go at as exhausting a rate as in any other large city, but there are one or two long-established places that won't let you down; most clubs open around 11pm, some stay open until sunrise. For listings of **what's on** in the city, there are two weekly guides, *Pariscope* and *L'Officiel des Spectacles*, which come out on Wednesdays; *Pariscope* (F3) is the handiest with a small *Time Out* section in English. The best places to get **tickets** for concerts are FNAC, main branch at Forum des Halles, 1–5 rue Pierre-Lescot, level 3, and the Virgin Megastore, 56–60 av des Champs-Élysées.

Live music

Le Bataclan, 50 bd Voltaire, 11e (bookings ☎01.43.14.35.35). One of the best larger rock venues.

Le Caveau de la Bolée, 25 rue de l'Hirondelle, 6e. Ancient place where Parisian luminaries used to go to hear their favourite singers. Still mainly *chansons* with occasional jazz.

La Cigale, 120 bd de Rochechouart, 18e. Old-fashioned theatre with an eclectic programme of rock. Long a fixture on the Pigalle scene.

Le Divan du Monde, 75 rue des Martyrs, 18e. A youthful venue in a café whose regulars included Toulouse-Lautrec. An eclectic and exciting programming policy.

L'Escale, 15 rue Monsieur-le-Prince, 6e. Hugely popular Latin American venue.

L'Eustache, 37 rue Berger, 1er. Cheap beer and very good jazz by local musicians in this young and friendly Les Halles café. Music from 10pm.

La **Guinguette Pirate**, quai de la Gare, 13e. Beautiful Chinese barge, moored alongside the quay in front of the Bibliothèque Nationale, hosting funk, reggae, rock and folk concerts.

New Morning, 7–9 rue des Petites-Ecuries, 10e. Famed jazz venue where blues, latin and world music now also hold sway.

Le Petit Journal, 71 bd St-Michel, 5e. A small, smoky bar, long frequented by Left Bank student types, with good, mainly French, traditional and mainstream jazz. Music starts 10pm.

Rex Club, 5 bd Poissonnière, 9e. Live music early on and disco from 11pm. House/techno, with a style-conscious crowd, on Thurs & Fri. Entrance F60. Open until 6am.

Satellit' Café, 44 rue de la Folie-Méricourt, 11e. Multicultural acoustic evenings – anything from swing to folk, Brazilian to Balkan. Entry is reasonable (F40–50) when bands are playing.

Utopia, 79 rue de l'Ouest, 14e. Good French blues singers interspersed with jazz and blues tapes.

Clubs and discos

Les Bains, 7 rue du Bourg-l'Abbé, 3e. A former Turkish bath house, this is currently one of the hippest clubs in Paris playing house, rap and funk and the odd rock band. If you can get past the door policy and afford the F100 entry, the spectacle of punters plunging into the pool by the dance floor awaits. Daily 11.30pm–6am.

Balajo, 9 rue de Lappe, 11e. Old-style music hall or *bal musette* with extravagant 1930s decor and music ranging from mazurkas and tangos to slurpy *chansons*. Entry around F100. Closed Aug.

Chapelle des Lombards, 19 rue de Lappe, 11e. Erstwhile *bal musette* that still plays the occasional waltz and tango but far more often salsa, reggae, rai and the blues. Entry F100–120 with a drink.

La Java, 105 rue du Faubourg-du-Temple, 11e. Live Latin bands Thurs–Sat followed by DJs playing Latin-American sounds. Older, energetic and friendly crowd.

La Locomotive, 90 bd de Clichy, 18e. Enormous hi-tech nightclub next to the legendary *Moulin Rouge* with two crowded dance floors and a very young crowd. Open until 6am.

Le Queen, 102 av des Champs-Élysées, 8e. Mainly gay club with women welcome except Thurs. Drag queens and model types mostly. "Disco inferno" on Mon, otherwise mainly house. Nightly 11pm–dawn.

Opera, ballet, classical and contemporary music

Paris is a stimulating environment for **classical music**, both established and contemporary. The **Cité de la Musique** project at La Villette has given Paris two new, major concert venues: the **Conservatoire**, the national music academy, av Jean-Jaurès (☎01.40.40.45.45), and, next door at no. 209, the **Salle des Concerts** (☎01.44.84.44.84) where ancient music, contemporary works, jazz, *chansons* and music from around the world are featured. Otherwise, the top **auditorium** is the **Salle Pleyel**, 252 rue du Faubourg-St-Honoré, 8e (☎01.45.61.06.30), home to the Orchestre de Paris, and there are also regular concerts at the **Théâtre des Champs-Élysées**, 15 av Montaigne, 8e (☎01.49.52.50.50) – home of the Orchestre National de France, and the **Théâtre Musical de Paris**, 1 place du Châtelet, 1er (☎01.40.28.28.40).

The ultra-modern Bastille hall, known as **Opéra-Bastille**, is the main place for **opera** (☎08.36.69.78.68). Tickets cost anything from F60 right up to F610, with the cheapest seats only available to personal callers; unfilled seats are sold at discount to students five minutes before the curtain goes up. The original opera house, now known as **Opéra-Garnier** or Palais Garnier (☎08.36.69.78.68), still has some small-scale operas, but its main feature now is **ballet** as home to the Ballet de l'Opéra National de Paris. Seats range from F30 to F380, and even if the cheapest provide a very restricted view, the splendid interior certainly makes for a memorable visit.

Film

There are over 350 **films** showing in Paris in any one week. Tickets cost around F44; most cinemas have lower rates on Monday, and reductions for students Monday to Thursday. Almost all of the huge selection of foreign films will be shown at some cinemas in the original – *vo* in the listings (as opposed to *vf*, which means it's dubbed into French). For the committed film freak, there are the small *cinémathèques*, which show a choice of over fifty movies a week; tickets are only F28. The Vidéothèque de Paris in the Forum des Halles, 2 Grande Gallerie, Porte Eustache, is an excellent-value venue for the bizarre or obscure on celluloid;

their repertoires are always based around a Parisian theme. There is also the Géode, the mirrored globe at La Villette, which, although it shows views of outer space, great cities, landscapes, etc, is mightily impressive. It has several screenings a day; tickets cost F57, or F92 as a combined ticket with Cité des Sciences. Also, look out for the following cinemas: Max Linder, 24 bd Poissonière, and Pathé Wepler, 140 bd de Clichy.

Gay Paris

Paris has a well-established **gay scene** concentrated in the Halles, Marais and Bastille areas, and there are numerous gay organizations. For **information** visit the main gay and lesbian bookshop, Les Mots à la Bouche, 6 rue Ste-Croix-de-la-Bretonnerie, 4e; or the Centre Gai et Lesbien, 3 rue Keller, 11e (daily 2–8pm; ☎01.43.57.21.47) – a handy drop-in information centre with its own café. They also produce a free guide map to gay Paris and a monthly publication, *Le 3 Keller*.

Bars and clubs

Bar Hôtel Central, 33 rue Vieille-du-Temple, 4e. Quiet bar for men, catering mainly to over-thirties. Open Thurs & Fri from 4pm, Sat & Sun from 2pm.

Le New Monocle, 60 bd Edgar-Quinet, 14e. Lesbian club with cabaret; some men also allowed in.

Le Piano Zinc, 49 rue des Blancs-Manteaux, 4e. A happy riot of songs, music-hall acts and dance, after 10pm nightly. One of the few venues patronized by both lesbians and gays. Closed Mon.

The Queen, 102 av des Champs-Élysées, 8e. Very trendy mainstream gay club, with a strict door policy. It's also one of the hippest spots in town for heterosexuals – if they can get in. Mainly house music with big-name guest DJs.

Le Quetzal, 10 rue de la Verrerie, 4e. A fashionable gay bar hosting a well-toned and stylish clientele, with space for dancing. Daily until 3am.

Les Scandaleuses, 8 rue des Ecouffes, 4e. Trendy and lively women-only bar in the Marais.

Le Squed, 35 rue Ste-Croix-de-la-Bretonnerie, 4e. Bar with pink furniture and a thumping beat; very popular with young foreigners.

Listings

Airlines Air France, 119 av des Champs-Élysées, 8e (information and reservations ☎08.02.80.28.02); British Airways, 12 rue de Castiglione, 1er (☎08.02.80.29.02).

Airport information Roissy-Charles de Gaulle (☎01.48.62.22.80); Orly (☎01.49.75.15.15).

Bike rental Paris Vélo, 2 rue du Fer-à-Moulin, 5e (☎01.43.37.59.22); Paris à Vélo C'est Sympa, 37 bd Bourdon, 4e (☎01.48.87.60.01).

Books English-language books from Shakespeare & Co, 37 rue de la Bûcherie, 5e; WH Smith, 248 rue de Rivoli, 1er; Village Voice Bookshop, 6 rue Princesse, 6e.

Car rental Dergi et Cie, 133 rue de Paris, 5e (☎01.43.68.55.55); Europcar, 145 av de Malakoff, 16e (☎01.45.00.08.06); Locabest, 104 bd de Magenta, 10e (☎01.44.72.08.05); Rent a Car, 79 rue de Bercy, 12e (☎01.43.45.98.99).

Embassies Australia, 4 rue Jean-Rey, 15e (☎01.40.59.33.00); Britain, 35 rue Faubourg-St-Honoré, 8e (☎01.44.51.31.00); Canada, 35 av Montaigne, 8e (☎01.44.43.29.00); Ireland, 4 rue Rude, 16e (☎01.44.17.67.00); New Zealand, 7 rue Léonard-de-Vinci, 16e (☎01.45.00.24.11); USA, rue St-Florentin, 1er (☎01.43.12.22.22).

Exchange Change money in banks if possible. The Crédit Commercial de France, 103 av des Champs-Élysées, 8e, is open Sat until 8pm. Otherwise, there are counters at the main train stations (daily 8am–9pm); and a 24-hour service at 150 av des Champs-Élysées, 8e.

Hospital SOS-Médecins (☎01.47.07.77.77 or 01.43.37.77.77) for 24hr medical help.

Left luggage Lockers at all train stations and *consignes* for bigger items.

Pharmacies Dérhy, 84 av des Champs-Élysées, 8e (☎01.45.62.02.41) has a 24hr service.

Police The main *Préfecture* is at 7 bd du Palais, 4e (☎01.42.60.33.22); ☎17 for emergencies.

Post office Main office at 52 rue du Louvre, 1er (daily 8am–7pm). Poste Restante, 52 rue du Louvre, 75001 Paris; to avoid confusion your surname should be in capitals and underlined.

Telephones The main post office is open 24hr for phone calls. Phonecards are available at *tabacs*.

Train information ☎08.36.35.35.35; Eurostar ☎08.36.35.35.39.
Travel agents USIT Voyages, 6 rue de Vaugirard, 6e (☎01.42.34.56.90); Nouvelles Frontières, 66 bd St-Michel, 6e (☎01.41.41.58.58). CTS Voyages, 20 rue des Carmes, 5e (☎01.43.25.00.76).

Around Paris

Like most Parisians, you may find there's enough in Paris to keep you from ever thinking about the world beyond. However, like any large city, Paris can get claustrophobic, and if it does there are one or two places in the countryside around that are worth making the trip out for. The most visited of these is undoubtedly **Versailles**, the most hyped currently **Disneyland Paris**, and the most rewarding is without question the cathedral at **Chartres**.

Versailles

The **Palace of Versailles** (Tues–Sun 9am–5.30/6.30pm; F45, gardens F21 on Sun otherwise free) is one of the three most visited monuments in France. It is not a beautiful building by any means, its decor a grotesque homage to two of the greatest of all self-propagandists, Louis XIV (the "Sun King") and Napoleon, and it's more impressive for its size than anything else, which, by any standards, is incredible. The most amazing room is perhaps the Hall of Mirrors, although the mirrors are not the originals. It is, more importantly, the room in which the Treaty of Versailles was signed, so bringing World War I to an end. You can also visit the state apartments of the king and queen, and the royal chapel, a grand structure that ranks among France's finest Baroque creations. Outside, the park is something of a relief, although it's inevitably a very ordered affair. You could wander for hours through its vast extent – the scenery gets better the further you go from the palace, and there are even informal groups of trees near the lesser outcrops of royal mania, the **Grand** and **Petit Trianons** (summer Tues–Sun 10am–6.30pm; winter Tues–Fri 10am–12.30pm & 2–5.30pm, Sat & Sun 10am–5.30pm; F25 and 15 respectively, F30 for both). Beyond is **Le Hameau** (the hamlet); several cute thatched cottages, a mill and a dairy set around a lake where Marie-Antoinette played at being a shepherdess.

To **get to Versailles**, take RER ligne C5 to Versailles-Rive Gauche (30min). You get maps of the park from the **tourist office** on rue des Réservoirs to the right of the palace.

Chartres

About 35km beyond Versailles, an hour by train from Paris-Montparnasse, **CHARTRES** is a small and relatively undistinguished town. However, its **Cathédrale Notre-Dame** (Mon–Sat 7.30am–7.15pm, Sun 8.30am–7.15pm) is one of the finest examples of Gothic architecture in Europe, and, built between 1194 and 1260, perhaps the quickest ever to be constructed. Its size and hilltop position are awe-inspiring, and there are more than enough visible wonders to enthral: the geometry of the building, unique in being almost unaltered since its consecration; the Renaissance choir screen and the hosts of sculpted figures above each transept door; and the shining symmetries of the stained glass, 130 windows in all, virtually all of which are original, dating from the twelfth and thirteenth centuries. It is the light coming through the rose windows which is one of the wonders of Chartres. There's also a treasury, and it's possible to climb the north tower (times vary, check in the cathedral; F25).

Though the cathedral is why you come here, Chartres town is not entirely without appeal, with a small old quarter of mazey streets and a picturesque district of bridges and old houses down by the river Eure. The **Musée des Beaux-Arts** in the former episcopal palace just north of the cathedral (Mon & Wed–Sat 10am–noon & 2–5/6pm, Sun 2–5/6pm; F10) has some beautiful tapestries, a room full of Vlaminck paintings, and Zurbarán's *St Lucy*, as well as good temporary exhibitions. The **tourist office** is in front of the cathedral, at place de la Cathédrale, and can supply free maps and help with rooms if you want to stay (Mon–Sat 9/10am–6/7pm; Sun 9.30/10am–4.30/5.30pm; winter closed daily 1–2pm for lunch). Rue du Cygne is a good place to look for **restaurants** or, if you want to splash out, have a meal at *Henri IV*, 31 rue Soleil-d'Or, which has one of the best selections of wines in France.

Disneyland Paris

Around 32km east of Paris, **Disneyland Paris** is a 5000-acre slice of the USA grafted onto a bleak tract of the Bassin Parisien. The ploy was to make the Disney empire more accessible to Europeans, but it seems that many Europeans are either not interested or would rather opt for the more reliable weather and better rides of Florida's Disneyworld, which is not much more expensive a proposition. But for all the jokes about "Euro-dismal" and "Disneybland", the theatricality and professionalism of the place elevate it head and shoulders above any other theme park.

The **Magic Kingdom** is divided into four "lands" radiating out from Main Street USA – Fantasyland, Frontierland, Discoveryland and Adventureland. **Fantasyland** appeals to the youngest kids (Sleeping Beauty's Castle, Peter Pan's Flight, Alice in Wonderland's Maze); **Adventureland** boasts the most outlandish sets and two of the best rides (Pirates of the Caribbean and Indiana Jones and the Temple of Doom); **Frontierland** has the *Psycho*-inspired Phantom Manor and the roller coaster Big Thunder Mountain; and **Discoveryland**, the hi-tech 3-D Michael Jackson film and a 360° Parisian exposé in Le Visionarium. The grand **parade** sallies down Main Street USA at 3pm sharp every day, and Snow White, Dumbo, Pinocchio, Mickey et al strut their stuff with unfoundering joviality. Night-time Electrical Parades and **firework displays** take place several times a week. The latest big-thrills highlight is Space Mountain.

The six themed Disney **hotels** may be out of many people's price range, the cheapest room off-season being F300 a night (2 adults, 2 children), rising to over F2500 peak season for a room in the *Disneyland Hotel* inside the Magic Kingdom on Main Street. The complexes are generally a mixed bag of hideous eyesores and over-ambitious kitsch, but they do offer an array of eating venues, as well as saunas, jacuzzis, gyms, golf, video games and even a children's theatre.

To reach **Disneyland** from Paris, take *RER ligne A* to Marne-la-Vallée Chessy/Disneyland – about a forty-minute journey from Gare de Lyon (F76 return). At the time of writing, peak season (April–Oct) **admission** charges are: one-day pass F200 (under-11s F155), two-day pass F385 (F300), three-day pass F545 (F420). Under 3s free. All credit cards welcome. Park **opening hours** are subject to change (mid-June to early Sept daily 9am–8/11pm; early Sept to end Oct Mon–Fri 10am–6pm, Sat & Sun 9am–8pm).

THE NORTH

When conjuring up exotic holiday locations, **northern France** is unlikely to get a mention, including as it does some of the most industrial and densely populated parts of the country. However, it is possible that you'll both arrive and leave France via this region, and there are curiosities within easy reach of the Channel ports – of which **Boulogne** is the nicest – and one of France's finest cathedrals at **Amiens**. Further south, the *maisons* and vineyards of the **Champagne** region are the main draw, for which the best bases are **Épernay** and **Reims**, the latter with another fine cathedral. Most of the champagne houses offer free visits and tastings, although beyond them the region is not the most enthralling.

Calais

CALAIS is less than 40km from England – the Channel's narrowest crossing – and is the busiest French passenger port. The ferry business dominates the town, for there's not much else here. In the last war the British destroyed Calais to impede its use as a port, fearing a German invasion. Seized by Edward III after the battle of Crécy in 1346, it remained English until 1558, and the association has been maintained across the centuries. Today, nine million British travellers per year pass through, in addition to one million day-trippers.

The town divides into two: **Calais-Nord**, the old town rebuilt after the war and, separated from it by canals, **Calais-Sud**. Once you've checked out the shopping on the central place d'Armes and rue Royale, Calais-Nord's charms wear thin. Calais-Sud is scarcely more significant, its focus the extravagant **Hôtel de Ville**, on the main shopping street of bd Jacquard, outside which Rodin's famous bronze **Burghers of Calais** records the self-sacrifice of these local dignitaries who offered their lives to assuage the English conqueror. Across the street in the **Parc St-Pierre**, the **Musée de la Guerre** (Feb–Nov Mon & Wed–Sun 10/11am–5/6pm; F15), installed in a former German blockhouse, records the town's wartime travails.

There is a **free bus service** during the day from the **ferry dock** at Calais-Maritime station to place d'Armes and the central Calais-Ville station in Calais-Sud; at night take a taxi, which will cost about F50. The **tourist office** is at 12 bd Clemenceau (Mon–Sat 9am–7pm, Sun 10am–1pm) and has an accommodation service, for which there is a small charge. There is a **youth hostel** near the seafront on av de Tassigny (☎03.21.34.70.20; ②), and a **camping municipal** at 26 av Poincaré, beyond the end of rue Royale. Affordable **hotels** include the *Bristol*, 13 rue du Duc-de-Guise, off rue Royale (☎03.21.34.53.24; ③), and the seafront *Albert 1er*, 51–53 rue de la Mer (☎03.21.34.36.08; ④). The place d'Armes area is good for **restaurants**. *Le Touquet's*, 57 rue Royale, and the slightly more expensive *Le Channel* at 3 bd de la Résistance, overlooking the yacht basin, are both recommended. Also worth a try is *Café de Paris*, 72 rue Royale, popular with both tourists and locals.

Boulogne

BOULOGNE is the one northern Channel port that might tempt you to stay. Its **Ville Basse**, centring on place Dalton, is home to some of the best *charcuteries* and *pâtisseries* in the north, as well as an impressive array of fish restaurants and, rising above, the **Ville Haute** is one of the gems of the northeast coast, flanked by grassy ramparts that give impressive views over the town and port. Inside the walls, the **Basilique Notre-Dame** is something of an oddity, raised in the nineteenth century without any architectural knowledge or advice by the town's vicar. Its crypt (Tues–Sun 2–5pm; F10) has frescoed remains of the previous Romanesque building and relics of a Roman temple to Diana, while the main part of the church has a curious statue of the Virgin and Child on a boat-chariot, drawn here on its own wheels from Lourdes.

Ferries dock within a few minutes' walk of the town centre. Arriving by **hovercraft**, a little further out, you'll be met by a free shuttle bus. The **tourist office** (summer Mon–Sat 9am–7pm, Sun 10am–1pm & 2–5pm; winter Mon–Sat 9am–6pm), over the bridge as you leave the ferry terminal, can advise on availability of rooms, which in summer fill early. Your best bet is probably the friendly **youth hostel** in front of the train station on place Rouget de l'Isle (☎03.21.99.15.30; ②). Most of the cheap **hotels** enclose the port area and include the *Hamiot*, 1 rue Faidherbe (☎03.21.31.44.20; ③), and *Hôtel des Arts*, 102 bd Gambetta (☎03.21.31.53.31; ③). For **eating**, there are dozens of possibilities around place Dalton and the cathedral, but be selective. The brasserie *Chez Jules*, on the square, is always a good bet and serves food all day. Opposite the cathedral on rue de Lille, *Estaminet du Château* offers inexpensive menus in a pleasant setting. The *Hamiot* restaurant is a decent alternative, and *La Houblonnière* on rue Monsigny has a vast international selection of brews to wash down its *plats du jour*.

Lille

By far the largest city in these northern regions, **LILLE** is the very symbol of French industry and working-class politics. There is some of the worst poverty and racial conflict here, and a crime rate rivalled only in Paris and Marseille. There is regionalism – the Lillois sprinkle their speech with a French-Flemish patois and, to an extent, assert a Flemish identity. But there is also classic French affluence here – the city has a lovely central heart, vibrant and prosperous, and it's a place that takes its culture and its restaurants very seriously. Though not a prime destination, if you're travelling through this region it's at least worth a night.

The busy **Grand Place** is the point to make for (also known as place du Général de Gaulle, who was born here in 1890). The **Hospice Comtesse**, roughly opposite the cathedral on rue de la Monnaie, is perhaps the main thing to see, a twelfth-century hospital that served as such right through to World War II. Its old ward, the Salle des Malades, can be visited (Mon, Wed–Sun 10am–12.30pm & 2–6pm; F15), where you'll see a selection of Dutch, Flemish and French paintings on loan from the Musée des Beaux-Arts. South of the old centre lies the modern place Rihour, south of which the stylish rue de Béthune leads into café-lined **place Béthune**, and beyond to bd de la Liberté and the city's **Musée des Beaux-Arts** on place de la République.

Arriving at the **train station**, you're only a few minutes' walk from Vieux Lille. The town **tourist office** is in the old Palais Rihour on place Rihour (Mon 1–6pm, Tues–Sat 10am–6pm, Sun 10am–noon & 2–5pm). Most of the inexpensive **hotels** are gathered around the train station. The *Hôtel des Voyageurs*, right opposite (☎03.20.06.43.14; ②), is basic but reasonable, or try the plusher *Hôtel de France,* 10 rue de Béthune (☎03.20.57.14.78; ③), in the centre. A good fall-back is the **youth hostel** near the Hôtel de Ville at 12 rue Malpart (☎03.20.57.08.94; ②). The nearest **campsite** is *Les Ramiers*, 10km north of the centre in Bondues (☎03.20.23.13.42). The main area for **restaurants** is around place Rihour and place Béthune. For mussels – a local speciality – the brasseries around the station are as good as any in town. *La Galetière*, 4 place Louise-de-Bettignies, is a nice creperie, *Brasserie Jean*, on place du Théâtre, a decent all-nighter. For **drinking**, Lille students with money hang around the groovy *Le Basse*, 57 rue Basse, or *L'Imaginaire*, next to *Hôtel Treille* in place Louis-de-Bettignies.

Amiens

Few travellers would stop at **AMIENS** unless they were visiting its Cathedral. Badly scarred during both world wars, it is not an immediately likeable place.

The **Cathédrale Notre-Dame** (Easter to Oct 8.30am–7pm; Nov to Easter 8.30am–noon & 2–5pm; free) provides the city's focus as the largest Gothic building in France. Begun in 1220 it was virtually complete by the end of the century. The interior is a light, calm space, its only real embellishments the sixteenth-century choir stalls (guided tours only), and the sculpted panels depicting the life of St Firmin, Amiens' first bishop, on the right-hand side of the choir screen. Close by the cathedral, the seventeenth-century **Musée de Hôtel de Berny** on rue Victor Hugo (Thurs–Sun 2–6pm; F10) has displays of local history collections, while another mansion five minutes' walk south of central place Gambetta houses the **Musée de Picardie** (Tues–Sun 10am–12.30pm & 2–6pm; F20), whose star exhibit is a collection of rare sixteenth-century paintings on wood, some in their original frames, carved by the same craftsmen who worked the choir stalls. You might also be interested in visiting the **Maison de Jules Verne**, devoted to the French writer who spent most of his life in this city, in his house at 2 rue Charles Dubois (Mon–Fri 9am–noon & 2–6pm, Sat 2–6pm; F15).

Amiens' **train station** is on place Alphonse Fiquet, five minutes from the cathedral. The **tourist office** is between the two, at 6 bis de Dusevel (summer daily 9am–6.30pm; winter Mon–Sat 9am–6.30pm, Sun 9am–5pm). The most affordable places to stay are the central hotels: *Hôtel Spatial*, 15 rue Alexandre-Fatton (☎03.22.91.53.23; ③) and *Victor Hugo*, 2 rue de l'Oratoire (☎03.22.91.57.91; ③). Good places to **eat** include a number of cheap brasseries in front of the station and around place Gambetta of which *Au Bureau*, 15 place de l'Hôtel de Ville, is perhaps the best.

Épernay

Though it's a pleasant enough town, the only real reason for coming to **ÉPERNAY** is to visit the **champagne** houses, whose free tours could keep you fully occupied for a couple of days. The largest and probably most famous is **Moët et Chandon** at 18 av de Champagne (summer daily 9.30–11.45am & 2–4.45pm; winter closed Sat & Sun; tour including tasting F25 Mon–Fri, F30 Sat & Sun) who own Mercier, Ruinart and a variety of other concerns. The cellars are adorned with mementoes of Napoleon, a good friend of the original M. Moët, and the vintage is named after the monastic hero of champagne history, Dom Pérignon. Of the other *maison* visits, the most rewarding are Mercier up the road at no. 70 (Mon–Sat 9.30–11.30am

& 2–4.30pm, Sun until 5.30pm; Dec–Feb closed Tues & Wed; F25 including tasting), and Castellane, over by the station at 57 rue de Verdun (May–Oct daily 10am–noon & 2–6pm). Mercier's glamour relic is a giant barrel that held 200,000 bottles, taken to the Paris Exposition of 1889 with the help of 24 oxen. Visits round the cellars here are by electric train, and again climax with a *dégustation*. The *Castellane* tour is much less gimmicky than Mercier's or Moët's, and the *dégustation* a lot more generous.

The **tourist office** is at 7 av de Champagne (Easter–Oct Mon–Sat 9.30am–12.30pm & 1.30–5.30/7pm, Sun 11am–4pm; Nov–Easter closed Sun), a short walk from the **train station**. **Accommodation** does not come cheap in Épernay. Your best bet is the *Foyer des Jeunes Travailleurs*, 2 rue Pupin (☎03.26.51.62.51; ②), a few minutes' walk from the station. As for **hotels**, the *St-Pierre*, 1 rue Jeanne d'Arc (☎03.26.54.40.80; ③), is probably the cheapest alternative, followed by *Le Chapon Fin* at 2 place Mendès-France (☎03.26.55.40.03; ④), and *Le Progrès*, 6 rue des Berceaux (☎03.26.55.24.75; ④). The **campsite** is just over 1km north in the Parc des Sports, on the south bank of the Marne along allée de Cumières (☎03.26.55.32.14; April–Sept). **Eating** is good and affordable at *La Terrasse*, 7 quai de Marne, across the river from the station, while *Le Messina*, 17 rue Gambetta, serves inexpensive pizzas and pasta. *La Table Kobus* at 3 rue du Dr-Rousseau is excellent but a bit more expensive, with a menu at F200.

Reims

Laid flat by World War I artillery, **REIMS** is a rather dreary city, although there are two good reasons for visiting: it's the best centre (with Épernay) for the Champagne region, and it's home to one of the most impressive Gothic cathedrals in the country, once scene of the coronations of French monarchs. The battered west front of the **Cathédrale** is still a rare delight, with an array of restored but badly mutilated statuary – although many of the originals have been removed to the former bishops' palace (see below). Inside, the stained glass includes stunning designs by Marc Chagall in the east chapel and glorifications of the champagne process in the south transept. Perhaps more famously, the building also preserves, in a state of somewhat absurd veneration, the paraphernalia of Charles X's coronation in 1824.

Next door to the cathedral, the **Palais du Tau** (daily: July & Aug 9.30am–6.30pm; rest of year 10am–noon & 2–5/6pm; F32), in the bishops' palace, is worth a visit to see some of the dislodged west-front figures – equally expressive at short range as in their intended positions on the cathedral. There are grinning angels, friendly-looking gargoyles and a superb Eve. Most of the early kings were buried in Reims' oldest building, the eleventh-century **Basilique St-Rémi** (daily 8/9am–dusk/7pm; closed during services; free), part of a former Benedictine abbey. Sited 1km east of the cathedral, it's an immensely spacious building, with side naves wide enough for a bus to drive through, and preserves its Romanesque choir and ambulatory chapels. You can also visit the adjacent monastic buildings, with more displays of stone sculpture and tapestries.

If you're in Reims for the champagne, head to **place des Droits-des-Hommes** and **place St-Niçaise**, around which are most of the Reims *maisons*; most charge a small fee for their tours. If you're limiting yourself to one, the **Maison Veuve Cliquot-Ponsardin**, 1 place des Droits-des-Hommes (by appointment only), is one of the least pompous and has the best video. The *caves*, with their horror-movie fungi, are old Gallo-Roman quarries. **Pommery**, too, at 5 place du Général-Gouraud (April–Oct daily 11am–5.30pm; Nov to March by appointment only; F20), has excavated Roman quarries for cellars. At **Taittinger**, 9 place St-Niçaise (March–Nov Mon–Fri 9.30am–noon & 2–4.30pm, Sat & Sun 9–11am & 2–5pm; rest of year closed Sat & Sun; F25) there are still more ancient *caves*, with statues of St Vincent and St Jean, patron saints respectively of *vignerons* and cellar hands.

Practicalities

The **train station** is on the northwest edge of the town centre, which centres on place Drouet d'Erlon. The **tourist office** is close to the cathedral at rue G-de-Machault (Mon–Sat 9am–6.30/8pm, Sun 9/9.30am–6.30pm). Among central **hotels**, the *Thillois*, 17 rue de

Thillois (☎03.26.40.65.65; ③), and the *Alsace*, 6 rue Général Sarrail (☎03.26.47.44.08; ③), are both cheap, and there's a *Centre International de Séjour* with dorm beds at Parc Léo Lagrange, Allée Polonceau, south of the city centre (☎03.26.40.52.60; ②) – twenty minutes from the station. For **food**, there are a number of reasonable places on place Drouet d'Erlon; try the *Colbert* at no. 64 or *aux Coteaux* at no. 86.

NORMANDY

To the French, the essence of **Normandy** is its produce: this is the land of butter and cream, famous cheeses and seafood, cider and calvados. Yet parts of Normandy are among the most economically depressed of the whole country. The Normans themselves have a reputation for being insular and conservative, with a hatred of Parisians with weekend homes in the region. Normandy's Channel ports, **Dieppe** and **Le Havre**, provide a better introduction to France than their counterparts to the north; the white cliffs put on an impressive show, and there are occasional surprises, notably the Benedictine distillery at **Fécamp** and the Beaux-Arts museum in Le Havre. Further along the coast, you may arrive at either **Caen**, which gives good access to the town of **Bayeux** with its famous tapestry, or **Cherbourg**, to the south of which is the much-photographed monastic site of **Mont St-Michel**. It's hard to pin down specific highlights in **inland Normandy**. The pleasures lie in the feel of particular landscapes – lush meadows and orchards, half-timbered houses, and the food and drink for which the region is famous. Of urban centres, **Rouen**, the Norman capital, is by far the most compelling.

Dieppe

Crowded between high cliff headlands, **DIEPPE** is an enjoyably small-scale port, but an industrious one, its docks unloading half the bananas of the Antilles and forty percent of all shellfish destined to slither down French throats. The town was the place where Parisians used to take the sea air before fast cars took them further afield, and its restaurants provide a marvellous introduction to the delights of French cooking.

The liveliest part of town, particularly for its Saturday market, is the pedestrianized **Grande-Rue**, although the obvious place to start exploring is the medieval **castle** overlooking the seafront from the west, home of the **Musée de Dieppe** (June–Sept daily 10am–noon & 2–6pm; Oct–May Mon & Wed–Sun 10am–noon & 2–5pm; F15) and two showpiece collections – a group of carved ivories plundered from Africa, and a hundred or so prints by the co-founder of Cubism, Georges Braque, who spent summers here and is buried just west of the town at Varangeville-sur-Mer. An exit from the western side of the castle takes you out onto a path up to the cliffs. On the other side, a flight of steps leads down to the **square du Canada**, originally a commemoration of the role played by Dieppe sailors in the colonization of Canada but since the last war dedicated to the Canadian soldiers who died in the 1942 raid on Dieppe.

The main **train station** is about 800m southwest of the ferry terminal; the **tourist office** is alongside the ferry terminal on Pont Ango (Mon–Sat 9am–noon/1pm & 2–6/8pm, Sun 10am–1pm & 3–6pm; closed Sun in winter), and can supply maps. For a **room**, try *Les Arcades*, 1–3 Arcades de la Bourse, on the curve of the port towards the ferry terminal (☎02.35.84.14.12; ③), or *Hôtel de la Jetée*, 5 rue de l'Asile Thomas (☎02.35.84.89.98; ①). The **youth hostel** (☎02.35.84.85.73; April–Sept; ①) is 2km to the south, on rue Louis Fromager, accessible by bus #2 from bd Général-de-Gaulle by the train station. The nearest **campsite**, *du Pré St-Nicolas*, is 3km down the coastal road to Pourville. For **food**, the *Arcades* has a good restaurant, *Les Écamias*, 129 quai Henri-IV, is one of the best for fresh fish, and there are several others along the quaysides.

Fécamp

About 25km west of Dieppe, **FÉCAMP** is another serious fishing port, with a seafront promenade and a **Benedictine distillery** on rue Alexandre-le-Grand (tours: May to mid-Sept daily

9.30am–6pm; mid-March to April & mid-Sept to mid-Nov 10am–noon & 2–5.30pm; mid-Nov to mid-Mar 10–11.15am & 2–5pm; F29), in the narrow strip of streets running parallel to the ports towards the town centre. Tours of the distillery last 90 minutes and start with a small **museum**, set firmly in the Middle Ages beneath a nightmarish mock-Gothic roof with props of manuscripts, locks, testaments, lamps and religious paintings. The boxes of ingredients are a rare treat for the nose and there's further theatricality in the old distillery, where boxes of herbs are thrown with gusto into copper vats and alembics. Hold on to your ticket to qualify for a *dégustation* in their bar across the road – neat, in a cocktail or on crepes.

The **tourist office** is opposite the distillery at 113 rue Alexandre-le-Grand (July & Aug Mon–Fri 10am–6pm; rest of year Mon–Fri 9am–12.15pm & 1.45–6pm, Sat 10am–noon & 2–6pm), with a seafront annexe on Quai de la Vicomte open daily during July and August. The **train station** is between the port and the town centre on av Gambetta. If you're staying, there are **hotels** set back away from the sea on odd side streets, though be warned that Fécamp is popular. The *Hôtel de l'Univers*, 5 place St-Étienne (☎02.35.28.05.88; ③), and the *Angleterre*, 93 rue de la Plage (☎02.35.28.01.60; ④), are both reasonable, although *Hôtel Moderne*, near the train station at 3 av Gambetta (☎02.35.28.04.04; ③) is slightly cheaper. There's a superb **campsite**, *Camping de Renneville*, a short walk away on the western cliffs. *Le Martin*, 18 place St-Étienne, behind the **post office**, does good basic Norman **food**, with menus at all prices.

Le Havre

On the whole, ferry passengers move straight out from the port of **LE HAVRE**. The port, the second largest in France after Marseille, takes up half the Seine estuary, extending far further than the town. Avenue Foch, the central street, runs east to west, looking onto the sea between the beach and the yacht harbour. On bd J.F. Kennedy, overlooking the port entrance, the **Musée des Beaux-Arts** (Mon & Wed–Fri 11am–6pm, Sat & Sun 11am–7pm; F25) is one of the best-designed art galleries in the country, with one of its finest collections of nineteenth- and twentieth-century paintings – fifty canvases by Eugène Boudin and works by Corot, Courbet, Monet and Dufy, a native of Le Havre, who has a room to himself.

The **tourist office** (May–Sept Mon–Sat 9am–7pm, Sun 10am–12.30pm & 2.30–6pm; Oct–April Mon–Sat 9am–6.30pm, Sun 10am–1pm) is on the seafront at 186 bd Clémenceau; the #3 bus makes the 2km journey from the **train station**, on cours de la République. For **accommodation**, try *Séjour Fleuri*, 71 rue Émile-Zola (☎02.35.41.33.81; ③), or *Hôtel Suisse*, 3 rue Racine (☎02.35.42.37.05; ③). The **campsite** is in the Forêt de Montgeon (☎02.35.46.52.39; Easter–Aug), take bus #1 or #14 from Hôtel de Ville. For food, head for the reasonable fish **restaurant**, *Huitrère*, 12 quai Michel Feré.

Honfleur

HONFLEUR, the best-preserved of the Normandy ports, is a near-perfect seaside town, missing only a beach: the accumulation of silt from the Seine has left the eighteenth-century waterfront houses stranded and a little surreal. The ancient port, however, still functions and although only pleasure craft now make use of the moorings in the harbour basin, fishing boats tie up alongside the pier close by, and there is usually freshly caught fish for sale either directly from the boats or from stands on the pier. It's all highly picturesque, and not so different from the town that had such appeal to artists in the late nineteenth century.

It's this artistic past – and its present concentration of galleries and painters – which dominates Honfleur. It owes most to Eugène Boudin, forerunner of Impressionism, who was born and worked in the town, trained the 15-year-old Monet, and was joined here for various periods by Pissarro, Renoir and Cézanne. There's a good selection of his work in the **Musée Eugène Boudin**, west of the port on place Erik-Satie (mid-March to Sept Mon & Wed–Sun 10am–noon & 2–6pm; Oct to mid-March Mon & Wed–Fri 2.30–5pm, Sat & Sun 10am–noon & 2.30–5pm; F28, F25 in winter) – quite appealing here in context, particularly the crayon seascapes, along with an impressive set of Dufys and Monets.

The **tourist office** is on place Arthur Boudin (July & Aug Mon–Sat 9.30am–7pm, Sun 10am–1pm; rest of year Mon–Sat 9.30–noon/12.30pm & 2–5.30/6.30pm). Honfleur is on the direct **bus** route between Caen and Le Havre (4 buses daily); the nearest **train station** is at Pont-l'Évêque, connected by the Lisieux bus, #50 (20min ride). None of the **hotels** are very affordable – the *Cascades*, 17 place Thiers (☎02.31.89.05.83; ③), is the best bet, or there's a **campsite**, *Le Phare*, at the west end of bd Charles V on place Jean de Vienne (☎02.31.89.10.26; April–Sept). The most reasonable **restaurants** and **bars** are on rue Haute, on the way up to the Boudin museum. Try *Taverne de la Mer* at no. 35 or the *Au P'tit Mareyeur* at no. 4. At the harbour itself, it's hard to beat *Le Vieux Honfleur*, 13 quai St Etienne.

Caen

CAEN, capital and largest city of Basse Normandie, was devastated during World War II. Its central feature is a ring of ramparts that no longer have a castle to protect, while roads and roundabouts fill the wide spaces where prewar houses once stood. Nonetheless, the favoured residence of William the Conqueror is still impressive. The **château** ramparts are dramatically exposed, having been cleared of their medieval houses by aerial bombardment. Within are two museums, the **Musée des Beaux Arts** (daily except Tues 10am–6pm; F20) and the **Musée de Normandie** (daily except Tues 9.30am–12.30pm & 2–6pm; F10), both devoted to Norman history and fine arts. They include masterpieces by Poussin, Géricault, Monet and Bonnard, as well as an exceptional collection of engravings by Dürer and Rembrandt. Below the ramparts to the south is the fourteenth-century church of **St-Pierre**, its facade reconstructed since the war, which spared the magnificent Renaissance stonework of the apse. To the west and east of the town centre respectively stand two great Romanesque constructions, the **Abbaye aux Hommes** with its church of **St-Étienne**, and the **Abbaye aux Dames** with **La Trinité** church. The first was founded by William the Conqueror to hold his tomb; the other by his wife, Queen Matilda. Hers is the more starkly impressive, with a gloomy pillared crypt, wonderful stained glass behind the altar, and odd sculptural details like the fish curled up in the holy-water stoup.

North of Caen, at the end of av Maréchal-Montgomery, there is a brand new museum, the **Caen Memorial**, standing on a plateau beneath which the Germans had their HQ in June and July 1944 (daily 9am–7/8pm; F72). One section deals with the rise of fascism in Germany, another with resistance and collaboration in France, while a third charts the major battles of World War II. There's also a film documentary covering all the conflicts since 1945. Bus #12 during the week or #14 on the weekend go direct to the museum from the Tour le Roi stop in the centre of town and take about twenty minutes.

These days, most of the centre of Caen is taken up with busy new shopping developments and pedestrian precincts, and the **port**, at the end of the long canal which links Caen to the sea, is where most life goes on, at least during the summer. The **tourist office** is located on the central place St-Pierre (July & Aug Mon–Sat 9.30am–7pm, Sun 10am–1pm & 2–5pm; Sept–June Mon–Sat 10am–1pm & 2–6pm, Sun 10am–1pm), and is connected by regular bus with the **train station** on the south side of the river. The **bus station** is on bd du Maréchal l'Éclair. Buses to Ouistreham, the Brittany Ferries **terminal**, connect with the train station and are timed to coincide with crossings to Portsmouth. The port is also the area where most of the **hotels** are situated, including a number of good, inexpensive ones like *Univers* at 12 quai Vendeuvre (☎02.31.85.46.14; ②) or *Rouen*, 8 place de la Gare (☎02.31.34.06.03; ③). Caen's **youth hostel** is a bit further out, southwest of the train station in the *Foyer Robert-Remé* at 68 bis rue E-Restout (☎02.31.52.19.96; ②; June–Sept). Close by the hostel is the town's **campsite**, down beside the River Orne on route de Louvigny (bus #13).

For **restaurants**, rue de Geôle, running alongside the western ramparts to place St-Pierre, is the most promising location, with some good Vietnamese and Chinese places as well as French. Another area worth trying is around the Abbaye aux Hommes. For a large traditional meal, go to *Le Boeuf Ferré* at 10 rue des Croisiers; for seafood try *Tongasoa* at 7 rue du Vaugueux.

Bayeux

BAYEUX's perfectly preserved medieval ensemble, magnificent cathedral and world-famous tapestry depicting the 1066 invasion of England by William the Conqueror make it one of the high points of Normandy. It's only fifteen minutes by train from Caen, and receives an influx of summer tourists that can make its charms pall somewhat.

The **Bayeux Tapestry** is housed in the **Centre Guillaume le Conquérant**, clearly signposted on rue de Nesmond (daily: May–Aug 9am–6.15pm; rest of year 9am–5.30pm; F39). Visits begin with a projection of slides on swathes of canvas, before moving on to an almost full-length reproduction of the original, complete with photographic extracts and detailed commentary. Upstairs in the plush theatre there's a film (French and English versions alternate) on the general context and craft of the piece, and beyond this the tapestry itself, a 70m strip of linen embroidered with coloured wools nine centuries ago. It records scenes from the Norman Conquest, as well as incidental details of domestic and daily life, which run along the bottom as a counterpoint. It was for the consecration in 1077 of the nearby **Cathédrale Notre-Dame** that the tapestry was commissioned – and, despite some eighteenth-century vandalism, the Romanesque plan of the church is still intact. The crypt, entirely unaltered, is a beauty, its columns graced with frescoes of angels playing trumpets and bagpipes.

Also well worth a visit while in Bayeux, is the **Memorial Museum to the Battle of Normandy** on bd Fabian Ware (May to mid–Sept 9.30am–6.30pm; mid-Sept to April 10am–12.30pm & 2–6pm; F32). The numerous original documents, life-size models, equipment and videos dramatically capture the war's most decisive chapter in the battle to re-establish peace in Europe.

Bayeux's **train station** is on the southern side of town, on bd Sadi Carnot. The **tourist office**, at Pont St Jean (Sept–June Mon–Sat 9am–noon & 2–6pm; July & Aug Mon–Sat 9am–6pm, Sun 9.30am–noon & 2.30–6pm; ☎02.31.51.28.28), might be able to help you find reasonable **accommodation**. Most affordable of the **hotels** are the *Notre-Dame*, 44 rue des Cuisiniers (☎02.31.92.87.24; ③), and *de la Gare*, 26 place de la Gare (☎02.31.92.10.70; ②). The *Family Home* at 39 rue du Général de Dais (☎02.31.92.15.22), north of the cathedral, functions as a friendly and decent **youth hostel** (②), and serves good **food** too. Otherwise, most of the restaurants are in the pedestrianized rue St-Jean – *La Rapière* at no. 53 is the most popular. Failing that, try the *Le Petit Normand*, 35 rue Larcher.

Cherbourg

Situated at the top end of the Cotentin Peninsula, the mucky metropolis of **CHERBOURG** may be your port of arrival, in which case you should head straight for the **train station** on av François-Millet – a ten-minute walk from the ferry terminal behind the inner dock. The town itself is almost devoid of interest. If you're waiting for a boat, the most enjoyable way of killing time is to settle into one of the **restaurants** around quai de Caligny. *Les Trois Capitaines*, 16 quai de Caligny, *La Moulerie*, specializing in mussels at 73 rue au Blé, and *Le Faitout* at no. 25 rue Tour-Carrée, are all excellent. If you need to stay overnight, *Hôtel de la Renaissance* (☎02.33.43.23.90; ②) has a good selection of rooms and there's a **youth hostel** (☎02.33.78.15.15; ②) at 55 rue de l'Abbaye, 1km away from the train station, near the town hall.

Mont St-Michel

One place many people hurry to is the island of **Mont St-Michel**, on the far western edge of Normandy, site of a marvellous Gothic abbey. The abbey church, long known as the Merveille, is visible from all around the bay, and it becomes more awe-inspiring the closer you get – as Maupassant said, it is "the most wonderful Gothic dwelling ever made for God on this earth". The abbey's granite was sculpted to match the exact contours of the hill, and though space was always limited, the building has grown through the centuries in ever more ingenious uses of geometry. To visit, you must join a tour (English-speaking; daily

9am–4.30/5.30pm; F40; night tour April & May weekends 10pm–midnight; June–Sept Mon–Sat 10pm–midnight/1am; F60); these last for about an hour, and the guides are real experts, pointing out – among much other useful information – that the current state of the stone walls is a far cry from the way the medieval monastery would have looked, brightly painted and festooned with tapestries. The most famous **hotel**, *La Mère Poulard* (☎02.33.60.14.09; ⑤) uses the time-honoured legend of its fluffy omelettes to justify extortionate charges. Higher up the one twisting street the *Hôtel Croix Blanche* (☎02.33.60.14.04; ⑥) has excellent rooms and an exceptional restaurant. Near the causeway on the mainland is a **campsite** (☎02.33.60.09.33; Feb–Nov).

The nearest **train station** is at **PONTORSON**, 6km south, a forgettable town where you can rent a bike from the station or take an expensive bus to the Mont. There's an HI **youth hostel** on rue Général-Patton, near the town's cathedral (☎02.33.60.18.65; ①; June–Sept). The best budget **hotel** is the *de France*, 2 rue de Rennes (☎02.33.60.29.17; ③ incl breakfast), next to the rail crossing; it has a late and youthful bar. Otherwise, you could stay at **AVRANCHES**, where there are a number of reasonable **hotels**, including *du Jardin des Plantes* at 10 place Carnot (☎02.33.58.03.68; ④) and *Le Croix d'Or*, 83 rue de la Constitution (☎02.33.58.04.88; ④). The **train station** is far below the town centre, but the views make up for that.

Rouen and around

You could spend a day wandering around **ROUEN** without realizing that the river Seine runs through the city. The war destroyed all the bridges, flattened the area between the cathedral and the *quais*, and razed much of the left bank industrial quarter. After repairing the damage, an enormous amount of money was spent on restoration to turn the centre into a largely fake medieval city. Still, the churches are extremely impressive and the whole place faintly seductive.

The nominal centre of the city, between place du Vieux-Marché and the cathedral, is the **Gros Horloge**, a colourful one-handed clock, which spans the street named after it. The belfry is closed for renovation, but when it reopens some time in 2000 you can climb up and see the surrounding towers and spires arraying themselves in startling density. Just off here, the **Cathédrale de Notre-Dame** remains at heart the Gothic masterpiece that was built in the twelfth and thirteenth centuries, although all kinds of vertical extensions have since been added. The west facade, intricately sculpted like the rest of the exterior, was Monet's subject for the series of celebrated studies of changing light. Inside, the carvings of the misericords in the choir provide a picture of fifteenth-century life in secular scenes of work and customs along with the usual mythical beasts.

The church of **St-Ouen**, in a park a short walk northeast, is larger than the cathedral and has far less decoration, so that the Gothic proportions have a more instant impact. Close by, the church of St-Maclou is more flamboyant, although perhaps the real interest is in its adjacent **Aître St-Maclou**, once a cemetery for plague victims, which still has its original macabre decorations, together with a mummified cat. The **Musée des Beaux-Arts** on the Square Vedrel (Mon & Wed–Sun 10am–6pm; F20) is not tremendously enthralling but it does include a number of works by the Rouennais Géricault, Boudin, Sisley and Monet, Dadaist pictures by Marcel Duchamp, and a collection of portraits by one Jacques Émile Blanche of Cocteau, Gide, Valéry, Mallarmé and others. Look in also on one of the city's smaller museums, the **Musée Flaubert et de l'Histoire de la Médicine** in the Hôpital Hôtel-Dieu on the corner of rue de Lecat and rue du Contrat-Social (Tues 10am–6pm, Wed–Sat 10am–noon & 2–6pm; F12), dedicated to Rouen's most famous novelist, Gustave Flaubert, whose father was chief surgeon at the medical school here. Some of the exhibits would have been familiar objects to him – a phrenology model, a childbirth demonstrator like a giant rag doll, and the sets of encyclopedias.

Practicalities

The **train station** is a five-minute bus (#8, #15) or metro ride from the centre; best place to get off is the Théâtre des Arts, one block east from the **bus station**. The **tourist office**, 25 place de la Cathédrale (Mon–Sat 9am–6.30/7pm; Sun & holidays 9.30/10am–12.30/1pm; summer also open Sun 2.30–6pm), has plenty of information, though cheap and central **hotel**

accommodation is in any case no problem: try the *Sphinx*, 130 rue Beauvoisine (☎02.35.71.35.86; ②), the old and beautifully decorated *des Carmes*, 33 pl des Carmes (☎02.35.71.92.31; ⑤), or the *Rochefoucauld*, 1 rue de la Rochefoucauld, near the train station (☎02.35.71.86.58; ③). The **camping municipal** is 5km northwest on rue Jules-Ferry in Déville-lès-Rouen (☎02.35.74.07.59; bus #2 from Théâtre des Arts).

Rouen has a reputation for good **food**, and its most famous dish, duckling (*caneton*), can be enjoyed quite reasonably at *Pascaline*, 5 rue de la Poterne. For good basic meals, the south side of place du Vieux-Marché and the north side of St-Maclou church are both lined with good-quality restaurants. Some specific recommendations include the traditional *Au Temps des Cerises* at 4–6 rue des Basnages and *Walsheim* at 260 rue Martainville, next to St-Maclou, with menus from around F60. Otherwise there's the *des Beaux-Arts*, 34 rue Damiette, which serves mountains of *couscous* and *paella* for very affordable prices or the *Jumbo*, 11 rue Guillaume-le-Conquérant, where you can pile up your own whopping salads.

Giverny

For a complete shift of mood the best place to visit around Rouen is **GIVERNY**, and the gardens which Monet laid out himself. Monet lived here from 1883 until his death in 1926 (April–Oct Tues–Sun 10am–6pm; F35 house and gardens, F25 gardens only). May and June, when the rhododendrons flower around the lily pond and the wisteria over the Japanese bridge is in bloom, are the best times to visit, but any month is overwhelmingly beautiful. Though you do get to see his famous water lilies in real life, there aren't any paintings on show, and the house is instead filled with Monet's collection of Japanese prints. It can get very busy, and the crowds and cameras can induce a feel that seems far removed from Monet's intentions, but really there's no place like it.

Giverny isn't easy to get to from Rouen by **public transport**. Your best bet is a train to Vernon and then either rent a bicycle or make the ten-minute ride on the *Gisor* bus from the station (departs Tues–Fri 9.10am/1pm/3.10pm, returning 2.10pm/5.15pm/6.55pm, Sat departs 11.30am/1.10pm/3.10pm returning at 2.10pm/5pm/5.15pm, Sun departs 10.55am/11.35am returning at 2.45pm/4.45pm/5.25pm; F23 return). Nearby **accommodation** is not much easier, with a **youth hostel** in Vernon at 28 av de l'Île-de-France (☎02.32.51.66.48; ②) or the *Hôtel d'Évreux* at pl d'Évreux (☎02.32.21.16.12; ③).

BRITTANY

For generations the people of **Brittany** risked their lives fishing and trading on the violent seas or struggling with the arid soil of the interior, and their resilience is tinged with Celtic culture: mystical, musical, sometimes morbid, sometimes vital and inspired. Unified with France in 1532, the Bretons have seen their language steadily eradicated, and the interior severely depopulated. Today, the people still tend to treat France as a separate country, even if few of them actively support Breton nationalism much beyond putting Breizh (Breton for "Brittany") stickers on their cars. The recent economic resurgence, helped partly by summer tourism, has largely been due to local initiatives, and at the same time a Celtic artistic identity has consciously been revived at festivals of traditional Breton music, poetry and dance.

For most visitors to this province, it is the **coast** that is the dominant feature. After the Côte d'Azur, this is the most popular summer resort area in France, and the attractions are obvious – white sand beaches, towering cliffs and offshore islands. Whether you approach across the Channel by ferry, or along the coast from Normandy, the Rance River, guarded by **St-Malo** on its estuary and **Dinan** 20km upstream, makes a spectacular introduction to Brittany. To the west stretches a varied coastline culminating in one of the most seductive of the islands, the Île de Bréhat; inland, most roads curl eventually to **Rennes**, the Breton capital. Brittany's **southern coast** takes in Europe's most famous prehistoric site, the alignments of **Carnac**, and although the beaches are not as spectacular as Finistère's, the water is warmer. Of the cities, **Vannes** has one of the liveliest medieval town centres.

Rennes

Capital and power centre of Brittany, **RENNES** seems, with its Neoclassical layout and the pompous scale of its buildings, uncharacteristic of the province. It was razed in a fire of 1720 and the task of remodelling was handed out to Parisian architects – not in deference to the capital but to rival it. The city's oldest and most central quarter is bordered by the canal to the west and the river to the south. The city's one central building to survive the great fire was, symbolically enough, the **Palais de Justice**, on place du Palais, home of the old Rennes *parlement*, which fought battles with the French governor from the reign of Louis XIV up until the Revolution (closed for renovation until Nov 1999; check with the tourist office for visiting hours and price). The seventeenth-century chambers are opulently gilded and adorned, culminating in the debating hall hung with Gobelin tapestries depicting scenes from the history of the duchy and the province.

South of here, at 3 quai Émile-Zola, the **Musée des Beaux-Arts** (Mon & Wed–Sun 10am–noon & 2–6pm; F20), contains an outstanding collection of pictures, from Leonardo drawings to 1960s abstracts. One room is dedicated to Brittany, with mythical and real-life scenes. The excellent **Musée de Bretagne** is currently being rehoused in what was the bus station on bd Magenta, but is not due to open until 2003.

The **train station** is linked with the central place de la République by buses #1, #17, #20. The **tourist office** is at 11 rue St Yves (Mon–Sat 9am–6/7pm, Sun 9am–6pm). **Hotels** are heavily concentrated around the station; the *Riaval*, 9 rue de Riaval (☎02.99.50.65.58; ②) is reliable, as is *Le Magenta*, 35 bd Magenta (☎02.99.30.85.37; ②) – if a little noisy. If you'd prefer to stay in the medieval quarter of town, the attractive *Rocher de Cancale*, 10 rue St-Michel (☎02.99.79.20.83; ④), fits the bill. The **youth hostel** is 3km out at 10–12 Canal St-Martin (☎02.99.33.22.33; ②), on bus route #18 towards St-Gregoire. Bus #3 takes you northeast to Gayeulles, from where it's a short walk to the city's **campsite**. The old town is the liveliest part of Rennes and stays up late, particularly in the vicinity of St-Aubin church. For food there's an excellent creperie at 5 place St-Anne, or for something more substantial and traditional, try *Ti-koz*, 3 rue St-Guillaume, or *Leon le Cochon* at 1 rue Maréchal-Joffre. Rennes is at its best in the first ten days of July, when the **Festival des Tombées de la Nuit** takes over the whole city to celebrate Breton culture with music, theatre, film, mime and poetry.

St-Malo and around

About 50km north of Rennes, **ST-MALO**, walled and built with the same grey granite as Mont St-Michel, presents its best face to the River Rance and the sea. If you're not arriving by ferry, it's still worth reaching it by boat – from either Dinard or Dinan. Once within the old ramparts, St-Malo can seem slightly grim and squat, and overrun by summer tourists. But away from the popular thoroughfares of the tiny **citadelle**, with its high seventeenth-century houses, random exploration is fun and you can surface to the light on the ramparts or pass through them to the nearby beaches. The **town museum**, in the castle to the right as you enter Porte St-Vincent (Tues–Sun 10am–noon & 2–6pm; in summer open daily; F26.50), glorifies on several exhausting floors St-Malo's sources of wealth and fame – colonialism, slave-trading and privateering among them.

Buses take you to the main city gate, the **Porte St-Vincent; trains** stop on the other side of the docks, a ten-minute walk away. If you have problems, the **tourist office** is on the corner of Esplanade St-Vincent and av Louis Martin beside the Bassin Duguay-Trouin (July & Aug Mon–Sat 8.30am–8pm, Sun 10am–7pm; Sept–June Mon–Sat 9am–noon & 2–6pm). It's always more difficult to find **accommodation** in the old city, despite its extraordinary number of hotels, but rooms at the *Univers*, 10 place Châteaubriand (☎02.99.40.89.52; ⑤), or *Du Louvre*, 2 rue des Marins (☎02.99.40.86.62; ③), are well worth trying for. Otherwise, there's an array near the station. In the suburb of Paramé there's an often crowded **youth hostel** at 37 av R.P. Umbricht, 2km northeast of the train station (bus #2; ☎02.99.40.29.80; ②). There's also a municipal **campsite**, *Les Nielles*, on av John Kennedy, near some shops and the beach. Most of the *citadelle*'s restaurants are pricey tourist traps, so you're better off at the creperies and mouleries such as *Chez Chantal*, 2 place aux Herbes, and *Brick*, 5 rue Jacques-Cartier.

Dinard and Dinan

Across the estuary from St-Malo, reachable by shuttle boat from below the southern wall of the citadel, **DINARD** has been transformed during this century from a simple fishing village to something along the lines of a Côte d'Azur resort, with a casino, shady villas and a glut of pricey hotels and restaurants. It's not a very welcoming place to stay, but is the start of some pleasant coastal walks, and pleasure trips by boat down the Rance to **DINAN**, whose citadel has been preserved, almost intact, within a three-kilometre circuit of walls, inside which lie street upon street of late medieval houses. It's almost too good to be true and time is easily spent rambling from creperie to café, admiring the houses on the way. Unfortunately, there's only one small stretch of the **ramparts** that you can walk along – from the gardens behind St-Sauveur to just short of the Tour Sillon – but you get a good general overview from the **Tour de l'Horloge** (daily: April, May & Sept 2–6.30pm; June–Aug 10am–7pm; F16) or from the top of the keep guarding the town from the south, known as the **Château Duchesse Anne** (summer daily 10am–5.45pm; winter Mon & Wed–Sun 1.30–5pm; F25). An inevitable target of any Dinan wanderings is the church of **St-Sauveur**, a real mix-up of periods, with a Romanesque porch and eighteenth-century steeple. Its nine Gothic chapels have five different patterns of asymmetrical vaulting; the most complex pair, in the centre, are wonderful.

Dinan's **train station** is a ten-minute walk away from place Duclos. The **tourist office** (winter Mon–Sat 9am–12.30pm & 2–5.45pm; summer Mon–Sat 9am–7.30pm, Sun 10am–12.30pm & 2.30–6pm) is opposite the Tour de l'Horloge in the *Hôtel Kératry*. The cheaper **hotels** are near the station – *De l'Océan*, 9 pl du 11 Novembre (☎02.96.39.21.51; ②), is as good as any. Within the walls there's *La Duchesse Anne* at 10 place du Guesclin (☎02.96.39.09.43; ③). Dinan's **youth hostel** (☎02.96.39.10.83; ②) is attractively set in the Moulin de Méen near the port at Taden, about 3km away, while the closest **campsite** is at 103 rue Châteaubriand (☎02.96.39.11.96), which runs parallel to the western ramparts. Among a wide choice of **eating places** in all price ranges on the old streets of Dinan, one of the best bets is *Crêperie Connetable*, 1 rue de l'Apport.

Roscoff

The opening of the deep-water port at **ROSCOFF** in 1973 was part of a general attempt by the government to revitalize the Breton economy. The ferry services to Plymouth and Cork are intended not just to bring tourists, but also to revive the traditional trading links that used to exist between the Celtic nations of Brittany, Ireland and southwest England. Roscoff itself has, however, remained a small resort with almost all activity confined to rue Gambetta and the old port. Until the last couple of centuries, the town made most of its money from piracy – like so many other ports along the Breton coast. There are a few reminders of that wealth in the ornate stone houses, and the **church** with its sculpted ships and protruding stone cannons, all dating from the sixteenth century.

To reach the town from the **ferry**, turn right leaving the terminal and follow the signs across a narrow promontory and down into Roscoff's harbour. The **tourist office** is at 46 rue Gambetta (July & Aug Mon–Sat 9.30am–12.30pm & 1.30–7pm, Sun 10am–12.30pm; rest of year Mon–Sat 9am–noon & 2–6pm). Later than 9pm it may be difficult to find a **restaurant** still serving, but **hotels** are used to clientele arriving on late sailings. The two most reasonable are both on rue Amiral-Réveillère – *Les Arcades* at no. 15 (☎02.98.69.70.45; ③), which has an unusually trendy bar and good food; and the quieter, more expensive *Les Chardons Bleus* at no. 4 (☎02.98.69.72.03; ④).

Quimper and around

QUIMPER, capital of the ancient diocese and kingdom of Cornouaille, is the oldest Breton city, founded according to legend by the original bishop of the town, St Corentin, who came here across the channel to the place they named Little Britain some time between the fourth and seventh centuries. It's a laid-back sort of place, with old granite buildings, two rivers and the rising woods of Mont Frugy overlooking the centre of town.

The town focuses on the enormous Gothic **Cathédrale St-Corentin**. The **Musée des Beaux-Arts** is next to the Hôtel de Ville (July & Aug daily 10am–7pm; rest of year Mon & Wed–Sat 10am–noon & 2–6pm, Sun 2–6pm; F25–30), with its amazing collections of drawings by Cocteau, Max Jacob and Gustave Doré (shown in rotation) and nineteenth- and twentieth-century paintings of the Pont-Aven school. If you're interested in seeing pottery made on an industrial scale, and an exhibition of the changing styles since the first Quimper *ateliers* of the late seventeenth century, the **Faïenceries de Quimper** (guided visits only Mon–Fri 9am–11.30am & 2–4.15pm; F20) and the **Musée de la Faïence** (May–Oct Mon–Sat 10am–6pm; F26) are both worth a visit. They're on rue Jean-Baptiste Bosquet, downstream from the tourist office on the south bank of the Odet.

A short walk west along the river brings you from the adjacent **train** and **bus stations** to the centre of town. The **tourist office** is on the south bank of the Odet at 7 rue de la Désse, place de la Résistance (July & Aug Mon–Sat 9am–7pm, Sun 10am–1pm & 3–6pm; rest of year Mon–Sat 9am–noon/12.30pm & 1.30–6/6.30pm, Sun 10am–1pm & 3–6pm; winter closed Sun). Budget **hotels** include the *Pascal*, near the station at 19 av de la Gare (☎02.98.90.00.81; ②), and the pleasant *de l'Ouest*, at 63 rue le Déan (☎02.98.90.28.35; ③). The **youth hostel** and **campsite** are downstream at 6 av des Oiseaux in the Bois du Seminaire – bus #1 from place de la Résistance. In the week preceding the last Sunday in July there's the **Festival Cornouailles**, a jamboree of Breton music, costume and dance; the town is packed, and every room booked.

Boats down the Odet to the coast leave from the end of quai de l'Odet, opposite the Faïenceries, a winding journey to the upmarket resort of **BENODET**, where there's a long sheltered beach. **Hotels** are comparatively expensive, but you could try *Le Minaret* overlooking the beach (☎02.98.57.03.13; ⑥) or the *Bains de Mer*, 11 rue du Kerguéleu (☎02.98.57.03.41; ⑤), and there are several large **campsites**. There are more beaches along the coast between Penmarch and Loctudy and beyond, about an hour by bus from Quimper. Another possibility is a trip to the **Pointe du Raz**, the Land's End of France, a series of plummeting fissures, filling and draining with deafening force, above which you can walk on precarious paths.

Carnac and Quiberon

About 10km along the coast from the functional port of **Lorient**, accessible only by way of the slightly dull town of Auray, **CARNAC** is home to one of the most important prehistoric sites in Europe, a congregation of some 2000 or so menhirs stretching for more than 4km to the north of the village, long predating the Pyramids or Stonehenge. The stones may have been part of an observatory for the motions of the moon, but no one really knows. Though many have been pillaged as ready-quarried stone, the stones remain an amazing site. The main alignments, fenced from the public, are viewed from a raised platform at one end of the plain, and you can get plenty of information at the **Musée de Préhistoire**, place de la Chapelle, near rue du Tumulus in Carnac-Ville (July & Aug daily 10am–6.30pm; rest of year Mon & Wed–Sun 10am–noon & 2–5/6pm; F30), which entertainingly traces the area's history from about 450,000 years ago.

Carnac, divided between the original **Carnac-Ville** and the more recent seaside resort of **Carnac-Plage**, is extremely popular. Buses to Quiberon and Vannes depart regularly from the main **tourist office** at 74 av des Druides in Carnac-Plage (July & Aug Mon–Sat 9am–7pm, Sun 3–7pm; rest of year Mon–Sat 9am–noon & 2–6pm). Among the town's innumerable **hotels**, the *Hoty*, 15 av de Kermario (☎02.97.52.29.78; ③), is the best deal you'll find near the beach; in town, try the *Chez Nous*, 5 pl de la Chapelle (☎02.97.52.07.28; ④). The best of Carnac's many **beaches** is the smallest, the **Men Dû**, just off the road towards La Trinité. If you're planning to **camp** by the sea, you should go to the *Men Dû*; otherwise, the best site is *La Grande Métairie*, opposite the stones, which organizes horse-riding and rents out bicycles.

South of Carnac, the **Presqu'île de Quiberon** is well worth visiting on its own merits. The town of **QUIBERON** itself is a lively port, and provides a jumping-off point for boats out to the nearby islands or simply a base for the peninsula. The ocean-facing shore, known as the **Côte Sauvage**, is a wild and unswimmable stretch, but the sheltered eastern side has safe and calm sandy beaches, and offers plenty of **campsites**. In Quiberon, Port Maria, the fishing harbour, is the most active part of town and has the best concentration of **hotels**, though they're often full in high season – try *Le Neptune* at 4 quai de Houat (☎02.97.50.09.62; ④), or *Pension au Bon Accueil*, 6 quai de Houat (☎02.97.50.07.92; ③). The **youth hostel**, *Les Filets Bleus*, 45 rue du Roch-Priol (☎02.97.50.15.54; ②), is set back from the sea about 1km southeast of the **train station**. A vast array of fish **restaurants** line the seafront, of which the best is at the *Pension au Bon Accueil*. The cafés by the long bathing beach are also enjoyable. The **tourist office** is at 14 rue de Verdun, downhill and to the left from the train station (July & Aug Mon–Sat 9am–8pm, Sun 9.30am–12.30pm & 3–7pm; rest of year Mon–Sat 9am–12.30pm & 1.30–6pm).

Vannes and the Golfe de Morbihan

VANNES is one of the most historic towns in Brittany, and it was here that the Breton assembly ratified the Act of Union with France in 1532. The old centre is a chaos of streets crammed around the cathedral and enclosed by ramparts and gardens. The building where the Act of Union was ratified, **La Cohue**, between rue des Halles and the cathedral square, is now the **Musée de Vannes** (June–Sept daily 10am–6pm; Oct–May Mon & Wed–Sat 10am–noon & 2–6pm, Sun 2–6pm; F26), with what was the local Beaux-Arts museum on its top floor, and a gallery downstairs for temporary exhibitions. Close by, the **Cathedral** is not the finest edifice in the town, but it does have one exquisite treasure, an early medieval wedding chest with beautifully painted figures (July & Aug 10.30am–6pm; June & Sept Mon–Sat 1.30–5.30pm; Oct–May by appointment only; F20).

Vannes' harbour is a channelled inlet of the ragged-edged **Golfe de Morbihan**, which lets in the tides through a narrow gap. By popular tradition, the **islands** scattered around this enclosure used to number the days of the year, though for centuries the waters have been rising and there are now fewer than one for each week. Of these, thirty are privately owned, while two – the Île aux Moines and Île d'Arz – have regular populations and ferry services and end up being crowded in summer. You can take a **boat tour** around the rest, a compelling trip through a baffling muddle of channels, megalithic ruins, stone circles and solitary menhirs on small hillocks. Full details from the Vannes tourist office.

It's twenty minutes' walk south from the **train station** to the centre at place de la République. South of here is the **tourist office** at 1 rue Thiers (July & Aug Mon–Sat 9am–7pm, Sun 10am–noon; rest of year Mon–Sat 9am–noon & 2–6pm). Vannes has the best choice of **hotels** anywhere around the Golfe de Morbihan: two good ones are *Le Bretagne*, 36 rue du Mené, in the old town (☎02.97.47.20.21; ②), and *Le Marina* overlooking the port at 4 place Gambetta (☎02.97.47.22.81; ③). For **food**, the *Villa Romana*, 16 rue des Vierges, serves great pizzas, pasta and fresh fish.

Nantes

Though the former capital, **NANTES**, is these days not officially a part of Brittany, it remains to its inhabitants an integral part of the province. Crucial to its self-image is **Château des Ducs**, subjected to a certain amount of damage over the centuries, but still preserving the form in which it was built by two of the last rulers of independent Brittany, François II, and his daughter Duchess Anne, who was born here in 1477. The most significant act in the castle's history was the signing of the Edict of Nantes by Henri IV in 1598, which ended the Wars of Religion and granted a certain degree of toleration to the Protestants. You can walk into the courtyard and up onto the low ramparts for free, and visit temporary exhibitions in the Harnachement building, but the rest of the castle is undergoing a huge renovation in order to become the **Museum of the History of Nantes and its Region**, projected to open completely by 2008, although parts may open before that. In 1800 the castle's arsenal exploded, shattering the stained glass of the **Cathédrale de St-Pierre et St-Paul**, 200m away, just one of many disasters that have befallen the church. Newly restored, its soaring heights are home to the tomb of François II and his wife, Margaret. Back past the château, the so-called **Île Feydeau**, once an island, was the birthplace of Jules Verne and has a **museum** dedicated to him at 3 rue de l'Hermitage (Mon & Wed–Sat 10am–noon & 2–5pm, Sun 2–5pm; F20).

The **train station** is on the south side of the centre, a short way east of the castle. For **places to stay**, try the *Hôtel St-Reine*, 3 rue Anatole-le-Braz (☎02.40.74.35.61; ③), *Hôtel de l'Océan*, 11 rue du Maréchal-de-Lattre-de-Tassigny (☎02.40.69.73.51; ③), or the *Fourcroy*, 11 rue Fourcroy (☎02.40.44.68.00; ③). The city's **youth hostel** is at 2 place de la Manu, and is reached by tram #1 to Beaujoire (summer only; ☎02.40.29.29.20; ②). The **tourist office** is in the *FNAC* on place du Commerce (Mon–Sat 10am–7pm), in an appealing, largely pedestrian area that's a good source of diverse **restaurants**.

THE LOIRE

Intimidated by the sheer density of châteaux, people tend to make bad use of their time spent in the Loire, which is a pity, for if you pick your castles selectively, this can be one of the most enjoyable of all French regions. The most salient features of the Loire itself are whirlpools, vicious currents and a propensity to flood. No one swims in or boats on the Loire, nor are any goods carried along it – it's just there, the longest river in France. The stretch above Saumur is the loveliest on the lower reaches, the land on the south planted with vines and sunflowers. Other than the châteaux, the best of which are those at **Chenonceaux**, **Azay-le-Rideau** and **Loches**, the region has few sights; of the towns, **Tours** can be tedious but is good for museums, while **Saumur** is perfect for indolence, but not hot on entertainment.

Saumur and around

The local sparkling wines for which **SAUMUR** is best known are based outside the town – in the suburb of St-Hilaire-St-Florent – and Saumur itself is simply peaceful and pretty, a good place to base yourself for a while, with Angers, Chinon and plenty of vineyards within easy reach. There is a **Château** (July & Aug daily 9.30–6pm, also Wed & Sat 8.30–10.30pm; June & Sept daily 9.30am–6pm; Oct–May Mon & Wed–Sun 9.30am–noon & 2–5.30pm; F35), where you can visit the dungeons and watchtower, and be guided around three museums within its walls – the **Musée des Arts Décoratifs**, with its huge collection of European china, the **Musée du Cheval**, with bridles, saddles and stirrups, and the **Musée de la Figurine-Jouet**, consisting of a display of antique toys.

Arriving at the **train station** leaves you on the north bank of the river; from here cross over the bridge to the island, then over another bridge to the main part of the town on the south bank. Saumur's main street, **rue d'Orléans**, cuts back through the south-bank sector; the **tourist office** is unmissable at the foot of the second bridge, on place de la Bilange (May–Sept Mon–Sat 9.15am–7pm, Sun 10.30am–12.30pm & 3.30–6.30pm; Oct–April Mon–Sat 9.15am–12.30pm & 2–6pm, Sun 10am–noon). The best **hotel** is *Le Cristal*, 10 place de la République (☎02.41.51.09.54; ④), with river views from most rooms and very friendly proprietors; other options include the *De Bretagne*, 55 rue St-Nicolas (☎02.41.51.26.38; ③), and the *Central*, 23 rue Daillé (☎02.41.51.05.78; ⑤). On the Île d'Offard, connected by bridges to both banks of the town, there's a good **youth hostel** at the eastern end of rue de Verden (☎02.41.40.30.00; ②), offering bike rental, and a **campsite** next door. The best area for **eating** is around place St-Pierre: *Auberge St-Pierre*, at no. 6, has a fairly cheap menu, as does *Les Forges de St-Pierre*.

Fontévraud

The **Abbaye de Fontévraud** (daily: June–Sept 9am–6.30pm; Oct–May 9.30am–noon & 2–5/6pm; F35), 13km southeast of Saumur (bus #16), was founded in 1099 as both a nunnery and a monastery with an abbess in charge – a radical move, even if the post was filled solely by queens and princesses. The premises had to be immense to house and separate not only nuns and monks but also the sick, lepers and repentant prostitutes. A prison from the Revolution until 1963, its most famous inmate was writer Jean Genet, but its chief significance is as the burial ground of the Plantagenet kings. Four tombstone effigies remain, of Henry II, Eleanor of Aquitaine, Richard the Lionheart and Isabelle of Angoulême (King John's wife).

Chinon

The first of the big Loire châteaux is at **CHINON** (daily: April–Oct 9am–6/7pm; Nov–March 9am–noon & 2–5pm; F28). It was one of the few places in which Charles VII could stay while Henry V of England held Paris and the title to the French throne. Charles' situation changed with the arrival here in 1429 of Joan of Arc, who persuaded him to give her an army. All that remains of the scene of this encounter, the Grande Salle, is a wall and first-floor fireplace. More interesting is the Tour Coudray, to the west, covered with intricate thirteenth-century graffiti carved by imprisoned and doomed Templar knights. Below the castle, the town is a tacky and rather sterile place, with very few **hotels** and everything closed up long before midnight. If you're looking for a room, the two cheapest alternatives are the *Point du Jour*, 102 quai Jeanne-d'Arc (☎02.47.93.07.20; ③), and the *Jeanne d'Arc*, 11 rue Voltaire (☎02.47.93.02.85; ③). There is a **youth hostel** (☎02.47.93.10.48; ②) close to the **train station** on rue Descartes and a **campsite** across the river at Île-Auger. The **tourist office** is on place Hofheim (summer Mon–Sat 9am–7pm, Sun 9am–12.30pm; winter Mon–Sat 9am–12.15pm & 1.30–6pm). The most reasonable **restaurant** is *Les Années 30* at 78 rue Voltaire.

Azay-le-Rideau

A few kilometres upstream from Chinon, **AZAY-LE-RIDEAU** is worth visiting for its serene setting, and for its **Château** (daily: April–Oct 9.30am–6/7pm; Nov–March 9.30am–12.30pm & 2–5.30pm; F35), which is one of the Loire's loveliest, at least from the outside. Its interior, furnished in Renaissance style, doesn't add much to the experience, but the portrait gallery has the whole sixteenth-century royal Loire crew – François I, Catherine de Médici et al – and includes a fine semi-nude painting of Gabrielle d'Estrées, Henri IV's lover. There is a large **campsite** a little way upstream from the château, although **hotels** don't come cheap. A possibility if you're stuck is *Le Balzac*, 4 rue A-Richer (☎02.47.45.42.08; ④).

Tours and around

A little way upriver, **TOURS** is a bourgeois, rather dull city, but a reasonable base for seeing a number of châteaux, a handful of decent museums and the pleasures of the nearby vineyards. The town's main street is **rue Nationale**, a short walk down which are two of the town's most compelling collections: the **Musée du Compagnonnage** (mid-June to mid-Sept daily 9am–12.30pm & 2–6pm; rest of year same hours but closed Tues; F25), which documents the origins and militant activity of the guilds that built the châteaux, and the **Musée des Vins**, next door (March–Dec Mon & Wed–Sun 9am–noon & 2–6pm; Jan & Feb reservation only; F15), which gives a pretty comprehensive treatment of the history, mythology and production of the wondrous liquid. Over beside the **Cathédrale St-Gatien** – with its crumbling, Flamboyant Gothic front – the city's third museum, the **Musée des Beaux-Arts** on place François Sicard (9am–12.45pm & 2–6pm; closed Tues; F30), has some beauties in its rambling collection – *Christ in the Garden of Olives* and the *Resurrection* by Mantegna, and Frans Hals' portrait of Descartes. The museum's top treasure, however, Rembrandt's *Flight into Egypt*, is difficult to see through the security glass. In the opposite direction, west of rue Nationale, Tours' **Old Town** crowds around place St-Pierre-le-Puellier, whose medieval half-timbered houses and bulging stairway towers are the city's showpieces.

The **tourist office** (May–Oct Mon–Sat 8.30am–7pm, Sun 10am–12.30pm & 2.30–5pm; Nov–April Mon–Sat 9am–12.30pm & 1.30–6pm, Sun 10am–1pm) is in front of the train station at 78 rue Bernard-Palissy. Finding **accommodation** isn't a problem in Tours. There's an official **youth hostel** on av d'Arsonval in Parc de Gramont (☎02.47.25.14.45; ②); bus #1, #6, #11 to Chambray from place Jean-Jaurès), and a **hostel** for under-25s, *Le Foyer*, 16 rue Bernard-Palissy (☎02.47.60.51.51; ②) – call first as they may be full. The nearest **campsite**, *Les Acacias*, is on the south bank of the Loire east of Tours. As for **hotels**, the *St-Éloi* is one of the cheapest options, at 79 bd Béranger (☎02.47.37.67.34; ③), while *Mon Hôtel*, near the cathedral at 40 rue de la Préfecture (☎02.47.05.67.53; ③), is similarly priced. Rue du Grand-Marché and rue de la Rôtisserie, on the periphery of old Tours, and rue Colbert – which runs down to the cathedral – are the most promising streets for **restaurants**. Try *Le Petit Patrimoine* at 58 rue Colbert or *Le Franglais*, at no. 27, for good French food. *Les Trois Rois* and *Le Vieux Mûrier* in place Plumereaux are good for late-night **drinking** and, for dancing, check out *Le Labo*, 18 rue de la Longue-Échelle.

Villandry, Chenonceaux and Loches

The most popular attraction close to Tours is the château of **VILLANDRY**, about 13km west, where there are some extraordinary Renaissance **gardens** set out on several terraces that give marvellous views over the river (château daily 9/9.30am–5/7pm; gardens daily 8.30/9am–5.30/8pm; F45 château & gardens, F32 gardens only). The château itself includes Spanish paintings and a Moorish ceiling from Toledo. There's no public transport, but if you can rent a bike it's a wonderful ride along the banks of the Cher.

Perhaps the finest of all the castles of the region is the river-straddling château at **CHENONCEAUX** (daily 9am–5/7pm; F45), about 15km away and connected with Tours by two daily buses. The building went up in the 1520s, and was the home of Diane de Poitiers, the lover of Henry II. You're allowed to roam around the place and there is lots to see – floors of tapestries, paintings and furniture, not least Zurbarán's penetrating depiction of Archimedes in the Salle François I.

The château at **LOCHES**, an hour by train southeast of Tours, is visually the most impressive of the Loire fortresses, with ramparts and a huddle of houses below still partly enclosed by the outer wall of the medieval town (daily: July & Aug 9am–7pm; rest of year 9am–noon & 2–5/6pm; F31). You can climb unescorted to the top of the keep, poke around in the dungeons and torture chamber, and visit the royal lodgings in the northern end of the castle, where Charles VII and his three successors had their residence.

Blois and Chambord

The **château** at **BLOIS**, 40km or so upriver from Tours (mid-March to Sept daily 9am–6.30/8pm; Oct to mid-March 9am–12.30pm & 2–5.30pm; F35), was another residence of Catherine de Médici, and she died here in 1589. All six French kings of the sixteenth century spent time here; Henri III murdered the Duc de Guise and his brother here, shortly before being knocked off himself by a monk. The building is a strange mixture of architectural styles. The oldest parts date from the thirteenth century, and are viewable in the Salle des États or the main hall; Louis XII built the later east wing in Flamboyant Gothic style, while the early sixteenth-century north wing shows the influence of the Italian Renaissance.

Blois is a modern, uninteresting town, the château girdled by a busy road. However, if you have to stay, the **tourist office** at 3 av Jean-Laigret (May–Sept Mon–Sat 9am–7pm, Sun 10am–7pm; rest of year Mon–Sat 9am–12.30pm & 2–6pm, Sun 9.30am–12.30pm) organizes private rooms for a small fee, and there are a few inexpensive **hotels**, including the *St-Jacques*, 7 rue Ducoux (☎02.54.78.04.15; ③) and the *Hôtel du Bellay*, 12 rue des Minimes (☎02.54.78.23.62; ③). The closest **campsite** (☎02.54.78.82.05; April–Sept) is 2km away across the river, on the Lac de Loire at Vineuil. There is a **youth hostel** 3km downstream at Les Grouets, 18 rue de l'Hôtel-Pasquier (☎02.54.78.27.21; ①); take bus #4 from the train station. Best bets for **food** are the many restaurants on rue Foulérie, rue St-Lubin and rue des Violettes.

A few kilometres southeast of Blois, **CHAMBORD** (daily 9.30am–5.15/7.15pm; F40), François I's little "hunting lodge", was one of the most extravagant commissions of the age –

its patron's principal object was to outdo the Holy Roman Emperor Charles V, and it would, he claimed, leave him renowned as "one of the greatest builders in the universe". It was begun in 1519 and the work was executed by French masons, so the overall result is essentially French medieval, something particularly evident in the massive round towers with their conical tops and the forest of chimneys and turrets. The details, however, are pure Italian: for example the double spiral Great Staircase (attributed by some to Leonardo), panels of coloured marble, niches decorated with shell-like domes, and freestanding columns. Irregular **buses** run daily from Blois, and from May to September there's a special train service from Blois (F60); otherwise you'll have to use the expensive château tour buses from Blois or Tours. Cycling is preferable – it's a beautiful ride.

Orléans

Directly below the turned-up nose of the capital, poor **ORLÉANS** feels compelled to recuperate its faded glory from 1429, when Joan of Arc delivered the city from the English. There is, however, enough to merit a stop. The **Cathédrale St-Croix** (daily 10am–noon & 2–6pm), battered for five and a half centuries, is wonderful. In the north transept, Joan's pedestal is supported by two golden leopards (representing the English) on an altar carved with the battle scene. The late nineteenth-century stained-glass windows in the nave tell the story of Joan's life, with caricatures of the loutish Anglo-Saxons and snooty French nobles. There's more on Joan of Arc in the **Maison de Jeanne d'Arc** on place Général-de-Gaulle (May–Oct Tues–Sun 10am–noon & 2–6pm; Nov–April Tues–Sun 2–6pm; F13); it's fun for children, with good models and displays of the breaking of the Orléans siege. If you've had your fill of Joan, the best escape is the modern art collection in the basement of the **Musée des Beaux-Arts**, opposite the Hôtel de Ville (Tues & Sun 11am–6pm, Wed 10am–8pm, Thurs–Sat 10am–6pm; F20), with canvases by Picasso, Miró, Dufy, Renoir and Monet.

The **train station** and **tourist office** (Mon 10am–6.30/7pm, Tues–Sat 9am–6.30/7pm, Sun 10am–noon) are next door to each other on place Albert I, north of the town centre, connected by rue de la République to the central place du Martroi. There are cheap **hotels** near the station – the pleasant *Hôtel de Paris*, 29 faubourg Bannier (☎02.38.53.39.58; ③), and in the centre, you could try the *Charles Sanglier*, 8 rue Charles-Sanglier (☎02.38.53.38.50; ④). The **youth hostel** is at 14 rue du faubourg-Madeleine to the west of town (☎02.38.62.45.75; ①) – bus #B from place Albert I, direction "Paulbert". Bus #D goes to the nearest **campsite** at St-Jean-de-la-Ruelle, 2km out on the Blois road, rue de la Roche (☎02.38.88.39.39). Rue de Bourgogne, parallel to the river, has a good choice of **restaurants** of which *Le Dakar*, serving African food, is one of the best. For decent French cuisine head for *La Chancellerie*, 95 rue Royale, on the corner of place du Martroi.

Bourges

The capital of the *département* of Berry, about 50km south of Orléans, **BOURGES** has strong medieval links and is an obvious stopoff if you're heading towards the Massif Central. There's not much to the town, but it's a pleasant enough place to spend the night, not least for its **Cathédrale St-Étienne** (daily 8am–6pm), which is one of the country's most distinctive cathedrals, with five great portals opening out of its west front, adorned by thirteenth-century sculpture. Beloved of Gothic purists, the interior is impressive too: light, large and airy, double-aisled with no transepts, setting off to best effect the marvellous stained glass in the choir and apsidal chapels – the finest in France after Chartres.

Old Bourges lies within a loop of roads northwest of the cathedral. On rue Jacques-Coeur stand the head office, the stock exchange, dealing rooms, safes and the home of Charles VII's finance minister, **Jacques Coeur**, a medieval shipping magnate, moneylender and arms dealer who dominates Bourges much as Joan of Arc does Orléans. The visit to his palace (tours daily: July & Aug 9am–7pm; Sept–June 9–11.10am & 2.15–4.10/5.10pm; F32) is fun and worthwhile, starting with the fake windows from which realistic sculpted figures look down. Though few furnishings remain, the decorations on the stonework, including numerous hearts and scallop shells (*coeurs* and *coquilles St-Jacques*), show the mark of the man who had it built.

The **train station** is 1km north of the centre on pl du G.Leclerc, just off av Pierre-Sémard, across the river. The **tourist office** (April–Sept Mon–Sat 9am–7pm, Sun 10am–7pm; March–Oct Mon–Sat 9am–6pm, Sun 10am–12.30pm) is close to the cathedral, at 21 rue Victor-Hugo. There is a **youth hostel** a short walk out of town at 22 rue Henri-Sellier (☎02.48.24.58.09; ②; red bus #1), and a **campsite** across the stream from the hostel on bd de l'Industrie; closer to the centre and the train station is the *Centre International de Séjour*, 17 rue Felix-Chédin (☎02.48.70.25.59; ②). Bourges' cheapest **hotel** is *Au Rendez-vous des Amis*, 6 av Marx-Dormoy (☎02.48.70.81.80; ②), a short walk from the station up av P-Sémard and right, while in the middle of town there's *Le Central*, 6 rue du Docteur-Témoin (☎02.48.24.10.25; ②). The main centre for **restaurants** is place Gordaine, an attractive medieval square where *Le Comptoir de Paris* makes a reasonable option; the *Arôme de Vieux Bourges* is a coffee shop selling all manner of edible delicacies – good for lunch.

POITOU-CHARENTE AND THE ATLANTIC COAST

The summer light, the warm air, the fields of sunflowers and the siesta-silent air of the farmhouses of **Poitou-Charente** give the first exciting promise of the south. The coast has great charm in places, although it remains distinctly Atlantic, with dunes, pine forests and misty mud flats, and it lacks the glamour of the Côte d'Azur. The principal port, **La Rochelle**, however, is one of the prettiest and most distinctive towns in France, and the islands of **Ré** and **Oléron**, out of season at least, are lovely, with kilometres of sandy beaches. **Poitiers** is a likely entry point to the region, a pleasant town with an attractive old centre. South of here, the valley of the Charente river, slow and green, epitomizes the blue-overalled, peasant France, accessible on boat trips from **Cognac**, famous for the eponymous spirit.

Poitiers

POITIERS is no seething metropolis, but a country town with a charm that comes from a long and sometimes influential history – as seat of the dukes of Aquitaine – discernible in the winding lines of the streets and the breadth of architectural fashions represented in its buildings.

The tree-lined **place Leclerc**, and **place de Gaulle** just a few streets north, are the two poles of communal life, flanked by cafés and bustling market stalls. Between is a warren of streets, with rue Gambetta cutting north past the **Palais de Justice** (Mon–Fri 9am–6pm; free), whose nineteenth-century facade hides the twelfth-century great hall of the dukes of Aquitaine. This magnificent room is where Jean, Duc de Berry, held his sumptuous court in the late fourteenth century, seated on the intricately carved dais at the far end of the room. In one corner, stairs give access to the old **castle keep**. The stairs lead out onto the roof with a fantastic view over the town.

Across from the Palais is one of the greatest and most idiosyncratic churches in France, **Notre-Dame-la-Grande**, whose west front is loaded with enthralling sculpture, typical of the Poitou brand of Romanesque – though the interior, crudely overlaid with nineteenth-century frescoes, is not nearly as interesting. There is another unusual church a little way east, literally in the middle of rue Jean-Jaurès as you head towards the River Clain. This is the mid-fourth-century **Baptistère St-Jean** (July & Aug daily 10.30am–12.30pm & 3–6pm; April–June & Sept–Oct same hours closed Tues; Nov–March Mon & Wed–Sun 2.30–5pm; F4), reputedly the oldest Christian building in France and until the seventeenth century the only place in town you could have a proper baptism; the font was the octagonal pool sunk into the floor. There are also some very ancient and faded **frescoes** on the walls, including the Emperor Constantine on horseback.

The **train station** is a ten-minute walk from the centre at the foot of the hill which forms the kernel of the town. Among cheap **hotels** the *Victor Hugo*, east of the train station at 5 rue Victor Hugo (☎05.49.41.12.16; ②), is a real bargain or there's the *Petite Villette*, 14 bd de l'Abbé de Frémont (☎05.49.41.41.33; ②). It's only a short uphill walk to the town centre, where you'll pay a bit more at the attractive *Hôtel du Plat d'Étain*, 7 rue du Plat d'Étain (☎05.49.41.04.80; ③). The **youth hostel** is at allée Roger-Tagault (☎05.49.30.09.70; ②) and there's a municipal **campsite** on rue du Porteau, 2km north of the town (bus #7). The **tourist office**'s main office is at 5 rue des Grandes-Écoles (July & Aug Mon–Fri 9am–7pm, Sat 9.45am–6.45pm Sun 9.45am–1pm & 3–6pm; Sept–June Mon–Fri 9am–noon & 1.30–6pm, Sat 9am–noon & 2–6pm), with a summer annexe by the station. As for **eating**, *Le St-Hubert*, 13 rue Cloche Perse, does regional food at reasonable prices, and *Le Cappuccino*, on rue de l'Université, is one of several good Italians in the area.

La Rochelle and around

LA ROCHELLE is the most attractive seaside town in France, with a seventeenth- and eighteenth-century centre and waterfront. The town has a long history. Eleanor of Aquitaine gave it a charter in 1199, and it rapidly became a port of major importance, trading in salt and wine, the principal terminus for trade with the French colonies in the West Indies and Canada. Indeed, many of the settlers, especially in Canada, came from this part of France.

From the visitor's point of view, everything worth seeing is in the area behind the waterfront, in effect between the harbour and place de Verdun. The heavy Gothic gateway of the **Porte de la Grosse Horloge** straddles the entrance to the old town, dominating the pleasure-boat-filled inner harbour, overlooked by two towers. Through the Grosse Horloge, the main shopping street, **rue du Palais**, is lined by eighteenth-century houses and arcaded shop fronts. To the west, especially in rue de l'Escale, are the discreet residences of the eighteenth-century shipowners and chandlers, while to the east, rue du Temple leads to the **Hôtel de Ville**, begun in the reign of Henri IV, whose initials, intertwined with those of Marie de Médici, are carved on the ground-floor gallery. It's a beautiful specimen of Frenchified Italian taste, adorned with niches and statues and coffered ceilings. There's more of this rich world in the **Musée du Nouveau Monde** on rue Fleuriau (Mon & Wed–Sat 10.30am–noon & 2–6pm, Sun 2–6pm; F21), which occupies the former residence of the Fleuriau family, who, like many of their fellow-Rochelais, made fortunes from slaving and West Indian sugar, spices and coffee.

From the **train station**, it's ten minutes down **av de Gaulle** to the town centre. The **tourist office** is by the harbour on place de la Petite Sirène, Quai de Gabut (June–Aug Mon–Sat 9am–7/8pm, Sun 10am–5pm; Sept–May Mon–Sat 9am–noon & 2–6pm, Sun 10am–noon), but finding **accommodation** can be a problem in season. There's a **youth hostel** in av des Minimes to the west (☎05.46.44.43.11; ②) – bus #10 from place de Verdun or the train station – and two **campsites**: the *Soleil* (☎05.46.44.42.53; May–Sept) by the hostel and a municipal site on the northwestern side of town, on bd A.-Rondeau, *Port Neuf* (☎05.46.43.81.20; bus #6 from Grosse Horloge). Of a handful of cheap **hotels** in the centre, the best bets are the *Bordeaux*, 43 rue St-Nicolas (☎05.46.41.31.22; ③), *Henri-IV*, 31 rue des Gentilshommes (☎05.46.41.25.79; ③), and the *Printania*, 9 rue Brave-Rondeau (☎05.46.41.22.86; ③). For **eating**, try the rue du Port/rue St-Sauveur area just off the waterfront and rue St-Nicolas. *Pub Lutèce* on rue St-Sauveur is a reasonably priced brasserie and *Café-Resto à la Villette*, behind the market, has good plats du jour, while *A Côté de Chez Fred*, at 34 rue St-Nicolas, has the freshest fish and a down-to-earth atmosphere. For **beaches**, you're best off crossing over to the **Île de Ré**, a long narrow island immediately west of La Rochelle (buses from place de Verdun or pricey boat trips with Ré-Croisières from the Vieux Port), which is surrounded by sandy strands. Out of season it has a slow, misty charm, with life in its little ports revolving around the cultivation of oysters and mussels.

Île d'Oleron

If you want to **swim**, south of La Rochelle is **ÎLE D'OLERON**, France's largest island after Corsica, joined to the mainland by toll bridge, which has kilometres of beautiful sandy beaches. The little towns, inevitably, have been ruined by the development of hundreds of holiday homes, and it can be a real battle in the summer season to find a place to stay, but, for all that, it's a pretty and distinctive island. With its pines, tamarisks and evergreen oaks, the stretch from Boyardville to St-Pierre – the most attractive of the towns – is the most appealing.

Cognac

COGNAC is a sunny, prosperous, little place, best-known for its brandy distilleries, which reveal themselves through the heady scent that pervades the air. The **tourist office**, close by the central place François I (summer Mon–Sat 9am–8pm, Sun 10.30am–4pm; winter Mon–Sat 9am–12.30pm & 2–6.15pm), has information on visiting the various cognac *chais*, most of which are situated at the end of Grand-Rue, which winds through the old quarter of town. Perhaps the best for a visit are those of **Hennessy** (March–Dec daily 10am–5pm; tours run every hour in winter, every 15min in summer; F30), a seventh-generation family firm of Irish origin, where tours begin with a film explaining what's what in the world of cognac. Hennessy alone keeps 180,000 barrels in stock; all are regularly checked and various blends made from barrel to barrel. Only the best is kept, a choice which depends on the taste buds of the *maître du chais*. At Hennessy the job has been in the same family for six generations; the present heir apparent has already been sixteen years under his father's tutelage and is still said to be not yet fully qualified.

From the **train station**, take rue Mousnier, then rue Bayard, which leads you up rue du 14-Juillet to the central place François I. There are a couple of **cafés** and a reasonable **brasserie** on the square or try the excellent *La Boîte-à-Sel*, 68 av Victor-Hugo. Upstream from the bridge, the oak woods of the Parc François I stretch along the riverbank to the town **campsite**; the cheapest **rooms** are at *Le Cheval Blanc*, 6–8 place Bayard (☎05.45.82.09.55; ②); while the *Hotel d'Orléans* at 25 rue d'Angoulême (☎05.45.82.01.26; ③) is more upmarket and characterful.

AQUITAINE, THE DORDOGNE AND THE LOT

Steamy, moist and green, the **southwest** of France can feel like a kind of lower-latitude England. In the Dordogne heartlands, the country is certainly beautiful, but the more famous spots, especially in the Dordogne valley, have become oppressively crowded in season. **Bordeaux** is a possible entry point to the region, though not really stimulating unless you're interested in wine.

East of Bordeaux, the northern half of the Dordogne *département*, the **Périgord Blanc**, is named for the light, white colour of its rock outcrops – undulating, fertile, wooded country, rising in the north and east to the edge of the Massif Central. The regional capital is **Périgueux** which, because of its central position and relative ease of access, makes the best base for the whole region, especially the cave paintings at **Les Eyzies** and around. The **Périgord Noir** is the stretch of territory from Bergerac to Brive. It's this area that people always think of when you say Dordogne, where most of the picture-book villages are, where the cuisine is at its richest and the prices at their highest. **Sarlat** is its capital and a good base for exploration. South from here lies the drier, poorer and more sparsely populated region through which the **Lot** river flows roughly parallel with the Dordogne, an ideal area to hike, bike and camp.

Bordeaux and around

The city of **BORDEAUX** is something of a disappointment. It's big, with a population of over half a million, and obviously rich, yet the only part you could call attractive is the relatively small eighteenth-century centre. The rest is scruffy and contains far fewer sights than many a lesser place. But if you are just passing through, its regional museum is worth seeing, cheap accommodation is plentiful, and it's a good place to eat, with numerous ethnic restaurants. The surrounding countryside is not the most enticing, and you definitely need your own transport to explore it; you go for the wines rather than the landscape. More interesting are the vast pine-covered expanse of Les Landes, to the south, and the huge wild Atlantic beaches.

Arrival and accommodation

Arriving by **train**, you find yourself at the **Gare St-Jean**, linked to the centre of town by bus #7/#8, and the heart of a convenient if insalubrious area for **accommodation**. Right outside the station, rue Charles-Domercq and cours de la Marne are full of one- and two-star **hotels** – try the *San Michel* at no. 32 rue Charles-Domercq (☎05.56.91.96.40; ②). Less seedily, there's the more central *Hôtel de la Boétie* at 4 rue de la Boétie (☎05.56.81.76.68; ③). The large **youth hostel** is near the station too, to the left off cours de la Marne at 22 cours Barbey (☎05.56.91.59.51; ②) – though there's an 11pm curfew. Less seedy than the main hostel, the *Maison des Étudiantes*, 50 rue Ligier (☎05.56.96.48.30; ②), at the end of cours de la Marne, sometimes has cheap rooms – and, although mainly for women, will accept men in July and August. The main **tourist office** is in the centre of town on cours du 30-juillet, just north of place de la Comédie (May–Oct Mon–Sat 9am–8pm, Sun 9am–7pm; Nov–April Mon–Sat 9am–7pm, Sun 9.45am–6.30pm), with an annexe at the station (May–Oct Mon–Sat 9am–noon & 1–7pm, Sun 10am–noon & 1–6pm; Nov–April Mon–Sat 9am–noon & 1–6pm). Though the city centre is walkable, you need to take **buses** to cover longer distances; tickets, valid for one journey only, are available on board but it's cheaper to buy packs of ten from a *tabac*.

The City

The centre of the city is the café-lined **place Gambetta**, a once majestic square conceived in the time of Louis XV. Its house fronts, arcaded at street level, are decorated with rows of carved masks, and in the middle an English-style garden soaks up some of the traffic fumes. In one corner, the eighteenth-century arch of the **Porte Dijeaux** spans the street. East, cours de l'Intendance, full of chic shops, leads to the impeccably classical **Grand Théâtre** on place de la Comédie, built in 1780 and faced with an immense colonnaded portico topped by Muses and Graces. From here, smart streets radiate out. Sanded and tree-lined allée de Tourny leads to a statue of Tourny, the eighteenth-century administrator who was prime mover of the city's golden age. Cours du 30-juillet leads into the bare expanse of **Esplanade des Quinconces**, said to be Europe's largest municipal square, with an enormous memorial to the Girondins, the influential local deputies to the Revolutionary Assembly of 1789, purged by Robespierre as counter-revolutionaries.

Rue Ste-Cathérine, the city's main shopping street, leads down from place de la Comédie towards the best of the city's museums, the **Musée d'Aquitaine** at 20 cours Pasteur (Tues–Sun 11am–6pm, Wed until 8pm; F20), an imaginative collection including drawings and writings that give some indication why eighteenth-century Bordeaux was compared to Paris by contemporary writers. Take a look, too, at the section on the wine trade before venturing off on a vineyard tour. A couple of blocks east is the cathedral of **St-André**, whose most eye-catching feature is the great upward sweep of the twin steeples over the north transept. The surrounding square is attractive, with enticing pavement cafés and the classical **Hôtel de Ville**. Just around the corner on cours d'Albert, the **Musée des Beaux-Arts** (Mon & Wed–Sun 11am–6pm, Wed until 8pm; F20) has a small but commendable collection, including works by Rubens, Matisse and Kokoschka.

Eating and drinking

There are a lot of cheap **eating** places in the station quarter, and ethnic restaurants along the left bank of the river near the station. In the centre of town, wholesome meals and terrace drinks are available from the very popular *Café des Arts* on the corner of rue St-Cathérine and cours Victor-Hugo. For typical French cooking try *Le Tire-Bouchon*, 15 rue des Bahutiers, and for French Bordelais specialities at *Le Bistro d'Édouard*, 16 place du Parlement, while *Aux Trois Arcades*, nearby at no. 10 place du Parlement, specializes in huge, unusual salads. The town has an excellent reputation for seafood restaurants: head for *Chez Joël D*, 13 rue des

Pilliers-de-Tutelle, for oysters. Home to a large university, Bordeaux has a good selection of studenty **bars**, such as *Chez Auguste*, place de la Victoire, *The Bus Stop*, 8 rue des Augustins, and the hip *Aviatic Bar*, place Général-Sarrail.

The vineyards

With Burgundy and Champagne, the wines of Bordeaux form the Holy Trinity of French viticulture. The reds in particular – known as claret to the English – have graced the tables of the discerning for many a century. The country that produces them stretches north, east and south of the city, and is the largest quality wine district in the world. North along the west bank of the brown, island-spotted Gironde are **Médoc** and **Haut-Médoc**, whose wines have a full-bodied, smoky taste and a reputation for improving with age. Across the Gironde – seven or eight ferries a day from Lamarque to Vauban-fortified Blaye – the green slopes of the *côtes* of **Bourg** and **Blaye** are home to heavier, plummier reds, cheaper than anything found on the opposite side of the river. South of the city is the domain of the great whites, the super-dry **Graves** and the sweet dessert wines of **Sauternes**, which get their flavour from grapes left to rot on the vine. East, on the other side of the River Garonne, are the **Premières Côtes de Bordeaux**, which form the first slopes of the **Entre-Deux-Mers** (by far the prettiest countryside in the Bordeaux wine region), whose wines are regarded as good but less fine than the Médocs and Graves – less fine also than the superlative reds of **Pomerol**, **Fronsac** and **St-Émilion**, just to the north of the River Dordogne.

The Bordeaux tourist office has a leaflet detailing all the châteaux that allow **visits and wine-tasting**. Since, however, getting to any of these places except St-Émilion without your own transport is hard work, the simplest thing is to take one of the tourist office's own **tours**, which leave daily between May and October at 1.30pm, and twice weekly between November and April. They are expensive (around F160) but are generally interesting and informative and well worth the money.

The beaches

On summer weekends the Bordelais escape to **ARCACHON**, a seaside resort forty minutes' train ride away across flat, sandy forest. The beaches of white sand are magnificent but inevitably crowded. **Hotels** tend to be expensive and fully booked in season – a good bet is *Hôtel St Christaud*, 8 allée de la Chapelle (☎05.56.83.38.53; ④), though there's also a campsite. Arcachon's chief curiosity is the **dune du Pyla** – at 114m the highest sand dune in Europe, a veritable mountain of wind-carved sand – about 8km down the coast. Buses run there from Arcachon **train station** every thirty minutes in July and August; there are about five a day at other times. From the end of the line the road continues on uphill for about fifteen minutes to the inevitable group of fast-food stands and a superb view of the bay of Arcachon and the forest of Les Landes stretching away to the south.

Les Landes

Travelling south from Bordeaux by road or rail, you pass for half a day through unremitting, flat, sandy pine forest – **Les Landes**. Until the nineteenth century this was a vast, infertile swamp, steadily encroached upon by the shifting sand dunes of the coast; today it supports over 10,000 square kilometres of trees. At **SABRES**, 18km east of Labouheyre on the N10 from Bordeaux to Bayonne, a resuscitated steam train runs to the **Éco-musée de Marquéze** (Easter–Oct Mon–Sat 2.40–4pm, last returning train 6pm, Sun 10.10am–12.20pm & 2.40–4pm, last returning train 7pm; F47 including train fare) run by the **Parc régional des Landes de Gascogne**. The museum illustrates the traditional *landais* way of life, where shepherds clomped around the scrub on long stilts.

Périgueux

PÉRIGUEUX is a busy and prosperous market town which makes a good base for seeing the best of the Dordogne's prehistoric caves. The centre of town focuses on **place Bugeaud**, a ten-minute walk from the train station. Ahead, down rue Taillefer, the **Cathédrale de St-Front** (daily 8am–12.30pm & 2.30–7.30pm), its square, pineapple-capped belfry surging above the roofs of the surrounding medieval houses, is one of the most distinctive Romanesque churches in France, modelled on the Holy Apostles in Constantinople. The big Baroque altarpiece is worth a look, too, depicting the Assumption of the Virgin. Outside, place de la Clautre gives on to Périgueux's renovated **old quarter**, with a number of fine Renaissance houses, particularly along rue Limogeanne. The **Musée du Périgord**, at the end of rue St-Front on the cours de Tourny (Mon & Wed–Fri 10am–noon & 2–6pm, Sat & Sun 1–6pm; F20), has some beautiful Gallo-Roman mosaics from local sites. There are some exquisite Limoges enamels near the exit; look especially at the portraits of the twelve Caesars.

There are some recommended cheap **hotels** right in front of the train station: try the *Hôtel du Midi et Terminus* (☎05.53.53.41.06; ③), whose good regional restaurant has menus for around F80. Alternatively, there is **hostel accommodation** at the *Résidence Lakanal*, 32 bd Lakanal (☎05.53.53.52.05; ②) – follow the rail track southeast from the station. The **tourist office** is at 26 place Francheville (June–Sept Mon–Sat 9am–7pm, Sun 10am–6pm; Oct–May Mon–Sat 9am–6pm), next to the Tour Mataguerre, the last remnant of the town's medieval defences. Surprisingly, Périgueux isn't greatly blessed with good **restaurants**. *Hercule Poireau*, 2 rue de la Nation, and *Au Petit Chef*, 5 place du Coderc, both serve up decent French meals. Failing that, you could try one of the **brasseries** around bd Montaigne.

The Vézère valley caves

Half an hour or so by train from Périgueux is a luxuriant cliff-cut region riddled with **caves** and subterranean streams. It was here that human skeletons were first unearthed in 1868, and an incredible wealth of archeological evidence of the life of late Stone Age people has since been found here. The paintings which adorn the caves – perhaps to aid fertility or hunting rituals – are remarkable not only for their age, but also for their exquisite colouring and the skill with which they are drawn.

LES EYZIES is the centre of the region, a rambling, unattractive village given over to tourism. Worth a glance before or after visiting the caves is the **Musée National de Préhistoire** (July & Aug 9.30am–7pm; rest of year 9.30am–noon & 2–5/6pm; closed Tues; F22), which exhibits prehistoric artefacts and art objects including copies of one of the most beautiful pieces of Stone Age art – two clay bison from the Tuc d'Audoubert cave in the Pyrenees. Just outside Les Eyzies, off the road to Sarlat, the tunnel-like **Grotte de Font de Gaume** (9/10am–noon & 2–5/6pm; closed Wed; F35) contains dozens of polychrome paintings. Most miraculous of all is a frieze of five bison discovered in 1966 during cleaning operations, the colour remarkably preserved by a protective layer of calcite. Maximum group size for admission at one time is twenty and **tickets** sell out fast. To be sure of a place in season, especially on a Sunday when they're half-price, get to the ticket office at least an hour before opening.

Not a cave but a rock shelter, **Abri du Cap-Blanc** (July & Aug daily 9.30am–7pm; April–June & Sept–Oct daily 10am–noon & 2–6pm; F30) is a steep but manageable bike ride 7km from Les Eyzies. Its sculpted frieze of horses and bison, dating from 12,000 BC, is polished and set off against a pockmarked background in extraordinary high relief. Of the ten surviving prehistoric sculptures in France, this is the best. The road up takes you past the **Grotte des Combarelles** (same hours & price as Grotte de Font de Gaume), whose engravings of humans, reindeer and mammoths dating from the Magdalanian period are also worth a visit.

Montignac and Lascaux

Heading up the valley of the Vézère river, northeast of Les Eyzies, **MONTIGNAC** (connected to Sarlat by bus) is more attractive than Les Eyzies. The **tourist office** (July & Aug daily 9am–7pm; Sept–Dec & Feb–June Mon–Sat 9am–noon & 2–6pm) is in the same building as a **museum** of local crafts and the ticket office for the nearby cave of **Lascaux** – or rather, for a tantalizing replica, **Lascaux II** (July & Aug daily 9am–7pm; Sept–Dec & Feb–June Tues–Sun 9.30am–noon & 1.30–6pm; F50); the original has been closed since 1963 due to deterioration from the body heat and breath of visitors. Executed 17,000 years ago, the paintings are said to be the finest prehistoric works in existence. There are five or six identifiable styles, and subjects include the bison, mammoth and horse, plus the biggest-known prehistoric drawing in existence, a 5.5-metre bull with astonishingly expressive head and face. The visit lasts forty minutes, and the commentary is in French, with English translations if requested.

Practicalities

Most facilities are situated in **Les Eyzies**. There's a riverside **campsite**, *La Rivière*, but **hotels** are pricey and likely to ask for *demi-pension*. The village **tourist office** has information on private rooms in the area and rents out **bikes**. If you're not staying in Périgueux, try **Le Bugue**, 10km down the River Vézère, where the friendly *Hotel de Paris* at 14 rue Paris (☎05.53.07.28.16; ②) has cheap rooms. Three or four **trains** run daily to Les Eyzies from Périgueux, and the Périgueux tourist office issues a sheet detailing how to get there and back in the day. **Montignac** (connected to Sarlat by bus) is short on even moderately priced accommodation, though *Hôtel de la Grotte*, 63 rue du 4-Septembre (☎05.53.51.80.48; ③) has a couple of cheap rooms and a good cheap menu. There is also a three-star **campsite**. The **tourist office** is on place Bertran de Born.

Bergerac and the Dordogne valley

Lying on the banks of the Dordogne southeast of Périgueux, **BERGERAC** is the main market centre for the surrounding maize, vine and tobacco farms. Devastated in the Wars of Religion, when most of its Protestant population fled overseas, it is essentially a modern town, yet it is still attractive. What is left of the old quarter has a lot of charm, with numerous late-medieval houses. In rue de l'Ancien-Pont, the seventeenth-century Maison Peyrarède houses a **tobacco museum** (Tues–Sat 10am–noon & 2–6pm, Sun 2.30–6.30pm; F17), detailing the history of the weed, with collections of pipes and tools of the trade. Bergerac is the mainstay of the French tobacco-growing industry, somewhat in the doldrums today since the traditional *brune* (brown cigarette tobacco) is gradually being superseded by the *blonde*, which is oven-cured and therefore a lot less labour-intensive to make. **Accommodation** in Bergerac isn't hard to find: there's a **campsite** west of the centre by the river, and several small hotels, among them the *Hôtel Pozzi*, 11 rue Pozzi (☎05.53.57.04.68; ②), and the *Family*, place du Marché-Couvert (☎05.53.57.80.90; ③), which has a good **restaurant**. The **tourist office** is at 97 rue Neuve-d'Argenson (summer daily 9am–7pm; winter Mon–Sat 9.30am–noon & 2–6.30pm).

To the east is **SARLAT**, capital of Périgord Noir, held in a hollow in the hills a few kilometres back from the Dordogne Valley. It has an alluring old medieval core, focusing on the central **place de la Liberté**, where you'll find the **tourist office** (May–Aug Mon–Sat 9am–7pm, Sun 10am–noon & 4–6pm; rest of year Mon–Sat 9am–noon & 2–6pm). Although there's not much to see, it makes a good base for the surrounding countryside and trips further upstream – the tourist office has details of organized trips if you don't have your own transport. There is a **youth hostel** on the Périgueux road at 77 av de Selves (☎05.53.59.47.59; ②; April–Oct), and a prettily sited **campsite** 2km beyond the rail viaduct. Hotels include the *Marcel*, 8 av de Selves (☎05.53.59.21.98; ④), which has a good restaurant, and the *Hôtel de la Mairie* on place de la Liberté (☎05.53.59.05.71; ③).

Among the places you might visit from Sarlat are **SOUILLAC**, further upstream, where the twelfth-century church of St-Marie has some marvellous Romanesque sculptures, and, about 10km southeast of there, **ROCAMADOUR**, wonderfully sited tucked under a cliff in a deep canyon. This has been visited for centuries by pilgrims for its miracle-working Black Madonna, housed in a votive-packed **Chapelle Miraculeuse**, to which the devout drag themselves on their knees. But be warned that it can sometimes get unbearably crowded these days, and is home to all manner of tourist junk.

THE PYRENEES

Basque-speaking and wet in the west, snowy and patois-speaking in the middle, dry and Catalan in the east, **the Pyrenees** are physically beautiful, culturally varied and a great deal less developed than the Alps. The whole range is marvellous walking country, especially the central region around the **Parc National des Pyrénées**, with its 3000-metre peaks, streams, forests, flowers and wildlife. If you're a serious hiker, it's possible to walk all the way across from Atlantic to Mediterranean between June and September, following the *GR10* or the more difficult *Haute Randonnée Pyrénéenne* – although bear in mind that these are big mountains, and to cover any of the main walks you'll need hiking boots and, despite the southerly latitude, warm and windproof clothing. As for more conventional tourist attractions, the **Basque coast** is lovely but very popular, suffering from seaside sprawl and a massive surfeit of campsites: **St-Jean-de-Luz** is by far the prettiest of the resorts; **Bayonne** the most attractive town, with an excellent Basque museum and art gallery, and **Biarritz** the most overrated. The foothill towns, on the whole, are dull, though **Pau** is worth a day or two, while **Lourdes** is a monster of kitsch that has to be seen.

Biarritz and Bayonne

Biarritz and Bayonne are virtual continuations of each other, but their characters are entirely different. **BIARRITZ** is a nineteenth-century resort once patronized by Queen Victoria; its ponderous architecture gives it an unfriendly air, but its waves provide some of the best surfing in Europe and ensure a kicking summer season. **BAYONNE**, on the other hand is a clean, sunny, southern town, workaday and very Basque: it stands back some 6km from the Atlantic, a position that's protected it from any real exploitation by tourism. This is fortunate, for with its half-timbered houses, their shutters and woodwork painted in the peculiarly Basque tones of green and red, it is one of the most distinctive and enjoyable towns in France.

The town of Bayonne is situated at the junction of the Nive and Adour rivers, with the centre grouped closely around the banks of the Nive. Close to the confluence of the two rivers, **place de la Liberté** is the main town square, full of cafés and *pâtisseries*. The **quays** nearby along the Nive are fun to wander, and on the opposite side of the river – in the area known as "Petit Bayonne" – at the corner of the second bridge, is the excellent **Musée Basque**, unfortunately closed at the time of writing, and not expected to reopen until 2002. The city's second museum, the **Musée Bonnat** on nearby rue Jacques-Lafitte (10am–noon & 2.30–6.30pm, Fri until 8.30pm; closed Tues; F20), is an unexpected treasury of art, with works by Rubens, Delacroix and Degas. Across the Nive, the **Cathédrale St-Marie** looks its best from a distance, its twin towers and steeple rising with airy grace above the houses. Up close, the stone reveals bad weathering, with most of the decorative detail lost, although the interior is more impressive due to the height of the nave and some stained sixteenth-century glass.

Practicalities

Bayonne's **train station** is in the shabby quarter of **St-Esprit** on the opposite bank of the Adour, connected to the city centre by the long Pont St-Esprit. For Biarritz and the **beaches**, you can hop on a bus by the Hôtel de Ville on place Liberté. The **tourist office** is located on place des Basques (July & Aug Mon–Sat 9am–7pm, Sun 10am–1pm; Sept–June Mon–Fri 9am–6.30pm, Sat 10am–6pm). The best cheap **accommodation** is at *Hôtel des Arceaux*, 26 rue Pont-Neuf (☎05.59.59.15.53; ③); if that's full, try *Paris-Madrid* by the station (☎05.59.55.13.98; ②), or *Hôtel des Basques*, place Paul-Bert, beside St-André (☎05.59.59.08.02; ②). The closest and nicest **campsite** is the well-equipped *La Chêneraie*, in the St-Frédéric quarter on the north bank of the Adour, while the nearest **youth hostel** (☎05.59.58.70.00; ②) is at 19 route des Vignes, Anglet, between Bayonne and Biarritz; to get there take bus #4 from the Hôtel de Ville to La Barre and change to the #9, direction La Bourd, getting off at the Auberge de Jeunesse stop. Biarritz has its own new youth hostel at 8 rue Chiquito de Cambo (☎05.59.41.76.00; ②) and is within walking distance from the train station, down towards the lake. The best area for **cafés and restaurants** in Bayonne is Petit Bayonne – try the tapas-style menu of the friendly *Xan Xan Gorri* at 9 rue des Cordeliers, or the *Bar des Amis*, 13 rue des Cordeliers, which does good cheap menus.

St-Jean-de-Luz

ST-JEAN-DE-LUZ is by far the most attractive resort on the Basque coast. Although it gets crowded and its main seafront is undistinguished, it has a long curving beach of beautiful fine sand. It is also a thriving fishing port, the most important in France for catches of tuna and anchovy, and the old houses around the harbour, both in St-Jean and across the water in Ciboure (effectively the same town) are very picturesque.

The focus of life for visitors is **place Louis XIV** near the harbour, with its cafés, bandstand and plane trees. The seventeenth-century **house** (June–Sept Mon–Sat 10.30am–noon & 2.30–5.30/6.30pm, Sun 2.30–5.30/6.30pm; F25) on the harbour side of the square was built by a shipowner called Lohobiague in 1635 and still belongs to the same family. It is also where Louis XIV stayed at the time of his marriage to Maria Theresa, Infanta of Castile, which took place in the town – an extravagant event at which Cardinal Mazarin alone presented the queen with 12,000 pounds of pearls and diamonds, a gold dinner service and a pair of sumptuous carriages drawn by teams of six horses. Maria Theresa lodged just along the quay in an Italianate mansion of faded pink brick. A short distance up rue Gambetta, on the town side of the square, is the church of **St-Jean-Baptiste**, the largest of the Basque churches and where Louis and Maria Theresa were married. It is a plain, fortress-like building from the outside; inside, the barn-like nave is roofed in wood and lined on three sides with tiers of dark oak galleries, a distinctive feature of Basque churches – they were reserved for the men, while the women sat in the nave.

The **tourist office** is in place du Maréchal-Foch (July & Aug Mon–Sat 9am–8pm, Sun 10am–1pm; rest of year Mon–Sat 9am–12.30pm & 2–6/7pm). There are several **hotels** near the station: try *Hôtel de Verdun*, 13 av de Verdun (☎05.59.26.02.55; ④) or the *Hôtel de Paris* at 1 bd du Comandant-Passicot (☎05.59.26.00.62; ⑤). There are lots of **campsites** in the vicinity, all grouped together a few kilometres northeast of the town; try the *Chibau-Berria*, one of the nearest, left off the N10.

Pau and the mountains

Capital of the viscounty of Béarn, **PAU** has had a more than usually turbulent history, maintaining its separatist leanings well into the seventeenth century; even today many of the Béarnais still speak *Occitan* rather than French. It's a university town, good-looking, lively and, partly thanks to tourism, with a fairly buoyant prosperity. It occupies a grand natural site on a steep scarp overlooking the Gave de Pau, and from its **boulevard des Pyrénées**, the promenade which runs along the rim of the scarp, there are superb views of the higher peaks. Not surprisingly, it has become the most popular starting point for the Parc National des Pyrénées Occidentales, and it's well-equipped for the purpose. As for its own sights, Pau's **Château** (guided tours: daily 9.30–11.45am & 2–5.15pm; F25), at the west end of bd des Pyrénées, was done up by Louis-Philippe in the nineteenth century after standing empty for 200 years.

From the **train station** down by the river, a free funicular shuttles you up to bd des Pyrénées. The **bus station** (for non-SNCF buses) is off place Clemenceau, on rue Gachet. The **tourist office** is at the end of place Royale (July & Aug Mon–Sat 9am–6pm; rest of year Mon–Fri 9am–noon & 2–6pm, Sat 9am–noon & 2–6pm). There is a **youth hostel** over the river in Gelos (☎05.59.06.53.02; ②), a *Foyer des jeunes travailleurs* at 30 rue Michel-Houneau (☎05.59.11.05.05; ②), and a similar *Maison Européenne de la Jeunesse* at 18 rue Bourbaki (☎05.59.62.50.50; ②). For **hotels**, try the quiet and hospitable *Hôtel d'Albret*, 11 rue Jeanne d'Albret (☎05.59.27.81.58; ③), or the *Hôtel Le Matisse*, 17 rue Mathieu-Lalanne (☎05.59.27.73.80; ③). There is a municipal **campsite** on bd du Cami-Salié, off av Sallenavem on the northern edge of town. **Restaurants** are numerous, too, especially towards the château. *La Brochetterie*, 16 rue Henri-IV, has reasonably priced menus and a pleasant family atmosphere; *Le Berry* on place Clemenceau is a popular brasserie with local students.

Into the mountains

Pau is probably the best large base for launching into the highest parts of the Pyrenees, as the **Parc National des Pyrénées Occidentales** lies to the south of the town. It is possible to hitch to the spectacular main passes of **Col d'Aubisque** and **Col du Tourmalet**, though you will find you invariably get left on the top by drivers coming up for the view and going back the same way. The **tourist office** supplies walking information and will recommend local organizations that run **guided hikes**. More specialist knowledge can be gleaned from the *Club Alpin Français*, 5 rue René Fournets (☎05.59.27.71.81).

Lourdes

LOURDES, about 30km southeast of Pau, has just one function. Over six million Catholic pilgrims arrive here each year, and the town is totally given over to looking after and exploiting them. Lourdes was hardly more than a village before 1858, when Bernadette Soubirous, the 14-year-old daughter of an ex-miller, had the first of eighteen visions of the Virgin Mary in a spot called the Grotte de Massabielle, by the Gave de Pau. Since then Lourdes has grown a great deal, and it is now one of the biggest attractions in this part of France, many of its visitors hoping for a miraculous cure.

Practically every shop is given over to the sale of religious kitsch – Bernadette in every shape and size adorning barometers, key rings, bottles, candles, plastic grottoes illuminated by coloured lights. The architecture of the **Cité Réligieuse**, by the river, which has grown up around the Gave de Pau, is scarcely any better. The **grotto** is a moisture-blackened overhang by the riverside with a statue of the Virgin in waxwork white and baby blue. Suspended in front are a row of rusting crutches, *ex votos* offered by the hopeful. Up above is the first church built here, dating from 1871, and below this a massive subterranean **basilica**, reputedly able to house 20,000 people at one time. For those with a particular fascination for the cult of Bernadette, F159 will buy you a *passeport touristique* which includes a range of museums and sightseeing tours; ask at the tourist office.

The **train station** is on the northeastern edge of town. The **tourist office** is on place Peyramale (Easter–Sept daily 9am–7pm; Oct–Easter Mon–Sat 9am–noon & 2–6pm) and can help with accommodation; turn right outside the station and then left down Chaussée Maransin. There is an abundance of cheap **hotels** around the station, and more en route to the Grotte and around the castle. **Hostel** accommodation can be had at the *Camp des Jeunes*, Ferme Milhas, rue Monseigneur-Rodhain (☎05.62.42.79.95; ①), which has ultracheap dorm beds and is on the western edge of town, ten minutes' walk from the centre. The nearest **campsite**, *La Poste*, is at 26 rue de Langelle, east off the Chaussée Maransin and near the post office. If everything is full, consider staying in **TARBES**, twenty minutes from Lourdes by train. There's a **youth hostel** at 88 av Alsace-Lorraine (☎05.62.38.91.20; ②), and cheap **hotels** around the train station.

LANGUEDOC AND ROUSSILLON

Languedoc is more an idea than a geographical entity. The modern region covers only a fraction of the lands where once *Occitan* or the *langue d'oc* was spoken, which stretched south from Bordeaux and Lyon into Spain and northwest Italy. Although things are changing, the sense of being Occitanian remains strong, a regional identity that dates back to the Middle Ages, when its castles and fortified villages were the final refuges of the Cathars, a heretical religious sect.

The old Roman town of **Nîmes** is an entry point; beyond, **Montpellier** and **Sète** are good bases, though otherwise the coast is not generally noteworthy, the beaches bleak strands for the most part, windswept and cut off from their hinterland by marshy lakes. There is the bonus of relatively unpolluted and uncrowded water, but even this is under threat from development. **Narbonne** and **Béziers** are enjoyable urban diversions, as is **Toulouse**, the cultural capital, though it lies some way west. South of Languedoc, **Roussillon**, or French

Catalonia, maintains much of its Catalan identity, though by contrast with the Basques there is little support nowadays for political independence or reunification with Spanish Catalonia, of which it was a part until the seventeenth century. Its countryside is its best feature, its hills and valleys providing some fine walking. The coast is again something of a disappointment, however, as is the region's main town, **Perpignan**.

Nîmes and around

NÎMES is inescapably linked to two things – denim and Rome. The latter's influence is manifest in some of the most extensive Roman remains in Europe, while the former (denim – *de Nîmes*, from Nîmes), equally visible on the backsides of the populace, was first manufactured in the city's textile mills and exported to the southern USA in the nineteenth century to clothe the slaves.

The central part of Nîmes spreads northwest from **boulevard de la Libération**, a few minutes from the station. The tall, narrow streets of the old town are dead ahead, while across to your left is the biggest and most spectacular edifice of all, the first-century **Arena** (daily: May–Sept 9am–7pm; Oct–April 9am–noon & 2–5.30pm; F26), one of the best-preserved Roman arenas in the world, with an arcaded two-storey facade concealing massive interior vaulting that supports tiers giving a capacity of more than 20,000. When Rome's sway was broken by the barbarian invasions, the arena became a fortress and eventually a slum, home to some two thousand people when it was cleared in the early 1800s. Today it has recovered something of its former role, and is a venue for bullfighting in summertime, and hosts opera and an international jazz festival. A short walk away, the **Maison Carrée** (daily 9am–noon & 2/2.30–6/7pm; free) is a compact little temple, built in 5 AD and celebrated for its harmony of proportion. It stands in a square opposite rue Auguste, where the Roman forum used to be. Around it are scattered pieces of Roman masonry, while inside are three enormous canvases donated by Julian Schnabel.

The **Cathedral** on place aux Herbes was mutilated in the Wars of Religion and significantly altered in the last century. Alphonse Daudet was born in its shadow, as was Jean Nicot, the doctor who introduced tobacco into France from Portugal in 1560, and gave his name to nicotine. Opposite the cathedral, in the Bishop's Palace, the **Musée du Vieux Nîmes** (Tues–Sun 11am–6pm; F26) has interesting displays of Renaissance furnishings and decor, while, backing onto Grande Rue in a seventeenth-century Jesuit chapel, the **Musée Archéologique** (same hours and price) gives further background on Roman Nîmes. Further out, across rue de la Libération, the **Musée des Beaux-Arts** on rue Cité-Foulc (same hours and price) prides itself on a huge Gallo-Roman mosaic showing the *Marriage of Admetus*.

Practicalities

The **train station** is at the end of av Feuchères, a few minutes from Esplanade de Gaulle, on the edge of the old centre; the **bus station** is opposite. The **tourist office** has an annexe at the train station (Mon–Fri 9.30am–12.30pm & 2–6pm), but the main office is at 6 rue Auguste, in the centre by the Maison Carrée (July & Aug Mon–Fri 8am–8pm, Sat 9am–7pm, Sun 10am–5pm; rest of year Mon–Fri 8.30am–7pm, Sat 9am–noon & 2–5pm, Sun 10am–noon), and has lots of information on what's on around town. There's a cluster of reasonable **hotels** around square de la Couronne at the beginning of bd Courbet – try *Hôtel Lisita* at 2 bis bd des Arènes (☎04.66.67.66.20; ④), or the *Concorde* at 3 rue des Chapeliers, next to the Palais de Justice (☎04.66.67.91.03; ③). If you want to stay in the heart of things, there's *Hôtel de la Maison Carrée*, 14 rue de la Maison Carrée (☎04.66.67.32.89; ④). There's a **youth hostel** on chemin de la Cigale (☎04.66.23.25.04; ②), reached on bus #2 from square Antonin, which also has tent space; otherwise, the main **campsite** is the *Domaine de la Bastide* on route de Générac, 5km or so from the station (bus #D from bd Gambetta). For **food**, bd de la Libération and bd Amiral-Courbet harbour a stock of reasonably priced brasseries and pizzerias, and the **café** scene is very lively. For something more substantial, try *Nicolas* at 1 rue Poise off bd Amiral-Courbet.

The Pont du Gard and Uzès

Several buses a day head east from Nîmes' bus station to Uzès via the **Pont du Gard**, the greatest surviving stretch of the Roman water supply system to the city, and a supreme piece of engineering. Three tiers of arches span the river, with the covered water conduit on the top waterproofed with a paint based on fig juice. The recently completed renovation work means you can walk across if the height does not bother you.

UZÈS is another 17km on, an attractive old town perched on a hill above the River Alzon, a bit of a backwater until renovation put its half-dozen medieval towers and narrow lanes of Renaissance and classical houses on the tourist circuit. From **Le Portalet**, with its view out over the valley, walk past the classical church of St-Étienne into the medieval **place aux Herbes**, where there's a Sunday morning market, and up the arcaded **rue de la République**. To the right of rue de la République, the castle of **Le Duché** (mid-June to mid-Sept daily 10am–6pm; rest of year 10am–noon & 2–6pm; F50), still inhabited by the same family a thousand years on, is dominated by its original keep, the Tour Bermonde. The **tourist office** is in av de la Libération, next to the bus station.

Montpellier

A thousand years of trade and intellect have made **MONTPELLIER** a teeming, energetic city. Benjamin of Tudela, the twelfth-century Jewish traveller, reported its streets crowded with traders – Arabs, merchants from Lombardy, and Rome, from every corner of Egypt and Greece. Little has dented this progress and the reputation of its university, founded in the thirteenth century, has shone untarnished.

At the town's hub is **place de la Comédie** – *L'Oeuf* to the initiated – a colossal oval square, paved with cream-coloured marble and surrounded by cafés. At one end bulks the **Opéra**, an enormous, ornate nineteenth-century theatre; the other opens onto the tree-lined promenade of **Esplanade** and, to the right, the **Polygone** shopping complex. On the Esplanade, Montpellier's most trumpeted museum, the **Musée Fabre** (Tues–Fri 9am–5.30pm, Sat & Sun 9.30am–5pm; F20), has a vast collection of seventeenth- to nineteenth-century European painting, some Delacroix, Courbet, Impressionists and a few moderns. Behind the Opéra lie the tangled, hilly lanes of Montpellier's **oldest quarter**, full of seventeenth- and eighteenth-century mansions, a curious mix of chic restoration and squalid disorder. Rue de l'Argenterie forks up to **place Jean-Jaurès**, with its morning **market** and cafés, a short walk from two local-history museums on place Petrarque: the **Musée du Vieux Montpellier** (Tues–Sat 9.30am–noon & 1.30–5pm; free), concentrating on the city's history, and the more interesting **Musée du Fougau** (Wed & Thurs 3–6/6.30pm; free), dealing with the folk history of Languedoc. On the western edge of the centre, at the end of rue Foch, are the formal gardens of the **Promenade du Peyrou** and a vainglorious **triumphal arch** showing Louis XIV-Hercules stomping on the Austrian eagle and the English lion. The **Jardin des Plantes**, just north of here, with its alleys of exotic trees, is France's oldest botanical garden (Tues–Sun 9am–7pm).

Practicalities

The **train station** is next to the *gare routière* on the southeastern edge of the centre, a short walk down rue Maguelone. The main **tourist office** is in the passage du Tourisme, at the top end of place de la Comédie (July & Aug daily 9am–7pm; rest of year Mon–Fri 9am–1pm & 2–6pm, Sat 10am–1pm & 2–6pm, Sun 10am–1pm & 2–5pm); there's also a desk in the station for July & August. There are numerous **hotels** between the station and place de la Comédie. The *Majestic*, 4 rue du Cheval-Blanc (☎04.67.66.26.85; ③), and the *Central*, rue Boussairolles/Bruyas (☎04.67.58.39.28; ③), are both clean and inexpensive, or there's the *Mistral*, 25 rue Boussairolles (☎04.67.58.45.25; ③), which is a little more salubrious. The grubby and overcrowded **youth hostel** is at 2 impasse de la Petite-Corraterie off rue des Écoles Laïques (☎04.67.60.32.22; ②). There's a **municipal campsite** 2km east of town on route de Mauguio (bus #15). The best general area for places to **eat** is around rue des Écoles–Laïques, and rue de l'Université. Try *Maison de la Lozére*, 27 rue de l'Aiguillerie, *Chez*

Marceau or *Le Vieil Écu* in the delightful place de la Chapelle-Neuve, or *Crêperie des Deux Provinces*, 7 rue Jacques Coeur.

Béziers

Though no longer the rich city of its nineteenth-century heyday, **BÉZIERS** is the capital of the Languedoc wine country and a focus for the Occitan movement. There were ugly events during the mid-1970s, when blood was shed in violent confrontations with the authorities over the importation of cheap foreign wines and the low prices paid for the essentially poorgrade local product. Things are calmer now, as the conservatism of Languedoc farmers has given way to public demands for something better than the traditional table wine.

The first view of the old town as you come in from the west is spectacular. From the Pont-Neuf across the River Orb, you look upstream at the sturdy golden arches of the **Pont-Vieux**, with the **Cathedral** crowning the steep-banked hill behind, more like a castle than a church. The building is mainly Gothic, in the northern style, the original having been burned in 1209, when most of the population was massacred for refusing to hand over about twenty Cathars. From the top of the cathedral's tower, there's a superb view out across the vine-dominated surrounding landscape, and next door an ancient **cloister** gives access to a terraced garden above the river. The narrow medieval streets make a pleasant stroll, with their mixture of sunny southern elegance and dilapidation. Centre of Béziers' life are the lively **allées Paul-Riquet**, a broad, leafy esplanade lined with cafés and restaurants. Laid out in the last century, the *allées* run from an elaborate theatre in the north to the gorgeous little park of the **Plateau des Poètes**, designed by the creator of Paris' Bois de Boulogne.

Arriving at the **train station**, the best way into town is through the Plateau des Poètes. The **tourist office** is at 29 av Saint-Saëns (July & Aug daily 9am–7pm; rest of year Mon 9am–noon & 2–6pm, Tues–Fri 9am–noon & 2–6.30pm, Sat 9am–noon & 3–6pm). For **hotels**, try the attractive *Hôtel des Poètes*, 80 allées Paul-Riquet (☎04.67.76.38.66; ③), the central *Angleterre*, 22 place Jean-Jaurès (☎04.67.28.48.42; ③), or the *Hôtel du Théâtre*, 13 rue de la Coquille (☎04.67.49.13.43; ④). For **eating**, there are several places on allée Paul-Riquet, or try *Le Cap d'Or* at 7 rue Viennet, which specializes in seafood.

Carcassonne

CARCASSONNE couldn't be easier to reach, sited on the main Toulouse–Montpellier train link, and for anyone travelling through this region it is a must – one of the most dramatic (if also most visited) towns in the whole of Languedoc. It owes its division into two separate "towns", the Cité and Ville Basse, to the Cathar wars of the Middle Ages. Following Simon de Montfort's capture of the town in 1209, its people tried to restore their traditional ruling family, the Trencavels, in 1240. In reprisal King Louis IX expelled them, only permitting their return on condition they built on the low ground by the River Aude.

The Ville Basse is enticing, but the main attraction is without question the **Cité**, a doublewalled and turreted fortress-town crowning the hill above the Aude. Viollet-le-Duc rescued it from ruin in 1844, and his "too-perfect" restoration has been furiously debated ever since. It is, as you would expect, a real tourist trap. There is no charge for admission to the main part of the city, or the grassy *lices* (moat) between the walls. However, to see the inner fortress of the **Château Comtal**, and to walk along the walls, you have to join a guided tour (summer daily 9am–7pm; rest of year daily 9.30/10am–12.30pm & 2–5/6pm; F35). In addition to wandering the narrow streets, don't miss the beautiful church of **St-Nazaire** at the end of rue St-Louis, a serene combination of Romanesque nave with carved capitals and Gothic transepts and choir adorned with some of the loveliest stained glass.

The **tourist office** is at 15 bd Camille-Pelletan, at the end of place Gambetta in the Ville Basse (July & Aug daily 9am–7pm; rest of year 9am–12.30pm & 2–6.30pm), with an annexe in the Cité's Tours Narbonnaises (daily June–Sept 9am–7pm; rest of year 9am–6pm). You can rent **bikes** at the **train station** in the Ville Basse. **Accommodation** in the Cité, as you would expect, is pricey, apart from the **youth hostel** on rue Trencavel (☎04.68.25.23.16; ②), and you're better off sleeping in the Ville Basse. Close to the station is the best of the cheap **hotels**, *Bonnafoux*, 40 rue de la Liberté (☎04.68.25.01.45; ③). *Le Cathare*, 59 rue Jean-Bringer (☎04.68.25.65.92; ③), is a reasonable alternative. The nearest **campsite** is *Les Campéoles* off route de St-Hilaire just west of the Cité. The only affordable **restaurant** in the Cité is the excellent *Auberge de Dame Carcas*, 3 place du Château, a traditional bistro with meals for below F100.

Toulouse

TOULOUSE, with its beautiful historic centre, is one of the most vibrant provincial cities in France, a result of a deliberate policy to make it the centre of hi-tech industry. Always an aviation centre – St-Exupéry and Mermoz flew out from here on their pioneering flights over Africa in the 1920s – Toulouse is now home to *Aérospatiale*, the driving force behind Concorde, Airbus and the Ariane space rocket. Added zest comes from its 60,000 students, who make it second only to Paris as a university centre.

The City

The centre of the city is a rough hexagon clamped around a bend in the wide, brown Garonne. At 21 rue de Metz, the **Musée des Augustins** (10am–6pm, Wed until 9pm; closed Tues; F12) incorporates the two cloisters of an Augustinian priory and houses collections of outstanding Romanesque and Gothic sculpture, much of it saved from the now-vanished churches of Toulouse's golden age. Outside the museum, the main shopping street, **rue Alsace-Lorraine**, runs north. West of here are the labyrinthine streets of the **old city**, lined with the ornate and arrogant *hôtels* of the merchants who grew rich on the woad trade, basis of the city's economy until the sixteenth century. The almost exclusive building material is the flat Toulousain brick, whose cheerful rosy colour gives the city its nickname of *ville rose*, and lends a small-scale, detailed finish to otherwise plain facades. Best known of these palaces is the **Hôtel Assézat**, towards the river end of rue de Metz (June–Sept Tues–Sun 10am–6pm; Oct–May Tues–Sat 10am–5.30pm, Sun 11am–6pm; F25), a vast brick extravaganza with classical columns.

The **place du Capitole** is the site of the huge classical town hall and today a great meeting place, with numerous cafés and a weekday market. North, rue du Taur leads to **place St-Sernin** and the largest Romanesque church in France, the **basilica de St-Sernin**. Begun in 1080 to accommodate the passing hordes of pilgrims, it is one of the loveliest examples of its genre, with an octagonal brick belfry with rounded and pointed arches, diamond lozenges, colonnettes and mouldings picked out in stone, and an apse of nine chapels. Inside, to get into the ambulatory you have to pay a small charge, but it's worth it for the exceptional eleventh-century marble reliefs on the end wall of the choir. Right outside on Sunday mornings is an impressively shambolic flea market. West of place du Capitole, on rue Lakanal, the church of **Les Jacobins** is another austere ecclesiastical building you cannot miss, started in 1230 by the Dominicans. It's a huge fortress-like rectangle of unadorned brick, but, inside, its single space is divided by a central row of ultraslim pillars from whose capitals spring an elegant splay of vaulting ribs. Beneath the altar lie the bones of the philosopher Saint Thomas Aquinas, while on the north side is a calming cloister.

Practicalities

Trains arrive at the **Gare Matabiau**, twenty minutes' walk or a five-minute metro ride from the centre down allées Jean-Jaurès. The **tourist office** is in the centre of town in place du Capitole (May–Sept Mon–Sat 9am–7pm, Sun 10am–1pm & 2–6.30pm; Oct–April Mon–Fri 9am–6pm, Sat 9am–12.30pm & 2–6pm, Sun 10am–12.30pm & 2–5pm). Best of the city's cheap **hotels** are the centrally placed *Hôtel du Grand-Balcon*, 8 rue Romiguières (☎05.61.21.48.08; ③), the *Hôtel des Arts*, on the corner of rue des Arts and rue Cantegril (☎05.61.23.36.21; ③), and the *Hôtel Anatole France*, 46 place A-France (☎05.61.23.19.96; ③). The closest **campsite** is on the chemin du Pont-de-Rupé, just north of the city – bus #2, #5 from place Jeanne-d'Arc. When the time comes to **eat**, there are numerous places around place Wilson, on rue de la

Colombette and on place Arnaud-Bernard, and several popular places open for lunch only in the food market on place Victor-Hugo. In the evening, try around place Arnaud-Bernard, in the rapidly gentrifying former Arab quarter on the north edge of the centre and, if you want music, *La Cav' Ragtime* is a lively jazz, salsa and blues bar. More centrally, the chic brasserie *Des Beaux-Arts*, opposite the end of the Pont Neuf, is good and reasonable, as is the nearby *La Tantina de Burgos*, 27 av de la Garonnette, with good tapas. Alternatively, there are pizzerias and brasseries aplenty on place St-Georges, behind the Musée des Augustins.

Albi

Though not itself an important centre of Catharism, **ALBI** gave its name to both the heresy and the crusade to suppress it. Today it is a small industrial town an hour's train ride northeast of Toulouse, with two unique sights. The first, the **Cathedral** (June to Sept daily 8.30am–7pm; Oct to May 8.30–11.45am & 2–5.45pm; F5 to enter the choir), is visible the moment you arrive at the train station, dwarfing the town. The brutal, fortress-like exterior expresses the power and authority of the church over the heretical townspeople; the vast hall-like nave is richly decorated with colourful Italian paintings. Opposite the east end of the cathedral, rue Mariès leads into the shopping streets of the **old town**, but the most interesting sight is next door in the powerful red-brick Palais de la Berbie, which houses Albi's other main attraction, the **Musée Toulouse-Lautrec** (9/10am–noon & 2–5/6pm; closed Tues; F20), with paintings, drawings, lithographs and posters by the artist (who was a native of the town). There is a huge range of exhibits, from the earliest work to the very last. The artist's birthplace, at 14 rue Toulouse-Lautrec, is a private house and is not open to the public.

The **tourist office** is on the corner of Palais de la Berbie (July & Aug Mon–Sat 9am–7.30pm, Sun 10am–1pm & 3.30–6.30pm; rest of year Mon–Sat 9am–noon & 2–6pm, Sun 10.30am–12.30pm & 3.30–5.30pm). There's a scruffy *Maison des Jeunes* at 13 rue de la République (☎05.63.54.53.65; ①), with ultracheap dorm beds, and cheap **hotels** include the *Terminus* on av Maréchal Joffre, by the station (☎05.63.54.00.99; ③), and the *Fouillade*, 12 place Pelloutier (☎05.63.54.21.86; ③). The closest **campsite** is the *Parc du Caussels* (☎05.63.60.37.06; April–Oct) about 2km east on the D999. For **eating**, try the *Casa Créole* or *Auberge Saint-Loup*, both on rue Castelviel at the west of the cathedral; the vegetarian *Le Tournesol*, in rue de l'Ort-en-Salvy, is also good.

Perpignan

PERPIGNAN is capital of French Catalonia and the only big city of the region. It's not, however, the most fascinating of places – its heyday was really during the thirteenth and fourteenth centuries, when the kings of Mallorca held their court here. For most of the Middle Ages its allegiance swung back and forth between France and Aragon, until finally it became part of the French state under Louis XIV in 1659.

The centre of Perpignan is marked by the palm trees and smart cafés of **place Arago**. From here rue Alsace-Lorraine and rue de la Loge lead past the massive iron gates of the classical Hôtel de Ville to the tiny **place de la Loge**, the focus of the renovated old core, dominated by the **Loge de Mer**, a late fourteenth-century Gothic building designed to hold the city's stock exchange and a maritime court. North up rue Louis-Blanc is one of the city's few remaining fortifications, the crenellated fourteenth-century gate of **Le Castillet**, now home to the **Casa Pairal**, a fascinating **museum** of Roussillon's Catalan folk culture (9/9.30am–6/7pm; closed Tues; F25). In the gloomy nave of the fourteenth-century **Cathédrale St-Jean**, down rue St-Jean and across place Gambetta, are some elaborate Catalan altarpieces; while a side chapel to the south, somewhat incongruously, houses a tortured Rhenish altarpiece dating from around 1400.

Through place des Esplanades, crowning the hill which dominates the southern part of the old town, is the **Palais des Rois de Majorque** (daily: June–Sept 10am–6pm; Oct–May 9am–5pm; F20). Vauban's walls surround it now, but the two-storey palace and its great arcaded courtyard date from the late thirteenth century. The Spanish-Moorish influence lends sophistication and finesse to the architecture and detailing, particularly the beautiful marble porch to the lower of the two chapels.

To get to the centre from the **train station**, follow av Général-de-Gaulle to place de la Catalogne, and then continue along bd Clemenceau as far as Le Castillet; the municipal **tourist office** is a short stroll from here, in the Palais des Congrès at the end of bd Wilson (June–Sept Mon–Fri 9am–7pm, Sat 10am–6pm, Sun 10am–noon & 2–5pm; Oct–May Mon–Fri 9am–6pm, Sat 9am–noon & 2–6pm). For **accommodation**, the best place to look is around the station: try the *Hôtel le Berry*, 6 av Général-de-Gaulle (☎04.68.34.59.02; ②), which is cheap and friendly. The **youth hostel** (☎04.68.34.63.32; ②) is about 1km from the station in Parc de la Pépinière, by the river. There are two **campsites**, *La Garrigole* on rue Maurice-Lévy (bus #2) and *Le Catalan* on route de Bompas, both signposted from the centre. The station is also a good area for inexpensive **food**. Nearer the centre, *Relais St Jean* in place Gambetta dishes up quality Catalan cuisine at low prices.

THE MASSIF CENTRAL

Thickly forested, and sliced by numerous rivers and lakes, the **Massif Central** is geologically the oldest part of France, and culturally one of the most firmly rooted in the past. Industry and tourism have made few inroads here, and the people remain rural and taciturn, with an enduring sense of regional identity. The heart of the region is the **Auvergne**, a wild, inaccessible landscape dotted with extinct volcanic peaks known as *puys*, much of it now incorporated into the **Parc Naturel Régional des Volcans d'Auvergne**, France's largest regional park. To the southeast are the gentler wooded hills of the **Cévennes**. This range, too, is now part of a national park, the **Parc National des Cévennes**. Only a handful of towns have gained a foothold in this rugged terrain. **Le Puy**, spiked with jagged pinnacles of lava and with a majestic cathedral, is the most compelling, but there is appeal, too, in the elegant spa city of **Vichy** and in the provincial capital, **Clermont-Ferrand**.

Clermont-Ferrand

CLERMONT-FERRAND is an incongruous capital for rustic Auvergne, a lively, youthful place, with a major university, and a manufacturing base (it's the HQ of the Michelin organization). As a base for this side of the Massif it's ideal, with a wide choice of rooms and some good restaurants and bars. And it is interesting in its own right too, for a well-preserved historic centre and for the nearby spectacle of Puy de Dôme and the Parc des Volcans.

Clermont and neighbouring Montferrand were united in 1631 to form a single city, but you're likely to spend most of your time in the former, since what is left of Vieux Montferrand stands out on a limb to the east. Clermont's "ville-noire" aspect – so-called after the local black volcanic rock used in the construction of many of its buildings – is its most immediate feature: dark and solid, it clusters untidily around the summit of a worn-away volcanic peak. On the edge of old Clermont, the huge and soulless **place de Jaude** is the hub of the city and its main shopping area. In the centre stands a rousing statue of the Gallic chieftain Vercingétorix, who in 53 BC led his people to their only – and indecisive – victory over Julius Caesar just south of the town. North from place de Jaude, **place St-Pierre** is the site of Clermont's principal market, with a morning food **market**, at its liveliest on Saturdays. The nearby **Musée du Ranquet**, in an impressive sixteenth-century building at 34 rue des Gras (Tues–Sat 10am–6pm; free), is one of the city's best museums, with displays on local history back to Roman times. Running roughly parallel, the quarter's other main street, rue de la Boucherie, is a fragrant bazaar of tiny shops selling all kinds of food and spices.

The streets gather up to the dark and soaring **Cathédrale Notre-Dame**, whose strong volcanic stone made it possible to build vaults and pillars of unheard-of slenderness and height. Off the nave, the **Tour de la Bayette** (Mon–Sat 2–6pm, Sun 3–6pm; F10) gives extensive views across the city, and provides some explanation as to why locals use the cathedral as a short cut – something the authorities have been trying to put a stop to for years. A short step northeast of the cathedral, on place Delille, stands Clermont's other great church, the **Basilique Notre-Dame du Port**: almost a century older, it's made from softer stone, which is corroding badly from exposure to Clermont's polluted air. For all that, it's a beautiful building, pure Auvergnat Romanesque; put a franc in the slot and you can light up the intricately carved ensemble of leaves, knights and biblical figures on the pillars and capitals.

Practicalities

The **train station** is on av de l'URSS, east of the city centre, and is connected by frequent buses with place de Jaude. The main **tourist office** is at pl de la Victoire (June–Sept Mon–Sat 8.30am–7pm, Sun 9am–noon & 2–6pm; Oct–May Mon–Fri 8.45am–6.30pm, Sat 9am–noon & 2–6pm, Sun 9am–1pm), with annexes at the train station and during summer on place de Jaude. The main tourist office also has an area devoted to information about local **hiking** and **mountain biking**. The **youth hostel** is at 55 av de l'URSS (☎04.73.92.26.39; ②; March–Oct), two minutes' walk right of the station; the *Foyer St-Jean*, 17 rue Gaultier-de-Biauzat (☎04.73.31.37.00; ②; March–Oct), charges a little more but is much nicer. There is a cluster of **hotels** outside the station, of which the *Grand Hôtel du Midi*, 39 av de l'URSS (☎04.73.92.44.98; ③), is one of the least expensive options. For something cheaper and nearer the centre there's *Blaise Pascal*, by the cathedral at 6 rue Massillon (☎04.73.91.31.82; ②), or *Hôtel Foch*, 22 rue Maréchal-Foch (☎04.73.93.48.40; ②). The nearest **campsite** is at Royat to the west (April–Oct; bus #14B from the *gare routière*). For **food**, the very popular *Crêperie 1513*, 3 rue des Chaussetiers, has a fine setting in a medieval mansion opposite the cathedral, and *Le Bistrot Vénitien*, 26 rue des Gras, dishes up good pizzas and pastas. The tiny place Renoux, off rue Maréchal-Joffre, and nearby place de Jaude make pleasant drinking spots. **Moving on**, *Le Cévenol*, a slow train through the mountains to Nîmes, is one of the most enchanting French rail journeys you can make.

Puy de Dôme

Frequent buses from Clermont run to **Puy de Dôme**, a few kilometres west of Clermont, one of the tallest of the *puys*, with sweeping views back towards the town and the Parc des Volcans. Close to the summit, ruins survive of a Roman temple to Mercury, in its time considered one of the marvels of the empire, fashioned from over fifty different kinds of marble and with an enormous bronze statue of Mercury where a TV antenna now stands. If you're walking here from Clermont, or even Royat, be sure to allow a good half-day – and take food. The restaurant on top enjoys a monopoly and makes full use of it.

Vichy

VICHY is famous for two things: its World War II puppet government under Marshal Pétain and its curative sulphurous springs. The population is largely elderly, genteel and rich, and swells several-fold in summer, and the town is almost entirely devoted to catering for visitors.

There's a real *fin-de-siècle* charm about the place. Life revolves around the **Parc des Sources**, a stately tree-shaded park that takes up most of the centre. At the north end stands the **Halle des Sources**, an enormous iron-framed greenhouse in which the various waters emerge from their spouts, people lining up to get their prescribed cupful. For a small fee you can join them, though bear in mind that only one of the five springs (the Célestin) is bottled and widely drunk; the others are progressively more foul and sulphurous, culminating in the Source de l'Hôpital, a truly despicable brew, which has its own building at the far end of the park.

After the waters, Vichy's curiosities are limited. Marshal Pétain's own offices were at the *Pavillon*, while the Gestapo had their headquarters at the *Hôtel du Portugal*, but, unsurprisingly, there's nothing to commemorate either.

Practicalities

The **train station** is on the west edge of the centre, at the end of rue de Paris. The **tourist office** is housed in Pétain's government building, at 19 rue du Parc (April–June & Sep

Mon–Sat 9am–12.30pm & 1.30–7pm, Sun 9.30am–12.30pm & 3–7pm; July & Aug Mon–Sat 9am–7.30pm, Sun 9.30am–12.30pm & 3–7pm; Oct–March Mon–Fri 9am–noon & 2–6.30pm, Sat 9am–noon & 2–6pm, Sun 2.30–5.30pm). There's a municipal **campsite** across the river – cross the pont de Bellerive from the Parc de l'Allier. Among hotels, try either the *Trianon*, 9 rue Desbrest (☎04.70.97.95.96; ③), or the *Azurea* in the same street at no. 14 (☎04.70.98.33.88; ③). For **food**, the junction of rue Clemenceau, rue de Pans, rue Lucas and rue Jean-Jaurès has plenty of places.

Le-Puy-en-Velay

A strange town in a strange setting, **LE-PUY-EN-VELAY** sprawls across a broad basin in the mountains, a muddle of red roofs barbed with poles of volcanic rock. Capital of the Haute-Loire, it isn't easy to get to – from Clermont or Nîmes you have to change trains at St-Georges-d'Aurac – but it's well worth the effort. In medieval times it was the assembly point for pilgrims to Santiago in Spain, and amid the cobbled streets of the old town are some of the most richly endowed churches in the land. The strange surrounding countryside is an added attraction.

The **old town**, reached by climbing the steep sequence of streets and steps that terrace the town's *puy* foundation, is dominated by the **Cathedral** – almost Byzantine in style, striped with alternate layers of light and dark stone and capped with a line of small cupolas. The Black Virgin inside is a copy of a revered original burned during the Revolution, and is still paraded through the town every August 15. Other, lesser treasures are displayed at the back of the church in the sacristy, beyond which is the entrance to the beautiful twelfth-century cloister (daily: July–Sept 9.30am–6.30pm; rest of year 9.30am–noon/12.30pm & 2–4.30/6pm; F25). At the highest point in the town is the giant crimson statue of the **Virgin and Child**, fashioned from the metal of guns captured in the Crimean War – you can pay F20 to climb to the top for some stunning views. The nearby church of **St-Michel** (daily: mid-June to mid-Sept 9am–7pm; rest of year 9/10am–noon & 2–5/7pm; F13), sitting on the peak of an even steeper *puy*, the Rocher d'Aiguilhe, is an eleventh-century construction that seems to grow out of the rock itself. It's a tough ascent, but one you should definitely make: it's a quirky little building decorated with mosaics, arabesques and trefoil arches, its bizarre shape following that of the available flat ground. Back down below, lacemakers – a traditional, though now commercialized industry – do a fine trade, doilies and lace shawls hanging enticingly outside shops for tourists. Le Puy's maze of old lanes is uncluttered and wonderful, while in the new part of town – beyond the squat **Tour Pannessac** – **place de Breuil** and **place Michelet** form the social hub, with spacious public gardens.

Practicalities

Arriving by **bus or train** you'll find yourself on place du Maréchal-Leclerc, a ten-minute walk from place de Breuil and the **tourist office** (July–Aug daily 8.30am–7.30pm; rest of year Mon–Sat 8.30am–noon & 1.30–6.15pm, Sun 10am–noon), and within easy striking distance of some reasonably priced **hotels**, including the *Régional*, 36 bd Maréchal-Fayolle (☎04.71.09.37.74; ③). There is a **youth hostel** at the Centre Pierre-Cardinal, 9 rue Jules-Vallès (☎04.71.05.52.40; ②), and a **campsite**, *Bouthézard*, thirty minutes from the station along chemin de Roderie – bus #6. For **food**, the restaurants around place Breuil and place Michelet are decent.

BURGUNDY

Peaceful, rural **Burgundy** is one of the most prosperous regions of modern France and was for a long time independent from the French state. In the fifteenth century its dukes ruled an empire that embraced much of northeastern France, Belgium, and the Netherlands, with revenues equalled only by Venice. Everywhere there is startling evidence of this former wealth and power, both secular and religious. **Dijon**, the dukes' capital, is a slick and prosperous town with plenty of remnants of old Burgundy; to the north, the town of **Sens** is a worthy stopoff on the way into the region, as is the great abbey of **Vézelay**. South, there are substantial Roman remains at **Autun**, and the ruins of the monastery of **Cluny**, whose influence was second only to that of Rome for a time, though wine devotees may head straight for the **vineyards**, whose produce has been a major moneymaker since Louis XIV's doctor prescribed the stuff for the royal dyspepsia. **Beaune** is a good centre for sampling the best of the wine, washed down with local specialities like *escargots à la bourguignonne, boeuf bourguignon* and *coq au vin*.

Sens

SENS, though never part of the Duchy of Burgundy, feels like a typically Burgundian town. Contained within a ring of tree-lined boulevards where the city walls once stood, its ancient centre, focusing on place de la République, is still dominated by the **Cathédrale de St-Étienne**. Begun around 1130, it was the first of the great French Gothic cathedrals and is a fine example of the space and weightlessness of the genre. The architect who completed it, William of Sens, was later to rebuild the choir of Canterbury Cathedral in England. Thomas à Becket spent several years in exile around Sens, and the story of his murder is told in the twelfth-century windows in the north aisle of the choir, just part of the cathedral's outstanding collection of stained glass. The treasury (June–Sept daily 10am–noon & 2–6pm; Oct–May Mon, Thurs & Fri 2–6pm, Wed, Sat & Sun 10am–noon & 2–6pm; F25, free Wed) is also uncommonly rich, containing Islamic, Byzantine and French vestments, jewels and embroideries. Just south is the thirteenth-century **Palais Synodal**, with its roof of Burgundian glazed tiles, restored like so many other buildings in this region by Viollet-le-Duc. Its vaulted halls, originally designed to accommodate the ecclesiastical courts, now house a small **museum** (same hours and ticket as treasury) of statuary from the cathedral and Gallo-Roman mosaics. Underneath is a medieval prison.

The **train station** is about ten minutes' walk from the cathedral, at the end of the main Grand Rue. The **tourist office** is on the north edge of the small centre, on place Jean-Jaurès (July & Aug Mon–Sat 9am–12.30pm & 2–7.30pm, Sun 10am–12.30pm & 2–5.30pm; rest of year Mon–Sat 9am–noon & 1–5.15/6.30pm;). For **accommodation**, try the *Hôtel Chemin de Fer* (☎03.86.65.10.27; ②) opposite the station or, in the centre, *Hôtel Esplanade*, 2 bd du Mail (☎03.86.83.14.71; ③). The closest **campsite** is *Entre-deux-Vannes*, on av de Sénigallia, just out of town – take bus #6 from the centre. For **eating**, rue de la République is a safe bet: *Restaurant de la Cathédrale*, at no. 13, does good traditional fare. Alternatively, there's a good creperie, *Au Petit Creux*, at 3 rue de Brennus.

Vézelay

The abbey church of **La Madeleine** at **VÉZELAY** (daily: summer 6am–8pm; winter 7am–7pm), one of the seminal buildings of the Romanesque period, was saved from collapse by Viollet-le-Duc in 1840. Home – it was thought – to the bones of Mary Magdalene, the church was a major pilgrimage site, and assembly point for pilgrims heading for Santiago de Compostela in Spain. Just inside, the colossal narthex was added to the nave around 1150 to accommodate the pilgrims, and is striking for the superb sculpture on its central doorway while on the outer arch there are small-scale medallions of the zodiac signs and labours of the months. The long body of the church is vaulted by arches of alternating black and white stone, edged with fretted mouldings, and the supporting pillars are crowned with finely cut capitals depicting scenes from the Bible, classical mythology, allegories and morality stories – in complete contrast to the clean, soaring lines of the early Gothic choir beyond.

The small **tourist office** is on the right in rue St-Pierre as you go up towards the abbey (summer daily 10am–1pm & 2–6pm; winter closed Thurs). Staying in Vézelay, there are a number of reasonable **hotels**, including *Le Cheval Blanc* (☎03.86.33.22.12; ③) on place Champ-du-foire, and an official HI **youth hostel** with camping space, about 1km along route d'Étang (☎03.86.33.24.18; ①).

Dijon

DIJON owes its origins to its strategic position in Celtic times on the merchant route from Britain up the Seine and across the Alps to the Adriatic. But it was as capital of the dukes of Burgundy from 1000 until the late 1400s that it knew its finest hour, under the auspices of Dukes Philippe the Bold, Jean the Fearless, Philippe the Good and Charles the Rash. They used their tremendous wealth and power to make Dijon one of the greatest centres of art, learning and science in Europe. Though it obviously lost some of this status with incorporation into the French kingdom in 1477, it has remained one of the pre-eminent provincial cities, especially since the rail and industrial boom of the mid-nineteenth century.

The City

You sense Dijon's former glory more in the lavish houses of its burghers than in the former seat of the dukes, the **Palais des Ducs**, an undistinguished building from the outside and one that has had many alterations, especially in the sixteenth and seventeenth centuries when it became the Parliament of Burgundy. In fact, the only outward reminders of the dukes' building are the fifteenth-century **Tour Philippe le Bon** (closed at time of writing but may reopen soon; check with the tourist office), from whose terrace on the clearest of days they say you can see Mont Blanc, and the fourteenth-century **Tour de Bar**, which now houses Dijon's **Musée des Beaux-Arts** (10am–6pm; closed Tues; F22), with a collection of paintings that represents many different schools and periods, from Titian and Rubens to Monet, Manet and other Impressionists, as well as religious artefacts, ivories and tapestries. Visiting the museum also provides the opportunity to see the surviving portions of the ducal palace, including the vast kitchens, the magnificent Salle des Gardes, and the relocated tombs of Philippe the Bold and of Jean the Fearless and his wife, Marguerite de Bavière.

The palace looks onto **place de la Libération**, a gracious semicircular space bordered by houses of honey-coloured stone, designed in the late seventeenth century. Behind the palace is a tiny, enclosed square, **place des Ducs**, and a maze of lanes flanked by beautiful old houses, best of which are those on **rue des Forges**. Parallel to rue des Forges, **rue de la Chouette** passes the north side of the impressive thirteenth-century Gothic church of **Notre-Dame**, whose north wall holds a small sculpted owl (*chouette*) which people touch for luck and which gives the street its name. At the end of the street is the attractive **place François-Rude**, a favourite summer hangout, crowded with café tables. Just south of here, the **Musée Archéologique**, 5 rue Docteur-Maret (June–Sept 9.30am–6pm; Oct–May 9am–noon & 2–6pm; closed Tues; F16), has interesting Gallo-Roman funerary bas-reliefs depicting the perennial Gallic preoccupation with food and wine and a collection of *ex-votos* from the source of the Seine, among them the little bronze of the goddess Sequana (Seine), upright in her bird-prowed boat. Back in the town centre at 4 rue des Bons-Enfants, the **Musée Magnin** (Tues–Sun 10am–noon & 2–6pm; F16) is a seventeenth-century *hôtel* with its original furnishings, more interesting than its paintings. Further south, the **Musée de la Vie Bourguignonne**, 17 rue St-Anne (9am–noon & 2–6pm; closed Tues; F18), documents Burgundian life in the last century and is housed in a stark modern setting inside a former convent. Being the mustard capital of France, Dijon of course has a museum dedicated to the unctuous condiment, the **Musée de la Moutarde Amora** on Quai Nicolas Rohin (tours at 3pm June–Aug Mon–Sat; rest of year Wed & Sat; F15).

Practicalities

The **train station** is at the end of av Maréchal-Foch, five minutes from place Darcy and the main **tourist office** (daily: summer 9am–7/9pm; winter closed for lunch). There's another tourist office at 34 rue des Forges (May to mid-Oct Mon–Sat 9am–noon & 1–6pm; rest of year Mon–Fri 9am–noon & 1–6pm). A general museum ticket for Dijon museums can be obtained for F45 from the tourist offices. The official **youth hostel** is at 1 bd Champollion (☎03.80.72.95.20; ②), 4km from the centre – bus #5 from place Grangier. As for **hotels**, try the *Monge* at 20 rue Monge (☎03.80.30.55.41; ③), or, in the same road, the *Hostellerie*

Sauvage, at no. 64 (☎03.80.41.31.21; ④) – both excellent value. The nearest **campsite** is by the lake off bd Kir – bus #12.

There is no problem finding a good **restaurant** in this centre of *haute cuisine*, though locating affordable places is harder. With a student card, you can fill up for less than F20 a head at the university restaurant, in the centre of town at 3 rue du Dr Maret, while the *Coum' Chez Eux*, 68 rue J.J. Rousseau, is good for those with a little more in their budget. If you're prepared to spend even more, *Le Clos des Capucines*, 3 rue Jeannin, serves excellent regional specialities. For a **drink**, *Café de la Cathédrale* and *Café au Carillon*, in front of the cathedral, are both lively bars, popular with students. *Le Café des Grand Ducs*, 96 rue de la Liberté, is another youthful hangout, open until 3am in summer, while *L'Univers* on rue Berbisey is a studenty club which regularly hosts live bands in its cellar.

Autun

AUTUN, today scarcely bigger than the circumference of its medieval walls, was one of the leading cities of Roman Gaul, founded by Augustus around 10 BC as part of his campaign to Romanize the Celts. Two of the city's four **Roman gates** survive, **Porte St-André** spanning rue de la Croix-Blanche in the northeast and **Porte d'Arroux** in Faubourg d'Arroux in the northwest, while in a field just across the River Arroux stands the so-called **Temple of Janus**, a lofty section of brick wall that was probably part of the sanctuary of some Gallic deity. Off av du 2ème-Dragon are the few remains of the largest **Roman theatre** in Gaul – a measure of the importance of the settlement.

Autun's main street is av Charles-de-Gaulle, leading to the main square, **Champ de Mars**, from which the narrow streets of the **old town** spread, converging towards the **Cathédrale de St-Lazare** in the most southerly and best fortified corner. Built in the twelfth century and much altered since, the church is uniquely important for its works by Gislebertus, one of the greatest of Romanesque sculptors. The tympanum of the *Last Judgement* above the west door bears his signature beneath the feet of Christ. The interior was also decorated by Gislebertus, who himself carved most of the capitals, some of the finest of which are now in the old chapter library. There are more pieces by Gislebertus outside the cathedral in the **Musée Rolin**, an old Renaissance *hôtel* on rue des Blancs (April–Sept Mon & Wed–Sat 9.30am–noon & 1.30–6pm; Oct–March Wed–Sat 10am–noon & 2–4pm, Sun 10am–noon & 2.30–5pm; F14), including his unashamedly sensual portrayal of Eve.

The **train station** is on av de la République, at the far end of av Charles-de-Gaulle, on which you'll find the **tourist office** at no. 2 (summer daily 9am–12.30pm & 2–7pm; winter Mon–Sat 9am–noon & 2–5pm). Opposite the station, the *Hôtel de France* (☎03.85.52.14.00; ③) and *Hôtel Commerce et Touring* (☎03.85.52.17.90; ③) are both decent and inexpensive, and the latter has a very acceptable, moderately priced **restaurant**. There's a **campsite** just across the river beyond Porte d'Arroux. Of a number of places to **eat**, the *Auberge de la Bourgogne* and the brasserie *Morvandiau* on place Champ-de-Mars, and *Le Châteaubriant*, 14 rue Jeannin, are recommended.

Cluny

The voice of the abbot of **CLUNY**, around 50km south of Dijon, once made monarchs tremble. His power in the Christian world was second only to that of the pope, his intellectual influence arguably greater. Founded in 910, the monastery was also one of the richest in France, and it was its wealth and secular involvement that led to the decline of its spiritual influence in the wake of the reforming zeal of Saint Bernard and his Cistercians.

Sadly, practically nothing of the complex remains. The Revolution suppressed the monastery, and the eleventh-century **church**, the largest building in Christendom until St Peter's in Rome, was dismantled in 1810. All you can see now is an octagonal belfry, the south transept and, in the granary of the former **abbey** (daily: July–Sept 9am–7pm; rest of year 9.30/10am–noon & 2–4/6pm; F32 incl entry to Musée Ochier), some capitals from its immense columns. The **Musée Ochier** (same hours & ticket), in the fifteenth-century palac of the last abbot to be freely elected, helps flesh out the picture with reconstructions and sculpture fragments.

If staying in the village, the cheapest option for groups of three or more is *Cluny Séjour*, a municipal **hostel** on rue Porte-de-Paris (☎03.85.59.08.83; ②), though it has a 10pm curfew, or there's a **campsite** on rue des Griottons across Pont de la Levée on the right. *Hôtel de l'Abbaye* on av Charles-de-Gaulle (☎03.85.59.11.14; ③) and *Hôtel du Commerce*, 8 place du Commerce (☎03.85.59.03.09; ②), have fairly cheap double rooms. The **tourist office** at 6 rue Mercière will reserve rooms for a small fee. *Marroniers* on av Charles-de-Gaulle is a reasonable **restaurant**, or you can check out the regional specialities at *Auberge du Cheval Blanc*, 1 rue Porte de Mâcon.

The Burgundy vineyards

Burgundy's best **wines** come from a narrow strip of hillside – the **Côte d'Or**, which runs southwest from Dijon to Santenay. It is divided into two regions – Côte de Nuits and Côte de Beaune. With few exceptions, the reds of the Côte de Nuits are considered the best: they are richer, age better and cost more. Côte de Beaune is known particularly for its whites – Meursault, Montrachet and Puligny. The countryside is attractive: the steep scarp of the *côte*, wooded along the top, is cut by deep little valleys called *combes*, where local rock climbers hone their skills. The villages, strung along N74 through the town of Beaune and beyond, are sleepy and exceedingly prosperous, full of houses inhabited by well-heeled *vignerons*. There are numerous *caves* to taste and buy at, but as usual the former is meant to be a prelude to the latter. If you are buying, be aware that the *Hautes Côtes* (Nuits and Beaune), from the top of the slope, are cheaper, although they don't have the cachet of the big guys.

Beaune

BEAUNE, the principal town of the Côte d'Or, has many charms, but it is totally devoted to tourism. The chief attraction is the fifteenth-century hospital, the **Hôtel-Dieu** on the corner of place de la Halle (daily April–Nov 9am–6.30pm; Dec–March 9–11.30am & 2–5.30pm; F32), whose vast paved hall has an impressive painted timber roof and until quite recently continued to serve its original purpose. It is here that the Hospices de Beaune's wines are auctioned during the annual *Trois Glorieuses*, the prices paid setting the pattern for the season. The private residence of the dukes of Burgundy on rue d'Enfer now contains the **Musée du Vin** (April–Nov daily 9.30am–6pm; Dec–March 9.30am–6pm, closed Tues; F25), with giant winepresses and an interesting collection of tools of the trade. At the other end of rue d'Enfer, the church of **Notre-Dame** has five **tapestries** from the fifteenth century depicting the Life of the Virgin, commissioned by the Rolin family.

From the **train station**, the town centre is 500m up av du 8-Septembre, across the boulevard, and left onto rue des Tonneliers. **Buses** leave from outside the walls at the end of rue Maufoux. The **tourist office** is opposite the Hôtel-Dieu on rue de l'Hôtel-Dieu (Mon–Sat 9am–6/8pm, Sun 9am–6/7pm) and has information on wine tours. **Accommodation** is pricey and it's cheaper to use Dijon or Chalon as a base, as both are easily accessible by train and Transco buses, which service all the villages down the N74. But if you want to stay, *Hôtel Foch* (☎03.80.24.05.65; ③), just to the west of town at 24 bd Foch, has cheapish rooms. There may be room at the *Foyer des Jeunes Travailleurs* opposite the hospital on av Guigone-de-Salins (☎03.82.48.80.00; ②), and there's a **campsite**, *Les Cent Vignes* (☎03.80.22.03.91), 1km out on rue Auguste Dubois off rue du Faubourg-St-Nicolas. **Eating** can also be expensive. The best places for cheap meals are rue Monge, place Carnot and rue de Lorraine. *Le Carnot* at 18 rue Carnot is a good cafeteria, and menus at the *Brelinette*, 6 rue Madeleine, start at F60. For **drinkers**, the massive number of wine sellers trying to lure you in to sample their wares can leave you feeling overwhelmed, tipsy or both, but one or two of the centrally located vendors are well worth a visit: try the *Caves des Cordeliers* on 6 rue de l'Hôtel-Dieu, for free tasting sessions (daily 9.30am–noon & 2–7pm).

Chalon, Mâcon and the Beaujolais

CHALON, around 30km south of Beaune on the banks of the Saône, has long been a thriving port and industrial centre, and its old riverside quarter has an easy charm. It is not a place you want to stay very long, however, although there are numerous **hotels** and it has a riverbank **youth hostel** on rue d'Amsterdam (☎03.85.46.62.77; ②), about a ten-minute walk north of the Pont St-Laurent, the last bridge upstream; the nearest **campsite** is 3km out of town in St Marcel. The one thing you might want to see is the **Musée Niepce** (July & Aug 10am–6pm; rest of year 9.30–11.30am & 2.30–5.30pm; closed Tues; F14), on the river quays just downstream from Pont St-Laurent. Local boy Niepce is credited with inventing photography in 1816, and the museum possesses a fascinating range of cameras from the first ever to those taken on the *Apollo* moon mission, plus a number of 007-type spy devices. SNCF buses go south to **MÂCON**, passing through some of the **Chalonnais** wine villages, best known for their whites. Mâcon itself is a large, modern town where again you are not likely to want to do more than stop over – most of the cheap hotels are near the Gare SNCF. The **Mâconnais** wine-producing country lies to the west. Its reds are good, but it is best known for the expensive white wines from the villages of Pouilly, Fuissé, Vinzelles and Prissé. South of here, the Mâconnais becomes the **Beaujolais**, a larger area of terraced hills producing light, fruity red wines. Of the three categories of Beaujolais, the superior *crus*, including Morgon and Fleurie, come from the northern part of the region; *Beaujolais villages*, which produces the best *nouveau*, comes from the middle; and *Beaujolais supérieur* comes from vineyards southwest of **Villefranche**. The **tourist office** at 290 rue de Thizy in Villefranche has detailed information about wine-tasting and cellar tours.

ALSACE-LORRAINE

France's eastern frontier provinces, Alsace and Lorraine, were for a thousand years a battleground. Disputed through the Middle Ages, in this century they became the scene of some of the worst fighting of two world wars. The democratically minded burghers of **Alsace** created a plethora of well-heeled semi-autonomous towns for themselves centuries before their eighteenth-century incorporation into the French state: neat, well-ordered places full of Germanic fripperies on the houses – though the Alsatians remain fiercely and proudly French, despite their German dialect. The combination of cultures is at its most vivid in the numerous little wine towns that punctuate the so-called "Route du Vin" along the eastern margin of the wet and woody **Vosges** mountains – at **Colmar**, in **Mulhouse**, and in the great cathedral city of **Strasbourg**. By comparison, **Lorraine**, though it has suffered much the same vicissitudes, is rather wan, apart from the elegant eighteenth-century provincial capital of **Nancy**.

Nancy

NANCY, capital of Lorraine, is lighter and more southern in feel than its close neighbour Metz, with a relatively untouched eighteenth-century core that was the work of the last of the independent dukes of Lorraine, Stanislas Leczinski, dethroned King of Poland and father-in-law of Louis XV. During the twenty-odd years of his office in the middle of the eighteenth century he ordered some of the most successful urban redevelopment of the period in all France.

The centre of this is **place Stanislas**, a supremely elegant, partially enclosed square at the far end of rue Stanislas from the station, the south side of which is taken up by the **Hôtel de Ville**, its roof line topped by florid urns and lozenge-shaped lanterns dangling from the beaks of gilded cocks. On the west side of the square, the excellent **Musée des Beaux-Arts** (Mon & Wed–Sun 10.30am–6pm; F30) boasts Bonnards, Dufys, Modiglianis and Matisses. A little north, on Grand Rue, is the **Musée Historique Lorrain** (May–Sept 10am–6pm; Oct–April 10am–noon & 2–5pm; closed Tues; F20), devoted to Lorraine's history and with a room of etchings by the seventeenth-century artist, Jacques Callot, whose concern with social issue presaged much nineteenth- and twentieth-century art. Alternatively, make your way to th

Musée de l'École de Nancy, a twenty-minute walk or #5/#25 bus ride away at 36 rue Sergent-Blandan (Mon 2–6pm & Wed–Sun 10.30am–6pm; F20). It's an exciting collection of Art Nouveau furniture and furnishings, arranged as if in a private house, and evidence of Nancy's prominence in the movement – a branch of which was founded here by Émile Gallé, a local manufacturer of glass and ceramics.

The **train station** is at the end of rue Stanislas, a five-minute walk from place Stanislas, where you'll find the **tourist office** (April–Oct Mon–Sat 9am–7pm, Sun 10am–5pm; Nov–March Mon–Sat 9am–6pm, Sun 10am–1pm). For cheap places to stay, there's the *Hôtel Poincaré*, 81 rue Raymond-Poincaré, west of the train station (☎03.83.40.25.99; ③), and the *Jean-Jaurès*, 14 bd Jean-Jaurès, south of the station (☎03.83.27.74.14; ③). There's a **youth hostel** out at the *Centre d'Accueil*, Château de Rémicourt, Villers-lès-Nancy (☎03.83.27.73.67; ②); bus #16, #32 or #42, plus a 15min walk. *Camping de Brabois* (☎03.83.27.18.28) is nearby. For **food**, Grande Rue and rue des Ponts offer the best choice. Try *Les Pissenlits*, at 25bis rue des Ponts. If you missed out on Nancy's Art Nouveau museum, the ornate café *L'Excelsior*, across place Thiers from the train station, is a nice place for coffee and, if you can afford it, a light meal.

Strasbourg

The capital of Alsace, **STRASBOURG** is prosperous, beautiful and modern, big enough to have a metropolitan air, but far from overwhelming. It has one of the loveliest cathedrals in France, one of the oldest and most active universities and is also the current seat of the Council of Europe and the European Court of Human Rights, and part-time base of the European Parliament. You may not be planning to spend time in eastern France, but if you're around the region it's the one city worth a detour.

The City

Strasbourg focuses on two main squares, the busy **place Kléber**, and, to the south, **place Gutenberg**, named after the pioneer of type, who lived here in the early fifteenth century. Close by, the **Cathédrale de Notre-Dame** (daily 7–11.30am & 1–7pm; free) soars out of a huddle of medieval houses, with a spire of such delicate, flaky lightness it seems the work of confectioners rather than masons. In the south transept the slender triple-tiered thirteenth-century column, the **Pilier des Anges**, is decorated with some of the most graceful and expressive statuary of its age. Look also at the enormous and tremendously complicated **astrological clock** built by Schwilgué of Strasbourg in 1842, a big hit with guided tours who roll up in droves to witness the clock's crowning performance of the day, striking the hour of noon with unerring accuracy at 12.30pm – noon, Strasbourg mean time.

South of the cathedral the **Musée de l'Oeuvre Notre-Dame** (Tues–Sat 10am–noon & 1.30–6pm, Sun 10am–5pm; F20) houses the original sculptures from the cathedral exterior, damaged in the Revolution and replaced today by copies. There's also the eleventh-century *Wissembourg Christ*, said to be the oldest representation of a human figure in stained glass, from the previous cathedral, as well as the present cathedral architect's original parchment drawings for the statuary, done in fascinating detail.

Just north of the old centre, across the river, **place de la République** is surrounded by vast German-Gothic edifices erected during the Prussian occupation (1870–1918), a few hundred metres beyond which is the **Palais de l'Europe**, home of the European Parliament and an imposing piece of contemporary architecture. The opposite edge of the city centre is more picturesque, where, around **quai Turckheim**, four square towers guard the so-called **Ponts Couverts** over a series of canals. The area is known as **La Petite France** and has winding streets bordered by sixteenth- and seventeenth-century houses with carved woodwork and decked with flowers. The brand new **Musée d'Art Moderne et Contemporain** (Tues, Wed & Fri–Sun 11am–7pm, Thurs noon–10pm; F30) stands on the west bank of the river and houses an impressive collection featuring Monet, Klimt, Ernst, Klee and Jean Arp. Just upstream you can see a dam built by Vauban to protect the city from waterborne assault.

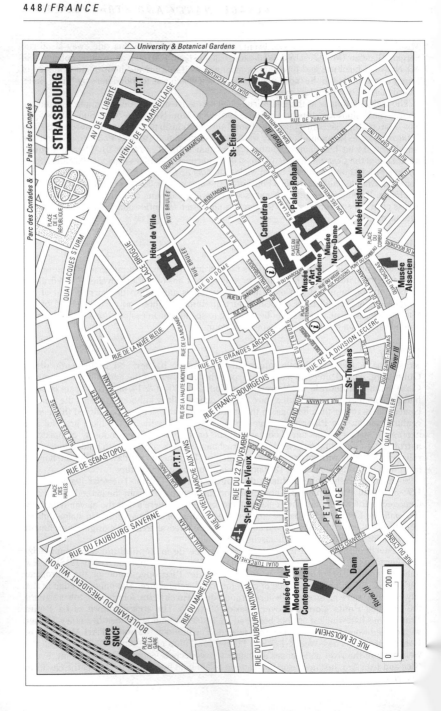

Practicalities

From the **train station** take rue du Maire-Kuss and cross the river onto rue du 22-Novembre, which leads to place Kléber, from where rue des Grandes-Arcades heads south to place Gutenberg and the **tourist office** at 17 place de la Cathédrale (daily 9am–6/7pm). The tourist office also has an annexe in the underground shopping centre in front of the train station. **Hotels** aren't cheap: close to the station there's the *Weber*, 22 bd de Nancy (☎03.88.32.36.47; ③), or more centrally and near the cathedral, try *Michelet* at 48 rue du Vieux Marché aux Poissons (☎03.88.32.47.38; ③), or the *Patricia*, 1a rue de Puits, in the backstreets of the old town (☎03.88.32.14.60; ③). There's a modern **youth hostel** on rue de l'Auberge-de-Jeunesse (#23 bus by the next bridge upstream from Pont Kuss; ☎03.88.30.26.46; ②), an HI hostel on rue des Cavaliers, close to the Pont de l'Europe over the Rhine (bus #21 from the station; ☎03.88.45.54.20; ②), and more central **hostel** beds at *CIARUS*, 7 rue Finkmatt (☎03.88.15.27.88; ②), which has a 1am curfew. For **food**, the *FEC* student canteen on place St-Étienne has rock-bottom prices and good meals, too. Otherwise, though, eating out can be pricey. *Flam's*, 27–29 rue des Frères, serves the local speciality, *tarte flambée*, a kind of onion tart, and *Le St-Sépulcre* on rue des Orfèvres is good traditional *winstub*. The city abounds in **wine bars** and **beer halls**: *L'Académie de la Bière*, 17 rue Adolphe Seyboth, is Strasbourg's most serious beer palace; *Le Java*, 6 rue Faisan, is a good place for live music, and is open until 1am.

Colmar

A fifty-minute train ride south of Strasbourg, **COLMAR** is at first sight an unattractive sprawl, but it merits a stop for its picturesque old centre and some remarkable paintings in its **Musée d'Unterlinden**, at the end of av de la République in a former Dominican convent (April–Oct daily 9am–6pm; Nov–March 10am–5pm, closed Tues; F35). The most notable of these is an altarpiece for St Anthony's monastery at Isenheim, painted by Mathias Grünewald, one of the most extraordinary of all Gothic paintings. Although displayed "exploded", the **Isenheim altarpiece** was designed to make a single piece. On the front was the *Crucifixion*, with an emaciated, tortured Christ flanked by his pale fainting mother, Saint John and Mary Magdalene. It was unfolded on Sundays and feast days to reveal an *Annunciation*, *Resurrection* and *Virgin and Child*, and a sculpted panel depicting the saints Anthony, Augustine and Jerome.

To get there from the **train station**, go straight ahead and turn left onto av de la République. There's a **tourist office** opposite the museum (April–Oct Mon–Sat 9am–6/7pm, Sun 9.30/10am–2pm; Nov–March Mon–Sat 9am–noon & 2–6pm, Sun 10am–2pm). Of the **hotels** on and around av de la République, *La Chaumière* at no. 74 (☎03.89.41.08.99; ③), and *Colbert*, at no. 2 rue des Trois-Épis (☎03.89.41.31.05; ④), are about the cheapest. There's also an HI **hostel** at 2 rue Pasteur (☎03.89.80.57.39; ②; bus #4 from the station), and a reasonable and more central *Maison des Jeunes* at 17 rue Camille-Schlumberger (☎03.89.41.26.87; ②), although the latter isn't always keen to take individuals. For **food**, *L'Amandine* on place de la Cathédrale has brasserie-type fare or, for a more upmarket Alsatian experience, try *Bartholdi* at 2 rue des Boulangers, near the Dominican church.

THE ALPS

Rousseau wrote in his *Confessions*, "I need torrents, rocks, pine trees, dark forests, mountains, rugged paths to go up and down, precipices at my elbow to give me a good fright." And these are, in essence, the principal joys of the **Alps**, made up of the *départements* of Dauphiné and Savoie. Along their western edge, **Grenoble** and **Annecy** are the gateways to the highest parts, although you really need to spend several days here to have time to do anything more strenuous than view the peaks from your hotel window. There are four national or **regional parks** – Vanoise, Ecrins, Queyras (the least busy) and Vercors (the gentlest) – each of which is ideal walking country, and the **Grande Traversée des Alpes**, which crosses all the major massifs from St-Gingolph on Lake Geneva to Nice. But on a quick tour you're best off doing as other people do and grabbing a taster at **Chamonix**, the best base for **Mont Blanc** on the French-Italian border, or simply doing day walks from the main centres. All **routes** are clearly marked and equipped with refuge huts and *gîtes d'étape*. The CIMES office in Grenoble can provide detailed information on GR paths, and local tourist offices often produce detailed maps of walks in their areas. Bear in mind that anywhere above 2000m will be snowbound until the beginning of July.

Grenoble

The economic and intellectual capital of the French Alps, **GRENOBLE** is a lively, thriving city, beautifully situated on the Drac and Isère rivers. The centre of town, by the river, is marked by the sixteenth-century **Palais de Justice**, with place St-André and the church of **St-André** behind, built in the thirteenth century and heavily restored. **Place Grenette** is the favourite resort of café loungers, and nearby at 14 rue J.J. Rousseau you can visit the house where **Stendhal** was born (Mon & Wed–Sat 10am–noon & 2–6pm; free), though the city's **museum** of Stendhaliana (Tues–Sun 2–6pm; free) is in a corner of the public gardens behind the St-André church. The **Musée de Grenoble**, situated in the Parc A. Michallon (Mon & Wed–Sun 11am–7pm, Wed until 10pm; F25), is worthwhile for its collection of representative works by the big names in twentieth-century art; it also has some good temporary exhibitions. For an insight into the region you should try and visit the **Musée Dauphinois** (10am–6/7pm; closed Tues; F20), which occupies the former convent of St-Marie-d'en-Haut, up a cobbled path opposite the Isère footbridge by the Palais de Justice. The French Resistance were particularly active in the Vercors Massif near Grenoble during World War II, and are commemorated – along with victims of the Holocaust – in the **Musée de la Résistance et de la Déportation** (9am–noon & 2–6pm; closed Tues; F20). Finally, the one thing you shouldn't miss is the trip by **téléférique** (Nov–March Mon 11am–6.30pm, Tues–Sun 10.30am–6.30pm; April, May & Oct Mon 11am–7.30pm Tues–Sat 9am–midnight, Sun 9am–7.30pm; June–Sept Mon 11am–midnight/0.30am, Tues–Sun 9am–midnight/0.30am; F35 return) from the riverside quai Stéphane-Jay up to **Fort de la Bastille** on the steep slopes above the north bank of the Isère. It's a hair-raising ride to an otherwise uninteresting fort, but the view over the surrounding mountains and valleys, and down onto the town, is fantastic.

Practicalities

The **train station** and **bus station** are on the western edge of the centre, at the end of av Felix-Viallet. The **tourist office**, at 14 rue de la République, near place Grenette (Mon–Sat 9am–6/7pm, Sun 10am–noon), can book rooms and rents out bikes for around F40 a day; while the CIMES desk in the same office will provide detailed information on hiking and climbing. There are numerous **hotels** in the station area, among them the *Alize* at 1 place de la Gare (☎04.76.43.12.91; ③) or the very good value *Lakanal* on the corner of rue des Bergers (☎04.76.46.03.42; ③). The *Bellevue* (☎04.76.46.69.34; ④), on the corner of quai Stéphane-Jay and rue Belgrade, has an attractive location but can be noisy. Alternatively, there's a **youth hostel** in Echirolles (☎04.76.09.33.52; ②; 10min by bus #1 or #8 from cours Jean-Jaurès); and summer-only hostel rooms at *Le Foyer de l'Étudiante*, 4 rue Ste-Ursule (☎04.76.42.00.84), and *Le Foyer de la Houille Blanche*, 2 av des Jeux Olympiques (☎04.76.54.56.01). There's also a **campsite** 5km away in Seyssins (☎04.76.96.45.73). For **food**, try anywhere on place St-André and place Notre-Dame, especially *Le Progrès* or *Le Tonneau de Diogène*.

Annecy

Sited at the edge of a turquoise lake, and close to some high peaks, **ANNECY** is very much a transit-point for hikers, offering good access to the Mont Blanc area and onto Lake Geneva and the northern foothills.

The most interesting part of the city lies at the foot of the castle mound, a warren of lanes and passages, between which flow branches of the Canal du Thiou, which drains the lake into the River Fier. It's a picture-book pretty place, and inevitably full of tourists. Opposite the Hôtel de Ville, in the main square, is the fifteenth-century church of **St-Maurice**, originally built for a Dominican convent, with attractive Flamboyant windows and walls leaning outwards to an alarming degree. South of here, across the canal bridge, is the grand old **Palais de l'Île** and **rue St-Claire**, the main street of the old town, with arcaded shops and houses. From rue de l'Île the narrow Rampe du Château leads up to the **Musée du Château** (June–Sept daily 10am–6pm; Oct–May Mon & Wed–Sun 10am–noon & 2–6pm; F30), the former home of the counts of Genevois, which now houses various archeological finds, Savoyard popular art, furniture and woodcarving and, on the top floor, an excellent display illustrating the geology of the Alps.

The **tourist office** is in the Centre Bonlieu, a modern shopping centre at the end of rue Paquier (July & Aug Mon–Sat 9am–6.30pm, Sun 9am–noon & 1.45–6.30pm; Sept–June Mon–Sat 9am–noon & 1.45–6.30pm, Sun 3–6pm; Nov–Easter closed Sun). The **youth hostel**, 4 route de Semnoz (☎04.50.45.33.19; ②), is a good 45-minute walk from the old town and often full. There's a municipal **campsite** off bd de la Corniche – turn right up a lane opposite Chemin du Tillier and it's on the left. **Hotels** need to be booked in advance – it's a popular place, expecially at weekends. For somewhere close to the centre and the lake, try the *Hôtel des Alpes* on rue de la Poste (☎04.50.45.04.56; ④). Failing that, head for the *Central*, 6 bis rue Royale (☎04.50.45.05.37; ③). A clutch of **eating places** can be found around the chateau – *Restaurant des Arts*, 4 passage de l'Île, occupies an especially pleasant position here. Also good are *Auberge de Savoie*, a fish restaurant at 1 place Saint-François, and the *Taverne de Maître Kanter* at 2 quai Perrière. For getting out of town, there are round-the-lake **boat trips**, at a reasonable price, from Compagnie des Bateaux (☎04.50.51.08.40) located by the mouth of the Thiou canal at 2 place aux Bois. The tourist office sells a 1:50,000 map of the Annecy area with **walking trails** marked, and **bikes** can be rented at Little Big Shop on rue Carnot.

Chamonix and Mont Blanc

Mont Blanc is the biggest tourist draw in the Alps, but by walking you can soon get away from the worst of the crowds. The two approaches come together at Le Fayet, where the **tramway du Mont-Blanc** begins its 75-minute haul to the **Nid d'Aigle**, a vantage point on the northwest slope. There's more exciting access 30km further on, at **CHAMONIX**, although there's little else to recommend the place. The **Musée Alpin** off rue Whymper (June–Oct daily 2/3–7pm; F20) will interest mountain freaks. The other thing you should do is take the expensive **téléférique** (return ticket F196) to the **Aiguille du Midi** (3842m), a terrifying granite pinnacle on which the *téléférique* dock and a restaurant are precariously balanced. The view of Mont Blanc from here is incredible. At your feet is the snowy plateau of the **Col du Midi**, with the glaciers of the Vallée Blanche and Géant crawling off left at their millennial pace. To the right, a steep snowfield leads to the "easy" ridge route to the summit with its cap of ice (4807m). You must, however, go before 9am, because the summits usually cloud over towards midday and the crowds become intolerable. Be sure also to take warm clothes: even on a summer day it can be well below zero at the top.

Finding **accommodation** can be a big problem. The best bet is the comfortable, largely modernized and welcoming **youth hostel** at 127 Montée Jacques-Balmat in Les Pèlerins d'en Haut (☎04.50.53.14.52; ②), just west of Chamonix proper (bus to les Houches – get off at Pèlerins École, from where the hostel is signposted). For other sporadic dormitory accommodation, ask at the **tourist office** (daily: July & Aug 8.30am–7.30pm; rest of year 8.30am–12.30pm & 2–7pm), near the church. **Campsites** are numerous, most convenient are *Les Molliases* on the left of the main road, going west from Chamonix towards the Mont Blanc tunnel entrance, and *Les Arolles* on the opposite side of the road – a fifteen-minute walk from the station.

RHÔNE VALLEY AND PROVENCE

Of all the areas of France, **Provence** is the most irresistible, with attractions that range from the high mountains of the southern Alps to the wild plains of the Camargue. Yet, apart from the coast (detailed in the following section), large areas remain remarkably unscathed by development. Its complete integration into France dates only from the nineteenth century and, although the Provençal language is rarely heard, the common accent is distinctive even to a foreign ear. The main problem is choosing where to go. The **Rhône valley**, north–south route of ancient armies, medieval traders and modern rail and road, is nowadays fairly industrialized, and other than the big city delights of **Lyon** – not strictly in Provence but the main gateway for the region – there's not much to detain you before the Roman city of **Orange** and the old papal stronghold of **Avignon**, the latter with a brilliant summer festival. Deeper into Provence, on the edge of the flamingo-filled lagoons of the **Camargue**, **Arles** is another ancient Roman settlement, retaining a superb amphitheatre, while **Aix**, a little way east, is perhaps Provence's most sophisticated city and for many years home to Cézanne, for whom the nearby **Mont St-Victoire** was an enduring subject. In eastern Provence it is the landscapes not the cities that dominate, the foothills of the Alps gradually closing in around the **Gorges du Verdon**.

Lyon

LYON is the third largest city in France, a long-established business centre – somewhat staid and very bourgeois, but not without its charms. Foremost of these is gastronomy: there are more restaurants per square metre than anywhere else on earth and the city could form a football team with its superstars of the international chef circuit. It also has a charming old quarter, and all the attractions you would expect of a city of its size (around half a million): a lively night scene and cultural life, including the famous Lyonnais puppets.

Arrival and accommodation

The centre of Lyon is the **Presqu'île**, the tongue of land between the rivers Saône and Rhône just before their confluence. Across the Saône is the **old town**, at the foot of **Fourvière**, on which the Romans built their capital of Gaul; to the north is the old silk weavers' district, **La Croix-Rousse**. Modern Lyon lies east of the Rhône, the city at its most self-assertive in the cultural and commercial centre of **La Part-Dieu**, beside the **TGV station**. Other **trains** arrive at the Gare de Perrache, along with **buses**, on what was once the tip of the peninsula. The **airport**, Satolas, is off the Grenoble *autoroute*, 45 minutes by *Satobus* from La Part-Dieu. There's a **tourist office** (summer only Mon–Fri 9am–6pm, Sat 9am–5pm) in the Centre Perrache in front of the station, where you can pick up transport maps for Lyon's **metro, tram and bus system**, or you can just hop two stops on the metro to place Bellecour, where the **central tourist office** is on the southeast corner (summer Mon–Sat 10am–8pm, Sun 10am–6pm; winter Mon–Sat 10am–7pm, Sun 10am–6pm). Transport tickets cost a flat F8, or you can buy them in *carnets* of ten for F68. Alternatively, the *liberté* ticket, sold at tourist offices, gives you one day's unlimited travel on trams, buses and metro for F24. For **accommodation**, close to Gare de Perrache, try the *Vaubecour*, 28 rue Vaubecour (☎04.78.37.44.91; ③), one block back from the Saône quays; the *d'Ainay*, 14 rue des Remparts d'Ainay (☎04.78.42.43.42; ③), which has decent-sized rooms; or the clean and convenient *De La Marne*, 78 rue de la Charité (☎04.78.37.07.46; ③). In Vieux Lyon, the *Celtic*, 10 rue François-Vernay (☎04.78.28.01.12; ③), is large, fairly pleasant and reasonably priced. There's a new state-of-the-art **youth hostel** in Vieux Lyon at 41–45 Montée du Chemin Neuf (04.78.15.05.51; ②), with great views over Lyon, and an alternative 4km southeast of the centre in Venissieux, 51 rue Roger-Salangro (☎04.78.76.39.23; ②) – take bus #53 from Perrache or #36 from Part-Dieu. The closest **campsite** is the *Porte de Lyon* at Dardilly, a ten-minute ride by #89 bus from the Hôtel de Ville.

The City

Directly in front of Gare de Perrache, **place Carnot** is a green square, linked by way of the pedestrian rue Victor-Hugo with the gravelly acres of the central **place Bellecour**, where even Louis XIV in the guise of a Roman emperor looks small. On rue de la Charité, which runs parallel to rue Victor-Hugo on the Rhône side, is the **Musée Historique des Tissus** (Tues–Sun 10am–5.30pm; F28), a brilliant collection of fabrics from ancient Egypt to the twentieth century. From here, push straight on up rue de la République, full of people jostling back and forth between cafés and shops, past place Bellecour. To the left, at the top of quai St-Antoine, the **quartier Mercière** is the old commercial centre of the town, with sixteenth- and seventeenth-century houses lining rue Mercière, while straight ahead, the monumental nineteenth-century fountain in front of the even more monumental **Hôtel de Ville** on place des Terreaux symbolizes rivers straining to reach the ocean. The building taking up the southern side of the square is one of the four wings of Lyon's **Musée des Beaux-Arts** (Wed–Sun 10.30am–6pm; F25), which has a great selection of works by among others Rubens, El Greco, Tintoretto. For more contemporary works head for the new **Musée d'Art Contemporain** (Wed–Sat noon–7pm; F25), 3km north of the city centre at 81 Cité Internationale, quai Charles-de-Gaulle.

North of here, the old silk weavers' district of **La Croix-Rousse** is still a working-class area, but only twenty or so people work on the computerized looms that are kept in business by the restoration and maintenance of the palaces and châteaux. You can watch the traditional looms in action at **La Maison des Canuts** at 10–12 rue d'Ivry, one block north of place de la Croix-Rousse (Mon–Sat 8.30am–noon & 2–6.30pm; F15), but otherwise you might as well cut down through the alleyways and narrow streets of the district to **Vieux Lyon**, across the river. The streets pressed close together beneath the hill of Fourvière on the right bank of the Saône form an operatic set of Renaissance facades, at night brightly lit and populated by well-dressed Lyonnais in search of supper. The **Musée Historique de Lyon** on place du Petit-Collège (Mon & Wed–Sun 10.45am–6pm; F25) has a good collection of Nevers ceramics, although the **Musée de la Marionnette** (same hours & ticket) on the first floor of the same fifteenth-century mansion is more engaging, containing the eighteenth-century Lyonnais creations, *Guignol* and *Madelon* (the French Punch and Judy, which you can see in action at *Théâtre Guignol*, rue Louis-Carrand; ☎04.78.28.92.57).

Rue St-Jean ends at the **Cathédrale St-Jean**, a much-damaged twelfth- to fifteenth-century construction, but one whose thirteenth-century stained glass above the altar and in the rose windows of the transepts is in perfect condition. Just beyond the cathedral, opposite av Adolphe-Max and Pont Bonaparte, is a **funicular station**, from which you ascend to a set of **Roman remains** on rue de l'Antiquaille, consisting of two theatres and an underground museum of Lyonnais life from prehistoric times to 7 AD. There's a **Musée de la Civilization Gallo-Romain** at 17 rue Cléberg (Wed–Sun 9.30am–noon & 2–6pm; F20), from where it's a short walk to the late nineteenth-century **Basilique de Notre-Dame**, a miasma of multi-coloured marble and mosaic. The belvedere behind the church affords an impressive view of Lyon and its curving rivers.

Reminders of the war are never far away in France and this is particularly true of Lyon where the **Centre d'Histoire de la Résistance et de la Déportation** at 14 av Berthelot (Wed–Sun 9am–5.30pm; F25) tells of the immense courage and ingenuity of the French resistance, and also serves as a poignant memorial to the city's Jews who were deported to concentration camps.

Eating, drinking and nightlife

Lyon is not a vegetarian's dream, its **food** specialities revolving around the different things you can do with meat and offal, most famously in *quenelles* – a bit like dumplings. Vieux Lyon has the greatest concentration of eateries, though you'll find cheaper and less busy ones between place des Jacobins and place Sathonay at the top of the Presqu'île. *L'Amphitryon*, 33 rue St-Jean, is open until midnight every night and gets packed, as does *La Grille*, 106 rue Sébastien-Gryphe, which is a good place to try local specialities. *La Meunière*, on rue Neuve, has a decent F90 menu, again of regional dishes, and is again normally very crowded, while

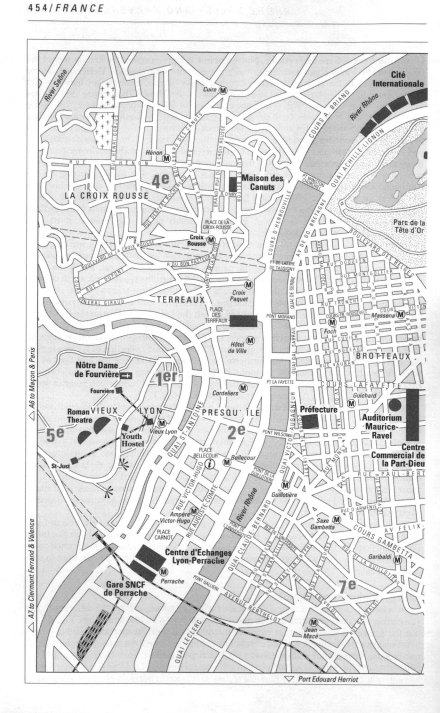

Cité
Internationale

River Saône

River Rhône

Cuire Ⓜ

CONS A. BRIAND

QUAI ACHILLE-LIGNON

Hénon Ⓜ

4e

LA CROIX ROUSSE

Maison des
Canuts

Parc de la
Tête d'Or

BOULEVARD DES BELGES

PLACE DE LA
CROIX-ROUSSE

Croix
Rousse Ⓜ

COURS D'HERBOUVILLE

AV DE GD BRETAGNE

PT WINSTON
CHURCHILL

R DU BON PASTEUR

PT DE LATTRE
DE TASSIGNY

RUE DUQUESNE

RUE MONTGOLFIER

BOULEVARD DE LA CROIX ROUSSE

COURS GENERAL GIRAUD

TERREAUX

Croix
Paquet Ⓜ

QUAI DE SERBIE

RUE TRONCHET

COURS FR. ROOSEVELT

COURS VITTON

Massena Ⓜ

PLACE
DES
TERREAUX

PONT MORAND

QUAI GAL SARRAIL

Foch Ⓜ

RUE CUVIER

BROTTEAUX

Hôtel
de Ville Ⓜ

RUE BUGEAUD

RUE VAUBAN

Nôtre Dame
de Fourvière ✠

1er

PT LA FAYETTE

COURS LAFAYETTE

Fourvière

Cordeliers Ⓜ

Guichard Ⓜ

Roman
Theatre

VIEUX LYON

PRESQU'ÎLE

Préfecture

Auditorium
Maurice-
Ravel

Youth
Hostel

Vieux Lyon Ⓜ

QUAI ST-ANTOINE

2e

PONT WILSON

QUAI VICTOR-AUGAGNEUR

Centre
Commercial de
la Part-Dieu

St-Just

PLACE
BELLECOUR

Bellecour Ⓜ ⓘ

RUE PAUL-BERT

RUE DE LA BARRE

RUE VICTOR-HUGO

PONT DE LA
GUILLOTIÈRE

RUE MONCEY

River Rhône

Guillotière Ⓜ

RUE D'ARMÉNIE

Ampère
Victor-Hugo Ⓜ

RUE AUGUSTE-COMTE

Saxe
Gambetta Ⓜ

COURS GAMBETTA

AV FÉLIX

PLACE
CARNOT

PONT DE
L'UNIVERSITÉ

Centre d'Échanges
Lyon-Perrache

QUAI CLAUDE-BERNARD

Garibaldi Ⓜ

RUE DE LA GUILLOTIÈRE

Gare SNCF
de Perrache

Perrache Ⓜ

PONT GALLIENI

7e

AVENUE BERTHELOT

Jean
Macé Ⓜ

QUAI LECLERC

△ A6 to Mâcon & Paris

△ A7 to Clermont Ferrand & Valence

▽ Port Edouard Herriot

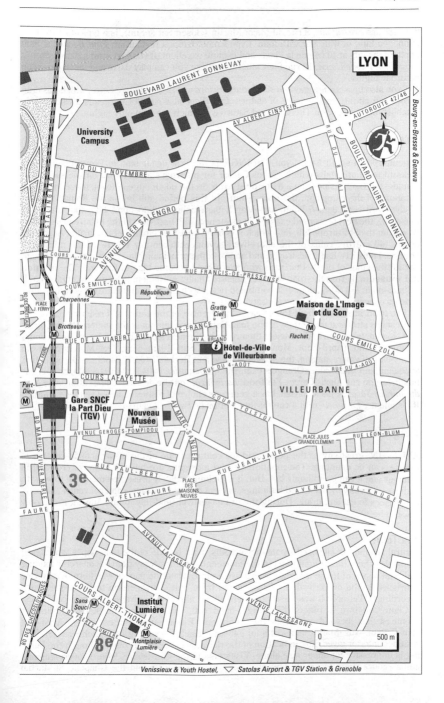

the *Café des Fédérations*, 8 rue du Major-Martin (closed Sat & Sun), is a typical Lyon "bouchon" – a kind of wine bar with food. Lyon's most famous restaurant, *Paul Bocuse*, is 9km north of the city at 40 rue de la Plage, and is quite excellent. If you just want a **drink**, there's the *Albion Public House*, 12 rue Ste-Cathérine, where you can play darts and listen to jazz on Saturday nights.

Lyon also boasts a few **gay bars** including *Mylord* at 112 quai Pierre-Scize, which has drag shows and an interesting decor of statues. *Le Village* at 8 rue St-Georges is a women-only establishment except on Tuesdays and Saturdays, which are men-only nights.

Orange

Around 100km south from Lyon, **ORANGE** is the first major stop in Provence proper, a pleasant town originally built by Julius Caesar for his troops as a reward for the successful conquest of Gaul. Aside from a **triumphal arch** on the north edge of town, friezed with celebrations of the campaign, the main feature of this period still left is the Roman **theatre** (daily: April–Sept 9am–6.30pm; Oct–March 9am–noon & 1.30–5pm; F30, incl municipal museum), the best-preserved example in existence. The best view of the theatre in its entirety is from the St-Eutrope hill, into which it is built, past the remains of the forum. At the top of the hill are the ruins of the short-lived seventeenth-century **castle** of the princes of Orange. Louis XIV had it destroyed and annexed the principality to France – a small price to pay for the ruler of the Netherlands who was also to become king of England. The **municipal museum**, across the road from the theatre (daily: April–Sept 9.30am–7pm; Oct–March 9.30am–noon & 1.30–5.30pm; F30 combined ticket with the Roman theatre), has various documents concerning the Orange dynasty.

The **train station** is about 1500m east of the centre, at the end of av Frédéric-Mistral; the nearest bus stop is at the bottom of rue Jean-Reboul, first left out of the station. Bus #2, direction Nogent, takes you to the ancient theatre and – the next stop – the **tourist office** on cours Aristide-Briand (April–Sept Mon–Sat 9am–7pm, Sun 10am–6pm; Oct–March Mon–Sat 9am–5pm). If you're staying, the *Arcotel*, 8 place aux Herbes (☎04.90.34.09.23; ③), is central, appealing and good-value. Orange's campsite, *Le Jonquier* (☎04.90.34.19.83; March–Oct), is northwest on rue Alexis-Carrel. For **food**, *La Fringale* on rue de Tourre does affordable *plats du jour*. *Le Yaca*, 24 place Silvian, has a generous choice of dishes in an old vaulted chamber. If it's full, try *La Roselière* at 4 rue du Renoyer or *Le Parvis*, 3 cours des Pourtoules.

Avignon

AVIGNON, great city of the popes and for centuries one of the major artistic centres of France, can be daunting. The monuments and museums are huge, it's always crowded in summer and it can be stiflingly hot. But, it is an immaculately preserved medieval town with endless impressively decorated buildings, ancient churches, chapels and convents, and plenty of places to eat and drink. During the drama festival (mid-July to mid-Aug), it is the only place to be.

The Town

Central Avignon is enclosed by medieval **walls**, built by one of the nine popes who based themselves here throughout most of the fourteenth century, away from the anarchic feuding and rival popes of Rome. Avignon was a lively place when the papacy was here. Every vice flourished in the overcrowded, plague-ridden town, full of hangers-on to the papal court; according to Petrarch it was "a sewer where all the filth of the universe has gathered".

Centre of town is **place d'Horloge**, lined with cafés and market stalls on summer evenings, just beyond which is the enormous **Palais des Papes** (daily: April–Oct 9am–7/9pm; Nov–March 9am–5.45pm; F40 with English-speaking headphone guide). The denuded interior gives little indication of the richness of the papal court, although the building is impressive for sheer size alone. Visits take in the Consistoire, where sovereigns and ambassadors were received. The adjacent Chapelle St-Jean, and the Chapelle St-Martial upstairs, were decorated by the Sienese artist Matteo Giovannetti on the orders of Clement VI, whose secular concerns are evident in the wonderful food-orientated murals of his bedroom and study – part of Clement's New Palace, whose Grande Chapelle has the proportions of a cathedral.

The **Cathédrale Notre-Dame-des-Doms**, north of the palace, might have been a luminous Romanesque structure once, but the interior has had a bad attack of Baroque. You could ignore it and wander instead around the **Rocher des Doms** park, which gives great views over the river. Along the river is the famous **Pont d'Avignon** of the song (daily: April–Sept 9am–6.30pm; Oct–March 9am–1pm & 2–5pm; F15). The struggle to keep the bridge in good repair despite the ravages of the Rhône was finally abandoned in 1660, three and a half centuries after it was built, and today just four of the original 22 arches survive. A combined ticket for F31 will also gain you entrance to the **Musée en Images** (daily: April–Sept 9am–7pm; Oct–March 10am–5pm), a panoramic screen history of Avignon.

Practicalities

The **train station** is beside porte de la République on bd St-Roch, on the southern edge of the centre. If you don't want to walk, you can also take bus #4 from the main post office, on the left through porte de la République. The **tourist office** is a short walk from the station at 41 cours Jean-Jaurès (Mon–Fri 9am–1pm & 2–6pm, Sat 9am–1pm & 2–5pm; April–Sept also open Sun 9am–1pm & 2–5pm) and there's another office at the Pont d'Avignon which is open daily. Outside festival time, finding **accommodation** can still be a problem. Off cours Jean-Jaurès between the station and the SI, rue Perdiguier has a couple of cheap hotels: *Le Parc* at no. 18 bis (☎04.90.82.71.55; ③) and the characterless *Splendid* at no. 17 (☎04.90.86.14.46; ④). The *Innova*, 100 rue Joseph-Vernet (☎04.90.82.54.10; ③), is nicer. There's a small **youth hostel**, the *Squash Club*, at 32 bd Limbert (☎04.90.85.27.78; ②; bus #2 from the Gare SNCF). The closest **campsite**, also with **dorm rooms**, is the *Bagatelle*, across the river on the Île de la Barthelasse – bus #10 to Porte de l'Oulle, then #20 to Bagatelle, or a ten-minute walk from the centre of town, across the Pont Daladier.

Eating on a budget is easy. The big brasseries on place d'Horloge all do well-priced meals and are nice places to sit outside – try *Le Venaissin* – and rue des Teinturiers is a good source of cheap restaurants. Specifically *Le Mesclun*, 46 rue Balance, does good plats du jour for around F50. Place d'Horloge is the liveliest place to sip an early evening **drink**, though place des Corps-Saints (near the tourist office) comes a close second.

The festival

Avignon's summer **festival** (mid-July to mid-Aug), is a great time to be in town. Theatre dominates, but opera, classical music, film and street theatre are also featured. Much of it takes place in the Palais des Papes and other interesting locations, while the streets are given over to the fringe. Around 200,000 spectators come here for the show, so doing any normal sightseeing becomes virtually impossible. The **festival headquarters** is at 8 rue de Mons (☎04.90.27.66.50) and, as well as providing the main festival programme and information, shows videos and a collection of festival memorabilia dating back to its inception in 1947.

Arles

Just 25km or so south from Avignon, **ARLES** was one of the most important settlements of Gaul, providing grain for most of the western empire, as well as being a crucial port and shipbuilding centre – indeed, in the fourth century it became the capital of Gaul, Britain and Spain. Today, Arles is a picturesque town with a laid-back Mediterranean atmosphere and well-preserved vestiges of its illustrious past – not least a marvellous Roman amphitheatre.

Boulevard des Lices is the main street, along with rue Jean-Jaurès and its continuation, rue Hôtel-de-Ville. The most obvious place to start exploring is the central **place de la République**, between rue Jean-Jaurès and rue Hôtel-de-Ville, highlight of which is the **Cathédrale St-Trophime**, whose doorway is one of the most famous bits of twelfth-century Provençal carving, depicting a *Last Judgement* trumpeted by angels playing with the enthusiasm of jazz musicians. Immediately east of the cathedral, the **Théâtre-Antique** (daily: July–Aug 9am–7pm; April–June & Sept 9am–12.30pm & 2–7pm; Oct–March 10am–noon & 2–4.30/5.30pm; F15) is fairly delapidated, and you'd do better to stroll just beyond to the **Arènes** (same times and price), the town's most impressive imperial structure. Built in the first century AD, it originally seated 20,000, and is still used for bullfights.

For a better insight into Roman Arles, head for the **Musée de l'Arles Antique** (daily: April–Sept 9am–7pm; Oct–March 9.30am–noon & 1.30–6pm; F35), west of the town centre on the spit of land between the Rhône and the Canal de Rhône, where fabulous mosaics, sarcophagi and sculpture illuminate Arles' early history. If you feel that life in Arles stopped with the Romans, you will be reassured by the **Musée Réattu** (same hours and price as Théâtre-Antique), opposite some Roman baths, which returns you to the twentieth century with a decent collection of modern paintings, not least a good array of work by Picasso, including sculpture and ink and crayon sketches he donated to the museum.

Practicalities

The **train station** is a few blocks north of the Arènes, close to the Porte de la Cavalerie. For **accommodation**, the *Regence* (☎04.90.96.39.85; ③), on rue Marius Jouveau, is a gloomy but adequate cheapie. Slightly more characterful are the *Terminus & Van Gogh* at 5 place Lamartine (☎04.90.96.12.32; ③) and *Le Rhône* on place Voltaire (☎04.90.96.43.70; ③). Perhaps the nicest choice is the *Gauguin*, also on place Voltaire (☎04.90.96.14.35; ④), which is comfortable, cheap and well run. There's a **youth hostel** at 20 av Maréchal-Foch (☎04.90.96.18.25; ②) – take bus #5 from place Lamartine – and six **campsites** in the vicinity of Arles, of which the most pleasant is *La Bienheureuse* (☎04.90.98.35.64), with a restaurant, 7km out on N453 at Rapheles-lès-Arles; regular buses run there. Closer to town is *Camping City* (☎04.90.93.08.86), 67 route de Crau. The **tourist office** is opposite rue Jean-Jaurès on bd des Lices (April–Sept daily 9am–7pm; Oct–March Mon–Sat 9am–6pm), and provides a hotel booking service; there's an annexe at the train station. **Bikes** can be rented from Peugeot, 15 rue du Pont. For a special treat, the place to **eat** is the *Hostellerie des Arènes*, 62 rue du Refuge; otherwise there are plenty of affordable brasseries on the main boulevards and around place du Forum – try the *Bistrot Arleésien*, on place du Forum, or *L'Affenage*, 4 rue Molière, which serves Provençal specialities in a pleasant atmosphere.

The Camargue

The flat, marshy delta area immediately south of Arles – the **Camargue** – is a unique area that is used as a breeding-ground for the bulls used in corridas around here, along with the horses that their herdsmen ride. Neither they nor the bulls are wild, though they run in semi-liberty, and the true wildlife of the area is made up of flamingos, marsh and seabirds, and a rich flora of reeds, wild flowers and juniper trees.

If you're interested in bird-watching or walking around the lagoons and have your own transport, your first stop should be *La Capelière* **information centre** on the eastern side of the Étang du Vaccarès on the small road leading south off the D37 from Villeneuve (Mon–Sat 9am–noon & 2–5pm). The imaginative **Musée Carmarguais**, halfway between Gimeaux and Albaron on the D570, documents the traditions and livelihoods of the Camarguais people, and its main products – rice and salt (April–Sept daily 9.15am–5.45/6.45pm; Oct–March Mon & Wed–Sat 10.15am–4.45pm; F25). The town that most people head for in the Camargue is **SAINTES-MARIES-DE-LA-MER**, on the western edge, where every May 24 and 25 gypsies gather to celebrate their patron saint, Sarah, who came to an island close by after being driven out of Palestine. There's a procession from the church to the sea, carrying the statue of Sarah, with the *gardiens* in full Camargue cowboy dress accompanying them. If you're in the area, it's not to be missed.

The rest of the year Saintes-Maries is a very commercialized town. However, there are kilometres of beaches and plenty of facilities, making it much the best resort close to Arles. The **tourist office** on 5 av Van-Gogh has more details (daily 9am–6/8pm). Exploring the region on **horseback** is a good way to get into the Camarguaise spirit of things and the tourist office has a list of places where you can arrange a day or half-day excursion. **Bikes** can be rented from Le Vélo Saintois, 19 av de la République (☎04.90.97.74.56). If you can stomach it, the **bullfighting** season is March to November when a number of festivals take place, although thankfully no animals are killed during Camargue bullfights.

Of **hotels**, *Le Mediterranée*, 4 rue F-Mistral (☎04.90.97.82.09; ③), has some of the cheapest rooms in town, and the *Dauphin Bleu*, overlooking the sea at 31 av G-Leroy (☎04.90.97.80.21; ③), is also pleasant, and has a decent **restaurant**, although you may be obliged to take half-board. There's a **youth hostel** at Pioch-Badet 10km along the Arles road, open all year (☎04.90.97.51.72; ②). The closest **campsite** is *La Brise*, on the Vacharel road just outside the village (☎04.90.97.84.67). There's also cheap accommodation along the coast at the more down-to-earth town of Salin-de-Giraud, and you can sleep on the beach near there at the **plage de Piemançon**.

MARSEILLE AND THE CÔTE D'AZUR

The **Côte d'Azur** is the most built-up, overpopulated, over-eulogized, and expensive stretch of coast anywhere in the world. What's more, along with the Provence region, it's become a leading stronghold for the extreme right party, Le Front National, who have made significant inroads in the recent French regional elections. There are only two industries to speak of – tourism and building plus the related services of estate agents, yacht traffic wardens and Rolls-Royce valets. However, in every gap between the monstrous habitations, the remarkable beauty of the hills and coastline, the scent of the plant life and the strange synthesis of the Mediterranean pollutants that make the water so translucent all devastate the senses. The coast's eastern reaches are its most spectacular, the mountains breaking their fall just a few metres before levelling off to the shore. **St-Tropez** is an expensive high spot, though only **Nice** has real substance – a major city far enough away from Paris to preserve a distinctive character. At the opposite end of the coast, the squalid naval base of **Toulon** and vast, seedy sprawl of **Marseille** are quite different. There is no continuous *corniche*, few villas in the Grand Style, and work is geared to an annual rather than summer cycle. All the way along, the **months to avoid** are July and August, when the overflowing campsites become health hazards, all hotels are booked up, the people are overworked and the vegetation is at its most barren.

Marseille

The most populated city in France after Paris, **MARSEILLE** has, like the capital, prospered and been ransacked over the centuries. It has suffered plagues, religious bigotry, republican and royalist terror and had its own Commune and Bastille storming. It was the presence of so many Marseillaise revolutionaries marching to Paris in 1792 that gave the name to the national anthem. Nowadays Marseille has every social, economic and political conflict of the country: it is a violent place and racism is rife, as is corruption and other lawlessness. Certainly it is not a glamorous city and you might not choose to live there, but it's a wonderful place to visit – a real port with a trading history going back over 2500 years. It's as cosmopolitan as Paris, with the advantages of being nearly 800km further south, with more down-to-earth, informal inhabitants and none of the tourist trappings of the rest of this coast.

Arrival and accommodation

Marseille's **airport**, de Marignane, is 25km northwest of the city, connected by bus (5.30am–10.50pm; every 20min; F46) with the main train station, **Gare St-Charles** – centrally situated on the northern edge of the 1er – around the corner from the **bus station** on place Victor-Hugo. The best way of getting around is to walk, although if you need to cover longer distances fast the **public transport** system – bus, tram and metro – is efficient enough; details are available at *L'Espace Infos*, 6 rue des Fabres. Tickets cost F9 each from metro stations and buses. The main **tourist office** is at 4 La Canebière, down by the harbour (Mon–Sat 9am–7/8pm, Sun 10am–5pm; ☎04.91.13.89.00), and offers a free **accommodation** booking service, although there are few budget **hotels**. Among cheaper places, the *Caravelle*, 5 rue Guy-Mocquet, 1er (☎04.91.48.44.99; ③), is friendly, quiet and close to the action; the *Edmond-Rostand*, 31 rue Dragon, 6e (☎04.91.37.74.95; ③), is further out but has great charm. Otherwise, there's the friendly and central *Pavillon*, at 27 rue Pavillon (☎04.91.33.76.90; ③); or, well worth the extra money, is *Le Corbusier* (☎04.91.16.78.00; ④), on the third floor of the architect's seminal tower block, Cité Radieuse, south of the city centre at 80 bd Michelet – take the metro to Rond Point du Prado, then bus #21 or #22. There are two official **youth hostels**: the *Bois Luzy*, 76 av de Bois-Luzy, 12e (☎04.91.49.06.18; ②), is perhaps the most pleasant, housed in an old château and easy to reach on bus #6 from Réformés, though it has an 11pm curfew; or the *Bonneveine*, 47 av J-Vidal, impasse du Dr-Bonfils, 8e (☎04.91.73.21.81; ②) – metro to Rond Point du Prado then bus #44 – which has a 1am curfew and is near a beach. You can also **camp** at *Bonneveine* (March–Oct), two stops before the hostel.

The City

Marseille is divided into *arrondissements*, sixteen in all, which spiral out from the focal point of the city, the **Vieux Port** – a good place to indulge in the sedentary pleasures of observing the city's street life. Two fortresses guard the entrance to the harbour, a little way south of which is the **Basilique St-Victor**, the city's oldest church. It looks and feels like a fortress – the walls of the choir are almost 3m thick – and for a small fee you can visit the crypt and catacombs (daily 8am–6pm; F10). Saint Victor himself, a Roman soldier, was slowly ground to death between two millstones. On the other, northern, side of the harbour is the former old town of Marseille, known as **Le Panier**, a densely populated area that was dynamited by the Nazis, who deported around 20,000 people from here. Nowadays it's a mainly Algerian quarter, especially over towards the train station, but it's fast being gentrified. After the war, archeologists reaped the benefits of the destruction by finding remains of the Roman docks equipped with vast storage jars for foodstuffs, which can be seen *in situ* at the **Musée des Docks Romains** on place Vivaux (Tues–Sun: summer 11am–6pm; winter 10am–5pm; F10). The new **Musée d'Art Contemporain**, nearby at 69 bd de Haifa (Tues–Sun: summer 11am–6pm; winter 10am–5pm; F15), boasts a strong collection, including works by Warhol, Christo and Buren.

Down below Le Panier, **La Canebière** is the city's main street, and one which more or less separates Arab Marseille from the rest. Just north, on busy cours Belsunce, the **Centre Bourse** is a fiendish giant mall, useful for mainstream shopping and home to a museum of finds from Roman Marseille, the **Musée d'Histoire de Marseille** (Mon–Sat noon–7pm; F10), including a third-century wreck of a Roman trading vessel. At the far eastern end, the **Palais Longchamp** (bus #80, #41) was the grandiose conclusion of an aqueduct bringing water from the Durance to the city. Water is still pumped into the middle of the central colonnade of the building, whose north wing houses the city's **Musée des Beaux-Arts** (Tues–Sun: summer 11am–6pm; winter 10am–5pm; F10), a stuffy museum but with a fair share of goodies, most notably three beautiful paintings by Françoise Duparc and a room of political cartoons by the nineteenth-century Marseille satirist, Honoré Daumier, along with a famous profile of Louis XIV by Pierre Puget.

South of La Canebière are Marseille's main shopping streets, rue Paradis, rue St-Ferréol and rue de Rome, and its principal collection of twentieth-century and contemporary art, the **Musée Cantini**, 19 rue Grignan (Tues–Sun: winter 10am–5pm; summer 11am–6pm; F10), with works by artists as diverse as Dufy, Léger, Bacon and Vasarely.

The only other thing to see while in Marseille is the **Château d'If**, the evil island fortress that figured in Dumas' great adventure story, *The Count of Monte Cristo*. No one ever escaped from here; most prisoners, incarcerated for political or religious reasons, went insane or died (usually both) before reaching the end of their sentences. Boats leave for the island roughly every two hours, on the hour, from the quai des Belges. The journey takes twenty minutes and costs F50.

Eating, drinking and nightlife

Even the takeaway **food** is excellent in Marseille. The main boulevards, and particularly cours Belsunce, are a source of wonderful filled baguettes, and the morning **markets** – at place Sébastopol near the Palais Longchamp and place Jean-Jaurès – sell mouth-watering edibles every day except Sunday. Among **restaurants** in the old town, *Chez Angèle*, 50 rue Caisserie, has a good *menu fixe* of standard French fare, and there's a branch of the international vegetarian restaurant *Country Life* at 14 rue Venture, 1er, which opens Monday to Friday lunchtimes for as-much-as-you-can-eat buffets for F62. Otherwise, the best low-priced meals can be found around cours Julien and place Jean-Jaurès, where you can sample various ethnic cuisines; *Ce Cher Arwell*, 96 cours Julien, is a popular place, serving good French food in generous portions. For authentic Provençal dishes, head for *Maurice Brun*, 18 quai de Rive Neuve, 7e, while *Chez Michel*, 6 rue des Catalans, 7e, is the best place to try *bouillabaisse*.

As for **nightlife**, the clubs around cours d'Estienne-d'Orves are for trendy kids from the upper-crust *arrondissements*, with prices to match. *Le Pourquoi Pas*, 1 rue Fortia, has Caribbean music and punch to get drunk on, while *New Cancan*, 20 rue Sénac, is a camp gay club. *Espace Julien* at 39 cours Julien puts on a wide range of live gigs, while *May Be Blues*, on rue Poggioli, is a relaxed blues/jazz club, with free entry. For night-clubbing *Le Trolleybus*, at 24 quai de Rive Neuve, is a warren-like club complete with funk, techno and rock rooms and even a *boules* area. FNAC in the Centre Bourse or the Virgin Megastore (see below) are the best places to find out **what's on**, and they also sell tickets. Otherwise, check the listings of the left-wing daily, *La Marseillaise*, or pick up a copy of the free weekly *Taktik*.

Listings

Airlines Air France, 14 La Canebière, 1er (☎08.02.80.28.02); British Airways, at the airport (☎04.42.14.21.24).

Beaches Best of the local beaches is the heavily landscaped plage du Prado, at the end of the Corniche du Président J.F. Kennedy – bus #83 from the Vieux Port.

Bike rental Both Cycles Do, 68 cours Lieutaud, 6e (☎04.91.54.33.14), and Tandem, on av du Parc Borély (☎04.91.22.64.80), have mountain bikes for around F100 a day.

Books Virgin Megastore, 75 rue St-Ferréol, stocks English books.

Consulates Britain, 24 av du Prado, 6e (☎04.91.15.72.10); USA, 12 bd Peytral, 6e (☎04.91.54.92.00).

Exchange 24 La Canetière (Mon–Sat 9am–6pm).

Hospital La Conception, 144 rue St-Pierre (☎04.91.38.36.52).

Internet Café 25 rue du Village, 6e.

Laundry Espace Lavarie, 8 rue Rodolphe-Pollak, 1er.

Pharmacy 44 Quai du Port, is open on Sundays; for 24hr service check on pharmacy doors for the rota.

Police Commissariat, 2 rue Antoine-Becker, 2e (☎04.91.39.80.00).

Post office 1 place de l'Hôtel-des-Postes (Mon–Fri 8am–7pm, Sat 8am–noon).

Travel agent Nouvelle Frontières, 11 rue Haxo, 1er (☎04.91.54.18.48).

Toulon

Home base to the French Mediterranean fleet and its arsenal, and until recently a major shipbuilding centre, the port of **TOULON** was half destroyed in World War II and doesn't offer much joy today. But since it is a major nexus you may well find yourself there, and it does have the advantage of being comparatively cheap for this coast. The old town, much besieged by bulldozers and planners intent on its gentrification, crams in between the main bd de Strasbourg and quai de Stalingrad, a pleasant enough place by day, though less appealing at night, especially towards the port. The **Musée d'Art** at 113 bd Maréchal-Leclerc (daily 1–6pm; free) has a good collection of paintings and sculpture including work by Bruegel,

Carracci, Vlaminck, Rodin and Francis Bacon. The most impressive public art work in the city is Pierre Puget's **Atlantes**, which hold up what's left of the old Town Hall on quai de Stalingrad. The best way to pass an afternoon in Toulon is to take bus #40 to bd Amiral-Vence, Super Toulon, and jump on the **funicular** (July & Aug daily 9.30am–7.45pm; rest of year Tues–Sun 9.30am–noon & 2–5.30pm; F38 return) to the summit of **Mont Faron**, 542m above.

The **train station**, on place de l'Europe, and **bus station**, on place Albert-1er, lie northeast of the town centre. To reach the old town, head down rue Vauban, turn left onto av Mal-Leclerc, which becomes bd de Strasbourg, then right by the theatre and you'll arrive in place Victor-Hugo. The **tourist office** is near the harbour on place Raimu (Mon–Sat 9am–6pm, Sun 10am–noon). One of the cheapest and nicest **hotels** is *Hôtel des Allées* at 18 allées Amiral-Courbet (☎04.94.91.10.02; ②). Close by, the *Little Palace*, 6 rue Berthelot (☎04.94.92.26.62; ②), is also a bargain and pleasant. For **hostel** accommodation between June and August there's a *Foyer de la Jeunesse* at 12 place d'Armes, on the west side of town, ten minutes from the station (☎04.94.22.62.00; ②).

St-Tropez

ST-TROPEZ is no more than a village really, gathered around a port founded by the ancient Greeks, and until recently was only easily accessible by boat. In the late nineteenth century, it became a favoured haunt of artists; later, in 1956, Roger Vadim arrived to film Brigitte Bardot in *Et Dieu Créa La Femme* (*And God Created Woman*), and the place has never looked back.

The road into St-Tropez splits in two as it enters the village, with the bus station between them and, a short distance beyond on place George Grammont, the **Musée de l'Annonciade** (10am–noon & 2/3–6/7pm; closed Tues and Nov; F30) – a reason in itself for coming here, with works by Matisse and most of the other artists who worked here. Beyond the museum, the **Vieux Port** is the centre of the town, the dockside café clientele face to face with the yacht-deck Martini-sippers, the latest fashions parading in between. Up from here, at the end of quai Jean-Jaurès, rue de la Mairie passes the **Town Hall**, with a street to the left leading down to the rocky Baie de la Glaye and, along rue de la Ponche, the fishing port with a tiny **beach**. Both these spots are miraculously free from commercialization. Beyond the fishing port, roads lead up to the sixteenth-century **Citadelle**, which has a drab maritime museum but marvellous views from the ramparts, or along to Les Graniers and further **beaches** on Baie des Canoubiers – accessible by a coastal path, frequent bus service, or on a **bike** or **moped** rented from 5 rue Quaranta.

The only vaguely affordable **hotels** are *Les Chimères*, Port du Pilon (☎04.94.97.02.90; ⑤), a short way back from the **bus station** towards La Foux, though it's likely to be booked for the summer, and *La Méditerranée*, 21 bd Louis-Blanc (☎04.94.97.00.44; ⑤). **Camping** poses similar problems. The two sites on the plage du Pampelonne are closest to St-Tropez but cost a fortune. Better is *Les Tournels* on route de Camarat, near Ramatuelle (☎04.94.79.80.54). The **tourist office**, on quai Jean-Jaurès, can help with reservations (daily: winter 9am–noon & 2–6pm; summer 9.30am–1pm & 3–10.30pm). For **eating**, try the takeaway places on rue G-Clemenceau and place des Lices, or make for *La Patate* on rue G-Clemenceau, which serves omelettes, pasta and so forth – nothing special but it may save you from starvation. Also worth checking out is *Le Gorille*, on quai Suffren, serving *moules-frites* and plats du jour.

St-Raphaël and Fréjus

There's a better choice of accommodation in **ST-RAPHAËL**, further north, and in the adjacent town of **FRÉJUS**, 3km inland. Both were established by the Romans and various remnants of this past lie scattered around the towns, including, in Fréjus, an **amphitheatre** on rue Henri-Vardon, used in its damaged state for bullfights and rock concerts, and a **theatre** on av du XV-Corps-d'Armées. Fréjus' **Cathedral** (9am–noon & 4–6pm; free), on place Formigé, has superb twelfth-century Romanesque cloisters and a late-medieval fantasy ceiling, as well as a **museum** with a complete Roman mosaic of a leopard (April–Sept daily 9am–7pm; Oct–March Mon & Wed–Sun 9am–noon & 2–5pm; F25).

St-Raphaël is served by a **youth hostel**, *Centre International Le Manoir*, 5km east at Chemin de l'Escale, Boulouris (☎04.94.95.20.58; ②), and has the better choice of **hotels**. *La Bonne Auberge*, close to the old port at 54 rue de la Garonne (☎04.94.95.69.72; ④) is fairly cheap, or try the *Mistral*, 80 rue de la Garonne (☎04.94.95.42.79; ④). The **tourist office** is on rue W. Rousseau (July & Aug daily 9am–7pm; Sept–June Mon–Sat 9am–12.30pm & 2–6.30pm), hard by the **train** and **bus station**. Between here and the seafront you'll have no trouble finding **restaurants**.

In Fréjus, *La Riviera*, 90 rue Grisolle (☎04.94.51.31.46; ③) is a cheap hotel and there's an HI **youth hostel** 2km northeast from the centre of town at Chemin du Counillier, where you can camp (☎04.94.53.18.75; ②) – bus #7 from St-Raphaël's bus station goes direct to the hostel at 6pm; the rest of the time take the same bus to Le Chênes stop, then it's a twenty-minute walk. **Campsites** are ubiquitous, with at least four on the Bagnols road and one close to the youth hostel. Somewhere to **eat** can be found on place Agricola, place de la Liberté and the main shopping streets.

Cannes

Fishing village turned millionaires' residence, **CANNES** is perhaps the most unpleasant town along the Côte d'Azur, with a fine sand beach that looks like an industrial production line for parasols. The seafront promenade, **La Croisette**, and the **Vieux Port** form the focus of Cannes life, especially during the frenzied two-week International Film Festival in May. The old town, **Le Suquet**, on the steep hill overlooking the bay from the west, masks its miserable passageways with quaint cosmetic streets; beyond Le Suquet there's another **beach**.

If you're compelled to **stay** in Cannes, the best concentration of **hotels** is in the centre, between the **train station** on rue Jean-Jaurès and La Croisette, around the main street of rue Antibes/Felix-Fauré. Possibilities include the unappealing *Bourgogne*, 11 rue du 24-août (☎04.93.38.36.73; ④), the adequate *National*, 8 rue Maréchal-Joffre (☎04.93.47.04.47; ④), and the *Chanteclair*, 12 rue Forville (☎04.93.39.68.88; ③) – the last close to the old town. More appealing is the excellent, new, year-round **youth hostel** at 35 av de Vallauris (☎04.93.99.26.79; ②) – a ten-minute walk from the station or take the bus towards Vallauris. The nearest **campsite** is *Le Grand Saule*, 24–26 bd Jean-Moulin, 4km west of town (bus from the Hôtel de Ville), though it's pretty exorbitant. If you're stuck, there is a **tourist office** at the train station (winter Mon–Sat 8.30am–noon & 2–6.30pm; summer daily 8.30am–7pm) and in the Palais des Festivals on the waterfront (Mon–Sat 9am–6.30pm). Le Suquet is full of **restaurants**, which get cheaper as you reach the top. *Au Bec Fin*, at 12 rue du 24-août, has superb traditional cooking and good plats du jour; *La Croisette*, at 15 rue du Commandant-André, serves excellent grilled fish; and *Le Bouchon d'Objectif*, 10 rue de Constantine, is a fabulous, reasonably priced local bistro.

Vallauris and Antibes

Just east of Cannes, **VALLAURIS**, reached by hourly bus, was home to Picasso for a while, where he was inspired by the local craft of ceramics. The main street, av George-Clemenceau, sells nothing but pottery; the **Madoura** pottery, where Picasso worked, is off rue 19-mars-1962, and has the sole rights on reproducing his designs. At the top of the main street, Picasso's bronze *Man with a Sheep* stands in the marketplace right opposite the **castle** courtyard, where an early medieval chapel (10am–noon/12.30pm & 2–5/6.30pm; closed Tues; F15) was painted by the artist as *La Guerre et la Paix* in 1952 – an initially slapdash-looking work, though its pacifism is unambiguous.

A few kilometres on lies **ANTIBES**, to which Picasso returned after the war and worked in a studio that has since been converted into a museum. Picasso left much of his output while here to what is now the **Musée Picasso** (summer Tues–Sun 10am–6pm; winter Tues–Sun 10am–noon & 2–6pm; sometimes closed Oct, Nov or Dec; F30), which displays numerous ceramics, still lifes of sea urchins, the wonderful *Ulysses et ses Sirènes*, and a whole room full of drawings. Antibes' **tourist office** (summer Mon–Sat 8.30am–7.30pm, Sun

10am–1pm; winter Mon–Sat 9am–noon/12.30pm & 2–6/6.30pm) is to the right of the **train station** at 11 place de Gaulle; the **youth hostel**, *Relais International de la Jeunesse*, by the sea on the corner of bd de la Garoupe and av l'Antiquité (☎04.93.61.34.40; ②; bus #2A from the bus station), is the best option for lodgings.

Cagnes and Vence

A little further on from Antibes, **CAGNES-SUR-MER** lies a little way inland but is walkable from the Cannes–Nice bus stop, and was home to Renoir for the last eleven years of his life. His house – *Les Collettes* – is a **museum** these days (10am–noon & 2pm–5/6pm; closed Tues; F20), and his studio, north-facing to catch the late afternoon light, is arranged as if he had just popped out.

On the other side of the town, to the north, is the ancient village of **HAUT-DE-CAGNES**, where the crenellated **château** (10am–noon & 2–5/6pm; closed Tues; F20) houses a number of museums covering local history, fishing, the cultivation of olives and the **Musée d'Art Moderne Méditerranéen**. This contains changing exhibitions of the painters who have worked on the coast in the last hundred years, and the Donation Suzy Solidor – wonderfully diverse portraits of the cabaret star from the 1920s to the 1960s by several great painters.

The next artistic treat, and one of the best in the region, is the **Fondation Maeght** (July–Sept daily 10am–7pm; Oct–June 10am–12.30pm & 2.30–6pm; F45) in **ST-PAUL-DE-VENCE**, reachable by taking the Nice–Vence bus from place de Gaulle in Cagnes-sur-Mer. It's a wonderful collection of the early works of Miró, Léger, Chagall and their contemporaries, as well as having an outdoor sculpture garden featuring Giacometti at his best. **VENCE**, a few kilometres north, is the site of the **Chapelle du Rosaire** (Tues & Thurs 10–11.30am & 2.30–5.30pm; closed Nov; F13), built between 1949 and 1951 under the direction of Matisse, who painted the black outline figures on plain matt tiles with a brush fixed to a 180cm bamboo pole specifically to remove his own signature from the lines. Colour comes from the light diffused through green, blue and yellow windows.

Vence is a lot more affordable than St-Paul. *La Closerie des Genets*, 4 impasse Maurel (☎04.93.58.33.25; ③), is a reasonably priced **hotel** and, in addition, there's a **campsite** about 3km west on the road to Tourettes-sur-Loup. The **tourist office** is near the main gate into the old town (July & Aug Mon–Sat 9.30am–12.30pm & 2–7pm, Sun 10am–noon; rest of year Mon–Sat 9am–12.30pm & 2–6pm). For a special **meal**, try *La Fariguoule,* 15 av Henri-Isnard or, on the same street but for half the price, *La Vieille Douve*.

Nice

NICE, the capital of the Riviera and fifth largest town in France, should be a loathsome place. A large portion of the population are either pensioners or fat-cat tycoons, and it can't even boast a sandy beach. And yet it is delightful, with the sun, sea, and affable Niçois compensating for a multitude of sins. The city also makes the best base for visiting the 30km of the Riviera coast to the border, and west as far as Cannes.

Arrival and accommodation

The main **train station** (Nice Ville) is a relatively short step from the centre, a couple of blocks left of the top of av Jean-Médecin. The helpful main **tourist office** is by the station on av Thiers (daily 7.30/8am–7/8pm) and offers an accommodation service; it also has maps and transport details. For **getting around the city**, you can buy a one-, five- or seven-day bus pass, or a *carnet* of ten tickets (reductions with ISIC) from Sunbus, 10 av Félix-Faure. *Carnets* can also be bought at kiosks and *tabacs*, and single tickets on the bus. The Sunbus office has free bus maps. Route #15, connecting the museums, the coast, Nice Ville station and place Masséna, is especially useful.

There are lots of affordable **hotels** around the train station, including *Les Orangers*, 10 bis av Durante (☎04.93.87.51.41; ③), popular with American students, and the light and spacious *d'Orsay*, 20 rue Alsace-Lorraine (☎04.93.88.45.02; ③). For something nearer the sea, you might try the *Hôtel du Danemark*, 3 av des Beaumettes (☎04.93.44.12.04; ③). The **youth hostel** is 4km out of town on route Forestière du Mont-Alban (☎04.93.89.23.64; ②) – take bus #14 from place Masséna. Slightly cheaper but further out, and with a 10.30pm curfew, is *Clairvallon Relais International de la Jeunesse* – north of Cimiez at 26 av Scudéri (☎04.93.81.27.63; ②); take bus #15. Another possibility close by on the south side of the urban highway is the *MJC Magnan*, 31 rue Louis-de-Coppet (☎04.93.86.28.75; ②; June to mid-Sept) – bus #12. The only **campsite** in Nice is the tiny *Camping Terry* on route de Grenoble, 6km north of the airport, and not on any bus route, but there are plenty of campsites in the area which can be reached by local train; the tourist office can furnish you with lists. In summer you'll find lots of people camping on the beach – the only stretch where it's tolerated on the whole of the Côte d'Azur.

The City

It doesn't take long to get a feel for the layout of Nice. The **old town** groups about the hill of Nice's former château, a previously rough but now fast-gentrifying pocket of narrow crammed streets centring on place Rossetti and the Baroque **Cathédrale St-Réparate**. Nearby is the entrance to the **parc du Château** (also reachable by lift from the eastern end of rue des Ponchettes), decked out in a mock-Grecian style harking back to the original Greek settlement of Nikea. The point of the climb, apart from the perfumed greenery, is the view stretching west and over the muddle of the old town's rooftops. The limits of the old town are marked by bd Jean-Jaurès, on which the **Musée d'Art Moderne et d'Art Contemporain** (Mon & Wed–Sun 11am–6pm, Fri until 10pm; F25) holds a collection of Pop Art and neo-Realist work, including pieces by Andy Warhol and Roy Lichtenstein. Beyond here, place Masséna, and the spine of the centre, av Jean-Médecin, represent the commercial heart of Nice, while, a short walk south, the **promenade des Anglais** was laid out by nineteenth-century English residents for their afternoon sea-breeze stroll.

Up above the city centre, **Cimiez**, a posh suburb reached by bus #15 from av Thiers, was the social centre of the town's elite some seventeen centuries ago, when the city was capital of the Roman province of Alpes-Maritimae. Excavations of the Roman baths are housed, along with accompanying archeological finds, in the **Musée d'Archéologie**, 160 av des Arènes (Tues–Sun 10am–noon/1pm & 2–5/6pm; F25). Overlooking the baths, the **Musée Matisse** (10am–5/6pm; closed Tues; F25) is home to a collection of work by the artist, who spent most of his life in Nice. The collection covers every period and includes models for the chapel in Vence, a nearly complete set of the bronze sculptures, and a complete set of the books that Matisse illustrated. Among the paintings are a 1905 portrait of Madame Matisse, *A Tempest in Nice*, and the 1947 *Still Life with Pomegranates*. At the foot of the hill, just off bd Cimiez on av du Docteur-Menard, there is more modern art in **Chagall's Biblical Message**, housed in a purpose-built museum opened by the artist in 1972 (10am–5/6pm; closed Tues; F30). The seventeen paintings, based on the Old Testament, are complemented by etchings, engravings, tapestries and mosaics, all perfectly set off by the light. Chagall himself contributed the stained-glass windows.

Eating, drinking and nightlife

The Old Town stays up the latest and is full of **restaurants**. *Café de Turin*, on place Garibaldi, is a good, basic place for mussels and clams, while *Chez René Socca*, 2 rue Miralhéti, serves, *socca*, a pancake made from chickpea flour and a speciality of Nice, *calamares*, and stuffed peppers at the counter. A locals' favourite is *Lou Pilha Leva*, a very inexpensive bar-restaurant on place du Central. Vegetarians could try *Passez á Table*, 30 rue Pertinax, which has meat-free options and organic produce. For **later carousing**, *Les 3 Diables*, on cours Saleya, is a smoky, posey dive with loud music; *Scarlett O'Hara*, 22 rue Droite, is an Irish place serving decent Guinness.

Monaco

Monstrosities are common on the Côte d'Azur, but nowhere, not even Cannes, can outdo **MONACO**. This tiny independent principality has lived off gambling and class for a century and is one of the greatest property speculation sites in the world. Finding out about the workings of the regime is not easy, but it is clear that Prince Rainier is the one autocratic monarch left in Europe. A copy of every French law is sent to Monaco, reworded, and put to the Prince. If he likes the law it is passed; if not, it's not. There is a parliament of limited function elected by Monagesque nationals – about sixteen percent of the population – and no opposition to the ruling family. What the citizens and residents like so much is that they pay no income tax.

The three-kilometre-long state consists of the old town of **Monaco-Ville** around the palace on a high promontory; the new suburb and marina of **Fontvieille** in its western shadow; **La Condamine** behind the harbour on the other side of the rock; **Larvotto**, the swimming resort with artificial beaches of imported sand to the east; and **Monte Carlo** in the middle. There's little in the way of conventional sights, only the toy-town palace and assorted museums in the old town, where every other shop sells Prince Rainier mugs and other junk. The only real must is the **Casino**, where the American Room is a riot of Rococo and the European Gaming Rooms have an atmosphere that's almost cathedral-like. You have to pay to get in (around F50) and you must look like a gambler, not a tourist; entrance is restricted to those over 21 and you may have to show your passport.

The **train station** is on av Prince-Pierre in La Condamine, a short walk from the *gare routière* on place d'Armes. Bus #4 takes you from the train station to the Casino-Tourism stop, with the **tourist office** at 2a bd des Moulins (Mon–Sat 9am–7pm, Sun 10am–noon). The one good free public service is the clean and efficient **lift system** for steep north–south journeys. If you must stay more than a day here, La Condamine is best for **hotels** – although they're expensive. You could try *Cosmopolite*, 4 rue de la Turbie (☎93.30.16.95; ④), or its neighbour *Hôtel de France* (☎93.30.24.64; ⑤). If you arrive early enough, and you're under 26 or a student under 31, you may be able to get a dorm bed at the *Centre de Jeunesse Princesse Stéphanie*, near the station at 24 av Prince-Pierre (☎93.50.83.20; ②). La Condamine and the Old Town are the places to look for **restaurants**, but good food and reasonable prices don't exactly match. You should be able to fill up on pizza at *Le Biarritz*, 3 rue de la Turbie. In Monte Carlo, try *Chérie's Café*, 9 av des Spélugues.

CORSICA

Despite two hundred years of French rule, **Corsica** has more in common culturally with Italy than with its governing country, as testified by a profusion of Italianate churches and a language that's closely related to the Tuscan dialect. A history of repeated invasion has strengthened the cultural identity of an island whose reputation for violence and xenophobia has overshadowed the more hospitable nature of its inhabitants.

Corsica, much of which is National Park, comprises an amazing diversity of landscapes: its magnificent rocky coastline is interspersed with outstanding beaches, while the inland mountains offer numerous opportunities for hiking. The extensive forests and sparkling rivers provide the islanders with a rich supply of game and fresh fish – regional specialities include wild boar, blackbird pâté, cured hams and sausages.

Two French *départements* divide Corsica, each with its own capital: Napoleon's birthplace, **Ajaccio**, is a sunny elegant town on the southwest coast, while **Bastia** faces Italy in the north. At the island's core, the old capital of **Corte** is one of many fortress villages which charac-

---

FERRIES TO CORSICA

To Ajaccio from Marseille (2–4 weekly; 10hr); Nice (1–6 weekly; 11hr); Toulon (May–Sept; 1–4 weekly; 10hr).

To Bastia from Livorno (2 weekly–4 daily; 4hr); Marseille (1–3 weekly; 10hr); Nice (1–12 weekly; 6hr); Savona (3 weekly–3 daily; 3hr); Toulon (June–Aug 1–3 weekly; 12hr).

To Calvi from Marseille (4 weekly; 8hr); Nice (1 daily; 5hr).

To Bonifacio from Sardinia (2 daily–4 daily; 1hr 30min).

terize the interior. The coastal resorts are equally superbly sited: **Calvi** draws in the tourists with its massive citadel and long sandy beach, and strung out at the southernmost point lies **Bonifacio**, perched on limestone cliffs that are buffeted by the clearest water in the Mediterranean. Ajaccio, Bastia, Corte and Calvi are connected by a slender **train** service; for Bonifacio you're reliant on **buses**.

Ajaccio

Set in a magnificent bay, **AJACCIO** combines all the ingredients of the archetypal Mediterranean resort with its palm trees, spacious squares, yachts and street cafés. There may not be a great deal to see here but Ajaccio is a pleasant place to spend some time. The town developed around a fifteenth-century Genoese citadel and the streets around remain appealingly ancient. Napoleon, who was born here in 1769, gave the town fame but did little else for the place except to make it capital of Corsica for the brief period of his empire. You can visit his family house, now a museum, and you'll find the town peppered with statues and streets named after the Bonaparte family.

Arrival and accommodation

Flying into Ajaccio you'll land at Campo dell'Oro **airport**, 6km southeast of town; buses depart hourly for the *gare routière*. **Ferries** come into the port at the town centre, but if you arrive by train from one of the other major towns you'll find yourself with about a ten-minute walk along the seafront. The **tourist office** (May–Oct Mon–Sat 8am–8.30pm, Sun 9am–1.30pm; Nov–April Mon–Fri 8am–6pm, Sat 9am–5pm) occupies the ground floor of the Hôtel de Ville opposite the port, directly opposite the port.

Cheap **accommodation** is pretty thin on the ground in Ajaccio, yet there are a few good addresses in the town centre. *Hotel Kalliste* at 51 cours Napoléon (☎04.95.51.34.45; ④) does a good deal whereby you can rent studios for one night, but the cheapest hotel is the tiny *Colomba* at 8 av de Paris (☎04.95.21.12.66; ③). Otherwise there's the pleasant *Marengo*, off bd Mme-Mère (☎04.95.21.43.66; ④), the *San Carlu*, close to the beach at 8 bd Danielle-Casanova (☎04.95.21.13.84; ⑤), or the *Bella Vista*, 20 bd Lantivy (☎04.95.21.07.97; ④).

The Town

Cours Napoléon is the main thoroughfare of Ajaccio, running parallel to the sea and culminating in place Général-de-Gaulle, which in turn leads onto **place Foch**, a shady, palm-lined square bordered by cafés and restaurants and open to the sea. The most rewarding visit in Ajaccio is to the **Musée Fesch** (mid-June to mid-Sept Mon & Wed–Sun 10am–5.30pm, Fri until midnight; mid-Sept to mid-June Tues–Sat 9.15am–12.15pm & 2.15–5.15pm; F25) the largest museum in Corsica, situated halfway down rue Cardinal-Fesch, an attractive winding shopping street that runs off place Foch. Apart from the **Chapelle Impériale** (F10 supplementary ticket), where the Bonaparte family vaults have been gathered, the building is home to an important collection of Italian paintings from the fifteenth and sixteenth centuries, the legacy of Napoléon's step-uncle Cardinal Joseph Fesch. Notable among the paintings is Botticelli's *Virgin and the Garland* and Veronese's startling *Leda and the Swan*.

Admirers of Napoleon will, no doubt, head straight for the **Maison Bonaparte** (Mon 2–4.45/5.45pm, Tues–Sat 9/10am–11.45am & 2–4.45/5.45pm, Sun 9/10am–noon; F22) located in place Letizia, off the west side of rue Napoléon in the heart of the old town. A disappointingly sparse museum, its exhibits include the chair Napoleon's mother lay on when in labour, and Napoleon's bed. For dedicated fans the **Salon Napoléonien** (Mon–Fri 9–11.45am & 2–4.45/5.45pm; F10) in the Hôtel de Ville houses the Bonaparte family portraits as well as other memorabilia such as a gold replica of Napoleon's death mask. Napoleon was baptized in Ajaccio's **Cathedral**, which dominates rue Forcioli-Conti, southwest of place Foch. Built in 1554, the church boasts a Delacroix *Virgin* which hangs in the chapel to the left of the altar. Napoleon's dying words are inscribed on a plaque adorning the pillar to the left of the entrance, expressing his wish to be buried in Ajaccio if they wouldn't have him in Paris.

For a fascinating insight into Corsican military history, the **Musée a Bandera** (May–Sept Mon–Sat 9am–noon & 3–7pm; Oct–April Mon–Fri 9am–noon & 2–6pm; 20F) is tucked away behind place Général-de-Gaulle in rue Général-Levie. Displays include an impressive collection of vendetta daggers and a room dedicated to bandits, displaying photographs and life-size models of the most notorious *bandits d'honneurs*.

Eating and drinking

Restaurants in Ajaccio vary from the simple bistro to pizzerias and expensive fish restaurants, most of which centre around the old town, east and west of place Foch. *A Cantina*, just above place Foch at 5 bd du Roi-Jérôme, does inexpensive Corsican snacks, while *20123*, 2 rue Roi-de-Rome, offers true Corsican country cooking. *Le Menestrel*, 5 rue Fesch, serves good food but its main attraction is the live local music which takes place most evenings. Young people hang out at *Snack Bar du Jetée* on the jetée de la Citadelle, overlooking the boats, or eat pizza at *Chez Paolo*, 8 rue Roi-du-Rome.

Bars and cafés take up much of the pavement space, with cocktail bars and *glaciers* lining the seafront behind the beach. *Safari* is a popular address, located by the beach at 18 bd Lantivy, and *Café du Flore*, opposite Palais Fesch, makes a change from the traditional bar and plays jazz.

Bastia

The port of **BASTIA** is a charismatic town, with its crumbling golden-grey buildings set against a backdrop of fire-darkened hills. Now a thriving commercial port, Bastia was capital of Corsica under the Genoese and has remained an authentic working town with few concessions to tourism. The place has much to recommend it: the dilapidated Vieux Port, a sprinkling of Baroque churches, the imposing citadel (or bastion) from which the town gets its name, and the vast place Saint-Nicolas, lined with trees and cafés open to the sea, where you can sit and absorb the Corsican way of life.

The most appealing part of Bastia is the **Vieux Port**, the site of the original fishing village around which the town grew, and nowadays a tranquil backwater. Dominating the harbour are the twin towers of **Église St-Jean-Baptiste**, the largest but not the most interesting church in Bastia, which shoulders the place du Marché, where a half-hearted market takes place each morning. The narrow streets around are known as **Terra Vecchia**, a flaking conglomeration of tenement blocks in attractive decay.

Close by, in rue Napoléon, are two Baroque churches whose dull facades belie their interiors. Halfway up the street stands the **Oratoire de l'Immaculée Conception**. Dating from 1611, this little church was a Genoese showplace used for state occasions, such as the inauguration of the Anglo-Corsican parliament in the 1760s. The Musée Ethnographique Corse is closed for renovation until 2001.

Practicalities

Bastia's **airport**, Poretta, is situated 16km south of town off the RN197. Shuttle **buses** into the town centre stop east of the train station, above place Saint-Nicolas (F50); other buses stop either at the top of boulevard Paoli, the main street, or outside the train station. **Ferries** use the Nouveau Port, just a five-minute walk from the centre. The **tourist office** in place St-Nicolas (June–Sept daily 8am–9pm; Oct–May Mon–Sat 8.30am–noon & 2–6pm) can give you bus timetables and lists of accommodation in the region; **bikes** can be rented from Cycles 20, by the Palais de Justice on rte du Fort La Croix.

Finding somewhere to **stay** in Bastia shouldn't be a problem even at the height of the season though the choice isn't great. About the cheapest place is the *Central*, 3 rue Miot (☎04.95.31.71.12; ④), or try the *Riviera* in the port at 1 rue du Nouveau Port (☎04.95.31.07.16; ⑤), a well-established place popular with travellers. *Hotel les Voyageurs* at 9 av du Maréchal-Sebastiani (☎04.95.34.90.80; ④) is handy for the Porto Vecchio bus. The best **campsite**, *Les Orangers* (☎04.95.33.24.09), is 4km north at Miomo, on the route to Cap Corse; take the Erbalunga bus.

The best **restaurants** are concentrated in and around the Vieux Port, with the emphasis on Italian food, though there are some authentic Corsican places; the best of these is *U Tianu* in rue Monsignor-Rigo, off place du Marché – they do an excellent selection of *charcuterie*. For good fish try *A Scaletta* and for Moroccan food there's *Le Zagora*; both are in the Vieux Port along with *U Cantarettu*, where you can eat excellent pizzas to live music. For a **drink** *Bar Corsica*, 2 rue Spinola, features traditional Corsican singing, or try *L'Impériale*, at the centre of place St-Nicolas, 6 bd Général-de-Gaulle.

Corte

Set amidst craggy mountains and gorges, the sleepy town of **CORTE** is known as the spiritual capital of Corsica, as this is where Pascal Paoli had his seat of government during the brief period of independence in the eighteenth century. Paoli founded a university here which was reopened in the early 1980s, but despite the weekly influx of students the town lacks much vibrancy – even its inhabitants call it a *trou perdu* (a lost hole).

The main street, **cours Paoli**, runs the whole length of the small town, culminating in place Paoli, a pleasant market square. A cobbled ramp leads from the square up to the Ville Haute, where in tiny **place Gaffori** you can still see the bullet marks that were made by Genoese soldiers during the War of Independence. The vigorously pointing statue is of General Gaffori, one of Paoli's right-hand men, who led the independent army in 1756. Continuing north you'll soon come to the gates of the extraordinary **Citadelle**, whose ramparts remain intact hiding the brand-new museum built inside it. The **Museu di a Corsica** (April–June Tues–Sun 10am–6pm; July–Sept daily 10am–8pm; Oct Tues–Sun 10am–5pm; Nov–March Tues–Sat 10am–5pm; F20) takes a look at the island's heritage through a display of traditional articles and activities, moving on to tackle the issue of contemporary Corsican identity. For the best view of the Citadelle and the town, you can climb up to the **Belvédère**, a platform opposite the tower, which affords panoramic vistas of the surrounding valley.

Corte's **train station** lies 1km out of town at the foot of the hill and near the university; **buses** to Ajaccio and Bastia stop at the north end of place Paoli. The **tourist office** (July & Aug daily 9am–1pm & 2–7pm; rest of the year Mon–Fri 9am–noon & 2–6pm) is situated within the Citadelle and has an annexe at the train station during July and August. The cheapest place to **stay** in Corte is at *Hôtel de la Poste*, 2 place Padoue (☎04.95.46.01.37; ③), a gloomy, functional building which has no restaurant. A preferable option is to venture out 1km out of town along the D623 to the *Auberge de la Restonica*, (☎04.95.46.20.13; ⑤); this sumptuous old-fashioned hunting-inn, set in the forest, overlooks a waterfall which provides its restaurant with delicious fresh trout. **Campsites** are also situated along this road: *U Sognu* (☎04.95.46.09.07) lies at the foot of the Restonica valley, about 500m from the town centre.

For **food** try *U Montagnone* on place Paoli for local specialities on menus from 59F, or *Le Gaffory* in place Gaffori-de-l'Église, for wild boar lasagne and F55 menus. *Café de la Place* in place Paoli is the best **café**.

Calvi

Seen from the water, the great *citadelle* of **CALVI** resembles a floating island, sharply defined against a hazy backdrop of snowcapped mountains. Corsica's third port, Calvi annually draws in thousands of tourists who come for the 6km of sandy beach, a semicircle of gold. Home to the Foreign Legion, Calvi today is a light-hearted holiday town. Hundreds of boats, many of them huge yachts belonging to European glitterati, find a mooring in the marina.

Calvi became a Genoese stronghold in 1268, when its inhabitants were granted special privileges for being loyal citizens; their motto *Civitas Calvis Semper Fidelis* is inscribed above the gate into the *citadelle* or **Haute Ville**, a labyrinth of tortuous cobbled lanes and stairways rising from place Christophe-Colomb, the square linking the two parts of town. Shops, restaurants and hotels are all found in the **Basse Ville**, which backs onto the marina, and the **beach** starts just beyond the boats.

Ste-Cathérine **airport** is 7km south of Calvi; there are **no buses** into town and a **taxi** costs around F70. **Trains** stop behind the marina and drive by is the stop for **buses** from Bastia and, on quai Landry, the **tourist office** (mid-June to Sept daily 9am–7pm; Oct to mid-June Mon–Fri 8.30am–noon & 2–6pm, Sat 9.30am–noon), which will help with accommodation for a small fee. **Ferries** come into port at the far end of the Quai Lantivy beneath the *citadelle*. **Bikes** can be rented from Location Ambrosini on place Christophe-Colomb.

Among **hotels** in Calvi, the *Hôtel du Centre*, 14 rue Alsace-Lorraine (☎04.95.65.02.01; ③), is about the cheapest and most central, but is closed in winter. Calvi boasts a rare **youth hostel** at 43 av de la République (April–Sept; ☎04.95.65.14.15; ②). *La Pinède*, 2km from Calvi along the N197 (☎04.95.65.17.80; summer only) is the closest **campsite**.

An abundance of **restaurants** cram the streets of the Basse Ville. *U San Carlo*, place St-Charles, serves excellent seafood at reasonable prices. *Le Santa Maria*, 5 rue Clemenceau, next to the church, may be touristy but there's a lively ambience and it turns out some unusual Corsican specialities such as *stifatu*, a tasty blend of stuffed meats. The famous piano bar and restaurant, *Chez Tao*, is worth a visit for its impressive views of the bay.

Bonifacio

The port of **BONIFACIO** enjoys a superbly isolated situation at Corsica's southernmost point, a narrow peninsula of dazzling white limestone creating an exceptional site for the town. For five hundred years Bonifacio was a virtually independent republic, and a sense of detachment from the rest of Corsica persists, with many Bonifaciens still speaking their own dialect. Be warned, though, that the town becomes unbearably overcrowded and expensive in midsummer, as Bonifacio has become a chic holiday spot as well as a sailing centre.

The first place to head for is the **Haute Ville**, connected to the marina by a steep flight of steps at the west end of the quay. Built within the massive fortifications of the *citadelle*, it's an alluring maze of dusty streets, its houses displaying pointed arches and closed arcades unique to Bonifacio – and from the edge of the ramparts there's a glorious view across the straits to Sardinia. In rue de Palais de Garde, straight in front of the drawbridge at the top of the steps, **Église Ste-Marie-Majeure**'s facade is hidden by the loggia where Genoese officers used to dispense justice in the thirteenth century. Whilst in the Haute Ville, another essential visit is to the **Cimetière Marin**, a captivating walled cemetery filled with elaborate mausoleums, strung out at the far end of the promontory.

Down in the marina, a worthwhile **boat excursion** (F75) to the **sea-caves**, wonderful grottoes where the rock glitters with rainbow colours and the turquoise sea is deeply translucent, also takes you round the base of the cliffs for a fantastic view of the town.

The closest **beach** to town is **plage de la Catena**, 1km west of the port. To get there follow the road to Ajaccio, go past the marina and then turn left down a track just before the *Araguina* campsite – a ten-minute walk then brings you to the cove. Some outstanding beaches lie to the north of Bonifacio: **plage de la Rondinara**, 10km north along the road to Porto Vecchio, is an almost circular cove of white dunes and clear sea, and the **Golfe de Santa Manza**, 5km back along the same road, is also sublime.

Practicalities

The nearest **airport** is Figari, 17km to the north, and as yet there's no public transport link to town, only cripplingly expensive **taxis** (around F230). **Ferries** from Sardinia dock at the far end of the quay; **buses** from Ajaccio, the only direct public transport to Bonifacio, stop in the car park by the marina, close to most hotels. The **tourist office** (July–Sept daily 9am–8pm; Oct–June Mon–Fri 8.30am–12.30pm & 1.30–5.15pm) is on Place de l'Europe. Hotels are all on the pricey side except *Étrangers*, 500m along the road to Ajaccio (☎04.95.73.01.09; ⑥). **Campers** have *L'Araguina*, 500m past the marina on the road to Ajaccio (☎04.95.73.02.96), or *Campo di Liccia*, opposite U Farniente, which is more likely to have space in summer. For **food** avoid the chintzy fish restaurants on quai Comparetti and head up to the Haute Ville where places are less pretentious and more reasonably priced. *Le Rustic*, 16 rue Fred-Scamaroni, offers good-value Corsican set menus at F75 and F85. *Pizza/Grill de la Poste*, at no. 6, is also very popular with the locals.

travel details

Trains

Paris to: Amiens (10 daily; 1hr 10min); Bordeaux (hourly; 3hr); Boulogne (7 daily; 3hr); Caen (hourly; 2hr 15min); Calais (7 daily; 3hr 10min); Clermont-Ferrand (8 daily; 4hr); Dieppe (5 daily; 2hr 20min); Dijon (hourly; 1hr 40min); Le Havre (12 daily; 2hr 20min); Lille (13 daily; 2hr 20min); Lyon (hourly; 2hr); Marseille (12 daily; 5hr); Montpellier (4 daily; 5hr); Nancy (11 daily; 2hr 30min); Nice (9 daily; 10hr); Nîmes (3 daily; 9hr); Poitiers (hourly; 1hr 45min); Reims (8 daily; 1hr 50min); Rennes (hourly; 2hr 30min); Rouen (hourly; 1hr 15min); Strasbourg (10 daily; 4hr); Toulouse (10 daily; 5hr 30min); Tours (8 daily; 2hr 30min).

Ajaccio to: Bastia (4 daily; 4hr); Calvi (2 daily; 3hr 30min); Corte (4 daily; 2hr).

Bastia to: Ajaccio (4 daily; 4hr); Calvi (2 daily; 3hr 30min); Corte (4 daily; 2hr).

Bergerac to: Périgueux (1 daily; 1hr 50min); Sarlat (3 daily; 1hr 30min).

Bordeaux to: Bayonne-Biarritz (11 daily; 2hr); Bergerac (6 daily; 1hr 20min); Marseille (5 daily; 6–7hr); Nice (4 daily; 9–10hr); Périgueux (11 daily; 1hr 20min); Toulouse (12 daily; 2hr).

Caen to: Rennes (2 daily; 2hr); Tours (3–6 daily; 3hr 10min).

Cahors to: Toulouse (4 daily; 1hr).

Calvi to: Ajaccio (2 daily; 3hr 30min); Bastia (2 daily; 3hr 30min); Corte (2 daily; 2hr 30 min).

Clermont-Ferrand to: Marseille (3 daily; 6hr); Nîmes (3 daily; 4hr 50min); Toulouse (4 daily; 6hr); Vichy (12 daily; 40min).

Corte to: Ajaccio (4 daily; 2hr); Bastia (4 daily; 2hr); Calvi (2 daily; 2hr 30 min).

Dijon to: Beaune (8 daily; 25min); Lyon (14 daily; 1hr 45min).

Le Puy to: Lyon (2 daily; 2hr 30min).

Lyon to: Avignon (6 daily; 3hr); Grenoble (8–10 daily; 1hr 45min); Marseille (6 daily; 4hr); Orange (6 daily; 2hr).

Nancy to: Strasbourg (2 daily; 1hr 20min).

Narbonne to: Carcassonne (frequent; 30min); Perpignan (hourly; 40min); Toulouse (12 daily; 1hr 30min).

Nice to: Marseille (20 daily; 2hr 30min); St-Raphaël (at least hourly; 1hr 30min).

Nîmes to: Arles (6 daily; 20min); Avignon (hourly; 30min); Clermont-Ferrand (3 daily; 5hr); Marseille (3–4 daily; 1hr); Montpellier (hourly; 30min); Narbonne (hourly; 1hr 30min)

Périgueux to: Les Eyzies (5 daily; 30min).

Poitiers to: Bordeaux (13 daily; 2hr); La Rochelle (8 daily; 1hr 30min).

Rennes to: Nantes (5 daily; 2hr); Quimper (7 daily; 2hr 30min); St-Malo (7 daily; 1hr 15min).

Rouen to: Amiens (3–6 daily; 1hr 30min); Caen (8 daily; 2hr); Fécamp (hourly; 1hr).

Sens to: Avallon (3–5 daily; 2hr); Dijon (7 daily; 2hr 10min).

Strasbourg to: Colmar (hourly; 30min); Mulhouse (hourly; 1hr).

Toulouse to: Albi (8 daily; 1hr); Bayonne-Biarritz (4 daily; 4hr); Bordeaux (12 daily; 2hr); Clermont-Ferrand (1 daily; 7hr); Lourdes (12 daily; 2hr 20min); Lyon (6 daily; 6hr); Marseille (10 daily; 4hr 30min); Pau (10 daily; 2hr 30min).

Tours to: Azay-le-Rideau (8 daily; 30min); Bourges (4 daily; 2hr); Chinon (8 daily; 1hr); Loches (6 daily; 1hr); Lyon (5 daily; 5hr).

Buses

Ajaccio to: Bastia (2 daily; 3hr); Bonifacio (2 daily; 3hr); Corte (2 daily; 2hr).

Bastia to: Ajaccio (2 daily; 3hr); Bonifacio (2 daily; 2hr 30min); Calvi (2 daily; 3hr); Corte (2 daily; 1hr 45min).

Bonifacio to: Ajaccio (2 daily; 3hr); Bastia (2 daily; 3hr).

Calvi to: Ajaccio (2 daily; 3hr); Bastia (2 daily; 3hr).

Corte to: Ajaccio (2 daily; 2hr); Bastia (2 daily; 2hr).

CHAPTER 11

GERMANY

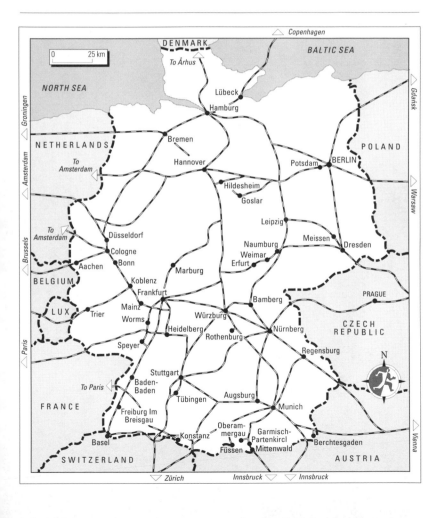

Introduction

The stereotype of **Germany** as the great monolith of western Europe has always been a long way from the truth, and is especially inaccurate now that postwar division of the country has been reversed. Regional characteristics are a strong feature of German life, and there are many hangovers from the days when the country was a patchwork of independent states. To travel from the ancient ports of the north, across the open fields of the German plain, down through the Ruhr conurbation and on to the forests, mountains and cosmopolitan cities of the south is to experience a variety as great as any continental country can offer.

Several of Germany's cities have the air of national capitals. **Cologne**, though enmeshed in one of Europe's most intensively industrialized regions, is one of the most characterful cities in the country, rich in historic monuments. Bavaria's capital, **Munich**, is another star attraction, boasting the best the country has to offer, whether in museums and galleries, beer, fashion or sport. **Berlin**, the nucleus of the turmoil of reunification, has an atmosphere at times electrifying, at times disturbing, while **Nürnberg** retains more than a trace of its bygone glory. **Hamburg**, burned to the ground by a firestorm in 1943, is now a pleasant city whose nightlife is comparable to that of Berlin. **Frankfurt**, the economic dynamo of postwar reconstruction, looks on itself as the "real" capital of the country, but **Stuttgart** and **Düsseldorf** contest the title of champion of German success, with their corporate skyscrapers and consumerist buzz. In the east, as well as Berlin, there's the Baroque splendour of **Dresden**.

Engaging as they are, these cities suffered considerable damage in World War II and have been subjected to some heavy-handed redevelopment, so in many respects it's the smaller towns of Germany that offer the richer experience. There's nowhere as well-loved as the university city of **Heidelberg**, guiding light of the Romantic movement, while **Trier, Bamberg, Regensburg, Rothenburg** and **Marburg** in the west and **Potsdam** and **Meissen** in the east are among the most attractive places in Europe.

Among the scenic highlights are the **Bavarian Alps** (on Munich's doorstep), the **Bodensee** (Lake Constance), the **Black Forest** and the valley of the **Rhine**, whose majestic sweep has spawned a rich fund of legends and folklore.

Information and maps

You'll find a **tourist office** (*Fremdenverkehrsamt*) in virtually every town in Germany. These are almost universally friendly and very efficient, providing large amounts of often useful literature and maps. The best general **maps** are those by RV or Kümmerly and Frey, whose 1:500,000 map is the most detailed single sheet of the country available. Specialist maps marking **cycling routes** or **alpine hikes** can be bought in the relevant regions.

Money and banks

German currency is the **Deutschmark**, which comes in notes of DM10, 20, 50, 100, 200, 500 and 1000; coins of DM0.01 (one Pfennig), 0.02, 0.05, 0.10, 0.50, 1, 2 and 5. **Exchange facilities** can be found in most banks and in post offices and commercial exchange shops called *Wechselstuben*. The Deutsches Reisebank has branches in the train stations of most main cities, which are generally open seven days a week, often until 10pm or 11pm. Basic **banking hours** are Mon–Fri 9am–noon & 1.30–3.30pm, with late opening on Thurs until 6pm, though these are often extended. Unusually, for such a consumer-orientated society, **credit cards** are used relatively infrequently, though they are becoming increasingly popular.

Communications

Post offices are normally open Mon–Fri 8am–6pm & Sat 8am–noon. **Poste restante** services are available at the main post offices in any given town: collect mail from the counter marked *Postlagernde Sendungen*. Mail is usually only held for a couple of weeks.

In the west you can **telephone abroad** from all pay phones except those marked "National"; coins of DM0.10, 1 and 5 are accepted, and only wholly unused ones are returned; telephone cards (DM12 or DM50) are widely used. Main post offices always have an international direct phone service facility. The **operator number** is ☎03.

Getting around

While it may not be cheap, getting around Germany is quick and easy. Barely an inch of the country is untouched by a reliable public transport system, and it's a simple matter to jump from train to bus on the integrated network.

■ Trains

By far the best form of public transport in **Germany** is the **train**, operated by the national company Deutsche Bahn (DB). **Fares** are DM26 per 100km second class, exclusive of supplements, and a return costs the same as two one-way tickets. The most luxurious service is the 250kph **InterCityExpress (ICE)**, where a supplement is charged according to the distance travelled up to a maximum cost of DM50. Otherwise, the fastest and most comfortable trains are the **InterCity (IC)** and **EuroCity (EC)**, with a supplement of DM8, or DM7 if bought before boarding. **InterRegio (IR)** trains offer a swift service along less heavily used routes (DM4 supplement for journeys of under 50km). Around major cities, the **S-Bahn** is a commuter network on which InterRail and Eurail cards are valid, as they are on all other services.

If you're making a lot of rail journeys and don't have an InterRail or Eurail pass, it's sensible to buy one of the discount passes exclusively for foreigners. The broadest-ranging is the **EuroDomino**, which entitles the holder to unlimited travel on all trains in Germany, and many buses and boats; it costs £116 for 3 days within any month, rising by an average £11 per day to £170 for 8 days. For under-26s, the **Youth Pass** costs £88 for 3 days, rising to £124 for 8 days.

Of the tickets available in Germany itself, by far the most useful is the *SchönesWochenende* ticket, which costs DM35 and allows up to five people travelling together to make unlimited journeys on local trains throughout the country on any given weekend.

The colossal national **timetable** (*Kursbuch*) can be bought from stations for DM25, though it's too bulky to be easily portable.

■ Buses

If you must forsake the trains for **buses**, you'll find no decline in efficiency. Many are run by regional co-operatives in association with DB, although there are a few privately operated routes on which rail passes cannot be used. You're most likely to need buses in remote rural areas, or along designated "scenic routes" where scheduled buses take the form of luxury coaches that pause at major points of interest.

■ Driving and hitching

German traffic moves fast. There are no legally enforced **speed limits** on the Autobahnen, but there is a recommended limit of 100–130kph. The speed limit on country roads is 80–100kph, in towns it's generally 50kph. A national or international driving licence is valid for a year's driving. **Car rental** rates begin at around DM350 per week. The Allgemeiner Deutscher Automobil Club (ADAC) runs a 24-hour **breakdown service**; they can be called from booths alongside the motorways or by dialling ☎19 211, with the prefix 01308 if you're outside the city limits.

Hitching is common practice all over Germany and with the excellent Autobahn network it's usually quite easy to cover long distances in a short time – though hitching on them or their access roads is illegal. The Germans have also developed an institutionalized form called Mitfahrzentralen, agencies that put drivers and hitchers in touch with each other for a nominal fee.

■ Cycling

Cyclists are well catered for in Germany: many smaller roads have marked cycle paths, and bike-only lanes are a common sight in cities and towns. Between April and October, the best place to **rent a bike** is from a railway station participating in the **Fahrrad am Bahnhof** scheme (DM10 per day). You can return it to any other participating station and holders of the various rail passes get a fifty percent discount.

Accommodation

Be it high-rise city hotels or half-timbered guesthouses in the country, **accommodation** of all types is easy to find in Germany, and it can often be good value.

■ Hotels

An immensely complicated grading system applies to western German **hotels**, but they're all more or less the same: clean, comfortable and functional. Just take care not to turn up in a large town or city during a trade fair, or *Messe* – hotels often double their rates and still get booked solid. In country areas, prices start at about DM35 for a single, DM50 for a double – at least DM10–15 extra for something similar in a

---

city. Hotels in eastern Germany are overwhelmingly geared to the business market, but the situation is much better for the budget traveller in holiday areas.

■ Pensions, guesthouses and private rooms

To escape the formality of a hotel, look for one of the plentiful **pensions**, which may be rooms above a bar or restaurant or simply space in a private house. In urban areas these cost roughly the same as hotels – they're usually a little cheaper in the countryside. An increasingly prevalent budget option is **bed & breakfast** accommodation in a private house (look for signs saying *Fremdenzimmer* or *Zimmer frei*). Prices vary but start at around DM25–30 for a single, DM45–50 for a double. Particularly plentiful along the main touring routes are **country inns** or **guesthouses** (*Gasthöfe* or *Gasthäuser*), charging upwards of DM50 per night for a double (more in popular areas).

The best budget option in the east is a room in a **private house**, of which thousands have now become available. Prices vary widely and may cost as much as DM50 per person in the cities. Nearly all **tourist offices** will book you a room for a fee and there are also a number of private agencies that may give a better deal. Private rooms in the west are not as common, but there are some in rural areas that provide reasonable accommodation.

■ Youth hostels

In Germany, you're never far away from a **youth hostel** (*Jugendherberge*), but at any time of the year (especially summer weekends) they're liable to be block-booked by school groups, so book as far in advance as possible. Most staff are courteous and helpful, but an unfortunate minority insist on rigid regimentation. Hostels divide into **categories** according to facilities and size of rooms, ranging from Grade I (basic affairs charging DM16–20) up to Grade VI, also known as youth guesthouses (DM27–45). HI members over 27 pay DM2.50–4 more per night; non-members, if admitted at all, will be charged an extra DM4 per night. Over-27s can't use the hostels in Bavaria at all, unless accompanying children.

■ Campsites

Big, well-managed **campsites** are a feature all over Germany. Even the most basic have toilets, washing facilities and a shop, while the grandest are virtually open-air hotels with swimming pools and supermarkets. Prices are based on facilities and location, comprising a fee per person (DM3–10) and per tent (DM3–6), plus extra fees for vehicles. Many sites are full from June to September, so arrive early in the afternoon. Most close down in the winter, but those in popular skiing areas remain open all year.

Food and drink

German food is both good value and high quality, but it helps if you share the national penchant for solid, fatty fare accompanied by compensating fresh vegetables.

■ Food

The vast majority of German hotels and guesthouses include **breakfast** in the price of the room. Typically, you'll be offered a small platter of cold meats and cheeses, with a selection of breads, marmalades, jams and honey, and sometimes muesli. If breakfast isn't included, you can usually do quite well by going to a local bakery – most have an area set aside for breakfast.

Elegant **cafés** are a popular institution in Germany, serving a choice of espresso, cappuccino and mocha to the accompaniment of cream cakes, pastries or handmade chocolates. More substantial food is available from **butcher's shops**; you can generally choose from a variety of freshly roasted meats to make up a hot sandwich. The easiest option for a quick snack is to head for the ubiquitous **Imbiss** stands and shops, serving a range of sausages, plus meatballs, hamburgers and chips; the better ones have soups, schnitzels, chops, spit-roasted chickens and salads as well.

All **restaurants** display their menus and prices by the door. Hot meals are usually served throughout the day. Most of the *Gaststätte, Gasthaus, Gasthof, Brauhaus* or *Wirtschaft* establishments belong to a brewery and function as a meeting point, drinking haven and cheap restaurant. Their cuisine resembles hearty German home cooking, and portions are usually generous. Standards in west German restaurants are amazingly high, but this is not the case everywhere in the east. Main courses are overwhelmingly based on pork, usually of very high quality, served with a variety of sauces. Sausages feature regularly, and can be surprisingly tasty, with distinct regional varieties. **Vegetarians** will find east Germany extremely difficult – menus are almost exclusively for carnivores, and even an innocent-sounding item like tomato soup will have meat floating around in it.

Germany's multicultural society is mirrored in its wide variety of **ethnic** eateries. Italian restaurants are generally the best, but there are also plenty offering Balkan and Greco-Turkish cuisine. All are worth heading for if you're on a tight budget. You'll also find restaurants offering spreads from Russia and other erstwhile Communist countries such as Hungary and the Czech and Slovak Republics.

■ Drink

For serious **beer** drinkers, Germany is paradise. The country has around forty percent of the world's breweries, with some 800 (about half the total) in Bavaria alone. It was in this province in 1516 that the *Reinheitsgebot* (Purity Law) was formulated, laying down stringent standards including a ban on chemical substitutes. A beer tour of Germany should really begin in **Munich**. The city's beer gardens and beer halls are the most famous drinking dens in the country, offering a wide variety of premier products, from dark lagers through tart *Weizens* to powerful *Bocks*. **Cologne** holds the world record for the number of city breweries, all of which produce the jealously guarded *Kölsch*. **Düsseldorf** has its own distinctive brew, the dark *Alt*, but wherever you go you can be fairly sure of getting a locally brewed beer.

Most people's knowledge of German **wine** starts and ends with *Liebfraumilch*, a medium-sweet easy-drinking wine. Sadly, its success has obscured the quality of other German wines, especially those made from the *Riesling* grape, which many consider one of the world's great white grape varieties. The vast majority of German wine is white, since the northern climate doesn't ripen red grapes reliably. If, after a week or so, you're pining for a glass of red, try a *Spätburgunder*.

Apart from beer and wine, there's nothing very distinctive about German drink, save for *Apfelwein*, a variant of cider. The most popular **spirits** are the fiery *Korn* and after-dinner liqueurs, which are mostly fruit-based.

Opening hours and holidays

By law, **shops** in Germany close at 8pm on weekdays, at 4pm on Saturdays, and all day Sunday (except for bakers, which may open for a couple of hours between 11am and 3pm). Exceptions are pharmacies and shops in and around train stations, which stay open late and at weekends. **Museums** and **historic monuments** are, with few exceptions, closed on Mondays. Most museums offer half-price entry for students with valid ID.

Public holidays are: Jan 1; Jan 6 (regional); Good Friday; Easter Monday; May 1; Ascension Day; Whit Monday; Corpus Christi (regional); Aug 15 (regional); Oct 3; Nov 1 (regional); Dec 25 & 26.

Emergencies

The German **police** (*Polizei*) are not renowned for their friendliness, but they usually treat foreigners with courtesy. Reporting thefts at local police stations is straightforward, but inevitably there'll be a great deal of bureaucracy to wade through. The level of theft in the former GDR has increased dramatically with unemployment, but, provided you take the normal precautions, there's no real risk. All drugs are illegal in Germany, and anyone caught with them will face either prison or deportation: consulates will not be sympathetic towards those held on drug charges.

German **doctors** are likely to be able to speak English, but to be certain, ask your consulate for a list of English-speaking doctors in the major cities. **Pharmacies** (*Apotheken*) can deal with many minor complaints and again will often speak English. In the west you'll find international *Apotheken* in most large towns, who will be able to fill a prescription in any European language. All pharmacies display a rota of 24-hour *Apotheken*.

EMERGENCY NUMBERS

Police ☎110; Ambulance & Fire ☎112.

NORTHERN GERMANY

The port of **Hamburg**, Germany's second city, is infamous for the sleaze of the Reeperbahn, but it has plenty more to offer, not least a sparkling nightlife and a city centre composed of enjoyably contrasting neighbourhoods. In this generally unprepossessing northernmost region of Germany, another maritime city, **Lübeck**, exerts the strongest pull, with the same sort of visual appeal as the finest mercantile towns of the Low Countries. To the north, Schleswig-Holstein's countryside mix of dyke-protected marsh, peat bog and farmland holds few rewarding sights, but to the south lies the more diverse region of Lower Saxony. **Hannover**, its capital, demands a visit for its museums and magnificent gardens. The province's smaller towns present a fascinating contrast – **Hildesheim**, with its grandiloquent Romanesque architecture is the most outstanding from an artistic point of view, while **Goslar** is a mining town quite unlike any other in the world. Near the centre of Lower Saxony sits the port of **Bremen**, the largest city of this region and, like Hamburg, a *Land* in its own right, a continuation of its age-long tradition as a free state.

Hamburg

A stylish media centre and the second largest port in Europe, **HAMBURG** has none of the sentimental-folklore tradition of the Rhineland and the south – rather it has a certain coolness, solidity and sense of openness. Hamburg's skyline is dominated by the pale green of its copper spires and domes, but a few houses and the churches are just about all that's left from before the last century. The Great Fire of 1842 was a main cause of this loss, followed by demolition to make way for the warehouse area, and bombing during World War II. Much of the subsequent rebuilding might not be especially beautiful, but at least it has preserved the human scale of the city. Two-thirds of Hamburg is occupied by parks, lakes or tree-lined canals, giving a refreshing rural feel to one of the country's major industrial centres.

Arrival and accommodation

Ferries from Harwich and Newcastle dock at Fischerhafen on Grosse Elbstrasse from where buses run to Altona Station, west of town. Ferries from other destinations dock at St Pauli Landungsbrücken. Buses run from the **airport** to the **train station** every twenty minutes, but it's a little cheaper to take the HVV airport bus to the U- and S-Bahn stop at Ohlsdorf, and then catch a train into town. The handiest **tourist office** is in the station (daily 7am–11pm; ☎040/300 51201), which has a full room-finding service; and there's another tourist office between bridges 4 and 5 (daily April–Sept 10am–7pm; Oct–March 10am–5.30pm). Rather than buy normal tickets or day passes for the integrated **public transport** network, it's best to invest in the Hamburg-Card which also gives free or reduced admission to most of the city's museums. This costs DM12.80 for a day (and can be used from 6pm the day before), or DM26.50 for three days; a group card for five people costs DM24.50, or DM43 for three days.

Near the St Pauli Landungsbrücken there's the *Auf dem Stintfang* **youth hostel**, Alfred-Wegener-Weg 5 (☎040/313488; ③). Another hostel, the *Jugendgästehaus Horner Rennbahn*, Rennbahnstr. 100 (☎040/6511671; ③), is out in the suburb of Horn; take the U-Bahn to Horner Rennbahn. **Hotels** are not cheap in Hamburg. The pick of the lower-cost places is *Steen's Hotel*, Holzdamm 43 (☎040/244642; ⑥), a delightful small hotel near the train station. *Annenhof*, Lange Reihe 23, (☎040/243426; ④), is a small, friendly place; *Sarah Petersen*, just down the road at no. 50 (☎040/249826; ④), is a good alternative. The nearest **campsite** is at Kieler Str. 374 (June–Sept); take the S-Bahn to Eidelstedt.

The City

Hamburg has no obvious centre, and it's probably best to begin an exploration in the oldest and liveliest area, the **harbour**. If you're arriving in Hamburg by ship, your landfall will be not far from the clock tower and green dome of the **St Pauli Landungsbrücken**. To the

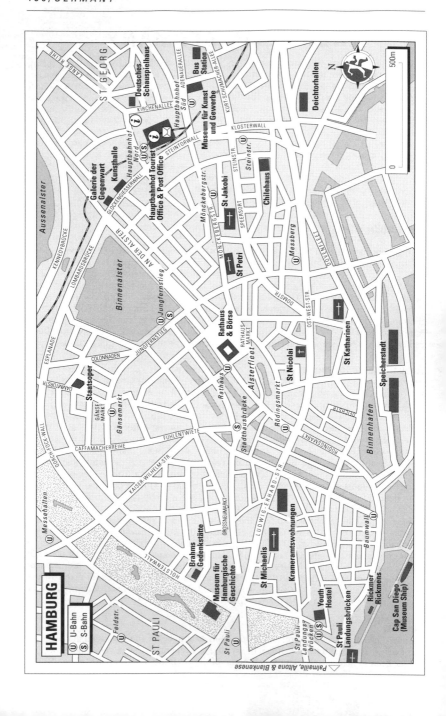

HAMBURG

Ⓤ U-Bahn
Ⓢ S-Bahn

ST GEORG
LANGE REIHE
KENNEDYBRÜCKE
Aussenalster
LOMBARDSBRÜCKE
Binnenalster
AN DER ALSTER
ESPLANADE
Galerie der Gegenwart
Kunsthalle
GLOCKENGIESSERWALL
Hauptbahnhof Nord
Ⓤ Ⓢ
Hauptbahnhof Süd
KIRCHENALLEE
Deutsches Schauspielhaus
ADENAUERALLEE
Bus Station
Hauptbahnhof Tourist Office & Post Office
STEINTORWALL
Museum für Kunst und Gewerbe
KURT-SCHUMACHER-ALLEE
KLOSTERWALL
Deichtorhallen
N
500m
0
Möenckebergstr.
St Jakobi
STEINSTR.
Steinstr.
Chilehaus
MÖNCKEBERGSTR
SPEERSORT
St Petri
Ⓤ
Messberg
DOVENFLEET
Jungfernstieg
Ⓤ Ⓢ
COLONNADEN
JUNGFERNSTIEG
Staatsoper
DAMMTORSTR
GÄNSE MARKT
Gänsemarkt
CAFFAMACHERREIHE
FUHLENTWIETE
KAISER-WILHELM-STR
Rathaus & Börse
RATHAUS-MARKT
Rathaus
Ⓤ
Alsterfleet
Stadthausbrücke
Ⓢ
DOMSTR.
OST-WEST-STR
St Nicolai
Rödingsmarkt
Ⓤ
St Katharinen
FISCHER
Speicherstadt
Binnenhafen
GORCH-DOCK-WALL
Messehallen
Ⓤ
GROSSNEUMARKT
HOLSTENWALL
Brahms Gedenkstätte
Museum für Hamburgische Geschichte
St Michaelis
LUDWIG-ERHARD-STR
Krameramtswohnungen
RÖDINGSMARKT
Baumwall
Feldstr.
Ⓤ
ST PAULI
St Pauli Landungsbrücken
Ⓤ
St Pauli Landungsbrücken
Ⓤ Ⓢ
Youth Hostel
St Pauli Landungsbrücken
Landungs- brücken
Rickmer Rickmers
Cap San Diego (Museum Ship)

▽ Palmaille, Altona & Blankenese

east, away from the ships and mighty cranes, is the late-nineteenth-century **Speicherstadt**, whose tall, ornate warehouses belong to a bygone era, but are still very much in use. You'll see bundles of Oriental carpets being hoisted, and smell spices and coffee wafting on the breeze. The Speicherstadt is within the **Freihafen** (customs-free zone), into which you can walk unrestricted. It's a magical place to stroll around and crisscross the bridges – Hamburg has more than Venice or Amsterdam.

Just to the north of the St Pauli Landungsbrücken is the nightlife centre of **St Pauli**, where music halls, bars and cafés sprang up in tandem with the growth of emigration to the USA. Nowadays this quarter is ruled by the sex industry, with its nerve centre on the notorious **Reeperbahn** – an ugly and unassuming street by day, ugly but sizzling with neon at night.

The main road running along the waterfront on St Pauli's edge is the **Hafenstrasse**, which runs west to the suburb of **Altona**, formerly a separate city ruled by the Holstein dukes. Its reputation for racial tolerance is one of the reasons it grew, and this part of the harbour still has a large Portuguese population – and good, very cheap Portuguese restaurants. Directly on Altona's waterfront one of Hamburg's main weekly events takes place: the **Fischmarkt**. Squeeze yourself out of bed early on a Sunday morning, or make Saturday night last, and you will find yourself in an amazing hubbub. If you want to buy bananas by the crate or a 2-metre-tall potted palm, this is the place to do it, for the market by no means sells only fish. The bars and restaurants are in full swing by 6am; by 10am trading has ceased; by 11am it's all over.

To all intents and purposes, Hamburg's core is the commercial and shopping district around the **Binnenalster** lake and the neo-Renaissance **Rathaus**, seat of Hamburg's government. When sessions aren't taking place you can go on a guided tour of the interior (Mon–Thurs 10am–3pm, Fri–Sun 10am–1pm; tours in English and German; DM2); it's a magnificently pompous demonstration of the city's power and wealth in the last century. The Rathaus has one of the six towers, each well over 100m tall, whose spires form a key feature of the skyline. All the other five belong to churches, two of which are a short walk to the east along Rathausstrasse: **St Petri**, the oldest building in the centre, and the far more impressive **St Jakobi**, in the late Gothic hall style typical of the Baltic regions.

Southeast of here, at the junction of Burchardstrasse and Pumpen, is Hamburg's most original building, the **Chilehaus**, designed by the Expressionist architect Fritz Höger. Rising like the prow of a huge ocean liner, the end of the Chilehaus is flanked by two small pavilions that symbolize the sea breaking against the ship. Across the street is the huge Sprinkenhof, begun by Höger immediately after the Chilehaus.

From here continue along Dovenfleet to the Gothic church of **St Katharinen**, whose Baroque tower rises high above the waterfront. To the west you'll find **Deichstrasse**, one of the few surviving streets of old Hamburg and to the north is the tallest of the six towers, rising above St Nicolai. West of here, along Ost-West-Strasse and Ludwig-Erhard Strasse, is **St Michaelis**, where the last and most imposing of the towers gives a grandstand view (May–Oct Mon–Sat 9am–6pm, Sun 11am–6pm; Nov–April Mon–Sat 10am–5pm, Sun 11am–5pm; DM4.50). Just up the Poststrasse, the **old post office** marks the heart of Hamburg's shopping area, where a number of classy arcades have been opened in the last few years. Architecturally they're stunning, and their exclusive shops put Bond Street in the shade: look out for Galleria and Hanseviertel.

Just north of the train station is the **Kunsthalle**, Hamburg's one unmissable art collection (Tues–Sun 10am–6pm, Thurs until 9pm; DM12). Upstairs, a room is devoted to three pieces by Master Bertram, the first German painter identifiable by name, and the layout continues in a broadly chronological order. After a Renaissance display in which the major work is Cranach's *The Three Electors of Saxony*, there's a Dutch and Flemish section where everything is overshadowed by two Rembrandts. The nineteenth-century German section is one of the museum's strengths: among the dozen works by Caspar David Friedrich are two of his most haunting creations, *Wanderer Above the Mists* and *Eismeer*. Among the Expressionists, look out for two masterpieces by Munch: *Girls at the Seaside* and *Girls on the Bridge*. Pick of the twentieth-century paintings is Otto Dix's *War* triptych, a powerful antiwar statement. Next door to the Kunstalle is the newly opened **Galerie der Gegenwart** (Gallery of the Present), where contemporary art is represented; Kunsthalle tickets are valid here.

On the other side of the train station, the **Museum für Kunst und Gewerbe** (Tues, Wed & Fri–Sun 10am–6pm, Thurs 10am–9pm; DM10) has excellent collections of art from ancient Egypt, Greece and Rome through to this century. The Jugendstil collection is extensive, and there are impressive sections dedicated to Chinese and Japanese art.

Eating, drinking and nightlife

Best places to **eat** are out of the city centre, in the Univiertel or the Schanzenviertel around Schulterblatt and Schanzenstrasse. For snacks, the stalls in front of the Rathaus are pricey but delicious, while most **café/bars** have food as well as drinks and sometimes music. Perhaps the best place for *Kaffee und Kuchen* is *Café Oertel*, Esplanade 29. *Eisenstein*, at Friedensallee 9, is a trendy café/bar popular with media types and serving very good food. Also worth trying is *Erika's Eck*, Sternstr. 98, open until 3am when it serves the largest and cheapest breakfast in the city. *Ahrberg*, Strandweg 33, down by the river in Blankenese, is one of the city's best **restaurants** for German dishes and fish, but main courses cost upwards of DM25. Cheaper options include *Atnali*, Rutschbahn 11, a Turkish restaurant with a large menu and friendly atmosphere; *Sagres*, Vorsetzen 42, a homely Portuguese place, popular with dock workers: and *Tre Fontane*, Mundsburger Damm 45, a well-priced and intimate Italian.

Hamburg's **nightlife** is among the best the country has to offer – for up-to-the-minute listings, get hold of a copy of *Szene* magazine. *Grosse Freiheit*, Grosse Freiheit 36, St Pauli, is the city's main venue for **live music**, with big-name bands mostly playing at weekends. *Logo*, Grindelallee 5, hosts mainly English and American underground bands. Hamburg's latest-opening **disco** is the *Top Ten Club*, Reeperbahn 136 (daily 10pm–9am). Rivals include the hard-rock *Grünspan* disco, Grosse Freiheit 58, and the massive *Kaiserkeller*, in the *Grosse Freiheit* basement.

Listings

American Express Ballindamm 39 (☎040/3039 3811).

Bike rental From the tourist office or Fahrrad Richter, Barmbeker Str. 16 (☎040/275095 or 273100; DM15 per day, DM75 per week).

Brewery tours The famous Holstenbrauerei, Holstenstr. 224, has regular free tours (Mon–Wed 9.30am–1pm & Thurs 9.30am; 2hr; bookings ☎040/3810 1782) which must be booked about three months in advance and are only for groups of three or more.

Consulates Britain, Harvestehuder Weg 8a (☎040/4480320); Ireland, Feldbrunnenstr. 43 (☎040/4418); USA, Alsterufer 28 (☎040/411 710).

Gay Hamburg The best way to find out what's on in the lively gay scene is through the magazine *Du und Ich* and the free sheet *Gay Express*.

Hitching Mitfahrzentrale at Ernst-Merck-Str. 8 (☎040/19440) and Gotenstr.19 (☎040/19444).

Post office At the Kirchenallee exit from the train station.

Women's Hamburg There's a café in the women's bookshop Frauenbuchladen, Bismarckstr. 98, plus a pub for women, *Frauenkneipe*, Stresemannstr. 60.

Lübeck

LÜBECK is just over thirty minutes from Hamburg by train – but as many north and southbound trains depart from here, it's not necessary to return to Hamburg to continue your tour. What's more, Scandinavia-bound ships leave from nearby Travemünde.

Most things of interest to see are in the **Altstadt**, an egg-shaped island surrounded by the water defences of the Trave and the city moat. Left out of the **train station** it's only five minutes' walk to the old town, passing the twin-towered **Holstentor**, the city's emblem. Built in 1477, it leans horrifyingly these days, but that shouldn't put you off calling in at its small **Historical Museum** (Mon–Sat 10am–4/5pm; DM5) – a useful introduction to the city and Hanseatic history. On the waterfront to the right of the Holstentor is a row of lovely gabled buildings – the **Salzspeicher** (salt warehouses).

Straight ahead over the bridge and up Holstenstrasse, the first church on the right is the Gothic **Petrikirche**, one of many buildings to suffer during the Allied bombing of March

1942. A lift goes 50 metres to the top of the spire (summer daily 9am–5/6pm; DM3.50) and a prime spot for an overview of the town's layout. Back across Holstenstrasse is the **Markt** and soaring above it the imposing **Rathaus**, or Town Hall, (guided tours Mon–Fri at 11am, noon & 3pm; DM4), displaying Lübeck's characteristic alternating rows of red unglazed and black glazed bricks. Opposite is the **Niederegger Haus**, renowned for its vast display of marzipan, which the town began producing in the Middle Ages; its old-style first-floor café is surprisingly affordable. Behind the north wing of the town hall is the **Marienkirche**, the earliest brick-built Gothic church in Germany. It was severely damaged in 1942, but the restored interior now makes a light and lofty backdrop for the church's treasures: a magnificent 1518 carved altar, a life-size figure of John the Evangelist dating from 1505, a beautiful Gothic gilded tabernacle and some fourteenth-century murals.

The best feature of the **Katharinenkirche** on the corner of Königstrasse and Glockengiesserstrasse is its exterior. The first three sculptures on the left of the west facade are by Ernst Barlach, who was commissioned to make a series of nine in the early 1930s, but had completed only these when his work was banned by the Nazis. Just north of Glockengiesserstrasse, sharing an entrance in Breite Strasse, are the **Behnhaus** and the **Drägerhaus**, two patricians' houses now converted into a museum (Tues–Sun 10am–4/5pm; DM5, free first Fri of the month). The former displays a good collection of paintings, including works by Kirchner and Munch, while in Drägerhaus it's the interiors that impress, along with nineteenth-century furniture, paintings and porcelain.

The nearby **Jakobikirche**, a sailors' church built in the thirteenth and fourteenth centuries, has Gothic wall paintings on its square pillars. On the other side of the Breite Strasse is a Renaissance house that used to belong to the sailors' guild, the **Haus der Schiffergesellschaft**. A tavern since 1535, it is decked out inside with all sorts of seagoing paraphernalia, and features on the programme of every tour group. East of here is the thirteenth-century **Heiligen-Geist-Hospital** (Tues–Sun 10am–4/5pm; free), one of the best-preserved hospices from this period, while if you carry on down Königstrasse you reach the **Burgtor**, an attractive square tower topped by a bell-shaped roof.

At the opposite end of the Altstadt are the **St-Annen-Museum** and the **Dom**. The museum (Tues–Sun 10am–4/5pm; DM5, free first Fri of the month) has a first-rate collection reflecting domestic, civic and church art and history from the thirteenth to the eighteenth century – including a magnificent *Passion* triptych by Memling. The large brick-built Dom, founded in 1173, contains an enormous triumphal cross by Bernt Notke, a celebrity throughout the Baltic in the late fifteenth century.

Practicalities

The **train station** is a few minutes west of the centre, off the Altstadt, and houses one of the **tourist offices** (Mon–Sat 10am–1pm & 2–6pm; ☎0451/864675); another can be found in the heart of the city at Breite Str. 62 (Mon–Fri 9.30am–6pm, Sat & Sun 10am–2pm). A Lübeck-Card, which can be used on public transport and for reduced entrance fees for museums and harbour-trips, costs DM9 for one day or DM18 for three days. The cheapest **hotel** in or near the centre is *Stadt Lübeck*, Am Bahnhof 21 (☎0451/83883; ④). The YMCA has a central **InterRail-Point-Sleep-In** at Grosse Petersgrube 11 (☎0451/71920; ②). If that's full, try the **youth hostel** at Gertrudenkirchhof 4 (☎0451/33433; ②), close to the Burgtor, or its more luxurious counterpart at Mengstr. 33 (☎0451/702 0399; ③) in the historic centre.

As a student town, Lübeck has a good choice of **cafés** and **eating places**. The *Ratskeller* serves a very good selection of vegetarian dishes, and *Schmidt's*, Dr. Julius-Leber-Str. 60–62, is a café/restaurant with a wide choice. *Tipasa*, Schlumacherstr. 12–14, has great cheap bistro-type dishes, highly popular with students. The Engelsgrube is the best street for **bars**, though the most enjoyable is probably the old, atmospheric *Im alten Zolln*, Mühlenstr. 93.

Bremen

Of the main north German cities, **BREMEN** is the most manageable, lacking the commercialism of Hamburg and the ugly redevelopment of Hannover. In 1949 Bremen was declared an autonomous *Land*, and since then it's had a reputation for being the most politically radical part of the country, electing the first Green MPs in 1979.

The main area of historical interest is the **Altstadt**, on the Weser's northeast bank, reached by walking straight ahead from the train station. At the top of Sögestrasse, Bremen's main shopping street, is the **Liebfrauenkirche**, a lovely hall church engulfed by a flower market; the single place worth stopping at on the way is the *Café Knigge*.

The **Marktplatz** ahead of the church is relatively small, and is dominated by the **Rathaus**, one of the most splendid buildings in northern Germany. You can only visit the interior as part of a guided tour (Mon–Sat 11am, noon, 3pm & 4pm, Sun 11am & noon; DM5), but it's worth it to see the extremes of Bremen's civic pride: rooms awash with gilded wallpaper and ornate carving. On the left as you face the Rathaus is a vast **statue of Roland**, erected in 1404 as a symbol of Bremen's independence from its archbishop; he now stares at the modern Parliament building, one of the ugliest edifices to disgrace a German town.

On a small rise beyond the Rathaus stands the **Dom**, its brooding interior ranging from Romanesque to late Gothic. You can climb one of the twin towers (Easter–Oct Mon–Fri 10am–5pm, Sat 10am–1pm, Sun 2–5pm; DM1). In the crypt are some fine works of art, notably an eleventh-century *Enthroned Christ* and a magnificent thirteenth-century font. Off the southeast corner is the **Bleikeller** (Easter–Oct Mon–Fri 10am–5pm, Sat 10am–1pm, Sun 2–5pm; DM2), where lead for the roofing was stored; a macabre attraction is provided by the corpses which were discovered here when the room was opened up, perfectly preserved as a result of the lack of air. Surviving buildings from Bremen's Hanseatic heyday are few – what's left include the line of restored patrician houses along the Marktplatz, and the **Schütting**, the ritzy, Flemish-inspired mansion where the guild of merchants convened.

Böttcherstrasse, off the south side of Marktplatz, was transformed in the 1920s by the Bremen coffee magnate Ludwig Roselius, who commissioned local artists to convert the alleyway into a Gothic-cum-Art Nouveau fantasy. Craft workshops are tucked in among the bronze reliefs, the arches and the turrets, and there's a musical clock depicting the history of transatlantic crossings. The only old house in the street is the **Roselius-Haus**, now a museum of art and furniture (Tues–Sun 11am–6pm; DM8); the best works are paintings by the Cranachs and an alabaster statue of *Saint Barbara* by Riemenschneider. Adjacent is the **Paula-Becker-Modersohn-Haus** (same entry ticket), containing a number of paintings by the artist, who lived in nearby Worpswede.

Tucked away between the Dom and the river is a small, extraordinarily well-preserved area of medieval fishing houses known as the **Schnoorviertel**. Though prettified, it has managed to avoid soulless gentrification. Just east of the Schnoorviertel at Am Wall 207, the **Kunsthalle** (Tues 10am–9pm, Wed–Sun 10am–5pm; DM8) houses a superb array of mainly nineteenth- and early twentieth-century paintings, including some forty works by Modersohn-Becker.

Practicalities

The **train station** is just north of the city centre, and immediately outside is the **tourist office** (Mon–Wed 9.30am–6.30pm, Thurs & Fri 9.30am–8pm, Sat & Sun 9.30am–4pm; ☎0421/30800). Bremen's **youth hostel** is in the western part of the old town at Kalkstr. 6 (☎0421/171369; ②). The densest and most convenient cluster of **hotels** is also near the train station, where prices start at DM60 per person. Less costly but still fairly close to the centre is *Heinisch*, Wachmannstr. 26 (☎0421/342925; ④), ten minutes' walk from the train station and on the #5 tramline. *Weidmann*, Am Schwarzen Meer 35 (☎0421/498 4455; ③), is a small, busy pension in the Ostertorviertel while *Weltevreden*, Am Dobben 62 (☎0421/78015; ④) is excellently located about halfway between the city centre and the Ostertorviertel, heart of Bremen's nightlife. There's a good central **campsite**, *Internationaler Campingplatz Freie Hansestadt Bremen*, Am Stadtwaldsee 1 – buses #28, #23 go in the right direction.

Bremen has a number of good **café/bars** and is also renowned for its fish specialities (particularly eel), best sampled in the *gemütlich* old restaurants of the Altstadt and Schnoorviertel. Try the *Ratskeller* underneath the Rathaus or *Flett*, Böttcherstr. 3. Bremen is home of Beck's, one of the most heavily exported **beers** in the country, but the products of Haake-Beck are the ones to go for in the city itself; a good place to sample them is the *Kleiner Ratskeller*, Hinter dem Schütting 11.

Hannover

HANNOVER has a closer relationship with Britain than any other German city, a consequence of the 1701 Act of Settlement, which resulted in Georg Ludwig of Hannover becoming King George I of the United Kingdom in 1714. As well as a monarch, Britain gained a great composer: anticipating the accession, the court director of music, Georg Friedrich Händel, had already established himself in London by the time his employer arrived, and went on to write his finest works there. Hannover's showpiece is not a great cathedral, palace or town hall, but a **series of gardens**, which are among the most impressive in Europe. Add to this a number of first-class museums and there's plenty here to keep you occupied for a couple of days. From June 1 to October 31, 2000 there's the added attraction of Expo 2000, the first World Fair to be staged in Germany.

The City

Hannover has had to reconstruct itself after almost total demolition by World War II bombing, and the view on arrival at the train station isn't prepossessing, with a bland pedestrian precinct stretching ahead. Underneath runs the **Passarelle**, a sort of subterranean bazaar-cum-piazza that at night is a little disconcerting.

Standing at Hannover's most popular rendezvous, the *Café Kröpcke*, the most imposing building in view is the Neoclassical **Opernhaus**, perhaps the finest of the city's public buildings. A short distance southwest, a few streets of rebuilt half-timbered buildings convey some impression of the medieval town; most notable is the high-gabled fifteenth-century **Altes Rathaus**, its elaborate brickwork enlivened with colourful glazed tiles. Alongside is the fourteenth-century **Marktkirche**, whose bulky tower has long been the emblem of the city; inside, there's some miraculously preserved stained glass in the east windows. Close by, at Pferdestr. 6, the **Historical Museum** (Tues 10am–8pm, Wed–Fri 10am–4pm, Sat & Sun 10am–6pm; DM5) incorporates the sole remnant of the city walls. The displays include some state coaches, a section illustrating the changing face of Hannover, and several reconstructed interiors from farmhouses in the province.

Southwards, across the Friedrichswall, is the **Neues Rathaus**, an Art-Deco-cum-neo-Gothic extravaganza whose dome gives the best views of the city (April–Oct daily 10am–12.45pm & 1.30–4.45pm; DM3). Next door, the **Kestner Museum** (Tues & Thurs–Sun 11am–6pm, Wed 11am–8pm; DM3, free Wed) is a compact and eclectic decorative arts museum. Round the back of the Rathaus, over the road from the artificial Maschsee, is the **Landesmuseum** (Tues, Wed & Fri–Sun 10am–5pm, Thurs 10am–7pm; DM6), housing an excellent collection of paintings from the Middle Ages to the early twentieth century. Centre stage is taken by an exquisite *Portrait of Philipp Melanchthon* by Hans Holbein the Younger. A decent display of Italian Renaissance work includes pictures by Botticelli and Raphael, and there's a good cross-section of Dutch work, including one of Rembrandt's rare nature paintings. On the first floor, the **archeology** department's showpieces are the bodies of prehistoric men preserved in the peat bogs of Lower Saxony, along with the contents of several graves and an array of Bronze Age jewellery.

A bit further down the road, the **Sprengel Museum** (Tues 10am–8pm, Wed–Sun 10am–6pm; DM7) is one of the most exciting modern art galleries in Germany. Much of the display space is given over to changing exhibitions of photography, graphics and experimental art-forms, but there's also a first-rate permanent display of twentieth-century painting and sculpture. Focal point is a huge range of work by Hannover's own Kurt Schwitters, the landscapes and still lifes coming as a surprise if you're familiar only with the famous Dada collages.

For Expo 2000, jump on a mainline train or U-Bahn #8 to Messegelände in the southeast of the city.

Herrenhausen

The royal gardens of **Herrenhausen**, summer residence of the Hannover court, can be reached by U-Bahn #1 or #2, but it's better to pick up the free tourist office plan of the complex and walk through it. Proceeding north from town along Nienburgerstrasse, the least remarkable of the gardens – the **Welfengarten** – lies to the right, dominated by the huge neo-Gothic **Welfenpalais**, now occupied by the university.

To the left, the dead straight Herrenhäuser Allee cuts through the **Georgengarten**, an English-style landscaped garden with an artificial lake. This garden was created as a foil to the magnificent formal **Grosser Garten** (daily 8am–4.30/8pm; DM3, free in winter), the city's pride and joy. If possible, time your visit to coincide with the playing of the fountains (May–Sept Mon–Fri 11am–noon & 3–4pm, Sat & Sun 11am–noon & 3–5pm) or when the illuminations are switched on (May–Sept Wed–Sun at dusk). Just inside the entrance gate is one of the most striking features, the **Hedge Theatre**, a permanent amphitheatre whose hedges double as scenery and changing rooms. Behind the **Grande Parterre**, eight small plots have been laid out to illustrate different styles of landscape gardening down the centuries, while the rear section of the Grosser Garten consists of a series of radiating avenues bounded by hedges and trees, each ending at a fountain. As a centrepiece, there's the **Grosse Fontäne**, which spurts a jet of water reaching 82m – Europe's highest after the Jet d'Eau in Geneva. In the adjoining Georgengarten is the **Wilhelm Busch Museum** (Tues–Sat 10am–5pm, Sun 10am–6pm; DM6), which features a brilliant collection by the eponymous father of the comic-strip cartoon, and hosts shows of other caricaturists.

Across Herrenhäuser Strasse to the north of the Grosser Garten is the **Berggarten**, set up to shelter rare and exotic plants. Some compensation for the loss of the palace in the last war is provided by a number of courtly buildings to the west along Herrenhäuser Strasse. One of these, the **Fürstenhaus**, is a sort of museum of the House of Hannover (Tues–Sun 10am–5/6pm; DM5).

Practicalities

The **train station** is right in the centre of town; behind is the **bus station** for long-distance routes. The **tourist office** is to the right of the train station in the **post office** building at Ernst-August-Platz 2 (Mon–Fri 9am–6pm, Sat 9.30am–3pm; ☎0511/30140).

There's a **youth hostel** at Ferdinand-Wilhelm-Fricke-Weg 1 (☎0511/322941; ②); take U-Bahn #3 or #7 towards Mühlenberg, and alight at Fischerhof, from where it's a five-minute walk to the left over the bridge, then right. Alongside is a **campsite**. For DM10 the tourist office will book you into a **hotel**. As a centre of the trade fair industry (the April fair is Europe's largest), Hannover charges fancy prices – for the duration of Expo 2000 accommodation will be at a premium and should be booked well in advance. Normally the lowest rates are at *Pension Indra*, Schiffgraben 46 (☎0511/810109; ③); *Flora*, Heinrichstr. 36 (☎0511/383910; ③); and *Gildehof*, Joachimstr. 6 (☎0511/363680; ④), or you could try the pricier *Reverey*, Aegidiendamm 8 (☎0511/883711; ⑤).

Hannover's major find for **snacks** is the Markthalle, where German, Italian, Spanish and Turkish stallholders sell wonderful examples of their cooking. Good **cafés** include the celebrated *Kröpcke* on the square of the same name, and, outside the city centre, *Klatsch*, at Limmerstr. 58. The *Brauhaus Ernst August* on Schmiedestr. 13 is a brewery serving hearty German **food**. *Weinloch*, Burgstr. 33, and *Hannen Fass* on Knochenhauerstr. 36, are youthful pubs serving cheap meals.

Hildesheim

Some of the finest buildings in Germany are to be found 30km southeast of Hannover at **HILDESHEIM**, where, during the eleventh century, the Romanesque style in architecture, sculpture and painting achieved its state of perfection. Much of what stands there now, however, is reconstructed: Hildesheim was bombed just a month before the German surrender in 1945, and the consequent fire caused damage which even exemplary restoration cannot disguise.

Throughout the 1980s restorers worked on the town's Marktplatz, re-creating what used to be Germany's most magnificent square. The fifteenth-century **Tempelhaus**, the only absolutely authentic structure here, is one of the country's finest secular medieval buildings. Hildesheim's supreme monument, the serene church of **St Michael**, is about ten minutes' walk south of the **train station**, perched on a little hill and girded with six towers. St Michael's was very much a personal creation of Bishop Bernward, confidant of Emperor Otto II and tutor to Otto III, and bishop here from 993 to 1022. Shortly after his canonization in 1192, seven elaborately carved capitals were made for the nave, and in the west transept a choir screen was erected; only part of this remains, but its stucco carvings rank among the masterpieces of German sculpture. An even more spectacular embellishment was the painted ceiling – three-quarters of the 1300 oak panels are original.

The **Dom**, reached via Burgstrasse, is largely fake on the outside, but the interior has been restored to its eleventh-century layout. Made for St Michael's by a bronze foundry which Bernward established, the doors inside the main entrance tell the story of Adam and Eve on the left-hand side, and of Christ on the right. Soon after, the same craftsmen made a triumphal column, now in the southern transept, illustrating the lives of Jesus and John the Baptist. Almost as impressive are the huge wheel-shaped chandelier, made around 1065, and the font in the baptismal chapel, made in 1225. The cloister (April–Oct Mon–Sat 9.30am–5pm, Sun noon–5pm; DM0.50) forms a protective shield round the apse, where the legendary thousand-year-old rosebush grows. A beautiful fourteenth-century miniaturization of a Gothic cathedral, the **St-Annen-Kapelle**, occupies the centre of the cloister garden.

Hildesheim's **Diocesan Museum** (Tues–Sat 10am–5pm, Sun noon–5pm; DM4) contains several works dating from Bernward's time, including the *Golden Madonna* and a pair of crucifixes. Adjoining the north side of the Dom's close is the old Franciscan friary, which now contains the archeological **Roemer-Pelizaeus Museum** (Tues–Sun 9am–4.30pm; DM3), with a collection of Egyptian antiquities that is one of the best in Europe. However, more often than not, this museum hosts a major temporary exhibition, when it's open daily (9am–5/6pm; DM12).

The southern part of Hildesheim was largely spared from war damage, and presents several streets of half-timbered houses as a reminder of what the whole of the old city once looked like. South of the Dom area stretches Hinterer Brühl, an almost completely preserved old street, at the end of which is **St Godehard**, built in the mid-twelfth century. East of St Godehard, Gelber Stern leads into Kesslerstrasse, arguably the most imposing of the old streets, lined with Renaissance and Baroque mansions.

The **tourist office** (Mon–Fri 9am–7pm, Sat 9am–4pm; ☎05121/15995) is currently located within the bookshop in the Tempelhaus. The **youth hostel** is sited above Moritzberg at Schirrmannweg 4 (☎05121/42717; ②), a good hour's walk from the centre (buses #1 and #4 go part of the way). The only budget option with a central location is a small **pension**, *Kurth*, on Küsthardtstr. 4 (☎05121/32817; ③). First choice among places to **eat** and **drink** is the *Ratskeller* on Marktplatz, which has cheap specials most lunchtimes.

Goslar

The stereotype of a mining town immediately conjures up images of grim terraced houses and lowering machinery. **GOSLAR**, superbly located at the northern edge of the gentle wooded **Harz mountains**, could not be more different. For one thing, the mining here was always of a very superior nature – silver was discovered in the nearby Rammelsberg in the tenth century, and the town soon became the "treasure chest of the Holy Roman Empire". The presence of a POW hospital during World War II spared it from bombing, and Goslar can claim to have more old houses than any other town in Germany.

Although it hosts an attractive market every Tuesday and Friday morning, the central **Marktplatz** is best seen empty to fully appreciate its gorgeous visual variety, with its elegantly Gothic **Rathaus** and roofs of bright red tiles and contrasting grey slate. The Huldigungssaal (Hall of Homage) in the Rathaus contains a dazzling array of medieval wall and ceiling paintings, with the most valuable items hidden in altar niches and closets behind the panelling. Long-term restoration work should be completed by late 1999, when the Rathaus will reopen.

Just behind the Rathaus is the **Marktkirche**, facing the sixteenth-century **Brusttuch**, with its top storey crammed with satirical carvings. Goslar's half-timbered beauty begins in earnest in the streets behind the church, the oldest houses lying in the Bergstrasse and Schreiberstrasse areas. An especially fine Baroque specimen is the **Siemenshaus** at their junction. Turning right into Bergstrasse, wind your way up to the roughly hewn **Frankenberger Kirche**, situated in tranquil solitude on the boundaries of the **Altstadt**. Some faint thirteenth-century frescoes compete in vain for attention against a Baroque pulpit.

Down Peterstrasse, past a variety of attractive buildings, lies the remarkable **Kaiserpfalz** (Imperial Palace). Built at the beginning of the eleventh century, the Kaiserpfalz continued to flourish until a fire gutted it in 1289 – it was rescued from disrepair by the future Kaiser Wilhelm I in 1868. Much of the **interior** (daily 10am–4/5pm; DM2.50) is occupied by the vast Reichssaal, decorated with romantic depictions of the emperors. Below the Kaiserpfalz, a large car park fills the former site of the **Dom**, pulled down in 1822 due to lack of funds for restoration. Only the entrance hall with its facade of thirteenth-century statues survived; you can peer at it through the recently installed glass doors. On Hoher Weg, which leads back to the Marktplatz, is the **Grosses Heiliges Kreuz** (daily 11am–4/5pm; free), a well-preserved thirteenth-century hospice. Down the Abzucht stream to the right is the **Goslar Museum** (Tues–Sun 10am–4/5pm; DM3.50), which contains the *Krodo* altar from the Dom and a section on mining.

A ten-minute walk northwest of Marktplatz brings you to the **Mönchehaus Museum** (Tues–Sat 10am–1pm & 3–5pm, Sun 10am–1pm; free). A black and white half-timbered building over 450 years old, it's the curious home to Goslar's modern art collection. East of here, the **Jakobikirche** contains a moving *Pietà* by the great but elusive sixteenth-century sculptor, Hans Witten. A little to the north is the **Neuwerkkirche**, which has impressive Romanesque carvings both inside and out. Finally, the **silver mine** in the Rammelsberg hill on the southern edge of town – the spot where silver was first discovered in this vicinity – has been opened to the public as a **mining museum** (tours daily 9.30am–6pm; DM10; rail tours DM15; combined ticket DM18).

Practicalities

The **tourist office** is at Marktplatz 7 (May–Oct Mon–Fri 9.15am–6pm, Sat 9.30am–4pm, Sun 9.30am–2pm; Nov–April Mon–Fri 9.15am–5pm, Sat 9.30am–2pm; ☎05321/28546). Just a few minutes' walk from the **train station** at the northern end of town is *Gästehaus Elisabeth Möller*, Schieferweg 6 (☎05321/23098; ③), an excellent **guesthouse** serving amazing breakfasts. The **youth hostel**, Rammelsberger Str. 25 (☎05321/22240; ②), is a bit of a trek from the centre. Of the **hotels** in historic buildings the eighteenth-century *Zur Börse*, Bergstr. 53 (☎05321/22775; ④), is one of the prettiest. The nearest **campsite** is the well-equipped *Sennhütte*, Clausthaler Str. 28, several kilometres along the B241 to the south – take the bus for Clausthal-Zellerfeld. As for **restaurants**, *Bistro Filou*, Worthstr. 10, does salads and baguettes, and *Worthmühle*, Worthstr. 4, is good for provincial cooking at very low prices.

CENTRAL GERMANY

Central Germany, the most populous region of the country, is the powerhouse of the economic miracle, and the zone of heaviest industrialization – the **Ruhrgebiet** – forms the most densely populated area in Europe. Within this conurbation, **Bonn**'s neighbour, **Cologne**, is the outstanding city, managing to preserve many of the splendours of its long centuries as a free state. The other city of top-class historical interest is **Aachen**, the original capital of the Holy Roman Empire. Swish, cosmopolitan **Düsseldorf** is the capital of present-day North Rhine-Westphalia (Nordrhein-Westfalen).

The adjoining province of Rhineland-Palatinate (Rheinland-Pfalz) is the land of the national epic, the *Nibelungenlied*, of the alluring Lorelei, of robber barons in their lofty fortresses, and of the traders who used the river routes to make the country rich. Nowadays pleasure cruisers run the length of the Rhine, through the **Rhine gorge**, past a wonderful landscape of rocks, vines, white-painted towns and ruined castles. Industry exists only in isolated pockets, and **Mainz**, the Palatinate's capital, only just ranks among the forty largest cities in Germany. Its monuments, though, together with those of the two other imperial cathedral cities of **Worms** and **Speyer**, merit more than a passing glance, while **Trier** preserves the finest buildings of classical antiquity this side of the Alps.

Occupying the geographical centre of the Federal Republic, the province of Hesse is focused on the American-style dynamism of **Frankfurt**. Although heavy industry still exists around the confluence of the Rhine and the Main, it's the serious money generated by Frankfurt's banking and communications industries that provides the region's real economic base. Of the region's historical centres, the place of particular interest is the old university town of **Marburg**.

Düsseldorf

DÜSSELDORF, which alongside Hamburg and Stuttgart claims to be the country's richest city, is the epitome of the economic miracle – orderly, prosperous and self-confident. Never as industrialized as its Ruhr neighbours, Düsseldorf has concentrated on its role as a financial and administrative centre: one of the country's largest stock exchanges is here, as are the headquarters and offices of innumerable multinationals. At least two of these, the **Thyssen-Haus** in the heart of the city and the **Mannesmann-Haus** on the banks of the Rhine, are dominant landmarks, in the way that towers of churches and town halls were in medieval cityscapes. Even for a short visit Düsseldorf is expensive, but on the plus side the **nightlife** is one of the most enjoyable in the country.

Arrival and accommodation

The **train station** is southeast of the city centre, with the shopping streets fanning out from it. S-Bahn trains leave at twenty-minute intervals for the **airport**. Düsseldorf's **tourist office** (Mon–Fri 8.30am–6pm, Sat 9am–12.30pm; ☎0211/172020) is on Konrad-Adenauer-Platz, facing the train station. The **youth hostel**, at Düsseldorfer Str. 1 in Oberkassel (☎0211/574041; ③), has singles as well as dormitory beds; from the station, take bus #835 or walk down Graf-Adolf-Strasse and continue over the Rheinkniebrücke – it's the first building on the other side. **Hotels** near the train station are about as reasonably priced as any, especially on Graf-Adolf-Strasse with *Manhattan* at no. 39 (☎0211/370247; ④), and *CVJM*, at no. 102 (☎0211/172850; ④). There are slightly cheaper options in the southern part of the city centre, such as *Diana*, Jahnstr. 31 (☎ 0211/375071; ③), or the nearby *Haus Hillesheim*, Jahnstr. 19 (☎0211/386860; ③). There are two **campsites** (April–Sept): *Oberlörick* is reached by U-Bahn #76, #705, #717 to Belsenplatz, then bus #828; for *Unterbachsee*, out at the eastern extremity, take bus #781.

The City

Though never one of Germany's great architectural attractions, Düsseldorf's **Altstadt** has a couple of churches to catch the eye: **St Lambertus**, a fourteenth-century brick building, is easily recognizable by its tall twisted spire, while a short walk to the east is the stuccoed **St Andreas**, mausoleum of the Electors Palatine – who were among the seven princes who elected the Holy Roman Emperor. The most popular of the Electors was Jan Wellem, commemorated in the huge open area named after him in the heart of the city, and by a masterly equestrian statue outside the Renaissance **Rathaus**. In the square immediately to the north is the **Schlossturm**, the only remnant of the old fortifications; it has been restored to house a small **Navigation Museum** (Wed & Sat 2–6pm, Sun 11am–6pm; DM4).

Jan Wellem's successors employed French gardeners to transform their city with parks, canals and miscellaneous urban improvements. This culminated in the creation of the main thoroughfare, the famously chic **Königsallee**. Only the Jugendstil Kaufhaus has any merits as a building; diagonally opposite its rear entrance is **Wilhelm-Marx-Haus**, the earliest visible expression of Düsseldorf's infatuation with the New World, hailed as the first skyscraper in Germany when it went up in the 1920s.

The largest of the parks is the **Hofgarten**, shaped like a great stiletto-heeled shoe, now crossed by several busy streets. At its far end is **Schloss Jägerhof**, a Baroque palace which has been refitted as the **Goethe Museum** (Tues–Fri & Sun 11am–5pm, Sat 1–5pm; DM4) – though unless you're an avid fan the contents will not thrill. Düsseldorf's own favourite son is another of Germany's most celebrated writers, **Heinrich Heine**, in whose honour a research institute and museum have been set up at Bilkerstr. 14 (Tues–Fri & Sun 11am–5pm, Sat 1–5pm; DM4).

The two large art museums each warrant a gentle browse. Housed in an ultramodern gallery in Grabbeplatz is the **Kunstsammlung Nordrhein-Westfalen** (Tues–Thurs, Sat & Sun 10am–6pm, Fri 10am–8pm; DM8–12). The collection began with an act of contrition: in atonement for the dismissal of Paul Klee from his professorship at the Düsseldorf Academy in the Nazi purges of 1933, around ninety of his works were bought by the city in 1960. Klee remains the big attraction, but later acquisitions have turned the museum into a who's who of modern painting.

The **Kunstmuseum** (Tues–Sun 11am–6pm; DM5), north of the Altstadt at Ehrenhof 5, has extensive displays on three floors. At ground level there's a fine collection of glass, much of it Art Nouveau and Art Deco. On the next floor, Rubens' altarpiece of *The Assumption* puts almost all its companions in the shade – exceptions being a *St Jerome* attributed to Ribera, and *St Francis in Meditation* by Zurbarán. Upstairs, there's a modern section that complements the Kunstsammlung, along with heavy stuff from the nineteenth-century Düsseldorf Academy.

Eating, drinking and nightlife

"The longest bar in Europe" is how the tourist office describes the Altstadt: the heart of the quarter – the parallel Kurze Str./Andreasstr. and Bolkerstr., and streets perpendicular to them – is almost entirely given over to places of entertainment. **Eating** is one of the few things it's possible to do cheaply in Düsseldorf, thanks to the variety of the city's ethnic communities, with the ubiquitous pizzerias leading the way. *Im Goldenen Kessel*, Bolkerstr. 44 is the flagship of the *Schumacher* **brewery**, and is equally renowned for its food. At no. 45 on the same street is *Zum Schlüssel*, a cavernous and popular bar/restaurant which brews its own beer on the premises. An even better-known boutique brewery is *Zum Uerige*, Bergerstr. 1. For **something wilder** there's *Ratinger Hof*, Ratinger Str. 10, the first punk bar in Germany, while at no. 18 is *Zum Goldenen Einhorn*, enduringly popular with the youth of the city. *Café Bernstein*, Oststr. 158 is a genuine local, tucked away in the shopping area between the Altstadt and the train station – a stylish place for a nightcap. The huge *Tor 3*, Rosendorfer Str. 143 – south of the centre in the Bilk district – is the city's best **disco**.

Cologne

Currently the fourth largest city in Germany, with a population of just over a million, **COLOGNE** (Köln) is the colossus of the Rhine–Ruhr sprawl. The huge Gothic **Dom** is the country's most visited monument, Cologne's medieval buildings are unsurpassed, and its museums bettered only by those in Berlin, Munich and Dresden. The annual **Carnival** in the early spring is one of Europe's major popular celebrations. The city also ranks high as a **beer** centre, with 24 breweries all producing the distinctive **Kölsch**.

Founded in 33 BC, Cologne owed much of its development to ecclesiastical affairs. A bishopric was established in the fourth century, and saints Severin, Gereon and Ursula were all martyred here. In the twelfth century Cologne acquired the relics of the Three Magi from Milan, thus increasing its standing as one of the greatest centres of pilgrimage in northern Europe. Situated on the intersection of the Rhine and several major trade routes, medieval Cologne became immensely rich – and the largest city in Germany. Later decline was partially reversed in the eighteenth century with the exploitation of an Italian recipe for distilling flower blossoms into almost pure alcohol. Originally created as an aphrodisiac, it was marketed here as a toilet water, achieving worldwide fame under its new name – eau de Cologne. In the twentieth century Cologne's great personality was Konrad Adenauer, deposed as mayor of the city by the Nazis, and the first chancellor of the country after the war.

Arrival and accommodation

The **train station** is immediately below the Dom; moving on is never a problem, as around a thousand trains stop here daily. The **bus station** is directly behind, with international services on the lower tier. For the **airport** take bus #170, which leaves every twenty minutes or so, and takes less than thirty minutes. The **tourist office**, at Unter Fettenhennen 19, in front of the Dom (May–Oct Mon–Sat 8am–10.30pm, Sun 9am–10.30pm; Nov–April Mon–Sat 8am–9pm, Sun 9.30am–7pm; ☎0221/221 3345), publishes a monthly guide to what's on, *Köln-Monatsvorschau* (DM2).

Cologne's **public transport** network, shared with Bonn, is a mixture of buses and trams, the latter becoming the U-Bahn around the centre. Fares are high, making it better to invest in a 24-hour ticket (DM9 for Cologne only) or a three-day pass (DM22.50). Finally, students can get half-price admission to all Cologne's museums. If you're not eligible, it might make sense to invest in the **Museums Pass** (DM20), which allows entry to all the city collections on any two consecutive days.

There are two **youth hostels**. The more central is the dingy and claustrophobic place at Siegesstr. 5a in Deutz (☎0221/814711; ②), about fifteen minutes' walk from the centre over the Hohenzollernbrücke. Much more enticing, and pricier, is the youth guesthouse in the northern suburb of Riehl (☎0221/767081; ③) – take U-Bahn #5, #16 or #18 from the train station to Boltensternstrasse. For a **hotel room**, best advice is to pay the DM5 the tourist office charges to find you a place, as they often offer special discounts. Accommodation is mainly geared to trade fairs, but it is plentifully scattered all over the city. If you prefer to look yourself, the homely *Rossner*, Jakordenstr. 19 (☎0221/122703; ③), is the pick of the cluster of hotels behind the station. Other bargain options with central locations include *Das Kleine Stapelhäuschen*, Fischmarkt 1–3 (☎0221/257 7862; ④), *Im Kupferkessel*, Probsteigasse 6 (☎0221/135338; ④), and *Jansen*, Richard-Wagner-Str. 18 (☎0221/251875; ③). The only all-year **campsite** is at Peter-Baum-Weg, in the northeastern suburb of Dünnwald.

The City

One of the most massive Gothic buildings ever constructed, the **Dom** is built on a scale that reflects its power – the archbishop was one of the seven Electors of the Holy Roman Empire, and the Dom remains the seat of the Primate of Germany. Impetus for its creation came with the arrival of the alleged relics of the Magi; when it came to commissioning a church of appropriate grandeur, it was decided to adopt the ethereal new Gothic style rather than the late Romanesque style still in vogue in the Rhineland.

The chancel was completed in 1322, but then the extravagant ambition of the plans began to take its toll. In 1560 the project was abandoned, to be resumed only in the nineteenth century. What you see today is substantially an act of homage from one age to another: taking guidance from recently discovered documents that showed the first designs for the facade, the masons continued the work in perfect imitation of the style of their precursors. Originally the **spires** were the tallest structures in the world, but were soon dwarfed by the Eiffel Tower and are no longer even the highest in Cologne. All the same, you need a fair bit of muscle to climb up the south tower for the panorama over the city and the Rhine (daily 9am–4/6pm; DM3).

From the west door your eye is immediately drawn down the length of the building to the high altar, with the spectacular golden **shrine** to the Magi, made in 1181. It's one of three masterpieces to be found here; the others are in the chapels at the entrance to the ambulatory. On the north side is the ninth-century **Gero crucifix**, the most important monumental sculpture of its period, while the corresponding chapel to the south has the greatest achievement of the fifteenth-century Cologne school of painters, the *Adoration of the Magi* by Stefan Lochner. Stained-glass windows are an essential component of a Gothic cathedral, and

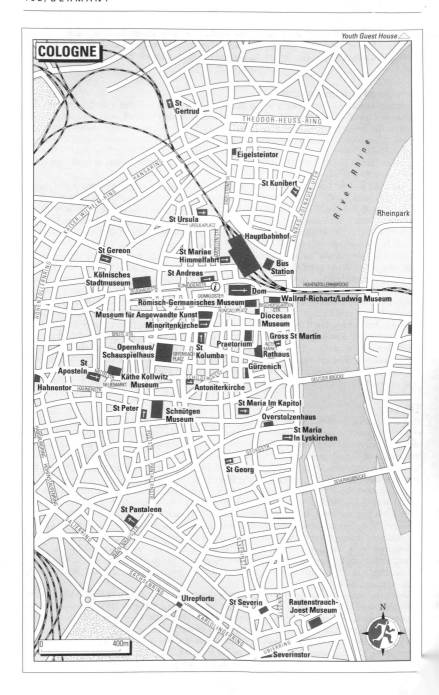

Youth Guest House

COLOGNE

St Gertrud

THEODOR-HEUSS-RING

Eigelsteintor

St Kunibert

River Rhine

Rheinpark

St Ursula
URSULAPLATZ

Hauptbahnhof

St Gereon

St Mariae Himmelfahrt

Kölnisches Stadtmuseum

St Andreas

ZEUGHAUSSTR.

KOMÖDIENSTR.

Bus Station

HOHENZOLLERNBRÜCKE

Dom

DOMKLOSTER

Römisch-Germanisches Museum

RONCALLIPLATZ

BISCHOFSGARTEN -STR.

Wallraf-Richartz/Ludwig Museum

Museum für Angewandte Kunst

Diocesan Museum

Minoritenkirche

BREITE STR.

Praetorium

Gross St Martin

Opernhaus/ Schauspielhaus

OFFENBACH PLATZ

St Kolumba

ALTER MARKT

Rathaus

St Aposteln

MITTELSTR.

Käthe Kollwitz Museum

NEUMARKT

SCHILDERGASSE

Gürzenich

Hahnentor

HAHNENSTR.

Antoniterkirche

St Peter

POST STR.

PANTALEONSTR.

Schnütgen Museum

St Maria Im Kapitol

Overstolzenhaus

St Maria In Lyskirchen

GEORGSTR.

St Georg

DEUTZER BRÜCKE

SEVERINSBRÜCKE

St Pantaleon

SACHSENRING

Ulrepforte

KAROLINGERRING

St Severin

Rautenstrauch-Joest Museum

N

UBIERRING

Severinstor

0   400m

Cologne has a marvellously varied set. The oldest, dating from 1260, is in the furthest chapel of the ambulatory.

The **Schatzkammer** (Mon–Sat 9am–4/5pm, Sun 12.30–4/5pm; DM3) is far less interesting than the **Diocesan Museum**, just outside in Roncalliplatz (11am–6pm; closed Thurs; free). Another beautiful Lochner, *Madonna of the Violets*, forms the centrepiece.

THE WALLRAF-RICHARTZ/LUDWIG AND RÖMISCH-GERMANISCHES MUSEUMS

Housed in an ultramodern building right next to the Dom, the **Wallraf-Richartz/Ludwig Museum** (Tues 10am–8pm, Wed–Fri 10am–6pm, Sat & Sun 11am–6pm; DM10) is an amazing picture hoard, comprising three distinct sections. Currently on the first floor, but due to move to its own separate premises beside the Rathaus in May 2000, the Wallraf-Richartz collection is centred on the fifteenth-century Cologne school. Stefan Lochner's *Last Judgement* is an especially inventive work, but the gems of the whole display are the two large triptychs by the Master of St Bartholomew, representing the school's final flowering at the beginning of the sixteenth century. Displayed alongside these Cologne masters are other German paintings, including a small Dürer and several Cranach pieces. There are also a number of Flemish panels, while the rich show of seventeenth-century Dutch artists includes what is probably the last of Rembrandt's great self-portraits.

The Ludwig Museum of twentieth-century art occupies the remainder of the galleries, providing a jolting gear-change to Andy Warhol, whose Brillo boxes and Campbell's cans are the centrepiece of the large Pop Art section. Among German works there's a fine group of Kirchners, a room full of Beckmanns, three superb portraits by Dix and a number of sculptures by Barlach. Two rooms are devoted to Picasso, with sculptures, ceramics and paintings from most phases of his career. The third collection, the **Agfa-Foto-Historama**, shows old photographic equipment and a selection of prints from the vast holdings of the company, whose headquarters are in nearby Leverkusen.

One of Germany's most important archeological museums, the neighbouring **Römisch-Germanisches Museum** (Tues–Sun 10am–5pm; DM5), was specially constructed around its star exhibit, the **Dionysus Mosaic**. The finest work of its kind in northern Europe, it was created for the dining room of a patrician villa in about 200 AD, and covers some 70 square metres. The other main item is the adjacent **Tomb of Poblicius**; dating from about 40 AD, it stands 15m high. The museum's collection of **glass** is reckoned to be the world's finest, but of more general appeal is the dazzling array of **jewellery** on the first floor, mostly dating from the so-called Dark Ages.

THE ALTSTADT

The vast **Altstadt** suffered grievous damage in the last war, and economic necessity meant that nondescript modern buildings were quickly raised to fill the bombsites. Where there wasn't a pressing need for reconstruction, as in the case of the churches, restoration projects were initiated, some of which are still going on. What has been achieved is so impressive that the Altstadt ideally requires two or three days' exploration.

For nearly 600 years, **Gross St Martin**'s tower, surrounded by four turrets, was the dominant feature of the Cologne skyline; the rest of the church seems rather truncated for such a splendid adornment, although the interior has a pleasing simplicity. A short distance beyond is the Alter Markt, one of three large squares in the heart of the city. From here, you can see the irregular octagonal tower of the **Rathaus**, a real fricassee of styles, the highlight being the graceful Renaissance loggia. Just in front of the entrance to the Rathaus, a door leads down into the **Mikwe** (ritual bathhouse), the only remnant of the Jewish ghetto, which was razed soon after the expulsion order of 1424 (Mon–Thurs 9am–5pm, Fri 9am–1pm, Sun 11am–1pm; free). More subterranean sights can be found in nearby Kleine Budengasse, in the form of the **Praetorium**, the foundations of the Roman governor's palace, and the **Roman sewer**, a surprisingly elegant vaulted passageway some one hundred metres long (Tues–Fri 10am–4pm, Sat & Sun 11am–4pm; DM3).

Proceeding south, you pass the burned-out **Alt St Alban**, left as a war memorial, and the tower which is all that survives of **Klein St Martin**. Behind, hemmed in by modern houses, is the severe **St Maria im Kapitol**, with a majestic interior – look out for the wooden doors, contemporary with the eleventh-century architecture. Its cloisters, unusually placed adjoining the facade, are the only ones left in Cologne.

Continuing in a southerly direction, go down Rheingasse to see the step-gabled **Overstolzenhaus**, the finest mansion in the city. A short walk from here is **St Maria in Lyskirchen**, where the vaults are covered with thirteenth-century frescoes. From here, head up Grosse Witschgasse and Georgstrasse to the eleventh-century **St Georg**, whose spacious interior contrasts markedly with the stumpy exterior.

The most southerly of the churches are **St Severin**, which was much altered in the Gothic era, and – northwest of it – **St Pantaleon**, the oldest church in the city. North up Poststrasse and Peterstrasse is **St Peter**, a Gothic church with gleaming stained-glass windows and a magnificent *Crucifixion of St Peter* by Rubens, whose childhood was spent in Cologne.

Next door, the St Cäcilien church now houses the **Schnütgen Museum** (Tues, Thurs & Fri 10am–5pm, Wed 10am–8pm, Sat & Sun 11am–5pm; DM5), a collection of all kinds of Rhineland religious art except paintings. There are some wonderful ivories, but the museum's most famous possession is a painted bust of a woman, carved by one of the Parler family and thought to be the portrait of a relative. Across the road and down Antongasse is the tiny Gothic **Antoniterkirche**, housing one of the most famous twentieth-century sculptures, Barlach's *Memorial Angel*. Around the church is the main shopping centre; the streets follow the same plan as their Roman predecessors, but almost all the buildings are modern.

A short distance west lies Neumarkt, dominated at the far end by the superb apse of **St Aposteln**, due north of which is **St Gereon**, a church without parallel in European architecture. Its kernel is an oval fourth-century chapel which, after various additions, became the basis of a four-storey decagon in the early thirteenth century – which is also when the frescoed baptistry was built.

From here you can return towards the Dom, passing a fragment of Roman wall and the Arsenal en route to the stately **St Andreas**, worth a look for its frescoes and the Maccabees shrine, a notable piece of early sixteenth-century craftsmanship. If you then strike north you'll come to **St Ursula**, with its prominent sturdy tower; unless you're squeamish, try to get hold of the sacristan, who will show you the **Goldene Kammer**, an ornate chamber gruesomely lined with reliquaries (Mon 9am–noon & 1–5pm, Wed–Sat 9.30am–noon & 1–5pm; DM2). From here the **Eigelsteintor**, an impressive survival of the medieval fortifications, is reached via the street of the same name. Dagobertstrasse then leads east to **St Kunibert**, the final fling of the Romanesque in the early thirteenth century, completed just as work began on the Dom. It's also the last church to be restored after war damage, with the nave and massive facade not yet joined up. Inside, note the stained-glass windows in the apse, which are contemporary with the architecture.

Drinking, eating and entertainment

Cologne crams over three thousand pubs, bars and cafés into a relatively small area. Their ubiquitous feature is the city's unique beer, **Kölsch**. Light and aromatically bitter, it's served in a tall, thin glass (*Stange*) which holds only a fifth of a litre – hence its rather effete image among other German beer drinkers. Best places to try it are the **Brauhäuser**, brewery-owned beer halls which, although staffed by horribly matey waiters called *Köbes*, are definitely worth sampling, as they offer some of the cheapest **eating** in the city. Three of the *Brauhäuser* are very close to the Dom: *Alt-Köln* at Trankgasse 7–9, *Früh am Dom* at Am Hof 12–14 and *Brauhaus Sion* at Unter Taschenmacher 5. For a more authentic atmosphere and better food, you'd be better trying those a bit further away – *Päffgen*, at Heumarkt 62 and Friesenstr. 64; *Haus Töller* at Weyerstr. 96, or *Zur Malzmühle* at Heumarkt 6.

Cologne's **nightspots** are concentrated in four distinct quarters. Most obvious of these is the area around Gross St Martin in the Altstadt, which catches the tourists and businessmen, yet manages to create a distinctive atmosphere in places. *Papa Joe's Klimperkasten*, Alter Markt 50, is a deservedly popular Altstadt bar for traditional live jazz; there's a cosier, smaller, equally good version called *Papa Joe's Em Streckstrumpf* at Buttermarkt 37. *Kauri*, Auf dem Rothenberg 11, is a conveniently sited disco which plays a good selection of funk an blues. Down the road from the university, in the southwestern zone, the **Quartier Lateng** is more like the real thing as far as mingling with locals is concerned, even if it has lost its trendy edge. At Zülpicher Str. 25, *Crimson* is a lovely café with kitsch decor, good food and cocktails, and occasional live music. Students make up most of the clientele at *Gilberts Pinte*, Engelbertstr. 1, a bar with plenty of atmosphere. One of the most popular late-night café/bars is the *Peppermint Lounge*, Hochenstauffenring 23, springing into action around midnight, while *Weinhaus Kyffhäuser Keller*, Kyffhäuser Str. 47, is one of the best places in Cologne for a glass of wine. The **Südstadt**, or St Severin quarter, now has the most stylish bars and cafés, and the biggest crowds. *Climax*, Ubierring 18, and *Chlodwig-Eck*, Annostr. 1, are the leaders of the pack. The more relaxed **Belgisches Viertel**, just to the west of the centre, is nowhere near as packed or self-consciously trendy. Currently dominated by arty types, it's also a centre of the **gay scene** and has the most original **discos**; try *Petit Prince* at Hohenzollernring 90 and Brabanter Str. 15.

THE CARNIVAL

Though the **Carnival** season actually begins as early as November 11, the real business begins with **Weiberfastnacht** on the Thursday prior to the seventh Sunday before Easter. A ceremony at 10am in the Alter Markt leads to the official inauguration of the festival, with the mayor handing over the keys of the city to "Prinz Claus III", who assumes command for the duration. At 3pm there's the first of the great **processions** and in the evening the great series of **costume balls** begins – with singing and dancing in the streets and taverns as an authentic alternative. On the Saturday morning there's the **Funkenbiwak**, featuring the *Rote und Blaue Funken*, men dressed up in eighteenth-century military outfits who disobey every order. On Sunday the **Schull- und Veedleszög**, largely featuring children, forms a prelude to the more spectacular **Rosenmontagzug** (Rose Monday Parade). After this, the festival runs down, but there are numerous smaller parades in the suburbs on Shrove Tuesday, while the restaurants offer special fish menus on Ash Wednesday. The grandstand seats along the route are expensive for the Rose Monday Parade, which falls on March 6 in 2000, but good value on the Sunday.

Listings

Airlines British Airways, Marzellenstr. 1 (☎0221/135081); Lufthansa, An Hof 30 (☎0221/9254 9921).

Car rental Avis, Clemensstr. 29 (☎0221/234333); Europ-Car, Christophstr. 24 (☎0221/9126 010); Hertz, Bismarckstr. 19–21 (☎0221/515084); Condor, Wilhelm-Mauser-Str. 53 (☎0221/581055).

Embassies The nearest British and US embassies are in Bonn: Britain, Friedrich-Ebert-Allee 119 (☎0228/234061); US, Deichmanns Aue 29, Bad Godesberg (☎0228/3391).

Doctor ☎0221/19292.

Hitching Mitfahrzentrale, Saarstr. 22 (☎0221/19444); women-only branch at Moltkestr. 66 (☎0221/523120).

Post office The main office with poste restante is at Breite Str. 6–26.

Bonn

BONN, Cologne's neighbour, served as West Germany's capital from the time the country was set up in 1949 until the unification of 1990, when Berlin was restored to its former role. However, it has managed to preserve an important administrative role, remaining the seat of seven ministries and a host of other governmental bodies. It is also a notable historic town in its own right, chiefly renowned, prior to its elevation as capital, as the birthplace of Ludwig van Beethoven.

The City

The small **Altstadt** is now predominantly a pedestrianized shopping area centred on two spacious squares. The square to the east is named after the huge Romanesque **Münster**, whose central octagonal tower with its soaring spire is the city's most prominent landmark. Below the chancel is a fine crypt, while there's an impressively severe and monumental cloister adjoining the southern side. The pink Rococo **Rathaus** adds a touch of colour to the other square, the **Markt**, which still hosts a market each weekday.

A couple of minutes' walk north of here, at Bonngasse 20, is the **Beethoven-Haus** (Mon–Sat 10am–4/5pm, Sun 11am–4pm; DM8), one of the few old buildings in the centre to have escaped wartime devastation. Beethoven served his musical apprenticeship at the Electoral court of his home town, but left it for good at the age of 22, though this hasn't deterred Bonn from building up the best collection of memorabilia of its favourite son. The Altstadt's second dominant building is the Baroque **Schloss**, an enormously long construction which was formerly the seat of the Archbishop-Electors of Cologne and is now used by the University.

Branching out from the Schloss is the kilometre-long avenue of chestnut trees which leads to the suburb of **Poppelsdorf**, where a second Electoral palace is now occupied by University departments, the grounds serving as the Botanical Gardens (April–Sept Mon–Fri 9am–6pm, Sun 9am–1pm; Oct–March Mon–Fri 9am–4pm; free). Not far from Poppelsdorf's Schloss, at Sebastianstr. 182, is the **Robert-Schumann-Haus** (Mon & Fri 10am–noon & 4–7pm, Wed & Thurs 10am–noon & 3–6pm, Sun 11am–1pm; free), containing a collection of memorabilia of the Romantic composer, who spent the last two years of his life in Bonn confined to the sanatorium adjoining his house.

Bonn's **government quarter** can be reached either by following Reuterstrasse from Poppelsdorf, or by taking Adenauerallee from the Hofgarten: the distance is about the same. Saddled with its "temporary status", it was not custom built, but utilized a series of existing structures – the Villa Hammerschmidt and the Palais Schaumburg, both pompous buildings from the last century, are now the official residences of the Federal President and Chancellor respectively. Planned as a cultural accompaniment to the government quarter, the **Museumsmeile** (Museum Mile), on its western edge, features the **Alexander-Koenig-Museum** (Tues–Fri 9am–5pm, Sat 9am–12.30pm, Sun 9.30am–5pm; DM4) one of the best natural history collections in the country, and the **Kunstmuseum** (Tues & Thurs–Sun 10am–6pm, Wed 10am–9pm; DM5), the municipal gallery of modern art, which is especially strong in its representation of the Expressionists. To the rear is the most attention-seeking of the three new museums, the **Kunst- und Ausstellungshalle der Bundesrepublik Deutschland** (Tues & Wed 10am–9pm, Thurs–Sun 10am–7pm; DM10), a space-age arts centre for temporary exhibitions.

When Bonn was officially expanded in 1969, it annexed the old spa town of **Bad Godesberg** (U-Bahn #16 or #63, or main-line train) to the south. Rearing high over the town is the Godesberg, the most northerly of the great series of castles crowning promontories above the Rhine, built in the thirteenth and fourteenth centuries by the archbishops of Cologne and blown up in 1583. Today it's chiefly a hotel, but the cylindrical keep is still intact and can be ascended (April–Oct Wed–Sun 10am–6pm; DM0.50) for a panoramic view.

Practicalities

The **train station** lies in the middle of the city; close by is the **bus station**, whose local services, along with the **trams** (which become the U-Bahn in the city centre), form part of a system integrated with that of Cologne. As the attractions are well spaced out, it's better to buy a 24-hour pass which costs DM9. The **tourist office** (Mon–Fri 9am–6.30pm, Sat 9am–4pm, Sun 10am–2pm; ☎0228/773466) is at Münsterstr. 20, at the entrance to the shopping area.

The city's **youth hostel** is at Haager Weg 42 (☎0228/289970; ③) in the suburb of Venusberg, served by bus #621. Good-value **hotels** in the centre of Bonn include: *Virneburg*, Sandkaule 3a (0228/636366; ③), *Deutsches Haus*, Kasernenstr. 19 (☎0228/633777; ④); *Mozart*, Mozartstr. 1 (☎0228/659071; ④); and *Savoy*, Berliner Freiheit 17 (☎0228/725970; ⑤).

Bonn has a fairly eclectic range of places to **eat**. *Cassius Garten*, Maximilianstr. 28d, offers a mouth-watering choice of vegetarian food, which you pay for by weight, while *Don Quijote*, Oxfordstr. 18, is the most convenient of a surprising number of Spanish restaurants, and *Grand' Italia*, Bischofsplatz 1, is the best of the many Italian places. *Em Höttche*, Markt 4, is a good traditional Gaststätte in the handiest of locations; *Im Bären*, Acherstr. 1–3, is an excellent brewery-owned Gaststätte.

Most of the best **bars** are conveniently located in the Altstadt. Try *Brauhaus Bönnsch*, Sterntorbrücke 4, which produces a distinctive blond ale and does good-value meals, and *Zebulon*, Stockenstr. 19, a big favourite with arts students, particularly for breakfast. Night owls should head south for *Zur Kerze*, Königstr. 25: open till 5am, it's frequented by a mixed age range, and serves excellent (if pricey) Italianate dishes.

Aachen

Now a frontier post – it borders both Belgium and the Netherlands – **AACHEN** once played a far grander role. Around the late eighth century the city became the hub of the great empire of **Charlemagne**, a choice made partly for strategic reasons but also because of the presence of hot springs – exercising in these waters was one of the emperor's favourite pastimes.

Aachen's centre is ten minutes from the train station – down Bahnhofstrasse then left into Theaterstrasse. Although the surviving architectural legacy of Charlemagne is small, Aachen retains its crowning jewel, the former **Palace chapel**. Now the heart of the **Dom**, the original octagon had to be enlarged by adding the Gothic chancel to accommodate the number of pilgrims that poured in. Some original furnishings – including the great bronze doors – survive, but these are overshadowed by the additions of Charlemagne's successors. Adorning the main altar is the **Pala d'Oro**, an eleventh-century altar front embossed with scenes of the Passion. Behind, and of similar date, is the ambo, a pulpit of gold-plated copper covered with precious stones. Suspended from the dome by a mighty iron chain is a massive twelfth-century chandelier. At the end of the chancel, the gilded shrine of Charlemagne, finished in 1215 after fifty years' work, contains the remains of the emperor. In the gallery is the **imperial throne**, perhaps made for the coronation of Otto I, which initiated the tradition of emperors being crowned at Aachen. In order to see the throne you have to join a **guided tour** (hourly in summer, at least twice daily for rest of year; DM3).

The **Schatzkammer** (Mon 10am–1pm, Tues, Wed, Fri & Sat 10am–5/6pm, Thurs 10am–8pm, Sun 10.30am–5pm; DM5) is the richest treasury in northern Europe. Prominent is the late-tenth-century Lothair cross, studded with jewels and bearing a cameo of Augustus, and the Roman sarcophagus which served as Charlemagne's tomb for 400 years.

Charlemagne's palace once extended across the Katsch Hof, now lined with ugly modern buildings, to the site of the fourteenth-century **Rathaus**, which incorporates two of the palace's towers. Fronting the **Markt**, which boasts the finest of the medieval houses left in the city, its facade is lined with the figures of fifty Holy Roman Emperors. The glory of the interior (daily 10am–1pm & 2–5pm; DM3) is the much-restored **Kaisersaal**, repository of the crown jewels – in reproduction. The originals have been in Vienna since the early nineteenth century, when they were commandeered by the Habsburgs for their new role as emperors of Austria.

Practicalities

The **tourist office** occupies the Atrium Elisenbrunnen on Friedrich-Wilhelm-Platz (Mon–Fri 9am–6pm, Sat 9am–2pm; ☎0241/152011). The **youth hostel** is in a suburban park to the southwest, at Maria-Theresa-Allee 260 (☎0241/71101; ②); take bus #2 as far as Brüsseler Ring or Ronheide. Cheapish **hotels** can be found near the **train station**: try *Hesse*, Friedlandstr. 20 (☎0241/34047; ④); *Rösener*, Theaterstr. 62 (☎0241/407215; ④); or *Dura*, Lagerhausstr. 5 (☎0241/40315; ④).

Many of the best places to **eat** and **drink** are found in and around the Markt. A spiced gingerbread called *Printen* is the main local speciality, and the place to eat it is the old coffee house *Leo van den Daele* at Büchel 18. The most celebrated **pub** is *Postwagen*, built onto the end of the Rathaus, with a cheerful Baroque exterior and wonderful cramped rooms inside. For a livelier atmosphere, try *Goldener Schwan* for good-value lunches, or *Goldener Einhorn*, offering a huge menu of German, Italian and Greek dishes. Both places are on the Markt.

The **student quarter** centres on Pontstrasse, where *Tangente* turns from an elegant café into a lively bar at night. Aachen's top **disco** is *B9* at Blondelstr. 9 on the eastern side of town, where music ranges from heavy metal to Europop until 5am on Fridays and Saturdays.

Mainz

Situated by the confluence of the Rhine and Main, **MAINZ** developed in the eighth century, when Saint Boniface made it the main centre of the Church north of the Alps. Later, the
local archbishop came to be one of the most powerful princes in the Holy Roman Empire,
and further prestige came through **Johannes Gutenberg**, who revolutionized the art of
printing here. Since the Napoleonic period it has never managed to recover its former status, and its strategic location inevitably made it a prime target of World War II bombers.
Nonetheless, it's an agreeable mixture of old and new, and makes a good place to stay if
you're flying in or out of Frankfurt, as the airport lies on the S-Bahn line between the two
cities.

Rearing high above the centre of Mainz is the red sandstone **Dom**, crowded in by eighteenth-century houses. Choirs at both ends of the building indicate its status as an imperial
cathedral, with one area for the emperor and one for the clergy. A few years ago it celebrated its 1000th anniversary, but most of what can be seen today is twelfth-century Romanesque.
The solemn and spacious interior makes a very superior cemetery for the archbishops,
whose tombs form an unrivalled panorama of sculpture from the thirteenth century to the
nineteenth. The **Diocesan Museum** (Mon–Wed & Fri 10am–4pm, Thurs 10am–5pm, Sat
10am–2pm; free), off the cloisters, houses the best sculptures of all.

On Tuesday, Friday and Saturday mornings the spacious **Markt**, with its riotously colourful fountain, is packed with market stalls and is unmissable. Dominating the adjoining
Liebfrauenplatz, the resplendent pink Haus zum Romischen Kaiser houses the offices of the
Gutenberg Museum (Tues–Sat 10am–6pm, Sun 10am–1pm; DM5, free Sun) – the actual
displays are in a modern extension behind. It's a fitting tribute to one of the greatest inven-
tors of all time, whose pioneering development of moveable type led to the mass-scale production of books. In 1978, the museum acquired the last Gutenberg **Bible** still in private
hands – made in the 1450s, it's one of only forty-odd surviving examples.

Despite war damage, the centre of Mainz contains many fine old streets and squares, such
as the magnificent **Knebelscher Hof** north of the Dom, and Kirschgarten and
Augustinerstrasse to the south. Just off the end of Augustinerstrasse is the sumptuous
church of **St Ignaz**, in front of which a monumental *Crucifixion* by Hans Backoffen stands
over his own tomb, which is even more imposing than those he had made for the archbishops. This marks the end of the historic quarter – beyond is the largest red-light district in the
Frankfurt conurbation.

Across Schöfferstrasse from the Dom, Ludwigstrasse runs to Schillerplatz and
Schillerstrasse, both lined with Renaissance and Baroque palaces. Up the hill by Gaustrasse
is the Gothic **St Stephan** (daily 10am–noon & 2–5pm), whose priest persuaded Marc Chagall
to make a series of stained-glass windows. Symbolizing the reconciliation between France
and Germany, Christian and Jew, the nine windows were finished in November 1984, a few
months before Chagall's death. Down Grosse Bleiche – which runs from the end of
Schillerstrasse to the river – are the old imperial stables, now home of the **Landesmuseum**
(Tues 10am–8pm, Wed–Sun 10am–5pm; DM5, free Sat). The outstanding archeology department includes a hall of Roman sculptural remains, dominated by the Jupitersäule, the most
important Roman triumphal column in Germany.

Further along is the **Schloss**, the enormous former palace of the Archbishop-Electors, a
superbly swaggering Renaissance building. The interior had to be completely rebuilt after
the war, and now contains the **Römisch-Germanisches Museum** (Tues–Sun 10am–6pm;
free), a confusing mix of original antiquities and copies.

Practicalities

The **train station** is northwest of the city centre, while the **tourist office** (Mon–Fri
9am–6pm, Sat 9am–1pm; ☎06131/286210) is in the Brückenturm am Rathaus at the corner
of Rheinstrasse. Near the station are many of the least expensive **hotels** – though even these
tend to charge upwards of DM100 for a double. Cheaper and with a better location very near

the Dom is *Stadt Coblenz*, at Rheinstr. 49 (☎06131/227602; ④). Alternatively, there's the **youth hostel** (☎06131/85332; ②), situated in the wooded heights of Am Fort Weisenau and reached by buses #1 and #22.

Mainz boasts more vineyards than any other German city, and you don't need to stray far from the Dom if you fancy a **wine** crawl. Some *Weinstuben* are open in the evenings only, such as the oldest, *Alt Deutsche Weinstube*, Liebfrauenplatz 7, which offers cheap daily dishes. Even better food is available at *Weinhaus Schreiner*, at Rheinstr. 38. Though Mainz is a wine rather than a **beer** city, it has the excellent brewery-owned *Gaststätte zum Salvator* at Grosse Langgasse 4. The hottest **nightspot** is *Terminus*, at Industriestr. 13, a former warehouse that now attracts punters from afar.

The Rhine gorge

North of Mainz, the Rhine bends westwards and continues its hitherto stately but undramatic journey – then suddenly, at **Bingen**, the river widens and swings north into the spectacular 80km **Rhine gorge**. This waterway may have become one of Europe's major tourist magnets, but the pleasure steamers are still outnumbered by commercial barges – a reminder of the river's crucial role in the German economy.

In summer, inexpensive **accommodation** is scarce and heavily booked. Spring and autumn are undoubtedly the best times to visit, and you could easily spend several days meandering. Rail and road lines lie on each side of the river and, although there are no bridges between Bingen and Koblenz, there are fairly frequent ferries, enabling you to hop from one side of the river to the other. However, it's undeniably most fun by **boat**. River cruises from Mainz depart from in front of the **Rathaus**, where there's also a K-D Line office (☎06131/24511). Fares aren't cheap but day returns sometimes work out cheaper than one-way tickets – Mainz to St Goar return costs DM54.80; both Eurail and EuroDomino train passes are valid (but not InterRail).

Bacharach and Kaub

At **BACHARACH**, 10km downstream from Bingen, the chunky castle of **Burg Stahleck** now houses the local **youth hostel** (☎06743/1266; ②), while moderately priced **hotels** are clustered in Blücherstrasse, Langstrasse and Oberstrasse. The local **campsite** is at Strandbadweg. From **KAUB**, a few kilometres on, you get a great view of the **Pfalz**, a white-walled toll fortress standing on a mid-river island which has become a famous Rhineland symbol (Tues–Sun 9am–1pm & 2–5/6pm; DM7 including ferry). This stronghold enabled the lords of **Burg Gutenfels** above Kaub to extract a toll from passing ships until well into the nineteenth century. Burg Gutenfels as you see it today is a late-nineteenth-century rebuild of the original thirteenth-century castle. There are **camping** facilities at *Am Elsleinband* on Blücherstrasse.

The Lorelei and Burg Rheinfels

On the way towards **ST GOARSHAUSEN** you'll pass the **Lorelei**, the famous outcrop of rock where the legendary siren of the Rhine lured passing sailors to watery graves. The rock is over-hyped, but there are outstanding views from the top; apart from a viewing platform, the summit has a **campsite**.

There's a regular ferry that crosses from St Goarshausen to the prettier and more touristy **ST GOAR**, over which looms the enormous **Burg Rheinfels** (daily 9am–5/6pm; DM5), that was founded back in 1245 by Count Dieter von Katzenelnbogen to secure his toll-collecting racket. St Goar features a **youth hostel** at Bismarckweg 17 (☎06741/388; ②), just outside the town centre, and has a number of reasonable hotels, including *Zur Post*, Bahnhofstr. 3 (☎06741/339; ③), and *Germania*, Heerstr. 47 (☎06741/1610; ③). Camping facilities can be found at Friedenau, Gründelbachstr. 103 (☎06741/368) and the *Loreleyblick* site, An der Loreley 29–39 (☎06741/2066).

Koblenz

Packed during the tourist season and deserted when it's over, **KOBLENZ** is a town that polarizes opinion – some enjoy the relaxed and faded charm that is typical of the place, while others find it smug and boring. The Rhine and Mosel meet here, and nearby the Lahn flows in from the east, so the town lies close to the four scenic regions separated by these rivers – the Eifel, Hunsrück, Westerwald and Taunus – and thus makes an ideal touring base.

Central Koblenz is at its best in the area around the confluence at **Deutsches Eck**, close to which stands the fine Romanesque church of **St Kastor**. However, the most commanding sights are to be found across the Rhine in Ehrenbreitstein, where the Baroque **Residenz** of the Electors of Trier is overshadowed by the **Festung**. One of the largest fortresses in the world, it is now home to the **Landesmuseum** (March to mid-Nov daily 9am–12.30pm & 1–5pm; DM3) and to one of the best and most popular **youth hostels** in Germany (☎0261/73737; ②, bus #8, #9, #10). Koblenz's main **tourist office** (May–Sept Mon–Fri 9am–8pm, Sat & Sun 10am–8pm; rest of year shorter and erratic hours; ☎0261/31304) is located opposite the **train station** and **bus station**, which are a little to the southwest of the centre. **Hotel rooms** are reasonably priced, the cheapest being in Ehrenbreitstein, where you'll find *Zur Kaul*, Helffensteinstr. 64 (☎02621/75256; ③), and *Mäckler*, Helffensteinstr. 63–65 (☎02621/73725; ③). Slightly more expensive, is *Jan van Werth* at Van-Werth-Str. 9, between the station and the centre (☎0261/36500; ④). The **campsite** is at Lützel, directly opposite Deutsches Eck, where the Mosel and Rhine join (April to mid-Oct); a ferry crosses the Mosel here in summer, while another crosses the Rhine further south.

Trier

The oldest city in Germany, **TRIER** was once the capital of the Western Roman Empire, and residence of the Emperor Constantine. Nowadays, it has the less exalted role of regional centre for the upper Mosel valley, its relaxed air a world away from the status it formerly held. Despite a turbulent history, an amazing amount of the city's past has been preserved, in particular the most impressive group of **Roman monuments** north of the Alps (daily: 9am–4/6pm; Dec opens 10am; Barbarathermen closed Dec and Mon all year; ticket for individual sites DM4; ticket for all sites DM9).

The City

The centre of modern Trier corresponds roughly to the Roman city and can easily be covered on foot. From the **train station**, it's a few minutes' walk down Theodor-Heuss-Allee to the **Porta Nigra**, northern gateway to Roman Trier, and the biggest and best-preserved city gate of its period in the world. The Porta Nigra probably owes its survival to the fact that Saint Simeon chose the east tower as his refuge from the world. After his death in 1035, the gate was made into a church in his honour; the Romanesque choir and some Rococo carvings remain from post-Roman embellishments. Next door is the **Simeonstift**, a monastery built in 1037 as another memorial to Simeon; its Brunnenhof is the oldest monastery courtyard in Germany. The neighbouring **Städtisches Museum** (Easter–Oct daily 9am–5pm; rest of year Tues–Fri 9am–5pm, Sat & Sun 9am–1pm; DM3) has a big selection of art from the fourteenth century to the twentieth, with the emphasis on devotional work.

From the Porta Nigra, Simeonstrasse runs down to the **Hauptmarkt**, roughly following the route of an old Roman street. Today it's a busy pedestrian shopping area, with stalls selling fruit and flowers, and gangs of kids and punks milling around. The finest of the Hauptmarkt's medieval monuments is the thirteenth-century **Dreikönigshaus**, once a secure home in uncertain times for a rich merchant family. At the southern end of the Hauptmarkt a Baroque portal leads to the Gothic **St Gangolf**, built by the burghers of Trier in an attempt to aggravate the archbishops, whose political power they resented.

If you go up Sternstr. from the Hauptmarkt you come to the magnificent Romanesque **Dom**, standing where Constantine had a huge church built in 325. The present building was started in 1030, and the facade has not changed significantly since then. Inside, the relative austerity is enlivened by devotional and decorative features added through the centuries. The **Schatzkammer** (Mon–Sat 10am–noon & 2–4/5pm, Sun 2–4/5pm; DM2) has many examples of the work of local goldsmiths, notably a tenth-century portable altar. Facing the north side of the Dom on Windstrasse is the **Bischöfliches Museum** (Mon–Sat 9am–1pm & 2–5pm, Sun 1–5pm; DM2) with a fourth-century ceiling painting from the palace which preceded the Dom and some important sculptures, including most of the original statues from the facade of the Liebfrauenkirche.

From the cloisters there's a good view of the ensemble of the Dom and the adjacent **Liebfrauenkirche**, one of Germany's first Gothic churches. From here, Liebfrauenstrasse goes past the ritzy Palais Kesselstadt to the **Konstantinbasilika**. Built as Constantine's throne hall, its dimensions are awe-inspiring: 30m high and 75m long, it has no pillars or buttresses and is completely self-supporting. It became a church for the local Protestant community in the nineteenth century, a role it still fills. Next door, the **Rokoko-Palais der Kurfürsten** was built in 1756 for an archbishop who felt that the adjoining old Schloss wasn't good enough for him. Its shocking pink facade overlooks the Palastgarten, setting for the **Landesmuseum** (Tues–Fri 9.30am–5pm, Sat & Sun 10.30am–5pm; DM5). Easily the best of Trier's museums, its collection of Roman relics brings to life the sophistication and complexity of Roman civilization; prize exhibit is the famous *Neumagener Weinschiff*, a Roman sculpture of a wine ship.

At the southern end of the gardens are the **Kaiserthermen**, once one of the largest bath complexes in the Roman world. The extensive underground heating system has survived, and you can walk around the service channels and passages. From the Kaiserthermen the route to the **Amphitheatre** is well signposted. The oldest of Trier's surviving Roman buildings, it was built around 100 AD and had a capacity of 20,000. You can inspect some of the animal cages and take a look under the arena, which has an elaborate drainage system cut into its slate base.

If you go back towards the town centre down Olewiger Strasse and then head down Südallee, you'll eventually come to the **Barbarathermen**, Trier's second set of Roman baths. Built in the second century, they look more like Roman ruins should – piles of rock, vaguely defined foundations and ruined walls. Midway between the baths and the Hauptmarkt, at Brückenstrasse 10, the **Karl-Marx-Haus** (April–Oct Mon 1–6pm, Tues–Sun 10am–6pm; Nov–March Mon 3–6pm, Tues–Sun 10am–1pm & 3–6pm; DM3) explicates the life and work of Trier's most influential son in detail that verges on the excruciating.

Practicalities

Trier's **tourist office** is at An der Porta Nigra (Mon–Sat 9am–5/6.30pm, Sun 9am–1/3.30pm; ☎0651/978080). The **youth hostel** is at An der Jugendherberge 4 (☎0651/146620; ②) on the banks of the Mosel. Central **hotels** are *Kolpinghaus*, Dietrichstr. 42 (☎0651/975250; ②), *Zur Glocke*, Glockenstr. 12 (☎0651/73109; ③), and there's a **campsite** on the western bank of the Mosel at Luxemburger Str. 81. There are plenty of places where you can get good and inexpensive **food**, thanks to the student population. The best bet is *Astarix*, Karl-Marx-Str. 11, a big, relaxed student bar which stays open until 2am at weekends. Other student haunts are to be found in the Viehmarktplatz area. *Abwärts* on Judengasse is a popular cellar bar-cum-Irish **pub**. On Pferdemarkt are *Blaues Blut*, where the "punk's not dead" crew congregate, and *Zapotex*, hangout of Trier's fashion victims.

Worms

Situated about 40km south of Mainz, **WORMS** achieved immense wealth during the Middle Ages and for a while was a venue for the Imperial Parliament. Terribly damaged in the Napoleonic Wars and the last war, it is now a medium-sized industrial town whose monuments stand out like oases amid modern rebuilding.

Foremost among the city's glories is the huge Romanesque **Dom**, with its distinctive pair of domes and four corner towers. These days the rich Gothic **Südportal** is the main entrance, but look out also for the **Kaiserportal**, on the north side of the building. As you enter the church, the sight of Balthasar Neumann's huge **high altar** – a tornado of technicolour marble and gilt – provokes a gasp. In marked contrast is the dank and eerie vault, where eight sinister sarcophagi sit in oppressive silence.

For over a millennium Worms had a large and influential Jewish population – so influential, in fact, that the city was long known as "Little Jerusalem". It all came to an end with the Nazis: in 1933 there were 1100 Jews in Worms, by 1945 all were either dead or had fled the country. The most famous and poignant reminder of the community is the **Heiliger Sand**, a short distance southwest of the Dom; the oldest Jewish cemetery in Europe, its crooked gravestones date as far back as 1076. To the southeast of the cemetery is the **Andreasstift**, comprising a Romanesque church and cloisters which now house the **Museum der Stadt Worms** (Tues–Sun 10am–5pm; DM4). The most significant exhibits are in the Lutherzimmer, which includes some of Luther's original writings.

The **Heylshofgarten**, just to the north of the Dom, marks the site of the now-vanished imperial palace, where an Imperial Diet was convoked in 1521 by Emperor Charles V; Luther refused to renounce his views there, and was forced into exile, setting the Reformation in motion. Within the park is the **Kunsthaus Heylshof** (closed for restoration in 1999; previously May–Sept Tues–Sat 9am–5pm; Oct–April Tues–Sat 2–4pm, Sun 10am–noon & 2–4pm; DM3), a fine collection of paintings, porcelain, glassware and ceramics. Beyond here lies Lutherplatz, where you'll find the **Lutherdenkmal**, a gang of bronze figures with Luther at the centre. Keep straight on and you'll come to the Romanesque **Martinskirche**; supposedly Saint Martin was once imprisoned in a dungeon underneath. Further north, around Judengasse, is the site of the old Jewish quarter. Here you'll find the Romanesque **Alte Synagoge** (daily 10am–noon & 2–4/5pm; free), reinaugurated in 1961 following its destruction on *Kristallnacht*. In the Raschi-Haus, a former school and meeting house, is the **Judaica Museum** (Tues–Sun 10am–noon & 2–5pm; DM2), with an extensive collection detailing the history of the Jews of Worms.

Practicalities

Worms' **tourist office** is at Neumarkt 14 (Mon–Fri 9am–6pm; April–Oct also Sat 9am–noon; ☎06241/25045). There's a **youth hostel** between the Dom and the Andreasstift at Dechaneigasse 1 (☎06241/25780; ②). Among the **hotels** in the town centre, try *Weinhaus Weis*, Färbergasse 19 (☎06241/23500; ③) or *Boos*, Mainzer Str. 5 (☎06241/947639; ④). **Camping** facilities are on the east bank of the Rhine near the Nibelungenbrücke. For typically hearty German **food**, head for *Kolb's Biergarten* or *Hagenbräu*, side-by-side on the west bank of the Rhine by the Nibelungenbrücke. There are also lively hangouts on Judengasse, such as the trendy *Café Jux*, and the *Kutscherschänke* **bar**.

Speyer

SPEYER is an outstanding little city, well worth a day of anyone's time. Chief attraction is its Dom, one of the largest and finest Romanesque buildings in Germany. Speyer can be reached by train from Heidelberg or from Worms by changing at Ludwigshafen. From the **train station**, head down Bahnhofstrasse and turn left into Maximilianstrasse, which leads straight to the centre.

The **Dom** was built in the mid-eleventh century and modified a generation later – the most significant alteration, the stone vault, was higher than any previously built. But even finer than the vaulting is the massive **crypt** – containing eight royal tombs, it has an almost Middle Eastern feel with its sandstone pillars and slabbed floor. Just to the south of the Dom, on Domplatz, is the palatial triple-towered **Historisches Museum der Pfalz** (Tues & Thurs–Sun 10am–6pm, Wed 10am–8pm; DM8). It includes objects found in the Dom's imperial graves, but the most celebrated exhibit is the Bronze Age *Golden Hat of Schifferstadt*, found in a nearby town. The same building also houses the **Weinmuseum**, featuring every conceivable kind of wine-related object and what is claimed to be the oldest bottle of wine in the world, dating from 300 AD. Not far from the museum, down Judengasse, is the **Judenbad**, a twelfth-century Jewish ritual bathhouse which is the oldest and best-preserved example in Germany (closed for restoration in 1999; previously daily April–Oct 10am–noon & 2–5pm; DM1.50).

The **tourist office** is at Maximilianstr. 11 (Mon–Fri 9am–5pm, Sat 10am–noon; ☎06232/14392). The **youth hostel** is at Leinpfad (☎06232/75380; ②), on the Rhine south of the centre, while the cheapest conveniently located **hotel** is *Zur Grünen Au*, Grüner Winkel 28 (☎06232/72196; ③). For *Kaffee und Küchen* try *Café-Konditorei Schumacher* at Wormser Str. 23; for something more substantial, go to the atmospheric old *Wirtschaft zum Alten Engel*, Mühlturmstr. 27.

Frankfurt

Straddling the Main just before it meets the Rhine, **FRANKFURT** is a city with two faces. On the one hand it's the cut-throat financial capital of Germany, with its fulcrum in the Westend district, and on the other it's a civilized place which spends more per year on the arts than any other city in Europe. In fact, Frankfurt is a thriving recreational centre for the whole of Hesse, with a good selection of theatres and galleries, and an even better range of museums. Over half of the city, including almost all of the centre, was destroyed during the war and the rebuilders opted for innovation rather than restoration. The result is a skyline that smacks more of Chicago than of Germany.

Arrival and information

Frankfurt **airport**, one of the world's busiest, is a major point of entry into Germany, and there are regular rail links between the airport and most west German cities. Trains leave the airport approximately every ten minutes for the **train station**, from where there are even more comprehensive services. The airport is also linked to the train station by two S-Bahn lines, run by the regional transport company (RMV), which is also responsible for **bus**, **tram** and **U-Bahn** services. **Ticket** prices vary according to the time of travel, making it better to invest in the DM8 24-hour ticket. Better still is the **Frankfurt Card**, which is available from tourist offices for DM19 and allows travel throughout Frankfurt for two days, plus reduced entry charges to most museums (a one-day version costing DM12 is also available). From the train station you can walk to the centre in fifteen minutes, or take tram #11.

Frankfurt has two main **tourist offices**: one in the train station (Mon–Fri 8am–9pm, Sat & Sun 9am–6pm; ☎069/2123 8849), and another at Römerberg 27 (Mon–Fri 9.30am–5.30pm, Sat & Sun 10am–4pm; ☎069/2123 8708). A free listings magazine, *Fritz*, is available at both.

Accommodation

Accommodation is pricey, thanks to the expense-account clientele. Best budget bet is the **youth hostel** at Deutschherrnufer 12 (☎069/619 058; ②), in Sachsenhausen, reached by bus #46 from the train station. As for cheap **hotels**, the majority of only a few reasonably priced options are in the sleazy environs of the train station, close to the Kaiserstrasse red-light district. The pick of the inexpensive hotels are listed below.

Atlas, Zimmerweg 1 (☎069/723946). Within walking distance of the station but away from the sleazier streets. ④.

Backer, Mendelssohnstr. 92 (☎069/747992). Pleasant place close to the University. U-Bahn to Westend or tram #19. ③.

Bruns, Mendelssohnstr. 42 (☎069/748896). Another option on the same street as the *Backer*. ③.

Goldener Stern, Karlsruher Str. 8 (☎069/233309). Acceptable place between the train station and the water. Prices may rise following renovation. ③.

Life, Weserstr. 12 (☎069/231014). Basic hotel near the station. ④.

The City

Almost all of the city's main sights lie within the bounds of the old city walls, which have now been transformed into a stretch of narrow parkland describing an approximate semicircle; from here it's an easy matter to cross the Main into Sachsenhausen, where most of the museums are located. As good a point as any to begin your explorations in the old city is the **Römerberg**, the historical and, roughly speaking, geographical centre of the city. Charlemagne built his fort on this low hill to protect the ford which gave Frankfurt its name – *Frankonovurd* (Ford of the Franks). At the start of this century the Römerberg was still the heart of the city, and an essentially medieval quarter. All this came to an end in March 1944 when two massive air raids flattened the historic core.

The most significant survivor was the thirteenth-century St Bartholomäus or **Dom**, and even that emerged with only its main walls intact. Before the construction of the skyscrapers it was the tallest building in the city, as befitted the venue for the election and coronation of the Holy Roman Emperors. Inside, to the right of the choir, is the restored **Wahlkapelle**, where the seven Electors used to make their final choice as to who would become emperor. For a fabulous panorama, climb the 95-metre tower (April–Oct daily 9am–1pm & 2.30–6pm; DM3).

Slightly to the north, in Domstrasse, looms the **Museum für Moderne Kunst** (Tues & Thurs–Sun 10am–5pm, Wed 10am–8pm; DM7, free Wed), its collection featuring most of the major names in postwar American and German art, with Joseph Beuys inevitably prominent. At the opposite end of the Römerberg is the building that gave the area its name – the **Römer**, formerly the Rathaus. Its distinctive facade, with its triple-stepped gables, fronts the **Römerplatz** market square, on whose southern side stands the former court chapel, the **Nikolaikirche**. The interior is refreshingly restrained, a real refuge from the noise and rampant commercialism of the Römerplatz; though the church was given a Gothic face-lift, the lines of the original Romanesque structure are visible on the inside.

For a long time the area between the Römer and the Dom remained little more than an ugly hole in the middle of the city. In 1978 the decision was taken to build replicas of some of the medieval buildings that had originally occupied the site, and fill the remaining space with an ultramodern complex. At its heart is the **Schirn Kunsthalle**, a general-purpose cultural centre known to the locals as the "Federal Bowling Alley".

The **Saalhof**, an amalgamation of imperial buildings now housing the **Historisches Museum**, is nearby on Mainkai, overlooking the river. Its twelfth-century chapel is all that remains of the old palace complex, which grew up in the Middle Ages. The museum (Tues & Thurs–Sat 10am–5pm, Wed 10am–8pm; DM5, free Wed) contains an extensive local-history collection, with an eye-opening section on the devastation caused by the bombing.

A short distance to the west, on Untermainkai, is the **Karmeliterkloster** (Tues & Thurs–Sun 11am–5pm, Wed 11am–8pm; DM3, free Wed), where Jerg Ratgeb's 80-metre-long fresco cycle of the life of Jesus occupies the cloister. The southern part of the complex houses the **Museum für Vor- und Frühgeschichte** (Tues & Thurs–Sun 10am–5pm, Wed 10am–8pm; DM5, free Wed), a collection devoted to early and prehistory. Just north of here, at Grosser Hirschgraben 23, is the **Goethehaus und Museum** (Mon–Sat 9am–4/6pm, Sun 10am–1pm; DM4), the house where Goethe was born and raised. It has been made to look as much as possible like it did when Goethe lived here, and there are even a few objects which somehow survived the war.

A couple of minutes away on the Liebfrauenberg is the fifteenth-century **Liebfrauenkirche** – look inside for the unusual altar, a huge alabaster and gilt affair which sits well in the dusky pink interior. A little to the northwest of the Hauptwache (originally a police station) is the **Börse**, Frankfurt's stock exchange. Appropriately enough, two of the most expensive shopping streets in the city are just around the corner. **Goethestrasse** is Frankfurt's Bond Street, all expensive jewellers and designer clothes shops, while **Grosse Bockenheimer Strasse** is home to upmarket delicatessens and smarter restaurants.

SACHSENHAUSEN

If you want to escape from the centre of Frankfurt, or have a laid-back evening out, then head for **Sachsenhausen**, the city-within-a-city on the south bank of the Main. Most people go here to eat, drink and be merry in the restaurants and bars of Alt Sachsenhausen, the network of streets around Affentorplatz, where the main attractions are the apple wine (*Ebelwei*) houses. There's entertainment of a different sort to be had on the **Museumsufer** (or Schaumainkai), which runs between the Eiserner Steg and the Friedensbrücke.

Schaumainkai's biggest draw is the **Städel** located at no. 63 (Tues & Fri–Sun 10am–5pm, Wed 10am–8pm; DM8, free Wed), one of the most comprehensive art galleries in Europe. The layout begins on the top floor, where virtually every big name in German art is represented: Dürer, Grünewald, both Holbeins, Cranach and Altdorfer. Van Eyck's *Lucca Madonna* stands out amid the gallery's wealth of early Netherlandish paintings, while another Madonna, an ethereal image by Fra Angelico, dominates the Italian section. Pride of place among the seventeenth-century paintings goes to Frankfurt's own Adam Elsheimer's *Altarpiece of the Cross*. Poussin, Claude and Rubens (all admirers of Elsheimer) are on display in the next section, which also includes Rembrandt's *Blinding of Samson* and a glorious Vermeer. Paintings from the late eighteenth century onwards occupy the first floor. Big French names such as Courbet, Degas and Monet appear, but German artists predominate – look out for Johann Heinrich Tischbein's celebrated portrayal of *Goethe in the Roman Campagna*.

The **Museum für Kunsthandwerk**, down at no. 15 (same times; DM6, free Wed), has a huge collection of applied art, divided into four sections: European, featuring a unique collection of furniture models, glassware and ceramics; Islamic, with some fine carpets; Far Eastern, with lots of jade and lacquer work plus a liberal sprinkling of porcelain and sculptures; and finally a section devoted to books and writing. Further along at no. 29, the **Museum für Völkerkunde** (same times; DM4, free Wed) is a small ethnographical museum with an extensive collection of masks and totems from all over the world. The **Deutsches Filmmuseum**, no. 41 (same times; DM5, free Wed), is Germany's biggest and best film museum, with its own cinema and a good little café in the basement. The **Deutsches Architekturmuseum**, no. 43 (same times; DM8, free Wed), is installed in a self-consciously avant-garde conversion of a nineteenth-century villa; the highpoint is the "house within a house" which dominates the museum like an oversized dolls' house. Finally, the **Liebieghaus**, no. 71 (same times; DM5, free Wed), is a step-by-step guide to the history of sculpture, going back to the third millennium BC.

Eating, drinking and nightlife

Not surprisingly, Frankfurt has a wealth of gastronomic possibilities, from the ultratrendy joints found in the Westend to the cheapo Italian **restaurants** of Bockenheim, the working-class/boho/student quarter. Whether it's vegan breakfast or Japanese afternoon tea you're after, you'll be able to find it somewhere in the city – though you might have to travel some distance to get it. Frankfurt's **nightlife** is pretty eclectic, too. Perhaps its best-known locale is Kleine Bockenheimer Strasse, aka Jazzgasse (Jazz Alley), the centre of Frankfurt's jazz scene.

CAFÉ/BARS AND CAFÉS

Café Bar, Schweizer Str. 14. The trendiest café in Sachsenhausen, all black and mirrored decor with a posey clientele.

Café Laumer, Bockenheimer Landstr. 67. One of Frankfurt's oldest cafés, halfway up the Westend's main thoroughfare.

RESTAURANTS

Atschel, Wallstr. 7/Abstgäschen. One of the ubiquitous Alsace speciality places in Sachsenhausen. Fish dishes and apple wine. Closed Mon.

Aubergine, Alte Gasse 14. Good food, good service; reasonable prices by central Frankfurt standards.

Iwase, Vibeler Str. 31. Reasonably priced Japanese, with seating at the counter or the few tables. Tues–Sun 6.30–10.30pm.

Knoblauch, Staufenstr. 39. Friendly, intimate little place where everything comes liberally laced with garlic.

Die Leiter, Kaiserhofstr. 11. Classy yet not too expensive. Pavement tables in the summer.

Nibelungenschänke, Nibelungenallee 55. Typical Greek food at very reasonable prices. The clientele tends to be young and the place is usually open until 1am. U-Bahn line #55 to Nibelungenallee.

Rosa, Grüneburgweg 25. Good food for Westend types not so keen on conspicuous consumption. Closed weekends.

Tse Yang, Kaiserstr. 67. One of several good Chinese restaurants in the vicinity of the train station.

PUBS, WINE CELLARS AND APPLE WINE TAVERNS

Club Voltaire, Kleine Hochstr. 5. Tasty, good food with a Spanish bias, and a fairly eclectic clientele including political activists, artists and gays. One of the best-established meeting places in Frankfurt.

Wagner, Schweizer Str. 71. A good tavern, with a lively clientele ranging from young to middle-aged. Frequently packed out.

Haus Wertheym, Fahrtor 1. A medieval inn on the Römerberg with *Bockbier*, traditional food and a friendly atmosphere. Closed Tues.

Zum Eichkatzerl, Dreieichstr. 29. A traditional Sachsenhausen apple wine tavern with a very popular restaurant. Closed Wed and first Thurs of every month.

MUSIC AND DISCOS

Brotfabrik, Bachmannstr. 2–4. One of the most innovative venues in the city, featuring live and disco music from all over the world, with salsa, African and Asian sounds particularly popular. Also has a café and a Spanish restaurant.

Jazzkeller, Kleine Bockenheimer Str. 18a. This atmospheric cellar is Frankfurt's premier jazz venue. Open Tues–Sun 9pm–3am.

Sinkkasten, Brönnerstr. 5. This place has a pool room, cabaret stage, disco and, most importantly, a concert hall as a venue for everything from jazz to avant-garde and indie. Open daily 9pm–2am.

Listings

Airlines Air Canada, Friedensstr. 11 (☎069/27115 111); Air New Zealand, Friedrichstr. 10 (☎069/9714 030); British Airways, Am Flughafen (☎069/698150); Lufthansa, Am Hauptbahnhof 2 (☎069/2554 511).

Consulates Britain, Bockenheimer Landstr. 42 (☎069/1700 020); US, Siesmayerstr. 21 (☎069/75350).

Hitching Mitfahrzentrale at Baseler Platz 7 (☎069/236444).

Post office The main post office is at Zeil 110.

Women's centre Am Weingarten 25 (☎069/707 8361).

Marburg

About 80km to the north of Frankfurt, **MARBURG**, the cradle of Hesse and its original capital, clusters up the slopes of the Lahn valley in a maze of narrow streets and medieval buildings, crowned by an impressive castle. Primarily a university town, Marburg has a relaxed and lively atmosphere, and has been touched by war less than almost any other city in the country.

The most important building is the **Elisabethkirche** (April–Oct Mon–Sat 9am–5/6pm, Sun 12.30–5/6pm; Nov–March Mon–Sat 10am–4pm, Sun 12.30–4pm; DM3), reached from the train station simply by following Bahnhofstrasse. The first Gothic church in Germany, it was erected to house the remains of St Elisabeth, who died here in 1231. Inside, the church is like a museum of German religious art, full of statues and frescoes; Elisabeth's thirteenth-century shrine is in the sacristy. From the Elisabethkirche, the Steinweg, a stepped street hemmed in by half-timbered buildings, leads up to the **Marktplatz**, the centre of the **Altstadt**. During term time the square is the focal point of Marburg's nightlife, but out of term it's very peaceful. The **Rathaus'** staircase tower features a statue of Elisabeth, holding a heraldic figure, said to be the arms of the count who financed the building.

From the Marktplatz make your way up Rittergasse to the thirteenth-century **Marienkirche**, just past which a flight of steps rises to the **Schloss**, towering 102 metres above the Lahn (Tues–Sun 10/11am–5/6pm; DM3). The present structure was begun by Sophie, the daughter of St Elisabeth, but the bulk of what can be seen today dates from the fifteenth and sixteenth centuries. Look out for the Gothic **Schlosskapelle** and the **Rittersaal**, the largest secular Gothic hall in Germany.

Marburg's **train station** is on the right bank of the Lahn at the northern end of town, and the **tourist office** is immediately outside the station (April–Sept Mon–Fri 9am–6pm, Sat 9.30am–1pm; rest of year Mon–Fri 9am–6pm; ☎06421/201262). The **youth hostel** is at Jahnstr. 1 (☎06421/23461; ②), a little to the south of the Altstadt. The central **hotels** are a little on the pricey side – *Gästehaus Müller*, Deutschhausstr. 29 (☎06421/65659; ④), is perhaps the best value. **Camping** facilities are over the river at Am Trojedamm. Quite a few little **pubs** are to be found on Hirschberg, the street leading off from the Marktplatz, and you could also try your luck on Untergasse.

SOUTHERN GERMANY

Theodor Heuss, the first Federal President, saw **Baden-Württemberg** as "the model of German possibilities", and it has remained the most prosperous part of the country. Weak in natural resources, the area has had to rely on ingenuity; the motor car was invented here in the late nineteenth century, and the region has stayed at the forefront of world technology ever since. Baden-Württemberg's largest city, **Stuttgart**, is the home of Mercedes and Porsche, and though extensively damaged in World War II it has plenty of good points. The historical centre of **Freiburg im Breisgau** was also bombed, but its Münster – one of Germany's greatest buildings – was spared. Germany's most famous university city, **Heidelberg**, was hardly touched, and the spa resort of **Baden-Baden** remains wonderfully evocative of its nineteenth-century heyday as the playground of Europe's aristocracy. The scenery of the province is wonderful too: its western and southern boundaries are defined by the Rhine and its bulge into Germany's largest lake, the **Bodensee** (Lake Constance); within the curve of the river lies the **Black Forest**, source of another of the continent's principal waterways, the Danube.

Bavaria (Bayern) is the home of all the German clichés: beer-swilling Lederhosen-clad men, sausage dogs, sauerkraut and wurst. But that's only a small part of the picture, and almost entirely restricted to the Alpine region south of the magnificent state capital **Munich**. In the state's western region, around its pristine capital **Augsburg**, the food is less pork and sausages and more pasta and sauces, and the landscape gentle farming country ideal for camping and cycling holidays. To the north lies **Nürnberg**, centre of a region of vineyards and nature parks, while eastern Bavaria – apart from its capital **Regensburg** – is relatively poor; life in its highland forests revolves around logging and workshop industries such as glass production.

One practical note: travellers over 27 are barred from using Bavarian youth hostels, but reasonable alternatives can usually be found, and you'll only be handicapped if you're on the tightest of budgets.

Heidelberg

Home to the oldest university on German soil, **HEIDELBERG** is a real-life fulfilment of the ideal German landscape, majestically set on the banks of the swift-flowing Neckar between ranges of wooded hills. Ever since the days of the Grand Tour it has seduced travellers to an extent no other German city comes close to matching.

Arrival and accommodation
First impressions are a letdown: the **train station** and **bus station** are in an anonymous quarter fifteen minutes' walk west of the centre, with the dreary Kurfürsten-Anlage leading towards town. The harassed **tourist office** is on the square outside (mid-March to mid-Nov Mon–Sat 9am–7pm, Sun 10am–6pm; rest of year Mon–Sat 9am–7pm; ☎06221/14220), and publishes the weekly *Heidelberg diese Woche*, which gives full details of what's on.

The **youth hostel** is on the north bank of the Neckar, about 4km from the centre, at Tiergartenstr. 5 (☎06221/412066; ②); take bus #11. Although a large number of **hotels** are dotted all over the city, they are often booked solid; however, there's a chart outside the tourist office detailing vacancies. The only real budget option is *Jeske*, located in the heart of the city at Mittelbadgasse 2 (☎06221/23733; ②, without breakfast), which offers doubles and beds in small dorms. The few other conveniently sited inexpensive hotels are *Elite*, Bunsenstr. 15 (☎06221/25734; ④); *Ballmann*, Rohrbacher Str. 28 (☎06221/24287; ④); and *Astoria*, Rahmengasse 30 (☎06221/402929; ④). Both **campsites** are east of the city by the river – *Heide* is between Ziegelhausen and Kleingemünd; *Neckertal* is in Schlierbach; both are served by local bus.

The City

Centrepiece of all the views of Heidelberg is the **Schloss**, a compendium of magnificent buildings, somehow increased in stature by its ruined condition. It was founded at the start of the thirteenth century, but its expansion gathered momentum in the middle of the sixteenth century, when the Electors converted to Protestantism, and began the construction of the most splendid **Renaissance buildings** in Germany. Friedrich V's ham-fisted attempt to establish a Protestant, anti-Habsburg majority in the Electoral college led to the Thirty Years' War, which devastated the country. However, it was French designs on the region in 1689 that led to the destruction of Heidelberg and its Schloss; after this, the Electorship passed to a Catholic branch of the family who, unable to establish a rapport with the locals, abandoned Heidelberg.

The Schloss can be reached by funicular from the **Kornmarkt** for DM4.70 return, but it's more fun to walk up via the Burgweg. At the southeastern corner is the most romantic of the ruins, now generally known as the **Gesprengter Turm** (Blown-up Tower); a collapsed section lies intact in the moat, leaving a clear view into the interior. In the **Schlosshof** (DM3 8am–5pm; free access outside these hours; guided tours of interiors daily 9am–4/5pm; DM4), what really catches your eye is the group of Renaissance palaces on the north and east sides. The triple loggia of the earlier **Saalbau** forms a link to the swaggering **Friedrichsbau**, which supports a pantheon of the House of Wittelsbach, beginning with Charlemagne, the alleged founder of the dynasty. The statues now on view are copies; the originals can be seen inside, along with a number of restored rooms which have been decked out in period style.

The finest surviving buildings in the **Altstadt** are grouped on **Marktplatz**, in the middle of which is the red sandstone **Heiliggeistkirche**, whose domed tower is one of the city's most prominent landmarks. Note the tiny shopping booths between its buttresses, a feature ever since the church was built. Inside, it's light, airy and uncluttered, but was not always so, as the church was built to house the mausoleum of the Palatinate Electors; only one tomb remains.

Facing the church is the only mansion to survive the seventeenth-century devastations, the **Haus zum Ritter**, so-called from the statue of St George on the pediment. The most striking Baroque building in Heidelberg is the **Alte Brücke**, reached from the Marktplatz down Steingasse; dating from the 1780s, it was blown up in the last war, but has been painstakingly rebuilt. The **Palais Rischer** on Untere Strasse was the most famous venue for one of the university's more risible traditions, the *Mensur*, or fencing match. Every vital organ was padded, but wounds were frequent and prized as badges of courage; for optimum prestige, salt was rubbed into them, leaving scars that would remain for life.

The **Jesuitenkirche**, across Hauptstrasse on Schulgasse, is in the sombre, classically inspired style favoured by this evangelizing order, who came here with the ill-fated intention of recapturing Heidelberg for Catholicism. Housed in its gallery and the adjoining monastery is a moderate **Museum of Sacred Art** (Museum für Sakralkunst; June–Oct Tues–Sat 10am–5pm, Sun 1–5pm; Nov–May Sat 10am–5pm, Sun 1–5pm; DM2.50).

One side of Universitätsplatz, the heart of the old town, is occupied by the **Alte Universität**, dating back to the first quarter of the eighteenth century. The rest of the square is occupied by the Neue Universität, erected in 1931 with American funding. The oddest of Heidelberg's traditions was that its students used not to be subject to civil jurisdiction: offenders were dealt with by the university authorities, and could serve their punishment at leisure. Now a protected monument, the **Students' Prison** (April–Oct Tues–Sat 10am–noon & 2–5pm; Nov–March Tues–Fri 10am–noon & 2–5pm, Sat 10am–1pm; DM1.50) is at the back of the Alte Universität on Augustinergasse; used from 1712 to 1914, the otherwise spartan cells are covered with graffiti.

Eating and drinking

The **student taverns** in Heidelberg are a must: known for serving basic dishes at reasonable prices, they are still regularly patronized by the university fraternities, even if tourists these

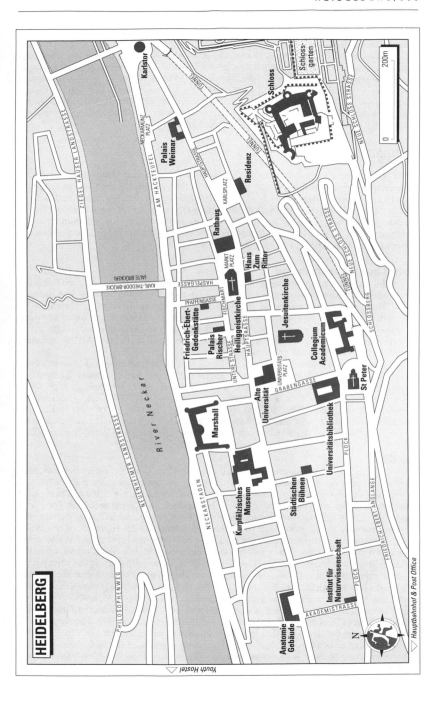

HEIDELBERG

Karlstor
Palais Weimar
Residenz
Rathaus
Schloss
Schlossgarten
NECKARMÜNZ PLATZ
KARLSPLATZ
Haus Zum Ritter
MARKT PLATZ
Jesuitenkirche
Friedrich-Ebert-Gedenkstätte
Palais Rischer
Heiliggeistkirche
Collegium Academicum
Alte Universität
St Peter
Marshall
Kurpfälzisches Museum
Städtischen Bühnen
Universitätsbibliothek
Institut für Naturwissenschaft
Anatomie Gebäude

AM HACKTEUFEL
HAUPTSTRASSE
HASPELGASSE
PFAFFENGASSE
FISCHMART
UNTERE STRASSE
HAUPTSTRASSE
UNIVERSITÄTS PLATZ
GRABENGASSE
PLOCK
AKADEMISTRASSE
PLOCK
FRIEDRICH-EBERT-ANLAGE
NEUE SCHLOSS STRASSE
SCHLOSSBERG
TUNNEL
ZIEGELHAUSER LANDSTRASSE
NEUENHEIMER LANDSTRASSE
PHILOSOPHENWEG
NECKARSTADEN
KARL-THEODOR-BRÜCKE (ALTE BRÜCKEN)

River Neckar

200m
0

N

△ Youth Hostel

▽ Hauptbahnhof & Post Office

days make up most of the clientele. At the eastern end of Hauptstrasse are the two most famous of these hostelries – *Zum Sepp'l* at no. 213, and *Roter Ochsen* at no. 217. Less touristy is the oldest of all the taverns, *Schnookeloch*, at Haspelgasse 8. Among other traditional **restaurants**, and for cheaper eating, try *Essighaus*, Plöck 97, or *Goldener Hecht*, Steingasse 2.

The *Biermuseum* at Hauptstr. 143 has 101 varieties of **beer** to choose from, while *Vetters*, Steingasse 9, has its own small house brewery. The mid-nineteenth-century *Knösel*, Haspelgasse 20, is the oldest of Heidelberg's **cafés**; its speciality is *Heidelberger Studentenkuss*, a dark chocolate filled with praline and nougat. For something more like a bistro setup, call in at the crowded *Café Journal*, Hauptstr. 162.

Stuttgart

STUTTGART breathes success. Firms like Bosch, Porsche and Daimler-Benz – whose three-pointed star beams down on the city – were in the vanguard of the German economic miracle, and have established the city at the forefront of European industry. Yet Stuttgart was slow to develop. Founded around 950 as a stud farm (*Stutengarten*), it became a town only in the fourteenth century, and lay in the shadow of its more venerable neighbours up to the early nineteenth century. Though not the comeliest of cities, Stuttgart has a range of superb museums, and a varied cultural and nightlife scene.

Arrival and accommodation

The **train station** is plumb in the centre of town and, immediately behind it, you'll find the **bus station**. The **airport** bus service #A runs every twenty minutes between 5am and midnight. There's a **tourist office** in front of the train station at Königstr. 1a (Mon–Fri 9.30am–8.30pm, Sat 9.30am–6pm, Sun 11am/1pm–6pm; 0711/2228240). The integrated **public transport** network comprises buses, trams, the U-Bahn and main-line and S-Bahn trains; given that the sights are scattered, it's worth investing in a 24-hour ticket (DM12 for the main part of the city, DM20 for the entire network).

The **youth hostel** is about fifteen minutes' walk east of the train station at Haussmannstr. 27 (☎0711/241583; ②). There's also an unofficial hostel, the *Jugendgästehaus Stuttgart*, at Richard-Wagner-Str. 2–4a (☎0711/241132; ②). Though average **hotel** rates are high, there are some bargains, such as *Eckel*, Vorsteigstr. 10 (☎0711/290995; ③); *Museumstube*, Hospitalstr. 9 (☎0711/296810; ③); and *Theaterpension*, Pfizerstr. 12 (☎0711/240722, ③). Alternatively, ask the tourist office to book a room; there's no charge. The **campsite** is on the banks of the Neckar in Bad Cannstatt – take a main-line train, or S-Bahn #1, #2 or #3.

The City

From the train station, Königstrasse passes the dull modern Dom and enters **Schlossplatz**, a welcome relief from the bustle, but favoured spot of Stuttgart's tramps and alcoholics. On the east side of the square, the colossal Baroque **Neues Schloss**, now used by the regional government, looks over at the Neoclassical **Königsbau**, its 135-metre facade lined with shops. To the south of the square is the Altes Schloss, which now houses the **Landesmuseum** (Tues 10am–1pm, Wed–Sun 10am–5pm; DM5). Highlight of this richly varied museum is the **Kunstkammer** of the House of Württemberg, displayed in one of the corner towers: the first floor has small bronze sculptures of mainly Italian origin, while the second is laid out in the manner of a Renaissance curio cabinet. Upstairs, in the main part of the building, is a large collection of Swabian devotional sculptures, arranged thematically rather than chronologically. On the same floor, the archeology section includes excavations from Troy, Roman antiquities, the grave of a Celtic prince and Frankish jewellery. The top floor has musical instruments and a wonderful array of clocks. The nearby **Galerie der Stadt Stuttgart** (Tues & Thurs–Sun 11am–6pm, Wed 11am–8pm; free) is a poor relation of the Staatsgalerie, but does contain some superbly acerbic works by Otto Dix.

To the north of Schlossplatz, facing the straggling complex of the Staatstheater across Konrad-Adenauer-Strasse, is the **Staatsgalerie** (Tues–Sun 11am–7pm, first Sat in month 11am–midnight; DM9, free Wed). The most startling work in the entire gallery is the huge, violently expressive *Herrenberg Altar* by Jerg Ratgeb, whose reputation rests almost entirely on this work. The equally idiosyncratic Hans Baldung is represented by his *Man of Sorrows* and *Portrait of Hans Jacob*. After some good examples of Cranach, Bellini, Carpaccio, Tintoretto and Tiepolo, Memling's sensual *Bathsheba at her Toilet* kicks off the Low Countries section, which also features Rembrandt's tender *Tobit Healing his Father's Blindness*. Nineteenth-century highpoints are *Bohemian Landscape* and *The Cross in the Woods* by Friedrich, and a decent cross-section of French Impressionism. The extension, a much-praised postmodern design by James Stirling, contains one of the two finest **Picasso** collections in Germany and traces the entire progress of German art this century. Avant-garde works occupy the end halls, while major temporary exhibitions are regularly featured downstairs.

On the other side of Schlossplatz, the **Altes Schloss** overlooks **Schillerplatz**, Stuttgart's sole example of an old-world square. Presiding in the middle is a pensive statue of Schiller himself, erected the year after his death by the Danish sculptor Bertel Thorwaldsen. Also here are two more Renaissance buildings – the **Alte Kanzlei** and the gabled **Fruchtkasten**. The latter preserves its fourteenth-century core, which has now been converted to house Landesmuseum's musical instruments collection (times and prices as above). At the back of Schillerplatz is the **Stiftskirche**, the choir of which is lined with one of the most important pieces of German Renaissance sculpture, an ancestral gallery of the counts and dukes of Württemberg.

THE MERCEDES-BENZ MUSEUM

Set up in 1986 to celebrate the centenary of the invention of the motor car by Gottlieb Daimler and Carl Benz, the **Mercedes-Benz Museum** (Tues–Sun 9am–5pm; free) is an absolute must, unless you rue the day the car was invented. Even entering here is an experience – you take S-Bahn #1 to Neckarstadion, then walk; or take bus #56 to the works entrance, from where you're whisked into a sealed minibus to the museum doors. The earliest vehicle on display is the Daimler Reitwagen of 1885, the first ever motorbike, which was capable of 12kph. The Daimler company's first Mercedes dates from 1902, its Spanish-sounding name being taken from the daughter of the firm's principal foreign agent, Emil Jellinek. Other exhibits include fire engines, motorboats, aeroplanes and buses, but the show is stolen by the luxury cars and the machines specially designed for world record attempts: so futuristic it's hard to believe they were made more than half a century ago.

THE PORSCHE MUSEUM

The **Porsche Museum**, right beside the Neuwirtshaus station on S-Bahn line #6 (Mon–Fri 9am–4pm, Sat & Sun 9am–5pm; free), is considerably more relaxed about visitors than Daimler-Benz. Not only can you wander at will around the factory site, but there are free **guided tours** of the production lines every working day. These are generally booked weeks in advance; a few extra visitors are allowed to tag on at short notice, but it's still best to phone first (☎0711/827 5685). **Ferdinand Porsche** made his name when Hitler commissioned him to create the original Volkswagen, precursor of the Beetle, the ultimate mass-market car. For his own enterprise, Porsche concentrated on the opposite end of the economic spectrum. The vehicles on show illustrate all the company's cars from the 356 Roadster of 1948 to current models.

Eating, drinking and nightlife

Though fancy restaurants abound in Stuttgart, there are a number of places offering traditional Swabian dishes at low cost, with plenty of ethnic eateries to stimulate the jaded palate. First recommendations for good-quality food and drink are the numerous **Weinstuben**, archetypally German establishments that are known for their solid cooking as well as for wine. *Zur Kiste*, Kanalstr. 2, is the best known, but the widest choice of wines is at *Weinhaus Stetter*, Rosenstr. 32. The best restaurant in a **beer hall** setup is *Ketterer*, Marienstr. 3b; the best **pub** in the city with an adjoining house brewery is *Stuttgarter Lokalbrauerei*, Calwer Str. 31; while the fullest range of **vegetarian** fare is at *Iden*, Eberhardstr. 1.

For **nightlife** details, pick up the tourist office's well-filled monthly programme, *Stuttgarter Monatsspiegel*, costing DM3.50. Alternative listings can be found in both *Lift Stuttgart* and *Prinz Stuttgart*, available from newsagents. *Schlesinger International*, Schloss Str. 28, is a popular, youthful hangout; the former punk haunt of *Exil*, Filderstr. 61, now belongs to arty types, with jazz and blues in a laid-back atmosphere. Jazz also features at *Laboratorium*, Wagenburgerstr. 147, popular with the Green Party contingent. Occupying an old rail tunnel, *Röhre*, Neckarstr. 34, platforms live bands playing everything from jazz to punk, and is also a disco patronized by fashion-conscious locals. *Café Stella*, Haupstätter Str. 57 is a trendy café/bar.

Listings

Airlines British Airways Kriegsbergstr. 28 (☎0711/299471); Lufthansa, Lautenschlagerstr. 20 (☎0711/227140).

Car rental Avis, Katharinenstr. 18 (☎0711/239320); Hertz, Im Hauptbahnhof (☎0711/226 2921).

Consulates Britain, Breite Str. 2 (☎0711/162690); US, Urbanstr. 7 (☎0711/210221).

Hitching Mitfahrzentrale at Lerchenstr. 65 (☎0711/636 8036).

Post office Main office is at the rear of the Königsbau on Schillerplatz.

Tübingen

"We have a town on our campus" runs the saying in **TÜBINGEN**, a peaceful town sited above the willow-lined banks of the Neckar, some 30km south of Stuttgart. Over half the population of 70,000 is in some way connected with the university, and the current size of the town is due entirely to the twentieth-century boom in higher education.

The old town is a visual treat, a mixture of brightly painted half-timbered and gabled houses grouped into twisting and plunging alleys. Two large squares provide a setting for communal activities. The first, **Holzmarkt**, is dominated by the **Stiftskirche St Georg**, a gaunt, late-Gothic church with a stunning interior. In the chancel (Easter–Oct daily 11am–5pm; DM2, incl ascent of the tower) an outstanding series of stained-glass windows casts reflections on the pantheon of the House of Württemberg, the thirteen tombs showing the development of Swabian sculpture in the Gothic and Renaissance periods.

Overlooking the banks of the Neckar on Bursagasse, the street immediately below, is the **Hölderlinturm** (Tues–Fri 10am–noon & 3–5pm, Sat & Sun 2–5pm; DM3). Originally part of the medieval fortifications, it's named after Friedrich Hölderlin, who lived here in the care of a carpenter's family, hopelessly but harmlessly insane, from 1807 until his death 36 years later. There's a collection of memorabilia of the poet, now regarded as one of the greatest Germany ever produced. At the end of the street is the **Evangelisches Stift**, a Protestant seminary established in a former Augustinian monastery in 1547.

The **Markt**, heart of old Tübingen, is just a short walk uphill from the Stift. It preserves many of its Renaissance mansions, along with a fountain dedicated to Neptune, around which markets are held on Mondays, Wednesdays and Fridays. Burgsteige, one of the oldest and handsomest streets in town, climbs steeply from the corner of the Markt to **Schloss Hohentübingen**, Renaissance successor to the original eleventh-century castle. One wing has recently been given over to the **Schausammlungen der Universität** (Wed–Sun 10am–5pm; DM4), one of the largest university museums in the world with archeology, history and ethnology displays. Only by taking a guided tour (April–Sept Sat 5pm, Sun 11am & 3pm) can you see the prison and the cellars, with their 18,700-gallon vat.

The northwestern part of town, lying immediately below the Schloss, has traditionally been the province of the non-academic community – especially the vine-growers. Here are some of the city's oldest and most spectacular half-timbered buildings, such as the old municipal **Kornhaus** on the alley of the same name, and the **Fruchtschranne**, formerly the storehouse for the yields of the ducal orchards, on Bachgasse.

The corresponding quarter northeast of the Markt is once more dominated by the university. Crossing Langegasse, and continuing along Metgergasse, you come to the **Nonnenhaus**, most photogenic of the half-timbered houses. Just outside the northeastern boundary of the old town are the former **Botanical Gardens**. These have been replaced by another complex, located amid most of the modern buildings of the university, a kilometre north by the ring road (Mon–Fri 7.30am–4.45pm, Sat & Sun 10–noon & 1.30–4.30pm).

Practicalities

The **train station** and **bus station** are side by side, just five minutes' walk from the old town. At the edge of Eberhardsbrücke is the **tourist office** (May–Oct Mon–Fri 9am–6.30pm, Sat 9am–5pm Sun 2–5pm; rest of year Mon–Fri 9am–6.30pm, Sat 9am–5pm; ☎07071/19440). **Hotels** aren't plentiful and tend to be expensive; the best bet is *Am Schloss*, Burgsteige 18 (☎07071/92940; ④), or try the **youth hostel** on the banks of the Neckar, a short walk from the station at Gartenstr. 22/2 (☎07071/23002; ②); the tourist office also has a list of **private rooms**. To reach the **campsite**, also with a riverside setting at Rappenberghalde, turn left on leaving the train station, and cross at Alleenbrücke. The best **restaurant** in the centre is *Forelle*, an old-world wine bar at Kronenstr. 8. Giant pancakes are the speciality of the *Ratskeller*, Haaggasse 4, while *Marktschenke*, Markt 11, is a lively student bar.

The Black Forest region

Stretching 170km north to south, and up to 60km east to west, the **Black Forest** (*Schwarzwald*) is the largest German forest and the most beautiful. As late as the 1920s, much of this area was an eerie wilderness, a refuge for boars and bandits. Nowadays most of the villages have been opened up as spa and health resorts, brimming with shops selling tacky souvenirs, while the old trails have become gravel paths smoothed down for easier walking. Yet by no means all the modernizations are drawbacks. **Railway** fans, for example, will find several of the most spectacular lines in Europe here. It should be noted, though, that the trains tend to stick to the valleys and that **bus services** are much reduced outside the tourist season.

Most of the Black Forest is associated with the Margraviate of Baden, whose old capital of **Baden-Baden** is at the northern fringe of the forest, in a fertile orchard and vine-growing area. The only city actually surrounded by the forest is **Freiburg im Breisgau**, one of the most enticing in the country.

Baden-Baden

In the present century, the social class that made **BADEN-BADEN** the "summer capital of Europe" has almost disappeared, yet the town still has a style that no other spa in the country can quite match. Buoyed by the postwar economic prosperity, people flock here to enjoy a taste of a lifestyle their parents could only dream about. Baden is on the fast Karlsruhe–Freiburg line, but the station is 4km northwest of the centre in the suburb of Oos; take bus #201, #205 or #216 into the centre.

The therapeutic value of Baden's hot springs was discovered by the Romans, but the town's rise to international fame only came about as a result of Napoleon's creation of the buffer state of Baden in 1806. The Grand Dukes promoted their ancestors' old seat as a modern resort, and began embellishing it with handsome buildings such as the **Kurhaus** and its integral **casino**. The easiest way to see these is to take a **guided tour** (daily 9.30/10am–noon; DM4); highlight is the Winter Garden, with its glass cupola, Chinese vases and solid gold roulette table. A day ticket, with no obligation to participate, is DM5.

South of the Kurhaus runs Baden-Baden's most famous thoroughfare, the **Lichtentaler Allee**, landscaped with exotic trees and shrubs and flanked by buildings such as the Parisian-style theatre and the **Kunsthalle**, which often hosts major exhibitions of twentieth-century art. Immediately north of the Kurhaus is the **Trinkhalle**, where varieties of spring water are dispensed from a mosaic fountain, under vast frescoes illustrating legends of the town and the nearby countryside.

Little remains today of the old town, almost completely destroyed in a single day in 1689, the result of a fire started by French troops. However, halfway up the Florintinerberg is the Marktplatz, and the **Stiftskirche**, a Gothic hall church containing one of the masterpieces of

European sculpture, an enormous sandstone *Crucifixion* by Nicolaus Gerhaert von Leyden. Hidden under the Stiftskirche are the remains of the Roman Imperial Baths; the more modest **Römerbad** (closed in 1999 for restoration; previously Easter–Oct daily 10am–noon & 1.30–4pm; DM2.50), just east on Römerplatz, was probably for soldiers. Above the ruins is the **Friedrichsbad** (Mon–Sat 9am–10pm, Sun noon–8pm), begun in 1869 and grand as a Renaissance palace. Speciality of the house is a two-hour "Roman-Irish Bath", which will set you back upwards of DM36, though the really broke need only fork out DM0.10 for a glass of thermal water.

From here you can climb the steep steps to the **Neues Schloss** (Tues–Sun 10am–12.30pm & 2–5pm; DM2), a mixture of Renaissance and Baroque buildings, housing displays on the history of the town. There's also the added attraction of the best view over Baden-Baden, a dramatic mix of rooftops, spires and the enveloping forest.

PRACTICALITIES

The **tourist office** is in the Kurverwaltung building on Augustaplatz (Mon–Fri 9.30am–5pm, Sat 9.30am–3pm; ☎07221/275200). A few rooms are available in **private houses** (②–④). Baden-Baden's **youth hostel** is between the **train station** and the centre at Hardbergstr. 34 (☎07221/52223; ②); take bus #201, #205 or #216 to Grosse-Dollen-Strasse, from where the way is signposted. The main group of cheap **hotels** is in Oos: try *Goldener Stern*, Ooser Hauptstr. 16 (☎07221/61509; ③), or *Zur Linde*, Sinzheimer Str. 3 (☎07221/61519; ③). The nearest **campsite** is in the Oberbruch park on the outskirts of Bühl, three stops by slow train. Among places to **eat** and **drink**, the *Münchener Löwenbräu*, Gernsbacher Str. 9 is a good choice; complete with beer garden, it's like a little corner of Bavaria, and serves excellent meals. For a trendy atmosphere, try *Leo's* on Luisenstr. 10, while for solid, low-cost German food, there's *Bratwurstglöckel* on Steinstr. 7.

Freiburg im Breisgau

"Capital" of the Black Forest, **FREIBURG IM BREISGAU** basks in a laid-back atmosphere which seems completely un-German. A university town since 1457, its youthful presence is maintained all year round with the help of a varied programme of festivals. Furthermore, the sun shines here more often, and there are more vineyards within the municipal area than in any other city in the country.

Though it rivals any of the great European cathedrals, the dark red sandstone **Münster** was built as a mere parish church, the costs being met entirely by the local citizens. The transepts were begun in about 1200, after which one of the architects of Strasbourg Cathedral took over and created a masterly Gothic nave, resplendent with flying buttresses, gargoyles and statues. At around this time the magnificent sculptures of the west porch were created, the most important German works of their time – note the *Prince of Darkness*, carved where the natural light is weakest. More sculptures adorn the portals of the chancel, which was begun in the mid-fourteenth century – look out for the unusual depiction of God resting on the seventh day. From the tower (March–Nov Mon–Sat 9.30am–5pm, Sun 1–5pm; DM2) you get a fine panorama over the city and the forest, and of the lacelike tracery of the spire, which rounds off the tower with a bravura flourish. Inside, the transept is lit by stained-glass windows of the early thirteenth century. Most of those in the nave date from a hundred years later, and were donated by the local trades and guilds, who incorporated their coats of arms. To get a decent look at Baldung's *Coronation of the Virgin* altarpiece, you have to take a guided tour of the ambulatory chapels (DM2), which contain some wonderful pieces – including a retable by the two Holbeins, and a silver crucifix from the first Münster.

The spacious **Münsterplatz**, the north side of which was flattened in the last war, holds one of the most diverting daily markets in Germany. The south side of the square is dominated by the blood-red **Kaufhaus**, a sixteenth-century merchants' hall, flanked by handsome Baroque palaces.

A peculiarity of Freiburg is the system of rivulets known as the **Bächle**, which run in deep gulleys all over the city. Formerly used for watering animals, and as a fire-fighting provision, they have their purpose even today, helping to keep the city cool. Following the main char nel of the Bächle southwards, you come to the **Schwaben Tor**, one of two surviving towers of the medieval fortifications. On Oberlinden, just in front, is **Zum Roten Bären**, which is generally considered to be Germany's oldest inn. Just to the west is Salzstrasse, where the **Augustinermuseum** (Tues–Sun 10am–5pm; DM4, free first Sun of month) houses works of art from the Münster and a few top-class pictures, including the most important paintings by the mysterious draughtsman known as Master of the Housebook. South of here, on Marienstrasse, the **Museum of Modern Art** (same times; free) has a good cross-section of twentieth-century German painting. From here, follow Fischerau, the old fishermen's street, and you come to the other thirteenth-century tower, the **Martinstor**, in the middle of Freiburg's central axis, Kaiser-Josef-Strasse.

Back on the west side of the Münster, the **Neues Rathaus**, **Altes Rathaus** and the plain Franciscan monastery church of **St Martin** stand around a shady chestnut-lined square. In the alley behind St Martin is the cheerful Gothic facade of the **Haus zum Wallfisch**, for two years the home of the great humanist Erasmus, who was forced to flee from Basel by the religious struggles there. A few minutes to the west, in the Columbipark opposite the tourist office, is the **Museum für Ur- und Frühgeschichte** (same times; DM3.50 donation requested), which has important archeological collections relating to the Black Forest region.

It's worth climbing one of the hills surrounding the city for the wonderful views. The **Schlossberg**, immediately to the east, is an easy ascent from the Schwaben Tor – or you could take the cable car. To the south, the **Lorettoberg** – where the stone for the Münster was quarried – makes a good afternoon or evening alternative.

PRACTICALITIES

The **train station**, with the **bus station** on its southern side, is about ten minutes' walk west from the city centre. Following Eisenbahnstrasse, you come to the **tourist office** on Rotteckring (Mon–Fri 9.30am–6/8pm, Sat 9.30am–2/5pm, Sun 10am–noon; ☎0761/388 1880). For DM3, they will find you a room; if you arrive after closing time, there's an electronic noticeboard equipped with a phone, which lists vacancies. Among **hotels** with a central location, the cheapest is *Schemmer*, Eschholzstr. 63 (☎0761/272424; ④). The **youth hostel** is at Karthäuserstr. 151 (☎0761/67656; ②), at the extreme western end of the city, reached by tram #1 to Hasemannstrasse. Nearby, slightly nearer town, is the *Hirzberg* **campsite** (open all year); *Mösle-Park* (mid-March to Oct) is on the opposite side of the river.

Freiburg has **restaurants** for all pockets. *Oberkirchs Weinstuben*, Münsterplatz 22 is a top-notch but not expensive wine cellar, and *Zur Traube* just behind at Schusterstr. 17 is equally good. Hearty South German cooking can be sampled at *Kleiner Meyerhof*, Rathausgasse 27 or *Grosser Meyerhof*, Grünwälderstr. 7. One of the trendiest places to be seen is *Uni-Café* Niemensstr. 7, which serves a wide selection of coffees and has good snacks. Freiburg now ranks as one of the leading German cities for **jazz**, thanks to the *Jazzhaus* at Schnewlinstr. 1, which has concerts every evening.

Konstanz and the Bodensee

In the far south of the province, **KONSTANZ** lies at the tip of a tongue of land sticking out into the **Bodensee** (Lake Constance), which is really a swelling in the River Rhine. The town itself is split by the water: the **Altstadt** is a German enclave on the Swiss side of the lake, which is why it was never bombed by the Allies, who couldn't risk hitting neutral Switzerland. It's a cosy little place, with a convivial atmosphere in summer, when street cafés invite long pauses and the water is a bustle of sails.

The most prominent church is the **Münster**, set on the highest point of the Altstadt. It was here in 1417 that the papal court tried the reformer Johannes Hus for heresy – the spot on which he stood during his trial is marked in the central aisle. Konstanz's major museum is the **Rosgartenmuseum** on the street of the same name (Tues–Thurs 10am–5pm, Fri–Sun 10am–4pm; DM3), which has a fine collection of local archeological finds, plus art and craft exhibits from the Middle Ages. Everything is as it was when the museum was designed in 1871, creating a pleasantly musty atmosphere.

The **tourist office** is located alongside the train station at Bahnhofplatz 13 (April–Oct Mon–Fri 9am–8pm, Sat 9am–4pm, Sun 10am–1pm; reduced hours out of season; ☎07531/133030); they can book accommodation for you in **private rooms** (②–④). The **youth hostel** is at Zur Allmannshöhe 18 (☎07531/32260; ②); take bus #4 from the train station to Jugendherberge, or #1 to Post Allmannsdorf. If you'd prefer a **hotel**, however, there's *Gretel* at Zollenstr. 6–8 (☎07531/23283; ③) or *Graf Zeppelin*, Am Stephansplatz 15 (☎07531/23780; ④). Information on **cruises and ferries** is available from the *Bodensee-Verkehrsdienst* at Hafenstr. 6 (☎07531/281398). Ferries regularly leave Konstanz for destinations all over the lake: perhaps the most worthwhile longer trip is to the **Rheinfall** in Switzerland – it costs DM34, but it's worth it to travel up one of the Rhine's most scenic stretches and to see Europe's largest waterfall.

Munich

Founded in 1158, **MUNICH** (München) has been the capital of Bavaria since 1503, and as far as the locals are concerned it may as well be the centre of the universe. *Münchener* pride themselves on their special status; even people who have made Munich their home for most of their lives are still called *Zugereiste* (newcomers). Next to Berlin, Munich is Germany's most popular city, with everything you'd expect in a cosmopolitan capital. Yet it's small enough to be digestible in one visit, and it's got the added bonus of a great setting, with the mountains and Alpine lakes just an hour's drive away. The best time of year to come here is from June to early October, when the beer gardens, street cafés and bars are in full swing.

Arrival, information and city transport

Munich's new airport, **Franz Josef Strauss Flughafen**, is connected to the **train station** (Hauptbahnhof) by S-Bahn #1 or #8. There are **tourist offices** at Bahnhofplatz 2 (Mon–Sat 9am–8pm, Sun 10–6pm; ☎089/233 30256) and in the Rathaus on Marienplatz (Mon–Fri 10am–8pm, Sat 10am–4pm; ☎089/233 30272). They will book rooms, and provide brochures about the city and what's on. The bus station is a stone's throw from the train station.

Day **tickets** for all public transport in the city centre cost DM9 (for the whole system DM18); a weekly pass covering the centre and most of Schwabing costs DM15.50. Note that these passes are valid from Monday to Monday, so buying midweek means losing out. Tickets for a week upwards require ID and two photos; all others can be bought from the automatic machines in all U-Bahn stations, at some bus and tram stops, and inside trams. If you're making several journeys across the city, it's far more economical to invest in a **strip card** (DM14 for ten strips), and stamp two strips for every zone crossed – the zones are shown on maps at stations and tram and bus stops. For journeys of up to two S- or U-Bahn stops, or up to four bus or tram stops, only one strip needs to be cancelled. There's also a DM6 children's strip card, for which it is only necessary to cancel one strip per trip. Tickets must be stamped before any journey – those without a validated ticket face an on-the-spot DM60 fine.

Accommodation

Cheap accommodation can be hard to find, especially during the high season in the summer, though prices are fairly constant throughout the year. If you're going to be in town during the Oktoberfest, it's essential to book your room well in advance. Details of the pick of the hotels, hostels and campsites are given below. Many pensions offer rooms with three to six beds, a much more pleasant way of saving money than hostel-type accommodation.

HOSTELS

Burg Schwaneck, Burgweg 4–6 (☎089/793 0643). HI hostel some way from the centre in an old castle on the river. Check-in 5pm–1am. S-Bahn #7 to Pullach, then follow signs to the *Jugendherberge*. ②.

DJH Jugendgästehaus, Miesingstr. 4 (☎089/723 6560). Smaller, more upmarket HI hostel with check-in 7am–11pm. U-Bahn to Harras, then tram #16 to Boschetsrlederstr. ②.

DJH München, Wendl-Dietrich-Str. 20 (☎089/131156). The largest, most central and most basic HI hostel, with 535 beds in dormitories. Check-in noon–1am. U-Bahn to Rotkreuzplatz. ②.

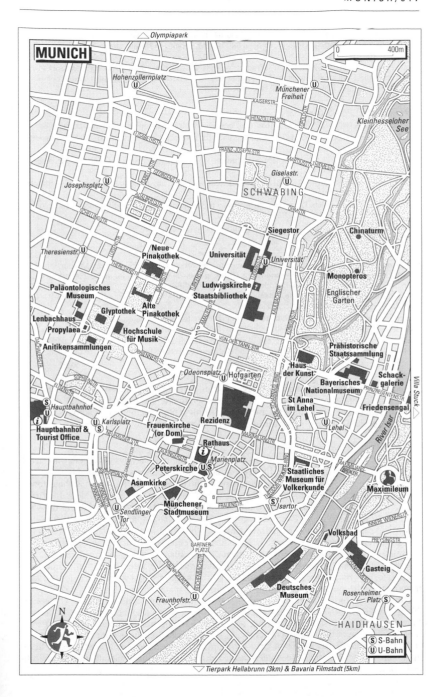

Haus International, Elisabethstr. 87 (☎089/1200 6224). Centrally located in Schwabing, rooms range from five beds to singles. No age limit, no need for HI card. U-Bahn to Hohenzollernplatz, then bus #33 or tram #12 to Barbarastrasse. ③.

Jump In, Hochstr. 51 (☎089/4895 3437). Friendly new privately owned hostel on the right bank of the Isar, not far from the Deutsches Museum. No age limit or curfew; doubles as well as dorm beds available. S-Bahn to Rosenheimer Platz, or tram #27 to Ostfriedhof. ②.

HOTELS AND PENSIONS

Eder, Zweigstr. 8 (☎089/554660). In a quiet road between the train station and Marienplatz. ③.

Frank, Schellingstr. 24 (☎089/281451). A good choice for both price and atmosphere. Mainly frequented by young travellers. ③.

Haberstock, Schillerstr. 4 (☎089/557855). Right beside the Hauptbahnhof with basic, no frills facilities, but it's good value nonetheless. ④.

Jedermann, Bayerstr. 95 (☎089/533617). Located well away from any noise and seediness, five minutes' walk from the Hauptbahnhof. ④.

Am Kaiserplatz, Kaiserplatz 12 (☎089/349190). Very friendly, good location and big rooms, each done in a different style – from red satin to Bavarian rustic. ③.

Steinberg, Ohmstr. 9 (☎089/331011). Friendly and in a good location. ④.

CAMPSITES

Kapuzinerhölzl Youth Camp. 500-berth tent with showers, canteen and information bureau. Price includes blankets, air mattress and morning tea. Check-in 5pm–9am. Officially for under-23s and for a maximum of three nights, but people in charge are very flexible. Open late June–end Aug. U-Bahn to Rotkreuzplatz, then tram #12 to the Botanischer Garten. Check with the tourist office whether it's open before setting out, as its future is uncertain.

Obermenzing, Lochhausenerstr. 59. In a posh suburb, close to Nymphenburg. Open mid-March to Oct. S-Bahn to Obermenzing, then bus #75 to Lochhausenerstrasse.

Thalkirchen, Zentralländstr. 49. Most central site, in an attractive part of the Isar valley. Very popular during the Oktoberfest as it's close to the fairground. Open mid-March to Oct. U-Bahn to Thalkirchen.

The City

Almost nothing is left of Munich's medieval city, but three of the gates remain to mark today's city centre. Bounded by the Odeonsplatz and the Sendlinger Tor to the north and south, and the Isartor and Karlstor to the east and west, it's only a fifteen-minute walk across – but it is so tightly packed it needs two or three days to explore thoroughly.

MARIENPLATZ AND AROUND

The central **Marienplatz** – the heart of the U-Bahn system – is always thronged, with street musicians and artists entertaining the crowds, and with youths lounging around the fountain. At 11am and noon, the square fills with tourists as the tuneless **carillon** in the Rathaus tower jingles into action. The **Rathaus** itself is a late nineteenth-century neo-Gothic monstrosity whose only redeeming features are the café in its cool and breezy courtyard and the view from the tower (ascent by elevator May–Oct Mon–Fri 9am–4pm, Sat & Sun 10am–7pm; Nov–April closed Fri pm and weekends; DM3). To the right is the plain Gothic tower of the **Altes Rathaus**, which was rebuilt in the fifteenth-century style after being destroyed by lightning; today it houses a **toy museum** (daily 10am–5.30pm; DM5). Close by, the **Peterskirche** looks out across the busy Viktualienmarkt; the oldest church in Munich, it's notable for its grisly relics of Saint Munditia, patron saint of single women, and for the view from its tower (Mon–Sat 9am–5/8pm, Sun 10am–5/7pm according to season; DM2.50).

Almost next to the Viktualienmarkt is the **Münchener Stadtmuseum** (Tues–Sun 10am–6pm; DM5), the excellent local-history museum, which also incorporates a Photo and Film Museum, a Museum of Brewing and a Puppet Museum. The last is highly recommended: it's one of the largest collections in the world, and includes puppets ranging from Indian and Chinese paper dolls to large mechanical European creations. Southwest of here, at Sendlinger Str. 62, stands the small **Asamkirche**, one of the most splendid Rococo churches in Bavaria.

St Paul's Cathedral, London, England

Judging sheep, Yorkshire Dales, England

Rathaus, Munich, Germany

Rhine gorge at Bingen, Germany

Castle in Aberdeenshire, Scotland

Erechtheion, Acropolis, Athens, Greece

Bay in Párga, Greece

Esterházy Palace, Fertőd, Hungary

Great Skellig, Co. Kerry, Ireland

White Island,
Co. Fermanagh, Ireland

Colosseum, Rome, Italy

Gondolas, Venice, Italy

Florence, Italy, in early morning

Following the pedestrian Kaufingerstrasse west from Marienplatz, you walk with the mainstream of shoppers, overlooked by the **Frauenkirche** or Dom. The red-brick Gothic cathedral is seen to its best advantage from a distance, its twin onion-domed **towers** (ascent by elevator April–Oct Mon–Sat 10am–5pm; DM6) forming the focus of the city's skyline. A little further up Kaufingerstrasse, the Renaissance facade of **St Michael** stands unassumingly in line with the street's other buildings. In the crypt (Mon–Fri 10am–1pm & 2–4.30pm, Sat 10am–3pm; DM2) you'll find the coffins of the Wittelsbach dynasty – a candle is always burning at the foot of mad castle-builder Ludwig II's.

NORTH OF MARIENPLATZ – THE RESIDENZ
North of Marienplatz is the posh end of the city centre. **Maximilianstrasse**, the Champs-Élysées of Munich, is where the fashion houses have their shops, and the *Hotel Vierjahreszeiten* is one of the best addresses in town. When the refinement gets too much, the little Kosttor road leads straight to the **Hofbräuhaus**, Munich's largest and most famous drinking hall. Nearby, with its Baroque facade standing proud on the Odeonsplatz, is one of Munich's most regal churches, the **Theatinerkirche**, whose golden-yellow towers and green copper dome add a splash of colour to the roofscape.

The palace of the Wittelsbachs, the **Residenz** (Tues–Sun 10am–4.30pm; DM7), stands across the square from the Theatinerkirche. One of Europe's finest Renaissance buildings, it was so badly damaged in the last war that it had to be almost totally rebuilt. To see the whole thing you have to go on two consecutive visits, as parts of the immense complex are shut in the morning and others in the afternoon. On the morning tour you see the Antiquarium, the oldest part of the palace; built in 1571 to house the ruling family's collection of antiquities, this cavernous chamber was transformed into a festive hall a generation later. The last stage of the morning tour – which can also be seen in the afternoon – includes the eight appropriately named Rich Rooms, and the Halls of the Nibelungs, in which medieval Germany's most famous epic is depicted in a series of paintings. The afternoon tour includes the two very contrasting chapels and the Baroque Golden Hall. A separate ticket is necessary to see the fabulous treasures of the **Schatzkammer** (same hours; DM7); star piece of the whole display, kept in a room of its own, is the dazzling stone-encrusted statuette of St George, made around 1590. Yet another ticket has to be bought for the glorious **Cuvilliés Theatre** (Mon–Sat 2–5pm, Sun 10am–5pm; DM3), the Wittelsbachs' private theatre.

ISARINSEL AND PRINZREGENTENSTRASSE
Munich's most overwhelming museum – the **Deutsches Museum** (daily 9am–5pm; DM10) – occupies much of the mid-stream island called the **Isarinsel**. Covering every conceivable aspect of technical endeavour, from the first flint tools to the research labs of modern industry, this is the most compendious collection of its type in Germany. Another gargantuan collection – the **Bayerisches Nationalmuseum**, Prinzregentenstr. 3 (Tues–Sun 9.30am–5pm; DM5, free Sun) – lies close to the first bridge to the north. This rambling decorative arts museum takes in arms and armour, ivories and sacred objects, with a superb display of German wood sculpture. The basement features Bavarian folk art and a collection of Christmas cribs, the first floor displays models of Bavarian towns as they appeared in the sixteenth century and the second floor has stained glass, crystal, ceramics and clocks. Close by, at Prinzregentenstr. 1, the Nazi-era **Haus der Kunst** hosts important temporary exhibitions and is also currently home to the **Staatsgalerie Moderner Kunst** (Tues–Thurs, Sat & Sun 10am–5pm, Fri 10am–8pm; DM7, free Sun), which takes up the story of twentieth-century European painting and sculpture where the Neue Pinakothek (see below) leaves off. In summer 2000, it is due to move to new custom-built premises alongside the two other galleries.

THE MUSEUM QUARTER
Tucked between the train station and Schwabing, the **museum quarter** contains enough treasures to keep you absorbed for days.

The **Alte Pinakothek**, Barerstr. 27 (Tues & Thurs 10am–8pm, Wed & Fri–Sun 10am–5pm; DM7, free Sun), is one of the largest galleries in Europe and the world's finest assembly of German art. Among the collection are Dürer's Christ-like *Self-portrait* and panels of SS. *Mark, John the Evangelist, Peter and Paul*; Lucas Cranach the Elder's *Lucretia* and *Venus and Cupid* – the first sensually explicit nudes in German art; and Albrecht Altdorfer's *Battle of Alexander*, a heaving mass of hundreds of soldiers, each painted in minute detail. In the Italian section works by Titian steal the show, notably the *Portrait of Charles V* and *Christ Crowned with Thorns*. Centrepiece of the entire museum is the collection of works by Rubens, with 62 paintings displaying the scope of the artist's prodigious output. There's also a haunting *Passion Cycle* by Rembrandt and, from an earlier period of Netherlandish art, Rogier van der Weyden's classic *Adoration of the Magi*.

The collection of eighteenth- and nineteenth-century European painting and sculpture in the **Neue Pinakothek** at Barerstr. 29 (Tues & Thurs–Sun 10am–5pm, Wed 10am–8pm; DM7, free Sun) seems a little thin after the Alte Pinakothek, but it's nonetheless worth an hour or so. Neoclassicism, the preferred style of the age of rationalism, is beautifully embodied in the sober portrait of the *Marquise de Sourcy de Thélusson* by David, while Romanticism is represented by Carl Spitzweg, whose everyday scenes have a wry sense of humour. Of the works by French Impressionists, Manet's *Breakfast in the Studio* is probably the most famous. Turn-of-the-century art is represented by a few paintings by Cézanne, Van Gogh and Gauguin, and the museum rounds off with a small selection of Art Nouveau.

The meticulously restored **Glyptothek** (Tues, Wed & Fri–Sun 10am–5pm, Thurs 10am–8pm; DM6, free Sun), the most striking structure on the majestically Neoclassical Königsplatz, contains a magnificent range of classical sculpture, the most striking exhibits being the ancient statuary plundered from the temple on Aegina. Facing the Glyptothek is the **Staatliche Antikensammlungen** (Tues & Thurs–Sun 10am–5pm, Wed 10–8pm; DM6, joint ticket with Glyptothek DM10, free Sun), displaying Greek vases from the fifth and sixth centuries BC, as well as beautiful jewellery and small statues from Greek, Etruscan and Roman antiquity.

Situated just off Königsplatz at Luisenstr. 30 is the **Lenbachhaus** (Tues–Sun 10am–6pm; DM8), the nineteenth-century villa that belonged to the Bavarian painter Franz von Lenbach. It's a pleasant setting for some of German art's most interesting modern painters, the highlights coming with the group known as *Der Blaue Reiter*, whose members included Kandinsky, Klee, Marc and Macke. In recent years the museum has also concentrated on temporary exhibitions of contemporary German art.

SCHWABING

Marienplatz might be the geographical centre of town but **Schwabing** is its social hub. A large part of Munich's northern sector, with Leopoldstrasse forming a straight axis through the middle, Schwabing splits into three distinct areas. Around the university and left of Leopoldstrasse, residential streets mix with student bars and restaurants. Along the centre and to its right, trendy shops and café/bars ensure permanent crowds, day and night – nightclubs are thick on the ground here, especially around the Wedekindplatz, near Münchener Freiheit station. The far north is a tidy residential area, uninteresting apart from the **Olympiapark**, built for the 1972 Olympics, and now used for free open-air rock concerts in July and August.

One diversion that unites everyone is beer drinking, especially in summer, and one of the most famous beer gardens is around the Chinesischer Turm (or China Tower) in the **Englischer Garten**. Not far off by the Kleinhesseloher See are a couple of more peaceful gardens – the lakeside one is the more attractive. The Eisbach meadow is the city's main playground, where people come to sunbathe (often nude), picnic, swim or ride horses.

NYMPHENBURG

Schloss Nymphenburg (Tues–Sun 9/10am–12.30pm & 1.30–4/5pm; DM5; combined ticket to pavilions and the Marschall DM11), the summer residence of the Wittelsbachs, is reached by taking the U-Bahn to Rotkreuzplatz and then tram #12. Its kernel is a small Italianate palace begun in 1664 for the Electress Adelaide, who dedicated it to the goddess Flora and her nymphs – hence the name. More enticing than the palace itself are the wonderful park and its four pavilions – all of a markedly different character. Three were designed by Joseph Effner: the **Magdalenenklause**, built to resemble a ruined hermitage; the **Pagodenburg**, used for the most exclusive parties thrown by the court; and the **Badenburg**, which, like the Pagodenburg, reflects an interest in the art of China. For all their charm, Effner's pavilions are overshadowed by the stunning **Amalienburg**, the hunting lodge built behind the south wing of the Schloss by his successor as court architect, François Cuvilliés. This supreme expression of the Rococo style marries a cunning design – which makes the little building seem like a full-scale palace – with the most extravagant decoration imaginable.

To the north of the Schloss, the **Botanical Gardens** (daily 9am–4.30/7pm; hothouses closed 11.45am–1pm; DM4) hide all manner of plants in their steamy hothouses, while the herbarium and other outdoor collections make a very fragrant landscape.

DACHAU

DACHAU, now reverted to a picturesque town on the northern edge of Munich, was site of Germany's first **concentration camp** (Tues–Sun 9am–5pm; free). The motto that greeted arrivals at the gates has taken its chilling place in the history of Third Reich brutality: *Arbeit Macht Frei*, "Work Brings Freedom". Of the original buildings, only the gas chambers, which were never used, remain. However, a replica hut gives an idea of the conditions under which prisoners were forced to live, and the permanent exhibition of photographs speaks volumes. Turn up at 11.30am or 3.30pm and you can also view the short, deeply disturbing, documentary *KZ-Dachau* in English. Get there by taking bus #722 from Dachau S-Bahn station.

Eating and drinking

It's not difficult to eat well for little money in Munich. *Mensas* are the cheapest places to get a good basic meal; you're supposed to have a valid student card to eat here, but no one seems to check. The most central one is at Leopoldstr. 15 (Mon–Thurs 9am–4.45pm, Fri 9am–3.30pm), and there are two more in the main building at Schellingstrasse and at the Technical University, Arcisstr. 17. Italian restaurants are especially cheap, and the Bavarian *Gaststätten* offer filling soups, salads and sandwich-type dishes. Not surprisingly, drinking is central to Munich social life and apart from the *Gaststätten* and beer gardens, Munich also has a lively café/bar culture, which carries on well into the early hours. The city's "alternative" district is the former working-class and immigrant quarter of **Haidhausen**, across the river to the southeast of the centre. Though tamer than Berlin's Kreuzberg and Prenzlauer Berg, it has a good mix of bars, cafés and restaurants, and makes a refreshing break from the glitz of the Schwabing nightspots.

CAFÉ/BARS, CAFÉS AND WINE BARS

Alter Simpl, Türkenstr. 57. Famous literary café/bar which spawned the satirical magazine *Simplicissimus*. Open daily 5pm–3am, 4am at weekends.

Café Kreuzkamm, Maffeistr. 4. Best and most expensive *Kaffee und Küchen* establishment.

Pfälzer Weinprobierstuben, Residenzstr. 1. Unpretentious place serving excellent wines.

Reitschule, Königinstr. 34. Typical haunt of the Schwabing *Schickies*.

Weintrödler, Briennerstr. 10. Late-night wine bar (5pm–6am); the last boozer to close.

RESTAURANTS

Adria, Leopoldstr. 19. Popular late-night Italian, with good food at reasonable prices.

Bella Italia, Weissenburger Str. 2. One of a chain of six Italian restaurants in Munich; a long-standing favourite.

Bernard & Bernard, Innere Wiener Str. 32. Great place for crepes, in Haidhausen.

Bodega Dalí, Augustenstr. 46. Best Spanish place in town, at lower-than-average Munich prices.

Donisl, Weinstr. 1. A fine old Munich *Gaststätte*, dating back to the early eighteenth century.

Haxnbauer, Munzstr. 6. Specializes in the delicious roasted pork knuckles that are such a high point of German cuisine; the lamb version is no less tasty.

Prinz Myshkin, Hackenstr, 2. Best vegetarian place in the centre.

Schelling Salon, Schellingstr. 54. Good for their large cheap breakfasts and also for playing pool.

BEER GARDENS AND BEER HALLS

Augustiner Keller, Arnulfstr. 52, near the Hackerbrücke S-Bahn stop. A shady island of green, hidden in one of Munich's grottier quarters.

Augustinerbräu, Neuhauser Str. 27. One of several beer halls and gardens on this central street, with an unusually long menu and wonderfully evocative turn-of-the-century decor.

Aumeister, Sondermeierstr. 1. At the northern end of the Englischer Garten; a good place for daytime breaks.

Hofbräuhaus, Platzl 9. The most famous, though nowadays, at least during the tourist season, it's by far the least authentic of any on this list.

Hofbräukeller, Innere Wiener Str. 19. Nestling under ancient chestnut trees; very popular in the evenings.

Paulaner-Keller, Hochstr. 77. High up on the Nockherberg, on the east bank of the Isar; one of the oldest havens for serious beer drinkers, and still known to the locals by its old name of *Salvator-Keller*.

Weisses Bräuhaus, Im Tal 10. Famous for the favourite Munich snack of *Weisswurst*, a white sausage which should traditionally only be eaten before noon.

Music, nightlife and festivals

Munich has a great deal to offer musically, from classical concerts to rock. Best sources for information on what's happening are the *Münchener Stadtzeitung* or *In München*, both available at any kiosk, or the monthly *Monatsmagazin* from the tourist office or the English-language *Munich Found*. For jazz concerts – a major feature of Munich nightlife – check the monthly *Münchener Jazz-Zeitung*. Munich has three first-rate symphony orchestras – the *Münchener Philharmonie*, the *Bayrisches Rundfunk Sinfonie Orchester* and the *Staatsorchester* – as well as eleven major theatres and numerous fringe theatres. Advance tickets for plays and concerts can be bought at the relevant box offices or commercial ticket shops such as the one located in the Marienplatz U-Bahn station. Opera tickets can be bought at the advance sales office at Maximilianstr. 11, or from the box office in the Nationaltheater one hour before performances begin.

ROCK AND JAZZ

Crash, Ainmillerstr. 10. Stage for heavy rock.

Drehleier, Rosenheimer Str. 123. Mainly jazz on weekdays from 8pm.

Kaffee Giesing, Bergstr. 5. Venue for small bands and solo artists.

Olympiapark. Free rock concerts by the lake in summer; they usually get going around 2pm at weekends.

Schwabinger Podium, Wagnerstr. 1. Chiefly Dixieland.

Unterfahrt, Einsteinstr. 42. Showcase for avant-garde jazz.

DISCOS

Nachtwerk, Landsberger Str. 185. Draws a young crowd on Friday and Saturday.

Oly-Club, Helene-Meyer-Ring 9. Mainly student disco, generally friendlier than the others.

Sugar Shack, Herzogspitalstr. 6. A trendies' favourite.

CLASSICAL MUSIC, OPERA AND THEATRE

Cuvilliéstheater, in the Residenz. Premier venue for drama, plus the occasional chamber music recital.

Deutsches Theater, Schwanthalerstr. 13. Home-grown and visiting spectaculars.

Gasteig, Rosenheimer Str. 5. One of the two main venues for classical concerts.

Herkulessaal, in the Residenz. The other big classical concert hall.

Staatsoper or **Nationaltheater**, Max-Josef-Platz 1. Munich's answer to Covent Garden, with grand opera and ballet.

Residenztheater, Max-Josef-Platz 1. Traditional dramatic fare.

Staatstheater Am Gärtnerplatz, Am Gärtnerplatz. Mixed programme of operetta, musicals and popular operas.

THE OKTOBERFEST AND OTHER EVENTS

The **Oktoberfest**, held on the Theresienwiese fairground from the penultimate Saturday in September for the next sixteen days, is an orgy of beer drinking, spiced up by fairground rides that are so hairy they're banned in the USA. The proportions of the fair are so massive that the grounds are divided along four main avenues, creating a boisterous city of its own, heaving from morning till night. **Fasching**, Munich's carnival, is an excuse for parades, fancy-dress balls and general shenanigans from mid-January until the beginning of Lent. More sedate is **Auer Dult**, a traditional market that takes place on the Mariahilfplatz during the last weeks of April, July and October each year; there are stalls selling food, craftware and antiques, and there's also a fairground.

Listings

Airlines British Airways, Promenadeplatz 10 (☎089/292121); Lufthansa, Lenbachplatz 1 (☎089/552 5050).

Airport information (☎089/9752 1313).

Bike rental In the Hauptbahnhof, opposite platform 31.

Car rental Avis (☎089/550 2251) and Europcar (☎089/549 0240) both have offices at the train station.

Consulates Britain, Bürkleinstr 10 (☎089/211 090); Canada, Tal 29 (☎089/219 9570); Ireland, Mauerkircherstr. 1a (☎089/985723); US, Königinstr. 5 (☎089/28 880).

Exchange The bank at the train station is open daily 6am–11pm.

Gay Munich Despite Bavaria's deep conservatism, Munich has one of the most active and visible gay scenes in Germany. Cafés that cater predominantly for lesbians are *Karotte*, Baaderstr. 13, *Frauencafé im Kofra*, Baaderstr. 8 and *Frauencafé*, Karlstr. 51. The following male gay bars are well known: *Cock*, Augsburger Str. 21; *Colibri*, Utzschneiderstr. 8; *Juice*, Buttermelcherstr. 2a; *Klimperkasten*, Maistr. 28.

Hitching Mitfahrzentrale at Adalbertstr. 10–12 (☎089/19444), and Lämnerstr. 4 (☎089/19440).

Laundry Amalienstr. 61; Ismaninger Str. 45.

Medical emergencies ☎089/551771.

Post office Bahnhofplatz 1, and Residenzstr. 2.

The Bavarian Alps

It's among the picture-book scenery of the Alps that you'll find the Bavarian folklore and customs that are the subject of so many tourist brochures, and the region also encompasses some of the most famous places in the province, such as the Olympic ski resort of **Garmisch-Partenkirchen**, and the fantasy castle of **Neuschwanstein**, just one of the lunatic palaces built for King Ludwig II of Bavaria. The western reaches are generally cheaper and less touristy, partly because they're not so easily accessible to Munich's weekend crowds. In contrast, much of the eastern region to **Berchtesgaden** is heavily geared to the tourist trade, but if you go outside the high season of July and August, you should have a good chance of avoiding the crowds and not straining your finances.

Garmisch and Mittenwald

GARMISCH-PARTENKIRCHEN is the most famous town in the German Alps, partly because it's at the foot of the highest mountain – the **Zugspitze** (2966m) – and partly because it hosted the Winter Olympics in 1936. Garmisch has excellent facilities for skiing, skating and other winter sports, but the town is irredeemably complacent and unfriendly. The ascent of Zugspitze by rack-railway and cable car (both DM61 in winter, DM76 in summer) is an exhilarating expedition, but far preferable to Garmisch is **MITTENWALD**, which remains a community rather than a resort; it's just 15km down the road and similarly on a main rail line from Munich. The **Karwendl** mountain towering above Mittenwald is a highly popular climbing destination, and the view from the top is one of the most exhilarating and dramatic in Germany; a cable car goes there for DM29 return. The **tourist office**, at Dammkarstr. 3 (Mon–Fri 8am–noon & 1–5pm, Sat 10am–noon; ☎08823/33981), will reserve rooms and provide free maps of the area. There are plenty of good **guesthouses** in the village, such as *Franziska*, Innsbrucker Str. 24 (☎08823/92030; ③) and *Bergfrühling*, Dammkarstr. 12 (☎08823/8089; ③). The nearest **campsite** is 3km north, on the road to Garmisch, and is open all year.

OBERAMMERGAU AND SCHLOSS LINDERHOF

From Murnau, midway between Munich and Garmisch-Partenkirchen, a branch line runs to **OBERAMMERGAU**, world-famous for its **Passion Play**, first performed in 1633 as thanks for being spared by a plague epidemic. The show takes place every ten years between May and October, with a cast of local villagers. All tickets for the year 2000 performances have long ago been sold out, so the only realistic chance of seeing the play, other than being lucky enough to obtain a last-minute cancellation, is to sign up for a package tour with an operator who has block-booked tickets. Many of Oberammergau's houses have traditional outside **frescoes** of religious or Alpine scenes, which you can see as either quaint or kitsch – that goes for the wood carvings in the local souvenir shops, too.

From here it's a short bus ride to the **Schloss Linderhof** (daily: April–Sept 9am–5.30pm; DM9; Oct–March 10am–4pm; DM7), one of the architectural fantasies conjured for dotty King Ludwig. Though built as a discreet private residence, it has a reception room with intricate gold-painted carvings, stucco ornamentation, and a throne canopy draped in ermine curtains. The real attraction is the delightful **park**: Italianate terraces, cascades and manicured flowerbeds give way to an English garden design that gradually blends into the forests of the mountain beyond. A number of romantic little buildings are dotted around the park, the most remarkable of which is the Venus Grotto. Based on the set for Wagner's opera *Tannhäuser* (Ludwig was the composer's principal patron), it has an illuminated lake supporting a huge floating golden conch in which the king would sometimes take rides.

Hohenschwangau and Neuschwanstein

Lying between the Forggensee reservoir and the Ammer mountains, around 100km by rail from Munich, **FÜSSEN** and the adjacent town of **SCHWANGAU** are the bases for visiting Bavaria's two most popular castles. **Schloss Hohenschwangau** (daily April–Oct 8.30am–5.30pm; Nov–March 10am–4pm; DM12), originally built in the twelfth century but heavily restored in the nineteenth, was where Ludwig spent his youth. A mark of his individualism is left in the bedroom, where he had the ceiling painted with stars that were spotlit in the evenings. **Schloss Neuschwanstein** (same times; DM12), the ultimate storybook castle, was built by Ludwig a little higher up the mountain. The architectural hotchpotch ranges from a Byzantine throne hall to a Romanesque study and an artificial grotto. Left incomplete at Ludwig's death, it's a bizarre monument to a very sad and lonely man.

The nearest **youth hostel** is in Füssen, at Mariahilferstr. 5 (☎08362/7754; ②). An inexpensive **guesthouse** near the castles is *Pension Weiher*, Hofwiesenweg 11 (☎08362/81126; ③). The **tourist office** at Kaiser-Maximilian-Platz (Mon–Fri 8am–noon & 2–6pm, Sat 10am–noon) in Füssen can book accommodation. Füssen is also the end of the much-publicized **Romantic Road** from Würzburg via Augsburg, served by special tour buses in season.

Berchtesgaden

Almost entirely surrounded by mountains at Bavaria's southeastern extremity, the area around **BERCHTESGADEN** has a magical atmosphere, especially in the mornings, when mists rise from the lakes and swirl around lush valleys and rocky mountainsides. The town is easily reached by rail from Munich and from Salzburg in Austria, which is just 23km to the north.

The town is famous for its **salt mine** (Salzbergwerk; May to mid-Oct daily 9am–5pm; mid-Oct to April Mon–Sat 12.30pm–3.30pm; DM21), where a small train will take you deep into the mountainside; you have to don protective clothing and descend on wooden slides. The region's other star attraction is **Königssee**, Germany's highest lake, which bends around the foot of the spiky Watzmann 5km south of the town and can be reached by regular buses. There are cruises on the Königssee all year round (DM22.50). You can also take a cable car up the **Jenner**, immediately above the lake (DM33 return). There are some great mountain trails to take you out of the crowds – maps of suggested walking routes can be bought at the **tourist office** opposite the train station (late June to mid-Oct Mon–Fri 8am–6pm, Sat 8am–5pm, Sun 9am–3pm; rest of year Mon–Fri 8am–5pm, Sat 9am–noon; ☎08652/9670).

The area's main historical claim to fame is its connection with Adolf Hitler, who rented a house in the nearby village of Obersalzberg, which he later enlarged into the **Berghof**, a stately retreat where he could meet foreign dignitaries. It was blown up by the Allies, and the ruins are now overgrown. High above the village on the Kehlstein, the **Kehlsteinhaus**, Hitler's "Eagle's Nest" survives as a restaurant, and can be reached by special bus from Obersalzberg (May–mid-Oct; DM20 return).

Berchtesgaden has plenty of reasonable **guesthouse** accommodation. Options include *Haus am Hang*, Göllsteinbichl 3 (☎08652/43590; ②), *Hansererhäusl*, Hansererweg 8 (☎08652/2523; ②), *Gästehaus Alpina*, Ramsauer Str. 6 (☎08652/2517; ③), and *Haus Achental*, Ramsauer Str. 4 (☎08652/4549; ③). The tourist office can help with booking rooms and will direct you to any of the five **campsites** in the valley.

Augsburg

Innovations, both religious and secular, have found fertile ground in **AUGSBURG**, 70km from Munich. Luther's reforms found their earliest support here, and in 1514 the city built the world's first housing estate for the poor, the Fuggerei – an institution still in use today. The citizens of Augsburg have gone to great lengths to restore the city's appearance to that of its medieval heyday, yet this isn't just a museum-piece. There's lively cultural action ranging from Mozart festivals to jazz and cabaret, and the university provides a thriving alternative scene to keep the place on its toes.

The City

Heart of the city is the spacious cobbled **Rathausplatz**, which turns into a massive open-air café during the summer and into a glittering market at Christmas. At the baseline of this great semicircle stands the massive **Rathaus**, perhaps Germany's finest secular Renaissance building. Inside, the spick-and-span **Goldener Saal** (daily 10am–6pm; DM2), with its gold-leaf pillars and marble floor, recalls the period when the Fugger banking dynasty made Augsburg one of the financial centres of Europe. Next to the Rathaus stands the **Perlachturm** (May to mid-Oct daily 10am–4/6pm; DM2), a good vantage point.

To the south, **Maximilianstrasse** is lined by merchants' palaces and punctuated by fountains. Soon after the Mercury fountain, the **Fuggerhäuser** stand proudly to the right; built in 1515 by Jacob Fugger "the Rich", they still belong to his loaded descendants, but you can walk through the main door to see the luxurious arcaded courtyard. Opposite the Hercules fountain is the **Schaezler Palais** (Wed–Sun 10am–4pm; DM4), through the courtyard of which is the Dominican nunnery of St Catherine and the **State Gallery** (same times and ticket), home of Dürer's portrait of Jacob Fugger. At the far end of Maximilianstrasse, Lutheran **St Ulrich** is dwarfed by the Catholic basilica of **St Ulrich-und-Afra**, resting place of the city's joint patron saints.

At the other end of the town's axis, the **Dom** stands in the grounds of the former episcopal palace, now the seat of the regional government. It was founded by Saint Ulrich in the tenth century, and the most interesting remains of its Romanesque origins are the enormous bronze doors at the southern entrance and the stained-glass windows – the oldest stained glass still in position. There are also a number of altarpieces by Hans Holbein the Elder.

The town's historical museum, the **Maximilianmuseum** (Wed–Sun 10am–4pm; DM4), is housed in a merchant's house at Philippine-Welser-Str. 24, and is currently being restored. Prehistoric and Roman remains are shown separately in the **Römisches Museum** (same hours and price), which occupies the old Dominican church at Dominikanergasse 15. The light and whitewashed interior makes an excellent setting for the Roman masonry and bronzes, and the uncluttered layout is a pleasure after the usual warehouse-like museums.

For a charge of one "Our Father", one "Hail Mary" and one Creed daily, plus DM1.72 per annum, good Catholic paupers can retire to the **Fuggerei** at the age of 55. With an entrance in the Jacoberstrasse, it's a town within a town, and compared with modern housing estates is a real idyll, the cloister-like atmosphere disturbed only by the odd ringing doorbell. **Number 13** (March–Oct daily 9am–6pm; Nov & Dec Sat & Sun only; DM1) in the Mittlere

Gasse is one of only two houses from the original foundation, and today it's full of furnishings that show how residents lived from the sixteenth to the eighteenth century.

On the other side of town, in Annastrasse, stands **St Anna**, where the **Fuggerkapelle** marks the belated German debut of the full-blooded Italian Renaissance style, a spin-off of the family's extensive business interests in Italy. An effect of overwhelming richness is created by the marble pavement, stained glass, choir stalls, a sculptural group of *The Lamentation over the Dead Christ*, and memorial tablets honouring the Fugger brothers made after woodcuts designed by Dürer. It was in St Anna that the final confrontation between the papal court and Luther took place in 1518. Luther found refuge with the Carmelites of St Anna when he was summoned to see the pope's legate, and today his room and several others in the old monastery have been turned into the **Lutherstiege** (Tues–Sun 10am–noon & 3–5pm; free), a museum of the reformer's life and times.

Practicalities

The **tourist office** (Mon–Fri 10am–5pm; ☎0821/502070) is a couple of minutes from the **train station** at Bahnhofstr. 7: there's also a branch on Rathausplatz (Mon–Fri 10am–5pm, Sat 10am–1pm). Good **pensions** are to be found in the suburb of Lechhausen, 1.5km from the city centre and connected by three bus routes and tram #1: *Bayerische Löwe*, Linke Brandstr. 2 (☎0821/702870; ③); *Linderhof*, Aspernstr. 38 (☎0821/713016; ③); and *Märkl*, Schillerstr. 20 (☎0821/791499; ③). The **youth hostel** is three minutes' walk from the Dom, at Beim Pfaffenkeller 3 (☎0821/33 909; ②). The nearest **campsite** is at motorway exit Augsburg-Ost, next to the Autobahnsee.

The cheapest places for **snacks** are the market and meat halls off Annastrasse, where you'll find several good *Imbiss* stands. Moving upmarket, excellent Swabian **meals** are served at the *Fuggerei-Stube*, Jakobergstr. 26. For **drinking**, *Kreslesmühle*, Barfüsserstr. 4, is a popular café/bar and arts centre; *Striese*, Kirchgasse 1, is also a theatre and music venue.

Regensburg

"Regensburg surpasses every German city with its outstanding and vast buildings," drooled Emperor Maximilian I in 1517. The centre of **REGENSBURG** has changed remarkably little since then; its undisturbed medieval panorama and its stunning location on the banks of the Danube make it a great place to spend a couple of days.

Maximilianstrasse leads straight from the train station to the centre. The best view of Regensburg's medieval skyline is from the twelfth-century **Steinerne Brücke**, which was the only safe and fortified crossing along the entire length of the Danube at the time it was built, and thus had tremendous value for the city as a trading centre. On the left, just past the medieval salt depot, the **Historische Wurstküche** (daily 8am–7pm) originally functioned as the bridge workers' kitchen. It's been run by the same family for generations and serves little else but delicious Regensburg sausages.

A short way south the **Dom** comes into full view. Bavaria's most magnificent Gothic building, it was begun around 1250, replacing a Romanesque church of which the **Eselsturm** is the only remaining part above ground. Highlights include the late thirteenth-century statues of the Annunciation and the fourteenth-century stained-glass windows in the south transept. In the cloisters – accessible only on guided tours (May–Oct Mon–Sat 10am, 11am & 2pm, Sun noon & 2pm; Nov–April Mon–Sat 11am, Sun noon; DM4) – the Allerheiligen Kapelle still has many Romanesque frescoes. Concerts and services are a musical treat in Regensburg, as the *Domspatzen* (Cathedral Sparrows) have some of the finest choristers in the country.

Perhaps the best of Regensburg's merchant and patrician houses are to be seen on the **Haidplatz**. The largest building on the square is the **Haus zum Goldenen Kreuz**, where Emperor Charles V used to meet a local girl called Barbara Blomberg: their son, John of Austria, was born here in 1547 and died Governor of the Netherlands in 1578. The nearby **Thon-Dittmer Palais** is one of the main cultural venues, concerts and plays being held in its courtyard in summer. A few minutes' walk away, the Neupfarrplatz is the centre of

Regensburg's commercial life: the **Neupfarrkirche**, standing forlorn in the middle of the car park, occupies the site of the old synagogue, which was wrecked during the 1519 expulsion of the Jews.

Apart from the Dom, the town's most important Gothic structure is the **Altes Rathaus** on the Kohlenmarkt. To appreciate its grand scale, you need to take a guided tour of the **Reichstagsmuseum** (tours in English May–Sept Mon–Sat 3.15pm; tours in German Mon–Sat 9.30am–11.30am/noon & 2–4pm, Sun 10am–noon, also 2–4pm April–Oct; DM5); the most significant room is the Imperial Diet Chamber, a parliamentary forum for the empire from 1663 to 1806.

On nearby Keplerstrasse, the **Kepler-Gedächtnishaus** (tours Tues–Sat 10am, 11am, 2pm & 3pm, Sun 10am & 11am, also 2pm & 3pm April–Oct; DM4) is dedicated to the astronomer Johann Kepler, who lived and worked in Regensburg in the early seventeenth century. Another museum worth looking into is the **Historical Museum** on Dachauplatz (Tues–Sun 10am–4pm; DM4) – especially the section on Albrecht Altdorfer, who, apart from being one of Germany's greatest artists, was also a leading local politician.

Schloss Thurn und Taxis (tours: April–Oct Mon–Fri 11am, 2pm, 3pm & 4pm, Sat & Sun also 10am; Nov–March Sat & Sun only 10am, 11am, 2pm & 3pm; DM12 combined entry to Schloss and cloisters), home of the Prince of Thurn and Taxis, is situated in the city's southern quarter. The palace isn't open to the public when the boss is at home, but when he's away a guide will show you the state rooms, with some wonderful Brussels tapestries on the walls recording the family's illustrious history. The former cloisters, now partly the library, represent some of the finest Gothic architecture to be found in Germany.

Practicalities

The **tourist office** is bang in the middle, in the Altes Rathaus (Mon–Fri 8.30am–6pm, Sat 9am–4pm, Sun 9.30am–2.30/4pm; ☎0941/507 4410). The **youth hostel**, Wöhrdstr. 60 (☎0941/57402; ②), is about five minutes' walk from the heart of things, on an island in the Danube. Cheapest **hotel** in the town centre is *Zum Fröhliche Türken*, Fröhliche-Türken-Str. 11 (☎0941/53651; ③). Just the other side of the Steinerne Brücke, *Spitalgarten*, St Katharinen-Platz 1 (☎0941/84774; ③) is conveniently sited next to the best beer garden. The **campsite** is about twenty minutes' walk from the centre, next to the Danube at Weinweg 40.

You're spoilt for places **to eat** in Regensburg. Two *Gaststätten* with good traditional and moderately priced Bavarian fare are *Alte Münz*, Fischmarkt 8, and *Kneitinger*, Arnulfsplatz 3. For more of a **bar**-type atmosphere, usually with good music, try *Rote Löwe*, Rote Löwengasse 10, or *Anopola*, Am Römling 1. Popular student hangouts are *Schwedenkugel*, Haaggasse 15, and *Goldene Ente*, Badstr. 32. For a traditional **beer garden**, take bus #6 south to *Kneitinger Keller*, at Galgenbergstr. 18 near the university, or for a great location on one of the Danube islands, try *Spitalgarten* on St Katharinen-Platz.

Nürnberg

Founded in the eleventh century, **NÜRNBERG** rapidly rose to become the unofficial capital of Germany, its position at the intersection of major trading routes leading to economic prosperity and political power. The arts flourished too, though the most brilliant period was not to come until the late fifteenth century, when the roll call of citizens was led by Albrecht Dürer. Like many other wealthy European cities, Nürnberg went into gradual economic and social decline once the sea routes to the Americas and Far East had been established; moreover, adoption of the Reformation cost the city the patronage of the Catholic emperors. It made a comeback in the nineteenth century, when it became the focus for the pan-German movement, and the Germanisches Nationalmuseum – the most important collection of the country's arts and crafts – was founded at this time.

Nürnberg is especially enticing in the summer, when the historic centre – the Altstadt – is alive with street theatre and music, and open-air concerts liven up the parks and stadiums; but there's always a wide and varied range of nightlife.

Arrival and accommodation

The main **tourist office** (Mon–Sat 9am–7pm; ☎0911/233632) is conveniently situated in the central hall of the **train station**, just outside the **Altstadt**. There's another office at Hauptmarkt 18, within the Altstadt (Mon–Sat 9am–6pm; May–Sept also Sun 10am–1pm & 2–4pm; ☎0911/233635). The official **youth hostel** has a wonderful location within the Kaiserburg, overlooking the Altstadt (☎0911/221024; ②). There's also a privately run *Youth Hotel* to the north of the city at Rathsbergstr. 300 (☎0911/521 6092; ③; no age restriction). Cheapest reasonably central **pensions** include: *Vater Jahn*, Jahnstr. 13 (☎0911/444507; ③), *Melanchthon*, Melanchthonplatz 1 (☎0911/412626; ③), and *Altstadt*, Hintere Ledergasse 4 (☎0911/2226102; ④). The **campsite** is in the Volkspark, near the Dutzendteich lakes (May–Sept; tram #12).

The City

On January 2, 1945, a storm of bombs reduced ninety percent of Nürnberg's centre to ash and rubble, but you'd never guess it from the meticulous postwar rebuilding. Covering about 4 square kilometres, the reconstructed medieval core is surrounded by its ancient **city walls** and neatly spliced by the River Pegnitz. To walk from one end to the other takes about twenty minutes, but much of the centre, especially the area around the castle (known as the **Burgviertel**), is on a steep hill. It's not all medieval pictures, either. Significant areas of modern architecture and open spaces are nearby, ensuring a refreshing mix of old and new.

One of the highest points of the city is occupied by the **Kaiserburg** (daily 9.30am–noon & 12.45–4/5pm; DM9), whose earliest surviving part is the eastern **Fünfeckturm**, which dates back to the eleventh century. A century later, Frederick Barbarossa extended the castle to the west: his **Sinwellturm**, built directly on the rock, can be ascended for the best of all the views. Another survivor of this period is the **Kaiserkapelle**, whose upper level was reserved for the use of the emperor, with the courtiers confined to the lower tier. At the extreme east end of the complex is the **Luginslandturm**, erected by the city council in the fourteenth century. At the end of the fifteenth century, the Luginslandturm was joined to the Fünfeckturm by the vast **Kaiserstallung** – originally a cereal warehouse and later a stable, it's now a perfect home for the youth hostel.

The area around the **Tiergärtner Tor** next to the Kaiserburg is one of the most attractive parts of the old town centre, a meeting point for summertime street vendors, artists and musicians. Virtually next door, the **Dürer Haus** (Tues, Wed & Fri–Sun 10am–5pm, Thurs 10am–8pm; DM5) is where the painter, engraver, scientist, writer, traveller and politician lived from 1509 to 1528, and is one of the very few original houses still standing. Don't come here looking for original Dürer paintings, though: there are only copies, plus works by artists paying homage to the great man. Dürer himself is buried in the St Johannisfriedhof, a few minutes' walk away, along Johannisstrasse.

Nürnberg's oldest and most important church, the twin-towered **Sebalduskirche**, is just down the road from the Fembohaus. Founded in the thirteenth century and altered a century later, it contains an astonishing array of works of art. Particularly striking are the bronze shrine of Saint Sebald and some pieces by Veit Stoss, Nürnberg's most famous sculptor: an expressive *Crucifixion* on the pillar behind the shrine and three stone reliefs in the chancel.

The **Hauptmarkt**, commercial heart of the city and the main venue for weekly markets (and the famous Christmas market), is a couple of minutes' walk away. Its east side is bounded by the **Frauenkirche**, on whose facade a clockwork mechanism known as the *Männleinlaufen* tinkles away at noon. Also on the Hauptmarkt is a replica of the famous **Schöner Brunnen**, looking like a lost church spire; the original parts are on display in the Germanisches Nationalmuseum.

Walking southwards from Hauptmarkt, you cross the river by Museumsbrücke, which gives you a good view of the **Fleischbrücke** to the right, and the **Heilig-Geist-Spital** – one of the largest hospitals built in the Middle Ages – on the left. Passing the oldest house in the city, the thirteenth-century **Nassauer Haus**, you shortly come to the **Lorenzkirche**, built about fifty years after the Sebalduskirche, its counterpart on the other side of the water. The nave has a resplendent rose window, while the chancel is lit by gleaming stained glass. The graceful late fifteenth-century **tabernacle**, some 20m high, was carved by Adam Kraft, who depicted himself as a pensive figure crouching at the base. Equally spectacular is the larger-than-life *Annunciation* by Veit Stoss, suspended above the high altar.

Further down Königstrasse in the direction of the train station is the massive and austere Renaissance **Mauthalle**, beyond which stands the Gothic **Marthakirche**, the hall of the *Meistersinger*. The distinctive form of lyric poetry known as *Meistergesang* flourished in Germany from the fourteenth century, and had a glorious final fling in Nürnberg, thanks above all to the shoemaker Hans Sachs, creator of some 6000 works.

West of the Mauthalle, the **Germanisches Nationalmuseum** occupies a fourteenth-century monastery on Kornmarkt (Tues & Thurs–Sun 10am–5pm, Wed 10am–9pm; DM6, free Wed 6–9pm). On the ground floor the displays follow a roughly chronological layout, beginning with Bronze Age items and moving onto medieval sculptures and carvings, outstanding among which are *The Seven Stations of the Cross* by Adam Kraft and works by Tilman Riemenschneider and Veit Stoss. German **painting** at its Renaissance peak dominates the first floor, with pieces by Dürer, Altdorfer, Baldung and Cranach. The following rooms focus on the diversity of Nürnberg's achievements during the Renaissance. The strong tradition of gold- and silversmithing is shown to best effect in the superb model of a three-masted ship, while the city's leading role in the fast-developing science of geography is exemplified by the first globe of the earth, made by Martin Behaim in 1491 – just before the discovery of America. This floor's south wing is entirely devoted to German folklore, and in particular to Catholic worship, notably weird votive offerings – look out for the wax toads offered for help with women's complaints.

THE ZEPPELIN FIELD AND MARS FIELD

In virtually everyone's mind, "Nuremberg" conjures up thoughts of Nazi rallies and war-crime trials. As the city council is eager to point out, the Nazis' choice of Nürnberg had less to do with local support of Nazi ideology, and more to do with what the medieval city represented in German history. The rallies were held on the **Zeppelin and Mars fields** in the suburb of Luitpoldhain (tram #9 from the centre), where today Albert Speer's Stadium and Congress Hall lie derelict, used only for the occasional rock concert or car rally. The tourist board has put together a multimedia presentation called **Fascination and Force** (mid-May to Oct Tues–Sun 10am–6pm; DM2), but the atmosphere of the stadium needs little explanation. The "Nürnberg Laws" of 1935 deprived Jews of their citizenship and forbade relations between Jews and Gentiles. It was through these laws that the Nazis justified their extermination of six million Jews, 10,000 of whom came from Nürnberg. Only ten remained here after the war. It was highly significant that the war criminals of the Nazi regime were tried in the city that saw their proudest demonstrations of power.

Eating, drinking and nightlife

Nürnberg is the liveliest Bavarian city after Munich, with a wealth of *Studentenkneipen* and café/bars catering for the students. The cheapest **meals** in town are to be found in the university **mensa**, in the northeastern corner of the Altstadt. Otherwise there are plenty of *Imbiss*-type snack-joints in the pedestrian zone between St Lorenz and the Ehekarussel. In the Altstadt, good places to **eat** include *Bratwurst-Häusle*, Rathausplatz 1, the most celebrated of the city's sausage restaurants, and the excellent and reasonable *Nassauer Keller*, Karolinerstr. 2, installed in an atmospheric thirteenth-century cellar. In Spitalgasse, *Heilig-Geist-Spital* serves hearty fare in the setting of a medieval hospital building. At Bergstr. 19 is *Schwarzer Bauer*, the pub of the Altstadthof's celebrated **house brewery**. Another place which brews its own beer is *Barfüsser*, which occupies the cavernous cellars of the Mauthalle at Hallplatz 2. For a combination of beer haven and music bar, make for *Starclub*, Maxtorgraben 33. *Ruhestörung*, Tetzelgasse 21, is one of the most fashionable café/bars. The tiny, excellent café-bar *Meisengeige*, Am Laufer Schlagturm 3, caters for a mixed crowd, and its small cinema shows an offbeat selection of films. The trendiest **nightclub** in Nürnberg is *Mach 1*, Kaiserstr. 1–9, with four different bars and some good lighting effects (Wed–Sun 9pm–4am). To find out what else is going on, get either the *Monatsmagazin* from the tourist office, or the *Plärrer* magazine from any kiosk.

Rothenburg ob der Tauber

The tourist itinerary known as the **Romantic Road**, which winds its way along the length of western Bavaria, runs through the most visited medieval town in Germany: **ROTHENBURG OB DER TAUBER**, 50km west of Nürnberg. It is connected by a branch railway with Steinach, on the Augsburg–Würzburg line – and there are scores of special buses ferrying tourists along the chain of half-timbered villages that comprise the Romantic Road.

It takes about an hour to walk around the fourteenth-century walls of Rothenburg, the ultimate museum piece. The promontory on the western side of town is the site of the **Burgtor** watchtower – the oldest of all the 24 towers – and the **Blasiuskapelle**, with murals from the fourteenth century. The nearby **Herrngasse** leads up to the town centre, and is the widest street in Rothenburg, once home to the local nobs. Also on this street is the severe early Gothic **Franziskanerkirche**, which houses a startlingly realistic altarpiece showing *The Stigmatization of St Francis*.

The sloping **Marktplatz** is dominated by the arcaded front of the **Renaissance Rathaus**, which supplanted the Gothic building that stands behind it. The sixty-metre **tower** of the **Gotisches Rathaus** (April–Oct daily 9.30am–12.30pm & 1–4pm; Nov–March Sat & Sun noon–3pm; DM1) is the highest point in Rothenburg and provides the best view of the town and surrounding countryside. The other main attractions on the Marktplatz are the figures on each side of the three clocks of the **Ratsherrntrinkstube**, which seven times daily re-enact an episode that occurred during the Thirty Years' War. The fearsome Johann Tilly agreed that Rothenburg should be spared if one of the councillors could drain in one draught a tankard holding over three litres of wine. A former burgomaster duly sank the contents of the so-called *Meistertrunk*, then needed three days to sleep off the effects. On the opposite side of the Marktplatz is Rothenburg's largest building, the Gothic **St Jakob-Kirche** (Easter–Oct Mon–Sat 9am–5.30pm, Sun 10.30am–5.30pm; Nov–Easter daily 10am–noon & 2–4pm; DM2.50), rising above the sea of red roofs like a great ship; the entrance fee is worth paying purely to see Tilman Riemenschneider's exquisite limewood *Holy Blood Altar*.

Of the local museums, the most fascinating is the **Kriminalmuseum** at Burggasse 3 (daily: April–Oct 9.30am–5.30pm; Nov, Jan & Feb 2–3.30pm; Dec & March 10am–3.30pm; DM5), which contains collections attesting to medieval inhumanity in the shape of torture instruments and related objects such as the beer barrels that drunks were forced to walk around in. The **Reichstadtmuseum** on Klosterhof (daily: April–Oct 10am–5pm; Nov–March 1–4pm; DM4) is most interesting for its original medieval workrooms.

There are many cheap **pensions** and **inns** in Rothenburg; worth trying are *Pension Pöschel*, Wenggasse 22 (☎09861/3430; ③), *Gästehaus Raidel*, on the same street at no. 3 (☎09861/3115; ③), and *Pension Hofmann*, Stollengasse 29 (☎09861/3371; ③). The two **youth hostels** – *Rossmühle* and its annexe *Spitalhof* (☎09861/4510; ②) – are in beautifully restored houses off the bottom of the Spitalgasse. **Private rooms** are the next cheapest option, with costs in the ②–③ range: details from the highly efficient **tourist office** on Marktplatz (Mon–Fri 9am–12.30pm & 2–6pm, Sat 9am–noon; also May–Sept Sat 2–4pm; ☎09861/40492).

Würzburg

Terminus of the Romantic Road, **WÜRZBURG** straddles the River Main some 60km north of Rothenburg, and can be reached either by bus from there or by train from Nürnberg, Augsburg or Munich. During the night of March 16, 1945, it got the same treatment from Allied bombers that Nürnberg had received two months earlier. Würzburg has been less successful in rebuilding itself, but a number of outstanding sights and the town's location among a landscape of vineyards easily justify a visit.

Bracketed by the river and the Residenz, the old town is focused on the **Marktplatz**, where a daily food market ensures a lively bustle. Just off the square, the **Haus zum Falken** is the city's prize example of a Rococo town house, perfectly restored to the very last stucco curl. Overlooking the Markt is the Gothic **Marienkapelle**, which has an intriguing *Annunciation* above the northern portal: a band leads from God to Mary's ear, a baby sliding towards her along its folds.

Halfway down the Kürschnerhof, leading off the Marktplatz, the **Neumünster**'s dusky pink facade stands out among the postwar houses. The church was built over the graves of saints Kilian, Kolonat and Totnan, Irish missionaries martyred in 689 for trying to Christianize the region. The Kiliani festival, at the beginning of July, is the region's most important religious event, drawing thousands of pilgrims to the crypt where the saints are buried. The **Dom**, again consecrated to St Kilian, is virtually next door; it was burned out in 1945, so only the exterior is true to the original Romanesque.

The **Residenz** (April–Sept Tues–Sun 9am–5pm; Oct–March daily 10am–4pm; DM7) was intended to show that the Würzburg bishops could hold their own among such great European courts as Versailles. Construction was left largely in the hands of the prolific Balthasar Neumann, whose famed staircase is covered by the largest fresco in the world. An allegory extolling the fame of the prince-bishops in the most immodest way imaginable, it was painted by the greatest decorator of the age, Giambattista Tiepolo. The tour of the palace goes through the plain stuccoed Weisser Saal, before plunging into the opulence of the Kaisersaal; once reserved for the use of the emperor, it now provides a glamorous setting for the June Mozart Festival. The marble, the gold-leaf stucco and the sparkling chandeliers produce an effect of dazzling magnificence, but finest of all are more frescoes by Tiepolo. Tucked discreetly into the southwest corner of the palace in order not to spoil the symmetry, the **Hofkirche** is a brilliant early example of Neumann's illusionism – the interior, based on a series of ovals, appears much larger than it really is. Both side altars are by Tiepolo.

On the other side of the Dom, the twelfth-century **Alte Mainbrücke** – the oldest bridge over the Main – leads towards the **Festung Marienberg**; if you don't fancy the climb to the castle, you can take the #9 bus from the bridge. This was home to the ruling bishops from the thirteenth century until 1750, when they shifted to the Residenz. The devastations of foreign armies – the Swedes, the Prussians, the Allies in the last war – have been so great that although much of the original structure has been restored, the interiors are largely missing. The medieval core contains the round **Marienkirche**, one of Germany's oldest churches, as well as the **Brunnenhaus**, whose 105-metre well was chiselled through the rock in around 1200. Surrounding this are a number of other buildings, including the Renaissance **Fürstenbau** (Tues–Sun 9am–12.30pm & 1–4/5pm; DM4). The **Mainfränkisches Museum** (Tues–Sun 10am–4/5pm; DM3.50) in the former arsenal contains sculptures by Riemenschneider and examples of all genres of art across the ages, as well as an interesting display on Franconian wine.

During work on the Residenz, Neumann also took time to build the **Käppele**, a pilgrimage church imperiously perched on the heights to the south of the Marienberg. Apart from the opportunity to see the interior, lavishly covered with frescoes and stucco, it's worth visiting for the **view** from the terrace – the finest in Würzburg.

Practicalities

There's a **tourist office** (Mon–Sat 10am–6pm; ☎0931/37436) just outside the **train station** at the northern end of the city centre and another in the Haus zum Falken (Mon–Fri 10am–6pm, Sat 10am–2pm; April–Oct also Sun 10am–2pm; ☎0931/37398). There are two reasonably priced **pensions** between the station and the centre: *Siegel*, Reisgrubengasse 7 (☎0931/52941; ④) and *Spehnkuch*, Röntgenring 7 (☎0931/54752; ④). The **youth hostel**, Burkarderstr. 44 (☎0931/42590; ②; tram #3), is situated below the Marienberg. The nearest **campsite** is about 4km south in Heidingsfeld (#16 bus from Barbarossaplatz).

Best places for Franconian **food** are *Bürgerspital*, Theaterstr. 19, and *Juliusspital*, Juliuspromenade 19. Both were founded as homes for the needy, and financed (as they still are) by their vineyards. *Zur Stadt Mainz*, Semmelstr. 39, though excellent, is the tourist spot in town, printing its menus in five languages as well as Braille. For **student bars** go to Sanderstrasse in the south of town – *Till Eulenspiegel*, Sanderstr. 1a, is particularly good.

Bamberg

The people of **BAMBERG**, which lies 60km north of Nürnberg and 95km east of Würzburg, knock back more beer per person than in any other town in the country: ten breweries produce thirty different kinds of ale, most notably the distinctive smoky *Rauchbier*. Bamberg's isolation has preserved it from the ravages of war, and today it is one of the most beautiful small towns in the world, where most European styles from the Romanesque onwards have left a mark.

Heart of the lower town is the **Maxplatz**, dominated by Balthasar Neumann's **Neues Rathaus**. A daily market is held here and on the adjoining Grüner Markt, which stands in the shadow of the huge Jesuit church of **St Martin**. On an islet anchoring the Obere Brücke to the Untere Brücke is the **Altes Rathaus**, almost too picturesque for its own good. Except for the half-timbered section overhanging the rapids, the original Gothic building was transformed into Rococo, and its walls are tattooed with exuberant frescoes. The famous **Klein-Venedig** (Little Venice) of medieval fishermen's houses is best seen from the Untere Brücke.

Uphill, the spacious, sloping **Domplatz** is lined with such a superb variety of buildings that it has no rival as Germany's finest square. The **Kaiserdom** was consecrated in 1012, but the present structure of golden sandstone is the result of a slow rebuilding that continued throughout the thirteenth century. The astonishing array of sculpture was initially executed in orthodox Romanesque style, best seen in the Fürstenportal on the north side of the nave, where figures of the Apostles are carved below a *Last Judgment*. The most famous sculpture is inside – the enigmatic **Bamberg Rider**, one of the first equestrian statues to be made since classical antiquity. Focus of the nave is the white limestone tomb of the canonized imperial couple Heinrich II and Kunigunde; Tilman Riemenschneider laboured away for fourteen years on this sarcophagus, whose reliefs depict scenes taken from the life and times of the couple. The south transept contains a contemporaneous masterpiece, the *Nativity Altar* by Veit Stoss, made when the artist was about eighty years old.

The **Diocesan Museum** (Tues–Sun 10am–5pm; DM4), entered from the square, houses some fascinating ecclesiastical vestments, notably the robes worn by Heinrich II and Kunigunde. Also here are statues of the ubiquitous emperor and his wife, in the company of the Dom's two patrons plus an erotic Adam and Eve.

Opposite the cathedral, the **Ratstube** is a Renaissance gem, now containing the **Historical Museum** (March–Oct Tues–Sun 9am–5pm; DM4), which covers local history from the Stone Age to the twentieth century, as well as Bamberg's rich art history. Adjoining it is the **Reiche Tor**, where Heinrich and Kunigunde appear once more, leading into the huge courtyard of the **Alte Hofhaltung**, the former episcopal palace. Across the street is the building which supplanted it, the huge Baroque **Neue Residenz** (tours daily 9am–noon & 1.30–4/5pm; DM5). Inside are richly decorated state rooms, and the **Staatsgalerie Bamberg**, with medieval and Baroque paintings by German masters.

From the rose garden behind the Neue Residenz is a view of Michaelsburg, crowned by a huge **Abtei**. Much of the Romanesque shell of the church remains, but the interior is an awesome hotchpotch: lavish Rococo furnishings, tombs of Bamberg bishops and a ceiling depicting over 600 medicinal herbs. The cellars house the **Fränkisches Brauereimuseum** (April–Oct Thurs–Sun 1–4pm; DM3) – even if you're not interested in beer, it's worth coming for the wonderful panorama of Bamberg's skyline and surrounding hills.

Another place for a great view is **Altenburg**, a ruined castle at the end of the very steep Altenburger Strasse. From here, up the Untere Kaulberg and past Karmelitenplatz, you'll find the **Karmelitenkloster**. The church is again Baroque, but the Romanesque cloister (daily 8–11am & 2.30–5.30pm; free), the largest in Germany, has been preserved.

Practicalities

The **train station** is fifteen minutes' walk northeast of the centre. The **tourist office** (Mon–Fri 9am–6pm, Sat 9am–3pm; May–Sept also Sun 10am–2pm; ☎0951/871161) is at Geyerswörthstr. 3. Among several inexpensive **hotels** are *Bamberger Weissbierhaus*, Obere Königstr 38 (☎0951/25503; ③) and *Zum Alten Goldenen Anker*, Untere Sandstr. 73

(☎0951/66505; ③). The **youth hostel** is 2km south of the centre at Oberer Leinritt 70 (☎0951/56002; ②), reached by buses #1, #7, #11 from the train station to ZOB Promenade, then bus #18 to Regnitzufer. The local **campsite** is another 2km downriver – also reached by bus #18.

Two **restaurants** worth trying are *Schlenkerla*, Dominikanerstr. 6, which is famous for its *Rauchbier*, and *Kaiserdom-Stuben*, Urbanstr. 18, which is good for vegetarian dishes. Three of the best **cafés** are *Am Dom*, Ringleinsgasse 2; *Michaelsberg*, Michaelsberg 10e; and the summer *Rosengarten* in the Neue Residenz. Good places to try the **local beers** are four beer cellar-cum-gardens: *Spezial*, on Obere Stephansberg 47; *Greiffenklau*, Laurenziplatz 20; *Keesmann*, Wunderburg 5; and *Mahr's-Bräu*, Oberer Stephansberg 36.

BERLIN

BERLIN is like no other city in Germany or the world. For over a century its political climate has mirrored or determined what has happened in the rest of Europe, and it's this sense of living in a place where all the dilemmas of contemporary Europe are embodied that gives Berlin its fascination. It was, of course, World War II that defined the shape of today's city. Bombing razed 92 percent of the shops, houses and industry, and at the end of the war the city was split. The Allies took the west of the city, traditionally an area of bars, hotels and shops fanning out from the Kurfürstendamm and the Tiergarten Park. The Soviet zone contained what remained of imperial Berlin, centred on Unter den Linden. After the building of the Wall in 1961, which sealed the Soviet sector and consolidated its position as capital of the young German Democratic Republic, the divided sections of the city developed in different ways.

For years its isolation in the middle of the GDR meant that **western Berlin** had a pressure-cooker mentality; this, combined with the fact that many young people came here to immerse themselves in alternative lifestyles, created a vivacious nightlife and a sense of excitement on the streets.

Over the last few years, this frisson has shifted to the **eastern Berlin** districts of Mitte and Prenzlauer Berg, where, in an explosion of redevelopment, the crumbling tenements are being transformed into bright new shops, restaurants and bars.

The refurbishment of the east is only part of a citywide building boom. With breathtaking speed, Berlin is transforming itself into capital city and top-rank European metropolis, and still emanates the unmistakable feel of history in the making.

Arrival and information

Most flights to Berlin arrive at **Tegel airport**, from where frequent #X9 express **buses** run to **Zoo Station** (Bahnhof Zoologischer Garten), located in the centre of the city (DM3.90); or take the #109 to Jakob-Kaiser-Platz and pick up the U-Bahn. **Taxis** cover it in half the time and cost DM30–35. Most international **coaches** stop at a station near the Funkturm, linked to the centre by #149 buses or U-Bahn from Kaiserdamm.

Berlin's **tourist office** is in the Europa Center on Budapester Strasse (Mon–Sat 8am–10pm, Sun 9am–9pm; ☎030/25 00 25), with additional offices in the Brandenburg Gate (daily 9.30am–6pm). Berlin has two **listings magazines**, *Zitty* (DM4) and *Tip* (DM4.50), published on alternate weeks.

City transport

The **U-Bahn** underground system covers much of central Berlin and the suburbs; trains run from 4am to approximately 12.30am, an hour later on Friday and Saturday. The **S-Bahn** system is better for covering long distances fast – getting out to the Wannsee, for instance. The city **bus network** – and the **tram** system in eastern Berlin – covers most of the gaps left by the U-Bahn: **night buses** run at intervals of around twenty minutes, although the

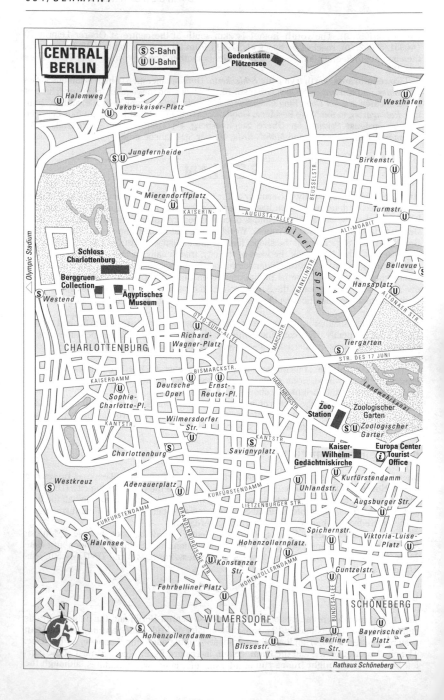

CENTRAL BERLIN

Ⓢ S-Bahn
Ⓤ U-Bahn

Gedenkstätte Plötzensee

Ⓤ Halemweg

Ⓤ Jakob-kaiser-Platz

Ⓤ Westhafen

ⓈⓊ Jungfernheide

Birkenstr.

Ⓤ Mierendorffplatz

KAISERIN-

-AUGUSTA-ALLEE

BEUSSELSTR

Turmstr. Ⓤ

ALT-MOABIT

River Spree

Schloss Charlottenburg

Berggruen Collection

Bellevue Ⓢ

Ⓢ Westend

Ägyptisches Museum

FRANKLINSTR

Hansaplatz Ⓤ

ALTONAER STR

OTTO-SUHR-ALLEE

Richard-Wagner-Platz

MARCHSTR

Tiergarten

CHARLOTTENBURG

Ⓢ STR. DES 17 JUNI

KAISERDAMM

BISMARCKSTR.

Landwehrkanal

Ⓤ Sophie-Charlotte-Pl.

Deutsche Oper

Ernst-Reuter-Pl.

HARDENBERGSTR

Zoo Station

Zoologischer Garten

KANTSTR.

Wilmersdorfer Str. Ⓤ

Ⓢ Ⓤ Zoologischer Garten

Ⓢ Charlottenburg

KANTSTR.

Ⓢ Savignyplatz

Kaiser-Wilhelm-Gedächtniskirche

Europa Center
ⓘ Tourist Office

Ⓢ Westkreuz

Adenauerplatz Ⓤ

Ⓤ Kurfürstendamm

KURFÜRSTENDAMM

Ⓤ Uhlandstr.

Augsburger Str.

LIETZENBURGER STR

Spichernstr. Ⓤ

Viktoria-Luise-Platz Ⓤ

KURFÜRSTENDAMM

BRANDENBURGISCHE STR

Ⓢ Halensee

Hohenzollernplatz Ⓤ

Ⓤ Konstanzer Str.

HOHENZOLLERNDAMM

Guntzelstr. Ⓤ

Fehrbelliner Platz Ⓤ

SCHÖNEBERG

N

WILMERSDORF

BUNDESALLEE

Bayerischer Platz Ⓤ

Ⓢ Hohenzollerndamm

Blissestr. Ⓤ

Berliner Str. Ⓤ

◁ Olympic Stadium

Rathaus Schöneberg ▽

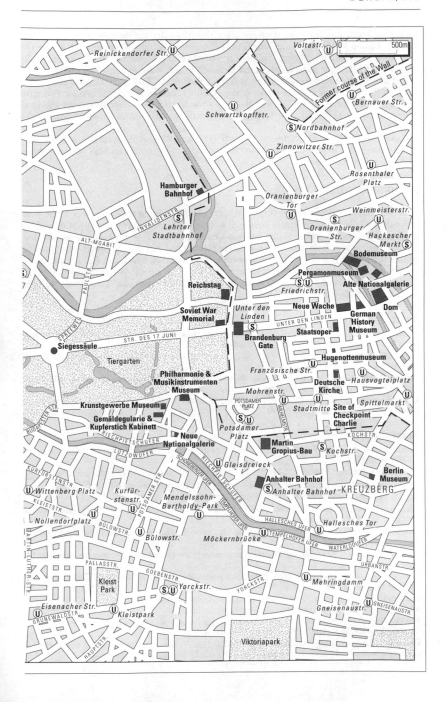

routes sometimes differ from daytime ones; the transport authority will supply a map. **Tickets** can be bought from machines at U-Bahn station entrances; common to all the systems they cost DM3.90, allowing you to travel in two of the three tariff zones, and are valid for two hours. Longer trips, from central Berlin to Potsdam for example, cost DM4.20. An *Einzelfahrschein Kurzstreckentarif*, or short-trip ticket, costs DM2.50 and allows you to travel up to three train or six bus stops. A **day ticket** (*Tageskarte*) is DM7.80 for two tariff zones, DM8.50 for all three. You can also buy a weekly ticket (*7-Tage-Karte*) for DM40 (2 zones) or DM48 (3 zones). There are on-the-spot fines of DM60 for those without a valid ticket or pass.

Taxis are plentiful and congregate at locations such as Savignyplatz and by the Zoo Station in the west, and at the northern entrance to Friedrichstrasse station and the *Forum Hotel* on Alexanderplatz in the east.

Accommodation

Accommodation in Berlin can be very hard to find, and if booking your own place in the western part it's best to call at least a couple of weeks in advance. If you turn up with nothing arranged, the tourist office in the Europa Center offers a free **hotel-booking service**, though their options tend to be pricey. If you're planning on a longer stay, the best way to find a place is through one of the **Mitwohnzentrale** organizations, which can find a room, usually for a minimum of seven nights, at roughly DM30–45 per person per night. Biggest of the Mitwohnzentrale is at Joachimstaler Str. 17 (Mon–Fri 9am–6pm, Sat 11am–2pm; ☎030/19 445), an easy walk from the Zoo Station.

Hostels

Bahnhofsmission, Zoo Station (☎030/313 8088). Dingy place with limited accommodation for rail travellers for one night only, including meagre breakfast. ②.

Jugendgästehaus, Kluckstr. 3 (☎030/261 1097). Bus #129, direction Oranienplatz. Fairly central, with 9am–noon lockout. Often full. ③.

Jugendgästehaus am Zoo, Hardenbergstr. 9a (☎030/312 9410). Zoologischer Garten U- and S-Bahn. Excellent location, extremely popular. No curfew. ④.

The Circus, Am Zirkus 2-3 (☎030/283 91433). Friedrichstrasse U- and S-Bahn. Clean and well-run hostel near the action in the east. No curfew. ④.

Hotels

Aacron, Friedrichstr. 124 (☎030/282 9352). About as central as you're likely to get at this price. The rooms are spartan but bearable. ③.

Alpenland, Carmerstr. 8 (☎030/312 3970). Well-situated and an excellent choice at this price. ⑥.

Artemisia, Brandenburgischestr. 18 (☎030/873 8905). The city's only women-only hotel. ⑧.

Bogota, Schlüterstr. 45 (☎030/881 5001). Pleasant luxury at sensible prices. ⑥.

Bregenz, Bregenzer Str. 5 (☎030/881 4307). A small family-run setup only a 10min walk from the Ku'damm. Children are welcome. ⑤.

Charlot, Giesebrechstr. 17 (☎030/323 4051). Neatly restored, efficiently run hotel near Adenauerplatz. Excellent value for money. ⑤.

Conti, Potsdamer Str. 67 (☎030/261 2999). Large pension in a tenement just a few minutes' walk from the Tiergarten museums. ④.

Cortina, Kantstr. 140 (☎030/313 9059). Reasonable rooms in a good area – one that's ideal for exploring the West End and Savignyplatz. ⑤.

Hansablick, Flotowstr. 6 (☎030/390 4800). A short hop from the Tiergarten, this is one of the few "alternative" hotels in town, being run by a collective; breakfast included. ⑦.

Merkur, Torstr. 156 (☎030/282 8297). Fairly comfortable rooms within easy walking distance of city centre attractions and local nightlife. Most rooms have showers. ⑤.

Unter den Linden, Unter den Linden 14 (☎030/238 110). Vintage East German hotel, now somewhat shopworn, located at the historic intersection of Unter den Linden and Friedrichstrasse. ⑦.

Campsite

Campingplatz Kohlhasenbrück, Neue Kreiss Str. 36 (☎030/805 1737). Closest of the Berlin sites. #118 bus in the direction of Drewitz. Facilities include a restaurant, showers and laundry room. DM7 per tent plus DM9.50 per person per night.

Western Berlin

Zoo Station is at the centre of the city's maelstrom: a short walk south and you're at the eastern end of the Kurfürstendamm or **Ku'damm**, a 3.5-kilometre strip of ritzy shops, cinemas, bars and cafés. The great landmark here is the **Kaiser-Wilhelm-Gedächtniskirche**, destroyed by British bombing in November 1943, and left as a reminder of wartime damage. There's little to do on the Ku'damm other than spend money, and there's only one cultural attraction nearby, the **Käthe Kollwitz Museum** at Fasanenstr. 24 (11am–6pm; closed Tues; DM8), devoted to the drawings and prints of the left-wing and pacifist artist Käthe Kollwitz.

The **Zoologischer Garten** itself (daily 9am–sunset; DM13) forms the beginning of the **Tiergarten**, a restful expanse of woodland and a good place to wander along the banks of the Landwehrkanal. At the centre of Strasse des 17 Juni, the broad avenue that cuts through the Tiergarten, rises the **Siegessäule** (daily 9am–6/8pm; DM2), a victory column celebrating Prussia's military successes; its summit offers one of Berlin's best views. Strasse des 17 Juni comes to an end at the **Brandenburg Gate**, built as a city gate-cum-triumphal arch in 1791. A little way north stands the **Reichstag**, the nineteenth-century home of the German parliament – it was remodelled by Norman Foster for the resumption of its historic role in April 1999. Immediately behind the Reichstag, it's now only just possible to make out the course of the **Berlin Wall**, which divided the city for 28 years until November 9, 1989.

The heart of Berlin used to be to the south of the Brandenburg Gate, its core formed by **Potsdamer Platz**. A huge commercial project now under construction hopes to bring back the area's former liveliness. Just to the east, near the corner of Wilhelmstrasse and An der Kolonnade, lies the site of **Hitler's bunker**, where the Führer spent his last days, issuing meaningless orders as the Battle of Berlin raged above.

West of Potsdamer Platz lies the **Tiergarten Complex**, a series of museums centred on the unmissable **Gemäldegalerie**, Matthäikirchplatz 8 (Tues–Sun 10am–6pm; DM8, free first Sun of month; the ticket also gives admission on the same day to all of Berlin's state-owned museums). In it the world-class collection of old masters, covering all the main European schools, ranges from the Middle Ages to the late eighteenth century. An outstanding display of early Netherlandish paintings includes the beautifully lit *Madonna in the Church* by Jan van Eyck, along with works by his successors Petrus Christus and Rogier van der Weyden, and two major paintings by Hugo van der Goes: *The Adoration of the Magi* and *The Adoration of the Shepherds* (the latter painted when the artist was in the first throes of madness). Later Dutch work includes Vermeer's *Man and Woman Drinking Wine* and a huge collection of Rembrandts; the famous *Man in the Golden Helmet* was recently proved to be the work not of Rembrandt, but of his studio, though this does little to detract from its elegance and power. Highlights of the German section include a marvellous group of portraits by Dürer, Cranach's tongue-in-cheek *The Fountain of Youth*, and Holbein's *The Danzig Merchant Georg Gisze*, which is celebrated for its virtuoso still-life background. Among the many Italian Renaissance masterpieces are works by Giotto, Masaccio, Lippi, Botticelli, Raphael, Correggio and Titian.

The interconnected building to the north houses the **Kunstgewerbemuseum** (same times; DM4 if visited separately, free first Sun of month), a sparkling collection of European arts and crafts from Byzantium to Bauhaus. Opposite are the **Philharmonie**, the home of the Berlin Philharmonic Orchestra, and the **Musikinstrumenten Museum** (Tues–Fri 9am–5pm, Sat & Sun 10am–5pm; DM4), a collection of weird and wonderful musical instruments. At Potsdamer Str. 50, a couple of minutes' walk to the south, is the **Neue Nationalgalerie** (Tues–Fri 10am–6pm, Sat & Sun 11am–6pm; DM8, free first Sun of month), which has a good collection of twentieth century German paintings, best of which are the Berlin portraits and cityscapes by George Grosz and Otto Dix.

Southeast of here, the **Martin-Gropius-Bau** at Stresemannstr. 110 (Tues–Sun 10am–8pm; admission varies) is now a venue for prestigious art exhibitions. An adjacent exhibition, **The Topography of Terror** (daily 10am–6pm; free), occupies the site of former Gestapo and SS headquarters. From here it's a ten-minute walk down Wilhelmstrasse and Kochstrasse to the site of the notorious Checkpoint Charlie; evidence of the trauma the Wall caused is still on hand in the **Haus am Checkpoint Charlie** at Friedrichstr. 44 (daily 9am–10pm; DM8), which tells the history of the Wall and the stories of those who tried to break through.

The checkpoint area marks the northern limit of **Kreuzberg**, famed for its large immigrant community, its self-styled "alternative" inhabitants and nightlife. The **Berlin Museum** at Lindenstr. 14 (due to reopen in early 2000), is the main daytime attraction for visitors. Its striking new extension by architect Daniel Libeskind houses a Jewish Museum documenting the culture, achievements, and tragic history of Berlin's Jewish community. Also meriting a visit is the **German Technology Museum** at Trebbiner Str. 9 (Tues–Fri 9am–5.30pm, Sat & Sun 10am–6pm; DM5), one of the city's most entertaining museums and a button-pusher's delight. Southwest in the other main nightlife zone, **Schöneberg**, the most famous attraction is the **Rathaus Schöneberg** on Martin-Luther-Strasse, where, in 1963, John F. Kennedy made his celebrated "Ich bin ein Berliner" speech.

Way over to the northwest of the Tiergarten stretches the district of **Charlottenburg**, its most significant target being the sumptuously restored **Schloss Charlottenburg** (Tues–Fri 10am–6pm, Sat & Sun 11am–6pm; DM15). Commissioned by the future Queen Sophie Charlotte in 1695, it was added to throughout the eighteenth and early nineteenth centuries, the master builder Karl Friedrich Schinkel providing the final touches. An inclusive ticket includes a guided tour of the main state apartments, self-guided visits to the private chambers, the Knobelsdorff-Flügel with its wonderful array of paintings by Watteau and other eighteenth-century French artists, and the Belvedere and Mausoleum in the park. Also housed in the Schloss is the **Galerie der Romantik** (same times; DM4, but included in state museums ticket), a collection of German Romantic paintings dominated by the brooding landscapes of Caspar David Friedrich and the meticulously observed Berlin cityscapes of Eduard Gaertner. Just to the south, at Schloss Str. 70, is the **Ägyptisches Museum** (same times; DM8; free first Sun of month), a fabulous collection of Egyptian antiquities; the famous bust of Nefertiti can be seen on the first floor. Also worth visiting is the **Berggruen Collection: Picasso and His Era** (same times; DM8, free first Sun of month) directly opposite, which houses some seventy paintings of the Spanish artist.

The southwestern suburb of **Dahlem**, reached by U-Bahn line #1 to Dahlem-Dorf, is home to the **Dahlem Museums** (Tues–Fri 10am–6pm, Sat–Sun 11am–6pm; DM4, free first Sun of month). Since the Gemäldegalerie moved to the Tiergarten, the Dahlem complex is no longer the must-see it once was, but it still impresses. Check out the rich and extensive and imaginatively laid out **ethnographic** treasures from Asia, the Pacific and South Sea Islands. The collections of **East Asian** and **Indian art** (the latter featuring a spectacular group of Buddhist cave paintings from the Silk Road) should be back on view in 2000.

West of Charlottenburg, U-Bahn line #2 runs to the Olympia Stadion station; a fifteen-minute, signposted walk brings you to the vast **Olympic Stadium** itself (daily 9am–sunset; DM1), one of the few Nazi buildings left intact in the city.

For a break from the city pressure, you could take a trip to the **Grunewald** forest and beaches on the **Havel** lakes. One possible starting point is the **Jagdschloss Grunewald** (Sat & Sun 10am–1pm & 1.30–4pm; DM4), a sixteenth-century hunting lodge reached by taking bus #115 from Fehrbelliner Platz U-Bahn in Wilmersdorf to Pücklerstrasse. Near the Pücklerstrasse stop you'll find the **Brücke Museum** at Bussardsteig 9 (11am–5pm; closed Tues; DM4.50), a fine collection of works by the Expressionist Brücke group. An alternative approach to the Grunewald is to take the #1 or #3 S-Bahn to Nikolassee station, from where it's a ten-minute walk to **Strandbad Wannsee**, a kilometre-long strip of pale sand that's the largest inland beach in Europe.

Eastern Berlin

The most atmospheric approach to eastern Berlin starts under the **Brandenburg Gate** and leads up **Unter den Linden**, a stately broad boulevard that is rapidly reassuming its prewar role as Berlin's most important thoroughfare. Beyond the equestrian monument to Frederick the Great are a host of historic buildings restored from the rubble of the war, starting with the Neoclassical Humboldt University, followed by the Alte Bibliothek, the flawless Deutsche Staatsoper and the domed St Hedwig's Cathedral, built for the city's Catholics in 1747. More than anyone, it was Karl Friedrich Schinkel who shaped nineteenth-century Berlin. One of his most famous creations can be found opposite the Staatsoper: the **Neue Wache**, a former royal guardhouse resembling a Roman temple. Next door, one of Berlin's finest Baroque buildings, the old Prussian Arsenal, is home to the **Museum of German History** (10am–6pm; closed Wed; free). While it's being refurbished over the next couple of years, temporary exhibitions on historical themes are being held in the Kronprinzenpalais across the road.

Following Charlottenstrasse south from Unter den Linden leads to the **Gendarmenmarkt**, much of whose appeal is derived from the **Französische Kirche** on the northern side of the square. Built as a church for Berlin's influential Huguenot community at the beginning of the eighteenth century, it also now houses the **Hugenottenmuseum** (Wed–Sat noon–5pm, Sun 11am–5pm; DM3), documenting their way of life. At the southern end of the square, the **Deutsche Kirche** was built around the same time for the city's Reformed community. It houses an engrossing though wordy historical exhibition, "Questions of German History" (Tues–Sun 10am–6pm; free). Schinkel's Neoclassical **Schauspielhaus** sits between the two churches.

At the eastern end of Unter den Linden lies the **Schlossplatz**, the former site of the imperial palace, the midpoint of a city-centre island whose northwestern part, Museumsinsel, is the location of the best of eastern Berlin's **museums**. An extensive reconstruction programme, however, has closed the **Bode Museum** and the **Alte Nationalgalerie** for several years. Until then, the **Altes Museum** (Tues–Sun 10am–6pm; DM8, free first Sun of month), perhaps Schinkel's most impressive surviving work, will display changing selections from the Alte Nationalgalerie's collection of nineteenth-century paintings. In addition, it devotes a floor to the city's excellent collection of Greek and Roman antiquities. The **Pergamonmuseum** (Tues–Sun 10am–6pm; DM8, free first Sun of month) houses the treasure trove of the German archeologists who plundered the ancient world in the nineteenth century, and includes the spectacular Pergamon Altar, which dates from 160 BC, and the huge Processional Way and Throne Room from sixth-century BC Babylon. Adjacent to the Altes Museum is the **Dom**, built between 1894 and 1905 to serve the House of Hohenzollern as a family church; its vault houses ninety sarcophagi containing the remains of various members of the line.

To reach **Alexanderplatz**, the commercial hub of eastern Berlin, head along Karl-Liebknecht-Strasse past the Neptunbrunnen fountain and the thirteenth-century **Marienkirche**, Berlin's oldest parish church. Like every other building in the vicinity, the church is overshadowed by the gigantic **Fernsehturm** or TV tower (daily 10am–1am; DM8), whose observation platform offers unbeatable views of the whole city on rare clear days. Southwest of here lies the **Nikolaiviertel**, a recent development that attempts to re-create this part of old prewar Berlin, which was razed overnight on June 16, 1944. At the centre of it all is the **Nikolaikirche** (Tues–Sun 10am–6pm; DM5), a thirteenth-century church now housing an exhibition about medieval Berlin. Not far away on Mühlendamm is the rebuilt Rococo **Ephraim-Palais** (same times; DM5), with a museum of nineteenth-century Berlin painters.

The one eastern district, or *Bezirke*, that should on no account be missed, is **Prenzlauer Berg**, radiating out from the northeastern edge of the city centre in a network of tenement-lined cobbled streets. Prenzlauer Berg, like Kreuzberg in western Berlin, has enjoyed a big influx of "alternative" lifestyle adherents and artists, a development which – coupled with the opening of various new cafés and galleries – has turned this into one of the most exciting parts of the city. The quickest way to get to Prenzlauer Berg is to take the U-Bahn from Alexanderplatz to either Eberswalder Strasse or Schönhauser Allee.

Eating, drinking and nightlife

Nowhere is more than a stone's throw from a **bar** in Berlin, and the range of **restaurants** in the west is wider than in any other German city. Cheapest way of warding off hunger is to use the **Imbiss** snack stands, or one of the **mensas**, officially for German students only but usually open to anyone who looks the part. Eating out in a proper restaurant won't break the bank, though, with prices for a main course usually between DM8 and DM20.

Western Berlin has four focal points for drinking: **Savignyplatz** is for conspicuous good-timers; **Kreuzberg** drinkers include political activists and punks; the area around **Nollendorfplatz** (northwestern Schöneberg) and **Winterfeldtplatz** is the territory of sped-out all-nighters and the pushing-on-forty crew; central **Schöneberg** bars are on the whole more mixed and more relaxed. Unless you're into pissed businessmen, avoid the Ku'damm and the rip-off joints around the Europa Center. In the **eastern part** of the city don't expect the variety or gloss found in the west, but there are a number of exciting new cafés and bars. Berlin is very much a city that wakes up when others are going to sleep – don't bother turning up before midnight for the all-night clubs in Kreuzberg and Schöneberg. For more sedate nightlife there are a number of theatres and one of Europe's great orchestras. To find out what's on, buy one of the listings magazines *Tip*, *Zitty* or *Prinz*, get the *Berlin Programm* leaflet, or look for the flyposters about town.

Snacks

Ashoka-Imbiss, Grolmanstr. 51. Situated off Savignyplatz, this is about the best of the lot, dishing up good portions of tremendous-bargain Indian food. Daily 11am–2am.

Ernst-Reuter-Platz Mensa, Ernst-Reuter-Platz. Small mensa of the nearby Technical University, with limited choice of meals. ISIC required. Mon–Fri 11.15am–2.30pm.

Fressco, Oranienburger Str. 48/49. Casseroles, salads and sandwiches for counter-top eating. Daily noon–1am.

Restaurants

Abendmahl, Muskauerstr. 9. Uniformly excellent food, a busy but congenial atmosphere, and reasonable prices make this one of the most enjoyable places to eat in the city.

Der Ägypter, Kantstr. 26. Egyptian falafel-type meals. Spicy, filling and an adventurous alternative to the safe bets around Savignyplatz. Good vegetarian selections.

Arche Noah, Fasanenstr. 79. Tucked inside the Jewish Community Centre, wonderful kosher delights in a good atmosphere.

Aroma, Hochkirchstr. 8 (☎030/782 5821). Well above average, inexpensive Italian. One of the best places to eat in east Schöneberg; it's advisable to book after 8pm.

Austria, Bergmannstr. 30. Delicious Austrian classics in a warm, woody atmosphere.

Cantamaggio, Alte Schönhauser Str. 4. A smart Scheunenviertel Italian run by Italians; excellent wines.

Carib, Motzstr. 30. Classical Caribbean cuisine, friendly service, lethal rum cocktails.

Chamisso, Willibald-Alexis-Str. 25. An intimate Italian restaurant with a reasonably priced menu; situated in a beautiful neighbourhood of restored prewar buildings.

Cour Carrée, Savignyplatz 5. Deservedly popular French restaurant with *fin-de-siècle* decor and garden seating.

Edd's Thailändisches Restaurant, Goebenstr. 20–21 (☎030/215 5294). Huge portions of Thai food make this a popular place: booking advised.

La Estancia, Bundesallee 45. Very good, value-for-money Latin American restaurant, patronized mainly by environmentally and politically conscious Berliners.

Gugelhof, Kollwitzstr. 59. Stylish and popular Alsatian restaurant in the trendy Kollwitzplatz neighbourhood.

Henne, Leuschnerdamm 25 (☎030/614 7730). Pub-style restaurant with the best chicken in Berlin. Reservation advisable.

Jimmy's Diner, Pariser Str. 41. American-style diner housed in an old dining carriage shipped from the USA. Popular with the under-30s crowd, who visit for chilled American beer and real hamburgers. Open daily till 3am, and 5am at weekends.

Keller Restaurant im Brecht Haus, Chauseestr. 125 (☎030/282 3843). A cellar restaurant decorated with Brecht memorabilia in the basement of Brecht's old house. Viennese specialities supposedly dreamt up by Brecht's wife, Helen Weigel, make this a very popular place. Worth booking.

Maothai, Wörther Str. 30. Despite being rather pricey, this Thai place is a welcome addition to the Prenzlauer Berg restaurant scene. Great food and service.

Merhaba, Hasenheide 39. Highly rated Turkish restaurant that's usually packed with locals. A selection of the starters here can be more interesting than a main course.

Osteria No.1, Kreuzbergstr. 71 (☎030/786 9162). Classy, inexpensive and therefore highly popular Italian run by a collective; booking advisable.

Publique, Yorckstr. 62 (☎030/786 9469). Friendly café-cum-restaurant serving superb food till 2am.

Restauration 1900, Husemannstr. 1. An institution even before reunification. Excellent if unsurprising German food.

Tegernseer Tönnchen, Berliner Str. 118. Bavarian cuisine – which means enormous dishes of *Würste* and schnitzels washed down with pitchers of beer. Excellent value.

Thürnagel, Gneisnaustr. 57. The ambience is a bit austere, but the kitchen of this vegetarian (with fish) restaurant shows flair.

Tuk-Tuk, Grossgörschenstr. 2 (☎030/781 1588). Amiable Indonesian near Kleistpark U-Bahn. Enquire about the heat of your dish before ordering. Booking advisable.

Vietnam, Suarezstr. 61. One of the city's most popular Vietnamese restaurants, quietly situated in a street of junk shops.

Bars and cafés

Café Adler, Friedrichstr. 206. Small café next to the site of the Checkpoint Charlie border crossing. Moderately priced breakfasts and meals.

Bar am Lützowplatz, Lützowplatz 7. The longest bar in the city. A dangerously great place.

Begine, Potsdamer Str. 139. Stylishly decorated women-only bar-bistro/gallery with limited choice of inexpensive food.

Blue Boy Bar, Eisenacher Str. 3. Tiny, convivial and relaxed gay bar.

Café Einstein, Kurfürstenstr. 58. Housed in a seemingly ancient mansion, this is about as close as you'll get to the ambience of the prewar Berlin *Kaffeehaus*, with international newspapers and breakfast served daily till 2pm. Occasional live music plus a good garden. Expensive.

Café M, Goltzstr. 34. Berlin's favoured rendezvous for creative types and the conventionally unconventional. Usually packed, even for breakfast.

Café Westphal, Kollwitzstr. 63. One of the best Prenzlauer Berg bars.

Fledermaus, Joachimstalerstr. 17. Bar and coffee shop popular with tourists and locals; one of the city's most relaxing gay bars.

O-bar, Oranienstr. 168. A landmark gay bar on one of the city's liveliest streets.

Obst & Gemüse, Oranienburger Str. 48. One of the anchors of the area's active nightlife; packed after 10pm.

Pinguin Club, Wartburgstr. 54. Tiny and cheerful Schöneberg bar with 1950–60s America supplying its theme and background music.

The Pips, Auguststr. 84. Very popular bar and dance club of bright colours and designer furnishings.

Schwarzes Café, Kantstr. 148. Kantstrasse's best hangout for the young and chic, with a relaxed atmosphere, good music and food. Open 24hr Wed–Sun, until 3am Mon, and from noon Tues.

Silberstein, Oranienburger Str. 27. One of eastern Berlin's trendiest bars, thanks to over-the-top designer furniture and fashion-conscious clientele.

VEB OZ, Auguststr. 92. A kind of East German theme bar serving Berliner Pilsener, a former Eastern brew that's still selling well. The decor includes a Trabant turned into a bench and various other bits of GDR ephemera.

Zillemarkt, Bleibtreustr. 48a. Wonderful if shabby bar that attempts a *fin-de-siècle* feel.

Zum Nussbaum, Am Nussbaum 3. In the heart of the Nikolaiviertel and overshadowed by the Nikolaikirche, this is a convincing replica of a prewar Kneipe.

Zur Letzten Instanz, Waisenstr. 14–16. Near the old city wall, this is one of the oldest city bars. Wine upstairs, beer downstairs, and in summer there's a beer garden.

Die Zwei, Spandauer Damm 168. The city's best lesbian bar, but non-exclusive.

Discos, clubs and rock venues

Boudoir, Brunnenstr. 192. A small but popular club with a bedroom motif, tucked away in a back courtyard.

Delicious Doughnuts, Rosenthaler Str. 9. A thinking person's club, featuring dance jazz, house music, and even occasional poetry readings.

Dunckerclub, Dunckerstr. 64. Indie gigs and frequent club evenings attract a youngish local crowd. A small but atmospheric venue with open-air gigs in the back yard in summer.

E-Werk, Wilhelmstr. 43. Flashy club in vast former east Berlin factory. Very popular and rather expensive.

Junction Club, Gneisenaustr. 18. Basement club featuring local talent from jazz guitarists to soul singers.

Metropol, Nollendorfplatz 5. Well-known, if not mega, names play frequently in this large dance space.

MS Sanssouci, Gröbenufer/Oberbaumbrücke. Party boat moored on the Spree River, offering a good mix – from house to soul.

Q-Club, Pücklerstr. 34. A dark and dank cellar that plays house and soul music to a sweating and happy crowd.

Sophienclub, Sophienstr. 6. Crowded central club playing host to the best local bands and often putting on discos.

Tacheles, Oranienburger Str. 53–56. Gigs, raves and a hangout in the ruins of a prewar department store.

Tempodrom, John-Foster-Dulles-Allee. Two tents, the larger hosting bands of middling fame.

Classical music

Deutsche Oper, Bismarckstr. 35 (☎030/341 0249). Good classical concerts, plus opera and ballet.

Komische Oper, Behrenstr. 55–57 (☎030/2026 0360). The house orchestra performs classical and contemporary music, and some very good opera productions are staged here.

Philharmonie, Herbert-von-Karajan-Str. 1 (☎030/254880). For years classical music in Berlin meant Herbert von Karajan's Berlin Philharmonic. Since Karajan's death in 1989 Claudio Abbado has maintained the orchestra's popularity, and tickets are extremely difficult to come by.

Konzerthaus Berlin, Schauspielhaus am Gendarmenmarkt, Gendarmenmarkt 2 (☎030/203 092101). Home to the Berlin Sinfonie Orchester and host to visiting orchestras.

Staatsoper, Unter den Linden 7 (☎030/203 54555). Excellent operatic productions in one of central Berlin's most beautiful buildings.

Theatre

Berliner Ensemble, Bertolt-Brecht-Platz 1 (☎030/282 3160). The official Brecht theatre.

Maxim Gorki Theater, Unter den Linden, Am Festungsgraben 2 (☎030/202 21115). Consistently good productions of modern works.

Schaubühne am Lehniner Platz, Kurfürstendamm 153 (☎030/890023). State-of-the-art theatre for performances of the classics and some experimental pieces.

Varieté Chamäleon, Rosenthaler Str. 40–41, Mitte (☎030/282 7118). Cabaret and variety theatre. Check out the *Mitternachtshow* at midnight on Friday and Saturday.

Listings

Airlines British Airways, Europa Center (☎030/254 0000); Lufthansa, Kurfürstendamm 220 (☎030/887588).

Airport enquiries ☎030/01805.

Bicycle rental Fahradstation, Möckernstr. 92 (☎030/216 9177). DM18 per day, DM70 per week; deposit and passport required.

Car rental ACS Rent a Car, Albrechtstr. 117 (☎030/792 0015); Allround, Kaiser-Friedrich-Str. 86 (☎030/342 5091).

Doctor ☎030/19242

Embassies and consulates Australia, Uhlandstr. 181-183 (☎030/880 0880); Britain, Unter den Linden 32–34 (☎030/201840); Canada, Internationales Handelzentrum, Friedrichstr. 95 (☎030/261 1161); Ireland, Ernst-Reuter-Platz 10 (☎030/348 00822); New Zealand, represented by the British embassy; US, Neustadtische Kirchstr. 4–5 (☎030/238 5174), visa section, Clayallee 170 (☎030/830 51200 or 832 9233).

Exchange At the main entrance to the Zoo Station (daily 7.30am–10pm).

Hitching Mitfahrzentrale, in Zoologischer Garten U-Bahn station (☎030/19440). Women's Mitfahrzentrale at Potsdamer Str. 139 (☎030/215 3165).

Laundry Uhlandstr. 53 (6.30am–10.30pm); Hauptstr. 151 (7.30am–10.30pm). Other addresses are listed under *Wäschereien* in the Yellow Pages.

Pharmacies Europa-Apotheke, Tauentzienstr. 9, is open 9am–8pm daily. Outside normal hours a notice on the door of any *Apotheke* indicates the nearest one open.

Police Platz der Luftbrücke 6 (☎030/6995).

Post office Budapester Str. 42 (Mon–Sat 8am–midnight, Sun 10am–midnight).

Women's centre Schokofabrik, Naunynstr. 72. (☎030/615 2999).

EASTERN GERMANY

By the time the former German Democratic Republic was fully incorporated into the Federal Republic of Germany, just one year after the peaceful revolution of autumn 1989 (the so-called *Wende*), most vestiges of the old political system had been swept away. Yet there is still a long way to go before the two parts of the country achieve parity, and the cities of **eastern Germany** are in the process of a major social and economic upheaval. While for visitors this transformation can be fascinating, for many citizens of the former GDR it is problematic.

Berlin stands apart from the rest of the east, but its sense of excitement finds an echo in the two other main cities – **Leipzig**, which provided the vanguard of the revolution, and **Dresden**, the beautiful Saxon capital so ruthlessly destroyed in 1945. Equally enticing are some of the smaller places, which retain more of the appearance and atmosphere of prewar Germany than anywhere in the west, notably **Erfurt**, capital of the ancient province of Thuringia, nearby **Weimar**, the small cathedral towns of **Naumburg** and **Meissen**, and the old Prussian royal seat of **Potsdam**. Although much of eastern Germany is monotonous – its heartland was once a vast swamp – it is by no means the drab industrial landscape you might imagine.

Potsdam

Site of the colossal palace of Frederick the Great, **POTSDAM** is an easy and excellent day-trip from Berlin. Bus #113 from S-Bahn station Wannsee will deposit you at **Bassinplatz** near the centre of Potsdam, or a continuation of S-Bahn line #3 or mainline train from western Berlin will drop you at S-Bahn station **Potsdam Stadt**, from where it's only a few minutes' walk north over the Lange Brücke and along Friedrich-Ebert-Strasse to the central Platz der Einheit.

Park Sanssouci (daily 9am until dusk; inclusive day ticket to all buildings DM20), fabled retreat of the Prussian king, stretches 2km west, a beautiful spectacle in spring when trees are in fresh leaf and flowers in bloom. These days it's too often overrun by visitors – to avoid the crowds, visit on a weekday. Frederick worked closely with his architect on designing the **Schloss Sanssouci** (tours every 20min Tues–Sun 9am–3/5pm; DM10), which was to be a place where the king could escape Berlin and his wife Elizabeth Christine, neither of whom he cared for. Begun in 1744, it's a surprisingly modest one-storey Baroque affair, topped by an oxidized green dome and ornamental statues looking out over vine terraces. Frederick loved the Schloss so much that he intended to be buried here, and had a tomb excavated for himself in front of the eastern wing; in 1991 his body was finally moved here. Inside is a frenzy of Rococo, spread through the twelve rooms where Frederick lived and entertained his guests. The most eye-catching rooms are the opulent **Marble Hall** and the **Concert Room**, where the flute-playing king had eminent musicians play his own works on concert evenings.

West of the palace, overlooking the ornamental **Holländischer Garten**, is the **Bildergalerie** (mid-May to mid-Oct Tues–Sun 10am–5pm; DM4), a restrained Baroque creation that contains paintings by Rubens, Van Dyck and Caravaggio. On the opposite side of the Schloss, steps lead down to the **Neue Kammern** (mid-May to mid-Oct 10am–5pm, closed Fri; rest of year Sat & Sun 10am–12.30pm & 1–5pm; DM4), the architectural twin of the Bildergalerie, originally used as an orangery and later as a guesthouse. Immediately to the west of the Neue Kammern is the prim **Sizilianischer Garten**, crammed with coniferous trees and subtropical plants, complementing the **Nordische Garten** just to the north.

From the west of the Sizilianischer Garten, the Maulbeerallee cuts through the park and ascends to the **Orangerie** (open for special exhibitions only), an Italianate Renaissance-style structure with belvedere towers. A series of terraces with curved retaining walls sporting water spouts in the shape of lions' heads leads to the sandy-coloured building, whose slightly down-at-heel appearance lends it added character.

To the west through the trees rises the **Neues Palais** (9am–12.30pm & 1–4/5pm, closed Fri; DM8), another massive Rococo extravaganza from Frederick's time. The main entrance is on the western facade, approached via gates flanked by stone sentry boxes. The interior is predictably opulent, though a couple of highlights stand out: the vast and startling **Grottensaal** on the ground floor decorated entirely with shells and semi-precious stones to form images of lizards and dragons, and the equally huge **Marmorsaal**, with its beautiful floor of patterned marble slabs. The southern wing (which these days houses a small café) contains Frederick's apartments and the theatre where the king enjoyed Italian opera and French plays.

Facing the Neues Palais entrance are the **Communs**, a couple of Rococo fantasies joined by a curved colonnade. They look grandiose, but their purpose was mundane: they were built for the serving and maintenance staff of the Palais.

Leipzig

Although never one of Germany's more visually appealing cities, **LEIPZIG** has always been among the most dynamic: its trade fairs have a tradition dating back to the Middle Ages and remained important during the communist years, so that there was never the degree of isolation from outside influences experienced by so many cities behind the Iron Curtain.

Arrival and accommodation

The **train station** – the largest dead-end passenger terminal in the world – is at the north-eastern end of the Ring, which encircles the old part of the city. The **tourist office**, directly opposite at Richard-Wagner Str. 1 (Mon–Fri 9am–7pm, Sat 9am–4pm, Sun 9am–2pm; ☎0341/224 1156), can book **private rooms** (③–④).

Other accommodation options include the brand-new **youth hostel** at Volksgartenstr. 24 (☎0341/245 7011; ③; tram #17, #27 or #37 to Löbauer Str.) and the **campsite**, *Am Auensee*, at Gustav-Esche-Str 5 (tram #10 or #28). Most **hotels** are prohibitively priced, apart from *Weisses Ross*, Ross Str. 20 (☎0341/960 5951; ④), and two pensions, both a short walk west from the train station: *Am Zoo*, Pfaffendorfer Str. 23 (☎0341/960 2432; ④) and *Am Nordplatz*, Nordstr. 58 (☎0341/960 3143; ⑤).

The City

Following Nikolaistrasse due south from the train station brings you to the **Nikolaikirche**, one of the two main civic churches and a rallying point during the *Wende*. Although a sombre medieval structure from outside, the church's interior is a real eye-grabber, its coffered vault supported by fluted columns whose capitals sprout like palm trees. A couple of blocks to the west is the open space of the **Markt**, whose eastern side is entirely occupied by the **Altes Rathaus** (Tues 2–8pm, Wed–Sun 10am–6pm; DM5), built in the grandest German Renaissance style with elaborate gables, an asymmetrical tower and the longest inscription to be found on any building in the world. The ground floor retains its traditional function as a covered walkway with shops; the upper storeys, long abandoned as the town hall, now house the local-history museum. However, the main reason for going in is to see the 53-metre-long *Festsaal* on the first floor, with its ornate chimneypieces and haughty portraits of the local mayors and Saxon dukes. On the north side of the square is another handsome public building from Renaissance times, the old weighing house or **Alte Waage**. To the rear of the Altes Rathaus, approached by a graceful double flight of steps, is the **Alte Handelsbörse**, a Baroque gem which was formerly the trade exchange headquarters. The nearby Handelshof at Grimmaische Str. 1–7 is the temporary home of the **Museum der Bildenen Künste** (Tues & Thurs–Sun 10am–6pm, Wed 1–9.30pm; DM5), a distinguished collection of old masters, including works by van der Weyden, Cranach, Hals and Rubens.

Following Barfussgässchen off the western side of the Markt brings you to Kleine Fleischergasse and the cheerful Baroque **Zum Coffe Baum**. One of the German pioneers in the craze for coffee which followed the Turkish invasion of central Europe in the late seventeenth century, it gained further fame courtesy of Robert Schumann, who came here regularly. Klostergasse leads southwards from here to the **Thomaskirche**, the senior of the two big civic churches, and the place where Johann Sebastian Bach served for the last 27 years of his life. Predominantly Gothic, the church has been altered down the centuries, notably by the addition of the galleries in line with the Protestant emphasis on preaching. However, the most remarkable feature remains its musical tradition: the *Thomanerchor*, which Bach once directed, can usually be heard on Fridays at 6pm, Saturdays at 3pm, and during the Sunday service at 9.30am. Directly across from the church is the **Bach Museum** (daily 10am–5pm; DM4), with an extensive show of mementoes of the great composer.

The southeastern part of the Altstadt is the academic quarter. On Schillerstrasse, east of the Neues Rathaus, is a surprisingly good **Egyptian Museum** (Tues–Sat 1–5pm, Sun 10am–1pm; DM3), containing finds from nineteenth-century excavations by archeologists from Leipzig University. Beyond is a fragment of the old fortifications, the **Moritzbastei**, now occupied by the leading student club. It's completely overshadowed by the 34-storey tower of the main **University** building itself. Beside it stands the **Gewandhaus**, the ultramodern home of the oldest orchestra in the world, and still one of the best.

Trams #15, #20 run southeast to the site of the **Battle of the Nations**, where Napoleon was defeated by a combined army of Prussians, Austrians, Russians and Swedes in 1813 – a defeat that led to his exile on Elba. A colossal and tasteless monument known as the **Völkerschlachtdenkmal** (daily May–Oct 10am–5pm; Nov–April 9am–4pm; DM5) was erected to commemorate the centenary of the victory. It can be ascended for a sweeping view over the city and the flat countryside.

Eating and drinking

Leipzig offers mainly traditional German taverns with the odd ethnic restaurant, giving a reasonable choice when it comes to **eating**. Many of the best spots are near the Markt. *Zum Coffe Baum*, Kleine Fleischergasse 4, is unmissable, whether for *Kaffee und Küchen* or a full meal. *Spizz*, at Markt 9, is a live music bar with regular jazz features. Tucked underneath the Mädler-Passage, one of the covered shopping malls off Grimmaischer Str. at the southeastern end of the Markt, is *Auerbachs Keller*, a historic and very formal restaurant that was the setting for a scene in Goethe's *Faust*. Good choices for a hearty, reasonably priced German meal are the rambling old *Thüringer Hof*, Burgstr. 19, *Apels Garten*, Kolonnadenstr. 2 or *Paulaner Palais*, Klostergasse 3. *Varadero*, Barfussgässchen 8, is a popular Cuban restaurant – a hangover of the political allegiances of the recent past – specializing in grills and cocktails. The city is also famous for its satirical political cabaret: if your German's up to it, try the *Pfeffermühle Club* in the same building as the Bach Museum.

Naumburg

The old cathedral city of **NAUMBURG** is situated on the fast rail line between Leipzig and Weimar, and reachable from both in well under an hour. Rather neglected in recent decades, it has already made giant steps in scraping off the grime which had smothered its buildings, and is well on the way to reclaiming its former status as one of Germany's most distinctive towns.

The historic part of Naumburg, set on heights overlooking the Saale valley, is dominated by the **Dom**, which shows medieval German architecture and sculpture at their peak. Though it was built as the seat of the local prince-bishop, with choirs at both ends of the building to emphasize its status as an imperial cathedral, it has been no more than a Protestant parish church since the Reformation. The thirteenth-century builders began by erecting the eastern choir, complete with its almost Oriental towers, in a florid Romanesque style. However, by the time the west choir was finished – minus one of the towers, which was finally built to the original plans a century ago – Gothic had taken over completely. Pride of the interior (April–Sept Mon–Sat 9am–6pm, Sun noon–6pm; reduced hours out of season; DM6) is the assemblage of sculptures by the so-called **Master of Naumburg**, one of the most original masons to have worked on a great European cathedral. His rood screen, illustrating the Passion, imbues the figures with a humanity and a realism previously absent from religious art, and the twelve life-size statues of the Dom's founders in the west choir are each given a distinctive characterization. Particularly outstanding are the couple Ekkehardt and Uta, who have come to symbolize the Germans' romantic view of their chivalric medieval past.

From the Dom, Steinweg and Herrenstrasse – each with its fair share of fine houses often complete with wrought-iron identification signs – lead eastwards to the central **Markt**. The square is dominated by the Renaissance **Rathaus**, whose huge curved gables served as a model for other mansions in the city. Rising behind the south side of the Markt is the curiously elongated **Wenzelskirche**, which was the burghers' answer to the prince-bishop's Dom. In the Baroque period, this late Gothic church was given an interior face-lift, including the provision of a magnificent organ; look out also for two paintings by Cranach. The **tower** (Wed–Sun 10am–5pm; DM3), home to a watchman until a few years ago, offers a superb panorama.

More fine mansions are to be seen on Jakobstrasse, which leads eastwards from the Markt. Also well worth going to see is the **Marientor**, at the edge of the inner ring road directly to the north of the Markt. This double gateway, one of the best preserved in the country, is the only significant reminder these days of the fifteenth-century fortifications.

Naumburg's **train station** is below and northwest of the historic centre. The **tourist office** at Markt 6 (March–Oct Mon–Fri 9am–1pm & 2–7pm, Sat 10am–4pm; Nov–Feb Mon–Fri 9am–1pm & 2–5pm; ☎03445/201617) can book **private rooms** (②–③). Alternatively, there's a **youth hostel** way to the south of the centre at Am Tennisplatz 9 (☎03445/5316; ②). **Hotels** include *Zum Akten Krug*, Lindenring 44 (☎03445/200 406; ④). Among **restaurants**, the *Ratskeller* in the Rathaus and *Domklause*, Herrenstr. 8, are recommendable.

Weimar

Despite its modest size, **WEIMAR** has played a role in the development of German culture that is unmatched: Goethe, Schiller, Herder and Nietzsche all made it their home, as did the Cranachs and Bach, and the architects and designers of the Bauhaus school. Its part in the politics of Germany is scarcely less significant: Weimar was chosen as the seat of government of the democratic republic established after World War I, a regime whose failure ended with the Nazi accession. One of the most notorious concentration camps was to be built here, and its preservation is a shocking reminder of Germany's double-edged contribution to the history of modern Europe. It served as **European City of Culture** in 1999, and for the years prior to this was subject to a frantic programme of restoration which has once again established its immaculate appearance.

The City

Weimar preserves the appearance and atmosphere of its heyday as the capital of the Duchy of Saxe-Weimar, whose population never rose much above 100,000. The seat of power was the **Schloss** (Tues–Sun 10am–6pm; DM6), set by the River Ilm at the eastern edge of the town centre, a Neoclassical complex of a size more appropriate for ruling a mighty empire. On the ground floor is a collection of old masters, including pieces by both the elder and younger Cranach, and Dürer's portraits of the Nürnberg patrician couple, Hans and Elspeth Tucher. Upstairs are some fine original interiors and German paintings from the Enlightenment era.

Just west of the Schloss on Herderplatz stands the **Stadtkirche St Peter und Paul** (May–Sept Mon–Sat 10am–noon & 2–4pm, Sun 11am–noon & 2–3pm; Oct–April Mon–Sat

11am–noon & ? 3pm, Sun 2–3pm), usually known as the Herderkirche in honour of the poet who was its pastor for three decades. Inside are several impressive tombs plus a large triptych by the Cranachs. South of Herderplatz is the spacious **Markt**, lined by an unusually disparate jumble of buildings, of which the most eye-catching is the green and white gabled **Stadthaus** on the eastern side, opposite the neo-Gothic Rathaus. Schillerstrasse snakes away from the southwest corner of the Markt to the **Schillerhaus** (9am–4/5pm; closed Tues; DM5), the home of the poet, dramatist and historian for the last three years of his life. Beyond lies Theaterplatz, in the centre of which is a large monument to Goethe and Schiller. The **Nationaltheater** on the west side of the square was founded and directed by Goethe, though the present building, for all its stern Neoclassical appearance, is a modern pastiche. Opposite is the **Wittumspalais** (Tues–Sun 9am–noon & 1–4/5pm; DM6), a Baroque palace containing some of the finest interiors of Weimar plus mementoes of the Enlightenment philosopher-poet, Christoph-Martin Wieland.

Last of the literary museums is **Goethewohnhaus und Nationalmuseum** (Tues–Sun 9am–4/5pm; DM8), on Frauenplan south of the Markt, where Goethe lived for some fifty years until his death in 1832. In the adjoining museum his achievement is chronicled with typically Teutonic detail. From the Goethewohnhaus, Marienstrasse continues to the **Liszthaus** (Tues–Sun 9am–1pm & 2–4/5pm; DM4), home of the Hungarian composer and virtuoso pianist for the last seventeen years of his life, when he was director of Weimar's orchestra and opera. A couple of minutes' walk west down Geschwister-Scholl-Strasse is the **Hochschule für Architektur und Bauwesen**, where in 1919 Walter Gropius established the original Bauhaus, which had a profound impact on architecture and design throughout Europe. Further to the west is the **Alter Friedhof** or Old Cemetery, site of the Neoclassical mausoleum of Goethe and Schiller (9am–1pm & 2–4/5pm; closed Tues; DM4).

The **Park an der Ilm** stretches from the Schloss to the southern edge of town on both sides of the river. Almost due east of the Liszthaus, on the opposite bank, is **Goethes Gartenhaus** (9am–noon & 1–4/5pm, closed Tues; DM4), where the writer stayed when he first came to Weimar in 1776 as a ducal administrator. Further south and back on the west bank is the ducal summer house, known as the **Römisches Haus** (9am–noon & 1–4/5pm; closed Tues; DM2). At the south edge of town, in the suburb of Oberweimar, there's the full-blown summer palace of **Schloss Belvedere** (April–Oct Tues–Sun 10am–6pm; DM5), whose light and airy Rococo forms a refreshing contrast to the Neoclassical solemnity of so much of the town. The **orangery** (April–Oct Tues–Sun 10am–1pm) contains a collection of historic coaches, while the surroundings were transformed under Goethe's supervision into a *jardin anglais*.

Finally, the **Konzentrationslager Buchenwald** (Tues–Sun 8.45/9.45am–5/6pm; free) is situated to the north of Weimar on the Ettersberg heights, and can be reached by buses which run every hour from just south of the train station. Over 240,000 prisoners were incarcerated in this concentration camp, with 65,000 dying here, among them the interwar leader of the German Communist Party, Ernst Thälmann. This gave the place a special significance for the GDR authorities, now tarnished by the emergence of evidence that the Russians used it after the war for their own political opponents.

Practicalities

Weimar's **train station**, on the main line between Leipzig and Erfurt, is a twenty-minute walk north of the main sights. One of the **tourist offices** is to be found there; another, much larger one is in the Stadthaus at Markt 10 (both April–Oct Mon–Fri 10am–7pm, Sat & Sun 10am–4pm; Nov–March Mon–Fri 10am–6pm, Sat 10am–1pm; ☎03643/24000). Both can arrange accommodation in **private rooms** (②–③). There are **youth hostels** at Humboldtstr. 17 (☎03643/850 792; ②), Carl-August-Allee 13 (☎03643/85 0490; ②) and, 5km south of the centre, at Zum Wilden Graben 12 (☎03643/850 750; ②). Reasonably priced **pensions** include *Am Berkaer Bahnhof*, Peter-Cornelius-Str. 7 (☎03643/202 010; ③), and *Savina*, Meyerstr. 60 (☎03643/86 690; ③). *Residenz-Café* on Grüner Markt is recommended for coffee and cakes. For a more substantial **meal**, try the places on the Markt, such as the inevitable *Ratskeller* or the surprisingly affordable *Elephantenkeller* under the *Hotel Elephant*, or go for a fish dish at *Gastmahl des Meeres* on Herderplatz.

Erfurt

Of all Germany's large cities, it's **ERFURT**, twenty minutes from Weimar by train, which is most redolent of prewar Germany. Although it lost a couple of important monuments in bombing raids, it was otherwise little damaged in World War II, while its streets of grandiose turn-of-the-century shops were saved by the communist authorities from the developers who would have demolished them had the city been on the other side of the Iron Curtain.

The vast open space of the Domplatz forms the heart of Erfurt. Imperiously set on the hill above, and reached via a monumental stairway, the **Dom** perches on a mighty fortress-like crypt. It's entered by a magnificent fourteenth-century porch which bears statues of the Apostles on one side, the Wise and Foolish Virgins on the other. Inside, the richly carved stalls and gleaming windows in the choir stand out, and the nave is jam-packed with works of art, the most notable being the so-called *Wolfram*, a Romanesque candelabrum in the shape of a man, and a spectacular font. Alongside the Dom is the **Severikirche**, a pure early Gothic hall church containing the tomb of the saint after whom it's named, a fourteenth-century masterpiece by an anonymous sculptor whose work adorns several of the city's churches.

From Domplatz, Marktstrasse leads east to Fischmarkt, lined by handsome Renaissance mansions and the nineteenth-century Rathaus. Just beyond is Erfurt's most singular sight, the **Krämerbrücke**. Walking along, you have the illusion of entering a narrow medieval alley; the fact that this is actually a bridge lined with shops and galleries only becomes obvious if you go down to the banks of the river. On the west bank, to the north of the Krämerbrücke, is the imposing Gothic facade of the **University**; the rest of the building was a casualty of World War II. However, its outstanding collection of old manuscripts survived, as did the academic church, the **Michaeliskirche**, which has a fine late Gothic chapel.

Across the river is the **Augustinerkloster** (tours April–Oct Tues–Sat 10am–noon & 2–4pm, Sun 10.45am; Nov–March Tues–Sat 10am, noon & 2pm, Sun 10.45am; DM5.50), one of a profusion of monasteries in Erfurt which earned it the nickname "little Rome". This one is best known – it was here that Luther served as a novice, then a monk, between 1505 and 1511. A visit to his cell forms part of the tour, which also includes the cloister and the typically austere church, which is enlivened by a fine stained-glass window depicting the life of St Augustine.

Of the other monasteries, pride of place goes to the **Predigerkirche** just south of Fischmarkt. Built by the Dominicans, it's extremely plain on the outside, but the interior is a masterpiece of spatial harmony in the purest Gothic style, and has preserved its layout and furnishings intact. Bombing wrecked the nave of the Franciscan **Barfüsserkirche**, over the river to the south, but the choir has been restored to house a small museum of religious art (April–Oct Tues–Sun 10am–1pm & 2–6pm; DM3, free Wed). This is a branch of the **Angermuseum** (Tues–Sun 10am–6pm; DM3, free Wed), in a Baroque mansion at the intersection of two of the main shopping streets, Bahnhofstrasse and Anger. Highlight here is the display of medieval artefacts, including more sculptures by the master who carved the tomb in the Severikirche. A fine collection of German painting from the Renaissance to modern times is also featured.

Practicalities

Erfurt's **train station** is situated at the southeastern corner of the city centre. The **tourist office** (Mon–Fri 10am–7pm, Sat & Sun 10am–4pm; ☎0361/562 3436) is at Fischmarkt 27. In addition to rooms in a **private house** (③), you can also consult their most recent list of **pensions** (③–⑤). There's a **youth hostel** at Hochheimerstr. 12 (☎0361/26705; ②), southwest of the centre: take tram #5 or #51.

Restaurants include *Bürenkeller*, Andreasstr. 26, or *Gildehaus*, Fischmarkt 13. *Haus zum Pfauen*, Marbacher Gasse 12–13, brews its own beer according to a sixteenth-century recipe and also has the cheapest **hotel rooms** in the city centre (☎0361/643 8099; ③).

Dresden

Generally regarded as Germany's most beautiful large city, **DRESDEN** survived World War II largely unscathed until the night of February 13, 1945. Then, in a matter of hours, it was reduced to ruins in the most savage saturation bombing ever mounted prior to Vietnam – according to official figures at least 35,000 civilians died (though the total was probably considerably higher), as the city was packed with people fleeing the advancing Red Army. With this background, it's all the more remarkable that Dresden is the one city in the former GDR which has slotted easily into the economic framework of the reunited Germany, and the post-communist authorities are now brilliantly restoring all the historic buildings left as rubble.

Arrival and accommodation

Dresden has two main **train stations** – the **Hauptbahnhof** is south of the Altstadt, while **Neustadt** is at the northwestern corner of the Neustadt district across the Elbe and only slightly further away from the main sights. The **tourist office** (Mon–Fri 9am–6/8pm, Sat 9am–4/6pm, Sun 9am–1/2pm; ☎0351/491920) is in the Schinkelwache on Theaterplatz, in the heart of the Altstadt. It sells the **Dresden Card** (DM26 for 48 hours), which covers public transport, entry to the main museums and sundry discounts. Otherwise, a 24-hour transport ticket costs DM8, and a day ticket for the museums costs DM12.

The tourist offices can book **private rooms** (③) and **pensions** (④). The main **youth hostel** is in a tower-block just a few minutes' walk southwest of the main Altstadt sights at Maternistr. 22 (☎0351/492 620; ③); two smaller hostels can be found just south of the Hauptbahnhof at Hübnerstr. 11 (☎0351/471 0667; ④) and well to the east at Sierksstr. 33 (☎0351/268 3672; ②; bus #84). Among the budget **hotels** are *Stadt Rendsburg*, Kamenzer Str. 1 (☎0351/804 1551; ④) and *Am Birkenhain*, Barbarastr. 76 (☎0351/85 140; ④). Unless you're travelling alone, the *Ibis* hotels on Prager Str. are good value; try *Königstein* (☎0351/4856 6662; ④). There are two **campsites** within the city boundaries, both with bungalows to rent: *Mockritz*, Boderitzer Str. 30 (bus #76 from the Hauptbahnhof), and *Wostra*, at Triekestr. 100 on the banks of the Elbe south of the tram terminus (tram #9, #14).

The City

If you arrive at the Hauptbahnhof, you see the worst of modern Dresden first: the **Prager Strasse**, a vast Stalinist pedestrian precinct with the standard cocktail of high-rise luxury hotels, public offices, boxlike flats and soulless cafés and restaurants, with a few fountains and statues thrown in for relief. At the far end, beyond the inner ring road, is the **Altmarkt**, which was much extended after its wartime destruction; the only building of note which remains is the **Kreuzkirche**, a church which mixes a Baroque body with a Neoclassical tower. On Saturdays at 6pm, and at the 9.30am Sunday service, you can usually hear the *Kreuzchor*, one of the world's leading church choirs. Behind stands the **Rathaus**, built early this century in a lumbering historicist style.

North of here, the **Albertinum** (10am–6pm; closed Thurs; DM7) houses the **Gemäldegalerie Neue Meister**, whose highlights include one of the greatest of Romantic paintings, Friedrich's *Cross in the Mountains*. Works by most of the French Impressionists and their German contemporaries precede a section devoted to the Expressionists of the Brücke group, which was founded in Dresden. Of the later pictures, two pacifist works stand out: *War* by Otto Dix and *The Thousand Year Reich* by Hans Grundig, a local artist who spent four years in a concentration camp. For the time being, the Albertinum is also home to the **Grünes Gewölbe** or Green Vault, a dazzling array of treasury items including the Baroque fancies created by the Saxon Electors' own jeweller, Johann Melchior Dinglinger. His *Court of Delhi on the Birthday of the Great Moghul* is a real *tour de force*, featuring 137 gilded and enamelled figures studded with 3000 diamonds, emeralds, rubies and pearls.

West of the Albertinum is the Neumarkt, formerly dominated by the round, domed **Frauenkirche**. Only a fragment of wall was left standing after the war, and the communists decided to leave it in this condition as a memorial. After fierce controversy, the decision was taken in 1991 to rebuild it completely, and you can now savour the slightly odd experience of watching a Baroque church rise from a modern building site.

The colossal **Residenzschloss** (Tues–Sun 10am–6pm; DM5) of the Electors of Saxony was also wrecked in the war, and the rebuilding programme now under way is a massive task: even the projected completion date of 2006 – the city's 800th anniversary – seems optimistic. Sooner or later, the miraculously preserved **Mirror Rooms** (currently closed) will contain the Grünes Gewölbe collection; in the meantime, you can see an exhibition of the history of the building in the Georgenbau. The main tower, the Hausmannsturm, can be ascended (April–Oct only; included in entrance ticket) for a view over the complex and the city. At the end of nearby Augustusstr. is the Baroque **Hofkirche** (or Dom) – the existence of this Catholic church in a staunchly Protestant province is explained by the fact that the Saxon rulers converted in order to gain the Polish throne. The church's gleaming white interior features an ornate pulpit by the great sculptor of Dresden Baroque, Balthasar Permoser. The plush **Opernhaus** opposite was built by the leading architect of nineteenth-century Dresden, Gottfried Semper, and saw the first performances of Wagner's *The Flying Dutchman* and *Tannhäuser*, and Richard Strauss' *Der Rosenkavalier*.

THE ZWINGER

Baroque Dresden's great glory was the palace known as the **Zwinger**, which was built facing the Residenzschloss; less severely damaged in the war, it was quickly restored. It's a daringly original building: a vast open space with fountains surrounded by a single-storey gallery linking two-storey pavilions, and entered by exuberantly grandiose gateways. The effect is further enhanced by superbly expressive decoration by Permoser.

The Zwinger contains several museums. Beautifully displayed in the southeastern pavilion, entered from Sophienstrasse, is the **Porzellansammlung** (10am–6pm; closed Thurs; DM3); products from the famous Meissen factory are extensively featured. A small natural history display, the **Tierkundemuseum** (July & Aug daily 9am–5pm; rest of year Tues–Sun 9am–4pm; DM2), is housed in the southern gallery. The southwestern pavilion is known as the **Mathematisch-physikalischer Salon** (9.30am–5pm; closed Thurs; DM3), and offers a fascinating array of globes, clocks and scientific instruments. In the northeastern part of the nineteenth-century extension by Semper is the **Armoury** (Rüstkammer; Tues–Sun 10am–6pm; DM3), featuring various weapons (including the sword of Elector Frederick the Valiant) and the coronation robes of Augustus the Strong.

The extension also contains the **Gemäldegalerie Alte Meister** (Tues–Sun 10am–6pm; DM7). The Saxon Electors' collection of old masters ranks among the dozen best in the world, and includes some of the most familiar Italian Renaissance paintings: Raphael's *Sistine Madonna*, Titian's *Christ and the Pharisees* and Veronese's *Marriage at Cana*. The German section includes Dürer's *Dresden Altarpiece*, Holbein's *Le Sieur de Morette* and Cranach's *Duke Henry the Pious*. Van Eyck's *Madonna and Child* triptych, executed with miniaturist precision, kicks off a distinguished Low Countries section in which Rubens and Rembrandt are extensively featured. The great artists of seventeenth-century France and Spain are all represented, though the gem of this section is the set of *The Parables* by a short-lived Italian, Domenico Feti. Finally, look out for the brilliantly detailed set of views by Bernardo Bellotto showing Dresden in all its eighteenth-century splendour.

THE NEUSTADT AND SCHLOSS PILLNITZ

Across the Elbe, the **Neustadt** was a planned Baroque town and its layout is still obvious, even if few of the original buildings survive. In the centre of the Markt rises the **Goldener Reiter**, a gilded equestrian statue of the Elector Augustus the Strong. The Neustadt's central axis, Hauptstrasse, preserves several Baroque houses by Pöppelmann, along with the same architect's **Dreikönigskirche**, only recently restored following war damage. In the park overlooking the Elbe is the most esoteric creation of Dresden Baroque, the **Japanisches Palais**, which now contains archeological and ethnographic museums (both Tues–Sun 10am–5pm; DM4). You don't have to pay to see the courtyard, a fantasy inspired by the eighteenth-century infatuation with the Orient.

Schloss Pillnitz, which lies up the Elbe at the extreme edge of the city boundary, is another Pöppelmann creation inspired by the mystique of the East; it's also the only part of the city's Baroque heritage to escape war damage altogether. There are actually two summer palaces here: the **Wasserpalais** (May–Oct Mon & Wed–Sun 9.30am–5pm; DM3), directly above the river, contains a museum of applied arts; the **Bergpalais** (May–Oct Tues–Sun 9.30am–5pm; DM3), across the courtyard, is an almost exact replica, whose apartments are themselves the main exhibits. Pillnitz can be reached by taking tram #9 or #14 to the terminus, then the ferry.

Eating, drinking and nightlife

In the old town, the city's most frequented venue is *Haus Altmarkt*, Wilsdruffer Str. 19–21. Just across the square, at Schloss Str. 2, there's a classy **restaurant** on the second floor of the *Kulturpalast*. Nearby at Wilsdruffer Str. 4 is *Szeged*, which serves both Hungarian and German dishes. In Neustadt, *Kügelgenhaus* at Hauptstr. 13 is probably Dresden's best café-cum-restaurant, in a Baroque building with a beer cellar. *Am Thor*, Hauptstr. 35, is the place in Dresden for good **beer**, and also serves excellent food. As for **nightlife**, the *Jazzclub Tonne*, Am Brauhaus 3, is the main jazz venue, with live music on Fridays, Saturdays and Sundays. *Bärenzwinger*, Brühlscher Garten, is a student club with a varied nightly programme of discos, films and music.

Meissen

Reachable from Dresden by a cruise down the Elbe or by S-Bahn train, the porcelain-producing town of **MEISSEN** is one of the most photogenic cities in Germany. Unlike Dresden, it survived World War II almost unscathed. Walking towards the centre from the **train station**, lying on the other side of the Elbe, you can immediately see the commandingly sited castle. The present building, the **Albrechtsburg** (daily 10am–5/6pm; closed Jan; DM6), is a late fifteenth-century combination of military fortress and residential palace. Cocooned within the castle precinct is the **Dom** (daily: 9/10am–4/6pm; DM3.50). For the most part it's a pure Gothic structure, but the distinctive openwork spires which dominate Meissen's skyline were added only in the first decade of the twentieth century. Inside, look out for the superb brass tomb plates of the Saxon dukes; the rood screen with its colourful altarpiece by Cranach; and the statues of the founders in the choir, made in the great Naumburg workshop.

Between the castle hill and the Elbe lies the atmospheric **Altstadt**, a series of twisting and meandering streets ideal for an aimless stroll. Centrepiece is the Markt, dominated by the Renaissance Rathaus. On its own small square to the side is the Flamboyant Gothic **Frauenkirche**, whose carillon, fashioned from local porcelain, can be heard six times daily. The church's **tower** (May–Oct daily 10am–12.30pm & 1–4pm; DM2) commands a superb view of the city and the Elbe. On the terrace just above is the celebrated **Gasthaus Vinzenz Richter**, a half-timbered old tavern which preserves an eighteenth-century winepress. The wines served here have the reputation of being the best in eastern Germany.

The **Staatliche Porzellan-Manufaktur Meissen** (tours daily 9am–noon & 1–5pm; DM5), about 1.5km south of the Markt, is most easily reached by going down Fleischer Gasse, then continuing straight down Neugasse; it's also close to the S-Bahn terminus, Meissen-Triebischtal. This is the latest factory to manufacture Dresden china, whose invention came about when Augustus the Strong imprisoned the alchemist Johann Friedrich Böttger, ordering him to produce some gold. Instead, he invented the first true European porcelain, according to a formula which remains secret. In addition to seeing the works, you can also view the **museum** (daily 9am–5pm; DM9), which displays many of the finest achievements of the factories, most notably some gloriously over-the-top Rococo fripperies made by the most talented artist ever employed here, Joachim Kaendler.

Practicalities

Meissen's **tourist office** is at Markt 3 (April–Oct Mon–Fri 10am–6pm, Sat & Sun 10am–3pm; Nov–March Mon–Fri 10am–5pm, Sat 10am–3pm; ☎03521/454470). If you're staying, the tourist office books **private rooms** (③) or there are several **hotels** costing far less than their Dresden counterparts, including two pensions: *Porsche*, Korbitzer Str. 186 (☎03521/457 479; ③); and *Burkhardt*, Neugasse 29 (☎03521/458 198; ④), which offers an unbeatable central location. There's a **youth hostel** at Wilsdruffer Str. 28 (☎03521/453 065; ②). For **eating** and **drinking**, the one unmissable place is the *Vinzenz Richter*; other possibilities include the *Sächsischer Hof*, Hahnemannsplatz 17 and *Winkelkrug*, Schlossberg 13.

travel details

Trains

Berlin to: Dresden (hourly; 2hr 30min); Erfurt (hourly; 4hr); Frankfurt (hourly; 7–8hr); Hamburg (hourly; 3hr 30min); Hannover (hourly; 4–5hr); Leipzig (hourly; 2hr 30min); Munich (hourly; 9–10hr); Weimar (hourly; 3hr 40min).

Bremen to: Hannover (every 30min; 1hr).

Cologne to: Aachen (every 20min; 45min); Düsseldorf (frequent; 25min); Frankfurt (hourly; 2hr 15min); Heidelberg (hourly; 2hr 50min); Mainz (hourly; 1hr 45min); Stuttgart (hourly; 3hr 25min).

Dresden to: Meissen (every 30min; 40min).

Frankfurt to: Baden-Baden (hourly; 1hr 30min); Berlin (hourly; 7–8hr); Cologne (hourly; 2hr 15min); Hamburg (hourly; 3hr 30min); Hannover (hourly; 2hr 20min); Heidelberg (every 30min; 1hr); Munich (hourly; 4hr); Nürnberg (hourly; 2hr); Würzburg (hourly; 1hr).

Hamburg to: Bremen (hourly; 1hr); Hannover (every 30min; 1hr 25min); Lübeck (every 30min; 40min).

Hannover to: Goslar (hourly; 1hr 20min); Hildesheim (every 20min; 25min).

Koblenz to: Trier (hourly; 1hr 30min).

Leipzig to: Dresden (hourly; 1hr 30min); Erfurt (hourly; 50min); Meissen (hourly; 2hr–3hr 30min); Naumburg (hourly; 40min); Weimar (hourly; 1hr 20min).

Mainz to: Koblenz (frequent; 50min); Worms (every 30min; 40min).

Munich to: Augsburg (every 20min; 30min); Nürnberg (hourly; 1hr 30min); Regensburg (hourly; 2hr); Würzburg (hourly; 2hr 20min).

Nürnberg to: Bamberg (every 30min; 45min); Munich (hourly; 1hr 30min).

Stuttgart to: Freiburg (hourly; 45min); Heidelberg (every 30min; 1hr 10min); Konstanz (hourly; 2hr 40min).

CHAPTER 12

GREECE

Introduction

With 166 inhabited islands and a landscape that ranges from Mediterranean to Balkan, **Greece** has enough appeal to fill months of travel. The historic sites span four millennia of civilization, encompassing the renowned – such as Mycenae, Olympia, Delphi and the Parthenon in **Athens** – and the obscure, where a visit can still seem like a personal discovery. The **beaches** are distributed along a convoluted coastline equal in length to that of France, and they range from islands where the boat calls once a week to resorts as cosmopolitan as they come.

Modern Greece is the sum of an extraordinary diversity of **influences**. Romans, Arabs, Franks, Venetians, Slavs, Albanians, Turks, Italians, to say nothing of the great Byzantine Empire, have all been here and gone since the time of Alexander the Great. All have left their marks: the Byzantines in countless churches and monasteries, and in ghost towns like **Mystra**; the Venetians in impregnable fortifications at **Monemvassía** in the Peloponnese; the Franks in crag-top castles, again in the Peloponnese but also in the east Aegean. Most obvious, perhaps, is the heritage of 400 years of Ottoman Turkish rule which, while universally derided, exercised an inestimable influence on music, cuisine, language and the way of life. The contributions, and continued existence, of substantial minorities – Vlachs, Muslims, Jews, Gypsies – round out the list of those who have helped to make up the Hellenic identity.

The Greek people – peasants, fishermen, shepherds – created perhaps the most vigorous and truly **popular culture** in Europe, which lives on in the songs and dances, costumes, embroidery, woven bags and rugs, furniture and the white cubist houses of popular image. Its vigour may be failing rapidly under the impact of Western consumer values, but much survives, especially in remoter regions.

The **landscape** of Greece encompasses an astonishing variety: the stony deserts of the Máni, the soft theatricality of the Peloponnesian coastal hills, the poplar-studded plains of Macedonia, the resin-scented ridges of Skíathos and Sámos, the wind-tormented rocks of the central Aegean. It's the simple pleasures of these landscapes and of the country's climate and food that make Greece special for most visitors.

Information and maps

The National Tourist Organization of Greece (Ellinikós Organizmós Tourismoú, or **EOT**) publishes an impressive array of free regional pamphlets, a reasonable fold-out map of Greece and a large number of sheets on special interests. You will find EOT offices in most of the larger towns and resorts. Where there is no EOT office, you can try municipally run tourist offices or the **Tourist Police**. The latter are basically a branch of the local police; they can sometimes provide you with lists of rooms to let, and in general are helpful and efficient.

The most reliable road **maps** of Greece are Geocenter's, *Greek Islands/Aegean Sea*, covering the whole country at 1:300,000. Alternatively, for a single sheet, go for Freytag-Berndt's 1:650,000 map. Freytag-Berndt also publishes a series of more detailed maps on various regions of Greece, such as the Peloponnese and Cyclades; these are issued by Efstathiadhis in Greece. Individual maps of islands are much less consistent, but are always available on the spot.

Money and banks

Greek currency is the **drachma**, most commonly circulated in notes of 100, 200, 500, 1000, 5000 and 10,000dr, and coins of 1, 2, 5, 10, 20, 50 and 100dr.

Travellers' cheques can be cashed at all banks and quite a number of hotels, agencies and tourist shops. Greek **banks** are normally open Mon–Thurs 8am–2pm and Fri 8am–1.30pm. Certain branches in the major cities and tourist centres are open extra hours in the evenings and on Saturday mornings to change money. Be prepared for at least one long queue, and possibly two. Commissions vary considerably: banks usually charge a flat 600–800dr; travel agencies may give a poorer rate, but often levy a sliding two percent commission, meaning you'll come out ahead on small amounts compared with banks.

Greece, especially in resort areas, has an increasing number of autoteller machines which accept foreign-issued cards; this is often the easiest and cheapest way of obtaining funds. Ethnikí Trápeza National Bank handles Access, Mastercard and Cirrus system cards; Emborikí Trápeza (Commercial Bank) caters to Visa; while Trápeza Písteos (Credit Bank) autotellers can be used with Visa and American Express cards.

Communications

Post offices are open Mon–Fri 7.30am–2pm or thereabouts; in big towns and important tourist centres, hours may extend into the evening and even weekends. **Stamps** (*grammatósimata*) can also be purchased at a corner kiosk (*períptero*), though staff tend not to know correct rates; a postcard or standard letter costs 170dr to post within the EU. If you are confronted by two slots on a post box, *esoterikó* is for domestic mail, *exoterikó* for overseas. The poste restante system is reasonably efficient, especially at the post offices of larger towns. American

Express holds mail at offices in Athens, Thessaloníki, Iráklio, Rhodes and Corfu.

Coin-operated **pay phones**, except for a very few red countertop models in big towns, are now almost extinct, replaced of late by card phones found in even the most unlikely places. The lowest-value card (sold at newsagents) costs 1000dr for 100 units; 500-unit and 1000-unit cards are 7000dr and 12000dr respectively. If you balk at this, keep in mind that phones at a *períptero* or kiosk will cost 20dr per unit.

For **international calls**, it's cheaper to visit the nearest **OTE** (Organizmós Tiliepikinoníon tis Elládhos) office, and you'll have to do this if you want to reverse charges. Operator-assisted calls can take over an hour to connect, but even dialling direct you should be prepared for a long wait. Note that direct dial calls from card-phones connect to the UK in seconds. It is also possible to call operators from these to make reverse-charge or charge-card calls – but this requires one credit on a card to begin. In major cities there is at least one branch open 24 hours; in smaller towns the OTE can close as early as 3pm; elsewhere count on service from 7am to 10pm. The **operator number** for domestic calls is ☎151, for international calls ☎161.

Getting around

Buses are the standard means of transport in Greece. They cover just about every route on the mainland and provide a basic service on the islands. The best way to supplement buses is to hire a moped or scooter, especially on the islands, where any substantial town or resort has rental outlets.

■ Buses

Bus services on the major routes – both on the mainland and islands – are highly efficient. On secondary roads they're a lot less regular, but even the most remote villages will be connected by a school or market bus, often leaving shortly after dawn. On the islands, buses usually connect the port and main town for ferry arrivals or departures. Most of these buses are run by a syndicate of companies known as the KTEL, and charge about 20dr per kilometre, with slight economies of scale taking effect after about 100km travelled.

■ Trains

The Greek **railway** network, run by **OSE** (State Railway Organization), is limited to the mainland, and trains are slower than the equivalent buses, except on the growing number of showcase IC (intercity) lines, for which fares are more expensive. However, most trains are cheaper than buses, and some of the lines are enjoyable in themselves. If you're starting a

journey at the initial station of a run you can reserve a seat at no extra cost; at most intermediate points, it's first come, first served. Timetables are sporadically available, printed in Greek only; the best places to obtain one are the OSE offices in Athens and Thessaloníki. Both Eurail and InterRail passes are valid in Greece, though holders must make reservations like other passengers.

■ Ferries

Ferries are of use primarily for travel to, and between, islands, though you may also want to make use of the routes between Athens and Monemvassía in the Peloponnese, and between the Peloponnese and Crete. Routes and the speed of the boats vary enormously: before buying a ticket it's wise to establish how many stops there'll be before your island, and the estimated time of arrival. Many agents act only for one specific boat, so you may have to ask around to uncover alternatives.

Schedules are notoriously erratic and out-of-season are severely reduced, with many islands served only once or twice a week. The most reliable, up-to-date information is available from the local **port police** (*limenarhío*), which maintains offices at Pireás and on all fair-sized islands.

Regular ferry tickets are, in general, best bought on the day of departure, unless you need to reserve a cabin, bunk or space for a car. There are only three periods of the year – March 23–25, Easter weekend and mid-August – when ferries need to be booked a couple of days in advance. The cheapest class of ticket, which you'll probably automatically be sold, is **deck class**. Motorbikes and cars get issued extra tickets, in the latter case up to four times as costly as simple passenger fares.

Ceres "Flying Dolphin" **hydrofoils** are roughly twice as fast and up to twice as expensive as ordinary ferries. They operate mainly among the Argo-Saronic islands close to Athens, and down the east coast of the Peloponnese to Monemvassía and Kíthira, and among the northern Sporades. There are also summer-only services in the Cyclades, the Dodecanese and between the northeast Aegean islands run by Ilio Lines plus several smaller companies such as Gianmar and Mamidhakis. If money is no object, there are now international hydrofoils between Turkey, Greece and Italy. It is only possible to buy one-way tickets on the Dolphins. In summer, if you have a tight schedule, it is worth buying your return (or onward) ticket on arrival at an island.

In season **kaíkia** (caiques) sail between adjacent islands and to a few of the more obscure ones. These are no cheaper than main services but can be useful and often very pleasant. Many depend on the whims of local boat-owners or fishermen – the only firm information is to be had on the quayside.

■ Moped and bike rental

Motorcycles, scooters, mopeds and bicycles are available to rent on many of the islands and in a few of the popular mainland resorts. Motorcycles and scooters cost from around £10/$16 a day; mopeds from £6/$10; bikes as little as £2/$3, but £5/$8 for a "mountain" model. All rates can be reduced with bargaining outside of peak season, or if you negotiate for a longer period of rental. To rent a motorcycle (usually 125cc) you will need to show a driver's licence. Make sure you check the bike thoroughly before riding off since many are only cosmetically maintained and repaired.

■ Driving and hitching

Cars have obvious advantages for getting to the more inaccessible parts of mainland Greece. Average cost for **rental** of the cheapest models is from £200/$320 per week with unlimited mileage, VAT and CDW included. In Greece, Rent-a-Reliable, EuroDollar, Payless and Just are reliable medium-sized companies with branches in many towns. Note that initial prices quoted may not include tax and supplemental insurance premiums, and check the fine print on your contract carefully.

If you drive your own vehicle through Greece you'll need international third-party insurance, and it's best to have an international driver's licence. Keep in mind that Greece has the highest accident rate in Europe after Portugal, and many of the roads, particularly if you're unfamiliar with them, can be quite perilous. Speed limits are 50kph in town, 100kph on motorways and 80kph on other roads. The Automobile and Touring Club of Greece (ELPA) operates a 24hr breakdown service on major roads, and a 7am–10pm service elsewhere; the number for assistance is ☎104.

Hitching is fine in Greece as long as you're not too bothered by time. Although Greek traffic is sparse, much of it is trucks and vans which are good for thumbing. Rides are easiest to come by in remote areas where most people know that buses are scarce.

Accommodation

There are huge numbers of beds for tourists in Greece, and most of the year you can rely on turning up pretty much anywhere and finding a room. Only in July and August are you likely to experience problems. At these times, it is worth striking a little off the standard tourist routes and turning up at each new place early in the day.

■ Hotels and private rooms

Hotels are officially categorized from "Luxury" down to "E-class", and all except the top category have to keep within set price limits. D- and E-class hotels are usually very reasonable, costing around £9–13/$14–21 for a double room, £7–10/$11–16 for a single. The better-value places tend to be in medium-sized resorts where limited custom encourages competition. In resorts and throughout the islands, you have the additional option of privately let **rooms** (*dhomátia*). These are again officially controlled and are divided into three classes (A–C). They are usually somewhat cheaper than hotels, and are in general spotlessly clean. These days the bulk of them are in new, purpose-built low-rises but some are in people's homes, where you'll often be treated with disarming hospitality. As often as not, rooms find you: owners descend on ferry or bus arrivals to fill any space they have. In smaller places you'll often see rooms advertised, or you can just ask at the local taverna or café.

Houses or flats – and, out of season, villas – can sometimes be rented by the week or month. If you have two or three people to share costs, and want to drop roots on an island for a while, it's an option well worth considering.

■ Hostels

Greece is not exactly packed with **youth hostels** (*ksenón neotítos*) but those that there are tend to be fairly easy-going affairs. Few ever ask for an HI card, and if they do you can usually buy one on the spot, or maybe just pay a little extra for your bed. Charges are

---

ACCOMMODATION PRICE CODES

Throughout this guide, accommodation is priced on a scale of ① to ⑨, the number indicating the lowest price per night a single person could expect to pay in that establishment in high season. With hostels this is the nightly rate per person; with hotels, the price is arrived at by dividing the cost of the cheapest double room by two. The prices indicated by the codes are as follows:

① under £5 / $8	④ £15–20 / $24–32	⑦ £30–35 / $48–56
② £5–10 / $8–16	⑤ £20–25 / $32–40	⑧ £35–40 / $56–64
③ £10–15 / $16–24	⑥ £25–30 / $40–48	⑨ £40 / $64 and over

around £4/$7 a night. In Athens there are also cheap dormitory-style "**Student Houses**", non-HI hostels which despite their name are in no way limited to students. These – and sometimes rural/island tavernas – will also sometimes let roof space, usually providing a mattress for you to lay a sleeping bag down on, or even full bedding.

■ **Camping**

Official **campsites** range from ramshackle compounds on the islands to highly organized EOT-run complexes. Cheap, casual places rarely cost much above £1.50/$2.50 a night per person; at the larger sites, though, it's possible for two people and a tent to add up to the price of a basic room.

Camping outside authorized campsites is such an established element of Greek travel that few people realize that it's officially forbidden, and once in a while the regulations get enforced. In effect this simply means you should exercise discretion.

■ **Monasteries**

Greek monasteries and convents have a tradition of putting up travellers of the appropriate sex. On the mainland, this is still customary practice; on the islands, much less so. Wherever, you should always ask locally before heading out to one for the night. Also, dress modestly – shorts on either sex, and short skirts on women, are anathema – and try to arrive no later than 8pm or sunset (whichever is earlier).

Food and drink

Greek cuisine and restaurants are simple and straightforward. There's no snobbery about eating out; everyone does it, and for foreigners with strong currencies it's reasonably priced – around £8/$12 per person for a substantial meal with house wine.

■ **Food**

Greeks generally don't eat **breakfast**. The only egg-and-bacon kind of places are in resorts where foreigners congregate; they're expensive compared to a taverna meal. The alternatives are the sort of bread/jam/yoghurt compromises obtainable in some *zaharoplastía* or *galaktopolía*.

Snacks can be one of the distinctive pleasures of Greek eating. Small kebabs (*souvlákia*) are on sale at bus stations, ferry crossings and all over the place in towns. The same goes for *tirópites* (cheese pies), which can almost always be found at the baker's, as can *koulouría* (crispy baked pretzel rings sprinkled with sesame seeds). Another city staple is *yíros* (doner kebab), served in píta bread with garnish.

In choosing a **restaurant**, the best strategy is to go where the Greeks go – and they go late: 2 to 3pm for lunch, 9 to 11pm for dinner. There are two basic types: the *estiatório* and the taverna. **Estiatória** specialize in the more complicated, oven-baked casserole dishes, like *moussakás* and *pastítsio*, stews like *kokinistó* and *stifádho*, *yemistá* (stuffed tomatoes or peppers), the oily vegetable casseroles called *ladherá*, and oven-baked meat and fish. The cooking is done in the morning and then left to stand, which is why the food is often lukewarm or even cold. Greeks don't mind this (most actually believe that hot food is bad for you), and in fact in summertime it hardly seems to matter.

Tavernas are much more common. The primitive ones have a very limited menu, but the more established will offer some of the main *estiatório* dishes mentioned above as well as the standard taverna fare, which essentially means *mezédhes* (hors d'œuvres) and *tis óras* (meat and fish fried or grilled to order).

The most interesting **mezédhes** are *tzatzíki* (yoghurt, garlic and cucumber dip), *melitzanosaláta* (aubergine dip), courgettes or aubergine fried in batter (*kolokithákia tiganitá*, *melitzánes tiganités*), *yígandes* (white haricot beans in vinaigrette sauce), small cheese and spinach pies (*tiropitákia*, *spanakópites*), *saganáki* (fried cheese), octopus (*okhtapódhi*) and *mavromátika* (black-eyed peas). Of **meats**, *souvláki* (shish kebab) and *brizóles* (chops) are reliable. *Keftédhes* (meatballs), *biftékia* (a sort of hamburger) and the spicy sausages called *loukánika* are cheap and good. Seaside tavernas of course also offer **fish**. *Kalamarákia* (fried baby squid) are a summer staple. The choicer fish, however, such as *barboúnia* (red mullet), *tsipoúra* (gilt-head bream) and *lavráki* (sea bass) are expensive. The price is quoted by the kilo, and the standard procedure is to go to the glass cooler and choose your own.

■ **Drink**

The *kafenío* is the traditional Greek coffee shop or café. Although its main business is Greek **coffee**, it also serves spirits such as **oúzo** (aniseed-flavoured grape distillate), and brandy, beer, tea or soft drinks. Like tavernas, *kafenía* range from the plastic and sophisticated to the old-fashioned, spit-on-the-floor variety. An important institution anywhere in Greece, they are the central pivot of life in the country villages. Take your pre-dinner *oúzo* around 6pm, as the sun begins to sink and the heat of the day cools. You will be served two glasses, one with the *oúzo*, and one full of water, to be tipped into your *oúzo* until it turns a milky white.

The **zaharoplastío**, a cross between café and patisserie, serves coffee, alcohol, yoghurt and a sometimes amazing variety of honey-soaked sweets. If you want a stronger slant toward the dairy products, find a **galaktopolío**, where you'll often find rizógalo (rice pudding), kréma (custard) and local yiaoúrti (yoghurt). Both zaharoplastía and galaktopolía are more family-orientated places than the kafenío, and many also serve proper tea (evropaïkó) and different kinds of coffee.

Bars – barákia – are a recent transplant, confined to big cities and holiday resorts. They range from clones of Parisian cafés to seaside cocktail bars and imitation English pubs (sic), with videos running all day. Drinks, at about £3/$5, are invariably more expensive than at a café.

Tavernas offer a better choice of **wines**. Cambas, Boutari Rotonda or Apelia are good brands among the cheaper bottled ones. If you want something better, the Boutari Naoussa is hard to beat. Otherwise, go for the local wines. Retsina – pine-resinated wine, an acquired taste – is invariably better straight from the barrel.

Opening hours and holidays

Shops generally open around 8.30 to 9.30am, then take a long break for the hottest part of the day. Things may then reopen in the mid- to late afternoon. Tourist areas tend to adopt a more northern timetable, though, with shops and offices probably staying open right through the day. Shopping hours during the hottest months are theoretically Mon, Wed & Sat 9am–2pm and Tues, Thurs & Fri 9am–1.30pm & 5.30–8.30pm. But there are so many exceptions to the rule that you can't count on getting anything done except from Monday to Friday from 9.30am to 1pm or so.

Opening hours for **museums and ancient sites** vary, and they change with exasperating frequency; we've given optimistic high-season hours, with winter hours where they are substantially different. Smaller sites generally close for a long lunch and siesta (even where they're not supposed to), as do monasteries. The latter are generally open 9am–1pm & 5–7pm for limited visits. All state-owned museums and sites are free on Sundays to EU citizens, and most are shut on Mondays. Many museums and archaeological sites – more so out of Athens – are free for students from EU countries. A valid card is

required but not necessarily an ISIC. Non-EU students generally only get a 50 percent discount, unless they can prove they are on a fine art or archaeology course, in which case they also get in free.

There's a vast range of **public holidays** and festivals. The most important, when almost everything will be closed, are: Jan 1; Jan 6; March 25; the first Monday of Lent; Easter weekend; May 1; Whit Monday (seven weeks after Easter); Aug 15; Oct 28; and Dec 24–27.

Emergencies

The most common causes of a run-in with the **police** are nude bathing or sunbathing and camping outside an authorized site – though topless bathing is now legal on virtually all the Greek beaches. Drug offences are a serious matter. The maximum penalty for "causing the use of drugs by someone under 18", for example, is life imprisonment and a ten-million-drachma fine. Theory is by no means usual practice but foreigners caught in possession do get jail sentences of up to a year. If you get arrested for any offence you have a right to contact your consulate who will arrange a lawyer for your defence. Beyond this, there is little they can, or in most cases will, do.

For **minor medical complaints** go to the local farmakío (pharmacy). In the larger towns there'll usually be one who speaks English. If you regularly use any **prescription drug** you should bring along a copy of the prescription together with the generic name of the drug. For serious medical attention you'll find moderately priced English-speaking doctors in any of the bigger towns or resorts; the Tourist Police or your consulate should be able to come up with some names if you have any difficulty. In emergencies, treatment – for cuts, broken bones – is given free in state hospitals, though you will only get the most basic level of nursing care.

> **EMERGENCY NUMBERS**
> Police ☎110; Ambulance & Fire ☎112.

ATHENS AND AROUND

ATHENS (Athína) has been inhabited continuously for over 7000 years. Its acropolis, supplied with springwater, protected by a ring of mountains and commanding views of all approaches from the sea, was a natural choice for prehistoric settlement. Its development into a city-state and artistic centre reached its apotheosis in the Classical period of the fifth century BC with a flourish of art, architecture, literature and philosophy that has pervaded Western culture ever since. Since World War II, the city's population has risen from 700,000 to 3.8 million – more than a third of the nation's people. The speed of this process is reflected in the city's chaotic mix of urban and rural: goats graze in yards, horse carts are pulled along streets thick with traffic, and Turkish-style bazaars vie for space with outlets for Armani and Benetton.

The ancient sites are only the most obvious of Athens' attractions. There are beautiful cafés, terraced tavernas and street markets; startling views from the hills of Likavitós and Filopáppou; and, around the foot of the Acropolis, scattered monuments of the Byzantine, medieval and nineteenth-century town. As you might expect, the city also offers the best eating to be found in Greece, as well as the most varied nightlife.

Outside the city, the Temple of Poseidon at **Sounion** is the most popular trip, and rightly so, with its dramatic clifftop position. **Pireás** (Piraeus), effectively an extension of Athens, is the main terminus for the island and international ferries, as well as for most Greek industry. The other two ports, **Rafína** and **Lávrio**, are on the east coast: the former is a useful departure point for many of the Cycladic islands; the latter serves only the islands of Kéa and Kíthnos.

Arrival and information

Athens **airport** (Ellenikóu) is 16km from the centre and has two terminals: **West**, which is used by Olympic Airways, and **East**, which is used by everyone else. Yellow #19 trolleybuses connect the two regularly from around 6am to midnight. **Buses** run every thirty minutes from both terminals: blue and white bus #91 from the West terminal through to the East terminal and on to Síndagma Square and Omónia; the #19 trolley, or identically numbered blue bus, into Pireás. Buy a ticket (250dr; 500dr at night) before boarding. A **taxi** should cost around 1800dr – the amount displayed on the meter plus a 300dr surcharge – at day rates (double that at night), but make sure the meter is working (fares begin at 200dr) and visible from the start – double or triple overcharging of newcomers is the norm.

International **trains** arrive at the Stathmós Laríssis in the northwest of the city centre; the virtually adjacent Peloponníssou Station handles traffic to and from the Peloponnese. The yellow trolleybus (#1), which leaves from outside Laríssis, goes to Síndagma. If you're coming into Athens **by bus from northern Greece or the Peloponnese**, you'll find yourself at **Kifissoú 100**, just a ten-minute ride from the middle of town by bus #051, or roughly a 1500dr trip by taxi. Routes into the city from **central Greece** arrive rather closer to the centre at **Liossíon 260**, north of the train stations; from here you take the blue city bus #024 to Síndagma. Most **international buses** will take you to the train station or to Kifissoú 100; a few drop passengers right in the city centre. If you arrive by boat at **Pireás**, the simplest access to Athens itself is by metro to Monastiráki, Omónia or Viktorías stations. **Taxis** from Pireás to central Athens should cost around 1000dr.

Once you've managed to find it, **central Athens** covers a mercifully small area. **Síndagma Square** (Platía Sindágmatos, "Constitution Square") is to all intents and purposes the focus of the city, and most things you'll want to see are within thirty minutes' walk. The city's main **tourist office**, the GNTO Hellenic Tourist Organization, is at Amerikis 2, near Síndagma Square (Mon–Fri 9am–5/7pm, Sat 10am–2pm; ☎01/331 0561).

City transport

All **public transport** systems operate from around 5am to midnight, with a skeleton service on some of the yellow trolleys in the small hours of the weekend. Athens' **bus network** is extensive but very crowded at peak times and unbearably hot in the unavoidable summer traffic jams.

The single-line **metro** is next to useless except for journeys to the termini of Pireás in the south or Kifissiá in the north; Monastiráki, Omónia and Platía Viktorías are the only central stops. You'll see ample evidence, though, of a huge extension project downtown, due to be completed sometime in 2000. The flat-fare 150dr tickets that you need for the buses are interchangeable with the metro system (75dr and 120dr, according to a zone system) and must be bought in advance from kiosks. **Taxis** in Athens are the cheapest in the EU: fares around the city will rarely come to more than 600dr. The officially licensed taxis are painted yellow with a special red numberplate – beware of cowboys at the train and bus stations. Taxi drivers will often pick up a whole string of passengers along the way, each passenger (or group of passengers) paying the full fare for their journey. So if you're picked up by an already occupied taxi, memorize the meter reading; you'll pay from then on, plus a 200dr minimum. Luggage is extra, at 50dr a piece (baggage over 10kg). The only central approximation of a **taxi rank** is on the National Gardens corner of Síndagma.

Accommodation

Hotels and **hostels** can be packed to the gills in midsummer – August especially – but for most of the year there are enough beds to go around, and to suit most wallets and tastes. On the **budget level**, expect to pay around £10/$16 for a double room in an E-class; as little as £5/$8 per person if you're prepared to share a three- to six-person room. If you have the money for a C-class hotel (or above) you can make a reservation at the tourist office. For cheaper places, you're on your own, but virtually every hotel and hostel in the city will have an English-speaking receptionist.

Many of the hotels around Pláka and Omónia are victim to around-the-clock noise; if you want uninterrupted sleep, better to head for the neighbourhoods south of the Acropolis (Pangráti, Veïkoú, Koukáki) or to the north between the National Archeological Museum and the train stations.

Hostels

Hostel Aphrodite, Inárdhou 12, cnr Mikhail Vódha 65, (☎01/88 10 589). Located between the main train station and Victoria Square, this friendly, clean hostel has a travel agency and a lively bar. ②.

International Youth Hostel, Victor Ougo 16 (☎01/523 4170). Cheapest option in Athens, with cheerful atmosphere and helpful staff. Buses #1 and #12 go to Karaiskaki Square nearby. ①.

John's Place, 5 Patroou, Plaka (☎01/322 9719). Dark rooms but nice enough. In a peaceful backstreet off Mitropoleous, with a good, cheap restaurant next door. ②.

The Student and Travellers' Inn, Kidathineon 16 (☎01/324 4808). Right in the centre of Plaka, this popular, clean and well-run hostel offers a ten percent discount to students. It also has Internet facilities, available to non-guests too. ②.

Tempi, Eolou 29 (☎01/321 3175). Cheerful hostel with helpful staff, set in an attractive, lively area on the #91 bus route. ②.

Youth Hostel #2, Alexandras av 87–89 (☎01/64 42 421). A bit of a trek to the north of the city, but the views make it worthwhile. Bus #15 takes you all the way. Open May–Sept. ①.

Youth hostel #5, Damaréos 75, Pangrati (☎01/75 19 530). Friendly place with no curfew in an appealing neighbourhood, but it's a bit out of the way; trolleys #2, #4 or #11 from downtown will get you most of the way there. ①.

Hotels

Acropolis House, Kódrou 6–8 (☎01/32 22 344). A very clean, well-sited pension, but the staff are notoriously rude and the rooms overpriced. ④.

Adonis, Kódrou 3 (☎01/324 9737). A classy hotel off Kidathineon, towards Voulis, with a stunning view of the Acropolis from the rooftop bar. Breakfast included. ④.

Dryades, (☎01/330 2387) next door to the *Orion Hotel* and under the same management. Has en-suite bathrooms and is consequently more expensive. ③.

Kouros, Kódrou 11 (☎01/32 27 431). On the same pedestrianized street as *Adonis* and *Acropolis House*, but more affordable, and very friendly. Most rooms have balconies, and the rooftop rooms face the Acropolis. ②.

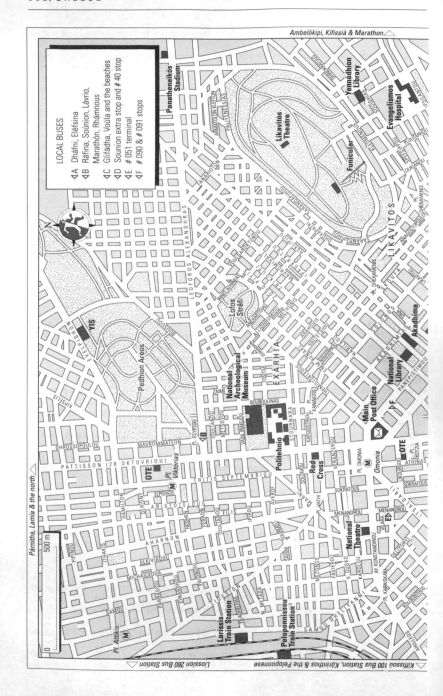

LOCAL BUSES

◁A Dháfni, Eléfsina
◁B Rafína, Soúnion, Lávrio, Marathón, Rhámnous
◁C Glifádha, Voúla and the beaches
◁D Soúnion extra stop and #40 stop
◁E #051 terminal
◁F #090 & #091 stops

Panathenaïkós Stadium

Yennádhion Library

Likavitós Theatre

Funicular

Evangelismós Hospital

LIKAVITOS

Akadhímia

National Library

National Archeological Museum

EXARHIA

Lófos Strefí

Pedhíon Áreos

YIS

LEOFOROS ALEXANDRAS

Main Post Office

OTE

Omónia

Politehnío

Red Cross

National Theatre

PL. Viktorías

OTE

PATTISSON (28 OKTOVRIOU)

TRITIS SEPTEMVRIOU

SOKRATOUS

MENANDROU

ATHINAS

PL. OMONIA

ARISTOTELOUS

AHARNON

ALKIVIADOU

MICHAIL VODA

SAMOU

Larissis Train Station

Pelopónnissou Train Station

500 m

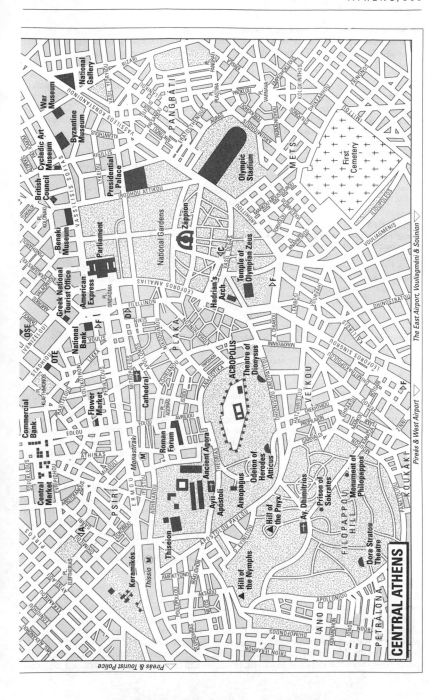

CENTRAL ATHENS

Marble House, in a quiet alley off A. Zínni 35 (☎01/92 34 058). Probably the best value in Koukáki, with helpful French/Greek management. Reservations essential. Nov–April rooms available by the month only. ③.

Hotel Museum, Bouboulínas 16 (☎01/360 5611), corner of Tossítsa. Nicely placed hotel right behind the National Archeological Museum, with a large café and bar. ③.

Orion, Emm. Benáki 105, corner Anexartisías, Exárhia (☎01/330 2388). Quiet, well-run budget hotel across from the Lófos Stréfi park – a steep walk to get there. Rooftop kitchen and common area with an amazing view. ③.

Palmyra, Marnis 42 (☎01/524 8471). Soulless and slightly seedy, but centrally placed. ③.

Pension Festos, Filellínon 18 (☎01/323 2455). Cheapest of the obvious options, right by Síndagma. The open dormitories are prey to thieves but storage facilities are on offer. ②.

Pension Myrto, Níkis 40 (☎01/32 27 237). Good value for its class, with baths in all rooms and a small bar. Just off Síndagma. ④.

Thisseus Inn, Thisséos 10 (☎01/32 45 960). Three blocks west of Síndagma, you don't get much more central than this – nor much cheaper. ②.

Tony's, Zaharítsa 26, Koukáki (☎01/92 36 370). Quiet and clean; slightly pricier than nearby *Marble House*, so fills last. ③.

Campsites

Camping Acropolis and **Camping Nea Kifissía**, set a kilometre apart in the leafy suburb of Kifissía, are both good bets, with swimming pools. #528 bus from near Omónia to reach either, or (less hassle) the metro to its last stop, catching #528 behind the station for the final leg.

Dhafni Camping, right beside Dhafni monastery and often crowded as a result; poor facilities. Clearly signposted on the left of the road next to the monastery; 20min by bus #862 or #853 from Platía Eleftherías. Prices include tent fee.

The City

Pláka, roughly the area between Síndagma, Odhós Ermoú and the Acropolis, is the best place to begin exploring. One of the few parts of Athens with charm and architectural merit, its narrow winding streets and stairs are lined with nineteenth-century Neoclassical houses, some grand, some humble and homemade. An attractive approach to Pláka is to follow **Odhós Kidhathinéon**, a pedestrian walkway starting near the English and Russian churches on Odhós Filellínon, south of Síndagma. It leads gently downhill close by the beautiful, small **Museum of Greek Folk Art** (Tues–Sun 10am–2pm; ☎01/321 3018; 500dr; student discounts) at Kidhathinéon 17. The first floor displays weaving, pottery and embroidery, revealing both the sophistication and the strong Middle Eastern influence on traditional Greek arts; the third and fourth levels display traditional and ceremonial costumes from almost every region of Greece. Odhós Kidhathinéon continues through café-crowded Platía Filomoúsis Eterías to Hadrian's street, **Odhós Adhriánoú**, running nearly the whole length of Pláka from the Thiseion to Hadrian's Arch.

The rightward section of Adhriánoú is largely commercial – souvenir shops and sandals – as far as the Roman Forum (see p.566). To the left, just a few metres on, there's a quiet and attractive sitting space around the fourth-century BC **Monument of Lysikrates**, erected to celebrate the success of a prize-winning dramatic chorus. Continuing straight ahead from the Kidhathinéon-Adhriánou intersection up **Odhós Thespídhos**, you reach the edge of the Acropolis precinct. Up to the right, the whitewashed Cycladic houses of **Anafiotiká** cheerfully proclaim an architect-free zone amidst the highest crags of the Acropolis rock.

The Acropolis

A craggy limestone plateau, watered by springs and rising an abrupt 100m out of the plain of Attica, the **Acropolis** (summer daily 8am–7pm; closes 2.30pm in winter; 2000dr; student discounts) was one of the earliest settlements in Greece, drawing a Neolithic community to its slopes around 5000 BC. In Mycenaean times it was fortified around a royal palace and temples where the cult of Athena was introduced. In the ninth century BC, the Acropolis became the heart of the first Greek city-state, and in the wake of Athenian military supremacy and a peace treaty with the Persians in 449 BC, Pericles had the complex reconstructed under the direction of architect and sculptor **Pheidias**, producing most of the monuments you see today, including the **Parthenon**.

Having survived more or less intact for well over two thousand years, the Acropolis finally fell victim to the demands of war. In 1687 besieging Venetians ignited a Turkish gunpowder magazine in the Parthenon, blasting off the roof, and in 1801 Lord Elgin removed the frieze, which he later sold to the British Museum, though there is hope it will soon be restored to Greece. Meanwhile, generations of visitors have slowly worn down the Parthenon's surfaces; and, more recently, sulphur dioxide-laden smog has been turning the marble to dust. Since 1981, visitors have been barred from the Parthenon's actual precinct and a major restoration scheme is in operation.

THE PROPYLAIA AND ATHENA NIKE TEMPLE

The Acropolis' monumental entrance, or **Propylaia**, was constructed upon completion of the Parthenon in 437 BC, and its axis and proportions were aligned to balance the temple. The ancient Athenians, awed by the fact that such wealth and craftsmanship should be used for a purely secular building, ranked this as their most prestigious monument. In front of the Propylaia, the simple and elegant **Temple of Athena Nike** was begun late in the rebuilding scheme and stands on a precipitous platform overlooking Pireás and the Saronic Gulf. The temple's frieze, with more attention to realism than triumph, depicts the Athenians' victory over the Persians at Plateia.

THE PARTHENON

The **Parthenon** was the first great building in Pericles' scheme. Designed by Iktinos, it utilizes all the refinements available to the Doric order of architecture to achieve an extraordinary and unequalled harmony. Built on the site of earlier temples, the Parthenon was intended as a new sanctuary for Athena and a house for her cult image, a colossal wooden statue decked in ivory and gold plate. Designed by Pheidias and considered one of the Seven Wonders of the Ancient World, the sculpture was lost in ancient times, but its characteristics are known through later copies – including a Roman one in the National Archeological Museum.

The name "Parthenon" means "virgins' chamber" and initially referred only to a room at the west end of the temple occupied by the priestesses of Athena. But the temple never rivalled the Erechtheion in sanctity and its role tended to remain that of treasury and artistic showcase. Originally its columns were painted and it was decorated by the finest frieze and pedimental sculpture of the Classical age. Of these, the best surviving examples are in the British Museum.

THE ERECHTHEION

To the north of the Parthenon, beyond the foundations of the Old Temple of Athena, stands the **Erechtheion**, the last of the great works of Pericles. Here, in symbolic reconciliation, Athena and the city's old patron of Poseidon-Erechtheus were both worshipped. Its elegant Ionic porticoes are all worth close attention, particularly the north one with its fine decorated doorway and frieze of blue Eleusinian marble. On the south side, in the Porch of the Caryatids, the Ionic line is transformed into six maidens (*caryatids*) holding the entablature on their heads. These are replicas: five of the originals are in the Acropolis Museum, and a sixth was looted by Elgin.

THE ACROPOLIS MUSEUM

Placed discreetly on a level below that of the main monuments, the **Acropolis Museum** (Mon noon–7pm, Tues–Sun 8am–7pm; winter daily 8am–2.30pm; free) contains nearly all of the portable objects removed from the Acropolis since 1834. In the first rooms to the left of the vestibule are fragments of pediment sculptures from the Old Temple of Athena, which give a good impression of the vivid colours that were used in temple decoration. Further on is the *Moschophoros*, a painted marble statue of a young man carrying a sacrificial calf, dated 570 BC and one of the earliest examples of Greek art in marble. Room 4 displays one of the chief treasures of the building, a unique collection of Korai, or maidens, dedicated as votive offerings to Athena sometime in the sixth century BC. The only pieces of Parthenon frieze left in Greece are in Room 7, while the adjoining room contains the graceful and fluid sculpture of Athena Nike adjusting her sandals. Finally, in the last room are the authentic and semi-eroded *caryatids* from the Erechtheion, displayed in a vacuum chamber.

THE WEST SLOPE

Rock-hewn stairs immediately below the entrance to the Acropolis ascend the low hill of the **Areopagus**, the site of the court of criminal justice. Following the road or path over the flank of the Acropolis, you come out on to Leofóros Dhionissíou Areopayítou, by the Odeion of Herodes Atticus (see below). Turning right, a network of paths leads up **Filopáppou Hill**, its summit capped by a grandiose monument to a Roman senator and consul, Filopappos, who is depicted on its frieze, driving his chariot. North, along the main path, which follows a line of truncated ancient walls, is the church of **Áyios Dhimítrios**, with Byzantine frescoes. Above the church, further to the north, rises the **Hill of the Pnyx**, an area used in Classical Athens as the meeting place for the democratic assembly. All except the most serious political issues were aired here, the hill on the north side providing a semicircular terrace from which to address the crowds of at least 6000 citizens that met more than forty times a year.

THE SOUTH SLOPE

The second-century Roman **Odeion of Herodes Atticus**, restored for performances of music and Classical drama during the summer festival, dominates the south slope of the Acropolis hill. It is open only for summer evening performances; dates can be obtained from Tourist Police (☎171), or from Athens Festival box office at Stadhíou 4 (☎01/322 3111). The main interest on the slope lies in the earlier Greek sites to the east. Pre-eminent among these is the **Theatre of Dionysus**, beside the main site entrance on Leof. Dhionissíou Areopayítou (daily 8am–7pm; winter closes 2.30pm; 500dr). One of the most evocative locations in the city, it was here that the masterpieces of Aeschylus, Sophocles, Euripides and Aristophanes were first performed. The ruins are impressive; rebuilt in the fourth century BC, the theatre could hold some 17,000 spectators. To the west of the theatre extend the ruins of the **Asclepion**, a sanctuary devoted to the healing god Asclepius and built around a sacred spring. The curative centre was probably incorporated into the Byzantine church of the doctor-saints, Kosmas and Damian, of which there are prominent remains. Nearer to the road are the foundations of the Roman **Stoa of Eumenes**, a colonnade of stalls which stretched to the Herodes Atticus Odeion.

The Agora

Northwest of the Acropolis, the **Agora** (Tues–Sun 8am–2.30pm; 1200dr, students 600dr) was the nexus of ancient Athenian city life, where the various claims of administration, commerce, market and public assembly competed for space. The site is a confused jumble of ruins, dating from various stages of building between the sixth century BC and the fifth century AD. For some idea of what you are surveying, the place to head for is the **Museum** (same hours; included in Agora entrance fee), housed in the rebuilt Stoa of Attalos. The stoa itself is, in every respect bar one, a faithful reconstruction of the original. What is missing is colour: in Classical times the exterior would have been painted bright red and blue.

The Forum area

The **Roman Forum**, or Roman Agora (Tues–Sun 8am–2.30pm; 500dr; students 300dr), was built as an extension of the city's Agora by Julius Caesar and Augustus, and its main entrance was through the relatively intact Gate of Athena Archegetis. The best-preserved and easily the most intriguing of the ruins, though, is the graceful, octagonal structure known as the **Tower of the Winds**. It was designed in the first century BC by a Syrian astronomer and served as a compass, sundial, weather vane and water clock powered by a stream from one of the Acropolis springs. Each face of the tower is adorned with a relief of a figure floating through the air, personifying the eight winds.

Síndagma and the National Gardens area

All roads lead to Platía Sindágmatos – **Síndagma Square**. Geared to tourism, with the main EOT branch, post office, American Express, airline and travel offices grouped around, it has convenience but not much else to recommend it. At the back of the parliament buildings, the **National Gardens** provide the most refreshing spot in the whole city, a luxuriant tangle of trees, shrubs and creepers, whose shade, duck ponds, cafés and sparkling irrigation channels bring relief from the heat and smog of summer. At the southern end of the park, beside one of the most hazardous road junctions in Athens, stands **Hadrian's Arch**, erected by the Roman emperor to mark the edge of the Classical city and the beginning of his own. Directly behind are the sixteen surviving columns of the 104 that originally comprised the **Temple of Olympian Zeus** (Tues–Sun 8am–2.30pm; 500dr; student discounts) – the largest in Greece, dedicated by Hadrian in 131 AD.

The Benáki Museum, the Cycladic Museum and Likavitós

At the northeast corner of the National Gardens, at Koumbári 1, is the fascinating **Benáki Museum** (temporarily closed). Overlooked by ninety percent of tourists, this constantly surprising collection ranges through Chinese ceramics, Mycenaean jewellery, Greek costumes and folk artefacts, memorabilia of the Greek War of Independence – even a reconstructed Muslim palace reception hall.

Taking the second left off Vassilísis Sofías after the Benáki Museum will bring you to the private **Museum of Cycladic and Ancient Greek Art** at Neofítou Dhouká 4 (Mon & Wed–Fri 10am–4pm, Sat 10am–3pm; 1000dr; student discounts), which in the quality of its display methods is streets ahead of anything else in Athens. Though the collections are restricted to covering the Cycladic civilization (third millennium BC), the pre-Minoan Bronze Age (second millennium BC), and the period from the fall of Mycenae to the beginning of historic times at around 700 BC (plus a selection of pottery), you come away having learned far more about these periods than from the equivalent sections of the National Museum.

North of the museum, past the posh shopping district of **Kolonáki**, a **funicular** begins its ascent to the summit of **Likavitós** at the corner of Dhorás Dhistría and Ploutárhou (Mon–Wed & Fri–Sun 8.45am–12.20am; Thurs 10.30am–12.20pm; one way 500dr, return 1000dr). For the more energetic, the principal path up the hill begins here, too, rambling up through the woods. On top, the chapel of Áyios Yióryios provides the main focus. There's a café on the adjacent terrace and another, less plastic one, halfway down; both have views spectacular enough to excuse the high prices and unenthusiastic service.

The National Archeological Museum

To get the most out of the treasure house of the **National Archeological Museum**, due north of the central market at Patissíon 44 (summer Mon 12.30–7pm, Tues–Sun 8am–7pm; winter Mon 10.30am–5pm, Tues–Sun 8am–2.30pm; 2000dr; student discounts), buy a detailed guide before you go in, as there's little in the way of explanatory captions. The biggest crowd-puller is the **Mycenaean hall** (Room 4), facing the main entrance, with all of Schliemann's gold finds from the grave circle at Mycenae, including the so-called **Mask of Agamemnon**, which is almost impossible to see in summer for the hordes of other tourists.

To the right of the Mycenaean hall, Room 6 houses a large collection of **Cycladic art** – pre-Mycenaean pieces from the islands; the most characteristic items are folded-arm figurines, among them a near full-sized nude. Most of the rest of the ground floor is occupied by sculpture. Beginning in Room 7, on the left of the main entrance, the exhibition evolves chronologically from the Archaic through the Classical and Hellenistic periods to the Roman-and Egyptian-influenced. Room 15 heralds the **Classical art** collection, with the mid-fifth-century BC **Statue of Poseidon**, dredged from the sea off Évvia in the 1920s. Found in the same shipwreck was the virtuoso **Little Jockey** (Room 21). The most reproduced of all the sculptures is in Room 31: a first-century statue of a naked **Aphrodite** about to rap Pan's knuckles for getting too fresh. The many **stelae** (carved gravestones) offer fascinating glimpses of everyday life and changing styles of craftsmanship and perception of the human form. Still on the ground floor, Room 32 contains the amazing **Helène Stathatos Collection** of gold jewellery from the ancient and Byzantine worlds.

Keep a reserve of energy for the reconstructed **Thíra rooms** upstairs. Discovered at Akrotiri on the island of Thíra, they date from around 1450 BC – contemporary with the Minoan civilization on Crete – and are frescoed with monkeys, antelopes and flowers, and furnished with painted wooden chairs and beds. The other upper rooms are occupied by a dizzying succession of **pottery**. In the south wing, entered separately from Tosítsa street, is the **Numismatic Collection**, taking in over 400,000 coins from Mycenaean times to Macedonian, though only a fraction are on display.

Eating, drinking and entertainment

As you'd expect, Athens has the best and the most varied **restaurants and tavernas** in the country. If it is character you are after, Pláka's hills and lanes can still provide a pleasant evening's setting for a meal, despite the touts and tourist hype. But for good-value, good-quality fare, it's best to strike out into the ring of neighbourhoods around: to Méts, Pangráti, Exárhia, Veïkoú/Koukáki, or the more upmarket Kolonáki. None is more than a thirty-minute walk or bus ride from the centre. The quintessentially Greek **ouzerí** are essentially bars selling *oúzo*, beer and wine, along with *mezédhes* (hors d'œuvres) to reduce the impact; in many **bars** and **pubs** you can similarly eat as well as drink. The more exciting of the city's bars, however, are music-orientated and tend to close down in the summer months. Bars, cinemas, exhibitions and nightlife venues change fast and often, so it's useful to have a copy of the monthly English-language *Atlantis* magazine and the daily *Athens News*, which between them have full **listings** of the city's clubs, galleries, concerts and films.

Restaurants

Dafni's, Ioulianou 65. Large, inexpensive portions of well-cooked, non-Greek dishes.

Eden, Lissiou 12. Athens' oldest vegetarian restaurant. Hugely popular and deservedly so. Closed Tues.

Ih Lefka, Mavromiháli 121, Neápoli. Traditional taverna with barrelled retsina and a garden. Moderate.

Kentrikon, Kolokotroni 3, in arcade. A lunchtime-only restaurant with a wide range of *mezédhes*; frequented by journalists, politicians and celebrities. Closed Sun. Moderate.

O Gavaons, Mitropoleos 73. Unpretentious and cheap kebab eatery in the tourist heart of Pláka.

O Ilias, corner Stasínou/Telesílis (near Leofóros Konstandínou), Pangráti. A very good and very popular taverna. Tables outside in summer. Moderately priced.

O Megaritis, Ferekídhou 2, corner Arátou. Cheap casserole food, barrel wine, indoor and outdoor seating.

Peristeria Taverna, Patroou 4, Plaka, next to *John's Place* hostel. No printed menu, but the owners are all too willing to give you a guided tour of the kitchens. Vegetable dishes especially good. Cheap.

Pozania, Valetsíou 58, Exárhia. The best hors d'œuvres, plus grilled fare, near the triangular plaza. Supper only; garden in summer. Moderate.

Ta Pergoulia, Márkou Moussoúrou 16, Méts. Delicious, unusual *mezédhes* – order seven or eight and you'll have a fair-sized bill but a big meal. Closed in summer.

Toh Kalivi, Empedhokleous 26, by Platía Varnáva, Pangráti. Excellent, traditional *mezédhes* fare. Closed June–Aug. Reasonable.

Vangelis, Sahíni, off Liossíon (100m up from Platía Váthis). One of the friendliest and most traditional tavernas in the city. Cheap.

Vlassis, Paster 8, by US Embassy, Kolonaki. Excellent home-style Greek cuisine and wines. Worth the trek out; bookings advised (☎01/642 5337). Moderate.

Ouzerí and bars

Brettos, Kidathineon 41. Small *ouzerí* right in the heart of Plaka, characterized by its colourful bottle-lined walls.

Café-Santé, Sólonos 54, parallel to Panepistimiou. Small and trendy bar.

Mezzo Mezzo, Singrou 58, Kolonaki. Fashionable art café/bar, south of the Acropolis crowds.

Ouzeri Euvia, G. Olimbíou 8, Koukáki. Large portions of rich food accompany drinks at this popular, reasonable place on a pedestrian street. Daily except Aug.

Toh Athinaikon, Themistokléous, near corner with Panepistimíou. An old *ouzerí* in a new location, but retaining its style, with marble tables and old posters. Variety of good-sized *mezédhes*. Closed Sun.

Toh Yerani/Kouklis/Skolarhio, Tripódhon 14, corner Epihármou, Pláka. Lively, triple-alias *mezé* bar with terrace. Open lunchtimes and evenings; moderate to pricey.

The Athens Festival

The summer **Athens Festival** has, over the years, come to encompass cultural events in just about every sphere: Classical Greek theatre most famously, but also established and contemporary dance, classical music, big-name jazz, traditional Greek music and a smattering of rock shows. As well as the Herodes Atticus theatre, which is memorable in itself on a warm summer's evening, the festival spreads to the open-air theatre on Likavitós hill, the Veákio amphitheatre in Pireás and (with special bus excursions) to the great ancient theatre at Epidaurus. The Festival runs from June 12 until October 5, and for theatre especially, you'll have to move fast to get tickets. The main **Festival box office** is in the arcade at Stadhíou 4 (Mon–Sat 8.30am–2pm & 5–7pm, Sun 10am–1pm; ☎01/32 23 111); theatre box offices open on the day of performance.

Listings

Airlines Alitalia, Vouliagmenis 577 (☎01/99 59 200); British Airways, Themistokleous 1 (☎01/89 06 655); Egyptair, Vouliagmenis 26 (☎01/92 12 818); Delta, Óthonos 4 (☎01/33 11 678); El Al, Voukourestiou 16 (☎01/36 38 681); Kenyan, Har. Trikoupi 6–10 (☎01/32 21 176); KLM, Vouliagmenis 41 (☎01/96 05 000); Olympic, Fillellínon 15 (☎01/92 67 444), main office at Andrea Singroú 96 (☎01/92 67 333); Qantas (see BA); TWA, Singroú 7 (☎01/92 13 400); United, Singroú 5 (☎01/92 42 646).

Bookshops Compendium, Níkis 28 off Síndagma, is the best organized and best value of the English-language bookstores. Eleftheroudhakis, Níkis 4, is probably the best for books about Greece (in English and Greek), with a good general English-language stock. Ih Folia tou Viviou, Panepistimíou 25, is best for fiction.

Car rental Most outlets are along Andrea Singroú: Just, at no. 43; Europcar/InterRent, no. 4; Hertz, no. 10; Alamo, no. 33; and Budget, no. 6.

Embassies and consulates Australia, Dhimitríou Soútsou 37 (☎01/64 50 404); Britain, Ploutárhou 1, Kolonáki (☎01/72 36 211); Canada, I Grenadiou 4 (☎01/72 73 400); Ireland, Vass. Konstantínou av 7 (☎01/72 32 771); Netherlands, Vass. Konstantínou av 7 (☎01/72 39 701); USA, Vass. Sofías av 91 (☎01/72 12 951); New Zealand, Xenias 24 (☎01/77 70 686).

Exchange National Bank of Greece in Síndagma, Mon–Thurs 8am–2pm & 3.30–6.30pm, Fri 8am–1.30pm & 3–6.30pm, Sat 9am–3pm, Sun 9am–1pm; General Bank on the west side of the square, with similar hours. American Express, Ermou 2 (☎01/32 44 975).

Flight information Olympic ☎01/96 66 666; other airlines ☎01/96 94 666.

Hospital Call the tourist police for the address of the nearest hospital. First Aid Ambulance ☎166.

Laundry Angélou Yerónda 10, off Platía Fillimoussís Eterías; at Dhidhótou 46, Exárhia; and at Veïkoú 107 (below Platía Koukakíou).

Luggage storage Best arranged with your hotel. Pacific Ltd, Níkis 26, stores luggage for 3000dr per item per month, 1500dr per week and 500dr per day (Mon–Sat 8am–8pm, Sun 8am–2pm).

Pharmacies Most pharmacists speak English. The Marinopoulos branches in Patissíon and Panepistimíou streets are very good; call ☎107 for details of after-hours pharmacies.

Post office The main offices with poste restante services are at Eólou 100, just off Omónia (Mon–Fri 7.30am–8pm, Sat 7.30am–2pm) and on Síndagma (same hours plus Sun 9am–1pm).

Telephones 24hr OTE office at Patissíon/Ikosiosdhóïs Oktovríou; the branch at Stahíou 15 is open 7am–midnight.

Tourist Police Head office at Pireós 158, corner Pétrou Rallí, near Thissío metro (☎171).

Train tickets The OSE office at Sína 6 (9am–3pm), by the university, gives out information and sells domestic tickets; international tickets and information at Filellínon 17.

Travel agencies Cheap ferry tickets to Italy and the Greek Islands can be found at Magic Bus, Filellínon 20 (☎01/32 37 471), Consolas next door at no. 18, and Sotiriou, the Council Travel representatives, Nikis 30 (☎01/32 20 503). Among other agencies, Himalaya (Filellínon 7) and Arcturus (Apóllonos 20) are worth scanning for air deals. Cheap train tickets and rail passes for under-26s at ISYTS, Nikis 11.

Around Athens

Attica (Attikí), the region encompassing the capital, is not much explored by tourists, except for the great romantic ruin of the **Temple of Poseidon at Sounion**. The rest tends to be visited for the functional reason of escaping to the islands from the ports of **Pireás** and **Rafína**.

Pireás (Piraeus)

PIREÁS, port of Athens since Classical times, is today a metropolis in its own right, containing much of Greater Athens' industries, as well as various commercial activities associated with a port. For most visitors it is Pireás's inter-island ferries that provide the reason for coming. The easiest way there is by metro – it's the last stop.

Perhaps the most fulfilling pursuit is to check out some of the port's excellent **eating** options – you'll find several budget restaurants around the market area, back from the waterside Aktí Miaoúli/Eth. Andistáseos. For more substantial meals, there is a string of *ouzerí* and seafood tavernas along Aktí Themistokléous, west of the Zéa Marina, most of them well priced. For a real blowout, there is *Vassilenas* at Etolikoú 72, providing *mezédhes* enough to defy all appetites; it's not cheap, but so many Athenians consider it worth the drive out that most evenings you'll need to book (☎01/46 12 457).

If you're staying in Athens prior to heading out to the islands, it is worth calling in at the EOT office near Síndagma to pick up a schedule of departures for the current week. Most of the boats leave between 8am and 9am for the main Cycladic islands, around 1pm for the major Dodecanese islands, between 5pm and 6pm for the northeast Aegean islands, and around 7pm for Crete. The best plan is to get to Pireás early and check with the various **shipping agents** around the metro station and in the quayside Platía Karaïskáki. Many of these act only for particular lines; for a full picture of the various boats sailing, ask at three or four outlets.

The Temple of Poseidon at Sounion

The 70km of coast south of Athens – the tourist-board-dubbed "**Apollo Coast**" – has some good but highly developed beaches. At weekends, when Athenians flee the city, the sands fill fast, as do the innumerable bars, restaurants and discos. If this is what you're after, then resorts like Glifádha and Vouliagméni are functional enough. But for most foreign visitors, the coast's attraction is at the end of the road, in the form of the temple at **Cape Sounion**. **Buses** to Sounion leave every thirty minutes from the KTEL terminal on Mavromatéon at the southwest corner of Áreos Park. They alternate between coastal (*paraliakó*) and inland (*mesoyiakó*) services, the latter slightly longer and more expensive. The coast route takes around two hours. For the main resorts there are more regular city buses from stops beside the Zappíon.

Cape Sounion (Akrí Soúnio) is one of the most imposing spots in Greece, and on its tip stands the fifth-century BC **Temple of Poseidon** (daily 8am–7pm; winter daily 10am–sunset; 800dr; student discounts), built in the time of Pericles as part of a sanctuary to the sea god. In summer there is faint hope of solitude, unless you slip into the site before the tours arrive, but the temple is as evocative a ruin as Greece can offer. Doric in style, it preserves sixteen of its thirty-four columns, and the view from the temple takes in the islands of Kéa, Kíthnos and Sérifos to the southeast, Éyina and the Peloponnese to the west. Below the promontory are several **coves**, the most sheltered of which is a five-minute walk east from the car park and site entrance. The main Soúnio beach is more crowded, but has a group of tavernas at the far end, which are fairly reasonably priced, considering the location. There are several **campsites** near the cape: *Camping Bacchus* and *Sounion Beach Camping* are both about 5km from the temple.

Rafína

The port of **RAFÍNA** has ferries and hydrofoils to a dozen of the Cyclades, as well as nearby Évvia. It connects regularly with Athens by an hour-plus bus route from the Mavromatéon terminal through the "gap" in Mount Pendéli. Much of the town has been spoilt by seaside development, but the little fishing harbour with its line of roof-terrace seafood restaurants remains one of the most attractive spots on the Attic coast. The town's half-dozen hotels are often full; the cheapest – *Corali* (☎0294/22 477; ③), *Kymata* (☎0294/23 406; ③) and *Rafina* (☎0294/23 460; ③) – are in the Platiá Nikifórou Plastíra. The beachside **campsite** at nearby Kókkino Limaneaki is a good fall-back.

THE PELOPONNESE

The appeal of the **Peloponnese** (Pelopónnissos) is hard to overstate. This southern peninsula, technically an island since the cutting of the Corinth Canal, seems to have the best of almost everything Greek. Its ancient sites include the Homeric palaces of Agamemnon at **Mycenae** and of Nestor at **Pílos** and the sanctuary of **Olympia**, host of the Olympic Games for a millennium. The medieval remains are scarcely less rich, with the fabulous castle at **Kórinthos**; the strange tower-houses and churches of the **Máni**; and the extraordinary Byzantine towns of **Mystra** and **Monemvassía**. The Peloponnesian **beaches**, especially along the west coast, are among the finest and least developed in the country. And, last but by no means least, the **landscape** itself is inspiring, dominated by range after range of forested mountains, and cut by lush valleys and gorges.

The usual approach from Athens to the Peloponnese is via Kórinthos; buses and trains run this way at least every hour. Alternatively – and attractively – you could go by ferry or hydrofoil, via the islands of the **Argo-Saronic**; routes run from Pireás, through the islands and then south to Monemvassía.

Kórinthos (Corinth)

The modern city of **KÓRINTHOS** was levelled by earthquakes in 1858, 1928 and again in 1981. It's a slightly grim industrial/agricultural centre, but it does have the attraction of easy access to its ancient predecessor, Arhéa Kórinthos, 7km southwest and served by hourly buses (7am–9pm; ☎0741/22 041) and by taxis.

The centre of Kórinthos is its **park**, bordered on the longer sides by Ermoú and Ethnikís Andístassis streets. The **bus station** for Athens and most local destinations is on the Ermoú side of the park; longer-distance buses use a terminal on the other side of the park. The **train station** is a couple of blocks toward the waterside. **Hotels** are quite easy to find, with two or three on the road into town from the train station and a couple of less expensive ones on or near the waterside, such as the basic *Acti* (②). If you get stuck, there's a **tourist police** post on Ermoú, just down from the bus station. There are also a couple of unenticing **campsites** along the gulf to the west: *Corinth Beach* at Dhiavakíta and *Blue Dolphin* at Léheo. **Eating** options in Kórinthos aren't spectacular. The few decent restaurants like *Neon* and *Axinos*, and fast-food/*souvlaki* places along the waterside, are all modestly priced. Buses to Agora and Náfplio leave from a café at Ethnikis Anexartisas 44; buses to Míkínes from Agora.

Ancient Corinth

The ruins of the **ancient city**, which displaced Athens as capital of the Greek province in Roman times, occupy a rambling site below the acropolis hill of Acrocorinth, itself littered with medieval remains. To explore both you will need to allow a full day, or better still, to stay close by. A modern **village** spreads back around the main archeological zone, and there is a scattering of **rooms** to rent in the backstreets – follow the signs or ask at the cafés. The two campsites detailed above are also within a three-kilometre walk.

Possession of Corinth gave control of trade between northern Greece and the Peloponnese, and a link between the Ionian and Aegean seas. Not surprisingly, the history of Corinth has been chequered with invasions and power struggles, but the city suffered only one break in its continuity, when the Romans razed it in 146 BC. For a century the site lay in ruins before being refounded, on a majestic scale, by Julius Caesar in 44 BC.

It is the remains of the Roman city that dominate the main excavated **site** (daily 8am–5/7pm; 1200dr; student discounts), just behind the road where buses pull in. You enter from the south side, which leads straight into the **Roman agora**, an enormous marketplace flanked by the foundations of a huge stoa, or covered walkway. To the north is a trace of the Greek city, a **sacred spring**, covered over by a grille at the base of a narrow flight of steps. More substantial is the elaborate Roman **Fountain of Peirene**, which stands below the level of the agora, to the side of a wide excavated stretch of what was the main approach to the city, the **Lechaion Way**. The fountain occupies the site of one of two natural springs in Corinth, and its cool water was channelled into a magnificent fountain and pool in the courtyard. The real focus, however, is a survival from the Classical Greek era: the fifth-century BC **Temple of Apollo**, whose seven austere Doric columns stand slightly above the level of the forum, and are flanked by the foundations of another marketplace and baths. To the west is the site **museum**, housing domestic pieces, some Roman mosaics and a frieze depicting the labours of Herakles.

Towering 575m above the lower town, **Acrocorinth** (Mon–Fri 8am–5/7pm, Sat & Sun 8.30am–3pm; 500dr; student discounts) is an amazing mass of rock still largely encircled by two kilometres of wall. During the Middle Ages the ancient acropolis of Corinth became one of Greece's most powerful fortresses, besieged by successive waves of invaders. It's a four-kilometre climb up – about an hour – but unreservedly recommended. Amid the sixty-acre site you wander through a jumble of semi-ruined chapels, mosques, houses and battlements, erected in turn by Greeks, Romans, Byzantines, Crusaders, Venetians and Turks.

Mikínes (Mycenae)

Tucked into a fold of the hills just to the east of the road from Kórinthos to Árgos is Agamemnon's citadel, "well-built **Mycenae**, rich in gold", as Homer wrote. It was uncovered in 1874 by the German archeologist Heinrich Schliemann, whose work was impelled by his belief that there was a factual basis to Homer's epics, and the brilliantly crafted gold and sophisticated architecture that he found bore out the accuracy of Homer's epithets.

Unless you have your own transport, you'll probably want to stay in the modern village of **MIKÍNES**, 2km east of the road and the train station and 2km from the ancient site. The cheapest options are the *Restaurant Iphigeneia*, halfway up the single street, which doubles up as a **youth hostel** (②), and the two **campsites**, *Camping Mycenae* and *Camping Atreus*, both fairly central. Alternatives include **rooms** to let in village houses or the C-class *Hotel Belle Hélène* (☎0751/66 225; ②), up the hill towards the site. The village has plenty of **restaurants**, all geared to the lunchtime bus-tour trade; don't expect too much in the way of first-rate cuisine.

The Site

The buildings unearthed by Schliemann show signs of having been occupied from around 1950 BC to 1100 BC, when the town, though still prosperous, was abandoned. No coherent explanation has been found for this event, but war among rival kingdoms was probably a major factor. The **Citadel of Mycenae** (daily 8am–5/7pm; 1500dr; student discounts) is entered through the mighty **Lion Gate** – the motif of a pillar supported by two lions was probably the symbol of the Mycenaean royal house, for a seal found on the site bears a similar device.

Inside the walls to the right is **Grave Circle A**, the cemetery which Schliemann believed to contain the bodies of Agamemnon and his followers, murdered on their triumphant return from Troy. In fact the burials date from about three centuries before the Trojan war, but they were certainly royal, and the finds (now in Athens' National Archeological Museum) are among the richest yet unearthed. Schliemann took the extensive **South House**, beyond the grave circle, to be the Palace of Agamemnon. But a much grander building, which must have been the **Royal Palace**, was later discovered on the summit of the acropolis. Rebuilt in the thirteenth century BC, probably at the same time as the Lion Gate, it is centred – as are all Mycenaean palaces – around a **Great Court**. The small rooms to the north are believed to have been royal apartments and in one of them the remains of a red stuccoed bath have led to its fanciful identification as the spot of Agamemnon's murder. Equally evocative are the ramparts and secret cistern at their east end, near the large, stately **House of Columns**.

Only the ruling elite were permitted to live within the citadel itself; outside its walls lay the main part of the town. The extensive remains of **merchants' houses** have been uncovered near to the road, beside a second grave circle. On the other side of the road from the main site is the startling **Treasury of Atreus**, a royal burial vault which is entered through a majestic fifteen-metre corridor. Set above the chamber doorway is a lintel formed by two immense slabs of stone – one of which, a staggering nine metres long, is estimated to weigh 118 tons.

Náfplio

NÁFPLIO – a lively, beautifully sited town with a fading elegance, inherited from when it was the fledgling capital of modern Greece – makes an attractive base for exploring the area and resting up by the sea. **Buses** arrive at Ódhos Singroú, just south of the interlocking main squares, **Platía Navárhon/Platía Kapodhistrías**, in turn just west of the **train station** for the recently reinstated service from Árgos. An alternative approach – or more likely a route onwards – is by the "Flying Dolphin" **hydrofoil** service; there are summer connections to Spétses and the other Argo-Saronic islands, or to Pireás and Monemvassía. Ferry services connect Náfplio to various Cycladic islands; details from Staikos Tours, Bouboulínas 50 (☎0752/27950).

The main fort – the **Palamídhi** (daily 8am–7pm; winter closes 2.30pm; 800dr; student discounts) – is most directly approached by 899 stone-hewn steps at the end of Polizídhou street, by the side of a Venetian bastion. Within the walls are three self-contained castles, all built by the Venetians in the 1710s – hence the Lion of Saint Mark above the gateways. The **Íts Kalé** ("Three Castles" in Turkish), to the west, occupies the ancient acropolis, whose walls were adapted by successive medieval occupants. The third fort, **Boúrtzi**, occupies the islet offshore from the harbour – accessible by *kaíkia* (800dr return) in summer. In the town itself, **Platía Sindágmatos**, the main square, is the focus of most interest. On and around it survive three converted **Ottoman mosques**: one is now a cinema; another, in the southwest corner, is Greece's original parliament building; the third has been reconsecrated as the cathedral of Áyios Yióryios.

Practicalities

Accommodation is generally overpriced, the most reasonable being *Hotel Epidhavros* on the corner of Kokkinou and Ipsilándou (☎0752/27 541; ③), which also has a pension up the road with cheaper rooms. *Hotel Acropole*, Vassilisis Ólgas 9 (☎0752/27 796; ③) is another option. If you're going to stay several nights, prices may work out lower in **private rooms**, most of which cluster on the slope south of the main square. The **youth hostel** on the corner of Vizandíou and Argonáfton (☎0752/246 720; ①; closed in winter) in the new town has been overhauled and is a good, friendly fall-back. For **eating**, try *Kakanarakis*, Vassilisis Ólgas 18, *Zorba* at Staïkopoúlou 30, and the *O Arapakos* and *Elatos*, both on Bouboulínas.

Epídhavros (Epidaurus)

From the sixth century BC to Roman times, **EPÍDHAVROS**, some 30km east of Náfplio, was a major spa and religious centre; its Sanctuary of Asclepius was the most famous of all shrines dedicated to the god of healing. The magnificently preserved 14,000-seat **theatre** (daily 8am–7pm; winter closes 5pm; 1500dr; student discounts), built in the fourth century BC, merges so well into the landscape that it was rediscovered only last century. Constructed with mathematical precision, it has near-perfect acoustics – from the highest of the 54 tiers of seats you can hear coins dropped in the circular orchestra. Close by is a small **museum** (Mon noon–5pm, Tues–Sun 8am–5pm; included in theatre entrance fee). The **Sanctuary** itself encompasses hospitals, dwellings for the priest-physicians, and hotels and amusements for the fashionable visitors. Its circular **Tholos**, one of the best-preserved buildings on the site, was designed, like the theatre, by Polycleitus.

Most people take in Epídhavros as a day-trip (4 buses daily from Náfplio), but if you want to stay you can **camp** near the car park. Alternatively, there are a couple of modestly priced places in Ligoúrio, 5km north – *Hotel Koronis* (☎0753/22 267; ②) and *Hotel Alkyon* (☎0753/22 002; ②). The nearest **restaurant** to the site is the *Oasis* on the Ligoúrio road, but *Leonidhas* in the village proper is better.

Trípoli

Unattractive **TRÍPOLI** is a major crossroads of the Peloponnese, from which most travellers either head northwest towards Olympia, or south to Spárti and Mystra, or Kalamáta. Alternatives include more direct routes to the coast – west to Kiparissía, or east to Náfplio or Ástros/Leonídhi – and the Peloponnese railway, which continues its meandering course from Kórinthos and Árgos to Kiparissía and Kalamáta. The major **bus terminal**, serving all destinations in Arcadia and the northern Peloponnese, is on Platía Kolokotrónis, one of the main squares. All other sevices – including those to Spárti, Kalamáta, the Máni and Pátra – leave from the café directly opposite the **train station**, five minutes' walk away at the eastern edge of town. If you need to spend a night, there's a good C-class **hotel**, the *Alex*, at Vassiléos Yioryíou 26 (☎071/22 34 65; ③).

Mistrás (Mystra)

A glorious, airy place, hugging a steep flank of Taíyettos, **MISTRÁS** is arguably the most exciting site that the Peloponnese can offer – an astonishingly complete Byzantine city which once sheltered a population of some 42,000. The castle on its summit was built in 1249 by Guillaume II de Villehardouin, fourth Frankish Prince of the Morea, and together with the fortresses of Monemvassía and the Máni it guarded his territory. In 1259 the Byzantines drove out the Franks and established the **Despotate of Mystra**. This isolated triangle of land in the southeastern Peloponnese enjoyed considerable autonomy from Constantinople, flowering as a brilliant cultural centre in the fourteenth and early fifteenth centuries and only falling to the Turks in 1460, seven years after the Byzantine capital.

The Byzantine city

The site of the **Byzantine city** (daily: summer 8am–7pm; winter 8am–2.30pm; 1200dr; free Sun and Nov–March; student discounts) has two entrances on the road up from Néos Mistrás: it makes sense to take the bus to the top entrance, then explore a leisurely downhill route. Following this course, the first identifiable building that you come to is the church of **Ayía Sofía**, erected in the fifteenth century as the burial place of the despot Mistrai Manouil Katakouzenes and which served as the chapel for the Despots' Palace. The chapel's finest feature is its floor, made from polychrome marbles; its frescoes have also survived reasonably well, protected until recently by whitewash applied by the Turks, who adapted the building as a mosque. The **Kástro**, reached by a path that climbs directly from the upper gate, maintains the Frankish design of its thirteenth-century construction, though modified by successive occupants.

Heading down from Ayía Sofía, there is a choice of routes. The right fork winds past the ruins of a Byzantine mansion, the **Palatáki** or "Small Palace", and **Áyios Nikólaos**, originally a Turkish building. The left fork is more interesting, passing the massively fortified **Náfplio Gate**, which was the principal entrance to the upper town, and the vast, multistoreyed complex of the **Despots' Palace**, parts of whose Gothic structures probably date to the Franks.

At the **Monemvassía Gate**, linking the upper and lower towns, turn right for the **Pantánassa convent**, whose nuns were the only people allowed to stay among the ruins after the village was evacuated in 1952. The church, whose name means "Queen of All", is perhaps the finest that survives in the town, a perfectly proportioned blend of Byzantine and

Gothic. Its frescoes date from various centuries, with some superb fifteenth-century work including **Scenes from the Life of Christ** in the gallery. Unfortunately, it is currently closed for restoration.

Further down on this side of the lower town stands the **House of Frangopoulos**, once the home of the Despotate's chief minister. Beyond it is the diminutive **Perívleptos monastery**, whose single-domed church, partly carved out of the rock, contains Mystra's most complete cycle of frescoes, almost all of which date from the fourteenth century. The **Mitrópolis**, or cathedral, immediately beyond the gateway, ranks as the oldest of Mystra's churches, built in 1309. A marble slab set in its floor is carved with the symbol of the Palaelogos dynasty, the double-headed eagle of Byzantium, commemorating the spot where Constantine XI Paleologus, the last emperor, was crowned in 1449.

A short way uphill lies the **Vrontohión monastery**, the centre of intellectual life in the fifteenth-century town, serving as the burial place of the despots as well. There are a couple of churches attached; **Afendikó**, built in 1311 and the further of the two, has been beautifully restored, revealing frescoes with startlingly bold juxtapositions of colour.

Practicalities

The modern town, **Néos Mistrás**, is a small roadside community whose half-dozen tavernas are crowded with tour buses by day and revert to a low-key life at night. **Accommodation**, however, is limited to the *Hotel Byzantion* (☎0731/83 309; ④). Nearby **Spárti** (ancient Sparta, though there's little left to see) is a good base, with a couple of cheaper **hotels** around the central square: D-class *Panelinion* on Paleológou 65 (☎0731/28 031; ②) and E-class, but less attractively situated, *Cecil*, at Paleológou 125 (☎0731/24 980; ③). The nearest **campsite**, 2.5km from Spárti, *Camping Mystra*, is pricey but has a swimming pool; closer to Mystra and less expensive is *Camping Castle View*. There are a couple of fair **restaurants** in Spárti: *Elyssé* at Paleológou 113, and a *psistariá* up at the north end of Stadhíou, just as it begins to bend into Tripoléos. All **buses** in and out of Spárti leave from the station marked KTEL on the last block of Likoúrgou going west from the centre.

Monemvassía

Set impregnably on a great eruption of rock connected to the mainland by a kilometre-long causeway, the Byzantine seaport of **MONEMVASSÍA** is a place of grand, haunted atmosphere. At the outset of the thirteenth century it was the Byzantines' sole possession in the Morea, eventually being taken by the Franks in 1249, after three years of siege. Regained by the Byzantines as part of the ransom for the captured Guillaume de Villehardouin, it served as the chief commercial port of the Despotate of the Morea. The city was eventually liberated from the Turks in 1823. Mystra, despite the presence of the court, was never much more than a large village; Monemvassía at its peak had a population of almost 60,000.

Monemvassía can be approached by road or, more enjoyably, by sea. There is a weekly **ferry** from Pireás, and Kastélli in Crete, and more or less daily **hydrofoils** in season, linking it to the north with Leonídhi, Spétses and Pireás, to the south with Neápoli and the island of Kíthira. Buses connect with Spárti and Athens three times daily and with Yíthio twice daily in season only. The boat or hydrofoil will drop you midway down the causeway; buses arrive in the town of **YÉFIRA** on the mainland, where most **accommodation** is found. By the causeway there are a couple of reasonable **hotels** – try the *Akroyiali* (☎0732/61 360; ②) – plus numerous pensions and **rooms**. The nearest **campsite**, *Camping Paradise*, is 3.5km south of Yéfira near a good beach. Rooms on the rock are a lot more expensive (④) and in short supply.

The **Lower Town** once sheltered forty churches and over 800 homes, an incredible mass of building threaded by an intricate network of alleys. A single main street harbours most of the restored houses, plus cafés, tavernas and a scattering of shops, adding much-needed life to the rock. The foremost building is the **Mitrópolis**, the cathedral built by Emperor Andronicus II Comnenus in 1293, and the largest medieval church in southern Greece. Across the square, the tenth-century domed church of **Áyios Pávlos** was transformed by the

Turks into a mosque and is now a small museum of local finds. Towards the sea is a third church, the **Hrissafítissa**, with its bell hanging from an old cypress tree in the courtyard. It was restored and adapted by the Venetians in the eighteenth century, when for twenty-odd years they took the Peloponnese from the Turks.

The climb to the **Upper Town** is highly worthwhile, not least for the solitude. Its fortifications, like those of the lower town, are substantially intact; within, the site is a ruin, though infinitely larger than you could imagine from below. Close to the gateway is the beautiful thirteenth-century **Ayía Sofía**, the only fully intact building. Beyond the church extend acres of ruins: the stumpy bases of Byzantine houses and public buildings, and, perhaps most striking, a vast **cistern** to ensure water in time of siege.

Yíthio and the Máni

YÍTHIO, Sparta's ancient port, is gateway to the dramatic **Máni peninsula** and one of the south's most attractive seaside towns. Its somewhat low-key harbour, with intermittent ferries or hydrofoils to Pireás, Kíthira and Crete, gives on to a graceful nineteenth-century waterside. Out to sea, tethered by a long narrow mole, is the islet of **Marathónissi** (ancient Kranae), where Paris and Helen of Troy spent their first night after her abduction from Sparta. Buses drop you close to the centre of town, and finding a **room** should be a matter of a stroll along the waterside. Just off the main square in Vassiléos Pávlou, there is the recently renovated D-class *Kranae* at no. 17 (☎0733/24 394; ③) and the C-class *Pantheon* at no. 33 (☎0733/22 166; ④). Four- or five-room establishments huddle by the port police; others are up the steps from the waterside and, cheapest of all, west along the seafront. If you want to **camp**, there are a couple of official summer sites at Mavrovoúni beach, which begins 3km south off the Areópoli road. For **eating**, *Petakos*, tucked against the sports stadium at the north end of town, or *Kostas*, by the bus station, tend to work out better than the obviously touristy fish tavernas on the quay.

The Máni

The southernmost peninsula of Greece, **the Máni**, stretches from Yíthio in the east and Kalamáta in the west down to Cape Ténaro, mythical entrance to the underworld. It is a wild and arid landscape with an idiosyncratic culture and history: nowhere in Greece does a region seem so close to its medieval past. The quickest way into it is to take a bus from Yíthio to **AREÓPOLI**, gateway to the so-called Deep Máni. **Rooms** are advertised at a number of ordinary houses, mostly grouped around the cathedral; or there's *Pension Kouris* in the main square (☎0733/51 340; ③). Taxis can be rented fairly easily here, and there are daily buses south to Yerolimín in summer (3 weekly out of season). More regular buses north to Khardhamíli and Kalamáta sometimes involve a change at Ítilo, 9km north.

SOUTH FROM AREÓPOLI

From Areópoli it is 8km to the village of **PÍRGOS DHIROÚ**, where the road forks off to the famed **caves**, 4km further on (daily: summer 8am–6pm; winter 8am–3pm; 2800dr). They are very much a packaged attraction, with long queues for admission, but it's worthwhile for the punt around the underground waterways of the **Glifádha caves** and the tour on foot of the huge **Alepótripa caves**, where recent excavation has unearthed evidence of prehistoric occupation.

YEROLIMÍN has an end-of-the-world air, but despite appearances was only developed in the 1870s. There are a few shops, a couple of cafés and two very simple E-class **hotels**; the *Akroyiali* (☎0733/54 204; ②) has slightly cheaper rooms. At the dock, occasional boat trips are offered around Cape Ténaro, passing the pebbly bay of Asomatíí, where a small **cave** is said to be the mythical gate to Hades.

NORTH FROM AREÓPOLI

The eighty kilometres or so of road between Areópoli and Kalamáta is as dramatic and beautiful as any in Greece, a virtual corniche between Mount Taíyettos and the Gulf of Messinía.

The beaches begin at **ÁYIOS NIKÓLAOS**, which has a few roadside rooms and tavernas, and extend more or less continuously through to Kardhamíli. **STOÚPA**, which has possibly the best sands, is now geared very much to tourism, with numerous **rooms** to let, several small hotels (cheapest is the C-class *Stoupa*; ☎0721/77 485; ③), a **campsite** five minutes' walk from Kalógria beach, a supermarket (which will change money and cheques) and a fair number of tavernas, the best of which is the *Mitar Kafenion*. **KARDHAMÍLI**, 10km north, remains a beautiful place despite its commercialization, with a long pebble beach and a ruined old tower-house quarter. Besides its ranks of prebooked self-catering apartments, there's the *Kardamyli Beach* hotel (☎0721/73 180; ④). **Eating** is best at *Kiki's* or *Lela's* (☎0721/73 541; ③), which also has some rooms.

Koróni and Methóni

At the end of the Messenian peninsula sprawling southwest of Kalamáta, **KORÓNI** and **METHÓNI** were the Venetians' longest-held possessions on the Peloponnese; today their castles shelter two attractive small resorts. Buses serve both places from Kalamáta, with a change at Pílos for Methóni, but they're linked directly only by the occasional bus in summer. Koróni's castle accents rather than dwarfs the picturesque town of tiled and pastel-painted houses spilling down to the harbour in a maze of stair-and-ramp streets. It is not undiscovered, though, the Germans having arrived in force in the 1980s, but outside summer – and the season is very long this far south – it is still a delightful place. On the opposite side of the castle from the town stretches two-kilometre **Zánga beach**. Most visitors stay in **rooms**, which are likely to be more pleasant and better value than Koróni's budget **hotel**, the friendly but poor-quality *Diana* (②).

By contrast, the **fortress** at Methóni (Tues–Sun 8.30am–3pm; 500dr; student discounts) is as imposing as they come: massively bastioned, washed on three sides by the sea, and cut off on the land side by a great moat. The village itself, dedicated more specifically to tourism than Methóni, isn't so appealing, but **accommodation** is at least reasonably priced and fairly abundant. Among less expensive hotels, *Iliodyssio* (☎0723/31 225; ③), near the moat, and *Alex* (☎0723/31 245; ③) on the beach are good choices. Behind the flat, hardpacked beach, devoted mostly to windsurfing, there's an official **campsite** (April–Oct).

Olimbía (Olympia)

The historic resonance of **OLIMBÍA**, which for over a millennium hosted the Panhellenic games, is rivalled only by Delphi or Mycenae. Its site, too, ranks with this company, for although the ruins are confusing, the setting is as perfect as could be imagined: a luxuriant valley of wild olive and plane trees, beside the twin rivers of Alfiós and Kládhios, and overlooked by the pine-covered hill of Krónos. Most people arrive at Olympia **via Pírgos**, which in addition to five daily trains has sixteen bus services to the site, plus numerous buses to Pátra and a couple daily to Kalamáta/Kiparissía.

Modern **OLIMBÍA** has grown up simply to serve the excavations and tourist trade. If you're travelling alone, the **youth hostel** on the main street at Kondhíli 18 (☎0624/22 580; ①) is the cheapest option; between two people, **rooms** in private houses can be better value – most are signposted on the road parallel to and above Kondhíli. Among **hotels**, the cheapest is generally the *Hermes*, Kondhili 63 (☎0624/22 577; ②). In the same price range, the pensions *Possidon* (☎0624/22 567; ②) and *Achilefs* (☎0624/22 562; ②), both on Stefanoloúlou, are worth noting. The closest **campsite**, *Diana*, just off the main road, has a pool and good facilities. For **eating**, most of the tavernas offer standard tourist meals at mildly inflated prices; honourable exceptions include the *Praxitelis*, a grill on Spiliopoúlou, and the *O Kladeos*, a beautiful and authentic taverna near the river, well worth seeking out.

The Site

The contests at Olympia probably began around the eleventh century BC, slowly developing over the next two centuries from a local festival to a major quadrennial celebration attended by states from throughout the Greek world. From the very beginning, the main **Olympic events** were athletic, but the great gathering of people expanded the games' importance: nobles and ambassadors negotiated treaties here, while merchants chased contacts, and sculptors and poets sought commissions. The games eventualy fell victim to the Christian Emperor Theodosius's crackdown on pagan festivities in 393 AD, and his successor ordered the destruction of the temples – a process completed by invasion, earthquakes and, lastly, by the River Alfiós changing its course to cover the sanctuary site. There it remained, covered by seven metres of silt and sand, until the 1870s.

The entrance to the **ancient site** (Mon–Fri 8am–5/7pm, Sat & Sun 8am–2.30pm; 1200dr; student discounts) leads along the west side of the sacred precinct wall, past a group of public and official buildings, including a structure adapted as a Byzantine church. This was originally the studio of Pheidias, the fifth-century BC sculptor responsible for the great cult statue in the focus of the precinct, the great Doric **Temple of Zeus**. Built between 470 and 456 BC, it was as large as the Parthenon and its decoration rivalled the finest in Athens – partly recovered, its sculptures are now exhibited in the museum. In the *cella* was displayed the great gold and ivory cult statue by Pheidias, and here, too, the Olympian flame was kept alight from the time of the games until the following spring – a tradition continued at an altar for the modern games. The smaller **Temple of Hera**, behind, was the first built here; prior to its completion in the seventh century BC, the sanctuary had only open-air altars, dedicated to Zeus and a variety of other cult gods. Rebuilt in the Doric style in the sixth century BC, it's the most complete structure on the site. Finally, though, what makes sense of Olympia is the 200-metre track of the **Stadium** itself. The start and finish lines are still there, as are the judges' thrones in the middle and seating banked to each side. The tiers here eventually accommodated up to 30,000 spectators, with a smaller number on the southern slope overlooking the **Hippodrome** where chariot races were held.

In Olympia's **archeological museum** (summer Mon noon–7pm, Tues–Sun 8am–7pm; winter Mon 10.30am–5pm, Tues–Fri 8am–5pm, Sat & Sun 8am–2.30pm; 1200dr; student discounts), a couple of hundred metres north, the centrepiece is the statuary from the Temple of Zeus, displayed in the vast main hall. Most famous of the individual sculptures is the **Hermes of Praxiteles**, dating from the fourth century BC; one of the best preserved of all Classical sculptures, it retains traces of its original paint. The best of the smaller objects, housed in Room 4, include several fine bronzes, among them the **helmet of Miltiades**, the Athenian general at the Battle of Marathon, and a superb terracotta group of *Zeus Abducting Ganymede*.

Pátra (Patras)

PÁTRA is the largest town in the Peloponnese and, after Pireás, the major port of Greece. You can go from here to Italy and Cyprus, as well as to the Ionian islands and Crete, and the city is a key to the transport network of the mainland too. It's not the ideal holiday retreat: there are no beaches, no particular sights, the hotels are on noisy streets and the restaurants are generally fairly wretched. Unless you arrive late in the day from Italy, you shouldn't need to spend more than a few hours in the city. If you do need to stay, the main concentration of low-budget **hotels** is on Ayíou Andhréou, a block back from Óthonos Keh Amalías. The cheapest, and possibly the grottiest, is the *Hotel Pantheon* on Ermou 25 (①), followed by the cheerful and well-run *Pension Nicos* (②), Ayíou Andhréou 121, on the corner of Patreas. The main low-budget alternative is the **youth hostel** at Iróon Politechníou 62 (☎061/427 278; ①), 1km north of the ferry terminal. For **eating** out, try the *Trikogial* on Amalias 48, or *Ouzo de Rapeythrio*, Karlour 11, a cosy, authentic bar selling cheap seafood snacks.

Innumerable agents along the harbour road, Óthonos Keh Amalías, sell different **ferry** tickets to Italy. En route to Italy it is possible to make stopovers on Kefalloniá, Páxi and, most commonly, Igoumenítsa or Corfu. Individual tickets to any of these islands are also available. The **EOT** office, by the customs house at the harbour, can be helpful for information. For **money exchange**, there is a Thomas Cook in the bus depot, an American Express on Amalias.

The main **bus** station, midway along the waterside, has services to Athens, Killíni, Pírgos and other towns in the Peloponnese, as well as to Ioánnina. Heading to **Delphi**, take local bus #6 (from Kandakári, five blocks back from the waterside) to the Río-Andírio ferry, cross over and take another local bus to Náfpaktos and then a regular bus from there. Finally, you can reach Kórinthos in two hours by bus or thirty minutes longer on the frequent **trains**.

CENTRAL AND NORTHERN GREECE

Central Greece has a slightly indeterminate character: vast agricultural plains occupy much of the land, dotted with rather drab market and industrial towns. For most visitors it's an area full of highlights – **Delphi** above all, and further to the north the unworldly rock-monasteries of the **Metéora**. Access to these monasteries is from **Kalambáka**, from where the **Katára pass** over the Píndhos Mountains brings you into **Epirus** (Ípiros), the region with the strongest identity in mainland Greece. En route is **Métsovo**, perhaps the easiest location for a taste of mountain life, though becoming increasingly commercialized. Nearby **Ioánnina**, once the capital of Ali Pasha, is a town of some character and the main transport hub for trips into the unspoilt villages of the **Zagóri** and the **Vikos gorge**. The rugged peaks, forested ravines and turbulent rivers of the Píndhos that helped to protect Epirus also kept it isolated. The region's role in ancient Greek affairs was peripheral, so there are few archeological sites of importance: the main one is at **Dodona**, where the sanctuary includes a spectacular Classical theatre. The Epirus coast is in general disappointing: **Igoumenítsa** is a useful ferry terminal but will win few admirers, while **Párga**, the region's major resort, has been developed beyond its capacity.

The northern provinces of **Macedonia** and **Thrace** have been part of the Greek state for little more than two generations. As such, the region stands slightly apart from the rest of the nation – an impression reinforced for visitors by scenery and climate that are essentially Balkan. Macedonia is characterized by lake-speckled vistas to the west, and, to the east, moving towards Thrace, by heavily cultivated flood plains and the deltas of rivers finishing courses begun in the former Yugoslavia or Bulgaria. The only areas to draw more than a scattering of summer visitors are **Halkidhikí** – which provides the city's beach-playground and shelters the "Monks' Republic" of Mount Áthos – and **Mount Olympus**. With a more prolonged acquaintance, the north may well grow on you – its vigorous day-to-day life, independent of tourism, is most evident in the relaxed Macedonian capital of **Thessaloníki** and its chief port **Kavála**.

Delphi

Access to the extraordinary site of **DELPHI**, 150km northwest of Athens, is straightforward: several buses run there from the capital daily, and services are as frequent from Livádhia, the nearest rail terminus. With its site raised on the slopes of a high mountain terrace and dwarfed by the ominous crags of Parnassós, it's easy to see why the ancients believed this to be the centre of the earth. But what confirmed its status was the discovery of a chasm that exuded strange vapours and reduced all comers to frenzied, incoherent and prophetic mutterings. For over a thousand years a steady stream of pilgrims worked their way up the dangerous mountain paths to seek divine direction in matters of war, worship, love or business, until the oracle eventually became defunct with the demise of paganism in the fourth century AD.

The modern village of **DHELFÍ**, like most Greek site villages, has a quick turnaround of visitors, so finding a place to stay should present few problems. There are upwards of thirty hotels and pensions, and various rooms to let, though all are expensive. Best value of the cheaper **hotels** is *Stadium* at Apollonos 21 (☎0265/82 251; ③) and *Athena* at Vassiléos Pavlou 55 (☎0265/82 239; ②), and, of the **pensions**, the *Odysseus* at Fillelínon 1 (☎0265/82 235; ②). The nearest official **campsite** is the *Apollon*, 1500m west towards Ámfissa. **Eating** is best at *Taverna Omfalos*, Apollonos 30, and *Taverna Vakhos*, next to the youth hostel, which is incredibly cheap and tasty, but only open from May to September.

The Site

The **Sacred Precinct** of Apollo (daily 8am–7pm; winter closes 2.30pm; 1200dr; student discounts) is entered by way of a small **Agora**, enclosed by ruins of Roman porticoes and shops for the sale of votive offerings. The paved **Sacred Way** begins after a few stairs and zigzags uphill between the foundations of memorials and treasuries to the **Temple of Apollo**. Of the main body of the temple only the foundations stood when it was uncovered by the French in the 1890s; they have, however, re-erected six Doric columns, giving a vertical line to the ruins and providing some idea of its former dominance over the sanctuary. In the innermost part of the temple was a dark cell where the priestess would officiate; no sign of cave or chasm has been found, but it is likely that it was closed by earthquakes. The theatre and stadium used for the main events of the Pythian games are on terraces above the temple. The **Theatre**, built in the fourth century BC with a capacity of 5000, was closely connected with Dionysus, god of the arts and wine, who reigned in Delphi over the winter months when the oracle was silent. A steep path leads up through cool pine groves to the **Stadium**, which was banked with stone seats only in Roman times.

Delphi's **museum** (summer Mon noon–7pm, Tues–Sun 8am–7pm; winter daily 8am–2.30pm; 1200dr; student discounts) contains a collection of archaic sculpture, matched only by finds on the Acropolis. Its most famous exhibit is the *Charioteer*, one of the few surviving bronzes of the fifth century BC. The charioteer's eyes, made of onyx and set slightly askew, lend it a startling realism while the demure expression sets the scene as a victory lap. Other major pieces include two huge *kouroi* (archaic male figures) from the sixth century BC, and a group of three colossal dancing women.

Following the road east of the sanctuary towards Aráhova, you reach a sharp bend. To the left, marked by niches for votive offerings and the remains of an archaic fountain house, the celebrated **Castalian spring** still flows from a cleft in the cliffs, which are swathed in scaffolding to prevent collapse. Visitors to Delphi were obliged to purify themselves in its waters, usually by washing their hair, though murderers had to take the full plunge. Across and below the road from the spring is the **Marmaria** or Sanctuary of Athena (Mon–Fri 8am–5/7pm, Sat & Sun 8.30am–3pm; free), the "Guardian of the Temple". The precinct's most conspicuous building is the Tholos, a fourth-century BC rotunda whose purpose is a mystery. Outside the precinct on the northwest side, above the Marmaria, is a **Gymnasium**, also built in the fourth century BC but later enlarged by the Romans.

Lamía and Vólos

LAMÍA is a busy provincial capital and an important transport junction, so you might have to stay here if you miss a connection. All **buses** – including the service from the **train** station (6km out) – arrive in the southeast quarter of the town, and most of the **hotels** are nearby. There's a pair of the cheapest places on Rozáki-Ángeli: *Thermopylae* at no. 36 (☎0231/21 366; ③) and the seedy but convenient *Neon Astron* (☎0231/26 245; ②) at Platía Laoú 5. The town's social hub is Platía Eleftherías, full of outdoor cafés and **restaurants**; a number of very cheap pasta-and-chicken restaurants can be found below Eleftherías in the vicinity of tree-shaded Platía Laoú, the site of more inexpensive hotels.

Southeast of Lárissa, **VÓLOS** is Greece's fastest-growing industrial city and is not a pretty sight: a modern, concrete sprawl, rebuilt after an earthquake in 1955 and now edging to its natural limits against the Pílion foothills. That said, you may well be spending some time here, as Vólos is the gateway to the Pílion and the main **port for the northern Sporades**. Ferries leave two to four times daily for Skiáthos and Skópelos, with at least one continuing to Alónissos; hydrofoils run two to three times daily to all three, occasionally proceeding to Skíros. **Hotels** are fairly plentiful with a concentration of inexpensive places in the grid of streets behind the port. *Iason*, Pávlou Melá 1 (☎0421/26 075; ②), is about as basic as you'd want, while the nearby *Ayra*, Sólonos 5 (☎0421/25 370; ③), is a bit more savoury. Two **restaurants** near the ferry jetty – *Ouzerí Axivos* at Argonáfron 9 and the *Chargrilled Restaurant* further on at no. 40 – are worth a try. If you've time to spare, the **Archeological**

Museum (Tues–Sun 8.30am–3pm; 500dr; student discounts) at the east end of the waterfront has arguably the best collection of Neolithic artefacts in Europe.

The Pílion (Pelion)

There is something decidedly un-Greek about the **Pílion Peninsula**, with its lush fruit orchards and dense broadleaf forests. Water gurgles from crevices beside every road, and summers are a good deal cooler than the rest of central Greece. Pílion villages are idiosyncratic too, sprawling affairs with sumptuous mansions and barn-like churches lining their cobbled streets. Add to the scenery and architecture a half-dozen or so excellent beaches, and equidistance from Athens and Thessaloníki, and it's no wonder that this is a well-loved corner of Greece – especially by Greeks; avoid July and August unless you wish to camp out.

The most visited part of the peninsula lies just north and east of Vólos, with bus services biased towards the twenty-odd villages here. If your time is limited, the best single targets are the EOT-recognized showcases of Makrinítsa and Vizítsa. **MAKRINÍTSA** is becoming a bit over-quaint, with expensive lodging in a bevy of restored mansions, though frequent connections to Vólos make day-trips easy. Remoter **VIZÍTSA** has equally good connections, with better possibilities of **staying and eating** cheaply – try *Kalliroi Dhimou* (☎0423/86 484; ④) and the taverna *O Yiorgaras*. Alternatively, the less homogeneous village of **MILIÉS**, 3km east, also has some accommodation and, down by the bus stop, the best bakery on the peninsula, cranking out every sort of pie, pastry and bread imaginable.

The largest village on the Pílion – virtually a small town – is **ZAGORÁ**, destination of fairly regular buses across the peninsula's summit. Unlike its seashore neighbours, it has a life independent of tourism, and is more appealing than first impressions suggest. You're also more likely to find a **room** here in season than down at **HOREFTÓ**, 8km below, though you can try there at the **hotels** *Votsala* (☎0426/22 001; ②) and *Erato* (☎0426/22 445; ②). There's also a good **campsite** at the south end of the main beach here; more coves beckon north of the resort.

Just before Zagorá, a junction funnels traffic southeast to **TSANGARÁDHA**, also the terminus of two daily buses from Miliés. Though nearly as large as Zagorá, it may not seem so, divided as it is into four distinct quarters along several kilometres of road. In the typical Pílion fashion, each is grouped around a parish church and tree-shaded *platía*. Reasonable **rooms** are difficult to come by, though you might start at *Villa ton Rodhon* (☎0426/49 340; ③) in Ayía Paraskeví. **Eating out** is frankly uninviting; most people do so at **MOÚRESSI**, a few kilometres north, where two adjacent **tavernas** dish out Pílion specialities at fairly moderate prices. **KISSÓS**, still further towards Zagorá, is another possibility for staying and dining, with its excellent *Ksenonas Kissos* (☎0426/31 214; ②).

Most visitors, however, stay at one of several nearby beaches, the best on this shore of the peninsula. **IOÁNNIS**, 6km below Kissós, is an overblown resort with twenty hotels – most reasonable is the friendly *Armonia* (☎0426/31 242; ③; no single rooms), also with a good restaurant. If it's too busy for your tastes, head south along the sand, past its crowded campsite, to **Papaneró** beach or further still to postcard-perfect **DAMOÚHORI** with its tiny ruined castle and fishing harbour. The area's most scenic beach is reached by following a winding seven-kilometre road from the south end of Tsangarádha to Milopótamos.

Lárissa and Tríkala

LÁRISSA stands at the heart of the Thessalian plain, a large market centre approached across a dull landscape of wheat and corn fields. For the most part modern and unremarkable, it retains a few old streets which hint at its recent past as a Turkish provincial capital. As another large **road and rail junction**, the town has efficient connections with most places you'd want to reach: Vólos to the east; Tríkala and Kalambáka to the west; and Lamía to the south. Should you need to stay in Lárissa, there are numerous **hotels**. The cheapest are in the square by the train station, 1km from the centre: *Diethnes* (☎041/234 210; ②) and *Pantheon* (☎041/236 726; ②).

West from Lárissa, five daily buses follow the Piniós river to **TRÍKALA**, where you may need to change buses for Kalambáka and the Metéora. The railway makes a similar number of connections between Lárissa and Tríkala, though it loops around to the south through Kardhítsa. A lively metropolis after the agricultural plains towns of central Thessaly, Tríkala retains many nineteenth-century Turkish houses, and a graceful old mosque. Around the **Fortress**, adapted by the Turks from a Byzantine structure, are some attractive gardens and the meagre remains of a **Sanctuary of Asclepius**, the healing god whose cult is said to have originated here. The liveliest part of town, with numerous cafés and restaurants, is around Platía Iróön Politechníou on the riverside. Accommodation should pose few problems, with two decent budget **hotels** near the square: the comfortable C-class *Palladion* at Víronos 4 (☎0431/28 091; ③) and the E-class *Panhellinion* above *Goody's* restaurant at Vassilísis Ólgas 2 (☎0431/27 644; ②), which should be in operation again after a major refurbishment. If not, try the pricier *Lithaeon*, adjacent to the bus station at Othonos 16 (☎0431/20 690; ④). Strangely, bona fide **tavernas** are scarce; good lunches and snacks can be had along Asklipíou.

Kalambáka and the Metéora

There are few more exciting places to arrive at than **KALAMBÁKA**. The shabby town itself you hardly notice, for the eye is immediately drawn up in an unremitting vertical ascent to the weird grey cylinders of rock overhead. These are the outlying monoliths of the extraordinary valley of the **Metéora**. To the right you can make out the monastery of Áyios Stéfanos, firmly entrenched on a massive pedestal; beyond stretches a chaotic confusion of spikes, cones and cliffs, beaten into bizarre shapes by the action of the sea that covered the Plain of Thessaly around fifty million years ago.

The earliest religious communities in the valley emerged in the eleventh century, when hermits made their homes in the caves that score many of the rocks. In 1336 they were joined by two monks from Mount Áthos, one of whom – Athanassios – established the first monastery here in 1389. Today, put firmly on the map by appearances in such films as James Bond's *For Your Eyes Only*, the four most accessible monasteries are essentially museums. Only two, Ayía Triádha and Áyios Stéfanos, continue to function with any real monastic purpose.

Visiting the Metéora demands a full day, which means staying at least one night at Kalambáka or at the village of Kastráki, right in the shadow of the rocks. Kalambáka is a characterless but pleasant enough base, with a fairly plentiful supply of rooms. Arriving by bus or train, in season, you are likely to be offered a **room** by waiting householders; if not, there are numerous signs on the road into town from the bus station. **Hotels** are pricier, with above-usual rates. Try the *Olympion*, Trikálon 97 (☎0432/22 792; ③), or ring Geiorgios Totis, who owns rooms in two separate hotels and will collect you from the bus or train station (☎0432/22 251; ②, beds on roof ①).

KASTRÁKI is twenty minutes' walk out of Kalambáka. Along the way you pass the busy *Camping Vrahos Kastraki*, the first of two **campsites** here; the other one, *Boufidhis*, is smaller but quieter and incomparably set under the pinnacles of the monasteries. The village also has a fair number of **private rooms**, as well as an extremely dilapidated E-class **hotel**, the *Kastraki* (☎0432/22 286; ③), not to be confused with the more luxurious hotel with the same name further up the road (☎0432/75 336; ④).

The Monasteries

If you want to see all the Metéora monasteries in a day, start early to take in Varlaám and Méga Metéoron before 1pm (when they close for two hours), leaving the rest of the day for the ten-kilometre walk from Kastráki to Áyios Stéfanos. Each monastery levies an admission charge of 500dr (students 300dr) and operates a strict **dress code**: skirts for women, long trousers for men and covered arms for both sexes.

From Kastráki the road loops around between huge outcrops of rock, passing below the chapel-hermitage of **Doúpiani** before reaching a track to the left, which winds up a low rock to the fourteenth-century **Áyiou Nikólaou**. A small, recently restored monastery, this has some superb sixteenth-century frescoes in its *katholikón* (main chapel). Next to it on a needle-thin shaft is **Ayía Moní**, ruined and empty since an earthquake in 1858. Bearing off to the right, fifteen minutes or so further on, a trio of well-signed cobbled paths lead to the tiny, compact convent of **Roussánou** (or Ayía Varvára), probably founded in 1288, approached across dizzying bridges from an adjacent rock. This has perhaps the most extraordinary site of all the monasteries, its walls built right on the edge of a sharp blade of rock. Its frescoes, particularly bloody scenes of martyrdom and judgment, were painted in 1561.

A short way beyond Roussánou the road divides, the left fork heading toward **Varlaám** (closed Fri), one of the oldest and most beautiful monasteries in the valley. The *katholikón* is small but glorious, supported by painted beams and with walls and pillars totally covered in frescoes. Varlaám also retains its old **Ascent Tower**: until 1923 the only way of reaching the monasteries was by being hauled up in a net drawn by rope and windlass, or by the equally perilous retractable ladders. Today, however, you can reach the monastery safely, if breathlessly, via the 195 steps cut into the side of the rock. From Varlaám a path cuts north to **Méga Metéoron** (closed Tues). This is the grandest of the monasteries and also the highest, built 415m above the surrounding ground. Its *katholikón* is the most magnificent, a beautiful cross-in-square church surmounted by a lofty dome.

It's just under an hour's walk from here to the fourteenth-century **Ayía Triádha** (Holy Trinity), approached up 140 steps carved into a tunnel in the rock. Although Ayía Triádha teeters above a deep ravine and its little garden ends in a precipitous drop, there is a trail at the bottom of the monastery's steps back to Kalambáka. This is about 3km long and well marked, saving a long trudge back around the circuit. **Áyios Stéfanou** (closed Mon), built in 1192, the last and easternmost of the monasteries, is a further twenty minutes' walk from Ayía Triádha – if you're pushed for time it's the obvious one to leave out.

The Katára pass: Kalambáka to Ioánnina

West of Kalambáka, the **Katára pass** cuts across the central range of the Píndhos to link Thessaly and Epirus. The route is one of the most spectacular in the country, and is covered by four buses daily between Tríkala and Ioánnina.

Métsovo

MÉTSOVO stands almost astride the Katára pass, a high mountain village built on two sides of a ravine and encircled by a mighty range of peaks. It is a startling site: from below the main road the eighteenth- and nineteenth-century stone houses, with their wooden balconies and tile roofs, wind down the ravine to the main *platía*, where the old men and women loiter, magnificent in full traditional dress. The town museum occupies the **Arhondíko Tossítsas** (tours: Mon–Wed & Fri–Sun 8.30am–1pm & 4–6pm; 300dr), a mansion restored to the full glory of its eighteenth-century past, with panelled rooms, rugs and a fine collection of crafts and costumes. The affiliated *Ídhrima Tositsa* down by the square also serves as a handicrafts centre, stocking what must be the most finely woven cloth, rugs and blankets in Greece – in a different class to the goods in the village shops.

Métsovo has quite a range of **accommodation**, and outside of the ski season or July 26, you should find little problem in getting a room. The cheapest are at the excellent *Acropolis*, Triados 22 (☎0656/41 672; ③), at the top end of town, to the right of the road down from the Kalambáka-Ioánnina road. For **eating**, try *O Kostas*, under the **post office**, or the *Platanakia*, just off the main square.

Ioánnina and around

Coming from Métsovo, you approach **IOÁNNINA** through more spectacular folds of the Píndhos Mountains, emerging high above the great lake of Pamvótis. The town, once the capital of Ali Pasha, stands upon its southern edge, a rocky promontory jutting out into the water, its fortifications punctuated by towers and minarets as if to declare its history. From this base Ali, "the Lion of Ioannina", carved from the Turks a kingdom encompassing much of western Greece, an act of rebellion that portended wider defiance in the Greeks' own War of Independence.

Disappointingly, most of the city is modern and undistinguished – a testimony not so much to Ali, who burnt much of it to the ground when under siege in 1820, as to the developers of the 1950s. However, the fortifications of his citadel, the **Froúrio**, survive more or less intact, and this is an obvious point to stroll towards. Once within, signs direct you to the **Byzantine Museum** (8.30am–3pm; closed Mon; 500dr; student discounts) inside the Its Kale citadel and dedicated to the Turkish influence on the area, and the **Municipal Museum** (Mon–Fri 8am–3pm, Sat & Sun 9am–3pm; 500dr; student discounts), a splendidly ramshackle collection of costumes and jewellery housed in the well-preserved Mosque of Aslan Pasha. East of here sprawls the **inner citadel**. Used for some years by the Greek military, most of its buildings have been adapted or restored past recognition.

Apart from the Froúrio, the most enjoyable quarter is the old **bazaar** area, outside the citadel's gate. This has a cluster of Turkish-era buildings, as well as a scattering of copper- and silversmiths, once a mainstay of the town's economy. The heart of town lies just south of the bazaar, grouped about the central platías of Pírrou, Akaohimias and Dhimokratías. Just off the last, beside a small park and the town's modern cathedral, is the **Archeological Museum** (Tues–Fri 8.30am–3/6pm, Sat & Sun 8.30am–3pm; 500dr; students 300dr), a must if you are planning a visit to Dodona. Displayed here, along with some exceptional bronze seals, is a fascinating collection of lead tablets inscribed with questions to the Dodona oracle.

The island of **Nissí**, on the polluted Lake Pamvótis, is connected by motor-launches every thirty minutes from the quay northwest of the Froúrio. Its village, founded in the sixteenth century by refugees from the Máni, is flanked by a beautiful group of five monasteries, providing the perfect focus for an afternoon's visit. The **Monastery of Pantelímonos**, just to the east of the village, is where Ali Pasha was assassinated in January 1822, his hiding place having been revealed to the Turks, who had finally lost patience with the wayward ruler. Stay on through the evening and you can eat at one of a string of restaurants on the waterfront, watching a superb sunset over the reed-beds.

Practicalities

If you arrive early enough in the day, it is worth heading straight out to Nissí, where the popular *Pension Della* (☎0651/84 494; ③) and adjacent *Pension Varvara* (☎0651/81 596; ③) offer the most attractive and the best-value **accommodation**. In the town, the most savoury budget lodging is in the area between the bazaar and the central plazas; best to start hunting at *Metropole*, Kristálli 2 (☎0651/26 207; ②) or *Tourist* nearby at the citadel, Kolétti 18 (☎0651/26 443; ③). The attractive *Limnopoula* campsite is 2km out of town on the road to Pérama. For **meals**, the three island tavernas are obvious choices. Back in town, more standard fare can be found in the bazaar near the Froúrio – try the *Pantheon*, or the excellent grill *Mandio*, immediately opposite the citadel gate. The main **bus station** is at Zozimádhou 4, serving most points north and west. A smaller terminal at Vizaníou 28 connects Árta, Préveza, Dodona and villages south and east. It is advisable to buy tickets the day before travelling, especially at weekends.

Dodona

At wildly mountainous **DODONA**, 22km southwest of Ioánnina, lie the ruins of the Oracle of Zeus, dominated by a vast theatre which was meticulously restored at the end of the last century. This is the oldest oracle in Greece: worship of Zeus and of the sacred oak tree of Dodona seems to have begun around 1900 BC. Entering the **ancient site** (daily 8am–5pm; 500dr; student discounts) you are immediately confronted by the massive western wall of the **Theatre**. Able to seat 17,000, it is one of the largest on the Greek mainland, built during the time of Pyrrhus (297–272 BC); later the Romans made adaptations necessary for their blood sports, building a protective wall over the lower seating and also a drainage channel. Nowadays in summer, plays are sporadically but atmospherically performed – ask at the ticket office for the current programme. At the top of the auditorium, a grand entrance gate leads into the

Acropolis, an overgrown and largely unexcavated area. Beside the theatre are the foundations of a **Bouleuterion** (council house), beyond which lie the complex ruins of the **Sanctuary of Zeus**, site of the ancient oracle. Worship centred upon Sacred Oak, within which the god was thought to dwell, and which was hacked down by Christian reformists. Remains of an early Christian **Basilica**, constructed over a Sanctuary of Herakles, are prominent nearby.

Transport to Dodona is sparse, with only two buses a day from Ioánnina, but hitching back should be feasible in summer, and a return trip by taxi from Ioánnina with an hour at the site is affordable in a group. Should you want to stay the night, there are some lovely spots to camp, a friendly if basic **taverna** in the neighbouring village, and a tiny, badly run C-class **pension** at the site, the *Xenia Andromachi* (☎0651/91 196; ③; closed Dec–Mar).

Zagóri and the Víkos Gorge

Few parts of Greece are more surprising or more beguiling than **Zagóri**, the wild, infertile region to the north of Ioánnina. This is the last place one would expect to find some of the most imposing architecture in Greece, yet the Zagorohória, as the 46 villages of Zagóri are called, are full of grand stone mansions, enclosed by semi-fortified walls and with deep-eaved porches opening onto immaculately cobbled streets.

In the northwest corner of the region, the awesome trench of the **Víkos Gorge** – its walls nearly 1000 metres high in places – cuts through the limestone tablelands of Mount Gamíla, separating the villages of western and central Zagóri. A hike through or around Víkos is the highlight of any visit to the area, the usual starting point being the handsome village of **MONODHÉNDRI**, perched right on the rim of the gorge near its south end. There is a twice-daily bus connection with Ioánnina (except Sat & Sun), as well as a pension and various rooms to let. If these are full, there's further choice at Vítsa, fifteen minutes' walk away.

Much the clearest **path into the gorge** starts beside the church; the route is fairly straightforward, and takes under five hours to reach the point where the gorge begins to open out. From here the best option is to follow the marked overland path to **MEGÁLO PÁPINGO**, two hours further on. A hillside of fifty or so houses along a tributary of the Voïdhomátis river, it has an inn with a café/grill (☎0653/41 138; ③) and a smaller inn offering comfortable but fairly pricey rooms with no singles (☎0653/41 081; ③). Around half the size of its neighbour, **MIKRÓ PÁPINGO** also has a few **inns** and **tavernas**, including the *O Dhias* (☎0653/41 257; ③), which provides both beds and meals. Returning to Ioánnina, there are buses four days a week from both the Pápingo villages. If there's no convenient connection, the best course is to walk to the village of Káto Klidhoniá, where there are regular buses along the Kónitsa–Ioánnina highway; the walk takes around two and a half hours.

Igoumenítsa and Párga

IGOUMENÍTSA is Greece's third passenger port after Pireás and Pátra, with almost hourly ferries to Corfu, several daily to Italy, and more sporadic connections to the Ionian islands of Páxi, Kefalloniá and Itháki. Levelled during the last war and rebuilt in a sprawling, functional style, it's a place most travellers aim to pass through, but since the majority of ferries leave early in the morning, an overnight stay is often necessary. Shop around carefully for **ferry tickets**, as prices vary greatly for similar services. Unlike sailings from Pátra, ferries from Igoumenítsa are not allowed to sell tickets with a stopover on Corfu. You can, however, take the regular Corfu ferry over and then pick up most routes from there – a more appealing option.

If you do **stay** the night, budget hotels are plentiful if uninspiring – most are to be found either along, or just back from, the waterside. The two cheapest are generally the *Egnatia*, at Eleftherias 1 (☎0665/23 648; ②), and *Stavrodhromi*, Souliou 14 (☎0665/22 343; ②). The beach villages of Kalámi and Platariá, respectively 10km and 12km south, both have **campsites** and **tavernas**.

The best **beaches** close to Igoumenítsa are at **PÁRGA** (4 buses daily), a small resort with a crescent of tiered houses below a Norman-Venetian castle. Párga's beaches line three consecutive bays, split by the headland of the fortress hill. **Váltos** and **Lihnós** beaches both have **campsites**. **Rooms** are plentiful if pricey: someone will probably approach you at the bus station or ferry quay. If you want to stay in a traditional building, try the *Vassilas House* or *Petros House* pensions, both in the market area – but hotels are generally reserved en masse in season. For **food**, the *Restaurant Panorama* up by the castle gate is okay, and not nearly as expensive as its location would suggest.

Thessaloníki

Second city of Greece and administrative centre for the north, **THESSALONÍKI** has a very different feel from Athens: more modern, cosmopolitan and for the most part wealthier. This "modern" quality is due largely to a disastrous fire, which in 1917 levelled most of the labyrinth of Turkish lanes; the city was rebuilt eight years later on a grid plan with long central avenues running parallel to the sea.

During the Byzantine era, **Salonica**, as it was then known, was the second city after Constantinople, remaining so until its sacking by Saracens in 904. It was restored to the empire in 1246, reaching a cultural "Golden Age" until Turkish conquest and occupation in 1430. Until just a few decades ago the city's population was as mixed as any in the Balkans. Besides the Turks, who had been in occupation for close on five centuries, there were Slavs, Albanians and the largest European **Jewish** community of the period – 100,000 at its peak. Numbers remained at around 70,000 up until World War II when all but a fraction were deported to the concentration camps, in the worst atrocity committed in the Balkans. You can get glimpses of "Old Salonica" in the walled **Kástra** quarter of the city, on the hillside beyond the modern grid of streets. For most visitors, however, it is Thessaloníki's excellent archeological museum that stands out, along with the unique array of churches dating from Roman times to the fifteenth century.

Arrival and accommodation

The **train station** on the west side of town is a short walk from the central grid of streets and the waterfront. If you're coming into Thessaloníki by bus you'll arrive at one of the KTEL terminals nearby (buses to Kavála leave from Langada 61; to Pella from Anagenisseos; and to Lárissa from Enotikon). Or, from the **airport**, 16km out, there's the #78 bus which runs every thirty minutes.

Outside of the fair-and-festival season (Sept–Nov), inexpensive **hotels** are reasonably easy to find – if not, as a rule, very attractive. The main concentration of D- and E-class places, along with a scattering of more upmarket hotels and the occasional bordello, are found along the busy Egnatía avenue. Congenial ones include the *Atlantis* at no. 14 (☎031/540 131; ③), the *Alexandria* at no. 18 (☎031/536 185; ③), and the *Acropol*, Tantalidou 4 on the corner of Egnatía (☎031/536 170; ②). If you're staying for more than a night or two, it is worth finding a more pleasant downtown location, such as *Bristol*, Ilía Oplopiou 2 (☎031/530 351; ③). Nearby are the *Pella* at Ionos Dragoumi 65 (☎031/524 221; ④) and the *Luxembourgo* at Komnínon 6 (☎031/278 449; ③).

The HI **youth hostel** at Svólou 44 (☎031/225 946; ②; March–Nov) is noisy, ill-equipped and seems to be run for minimum inconvenience to the wardens. The closest **campsites** are at the uninspiring beaches of Peréa and Ayía Triádha, 28km distant; take bus #72 from Platía Dhikastiríon or, in summer, a boat from the White Tower.

The City

The obvious place to begin a wander is the **White Tower** (Mon 12.30–7pm, Tues–Fri 8am–7pm, Sat & Sun 8.30am–3pm; 800dr; student discounts), a corner of the city defences; it now looks a little stagey, isolated on the seafront, but is a graceful symbol nonetheless, and you can climb to the top for the view. The tower is a couple of minutes' walk from the **Archeological Museum** (summer Mon noon–7pm, Tues–Sun 8am–7pm; winter Mon

10.30am–5pm, Tues–Sun 8am–2.30pm; 1500dr; student discounts), containing almost all of the finds from the tombs of Philip II of Macedon and others at the ancient Macedonian capital of Aegae (modern Veryína). They include startling amounts of gold – masks, crowns, wreaths, pins and figurines – all of extraordinary craftsmanship. Thessaloníki's other main museum, the **Folklore Museum** (due to reopen in 2000 after lengthy restoration; check with GNTO first), is a fifteen-minute walk east at Vassilísis Ólgas 68 (#5 bus). It is the best museum of its kind in Greece, with well-written commentaries accompanying displays on housing, costumes, day-to-day work and crafts. There is a sharp, highly un-folkloric emphasis on context: on the role of women in the community, the clash between tradition and progress, and the cycle of agricultural and religious festivals.

The closest of the city's major churches to the White Tower is **Ayía Sofía**, built early in the eighth century on the model of its illustrious namesake in Istanbul. Its dome, ten metres in diameter, bears a splendid mosaic of *The Ascension*, currently being restored. A short distance to the northwest, the eleventh-century **Panayía Halkéon** is a classic example of the Greek cross-in-square form, but far more beautiful is the church of **Dhódheka Apóstoli** at the western end of Ayíou Dhimitríou, built three centuries later; its five domes rise in perfect symmetry above walls of fine brickwork, though its interior no longer does it justice.

Northeast of Ayía Sofía, the church of **Áyios Yióryios**, popularly known as the **Rotunda**, is the oldest and strangest of the churches. It was designed, but never used, as a Roman imperial mausoleum and converted to Christian use in the fourth century. Later it became one of the city's major mosques; the minaret remains. Sadly, the church's interior has been closed since the 1978 earthquake.

Rising in the centre of Ayíou Dhimitríou is the largest church in Greece, **Áyios Dhimítrios** (daily 8am–10pm). Founded in the fifth century, it's dedicated to the city's patron saint and stands on the site of his martyrdom. The church interior was badly damaged by fire in 1917, and, in 1948, careful restoration work was undertaken, conforming to the original five-aisled basilica design. The few small mosaics that survived the fire now make an easy focal point amid the white plaster. The best are grouped to the side of the iconostasis and date back to the church's second building in the late seventh century; they include the celebrated *Saint Dimitrios with the Church's Founders* and a contrastingly humane scene of the saint with two young children. The **crypt** (Mon 12.30–7pm, Tues–Sat 8am–8pm, Sun 10.30am–8pm; free) contains the *martyrion* of the saint, and was probably adapted from the original Roman baths where he was imprisoned.

Finally, tucked into the heart of the old Turkish quarter, there's the fourteenth-century **Áyios Nikólaos Orfanós** (Tues–Sun 8.45am–3pm), preserving its original frescoes. Five minutes' walk northwest, **Óssios Davíd** (daily 8am–noon & 5–7pm) is a tiny late fifth-century church overzealously converted by the Turks. However, it has arguably the finest mosaic in the city, depicting a clean-shaven Christ appearing in a vision to the prophets Ezekiel and Habakkuk.

Eating, drinking and nightlife

Recently there's been an explosion of interesting places to **eat** and **drink** in Thessaloníki, few of them as obvious as the fast-food outlets dominating the city centre. Most central are *Pazar Hamami*, Komninón 15A, a converted Turkish bath with tables on the pavement, which serves excellent fish, and *Tsarouhas*, Olímbou 78, a famous outlet for local speciality *patsas* (tripe and trotter soup). Up in the medieval Eptapirgíou quarter, try *Kastroperpatimata*, Steryíolu Polidhórou 15, for Cypriot-style dishes, or two grills at Graviás 2, inside the eastern gate, for carnivorous fare. For excellent fish dishes, try one of the tavernas east at Aretsou. Finally, for a gourmet splurge, *Ta Pringiponissia*, in the eastern part of town at Krítis 60, fits the bill with Turkish-style *mezédhes*. **Bars** and **clubs** tend to be concentrated in the narrow streets behind the quayside boulevard Níkis; good examples are *Zythos*, Katoúni 5, *Corner*, Agias Sofias 6, and *Stala*, Nikis 3. There are many cafés up by the castle that keep going until late into the night. The city's main music venue is the multidisciplinary complex *Milos*, out in an old warehouse at Andreou Yioryíou 56 (☎031/525 968 for what's on); there are several tavernas, cafés and bars here as well.

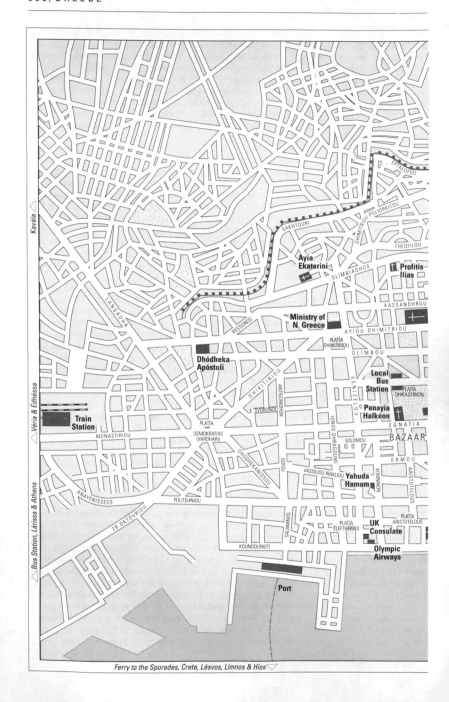

Kavála ◁

◁ Véria & Édhessa

◁ Bus Station, Lárissa & Athens

EPTALOFOU

SAKHTOURI

DHIMITRIOU POLIORKITOU

THEOFILOU

Ayia Ekaterini

Profitis Ilias

OLIMBIADHOS

KASSANDHROU

Ministry of N. Greece

AYIOU DHIMITRIOU

PLATÍA DHIKITIRIOU

OLIMBOU

LANGADHA

Dhódheka Apóstoli

DHIKITIRIOU

ANTIGONIDHON

VENIZELOU

Local Bus Station

PLATÍA DHIKASTIRION

Panayía Halkéon

RESTNONOS

E. SVORONOU

IONOS DHRAGOUMI

EGNATIA

BAZAAR

Train Station

MONASTIRIOU

PLATÍA DEMOKRATIAS (VARDHARI)

DHODHEKANISSOU

SOFOU

SOLOMOU

ERMOU

ARISTOTELOUS

ANAYENISSEOS

POLITEHNIOU

VASSILIOU IRAKLIOU

Yahuda Hamam

KOMNINON

28 OKTOVRIOU

SALAMINOS

PLATÍA ELEFTHERIAS

PLATÍA ARISTOTELOUS

UK Consulate

KOUNDOURIOTI

Olympic Airways

Port

Ferry to the Sporades, Crete, Lésvos, Límnos & Híos ▽

Folklore Museum, Airport & Halkidhikí ▽

Listings

Bookshops Molho, Tsimíski 10; Promitheus, Ermoú 75.

Car rental Ansa, Laskárata 19; Budget, Angeláki 15; Europcar/InterRent, G. Papandhréau 5.

Consulates Britain and all Commonwealth citizens are represented by the Honorary Consul at Venizélou 8 (open to public Mon–Fri 8am–1pm; meeting by appointment only, call ☎031/278 006); Netherlands, Komnínon 26; USA, Níkis 59.

Exchange The National Bank of Greece, Tsimíski 11 (Mon–Thurs 8am–2pm & 6–8pm, Fri 8am–1.30pm & 6–8pm, Sat 8.30am–2pm, Sun 9.30am–noon); American Express, Tsimíski 19; also at the post office.

Ferries In high season there are "Flying Dolphin" hydrofoils to Skíathos, Skópelos and Alónissos; details and tickets from Egnatía Tours, Kamboínion 9 (☎031/223 811). For the three or four ferries a week to the north Aegean islands, Sporades, Cyclades and Crete, buy tickets at Nomikos, Koundourióti 8, corner Vótsi, by the harbour gate.

Laundry Bianca, Antoniádhou 3; Zerowatt, Episkópou 2; Canadian, Platía Navarínou.

Post office Main office at Aristotelous 26 (Mon–Fri 7.30am–8pm).

Telephones 24hr OTE office on Ermoú, corner Karólou Díehl.

Tourist office Main EOT office at Platía Aristotélous 8 (Mon–Fri 8am–8pm, Sat 8am–1.30pm; ☎031/271 888).

Train tickets For tickets and reservations, the OSE office at Aristotélous 18 is more central and more helpful than the main terminal.

Travel agents Most travel agents are on Nikis. Flights out of Thessaloníki are not cheap, but such bucket shops as exist cluster in the side streets around Platía Eleftherías.

Pella

PELLA was the capital of Macedonia throughout its greatest period, and the first real capital of Greece after Philip II forcibly unified the country around 338 BC. It was founded some sixty years earlier by King Archelaus, and from its beginnings was a major centre of culture. The royal palace was said to be the greatest artistic showplace since Classical Athens: Euripides wrote and produced his last plays at the court, and Aristotle was tutor to the young Alexander the Great – born, like his father Philip II, in this city. The site, less than 50km away, is an easy day-trip from Thessaloníki: take the Édhessa-bound **bus** – they run more or less every thirty minutes.

The **ruins** (8am–2.30pm; closed Mon; 500dr; student discounts) cover around four square kilometres and as yet only a few blocks of the city have been fully excavated. To the right of the road is a grand official building, probably a government office. The three main rooms of the first court have patterned geometric floors, in the centre of which were found superb, intricate pebble-mosaics depicting scenes of a lion hunt, a griffin attacking a deer, and Dionysus riding a panther. These are now in the **museum** (8am–2.30pm; closed Mon; 500dr; student discounts), but in the third court three mosaics have been left in situ; one of these, a stag hunt, is complete, and it is astounding in its dynamism and use of perspective.

Mount Olympus

Highest, most magical and most dramatic of all Greek mountains, **Mount Olympus** – the mythical seat of the gods – rears high on 3000 metres straight from the shores of the Thermaíkos gulf, south of Thessaloníki. Dense forests cover its slopes and its wild flowers are without parallel even by Greek standards. If you are equipped with decent boots and warm clothing, no special expertise is necessary to get to the top in summer, though it's a long hard pull, and at any time of year Olympus must be treated with respect: its weather is notoriously fickle and it does claim lives.

The best base for a walk up the mountain is the village of **LITÓHORO** on the eastern side. The station for trains from Thessaloníki is 9km from the village, with rare connecting buses; or you can get a bus direct from Thessaloníki. Cheapest lodgings are at the **youth hostel** (☎0352/22 580; ①) or D-class *Hotel Enipeas* near the National Bank and above the post office (☎0352/84 328; ②), respectively above and below the square. For a more comfortable **hotel**, well heated in winter and only marginally more expensive, try the *Myrto* (☎0352/81 398; ③) near the main square. Best **eats** are at *Dhamaskinia*, uphill on Vassiléos Konstandínou.

Buy a proper map of the range at the youth hostel, which is also the start of the well-marked scenic E4 path up the Mavrólongos canyon. Four to five hours' walk brings you to Priónia, the end of the road and last reliable water source; from here begins the sharper three-hour climb along a track to the *Spílios Agapitós* refuge (☎0352/81 800; ①; mid–May to Oct), which perches on the edge of an abrupt spur, surrounded by huge storm-beaten trees. It's best to stay overnight here, as you need to make an early start for the three-hour ascent to **Mítikas**, the highest peak at 2917m – the summit frequently clouds up towards midday, to say nothing of the danger of catching one of Zeus' thunderbolts. The path continues behind the refuge, reaching a signposted fork above the tree line in about an hour. Straight on takes you to Mítikas via the ridge known as Kakí Skála, while the right goes via the *Yiósos Apostolídhis* hut in one hour (☎0352/82 300; ②; July to mid-Sept). From the latter you can enjoyably loop down in another day's walk to the Gortsia trail head and from there back down into the Mavrólongos canyon.

Halkidhikí

The squid-shaped peninsula of Halkidhikí begins at a perforated edge of lakes east of Thessaloníki and extends into three prongs of land – Kassándhra, Sithonía and Áthos – trailing like tentacles into the Aegean Sea. **Kassándhra** and **Sithonía** are Thessaloníki's beach-playground, hosting some of the fastest-growing holiday resorts in Greece. Both are connected to Thessaloníki by buses, but neither peninsula is that easy to travel around if you are dependent on public **transport**. You really have to pick a place and stay there, perhaps hiring a moped for local excursions. Sithonía is marginally less packaged, with low-key resorts at **Pórto Kouféa** and **Toróni**.

Mount Áthos, the easternmost peninsula, is in all ways separate: a "Holy Mountain" whose monastic population, semi-autonomous from the Greek state, excludes all women – even as visitors. For men who wish to experience Athonite life, a visit involves suitably Byzantine procedures – your consulate in Athens or Thessaloníki will explain the full rigmarole.

However, **boat tours** leave **IERISSÓS** daily in summer on a loop around the Holy Mountain – both Ierissós and Ouranópoli (see below) are served by several daily buses from Thessaloníki. Unless they are all-male parties (in which case they're allowed to dock at the monastery of Ivíron) they have to stay 500m from the coast, but the views of the monasteries are impressive anyway. Ierissós has many rooms to let and two **hotels** – the basic *Akanthos* (☎0377/22 359; ②) and *Marcos* (☎0377/22 518; ②).

The last settlement before you reach the monastic domains is the package resort of **OURANÓPOLI**, overrun by both Germans and Greeks in summer. **Accommodation** is plentiful, with numerous rooms and two budget hotels – the *Galini* (☎0377/71 217; ②) and *Akrogiali* (☎0377/71 201; ②). It's from here that the most reliable ferries depart for monastic Áthos, usually by 10am. You'll need the earliest bus of the day out of Thessaloníki to coincide.

Mount Áthos

Equipped with the suitable paperwork proving religious or scholarly intent, foreign, non-Orthodox men over the age of eighteen may stay for up to four days on the Holy Mountain, moving to a different monastery or monastic dependency each night. There are some possibilities of **moving about** by boat or bus, but walking between the communities is an integral part of the Athonite experience, so you should be reasonably fit and self-sufficient in trail **food**, as the two meals offered each day tend to be spartan. Most monks pay scant attention to foreigners, so you get more of an idea of the magnificent scenery and engaging architecture than of the religious life, though it's hard to avoid tangling with the disorientating daily schedule, dictated by the hours of sun and darkness.

That said, a visit is highly recommended, though you can't hope to see more than a fraction of the twenty fully fledged monasteries or their satellites in the time allotted. Choose between the "museum monasteries" of **Meyístis Lávras**, **Vatopedhíou**, **Ivíron** or **Dhioníssiou** with their wealth of treasures and art, and the more modestly endowed cloisters where the brothers will make more time for you, such as **Osíou Grigíou**, **Pandokratoros** and **Ayíou Pávlou**.

Kavála

KAVÁLA, backing on to the lower slopes of Mount Simbólon, is the second largest city of Macedonia and a principal port for northern Greece. Coming in through the suburbs there seems little to commend a stay, but the **Panayía** quarter above the port preserves a scattering of eighteenth- and nineteenth-century buildings, and considerable atmosphere. It is by far the most attractive part of town to explore, wandering amid the twisting wedge of lanes and up towards the citadel.

Mehmet Ali, the Pasha of Egypt and founder of the dynasty which ended with King Farouk, was born in Kavála in 1769 and his birthplace, at the corner of Pavlídhou and Méhmet Alí, is maintained as a monument. To visit its wood-panelled reception rooms, ground-floor stables and first-floor harem, ring for the caretaker. Another caretaker may escort you through the **Citadel** (daily summer 10am–7pm) so you can explore the Byzantine ramparts and dungeon; in season it hosts a few festival performances, mainly dance, in its main court.

The **Archeological Museum** (Tues–Sun 9am–3pm; 800dr; student discounts) at the west end of the waterfront, just off Erithroú Stavroú, contains a fine dolphin mosaic, a reconstructed Macedonian funeral chamber and many terracotta figurines decorated in their original paint. Close by, on Odhós Filíppou, is the **Folk Art Museum** (daily 9–11am & 6–9pm; free), which, as well as traditional costumes and household utensils, has some interesting rooms devoted to the locally born sculptor Polignotos Vigis.

In the main square, Platía Eleftherías, is an **EOT** office (☎051/222 425), which can provide schedules for daily **ferries** from Kavála to Thássos and other east Aegean islands (the latter usually Wed & Sat); tickets are sold at Nikos Miliadhes, Platía Karaóli Dhimitríou 36 (☎051/226 147).

Hotels are in short supply and in season it's wise to phone ahead and book. The cheapest places are in the grid of streets around Eleftherías: *Attikon*, Megaloú Alexándhrou 8 (☎051/222 257; ②), *Parthenon*, Spetsón 14 (☎051/223 205; ②), and *Acropolis*, El. Venizelou 29 (☎051/223 543; ②), with private rooms in the centre of town. The nearest **campsite** is *Camping Irini*, 2km east and reached by city bus #2. When **eating out**, it's wisest to ignore waterfront tourist traps in favour of a row of locally favoured tavernas on Theodhórou Poulídhou, up in the Panayía district.

Crossing the border

The border town and military garrison of **ALEXANDHROÚPOLI** has little to recommend it, but it can get very crowded in season, with overland travellers and Greek holidaymakers competing for space in the few hotels and gritty beach campsites. The best places to stay are the fairly inexpensive **hotels** around the train station: the D-class *Majestic*, Platía Troúman 7 (☎0551/26 444; ②), and the D-class *Metropolis*, Ath. Diakou 11 (☎0551/26 443; ②). The municipal *Camping Alexandhroupoli* is a thirty-minute walk from the train station, or take the #5 bus. Excellent **meals** are to be had at *I Neraidha*, a couple of blocks from the train station and across from the town hall. Tickets for daily **ferries** to Samothráki are sold at a cluster of waterfront agencies opposite the dock, within sight of the train station.

There are several **buses** from here **to Istanbul**, but most start in Thessaloníki and by this stage are full. An alternative is to take a local bus to the border at **KÍPI** (6 daily). You are not allowed to cross the frontier here on foot, but it is generally no problem to get a driver to shuttle you the 500m across to the Turkish post – and possibly to give you a lift beyond. The nearest town is Ipsala (5km), but if possible get as far as Kesan (30km), from where buses to Istanbul are much more frequent. There's only one **train to Istanbul** per day from Alexandhroúpoli; services are more frequent to Kastaniés, but get an early one to ensure arrival at the frontier before it shuts at 1pm. Once over – again, no walking – there's a bus service the remaining 7km to Edirne.

There is one early-morning train daily into **Bulgaria**, reaching Svilengrad in five hours. From Svilengrad, it is best to move on immediately towards Plovdiv.

THE SOUTHERN AEGEAN ISLANDS

The rocky, volcanic chain of **Argo-Saronic** islands is the nearest group to Athens and among the busiest. **Éyina** is most frenetic, but **Ídhra** and **Spétses** aren't far behind in summer: more than any other group, these islands are at their best out of season. To the east, the **Cyclades** is the most satisfying Greek archipelago for island-hopping. The majority of the islands are arid and rocky, with brilliant-white, cubist architecture. The impact of tourism is haphazard, and though some English is spoken on most islands, a slight detour could have you groping for your Greek phrasebook. **Íos**, the original hippie island, is still a backpackers' paradise, while **Míkonos** – with its teeming old town, nude beaches and highly sophisticated clubs and bars – is by far the most visited of the group. After these, **Páros**, **Sífnos**, **Náxos** and **Thíra** are currently most popular, their beaches and main towns drastically overcrowded in July and August. The one major ancient site worth making time for is **Delos**: the commercial and religious centre of the Classical Greek world. Almost all of the Cyclades are served by boats from Pireás, but there are also ferries from Rafína for Síros, Míkonos, Páros and Náxos, among others.

Further east still, the **Dodecanese** lie so close to the Turkish coast that some are almost within hailing distance of the shore. The islands were only included in the modern Greek state in 1948 after centuries of occupation by Crusaders, Turks and Italians. Medieval **Rhódos** is the most famous, but almost every island has its Classical remains, its Crusaders' castle, its traditional villages and grandiose public buildings. The dry limestone outcrop of **Sími** has always been forced to rely on the sea for its livelihood, while the sprawling, relatively fertile giants, Rhódos and Kós, have recently seen their traditional agricultural economies almost totally displaced by tourism. **Kárpathos** lies somewhere in between, with a once-forested north grafted onto a rocky limestone south. **Pátmos**, at the fringes of the archipelago, boasts architecture and landscapes more appropriate to the Cyclades. The main islands are connected almost daily with each other, and none is hard to reach. Rhódos is another transport hub, with services to Turkey, Israel, Egypt and Cyprus, as well as connections with Crete, the northeastern Aegean islands, the Cyclades and the mainland (both Rafína and Pireás).

Éyina (Aegina)

It seems incredible today, but ancient **Éyina** was a major power in Classical times, with trade carried on to the limits of the known world. Today the island is essentially regarded as a beach annexe of Athens, and a solitary column of a Temple of Apollo beckons as your ferry steams around the point into the harbour at **ÉYINA TOWN**. The bus stop is at Platía Ethneyersías, while moped rental is also handy for a day-trip exploration of the island. There are a few moderately priced **hotels** scattered throughout town, particularly in the streets behind Ethneyersías – try the *Toghia Hotel* (③), visible from the jetty. The helpful Aegina Tourist Board (☎0297/22334) opposite the boat jetty will book hotels and private rooms.

The **Temple of Aphaia** (Mon–Fri 8am–3/5pm, Sat & Sun 8.30am–3pm; 800dr; student discounts), dating from the sixth century BC, stands 17km east of town among pines tapped to make the excellent local retsina. To get to the temple from Éyina town you can go by bus, though the best approach is by hired bicycle; if under your own power, take the inland road which passes deserted **Paleohóra**, the island's old capital.

The only really sandy beach is at the overblown resort of **AYÍA MARÍNA**, close to the temple and mobbed due to its role as a stopoff for ferries; otherwise the best bet is in the vicinity of **PÉRDHIKA**, a fishing village twenty minutes by bus from Éyina town, with a small beach. It is certainly the best place to stay on the island besides the main town, with a pension and a few rooms to rent. Alternatively, there are *kaíkia* from here across to **Moní Islet**, where there's an official campsite and a seasonal taverna.

Ídhra (Hydra)

The port and town of **ÍDHRA**, with its tiers of stone mansions and white, tiled houses climbing up from a perfect horseshoe harbour, is a very beautiful spectacle. Unfortunately, thousands of others think so too; from Easter to September it's packed to the gills, and the front becomes one uninterrupted outdoor café. The town's dozens of mansions were built mostly during the eighteenth century, on the accumulated wealth of a merchant fleet which traded as far afield as America. By the 1820s the town's population stood at nearly 20,000, seven times what it is today. Ídhra is reputedly hallowed by no fewer than 365 churches; the most important is the cathedral of **Panayía Mitropóleos**, with its distinctive clock tower, down by the port.

There is no shortage of inexpensive **restaurants** on the waterfront – try *Art Café* or the *Isalos* – along with a number of **pensions**, most charging thirty percent or so above usual island rates, with single rooms rare. Reasonable-value places include *Pension Antonios* (☎0298/53 227; ③), *Theresa Pension* (☎0298/53 983; ③), *Dina* (☎0298/52 248; ③) or *Sofia* (☎0298/52 313; ②), and the pleasant, C-class *Amarillis* (☎0298/53 611; ③).

The island's only sandy beach is the private one at Mandhráki, 2km east of town. On the opposite side of the harbour a coastal path leads to a pebbly but popular stretch, just before **KAMÍNI**, where there's a good year-round taverna, *Christina*. Thirty minutes' walk beyond Kamíni (or a boat ride from the port) will bring you to **VLÍHOS**, a small hamlet with **rooms** and three tavernas. **Camping** is tolerated here (the closest to town) and the swimming is good.

Spétses (Spetsai)

Spétses is very green, very small and alarmingly popular, but it absorbs its tourists with grace. The port and town of **SPÉTSES** (or Kastélli) shares with Ídhra a history of nineteenth-century mercantile prosperity, and pebble-mosaic courtyards and streets sprawl between mansions whose architecture is quite distinct from the Peloponnesian styles across the straits. Horse-drawn cabs connect the various quarters of town, spread out along the waterfront.

Most visitors stay in Spétses town, where all kinds of **accommodation** are available. Well worth trying are the *Hotel Star* (☎0298/72 214; ④) and *Hotel Faros* (☎0298/72 613; ③). If you don't fancy pounding the streets yourself, then go to Takis' Tourist Office, 50m from the end of the jetty, and see what they can come up with. For **camping**, head out to the shade of tamarisks behind Lámpara Beach, 700m northwest of the dock. **Food and drink** can be expensive. Among cheaper places are *Rousos*, 300m south of Dápia, and *Taverna Haralambos*, on the waterfront leading to the Baltíza inlet, by the smaller harbour; the only traditional taverna is *Lazaros's*, 400m inland and uphill from Dápia.

Ayii Anaryiri, on the south side of the island, is the best, if also the most popular, beach: a beautiful, long, sheltered bay of fine sand. There's a self-service taverna on the beach, and, just behind, the moderately priced *Tassos*, Spétses' finest eating establishment. It's only about an hour's walk through the woods from the town, or accessible by *káiki* from Dápia or on the island bus.

Sífnos

Although **Sífnos** often gets crowded, its modest size means that wherever you stay, you can reach the rest of the island by the excellent bus service to all points or on foot over a network of old stone pathways. **KAMÁRES**, the port, is tucked at the base of high bare cliffs in the west. It can be expensive – the budget option is a **room** above the Katsoulakis Tourist Agency close to the quay. There are other places behind the beach, including a **campsite**, and the reasonable *Hotel Stavros* (☎0284/31 641; ②), just past the church. The best **meals** are at the quayside *Meropi*.

An excitingly steep twenty-minute bus ride takes you up to **APOLLONÍA**, a rambling collage of flagstones, belfries and flowered courtyards. The island bank, post office and Tourist Police are all here, but **rooms**, though plentiful, are even more likely to be full than at Kamáres. Outside of high season, there will be vacancies at establishments lining the road to Fáros; quieter, and pricier, digs are found along the stair-street north of the main square. The **Folk Museum** (open on request only) in the square by the bus stop is also well worth a look since Sífnos produces some of the finest pottery and fabrics in Greece. As an alternative base, with a number of rooms, you could try **KÁSTRO**, a forty-minute trail walk or regular bus ride below Apollonía on the east coast. Built on a rocky outcrop with an almost sheer drop to the sea on three sides, the ancient capital of the island retains much of its medieval character.

At the southern end of the island, around 10km from Apollonía, lies the growing beach resort of **PLATÍS YIALÓS**. It has another (poor) campsite and numerous rooms to let, as well as tavernas, of which the best are *Toh Steki* and *Bus Stop*. Far less crowded sand is to be found just to the northeast at **FÁROS**, which has regular buses from Apollonía, rooms to let and good, cheap tavernas. Perhaps the finest walk is to **VATHÍ**, around three hours from Apollonía. A fishing and pottery village on a stunning funnel-shaped bay, Vathí is the most attractive base on the island: there are **rooms** to let and summer tavernas, the best and cheapest being *Manolis*, which serves its own home-grown vegetables and home-made wine. An alternative route here is by the twice-daily boat from Kamáres.

Míkonos (Mykonos)

Míkonos has become the most popular and expensive of the Cyclades, visited by nearly a million tourists a year. But if you don't mind the crowds – or you come out of season – the prosperous capital is one of the most beautiful of all island towns. Dazzlingly white, it's the archetypal postcard image, with sugar-cube buildings stacked around a cluster of seafront fishermen's dwellings. The labyrinthine design was intended to confuse the pirates who plagued Míkonos in the eighteenth and early nineteenth centuries and it remains effective – everyone gets lost.

The **airport** is about 3km out of town, a short taxi ride away. **Ferries** and cruise ships dock at the northern jetty, where you'll be met by a horde of owners hustling hotels and **rooms**. If you balk at the prices, be warned that a private room here is likely to be cheaper than staying in a hotel on any of the nearby beaches. As for **hotels** in town, out of season you might consider *Hotel Delfines* on Mavroyéni (☎0289/22 292; ④); *Hotel Karboni* on Matoyiánni (☎0289/22 217; ④); *Hotel Apollon* on Mavroyénous (☎0289/22 223; ③); *Hotel Maria* at Kaloyéra 24 (☎0289/24 670; ④); *Hotel Marios* at Kaloyéra 5 (☎0289/22 704; ④); *Hotel Philippi* at Kaloyéra 32 (☎0289/22 294; ④); or *Hotel Karbonaki* at Panahrándou 21 (☎0289/22 461; ⑥). *Zorzis Hotel* on Kaloyéra (☎0289/22 167; ⑤) can also offer rooms in nearby apartments and pensions. Otherwise there are official **campsites** at Paradise and Paránga beaches (see overleaf), and every other bay on the island has some sort of taverna.

The harbour curves around past the dull, central Polikandhrióti beach, behind which is the **bus station** for Toúrlos, Áyios Stéfanos and Áno Méra. Continue along the seafront to the southern jetty for the **Tourist Police** and *kaíkia* to Delos. A second bus terminus, for beaches to the south of town, is right at the other end of Hóra, beyond the windmills.

Around Kaloyéra is a promising area for **food**: the *Edem Garden* is a popular gay restaurant with an adventurous menu, and *El Greco* and *The Sesame Kitchen* are two other fairly reasonable eateries. Cheaper eating can be had at *Nikos*, behind the town hall, while *Rendez-Vous* serves pizzas, and *Dynasty* is a Chinese takeaway. **Drinking** haunts are over in the Alefkándhra area in the south of the town – or "Little Venice" as it's known. Try *Kástro's* for an early-evening cocktail, moving on later to *Montparnasse*, which is fairly swanky – to the extent of boasting a visitors' book. In K. Yiorgoúli street, off Mitropóleos, the *City Bar* is the campest spot in town; close by, *Scandinavia Bar* is a cheap, jovial and nonstop party bar. The *Famous Mykonos Dance Bar* and the *Rainbow* are young, mixed and sweaty. The **nightlife** in town is every bit as good – and expensive – as it's cracked up to be. It's impossible to list every hot spot, but among the most durable are *Remezzo*, near the OTE and with sunset views, or *Pierro's*, once mecca for the island's substantial gay contingent, but now mixed.

The beaches

The closest decent **beach** is **ÁYIOS STÉFANOS** (4km north), connected by a very regular bus service. Other nearby, mainstream destinations are the resorts on the southwest peninsula, with fairly undistinguished beaches tucked into pretty bays at Áyios Yiannis and Órnos. Better to make for **PLATÍS YIALÓS**, 4km south, though you won't be alone. A **kaíki service** from Míkonos town connects almost all the beaches east of Platís Yialós: gorgeous, pale-sand **Paránga** beach, popular with campers; **Paradise Beach**, well sheltered by its headland, predominantly nudist, with another official **campsite** (April–Oct) and two tavernas; and **Super Paradise**, which has a friendly atmosphere and a couple of tavernas. Probably the best beach on Míkonos is **Elía**, the last port of call for the *kaíkia*. The longest on the island, it's a broad sandy stretch with a verdant backdrop, split in two by a rocky area. Almost exclusively nudist, it boasts an excellent restaurant, *Matheos*.

Dhílos (Delos)

The remains of ancient **Dhílos** (Tues–Sun 8am–2.30pm; 1200dr), though skeletal and swarming now with lizards and tourists, give some idea of the past grandeur of this sacred isle a few sea-miles west of Míkonos. The *kaíki* to Dhílos gives you three hours on the island – barely enough time to take in the main attractions, but it's no longer possible to stay the night.

Dhílos' ancient fame was due to the fact that Leto gave birth to the divine twins Artemis and Apollo on the island, and one of the first things you see is the **Sanctuary of Apollo**, while three Temples of Apollo stand in a row along the Sacred Way. To the east towards the museum you pass the **Sanctuary of Dionysus** with its marble phalli on tall pillars. To the north is the **Sacred Lake** where Leto gave birth: guarding it is a group of superb lean lions, masterfully executed in the seventh century BC. Set out in the other direction from the agora and you enter the residential area, known as the **Theatre Quarter**. Many of the walls and roads remain but there is none of the domestic detail that makes Pompeii, for example, so fascinating. Some colour is added by the mosaics: one in the **House of the Trident**, better ones in the **House of the Masks**, including a vigorous portrayal of Dionysus riding on a panther's back. The **Theatre** itself, though much ravaged, offers some fine views.

Páros and Andíparos

With a little of everything – old villages, monasteries, fishing harbour and a labyrinthine capital – **Páros** is a good point to begin your island wanderings, with boat connections to virtually the entire Aegean, though things are nearly as expensive and commercialized here as on Míkonos. **PARIKÍA**, the main town, sets the tone for the rest of Páros, with its ranks of white houses punctuated by the occasional Venetian-style building and church domes. All ferries dock here, and the waterfront is packed with bars, restaurants, hotels and ticket agencies.

Just outside the central clutter, the town also has one of the most interesting churches in the Aegean – the **Ekatondapiliani**, or "Church of One Hundred Gates" (daily 8am–1pm & 4–9pm). The original construction was overseen in the sixth century by Isidore of Miletus but the work was carried out by his pupil Ignatius. Behind the Ekatondapiliani, the **Archeological Museum** (Tues–Sun 8.30am–2.30pm; 500dr; student discounts; free Sun) has a fair collection of antique pieces, its prize exhibit a portion of the *Parian Chronicle*, a social and cultural history of Greece up to 264 BC, recorded on marble.

Páros is fast becoming a major hub of inter-island **ferry** services. Boats dock by the windmill, which houses a summer tourist **information centre**. The bus stop is 100m or so to the left – routes extend to Náoussa in the north, Alikí in the south, and Dhríos on the island's east coast (with another very useful service between Dhríos and Náoussa). You'll be met off the ferry by locals offering **rooms**, and it's a good idea to capitulate straight away. Most of the **hotels** tend to be reserved by tour operators, and you'll have to be quick to grab space in the remaining cheaper places, many north of the post office. Try the *Hotel Dina* near Platía Valéntza (☎0284/21 325; ③), or, as a last resort, the jail-like *Hotel Kondes* behind the windmill (☎0284/21 096; ③). For a touch of luxury, treat yourself to the friendly and comfortable *Sophia Rooms* behind Cinema Paros (☎0284/22 085; ④).

For what may easily be the best **food** you will have in Greece, try the exceptional *Trata* to the left of the cemetery of the ancient city. The *Paros Family Taverna*, opposite *Hotel Galinos Louiza*, is another reasonable choice. There's a crowded **campsite**, the *Parasporos*, at the northern end of the town beach. Parikía has a wealth of **pubs**, **bars** and low-key **discos**, not as pretentious as on Míkonos or as raucous as on Íos, but certainly everything in between. The most popular cocktail bars extend along the seafront, tucked into a series of open squares.

The second port of Páros, **NÁOUSSA** was recently an unspoilt town, but a rash of new concrete hotels has all but swamped its character. Despite the development, the town is a good place to head for as soon as you reach Páros; there are some good-to-excellent **beaches** nearby, while **rooms** are marginally cheaper than in Parikía – track them down with the help of Katerini Simitzi's **tourist office** on the main square. **Hotels** are more expensive, though haggle for reduced prices out of season at the *Madaki* (☎0284/51 475; ②) and the *Stella* (☎0284/51 317; ③). There's a **campsite**, too, out of town towards Kolimbíthres, much better than the mosquito-plagued one in Parikía, and various tavernas – all of which are pretty good, specializing in fresh fish and seafood: *Diamante* and *Limanakis* are recommended.

Andíparos

There's little to stop for south of Parikía until **POÚNDA**, 6km away, and then only to catch the ferry to **Andíparos**. In recent years this islet has become something of an open secret, and in high season can be very full. Most of the population of 500 live in the single northern village where the barge-ferry from Poúnda and *kaíkia* leave daily (every 30min 9.15am–12.15am) from Parikía dock. There are a dozen tavernas and some small hotels – the cheapest are *Korali* (☎0284/61 236; ②) and *Anargyros* (☎0284/61 204; ③) – and a very popular campsite with a nudist beach. It's the great **cave** in the south of the island that is the chief attraction for day-trippers: four buses a day run there from the port, or it's a stony ninety-minute hike.

Náxos

Náxos is the largest and most fertile of the Cyclades, and with its bushy and mountainous interior seems immediately distinct from many of its neighbours. The Venetian occupation left towers and fortified mansions scattered throughout the island, while late medieval Cretan refugees bestowed a singular character upon the eastern settlements.

A long causeway protecting the harbour connects **NÁXOS** town with the islet of Palátia, where the huge stone portal of an unfinished **Temple of Apollo** still stands. Most of the town's life goes on down by the port or in the streets just behind it; stepped lanes behind lead up past crumbling balconies and through low arches to the fortified **Kástro**, from where the Venetians ruled over the Cyclades. Other brooding relics survive in the same area: a seventeenth-century Ursuline convent, the Catholic cathedral and one of Ottoman Greece's first schools, now housing an excellent **Archeological Museum** (Tues–Sun 8am–2.30pm; 500dr; students 300dr), worth visiting just for the stunning view of Naxos from its balcony.

Tourism has now reached such a pitch that an annexe of purpose-built accommodation extends south of the town centre. **Rooms** downtown are uniformly poor standard and overpriced; **hotels** are better on the cooler north slope of the Kástro: best of these are the *Panorama* on Amfitrítis (☎0285/22 330; ③), the *Anixix* nearby (☎0285/22 112; ③) or try the *Hermes* on Papavassiliou (☎0285/22 220; ③). Along the quayside, cafés and restaurants are abundant enough, if a bit on the expensive side. The *Manolis Garden Taverna*, behind the church, near the *Anixix*, gives enormous portions, while *Popi's Grill* on the waterfront is also worth a visit.

The island's best **beaches** line the southwest coast a few kilometres from town, and are regularly served by buses. ÁYIOS YIÓRYIOS, a lengthy sandy bay on the south of the hotel "ghetto", is within walking distance. There are several tavernas here and you can **camp** officially just off the beach in the first of three organized sites on this coast, although the second site, the *Appollo*, has the best facilities, including a swimming pool, and offers free daily kung-fu classes. A pleasant hour's walk south through the salt marshes brings you to PROKÓPIOS beach (cheapish hotels and basic tavernas), or follow the tracks a little further to AYÍA ÁNNA, a small port where there are plenty of **rooms** to let and a few modest tavernas (plus summer *kaíkia* to Píso Livádhi on Páros). Beyond the headland stretch the five barely developed kilometres of PLÁKA beach, a vegetation-fringed expanse of white sand which comfortably holds the summer crowds of nudists and campers.

Íos

No other island attracts the same vast crowds of young people as ÍOS, yet the island hasn't been commercialized in quite the same way as, say, Míkonos – mainly because few of the visitors have much money. You might be tempted to grab a **room** in YIALÓS as you arrive, though it's the most expensive place on the island to stay. The newly refurbished official campsite is to the right of the harbour, although there are also two other decent sites further off. Yialós **beach**, five minutes' walk from the harbour, is backed by hotels and lodgings, but loud music seems to be accepted on the beach and obligatory in the tavernas.

Most of the cheaper **rooms** are in HÓRA, a twenty-minute walk up the mountain behind the port. There's dormitory space as well as the usual rooms and hotels – though for the latter two options you've a better chance of getting a good deal if you're staying for several days. Every evening the streets throb to music from competing clubs – mostly free or with a nominal cover charge. Drinks tend to be expensive, although haggling can be rewarding, especially out of season. There are plenty of places **to eat** too: the restaurant most popular with Greeks and non-Greeks in the know is the *Fiesta*, on the second bend of the road up from the harbour. The *Far Out Café*, in the *Far Out* camping site – so named for the standard reaction to the view on the ride in – is a good self-service café. Also try *Ikoyeniaki Taverna Stani*, at the heart of town.

The most popular stop on the island's bus routes is MILOPÓTAMOS, site of a magnificent beach and a mini-resort. By day, bodies cover every inch of the bus-stop end of the sand – for a bit more space head the other way, where there are dunes behind the beach. There are two decently equipped **campsites**, *Camping Stars* and *Far Out Camping*; for **rooms**, try *Draco Pension* to the right of the bus stop.

From Yialós, daily boats depart at around 10am (returning in the late afternoon) to MAN-GANÁRI on the south coast, the beach to go to for serious tans. There's a better atmosphere, though, at ÁYIOS THEODHÓTIS, up on the northeast coast; a daily **bus** service runs from Yialós.

Santoríni

As the ferryboat manoeuvres into **Santoríni**, gaunt, sheer cliffs loom hundreds of feet above. Nothing grows to soften the view, and the only colours are the reddish-brown, black and grey pumice striations of the cliff face. As early as 3000 BC Santoríni developed as an outpost of Minoan civilization until, around 1450 BC, the volcano-island erupted; it was destroyed and, it is thought, the great Minoan civilizations on Crete fell with it.

Ferries dock at either SKÁLA FIRÁ or more often at the somewhat grim port of ÓRMOS ATHINIÓS. Half-rebuilt after a devastating earthquake in 1956, Firá lurches dementedly at the cliff's edge. Besieged by day-trippers, it's become incredibly tacky of late, the most grossly commercial spot on what can – in summer, at least – seem a grossly commercial island. There is no shortage of **rooms**, no matter what is shouted at you by the touts as you arrive. There is, however, a large and unscrupulous Santoríni mafia who have been responsible for a number of attacks on lone women. Find your room here without the "help" of touts, or if you arrive late, go to one of the three **youth hostels**. The unofficial *Kamaras* (②), directly behind the official hostel, is the best of these. The **campsite** is 500m from the bus terminal and is well signposted. Firá is not a place to linger, but make time for the **Archeological Museum** (Tues–Sun 8am–2.30pm; 800dr; student discounts), near the cable car to the north of town. An excellent collection, it includes a curious set of autoerotic figures. **Buses** from Firá are plentiful enough to get around between the town and beaches, but if you want to see the whole island in a couple of days, hiring a **moped** is useful – try any of the firms on the main road to Ía from the bus station square.

At the northwest of the island is one of the most dramatic towns of the Cyclades, **ÍA**, a curious mix of pristine white reconstruction and tumbledown ruins clinging to the cliff face. It's also much the calmest place on Santoríni, and with the recent introduction of a post office, part-time bank and bike-hire office, there's no longer any reason to feel stuck in Firá. However, **rooms** aren't too easy to come by; the most reasonable choices are the *Hotel Anemones* (☎0286/71 220; ②) and the *Hotel Fregata* (☎0286/71 221; ③). Best-value **eating** is at the *Dixti*, or *Markozanes*, 1km east in Finikiá hamlet.

Beaches on Santoríni are bizarre: long black stretches of volcanic sand which get blisteringly hot in the afternoon sun. There's little to choose between Kamári and Périssa, the two main resorts: both have long beaches and a mass of restaurants, rooms and apartments; neither is for those seeking solitude. Périssa gets more backpackers, and has the well-run **hostel** *Anna* (②). Those camping rough may be rousted by police. Kamári and Périssa are separated by the Mésa Vounó headland, on which stood **ancient Santoríni** (Tues–Sun 8am–2.30pm; free). Most of the ruins are difficult to place, but the theatre is awesome – beyond the stage there's a sheer drop to the sea.

Evidence of the Minoan colony was found at **Akrotíri** (Tues–Sun 8am–2.30pm; 1200dr; student discounts), a village buried under banks of volcanic ash at the southwest tip of the island, and reached by bus from Firá or Périssa. Tunnels through the ash uncovered structures two and three storeys high; lavish frescoes adorned the walls and Cretan pottery was found stored in a chamber. The frescoes are currently exhibited in Athens, but there are plans to bring them back when a new museum is built.

Kárpathos

Kárpathos has always been something of a backwater, and despite a magnificent coastline of cliffs and rocky promontories constantly interrupted by little beaches, it has succumbed surprisingly little to tourism. **PIGÁDHIA**, the capital, is now more often known simply as Kárpathos. It curves around one side of Vróndis Bay, a long sickle of sandy beach stretching north. **Hotels** such as the *Karpathos* (☎0245/22 347; ②) and **rooms** like those at *Sofia's* (☎0245/22 154; ③) in town often get full in midsummer, when you may have to head west to Arkássa or Finíki. Tavernas tend to be expensive, especially on the waterfront, with the *Olympia* and *Kali Kardhia* as honourable exceptions.

Many of the ferries calling at Pigádhia stop also at **DHIAFÁNI**, the northern port, which is also served by a daily *kaíki* from Pigádhia. Although its popularity is growing, rooms in Dhiafáni are still cheap and life slow. Paths lead north to the stony Vanánda beach, thirty minutes away, and south to more isolated strands, while both road and path climb to **ÓLIMBOS**, two hours' walk into the mountains and the one essential sight on the island. The older women, in their magnificent traditional dress, dominate the village, working in the gardens, carrying goods on their shoulders, or tending mountain sheep. The long-isolated villagers also speak a unique dialect, and traditional music is still heard regularly. There are several cheap places **to stay**, such as *Olimbos* (☎0245/51 252; ②) or *Aphrodite* (☎0245/51 307; ③), and a couple of tavernas – but it is almost impossible to get a room around the dates of any festival.

Ródhos (Rhodes)

It's no surprise that **RÓDHOS** is among the most visited of Greek islands. Not only is its east coast lined with sandy beaches, but the core of the capital is a beautiful and remarkably preserved medieval city. **RÓDHOS TOWN** divides neatly into two: the old walled city, and the tourist-orientated new town which has oozed out around it. The **old town** is infinitely more rewarding. First thing to meet the eye, and dominating the northeast sector of the city's fortifications, is the **Palace of the Grand Masters** (Mon 12.30–7pm, Tues–Fri 8am–7pm, Sat & Sun 8am–3pm; medieval walls Tues & Sat 2.30pm; palace 1200dr; student discounts). Destroyed by an explosion in 1856, it was reconstructed by the Italians as a summer home for Mussolini and Victor Emmanuel III, neither of whom used it much. Inside, a marble staircase leads up to rooms paved with mosaics from Kós, and the furnishings rival many a grand northern European palace.

The heavily restored **Street of the Knights** (Odhós Ippotón) leads due east from the front of the palace. The "Inns" lining it housed the Knights of St John for two centuries, and at the bottom of the slope the Knights' Hospital has been restored as the **Archeological Museum** (Tues–Sun 8.30am–3pm; 800dr; student discounts), where the star exhibits are two statues of Aphrodite. Across the way is the recently restored **Byzantine Museum** (same hours; 600dr; student discounts), housed in the knights' chapel and devoted to the island's icons and frescoes.

Leaving the Palace and heading south, it's hard to miss the most conspicuous Turkish monument in Rhodes, the candy-striped **Süleymaniye Mosque**. Downhill and east from the mosque is **Odhós Sokrátous**, once the heart of the old bazaar, and now packed with souvenir shops and milling foreigners. The most enduring civic contribution of Rhodes' Muslims is the **bathhouse** on Platía Ariónos, up in the southwest corner of the old city. One of only a couple of working public baths in Greece, it's a great place to go on an off-season day (Tues 1–7pm; Wed–Fri 11am–7pm, Sat 8am–7pm; 500dr; Wed & Sat 300dr).

Cheap **pensions** abound in Ródhos and are contained almost entirely in the quad bounded by Odhós Omírou on the south, Sokrátous on the north, Perikléos to the east and Ippodhámou in the west. Outside peak season lodging is the one thing still reasonably priced, but at crowded times it's wise to accept the offers of proprietors meeting the ferries. *Hotel Spot*, Perikleous 21 (☎0241/34 737; ③), is not an authentic building, but the rooms are clean with private bathrooms. There is a **youth hostel** at Ergiou 12, just off Sokrátous (☎0241/30 491; ①). **Eating cheaply** can be more of a problem; try the little alleys and backstreets well south of Sokrátous. Here you'll find *Yiannis*, Apéllou 41, *Akropolis*, Sofokleous 13, and for late-night eating *O Meraklis* at Aristotélous 32.

OTE, the **post office**, **banks**, **EOT** and the **police** are all in the new town, mostly northwest of the Italian-built New Market. **Buses** for the rest of the island leave from two terminals within sight of the market, one for the east coast, the other for the western shore.

Around the island

Heading down the east coast from Ródhos, the giant volcanic promontory of **TSAMBÍKAS**, 26km south, is the first place to seriously consider stopping – it has an excellent beach on the south of the headland, and another, more developed, one just north at Kolímbia. The best overnight base on this stretch of coast is probably **HARÁKI**, a tiny port with rooms and tavernas overlooked by a very ruinous castle.

LÍNDHOS, Rhódos' number-two tourist draw, erupts 12km south of here. Like Ródhos town itself, its charm is undermined by commercialism and crowds, and there are only two places to stay that are not booked semi-permanently by tour companies – *Pension Electra* (③) and *Pension Katholiki* (③), next door to each other on the way to the north beaches. Nevertheless, if you can arrive before or after the tours, Líndhos can still be a beautiful and atmospheric place. Its **Byzantine church** is covered with eighteenth-century frescoes, and several of the older houses are open to the public; entrance is free but they tend to expect you to buy something. On the hill above the town, the scaffolding-swathed **Temple of Athena** stands inside the castle (summer Mon 2.30–6.40pm, Tues–Fri 8am–6.40pm, Sat &

Sun 8.30am–2.40pm; 1200dr; student discounts). Líndhos' beaches are crowded and overrated, so head for **LÁRDHOS BAY**, 10km south, the start of 15km of intermittent coarse-sand beach up to and beyond the growing resort of **Yennádhi**. Inland near here, the medieval frescoes in the village church of **ASKLIPÍO** are the best on Rhódos.

Sími

Sími's great problem, lack of water, is in many ways also its greatest asset, as the island can't hope to support more than two or three large luxury hotels. Instead, hundreds of people are shipped in daily from Rhódos, relieved of their money and sent back. The island's capital consists of **Yialós**, the port, and **Horió**, on the hillside above, collectively known as **SÍMI**. Less than a century ago the town was richer and more populous than Rhódos, but the magnificent nineteenth-century mansions are now for the most part roofless and deserted, their windows gaping blankly across the harbour. There is an excellent island **museum**, which highlights Byzantine and medieval Sími, while at the very pinnacle of the hill a castle occupies the site of Sími's acropolis, surrounded by a dozen chapels.

Rooms are outnumbered by studios and both are hard to come by in high season; best try a booking agency such as Sunny Land (☎0241/71 320) for a week's minimum stay. Otherwise, try *Katerina Tsakiris* (☎0241/71 813; ③). Other good, reasonable stand-bys are *Glafkos* (☎0241/71 358; ②) and *Egli* (☎0241/71 392; ③). For **eating out**, shun the north quay in favour of *Tholos*, beyond Haráni boatyard, and *Neraïdha*; in the Horió, *Georgios* is a long-standing, good-value choice.

Sími has no big sandy beaches, but there are plenty of pebbly stretches at the heads of the coastline's deep narrow bays. **PÉDHI**, 45 minutes' walk or a ten-minute regular bus ride from Yialós, is a hamlet in one of Sími's only farming valleys, with an average beach, some seasonal rooms and an exorbitant new hotel. Many will opt for a twenty-minute walk via a goat track on the south shore to **Áyios Nikólaos**, sandy and with fine swimming. Further afield, excursion boats tout day-trips to the southeasterly bays of **Marathoúnda, Nanoú** and **Áyios Yióryios Dhissálona**, or the giant **Monastery of Taxiárhis Mihaél Panormítis** at the far south of the island.

Kós

After Rhódos, **Kós** is easily the most popular island in the Dodecanese, and there are remarkable similarities between the two. On Kós as on Rhódos the harbour is guarded by a castle of the Knights of St John, the waterside is lined with grandiose Italian public buildings, and minarets and palm trees punctuate extensive Greek and Roman remains. Dutch, German and Scandinavian package tourists predominate, filling the hotels behind the beaches – in midseason you'd be lucky to find any sort of room at all, except perhaps at the far west end of the island.

The town of **KÓS** spreads in all directions from the harbour. The municipal **tourist office** (July & Aug daily 7am–9pm; spring & autumn Mon–Fri 7.30am–8pm, Sat & Sun 8am–3pm; winter Mon–Fri 8am–3pm), 500m south of the ferry dock on the shore road, offers maps and ferry schedules; long-distance **buses** arrive at a park another 500m west of the tourist office. Among budget **accommodation**, the clean and friendly, co-managed *Pension Alexis* at Irodhótou 9 (☎0242/28 798; ②) and *Hotel Afendoulis*, 600m south at Evripilou 1 (☎0242/25 321; ③), are long-running favourites, and deservedly so. The official **campsite** is thirty minutes' walk along the scrappy beach to the southeast of town, served by city buses. Avoid the waterfront **restaurants** in favour of such inland outfits as *Olimpiadha* at Kleopátras 2, *Antoni's* behind *Hotel Anna* on Koutary and *Hellas* at Psaron 7.

Apart from the **castle** (Tues–Sun 8.30am–3pm; 800dr; student discounts), the town's main attraction is its wealth of Hellenistic and Roman remains, the largest single section of which is the ancient **agora**, reached from the castle or the main square next to the **Archeological Museum** (same hours; 800dr; student discounts). The best pieces have been taken for safekeeping into the castle, where most are piled up, unmarked and unnoticed. A couple of pillars, now replaced by scaffolding, once propped up the branches of **Hippocrates' plane tree**, which has a fair claim as one of the oldest trees in Europe.

Not only does Hippocrates have a tree named after him, but the star exhibit in the museum is his statue, and he is also honoured by the **Asclepion** (Tues–Sun 8.30am–3pm; 800dr; student discounts), a temple to Asclepius and renowned centre of Hippocratic teaching, 45 minutes on foot (or a short bus ride) from town. The road to the Asclepion passes through the bi-ethnic village of **PLATÁNI** (or Kermeté), where the Muslim minority run the several establishments dominating the crossroads. *Arap* and *Gin's Place*, in particular, serve excellent, cheap, Turkish-style food, far better than you generally get in Kós town.

If you're looking for anything resembling a deserted **beach** near the capital, you'll need to ride the long-distance buses, or else find your own transport. Around 12km west of Kós town, **TIGÁKI** is easily accessible and thus oversubscribed, though the crowds thin out in the dunes between it and Marmári, another, smaller resort 3km southwest. **MASTIHÁRI**, 30km from Kos town, is an actual village with a decent beach and non-package-tour rooms, as well as regular *kaíkia* to Kálimnos.

KARDHÁMENA, halfway down the southeast coast, is the island's second largest tourist playpen, and runaway development has banished whatever qualities it may once have had. Continuing west, buses run as far as **KÉFALOS**, which squats on a mesa-like hill looking back down the length of Kós. However, most visitors will have descended long before, either at **ÁYIOS STÉFANOS**, where the exquisite remains of a mosaic-floored fifth-century basilica overlook tiny Kastrí islet, or at **KAMÁRI**, the resort just below Kéfalos. Beaches begin at Kamári and extend virtually without interruption, past Ayios Stéfanos, for 7km; "Paradise" has the most facilities, and "Sunset" and "Camel" are calmer.

Pátmos

It was in a cave on **PÁTMOS** that St John the Divine wrote the Book of Revelation, and the monastery which commemorates him, founded here in 1088, dominates the island both physically and politically. While the monks no longer run the island as they did for more than 700 years, their influence has stopped most of the island going the way of Rhódos or Kós. **SKÁLA**, the port and main town, is the chief exception, crowded on summer days with excursionists from Kós and Rhódos or cruise-ship shoppers, and by night with well-dressed cliques of French, Germans, Italians, Brits and Americans.

The boat docks are right opposite the police station, the **tourist office** just behind it. **Accommodation** here is in demand but there's a reasonable amount of it: the *Blue Bay Hotel* (☎0247/31 165; ④), just east of town, is a fine choice, as is the *Hellenis* on the waterfront (☎0247/312 75; ③), and there are dozens of cheaper pensions. More likely, however, you'll end up in **rooms**, hawked vociferously as ever on the quay; they are mostly better-than-usual quality, though at higher-than-usual prices too. Among **restaurants**, try *O Grigoris*, the top choice; the *Skorpios Creperie*, around the corner on the main road to Hóra; or *O Kipos*, at the back of town, just before the OTE. North around the bay lies **Méloï Beach**, with a good, but overpriced, **campsite**; for swimming, the next beach, **Agriolivádhi**, is usually preferable.

The **Monastery of St John** shelters behind massive defences in the hilltop capital of Hóra. There is a bus up, but the thirty-minute walk by a beautiful old cobbled path puts you in a more appropriate frame of mind. Just over halfway is the Monastery of the Apocalypse, built around the cave where St John heard the voice of God issuing from a cleft in the rock. This is merely a foretaste, however, of the main monastery, behind whose fortifications have been preserved a fantastic array of religious treasures dating back to medieval times. Opening hours are incredibly erratic – the best advice is to go any morning between 8am and 2pm.

HÓRA itself is a beautiful little town whose antiquated alleys shelter over forty churches and monasteries. The churches, many of them containing beautiful icons and examples of the local skill in woodcarving, are almost all locked, but someone living nearby will have the key. If you're determined to stay here – and there are only a total of about fifty beds – it's best to make enquiries at the recommended taverna *Vangelis*, on Platía Levías, early in the day.

From Hóra a good road runs above the forgettable package resort of **Gríkou** to the isthmus of **Stavrós**, from where a thirty-minute trail leads to the much better beach, with one seasonal taverna, at **Psilí Ámmos** (there's also a summer *kaíki* service from Skála). More good beaches are found in the north of the island, particularly **Livádhi Yeránou**, shaded by tamarisk groves, and **Lámbi** with volcanic pebbles and two quality tavernas.

THE NORTHERN AEGEAN ISLANDS

In the northeasternmost part of the Aegean, the seven islands scattered off the coast of Asia Minor and Greece form a rather arbitrary archipelago. Despite their proximity to Turkey, members of the group bear few signs of an Ottoman heritage apart from the odd minaret. International tensions are high, and the resulting heavy military presence can be disconcerting. But, as in the Dodecanese, local tour operators do a thriving business shuttling passengers for absurdly high tariffs between the easternmost islands and the Turkish coast.

Sámos is the most visited of the "group", but, if you can leave the crowds behind, perhaps also the most verdant and beautiful. **Híos** is culturally interesting, but its natural beauty has been ravaged and the development of tourism has – so far – been deliberately retarded. **Lésvos** is more of an acquired taste, though once you get a feel for the island you may find it hard to leave. The appeal of **Thássos** is rather broader, with a varied offering of sandy beaches, forested mountains and minor archeological sites; cheaply accessible from the mainland, it can, however, be rather overrun in high season. The **Sporades**, in the northwestern Aegean, are a very easy group to island-hop and well connected by bus and ferry with Athens via Áyios Konstandínos or Kími, and with Vólos.

Sámos

Lush and seductive, Sámos was the wealthiest island in the Aegean during the seventh century, but fell on hard times thereafter; today the Samian economy is increasingly dependent on package tourism. The more rugged western part of Sámos has retained much of its undeveloped grandeur, but the eastern half has surrendered to the onslaught of holiday-makers. It's a rather staid, Nordic, thirtysomething clientele – the absence of a campsite indicates what sort of visitor is expected.

All main-line **ferries** call at both Karlóvassi in the west and Vathí, the capital, in the east; additionally there are services to the Dodecanese out of Pithagório in the south. **VATHÍ** itself lines the steep-sided shore of its namesake bay and is of minimal interest except for its hill quarter of tottering, tile-roofed houses, Áno Vathí, and an excellent **archeological museum** (Tues–Sun 8.30am–3pm; 600dr; students 300dr). A wealth of peculiar votive offerings balances the star exhibit: a huge, five-metre *kouros* or statue of an idealized youth.

Pensions and **hotels** without tour-group allotments include the basic *Ionia*, Manóli Kalomíri 5 (☎0273/28 782; ②) and the *Hotel Artemis* on the "Lion Square" (☎0273/27 792; ②). When **eating out**, avoid the obvious tourist traps in favour of *Taverna Gregory*, inland near the post office, or in exchange for a bit more cash, *Ta Dhiodhia*, down at the south end of the front past the Credit Bank. **Bus services** off the main corridors to Kokkári and Pithagório are skimpy; you're expected to rent a **moped** or motorbike, for which there are a dozen outlets in town.

After Vathí, **PITHAGÓRIO** is the island's main resort; its views across to Turkey are more attractive than the surroundings, though the village and its relentlessly commercialized harbour retain some charm. It's built atop the ancient capital of the island, of which evidence abounds: Roman baths, an ancient subterranean aqueduct (the Evapalinio tunnel; Tues–Sun 8am–2.30pm; 500dr; student discounts), an amphitheatre, and, 8km west, the **Sanctuary of Hera** (Tues–Sun 8am–2.30pm; 600dr; student discounts), marked by a single standing column. Pithagório has little to hold you in the way of good-value accommodation or food, however; just show up for your ferry or hydrofoil to the Dodecanese.

Heading west from Vathí, the first place of any note is the growing resort of **KOKKÁRI**, enchantingly set between twin headlands at the base of forested mountains. Nearby beaches are pebbly and exposed, prompting its role as a major windsurfers' resort. You've slightly more chance of finding a free room here than in Pithagório; **eating out**, try *Farmers Restaurant* in the town centre. Less than an hour's walk west from **Karlóvassi**, the island's second town, **Potámi** is a popular beach ringed by forest and weird rock formations; for more solitude you can continue another hour or so to the two bays of **Mikró Seitáni** (pebbles) and **Megálo Seitáni** (sand). But for an actual amenitied beach resort in the west of the island, you'll need to shift south to **VOTSALÁKIA**, almost 2km of sand and pebbles lined with **accommodation**, under the shadow of brooding Mount Kérkis. *Emmanuel Dhespotakis* (☎0273/31 258; ③) has two premises on the westerly and more peaceful of two bays here; among **tavernas**, *Akroyialia* is the most reasonable and filling.

Híos

Increasing numbers of foreigners are discovering **Híos** beyond its port city – fascinating villages, an important Byzantine monument and a healthy complement of beaches. In August there may not be enough beds to go around, but at other times you'll find the island blissfully tourist-free.

HÍOS town is always full of life, with a shambling old bazaar district, some excellent authentic tavernas, and a regular evening promenade along the waterfront. Relatively cheap **accommodation** is beginning to proliferate along the waterfront and just behind; the helpful **tourist office** at Kanári 18 has comprehensive lists. Currently the best value and quietest (a big issue here) include *Rooms Alex* at Miháli Livanoú 29 (☎0271/26 054; ②) and *Rooms Alexios* at Rodhokanáki 34 (☎0271/41 721; ②).

Eating out is better than the glut of shoreline bars would suggest. There are still two decent beach tavernas here, *Yiamos'* and *Karazas*. You can get good, cheap, cooked lunches at *Estiatorio Dhimitrakopoulos* on the corner of Sgoutá and Valtarías, a few steps from the bus terminal. The milk shops by the *Hotel Apollonio* have good puddings and breakfast yoghurts.

Green long-distance **buses** run from the terminal south of the central park to most of the villages on Híos, though services to the north are sparse. The closest good **beach** is **Karfás** (7km; very frequent blue bus), a long sweep of fine sand unfortunately overwhelmed by recent development.

Around the island

The monastery of **NÉA MONÍ**, founded by the Byzantine emperor in 1049, is the most beautiful and important medieval building on the Greek islands. Its mosaics rank among the finest artistic expressions of their age, and its setting, high in the mountains west of the port, is no less memorable. There's a direct green bus only on Wednesday mornings for mass; at other times you have to take a local blue bus as far as Karyés (7km) and walk or hitch an equal distance further. Once a community of 600 monks, Néa Moní was pillaged during Turkish atrocities in 1822 and most of its inmates put to the sword. Today the monastery, with its giant refectory and vaulted water cisterns, is maintained by just two nuns and a few lay workers.

The dry valleys of **southern Híos** are home to the mastic bush, whose resin – for centuries the base of paints and cosmetics – was the source of the island's wealth before petrochemicals came along. **PIRGÍ**, 24km from the port, is one of the liveliest and most colourful of the villages, its houses elaborately embossed with geometric patterns cut into the plaster and then outlined with paint. On the northeast corner of the central *platía*, the fresco-embellished Byzantine church of **Áyii Apóstoli** is tucked under an arcade (erratic hours). Pirgí has a handful of rooms, a couple of tavernas, and some good beaches nearby – the closest being Emborió, 5km from Pirgí and served by occasional buses in summer.

The villages of **northern Híos** never recovered from the Turkish massacres of the War of Independence, and many are now virtually deserted. Perhaps the best target is eerie **VOLISSÓS**, a large, half-inhabited village guarded by a castle. Just over a kilometre away there's **LIMNIÁ**, a lively and authentic little fishing village with two good tavernas, plus a few more studios on the slopes inland. One kilometre southeast, at Managrós, begins an almost boundless sand-and-pebble **beach**, while the more intimate cove of Lefkáthia is just a ten-minute walk over the headland north of the harbour. **AYÍA MARKÉLLA**, 5km further north, stars in many of the local postcards: a long, stunning beach fronting the monastery of the same name – not particularly interesting but with a summer taverna and lodging in the grounds.

Lésvos

Lésvos, birthplace of Sappho, the ancient world's foremost woman poet, may not at first strike the visitor as particularly beautiful, but the rocky volcanic landscape of pine and olive groves grows on you. Despite the inroads of tourism, this is still by and large a working island, with few large hotels outside the capital, Mitilíni, and the resort of Mólivos. Moreover, buses from Mitilíni are run for the benefit of the locals, not tourists, and journeys are often slow and tortuous – it's wise to base yourself at one of the several resorts and explore its surroundings. **MITILÍNI** itself has little to detain you, other than a good **archeological museum** (Tues–Sun 8am–2.30pm; 400dr; student discounts); **rooms** are expensive and most restaurants substandard. Worth a detour at **VARIÁ**, 5km south, are the adjacent **Theophilos** (summer Tues–Sun 9am–1pm & 4.30–8pm; winter Tues–Sun 9am–1pm; 250dr; student discounts) and **Thériade museums** (summer Tues–Sun 9am–2pm & 5–8pm; winter Tues–Sun 9am–2pm; 500dr; student discounts), with astonishing collections of folk and modern art respectively.

MÓLIVOS, on the northwestern coast, is easily the most attractive spot on Lésvos. Tiers of sturdy, red-tiled houses mount the slopes between the picturesque harbour and the Genoese castle. Closer examination reveals a dozen weathered Turkish fountains along shady, stone-paved alleyways. There are plenty of **rooms** to let, a **tourist office** by the bus stop to help you find them if necessary, and a **campsite** east of town. The main lower road, straight past the tourist office, heads towards the picturesque harbour, where *The Captain's Table* is the one affordable **taverna**; back up in town, try *Melinda's*. What with a **bank**, **post office** and **OTE** station, there's no need to move far to transact essential business.

The island's best **beach** is at **SKÁLA ERESSOÚ** on the west coast. There are rooms to let here, but sometimes not enough, so **camping** is tolerated at a quasi-official site to the west; **tavernas** with wooden terraces line the beach – best of these are *Iy Gorgona* and *Bennetts*, with *Aphrodite* recommended inland. Visitors include gay women paying homage to **Sappho**, who supposedly lived in ancient Eressós – all that remains of the old town crumbles away atop a bluff to the east. The southeastern peninsula also offers its share of attractions. Foremost is the huge beach at **VATERÁ** – the equal of Skála Eressoú's and provided with a new **campsite** and good shoreline **tavernas**.

Thássos

Just 12km from the mainland, **Thássos** has long been a popular resort for northern Greeks, and in recent years has been attracting considerable numbers of foreign tourists. Without being spectacular it is a very beautiful island, its almost circular area covered in gentle slopes of pine, olive and chestnut which rise to a mountainous backbone and plunge to a line of good sand beaches.

THÁSSOS TOWN is the island capital and nexus of life, though not the main port: ferries from Kavála usually stop down the coast at Órmos Prínou, but a few each day continue to Thássos town. The largely modern town is partly redeemed by its pretty harbour and popular sand beach just east, and the substantial remains of the ancient city. If you want to stay there are several cheap **hotels** – the *Astir* (③), *Diamando* (③), *Viky* (③) and *Angelika* (③) – plus reasonably plentiful rooms, though in summer you should take the first offered on arrival. **Eating out**, menus tend to be expensive and bland. There's a privately run Thassos Tours **tourist information office** on the main street parallel to the seafront, and a high-season **Tourist Police** office near the bus station.

The main excavated area of ancient Thássos is the **agora**, entered beside the town **museum** (daily 8am–2.30pm; 400dr; student discounts), a little way back from the modern harbour. Prominent here are two Roman stoas, but you can also make out shops, monuments, passageways and sanctuaries from the remodelled Classical city. Above the town, roughly in line with the smaller fishing port, steps spiral up to a **Hellenistic theatre**, fabulously positioned above a broad sweep of sea. Beyond the theatre, a path winds on to a **Genoese fort**, constructed out of stones from the acropolis. From here you can follow the circuit of **walls** to a high terrace supporting the foundations of a Temple of Apollo and onwards to a rock-hewn sanctuary of Pan. Below it a precarious sixth-century BC "secret stairway" descends to the outer walls and back into town.

About five **buses** per day do the full island circuit in season, and there are several more to and from different villages, with a bias towards the west coast. The south-facing coast has most of the best beaches. Above the east coast, **PANAYÍA** village, with its **accommodation** and proximity to **Hrissí Amnoudhísa Beach**, makes the best base; **KÍNIRA**, 11km south, is quieter and right on the seaside. **ALIKÍ** faces a double bay which almost pinches off a headland. The mixed sand-and-pebble spit gets too popular for its own good in high season, but the water is crystal-clear and the beachside taverna offers good food. The hamlet here has one place with rooms. At the south tip of Thássos, **ASTRÍS** has two excellent beaches set in a stunning cliffscape, but the best-appointed local resort – and virtually the only one to function outside of summer – is **POTÓS**, where there's a **campsite** plus a fine, kilometre-long sand beach facing the sunset.

The Sporades

The three northern Sporades – package-tourist haven Skíathos, Alónissos and **Skópelos**, the pick of the trio – have good beaches, transparent waters and thick pine forests. **Skíros**, the fourth island, is slightly isolated from the others, less scenic, but with perhaps the most character; for a relatively uncommercialized island within a day's travel of Athens it is hard to beat.

SKÓPELOS

More rugged and better cultivated than neighbouring Skíathos, **Skópelos** is also very much more attractive. Most boats call first at the small port of Loutráki, below the western village of Glóssa, but it's best to stay on board until **SKÓPELOS TOWN**, sloping down one corner of a huge, almost circular bay. **Hotels** here are ever increasing in quantity, but occupied mainly by package tourists; tucked away on the far side of the bay, in the main body of the town there are dozens of **rooms** to let – take up one of the offers when you land. **Nightlife** is fairly subdued, though there are several discos and a dozen or so bars. The three tavernas opposite where the ferries dock are acceptable, though hardly cheap. Within the town, spread below the oddly whitewashed ruins of a Venetian **kástro**, are an enormous number of churches – 123 reputedly, though some are small enough to be mistaken for houses.

Buses cover the island's one asphalt road between Skópelos and Loutráki about six times daily, stopping at the turn-offs to all the main beaches and villages. **Stáfilos Beach**, 4km out of town, is the closest, but it's small, rocky and increasingly crowded – the overflow, much of it nudist, flees to Velánio, just east. Much more promising, if you're after isolation and happy to walk to a nearby beach, is **PÁNORMOS**, a pleasant little hamlet with rooms, tavernas and a **campsite**. The beach here is gravelly and steeply shelving, but there are small secluded bays close by and, slightly further on at **MILIÁ**, a tremendous, 1500-metre sweep of tiny pebbles beneath a bank of pines.

SKÍROS

Skíros was until recently a very traditional and idiosyncratic island. Though it has definitely been "discovered" since 1980, it still ranks as one of the most interesting places in the Aegean. The older men still wear the vaguely Cretan costume of cap, vest, baggy trousers, leggings and clogs, while the women favour yellow scarves and long embroidered skirts.

Skíros also has some particularly lively **festivals** – notably the *Apokriatiká* (pre-Lenten) carnival's "Goat Dance", performed by masked revellers in the village streets.

A **bus** service connects Linariá – a functional little port with a few tourist facilities – to **HÓRA**, the island capital, perched on a high rock rising precipitously from the coast. Traces of Classical walls can still be made out among the ruins of the Venetian **kástro**; within the walls is the crumbling, tenth-century monastery of Áyios Yióryios. At the north end of town, the **Memorial to Rupert Brooke** – a splendidly incongruous bronze nude of "Immortal Poetry" – commemorates the World War I poet who died on a hospital ship anchored offshore in 1915.

Back in town, there are several **hotels** and plenty of **rooms to let** in private houses. The latter are preferable, and you'll be met with offers as you descend from the bus. **Eating out**, you'll find most **tavernas** overpriced and mediocre, *O Glaros* being the exception. The **campsite** is down the hill from the Rupert Brooke statue, at the fishing village of **MAGAZIÁ**, with rooms and tavernas fronting the best beach on the island.

The only practical ways of getting around Skíros are on foot or by moped (there are several rental places in the main town), though in summer the whimsical bus service also visits the more popular beaches. The most rewarding walk is a four-hour traverse of the island by rough jeep track to Atsítsu on the west coast.

THE IONIAN ISLANDS

The six **Ionian islands** are both geographically and culturally a mixture of Greece and Italy. Floating on the haze of the Adriatic, their green, even lush, silhouettes come as a shock to those more used to the stark outlines of the Aegean. The islands were the Homeric realm of Odysseus and here alone of all modern Greek territory (except for Lefkádha) the Ottomans never held sway. After the fall of Byzantium, possession passed to the Venetians, and the islands became a keystone in that city-state's maritime empire from 1386 until its collapse in 1797. Most of the population must have remained immune to the establishment of Italian as the official language and the arrival of Roman Catholicism, but Venetian influence remains evident and beautiful despite a series of earthquakes.

Tourism has hit **Corfu** in a big way – so much so that it's the only island besides Crete known to locals and foreigners by different names. None of the other islands has endured anything like Corfu's scale of development, although the process seems well advanced on parts of **Zákinthos**. For a less sullied experience, the duo of **Kefalloniá** and **Itháki** is recommended.

Kérkira (Corfu)

Corfu's natural appeal remains an intense experience, if sometimes a beleaguered one, for Corfu has more package hotels and holiday villas than any other Greek island. The commercialism is apparent the moment you step ashore at the ferry dock, or cover the two kilometres from the **airport** to the city. From the latter you can walk, get a taxi, or catch the local #2 or #3 buses which leave 500m north of the terminal gates.

KÉRKIRA TOWN has a lot more going for it than first exposure to the summer crowds might indicate. The cafés on the Spianádha (Esplanade) and in the arcaded Listón have a civilized air, and the **Palace of St Michael and St George** (daily 8am–2.30pm; 800dr; student discounts) on the Spianádha houses a collection of Asiatic art. The **Byzantine Museum** (Tues–Sat 8am–2.30pm, Sun 9.30am–2.30pm; 500dr; student discounts) and the cathedral are also worth visiting, as is the **Archeological Museum** at Vraíla 3 (Tues–Sun 9am–3pm; 800dr; student discounts), where the small but interesting collection features a 2500-year-old pediment of Medusa. The island's patron saint, **Spirídhon**, is entombed in a silver-covered coffin in his own church on Odhós Vouthrótou, and four times a year, to the accompaniment of much celebration and feasting, the relics are paraded through the streets. Finally, 5km south of town lies one of Greece's most popular excursion targets, the picturesque island of

Vlahérna, which is capped by a small monastery and joined to the plush mainland suburb of **Kanóni** by a short causeway, spoilt by airport noise.

There are several agencies along Vassiléos Konstandínou who can arrange your **accommodation**. Otherwise, try the cheapest old-town **hotel**, the *Europa*, at Yitsaiali 10, near the new port (☎0661/39 304; ②); *Hotel Hermes*, at Makóra 14, behind the daily market in the old town (☎0661/39 321; ③); or the more upmarket *Hotel Ionion*, Xen Stratigou 46 (☎0661/39 915; ②). For real budget accommodation, try *Kerkyra Youth Hostel* on Kontokali Beach (☎0661/91 202; ①), an hour's walk north of the town. For **eating out**, two authentic restaurants are *Porta Remounda*, off Kapodhistriou at Moustoxidi 14, and the more expensive *Rex*, at Kapodhistríou 66.

There are two **bus terminals**: one on Platía San Rócco for blue-vehicle routes through the middle of the island, the other on Platía Néou Frouríou, just below the fort, for green buses to more remote destinations. There is also a KTEL station, with buses to Thessaloníki and Athens, near the New Port. **Mopeds** are also available nearby, and at most other resorts on the island.

Around the island

The coast north of the port has been remorselessly developed as far as Pyrgi, and much of it is best written off. West of Kassiópi, the first substantial place to stay is **ÁYIOS SPIRÍDHON**, where there are restaurants and a few campers ignoring the "No camping" signs on the small beach. A little way on you'll see a sign to Almirós beach, start of the continuous strand that sweeps around to **RÓDHA** – once a small village but now taken over by British travel companies. The best spot on this northern coast is beyond Sidhári at **PEROULÁDHES**, a genuine, somewhat run-down village with a spectacular beach of brick-red sand below wind-eroded cliffs.

On the west coast, **PALEOKASTRÍTSA** has gone the way of all package locations, though its coves are on a beautiful stretch of coast. Expensive villas and hotels are present in abundance, plus a few **campsites**, which are, however, some distance from the town. If you just want a **room**, look uphill in the villages of Lákones and Makrádhes, three to four miles away.

The tiny village of **VÁTOS**, just inland from west-coast Ermónes, seems to be the one place within easy reach of Kérkira town that has an easy, relaxed feel to it. There are reasonable **rooms** and two **tavernas** here, both (as so often on Corfu) called *Spiro's*. The best by far is the one furthest from the road. Campers pitch tents down towards **Mirtiótissa Beach**, though they sometimes get encouraged to use the official site, *Vátos Camping*, near the village. The dirt track down to the sand is steep and has so far prevented development. Nearby **GLIFÁDHA** is dominated by a huge hotel, and adjacent **PÉLEKAS** is likewise busy, as the main crossroads in the west-centre of the island; but it's a good alternative base, with simple **tavernas**, a **hostel** and **rooms**. Continuing south, **ÁYIOS GÓRDHIS** beach is more remote but that hasn't spared it from the crowds who come to admire the cliff-girt setting or patronize the *Pink Palace*, a foreign-run combination holiday village/disco right on the sand.

Beyond Messongí extends the flat, sandy southern tip of Corfu. **ÁYIOS YIÓRYIOS**, on the southwest coast, consists of a developed area just before its beautiful beach, and a campsite. **KÁVOS**, near the cape itself, rates with its many **clubs** and **discos** as the nightlife capital of the island; for daytime solitude and swimming, you can walk to **beaches** beyond the nearby hamlets of Spartéra and Dhragotína.

Kefalloniá (Kefallinía, Cephalonia)

KEFALLONIÁ is the largest, and at first glance least glamorous, of the Ionian islands; the 1953 earthquake which rocked the archipelago was especially devastating here, with almost every town and village levelled. Couple that with the islanders' legendary eccentricity, and with poor infrastructure – many roads are still unpaved – and it's no wonder tourism didn't take off until the late Eighties. Nonetheless, there's plenty here of interest: beaches to compare with the best on Corfu or Zákinthos, a good local wine, and the partly forested mass of 1632-metre Mount Énos. The island's size, skeletal bus service and persistent shortage of summer accommodation make **motorbike or car rental** a must for explorations; mopeds may not cope with some grades or surfaces.

Ferries from Pátras, other Ionian islands or overseas dock at Sámi, a drably functional port on the northeast coast; few people linger, especially when Ayía Evfimía, 10km north, makes a far more attractive base – ferries also call here from Astakós on the mainland, and you can **eat** at *Stavros Dhendhrinos*, arguably the best taverna on Kefalloniá. Between the two, 3km from Sámi, the **Melissáni cave**, a partly submerged Capri-type "blue grotto", is well worth a stop.

Southeast from Sámi you find the resorts of **POROS**, with ferries to Killíni on the Peloponnese, and **SKÁLA**, whose remains of a **Roman villa** boast fine mosaics. Rooms are difficult to find here in season, being block-booked by tour operators. You may have to continue around the cape, past excellent beaches, to find accommodation in the coastal village of Lourdáta, about halfway between Skála and the island capital of Argostóli. Just inland, detour to the Venetian **castle of Áyios Yióryios**.

ARGOSTÓLI, with occasional ferries to Killíni and Zákinthos, is the bustling island capital: inevitably concrete, very Greek. The waterfront **tourist office** keeps comprehensive lists of **accommodation** and, unusually, may book private rooms for you – hotels are expensive. **Eating out**, a good if unromantically set fall-back is the *Adherfi Tzirvas*, on Vandárou near the bus station; they also have rooms to rent. Argostóli is perhaps the best place to rent your **own transport**, with a dozen agencies on the waterfront.

Heading north from Argostóli, there's little to stop for on the west coast until you emerge, along a dizzying corniche road, above **Mírtos**, considered the best beach on the island. There are almost no facilities, though – closest place to **stay** is the almost bus-less **ÁSSOS**, a fishing port perched on a narrow isthmus linking it to a castellated headland. End of the line means **FISKÁRDHO**, with its eighteenth-century houses, notable mainly for having escaped damage in the earthquake. It's the most expensive place on the island, and in July available rooms are as rare as snowflakes. The main reason to come here would be for the daily **ferry** to Lefkádha island, and sometimes Itháki.

Itháki (Ithaka)

Despite its proximity to Kefalloniá, there's still very little tourist development to spoil **Itháki**, Odysseus' capital. There are few sandy beaches, but the island is good walking country, with a handful of small fishing villages and various pebbly coves to swim from. Ferries from Pátra, Kefalloniá, Astakós, Corfu, Igoumítsa and Italy land at the main port and the village-sized capital of **VÁTHI**, at the back of a deep bay which seems to close completely around it. **Rooms** remain fairly easy to come by except during the July music festival and the August/September theatre events; they tend, however, to be inconspicuous, and are best sought by nosing around the backstreets south of the ferry dock. There are just two mid-range **hotels** at opposite ends of the long quay, the *Odysseus* (④) and the *Mentor* (④). There's more choice for **food**, with seven or eight tavernas, though all seem remarkably similar in price and fare.

In season the usual small boats shuttle tourists from the harbour to a series of tiny coves along the peninsula northeast of Váthi. The pebble-and-sand **beaches** between Cape Skinós and Sarakinikó Bay are excellent; most of those closer to town are little more than concrete diving platforms. Three daily **buses** run north along the main road out of Váthi to **STAVRÓS**, a fair-sized village with a couple of relatively expensive tavernas and some rooms. **FRÍKES**, a thirty-minute walk downhill beyond Stavrós, is smaller but has a handful of tavernas, rooms and a pebbly strip of beach. This is where the seasonal ferries dock, to and from Lefkádha and Fiskárdho on northern Kefalloniá; the port is linked by bus and occasional *kaíki* to Váthi.

Zákinthos (Zante)

Zákinthos, which once exceeded Corfu in architectural distinction, was hit hardest by the 1953 earthquake, and the island's grand old capital was completely destroyed. Although some of its beautiful Venetian churches have been restored, it's a rather sad town, and the attraction for travellers lies more in the thick vineyards, orchards and olive groves of the interior, and some excellent beaches. Under two hours from Killíni on the mainland, Zákinthos now gets close to half a million visitors a year. Most tourists, though, are conveniently housed in one place, Laganás, on the south coast; if you avoid July and August, and steer clear of Laganás and the developing villages of Argássi and Tsilívi, there is still a peaceful Zákinthos to be found.

The most tangible hints of the former glory of **ZÁKINTHOS TOWN** are in **Platía Solómou**, the grand and spacious main square. At its waterside corner stands the beautiful fifteenth-century sandstone church of **Áyios Nikólaos**, whose paintings and icons, along with those from other island churches, are displayed in the imposing **Neo-Byzantine Museum** (Tues–Sun 8.30am–3pm; 800dr; student discounts) by the town hall. The large church of **Áyios Dhioníssios** was one of the few buildings left standing after the earthquake, and murals still cover the interior. If you've a couple of hours to fill, walk up the cobbled path to the town's massive **Venetian fortress** (Tues–Sun 8.30am–2.30pm; 500dr; student discounts).

As there is no tourist office, the **tourist police** on Platía Solómou have information about accommodation and bus services; they're in the police station on the waterfront. **Accommodation** in Zákinthos town is relatively plentiful and reasonably priced, but tends to be hotel-based. Cheaper **hotels** include *Diethnes* at Agiou Lazarou 102 (☎0695/22 286; ②) and *Omonia* at Xanthopoulou 4 (☎0695/22 113; ②). **Restaurants** or tavernas are a bit thin on the ground. *Taverna Arekia* is strongly recommended, but it's a fair walk north along the east road. You can also work up an appetite by walking a good way in the opposite direction to the *Malavetis Restaurant* at Ayíou Dhionissíou 4. More central is the *Kalliniko*, best value of the places on the Platía Solómou.

To get to the beaches, there is a **bus service** from the station on Odhós Filitá (one block back from the Fina pump on the main waterside road), but since the island is mostly flat, this is an ideal place to rent a **bike** available from Motorakis (which also has mopeds and motorcycles) on Leofóros Dhimokratías, opposite the phone office.

CRETE

With its flourishing agricultural economy, **Crete** is one of the few islands which could probably support itself without tourists. Nevertheless, tourism is heavily promoted here. The northeast coast in particular is overdeveloped and, though there are parts of the south and west coasts that have not been spoiled, they are getting harder and harder to find. By contrast, the high mountains of the interior are still barely touched, and one of the best things to do is to hire a moped and explore the remoter villages.

Crete is distinguished as the home of Europe's earliest civilization, the **Minoan**, which made the island the centre of a maritime trading empire as early as 2000 BC, and produced art works unsurpassed in the ancient world. Control of the island passed from Greeks to Romans to Saracens, through the Byzantine Empire to Venice, and finally to Turkey for more than two centuries. Almost wherever you go, you'll find some reminder of the island's history. The first priority is to get away from **Iráklio** as quickly as possible, having paid a visit to nearby **Knossos**. There's another great Minoan site at **Mália** on the north coast, while the Roman ruins at **Gortys** lie to the south. For many people, unexpected highlights turn out to be Crete's Venetian forts, dominant at **Réthimno**, and its Byzantine churches, most famously near **Krítsa**. And if you want to get away from it all you should head west, towards **Haniá** and the smaller, less well-connected places along the south and west coasts. It is in this part of the island also that the White Mountains rise, while below them yawns the famous **Samarian Gorge**.

Iráklio (Heraklion)

The best way to approach **IRÁKLIO** is by sea; that way you see the city as it should be seen, with Ioúktas rising behind and the Psilorítis range to the west. As you get closer, it's the city walls which first stand out, still dominating and fully encircling the oldest part of town, and finally you sail in past the great fort defending the harbour entrance. Unfortunately, big ships no longer dock in the old port but at great modern concrete wharves alongside – which neatly sums up Iráklio itself: many of the old parts have been restored, but they're of no relevance to the dust and noise which characterize the city today.

Platía Eleftherías is very much the traditional heart of the city, both in terms of traffic, which swirls around it constantly, and for life in general: lined with expensive cafés and restaurants, and jammed in the evening with strolling hordes. Most of Iráklio's more expensive shops are in the streets leading off the square. The **Archeological Museum** (Mon noon–5/7pm, Tues–Sun 8am–5/7pm; 1500dr; student discounts) is also just off here, directly opposite the EOT office. Almost every important prehistoric and Minoan find on Crete is part of this fabulous, if bewilderingly large, collection. Remember to save some energy for upstairs, too, where the **Hall of the Frescoes**, with its intricately reconstructed fragments of wall paintings from Knossos and other sites, is especially wonderful.

Practicalities

Finding a **room** can be very hard in season: the best place to look is in the area below Platía Venizélou. *Vergina*, Hortátson 32 (☎081/242 739; ②), and *Rea*, Kalimeráki 1 (☎081/223 638; ②), are both good and are close to each other. The former official youth hostel has been transformed into the clean and well-maintained *Rent Rooms Hellas*, on Chandákos 24 (☎081/280 858; ①), and overall it's better than the friendly and comfortable Greek **youth hostel** on Vironos 5 (☎081/286 281; ①). There are a number of campsites in Iráklio. Try the *Creta* on Gournes (☎0897/41 400), or the *Komos* on Pitsidia (☎0892/42 596). Official **camping** is at the expensive and regimented *Camping Iráklio*, about 6km west on the beach at Amoudhári (bus #6).

There are plenty of places to **eat**, but in general eating out is expensive. For substantial meals the best bets are *Kale Orexi* and *Minos* at Dedalou no. 24 and no. 10, while the *Ionia*, on the corner of Evans and Yianári, is also good. Other scattered possibilities include the *Kiriakos*, Dimokratias 51, and the pizzeria *Tartuffo* on Dimokratias 83.

Iráklio's **tourist office** is just below Platía Eleftherías, opposite the archeological museum. The **Tourist Police** are on Dhikeosínis, halfway between Platía Eleftherías and the market, and the **post office** is just behind here, on Platía Dhaskaloyiánni. The 24-hour **OTE** office is next to El Greco Park, in the square immediately north of Venizélou. You can find several **banks** down Ikosipémptis Avgoústou, where the **shipping and travel agents** are. You'll also find **motorbikes and cars to rent** down here, but places off the main road offer better prices; try Ariadne, opposite the Venetian Loggia town hall for bikes, Ritz at Kalimeráki 1 for cars.

Buses for all points along the coast road leave from the new station by the harbour; south and east to Áno Viános, Mírtos and Árvi, from just outside the walls on Platía Kíprou, at the end of Odhós Evans; southwest to Festos, Mátala, Léndas and Ayía Galíni, or along the old road west, from just outside the Haniá Gate. For Knossos, the #2 local bus sets off from the stop adjacent to the harbour bus station, runs up Ikosipémptis Avgoústou and out of town on Odhós Evans.

Knossos

The largest of the Minoan palaces, **KNOSSOS** reached its cultural peak over 3500 years ago, though a town of some importance persisted here until well into the Roman era. It lies on a low, largely artificial hill some 5km southeast of Iráklio amid hillsides rich in lesser remains spanning 25 centuries. As soon as you enter the **Palace of Knossos** (daily 8am–7pm; winter closes 5pm; 1500dr; student discounts) through the West Court, the ancient ceremonial entrance, it is clear how the legends of the Labyrinth of the Minotaur grew up around it. Even with a detailed plan, it's almost impossible to find your way around the site systematically – but wander around for long enough and you'll eventually stumble upon everything.

Evidence of a luxurious lifestyle is plainest in the **Queen's Suite**, off the grand **Hall of the Colonnades** at the bottom of the staircase. The main living room is decorated with a reproduction of the celebrated dolphin fresco, though the original, now in the Iráklio Archeological Museum, was actually found in the courtyard. Going up the **Grand Staircase** to the floor above the Queen's domain, you come to a set of rooms in a sterner vein, generally regarded as the **King's quarters**. The staircase opens into a grandiose reception chamber known as the **Hall of the Royal Guard**, its walls decorated in repeated shield patterns. Continuing to the top of the staircase you emerge onto the broad **Central Court**, which would once have been enclosed by the walls of the buildings all around. On the far side, in the northwestern corner of the courtyard, is the entrance to one of Knossos' most atmospheric survivals, the **Throne Room**, in all probability the seat of a priestess rather than a ruler.

Gortys and Mátala

The three major sites south of Iráklio – **Gortys**, **Festos** and **Ayía Triádha** – can be visited on a day's tour from the city, probably with a lunchtime swim at **Mátala** thrown in. Doing it by public transport you'll be forced into a rather more leisurely pace, but there's still no reason why you shouldn't get to all three sites and reach Mátala within the day; if necessary, it's easy enough to hitch the final stretch.

GORTYS (daily 8.30am–5/7pm; 800dr; student discounts) is the ruined capital of the Roman province which included not only Crete but also much of North Africa. Cutting across the fields will give you some idea of the scale of this city at its zenith, approximately the third century AD; an enormous variety of other remains, including an impressive theatre, are strewn across your route. At the main entrance to the fenced site, alongside the road, is the ruinous but still impressive basilica of **Áyios Títos**, the saint who converted Crete and was also its first bishop. Beyond this is the **Odeion**, which houses the most important discovery on the site, the **Law Code** – an inscription measuring about thirty feet by ten feet in all.

MÁTALA is by far the best known beach in Iráklio province, widely promoted and included in tours mainly because of the famous caves cut into the cliffs (daily 8.30am–3.30pm; free) above its beautiful beach. These ancient tombs used to be almost permanently inhabited by a sizeable hippie community; nowadays the town is full of package tourists and tries hard to present a respectable image: the cliffs are now cleared and locked up every evening.

Early afternoon, when the tour buses pull in for their swimming stop, the beach is packed to overflowing. If the crowds get too much, it's a twenty-minute clamber over the rocks to another excellent stretch of sand, known locally as "Red Beach". In the evening, when the trippers have gone, there are waterside bars and restaurants looking out over invariably spectacular sunsets. The chief remaining problem concerns prices: **rooms** are both expensive (③) and oversubscribed, and food, though good, is not cheap either.

Mália

The resort of **MÁLIA**, 31km east of Iráklio, is very commercial, and the long sandy beach becomes extremely crowded at times, but it's fun if you're prepared to enter into the sybaritic spirit of things. There are dunes at the end of the beach where people sleep out, plus a **youth hostel** signposted just off the main road. The cheapest rooms are in the old town – the hostel has lists. Ditto for tavernas, but avoid the ones lining the road to the beach, which is better as a raucous nightlife venue.

The **Palace of Mália** (Tues–Sun 8.30am–3pm; 800dr; student discounts) lies forty minutes' walk east of Mália town along the beach or on the main road – any bus will stop there. It's a great deal easier to comprehend than Knossos, and if you've seen the reconstructions there, it's easy to envisage this seaside palace in its days of glory. Look out for the strange indented stone in the central court, which probably held ritual offerings; for the remains of ceremonial stairways; and for the giant *pithoi* (ceramic jars) which stand like sentinels around the palace. Moving on, you should have no difficulty flagging down a bus headed towards Áyios Nikólaos.

Áyios Nikólaos and around

ÁYIOS NIKÓLAOS is set around a supposedly bottomless salt lake, now connected to the sea to form an inner harbour. It is supremely picturesque, and exploits this fact to the full. Both the lake and the port are surrounded by restaurants and bars, all of which charge well above normal, and the town itself is permanently crammed with tourists, many of whom are distinctly surprised to find themselves in a place with no decent beach. If you're after clubs, crowds and souvenirs, though, this is the place for you. Finding a cheap **room**, however, is virtually impossible in mid-season. Undeniably central, but a grim last resort, is the **youth hostel** at Stratigoú Koráka 3 (②), immediately northeast of the lake. Better to walk up the hill on one of the roads leading out northeast of town and try for rooms in all the side streets. There's also a collection of somewhat run-down places on the other side of town near the bus station. The **tourist office**, at the outlet of the lake, has exhaustive accommodation lists.

The riviera set tends to hang out along the coast road north towards ELOÚNDA, a resort on a more acceptable scale. Buses cover the 8km regularly, and it's a spectacular ride with a series of impeccable views over a gulf dotted with islands and moored supertankers. From Eloúnda *kaíkia* run to the fortress-rock of SPINALÓNGA. As a bastion of the Venetian defence, this tiny islet withstood the Turkish invaders for 45 years after the rest of Crete had fallen; in more recent decades it served as a leper colony.

The other bus excursion most visitors to Áyios Nikólaos take goes inland to KRITSÁ, about 10km away. Despite the rampant commercialization it's still a good trip: the local crafts are fair value and it provides a welcome break from living in the fast lane at "Ag Nik", with the possibility of staying in **rooms** here. On the approach road some 2km before Kritsá stands the lovely Byzantine church of **Panayía Kirá** (Mon–Sat 9am–3pm, Sun 9am–2pm; 800dr; student discounts), whose fourteenth- and fifteenth-century frescoes have been much retouched, but still make the visit worth the effort.

Sitía and Vái beach

The port and main town of the relatively unexploited eastern edge of Crete, SITÍA offers a plethora of waterside restaurants, a long sandy beach and a lazy lifestyle little affected even by the thousands of visitors in peak season. You pass the excellent **youth hostel** (②) as you come into Sitía from Áyios Nikólaos on the main road, and there are a few rooms between here and the town. More pleasant options, though, can be found in the streets behind the northern stretch of the waterside, especially around the OTE. For **food**, the waterside places are expensive enough to make you careful about what you eat; there are cheaper options in the streets behind, such as *Erganos* at Dhimokrátou 4 or *Mixos* at Kornárou 117, while the two bars next to *Zorbas* do good *meze* deals.

Vái beach features on almost every Cretan travel agent's list of excursions and for years has also been a popular hangout for backpackers camping on the sands. This dual role has created something of a monstrosity, with the vast crowds divided into two hostile camps. The beach itself is famous above all for its palm trees, creating an illusion of a Caribbean island. If you do sleep out, watch your belongings – this seems to be the one place on Crete with crime on any scale. All this admitted, it is a superb beach, and the trip there is an enjoyable one, passing the **Monastery of Tóplou**, which has a gorgeous flower-decked cloister and one of the masterpieces of Cretan art, the eighteenth-century icon *Lord Thou Art Great*.

Réthimno

Since the mid-1980s, RÉTHIMNO has seen a greater influx of tourists than perhaps anywhere else on Crete, with the development of a whole series of large hotels extending almost 10km along the beach to the east. For once, though, the middle of town has been spared, so that at its heart Réthimno remains one of the most beautiful of Crete's major cities. A wide sandy beach and palm-lined promenade border a labyrinthine tangle of Venetian and Turkish houses lining streets where many of the old men still dress proudly in high boots, baggy trousers and black head-scarves. Medieval minarets lend an exotic air to the skyline, while dominating everything from the west is the superbly preserved outline of the fortress built by the Venetians after a series of pirate raids had devastated the town.

When you get off the bus, walk east around the fortress to get to the beach and the centre; the waterside **tourist information office** will be in front of you when you get to the beach. The best bet is probably to follow Arkadhíou, the street which curves around immediately inland from the beach, and then continue towards the fortress (Tues–Sun 8.30am–3pm). A good option among many is *Pension Anna* on Kateháki, by the fortress (☎0831/25 586; ②). If you can't find a room – quite likely in midsummer – the **youth hostel** at Tombázi 45 (☎0831/22 848; ①) is a passable alternative, or there are two **campsites** right next to each other about 4km east along the beach, with a frequent bus service.

There's an unbroken line of **tavernas**, cafés and cocktail bars right around the waterside and into the area around the old port, but the sea view comes at a price. You'll find an assortment of better-value tavernas around the Rimóndi Fountain; or try *Soumbousakis* at Nikifórou Fóka 98. Bars and **nightlife** concentrate in the same general area, particularly towards the western end of the town beach.

Haniá

HANIÁ, as any of its residents will tell you, is the spiritual capital of Crete; for many it is also by far the island's most attractive city – especially if you can catch it in spring, when the Lefká Óri's snowcapped peaks seem to hover above the roofs. Although it is for the most part a modern city, the small outer harbour is surrounded by a wonderful jumble of half-derelict Venetian streets which survived the wartime bombardments.

The **bus station** is on Odhós Kidhonías, within easy walking distance of the action – turn right, then left down the side of Platía 1866 and you'll emerge at a major road junction opposite the top of Hálidhon, the main street of the old quarter. **Arriving by boat**, you'll anchor about 10km from Haniá at the port of Soúdha: there are frequent city buses which will drop you by the market on the fringes of the old town.

The **port area** is as ever the place to start, the oldest and the most interesting part of town. The little hill which rises behind the tourist office/mosque is **Kastélli**, site of the earliest habitation and core of the Venetian and Turkish towns. Beneath the hill, on the inner harbour, the arches of sixteenth-century Venetian arsenals survive alongside remains of the outer walls. Following the esplanade around in the other direction leads to a hefty bastion which now houses Crete's **Maritime Museum** (Tues–Sun 10am–4pm; 500dr; students 300dr) – not exactly riveting, but wander in anyway for a look at the seaward fortifications. Walk around the back of these restored bulwarks to a street heading inland and you'll find the best-preserved stretch of the outer walls.

Behind the harbour lie the less picturesque but more lively sections of the old city. First, a short way up Hálidhon on the right is Haniá's **Archeological Museum** (summer Mon 12.30am–7pm, Tues–Fri 8am–7pm, Sat & Sun 8.30am–3pm; winter Tues–Fri 8am–3pm, Sat & Sun 8.30am–3pm; 500dr; students 300dr), housed in the Venetian-built church of San Francesco. Damaged as it is, this remains a beautiful building and a fine little display, even though there's nothing of outstanding interest. In the garden, a huge fountain and the base of a minaret survive from the period when the Turks converted the church into a mosque.

Around the nearby **Cathedral** – ordinary and relatively modern – are some of the more animated shopping areas, particularly leather-dominated **Odhós Skrídlof**, with streets leading up to the back of the market beyond. In the direction of the Spiántza quarter are ancient alleys which have yet to feel much effect of the city's modern popularity, still with tumbledown Venetian stonework and overhanging wooden balconies.

Haniá's **beaches** all lie to the west: the packed **city beach** is a ten-minute walk beyond the naval museum, but for good sand you're better off taking the local bus from the east side of Platía 1866 along the coast road to Kalamáki. In between you'll find emptier stretches if you're prepared to walk from Haniá.

Practicalities

The extremely helpful **tourist office** is in the new town at Kriari 40, by the front door. There seem to be thousands of **rooms** on offer in Haniá but high taxes have recently forced many of the cheaper ones out of business. *Pension Fidias* on Kalinikou Sarpaki 6, behind the cathedral (☎0821/524 94; ②), is exceptionally friendly and comfortable and, since the youth hostel closed down, is the only place in town to also offer dormitory beds (①). The *Kastelli*, Kanevário 39 (☎0821/57 057; ②), is another favourite, and the owner also rents out apartments for two to four people. There are two **campsites** to the west: *Camping Hania* (☎0821/31 138), just about within walking distance, and the bigger and better *Camping Ayia Marina* (☎0821/68 556), 10km out in the village of the same name.

Both the inner and outer harbours are circled by **cafés, tavernas** and **bars**, although most are totally overpriced. Heading east, around the port restaurants become noticeably cheaper. An excellent restaurant, well worth seeking out, is the *Tamam*, set in a Turkish bathhouse on Zambeliu, a small street just off Karaoli. Haniá's **market**, the finest in Crete, is not to be missed.

For **nightlife**, most of the action takes place in a series of bars around the harbour, particularly near Sarpidhóna on the inner port. If it all seems a bit raunchier than you'd expect, remember that these places cater to servicemen from the nearby NATO bases at least as much as to visitors. Haniá can also be a good place to catch **local music**, especially at the *Café Kriti*, Kallérgon 22.

The Samarian Gorge

From Haniá the beautiful **Gorge of Samariá** – Europe's longest – can be visited as a day-trip or as part of a longer excursion to the south. It's well worth catching the early bus at 6.15am to avoid the full heat of the day while walking through the gorge, though be warned that you will not be alone – there are often as many as four coachloads setting off before dawn for the nail-biting climb into the White Mountains.

The gorge (1200dr; children free) begins at a stepped path descending steeply from the southern lip of the Omalós Plain through almost alpine scenery of pines, wild flowers and un-Cretan greenery. At an average pace with regular stops, the eighteen-kilometre walk down takes four to six hours; solid shoes are vital. There's plenty of water from springs and streams (except in Sept & Oct some years), but nothing to eat. Small churches and viewpoints dot the route, and about halfway down you pass the abandoned village of **Samariá**, now home to a wardens' station, with picnic facilities and filthy toilets. Further down, the path levels out and the walls close in until at the narrowest point – the *Sidherespórtes* or "Iron Gates". Here one can practically touch both rock faces at once where the gorge narrows to a mere three-metre width, and, looking up, see them rising sheer for almost a thousand feet.

When you finally get down, the village of **AYÍA ROÚMELI** is all but abandoned until you reach the beach, a mirage of iced drinks and a cluster of expensive tavernas with equally pricey rooms to let. If you want to get back to Haniá, buy your **boat** ticket immediately, especially if you want an afternoon on the beach – the last boat tends to sell out first. You may find boats going to Soúyia rather than Hóra Sfakíon, owing to a local dispute; count your blessings, as Soúyia's a much better beach resort at which to wait for the bus to Haniá – or even stay.

travel details

Buses

Athens to: Corfu (4 daily; 11hr); Delphi (5 daily; 3hr); Halkídha (every 30min; 1hr 30min); Igoumenítsa (4 daily; 8hr 30min); Ioánnina (8 daily; 7hr 30min); Kefallonía (3 daily; 8hr); Kími (5 daily; 3hr 30min); Kórinthos (hourly; 1hr 30min); Lefkádha (4 daily; 5hr 30min); Mycenae (13 daily; 2hr 30min); Náfplio (13 daily; 2hr 30min); Olympia (10 daily; 5hr 30min); Pátra (every 30min; 3hr); Pílos (2 daily; 5hr 30min); Rafína (every 30min; 1hr 30min); Sounion (every 30min; 2hr); Spárti (9 daily; 4hr 30min); Thessaloníki (10 daily; 7hr 30min); Tríkala (7 daily; 5hr 30min); Trípoli (12 daily; 2hr 15min); Vólos (10 daily; 5hr 15min); Zákinthos (3 daily; 7hr).

Ioánnina to: Athens (14 daily; 7hr 30min); Igoumenítsa (10 daily; 2hr 30min); Metsovo (4 daily, 1hr 30min); Dodona (2 daily; 40min).

Igoumenítsa to: Párga (4 daily; 1hr 30min); Préveza (2 daily; 3hr).

Kalamáta to: Areópoli (4 daily; 1hr 30min); Kóroni (7 daily; 1hr 30min); Megalópoli (10 daily; 1hr); Methóni via Pílos (5 daily; 1hr 30min); Pátra (2 daily; 4hr); Pílos (8 daily; 1hr); Trípoli (10 daily; 1hr 45min).

Kórinthos to: Árgos (hourly; 1hr); Kalamáta (7 daily; 4hr); Mycenae (hourly; 30min); Náfplio (hourly; 1hr 30min); Spárti (8 daily; 4hr); Tíryns (hourly; 15min); Trípoli (9 daily; 1hr 30min).

Lamía to: Lárissa (4 daily; 3hr 30min); Tríkala, via Kardhítsa (4 daily; 3hr); Vólos (2 daily; 3hr).

Lárissa to: Kalambáka (hourly; 30min); Litóhoro junction (hourly; 1hr 45min); Tríkala (every 30min; 1hr 25min).

Náfplio to: Epidaurus (4 daily; 45min); Mycenae (3 daily; 30min); Trípoli (4 daily; 1hr).

Pírgos to: Kalamáta (2 daily; 2hr); Kiparissía (2 daily; 1hr); Olympia (hourly; 45min).

Thessaloníki to: Ierissós (7 daily; 3hr 30min); Ioánnina (6 daily except Tues; 7hr 30min); Kalambáka (4–5 daily; 4hr 30min); Kateríni for Mount Olympus (hourly; 1hr 30min); Kavála (hourly; 2hr); Ouranópoli (7 daily; 3hr 30min); Pella (hourly; 1hr); Vólos (4 daily; 4hr).

Tríkala to: Ioánnina (2 daily; 4hr); Kalambáka (hourly; 30min); Métsovo (2 daily; 2hr).

Trípoli to: Kalamáta (6 daily; 2hr); Kiparissía (2 daily; 2hr); Olympia (3 daily; 5hr); Pílos (2 daily; 3hr); Pírgos (3 daily; 3hr); Spárti (8 daily; 1hr 30min).

Vólos to: Lárissa (hourly; 1hr 30min); Makrinítsa (9 daily; 50min); Milés (6 daily; 1hr–1hr 10min); Portaría (9 daily; 40min); Thessaloníki (4 daily; 3hr 20min); Tríkala (4 daily; 2hr 30min); Vizitsu (6 daily; 1hr–1hr 10min); Zagorá (4 daily; 1hr 40min).

Trains

Athens to: Halkídha (17 daily; 1hr 30min); Kalamáta (3 daily; 7hr); Kalambáka via Pateofársala (7 daily; 5hr 30min); Kórinthos (14 daily; 1hr 30min–2hr); Mikínes (5 daily; 2hr 45min); Náfplio (5 daily; 3–3hr 30min); Pátra (9 daily; 3hr 30min); Thessaloníki (10 daily, 1 sleeper; 4–8hr); Vólos (8 daily; 5–6hr 30min).

Thessaloníki to: Alexandhroúpoli (2 daily; 7hr); Litóhoro (6 daily; 1hr 40min); Vólos (4 daily; 30min).

Vólos to: Athens (8 daily; 5–7hr); Kalambáka (4 daily; 4hr); Lárissa (13 daily; 1hr).

Ferries

Astakós to: Itháki (1 daily; 1hr 45min); Kefalloniá (2 daily; 3hr 30min).

Áyios Konstantínos to: Skópelos (11 weekly; 5hr).

Híos to: Lésvos (7 weekly; 4hr); Sámos (2 weekly; 4hr).

Íos to: Náxos (1 daily; 3hr); Páros (1 daily; 5hr); Thíra (1 daily; 2hr).

Iráklio to: Páros (3 weekly; 7hr); Ródhos (2–3 weekly; 11hr).

Kavála to: northeast Aegean and Dodecanese islands (1–3 weekly); Thássos (7–11 daily).

Kefalloniá to: Zákinthos/Porros (2–4 weekly in summer).

Killíni to: Kefalloniá (3 daily; 1hr 30min); Zákinthos (6 daily; 1hr 30min).

Kími to: Skíros (1 daily; 2hr 30min).

Kós to: Pátmos (4 weekly; 5hr); Ródhos (2 daily; 4hr).

Lésvos Híos (5–7 weekly; 4hr); Kávala (2 weekly; 15hr); Thessaloníki (2 weekly; 15hr).

Náxos to: Íos (1 daily; 3hr); Iráklio (2 weekly; 6hr); Páros (1 daily; 1hr); Thíra (1 daily; 4hr).

Pátra to: Corfu (3 daily; 7–9hr); Itháki (1 daily; 4–5hr); Kefalloniá (1 daily; 4–5hr).

Pireás to: Crete (2–4 daily; 12hr); Híos (3 weekly; 10hr); Íos (3–6 daily; 10hr); Kós (16 weekly; 12hr); Lésvos (5–7 weekly; 14hr); Míkonos (2 daily; 5hr); Náxos (4 daily; 8hr); Páros (4 daily; 7hr); Ródhos (19 weekly; 18–23hr); Sámos (13 weekly; 11–14hr); Sífnos (12 weekly; 6hr); Thíra (2–7 daily; 10–12hr).

Rafína to: Míkonos, Síros, Páros, Náxos (2 daily; 3–7hr); Kós & Ródhos (3 weekly; 18hr total).

Ródhos to: Crete (2 weekly; 13hr); Kálimnos (2 weekly; 5hr); Kós (2 daily; 4hr); Pátmos (2 weekly; 8hr).

Sámos to: Kálimnos (2–3 weekly; 8hr); Pátmos (6 weekly; 5hr).

Thessaloníki to: Híos (2 weekly; 15hr); Iráklio (3 weekly; 21hr); Lésvos (2 weekly; 15hr); Skíros (2 weekly; 7hr); Skópelos (3 weekly; 6hr).

Thíra to: Íos (1 daily; 2hr); Iráklio, Crete (3 weekly; 5hr); Míkonos (1 daily; 7hr); Náxos (1 daily; 4hr); Páros (2 daily; 5hr).

Vólos to: Skíathos (3–4 daily; 3hr); Skópelos (2–3 daily; 4hr).

Zákinthos to: Killíni (6 daily; 1hr 30min).

CHAPTER 13

HUNGARY

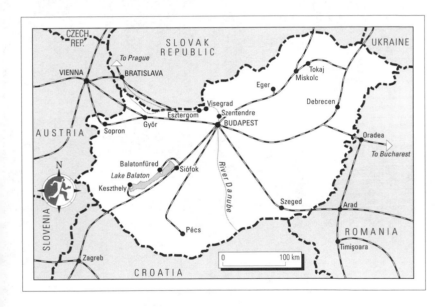

Introduction

Visitors who refer to **Hungary** as a Balkan country risk getting a lecture on how this small, landlocked nation of 10,136,000 people differs from "all those Slavs": locals are strongly conscious of themselves as Magyars – a race that transplanted itself from Central Asia into the heart of Europe. Hungary was in the vanguard of the dissolution of communist hegemony in eastern Europe. Its decision to open its borders in 1989 and let East Germans out to the West precipitated the fall of the repressive regimes in East Germany, Romania and Czechoslovakia.

The magnificent capital, **Budapest**, with its coffee houses, Turkish baths, and the fad for Habsburg bric-a-brac, has a strong whiff of *Mitteleuropa* – that ambient culture that welcomed Beethoven in Budapest and Hungarian-born Liszt in Vienna, a culture currently being revived in a new form by writers, film directors, artists and other media figures. But there is also a hungry modern feel as international fashions are snapped up and adapted to local tastes.

After Budapest, **Lake Balaton** and the **Danube Bend** vie for popularity. The Balaton, with its string of brash resorts, styles itself as the "Nation's Playground" and enjoys a fortuitous proximity to the Badacsony wine-producing region. The Danube Bend has more to offer in terms of scenery and historic architecture, as do the Northern Uplands and Transdanubia. **Sopron** and **Pécs** are rightfully the main attractions in Transdanubia, while in the uplands it's the famous wine centres of **Tokaj** and **Eger** that draw most visitors.

Information and maps

A large number of photo-packed brochures, maps and leaflets are available from **Tourinform**, the Hungarian National Tourist Office's chain of offices that you will find in Budapest and in larger towns across the country. The Tourinform staff have a reputation for being helpful and speaking English and are the recommended source of information wherever they have an office. The office in Budapest is at Sütő utca 2, behind the big yellow Lutheran church at Deák tér (May–Oct daily 9am–7pm; Nov–April Mon–Fri 9am–7pm, Sat & Sun 9am–4pm). Most Tourinform offices do not handle booking of accommodation, though they do have information on where rooms and beds are available. The most useful publications they produce are the booklet detailing the year's festivals and events, and two national lists of accommodation – *Hotel*, a small booklet, and *Camping*, a map of the country with a comprehensive list of camping facilities. These are now comple-mented by increasingly well-produced leaflets on accommodation and events in each region. Information is also available at the **local tourist offices** in larger towns (Savaria Tourist, Balaton Tourist, etc, according to the region), where you can also book rooms; opening hours are generally Mon–Fri 9am–6pm and Sat 8am–1pm, though in the winter months they may be closed at 4pm on weekdays and not open at all on Saturdays. Some good **map shops** in Budapest include: Cartographia, Pest VI, Bajcsy-Zsilinszky utca 37; Térképbolt, Pest VII, Nyár utca 1; and Térképkirály, Pest V, Sas utca 1.

Money and banks

Hungarian **forints** (Ft) come in notes of 200, 500, 1000, 2000, 5000 and 10,000Ft, with 1, 2, 5, 10, 20, 50, and 100 coins. The 50Ft coin is easily confused with the 10Ft coin, so watch your change. Changing money is best done at any regional tourist office, or at a bank; these usually give the best rates. You can also change at most large hotels, and there is a growing number of exchange offices, but these are often a rip-off – as is American Express. The black market offers little benefit and you can easily be cheated.

Budapest has a large number of ATMs, so that you can get money straight from the wall. More are appearing in larger towns across the country too, though you should not rely on finding one. Most brands of travellers' cheques and Eurocheques are accepted. Credit cards can be used to rent cars, buy airline tickets or pay your bills directly in many hotels, restaurants and tourist shops. Outside the main tourist centres their usefulness is more restricted.

Communications

Larger **post offices** (*posta*) are usually open Mon–Fri 8am–6pm, Sat 8am–1pm. Smaller branches close at 3pm and don't always open Saturdays. Mail from abroad should be addressed "Poste restante, Posta", followed by the name of the town – in Budapest you can use the main post office at V, Petőfi Sándor utca 13 (Mon–Fri 8am–8pm): Poste restante, Magyar Posta, 1364, Budapest. A more secure "drop" – for American Express cardholders, or those using their services – is the American Express bureau at V, Deák Ferenc utca 10. It's quicker to buy stamps (*bélyeg*) at tobacconists (*trafik*) – post offices often have long queues and staff are not always helpful.

Local calls can be made from public **phones**, where 20Ft is the minimum charge (40Ft if you are calling a mobile phone number). **Cardphones** are better – they are increasingly common, and you have less chance of losing your money; you can buy cards of 50 or 120 units in post offices and newsstands. Alternatively you can use the Countrydirect phone services offered by the Hungarian or other telephone companies. To call direct to other parts of the country, dial ☎06, wait for the buzzing tone, then dial the area code and subscriber number. All phones can be used for direct **international calls**, or alternatively you can phone through the Telephone Bureau, upstairs at Petőfi Sándor utca 17–19, in Budapest or through hotels.

Getting around

Although it doesn't break any speed records, **public transport** reaches most parts of Hungary, and fares remain very cheap. The only problem is getting information, for staff rarely speak anything but Hungarian, although German is spoken around Lake Balaton.

■ Trains

The centralization of the MÁV rail network means that many cross-country journeys are easier if you travel via Budapest. The new network of intercity **trains** is the fastest way of getting from Budapest to Debrecen, Eger, Esztergom, Keszthely, Miskolc, Pécs, Sopron, Tokaj and other destinations. Seat reservations are compulsory on intercity trains (the charge is an extra 320Ft) and all international trains, but not for *személyvonat*, which halt at every hamlet en route; reservations can be made through any MÁV office. Most international, intercity and some express trains have buffets – but it is best to take food and drink with you if you are going on a long trip; except for some slower trains there is usually a first-class (*elsőosztály*) section; international services through Budapest have sleeping cars and couchettes (*hálókocsi* and *kusett*). **Tickets** (*jegy*) for domestic services can be bought at the station (*pályaudvar* or *vasútállomás*) on the day of departure, but it's best to buy tickets for **international trains** (*nemzetközi gyorsvonat*) at least 36 hours in advance. You can break your journey once between the point of departure and the final destination. When buying your ticket, specify whether you want a one-way ticket (*egy útra*), or a return (*retur* or *oda-vissza*).

InterRail and Eurail passes are both valid. MÁV itself issues various **season tickets**, valid on domestic lines for one week or ten days, but you'd need to travel intensively to make savings with a seven-day national Runaround (8940Ft).

■ Buses

Regional **Volán** ("Wheel") companies run the bulk of Hungary's **buses**, which are often the quickest way to travel between towns. Schedules are clearly displayed in bus terminals; arrive early to confirm the departure bay and ensure getting a seat. For long-distance services originating from Budapest or major towns, you can buy tickets with a seat booking up to 30min before departure; after that you get them from the driver and risk standing throughout the journey. Services in rural areas may be limited to one a day, and tickets are only available on board.

■ Driving and hitching

To **drive** in Hungary you'll require an international driving licence, Green Card insurance and third-party insurance. Speed limits are 50kph in town, 80–100kph on main roads and 120kph on motorways. You can get 24hr breakdown assistance from the Magyar Autóklub (☎088 national breakdown service) provided you are insured. **Car rental** costs from $500 per week with unlimited mileage. Cars are available through Budget, Avis, Hertz and a number of others as well as from hotel reception desks, both the Budapest airport terminals and certain tourist offices.

Hitchhiking is widely practised by young Magyars, and only forbidden on motorways.

Accommodation

The cost of **accommodation** in Hungary has gone up dramatically in recent years, but there is plenty of it. More upmarket accommodation tends to quote prices in Deutschmarks; private rooms and hostels charge in local currency. The cheapest places tend to fill up during high season (June–Sept), so it's wise to make bookings if you're bound for somewhere with limited accommodation.

■ Bungalows and campsites

Throughout Hungary, campsites and bungalows come together in complexes. **Bungalows** (*faház*) proliferate around resorts and on the larger campsites; prices depend on their amenities and size. The first-class bungalows – with well-equipped kitchens, hot water and a sitting room or terrace – are excellent, and will cost a few thousand Forint, while the most primitive at least have clean bedding and don't leak. **Campsites** – usually signposted *Kemping* – likewise range across the spectrum from "de luxe" to third class. The more elaborate places include a restaurant and shops and tend to be overcrowded; second- or third-class sites often have a nicer ambience. Expect to pay anything up to 1500 Ft (more around Lake Balaton) in high season.

ACCOMMODATION PRICE CODES

Throughout this guide, accommodation is priced on a scale of ① to ⑨, the number indicating the lowest price per night a single person could expect to pay in that establishment in high season. With hostels this is the nightly rate per person; with hotels, the price is arrived at by dividing the cost of the cheapest double room by two. The prices indicated by the codes are as follows:

① under £5 / $8	④ £15–20 / $24–32	⑦ £30–35 / $48–56
② £5–10 / $8–16	⑤ £20–25 / $32–40	⑧ £35–40 / $56–64
③ £10–15 / $16–24	⑥ £25–30 / $40–48	⑨ £40 / $64 and over

■ Hostels

A cheaper option is **hostels**, which go under various names. In provincial towns they're called *Túristaszálló*, but in the highland areas they go by the name of *Túristaház*. Local tourist offices can give you details and handle bookings. They can also guide you to college dormitories, which are usually even better budget-wise: rooms are rented out in July and August, but can often be taken at weekends throughout the year too.

■ Private rooms

Private rooms (*fizető vendégszoba*) are a cheaper way of staying near the centre, and often quite appealing. Such accommodation can be arranged by local tourist offices for a small fee; otherwise deal direct with the owner (who'll advertise *szoba kiadó* or *Zimmer Frei*). Doubles range from 1500Ft in provincial towns to around 4500Ft in Budapest or around the Balaton; singles usually pay the full double rate, though there may be a small reduction. Rooms in a town's Belváros (inner sector) are likely to be much better than those in outlying zones.

It's possible to rent whole apartments in some towns and resorts, while regional tourist offices can arrange home accommodation through the village tourism (*Falusi turizmus*) network, the central office of which is in Budapest at VII, Király utca 93 (☎1/352-1433).

■ Hotels

Three-star **hotels** (*szálló* or *szállóda*) have become the most common category, with de luxe four- and five-star establishments still mainly confined to Budapest and major resorts, and humble one- and two-star joints getting rarer. Outside Budapest and Lake Balaton (where prices are thirty percent higher), a three-star hotel will charge from around DM70–100 for a double room with bath, TV, etc; solo travellers often have to pay this too, since singles are rare. The same goes for four-star or two-star hotel rooms; luxury hotels in Budapest charge cheaper rates during winter. A similar rating system is used

for **inns** (*fogadó*) and **pensions** (*panzió*), which charge a little less than hotels, though prices in the middle range often turn out very similar.

Food and drink

For foreigners the archetypal Hungarian dish is "goulash" – historically a soup made of potatoes and whatever meat was available, which was later flavoured with paprika and beefed up into a variety of stews, modified over the centuries by various foreign influences.

■ Food

As a nation of early risers, Hungarians like a calorific **breakfast** (*reggeli*) that includes cheese, eggs or salami plus bread and jam. Though **coffee houses** are no longer at the centre of Budapest's cultural and political life, you'll find plenty of *kávéház* serving the beverage with milk (*tejeskávé*) or whipped cream (*tejszínhabbal*).

A whole range of places sell **snacks**, including the delicatessens (*Csemege*) and the bakeries, which display a tempting spread of salads, open sandwiches, pickles and cold meats. Numerous **patisseries** (*cukrászda*) pander to the Magyar fondness for sweet things. Pancakes (*palacsinta*) with fillings are very popular, as are strudels (*rétes*) and a staggering array of cakes and other sticky items.

On the streets you can buy corn on the cob (*kukorica*) in summer or roasted chestnuts (*gesztenye*) in winter; while fried fish (*sült hal*) stalls are common in towns near rivers or lakes. Sandwich (*szendvics*) and hamburger stands are mushrooming in the larger towns, and **in markets** you'll also find various greasy spoons.

Traditionally, Hungarians take their main meal at midday. At lunchtime, some eating places offer **set menus** (*napi menü*), a basic meal at moderate prices. Keep an eye on prices – you can pay exorbitant amounts for not very much, and gone are the days when even the top restaurants were cheap; but there are still plenty of places where you can eat well and sink a few beers for 1000Ft. Always check your bill carefully as foreigners are a common target for being ripped off. (A recent series of scandals has revealed foreigners being lured into bars and restaurants in central Budapest and being charged exorbitant rates and then being threatened when they refused to pay. So check the menu prices beforehand too.)

Starters (*előételek*) range from soup (*leves*) to the popular *Hortobágyi palacsinta* (pancakes stuffed with mince and doused in a creamy paprika sauce) and the more extravagant *Libamáj* (goose liver), though nobody will mind if you just have a **main course** (*főételek*). The outlook for **vegetarians** is poor: aside from cooked vegetables (notably *rántott gomba* or *rántott sajt* – mushrooms or cheese in breadcrumbs), often the only meatless dishes are various permutations of eggs.

Hungarians have a variety of words implying fine distinctions among restaurants. In theory an *étterem* is a proper restaurant, while a *vendéglő* approximates to the Western notion of a bistro; however, these distinctions are very thin now. The old word for a roadside inn, *csárda*, is often used today of touristy, folksy restaurants.

■ Drink

Hungary's mild climate and diversity of soils is perfect for **wine** (*bor*), which is perennially cheap, whether you buy it by the bottle (*üveg*) or the glass (*pohár*). **Wine bars** (*borozó*) are ubiquitous and generally far less pretentious than in the West; while true devotees of the grape make pilgrimages to the extensive **wine cellars** (*borpince*) around towns like Tokaj and Eger. **Spirits** are cheap, if you stick to native brands. The best-known types of **brandy** (*pálinka*) are distilled from apricots (*barack*) and plums (*szilva*), the latter often available in private homes in a mouth-scorching home-distilled version. **Beer** (*sör*) of the **lager** type (*világos*) predominates, although you can also find **brown ale** (*barna*): these come in draught form (*csapolt sör*) or in bottles (*üveges sör*). Local brands to look out for are *Pécsi Szalon sör* and *Soproni Ászok*. Western brands are imported or brewed under licence.

Opening hours and holidays

Opening times for most public buildings are Mon–Fri 8.30am–4pm; smaller places usually close for an hour at lunchtime. Museums are generally open Tues–Sun 10am–6pm or 9am–5pm, and some have free admission over the weekends. **Public holidays** are: Jan 1; March 15; Easter Monday; May 1; Whitsun Monday; Aug 20; Oct 23; Dec 25 & 26.

Emergencies

The Hungarian **police** (*Rendörség*) are badly paid and under-trained which doesn't make for good policing. However, foreign tourists are handled with kid gloves unless they're suspected of black-marketeering, drug smuggling or driving under the influence of alcohol. Most police officers have at least a smattering of German, but rarely any other foreign language. Should you be arrested or need legal advice, ask to contact your embassy or consulate.

All towns and some villages have a **pharmacy** (*gyógyszertár* or *patika*), with staff – often German-speaking – authorized to issue a wide range of drugs. However, anyone requiring specific medication should bring a supply with them. Opening hours are normally Mon–Fri 9am–6pm, Sat 9am–noon/1pm; signs in the window give the location or telephone number of all-night (*éjjel*) pharmacies

Tourist offices can direct you to local medical centres or doctors' surgeries (*orvosi rendelő*), while your embassy in Budapest will have the addresses of **doctors** and **dentists**, who'll probably be in private (*magán*) practice, so you should check on prices.

EMERGENCY NUMBERS
Police ☎107; Ambulance ☎104; Fire ☎105.

BUDAPEST

The importance of **BUDAPEST** to Hungary is difficult to overestimate. Around two million people – one-fifth of the population – live in the city, and everything converges here: wealth, political power, cultural life and transport. Surveying the city from Castle Hill, it's obvious why Budapest was dubbed the "Pearl of the Danube". Its grand buildings and sweeping bridges look magnificent, especially when floodlit or illuminated by the barrage of fireworks launched from Gellért Hill on St Stephen's Day. The inner city and the nineteenth-century boulevards are now under siege from Western fashions and advertising, but they retain a distinctively Hungarian character, which for visitors is highlighted by the sounds and appearance of the distinctive Magyar language.

Castle Hill (Várhegy) is the most prominent feature of the Buda district, a plateau one mile long laden with bastions, old mansions and a huge palace, commanding the Watertown. Its grandiosity and strategic utility have long gone hand in hand: Hungarian kings built their palaces here because it was easy to defend, a fact appreciated by the Turks, Habsburgs, and most recently the Nazis, so that the castle has had to be almost wholly reconstructed from the rubble of 1945.

Buda and its twin, Pest, have a surfeit of other fine sights; museums and galleries, restaurants and bars abound, and there's a wide variety of entertainments accessible by efficient, cheap public transport. A host of new nightclubs and rave haunts mean that the city is making up for its dreary postwar past, though it is still true to say that many people rise early and call it a day at around 10pm, interrupting their labours with breaks in patisseries and *eszpresszó* bars. Perhaps the best way to ease yourself into the life of Budapest is to wallow away an afternoon in one of the city's **thermal baths** (*gyógyfürdő*). For 2000 years people have appreciated the relaxing and curative effects of the mineral water from the Buda Hills, currently gushing at a rate of about 70,000,000 litres per day, at temperatures of up to 80°C. A basic ticket covers three hours in the pools, sauna and steamrooms (*gözfürdő*) while supplementary tickets are available for such delights as the mud baths (*iszapfürdő*) and massages (*masszázs*).

Arrival and information

The Danube (Duna) determines basic **orientation**, with Pest sprawled across the eastern plain and Buda reclining on the hilly west bank. The Belváros constitutes the city centre and the hub of Pest, while Castle Hill is the historic focal point of Buda. Each of Budapest's 23 districts (*kerületek*) is designated on maps, street signs and addresses by a Roman numeral – V is Belváros, I the Castle district. Most points of arrival are fifteen to thirty minutes from the centre. Keleti, Déli and Nyugati, the main **train stations**, are directly connected by metro to Deák tér in the Belváros. Across the road from Deák tér metro lies the Erzsébet tér **bus station**, where the half-hourly shuttle from **Ferihegy airport** (600Ft from Ferihegy Terminals 2A and 2B) and international buses arrive. Pest's Népstadion and Árpád híd bus terminals are further out, but still on the metro; while hydrofoils from Vienna dock right alongside the Belváros embankment.

At the earliest opportunity, get hold of a proper **map of the city**; tourist offices supply small freebies, but far better is the Budapest Atlas, available from newsstands in Deák tér metro, or some bookshops. Leaving aside the business of finding accommodation, the best source of practical information is the friendly polyglot staff of **Tourinform** (May–Oct daily 9am–7pm; Nov–April Mon–Fri 9am–7pm, Sat & Sun 9am–4pm; ☎1/317-9800), just around the corner from Deák tér metro at Sütő utca 2. Other useful offices are those of the **IBUSZ** tourist office at Ferenciek tere 10 (Mon–Fri 8.15am–5pm; ☎318-1120) and **Budapest Tourist**, at Roosevelt tér 5 by the Chain Bridge (☎317-3555), and Baross tér 3 (☎333-6587), across from Keleti train station (both Mon–Fri 9am–4pm). For the latest on what's on, check out the weekly *Budapest Sun* or *Where Budapest*, a free guide to the month's events available in many hotel foyers.

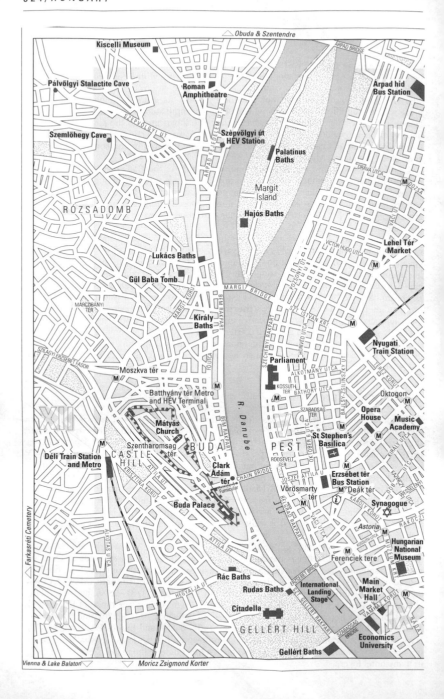

△ *Obuda & Szentendre*

Kiscelli Museum

Pálvölgyi Stalactite Cave

Roman Amphitheatre

ARPAD BRIDGE

Árpad hid Bus Station

Szemlöhegy Cave

SZEPVÖLGYI UT

Szépvölgyi út HÉV Station

Palatinus Baths

XIII

DRAVA UTCA

Margit Island

RÓZSADOMB

Hajós Baths

II

Lehel Tér Market

Lukács Baths

VICTOR HUGO UTCA

VI

Gül Baba Tomb

MARCZIBANYI TER

MARGIT BRIDGE

Nyugati Train Station

Király Baths

SZILAGYI ERZSEBET FASOR

Moszkva tér

Parliament

KOSSUTH TER

BATHORY UTCA

Oktogon

Batthyány tér Metro and HÉV Terminal

R. Danube

SZABADSAG TER

Opera House

Music Academy

XII

Mátyás Church

BUDA

PEST

St Stephen's Basilica

Szentharomsag tér

CASTLE HILL

Déli Train Station and Metro

Clark Adám tér

ROOSEVELT TER

CHAIN BRIDGE

JOZSEF ATTILA U

Erzsébet tér Bus Station

Deák tér

Vörösmarty tér

Buda Palace

Synagogue

Astoria

Farkasréti Cemetery

Ferenciek tere

Hungarian National Museum

ALKOTAS UTCA

KRISZTINA KORUT

ATTILA UT

Rác Baths

HEGYALJA UT

Rudas Baths

International Landing Stage

Main Market Hall

XI

Citadella

ELZEBET BRIDGE

GELLÉRT HILL

IX

Economics University

▽ *Moricz Zsigmond Korter*

Gellért Baths

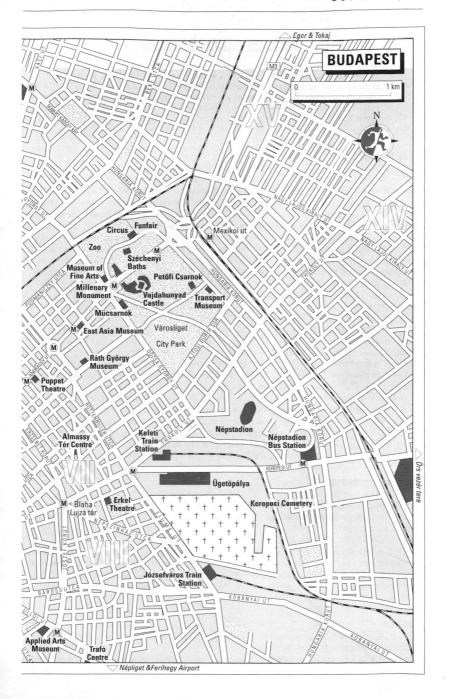

△ *Eger & Tokaj*

BUDAPEST

M3

0   1 km

XV

N

XIV

NAGY LAJOS KIRÁLY ÚT

NAGY LAJOS KIRÁLY ÚT

Mexikoi ut Ⓜ

Circus   Funfair

Zoo

Széchenyi Ⓜ
Baths

Museum of
Fine Arts

Petőfi Csarnok

Millenary Ⓜ
Monument

Vajdahunyad
Castle

Transport
Museum

Mücsarnok

Ⓜ East Asia Museum   Városliget

City Park

Ⓜ

Ráth György
Museum

Ⓜ Puppet
Theatre

Almassy
Tér Centre

Keleti
Train
Station

Népstadion

Népstadion
Bus Station

Ⓜ

KEREPESI ÚT   Ⓜ

Ⓜ

Ügetőpálya

Ⓜ< Blaha
Lujza tér

Erkel
Theatre

+ + + + + + +
+ + + + + + +
+ + + + + + +
+ + + + + + +
+ + + + + + +
+ + + + + + +

Kerepesi Cemetery

VIII

Józsefváros Train
Station

KÖBÁNYAI ÚT

BÁROSS UTCA

Ⓜ

Applied Arts
Museum

Trafó
Centre

▽ *Népliget &Ferihegy Airport*

▷ *Őrs vezér tere*

HUNGÁRIA KÖRÚT

HUNGÁRIA KÖRÚT

KÖBÁNYAI ÚT

THE BUDAPEST CARD

If you are cramming in a lot of sightseeing and making plentiful use of public transport, you might consider investing in a **Budapest Card**. A three-day card costs 2950 Ft and gives you unlimited travel on public transport, free admission to a long list of museums, reductions on the airport minibus, car rental, certain sightseeing tours and cultural events, and discounts in some shops, restaurants and thermal baths. There is also a two-day card for 2450 Ft. Cards are available at tourist offices, hotels and major metro station ticket offices.

City transport

Running between 4.30am and 11.15pm, the metro is the easiest way of getting around. Its three lines intersect at Deák tér, and there's little risk of going astray once you've learned to recognize the *bejárat* (entrance), *kijárat* (exit), *vonal* (line) and *felé* (towards) signs. A basic 90Ft ticket is valid for a journey along one line, and is also valid for a single journey on **buses** (*busz*), **trolley-buses** (*trolibusz*), **trams** (*villamos*) and the **HÉV suburban train** as far as the city limits. On the metro you can get various other kinds of tickets for short journeys, and combination tickets for transferring to another metro line. Rather than queueing at a metro station, it's quicker to buy tickets from street stands, tobacconists or newsagents. Tickets have to be punched in the machines at the entrances of metro stations, or once on board buses, trolleybuses and trams.

Buses with red numbers make limited stops, while the red suffix "E" denotes buses running nonstop between termini. Buses run every ten minutes or so during the day (as do trams and trolleybuses) and every thirty to sixty minutes between 11pm and dawn along those routes with a **night service** (denoted with the black suffix "É"). When the metro or trams are not running on a line, you'll find buses (*potlóbusz*) operating in their place.

If you plan to travel round the city a lot, it might be worth getting a day pass (700Ft) or buying a book of ten tickets (810Ft) – do not tear the tickets out, as they are only valid if kept together in the book. For longer stays there are travel passes for three days (1400Ft), a week (1750Ft) or a month (3400Ft). For the last two you will also need a passport-size photo for an identity card. They are available from metro stations.

Taxis are cheap, but are also a common rip-off. The ones from the airport are most notorious – take the **airport minibus**, which takes you to where you are staying (1200Ft), or the bus that runs between the airport and the centre. If you do use a taxi, go for Fötaxi (☎1/322-2222), Teletaxi (☎1/355-5555), or English-speaking Citytaxi (☎1/211-1111), charging a basic fee of 100Ft plus 150–170Ft per kilometre; they can be hailed in the street, but are cheapest if you order them by phone, giving the number you are phoning from.

Accommodation

Hotels are generally expensive in Budapest, and many of the better places expect payment in Deutschmarks. For **hotel bookings**, you should contact Danubius-HungarHotels, V, at Petőfi Sándor utca 16 (☎1/318-3018), and V, Szervita tér 8 (☎1/317-3652); IBUSZ, V, Ferenciek tere 10 (☎1/318-1120); or American Express, V Deák Ferenc utca 10 (☎1/235-4330), which charges a $20 service fee. For inexpensive **private rooms**, go to the IBUSZ or Budapest Tourist offices (see "arrival and information"). Another budget option is to book a **hostel** bed through the Tourist Information Centre (☎1/343-0748) in Keleti Station, or the youth travel agency Express at V, Semmelweis utca 4 (Mon–Thurs 8.30am–noon & 12.45–4.30pm, Fri 8.30am–noon & 12.45–3pm; ☎1/317-8600).

Hostels

Back Pack, XI, Takács Menyhért utca 33 (☎1/385-8946). Tram #49 or Bus #7 to Tétényi út stop, out in Buda. Five- and eight-bed dorms. ③.

Citadella, I, Citadella sétány (☎1/466-5794). First-choice hostel, with breathtaking views of the city, but you have to get there early to get a bunk. Bed in dorms ③, bed in double ④.

Diáksport Szálló, XIII, Dózsa György út 152 (☎1/340-8585). Open all year. Bed in dorms ②, bed in double ②.
Landler, XI, Bartók Béla út 17 (☎1/463-3621). Tram #47 or #49 from Deák tér (M1/2/3). An older hostel with high ceilings near the Gellért Baths, housed in the Baross Gábor Kollégium. Open July & Aug. ②.
Strawberry Youth Hostel, IX, Ráday utca 43–45 (☎1/218-4766, booking on ☎06-209/528-724). Kálvin tér on the blue metro line. The older of two *Strawberry Hostels* near Kálvin tér, with basic student hostel furniture but tall spacious rooms with rooms of two to six beds or dormitories. Internet access and discounts for HI card holders. Open July & Aug. ②.
Teréz Guest House, VIII, Bezerédj utca 6 (☎1/333-2452). Best budget option, with home cooking too. On the second floor of a big old block near Blaha Lujza tér on the red metro line, it consists of two rooms in a private flat, jam-packed with beds and mattresses on the floor. Parking available in courtyard. ①.

Hotels and pensions

ELTE Peregrinus Vendégház, V, Szerb utca 3 (☎1/266-4911). Located in a quiet back street in central Pest, this is a friendly, elegant place attached to the university; 25 rooms. ④.
Jager-Trio Panzió, XI, Ördögorom út 20 (☎1/246-4558). Small pension on the edge of the city in the Buda hills, close to the end of the bus #8 route. Open all year. ②.
Medosz, VI, Jókai tér 6 (☎1/374-3000). Ugly building, but comfortable – and in a good location near the Octogon. ③.
Victoria, I, Bem rakpart 11 (☎1/201-8644). Pleasant, small hotel on the embankment directly below the Mátyás Church, with excellent views of the Chain Bridge and the river. Rooms have minibar, TV and air-conditioning. Sauna and garage facilities. ⑦.
San Marcó Panzió, III, San Marcó utca 6 (☎1/388-9997). Small, friendly pension in northern Buda. ②.

Private rooms and apartments

Private rooms in downtown areas cost only 2500–4000Ft a night and are often the cheapest option. Besides the above agencies (see under hotels) you can also try the small To-Ma Travel Agency at V, Október 6, utca 22 (☎1/353-0819). A copy of the Budapest Atlas is handy for checking the location of prospective sites: preferable locales are Pest's V, VI and VII districts, and the parts of Buda nearest Castle Hill. **Apartments**, rented out for 7000Ft a night, are perfect if there are several of you. They're not as common as rooms, but you should be able to find a tourist office with one on its books.

Campsites

Csillebérci Camping, XII, Konkoly Thege M. út 21 (☎1/395-6537). A short walk from the last stop of the #21 bus from Moszkva tér. Large, well-equipped site with space for 1000 campers, open year-round. A range of bungalows also available.
Zugligeti Niche Camping, XII, Zugligeti út 101 (☎1/200-8346). Bus #158 from Moszkva tér. Occupies a disused tram cutting in the hills – the site restaurant used to be the terminus. Open April–Oct.

Buda

Seen from the embankments, **Buda** looks irresistibly romantic with its palatial buildings, archaic spires and outsize statues rising from rugged hills. To experience its centre – Castle Hill – at its quasi-medieval best, come in the early morning before the crowds arrive. Then you can beat them to the museums, wander off for lunch or a Turkish bath, and return to catch streetlife in full swing during the afternoon.

Castle Hill

There are several approaches to **Castle Hill** from Pest, starting with a breezy walk across the Chain Bridge to Clark Ádám tér, where you can ride up to the palace by the nineteenth-century funicular or **Sikló** (daily 7.30am–10pm; 200-250Ft). Otherwise, take the red metro line to Moszkva tér and the mini *Várbusz* from there; or get off at the previous stop, Batthyány tér, and start walking.

By midday, **Trinity Square** (Szentháromság tér), the heart of the Castle district, is crammed with tourists, buskers, handicraft vendors and other entrepreneurs, a multilingual spectacle played out against the backdrop of the wildly asymmetrical **Mátyás Church** (Mátyás templom). The church is a riotous nineteenth-century re-creation of the medieval spirit, grafted onto those portions of the thirteenth-century structure that survived the siege of 1686, having served as a mosque during the Turkish occupation. An equestrian statue of **King Stephen** stands just outside the church, commemorating this ruler who forced Catholicism onto his subjects, thus aligning Hungary with the culture of Western Europe. The **Fishermen's Bastion** (Halászbástya; 100Ft) nearby is an undulating white rampart with gargoyle-lined cloisters and seven turrets, which frames the view of Parliament across the river.

Medieval architectural features have survived along **Országház utca** (Parliament Street), at the northern end of which the quasi-Gothic **Mary Magdalene Tower** still dominates Kapisztrán tér, albeit gutted and transformed into an art gallery. To the south of Szentháromság tér the street widens as it approaches the **Buda Palace**. The fortifications and dwellings built by Béla III after the thirteenth-century Mongol invasion were replaced by ever more luxurious palaces; the most recent reconstruction dates from after the devastation wrought by World War II. Grouped around two courtyards, the sombre wings of the palace contain a clutch of museums and portions of the medieval structures discovered in the course of excavation. The northern wing (Wing A) houses the **Museum of Contemporary Art (Ludwig Collection)** (Tues–Sun 10am–6pm; 100Ft, free Tues), with a collection that includes well-known names like Picasso, Hockney and Lichtenstein as well as pieces by younger Hungarian artists such as Attila Szűcs. The **National Gallery** (Tues–Sun 10am–4/6pm; 300Ft, free Wed), occupying the central wings B, C, & D, contains Hungarian art since the Middle Ages. Gothic stone-carvings, altars and painted panels fill the ground floor, while nineteenth-century painting, including major Hungarian artists such as Csontváry, Rippl-Rónai, and Munkácsy, dominates the floor above. On the far side of the Lion Courtyard, the **Budapest History Museum** in Wing E (Mon & Wed–Sun 10am–4/6pm; 250Ft, free Wed) gives the whole history of the territory that makes up the city, from its pre-history on the top floor down to the marbled and flagstoned halls of the Renaissance palace deep underground.

The Watertown and Gellért Hill

The busy square at the foot of the Sikló takes its name from Adam Clark, the engineer who completed the **Chain Bridge**, which was opened in 1849 and was the first permanent bridge between Buda and Pest. To the north of the bridge lies the **Watertown** (Víziváros) district, a wedge of narrow streets, some gas-lit, that was once a poor quarter housing fishermen, craftsmen and their families. Today it's a reclusive neighbourhood of old blocks and mansions meeting at odd angles upon the hillside, reached by alleys which mostly consist of steps rising from the main street, Fő utca. North along Fő utca stand the **Király baths** (Mon–Fri 6.30am–7pm & Sat 6.30am–noon; men only Mon, Wed & Fri; women only Tues, Thurs & Sat; 450Ft), distinguishable by the four copper cupolas shaped like tortoise shells.

To the south of Watertown, the tall Liberation Monument crowns the summit of **Gellért Hill** (Gellérthegy), named after Bishop Ghirardus, who converted the Magyars to Christianity at the behest of King Stephen. A statue of the bishop bestrides a waterfall facing the Erzsébet Bridge, marking the spot where he was murdered in 1064 by vengeful heathens following the demise of his royal protector. Near the foot of the bridge, puffs of steam and cute little cupolas surmount the **Rudas baths** (for men only Mon–Fri 6.30am–7pm & Sat 6am–1pm; 450Ft), Budapest's most atmospheric Turkish baths, whose interior has hardly changed since they were constructed in 1556. On the other side of the Hegyalja út flyover, the **Rác baths** (Mon–Sat 6am–6pm; 450Ft) were also built during the Turkish occupation, but largely modernized with the exception of the pool; unlike the Rudas it's open to women (Mon, Wed, Fri) as well as men (Tues, Thurs, Sat).

Every August 20 an amazing barrage of fireworks is launched from the hilltop **Citadella**, a low fortress built by the Habsburgs to cow the population after the 1848–49 revolution. Nowadays the fort contains nothing more sinister than a few exhibits, a tourist hostel, a dismal disco/bar, and an overpriced restaurant. The **Liberation Monument** thrusts over a hundred feet into the sky, a stark female figure holding aloft the palm of victory. Originally commissioned by Admiral Horthy – a reluctant ally of the Reich – in memory of his own son, it was adapted to suit the requirements of the Soviet liberators.

Descending the hillside through the playgrounds of Jubileumi Park, you'll see rough-hewn stone figures seemingly writhing from the massive portal of the **Gellért baths**, at the side of the *Hotel Gellért*. The best-publicized of the city's baths, they were built in 1913, and the grandeur of the entrance hall is continued in the main pool (Mon–Fri 6am–7pm, Sun 6am–5/7pm; thermal baths Oct–April 6am–2pm; May–Sept 6am–5pm; 1200Ft). In summer its terrace and wave pool are packed.

Pest

Pest, busier and more vital than Buda, is the place where things are decided, made and sold. Much of the architecture and general layout dates from the late nineteenth century, when boulevards, public buildings and apartment houses were built on a scale appropriate to the Habsburg Empire's second city and the capital of Hungary, which celebrated its 1000th anniversary in 1896. The **Belváros** revels in its cosmopolitanism, with shops selling Nikons and French perfume, posters proclaiming the arrival of Western films and rock groups, and streets noisy with the sound of foreign cars and languages. **Ferenciek tere** is the area's centre, its approach from the Erzsébet Bridge flanked by the twin Clothild palaces, a last flourish of the empire. Overlooking the square stands a slab of gilt and gingerbread architecture, the Párisi udvar, home to an ice cream parlour and a big IBUSZ office, but chiefly known for its "Parisian arcade" adorned with arabesques and stained glass.

The city's most chic shopping street is **Váci utca**, running parallel to the river and thronged with people strolling past its cafés and boutiques. Passing the Pesti Theatre, where twelve-year-old Liszt made his concert debut, the crowds flow onto **Vörösmarty tér**, haunt of portraitists, conjurers, violinists and other performers. While children play in the fountains, their elders congregate around the statue of the poet and translator Mihály Vörösmarty (1800–1855). Underfoot lies continental Europe's first underground train system, opened in 1896: the **Millennial Railway** (metro line 1), which runs beneath Andrássy utca up to Heroes' Square. However, the most venerable institution on Vörösmarty tér is the *Gerbeaud* patisserie, the favourite of Budapest's high society since the late nineteenth century, and now packed with tourists.

The quieter part of Váci utca runs south of Ferenciek tere: more recently pedestrianized, it has yet to acquire the touristy commercialism of the northern section. The southern end of the street opens out to reveal the **Main Market Hall** (*Nagycsarnok*) with its fancy ironwork, porcelain tiles, and stalls festooned with strings of paprika and garlic. Ever since the visit of Mrs Thatcher in 1984, who impressed the locals by haggling with the stallholders, this has been a regular port of call for visiting statespersons.

Peering over the rooftops to the north of Vörösmarty tér is the dome of **St Stephen's Basilica**; like that of the Parliament, its dome is 96m high – an allusion to 896, the year of the Magyar conquest, and in summer you can get a good view over the city from the top (daily: April & May 10am–5pm; June–Aug 10am–7pm; Sept & Oct 10am–6pm; 300Ft). On his name day, August 20, St Stephen's mummified hand and other holy relics are paraded round the building; the rest of the year, the hand is on show in a chapel behind the altar (100Ft to illuminate the relic).

To the east of the Basilica, **Andrássy utca** runs dead straight for two and a half kilometres, a parade of grand buildings laden with gold leaf, dryads and colonnades, including the magnificent Opera House at no 22. Its shops and sidewalk cafés retain some of the style that made the avenue so fashionable in the 1890s. The boulevard culminates at **Heroes' Square** (Hősök tere), erected to mark the thousandth anniversary of the Magyar conquest. Its centrepiece is the **Millennary Monument**, portraying Prince Árpád and his chieftains grouped around a 36-metre-high column topped by the Archangel Gabriel, and half encircled by a colonnade displaying statues of Hungary's most illustrious leaders, from King Stephen to Kossuth. The **Museum of Fine Arts** on the square (Tues–Sun 10am–4/6pm; 500Ft) contains Egyptian funerary relics, Greek and Roman ceramics, and paintings and drawings by European masters from the thirteenth to the twentieth century – including Dürer, El Greco, Velázquez and Bronzino.

Back towards the centre of the Belváros, on the corner of Wesselényi and Dohány utca, stands the dramatic main **Synagogue**, whose Byzantine-Moorish architecture has been undergoing much-needed restoration; the interior is now complete and utterly magnificent. In the **National Jewish Museum** next door (Mon–Fri 10am–2pm, Sun 10am–1pm), exhibits dating back to the Middle Ages are opposed by a harrowing Holocaust exhibition, which casts a chill over the third section, portraying Jewish cultural life today. In the streets behind the synagogue lies Pest's main **Jewish quarter**. In recent years the small Jewish community that survived the Holocaust has become much more visible in the city, although even here, where the community is strongest, it keeps a low profile. Along Dob utca there is a kosher coffee shop at no. 22, and at no. 35, by the entrance to the orthodox community buildings, a kosher butcher's; in Kazinczy utca you can get kosher bread (at no. 28) and sausage (at no. 41) and the wine merchant in the basement at Klauzál tér 16 also sells excellent kosher plum brandy (*slivovitz*).

South of the synagogue, **Múzeum körút** (Museum Boulevard) resembles Andrássy út in miniature, with its trees, shops and grandiose stone buildings. The **Hungarian National Museum** at no. 14 (Magyar Nemzeti Múzeum; Tues–Sun 10am–4/6pm; 250Ft) covers the history of Hungary since the Magyar conquest, with an excellent section on the twentieth century. There are captions and explanatory texts in English, as well as info-touch machines giving extra information on exhibits. The most prestigious exhibit is the Coronation Regalia, reputedly the very crown, orb and sceptre used by King Stephen. The regalia is now thought to be a combination of two crowns used by Stephen's successors, but has come to be seen as a symbol of Hungarian statehood.

Eating and drinking

Magyar cooking naturally predominates in Budapest, but the capital has a growing number of places devoted to international cuisine. Prices by Western standards are very reasonable, and your budget should stretch to at least one binge in a top-flight place providing you're otherwise Forint-conscious. The following categories – patisseries (for non-alcoholic drinks and a sweet tooth), restaurants (for eating), and taverns and brasseries (for drinking) – are to an extent arbitrary, since all restaurants serve alcohol and all bars serve some food, while *eszpresszós* (cafés) feature both, plus coffee and pastries.

Patisseries

Angelika, I, Batthyány tér 7. Quiet atmosphere in former convent. Daily 10am–8pm.

Bécsi Kávéház (Viennese Coffee House) *Inter-Continental Hotel*, V, Apáczai Csere János utca 12–14. Excellent cakes in not so tasty surroundings. Daily 9am–9pm.

Eckermann, VI, Andrássy út 24. Big coffees and Internet terminals in this café next to the Goethe Institute. Mon–Fri 8am–10pm, Sat 9am–10pm.

Fröhlich, VII, Dob utca 22. A kosher patisserie five minutes' walk from the Dohány utca synagogue, presided over by the cheery Mrs Fröhlich and her daughter. Mr Fröhlich appears from time to time covered in flour in his cake-stained overalls bearing specialities like *flodni* (an apple, walnut and poppy-seed cake). Tues–Thur 8am–5pm, Fri 8am–2pm, closed Jewish holidays.

Gerbeaud's, V, Vörosmarty tér 7. Now in private hands, which has meant improvements in service and cakes, as well as a glossy refurbishment. A coffee and a torte will set you back around 500Ft; the same rich pastries are cheaper in *Kis Gerbeaud* around the corner, a less sumptuous annexe. Gets unbearably full in summer. Daily 9am–9pm.

Múzeum Cukrászda, VIII, Múzeum körút 10. Friendly 24-hour hangout by the National Museum. Fresh pastries arrive at 6–7am.

Müvész, VI, Andrássy út 29. Another grand coffee house – less crowded and cheaper than *Gerbeaud's*. Daily 8am–midnight.

Ruszwurm's, I, Szentháromság utca 7. Excellent cakes, served production-line fashion to those taking a break from sightseeing on Castle Hill, who crowd its diminutive interior. Daily 10am–8pm.

Fast food, self-service and snack bars

Duran Sandwich bar, V, Október 6 utca 15. A sandwich and coffee bar – still a rare combination in Budapest, oddly enough. Mon–Fri 8am–6pm, Sat 9am–1pm.

Falafel, VI, Paulay Ede utca 53. Best of the city's falafel joints. Mon–Fri 10am–8pm, Sat 10am–6pm.

Gresham Borozó, V, Mérleg utca 2. Good Hungarian food and fast service in this popular place by the Pest end of the Chain Bridge. It's usually packed at lunchtime and you may have to wait or share a table. Mon–Fri 7am–10pm, Sun 8am–4pm.

Izes Sarok, V, Bajcsy-Zsilinszky út 1. On the edge of Erzsébet tér. If you don't mind standing up, this is a nice place to breakfast on sandwiches, coffee and juice. Mon–Fri 8am–5pm

Marie Kristensen Sandwich Bar, IX, Ráday utca 7. The Danish flavour is hard to spot, but this is basically a decent regular sandwich bar behind Kálvin tér. Mon–Fri 10am–8pm.

New York Bagels, Bajcsy Zsilinszky út 21 and (for a great view) 8th floor of the East–West Centre opposite the *Astoria Hotel*. Serves New-York-style bagels and fillings. Bajcsy Zsilinszky út Mon–Fri 8am–10pm, Sat & Sun 9am–10pm; East–West Centre Mon–Fri 8am–6pm.

Self-service canteen, V, Szende Pál utca 3. Standard Hungarian food at this super-cheap lunch spot just round the corner from Vörösmarty tér. Mon–Fri noon–3pm.

Restaurants

Al-Amir, VII, Király utca 17 (☎352-1422). Syrian restaurant serving excellent salads and hummus, making it a haven for vegetarians in a city of carnivores. If that isn't enough, the array of Arabic sweets is very enticing. No alcohol served. Daily 11am–11pm.

Bagolyvár, XIV, Állatkerti körút 20 (☎1/321-3550). Sister to the expensive top-bracket *Gundel* next door, but offering traditional Hungarian family-style cooking at lower prices. Daily noon–11pm.

Berlini Sörkatakomba, IX, Ráday utca 9. Smoky cellar restaurant by the Kálvin tér metro. Genial atmosphere; popular with a student crowd. Daily 11am–2am.

Café Kör, V, Sas utca 17 (☎311-0053). Popular establishment near the Basilica with a continental feel, airy open plan and fine street view. Menu supplemented by specials written up on the wall. Essential to book. Mon–Sat 10am–10pm.

Chez Daniel, VI, Szív utca 32 (☎1/302-4039). Excellent French restaurant, the best in town, run by idiosyncratic master chef. Booking recommended. Daily noon–3pm & 7–10.30pm.

Csarnok, V, Hold utca 11. Unshowy and inexpensive, serving traditional Hungarian food. Small terrace in summer. Close to Arany Janos utca on the blue metro line. Open daily 10am–midnight.

Fausto's, VII, Dohány utca 5 (☎1/269-6806). Stylish and expensive Italian joint with homemade pasta and fine wines. Daily noon–3pm & 7pm till midnight.

Gandhi, V Vigyázó Ferenc utca 4. An oasis of spiritual calm in the city serving a range of international vegetarian dishes. Daily noon–10.30pm.

King's Hotel, VII Nagydiófa utca 25–27 (☎352-7675). Mehadrin kosher food in the old Jewish ghetto, five minutes' walk from the Dohány utca synagogue. Daily noon–9.30pm.

Kiskacsa, VII, Dob utca 26. Friendly small joint ten minutes up from the big synagogue, serving traditional Hungarian fare. You get three dice with your bill and if you roll three sixes your meal is on the house. Mon–Sat noon–midnight.

Krónikás, XIII, Tátra utca 2 (☎269-5048). Excellent, moderately priced cellar-restaurant just off the Szent István körút near the Margit híd. Good range of vegetarian dishes. Mon–Sat noon–midnight.

Márkus Vendéglő, II, Lövőház utca 17. Friendly and cheap Hungarian restaurant near Moszkva tér. Daily 11am–1am.

Marquis de Salade, VI, Hajos utca 43, just off Bajcsy Zsilinszky út. Large portions of foods from a wide range of cuisines in a cellar grandly decorated with oriental carpets. No credit cards. Daily 11am–midnight.

Náncsi Néni, II, Ördögárok út 80 (☎1/397-2742). Popular garden restaurant in the leafy Hsvösvölgy, ten minutes' walk from the terminus of bus #56. Live music and excellent food. Booking advisable. Daily noon–11pm.

Múzeum Kávéház, VIII, Múzeum körút 12 (☎1/338-4221). Excellent, pricey food in this beautiful nineteenth-century coffee house next to the National Museum. Booking essential. Mon–Sat 10am–1am.

Okay Italia, XIII, Szent István körút 20. Italian-run place, serving pizzas and fresh pasta. Daily noon–midnight; kitchens close at 11.30pm.

Bars, wine bars and beer halls

Bambi, I, Bem tér. Wonderful old socialist bar serving breakfast, snack lunches, dry-looking cakes, and alcohol. Open till 8/9pm.

Cafe Mediterrán, VI Liszt Ferenc tér. Laid-back bar right near the Music Academy with the Undergrass nightclub right underneath it. Open till 2am.

Café Miro, I, Uri utca 30. A trendy bar in the Castle district which often has live music and is open till midnight.

Darshan Udvar, VIII, Krudy Gyula utca 7. The largest bar in a growing complex of bars, cafés and shops. Set at the back of the courtyard, with oriental/hippie decorations, good food and world music, but leisurely service. Mon–Wed 11am–midnight, Thurs & Fri 11am–2am, Sat & Sun 6pm–midnight

Gusto's, II, Frankel Leo utca. Minute bar near Buda side of Margit Bridge, serving the best tiramisu in town. Open till 10pm.

Kisposta, XII, Krisztina körút 6. Atmospheric local dating from the Sixties with regulars dancing to old-style music. Open till 1am.

Libella, XI, Budafoki út 7. Friendly bar near the Gellért Baths with bar snacks, chess and draughts. Attracts a younger alternative crowd. Mon–Sat 8am–11pm, Sun 10am–11pm.

Miniatűr Eszpresszó, II, Rózsahegy utca 1. Small bohemian bar with red velvet furnishings and piano music after 9pm. If you win approval from the woman who presides over the place, you get to sit in the inner room by the pianist. Open till 3am.

Móri Borozó, I, corner of Hattyú utca and Fiáth János utca. Typical inexpensive and cheerful neighbourhood wine-bar, in the backstreets north of Castle Hill. Mon–Sat 2–11pm, Sun 2–9pm (June–Aug 4–11pm).

Rácz Kert Söröző, I, Hadnagy utca 12, by the Rác Baths. This place on the edge of the Tabán is one of the few places where you can drink outside after 10pm. Excellent atmosphere and good bar snacks and food – that is, if the licence is reissued this year. March–Oct daily from 5pm until customers leave.

Sixtusi Kápolna, VII, Nagydiófa utca 24. The "Sistine Chapel" is rather like the brown bars of Amsterdam, attracting a friendly crowd of non-business ex-pats. There is no street sign announcing the place, just two steamed up windows. Mon–Sat 6pm–1am. Usually closed in mid-August during the Sziget Festival.

Entertainment and nightlife

Star events in the capital's cultural year are the **Budapest Spring Festival** (two weeks in March or April) and the **Autumn Music Weeks** (late Sept to late Oct), both of which attract the cream of Hungary's artists and top international acts. There's hardly less in the way of concerts and the like during the summer months. On **St Stephen's Day** (Aug 20) the area around the Royal Palace becomes one big folk and crafts fair, and in the evening the population lines the embankments to watch a fantastic display of fireworks from Gellért Hill.

You'll have to check the posters and listings publications for information regarding rock concerts. The **Petőfi Csarnok** in the Városliget (✆1/342-4327), the **Almássy tér Cultural Centre** at VII, Almássy tér 6 (✆1/267-8709), the **Trafó** at IX, Liliom utca 41, a revamped transformer station in Pest, and the **Fonó** at XI, Sztregova utca 3 (✆1/206-5300) in Buda are four of the main venues for alternative concerts, folk music and modern dance events, while big foreign acts merit an athletics stadium. Tickets for most events can be obtained through the Filharmonia Ticket office, Mérleg utca 10 (Mon–Fri 10am–6pm; ✆1/318-0281); the Central Booking Office, VI, Andrássy út 18, for classical music; Music Mix at V, Váci utca 33 (✆1/338-2237); and Publika at VII, Károly körút 9 (✆1/322-2010) for rock and jazz.

New **clubs and discos** are opening all the time, and the rave and floating party scene is growing constantly – check flyers and posters around town. In the summer there are weekend parties outside the city in the Buda hills and caves (special buses shuttle people to and fro), and Tilos raves, organized by the pirate Tilos Radio, at the Petőfi Csarnok and other venues, which are worth looking out for. There are also a variety of **student clubs**, where drinks are cheap and the crowd young.

Nightclubs

Angyal, VII Szövetség utca 33, Budapest's premier gay club, looks like an airport lounge but has an interesting crowd.

Capella, V Belgrád rakpart 23. Drag queens, jungle music and lots of tat: just the place for Friday night on the town.

E-Play, VI Teréz krt 55. Housed in the top of the magnificent Nyugáti Station, this newly decked-out techno haunt is for the fast and flashy.

Franklin Trocadero Café, V, Szent István körút 15. Excellent Latin music and dancing just up from Nyugáti Station.

Garage Café, V, Arany János utca 9. Cool, spacious and hip bar with a restaurant serving excellent food. Wednesday night, featuring house DJ Tommy Boy and other top DJs, is the best night for dancing. Daily 11am–2am.

Nincs Pardon, VIII Almássy tér 11. Unpretentious cellar with Seventies hits and friendly service.

Süss Fel Nap, V, Honvéd utca 40. Heaving, lively place attracting a young crowd.

Vox, II Márcibányi tér 5/a. Live acts and funky music in this popular dive on the Buda side.

Listings

Bus terminals The central bus station is at Erzsébet tér, by the Deák tér metro station, with services to Ferihegy airport, international destinations and routes to Transdanubia (☎1/317-2318); Népstadion (red metro; ☎1/252-4498) serves areas east of the Danube; and Árpád híd (blue metro) serves the Danube Bend.

Car rental All the main car rental companies also have offices in both the airport terminals. Those with offices in town include: Budget at the *Hotel Mercure Buda*, I, Krisztina körút 41-43 (☎1/214-0420); Europcar at VIII, Üllői út 60-62 (☎1/313-1492); and Hertz at Marriott Hotel, V, Apáczai Csere János utca 4 (☎1/266 4361).

Cybercafés Internet connections are on the increase in Budapest, although the experience at cybercafés can be frustrating, with long queues and very slow machines. *Eckermann Café*, VI, Andrássy út 24, near the Opera House (Mon–Fri 2pm–10pm, Sat 10am–10pm), offers access to the Internet at no charge. Other cybercafés include *Kommunikációs Szaküzlet Internet Rock Café*, IX, Mester utca 57 (*www.comfort.hu/*); *Internext Studio*, VIII, Horánszky utca 26 (*www.inext.hu/*); *Matávnet*, V, Petőfi Sándor utca 17-19 (Mon–Fri 8am–8pm, Sat 9am–3pm; ☎1/318-1897), which is a cyber office rather than café; and the *Teleport Internet Café*, VIII, Vas utca 7 (Mon–Sat noon–10pm; ☎1/267-6361), a café with snacks, just off Rákóczi út, which has the advantage of the use of a printer.

Dry cleaning at Ametiszt, East-West Business Center, VIII, Rákóczi út 1-3.

Embassies and consulates Australia, XII, Királyhágó tér 8-9 (☎1/201 8899); Canada, XII, Budakeszi út 32 (☎1/275-1200); Great Britain, V, Harmincad utca 6 (☎1/266-2888); USA, V, Szabadság tér 12 (☎1/267-4400).

Exchange Best rates are at the Gönc és vidék bank at V, Rákóczi út 5, while around Vörösmarty tér in central Pest you are best advised to head for the Magyar Külkereskedelmi Bank at Türr István utca at the top of Váci utca. There is a 24hr service in the tourist office at V, Apáczai Csere János utca 1 by the *Marriott Hotel*.

Hospital There are 24hr casualty departments at V, Hold utca 19, behind the US embassy (☎1/311-6816), and at II, Ganz u 13-15 (☎1/202-1370). Profident, VII, Károly krt 1 is a round-the-clock English-speaking dentist. Embassies can also recommend private, English-language-speaking doctors and dentists.

Pharmacy There's a 24-hour service in each district – details are posted on pharmacy doors. Central 24hr pharmacies are at Alkotás utca 1/b, opposite Déli station, and at Rákóczi utca 86, near Keleti station.

Post offices Main office at V, Petőfi utca 13 (Mon–Fri 8am–8pm, Sat 8am–2pm). The post office by Keleti Station at VII, Baross tér 11C is open daily 7am–9pm.

Telephones International calls can be made from most phone boxes, though you can do it without feeding in coins and cards at the Telephone and Telegram Bureau, V, Petőfi utca 17–19 (Mon–Fri 7am–9pm, Sat 7am–8pm, Sun 8am–1pm), or, more expensively, from the more up-market hotels.

Travel agents Vista Travel, VI, Andrássy út 1(☎1/269-6032); Travel Unlimited, VIII, Rákóczi út 1/3 (☎1/266-8919).

THE DANUBE BEND

Entering the Carpathian Basin, the Danube widens hugely, only to be forced by hills and mountains through a narrow, twisting valley – almost a U-turn – before parting for the length of Szentendrei Island and flowing into Budapest. To escape Budapest's humid summers, people flock to this region, known as the **Danube Bend** (Dunakanyar), where the historic attractions are **Szentendre**, **Esztergom** and **Visegrád**. Szentendre, forty minutes' journey by HÉV **train** from Batthyány tér in Budapest, is the logical place to start, though with hourly **buses** from the capital's Árpád híd terminal, you could travel directly to Visegrád or Esztergom, the heart of Hungarian Catholicism. Travelling **by boat** can be fun, but it takes five hours from Budapest to Esztergom. It's better to sail only part of the way, say between the capital and Szentendre (1hr 40min), or Visegrád and Esztergom (1hr 30min), or take the hydrofoil to Esztergom (weekends only, June–Aug.)

Szentendre

Having cleared the bus and HÉV stations and found their way into its Baroque heart, visitors are seldom disappointed by **SZENTENDRE**. Ignoring the outlying housing estates and the rash of Nosztalgia and Folklór boutiques in the centre, it's a friendly maze of houses painted in autumn colours, secretive gardens and alleys leading to hilltop churches – the perfect spot for an artists' colony. Before the artists moved in at the turn of the century, Szentendre's character was largely shaped by Serbians seeking refuge from the Turks. Their town houses – now converted into galleries, shops and cafés – form a set piece around Fő tér, a stage for musicians, mimes and other events.

The **Blagovestenska Church** – whose iconostasis by Mikhail Zivkovia suggests the richness of the Serbs' artistry and faith – is first stop on the heritage trail, while just around the corner at Vastagh György utca 1 stands the wonderful **Margit Kovács Museum** (Tues–Sun 10am–6pm), displaying the lifetime work of Hungary's best-known ceramicist, born in 1902. Above Fő tér there's a fine view of Szentendre's steeply banked rooftops and gardens from the hilltop **Templom tér**, where frequent craft fairs help finance the restoration of the parish church. Opposite this, paintings whose fierce brush strokes and sketching were a challenge to the canons of classicism during the 1890s hang in the **Béla Czóbel Museum** (mid-March to Oct Tues–Sun 10am–4pm; Nov to mid-March Fri–Sun 10am–4pm), beyond which the spire of the **Serbian Orthodox Cathedral** pokes above a walled garden. Tourists are generally not admitted, but you can see the cathedral iconostasis and treasury in the adjacent museum (mid-March to Oct Wed–Sun 10am–4pm; Nov to mid-March Fri–Sun 10am–4pm).

An hourly bus runs from the HÉV terminal out along Szabadságforrás út to Szentendre's **Village Museum** (Szabadtéri Múzeum; April–Oct Tues–Sun 9am–5pm), which has reconstructed villages from four regions of Hungary (more are planned) – and is already a fascinating place. The brochure on sale at the gate points out the finer distinctions between humble peasant dwellings like the house from Kispalad and the cottage from Uszka, formerly occupied by petty squires. During the summer, on alternate weekends, people demonstrate traditional craft techniques, like pottery, baking and basket-making.

The best place for information is **Tourinform**, Dumsta Jenő utca 22 (Mon–Fri 9am–5pm, Sat & Sun 10am–4pm; ☎26/317-965). The staff are friendly, speak English and can provide information about accommodation, though they don't make bookings. While fast-food joints and **restaurants** – such as the *Aranysárkány* at Alkotmány utca 1/a and the *Rab Ráby* at Péter-Pál utca 1 – are concentrated around the station and the centre, **accommodation** is mainly in the north of town: the best budget options are the *Aradi Panzió*, Aradi utca 4 (☎26/314-274; ①) near the HÉV station; and *Ilona Panzió*, Rákóczi F. utca 11 (☎26/313-599; ②), in a pleasant location in the centre of town – or whatever IBUSZ, Bogdányi utca 11 (☎26/310-181), can arrange in the way of private rooms. A lot of people end up camping, either on Szentendrei Island or on Pap Island to the north of town – accessible by ferry and bus respectively. Although ferries, leaving from the pier ten minutes' walk upriver from the centre, are the coolest way of travelling north, buses are quicker and more frequent.

Visegrád

During the fifteenth-century reign of Mátyás and Beatrice the palace at **VISEGRÁD** was famed throughout Europe. After the Turkish occupation Visegrád declined, gradually turning into the humble village that it is today. However, the basic layout of the settlement – the stunning Citadel on the hill, and the ruins of the once grand palace down by the river – hasn't altered significantly.

The ruins of the **Palace** are spread over four levels behind the gate of 27 Fő utca. Nothing remains of the building founded by the Angevin king Charles Robert, but the *cour d'honneur* built for his successor Louis can still be seen on the second terrace. Its chief features are a

Renaissance loggia and two panels from its Hercules Fountain. From the decrepit **Water Bastion** just north of the main landing stage – where the boats from Budapest and Esztergom arrive – a rampart ascends the slope to **Solomon Tower**, a mighty hexagonal keep buttressed by concrete slabs. Inside, the tower's **Mátyás Museum** (May–Oct Tues–Sun 9am–4pm) houses finds from the excavated palace, including the white Anjou Fountain and the red marble *Visegrád Madonna*.

Visegrád's most dramatic feature is the imposing **Citadel** on the mountain top; though only partly restored, it is still mightily impressive, commanding a superb view of Nagymaros and the Börzsöny Mountains to the east bank. You can reach it by the Kálvária footpath which begins behind the church on Fő tér, or by catching a bus from the Mátyás statue on Fő utca, which follows the scenic Panorama út. From the car park on the summit, the road leads on up to the luxury *Hotel Silvanus*, and then to the Nagy-Villám observation tower, where you'll get a view that stretches into the Slovak Republic.

During high summer you might have problems finding somewhere to **stay** – ask at the only **tourist office** in the place, the rather unfriendly Visegrád Tours (April–Oct daily 8.30am–5.30pm; Nov–March Mon–Fri 10am–4pm; ☎26/398-160), next to the touristy *Sirály* restaurant near the Nagymaros ferry pier in the centre of town; or try Bauer Folk Art (☎26/316 469; May–Sept 10am–5pm), Fő utca 46. If the grander *Mátyás tanya* at Fő utca 47, near the palace (☎26/398-309; ④), does not appeal, there is the more homely *Haus Honti* at Fő utca 66, which also rents out bikes (☎26/398-120; ②); or one of the many private rooms advertised all over the place – look for the *Zimmer Frei* signs. The best two **restaurants** in the centre of town are the *Gulás Csárda* in Rév utca (just across from the church) and the less touristy *Diófa* restaurant nearby at Fő utca 48.

Esztergom

Beautifully situated in a crook of the Danube facing the Slovak Republic, enclosed by glinting water and soft hills, **ESZTERGOM** is dominated by its great basilica, whose dome is visible for miles around. The sight is richly symbolic, for although the royal court abandoned Esztergom for Buda after the Mongol invasion, this has remained the centre of Hungarian Catholicism since 1000, when Stephen – who was born and crowned here – imposed Christianity.

Completed in 1869, Esztergom's is the largest **Basilica** in Hungary: 118m long and 40m wide, capped by a dome 71.5m high. Its nave is on a massive scale, clad in marble, gilding and mosaics, with a collection of saintly relics in the chapel to the right as you enter. A ticket is required to visit the crypt, which resembles a set from an old horror movie, with giant stone women flanking the stairway that descends to gloomy vaults full of prelates' tombs – including that of the conservative Cardinal Mindszenty, whose opposition to the liberalizing Kadar regime in the Sixties greatly embarrassed the Vatican. The treasury entrance is north of the altar, and having seen its overpowering collection of bejewelled crooks and chalices, it's almost a relief to climb the seemingly endless stairway to the bell tower and cupola.

On the same craggy plateau you'll find the ruins of the medieval **Palace** (Tues–Sun 9am–5pm) once occupied by Béla III, the widowed Queen Beatrice and sundry archbishops. You can visit the remains of a chapel with its rose window and Byzantine-style frescoes, Beatrice's suite and the study of Archbishop Vitéz – known as the Hall of Virtues after its allegorical murals. Below, the Baroque streets of the Watertown are connected by the sloping Bajcsy-Zsilinszky út to Rákóczi tér, the centre of downtown Esztergom. South of the Basilica, separated by a tributary of the Danube, is Primás-Sziget, where you'll find a hotel, a restaurant, boats to Budapest, ferries across the river to Sturovo in Slovakia, and the remains of a bridge that was destroyed at the end of World War II.

Practicalities

The Gran Tours **tourist office** (Mon–Fri 8am–4/6pm, Sat 9am–noon; ☎33/417-052) and the post office stand a short way south of the Basilica in Széchenyi tér. For **accommodation**, private rooms are probably the best budget option – ask at the tourist office or at IBUSZ at

Kossuth utca 5 (Mon–Fri 8am–4pm, Sat 9am–noon; ☎33/411-643). There are also student hostels in summer and pensions in the town: of these, *St Kristóf Panzió*, Dobozi Mihály utca 11 (☎33/416-255; ③), is the nicest and has a good restaurant attached, while the more basic *Platán Panzió*, Kis-Duna sétány 11 (☎33/411-355; ①) is attractively situated opposite Primás-Sziget. The nearest campsite is Gran Tours, on the Prímás-Sziget by the river (book through the Gran Tours office). There are some pleasant pavement **cafés** around Széchenyi tér; for **restaurants** try the *St Kristóf Panzió* (see above for address), the *Hotel Esztergom* on Nagy Duna sétány on the northern tip of Primás-Sziget, the *Csülök Csárda* offering gargantuan portions on Batthyány utca, or the *Szálma Csárda*, serving traditional Hungarian fare by the river, down past the truncated bridge.

WESTERN HUNGARY

The major tourist attraction to the west of the capital is **Lake Balaton**, over-romantically labelled the "Hungarian sea". Despite the fact that rising prices are pushing out natives in favour of Austrians and Germans, this is still very much the nation's playground, with vacation resorts lining both shores. On the northern bank, development has been limited to some extent by reedbanks and cooler, deeper water, giving tourism a different slant. Historic **Tihany** and the wine-producing **Badacsony Hills** offer fine sightseeing, while anyone whose social life doesn't take off in **Keszthely** can go soak themselves in the thermal lake at **Hévíz**.

More than other regions in Hungary, the western region of **Transdanubia** (Dunántúl) is a patchwork land, an ethnic and social hybrid. Its valleys and hills, forests and mud flats have been a melting pot since Roman times: settled by Magyars, Serbs, Slovaks and Germans; torn asunder and occupied by Turks and Habsburgs; transformed from a state of near feudalism into brutal collectives; and now operating under a modern capitalist form. All the main towns display evidence of this evolution, especially **Sopron**, with its well-preserved medieval centre, and **Pécs**, which boasts a Turkish mosque and minaret.

Lake Balaton

Given the over-development of the southern shore, you'll get the best out of **Lake Balaton** by catching one of the **trains** from Déli station to Balatonfüred; from there the route follows the northern shore to the Badacsony Hills, then north to Tapolca. Alternatively, catch one of the **buses** from Budapest's Erzsébet tér to the major lakeside towns. Hotels cost about the same as in Budapest, and private rooms cost 3000–5000Ft for a double. In addition, the shore is ringed with company holiday homes; it's always worth asking about spare rooms at these places, as they are often rented out at a reasonable price. Balaton campsites are Hungary's most expensive, though some sites drop their prices out of season. The lake goes quite dead out of season (Oct–March), which makes it pleasantly peaceful – but also means that most places are shut.

Balatonfüred

The Romans were the first to imbibe the curative waters of **BALATONFÜRED**, and nowadays some 30,000 people come every year for treatment in its sanatoriums. A busy harbour and skyscraper hotels dominate approaches to the town, but the centre has a sedate, convalescent atmosphere, typified by the embankment promenade, Rabindranath Tagore sétány, named after the Bengali poet who came here in 1926. Above the tree-lined promenade lies **Gyógy tér** (Healing Square), where you can drink the Kossuth spring's carbonic water at a pagoda-like structure. Four other springs feed the mineral baths on the eastern side, but these are only open for patients at the adjoining hospital.

For information on the town and surrounding region there is a **Tourinform** office at Petőfi utca 8 (☎87/342-237) and a Balatontourist office down by the pier (☎87/342-822). Balatonfüred's least expensive **accommodation** includes the *Korona Panzió*, Vörösmarty utca 4 (☎87/343-278; ③), a decent pension open year-round; the *Tagore*, by the lakeside at

Deák Ferenc utca 56 (☎87/343-173; ③; May–Oct); the *Blaha Lujza*, Blaha Lujza sétány 4 (☎87/343-700; ③); and the *Fortuna*, Huray utca 6 (☎87/343-037; ③). Better value private rooms can be arranged through Balatontourist, or IBUSZ, a few blocks from the station at Petőfi utca 4A (☎87/342-028). There are dormitory rooms at *Széchenyi Ferenc Kollégium* in Iskola utca, though those in the old town can be a long way from the water. There's a big **campsite** to the west of town, beyond the *Füred* and *Marina* hotels by the lakeside.

Tihany

The historic centre of **TIHANY**, the self-proclaimed "Pearl of the Balaton", sits above the harbour where the **ferries** from Siófok and Balatonfüred pull in; you'll find it by following the winding steps up between a screen of trees, and you'll know you've arrived by the mass of tourist boutiques and stalls that crowd the streets. The rail line bypasses the peninsula, so the alternative way of getting to the town is by **bus** from Balatonfüred.

Tihany's **Benedictine Abbey** was established in 1055 at the request of Andrew I, whose body now lies in the crypt. The church is embellished by the virtuoso woodcarvings of Sebestyén Stulhoff, who preserved the features of his fiancée in the face of the angel kneeling to the right of the altar of the Virgin. A few minutes' walk north from the abbey brings you to the **Open-Air Museum**, a collection of old cottages giving a feel of life in the village in the early twentieth century (Easter–Sept Tues–Sun 10am–6pm; 100Ft). Around Petőfi and Csokonai streets, houses are built of grey basalt tufa, with windows and doors outlined in white, and porticoed terraces. Even without a map it's easy to stumble upon **Belső-tó lake**, whose sunlit surface is visible from the abbey. From its southern bank, a path runs through vineyards, orchards and lavender fields past the Aranyház geyser cones and down to Tihanyi-rév.

Hotel prices, like everything else in Tihany, are exorbitant by Hungarian standards. The neighbouring campsite or private rooms are the only affordable **accommodation** – book at Balatontourist, Kossuth utca 20 (April–Oct Mon–Sat 8am–6.30pm, Sun 8am–1pm; Nov–March Mon–Fri 8am–4.30pm, Sat 8am–1pm; ☎87/448-519) or Tihany Tourist at Kossuth utca 11 (April–Oct Mon–Sat 9am–7pm; ☎87/448-481), up in the old town.

The Badacsony

For 30km west of Tihany the shoreline is lined with holiday homes and small resorts. The next main stop is the **Badacsony**, a hulk of rock with four villages prostrated at its feet, backed by extinct volcanoes ranged across the Tapolca basin. A great semicircle of basalt columns, 210m high, forms the Badacsony's southeastern face, while Kőkapu (Stone Gate) cleaves the northeast side, its two natural towers flanking a precipitous drop. The rich volcanic soil of the mountain's lower slopes has supported vineyards since the Avars buried grape seeds with their dead to ensure that the afterlife wouldn't lack wine. The region's (predominantly white) wine is celebrated in the annual wine festival (second week of Sept), when there is a procession, lots of folk-dancing – and, of course, lots to drink.

Developments are clustered around the southern tip of the hill where the crowds mill around in the summer. You'll find two **tourist offices** in the Capitano Shopping centre by the quay: Balatontourist (☎87/431-249) and IBUSZ, at the same place (☎87/431-292) can help with private rooms; as can Miditourist at Park utca 6 and 53 (☎87/431-028); and Cooptourist at Egry sétány 1 (☎87/431-134). The cheapest **accommodation** close to the centre is the *Hársfa Panzió* at Szegedi Róza utca 1 (☎87/431-293; May–Sept ①), while the flashier *Volán Panzió*, a neo-Baroque heap with a 1980s annexe, is five minutes' walk further on at Római út 168 (☎87/431-013; April–Nov; ③). The campsite is fifteen minutes' walk west of the pier.

Maps and **information** are available from Tourinform, inconveniently placed 1km to the east in **Badacsonytomaj** at Római út 55 (☎87/472-023). But nearby there is cheap accommodation: the friendly *Egry József Fogadó* at Római út 1 offers simple accommodation with shared bathrooms (☎87/471-057; ①; April–Sept), or the *KSH Üdülője* (☎87/471-245; ①), the holiday home of the Central Statistical Office at Római út 42–44. A few steps along the same road, opposite the Tourinform office, the smarter *Borbarátok* ("Wine Friends") pension at no. 78 (☎87/471-597; ②) also has a good restaurant.

Keszthely and around

Though you can change trains at Tapolca and ride back down to **KESZTHELY** – the Balaton's best hangout – it's easier to continue around the northern shore by **bus**. Absorbing thousands of visitors gracefully, Keszthely has some good bars and restaurants, a thermal lake at nearby Hévíz, and a university to give it some life of its own. The centre is roughly ten minutes' walk from the dock (follow Erzsébet királyné útja), or from the **train station** at the bottom end of Mártirok útja, where some intercity buses terminate. Most buses, however, drop passengers on Fő tér, halfway along Kossuth utca, the main drag.

Walking up from the train station you'll pass the **Balaton Museum** (Tues–Sun 9/10am–5pm; 150Ft), with exhibits dating back to the first century AD. From Fő tér onwards, with its much-remodelled Gothic church, Kossuth utca is given over to cafés, vendors, buskers and strollers – a cheerful procession towards the **Festetics Palace**. Founded in 1745 by Count György Festetics, the palace (July & Aug daily 9am–6pm; rest of year Tues–Sun 9/10am–5pm; 700Ft) attracted the leading lights of Magyar literature from the nineteenth century onwards. The building's highlights are its gilt, mirrored ballroom and the Helikon Library, a masterpiece of joinery and carving. Regular concerts are held in the palace during the summer.

Keszthely's waterfront has two moles (one for swimming, the other for ferries), a slew of parkland backed by plush hotels and miniature golf courses, and dozens of fast-food joints and bars. In the evening, action shifts to the centre, where the **bars and restaurants** work at full steam. The friendly *Oasis* restaurant, down Szalasztó utca from the palace at Rákóczi tér 3 (Mon–Fri 11am–6pm, Sat & Sun 11am–4pm), has an excellent salad and vegetarian self-service bar, while from June until August, the *Borház* at Helikon utca 4 offers Hungarian food cooked in the traditional way on an open fire. Local student hangouts are the trio of **bars** opposite the post office on Kossuth Lajos utca.

The best source for **information** in town is Tourinform at Kossuth utca 28 (Mon–Fri 9am–4/5pm; May–Aug also Sat & Sun 9am–1pm; ☎83/314-144). For budget **accommodation**, private rooms are your best bet. They are available from the cluster of tourist offices on Kossuth utca, including IBUSZ at no. 27 (☎83/314-321) and Zalatour at no. 1 (☎83/312-560) – or just look out for houses with *Zimmer Frei* signs. Rooms in college dormitories are available throughout July and August, and at weekends throughout the year – ask at the tourist offices. Campers have the option of two sites just south of the station or the big and expensive *Castrum* site 1500m along the shore in the other direction.

HÉVÍZ

Half-hourly buses from outside Keszthely train station run to **HÉVÍZ**, a spa based around Europe's largest **thermal lake**. The wooden terraces surrounding the **Tófürdő** (Lake Baths; daily 8am–5pm; 400Ft) have a vaguely *fin-de-siècle* appearance, but the ambience is contemporary, with people sipping beer while bobbing on the lake in hired inner tubes. Otherwise, Hévíz seems to comprise of rest homes and costly hotels, with a late-night bar and a casino in the *Hotel Thermál*. Should you wish **to stay**, a budget option is the *Amazon*, Széchenyi utca 23 (☎83/340-482; ②) near the centre of town, or you could try the slightly smarter *Piroska Panzió* at Kossuth utca 10 (☎83/342-698; ②). Otherwise the tourist offices – Zalatour at Rákóczi utca 8 (☎83/341-048), a block behind the bus station, or Héviz Tourist at Rákóczi utca 2 (☎83/341-348) – can book private rooms.

Sopron and around

SOPRON is the nearest big Hungarian town to Vienna – one reason why there are the crowds of Austrians strolling around on summer weekends. The other is the town's 240 listed buildings, which allow it to claim to be "the most historic town in Hungary". The horseshoe-shaped Belváros (old town) is north of Széchenyi tér and the main train station. At the southern end, Orsolya tér features Renaissance edifices dripping with loggias and carved protrusions, and a Gothic church. For more atmosphere there's the **Cezár Borozó**, a cellar with oak butts and leather-aproned waiters, serving local wines and platters of *wurst*. Heading north towards the main square, Új utca (New Street) is a gentle curve of arched dwellings painted in red, yellow and pink, with chunky cobblestones and pavements. Despite its name this is one of the town's oldest thoroughfares. At no. 22 stands one of the synagogues that flourished when the street was known as Zsidó utca (Jewish Street); its collection serves as a reminder that Sopron's Jewish community survived the expulsion of 1526 only to be all but annihilated during World War II.

The main source of interest is up ahead on Fő tér, a parade of Gothic and Baroque architecture partly overshadowed by the **Goat Church** – so called, supposedly, because its construction was financed by a goatherd whose flock unearthed a cache of loot. The Renaissance **Storno House**, once visited by King Mátyás and Count Széchenyi, now exhibits Roman, Celtic and Avar relics, plus mementoes of Liszt.

North of the square rises Sopron's symbol, the **Firewatch Tower** (Tues–Sat 9am–6pm), founded upon the stones of a fortress originally laid out by the Romans. From the top there's a stunning view of Sopron's narrow streets and weathered rooftops. Offered the choice of Austrian citizenship in 1921, the townsfolk voted to remain Magyar subjects and erected a "Gate of Loyalty" at the base of the tower to commemorate this act of patriotism. Walk through it and you'll emerge onto Előkapu (outer gate), a short street where the houses are laid out in a saw-toothed pattern. Beyond Várkerület, atmospheric Balfi utca leads directly to the privately owned **Zettl-Langer Collection** of porcelain, earthenware and weaponry at no. 11 (daily 10am–noon), while Szent Mihály utca wends uphill past the "House of the Two Moors" to the partly Gothic **church of Saint Michael**, whose gargoyles leer over the chapel of Saint Jacob decaying in the graveyard. Nearby stand the crossless tombstones of Russians killed liberating Sopron from the Nazis.

Information is offered by Tourinform at Előkapu 11, just north of the Firewatch Tower (May–Sept Mon–Sat 9am–6pm; Oct–April Mon–Fri 9am–4pm, Sat 9am–noon; ☎99/338-892); Ciklámen Tourist, Ógabona tér 8 (Mon–Fri 8am–4.30pm, Sat 8am–1pm; ☎99/312-040); and IBUSZ at Füredi sétány 9 (May–Sept Mon–Fri 8am–5pm, Sat 8am–1pm; Oct–April Mon–Fri 9am–5pm; ☎99/338-695). **Private rooms** can be arranged at Lokomotiv Tourist at Új utca 1 (Mon–Fri 9am–5pm; ☎99/311-111); IBUSZ and Ciklámen Tourist. They can also arrange student hotel accommodation in July and August. The *Lövér* **campsite**, 4km south of town, is served by bus #12 hourly from Deák tér – booking is advisable through Ciklámen Tourist. The *Stefánia Cukrászda* at Szent György utca 12 offers excellent cakes and coffee. Aside from hotel restaurants the best places **to eat** are the *Várkerület Söröző* at Várkerület 83, and the *Corvinus Söröző* on Fő tér, which does good pizza. Up on Fövényverem utca the *Sopron Halászcsárda* at no. 15 is a charming fish restaurant with a garden (☎1/338-403; closed Sun), or the *Fekete Bárány* opposite. To sample the **local wines**, head for the *Cezár* cellar on Orsolya tér or the *Gyögygödör Borozó* on Fő tér.

Four **trains** daily leave Sopron for Vienna, and there are also a dozen Volán **buses** to Vienna each week.

The Esterházy Palace

Twenty-seven kilometres from Sopron (hourly buses Mon–Sat) lies a monument to one of the country's most famous dynasties: the **Esterházy Palace** at Fertőd (guided tours run hourly Tues–Sun 9am–noon & 1–4/5pm; 600Ft). Originally of the minor nobility, the Esterházy family began its rise thanks to Miklós Esterházy I (1583–1645), who married two rich widows, sided with the Habsburgs, and got himself elevated to count. The palace itself was begun by his grandson, Miklós the Ostentatious, who inherited 600,000 acres and a dukedom in 1762. With its 126 rooms, fronted by a vast horseshoe courtyard where Hussars once pranced to the music of Haydn – Esterházy's resident maestro for many years – the palace was intended to rival Versailles. It now lies in a sad state of decaying splendour, but highlights of the guided tour – which only covers 25 of the rooms – include salons of blue and white chinoiserie, gilded rooms lined with mirrors, and a hall where concerts are held beneath a splendid fresco of Hermes, so contrived that from whichever angle you view it his chariot seems to be careering towards you across the sky. And, of course, there's also a room full of Haydn memorabilia.

The prospect of staying in the palace is almost irresistible – even if the accommodation is all in socialist-realist style: rooms with shared showers are available in the east wing all year round (booking essential; ☎99/370-971; ①) and have delightful views over the neglected gardens. Alternatively there is the Újvári Vendégház at Kossuth utca 57/a (☎99/371-828; ②). There are a couple of restaurants outside the gates of the palace, but if you can arrange transport to the village of Fertőszéplak, a couple of kilometres west, you'll find the excellent *Polgármester Vendéglő* behind the church at Széchenyi utca 39. If you need information, next to the palace is the Tourinform office at Madách sétány 1 (Mon–Fri 8am–4/6pm; mid-April to mid-Oct also open Sat 8am–noon; ☎99/370-544).

Pécs

The town of **PÉCS** is not only one of Transdanubia's largest towns, but is also one of the most attractive; indeed, it lays claim to being the finest town in the country, with its tiled rooftops climbing the vine-laden slopes of the Mecsek range. And being so far south, it also tends to be a couple of degrees warmer than the capital. It is also a leading centre of education, having the fifth oldest university in Europe, founded in 1367. Besides some fine museums and a great market, Pécs contains Hungary's best examples of Islamic architecture – a legacy of the long Turkish occupation.

Heading up Bajcsy-Zsilinszky út from the bus terminal, or by bus #30 from the train station towards the centre, you'll pass Kossuth tér and Pécs' **Synagogue** (Sun–Fri May–Oct 9am–1pm & 1.30–5pm). The beautiful nineteenth-century interior is a haunting place, with Romantic frescoes swirling around space emptied by the murder of almost 4000 Jews – ten times the number that live in Pécs today. During the Turkish occupation (1543–1686) a similar fate befell the Christian population, whose principal church was replaced by the **Mosque of Gazi Kasim Pasha** (summer Mon–Sat 10am–4pm, Sun 10.30am–4pm; winter Mon–Sat 11am–noon, Sun 11.30am–2pm), to the north on Széchenyi tér – an otherwise modern square, with an ice cream parlour and tourist offices. Also on the square there's a gallery of contemporary work by local artists and an **Archeological Museum** (April–Sept 10am–6pm; Oct–March 10am–2pm) displaying items testifying to a Roman presence between the first and fifth centuries.

From here you can follow either Káptalan or Janus Pannonius utca towards the **Cathedral**. Though its architects have incorporated a crypt and side chapels from eleventh- to fourteenth-century churches, the church is predominantly nineteenth-century neo-Romanesque, with four spires, three naves and a lavish decor of blue and gold and floral motifs. The site has been used for religious and funerary purposes since Roman times, and remnants of an early Christian basilica are sunk into the park-like square below Dóm tér. Behind the Bishop's Palace, a circular **barbican** occupies a gap in the decrepit **town walls** – once a massive rampart 5500 paces long, buttressed by 87 bastions erected after the Mongol invasion. South of the barbican, Szepessy Ignác utca slopes down to meet Rákóczi út, where grubby buildings almost conceal the sixteenth-century **Jakovali Hassan Mosque** (10am–1pm & 1.30–6pm; closed Wed), with friezes and Turkish carpets adorning the cool white interior.

Practicalities

Central **hotels** are expensive: central **private rooms** and student **hostel** beds from Mecsek Tours (☎72/213-300) at Széchenyi tér 1 or IBUSZ at Apáca utca 1 (☎72/212-157) are a better deal. The *Hotel Laterum* offers basic rooms west of the centre at Hajnóczy utca 37 (☎72/315-829; ①) while the *Mandulás* campsite on the hill above town has rooms at Ángyán János utca 2 (☎72/315-981; mid-April to mid-Oct ②). Bus #34 stops outside. The *Familia Privát Camping* at Gyöngyösi utca 6 (☎ 72/329-938) is the nearest official **campsite**. **Tourinform**, Széchenyi tér 9 (summer Mon–Fri 9am–7pm, Sat & Sun 9am–4pm; winter Mon–Fri 9am–7pm; ☎72/213-315), is the best source of **information** and also has a complete list of hotels, dormitories and pensions, but does not book private rooms. When it comes to **eating**, the *Aranykacsa* at Teréz utca 4 is excellent, while wholesome Hungarian food is the order of the day at the magnificently decorated *Dóm Étterem*, Király utca 3. The *Virág Cukrászda* serves up good coffee and cakes, and Király utca abounds with pizzerias and cafés. In summer the beer garden of the *Rózsakert* on Janus Pannonius utca is very pleasant; **bars** are more numerous in the western part of the Belváros, south of the centre. Pécs has its own brewery in Rókusalja utca, and the local beer is served up in the *Kiskorsó* restaurant there.

The **Pécs Fair**, held on the morning of the first Sunday of each month, sees some hard bargaining and hard drinking, and there are smaller flea markets on the same site every Sunday. Bus #50 runs to the market site from outside the Konzum store in Rákóczi utca; get a ticket from a newspaper stall or the train station before boarding. Pécs is also an excellent starting point for heading to the nearby **wine region** of Villány to the south – for which the tourist offices can provide more information.

EASTERN HUNGARY

The hilly and forested northern region of eastern Hungary will not feature prominently in any hurried tour of the country, but nobody should overlook the famous wine-producing towns of **Eger** and **Tokaj**, mellow, historic places whose appeal goes beyond the local beverage.

Eger

Its colourful architecture suffused by sunshine, **EGER** seems a fitting place of origin for Egri Bikavér, the famous red wine marketed as Bull's Blood abroad, which brings hordes of visitors to the town. Despite occasional problems with accommodation, it's a fine place to hang out and wander around, not to mention all the opportunities for drinking. There are five **trains** a day from Budapest; from the station, walk up the road to Deák Ferenc út, catch a #10 or #12 bus and get off when the cathedral appears.

Inside the cupola of the Neoclassical **Cathedral** – József Hild's rehearsal for the still larger basilica at Esztergom – the "City of God" rises triumphantly, while St Rita's shrine is cluttered with supplications and testimonials. The florid **Lyceum**, opposite the cathedral, was founded by two enlightened bishops whose proposal for a university was rejected by Maria Theresa. Now a teacher training college (named after Ho Chi Minh during the communist era), the building is worth visiting for its **library** (Mon–Fri 9.30am–1pm, Sat & Sun 9.30am–noon; 150Ft), whose beautiful floor and fittings are made of polished oak. There is also a huge trompe l'oeil ceiling fresco of the Council of Trent by Kracker and his son-in-law. The lightning bolt and book in one corner symbolize the Council's decision to establish an Index of forbidden books and suppress all heretical ideas.

While in the building, it's definitely worth checking out the **observatory**, at the top of the tower in the east wing (same hours and ticket as the library), where a nineteenth-century **camera obscura** projects a view of the entire town from a bird's-eye perspective. The camera's monocled curator gleefully points out lovers kissing in the backstreets, unaware of surveillance.

Close by, facing Széchenyi utca, stands the **Archbishop's Palace**, a U-shaped Baroque pile with fancy wrought-iron gates. In the right wing of the palace you'll find the treasury and a history of the bishopric of Eger (April–Oct Mon–Sat 9am–5pm; Nov–March Mon–Sat 10am–2pm; 80Ft).

Heading towards the centre you pass several tourist offices and restaurants before reaching **Dobó István tér**. With its wine bars and statues facing a stately Minorite church, the main square is a pleasant spot and the starting point for further sightseeing. Cross the bridge and head to the left to find Eger's most photographed structure, a slender fourteen-sided **minaret** (daily 9am–5pm), looking rather lonely without its mosque, which was demolished during a nineteenth-century building boom.

Alternatively, head uphill from the square past the *Senator Ház Hotel* to the gates of the **Castle** (daily 8am–5/8pm; 250Ft, half-price on Mon, when only the underground galleries and the Hall of Heroes are open). From the bastion overlooking the main gate, a path leads up to the ticket office and the fifteenth-century Bishop's Palace. Tapestries, ceramics, Turkish handicrafts and weaponry fill the museum upstairs in the palace, while downstairs are temporary exhibits and a Hall of Heroes (Hősök terme), where a life-size marble István Dobó lies amid a bodyguard of heroes of the 1552 siege in which 2000 soldiers and Eger's women repulsed a Turkish force six times their number. From the ticket office a guide will take you into the Kazamata underground galleries, a labyrinth of sloping passageways, gun emplacements and mysterious chambers.

Wine tasting and other practicalities

Local vineyards produce four types of **wine** – Muskotály (Muscatel), Bikavér (Bull's Blood), Leányka (medium dry white with a hint of herbs) and Medoc Noir (rich, dark and sweet) – all of which can be sampled in the cellars of the Szépasszony Valley (Valley of Beautiful Women) just west of town – around 600Ft by taxi. Finding the right cellar is a matter of luck and taste – but recommended are Medoc Noir in English-speaking Mr Szilágyi's cellar at no. 31, and the old wines of János Birincsik at no. 32. The cellars tend to close by 8pm and getting a taxi back into town can be a challenge; it's only a twenty-minute walk, which might be easier than arranging with a taxi to come and pick you up at an agreed time. Later hours are kept in town, where the **Wine Museum**, Városfal utca 1, gives you the chance to sample the stuff until 10pm from Tuesday to Saturday.

The first port of call for **information** is Dobó István tér, where there's a Tourinform office at no. 2 (May–Oct daily 9am–6pm; Nov–April Mon–Fri 9am–5pm, Sat 9am–2pm; ☎36/321-807). Eger's cheapest **accommodation** is the summer student hostels: details of these and of private rooms are obtainable from the tourist offices – Eger Tourist at Bajcsy-Zsilinszky utca 9 (☎36/411-724), IBUSZ at Széchenyi utca 9 (☎36/311-451), or Express at Széchenyi utca 28 (☎36/427-757). Along from the castle is the *Tourist Motel* at Mekcsey utca 2 (☎36/429-014; ①). For more comfort, try the *Hotel Minaret*, Harangöntő utca 5 (☎36/410-020; ③), or the classier *Senator Ház Hotel*, Dobó István tér 11 (☎36/320-466; ④). There are two **campsites**: *Autós Caraván Camping* to the north at Rákóczi út 79 (mid-April to mid-Oct; bus #10 or #11), and the *Tulipán* site in the Szépasszony Valley. The best of Eger's **restaurants** is the *Talizmán*, Kossuth utca 19, and the town has two elegant patisseries: the *Kopcsik* at Kossuth utca 28 and the *Dobos* at Széchenyi utca 6.

Tokaj

TOKAJ is to Hungary what Champagne is to France, and this small town has become a place of pilgrimage for wine lovers. Perched beside the confluence of the rivers Bodrog and Tisza, Tokaj is a place of sloping cobbled streets and faded ochre dwellings with nesting storks and wine cellars, overlooked by lush vineyards climbing the hillside towards the "Bald Peak" and the inevitable TV transmission tower. It's fifteen minutes' walk left out of the station and left under the bridge to the old town centre. Tokaj has a few architectural "sights" – the old Town Hall and Rákóczi-Dessewffy mansion, the large half-restored synagogue and Jewish cemetery (reminders of the large Jewish population that lived here till the Holocaust), and a ruined castle by the river – but inevitably it's the wine that attracts most people's attention.

Tokaj wines derive their character from the local soil, the prolonged sunlight and the wine-making techniques developed here. The two main Tokaj grape varieties are Furmint and Hárslevels (linden leaf). While these are used to make straight wines, what gets most of the attention are the special golden wines bottled in characteristic short, stubby bottles: Szamorodni (a word of Polish origin meaning "as it comes"), which can be dry or sweet, and the far sweeter Aszú. Heat is trapped by the volcanic soil, allowing a delayed harvest in October, when many over-ripe grapes have a sugar content approaching sixty percent. Their juice and pulp is added to 136-litre barrels of ordinary grapes, the volume of the addition determining the qualities of the wine. The **Tokaj Museum** at Bethlen Gábor utca 7 (Tues–Sun 9am–3/5pm) complacently displays wine labels from Crimea, France and the Rhineland, where attempts to reproduce Tokaj all failed. The favourite place for oenophiles is the **Rákóczi cellar** in the centre of the town at Kossuth tér 15 (daily 8am–noon &

12.30–7pm), but you can get more personal service in the small private cellars that line the hill, for example at the friendly Himesudvar at Bem utca 2, a former hunting lodge five minutes' walk up from the square.

Tourinform at Serház utca 1 (☎47/353-390) has all the **information** you need about Tokaj and the surrounding wine-producing villages. If you want to indulge in a binge, **private rooms** are available through Tokaj Tours next door (☎47/353-323), or there are *Zimmer Frei* signs all over the town. Also worth trying are the *Kollégium* at Bajcsy-Zsilinszky utca 15–17 (☎47/352-355; June–Aug; ①); *Lux Panzió* at Serház utca 14 (☎47/352-145; ②) and the *Hotel Tokaj*, Rákóczi utca 5 (☎47/352-344; ③), an extraordinarily hideous building, but the rooms overlooking the river have an excellent view. At the north end of the town, the *Torkolat Panzió* (☎42/314-517; ②) loans bikes and canoes to guests free of charge; bikes cost 1000Ft a day for non-residents. There are two **campsites**, *Tisza* and *Pelsöczi*, opposite each other on the far side of the river, and the *Unió Vízitelep* up the river at Bodrogkeresztúri út 5. For **meals**, your options are the *Róna Étterem* on Bethlen Gábor utca, or the *Hotel Tokaj*, both of which serve up reasonable fare.

travel details

Trains

Budapest to: Balatonfüred (every 1–2 hr; 2hr 15min); Esztergom (every 40min; 1hr 20min); Pécs (8 daily; 2hr 30min); Sopron (8 daily; 2hr 50min); Szentendre (every 15–30min; 45min); Tokaj (2 direct daily; 2hr 30min–3hr).

Buses

Budapest to: Balatonfüred (2 daily); Eger (hourly from the Népstadion bus station); Esztergom from the Árpád híd bus station via the Danube Bend (hourly) or Dorog (every 30min); Hévíz (2 daily); Keszthely (2 daily); Sopron (4 daily); Szeged (5 daily); Szentendre from the Árpád híd bus station (every 30min–1hr); Visegrád from Árpád híd bus station (hourly).

Badacsony to: Keszthely (hourly).
Balatonfüred to: Tihany (hourly).
Esztergom to: Visegrád (hourly).

Keszthely to: Hévíz (every 30min).
Szentendre to: Esztergom & Visegrád (hourly).
Visegrád to: Esztergom (hourly).

Ferries

(operating April–Oct or Nov, as weather permits, with more running June–Aug. Times running downstream are quicker, naturally.)

Budapest to: Esztergom (1–2 daily; 5hr 20 min); Szentendre (1–3 daily; 1hr 40min); Visegrád (2–4 daily; 3hr 20 min).

Esztergom to: Budapest (as above, boat takes 4hr); Szentendre (June–Aug 2 daily; 3hr).

Hydrofoils

Budapest to: Esztergom (June–Aug 2 daily, weekends only; 1 hr 20 min); Vienna (April–Oct 1–2 daily; 6hr 20 min); Visegrád (June–Aug 1 daily, weekends only; 50 min).

CHAPTER 14

IRELAND

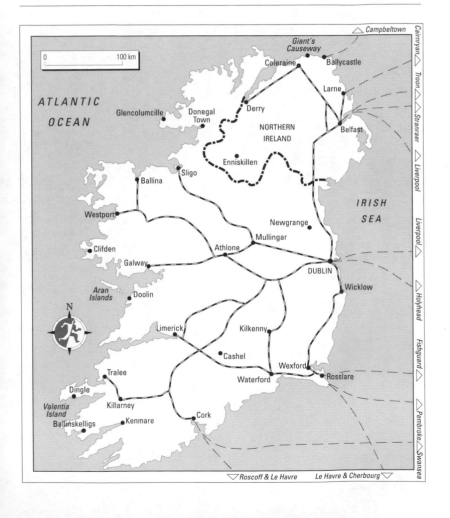

Introduction

Ireland's attractions are its landscape and people – both in the **Republic** and **Northern Ireland** – and few visitors are disappointed by the reality of the stock Irish images: the green, rain-hazed loughs and wild, bluff coastlines, the inspired talent for conversation, the easy pace of life and wealth of traditional music. Ireland has become increasingly integrated with the industrial economies of western Europe, yet the modernization of the country has to date made few marks. It's a place to explore slowly, roaming through agricultural landscapes scattered with farmhouses, or along the endlessly indented coastline. In town, too, the pleasures are unhurried: evenings over Guinnesses in the snug of a pub, listening to the chat around a turf fire.

Especially in the Irish-speaking Gaeltacht areas, you'll be aware of the strength and continuity of the island's **oral tradition**. The speech of the country, moulded by the rhythms of the ancient tongue, has fired such twentieth-century greats as Yeats, Joyce, Beckett and Heaney. **Music**, too, has always been at the centre of Irish community life, and you can expect to find traditional music sessions in the pubs of all towns of any size and along the west coast. Side by side with this is a romping rock scene that has spawned Van Morrison, U2, Sinead O'Connor and The Corrs.

The area that draws most visitors is the **west coast**, whose northern reaches are characterized by the demonically daunting peninsulas and the mystical lakes and glens of **Donegal**. The midwest coastline and its offshore islands – especially the **Aran Islands** – are just as attractive, combining vertiginous cliffs, boulder-strewn wastes and violent mountains. In the south, the melodramatic peaks of the **Ring of Kerry** fall to lake-pools and seductive seascapes, while in the north of the island, the principal draw is the bizarre basalt formation of the **Giant's Causeway**. The **interior** is less spectacular, but the southern pastures and low wooded hills, and the wide peat bogs of the midlands, are the classic landscapes of Ireland. Of the **inland waterways**, the most alluring is the island-studded **Lough Erne**, easily reached from Enniskillen.

For anyone with strictly limited time, one of the best options is to combine a visit to **Dublin** with the mountains and monastic ruins of County Wicklow. Dublin is an extraordinary mix of youthfulness and tradition, a human-scale capital of rejuvenated Georgian squares and vibrant pubs. **Belfast**, victim of a perennial bad press, vies with Dublin in the vitality of its nightlife, while the cities of Cork, Limerick and, most of all, Galway, have a rediscovered energy about them.

No introduction can cope with the complexities of Ireland's **politics**, which permeate every aspect of daily life, most conspicuously in the North. Suffice it to say that, regardless of partisan politics, Irish hospitality is as warm as the brochures say, on both sides of the border.

Information and maps

In the Republic, tourist information is handled by **Bord Fáilte**, while in the North it's administered by the **Northern Ireland Tourist Board**. You'll find branches of one or the other almost anywhere that has a reasonable number of visitors, and they'll frequently be able to assist in finding accommodation.

For a good **road map** either the Michelin 1:400,000, #405, or the AA 1:350,000 is worth getting. The four Ordnance Survey 1:250,000 regional Holiday Maps are useful but for more detail, and for walking, their 1:50,000 Discovery series maps are generally the best option. Locally produced specialist maps, such as the Folding Landscapes series for Connemara, the Burren and the Aran Islands are worth buying for areas high in archeological interest.

Money and banks

The **currency in the Republic** is the Irish pound, or **punt**, which is divided into 100 pence. The currency comes in coin denominations of 1p, 2p, 5p, 10p, 20p, 50p and IR£1, and in notes of IR£5, IR£10, IR£20, IR£50 and IR£100. Standard bank hours in the Republic are Mon–Fri 10am–4pm and most have a late opening till 5pm one day a week. In less populated areas banks may close for one hour at lunchtime and, in some cases, may only be open certain days of the week, so it makes sense to change your money while in the large towns.

In the North the currency is the pound sterling. In Belfast, Derry and other main towns, most banks are open Mon–Fri 9.30am–4.30pm. Some may open longer and on Saturdays. Elsewhere they may close 12.30–1.30pm, and in small villages the bank may not be open every day. As in the Republic, aim to get your cash in the bigger centres.

Automatic Teller Machines (ATMs) are widely available throughout the island – but not in all villages – and most accept a variety of cards.

Communications

Main **post offices** in Ireland are open Mon–Fri 9am–5.30pm, Sat 9am–1pm. Stamps are sometimes available in newsagents and in shops selling postcards. Domestic and international calls can easily be made from **pay phones** and **card phones** throughout Ireland. It's worth carrying a phonecard since coin-operated phones are rare in rural areas – expect a hefty premium charged on top of the normal price when making a call from a hotel. International calls are cheapest after 6pm on weekdays, and at weekends. The **operator number** in the Republic is ☎10 for domestic calls and ☎114 for international; in the North it's ☎100 for both.

Getting around

Reliable, albeit infrequent and slow, public transport is run in the Republic by the state-supported train and bus companies. There are, however, anomalies – never assume that two nearby towns are necessarily going to be connected. Transport in the North is rather more efficient.

■ Trains

In the **Republic**, Irish Rail (Iarnród Éireann) operates **trains** to most major cities and towns en route, and on direct lines it's by far the fastest way of covering long distances. In general, rail lines fan out from Dublin, with few routes running north–south across the country, so, although you can get to the west easily by train, you can't use the railways to explore the west coast. The only service **between the Republic and the North** is the Belfast–Dublin express.

Train travel is by no means cheap, but there's a complex system of peak and off-peak fares – it's always worth asking about special deals. InterRail passes entitle you to a fifty percent reduction in train travel, while Eurail passes are valid only in the Republic. Student ISIC card holders can buy a Travelsave stamp for £7 (both currencies) from any USIT office giving discounts of fifty percent off standard train fares and thirty percent off bus fares in the Republic; in the North the discounts are half-price single fares and returns for the price of singles, for trains and buses – no private buses, however, will offer discounts. If you don't have any of these cards, you can still get one of a range of **travel passes**. For travel within the Republic, the Irish Explorer rail pass costs IR£67 for five days' travel out of fifteen, while the Rover pass covers all of Ireland (IR£83 for five days out of fifteen). More comprehensive is the Explorer pass, which covers all **rail** and **bus** travel in the Republic and costs IR£100 for eight days out of fifteen, and, if you want to go the whole hog, the Emerald Card covers rail and bus services in both Northern Ireland and the Republic (IR£115 for eight days out of fifteen, IR£200 for fifteen out of thirty).

■ Buses

A **national bus service** (Dublin Bus in the capital, Bus Éireann elsewhere) operates throughout the Republic, but routeings can be complex and slow. Fares are generally far lower than the train, especially in midweek; if you travel on Tuesday, Wednesday or Thursday, ask for a Boomerang ticket, which will buy you the return journey free and is valid for one month. If you are going to be using buses a lot it makes sense to buy a **timetable** from any major bus station; remote villages may only have a couple of buses a week, so knowing when they run is essential. It's also worth buying a **pass**: for buses within the Republic there are various Rambler tickets (IR£28 for three days out of eight, IR£68 for eight days out of fifteen, IR£98 for fifteen days out of thirty), as well as Rover tickets that cover the North as well (IR£36 for three days out of eight, IR£85 for eight days out of fifteen, IR£130 for fifteen days out of thirty).

Private buses, which operate on many major routes, are often cheaper than the national services, and sometimes faster – look out for local advertisements. They're very busy at weekends, so it makes sense to book ahead; during the week you can usually pay on the bus. Prices for parts of their journeys are often negotiable, and bikes can sometimes be carried if booked with your seat. Note that travel passes will not be accepted on any private buses.

In the **North**, Ulsterbus runs regular and reliable services, particularly to towns not served by the rail network. The Freedom of Northern Ireland pass covers Belfast Citybus and Ulsterbus services, and all NI Railways, and costs £10 for one day or £35 for seven days.

■ Driving and hitching

Uncongested roads in the **Republic** make driving a very relaxing option – but watch out for unmarked junctions, appalling minor roads, and unlit cycles late at night. Watch out too for passing lanes or slow lanes, indicated by a broken yellow line: you are expected to pull over to the left to let someone overtake, but these lanes are best used with care since they often have poor surfaces and can suddenly come to an end with little or no warning. As in Britain you drive on the left, and most of the road signs and markings are similar. Speed limits are 30–40mph in town, 60mph outside and 70mph on motorways. Breakdown services are operated by the Irish Automobile Association (☎1800/667 788☎; members only).

Roads in the **North** are in general notably superior to those in the Republic. Driving is on the left, and rules of the road are as in mainland Britain. Breakdown numbers are ☎0800/88 77 66 (freephone) for the AA and ☎0800/82 82 82 for the RAC (members only). Some towns have no-parking control zones in the centre, indicated by prominent yellow or pink signs: these are to prevent car-bombs being left.

International **car rental** companies have outlets in all major cities, airports and ferry terminals: costs are from around IR£170–£220 a week, although smaller local firms can almost always offer better deals, and booking in advance can produce huge discounts – it's worth shopping around. In the North, expect to pay around £170–240 a week. Companies insist you have held a full, endorsement-free driving licence for two years, and most won't rent cars to under-21s or over 75s. Check in advance if you intend to rent a car in the Republic and drive into the North – many companies will charge extra.

The **Republic** is one of the easiest European countries in which to **hitch**, though women especially should be cautious; for locals it's almost as much a normal part of getting around as using the buses and trains. The chief problem is the lack of traffic, especially off the main roads; and if you are travelling around the tourist-swamped west you may find there's a reluctance to pick up foreigners. In the **North** the best way to hitch is to make sure you look like a tourist – and even then, it's never easy. Men travelling alone or in pairs may be viewed with suspicion, and may even find it impossible to get a lift. Men and women travelling together are at least in with a chance. Getting a lift across the border can be difficult.

■ Cycling

If you are lucky enough to get decent weather, **cycling** is one of the most enjoyable ways to see Ireland. Roads are generally empty, though very poor surfaces may slow you down. It's easy and relatively cheap to **rent a bike** in most towns in the Republic, and at a limited number of places in the North; you can't take a rented bike across the border. Raleigh is the biggest national operator (about IR£7 per day, IR£35 per week plus around IR£40 deposit; call ☎01/626 1333 for information on your nearest Raleigh outlet), but local dealers (including some hostels) are often less ☎expensive. If you arrive with your own bike, it will cost you an extra IR£5 to carry it on each single bus journey or IR£3–6 on each single train journey in the Republic, though not all buses or trains have the capacity to carry bikes so check in

advance. To take a bike on a train in the North, add 25 percent extra to the price of each journey.

Accommodation

Though it's obviously the cheapest way to sleep in Ireland, camping can be hampered by tricky terrain and the possibility of continual rain. Next up in price, hostels vary a lot, but all offer the essential basics, and some are very good indeed. Above these come bed and breakfasts, guesthouses and hotels, usually – but not necessarily – registered with and graded by the tourist boards.

■ Bed and breakfasts and hotels

In the South, the least expensive form of comfortable accommodation is a **bed and breakfast**. They vary enormously, but most are welcoming, warm and clean, with huge breakfasts. Registered B&Bs are generally pretty good, though it's not an absolute guarantee. Expect to pay from around IR£15 per person (from IR£12 for nonregistered houses); those advertising en-suite facilities are usually a few pounds more expensive. Bookings for registered B&Bs can be made through tourist offices for an extra £1–3 (Punts or Sterling), or by telephoning ☎00 800 668 668 66 (in the Republic) and 0800 783 5740 (in the North). Even the lowliest regular hotels are generally dearer, though small village hotels can cost about the same as private B&Bs. Bed and breakfast accommodation is expanding in the North, but you will probably need to ring ahead if you want to guarantee a bed during the summer months.

■ Hostels

An Óige hostels – those of the official Irish Youth Hostel Association – and **YHA of Northern Ireland** hostels are run like youth hostels throughout Europe (some close during the daytime and have evening curfews) – at least officially. In fact, you'll find many are more flexible than the rule book

---

ACCOMMODATION PRICE CODES

Throughout this guide, accommodation is priced on a scale of ① to ⑨, the number indicating the lowest price per night a single person could expect to pay in that establishment in high season. With hostels this is the nightly rate per person; with hotels, the price is arrived at by dividing the cost of the cheapest double room by two. The prices indicated by the codes are as follows:

① under £5 / $8	④ £15–20 / $24–32	⑦ £30–35 / $48–56
② £5–10 / $8–16	⑤ £20–25 / $32–40	⑧ £35–40 / $56–64
③ £10–15 / $16–24	⑥ £25–30 / $40–48	⑨ £40 / $64 and over

would suggest, particularly in out-of-the-way places. IYHA membership is required at most hostels, and overnight fees for members start at IR£6.50 in the country, IR£8 in Dublin and larger cities. Full lists of places and prices are available from An Óige, 61 Mountjoy St, Dublin 7 (☎01/830 4555) and YHANI, 22 Donegall Road, Belfast BT12 5JN (☎028/90 324 733).

Across the island, **independent hostels** are often more interesting places to stay, as each reflects the character and interests of its owner, and some are tucked away in beautiful countryside. Very often the atmosphere is cosy and informal: you can stay in all day if you want and there are no curfews or chores, though some hostels cram people in to the point of discomfort. The Independent Holiday Hostels organization (☎01/836 4700) will send you a comprehensive list of their hostels. It is worth using their book-ahead system during high season; although most won't let you book over the phone, some may reserve you a bed up to a certain time in the early evening. Other hostels may be members of the Independent Hostels Ireland network (☎073-30130 for a list). In tourist hot spots, you may be hassled at railway stations to book a bed: there are a very small number of dangerous and disreputable hostels around, so it's a good idea to check *The Rough Guide* or ask around locally before booking in at a non-approved hostel. Expect to pay around IR£7 for a dormitory bed (more in Galway, Cork and Dublin), IR£8–16 per person for private rooms where available, and similar prices in sterling in the North.

■ Camping

The cost of staying on **organized campsites** varies: usually about IR£3–6 a night. In out-of-the-way places nobody minds where you pitch – the only place in the Republic you definitely can't camp is in state forests, though the North's forest parks contain some of its best campsites. Farmers in heavily touristed areas may ask for a pound or two to use their land, but other than this you can expect to camp for free in areas where there's no official site. Some hostels will also let you camp on their land for around IR£4.

Food and drink

Although Ireland still has no great tradition of eating out, the island has undergone a major transformation during the 1990s and you will now find a wide choice of sophisticated cuisine in most towns and resorts. In smaller, rural places, the food you'll find as a traveller will tend to be simple and hearty at best.

■ Food

Irish food is generally highly meat-orientated. If you're staying in B&Bs, it's almost impossible to avoid the "traditional" Irish **breakfast** of sausages, bacon and eggs, although this usually comes accompanied by generous quantities of delicious soda bread. Pub lunch staples are usually meat and two veg, with plenty of gravy, although you can almost always get freshly made soup and sandwiches. Most larger towns have good, simple cafés (open daytimes only) serving soup, sandwiches and cakes as well as slightly more ambitious dishes. Hotels are usually a good bet for a sandwich and a cup of coffee at any reasonable hour; you can generally order a plate of sandwiches and a pot of tea in pubs, too.

The **fast-food** revolution has brought kebabs and burgers to every town of any size, but old-fashioned fish and chips are a better bet, especially in coastal towns. For the occasional binge, there are some very good seafood restaurants, particularly along the southwest and west coast, serving fresh seafood and, often, home-grown vegetables. Irish oysters are the country's most refined and celebrated culinary treat. **Wholefood** and **vegetarian restaurants** or cafés are thin on the ground outside Belfast, Dublin, Galway, Cork and some of the more tourist-influenced areas in the west and southwest.

■ Drink

To travel through Ireland without visiting a **pub** would be to miss out on a huge chunk of Irish life. Especially in rural areas, the pub is the social heart of the community, and often the political and cultural centre, too. Talking is an important business here, and drink is the great lubricant of social discourse. In major cities you'll find pubs heaving with life, and out in remote country villages it can be great fun drinking among the fig rolls and trifle sponges of the grocery-shops-cum-bars you'll find dotted around. While women will always be treated with genuine civility, it's true to say that most bars are a predominantly male preserve. In the evening, especially, women travellers can expect occasional unwanted attention, though this rarely amounts to anything too unpleasant.

In the Republic, **pub opening hours** are Mon–Sat 10.30am–11pm (11.30pm in summer), Sun 12.30–2pm & 4–11pm; some pubs, especially in the cities, may close for a couple of hours in the afternoon. In the **North** pubs are open Mon–Sat 11am–11pm, Sun 12.30–10pm. Many pubs, both North and South, now have late licences on certain nights until 1am.

The classic Irish drink is, of course, **Guinness**, which, as anybody will tell you, is simply not the same as the drink marketed as Guinness outside Ireland. It's best in Dublin, home of the brewery. "A Guinness" is a pint; if you want a half-pint of any beer, ask for "a glass". Other local stouts, like Beamish and Murphy's, make for interesting comparison: they all have their faithful adherents.

If you want a pint of English-style keg **bitter**, try Smithwicks, which is not so different from what you'd get in an English pub. As everywhere, of course, lager is also increasingly popular: mostly Harp (made by Guinness) or Heineken, though more exotic Continental brews are appearing now. Whatever your tipple, you're likely to find drinking in Ireland an expensive business at over IR£2 a pint, and IR£2.50 or more in Dublin. Irish **whiskeys** – try Paddy's, Powers or, from the North, Bushmills – also seem expensive, but the measures are large.

Opening hours and holidays

Business and shop **opening hours**, both North and South, are approximately Mon–Sat 9am–6pm, with a smattering of late openings (usually Thurs or Fri) and half-days. In the South, particularly away from the bigger towns, hours are much more flexible, with later closing times. There's no rigid pattern to the opening and closing of **museums** and the like, though most are closed at least one day a week, often Monday, and many will close between 1pm and 2pm. The bigger attractions will normally be open regular shop hours, while smaller places may open only in the afternoon. Many sites away from the main tourist trails are open only during the peak summer months.

Public holidays in the Republic are: Jan 1; March 17 (St Patrick's Day); Easter Mon; first Mon in May; first Mon in June; first Mon in Aug; last Mon in Oct; Dec 25 & 26. In the North: Jan 1; March 17; Easter Mon; May 1; last Mon in May; July 12; last Mon in Aug; Dec 25 & 26.

Emergencies

In the Republic, people generally have a healthy indifference to law and red tape, perhaps in part a vestige of pre-Independence days, when any dealings with the police smacked of collusion with the British. The **police** – known as the **Gardaí** (pronounced "gar-dee") – or the Guards, accordingly have a low profile. If you have any dealings with the Gardaí at all, the chances are you'll find them affable enough.

In the **North**, the **Royal Ulster Constabulary** (RUC) deals with all general civic policing: contact them if in difficulties. The North is subject to British law and heavily policed, with several "emergency measures" permanently in effect. Despite a gradual relaxation in security measures you may occasionally find yourself being quizzed about where you are going, what you are doing, and so forth, especially in border areas. Be co-operative and polite and you should have no difficulties. Again, whatever their reputation, you'll find that the RUC are helpful enough in matters of everyday police activity.

In the North and South, as in Britain, **pharmacists** can dispense only a limited range of drugs without a doctor's prescription. Most pharmacies are open standard shop hours, though in large towns some may stay open as late as 10pm.

EMERGENCY NUMBERS
All emergencies, in both North and South, ☎999.

DUBLIN AND AROUND

Clustered on the banks of the River Liffey, **DUBLIN** is a splendidly monumental city, but it's also a youthful city. Of roughly one and a half million people in greater Dublin, about half are under 25, with the drift of population from the countryside continuing. Membership of the European Union has infused money into the city, and you'll see new building everywhere, but you'll also witness deprivation as bad as any in Europe. It's the collision of the old and the new, the slick and the tawdry, that makes Dublin the exciting, aggravating, energetic place it is.

Dublin really began as a Viking trading post called **Dubh Linn** (Dark Pool), which soon amalgamated with a Celtic settlement called **Baile Átha Cliath** (Town of the Hurdle Ford) – still the Gaelic name for the city. Because most of the early city was built of wood, only the two cathedrals, part of the castle and several churches have survived from before the seventeenth century. The fabric of the city dates essentially from the Georgian period, when the Anglo-Irish gentry began to invest their income in new town houses. After the Act of Union Dublin entered a long economic decline, but it was the focus of much of the agitation that eventually led to independence. In 1829 Daniel O'Connell secured a limited role for Catholics in the administration of the city, and Dublin was later the birthplace of the Gaelic League, which encouraged the formation of an Irish national consciousness by nurturing the native language and culture. The long struggle for independence came to a head as open warfare hit the streets during Easter Week of 1916, an uprising commemorated by a host of monuments in Dublin.

Arrival and information

From the **airport**, six miles north of the centre, you can take the official airlink bus #747 or #748 (IR£3), which takes thirty minutes to reach **Busáras**, the Central Bus Station (☎01/836 6111), or a slower city bus #41 or #41C (IR£1.10), terminating on Abbey Street Lower. The twenty-minute ride by taxi will cost around IR£15. If you arrive by **boat**, you'll come in at either **Dún Laoghaire** (for Stena Line services), six miles out, from where the DART (Dublin Area Rapid Transport) train will whisk you into town in about twenty minutes, or at the closer **Dublin Port** (Irish Ferries), served by bus #53 – though coaches from Britain usually end up at the Busáras. **Trains** arrive either at Heuston Station on the south side of the city (from Cork, Waterford, Limerick, Killarney, Tralee, Athlone, Galway, Westport, Ballina) or at Connolly Station on the North Side (from Belfast, Sligo, Wexford, Rosslare Harbour). Both areas are quite risky after dark. For train information call ☎01/836 62222. **Buses** from all parts of the Republic and Northern Ireland arrive at Busárus, the central bus station off Beresford Place, just behind the Customs House and within easy walking distance of O'Connoll Street.

Dublin's main **tourist office** is in a converted church on Suffolk St, off Dame St (July–Aug Mon–Sat 9am–8.30pm & Sun 11am–5.30pm; rest of year Mon–Fri 9am–5.30pm). There are other branches at the airport (daily 8am–10pm) and Dun Laoghaire (Mon–Sat 10am–9pm). Their room booking service (☎01/605 7777) costs IR£1 per booking. The **USIT** office on Aston Quay, near O'Connell Bridge on the south side (Mon–Fri 9am–5.30pm, Sat 10am–1pm; ☎01/602 1600), also books B&Bs during the summer, and has its own hostel and a travel agency offering student discounts on ferries and flights. For **listings** of events, see the free *Events in Dublin* or *In Dublin* (IR£1.95) or, for music events, *Hot Press* (IR£1.95). All three are published fortnightly.

City transport

Dublin has an extensive and reasonably priced bus network that makes it easy to hop around. The maximum fare is IR£1.10, a one-day bus pass is IR£3.30, a bus and rail pass (including DART) is IR£4.50, and a four-day bus and rail ticket costs just IR£10. A weekly student bus

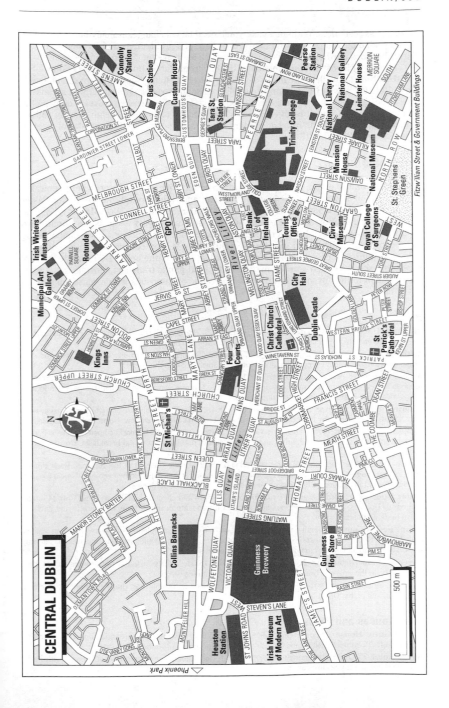

CENTRAL DUBLIN

△ Phoenix Park

Fitzwilliam Street & Government Buildings ▷

Connolly Station
Bus Station
Custom House
City Quay
Pearse Station
National Gallery
Leinster House
MERRION SQUARE
Tara St. Station
Trinity College
National Library
National Museum
Mansion House
Irish Writers' Museum
Rotunda
O'Connell Street
GPO
Bank of Ireland
Tourist Office
Civic Museum
Royal College of Surgeons
St. Stephens Green
Municipal Art Gallery
River Liffey
City Hall
Capel Street
Dame Street
Kings Inns
Four Courts
Christ Church Cathedral
Dublin Castle
St Patrick's Cathedral
St Michan's
Church Street
Collins Barracks
Heuston Station
Irish Museum of Modern Art
Guinness Brewery
Guinness Hop Store

500 m
0
N

cltizone pass costs IR£9. Without a pass, you'll need lots of change, as many buses are exact-fare-only. Finding your way round may prove more of a problem, as there's often no indication at the stops of where the buses go. Either ask an inspector – there usually seems to be one around – or invest in a bus timetable (IR£1.20 from Dublin Bus, 59 Upper O'Connell St). The **DART** links Howth to the north of the city with Bray to the south. The maximum fare is again IR£1.10. Taxis in Dublin don't generally cruise the streets, but instead wait at ranks in central locations, such as outside the Shelbourne Hotel on St Stephen's Green, or along the Quays near the O'Connell Bridge. However, demand for taxis far outweighs supply and it's virtually impossible to find one late at night when many people use the network of Nitelink buses, costing IR£2.50 or IR£4 depending on your destination.

Accommodation

Although Dublin has lots of **accommodation** in all price ranges, everywhere central is liable to be full at weekends throughout the year, and right through the week over Easter or summer. Finding a bed may also be difficult around St Patrick's Day (March 17) and on the days of major sporting and musical events, so it's always wise to **book ahead** (two weeks to a month, depending on the season). Hotels are generally expensive, and often no more comfortable than good guesthouses, but out of season reductions can be considerable – the tourist office in Suffolk St will have a list. Most of the better B&Bs are in the suburbs – but this isn't such a problem, given the good public transport. Hostels range from the excellent to the abysmal, and there are a couple of campsites within reasonable reach of the city.

Hostels

Abraham House, 82 Lower Gardiner St (☎01/855 0600). Large, well-run complex of rooms and dorms with en-suite and shared facilities. Kitchen and launderette. Dorm beds ③, doubles ④.

Ashfield House, 19–20 D'Olier St (☎01/679 7734). Handily located near Trinity College. Clean and spacious, with a bathroom in every room, and a kitchen. Dorm beds ③, doubles ⑥.

Avalon House, 55 Aungier St (☎01/475 0001). Impressive Victorian building 5 minutes' walk from St Stephen's Green. Cramped dorms and twin or four-bedded rooms, sharing unisex bathrooms. Friendly and noisy, with a good café. Dorm beds ③, doubles ④.

Belgrave Hall, 34 Belgrave Sq, Monkstown (☎01/284 2106). Fine Neoclassical Victorian mansion with easy access to the centre by DART. Small dorms, all rooms en-suite. No curfew. Dorm beds ③, doubles ⑤.

Globetrotters Tourist Hotel, 46 Lower Gardiner St (☎01/873 5893). Upmarket hostel where security-locked dorms and individual bed lights make for a peaceful night's sleep. Great breakfasts. Dorm beds ③, doubles ⑨.

Isaac's Hostel, 2–4 Frenchman's Lane (☎01/855 6215). Opposite Gate 15 of the Busáras. Basic dorms (very noisy), singles and doubles, with a good, cheap restaurant and music some evenings. No curfew, but lockout from 11am–2.30pm. Breakfast not included. Dorm beds ③, doubles ④.

Kinlay House, 2–12 Lord Edward St (☎01/679 6644). Bright and cheerful USIT hostel near Christ Church Cathedral. Doubles, quadruples and six-bed dorms with en-suite facilities. Café, launderette and kitchen. Dorm beds ③, doubles ④.

Mount Eccles Court, 42 North Great George's St (☎01/878 0071). A splendid converted house in what is probably the Northside's finest Georgian street. Has a great kitchen, helpful staff and concessions for long stays. There's no lockout or curfew. Dorm beds ③, doubles ④.

Oliver St John Gogarty, 18–21 Anglesea St (☎01/671 1822). Stylish dorms, private rooms and rooftop apartments, in the heart of Temple Bar. Dorm beds ④, doubles ④.

Strollers, 29 Eustace St (☎01/677 5614). Another new place in Temple Bar, that's slightly less chic and without private baths. Dorm beds ③, doubles ④.

Guesthouses and B&Bs

Anchor Guest House, 49 Lower Gardiner St (☎01/878 6913). Refurbished Georgian house close to the Busáras and O'Connell St. All rooms en-suite. Discount for under 12s, infants free. ⑥.

Maple Hotel, 75 Lower Gardiner St (☎01/874 0225). Cosy family-run guesthouse. All rooms with bathrooms, TV and phone. Secure car park. ⑧.

Marian Guesthouse, 21 Upper Gardiner St (☎01/874 4129). Friendly guesthouse offering the best value for money in the area. ④.

Mrs M. Bermingham, 8 Dromard Terrace, Sandymount (☎01/668 3861). Period-style house close to a sandy beach. On the #3 bus route, and near the DART. Open May–Sept. ④.

Mrs R. Casey, Villa Jude, 2 Church Ave, Sandymount (☎01/668 4982). Quiet rooms in a convenient location for the ferries. Bus #3 or DART to Sandymount. ④.

Othello House, 74 Lower Gardiner St (☎01/855 4271). Pleasant family-run establishment with en-suite facilities and TV in the rooms. ⑥.

The Townhouse, 47–48 Lower Gardiner St (☎01/878 8808). Attractive Georgian house with period decor; most rooms have TV and en-suite baths. Good breakfast. ⑦.

Hotels

Bewley's Hotel, 19–20 Fleet St (☎01/670 8122). Comfy, cosy hotel on the edge of Temple Bar, bearing the name of Dublin's famous chain of cafés. No service charge though breakfast is extra. ⑨.

Central Hotel, 1/5 Exchequer St (☎01/679 7302). Refurbished nineteenth-century pile with modern art on the walls. All rooms en-suite with TV. Excellent breakfasts. ⑨.

Georgian House Hotel, 18 Baggot St Lower (☎01/661 8832). Occupying a beautiful old building just five minutes' walk from St Stephen's Green. All rooms en-suite with TV. ⑨.

Harding Hotel, Copper Alley, Fishamble St (☎01/679 6500). Attractive USIT-run hotel next to the Kinlay House hostel. All rooms en-suite. Café, bar and pool tables. Breakfast not included. ⑨.

Parliament Hotel, Lord Edward St (☎01/670 8777). A converted Edwardian bank overlooking Dame St; rooms are soundproofed. Bar and restaurant; disabled access. ⑨.

Temple Bar Hotel, Temple Bar (☎01/677 3333). A larger version of Bewley's Hotel on the same street. ⑨.

Wellington Hotel, 21–22 Wellington Quay (☎01/677 9315). New, smart and overlooking the Ha'Penny Bridge – but a bit noisy thanks to the traffic. Breakfast and service charges included. ⑨.

Campsites

Comac Valley Caravan and Camping Park, Corkegh Regional Park (☎01/464 0644). Off the Naas Rd, Clondalkin; bus #68, #68A or #69. Pleasant site with views of the Dublin Mountains. ②.

Shankill (☎01/282 0011). Close to the DART stop at Shankill – or take bus #45, #45A or #84 from the city centre. ②.

The City

Two areas have a claim to be Dublin's centre of gravity – Grafton Street, the pedestrianized shopping street which links Trinity College with St Stephen's Green, and O'Connell Street, north of the river – but most of the city's historic monuments are on the South Side, where College Green is as good a place as any to start.

The South Side

The Vikings sited their assembly and burial ground near what is now **College Green**, where **Trinity College** is the most famous landmark. Founded in 1591, it played a major role in the development of a Protestant Anglo-Irish tradition. Right up to 1966 Catholics had to obtain a special dispensation to study here, though nowadays roughly seventy percent of the students are Catholics. The stern grey and mellow red-brick buildings are ranged around cobbled quadrangles in a grander version of the quads at Oxford and Cambridge. **The Old Library** (Mon–Sat 9.30am–5.30pm, Sun 12–4.30pm; IR£4.50, students IR£4) owns numerous priceless Irish manuscripts, and gives pride of place to the eighth-century **Book of Kells**. Totalling 680 pages, it was rebound in the 1950s into four volumes, of which two are on show at any one time, one open at a completely illuminated page, the other at a text page, itself adorned with patterns and fantastic animals intertwined with the capitals. The **Book of Durrow** is equally interesting – it is the first of the great Irish illuminated manuscripts, dating from between 650 and 680, and has, unusually, a whole page given over to abstract ornament. In summer there are guided tours of Trinity, and an audio-visual presentation of Dublin's history, The Dublin Experience, in the arts block (June–Sept daily 10am–5pm; IR£5).

Facing Trinity across the busy interchange, the imposing **Bank of Ireland** was originally built in 1729 as the parliament of independent Ireland. After the Act of Union in 1801, the building was sold to the bank, which still adheres to tradition by having a guard in a top hat and tailcoat, and a coal fire in the lobby. You can visit the former House of Lords (Tues 10.30am, 11.30am & 1.45pm) and the grand Cash Hall for free during working hours; and look out for lunchtime **concerts** in the bank's Arts Centre (Tues–Fri 10am–4pm; IR£1.50).

The streets around **Grafton Street** frame Dublin's quality shopping area – chic, sophisticated and expensive. After spotting the statue of Molly Malone – nicknamed the "Tart with the Cart" – drop into **Bewley's** coffee house, whose dark wood and marble-tabled interior is a great place to sit and watch people; there's even a small **museum** tracing the history of this Dublin institution. Grafton Street's **buskers** are the best in town.

Following the pedestrianized Grafton Street from Trinity you'll emerge at the northwest corner of **St Stephen's Green**, whose pleasant gardens are the focus of Georgian city planning. Running off beside the swanky *Shelbourne Hotel*, **Kildare Street** harbours the imposing **Leinster House**, built in 1745 as the Duke of Leinster's town house, and now the seat of the Irish parliament, the **Dáil** (open when in session Tues 2.30–8.30pm, Wed 10.30am–8.30pm & Thurs 10.30am–5.30pm; bring your passport). Alongside are the rotundas of the **National Library** and the **National Museum** (Tues–Sat 10am–5pm, Sun 9am–5pm; free), the repository of the treasures of ancient Ireland. Much of its **prehistoric gold** was found in peat-bogs, as were a sacrificed human and the Lurgan Longboat. The **Treasury** and the **Viking exhibition** display such masterpieces as the Ardagh Chalice and Tara Brooch, St Patrick's Bell and the Cross of Cong. The brooch is perhaps the greatest piece of Irish metalwork and is decorated both on the front and the back, where the intricate filigree could be seen only by the wearer.

Around the block, the other side of Leinster House overlooks **Merrion Square**, the finest Georgian plaza in Dublin, whose park railings are used on Sundays by artists flogging their wares. Here, Ireland's **National Gallery** (Mon–Sat 10am–5.30pm, Thurs till 8.30pm, Sun 2–5pm; free) owns a fair spread of European old masters and French Impressionists, but the real draw is the trove of Irish paintings, ranging from formal portraits and landscape paintings of the Anglo-Irish era to the modernist creations of Mainie Jellett, Evie Hone and Roderic O'Conor. Best of all, however, is the new permanent exhibition devoted to the work of Ireland's best-known painter, Jack B. Yeats, tracing his development from Dublin illustrator to expressionist interpreter of Connemara sea- and landscapes.

Don't miss the guided tours of **No. 29 Lower Fitzwilliam Street** (Jan to mid-Dec Tues–Sat 10am–5pm, Sun 2–5pm; IR£2.50) – a sumptuously re-created Georgian household that includes a giant doll's house and an eighteenth-century exercise machine – or the **Government Buildings** (Sat 10am–3.30pm; free; tickets from the National Gallery) on Merrion St Upper, featuring the Taoiseach's office (with a private lift to a rooftop helipad or basement limo) and Cabinet Room.

Dame Street, the main thoroughfare leading west from College Green, marks the southern edge of the redeveloped **Temple Bar** quarter, whose fashionable restaurants, pubs, boutiques and arts centres make this one of the liveliest parts of town. Dublin's **Viking Adventure** (March–Oct Tues–Sat 10am–4.30pm; IR£4.75), on the corner of Essex St West and Exchange St Upper, beside Essex Quay, is an interactive exhibition on the Viking settlement that once existed on Wood Quay, where the Dublin Corporation has built its ugly Civic Offices.

Uphill, tucked away behind City Hall, **Dublin Castle** (Mon–Fri 10am–5pm, Sat & Sun 2–5pm) was founded by the Normans, and symbolized British power over Ireland for 700 years. Though parts date back to 1207, it was largely rebuilt in the eighteenth century. Tours of the State Apartments (IR£3) reveal much about the tastes and foibles of the Viceroys and while you can see the lovely **Chapel Royal**, the real highlights are the excavations of Norman and Viking fortifications in the Lower Yard. Over the brow of Dublin Hill, **Christ Church Cathedral** (daily 10am–5pm; IR£1 donation) is a resonant monument built in 1190 by the Norman baron, Richard de Clare "Strongbow". The north wall of the nave has leaned eighteen inches outwards since the roof collapsed in 1562. The former Synod Hall, connected to Christ Church by an overhead bridge, contains **Dublinia** (April–Sept daily 10am–7pm;

Oct–March Mon–Sat 11am–4pm & Sun 10am–4.30pm; IR£3.95; includes entry to Christ Church), an array of presentations, models and tableaux depicting Dublin's medieval past and Viking and Norman artefacts excavated at nearby Wood Quay. A substantial section of the Norman city walls runs along Cook Street, further to the west.

Five minutes' walk south from Christ Church is Dublin's other great Norman edifice, **St Patrick's Cathedral** (Mon–Fri 9am–6pm, Sat 9am–4/5pm, Sun 10am–4.30pm; IR£1 donation). Founded in 1172, the cathedral is replete with relics of Jonathan Swift, its dean from 1713 to 1745. To the right of the entrance are memorials to both him and Esther Johnson, the "Stella" with whom he had a passionate though apparently platonic relationship, while the north pulpit contains Swift's writing table, chair, portrait and death mask. Of the other memorials, at the west end is one of the most interesting and elaborate – the seventeenth-century monument to the Boyle family, teeming with painted figures of the clan, including the physicist Robert Boyle.

A mile west of Christ Church, the **Guinness Brewery** covers 64 acres on either side of James's St. Founded in 1759, Guinness has the distinction of being the world's largest single beer-exporting company, dispatching some 300 million pints a year. Although you can't tour the brewery, the former **Guinness Hop Store** on Crane St houses an exhibition centre (April–Sept Mon–Sat 9.30am–5pm, Sun 10.30am–4.30pm; Oct–March Mon–Sat 9.30am–4.30pm, Sun 12–4pm; IR£4) where you can taste the best Guinness in Dublin. The upper floors of this airy, four-storey building are given over to exhibitions of contemporary art, and offer fine views over the city.

Regular buses (#24, #51, #63, #69, 78, #79 and #90) ply the road out to Heuston Station and the **Royal Hospital Kilmainham**, Ireland's first Neoclassical building, dating from 1680, which now houses the **Irish Museum of Modern Art** (Tues–Sat 10am–5pm, Sun noon–5.30pm; free), used for temporary exhibitions. If you exit via the west wing and head towards the gateway at the end of the avenue, you'll emerge near **Kilmainham Gaol** (May–Sept daily 10am–6pm; Oct–April Mon–Fri 1–4pm, Sun 1–6pm; IR£2), where the British incarcerated such patriots as Parnell, Padraig Pearse and James Connolly (both executed here). A superb museum on crime and punishment sets the tone for guided tours of the gaol.

The North Side

Crossing O'Connell Bridge, the view of the Georgian Custom House is marred by a railway viaduct, and many of the handsome buildings on **O'Connell Street** – the main avenue on the North Side – have been spoiled by tacky facades. One major exception is the **General Post Office**, the insurgents' headquarters in the 1916 Easter Rising; only the facade survived the fighting – its pillars are still scarred by bullets. There's a **statue of James Joyce** across the road by the corner of Essex St North.

At the northern end of O'Connell St lies Parnell Square, one of the first of Dublin's Georgian squares. Its plain red-brick houses are broken by the grey stone **Municipal Art Gallery** (Tues–Thurs 9.30am–6pm, Fri–Sat 9.30am–5pm, Sun 11am–5pm; free), originally the town house of the Earl of Charlemont and the focus of fashionable Dublin before the city centre moved south of the river. The gallery was set up in 1908 and features work from the Pre-Raphaelites onwards, with an excellent section of modern Irish painters such as Jack B. Yeats and Roderic O'Conor.

Nearby at nos. 18–19, the **Dublin Writers Museum** (Mon–Sat 10am–5pm, Sun 11am–5pm; IR£3) whisks you through Irish literary history from early Christian writings up to Samuel Beckett and Brendan Behan. The exhibits are fairly dull, though the house itself is richly decorated by Georgian stuccadores, especially the magnificent gilded Gallery of Writers. Worth visiting are its well-stocked bookshop, where you can browse through works by all the authors in the exhibition, and the summertime Zen garden.

Two blocks east of Parnell Square, the **James Joyce Centre** (April–Sept Mon–Sat 9.30am–5pm, Sun noon–5pm; Oct–March Tues–Sat 10am–4.30pm, Sun 12.30–4.30pm; IR£2.75) at 35 North Great George's St is devoted to the novelist and runs intriguing walking tours of his haunts (☎01/878 8547). Down Church St, you'll pass **St Michan's Church** (Mon–Fri 10am–1pm & 2–5pm, Sat 10am–1pm; IR£1.50), the oldest on the North Side, founded in 1095. The crypt is famous for its **"mummified" bodies**, preserved by the constant temperature and dry air pervaded by methane gas. The oldest – thought to have been a Crusader – dates back 700 years. The church organ was played by Handel in 1742. At the bottom of Church Street, on the bank of the Liffey, stands the **Four Courts**. Like the Custom House downriver, it's a grand eighteenth-century edifice by James Gandon that has been restored after serious damage during the Civil War which followed the 1921 treaty.

One block west, tours of the **Irish Whiskey Corner** (May–Oct Mon–Fri 11am, 2.30pm & 3pm; Nov–April Mon–Fri 3pm; IR£3) on Bow Street cover the history and method of distilling what the Irish called *uisce beatha* (water of life) – anglicized to "whiskey" – which differs from Scotch whisky by being thrice-distilled and lacking a peaty undertone. Tours end with a tasting session involving five different types of whiskey, Scotch and bourbon. On the first Sunday of each month, the nearby cobbled **Smithfield** is the site of **horse-sales** (from 9am to 4pm; best at midday) attended by Travellers who race their ponies bareback through the streets. Further west is the **Collins Barracks** (Mon–Sat 10am–5.30pm, Thurs till 8.30pm, Sun 2–5pm; free), an annexe of the National Museum housing its decorative arts collection and occasional special exhibitions.

Finally, there's **Phoenix Park**, one of the largest urban parks in the world. Originally priory land, later made into a royal deer park after the Reformation, it contains **Dublin's Zoo** (Mon–Sat 9.30am–6pm, Sun 10.30am–6pm; IR£6), the Presidential Lodge, the old duelling grounds or **Fifteen Acres** – now the venue for Gaelic football, cricket, soccer and occasionally polo, as well as a racecourse. As it's too far to walk from the centre, take bus #10 from O'Connell St or #23 or #26 from Abbey St Middle.

Eating, drinking and entertainment

Thanks to a gastronomic revolution most kinds of cuisine are now widely available in Dublin's centre, especially in Temple Bar. Take advantage of the fact that many cafés and restaurants serve lunch at much lower prices than they'll charge in the evening (when it's wise to reserve a table); while Dublin's eight hundred pubs offer anything from soup and sandwiches to a full carvery at lunchtime. The music scene – much of which is based in the pubs – is volatile, so it's always best to check on the latest action by reading *In Dublin* or *Hot Press*, the national music paper. Nightclubs along Leeson Street (known as "The Strip"), at the southeastern corner of St Stephen's Green, are mostly pretty dire and directed single-mindedly at the tourist or business trade; the trendier clubs closer to Dame Street are a better bet. Dublin's theatres, however, can hold their own with many of Europe's best.

Restaurants and cafés

Auriga, Temple Bar Square (☎01/671 8228). Glass-fronted restaurant overlooking the square; modern interior, varied menu at reasonable prices. Main courses are around IR£10. Open from 6pm.

Bad Ass Café, 9 Crown Alley, Temple Bar. No longer hip, but still one of the best of Dublin's many pizza joints, with a lively atmosphere and reasonable prices. Open daily, with last orders around 11pm.

Bewley's, 78 Grafton St, 11/12 Westmoreland St and 13 South Great George's St. An essential food experience in Dublin, serving everything from a sticky bun to a full meal. Mon–Sat 7.30am–9pm, Sun 8.30am–9pm; the Great George's St branch keeps shorter hours.

Blazing Salads II, Powerscourt Townhouse Centre, off Grafton St. Delicious vegetarian food, on tables overlooking the atrium. Mon–Sat 9am–6pm.

The Chameleon, 1 Fownes St (☎01/671 0362). Temple Bar's only specialist Indonesian restaurant whose highlight is the *rijstaffel* (rice table), a tasty banquet of assorted dishes and dips. Lots of vegetarian options. Wed–Sat 6–11pm, Sun 3–11pm.

Cornucopia, 51 Wicklow St. A wholefood shop with one of the city's few vegetarian cafés, serving daily 8am–9pm.

Chez Jules, D'Olier Chambers, D'Olier St (☎01/677 0499). Decent French food sans frills. Mon–Fri noon–3pm & 5–11pm, Sat 1–11pm, Sun 1–10pm.

Da Pino, 38/40 Parliament St, Temple Bar (☎01/671 9308). Marvellous pasta and good-value set lunches. Daily noon–11.30pm.

Elephant and Castle, 18 Temple Bar (☎01/679 3121). Busy diner-cum-brasserie with burgers and Cajun-Creole dishes; classy without being posey. Mon–Fri 8am–11.30pm, Sat 10.30am–midnight, Sun 12pm–11.30pm.

Fitzer's, 51 Dawson St (☎01/660 1644). Cool, airy café/restaurant with light new-wave food and outdoor tables in summer (Mon–Sat 8am–11pm). There's also a branch in the National Gallery on Merrion Square.

Gallagher's Boxty House, 20 Temple Bar (☎01/667 2762). Traditional Irish food and a friendly atmosphere, popular with tourists rather than Dubliners. Try the savoury pancakes, followed by brown bread ice-cream. Daily noon–11.30pm.

Irish Film Centre, 6 Eustace St, Temple Bar (☎01/667 8788). Delicious inventive food in elegantly minimal surroundings. Daily lunches; evening meals Mon–Sat from 6pm. You can see a film or just soak up the atmosphere in the bar.

Leo Burdock's, 2 Werburgh St. The best fish and chips in Dublin – take-away only. Mon–Fri 12.30–11pm, Sat 2–11pm.

Mao Café and Bar 2–3 Chatham Row (☎01/670 4899). Communist-chic themed restaurant serving reasonably priced rice- and noodle-based dishes with the best service in town. Daily 9am–10.30pm

Mongolian Barbecue, 7 Angelsea St, Temple Bar (☎01/670 4154). Choose your own meats, noodles and sauces and watch the chef cook them in front of you. Mon–Fri noon–3pm & 6.30 11pm, Sat noon–11pm, Sun 1–10pm. Sadly, no vegetarian options.

Nico's, 53 Dame St (☎01/677 3062). Highly successful Italian restaurant that's significantly dearer than other places around Temple Bar. Mon–Fri 12.30–2.30pm & 6pm–12.30am, Sat 6pm–12.30am.

Tosca, 20 Suffolk St (☎01/66796744). A chic modernist temple to Southern European food and wine, owned by Bono's brother. Laid-back by day, busy at night. Daily 12–3.30pm, 5.30pm–12am, Fri & Sat until 1am.

Pubs

Davy Byrne's, 21 Duke St. An object of pilgrimage for Ulysses fans, since Leopold Bloom stopped by for a snack. Despite the pastel-toned refit, it's still a good pub, and serves oysters at lunch.

Doheny and Nesbitt's, 5 Lower Baggot St. Tiny, atmospheric, smoke-filled rooms; often crowded.

The Duke, Duke St. The starting point for "Dublin's Literary Pub Crawl" (April–Oct Mon–Sat 7.30pm, Sun noon; Nov–March Thurs–Sat 7.30pm, Sun noon; IR£6.50).

Keogh's, South Anne St. Wonderful snugs for comparative privacy to sip your pint.

The Long Hall, South Great George's St. Victorian pub encrusted with mirrors and antique clocks.

McDaid's, 3 Harry St. Excellent Guinness in Brendan Behan's former local. Often has traditional music.

Mulligan's, 8 Poolbeg St. Shabby and smoky, but always packed in the evenings; many claim that it serves the best Guinness in Dublin.

Neary's, 1 Chatham St. Plenty of bevelled glass and shiny wood, plus Liberty-print curtains to demonstrate a sense of style to suit the theatre people who frequent it.

The Porter House, Parliament St. Trendy micro-brewery in Temple Bar, serving its own beers and attracting a cosmopolitan crowd.

Pravda, Lower Liffey St. Communist-chic bar north of the river. Airy upper lounge for quieter conversations.

Ryan's, Parkgate St, near Heuston Station. Another pub famous for its wood-lined snugs.

Stag's Head, Dame Court, Dame St, almost opposite the Central Bank. Wonderfully intimate pub, all mahogany, stained glass and mirrors. Good lunches, too.

Music pubs and venues

Bad Bob's Backstage Bar, Essex St East. Temple Bar's main late-night venue, with a live band downstairs, a lounge on the middle floor and a disco up top.

Brazen Head, 20 Lower Bridge St. The oldest pub in Dublin, with traditional music most nights from 9.30pm.

Break for the Border, Lower St Stephen's St. Regular gigs sometimes serve merely as a soundtrack to young Dubliners' courting rituals.

International Bar, 23 Wicklow St. Large smoke-filled saloon with gigs upstairs – mostly rock bands, but also solo acts on Tuesdays.

The Kitchen, Essex St East. Curved walls, moat-surrounded dance floor and a sometimes-strict entry policy for a club offering some of Dublin's best dance sounds.

The Mean Fiddler, 26 Wexford St. One of Dublin's best smaller venues with great decor and a usually excellent line-up of live bands.

Mother Redcap's Tavern, Back Lane, off High St. Traditional and country music. Get your chips around the corner at Leo Burdock's, then come here for a great Friday night.

Oliver St John Gogarty's, 57/58 Fleet St. Lively tourist pub with Irish music upstairs, the starting point for "Dublin's Musical Pub Crawl" (Sat–Thurs 7.30pm; IR£6.50). The adjoining Left Bank Bar often has live jazz and blues.

The Olympia, 74 Dame St. A theatre most of the time, but also hosts regular top-name gigs.

Slattery's, 129 Capel St. Down-to-earth North Side pub with trad or rock music.

Temple Bar Music Centre, Curved St. Everything from traditional acts to salsa, with live recording of all gigs.

Whelans, 25 Wexford St. Very lively pub with nightly gigs and frequent bar extensions.

Theatre

Abbey Theatre, Lower Abbey St (☎01/878 7222). Founded in 1904 by W.B. Yeats and Lady Gregory, the Abbey had its golden era in the days when writers like Yeats, J.M. Synge and later Sean O'Casey were its house playwrights. It's still known for its productions of older Irish plays, but does encourage younger writers. The building also houses the **Peacock Theatre**, which sometimes has more experimental shows.

Gaiety Theatre, South King St (☎01/677 1717). Dublin's oldest theatre stages a mix of musical comedy, revues and occasional opera, plus popular dance clubs on Fridays and Saturdays.

Gate Theatre, Cavendish Row, Parnell Square (☎01/874 4045). Another of Dublin's literary institutions, staging more modern Irish plays.

Project Arts Centre, Henry Place, off Henry St near the GPO (☎01/671 2321). Temporary home to Temple Bar's long-standing project mounting experimental or politically sensitive theatre; may have returned to its former home on Essex Street East by the time of publication.

Listings

Airlines Aer Lingus, 41 Upper O'Connell St and 42 Grafton St (☎01/844 4777); British Airways, 60 Dawson St (☎1800/626742); British Midland, Merrion Centre (☎01/283 8833); Ryanair, 3 Dawson St (☎01/677 4422). **Airport information** ☎01/704 4222.

Bicycle rental 58 Lower Gardiner St, near Isaac's Hostel (Mon–Sat 9am–6pm; ☎01/870 5399).

Buses National services leave from around Busáras, local services from the Quays and Abbey St Middle.

Car rental Argus Rent-a-Car, in the tourist office on Suffolk St (☎01/605 7701); Budget, 29 Abbey St Lower (☎01/878 7814); Dan Dooley, 42 Westland Row (☎01/677 2723); Thrifty Rent-a-Car, 14 Duke St (☎01/679 9420).

Embassies Australia, Fitzwilton House, Wilton Terrace (☎01/676 1517); Britain, 31/33 Merrion Rd (☎01/269 5211); Canada, 64/65 St Stephen's Green (☎01/478 1988); Netherlands, 160 Merrion Rd (☎01/269 3444); US, 42 Elgin Rd, Ballsbridge (☎01/668 8777).

Exchange Thomas Cook, 118 Grafton St or most city centre banks.

Ferry companies Irish Ferries, 16 Westmoreland St (☎01/661 0511); Stena Line, 15 Westmoreland St (☎01/204 7777).

Gay Switchboard Sun–Fri 8–10pm, Sat 3.30–6pm; ☎01/872 1055.

Hospital South Side: Meath Hospital, Heytesbury St (☎01/453 6555); North Side: Mater Misericordae Hospital, Eccles St (☎01/830 1122).

Laundry Nova Launderette, 2 Belvedere St; Powder Launderette, 42a South Richmond St.

Left luggage At the stations: Busáras (Mon–Sat 8am–8pm, Sun 10am–6pm); Heuston (Mon–Sat 7.15am–8.35pm, Sun 8am–3pm & 5–9pm); Connolly (Mon–Sat 7.40am–9.30pm, Sun 9.15am–1pm & 5–9pm).

Pharmacy O'Connell's, 55 O'Connell St, is open till 10pm daily.

Police The most centrally located station is on Pearse St, near Trinity College; the main Gardaí station is on Harcourt Sq (01/873 2222). In an emergency call ☎999.

Post office General Post Office, O'Connell St (Mon–Sat 8am–8pm, Sun 10.30am–6pm).

Taxis Taxi ranks throughout central Dublin. Metro Cabs can be booked on ☎01/668 3333, 24 hours a day.

Telephones International booths at the General Post Office, or buy a phonecard for use in kiosks.

Transport information Dublin Bus, 59 Upper O'Connell St (Mon 8.30am–5.30pm, Tues–Fri 9am–5.30pm, Sat 9am–1pm; ☎01/836 6111); Bus Éireann, Busáras (☎01/836 6111); Iarnród Éireann (trains) 35 Abbey St Lower (☎01/836 6222), or the tourist office on Suffolk St.

Travel agents USIT, 19 Aston Quay (☎01/679 8833).

Around Dublin

County Wicklow, easily accessible to the south of Dublin, has some of the wildest, most spectacular mountain scenery in Ireland, the impressive monastic monuments of **Glendalough**, and the Neoclassical splendour of **Russborough**. To the north of the city is the Brú na Bóinne complex of prehistoric remains, the most important and spectacular of which is **Newgrange**.

Glendalough

The early Celtic monastery of **GLENDALOUGH**, eighteen miles south of Dublin, is one of the most important monastic sites in Ireland, with a tangible quality of peace and spirituality that's only marginally disturbed by coach parties. Transport from the city is easy – the St Kevin's Bus Service leaves from outside the Royal College of Surgeons, St Stephen's Green, at 11.30am every day and returns in the late afternoon. Founded by St Kevin in the sixth century, the **Monastery** (daily 10am–6.00pm; free) became famous throughout Europe for its learning. The **Cathedral**, which dates from the early ninth century, has an impressive ornamental east window; the saint's burial spot is marked by the massive granite **St Kevin's Cross**, carved around 1150. The **round tower**, whose door is ten feet above the ground, was probably used as a refuge in times of trouble. Glendalough's most famous building, though, has to be the solid barrel-vaulted stone oratory of **St Kevin's Church**. Although the church may well date from St Kevin's time, the round-tower belfry is eleventh-century, and the structure has clearly been altered many times. The huge visitors' centre (daily: June–Aug 9am–6.30pm; rest of year 9.30am–5/6pm; IR£2, students IR£1) features an excellent exhibition and video show; entrance includes a guided tour of the site itself.

There are more monastic antiquities among the cliffs around the **Upper Lake**. The site of St Kevin's original church, the **Temple-na-Skellig**, is on a platform approached by a flight of stone steps, accessible only by boat. **St Kevin's Bed**, a rocky ledge high up the cliff, is said to be where the holy man used to sleep in an attempt to escape the unwelcome advances of a young girl. If you want to stay in the middle of this amazing place, the *Brocagh Heights B&B* overlooks the Upper Lake (☎0404/45243; ④). Otherwise you can stay at the *An Óige* **hostel**, about half a mile up the valley (☎0404/45342; ②).

Russborough

Forty minutes from Dublin on the Waterford bus is the Neoclassical splendour of **RUSS-BOROUGH HOUSE** (June–Aug daily 10.30am–5.30pm; May & Sept Mon–Sat 10.30am–2.30pm, Sun & bank holidays 10.30am–5.30pm; Easter, April & Oct Sun & bank holidays 10.30am–5.30pm; IR£3) and its impressive art collection. A classic Palladian building, Russborough was constructed for Joseph Leeson, MP for Rathcormack in the eighteenth century during the days of the semi-independent Irish parliament. No expense was spared – the fashionable architects of the day were employed, and the plasterwork is by the virtuoso Francini brothers. The chief reason to visit Russborough, however, is its collection of paintings, which includes works by Goya, Murillo, Velázquez, Gainsborough, Rubens and Frans Hals. You can stay at the *An Óige Baltyboys* **hostel** in a tranquil location on the wooded shore of the reservoir just outside Blessington (March–Nov; ☎045/867266; ②).

Newgrange

The main N1 Belfast road and the railway provide rapid access from Dublin to Drogheda, from where it's a short bus hop to the great **NEWGRANGE** tumulus (enter by the Brú na Bóinne visitor centre; daily: June–Sept 9am–7pm; Nov–Feb and mid-March–April 9.30am–5pm, May 9.30am–6pm; IR£5; advance booking is not possible and, since it's very popular, there may be long waits). Raised around 5000 years ago and completely restored, the mound of earth and loose stone covers the chambers of a remarkable passage grave. The outer ring of **standing stones**, of which only twelve uprights now remain, was unique among passage grave tombs. Perhaps the most important feature – again unique – is the **roof-box** several feet in from the tunnel mouth. This contains a slit through which, at the **winter solstice**, the light of the rising sun fills the chamber with a sudden blaze of orange light. The entry passage, about three feet wide, leads into the **central chamber**, where the stones are carved with superbly intricate decorations.

SOUTHERN IRELAND

The southeast of Ireland is not the most immediately attractive area of the country, but this is often Ireland's sunniest and driest corner, and it does have a couple of rewarding and contrasting towns. Inland, the region's medieval and Anglo-Norman history is richly concentrated in **Kilkenny**, a bustling, quaint favourite, while on the coast there's **Waterford** city, which preserves an ancient heart but is also a thriving commercial centre, young and enjoyably lively. To the west, County Tipperary consists largely of prosperous, contented farming country, with little to offer visitors. There is, however, one site of outstanding interest at the very heart of the county – the **Rock of Cashel**, a spectacular natural formation topped with Christian buildings from virtually every period. Moving towards the southwest, **County Cork** – Ireland's largest county – is the perfect place to ease yourself into the exhilarations of the west coast, and **Cork** city manages to be a relaxed as well as a spirited place.

Coming from abroad, there's ready access to the south through **Rosslare Harbour/Europoort**, which serves ferries from Cherbourg, Roscoff, Fishguard and Pembroke. There's a **tourist desk** in the terminal open for all incoming sailings (May–Sept, except early mornings ☎053/33622), or try the Kilrane tourist office, just over a mile from the ferry along the N25 (May–Sept daily 11am–8pm, Oct–April Tues–Sun 2–8pm; ☎053/33232). There's an *An Óige* hostel in Goulding St (open all year; ☎053/33399; ②), a short walk from the ferry, though *Kirwan House* **hostel**, 3 Mary St, Wexford, 13 miles away (open all year; ☎053/21208; ②), is a more appealing place to spend your first night in Ireland. Moving on from Rosslare Harbour is fairly straightforward: trains from the pier for Wexford, Waterford and Dublin depart daily and there's also a daily bus service to Dublin.

Kilkenny

KILKENNY is Ireland's finest medieval city, its castle set above the broad sweep of the River Nore and its narrow streets laced with carefully maintained buildings. In the mid-seventeenth century, the city became virtually the capital of Ireland, with the founding of a parliament in 1641 known as the Confederation of Kilkenny. The power of this short-lived attempt to unite the resistance to English persecution of Catholicism had greatly diminished by the time Cromwell's wreckers arrived in 1650. Kilkenny never recovered its prosperity, but enough remains to attest to its former importance.

The **bus and train stations** are a short distance north of the city, at the top of John St. Following this road over the river and climbing Rose Inn St brings you to the **tourist office** (July–Aug Mon–Sat 9am–8pm; Sept–June Mon–Sat 9am–5/6pm; also May–Sept Sun 11am–5pm; ☎056/51500), housed in the sixteenth-century **See Alms House**, one of the very few Tudor almshouses in Ireland. At the top of Rose Inn St to the left is the broad **Parade**, which leads up to the castle. To the right, the High St passes the eighteenth-century **Tholsel**, once the centre of the city's financial dealings and now the town hall. Beyond is **Parliament Street**, the main thoroughfare, where the **Rothe House** (March–Oct Mon–Sat 10.30am–5pm, Sun 3–5pm; Nov–Feb Mon–Sat 1–5pm, Sun 3–5pm; IR£2, students IR£1.50) provides a unique example of an Irish Tudor merchant's home, comprising three separate houses linked by courtyards.

The highlight of this end of town is, without doubt, the thirteenth-century **St Canice's Cathedral** (Mon–Sat 9/10am–1pm & 2–4/6pm, Sun 2–4/6pm; donations accepted). Rich in carvings, it has a fine array of sixteenth-century monuments, many in black Kilkenny limestone, which looks remarkably like marble. The **round tower** next to the church (weather

A ROUGH GUIDE TO

Europe's Millennium Events

written and researched by

Nick Hanna

Adapted from The Rough Guide to the Year 2000

The year 2000 is a fascinating time to be in Europe. The millennium year will witness a host of special events, from street festivals of hip-hop to celebratory classical concerts and major art retrospectives. This fever of activity is largely fuelled by the designation of nine European cities as **Cultural Capitals** for the year 2000. Since the EC-funded programme began in 1985, one city has been selected each year, but to mark the millennium nine were chosen: three from the north (Helsinki, Bergen and Reykjavik), three from the centre (Brussels, Prague and Krakow) and three from the south (Avignon, Bologna and Santiago de Compostela). The aim of the programme is to open up the cultural riches of each city to a wider audience, but in 2000 the programme will also involve numerous projects designed to foster an international, pan-European identity. Thus, **Voices of Europe** is a choir of ninety young people, ten from each city, who will perform music from all nine countries in nine languages (it will tour in the autumn); the **ARCEUnet** project aims to link up museums and cultural institutions from four of the cities (Bergen, Bologna, Krakow and Santiago) into a vast "virtual museum"; and the **Transeuropean Literary Express** will see a train packed with 100 writers travel across the continent on a seven-week journey of literary exploration.

To mark the two-thousand-year anniversary (more or less) since the birth of Jesus Christ, the Vatican has declared 2000 a Holy Year or **Great Jubilee**. The first Jubilee was declared in 1300, when the first mass pilgrimages to Rome took place; it marks a year of forgiveness for all sins. Millions of pilgrims are expected in the Holy Land, but there will also be celebrations in the Catholic countries of southern Europe. Rome is expecting a vast influx, and is creating many special exhibitions and events to mark the occasion. As well as taking on the role of a Cultural Capital, Santiago de Compostela will be a major centre for pilgrimages to the shrine of St James.

The millennium year has more secular overtones elsewhere in Europe. In Germany the first world fair of the twenty-first century, **Expo 2000**, in Hannover, aims to be a "laboratory for the future", with hi-tech displays on the theme of sustainability. France is toasting the millennium with an extravaganza of new exhibitions, fairs, feasts and street theatre, and a thirty-kilometre-long music party. In Britain a millennium boom is underway, fuelled by £2 billion of lottery money, with state-of-the-art visitor attractions opening up and special festivals taking place in many towns and cities. London is home to the famous **Millennium Dome**, the most ambitious millennium project in the world, and this is the only year to experience it – the Dome closes on December 31, 2000. Whatever your interests or tastes, it's a great year to travel around Europe.

BELGIUM

Brussels

Brussels' overall theme as one of the nine Cities of Culture in 2000 is "the city". Some of the highlights of the programme include **Time is a Circle** (citywide; *monthly*), a series of performances at various venues by the contemporary chamber music group, Q-02; **The Second International Festival of Hip-Hop and Urban Culture** (Halles de Schaerbeek; *March*), a four-day extravaganza of rap, hip-hop, breakdance and street art; **Twelve World Music Creations** (Botanique; *March 23–24*), in which new compositions collaborated on by young composers of world music from France, Italy, Spain and Belgium are premiered in a series of twelve performances and recordings; **Bruxelles, Ville d'Afrique** (Palais des Beaux-Arts; *April 5–15*), a theatrical journey into the former Belgian Congo (now the Democratic Republic of Congo); **Scar Stories** (venue TBA; *May*), an exploration by the Sheffield-based Forced Entertainment group, via video montage and public performance, of the scars left by city life on its inhabitants; **Make Haste Slowly** (Maison d'Érasme; *May 25–Oct 7*), which applies the writer Erasmus' favourite motto to the creation of a "Garden of Slowness" created by various contemporary artists, geared towards "metaphysical perambulation"; and **We Are So Happy** (citywide; *May–June*), an exhibition from the archives of the famous Magnum agency, depicting happiness in all its manifestations, which will be projected onto buildings to turn the city into a giant outdoor photographic gallery.

There will also be a **Festival of Science** (Campus of the Vrije Universiteit Brussel; *Aug–Nov*); **French In All Its Forms** (venue TBA; *Sept 26–Dec 31*), a multimedia installation which will link Brussels, Paris and Montreux, exploring the changing nature of the French language; and **Voici** (venue TBA; *Sept–Dec*), a major exposition on contemporary art, exploring the links between figurative and abstract art in the twentieth century. Other events planned include **Stockhausen 2000** (Théâtre des Tanneurs; dates TBA), a choreographic interpretation of Stockhausen's work; and **Hidden Mates** (Institut Royal des Sciences Naturelles; *Oct 18*), looking at the secret wildlife in the city. Brussels is also a key city in the new circus renaissance and will be hosting performances of **Kayassine** by the French group Les Arts Sauts (venue TBA; *Oct 24–Nov 4*).

THE CZECH REPUBLIC

Prague

After half a century of isolation, Prague is planning to once more take its place as a cradle of European culture, opening up its rich heritage with a series of one-off events as well as special editions of traditional festivals such as the **Prague Spring Festival** (*May/June*) and **Dance Prague** (*June/July*). There will also be two sessions of an **International Week of Dance** (State Opera; *Jan 8–16 & Nov 24–29*), a **Festival of Street Theatre** (citywide; *June–Aug*), the world premiere of the opera **Dracula** by the composer Hayden Wayne (National Theatre; *Sept 5*); and the **Prague German Language Theatre Festival** (Vinohrady Theatre and Estates Theatre; *Nov*).

Other performances include an international festival of rock and alternative music, **ET Jam 2000** (Trade Exhibition Centre; *July*); concerts by the **New York Philharmonic** (Rudolfinum; *June 23–24*); a production of **Don Giovanni** that harks back to its original setting (Estates Theatre; *July*); the **WOMAD** International Festival of ethnic music (Letenska plan; *Sept 8–19*); and an international Jewish music festival, **Musica Iudaica 2000** (venue TBA; *Nov*).

Exhibitions include **Birth of the Metropolis**, focusing on architecture and the city in central Europe 1890–1937 (The Municipal House; *until March 1*); **Prague Passageways** (Jaroslav Fragner Gallery; *Jan–March*); and several exhibitions on Czech photography. There will be a major **Writer's Festival** (*April*); a **Prague Indies Film Festival** (*Oct*); and a celebration of boats and sailing vessels, with concerts and theatrical presentations, during **Prague – City on the River** (*summer*).

FINLAND

Helsinki

Helsinki will be staging a wide range of musical events, among them **Placido Domingo In Concert** (Olympic Stadium; *Aug 26*); a series of ten **Culinary Summer Concerts** (Suomenlinna; *July*) on the eighteenth-century fortified island just outside Helsinki, in which "the pleasures of taste unite with the joys of music"; an **International Festival of Baroque Music** (Aug 5–13); the **Kuhmo Chamber Music Festival** (*Feb 1–5*); a **Church Music Festival** (March 19–23); and the **Millennium Clubs** (*all year*), a hundred rock, dance, jazz and world music clubs all over the city featuring the latest talents, cross-border inspiration and discussions between audiences and musicians. There will also be film festivals, performance art and photography exhibitions.

Considerable emphasis is being placed on events for children, "the forthcoming generations of the third millennium". These include **Bravo!**, a theatre festival for children (*March 20–26*), with ten Finnish premieres and eight performances from the other eight Cities of Culture; a puppet version of Hans Christian Andersen's moving tale **The Snow Queen** (venue TBA; *Feb*); **Historical Tours** (*spring*), with actors and performers bringing the city's history to life on the streets; a new exhibition of **Theatre Puppets** (Horseshoe Gallery; *May*); the **Nouveau Cirque** (*July & Aug*); and a series of hands-on **Art Education** events produced by the Annantalo Arts Centre.

General events being staged include **Sauna of the Month**, with each month one of the thousands of saunas in the Helsinki area – some previously hidden from public view – opening its doors to steam-bath enthusiasts; **Dancing in the City**, which will take place throughout the year in squares, parks and shopping centres, with coaching for couples, and live music including polkas, the samba, and the exotic Finnish humppa; and **Fish and Ships** (*May 8–10*), a weekend-long event opening the season for old sailing ships, with sea shanties, accordion playing, jetty dances and sailings for the public. An **Iron Age Village** will be built on a small island within the city harbour, with a market for Iron Age products and a chance for the public to experience Iron Age culture and lifestyles. **Stop and Look!** is a series of environmental art installations erected in the streets and on buildings in the city centre, while the **Snow Church** (*Feb 7–March 7*) will be a splendid structure built in Senate Square, with church services and weddings being performed inside.

There are also several international projects involving the nine European Cities of Culture initiated by Helsinki. **Communication** is a hands-on exhibition staged by Heureka, the Finnish Science Centre, which will appear in the other eight cities too; its theme is "interpersonal communications, mobile phones and the Internet". **Transplant/Heart** involves eight pairs of artists, one from each of the nine cultural cities, producing works which are then brought to Helsinki for display. **ArtGenda** brings together young artists from sixteen northern European countries to work on the theme of "the city and its identity". Finally, there is **Kide** (or Crystal), a sound-and-light artwork made from glass which is intended to symbolize the connections between peoples and cultures. In 1999, the crystal was divided into separate parts to tour the other eight cities and then brought together again in Helsinki and reassembled as an eighteen-metre-long tunnel of light, which people can walk through. The shimmering, shining structures react to the touch, brightening if a hand is left on them, dimming again when it is taken off.

FRANCE

France's biggest national project is the creation of the **Meridian Verte** ("the Green Meridian"), which stretches over 1000km along the meridian from Dunkerque through Paris to the south coast. Its big celebration is planned for Bastille Day, France's most important national holiday (*July 14*), when millions of people are being invited to join the world's largest picnic along the meridian line. With fields especially planted with poppies and clover for the occasion, some 337 cities and villages along the route will be serving fine regional food and wines and playing traditional music, while in the skies above, an air show, featuring everything from Concorde to hot-air balloons, will perform from the Channel to the Mediterranean.

Paris

The world's largest tethered balloon is open for rides of up to 300m in the futuristic Parc André Citroen in the southwest of the city, giving unrivalled views over the city (*all year*; daily 9am–sunset). In the centre, the **Georges Pompidou Centre** has reopened after a two-year renovation programme; the inaugural exhibition at the new centre is **Le Temps Vite** ("fast time"), which will show how mankind has dealt with time and speed in the twentieth century, embracing everything from microprocessors to soundbites, calendars and rituals connected to time (*Jan 19–April 24*); it will be followed by an exhibition of **Picasso** sculptures (*May 31–Sept 11*) and **Regards d'un Siècle** ("glimpses of a century"), a multimedia presentation (*mid-Sept to early Dec*). The huge space of the Grand Halle de la Villette has been transformed into **The Planetary Garden** (*until Jan 23*), an immense indoor garden which will propose a new vision of the relationship between humankind and nature, conceived by landscape artist Gilles Clément. The motorway which encircles Paris, the boulevard périphérique, will be converted into a giant outdoor rock stage for **Périphérok** (*June 21*), with most lanes closed to allow dancers to groove the night away to big-name rock bands as well as local musicians; there will be several sound stages around the 32km route, while other bands will travel around on lorries. The event will be mirrored on ring roads around all the main regional cities in an attempt to create the largest musical show in the world.

Photographer Bernard Faucon will be staging an exhibition on **The Most Beautiful Day of My Childhood** (Maison Européene de la Photographie; *Nov*), with pictures taken by over a hundred children from all over Europe. Other events planned include a new dramatic production, **The Nativity for the Third Millennium** (Théâtre du Châtelet; *Dec*); and **A Wall of Peace** (venue TBA), co-sponsored by UNESCO, inspired by the Wailing Wall of Jerusalem, which will be inscribed with the word "peace" written in all the languages of the world.

Avignon

Avignon's theme as a City of Culture for the year 2000 is "passages" – the passage from one millennium to the next, passage from one shore to another, and passages between neighbourhoods inside and outside the city's famous medieval ramparts. Its major exhibition for the year is **Beauty** (*April 15–Sept 15*), which will be presented in four parts: The Experience of Beauty (a visual spectacular at the Palace of the Popes); New Beauties (great beauties of the twentieth century, at twenty different locations); Natural Beauty (masterpieces of nature which have inspired artists; venue TBA); and Beauty in Our Daily Life (throughout the city).

The city will also be hosting a special edition of the **Avignon Festival** (*July*), featuring extensive collaboration with artists from Eastern European countries. Another major project is **AvignoNumérique**, a multidisciplinary development project which aims to engage residents through living theatre, technology displays, interactive workshops and performances to create a "new cultural space" for urban growth. There will also be a chance to see the four hundred works of contemporary art currently held privately by the **Yvon Lambert Foundation** (venue and dates TBA), and a major exhibition on the **Arts de la Table** (various museums; *Sept*).

The rest of southern France

AIX-EN-PROVENCE is staging **Music of the Millennium**, a special edition of the annual International Festival of Lyric Art (*June & July*). In ARLES, the annual Rencontres Internationales de la Photographie (*July*) will be devoted to **Voyages in the Mediterranean**, examining the exchange of commerce, mythology, religion and ideology as reflected in this contemporary medium. LYON is staging its fifth **Biennial of Contemporary Art** (Halle Tony Garnier; *July–Oct*), which will reflect on the flow of ideas between occidental and non-occidental art forms at the turn of the millennium; the city's **Dance Biennial** (*Sept 8–30*) will also explore the orient, with a theme of "the Silk Road".

Southwestern France

The city of BORDEAUX is staging a major exhibition on **Urban Transformations** at the Centre d'Arts Plastiques Contemporain (*June–Oct*), directed by the Dutch artist Rem Koolhaas. In the border town of PERPIGNAN, the **Ida y Vuelta** ("coming and going") is a celebration of world music, particularly the links between Catalan and Latin American music (citywide; *June 1–3*).

The aeronautically oriented city of TOULOUSE is staging several exhibitions on the theme of "sky and space". The newly opened Cité de l'Espace will host **Earth, Living Planet** (*until May 2001*), an audiovisual spectacular which will take you on a tour of earth through time and space. Events at the Musée Aéronautique focus on aviation history and the conquest of skies. The Musée d'Art Moderne and the Musée des Beaux Arts will both host expositions on the theme of space in art. The programme for the annual **Garonne Festival** (*summer*) will focus on space, air, sky and gravity.

West and Northwest France

BREST is celebrating its role as a seaport with an **International Festival of the Sea and Sailors** (*July 13–17*). The city of NANTES will be honouring its most celebrated citizen, Jules Verne, with a series of events on the theme of "invented worlds". The title exhibition (Musée des Beaux-Arts; *April 20–Aug 20*) will present impossible worlds and utopias as imagined by twentieth-century artists. **Extraordinary Voyages** (Château des Ducs de Bretagne; *April 20–Jan 7, 2001*) examines the imagined worlds of Jules Verne, while a simultaneous exhibition (Municipal Library; *April 20–Jan 7, 2001*) will feature rare original manuscripts and look at his work in the wider context of sci-fi writing.

In BLOIS and the Parisian region a project entitled **Children of Today, Musicians of Tomorrow** (*spring–autumn*) will bring together young musicians and their families from Brazil, Bali, Namibia, Rajasthan, Mauritania, Congo and Trinidad with those from the Parisian region. Over the months they will meet up in a specially built village in Blois, inside a former factory, to explore music.

Northern France

Over a hundred artists are taking part in AMIENS' **Colours of the World** project, which will involve exchanges with artists in Turkey, Australia, China, Mexico and Mali to create works in dance, music, puppetry, street theatre and other media. LILLE is exploring the creativity of urban Africa in **African Presences** (*Aug 1–Nov 15*).

Eastern France

In the **Champagne-Ardenne** region, an ambitious project aims to take over 60km of the River Meuse between Nouzonville and Givet and turn it into a permanent **Valley of Light** (*from July*). The illuminations will embrace natural sites (such as the local blue-stone quarries), as well as specially commissioned sculptures illustrating local legends. STRASBOURG's theme for the millennium is "links" – between the past and the future, between countries and between people. The city will host the eighth annual **Festival of the Union of European Theatres** (Théâtre National de Strasbourg; *Oct 7–Nov 7*), as well as celebrations surrounding the Pont d'Europe (the first postwar bridge linking France and Germany) and an exhibition on Strasbourg 1900–2000 (venue and dates TBA).

GERMANY

Berlin

The long-standing **Berliner Festspiele** (Berlin Festival) will be staging a special millennium edition under the slogan "The New Berlin". Events include **Berlin: Open City** (citywide; *until Jan 2001*), which puts the metropolis itself on show through a series of ten signposted routes encouraging people to explore the cityscape; **Forum City** (venue TBA; *April–Oct*), which looks at the logistical infra-structure of the city; **Architecture and Town Planning 1900–2000** (Neues Museum; *May–Oct*); and **Urban 21** (International Congress Centre; *July 4–6*), bringing together representatives of the 21 megacities of the world to discuss sustainable urban development.

Under the rubric "Seven Hills", various programmes will cast an eye over the intellectual, cultural and scientific landscape at the threshold of the twenty-first century; all events will be staged at the Martin-Gropius-Bau. In **Images and Signs of the 21st Century** (*May 14–Nov 5*), the galleries will be turned into "a magic chamber of the twenty-first century", filled with natural objects and art objects, as well as visualizations of natural processes and multimedia creations. **Theatrum Naturae et Artis** (*May 14–Nov 5*) looks at which powers have determined the history of science in the last two centuries.

The theme "A Time for Children" includes **TimeJourney** (Akademie der Künste; *May 14–June 25*), which allows children to investigate the great mysteries of the past; **Stories on Time** (*May 20–26*), a week of European children's and youth theatre; **My Times** (*June 5–17*), featuring works by children from all over the world, as well as meetings with artists, scientists and journalists; **Z 2000** (*July 15–Aug 20*), bringing together young artists from different regions of Europe for exhibitions, installations, concerts, readings, workshops and theatre performances; and **Musical Summer** (*Aug 1–27*), involving meetings of international youth orchestras.

Other events planned include the fiftieth **Berlin International Film Festival** (*Feb 9–20*); a **Kurt Weill Festival** (*March 2–April 3*); a drumming festival, the

Carnival of Cultures (*June 9–12*); the **Mozart Festival** (*June 9–12*), in conjunction with New York and Paris; **Key Composers of the Twentieth Century** (*Sept 1–Oct 4*), a series of eighty concerts with works by eighty composers; and the **Festival of the Continents** (*July*).

The city is expecting an influx of visitors staying here in order to visit Expo 2000 or making side-trips from the exposition in Hannover (1hr 40min by high-speed train). In view of this, museums and galleries will be opening late throughout the duration of Expo (*June–Oct*) to allow returning Expo visitors a chance to look in.

Hannover

The first of its kind to take place in Germany, **Expo 2000** will be held at the refurbished Hannover Exhibition Ground and the adjacent Kronsberg area from June 1 to Oct 31. It is hoping for forty million visitors, and its theme, "humankind-nature-technology", aims to promote and implement the principles of Agenda 21, the programme for global action which was signed by 176 nations at the UN Earth Summit in Rio in 1992. The idea is to make tangible the concepts behind Agenda 21, creating a visual and interactive experience which will be a "laboratory for the future in the year 2000".

Expo comes in four parts. The flagship is the **Theme Park**, a 100,000-square-metre display which will be "an adventure journey through an experiential landscape" under the supervision of French virtual reality wizard Francois Confino. Within this area different zones will focus on themes such as the twentieth century, the future of work and humankind. The designers are promising journeys through a virtual body, virtual tours of the cities of the world, subterranean voyages through energy systems, links to space, and many other hi-tech goodies; these will all be linked into scenarios exploring sustainable options for the next millennium.

The second leg is the **National Pavilions** zone, which promises some unusual structures: the Japanese pavilion will be built entirely from rice paper and the six-floor Dutch pavilion features a different natural landscape on each level, topped off by a rooftop lake flanked by wind turbines. The German pavilion and the EU pavilion will be built flanking the entrance to the Europa Boulevard, which will feature the pavilions of EU member states in order to "jointly present Europe in a way that will send a clear political signal".

The third strand is the **Culture Programme**, which features an extensive array of international performances in opera, rock and pop, theatre, film, the plastic arts, multimedia and much more. Finally, there are the **Worldwide Projects**, which aim to extend Expo's principles on sustainable development globally – the first time that an exposition has reached outside its boundaries in this way to projects of ecological and social significance worldwide.

Leipzig

The city of Leipzig will be celebrating the 250th anniversary of Johann Sebastian Bach during July. Events planned include a **Bach Festival** (*July 24–30*), the **Twelfth International Bach Competition** (*July 9–20*), and lectures and exhibitions at the Bach Museum.

Mainz

The city will be celebrating the 600th anniversary of Gutenberg; highlights include a performance of the *Gutenberg Oratorium* (venue and dates TBA) and a major exhibition, **Gutenberg's Time** (*April–Oct*).

Oberammergau

Once every decade the citizens of the Bavarian village of Oberammergau perform a **Passion Play**, focusing on the life and death of Jesus. In 2000, the season starts on May 20 with the final performance on Oct 8. Over 2200 villagers will be involved in the production, which runs daily from 9am–5.30pm with a three-hour lunch break. There is covered seating for 4700 spectators, but tickets will be hard to come by and black market prices are expected to escalate.

ITALY

Rome

Rome will be staging various exhibitions looking back at the pilgrimages and jubilees of the past. **Pilgrims and Jubilees in the Middle Ages** (Museum of Palazzo Venezia; *Feb 26–Oct 21*) looks at medieval pilgrimages to St Peter's tomb not only in terms of journeys of faith, but also how the journeys joined together different peoples and cultures. **1300: the First Jubilee, Bonifacio VIII and his Period** (Museum of Palazzo Venezia; *March 30–July 10*) is a major exhibition examining the first jubilee through the works of artists such as Giotto, Arnolfo di Cambio, and Pietro Cavallini; there will be numerous other events in the Lazio region relating to this exhibition. **Plants of Christian Religious Tradition** (National Museum of Popular Arts and Traditions; *May 1–Sept 30*) examines the symbolic meanings given to plants by early Christians. There is also an exhibition on **Women in the Jubilee Age** (Arce Capitolina; *May 3–Aug 31*).

Other exhibitions include **Cleopatra** (Palazzo Ruspoli; *Oct 1–Dec 31*), in collaboration with the British Museum in London and the National Gallery of Washington, billed as the first ever complete exposition about Cleopatra; **The Borgia Family** (Palazzo Ruspoli; *July 1–Sept 30*), the first great exhibition tracing the story of the most important members of the Borgia dynasty; **Goya** (National Gallery of Ancient Art/Palazzo Barberini; *Feb 1–April 30*); **Raphael's Paintings of the Borghese Family** (Borghese Gallery; *Oct 1–Feb 28, 2001*); **Crossing the Threshold** (Villa Glori; *Oct 10–Dec 31*), an exhibition of works by Kounellis, Mauri, Mattiacci, Dompè, Mochetti, Caruso, Nunzio, Staccioli and Dorazio; **Machines and Gods** (Centrale Acea Montemartini; *Oct 1–Dec 31*), an exhibition of ancient sculptures set in an old power plant, juxtaposing ancient Roman and modern technology; and **Goethe in Rome** (House of Goethe; *March 24–Dec 31*), an exhibition of graphics, manuscripts, sculptures and books relating to the writer's time in Rome.

Performances taking place include **The Passion Voices** (*March 31–April 13*), a series of six special concerts organized by the Rome Philharmonic Academy tracing the Passion from the seventeenth century through to contemporary composers.

Bologna

The city's theme as a Cultural Capital 2000 is "communication". As part of its programme, Bologna will be opening a number of new or refurbished museums and other cultural institutions at a cost of 150 billion lire. These include the conversion of the former Stock Exchange into the Library-Mediatheque, which will be the largest library in Italy and will also house a multimedia project presided over by Umberto Eco; the opening of a new Museum of Jewish Culture; the restoration of the Palace of King Enzo and the Podestà; the creation of a National Library and

Documentation Centre for Women; and the conversion of a derelict area around the former tobacco factory into a Centre for the Visual Arts.

Exhibitions include **The European Spirit** (Gallery of Modern Art; *spring*), a wide-ranging exhibition exploring the notion of spirituality as a possible source of common European identity; **The Etruscan Princes** (*autumn*), revisiting Bologna's Etruscan origins in a new exhibition examining the ideologies and lifestyles of the aristocratic Etruscan and Italic communities; **Made in Bologna** (Museum of Industrial Heritage; *autumn*), with new perspectives on Bolognese industry, from the Renaissance to today's hi-tech industries; **The Bibienas** (*spring*), in which the Italian architectural tradition will be explored concentrating on the work of the Bibienas, a famous Bolognese family of architects and set designers who worked in the seventeenth and eighteenth centuries throughout Europe; and **Italia Dipinta** (*autumn*), a show about images of Italy, its monuments and countryside, with landscape painting from Valenciennes to Corot.

NORWAY

The Norwegian government's Department of Culture has set up a company, Norway 2000 Ltd, with a budget of £25 million (US$40m) to promote cultural initiatives across the country. More than 250 projects have been identified in areas as diverse as art, architecture, technology, science, multicultural relations, and the environment. On Jan 1, 2000, more than four hundred millennium squares are being inaugurated across the country (one in each borough); January 2 sees the launch of a year-long cultural festival for young people on the theme of international and multicultural solidarity. Other events planned include cultural exchanges with Latin America; the **Sixth European Youth Music Festival** (Trondheim; *June*); an international exhibition on the Norwegian cultural heritage and its relationship to Europe (venue TBA; *Aug*); a display on industrial design in the new millennium, **The Luggage of Noah** (venue and dates TBA); and workshops on the environment throughout the country. The celebrations will also embrace 200 years of friendly relationships with Sweden.

Oslo

The capital, Oslo, will be celebrating its thousand-year jubilee with a series of themed events emphasizing the diversity and contrasts to be found within the city. **The Challenges and The Records** (*March 5–12*) will focus on the Holmenkollen ski arena, just outside the city, with a huge festival, snow games, skiing across Grønland, and overnight camping in the woods. **The King and the Contrasts** (*May 13–17*) will focus on the past, with historical processions and a specially constructed medieval town; it will also celebrate the birthday of Oslo's patron saint, Saint Hallvard, with a gigantic birthday party for all the children of Oslo (*May 17*). **The Dreams and the Night** (*Aug 11–13*) will be a "mad weekend where everything is turned upside down", with shops, restaurants and bars open all day and night, and music and concerts on every street and in every square; there will be brunches in city parks the morning after. An outdoor opera, **Carmina Burana**, performed in the City Hall Square on August 19, will close this "voyage through dreams and the night". **The Power and the Possibilities** (*autumn*) will feature a series of cultural events, and **The Finale** (*New Year's Eve, 2000*) will celebrate the enduring values of the jubilee celebrations.

Bergen

Bergen is one of the nine European Cities of Culture and has developed its programme around three themed seasons. As well as the events highlighted here, Bergen will be staging events as diverse as a philosophy symposium, a snowboarding display and tastings of Norwegian seafood. Throughout the year, light formations projected onto Mount Ulriken, above the city, will serve as a constant reminder of Bergen's role as a Cultural Capital.

The first season is called "Dreams" (*Feb 17–June 4*), which will feature **The Land Within**, a three-dimensional sculpture where the public can wander through a "fairytale world" inside a giant steel cube (DnB Fresco Hall; *spring*). In March, highlights include **Time, Suspend Your Flight**, an exhibition looking at how artists have represented time, as well as the relationship between time and architecture (Bergen Art Museum), and an **International Festival of Dance**, in collaboration with visiting troupes from France, Belgium and Finland. April sees the opening of the **Heureka Communications Exhibition**, a large-scale travelling exhibition about communications technology (Bergen Museum; *April 28–Aug 28*). Nordic fashion and fashion designers come under the spotlight in **A La Mode Eskimo** (venue and dates TBA), which will combine music, fashion and drama created by artists in Bergen, Helsinki and Reykjavik; while **White Axis** is a silent, white exhibition which aims to "make visible the invisible" (Bergen Art Gallery). One of the major events of the year is a greatly expanded edition of the **Bergen International Festival** (*May 24–June 4*), incorporating music, dance and theatre; running alongside it is the **Literature Festival** (*May 24–June 4*), which will place particular emphasis on European literature and dialogue with writers in the other eight Cities of Culture; around the same time there will also be an **International Festival of Contemporary Music** (Music Factory; *May 25–June 6*).

"Roaming" (*June 8–Sept 3*), Bergen's summer season, will embrace the whole of the western fjord region of Norway. **The Norwegian Fjords** (Bergen Museum, University of Bergen and Bergen Aquarium; *June 12–Dec 31*) will examine the geology, zoology, botany and cultural history of this area. The **Hordaland Coastal Cultural Meeting** (Moster; *June 10–11*) will see the harbour re-created as it was a century ago, complete with old wooden boats. Bergen Harbour will be the setting for a musical production, **The Steamer** (*June 20–30*), which will re-create life on the harbour's waterways during the 1950s. **Living on the North Atlantic** is a major exhibition honouring the fishing communities of the North Atlantic (Coastal Culture Centre, Sandviken; *July 15–Sept 15*; see "Santiago de Compostela", p.13). **Nordstream 2000** is a festival of veteran ships in Bergen's harbour (*Aug 3–6*).

The autumn season, **"Spaces"** (*Sept 7–Dec 3*), will involve several projects based around the theme of the city and urban spaces, with exhibitions and displays both outdoors in Bergen itself and at several cultural institutions. In September, the Icelandic star Bjork is performing with a choir of singers from all the European Cities of Culture in **Voices of Europe** (Grieg Hall); European Figurative Art from the 1960s will be presented in **La Figuration Narrative** (Bergen Museum of Art); and Bergen's trademark rainy weather will be celebrated in a monumental sculpture, the **Rain Hut**, which can be experienced "as a temple or musical instrument for the rain". Contemporary art comes under the spotlight in **BergART**, the Bergen Art Festival (*Oct 8–Nov 7*), which will also include the Bergen International Film Festival (*Oct 20–27*), Oct Dance, Flazz (several days of jazz), the Bergen International Guitar Festival (*Oct 5–8*), a Roald Dahl Weekend and a Literary Festival (*Nov 1–4*).

POLAND

Krakow

As one of the nine Cities of Culture, Krakow's theme is "thought–spirituality–creativity", intended to provide "a meeting point for tradition and modernity, for the East and the West". Events planned include a photographic exhibition, **The Gothic – Shape and Light** (Dominican Cloister; *Aug 10–Nov 30*); **The Stanislaw Wyspianski Festival** (*Sept–Oct*), with performances, exhibitions, open-air shows and drama contests centred on the playwright's work; **Wianki 2000** (Wawel Hill; *June 23–25*), a traditional open-air performance of Wyspianski's plays, *The Legend* and *Acropolis*; **A Happier Ending to a Legend** (*June 20–22*), in which descendants of Tartars now living in Poland have been invited to a performance of one of Krakow's most dramatic legends, based on a Tartar invasion in the thirteenth century; **Wawel 1000–2000** (Cathedral Museum and western wing of the Castle; *May 5–July 30*), an exhibition focusing on the one-thousandth anniversary of the royal and ecclesiastical seat of Wawel Castle; and **The Lanckoronski Exhibition** (various museums; *from Jan 2000*), featuring a set of unusual Italian paintings from the fourteenth to sixteenth centuries. The 600th anniversary of Jagiellonian University features an exhibition on the university's role in European history (*Sept 25–Oct 30*).

Krakow will also be staging three exhibitions on aspects of God: **Gods of Ancient Egypt** (Archeological Museum; *from Feb*); **Treasures of St Francis** (Historical Museum and Franciscan Monastery; *March–May*); and **The Cradle of Slavic Christianity** (Archeological Museum; *Jan–April*). Composers from the former Soviet Bloc will be featured in **The Velvet Curtain** (*Oct 20–28*), while **Encounters 2000** (*July*) will feature folk music from all over Europe.

SPAIN

As a predominantly Catholic country, Spain will be celebrating **The Great Jubilee** in the year 2000 in churches and cathedrals nationwide, with magnificent processions during Semana Santa (*Easter week*) and Corpus Christi (*early June*). The Spanish belatedly began drawing up a two-year programme of millennium events in June 1999, covering concerts, theatre, exhibitions and scientific congresses. Events will take place all over Spain and in countries with a related history including Belgium, Italy, Portugal, Mexico and Argentina. The programme was still not finalized at the time of going to press although it has been announced that events in 2000 will focus on the past, while those in 2001 will look to the future. The first major event will be a classical concert in Seville on January 1. Other events planned will celebrate the 25th Jubilee of King Carlos I and major retrospectives on a millennium of Spanish history and art.

Madrid

The city is undergoing a massive clean-up in honour of the millennium. The Museo del Prado is staging several major exhibitions on the painter **Velazquez** (*June 1999–June 2000*) to mark the 400th anniversary of his birth. In 2000 the city will also be celebrating the 500th anniversary of the birth of Charles V.

Barcelona

Most of Barcelona's museums are staging exhibitions over the millennium itself, including **Charlemagne and the Conquest of Europe** (Museo Nacional d'Art de Catalunya; *until Feb 28*); **Catalan Monasteries from the Year 1000** (Museu d'Historia de Catalunya; *until Feb 28*); and **From Impressionism to the Future: Works from the Thyssen-Bornemisza Collection** (Fundacio Caixa Catalunya, La Pedrera; *until Feb 20*).

Santiago de Compostela

The Camino de Santiago (Road to St James) will be particularly busy during the Great Jubilee year as pilgrims stream in on the traditional walking route from France. The first guide to the Camino de Santiago was the **codex calixtinus**, a twelfth-century manuscript which also includes a rich legacy of liturgical songs which have been performed during important ceremonies in Santiago; in 2000 there will be a special performance (*May 10*) with processions and use of the *botafumeiro*, a giant incense burner which swings from the ceiling.

Santiago is also one of the European Cities of Culture 2000 and is creating new gardens, parks and museums to commemorate the event, with a theme of "Europe and the world". Events planned include **Faces of the Gods** (venue and dates TBA), which explores representations of various deities through seven millennia, across many different cultures and religions, using artefacts and iconography from prehistoric times up until the present day. **The Faces of the Earth** (venue and dates TBA) is an exhibition "showing us our physical world on a fantastic journey through time". The "face of the earth" will be examined from two different perspectives: first, from cartography (both ancient and modern), and second, through paintings and photographs. Other areas which will be explored through projections and audiovisual aids include the birth of the universe, the evolution of the planet, maps for travelling and modern high-resolution cartography. Finally, the **European City as a Model** (venue and dates TBA) is a complex programme which uses exhibitions, publications, and seminars to examine the effectiveness of the European city as an urban planning model for Ibero-American cities.

Living on the North Atlantic (in conjunction with Bergen and Reykjavik) honours the fishing communities of the North Atlantic, exploring the differences and similarities between the coastlines of Iceland, west Norway and northwest Spain, as well as looking at boat-building and fishing techniques, salting and freezing fish, markets, the role of women, beliefs and traditions. In each city the first part of the exhibition will look at common topics (including the historical perspective), while the second part will deal with local customs and fishing cultures. Finally, the future of fishing in the North Atlantic will be explored. The exhibition will be staged in Reykjavik (*spring*), Bergen (*summer*) and Santiago (*autumn*).

Valencia

The city is celebrating the millennium with the completion of a futuristic **City of Arts and Sciences**. It includes a Science Museum built in the shape of a gigantic animal carcass, a Universal Oceanographic Park (*opens summer 2000*), and an Arts Palace (*opens summer 2000*). The city will have a gigantic fireworks display, with the burning of huge papier-mâché figures, on the last day of the **Fallas Festival** (*March 12–19*).

SWEDEN

Sweden's national Millennium Committee has initiated activities throughout the country to set a debate going on the future. The focus will be on issues such as democracy, equality amongst humans, the environment and the distribution of wealth. Events scheduled include **World Music in Halland** (Halland; *Jan–Aug*), with performances of local, national and international music, as well as film, dance and seminars to create an "all-round experience" of world music; **God Has 99 Names** (tours nationwide throughout 2000 and 2001), exploring religious diversity in what is acknowledged as the most secular country in the world; **The Global Environment in the Future** (Royal Swedish Academy of Sciences, Stockholm; *spring*), a series of public lectures and seminars with leading international scientists; **What Do We Need Sweden For?** (nationwide; *Jan–summer*), which aims to establish a dialogue on potential futures for Sweden; **The Youth Futures Exhibition** (Stockholm; *spring*); and **Brave New World** (nationwide; *Jan–May*), a series of music, dance and drama events revolving around issues such as globalization, national identity, culture and ethnicity.

Framstidstro ("Faith in the Future") is a collaborative venture organized by the 26 regional museums of cultural history in Sweden together with Stockholm's national cultural history museum, the Nordiska Museet. Some thirty exhibitions around the country will examine the many images of the future that have existed in the past and the roles that these images have in society – both the optimistic and pessimistic ones, dreams and visions as well as nightmare scenarios. The project involves museums, schools, music and theatre groups in a wide variety of activities including exhibitions, festivals, interactive workshops, discussions and art projects. Special projects include Soap for the Future, which involves mobile animation boxes for people to make their own films; and Write a Letter to Your Grandchild!, which invites people to write letters to future family members. Other events scheduled include a Gala for the Future (Stockholm; *May*), the Global Environment Youth Convention 2000 (Kutluren; *June*), plus And What Then? (museums nationwide; *Jan*).

THE UNITED KINGDOM

London

The **Millennium Dome** at Greenwich will undoubtedly be a "must-see" in the millennium year, but there is plenty going on elsewhere in the capital. The new **Tate Gallery of Modern Art** is a dramatic conversion of a former power station on the South Bank into one of the city's most spectacular exhibition spaces (*opens May*), and from the spring onwards you'll be able to cross the river from here to St Paul's across the eye-catching **Millennium Bridge**, the first pedestrian-only bridge to be built across the Thames in a hundred years. The world's highest observation wheel, the **BA London Eye**, will provide unparalleled views across London from its position opposite the Houses of Parliament (*opens Jan*). At the **British Museum** the inner courtyard, housing the famous Reading Room, will open up to the public for the first time in 150 years with the completion of their Great Court project (*opens Sept*).

Other projects reaching fruition during the year include the Wellcome Wing at the **Science Museum**, devoted to contemporary science, medicine and technology (*opens summer*), a new **Docklands Museum** (*opens spring*), and a redevelopment of the **National Portrait Gallery**, which will include a rooftop restaurant with views over Trafalgar Square and Whitehall (*opens spring*).

The Barbican Art Gallery is staging **Magnum: New Worlds** (*until March 31*), documenting the events of the last decade that raise global issues for the millennium; the British Museum is mounting a major exhibition on the Book of Revelations, entitled **Apocalypse and the Shape of Things to Come** (*until April 24*); the National Gallery is featuring an exhibition on **Kingdom Come: Botticelli's "Mystic Nativity"** (*until Feb 6*), examining this controversial work in relation to the half-millennium in 1500; the National Maritime Museum's **Story of Time** (*until Sept 24*) is a prestigious exhibition bringing together hundreds of artefacts from around the world connected to our collective fascination with the concept of time; and the National Portrait Gallery's **Faces of the Century** (*until Jan 30*) features one hundred of the most important photographic portraits of the last century. The Victoria and Albert Museum is mounting **Art Nouveau 1890–1914** (*April 6–July 30*), which will highlight the major concerns of art and design at the turn of the century and compare them with contemporary urban attitudes to the millennium; and the Mall Galleries will feature **People's Portraits** (*Jan 11–22*), with members of the Royal Society of Portrait Painters creating "a visual time capsule of Britain at the end of the millennium".

A major initiative taking place between over thirty national institutions, most clustered along the banks of the Thames, is the **String of Pearls Millennium Festival** (*until Dec 31*). Intended to reflect the social, political, cultural and technological achievements of the last thousand years, the festival will see the opening up of many of these organizations to the public for the first time, as well as the staging of special exhibitions. Some of the institutions involved include the Royal Court of Justice, the Palace of Westminster, Lambeth Palace, Custom House, Somerset House, and many other establishment landmarks. As part of the String of Pearls, the National Gallery will be staging **Close Encounters – New Art from Old** (*June 14–Sept 10*), with work by major contemporary artists inspired by paintings from the Gallery's collection; Goldsmiths Hall will be displaying silver, jewellery and art medals in **Treasures of the Twentieth Century** (*May 25–July 21*); and the Tower of London will have the Domesday Book on show, as well as art works representing two thousand years of the Tower's history in the **Royal Armouries Millennium Exhibition** (*April 15–Dec 31*).

London's East End, a major focus of the millennium celebrations thanks to the presence of Greenwich and the Millennium Dome, is staging other special events including **Drum 2000** (Woolwich Parade Ground; *March*), a pageant with 2000 military orchestra drummers; a big Caribbean-style carnival **MAS2000** (Greenwich; *March*); the **Easter Passion Play** (Greenwich Park; *April*); the **Global Market** (Hackney Marshes; *July*), a showcase of world culture; and the **Greenwich and Docklands International Festival** (*July*), a two-week-long extravaganza of theatre, spectacle, music, art and fireworks; there will also be a **Millennium Maritime Festival** (*May 26–June 4*) in Docklands.

The rest of southern England

In the rest of southern England, the disused naval dockyards of PORTSMOUTH are undergoing a transformation into a vast maritime leisure complex in the **Renaissance of Portsmouth Harbour** (*opens June*), and in **Cornwall** a huge worked-out china clay pit is being transformed into a spectacular series of "biomes" containing rainforest, desert, temperate and Mediterranean plants (*opens April*). The Royal Cornwall Museum in TRURO will be relating **The Story of Christianity in Cornwall: 500–2000** (*until Sept 30*). In BRISTOL much of the city centre and adjacent docklands is being revamped as part of **@Bristol**, an imaginative project which incorporates a hands-on science centre, Explore@Bristol, and an innovative wildlife centre, Wildscreen@Bristol (*opens June*). **Glastonbury Abbey** is staging **Voices of Glastonbury** (*Sept 13–17*), a three-day programme celebrating the abbey's history, with dramatic performances of key events. BATH's Museum of East Asian Art is staging **One Hundred Treasures: Neolithic to the 20th Century** (*until March 31*). In CAMBRIDGE the millennium music festival, **Sounds and Spaces** (*Nov 11–29*) will involve a host of performances in unusual outdoor locations as well as in industrial venues and heritage buildings.

Northern England

One of the first millennium projects to open in the UK was the **Earth Centre**, near DONCASTER in Yorkshire, which aims to be a world centre for sustainable technologies and future lifestyles. In NEWCASTLE, the **International Centre for Life** explores issues surrounding biotechnology and genetic research (*opens April*), while in LIVERPOOL a **National Discovery Park**, focusing on the history of exploration, is being built (*opens Dec*). YORK is staging the **York Millennium Mystery Plays** (*June 22–July 22*), a high-profile production of Britain's oldest cycle of mystery plays, which date back to the fourteenth century. For the first time ever they will be staged inside York Minster, and will involve 200 actors and 2500 local schoolchildren. Visitors to York will also be able to pick over four hundred years of culinary history (1600–2000) in a special exhibition, **Eat, Drink and Be Merry** (*Feb 26–June 4*). BIRMINGHAM's Museum and Art Gallery is bringing together paintings, sculpture, photographs, prints and drawings for **20th Century Art** (*until March 26*). LEEDS' summer season of free, open-air events will include millennium-themed opera, ballet, pop and classical performances under the rubric "A Sense of Occasion"; the city will also be staging a visual arts project called **The Idea of the North** (*Oct–Dec*); and throughout the year there will be a multicultural celebration, the **Festival of Festivals**.

Wales

In Wales, CARDIFF has acquired a Millennium Stadium at Cardiff Arms Park, while Cardiff Bay is being redeveloped to include the new Welsh Assembly and the Welsh Millennium Centre, a multipurpose arts centre focusing on Welsh culture (*opens late 2001*). In **Carmarthenshire** the National Botanic Gardens of Wales will be dedicated to the protection of threatened plant species (*opens April*).

Scotland

In Scotland, the **Dynamic Earth** in EDINBURGH, the "world's first geological visitor centre", is already open. GLASGOW is creating **X-Site**, an interactive science centre (*opens Oct*).

Northern Ireland

In Northern Ireland, the **Odyssey Project** is the biggest development in the region, encompassing education, entertainment and sporting facilities (*opens Nov*); in County Down the **Strangford Stone** now stands in the Delamont Country Park, a 12m-high megalith, which was erected on Midsummer's Day 1999 using the muscle-power of over a thousand young people.

permitting; IR£1) is all that remains of the monastic settlement reputedly founded by St Canice in the sixth century; there are superb views from the top.

It's the **Castle**, though, that defines Kilkenny, an imposing building standing high and square above the river (guided tours: April–Sept daily 10/10.30am–5/7pm; Oct–March Tues–Sun 10.30/11am–12.45pm & 2–5pm; IR£3). Founded in the twelfth century, the castle was radically altered by a nineteenth-century restoration – hence the folksy, pre-Raphaelite decoration on the flimsy wooden hammer-beam roof of the picture gallery. Also within the castle is the **Butler Gallery**, housing an exhibition of modern art. The castle's kitchen is a tearoom in summer.

Practicalities

Kilkenny is well served by **B&Bs**, although in the summer the city can get crowded and during the comedy and arts festival weeks in June and August you'll need to book in advance. There are several along Dean St, just off the end of Parliament St: *Bregagh* (☎056/22315; ④), *The Deanery* (☎056/52822; ③) and *Kilkenny B&B* (☎056/64040, ④) are all worth trying. There's an *An Óige* **hostel**, *Foulksrath Castle*, at Jenkinstown (☎056/67144; ②), eight miles north along the N77 – Buggy's buses (☎056/41264 for details) run to the hostel from the Parade near the castle three times a day. The friendly *Kilkenny Tourist Hostel*, 35 Parliament St (☎056/63541; ②), is a more central independent hostel, or try the *Ormonde Accommodation Centre* on Wolfe Tone St (☎056/52733; ②). There's **camping** at the *Tree Grove* (☎056/70302; ①), a mile outside the city, or further south near Bennettsbridge at the *Nore Valley Park* (☎056/27229; ①).

Kilkenny has taken off in recent years – an influx of artists and craftspeople to the area in pursuit of the good life has boosted restaurant and pub life. Among popular **eating** places are *Café Sol* on William St, great for lazy breakfasts, and *Fl'éva* on High St, while the garden of *The Basement Restaurant*, Butler House, Patrick St, is just about the prettiest spot for lunch in fine weather. The **café** in the Kilkenny Design Centre, opposite the castle, serves excellent home-cooked lunches. There are several other good spots for **bar food** – *Paris Texas*, High St, and, for a more medieval atmosphere, *Kyteler's Inn*, St Kieran St; *Lautrec's*, St Kieran St is the best bistro in town. Bars are as alluring in Kilkenny as anywhere in Ireland, and you won't be hard pushed to find **music** here: try *Widow McGrath's* or *Cleere's* both on Parliament St, or *Maggie's* on St Kieran St and *Ryan's* in Friary St. In early June, the popular **Kilkenny Cat Laughs Comedy Festival** commandeers every pub, music venue, restaurant and theatre to house a host of comedians. Pick up a copy of the weekly *Kilkenny People* for information about what's on.

Waterford City

WATERFORD is a modern European port wrapped around an ancient Irish city. It's an important commercial centre and this, coupled with a large student population, makes it a fairly lively place. Alongside the city's modernity, though, there's plenty that's traditional, most obviously the place of the pub as a focal point of social activity, and the persistence of traditional music.

The layout of the city, with its long quays and adjacent narrow lanes, dates back to its origin as a Viking settlement in the mid-ninth century. Waterford flourished as a European port into the eighteenth century – the period when the famous Waterford crystal was first produced – and there's plenty of architectural evidence of this prosperity.

The **train and bus stations** are just across the river from the city, a good twenty minutes' walk from Waterford's most historic building – **Reginald's Tower** (June–Aug daily 10am–8pm; May & Sept Mon–Fri 10am–5pm, Sat & Sun 2–5pm; IR£1.50, combined ticket with the Heritage Centre IR£2), a large, cylindrical, late-twelfth-century tower at the far end of the quays. It houses the city's **museum**, which has an impressive collection of royal charters showing the central role of Waterford's allegiance to the English Crown from the arrival of Henry II in 1171 onwards. Wander up Bailey's New St just behind the tower and you'll immediately come to Waterford's other important medieval building, the ruined **French**

Church, or Greyfriars. Founded by Franciscans in 1240, it was used as a place of worship by French Huguenot refugees from 1693 to 1815. Nearby is the **City Heritage Centre** (April–Oct daily 10am–5pm; Nov–March Mon–Fri 10am–5pm; IR£1.50), a showcase for recently excavated Viking and Norman artefacts of outstanding quality and design.

Further up Bailey's New St, you enter Waterford's next significant period of church-building at **Christ Church Cathedral**, which currently hosts a sound and light presentation of the city's history (April, May, Sept & Oct Mon–Fri 11.30am, 2.15pm & 3.30pm; June–Aug Mon–Sat 10.30am, 2.15pm, 3.30pm & 4.30pm, Sun 2.30pm & 4pm; IR£2). Built in the 1770s by John Roberts, who did much work in Waterford for both Catholics and Protestants, it's a nicely proportioned building, with some fine monuments inside – look out for the tomb of James Rice (1482), an effigy of a corpse in an advanced state of decay. Roberts was also responsible for **Holy Trinity Cathedral** in Barron Strand St. Originally built in 1793, this was greatly altered during the nineteenth century to become the curvaceous extravaganza it is today. Christ Church Cathedral looks down over The Mall, where the **City Hall** – again by Roberts – was once used as a merchants' exchange. By far the finest eighteenth-century architectural detail in the city, though, is the beautiful oval staircase inside the **Chamber of Commerce** in George St, yet again by John Roberts. Georgian housing continues down O'Connell St, where the Garter Lane Arts Centre has a gallery, a theatre and a good events noticeboard.

Practicalities

The **tourist office**, at 41 Merchants Quay (April–Oct Mon–Sat 9am–5/6pm, also July & Aug Sun 11am–5pm; Nov–March Mon–Fri 9am–5pm, ☎051/875823), has a comprehensive list of recommended **B&Bs**. Good, central options include the *Portree Guest House* in Mary St (☎051/74574; ④); *Brown's Town House*, 29 South Parade (☎051/870594; ⑤); and *Avondale*, 2 Parnell St (☎051/852267, ④). On the Quay, *Barnacles Viking House* (☎051/853827; ②) is an excellent **hostel**. For your own safety – especially women – we strongly recommend that you call at the tourist office and ask for details before approaching any other places offering budget accommodation.

There are plenty of fast-food joints down Michael St and John St. *Haricot's* on O'Connell St is a cosy, reasonably priced wholefood restaurant, and *Café Luna*, John St, serves a good range of baguettes and hot lunches. For **pub food** try *Egan's*, Broad St, *Dooley's Hotel*, The Quay or *T.H. Doolan's*, George St. John St has two of the city's favourite **pubs** – *Geoff's* and *The Pulpit* – both lively, young places with a good social mix, and useful for keying into what's happening in the city; after hours head for *Preachers*, a wacky club behind *The Pulpit*, or *Club LA* on Manor St. For **traditional music** there are a couple of regular spots: *T.H. Doolan's* in George St and *Muldoon's* on the corner of Manor and Parnell streets.

The Rock of Cashel

Approached from the north or west, **The Rock of Cashel** (daily: mid-June to mid-Sept 9am–7.30pm; rest of year 9.30am–4.30/5.30pm; IR£3, students £1.25, Heritage Card) appears as a mirage of crenellations rising bolt upright from the vast encircling plain. The rock, less than a quarter of a mile wide, is arguably the most extraordinary architectural site in Ireland and is also the place where St Patrick is supposed to have picked a shamrock in order to explain the doctrine of the Trinity. Cashel town is easily reached by bus from Waterford, changing at Cahir, and has two excellent **hostels**: *O'Brien's Farmhouse Hostel* (☎062/61003; ②; camping available), off the Dundrun Rd, and *Cashel Holiday Hostel*, 6 John St (☎062/62330; ②), both a short walk from the Rock. For **B&B**, try *Abbey House*, 1 Dominic St (☎062/61104; ④), or *Maryville*, Bank Place (☎062/61098; ④). The **tourist office** (April–Sept Mon–Sat 9am–6pm, also June & July Sun 9am–6pm; ☎062/61333) is in the market house on Main St alongside the **Cashel of the Kings Heritage Centre** (July–Aug daily 9.30am–8pm; April–June daily 9.30am–5.30/6pm; Sept–March Mon–Fri 9.30am–5.30pm; IR£1, students 50p) where a small exhibition covers the history of the town and you can take a ride on the Heritage Tram (June–Sept Tues–Sat noon–6pm; IR£3; student IR£1.50). The **Bolton Library**

(June–Aug Mon–Fri 11am–4.30pm, IR£2.50), up a lane opposite the Cashel Palace Hotel on Main Street, houses a fine collection of early manuscripts and rare maps.

The first thing you'll encounter on the Rock, approached from Cashel town, is the fifteenth-century **Hall of the Vicars**, whose vaulted undercroft today contains the original **St Patrick's Cross**. Tradition has it that the cross's huge plinth was the coronation stone of the High Kings of Munster. **Cormac's Chapel**, built in the 1130s, is the earliest and most beautiful of Ireland's Romanesque churches. Both north and south doors feature intricate carving, while inside the alleged sarcophagus of King Cormac has an exquisite design of interlacing serpents and ribbon decoration. The graceful limestone **Cathedral**, begun a century after Cormac's chapel, is Anglo-Norman in conception, with its Gothic arches and lancet windows. A door in the south transept gives access to the tower, and in the north transept some panels from sixteenth-century altar-tombs survive, one with an intricately carved retinue of saints.

The tapering **Round Tower** is the earliest building on the Rock, perhaps dating back to the tenth century, though the officially accepted date is early twelfth century. From the grounds of the Rock you can look down at the thirteenth-century Hore Abbey on the plain below.

Cork City

Everywhere in **CORK** there's evidence of the city's history as a great mercantile centre, with grey stone quaysides, old warehouses, and elegant, quirky bridges spanning the River Lee to each side of the island core. Cork had its origins in the seventh century, when **St Finbarr** founded an abbey and school here. A settlement grew up around the monastic foundation, but in 820 the **Vikings** arrived and wrecked both abbey and town. They built a new settlement on one of the islands in the marshes, and eventually integrated with the native Celts. The twelfth century saw the invasion of the **Normans**, who fortified the place with massive stone walls which were destroyed by Williamite forces at the **Siege of Cork** in 1690. From this time on the city began to take on the shape recognizable today. Waterborne trade brought increasing prosperity, as witnessed by the city's fine eighteenth-century bow-fronted houses and ostentatious nineteenth-century churches.

The graceful arc of **St Patrick's Street** – which with **Grand Parade** forms the commercial heart of the centre – is crammed with major chain stores and modest traditional businesses. A hundred yards north of St Patrick's St you'll find **Coal Quay Market** in Cornmarket St – a flea market, worthy of the name, with organic veg and local crafts. A minute's walk from here down the ever-smarter Paul St brings still more variety in the bijou environs of French Church St and Carey's Lane. The downstream end of the island, where many of the quays are still in use, gives the clearest sense of the old port city. In the west the island is predominantly residential, though Fitzgerald Park is the home of the **Cork Public Museum** (Mon–Sat 11am–1pm & 2.15–5/6pm, Sun 3pm–5pm; free, except Sun 75p), which focuses on Republican history with side exhibits on the city trades and guilds, silver and glassware and local natural history.

North of the River Lee is the area of **Shandon**, a reminder of Cork's eighteenth-century status as the most important port in Europe for dairy products. The most striking survival is the **Cork Butter Exchange**, stout nineteenth-century classical buildings recently given over to craft workshops. The old butter market itself sits like a generously proportioned butter tub in a cobbled square; recently renovated, it now houses the **Firkin Crane Theatre**. To the rear is the pleasant Georgian church of **St Anne's Shandon** (Mon–Sat 10am–4/5pm), easily recognizable from all over the city by its weather vane – an eleven-foot salmon. The church tower (IR£2, students IR£1.50) gives excellent views and an opportunity to ring the bells – a good stock of sheet tunes is provided.

To the west of here in the area known as Sunday's Well is **Cork City Gaol** (March–Oct daily 9.30am–6pm; Nov–Feb daily 10am–5pm; last admission 1hr before closing; IR£3, students IR£2.50), built in the nineteenth century; the animated taped tour, focusing on social history, is excellent. From here it's possible to walk back to the town centre via the Shaky Bridge and Fitzgerald Park.

Practicalities

The **bus station** (☎021/450 8188) is at Parnell Place alongside Merchant's Quay, while the **train station** (☎021/450 6766) is about one mile out of the city centre on the Lower Glanmire Road. **Ferries** from Swansea and Roscoff come in at Ringaskiddy, some ten miles out, from where there's a bus into the centre.

The **tourist office** on Grand Parade (June–Sept Mon–Sat 9am–6pm, also July & Aug Sun 10am–1pm; March–May & Oct Mon–Sat 9.15am–5.30pm; Nov–Feb Mon–Sat 9.15am–1pm & 2.15pm–5.30pm; ☎021/427 3251) will book rooms in **B&Bs**; there are plenty strung out along the Western Road, near the university, and along Lower Glanmire Road, near the train station. For **hostels** try *Sheila's*, 4 Belgrave Place, Wellington Rd (☎021/450 5562; ②); *Isaac's*, 48 MacCurtain St (☎021/450 8388; ③); or, just opposite the train station, the *Cork City Independent Hostel* (☎021/450 9089; ②) on Lower Glanmire Rd. Over on the south side of the city is *Kelly's Hostel* (☎021/431 5612; ②), 25 Summerhill South; and, to the west, the newly refurbished *An Óige* hostel, at 1–2 Redcliffe along the Western Rd (☎021/454 3289; ②) – a fifteen-minute walk from the centre of town, and just over a mile from the train station, or take bus #8 from the bus station and ask to be put down at University College Cork.

For **food**, the *Quay Co-op*, 24 Sullivan's Quay, and *Café Paradiso*, on Lancaster Quay, both offer excellent vegetarian meals, while the eminently fashionable *Bodega*, Cornmarket St, and the hugely imaginative *Ivory Tower*, 35 Princes St, both have appealing, reasonably priced lunch menus. *The Farm Gate*, upstairs in the English Market, Princes St, serves wonderfully fresh light lunches, while *The Gingerbread House*, on Paul St, has superb coffee and baguettes.

There's plenty of **traditional Irish music** around town: try *An' 'Spáilpín Fánac*, South Main St (Sun & Wed); *The Lobby*, Union Quay (various nights, with rock and indie too); *The Office*, Sullivan's Quay (Wed); or *Sin É*, Coburg St (Sun). For **clubs**, there's *Zoe's*, Oliver Plunkett St (nightly) or the nearby *Temple of Sound* (Thurs, Sat & Sun). *The Half Moon Theatre* (☎021/427 4308) acts as both a theatre and a club, and has a varied programme of drama and poetry readings (starting around 7.30pm). The hub of artistic activity in Cork is the **Triskel Arts Centre** in Tobin St, off South Main St. It has contemporary art shows, a cinema, poetry readings, concerts and a very good wholefood café. The *Kino Cinema* on Washington St screens art house and independent films and hosts some of the shows during Cork's excellent film **festival** in October. Cork also has an international jazz festival towards the end of October. For the latest details about what's on, buy the *Cork Examiner*, or pick up a copy of the fortnightly freebie *Cork List*.

THE WEST COAST

If you've come to Ireland for scenery, mountains, sea and remoteness, you'll find them all in **County Kerry** – miles of mountain-moorland where the heather and the bracken are broken only by the occasional lake – a landscape whose smooth hills of fragrant, tussocky grass and wildflowers fragment into jagged rocks as they near the ocean. By far the most visited area – indeed, the most visited in the whole of Ireland – is **Killarney and the Ring of Kerry**, a route around the perimeter of the Iveragh Peninsula. This region is predictably geared up for tourism, but whether you head for the mountains or the sea, you can soon lose all contact with modern civilization. The **Dingle Peninsula**, to the north, is on a smaller scale, but equally magical and peppered with ancient remains.

Across the Shannon estuary, beyond the busy city of Limerick, lies **County Clare**, bordered by Galway Bay to the north and the massive Lough Derg to the east. The county is sometimes glossed over as an interval between the magnificent scenery of Kerry and Galway, but Clare has its own distinctive flavour, especially on the stark and barren heights of the **Burren**.

The easiest approach to the Burren is from **Galway City**, an exceptionally enjoyable, free-spirited sort of place, and a gathering point for young travellers. The city sits at the foot of Lough Corrib, which splits County Galway in two: to the east stretches tame, fertile land which people have farmed for centuries, while to the west lies **Connemara**, a magnificently wild terrain of wind and rock and water. The **Aran Islands**, in the mouth of Galway Bay, resemble Connemara in their elemental beauty and in their culture, and offer some of the most thrilling cliff scenery in Ireland.

If you carry on up the coast you'll enter **Mayo**, where the landscape softens and the historic town of **Westport** provides the main base. Neighbouring counties **Sligo** and **Leitrim** both feature a more luscious and gentle scenery, but Sligo is the more enticing of the two, having the beautiful mountain of **Benbulben** and the enchanting **Glencar Lough**. Not many people would disagree with the assertion that **County Donegal** has the richest scenery in the whole country. Second only in size to Cork, it has a spectacular two-hundred-mile coastline whose highlight is **Slieve League** with its spectacular sea cliffs, the highest in Europe.

Killarney and around

Although **KILLARNEY** has been commercialized to saturation point and has little in the way of architectural interest, its location amid some of the best lakes, mountains and woodland in Ireland more than compensates. The town is essentially one main street and a couple of side roads, full of souvenir shops, cafés, pubs, restaurants and B&Bs. Pony traps and jaunting cars line up while their owners talk visitors into extortionate trips through the surrounding country. It's all done with bags of charm, true to Killarney's long tradition of profitably hosting the visiting masses ever since its establishment as a resort in the mid-eighteenth century.

The real reason for coming to Killarney is, without doubt, the surrounding landscape where three spectacular lakes – Lough Leane, Muckross Lake and the Upper Lake – form an appetizer for MacGillycuddy's Reeks, the highest mountains in Ireland. **Cycling** is a great way of seeing the terrain, and makes good sense because local transport is sparse. O'Callaghan Brothers in College St, O'Neill's in Plunkett St and O'Sullivan's in Main St all offer **bike rental.**

B&Bs abound in Killarney, though in high season the town fills up and it's worth calling the **tourist office** (July & Aug Mon–Sat 9am–8pm, Sun 10am–6pm; June & Sept daily 9am–6pm; Oct–May Mon–Sat 9.15am–5.30pm; ☎064/31633), on Beech Rd, off New St, to make advance bookings. The *An Óige* **hostel** (☎064/31240; ②) is three miles west of town along the Killorglin road, at Aghadoe, but there are several independent hostels in Killarney itself: try the extrovert and noisy *Four Winds Hostel*, 43 New St (☎064/33094; ②); *The Súgan Kitchen* on Lewis Rd, minutes from the station (☎064/33104; ②), a cosy little place where the owners play traditional music; the *Bunrower House* (☎064/33914, ②) near Ross Castle; or the *Park Hostel* (☎064/32119; ②) up the hill off Cork Rd, opposite the petrol station. There's a **campsite** at the *Fossa Hostel and Caravan Park*, (☎064/31497; ②; March–Oct), just past the Aghadoe youth hostel. Places to **eat and drink** are thick on the ground: one of the best is *Bricín*, on High St, or try *Taste of Eden* (closed Mon), Bridewell Lane, for delicious vegetarian fare or the *Celtic Cauldron*, also on High St, for Italian food. Evening **entertainment** is everywhere as you walk along the streets; latest news on the music venues is available from *The Súgan Kitchen* hostel.

Knockreer Estate

The gates of the **Knockreer Estate** are just over the road from Killarney's cathedral, and a short walk through the grounds takes you to the banks of **Lough Leane**, where tall wooded hills plunge into the water, with the peaks rising behind to the highest, **Carrauntoohill** (3414ft). The main path through the estate leads to the restored fourteenth-century tower of **Ross Castle**, (Easter–May & Sept daily 10/11am–6pm; June–Aug daily 9am–6.30pm; Oct Tues–Sun 10am–5pm; IR£2.50, students IR£1; gardens free) the last place in Munster to succumb to Cromwell's forces in 1652. From Ross Castle you can tour the lake in large glassed-over boats, but these don't make stops; an alternative is to get a fisherman to take you out in a little craft with an outboard motor, or hire one yourself. This way, you can land on and explore the island of **Inisfallen**, the biggest and the most enchanting of the thirty-odd small islands that dot Lough Leane. Wandering around the island is a delight: heavily wooded, it's also scattered with monastic buildings – nothing from the original seventh-century foundation, but there's a small Romanesque church and an extremely ruined Augustinian priory.

Muckross and the lakes

The first place to head for in the **Muckross Estate** – a mile and a half south of Killarney – is **Muckross Abbey**, not only for the ruin itself but also for its calm, contemplative location. Founded by the Franciscans in the mid-fifteenth century, it was suppressed by Henry VIII; the friars returned, but were finally driven out by Cromwell in 1652. Back at the main road, signposts direct you to **Muckross House** (daily 9am–6pm; IR£3.80, students IR£1.60), a solid nineteenth-century neo-Elizabethan mansion with a dullish crafts museum in the basement but wonderful gardens. There's also a traditional working farm on the grounds (IR£3.80, students IR£1.60; combined ticket with house IR£5.50, students IR£2.75). The estate gives access to well-trodden paths along the shores of the Muckross Lake, and it's here that you can see one of Killarney's celebrated beauty spots, the **Meeting of the Waters**. Actually a parting, it has a profusion of indigenous and flowering subtropical plants on the left of the Old Weir Bridge. Close by is the massive shoulder of Torc Mountain, shrugging off **Torc Waterfall**. The Upper Lake is beautiful, too, but still firmly on the tourist trail, with the main road running along one side up to **Ladies' View**, from where the view is truly amazing.

The Gap of Dunloe

A natural defile formed by glacial overflow that cuts the mountains in two, the **Gap of Dunloe** is one of Kerry's prime tourist attractions, attracting a continual stream of expensive jaunting cars from Killarney. A better option is to walk the four miles in the late afternoon, when the cars have gone home and the light is at its most magical. **Kate Kearney's Cottage**, a small hamlet at the foot of the track leading up to the Gap, is the last place for food and water before **Lord Brandon's Cottage**, a summer tearoom (June–Aug), way over the other side of the valley. The track – closed to motor traffic – winds its way up the desolate valley between high rock cliffs and waterfalls, past a chain of icy loughs and tarns, to the top, where you find yourself in what feels like one of the remotest places in the world: the **Black Valley**. Named after its entire population perished during the potato famine (1845–49), it's now inhabited by a mere handful of families, and was the very last valley in Ireland to get electricity. There's a wonderfully isolated *An Óige* **hostel** here too (March–Nov; ☎064/34712, ②); booking advisable). From here, the quick way back to Killarney is to carry on down to Lord Brandon's Cottage and take the boat across the Upper Lake.

The Ring of Kerry

Most tourists view the spectacular scenery of the 110-mile **Ring of Kerry** without ever leaving their coach or car. Consequently, anyone straying from the road or waiting until the buses knock off in the afternoon will be left to experience the slow twilights of the Atlantic seaboard in perfect seclusion. **Cycling** the Ring takes three days, and a bike will let you get on to the largely deserted mountain roads. Buses from Killarney go right around the Ring during July and August (2 daily); for the rest of the year they travel along the northern coast as far as Cahersiveen; for bus times, call ☎066/23566.

Valentia Island

At **Kells Bay** the road veers inland towards **CAHERSIVEEN**, a long, narrow street of a town and also the main shopping centre for the western part of the peninsula, giving itself over cheerfully to the tourist trade in summer. It has an independent **hostel**, *Sive*, at 15 East End (☎066/72717; ②), with camping facilities. Beyond Cahersiveen, lanes lead out to **VALENTIA ISLAND**, Europe's most westerly harbour, its position on the Gulf Stream giving it a mild, balmy climate – hence the abundance of fuchsias on the intensively cultivated land. Access to the island is by **ferry** from Reenard Point (two and a half miles from Cahersiveen) to **Knightstown** or across the Maurice O'Neill Bridge from Portmagee, seven miles from the main N70, and a difficult hitch along the R565 coast road (there's no public transport on the island). Knightstown is the focal village, with about a thousand houses clustered around a slate church hidden within a dark rookery. The main street has a few well-stocked shops, a post office offering free maps of the island, and a couple of bars. The much-touted **Grotto** – the highest point on the island – is a gaping slate cavern with a crude statue of the Virgin perched two hundred feet up, amid dripping icy water. More exciting by far is the cliff scenery to the northwest, some of the most spectacular of the Kerry coast.

Accommodation is at a premium during the summer season, so book ahead. The Knightstown *An Óige* **hostel** (☎066/947 6154; ②; June–Sept) has space for forty at the Coastguard Station, though facilities are spartan. Alternatively, there's **B&B** in the village at homely *Walsh's* (☎066/947 6155; ④) or *Spring Acre* (☎066/947 6377; ④).

The Skellig Islands

From Valentia there's a tantalizing view across a broad strip of sea to the **Skellig Islands**. Little Skellig is a bird sanctuary where landing isn't permitted, but you can visit Great Skellig, or **Skellig Michael** as it's also called, and climb up to its ancient monastic site. **Boat trips** depart from Knightstown, Portmagee (May–Sept; contact Owen Walsh, ☎066/947 6327, or Sean Murphy, ☎066/947 6214) and from Ballinskelligs (Joe Roddy; ☎066/947 4268). Trips cost around IR£20, and it's wise to book in advance for the dramatic voyage to the gargantuan slatey mass. From the sea there's no visible route to the summit, but from the tiny landing stage the cliff reveals steps cut into the rock that were formerly the monks' path. Nowadays there's also a path leading to Christ's Saddle, the only patch of green on this savage island. From here, a narrow path leads to the remains of the sixth-century **St Finian's Abbey** with its extraordinary cluster of beehive huts. If the weather is poor, pop into **The Skellig Experience Heritage Centre** (May–Sept daily 10am–6pm; IR£3) just over the Maurice O'Neill Bridge on Valentia, where you can see a sixteen-minute film of the experience – though it can never match the real thing.

Ballinskelligs and Waterville

The stretch of coast between Valentia and Waterville is wild and almost deserted, apart from a scattering of farms and fishing villages. Sweet-smelling, tussocky grass dotted with wild flowers is raked by Atlantic winds, ending in abrupt cliffs or sandy beaches – a beguiling landscape where you can wander for days. The *An Óige* **hostel** (☎066/947 9229; ②; April–Sept) in **BALLINSKELLIGS** is pretty basic but sells supplies. The village is something of a centre of Gaelic culture: monks from the Skellig islands retreated to Ballinskelligs Abbey in the thirteenth century, while the village itself is busy in summer with schoolchildren and students learning Gaelic. **WATERVILLE** may be touristy, but it does have a certain grace. Popular as a Victorian and Edwardian resort and angling centre, it still has an air of consequence that oddly contrasts with the wild Atlantic views. Its few bars and hotels aside, the town is chiefly notable as the best base on the Ring for exploring the coast and the mountainous country inland. There's a very welcoming **B&B** at *Lake Rise*, Lake Rd (☎066/947 4278; June–Aug; ③); *Ashling House* (☎066/74247; April–Oct; ④) is another inexpensive option. Hostellers can muck in at the inimitable and recently expanded *Peter's Place*, Main St (☎066/947 4608; ②).

Kenmare

With its delicatessens, designer boutiques and arty second-hand clothes shops, **KENMARE** is something of a cosmopolitan anomaly, where you're more likely to hear English or German tones than Irish. Kenmare was established by Sir William Petty, Cromwell's surveyor general, who laid the foundations of the mining and smelting industries in this area, encouraged fishing and founded the enormous Lansdowne estate, many of whose buildings still surround the town. Evidence of much more ancient settlement is the stone circle just outside the centre, on the banks of the river. Kenmare has a **hostel**: the *Fáilte* in Shelbourne St (☎064/42333; March–Oct; ②). There are also plenty of **B&Bs**, both in and just outside town: try *Sunville* on Cork Rd (☎064/41169; ③; Feb–Nov) or the excellent *Druid Cottage*, a mile along Sneem Rd (☎064/41803, ④). Alternatively, check vacancies at the **tourist office** on

The Square (July–Aug Mon–Sat 9am–7pm, Sun 9.15am–1pm & 2.15pm–5.30pm; April–June & Sept to mid-Oct Mon–Sat 9.15am–1pm & 2.15pm–5.30pm; ☎064/41233).

The Dingle Peninsula

The remote beauty and poverty of the Dingle Peninsula, and the prevalence of the Gaelic language here, have all lent fuel to romanticizing, the myth being strengthened by the wealth of Gaelic literature once created on the now uninhabited Blasket Islands – and the fact that *Ryan's Daughter* was filmed here. There's one other component to the Dingle's irresistible appeal: outside the Aran Islands, the peninsula has the greatest concentration of monastic ruins in Ireland.

Dingle Town

Served by a morning bus from Killarney's train station, **DINGLE** makes the best base for exploring the peninsula. Though essentially little more than just a few streets by the side of **Dingle Bay**, the town has a solidity that suggests this was a place of some consequence, and Dingle was indeed Kerry's leading port in the fourteenth and fifteenth centuries. It later became a centre for smuggling, and even minted its own coinage during the eighteenth century when the revenue from contraband was at its height.

There's no shortage of **accommodation**, although many of Dingle's B&Bs are fairly expensive; the **tourist office** in Strand St (July–Aug daily 9.30am–6pm; March–June, Sept & Oct daily 9am–1pm & 2.15–6pm; ☎066/915 1188) has an accommodation-booking service. For **hostel** accommodation, try the friendly *Grapevine*, Dykegate St (☎066/915 1434; ②); the *Rainbow* (☎066/915 1044; ②), one mile out west; the haunted *Ballintaggart House*, one mile before Dingle Town (☎066/915 1454; ②), which also offers camping; or the beautifully situated *Seacrest* (☎066/915 1390; ②), near Lispole. Dingle's top **restaurants** serve excellent seafood, landed just a few hundred yards away. Try *Doyle's* or the *Half Door* on John St for a good lunch or dinner. *Greaney's*, on the corner of Dykegate and Strand streets, does good cheap lunches and dinners. Life in the evenings is centred on Dingle's **pubs**, with many of them running traditional music sessions. *An Droichead Beag* on Main St and *O'Flaherty's* on Bridge St are good places to start – there's music most nights, and advice on where to find it elsewhere.

Cycling is the best way to explore the area beyond Dingle, as public transport in the west of the peninsula amounts to a bus from Dingle to Dunquin (July–Aug daily; Sept–June Mon & Thurs; call ☎066/912 3566 for a schedule). Mountain bikes are available from Moriarty's on Main St and Paddy's on Dykegate St.

To Slea Head – and the Blaskets

The Gaelic-speaking area west of Dingle is rich with relics of the ancient Gaelic and early Christian cultures. The main concentration of ancient monuments is to be found between **VENTRY**, now a small village, though once the main port of the peninsula, and Slea Head. First off there's the spectacular **Dun Beag** (IR£1), a scramble down from the road about four miles out from Ventry. A promontory fort, its defences include four earthen rings, with an underground escape route by the main entrance. It's a magical location, overlooking the open sea – into which some of the building has tumbled.

Between Dun Beag and Slea Head, the hillside above the road is studded with stone beehive huts, cave dwellings, souterrains, forts, churches, standing stones and crosses – over 500 of them in all. The beehive huts were being built and used for storing farm tools and produce until the late nineteenth century, but among ancient buildings like the **Fahan group** you're looking over a landscape that's remained essentially unchanged for centuries.

At **Slea Head** the view opens up to include the desolate, splintered masses of the **Blasket Islands**, which have been uninhabited since 1953 though there are some summer residents. In the summer, boats bound for **Great Blasket** leave the pier just south of Dunquin (9.30am–5pm every 30min, weather permitting; IR£10 return). Great Blasket's delights are simple ones: tramping the footpaths that crisscross the island, sitting on the beaches watching the seals and dolphins, or the amazing spectacle of the sun sinking into the ocean. There is no accommodation, but camping is no problem and the café (noon–5pm) serves good, cheap vegetarian meals. At **Dunquin**, there's an *An Óige* **hostel** (☎066/915 6121; ②), and **B&B** accommodation in Kruger's pub (☎066/915 6127; ③).

Ballyferriter and around

A couple of miles around the headland from Dunquin stands **BALLYFERRITER**, where the little northward lanes lead to the 500-foot cliffs at Sybil Head or to Smerwick Harbour and **Dún án Óir** (Golden Fort). The single most impressive early Christian monument on the Dingle Peninsula is the **Gallarus oratory**, three miles further east, constructed some time between the ninth and twelfth centuries. It's the most perfectly preserved example of around twenty such oratories in Ireland and represents a transition between the round beehive huts and the later rectangular churches, an example of which is to be found a mile to the north at **KILMAKEDAR**. Its nave dates from the mid-twelfth century, and the corbelled stone roof was an improvement on the unstable structure at Gallarus. The site also marks the beginning of the **Saint's Road**, dedicated to St Brendan, patron saint of Kerry, which leads to his shrine on the top of Brandon Mountain. For **hostel** accommodation in Ballyferriter try *The Black Cat* (☎066/9156286; ②; May–Sept).

The Burren

A huge plateau of limestone and shale covering over a hundred square miles of northwest Clare, **The Burren** will come as a shock to anyone associating Ireland with all things green. Barely capable of sustaining human habitation, it is bone white in sunshine, becoming dark and metallic in the rain, its cliffs and canyons blurred by mists. Yet this is a botanist's delight, with an astounding variety of arctic, alpine and Mediterranean **flora** – a mixture that nobody can account for. The area's lack of appeal to centuries of speculators and colonizers has meant that evidence of many of the Burren's earlier inhabitants remains. The place buzzes with the prehistoric and historic past, having over sixty Stone Age burial monuments, over four hundred Iron Age ring forts, and numerous Christian churches, monasteries, round towers and high crosses.

For a quick exploration, there's a **Bus Éireann** service from Galway to the village of **DOOLIN**, lodged beside a treacherous sandy beach and famed for a steady supply of **traditional music** throughout the summer. Bold shelves of limestone pavement step into the sea by the pier, from where a ferry runs to all three of the **Aran Islands**. An otherwise forlorn place, Doolin has long been renowned for music, though it's now largely fuelled by tourism. Still, whatever day of the week you arrive in the summer, traditional music will be playing in the three bars, and all in all the place has a lively atmosphere. There is plenty of **accommodation** available here and several budget options: *Paddy's Doolin Hostel* (☎065/707 4006; ②); the *Rainbow Hostel* (☎065/707 4415; ②); *Flanagan's Village Hostel* (☎065/707 4564; ②); and the *Aille River Hostel* (☎065/707 4260; ②). The last two both offer **camping**; there's also a summer **campsite** by the pier, and *O'Connor's* campsite in the village by the *Aille River Hostel*. Walking tours of the Burren are available locally.

The Cliffs of Moher, beginning four miles south of Doolin and stretching for five miles, are Clare's most famous tourist spot, their great bands of shale and sandstone rising 660 feet above the waves.

Galway City

The city of **GALWAY** can be difficult to leave: it has become a playground for disaffected Dubliners, and folksy young Europeans return each year with an almost religious devotion. University College Galway guarantees a high number of young people in term time, but the energy is never more evident than during Galway's **festivals**, especially the Arts Festival in the last two weeks in July. For the locals, however, the most important event in the social calendar is the **Galway Races**, usually held in the last week of July. Accommodation has to be pre-booked during these weeks.

Galway originated as a crossing point on the River Corrib, and developed as a strong Anglo-Norman colony. Granted a charter and city status in 1484 by Richard III, it developed a flourishing trade with the Continent, especially Spain. When Cromwellian forces arrived in 1652, however, the city was besieged for ninety days and went into a decline from which it has only recently recovered.

Arrival and accommodation

The **bus and train stations** are off Eyre Square, on the northern edge of the city centre. The **tourist office** (May–June Mon–Sat 9am–5.45/6.45pm; July–Aug daily 8.30am–7.45pm; Sept–April Mon–Fri 9am–5.45pm, Sat 9am–12.45pm; ☎091/563081) is off the south side of the square, and has an accommodation service. Single travellers and women are strongly advised to ignore any hotel touts they meet at the station; there is decent budget **accommodation** opposite the station at *Great Western House* (☎091/561139; ②) and *The Galway Hostel* (☎091/566959; ②). Other options include: *Kinlay House*, Merchants Rd, Eyre Square (☎091/565244; ②), near the tourist office; *Arch View Hostel*, Dominick St (☎091/586661; ②); *Corrib Villa*, 4 Waterside (☎091/562892; ②); *Woodquay Hostel*, 23–24 Woodquay (☎091/562618; ②); *Salmon Weir Hostel*, St Vincent's Ave, Woodquay (☎091/561133; ②); and the popular, if small, *Mary Ryan's*, 4 Beechmont Rd, Highfield (☎091/523303; ②; summer only). For **B&Bs** head for *Joan Sullivan's*, 46 Prospect Hill (☎091/566324; ④), or *Villa Maruea*, 94 Father Griffin Rd (☎091/589033; ④). There are **campsites** at *Ballyloughane Caravan Park* on Dublin Rd (May–Sept), and several in Salthill, the most pleasant being *Hunter's Silver Strand*, four miles west on the coast road (Easter–Sept).

The City

The prosperity of maritime Galway and its sense of civic dignity were expressed in the distinctive town houses of the merchant class, remnants of which are littered around the city, even though recent development is rapidly destroying the character of the place. The **Browne doorway** in Eyre Square is one such monument, a bay window and doorway with the coats of arms of the Browne and Lynch families, dated 1627. Just about the finest medieval town house in Ireland is **Lynch's Castle** in Shop St – along with Quay St, the social hub of Galway. Now housing the Allied Irish Bank, it dates from the fifteenth century and has a stone facade decorated with carved panels, gargoyles and a lion devouring another animal.

There are two churches of interest: the **Collegiate Church of St Nicholas** and the **Cathedral of Our Lady Assumed into Heaven and St Nicholas**. The former, founded in 1320, is the largest medieval church in Ireland. The Cathedral, in hideous contrast, was commissioned about 25 years ago by the then Bishop of Galway, Mícheal (pronounced Me-hile) Brown – hence its nickname, "The Taj Mícheal". It sits on the banks of the river like a huge toad, its copper dome seeping green slime down the formica-bright limestone walls.

Down by the harbour stands the **Spanish Arch**: more evocative in name than in reality, it's a sixteenth-century structure that was used to protect galleons unloading wine and rum. Next door is housed the uninspiring **Galway Museum** (daily 10am–1pm & 2.15–5.15pm; IR£1), where the only things of real interest are the old photographs of the Claddagh district of the city.

Salthill

To the west of the city lies **SALTHILL**, Galway's seaside resort, complete with amusement arcades, discos, seasonal cafés and a fairground. The huge **Leisureland** amusement complex is used as a venue for big gigs, and also has a swimming pool (summer daily 8.00am–10pm; IR£3.30, IR£2.20 for students). Lower Salthill has a long promenade with a series of safe and sandy beaches, giving a great view over the glittering expanse of water to the Burren, though probably the best in the vicinity is the small beach at **White Strand**, nestling beneath a grassy headland immediately west of Salthill.

Eating, drinking and entertainment

If the "craic" has eluded you so far, this is where you're going to find it. The bars are the lungs of this town, and even the most abstemious travellers are going to find themselves sucked in. You are guaranteed to find music somewhere and similarly there's absolutely no problem finding places to eat. Good-value **pub food** is served around midday at *The Quays*, Quay St, *Tigh Neachtain's*, Cross St, and *MacSwiggan's* in Eyre St. In Quay St, *McDonagh's Seafood Bar* is a must for seafood at any time of day, *Fat Freddy's* is a great place for pizzas, and *Café du Journal* is a coffee-head's heaven while *Sev'nth Heaven*, in nearby Courthouse Lane, serves Tex-Mex, Italian, Cajun and vegetarian meals. The *Get Stuffed Olive*, St Anthony's Place, Woodquay serves excellent vegetarian nosh; *Java's* on Upper Abbeygate St is the place to go for a cheap but healthy breakfast or lunch and *The Home Plate*, Mary Street, serves tasty pizza, pasta and Thai meals at budget prices; *An Chistin* (the Kitchen) West William St has all-day Irish breakfasts for IR£3 and student menus for under IR£2.

Shop and Quay streets offer great traditional-style **bars**, such as *The Quays*, *Tig Neachtain's* and *Busker Browne's*. *Roísín Dubh*, in Dominick St, is a lively spot for solo artistes and bands, *The Blue Note*, Sea Rd, has great jazz at Sunday brunch, and nearby *The Crane Bar* is renowned for its traditional sessions. Galway has its fair share of **clubs and discos**: the *Warwick Hotel*, Salthill, and the *GPO*, Eglinton Street, are a couple of favourites; the latter also has an excellent Friday night comedy club.

The Aran Islands

The Aran Islands – Inishmore, Inishmaan and Inisheer – lying thirty miles out across the mouth of Galway Bay, are spectacular settings for a wealth of pre-Christian and early Christian remains and some of the finest archeological sites in Europe. The islands are Gaelic-speaking, and their isolation allowed the continuation of a unique, ancient culture into the early twentieth century. In 1934 Robert Flaherty made his classic semi-documentary *Man of Aran*, recording the life he found – the film can be seen every day during the summer in Halla Ronain, Kilronan. While the folklore and traditions it depicts have waned considerably, fishing and farming do remain central to the way of life: look out for **currachs**, the light wood-framed boats still used for fishing and for getting ashore on the smaller islands.

Several **ferry** companies operate to the Aran Islands, embarking from Galway City, Rossaveel (20 miles west; bus IR£4) or Doolin in County Clare; the cost of a return trip ranges from IR£12–20, with some student reductions and some good-value accommodation packages, particularly during high season. There are daily sailings to **Inishmore** throughout the year, but less frequently to the other islands. Book through Island Ferries, Victoria Place, Eyre Square, Galway City (☎091/568903 or evenings 561767), O'Brien Shipping, in the Galway tourist office (☎091/567283) or Doolin Ferry Company (☎065/74455), which only operates between mid-April and the end of September. Alternatively, you can **fly** with *Aer Árann* (☎091/593034) for IR£35 return (students IR£29); book tickets and package tours at their desk in the Galway City tourist office.

Inishmore

Although **Inishmore** is the most tourist-orientated of the Aran Islands, its wealth of dramatic ancient sites overrides such considerations. It's a long strip of an island, a great tilted plateau of limestone, with a scattering of villages along the sheltered northerly coast. The land slants up to the southern edge, where tremendous cliffs rip along the entire shoreline. As far as the eye can see is a tremendous patterning of stone, some of it the bare pavementing of grey rock split in bold diagonal grooves, gridded by dry-stone walls that might be contemporary, or might be pre-Christian.

The ferry comes in at **KILRONAN**, where the cheapest place to stay is the *Aran Islands Hostel* (April–Oct; ☎099/61255; ②). B&Bs can be booked through the **tourist office**, across the lane from the hostel (June to mid-Sept daily 10am–6pm; ☎099/61263), or when you buy your ferry ticket. Not surprisingly, seafood is the great speciality on the island: *Dún Aonghasa* has probably the most varied and reasonably priced menu; *Joe Watty's* bar serves good soups and stews, *Dormer House* in Kilronan cooks great seafood and steaks, and *Pota Stair*, based in the Heritage Centre, does delicious homemade soups and cakes.

The best ways to **get about** Inishmore are cycling and walking. For **bicycle rental**, there's Aran Bicycle Hire, beside the ferry dock, Costello's Bike Hire, opposite the *American Bar* further up the lane, or Mullin & Burke, by the *Aran Islands Hostel*. Alternatively, take the **minibus** up the island through the villages that stretch over seven miles to the west – Mainistir, Eochaill, Kilmurvey, Eoghannacht and Bun Gabhla – and walk back from any point.

Most of Aran's sites are to the northwest of Kilronan. The first hamlet in this direction is Mainistir, from where it's a short signposted walk to the simple twelfth-century church of **Teampall Chiaráin**, the most interesting of the ecclesiastical sites on Inishmore. Alongside is **St Kieran's Well**, a long U-shaped spring backed by huge blocks of plant-covered stone. Back on the main road, three miles or so further is Kilmurvey, a fifteen-minute walk from the most spectacular of Aran's prehistoric sites, **Dún Aengus**. This massive ring fort, lodged on the edge of cliffs that plunge three hundred feet into the Atlantic, has an inner citadel of precise blocks of grey stone, their symmetry echoing the almost geometric regularity of the land's limestone pavementing. Nearby **Dún Eoghannachta** is a huge drum of a fort, a perfect circle of stone settled in a lonely field with the Connemara mountains as a backdrop. It's accessible by tiny lanes from Dún Aengus if you've a detailed map; otherwise retrace your steps to Kilmurvey and follow the road west for just over a mile. At the **seven churches**, just east of Eoghannacht, there are ancient slabs commemorating seven Romans who died here, testifying to the far-reaching influence of Aran's monasteries. The site is, in fact, that of two churches and several domestic buildings, dating from the eighth to the thirteenth centuries, and includes Saint Brendan's grave, adorned by an early cross with interlaced patterns. A two-mile walk **south of Kilronan** brings you to **Dún Ducathair**, the massive remains of a fort straddling an ever-shrinking headland. The eastern gateway fell into the sea early in the last century, leaving the entrance a perilous twelve inches from the sheer drop.

Inishmaan

Coming from Inishmore you are immediately struck by how lush **Inishmaan** is, the stone walls forming a maze that chequers off tiny fields of grass and clover. Yet at the same time it's a dour island, where farming is at subsistence levels and cottages are overhung by soggy thatch. The island's main sight is **Dún Conchúir**: built some time between the first and seventh centuries, its massive oval wall is almost intact and commands great views. Inishmaan's indifference to tourism means that amenities for visitors are minimal; if you arrive on spec ask at the pub for information (☎099/73003) – it's a warm and friendly haven which also serves snacks in summer. **B&Bs** are cheaper than on the mainland; try *Mrs A. Faherty* (☎099/73012; ③); or *Máire Bu Uí Mhaolchairáin* (☎099/73016; ③) which also offers free **camping**. Farmers will also let you camp if you ask them.

Inisheer

Inisheer, at just under two miles across, is the smallest of the Aran Islands. Tourism has a key role here; Inisheer doesn't have the archeological wealth of Inishmore, nor the wild solitude of Inishmaan, but regular day-trip ferry services from Doolin during the summer ensure a steady flow of visitors.

A great plug of rock dominates the island, its rough, pale-grey stone dripping with greenery. At the top, the fifteenth-century **O'Brien's Castle** stands inside an ancient ring fort. Set around it are low fields, a small community of pubs and houses, and windswept sand dunes. Half buried in sand just south of the beach is the ancient **Church of St Kevin**, the patron saint of the island. The **tourist office** by the pier (June–Sept daily 10am–7pm) will give you a map and a list of **B&Bs** or you could try *Uí Chongaile's*, Lioseine, West Village (☎099/75025; ③). There's also a **hotel**, *Óstán Inis Oírr* (Hotel Inisheer; ☎099/75099, April–Sept; ④), a **hostel**, *Brú Radharc na Mara* (☎099/75087; ②) and a **campsite** near the pier. **Meals** are available all day at *Radharc na Mara* (June–Sept) beside the hotel. For **live music**, head for the bar or *Tigh Ned's*.

Clifden

The great asset of **CLIFDEN** – known as the capital of Connemara – is its position, perched high above the deep sides of the boulder-strewn estuary of the Owenglin River, with the circling jumble of the Twelve Bens providing a magnificent backdrop. Clifden seems to be trying hard to cultivate the cosmopolitan atmosphere of Galway, and it attracts a fair number of young Dubliners, too, revving up the life of this rural town.

The **tourist office** on Market St (April–Sept Mon–Sat 9/10am–6pm; ☎095/21163) has lists of the plentiful **B&B** accommodation around Clifden, though these can be very busy in July and August and there are few budget options in the town itself. Just outside are *Winnowing Hill*, Ballyconneely Rd (March–Nov; ☎095/21281; ④) and *Hylands Bay View*, Westport Rd (March–Nov; ☎095/21286; ④). Clifden has several **hostels** including the excellent *Clifden Town Hostel*, Market St (☎095/21076; ②); or cosy *Leo's Hostel*, Beach Rd (☎095/21429; ②) which also has **camping** facilities.

Mannion's and *E.J. King's* on Market St are two of the nicest **bars** for drink and music; for evening meals at IR£11 and upwards, try *O'Grady's Seafood Restaurant* or the *Crannmer Restaurant* off Church Hill (evenings; May–Oct). Clifden is the only real base for getting out into the Connemara countryside, and to do this you really need your own transport. There are plenty of places for **bike rental**: try John Mannion on Bridge St.

Westport

Set on the shores of Clew Bay at the end of a rail line from Dublin, the comfortable, relaxed town of **WESTPORT** was planned by the eighteenth-century architect James Wyatt, and its formal layout comes as quite a surprise in the midst of the west. Wyatt's scheme was backed by money from Westport's trade in linen and cotton, but after the Act of Union of 1801 its hand looms could not compete with Britain's or Belfast's industrial mills, and Westport's economy was ruined.

Its quiet Georgian beauties apart, the town's major attraction is **Westport House** (summer Mon–Sat 10.30am–6pm, Sun 2–6pm; IR£6, combined ticket with the zoo IR£8), a mile or so out of town towards the bay. The house was beautifully designed in 1730 by the ubiquitous Richard Castle and was one of the first Irish houses opened to the public. There's a zoo park in the grounds and horse-drawn caravans for hire, while the dungeons have gimmicks such as a trace-your-ancestor service. Inside, however, the house is a little disappointing. There's a *Holy Family* by Rubens, a violin which used to belong to J.M. Synge, and an upstairs room with intricate Chinese wallpapers dating from 1780.

Westport makes a great base for soaking up some urban comforts while you explore the milder country to the north and south. For **accommodation**, you have a choice between three independent hostels: the central *Old Mill Hostel* on James St (☎098/27045; ②), converted from part of an eighteenth-century complex of mills and warehouses; the enormous *Club Atlantic* (☎098/26644; March–Oct; ②), on Altamount St, convenient for the railway station and affiliated to both *An Óige* and IHH; and, a little further out of town, the *Granary* on Quay Rd (☎098/25903; April–Oct; ②). There are plenty of **B&Bs** about, too – check at the **tourist office** (April–Sept Mon–Sat 9am–6pm; also July–Aug Sun 9am–6pm; Oct–March Mon–Fri 9am–5.15pm; ☎098/25711) in the Mall for availability. *O'Malley's* on Bridge St is a popular **eating** choice while the *Lemon Peel*, just off the Octagon, has a burgeoning reputation for its evening meals. Alternatively, *The Continental Café and Healthfood Shop*, High St, serves organic dishes in an old-fashioned New Age environment. The restaurant at *Quay Cottage*, the entrance to Westport House, serves enormous salmon salads and plenty of vegetarian food; the nearby complex of refurbished waterside buildings brims with people, pubs and more expensive restaurants. The best **music** pubs are on Bridge St – *The West* is hugely popular and *Matt Molloy's Bar*, owned by the eponymous Chieftains' flautist, occasionally features visiting celebrities and livens up considerably during Westport's **Arts Festival** at the end of September.

Sligo Town and around

SLIGO is, after Derry, the biggest town in the northwest of Ireland and a focal point for the area. During the Famine its population fell by a third through death and emigration, but a recovery began at the end of the nineteenth century and the upswing has continued to the present day. This said, it still has a small-town atmosphere with a compact centre barely affected by the country's recent economic boom.

The town's main sight, the thirteenth-century **Dominican Friary** (mid-June to mid-Sept daily 9.30am–6.30pm; IR£1.50), ceased its life as a religious foundation in 1641, when the whole town was sacked. These days it's a fine place to have a picnic, as its walls still stand and the chancel and high altar, with fine carvings, are in a good state of preservation. There are two museums of interest along Stephen Street: the **Sligo County Museum** (Mon–Sat 10am–noon & 2–4.50pm; free) with an interesting collection on local history; and **The Yeats Memorial Museum** (same hours; free), a celebration of the life and works of W.B. Yeats, arguably Ireland's most loved poet – among the memorabilia is the Nobel Prize medal awarded him in 1923. Before you rush out, read a bit of the long article on Michael Coleman, one of Ireland's most famous fiddle players; Fritz Kreisler, the greatest of classical violinists, wrote that even he could not attempt the kind of music Coleman played, even if he practised for a thousand years. **The Model Arts Centre** (daily 11am–5pm) on The Mall is home to the Niland Collection and includes paintings and pencil drawings by Jack B. Yeats. His work has a strong local flavour, and his later efforts like *The Graveyard Wall* and *The Sea and the Lighthouse* are especially potent evocations of the life and atmosphere of the area.

Sligo's **tourist office** is on Temple St (July–Aug Mon–Sat 9am–8pm, Sun 10am–2pm; Sept–June Mon–Fri 9am–5pm; ☎071/61201). There are several **B&Bs** in town: try *Renaté House*, 9 Upper John St (☎098/62014; ④); or *St Anne's* (☎071/43188, ④) or *St Theresa's* (☎071/62230, ④), two good choices from the many options on Pearse Rd. **Hostels** include the central and popular *White House Hostel* (☎071/45160; ②) on Markievicz Rd, which gets overcrowded in the summer; *Eden Hill Hostel* on Pearse Rd (☎071/43204; ②) where there's a cosy sitting room, though the beds have seen better days; *The Yeats County Hostel*, Lord Edward St (☎071/46876, ②), clean, well-run, and handy for the train station; or the *Harbour House*, Finisklin Rd, (☎071/71547, ②), which offers very comfortable budget accommodation, though it's a lonely, mile-long walk from the centre – not recommended if you're a woman walking alone. For **bike rental**, try Gary's Cycles on Lower Quay St (☎071/45418).

Every pub in Sligo seems to serve a decent **bar lunch**, though there are plenty of **eating** alternatives. *Café Cairo*, Rockwood Parade, has an imaginative menu with good vegetarian options, while *Bistro Bianconi* on O'Connell St does upmarket pizza and pasta, and *The Loft Restaurant*, above *M.J. Carr's* on Lord Edward St, has a varied menu of burgers, fish and Mexican dishes. Sligo does well for **pubs**: *Hargadon's* on O'Connell St is a fine old traditional place, with dark recesses, snugs and shelves of nineteenth-century earthenware jugs; *Shoot the Crown*, Castle St, is a livelier alternative. The best spots for **traditional music** are *T.D.'s*, Adelaide St, and *The Leitrim Bar*, across the river on The Mall – check the weekly *Sligo Champion* for listings of these and other events. Sligo's biggest **club** is *Taff's* at the Embassy Rooms, John F. Kennedy Parade (Thurs–Sun).

Drumcliff, Benbulben and Glencar Lough

Heading north from Sligo, bus #480 or #64 will take you to **DRUMCLIFF**, a monastic site probably better known as the last resting place of **W.B. Yeats**. His grave is in the grounds of an austere nineteenth-century Protestant church, within sight of Benbulben, as the poet wished. In 575 St Columba founded a monastery here, and you can still see the remnants of a round tower on the left of the roadside and a tenth-century high cross – the only one in County Sligo – on the right. Local excavations have turned up a wealth of Iron and Bronze Age remains, too.

There are no hostels, but probably the best **B&B** in the area is *Urlar House* (March–Oct; ☎071/63110; ④), one mile north of Drumcliff graveyard. It makes the best base for the climb of **Benbulben**, which at 1730 feet is one of the most spectacular mountains in the country, its profile changing dramatically as you round it. Access to its slopes is easy, but avoid it after dark as there are a lot of dangerous clefts.

Just to the east of Drumcliff, set into the back of Benbulben, is **Glencar Lough**. For the best of the lake, follow the road around its northern edge until you see the "Waterfall" signpost. From the nearby car park a path leads up to the waterfall itself, which is especially impressive after heavy rain. For an excellent mountain walk, continue along the road to the eastern end of the lake where a track rises steeply northwards to the **Swiss Valley**, a deep rift crowned with silver fir. To reach Glencar Lough from Sligo (around 10 miles) take the #64 Manorhamilton bus and ask to be dropped at the junction for the lake from where it's a two-mile walk (for Sligo bus times call ☎071/60066).

Donegal Town

Regular buses connect Sligo to **DONEGAL TOWN**, a bustling place with traffic usually jammed around its busy Diamond, the old marketplace. Donegal is a fine base from which to explore the stunning coastal countryside and inland hills and loughs, though just about the only thing to see in the town itself is the well-preserved shell of **O'Donnell's Castle** (daily May–Oct 9.30am–5.45pm; IR£2) on Tirchonaill St by the Diamond, a fine example of Jacobean architecture. On the left bank of the River Eske stand the few ruined remains of **Donegal Friary**, while on the opposite bank a woodland path known as **Bank Walk** offers wonderful views of **Donegal Bay** and towards the **Blue Stack Mountains**, which rise at the northern end of **Lough Eske**.

There are dozens of **B&Bs** in town, and to avoid a lot of walking it's simplest to call at the **tourist office** on the Quay (July–Aug daily 9am–8pm; Easter–June & Sept Mon–Sat 9am–5pm; ☎073/21148). There are also three **hostels** on or near the Killybegs road: nearest is *Cliffview Hostel* (☎073/21684; ②), followed by *Donegal Town Independent Hostel* (☎073/22805; ②); both offer **camping** facilities. Finally, the *An Óige Ball Hill Hostel* is about three miles out on the north side of Donegal Bay (Easter–Sept; ☎073/21174; ②).

Eating places are plentiful. You'll find excellent fast food at the *Harbour*, opposite the tourist office, a substantial cheap meal at the *Atlantic Café* at the town end of Main St and fish from Killybegs further up at *The Errigal Restaurant*. As for **pubs**, many do good lunches and are good evening watering holes. The *Olde Castle Bar*, next to the castle, is fine for a quiet daytime drink and often has evening music. *McGroarty's*, a few doors down, has a Thursday night traditional session. Several of the pubs on Main St also offer regular **music** while *The Abbey Hotel* on the Diamond hosts an incredibly popular Sunday **disco** and other events. **Bikes** can be rented from the Bike Shop on Waterloo Place or O'Doherty's on Main St, which is also useful for supplementary information about the region.

Slieve League and Glencolmcille

To the west of Donegal Town lies one of the most stupendous landscapes in Ireland – the elementally beautiful **Teelin Bay** and the awesome **Slieve League** cliffs. An ideal base for exploring the region is one of the most welcoming independent **hostels** in the country, the *Derrylahan Independent Hostel* (☎073/38079; ②) on the seaside road between Kilcar and Carrick, which also has a campsite. If you're arriving by bus (daily from Donegal to Glencolmcille), ask to be put down at The Rock and walk from there – otherwise it's two miles from Kilcar.

There are two routes up to the ridge of Slieve League: a back route following the signpost to Baile Mór just before you come into Teelin, and the road route from Teelin to Bunglass, which is one thousand sheer feet above the sea. The former path, which in places is only a few feet wide and can be extremely dangerous in windy weather, has you looking up continually at the ridge known as One Man's Path, on which walkers seem the size of pins, while the frontal approach swings you up to one of the most thrilling cliff scenes in the world, the **Amharc Mór** (Great View). The sea moves so far below it seems like a film that has lost its soundtrack, and the two-thousand-foot-high face of Slieve League glows with mineral deposits in tones of amber, white and red. On a good day it's possible to see one third of Ireland from the summit.

From Amharc Mór you can walk via Malinbeg and Malinmore to **GLENCOLMCILLE** – the Glen of St Columbcille, the name by which Columba was known after his conversion. Approaching it by road, you cross a landscape of desolate upland moor, after which the rich verdant beauty of the Glen (as it's invariably known) comes as a welcome shock.

Glencolmcille has been a place of pilgrimage since the seventh century AD, following the saint's stay in the valley. Every June 9 at midnight the locals commence a three-hour barefoot itinerary of the cross-inscribed slabs that stud the valley basin, finishing up with Mass at 3am in the small church. For the rest of the summer, the **Folk Village Museum and Heritage Centre** next to the beach usually has tourists tripping over one another on the strictly guided tours (Easter–Sept Mon–Sat 10am–6pm, Sun noon–6pm; IR£1.50) through a clustered *clachan* of replica thatched cottages, each decked out with furniture and artefacts from the era it represents. There's a new reception area with information on the area's history and heritage, a National School replica with a section on American artist Rockwell Kent, who painted marvellous landscapes of the area, and a **Shebeen** house where you can sample seaweed wine and other concoctions.

A path up to the left from the Folk Village leads to the *Dooey Hostel* (☎073/30130; ②), which also caters for wheelchairs and has a **campsite** and a staggering view; from behind the hostel cliff walks steer off around the south side of the bay above a series of jagged drops. Rising from the opposite end of the valley mouth, the promontory of Glen Head is surmounted by a Martello tower. On the way out, you pass the ruins of **St Columbcille's Church**, with a "resting slab" where Saint Columba lay down exhausted from prayer. The place to **eat** in the village is *An Bradán Feasa*, part of the Foras Cultúir Uladh complex (Ulster Studies Centre), or there's the *Lace House Restaurant* on the main street above the **tourist office** (June–Aug daily 10am–6pm; ☎073/30116). **B&B** accommodation is available at *Brackendale* (☎073/30038; ③) or *Corner House* (☎073/30021; April–Sept; ④) both near *Biddy's Bar* in Cashel, the village centre.

NORTHERN IRELAND

Nowhere is the pace of political change more rapid, nor the future more uncertain, than in Northern Ireland. In May, 1998, after thirty years of "The Troubles", its people overwhelmingly voted in support of the peace process and, in consequence, an end to sectarian violence. The fragility of the peace settlement was demonstrated by the bombing of Omagh town centre in August 1998 and there remains considerable uncertainty around the future of the elected Northern Ireland Assembly and the decommissioning of paramilitary weaponry. Nevertheless, the North remains a relatively safe place for visitors. Nowadays it's possible to visit **Belfast** and **Derry** – two lively cities that should be on every visitor's list of must-see places – without ever being aware of a security presence. Despite the fact that the North is generally more hospitable than the Republic, it's little frequented by tourists, even though the northern coastline of **County Antrim** – expecially **Glens** and the weird geometry of the **Giant's Causeway** – is as spectacular as anything you will find in Ireland. **Counties Tyrone** and **Fermanagh** form the bulk of inland Northern Ireland; Tyrone is largely dull farming country, but Fermanagh has at its core the great **Lough Erne**, a huge lake complex dotted with islands and surrounded by richly beautiful countryside. **Enniskillen**, its county town, is resonant with history, as are many of the ancient sites within the waterways of Lough Erne.

Belfast

A quarter of the population of Northern Ireland live in the capital, **BELFAST**. While the legacy of "The Troubles" is clearly visible in the landscape of areas like West Belfast – the peace walls, derelict buildings and political murals – security measures have been considerably eased and the place still buzzes with a tangible sense of optimism engendered by the peace process and economic rejuvenation.

Belfast began its life as a cluster of forts built to guard a ford across the River Farset, which nowadays runs beneath the High Street. However, Belfast was very slow to develop, and its history as a city doesn't really begin until 1604, when Sir Arthur Chichester was "planted" in the area by James I. By the eighteenth century the cloth trade and shipbuilding had expanded tremendously, and the population increased ten-fold in a hundred years. It was then a city noted for its liberalism, but in the nineteenth century the sectarian divide became wider and increasingly violent. Although Partition and the creation of Northern Ireland with Belfast as its capital inevitably boosted the city's status, the Troubles exacerbated the industrial decline which hit most of the British Isles during the 1980s. However, a massive programme of regeneration commenced in the 1990s at the first signs of peace, fuelled by the billions of pounds being pumped in from Britain, the European Union and the International Fund for Ireland in the hope that political stability would ensue. New businesses were attracted and old ones – such as the linen and shipbuilding industries – reinvigorated. As yet, there's no sign of the bubble bursting and there's a real sense of liveliness; Belfast is no longer a city under siege.

Arrival and information

Flying into Belfast you arrive either at **Belfast International Airport** (☎028/94 422888) in Aldergrove, nineteen miles from the city (airport coaches every 30min to the Europa Bus Station; £4.50), or at **Belfast City Airport** (☎028/90 457745), four miles out (bus #21 to city centre; 90p). Of the **ferries** to Northern Ireland, the ninety-minute journey with Seacat (☎08705/523523) from Stranraer to Belfast Harbour is the quickest and most convenient, docking at Donegall Quay; from here it's a fifteen-minute walk into the centre. Seacat's new services from Troon and Heysham (April–Sept) also dock here. The Stena Line high-speed ferry (☎0990/707070) from Stranraer docks further north at Ballast Quay – a taxi from here will cost around £4. Norse Irish Ferries (☎028/90 779090) arrive from Liverpool even further north on West Bank Rd – expect to pay a taxi fare of at least £5. Finally, P&O ferry services from Cairnryan (☎0990/980777) dock at Larne, twenty miles north, connected to the Laganside Bus Station by Ulsterbus and to Yorkgate and Central Stations by train. All **trains** pass through or terminate at the Central Railway Station on East Bridge St (☎028/90 899411). **Buses** from the west and the Republic arrive at the Europa Bus Station, Great Victoria St, whereas buses from the north and east use the Laganside Buscentre in Queen's Square. A Centrelink bus service connects bus and train stations.

The **Northern Ireland Tourist Information Centre** is at 59 North St (July–Aug Mon–Fri 9am–6.30pm, Sat 9am–5.15pm, Sun noon–4pm; Sept–June Mon–Sat 9.30am–5.15pm; ☎028/90 246609). **Bord Fáilte**, for information about the Republic, can be found at 53 Castle St (☎028/90 327888 Mon–Fri 9am–5pm, Sat 9am–12.30pm).

Accommodation

Many of Belfast's numerous **B&Bs** are on the south side of the city in the university area – the tourist office or information centre can make bookings – and there are now a number of budget options.

The Ark, 18 University St (☎028/90 329626). Friendly, comfortable hostel close to Queen's. ②.

Arnie's Backpackers, 63 Fitzwilliam St (☎028/90 242867). Cheerful and relaxed independent hostel near the university. ②.

Belfast International Youth Hostel, 22 Donegall Rd (☎028/90 315435). Large, well-equipped but characterless new hostel in the city centre. ②.

Botanic Lodge Guest House, 87 Botanic Ave (☎028/90 327682). Popular, family-run B&B, seventeen rooms, but only two en-suite. ⑤.

Eglantine Guest House, 21 Eglantine Ave (☎028/90 667585). Homely accommodation in Victorian house, with seven rooms, including one family room. ④.

The Linen House, 18 Kent St (☎028/90 586400). New 130-bed independent hostel off Royal Avenue in the city centre. ②.

Liserin Guest House, 17 Eglantine Ave (☎028/90 660769). Another well-run B&B in the University area. Seven rooms including one family room. ④.

City transport

The excellent **City Bus** service covers nearly everywhere you'll want to go, with Ulsterbus serving the outlying areas from depots at the Laganside Buscentre and the Europa Bus Station. There are also special **late-night buses** running drop-off services from 1am to 2am (Fri & Sat; £2.50) from Shaftesbury Square. Ticket prices on most services vary according to length of journey. If you're planning on visiting sites outside the inner zone, it's worth buying a multi-journey ticket (£2.70) in advance, available from newsagents and the CityBus kiosk in Donegall Square West, which can also provide a free bus map. **Taxis**, based at ranks in Donegall Square and others throughout the city, charge a minimum £2.

The City

The **City Hall**, presiding over central **Donegall Square**, is an austere building (guided tours June–Sept Mon–Fri 10.30am, 11.30am & 2.30pm, Sat 2.30pm; Oct–May Mon–Sat 2.30pm; free), its civic purpose almost subservient to its role in propagating the ethics of Presbyterian power. From the main entrance Queen Victoria, portrayed as empress, gazes maternally across the rooftops towards the Protestant Shankill area. At the northwest corner of the square stands **Linenhall Library** (Mon–Wed & Fri 9.30am–5.30pm, Thurs till 8.30pm, Sat till 4pm), where the Political Collection houses over 80,000 publications dealing with every aspect of Northern Irish political life since 1966. The streets leading north off Donegall Square North take you into the main shopping area. Towards the river, either side of Ann St, you're in the narrow alleyways known as the **Entries**. Here you'll find some great old saloon bars. At the end of **High Street** the clock tower is a good position from which to view the world's second and third largest cranes, Goliath and Samson, across the river in the Harland & Wolff shipyard where the Titanic was built. Down Oxford St, to the south, lies the massive Laganside redevelopment, focusing on the impressive **Waterfront Hall** theatre complex.

North of the clock tower is a series of grand edifices which grew out of a similar civic vanity to that invested in the City Hall. The recently restored **Customs House**, a Corinthian-style building, is the first you'll see, but the most monolithic is the Protestant **Cathedral of St Anne** at the junction of Donegall and Talbot streets, a neo-Romanesque basilica started in 1899. Entrance is via a huge west door, but there's little else of interest except for the body of Lord Edward Henry Carson, the leading opponent of Home Rule, entombed underneath the nave floor.

The **university area** inhabits part of the stretch of **South Belfast** known as "The Golden Mile", starting at the **Grand Opera House** on Great Victoria St. The area is littered with eating places, pubs and bars, B&Bs and guesthouses; dozens of restaurants have sprung up, triggered by the refurbishment of the grandiose, turn-of-the-century Opera House in 1980. Among the attractions is the **Crown Liquor Saloon**, one of the greatest of the old Victorian gin palaces and now a National Trust property, though still open for drinking. Before heading straight into the university quarter, sidestep off Great Victoria St into **Sandy Row**, which runs parallel to the west. A strong working-class, Protestant quarter, with the tribal pavement painting to prove it, it's one of the most glaring examples of Belfast's divided worlds, wildly different from the cosmopolitan Golden Mile. Just past the southern end of Sandy Row, three church steeples frame the entrance to the university quarter, of which **Queen's University** is the architectural centrepiece, flanked by the most satisfying Georgian terrace in Belfast, **University Square**.

Just to the side of the University are the verdant **Botanic Gardens**, whose **Palm House** (Mon–Fri 10am–4/5pm, Sat & Sun 2–4/5pm; free) was the first of its kind in the world. Also in the Botanic Gardens you'll find the **Ulster Museum** (Mon–Fri 10am–5pm, Sat 1–5pm, Sun 2–5pm; free, except for some major exhibitions; buses #69, #70 & #71), where the displays run from an Early Ireland gallery to the Living Sea's interactivity, while the Girona exhibition shows treasures salvaged from the Spanish Armada ships which foundered off the Giant's Causeway in 1588. The excellent art exhibitions on the top floor embrace a variety of modern Irish art drawn from the museum's extensive collection and there are also regular special shows.

Eating, drinking and entertainment

Belfast is a big city, and it's never hard to keep yourself amused in the evenings. Many of the best places to eat and the liveliest **pubs** can be found around Great Victoria St and in the university area. As so often in Ireland, the best entertainment you'll find in Belfast is **music** in the pubs. Some of the main sessions and venues are listed below; other good sources of information are the free papers *The Big List* (fortnightly) and *Wipeout* (monthly), both available in pubs and record shops, the monthly *Northern Entertainment* and *Arts Link* available from the tourist office, and the *Belfast Evening Telegraph*.

RESTAURANTS AND CAFÉS

Archana, 53 Dublin Rd. Reasonably priced Indian restaurant specializing in balti dishes.

Bewley's, Donegall Arcade. Branch of the famous Dublin coffee house serving good-value breakfasts, lunches and snacks.

Bonnie's Museum Café, 11a Stranmillis Rd. Trendy café opposite the Ulster Museum, serving a fine fisherman's pie and open till 1.30 am Fri–Sun.

Chez Delbart (aka *Frogities*), 10 Bradbury Place. French food at good prices, though you often have to queue.

Láziz, 99 Botanic Avenue. Splendid new Moroccan restaurant serving beautifully presented and extremely tasty specialities.

Maggie May's, 45 Botanic Ave. Huge, economically priced portions with lots of veggie choices.

Mogwai, 45 University Rd. Belfast's first all-night café, part-owned by local music star David Holmes, who also selects the background sounds.

Nick's Warehouse, 35 Hill St. Good-value food in the downstairs winebar, chic restaurant upstairs.

Roscoff Café, 21 Fountain St. Sublime sandwiches in this down-to-earth branch of the internationally acclaimed restaurant.

Sun Kee, 38 Donegall Pass. No-frills decor, but superbly adventurous Chinese food. BYOB.

Villa Italia, 39 University Rd. Queues outside are the best indicator of this reasonably priced Italian restaurant's popularity.

PUBS & MUSIC

The Beaten Docket, 48 Great Victoria St. Packed with fashion-conscious youngsters; discos at weekends.

The Crown Liquor Saloon, 46 Great Victoria St. The city's most famous pub, decked out like a spa bath, with a good range of Ulster food and Strangford oysters in season.

The Empire, 42 Botanic Ave. Cellar bar in converted church with regular music and popular Tuesday-night comedy club.

The Front Page, 108 Upper Donegall St. Packed with journalists during the day – major club nights on Saturday.

Katy Daly's, Ormeau Ave. Singers most evenings and regular club nights.

Kelly's Cellars, 30 Bank St. Traditional bar with live bands on Friday and sessions Saturday.

The Kitchen Bar, 16 Victoria Sq. Fine old bar, tucked away behind Ann St – great value lunches and traditional sessions Friday and Saturday.

The Liverpool, Donegall Quay. Worth the trek for the traditional music on Sunday nights.

Madden's, Smithfield. Unpretentious and atmospheric pub – regular traditional sessions.

The Morning Star, 17 Pottinger's Entry. Once the Dublin–Belfast mail coach stop, this comfortable and old-fashioned bar serves great food in the restaurant upstairs.

Morrison's Spirit Grocer's, 21 Bedford St. Retro bar with interesting lunchtime food.

The Rotterdam, 54 Pilot St. Major and minor music names play in this docklands venue. First-class stuff.

Listings

Airlines Aer Lingus, 46 Castle St (☎0645/737747); British Airways (☎0345/222111); British Midland, Suite 2, Fountain Centre (☎0345/554554); Jersey European (☎0990/676676).

Airports Belfast City Airport (☎028/90 457745); Belfast International Airport (☎028/94 422888).

Buses CityBus (☎028/90 246485); Ulsterbus (☎028/90 333000).

Car rental Avis (☎028/90 240404); Budget (☎028/90 230700).

Exchange Most city centre banks; Thomas Cook, 11 Donegall Place (Mon–Sat 9am–5pm; ☎028/90 550030) and at the Tourist Information Centre.

Ferries Seacat, Donegall Quay (☎08705/523523); Stena Line, Ballast Quay (☎0990/707070); Norse Irish Ferries, West Bank Rd (☎028/90 779090); P&O European Ferries at Larne Harbour (☎0990/980777).

Hospitals Belfast City Hospital, Lisburn Road (☎028/90 329241); Royal Victoria, Grosvenor Rd (☎028/90 240503).

Left luggage Due to security considerations, there is no official place to leave your luggage.

Police Main police station is in North Queen St (☎028/90 650 222); in emergencies call ☎999.

Post office General Post Office, Castle Place.

Trains Central Station information (☎028/90 899491).

Travel agents USIT, Fountain Centre (☎028/90 324073); Thomas Cook, 11 Donegall Place (☎028/90 550030).

The Giant's Causeway and Dunluce Castle

Since 1693, when the Royal Geographical Society publicized it as one of the great wonders of the natural world, the **Giant's Causeway** has been a major tourist attraction. Made up of an estimated 37,000 polygonal basalt columns, it's the result of a massive subterranean explosion some sixty million years ago, which stretched from here to Staffa (see p.218), where it was responsible for the formation of Fingal's Cave. A huge mass of molten basalt spewed out onto the surface and, as it cooled, solidified into what are, essentially, massive polygonal crystals. Public transport to and from the Causeway is well organized in summer: the train line from Belfast ends at Portrush (change at Coleraine), where you can either catch the open-top bus or the regular #172; or take the once-daily coach service, Antrim Coaster Express, from Belfast.

The Causeway's **visitor centre** (April–Oct daily 10am–6/7pm; Nov–March 10am–4.30/5pm; free; car parking IR£3) is not a place to linger unless you're very cold or very wet. There's an exhibition (IR£1) that doesn't tell you a great deal, its single engaging exhibit being a tram that used to run between Portrush and the Causeway. Taking the path from the visitor centre brings you to the **Grand Causeway**, where you'll find some of the most spectacular of the blocks, and where most of the crowd lingers. A shuttle bus (every 15 minutes; £1 return) operates between the centre and the Causeway, but if you push on, you'll be rewarded with relative solitude and views of some of the more impressive formations high in the cliffs. One of these, **Chimney Point**, has an appearance so bizarre that it persuaded the ships of the Spanish Armada to open fire on it, believing that they were attacking Dunluce Castle, a few miles further west. Tucked into the coastline are some spectacular caves, inaccessible from land, including Runkerry Cave, an amazing 700ft long and 60ft high. Your best option, if you wish to explore them, is to persuade a fisherman in Portballintrae or Dunseverick Harbour to take you (£40 is considered a persuasive offer).

Dunluce Castle

Seven miles west of the Causeway – just beyond Portballintrae, where the bus from the Causeway to Portrush stops – sits sixteenth-century **Dunluce Castle** (April–Sept Mon–Sat 10am–7pm, Sun 2–7pm; Oct–March Mon–Sat 10am–4pm, Sun 2–4pm; £1.50), the most impressive ruin along this entire coastline. Sited on a fine headland high above a cave, it looks as if it only needs a roof to be perfectly habitable once again. Its original owner, **Sorley Boy MacDonnell**, was driven from the castle by the English in 1584, but soon returned, using the salvage from a Spanish Armada wreck to finance the repairs. His son was made Viscount Dunluce and Earl of Antrim by James I, but in 1639 Dunluce Castle paid the penalty for its precarious position when the kitchen, complete with cooks and dinner, fell off during a storm. Shortly afterwards the MacDonnells moved to more comfortable lodgings in Glenarm.

Derry

Lying at the foot of Lough Foyle, immediately before the border, **DERRY** presents a beguiling picture, the city's two hillsides terraced with pastel-shaded houses punctuated by stone spires. However, the reputation of the North's second city has more to do with its politics than its scenic appeal. Until recently Derry's two-thirds Catholic majority was denied its civil rights by gerrymandering, which ensured that the Protestant minority maintained control of all important local institutions. The situation came to a head after the Protestant Apprentice Boys' March in August 1969, when the RUC attempted to storm the Catholic estates of the Bogside. In the tension that ensued, British troops were for the first time widely deployed in the North. On January 31, 1972, the crisis reached a new pitch when British paratroopers opened fire on civilians, killing thirteen unarmed demonstrators in what became known as **Bloody Sunday**. Derry is now greatly changed: tensions eased considerably here long before Belfast, thanks in part to a determinedly even-handed local council, although defiant murals remain and marching is still a contentious issue. The city centre has undergone significant regeneration too, with the construction of several new shopping malls, and Derry has gained a justifiable reputation for innovation in the arts.

The City

The entire circuit of Derry's **city walls** – some of the best-preserved defences left standing in Europe – is open to the public and makes the best starting point for a walkabout of the city. A mile in length and never higher than a two-storey house, the walls are reinforced by bulwarks, bastions and a parapeted earth rampart as wide as a thoroughfare. Within their circuit, the medieval street pattern has remained, with four gateways – Shipquay, Butcher, Bishop and Ferryquay – surviving from the first construction, in slightly revised form.

You're more than likely to make your approach from the Guildhall Square, once the old quay. Most of the city's cannon are lined up here, between Shipquay and Magazine gates, their noses peering out above the ramparts. A reconstruction of the medieval **O'Doherty Tower** houses an excellent museum of local history (Tues–Sat 10am–5pm; £3.50) with artefacts from Spanish Armada wrecks on show on the upper storey.

Turning left at Shipquay Gate, you follow the promenade as it doglegs at Water Bastion where the River Foyle once lapped the walls at high tide. Continue on to Newgate Bastion and Ferryquay Gate, where you can look out across the river to prosperous and largely Protestant Waterside. En route you'll come across a cast-iron cruciform mould of two figures back to back. Several sculptures have been placed at strategic points on the walls by the English artist Antony Gormley, their gaping eye sockets looking out in diametrically opposite directions from a single body – a frank comment on the city's ideological split.

Between Ferryquay and Bishop's Gate the major sight of interest is the Protestant cathedral, just within the south section of the walls. It overlooks the Fountain, the Protestant enclave immediately outside the same stretch of walls, named after the freshwater source that once supplied the city. **St Columb's Cathedral** (Mon–Sat 9am–1pm & 2–4/5pm; £1 donation) was built in 1633, the first post-Reformation cathedral to be constructed in the British Isles. In 1688–89 Derry played a key part in the Williamite victory over the Catholic King James II by holding out against a fifteen-week siege that cost the lives of one-quarter of the city's population. The cathedral was used as a battery during the siege, its tower serving as a lookout post; today it provides the best view of the city. The present spire dates from the late Georgian period, its lead-covered wooden predecessor having been stripped to fashion bullets and cannon shot. Inside, flags brought back from military expeditions give the interior a strong sense of British imperialism. Other things to look out for are the finely sculpted reredos behind the altar, the eighteenth-century bishop's throne, and the window panels showing scenes as diverse as the relief of the city on August 12, 1689, and Saint Columba's mission to Britain.

Back on the walls, you'll pass the white sandstone **courthouse** next to Bishop Gate and you'll see, downhill to the left, the only remaining tower of the old Derry jail. At the Double

Bastion sits the Roaring Meg cannon, used during the siege, while down in the valley below are the streets of the Bogside, once the undisputed preserve of the IRA, and a more recent symbol of defiance, **The Free Derry Mural**, painted in 1968 – nearby to its right is the Bloody Sunday memorial. Clearly visible from the **Royal Bastion** are the words "No Sectarian Marches" printed out across the balconies of a block of flats just below. The Bastion used to be topped by a nine-foot statue of Rev. George Walker, "the defender of Derry", until it was blown up in 1973 – it is in Walker's and their predecessors' memory that the Protestant Apprentice Boys march on August 12.

Practicalities

The **tourist information office** is situated in a new building at the far end of Foyle St (☎028/71 267284) and contains both a Bord Fáilte office and a branch of the Northern Ireland Tourist Board (July–Sept Mon–Fri 9am–7pm, Sat 10am–6pm, Sun 10am–5pm; rest of year Mon–Thurs 9am–5.15pm, Fri 9am–5pm). There is a 150-bed YHANI **hostel** in the city centre at *Oakgrove Manor*, 4 Magazine St (☎028/ 71 372273; ②), which also has **bikes** for rent, and an independent hostel, *Steve's Backpackers*, at 4 Asylum Rd, half a mile from town down Strand Rd (☎028/71 377989; ②). **B&Bs** are fairly thin on the ground within the city itself, but *Saddler House*, 36 Great James St (☎028/71 269691; ④) is excellent value, with *Clarence House*, 15 Northland Rd (☎028/71 265342; ④), as a good alternative.

Eating out in the city has improved dramatically over the last few years, though the choice is still not what you would call bewildering. Shipquay St has the widest variety, including *The Galley*, which does very tasty and reasonably priced home-baked food. Even cheaper are *Anne's Hot Bread Shop*, 8 William St, and the very sociable *Leprechaun*, 23 Strand Road. Further on is *Reggie's*, 145 Strand Rd, for seafood treats including chowder. For entertainment, the **pubs** once again are the best bet. The student set congregates at the *College Arms* at the bottom of the Rock Road and, of course, in the campus bar in Magee College grounds. Congenial and conversational pubs are: *Badgers*, 16 Orchard St, and the *Clarendon Bar*, 48 Strand Rd; livelier pubs are the *Metro*, 3 Bank Place, the *Monico*, 4 Customs House St and *Mullan's*, 13 Little James St. **Traditional music** venues that remain are mostly on Waterloo St, just outside the northern section of the walls: The *Dungloe Bar* (pronounced Dun-Low) and *Peadar O'Donnell's* have regular sessions and you'll also find music at *The Gweedore* and the *Rocking Chair*.

Enniskillen and around

ENNISKILLEN – served by regular buses from Belfast, Derry and Dublin – is the only place of any size in Fermanagh, and although you can see all that it has to offer in a day, it makes a good base for wider exploration. The town sits on an island like an ornamental buckle, a narrow ribbon of water passing each side connecting the Lower and Upper Lough complexes. The water loops its way around the core of the town, its glassy surface lending Enniskillen a sense of calm and reflecting the mini-turrets of **Enniskillen Castle**. Rebuilt by William Cole, to whom the British gave Enniskillen in 1609, the castle houses the **Watergate History and Heritage Centre** and the **Regimental Museum of the Royal Inniskilling Fusiliers** in the keep (both museums all year Mon 2–5pm, Tues–Fri 10am–5pm; plus May–Sept Sat 2–5pm, July–Aug Sun 2–5pm; £2), a proud, polished display of the uniforms, flags and paraphernalia of the town's historic regiments.

A mile along the Belfast road stands **Castle Coole**, the eighteenth-century home of the Earls of Belmore (May–Aug Mon–Wed & Fri–Sun 1–6pm; April & Sept Sat, Sun & bank holidays only 1–6pm; gardens open all year; £2.80; grounds free to pedestrians, but £2 per car). A perfect Palladian building of Portland stone, with an interior of fine plasterwork and superb furnishings, it sits in a beautiful landscaped garden, whose cultivated naturalness reinforced its owners' belief that the harmony of God's creation mirrored that of society.

Opposite the **bus station** on Wellington Rd is the **Fermanagh Tourist Information Centre** (Easter–Sept Mon–Fri 9am–5.30/6.30pm, Sat 10am–6pm, Sun 11am–5pm;

Oct–Easter Mon–Fri 9am–5.30pm; ☎028/66 323110). The office has comprehensive accommodation lists and will book rooms for a small charge. Alternatively, **B&B** is easily found across the town's western bridges, along the A46 Derrygonnelly road and along the Sligo road. The nearest **hostel** is at Castle Archdale (see below). Currently everybody's favourite **place to eat** is *Franco's* in Queen Elizabeth Rd, north and parallel to High St. The best Indian is *Kamal Mahal* in Water St, off High St. A lot of the bars along High St and its continuation, Townhall St, do decent pub food, particularly *The Vintage* and *Pat's Bar*, but, further down on East Bridge St, the *Barbizon Café* has the most imaginative menu available during the day. **Country music** is big in Enniskillen, but you'll find regular **traditional sessions** at the *Bush*, Townhall St (Mon) and the *Railway Hotel*, Forthill Rd (Sun).

Lough Erne

The earliest people to settle in this region lived on and around the two lakes of Lough Erne, and many of the islands here are in fact *crannogs* – Celtic artificial islands. Its myriad waterways were impenetrable to outsiders, protecting the settlers from invaders and creating an enduring cultural isolation. Evidence from stone carving suggests that Christianity was accepted far more slowly here than elsewhere: several pagan idols have been found on Christian sites, and the early Christian remains to be found on the islands show strongly the influence of pagan culture.

The easiest place to visit from Enniskillen is **Devenish Island**, two miles downstream from Enniskillen in the south of the Lower Lough. A monastic settlement was founded here by Saint Molaise in the sixth century, and despite being plundered by Vikings in the ninth century and again in the twelfth, it continued to be an important religious centre up until the Plantations. It's a delightful setting, not far from the lough shore, and the considerable ruins span the entire medieval period. Devenish Island Ferries run regular services from Trory Point, three miles north of Enniskillen off the Omagh road (April–Sept; £2.25 including entrance fees; check times with tourist office); a two-hour **cruise** of Lough Erne, stopping at Devenish for thirty minutes, is operated by Erne Tours (☎028/66 322882; May–Sept; £5) from the Round "O" pier, off the Derrygonnelly road.

To immerse yourself thoroughly in the beauty of the lough scenery, you could hardly do better than stay in the YHANI **hostel** (☎028/686 28118; ②) set in the **Castle Archdale** forest park near Lisnarrick on the eastern shore. A bus service runs from Enniskillen to Pettigo (4 daily), which will put you down at the park gates, a mile from the hostel. From near the hostel you can get a ferry (June–Sept) to **White Island**, whose ruined abbey bears early Christian carvings that look eerily pagan. The most disconcerting is the lewd female figure known as a *sheila na gig*, with bulging cheeks, a big grin, open legs and arms pointing to her genitals. This could be a female fertility figure, a warning to monks of the sins of the flesh, or an expression of the demoniacal power of women, designed to ward off evil.

travel details

Trains

Details given below refer to weekday services; extra services may run on Fridays, fewer on Sundays.

Dublin to: Belfast (8 daily; 2hr 10min); Cork (8 daily; 2hr 30min–3hr); Galway (5 daily; 2hr 45min); Killarney (4 daily; 3hr 30min); Limerick (11 daily; 2–2hr 30min); Rosslare (3 daily; 3hr); Sligo (3 daily; 3hr 15min); Waterford (4 daily; 2hr 40min); Westport (3 daily; 3hr 40min).

Belfast to: Derry (7 daily; 2hr 40min); Dublin (8 daily; 2hr 10min); Larne Harbour (15 daily; 55min). Coleraine to Portrush (for Giant's Causeway) (7 daily; 15min)

Cork to: Dublin (7 daily; 2hr 30min–3hr); Killarney (5 daily; 2 hr).

Derry to: Belfast (7 daily; 2hr 40min); Coleraine (7 daily; 40min).

Galway to: Dublin (5 daily; 2hr 45min).

Killarney to: Cork (5 daily; 2hr); Dublin (4 daily; 3hr 30min).

Sligo to: Dublin (3 daily; 3hr 15min).

Waterford to: Dublin (4 daily; 2hr 40min).

Westport to: Dublin (3 daily; 3hr 40 min).

Buses

The details given are for Bus Éireann or Ulsterbus services on summer weekdays; extra services may run on Fridays, fewer in winter and on Sundays.

Dublin to: Belfast (7 daily; 3hr); Cork (4 daily; 4hr 30min); Derry (4 daily; 4hr 30min); Donegal (5 daily; 4hr 30min); Enniskillen (4 daily; 3hr 40min); Galway (13 daily; 3hr 30min); Killarney (5 daily; 6hr); Sligo 3 daily; 4hr); Waterford (5 daily; 2hr 45min); Westport (3 daily; 5hr).

Belfast to: Derry (6 daily; 1hr 40min); Dublin (7 daily; 3hr); Enniskillen (9 daily; 2hr 40min); Galway (1 daily; 7hr); Sligo (3 daily; 4hr).

Cork to: Dublin (4 daily; 4hr 30min); Killarney (7 daily; 2hr 30min).

Derry to: Donegal (4 daily; 1hr 30min); Dublin (5 daily; 4hr 15min); Enniskillen (6 daily; 1hr 30min); Sligo (3 daily; 2hr 45min).

Donegal to: Derry (4 daily; 1hr 30min); Dublin (4 daily; 4hr 30min); Galway (3 daily; 5hr); Glencolmcille (2 daily; 2hr); Sligo (3 daily; 1hr 30min).

Enniskillen to: Belfast (9 daily; 2hr 35min); Derry (6 daily; 1hr 30min); Dublin (4 daily; 3hr 40min).

Galway to: Clifden (2–5 daily; 1hr 45min–2hr 20min); Doolin (1–7 daily; 1hr 35min); Dublin (13 daily; 3hr 30min).

Killarney to Dingle (5 daily; 2hr 15min); Waterville via Cahersiveen (1–2 daily; 2hr).

Sligo to: Belfast (3 daily; 4hr); Galway (4 daily; 2hr 45min).

CHAPTER 15

ITALY

Introduction

Of all the countries in Europe, **Italy** is perhaps the hardest to classify. It is a modern, industrialized nation; it is the harbinger of style, its designers leading the way with each season's fashions. But it is also a Mediterranean country, with all that that implies. Agricultural land covers much of the country, a lot of it, especially in the south, still owned under almost feudal conditions. In towns and villages all over the country, life stops during the middle of the day for a siesta. It is also strongly family-orientated, with an emphasis on the traditions and rituals of the Catholic Church. If there is a single national characteristic, it's to embrace life to the full, manifest in the hundreds of local festivals taking place on any given day; in the importance placed on good food; and above all in the daily domestic ritual of the collective evening stroll or *passeggiata*. There is also, of course, the country's enormous cultural legacy: Tuscany alone has more classified historical monuments than any country in the world and every region retains its own relics of an artistic tradition generally acknowledged to be the world's richest.

Italy wasn't a unified state until 1861, something borne out by the regional nature of the place today. The country breaks down into nineteen often very distinct *regione*, but the sharpest division is between north and south. The north is one of the most advanced industrial societies in the world; the south, known as *il mezzogiorno*, is by contrast one of the economically most depressed areas in Europe. In the northwest, the regions of Piemonte and Lombardy – and the two main centres of **Turin** and **Milan** – epitomize the wealthy north. Liguria, the small coastal province to the south, has long been known as the "Italian Riviera" and is accordingly crowded with sun-seeking holidaymakers for much of the summer season. But it's a beautiful stretch of coast, and its capital, **Genoa**, is a bustling port with a long seafaring tradition. The interest of the north-eastern regions of the Veneto and Friuli-Venezia Giulia is of course Venice itself, a unique city, and every bit as beautiful as its reputation would suggest – though this means you won't be alone in appreciating it. If the crowds are too much, there's also the arc of historic towns outside the city – **Verona**, **Padua** and **Vicenza**. To the south, the region of Emilia-Romagna has been at the heart of Italy's postwar industrial boom. Its coast is popular among Italians, especially **Rimini**, Italy's brashest seaside resort; and there are also the ancient centres of **Ravenna**, **Ferrara**, **Parma** and **Bologna**, the capital – one of Italy's liveliest but least appreciated cities. Central Italy perhaps represents the most commonly perceived image of the country, and

Tuscany, with its classic rolling countryside and the art-packed towns of **Florence**, **Pisa** and **Siena**, is one of its most visited regions. Neighbouring **Umbria** is similar in all but its relative emptiness, though it gets fuller every year, as visitors flock into towns such as Perugia, Spoleto and Assisi – and unspoilt Urbino in adjacent Marche. Lazio, to the west, is a poor and desolate region whose real focal point is **Rome**, Italy's capital, the one city in the country which owes allegiance neither to the north nor south. Beyond Rome, **Naples**, capital of Campania, a petulant, unforgettable city, is the spiritual heart of the Italian south, and is close to some of Italy's finest ancient sites in **Pompeii** and **Herculaneum**, not to mention its most spectacular stretch of coast around **Amalfi**. Puglia, the "heel" of Italy, has underrated pleasures, notably the souk-like quality of its capital, **Bari**. As for **Sicily**, the island is really a law unto itself, a wide mixture of attractions ranging from some of the finest preserved Hellenistic treasures in Europe, to the drama of Mount Etna and one of the country's fanciest beach resorts in **Taormina**. **Sardinia**, too, feels far removed from the mainland, especially in its relatively undiscovered interior, though you may be content to just explore its fine beaches.

Information and maps

Most Italian towns, major train stations and airports have a **tourist office** – usually either an APT (Azienda Promozione Turistica), an EPT (Ente Provinciale per il Turismo), a provincial branch of the state organization, an IAT (Ufficio di Informazione e Accoglienza Turistica) or an AAST (Azienda Autonoma di Soggiorno e Turismo), a smaller local outfit. Very small or out-of-the-way villages may have a tiny office known as a Pro Loco. All offer much the same mix of general advice and bumph, free maps and accommodation lists, though rarely do they book accommodation. **Opening hours** vary, but larger city offices are likely to be open Mon–Sat 9am–1pm & 4–7pm, and sometimes for a short period on Sun mornings; smaller offices may open weekdays only.

Most tourist offices will give out **maps** of their local area for free, but if you want an indexed town plan, Studio FMB cover the country's towns and cities; Falk also sell decent plans of the major cities. For road maps, the Automobile Club d'Italia issue a reasonable free map, available from the State Tourist Office; the clearest and best-value large-scale commercial road map of Italy is the Michelin 1:1,000,000, or you have the choice between the TCI 1:800,000 North and South maps. Michelin also produce 1:400,000 maps of the north and south, as well as Sicily and Sardinia, and TCI do maps of the individual regions, scale 1:200,000.

Money and banks

The Italian unit of currency is the **Lira** (abbreviated to L). Notes come in denominations of L1000, L2000, L5000, L10,000, L50,000 and L100,000, and coins of L50, L100, L200 and L500. The best place to change money or travellers' cheques is at a **bank**; hours are normally Mon–Fri 8.30am–1pm, and an hour in the afternoon (usually 3–4pm), though there are local variations on this; before a public holiday banks are usually open in the morning. Outside banking hours, the larger hotels will change money and travellers' cheques, but if you stay in a reasonably large city the rate is invariably better at the train station exchange bureau – normally open evenings and weekends. If you have a debit or credit card with a PIN number, then you can use the cash dispensers (*bancomat*) which are found everywhere.

Communications

Post office opening hours are usually Mon–Sat 8am–6.30pm (smaller towns have no service on Sat). If you want stamps, you can also buy them in *tabacchi*. Public **telephones**, run by Telecom Italia, come in various forms. For the most common type, you'll need L100, L200 or L500 coins, or a phonecard, available from Telecom Italia offices, *tabacchi* and newsstands for L5000, L10,000 or L15,000. In larger towns you can also use the international phone card. If you can't find a call box, bars will often have a phone you can use. Alternatively, Telecom Italia have offices where you can make a metered call from a kiosk, though these are being phased out now. For calls within Italy – local, long-distance and international – dial all digits, including 0 and the area code.

Getting around

The easiest way of travelling around Italy is by train. The Italian train system is relatively inexpensive, reasonably comprehensive, and in the north of the country at least, fairly efficient – far preferable to the fragmented and sometimes grindingly slow buses.

■ Trains

Apart from a few private lines, Italian **trains** are operated by Italian State Railways (Ferrovie dello Stato or FS). There are seven types of train. At the top of the range is the ETR 450 Pendolino, an exclusively first-class intercity service whose ticket prices include reservation, newspapers and a meal.

Eurostar trains connect the major Italian cities with centres such as Paris, Vienna, Hamburg and Barcelona, while Intercity trains link the major Italian centres; a supplement of around thirty percent of the ordinary fare is payable on both services, while a reservation is obligatory only on Eurostar services. Espresso, Diretto and Interregionale are long-distance expresses stopping at most major stations, and a Regionale stops just about everywhere and is usually worth avoiding. In summer it's often worth making a seat reservation on the main routes. Fares are very reasonable, calculated by the kilometre and thus easy to work out for each journey. The single second-class fare from Milan to Bari, one of the longest journeys you're ever likely to make, currently costs about L91,000.

As with most other European countries, you can cut **costs** greatly by using a rail pass. InterRail and Eurail passes give free travel on the whole FS network (though you'll be liable for supplements on the fast trains), and there are specific Italian passes available. A Euro-Domino pass can benefit travellers from the UK with 3 days of unlimited travel for £99 (£79 for under-26s), 5 days for £89/$95 or 8 days for £109/$157. The Italy Railcard/Biglietto Turistico Libera Circolazione entitles you to unlimited travel on consecutive days on the entire network, including Intercity services, and for 8 days costs £150/$172, for 15 costs £153/$213, for 21 costs £167/$248, and for 30 costs £200/$297. The Italy Flexi-Rail allows you to travel for 24 hours (from midnight to midnight) on 4, 8 or 12 days of your choice within a one-month period, and costs £91/$135 for 4 days, £126/$189 for 8 days and £162/$365 for 12 days. A Chilométrico ticket, valid for up to five people at once, gives 3000km worth of free travel on a maximum of twenty separate journeys and costs £88/$150. Under-26s can also buy a Cartaverde, which for L40,000 entitles you to twenty percent off train fares for a year; it's available from any main train station in Italy. Children under four years old (not occupying a seat) travel free, while those aged four to twelve qualify for a fifty-percent discount on all journeys.

■ Buses

Almost everywhere is connected by some kind of **bus** service, but schedules can be sketchy, and are drastically reduced – sometimes nonexistent – at weekends. Bear in mind also that in rural areas timetables are often designed with the working or school day in mind, making for some frighteningly early starts and occasionally no buses at all during school holidays. Even if there are plentiful buses, bear in mind that the journey will be long and full of stops and starts. Bus terminals are often next door to the train station in larger towns. Tickets are bought on board, though on longer hauls you can try to buy them in advance direct from the bus company; seat reservations are, however, not possible.

■ Driving

Travelling by **car** in Italy is relatively painless. The roads are good, the highway (*autostrada*) network very comprehensive, and the notorious Italian drivers rather less erratic than their reputation suggests. Most highways are toll-roads, but rates aren't especially high: as a general reference, you'll pay L19,000 for a small car from Milan to Bologna. As for documentation, if bringing your own car you need a valid **driving licence** and you're advised to get an International Green Card of insurance. You drive on the right, and at junctions give precedence to vehicles coming from the right. Speed limits are 50kph in built-up areas, 110kph on country roads, 130kph on highways. If you break down, dial ☎116 and the nearest office of the Automobile Club d'Italia (ACI) will be informed.

Car rental in Italy is pricey, currently around £200 a week for a small car with unlimited mileage. Italy is also one of the most expensive countries in Europe in which to buy petrol. **Hitchhiking** is seldom practised, particularly not in the south, and is definitely not advisable for women travelling alone.

Accommodation

Accommodation in Italy is never especially cheap, but it is at least fairly reliable: hotels are star-rated and required to post their prices clearly in each room. Most tourist offices have details of hotel rates in their town or region, and you can usually expect them to be broadly accurate. In the major cities and resorts, booking ahead is often a good idea, particularly during July or August.

One peculiar Italian institution is the confusingly named *albergo diurno* or day hotel, an establishment providing bathrooms, showers, hairdressers and the like – but no accommodation. You'll often find them at train stations and they're usually open daily 6am–midnight – useful for a fast clean-up if you're on the move.

■ Hotels

Hotels in Italy come with a confusing variety of names. *Locanda* are historically the most basic option, although the word is sometimes used to denote something quite fancy these days; *pensione* too can be little different from the regular *alberghi* or hotels. Prices do vary greatly between the poor south and the wealthy north, but on average, you can expect to pay L50–60,000 for a double without private bathroom in a one-star hotel, and a minimum of L120,000 a double in a three-star. In very busy places it's not unusual to have to stay for a minimum of three nights, and many proprietors will add the price of breakfast to your bill whether you want it or not; try to resist this – you can eat more cheaply in a bar. Whatever happens, establish the full price of your room before you accept it.

■ Hostels and student accommodation

There are around sixty **youth hostels** in Italy, charging between L13,000 and L30,000 for a dorm bed for HI members, and if you're two people travelling together, they don't represent a massive saving on the cheapest double hotel room. Whether or not you're a member, you'll need to book ahead in the summer months. You can get a full list of Italian youth hostels from the Associazione Italiana Alberghi per la Gioventù, Via Cavour 44, 00184 Roma (☎06.487.1152). In some cities it's also possible to stay in **student accommodation** during the summer; accommodation is generally in individual rooms and can work out cheaper than a straight hotel room. Again, you'll need to book in advance.

■ Campsites

Camping is not really as popular in Italy as it is in some other European countries, but there are plenty of sites, and most of them are well equipped. The snag is that they're expensive, and, once you've

---

ACCOMMODATION PRICE CODES

Throughout this guide, accommodation is priced on a scale of ① to ⑨, the number indicating the lowest price per night a single person could expect to pay in that establishment in high season. With hostels this is the nightly rate per person; with hotels, the price is arrived at by dividing the cost of the cheapest double room by two. The prices indicated by the codes are as follows:

① under £5 / $8	④ £15–20 / $24–32	⑦ £30–35 / $48–56
② £5–10 / $8–16	⑤ £20–25 / $32–40	⑧ £35–40 / $56–64
③ £10–15 / $16–24	⑥ £25–30 / $40–48	⑨ £40 / $64 and over

added the cost of a tent and vehicle, don't always work out a great deal cheaper than staying in a hostel. Prices are around L6000–10,000 per person daily, plus L7000–17,000 for a caravan or tent, and around L6000 for a vehicle. If you're camping extensively it might be worth investing in the TCI's *Campeggi e Villaggi Turistici* or the free abridged version from Centro Internazionale Prenotazioni, Federcampeggio, Castella Postale 23, 50041 Calenzano, Florence (☎055.882.391).

Food and drink

Though it has long been popular primarily for its cheapness and convenience, Italian **food** is finally beginning to wrest some of the attention it deserves as one of the world's great cuisines. Indeed, there are few national cuisines that can boast so much variety in ingredients and cooking methods. **Wine**, too, is becoming more respected, as the Italian industry's devotion to fizzy pop and characterless plonk is replaced by a new pride and a better product.

■ Food

Most Italians start their day in a bar, their **breakfast** consisting of a cappuccino, and a *cornetto* – a jam, custard or chocolate-filled croissant. At other times of day, **sandwiches** (*panini*) can be pretty substantial. There are sandwich bars (*paninoteche*) in larger towns and cities, and in smaller places grocer's shops (*alimentari*) will normally make you up whatever you want for about L3000–L5000 a sandwich. Bars may also offer *tramezzini*, ready-made sliced white bread with mixed fillings – less appetizing than the average *panino* but still tasty, and slightly cheaper at around L2000 a time. You can get hot **take-away food** in a *távola calda*, a snack bar that sometimes has limited seating. The bigger towns have these, and there's often one inside larger train stations. Try also a *rosticceria*, serving spit-roast chicken, slices of pizza, fries and burgers. Italian ice cream (*gelato*) is justifiably famous: a cone (*un cono*) is an indispensable accessory to the evening *passeggiata*. Most bars have a fairly good selection, but for real choice go to a *gelateria*.

As for sit-down food, the cheapest thing you can eat is **pizza**. This is now a worldwide phenomenon but Italy remains the best place to eat it – thin and flat, and, if you're lucky, cooked in the traditional way in wood-fired ovens. Pizzerias range from stand-up counters selling slices (*pizza al taglio*) to fully fledged restaurants. A basic cheese and tomato pizza (*margherita*) costs around L6000–8000, a fancier variety L8000–15,000. Full meals are generally served in a trattoria or a ristorante. Traditionally, a

trattoria is a cheaper purveyor of home-style cooking, a **ristorante** more upmarket, though these days there's a fine line between the two. In either, pasta dishes go for around L8000–12,000, and there's usually not a problem just having this; the main fish or meat courses will normally be L10,000–15,000. Bear in mind that almost everywhere you'll pay a cover charge on top of your food (*pane e coperto*) of around L3000 a head. Watch out when ordering fish, which will either be served whole or by weight: 250g is usually plenty for one person. Vegetables or salads – *contorni* – are ordered separately: potatoes will invariably be fries, salads either green (*verde*) or mixed (*mista*). Afterwards you nearly always get a choice of fresh fruit (*frutta*) or a selection of desserts (*dolci*). At the end of the meal ask for the bill (*il conto*). As well as the cover charge, service (*servizio*) will often be added, generally about ten percent. If service isn't included you should tip about the same amount, though trattorias outside the large cities won't necessarily expect this.

■ Drink

Although many Italian children are brought up on wine, there's not the same emphasis on dedicated drinking as there is in Britain or the US. Bars are less social centres than functional places for a quick coffee or beer. You pay first at the cash desk (*la cassa*), present your receipt (*scontrino*) and give your order. In the south of the country it's customary to leave a tip of about L50 or L100 on the counter, though no one will object if you don't. Bear in mind that sitting down sometimes costs twice as much, especially if you sit outside. Coffee is always excellent, small and black (espresso, or just *caffè*), or white and frothy (cappuccino); try also a *granita* – cold coffee with crushed ice, usually topped with cream. If you don't like coffee, tea (*te*) comes with lemon (*con limone*) unless you ask for milk (*con latte*); it's also served cold (*té freddo*). As for soft drinks, a *spremuta* is a fresh fruit juice; there's also crushed-ice fruit *granitas*, and the usual range of fizzy drinks and concentrated juices.

Beer (*birra*) usually comes in one-third or two-third litre bottles. Commonest and cheapest are the Italian brands, *Peroni* and *Dreher*, both of which are very drinkable; in most bars you have a choice of this or draught beer (*alla spina*). All the usual spirits are on sale and known mostly by their generic names, as well as Italian brandies like Stock and Vecchia Romagna. A generous shot of these costs about L3000, more for imported stuff. There's also **grappa**, made from the leftovers from the wine-making process and something of an acquired taste. You'll also find **fortified wines** like Martini, Cinzano and Campari and a daunting selection of liqueurs. Amaro is a bitter after-dinner drink,

Amaretto much sweeter with a strong taste of marzipan, Sambuca a sticky-sweet aniseed concoction. Wine is invariably drunk with meals, and is still very cheap. If you're unsure about what to order, don't be afraid to try the local stuff: ask for *vino sfuso* or simply *un mezzo* (a half litre), or *un quarto* (a quarter), sometimes served straight from the barrel, particularly down south, and often very good for just L6000 a litre. Bottled wine is pricier but still good value; expect to pay around L12,000 a bottle in a restaurant, less than half that from a shop or supermarket.

Opening hours and holidays

Most **shops and businesses** in Italy open Mon–Sat from 8 or 9am until around 1pm, and from about 4pm until 7pm or 8pm, though in the north offices work to a more standard European 9am–5pm day. Everything, except bars and restaurants, closes on Sunday, though you might find fish shops in some coastal towns and *pasticcerias* or bakers open until Sunday lunchtime. Most **churches** open early morning and close around noon, opening again at 4pm until 7pm or 8pm. **Museums** generally open Tues–Sat from 9am until 2pm, and from 9am to 1pm on Sunday, and are closed on Mondays. Be prepared to queue in Rome, Venice and Florence, where last tickets are usually issued 30min before closing. It's also worth checking out the main museums for late-night openings in summer. Most archaeological sites open every day, 9am until late evening – usually one hour before sunset. Everything closes on the following **national holidays**: Jan 1; Jan 6; Easter Monday; April 25; May 1; Aug 15; Nov 1; Dec 8; Dec 25 and 26.

Emergencies

Despite what you hear about the mafia, most of the crime you're likely to come across in Italy is of the small-time variety, prevalent in the major cities and the south of the country, where gangs of *scippatori* operate, snatching handbags, wallets, jewellery, etc. You can minimize the risk of this by being discreet, not flashing anything of value, keeping a firm hand on your camera and bag, and never leaving anything valuable in your car. If it comes to the worst, you'll be forced to have some dealings with the **police**. In Italy these come in many forms: the *Polizia Urbana/Vigili Urbani* are mainly concerned with directing the traffic and punishing parking offences; the Polizia Stradale patrol highways; the Carabinieri, with their military-style uniforms and white shoulder belts, deal with general crime, public order and drug control; and the *Polizia Statale* are the branch you'll perhaps have most chance of coming into contact with, since it's to them that thefts should generally be reported.

If you need medical treatment, Italian **pharmacies** (*farmacia*) are well qualified to give you advice on minor ailments, and to dispense prescriptions, and there's generally one open all night in the bigger towns and cities. They work on a rota system; you'll find the address of the nearest open one on any *farmacia* door. If you are more seriously ill, call an **ambulance** or go to the *Pronto Soccorso* (casualty) section of the nearest hospital.

> **EMERGENCY NUMBERS**
> Ambulance ☎113; police ☎112; fire ☎115.

THE NORTHWEST

The **northwest** of Italy is many people's first experience of the country, and in many ways represents its least "Italian" corner, at least in the regions of **Piemonte** and **Val d'Aosta**, where French is still spoken by some as a first language. **Turin**, on the main rail and road route from France to Milan, is the obvious first stop, the first capital of Italy after the Unification in 1860 and a grand city with many remnants of its past as seat of the Savoy dukes, later the Italian royals. To the east, **Lombardy** was long viewed by northerners as the heart of Italy – emperors from Charlemagne to Napoleon came here to be crowned – and northern European business magnates continue to take its capital, Milan, more seriously than Rome, the region's big businesses and banks wielding political as well as economic power across the nation. Lombardy's landscape has paid the price for economic success: industry chokes the peripheries of towns and even spreads its polluting tentacles into the northern lakes and mountain valleys. Nonetheless, Lombardy has its attractions. **Milan** is a natural gateway to the region, an upbeat city with plenty to see, dominating the plain that forms the southern part of Lombardy, the towns of which – such as **Mantua** – flourished during the Middle Ages and Renaissance, and retain their historical character today. To the north, the lakes and low mountains shelter fewer historic towns, though **Brescia** and especially **Bergamo** are notable exceptions. The region of **Liguria** to the south provides light relief, an unashamedly touristy strip, and perhaps the country's most spectacular stretch of coastline. Chief town of the province is the sprawling port of **Genoa**, west of which the **Riviera del Ponente** is one long ribbon of hotels, though **Finale Ligure** is a pleasant resort. Southeast, towards Tuscany, the **Riviera del Levante** is more rugged, its mix of mountains and fishing villages "discovered" by the Romantics in the late eighteenth century, preparing the way for the first package tourists earlier this century. Now the whole area explodes into a ruck every July and August, with people coming to resorts like **Portofino** strictly for pose value – although stretches like the **Cinque Terre** are still well worth discovering.

Turin

"Do you know Turin?" wrote Nietzsche, "It is a city after my own heart…a princely residence of the seventeenth century, which has only one taste giving commands to everything, the court and its nobility. Aristocratic calm is preserved in everything: there are no nasty suburbs." Although **TURIN**'s traffic-choked streets are no longer calm, and its suburbs, built by the vast Fiat empire that virtually owns the city, are as nasty as any in Italy, the city centre's gracious Baroque avenues, opulent palaces, sumptuous churches and splendid collections of Egyptian antiquities and northern European paintings are still here – a pleasant surprise to those who might have been expecting satanic factories and little else.

Arrival and accommodation

Turin's main **train station**, Porta Nuova, is on Corso Vittorio Emanuele, at the foot of Via Roma, convenient for the city centre and hotels. There are two **tourist offices** – the main one at Piazza Castello 161 (daily 8.30am–7.30pm) and a smaller one at the train station (same hours). Many of Turin's **cheap hotels** are in the sleazy quarter off Via Nizza, convenient enough but not an advisable choice, particularly for solo women. Somewhat safer, but more expensive, are the streets opposite Porta Nuova, close to Piazza Carlo Felice. There are also a number of fairly reasonably priced hotels west of Piazza Castello. As for specific **hotels**, the *Paradiso*, Via Berthollet 3 (☎011.669.8678; ②), is extremely clean and does doubles without bath. The *Canelli*, Via San Dalmazzo 7, close to the pedestrian area of Via Garibaldi (☎011.546.078; ②), is the cheapest option and very central, while *Hotel Mobledor*, Via Accademia Albertina 1 (☎011.812.5805; ③), is a small friendly hotel and also in an excellent location. The **youth hostel**, *Ostello Torino*, is at Via Alby 1 (☎011.660.2939; ②) – take bus #52 from Porta Nuova. If you're **camping**, the *Villa Rey* is the most convenient site, on the far side of the river south of the youth hostel – take bus #61 from Porta Nuova, and then bus #56.

The City

The grid street-plan of Turin's Baroque centre makes finding your way about easy. **Via Roma** is the city's central spine, a grand affair lined with designer shops and ritzy cafés and punctuated by the city's most elegant piazzas, most notably **Piazza San Carlo**, a little way north of Porta Nuova station – known with some justification as the parlour of Turin. This is a grand and stylish open space, flanked with symmetrical porticoed buildings housing opulent cafés and centring on an equestrian statue of the Savoy Duke, Emanuele Filiberto, its entrance guarded by the twin Baroque churches of **San Carlo** and **Santa Cristina**, whose languishing nude statues represent Turin's two rivers – the Po and the Dora. Around the corner, the **Museo Egizio** (Tues–Sat 9am–7pm, Sun 9am–2pm; L12,000) holds a superb collection of Egyptian antiquities, gathered together in the late eighteenth century under the aegis of Carlo Emanuele III. There are gorgeously decorated mummy cases, an intriguing assortment of everyday objects and, the undoubted highlight, the Tomb of Kha, the burial chamber of a 1400 BC architect, Kha, and his wife Merit, discovered in 1906 at Deir-el-Medina. Above the museum, the **Galleria Sabauda** (Tues, Wed, Fri, Sat & Sun 9am–2pm, Thurs 10am–7pm; L8000) was built around the Savoys' private collection and is still firmly stamped with their taste – a miscellany of Italian paintings, supplemented by a fine Dutch and Flemish collection, including works by Memling, Bruegel, David Teniers Jnr and Van Dyck. Almost opposite, the **Museo del Risorgimento** (Tues–Sat 9am–7pm, Sun 9am–1pm; L8000), housed in the double-fronted **Palazzo Carignano**, is worth a brief visit even if you usually give such things a miss. The **Palazzo Madama** on Piazza Castello is an appealing building with an ornate Baroque façade by the early eighteenth-century architect, Juvarra. Inside, the originally fifteenth-century palace incorporates parts of a thirteenth-century castle and a Roman gate. Opposite is the **Armeria Reale** (Tues & Thurs 1.30–7pm, Wed 9am–7pm, Fri & Sat 9am–2pm; L8000), a collection of armour and weapons spanning seven centuries and several continents started by King Carlo Alberto in 1837.

Around the corner, the fifteenth-century **Duomo** (daily 8.30am–noon & 3–7pm) houses the **Turin Shroud** (pre-booked visits 26 Aug–22 Oct only; ☎011.436.1540), a piece of cloth imprinted with the image of a man's body that has been claimed as the shroud in which Christ was wrapped after his crucifixion. In 1989 it was announced that carbon-dating tests showed it to be a fake, made between 1260 and 1390 – although no one is any the wiser about how the medieval forgers actually managed to create the image. The shroud had a narrow escape in April 1997 when the church was gutted by fire. Beyond the Duomo, the massive **Piazza della Repubblica** is another Juvarra design, though his grand plan for it is marred nowadays by seedy market buildings. The scruffy porticoes of Via Po lead down to the river, ending just before the bridge in the vast arcaded **Piazza Vittorio Veneto**. Along the river from here, the massive **Parco del Valentino** is one of Italy's largest parks, home to the **Castello e Borgo Medioevale** (daily 9am–7pm; castle closes at 6pm; L5000), a synthesis of the best houses and castles of Piemonte and Val d'Aosta, built with the same materials and techniques as the originals. Further south still, the **Museo dell'Automobile** at Corso Unità d'Italia 40 (Tues–Sun 9am–7pm; L10,000; bus #34 from Piazza Marconi) traces the development of the motor car, with one of the first Fiats, a bulky 1899 model, the gleaming Isotta Fraschini driven by Gloria Swanson in *Sunset Boulevard*, and, the pride of the collection, the 1907 Itala which won the Peking to Paris race in the same year.

Eating, drinking and nightlife

There are **snack bars** and takeaways on Via Nizza, some tempting delicatessens on Via Lagrange and a superb *rosticcerie* on Corso Vittorio Emanuele for do-it-yourself lunches. *Cossolo*, Via Roma 68, does great pastries, sandwiches and other snacks. *Frullati Varturi*, Piazza Castello 15, is in a good central location for sandwiches, and there's a branch of the quality self-service chain, *Brek*, at Piazza Carlo Felice 22. For more substantial **meals** try *L'Arcimboldo*, Via Santa Chiara 54, a restaurant specializing in pasta fresca with a choice of a hundred different sauces. *Trattoria Alba*, at Via S. Pio V 8, serves wholesome food at low prices, as does the cheerful *Porto di Savona*, Piazza Vittorio Veneto 2, which is popular with students. Make sure you at least look in on one of the city's *fin-de-siècle* **cafés**, most of which have an atmosphere that more than compensates for the steep prices. In *Baratti and Milano*, Piazza Castello 29, genteel Torinese sip tea in a rarefied ambience of mirrors, chandeliers and carved wood. The glitzy *Caffè San Carlo*, Piazza San Carlo 156, is reputedly a favoured hangout of politicians and industrialists. *Fiorio*, Via Po 8, was once the haunt of Cavour, and is now visited mostly for its ice cream. Later on in the **evening**, Via Carlo Alberto, Via San Quintino and Corso Matteotti is the area to hang out. Otherwise try *Doctor Sax*, Murazzi di Lungo Po Cadorna 4, a live-music bar (Afro, jazz and rock), or *La Contea*, Corso Quintino Sella 132, across the river, featuring live jazz most nights. For something a bit more clubby, try *AEIOU*, Via Spanzotti 3, housed in a former warehouse with a wide selection of music.

Milan

The dynamo behind the country's economic miracle, **MILAN** is a city like no other in Italy. A fast-paced business city in which consumerism and the work ethic rule, it's foggy in winter, muggy in summer, and is closer in outlook as well as distance to London than Palermo. Because of this most people pass straight through, and if it's summer and you're keen for sun and sea this might well be best. But at any other time of year it's worth giving Milan a bit more of a chance. It's a historic city, with enough churches and museums to keep you busy for a week, much of the city a testament to the prestige-building of the Visconti dynasty and their successors, the Sforzas, who ruled here in Renaissance times; and the contemporary aspects of the place represent the leading edge of Italy's fashion and design industry, not to mention a nightlife scene which is perhaps Italy's most varied.

Arrival, information and city transport

Most international **trains** pull in at the monumental Stazione Centrale, northeast of the centre on Piazza Duca d'Aosta, on metro lines 2 and 3 (MM2 or MM3). International and long-distance **buses** arrive at and depart from Piazza Castello, in front of the Castello Sforzesco. Of Milan's two **airports**, Linate is the closer, 7km from the city centre, and connected with the airport bus terminal at Stazione Centrale every twenty minutes between 5.40am and 7pm and then every half-hour until 9pm; it's a twenty-minute journey (L4500). There are also ordinary **city buses** (#73) until around midnight from Linate to Piazza San Babila. The other airport, Malpensa, is 50km away towards Lago Maggiore, connected by bus with Stazione Centrale to coincide with flight arrivals and departures. The journey takes an hour and costs L13,000.

Information and city maps are available from Milan's main **tourist offices**, at the Stazione Centrale (Mon–Sat 8am–7pm, Sun 9am–12.30pm & 1.30–6pm) and at Via Marconi 1, off Piazza Duomo (summer Mon–Fri 8.30am–8pm, Sat 9am–1pm & 2–7pm, Sun 9am–1pm & 2–5pm; winter Mon–Fri 8.30am–7pm, Sat 9am–1pm & 2–6pm, Sun 9am–1pm & 2–5pm). At some point you'll want to make use of the **public transport** system – an efficient network of trams, buses and metro. The metro is the most useful, made up of three lines, the red MM1, green MM2 and yellow MM3, converging at Duomo, Centrale FS, Loreto and Cadorna. Buses, trams and the metro run from around 6am to midnight, when night buses take over, following the metro routes until 1am. Tickets, valid for 75 minutes, cost a flat L1500 from tobacconists, bars and metro station newsagents. The 75-minute ticket is valid for one journey only on the Metro regardless of journey length. You can also buy a *blochetto* of ten tickets for L14,000, or a 24-hour ticket for L5000, from the Centrale or Duomo metro stations.

Accommodation

Milan is more a business than a tourist city, and its **accommodation** is geared to the expense-account traveller. However, there are plenty of one-star **hotels**, mostly concentrated in the area around Stazione Centrale, and along Viale Vittorio Veneto and Corso Buenos Aires. Close to the station, the *Casa Mia*, Viale V. Veneto 30 (☎02.657.5249; ⑤), is the best, and *San Tomaso*, Viale Tunisia 6 (☎02.295.14747; ④), is a popular *pensione*; the *Arno*, Via Lazzaretto 17 (☎02.670.5509; ④), off Viale Tunisia not far from Stazione Centrale, gets packed from March to July; at the same address is the similar *Pensione Eva* (☎02.670.5907;

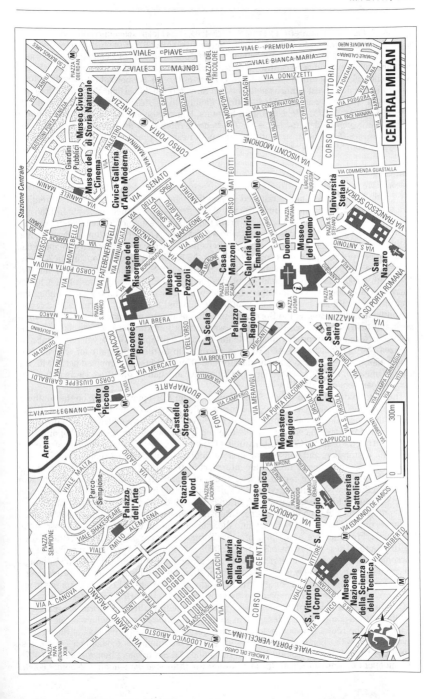

⑨). The *Arthur*, Via Lazzaretto 14 (☎02.204.6294; ④), has clean, spacious rooms with a touch of fading splendour, and *Speronari*, Via Speronari 4 (☎02.864.61125; ⑤), is friendly, and very close to the cathedral; *Manzoni*, Via Senato 45, off Corso Venezia (☎02.760.21002; ⑤), is near the public gardens and very central. *Trieste*, Via M. Polo 13 (02.65.54405; ⑤) is near Piazza della Repubblica. The official **youth hostel**, *Piero Rotta*, Via Salmoiraghi 2 (☎02.392.67095; ②), out in the northwest suburbs near the San Siro stadium, is perhaps the cheapest option but has a 12.30am curfew (MM Lotto). Failing that, *ACISJF*, Corso Garibaldi 121 (☎02.290.00164; ③; MM Moscova), run by nuns, is a reasonable option for women under twenty-five; accommodation here is in four-bedded rooms. As for **campsites**, there's the *Autodromo* site (April–Sept) in Monza, in the park near the renowned Formula One circuit; take a bus from Stazione Centrale.

The City

Historic Milan lies at the centre of a web of streets zeroing in on **Piazza del Duomo**, the city's main hub, a mostly pedestrianized square that's home to the best of Milan's streetlife, and, on its eastern side, the **Duomo**, the world's largest Gothic cathedral, begun in 1386 and taking nearly five centuries to complete. From the outside it's an incredible building, notable as much for its decoration as its size and with a front that's a strange mixture of Baroque and Gothic. The gloomy interior holds, among other things, a large crucifix which contains a nail from Christ's cross, crafted to become the bit for the bridle of Emperor Constantine's horse, while close by, beneath the presbytery, the **Scurolo di San Carlo** (daily 9am–noon & 2.30–6pm; L2000) is an octagonal crypt designed to house the remains of St Charles Borromeo, a zealous sixteenth-century cardinal who was canonized for his work among the poor of the city. He lies here in a glass coffin, clothed and bejewelled, wearing a gold crown attributed to Cellini. Adjacent to Borromeo's resting place, the treasury has Byzantine ivory-work and heavily embroidered vestments, while, back towards the entrance, is the cathedral's fourth-century **baptistry** (daily 9.45am–12.45 & 2–5.45pm; L3000), where St Ambrose baptized St Augustine in 387 AD. You can also get up to the cathedral **roof** (March–Nov 9am–5.45pm; Nov–Feb 9am–4.15pm; elevator L8000, on foot L6000, combined ticket with the Duomo museum L12,000), whose forest of pinnacles and statues gives fine views of the city, and on clear days even the Alps.

The **Museo del Duomo** (Tues–Sat 9.30am–12.30pm & 3–6pm; L10,000), on the southern side of the piazza, holds casts of a good many of the three thousand or so statues and gargoyles that spike the Duomo. You can also see how it might have ended up, in a display of entries for a nineteenth-century competition for a new facade. In the same building, the **Civico Museo di Arte Contemporanea** (Tues–Sun 9.30am–5.30pm; free) is at present closed for restoration, and houses temporary exhibitions only. When it reopens, you can see a wide-ranging collection of twentieth-century art, with works by De Chirico, Boccioni and Morandi, as well as more recent artists. South of Piazza del Duomo, the church of **San Satiro**, on the busy shopping street of Via Torino, is a study in ingenuity, commissioned from Milan's foremost Renaissance architect, Bramante, in 1476. Originally the oratory of the adjacent ninth-century church of San Satiro, Bramante transformed it into a long-naved basilica by converting the long oblong oratory into the transept and adding a trompe l'oeil apse to the back wall. Five minutes away, just off Via Torino at Piazza Pio XI 2, the **Pinacoteca Ambrosiana** (Tues–Sun 10am–5.30pm; L12,000) was founded by another member of the Borromeo family, Cardinal Federico, and is one of the largest libraries in Europe – though what you come here for now is his art collection, stamped with his taste for Jan Bruegel, sixteenth-century Venetians and some of the more kitschy followers of Leonardo. Among many mediocre works, there is a rare painting by Leonardo himself, *Portrait of a Musician*.

On the opposite side of the piazza is the gaudily opulent **Galleria Vittorio Emanuele**, a cruciform glass-domed gallery designed in 1865 by Giuseppe Mengoni, who was killed when he fell from the roof a few days before the inaugural ceremony. Take a look at the circular mosaic of the zodiac beneath the cupola – it's considered good luck to stand on Taurus' testicles. The Galleria leads through to the world-famous **La Scala** opera house, opened in 1778 with an opera by Antonio Salieri. Its small **museum** (Mon–Sat 9am–noon & 2–5pm; L6000), with composers' death masks, plaster casts of conductors' hands and a statue of Puccini in a capacious overcoat, may be the only chance you get to see the interior.

North of La Scala, **Via Brera** sets the tone for the city's arty quarter with its fancy galleries and art shops, and, at its far end, Milan's most prestigious gallery, the **Pinacoteca di Brera** (Tues–Sat 9am–5.30pm, Sun 9am–12.15pm; L8000), filled with works looted from the churches and aristocratic collections of French-occupied Italy. There's a good representation of Venetian painters – works by Paolo Veronese, Tintoretto, Gentile Bellini and his follower, Carpaccio, and a *Pietà* by Gentile's more talented brother, Giovanni, deemed one of the most moving paintings in the history of art. Look out also for Mantegna's *The Dead Christ*, an ingenious painting of Christ on a wooden slab, viewed from the soles of his feet upwards; Piero della Francesca's chill *Madonna*, perhaps the most famous painting here; and Raphael's *Marriage of the Virgin*, whose languid Renaissance mood is in sharp contrast to the grim realism of Caravaggio's *Supper at Emmaus,* painted a century later.

West of the Accademia down Via Pontaccio, **Castello Sforzesco** rises imperiously from the mayhem of Foro Buonaparte, laid out by Napoleon in self-tribute as part of a grand plan for the city. An arena and triumphal arch remain from the scheme, behind the castle in the **Parco Sempione**, a notorious hangout for junkies and prostitutes, but otherwise the redbrick castle is the main focus of interest, with its crenellated towers and fortified walls one of Milan's most striking landmarks. Begun by the Viscontis and rebuilt by their successors, the Sforzas, whose court was one of the most powerful and cultured of the Renaissance, the castle houses – along with a number of run-of-the-mill collections – the **Museo d'Arte Antica** and **Pinacoteca** (daily 9.30am–1pm & 2–5.30pm; free), the former including Michelangelo's *Rondanini Pietà*, which the artist worked on for the last nine years of his life. The latter contains a cycle of monochrome frescoes illustrating the Griselda story from Boccaccio's *Decameron;* one of Mantegna's last works, *Madonna in Glory among Angels and Saints*; and paintings by Vincenzo Foppa, the leading Milanese artist before Leonardo da Vinci.

South of the castle, the **Museo Archeologico** at Corso Magenta 15 (Tues–Sun 9.30am–5.30pm; free) is worth a visit for its displays of kitchen utensils and jewellery from Roman Milan, as well as a colossal head of Jove, found near the castle. But what really brings visitors into this part of town is the church of **Santa Maria delle Grazie**, an originally Gothic pile, partially rebuilt by Bramante (who added the massive dome), that is famous for its mural of the *Last Supper* by Leonardo da Vinci, now restored, which covers one wall of the refectory (Tues–Fri 9am–9pm, Sat 9am–midnight, Sun 9am–8pm; L12,000; ☎02.89.42.11.46).

Eating, drinking and nightlife

Food in workaholic Milan, at lunchtime at least, is more of a necessity than a pleasure, with the city centre dominated by *paninoteche* and fast-food outlets. *Crota Piemunteisa*, Piazza Beccaria 10, has a vast array of chunky sandwiches for around L5000, and a few tables, or try out *Il Fornaio* on the opposite side of the piazza, for sandwiches and pizzas. Among **restaurants**, *Brek*, on Piazza Cavour, is a good-value and central self-service place, as is *Ciao*, a citywide chain with branches on the corner of Via Dante and Via Meravigli and at Via Fabio Filzi 8, near Stazione Centrale. *Autogrill* is another chain, with self-service restaurants and good sandwiches; branches are located at Piazza Duomo and Piazza Cinque Fiornate amongst others. Moving upmarket a little, *Il Cantinone*, Via Agnello 19, is a famous old trattoria and bar, with homemade pasta and some choice wines; *La Bruschetta*, Piazza Beccaria 12, is one of the best city-centre pizzerias, though you'll have to wait for a table. *Grand Italia*, Via Palermo 5, is cheaper and just as good. On the other side of the centre, *Latteria Unione*, Via Unione 6, close to the Duomo, dishes up excellent and varied vegetarian food, with friendly service, though it closes at 8pm. Further out, there's *Da Abele*, Via della Temperanza 5 (MM Pasteur), a long-established, cosy haunt that specializes in risotto, and *La Stella d'Oro*, Via Donizetti 3, an institution among Milanese cheapo restaurants – take bus #60. In the Città Studi, *Lo Smeraldo*, Via Ajaccio 1, serves thirty types of pizza.

Milan's **nightlife** centres on two areas – the streets around the Brera gallery and the Navigli and Ticinese quarters, where there's a hip, late-night **bar** scene. *Bar Magenta*, Via Carducci 13, is extremely trendy and usually packed. As for **live music**, *Capolinea*, Via

Lodovico Il Moro 119, named after its position at the terminal of tram #19, is a long-established jazz venue that hosts top-notch performers; *Scimmie*, Via Ascanio Sforza 49, is another popular stage, small and buzzy and mainly hosting jazz; while *Tunnel*, Via Sammartini, right by Stazione Centrale puts on alternative rock. Among many **clubs**, *Plastic*, Viale Umbria 120, is a Gothic hangout; *SplashDown*, Via Natale Battaglia 12, plays a wide range of music, as does *Rolling Stone*, Corso XXII Marzo, an enormous place and sometime host to big-name rock bands. *Hollywood*, Corso Como 15, is a long-established club with an airport theme. There's also, of course, La Scala, one of the world's most prestigious **opera** houses, whose season runs from December to July. Although seats are expensive and can sell out months in advance, there is often a reasonable chance of picking up a seat in the gods on the day – get there an hour or so before the performance. The pull-outs in Wednesday's *Corriere della Sera* or Thursday's *La Repubblica* give the rundown on **what's on**. The city **information office** in the Galleria Vittorio Emanuele (Mon–Sat 8am–7pm) also has details of cultural events and can book tickets.

Listings

Airlines Air Canada, Piazza VIII Novembre 6 (☎02.294.09189); Alitalia, Corso Como 15 (☎02.249.92500 or 147.865.643); American Airlines, Via V. Pisani 19 (☎02.6791.4400); British Airways, Corso Italia 8 (☎02.809.892 or 147.812.266); Qantas, Piazza Velasca 4 (☎02.864.50168).

Airport enquiries ☎02.748.52200.

American Express Via Brera 3 (Mon–Fri 9am–5pm).

Books A wide array of English-language books is available at the American Bookstore, Largo Cairoli.

Car rental Avis, Piazza Diaz 6 (☎02.863.494); Europcar, Piazza Diaz 6 (☎02.864.63454); Hertz, Via Gonzaga 5 (☎02.720.04562).

Embassies Australia, Via Borgogna 2 (☎02.77.70421); Canada, Via V. Pisani 19 (☎02.67.581); Great Britain, Via San Paolo 7 (☎02.723.001); USA, Via Principe Amedeo 2/10 (☎02.290.351).

Exchange The office in Stazione Centrale is your best bet: open Mon–Fri 7.05am–8pm, it also has a 24hr automatic currency exchange machine.

Hospital 24hr casualty department at the Fatebenefratelli hospital, Corso Porta Nuova 23 (☎02.63.631), or Ospedale Maggiore Policlinico, Via Francesco Sforza 35 (☎02.55.031), a short walk from Piazza Duomo.

Pharmacy 24hr service at Stazione Centrale.

Police Head office at Via Fatebenefratelli 11, near the Brera (☎02.62.261).

Post office Via Cordusio 4, off Piazza Cordusio (Mon–Fri 8.15am–7pm, Sat 8am–noon).

Telephones Telecom, Galleria V. Emanuele II (daily 8am–9.30pm), Stazione Centrale (daily 8am–8pm).

Train enquiries ☎02.63.711 or 147.888.088.

Bergamo

Just 50km north of Milan, yet much closer to the mountains in look and feel, **BERGAMO** is made up of two distinct parts – **Bergamo Bassa**, the lower, modern centre, and **Bergamo Alta**, clinging to the hill 400m above the Lombardian plain. Bergamo Bassa is no great shakes, a mixture of faceless suburbs and pompous Neoclassical town planning, but Bergamo Alta is one of northern Italy's loveliest city centres, a favourite retreat for the work-weary Milanese, who flock here at weekends seeking solace in its fresh mountain air, wanderable streets and lively, easy-going pace.

You can get up to Bergamo Alta by funicular from the top end of Viale Vittorio Emanuele II, or by taking a #1A bus from the train station (L1600, valid for 1 hour). Its centre **Piazza Vecchia** is a harmonious square rather enthusiastically dubbed by Stendhal as "the most beautiful place on earth", and flanked by the Venetian-Gothic **Palazzo della Ragione**; to the right is the massive **Torre Civica** (March daily 10am–noon & 2–6pm; April–Sept Mon–Thurs 9am–noon & 2–8pm, Fri & Sat 9am–noon & 2–11pm, Sun 9am–8pm; Oct Sat & Sun 10am–noon & 2–6pm; Nov–Feb Sat & Sun 10am–noon & 2–4pm; L2000). Through the palazzo's arcades is the **Duomo**, and, of more interest, the church of **Santa Maria Maggiore**, an extraordinarily elaborate church, with a ceiling in the worst tradition of Baroque excess and a piece of nineteenth-century kitsch in its monument to Donizetti, the Bergamo-based composer of highly popular romantic comedies. Next door, the Renaissance **Cappella Colleoni** (Tues–Sat 9am–12.30pm & 2–4.30/6.30pm; free), built onto the church in the 1470s, is equally extravagant, a confection of marble carved into an abundance of miniature arcades, balustrades and twisted columns, and capped with a mosque-like dome. Its opulent interior has a ceiling frescoed in the eighteenth century by Tiepolo and the ornate sarcophagus of the Venetian military hero, Bartolomeo Colleoni, topped with a gleaming gilded equestrian statue.

Leading out of Piazza Vecchia, the narrow **Via Colleoni** is the upper city's main thoroughfare, leading to the remains of Bergamo's **Cittadella**, home to museums of archeology and natural history and offering good views across to Bergamo Bassa – though for really outstanding views you should stroll (or take the funicular) up to the **Castello** on the summit of San Vigilio. In the opposite direction, down Via Porta Dipinta and through the Porta Sant'Agostino, just below the upper town, the **Accademia Carrara** (Tues–Sun 9.30am–12.15pm & 2.30–5.15pm; L5000) is among Lombardy's top quality collections of art, with portraits by Pisanello and Botticelli, works by Crivelli, Carpaccio and Lotto, the Lombard realists Foppa and Bergognone, and Venetians Titian and Palma il Vecchio.

Practicalities

The **train station** is right at the end of Bergamo Bassa's central avenue, on Piazzale Marconi. The **tourist office** at Vicolo Aquila Nera 2, off Piazza Vecchia in the upper town (daily 9am–12.30pm & 2–5.30pm; ☎035.232.730), has maps and information; the other APT in Bergamo Bassa is at Viale Vittorio Emanuele 20 (Mon–Fri 9am–12.30pm & 3–5.30pm). For the **youth hostel**, Via Galileo Ferraris 1 (☎035.361.724; ②), take bus #14, and get off at the stop after the modern church and the *Red Mountain Café*. The cheapest **hotel** in the upper town is the *Agnello d'Oro*, Via Gombito 22 (☎035.249.883; ⑤); *Sole*, also in the old town at Via Rivoli 2 (☎035.218.238; ⑤), is also worth trying. Otherwise most of Bergamo's cheaper hotels are in Bergamo Bassa. The *Antica Trattoria della Brianza*, Via Broseto 61a (☎035.253.338; ③), is a fifteen-minute walk west of the train station or take bus #11 from Porta Nuova. For **eating**, the *Cooperativa Citta Altà* off Via Colleoni, at Vicolo Sant'Agata 19, in the upper town is excellent value, as is *Da Mimmo*, Via Colleoni 17, which serves good pizzas and a decent four-course menu for around L30,000.

Mantua

Aldous Huxley called it the most romantic city in the world, and with an Arabian nights skyline rising above its three encircling lakes, **MANTUA** is undeniably evocative. It was the scene of Verdi's *Rigoletto*, and its history is one of equally operatic plots, most of them perpetuated by the Gonzagas, who ruled the town for three centuries and left two splendid palaces – the Palazzo Ducale, with Mantegna's stunning fresco of the Gonzaga court, and Palazzo del Tè, whose frescoes have entertained generations of visitors with their combination of steamy erotica and illusionistic fantasy.

The City

Historic Mantua centres on four interlinking squares. Of these, **Piazza Mantegna** is dominated by the facade of Alberti's **Sant'Andrea**, an unfinished basilica commissioned by Lodovico II Gonzaga, who felt that the existing medieval church was neither impressive enough to represent the splendour of his state, nor large enough to hold the droves of people who flocked here to see the holy relic of Christ's blood that had been found on the site. Inside, an octagonal balustrade stands above the crypt where the holy relic is kept in two vases, copies of originals designed by Cellini and stolen by the Austrians in 1846. There are also wall-paintings designed by Mantegna and executed by his students, one of whom was Correggio; Mantegna himself is buried in the church, in one of the north aisle chapels, his tomb topped with a bust that's said to be a self-portrait. Opposite Sant'Andrea and sunk below the present level of the busy **Piazza dell'Erbe**, Mantua's oldest church, the eleventh-century **Rotonda**, narrowly escaped destruction under Lodovico's city-improvement plans, and still contains traces of twelfth- and thirteenth-century frescoes.

The dark underpassage beneath the red-brick **Broletto**, or medieval town hall, leads into **Piazza Broletto**, beyond which the sombre Piazza Sordello is flanked by the Baroque facade of the **Duomo**, which conceals a rich interior designed by Giulio Romano, and the **Palazzo Ducale** (Tues–Sat 9am–6pm, Sun 9am–2pm; L12,000), an enormous complex that was once the largest palace in Europe, with a population of over a thousand. When it was sacked by the Habsburgs in 1630, eighty carriages were needed to carry the two thousand works of art contained in its five hundred rooms. Only a proportion of these are open to visitors, and to see them you have to take a guided tour. In the Salone del Fiume there's a trompe l'oeil garden complete with painted creepers and two ghastly fountains; the Sala degli Specchi, further on, has a notice outside signed by Monteverdi, who worked as court musician to Vincenzo I and gave frequent concerts of new works. Vincenzo also employed Rubens, whose *Adoration of the Magi* in the Salone degli Arcieri shows the Gonzaga family of 1604. However, the palace's real treasure is in the Castello di San Giorgio beyond, where you can see Mantegna's frescoes of the Gonzaga family, splendidly restored in the so-called Camera degli Sposi. In the main one Lodovico discusses a letter with a courtier while his wife looks on; their youngest daughter leans on her mother's lap, about to bite into an apple. The other fresco, *The Meeting*, shows Gonzagan retainers with dogs and a horse in attendance on Lodovico who is welcoming his son Francesco back from Rome, where he had just become the first Gonzaga to be made a cardinal.

Mantua's other main sight, the **Palazzo Tè**, on the opposite side of town (Mon 1–5.30pm, Tues–Sun 9am–5.30pm; L12,000), was designed for Federico Gonzaga and his mistress, Isabella Boschetta, by Giulio Romano, and a tour of it is like a voyage around Giulio's imagination, a sumptuous world where very little is what it seems. In the Sala dei Cavalli, portraits of horses stand before an illusionistic background in which simulated marble, fake pilasters and mock reliefs surround views of painted landscapes through nonexistent windows. The function of the Salotta di Psiche, further on, is undocumented, but the sultry frescoes, and its proximity to Federico's bedroom, might give a few clues, the ceiling paintings telling the story of Cupid and Psyche with some dizzying *sotto in su* (from the bottom up) works by Giulio. On the walls, too, are racy pieces, covered with orgiastic wedding-feast scenes, watched over by the giant Polyphemus, perched above the fireplace, while, beyond, the extraordinary Sala dei Giganti shows the destruction of the giants by the gods, with cracking pillars, toppling brickwork and screaming giants appearing to crash down into the room.

Practicalities

The city centre is a ten-minute walk from the **train station** down Via Solferino. There is only one cheap **hotel** in Mantua, the *Peter Pan*, at Citadella Piazza Giulia 3 (☎0376.392.638; ④). Otherwise try the *ABC*, Piazza Don Leoni 25 (☎0376.322.329; ⑤) or the *Bianchi Stazione*, next door (☎0376.326.465; ⑤), both opposite the station, or *Ai Due Guerrieri*, Piazza Sordello 52 (☎0376.325.596; ⑤), in the town centre overlooking the Palazzo Ducale. The **tourist office** (Mon–Sat 8.30am–12.30pm & 3–6pm, Sun 9am–noon; ☎0376.328.253) is around the corner from Sant'Andrea, and has maps and accommodation lists. For inexpensive **food**, the cheapest place is the *Il Punto* self-service at Via Solferino 36, near the train station (closed Sun). Failing that, try the *Bella Napoli*, Piazza Cavalotti 14, which serves good pizza (closed Tues), or the *Leoncino Rosso* Via Giustiziati 33, off Piazza Broletto (closed Sun).

Genoa

GENOA is "a place that grows upon you every day…it abounds in the strangest contrasts; things that are picturesque, ugly, mean, magnificent, delightful and offensive break upon the view at every turn", wrote Dickens in 1844, and the description still fits. Genoa is a marvellously eclectic city, centring on the port that made it one of the five Italian maritime republics by the thirteenth century. Later, during the unification era, the city was a base for radical thought. Mazzini, one of the main protagonists in Italy's unification was born here, and in 1860 Garibaldi set sail for Sicily with his "Thousand" from the city's harbour. The city is now in economic decline, but it remains a wonderfully vibrant place, with a warren-like medieval centre that has more zest than all the nearby coastal resorts put together.

Arrival and accommodation

Trains from Ventimiglia and points west arrive at Stazione Principe in Piazza Acquaverde, just above the port; and trains from La Spezia, Rome and points south arrive at Stazione Brignole, Piazza Verdi, on the other side of the city centre; trains from Milan and Turin usually stop at both, but if you have to travel between the two, take bus #18 or #37. **Ferries** arrive at the Stazione Maríttima, ten minutes' walk downhill from Stazione Principe. **Getting around** is best done on foot; if you do need to take a **bus**, a basic ticket, available from *tabacchi* and newspaper stands, costs L1500 and is valid for ninety minutes. There is a **tourist office** at Stazione Principe (Mon–Sat 8am–8pm, Sun 9am–noon), and another at Porto Antico, Palazzina S. Maria (Mon–Sat 8am–6.30pm, Sun 9am–noon).

There are plenty of cheap **hotels** in the city centre, but many are grimy and depressing and you need to look hard to find the exceptions. Good areas to try are the roads bordering the old town, and Piazza Colombo and Via XX Settembre, near Stazione Brignole. The *Soana*, about ten minutes' walk from Stazione Brignole, at Via XX Settembre 23/8/a (☎010.562.814; ⑤), is a very friendly place with a mixture of plain unmodernized rooms and others with TV and telephone; nearby, the *Carletto*, Via Colombo 16/4 (☎010.588.412; ④), is a good fallback option if the *Soana* is full. In the old town, the *Major*, close to Piazza del Ferro, at Vico Spada 4 (☎010.247.4174; ③), has a more atmospheric location and better-equipped rooms at similar prices, but if you have a bit more money to spend, the *Cairoli*, Via Cairoli 14/4 (☎010.246.1454; ⑤), is a very pleasant option and is handy for the old town and Stazione Principe. Genoa's official **youth hostel** is a clean and well-run place with great views up in the hills, north of the centre at Via Costanzi 120 (☎010.242.2457; ②) – take bus #40 from Stazione Brignole or bus #35 from Stazione Principe then #40 from Piazza Nunziata, three minutes downhill from Stazione Principe. Campers should bear in mind that Genoa's **campsites** are without exception ghastly; it's far better to stay out at one of the nearby coastal resorts and commute into the city from there.

The City

Genoa spreads outwards from its **old town** around the port in a confusion of tiny alleyways and old palaces in which people speak the impenetrable Genoese dialect – a mixture of Neapolitan, Calabrese and Portuguese. From 1384 to 1515, except for brief periods of foreign domination, the doges ruled the city from the **Palazzo Ducale** in Piazza Matteotti (Tues–Sun 9am–8pm; prices vary), across from which the dour **Gesù** church, designed by Pellegrino Tibaldi at the end of the sixteenth century, contains Guido Reni's *Assumption* and two paintings by Rubens. Close by, the Gothic **Cattedrale di San Lorenzo** is home to the Renaissance chapel of St John the Baptist, whose remains once rested in the thirteenth-century sarcophagus. After a particularly bad storm, priests carried his casket through the city to placate the sea, and a commemorative procession takes place each June 24 to honour him. His reliquary is in the treasury (daily 9am–noon & 3–6pm; L10,000), along with a polished quartz plate on which, legend says, Salome received his severed head. Also on display is a glass dish said to have been given to Solomon by the Queen of Sheba, and used at the Last Supper. East from the adjacent Piazza Ferrari leads **Via XX Settembre**, Genoa's commercial nucleus, with big department stores and pavement cafés in the arcades.

Heading south across **Via San Bernardo**, another busy street, the mosaic spire of the church of **Sant'Agostino** marks the adjacent **Museo dell'Architettura e Scultura Ligure** (Tues–Sat 9am–7pm, Sun 9am–12.30pm; L6000), built around the cloister of a thirteenth-century monastery, with a collection of Roman and Romanesque fragments from other churches, as well as woodcarvings and ancient maps of Genoa. Down on the waterfront, the sea once came up to the vaulted arcades of **Piazza Caricamento**, a hive of activity, fringed by café-restaurants and the stalls of its market. Customs inspectors, and subsequently the city's elected governors, set up in the **Palazzo San Giorgio** on the edge of the square, some rooms of which are open to the public (Sat 10am–6pm; free). Beyond, the waterfront has been the subject of a massive restoration project manifest most obviously in the huge **Aquarium** (April–Sept Mon–Fri 9.30am–6.30pm, Sat & Sun 9.30am–8pm; Oct–March Tues–Fri 9.30am–6.30pm, Sat & Sun 9.30am–8pm; last ticket 1hr 30min before closing; L19,000), which contains sea creatures from all the world's habitats. Behind Piazza Caricamento is a thriving commercial zone centred on **Piazza Banchi**, formerly the heart of the medieval city, off which the long Via San Luca leads to the **Galleria Nazionale di Palazzo Spinola** (Tues–Sat 9am–7pm, Sun 2–7pm; L8000), whose collection includes work by the Sicilian master Antonello da Messina and an *Adoration of the Magi* by Joos van Cleve.

North of here, **Via Garibaldi** is lined with Renaissance palaces, two of which have been turned into art galleries. The **Palazzo Bianco** (Tues, Thurs, Fri 9am–1pm, Wed & Sat 9am–7pm, Sun 10am–6pm; L6000) holds paintings by Genoese artists and others, including Van Dyck and Rubens, and a good general gathering of Flemish art. The paintings in the **Palazzo Rosso** across the road (same hours as Palazzo Bianco; L6000) include works by Titian, Caravaggio and Dürer, but it's the decor which really impresses – fantastic chandeliers, mirrors, an excess of gilding, and frescoed ceilings. Behind, Genoa heaps up the hill like the steps of an amphitheatre, a part of town best seen by way of the **funicular** from Piazza del Portello up to Sant'Anna. The view from up here is much hyped, but the trip is more absorbing than anything you'll see when you arrive.

Eating, drinking, nightlife and beaches

For cheap **lunches**, **snacks** and **picnic** ingredients, try the side streets around Stazione Brignole and Piazza Colombo, and the covered Mercato Orientale, halfway down Via XX Settembre in the old cloisters of an Augustinian monastery. There are also a lot of good cheap alternatives on Piazza Caricamento. For full **meals**, *Sâ Pesta*, Via Giustiniani 16, is a well-known source of good local cooking, including *farinata*, a thin chickpea-based pancake, but it closes early. *Corona di Ferro*, Vico Inferiore del Ferro 9, off Via di Macelli di Soziglia, is a long-established old-town restaurant that serves a good array of low to moderately priced local dishes, mainly pasta with seafood sauces; the *Ostaja do Castello*, Salita Santa Maria di Castello 32, on the other side of the old town, closer to the water, is a similar small, family-run trattoria. If you've had enough of Italian food, try the *Circolo Latino Americano*, Via della Maddalena 50 (Wed–Sat only), which serves chilli, enchiladas, tacos, and above all lots of meat. For a **drink**, the *Brittania* in Vico Casana, just off Via XX Aprile and Piazza di Feurni, is open all day, but its pseudo-English pub atmosphere is liveliest at night, when it's fraternized by Italians as well as expats dying for a Guinness or a hamburger.

As for **beaches**, you need to travel some way before you really feel free of the Genoa sprawl, and it's probably best to accept that sunbathing isn't part of the Genoese experience. If you fancy a swim, though, the small suburb-cum-resort of **Nervi**, on the eastern side of the city, is probably the most attractive spot that can be easily reached – take bus #15 from Piazza Caricamento; failing that take bus #3, also from Piazza Caricamento, to **Pegli**, on the opposite side of the city.

The Riviera di Ponente

You get the most positive impression of the coast west of Genoa – the **Riviera di Ponente** – as you speed along the *autostrada*, from where the marinas and resorts are mere specks in a panorama of glittering sea and acres of glasshouses. Close up, the seaside towns from Genoa to the French border are fairly functional places, yet they have their good points – chiefly the sandy beaches and an exceptionally mild climate, which means that flowering plants grow here all year round.

With nearly a hundred hotels in and around its centre, **FINALE LIGURE**, about 40km west of Genoa, is committed to tourism, yet manages to remain an attractive place. It is well known for its nearby Grotte delle Arene Candide, finds from which are on display at the **Museo Archeologico** (Tues–Sat 9am–noon & 2.30–4.30pm, Sun 9am–noon; L5000) in the cloisters of Santa Caterina in the old appealing upper town – **Finale Borgo**; the main and tourist part of town, **Finale Marina**, is about a kilometre below here, along the seafront. Above all, it's a pleasant place to stay and see this part of the coast. There's a **youth hostel**, the *Wuillermin*, in a castle high above the train station at Via Generale Caviglia 46 (☎019.690.515; ②; mid-March to mid-Oct), and a vast number of **hotels**, though many get booked up well in advance in high season and insist on you taking full pensions. Try the

Marco at Lungomare Concezione 22 (☎019.629.533; ③), which has cheap clean, if basic, rooms and is right across from the beach, or the more upmarket *Medusa* (☎019.692.545; ⑤), just the other side of the main square and tucked down the tiny Vico Bricchieri. The **tourist office**, on the seafront at Via San Pietro 14 (Mon–Sat 9am–12.30pm & 3.30–6.30/7pm, Sun 9am–noon; ☎019.681.019), has details of other possibilities, including **rooms in private houses**. On the food side, there's a similarly wide range of places to **eat**, even if the quality isn't always high. In Finale Marina, the fairly typical *La Grotta*, on the seafront next to the tourist office, is a so so lively spaghetteria serving pasta and pizza at reasonable prices. The pizzas at *Pizzeria da Tonino*, Via Bolla 5, are better – and you can sit outside – while if you want something a little more adventurous try the *Gnabbri Trattoria* up behind the church off Via Roma, bang in the centre of Finale Marina – its friendly neighbourhood atmosphere and regularly changing small menu of *linguini* specialities are excellent value.

One of the other main resorts of this stretch of coast is **SAN REMO**, a grand old place whose heyday was the early twentieth century, when wealthy Europeans paraded up and down the Corso Imperatrice and filled the large hotels overlooking the sea. There isn't a lot to see, and even the small **beach** by the train station is a bit mucky, but the place has a certain seedy charm and big-town feel that's refreshing after the resortiness of much of the rest of the coast. It also has an amazing old town – known as **La Pigna** – a kasbah-like maze of tunnels and blind alleys that makes for hours of happy clambering. The **train station** is right in the centre of town by the sea, just across the road from which is the **tourist office**, Via Nuvaloni 1 (Mon–Sat 8am–7pm; Sun 9am–1pm). There are loads of **places to stay**, including a number of handily placed budget **hotels** along the streets to the right as you come out of the station. Cheap options are the *Arenella*, Corso Raimondo 2 (☎0184.503.639; ④), or opposite the fish market, the *Saracena* at Via Francia 17 (☎0184.502.416; ③). Slightly pricier is the *Matuzia*, around the corner at Corso Matteotti 121 (☎0184.577.070; ④). For **food**, the *Cantine San Remo* Via Palazzo 7, is a good place for lunch or an evening meal – it's a bar that serves snacks and has a few tables out back for more substantial fare; around the corner, Piazza Eroi San Remesi has a number of decent pizzerias – try the *Graziella*, on the left looking away from the sea. Up in the old town the tiny *Osteria della Costa* serves an excellent rabbit stew.

The Riviera di Levante

The stretch of coast east from Genoa, the **Riviera di Levante**, is not the place to come for a relaxing beach holiday. The ports which once survived on navigation, fishing and coral diving have now experienced thirty years of tourism; the coastline is still wild and beautiful in parts, but the sense of remoteness has gone.

CAMOGLI was in its day an important seafaring town, supporting a fleet of seven hundred vessels. But it declined in the age of steam, and these days the harbour is mostly busy with ferries along the coast. **Punta Chiappa**, across the bay, was once famous for the "ever changing colours of the sea" but is now murky in places with rubbish from the yachts moored off the promontory. The flat rocks are still a popular place to bask, and plenty of people swim from here. It's also the starting point for trails around the edge of **Monte di Portofino**, and is accessible by ferry or by taking the path from San Rocco church, on the edge of Camogli. From Punta Chiappa it takes three hours to walk to San Fruttuoso and five to Portofino, along wild and beautiful clifftops. For **places to stay**, try *La Camogliese*, Via Garibaldi 55 (☎0185.771.402; ④), which has a decent, fair-priced **restaurant**, a few steps along the seafront.

PORTOFINO, at the extremity of the Monte Portofino headland, manages to be both attractive and offputting at the same time, a wealthy resort but a beautiful one. The two-and-a-half-hour walk to **San Fruttuoso**'s thirteenth-century **Abbey** (March, April & Oct daily 10am–4pm; May–Sept daily 10am–6pm; Jan, Feb & Dec Sat & Sun only 10am–4pm; L5000) and beach is well worth doing. Boats go from San Fruttuoso to Camogli, Portofino, Santa Margherita and Rapallo. Three kilometres out of Portofino, on the corniche road, the sparkling cove at **PARAGGI** is a good place for a swim, with a couple of bars set back from the beach, and you can take a bus to Ruta, from where you can either slog on foot to the summit of Monte Portofino or catch another bus to Portofino Vetta, from where it's twenty minutes' walk to the top. On very clear days the views are fantastic.

SANTA MARGHERITA LIGURE is a small, thoroughly attractive resort, with palm trees along the front and a minuscule pebble beach and concrete jetties to swim from; it also has plenty of cheapish accommodation, making it a convenient base for visiting Portofino and the other coastal towns. The **hotels** are friendly and pleasant: try *Albergo Annabella* at Via Costasecca 10, just off Piazza Mazzini (☎0185.286.531; ③), or the more expensive *Albergo Fasce*, a little further up the road at Via L. Bozzo 3 (☎0185.286.435; ⑤), run by a friendly Anglo-Italian couple, and which has a dozen bikes guests may use free of charge. The **tourist office** on Via XXV Aprile (summer Mon–Sat 9am–12.30pm & 3.30–6.30pm, Sun 9am–12.30pm; winter Mon–Sat 9am–12.30pm & 2.30–5.30pm) has free footpath maps of the area. For **food**, either try *Trattoria Baicin*, just off the seafront square at Via Algeria 9, or the long-established *Da Pezzi*, around the corner at Via Cavour 21, a canteen-like locals' hangout serving a basic formula of pasta and grills, and takeaway snacks for lunch.

RAPALLO crowds around the first bay and along in the gulf, a highly developed though still attractive resort that used to be patronized by a number of writers, drawn here by the bay's extraordinary beauty. Caricaturist and ferocious critic of British imperialism Max Beerbohm lived in Rapallo, attracting a vast coterie, and Ezra Pound wrote the first thirty of his *Cantos* here between 1925 and 1930. There are decent **places to stay** in the centre of town, most notably the extremely welcoming *Pensione Bandoni*, Via Marsala 24/3 (☎0185.50.423; ③); if it's full, try the *Fernanda*, along the front at Via Milite Ignoto 9 (☎0185.50.244; ④), cosy enough, but more expensive for less pleasant rooms. There are a couple of **campsites**, *Rapallo* (☎0185.262.018) at Via San Lazzaro 4 and the *Miraflores* (☎0185.263.000) at Via Savagna 10. Perhaps the least expensive and most authentic place **to eat** is *Bansin*, right in the heart of the old town at Via Venezia 49, though it closes early; with a little money, *Da Mario*, Piazza Garibaldi 23, is a good, moderately priced fish restaurant.

A number of paths lead down from the main Rapallo–Chiávari road to some small coves – to investigate them, take the bus and get off when you see signs pointing to the sea. **CHIÁVARI** itself faces a featureless bit of coastline, but does boast a reasonable beach. The **bus** and **train** stations are next to each other, just off the main Corso della Libertà, which bisects a grid pattern of medieval arcades. Off the Corso, at Via Costaguta 2, is the **Civico Museo Archeologico** (daily 9am–1.30pm; closed alternate Mon and Sun; free), with graphics explaining such matters as the triple flint arrowhead, backed by finds from a vast seventh- to eighth-century necropolis on the outskirts of town. There is a **tourist office** opposite the station (Mon–Sat 9.30am–12.30pm & 3.30–6.30pm), as well as others dotted throughout the city.

The road sweeps around the bay to **SESTRI LEVANTE**, one of the largest resorts this side of Genoa. It consists of two bays separated by a narrow isthmus: the Baia delle Favole (Bay of Fables), said to be so named by Hans Christian Andersen, and the Baia del Silenzio (Bay of Silence). On the Bay of Fables side, the beach is wide and sandy but is packed with sunbeds and overlooked by ranks of hotels. The Bay of Silence, on the other hand, might not exactly live up to its name in high season, but is far more pleasant, with a narrow beach and lots of fishing boats. Among **places to stay** are *Villa Jolanda*, Via Pozzetto 15 (☎0185.41.354; ③), which enjoys a lovely location on the headland; the *San Pietro* on Via Palestro (☎0185.41.279; ③), just off the main street; and *La Neigra*, Viale Roma 49 (☎0185.41.756; ③), near the station and with a great trattoria, though its location isn't necessarily what you come to Italy for. Via XXV Aprile, which runs through the narrow peninsula and widens out onto Corso Colombo, is where you'll find the best places to **eat and drink**. *Polpo Mario*, at Via XXV Aprile 163, specializes in fish and reckons itself something of a gourmet mecca, and *Buon Geppin* on Corso Colombo has good antipasti, though neither are especially cheap. For a **pizza** try the *Leda* restaurant, near the tourist office on the corner of Piazza San Antonio.

The Cinque Terre

If you're travelling on a fast train, you'll speed through the five villages of the **Cinque Terre** without seeing much more than a few tantalizing glimpses of sheer cliff as the train dashes from one tunnel to the next. However, the stopping services on the Genoa to La Spezia line call at each one, and there is a ferry service linking them with La Spezia. Their comparative remoteness, and the drama of their position on tiny cliff-bound inlets, make a visit to the area a real attraction. **RIOMAGGIORE**, closest to La Spezia and one of the larger villages, is the best place to head for, wedged impossibly into a hillside, with no two buildings on the same level. Along the cliff path which winds its way to **MANAROLA**, lemon trees flourish in every backyard, and in spring the cliffs are covered with wild flowers. From Manarola a spectacular path passes rock-cut steps leading down to the water all the way to **MONTEROSSO** (12km), largest and least charming of the villages, and the only one with a recognizable beach. **CORNIGLIA** and **VERNAZZA** are similar to Riomaggiore, but on a smaller scale. Hotels aren't too difficult to find – Monterosso and Riomaggiore present the best opportunities – but they can be pricey; you could base yourself in **LEVANTO**, a little way west, which has plentiful reasonable accommodation and food options, including a decent **campsite**, the *Aquadolce*, in the centre of town, plus a long stretch of sandy **beach** – and it's on the main rail line. If you do decide to stay, try the *Pensione Garden*, the cheapest **hotel**, located right by the sea at Corso Italia 8 (☎0187.808.173; ③); if that's full, or you have a little more money, try the slightly cosier atmosphere of the *Europa*, up the street at Via Dante 41 (☎0187.808.126; ⑤; half board obligatory in July and Aug). For **food** and late-night **drinks**, the *Caffè Roma*, on the square round the corner from the *Pensione Garden*, has a small reasonably priced **restaurant** out the back.

THE NORTHEAST

Italy's **northeast** is one of the country's most appealing – and versatile – regions. The appeal of **Venice** hardly needs stating: it's one of Europe's truly unique urban landscapes, and, despite its equally unique huge number of visitors, really unmissable on any European – let alone Italian – tour. The region around Venice – the **Veneto** – is a prosperous one, where virtually every acre still bears the imprint of Venetian rule. **Padua** and **Verona** are the main attractions, with their masterpieces by Giotto, Donatello and Mantegna, and a profusion of great buildings from Roman times to the Renaissance. Much of the countryside is dull and flat, only perking up to the north with the high peaks of the Dolomite range. East, on the former Yugoslav border, **Trieste** is capital of the partly Slav region of **Friuli-Venezia Giulia**, a Habsburg city only united with Italy after World War II. South, between Lombardy and Tuscany, stretching from the Adriatic coast almost to the shores of the Mediterranean, **Emilia-Romagna** is the heartland of northern Italy, a patchwork of ducal territories formerly ruled by a handful of families, whose castles and fortresses remain in well-preserved medieval towns. Carving a straight route through the heart of the region, from Milan to Rimini on the coast, the Via Emilia is a central and obvious reference point, a Roman military road constructed in 187 BC that was part of the medieval pilgrim's route to Rome and the way east for crusaders to Ravenna and Venice. **Bologna**, the region's capital, is one of Italy's largest cities, but despite having one of the most beautifully preserved city centres in the country and some of its finest food, it's relatively neglected by tourists – definitely a mistake. Bologna also gives easy access to **Parma**, just an hour or so away by train, a wealthy provincial town that is worth visiting for its paintings by Parmigianino and Correggio. The coast is less interesting, and the water polluted, although **Rimini** provides a spark of interest, its oddly attractive seaside sleaze concealing a historic town centre, and, just south of the Po delta, **Ravenna** boasts probably the world's finest set of Byzantine mosaics in its churches and mausoleums. **Ferrara**, a little way inland, is, as the domain of the Este family, one of the most important Renaissance centres in Italy.

Venice

The first-time visitor to **VENICE** arrives with a heavy freight of expectations, most of which turn out to have been well founded. It is an extraordinarily beautiful city, an urban landscape so rich that you can't walk for a minute without coming across something that's worth a stop;

and the major sights like the basilica and piazza of San Marco are all they are cracked up to be, as are most of the lesser-known ones. The downside is that Venice is deluged with tourists, the annual influx exceeding the city's population two-hundredfold; and it is expensive – the price of a good meal anywhere else in Italy will get you a lousy one in Venice, and its hoteliers make the most of a situation where demand will always far outstrip supply. However, the crowds thin out beyond the magnetic field of San Marco, and in the off-season it's still possible to have parts of the centre virtually to yourself. As for keeping your costs down, there are a few inexpensive eating places, and it is still possible to find a bed for the night without spending a fortune.

Venice first rose to a kind of prominence when the traders of what was then a small settlement on the lagoon signalled their independence from Byzantium through a great symbolic act – the theft from Alexandria in 828 of the body of St Mark, who became the city's patron. Venice later exploited the trading networks and markets of Byzantium and the East, aided by the Crusades, by the twelfth century achieving unprecedented prosperity and benefiting especially from the Sack of Constantinople in 1204, which left much of the Roman Empire under the city's sway. Following the defeat of Genoa in 1380, Venice consolidated its position as the unrivalled trading power of the region, and by the middle of the fifteenth century was in possession of a mainland empire that was to survive virtually intact for several centuries – although its eastern dominions were increasingly encroached on by the Ottomans. Decline set in in the eighteenth century, when, politically moribund and constitutionally ossified, Venice became renowned as a playground of the rich, a position consolidated in the nineteenth century with the growth of tourism and the development of the Lido as Europe's most fashionable resort. This turns out to have been a wise move, despite the drawbacks. Nowadays some twenty million people visit the city each year, around half of whom don't even stay a night. Without them, however, Venice would barely exist at all.

Arrival and information

Flights arrive at the city's **Marco Polo** airport, on the edge of the lagoon, linked to the city centre by ACTV bus #5 (every 30min; L1500); alternatively you can catch an ATVO bus (L5000) or more expensive waterbus (L17,000). All road traffic comes into the city at **Piazzale Roma**, at the head of the Canal Grande, from where waterbus services run to the San Marco area, stopping off at Santa Lucia **train station**, the next stop along the Canal Grande. If you're coming right into Venice by **car**, you'll have to park in either the Piazzale Roma multistorey car park, or on the adjoining Tronchetto, a vast artificial island. The queues for both can be huge – a better option in summer is to park in Mestre's municipal car park, then take a bus over the causeway.

The main **tourist office** (daily 9.40am–3.20pm) is in the Casinò da Caffè, on the edge of the Giardinetti Reali, by the San Marco waterbus stop; there are desks at the train station, at the airport and at San Marco 71/f. Pick up their free map and English/Italian magazine, *Un Ospite di Venezia*, which gives up-to-date what's-on information and waterbus timetables.

City transport

In most cases the speediest way of getting around Venice is **on foot**. Distances between major sights are short (you can cross the whole city in an hour), and once you've got your general bearings navigation is not as daunting a prospect as it seems. To get between two points quickly, however, it's sometimes faster to take a waterbus (*vaporetto*). **Tickets** are available from most landing stages and all shops displaying the ACTV sign. Flat-rate fares are L6000 for any one continuous journey, except for most one-stop journeys, which cost L3000. Tickets bought on board are subject to a surcharge, and the spot-fine for not having a valid ticket is L30,000, so it's a good idea to buy a block of ten (*un blochetto*) or a tourist ticket: a 24-hour ticket costs L18,000, a three-day pass is L35,000, and a weekly ticket costs L60,000. Timetables are posted at each stop, the tourist office's city map has a route plan, and *Un Ospite di Venezia*, the listings magazine, has details of the important lines. In addition, there are the **traghetti** that cross the Canale Grande, which cost L800 a trip and are the only cheap way of getting a ride on a gondola. In summer they run from early morning to around 7–9pm daily with a two-hour break for lunch. Otherwise the **gondola** is an adjunct of the tourist industry: to hire one costs L120,000 for 50 minutes, rising to L150,000 between 8pm and 8am, plus L60,000 for each additional 25 minutes – be sure to confirm the charge beforehand.

Accommodation

Accommodation is the major expense in Venice, although there are inexpensive options, not least a number of **hostels**, most owned by religious foundations, which are generally comfortable and well run. Unless you're coming during winter (when many hotels close), you should always book ahead; if you haven't, there are **booking offices** at the train station (daily 8am–9pm), on the Tronchetto (daily 9am–8pm), at Piazzale Roma (daily 9am–9pm), at Marco Polo airport (daily summer 9am–7pm; winter noon–7pm), and at the *autostrada*'s Venice exit (8am–8pm). They only deal with hotels and take a deposit, deductable from your first night's bill.

HOSTELS

Domus Cavanis, Rio Terrà Foscarini, Dorsoduro 912 (☎041.528.7374). Catholic-run, with separate rooms for men and women. Open mid-June to end Sept. ③.

Domus Civica, Calle Campazzo, San Polo 3082 (☎041.721.103). A student house in winter, open to women travellers June, July, Sept & Oct. 11.30pm curfew. ③.

Foresteria Valdese, Santa Maria Formosa, Castello 5170 (☎041.528.6797). Difficult to find – go from Campo Santa Maria Formosa along Calle Lunga, and it's at the foot of the bridge at the far end. Two large dorms, and a few rooms for 2 to 4 people; open for registration 9am–1pm & 6–8.30pm. ③.

Ostello Venezia, Fondementa delle Zitelle, Guidecca 86 (☎041.523.8211). The official HI hostel, in a superb location looking towards San Marco from the island of Giudecca. Opens at 2pm for registration, and it's a good idea to get there early, but if it's full, don't panic: they use a local school with camp-beds as an annexe. Curfew 11.30pm. ②.

HOTELS

Ai Do Mori, Calle Larga S. Marco 658, San Marco (☎041.520.4817). Very friendly one-star, a few steps from the Piazza. ④.

Albergo Bernardi Semenzato, Calle dell'Oca, Cannaregio 4366 (☎041.522.7257). Recently renovated place with very welcoming and helpful English-speaking owners. ⑤.

Antica Casa Carettoni, Lista di Spagna, Cannaregio 130 (☎041.716.231). By a long way the most comfortable one-star in the vicinity of the train station. ⑤.

Antico Capon, Campo S. Margherita, Dorsoduro 3004 (☎041.528.5292). Situated on one of the city's most atmospheric squares, in the heart of the student district. ⑤.

Ca' Fóscari, Calle della Frescada, Dorsoduro 3887B (☎041.710.401). Tucked away in a micro-alley near San Tomà, near the university. Quiet, well decorated and relaxed. ④.

Caneva, Ramo della Fava, Castello 5515 (☎041.522.8118). Overlooking the Rio della Fava on the approach to the busy Campo San Bartolomeo, yet very peaceful. ⑤.

Casa Gerotto Calderan, Campo S. Geremia 283, Cannaregio (☎041.715.361 or 041.715.562). Tremendous value, very welcoming and not far from the train station. Dormitory accommodation also available. ③.

Casa Petrarca, Calle delle Colonne, San Marco 4394 (☎041.520.0430). Friendly place, and the cheapest near the Piazza. Phone first, as they only have 6 rooms. ④.

Fiorita, Campiello Nuovo, San Marco 3457 (☎041.523.4754). Just 9 rooms, so it's important to book. Welcoming management. ⑤.

Sant'Anna, Corte del Bianco, Castello 269 (☎041.528.6466). A fair way out from the centre but good for families with kids, as it has rooms for 3–4 people and is near the Giardini Pubblici; book in early. ④.

Toscana-Tofanelli, Via Garibaldi, Castello 1650 (☎041.523.5722). Spartan hotel but a good location and excellent trattoria attached; midnight curfew. ③.

CAMPSITES

There are a number of fairly expensive **campsites** along the **Litorale del Cavallino**, accessible on waterbus #14 from the Riva degli Schiavoni, a forty-minute trip. Two to try are *Marina di Venezia*, Via Montello 6 (☎041.530.0955; April–Sept; minimum stay 3 nights), and *Miramare*, Lungomare Dante Alighieri 29 (☎041.966.150; March–Oct). There's an all-year

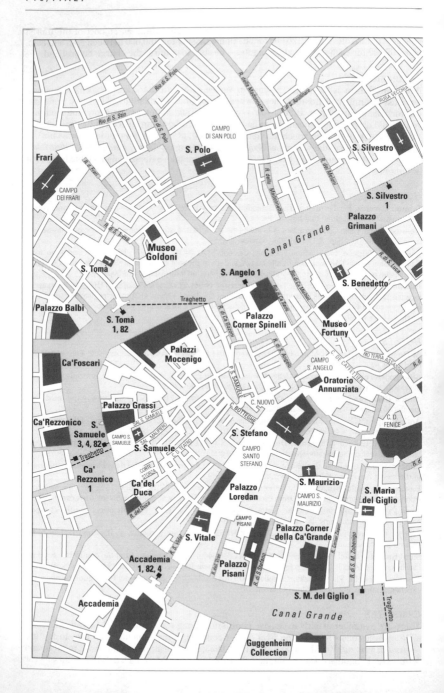

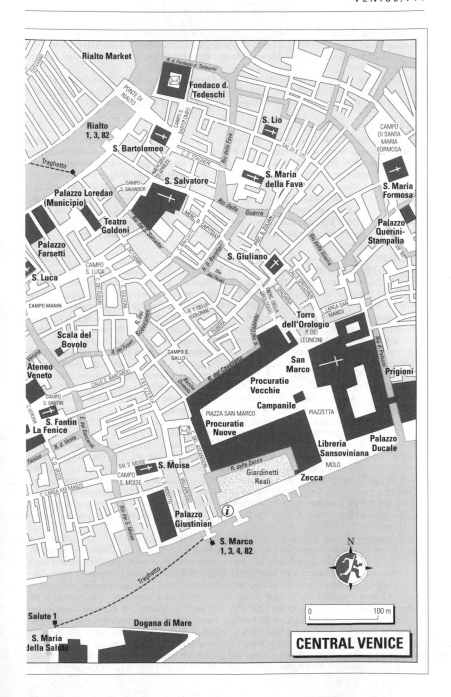

CENTRAL VENICE

site at Fusina, *Mestre Fusina* (☎041.547.005), on Via Moranzani – better in summer when there's a direct *vaporetto* (#16); at other times get the bus to Mestre and change there. The two sites out by the airport, the *Marco Polo* and the *Alba d'Oro*, are expensive and not particularly attractive.

Self-sufficient travellers used to spread their sleeping bags in front of the train station in summer, an expedient that was banned in 1987. Ask at the tourist office if there's a makeshift dormitory anywhere to absorb the overspill – there normally is somewhere in the city.

The City

The 118 islands of central Venice are divided into six districts known as *sestieri*. The *sestiere* of **San Marco** is home to the majority of the essential sights, and is accordingly the most expensive and most crowded district of the city. On the east it's bordered by **Castello**, on the north by **Cannaregio** – both of which become more residential the further you go from the centre. On the other side of the Canal Grande, the largest of the *sestieri* is **Dorsoduro**, which stretches from the fashionable quarter at the southern tip of the canal to the docks in the west. **Santa Croce**, named after a now-demolished church, roughly follows the curve of the Canal Grande from Piazzale Roma to a point just short of the Rialto, where it joins the smartest and commercially most active of the districts on this bank – **San Polo**.

SAN MARCO

The section of Venice enclosed by the lower loop of the Canal Grande is, in essence, the Venice of the travel brochures. The **Piazza San Marco** is the hub of most activity, signalled from most parts of the city by the **Campanile** (daily summer 9.30am–10pm; winter 9.30am–4.15pm; L8000), which began life as a lighthouse in the ninth century and was modified frequently up to the early sixteenth century. The present structure is in fact a reconstruction: the original tower collapsed on July 14, 1902. At 99m, it is the tallest structure in the city, and from the top you can make out virtually every building, but not a single canal. The other tower in the Piazza, the **Torre dell'Orologio**, was built between 1496 and 1506, although the panorama can't compete with the Campanile's and you can watch the Moors at the top strike the hour perfectly well from the ground; it's also currently closed for restoration. Away to the left stretches the **Procuratie Vecchie**, an early sixteenth-century structure that was converted into a palace by Napoleon, who connected the building with the other side of the piazza – the **Procuratie Nuove** – by way of a new wing for dancing. Generally known as the **Ala Napoleonica**, this short side of the Piazza is partly occupied by the **Museo Correr** (daily summer 9am–7pm; winter 9am–5pm; L17,000 joint ticket for Piazza Ducale), whose vast historical collection – coins, weapons, regalia, prints, mediocre paintings – is heavy going unless you have an intense interest in Venetian history. The **Quadreria** on the second floor is no rival for the Accademia's collection, but does set out clearly the evolution of painting in Venice from the thirteenth century to around 1500, and contains some gems – a *Pietà* by Cosmé Tura, the *Transfiguration* and *Dead Christ Supported by Angels* by Giovanni Bellini, along with a Carpaccio picture known as *The Courtesans*. There's also an appealing exhibition of applied arts, featuring a print of Jacopo de'Barbari's astonishing aerial view of Venice, engraved in 1500.

The **Basilica di San Marco** (Mon–Sat 9.45am–5.30pm, Sun 3–5.30pm) is the most exotic of Europe's cathedrals, modelled on Constantinople's Church of the Twelve Apostles, finished in 1094 and embellished over the succeeding centuries with trophies brought back from abroad – proof of Venice's secular might and thus of the spiritual power of St Mark. The Romanesque carvings of the central door were begun around 1225 and finished in the early fourteenth century, while the mosaic above the doorway on the far left – *The Arrival of the Body of St Mark* – was made around 1260 (the only early mosaic left on the main facade) and includes the oldest-known image of the basilica. Inside, the narthex holds more mosaics, Old Testament scenes on the domes and arches, together with *The Madonna with Apostles and Evangelists* in the niches of the bay in front of the main door – dating from the 1060s, the oldest mosaics in San Marco. A steep staircase goes from the church's main door up to the **Museo Marciano** and the **Loggia dei Cavalli** (daily 9.45am–4.30pm; L3000), where you can enjoy fine views of the city and the Gothic carvings along the apex of the facade, as well as the horses in question, replicas of Roman works thieved from the Hippodrome of Constantinople (the genuine articles are inside). Downstairs, beyond the narthex, the interior proper is covered with more mosaics, most dating from the middle of the thirteenth century, although the **Sanctuary**, off the south transept (Mon–Sat 9.45am–4.30pm, Sun 2–5pm; L3000), holds the most precious of San Marco's treasures, the **Pala d'Oro** or golden altar panel, commissioned in 976 in Constantinople and studded with precious stones. The **Treasury** (same times; L4000) nearby is a similarly dazzling warehouse of chalices, reliquaries and candelabra, a fair proportion pillaged from Constantinople in 1204. Back in the main body of the church, there's still more to see on the lower levels of the building. Don't overlook the **rood screen**'s marble figures of *The Virgin, St Mark and the Apostles*, carved in 1394 by the dominant sculptors in Venice at that time, Jacobello and Pietro Paolo Dalle Masegne. The **pulpits** on each side of the screen were assembled in the early fourteenth century from miscellaneous panels, some from Constantinople; the new doge was presented to the people from the right-hand one. The tenth-century **Icon of the Madonna of Nicopeia** (in the chapel on the east side of the north transept) is the most revered religious image in Venice, and was one of the most revered in Constantinople.

The adjacent **Palazzo Ducale** (daily summer 9am–7pm; winter 9am–5pm; L17,000 joint ticket for Museo Correr) was the residence of the doge, as well as housing Venice's governing councils, courts, a sizeable number of its civil servants and even its prisons. Like San Marco, the Palazzo Ducale has been rebuilt many times since its foundation in the first years of the ninth century, but the earliest parts of the current structure date from 1340. The principal entrance, the **Porta della Carta**, is one of the most ornate Gothic works in the city, commissioned in 1438 by Doge Francesco Fóscari; the figures of Fóscari and his lion are replicas – the originals were pulverized in 1797 by the head of the stonemasons' guild, as a favour to Napoleon. The passage inside ends under the **Arco Fóscari**, also commissioned by Doge Fóscari but finished a few years after his death. Parts of the Palazzo Ducale can be marched through fairly briskly, its walls covered with acres of wearisome canvas, although you should linger in the **Anticollegio**, one of the palace's finest rooms and home to four pictures by Tintoretto and Veronese's characteristically benign *Rape of Europa*. The cycle of paintings on the ceiling of the adjoining Sala del Collegio is also by Veronese, and he features strongly again in the most stupendous room in the building – the Sala del Maggior Consiglio, where his ceiling panel of the *Apotheosis of Venice* is suspended over the dais from which the doge oversaw the sessions of the city assembly. The backdrop is the immense *Paradiso* painted at the end of his life by Tintoretto, with the aid of his son, Domenico. From here you descend quickly to the underbelly of the Venetian state, crossing the **Ponte dei Sospiri** (Bridge of Sighs) to the **prisons**, and then back over the water to the Pozzi, the cells for the most hardened malefactors.

Facing the Palazzo Ducale across the Piazzetta is Sansovino's masterpiece and the most consistently admired Renaissance building in the city – the **Libreria Sansoviniana**, part of which is given over to the **Museo Archeologico** (daily 10am–2pm; L4000), a collection of Greek and Roman sculpture that's best left for a rainy day.

DORSODURO

Some of the finest architecture in Venice is in the *sestiere* of **Dorsoduro**, yet for all its attractions, not many visitors wander off the strip that runs between the main sights of the area, the first of which, the **Galleria dell'Accademia** (Tues–Sat 9am–10pm, Mon 9am–2pm, Sun 9am–8pm; L12,000), is one of the finest specialist collections of European art, following the history of Venetian painting from the fourteenth to the eighteenth centuries. Housed in the church of Santa Maria della Carità and the incomplete Convento dei Canonici Lateranensi, partly built by Palladio in 1561, the gallery is laid out in roughly chronological order. The early sections include paintings by Paolo Veneziano, Carpaccio's strange and gruesome *Crucifixion and Glorification of the Ten Thousand Martyrs of Mount Ararat*, an exquisite *St George* by Mantegna, a series of Giovanni Bellini *Madonnas*, and one of the most mysterious of Italian paintings, Giorgione's *Tempest*. Tintoretto weighs in with three typically energetic pieces illustrating the legend of St Mark, and an entire wall is filled by Paolo Veronese's *Christ* *in the House of Levi* – called *The Last Supper* until the authorities objected to its lack of reverence. Among the most impressive pieces in the Accademia is the magnificent cycle of pictures painted around 1500 for the Scuola di San Giovanni Evangelista, of which Carpaccio's *Cure of a Lunatic* and Gentile Bellini's *Recovery of the Relic from the Canale di San Lorenzo* and *Procession of the Relic in the Piazza* stand out. There's also a cycle of pictures by Carpaccio illustrating the *Story of Saint Ursula*, painted for the Scuola di Sant'Orsola at San Zanipolo, which is one of the most unforgettable groups in the entire country. Finally, in room 24 there's Titian's *Presentation of the Virgin*, painted for the place where it hangs.

Five minutes' walk from the Accademia is the unfinished Palazzo Venier dei Leoni, home of the **Guggenheim Collection** (11am–6pm; closed Tues; L12,000), and of Peggy Guggenheim for thirty years until her death in 1979. Her private collection is an eclectic choice of (mainly) excellent pieces from her favourite modernist movements and artists, including works by Brancusi, De Chirico, Max Ernst and Malevich. Continuing along the line of the Canal Grande, the church of Santa Maria della Salute, better known simply as the **Salute** (daily 10am–noon & 4–6pm), was built to fulfil a Senate decree of 1630 that a new church be dedicated to Mary if the city were delivered from plague. Every November 21 there's still a procession from San Marco to the church, over a specially constructed pontoon bridge, to give thanks for the city's good health, a major event on the Venetian calendar. In 1656, a hoard of Titian paintings were moved here and are now housed in the sacristy (L2000), most prominent of which is the altarpiece of *St Mark Enthroned with Saints Cosmas, Damian, Sebastian and Rocco*. The *Marriage at Cana*, with its dramatic lighting and perspective, is by Tintoretto, featuring portraits of a number of the artist's friends.

SAN POLO

North of Dorsoduro is the *sestiere* of **San Polo**, on the northeastern edge of which the **Rialto** district was in former times the commercial zone of the city, home to the main Venetian banks and maritime businesses. It's the venue of the Rialto market on the far side of the Rialto Bridge, a lively affair and one of the few places in the city where it's possible to hear nothing but Italian spoken. The main reason people visit San Polo, however, is to see the mountainous brick church of the **Frari** west of here (Mon–Sat 10am–5.30pm, Sun 3–5.30pm; L3000), whose collection of art works includes a rare couple of paintings by Titian – most notably his *Assumption*, painted in 1518, a swirling piece of compositional bravura for which there was no precedent in Venetian art. Look also at the Renaissance tombs of the doges flanking the *Assumption*, dating from the late fifteenth century; the wooden *St John the Baptist*, in the chapel to the right, commissioned from Donatello in 1438; and, on the altar of the sacristy, a marvellous *Madonna and Child with Saints* by Giovanni Bellini. Titian is buried in the church, the spot marked by a bombastic nineteenth-century monument, opposite which the equally pompous mausoleum of Canova was erected by pupils of the sculptor, following a design he himself had made for the tomb of Titian.

At the rear of the Frari is the **Scuola Grande di San Rocco** (April–Oct daily 9am–5.30pm; Dec–Feb Mon–Fri 10am–1pm, Sat & Sun 10am–4pm; Mar & Nov daily 10am–4pm; L8000), a sixteenth-century building that is home to a cycle of more than fifty major paintings by Tintoretto. These fall into three main groups. The first, painted in 1564, adorns the upper Sala dell'Albergo – a *Glorification of St Roch*, painted for a competition, and a stupendous *Crucifixion*, which Ruskin claimed to be "above all praise". In the building's main hall, Tintoretto covered three large panels of the ceiling with Old Testament references to the alleviation of physical suffering – coded declarations of the Scuola's charitable activities – while around the walls are New Testament themes, an amazing feat of sustained inventiveness, in which every convention of perspective, lighting, colour and even anatomy is defied. The paintings on the ground floor were created between 1583 and 1587, when Tintoretto was in his late sixties, and include a turbulent *Annunciation*, a marvellous Renaissance landscape in *The Flight into Egypt* and two small paintings of *St Mary Magdalene* and *St Mary of Egypt*.

CANNAREGIO

In the northernmost section of Venice, **Cannaregio**, you can go from one extreme to another in a matter of minutes: it is a short distance from the bustle of the **train station** to areas which are among the quietest and prettiest parts of the whole city. The district also has the dubious distinction of containing the world's first **Ghetto**: in 1516, all the city's Jews were ordered to move to the island of the Ghetto Nuovo, an enclave which was sealed at night by Christian curfew guards. Even now it looks quite different from the rest of Venice, many of its buildings relatively high-rise due to the restrictions on the growth of the area. A couple of the oldest synagogues – the **Scola Levantina**, founded in 1538, and the **Scola Spagnola**, founded twenty years later – are still in use and can be viewed on an informative and multilingual guided tour that leaves on the half-hour, organized by the **Jewish Museum** in Campo Ghetto Nuovo (Mon–Fri & Sun 10am–5.30pm, closed Sat and Jewish holidays; museum and synagogue L5000; tours 10.30am–4.30pm; L12,000), where you can also see a collection of silverware and fabrics.

Northeast of the ghetto, the church of **Madonna dell'Orto** (Mon–Sat 10am–5.30pm, Sun 3–5.30pm; L3000) contains several paintings by Tintoretto, including the colossal *Making of the Golden Calf* and *The Last Judgment* which flank the main altar; the artist is buried in the chapel to the right.

CASTELLO

Northeast of San Marco, **Castello** is home among other things to the **Miracoli** church, built in the 1480s to house a painting of the Madonna which was believed to have performed a number of miracles, such as reviving a man who'd spent half an hour lying at the bottom of the Giudecca canal. The church is thought to have been designed by Pietro Lombardo, who with his two sons Tullio and Antonio oversaw the building and executed much of the carving, which ranks as some of the most intricate decorative sculpture in Venice.

East of here, the **Campo San Zanipolo** (a contraction of Santi Giovanni e Paolo) is the most impressive open space in Venice after Piazza San Marco, dominated by the huge brick church of **San Zanipolo** (Mon–Sat 8am–12.30pm & 3–8pm, Sun 3–5.30pm), founded by the Dominicans in 1246, rebuilt and enlarged from 1333 and finally consecrated in 1430. The church is perhaps best known for the tombs and monuments around the walls, the memorials of some 25 doges, most impressive of which is perhaps the tomb of Doge Michele Morosini on the right of the chancel, selected by Ruskin as "the richest monument of the Gothic period in Venice". On the square outside the church, Verrochio's statue of the Venetian military hero **Bartolomeo Colleoni** is one of the finest Renaissance equestrian monuments in Italy, commissioned in 1481.

The other essential sight in this area is over to the east of San Marco – the **Scuola di San Giorgio degli Schiavoni** (Tues–Sat 10am–12.30pm & 3–6pm, Sun 10am–12.30pm; L5000), set up by Venice's Slav population in 1451. The building dates from the early sixteenth century, and its interior looks more or less as it would have then, with a superb ground-floor room decorated with a cycle painted by Vittore Carpaccio between 1502 and 1509.

THE SOUTHERN ISLANDS

Immediately south of the Palazzo Ducale, Palladio's church of **San Giorgio Maggiore** stands on the island of the same name (Mon–Sat 10am–12.30pm & 2.30–4.30pm, Sun 9.30–10.30am & 2.30–4.30pm). This proved one of the most influential Renaissance church designs, and it has two pictures by Tintoretto in the chancel – *The Fall of Manna* and *The Last Supper*, perhaps the most famous of all his images, painted as a pair in 1592–94, the last years of the artist's life. On the left of the choir a corridor leads to the **Campanile**, rebuilt in 1791 after the collapse of its predecessor and one of the two best vantage points in the city.

The long island of **La Giudecca**, to the west, was where the wealthiest aristocrats of early Renaissance Venice built their villas, and in places you can still see traces of their gardens, although the present-day suburb is a strange mixture of decrepitude and vitality, boatyards and fishing quays interspersed with half-abandoned factories and sheds. Unless you're staying at the *Cipriani*, the most expensive hotel in Venice, the main reason to come is the Franciscan church of the **Redentore** (Mon–Sat 10am–5.30pm, Sun 3–5.30pm; L3000), designed by Palladio in 1577 in thanks for Venice's deliverance from a plague that killed a third of the population. Sadly, the church is in a bad state of repair, and a rope prevents visitors going beyond the nave, but you can see its best paintings, including a *Madonna with Child and Angels* by Alvise Vivarini, in the sacristy, as well as a curious gallery of eighteenth-century wax heads of illustrious Franciscans.

Sheltering Venice from the open sea, the thin strand of the **Lido** used to be the focus of the annual hullaballoo of Venice's "Marriage to the Sea", when the doge went out to the Porto di Lido to drop a gold ring into the brine and then disembarked for mass at San Nicolò al Lido. Later it became the smartest bathing resort in Italy, and although it's no longer as chic as it was when Thomas Mann set *Death in Venice* here, there's less room on its beaches now than ever before; indeed, unless you're staying at one of the flashy hotels on the seafront, or are prepared to pay a ludicrous fee to hire a beach hut, you won't even be allowed to get the choicest Lido sand between your toes. There are public beaches at the northern and southern ends of the island – though the water is, as you would expect, filthy.

THE NORTHERN ISLANDS

The major islands lying to the north of Venice – **Murano**, **Burano** and **Torcello** – can be reached by waterbus from the **Fondamente Nuove**, the #52, which runs about every fifteen minutes, will take you to San Michele and Murano; for Burano and Torcello there is the #12 (roughly hourly), which takes forty minutes to Burano, from where it's a short hop to Torcello. This service can also be caught from Murano, at the Faro landing stage.

Chiefly famed as the home of Venice's glass-blowing industry, **Murano**'s main *fondamente* are crowded with shops selling the mostly revolting products of the furnaces, but the process of manufacture is more interesting. There are numerous **furnaces** to visit, all free of charge on the assumption that you will then want to buy something, though you won't be pressed too hard to do so. Many of the workshops are along Fondamenta dei Vetrai. There's also the **Museo Vetrario** in the Palazzo Giustinian (10am–4pm; closed Wed; L8000), which displays Roman pieces and the earliest surviving examples of Murano glass from the fifteenth century. Other attractions include the church of **San Pietro Martire**, a Dominican Gothic church which houses an elegant *Madonna* by Giovanni Bellini, and the Veneto-Byzantine church of **Santi Maria e Donato**, founded in the seventh century and rebuilt in the twelfth (daily 9am–noon & 4–7pm), which has a beautiful mosaic floor.

Burano is still largely a fishing community, although there is also a thriving trade in **lace-making** here, and the main street is crammed with shops selling Burano-point and Venetian-point lace. The skills are taught at the **Scuola dei Merletti** in Piazza Baldessare Galuppi (10am–4pm; closed Mon; L5000), which also houses a small museum with work dating back as far as the sixteenth century.

The island of **Torcello** was settled as early as the fifth century, and once had a population of some twenty thousand. Nowadays, however, the population is about one hundred, and there is little visible evidence of the island's prime except for Venice's first cathedral, **Santa Maria Assunta** (daily 10am–12.30pm & 2–5pm; L4000). A Veneto-Byzantine building on the site of a seventh-century church (only the crypt of which survives), the cathedral has a stunning twelfth-century mosaic of the Madonna and Child in the apse. Look in also on the church of **Santa Fosca**, built in the eleventh and twelfth centuries to house the body of the saint, brought from Libya some time before 1011 and now resting under the altar. In the square outside sits the curious **chair of Attila**: sit in it and – local legend says – you will be wed within a year. Behind, the **Museo dell'Estuario** (Tues–Sun 10am–12.30pm & 2–4pm; L3000) displays thirteenth-century beaten gold figures, sections of mosaic heads and pieces of jewellery.

Eating and drinking

Virtually every **restaurant** in Venice advertises a set-price *Menu Turistico*, which can be a cheap way of sampling Venetian specialities, but the quality and certainly the quantity won't be up to the mark of an *à la carte* meal. As a general rule, value for money tends to increase with the distance from San Marco; plenty of restaurants within a short radius of the Piazza offer menus that seem to be reasonable but you'll probably find the food unappetizing and the service abrupt. Most bars will also serve some kind of food, ranging from *tramezzini* through to more exotic nibbles called *cicheti*.

TAKEAWAYS AND PICNIC FOOD

Cip Ciap, close to the church of Santa Maria Formosa in Calle Mondo Nuovo, Castello, has perhaps the city's best range of takeaway pizzas, with a wonderfully tasty spinach and ricotta variety (closed Thurs). *Aliani Gastronomia*, Ruga Vecchia S. Giovanni, San Polo, is a good source of picnic fare, as are the fruit and veg **markets** at Santa Maria Formosa and Santa Margherita, and the general market at the Rialto, where you can buy everything you need for an impromptu feast – it's open Monday to Saturday from 8am to 1pm.

RESTAURANTS

Al Cugnai, Piscina del Forner, Dorsoduro. Immensely welcoming trattoria close to the Accademia – get there by 8pm or be prepared to wait in line. Closed Mon.

Alle Oche, Calle del Tintor (south side of Campo S. Giacomo dell'Orio), San Polo. Has about 80 varieties of inexpensive pizza to choose from.

Altanella, Calle dell'Erbe, Giudecca. Beautiful fish dishes, and a terrace overlooking the island's central canal. Good for a treat; closed Mon & Tues.

Antico Mola, Fondamenta degli Ormesini, Cannaregio. Originally a family-run, local place, but becoming trendier by the year. Good food, good value; closed Wed.

Casa Mia, Calle dell' Oca, Castello. Very popular trattoria-pizzeria close to Santi Apostoli church. Closed Tues.

Paradiso Perduto, Fondamenta della Misericordia, Cannaregio. Fronted by a popular bar, with a lively relaxed atmosphere and sometimes live music. Full meals start at around L20,000; closed Wed & Sun.

Rosticceria San Bartolomeo, Calle della Bissa, San Marco. A glorified snack bar serving low-priced full meals. Good if you need to refuel quickly and cheaply; closed Mon.

BARS, CAFÉS AND PASTICCERIE

Al Volto, Calle Cavalli (near Campo S. Luca), San Marco. Stocks 1300 wines from Italy and elsewhere, some cheap, many not; good snacks, too; closed Sun.

Cantina del Vino gia Schiavi, Fondamenta Maravegie, Dorsoduro. Great wine shop and bar opposite San Trovaso church; closed Sun.

Do Mori, Calle Do Mori, San Polo. Narrow, standing-only bar, catering for the Rialto traders, office-workers, and locals just out for a stroll. One of the best of a number of bars in the market area, it serves delicious snacks; closed Wed afternoon & Sun.

Il Golosone, Salizzada San Lio, Castello. *Pasticceria* and bar with a glorious spread of cakes; does a delicious apple *spremuta*; closed Mon.

Marchini, Ponte San Maurizio, San Marco. The most delicious and expensive of Venetian *pasticcerie*, where people come on Sun morning to buy family treats.

Nico, Záttere ai Gesuati, Dorsoduro. Highspot of a wander in the area, celebrated for an artery-clogging creation called a *gianduiotto* – a block of praline ice cream in whipped cream; closed Thurs.

Paolin, Campo Santo Stefano, San Marco. Thought by many to be the makers of the best ice cream in Venice; the outside tables also have one of the finest settings in the city; closed Fri.

VinoVino, Ponte delle Veste, San Marco. Slightly posey bar stocking over 100 wines; open until midnight; closed Tues.

The Carnevale, Regata Storica and Biennale

Perhaps the city's most famous annual event is the **Carnevale**, which occupies the ten days leading up to Lent, finishing on Shrove Tuesday with a masked ball for the glitterati and dancing in the Piazza for the plebs. It was revived in the late Seventies, and after three years gained support from the city authorities, who now organize various pageants and performances. It's also very much a time to see and be seen: people don costumes and in the evening congregate in the squares. Masks are on sale throughout the year in Venice, but new mask and costume shops suddenly appear during Carnevale, and Campo San Maurizio sprouts a marquee with mask-making demonstrations and a variety of designs for sale. Another big event is the **Regata Storica**, held on the first Sunday in September, an annual trial of strength and skill for the city's gondoliers which starts with a procession of richly decorated historic craft along the Canal Grande course, their crews all decked out in period dress. Bystanders are expected to join in the support for the contestants in the main event, and may even be issued with appropriate colours. There's also the **Venice Biennale**, set up in 1895 as a showpiece for international contemporary art and held every odd-numbered year from June to September. Its permanent site in the Giardini Pubblici has pavilions for about forty countries, plus space for a thematic international exhibition. The *Aperto* ("Open") section, a mixed exhibition showing the work of younger or less-established artists, takes over spaces all over the city, and various sites throughout the city host fringe exhibitions, installations and performances, particularly in the opening weeks.

Listings

Airlines Alitalia, Salizzada San Moisè, San Marco 1463 (☎041.520.0355); British Airways, Riva degli Schiavoni, Castello 4191 (☎041.528.5026).

Airport enquiries Marco Polo airport, ☎041.260.6111.

Books A good general bookshop is Goldoni, Calle dei Fabbri, San Marco.

Car rental All the major companies have desks at the airport and Piazzale Roma.

Consulates Great Britain, Palazzo Querini, Accademia, Dorsoduro 1051 (☎041.522.7207). The nearest US consulate is in Milan; travellers from Canada, Australia, New Zealand and Ireland should contact the embassy in Rome.

Exchange American Express, Salizzada San Moisè, San Marco (Mon–Fri 9am–5.30pm, Sat 9am–12.30pm; ☎041.520.0844).

Hospital Ospedale Civili Riuniti di Venezia, Campo Santi Giovanni e Paolo (☎041.523.0000).

Laundry Ai Tre Ponti, Santa Croce 274; Salizzada del Pistor, Cannaregio 4553, near Santi Apostoli.

Left luggage Train station left-luggage desk open 24hr; L5000 per item.

Pharmacies Consult *Un Ospite di Venezia*.

Police The Questura is on Via Nicoldi 24, Marghera (☎041.271.5511).

Post office Central office in the Fondaco dei Tedeschi, by the Rialto Bridge (Mon–Sat 8.15am–7pm, poste restante 8.15am–6.45pm); 24hr telegram service.

Train enquiries ☎147.888.088, or 041.524.2303 for reservations.

Padua

Extensively rebuilt after damage caused by bombing during World War II, and hemmed in by the sprawl which accompanied its development as the Veneto's most important economic centre, **PADUA** is not immediately the most alluring city in northern Italy; however, it is one of the most ancient, and plentiful evidence remains of its lineage. A former Roman settlement, the city was a place of pilgrimage following the death of St Anthony here, and it later became an artistic and intellectual centre: Donatello and Mantegna both worked here, and in the seventeenth century Galileo researched at the university, where the medical faculty was one of the most ambitious in Europe.

The City

Just outside the city centre, through a gap in the Renaissance walls off Corso Garibaldi, the Giotto frescoes in the **Cappella degli Scrovegni** (summer daily 9am–7pm; winter 9am–6pm; L10,000 for joint ticket with Musei Civici) are for many the reason for coming to Padua. Commissioned in 1303 by Enrico Scrovegni in atonement for his father's usury, the chapel's walls are covered with illustrations of the life of Mary, Jesus and the story of the Passion – a cycle, arranged in three tiers and painted against a backdrop of saturated blue, that is one of the high points in the development of European art in its innovative attention to the inner nature of its subjects. Beneath the main pictures are shown the vices and virtues in human (usually female) form, while on the wall above the door is the *Last Judgment*.

Directly above the door is a portrait of Scrovegni presenting the chapel; his tomb is at the far end, behind the altar with its statues by Giovanni Pisano. The adjacent **Musei Civici** (Tues–Sun 9am–6/7pm) contains an assembly of fourteenth- to nineteenth-century art from the Veneto and further afield, the high point being a *Crucifixion* by Giotto that was once in the Scrovegni chapel, a fine *Portrait of a Young Senator* by Bellini, and a sequence of devils overcoming angels by Guariento. In addition to the vast picture galleries, the museum complex also features a superbly presented archeological museum and one of the world's largest collections of coins and medals. Nearby, the church of the **Eremitani**, built at the turn of the fourteenth century but almost completely wrecked by bombing in 1944, has been fastidiously rebuilt (Mon–Sat 8.15am–12.15pm & 4–6pm, Sun 9.30am–12.15pm & 4–6pm), although the frescoes by Mantegna that used to be here were almost totally lost, and can now be assessed only from a few fuzzy photographs and some fragments on the right of the high altar.

South of here, on the other side of the centre, the main sight of the Piazza del Santo is Donatello's **Monument to Gattamelata** ("The Honeyed Cat"), as the *condottiere* Erasmo da Narni was known. He died in 1443 and this monument was raised ten years later, the earliest large bronze sculpture of the Renaissance, and a direct precursor to Verrocchio's monument to Colleoni in Venice. On one side of the square, the basilica of San Antonio or **Il Santo** (daily 6.30am–7/7.45pm) was built to house the body of St Anthony, and its Cappella del Santo has a sequence of panels showing scenes from his life, carved between 1505 and 1577. Take a look, too, at Padua's finest work by Pietro Lombardo, a monument to Antonio Roselli, and the high altar's sculptures and reliefs by Donatello. The Cappella del Tesoro (8am–noon & 2.30–7pm), off the ambulatory, houses the tongue and chin of St Anthony in a head-shaped reliquary.

From the basilica, Via Umberto leads you back towards the **University**, established in 1221, and older than any other in Italy except Bologna. The main block is the **Palazzo del Bò**, where Galileo taught physics from 1592 to 1610, declaiming from a lectern that is still on show, though the major sight is the sixteenth-century anatomy theatre (guided tours: March–Oct Tues & Thurs 9am, 10am & 11am, Mon, Wed, Thurs & Fri 3pm, 4pm & 5pm; L5000). The area west of here, around the **Piazza della Frutta** and **Piazza delle Erbe**, is effectively the hub of the city. Separating the two squares is the extraordinary **Palazzo della Ragione** (summer Mon–Sat 9am–7pm; winter 9am–6pm; L7000), which, at the time of its construction in the early 1200s, sported frescoes by Giotto and his assistants. These were destroyed by fire in 1420 and most of the extant frescoes (1425–40) are by Nicola Miretto. Close by, Padua's **Duomo** (daily 9.30am–1.30pm & 3–6/7pm; L3000) is an unlovely church whose design was cribbed from drawings by Michelangelo, though the adjacent Romanesque **Baptistry** (same times) is one of the unproclaimed delights of Padua, lined with some fourteenth-century frescoes by Giusto de'Menabuoi – a cycle which makes a fascinating comparison with Giotto's in the Cappella degli Scrovegni.

Practicalities

The main **tourist office** is at the **train station**, at the far end of Corso del Popolo (summer Mon–Sat 9am–7pm, Sun 9am–1pm; winter Mon–Sat 9.15am–5.45pm, Sun 8.30am–12.30pm). Of many affordable **hotels**, *Pavia*, Via Papafava 3 (☎049.661.558; ④), and the *Verdi*, Via Dondi dell'Orologio 7 (☎049.875.5744; ③), are clean and friendly. The **youth hostel** is at Via A. Aleardi 30 (☎049.875.2219), and has an 11pm curfew – take bus #3, #8, #12, #18 or #22 from the station. The nearest **campsite** is 15km away in Montegrotto Terme (Via Roma 123), served by frequent trains – a fifteen-minute trip, or Bus M. As for **food**, the *rosticceria* in Via Daniele Manin offers a wide variety of snacks or, if you want to sit down, there's *La Mappa*, Via Matteotti 17, with decent self-service fare (closed Sat) or *Brek*, at the corner of Piazza Cavour. For a more relaxed session at only slightly greater expense, three good cheap restaurants are *Da Giovanni* at Via De Cristoforis 1, *7 Teste* at Via C. Battisti 44, and *Pago Pago* at Via Galilei 59. On Piazza Cavour, *Pepen* (closed Sun) has a wonderful range of pizzas, with seats on the square in summer. The *Dotto*, Via Randaccio 23, is a superb mid-range restaurant – allow around L50,000 per person.

Verona

The easy-going city of **VERONA** is the largest city of the Veneto, and, with its wealth of Roman sites and streets of pink-hued medieval buildings, one of its most interesting. First settled by the Romans, it later became an independent city-state, reaching its zenith in the thirteenth century under the Scaligeri family. Ruthless in the exercise of power, the Scaligeri were at the same time energetic patrons of the arts, and many of Verona's finest buildings date from the century of their rule. With their fall, the Viscontis of Milan assumed control of the city, which was later absorbed into the Venetian empire.

The City

The city centre clusters into a deep bend in the River Adige, the main sight of its southern reaches the central hub of **Piazza Brà** and its mighty Roman **Arena** (Tues–Sun 9am–6.30pm, July & Aug 9am–3pm; L6000, first Sun of month L2000). Dating from the first century AD, and originally with seating for some twenty thousand, this is the third-largest surviving Roman amphitheatre, and offers a tremendous panorama from the topmost of the 44 marble tiers. North, **Via Mazzini**, a narrow traffic-free street lined with expensive shops, leads to a grouping of squares, most noteworthy of which is the **Piazza dei Signori**, flanked by the medieval **Palazzo degli Scaligeri** – the residence of the Scaligeri. At right angles to this is the fifteenth-century **Loggia del Consiglio**, the former assembly hall of the city council and Verona's outstanding early Renaissance building, while, close by, the twelfth-century **Torre dei Lamberti** (Tues–Sun: summer 9am–6pm; winter 10am–1pm & 1.30–4pm; L4000 by elevator, L3000 on foot) gives dizzying views of the city. Beyond the square, in front of the Romanesque church of Santa Maria Antica, the **Arche Scaligere** are the elaborate Gothic funerary monuments of Verona's first family, in a wrought-iron palisade decorated with ladder motifs, the emblem of the Scaligeri. Mastino I ("Mastiff"), founder of the dynasty, is buried in the simple tomb against the wall of the church; Mastino II is to the left of the entrance, opposite the most florid of the tombs, that of **Cansignorio** ("Top Dog"); while over the side entrance of the church is an equestrian statue of **Cangrande I** ("Big Dog") – a copy of the original now in Verona's Castelvecchio. Towards the river from here is the church of **Sant'Anastasia** (Tues–Sat summer 8.30am–5.30pm, Sun 1–5.30pm, winter 10am–4pm, Sun 1–5pm; L3000, combined ticket for the duomo & San Zeno Maggiore L8000), a mainly Gothic church, completed in the late fifteenth century, with Pisanello's delicately coloured fresco of *St George and the Princess* in the sacristy. Verona's **Duomo** (same hours as Sant'Anastasia; L3000) lies just around the river's bend, a mixture of Romanesque and Gothic styles that houses an *Assumption* by Titian in an architectural frame by Sansovino, who also designed the choir.

In the opposite direction, off Piazza delle Erbe at Via Cappello 23, is the **Casa di Giulietta**, a fourteenth-century structure that's in a fine state of preservation, though there's no connection between this house and the historical character to whom Shakespeare's Juliet is distantly related (Tues–Sun 9am–7pm; L6000). South of here, on the junction of Via Diaz and Corso Porta Borsari, the **Porta dei Borsari** is a fine Roman monument, with an inscription that dates it to 265 AD, though it's almost certainly older than that. Some way down Corso Cavour from here, the **Arco dei Gavi** is a first-century Roman triumphal arch, beyond which the **Castelvecchio** (Tues–Sun 9am–6.30pm; L6000) houses a collection of paintings, jewellery and weapons, as well as the equestrian figure of Cangrande I, removed from his tomb, strikingly displayed on an outdoor pedestal. Outstanding among the paintings are works by Jacopo and Giovanni Bellini, a *Madonna* by Pisanello, Veronese's *Descent from the Cross*, a Tintoretto *Nativity*, and works by the two Tiepolos.

A kilometre or so northwest of here, the **Basilica di San Zeno Maggiore** (same hours as Sant'Anastasia; L3000) is one of the most significant Romanesque churches in northern Italy, put up in the first half of the twelfth century. Its rose window, representing the Wheel of Fortune, dates from then, as does the magnificent portal, whose lintels bear sculptures representing the months while the door has bronze panels depicting scenes from the Bible and the miracles of San Zeno. The simple interior is covered with frescoes, although the church's most compulsive image is the altar's luminous *Madonna and Saints* by Mantegna.

Practicalities

The **train station** is twenty minutes outside the city centre, connected with Piazza Brà by a #1 or #8 bus. There's a **tourist office** at the train station (summer Mon–Sat 8am–7.30pm, Sun 9–noon; winter Mon–Sat 9am–6pm; ☎045.800.0861) and at the Cortile del Tribunale, close to the Arche Scaligere (Tues–Sun 10am–7pm). Of **hotels**, the *Al Castello*, Corso Cavour 43 (☎045.800.4403; ④), has recently refurbished rooms, *Catullo*, Via Catullo 1 (☎045.800.2786; ④), is in a central position just off Via Mazzini, and the *Aurora*, Piazzetta XIV Novembre 2 (☎045.594.717; ⑤), has many rooms overlooking the Piazza delle Erbe. Verona's **youth hostel** is at Via Fontana del Ferro 15 (☎045.590.360; ②), on the north side of the river behind the Teatro Romano (bus #2), close to which there's a pleasant summer **campsite**. There's also the *Casa della Giovane*, Via Pigna 7 (☎045.596.880; ②), in the old centre, for women only.

Among **eating** options, *Alla Costa*, Via della Costa 2, serves good pizzas, as does *Pizzeria Arena*, Vicolo Tre Marchetti 1, which is open until 1am, and there's a *Brek* self-service on Piazza Brà. Otherwise, the most plentiful source of cheap places is over the river: especially good is the *Dal Ropeton*, below the youth hostel at Via S. Giovanni in Valle 46. On the other side of the Teatro Romano, *Pero d'Oro*, Via Ponte Pignolo 25, serves inexpensive but genuine Veronese dishes. For evening drinks, the ultra-friendly *Bottega del Vino* in Vicolo Scudo di Francia, just off the north end of Via Mazzini, is an old **bar** with a selection of wines from all over Italy. For a less touristy ambience, try *Al Carro Armato*, Vicolo Gatto 2a, or *Osteria Al Duomo*, Via Duomo 7a.

Trieste

Backed by a white limestone plateau and facing the blue Adriatic, **TRIESTE** is in a potentially idyllic setting – get close up, however, and you see that a lot of the place is run-down, and the water uninviting, confirming that most visitors just pass through Trieste, and few actually stop. The city itself is a strange place, its massive Neoclassical architecture dating from the time when it was the Habsburg Empire's southern port. Lying as it does on the political and ethnic fault-line between the Latin and Slavic worlds, Trieste has long been a city of political extremes. Yugoslavia and the Allies fought over it until 1954, when the city and a connecting strip of coast were secured for Italy. The neo-Fascist MSI party has always done well here, and there's even a local anti-Slav party, Lista per Trieste.

The City

The social centre of Trieste is the huge **Piazza dell'Unità d'Italia**, opening onto the harbour and flanked by the vast bulks of the **Palazzo del Comune** and **Palazzo di Governo**. The focal point of the city's history, however, and its prime tourist site, is the hill of **San Giusto**, with its castle and cathedral, accessible on bus #24. The **Castello** (daily 9am–sunset; L2000) is a fifteenth-century Venetian fortress, built near the site of the Roman forum, whose ramparts are worth a walk and whose museum (Tues–Sun 9am–1pm; L3000) houses a collection of antique weaponry. The **Cattedrale di San Giusto** (8am–noon & 3.30–6.30pm) is a typically Triestine synthesis of styles, with a predominantly Romanesque facade including five Roman columns and a Gothic rose window. Inside, between Byzantine pillars, there are fine thirteenth-century frescoes of St Justus, a Christian martyr killed during the persecutions of Diocletian. Trieste's principal museum, the **Museo Revoltella** at Via Diaz 27 (Mon & Wed–Sun 10am–7pm; L5000), is housed in a nineteenth-century Viennese-style palace and displays dull nineteenth-century and decent modern art collections. More disturbingly, on the southern side of the city, the **Risiera di San Sabba** at Rattodella Pileria 43 (Tues–Sun 9am–1pm; April & May Tues–Sat 9am– 6pm, Sun 9am–1pm; free), on the #10 bus route, was one of Italy's two concentration camps (the other is near Carpi in Emilia Romagna). A permanent exhibition serves as a reminder of Fascist crimes in the region.

Practicalities

The central **train station** is on Piazza Libertà, on the northern edge of the city centre. There's a **tourist information** desk here, and a main office at Via S. Nicolo 20 (Mon–Sat

9am–7pm, Sun 10am–1pm & 4–7pm; ☎040.420.182). There are many reasonable **hotels**, nicest of which are the *Centro*, Via Roma 13 (☎040.634.408; ③); the *Rino*, Via Boccardi 5 (☎040.300.608; ③); and the *Blaue Krone*, Via XXX Ottobre 12 (☎040.631.882; ③). The **youth hostel** is 8km out of the city at Viale Miramare 331 (☎040.224.102; ②) – take bus #6 from the tourist office, then bus #36. The nearest **campsite** is in nearby Obelisco, on the #4 bus route.

For **snacks and light meals**, *Da Bepi* in Via Cassa di Risparmio is a favourite student lunch-stop, with excellent sausages and sauerkraut. Another student hangout is *Notorious* in Via del Bosco – sandwiches and salads on the ground floor and a good cheap trattoria on the first floor. Decent pizzas can be had at *Il Barattolo* in Piazza Sant'Antonio Nuovo, and there are *Brek* self-service places in Via San Francesco and Via Campi Elisi. For **more substantial food**, try the excellent *Da Giovanni* at Via Lazzaro 14 or the very popular but basic *Trattoria All'Antica Ghiacceretta* in Via dei Fornelli, or the *Arco di Riccardo* at Via del Trionfo 3. The city's favourite **café** is the *Caffè San Marco*, which has occupied its Liberty-style premises on Via G. Battisti for some eighty years. The *Caffè Tommaseo* on Piazza Tommaseo was a rendezvous for Italian nationalists in the last century and although refurbished still makes a pleasant, if pricey refuge in the summer heat. For **bars**, try the *Birreria Spofford* in Via Rossetti, a youthful place attracting a student clientele, *Mariuccia* at Via Madonna del Mare 18, or *Osteria de Libero*, Via Risorta 8, an atmospheric place for both eating and drinking.

Bologna

The capital of Emilia-Romagna, **BOLOGNA** is a boom town of the Eighties whose computer-associated industries have brought conspicuous wealth to the old brick palaces and porticoed squares. Previously, it was best known for its food, undeniably the richest in the country, and for its politics – "Red Bologna" has been the Italian Communist Party's stronghold and spiritual home since World War II. The city centre is among the best-looking in the country, still startlingly medieval in plan, and has enough curiosities to warrant several days' exploration. However, Bologna is really enjoyable just for itself, with a busy cultural life and a café and bar scene that is one of the most convivial in northern Italy.

Arrival and accommodation

Bologna's **airport** is northwest of the centre, linked to the **train station** on Piazza delle Medaglie d'Oro, at the end of Via dell'Indipendenza, by the Airobus (L7000). There are **tourist information** booths at the airport (Mon–Sat 9am–1pm & 2–6pm) and at the train station (Mon–Sat 9am–7pm), and a main office at Piazza Maggiore 6 (Mon–Sat 9am–7pm, Sun 9am–2pm), with what's-on booklets, maps and a hotel-booking facility. In terms of **places to stay**, Bologna is not geared up for tourists, least of all for those travelling on a tight budget, and the trade fairs during high season make booking ahead imperative. The most inexpensive are the city's official **youth hostels**, 6km outside the centre of town at Via Viadagola 14 (☎051.519.202; ②) and Via Viadagola 5 (☎051.501.810; ②), both with a midnight curfew. Bus #93 from Via Irnerio, a short walk southeast from the train station, takes you within 800m of the hostels. Among the few affordable **hotels** are the centrally positioned *Garisenda*, Via Rizzoli 9, Galleria del Leone 1 (☎051.224.369; ④), *Minerva*, Via De Monari 3 (☎051.239.652; ④), and the *Panorama*, Via Livraghi 1 (☎051.221.802; ④). More expensive is the *Accademia*, nicely situated at Via Belli Arti 6 (☎051.232.318; ⑥), and the popular *Orologio*, Via IV Novembre 10 (☎051.231.253; ⑧), which should be booked in advance.

The City

Bologna's city centre is quite compact, with most things of interest within the main ring road. **Piazza Maggiore** is the obvious place to make for first, buzzing with almost constant activity. On its western side, the **Palazzo Comunale** has two galleries: the Museo Morandi and the Collezioni Comunali D'Arte (10am–6pm; closed Mon; L10,000 joint ticket), and apartments open for public viewing when not in use for concerts and other events, and it is well worth visiting for the view over the square. On the square's south side, the church of **San Petronio** (7.15am–1.30pm & 2.30pm–6.30/6.45pm) is the city's largest, intended originally to have been larger than St Peter's in Rome, and one of the finest Gothic brick buildings in Italy; money and land for the side aisle were diverted by the pope's man in Bologna towards a new university, and the architect Antonio di Vicenzo's plans had to be modified. You can see the beginnings of the planned side aisle on the left of the building and there are models of what the church was supposed to look like in the museum (10am–12.30pm; closed Tues); otherwise the most intriguing features are a beautiful carving of *Madonna and Child* by Jacopo della Quercia, above the central portal, and an astronomical clock – a long brass meridian line set at an angle across the floor, with a hole left in the roof for the sun to shine through on the right spot. The adjacent **Piazza Nettuno** has an extravagant **statue of Neptune** that was fashioned by Giambologna in 1566.

Across Via dell'Archiginnasio from here, the **Museo Civico Archeologico** (Tues–Fri 9am–2pm, Sat & Sun 9am–1pm & 3.30–7pm; L8000) is a rather stuffy museum but its displays of Egyptian and Roman antiquities are good ones, and the Etruscan section is one of the best outside Lazio. Down the street, Bologna's university – the **Archiginnasio** – was founded at more or less the same time as the Piazza Maggiore was laid out, predating the rest of Europe's universities, though it didn't get a special building until 1565. The most interesting part is the recently renovated **Teatro Anatomico** (Mon–Sat 9am–1pm; free), the original medical faculty dissection theatre, whose tiers of seats surround an extraordinary professor's chair, covered with a canopy supported by figures known as *gli spellati* – the skinned ones. South, down Via Garibaldi, **Piazza San Domenico**, with its strange canopied tombs holding the bones of medieval law scholars, is the site of the church of **San Domenico** (daily 7am–1pm & 2–7pm), built in 1251 to house the relics of St Dominic. The bones rest in the so-called *Arca di San Domenico*, a fifteenth-century work that was principally the creation of Nicola Pisano – though many artists contributed to it. Pisano and his pupils were responsible for the reliefs illustrating the saint's life; the statues on top were the work of Pisano himself; Nicola dell'Arca was responsible for the canopy; and the angel and figures of saints Proculus and Petronius were the work of a very young Michelangelo.

North of here, the eastern section of Bologna's *centro storico* preserves many of the older **University** departments, housed for the most part in large seventeenth- and eighteenth-century palaces. At Piazza di Porta Ravegnana, the Torre degli Asinelli (daily 9am–5/6pm; L3000) and perilously leaning Torre Garisenda are together known as the **Due Torri**, the only survivors of literally hundreds of towers that were scattered across the city during the Middle Ages. From here, Via San Stefano leads down past a complex of four – but originally seven – churches, collectively known as **Santo Stefano**. The striking polygonal church of **San Sepolcro**, reached through the church of **Crocifisso**, is about the most interesting: the basin in its courtyard is by tradition the one used by Pilate to wash his hands after he condemned Christ to death, while, inside, the bones of St Petronius provide a pleasingly kitsch focus, held in a tomb modelled on the Church of the Holy Sepulchre in Jerusalem. A doorway leads from here through to **San Vitale e Agricola**, Bologna's oldest church, built from discarded Roman fragments in the fifth century; while the fourth church, the **Trinità**, lies across the courtyard and is home to a small museum (daily 9am–noon & 3.30–6pm) containing a reliquary of St Petronius and a handful of dull paintings.

Eating, drinking and nightlife

Bologna is one of the best places in Italy to **eat**, and not just in restaurants. There are any number of places to put together delicious **picnics**, best of which is the Mercato delle Erbe, Via Ugo Bassi 2, biggest and liveliest of the city's markets, or the small but inviting Mercato Clavature, Via Clavature, just off Piazza Maggiore. For **snacks**, the *Impero*, Via Indipendenza 39, does excellent croissants and pastries; *Altero*, at Via Indipendenza 33 or Via Ugo Bassi 10, is best for pizza by the slice; *La Torinese*, under the vaults of Palazzo del Podestà in Piazza Maggiore, does daily quiches and stuffed vegetables. Of **restaurants**, *C'entro*, Via Indipendenza 45 (open until 2am), and *Bassotto*, Via Ugo Bassi 8 (lunchtimes only), serve quality fast food in comfortable surroundings; *Boni*, Via Saragozza 88, has very good Emilian cuisine, likewise *Lamma* at Via dei Giudei 4 – a popular place with a pub atmosphere. For family-style Bolognese food, go to *Fantoni* at Via del Pratello 11, one of the oldest streets in the city. *Nino's*, Via Volturno 9 (off Via dell'Independenza), serves inexpensive pizza and pasta; *Clorofilla*, Strada Maggiore 64, is a good place for vegetarians though it's expensive, and the self-service *Lazzarini*, Via Clavature 1 (Mon–Sat 7am–8pm), is cheap but more stylish than many self-service places.

To **drink**, there are plenty of good bars on and around Via Zamboni, in the student quarter, and plenty of *osterie* all over town – pub-like places, that have been the mainstay of Bolognese **nightlife** for a few hundred years, and stay open till late. *Matusel*, at Via Bertolini 2, close to the university, is a lively and noisy example, with reasonably priced full meals; *Del Montesino*, at Via del Pratello 74b, is a convivial haunt, open until 2am; *Senzanome*, Via Senzanome 42, serves good meals and has a wide choice of beers and wines; and *Marione*, at Via San Felice 137, close to the city gate, is old and dark, with good wine and snacks. The tiny *Osteria dell'Infidele*, on Via Gerusalemme, has good economic food but is better for just drinking.

Parma

PARMA is about as comfortable a town as you could wish for. The measured pace of its streets, the abundance of its restaurants and the general air of provincial affluence are almost cloyingly pleasant, especially if you've arrived from the south. But it's a friendly enough place with plenty to see, not least the works of two key late Renaissance artists – Correggio and Parmigianino.

The Town

Piazza Garibaldi is the fulcrum of Parma, its packed-out cafés, along with the narrow streets and alleyways which wind south and west of the piazza, home to much of the town's nightlife. The mustard-coloured **Palazzo del Governatore** flanks the square, behind which the Renaissance church of the **Madonna della Steccata** stands, apparently using Bramante's original plan for St Peter's as a model. Inside there are frescoes by a number of sixteenth-century painters, notably Parmigianino, who spent the last ten years of his life on this work, eventually being sacked for breach of contract by the disgruntled church authorities. Five minutes' walk away, the beautiful Romanesque **Duomo** (daily 9am–12.30pm & 3–7pm), dating from the eleventh century, holds earlier work by Parmigianino in its south transept, painted when the artist was a pupil of Correggio – one of whose most famous works, a 1534 fresco of the *Assumption*, can be seen in the central cupola. There's more by Correggio in the cupola of **San Giovanni Evangelista** behind the Duomo – a fresco of the *Vision of St John*. You should also visit the Duomo's octagonal **Baptistry** (daily 9am–12.30pm & 3–6pm; L5000), considered to be Benedetto Antelami's finest work, built in 1196 and bridging the gap between the Romanesque and Gothic styles. Antelami sculpted the frieze which surrounds the building, and was also responsible for the reliefs inside, including a series of fourteen statues representing the months and seasons. Take the spiral staircase to the top for a closer view of the frescoes on the ceiling; they are by an unknown thirteenth-century artist. Correggio was also responsible for the frescoes in the **Camera di San Paolo** of the former Benedictine convent off Via Melloni, a few minutes north; he portrayed the abbess who commissioned the work as the goddess Diana, above the fireplace.

East of the cathedral square, the **Museo Glauco-Lombardi** at Via Garibaldi 15 (closed for restoration but due to reopen early 2000) recalls later times, with a display of memorabilia relating to Marie-Louise of Austria, who reigned here after the defeat of her husband Napoleon at Waterloo, setting herself up with another suitor (much to the chagrin of her exiled spouse) and expanding the Parma violet perfume industry. Just across Piazza Marconi from here, it's hard to miss Parma's biggest monument, the **Palazzo della Pilotta**, begun for Alessandro Farnese in the sixteenth century and rebuilt after World War II bombing to house a number of Parma's museums, notably the city's main art gallery, the **Galleria Nazionale** (Tues–Sun 9am–2pm; L12,000, includes admission to Teatro Farnese). The hi-tech display includes more work by Correggio and Parmigianino, and the remarkable *Apostles at the Sepulchre* and *Funeral of the Virgin* by Caracci – massive canvases suspended each side of a gantry at the top of the building. The **Teatro Farnese**, which you pass through to get to the gallery, was almost entirely destroyed in 1944 and has been virtually rebuilt. An extended semicircle of seats three tiers high, made completely of wood, it's a copy of Palladio's Teatro Olimpico at Vicenza, and as well as being (temporarily) the biggest theatre of its kind, sported Italy's first revolving stage. Up a floor, the **Museo Archeologico Nazionale** (Tues–Sun 9am–7pm; L4000) is less enticing but still worth a glance, with finds from the Etruscan city of Velleia and the prehistoric lake villages around Parma, as well as the tabletop on which the emperor Trajan notched up a record of his gifts to the poor.

Practicalities

Parma's **train station** is fifteen minutes' walk from the central Piazza Garibaldi, or a short ride on bus #7, #8, #9 or #10. The main **tourist office** is on Via Mellini (Mon–Sat 9am–7pm, Sun 9am–1pm). Finding a **place to stay** can be tricky. There's an official **youth hostel** with **camp-site** at Parco Cittadella 5 (☎0521.961.434; ②; April–Oct; 11pm curfew), take bus #9 or, after 8pm, #E. Among **hotels** near the station, the *Brozzi*, Via Trento 11 (☎0521.272.717; ③), is reasonable; the *Leon d'Oro*, a few minutes away at Viale A. Fratti 4 (☎0521.773.182; ③), has a **restaurant** attached. In the centre, the *Lazzaro*, Via XX Marzo 14 (☎0521.208.944; ④), is a small *locanda*. On the other side of the river (bus #3 from Piazza Garibaldi), try *Il Sole*, Via Gramsci 15 (☎0521.995.107; ③). *Pizzeria/ristorante L'Artista*, Via Bruno Longhi 3/a, does good pizzas and has friendly English-speaking owners, and *Taverna San Ambrogio*, off Borgo Piero Torrigiani, has a meaty menu that leans towards game. At night, **opera** is the biggest deal; the Teatro Regio on Via Garibaldi (☎0521.218.678) is renowned for its discerning audiences.

Ferrara

Half an hour by train from Bologna, **FERRARA** was the residence of the Este dukes, an eccentric dynasty that ranked as a major political force throughout Renaissance times. The Este kept the main artists of the day in commissions and built a town which, despite a relatively small population, was one of the most elegant urban creations of the period. It's a popular stop for tourists travelling up from Bologna to Venice, but they rarely stay, leaving the centre enjoyably crowd-free by the evening.

Dominating the centre of town, the bulky **Castello Estense** (Tues–Sun 9.30am–5.30pm; L8000, price changes for exhibitions) was home to the Este court, and its rooms go some way to bringing back the days of Este magnificence, although it's a cold, draughty place on the whole, at its most evocative in the dungeons, where the numerous Este enemies were incarcerated. Just south, the **Palazzo Comunale**, built in 1243 but much altered since, holds statues of Nicolò III and his son Borso on its facade, though they're twentieth-century reproductions. A little way beyond, Ferrara's **Duomo** is a mixture of Romanesque and Gothic styles, with a carved central portal and a **museum** (Tues–Sat 10am–noon & 3–5pm, Sun 10am–noon & 4–6pm; donation requested) which has a set of bas-reliefs illustrating the labours of the months that formerly adorned the outside. There are also illuminated manuscripts, two organ shutters decorated by Cosme Turà, one of the *Annunciation*, another showing St George killing the dragon, and a beautiful *Madonna* by della Quercia. Corso Ercole I d'Este leads north from the castle to the **Palazzo dei Diamanti**, on the left, named after the diamond-shaped bricks that stud its facade and home to the **Pinacoteca Nazionale** (Tues–Sun 9am–2pm; L8000), which holds works from the Ferrara and Bologna Schools, notably paintings by Dossi and Guercino, and a spirited *St Christopher* by Sebastian Filippo.

More Renaissance palaces lie in the southeastern quarter of the city centre, lining the wider streets above the tangled medieval district, one of which, the **Casa Romei** on Via Savonarola (Tues–Sat 8.30am–6.30pm, Sun and Mon 8.30am–2pm; L4000), is typical of the time, with frescoes and graceful courtyards alongside artefacts rescued from various local churches. Two minutes away, the **Palazzo Schifanoia** on Via Scandiana (daily 9am–7pm; L8000) is one of the grandest of Ferrara's palaces. It belonged to the Este family, and Cosimo Turà recorded their court in the frescoes in its Salone dei Mesi, decorated with hunting scenes, groups of musicians, signs of the zodiac and classical legends.

Practicalities

Ferrara's **train station** is just west of the city walls, ten minutes' walk (or a #1, #2 or #9 bus ride) along Viale Cavour from the centre of town. The **tourist office** at Corso Giovecca 21 (Mon–Sat 9am–1pm & 2.30–6pm, Sun 9am–1pm) has maps. Behind the duomo, the labyrinth of alleyways that makes up Ferrara's medieval quarter is the best area to look for cheap **hotels**. The best of these is the *San Paolo*, Via Baluardi 9 (☎0532.762.040; ④); if this is full there's the *Casa degli Artisti*, Via Vittoria 66 (☎0532.761.038; ③), or the *Nazionale*, Corso Porta Reno 32 (☎0532.209.604; ④). Ferrara's **campsite**, *Estense*, is off the ring road just outside the city walls in Via Gramicia (☎0532.752.396). Ferrara isn't an especially cheap place to eat. *Pizzeria-Gelateria Giuseppe* at Via Carlo Mayr 71 has decent pizzas, *Osteria Al Postiglione* at Vicolo Chiuso del Teatro 4 has good homemade pasta and sandwiches; try *Osteria degli Angeli,* Via delle Volte 4. There's also a rather dour student mensa at Corso della Giovecca 145.

Ravenna

When **RAVENNA** became capital of the Western Roman Empire 1500 years ago, it was more by quirk of fate than design. The emperor Honorius, alarmed by armies invading from the north, moved his court from Rome to this obscure town on the Romagna coast because it was easy to defend, being surrounded by marshland, and situated close to the port of Classis – the biggest Roman naval base on the Adriatic. Honorius' anxiety proved well founded – Rome was sacked by the Goths in 410 – but Ravenna's days of glory were brief, and it, too, fell in 473. Yet the Ostrogoth King Theodoric continued to beautify the city, and it wasn't long before it was taken by the Byzantines, who were responsible for Ravenna's most glorious era – the city's mosaics are generally acknowledged to be one of the crowning achievements of Byzantine art.

The City

The best of the mosaics are in the basilica of **San Vitale**, ten minutes northwest of the centre (daily 9am–4.30/5.30pm; L6000 includes entry to Mausoleo Galla Placidia), a fairly typical Byzantine church, begun in 525 AD under Theodoric and finished in 548 under Justinian, which formed the basis for the great church of Aya Sofia in Constantinople fifteen years later. The mosaics are in the apse, arranged in a rigid hierachy, with Old Testament scenes across the semicircular lunettes of the choir, Christ, the Apostles and sons of San Vitale on the arch, and, on the semidome of the apse, a beardless Christ presenting a model of the church to San Vitale and Bishop Ecclesius. On the side walls of the apse are portraits of the emperor Justinian and his wife Theodora, Justinian's foot resting on that of his general, Belisarius, who reclaimed the city from the Goths, while Theodora looks on, her expression giving some hint of the cruelty that she was apparently notorious for.

Across from the basilica is the tiny **Mausoleo di Galla Placidia** (same hours and ticket as San Vitale), named after the half-sister of Honorius, who later became regent of the Western Empire and was responsible for much of the grandeur of Ravenna's early days, though it's unlikely that the building ever held her bones. Inside, the mosaics glow with a deep blue lustre, most in an earlier style than San Vitale's, full of Roman and naturalistic motifs. Stars around a golden cross spread across the vaulted ceiling, while at each end are representations of St Lawrence, with the gridiron on which he was martyred, and the Good Shepherd, with one of his flock. Adjacent to San Vitale, housed in the former cloisters of the church, the **National Museum of Antiquities** (Tues–Sun 8.30am–7pm; L8000) contains various items from this and later periods, most notably a sixth-century statue of Hercules capturing a stag, possibly a copy of a Greek original, and the so-called "Veil of Classis", decorated with portraits of Veronese bishops of the eighth and ninth centuries.

There are more fine mosaics east of here, on the busy Via di Roma, in the basilica of **Sant'Apollinare Nuovo** (daily 9.30am–4.30/6.30pm; L5000), another building of the sixth century, again built by Theodoric. The mosaics run the length of the nave and depict ceremonial processions of martyrs bearing gifts for an enthroned Christ and the Virgin through an avenue of date palms. Some of the scenery is more specific to Ravenna: you can make out what used to be the harbour at nearby Classe against the city behind, out of which rises Theodoric's palace. Five minutes' walk up Via di Roma, the **Arian Baptistry**, also known as the **Basilica dello Santo Spirito** (Mon–Sat 9.30am–12.30pm & 3–6pm, Sun 9.30am–12.30pm & 3–5pm; L5000), has a fine mosaic ceiling showing the twelve Apostles and the baptism of Christ. Via Diaz leads from here down to **Piazza del Popolo**, the centre of Ravenna, a few blocks south of which the **Tomba di Dante** was put up in the eighteenth century to enclose a previous fifteenth-century tomb. Dante died here in exile from Florence in 1321 and was laid to rest in the adjoining church of **San Francesco**, a much-restored building, elements of which date from the fourth century.

A couple of minutes away on Piazza Duomo, the **Museo Arcivescovile** (daily 9.30am–4.30/6.30pm; L5000) has mosaic fragments from around the city and the sixth-century Oratorio Sant'Andrea, adorned with mosaics of birds above a Christ dressed in the uniform of a Roman centurion. There are also fragments from the original cathedral (the present one is an uninteresting reconstruction), and an ornate ivory throne from Alexandria which belonged to Bishop Maximian in the sixth century. The **Neonian Baptistry** (daily 9.30am–4.30/6.30pm; same ticket as Museo Arcivescovile), next door, is a conversion from a Roman bathhouse. The original floor level has sunk into the marshy ground, and you can see the remains of the previous building, 3m below.

Note that a ticket to all six of Ravenna's monuments plus the Ceramics Museum of Faenza costs L10,000 and is valid for a year.

Practicalities

Ravenna has a compact city centre, and it's only a short walk from the **train station** on Piazza Farini, along Viale Farini and Via A. Diaz, to the central Piazza del Popolo. The **information office** at Via Salara 8 (June–Sept Mon–Sat 8.30am–7pm, Sun 9.30am–12.30pm & 3.30–6.30pm; Oct–May Mon–Sat 8.30am–6pm, Sun 10am–4pm) has maps and accommodation lists. The slightly unsavoury district around the station is the best place for cheap **hotels** like the *Roma*, Via Candiano 26 (☎0544.421.515; ⑤), and *Al Giaciglio*, Via Rocca Brancaleone 42 (☎0544.39.403; ③), which has a decent restaurant, although it's further to walk. There's a **youth hostel**, the *Ostello Dante*, a ten-minute walk out of town at Via Nicolodi 12 (☎0544.421.164; ②), or take bus #1 from outside the station. Ravenna's best **places to eat** are between the duomo and Piazza San Francesco. *Ca' De Ven*, at Via C. Ricci 24, has a large selection of Emilia-Romagnan wine, and decent food. Back towards the square, on Via Mentana, *Da Renato*, and its sister restaurant next door, *Guidarello*, on Via R. Gessi, both do traditional local food. *Ristorante Scai*, Piazza Baracca 20, close to San Vitale, specializes in roast meat and game for those so inclined; it's reasonably priced and also serves pizzas in the evening. There are also mensas at the station and Via G. Oberdan 8, as well as a branch of the *Pizza Altero* chain on Via Camillo B. Cavour.

Rimini

RIMINI is the least pretentious town in Italy, the archetypal seaside city, with a reputation for good – if slightly sleazy – fun. Brash and high-rise, it's a traditional family resort, to which some Italians return year after year, but there's another, less savoury side to the town: Rimini is known across Italy for its fast-living and chancy nightlife, and there's a very active hetero- and transsexual prostitution scene.

In summer most activity is concentrated on the main seafront drag of souvenir shops, restaurants and video arcades, which stretches 9km north to the suburbs of Viserba and Torre Pedrera and 7km south to Miramare. Out of season, though, you'll find most life a little way inland in the older part of town, clustered around the main squares of **Piazza Tre Martiri** and **Piazza Cavour**. The latter is home to the Gothic **Palazzo del Podestà**; the square was rebuilt in the 1920s and bristles with fishtail battlements. **Castel Sigismondo** in the adjoining **Piazza Malatesta** holds a museum of ethnography, the **Museo delle Culture Extraeuropee** "Dinz Rialto" (Tues–Fri 8.30am–12.30pm, Sat & Sun 3–7pm; L4000) is worth a look for its fine collection of Oceanic and pre-Colombian art. Less interesting are the Roman **Ponte di Tiberio** and **Arco d'Augusto**, just inside the old town ramparts. Rimini's best-known monument, however, is the strange-looking **Tempio Malatestiano** on Via 4 Novembre (Mon–Sat 7.15am–12.30pm & 3.30–6.30pm, Sun 9am–1pm & 3.30–6pm; free), one of the masterworks of the Italian Renaissance. Originally a Gothic Franciscan church, in 1450 it was transformed for the savage Sigismondo Malatesta by Leon Battista Alberti, and is an odd mixture of private chapel and personal monument. Sigismondo treated the church as a memorial chapel to his great love, Isotta degli Atti, and their initials are linked in emblems all over the building; the Malatesta armorial emblem – the elephant – appears almost as often, alongside chubby putti, nymphs and shepherds in a decidedly unchristian celebration of excess. There are some fine artworks – one by Piero della Francesca, and a *Crucifix* attributed to Giotto – although even now you get the feeling the authorities are slightly embarassed by the place. It is, however, an appropriate attraction for a town that thrives on excess.

Practicalities

The **train station** is in the centre of Rimini, on Piazzale Cesare Battisti, ten minutes' walk from the sea and the old centre. There's a **tourist office** by the station and in Piazzale Fellini on the seafront (daily summer 8am–7pm; winter 9am–noon & 3.30–6.30pm). Both these offices can help with **accommodation**, which can be a problem during the season, when you may have to take full or half board. Try *Nancy*, a lovely villa with garden five minutes' walk from the beach at Viale Leopardi 11 (☎0541.381.731; ⑤), or the cheaper *Alfieri* at Viale Alfieri 10 (☎0541.381.436; ④). You could also **camp**: on sites next to the rail line at Viserba (Via Toscanelli), and Viserbella (off the main road), and south towards Miramare (Viale Principe di Piemonte).

The seafront is the best place to **eat** cheaply, with hundreds of takeaway pizza places. Most of the nicer restaurants are in the old town – try *Osteria dë Börg*, at Via Forzieri 12, just the other side of the old port from the town centre, or the *Rimini Key* at Piazzale Croce by the seafront. There's also a good student mensa by the train station at Via Roma 70. Rimini's **nightlife** also happens along the seafront, out towards Riccione.

CENTRAL ITALY

The Italian heartland region of **Tuscany** represents perhaps the most archetypal image of the country – its walled towns and rolling, vineyard-covered hills the classic backdrops of Renaissance art. Of Tuscany's urban centres, few people react entirely positively to **Florence**. But however unappealing some of the central streets might look, there are plentiful compensations – the Uffizi gallery's masterpieces, the great fresco cycles in the churches, the wealth of Florentine sculpture in the city's museums. **Siena** provokes less ambiguous reactions: one of the great medieval cities of Europe, it's also the scene of Tuscany's one unmissable festival – the *Palio* – which sees bareback horse riders careering around the cobbled central square. The other major cities, **Pisa** and **Lucca**, both have medieval splendours – Pisa has its Leaning Tower and cathedral ensemble, Lucca a string of Romanesque churches – and there are, of course, the smaller hill towns, of which **San Gimignano**, the "city of the towers", is the best known. The provincial capital of the upper Arno region, **Arezzo**, an hour's train ride from Florence, is also worth a stop, if only for its marvellous series of paintings by Piero della Francesca, while to the east lies **Umbria**, a beautiful region of rolling hills, woods and valleys – not unlike Tuscany but as yet less discovered. Most visitors head for the capital, **Perugia**, for **Assisi** – with its extraordinary frescoes by Giotto in the Basilica di San Francesco – or **Orvieto**, where the Duomo is one of the greatest Gothic buildings in the country, though lesser-known places like **Gubbio**, ranked as the most perfect medieval centre in Italy, and **Spoleto**, for many the outstanding Umbrian town, are worth taking in, too. Further east still, the **Marche** repeats much the same sort of pleasures, the town of **Urbino** in the north of the region, with its superb Renaissance ducal palace, providing a deserved highlight, and the port of **Ancona** useful ferry links to Greece.

Florence

Ever since the nineteenth-century revival of interest in the art of the Renaissance, **FLORENCE** has been a shrine to the cult of the beautiful. Close up, however, it does not immediately impress visitors as a beautiful city. The marble-clad baptistry and Duomo are stupendous, of course, the architectural perfection of the latter's dome as celebrated now as it ever was. But these colourful monuments are not typical of the city as a whole: the streets of the historic centre are often narrow and dark, their palaces robust and intimidating, and few of the city's squares are places where you'd want to pass an idle hour. However, Florence is a city of incomparable indoor pleasures, its chapels, galleries and museums an inexhaustible treasure, embodying the complex, exhilarating and often elusive spirit of the Renaissance more fully than any other place in the country, and few leave completely disappointed.

Florence became the centre of artistic patronage in Italy under the Medici family, who made their fortune in banking and ruled the city as an independent state for some three centuries, most auspiciously during the years of Lorenzo de' Medici, tagged "Il Magnifico", who held fiercely onto Florentine independence in the face of papal resentment. Later, in the late eighteenth century, Florence fell under Austrian and then French rule, and in the nineteenth century was for a short time the capital of the kingdom of Italy. The story of Florence since then has been fairly low-key, and nowadays the monuments and paintings of the city's Renaissance heyday are the basis of its survival.

Arrival, information and city transport

The nearest major international **airport** to Florence is at Pisa, connected by a regular train service to Florence's Santa Maria Novella **train station** in the city centre; the journey takes an hour. An increasing number of flights now come into Florence's tiny Perètola airport, 5km out of the city and connected by bus to the main **bus station**, alongside Santa Maria Novella. The main **tourist offices** are at Via Cavour 7r, just north of the Duomo (summer Mon–Sat 8.15am–7.15pm, Sun 8.15am–1.45pm; winter Mon–Sat 8.15am–1.45pm), at Borgo San Croce 29r, near Piazza Santa Croce (summer daily 8.30am–7.15pm; winter Mon–Sat 8.30am–1.45pm), and Piazza della Stazione (June–Sept Mon–Sat 8.30am–7.15pm, Sun 8.30am–1.45pm; Oct–May Mon–Sat 8.30am–1.45pm). All have free maps and the useful *Concierge Information* booklet. **Walking** is generally the most efficient way of getting around, but if you want to cover a long distance in a hurry, take one of the orange ATAF **buses**; tickets, valid for sixty minutes, cost L1500 from *tabacchi* and machines all over Florence. Alternatively you can hire a bike for just L1000 per day under the "Mille e una bici" scheme; ask at the tourist office for details.

Accommodation

Florence's most affordable **hotels** are close to the station, in particular along and around Via Faenza and the parallel Via Fiume, and along Via della Scala and Piazza Santa Maria Novella; you could also try the slightly more salubrious Via Cavour, north of the Duomo. However, availability is a problem at most times of year, and between Easter and the start of October you're taking a risk in turning up without a pre-booked room. If you do, the Informazioni Turistiche Alberghiere **accommodation office** at the station (daily 8.45am–8pm) can make last-minute reservations for a fee, though in high season the queues here can be a nightmare. They will also give details of the **emergency camping area** or *Area di Sosta* provided by the city authorities in high season.

HOSTELS AND DORMITORY ACCOMMODATION

Istituto Gould, Via dei Serragli 49 (☎055.212.576). Over in Oltrarno, and open Mon–Fri 9am–1pm & 3–7pm, Sat 9am–1pm. It's wise to book in advance. ③.

Ostello Villa Camerata, Viale Righi 2 (☎055.601.451). The official HI hostel lies in a beautiful park, a 30-min journey on bus #17b from the train station. Doors open at 1pm; if you can't be there by then, ring ahead to make sure there's space left. ②.

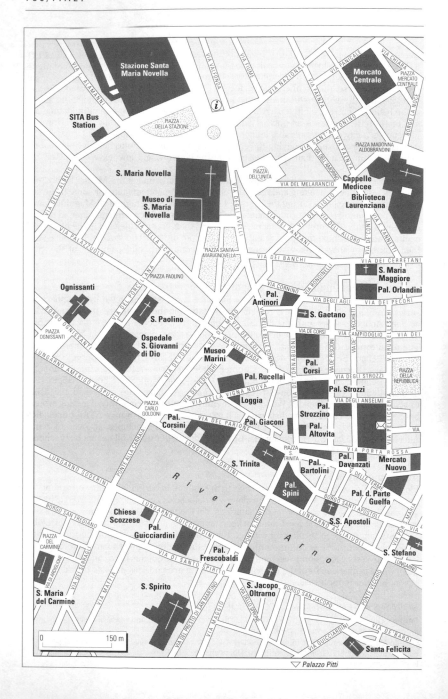

▽ *Palazzo Pitti*

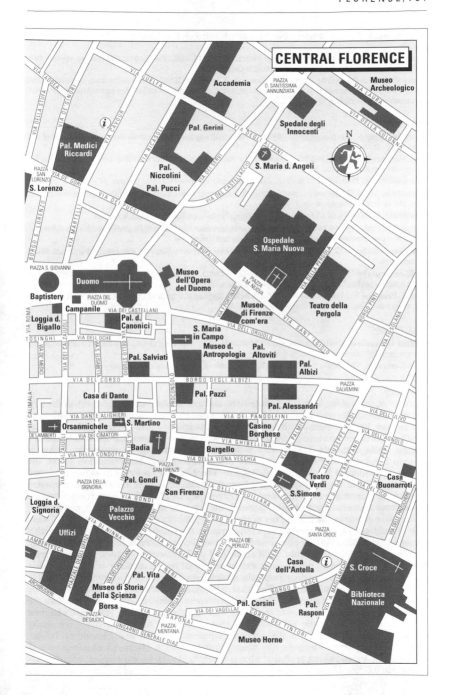

CENTRAL FLORENCE

Santa Monaca, Via Santa Monaca 6 (☎055.268.338). In Oltrarno. Free hot showers, 1am curfew. Very popular. ②.

Suore Oblate dell'Assunzione, Via Borgo Pinti 15 (☎055.248.0582). Not far from the Duomo, open to men and women. Single and double rooms; midnight curfew. ④.

Suore Oblate dello Spirito Santo, Via Nazionale 8 (☎055.239.8202). A few steps from the station, and open to women mid-June to Oct. Very clean and pleasant; single, double and triple rooms; 11pm curfew and minimum stay of 2 nights. ③.

HOTELS

Ausonia e Rimini, Via Nazionale 24 (☎055.496.547). Halfway between the train station and the market and welcoming. ⑤.

Azzi, Via Faenza 56 (☎055.213.806). Probably the most pleasant of six reasonably priced *pensioni* on the upper floors of this building. ④.

Brunetta, Borgo Pinti 5 (☎055.240.360). Cheap and central, just east of the Duomo. ③.

Concordia, Via dell'Amorino 14 (☎055.213.233). Extremely convenient, right in the heart of the market area and beautifuly decorated. ⑤.

Costantini, Via Calzaiuoli 13 (☎055.213.995). Friendly place on the city's main street. ⑥.

Donatello, Via V. Alfieri 9 (☎055.245.870). In a quiet area between Piazzale Donatello and Piazza d'Azeglio; strongly recommended – smartly renovated, young and friendly. ④.

Elite Via della Scala 12 (☎055.215.395). Two-star hotel with very pleasant management in Santa Maria Novella area. ⑤.

La Romagnola (☎055.211.597) and **Gigliola** (☎055.287.981), both at Via della Scala 40. Best of the Via della Scala hotels – midnight curfews are the only drawback. Both ④.

Teti & Prestige, Via Porta Rossa 5 (☎055.239.8435). Right in the thick of things between Via Tornabuoni and Piazza della Signoria. Good value and friendly. ⑤.

CAMPSITES

Italiani e Stranieri, Viale Michelangelo 80 (☎055.681.1977). Open April–Oct, and always crowded owing to its superb hillside location. Bus #13 from the train station.

Villa Camerata, Viale Righi 2 (☎055.600.315). Basic site in hostel grounds, open all year.

The City

Florence sprawls along both sides of the Arno and into the hills north and south of the city, but the major sights are contained within an area that can be crossed on foot in a little over half an hour. Perhaps the most obvious place to start exploring is the **Piazza della Signoria**, a rather charmless open space, fringed on one side by the graceful late fourteenth-century **Loggia della Signoria**. Dotted with statuary, like Giambologna's equestrian statue of Cosimo I and copies of Donatello's *Judith and Holofernes* and Michelangelo's *David*, the square is dominated by the colossal **Palazzo Vecchio**, Florence's fortress-like town hall (Mon–Wed, Fri & Sat 9am–7pm, Thurs 9am–2pm, Sun 8am–1pm; L10,000; last admission 45min before closing; a L10,000 *carnet* for 6 city museums gives you a 50 percent reduction on entrance fees plus a guidebook), begun in the last year of the thirteenth century as the home of the *Signoria*, the highest tier of the city's republican government. The Medici were only in residence here for nine years, but the layout of the palace owes much to them, notably Cosimo I, who decorated the state rooms with relentless eulogies to himself and his family. The huge Salone dei Cinquecento, built at the end of the fifteenth century, is full of heroic murals by Vasari, though it is to some extent redeemed by the presence of Michelangelo's *Victory*, facing the entrance door, originally sculpted for Pope Julius II's tomb but donated to the Medici by the artist's nephew. The bizarre Studiolo di Francesco I was also created by Vasari, and decorated by several of Florence's prominent Mannerist artists as a retreat for the introverted son of Cosimo, most of the bronzes and paintings reflecting Francesco's interest in the sciences, though the best ones are those that don't fit the scheme – principally Bronzino's glacial portraits of the occupant's parents, Cosimo and Eleanor of Toledo. Bronzino also painted Eleanor's tiny chapel upstairs, and a Mannerist contemporary of Bronzino, Cecchino Salviati, produced what is widely held to be his masterpiece with the fresco cycle in the Sala d'Udienza, once the audience chamber of the Republic. The adjoining Sala dei Gigli was frescoed by Ghirlandaio, although the main focus is Donatello's restored *Judith and Holofernes*.

Immediately south of the piazza, the **Galleria degli Uffizi** (summer Tues–Sat 8.30am–10pm, Sun 8.30am–8pm; winter Tues–Sat 8.30am–6.50pm, Sun 8.30am–1.50pm; L12,000, last admittance 45min before closing) is the greatest picture gallery in Italy, with a collection of masterpieces that is impossible to take in on a single visit. The early Renaissance is represented by three altarpieces of the *Madonna Enthroned* by Cimabue, Duccio and Giotto, and a luscious golden *Annunciation* by the fourteenth-century Sienese painter, Simone Martini. There's also Uccello's *Battle of San Romano* – demonstrating the artist's obsessional interest in perspectival effects – which once hung in Lorenzo il Magnifico's bed chamber, in company with depictions of the skirmish now in the Louvre and London's National Gallery. Among plentiful works by Filippo Lippi is his *Madonna and Child with Two Angels*, one of the best-known Renaissance images of the Madonna. Close by, there's a fine *Madonna* by Botticelli, who in the next room is represented by some of his most famous works, notably *Primavera* and the *Birth of Venus*; look also at the huge *Portinari Altarpiece* by Botticelli's Flemish contemporary Hugo van der Goes, a work whose naturalism greatly influenced the artists of Florence. The Uffizi doesn't own a finished painting that's entirely by Leonardo da Vinci, but there's a celebrated *Annunciation* (mainly by him) and the angel in profile that he painted in Verrocchio's *Baptism*. Room 18, the octagonal Tribuna, where the cream of the collection used to be exhibited, houses the most important of the Medici sculptures, first among which is the *Medici Venus*, along with some chillingly precise portraits by Bronzino and Vasari's portrait of Lorenzo il Magnifico, painted long after the death of its subject. Michelangelo's *Doni Tondo* is his only completed easel painting, its contorted gestures and virulent colours studied and imitated by the Mannerist painters of the sixteenth century, as can be gauged from the nearby *Moses Defending the Daughters of Jethro* by Rosso Fiorentino, one of the pivotal figures of the movement. Separating the two Mannerist groups are a number of compositions by Raphael, including *Pope Leo X with Cardinals Giulio de' Medici and Luigi de' Rossi* – as shifty a group of ecclesiastics as ever was gathered in one frame – while Titian weighs in with his fleshily provocative *Venus of Urbino*. Later rooms include some large works by Rubens and Van Dyck; Caravaggio has a cluster of pieces, including a severed head of Medusa; while another room has portraiture by Rembrandt, notably his melancholic *Self-Portrait as an Old Man*, painted five years before his death.

To get a comprehensive idea of the Renaissance achievement in Florence, you need also to visit the **Museo Nazionale del Bargello** (Tues–Sat 8.30am–1.50pm, also second & fourth Sun and first, third & fifth Mon of each month; L8000), a short step north in Via del Proconsolo, where there is a full collection of sculpture from the period, housed in a thirteenth-century palace that was formerly the HQ of the city's chief of police (the *Bargello*). The first part of the collection focuses on Michelangelo, represented by among others his first major sculpture, the lurching figure of *Bacchus*, carved at the age of 22. Beyond, the more flamboyant art of Cellini and Giambologna is exhibited, notably a huge *Bust of Cosimo I*, Cellini's first work in bronze, a sort of technical trial for the casting of the *Perseus* nearby, and Giambologna's best-known creation, the nimble figure of *Mercury*. Out in the courtyard, at the top of its external staircase, the first-floor loggia has been turned into an aviary for Giambologna's bronze birds, imported from the Medici villa at Castello, while a nearby room displays work by Donatello – the mildly Gothic *David* and the alert figure of *St George*. His sexually ambiguous bronze *David*, the first freestanding nude figure since classical times, was cast in the early 1430s. Donatello's master, Ghiberti, is represented by his relief of *The Sacrifice of Isaac*, his successful entry in the competition for the baptistry doors. The treatment of the theme submitted by Brunelleschi, the runner-up, is hung close by. Upstairs the Sala dei Bronzetti has Italy's best assembly of small Renaissance bronzes, with plentiful evidence of Giambologna's virtuosity, and a further room holds Renaissance portrait busts, including Mino da Fiesole's busts of *Giovanni de' Medici* and *Piero il Gottoso*, and a couple of pieces by Verrocchio, including a *David* clearly influenced by Donatello.

Parallel to Via del Proconsolo on the opposite side of Piazza della Signoria is **Via dei Calzaiuoli**, one of the city's more animated streets and home to the church of **Orsanmichele** (daily 9am–noon & 4–6pm; closed first and last Mon of the month). Its exterior is decorated by a number of early Renaissance sculptures, including a *John the Baptist* by Ghiberti, the first life-size bronze statue of the Renaissance, and an *Incredulity of St Thomas* by Verrocchio. Inside a vast tabernacle by Orcagna frames a *Madonna* painted by Bernardo Daddi in 1347 to replace a miraculous image of the Virgin destroyed by a 1304 fire.

The streets west of the Signoria retain a medieval character, lined with palaces like the fourteenth-century Palazzo Davanzati on Via Porta Rossa which houses the **Museo della Casa Fiorentina Antica** (presently closed for restoration). Inside, virtually every room of the reconstructed interior is furnished and decorated in medieval style. About 500m north-west, off Via della Scala, the partly Gothic church of **Santa Maria Novella** (Mon–Sat 7am–12.15pm & 3–6pm, Sun 3–5pm) was the Florentine base of the Dominican order. Halfway down the left aisle of the nave is Masaccio's extraordinary fresco of *The Trinity*, one of the earliest works in which perspective and classical proportion were rigorously employed. The church's **cloisters** (Mon–Thurs & Sat 9am–2pm, Sun 8am–1pm; L5000) are richly decorated with frescoes by Uccello and his workshop.

THE DUOMO AND AROUND

North of the Signoria on **Piazza del Duomo**, the **Duomo** (Mon–Sat 10am–5pm, Sun 1–5pm) was built between the late thirteenth and mid-fifteenth centuries to an ambitious design, originally the brainchild of Arnolfo di Cambio and realized finally by Filippo Brunelleschi, who completed the majestic dome – the largest in existence until this century. The fourth largest church in the world, its ambience is more that of a great assembly hall than of a devotional building, its most conspicuous pieces of painted decoration two memorials to *condottieri* – Uccello's monument to Sir John Hawkwood, painted in 1436, and Castagno's monument to Niccolò da Tolentino, created twenty years later. Just beyond, Domenico do Michelino's *Dante Explaining the Divine Comedy*, painted in 1465, gives the recently completed dome a place only marginally less prominent than the *Mountain of Purgatory*. Above, the fresco of *The Last Judgment* in the dome is the work of Vasari and Zuccari, below which are seven stained-glass roundels designed by Uccello, Ghiberti, Castagno and Donatello – best inspected from a gallery which forms part of the route to the top of the dome (Mon–Fri 8.30am–6.20pm, Sat 8.30am–5pm; L10,000). The views at the very top are as stupendous as you would expect.

Next door to the Duomo, the **Campanile** (summer daily 9am–6.50pm; winter daily 9am–4.20pm; L10,000) was begun in 1334 by Giotto and continued after his death by Andrea Pisano and Francesco Talenti. The only part of the tower built exactly as Giotto designed it is the lower storey, studded with two rows of remarkable bas-reliefs, the lower one illustrating the *Creation of Man* and the *Arts and Industries* carved by Pisano. The figures of *Prophets* and *Sibyls* in the second-storey niches are by Donatello and others. Opposite, the **Baptistry** (Mon–Sat noon–6.30pm, Sun 8.30am–1.30pm; L5000), generally thought to date from the sixth or seventh century, is the oldest building in the city. Its most famous embellishments, the gilded bronze doors, were cast in the early fifteenth century by Lorenzo Ghiberti, and were described by Michelangelo as "so beautiful they are worthy to be the gates of Paradise". They're a primer of early Renaissance art, innovatively using perspective, gesture and sophisticated grouping of subjects to convey the human drama of each scene. Ghiberti included a self-portrait in the frame of the left-hand door – his is the fourth head from the top of the right-hand band. Inside, the baptistry is equally stunning, with a thirteenth-century mosaic floor and ceiling and the tomb of Pope John XXIII, draped by a superb marble canopy, the work of Donatello and his pupil Michelozzo.

Since the early fifteenth century the maintenance of the Duomo has been supervised from the building at Piazza del Duomo 9, nowadays housing the **Museo dell'Opera del Duomo** (Mon–Sat 9am–6.20/6.50pm; L10,000), the repository of the most precious and fragile works of art from the buildings around, including a series of sculptures by Arnolfo di Cambio; Brunelleschi's death mask; models of the dome and a variety of tools and machines devised by the architect; Michelangelo's anguished late *Pietà*; Pisano's bas-reliefs and Donatello's figures for the Campanile; and four of Ghiberti's door panels and a dazzling silver-gilt altar from the baptistry, completed in 1480.

NORTH OF THE DUOMO

The church of **San Lorenzo** (daily 7am–noon & 3.30–6.30pm), north of the baptistry, has good claim to be the oldest church in Florence, and for the best part of three hundred years was the city's cathedral. Rebuilt by Brunelleschi in the mid-fifteenth century under the patronage of the Medici, the interior is a fine example of early Renaissance church design. Inside are two bronze pulpits by Donatello; close by, a large disc of multicoloured marble marks the grave of Cosimo il Vecchio, the artist's main patron, while further pieces by Donatello adorn the neighbouring Sagrestia Vecchia by Brunelleschi – the two pairs of bronze doors, the large reliefs of *SS Cosmas and Damian* and *SS Lawrence and Stephen*, and the eight terracotta tondoes. At the top of the left aisle and through the cloisters, the **Biblioteca Medicea-Laurenziana** (Mon–Sat 9am–1pm; free) was designed by Michelangelo in 1524; its most startling feature is the vestibule, a room almost filled by a flight of steps resembling a solidified lava flow. Michelangelo's most celebrated contribution to the San Lorenzo buildings, however, is the Sagrestia Nuova, part of the **Cappelle Medicee** (Tues–Sun 8.30am–1.50pm; also second & fourth Mon of each month; L13,000). Begun in 1520, in part as a tribute to Sagrestia Vecchia, it contains the fabulous Medici tombs, carved between 1524 and 1533. To the left is the tomb of Lorenzo, duke of Urbino, the grandson of Lorenzo il Magnifico, bearing figures of *Dawn* and *Dusk* to sum up his contemplative nature. Opposite is the tomb of Lorenzo il Magnifico's youngest son, Giuliano, his supposedly more active character symbolized by *Day* and *Night*. Their effigies were intended to face the equally grand tombs of Lorenzo il Magnifico and his brother Giuliano, though the only part of this actually realized by Michelangelo is the serene *Madonna and Child*.

The **Museo di San Marco**, in a former convent in the piazza of the same name, is dedicated to the work of Fra Angelico. Just east of here, the **Galleria dell'Accademia** (Mon–Fri 9am–9pm, Sat 9am–11pm, Sun 9am–8pm; shorter hours in winter; L12,000) was Europe's first school of drawing. Its collection of paintings is impressive, but most people come to view the sculpture of Michelangelo, specifically his *David*. Finished in 1504, when Michelangelo was just 29, and carved from a gigantic block of marble, it's an incomparable show of technical bravura. The gallery also houses his remarkable unfinished *Slaves*.

THE SANTA CROCE DISTRICT

Down by the river, the Franciscan church of Florence, **Santa Croce** (summer Mon–Sat 8am–6.30pm, Sun 3–6pm; winter Mon–Sat 8am–12.30 & Sun 3–6.30pm), was begun in 1294, possibly by the architect of the Duomo, Arnolfo di Cambio, and is full of tombstones and commemorative monuments, including Vasari's monument to Michelangelo, and, on the opposite side of the church, is the tomb of Galileo, built in 1737 when it was finally agreed to give the great scientist a Christian burial; most visitors come to see the frescoes by Giotto in the Cappella Peruzzi and the Cappella Bardi (on the right of the chancel). The former shows scenes from the lives of St John the Baptist and St John the Evangelist; the latter, painted slightly earlier with some assistance, features the life of St Francis. Agnolo Gaddi was responsible for all the frescoes around and above the high altar and for the design of the stained glass in the lancet windows. At the end of the left chancel, a second Cappella Bardi houses a wooden *Crucifix* by Donatello. Also visit Brunelleschi's **Cappella dei Pazzi**, at the end of the first cloister (summer 10am–12.30pm & 2.30–6.30pm, winter 10am–12.30pm & 3–5pm; closed Tues; L4000), designed in the 1430s and completed in the 1470s, several years after the architect's death, with decorations by Luca della Robbia. The **Museo dell'Opera di Santa Croce**, off the first cloister (same times), also houses a miscellany of works of art, the best of which are Cimabue's flood-damaged *Crucifixion*, Gaddi's fresco of the *Last Supper and Crucifixion*, and Donatello's enormous gilded *St Louis of Toulouse*, made for Orsanmichele. North of Santa Croce at Via Ghibellina 70, the **Casa Buonarroti** (Mon & Wed–Sun 9.30am–1.30pm; L12,000) is enticing in name, but Michelangelo Buonarroti never actually lived here, and there is little to see of his work. The most exciting items are an early *Madonna of the Steps*, and the unfinished *Battle of the Centaurs*.

OLTRARNO AND SAN MINIATO

The thirteenth-century **Ponte Vecchio**, loaded with jewellers' shops which overhang the water, leads from the city centre across the river to **Oltrarno**. The district is dominated by the massive bulk of the **Palazzo Pitti**. Nowadays the fifteenth-century palace and its stupendous garden – the Giardino di Bóboli – contain six separate museums. The **Galleria Palatina** (summer Tues–Sat 8.30am–10pm, Sun 8.30am–8pm; winter Tues–Sat 8.30am–6.50pm, Sun 9am–1.50pm; L12,000) has superb displays of the art of Raphael and Titian, including a number of Titian's most trenchant portraits. Andrea del Sarto is represented in strength, too, as is Rubens, whose *Consequences of War* packs more of a punch than most other Baroque allegories. Much of the rest of the first floor comprises the **Appartamenti Monumentali** (included in the Galleria Palatina ticket), the Pitti's state rooms, while on the floor above, the **Galleria d'Arte Moderna** (Tues–Sat 8.30am–1.50pm, also second & fourth Sun and first, third & fifth Mon of each month; L8000) is a chronological survey of primarily Tuscan art from the mid-eighteenth century to 1945. The Pitti's enormous formal garden, the **Giardino di Bóboli** (April, May, Sept Tues–Sun 9am–6.30pm, also second & third Mon of each month; June–Aug closes 7.30pm; Oct closes 5.30pm, Nov–Feb 4.30pm; L4000) is full of Mannerist embellishments including the Grotta del Buontalenti, close to the entrance to the left of the palace facade; among its fake stalactites are shepherds and sheep and replicas of Michelangelo's *Slaves*, replacing the originals that were here until 1908. In the deepest recesses of the cave stands Giambologna's *Venus*, leered at by attendant imps. In the eastern corner of the gardens is **Forte di Belvedere** (daily 9am–6/7pm; free), a star-shaped fortress built in 1590, which can only be entered through Porta San Giorgio at the top of the hill.

About 500m northwest of the Palazzo Pitti, the church of **Santa Maria del Carmine** is visited for the frescoes in its Cappella Brancacci (Mon & Wed–Sat 10am–5pm, Sun 1–5pm; L5000) by Masaccio – recently, and controversially, restored. The cycle was completed by Filippino Lippi, his most distinctive contribution being the affecting *Release of St Peter* on the right-hand side of the entrance. In the opposite direction, the multicoloured facade of **San Miniato al Monte** lures troops of visitors up the hill. The interior (daily: summer 8am–noon & 2–7pm; winter 8am–noon & 2.30–6pm) is like no other in the city, and its general form has changed little since the mid-eleventh century. In the lower part of the church, don't overlook the intricately patterned panels of the pavement, from 1207, and the tabernacle between the choir stairs, designed in 1448 by Michelozzo.

Eating and drinking

Although Tuscan cuisine is distinguished by its simplicity, in recent years Florence's gastronomic reputation has suffered under the pressure of mass tourism. Certainly there's a dearth of good places to eat if you're on a limited budget, although a decent meal isn't hard to come by if you explore the remoter quarters. The best place to find **picnic food** and **snacks** is the **Mercato Centrale** (summer Mon–Sat 9am–7pm; winter Tues–Sat 9am–5pm), just east of the train station, which is full of greengrocers, pasta stalls and bars charging prices lower than elsewhere in the city. There are also plenty of city-centre **bars**, along Via de' Panzani, Via de' Cerretani, Via Por Santa Maria and Via Guicciardini, whose snacky food offers ample compensation for their lack of character. Otherwise, try a **vinaio**, a wine cellar/snack bar that serves *crostini* and other snacks. The *vinaio* at Via Cimatori 38 is a perfect example, as is the place at Via Alfani 70, in the university area, which serves stuffed tomatoes and a range of other vegetables in addition to the traditional *crostini*. For classier snacks, try the *panini* and pasta at *Fiaschetteria*, Via de' Neri 17, or the similar fare at *Fiaschetteria da 11 Latin*, Via del Palchetti 6/r, behind Palazzo Rucellai. Another Florentine speciality is the **friggitoria**, serving *polenta*, potatoes and apple croquettes – try the one at Via Sant'Antonino 50, which also sells pizza, or *Antico Noê* at Volta di San Piero 6, which does burgers and salads and has a restaurant next door. *Giuliano* is a superb *rosticceria*, with seats, at Via de' Neri 74. For **ice cream**, leader of the pack is *Vivoli*, near Santa Croce at Via Isola delle Stinche 7/r.

RESTAURANTS

Alle Mossacce, Via del Proconsolo 55. Once the haunt of Florence's young artists; the bohemian element has since dispersed, but the food remains excellent. Closed Sun.

Bar Santa Croce, Borgo Santa Croce 31. Good lunchtime menu and marvellous pasta.

Benvenuto, Via Mosca 16/5, off Via de' Neri. Looks more like a delicatessen than a trattoria from the street, but the groups waiting for a table give the game away; the *gnocchi* and *arista* are delicious.

Dante, Piazza Nazario Sauro 10. Busy pizzeria with around a dozen types of spaghetti on the menu too.

Da Mario, Via Rosina 2. Popular with students and market workers – be prepared to queue and share a table. Closed evenings.

Dei Quattro Leoni, Via Vellutini 1. Atmospheric trattoria in the Oltrarno district.

Palle d'Oro, Via Sant'Antonio 43. Station area eatery that's halfway between a *rosticceria* and a trattoria. Besides full meals, they do sandwiches to take away.

Trattoria Casalinga, Via Michelozzi 9r. Oltrarno restaurant, off Via Maggio, that offers just about the best low-cost authentic Tuscan dishes in town. Always crowded.

Za-Za, Piazza del Mercato 26. A few tables on ground level, but a bigger canteen below.

Nightlife

Florence enjoys a reasonably vibrant **nightlife** by Italian standards. Of **places to drink**, *Rifrullo*, Via San Niccolò 55, attracts an affluent young clientele; *Dolce Vita*, on Piazza del Carmine, is a trendy hangout that also stages small-scale art exhibitions; the nearby *Tiratoio*, on Piazza de' Nerli, is a large easy-going place, with a couple of video jukeboxes and a wide range of food. In the Santa Croce district, *Rex*, Via Fiesolana 25r has good music, a varied clientele, and serves snacks and cocktails. For a quiet drink in a beautifully situated bar, try *Chalet Fontana* on Viale Michelangelo – pricey but worth it. *Tenax*, on Via Pratese 47, is the city's biggest **disco** and one of its leading venues for new and established bands. *Yab Yum*, Via de' Sassetti 5r, is a city-centre disco with a vast dance floor playing the best of new dance music; and *Space Electronic*, Via Palazzuolo 37, is the favourite disco of young foreigners, open nightly; but *Meccanò*, Piazza Vittorio Veneto, is the in place to be seen. For **information** on what's on, call in at Box Office, Via Faenza 139r (☎055.210.804), or consult the listings magazines *Firenze Spettacolo*, and *Informa Città*.

Listings

Airlines Alitalia, Lungarno Acciaiuoli 10–12 (☎055.27.881); British Airways, Via della Vigna Nuova 36r (☎055.218.655 or 218.659 or 147.812.266).

Airport enquiries G. Galileo Airport, Pisa (☎050.500.707); A. Vespucci airport, Florence (☎055.373.498).

American Express Via Dante Alighieri 22r (Mon–Fri 9am–5.30pm, Sat 9am–12.30pm; ☎055.50.981).

Books Paperback Exchange, at Via Fiesolana 31r and Feltrinelli International, at Via Cavour 12r, stock a wide selection of English-language books.

Car rental Avis, Borgo Ognissanti 128r (☎055.213.629), airport (☎055.315.558); Hertz, Via Maso Finiguerra 33r (☎055.282.260); Maggiore, Via Maso Finiguerra 31r (☎055.210.238).

Consulates Great Britain, Lungarno Corsini 2 (☎055.284.133); USA, Lungarno Vespucci 38 (☎055.239.8276).

Exchange Esercizio Promozione Turismo, Via Condotta 42 (Mon–Sat 10am–7pm, Sun 10am–6pm).

Hospital Santa Maria Nuova, Piazza Santa Maria Nuova 1 (☎055.27.581). The Tourist Medical Service, Via Lorenzo il Magnifico 59 (☎055.475.411), has English-speaking doctors on 24hr call.

Laundry Onda Blu, at Via degli Alfani 24r; Wash & Dry, at Via della Scala 52-54r.

Pharmacies All-night pharmacy at the train station, and Molteni, Via dei Calzaiuoli 7r.

Police Main office at Via Zara 2 (☎055.49.771).

Post office Central office at Via Pellicceria (Mon–Fri 8.20am–6pm, Sat 8.20am–12.30; ☎055.211.147).

Telephones Booths at the train station (24hr), Via San Piero Maggiore 10r (7–10pm)and Telecom Italia – which also has a fax service – at Via Cavour 21r (7am–11pm).

Train enquiries ☎055.288.785, 055.23.521 or 147.888.088.

Fiesole

A long-established Florentine retreat from the summer heat and crowds, **FIESOLE** spreads over a cluster of hilltops some 8km northeast of Florence. It rivalled its neighbour until the early twelfth century, when it became favoured as a semirural second home for Florence's wealthier citizens. The #7 ATAF bus runs there every fifteen minutes from Florence's train station, a twenty-minute journey.

Fiesole's central **Piazza Mino da Fiesole** is home to the **Duomo**, in which the Cappella Salutati, right of the choir, contains two fine pieces carved by Mino da Fiesole in the mid-fifteenth century – an altar frontal of *The Madonna and Saints* and the tomb of Bishop Salutati. From here, Via San Francesco leads up to a terrace which gives a remarkable panorama of Florence, just above which the church of **Sant'Alessandro** (daily 10am–noon & 3–5pm), founded in the sixth century on the site of Etruscan and Roman temples, has a beautiful basilical interior with onion marble columns. Around the back of the duomo, in Via Marini, is the entrance to the **Teatro Romano** and **Museo Archeologico** (daily: April–Sept 9am–6/7pm; Nov–Feb 9.30am–5pm; Mar & Oct 9.30am–6pm; L6000). Built in the first century BC, the 3000-seater theatre is still used for performances during the *Estate Fiesolana* festival. Most of the museum exhibits were discovered in this area, and encompass pieces from the Bronze Age to the Roman occupation. The narrow Via Vecchia Fiesolana leads from just west of the main square to the hamlet of **SAN DOMENICO**, 1500m southwest. Fra Angelico was once prior of the Dominican **monastery** here, and the church retains a *Madonna and Angels* by him; the chapterhouse also has a Fra Angelico fresco of *The Crucifixion*. Five minutes' walk northwest from San Domenico brings you to the **Badia Fiesolana**, formerly Fiesole's cathedral and altered by Cosimo il Vecchio in the 1460s, who left the magnificent Romanesque facade intact while transforming the interior into a superb Renaissance building.

San Gimignano

SAN GIMIGNANO – "delle Belle Torri" – is one of the best-known towns in Tuscany. Its image as a "Medieval Manhattan", with its skyline of towers, has caught the tourist imagination, helped along, no doubt, by its convenience as a day-trip from Florence or Siena. However, from May through to October, San Gimignano is very busy, and to really get any feel for the place you need to come out of season. If you can't, aim to spend the night here – in the evenings the town takes on a very different pace and atmosphere.

Founded around the eighth century, San Gimignano was a force to be reckoned with in the Middle Ages, with a population of fifteen thousand (twice the present number). Nowadays it's not much more than a village: you could walk across it in fifteen minutes, around the walls in an hour. The main entrance gate, facing the bus terminal on the south side of town, is **Porta San Giovanni**, from where Via San Giovanni leads to the town's interlocking main squares, Piazza della Cisterna and Piazza del Duomo. You enter the **Piazza della Cisterna** through another majestic gateway, the **Arco dei Becci**, part of the original fortifications before the town expanded in the twelfth century. The more austere **Piazza Duomo**, off to the left, is flanked by the **Collegiata** church, frescoed with Old Testament scenes by Bartolo di Fredi on the left wall, from around 1367, and, opposite, slightly later New Testament scenes by Barna da Siena. Best, though, is the fresco cycle by Ghirlandaio in the Cappella di Santa Fina, depicting the trials of a local saint – a superb work, access to which is included on a general tourist ticket (L18,000) that includes entry to all the town's museums. There's more work by Ghirlandaio to the left of the cathedral – a fresco of the *Annunciation* on the courtyard loggia – while the **Palazzo del Popolo**, next door (Tues–Sun: summer 9.30am–7.20pm; winter 9.30am–12.50pm & 2.30–4.50pm; L7000), gives you the chance to climb the **Torre Grossa** (L8000), the town's highest surviving tower and the only one you can ascend. The same building is home to a number of rooms given over to the **Museo Civico**, the first of which, frescoed with hunting scenes, is known as the Sala di Dante and houses Lippo Memmi's *Maestà*, modelled on that of Simone Martini in Siena.

Search out also the delightful frescoes of wedding scenes in a small room off the stairs, completed early in the fourteenth century by the Sienese painter Memmo di Filipuccio. North from Piazza Duomo, **Via San Matteo** is one of the grandest and best preserved of the city streets, with quiet alleyways running down to the walls. The street ends at the **Porta San Matteo**, just inside which, in a corner of walls, is the large hall church of **Sant'Agostino** (daily 7am–noon & 3–6/7pm), with a much-damaged fresco series of the *Life of the Virgin* by Bartolo di Fredi and a cycle of seventeen scenes of the *Life of St Augustine* by Gozzoli, behind the high altar. At the **Museo Criminale Medioevale** (summer daily 10am–8pm; winter Mon–Sat 10am–5.30pm, Sun 10am–7pm; L10,000) at Via del Castello 1, you get a no-holds-barred exploration of the medieval torturer's mind, aided and abetted by explicit explanations in good English.

Practicalities

Accommodation lists are available from the **tourist office** on Piazza del Duomo, but from May to September you'll save a lot of frustration by using the Associazione Extralberghiere at Piazza della Cisterna 6 (☎0577.943.190; March–Oct daily 9.30am–7.30pm), which can arrange **private rooms** without commission, or the Cooperativa Turistiche office at Via S. Giovanni 125 (summer Mon–Sat 9.30am–7pm, Sun 3–7pm; winter Mon–Sat 9.30am–12.30pm & 3–5.30pm), which arranges hotel accommodation for L3000 commission. San Gimignano's **hotels** are expensive, two of the cheapest being the three-star *Da Graziano* at Via Matteotti 39/a (☎0577.940.701; ⑤), and the beautifully situated *Leon Bianco*, Piazza della Cisterna 13 (☎0577.941.294; ⑦). The **youth hostel** is at Via delle Fonti 1 (☎0577.941.991; ②) and for **camping**, the nearest site is *Il Boschetto*, 3km downhill at Santa Lucia (☎0577.940.352). One of the most popular **restaurants**, and a fraction cheaper than most, is *Le Vecchie Mura* at Via Piandornella 15, off Via San Giovanni. For **snacks**, pizza is served by the slice at Via San Giovanni 38.

Arezzo

About 50km southeast of Florence, **AREZZO** was one of the most important settlements of the Etruscan federation and a prosperous independent republic in the Middle Ages, later falling under the sway of Florence. During the Renaissance, Petrarch, Pietro Aretino and Vasari brought lasting prestige to the city, yet it was an outsider – Piero della Francesca – who gave Arezzo its permanent Renaissance monument, the glorious fresco choir in the church of **San Francesco** (daily 8.30am–noon & 2.30–6.30pm; reservation necessary to see restored part of frescoes; ☎0575.355.668; L10,000). Located to the left of Corso Italia, which leads from the **lower town** to the more interesting **older quarter** at the top of the hill, the church was built in the early fourteenth century. A century later Piero della Francesca was commissioned to paint the choir with a cycle depicting *The Legend of the True Cross*, one of the most radiant creations of the period.

Further up the Corso, the twelfth-century **Pieve di Santa Maria** is one of the finest Romanesque structures in Tuscany, with some wonderful early thirteenth-century carvings of the months over the portal. The fourteenth-century campanile, known locally as "the tower of the hundred holes", has become the emblem of the town. On the other side of the church, the dramatically sloping Piazza Grande is bordered by the tiered facade of the **Palazzetto della Fraternità dei Laci**, with a Gothic ground floor and fifteenth-century upper storeys, and **Vasari's loggia**, occupied by shops that in some instances still have their original stone counters. At the highest point of the town, the large unfussy **Duomo** (daily 7am–12.30pm & 3–6.30pm), begun in the late thirteenth century, has stained-glass windows from around 1520, terracottas by the della Robbia family, and a tiny fresco of the *Magdalene* by Piero della Francesca. A short distance in the opposite direction from the duomo, the church of **San Domenico** (8am–1pm & 3.30–5.30pm) has a dolorous *Crucifix* by Cimabue. Signs point the way to the nearby **Casa di Giorgio Vasari** (Mon & Wed–Sat 9am–7pm, Sun 9am–12.30pm; free), designed by the celebrated biographer-architect-painter for himself and coated with his own lurid frescoes.

Practicalities

The **tourist office** is in front of the train station (summer Mon–Sat 9am–1pm & 3–7pm, Sun 9am–1pm; winter Mon–Sat 9am–1pm & 3–6.30pm, also first Sun of the month 9am–1pm). **Rooms** are hard to come by on the first weekend of every month (because of the massive antiques fair), and at the end of August and beginning of September. The most convenient affordable **hotel** is at *La Toscana*, Via M. Perennio 56 (☎0575.21.692; ③), on the main road coming in from the west. Alternatively try the centrally located, good-value *Astoria*, Via Guido Monaco 54 (☎0575.24.361; ③), or the *Cecco*, at Corso Italia 215 (☎0575.20.986; ④). Otherwise, there's a **youth hostel** occupying the Ostello Villa Severi, Via Redi 13, some way out of town (☎0575.299.047; ②; reception open 8am–2pm & 6pm–midnight); take bus #4 from the train station. For **restaurants**, *Da Guido*, Via Madonna del Prato 85, is a basic local trattoria, and for more pricey but high-quality Tuscan cuisine, try *La Buca di San Francesco*, by San Francesco church.

Siena

During the Middle Ages **SIENA** was one of the major cities of Europe. Virtually the size of Paris, it controlled most of southern Tuscany and its flourishing wool industry dominated the trade routes from France to Rome. The city developed a highly sophisticated civic life, with its own written constitution and a quasi-democratic government. Nowadays it's the perfect antidote to Florence. Self-contained and still rural in parts behind its medieval walls, its great attraction is its own cityscape – a majestic Gothic whole that could be enjoyed without venturing into a single museum. To get the most from it you'll need to stay, especially if you want to see its spectacular horse race, the *Palio* – though you'll definitely need to book during this time (July & Aug).

Arrival and accommodation

Arriving by **bus**, you are dropped along Via Curtatone, by the church of San Domenico; the **train station** is less convenient, 2km northeast, connected with Piazza Matteotti, at the top end of Via Curtatone, by shuttle bus. **Accommodation** is less of a struggle than in Florence, though it still pays to phone ahead. If you haven't, make your way either to the Cooperativa Hotels Promotion booth opposite San Domenico on Via Curtatone (Mon–Sat 9am–7/8pm; ☎0577.288.084), which can book you a room in a hotel or at one of three *residenze turistico*; or to the **tourist office** at Piazza del Campo 56 (summer Mon–Sat 8.30am–7.30pm, Sun 8.30am–2pm; winter Mon–Fri 8.30am–1.30pm & 3.30–7pm, Sat 8.30am–1.30pm), which provides an accommodation list including **private rooms** from L50,000 a double, and has good free maps. Otherwise, the *Tre Donzelle* (☎0577.280.358; ③), Via Donzelle 5, which has good clean rooms, and the small smart *Piccolo Hotel Etruria* at Via Donzelle 3 (☎0577.288.088; ④), right in the heart of town are good no-nonsense locandas. *La Perla*, Via delle Terme 25 (☎0577.47.144; ④), is a regular *pensione* in a very central location, just two blocks north of the Campo, and the *Bernini* (☎0577.289.047; ④), at Via della Sapienza 15, has stunning views to the duomo. The *Alma Domus*, Via di Camporegio 37 (☎0577.44.177; ④), is in a quiet spot, also with great views. Alternatively, you can try the official **youth hostel** at Via Fiorentina 89 (☎0577.522.12; ②), 2km northwest of the centre; take bus #10 or #15 from Piazza Gramsci or, if you're coming from Florence, ask the bus driver to let you off at "Lo Stellino". The nearest **campsite** is the well-maintained *Campeggio Siena Colleverde*, Strada di Scacciapensieri 47, 2km north (☎0577.280.044; mid-March to late-Nov); take bus #3 from Piazza Gramsci (last one at 11.45pm).

The City

The centre of Siena is almost entirely medieval in plan and appearance, and has been effectively pedestrianized since the 1960s. At its heart, the **Campo**, with its amphitheatre curve, is an almost organic piece of city planning, and is still the focus of city life. The **Palazzo Comunale**, with its 107-metre-tall bell tower, the **Torre del Mangia** (summer Mon–Sat 10am–6pm, Sun 9.30am–1.30pm; winter Mon–Sat 10am–4pm, Sun 9.30am–1.30pm; open till

11pm July & Aug; L7000), occupies virtually the entire south side, and although it's still in use as Siena's town hall, its principal rooms have been converted into a **Museo Civico** (L8000), a series of former public rooms, frescoed with themes integral to the secular life of the medieval city. Best of these are the Sala del Mappamondo, on the wall of which is the fabulous *Maestà* of Simone Martini, an acknowledged masterpiece of Sienese art, painted in 1315 and touched up (the site was damp) six years later, and the former Sale dei Nove, the "Room of the Nine", decorated with Lorenzetti's *Allegories of Good and Bad Government*, commissioned in 1377 to remind the councillors of their duties. Look, too, at the fine panel paintings by Lorenzetti's contemporaries, Guido da Siena and Matteo di Giovanni, in the adjacent Sala della Pace. At the top end of the Campo, the fifteenth-century **Loggia di Mercanzia**, built as a dealing room for merchants, marks the intersection of the city centre's principal streets. From here Via Banchi di Sotto leads up to the **Palazzo Piccolomini**, housing the **state archive** (Mon–Sat 9am–1pm; free), which displays the painted covers of the *Tavolette di Biccherna*, the city accounts.

Further south, following Via di Pantaneto then Via Roma, the church of **Santa Maria dei Servi** houses two contrasting frescoes of the *Massacre of the Innocents* – a Gothic version by Lorenzetti, in the second chapel behind the high altar, and a Renaissance treatment by Matteo di Giovanni in the fifth chapel on the right. On the other side of the Campo, **Via di Città** cuts across the oldest, cathedral quarter of the city, fronted by some of Siena's finest private palazzi. At the end of the street, Via San Pietro leads to the **Pinacoteca Nazionale** (summer Mon 8.30am–1.30pm, Tues–Sat 9am–7pm, Sun 8am–1pm; winter Tues–Sat 8.30am–1.30pm; guided visits only at 2.30, 4 & 5.30pm; L8000), a roll call of Sienese Gothic painting housed in a fourteenth-century palace, while in the opposite direction Via di Capitano leads up to the **Duomo** (daily: summer 9am–7.30pm; winter 7.30am–1pm & 2.30–5pm), completed to virtually its present size around 1215; plans to enlarge the church withered with Siena's medieval prosperity, and the vast skeleton of an unfinished extension still stands at the north end of the cathedral square. The Duomo is in any case a delight, its style an amazing conglomeration of Romanesque and Gothic, delineated by bands of black and white marble on its facade. This theme is continued in the sgraffito marble pavement, which begins with geometric patterns outside the church and takes off into a startling sequence of 56 panels within, completed between 1349 and 1547; virtually every artist who worked in the city tried his hand at a design. The finest are reckoned to be Beccafumi's *Moses Striking Water from a Rock* and *Sacrifice of Isaac*, just beyond the dome area. The rest of the interior is equally arresting: among its greatest treasures are Nicola Pisano's font with its high relief details of the *Life of Jesus* and *Last Judgment*, and a bronze Donatello statue of *St John the Baptist* in the north transept. Midway along the nave, the **Libreria Piccolomini** (daily: summer 9am–7.30pm; winter 10am–1pm & 2.30–5pm; L2000), signalled by Pinturicchio's brilliantly coloured fresco of the *Coronation of Pius II*, has further frescoes by Pinturicchio and his pupils (including Raphael).

Behind the cathedral, the **Baptistry** (daily: April–Sept 9am–7.30pm, Oct 9am–6pm, Nov–March 10am–1pm & 2.30–5pm; L3000) houses a Renaissance font with panels illustrating John the Baptist's life by della Quercia and Donatello. Visit also the **Museo dell'Opera del Duomo** (daily 9am–6.30pm; L10,000), which occupies part of the cathedral's planned extension and houses Pisano's original statues from the facade. Upstairs is a fine array of panels, including works by Simone Martini, Pietro Lorenzetti and Sano di Pietro, and the cathedral's original altarpiece, a haunting Byzantine icon known as the *Madonna dagli Occhi Grossi* (Madonna of the Big Eyes). The painting that repays a visit most, however, is the cathedral's second altarpiece, Duccio's *Maestà*, completed in 1311 and generally thought to be the climax of the Sienese style of painting. The church to the north of the cathedral is **San Domenico**, founded in 1125 and closely identified with Saint Catherine of Siena. Her chapel, on the south side of the church, has frescoes by Sodoma, and a reliquary containing her head.

Eating and drinking

Restaurants cost a bit over the odds in Siena, especially if you want to eat out in the Campo. If you just want a **snack,** there's pizza by weight at Via delle Terme 10, and an extravagant-

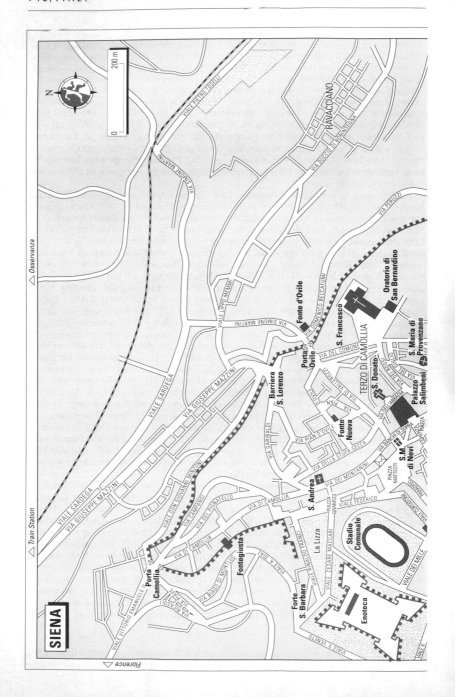

SIENA

200 m

N

△ Osservanza

△ Train Station

▽ Florence

VIALE PIETRO TOSELLI

RAVACCIANO

VIA BUCCIO DI RINASEGNA

VIA SIMONE MARTINI

VIA PERUZZI

VIA TIPPO MEMMI

VIALE SIMONE MARTINI

Fonte d'Ovile

VIA DOMENICO BECCAFUMI

Oratorio di
San Bernardino

S. Francesco

Porta
Ovile

VIA DEL COMUNE

TERZO DI CAMOLLIA

S. Maria di
Provenzano

S. Donato

Palazzo
Salimbeni

Barriera
S. Lorenzo

VIALE SARDEGNA

VIALE GIUSEPPE MAZZINI

VIA D'OVILE

VIA VAL DI MONTONE

VIA DEL OPERA

VIA GARIBALDI

VIA PIAN D'OVILE

Fonte
Nuova

VIA DEI BANCHI DI SOPRA

S.M.
di Nevi

VIA DELLA STUFA SECCA

PIAZZA
MATTEOTI

VIALE SARDEGNA

VIA GIUSEPPE MAZZINI

VIA DON GIOVANNI MINZONI

VIA CAMPANSI

VIA DEL PIGNATELLO

S. Andrea

VIA DI MONTANINI

PIAZZA
GRAMSCI

Viale Federico

VIA DI CAMOLLIA

La Lizza

VIALE MACCARI

Stadio
Comunale

VIA DI CAMOLLIA

VIALE RINALDO FRANCI

VIALE CESARE MACCARI

VIALE DEI MILLE

Fonteguista

VIA BIAGIO DI MONTLUC

Porta
Camollia

VIALE VITTORIO EMANUELE II

VIA RICASOLI

VIA STAT

Forte
S. Barbara

VIALE V. VENETO

Enoteca

VIALE V

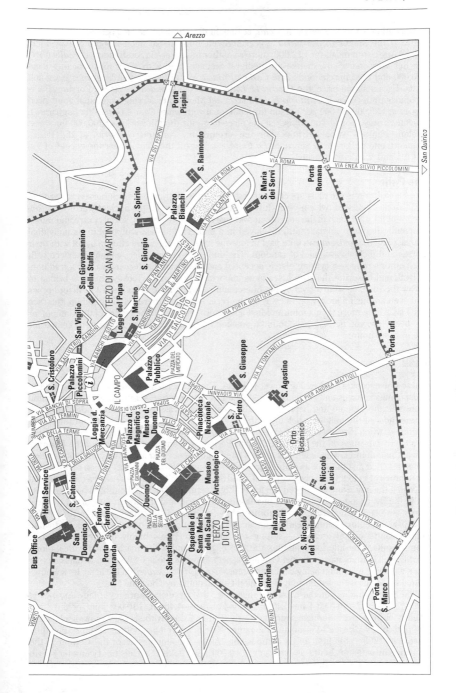

ly stocked deli, the *Pizzicheria Morbidi*, at Banchi di Sotto 27. The cheapest **sit-down** alternative is the *Mensa Universitaria*, Via Sant'Agata 1 (Mon–Sat noon–2.30pm & 6.30–9pm; closed Aug), with meals for L12,000; there's another mensa at Via San Bandini 47. *Gallo Nero*, Via del Porrione 65–67, dishes up medieval Sienese fare, with a set meal starting from L20,000 and the unpretentious café *Carlo e Franca*, Via di Pantaneto 138, serves pizza and pasta. Up a notch in price, the *Osteria Le Logge*, in an old *farmacia* in Via del Porrione 33, is a popular trattoria, as is *Trattoria Papei* Piazza del Mercato 6, serving traditional good-sized dishes at L25,000–30,000 per person for a full meal with wine. *Cane e Gatto*, Via Pagliaresi 6 (evenings only; closed Thurs), is just the place to go for the full works – L100,000 for seven sublime courses without drinks. For **ice cream**, try *Nannini Gelateria*, at the Piazza Matteotti end of Banchi di Sopra, or *La Costarella* just off the Campo near the corner of Via di Città and Via dei Pellegrini.

The Palio

The Siena **Palio** is the most spectacular festival event in Italy, a bareback horse race around the Campo contested twice a year (July 2 and Aug 16) between the ancient wards – or *contrade* – of the city. Each of the seventeen *contrade* has its own church, social centre and museum, and a heraldic animal motif, displayed in a modern fountain-sculpture in its individual piazza. Only ten *contrade* can take part in any one race, and these are chosen by lot with their horses and jockeys assigned at random. The only rule is that riders cannot interfere with each other's reins; everything else is accepted and practised. Each *contrada* has a traditional rival, and ensuring the rival loses is as important as winning. Jockeys may be bribed to throw the race, or whip a rival or his horse; and *contrade* have been known to drug horses and even ambush a jockey on his way to the race. Although there's a big build-up, the race itself lasts little more than a minute. Most spectators crowd into the centre of the Campo; for the best view, you need to have found a position on the inner rail by 2pm and to keep it for the next six hours.

Pisa

There's no escaping the Leaning Tower in **PISA**. The medieval bell tower is one of the world's most familiar images and yet its beauty still comes as a surprise, set in chessboard formation alongside the Duomo and baptistry on the manicured grass of the **Campo dei Miracoli** where most of the buildings belong to the city's "Golden Age" of the twelfth and thirteenth centuries, when Pisa, then still a port, was one of the great Mediterranean powers (admission to all four museums on the Campo L18,000). Perhaps the strangest thing about the **Leaning Tower**, begun in 1173, is that it has always tilted; subsidence disrupted the foundations when it had reached just three of its eight storeys. For the next 180 years a succession of architects were brought in to try and correct the tilt, until around 1350 Tomasso di Andrea da Pontedera accepted the angle and completed the tower. Eight centuries on, it is thought to be nearing its limit: the overhang is over 5m and increasing each year, and the tower, supported by steel wires, is closed to the public. The **Duomo** (Mon–Sat 10am–4.40/7.40pm, Sun 1–5.40/7.40pm; L3000) was begun a century earlier, its facade – with its delicate balance of black and white marble, and tiers of arcades – setting the model for Pisa's highly distinctive brand of Romanesque. The interior continues the use of black and white marble, and with its long arcades of columns has an almost Oriental aspect. Most of the art works are Renaissance or later, a notable exception being Cimabue's mosaic of *Christ in Majesty* in the apse. Its acknowledged highlight is the astonishingly detailed Gothic pulpit by Giovanni Pisano.

The third building of the Miracoli ensemble, the circular **Baptistry** (daily April–Sept 8am–7.40pm, March–Oct 9am–5.40pm, Nov–Feb 9am–4.40pm; L10,000 joint ticket), is a slightly bizarre mix of Romanesque and Gothic, embellished with statuary (now displayed in the museo) by Giovanni Pisano and his father Nicola, as well as another pulpit, sculpted by Nicola in 1260 – his first major commission. Along the north side of the Campo is the **Camposanto** (same hours as baptistry; L10,000 joint ticket), a cloistered cemetery built towards the end of the thirteenth century. Most of the cloister's frescoes were destroyed by

Allied incendiary bombs in World War II, but two masterpieces survived relatively unscathed – a fourteenth-century *Triumph of Death* and *Last Judgment* in the Cappella Ammanati, a ruthless catalogue of horrors painted around the time of the Black Death. It also has a number of sculptures and numerous Roman sarcophagi – Nicola Pisano's original sources of inspiration. At the southeast corner of the Campo, a vast array of pieces from the cathedral and baptistry are displayed in the **Museo dell'Opera del Duomo** (daily same hours as baptistry; L10,000 joint ticket), a huge collection which includes statuary by each of the Pisano family and examples of *intarsia*, the art of inlaid wood.

Away from the Campo dei Miracoli, Pisa takes on a very different character, as tourists give way to students at the still-thriving university. It's nonetheless a quiet place, eerily so at night, set about a series of erratic squares and arcaded streets, and with clusters of Romanesque churches and, along the banks of the Arno, a number of fine palazzi. The **Piazza dei Cavalieri** is an obvious first stop, a large square that was the centre of medieval Pisa, before being remodelled by Vasari as the headquarters of the Knights of St Stephen, whose palace, the curving **Palazzo dei Cavalieri**, topped with busts of the Medici, faces the order's church of **San Stefano**. A short walk east along the river, the **Museo Nazionale di San Matteo** (Tues–Sat 9am–7pm, Sun 9am–2pm; L8000), housed in a twelfth-century convent, displays fourteenth-century panels by the Maestro di San Torpè, a Simon Martini polyptych and a panel of *San Paolo* by Masaccio. Also in the museum are the antique armour and wooden shields used in the annual *Gioco del Ponte* pageant (see below).

Practicalities

Pisa's **train station** is south of the centre on Piazza della Stazione, a twenty-minute walk from the Campo dei Miracoli; or catch bus #3. From the **airport**, take the hourly Florence train. There are two **tourist offices**: one to the left of the station as you leave (Mon–Fri 8.30am–5.30/7pm, Sat & Sun 9am–5pm), and another in the northeast corner of the Campo dei Miracoli (Mon–Sat 8.30am–5.30/7pm, Sun 10.30–4.30pm, with maps and accommodation lists. The most attractive budget **hotels** are grouped around the Campo dei Miracoli, and the best of the lot is the elegant old *Albergo Gronchi* in Piazza Arcivescovado (☎050.561.823; ②). Others include the *Locanda Galileo*, Via Santa Maria (☎050.40.621; ③); the *Hotel Giardino*, behind a self-service restaurant on Via Cammeo (☎050.562.101; ③); and *Pensione Helvetia*, Via Don G. Boschi 31, off Piazza Arcivescovado (☎050.553.084; ③). You could also try the *Serena*, Via D. Cavalca 45 (☎050.580.809; ③); the *Rinascente*, Via del Castelleto 28 (☎050.580.460; ③); or one of a number of places in the station area, best of which is the *Albergo Milano*, Via Mascagni 14, off Piazza della Stazione (☎050.23.162; ③). A good **women-only** alternative, five minutes' walk from the station (first right), is the *Casa della Giovane*, Via Corridoni 31 (☎050.43.061; ③). The nearest **youth hostel**, Via Pietra Santina 15 (☎050.890.622; ②), is 2.5km from the centre past the cemetery. The city **campsite**, *Campeggio Torre Pendente*, is 1km west of the Campo dei Miracoli at Viale delle Cascine 86 (☎050.561.704; April–Oct) – a large, well-maintained site, with a restaurant and shop.

Restaurants in the environs of the Leaning Tower are not good value, but a few blocks south, around Piazza Cavalieri and Piazza Dante, are a number of reasonably priced places. One of the most popular is *Trattoria Stelio*, Piazza Dante 11, or there's a cheaper, unnamed pizzeria on the same square. Over to the west, *Pizzeria da Cassio*, Piazza Cavallotti 14, is a good *tavola calda*, and the university building on Via Martiri, off Piazza Cavalieri, houses a student **mensa** (mid-Sept to mid-July Mon–Fri noon–2.30pm & 7–9pm, Sat & Sun noon–2.30pm). The city's big traditional event is the **Gioco del Ponte**, held on the last Sunday in June, when teams from the north and south banks of the city stage a series of "battles", pushing a seven-tonne carriage over the Ponte di Mezzo. The event has taken place since Medici times and continues in Renaissance costume.

Lucca

LUCCA is as graceful a provincial capital as they come, set inside a thick swathe of Renaissance walls, and with a quiet, almost entirely medieval street plan. Palazzi and the odd tower dot the streets, at intervals overlooked by a brilliantly decorated Romanesque facade. It's not exactly undiscovered, but for once the number of tourists seems to fit.

The most enjoyable way to get your bearings is to follow the path around the top of the **Walls** – nearly 4km in extent and built with genuine defensive capability in the early sixteenth century, before being transformed to their present, garden aspect by the Bourbon ruler, Marie Louise. In the centre of town, just east of the main Piazza Napoleone on Piazza San Martino, the **Duomo of San Martino** (daily 7am–5/7pm) was in part sculpted by Nicola Pisano. The great hall-like interior includes paintings by Tintoretto, Ghirlandaio and Filippino Lippi. The most famous item, however, Jacopo della Quercia's **Tomb of Ilaria del Carretto** (summer daily 10am–6pm; winter Mon–Fri 10am–4.45pm, Sat 9.30am–6.45pm, Sun 9–10am & 3–5pm; L3000), has been restored so vigorously that one expert declared it had been ruined – prompting a libel action from the restorer. Lucca's finest sculptor was perhaps Matteo Civitali, whose *Tempietto* in the north aisle was sculpted to house the city's most famous and lucrative relic, the *Volto Santo* – said to be the "true effigy of Christ" and the focus for international pilgrimage.

Northwest of the Duomo across Via Fililungo, the facade of **San Michele in Foro** church (7.30am–12.30pm & 3–8pm) is a triumph of eccentricity, each of its loggia columns different, some twisted, others sculpted or candy-striped. The interior is relatively plain, though there's a good Andrea della Robbia terracotta and a painting by Filippino Lippi. Giacomo Puccini was born almost opposite at Via di Poggio 30, and his home, the **Casa di Puccini** (Jan–Feb Tues–Fri 10am–1pm, Sat & Sun 10am–1pm & 3–6pm; March–June & Oct–Dec Tues–Sun 10am–1pm & 3–6pm; July–Sept Tues–Sun 10am–6pm; L3000), is now a school of music with a small museum, featuring the Steinway piano on which he composed *Turandot*, along with original scores and photographs from premieres. At the end of the street in Via Galli Tassi is the seventeenth-century **Palazzo Mansi**, which houses a **Pinacoteca Nazionale** (Tues–Sat 9am–7pm, Sun 9am–2pm; L8000), an indifferent collection of pictures, although the Rococo palace itself is a sight, at its most extreme in a spectacularly gilded bridal suite.

Northeast of here, the basilica of **San Frediano** (Mon–Sat 7.30am–12.30pm & 3–8pm, Sun 9am–1pm & 3–6pm) has a facade with a brilliant thirteenth-century **mosaic** of *Christ in Majesty* and fine treasures inside, most enjoyable of which is the font carved with Romanesque scenes of Moses, the Good Shepherd and Apostles; set behind it is a ceramic *Annunciation* by Andrea della Robbia.

Be sure to visit the remarkable **Piazza Anfiteatro**, a circuit of medieval buildings whose foundations are the arches of the Roman amphitheatre. Just southeast, the strangest sight in Lucca is perhaps the **Casa-Torre Guinigi** (March–Sept daily 9am–7.30pm; Oct 10am–6pm; Nov–Feb 10am–4.30pm; L4500), the fifteenth-century home of Lucca's leading family, with a battlemented tower surmounted by holm oaks whose roots have grown into the room below. Much of it is being restored, but from Via San Andrea you can climb it for one of the best views over the city. Across the narrow canal on Via della Quarquonia, the fifteenth-century **Villa Guinigi** is now the home of Lucca's major museum of art and sculpture, the **Museo Nazionale Guinini** (Tues–Sat 9am–7pm; Sun 9am–2pm; L4000), with a good deal of lively Romanesque sculpture from the city and some good work by the cathedral's maestro, Matteo Civitali.

Practicalities

The **train station** is just outside the city walls to the south, an easy walk or short bus ride to the centre. The **tourist office** is on the north side of Piazza Verdi (daily: summer 9am–7pm; winter 9.30am–4.30pm), a swish affair with plenty of information. Finding **accommodation** is a problem at almost any time of year, but of the **hotels**, the *Melecchi* at Via Romana 37 (☎0583.950.234; ③), *Stipino* at Via Romana 95 (☎0583.495.077; ③), and *Diana* at Via del Molinetto 11 (☎0583.492.202; ④), are all good. After these the best bet is the *Moderno*, in the centre at Via Civitali 38 (☎0583.558.40; ④). There's a **youth hostel** with **campsite** at Via del Brennero 673 (☎0583.341.811; ②), 3km north of the centre. For **food**, try the *Trattoria da Guido*, Via C. Battisti 28, the cheapest place in town, or *Trattoria da Leo*, Via Tegrimi 1. *Trattoria da Giulio*, Via delle Conce 47, is also good and very popular, as is *Ristorante* *all'Olivo*, Piazza S. Quirico 1. For excellent pizza, with good beer, try the *Gli Orti di Via Elisa*, Via Elisa 17; *Le Salette*, Piazza S. Maria 15, is another good pizzeria – a big friendly place with tables outside.

Perugia

The provincial capital, **PERUGIA** is the most obvious base to kick off a tour of Umbria. It's an oddly mixed town, with a medieval centre and not a little industry: Buitoni, the pasta people, are based here, and it's also where Italy's best chocolate, Perugini, is made. It can get very busy in summer, but there's a day's worth of good sightseeing to be done and the presence of the Italian University for Foreigners, set up by Mussolini to improve the image of Italy abroad, lends a dash of cosmopolitan style.

Perugia hinges on a single street, **Corso Vannucci**, a broad pedestrian thoroughfare constantly buzzing with action. At the far end, the austere **Piazza Quattro Novembre** is backed by the plain-faced **Duomo** (8am–noon & 4pm–sunset), recently reopened after damage caused by the 1983 earthquake, although the interior, home to the so-called Virgin's "wedding ring", an unwieldy one-inch-diameter piece of agate that changes colour according to the character of the person wearing it, isn't especially interesting. The Perugians keep the ring locked up in fifteen boxes fitted into one another like Russian dolls, each opened with a key held by a different person; it's brought out for public viewing every July 30. The centrepiece of the piazza is the **Fontana Maggiore**, sculpted by the father-and-son team Nicola and Giovanni Pisano and describing episodes from the Old Testament, classical myth, Aesop's fables and the twelve months of the year. Opposite rises the gaunt mass of the **Palazzo dei Priori**, worth a glance inside for its frescoed **Sala dei Notari** (Tues–Sun 9am–1pm & 3–7pm; free). A few doors down at Corso Vannucci 25 is the **Collegio di Cambio** (summer Tues–Sat 9am–12.30pm & 2.30–5.30pm; winter Tues–Sat 8am–2pm, Sun 9am–12.30pm; L5000), the town's medieval money-exchange, frescoed by Perugino. The palace also houses the **Galleria Nazionale di Umbria** (Mon–Sat 9am–7pm, Sun 9am–1pm, closed first Mon of each month; L8000), one of central Italy's best galleries – a twelve-room romp through the history of Umbrian painting, with work by Perugino and Pinturrichio along with one or two stunning Tuscan masterpieces (Fra Angelico, Piero della Francesca) and early Sienese works (Duccio).

The best streets to wander around to get a feel of the old city are either side of the Duomo. **Via dei Priori** is the most characteristic, leading down to Agostino di Duccio's colourful **Oratorio di San Bernardino**, whose richly embellished facade is by far the best piece of sculpture in the city. From here you can wander through the northern part of the centre, along Via A. Pascoli, to the **Arco di Augusto**, whose lowest section is now one of the few remaining monuments of Etruscan Perugia. The upper remnant was added by the Romans when they captured the city in 40 BC. On the other side of town, along **Corso Cavour**, is the large church of **San Domenico**, one of whose chapels holds a superb carved arch by Agostino di Duccio, and, to the right of the altar, the tomb of Pope Benedict XI, an elegant piece by one of the period's three leading sculptors: Pisano, Lorenzo Maitini or Arnolfo di Cambio – no one knows which. There are also some impressive stained-glass windows, the second biggest in Italy after those in Milan Cathedral. In the church's cloisters, the **Museo Archeologico Nazionale dell'Umbria** (Mon–Sat 9am–7pm, Sun 9am–1pm; L4000) has one of the most extensive Etruscan collections around. Further on down the Corso Cavour, advertised by a rocket-shaped bell tower, the tenth-century basilica of **San Pietro** is the most idiosyncratic of all the town's churches. Its choir has been called the best in Italy, and there is a host of works by Perugino and others.

Practicalities

Arriving by **train**, you'll find yourself well away from the centre of Perugia on Piazza V. Veneto; buses #6, #7 and #11 run to Piazza Italia (15min journey) and you'd do well to take one rather than attempt the long walk.

The **tourist office** is on Piazza IV Novembre 3 (Mon–Sat 8.30am–1.30pm & 3.30–6.30pm, Sun 9am–1pm). There's a youth **hostel** two minutes from the Duomo at Via Bontempi 13

(☎075.572.2880; ②), with dorm beds and a midnight curfew. As for **hotels**, try *Rosalba* at Via del Circo 7 (☎075.572.0626; ④); *Etruria*, just off the Corso at Via della Luna 21 (☎075.572.3730; ③); or *Anna*, centrally placed at Via dei Priori 48 (☎075.573.6304; ③). On the **food** front, *Osteria del Gambero*, Via Baldeschi 17, has healthy Umbrian specialities, and *Lo Scalino*, Via S. Ercolano 2, and *La Botte*, Via Volte della Pace 33, are decent pizzerias, the latter with a tourist menu at L15,000. On Via dei Priori, *Papaia* is a good bar with plenty of seating and decent *panini*. The reasonably priced *Dal mì Cocco*, Corso Garibaldi 12, with a student clientele, offers traditional cuisine near the university. *Café del Cambio* at Corso Vannucci 29 is one of the trendiest **bars** in the centre, and does snacks and light meals at lunchtime. For **evening** entertainment, *Zooropa* at Pozzo Etruria, off Via Bontempi, has live music on selected nights, as does *Bratislava* at Via Fiorenzuola 12, near Corso Cavour.

Gubbio

GUBBIO is the most thoroughly medieval of the Umbrian towns, an immediately likeable place that's hanging onto its charm despite an ever-increasing influx of tourists. The first high peaks of the Apennines rising behind give the place the feel of a mountain outpost – something it's always been, in fact. The best (and most scenic) approach is by frequent bus from Perugia, or by train from Foligno to Fossato di Vico, 19km away but with an hourly connecting bus.

Centre-stage on the windswept Piazza della Signoria is the immense fourteenth-century **Palazzo dei Consoli** (daily: summer 10am–1pm & 3–6pm; winter 10am–1pm & 2–5pm), whose crenellated outline and campanile command your attention for miles around. Council officials and leading citizens met to discuss business here in the cavernous Salone dell'Arengo, from which the word "harangue" is derived. The building also holds the **Museo Civico** (same times; L7000), unremarkable except for the famous Eugubine Tablets, Umbria's most important archeological find and the only extant record of the ancient Umbrian language. Admission to the museum also gets you into the three-roomed **Pinacoteca** upstairs, worth a look for works by the Gubbian School, notably Ottaviano Nelli, who painted seventeen frescoes on the life of the Virgin in the church of **San Francesco** on Piazza dei Quaranta Martiri. There's also an unusually lovely *Madonna del Belvedere* by him in the church of **Santa Maria Nuova**, off Corso Garibaldi. On the hillside above the town, the **Basilica of Sant'Ubaldo** is the place Gubbians drive to on Sunday mornings, a pleasant spot with a handy bar and great views, connected with the town's Porta Romana by a slightly scary **funicular** (L6000). There's not much to see in the basilica itself, except the body of the town's patron saint, Ubaldo, who's missing three fingers, hacked off by his manservant as a religious keepsake. You can't miss the big wooden pillars (*ceri*), though, featured in Gubbio's annual *Corsa dei Ceri* (May 15), a race to the basilica from the town that's second only to Siena's Palio in terms of exuberance.

You shouldn't have any problem **staying** in Gubbio, though the place does get busy. The **tourist office**, Piazza Oderisi 6 (Mon–Sat 8.30am–1.30pm & 3–6pm, Sun 9am–12.30pm), may be able to help; or try the *Locanda Galletti*, Via Piccardi 3 (☎075.927.7753; ③), or the *Grotta dell'Angelo*, Via Gioia 47 (☎075.927.1747; ③), which has an excellent restaurant. There's a good selection of **eateries**, including an excellent cheap pizzeria, *Il Bargello*, Via dei Consoli 37, and if you want to be outdoors, the *Trattoria San Martino* at Via dei Consoli 8. Failing that, you could try the classier *Taverna del Lupo*, Via Baldassini 60. There are two **campsites** for Gubbio, both in Loc. Ottoguidone – *Villa Ortoguidone* (☎075.927.2037) and *Città di Gùbbio* (☎075.927.2037), both open April–Sept.

Assisi

Thanks to Saint Francis, Italy's premier saint and founder of the Franciscan order, **ASSISI** is Umbria's best-known town, and suffers as a result, crammed with people for ten months of the year. It quietens down in the evening, and does retain some medieval hill-town charm, but you may not want to hang around once you've seen all there is to see. An earthquake in

September 1997 caused extensive damage to parts of the town, most notably to the Basilica di San Francesco. Restoration is due for completion for 2000.

The **Basilica di San Francesco** (daily 7am–7pm, except Sun morning), at the end of Via San Francesco, is justly famed as Umbria's single greatest glory, and one of the most overwhelming collections of art outside a gallery anywhere in the world. Begun in 1228, two years after the saint's death, it was financed by donations that flooded in from all over Europe. The sombre **Lower Church** is the earlier of the two churches that make up the basilica, its complicated floor plan and claustrophobic vaults intended to create a mood of meditative introspection – an effect added to by brown-robed monks, strict rules on silence and no photography. Francis lies under the floor in a crypt only brought to light in 1818. Frescoes cover almost every available space, and span a century of continuous artistic development, from the anonymous early works above the altar, through Cimabue's over-restored *Madonna, Child and Angels with St Francis* in the right transept to work by the Sienese School painters, Simone Martini and Pietro Lorenzetti. Martini's frescoes are in the Cappella di San Martino, the first chapel on the left as you enter the nave, while Lorenzetti's works, dominated by a powerful *Crucifixion*, are in the transept and small chapel to the left of the main altar. The **Upper Church**, built to a light and airy Gothic plan, is richly decorated, too, with Giotto's dazzling frescoes on the life of St Francis. The **treasury** contains a rich collection of paintings, reliquaries and religious clutter.

There's not a great deal worth seeing in Assisi's small centre – only a nondescript **Museo Civico** in the central Piazza del Comune (daily 10am–1pm & 3–5/7pm; L4000), housed in the crypt of the now defunct church of San Nicolo, whose collection includes Etruscan fragments and the so-called **Tempio di Minerva**, six columns and a pediment from a Roman temple of the first century. A short trek up the steep Via di San Rufino from here, the thirteenth-century **Duomo** has the font used to baptize St Francis and St Clare, and close by is the **Basilica di Santa Chiara**, burial place of St Francis's devoted early companion. Consecrated in 1265, the church is a virtual facsimile of the basilica up the road, and is home to the macabrely blackened body of Clare herself and a Byzantine crucifix famous for having bowed to Francis and commanded him to embark on his sacred mission.

Practicalities

The **train station** is 5km south of Assisi, connected to the centre by half-hourly buses. The **tourist office** is at Piazza del Comune 12 (Mon–Fri 8am–2pm & 3.30–6.30pm, Sat 9am–1pm & 3.30–6.30pm, Sun 9am–1pm) and has accommodation lists, including details of **private rooms**. There are plenty of cheap places to **stay** but they can get full. The functional *Italia*, off the central Piazza del Comune at Vicolo della Fortezza 2 (☎075.812.625; ③; March–Nov), is about the cheapest option; *La Rocca*, Via Porta Perlici 27 (☎075.812.284; ③), is also a fair option, as is the *Anfiteatro Romano*, close by at Via Anfiteatro Romano 4 (☎075.813.025; ③). There are also **pilgrim hostels** (*Case Religiose di Ospitalità*) all over town, charging L20,000–40,000 depending on the type of accommodation; the *Suore del Giglio*, Via San Francesco 13 (☎075.812.267; ③), is perhaps the best as far as location goes. There's a big **campsite** and **youth hostel** at Fontemaggio (☎075.813.636; ②), 3km out on the road to the monastery of Eremo di Carceri. For **food**, try the reasonably-priced *Spadini* on Via Sant'Agnese near Santa Chiara; *Pallotta*, Via San Rufino 4, which is reasonable and friendly; or the excellent *I Monaci*, off Via Fontebella at Via A Fortini 10. The *La Rocca* hotel (see above) has a good no-frills restaurant, and *Buca di San Francesco*, Via Brizi 1, is busy but expensive.

Spoleto

SPOLETO is Umbria's most compelling town, remarkable for its extremely pretty position and several of Italy's most ancient Romanesque churches. For several centuries it was among the most influential of Italian towns, the former capital of one of the Lombards' three Italian dukedoms, which at one time stretched as far as Rome. Barbarossa flattened the city in 1155, and in 1499 the nineteen-year-old Lucrezia Borgia was appointed governess by her father, Pope Alexander VI.

Spoleto's lower town, where you arrive, was badly damaged by World War II bombing, and doesn't hold much of interest, so it's best to take a bus straight to the upper town. There's no single, central piazza, but the place to head for is **Piazza Libertà**, site of a much-restored first-century **Roman Theatre**, visible at all times, but also visitable more closely in conjunction with the **Museo Archeologico** (Mon–Sat 9am–7pm, Sun 9am–1pm & 3–7pm; L4000). The adjoining Piazza della Fontana has more Roman remains, best of which is the **Arco di Druso**, built to honour the minor campaign victories of Drusus, son of Tiberius. The homely **Piazza del Mercato**, beyond, is a fine opportunity to take in some streetlife, and from there it's a short walk to the **Duomo** (daily 8am–1pm and 3–5.30/6.30pm), whose facade of restrained elegance is one of the most memorable in the region. Inside, various Baroque embellishments are eclipsed by the superlative apse fres-coes of the fifteenth-century Florentine artist Fra Lippo Lippi, dominated by his final mas-terpiece, a *Coronation of the Virgin*. He died shortly after their completion (amid rumours that he was poisoned for seducing the daughter of a local noble family) and was interred here in a tomb designed by his son, Filippino. You should also take the short walk out to the **Ponte delle Torri**, a picture-postcard favourite, and an astonishing piece of medieval engineering, best seen as part of a circular walk around the base of the **Rocca** – everyone's idea of a cartoon castle, with towers, crenellations and sheer walls; it served until recently as a high-security prison, home to Pope John Paul II's would-be assassin and leading mem-bers of the Red Brigades. The church of **San Pietro**, 1km or so beyond the bridge on a hill-side, is also worth the walk for the splendid sculptures on its facade, among the best Romanesque carvings in Umbria.

Spoleto's **train station** is around 1km north of the town centre and the central Piazza Libertà, where you'll find the **tourist office** (Mon–Fri 9am–1pm & 4–7pm, Sat & Sun 10am–1pm & 4–7pm). If you're planning on **staying** in town, there's the central and reason-ably priced *Pensione dell'Angelo*, Via Arco del Druso 25 (☎0743.222.385; ④). If that's full, then the only other vaguely affordable place in the upper town is the *Pensione Aurora*, off Piazza Libertà at Via dell'Apollinare 4 (☎0743.220.315; ④). The lower town is very much a second choice, but there are more likely to be rooms available; try the *Anfiteatro*, Via dell'Anfiteatro 14 (☎0743.49.853; ③). The closest **campsite** is the small *Camping Monteluco*, behind San Pietro (☎0743.220.358; April–Sept); tiny but very pleasant. For **food**, the best basic trattoria, always full of locals, is the *Trattoria del Festival* at Via Brignone 8, as well as *Il Panciolle*, Via del Duomo 3–4, which has a wonderful terrace. *Pecchiarda*, in Vicolo S. Giovanni off Via delle Postierno in the lower town has a pleasant enclosed garden, but if you want something more special, go to *Pentagramma*, off Piazza Libertà at Via T. Martani 4.

In June and July Spoleto plays host to the country's leading international arts festival, the **Festival dei Due Mondi**. The jet-set audiences – and ticket prices to match – can be off-putting, but there's also an Edinburgh-type fringe with lots of film, jazz, buskers and so on. **Tickets and information** are available from the festival's information office at Via del Duomo 8 (☎0743.45.028).

Orvieto

Out on a limb from the rest of Umbria, **ORVIETO** is flooded wth tourists in summer, most of whom are drawn by its **Duomo** (daily 7.30am–12.45pm & 2.30–5.15/7.15pm, one of the greatest Gothic buildings in Italy, built, according to tradition, to celebrate the so-called Miracle of Bolsena (1263), in which a doubting priest celebrating Mass in a church on the nearby Lago di Bolsena noticed real blood dripping from the Host onto the altarcloth. The stained linen was whisked off to Pope Urban IV, who was in Orvieto to escape the heat and political hassle of Rome, and the building was constructed over the ensuing three centuries, in a surprisingly unified example of the Romanesque-Gothic style. The star turn is the facade, a riot of columns, spires, bas-reliefs, sculptures and dazzling colour, just about held together by four enormous fluted columns, the work of the master mason Lorenzo Maitini and his pupils, describing episodes from the Old and New Testaments in staggering detail.

Inside, the church is surprisingly plain by comparison, mainly distinguished by the **Cappella di San Brizo** (Mon–Sat 7.30am–12.45pm & 2.30–5.15/7.15pm, Sun 2.30–5.45/6.45pm; L3000; tickets from the tourist office), which holds Luca Signorelli's fresco of the *Last Judgment*, a realistic yet grotesque work, full of beautifully observed muscular figures which greatly influenced Michelangelo's celebrated cycle in the Vatican's Sistine Chapel. Signorelli, suitably clad in black, includes himself with Fra Angelico in the lower left-hand corner of *The Sermon of the Antichrist*, both calmly looking on as someone is garrotted at their feet. The twin Cappella del Corporale contains the sacred *corporale* (altar cloth) itself, locked away in a massive, jewel-encrusted casket (an accurate facsimile of the facade), and some appealing frescoes by local fourteenth-century painter Ugolino di Prete, describing the events of the miracle.

Next to the duomo, the **Museo dell'Opera del Duomo** (closed for restoration at time of writing) has paintings by Martini, several important thirteenth-century sculptures by Arnolfo di Cambio and Andrea Pisano, and a lovely font filled with Escher-like carved fishes. Opposite, the **Museo Greco** (summer daily 10.30am–1pm & 3–7pm; winter 10.30am–1pm & 2–6pm; L5000) features a fairly predictable collection of vases and assorted fragments excavated from local tombs. Moving north up Via del Duomo, you come to **Corso Cavour**, the town's pedestrianized main drag, at the far end of which, across Piazza Cahen, is **Il Pozzo di San Patrizio** (summer daily 9.30am–6.45pm; winter 10am–5.45pm; L6000), the novelty act of the town, a huge cylindrical well, commissioned in 1527 by Pope Clement VII to guarantee the town's water supply during an expected siege by the imperial army. It's a dank but striking piece of engineering, 62m deep, named after its alleged similarity to the Irish cave where St Patrick died in 493, supposedly aged 133 – though, apart from a small Etruscan tomb halfway down, it's really just an impressive hole in the ground.

Practicalities

Bus #1 makes a regular trip from the distant **train station** to Piazza XXIX Marzo, a short way north of the Duomo. An alternative is the funicular up to Piazza Cahen, from where minibuses wind through the twisting streets to Piazza del Duomo. The **tourist office** at Piazza del Duomo 24 (Mon–Fri 8.15am–1.50pm & 4–7pm, Sat 10am–1pm & 4–7pm, Sun 10am–noon & 4–6pm) has plenty of information and an accommodation service. Of **hotels**, the *Duomo*, Via Maurizio 7 (☎0763.341.887; ③), is a good central option, as is the pleasant *Posta*, Via Luca Signorelli 18 (☎0763.341.909; ③). Slightly pricier, the *Corso*, Corso Cavour 343 (☎0763.342.020; ⑤), is the best hotel near Piazza Cahen. The nearest **campsite** is the *Orvieto*, 10km away on Lago di Corbara (take the bus to Baschi/Civitella). There's a group of cheap **restaurants** at the bottom of Corso Cavour, though the best-value eating is close to the Duomo *Al Francesco*, Via B. Cerretti 10, a canteen affair run by the CRAMST co-operative offering a choice between a restaurant and self-service trattoria. The *Grotta*, Via Signorelli 5, off Via del Duomo, is a standard, friendly trattoria, and the *Antico Bucchero*, Via de' Cartari 4, is a popular restaurant with reasonable prices. The *Bottega del Buon Vino*, Via della Cave 26, is a wine bar that's good for staples and has a few outside tables.

Urbino

For the second half of the fifteenth century, **URBINO** was one of the most prestigious courts in Europe, ruled by the remarkable Federico da Montefeltro, who employed a number of the greatest artists and architects of the time to build and decorate his palace in the town. At one time it was reckoned the most beautiful in all Italy, and it does seem from contemporary accounts that fifteenth-century Urbino was an extraordinarily civilized place, a measured and urbane society in which life was lived without indulgence.

In the centre of Urbino, the **Palazzo Ducale** is a fitting monument to Federico, home now to the **Galleria Nazionale delle Marche** (daily 9am–2pm, Sun 9am–1pm; L8000), although it's the building itself that makes the biggest impression. Among the paintings in the

Appartamento del Duca are Piero della Francesca's strange *Flagellation*, and the *Ideal City*, a famous perspective painting of a symmetrical and deserted cityscape long attributed to Piero but now thought to be by one of his followers. There's also Paolo Uccello's last work, the six-panelled *Profanation of the Host*, and, in the same room, a portrait of Federico da Montefeltro by the Spanish artist Pedro Berruguete. The most interesting and best preserved of the palazzo's rooms is Federico's Studiolo, a triumph of illusory perspective created by *intarsia*. Shelves appear to protrude from the walls, cupboard doors seem to swing open to reveal lines of books, a letter lies in an apparently half-open drawer. Even more remarkable are the deli-cately hued landscapes of Urbino as it might appear from one of the surrounding hills, and the life-like squirrel perching next to a bowl of fruit.

Urbino is a lively university town, and its bustling streets – a pleasant jumble of Renaissance and medieval houses – can be a welcome antidote to the rarefied atmosphere of the Palazzo Ducale. You can wind down in one of the many bars and trattorias, or take a pic-nic up to the gardens within the **Fortezza Albornoz**, from where you'll get great views of the town and the countryside out to **San Bernardino**, a fine Renaissance church 2km away that is the resting place of the Montefeltros.

Urbino is notoriously difficult to reach – the best approach is by bus from Pésaro, about 30km away on the coast (the last one leaves at around 8pm). Buses stop in Borgo Mercatale, at the foot of the Palazzo Ducale, which is reached either by lift or by Francesco di Giorgio Martini's recently restored spiral staircase. For **accommodation**, the cheapest options are **private rooms**, most of which are on Via Budassi – details from the **tourist office** on Piazza Rinascimento (summer Mon–Fri 9am–6pm, Sat 9am–1pm & 3–6pm, Sun 9am–1pm; winter Tues–Sat 9am–7pm, Sun & Mon 9am–2pm). The most convenient **hotels** are the *Italia*, Corso Garibaldi 32 (☎0722.2701; ③), and the *San Giovanni*, Via Barocci 13 (☎0722.2827; ③). The best deals for **food** are at the university mensa on Piazza San Filippo, or the *Self-Service Franco* on Via del Poggio. If your budget's not too tight, *Il Girarrosto*, off Via Raffaello on Piazza San Francesco, serves good traditional food.

Ancona

ANCONA is a depressing place, severely damaged by war and earthquakes, with a modern centre of bland broad avenues and palm-shaded piazzas. However, it's the mid-Adriatic's largest port, with regular ferries to Greece, and you may well pass through. Regular buses run along the seafront from the train station to the port, so it's easy enough to miss the place altogether, but if you are hanging around between connections there are a couple of things to see. The port itself is headed by a well-preserved Roman arch, the **Arco di Traiano**, raised in honour of Emperor Trajan, under whose rule Ancona first became a major port. Behind it is the **Arco Clementino**, a piece of architectural self-congratulation by Pope Clement XII, who made Ancona a free port in the eighteenth century, and thus considered himself Trajan's equal. On Via Pizzecolli is the town's **art gallery** (Tues–Sat 9am–7pm, Sun 3–7pm, Mon 9am–1pm; L5000), highlights of which are Titian's *Apparition of the Virgin*, a glorious *Sacra Conversazione* by Lotto and an exquisite *Madonna and Child* by Crivelli. Further up the hill is the **Museo Nazionale delle Marche** (daily 8.30am–1.30pm; L4000), worth a visit for its frescoed ceilings by Tibaldi and a magnificent first-century gilded bronze sculpture of two Roman emperors on horseback.

Tickets for **ferries to Greece** are on sale at the Stazione Maríttima, as well as at the numerous agencies that line the road to the port. Most operators run services to Igoumenitsa, Corfu and Patras; Marlines also go to Crete and Turkey. In peak season ferries tend to run at least daily; two to four times a week at other times of the year. As most ferry departures are at night, you're unlikely to need to stay over in Ancona. However, if you do, the most convenient **hotels** are opposite the train station – the *Dorico* (☎071.42.761; ③) and *Fiore* (☎071.43.390; ③). **Bars** and **pizzerias** are plentiful along the port, or *Osteria del Pozzo*, in the old town on Via Bonda, and *Trattoria Vittoria* at Via Calatafini 2, off Piazza Cavour, are both quite reasonable.

ROME

Of all Italy's historic cities, it's **ROME** which exerts the most compelling fascination. There's arguably more to see here than in any other city in the world, with the relics of more than two thousand years of continuous occupation packed into its sprawling urban area; and as a contemporary European capital, it has a feel which is quite unique. Rome is, in many ways, the ideal capital of Italy, perfectly placed between Italy's warring north and south factions and heartily despised by both. For the traveller, it is the sheer weight of history in the city that is most evident, its various eras crowding in on each other to an almost breathtaking degree. There are the classical features – the Colosseum, the rubbly Forum and Palatine Hill – and relics from the early Christian period in ancient basilicas, while the fountains and churches of the Baroque period go a long way to determining the look of the city centre. But these are just part of the picture, which is an almost continuous one right up to the present day, taking in Romanesque churches, Renaissance palazzi, Rococo fountains and the ponderous buildings of post-unification, often all found within a few paces of each other.

Rome is not an easy place to absorb on one visit, and you need to approach things slowly, taking care not to try and see too much too quickly, even if you only have a few days here. On foot it's easy to lose a sense of direction in the twisting old streets, and in any case you're so likely to see something interesting that detours and stop-offs are inevitable. Stout, comfortable shoes and loose, cool clothes – Rome can get very sticky in summer – will be your greatest assets.

One other thing to be aware of is that the year 2000 is a **Giubileo** year in the Catholic Church. Inaugurated by Pope Boniface VIII in 1300, such a year only occurs once in every twenty-five, and gives an opportunity for making a pilgrimage as a physical act of penance in order to gain an indulgence (a sort of extra plea for God's mercy). The focus is on St Peter's in Rome where on 24 December 1999 the Pope, as the first pilgrim, will walk through the special Holy Door, which remains open until 6 January 2001, when it will be blocked up for the next twenty-four years. As a consequence Rome will be extremely full during this time, so make sure you book your accommodation as far in advance as possible.

Arrival and information

Travelling by train, you arrive at the central **Stazione Termini**, meeting-point of the metro lines and city bus routes. Rome has two **airports**: Leonardo da Vinci, better known as Fiumicino, which handles all scheduled flights, and Ciampino, where charter flights land. Two train services link **Fiumicino** to Rome: one leaves every hour and arrives at Termini (L15,000), the other leaves every twenty minutes and links Fiumicino with Trastevere, Ostiense and Tiburtina stations. At night (1.15–5am) you can catch a bus to Piazzale Stazione Tiburtina (L7000); nightbus #42 connects Tiburtina with Termini. A taxi will cost at least L70,000. From **Ciampino**, take a Cotral bus to Anagnina on metro line A (L1500), from where it's a twenty-minute ride to Termini. Taxis cost around L50,000.

There are **tourist information booths** at Fiumicino airport (Mon–Sat 8am–7pm) and at Termini (daily 8am–9pm), though heavy queues mean you're usually better off heading straight for the **main office** at Via Parigi 5 (Mon–Fri 8.15am–7pm, Sat 8.15am–1.45pm; ☎06.488.991). They can help with accommodation, give out free maps, general information, and the *Musei e Monumenti* pamphlet which gives a listing of visitable sites. There are also information kiosks dotted around the city, open from 9am–6pm. The privately run and more helpful Enjoy Rome tourist information service by the station at Via Varese 39 (Mon–Fri 8.30am–1pm & 3.30–6pm, Sat 8.30am–1pm; ☎06.445.1843) has a free hotel booking scheme, publishes a handy free guide, and runs bus, bike and walking tours which take in the essential sights of Rome.

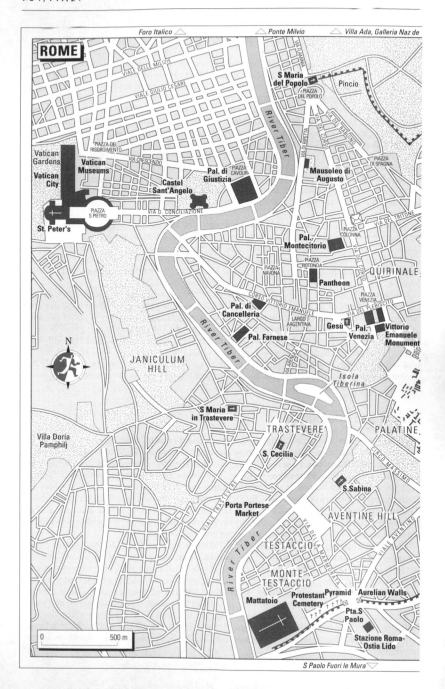

ROME

VIALE DELLE MILIZIE

VIALE GIULIO CESARE

S Maria del Popolo

PIAZZA DEL POPOLO

Pincio

River Tiber

VIA FLAMINIA

PIAZZA DEL RISORGIMENTO

VIA CRESCENZIO

VIA DI RIPETTA

VIA DEL CORSO

PIAZZA DI SPAGNA

Vatican Gardens

Vatican Museums

Vatican City

Pal. di Giustizia

PIAZZA CAVOUR

Castel Sant'Angelo

Mausoleo di Augusto

PIAZZA S PIETRO

St. Peter's

VIA D. CONCILIAZIONE

VIA DEL TRITONE

PIAZZA COLONNA

Pal. Montecitorio

PIAZZA ROTONDA

QUIRINALE

PIAZZA NAVONA

Pantheon

PIAZZA VENEZIA

CORSO VITTORIO EMANUELE

River Tiber

Pal. di Cancelleria

LARGO ARGENTINA

Gesù

VIA DEL PLEBISCITO

Vittorio Emanuele Monument

Pal. Farnese

Pal. Venezia

Isola Tiberina

N

JANICULUM HILL

PALATINE

Villa Doria Pamphilj

S Maria in Trastevere

TRASTEVERE

S. Cecilia

CIRCO MASSIMO

VIALE DI TRASTEVERE

S.Sabina

Porta Portese Market

AVENTINE HILL

VIALE AVENTINO

River Tiber

TESTACCIO

VIA DELLA MARMORATA

MONTE TESTACCIO

Mattatoio

Protestant Cemetery

Pyramid

Aurelian Walls

Pta.S Paolo

0   500 m

Stazione Roma-Ostia Lido

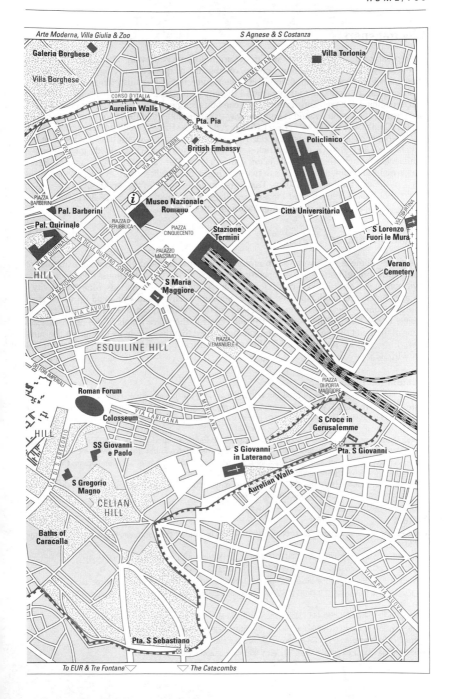

Arte Moderna, Villa Giulia & Zoo   S Agnese & S Costanza

Galeria Borghese
Villa Borghese
Villa Torlonia

CORSO D'ITALIA

VIA NOMENTANA

Aurelian Walls

Pta. Pia

Policlinico

British Embassy

VIA XX SETTEMBRE

VIA CERNA

PIAZZA
BARBERINI

Museo Nazionale
Romano

Città Universitària

Pal. Barberini

PIAZZA D'
REPUBBLICA

PIAZZA
CINQUECENTO

Stazione
Termini

S Lorenzo
Fuori le Mura

Pal. Quirinale

VIA D QUIRINALE

VIA DELLE QUATTRO FONTANE

PALAZZO
MASSIMO

Verano
Cemetery

HILL

VIA NAZIONALE

S Maria
Maggiore

VIA CAVOUR

ESQUILINE HILL

PIAZZA
V.EMANUELE II.

VIA MERULANA

PIAZZA
DI PORTA
MAGGIORE

DEI FORI IMPERIALI

Roman Forum

VIA LABICANA

S Croce in
Gerusalemme

Colosseum

HILL

VIA D S GREGORIO

SS Giovanni
e Paolo

S Giovanni
in Laterano

Pta. S Giovanni

S Gregorio
Magno

Aurelian Walls

CELIAN
HILL

Baths of
Caracalla

VIA APPIA NUOVA

Pta. S Sebastiano

To EUR & Tre Fontane   The Catacombs

City transport

As in most Italian cities, the best way to get around Rome is to **walk**. That said, its **bus service**, run by ATAC, is a good one – cheap, reliable and as quick as the clogged streets allow. Rome also has a **metro**, and although it is more directed at ferrying commuters out to the suburbs than transporting tourists around the city centre, there are a few useful stations. If you're planning to cover some ground, you can buy a single ticket combining different modes of transport (bus, metro A and B and one-way urban trains), valid for 75 minutes and costing L1500; a book of eleven tickets costs L15,000. A day pass (BIG) valid for 24 hours costs L6000 and a weekly pass (CIS) costs L24,000. You can make savings by purchasing a block of ten tickets for L15,000 or a one-day ticket for L6000 from the ATAC booth on Piazza dei Cinquecento, where they also sell decent transport maps for L1000. The buses and the metro stop around 11.30pm, after which a network of **night buses** clicks into service, serving most parts of the city until about 5.30am. **Taxis** are costly; hail one in the street, or try the ranks at Termini, Piazza Venezia, and Piazza San Silvestro; alternatively call ☎06.3570, 06.4494 or 06.6645 to book one. The meter should start at L4500.

Accommodation

In summer Rome is as crowded as you might expect, and although the city's huge number of **hotels and hostels** offers a vast capacity for absorbing visitors, you should book in advance if you can; if you can't, make straight for the tourist office to save your legs. Many of the city's cheaper hotels are handily located close to Stazione Termini, and you could do worse than hole up in one of these: the streets both sides of the station square are stacked full of cheap places. If you want to stay somewhere more central, there are hotels in the *centro storico*, some of them not that expensive, but again be warned that they might be full during the summer. For current details ask at the tourist office or contact AIG, Via Cavour 44 (☎06.487.1152).

Hostels

Fawlty Towers, Via Magenta 39 (☎06.445.4802). Great value for money, situated near the station. ②.

Ostello del Foro Italico, Viale delle Olimpiadi 61 (☎06.324.2571). Rome's official hostel is vast though not especially central. Take bus #492 or metro line A from Termini to Ottaviano, then bus #32. Midnight curfew. ②.

Hotel Ottoviano, Via Ottaviano 6 (☎06.397.37253). Excellently situated private hotel/hostel, just outside the Vatican walls. Friendly, helpful staff, and no curfew. Take Metro line A from Termini to Ottaviano. ③.

Hotel Sandy, Via Cavour 136 (☎06.488.4585). Young people's hotel/hostel accommodation. Good value central location between the station and the Colosseum. No curfew.②.

YWCA, Via C. Balbo 4 (☎06.488.3917). For women only, and more conveniently situated than the HI hostel, ten minutes' walk from Termini. Midnight curfew. ②.

Hotels

Abruzzi, Piazza della Rotonda 69 (☎06.679.2021). Bang in front of the Pantheon, and as such you pay for the location. ⑤.

Alimandi, Via Tunisi 8 (☎06.397.23948). Close to the Vatican with good facilities. ⑦.

Capitol, Via G. Amendola 77 (☎06.488.2617). Comfortable hotel close to the station. ⑥.

Della Lunetta, Piazza del Paradiso 68 (☎06.686.1080). Close to Campo dei Fiori, an unspectacular hotel. ④.

Di Rienzo, Via P. Amadeo 79 (☎06.446.7131). Spacious clean rooms within spitting distance of the train station. ③.

Katty, Via Palestro 35 (☎06.444.1216). One of the cheaper options east of the station. ③.

Kennedy, Via F. Turati 62 (☎06.446.5373). Young management and well kept. ⑤.

Marsala, Via Marsala 36 (☎06.444.1262). Pleasant, clean hotel 50m from the station. ④.

Monaco, Via Flavia 84 (☎06.474.4335). Very welcoming and clean cheapie. ③.

Navona, Via dei Sediari 8 (☎06.686.4203). Perfectly placed *pensione* run by a friendly Italian-Australian couple. ④.

Perugia, Via del Colosseo 7 (☎06.679.7200). On a peaceful but central street. ④.

Piccolo, Via dei Chiavari 32 (☎06.688.02560). Reasonably priced hotel handily located for Piazza Navona. ④.

Prati, Via Crescenzio 87 (☎06.687.5357). Two-star hotel across the river with a nice, family-run feel. ④.

Romano, Largo C. Ricci 32 (☎06.679.5851). Good central location. ⑥.

Rosetta, Via Cavour 295 (☎06.488.1598). Nice location close to the Colosseum. ⑤.

Smeraldo, Via dei Chiodaroli 11 (☎06.687.5929). Popular place with lovely doubles. ④.

Sole, Via del Biscione 76 (☎06.688.06873). Near Piazza del Campo dci Fiori, one of the nicest city-centre locations. ⑥.

Campsites

Camping Flaminio, Via Flaminia Nuova. 8km north of the city; bus #202, #204 or #205 from Piazzale Flaminio, which is connected with Termini by metro line A.

Camping Tiber, Via Tiburina (☎06.3361.0733). Offers a free shuttle service to Prima Porta station which has train connections to Piazzale Flaminio.

The City

Piazza Venezia is a good central place to start your wanderings, flanked by the **Palazzo di Venezia** and overlooked by the hideous **Vittorio Emanuele Monument** or Altar of the Nation, erected at the turn of the century to commemorate the Roman unification. Behind, the **Capitoline Hill**, formerly the spiritual and political centre of the Roman Empire, is home to one of Rome's most elegant squares, **Piazza del Campidoglio**, designed by Michelangelo in the 1550s for Pope Paul III, and flanked by the two branches of one of the city's most important museums of antique art – the **Capitoline Museums** (Tues–Sat 9am–7pm, Sun 9am–1.30pm; L10,000). On the left, the **Palazzo Nuovo** concentrates some of the best of the city's Roman and Greek sculpture into half a dozen or so rooms. There's a remarkable, controlled statue of the *Dying Gaul*, a Roman copy of a Hellenistic original; an original grappling depiction of *Eros and Psyche*; a *Satyr Resting*, after a piece by Praxiteles; and the red marble *Laughing Satyr*, another Roman copy of a Greek original. Walk through to the so-called Sala degli Imperatori, with its busts of Roman emperors and other famous names, and don't miss the coy *Capitoline Venus*, housed in a room on its own, again based on a work by Praxiteles. The same ticket will get you into the **Palazzo dei Conservatori** across the square, a larger, more varied collection, with more ancient sculpture, including the exquisite *Spinario* – a Hellenistic work from the first century BC showing a boy plucking a thorn from his foot – and the sacred Roman statue of the she-wolf suckling the twins, thought to be originally an Etruscan work. The second floor holds Renaissance painting – numerous works by Reni and Tintoretto, a vast picture by Guercino that used to hang in St Peter's, some nice small-scale work by Annibale Carracci, an early work by Ludovico Carracci, *Head of a Boy*, and Caravaggio's *St John the Baptist*. Behind the square, a road skirts the Forum down to the small church of **San Giuseppe dei Falegnami** (daily 9am–noon & 2–6.30pm), built above the prison where St Peter is said to have been held – you can see the bars to which he was chained, along with the spring the saint is said to have created to baptize other prisoners here, and, at the top of the staircase, an imprint claimed to be of St Peter's head as he was tumbled down the stairs.

Via del Plebiscito forges west from Piazza Venezia past the church of **Gesù** (daily 7am–12.30pm & 4–7.15pm), a high, wide Baroque church of the Jesuit order that has served since as the model for Jesuit churches everywhere. Still well patronized, it's notable for its size (the left transept is surmounted by the largest single piece of stone in existence) and the richness of its interior, especially the paintings of Baciccia in the dome and the ceiling's ingenious trompe l'oeil, which oozes out of its frame in a tangle of writhing bodies, flowing drapery and stucco angels. Crossing over, streets tangle down to **Piazza di Campo de' Fiori**, Rome's most appealing and unpretentious square, home to a morning market and surrounded by restaurants and bars. South of the Campo, at the end of Vicolo di Grotte, the **Galleria Spada** (Tues–Sat 9am–7pm, Sun 9am–1pm; L10,000) is decorated in the manner of a Roman noble family and displays a small collection of paintings, best of which are a couple of portraits by Reni. To the left off the courtyard is a crafty trompe l'oeil tunnel by Borromini, whose trick perspective makes it appear to be about four times its actual length. Across Via Arenula, the broad open space of **Piazza della Bocca di Verità** is home to two of the city's better-preserved Roman temples, the **Temple of Fortuna Virilis** and the circular **Temple of Vesta**, both of which date from the end of the second century BC, though the church of **Santa Maria in Cosmedin**, on the far side of the square (daily10am–noon & 3–6/7pm), is more interesting, a typically Roman medieval basilica with a huge marble altar and surround and a colourful and ingenious Cosmati mosaic floor – one of the city's finest. Outside in the portico, the **Bocca di Verità** (Mouth of Truth) gives the square its name, an ancient Roman drain cover in the shape of an enormous face that in medieval times would apparently swallow the hand of anyone who hadn't told the truth.

The Centro Storico

You need to walk a little way north from the Capitoline Hill to find the real city centre of Rome, the **Centro Storico**, a roughly triangular knob of land that bulges into a bend in the Tiber, above Corso Vittorio Emanuele. The old Campus Martius of Roman times, it later became the heart of the Renaissance city, and is now an unruly knot of narrow streets holding some of the best of Rome's classical and Baroque heritage, and its street- and nightlife.

The boundary of the historic centre to the east, **Via del Corso**, is Rome's main street, holding its principal shops and cutting straight through the heart of the city centre. Walking north from Piazza Venezia, the first building on the left is the **Galleria Doria Pamphilj** (10am–5pm; closed Thurs & Aug 15–31; L13,000), one of many galleries housed in palaces belonging to Roman patrician families. Its collection includes Rome's best cache of Dutch and Flemish paintings, canvases by Caravaggio and Velázquez's painting of Pope Innocent X. The next left after the palace leads into Piazza Sant'Ignazio, an odd little square dominated by the church of **Sant'Ignazio** (daily 7.30am–12.30pm & 4–7.15pm), which has a marvellous ceiling by Pozzo showing the entry of St Ignatius into paradise, employing sledgehammer trompe l'oeil effects, notably in the mock cupola painted into the dome of the crossing. Stand on the disc in the centre of the nave for the truest sense of the ingenious rendering of perspective.

Through Via di Seminario from here and you're standing in front of the **Pantheon** (Mon–Sat 9am–6.30pm, Sun 9am–1pm; free) on Piazza della Rotonda, the most complete ancient Roman structure in the city, finished around 125 AD. A formidable architectural achievement even now, its dome still has the second widest diameter in Rome. Inside, the width and height of the dome are precisely equal, and the hole in the dome's centre is a full 9m across; there are no visible arches or vaults to hold the whole thing up; instead, they're sunk into the concrete of the walls of the building. It would have been richly decorated, the coffered ceiling heavily stuccoed and the niches filled with statues of the gods. Now, apart from the sheer size of the place, the main thing of interest is the tomb of Raphael, inscribed by the writer and priest Bembo: "Living, great Nature feared he might outvie Her works, and dying, fears herself may die."

There's more artistic splendour on view behind the Pantheon, in the church of **Santa Maria sopra Minerva** (daily 8am–1pm & 4–7pm), one of the city's art-treasure churches, crammed with the tombs and self-indulgences of wealthy Roman families. Of these, the Carafa chapel, in the south transept, is the best known, holding Filippino Lippi's recently restored fresco of *The Assumption*, below which one painting shows a hopeful Oliviero Carafa being presented to the Virgin Mary by Thomas Aquinas; another depicts Aquinas confounding the heretics in the sight of two beautiful young boys – the future Medici popes Leo X and Clement VII. You should look, too, at the figure of *Christ Bearing the Cross*, on the left-hand side of the main altar, a serene work that Michelangelo completed in 1521 especially for the church.

In the opposite direction from the Pantheon, **Piazza Navona** is in many ways the central square of Rome, an almost entirely enclosed space fringed with cafés and restaurants that follows the lines of the Emperor Domitian's chariot arena, whose overgrown ruins survived here until the mid-fifteenth century. The square was given a face-lift in the mid-seventeenth century by Pope Innocent X, who built most of the grandiose palaces that surround it and commissioned Borromini to design the church of **Sant'Agnese** on the west side. The church, typically squeezed into the tightest of spaces by Borromini, supposedly stands on the spot where Saint Agnes, exposed naked to the public in the stadium, miraculously grew hair to cover herself. The **Fontana dei Quattro Fiumi** opposite, one of three that punctuate the square, is by Borromini's arch-rival, Bernini; each figure represents one of the four great rivers of the world – the Nile, Danube, Ganges and Plate – though only the horse, symbolizing the Danube, was actually carved by Bernini himself.

North of Piazza Navona, the Renaissance facade of the church of **Sant'Agostino** (daily 8am–noon & 4.30–7.30pm) is not much to look at but the church's handful of art treasures might draw you in – among them Raphael's vibrant *Isaiah*, on the third pillar on the left, Sansovino's craggy *St Anne, Virgin and Child*, and, in the first chapel on the left, a *Madonna and Pilgrims* by Caravaggio, which is badly lit, so come prepared with L500 coins for the light box if you want to appreciate the work. There's more work by Caravaggio down Via della Scrofa, in the French national church of **San Luigi dei Francesi** (daily except Thurs afternoon 8am–12.30pm & 3.30–7pm), in the last chapel on the left: early works, describing the life and martyrdom of St Matthew, best of which is the *Calling of St Matthew* on the left wall – Matthew is the dissolute-looking youth on the far left, illuminated by a shaft of sunlight. A little way up Via della Ripetta from here, the **Ara Pacis Augustae** (Tues–Sat 9am–4.30/7pm, Sat & Sun 9am–1.30pm; L3750) was built in 13 BC to celebrate Augustus' victory over Spain and Gaul. It supports a fragmented frieze showing Augustus himself, his wife Livia, Tiberius, Agrippa, and various children clutching the togas of the elders, the last of whom is said to be the young Claudius.

At the far end of Via di Ripetta the **Piazza del Popolo** provides an impressive entrance to the city, all symmetry and grand vistas, although its real attraction is the church of **Santa Maria del Popolo** (daily 7am–noon & 4– 7pm), which holds some of the best Renaissance art of any Roman church, including frescoes by Pinturicchio in the south aisle and two fine tombs by Andrea Sansovino. The second chapel in the northern aisle, the Chigi chapel, was designed by Raphael for Antonio Chigi in 1516 – though most of the work was accomplished by other artists and not finished until the seventeenth century. Michelangelo's protégé, Sebastiano del Piombo, was responsible for the altarpiece; the two sculptures in the corner niches of Daniel and Habakkuk are by Bernini. Two pictures by Caravaggio get most attention – one, the *Conversion of St Paul*, showing Paul and horse bathed in a beatific radiance, the other, the *Crucifixion of St Peter*, showing Peter as an aged figure, dominated by the muscular figures hoisting him up.

East of Via del Corso

The area immediately southeast of Piazza del Popolo is travellers' Rome, historically the artistic quarter of the city, for which eighteenth- and nineteenth-century Grand Tourists would make, lending the area a distinctly cosmopolitan air, even today. At the centre of the district, **Piazza di Spagna** is a long, thin square centring on the distinctive boat-shaped **Barcaccia** fountain, the last work of Bernini's father. Opposite, the **Keats-Shelley Memorial House** (summer Mon–Fri 9am–1pm & 3–6pm, Sat 11am–6pm; winter Mon–Fri 9am–1pm & 2.30–5pm, Sat 11am–5pm; L5000), where John Keats died in 1821, now serves as an archive of English-language literary and historical works and a museum of literary mementoes. Beside the house, the **Spanish Steps** – a venue for international posing and fast pick-ups late into the summer nights – sweep up to the **Trinità dei Monti**, a largely sixteenth-century church that holds a couple of works by Daniel da Volterra, notably a soft flowing fresco of *The Assumption* in the third chapel on the right, which includes a portrait of his teacher Michelangelo. His *Deposition*, across the nave, is also worth a glance; it was painted from a series of cartoons by Michelangelo.

From the church, follow Via Sistina to **Piazza Barberini**, a busy traffic junction, in the centre of which is Bernini's **Fontana del Tritone**. **Via Veneto** bends north from here, with its pricey bars and restaurants once the haunt of Rome's Beautiful People but now home of high-class tack and overpriced sleaze. A little way up, the Capuchin **Church of the Immaculate Conception** is not particularly notable, but is worth visiting for its **Cemetery** (9am–noon & 3–6.30pm, closed Thurs; donation requested), one of the more macabre sights of Rome, somewhere between the chilling and the ludicrous; the bones of four thousand monks coat the walls of a series of chapels in abstract patterns or as fully clothed skeletons, their faces peering out of their cowls in expressions of agony.

Retracing your steps back across Piazza Barberini, the **Palazzo Barberini** is home to the **Galleria d'Arte Antica** (Tues–Sat 9am–7pm, Sun 9am–1pm; L8000), which displays a rich patchwork of mainly Italian art from the early Renaissance to late Baroque period. In addition to canvases by Tintoretto, Titian and El Greco, highlights include Filippo Lippi's warmly maternal *Madonna and Child*, painted in 1437, and Raphael's beguiling *Fornarina*. But perhaps the most impressive feature of the gallery is the building itself, the epitome of Baroque grandeur worked on at different times by the most favoured architects of the day: Bernini, Borromini and Maderno. The Salone (L2000) is guaranteed to impress, its ceiling frescoed by Pietro da Cortona in one of the best examples of exuberant Baroque trompe l'oeil work, a manic rendering of *The Triumph of Divine Providence* that almost crawls down the walls.

East down Via del Tritone from Piazza Barberini, hidden among a tight web of narrow, apparently aimless streets, is one of Rome's more surprising sights, easy to stumble upon by accident – the **Fontane di Trevi**, a huge Baroque gush of water over statues and rocks built onto the backside of a Renaissance palace. Originally commissioned from Bernini by Pope Urban VIII, it wasn't begun until Niccolo Salvi took up the project in 1723. The Trevi fountain is now, of course, the place you come to chuck in a coin if you want to guarantee your return to Rome, and it's one of the city's most vigorous outdoor spots to hang out in of an evening. A short stroll directly south from here brings you to the **Galleria Colonna**, Via della Pilotta 17 (Sat 9am–1pm; closed Aug; L10,000), worth forty minutes or so if only for the chandelier-decked Great Hall, where a display of paintings includes Carracci's early *Bean Eater*, a *Narcissus* by Tintoretto, and a *Portrait of a Venetian Gentleman* caught in supremely confident pose by Veronese.

Five minutes from the gallery, **Via Nazionale**, Rome's main shopping street, lined with boutiques, leads up to **Piazza della Repubblica**, a stern but rather tawdry semicircle of buildings that occupies part of the site of Diocletian's Baths, the scanty remains of which lie across the square in the church of **Santa Maria degli Angeli** (daily 7am–12.30pm & 4–7pm). This is a huge, open building, with an interior standardized after a couple of centuries of piecemeal adaptation (started by an aged Michelangelo) by Vanvitelli in a rich eighteenth-century confection. The pink granite pillars are, however, original, and the main transept formed the main hall of the baths – though only the crescent shape of the facade remains from the original *caldarium*. Michelangelo is also said to have had a hand in modifying another part of the baths, the courtyard which makes up part of the **Museo Nazionale Romano** behind the church (closed for restoration). The museum's collection of Greek and Roman antiquities is second only to the Vatican's and is now partly housed in the **Palazzo Massimmo** (Tues–Sat 9am–7pm, Sun 9am–2pm; L12,000), across the square at Piazza dei Cinquecento 68, a recently restored air-conditioned building featuring on the ground floor a series of Roman busts, mosaics and fresco fragments, and the star attraction of the Ludovisi Throne (5 BC) depicting the birth of Aphrodite. The top floor gallery contains stunning, sylvan frescoes from a country villa that belonged to the emperor Augustus's wife Livia, and some of the best examples of mosaics from Roman villas around the world. Close by on Via XX Settembre, the church of **Santa Maria della Vittoria** (daily 7am–noon & 4.30–7pm) was built by Carlo Maderno and its interior is one of the most elaborate examples of Baroque decoration in Rome, its ceiling and walls pitted with carving, and statues crammed into remote corners like an overstuffed attic. The church's best-known feature is Bernini's melodramatic carving of the *Ecstasy of St Theresa*, the centrepiece of the sepulchral chapel of Cardinal Cornaro.

South of Piazza Venezia

From Piazza Venezia **Via dei Fori Imperiali** cuts south, a soulless boulevard whose main pedestrians are tourists rooting about among the ancient sites. Just off Piazza Venezia, **Trajan's Column** was erected to celebrate the emperor's colonization of Dacia (modern-day Romania), and its reliefs illustrate the highlights of the Dacian campaign. Across the road is the main part of the **Roman Forum and Palatine Hill** (Mon–Sat 9am–3.30/6pm, Sun 9am–1pm; L12,000; forum area free), in ancient times the centre of what was a very large city. Following the downfall of the city to various barbarian invaders, the area was left in ruin, its relics quarried for construction in other parts of Rome during medieval and Renaissance times. Excavation of the site didn't start until the beginning of the nineteenth century, since when it has been pretty much continuous: you'll notice a fair part of the site closed off for further digs.

Running through the core of the Forum, the **Via Sacra** was the best-known street of ancient Rome. At the bottom of the Capitoline hill, the **Arch of Septimus Severus** was built in the early third century AD to commemorate the emperor's tenth anniversary in power, and the grassy, wide-open scatter of paving and beached columns in front of it was the place where most of the life of the city was carried on. Nearby, the **Curia** is one of the few whole structures here, a huge barn-like building that was begun in 80 BC, restored by Julius Caesar soon after and rebuilt by Diocletian in the third century AD. The Senate met here during the Republican period, and augurs would come to announce the wishes of the gods. On the opposite side is the **House of the Vestal Virgins**, where the six women charged with the responsibility of keeping the sacred flame of Vesta alight lived: four floors of rooms around a central courtyard, with the round **Temple of Vesta** at the near end. On the far side of the site, the **Basilica of Constantine and Maxentius** is, in terms of size and ingenuity, probably the Forum's most impressive remains. It's said that Michelangelo studied the hexagonal coffered arches here when grappling with the dome of St Peter's. From the basilica, the Via Sacra climbs to the **Arch of Titus** on a low arm of the Palatine Hill – although it's covered for restoration – its reliefs showing the spoils of the sacking of Jerusalem being carried off by eager Romans. To the left of the arch is the Forum Museum Antiquarian Firense – a small collection of iron-age burial urns and pre-Roman artefacts.

Turning right at the Arch of Titus takes you up to the **Palatine Hill**, a pleasanter and greener site than the Forum. In the days of the Republic, the Palatine was the most desirable address in Rome (from it is derived our word "palace"), and the big names continued to colonize it during the imperial era, trying to outdo each other with ever larger and more magnificent dwellings. The gargantuan **Domus Augustana** spreads to the far brink of the hill. You can look down from here onto its vast central courtyard and maze-like fountain, and wander through a handful of its bare rooms. From close by, steps lead down to the **Cryptoporticus**, a passage built by Nero to link the Palatine with his palace on the far side of the Colosseum, and decorated along part of its length with well-preserved Roman stuccowork. **Nero's Palace** itself has recently been opened to the public after twenty years of restoration. Known as the Golden House because of the extensive use of gold leaf, its many rooms boast jewel-studded ceilings and frescoes that were admired by Raphael and Michaelangelo. A left turn leads to the **House of Livia**, originally believed to have been the residence of the wife of Augustus, whose courtyard and rooms are decorated with scanty frescoes. Turn right down the passage and up some steps and you're in the **Farnese Gardens**, among the first botanical gardens in Europe, laid out by Alessandro Farnese in the mid-sixteenth century and now a tidily planted refuge from the exposed heat of the ruins. The terrace here looks back over the Forum, while the terrace at the opposite end looks down on the real centre of Rome's ancient beginning – an Iron Age hut, known as the **House of Romulus**, that is the best preserved of a ninth-century Iron Age village discovered here, and the so-called **Lupercal**, beyond, which is traditionally believed to be the cave where Romulus and Remus were suckled by the she-wolf.

Immediately outside the Forum site, the fourth-century **Arch of Constantine** marks the end of the Via Sacra. Across from here, the **Colosseum** (daily 9am–3.30/6pm; L10,000) is Rome's most awe-inspiring ancient monument, begun by the Emperor Vespasian around 72 AD and finished by his son Titus about eight years later – an event celebrated by one hundred days of continuous games. The Romans flocked here for gladiatorial contests and other equally cruel spectacles that pitted man against animal, animal against animal; they even had mock sea battles – the arena could be flooded in minutes. After the games were outlawed in the fifth century, the Colosseum was pillaged over the centuries for building stone, and is now little more than a shell. But the basic structure of the place is easy to see, and has served as a model for stadiums around the world ever since.

It's a short walk from here down Via San Giovanni in Laterano to the church of **San Clemente**, a light, twelfth-century basilica that encapsulates better than any other the continuity of history in the city. It's in fact a conglomeration of three places of worship. The ground-floor church is a superb example of a medieval basilica, with some fine mosaics in the apse. Downstairs (Mon–Sat 9am–12.30pm & 3–6pm, Sun 10am–noon & 3–6pm; L2000), there's the nave of an earlier church, dated back to 392 AD. And at the eastern end and down another level of this church, are the remains of a Roman apartment building – a labyrinthine set of rooms including a Mithraic temple of the late second century standing next to a first-century imperial block. The same street leads to the basilica of **San Giovanni in Laterano** (daily 7am–6/7pm), Rome's cathedral and the seat of the pope until the unification of Italy. There has been a church on this site since the fourth century, the first established by Constantine. The present building, reworked by Borromini in the mid-seventeenth century, evokes Rome's staggering wealth of history. The doors were taken from the Curia of the Roman Forum. Inside, the first pillar on the left of the right-hand aisle shows a fragment of Giotto's fresco of Boniface VIII, proclaiming the first Holy Year in 1300, while further on, a more recent monument commemorates Sylvester I, bishop of Rome during much of Constantine's reign, and incorporates part of his original tomb, said to sweat and rattle its bones when a pope is about to die. Kept secure behind the papal altar are the heads of St Peter and St Paul, the church's prize relics. Outside, the cloisters (L4000) are one of the most pleasing parts of the complex, decorated with early thirteenth-century Cosmati work. Next door to the church, the **Baptistry** is the oldest surviving baptistry in the Christian world, an octagonal structure built by Constantine, rebuilt during the fifth century, and currently being restored after a 1993 car bomb damaged the stonework and some of the frescoes. On the other side of the church the **Scala Santa** is claimed to be the staircase from Pontius Pilate's house down which Christ walked after his trial. The 28 steps are protected by boards, and the only way you're allowed to climb them is on your knees – which pilgrims do regularly.

On the far side of the road from the Colosseum, the one feature of interest on the **Esquiline Hill** is the church of **San Pietro in Vincoli** (daily 7am–12.30pm & 3.30–6/7pm), one of Rome's most delightfully plain churches, built to house an important relic: the chains of St Peter from his imprisonment in Jerusalem, along with those that bound him when a prisoner in Rome. These can still be seen in the glass case on the altar, but most people come for Michelangelo's unfinished Tomb of Pope Julius II in the southern aisle. The figure of Moses, pictured as descended from Sinai to find the Israelites worshipping the golden calf, and flanked by the gentle figures of Leah and Rachel, is one of the artist's most arresting works. Steps lead down from San Pietro to **Via Cavour**, a busy central thoroughfare which carves a route up to Termini past the basilica of **Santa Maria Maggiore** (daily 7am–6/7pm), one of the city's four great basilicas, with a broad nave fringed on both sides with strikingly well-kept mosaics, most of which date from the church's construction and tell of incidents from the Old Testament. The Sistine chapel, on the right, holds the elaborate tomb of Sixtus V, while the equally fancy Pauline chapel opposite has a venerated twelfth-century *Madonna* topped with a panel showing the legendary tracing of the church's plan after a miraculous August snowfall.

Villa Borghese

At the northern edge of the city centre, the **Villa Borghese** (now beautifully restored) is made up of the grounds of the seventeenth-century palace of Cardinal Scipione Borghese – a vast area, whose woods, lakes and grass are about as near as you can get to a tranquil spot in Rome. Apart from the peace, the main attraction is the **Galleria Borghese** (Tues–Sat 9am–7pm, Sun 9am–1pm; L10,000), with an assortment of works collected by Scipione Borghese. The ground floor contains sculptures, where the work of Bernini, a protégé of Borghese, dominates: there's an *Aeneas and Anchises*, carved with his father when he was fifteen; an ingenious *Rape of Proserpine*, amid busts of Roman emperors; his dramatic *Apollo and Daphne*; and, in the next room, his *David* – a self-portrait.

The Villa Borghese's two other major museums are on the other side of the park, along the Viale delle Belle Arti. Of these, the **Galleria Nazionale d'Arte Moderna** (Tues–Sun 9am–7pm; L10,000) is probably the least compelling, housing a wide selection of nineteenth-

and twentieth-century Italian names, most undistinguished; artists you might recognize include Modigliani, De Chirico, Boccione and other futurists, along with the odd Cézanne, Mondrian and Klimt. The **Villa Giulia**, ten minutes away, is more of an essential stop, a collection of courtyards, loggias and gardens that is home to the **Museo Nazionale di Villa Giulia** (Tues–Sat 9am–7pm, Sun 9am–2pm; L8000) – the world's primary collection of Etruscan treasures. Best among the sculpture is the group of *Apollo and Herakles*, from the site of Veio, north of Rome, and the remarkable *Sarcophagus of a Married Couple* from Cerveteri. Other highlights include the *Cistae* recovered from tombs around Praeneste – drum-like objects, engraved and adorned with figures, that were supposed to hold all the things needed for the care of the body after death – and marvellously intricate pieces of gold jewellery, delicately worked into tiny animals.

South of the centre

On its southern side, the Palatine Hill drops suddenly down to the **Circo Massimo**, a long green expanse that was the ancient city's main venue for chariot races. The arena could apparently hold a crowd of around two hundred thousand betting punters, and if it was still even half intact could no doubt have matched the Colosseum for grandeur. As it is, a litter of stones at the Viale Aventino end is all that remains. Across the far side of Piazza di Porta Capena, the **Baths of Caracalla** (summer Mon & Sun 9am–1pm, Tues–Sat 9am–6pm, winter daily 9am–3pm; L8000) are better preserved, and give a much better sense of the scale of Roman architecture than most of the ruins in the city. It's a short walk from behind the baths down Via Gitto to the **Protestant Cemetery** (Tues–Sun, 9am–5pm; donations expected), accessible direct on metro line B (Piramide stop), the burial place of Keats and Shelley, along with a handful of other well-known names – a small, tranquil enclave, crouched behind the mossy pyramidal tomb of Caius Cestius.

Two kilometres or so south, **San Paolo fuori le Mura** (daily 7am–6.45pm) is one of the four patriarchal basilicas of Rome, occupying the supposed site of St Paul's tomb. Of the four, it has probably fared least well over the years, and the church you see is largely a nineteenth-century reconstruction. It is a huge, impressive building, and home to a handful of ancient features: in the south transept, the Paschal Candlestick is a remarkable piece of Romanesque carving, supported by half-human beasts and rising through entwined tendrils and strangely human limbs and bodies to scenes from Christ's life; the bronze aisle doors date from 1070, and the Cosmati cloister, just behind here, is probably Rome's finest, its spiralling, mosaic-encrusted columns enclosing a peaceful rose garden.

Further south still, on the edge of the city, the **Via Appia** was the most important of all the Roman trade routes. Its sides are lined with the underground burial cemeteries or **Catacombs** of the first Christians. There are around five complexes in all, dating from the first to the fourth centuries, almost entirely emptied of bodies now but still decorated with the primitive signs and frescoes that were the hallmark of the then-burgeoning Christian movement. You can get to the main grouping on bus #218 from the Colosseum (Via San Gregorio in Laterano), but the only ones of any significance are the catacombs of **San Callisto** (Thurs–Tues 8.30am–noon & 2.30–5.30pm, closed Feb; L8000), burial place of all the third-century popes, whose tombs are preserved in the papal crypt, and the site of some well-preserved seventh- and eighth-century frescoes; and those of **San Sebastiano** (Mon–Sat 8.30am–noon & 2.30–5.30pm; closed mid-Nov to mid-Dec; L8000), 500m further on, situated under a basilica that was originally built by Constantine on the spot where the bodies of the Apostles Peter and Paul are said to have laid for a time. Thirty-minute tours take in paintings of doves and fish, a contemporary carved oil lamp and inscriptions dating the tombs themselves – although the most striking features are three pagan tombs discovered when archeologists were burrowing beneath the floor of the basilica upstairs. The nearby graffiti record the fact that this was indeed, albeit temporarily, where the Apostles Peter and Paul rested.

Trastevere

Across the Tiber from the centre of town, the district of **Trastevere** has traditionally been a place somewhat apart from the rest of the city centre, a small, tightly knit neighbourhood that was formerly the artisan quarter of the city and has since become rather gentrified, home to much of its most vibrant and youthful nightlife – and some of Rome's best and most affordable restaurants. The best time to come is on Sunday morning, when the **Porta Portese** flea market stretches down Via Portuense to Trastevere station in a congested medley of antiques, old motor spares, trendy clothing and assorted junk. Afterwards, stroll north up Via Anicia to the church of **Santa Cecilia in Trastevere** (daily 8am–6pm; excavations Mon–Sat 8am–6pm), built over the site of the second-century home of the patron saint of music. Locked in the hot chamber of her own baths for several days, she refused to die, singing her way through the ordeal until her head was hacked half off with an axe. At the back of the church you can descend to the excavations of the baths, though hints at restoration have robbed these of any atmosphere. On Tuesday and Thursday mornings the Singing Gallery's beautifully coloured and tender frescoes by Piero Cavallini (c.1293) can be viewed (donation expected).

Santa Cecilia is situated in the quieter part of Trastevere, on the southern side of **Viale Trastevere**, the wide boulevard which cuts through the centre of the district. There's more life on the far side of here, centred around **Piazza Santa Maria in Trastevere**, named after the church of **Santa Maria in Trastevere** (daily 9.30am–12.30pm & 4–7pm) – held to be the first official church in Rome, built on a site where a fountain of oil is said to have sprung on the day of Christ's birth and sporting some of the city's most impressive mosaics, also by Cavallini. North towards the Tiber, the **Villa Farnesina** is known for its Renaissance murals, including a Raphael-designed painting of *Cupid and Psyche*, completed in 1517 by the artist's assistants. Raphael did, however, manage to finish the *Galatea* next door. The other paintings in the room are by Sebastiano del Piombo and the architect of the building, Peruzzi, who also decorated the upstairs Salone delle Prospettive, which shows trompe l'oeil galleries with views of contemporary Rome – one of the earliest examples of the technique.

Castel Sant'Angelo, St Peter's and the Vatican Museums

Across the Tiber from Rome's old centre, the **Castel Sant'Angelo** (Tues–Sun 9am–8pm; L8000) was the burial place of the emperor Hadrian. Later, the papal authorities converted the building for use as a fortress and built a passageway to link it with the Vatican as a refuge in times of siege. Inside, rooms hold swords, armour, guns and the like, while below, dungeons and storerooms are testament to the castle's grisly past as the city's most notorious Renaissance prison. Upstairs, the official papal apartments, accessible from the terrace, are extravagantly decorated with lewd frescoes amid paintings by Poussin, Jordaens and others.

Via della Conciliazione leads up from here to the **Vatican City**, a tiny territory surrounded by high walls on its far side and on the near side opening its doors to the rest of the city and its pilgrims in the form of Bernini's **Piazza San Pietro**, whose two arms extend a symbolic welcome to the lap of the Catholic Church. The basilica of St Peter's (daily 7am–6/7pm; free) is the replacement of a basilica built during the time of Constantine, to a plan initially conceived at the turn of the fifteenth century by Bramante and finished off, heavily modified, over a century later by Carlo Maderno, making it something of a bridge between the Renaissance and Baroque eras. The inside is full of features from the Baroque period, although the first thing you see, on the right, is Michelangelo's *Pietà*, completed when he was just 24 and, following an attack in 1972, displayed behind glass. To the right is the Holy Door, opened by the pope on 24 December 1999 for the Jubilee year (see p.753); in all other years it remains bricked up. On the right-hand side of the nave, the bronze statue of St Peter was cast in the thirteenth century by Arnolfo di Cambio and has its right foot polished smooth by the attentions of pilgrims. Bronze was also the material used in Bernini's massive 28m-high *baldachino*, the centrepiece of the sculptor's embellishment of the interior. Bernini's feverish sculpting decorates the apse, too, his *cattedra* enclosing the supposed chair of St Peter in a curvy marble and stucco throne. An entrance off the aisle leads to the **treasury** (daily 9am–5.30/6.30pm; L8000), which, along with more recent additions, holds artefacts left from the earlier church – principally a wall-mounted tabernacle by Donatello, and the massive, though fairly ghastly, late fifteenth-century bronze tomb of Sixtus IV by Pollaiuolo, which as a portrait is said to be very accurate. Back at the central crossing, steps lead down to the

Vatican Grottoes (daily: summer 8am–6pm; winter 7am–5pm), where a number of popes are buried in grandiose tombs – in the main, those not distinguished enough to be buried up above. Under the portico, to the right of the main doors, you can ascend to the roof and dome (on foot L5000, by lift L6000) – though you'll probably need to queue – from where the views over the city are as glorious as you'd expect.

A five-minute walk out of the northern side of the piazza takes you up to the only part of the Vatican Palace you can visit independently, the **Vatican Museums** (March–Oct & 20th–30th Dec Mon–Fri 8.45am–4.45pm, Sat 8.45am–1.45pm; rest of year Mon–Sat 8.45am–1.45pm; L18,000; also open last Sun of each month 8.45am–3.45pm; free; last ticket issued 1hr before closing) – quite simply the largest, richest, most compelling museum complex in the world, stuffed with booty from every period of the city's history. There's no point in trying to see everything on one visit; you'd do far better to select what you want to see and aim to return another time if you can. It's worth also taking account of the official, colour-coded routes which are constructed for varying amounts of time and interest and can take you anything from 45 minutes to the best part of a day.

Start off at the **Raphael Stanze**, at the opposite end of the building to the entrance, a set of rooms decorated for Pope Julius II by Raphael among others. Of the two most interesting rooms, the **Stanza Eliodoro** is home to the *Expulsion of Heliodorus from the Temple*, an allusion to the military success of Julius II, depicted on the left in portrait. Not to be outdone, Leo X, Julius' successor, in the *Meeting of Atilla and St Leo* opposite, ordered Raphael to substitute his head for that of Julius II, turning the painting into an allegory of the Battle of Ravenna at which he was present; thus he appears twice, as pope and as the equally portly Medici cardinal just behind. In the same room, the *Mass at Bolsena* shows Julius again on the right, pictured in attendance at a famous thirteenth-century miracle in Orvieto. The next room, the **Stanza della Segnatura** or pope's study, was decorated between 1512 and 1514, and its *School of Athens*, on the rear wall as you come in, is perhaps Raphael's most renowned work, a representation of the "Triumph of Scientific Truth" in which all the great minds from antiquity are present. Plato and Aristotle discuss philosophy in the background, and spread across the steps is Diogenes, lazily ignorant of all that is happening around him; to the right, Raphael cheekily added a solitary, sullen portrait of his rival Michelangelo, who was working practically next door on the Sistine Chapel at the time.

Steps lead down from the Raphael Stanze to the **Sistine Chapel**, a huge barn-like structure, built for Pope Sixtus IV in 1481, which serves as the pope's private chapel and is scene of the conclaves of cardinals for the election of each new pontiff. The **paintings** down each side wall are contemporary with the building, depictions of scenes from the lives of Moses and Christ by Perugino, Botticelli and Ghirlandaio among others. But it's the **ceiling frescoes** of Ghirlandaio's pupil, Michelangelo, depicting the *Creation*, that everyone comes to see, executed almost single-handedly over a period of about four years, again for Pope Julius II. Whether the ceiling has been improved by the controversial recent restoration is a moot point, but the virtuosity of the work remains stunning. The *Last Judgment*, on the west wall of the chapel, was painted by Michelangelo over twenty years later, and is quite possibly the most inspired large-scale painting you'll ever see. The nudity caused controversy from the start, and the pope's zealous successor, Pius IV, would have had the painting removed had not Michelangelo's pupil, Daniele da Volterra, carefully added coverings – some of which have been left by the restorers – to the more obvious nudes, earning himself the nickname of the "breeches-maker".

Having seen the Raphael rooms and the Sistine Chapel, you've barely scratched the surface of the Vatican. At the opposite end of the Vatican Palace are grouped most of the other museums. In the main body of the palace, the small **Museo Pio-Clementino** holds some of the best of the Vatican's classical statuary, including the serene *Apollo Belvedere*, a Roman copy of a fourth-century BC original, and the second-century BC *Laöcoön*, which depicts the treacherous priest of Apollo being crushed with his sons by serpents. Near the Pio-Clementino museum, the **Museo Chiaramonti** and **Braccio Nuovo** hold more classical sculpture, the **Museo Egizio** has lots of mummies, and the **Museo Gregoriano Etrusco** offers sculpture, funerary art and applied art from the sites of southern Etruria. In a separate building, the **Pinacoteca** has works from the early to High Renaissance: pieces by Crivelli, Lippi and Giotto; the rich backdrops and elegantly clad figures of the Umbrian painters Perugino and Pinturrichio; Raphael's unfinished *Transfiguration*, which hung above the artist as he lay in state; Leonardo's *St Jerome*; and Caravaggio's *Descent from the Cross* – a warts 'n' all canvas that is imitated successfully by Reni's *Crucifixion of St Peter* in the same room. Nearby, the **Museo Gregoriano Profano** holds more classical sculpture, mounted on scaffolds for all-round viewing, and mosaics of athletes from the baths of Caracalla; the adjacent **Museo Pio Cristiano** has intricate early Christian sarcophagi, and, most famously, an expressive third-century statue of the *Good Shepherd*. Finally, the **Museo Missionario Etnologico** displays art and artefacts from all over the world, collected by Catholic missionaries.

Eating and drinking

It's relatively simple to **eat** cheaply and well in Rome, certainly easier than in Venice or Florence. Prices – even in the city centre – are reasonable, and the quality remains of a fair standard. You'll find a good array of places in the *centro storico*, not all of them tourist traps by any means, and Via Cavour and up around Stazione Termini is a good source of cheaply priced restaurants – though the area isn't renowned for its food quality rating. Similarly, you can eat cheaply in the Borgo district around the Vatican. Trastevere is Rome's traditional restaurant ghetto – touristy now, inevitably, but still the home of some fine and reasonably priced eateries, and Testaccio is also a popular evening place with a good selection of restaurants and pizzerias to choose from.

Snacks, cakes and ice cream

Corso Chianti, Via del Gesù 88. Sit-down snacks or full meals in this small, friendly and popular place. Arrive early.

Il Delfino, Corso V. Emanuele 67. Central and very busy cafeteria with a huge choice of snacks and full meals. Good for a fast fill-up between sights.

Giolitti, Via Offici del Vicaro 40. An Italian institution which once had a reputation for the country's top ice cream. Still pretty good, however, with a choice of 70 flavours.

Il Forno del Ghetto, Via del Portico d'Ottavia 2. Unmarked Jewish bakery with marvellous ricotta and dried fruit-filled cakes.

Il Gelato di San Crispino, Via della Panetteria 42. Close to the Trevi fountain and considered Rome's best.

Tre Scalini, Piazza Navona. Renowned for its absolutely remarkable *tartufo* – death by chocolate.

Restaurants

Hosteria Africa, Via Gaeta 28. One of Rome's few African restaurants.

Hosteria Angelo, Via P. Amedeo 104. Appealing atmosphere, average prices and above-average menu. Probably the best choice this side of the Termini tracks.

Da Augusto, Piazza de Renzi 15. Relaxed and genuine restaurant in a quiet piazza off the tourist beat.

Da Baffetto, Via Governo Vecchio 114. Authentic pizzeria that has long been a Rome institution, though it now tends to be swamped by tourists. Amazingly, it's still good value – although service can be off-ish – but you'll always have to queue. Open evenings only.

Il Boscaiolo, Via degli Artisti 137. Good-value pizzeria close by the Spanish Steps. Open until 2.30am.

Il Corallo, Via del Corallo 10. Friendly restaurant which attracts a lively crowd and serves way above average quality food – especially pizzas – though it isn't cheap. Open evenings only.

La Diligenza Rossa, Via Merulana 271. Low-priced, convivial eatery full of locals.

Dragon Garden, Via del Boschetto 41. Run by an Italian-Chinese couple, and probably the best-value Chinese in the city. Slow service but worth waiting for.

Filetti di Baccala, Largo dei Librari 88. Paper-covered Formica tables, cheap wine and beer, and fried fish dishes for L3000.

Da Giggetto, Via del Portico d'Ottavia 21a. Slightly more pricey than most, but worth it for genuine Roman–Jewish cooking.

Gino e Pietro, Via Governo Vecchio 106. Osteria serving wonderful food at the right price in a modest setting.

Grappola d'Oro, Piazza della Cancelleria 80. Curiously untouched place with genuine Roman cuisine and a traditional trattoria feel. Prices in upper bracket.

L'Insalata Ricca, Largo di Chiavari 85. Relaxed and slightly out-of-the-ordinary place, with interesting salads and healthy Italian food.

Ivo, Via di San Francesco a Ripa 157. The top Trastevere pizzeria. Arrive early to avoid a chaotic queue. Still worth experiencing, but in danger of becoming a caricature.

Al Leoncino, Via del Leoncino 28. Inexpensive and genuine city-centre pizzeria, little known to out-of-towners.

Il Piccolo Alpino, Via Orazio Antinori 5. Testaccio neighbourhood restaurant with good pizzas and great *spaghetti alle vongole*.

Il Piccolo Arancio, Vicolo Scanderberg 112. Handily placed restaurant just around the corner from the Trevi fountain. Excellent low-priced food and a cosy atmosphere.

Dar Poeta, Vicolo del Bologna 45. One of the best pizzerias in Rome and with good beer, too.

Remo, Piazza Santa Maria Liberatrice 44. Cheap, crowded and chaotic pizzeria in the heart of Testaccio.

Da Vittorio, Via San Cosimato 14a. Neopolitan pizza in the heart of Trastevere. Closed Mon.

Bars and birrerias

Bar della Pace, Via della Pace 5. Just off Piazza Navona, this is the summer bar to be seen in, with outside tables full of Rome's self-consciously beautiful people.

Bar San Calisto, Piazza San Calisto 4. Basic Trastevere bar that attracts an eclectic bunch of late-night drinkers. Outside tables in summer.

Druid's Den, Via San Martino ai Monti 28. Appealing Irish pub with a mixed expat/Italian clientele. Cheap and lively, with occasional impromptu music.

Enoteca Cavour, Via Cavour 313. At the Forum end of Via Cavour, a handy retreat with an easy-going studenty feel, lots of wine and bottled beers and (slightly overpriced) snacks.

Fiddler's Elbow, Via dell'Omertà 43. Irish bar, roomier than *Druid's* and with a decidedly more Latin feel.

Four Green Fields, Via C. Morin 42. Versatile pub with cocktail bar and live music in basement.

La Scala, Piazza della Scala. The most popular Trastevere birreria – big, bustling and crowded. Pub food, cheap beer and occasional (dire) music.

Trasté, Via della Lungheretta 76. Refined meeting place for the young and cultured Trastevere crowd. Emphasis more on fancy teas then alcohol.

Vineria, Campo de' Fiori. Small vineria which spills out into the square during the summer months.

Nightlife

Roman **nightlife** still retains some of the smart ethos satirized in Fellini's *Dolce Vita*. **Discos and clubs** cover the range: there are vast glittering palaces with stunning lights and sound systems, places that are not much more than upmarket bars with music, and other, more down-to-earth places to dance, playing a more interesting selection of music to a younger crowd, with the new *centri sociali* (see below) offering an innovative alternative to the mainstream scene, usually on a "pay what you can" basis. Whichever you prefer, all tend to open and close late. Some charge a heavy entrance fee (L10,000–L40,000) – though the more expensive places often include one free drink. Rome's **rock scene** is a fairly limp affair, and the city is much more in its element with **jazz**, with lots of venues and a wide choice of styles performed by a healthy array of local talent. Most clubs close during July and August, or move to locations on the coast but *Estate Romana* organizes many outdoor locations all over Rome for concerts, discos, bars and cinemas. Many top international groups participate. Bear in mind, too, that you may have to pay a membership fee on top of the admission price. Drinks, though, are generally no more expensive than you'd pay in the average bar.

The city's best source of **listings** is the magazine *Roma C'e* issued on Thursday with a section in English, or the *TrovaRoma* supplement published with the Thursday edition of *La Repubblica*. For English-language information, there's *Wanted in Rome* or *Time Out*. First stop for **tickets** should be *Orbis* at Piazza Esquilino 37 (☎06.474.4776).

Centri sociali

In the suburbs of Rome, new *centri sociali* are being opened in abandoned public buildings mostly by students who offer a cheap, alternative programme of concerts, films and parties.

The students are politically active, and work for and with newly arrived immigrants, the events they organize being among the more interesting that take place in Rome. The numerous *centri sociali* are listed in *Roma C'e* and *Il Manifesto*.

Forte Prenestino, Via F. del Pino. One of the most established *centri* situated in an abandoned nineteenth-century fortress. Offers two big arenas for concerts and a beehive of smaller spaces used for exhibitions, cinema, a disco and a bar.

Villaggio Globale, Ex-Mattatoio (☎06.573.00329) Located in the old slaughterhouse in Testaccio this *centro* is partly run by the Senagalese community in Rome, which organizes concerts, parties and exhibitions, helped by a grant from local authorities.

Discos and clubs

L'Alibi, Via Monte Testaccio 44. Predominantly but not exclusively male venue that's one of Rome's best gay clubs. Downstairs cellar disco and upstairs open-air bar.

Alien, Via Velletri. Rome's trendiest club, this place is host to the best dance DJs.

Angelo Azzurro, Via Cardinale Merry del Val. Relaxed gay club with a mixed crowd.

Black Out Club, Via Saturnia 18. Popular disco playing a mix of house, trash and grunge.

B-Side, Via dei Funari 21a. Small nightclub playing black music until 5am.

Gilda, Via Mario de' Fiori 97. Slick, stylish club, the focus for the city's minor (and would-be) celebs.

Heaven, Viale di Porta Ardeatina 218. Large disco in southern suburbs playing dance and underground.

Krylon, Via Aurelia 601. Mixture of Latin-American on Thursday, jungle on Friday and underground on Saturday.

Piper, Via Tagliamento 9. One of the oldest discos in Rome, with live music, videos and different nightly events.

Live music: rock, jazz and Latin

Alexanderplatz, Via Ostia 9. Rome's foremost jazz club/restaurant. Reservations recommended.

Alpheus, Via del Commercio 36–38. A four-roomed venue with simultaneous concerts, a disco, theatrical performances and a bar.

Big Mama's, Vicolo San Francesco a Ripa 18. Trastevere-based jazz/blues club of long standing. Closed July–Sept.

Caffè Latino, Via di Monte Testaccio 96. Multi-event club in the newly hip area near the Protestant cemetery. Best at weekends when it's crowded and more atmospheric.

Circolo degli Artisti, Via Lamarmora 28. Bar and disco with more alternative live music. Cheap and fun.

Fonclea, Via Crescenzio 82a. Long running jazz/salsa outfit, with live music most nights.

Palladium, Piazza B, Romano 8. International groups come to this old cinema in the southern suburbs. One of the few live-music venues where dancing is encouraged.

St Louis, Via del Cardello 13a. Modern club known for serious, high-quality music. Membership is L20,000 a year. Live jazz, restaurant and cocktail bar. Closed July–Oct.

Berimbau, Via dei Fienaroli 30/b. Live Latin-American music and Brazilian drinks.

Classical music, opera and film

During the summer there are quite a few places you can hear **classical music**. The city's churches host a wide range of choral, chamber and organ recitals, many of them free. Year-round, the *Accademia di Santa Cecilia* (☎06.6880.1044) stages concerts by its own or visiting orchestras at Via delle Conciliazione 4 (☎06.678.0742) and in summer in the gardens of the Villa Giulia. Rome's **opera** scene concentrates on the *Teatro dell'Opera*, on the Via Firenze, Piazza B. Gigli, from November to May (box office Mon–Sat 10.45am–5pm; ☎06.481.601); check for information on outdoor summer venues. Purists should be prepared for a carnival atmosphere and plenty of unscheduled intervals. Rome's two **English-language cinemas** are the Pasquino on Vicolo del Piede in Trastevere (☎06.580.3622), which shows recent general releases, and the Quirinetta at Via Minghetti 4. Tickets are currently L10,000 for evening performances, L8000 afternoons. Other cinemas show foreign-language films usually on Monday or Tuesday nights. Look in local papers for a list: the *Nuovo Sacher*, Largo Ascianghi 1 (☎06.581.8116), and *Alcazar*, Via Cardinal Merry del Val 14 (☎06.588.0099), are two.

Listings

Airlines Alitalia, Via Bissolati 13 (☎06.65.643); British Airways, Via Bissolati 54 (☎147.812.266 or 06.6501.1513); TWA, Via Barberini 67 (☎06.47.241).

American Express Piazza di Spagna 38 (Mon–Fri 9am–5.30pm, Sat 9am–12.30pm; ☎06.67.641).

Books The Lion Bookshop, Via dei Greci 33 (☎06.3265.0437), is the city's biggest and best-stocked English-language bookstore. Try also the Economy Book Center, Via Torino 136 (☎06.474.6877), which has a good stock of new and used English-language paperbacks.

Car rental At Fiumicino Airport a shuttle bus takes you to the car-rental depot with all main firms. In the foyer at Termini there are car-rental booths. Avis, Via Sardegna 38a (☎06.4282.4728); Europcar, Via Lombardia 7 (☎06.481.9103); Hertz, Via Gregorio VII 207 (☎06.3937.8807); Maggiore, Via Po 8 (☎06.884.0137).

Embassies Australia, Via Alessandria 215 (☎06.852.721); Canada, Via Zara 30 (☎06.445.981); Great Britain, Via XX Settembre 80 (☎06.482.5441); New Zealand, Via Zara 28 (☎06.440.2928); USA, Via V. Veneto 121 (☎06.46741).

Exchange Two offices at Termini station operate out of banking hours; try also Thomas Cook, Via Barberini 21 (☎06.482.8082), Cambio Rosati, Via Nazionale 186 (☎06.488.5498), or look for booths which advertise no commission.

Hospital Call ☎06.884.0113 for 24hr assistance. The most central hospital is the Santo Spirito, Lungotevere in Sassia 1 (☎06.68.351). The International Medical Centre (☎06.488.2371) has an English-speaker on hand.

Laundry Bolle Blu, Via Palestro 59 and Via Milazzo 20 (8am–10pm).

Left luggage At Stazione Termini 7am–9pm; L5000 per item for 12hrs only.

Pharmacies Try PIRAM at Via Nazionale 228 (☎06.488.0754) or at Stazione Termini (☎06.488.0019). A list of late-opening pharmacies is posted on pharmacists' doors.

Police The police station/foreign office is Questura, Via Genova 3 (☎06.4686).

Post office The main office is on Piazza San Silvestro 6771 (Mon–Fri 8.30am–7pm, Sat 8.30am–noon; ☎06.160 for information).

Telephones Phone booths at Stazione Termini (Mon–Fri 9am–6pm & Sat 9am–2pm).

Train enquiries ☎147.888.088. The information booth at Stazione Termini is open daily 7am–11.30pm.

Travel agents CTS, Via Genova 16 (☎06.462.0431), and Corso Vittorio Emanuele II 297 (☎687.2672); Elsy Viaggi, Via di Torre Argentina 80 (☎06.689.6460).

Around Rome

You may find there's quite enough of interest in Rome to keep you occupied during your stay; but it can be a hot and oppressive city, and you really shouldn't feel any guilt about freeing yourself from its weighty history to see something of the countryside around. Two of the main attractions visitable on a day-trip are, it's true, Roman sites, but just the process of getting to them can be energizing.

Tivoli

Just 40km from Rome, **TIVOLI** has always been something of a retreat from the city. In classical days it was a retirement town for wealthy Romans; later, during Renaissance times, it again became the playground of the monied classes, attracting some of the city's most well-to-do families.

Most people head first for the **Villa d'Este** (Tues–Sun 9am–4/7pm; L8000), the country villa of Cardinal Ippolito d'Este, across the main square of Largo Garibaldi. It's the gardens rather than the villa itself that they come to see, peeling away down the hill in a succession of terraces – probably the most contrived gardens in Italy, interrupted at decent intervals by one playful fountain after another, unfortunately not all in working order. In their day some of these were quite ingenious – one played the organ, another imitated the call of birds – though nowadays the emphasis is on the quieter creations. There's the central *Fontana del Bicchierone* by Bernini, one of the simplest and most elegant; on the far left, the *Rometta* or "Little Rome" has reproductions of the major buildings of the city; while the *Fontana del Ovato*, on the opposite side of the garden, has statues and an arcade in which you can walk. The town's other attraction, the **Villa Gregoriana** (daily 9am to 1hr before sunset; L3500), is a park with waterfalls created when Pope Gregory XVI diverted the flow of the river here in 1831 to ease periodic flooding of the town. The lush, overgrown vegetation descends into a gorge over 60m deep. There are two main waterfalls – the *Grande Cascata* on the far side, and a small Bernini-designed one at the neck of the gorge. The path winds down to the bottom of the canyon, where you can get right up close to the pounding water, the dark shapes of the rock glowering overhead. From here the path leads up on the far side to an exit and the substantial remains of a **Temple of Vesta**, clinging to the side of the hill.

Once you've seen these two sights you've really seen Tivoli. But just outside at the bottom of the hill, fifteen minutes' walk off the main Rome road (CAT bus #4 from Largo Garibaldi), the **Villa Adriana** (daily 9am to 1hr 30min before sunset; L8000) casts the inventions of the Tivoli popes and cardinals very much into the shade. This was probably the largest and most sumptuous villa in the Roman Empire, the retirement home of the emperor Hadrian for a short while between 135 AD and his death three years later, and it is now one of the most soothing spots around Rome. Hadrian was a great traveller and a keen architect, and parts of the villa were inspired by buildings he had seen around the world. The massive Pecile for instance, through which you enter, is a reproduction of a building in Athens. And the Canopus, on the opposite side of the site, is a liberal copy of the sanctuary of Serapis near Alexandria, its long, elegant channel of water fringed by columns and statues. Nearby, a museum displays the latest finds from the excavations, though most of the extensive original discoveries have found their way back to Rome. Back towards the entrance, there's a fish pond with a *cryptoporticus* winding around underneath, and – perhaps the most photographed part of the site – the Teatro Marittimo, with its island in the middle of a circular pond, to which it's believed Hadrian would retire at siesta time.

Buses leave Rome for Tivoli frequently (every 10–15min) from Rebibbia Metro Station; tickets cost L6000 return from the office on the right – journey time 45 minutes. In Tivoli they stop at and leave from the main Largo Garibaldi, opposite the **tourist office** (Mon & Sat 9am–3pm, Tues–Fri 9am–6.30pm), which has information on accommodation if you're planning to stay over.

Ostia

There are two Ostias, both reachable in around thirty minutes by regular metro from Magliana, then train: one, Lido di Ostia, is an over-visited seaside resort that is well worth avoiding; the other, the excavations of the port of **OSTIA ANTICA**, is on a par with anything you'll see in Rome itself and easily merits a half-day's outing (Tues–Sun 9am to 1hr before sunset; L8000). The site groups around the town's commercial centre, otherwise known as the **Piazzale di Corporazione** for the remains of shops and trading offices that still fringe it, the mosaics in front of which denote their trade. Flanking one side of the square, the **Theatre** has been much restored but is nonetheless impressive, enlarged in the second century to hold up to four thousand people. On the left of the square, the **House of Apulius** preserves mosaic floors and, beyond, a dark-aisled *mithraeum* with more mosaics illustrating the cult. Behind here, the **Casa di Diana** is probably the best-preserved private house in Ostia, with a dark set of rooms around a central courtyard, and again with a *mithraeum* at the back. You can climb up to its roof for a fine view of the rest of the site, afterwards crossing the road to the **Thermopolium** – an ancient Roman café, complete with seats, counter, display shelves and even wall paintings of parts of the menu. North of the Casa di Diana, the **Museum** (Tues–Sun 9am–1.30pm & 3–6pm) holds a variety of articles from the site, including wall paintings depicting domestic life in Ostia and some fine sarcophagi and statuary. Left from here, the **Forum** centres on the **Capitol** building, reached by a wide flight of steps.

Anzio

About 40km south of Rome, **ANZIO** is much the best bet for a day by the sea if you're staying in Rome. Much of the town was damaged during a difficult Allied landing here on January 22, 1944, to which two military cemeteries (one British, the other, at nearby Nettuno, American) bear testimony. But despite a pretty thorough rebuilding it's a likeable resort, still depending as much on fish as tourists for its livelihood. The town's seafood **restaurants** are reason enough to come, crowding together along the harbour and not unreasonably priced, and the **beaches**, which edge the coast on either side, don't get unbearably stuffed outside August. Anzio is also a possible route onto the island of Ponza, for which **hydrofoils** leave daily in summer – ask for timings at the **tourist office** in the harbour (daily 9am–1pm & 3.30–6pm).

THE SOUTH

The Italian south or *mezzogiorno* is quite a different experience from the north; indeed, few countries are more tangibly divided into two distinct, often antagonistic, regions. While the north is rich, the south is by contrast one of the most depressed areas in Europe. Its rate of unemployment (about 25 percent) is around twice that of the north, its gross regional product about a third. Its people are dark-skinned and speak with the cadences of the Mediterranean, the dialect down here sounding almost Arabic sometimes. Indeed the south's "capital", Naples, is often compared to Cairo.

For most people, **Naples**, regional capital of **Campania** and only a couple of hours south of Rome, is the obvious focus, an utterly compelling city, dominating the region in every way. The **Bay of Naples** is dense in interest, with the ancient sites of Pompeii and Herculaneum just half an hour outside – probably Italy's best-preserved and most revealing Roman remains – and the island of Cápri, swarmed over by tourists these days but so beautiful that a day there is by no means time squandered. South of Naples, **Sorrento**, at the far east end of the bay, has all the beer 'n' chips trappings you'd expect from a major Brit package destination, but is a likeable place for all that; and the **Amalfi Coast**, across the peninsula, is probably Europe's most dramatic stretch of coastline, harbouring some enticing – if crowded – beach resorts. **Puglia** – the long strip of land that makes up the "heel" of Italy – was for centuries a strategic province, invaded and colonized by just about every major power of the day. There's no escaping these influences in the Saracenic kasbah-like quarters of cities such as **Bari**, and the Baroque exuberance of **Lecce**. All the same, Puglia is still very much a province you pass through on the way elsewhere, not least to **Bríndisi** with its ferry connections with Greece. **Basilicata** and **Calabria** are also to some extent transit regions, although in many ways they represent the quintessence of the *mezzogiorno* – culturally impoverished, underdeveloped and – owing to emigration – sparsely populated. Artistically they are the most barren regions in Italy, but the combination of mountain grandeur and a relatively unspoilt coastline, often in close proximity, is a unique attraction, only now beginning to be exploited by the tourist industry.

Naples

Wherever else you travel south of Rome, the chances are that you'll wind up in **NAPLES** – capital of the whole Italian south. It's the kind of city people visit with preconceptions, and it rarely disappoints: it is filthy, large and overbearing; it is crime-infested; and it is most definitely like nowhere else in Italy – something the inhabitants will be keener than anyone to tell you. In all these things lies the city's charm. Perhaps the feeling that you're somewhere unique makes it possible to endure the noise and constant harassment, perhaps it's the feeling that you've travelled from an ordinary part of Europe to somewhere that feels like an Arab bazaar in less than three hours. One thing, though, is certain: a couple of days here and you're likely to be as staunch a defender of the place as its most devoted inhabitants. No city on earth, except perhaps New York, excites fiercer loyalties.

Arrival and information

Naples' **Capodochino Airport** is northwest of the city centre at Viale Umberto Maddalena, connected with Piazza Garibaldi by bus #14 (every 15min; L1500). The bus journey takes about thirty minutes – not much more than a taxi, for which you'll pay up to L40,000; there's also a blue official airport bus (every 50min 6am–midnight; L3000) which will take you

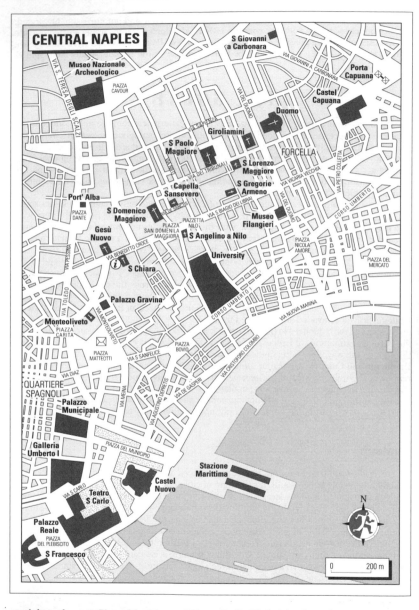

CENTRAL NAPLES

straight to the port, Piazza Municipo and Piazza Garibaldi. Arriving by **train**, Napoli Centrale is on Piazza Garibaldi, at the main hub of all transport services. The main **tourist office** is at Piazza dei Martiri 58 (Mon–Fri 8.30am–4pm; ☎081.405.311), and there are branches at Capodichino Airport (daily 8.30am–7.30pm), and another on Piazza del Gesù, but the most convenient is at the Stazione Centrale (Mon–Sat 9am–7pm, Sun 9am–2pm). All have free maps of the city, information on accommodation, and copies of the free monthly booklet *Qui Napoli*, handy for current events, ferry and bus times.

City transport

The only way to really get around Naples and stay sane is to walk. However, Naples is a large, sprawling city, and its transport services extend to the Bay as a whole, which means you'll definitely need to use some form of public transport sooner or later. City **buses** are much the best way of crossing the city centre: fares are a flat L1500 per journey (valid for 90min); buy tickets in advance from tobacconists or the booth on Piazza Garibaldi; one-day tickets are also available for L4500. The bus system is supplemented by the **metropolitana**, a small underground network which crosses the centre and runs around the Bay, and **funiculars** scaling the hill of the Vómero from stations at Piazzas Montesanto, Amadeo and Augusto. For **trips around the bay** in either direction, there are three rail systems, the most useful of which is the **Circumvesuviana**, which runs from its station on Corso Garibaldi around the Bay of Naples about every half-hour as far as Sorrento, which it reaches in about an hour. The minimum **taxi** fare in the city is L6000.

Accommodation

A good many of the city's cheaper **hotels** are situated around Piazza Garibaldi, within spitting distance of the train station and not badly placed for the rest of town. The *San Pietro*, Via San Pietro ad Aram 14 (☎081.553.5914; ③), has clean if characterless rooms; off Piazza Garibaldi to the right is the pleasant *Casanova*, Corso Garibaldi 333 (☎081.268.287; ③). With a little more money, try the *Odeon*, on Via Silvio Spaventa (☎081.285.656; ③), a two-star hotel two minutes from the station. Enjoying a nicer location over in the *centro storico*, the small *Imperia*, Piazza Miraglia 386 (☎081.459.347; ⑤), is a homely, clean and fairly comfortable hotel. *Pensione Eden* (☎081.285.656; ③) is friendly and within a stone's throw of the station, and the welcoming *Bella Capri* (☎081.552.9494; ③) is right on the seafront and has nicely furnished rooms on the top floor of a modern block with a great view of the bay. Don't, whatever you do, go with one of the touts outside the station. There's an official **youth hostel**, *Ostello Mergellina*, Salita della Grotta 23 (☎081.761.2346; ②), in a nice location, but a long way out and there's also a midnight curfew and a three-day maximum stay during July and August; take the metropolitana to Mergellina or bus #152 from Piazza Garibaldi. There's also a small, accommodating hostel close to Piazza Garibaldi, *Pensione Mancini*, at Via Mancini 33 (☎081.553.6731; ②). The closest **campsite** is *Vulcano Solfatara* in nearby Pozzuoli at Via Solfatara 161 (☎081.526.7413; April–Nov); bus #152 runs right there from Piazza Garibaldi, or take the metropolitana to Pozzuoli and walk ten minutes up the hill. During the winter months, you're probably best off going to one of the other sites around the Bay – at Pompeii or Sorrento, both of which are less than an hour out from the city.

The City

Naples is a large city, with a centre that has many different focuses. The area between the vast and busy Piazza Garibaldi, where you will arrive, and Via Toledo, the main street a mile or so west, makes up the old part of the city – the **centro storico**. Buildings rise high on either side of the narrow, crowded streets, cobwebbed with washing; there's little light, not even much sense of the rest of the city outside – certainly not of the proximity of the sea. The two main drags of the *centro storico* are **Via dei Tribunali** and **Via San Biagio dei Librai** – two narrow streets, lined with old arcaded buildings, that are a maelstrom of hurrying pedestrians, revving cars and buzzing, dodging scooters. Via dei Tribunali cuts through to **Via Duomo**, where you'll find the tucked-away **Duomo** (Mon–Sat 9am–noon & 4.30–7pm, Sun 9am–1pm), a Gothic building from the early thirteenth century dedicated to San Gennaro, the patron saint of the city. San Gennaro was martyred in 305 AD. Two phials of his blood miraculously liquefy three times a year – on the first Saturday in May (when a procession leads from the church of Santa Chiara to the cathedral) and on September 19 and December 16. If the blood refuses to liquefy – which luckily is rare – disaster is supposed to befall the city. The first chapel on the right as you walk into the cathedral holds the precious phials and Gennaro's skull in a silver bust-reliquary from 1305. On the other side of the church, the basilica of **Santa Restituta** is officially the oldest structure in Naples, erected by Constantine in 324 and supported by columns taken from a temple to Apollo on this site. Downstairs, the **Crypt of San Gennaro** is one of the finest examples of Renaissance art in Naples, founded by Cardinal Carafa and holding the tombs of both San Gennaro and Pope Innocent IV.

Across Via Duomo, Via dei Tribunali continues on into the heart of the old city: the **Spaccanapoli** ("split-Naples"), the city's busiest and architecturally richest quarter. Cut down to its other main axis, **Via San Biagio dei Libra**, which leads west to **Piazza San Domenico Maggiore**, marked by the **Guglia di San Domenico** – one of the whimsical Baroque obelisks that pop up all over the city, built in 1737. The **Church** of the same name flanks the north side of the square, an originally Gothic building from 1289, one of whose chapels holds a miraculous painting of the *Crucifixion* which is said to have spoken to St Thomas Aquinas during his time at the adjacent monastery. North, Via de Sanctis leads off right to one of the city's odder monuments, the **Cappella Sansevero** (Mon & Wed–Sat 10am–5pm, Sun 10am–1.30pm; L8000), the tomb-chapel of the di Sangro family, decorated by the sculptor Guiseppe Sammartino in the mid-eighteenth century with some remarkable carving including a starkly realistic dead *Christ*. The chapel downstairs, commissioned by alchemist Prince Raimondo, contains the gruesome results of some of his experiments: two bodies under glass, their capillaries and organs preserved by a mysterious liquid developed by the prince.

Continuing west, the **Gesù Nuovo** church is most notable for its lava-stone facade. Originally part of a fifteenth-century palace which stood here, its prickled with pyramids that give it an impregnable, prison-like air. The inside is in part decorated by the Neapolitan-Spanish painter Ribera. Facing the Gesù church, the church of **Santa Chiara** is quite different, a Provençal-Gothic structure built in 1328 and rebuilt after World War II with an austerity that's pleasing after the excesses opposite. The attached **cloister** (Mon–Sat 9.30am–1pm & 2.30–5.30pm; L6000, including entrance to museum), lushly planted and covered with colourful majolica tiles depicting bucolic scenes of life outside, is one of the gems of the city.

Piazza del Municipio is a busy traffic junction that stretches down to the waterfront, dominated by the brooding hulk of the **Castel Nuovo**. Built in 1282 by the Angevins and later the royal residence of the Aragon monarchs, it now contains the **Museo Civico** (Mon–Sat 9am–7pm; L10,000), which holds periodic exhibitions in a series of elaborate Gothic rooms. The entrance of the Castel incorporates a triumphal arch built in 1454 to commemorate the taking of the city by Alfonso I, the first Aragon ruler. Just beyond the castle, on the left, the **Teatro San Carlo** (guided tours Sept–June, Sat & Sun 2–3.30pm; L5000)) is still the largest opera house in Italy, and one of the most distinguished in the world. Beyond, at the bottom of the main shopping street of Via Toledo, the dignified **Palazzo Reale** (Sun–Tues, Thurs & Fri 9am–2pm, Sat 9am–7pm; L8000) was built in 1602 to accommodate a visit by Philip III of Spain. Upstairs, the palace's first-floor rooms are decorated with gilded furniture, trompe l'oeil ceilings, overbearing tapestries and lots of undistinguished seventeenth- and eighteenth-century paintings. Best are the chapel, with its finely worked altarpiece, and the little theatre which is refreshingly restrained after the rest of the palace. The original bronze doors of the palace, at the bottom of the main staircase, were cast in 1468 and show scenes from Ferdinand of Aragon's struggle against the local barons. The cannonball wedged in the bottom panel dates from a naval battle between the French and the Genoese.

Via Toledo leads north from Piazza Trieste e Trento to the **Museo Archeologico Nazionale** (daily: summer 9am–7pm; winter 9am–2pm; L12,000; bus #110 from Piazza Garibaldi) – perhaps Naples' most essential sight, home to the Farnese collection of antiquities from Lazio and Campania, and the best of the finds from the nearby Roman sites of Pompeii and Herculaneum. The ground floor concentrates on sculpture, including the *Farnese Bull* and *Farnese Hercules* from the Baths of Caracalla in Rome – the former the largest piece of classical sculpture ever found. The mezzanine floor at the back houses the museum's collection of mosaics, remarkably preserved works giving a superb insight into ordinary Roman customs, beliefs and humour. Upstairs, the wall paintings from the villas of

Pompeii and Herculaneum are the museum's other major draw, rich in colour and invention. Look out for the group of four small pictures in the first main room, best of which is a depiction of a woman gathering flowers entitled *Primavera*. There are also everyday items from the Campanian cities – glass, silver, ceramics, charred pieces of rope, even foodstuffs – together with a model layout of Pompeii in cork. The other side of the first floor has sculptures in bronze from the **Villa dei Papiri** in Herculaneum, including a superb *Hermes at Rest*, a languid *Resting Satyr* and a convincingly woozy *Drunken Silenus*.

At the top of the hill is the city's other major museum, the **Palazzo Reale di Capodimonte** (Tues–Sat 10am–7pm, Sun 9am–2pm; L9500; bus #24 from Piazza Municipio, #110 from Piazza Garibaldi, or #137 from Piazza Dante), the former residence of the Bourbon King Charles III, built in 1738 and now housing the **Museo Nazionale di Capodimonte**. This has a superb collection of Renaissance paintings, including a couple of Bruegels, *The Misanthrope* and *The Blind*, canvases by Perugino and Pinturicchio, an elegant *Madonna and Child with Angels* by Botticelli and Lippi's soft, sensitive *Annunciation*. Later paintings include a room full of Titians, with a number of paintings of the shrewd Farnese Pope Paul III in various states of ageing, Raphael's austere portrait of *Leo X*, and Bellini's impressively composed *Transfiguration*.

Vómero, the district topping the hill immediately above the old city, can be reached on the Montesanto funicular. Go up to the star-shaped fortress of **Castel Sant'Elmo** (Tues–Sun 9am–sunset; L4000), occupying Naples' highest point. Built in the fourteenth century, it now hosts exhibitions and concerts, and boasts the very best views of Naples.

Eating, drinking and nightlife

Neapolitan cuisine is among Italy's best – simple dishes cooked with fresh, healthy ingredients that have none of the richness or pretensions of the north. It's also the best place in the country to eat **pizza**, which originates from here. If you're just after a **snack**, you can pick something up from the city's **street markets** – the Forcella quarter market on the far side of Piazza Garibaldi or the fish market at Porta Nolana, off to the left – and there are plenty of snack places around Piazza Garibaldi, not to mention **restaurants**, though most of these are of indifferent quality. *La Nova Club*, at Piazza San Maria La Nova 9, is one of Naples best restaurants where you can eat within a specified budget, while *Da Peppino Avellinese*, Via Spaventa 31, is the most welcoming and best value of the many options on and around Piazza Garibaldi. Also in the centre, *Di Matteo*, Via dei Tribunali 94, is a cheap, unpretentious pizzeria, as is *Lombardi*, not far away at Via B. Croce 59. Next door to *Di Matteo*, *Da Carmine* is a simple trattoria with an extensive menu and low prices.

Bellini, Via Santa Maria di Constantinopoli 80, is a good place for a splurge, one of the city's longest-established restaurants, also with great pizzas. A little further on, on Piazza Dante, *Leon d'Oro* is a pleasant, centrally placed restaurant with outdoor seating and reasonably priced food. On the other side of Via Toledo, *Brandi*, Salita Sant'Anna di Palazzo 1–2, off Via Chiaia, is possibly Naples' most famous pizzeria – very friendly, and serving pasta too. *California*, Via Santa Lucia 101, is an institution of a rather different kind, with a menu that's an odd hybrid of American and Italian specialities. It's perhaps best known for its full American breakfasts.

As for **nightlife**, the beautiful Piazza Bellini is a trendy drinking spot, where tables spill out from the surrounding bars. Of these *Intra Moenia* serves a bite to eat, *Libreria Bar 1799 Club* sells books as well, and *Gauguin* goes in for a spot of live music.

Listings

Airlines Alitalia, Via Medina 41–42 (☎081.542.5111); British Airways, Capodichino Airport (☎081.780.3087 or 147.812.266)

Car rental Avis, Via Partenope 23 (☎081.764.5600); Europcar, Via Partenope 38 (☎081.764.5070); Hertz, Via N. Sauro 21a (☎081.764.5323); Maggiore, Via Cervantes 92 (☎081.552.1900). All have desks at the airport and Stazione Centrale.

Consulates Great Britain, Via Crispi 122 (☎081.663.511); USA, Piazza della Repubblica (☎081.583.8111).

Exchange Outside banking hours at Stazione Centrale (daily 7am–9pm).

Hospital ☎081.747.1111 or go to the 24hr Guardia Medica Permanente in the train station.
Laundry Bolle Blu at Corso Novara 62 (Mon–Sat 9am–8pm).
Pharmacy At Stazione Centrale (Mon–Sat 24hr)..
Police The main station is at Via Medina 75 (☎081.794.1111); for emergencies call ☎112.
Post office Main office on Piazza Matteotti, off Via Toledo (Mon–Fri 8am–7.40pm, Sat 8.30am–noon).
Telephones The Telecom Italia office at Via Depretis 40 (Mon–Fri 9.30am–1pm & 2–5.30pm).
Train enquiries ☎147.888.088 (daily 7am–9pm). Station booths are open daily 7am–10pm, but be prepared to queue.
Travel agents CTS, Via Mezzocannone 25 (☎081.552.7960).

The Bay of Naples

For the Romans, the **Bay of Naples** was the land of plenty, a blessed region of mild climate, gorgeous scenery and an accessible location that made it a favourite vacation and retirement area for the city's nobility. Later, when Naples became the final stop on northerners' Grand Tours, the relics of its heady Roman period only added to the charm for most travellers. However, these days it's hard to tell where Naples ends and the countryside begins, the city sprawling around the Bay in an industrial and residential mess that is quite at odds with the region's popular image. It's only when you reach **Sorrento** in the east, or the islands that dot the Bay, that you really feel free of it all. Of the islands, **Cápri** is the best place to visit if you're here for a short time. There's also, of course, the ever-brooding presence of **Vesuvius**, and the incomparable Roman sites of **Herculaneum** and **Pompeii** – each of which is well worth extending your stay in the city for.

Herculaneum and Vesuvius

The first point of any interest travelling east is the town of **ERCOLANO**, the modern offshoot of the ancient site of Herculaneum, which was destroyed by the eruption of Vesuvius on August 2, 79 AD. It's worth stopping here for two reasons: to see the excavations of the site and to climb to the summit of Vesuvius – to which buses run from outside the train station. If you're planning both to visit Herculaneum and scale Vesuvius in one day, though, be sure to see Vesuvius first, and set off reasonably early – buses stop running up the mountain at lunchtime, leaving you the afternoon free to wander around the site.

Situated at the seaward end of Ercolano's main street, **Herculaneum** (June–Sept daily 9am to 1hr before sunset; Oct–May 9am–2.45pm; L12,000) was a residential town in Roman times, much smaller than Pompeii, and as such it's a more manageable site, less architecturally impressive but better preserved and more easily taken in on a single visit. Because it wasn't a commercial town, there is no central open space or forum, just streets of villas and shops, cut as usual by two very straight main streets. The **House of the Mosaic Atrium** (closed at time of writing) at the bottom end of the main street, Cardo IV, retains its mosaic-laid courtyard, corrugated by the force of the tufa, behind which the **House of the Deer** contains corridors decorated with richly coloured still lifes and a bawdy statue of a drunken Hercules seemingly about to piss all over the visitors. There's also a large **Thermae** or bath complex (partly closed) with a domed *frigidarium* decorated with frescoes of fish and a *caldarium* containing a plunge bath at one end and a scallop-shell apse complete with washbasin and water pipes. The women's bath complex has a mosaiced floor of Triton and sea creatures. Opposite, the **House of Neptune and Amphitrite** holds a sparklingly preserved wall mosaic of the god and goddess, and frescoes of flowers and vegetables, served in lieu of a garden. Next door is a wine shop, stocked with amphorae in wooden racks, left as they lay when disaster struck. Close by in the **Casa del Bel Cortile** are some skeletons poignantly lying in the same attitude as they were in 79 AD. Further down on the opposite side of the road in **House of the Wooden Partition**, there's a room with the marital bed still intact, and in the house nearby a perfectly preserved coiled rope.

Since its first eruption in 79 AD, when it buried the towns and inhabitants of Pompeii and Herculaneum, **Vesuvius** has dominated the lives of those who live on the Bay of Naples. It's still an active volcano, the only one on mainland Europe, and there have been more than a hundred eruptions over the years, but only two of real significance: one in December 1631 that engulfed many nearby towns and killed three thousand people; and the last, in March 1944, which caused widespread devastation, though no one was actually killed. The people who live here still fear the reawakening of Vesuvius, and with good reason – scientists calculate it should erupt every thirty years or so, and it hasn't since 1944.

There are two ways to make the **ascent**. Trasporti Vesuviani run bus services (around 6 daily in summer; L6000 return) from Ercolano train station to a car park and huddle of souvenir shops and cafés close to the crater; don't listen to the taxi drivers at the station who will try and persuade you there is no bus. If you've more energy, or have missed the bus, you can also take a local bus (#5) from the roundabout near the station to the end of the line and walk the couple of hours to the car park from there. The walk up to the crater from the car park where the bus stops takes about half an hour, across barren gravel on marked-out paths. At the top (admission L9000), the crater is a deep, wide, jagged ashtray of red rock emitting the odd plume of smoke, though since the last eruption effectively sealed up the main crevice this is much less evident than it once was. You can walk most of the way around, but take it easy – the fences are old and rickety.

Pompeii

The other Roman town destroyed by Vesuvius, **Pompeii** (daily 9am to 1hr before sunset; L12,000) was much larger than Herculaneum, and one of Campania's most important commercial centres. Out of a total population of twenty thousand, it's thought that only two thousand actually perished, asphyxiated by the toxic fumes of the volcanic debris, their homes buried in several metres of volcanic ash and pumice. In effect, the eruption froze the way of life in Pompeii as it stood at the time, and the excavations here have probably yielded more information about the life of Roman citizens during the imperial era than any other site. The full horror of their way of death is apparent in plaster casts made from the shapes their bodies left in the volcanic ash. Bear in mind, however, that most of the best mosaics and murals have found their way to the Archeological Museum in Naples.

The site covers a wide area, and seeing it properly takes half a day at least. Entering the site from the Pompeii-Villa dei Misteri side, the **Forum** is the first real feature of significance, a slim open space surrounded by the ruins of what would have been some of the town's most important official buildings. North from here, the **House of the Tragic Poet** is named for its mosaics of a theatrical production and a poet inside, though the "Cave Canem" (Beware of the Dog) mosaic by the main entrance is more eye-catching. Close by, the residents of the **House of the Faun** must have been a friendlier lot, its "Ave" (Welcome) mosaic outside beckoning you in to view the atrium and the copy of a tiny bronze dancing faun that gives the villa its name. On the street behind, the **House of the Vettii** is one of the most delightful houses in Pompeii, a merchant villa ranged around a lovely central peristyle that gives the best possible impression of the domestic environment of the city's upper middle classes. The first room on the right off the peristyle holds the best of Pompeii's murals viewable in situ: the one on the left shows the young Hercules struggling with serpents, while, through the villa's kitchen, a small room that's normally kept locked has erotic works showing various techniques of lovemaking, together with a potent-looking statue of Priapus from which women were supposed to drink to ensure fertility.

On the other side of the site, the **Grand Theatre** is very well preserved and still used for performances, as is the **Little Theatre** on its far left side. Walk up to the **Amphitheatre**, one of Italy's most intact and also its oldest, dating from 80 BC. Next door, the **Palestra** is a vast parade ground that was used by Pompeii's youth for sport and exercise. One last place you shouldn't miss is the **Villa dei Misteri**, outside the main site, a short walk from the Porta Ercolano and accessible on the same ticket. This is probably the best preserved of all Pompeii's palatial houses, and it derives its name from a series of excellently preserved paintings in one of its larger chambers: depictions of the initiation rites of a young woman into the Dionysiac Mysteries, an outlawed cult of the early imperial era.

To **reach Pompeii from Naples**, take the Circumvesuviana to Pompeii-Scavi-Villa dei Misteri (direction Sorrento) for about thirty minutes; this leaves you right outside the western entrance to the site. The Circumvesuviana also runs to Pompeii-Santuario, outside the site's eastern entrance (direction Sarno), or you can take the roughly hourly main-line train (direction Salerno) to the main Pompeii FS station, on the south side of the modern town. It makes most sense to see the site from Naples, and there's really no need to stay overnight, though if you get stuck or are planning to move on south after seeing Pompeii, there are plenty of **hotels** in the modern town, and a large and well-equipped **campsite**, *Zeus*, right outside the Pompeii-Villa dei Misteri station. The **tourist office** on Piazza Esedra (turn right outside Pompeii-Villa dei Misteri station) has full details and plans of the site.

Sorrento

Topping the rocky cliffs close to the end of its peninsula, **SORRENTO** is unashamedly a resort, its inspired location and mild climate having drawn foreigners from all over Europe for close on two hundred years. Nowadays it's strictly package-tour territory, but really none the worse for it, a bright, lively place that retains its southern Italian roots. Cheap restaurants aren't hard to find; neither is reasonably priced accommodation; and there's really no better place outside Naples itself from which to explore the rugged Amalfi shore and the islands of the Bay.

Sorrento's centre is **Piazza Tasso**, five minutes from the train station along the busy Corso Italia, the streets around which are pedestrianized for the lively evening *passeggiata*. Strange as it may seem, Sorrento isn't particularly well provided with **beaches**: most people make do with the rocks and a tiny, crowded strip of sand at **Marina Grande** – fifteen minutes' walk or a short bus ride from Piazza Tasso – or simply use the wooden jetties. If you don't fancy this, try the beaches further along, like the tiny **Regina Giovanna** at Punta del Capo, again connected by bus from Piazza Tasso, where the ruins of the Roman Villa Pollio Felix make a unique place to bathe. There's a **tourist office** in the large yellow Circolo dei Foresteri building at Via de Maio 35, just off Piazza San Antonino (Mon–Sat 8.45am–2.15pm & 3.45–6.15pm), which has maps and details on accommodation. There's a **youth hostel** close to the station at Via degli Aranci 156 (☎081.807.2925; ②); walk out of the station, turn left on the main road and it's a little way down on your left. Among a number of centrally placed **hotels**, the cheapest are the *City*, Corso Italia 221 (☎081.877.2210; ④), and the *Astoria* on Via Santa Maria delle Grazie (☎081.807.4030; ⑤). The cheapest and closest **campsite** is *Nube d'Argento* (April–Oct), ten minutes' walk from Piazza Tasso in the direction of Marina Grande at Via del Capo 12. For **eating**, the *Ristorante San Antonino*, off Piazza Antonino, is good value. For late-night boozing and **nightlife**, there are the town's English-style pubs: try the *English Inn*, or *Chaplin's*, almost opposite, on Corso Italia.

Cápri

Sheering out of the sea off the far end of the Sorrentine peninsula, the island of **Cápri** has long been the most sought-after part of the Bay of Naples. During Roman times the emperor Tiberius retreated here to indulge in legendary debauchery until his death in 37 AD. Later, the discovery of the Blue Grotto and the island's remarkable natural landscape coincided with the rise of tourism; the island has attracted a steady flow of artists and writers and, more recently, inquisitive tourists, ever since. Inevitably, Cápri is a crowded and expensive place, and in July and August it's perhaps sensible to give it a miss. But it would be hard to find a place with more inspiring views, and it's easy enough to visit on a day-trip.

From Naples, there are regular ferries to Cápri from the Molo Beverello, at the bottom of Piazza Municipio (at least 6 daily in summer; journey time 1hr 15min); there are also regular hydrofoils from the Mergellina jetty a couple of miles north of here and from Sorrento: these are quicker, but are much more expensive. For more information, consult the daily newspaper, *Il Mattino*.

Ferries and hydrofoils dock at **MARINA GRANDE**, the waterside extension of Cápri town, which perches on the hill above, connected by **funicular** (L1700 one way). There's not much to actually see, but it's very pretty, its winding, hilly alleyways converging on the dinky main square of **Piazza Umberto**. The **Certosa San Giacomo** (Mon–Fri 9am–2pm, Sun 9am–1pm; free) on the far side of the town is a run-down old monastery with a handful of paintings, and the **Giardini Augustos** next door give tremendous views of the coast below and the towering jagged cliffs above. From here you can wind down to **MARINA PICCOLA**, a huddle of houses and restaurants around a few patches of pebble beach – pleasantly uncrowded out of season, though in season you might as well forget it. You can also reach the ruins of Tiberius' villa, the **Villa Jovis** (daily 9am to 1hr before sunset; L4000), from Cápri town, a steep thirty-minute trek east. The site is among Cápri's most exhilarating, with incredible vistas of the Bay, although there's not much left of the villa.

The island's other main settlement, **ANACÁPRI**, is less picturesque than Cápri town, its tacky main square flanked by souvenir shops, boutiques and touristy restaurants. But during the season, a chair lift operates from here up **Monte Solaro**, at 596m the island's highest point, and you can also get to the island's most famous attraction, the **Blue Grotto** ("Grotta Azzurra"), from here – a good 45-minute trek down Via Lo Pozzo or reachable by bus every twenty minutes from the main square. This is a bit of a rip-off, with boatmen whisking visitors through the grotto in five minutes flat, but you may want to do it just to say you've been, despite the L23,000 fee. In the late afternoons after the tourists have gone you can swim into the cave for nothing – change at the bar next to the entrance. It's also possible to take a boat trip to the Grotto direct from Marina Grande, though at L8000 a head, not including entrance to the cave, it's a pricey outing. Time is better spent walking in the opposite direction from Piazza Vittoria to Axel Munthe's **Villa San Michele** (daily 9am to 1 hr before sunset; L8000), a light, airy house that was home to the Swedish writer for a number of years, and is filled with his furniture and knick-knacks, as well as Roman artefacts ingeniously incorporated into the villa's rooms and gardens.

There are **tourist offices** in Marina Grande, on Piazza Umberto in Cápri town, and on Via G. Orlandi in Anacápri. You'd be advised not to **stay** overnight, but if keen you could try the centrally placed *Quattro Stagioni*, Via Marina Piccola 1 (☎081.837.0041; ⑤; March–Oct), *Stella Maris*, Via Roma 27 (☎081.837.0452; ⑥), or *Pensione Esperia*, Via Supramonte (☎081.837.0262; ⑧). Even if you don't stay, **eating** is an expense, and you might prefer to fix a picnic: in Cápri town there is a supermarket and bakery a little way down Via Botteghe off Piazza Umberto, and well-stocked food stores at Via Roma 13 and 30. For sit-down food, *Di Giorgio* in Via Roma is inexpensive. For a good pizza, try *Da Gemma* in Via Madre Serafina 6, just off the south side of the piazza, up the steps, past the church and bearing right through the tunnel.

The Amalfi Coast

Occupying the southern side of Sorrento's peninsula, the **Amalfi Coast** lays claim to being Europe's most beautiful stretch of coast, its corniche road winding around the towering cliffs. It's an incredible ride, and if you're staying in Sorrento shouldn't be missed on any account; in any case, the towns along here hold the beaches that Sorrento lacks. It's become rather developed, but the cliffs are so steep and the towns' growth so constrained it seems unlikely that it can ever become completely spoilt.

Positano

There's not much to **POSITANO**, only a couple of decent beaches and a handful of clothing and souvenir shops. But its location, heaped up in a pyramid high above the water, has inspired a thousand picture postcards, and helped to make it a moneyed resort that runs a close second to Cápri in the celebrity stakes. It's inevitably pricey – an overnight stay isn't recommended. But its beaches – a small one to the right of the pyramid, a larger one to the left, ringed with overpriced bars and restaurants – are rarely unpleasantly crammed. And if you can't bring yourself to get back on the bus, there are summer hydrofoil connections with Cápri, Amalfi and Salerno. For food, try the *salumeria*, next to the *tabacchi* which sells hydrofoil tickets.

Amalfi

For affordable food and accommodation, you'd do better to push on to **AMALFI**, the largest town along this coast and an established seaside resort since Edwardian times, when the

British upper classes spent their winters here. An independent republic in Byzantine times, Amalfi was one of the great naval powers with a population of some seventy thousand. Vanquished by the Normans in 1131, it was devastated by an earthquake in 1343. A few remnants of Amalfi's past glories survive, and the town has a crumbly attractiveness that makes it fun to wander through.

The **Duomo**, at the top of a steep flight of steps, dominates the town's main piazza, its decorated, almost gaudy facade topped by a glazed tiled cupola that's typical of the region. Inside, it's a mixture of Saracen and Romanesque styles, though now heavily restored, with a major relic in the body of St Andrew buried in its crypt. The most appealing part of the building is the cloister – oddly Arabic in feel, with its whitewashed arches and palms. Close by, the **Museo Civico** displays the original *Tavoliere Amalfitane* – the book of maritime laws which governed the republic, and the rest of the Mediterranean, until 1570. Beyond these, the focus is along the busy seafront, where there's an acceptably crowded **beach**. There's a rather unhelpful **tourist office** at Corso delle Repubbliche 27, next door to the **post office** (Mon–Sat 8am–2pm & 4–7pm; ☎089.872.619). The cheapest **hotels** are the *Proto*, off Via Genova down Salita dei Curiali (☎089.871.003; ④), and the *Sant'Andrea*, Piazza Duomo 26, (☎089.871.145; ④). For **eating**, try *Trattoria Vincola*, on the main street, where you can sit outside; *Trattoria Gemma*, back towards the sea on the opposite side, with a lovely terrace overlooking the street; or *Il Tari*, also on the left side of the street, a small and inexpensive eatery.

Ravello

The best views of the coast can be had inland from Amalfi, in **RAVELLO**: another renowned spot, "closer to the sky than the seashore," wrote André Gide – with some justification. Ravello was also an independent republic for a while, and for a time an outpost of the Amalfi city-state; now it's not much more than a large village, but its unrivalled location, spread across the top of one of the coast's mountains, makes it more than worth the thirty-minute bus ride up from Amalfi.

Buses drop off on the main **Piazza Vescovado**, outside the **Duomo**: an eleventh-century church dedicated to St Pantaleone, a fourth-century saint whose blood – kept in a chapel on the left-hand side – is supposed to liquefy like that of Naples' San Gennaro, twice a year on May 19 and August 27. It's richly decorated, with a pair of twelfth-century bronze doors, cast with 54 scenes of the Passion; inside, attention focuses on a monumental ambo of 1272, adorned with mosaics of dragons and birds on spiral columns, and with the coat of arms and the vivacious profiles of the Rufolo family, the donors, on each side. The Rufolos figure again on the other side of the square, where various leftovers of their **Villa Rufolo** (daily 9am–6/8pm; L5000) scatter among gardens overlooking the precipitous coastline. Ten minutes away, the gardens of the **Villa Cimbrone** (daily 8.30am–4.30/7pm; L6000), laid out by a Yorkshire aristocrat earlier this century, spread across the furthest tip of Ravello's ridge. Most of the villa itself is not open to visitors, though it's worth peeking into the crumbly, flower-hung cloister as you go in, and the open crypt down the steps from here. Best bit of the gardens is the belvedere at the far end of the main path, giving marvellous views over the sea below.

Bari

Commercial and administrative capital of Puglia, and the second city of the *mezzogiorno*, **BARI** has its fair share of interest. But although an economically vibrant place, it harbours no pretensions about being a major tourist attraction. Primarily people come here to work, or to leave for Greece on its many ferries.

There's not a lot to the new part of the city so you should head straight for tree-lined **Corso Cavour**, Bari's main commercial street, which leads down to the waterfront and the **old city**, an entrancing labyrinth of seemingly endless passages weaving through courtyards and under arches that was originally designed to spare the inhabitants from the wind and throw invaders into a state of confusion. The **Basilica di San Nicola** (daily 7am–2pm & 4–7pm), in the heart of the old city, was consecrated in 1197 to house the relics of the saint. Inside, its twelfth-century altar canopy is one of the finest in Italy, the motifs around the capitals the work of stonemasons from Como. The twelfth-century carved doorway and the simple, striking mosaic floor of the choir are lovely, and the twelfth-century episcopal throne behind the altar is a superb piece of work, supported by small figures wheezing beneath its weight. Close by, the **Cattedrale di San Sabino** (daily 7am–2pm & 4–7pm), off Piazza Odegitria, was built at the end of the twelfth century, and is a plain church by contrast, home to an eighth-century icon known as the *Madonna Odegitria* that's said to be the most authentic likeness of the Madonna in existence, taken from an original sketch by Luke the Apostle. Across the piazza, the **Castello Normanno-Svevo** (Tues–Sat 9am–1pm & 3.30–7pm, Sun 9am–1pm; L4000) sits on the site of an earlier Roman fort. Built by Frederick II, much of it is closed to the public, but it has a vaulted hall that provides a cool escape from the afternoon sun.

Practicalities

The **tourist office** on Piazza Aldo Moro (Mon–Fri 8am–2pm) by the train station, a kilometre south of the old city, has maps and a list of **private rooms**. All **ferries** use the Stazione Maríttima, next to the old city. Looking for somewhere **cheap to sleep** can be tricky, and if you're stuck, you should find a room in *Pensione Giulia*, Via Crisanzio 12 (☎080.521.8271; ③). The nearest campsite is 6km south of the city on the SS16 – bus #12 from Teatro Petruzzelli. **Eating out**, *Le Travi del Buco* (closed Mon), on Largo Chiurlia in the old part of town, is good, or there's a characterful and cheap wine-shop-cum-fish-restaurant on the edge of the old quarter at Strada Vallisa 23.

Ferries to Greece

For details of ferry services to **Greece**, contact Ventouris, c/o Lorusso, Via Piccini 133 (☎080.521.2840), who run services to Corfu or Igoumenitsa (L70,000 one way); there are four sailings a week between May and September. Superfast, Corso Tullio 6 (☎080. 528.2828) run daily sailings to Patras (L98,000 one way) and Igoumenitsa (L68,000 one way). Travel agents around town often have a wide variety of offers on **tickets**, including CTS, Via Fornari 7 (☎080.521.3244), who give a discount on student/youth fares; InterRail pass holders get discounts too. Once you've got your ticket, you must report to the Stazione Maríttima at least two hours before departure.

Bríndisi

BRÍNDISI, about 100km southeast of Bari, was once the main crossing point between the eastern and western empires, and later, under the Normans, on the route of pilgrims heading east towards the Holy Land – and it is still strictly a place for passing through, mainly for tourists on their way to Greece. There's not much to see, but the old centre has a pleasant, almost Oriental flavour, with a *passeggiata* that's one of the south's best.

   Ferries dock at the **Stazione Maríttima** on Via del Mare, from where it's a few minutes' walk to the bottom of Corso Garibaldi, and another twenty minutes to the **train station** in Piazza Crispi. Lots of **buses** run down Corso Umberto and Corso Garibaldi (L1500 a ride). There's a **tourist office** on Viale Regina Margherita (summer daily 8am–7pm; winter Mon–Sat 8am–2pm). As most ferries leave in the evening, **accommodation** isn't usually a problem: try the central *Venezia*, Via Pisanelli 6 (☎0831.527.511; ②). There's also a **youth hostel**, 2km out of town at Via Brandi 2 (☎0831.413.123; ②) – take bus #3 or #4 from the train station. It's not difficult to **eat** cheaply, the whole of Corso Umberto and Corso Garibaldi (particularly the port end) being smothered in bars and restaurants in which you should be able to grab a reasonably priced if average meal. Try *Pizzeria L'Angoletto*, Via Pergola 3, just off Corso Garibaldi, which has outdoor tables and cheap local wine.

Ferries to Greece

There is a huge array of **agents** selling ferry tickets **to Greece**, and you must take care to avoid getting ripped off. The most reliable are Grecian Travel, Corso Garibaldi 65

(☎0831.597.884), and UTAC Viaggi, Via Santa Lucia 11 (☎0831.524.921). There's usually at least one daily service to the main Greek ports throughout the year; services increase between April and September, and mid-June to August is peak season, with several sailings a day to most destinations, though you still should book in advance if possible. The most reliable ferry companies are Adriatica, on the first floor of the Stazione Maríttima (☎0831.523.825), who sail to Corfu, Igoumenitsa and Patras; Hellenic Mediterranean Lines, Corso Garibaldi 30 (☎0831.528.531), who go to the same destinations; plus Cefalonia and Fragline, Corso Garibaldi 88 (☎0831.590.310), with sailings to Corfu and Igoumenitsa. All these companies' ferries sail at night (between 9pm and 10.30pm). **Prices** vary according to season: you're looking at around L55,000–65,000 one way to Corfu/Igoumenitsa or Patras, though less than double that for returns. In general, Adriatica are the most expensive, Fragline the cheapest. InterRail and Eurail passes are valid on the Corfu/Patras crossing with Adriatica and Hellenic Mediterranean lines. Everyone pays an **embarkation tax** – currently L12,000. Don't forget to stock up on **food and drink**, as there are serious mark-ups once on board. For exchanging to Greek drachmas, the most central **banks** are Banco di Napoli and Credito Italiano on Corso Garibaldi; the Cambio at the Stazione Maríttima is open on Saturdays until 9pm.

SICILY

Coming from the Italian mainland, **Sicily** feels socially and culturally all but out of Europe. Occupying a strategically vital position, and as the largest island in the Mediterranean, Sicily's history and outlook is not that of its modern parent but of its erstwhile foreign rulers – from the Greeks who first settled the east coast in the eighth century BC, through a dazzling array of Romans, Arabs, Normans, French and Spanish, to the Bourbons seen off by Garibaldi in 1860. Substantial relics of these ages remain: temples, theatres and churches are scattered about the whole island. But there are other, more immediate hints of Sicily's unique past. A hybrid Sicilian language is still widely spoken in the countryside; the food is noticeably different, spicier and with more emphasis on fish and vegetables; and there is, of course, the **mafia** – though this is not something which impinges upon the lives of tourists.

Inevitably perhaps, most points of interest are on the coast: the interior of the island is often mountainous, sparsely populated and relatively inaccessible. The capital, **Palermo**, is a memorable first stop, a bustling city with an unrivalled display of Norman art and architecture and Baroque churches. The most obvious other trips are to the chic resort of **Taormina** and the lava-built second city of **Catania**, close by which you can skirt around the foothills and even up to the craters of **Mount Etna**. To the south, the greatest draw is the grouping of temples at **Agrigento**, the best of the island's Greek remnants.

Palermo and around

In its own wide bay underneath the limestone bulk of Monte Pellegrino, **PALERMO** is stupendously sited. Originally a Phoenician, then a Carthaginian colony, this remarkable city was long considered a prize worth capturing, and under Saracen and Norman rule in the ninth to twelfth centuries Palermo became the greatest city in Europe, famed for the wealth of its court and peerless as a centre of learning. Nowadays it's a fast, brash and exciting city, a fascinating place to be as much for just strolling and consuming as for specific attractions. But Palermo's monuments, its unique series of Baroque and Arabo-Norman churches, the unparalleled mosaic work and excellent museums are also the equal of anything on the mainland.

Incidentally, to **get to Sicily**, you can simply take a train from the mainland – they travel across the Straits of Messina on the ferries from Villa San Giovanni and continue on the other side. Travelling by car, there are also direct ferries from Reggio di Calabria, Naples, Genoa and Livorno.

Arrival and accommodation

Trains all pull in at the Stazione Centrale, at the southern end of Via Roma, connected with the modern centre by almost any bus. **Ferry and hydrofoil** services dock at the Stazione Maríttima, just off Via Francesco Crispi, from where it's a ten-minute walk up Via E. Amari to Piazza Castelnuovo. There are **tourist offices** at Stazione Centrale (Mon–Fri 8.30am–2pm & 3–6pm, Sat 8.30am–2pm) and the Stazione Maríttima, and a main **office** at Piazza Castelnuovo 34 (same hours as station; ☎091.583.847), with free maps, accommodation and entertainment guides.

You'll find getting around exclusively on foot exhausting and impractical. City **buses** are easy to use, covering every corner of Palermo and stretching out to Monreale and Mondello. There's a flat fare of L1500 (valid for 60min) or L5000 (for a day) and you can buy tickets from the glass booths outside Stazione Centrale, at the southern end of Viale della Libertà, or from *tabacchi*.

Most of the budget **hotel accommodation** in Palermo is on and around the southern ends of Via Maqueda and Via Roma, in the area between Stazione Centrale and Corso Vittorio Emanuele. On Via Roma, there's the *Concordia* at no. 72 (☎091.617.1514; ③); or off to the right, just before Corso Vittorio Emanuele, the *Olimpia* (☎091.616.1276; ②) has rooms overlooking Piazza Cassa di Risparmio. At Via Maqueda 8, there's the *Vittoria* (☎091.616.2437; ②), and the atmospheric *Orientale* lies a little further up at no. 26 (☎091.616.5727; ②) – mostly pokey rooms in a marble-studded palazzo. Signposted left just before Corso Vittorio Emanuele, the *Cortese* (☎091.331.722; ②) has clean rooms in a murky neighbourhood, near the Ballarò market. Off Corso V. Emanuele, at Via Bottai 30, the *Letizia* (☎091.589.110; ③), is good, clean and safe. If you want to stay central and pay a little more, the *Grande Albergo Sole* (☎091.581.811; ⑤) offers plenty of old-fashioned comfort. If you're **camping**, take bus #616 from Piazza Vittorio Veneto (for which take any bus up Via Libertà from Piazza Castel-Nuovo) out to Sferracavallo, 13km northwest of the city, where there are two sites: the *Campeggio Internazionale Trinacria* on Via Barcarello (☎091.530.590), with two-bedded **cabins**, and the cheaper *degli Ulivi* (☎091.533.021), on Via Pegaso, both open all year.

The City

The heart of the old city is the dingy Baroque crossroads of the **Quattro Canti**, erected in 1611, across from which is **Piazza Pretoria** and the church of **La Martorana** (Mon–Sat 9.30am–1pm & 3.30–5.30/6.30pm, Sun 8.30am–1pm), one of the finest survivors of the medieval city, with a slim twelfth-century campanile and a series of spectacular mosaics, animated twelfth-century Greek works. In the district southwest of here, the **Albergheria**, a warren of tiny streets, the deconsecrated church of **San Giovanni degli Eremeti** (daily 9am–1pm & 3–6.30pm, Sun 9am–12.30pm; L4000) was built in 1148, and is the most obviously Arabic of the city's Norman relics, with five ochre domes topping a small church that was built upon the remains of an earlier mosque. A path leads up through citrus trees to the church, behind which lie its celebrated late thirteenth-century cloisters. From here it's a few paces north to the **Palazzo dei Normanni** whose entrance is on Piazza Indipendenza; it was originally built by the Saracens and was enlarged considerably by the Normans, under whom it housed the most magnificent of medieval European courts. Sadly, there's little left from those times, and most of the interior is now taken up by the Sicilian parliament, but you can visit beautiful **Cappella Palatina** (Mon–Fri 9am–11.45 & 3–4.45pm, Sun 9–10am & noon–1pm), the private royal chapel of Roger II, built between 1132 and 1143 and almost entirely covered with twelfth-century mosaics.

On the far side of Corso V. Emanuele from here, the **Cattedrale** (Mon–Sat 7am–7pm, Sun 8am–1.30pm & 4–7pm) is a more substantial Norman relic, an odd building mainly because of the eighteenth-century alterations which added the dome and spoiled the fine lines of the tawny stone. Still, the triple-apsed eastern end and the lovely matching towers are all original and date from 1185; the interior is cold and Neoclassical, the only items of interest the fine portal and wooden doors and the royal tombs, containing the remains of some of Sicily's most famous monarchs.

Across Via Roma, the **Museo Archeologico Regionale** (daily 9am–1.30pm, also Tues & Fri 3–6.30pm, Sun 9am–1pm; L8000) is a magnificent collection of artefacts, mainly from the island's Greek and Roman sites. Two cloisters hold anchors and other retrieved hardware from the sea off the Sicilian coast, and there are rich stone carvings from the temple site of Selinunte. In the opposite direction from Santa Zita lies the depressed area around the old harbour, **La Cala**, and, across Corso V. Emanuele on Via Alloro, Sicily's **Galleria Regionale** (daily 9am–1.30pm, Tues & Thurs also 3–6.30pm, Sun 9am–12.30pm; L8000), a stunning medieval art collection that includes a magnificent fifteenth-century fresco of the *Triumph of Death*, the works of fifteenth-century sculptor Francesco Laurana and paintings by Antonello da Messina.

The third of Palermo's showpiece museums – the **Museo Etnografico Pitre** (9am–8pm; closed Fri; L5000) – lies on the edge of **La Favorita**, a large park around 3km from Piazza Castelnuovo (bus #806 from Piazza Sturzo, behind the Politeamar, or from Viale della Libertà). This is the key exhibition of Sicilian folklore and culture on the island, with a wealth of carts painted with bright scenes from the story of the Paladins, a reconstructed puppet theatre and dozens of the expressive puppets, and a whole series of intricately worked terracotta figures, dolls and games.

For real attention-grabbing stuff, take bus #327 from Piazza Indipendenza southwest to Via Pindemonte (a 20min walk), where the **Convento dei Cappuccini** (daily 9am–noon & 3–5pm; donation expected) has a warren of catacombs under its church that's home to some eight thousand bodies, preserved by various chemical processes and placed in niches along corridors, dressed in the suits of clothes they provided for the purpose. The bodies that aren't lined along the walls lie in stacked glass coffins, and – to say the least – it's an unnerving experience to walk among them.

Eating, drinking and nightlife

For authentic Sicilian fast **food**, *Antica Focacceria San Francesco*, Via A. Paternostro 58, off Corso Vittorio Emanuele, is an old-time pizzeria with marble-topped tables and pizza slices. Otherwise, the best pizzerias are *Pizzeria Italia*, Via Orologio 54, off Via Maqueda, where large queues develop quickly, and the slightly fancier *Trattoria dal Pompiere* at Via Bara 107, the next parallel street north. For full-blown **meals**, the city's best bargain is *Trattoria-Pizzeria Enzo*, Via Maurolico 17/19, close to the station, or the small *Trattoria Azzurra*, Via dei Bottai 54, off Corso V. Emanuele, with a long list of pasta dishes and healthy fish portions. Failing that, try *Il Cotto e il Crudo*, on Piazza Marina.

Come the **evening**, most young people head for the resort of **Mondello**, 11km away and connected by regular bus #806. During the day it's the nearest decent place to **swim**, too. Right in the centre of Palermo, *Au Dominò*, on trendy Via Principe di Belmonte, is a pleasant place for a **drink**; *Pinguino*, Via Ruggero Settimo 86, has excellent ice cream, famous milk shakes and a range of non-alcoholic cocktails.

Monreale

Sicily's most extraordinary medieval mosaics are to be seen in the Norman cathedral at **Monreale**, a small hill-town 8km southwest of Palermo and accessible on bus #389 from Piazza dell'Indipendenza, a twenty-minute journey. The **Duomo** mosaics (daily 8am–6pm) represent the apex of Sicilian-Norman art, and were almost certainly executed by Greek and Byzantine craftsmen, revealing a unitary plan and inspiration: your eyes are drawn to the all-embracing figure of Christ in the central apse – an awesome and pivotal mosaic, the head and shoulders alone almost 20m high. Underneath sit an enthroned Virgin and Child, attendant angels and ranks of saints, each individually and subtly coloured and identified by name. No less remarkable are the nave mosaics, an animated series starting with the Creation to the right of the altar and running around the entire church. Ask at the desk by the entrance to climb the **tower** in the southwest corner of the cathedral – an unusual and precarious vantage point. The **cloisters** (Mon–Sat 9am–1pm & 3–6.30pm, Sun 9am–12.30pm; L4000), part of the original Benedictine monastery, form an elegant arcaded quadrangle, with some 216 twin columns that are a riot of detail and imagination.

Taormina

TAORMINA, high on Monte Tauro and dominating two grand sweeping bays below, is Sicily's best-known resort. The outstanding remains of its classical theatre, with Mount Etna as an unparalleled backdrop, arrested passing travellers when Taormina was no more than a medieval hill village, and these days it's virtually impossible to find anywhere to stay between June and August. Despite this, Taormina retains much of its small-town charm, the main traffic-free street, Corso V. Emanuele, an unbroken line of fifteenth- to nineteenth-century palazzi and small, intimate piazzas.

The **Teatro Greco** (daily 9am to 1hr before sunset; L4000) – signposted from just about everywhere – is the only real sight, founded by Greeks in the third century BC, though most of what's left is a Roman rebuilding from the first century AD, when the stage and lower seats were cut back to provide room and a deep trench dug in the orchestra to accommodate the animals and fighters used in gladiatorial contests.

Trains pull up at Taormina-Giardini station, way below town, from where it's a steep thirty-minute walk up or a short bus ride to the centre of town. The central **tourist office** (Mon–Fri 8am–2pm & 4–7pm, Sat 9am–1pm; April–Sept also Sun 9am–1pm; ☎0942.23.243) in Piazza Santa Caterina, Palazzo Corvaja, has free maps. There are good **accommodation** possibilities along Via Bagnoli Croce: private rooms at no. 66 (③), with incredible roof-terrace views, or *Il Leone* at no. 124–126 (☎0942.23.878; ③). You could also try the *Pensione Svizzera*, at Via Pirandello 26 (☎0942.23.790; ⑤), just up from the bus terminal. If everywhere is full, you'll have to try nearby Giardini-Naxos. The **campsite**, *San Leo*, on the cape below town, is open all year, though it's not particularly good; take any bus running between Taormina and the station. **Eating** can be terribly expensive – if money is tight, try a couple of unspectacular pizzerias outside Porta Messina. The only vaguely inexpensive trattoria is *Da Nino*, Via Pirandello 37, or try *Il Baccanale* in Piazza Filea (end of Via Bagnoli Croce), which has outdoor tables and similar prices.

The closest beach to town is at **MAZZARO**, with its much-photographed islet. There's a **cable car** (L3000) every fifteen minutes from Via Pirandello, and a steep path which starts just below the cable car station. The beach-bars and restaurants at **SPISONE**, north again, are also reachable by path from Taormina, this time from below the cemetery in town. From Spisone, the coast opens out and the beach gets wider. With more time, **LETOJANNI** is a little resort in its own right, with a few fishing boats on a sandy beach, two campsites and regular buses and trains back to Taormina. Roomier and better for swimming are the sands south of Taormina at **GIARDINI-NAXOS**, which is an excellent alternative source of **accommodation** and food. Prices tend to be a good bit cheaper than in Taormina and in high season it's worth trying here first. Immobiliare Naxos, Via V. Emanuele 58 (☎0942.51.184), can arrange apartments – good value if you're a group of four or more; recommended **hotels** include *Villa Pamar*, Via Naxos 23 (☎0942.52.448; ④). For **eating**, good pizzas and fresh pasta can be had at *Fratelli Marano*, Via Naxos 181. *Da Angelina*, on Via Schisò by the pier, does marvellous well-priced pizzas and has good service and great views. Also good are *Arcobaleno*, Via Naxos 169, and *La Conchiglia*, Via Naxos 221, specializing in Sicilian meat dishes and good pizzas.

Mount Etna

Mount Etna's massive bulk looms over much of the coastal route south of Taormina, and, if you don't have the time to reach the summit, rail services provide some alternative volcanic thrills in a ride around the base of the volcano from **GIARRE-RIPOSTO**, thirty minutes by train or bus from Taormina; InterRail passes are not valid, and if you make the entire trip to Catania, allow five hours; tickets cost L9800 one way. As for the ascent, this is a spectacular trip worth every effort to make – though without your own transport that effort can be considerable. At 3323m, Etna is a fairly substantial mountain, the fact that it's also one of the world's biggest volcanoes (and still active) only adding to the draw. Some of the eruptions have been disastrous: in 1669 Catania was wrecked; this century the Circumetnea rail line has been repeatedly ruptured by lava flows, and, in 1979, nine people were killed on the edge of the main crater. In 1997 and 1998 the eruptions were high, but not life-theatening. This is not to say you'll be in any danger, provided you heed the warnings as you get closer to the top. There are several approaches. On public transport, you'll need to come via **NICOLOSI**, an hour from Catania by frequent bus, one of which (8am from Catania train station) continues on to a huddle of souvenir shops and restaurants around the *Rifugio Sapienza* (☎095.911.062; ③). Arriving on the early morning bus, you'll have enough time to make it to the top and get back for the return bus to Catania – it leaves around 4pm. To get up the volcano from the refuge, you can take the cable car up to about 2500m (L34,000 return) from where a guide takes you by jeep to the Torre del Filò sofo (April–Oct; L30,000 return) or you can **walk**, following the rough minibus track (3–4hr each way). However you go, take warm clothes, good shoes and glasses to keep the flying grit out of your eyes. The highest you're allowed to get is 2900m, and though there's only a rope across the ground to prevent you from climbing further, it would be foolish to do so.

Catania

First impressions don't do much for **CATANIA**, on an initial encounter possibly the island's gloomiest spot. Built from black-grey volcanic stone, its central streets can feel suffocating. Yet fight the urge to change buses and run: Catania is one of the most intriguing and historic of Sicily's cities. Some of the island's first Greek colonists settled the site as early as 729 BC, becoming so influential that their laws were eventually adopted by all the Ionian colonies of Magna Graecia. Later, in the seventeenth century, Etna swamped the city, leading to a swift rebuilding under the architect Giovanni Vaccarini that gave the city a lofty, noble air.

Catania's main square, **Piazza del Duomo**, is a handy orientation point and one of Sicily's most attractive city squares, surrounded by fine Baroque structures, including the **Duomo** (daily 7am–noon and 4–7pm), which incorporates granite columns from Catania's Roman amphitheatre. A short way west, at the bottom of Via Crociferi, the house where the composer Vincenzo Bellini was born in 1801 now houses the **Museo Belliniano** (Mon–Fri 9am–1.30pm, Sun 9am–12.30pm; free), an agreeable collection of photographs, original scores and other memorabilia; beyond it, the **Teatro Romano** (Mon–Sat 9am–1pm & 3–7pm, Sun 9am–1pm; L4000) was built on the site of an earlier Greek theatre, and preserves much of its seating and underground passageways. A few minutes' walk north, the enormous **Piazza Stesicoro** marks the modern centre of Catania, one half of which is almost entirely occupied by the sunken, black remains of another Roman theatre, the **Antifeatro Romano**, dating back to the second or third century AD.

Catania's main **train station** is in Piazza Giovanni XXIII, northeast of the centre; the **Circumetnea terminus** is on Corso delle Province, off Corso Italia. There's a **tourist office** inside the train station (summer daily 7am–9.30pm; winter Mon–Fri 9am–1pm & 4–7pm; ☎095.730.6255), with accommodation listings and maps. There are lots of **places to stay**, and some real bargains if you hunt around. One of the best is the clean and friendly *Pensione Gresi*, Via Pacini 28 (☎095.322.709; ③), and the *Rubens* at Via Etnea 196 (☎095.317.073; ③) is also good, though always busy; there's also the *Holland International*, Via V. Emanuele 8 (☎095.533.605; ③), with rooms above a courtyard in a palazzo. There are three **campsites** with cabins a short way south of the city on Viale Kennedy; take bus #27 from the station. For **eating**, the *Centrale* at Via Etnea 123 is a great place for a snack; the *Ristorante Rapido*, Via Corridoni 17, off Via Pacini, is cheap, if rather average. Worth trying, too, is the *Trattoria Calabrese*, on Via Penninello, down the steps at the end of Via Crociferi. *Le Collegiata* pub/pizzeria, Via Collegiata 3 overlooking the Piazza dell'Università, is a good place for a **drink**, full of young, studenty Catanese.

Agrigento

Though it's handsome, well sited and awash with medieval atmosphere, no one comes to **AGRIGENTO** for the town. The interest instead focuses on the substantial remains of

Pindar's "most beautiful city of mortals", a couple of kilometres below. Here, strung out along a ridge facing the sea, is a series of Doric temples – the most captivating of Sicilian remains and unique outside Greece – built during the fifth century BC.

A road winds down from the modern city to the **Valle dei Templi**, buses (#1, #2 or #3) dropping you at a car park between the two separate sections of archeological remains. The **eastern zone** is unenclosed, and home to scattered remains of the oldest of the temples, the **Tempio di Ercole**, probably begun in the last decades of the sixth century BC, and the better-preserved **Tempio della Concordia**, dated to around 430 BC, with fine views of the city and sea. There's also the **Tempio di Giunone**, an engaging half-ruin standing at the very edge of the ridge. The **western zone** (daily 9am to 1hr before sunset; L4000), back along the path and beyond the car park, is less impressive, a vast tangle of stone and fallen masonry from a variety of temples. Most notable is the mammoth construction that was the **Tempio di Giove**, or Temple of Olympian Zeus, the largest Doric temple ever known, though never completed, left in ruins by the Carthaginians and further damaged by earthquakes. Via dei Templi leads back to the town from the car park via the excellent **Museo Nazionale Archeologico** (Wed–Sat 9am–1pm & 2–6pm, Mon, Tues & Sun 9am–12.30pm; L8000) – an extraordinarily rich collection devoted to finds from the city and the surrounding area.

Trains arrive at the edge of the old town, outside which – on Piazza Marconi – buses leave for the temples. The **tourist office** (Mon–Sat 8am–2pm & 4–8pm; ☎0922.204.54) is nearby at Via Cesare Battisti 15, at the eastern end of Via Atenea, and has hotel listings and maps. Among **hotels** worth trying are the *Concordia*, behind the station at Piazza San Francesco 11 (☎0922.596.266; ②); the *Bella Napoli*, Piazza Lena 6 (☎0922.20.435; ②); and the *Belvedere*, Via San Vito 20 (☎0922.20.051; ③). You can **camp** 5km away at the coastal resort of San Leone; take bus #2 from outside the train station. For **eating**, the food is excellent at *La Forchetta*, next door to the *Concordia* hotel, but not particularly cheap. If you're budgeting, you can get reasonable food at the *Atenea*, Via Ficani 12, an alley above Via Atenea.

SARDINIA

A little under 200km from the Italian mainland, slightly more than that from the North African coast at Tunisia, **Sardinia** is way off most tourist itineraries. Relatively free of large cities or heavy industry, the island boasts some of the country's cleanest, least crowded beaches, and, though not known for its cultural riches, holds some fascinating vestiges of the various civilizations that passed through. In addition to Roman and Carthaginian ruins, Genoan fortresses and a string of lovely Pisan churches, there are striking remnants of Sardinia's only significant native culture, known as the **nuraghic** civilization after the 7000 or so stone constructions which litter the landscape.

On the whole, Sardinia's smaller centres are the most attractive, but the capital, **Cágliari** – for many the arrival point – shouldn't be written off. With good facilities for eating and sleeping, it makes a useful base for exploring the southern third of the island. The other main ferry port and airport is Olbia in the north, little more than a transit town for visitors to the nearby Costa Smeralda, though budget travellers are unlikely to want to spend time in this uncomfortable mix of opulence and suburbia.

In the northwest of the island, **Sássari** and **Alghero** manifest the deepest imprint of the long Spanish presence in Sardinia, with the latter having developed into the chief package resort. Inland, **Nuoro** has impressive literary credentials and a good ethnographical museum. As Sardinia's biggest interior town, it also makes a useful stopover for visiting some of the remoter mountain areas, in particular the **Gennargentu** range, covering the heart of the island. This is where you can find what remains of the island's traditional culture, best embodied in the numerous village **festivals**.

The island boasts a good network of public transport to get you round all but the remoter areas. On the roads there is the island-wide bus network run by ARST and the private PANI for longer hauls between towns, while trains connect the major towns of Cágliari, Sássari and Olbia, with smaller lines linking with Nuoro and Alghero.

Getting to Sardinia

There are frequent daily **flights** from the Italian mainland to the island's three airports, at Cágliari, Olbia and Fertília (for Alghero and Sássari). The flights, which take about an hour, are run by Alitalia, and Sardinia's own Meridiana. Cheaper but slower are the overnight **ferries** from mainland Italy (Civitavecchia, Genoa, Livorno, Naples) – as well as from Sicily, Tunis, Corsica and France. If you're travelling by car, it's essential to book well in advance: sailings in July and August can be fully booked by May. Prices range from L40,000 to L150,000 per person, depending on season and route taken: a berth costs a minimum of L16,000 extra. A vehicle will cost a minimum of L70,000 for a small car in low season. Note that Navarma and Sardinia Ferries offer fifty-percent discounts for vehicles on certain dates if you book your return when you buy your outward-bound ticket.

Cágliari

Rising up from its port and crowned by an old centre squeezed within a protective ring of Pisan fortifications, **CÁGLIARI** has been Sardinia's capital at least since Roman times and is still the island's biggest town. Nonetheless, its centre is easily explored on foot, and offers sophistication and charm in its raggle-taggle of narrow lanes. The main attractions here are the **museum** with its unique collection of nuraghic statuettes, the city walls, with their two **Pisan towers** looking down over the port, and the **cathedral**.

Arrival, information and accommodation

Cágliari's **port** lies in the heart of the town, opposite Via Roma. The **airport** sits beside the Stagno di Cágliari, the city's largest lagoon, fifteen minutes' bus ride west of town. The airport has a bureau de change and a **tourist office** (Mon–Fri 9am–1pm & 4–6pm; ☎070.240.200), with maps and information on accommodation; there's another at the Stazione Maríttima (open 2hr most mornings; ☎070.668.352), but the main office is at Via Mameli 97 (mid-May to Sept daily 8am–8pm; Oct–Nov Mon–Sat 9am–7pm, Sun 9am–2pm; Dec–March Mon–Sat 9am–5pm; April to mid-May daily 9am–7pm; ☎070.664.195). A **bus** service into town runs at least every ninety minutes from 6.20am until midnight to Piazza Matteotti; otherwise a taxi ride costs around L20,000. Piazza Matteotti also has the **bus and train stations** and a tourist information kiosk (July & Aug daily 8am–8pm; Sept–June Mon–Sat 8am–2pm; ☎070.669.255).

Cágliari has a good selection of budget **hotels**, though availability may be restricted in high season, and single rooms are always at a premium. In Via Roma, try the *Vittoria* at no. 75 (☎070.657.970; ③) or the nearby *La Perla* at no. 18 (☎070.669.446; ③). At the far end of Via Sardegna, the cramped but clean *Londra* at Viale Regina Margherita 16 (☎070.669.083; ②) is run by a London woman who's lived on the island for twenty years. The central *La Terazza* at Via S. Margherita 21 (☎070.668.652; ③) is another option. The nearest **campsite** is at Quartu Sant'Elena, a 45-minute bus ride east along the coast, where the *Pini e Mare* (☎070.803.103; July & Aug) has bungalows as well.

The City

Almost all the wandering you will want to do in Cágliari is encompassed within the old quarter. The most evocative entry to this is from the monumental **Bastione San Remy** on Piazza Costituzione. It's worth the haul up the grandiose flight of steps inside for Cágliari's best views over the port and the lagoons beyond — especially at sunset.

From the bastion, you can wander off in any direction to enter the intricate maze of Cágliari's citadel, traditionally the seat of the administration, aristocracy and highest ecclesiastical offices. It has been little altered since the Middle Ages, though the tidy Romanesque facade on the **Cattedrale** (daily 8am–12.30pm & 4–8pm) in Piazza Palazzo is in fact a fake, added in this century in the old Pisan style. The structure dates originally from the thirteenth century but has gone through what D.H. Lawrence called "the mincing machine of the ages, and oozed out Baroque and sausagey".

Inside, a couple of massive stone **pulpits** flank the main doors: they were crafted as a single piece around 1160 to grace Pisa's cathedral, but were later presented to Cágliari along with the same sculptor's set of lions, now adorning the outside of the building. Other features of the cathedral include the ornate seventeenth-century tomb of Martin II of Aragon (left transept), the presbytery, which is the entrance to a small museum, and the **crypt** (appointment only). Hewn out of the rock, little of this subterranean chamber has been left undecorated, and there are carvings by Sicilian artists of Sardinian saints.

At the opposite end of Piazza Palazzo a road leads into the smaller Piazza dell'Arsenale, site of the **Museo Archeologico Nazionale** (daily 8.30am–7pm; L4000), a must for anyone interested in Sardinia's past. The island's most important Phoenician, Carthaginian and Roman finds are gathered here, but everything pales beside the museum's greatest pieces, from Sardinia's **nuraghic** culture. Of these, the most eye-catching is a series of bronze statuettes, ranging from about 15 to 45cm in height, spindly and highly stylized, but packed with invention and quirky humour. The main source of information about this phase of the island's history, the figures were mostly votive offerings, made to decorate the inside of temples, later buried to protect them from the hands of foreign predators.

Off the piazza stands the **Torre San Pancrazio**, from which it's only a short walk to Via dell'Università and the **Torre dell'Elefante** (Tues–Sun 9am–4.30pm) named after the small carving of an elephant on one side. The towers were erected by Pisa after it had wrested the city from the Genoans in 1305 and formed the main bulwarks of the city's defences. Both have a half-finished look about them, with the side facing the old town completely open. Nearby, Viale Buon Cammino leads to the **Anfiteatro Romano** (Tues–Sun: summer 9am–1pm & 5–9pm; winter 9am–1pm & 4–6pm; free). Cut out of solid rock in the second century AD, the amphitheatre could hold the entire city's population of twenty thousand.

The only item of interest in Cágliari's traffic-thronged modern quarters is the fifth-century church of **San Saturnino**, Sardinia's oldest and one of the most important surviving examples of early Christian architecture in the Mediterranean. Stranded on the busy Via Dante, and surrounded by various pieces of flotsam from the past, the basilica was erected on the spot where the Christian martyr Saturninus met his fate.

Eating and drinking

Most of Cágliari's **restaurants** are clustered around Via Sardegna. *Da Serafino*, at Via Sardegna 109, is extremely good value and popular with the locals. *Da Lillicu* at Via Sardegna 78 (closed Sun) is plain but authentic, offering Sardinian specialities and delicious fish. Seafood-lovers will do well at the *Stella Marina di Montecristo*, at the end of Via Sardegna, where it meets Via Regina Margherita. Away from the port area, try *Il Gatto*, just off Piazza del Cármine at Viale Trieste 15, for seafood or meat dishes, all immaculately prepared.

For a **snack** and a beer, drop in on *Il Merlo Parlante* in Via Portascalas, an alley off Corso Vittorio Emanuele, where you can find drink, music and *panini* (open evenings only). Down by the port, the bars on Via Roma make good breakfast stops, while there are several decent pizza and sandwich joints in the alleys running off it.

Su Nuraxi

If you have no time to see any other of Sardinia's ancient stone *nuraghi*, make a point of visiting **SU NURAXI**, the biggest and most famous of them and a good taste of the primitive grandeur of the island's only indigenous civilization. The snag is access: the site lies a kilometre outside the village of Barúmini, 50km north of Cágliari, to which there are only two daily ARST buses, which stop here en route to Désulo and Samugheo.

At Barúmini, turn left at the main crossroads and walk the last leg to Su Nuraxi (open daily 9am–sunset; free). Its dialect name means simply "the *nuragh*" and not only is it the biggest *nuraghic* complex on the island, but it's also thought to be the oldest, dating probably from around 1500 BC. Comprising a bulky fortress surrounded by the remains of a village, Su Nuraxi was a palace complex at the very least – possibly a capital city. The central tower once reached 21m (now shrunk to less than 15m), and its outer defences and inner chambers are connected by passageways and stairs. The whole complex is thought to have been covered with earth by Sards and Carthaginians at the time of the Roman conquest, which may account for its excellent state of preservation.

Nuoro and around

Superbly sited beneath the soaring peak of Monte Ortobene opposite the stark heights of Sopramonte, **NUORO** is, in many respects, merely a bigger version of the other villages of the region. No place on the island, though, can match its extraordinary literary fame. The best-known Sard poet, **Sebastiano Satta** (1867–1914), was Nuorese, as was the author **Grazia Deledda** (1871–1936), who won the Nobel Prize for Literature in 1927. For **Salvatore Satta** (1902–75), "Nuoro was nothing but a perch for the crows," and the twentieth century has done little to change this insular town, despite the unsightly apartment blocks, administrative buildings and banks.

Nuoro's **old quarter** is the most compelling part of town, spread around the pedestrianized hub of **Corso Garibaldi**, along which the *passeggiata* takes place. Otherwise the only attraction is the impressive **Museo Etnografico** (summer daily 9am–7pm; winter Mon–Sat 9am–1pm & 3–6pm, Sun 9am–1pm; L3000) on Via Antonio Mereu, a ten-minute walk from the Corso on the other side of Piazza Vittorio Emanuele, which contains Sardinia's most comprehensive range of local costumes, jewellery, masks, carpets and other handicrafts.

As many as three thousand of the costumes are aired at Nuoro's biggest annual **festival**, the **Sagra del Redentore**, usually taking place on the penultimate Sunday of the month and involving participants from all over the island, but especially the villages of the Barbágia. The religious festivities usually take place on August 29, when a procession from town weaves up to the 955-metre summit of **Monte Ortobene**, 8km away, where a bronze **statue** of the Redeemer stands, poised in an attitude of swirling motion with stunning views of the gorge separating Nuoro from the Sopramonte.

From Nuoro there are numerous routes weaving through Barbágia and the Gennargentu range, though the bus service is slow and sporadic. **ORGÓSOLO**, a straggly 30km from Nuoro, is famous for its history of violent feuding and the vivid **murals** which adorn the houses and shops, depicting village culture and the oppression of the landless. **MAMOIADA**, 11km west of Orgósolo, and **OTTANA** – reckoned to be the dead centre of Sardinia – stage masked and horned carnival romps that go back to pagan times. **FONNI**, due south of Mamoiada and at 1000m the island's highest village, has a less gruesome costumed procession in its festival of the Madonna dei Mártiri, held on the Monday following the first Sunday in June.

Practicalities

Nuoro's **train station** is a twenty-minute walk from the centre of town along Via Lamármora. ARST buses stop outside, while PANI buses stop at Via Brigata Sássari (parallel to Via Lamarmora). Nuoro's few **hotels** are antiquated, grubby and usually full. The **tourist office** on Piazza Italia (Mon–Fri 9am–1pm, also Tues & Wed 3.30–6.30pm; ☎0784.30.083) has a list of private rooms that may be the best option for a short stay. Otherwise try Signora Iacobini's unofficial hotel at Via Cedrino 31, off Piazza Italia (☎0784.30.675; ③), or the *Mini Hotel* in the centre of town, at Via Brofferio 31 (☎0784.33.159; ③). The best **restaurant** is the excellent pizzeria *Ciusa*, at Viale Ciusa 53, on the western end of town. Alternatively try *Sa Bertula* at Via Sicilia 119, near the station. For a lunch-time snack, there's a handy sit-down **bar** on Via Mereu, between the museum and the Duomo.

Sássari and around

Historically, while Cágliari was Pisa's base of operations during the Middle Ages, **SÁSSARI** was the Genoan capital, ruled by the Doria family, whose power reached throughout the Mediterranean. Under the Aragonese it became an important centre of Spanish hegemony, and the Spanish stamp is still strong.

The **old quarter**, a network of alleys and piazzas bisected by the main Corso Vittorio Emanuele, is a good area for aimless wandering, but take a look at the **Duomo**, whose florid facade is Sardinia's most imposing example of Baroque architecture, added to a simpler Aragonese-Gothic base from the fifteenth and sixteenth centuries. The only other item worth searching out is the late Renaissance **Fonte Rosello**, at the bottom of a flight of dilapidated steps accessible from Corso Trinità, in the northern part of the old town. The fountain is elaborately carved with dolphins and four statues representing the seasons, the work of Genoese stonemasons.

Connected by a series of squares to the old quarter, the **newer town** is centred on the grandiose Piazza Italia. Leading off the piazza is Via Roma, site of the **Museo Sanna** (Tues–Sat 9am–7pm, Sun 9am–1pm; also July–Sept Thurs–Sat 8.30am–11.30pm; L4000), Sardinia's second archeological museum; it's a good substitute if you've missed the main one at Cágliari, and like the Cágliari museum its most interesting exhibits are *nuraghic* sculptures.

Roughly 15km inland from Sássari, right on the main Sássari–Olbia road (the SS597), rises the tall bell tower of **Santa Trinità di Saccárgia**, its conspicuous zebra-striped facade marking its Pisan origins. Built in 1116, the church owes its remote location to a divine visitation, informing the wife of the *giudice* of Logudoro that she was pregnant. It has survived remarkably well, with lovely Gothic capitals at the top of the entrance porch.

Practicalities

The **train station** is at the bottom of the old town's Corso Vittorio Emanuele. All local and ARST **buses** arrive at and depart from the semicircular Emiciclo Garibaldi, south of the tourist office. PANI buses run from Via Bellini 5, just off Via Roma. Buses connect **Fertília airport** with the bus station (L5000), scheduled to coincide with incoming and outgoing flights.

Sássari's **tourist office** is at Viale Umberto 72 (Mon–Wed 8am–2pm & 4–7pm, Thurs & Fri 8am–2pm; ☎079.231.331), a couple of blocks up from the museum. **Staying** in Sássari can be a real problem, and you'd do well to ring ahead to ensure availability. The best budget option is the tumbledown *Sássari Hotel* at Viale Umberto 65 (☎079.239.543; ②); otherwise try the *Giusy* (☎079.233.327; ③), conveniently near the station on Piazza Sant'Antonio. Among a range of **restaurants** in town try *Da Peppina*, in Vícolo Pigozzi, an alley off Corso Vittorio Emanuele – a good place to sample the local speciality of horsemeat. For a bit more class, try *Da Gesuino*, at Via Torres 17, which is popular with locals.

Alghero

ALGHERO owes its predominantly Catalan flavour to a wholesale Hispanicization that followed the overthrow of the Doria family by Pedro IV of Aragon in 1354. The traces are still strong in the old town today, with its flamboyant churches, wrought-iron balconies and narrow cobbled streets named in both Italian and Catalan.

A walk around the old town should include the seven defensive **towers** which dominate Alghero's centre and surrounding walls. From the **Giardino Púbblico**, the **Porta Terra** is the first of the massive bulwarks: known as the Jewish Tower, it was erected at the expense of the prosperous Jewish community before their expulsion in 1492. Beyond is a puzzle of lanes, at the heart of which the pedestrianized Via Carlo Alberto, Via Principe Umberto and Via Roma have most of the bars and shops. At the bottom of Via Umberto stands Alghero's sixteenth-century **Cattedrale**, where Spanish viceroys stopped to take a preliminary oath before taking office in Cágliari. Its unprepossessing entrance is round the other side on Via Manno; inside, the lofty nave's alternating pillars and columns rise to an impressive octagonal dome. In fact, most of Alghero's finest architecture dates from the same period, and is built in a similar Catalan-Gothic style. Two of the best examples are a short walk away: the **Palazzo d'Albis** on Piazza Cívica, and the elegantly austere Jewish palace **Palau Reial** in Via Sant'Erasmo.

The best of the excursions you can take from the port is to **Neptune's Grotto**, with hourly departures each day during summer: tickets cost L16,000, not counting the entry charge to the grotto. The ride takes you west along the coast past the long bay of Porto Conte as far as the point of **Capo Caccia**, where the spectacular sheer cliffs are riddled by deep marine caves. The most impressive is the **Neptune's Grotto** (daily: April–Sept 9am–7pm; Oct 10am–5pm; Nov–March 9am–2pm; L13,000), a long snaking passage delving far into the rock, into which thirty-minute tours are led, single-file, on the hour every hour, past dramatically lit and fantastical stalagmites and stalactites. A cheaper alternative to the boat tour is by bus to Capo Caccia.

Practicalities

Trains to Alghero from Sássari arrive some way out of the centre, connected to the port by shuttle buses. **Buses** arrive in Via Catalogna, on the Giardino Púbblico. Alghero's efficient **tourist office** is on the corner of the Giardino Púbblico (May–Sept Mon–Sat 8am–8pm; July & Aug also Sun 8am–noon; Oct–April Mon–Sat 8am–2pm; ☎079.979.054).

The best-value **hotel** in town is the *San Francesco* (☎079.980.330; ③), in the heart of the old town at Via Machin 2, just behind San Francesco church; each of its clean, quiet rooms has a bathroom. If it's full, try the *Normandie*, on Via Enrico Mattei in the newer part of town, between Via Kennedy and Via Giovanni XXIII (☎079.975.302; ③). Two kilometres out of town, *La Mariposa* **campsite** (☎079.950.360; April–Oct) has direct access to the beach. Alghero's *Giuliani* **youth hostel** (☎079.930.353; ②) is actually 6km along the coast at Fertília, reachable by local bus. Ring first to check availability.

Alghero's **restaurants** are renowned for fish and seafood, always fresh, inventively prepared and well presented – spring and winter are the best seasons. *Il Pavone* on Piazza Sulis is excellent (expect to pay at least L45,000 a head), as are *La Lépanto* on Via Carlo Alberto and *Da Pietro*, at Via Machin 20, though none could be described as budget places. For cheaper meals, you're better off trying the right-angled streets of the new town, like Via Mazzini, where the *Ristorante Mazzini* at no. 59 serves decent fare at modest prices and has a wood-fired oven for pizzas. For snacks, the fast-food joints by the port aren't bad.

There is an abundant supply of decent **bars**: at the *Bar Granada,* at Bastioni Marco Polo you can sip cappuccinos or cocktails.

travel details

Trains

Bari to: Bríndisi (hourly; 2hr).

Bergamo to: Brescia (19 daily; 1hr).

Bologna to: Ferrara (every 30min; 30min); Florence (hourly; 1hr 30min); Milan (hourly; 2hr–2hr 35min); Ravenna (15 daily; 1hr 25min); Rimini (hourly; 1hr 20min).

Cágliari to: Arbatax (1–2 daily; 7hr); Macomer (6 daily; 2–3hr); Olbia (4 daily; 4hr 30min); Oristano (hourly; 1hr–1hr 30 min); Sássari (3 daily; 3hr 40min).

Ferrara to: Rimini (10 daily; 2hr 15min).

Florence to: Arezzo (hourly; 1hr); Bologna (hourly; 1hr 30min); Genoa (6 daily; 3–4hr 30min); Lucca (hourly; 1hr 5min–1hr 50min); Milan (hourly; 3–4hr 30min); Naples (9 daily; 4hr); Perugia (5 daily; 2hr 10min); Pisa (hourly; 55min); Rome (hourly; 2hr 15min–3hr 30min); Venice (hourly; 3hr 15min); Verona (15 daily; 2–3hr).

Genoa to: Bologna (3 daily; 3hr); Milan (hourly; 2hr); Naples (4 daily; 8hr); Pisa (every 2hr; 2hr 30min); Rome (every 2hr; 6hr).

Milan to: Bergamo (5 daily; 50min); Bologna (hourly; 2hr–2hr 35min); Brescia (32 daily; 45min–1hr 10min); Como (12 daily; 30min); Rome (10 daily; 4hr); Venice (hourly; 3hr).

Naples to: Bríndisi (1 daily; 6hr 30min); Palermo (4 daily; 9hr 30min).

Padua to: Bologna (34 daily; 1hr 25min); Milan (25 daily; 2hr 30min); Verona (hourly; 50min); Vicenza (25 daily; 55min).

Palermo to: Agrigento: (11 daily; 2hr); Catania (5 daily; 3hr 10min).

Parma to: Brescia (8 daily; 1hr 45min).

Perugia to: Assisi (hourly; 25min); Florence (4 daily; 2hr 15min); Rome (6 daily; 2hr 20min).

Pisa to: Florence (hourly; 1hr); Livorno (every 30min; 15min); Lucca (hourly; 30min).

Rome to: Ancona (9 daily; 3hr 15min–6hr); Bologna (12 daily; 3hr 20min); Florence (10 daily; 2–3hr 30min); Milan (hourly; 3hr–5hr 40min); Naples (hourly; 2hr 30min).

Sássari to: Alghero (11 daily; 35min); Cágliari (3 daily; 3hr 40min); Macomer (4 daily; 1hr 35min); Olbia (4 daily; 2hr); Oristano (4 daily; 2hr 35min).

Turin to: Genoa (12 daily; 2hr); Milan (19 daily; 1hr 45min).

Venice to: Bologna (hourly; 2hr); Florence (hourly; 3hr 15min); Milan (hourly; 3hr); Padua (hourly; 30min); Trieste (hourly; 2hr 10min); Verona (hourly; 1hr 30min); Vicenza (hourly; 55min).

Verona to: Milan (hourly; 1hr 30min); Padua (hourly; 55min); Rome (6 daily; 6hr); Venice (hourly; 1hr 30min).

Vicenza to: Milan (hourly; 2hr); Verona (hourly; 30min).

Buses

Cágliari to: Macomer (5 daily; 2hr 30min); Nuoro (4 daily; 3hr 30min); Oristano (5 daily; 1hr 30min); Sássari (7 daily; 3hr 15min–4hr).

Sássari to: Alghero (hourly; 1hr); Bosa (1–4 daily; 2hr 15min); Cágliari (7 daily; 3hr 15min–3hr 45min); Olbia (2 daily; 1hr 45min); Stintino (2–6 daily; 1hr 15min).

Ferries

Arbatax to: Civitavécchia (2 weekly; 10hr 30min); Genoa (2 weekly; 19hr).

Cágliari to: Civitavécchia (1 daily; 14hr); Genoa (1 weekly in summer; 21hr); Naples (1 weekly; 16hr);

Palermo (1 weekly; 13hr 30min); Trápani (1 weekly; 11hr); Tunis (1 weekly; 35hr 30min).

Genoa to: Palermo (4 weekly; 23hr).

Naples to: Cápri (5 daily; 1hr 15min); Palermo (1 daily; 11hr); Sorrento: (3 daily; 1hr 15min).

Olbia to: Civitavécchia (1daily; 8hr); Genoa (3–14 weekly; 13hr 30min); Livorno (1 daily; 10hr).

Porto Torres to: Genoa (June–Sept 1–2 daily; 10hr); Toulon, France (May–Sept 1 weekly; 9hr; Oct–Apr 1 weekly; 16hr).

Reggio di Calabria to: Messina (15–25 daily; 45min).

Santa Teresa di Gallura to: Bonifacio (2–12 daily; 50min).

Sorrento: to: Cápri (4 daily; 50min).

Villa San Giovanni to: Messina (every 30min; 35min).

Hydrofoils

Naples to: Cápri (6–9 daily; 40min); Sorrento: (5 daily; 40min).

Olbia to: Civitavécchia (6–7 weekly; 4–6 hr)

Palermo to: Naples (3 weekly; 5hr 20min).

Reggio di Calabria to: Messina (every 40min; 15min); Naples (summer 1 daily; 6hr).

Sorrento: to: Cápri (5 daily; 20min).

CHAPTER 16

LATVIA

Introduction

The history of **Latvia**, like that of its neighbour Estonia, is largely one of foreign occupation. The indigenous Balts were overwhelmed at the start of the thirteenth century by German crusading knights, who massacred and enslaved them in the name of converting them to Christianity. The Germans continued to dominate both land and trade even after political control passed to the Polish-Lithuanian Commonwealth, then Sweden and finally Russia. During the second half of the nineteenth century the Latvians began to reassert their identity, achieving independence in 1918–20 after a war in which – with Estonian help – they beat off both the Soviets and the Germans. This hard-won independence was extinguished by Soviet annexation in 1940. As conditions in the Soviet Union relaxed during the late 1980s demands for increased autonomy turned into calls for outright independence, and on August 21, 1991, as the attempted coup against Gorbachev disintegrated in Moscow, Latvia declared its independence for the second time.

These days Latvia is engaged in turning over the economy to private ownership and struggling to put to rights the results of Soviet-era stagnation and neglect. Environmental damage aside, the most enduring legacy of Soviet occupation in Latvia is a Russian minority population of 30 percent.

The most obvious destination in Latvia is **Rīga**, a city whose architectural treasures have largely survived five decades of isolation. Places within easy reach of the capital include the resort area of **Jūrmala**, and the gently scenic **Gauja Valley** with the attractive small towns of **Sigulda** and **Cēsis**. The **palace of Rundāle**, 80km to the south of Riga, also makes a great day-trip. These are just a few possibilities, with much more waiting to be discovered along Latvia's hundreds of miles of unspoilt coast and amid the forests of the countryside.

Information and maps

Rīga has a privately run **tourist information office** in the old town and another office at the airport (Mon–Fri 10am–6pm). At the time of writing there are plans to relocate the privately run office to a nearby Old Town location and establish an office at the train station. The Kümmerly & Frey 1:1,000,000 map of the Baltic States includes Latvia, and has a basic street plan of Rīga. If you're planning to travel extensively in Latvia it's worth investing in the 1:300,000 Euromap of Latvia. Jāņa Sāta, Elizabetes 83–85, Rīga, is well-stocked with maps and guides, and also publishes its own excellent maps of the region. The Falk Plan of Rīga includes

enlarged city-centre and old-town sections and also shows public transport routes. *Rīga in your Pocket* is an excellent English-language listings guide to the capital, with details on everything you could possibly need to know. In Latvia (as in Estonia and Lithuania) you can usually get into museums at a reduced price, without having to show ID, if you look like a student.

Money and banks

Latvia's unit of currency is the **lat** (plural lati), normally abbreviated to Ls, which is divided into 100 santimi. Coins come in 0.01, 0.02, 0.05, 0.10, 0.20, 0.50, 1 and 2Ls and notes in 5, 10, 20, 50, 100 and 500Ls. At the time of writing £1 was worth 1Ls and $1 was worth 0.6Ls.

Bank (*banka*) **opening times** vary, but in Rīga you should be able to find ones that are open between 10am and 5pm, and some stay open later. Outside the capital many banks close at 1pm and all banks are closed on Saturday and Sunday. Most major banks like the Hansabank, Rigas Komercbanka, and Unibank will cash **travellers' cheques** (Thomas Cook and American Express preferred) and some give advances on major credit cards.

In Rīga some major hotels will also cash travellers' cheques and accept credit cards. **Exchanging cash** presents few problems, even outside banking hours, as Rīga is full of currency exchange offices (*valūtas apmaiņa*), many of which are little more than kiosks and often in unlikely locations like food shops. There are also cash machines around town. **Credit cards** can be used in Rīga's more expensive restaurants and stores, and also in some petrol stations, but are not widely accepted outside the capital.

Communications

Post office (*pasts*) opening times are generally Monday to Friday 8am–7pm. For **telephone** calls there are modern digital call boxes which are operated using magnetic cards and analogue ones (now rare) that take tokens (*žeton*). You can also make long-distance calls from post offices and telephone centres. Magnetic **phone cards** come in 2, 5 and 10Ls denominations and can be bought at the post office and most stores. As Latvia is in the process of switching from analogue to digital the whole telephone system, while good, is confusing and area codes are in flux. When in Latvia, for all calls to analogue phones (those with six-digit numbers) you should dial 2 before the six-digit number. For long-distance calls dial 8, wait for the new dial tone, then dial the area code (preceded by a 2 if calling an analogue phone) and number, and for international calls dial 8, wait for the new tone then dial 00 followed by the country code, area code and number.

Getting around

The destinations covered in this chapter are all easily reachable by bus and/or rail. Travelling by bus is generally slightly quicker, but also slightly more expensive, than by train.

■ Trains and buses

Train tickets should be bought in advance – stations have separate windows for long-distance (*starpilsetu*) and suburban (*pirpilsetu*) trains. Long-distance services are divided into the following categories: "passenger" (*pasažieru vilciens*) and fast (*ātrs*). Both are painfully slow but the latter, usually requiring a reservation, won't stop at every second village. Train information is available from station timetable boards – the Latvian for departure is *atiet*, and arrival is *pienāk*.

A useful **rail pass** if you're planning to travel extensively by train in Latvia and the other Baltic Republics is the Baltic Explorer, giving you unlimited travel throughout the region. For information on the latest prices and conditions of use, contact the International Rail Centre or USIT Campus in London. It's available to ISIC-card holders, under-26s, and ITIC-card holders and their accompanying spouses.

It's best to buy long-distance **bus** tickets in advance. Opt for an express (*ekspresis*) bus if possible to avoid frequent stops. Ensure that your ticket entitles you to a seat, or you may have to stand in the aisle for the whole journey. You can also pay for your ticket on board, but again this means you risk having to stand. Normally luggage is taken on board – if you have a particularly large bag you may have to pay extra to have it stowed in the luggage compartment. Buses are also useful for travelling to other Baltic countries, with services linking Rīga with Tallinn and Vilnius.

■ Driving and hitching

If you're **driving** in Latvia you'll soon notice that road conditions can vary dramatically. There's no highway apart from a brief stretch linking Rīga and Jūrmala. Roads linking major towns are usually in a reasonable state, but off the beaten track conditions deteriorate rapidly. The biggest hazard is reckless drivers – Latvia's road casualty rate is shocking. Though most towns are well provided with petrol stations, there are few in rural areas – carry a spare can. Speed limits are 50kph in built-up areas and 90kph on the open road. In towns it's forbidden to overtake stationary trams (allowing passengers to alight in safety) and it's against the law to drive after drinking any alcohol.

For **car rental**, Western rates apply, though you may get a better deal from small local firms – bear in mind though that with the latter contracts can be dubious, insurance coverage sketchy and the cars themselves not necessarily maintained properly.

Hitching is fairly common between major centres and holiday destinations; you should offer to make a contribution towards petrol.

Accommodation

Outside of Rīga and Jūrmala **accommodation** possibilities are fairly limited and even in tourist areas towns will often only have a couple of hotels and perhaps a campsite to their name.

■ Hotels and private rooms

Rīga has **hotels** at both the opulent and fleapit end of the scale, but not much in between. Away from the capital, even in tourist areas like Jūrmala and the Gauja Valley, your only choice is likely to be either cheap Soviet-era dives with no facilities or overpriced Soviet-era places where higher rates are justified by leaky en-suite plumbing and the presence of a broken TV in your room. Small, pension-type places

---

ACCOMMODATION PRICE CODES

Throughout this guide, accommodation is priced on a scale of ① to ⑨, the number indicating the lowest price per night a single person could expect to pay in that establishment in high season. With hostels this is the nightly rate per person; with hotels, the price is arrived at by dividing the cost of the cheapest double room by two. The prices indicated by the codes are as follows:

① under £5 / $8
② £5–10 / $8–16
③ £10–15 / $16–24
④ £15–20 / $24–32
⑤ £20–25 / $32–40
⑥ £25–30 / $40–48
⑦ £30–35 / $48–56
⑧ £35–40 / $56–64
⑨ £40 / $64 and over

are starting to appear but for the time being, they are few and far between. In Rīga there are also a number of **private room** agencies that generally represent good value for money.

■ Hostels, student accommodation and camping

Hostel accommodation exists in Rīga and in the capital it's also possible to find rooms in student halls of residence during college vacations. Such options don't really exist elsewhere in the country, where the only choice open to budget travellers is to head for a **campsite** (*kempings*), where accommodation consists of basic cabins, with shared toilets and washing facilities. Most campsites also have space for tents.

Food and drink

Latvian cooking is based around meat, fish, potatoes and dairy products, with vegetables of the kind people can grow on their own plots. For drinking, Rīga has some excellent bars, and though some are expensive, you shouldn't have trouble finding somewhere affordable.

■ Food

Popular **starters** include cabbage soup (*svaigu kāpostu zupa*) – often almost a meal in itself – and sprats with onions (*šprotes ar sīpoliem*). Most **main courses** are meat- or fish-based – if you want to try something indigenous go for *cūkas galerts* (pork in aspic) or *rasols* (potato salad with herring, beetroot and apple). Popular fish dishes include herring (*siļķe*) and fried, smoked or salted eel (*zutis*). **Desserts** are normally based around forest berries – try *debess manna* (cranberry sauce and creamed wheat with vanilla sauce).

Eating out in Latvia, particularly in Rīga, is often very expensive; two people can easily run up a bill of 20Ls. Keep costs down by dining in **fast-food** places serving pizza and chicken (avoid burgers unless you're a culinary masochist). In Rīga you'll also find a few **ethnic** restaurants offering vegetarian options. Eating in **cafés** and **bars** is another cheap option, and self-catering should be no problem as food shops are well stocked with picnic staples.

■ Drink

The main alcoholic drink in Latvia is **beer** (*alus*). A lot of places serve imported beer but the local brews are

fine, and usually cheaper – the most common brand is Aldaris. Worth trying once (and probably once only) is Rīgas Melnais Balzāms, or Rīga Black balsam, a kind of bitter made according to a secret recipe that combines various roots, grasses and herbs.

Outside the capital there isn't a great choice of watering-holes, but most places will have at least one bar, café or restaurant. If you want to sample local drinking culture head for a **beer bar**, though these are mostly male-only hangouts dedicated to serious imbibing. For something more civilized try **cafés** where, though alcohol is usually served, abstainers won't feel out of place. **Coffee** (*kafiju*) and **tea** (*tēja*) are usually served black – if you want milk and/or sugar you'll have to ask.

Opening hours and holidays

Shops are usually open Monday to Friday 8/10am–6/8pm, though some close for an hour around lunchtime. A few food shops stay open until 10pm and also open on Sunday. Most shops and all banks will be closed on the following **public holidays**: Jan 1; Good Friday; Easter Day; May 1; Mothers' Day (second Sunday in May); June 23 (Midsummer); June 24 (St John's Day); Nov 18 (National Day); Dec 25 & 26; and Dec 31.

Emergencies

Latvia has a major organized crime problem, but though the mafia are highly visible in the smart bars and restaurants of Rīga, their activities are unlikely to impinge on the average visitor. Theft is the biggest hazard you're likely to face, and if you're staying in a cheap hotel it's better not to leave valuables in your room. Muggings and casual violence are not unknown in Rīga, but you can minimize the risks by avoiding the backstreets after dark. Latvian police (*policija*) are unlikely to speak much, if any, English.

No immunizations are necessary for Latvia and emergency medical care is free, though if you fall ill it's best to head for home if you're able to do so as the country's medical facilities are run-down.

> **EMERGENCY NUMBERS**
> Fire ☎01; Police ☎02; Ambulance ☎03.

RĪGA

RĪGA is the undisputed Baltic metropolis, a major port and industrial centre of nearly a million people. The city was founded by Albert von Buxhoeveden, a German canon who arrived in 1201 with twenty shiploads of crusaders to convert the Latvian tribes to Christianity. The main Hanseatic outpost in the region, Rīga was run by German nobles and merchants even when wider political control passed to other powers, starting with the Polish-Lithuanian Commonwealth in the late sixteenth century. After a subsequent period of Swedish rule Rīga became part of the Russian Empire in 1710 and during the second half of the nineteenth century it developed into a major manufacturing centre. Badly damaged during World War I, the city made a comeback during the first Latvian independence and remained a major centre after the country was swallowed up by the Soviet Union in 1940. Under the Soviets, the influx of Russian immigrants reduced the Latvians to a minority in their own capital – forty-seven percent of the city's population is now Russian, with a further sixteen percent made up of other non-Latvian nationalities. These days Rīga has a boom-town feel with a small but conspicuous section of the population making big bucks from the get-rich-quick opportunities thrown up by the switch to full-blown market economics.

Arrival, information and city transport

Rīga's main **train station** (Centrālā Stacija) and **bus station** (Autoosta) are just south of Old Rīga and within easy walking distance of the centre. The sea passenger terminal (Jūras pasažieru stacija) is to the north of the centre. **Trams** #5, #7 or #9 run from the stop in front of the terminal on Ausekla iela into the centre of town (2 stops). Rīga **airport** (Lidosta Rīga) is at Skulte, 8km southwest of the centre, with a currency exchange office (6am–10pm) on the left after you exit customs. Bus #22 runs approximately every thirty minutes from the airport to Arhitektu iela, off Raiņa bulvāris. Tickets cost 0.18Ls and are available from the kiosk in the terminal building or from the driver.

There is a tourist office based at the airport (☎2/720 7800; Mon–Fri 10am–6pm), or you can go to the privately run **tourist office** at Skārņu 22, which has maps and guides and can also book rooms and tours. At the time of writing, there were plans to establish more tourist offices in Rīga and relocate the privately run office to a nearby building; check the free magazine *Riga This Week*, available from the tourist office, for more information. In addition, the excellent English-language guide *Rīga in Your Pocket*, available from newsstands and hotel foyers, contains all the information you could possibly require. Old Rīga is easily walkable, and you can cover the New Town on foot without much effort too. Outlying attractions are easily reached by bus, tram or trolleybus. **Tickets** cost 0.18Ls – bus tickets are bought on board from the conductor, tram and trolleybus tickets are available from kiosks. Different tickets are needed for each mode of transport. **Taxis** should cost 0.25Ls per kilometre during the day and 0.35Ls between 10pm and 6am, but watch out for rip-offs, particularly if taking taxis from the airport and train or bus stations. The black and orange taxis are usually reliable.

Accommodation

Rīga has no shortage of expensive **hotels** and there are a number of very basic budget places too. What's lacking are comfortable, reasonably priced mid-range places. If you're looking for something in this bracket you may want to consider **bed and breakfast** accommodation in a private apartment. Patricia Ltd, Elizabetes 22–6 (☎2/728 4868), has private rooms from 9Ls, mostly within walking distance of the centre. The Rīga Tourism Information Bureau, Skārņu 22 (☎2/722 1731), has **private rooms** too and they can also direct you to rooms in student accommodation starting at 3Ls per person. The *Rīga Technical University Hostel*, Azenes 22a (☎2/708 9261), has double and triple rooms at 3Ls per person (trolleybus #7 or #21 to Kipsala, the first stop across the river); and *Placis*, Laimdotas 2a (☎2/755 1824), has decent

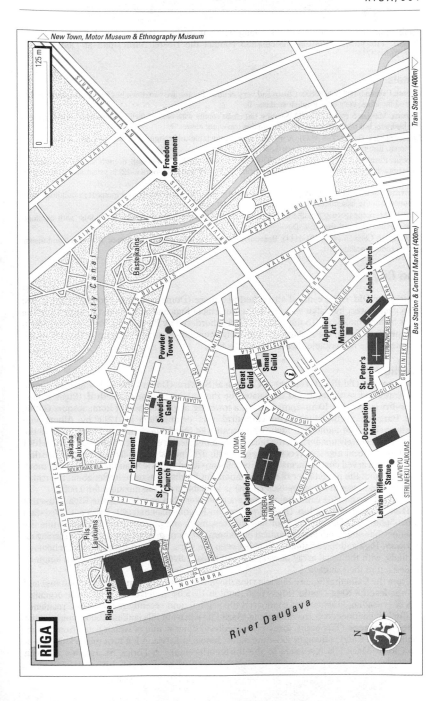

RĪGA

New Town, Motor Museum & Ethnography Museum

Train Station (400m)

Bus Station & Central Market (400m)

125 m

0

STABU IELA

KALPAKA BULVARIS

RAINA BULVARIS

BRIVIBAS BULVARIS

Freedom Monument

City Canal

Bastejkalns

BASTEJA BULVARIS

ASPAZIJAS BULVARIS

VALNU IELA

R. VAGNERA IELA

KALEJU IELA

JANA IELA

St. John's Church

Powder Tower

SMILSU IELA

MAZA SMILSU IELA

ZIRGU IELA

MEISTARU IELA

TROKSNU IELA

ALDARU IELA

Applied Art Museum

SKARNU IELA

PETERBAZNICAS IELA

GRECINIEKU IELA

Great Guild

Small Guild

St. Peter's Church

KUNGU IELA

JEKABA IELA

Swedish Gate

TORNA IELA

Jekaba Laukums

NOLIKTAVAS IELA

VALDEMARA IELA

Parliament

St. Jacob's Church

ARSENALA IELA

MAZA PILS IELA

PILS IELA

DOMA LAUKUMS

Occupation Museum

JAUNA IELA

TIRGONU IELA

KALKU IELA

AMATU IELA

SKUNU IELA

ZIRGU IELA

Riga Cathedral

HERDERA LAUKUMS

Latvian Riflemen Statue

LATVIEŠU STRELNIEKU LAUKUMS

PALASTA IELA

Pils Laukums

Riga Castle

DAUGAVAS GATE

11 NOVEMBRA

PUTU GATE

POLU GATE

ANGLIKANU IELA

MINSTEREJAS IELA

River Daugava

N

RĪGA

doubles at 3Ls per person but it's a long way out (trolleybus #4 or bus # 1, #14 or #32 to Teika). For **youth hostels** information contact the Hostel Association at Laimdotas 2a (☎2/755 1271).

Hotels

Arena, Palasta 5 (☎2/722 8583). Cheap and very central. Rooms are run-down but just about bearable with shared facilities. Very little English spoken. ①.

Aurora, Marijas 5 (☎2/722 4479). Shabby but clean rooms with shared facilities near the station. Best of the budgets, but not recommended for females travelling alone. ①.

Laine, Skolas 11 (☎2/728 9823). A friendly and comfortable mid-range hotel, ten minutes' walk from the old town. Enter through the courtyard. ③.

Latvija, Elizabetes 55 (☎2/722 2211). The rooms are comfortable enough though a residual patina of Soviet-era drabness makes them seem overpriced. The VIP section (floors 6–12) is swish and more expensive. ⑦.

Konventa Sēta, Kalēju 9/11 (☎2/708 7501). A charming, cosy hotel in restored monastery buildings, with a museum in the basement. Ideal location in the heart of the old town. ⑦.

Saulīte, Merķeļa 12 (☎2/722 4546). The renovated rooms are quite presentable. Rooms "with comfort" have en-suite WC and showers. ①.

Viktorija, A Čaka 55 (☎22/701 4111). Reasonable place about 1km from the station. Renovated and unrenovated rooms available. ④.

The City

Vecirīga or **Old Rīga**, centred on Cathedral Square (Doma laukums) and neatly cut in two from east to west by Kaļķu iela, forms the nucleus of Rīga and is home to the majority of the city's historic buildings. To the east Old Rīga is bordered by Bastejkalns Park, beyond which lies the **New Town**, the nineteenth- and early twentieth-century extension of the city which contains some remarkable *Jugendstil* architecture.

Old Rīga

At the core of Old Rīga (Vecirīga) is **Cathedral Square** (Doma laukums), edged by expensive cafés and restaurants and dominated by the red-brick **Rīga Cathedral** (Rīgas Dome; Tues–Fri 1–5pm, Sat 10am–2pm; 0.50Ls), a towering agglomeration of Romanesque, Gothic and Baroque architecture. The cathedral was established in 1211 by Albert von Buxhoeveden, the founder of Rīga, who became its first bishop. In true Lutheran style the interior is relatively unadorned, the most eye-catching features being a florid pulpit from 1641 and a magnificent nineteenth-century organ with 6768 pipes. The pillars of the nave are decorated with carved coats of arms while its walls are lined with German memorial slabs, mostly dating from the period after the Reformation. An English-language leaflet about the cathedral and the museum it houses (see below) is available from the musuem for 0.60Ls.

The east wing of the cathedral was once a monastery but now houses the **Rīga Museum of History and Navigation** (Rīgas Vestures un Kuģniecības muzejs), Palasta 4 (Wed–Sun 11am–5pm; 1Ls). The ground floor has pictures, maps and postcards of Old Rīga, while the first-floor has ship models and nautical ephemera. Of more general interest is the display on *Jugendstil* Rīga and the section on Rīga between the wars. The next floor houses archeological finds, with the usual array of weapons and tools enlivened by the remains of a longboat hauled out of the Daugava.

From the Cathedral Square Pils iela runs down to leafy **Castle Square** (Pils laukums) and the nondescript **Rīga Castle** (Rīgas pils), built in 1515 by the Livonian Order (the organization of crusading knights who conquered the region), and recently restored as a residence for the Latvian president. Heading along Mazā Pils iela from Pils laukums takes you past the **Three Brothers** (Trīs brāli), three plain medieval houses, one of which dates from the fifteenth century and is thought to be the oldest house in Latvia. A left turn into Jēkaba iela at the end of Mazā Pils iela leads to the thirteenth-century red-brick **St Jacob's Church**

(Jēkaba baznīca), the seat of Rīga's Roman Catholic archbishop. Next door at Jēkaba 11 is Latvia's **Parliament** (Latvijas augstākā padome), housed in a pompous Renaissance-style building. In January 1991 barricades were erected around the building to protect it from an expected Soviet attack and these remained in place for a year, even after the collapse of the Soviet Union and the recognition of Latvian independence by Russia.

Nearby on Torņa iela you'll find the seventeenth-century **Swedish Gate** (Zviedru vārti). This simple archway beneath a three-storey townhouse was built when Rīga was ruled by the Swedes, and is the sole surviving city gate. A more impressive relic can be found at the end of Torņa iela in the shape of the **Powder Tower** (Pulvertornis), a vast, fourteenth-century bastion whose red-brick walls are still embedded with cannonballs from various sieges. Today, it's home to the **Museum Of War** (Kara Muzejs; Wed–Sun 10am–5pm; 0.50Ls; English-language leaflet 0.40Ls.) with sections on the War of Liberation (1918–20) when the Latvians beat off the Soviets and the Germans, and on the Latvian Legion of volunteers who served with the German Waffen SS during World War II.

Though it's not readily apparent, **Bastion Hill** (Bastejkalns) – the park that slopes down to the city canal on the eastern edge of Old Rīga – is actually a vast earthworks built as part of the city's outer defences. It is also a reminder of Rīga's more recent history: on January 20, 1991 four people were killed here by sniper fire as Soviet OMON troops stormed the Latvian Ministry of the Interior on nearby Raiņa bulvaris during an attempted crackdown on Latvia's independence drive. Stones bearing the names of the victims mark where they fell near the Bastejas bulvaris entrance to the park.

From the Swedish Gate Meistaru iela runs down to the **Great Guild Hall** (Lielā Ģilde) at Amatu 6, once the centre of commercial life in Hanseatic Rīga. Though it dates from the fourteenth century the building owes its present neo-Gothic appearance to a nineteenth-century facelift and now houses the Latvia State Philharmonic. South of Kaļķu iela on Skārņu iela is **St Peter's Church** (Pētera Baznīca; Tues–Sun 10am–7pm), a large red-brick church with a graceful three-tiered spire, dedicated to the city's patron saint. Construction began in 1408 to replace a wooden church built two hundred years earlier. The new church boasted the highest wooden spire in Europe. This was rebuilt in 1746 after it was struck by lightning, only to be destroyed once more by German shelling in 1941. Today, the 123-metre spire is a steel replica, completed in 1973, with a lift (1.20Ls) taking visitors to a gallery in its upper reaches. A panoramic view of the city can be had from the observation platform.

More or less opposite the church, on Skārņu iela, are a clutch of restored medieval buildings. At nos. 10–16 a former chapel of the Knights of the Sword, built in 1208, now houses the **Museum of Decorative and Applied Arts** (Dekoratīvās Mākslas Muzejs; Tues–Sun 11am–5pm; 0.50Ls) with a collection of pottery, ceramics, glass and sculpture, while at no. 22 is the Ekes konvents, a fifteenth-century convent, and today home to the tourist office. Next door is the thirteenth-century **St John's Church** (Jāņa Baznīca), whose sober Gothic exterior conceals a fanciful Baroque altar.

Before World War II the late-Gothic **House of the Blackheads** (Melngalvju nams), headquarters of a guild of bachelor merchants and one of Rīga's most famous medieval buildings, stood to the west of St Peter's on what used to be the town hall square (Rātslaukums), which was destroyed in 1941, but is now being rebuilt to coincide with Rīga's 800-year anniversary in 2001. These days the square, bereft of historic buildings, is known as **Latvian Riflemen's Square** (Latviesu Strēlnieku Laukums) in honour of the Latvian soldiers who fought with the Imperial Russian army during World War I, and then with the Bolsheviks, as the Latvian Red Riflemen, during the Russian Civil War. They are commemorated by a red marble statue depicting three stern figures clad in greatcoats and caps near the bridge at the western end of the square. Also on the square is the **Occupation Museum of Latvia** (Latvijas Okupācijas Muzeja; Tues–Fri, Sun 11am–5pm; free), formerly the Latvian Riflemen's Museum, but now devoted to Latvia's occupation by the Bolsheviks, Nazis and Soviets. Nearby at Grēcinieku 18 is **Menzendorff's House** (Mencendorfa nams; Wed–Sun 10am–5pm; 1Ls), an impeccably restored late seventeenth-century merchant's house decorated in grand style and adorned with period furniture and artefacts.

The New Town

The boulevards of the **New Town**, rolling east from Old Rīga, bear witness to a period of rapid urban expansion that began in 1857, when the city's medieval walls were demolished, and lasted right up until World War I. As Rīga grew into a major industrial centre and country-dwellers flocked to the city, four- and five-storey apartment buildings – many of them decorated with extravagant *Jugendstil* motifs – were erected to house the expanding middle-class.

As you head east out along Kaļķu, which widens out and becomes Brīvības bulvāris, the defiantly modernist **Freedom Monument** (Brīvības piemineklis) dominates the view. This stylized female figure, placed here in 1935 and known as "Milda", holds aloft three stars symbolizing the three regions of Latvia. Incredibly, the monument survived the Soviet era, and nowadays two soldiers stand guard here in symbolic protection of Latvia's independence.

Running north from Brīvības bulvāris to the east of the Freedom Monument is the formal **Esplanade Park** with the **Cathedral of Christ's Nativity** (Kristus dzimsanas katedrāle) just inside its grounds. This late nineteenth-century mock-Byzantine creation was recently returned to the city's Orthodox community after serving as a planetarium during the Soviet period. At the far end of the park is the **State Museum of Latvian Art** (Valsts Mākslas Muzejs), Valdemāra iela 10A (Tues–Sun 11am–5pm; 0.50Ls), housed in a grandiose Baroque building. The ground floor features conventional Russian art from the eighteenth to the twentieth century; while on the first floor you'll find nineteenth- and twentieth-century Latvian works. The odd, stylized street scenes and portraits of Jānis Tīdemanis (1897–1964) make the most lasting impression. Beyond the park it's worth continuing along Brīvības bulvāris as far as the **Alexander Nevsky Church** (Aleksandra Nevska Baznīca) at no. 56, an attractive little Orthodox church from the 1820s, partly concealed by trees on the southern side of the street.

Jugendstil architectural embellishments – florid stucco swirls surrounding doorways, stylized human faces incorporated into facades, and towers fancifully placed on top of buildings – can be seen on virtually every street of the New Town and, while walking through the area, it always pays to look up to catch details that might otherwise pass by unnoticed. One of the most famous *Jugendstil* creations in the city is at **Elizabetes** 10a and 10b, an apartment building adorned with plaster flourishes and gargoyles, and topped by two vast impassive faces. It was designed by Mikhail Eisenstein, the architect father of Sergei, director of the *Battleship Potemkin*; more of Eisenstein's creations can be seen at Alberta iela 2, 2a, 4, 6, 8 and 13.

Elsewhere in central Rīga

A few hundred metres south of Old Rīga, near the bus and train stations, is the bustling **Central Market** (Centrālais tirgus), housed in a couple of hulking 1930s Zeppelin hangars. As well as being a useful source of fruit and vegetables, the market is an interesting place to wander round – but keep an eye on your possessions. Five run-down blocks southeast of the market on Elijas iela, the white-painted **Jesus Church** (Jēzus Baznīca), is surrounded by a neighbourhood of decaying timber houses. Dating back to 1635, this is Rīga's oldest wooden church, though it's been rebuilt following fires a couple of times since then. The interior is unusual, with a circular central hall supported by wooden pillars. The church is overshadowed by the **Academy of Sciences** (Latvijas Zinātņu Akedemija) at Turgeņeva 19, a Soviet-era pile built in monumental "wedding-cake" style during the early 1960s and nicknamed "Stalin's Birthday Cake".

Rīga's **Ghetto**, the area originally inhabited by the city's Jews and to which the Nazis later restricted Rīga's Jewish inhabitants, was located about 1km southeast of the train station, in an area now bounded by Lāaplēsa iela, Maskvas iela, Lauvas iela and Kalna iela. Most of its original inhabitants were murdered at Salaspils concentration camp, outside the city, between November 30 and December 8, 1941. The ghetto remained in operation, occupied by Jews from elsewhere in Europe until 1943, when it was liquidated on the orders of Himmler after the Warsaw Ghetto uprising. Rīga still has a several-thousand strong Jewish community and their synagogue is at Peitavas 6–8 in the old town.

On the edge of the former ghetto at Krasta 73, is the gold-domed **Grebenščikova Church** (Grebenščikova Baznīca), a wooden church dating from 1814 with a congregation of Old

Believers, a dissenting sect which broke away from the Orthodox church during the seventeenth century, many of whose members had fled Russia to escape persecution. To the south of the former ghetto area on **Rabbit Island** (Zaķu Salu) is Rīga's TV Tower, a 368-metre concrete tripod, with a viewing platform and restaurant halfway up, which ranks as one of the highest buildings in the world.

Eating, drinking and nightlife

You can **eat** very well in Rīga's restaurants, but at a price. If you're on a budget, many bars and cafés do food that is less expensive and often just as good as restaurant dishes. There are also plenty of inexpensive fast-food places. For **drinking**, most of the Old Town bars, particularly those around Cathedral Square, tend to be expensive and geared towards tourists and the local nouveaux riches. A number of cheaper and more off-beat places can be found in the New Town. The majority of locals can't afford Rīga bar prices so they buy beer from kiosks and wander the streets clutching bottles. Many places have English-language menus.

Rīga has a reasonable number of live **music venues**, a few discos and some excellent clubs. **Gambling** is very big in the city with a number of casinos and numerous bars devoted to gaming.

Cafés and snacks

Andalūzijas Suns, Elizabetes 83–85. Named after Dalí and Buñuel's collaboration *Un Chien Andalou,* this arty café is one of the most recommendable places in town. The menu lists some eclectic dishes, with main courses from around 3Ls and some good vegetarian options. Sun 4pm–midnight, Mon–Sat noon–midnight.

Elektroniskā Kafejnīca, 81/85 Elizabetes. Moodily atmospheric café, with Internet access at 1.80Ls per hour. Daily noon–10pm.

Ice Queen, Ģertrūdes 20. The best ice cream in the Baltics – try the "spaghetti" ice. They also do a decent cappuccino. Expensive but worth it. Daily 11am–10pm.

Kolonāde, Brīvības 26. Central café in the shadow of the Freedom Monument, with outside seating to the rear. Cheap food and drinks – order from the counter. Daily 8am–10pm.

Lido, Ģertrūdes 54. No-smoking place where you can eat in or take away. Daily 24hr.

Monte Kristo, Ģertrūdes 27. Excellent little coffee-house that also serves pastries. Sun noon–9pm, Mon–Sat 9am–9pm.

Pie Kūma, A. Čaka 65. Ukrainian café with good *borscht*. Sun 11am–6pm, Mon–Sat 11am–10pm.

Pizza Lulū, Ģertrūdes 27. Fashionable little pizzeria where you can eat well at a reasonable price. Can get crowded. Daily 8am–midnight.

Šefpavārs Vilhelms, Sķūņu 6. Self-service, create your own pancake place near the Cathedral Square. Mon–Fri 8am–10pm, Sat & Sun 10am–10pm.

Sala, Dzirnavu 49. Light meals and cakes amid decor best described as rustic meets 1950s sci-fi. Daily 11am–11pm.

Restaurants

Arve, 12–14 Aldaru. Pleasant little restaurant near the Swedish Gate with a menu that's a little more varied than most. Good quality, but small portions. Daily 11am–11pm.

Ļidojošā Varde, Elizabetes 31a. A basement restaurant in the New Town with *Jugendstil*-pastiche decor. Not as expensive as the atmosphere might lead you to imagine. Main courses from around 3Ls. Mon–Thurs & Sat 10am–1am, Fri & Sun 10am–3am.

Put Vējiņ!, Jauniela 18. Serving Latvian specialities in a low-key atmosphere. Moderate prices, but you'll probably need to book. Daily 11am–midnight.

Pulkvedim Neviens Neraksta, Peldu 26/28. Serves meat and pasta during the day, but becomes a club at night. Sun–Thurs noon–3am, Fri & Sat noon–5am. Fri & Sat 1–3Ls.

Rāma & Svāmīdži's Space Station, Barona 56. Hare-Krishna-run veggie place in the New Town. Downstairs it's so cheap that pensioners line up in soup-kitchen style. Daily 8am–10pm.

Rozamunde, Maza Smilsu 8. The atmosphere of prewar Rīga, with live music from 7pm onwards. Daily 11am–11pm.

Saigona, Dzirnavu 87/89. Excellent and inexpensive little Vietnamese restaurant. Daily 10am–2am.

Šanhaja, Grēcinieku 26. Chinese cuisine without a hint of Latvia. Daily noon–10pm.

Senā Rīga, Aspazijas 22. Dine in rustic cabins while accordionists entertain you from on board a mocked-up pirate galleon, in a restaurant that forms part of the *Rīga Hotel*. The food is Latvian, portions are large and if you choose carefully, the bill won't clean you out. Daily noon–midnight.

Slepenais Eksperiments, Šķūņu 15 (entrance on Amatu). Salads and savoury meals during the day and techno at night. Sun–Thurs noon–5am, Fri & Sat 8pm–6am; 1–2Ls.

Staburags, Čaka 55. Traditional Latvian food served amidst old-fashioned oak rooms. Large portions at reasonable prices. Daily noon–1am.

Vincents, Elizabetes 19. The nouveau-ish cuisine is excellent, but you're unlikely to escape with a bill of less than 12Ls per person. Daily noon–midnight.

Zilais Putns, Tirgoņu 4. Excellent Italian just off Cathedral Square. Reasonably expensive. Daily 11am–1am.

Bars

13 Krēsli, Jauiela 11. A trendy little bar on Cathedral Square, with chrome and leatherette decor, and techno pumping from the speakers. Expensive. Daily 11am–midnight.

Ala, Audēju 11. Popular with young locals. Good, inexpensive cocktails, but the steep stairs may prove to be an obstacle after a few drinks in "the cave". Open 10am–4am.

Alus Sēta, Tirgotu iela 6. Justifiably popular pub with huge meals served from the grill and good, cheap beer. Outdoor seating in warm months. Daily 11am–1am.

DECO Bars, Dzirnavu 84. Snacks, great cocktails, music, dancing and excellent service. Daily 11am till the last person leaves.

Fredis, Ģertrūdes 62. A friendly little bar that's popular with tourists, expats and young locals eager to try out their English. A good place for a cheapish meal with dishes for around 1.80Ls. Daily 9am–11pm.

Možums, Šķūņu 19. Guinness on tap and reasonable, albeit pricey food. Attracts a business crowd. Sun noon–1am, Mon–Thurs 11am–1am, Fri 11am–3am, Sat noon–3am.

Paddy Whelan's Bar, Grēcinieku 4. Big, lively Irish pub that seems to attract every expat, tourist and visiting sailor in town. Sat–Thurs 10am–1am, Fri 10am–2am.

Live music

Hamlet Club, Jāņa Sēta 5. Political cabaret and jazz. Daily 7pm–5am.

Kabata, Peldu 19. A basement club in Old Rīga, with a small dance floor and live bands. Daily noon–5pm & 6pm–5am; 2Ls.

Karakums, Lāčplēša 18. A popular café/bar with acoustic bands playing on the ground floor, and a dance floor upstairs with live bands or DJs providing the sounds. Mon–Thurs 11am–3am, Sat & Sun 1pm–5am.

Reformātu Klubs, Mārstaļu 10. A jazz club in a former church. Drinks are expensive, but you can also eat here. Daily 5pm–1am; 10Ls.

Saksofons, Stabu 43. Small jazz and blues venue with a bohemian clientele. The cocktails are cheap and potent. Daily 4pm–4am; 0.50–1.50Ls.

Clubs and discos

Pepsi Forums, Ķaļķu 24. Popular with Russian speakers, expats and beautiful young things. Bar, billiards and dancing. Daily 8pm–5am; 5Ls.

Slepenais Eksperiments, Šķūņu 15, entrance at Amatu 4. Hippest club in town with great interior decor (check out the motif on the dancefloor), live bands and DJs. Go before midnight to avoid the queues. Fri midnight–5am, Sat 8pm–6am. 2Ls, 1Ls after 4am. Thurs is student night (0.5Ls).

Underground, Slokas 1. A Latvian-Swedish joint-venture on the ground floor of the *Turists Hotel*. Despite the arty decor the place feels more like a disco than a club. Cloakroom doesn't accept bags. Daily 9pm–6am. 2–3Ls.

Classical music, opera and ballet

The Philharmonic Concert Hall at Amatu iela 6 in the Lielā Ģilde is the home of the Latvian National Symphony Orchestra and is Rīga's main classical venue. The National Opera House at Aspazijas bulvaris 3, stages classic operatic productions and is home to the Rīga Ballet (Rīgas Balets), where Mikhail Baryshnikov had his first break; the building is currently under restoration, but both companies perform there – check *Rīga in Your Pocket* for details. There are regular organ and other recitals in the cathedral – tickets can be obtained from the office opposite the west door. Another Rīga attraction is the celebrated Ave Sol, Citadeles 7, one of the best choral ensembles in the Baltic States.

Listings

Airlines Aeroflot, Ģertrūdes 6 (☎22/278 774); Air Baltic, Kaļķu 15 (☎2/722 9166); British Airways, Tornu 4/IIIa (☎2/732 6737); Finnair, Barona 36 (☎2/724 3008); LOT, M. Pils 5 (☎2/722 7234); Lufthansa at the airport (☎2/720 7183); Riair, Mellužu (☎2/424 283); SAS, Kaļķu 15 (☎2/721 6139).

Airport enquiries ☎2/720 7888.

Bike rental Gandrs. Kalnciema 28 (☎2/7614 775).

Books Aperto Libro, Barona 31. For maps and travel guides, Jāna Sēta, Elizabetes 83/85. Mon–Fri 10am–7pm, Sat 11am–5pm.

Car rental Avis, at the airport (☎2/720 7353); Hertz at the airport (☎2/720 7980).

Embassies Canada, Doma laukums 4 (☎2/783 0141); United Kingdom, Alunana 5 (☎2/733 8126); USA, Raina bulvaris 7 (☎2/721 0055).

Exchange Round-the-clock service at Marika, Basteja 14, Brīvības 30, Marijas 5 & 14, Merķeļa 10.

Hospital Ars, Skolas 5 (☎2/720 1001). Some English-speaking doctors.

Internet Access Elektroniskā Kafejnīca, Elizabetes 83/85 (2/724 2826; daily noon–10pm); Internet Kafejnīca, Jekaba 20 (2/732 3361; daily 10am–9pm).

Laundry Miele, Elizabetes 85a. Open 24hr.

Left Luggage There are 24hr lockers at Rokas Bagāīas in the basement of the long-distance rail terminal (0.50–1Ls per day). Lockers next to track 6.

Pharmacies Ring the bell for 24hr service at Brīvības bulvāris 121 & 230.

Police Emergency number ☎02.

Post office 24hr service on Brīvības bulvāris 19.

Telephones Telephone Centre at Brīvības bulvāris 19. Open 24hr. Fax service at Brīvības bulvāris 19.

Day-trips from Rīga

For a taste of the rest of Latvia, a number of destinations within easy reach of Rīga make feasible day-trips from the capital. Northeast of Rīga are the small towns of **Sigulda** and **Cēsis**, which lie at the heart of the **Gauja National Park** (Gaujas Nacionālais Parks), a 920-square-kilometre forested region, while **Rundale Palace**, 80km to the south of the city, is one of the architectural highlights of Latvia.

Salaspils

The concentration camp at **SALASPILS**, 22km southeast of Rīga, is where most of Rīga's Jewish population perished during World War II. Around 100,000 people died here, including Jews from other countries who had been herded into the Rīga Ghetto after most of the indigenous Jewish population had been wiped out. Today the site is marked by monumental sculptures and a museum, with the former locations of the barrack buildings outlined by white stones. To get there take a suburban train in the direction of Ogre and alight at Dārziņa station from where a clearly signposted path leads to the memorial, a walk of about fifteen minutes.

Jūrmala

JŪRMALA or "Seashore" is the collective name for a string of small seaside resorts that straggle along the Baltic coast for about 20km west of Rīga. Originally favoured by the tsarist nobility, it became the haunt of Latvian intellectuals between the wars. Today, its sandy beaches backed by dunes and pine woods seethe with people at weekends and on public holidays. Beyond the beach, however, Jūrmala is quite dull – decaying wooden houses punctuated by gargantuan Soviet-era sanatoria complexes, while most of the hotels and restaurants are pretty lacklustre.

Trains to Jūrmala leave the suburban terminus of Rīga's central station (every 30min 5am–11pm) from platforms 3 and 4. Majori, about 10km beyond Rīga city limits, is the main stop and a service centre of sorts, with a number of restaurants and cafés along Jomas iela, the pedestrianized main street running east from the station square. Head north to Jūras iela, from where a few paths lead to the beach.

Sigulda and Cēsis

SIGULDA, dotted with parks and clustered above the southern bank of the River Gauja, around 50km northeast of Rīga, is the Gauja National Park's main centre and makes a good jumping-off point for exploring the rest of the Gauja Valley.

From the train station Raiņa iela runs north into town. After about 800m a right turn into Baznīca iela brings you to **Sigulda Church** (Siguldas Baznīca), built over seven hundred years ago, though much altered since. A left turn after the church leads, by way of **Sigulda New Castle** (Siguldas Jaunā Pils), a nineteenth-century manor house masquerading as a medieval castle, to the ruins of Sigulda Castle (Siguldas Pilsdrupas), a former stronghold of the Knights of the Sword. From here you can admire **Turaida Castle** (Turaidas Pils), perched on a bluff at the far side of the densely wooden Gauja Valley. The most atmospheric way to reach it is to take the cable car that runs from Baumaņu iela, west of Raiņa iela, to the scant remains of the thirteenth-century Krimulda Castle; Turaida Castle is close by. Built on the site of an earlier stronghold by the bishop of Rīga in 1214, it was destroyed when lightning hit its gunpowder magazine during the eighteenth century. The pristine state of much of its brickwork attests to the fact that it has been extensively restored, and these days it houses a local history **museum** (Tues–Sun 10am–5/6pm; 0.80Ls). Just before the castle is the eighteenth-century **Turaidas Church** (Turaidas Baznīcas), an appealing little wooden church with a Baroque tower that's one of the best-preserved examples of Latvian native architecture in the country.

The well-preserved little town of **CĒSIS**, 35km northeast of Sigulda, is considered by many Latvians to have an atmosphere as close to that of prewar smalltown Latvia as it's possible to get. One of the oldest towns in the country, it's the former seat of the master of the Livonian order and was also a member of the Hanseatic League. More recently Cēsis was the site of a crucial battle during the War of Independence, when a combined Latvian/Estonian force defeated the Iron Division of the German *Landeswehr* between June 19 and June 24, 1919.

From the **train** and **bus stations** walk down Raunas iela to Vienības Laukums, the town's main square. The attractive but run-down old town – a few narrow streets lined with flaking wooden buildings – lies to the south of here. On Rīgas iela just south of the square the remains of the old town gates have been excavated. Nearby, on Skolas iela, is the thirteenth-century **St John's Church** (Svēta Jāņa Baznīca), which contains the tombs of several masters of the Livonian order. East of the square are the remains of **Cēsis Castle** (Cēsu Pils) founded by the Knights of the Sword in 1209. Apart from a couple of towers, not much survives, but in the adjoining manor house you'll find a small regional history **museum** (Cēsu Vēstures; Tues–Sun 10am–4pm; 0.50Ls). More appealing perhaps are the grounds, with their small lake and Orthodox church.

Rundāle Palace

RUNDĀLE PALACE or Rundāles Pils (summer Wed–Sun 10am–6pm; winter 1–5pm; 1Ls), 77km south of Rīga, is one of the architectural wonders of Latvia. This 138-room Baroque palace, built in two phases during the 1730s and 1760s, was designed by Bartolomeo Rastrelli, the architect who created the Winter Palace in St Petersburg. It was privately owned until 1920 when it fell into disrepair, but meticulous restoration, begun in 1973, has largely returned it to its former glory. Highlight of the interior is the eastern wing, where a spectacular staircase leads to the most opulent rooms in the whole building – the Zelta zāle, or Gold Hall, throne room, and the Baltā zāle, or White Hall, ballroom featuring a dazzling stucco ceiling. To get there take the bus to **Bauska** and then a bus for Rundāles Pils (no service between 10.30am and 2pm so plan accordingly) from where it's a twenty-minute walk to the palace. Should you want to stay overnight try the *Viesnīca Bauska*, Slimnīcas 7, Bauska (☎239/23027; ①) adjacent to the bus station.

travel details

Trains

Rīga to: Cēsis (9 daily; 1hr 30min); Moscow (2 daily; 17hr 30min); Sigulda (14 daily; 1hr); St Petersburg (1 daily; 14hr); Tallinn (1 daily; 7hr); Vilnius (1 daily; 6hr).

Buses

Rīga to: Bauska (4 daily; 2hr); Cēsis (14 daily; 2hr), Sigulda (2 daily; 1hr), Tallinn (7 daily; 5hr 30min), Vilnius (5 daily; 6hr).

CHAPTER 17

LITHUANIA

Introduction

Unlike its Baltic neighbours, **Lithuania** once enjoyed a period of sustained independence. Having driven off the German Knights of the Sword in 1236 at Yiaulai, the Lithuanians emerged as a unified state under Grand Duke Gediminas (1316–41). The 1569 Union of Lublin established a combined Polish-Lithuanian state which reached its zenith under King Stefan Batory. But the Great Northern War of 1700–21, in which Poland-Lithuania, Russia and Sweden battled for control of the Baltics, left the country devastated, and by the end of the eighteenth century most of Lithuania had fallen into Russian hands. Uprisings in 1830 and 1863 presaged a rise in nationalist feeling, and Russia's collapse in World War I enabled the Lithuanians to re-establish their independence. In July 1940, however, the country was effectively annexed by the USSR. German occupation from 1941 to 1944 wiped out Lithuania's Jewish population and wrecked the country, and things scarcely improved when the return of the Soviets resulted in executions and deportations. When Moscow eventually relaxed its hard line in the late 1980s, demands for greater autonomy led to the declaration of independence on March 11, 1990, way ahead of the other Baltic States. A prolonged stand-off came to a head on January 11, 1991 when Soviet forces killed fourteen people at Vilnius TV Tower, but as the anti-Gorbachev coup foundered in August 1991, the world – soon followed by the disintegrating Soviet Union – recognized Lithuanian independence.

Lithuania is perhaps not the most visitor-friendly of the Baltic Republics but travelling here presents no real hardships, and even in well-trodden destinations the volume of visitors is low, leaving you with the feeling that there's still much to discover here. **Vilnius**, with its Baroque old town, is the most architecturally beautiful of the Baltic capitals, with an easy-going charm all of its own. Lithuania's second city **Kaunas** also has an attractive old town and a couple of unique museums, along with a handful of surprisingly good restaurants and bars. The port city **Klaipėda**, despite its restored old town, is more a stopping-off point en route to the low-key resorts of **Neringa**, a unique spit of sand dunes and forest that shields Lithuania from the Baltic.

Information and maps

Although Vilnius and Klaipėda both have **tourist offices**, the *In Your Pocket* guide series is the most indispensable source for practical information, with separate publications covering Vilnius, Kaunas, Klaipėda and all regions of the country. The soft-cov-ered A5-sized guides cost 4Lt and are available from bookshops, news stands, tourist offices and in some hotels. The Kümmerly & Frey 1:1,000,000 **map** of the Baltics, includes Lithuania in some detail along with a basic street plan of Vilnius. If you're planning to travel extensively in Lithuania the Euromap 1:300,000 map of the country is a useful investment. The Falk Plan of Vilnius has an enlarged Old Town section but does not include public transport – the Vilnius Maps plan available from bookstores in the city does include public transport routes. Locally produced maps are excellent, as are those produced by Jāṇa Sēta, in Latvia.

Money and banks

Lithuania's unit of **currency** is the *litas* (usually abbreviated to Lt) which is divided into 100 *cento*. Coins come in denominations of 0.01, 0.02, 0.05, 0.10, 0.20, 0.50Lt and bank notes in 1, 2, 5, 10, 20, 50 100 and 200Lt denominations. **Bank** (*bankas*) opening hours vary, though branches of the Vilniaus Bankas are usually open Monday to Friday 8am–3/4pm. They'll usually give you an advance on your Visa/Mastercard or American Express card and cash **travellers' cheques** (commission 2–3 percent). If you want to exchange cash outside banking hours head for a **currency exchange** office (*valiutos keitykla*). **Credit cards** are most likely to be accepted in Vilnius where big hotels, restaurants, luxury stores and petrol stations may let you pay with plastic. Outside the capital, apart from a handful of places in Kaunas and Klaipėda, you're unlikely to have much luck.

Communications

In major towns, **post offices** (*paštas*) are usually open Monday to Friday 8am–6pm, Saturday 8am–4pm; in smaller places hours are more restricted. Post offices are the best places to buy stamps, but it's also possible to obtain them from some newspaper kiosks and tourist offices. Lithuania has standard international rates for both airmail and surface letters and postcards. Virtually all public telephones now operate on cards (8.74Lt, 12.96Lt, 16.50Lt and 30.66Lt) from post offices and some hotel lobbies, but you have to make sure you insert the old phone cards and the new phone cards into the appropriate phone. For long-distance or international **phone calls** go to a post office or telephone centre and buy a phone card (*telefono kortel*) – you have to snap off the left-hand corner before using the old-style ones. Where no card phones are available book your call through the operator and pay afterwards. You may also occasionally find card phones in hotel lobbies. To make a long-distance call first dial 8, then wait for the tone before dialling the area code and phone number. For international calls dial 8, wait for the tone, followed by 10, then the country code, area code and phone number. It's worth remembering that, unlike its Baltic counterparts, Lithuania has adopted central European time and is now GMT + 1hr.

Getting around

The destinations covered in this chapter are all easily reachable by bus and/or rail. Travelling by bus is generally slightly quicker but also slightly more expensive than travelling by train.

■ Trains and buses

Train tickets should be bought in advance – stations have separate windows for long-distance and suburban (*priemiestinis* or *vietinis*) trains. Long-distance services are divided into the following categories: passenger (*keleivinis traukinys*) and fast (*greitas*). Both are painfully slow but the latter, usually requiring a reservation, won't stop at every second village. Train information is available from station timetable boards – the Lithuanian for departure is *izvyksta*, and arrival is *atvyksta*.

A useful **rail pass** if you're planning to travel extensively by train in Lithuania and other Baltic Republics is the Baltic Explorer, giving you unlimited travel throughout the region. For information on the latest prices and conditions of use contact the International Rail Centre or USIT Campus in London. It's available to ISIC-card holders, under-26s and ITIC-card holders and their accompanying spouses.

It's best to buy long-distance **bus** tickets in advance, and opt for an express (*ekspresas*) bus if possible to avoid frequent stops. Ensure that your ticket actually entitles you to a seat, or you may have to stand in the aisle for the whole journey. You can also pay for your ticket on board, at the risk of having to stand. Normally luggage is taken on board – if you have a large bag you may have to pay extra to have it stowed in the luggage compartment. As well as being a viable means of getting around Lithuania, buses are also useful for travelling to other Baltic countries with services linking Vilnius, Rīga and Tallinn.

■ Driving and hitching

Driving in Lithuania throws up a number of hazards. Along with people showing off in high-powered Western cars and four-wheel drives there are also some spectacularly decrepit cars on the roads, and in country areas you may have to contend with slow-moving tractors, horses and carts, stray farm animals and the odd drunk wandering onto the road. There's no motorway, though the road linking Vilnius and Kaunas is a fairly respectable two-lane highway for much of its length.

Most main roads are in reasonable repair, but many minor roads are little more than dirt tracks. Though most towns are well provided with petrol stations, there are few in rural areas – carry a spare can. Speed limits are 60kph in built-up areas and 90kph on the open road. The limit on highways is 100kph and the police are extremely vigilant. In towns it's forbidden to overtake stationary trams, allowing passengers to alight in safety, and it's against the law to drive after drinking any alcohol.

Car rental will be around $79 per day from one of the big companies, half that from some local firms – bear in mind though that with the latter contracts can be dubious, insurance coverage sketchy and the cars may not be well maintained. The car's registration papers and, if you don't own the car, a note of authorization should be carried at all times. **Hitching** is fairly common between major centres and it isn't necessary to make a contribution towards petrol. As in any country, women are advised not to hitch alone.

Accommodation

Accommodation in Lithuania is generally cheaper than in western Europe, but it's still a good idea to look around first. The best way to keep costs down is by staying in private rooms, as budget hotels tend to be pretty grim. If money isn't a major issue, you'll have few problems finding a decent place to stay.

■ Bed and breakfast and hotels

For budget travellers **private room** accommodation is often the best option, usually costing around 70Lt per person. The most ubiquitous and reliable agency is Litinterp with offices in Vilnius, Klaipėda and Kaunas. Budget **hotels** tend to be fairly grim, though if you don't mind spartan conditions you may be able to find rooms in Soviet-era fleapits for as little as 40Lt for a double. Some cheap hotels can be dodgy – if things don't feel right (rooms show signs of past forced-entry, etc) don't stay. A few smaller, mid-range places are starting to appear, usually charging upwards of 280Lt a double, and where they exist they are usually preferable to similarly priced Soviet-era hotels which tend to be large and impersonal. In Vilnius you'll also find a few very luxurious places charging 380Lt and upwards for a double; these are about as good as anything you'll find in Lithuania.

ACCOMMODATION PRICE CODES

Throughout this guide, accommodation is priced on a scale of ① to ⑨, the number indicating the lowest price per night a single person could expect to pay in that establishment in high season. With hostels this is the nightly rate per person; with hotels, the price is arrived at by dividing the cost of the cheapest double room by two. The prices indicated by the codes are as follows:

① under £5 / $8	④ £15–20 / $24–32	⑦ £30–35 / $48–56
② £5–10 / $8–16	⑤ £20–25 / $32–40	⑧ £35–40 / $56–64
③ £10–15 / $16–24	⑥ £25–30 / $40–48	⑨ £40 / $64 and over

■ Hostels and camping

Lithuania has a few **youth hostels** where you'll pay 24-32Lt per night. Space is limited and it's best to try and book in advance – contact the youth hostels **head office** at Filaretų gatvė 17, Vilnius (☎2/254 627). An ex-Soviet phenomenon is the cabin **campsite** (*kempingas*), offering accommodation in three- to four-bed cabins (WC and washing facilities, which can be on the primitive side, are shared with other cabins) for around 20Lt per person. Many of these places will also let you pitch a tent, an option which works out slightly cheaper than sleeping under a roof. The downside is that they're often located a long way out of town. You can also camp wild in the countryside, subject to the approval of the landowner (if there is one).

Food and drink

Lithuanian cuisine, based on traditional peasant dishes, is less bland than that of its Baltic neighbours, partly as a result of Polish influence. Typical **starters** include marinated mushrooms (*marinuoti grybai*), herring (*silke*) and smoked sausage (*rukyta dešra*) along with cold beetroot soup (*šaltibarščiai*). Potatoes play a major role; one of the most commonly encountered dishes is *cepelinai* or zeppelins – cylindrical potato dumplings stuffed with meat, mushrooms or cheese and topped with pieces of fried bacon. Also popular are potato pancakes (*bulviniai blynai*), and cabbage leaves stuffed with minced meat (*balandėlai* or "pigeons"). **Desserts** include stewed fruit (*kompotas*), sweet fruit sauce (*kiselius*), and pancakes filled with curd cheese (*varškečia*) – a real treat.

Some **restaurants** serve indigenous cuisine, and even the ubiquitous post-Soviet chops (*karbonadas*) and roast meat (*kepsnys*), tend to be better than in the other Baltic States. Even in a fairly upmarket place a meal shouldn't work out much more expensive than in a mid-range restaurant in western Europe, and it's possible to eat really well for much

less. At the cheapest end, the food in the Soviet-era canteens (*valgykla*) is edible if you're not over-fussy. Western fast food is making inroads, and Vilnius has a few ethnic places and although vegetarianism has yet to establish itself here, it is possible to find meat-free options on most menus. As an alternative to restaurant dining many cafés and bars do reasonably priced food.

Beer (*alus*) is the most popular alcoholic drink. The most common local brand is Utenos alus, a fairly heavy beer with a distinctive taste. For something different try Utenos Porteris, a dark porter. Imported beer (mainly German) is widely available, but expensive – stick to bottles and cans as imported draught beer is often suspiciously watery. The leading Lithuanian **vodka** brands are Kvietinė and Kristalinė.

Vilnius has some lively **bars**, and Kaunas and Klaipėda can muster a few decent places. Serious drinking goes on in beer halls; these can be pretty rough and ready, though a few of the more civilized ones are listed in this chapter. For an altogether different atmosphere head for a **café**, though some of these are on the chintzy side. **Coffee** (*kava*) and **tea** (*arbata*) are usually served black.

Opening hours and holidays

Opening hours for **shops** are 9 or 10am until 6 or 7pm. Outside of Vilnius, some places take an hour off for lunch; most usually close on Sun (though some food shops stay open). Most shops and all banks will be closed on the following **public holidays**: Jan 1; Feb 16 (Old Independence Day); March 11 (New Independence Day); Easter Sunday; Easter Monday; July 6 (Statehood Day); Nov 1 (All Saints Day); Dec 25 and 26.

Emergencies

Though many Lithuanians claim that the streets are unsafe, you're unlikely to meet trouble if you're sensible. Nor is organized **crime** likely to affect the average visitor; you'll spot huddles of "mafia" types in bars and restaurants but you only need to think about going elsewhere if they're in the majority. Car theft and vandalism are the most common crimes.

The cash-starved Lithuanian **police** drive some of the most beaten-up squad cars in Europe, but they expect to be taken seriously – be polite if you have any dealings with them and you should have no problems. There's little chance that police officers will speak any language other than Lithuanian or Russian; a few of the younger ones may speak a little English. Emergency **health care** is free in Lithuania but if you get seriously ill it's best to head for home (or at least western Europe) if you can.

EMERGENCY NUMBERS

Fire ☎01; Police ☎02; Ambulance ☎03.

VILNIUS

"Narrow cobblestone streets and an orgy of Baroque: almost like a Jesuit city somewhere in the middle of Latin America," wrote the author Czesław Milosz of prewar **VILNIUS**. Soviet-era satellite suburbs aside, it's a description which still rings true today, though the city Milosz knew was, in many ways, a different one to modern Vilnius. Between the wars Vilnius, known as **Wilno**, belonged to Poland and was inhabited mainly by Poles and Jews, who played such a prominent role in the city's life that it was known as the "Northern Jerusalem". Though now firmly part of Lithuania, Vilnius is still a cosmopolitan place – around twenty percent of its population is Polish and another twenty percent is Russian – though with just 578,600 inhabitants it has an almost village-like atmosphere, making it an easy place to get to know.

Arrival, information and city transport

The main **train station** (*Stotis*) is at Gelžinkelio 16, just south of the Old City, and the main **bus station** (*Autobusu Stotis*) is nearby at Sodų 22. There are exchange facilities at the train station though it's probably better to use a bank in town for greater security. Trolleybus #2 will take you from the square in front of the train station to Arkikatedros aikstė in the centre of town. Walking into the Old Town is feasible too – avoid taxis as they tend to overcharge. The **airport** (*Oro Uostas*) is around 5km south of the city centre at Rodųnės kelias (☎2/306 666) with exchange facilities in the arrival hall. From outside the main entrance bus #2 runs a couple of times an hour to Lukiskiu aikstė in the city centre, and takes approximately 25 minutes. Bus #1 will take you to the train and bus station area. **Tickets** for both buses (available from a kiosk on the right before the arrival-hall exit) cost 0.60Lt or 0.75Lt from the driver. The burgundy Hondas of Ekspres Taksi, the official airport taxi, will charge 10–15Lt for the 5km journey to the old town; other taxis don't always adhere to the regulations, so it's best to fix a price beforehand.

The **tourist offices** at Vilniaus 22 (May–Sept Mon–Fri 9am–7pm, Sat 12am–6pm; Oct–April Mon–Fri 9am–6pm; ☎2/629 660), and at Pilies 42 (Mon–Fri 9am–6pm; ☎2/620 762) offer maps, tours and information on hotels and museums, but your best bet is to pick up a copy of the excellent *Vilnius in Your Pocket* city guide which costs 4Lt from newspaper kiosks, tourist offices or hotels. It's also available from a special *Vilnius in Your Pocket* booth in the airport arrival hall. Vilnius is well served for **public transport** with buses and trolleybuses covering most of the city. Tickets cost 0.60Lt from newspaper kiosks (*kioskas*) and 0.75Lt from the driver. Buses and trolleybuses need different tickets so make sure you have the right one; and remember to validate your ticket by punching it in the machine on board. Alternatively, hail a minibus at any bus stop in the direction you're going, pay the driver 2Lt and you'll be dropped off at the stop you require. **Taxi** prices can be a rip-off – make sure the meter is switched on and that the fare costs no more than around 1–2Lt per kilometre. Telephoning for a taxi (☎2/250 000) is the only way to ensure getting a meter and a fair rate.

Accommodation

There's a shortage of good, cheap **accommodation** in Vilnius, and though there are a few very cheap hotels they're best avoided. Best value for money is offered by **private rooms**. *Litinterp*, Bernardinų 7/2 (Mon–Fri 8.30am–5.30pm, Sat 8.30am–3.30pm; ☎2/223 850), have rooms in the Old Town with singles from 70Lt and doubles from 120Lt. Vilnius has two **youth hostels**. The Old Town Hostel is at Aušros Vartų 20–15a (☎2/625 357), follow the signs from outside the train station, which costs 32Lt per person; reservations are essential due to the very limited number of beds. There is also a comfortable and exceedingly friendly youth hostel at Filaretų 17, east of the Old Town (☎2/254 627), reached by bus #34 from the train station, opposite *McDonald's*. It costs 24–32Lt per person with the first night being 5Lt extra. The *Teacher's University Hotel* at Vivulskio 36 (☎2/230 509), is a twenty-minute walk west of

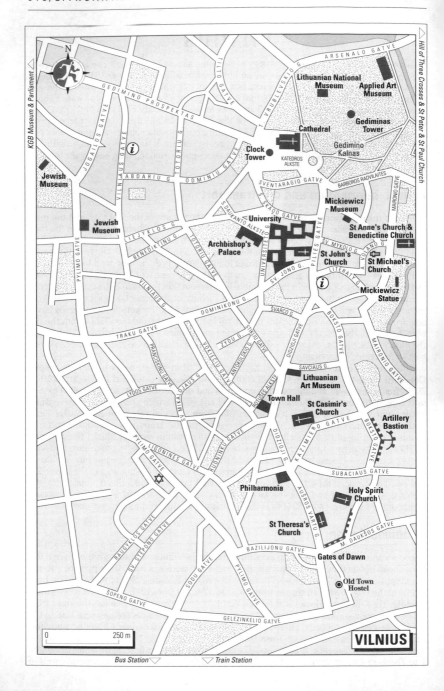

VILNIUS

the Old Town in a dull neighbourhood but rooms are decent at 27Lt for student dorms and 65Lt for a single. The *JNN Hostel*, Ukmergės 25 (☎2/722 270) is a slightly more upmarket place with modern and clean rooms which come complete with their own showers and toilets. Singles cost 80Lt and doubles 120Lt. The **campsite** *Rytų kempingas* (☎2/651 195) in Rukainiai is a bit of a trek from town, on the road to Minsk 25km east of the city – the cost is 25Lt per person for accommodation in cabins sleeping three to four people and is only feasible if you have your own transport.

Hotels

Gintaras, Sodų 14 (☎2/738 003). Scruffy place near the station. Don't leave valuables in your room. Little English spoken. ②.

Grybas House, Aušros Vartų 3A (☎2/619 695). Congenial and usually fully booked place in the Old Town. ⑨.

Jaunųjų Turistų Centras, Polocko 7 (☎2/611 547). Cheap spartan rooms. Cooking facilities available. Don't walk there alone after dark. ①.

Mabre Residence Hotel, Maironio 13. (☎2/222 087). Fine courtyard and elegant quarters, right in the centre. ⑨.

Naujasis Vilnius, Ukmergės 14 (☎2/726 756). Renovated Lithuanian-Swiss hotel, north of the river. Probably the best mid-range place, with friendly service and comfortable rooms. ⑤.

Neringa, Gedimino 32 (☎2/610 516). Clean and comfortable mid-range place though perhaps a little overpriced for what it provides. Car rental service available. ⑥.

Šauni Vietelė, Pranciskonų 3/6 (☎2/222 189). Tiny, cosy place with parquet floors. Excellent value; reservations essential. ④.

Victoria, Saltoniskių 56 (☎2/724 013). Pink exterior but pleasant rooms and friendly service inside. Showers in each room. ⑤.

Žaliasis Tiltas, Gedimino 12 (☎2/615 460). Clean and central, if a little worn. ②.

The City

At the centre of Vilnius, poised between the medieval and nineteenth-century parts of the city is **Cathedral Square** (Katedros aikstė). To the south of here along Pilies gatvė and Didžioji gatvė is the **Old Town**, containing perhaps the most impressive concentration of Baroque architecture in northern Europe. West of the square in the New Town is **Gedimino prospektas**, a nineteenth-century boulevard that's the focal point of the city's commercial and administrative life.

Cathedral Square and around

Cathedral Square (Katedros aikstė), dominated by the Neoclassical **Cathedral** (Arkikatedra bazilika; Mon–Fri 11am–5pm), is the point where modern and old Vilnius meet. The cathedral belongs firmly in the old part, its origins going back to the thirteenth century, when a wooden church is thought to have been built here on the site of a temple dedicated to Perkūnas, the god of thunder. Today's structure is based on a more substantial stone building erected during the fifteenth century, and given a facelift over the next three hundred years that's left it looking more like a piece of grandiose Neoclassical civic architecture than a place of worship. The highlight of the airy, vaulted interior is the opulent **Chapel of St Kazimieras** (Kazimiero koplyčia), dedicated to the patron saint of Lithuania, who lies buried in the crypt of the cathedral. Created between 1623 and 1636, the chapel is a riot of marble, stucco and silver statuary, with frescoes on the ceilings and side walls depicting episodes from the saint's life. Next to the cathedral on the square is the white **Clock Tower** (Boksto laikrodis) once part of the fortifications of the vanished Lower Castle but now looking like a stranded Baroque lighthouse.

Rising behind the cathedral is the tree-clad **Gediminas Hill** (Gedimino kalnas), its summit crowned by the red-brick octagon of **Gediminas Tower** (Gedimino bokštas), one of the city's best-known landmarks. The first substantial fortification here was founded by Grand Duke Gediminas, the Lithuanian ruler who consolidated the country's independence. According to legend Gediminas dreamt of an iron wolf howling on a hill overlooking the River

Vilnia and was told by a pagan priest to build a castle on the spot. These days the castle hous-es the **Vilnius Castle Museum** (Vilnius Pilies muziejus; May–Sept Wed–Sun 11am–6pm; Oct–April Tues–Sat 11am–5pm; 4Lt; free on Wed in winter), showing the former extent of the Vilnius fortifications.

A hundred metres or so north of the cathedral in a former arsenal building is the **Lithuanian National Museum** (Lietuvos Nacionalinis muziejus), Arsenalo 1 (May–Sept Wed–Sun 11am–6pm; Oct–Apr 11am–5pm; 4Lt; free Wed in winter), covering the history of Lithuania from prehistoric times to 1940. Though most items are labelled in Lithuanian and Russian only, the exhibits, ranging from a pair of mammoth tusks to re-created domestic inte-riors from the eighteenth and nineteenth centuries, are worth a visit. Nearby is the less note-worthy **Applied Art Museum**, Arsenalo 3 (Taikomosis Dailės muziejus; Tues–Sun noon–5/6pm; 4Lt: free Wed in winter) with French and German furniture and ceramics, and jewellery from the thirteenth to the nineteenth century.

The Old Town

The **Old Town** (Senamiestis), just south of Cathedral Square, is a network of narrow, often cobbled streets that forms the Baroque heart of Vilnius, with the theoretically pedestrianized **Pilies gatvė** (Castle Street) cutting into it from the south-eastern corner of the square. To the right of this street is **Vilnius University** (Vilniaus Universitetas), a jumble of buildings constructed between the sixteenth and eighteenth centuries around nine linked courtyards that extend west as far as Universiteto gatvė. The university was founded by the Jesuits in 1579 at the behest of the Polish king, Stefan Batory, and by the time Lithuania was annexed by tsarist Russia in 1795, it ranked as the oldest in the Russian Empire, though this didn't deter the Russians from closing it down in 1832. Reopened during the first independence, the university survived the Soviet era and now has fourteen thousand students.

Within its precincts you'll find the ornate **St John's Church** (Šv Jono bažnyčia), standing out from the crowd even in this city of beautiful churches – access from Šv Jono gatvė. Founded during the fourteenth century, St John's was taken over by the Jesuits in 1561 and given to the university in 1737. Reconstruction after a fire in the same year has left it with its present Baroque facade, and a no-holds-barred Baroque altar inside. The side-chapel dedi-cated to St Anne is comparatively restrained, with an unusual wooden altar showing Christ on the Cross with the disciples represented as bunches of grapes. Some recently uncovered ceiling frescoes depict the biblical story of Esther. St John's **bell tower**, separate from the main building, gives excellent views of the city.

The **Archbishop's Palace** (Vyskupų rūmai), just west of the university on **Daukanto aikstė**, was originally built during the sixteenth century as a merchant's residence and remodelled into its present Neoclassical form at the end of the eighteenth century. More interesting than the building itself are its grounds (reached via a gateway on Universiteto gatvė, but also under reconstruction), and the fact that Napoleon Bonaparte stayed here dur-ing his ill-fated campaign against Russia in 1812. The emperor's sojourn excited hopes that a French victory might bring a revival of Lithuanian independence, but in the event resulted in nothing more than a bout of plundering as his defeated army straggled westwards.

The emperor is said to have been so impressed by **St Anne's Church** (Šv Onos bažnyčia; Sun 8am–1pm & 5–7pm, Tues–Sat 10am–3pm & 5.30–9pm) on Maironio gatvė, to the east of Pilies gatvė, that he wanted to take it back to Paris on the palm of his hand. Studded with skeletal, finger-like towers, and its facade overlaid with intricate brick traceries and fluting, this late sixteenth-century structure is the finest Gothic building in Vilnius. Rising behind St Anne's is the Gothic facade of the much larger **Bernardine Church** (Bernardinų vienuoly-no bažničia) from 1520. Its once fine Baroque interior suffered during its Soviet-era incarna-tion as home to the Vilnius Art Academy, and the building is now undergoing a much-need-ed overhaul.

Just south of St Anne's and the Benedictine church is a **statue** commemorating the Polish Romantic poet Adam Mickiewicz (1798–1855), author of *Pan Tadeusz,* the Polish national epic. Nearby is the **A. Mickievičius Memorial Apartment** (A. Mickievičius Memorialinis butas; Tues–Fri 11am–5pm, Sat & Sun 10am–2pm; free), Bernardinų 11, a small **museum** whose rather paltry exhibits include a couple of chairs and a desk owned by Mickiewicz and a number of Polish and Lithuanian first editions of his works. **Bernardinų gatvė** itself is one of the Old Town's more appealing back streets, a narrow lane lined by seventeenth- and eighteenth-century houses that runs back to Pilies.

Heading south Pilies becomes Main Street (Didžioji gatvė). The restored Baroque palace on the corner with Saviaiaus is the **Vilnius Picture Gallery** which houses the Lithuanian Art Museum (Tues–Sun 11am–5pm; 4Lt; free on Wed in winter), a marvellous collection of sixteenth- to nineteenth-century paintings and sculptures, gathered from around the country. The colonnaded Neoclassical building standing firmly at the end of **Town Hall Square** has recently been restored to its original function as the town hall. The modern building behind it and to the right houses the **Contemporary Art Centre** (Tues–Sun 11am–6.30pm; 4Lt, free on Wed in winter), an eclectic collection of works by Lithuanian artists from the last half of the twentieth century.

Just east of the square, **St Casimir's Church** (Šv Kazimiero bažnyčia; Mon–Fri 4pm–6.30pm, Sun 8am–2pm) dating from 1604 and the oldest Baroque church in the city remains a striking building – its central cupola topped by an elaborate crown and cross symbolizing the royal ancestry – of St Casimir, the son of King Casimir IV of Poland. The interior is, however, disappointingly ugly with a startlingly tacky-looking main altar, a legacy of a chequered history that saw the building remodelled as an Orthodox church in tsarist times and converted into a Museum of Atheism and the History of Religion under the Soviets.

Continuing along Didžioji leads to the **Philharmonic** building where Lithuania's independence was proclaimed in February 1918. Beyond here, Didžioji becomes **Aušros Vartų gatvė**, a short distance along which a gateway on the left-hand side leads to the seventeenth-century **Church of the Holy Spirit** (Šv Dvasios Cerkvė), Lithuania's main Orthodox church, a Baroque structure built on a low hill in the grounds of a monastery. The interior is surprisingly airy and in front of the large iconostasis a flight of steps leads down to a crypt, where the bodies of three fourteenth-century martyrs are displayed in a glass case, their faces swathed in cloth.

A little further along Aušros Vartų gatvė the seventeenth-century **St Theresa's Church** (Šv Teresės Bažničia) rises to the left of the street, another soaring testimony to the city's dominating architectural style. The end of the street is marked by the **Gates of Dawn** (Aušros Vartai), the sole survivor of nine city gates that once studded the walls of Vilnius. A **Chapel** above the gate houses the city's most celebrated religious monument, the **White Madonna**, an image of the Virgin Mary said to have miraculous powers and revered by Polish Catholics. Only the Madonna's hands and face are visible, the rest of the likeness being overlaid by a gilt covering. Entrance to the chapel is via a small door in the walls of St Theresa's from where steps lead up to the room containing the White Madonna, which is usually surrounded by rapt worshippers. During the day the chapel windows are often left open and the Madonna is visible from the street below.

East of Aušros Vartų gatvė on Boksto 20/18 is the **Artillery Bastion** (Artilerijos Bastėja), a seventeenth-century bastion that was once part of the city's outer fortification ring and which now houses a **museum** (May–Sept Wed–Sun 10am–5pm; Oct–April Wed–Sun 11am–5pm; 4Lt, free on Wed in winter) of weapons and armour. The museum is more interesting for its setting than its contents: exhibits are housed in a long brick passageway leading to the outer part of the bastion, where cannons similar to those used to defend the city have been placed in the embrasures. Labels are in Lithuanian and Russian, with some English.

Jewish Vilnius

Before World War II Vilnius was one of the most important centres of Jewish life in eastern Europe. The Jews – first invited to settle in 1410 by Grand Duke Vytautas – made up around a third of the city's population, mainly concentrated in the eastern fringes of the Old Town around present-day Vokiečių gatvė, Žydų gatvė and Antokolskio gatvė. The **Great Synagogue** was located just off Žydu gatvė, on a site now occupied by a kindergarten.

Massacres of the Jewish population began soon after the Germans occupied Vilnius on June 24, 1941, and those who survived the initial killings found themselves herded into two

ghettos. The smaller of these ghettos centred around Žydų, Antokolskio, Stiklių and Gaono streets and was liquidated in October 1941, while the larger occupied an area between Pylimo, Vokiečių, Lydos, Mikalojaus, Karmelitų and Arklių streets and was liquidated in September 1943. Most of the Jews of Vilnius perished in Paneriai forest on the southwestern edge of the city (see p.825).

Today, the Jewish population of Vilnius numbers only a few thousand. The city has one surviving **synagogue** (Mon–Thurs 8am–10am, Sun 7pm–9pm) at Pylimo 39, out of the 96 that once existed. To find out about the history of Jewish Vilnius head for the **Lithuanian State Jewish Museum** (Lietuvos valstybnis žydų muziejus), Pylimo 4 (Mon–Thurs 10am–5pm, Fri 9am–4pm; 1Lt, free on Wed in winter), which displays items salvaged from the Great Synagogue, including puppets used during the Purim festival and pictures of wooden synagogues from small towns in Lithuania. Some of the museum staff speak English and exhibits are captioned in English. The museum can also arrange "history of Jewish Vilnius" tours (☎2/620 730). A second branch of the museum (Mon–Thurs 9am–5pm, Fri 9am–4pm) at Pamenkalnio 12 contains a harrowing display about the fate of Vilnius Jews during the war. Captions are in Lithuanian, Russian and English, but by and large the exhibits speak for themselves.

Gedimino prospektas

Gedimino prospektas, running west from Cathedral Square, was the main thoroughfare of nineteenth-century Vilnius, and remains the most important commercial street of the city centre. The city's largest department store and main post office, along with various government ministries and public buildings, are all situated here. Now bearing the name of the founder of the city, in the past this broad boulevard of flaking stuccoed buildings has been named after St George, Mickiewicz, Stalin and Lenin, reflecting the succession of foreign powers that have controlled the city.

Lukiškių aikštė, around 600m west of Cathedral Square, is the former location of the city's Lenin statue, removed after the failed 1991 coup which precipitated the final break-up of the Soviet Union. The square has long played an infamous role in city history. After the 1863–64 uprising against the Russians, a number of rebels were publicly hanged here, while Gedimino 40, on the southern side of the square, was Lithuania's **KGB Headquarters**. The building also served as Gestapo headquarters during the German occupation and more recently the Soviets incarcerated political prisoners in the basement. It has now been turned into the **Genocide Museum** (Genocido Aukų Muziejus; entrance on Aukų 2a; mid-May to mid-Sept Tues–Sun 10am–6pm; mid-Sept to mid-May Tues–Sun 10am–4pm; donation expected). The dank green cells and courtyard where some prisoners were tortured and executed are preserved in their pre-1991 state. A former inmate who survived Soviet imprisonment here now gives a moving personal tour of the museum – in Russian.

At the far end of Gedimino prospektas stands Lithuania's ugly **Parliament Building** (Aukščiausiosios tarybos rūmai). Thousands gathered here on January 13, 1991, when Soviet troops threatened to occupy it following the killing of a dozen people at the TV Tower (see below). On the side of the parliament facing the river some of the barricades built to defend the building have been preserved, complete with anti-Soviet graffiti; there's also a moving memorial of traditional wooden crosses commemorating those who died at the TV Tower and the seven border guards killed by Soviet special forces in July 1991. The 326-metre **TV Tower** (Televizijos bokštas; 10am–9pm; 10–15Lt) itself is around 3km west of the centre in the Karoliniškės district – trolleybus #16 from the train station or #11 from Lukiskių aikstė; alight at the Televizijos bokštas stop on Sausio 13-Osios gatvė. At the tower's base, wooden crosses commemorate those killed here in the bloodiest event of the struggle for Baltic independence.

Eating, drinking and nightlife

White-tablecloth **restaurants** tend to be pricey and the expense is not always a guarantee of quality. Many **bars** and **cafés** serve snacks and meals and these often represent better value for money. *McDonald's* has arrived in Vilnius and can be found at Gedimino 15 and Seinų 3, across from the train station. If you're on a really tight budget head for *Valgykla* canteens, still dishing up stodge for the masses as in Soviet times. Vilnius has a few **clubs** and **discos** that are worth investigating, though you may find you have a better (and cheaper) time in some of the bars mentioned below, where people tend to start dancing after a few beers.

Cafés and snacks

Baras, Gedimino 10. Cheap, simple café with basic food. Mon–Fri 7am–9pm, Sat & Sun 10am–9pm.

Gabi, Šv Mykolo 6. Inexpensive drinks and good solid home-cooking in a relaxed atmosphere. 10am–10pm.

Ida Basar, Gedimino Vrublevskio. Pleasant café conveniently located across from the Cathedral. Light meals and alcoholic and non-alcoholic beverages available. 8am–midnight.

Kavine, Aušros vartų 5. A smart and pricey (8Lt for 0.33l of imported beer) café in the Philharmonic building; a pleasant place to watch Old Town life passing by. 9am–11pm.

Pakeleivio Užeiga, Bazilijonų 3. If your budget's really stretched, this place has cheap large beers (2.50Lt) and fat *cepelinai* (potato dumplings stuffed with meat; 5Lt). Open 9am–9pm.

Pieno Baras, Didžioji 21. Roomy, old-style café serving pastries and warm drinks. Eat in or take away. Sun 9am–6pm, Mon–Sat 8am–8pm.

Restaurants

Geležinis Vilkas, Lukiškių 3. Tacky black-and-neon decor but the menu is extensive and the staff eager to please. Mon–Fri noon–6pm, Sat & Sun 6pm–6am.

Lokys, Stiklių 8/10. Reasonably priced and highly recommended Lithuanian cellar restaurant serving boar and elk. Daily noon–midnight.

Medininkai, Aušros vartų 8. Dine on *karbonade*, chicken cutlet and similar meat and potatoes staples in an atmospheric cellar setting. Main courses start at 11–17Lt. Service is polite but slow. Daily 11am–11pm.

Neringa, Gedimino 23. A Soviet-era hotel restaurant with a band playing Wed–Sat evening. Meals 15–20Lt. 8am–10.30pm.

Naujasis Vilnius, Ukmergės 14. A restaurant in the hotel of the same name. Low on atmosphere, but the service and food (variations on meat and potatoes) are good. Non-smoking environment. Daily 7am–10pm.

Ponių Laimė, Gedimino 31. Upmarket Burgundy and gold decor, very popular with the moneyed crowd. You can also just have a drink or coffee and cake. Big windows and outdoor seating make it a prime spot for watching the world go by. Mon–Fri 10am–midnight, Sat 11am–midnight, Sun 1pm–midnight.

Ritos Sléptuvé, Goštauto 8. Immensely popular pizza place run by a Lithuanian-American. The pizzas are excellent and they also do dishes like quiche and spaghetti and have a few vegetarian options. Order local beer to keep your bill manageable. Good place for breakfasts. Mon–Fri 2.30am–2am, Fri & Sat 7.30am–6am, Sun 9am–midnight.

Sidabrinis Drakonas, Šv Kazimiero 2. Decent Chinese food; large portions. 11am–11pm.

Stiklai Aludé, Gaono 7. French food plus a range of potato dishes. Live Lithuanian folk music every evening bar Sunday. Expect to pay from 20Lt for a decent meal. Dinner reservations recommended. Noon–midnight.

Šavarma, Aušros Vartų 8. Good Lebanese fare at reasonable prices. Mon–Fri 10am–midnight, Sat & Sun noon–midnight.

Bars

Great new bars are opening up all over town. Check *Vilnius in Your Pocket* for a complete list but here are a few possibilities.

Amatininkų Užeiga, Didžioji 19/2. Great bar for dancing, conversation, and drinking. Mon–Fri 8am–5am, Sat & Sun 11am–5am.

Amerika, Šv. Kazimiero 3. Saloon bar in a courtyard. Pool, cocktails and jazz nights. Mon–Fri noon–2am, Sat & Sun noon–5am.

Bix, Etmonų 6. Great bar with wild decor and a lively atmosphere and live bands on some nights – run by members of local rock band *Bix*. Serves meals too. Sun–Thurs 11am–2am, Fri & Sat 11am–5am.

Gero Viskio Baras, Pilies 34. Chicken and fish dishes on the menu. Cellar disco after 8pm. Thurs–Sat 10am–midnight.

Prie Parlamento, Gedimino 46. A restaurant with the feel of a pub. The menu offers cooked breakfasts, salads, and desserts and has an excellent vegetarian selection. Popular with expats. Sun 10am–3am, Mon–Thurs 8am–3am, Fri 8am–5am, Sat 10am–5am. Thirty-percent discount on all food and alcoholic drinks Mon–Fri 4.30–6.30pm.

Ritos Slėptuvė, Goštauto 8. Lively bar to the rear of the pizza restaurant. Pulls in lots of expats and better-off locals, and there tends to be dancing here as the evening wears on. Mon–Thurs 7.30am–2am, Fri & Sat 7.30am–6am, Sun 9am–midnight.

Savas Kampas, Vokiečių 4. The dark interior sets a good mood in which to peruse the extensive list of alcohol available. Daily 11am–5am.

The PUB, Domini Konų 9. Popular bar serving food and drinks. Comfortable coffee-drinking and postcard-writing place. Daily 11am–2am.

Clubs and discos

Indigo, Traku 3/2. Bizarre metallic and mosaic interior decoration. Special events featuring international entertainers on occasions. Tues–Thurs 9pm–3am, Fri & Sat 9pm–5am. 10–25Lt.

Ministerija, Gedimino 46. Located in the cellar below Prie Parlimento. Dance and popular classics on weekends. Sun–Thurs 6pm–3am, Fri & Sat 6pm–5am. 5–15Lt.

Naktinis Vilkas, Lukiskiu 3. Chandeliers, Lenin artefacts and velvet booths. Go early if you want a seat. Daily 7pm–6am. 5–10Lt.

Ultra, Goštauto 12. Trendy place catering for a younger age group. Pop during the week and techno on Sat. Thurs–Sat 8pm–5am. 5–15Lt.

Classical music, opera and ballet

Music Academy, Gedimino pr. 42 (☎2/610 144). Venue for concerts by local music students.

National Philharmonic (Nacionalų Filharmonija), Aušros Vartų 5 (☎2/626 832). A reliable venue for classical standards along with occasional forays into more unusual modern territory. Occasional guest appearances by international artists.

Opera and Ballet Theatre (Operos ir baletos teatras; ☎2/620 636), Vienuolio 1. Hugely popular, it stages excellent productions and is usually a sell-out, so book well in advance.

Listings

Airline offices Aeroflot, Tauro 8/30 (☎2/621 834); British Airways at the airport (☎2/262 167); Estonian Air at the airport (☎2/261 559); Lithuanian Airlines, Ukmergės 12 (☎2/752 588); LOT, room 104, *Hotel Skrydis* (☎2/739 020); Lufthansa at the airport (☎2/262 222); SAS at the airport (☎2/236 000).

Airport information Rodųnės kelias (☎2/306 666).

Bike rental Litinterp, Bernardinų 7–2 (☎2/223 850). Bikes for 20Lt per day.

Books and papers America Center, Pranciskonų 3/6 (☎2/222 658) has American papers and magazines plus a well-stocked library; the British Council, Vilniaus 39-6 (☎2/616 607) also has books and papers.

Car rental Cheapest is local company A & A Litinterp, Bernardinų 7–2 (☎2/223 850) with cars from around 190Lt per day. Otherwise try Avis, Ukmergės 14 (☎2/724 275); Europcar, Stuokos-Gucevičiaus (☎2/222 739); Hertz, Ukmergės 2 (☎2/726 940).

Embassies; Canada, Gedimino 64 (☎2/220 898); USA, Akmenų 6 (☎2/223 031), United Kingdom, Antakalnio 2 (☎2/222 070).

Exchange Main post office, Gedemino prospektas 7. Gelezinkelio 6. Open 24hr.

Hospital Vilnius University Emergency Hospital, Siltnamių 29 (☎2/269 069). Open 24hr.

Internet Access Ralinga Internet Centre, Pylimo 20 (☎2/611 966). Open Mon–Fri 9am–6pm, Sat 10am–3pm; 15Lt/hr.

Laundry Vikdagis, Tuskulerų 35. Self-service. Open Mon–Fri 7am–8pm, Sat 7am–2pm.

Pharmacies Gedimino Vaistine, Gedimino prospektas 27 (☎2/624 930; Mon–Sat 7.30am–9pm, Sun 11am–6pm).

Police Jogailos 3 (☎2/616 208).

Post office Main office, Gedimino prospektas 7 (Mon–Fri 8am–8pm, Sat 10am–5pm). International phone calls and currency exchange facilities available.

Taxis Express Taxi (☎2/250 000).

Telephones Central Telegraph Office, Vilniaus 33. Open 24hr.

Around Vilnius

In the area surrounding Vilnius the two most accessible destinations are **Paneriai**, where the Jewish inhabitants of the city were murdered by Nazis during World War II, and **Trakai**, the medieval capital of Lithuania, now a recreation centre for the citizens of the present-day capital.

Paneriai

PANERIAI, the site where the Nazis and their Lithuanian accomplices murdered one hundred thousand people during World War II, lies within Vilnius city limits in a forest at the edge of a suburb 10km southwest of the centre. Seventy thousand of those killed here were Jews from Vilnius, who were systematically exterminated from the time the Germans arrived in June 1941 until they were driven out by the Soviet army in 1944.

The killing grounds are about 1km into the woods due west of Aukstieji Paneriai train station and marshalling yards. The entrance to the site is marked by the **Paneriai Memorial** (Panerių Memorialas). Here, two stone slabs with Russian and Lithuanian inscriptions commemorate the hundred thousand murdered "Soviet citizens", flanking a central slab with an inscription in Hebrew commemorating "seventy thousand Jewish men, women and children". From the memorial a path leads to the **Paneriai Museum** (Panerių muziejus, Agrastų 15; Mon & Wed–Sat 11am–6pm, to check times, call ☎2/620 730) with a small display detailing what happened here. Nearby are two monuments, one with a Hebrew inscription (English on the obverse) honouring the seventy thousand Vilnius Jews, the other a Soviet obelisk recalling the "victims of fascist terror". From here paths lead to the pits in the woods where the Nazis burnt the bodies of their victims and to another eight-metre pit where the bones of the dead where crushed.

To get to Paneriai take a southwest-bound suburban train from Vilnius station and alight at Aukštieji Paneriai. From the station platform descend onto Agrastų gatvė, turn right and follow the road through the woods for about a kilometre.

Trakai

Lakeside **TRAKAI**, 25km west of Vilnius, founded during the fourteenth century and the site of two medieval castles, is the former capital of the Grand Duchy of Lithuania. The town's island castle built by Grand Duke Vytautas, under whom Lithuania reached the pinnacle of its power during the fifteenth century, is one of Lithuania's most famous monuments, though for many Vilnius inhabitants boating and swimming in the town's lakes is as much of an attraction as reminders of past glories.

Trakai stands on a peninsula jutting out between two lakes. From the **train** and **bus stations** follow Vytauto gatvė to reach the main sights. After about 500m turn right down Kęstuaio gatvė to the remains of the **Peninsula Castle**, thought to have been built by Duke Kęstutis, son of Gediminas and father of Vytautas. These days only the walls and a couple of towers remain.

Trakai is home to the **Karaites**, members of a Judaic sect whose ancestors were brought here from the Crimea by Grand Duke Vytautas to serve him as bodyguards, and whose distinctive wooden cottages line Karaimų gatvė, the northern continuation of Vytauto gatvė. Around two hundred inhabitants of Trakai are Karaites; Lithuania's smallest ethnic minority, they recognize only the laws of the Old Testament. Down the street at no. 30 is their wooden **Kenessa** or prayer house, built in the early nineteenth century.

A hundred metres or so beyond the Kenessa two wooden footbridges lead to the **Island Castle**, a cluster of red-brick towers built around 1400 on a small offshore island by Grand Duke Vytautas to provide stronger defences than those of the peninsula castle. Though it fell into ruin from the seventeenth century, a 1960s restoration has returned it to its former glory, and it now houses a **museum** (May–Sept Tues–Sun 10am–7pm, Oct–April 10am–5pm; 5Lt). The main **tower**, built around a galleried courtyard, is separated from the outer buildings by a moat – you cross a footbridge to enter. Within are exhibits covering the history of the castle, plus examples of medieval weaponry and wooden carvings. Captions are in Lithuanian. The castle's outer buildings contain further exhibits, mostly furniture, including a bizarre table-and-chair set made from antlers in the "Hunters' Room". Some captions in this section are in English and German.

Trakai's **dining** experience is the *Kibinine* a hundred metres or so beyond the castle on the right-hand side of Karaimų, where people queue to consume Cornish-pasty-like creations filled with grey meat, that unleash a deadly drip of hot fat after a few bites.

THE REST OF LITHUANIA

Kaunas

KAUNAS, 80km west of Vilnius and easily reached by bus or rail, is Lithuania's second city and seen by many Lithuanians as the true heart of their country. It served as provisional capital during the interwar independence when Vilnius was part of Poland, and remains a major commercial and industrial centre. Nevertheless it's an attractive, easy-going city well served by road and rail, with enough sights to make it worth at least a full day's visit.

The Old Town

The most interesting part of town is predictably the **Old Town** or **Senamiestis**, centred around **Town Hall Square** (Rotušės aikstė), on a spur of land between the Neris and Nemunas rivers. The square is lined with fifteenth- and sixteenth-century merchants' houses in pastel stucco shades, but the overpowering feature is the magnificent **Town Hall**, its tiered Baroque facade rising to a graceful 53-metre tower. Known as "White Swan" for its elegance, this building dates back to the sixteenth century and during its history has been used as an Orthodox church, a theatre and university department, though these days it houses a "Palace of Weddings" with a ceramics museum in the basement. After the town hall the most eye-catching structure on the square is the seventeenth century **Jesuit Church** (Jėzuitų bažnyčia) on the southern side. Originally part of a larger college and monastery complex, the church was built in 1666. In 1825 the Russians handed it over to the Orthodox church. Later, the Soviets turned it into a trade school, but the Baroque interior remains intact, and the church has recently been reconsecrated.

Northeast of the square, the red-brick tower of Kaunas' austere **Cathedral** (Katedra Basilika) can be seen at the start of Vilniaus gatvė. Dating back to the reign of Vytautas the Great, the cathedral was much added to in subsequent centuries. After the plain exterior, the lavish gilt and marble interior comes as a surprise. There are nine altars in total, though the large, statue-adorned Baroque high altar (1775) steals the limelight.

Predating the cathedral by several centuries is **Kaunas Castle** (Kauno pilis), whose scant remains survive just northwest of the square. Little more than a restored tower and a couple of sections of wall are left, the rest having been washed away by the Neris, but in its day the fortification was a major obstacle to the Teutonic Knights. The fifteenth-century **St George's Church** (Šv. Jurgio bažnyčia) next door is an impressive Gothic pile in crumbling red-brick, where restoration has so far done little to arrest fifty years of decay.

There's better-preserved Gothic finery south of the town square. The **Perkūnas House** (Perkūno namas) at Aleksoto 6 is an elaborately gabled red-brick structure, thought to have been built as a Hansa office or possibly a Jesuit chapel, standing on the reputed site of a temple to Perkūnas, the pagan god of thunder. From here Aleksoto descends to the banks of the Nemunas and the glowering **Vytautas Church** (Vytauto bažnyčia), built by Vytautas the Great in around 1399. During its long existence it has suffered various indignities, including use as a munitions magazine and potato store, and, like many other Lithuanian churches, it also had a stint as an Orthodox place of worship.

The New Town

The main thoroughfare of Kaunas' **New Town** (Naujamiestis) is **Freedom Avenue** (Laisvės alėja), a broad pedestrianized shopping street running east from the Old Town, which is, bizarrely, a no-smoking zone. At the junction with L. Sapiegos the street is enlivened by a bronze **statue of Vytautas the Great**, which faces the **City Garden** (Miesto sodas) where, on May 14, 1972, the 19-year-old student Romas Kalanta immolated himself in protest against Soviet rule. Kalanta's death sparked several days of anti-Soviet rioting, and today he is commemorated by a memorial stone in the gardens.

Towards the eastern end of Freedom Avenue the silver-domed **Church of St Michael the Archangel** (Igulos bažnyčia) looms over Independence Square (Nepriklausomybes aikštė). Originally an Orthodox church built for the tsarist garrison in the 1890s, this neo-Byzantine structure is now Catholic, its bare interior a reflection of the fact that it was an art gallery for most of the Soviet period. The striking modern building in the northeast corner of the square is one of the best art galleries in the country, the **Mykolas Žilinskas Art Museum** (Summer Tues–Sun noon–6pm; winter 11am–5pm, closed last Tues of every month; 3Lt), which houses a fine collection including artifacts from Egypt, Renaissance paintings from Italy, Chinese porcelain, and Lithuania's only Rubens.

Kaunas celebrates its role in sustaining Lithuanian national identity on **Unity Square** (Vienybės aikštė), at the junction of S. Daukanto and K. Donelaiaio, a block north of Laisvės. Here a **monument** depicting liberty as a female figure faces an eternal flame flanked by traditional wooden crosses, with busts of prominent Lithuanians from the nineteenth century between the two. Overlooking all this is the **Military Museum of Vytautas the Great** (Vytauto Didžiojo karo muziejus; winter Wed–Sun 10am–4.30pm; summer Wed–Sun noon–6pm; closed last Thurs of every month; 2Lt; English leaflets available), with a display that covers local archeological finds and Lithuanian military history.

Behind the museum at Putvinskio 55 is the **M.K. Čiurlionis Art Museum** (M. K. Čiurlionio dailės muziejus; summer Tues–Sun noon–6pm, winter Tues–Sun 11am–5pm, closed last Tues of every month; 3Lt). The collection has a large display of pre-1940 Lithuanian art, but its *raison d'être* – and one of the highlights of Kaunas – is the section dedicated to **Mikalojus Konstantinas Čiurlionis** (1875–1911), Lithuania's best-known artist. During his short career (his most significant works were completed during the first decade of the twentieth century) Čiurlionis created a unique body of work, producing enigmatic mystical paintings, many of them suffused with religious imagery.

Kaunas has a second unique art collection nearby in the **A. Žmuidzinavičius Art Museum** Putvinskio 64 (A. Žmuidzinavičius kurinių ir rinkinių muziejus; summer Tues–Sun noon–6pm, winter Tues–Sun 11am–5pm; closed last Tues of every month; 4Lt). Better known as the **Devil's Museum** (Velnių muziejus), this houses a vast collection of devil figures put together by the artist Antanas Žmuidzinavičius. Though most of the images are comic, there's also a sinister representation of Hitler and Stalin as devils dancing on a Lithuania composed of skulls.

Heading east down Putvinskio brings you to the 1930s **funicular railway** (funikulierius) which climbs up to the **Žaliakalnis** district to the north of the city centre, allowing views across the rest of the city (0.50Lt). Near the upper terminal is the **Church of Christ's Resurrection** (Prisikėlimo bažnyčia), a striking 1930s modernist edifice with a very tall tower topped by a white cross. The church was under restoration, having been a radio factory during Soviet times, but funds ran out and work has stopped, leaving it looking like a rundown warehouse.

Before World War II Kaunas, like Vilnius, had a large **Jewish population**. Nearly all were killed during the war and little remains to remind of their presence. From medieval times, Kaunas' **ghetto** was in Viljampolė (then known as Slobodka) on the opposite side of the Neris to the Old Town. After 1858 restrictions on where Jews could live were eased, and many moved into other parts of the city. When the Nazis arrived the Jews were forced to return to Viljampolė. The city's sole surviving **synagogue** is at Ožeskienės 17 in the New Town and the ruins of two more are at Zamenhofo 7 and 9. To find out more about the fate of the Jews of Kaunas head out of town to the **Ninth Fort Museum** (Devintojo Forto Muziejus), Žemaiaių plentas 73 (Wed–Mon 10am–5/6pm; 14Lt to see all three parts), housed in the tsarist-era fortress where the Jews were kept while awaiting execution. Get there via bus #23 or #35 from Šv. Gertrūdos just north of the Old Town.

Practicalities

There's no **tourist office** in Kaunas but you should be able to pick up a copy of *Kaunas in Your Pocket* (4Lt), a very handy little publication produced by the *Vilnius in Your Pocket* people, from bookstores, newspaper kiosks and some hotel foyers. For **accommodation** the ever-reliable *Litinterp*, Kumelių 15–4 (☎27/228 718) can sort you out with a room in the centre for 60Lt single, 100Lt double. There is no longer a **youth hostel** in Kaunas. The cheapest **hotels** include the drab *Baltija*, Vytauto 71 (②) and the grimy *Lietuva II*, Laisvės 35 (②). Moving up the scale, the hulking *Neris*, Donelaičio 27 (☎27/204 224; ③) is reasonable and the *Lietuva I*, Daukanto 21 (☎27/205 992; ④) is comfortable but gloomy. The best places in town are the *Perkjno Namai* (☎27/209 386; ⑤) and the *Minotel*, Kuzmos 8 (☎27/203 759; ⑨), in the Old Town.

To **eat** in style head for *Chez Eliza*, Vilniaus 30, with an international, French-influenced menu (main courses from 12Lt). For something a little more indigenous try the *Gildija*, Rotuses aikste 2, set in an old merchant's house where you can dine on meat and potatoes at large wooden tables (closes at 10pm). **Cafés** and **bars** are often a good bet for eating too and Laisvės aleja is full of them. Try the *Café Astra*, Laisvės 76, a bit pricey but with fine food and drink attracting all types of people. The *Skliautas*, Rotuses aikšte 26, is an arty jazz bar with a youngish clientele and a great atmosphere (11am–11pm). *Pizza Jazz*, Laisvės aleja 68, does delicious thin-crust pizzas and Mexican dishes at reasonable prices. The *Kavine Internetas* (☎27/225 364; daily 10am–10pm), Vilniaus 26/Dauksos 12, is a pleasant place where you can drink a coffee and surf the Web for 8Lt/hr.

Klaipėda and around

KLAIPĖDA, Lithuania's third largest city and most important port, lies on the Baltic coast, a long and tedious 275km by road or rail northwest of Vilnius. Though it has a handful of sights the city is of more interest as a staging post en route to **Neringa**, the Lithuanian name for the Kurland Spit which shields much of Lithuania's coast from the open Baltic.

The City

Until 1919 the city was part of Germany and known as **Memel**, and its population remained largely German until 1945. The neatly restored Old Town draws quite a few visitors (mainly German), but there's not much to keep you here for more than a few hours.

Klaipėda is bisected by the River Danė and the main sights are in the **Old Town** (Senamiestis) on its southern bank, an area of half-timbered buildings and cobbled streets. At the heart of the Old Town is **Theatre Square** (Teatro aikstė) named after the ornate Neoclassical **Theatre** building on its northern side. Hitler spoke from the balcony in March 1939 after Germany annexed Klaipėda in its last act of territorial aggrandizement before the outbreak of war. In front of the theatre is **Anna's Fountain** (Anikės fontanas), a replica of a famous prewar monument to the German poet Simon Dach (1605–59), which depicts the heroine of his folksong *Ännchen von Tharau*.

Southeast of the square, the **History Museum of Lithuania Minor**, Didžioji vandens 6 (Mažosios Lietuvos istorijos muziejus; Wed–Sun 11am–7pm; 2Lt), has local archeological finds, national costumes and ancient domestic implements, while the nearby **Blacksmiths' Museum of Lithuania Minor**, Saltaklvių 2 (Mažosios Lietuvos kalvystės muziejus; Wed–Sun 11am–7pm; 2Lt), has a display of wrought-iron work, a traditional Lithuanian folk art form, including some ornate grave memorials.

In the **New Town** (Naujamiestis), on the northern side of the Danė, at Liepų 16, is Klaipėda's splendid red-brick Gothic-revival **Post Office**. Built between 1883 and 1893, it is a vivid reminder of imperial German civic pride. A few doors along at Liepų 12, the **Clock Museum** (Laikrodžių muziejus; Tues–Sun noon–5/6pm; 4Lt) is stuffed with timepieces from the earliest candle clocks onwards, and includes some magnificent seventeenth- and eighteenth-century examples.

Klaipėda's other main attraction is the **Maritime Museum and Aquarium** (Jūrų muziejus ir akvariumas; May–Sept Wed–Sun 11am–7pm, June–Aug Tues–Sun 11am–7pm; Oct–April Sat & Sun 11am–6pm; 5Lt) on the northern tip of Neringa, a short ferry-ride from town across the **Kurland Lagoon** (Kusių marios) and housed in a red-brick German fort. Nearby is a dolphinarium where captive Black Sea Dolphins are put through the hoops (May–Sept noon, 2pm & 4pm; 10Lt). To get there take a ferry from the quayside towards the end of Žvejų (1Lt each way). Between the landing point and the aquarium is a re-created thatched wooden fishing village.

Practicalities

Klaipėda in Your Pocket (4Lt) is your best source of information about what's going on in town. *Litinterp*, Šimkaus 21/8 (☎26/216 962), have central singles for 60Lt and doubles for 100Lt, and they can also help with rooms in Nida. The most bearable bottom-end **hotel** is the *Viktorija*, Šimkaus 2 (☎26/213 670; ②), though if you can stretch to it you'd be better off in the *Fortuna*, Poilsio 64 (☎26/275 242; ④), a small pension best booked in advance. Nearer the centre and equally good is *Prjsija*, Šimkaus 6 (☎26/255 963; ⑤), a wonderful family-run pension with plenty of character. There's an unofficial **campsite** at Giruliai, 8km north of Klaipėda next to the sanatorium, *Pajuris*, on Slaito. There are no facilities at all but it's free (shuttle bus #8 from the centre).

Good places to **eat** are *Cafe Antika*, Liepų 1, which dishes up well-presented meat and fish dishes from 13Lt and *Galerija Pėda*, Turgaus 10, whose tasty food looks as arty as the gallery it occupies. For drinking your best bets are *Baras Flamingo*, H. Manto 38, a hip hangout with big windows for optimum see-and-be-seen effect (10am–11pm), or the *Bohema Bar*, Aukstoji 3/3 (11am–11pm), an arty little place with outdoor seating in the yard.

Neringa

NERINGA or the Kursių Nerija is the Lithuanian section of the Kurland Spit (known as Kurische Nehrung when the region was part of Germany), a 97-kilometre spit of land characterized by vast sand dunes and pine forests. To get there take a ferry from the quayside towards the end of Žvejų gatvė in Klaipėda (sailings every thirty minutes between 6am and 11pm) to **Smyltinė**. From the landing point buses (8 daily 7am–midnight; 7Lt) and minibuses (frequent services; 10Lt) run the length of the spit as far as Nida. If you can't get a bus or minibus, taxis also cover the distance, charging 40Lt per car. At the National Park Station you will have to pay an entrance fee (2Lt/person, 10Lt/car without a trailer). Keep the receipt for your return journey. The speed limit is 40km/hr.

NIDA, 35km or so south of Smyltinė, is the most famous village on the spit. Inhabited since 3500 BC, this small fishing village has several streets of attractive wooden houses but is disfigured by some lumpen Soviet resort architecture at its heart. To get a feel for the old fishing settlement head for **Naglių gatvė** and **Lotmisko gatvė**, (5min south of the village centre bus stop), lined by single-storey blue- and brown-painted wooden houses with thatched roofs and kitchen gardens. The **Etnografinė Žvejo Sodyba**, Naglių 4 (May–Sept Wed–Sun 11am–5pm; 2Lt), is a re-created nineteenth-century fisher cottage with simple wooden furnishings and explanations in Lithuanian, Russian and German of fishing-village development and architectural styles. Outside, between the building and the sea, are a couple of old fishing boats.

From the end of Naglių a shore path runs to a flight of wooden steps leading up to the top of the **dunes** south of the village. From the summit you can gaze out across a Saharan sandscape to the Kaliningrad *oblast*, part of German East Prussia until 1945 but now belonging to the Russian Federation. At the northern end of the village is **Thomas Mann's House** (Tomo Mano Namelis; May–Sept Tues–Sun 10am–5pm; 2Lt), his summer residence from 1930 to 1932. An uneventful museum within contains a few photos of the man himself and various editions of his books.

For **accommodation** the best place in town is the *Rasytė*, Lotmiskio 11 (☎259/52592; ③), a wooden hotel in the heart of the old fisher settlement. Nida gets very busy in summer so it's essential to book accommodation in advance by calling the hotel or Litinterp (☎26/216 962), in Klaipėda, who can help with bookings. For **food** head for *Seklyčia*, Lotmiškio 1 (summer 9am–11pm; winter 9am–3pm), a bar in a wooden house that does dishes like *cepelinai*. If you want to sample the excellent local smoked fish try the *Žuvis* kiosk at Naglių 18.

travel details

Trains

Vilnius to: Kaunas (12 daily; 1hr 15min–2hr); Klaipėda (3 daily; 5hr); Rīga (2 daily; 9hr); Tallinn (1 daily; 16hr); Warsaw (1 daily; 11hr). The only way to get from Vilnius to Warsaw without passing through Belarus, for which you will need an expensive visa, is to travel indirectly via Sestokai and Suwalki.

Kaunas to: Klaipėda (2 daily; 8hr); Rīga (1 daily; 7hr); Vilnius (hourly; 1hr 30min–2hr).

Klaipėda to: Kaunas (1 daily; 8hr 20min); Nida (departures from Smiltynė; 8 daily; 50min); Vilnius (3 daily; 5–9hr).

Buses

Vilnius to: Kaunas (39 daily; 1hr 30min–2hr); Klaipėda (9–11 daily; 5hr); Rīga (3 daily; 8hr); Tallinn (2 daily; 11hr 40min); Warsaw (4 daily; 12hr).

Kaunas to: Klaipėda (10 daily; 3hr); Rīga (2 daily; 4hr 30min); Vilnius (12 daily; 1hr 30min).

Klaipėda to: Kaliningrad (2 daily, 3hr 50min); Kaunas (10 daily; 3hr); Vilnius (10–12 daily; 5hr).

Ferries

Kaunas to: Nida (hydrofoil service; June–Aug 1 daily; 4hr).

CHAPTER 18

MOROCCO

Note: This chapter covers only the most easily accessible towns in northern Morocco. The map therefore shows only the northern regions, not the whole of the country

Introduction

Though just an hour's ferry ride from Spain, **Morocco** seems very far from Europe, with a deeply traditional Islamic culture. Throughout the country, despite the 44 years of French and Spanish colonial rule, a more distant past constantly makes its presence felt. Travel here is an intense and rewarding – if not always easy – experience.

Geographically, the country divides into five zones: the coast; the great cities of the plains; the Rif; the Atlas; and the oases and desert of the pre-Sahara and Sahara. Contrary to general misconceptions, it is actually the Berbers, the indigenous population of the mountains, who make up over half of the population; only around ten percent of Moroccans claim to be "pure" Arabs, although with the shift to the industrialized cities, such distinctions are becoming less significant. A more current distinction, perhaps, is the legacy of the colonial period: before Morocco reclaimed its independence in 1956, the country was divided into Spanish and French zones. It was the French, who ruled the main cities and governed their "protectorate" more closely, who had the most lasting effect, imposing their language, which is spoken today by all educated Moroccans (after Moroccan Arabic or one of the three local Berber languages). They built Villes Nouvelles alongside the four Imperial Cities, created **Casablanca** – the commercial capital – in the image of Marseille and chose **Rabat**, on the Atlantic coast and one of the Imperial Cities, to be the new seat of government.

Broadly speaking, on a brief visit the coast is best enjoyed in the north around **Tangier**, pleasant and still shaped by its old "international" port status. Inland, where the real interest of Morocco lies, the outstanding cities are **Fes** and **Marrakesh**. The greatest of the four imperial capitals of the country's various dynasties, they are unique in the Arab world for the chance they offer to witness a city life that, in patterns and appearance, remains in large part medieval. For monuments, Fes is the highlight, though Marrakesh, the "beginning of the south", is for most visitors the more enjoyable and exciting – and it gives easy access to the laid-back resort of **Essaouira** on the coast.

Travel in the south – roughly beyond a line drawn between Casablanca and **Meknes**, the fourth Imperial City – is, on the whole, more relaxing than in the sometimes frenetic north. This is certainly true of the **mountain ranges**. The Rif, in the north, is really for hardened travellers; only **Chaouen**, on its periphery, could be counted a "tourist spot". Hiking in the **High Atlas**, especially around North Africa's highest peak, **Djebel Toubkal**, is something of a

growth industry. Even if you're just a casual walker, it's worth considering, with summer treks possible at all levels of experience and altitude. And, despite inroads made by commercialization, it remains essentially "undiscovered" – like the Alps must have been in the last century.

Beyond here, in the two-thirds of Morocco lying south of Marrakesh and the High Atlas, is the sub-Sahara with its palm trees and camels (and not covered in this chapter). Here, peopled by proud tribes who kept the French foreign legion at bay, the land provides the backdrop to fabled films of the south which are still made in **Ouarzazate**, staging post for the southern oases.

Information, guides and maps

The **Office National Marocain du Tourisme (ONMT)** has an office in every major city. Each is correctly referred to as the Délégation du Tourisme, but locally it may be called the **ONMT** or **tourisme** office. In addition, there is sometimes a locally funded **Syndicat d'Initiative et de Tourisme**. In smaller towns, which do not justify a Délégation, there may be a Syndicat only. Occasionally, these offices can supply you with local information sheets and lists of classified hotels and restaurants. There are also nationally produced pamphlets on the four imperial capitals, the fortified towns of the coast and on trekking; as well as leaflets with good maps of the other major cities and towns. Local offices can also put you in touch with an officially recognized **guide** and *La Grande Traversée* lists qualified **mountain guides** area by area.

In addition to the guides trained by the government, there are scores of young Moroccans offering their services to show you around the *souks* (markets) and sights. Some of these "unofficial guides" are genuine students, who may want to earn a small fee but may equally be interested in practising their English. Others are out-and-out hustlers. Deal with them politely at all times and do not be intimidated. In Marrakesh and Fes, "tourist police" operate to protect visitors from the worst of the hustlers.

Maps of Moroccan cities are hard to obtain locally. The most functional are those in the *Rough Guide to Morocco* – beg or borrow or photocopy from travellers you meet. The best road map is the Michelin 1:1,000,000 sheet #959.

Money and banks

Once you've arrived, Morocco is an inexpensive and excellent-value destination, although you'll find the poverty demands some response – small tips can make a lot of difference to an individual's family life.

Morocco's basic unit of **currency** is the **dirham** (dh), which is divided into 100 **centimes** (10-, 20- and 50-centime coins are in circulation), and in markets you may well find prices written or expressed in centimes rather than dirhams. There are also 1-, 5- and 10-dirham coins and 10-, 20-, 50-, 100- and 200-dirham notes.

Moroccan currency is not yet available, nor exchangeable outside the country. This can cause difficulties on arrival and departure. You can usually change foreign notes into dirhams on arrival at major sea- or airports, but you will find it difficult to change travellers' cheques or Eurocheques until you reach a bank or bureau de change in the town centre. When you're nearing the end of your stay, it's best to get down to as little Moroccan money as possible, especially if you're leaving from the sea- or airport outside normal banking hours.

For **exchange** purposes, by far the most useful and efficient chain of banks is the **BMCE** (Banque Marocaine du Commerce Extérieur). Their major bureaux de change (often in the form of a small office or guichet next to the bank itself) are open 8am–8pm daily. They handle travellers' cheques (3dh commission) and Eurocheques (no commission on the spot, but your bank account may be debited by between 5 and 8 percent), and give cash advances on Visa and Access credit cards, which can also be used in payment at most classified hotels (though rarely at pensions), restaurants, tourist shops, and for car rental.

Hours for **banks** other than the BMCE are normally Mon–Fri 8.30–11.30am & 3–4.30pm in winter, 8.30am–2pm in summer and during Ramadan (the Muslim month of fasting). In major resorts there is usually at least one bank that keeps flexible hours to meet tourist demand; and a growing number of banks have 24-hour cashpoints (ATMs).

In smaller towns, particularly in the south, the state-run Banque Populaire is more common; where it is the only bank queuing is likely, especially on market days.

Communications

Stamps can often be bought alongside postcards or at a **PTT** (post office), and sometimes at tobacconists (look for the sign: three interlocking blue circles); always post letters at a PTT. Post office hours are Mon–Fri 8am–noon & 3–6pm in winter, 8am–3pm in summer. Receiving letters **poste restante** can be a bit of a lottery, as Moroccan post office workers don't always file letters under the name you might expect. The alternatives are to pick a big hotel (anything with three or more stars should be reliable) or have things sent c/o American Express – represented in Morocco

by Voyages Schwartz in Tangier, Fes, Casablanca and with irregular hours in Marrakesh; there is no American Express in Rabat.

The **public telephone** section is usually housed in the main post office, often with a separate entrance and sometimes open longer hours – 24 hours in some of the main cities. In most major towns you can also make international calls from centrally placed **phone boxes** (*cabines*). Alternatively, there are an increasing number of privately run **Téléboutiques** and state-run Technopubs; here you can phone, use a fax and sometimes photocopy. They remain open late – often until midnight.

You can also make calls through a hotel: even fairly small places will normally do this, but be sure to ask in advance about possible surcharges and the chargeable rate. All **pay phones** accept 50-centime or 1-dirham and the old, larger 5-dirham coins – a few dirhams are enough for a call within Morocco, and a brief short call across town can cost 50-centimes only; so, to economize, carry a range of coins.

Getting around

Moroccan public transport is, on the whole, good. There is an efficient rail network linking the main towns of the north, the coast and Marrakesh, and elsewhere you can travel easily enough by bus or collective *grand taxi* between towns and to outlying villages. Renting a car can be a good idea, at least for part of your trip, opening up routes that are time-consuming or difficult on local transport.

■ Trains

Trains cover a limited network of routes, but for travel between the major cities they are the best option – comfortable, efficient and fairly fast. Free **timetables**, printed by ONCF, the national railway company, are usually available – or at least on display – at major stations; they are updated from time to time but, over the years, the timing and frequency of trains have altered little.

There are three classes of **tickets** – confusingly, first, second and fourth (*économique*). **Costs** for a second-class ticket are comparable to what you'd pay for buses; on certain "express" services, which are first- and second-class only, they are around 30-percent higher. In addition, there are **couchettes** (50dh extra) available in summer on the Tangier–Marrakesh and the Tangier–Fes–Oujda trains; these are worth the money for the sake of security, as passengers are locked into a carriage with a guard.

Fares follow a reasonably consistent pattern – around 2dh for each 10km, 2.5–3dh for an express service. InterRail **passes** are valid, Eurail are not.

■ Grands taxis and petits taxis

Collective **grands taxis** are one of the best features of Moroccan transport. They operate on a variety of routes, are much quicker than the buses (often quicker than trains, too), and fares are very reasonable. Most business is along specific routes, many served by almost continuous departures throughout the day. As soon as six (or, if you're willing to pay extra, five or even four) people are assembled, the taxi sets off. On established routes *grands taxis* keep to fixed **fares** for each passenger – as a general guideline, around 2.5dh per person for each 10km. If you or your group want to take a non-standard route, or an excursion, it is possible to pay for a whole *grand taxi* (*une course*) – bargain hard to get the price down to around 12.5–16dh per 10km.

Within towns **petits taxis** do short trips, carrying up to three people, with luggage on the roof. They queue in central locations and at stations and can be hailed on streets when they're empty. Payment – usually no more than 10dh – relates to distance travelled.

■ Buses

Bus travel is marginally cheaper than taking a *grand taxi*, and there are far more regular routes, particularly over longer distances. Where you can take a *grand taxi* rather than a bus, however, do so. The difference in fare is small, and all except the express buses such as **SATAS** are very much slower and less comfortable than *grands taxis*.

There are a variety of bus services and companies. Buses run by **CTM** (the national company) are usually more reliable, with numbered seats and fixed schedules. An additional service, on certain major routes, is the express buses run by **Supratours**, on behalf of the train company ONCF, where there are now no trains – or never have been. These are fast and comfortable and compare, both in terms of time and cost, with *grands taxis*. CTM and ONCF look after your luggage on airport lines, and at no extra cost. Bear in mind that such companies may insist that

your luggage is padlocked, especially if it is deposited in left luggage (*consigne*).

On small private-line buses, you generally have to pay for your **baggage** to be loaded onto the roof (and taken off). Moroccans pay just a small tip for this but tourists are expected to pay 3–5dh.

■ Driving, trucks and hitching

Car rental – costing from £200/$320 a week with unlimited mileage to which you must add insurance and tax (currently 19 percent) – pays obvious dividends if you are pushed for time or want to explore the south, where getting to see anything can be quite an effort if you have to rely on public transport. However, wherever buses are sporadic or even nonexistent, it is standard practice for **vans**, **lorries** and **pick-up trucks** to carry and charge passengers. You may be asked to pay a little more than the locals, and you may be expected to bargain over this price. In parts of the Atlas, the Berbers run more or less scheduled truck services to coincide with local *souks*.

Hitching is not very big in Morocco: most people, if they own any form of transport at all, have mopeds which they use even for long journeys. However, it is often easy to get rides from other **tourists**, particularly if you ask around at the campsites, and for **women travellers** this can be an effective and positive option for getting around. Out on the road, it's inevitably a different matter – and hitching is definitely not advisable for women travelling alone.

Accommodation

Accommodation in Morocco is generally cheap, good value and usually pretty easy to find. The only times you might have any problems in getting a room are in the peak seasons (August, Christmas and Aïd el Kebir), and even then only in a handful of main cities and resorts.

Hotels are classified in accordance with national criteria which reflect the type and quality of accom-

---

ACCOMMODATION PRICE CODES

Throughout this guide, accommodation is priced on a scale of ① to ⑨, the number indicating the lowest price per night a single person could expect to pay in that establishment in high season. With hostels this is the nightly rate per person; with hotels, the price is arrived at by dividing the cost of the cheapest double room by two. The prices indicated by the codes are as follows:

① under £5 / $8	④ £15–20 / $24–32	⑦ £30–35 / $48–56
② £5–10 / $8–16	⑤ £20–25 / $32–40	⑧ £35–40 / $56–64
③ £10–15 / $16–24	⑥ £25–30 / $40–48	⑨ £40 / $64 and over

modation, but the corresponding price scales are determined locally. Unclassified hotels and pensions charge according to market forces which means there are seasonal variations. Note also that the exchange rate, which you are unlikely to know until you arrive and obtain local currency, does fluctuate. Price codes given throughout this chapter are based on a rate of 15.5dh to £1(Sterling) and 9.7dh to $1(US).

■ Unclassified hotels and pensions

Unclassified hotels and pensions (charging from about £5/$8 for a double) are mainly to be found in the older, Arab-built parts of cities – the **Medinas** – and are almost always the cheapest options on offer. At their best, unclassified Medina hotels and pensions are beautiful, traditional houses with white-washed rooms grouped around a central patio. On the down side, they regularly have a problem with **water**. Most of the Medinas remain substantially unmodernized – hot showers are a rarity and the toilets are occasionally nauseating. Local tourisme officials prefer tourists not to use unclassified hotels for a number of reasons, one being that they have no control over the prices charged; in any case, they will not accept responsibility for any problems encountered by tourists staying there.

■ Classified hotels

Classified hotels – whose prices are decided by local tourisme offices – are almost always concentrated in a town's **Ville Nouvelle** – the "new" or administrative quarter, built by the French and usually set apart from the Medina. Star-ratings are fairly self-explanatory and prices are reasonable for all except the five-star categories. At the lower end, there's often little difference between officially classified one-star B and one-star A, either of which will offer you a basic double room with a washbasin for around £8.25/$11, depending on the local price scales which should be on display in the hotel; expect to pay a little more for an en-suite room. Going up to two- and three-star, there's a definite progression in comfort, and you can find a few elegant, old hotels in these categories. However, if you're in search of a touch of luxury, you'll most likely be looking for a room with access to a swimming pool – which means, on the whole, four stars.

■ Hostels, refuges and campsites

At the lower price levels – though often no cheaper than a shared room in the Medina – there are seven **youth hostels**, or **auberges de jeunesse**. One, in Asni in the High Atlas, is a hiking base – useful and

recommended. The other six are all in major cities: Tangier, Meknes, Fes, Rabat, Casablanca and Marrakesh. In the High Atlas Mountains, you will also find a number of huts, or **refuges**, equipped for hikers. These provide dormitory beds and sometimes meals and/or cooking facilities.

Campsites can be worth visiting in order to find a lift or people to share car costs. Most sites have limited facilities and are very cheap, at around 75p/$1 per person and per tent; the fancier places charge around double this, but offer swimming pools and better facilities.

Food and drink

Like accommodation, **food** in Morocco falls into two basic categories: ordinary Moroccan meals served in the Medina cafés (or bought from stalls), and French-influenced tourist menus in most of the hotels and Ville Nouvelle restaurants. If funds are limited, it's best to stick to the Medina places (most are cleaner than they look), with an occasional splurge in the better restaurants.

■ Food

For **breakfast** or a **snack**, you can always buy a half **baguette** – plus packs of butter and jam, yoghurt, cheese or eggs, if you want – from many bread or grocery stores, and take it into a café to order a drink.

Basic Moroccan meals centre on a thick, very filling soup – most often the spicy, bean-based **harira**, which can be a meal in itself. To this you might add a plateful of kebabs and perhaps a salad, together with dates, or other fruit in season, bought at a market stall. Alternatively, you could go for a **tajine** – essentially a stew, steam-cooked slowly over a charcoal fire. Either alternative will set you back about £4/$6 for a hearty meal at a stall or simple place in the Medina.

More expensive dishes, available in some of the Medina cafés as well as in the dearer restaurants, include **fish**, particularly on the coast, and **chicken** (*poulet*), either spit-roasted (*rôti*) or with olives and lemon (*poulet aux olives et citron*). A particular speciality of Fes is **pastilla**, a succulent pigeon pie, made with filo pastry coated with sugar and cinnamon. The most famous Moroccan dish, of course, is **couscous**, a huge bowl of steamed semolina piled with vegetables and mutton, chicken, or occasionally fish. Tourist restaurants also have a few **French dishes** – steak, liver, various fish and fowl, etc – and the ubiquitous **salade marocaine**, based on a few tomatoes, cucumbers and other greens. With a dessert of fruit or pastry, these meals usually come to around £6/\$10.

Excellent **cakes and desserts** are available in some Moroccan cafés, but more often at pastry shops or street stalls. The most common are *cornes de gazelles*, sugar-coated pastries filled with a kind of marzipan, but there are infinite variations. **Yoghurt** (*yaourt*) is also delicious, and Morocco is surprisingly rich in seasonal **fruits**. In addition to the various kinds of **dates** – sold all year but at their best fresh from the October harvests – there are grapes, melons, strawberries, peaches and figs, all advisably washed before eaten. Or for a real thirst-quencher (and a good cure for a bad stomach), you can have quantities of **prickly pear**, cactus fruit, peeled for you in the street for a couple of dirhams.

Eating in local cafés, or if invited to a home, you may find yourself using your hands rather than a knife and fork. Muslims eat only with the **right hand**, and you should do likewise. Eating from a **communal bowl** at someone's home, it is polite to take only what is immediately in front of you, unless specifically offered a piece of meat by the host.

■ Drink

The national drink is **thé à la menthe** – green tea flavoured with sprigs of mint and with a minimum of four cubes of sugar per cup. If you want unsweetened tea, European-style, ask for *thé noir* (black), *thé citron* (with lemon) or *thé Lipton* (tea bags). You can also occasionally get varieties of red or amber tea – more expensive and rarely available, but delicious and well worth trying. **Coffee** (*café*) is best in French-style cafés – either *noir* (black), *cassé* (with a drop of milk), or *au lait* (white). Wonderful, too, and easily found at cafés or street stalls, are the fresh-squeezed **juices**: *jus d'orange*, *jus d'amande* (almond), *jus des bananes* and *jus de pomme* (apple), the last three all milk-based and served chilled. *Leben* – yoghurt and water – is often sold at train and bus stations, and can do wonders for an upset stomach. Though water is generally safe to drink, it's good to get accustomed to it slowly. **Mineral water**, available throughout the country, is usually referred to by brand name: the ubiquitous *Sidi Harazem*, the much lauded *Sidi Ali*, or the naturally sparkling *Oulmès*.

As an Islamic nation, Morocco gives **alcohol** a low profile. It is not generally possible to buy any alcohol at all in the Medinas, and for beer or wine you always have to go to a tourist restaurant or hotel, or a bar in the Ville Nouvelle. Moroccan **wines**, however, can be very good, if a little heavy for drinking without a meal; most come from the area around Meknes and, generally speaking, reds are better than whites. Those Moroccans who drink in **bars** – a growing number in the major cities – tend to stick to **beer**, which should cost around 12dh a bottle in ordinary bars. Bars are totally male domains, except in tourist hotels – but even then they can be a bit rowdy.

Opening hours and holidays

Shops and stalls in the *souk* areas stay open just about every hour of the day, though the shop owners might be found sleeping through the midday hours. The exception to all this is Friday, when most vendors close at least for morning prayers, with some staying shut all day. **Museums** in Morocco are generally open 9am–noon & 2–6pm, closing on Friday morning and sometimes all day Sunday, Monday or Tuesday as well. Bear in mind that non-Muslims are forbidden entry to virtually all **religious buildings**. Entrance to museums and to most secular buildings and historical sites is either free or costs only 10dh (80p). Where admission fees cost more, it is indicated in the text accordingly.

Islamic **religious holidays** are calculated on the lunar calendar, so their dates tend to rotate through the seasons. During **Ramadan**, the ninth month of the Islamic calendar, all Muslims observe a total fast lasting from sunrise to sunset. Non-Muslims are not expected to observe Ramadan, but it is a good idea to be sensitive about not breaking the fast (particularly smoking) in public. Ramadan begins on December 2 in 2000; exact dates in the calendar are set by the Islamic authorities in Fes, and depend on sighting the "new" moon.

The other main religious holidays in the Islamic year are **Aïd el Kebir**, otherwise known as Aïd al Adhar or even Fête des Moutons (the celebration of Abraham's willingness to sacrifice his son Ishmael, known among Christians as Isaac), **Moharem** (the Muslim new year) and **Mouloud** (the birthday of the Prophet), each of which is usually marked by two official days off.

Secular holidays are considered less important, with most public services (except banks and offices) operating normally even during the two biggest ones – the Feast of the Throne that takes place on March 3 and Independence Day on November 18.

Emergencies

Keeping your luggage and money secure is an important consideration in Morocco – it is obviously not wise to carry large sums of cash or valuables on your person, especially in the main tourist cities. **Hotels** are generally secure for depositing money; **campsites** are considerably less secure, and many campers advise wearing a money belt even while sleeping.

There are two main types of **police**. The grey-clad **gendarmes**, who staff the road checkpoints, are the ones with whom foreigners should deal. The navy-clad military police have limited authority and are usually none too helpful, except where they are designated "tourist police" (as in Marrakesh).

Moroccan **pharmacists** are well trained and dispense a wide range of drugs. If they feel you need a full diagnosis, they can usually recommend a **doctor**, or a list of English-speaking doctors in major cities can be obtained from consulates.

The smoking of **kif** (hashish) has for a long time been a regular pastime of Moroccans and tourists alike. There is no real effort to stop Moroccans from using *kif*, but nonetheless it is illegal to trade in it. As a tourist you are peculiarly vulnerable to the rip-offs and scams of dealers. Many have developed aggressive tactics, selling people hash and then turning them in to the police or threatening to do so.

EMERGENCY NUMBERS

Police ☎19; Hospital ☎15.

TANGIER TO FES

The two chief cities of northern Morocco, Tangier and Tetouan, are by reputation difficult, with guides and hustlers preying on first-time travellers. However, it doesn't take long to get the measure of them – and to enjoy the experience. **Tangier**, hybridized and slightly seedy from its long European contact, has a setting and skyline the equal of any Mediterranean resort, and is immediately compelling in its long-time role as the meeting point of Europe and Africa. **Tetouan**, in the shadow of the barren foothills of the Rif Mountains, feels more Moroccan – its Medina a glorious labyrinth, dotted with squares and *souks*. Moving on from either city, the mountain town of **Chaouen** is a small-scale and enjoyably laid-back place to come to terms with being in Morocco. South from Tangier – which stands at the beginning of the railway line to Fes and Meknes and to Rabat, Casablanca and Marrakesh – the seaside resort of **Asilah** is another good place to get acclimatized.

Inland, **Fes** has for over a thousand years been at the heart of Moroccan history and is today unique in the Arab world, preserving the appearance and much of the life of a medieval Islamic city. **Meknes** is another city of bygone ages – its enduring impression being that of an endless series of high unbroken walls – though it is also a thriving market centre. There are, too, the local attractions of **Volubilis**, the best preserved of the country's Roman sites, and the hilltop town of **Moulay Idriss**, the oldest and most important Moroccan shrine.

Tangier (Tanger, Tangiers)

For the first half of this century **TANGIER** was one of the stylish resorts of the Mediterranean – an "International City" with its own laws and administration, plus an eclectic community of exiles, expatriates and refugees. When Moroccan independence was gained in 1956, however, Tangier's special status was removed. Almost overnight, the finance and banking businesses shifted to Spain and Switzerland, and the expatriate colony dwindled as the new national government imposed bureaucratic controls. These days there's an air of decay about the city, most tangible in the older hotels and bars, and a somewhat uncertain overall identity: a city that seems halfway to becoming a mainstream tourist resort yet still retains hints of its decadent past amid the shambling 1930s architecture and the modern high-rise apartment blocks and tall featureless four-star hotels.

Arrival and accommodation

The Gare du Port **train station** is almost directly by the **ferry terminal**; most trains leave from here as well as from the Gare de Ville, 300m past the port gates. Nearby there are ranks for *grands* and *petits taxis*; they are best engaged at the latter, rather than amid the hustle of the port gates. The Gare Routière **bus station** is 1.5km inland near the Syrian Mosque; from here you can catch long-distance buses and *grands taxis*. Tangier's **airport** is about 15km outside the city; alternatives to the very sporadic bus are to take a taxi or to walk the two kilometres to the main road, where you can pick up a local bus to the Grand Socco. The **tourisme** office is at 29 bd Pasteur (Mon–Fri 8.30am–noon & 2.30–6.30pm; ☎09/94.80.50), just down from the place de France and opposite the *Hôtel de Paris*; despite its recent facelift, don't expect too much from it.

Tangier has dozens of **hotels and pensions**, and finding a room is never much of a problem: if the first place you try is full, ask them to phone and reserve you a place elsewhere – most will be happy to do so. The city does, however, get crowded during July and August, when some places double their prices.

The *Pension Mauretania*, 2 rue des Almohades, aka rue des Chrétiens (☎09/93.46.77; ①), is just off the Petit Socco; it has cold showers and shared toilets, but is clean. *Hôtel Olid*, 12 rue Mokhtar Ahardane, aka rue des Postes (☎09/93.13.10; ①), has seen better days, but is still value for money, while the *Pension Palace*, 2 rue Mokhtar Ahardane (☎09/93.61.28; ①), is more attractive with balconies and a lovely courtyard – certainly one of the best hotels in

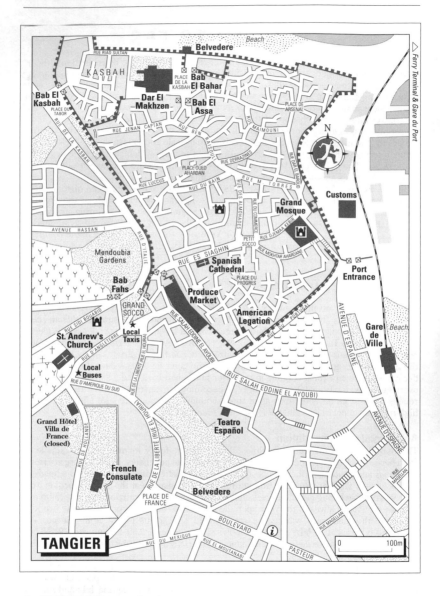

On map: Belvedere, Beach, RUE RIAD SULTAN, KASBAH, PLACE DE LA KASBAH, Bab El Bahar, Bab El Kasbah, PLACE DU TABOR, Dar El Makhzen, Bab El Assa, PLACE DE ARSENAL, RUE JENAN CAPTAN, RUE BEN RAISOULI, RUE MAIMOUNI, N, RUE DERRAZINES, RUE M TORRES, PLACE OUED AHARDANE, RUE DE LA KASBAH, RUE LUCCUS, RUE DU BAIN, RUE DES AMOUADES, Grand Mosque, Customs, AVENUE HASSAN I, RUE D'ITALIE, RUE DU COMMERCE, RUE DJEMAA KEBIR, RUE MOKHTAR AHARDANE, Mendoubia Gardens, PETIT SOCCO, RUE ES SIAGHIN, Spanish Cathedral, Port Entrance, Bab Fahs, PLACE DU PROGRES, GRAND SOCCO, Produce Market, RUE SALAH EDDINE EL AYOUBI, American Legation, AVENUE D'ESPAGNE, Gare de Ville, Beach, St. Andrew's Church, Local Taxis, RUE D'ANGLETERRE, RUE DE LA LIBERTE (RUE EL HOURIA), Local Buses, RUE D'AMERIQUE DU SUD, RUE DU PORTUGAL, (RUE SALAH EDDINE EL AYOUBI), AVENUE D'ESPAGNE, RUE SIDI BOUABID, Grand Hôtel Villa de France (closed), RUE DE HOLLANDE, Teatro Español, RUE MAGELLAN, French Consulate, PLACE DE FRANCE, Belvedere, TANGIER, BOULEVARD, RUE DU MEXIQUE, RUE EL MOUTANABI, PASTEUR, 0 100m, Ferry Terminal & Gare du Port

the Medina. More expensive, but still good value, is the *Mamora Hôtel*, 19 rue Mokhtar Ahardane (☎09/93.41.05; ②).

In the Ville Nouvelle are the *Hôtel Magellan*, 16 rue Magellan (☎09/37.23.19; ①), and *Hôtel El Muniria*, 1 rue Magellan (☎09/93.53.37; ①), good value and helpful, with a late-night bar. *Hôtel de Paris*, 42 bd Pasteur (☎09/93.18.77; ②) on the main street opposite the tourisme office, is well maintained and the best value in the area. Best value on the seafront are the

Hôtel Miramar, 168 av des FAR (☎09/94.17.15; ②), friendly, old and a little shabby with a bar and restaurant; and *Hôtel Marco Polo*, on the corner of av d'Espagne and rue El Antaki (☎09/94.11.24; ②), well established and popular with a bar and good restaurant. The closest and most popular **campsite** is *Camping Miramonte* aka *Camping Marshan* (☎09/93.71.33), 3km to the west of the centre (signposted from place de France, or take bus #1 from the local bus station near the Grand Socco), and near a small beach. The **youth hostel**, 8 rue El Antaki (8–10am, noon–3pm & 6–10.30pm; open until midnight in summer; ☎09/94.61.27; ①), near the seafront, is clean and well run.

The City

Together with the **beach** and the seafront **Avenue d'Espagne** and its continuation as **Avenue des FAR**, the easiest reference points are the city's three main squares – the Grand Socco, Petit Socco and place de France. The **Grand Socco** – once the main market square (and, since Independence, officially place 9 Avril 1947) – offers the most straightforward approach to the **Medina**. The arch at the northwest corner of the square opens onto rue d'Italie, which becomes rue de la Kasbah, the northern entrance to the Kasbah quarter. To the right, there is an opening onto rue es Siaghin, off which are most of the *souks* and at the end of which is the **Petit Socco**, the Medina's principal landmark and square, seedy and slightly conspiratorial in feel. Heading past the Petit Socco toward the sea walls are two small streets straddled by the Grand Mosque, which, as throughout Morocco, is strictly closed to non-Muslims. If instead you follow **rue des Almohades** (aka rue des Chrétiens) and its continuation **rue Ben Raisouli** you'll emerge, with luck, around the lower gate to the Kasbah.

The **Kasbah**, walled off from the Medina on the highest rise of the coast, has been the palace and administrative quarter since Roman times. It is a strange, somewhat sparse area of walled compounds, occasional colonnades and a number of luxurious villas built in the 1920s. The main point of interest is the former Sultanate Palace, or **Dar El Makhzen** (summer Mon–Sat 9am–3.30pm; winter Mon–Sat 9am–noon & 3–6pm), now converted to an excellent two-part museum of crafts and antiquities. At the entrance to the main part of the palace is the **Bit El Mal**, the old treasury, and adjoining it a small private **mosque**, near to which is the entrance to the herb- and shrub-lined palace **gardens**, shaded by jacaranda trees. If you leave this way, you will come out by the stairway to the **Café-Restaurant Detroit**, set up in the 1960s by Beat writer Brion Gysin. The café is now an overpriced tourist spot but worth the price of a mint tea for the views.

Eating, drinking and nightlife

As with most Moroccan cities, the cheapest places to **eat** are in the **Medina**. There's a choice of several basic cafés on rue du Commerce and rue des Almohade (aka rue des Chrétiens). *Restaurant Andaluz*, 7 rue du Commerce, off the Petit Socco, is small and simple, and the food is good and cheap. Try fried swordfish, grilled *brochettes* and salad. Also good is *Grèce Restaurant*, 21 rue du Commerce, which serves traditional Moroccan – but no Greek – dishes. The **cafés** around the Grand Socco are worth a look too; most stay open until midnight or later. Alcoholic drinks are not served in the Medina or Grand Socco restaurants.

In the **Ville Nouvelle**, the *Restaurant Africa*, 83 rue Salah Eddine El Ayoubi (aka rue de la Plage) has a plat du jour for 50dh and is licensed to serve beer and wine with meals. Also recommended, is *Restaurant Hassi Baida*, next door at no. 81; with a traditional Moroccan menu, but no licence. They are at the bottom of the hill, almost opposite *Hôtel Valencia*; often crowded, both offer generous portions of highly recommended dishes. *Restaurant Agadir*, 21 rue Prince Héretier Sidi Mohammed, uphill from place de France, is small and friendly, serving French and Moroccan dishes, and *San Remo*, 15 rue Ahmed Chaouki, opposite the terrace belvedere on bd Pasteur, specializes in Italian dishes and runs a takeaway pizzeria opposite. For Spanish seafood, including vast portions of fine paella, try the pricier *Romero*, 12 rue Prince Moulay Abdallah, off bd Pasteur around the corner from the tourisme office.

On the **seafront**, many of the hotels have reliable European restaurants, among which is the *Marco Polo* whose generous servings come at a fair price. As an alternative, try *Hôtel Restaurant L'Marsa*, 92 av d'Espagne, with a roof terrace, open-air patio and indoor restaurant offering excellent pasta and pizzas, with homemade ice cream to follow. Finally, back in town, the long-established *Rubis Grill*, at 3 rue Ibn Rochd off rue Prince Moulay Abdallah, serves Spanish and other European dishes; the candlelit hacienda decor is a bit over the top but the food and service are exemplary.

For **drinking**, the *Tanger-Inn*, the late-night bar of the *Hôtel El Muniria* at 1 rue Magellan, is an imitation Brighton pub and quite an institution, run by an ex-trooper and serving the expats for the last twenty years (daily 9pm–2am). The *Hôtel Miramar* on av des FAR is a hard-drinking seafood spot. Traditionally a gay **disco**, *Scott's* on rue El Moutanabi is worth a look for its decor, although nothing much happens here before midnight; take care leaving late at night – the best idea is to tip the doorman 5dh to order you a taxi. Finally, the *Morocco Palace*, av du Prince Moulay Abdallah, is a strange, sometimes slightly manic place that puts on traditional Moroccan music for Westerners until around 1am, then a Western disco for the Moroccans.

Listings

Airlines Royal Air Maroc, place de France (☎09/93.47.22); British Airways, 83 rue de la Liberté, aka El Houria (☎09/93.52.11 or 09/93.58.77).

American Express Represented by Voyages Schwartz, 54 bd Pasteur (☎09/93.34.59 & 09/93.34.71; Mon–Fri 9am–12.30pm & 3–7pm, Sat 9am–12.30pm).

Car rental Most big companies – Avis, Europcar, InterRent, Hertz – have offices along bd Pasteur/bd Mohammed V. For a more local and personal service visit Harris Rent-a-Car, 1 rue Zerktouni, just off bd Mohammed V (☎09/94.21.58).

Consulates Britain, 41 bd Mohammed V (☎09/94.15.57).

Exchange BMCE on bd Pasteur is the most efficient and accessible; there is a separate exchange guichet alongside and an ATM cashpoint (both daily 9am–12.30pm & 3–7pm).

Pharmacies There are several English-speaking pharmacies in the place de France and along bd Pasteur.

Post office Main PTT, 33 bd Mohammed V (Mon–Sat 8.30am–12.15pm & 2.30–6.45pm).

Police Main station is on rue Ibn Toumert.

Telephones At the main post office; also along and around bd Pasteur/bd Mohammed V and on the seafront.

Asilah

The first stop on the railway beyond Tangier, **ASILAH** is one of the most elegant of the old Portuguese Atlantic ports, with its square, stone ramparts flanked by palms. Its beach is also outstanding – the most popular stretches are to the north of the town. The **train station** is 2km north of the town – an easy enough walk if you can't hitch a lift. Arriving by **grand taxi** (1hr from Tangier), you're dropped in place Mohammed V, a small square about 100 metres north of the ramparts and the northern entrance, Bab El Kasaba; buses drop you in an adjacent street.

The circuit of **towers and ramparts**, built by the Portuguese in the sixteenth century, makes for a pleasant stroll. Along here, the main keep, **El Hamra**, has been restored as one of the venues for the International Festival of the Arts (usually mid-July to mid-Aug) and has the occasional exhibition at other times of the year. The modern international arts centre is opposite the restored Grand Mosque, just inside the Bab El Kasaba. Asilah's focal sight – stretching over the sea from the heart of the Medina – is the **Palais de Raisuli**, built in 1909 by one Er Raisuli, a local bandit who was eventually appointed governor over the tribes of northwest Morocco. It is closed outside festival times, but you may strike lucky with the caretaker. Failing that, and if you are keen, you could get a note in Arabic from the Hôtel de Ville; this should do the trick.

Practicalities

Asilah can be packed full during the International Festival, but most of the year **accommodation** is easy enough to find and generally inexpensive. The small *Pension Ennasr*, 3 rue Ahmed M'dem (☎09/41.73.85; ①), is a basic but pleasant hotel on a side street just off place

Mohammed V. *Hôtel Ouad El Makhazine*, av Melilla (☎09/41.70.90; ②), close to the seafront, is pleasant and comfortable. *Hôtel las Palmas*, 7 rue Imam Assili (☎09/41.76.94; ②), is modern but some distance from the seafront, albeit well signposted from the town centre. The refurbished *Hôtel El Mansour*, at 49 av Mohammed V on the northern approach into town (☎09/41.73.90; ②), has a good restaurant.

There is a string of **campsites** north of the town but those between the train station and the centre are more convenient. *Camping Echrigui*, Asilah BP 23 (☎09/41.71.82), and *Camping As Saada*, Asilah BP 34 (☎09/41.73.17), are well equipped; both have thatched bungalows (①).

The two most prominent **restaurants** are on place Zallaka facing Bab El Kasaba; *Casa Pepe*, (aka *El Oceano*), with a roof terrace overlooking the ramparts, is marginally better than its rival and next-door neighbour, *Al Kasaba*; both have pavement tables and serve Spanish-style fried fish. At the northern end of the seafront, and convenient for the campsites, *El Espignon* has an extensive seafood menu and attentive staff – on high season weekends it's worth booking in advance (call ☎09/41.71.57). Back in town near *Hôtel las Palmas*, the *Sevilla* serves generous helpings of Spanish-style dishes.

Ceuta (Sebta)

A Spanish enclave which dates back to the sixteenth century, **CEUTA** is a curious political anomaly but, since the Algeciras–Ceuta ferries and hydrofoils are quicker than those going to Tangier, this drab outpost has become a popular point of entry to Morocco. Try to arrive early in the day so that you have plenty of time to move on to Tetouan or beyond. You don't officially enter Morocco until the border at **FNIDEQ**, 3km out of town, reached by local bus from the seafront. Once across, the easiest transport is a shared *grand taxi* to Tetouan; buses are infrequent, though a couple of dirhams cheaper. There are **exchange facilities** (cash only) at the frontier.

It isn't easy to find a room in Ceuta – and not cheap when you do. A complete list is available from the **tourisme** office by the ferry dock; if it is closed, you can consult the list displayed in its window. The **youth hostel**, at Plaza Rafael Gilbert 27 (②), is open in July and August only and is often full.

Leaving Ceuta **by ferry** for Algeciras, you can usually turn up at the port, buy tickets, and board a ferry within a couple of hours. The one time to avoid, as at Tangier, is the last week of August. If you intend to use the quicker **hydrofoil service**, it's best to book the previous day in high season; details and tickets for the hydrofoil are available from travel agents around town, and from 6 Muelle Caõnero Dato, by the ferry terminal.

Tetouan

If you're a first-time Moroccan visitor coming from Ceuta, **TETOUAN** can be intimidating. The Medina seems overwhelming, and the hustlers, sometimes trading large quantities of *kif*, have the worst reputation in Morocco. Physically, though, Tetouan is strikingly beautiful, poised atop the slope of an enormous valley against a dark mass of rock. The town was hastily constructed by Andalusian refugees in the fifteenth century, and their houses, full of extravagant detail, seem more akin to the old Arab quarters of Córdoba and Seville than to other Moroccan towns.

Arriving by bus or *grand taxi*, you'll find yourself on the edge of the **Ville Nouvelle**, which follows a fairly straightforward grid. At its centre is **place Moulay El Mehdi**, with the post office and main banks. From here the grid stretches east toward **place Hassan II**, the old meeting place and market square, recently remodelled with a pavement of Islamic motifs, minaret-like floodlights and a brand-new Royal Palace. The usual approach to the Medina is through **Bab El Rouah** (Gate of the Wind), the archway just south of the Royal Palace. You then find yourself on **rue Terrafin**, a relatively wide lane which, with its continuations, cuts straight across to the east gate, **Bab Okla**. To the left of rue Terrafin, a series of alleys gives access to most of the town's food and craft **souks**, packing the mass of alleys and passageways leading toward Bab Sebta, the northern gate. The quarter to the north of Bab Okla, below the Grand Mosque, was the Medina's most exclusive residential area and contains some of its finest mansions. Walking towards the gate you'll see signs for a *Palais*, one of the best of the buildings, now converted into a carpet and crafts warehouse aimed at tourists. Considerably more authentic is the **Museum of Moroccan Arts** (Mon–Fri 8.30am–noon & 2.30–6.30pm), just outside Bab Okla. A former arms bastion, the museum has one of the more impressive collections around of traditional crafts and ethnographic objects. Take a look particularly at the *zellij* – enamelled tile mosaics – and then cross the road to the **Crafts School** (open to the public during school terms only; same hours as museum) where you can see craftsmen producing them in ways essentially unchanged since the fifteenth century.

Practicalities

The **tourisme** office, at 30 bd Mohammed V, a few metres from place Moulay El Mehdi (Mon–Fri 8.30am–noon & 2.30pm–6.30pm; ☎09/96.19.16), has lots of useful information about the province, including Chaouen (see below). Pick of the **hotels** is the comfortable *Principe*, 20 av Youssef Ibn Tachfine (☎09/96.27.95; ③), midway between the bus station and place Moulay El Mehdi. Failing that, there is the *National* at 8 rue Mohamed Ben Larbi Torres (☎09/96.32.90; ①). Two other possibilities are *Hôtel Trebol*, 3 av Yacoub El Mansour (no phone; ①), behind the bus station, and *Paris Hôtel*, 11 rue Chakib Arssalane (☎09/96.67.50; ②), which is more central, but can be noisy. The nearest **campsites** are on the coast at Martil, 11km to the east.

As ever, the cheapest **food** is to be found in the Medina, particularly the stalls inside Bab El Rouah and along rue Luneta. For variety, try one of the many places on or around bd Mohammed V/bd Mohamed Ben Larbi Torres in the Ville Nouvelle. Good choices here include *Restaurant La Union* in Pasaje Achaach (off rue Mohamed Ben Larbi Torres); *Restaurant Café Saigon*, 2 rue Mohamed Ben Larbi Torres, at the junction with rue Abdelkrim El Kattabi; and the licensed *Restaurant Restinga*, 21 bd Mohammed V, alongside Alcaraz bookshop, almost facing the tourisme office, where you can eat outdoors or inside – either way the food and service are excellent.

For **moving on**, there are regular **buses** to Chaouen, Meknes, Fes and Tangier, but for Tangier or Ceuta it's easiest to travel by **grand taxi**. The ONCF office on rue Achrai Mai, alongside place Al Adala, sells **train** tickets that include connecting buses to the stop at Tnine Sidi Lyamani, south of Asilah.

Chaouen (Chefchaouen, Xaouen)

Shut in by a fold of mountains, **CHAOUEN** becomes visible only once you have arrived – a dramatic approach to a town which, until the arrival of Spanish troops in 1920, had been visited by just three Europeans. The region is sacred to Muslims due to the presence of the tomb of Moulay Abdessalam Ben Mchich – one of the "four poles of Islam". These days, Chaouen is becoming a little over-concerned with tourism, but like Tetouan, its architecture has a strong Andalusian character, and it's a town of extraordinary light and colour, its whitewash tinted with blue and edged by golden stone walls. Pensions are among the friendliest and cheapest around, and to stay here a few days is one of the best possible introductions to Morocco.

With a population of around 25,000 – an eighth of Tetouan's – Chaouen is more like a large village, confusing only on arrival. **Buses** and **grands taxis** drop you outside the town walls; to reach the Medina, walk up across the old marketplace to the tiny arched entrance, **Bab El Ain**. Through the gate a dominant, but narrow, lane winds up to the main square, the elongated **place Outa El Hammam**. This is where most of the town's evening life takes place, its cafés overhung by upper rooms – some still the preserve of *kif* smokers. By day, the town's focus is the **Kasbah**, a quiet ruin with shady gardens which occupies one side of the square. Beyond, the smaller **place El Makhzen** is in some ways a continuation of the downtown marketplace, an elegant clearing with an old fountain and pottery stalls set up for package tourists.

Along and just off the main route through the Medina is a series of small **hotels**, possibly the quietest of which is the *Hôtel Abi Khancha*, 75 rue Lala El Hora (☎09/98.68.79; ①), a converted house with an open courtyard, salon and high terrace. Outside the Medina, and nearer to transport, are the immaculate *Hôtel Madrid*, av Hassan II (☎09/98.74.96; ②), and the cheaper *Hôtel Sevilla*, av Allal Ben Abdallah (☎09/98.72.85; ①). For more comfort, there is the *Hôtel Rif*, 29 av Hassan II (☎09/98.69.82; ①) below the old walls. Chaouen's **campsite** (☎09/98.69.79) is up on the hill above the town, by the modern *Hôtel Asma*; it is inexpensive but can be crowded during summer. The adjoining **youth hostel** (☎09/98.60.31; ①) is open intermittently, but you can live in the Medina for a little more and be at the centre of things.

A few of the cafés in the place Outa El Hammam serve regular Moroccan **meals**; the best is the *Ali Baba*. Better still is the *Restaurant Tissemlal* (aka *Casa Hassan*), 22 rue Targui, just up from place Outa El Hammam which serves delicious food in elegant surroundings. Outside the Medina, up from Bab El Ain on rue Moulay Ali Ben Rachid, is the *Restaurant Zouar*, a favourite with the locals – a sure sign of excellence.

Bus departures to Fes, and to a lesser degree Meknes, are quite often full, so when **moving on**, try to buy tickets a day in advance. If you can't get on a direct bus, an alternative is to take a *grand taxi* or local bus to Ouezzane and another from there, or to return to Tetouan, where most of the buses originate. For Tetouan, buses leave at least six times a day – much less of a problem – or you can share a *grand taxi*. Daily buses also run to the Ceuta border.

Meknes

Cut in two by the wide river valley of the Oued Boufekrane, **MEKNES**, on the main rail line south from Tangier, is a sprawling, prosperous provincial city. Monuments from its past well reward a day's exploration, as do the varied and busy *souks* of its Medina: getting a grasp of Meknes prepares you a little for the drama of Fes, and certainly helps give an idea of quality and prices for crafts shopping.

Arrival and accommodation

There are two **train stations**, both of which are situated in the Ville Nouvelle on the east bank. The **Gare El Amir Abdelkadir** is the more convenient, being only a couple of blocks from the centre – the **Gare de Ville** is further out. All trains stop at both stations. **Petits taxis**, **grands taxis** and **buses** arrive close to the focal point of the Medina, place El Hedim; CTM buses arrive at either 47 av Mohammed V in the Ville Nouvelle, or at the new terminal on av de la Gare, near the Gare de Ville and opposite *Hôtel Bordeaux*. For bus connections onwards from Meknes, and other matters, check at the helpful **tourisme** office on the place d'Administrative (Mon–Thurs 8.30am–noon & 2.30–6.30pm, Fri 8.30–11.30am & 3–6.30pm; ☎05/52.44.26).

Hotels are concentrated in the Ville Nouvelle, and if you're looking for comfort and proximity to bars and restaurants, this is definitely the place to stay. However, it's a fairly long walk from the Ville Nouvelle to the Medina and, if you're here for only a short stay, there are some advantages in being close to the monuments and *souks*. Pick of the Medina hotels are the *Hôtel Maroc*, 7 rue Rouamzine (☎05/53.00.75; ①), one of the best, with hot showers, and further up the street at no. 58, the *Hôtel de Paris* (no ☎; ①). The best cheap choice in the Ville Nouvelle is the *Hôtel Bordeaux*, 64 av de la Gare (☎05/52.25.63; ①), with a friendly atmosphere and shady garden, and for which the Gare de Ville is the nearer station. *Hôtel Touring*, 34 av Allal Ben Abdallah (☎05/52.23.51; ①) is the best of the one-star places, followed by the modern and standard *Hôtel Ouislane*, 54 av Allal Ben Abdallah (☎05/52.17.43; ②), and the friendly, clean and comfortable *Hôtel Majestic*, 19 av Mohammed V (☎05/52.20.35; ①), handy for the Gare El Amir Abdelkadir.

The **youth hostel**, av Okba Ben Nafi (8am–10pm/midnight; ☎05/52.46.98; ①), is 1.5km from the city centre – take bus #15. The town's pleasant **campsite**, *Camping Aguedal* (☎05/55.53.96), to the south of the Imperial City, is a twenty-minute walk from place El Hedim, opposite the Heri as-Souani. At 44dh for a tent sleeping two, it's pricey, but arguably the best site in Morocco.

The City

More than any other Moroccan town, Meknes is associated with a single figure, the **Sultan Moulay Ismail**, in whose reign (1672–1727) the city was built up from a provincial centre to a spectacular capital with over fifty palaces and some fifteen miles of exterior walls. The principal remains of Ismail's creation – the Imperial City of palaces and gardens, barracks, granaries and stables – sprawl below the Medina amid a confusing array of enclosures. **Place El Hedim** (the Square of Demolition and Renewal) originally formed the western corner of the Medina, but the sultan demolished the houses here to provide a grand approach to his palace quarter. Beyond the magnificent **Bab Mansour**, and straight ahead through a second gate, you will find yourself in an open square, on the right of which is a domed **Koubba**, once a reception hall for ambassadors to the imperial court. Below it, a stairway descends into a vast series of subterranean vaults, known as the **Prison of Christian Slaves** (daily 9am–noon & 3–5.30pm), though it was probably a storehouse or granary.

Ahead of the Koubba, within the wall and at right angles to it, are two modest gates. The one on the left opens onto an apparently endless corridor of walls and, a few metres down, the entrance to **Moulay Ismail's Mausoleum** (9am–12.30pm & 3pm–sunset, closed Fri pm). The fact that this tyrannical ruler's tomb has remained a shrine might seem puzzling, but his extreme Islamic orthodoxy and success in driving the Spanish from Larache and the British from Tangier have conferred a kind of magic on him. Entering the mausoleum, you are allowed to approach the sanctuary; decorated in bright *zellij* tilework and spiralling stucowork, it is a fine if unspectacular series of courts and chambers.

Past the mausoleum, a gate to your left gives access to the dilapidated quarter of **Dar El Kebira**, Ismail's palace complex. The imperial structures – the legendary fifty palaces – can still be made out between and above the houses here: ogre-like creations, whose scale is hard to believe. They were completed in 1677 and dedicated at an astonishing midnight celebration, when the sultan personally slaughtered a wolf so that its head might be displayed at the centre of the gateway. On the opposite side of the long-walled corridor, beyond the Royal Golf Gardens, more immense buildings are spread out, making up Ismail's last great palace, the **Dar El Makhzen**. At its end, and the principal "sight" of the Imperial City, is the **Heri as-Souani** – a series of storerooms and granaries that were filled with provisions for siege or drought. From the roof garden, with its café, you can gaze out across much of the Dar El Makhzen and the wonderfully still **Agdal Basin** – built as an irrigation reservoir and pleasure lake.

The Medina, although taking much of its present form and size under Moulay Ismail, bears less of his stamp. The **Dar Jamai** (9am–noon & 3–6pm, closed Tues), at the back of place El Hedim, is one of the best examples of a nineteenth-century Moroccan palace and the museum inside one of the best in Morocco. Its exhibits, some of which have been used to re-create the reception rooms, are predominantly of the same age, though some of the pieces of Fes and Meknes pottery date back to around Ismail's reign. The best display, however, is of Middle Atlas carpets, particularly those of the Beni Mguild tribe.

To get down into the **souks** from place El Hedim, follow the lane immediately behind the Dar Jamai. You will come out right in the middle of the Medina's major market street: on your left is **Souk en Nejjarin**, with the carpet *souk*; on your right, leading to the Grand Mosque and Bou Inania Medersa, are the fancier goods offered in the **Souk es Sebbat**. The **Bou Inania Medersa** (daily 9am–noon & 3–6pm) was constructed around 1340–50, and its most unusual feature is a ribbed dome over the entrance hall, an impressive piece of craftsmanship which extends right out into the *souk*. From the roof, to which there's usually access, you can look out to the tiled pyramids of the Grand Mosque; the *souk* is mostly obscured from view, but you can get a good, general panorama of the town.

Eating and drinking

For straight Moroccan **food** the *Restaurant Économique*, 123 rue Dar Smen, opposite Bab Mansour, is one of the better of the Medina's café/restaurants. In the heart of the Medina is the *Zitouna*, 44 rue Djemaa Zitouna, a bit fancier with good traditional food, while at the *Restaurant Riad*, in an old town house on 79 Ksar Chaacha, well-prepared Moroccan dishes are served in beautifully restored rooms or outdoors beside a sunken garden. The *Collier de la Colombe*, 67 rue Driba, is in an ornate mansion on the edge of the Medina; the international cuisine is outstanding and the prices reasonable. In the Ville Nouvelle, there is the reasonably priced *La Coupole*, on the corner of av Hassan II and rue Ghana, serving Moroccan and European food and with a bar and **nightclub**. On rue Atlas, near the *Hôtel Majestic*, off av Mohammed V, is the reliable *Pizzeria Le Four* (pasta and pizzas). Almost opposite is *La Gringote*, serving a mixture of French and Moroccan dishes at modest prices. There are also a surprising number of **bars**, several of them in Ville Nouvelle hotels. Swing doors and sawdust on the floor are the self-image of *Club de Nuit,* near the *Hôtel Excelsior* on av des FAR.

Volubilis and Moulay Idriss

The classic excursions from Meknes, **Volubilis** and **Moulay Idriss** embody much of Morocco's early history – Volubilis as its Roman provincial capital, Moulay Idriss as the source of the country's first Arab dynasty. The sites stand 4km apart, at either side of a deep and very fertile valley, about 30km north of Meknes. You can take in both on a leisurely day trip from Meknes by *grand taxi* or bus – non-Muslims have no choice when it comes to Moulay Idriss, as only Muslims are allowed to stay there. It is simplest to visit Volubilis first, then go on to Moulay Idriss, where you can pick up a bus or *grand taxi* returning to Meknes.

Volubilis

Visible for miles from the bends in the approach road, **VOLUBILIS** occupies the ledge of a long, high plateau. Volubilis was the Roman Empire's remotest city, but direct Roman rule lasted little more than two centuries – the garrison withdrew in 285 AD, to ease pressure elsewhere. The city itself remained active well into the eighteenth century, when its marble was carried away by slaves for the building of Meknes. What you are able to see today, well excavated and maintained, are largely the ruins of second- and third-century AD buildings – impressive and affluent creations from its period as a colonial capital. The entrance to the site (daily 9am–sunset; 20dh) is through a minor gate set into the city wall, built in 168 AD following a series of Berber insurrections. Just inside are the ticket office, a shaded café/bar and a small, open-air **museum** of sculpture and other fragments. The best of the finds made here – which include a superb collection of bronzes – have all been taken to the Rabat museum. Volubilis has, however, retained the great majority of its **mosaics**, some thirty or so in a good state of preservation.

Moulay Idriss

MOULAY IDRISS takes its name from its founder, Morocco's most venerated saint and the creator of its first Arab dynasty. His tomb and *zaouia* (sanctuary) – the object of constant pilgrimage – lie right at the heart of the town. Even today, open to non-Muslims for almost seventy years, it is still a place which feels closed and introspective. On arrival you find yourself below an elongated square near the base of the town; above you, almost directly ahead, stand the green-tiled pyramids of **Moulay Idriss' shrine and zaouia**. Rebuilt by Moulay Ismail, the shrine stands cordoned off from the street by a low, wooden bar to keep out Christians and beasts of burden. To get a true sense of it, you have to climb up towards one of the vantage points near the pinnacle of each quarter.

Fes

The most ancient of the imperial capitals, **FES** is a place that stimulates your senses – with haunting and beautiful sounds, infinite visual details and unfiltered odours – and seems to exist suspended somewhere between the Middle Ages and the modern world. Some 200,000 of the city's approximately half-million inhabitants continue to live in an extraordinary Medina "city" – Fes El Bali – which owes absolutely nothing to the West besides its electricity, video-rental shops and tourists. By building a new European city– the Ville Nouvelle –

nearby, and then transferring Fes' economic and political functions to Rabat, the French ensured both the city's eclipse and the preservation of its Medina. The decline of the city notwithstanding, **Fassis** – the people of Fes – have a reputation throughout Morocco for being successful and sophisticated.

Arrival and information

The **train station** is situated in the Ville Nouvelle, fifteen minutes' walk from the concentration of hotels around place Mohammed V. If you prefer to stay in the Medina, either take a *petit taxi* or walk down to av Hassan II, where you can pick up the #9 bus to Dar Batha/place de l'Istiqlal, near Bab Boujeloud – the western gate to Fes El Bali. Be prepared for hustlers: Fes rivals Marrakesh in this respect, and here the station is the key locale. The new Gare Routière **bus station** is outside the walls of Fes El Bali, above Bab Mahrouk. The new terminal for CTM buses is off rue Atlas, which links the far end of av Mohammed V with place d'Atlas. **Grands taxis** operate from both bus stations, from place Baghdadi by Bab Boujeloud and from place de la Résistance (aka La Fiat) in the Ville Nouvelle – depending on the destination.

The Medina is actually two separate cities: Fes El Bali, the oldest part, and Fes El Djedid, the "New Fes" established in the thirteenth century. Fes El Bali, where you'll want to spend most of your time, is an incredibly intricate web of lanes, blind alleys and *souks*. A half-day **tour** with an official guide is a useful introduction to Fes El Bali; they can be hired from the tourisme office or outside the upmarket hotels – look for the official guide medallion worn round the neck. The **tourisme** office is on place de la Résistance (Mon–Fri 8.30am–noon & 2.30–6.30pm; ☎05/62.34.60), where you can find out about the *Son et Lumière* shows started in 1994 in Fes El Bali (currently March, April, Oct & Nov 7.15pm; May–Sept 9.30pm). Ask too about the seven-day **Festival of World Sacred Music** (May–June), which includes concerts, films, lectures and exhibitions; more details can be obtained from Association Fes-Saïss, Sidi El Khayat, BP629 (☎05/63.54.00).

Accommodation

There is a shortage of **hotel** space in all categories, so be prepared for higher than usual prices and try to phone ahead. If you are not overly concerned about the size and cleanliness of your room, then the **Medina** is the place to be, but you will be paying well over the odds for a distinctly flea-pit environment. In the **Ville Nouvelle**, there is a much wider choice of hotels – most of them adequate, if unexciting, but close to the restaurants and bars, and the train station and CTM terminal.

One of the best Moroccan **youth hostels**, at 18 rue Abdeslam Serghini, is currently closed for renovation. The nearest **campsite** is *Camping Diamant Vert*, Aïn Chkeff (☎05/60.83.67), 6km south of the city and off the road to Ifrane.

HOTELS IN MEDINA

Du Commerce, place des Alaouites, Fes El Djedid, and facing the golden doors of the royal palace (☎05/62.22.31). Still owned by a Jewish family; old, but comfortable and friendly, with a lively café at street level. ①.

Cascade, on the square just inside the Bab Boujeloud, Fes El Bali (☎05/63.84.42). An old building, which incorporates a useful public *hammam*. Small rooms, but clean and friendly; the first to fill daily. ①.

Erraha, place Boujeloud, Fes El Bali (☎05/63.32.26). The cheapest place around and, for the price, reasonable enough. ①.

Lamrani, Talâa Seghira, Fes El Bali (☎05/63.44.11). Friendly with small but acceptable rooms, mostly doubles. Opposite an old *hammam*, it's in the heart of the Medina. ①.

HOTELS IN VILLE NOUVELLE

Amor, 31 rue Arabie Saoudite, formerly rue du Pakistan (☎05/62.33.04). One block from av Hassan II, behind the Banque du Maroc. Attractive tiled frontage, bar, restaurant and reasonable rooms. ②.

Grand, bd Abdallah Chefchaouni (☎05/93.20.26). Old colonial hotel opposite the sunken park on place Mohammed V. Prices vary according to season and length of stay. ②.

Ibis (previously *Moussafir*), place de la Gare (☎05/65.19.02). One of a new chain of hotels built beside train stations, with restaurant, bar and small swimming pool. Look for the blue and white house style. ③.

Mounia, 60 rue Asilah (☎05/62.48.38). Modern hotel with friendly management. Restaurant and popular bar which can be noisy. ②.

Nouzha, 7 av Hassan Dkhissi (☎05/64.00.02). Splendid new hotel with mosaic tilework, rich carpeting and natural wood. In an out-of-centre district unknown to tourists but only twenty minutes' walk from the centre and convenient for the new CTM terminal. ②.

Olympic, on a small street off av Mohammed V (known in colonial days as rue 3), facing one side of the covered market (☎05/93.26.82). Newly renovated, and with a unique collection of colonial travel posters; used by Explore and young groups. ②.

Du Pacha, 32 av Hassan II (☎05/65.22.90). An old-style downmarket hotel, favoured by Moroccans in town; useful as backup if the others are full or funds are low. ①.

Rex, 32 place Atlas (☎05/64.21.33). Built in 1910, small and congenial. The new CTM terminal nearby has given *Rex* a new lease of life. ①.

Royal, 36 rue es Soudan (☎05/62.46.56). In no-man's land, near – and preferable to – the *Kairouan*. All rooms have a toilet, and some have showers too. ①.

Fes El Bali

The area around **Bab Boujeloud** is today the principal entrance to Fes El Bali: a place with a great concentration of cafés and stalls where people come to talk and stare. Before heading into the Medina proper, take a look at the elegant **Dar Batha** palace, designed for the reception of ambassadors and now a **Museum of Moroccan Arts and Crafts** (8.30am–noon & 2.30–6.30pm, closed Tues). The collections are probably the finest of their kind in Morocco, and the courtyards and gardens a good respite from the general exhaustion of the Medina.

Talâa Kebira (or rue du Grand Talâa) is the major artery of the Medina, and with its continuations runs through to the Kairaouine Mosque and is lined with shops and stalls for virtually its whole length. About one hundred metres down is the most brilliant of Fes' monuments, the **Medersa Bou Inania**. Established as a rival to the Kairaouine university, and for a while the most important religious building in the city, it comes close to perfection in every aspect of its construction. In addition, it is the city's only building still in religious use that you are allowed into; you cannot enter the prayer hall but you can sit in the marble courtyard and gaze across to it (8am–noon & 2–6pm, closed Fri am).

Making your way down Talâa Kebira you will come to an arched gateway marked **Souk El Attarin** (Souk of the Spice Vendors); this is the formal heart of the city, and its richest and most sophisticated shopping district. The principal landmark to the south of the Souk El Attarin is the **Zaouia Moulay Idriss II**, one of the holiest buildings in the city. As you look in from the doorway, the tomb of Moulay Idriss II is over on the left, and a scene of intense devotion is usually going on around it.

Standing at the women's entrance to the *zaouia*, you'll see a lane off to the left – **rue du Bab Moulay Ismail** – full of stalls selling candles and silverware for devotional offerings. If you follow this lane around to the wooden bar, go under the bar (turning to the right), and then keep to your left, you should come out in the picturesque square of **place Nejjarin** (Carpenters' Square). Here is the very imposing **Nejjarin Fondouk**, built in the early eighteenth century along with a beautiful canopied fountain on one side of the square. In the alleys off the square, you'll find the **Nejjarin Souk**, easily located by the sounds and smells of the carpenters chiselling away at cedar wood. The nearby **Souk El Henna**, a tree-shaded square adjoining what was once the largest madhouse in the Merenid Empire, sells henna and the usual cosmetics, as well as more esoteric ingredients for aphrodisiacs and other magical spells. Pottery stalls are gradually encroaching on the traditional pharmaceutical business.

All roads in Fes El Bali lead to **El Kairaouine**, the largest mosque in the country until the completion of the Grande Mosquée Hassan II in Casablanca, one of the oldest universities in the world, and the fountainhead of Moroccan religious life. The mosque was founded in 857 by a Tunisian woman, a wealthy refugee from the city of Kairouan, but its present dimensions, with sixteen aisles and room for 20,000 worshippers, are essentially the product of tenth- and twelfth-century reconstructions. The mosque is enmeshed in houses and shops –

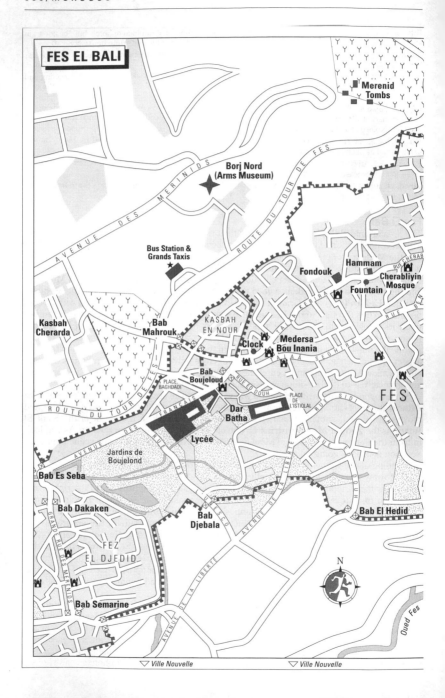

FES EL BALI

Merenid Tombs

Borj Nord
(Arms Museum)

Bus Station &
Grands Taxis

Fondouk

Hammam

Cherabliyin
Mosque

Fountain

Kasbah
Cherarda

Bab
Mahrouk

KASBAH
EN NOUR

Clock

Medersa
Bou Inania

FES

Bab
Boujeloud

PLACE
BAGHDADI

Dar
Batha

PLACE
DE
L'ISTIQLAL

Lycée

Jardins de
Boujelond

Bab Es Seba

Bab Dakaken

Bab
Djebala

Bab El Hedid

FEZ
EL DJEDID

Bab Semarine

N

▽ *Ville Nouvelle* ▽ *Ville Nouvelle*

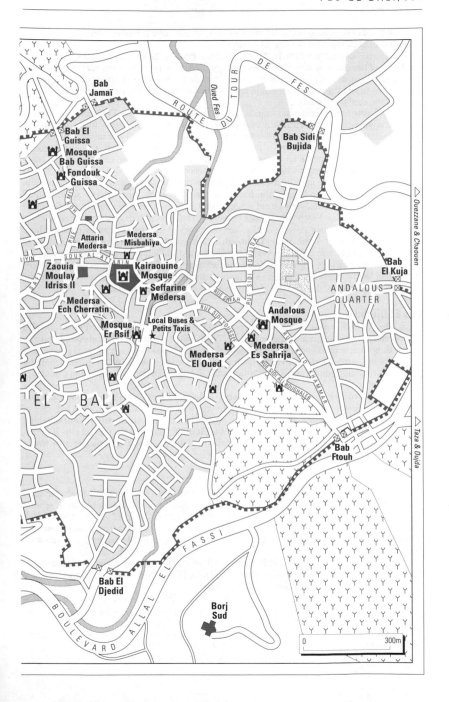

the best point of reference is the Attarin Medersa, whose fairly prominent bronze door is just to the north at the far end of Souk El Attarin.

The fourteenth-century **Attarin Medersa** (8am–noon & 2–6pm) is, after the Bou Inania, the finest of the city's medieval colleges, with an incredible profusion and variety of patterning. Its lightness of feel is achieved by the relatively simple device of using pairs of symmetrical arches to join the pillars to a single lintel – a design repeated in the upper floors and mirrored in the courtyard basin.

The east gate to the Kairaouine stands right opposite the **Palais de Fes**, a nineteenth-century mansion now converted into a restaurant and rug shop. Nearby is **place Seffarine**, almost wilfully picturesque with its faience fountain, gnarled fig trees and metalworkers hammering away. Just off the square is the entrance to the **Seffarine Medersa**. Built around 1285, the Seffarine is unlike all the other *medersas* in that it takes the exact form of a traditional Fassi house, with an arched balcony above its courtyard.

If you're beginning to find the medieval prettiness of the central *souks* and *medersas* slightly unreal, then the region beyond the Kairaouine, with its dyers' and tanners' *souks*, should provide the antidote. The dyers' street – **Souk Sabbighin** – is directly south of the Seffarine Medersa, and is draped with fantastically coloured yarn and cloth drying in the heat. Below, workers in grey, chimney-sweep's clothes toil over ancient cauldrons of multicoloured dyes. The tanneries quarter – the **Souk Dabbaghin** – is constantly being visited by groups of tourists, with whom you could discreetly tag along for a while if you get lost. Otherwise, follow your nose or accept a guide up from the Seffarine. Inside the tanneries, water deluges through holes that were once windows of houses, and hundreds of skins lie spread out on the rooftops, above vats of dye and the pigeon dung used to treat the leather.

Fes El Djedid

Unlike Fes El Bali, whose development seems to have been almost organic, **Fes El Djedid** was an entirely planned city, begun around 1273 by Sultan Abou Youssef and completed in a manic three years. It was occupied largely by the **Dar El Makhzen**, a vast royal palace, and by a series of army garrisons. The French Protectorate left Fes El Djedid greatly changed and somewhat moribund – as a "government city" it had no obvious role after the transfer of power to Rabat.

Walking down to Fes El Djedid from **Bab Boujeloud** involves a shift in scale. Gone are the labyrinthine alleyways and *souks* of the Medina, to be replaced by a massive expanse of walls. Within them, to your left, are a series of gardens: the private **Jardins Beida**, behind the Lycée, and then the public **Jardins de Boujeloud**, a vital lung for the old city. If everything gets to be too much, wander in, lounge about on the grass and spend an hour or two at the tranquil **café**, by an old waterwheel at their west corner.

Eating and drinking

Cafés are plentiful in the Ville Nouvelle, with some of the most popular along av Mohammed es Slaoui and av Mohammed V. Fes El Bali has two main areas for **budget eating**: around Bab Boujeloud and along rue Hormis (which runs up from Souk El Attarin toward Bab Guissa), but for a cheap, solid option, it's best to try one of the café/restaurants near the municipal market in the Ville Nouvelle – on the left-hand side of av Mohammed V as you walk from the post office.

For **bars**, you have to look a little harder. There are the usually lively *Es Saada* on av Mohammed es Slaoui and the seedy but cheap *Dailla*, 17 av Mohammed V. Failing those, try the hotel bars: the *Lamdaghri*, *Mounia* or *Splendid*.

Café Restaurant des Jeunes (aka Chez Hamid), place Boujeloud. Cheap and basic – soups and kebabs.

Chamonix, 5 rue Moukhtar Soussi, off av Mohammed V. A reliable restaurant serving Moroccan and European dishes. Attracts a young crowd, and stays open until late in summer.

La Cheminée, 6 av Lalla Asma (aka rue Chenguit) on the road to the train station. Small and friendly licensed restaurant, moderate prices. Open noon–3pm & 7–11pm, closed Sun in low season.

Chez Vittoria Pizzeria, 21 rue du Nador, opposite *Hôtel Central*. Pizza and pasta; reliable and value for money, but not very exciting.

Fish Friture, 138 av Mohammed V, at the far end of a short passageway off the main street. Fish dishes are the mainstay, but there is much else on offer. Courteous and quick.

Marrakesh, 11 rue Abes Tazi (between *Hôtel Mounia* and the old CTM terminal). Small, but good and cheap, with a limited menu; recently done up.

Nautilis, in the basement of *Hôtel le Paix* on av Hassan II. Renowned for its seafood.

Zagora, 5 av Mohammed V in a small arcade, behind the Derby shoe shop. New, and a little pretentious, but the food and service are well above average.

Listings

Car rental Avis, 50 bd Abdallah Chefchaouni (☎05/62.67.46); Budget, corner of rue Bahrein and av Hassan II (☎05/62.09.19) and alongside *Hôtel Palais Jamai*, Bab Guissa (☎05/63.43.31); Hertz, bd Lalla Meryem, 1 Kiwsariat de la Foire (☎05/62.28.12); Tourvilles, 15 rue Houmam Fetouaki, off bd Mohammed V (☎05/62.66.35).

Exchange The BMCE on place Mohammed V is the best of the banks.

Pharmacies Pharmacie du Municipalité, just up from place de la Résistance (aka La Fiat), on av Abdelkrim El Khattabi (☎05/62.33.80; open 24hr).

Police Commissariat Central is on av Mohammed V (☎19).

Post office The main PTT is on the corner of avenues Mohammed V and Hassan II (summer 8am–2pm; winter 8.30am–noon & 2.30–6pm). Poste restante is in the main building; the phone section (open until 9pm) has a separate side entrance.

RABAT AND THE SOUTH

Rabat and **Casablanca** are the power axis of the nation – respectively the seats of government and of industry and commerce. They've acquired their pre-eminence almost entirely in the last sixty years, so French and post-colonial influences are dominant. Don't show up in "Casa" expecting it to look "Moroccan" – it looks like Marseille. Likewise Rabat, though this is one of the best places to make for as soon as you arrive in the country: the city is well connected by train with Tangier, Fes and Marrakesh, and in addition, it makes an easy cultural shift in which to gain confidence. With the old port of **Salé**, facing Rabat across the estuary, it also has some of Morocco's finest and oldest monuments.

Marrakesh has always been something of a pleasure city, a marketplace where the southern tribesmen and Berber villagers bring their goods, spend their money and find entertainment. For tourists it's an enduring fantasy, given added allure by the **High Atlas**, the grandest Moroccan mountain range, and the proximity of **Essaouira**, the country's best resort.

Rabat

Capital of the nation since independence – and, before that, from 1912 to 1956, of the French Protectorate – **RABAT** is elegant in its spacious European grid, slightly self-conscious in its modern ways, and, as an administrative centre, a little bit dull. However, Rabat's monuments punctuate the span of Moroccan history, for both the Phoenicians and Carthaginians established trading posts here. The Arab city was largely the creation of the Almohad Caliph Yacoub El Mansour, whose twelfth-century legacy includes the superb Oudaïa Gate, Bab er Rouah at the southwest edge of town, and the early stages of the Hassan Mosque. After Mansour's death, Rabat fell into neglect until it was resettled by fifteenth-century Andalusian refugees, who rebuilt the Medina in a style reminiscent of their homes in Spanish Badajoz. Their pirate state survived until the time of Moulay Rashid, when Rabat finally reverted to government control.

Arrival and accommodation

The **Rabat Ville train station** is at the heart of the Ville Nouvelle, with most of the classified hotels situated only a few minutes' walk away; if you are coming from Casablanca, the train passes through the smaller Rabat Agdal train station, which is 2km from the centre –

don't get off here. The main **bus** terminal is in place Zerktouni, roughly 3km out from the centre; to get into the town itself, you'll have to take a local bus or compete for a *grand taxi* from there into Rabat. An easier option, if you are coming by bus from the north, is to get off in Salé and take a *grand taxi* from there into Rabat. **Taxis** for non-local destinations operate from outside the main bus station. Those to Casa cost only a couple of dirhams more than the bus and leave more or less continuously. Local bus services radiate from the corner of rue Nador and bd Hassan, where *petits taxis* and *grands taxis*, particularly for Salé and beyond, can also be found.

Accommodation can be a little difficult to find in midsummer and during festivals. It's perhaps best, arriving at any time of year, to make an advance reservation by phone if at all possible. Unless stated otherwise, the places listed below are in the Ville Nouvelle. The adequate **youth hostel**, 43 rue Marrassa (☎07/72.57.69; ①; daily 8–10am, noon–3pm & 6–10.30pm), is sited just outside the Medina walls and north of bd Hassan II; it's hard to find as the space between it and the boulevard has become a truck park and is overrun by shacks – if you arrive at night, don't come alone. The nearest **campsite** is *Camping de la Plage* (☎07/78.23.68), across the river at Salé. There are more, and better, campsites south of Rabat on the beaches between Rabat and Mohammedia. The nearest are at Erg Chiana, 24km south of Rabat.

Berlin, 261 av Mohammed V (☎07/72.34.35). Small hotel with hot showers. Centrally located above the Chinese *Restaurant Hong Kong*. Good value for money. ①.

Central, 2 rue Al Basra (☎07/70.73.56). Central position near train station and alongside better-known *Hôtel Balima* on av Mohammed V. A reasonable budget choice and, with 34 rooms, likely to have space. ①.

Dorhmi, 313 av Mohammed V, Medina, just inside Bab Djedid (☎07/72.38.98). Above the *Café Essalem* and Banque Populaire. Well furnished and maintained; highly recommended. Hot showers cost extra. ①.

Gaulois, corner of rue Hims and av Mohammed V (☎07/72.30.22). One of a cluster of budget hotels around the bottom end of av Mohammed V; reasonable for the price. ②.

Majestic, 121 av Hassan II (☎07/72.29.97). Once an old hotel with fading charm, it has undergone a complete make-over and is still popular and good value; across the road from the Medina. ②.

D'Orsay, 11 av Moulay Youssef, on place de la Gare (☎07/70.13.19). Convenient for train station and café-restaurants, this is a friendly, helpful and efficient hotel, and a good mid-range alternative to older *Hôtel Balima*. Breakfast included. ②.

Splendid, 8 rue Ghazza (☎07/72.32.83). Old hotel which has a sense of better days; the best rooms overlook a courtyard. Opposite is *Café-Restaurant Ghazza*, good for breakfast and a snack any time. ②.

Terminus, 384 av Mohammed V (☎07/70.52.67). A good alternative to the *Hôtel D'Orsay* round the corner. A large, featureless block, but the interior has been updated. ③.

Des Voyageurs, 8 Souk Semarine, Medina, near Bab Djedid (☎07/72.37.20). Incredibly cheap, popular, and often full. There are no showers. ①.

The City

Rabat's **Medina** – all that there was of the city until the French arrived in 1912 – is a compact quarter, wedged on two sides by the sea and the river, on the others by the Almohad and Andalusian walls. From **bd Hassan II**, a series of streets give access to the Medina, all of them leading more or less directly through the quarter, to emerge near the Kasbah and the old cemetery. At right angles to these run the main market street, **rue Souika**, and its continuation **Souk es Sebbat**, behind which lies a residential area scattered with smaller *souks* and "parish" mosques.

North lies **Kasbah des Oudaïas**, a striking quarter whose principal gateway – **Bab El Kasbah** or Oudaïa Gate – is perhaps the most beautiful in the Moorish world. Built around 1195, the gate was the heart of the Kasbah, its chambers acting as a courthouse and state-rooms, with everything important taking place within its confines. It impresses not so much by its size as by the strength and simplicity of its decoration, based on a typically Islamic rhythm which establishes a tension between the exuberant, outward expansion of the arches and the heavy, enclosing rectangle of the gate itself.

You can get into the **Kasbah** proper through the Oudaïa Gate or by means of a lower, horseshoe arch that you'll find at the base of the ceremonial stairway. This latter approach leads directly to the **Palace** built by Moulay Ismail, now housing a **Museum of Moroccan**

Arts (9am–noon & 3–5.30pm, closed Tues), which features Berber and Arab jewellery from most regions of Morocco and traditional costumes which reveal the startling closeness of the medieval past. However, be warned that, at any one time, some of the exhibits are undergoing restoration or are out on loan and collections described in the publicity are often inexplicably absent. The adjoining **Andalusian Garden** – one of the most delightful spots in the city – was actually constructed by the French in the present century, though true to Spanish-Andalusian tradition, with deep, sunken beds of shrubs and flowering annuals. It has a pleasant Mauresque café.

The most ambitious of all Almohad buildings, the **Hassan Mosque** with its vast minaret dominates almost every view of the capital. Designed by El Mansour as the centrepiece of the new capital, the mosque seems to have been more or less abandoned at his death in 1199. The minaret, despite its apparent simplicity, is perhaps the most complex of all Almohad structures; each facade is different, with a distinct combination of patterning, yet the whole intricacy of blind arcades and interlacing curves is based on just two formal designs. Facing the tower are the **Mosque** and **Mausoleum of Mohammed V**, begun on the sultan's death in 1961 and dedicated six years later. The mosque, extending between a pair of stark white pavilions, gives a somewhat foreshortened idea of how the Hassan Mosque must once have appeared, roofed in its traditional green tiles. The Mausoleum, with its brilliantly surfaced marbles and spiralling designs, pays homage to traditional Moroccan techniques, though fails to capture their rhythms and unity. It is, nevertheless, an important shrine for Moroccans – and one which, unusually, non-Muslims are permitted to visit.

On the opposite side of the Ville Nouvelle from the mausoleum is the **Archeological Museum**, rue Brihi (9–11.30am & 2.30–5.30pm, closed Tues), the most important in Morocco. Although small, it has a quite exceptional and beautiful collection of Roman-era bronzes, found mainly at Volubilis, including superb figures of a guard dog and a rider, and two magnificent portrait heads, reputedly Cato the Younger and Juba II – the last significant ruler of the Romanized Berber kingdoms of Mauretania and Numidia.

The most beautiful of Moroccan ruins, the royal burial ground called the **Chellah** (daily 8.30am–6.30pm), is a startling sight as you emerge from the long avenues of the Ville Nouvelle, with its circuit of fourteenth-century walls – the legacy of **Abou El Hassan** (1331–51), the greatest of Merenid rulers. Off to the left of the main gate – whose strange turreted bastions create an almost Gothic appearance – are the partly excavated ruins of the Roman city that preceded the necropolis. A set of Islamic ruins are further down to the right, situated within a second inner sanctuary which is approached along a broad path through half-wild gardens. You enter directly into the courtyard of Abou Youssef's Mosque, behind which is a series of scattered royal tombs, each aligned so that the dead, dressed in white and lying on their right-hand sides, may face Mecca to await the Call of Judgment. The nearby *zaouia* – a kind of monastery-shrine – is in a much better state of preservation, its long, central court enclosed by cells, with a small oratory at the end.

Eating and drinking

Rabat has a wide range of good **restaurants** serving both Moroccan and international dishes. As ever, the cheapest ones are to be found in the Medina. Just on the edge of the quarter, down rue Mohammed V and along rue Souika, there is a string of good everyday café/restaurants – clean enough and serving regular Moroccan fare. In the Ville Nouvelle, restaurants are grouped around the train station, place de la Gare and av Moulay Youssef.

Try *Café-Restaurant de la Paix*, 1 av Moulay Youssef, place de la Gare, with a bar downstairs and a brasserie on the first floor – or eat outside in an old French-style glass corridor. *Café Français*, 3 av Moulay Youssef, is another upstairs restaurant, and arguably the best around the train station. *La Clef*, alongside *Hôtel d'Orsay* on rue Hatim, serves good French and Moroccan dishes upstairs, and has a small bar downstairs. Worthwhile, but more expensive, choices include *Restaurant Saïdoune*, in the mall at 467 av Mohammed V, opposite *Hôtel Terminus*, a good Lebanese restaurant run by an Iraqi, and *Fouquet*, 285 av Mohammed V, which, despite several changes of management, is still worth a visit. *Restaurant Hong Kong*, 261 av Mohammed V, does a good range of Chinese and Vietnamese dishes. For Spanish food try *La Bamba*, and for Italian specialities, go to *La Mamma* (with take-away and home delivery options); both are on rue Tanta, behind *Hôtel Balima*. Also on rue Tanta is the new and stylish *Restaurant Equinox*, with set and à la carte menus. All of these serve beer and wine with meals.

Unlicensed, better suited for lunch, and both on bd Hassan II, are *Café/Restaurant Shahrazade*, next to the *Hôtel Majestic*, with quick, friendly service in or out of doors, and *Café/Restaurant El Bahia*, set into the Andalusian wall, with reasonably priced Moroccan dishes served in a pleasant courtyard, upstairs or on the pavement outside. If you're looking for a treat, get away from the city centre at *L'Entrecôte* in Agdal at 74 bd Al Amir Fal Ould Omar (☎07/67.11.08) or the more expensive *Restaurant de la Plage* on the beach, below the Kasbah des Oudaïas (☎07/72.31.48); both specialize in fish.

Avenues Mohammed V and Allal Ben Abdallah have some good **cafés**, but **bars** are few and far between outside the main hotels. The one at the *Hôtel Balima* is as good a place as any. After the *Balima* has closed, late-night options include a string of disco/bars around place de Melilla and on rue Patrice Lumumba.

Listings

Airlines Royal Air Maroc (☎07/70.97.66) is just across from the train station on the opposite side of av Mohammed V; Air France (☎02/29.40.40) is on the same avenue at no. 281, just below *Hôtel Balima*.

Car rental. Try Avis, 7 rue Abou Faris Al Marini (☎07/76.79.59); Budget, Ville train station (☎07/70.57.89); Europcar-InterRent, 25 bis rue Patrice Lumumba (☎07/72.23.28); Hertz, 467 av Mohammed V (☎07/70.73.66); or Visacar, av Moulay Youssef, behind *Café Français*. But cheaper deals can be found in Casablanca.

Embassies Australia, at the British embassy; Britain, 17 bd Tour Hassan (☎07/72.09.05); Canada, 13 bis rue Jaafar as Sadiq, Agdal (☎07/67.28.80); Ireland, at the British embassy; USA, 2 av de Marrakesh (☎07/76.22.65).

Exchange Most banks are along av Allal Ben Abdallah and av Mohammed V. BMCE, 260 av Mohammed V (Mon–Fri 8am–noon & 2–7pm, Sat & Sun 10am–2pm & 4–7pm) and Ville train station (Mon–Fri 8am–noon & 3–7pm, Sat & Sun 9am–noon & 3–6pm), handles VISA, Mastercard, travellers' cheques, Eurocheques and cash.

Police Central office, rue Soekarno, a couple of blocks from av Mohammed V. Manned police post at Bab Djedid.

Post office The main PTT office is halfway down av Mohammed V, on the left-hand side and is open 24hr for telephones. The poste restante section, however, is across the road from the main building.

Salé and around

Although it is now essentially a suburb of Rabat, **SALÉ** was the pre-eminent of the two right through the Middle Ages. Today, largely neglected since the French creation of a capital in Rabat, it looks and feels very distinct. The spread of a Ville Nouvelle outside its walls has been restricted to a small area around the bus station and main gates, and the *souks* and life within its medieval limits remain surprisingly traditional. From Rabat you can cross to Salé by **boat** or take a **bus** (#6 or #12) from bd Hassan II.

As far as buildings go, the **Grand Mosque** marks the most interesting part of town, its surrounding lanes fronting a concentration of aristocratic mansions and religious foundations. Almohad in origin, the mosque is one of the largest and oldest in Morocco, though what you can see as a non-Muslim (the gateway and minaret) are recent additions. You can, however, visit its **Medersa** (10dh plus tip), opposite the mosque's monumental main entrance. Salé's main monument, it was founded in 1341 by Sultan Abou El Hassan, and is intensely decorated in carved wood, stucco and *zellij* tilework. Close to its entrance there is a stairway up to the windowless student cells and to the roof, where, looking out across to Rabat, you sense the enormity of the Hassan Tower.

The best beach in the area is the **Plage des Nations**, 18km north and reached by taking the #28 bus to the village of Bouknadel and then following the crowds. Flanked by a couple of beach cafés and the refurbished four-star *Hôtel Firdaous* (☎07/82.21.31) – a slick modern complex with a freshwater pool that's open to all for a small charge – the beach seems more

Westernized than Rabat itself. The waves are big and exciting, but there are dangerous currents, hence the lifeguards along the central strip.

Casablanca

Principal city of Morocco, and capital in all but administration, **CASABLANCA** is the largest port of the Maghreb – busier even than Marseille, on which it was modelled by the French. Casa's Westernized image – with the almost total absence of women wearing veils, and its fancy beach clubs – masks what is still substantially a "first generation" city and one which inevitably has some of Morocco's most intense social problems.

Some **trains** terminate at the **Gare des Voyageurs** (2km from the centre) rather than continuing on to the far better situated **Gare du Port**. Bus #30 runs into town from the Voyageurs – if you don't grab a seat, it's a twenty-minute walk or a *petit taxi* ride. All CTM **buses** arrive at the CTM Gare Routière on rue Léon l'Africain, behind the *Hôtel Safir* on av des FAR; **grands taxis** usually queue behind the CTM terminal.

It used to be said that Casa had not a single "real" monument. This was never quite true, but the city did undoubtedly lack any one single, great building: a position that, in part, prompted King Hassan II's decision to construct here the world's second largest mosque. The **Grande Mosquée Hassan II** (guided tours 9am, 10am, 11am & 2pm, except Fri; 100dh) has space for 100,000 worshippers (80,000 in the courtyard and 20,000 indoors) and a minaret that soars to a record 172 metres. Equally extraordinary is its cost – an estimated £320 million – and the fact that this was raised entirely by public subscription. It's a twenty-minute walk from the town centre.

The French city centre and its formal colonial buildings already seem to belong to a different and distant age. Grouped around **place Mohammed V**, they served as models for administrative architecture throughout Morocco. Their style, heavily influenced by Art Deco, is known as *Mauresque* – a French idealization and "improvement" on Moorish design. The **Old Medina**, above the port and recently gentrified, is largely the product of the late nineteenth century, when Casa began its modest growth as a commercial centre. It has a fairly affluent air, and is said to be the place to go to look for any stolen goods you might want to buy back.

You can get out to the beach suburb of **Aïn Diab** by bus #9 from bd de Paris, by *petit taxi* from around place des Nations Unies, or on foot. The beach starts around 3km out from the port and Old Medina, past the Grande Mosquée Hassan II, and continues for about the same distance. Aïn Diab's big attraction is not so much the sea as the **beach clubs** along its front. Each of these has one or more pools, usually filled with filtered seawater, plus a restaurant and a couple of snack bars.

Practicalities

Hotels are plentiful in Casa, though they run near capacity for much of the year. There are some unclassified hotels in the Medina, but there are better ones, and no dearer, in the centre: for example, *Mon Rêve*, 7 rue Chaouia (☎02/31.14.39; ①), is the best option in an area of cheap hotels. *Hôtel du Centre*, 1 rue Sidi Belyout/corner av des FAR (☎02/44.61.80; ②), is another golden oldie, with an antique lift and dicey wiring in the rooms. *Terminus*, 184 bd Ba Hamad (☎02/24.00.25; ①), is handy for the Gare des Voyageurs, and for eating places nearby. *Foucauld*, 52 rue Araibi Jilali (☎02/22.26.66; ①), is lauded as great value and is near several good café/restaurants. Very central are two old hotels which keep up appearances and are value for money: *Excelsior*, 2 rue El Amraoui Brahim, off place des Nations Unies (☎02/20.02.63; ②), which can get bad traffic noise, and *Plaza*, 18 bd Houphouët Boigny (☎02/29.78.22; ②), which has good facilities and front rooms offering views of the Grande Mosquée Hassan II.

The **youth hostel**, 6 place Ahmed Bidaoui (daily 8–10am & noon–11pm; ☎02/22.05.51; ①), is a friendly, well-maintained, airy place situated just inside the Medina, facing a small leafy square and signposted from the nearby Gare du Port. The nearest **campsite** – *Camping Oasis*, av Jean Mermoz, Beauséjour (☎02/25.33.67) – is 8km out on the P8 road to Azemmour and El Jadida (buses #19 & #35; car drivers should ask for the street market – Marché Beauséjour).

Casa has the reputation of being the best place to eat in Morocco, and if you can afford the fancier **restaurant** prices, this is certainly true. For anyone keeping to a budget, some of the best possibilities lie in the smaller streets off bd Mohammed V. *L'Étoile Marocaine*, 107 rue Allal Ben Abdallah (evenings only), has an ambitious menu and a good atmosphere, but is only open in the evenings. There are grills across the street on rue Chaouia (aka rue Colbert) – the best of these is *Rotisserie Centrale*. *La Corrida*, 85 rue El Araar, near the main post office, is an informal tapas-style Spanish restaurant run by a Spanish-French couple; and the stylish *Petit Poucet*, 86 bd Mohammed V, which still looks like a 1920s Parisian saloon, has a much cheaper snack bar next door – one of the best places for some serious drinking.

Down near the port is *Centre 2000*, with five good ethnic restaurants serving Spanish, French, Italian and Moroccan food; nearby the *Chiang Mai* serves Asiatic dishes. *Taverne du Dauphin*, 115 bd Houphouët Boigny, is a long-established and very popular fish restaurant – well worth the queue. *Restaurant des Fleurs*, 42 av des FAR, has a snack-bar/café, which is good for breakfast and serves evening meals upstairs.

Despite a scattering of more or less seedy clubs and **bars** on bd Mohammed V and bd Houphouët Boigny, nightlife in Casa is elusive. Given transport, it is better to explore the Aïn Diab coast road, bd de la Corniche. Look for *Le Balcon*, *Le Tube*, *La Notte*, *Calypso* and the lively *Palm Beach Club*.

Marrakesh

MARRAKESH is a city of immense beauty, low, pink and tent-like before a great shaft of mountains. It's an immediately exciting place, especially around the vast space of the Djemaa El Fna, the stage for a long-established ritual in which shifting circles of onlookers gather around groups of acrobats, drummers, pipe musicians, dancers, storytellers and comedians. Unlike Fes, for so long its rival as the nation's capital, Marrakesh exists very much in the present: its population is rising, it has a thriving industrial area and it remains the most important market and administrative centre of southern Morocco.

The **Djemaa El Fna** (referred to simply as "Djemaa", or even "la place") lies right at the heart of the Medina, and almost everything of interest is concentrated in the web of alleyways around it. Just to the west of the Djemaa, an unmistakable landmark, is the minaret of the great **Koutoubia** mosque (enchanting under floodlights at night) – in the shadow of which begins **avenue Mohammed V**, leading out of the Medina and up the length of the new city, **Gueliz**. It is a fairly long walk between Gueliz and the Medina, but there are plenty of **petits** and **grands taxis** and a regular **bus** (#1) between the two.

Arrival and information

From the **train station**, alongside Gueliz, you should take bus #3 or #8 or a *petit taxi* to get to the Djemaa. The **bus** terminal is just outside the northwestern walls of the Medina by Bab Doukkala – a 25-minute walk to the Djemaa, or again a ride on the #3 or #8 bus or *petit taxi* (8–10dh). The city's **airport** is 5km to the southwest; the #11 bus is supposed to run every thirty minutes to the Djemaa, but it is very erratic – *petits taxis* or *grands taxis* are a better option.

The tourist-friendly **GRIT** (Groupement Régional d'Interêt Touristique) at 170 av Mohammed V (Mon–Fri 8.30am–noon & 2.30–6pm, Sat 8.30am–noon; ☎04/43.10.16) has replaced the Syndicat d'Initiative previously at that address. It contains a Banque Populaire kiosk for changing money, travellers' cheques and Eurocheques. The **tourisme** office, place Abdelmoumen Ben Ali, is still open but has little to offer; for an official guide you'd be better off asking at your hotel. You can ask at either for details of the two-week Festival National des Arts Populaires, which is sometimes held in June.

Accommodation

The Medina, as ever, has the main concentration of cheap places – most of them quite pleasant – and, unusually, has a fair number of classified hotels too. Given the attractions of the Djemaa El Fna and the *souks*, this is the first choice. The main advantages of Gueliz and

Hivernage hotels are their convenience for the train station and their swimming pools, a major consideration in a city where the midday temperature can hit 130°F. At certain times of year, for example during religious festivals and when the king is in residence, the city has a shortage of accommodation, so **advance bookings** are a wise idea. All hotels are in the Medina unless stated otherwise. The improved **youth hostel** is on rue El Jahid, Gueliz (8–9am & 2–10pm; IYHF card holders given priority; ☎04/44.77.13; ①), close to the train station. The nearest **campsite**, *Camping Ferdaous* (☎04/31.31.67), 13km out of town on the P7, direction Casablanca, is a feasible option only if you have your own transport.

HOTELS

Ali, rue Moulay Ismail (☎04/44.49.79). Popular – almost legendary – small hotel with showers in rooms. Has a good, inexpensive restaurant serving à la carte lunch and buffets in the evenings. ③.

CTM, Djemaa El Fna (☎04/44.23.25). Located above the old bus station; decent-sized rooms, which are clean and relatively cheap. ①.

Farouk, 66 av Hassan II, on the corner with rue Mauretania, Gueliz (☎04/43.19.89). Excellent hotel with popular restaurant, within walking distance of the train station. ①.

Gallia, 30 rue de la Recette (☎04/44.59.13). Pleasant building in a quiet road; airy and spotless rooms off two tiled courtyards. Highly recommended – reserve ahead if possible. ②.

La Gazelle, 12 rue Bani Marine (☎04/44.11.12). A modern hotel with bright airy rooms and hot showers, on a street with a row of outdoor foodstalls. Reductions for long stays. ①.

Ichbilia, off rue Bani Marine (☎04/32.04.86). Quite new, and wearing well, with rooms off a courtyard and balcony; sometimes called *Sevilla* by Moroccans (*Ichbilia* is Arabic for Seville). ①.

Islane, 279 av Mohammed V, facing the Koutoubia minaret (☎04/44.00.81). The traffic outside makes it a bit noisy, but the view of Koutoubia and the comfortable modern rooms compensate. ②.

Medina, 1 Derb Sidi Bouloukat (☎04/44.29.97). A real gem: small, clean, family-run. Good value, too, with hot showers included. Breakfast on the terrace. ①.

Du Pacha, 33 rue El Houria, aka de la Liberté, Gueliz (☎04/43.13.26), near the old covered market. Another old hotel, recently renovated and extended, with a reliable restaurant. ②.

Sherazade, 3 derb Djama, off rue Zitoun Kadem (☎04/42.93.05). Beautifully restored merchant's town house with a rooftop restaurant by arrangement. Seen as an overspill for the *Gallia*, but generally more expensive. ③.

Souria, 17 rue de la Recette (☎04/42.67.57). Deservedly popular and over one hundred years old. ①.

Toulousain, 44 rue Tariq Ben Ziad, Gueliz (☎04/43.00.33), near the old covered market. A bargain and famous locally as the hotel used by the Peace Corps. ②.

Des Voyageurs, 40 bd Mohammed Zerktouni, Gueliz (☎04/44.72.18). An old respectable hotel; unexciting, but good value. ①.

The City

There's nowhere in North Africa like the **Djemaa El Fna**: by day it's basically a market, with a few snake charmers and an occasional troupe of acrobats; in the late afternoon it becomes a whole carnival of musicians, clowns and entertainers and in the evening a couple of dozen "kitchens" are set up dispensing hot food. If you get tired of the spectacle, or if things slow down, you can move over to the rooftop terraces of the *Café de France* or the *Restaurant Argana* to gaze at it all from above. The absence of any architectural feature in the Djemaa serves to emphasize the drama of the **Koutoubia Minaret**, the focus of any approach to the city. Nearly seventy metres high and visible for miles on a clear morning, it was begun shortly after the Almohad conquest of the city, around 1150. It displays many of the features that were to become widespread in Moroccan architecture – the wide band of ceramic inlay near the top, the pyramid-shaped, castellated *merlons*, and the alternation of patterning on the facades.

THE NORTHERN MEDINA

On the northern corner of Djemaa El Fna itself there is a small potters' market, but the main **souk** area begins a little further beyond this. Its entrance is initially confusing. From the *Café de France*, look across the street and you'll see the *Café El Fath* and, beside it, a building with the sign "Tailleur de la place" – the lane between them will bring you out at the beginning of

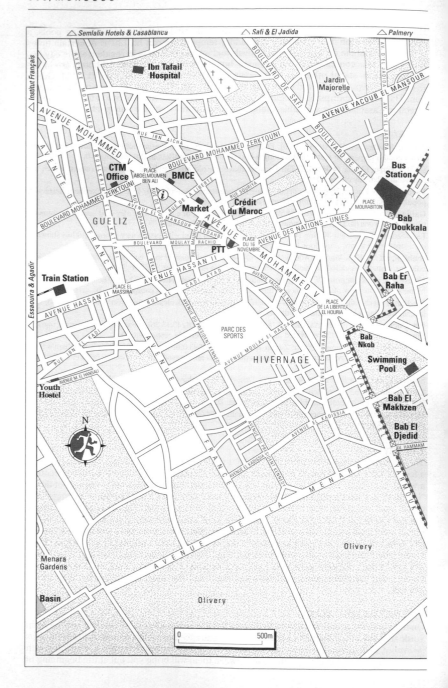

△ Semlalia Hotels & Casablanca   △ Safi & El Jadida   △ Palmery

Ibn Tafail Hospital

Jardin Majorelle

△ Institut Français

BOULEVARD DE SAFI

AVENUE YACOUB EL MANSOUR

AV DE L JADIDA

AVENUE MOHAMMED V

RUE IBN AICHA

BOULEVARD MOHAMMED ZERKTOUNI

BOULEVARD DE SAFI

Bus Station

CTM Office

PLACE ABDELMOUMEN BEN ALI

BMCE

PLACE MOURABITON

BOULEVARD MOHAMMED ZERKTOUNI

RUE DE LA LIBERTE

RUE SOURIYA

Market

Crédit du Maroc

Bab Doukkala

GUELIZ

AVENUE DE FRANCE

AVENUE DES NATIONS - UNIES

△ Essaouira & Agadir

BOULEVARD MOULAY RACHID

PLACE DU 16 NOVEMBRE

PTT

AVENUE HASSAN II

Bab Er Raha

Train Station

PLACE EL MASSIRA

AVENUE MOHAMMED V

PLACE DE LA LIBERTE EL HOURIA

AVENUE HASSAN II

RUE EL CADI AYAD

PARC DES SPORTS

Bab Nkob

RUE IBN EL KADI

HIVERNAGE

AVENUE MOULAY EL HASSAN

Swimming Pool

AVENUE M. EL HANGALI

Youth Hostel

AVENUE DE FRANCE

Bab El Makhzen

Bab El Djedid

AV HAMMAM

N

AVENUE DU PRESIDENT KENNEDY

AVENUE EL KADISSIA

AVENUE YARMOUK

Menara Gardens

AVENUE DE LA MENARA

Olivery

Basin

Olivery

0   500m

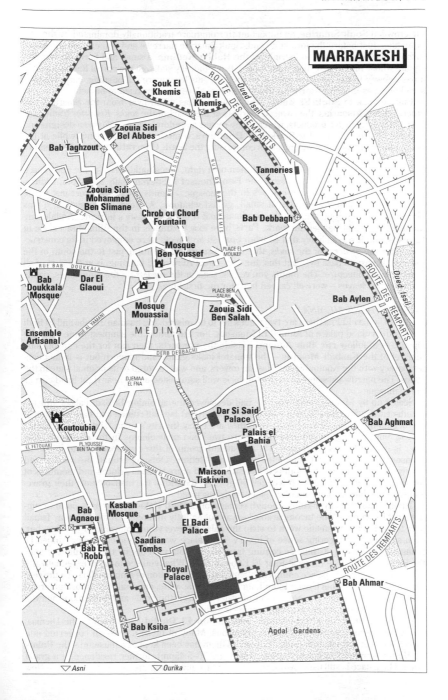

the crowded **Souk Smarine**, an important thoroughfare traditionally dominated by the sale of textiles. Just before the fork at its end, Souk Smarine narrows and you can get a glimpse through the passageways to its right of the **Rahba Kedima**, a small and fairly ramshackle square whose most interesting features are its apothecary stalls. At the end of Rahba Kedima, a passageway to the left gives access to another, smaller square – a bustling, carpet-draped area known as **la Criée Berbère**, which is where slave auctions used to be held.

Cutting back to **Souk El Kebir**, which by now has taken over from the Smarine, you emerge at the **kissarias**, the covered markets at the heart of the *souks*. *Kissarias* traditionally sell more expensive products, which today means a predominance of Western designs and imports. Off to their right is **Souk des Bijoutiers**, a modest jewellers' lane, while at the north end is a convoluted web of alleys comprising the **Souk Cherratin**, essentially a leather workers' *souk*.

If you bear left through this area and then turn right, you should arrive at the open space in front of the Mosque Ben Youssef. The **Ben Youssef Medersa** (daily 9am–5pm; 10dh) – the annexe for students taking courses in the mosque – stands off a side street just to the east, distinguishable by a series of small, grilled windows. A Merenid foundation, it was almost completely rebuilt under the Saadians, and it is this dynasty's intricate, Andalusian-influenced art that has left its mark. Parts have exact parallels in the Alhambra Palace in Granada, and it seems likely that Muslim Spanish architects were employed in its construction. After the *medersa* or the *souks*, the small **Almoravid Koubba**, just to the south of the mosque, is easy to pass by – but this, the only intact Almoravid building, is at the root of all Moroccan architecture. The motifs you've just seen in the *medersa* – the pine cones, palms and acanthus leaves – were all carved here for the first time.

THE SOUTHERN MEDINA

South of Djemaa El Fna there are two places not to be missed: the Saadian Tombs and El Badi Palace, the ruined palace of Ahmed El Mansour. For the tombs, the simplest route from the Djemaa is to follow **rue Bab Agnaou** outside the ramparts, then aim for the conspicuous minaret of the **Kasbah Mosque** – the minaret looks gaudy and modern but is in fact contemporary with the Koutoubia and Hassan towers, and was restored to its original state in the 1960s. The narrow passageway to the tombs is well signposted at the near right-hand corner of the mosque.

Sealed up by Moulay Ismail after he had destroyed the adjoining El Badi Palace, the sixteenth-century **Saadian Tombs** (daily 9am–5pm; 10dh) lay half-ruined and half-forgotten at the beginning of this century. Restored, they are today the city's main "sight" – overlavish, maybe, but dazzling nonetheless. There are two main mausoleums in the enclosure. The finer is on the left as you come in – a beautiful group of three rooms, built to house El Mansour's own tomb and completed within his lifetime. Outside, around the garden and courtyard, are scattered the tombs of over a hundred more Saadian princes and members of the royal household. Like the privileged 66 given space within the mausoleums, their gravestones are brilliantly tiled and often elaborately inscribed.

Though substantially in ruins, enough remains of **El Badi Palace** (daily 9am–5pm) to suggest that its name – "The Incomparable" – was not entirely immodest. It took Moulay Ismail over ten years of systematic work to strip the palace of everything movable or of value, but, even so, there's a lingering sense of luxury. The palace was begun shortly after Ahmed El Mansour's accession, its finance coming from the ransom paid out by the Portuguese after the Battle of the Three Kings at Ksar El Kebir in 1578. What you see today is essentially the ceremonial part of the palace complex, planned for the reception of ambassadors. To the rear extends the central court, over 130m long and nearly as wide, and built on a substructure of vaults in order to allow the circulation of water through the pools and gardens. When the pools are filled they are an incredibly majestic sight.

Heading north from El Badi Palace, **rue Zitoun El Djedid** leads back to the Djemaa, flanked by various nineteenth-century mansions. Many of these have been converted into carpet shops or tourist restaurants, but one of them has been kept as a museum – the **Palais El Bahia** (guided tours daily 8.30–11.45am & 2.30–5.45pm), former residence of a grand vizier. The palace is still used by the royal family (usually during the time of the Western New

Year) and there is no public admission at these times. The name of the building means "The Effulgence" or "Brilliance", but after the guided tour around the rambling palace courts and apartments you might feel this to be a somewhat tall claim. There is reasonable craftsmanship in the main reception halls, and a pleasant arrangement of rooms in the harem quarter, but for the most part it is all fabulously vulgar.

Also on this route is the Dar Si Said palace, which houses the **Museum of Moroccan Arts** (Mon, Wed, Thurs, Sat & Sun 9–11.45am & 2.30–5.45pm, Fri 9–11am & 3–5.45pm), particularly strong on its collections of southern Berber jewellery and weapons – large, boldly designed objects of great beauty. There are also fine displays of eighteenth- and nineteenth-century carving, modern Berber rugs and a curious group of traditional wedding chairs – once widely used for carrying the bride, veiled and hidden, to her new home.

A further superb collection of Moroccan art and artefacts is housed in the **Maison Tiskiwin** (daily 9.30am–12.30pm & 3–6pm), which lies between the El Bahia and Dar Si Said palaces at 8 rue de la Bahia; each room displays carpets, fabrics, clothes and jewellery from a different town or region.

If you are keen to buy the best in the *souks*, you should study the more or less fixed prices in the excellent **Ensemble Artesenal** (daily 9am–1pm & 3–7pm) just inside the ramparts on av Mohammed V.

THE GARDENS

With summer temperatures peaking in excess of 100°F it seems best to devote at least the middle of a Marrakesh day to inactivity. If you want to do this in style, it means finding your way to one of the two gardens – **Agdal** and **Menara** – designed for just this purpose. Each rambles through acres of orchards and olive groves, and has, near its centre, an immense, lake-size pool. This is all – they are not flower gardens, but, cool and completely still, they are a luxurious contrast to the close city streets. To get to either, take a *petit taxi* or a horse-drawn *calèche* from El Badi Palace or the Koutoubia.

A smaller garden, only twelve acres, is the meticulously planned botanical haven, created by the French painter Jacques Majorelle (1886–1962). **Jardin Majorelle** (daily: winter 8am–noon & 2–5pm; summer 8am–noon & 3–7pm; 15dh) – not to be missed – is entered from a small cul-de-sac off av Yacoub El Mansour, north of the bus station.

Eating and drinking

Gueliz, naturally enough, is where you'll find French-style **cafés** and **restaurants**, and virtually all of the city's **bars** – av Mohammed V is the busiest area. In the Medina, in addition to the spectacle of the Djemaa El Fna foodstalls, there's a fair range of inexpensive café/restaurants just off the Djemaa El Fna in rue Bani Marine.

In the **Medina**, three of the upmarket hotels have restaurants. The best of these is undoubtedly the *Hôtel Ali*, while second best is *Hôtel de Foucauld*, on av El Mouahidine. The *Grand Hôtel Tazi*, on nearby rue Bab Agnaou has a restaurant and the only bar in the Medina, but recently the cuisine has disappointed and the bar is no longer attractive.

Café Étoile de Marrakesh, on rue Bab Agnaou, is justifiably popular with the locals; eat upstairs on the balcony. Nearer to the Djemaa El Fna is the refurbished *L'Étoile Glacier*, which attracts a younger crowd, while – besides the terrace café of the *Hôtel CTM* – two other rooftop cafés overlook the Djemaa El Fna itself. There is the *Argana*, with regular French-Moroccan food, and the *Hôtel du Café de France*, where the restaurant is reasonable but the hotel itself is wretched – not to be confused with the *Hôtel de France*, at 197 rue Zitoun El Kadem.

Better – and dearer – than either of these is the *Restaurant al Baraka*, 1 Djemaa El Fna, by the Commissariat de Police; a French-Moroccan restaurant in a beautiful fountain courtyard (no credit cards accepted). Not far away from here, and facing the Koutoubia, is the *Pizzeria Venetia* on the roof terrace of the *Hotel Islane*, 279 Mohammed V; the food and view can be superb.

In **Gueliz**, there are many pavement **cafés** on av Mohammed V, particularly around place Abdelmoumen ben Ali, where bd Mohammed Zerktouni crosses av Mohammed V. The *Restaurant le Jacaranda*, 32 bd Mohammed Zerktouni, is an upmarket French restaurant;

Chez Jack'Line, 63 av Mohammed V, serves Italian, French and Moroccan dishes at competitive prices; *L'Entrecôte*, 55 bd Mohammed Zerktouni, is new and, despite the Hollywood decor, has an international menu well worth checking out; and *Le Catanzaro*, behind the old covered market on rue Tarik Ben Ziad, serves Continental fare and is popular with locals, particularly on weekends.

Listings

Airport information ☎04/44.78.26.

American Express c/o Voyages Schwarz, Immeuble Moutaoukil, 1 rue Mauritania (☎04/43.66.00). Open irregular hours.

Car rental Golden Tours, 113 av Abdelkrim El Khattabi (☎04/44.91.61), is a reliable agency, with branches in Agadir, Casablanca and Ouarzazate; they'll provide drivers if you want. Similar are Rabia Car, 11 rue Rahal Ben Ahmed (☎04/43.00.35), with a branch in Ouarzazate, and Najim Car, 21 rue Loubnane (☎04/43.78.91), with outlets in several hotels. Others can be found around av Mohammed V and bd Mohammed Zerktouni.

Doctor Dr Abdelmajid Bentbib, 171 av Mohammed V (☎04/43.10.30), is reliable and speaks English.

Exchange BMCE is the best bet for exchange and has branches in both the Medina (rue Moulay Ismail, facing place de Foucauld) and Gueliz (144 bd Mohammed V). Open daily 8am–8pm.

Pharmacies There are several along av Mohammed V, including Pharmacie de la Liberté just off place de la Liberté (or Houria), which has a doctor on call.

Post office The main PTT is on place du 16 Novembre, midway along av Mohammed V (Mon–Thur 8.30am–12.15pm & 2.30–6.30pm, Fri 8.30–11.30am & 3–6.30pm, Sat 8.30am–12.15pm; telephone section open until 9pm). The branch office on Djemaa El Fna is open similar hours.

The High Atlas

The **High Atlas**, the greatest mountain range of North Africa, is for many travellers the most beautiful and intriguing part of Morocco. A historical and physical barrier between the northern plains and the pre-Sahara, its Berber-populated valleys, Kasbahs and villages are very remote from the country's mainstream or urban life. When the French began their "pacification" in the 1920s, the Atlas way of life was essentially feudal, and even today, with the region under government control through a system of local *caids*, the Atlas Berbers are not taxed, nor do they receive any national benefits or services.

The **Toubkal National Park**, a rugged area enclosing the Atlas' highest peaks, is the goal of 95 percent of people who hike in Morocco. Unless you're undertaking a particularly long or ambitious hike – or are here in winter conditions – you don't need any special equipment, nor will you need to do any actual climbing. The main physical problems you'll find are the high altitudes (over 4000m in the Toubkal region), the midday heat and the tiring process of walking over long sections of scree.

Asni, Imlil and the ascent of Djebel Toubkal

The end of the line for the Marrakesh buses and *grands taxis*, **ASNI** is really little more than a roadside village and Saturday market – and a spot many hikers pass straight through to get up into the mountains. If you're in a hurry, this is good reasoning, though it's no disaster if you have to stay overnight. The all-year **youth hostel** (①) has no cooking facilities and you'll need your own sleeping bag. Heading on, the place you need to get to is **IMLIL**, 17km into the mountains on a rough road; pick-up vans and minibuses shuttle back and forth from Asni, along with larger lorries on Saturdays for the Asni *souk*. The established trailhead for Toukbal, Imlil comprises a small cluster of houses, along with many provisions shops, a prominent CAF (French Alpine Club) refuge and several cafés. Most hikers choose to stay at the **CAF refuge**, which is open all year round and provides bunk beds, camping mattresses and blankets, as well as kitchen and washing facilities and luggage storage. In addition, Imlil has two **hotels**, the *Étoile de Toubkal* (③) and the more basic *Hôtel-Café Soleil* (②), while several houses offer **rooms** and there are several official **gîtes**. A guides office can arrange mules, guides and the like for treks here and elsewhere in the mountains.

The ascent of **Djebel Toubkal** is a walk rather than a climb after the snows have cleared, but a serious business nonetheless: this is North Africa's highest mountain (4167m). The walk to the base is enjoyable in its own right, following the Mizane Valley to the village of **Aroumd** (4km from Imlil) and thence through the hamlet of **Sidi Chamcharouch** to the Toubkal refuge hut (12km from Imlil, 5/6hr in all), at the foot of the mountain. The *refuge gardien* is usually prepared to cook meat or vegetable *tajine* for guests, though beware that the hut can be very busy – and crowded. Most people set out early to mid-morning from Imlil to stay the night at the main Toubkal refuge, setting out on the ascent at first light the next morning in order to get the clearest panorama. At the refuge you're almost bound to meet people who have just come down – and you should certainly ask them and the *gardien* for a description of the routes and the current state of the (South Cirque) trail to the summit.

Essaouira

ESSAOUIRA is Morocco's most congenial resort: an eighteenth-century town, enclosed by almost Gothic battlements, facing a cluster of rocky offshore islands, and fringed by a vast expanse of empty sands and dunes. Its whitewashed and blue-shuttered houses and colonnades, its wood workshops and art galleries, its boat-builders and sardine fishermen all provide a colourful and very pleasant backdrop to the beach. The life of the resort, too, is easy and uncomplicated, and very much in the image of the predominantly youthful Europeans and Marrakchis who come here on holiday – many of them for **windsurfing** and **surfing**, for which the town hosts international contests.

Arrival and accommodation

Still largely contained within its ramparts, Essaouira is a simple place to get to grips with. At the northeast end of town is the **Bab Doukkala**; at the southwest is the town's pedestrianized main square, **place Prince Moulay El Hassan**, and the fishing **harbour**. Between them run two main parallel streets: av de l'Istiqlal/av Mohammed Zerktouni and rue Sidi Mohammed Ben Abdallah.

Buses (both CTM and private lines) arrive at a new bus station, inconveniently sited on the outskirts of the town, about 1km (ten minutes' walk) northeast of Bab Doukkala. Especially at night, it's well worth taking a *petit taxi* or horse-drawn *calèche* into or out from town; the charge is around 8dh (10dh at night). **Grands taxis** also operate from the bus station, though they will drop arrivals at Bab Doukkala or place Prince Moulay El Hassan. There is a **petit taxi rank** by the clocktower east of place Prince Moulay El Hassan and *calèches* wait at Bab Doukala.

Leaving Essaouira for **Marrakesh**, there is an early morning nonstop Supratours bus which leaves from av Lalla Aicha, round the corner from the *Hôtel des Iles* on the seafront, at 6.15am, arriving in Marrakesh at the train station; tickets for this should be bought from the nearby kiosk the day before. The best buses direct to **Casablanca** are the CTM Mumtaz Express (leaves Essaouira bus station daily at 11pm, arriving Casa at 5am) and the night Pullman du Sud; they cost only around 10dh more than other departures.

Accommodation can be tight over Easter and in summer– when advance booking is recommended – but at the end of the day there are usually rooms available. A limited number of apartments, suitable for families or small groups, are available. Enquire at *Jack's Kiosk* or *Restaurant Essalam*, both on place Prince Moulay El Hassan. There is also a small and central **campsite**, *Camping d'Essaouira*, bd Mohammed V (☎04/47.21.00), just 300m out from the walls, past the *Hôtel des Îles*; if threatened closure goes ahead, however, the nearest campsite will be next door to the *Auberge Tangaro* south of Essaouira, with a half-hour hike to the beach. The following **hotels** are good value:

Beau Rivage, place Prince Moulay El Hassan (☎04/47.59.25). Attractive, old-established hotel, above the *Café de France*. Rooms (some with private showers) look out onto the main square. ③.

Majestic, 40 rue Laâlouj (☎04/47.49.09). Opposite the museum. Good, clean rooms and hot showers, though a little cheerless. ③.

Sahara, av Okba Ibn Nafia (☎04/47.52.92). Big rooms around a central well, and hot showers in the rooms – if the plumbing is in the mood. ③.

Shahrazed, 1 rue Youssef El Fassi (☎04/47.64.36). New, spacious, and very comfortable hotel, alongside the Syndicat d'Initiative and opposite police headquarters. ②.

Souiri, 37 rue Latterine (☎04/47.53.39). New and colourful hotel in the Medina, good value and the price includes breakfast. ①.

Riad al Madina, 9 rue Latterine (☎04/47.57.27). A nineteenth-century house, now beautifully restored, which, in the 1960s as the *Hôtel du Pasha*, counted the likes of Jimi Hendrix and Cat Stevens among its guests. ⑤.

The town and beach

There are few formal "sights" in Essaouira, but it's a great place just to walk around, exploring the **ramparts**, the **harbour** and the **souks** – above all the **thuya wood workshops** – or wandering along the immense windswept **beach**.

The ramparts are the obvious place to start. If you head north along the lane at the end of place Prince Moulay El Hassan, you can gain access to the **Skala de la Ville**, the great sea bastion which runs along the northern cliffs. Along the top of it are a collection of European cannons, presented to Sultan Sidi Mohammed Ben Abdallah by ambitious nineteenth-century merchants, and at its end is the circular **North Bastion**, with panoramic views.

Along the rue de Skala, built into the ramparts, are the **marquetry and woodcarving workshops**, long established in Essaouira. These artisans produce painstaking and beautiful work from **thuya**, a local mahogany-like hardwood. You will see their wares – boxes and chess sets – elsewhere in Morocco but if you're thinking of buying this is the place to do it. There are further displays of marquetry, past and present, at the **Musée Sidi Mohammed Ben Abdallah** (8.30am–noon & 2.30–6pm, closed Tues), a nineteenth-century mansion on rue Derb Laâlouj, the road running down from the ramparts to av de l'Istiqlal. The museum also houses displays of carpets, costumes, jewellery and musical instruments, some of which are decorated with local marquetry, and there is an interesting gallery of old pictures of Essaouira.

The town's **other souks** spread around and to the south of two arcades, on either side of rue Mohammed Zerktouni, and up towards the Mellah. Worth particular attention are the **Marché d'Épices** (spice market) and **Souk des Bijoutiers** (jewellers' market). The jewellery business was one of the traditional trades of Essaouira's Jewish community, who have long since deserted the **Mellah**, in the northwest corner of the ramparts.

At some point, perhaps around lunchtime or early evening, make your way down to the **harbour,** where fresh sardines (and all variety of other fish) are cooked on the quays. There is also an impressive sea bastion here, the **Skala du Port**, and a busy boatbuilding and repairs industry. The port is entered by a small gate to the left of its main **Marine Gate**.

Essaouira has **beaches** to the north and south. The **northern** one, known as the Plage de Safi, is good in hot weather and with a calm sea, but unattractive and dangerous if the winds are up. The **southern beach** extends for miles, often backed by dunes, out towards Cap Sim. On its early reaches, the main activity, as ever, is football; it's also the better beach for surfing. Further along, you pass the riverbed of the **Oued Ksob** – and then the ruins of an old fort and royal summer pavilion known as the **Bordj El Berod** – the inspiration for Jimi Hendrix's song *Castles in the Sand*. The fort is an excellent viewing spot for the **Îles Purpuraires**, which are protected as a birdlife reserve. The Île de Mogador, the main island, topped with a ruined prison and mosque, can be visited but you need to get permission from the province authorities and the harbour master.

Eating

For an informal lunch, or early-evening meal, you can do no better than eat at the line of grills down at the port, an Essaouira institution. Among the regular **restaurants**, try the budget *Restaurant Essalam*, on place Prince Moulay El Hassan or the pricier *Petite Perle*, just off the clocktower square, with well-prepared dishes in a traditional setting. For a seafood splurge, you can't beat *Chez Sam's*, down by the port, or *Chalet de la Plage* on the seafront just above the high-tide mark. For Continental cuisine try *Dar Loubane*, signposted from the clocktower square, where there are also three rooms to let (☎04/47.62.96; ①). Finally, the new *Le Coquillage*, at the port entrance on the way to *Chez Sam's*, has already made its name as a first-class fish restaurant.

travel details

Trains

Casablanca Port to: Fes (2 daily; 4hr 45min); Meknes (2 daily; 3hr 45min); Rabat (14–18 daily; 50min–1hr).

Casablanca Voyageurs to: Marrakesh (8 daily; 3hr 30min); Meknes (6 daily; 4hr); Mohammed V airport (12 daily; 35min); Tangier (4 daily; 6hr).

Fes to: Asilah (5 daily; 5hr); Casablanca Voyageurs (6 daily; 5hr); Marrakesh (6 daily; 8hr 30min–10hr); Meknes (12 daily; 50min), Rabat (8 daily; 3hr 45min–4hr 15min); Tangier (5 daily; 5hr 50min).

Marrakesh to: Casablanca Voyageurs (8 daily; 3hr 30min); Fes (6 daily; 8hr–9hr 45min); Meknes (6 daily; 7hr 30min); Rabat (6 daily; 4hr 20min); Tangier (4 daily; 10–11hr).

Rabat to: Casablanca Port (14–18 daily; 50min–1hr).

Tangier to: Asilah (4 daily, 50min); Casablanca Port (1 daily; 6hr); Casablanca Voyageurs (4 daily; 5hr 30min–6hr); Fes (5 daily; 5hr 40min); Marrakesh (4 daily; 10hr); Meknes (5 daily; 4hr 45min); Rabat (5 daily; 5hr).

Buses

Casablanca to: Marrakesh (5 daily; 4hr); Rabat (19 daily; 1hr 40min); Tangier (6 daily; 6hr 30min).

Chaouen to Al Hoceima (3 daily; 8hr); Ketama (3 daily; 5hr); Meknes (2 daily; 5hr 30min); Tetouan (6 daily; 3hr).

Fes to: Casablanca (8 daily; 7hr); Marrakesh (2 daily; 11hr); Rabat (7 daily; 5hr 30min); Tangier (2 daily; 8hr); Tetouan (2 daily; 5hr).

Marrakesh to: Agadir (5 daily; 3hr 30min); Asni (frequent; 1hr 30min); Casablanca (5 daily; 4hr); Essaouira (6 daily; 3–4hr); Fes (2 daily; 11hr); Rabat (9 daily; 5hr 30min).

Meknes to Chaouen (2 daily; 5hr 30min); Fes (hourly; 50min); Marrakesh (2 daily; 9hr); Rabat (9 daily; 4hr); Tangier (1 daily; 7hr).

Rabat to: Casablanca (19 daily; 1hr 40min); Fes (7 daily; 5hr 30min); Meknes (9 daily; 4hr); Salé (frequent; 15min); Tangier (6 daily; 5hr).

Tangier to Asilah (9 daily; 1hr); Fes (2 daily; 8hr); Meknes (1 daily; 7hr); Rabat (6 daily; 5hr); Tetouan (4 daily; 1hr 30min).

Tetouan to Chaouen (6 daily; 3hr); Tangier (4 daily; 1hr 30min).

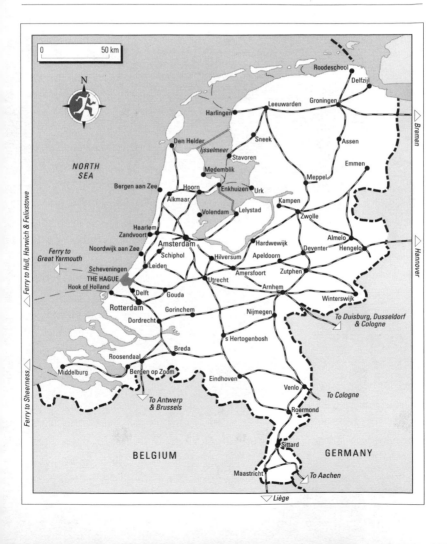

Introduction

The Netherlands is a country partly reclaimed from the waters of the North Sea, and around half of it lies at or below sea level. Land reclamation has been the dominant motif of its history, the result a country of resonant and unique images – flat, fertile landscapes punctured by windmills and church spires; ornately gabled terraces flanking peaceful canals; and mile upon mile of grassy dunes, backing onto stretches of pristine sandy beach.

A leading colonial power, its mercantile fleets once challenged the best in the world for supremacy, and the country enjoyed a so-called "Golden Age" of prosperity in the seventeenth century. These days, the Netherlands is one of the most developed countries in the world, with the highest population density in Europe, its fifteen million or so inhabitants (most of whom speak English) concentrated into an area about the size of southern England.

Most people travel to the capital, **Amsterdam**, and the rest of the country, despite its relative accessibility, is comparatively untouched by tourism. The provinces of **North** and **South Holland**, in the west of the country, are the most populated and most historically interesting region: unrelentingly flat territory, much of it reclaimed, that has since become home to a grouping of towns known collectively as the **Randstad** (literally "rim town"). It's a good idea to forsake Amsterdam for a day or two and investigate places like **Haarlem**, **Leiden** and **Delft** with their old canal-girded centres, the gritty port city of **Rotterdam**, or **The Hague**, stately home of the government and the Dutch royals. Outside the Randstad, life moves more slowly. The province of **Friesland**, to the north, is probably the Netherlands at its most remote, its inhabitants speaking Frysk, a language neither spoken nor understood elsewhere in the country. Friesland's capital, **Leeuwarden**, is a likeable city, and neighbouring **Groningen** is one of the country's busiest cultural centres, lent verve by its large resident student population. To the south, the landscape undulates into heathy moorland around the town of **Arnhem**, best experienced in the country's only national park, the **Hoge Veluwe**. Further south still lies the compelling city of **Maastricht**, capital of the province of Limburg, squeezed between the German and Belgian borders.

Information and maps

A nationwide network of **VVV tourist offices** dispenses information, usually from offices conveniently sited in the town centre or by the train station. They have plenty of information in English, maps and accommodation lists, usually for a small fee, and will book rooms for you, again for a few guilders. Most can be reached on ☎0900 premium-rate phone numbers, charged at 50c–f1 per minute from within the Netherlands, and normal international rates from outside. Most carry information on the rest of the country too. For travelling purposes, the best general **map** of the Netherlands is Kümmerley and Frey's. For more detailed regional maps, the Dutch motoring organization ANWB publishes an excellent 1:100,000 series that covers the whole country.

Money and banks

Dutch currency is the guilder, written as "f" and made up of 100 cents ("c"). It comes in coins worth 5c (thin bronze), tiny 10c pieces, 25c, f1 and f2.50 (all silver) and f5 (thick bronze); denominations of notes are f10, f25, f50, f100, f250 and f1000. Banking hours are Mon–Fri 9am–4/5pm; in larger cities some banks also open Thurs 7–9pm and occasionally on Saturday mornings. There are also the GWK exchange offices, usually at train stations, which are open late hours every day (24hr at Schiphol airport and Amsterdam Centraal Station), change money and travellers' cheques, and give cash advances on all the major credit cards, for similar rates – though there's normally a f300 or so minimum. You can also change money at most VVV tourist offices and numerous bureaux de change, though the rates will be less favourable – many, such as Chequepoint, charge exorbitant commissions. ATMs dispense cash advances, though Visa card holders may have to search for a compatible machine. Only the more expensive shops and restaurants accept credit cards.

Communications

Dutch post offices are usually open Mon–Fri 8.30am–5pm, plus Sat 8.30am–noon, or later, in the larger cities. Post boxes are everywhere, though make sure you use the correct slot for foreign destinations, marked "Overige".

Public phones are widespread. Although there are some coin-phones left (most requiring 25c as a minimum), most public phones in the street now take phonecards only – these can be bought at post offices and VVV tourist offices in denominations of f10, f25 and f50, and can be used in Germany, as well as the Netherlands. Card phones also accept credit cards. Discount rates apply all weekend and Mon–Fri 8pm–8am. The operator number is ☎0800/0410: international directory enquiries is on ☎0900/8418.

Getting around

Getting around is never a problem: distances are short, and the longest journey you'll ever make – say from Amsterdam to Maastricht – takes under three hours by train or car. Public transport in and around towns and cities, too, is efficient and cheap, running on an easy-to-understand ticketing system that covers the whole country. The bus and train networks link up together neatly, with bus terminals almost always next door to the train station.

■ Trains

The best way of travelling around Holland is to take the train. The system, run by Nederlandse Spoorwegen (Dutch Railways), is one of the best in Europe: trains are fast, modern and frequent, fares relatively low, and the network of lines extremely comprehensive. Ordinary fares are calculated by the kilometre, diminishing proportionally the further you travel. NS publish a booklet detailing costs and distances, so it's easy to work out how much a ticket will cost; reckon on spending about f15 to travel 50km or so, up to a maximum one-way fare of f73.50. With any ticket, you're also free to stop off en route and continue your journey later that day.

InterRail and Eurail **passes** are both valid, as is the EuroDomino ticket, which is valid for unlimited travel on a certain number of days within a specified period: a pass for 3 days (not necessarily consecutive) in a month costs £34 (£25 if you are under 26); for 5 days costs £54 (£38 under 26); for 10 days £96 (£67). The Holland Rail Pass is now available to foreigners on production of a passport; 3 days in the month costs f130 (f104 if you are under 26), and 5 days costs f196 (f158).

Of a number of ways of saving money, the **day return** (*dagretour*), is the most commonly used, valid for 24 hours and costing around ten percent less than two ordinary singles. A **Daypass** (*OV Dagkaart*) entitles the holder to unlimited travel anywhere in Holland at a cost of f81.75 (second-class) for one day or f349 for five days.

Stations are well equipped and usually have a reasonably priced restaurant, left-luggage lockers (around f4 for 24 hours), and a GWK change office. NS have also devised a **treintaxi** scheme, whereby for f7 a taxi will take you anywhere within the city limits from your destination train station – very useful for smaller towns, although it doesn't apply to Amsterdam, The Hague, Rotterdam or Utrecht. Vouchers for treintaxis must be purchased when you buy your ticket. NS publish mounds of **information** annually, including a free timetable detailing intercity services, and a full timetable available from any station.

■ Buses

For local transport you need to use buses, again very efficient, and almost always running from ranks of bus stops next to the train station. Ticketing is simple, organized on a system that covers the whole country. You need buy just one kind of ticket, a **strippenkaart**, wherever you are. The country is divided into zones: the driver will cancel two strips on your *strippenkaart* for your journey plus one for each extra zone you travel through. Two strips will get you around the centre of most cities, three strips will take you out into the suburbs, travelling between towns will use up proportionally more. Additional people can travel on the same *strippenkaart* by cancelling the requisite number of strips. You can buy 2-, 3- or 8-strip *strippenkaarts* from bus drivers, or the better-value 15-strip (f11.75) or 45-strip (f33.75) *strippenkaarts* in advance from train stations, tobacconists and local public transport offices.

■ Driving and hitching

The country has a good and comprehensive **road network**. You drive on the right; speed limits are 50kph in built-up areas, 80kph outside and 120kph on motorways, though some motorways have a speed limit of 100kph. Drivers and front-seat passengers are required by law to wear seatbelts, and crackdowns on drunken driving are severe. There are no toll roads, and although petrol isn't particularly cheap at around f2 a litre, once again the distances involved mean this isn't much of a factor. You need an ordinary driver's licence, and, if you bring your own car, Green Card insurance, though you can obtain last-minute insurance cover at border exchange offices. If you break down, the ANWB offers reciprocal repair and breakdown services to members of foreign motoring organizations; their nationwide number is ☎0800/0888. **Car rental** is fairly expensive: reckon on paying upwards of f700 per week with unlimited mileage, or around f50 a day plus 60c per kilometre – though there are much cheaper weekend deals available.

Hitching is feasible throughout the country: the Dutch are usually well disposed towards giving lifts. Bear in mind, though, that motorways are hard to avoid, and that it's only legal to hitch on slip roads or at the special marked places you'll find on the outskirts of some larger cities, known as *liftplaatsen*.

■ Cycling

If you're not pushed for time, **cycling** is the best way to see the country. There's a nationwide system of well-signposted cycle paths, which often divert away from the main roads into the countryside. Bikes can be **rented** from all main train stations for f10 a day or f35 per week, plus a f100 or f200 cash deposit; if you have a valid train ticket, rental costs just f6 a day (f24 per week) with a *treinfiets* voucher. You'll also need some form of ID. The snag is that cycles must be returned to the station from which they were rented. In high season you may need to book ahead (☎0900/9292). As an alternative, you can rent bikes from outlets in almost any town and village (some may take a credit card imprint as a deposit). It is possible to take your bike on trains, but it isn't encouraged; a ticket costs f10 single, f17.50 return – more for journeys over 80km – and you're not allowed to take your machine on board during the rush hour. Never leave your bike unlocked: most stations have somewhere you can store it for around f2 a day.

Accommodation

Accommodation is not particularly cheap in the Netherlands, though a wide network of youth hostels and well-equipped campsites can help to cut costs. Wherever you stay, you should book ahead during the summer and over holiday periods, especially Easter, when places can run short.

■ Hotels and private rooms

Rates for the cheapest one- or two-star **hotel** room start at around f120 for a double without private bath or shower; count on paying upwards of f85 if you want your own facilities; three-star hotels cost f120–225. Prices usually include a reasonable breakfast. You can make reservations for free anywhere in the country through the Netherlands Reservation Centre (NRC), PO Box 404, 2260 AK Leidschendam (☎070/419 5533), although they don't deal with rooms cheaper than f150. You can also make reservations in person through VVV offices, for a fee of f5 per person, with an 11 percent deposit payable at the VVV which is then deducted from the hotel bill.

One way of cutting costs is, wherever possible, to use **private accommodation** – rooms in private homes that are let out to visitors on a bed-and-break-

fast basis; they're sometimes known as pensions. Prices are usually quoted per person and normally come to f30–35; breakfast is usually included, but if not it will cost you about f5 extra. You have to go through the VVV to find private rooms: they will either give (or, more likely, sell) you a list or will insist they book the accommodation themselves and levy the appropriate fee.

■ Hostels and student rooms

There are about 40 HI **youth hostels** in Holland, charging f21–35 per person per night, including breakfast – f5 extra for nonmembers and an extra charge (f6.25) for bedding. Accommodation in these places is usually in dormitories, though some of the hostels do have single and double rooms available. Meals are also often possible – about f16.50 for a filling dinner – and in some hostels there are kitchens where you can self-cater. For a full list of Dutch hostels, contact the Nederlandse Jeugdherberg Central (NJHC), Prof. Tulpstraat 2, 1018 HA Amsterdam (☎020/551 3155). In addition to official hostels, the larger cities often have a number of **unofficial hostels** with dormitory accommodation at broadly similar prices, though standards are sometimes not as reliable. In some cities you may also come across something known as a **sleep-in** – dormitory accommodation run by the local council that's often cheaper than regular hostels and normally only open during the summer. **Student accommodation** is sometimes open to travellers during the holidays, but only in a few cities.

■ Campsites and cabins

Camping is a serious option in Holland: there are plenty of sites, most well equipped, and they represent a good saving on other forms of accommodation. Prices vary greatly, but you can generally expect to pay around f7.50 per person, plus f5–10 for a tent, and f7.50 or so for a car or f5 for a motorcycle. There's a tourist board list of selected sites, and the ANWB publishes an annual guide (f19.95). Some sites also have **cabins**, spartan affairs that can

---

ACCOMMODATION PRICE CODES

Throughout this guide, accommodation is priced on a scale of ① to ⑨, the number indicating the lowest price per night a single person could expect to pay in that establishment in high season. With hostels this is the nightly rate per person; with hotels, the price is arrived at by dividing the cost of the cheapest double room by two. The prices indicated by the codes are as follows:

① under £5 / $8	④ £15–20 / $24–32	⑦ £30–35 / $48–56
② £5–10 / $8–16	⑤ £20–25 / $32–40	⑧ £35–40 / $56–64
③ £10–15 / $16–24	⑥ £25–30 / $40–48	⑨ £40 / $64 and over

house a maximum of four people, for around f75 a night. Again both the VVV and ANWB can provide a list of these, and you should normally book in advance.

Food and drink

Holland is not renowned for its cuisine, but although much is unimaginative it's rarely unpleasant. The country also has a good supply of ethnic restaurants, especially Indonesian and Chinese, and if you're selective prices needn't break the bank. Drinking, too, is easily affordable: Dutch beer is one of the real pleasures of the country.

■ Food

Dutch food tends to be fairly plain, mainly consisting of steak, chicken or fish, along with filling soups and stews. In all but the very cheapest hostels or most expensive hotels **breakfast** (*ontbijt*) will be included in the price of the room. Though usually nothing fancy, it's generally very filling: rolls, cheese, ham, hard-boiled eggs, jam and honey or peanut butter are the principal ingredients. If you don't have a hotel breakfast, many bars and cafés serve at least rolls and sandwiches, and some offer a set breakfast. The **coffee** is normally good and strong, around f3 a cup, served with a little tub of evaporated milk (*koffiemelk*). **Tea** generally comes with lemon if anything; if you want milk you have to ask for it. **Chocolate** (*chocomel*) is also popular, served hot or cold.

For the rest of the day, **fast food** options include chips – *frites* or *patat* – sprinkled with salt and smothered with mayonnaise, curry, sate, goulash or tomato sauce. If you just want salt, ask for *patat zonder*; chips with salt and mayonnaise are *patat met*. Often chips are complemented with *kroketten* – spiced minced meat coated in breadcrumbs and deep fried – or *fricandel*, a frankfurter-like sausage. Tastier, and good both as a snack and a full lunch, are the fish specialities that you see being sold from street kiosks: salted raw herrings, smoked eel (*gerookte paling*), mackerel in a roll (*broodje makreel*), mussels and various kinds of deep-fried fish. A nationwide chain of fish restaurants, *Noordzee*, serves good-value fish-based sandwiches and light fish lunches. Another fast snack you'll see everywhere is *shoarma* or kebab, sold in numerous Middle Eastern restaurants and takeaways which traditionally also offer the chick-pea based falafel, a good vegetarian stand-by. Pizza is, as ever, widely available.

The majority of **bars** serve some kind of food, sometimes a full menu, in which case they may be known as an **eetcafé**. Most serve at least sandwiches and rolls (*boterham* and *broodjes* – *stokbrood* if made with French bread); in winter they serve *erwtensoep*, a thick pea soup with smoked sausage, for about f7.50, and *uitsmijters* (literally "bouncer"), fried eggs on buttered bread, topped with ham or roast beef for about f9.50. Full-blown **restaurants** tend to open in the evening only, until around 11pm. If you're on a tight budget, stick to the dish of the day (*dagschotels*), for which you pay f15–20 for a meat or fish dish heavily garnished with vegetables. Otherwise, meat dishes go for f20-25, fish for f25–30. **Train station restaurants** are a good stand-by, as they are generally able to supply full meals for f15, and in university towns **student mensa restaurants** serve meals for under f10. Vegetarian food isn't a problem. Many *eetcafés* and restaurants have at least one meat-free item, and you'll find vegetarian restaurants in most towns, offering full-course set meals for f15–20, though they often close early. Of **foreign cuisines**, Surinamese restaurants are a good bet for food on a budget, as are Chinese and Indonesian restaurants (sometimes combined).

■ Drink

Most drinking is done either in the cosy environs of a **brown café** (*bruin kroeg*) – so named because of the colour of the walls – or in more modern-looking **bars**, usually catering to a younger crowd. Most bars are open till around 1am during the week, 2am at weekends. You may also come across *proeflokalen* or **tasting houses**, small, old-fashioned bars that once only served spirits – though most now serve beer and, usually, coffee – and close around 8pm. The most commonly consumed beverage is **beer**, usually served in small measures; ask for *een pils*. Prices are fairly standard; reckon on paying about f3 a glass pretty much everywhere. From a supermarket you'll pay f1–2 for a half-litre bottle. The most commonly seen names are Heineken, Amstel, Oranjeboom and Grolsch, though there are other regional brews and you will also come across plenty of the better-known Belgian brands. **Wine** is reasonably priced – expect to pay around f7 or so for an average bottle of French white or red. As for **spirits**, the indigenous drink is **jenever** or Dutch gin, served in small glasses and traditionally drunk straight. *Oud* (old) is smooth and mellow, *Jong* (young) packs more of a punch, though neither is extremely alcoholic. A glass in a bar costs around f2.90.

Opening hours and holidays

The Dutch weekend fades painlessly into the working week with many **shops** staying closed on Monday morning, even in major cities. Otherwise, opening hours tend to be 9am to 5.30 or 6pm, though certain shops stay open later on Thursday or Friday evenings. Outside these hours night shops (*avonwinkels*) can be found in major cities, usually opening at 4pm and closing at 1 or 2am. In general, things shut a little earlier on Saturday.

Opening times of **museums** are fairly uniform – generally Tues–Sat 10am–5pm, Sun 1–5pm; entry prices for the more ordinary collections are f5, although the major museums can be around f15. If you're intending to visit more than a handful of museums, it's worth investing in a **museumcard** – available from the VVV tourist offices or direct from museums for f25 if you're 24 or under, f55 otherwise, and granting free or drastically reduced access to all state and municipally run museums and galleries for a year. An alternative for the under-26s is the Cultureel Jongeren Paspoort or **CJP** (f22.50), also available from the VVVs, which gets reductions in museums and on theatre, film and concert tickets – though the discounts vary wildly.

Shops and banks are closed and museums adopt Sunday hours on the following **public holidays**: Jan 1; Good Fri; Easter Sun & Mon; April 30; May 5; May 13; Whit Sun & Mon; Dec 5; Dec 25 & Dec 26.

Police and drugs

There's little reason ever to come into contact with the **police force** in the Netherlands, and, as far as personal safety goes, it's normally possible to walk anywhere in the larger cities at any time of day, though you should obviously be wary of badly lit or empty streets. If you're detained by the police, you don't automatically have the right to a phone call, although they'll probably phone your embassy for you. As for **drugs**, people over the age of eighteen are legally allowed to buy five grams of hashish or marijuana (less than one-fifth of one ounce) for personal use at any one time. Possession of amounts less than 28 grams (one ounce) is ignored by police, although bear in mind that the liberal attitude exists only in Amsterdam and the larger cities of the Randstad. All other narcotics – except fresh magic mushrooms – are illegal. Regarding health, an *apotheek* or pharmacy is the place to get a prescription filled; all are open Mon–Fri 8.30am–5.30pm – outside this time there'll be a note of the nearest open pharmacy on the door.

EMERGENCY NUMBERS
Police, Ambulance and Fire ☎112.

AMSTERDAM

AMSTERDAM is a beguiling capital, a compact mix of the provincial and the cosmopolitan. It has a welcoming attitude towards visitors, and a uniquely youthful orientation. For many, however, its world-class museums and galleries – notably the Rijksmuseum, with its collection of seventeenth-century Dutch paintings, and the Van Gogh Museum – are reason enough to visit.

As the name suggests, Amsterdam was founded on a dam on the river Amstel, in the thirteenth century. During the Reformation it rose in stature, taking trade from Antwerp and becoming a haven for its religious refugees. Having shaken off the yoke of the Spanish, the city went from strength to strength in the seventeenth century, becoming the centre of a vast trading empire with colonies in southeast Asia. Amsterdam accommodated its expansion with the cobweb of canals that gives the city its distinctive and elegant shape today.

Come the 1700s, Amsterdam went into gentle decline, re-emerging as a fashionable focus for the alternative movements of the 1960s. Despite an Eighties backlash, the city still fulfils this role with its buzz of open-air summer events, intimate clubs and bars, and relaxed attitude to soft drugs.

Arrival and information

Amsterdam's airport, **Schiphol**, is connected by train with the city's Centraal Station (every 15min during the day, hourly at night). **Centraal Station** is at the hub of all bus and tram routes and just five minutes' walk from Dam Square. Eurolines long-distance **buses** arrive at Amstel Station, ten minutes from Centraal Station by metro. For **information**, the VVV have a main branch right outside Centraal Station (daily 9am–5pm; information line, charging f1/min: ☎0900/400 4040), another branch inside the station itself (Mon–Sat 8am–8pm, Sun 9am–5), and a smaller kiosk on Leidsestraat at the corner with Leidseplein (Mon–Fri 9am–8pm, Sat & Sun 9am–5pm; Aug 9am–9pm); there are also offices at Schiphol Airport (daily 7am–10pm) and at Stadionplein, Serookerkenweg 125 (9am–5pm, July & Aug 10am–6pm). Any of these offices can sell you a map, book accommodation and provide answers to most enquiries, though summer queues can be a nightmare; they can also sell you an **Amsterdam Culture & Leisure Pass** (f39.50), which gives free or discounted entry to a selection of major attractions as well as reductions on public transport and some restaurant prices. The bi-weekly **listings guide**, *What's On In Amsterdam*, published by VVV, is available direct from their offices for f4 or free from some hotels, hostels and restaurants.

City transport

Amsterdam's excellent **public transport** network of **trams**, **buses** and a small **metro** system isn't expensive; as with the rest of the country, you can use a *strippenkaart* on all services – available from any GVB public transport office, post office, selected tobacconists, train station ticket counters and VVV offices. Since you rarely need to travel outside the central zone, cancelling two strips is normally sufficient. Instructions in English are displayed inside all trams. *Dagkaarten* – **day tickets** – are also available, valid for as many days as you need for a cost of f10 for one day, going up to f23 for four, then f4 for each additional day. If caught without a ticket, you're liable for a f60 spot fine plus the journey fare. All standard services stop around 12.30am, when **night buses** take over, running roughly hourly through the night from Centraal Station to most parts of the city. The GVB office in front of Centraal Station (Mon–Fri 7am–9pm, Sat & Sun 8am–9pm; winter until 7pm; ☎0900/9292) has free route maps and an English guide to the ticketing system. **Taxis** are expensive, and are found in ranks on main city squares (Stationsplein, Dam Square, Leidseplein); to book one call ☎020/677 7777. **Bicycles** can be rented from Centraal Station or from a number of similarly priced bike-rental firms scattered around town (see "Listings").

Accommodation

Hotels in Amsterdam can be expensive, although the city's size means that you'll inevitably end up somewhere central. A viable alternative is to stay in one of the many hostels offering dormitory beds and usually a few rooms. They're scattered all over the city, most densely in the red-light district along Warmoestraat, which is five minutes' walk from Centraal Station, and not as seedy as it sounds. At peak periods throughout the year (April–August, but especially Easter) it's advisable to book ahead. The Amsterdam Reservation Centre (charging 25c/min: ☎ & fax 31/77700 0888) can book accommodation for a f5 fee and is especially useful for last-minute bookings. Directions given are from Centraal Station (CS).

Hostels

Arena, 's-Gravesandestraat 51 (☎020/694 7444). A little way east of the centre, but probably the best value in the city. On-site facilities include live music, tourist and cultural information, bike rental, a great bar & restaurant and even parking. Women-only dorms available. Metro Weesperplein or tram #6, #7 or #10 from Leidseplein to Korte 's-Gravesandestraat. ②.

Bob's Youth Hostel, Nieuwezijds Voorburgwal 92 (☎020/623 0063). An old favourite of backpackers; lively and smoky, with small, clean dorms and cheap meals. Ten-minute walk from CS; 3am curfew. ②.

Eben Haezer, Bloemstraat 179 (☎020/624 4717). A non-evangelical Christian hostel in a beautiful part of the Jordaan. About the cheapest beds in the city, in single-sex dorms. Tram #13, #17 to Marnixstraat. ②.

Flying Pig Downtown, Nieuwendijk 100 (☎020/420 6822). Clean, large and well run by ex-backpackers. Free kitchen facilities and Internet access, no curfew, all-night bar. Not for faint-hearted anti-smokers. Five-minute walk from CS. ②.

Flying Pig Palace Vondelpark, Vossiusstraat 46 (☎020/400 4187). Tram #1, #2, #5 to Leidseplein, then walk. On the edge of the city's major park; clean and well maintained. Free kitchen facilities and Internet access, no curfew, good tourist information. Use the Safe service provided to store valuables. ②.

Kabul, Warmoesstraat 38 (☎020/623 7158). Huge, bustling hostel with multilingual staff, three minutes' walk from the station. Rooms sleep between 1 and 16 people. Immaculately clean. ③.

Keizersgracht, Keizersgracht 15 (☎020/625 1364). Terrific location on a major canal five minutes' walk from CS, with a good mix of small dorms, singles and doubles. Spotless. ③.

Meeting Point, Warmoestraat 14 (☎020/627 7499). Youth hostel open 24hrs. Breakfast not included. Two-minute walk from CS. ②.

The Shelter, Barndesteeg 21 (☎020/625 3230). A non-evangelical Christian hostel smack in the middle of the red-light district: single sex dorms, lockers (f10 deposit), midnight curfew (1am w/ends) and sizeable breakfast included. Metro Nieuwmarkt. ②.

Stadsdoelen, Kloveniersburgwal 97 (☎020/624 6832). The closer of the two HI hostels, with clean semi-private dorm rooms. Sheet hire is a steep f6.25. HI members have priority in high season. Tram #4, #9, #16, #24, #25 to Muntplein. ②.

Vondel Park, Zandpad 5 (☎020/589 8996). For facilities, the better of the two HI hostels, with bar, restaurant, TV lounge and kitchen; also well located on the edge of the park. Secure lockers and a lift. Curfew 2am. Tram #1, #2, #5 to Leidseplein, then walk. ②.

Hotels

Asterisk, Den Texstraat 16 (☎020/626 2396). Good-value budget hotel on the edge of the centre, just across the canal from the Heineken Brewery. Tram #16, #24, #25 to Weteringcircuit. ④.

Bema, Concertgebouwplein 19b (☎020/679 1396). Small place, kept very clean by the English-speaking manager. The rooms are not modern, but are full of character. Handier for concerts and museums than nightlife. Tram #2 or #5 to Museumplein. ④.

Clemens, Raadhuisstraat 39 (☎020/624 6089). One of the many options on this hotel strip. Clean neat and good value for money. Ask for a room at the back. Tram #13, #17 to Westermarkt. ④.

Euphemia, Fokke Simonszstraat 1 (☎020/622 9045). A likeable laid-back atmosphere: rooms are big and basic, with free showers and TVs. Very reasonable prices, which means it's usually full. Trams #16, #24, #25 to Weteringcircuit. ③.

Hans Brinker, Kerkstraat 136 (☎020/622 0687). Well-established and raucously popular cheapie, though a little more upmarket than some. Good, basic and clean, and close to the Leidseplein buzz. Tram #1, #2, #5 to Prinsengracht. ③.

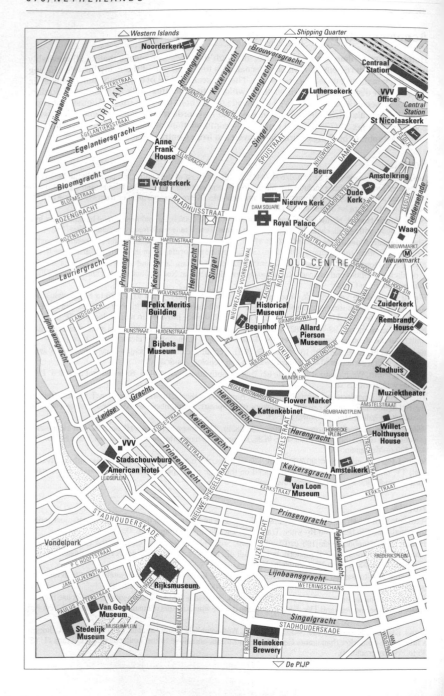

△ Western Islands △ Shipping Quarter

Noorderkerk

Brouwersgracht

Centraal Station

VVV Office   Central Station

Luthersekerk

St Nicolaaskerk

Egelantiersgracht

Anne Frank House

Singel

SPUISTRAAT

Beurs

Amstelkring

Oude Kerk

Bloemgracht

Westerkerk

RAADHUISSTRAAT

Nieuwe Kerk

DAM SQUARE

Royal Palace

Waag

NIEUWMARKT

Nieuwmarkt

ROZENGRACHT

OLD CENTRE

Lauriergracht

Felix Meritis Building

Historical Museum

Begijnhof

Allard Pierson Museum

Zuiderkerk

Rembrandt House

Bijbels Museum

Stadhuis

Muziektheater

Flower Market

Kattenkebinet

REMBRANDTPLEIN

Willet-Holthuysen House

Gracht

Leidse

VVV

Stadschouwburg

American Hotel

LEIDSEPLEIN

Amstelkerk

Van Loon Museum

Prinsengracht

STADHOUDERSKADE

Vondelpark

P.C. HOOFTSTRAAT

FREDERIKSPLEIN

Lijnbaansgracht

WETERINGSCHANS

Rijksmuseum

Van Gogh Museum

Stedelijk Museum

MUSEUMPLEIN

Singelgracht

STADHOUDERSKADE

Heineken Brewery

▽ De PIJP

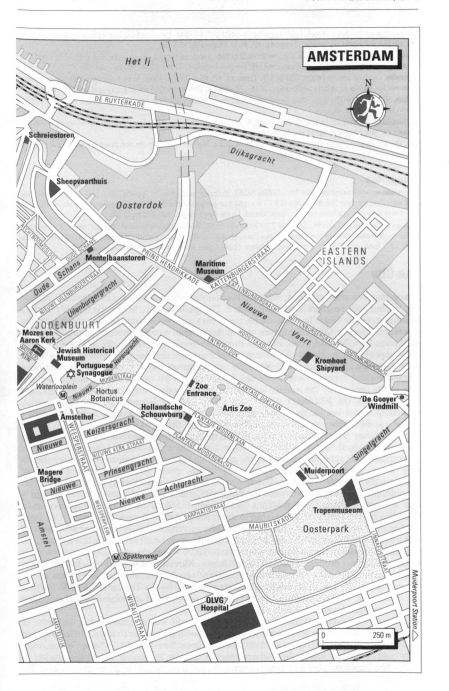

International Budget Hotel, Leidsegracht 76 (☎020/624 2784). Excellent budget option on a peaceful little canal in the heart of the city. Tram #1, #2, #5 to Prinsengracht. ③.

Nova, Nieuwezijds Voorburgwal 276 (☎020/623 0066). Spotless rooms, all en-suite and with fridge and TV. Friendly staff, secure access and internal lift. Perfect location. Tram #1, #2, #5 to Spui. ⑦.

Quentin, Leidsekade 89 (☎020/626 2187). Tram #1, #2, #5 to Leidseplein. Very friendly small hotel, often a stopover for bands or artists performing at the Melkweg. Well regarded among gay and lesbian visitors. ④.

Rokin, Rokin 73 (☎020/626 7456). Something of a bargain considering the location. Tram #4, #9, #16, #24, #25 to Dam or Spui. ⑤.

St Nicolaas, Spuistraat 1a (☎020/626 1384). Very pleasant well-run little hotel housed in a former mattress factory (with a king-size lift to prove it). ⑥.

Van Onna, Bloemgracht 102 (☎020/626 5801). A quiet, comfortable, family-run place on a tranquil canal in the Jordaan. Tram #13, #17 to Westermarkt. ⑤.

Campsites

Vliegenbos, Meeuwenlaan 138 (☎020/636 8855). Relaxed and friendly "youth" site, just a ten-minute bus ride into Amsterdam North. Costs f13.75 a night per person including tent charge and hot showers. Also has a few four-person huts for f77; book ahead. Open April–Sept. Bus #32 from CS.

Gaasper Camping, Loosdrechtdreef 7 (☎020/696 7326). Amsterdam's newest "family" campsite, way out in the southeast, close to the Gaasperplas Park, though with a fast metro link. Rates are f6.25 per person, f6.50 for a tent and f5.50 for a car. Hot showers f1.50. Open March–Dec. Metro Gaasperplas.

The City

Amsterdam is a small city, and, although the concentric canal system can be initially confusing, finding your bearings is straightforward. The medieval core boasts the best of the city's bustling streetlife and is home to shops, many bars and restaurants, fanning south from the nineteenth-century Centraal Station, one of Amsterdam's most resonant landmarks and a focal point for urban life. Come summer there's no livelier part of the city, as street performers compete for attention with the trams that converge dangerously from all sides. From here, **Damrak** storms into the heart of the city, an unenticing avenue lined with overpriced restaurants and bobbing canal boats and flanked on the left by the **Beurs**, designed at the turn of the century by the leading light of the Dutch modern movement, H.P. Berlage, and the enormous **De Bijenkorf** department store. Left off Damrak, the red-light district, stretching across two canals – **Oudezijds Voorburgwal** and **Oudezijds Achterburgwal** – is perhaps inevitably one of the real sights of the city, thronged with people in high season just to discover how shocking it all is. A little way up **Warmoesstraat**, the precincts of the **Oude Kerk** (April–Sept Mon–Sat 11am–5pm, Sun 1–5pm, Oct–March 1pm–5pm; f5) offer a reverential peace after the excesses of the area; it's a bare, mostly fourteenth-century church with some beautifully carved misericords in the choir and the memorial tablet of Rembrandt's first wife, Saskia van Uylenburg. Nearby, the **Amstelkring**, at the northern end of Oudezijds Voorburgwal, was once the principal Catholic place of worship in the city and is now a museum (Mon–Sat 10am–5pm, Sun 1–5pm; f7.50) commemorating the days when Catholics had to confine their worship to the privacy of their homes. Known as "Our Dear Lord in the Attic", it occupies the loft of a wealthy merchant's house, together with those of two smaller houses behind it. Just beyond, **Zeedijk**, once haunt of Amsterdam's drug dealers, leads through to **Nieuwmarkt**, where the turreted **Waag** was originally part of the city's fortifications, later becoming the civic weigh-house. **Kloveniersburgwal**, which leads south, was the outer of the three eastern canals of sixteenth-century Amsterdam, and boasts, on the left, one of the city's most impressive canal houses, built for the Trip family in 1662. Further up on the right, the **Oudemanhuispoort** passage, once part of an almshouse and now filled with secondhand bookstalls, leads to O.Z. Achterburgwal.

At the end of Damrak, **Dam Square**, where the Amstel was first dammed, is the centre of the city, its tusk-like **War Memorial** serving as a meeting place for tourists. On the western side, the **Royal Palace** (June–Oct daily 11am–5.30pm; Nov–May 12.30–5pm; f7) was originally built as the city hall in the mid-seventeenth century. It received its royal monicker in 1808 when Napoleon's brother Louis commandeered it as the one building fit for a king. He was forced to abdicate in 1810, leaving behind a sizeable amount of the Empire furniture. Vying for importance is the **Nieuwe Kerk** (daily 10am–5pm; f3), a fifteenth-century structure rebuilt several times that is now used only for exhibitions and state occasions. Inside, rest numerous names from Dutch history, among them the seventeenth-century naval hero Admiral de Ruyter, who lies in an opulent tomb in the choir, and the poet Vondel, commemorated by a small urn near the entrance.

South of Dam Square, **Rokin** follows the old course of the Amstel River, lined with grandiose nineteenth-century mansions. Running parallel, **Kalverstraat** is an uninspired strip of monotonous clothes shops, halfway down which, at no. 92, a gateway forms the entrance to the former orphanage that's now the **Amsterdam Historical Museum** (Mon–Fri 10am–5pm, Sat & Sun 11am–5pm; f11), where artefacts, paintings and documents survey the city's development from the thirteenth century. Directly outside, the glassed-in Civic Guard Gallery draws passers-by with free glimpses of the large company portraits. Just around the corner, off Sint Luciensteeg, the **Begijnhof** is a small court of seventeenth-century buildings; the poor and elderly led a religious life here, celebrating Mass in their own, concealed, Catholic Church. The plain and unadorned English Reformed Church, which takes up one side of the Begijnhof, has pulpit panels designed by the young Piet Mondrian. Close by, the **Spui** is a lively corner of town whose mixture of bookshops and packed bars centres around a small statue of a young boy known as 't **Lieverdje** (Little Darling). In the opposite direction, Kalverstraat comes to an end at **Muntplein** and the **Munttoren** – originally a mint and part of the city walls, topped with a spire by Hendrik de Keyser in 1620. Across the Singel is the **Flower Market**, while in the other direction Reguliersbreestraat turns left toward the loud restaurants of **Rembrandtplein**. To the south is **Reguliersgracht**, an appealing stretch of water with distinctive steep bridges; it was to have been filled in at the beginning of the century but was saved by public outcry.

Across the Amstel from here, the large squat **Muziektheater and Town Hall** – dubbed the Stopera after the 1980s campaign to "Stop the Opera" – flank **Waterlooplein**, home to the city's excellent **flea market**. Behind, **Jodenbreestraat** was once the main street of the Jodenhoek, the city's Jewish quarter, and is the site of the **Rembrandt House**, no. 4–6 (Mon–Sat 10am–5pm, Sun 1–5pm; f7.50), which the painter bought at the height of his fame, living here for over twenty years. The interior is mostly a disappointing reconstruction, but it does display a huge number of the artist's engravings. Close by, the most tangible mementoes of the Jewish community are shown in the **Portuguese Synagogue** (Mon–Fri & Sun 10am–4pm; closed Yom Kippur; f7.50), completed in 1675 and once the largest synagogue in the world. Across the way, the **Jewish Historical Museum** (daily 11am–5pm; closed Yom Kippur; f8) is cleverly housed in a complex of Ashkenazi synagogues dating from the late seventeenth century and gives a broad and imaginative introduction to Jewish life and beliefs.

Down Muiderstraat from here, the prim **Hortus Botanicus**, Plantage Middenlaan 2 (April–Oct Mon–Fri 9am–5pm, Sat & Sun 11am–5pm, Nov–March Mon–Fri 9am–4pm, Sat & Sun 11am–4pm; f7.50), is a pocket-sized botanical garden whose 6000 plant species make a wonderfully relaxed break from the rest of central Amsterdam; stop off for coffee and cakes in the orangery. Four hundred metres down Plantage Middenlaan and entered off Plantage Kerklaan is Amsterdam's **Zoo** (daily 9am–5pm; f25, children f17.50), beyond which the **Kromhout Shipyard** at Hoogte Kadijk 147 (Mon–Fri 10am– 4pm; free), one of the few survivors of the shipbuilding industry that flourished during the nineteenth century, is a combination of industrial monument, operating shipyard and museum. A short walk northwest, the **Maritime Museum** on Kattenburgerplein (Tues–Sun 10am–5pm, mid–June to mid–Sept also Mon 10am–5pm; f14.50), housed in a fortress-like seventeenth-century arsenal, has more marine attractions – maps, navigational equipment and weapons – though the most impressive exhibits are the large models of sailing ships and men-of-war.

The main canals

The city's expansion in the seventeenth century was designed around three new canals, **Herengracht, Keizersgracht** and **Prinsengracht**, which formed a girdle of canals, or *grachtengordel*, around the centre. Development was strictly controlled: even the richest burgher had to conform to a set of stylistic rules, and taxes were levied according to the width of the properties. The result was the tall, narrow residences you see today, with individualism restricted to decorative gables and sometimes a gablestone to denote name and occupation. It's difficult to pick out any particular points to head for: most of the houses have been turned into offices or hotels. Rather, the appeal lies in wandering along selected stretches admiring the gables while taking in the calm of the tree-lined waterways. For shops, bars and restaurants, explore streets connecting the canals.

Herengracht remains the city's grandest canal, especially between Leidsestraat and Vijzelstraat, a stretch known as the "Golden Curve". To see the interior of one of the canal houses you should head for the **Willet-Holthuysen House**, Herengracht 605 (Mon–Fri 10am–5pm, Sat & Sun 11am–5pm; f7.50), splendidly decorated in Rococo style and containing Abraham Willet's collection of glass and ceramics, and a well-equipped seventeenth-century kitchen. Perhaps more likeable, with a pleasantly down-at-heel interior of peeling stucco and shabby paintwork, is the **Van Loon House**, Keizersgracht 672 (Fri–Mon 11am–5pm; f7.50), built in 1672 for the artist Ferdinand Bol. The Van Loon family bought the house in 1884, bringing with them a collection of family portraits and homely bits and pieces dating from between 1580 and 1949.

On the corner of Keizersgracht and Leidsestraat, the designer department store **Metz & Co** has a top-floor café with one of the best views of the city. **Leidsestraat** itself is a long, slender passage across the main canals that broadens into **Leidseplein** at its southern end in the area that's the focus of Amsterdam's nightlife, with a concentration of bars and restaurants. On the far corner, the **Stadsschouwburg** is the city's prime performance space after the Muziektheater, while behind, the fairy-castle **American Hotel** has a bar whose carefully co-ordinated furnishings are as fine an example of Art Nouveau as you'll find.

The area immediately north of here, along Prinsengracht, is one of the city's loveliest neighbourhoods, focusing on the gracious tower of the **Westerkerk** (April–Sept Mon–Sat 10am–4pm; f3), designed by Hendrik de Keyser in 1631, though there's little within of special note – only a small memorial to Rembrandt, who died in the neighbourhood. Directly outside the church, a statue of Anne Frank, by the Dutch sculptor Mari Andriessen, signals the fact that the house where the young diarist lived is just a few steps away at Prinsengracht 263. This is now open as the **Anne Frank House** (April–Aug daily 9am–9pm, Sept–March 9am–7pm; closed Yom Kippur; f10) and is deservedly one of the most popular tourist attractions in town. The story of Anne Frank, her family and friends is well known. They went into hiding from the Nazis in July 1942, staying in the annexe behind the house for two years until they were betrayed and taken away to labour camps, an experience which only Anne's father survived. Anne Frank's diary was among the few things left behind here, and was published in 1947, since when it has sold over thirteen million copies worldwide. The rooms the Franks lived in are left much as they were, even down to the movie-star pin-ups in Anne's bedroom and the marks on the wall recording the children's heights. A number of other rooms offer background detail on the war and the atrocities of Nazism, giving some up-to-date and pertinent examples of fascism in Europe.

Across Prinsengracht, the **Jordaan** is a beguiling area of narrow canals, narrower streets and simpler, architecturally varied houses, originally home of artisans and religious refugees, and later the inner-city enclave of Amsterdam's industrial working class – which, in spite of widespread gentrification, to some extent remains. Other than a handful of bars and restaurants, some posh clothes shops and the odd outdoor market (including the popular Saturday farmers' market, in the square outside the Noorderkerk) there's nothing specific to see, though it's a wonderful area to wander through, focusing on **Tweede Anjelierdwarsstraat** and **Tweede Tuindwarsstraat**, which hold the bulk of the neighbourhood's trendy stores and some of its liveliest bars and cafés.

The Old South and the major museums

Immediately south of Leidseplein, the **Vondelpark** is the city's most enticing park, named after the seventeenth-century Dutch poet Joost van der Vondel and a regular forum for drama and other performance arts on summer weekends, when young Amsterdam flocks here to meet friends, laze by the lake and listen to music – in June, July and August bands give free **concerts** here every Sunday at 2pm. Southeast of the park is one of Amsterdam's better-heeled residential districts, with designer shops and delis along chic **P.C. Hooftstraat** and **Van Baerlestraat** and some of the city's major **museums** grouped around the grassy wedge of **Museumplein**.

The **Rijksmuseum**, Stadhouderskade 42 (daily 10am–5pm; f15), is the one museum you shouldn't leave Amsterdam without visiting, with fine collections of medieval and Renaissance applied art, displays on Dutch history, a fine Asian collection, and, most importantly, an array of seventeenth-century Dutch paintings that is far and away the best in the world. Most people head straight for one of the museum's great treasures, Rembrandt's *The Night Watch*, but there are many other, perhaps more interesting, examples of his work, not least the *Staalmeesters*, the late *Jewish Bride*, and some private and beautifully expressive works – a portrait of his first wife Saskia, a couple of his mother, a touching depiction of his son, *Titus*, and a late *Self-portrait*, caught in mid-shrug as the Apostle Paul. There are also portraits by Frans Hals, landscapes by Jan van Goyen and Jacob van Ruisdael, the riotous scenes of Jan Steen and the peaceful interiors of Vermeer and Pieter de Hooch.

Just south, the **Vincent Van Gogh Museum**, Paulus Potterstraat 7 (daily 10am–5pm; f15), comprises the collection of the artist's art-dealer brother Theo, with drawings, notebooks and letters displayed on a rotating basis, and a collection arranged chronologically, from the early years in Holland and works like the dour *Potato Eaters*, to the brighter works he painted after moving to Paris and then Arles, where he produced vivid canvases like *The Yellow House* and the *Sunflowers* series. Later, more expressionistic works include the *Garden of St Paul's Hospital*, painted at the asylum in St-Rémy, and his final, tortured paintings, including *The Reaper* and *Wheatfield with Crows*.

Further up the street at Paulus Potterstraat 13 is the **Stedelijk Museum** (April–Sept daily 10am–6pm, Oct–March 11am–5pm; f9), Amsterdam's modern art museum. Much of its wide-ranging permanent collection is on display in July and August, and parts of it year-round. There's normally a good showing on the first floor, starting off with drawings by Picasso, Matisse and their contemporaries, and moving on to paintings by the major Impressionists – Manet, Monet, Bonnard – and Post-Impressionists such as Ensor, Van Gogh and Cézanne. There's also work by Mondrian and Malevich, a good stock of Marc Chagall's paintings, and a number of American Abstract Expressionists – Mark Rothko, Ellsworth Kelly and Barnett Newman. Two additional large-scale attractions are on the ground floor: Karel Appel's Bar in the foyer, installed for the opening of the Stedelijk in the 1950s, and the same artist's wild daubings in the museum's restaurant.

Further along Stadhouderskade from the Rijksmuseum, the **Heineken Brewery** (Mon–Fri 9.30am & 11am and June–Sept also 2.30pm, July & Aug additional tours Sat 11am, 1pm & 2.30pm; over 18s only; f2), though no longer in production, runs tours of the characteristic red-copper brewery providing a résumé of Heineken's history and the methods involved in the brewing process; afterwards you are given snacks and free beer. Beyond here, the neighbourhood is known as **"De Pijp"** (The Pipe) after its long, sombre canyons of brick tenements that went up in the nineteenth century as the city grew out of its canal-girded centre. De Pijp has always been one of the city's closest-knit communities, and one of its liveliest, with numerous inexpensive Surinamese and Turkish restaurants and a cheerful hub in the long slim thoroughfare of **Albert Cuypstraat**, whose daily general market is the largest in the city.

Eating and drinking

Amsterdam may not be the culinary capital of Europe, but there's a good supply of ethnic restaurants, especially Indonesian and Chinese, as well as *eetcafés* and bars which serve decent, well-priced food in a relaxed and unpretentious setting. We've also listed a handful of places to get just a snack (though you can do this easily enough in many bars), as well as the best of the city's coffeeshops, where smoking dope is the primary pastime (all sell a range of hash and grass). Restaurants have been divided into budget (under f20), inexpensive (f20–f30) and moderate (f30–f40) and denote the average cost per person for a starter and main course without drinks.

Cafés and snacks

Café Esprit, Spui 10a. Swish modern café, with wonderful sandwiches and superb salads.

Gary Muffins, Prinsengracht 454, near Leidseplein; Reguliersdwarsstraat 53, near Koningsplein. The best muffins and bagels in town, with big cups of coffee (and half-price refills).

Greenwoods, Singel 103 near Dam Square. Small English-style teashop, with a decent breakfast.

Maoz Falafel, Reguliersbreesstraat 45, near Rembrandtplein. The best street-food in the city – falafel with bread and as much salad as you can eat for the grand sum of f6.

Mr Hot Potato, Leidsestraat 44. Baked potatoes – nothing fancy, but cheap.

The Pancake Bakery, Prinsengracht 191. A large selection of pancakes from f8.95.

Puccini, Staalstraat 17–21, near Waterlooplein. Dreamy cakes, pastries and chocolates, all hand-made.

Studio 2, Singel 504. Pleasantly situated, airy tearoom with a delicious selection of rolls and sandwiches.

Toko Sari, Kerkstraat 161. Fabulous Indonesian takeaway. Tues–Sat 11am–6pm.

Villa Zeezicht, Torensteeg 3, at Singel. Small place, all in wood, with excellent sandwiches and some of the best apple-cake in the city.

Restaurants

Akbar, Korte Leidsedwarsstraat 33, near Leidseplein. Fabulous South Indian food, with a fine choice across the board. Plenty for vegetarians. Moderate.

An, Weteringschans 199, near Frederiksplein. Excellent Japanese cooking in this family-run place with an open kitchen. Moderate.

Beyrouth, Kinkerstraat 18, Old West (tram #7 or #17 to Bilderdijkstraat). Small Lebanese place well off any beaten tracks; highly acclaimed food. Inexpensive.

De Blauwe Hollander, Leidsekruisstraat 28, near Leidseplein. Dutch food in generous quantities. Expect to share a table. Inexpensive.

Burger's Patio, 2e Tuindwarsstraat 12, Jordaan. Trendy but convivial Italian restaurant. Despite the name, not a burger in sight. Inexpensive.

Casa di David, Singel 426. Solid-value Italian wtih a long-standing reputation. Pizzas from wood-fired ovens and fresh hand-made pasta. Moderate.

Dionysos, Overtoom 176. Fine Greek restaurant with live music every Sunday, a little to the south of Leidseplein; serves until 1am. Inexpensive.

Duende, Lindengracht 62, Jordaan. Good Spanish bar with cheap tapas to help your drink go down. Budget. Roughly 4pm–1am.

De Eetuin, 2e Tuindwarsstraat 10, Jordaan. Hefty portions of Dutch food. Inexpensive.

Golden Temple, Utrechtsestraat 126, near Frederiksplein. Laid-back vegetarian place with attentive service; the only non-smoking restaurant in the city. Inexpensive.

Hoi Tin, Zeedijk 122, near Nieuwmarkt. One of the best places in the rather dodgy Chinatown, with an enormous menu (in English too) and some vegetarian dishes. Always busy. Moderate.

Kam Yin, Warmoestraat 6. Excellent option for large portions of Chinese and Surinamese dishes. Budget.

Kilimanjaro, Rapenburgerpin 6. Small, friendly place serving North African specialities. Open Tues–Sun from 5pm. Moderate.

Keuken van 1870, Spuistraat 4. Former soup kitchen still serving Dutch meat-and-potato staples. Budget.

Lokanta Ceren, Albert Cuypstraat 40, Old South. Authentic local Turkish place, with a welter of meze and fine kebab dishes. Inexpensive.

Mensa Atrium, Oudezijds Achterburgwal 237. Central self-service cafeteria attached to the university (but open to all). Budget. Mon–Fri noon–2pm & 5–7pm.

De Rozenboom, Rozenboomsteeg 6. Quaint little Dutch restaurant with good traditional food and a menu in English. Ideally situated, just off Spui Centrum. Inexpensive.

Shiva, Reguliersdwarsstraat 72. Outstanding Indian restaurant, with well-priced, expertly prepared food. Vegetarians well catered for. Inexpensive.

Sisters, Nes 102, city centre. A busy vegetarian restaurant serving delicious balanced meals, as well as plenty of snack-type items. Budget.

Tempo Doeloe, Utrechtsestraat 75, near Rembrandtplein. Reliable, quality Indonesian place. Moderate.

De Vliegende Schotel, Nieuwe Leliestraat 162, Jordaan. Perhaps the best of the city's vegetarian restaurants, serving delicious food in large portions. Budget.

Bars

Cul de Sac, Oudezijds Achterburgwal 99. Down a long alley, in what used to be a spice warehouse, this is a handy retreat from the red-light district.

De Drie Fleschjes, Gravenstraat 18, near Dam. Tasting house for spirits and liqueurs. No beer, and no seats either. Closes 8pm.

Durty Nelly's, Warmoesstraat 117. Irish pub in the heart of the red-light action, packed if there's weekend football.

De Engelbewaarder, Kloveniersburgwal 59. Once a meeting place of Amsterdam's bookish types, with live jazz on Sunday afternoons.

Flying Dutchman, Martelaarsgracht 13, near Centraal Station. Principal watering hole of British expats, and not a word of Dutch to be heard.

't IJ, Funenkade 7. Situated in the base of a windmill to the east of the centre. The home-brewed beers are extremely strong. Wed–Sun 3–8pm.

De Jaren, Nieuwe Dolenstraat 20–22, near Muntplein. Grand café overlooking the river – one of the best places to nurse the Sunday paper. From 10am.

Koophandel, Bloemgracht 49, Jordaan. Empty before midnight, this is the early-hours bar you dreamt about, in an old warehouse on one of Amsterdam's most picturesque canals. Open until at least 3am.

Lokaal 't Loosje, Nieuwmarkt 32. Quiet old-style brown café that's been here for 200 years and looks its age.

Mulligans, Amstel 100, near Rembrandtplein. By far the best Irish pub in the city, with superb Gaelic music.

O'Donnells, Ferdinand Bolstraat 5, Old South. The best Guinness in town, just behind the Heineken Brewery.

Saarein, Elandsstraat 119, Jordaan. No longer women-only; though some of the former glory of this café is gone, still a peaceful, relaxed place to take it easy.

Sound Garden, Marnixstraat 164, Jordaan. Grunge bar, packed with people and noise, with a canalside terrace to retreat to.

Tara, Rokin 89. Excellent Irish bar with regular live music.

De Tuin, 2e Tuindwarsstraat 13. The Jordaan has some marvellously unpretentious bars, and this is one of the best. Agreeably unkempt.

De Twee Zwaantjes, Prinsengracht 114. Tiny odd-ball Jordaan bar where locals sing along raucously to accordian music – you'll either love it or hate it.

Café Vertigo, Vondelpark 3. Attached to the Film Museum, a wonderful place to while away a sunny afternoon (or take refuge from the rain) with a spacious interior and a large terrace overlooking the park.

Vrankrijk, Spuistraat 216. The best of Amsterdam's few remaining squat bars. Buzz to enter. From 10pm.

Smoking coffeeshops

The Bulldog, Leidseplein 15 and a couple of other outlets. The oldest and biggest, not at all the place for a thoughtful smoke.

Global Chillage, Kerkstraat 51. Celebrated slice of tie-dyed dope culture.

Grasshopper, Oudebrugsteeg 16 and other outlets. One of the more welcoming large coffeeshops.

Greenhouse, Tolstraat 4; Waterlooplein 345. Top quality dope. Tolsraat is a way down to the south (tram #4), but if you're only buying once, buy here.

't Kruydenhuys, Keizersgracht 665. Perhaps the best general coffeeshop in the city, in an old house on a quiet stretch of water.

Paradox, 1e Bloemdwarsstraat 2. Satisfies the munchies with outstanding natural food, including spectacular fresh-fruit concoctions. Closes 7pm.

Siberië, Brouwersgracht 11. Relaxed, and worth a visit whether you want to smoke or not.

Tweede Kamer, Heisteeg 6. Pleasant coffeeshop near Spui where you can chill out over a game of chess or draughts.

Nightlife

Amsterdam is a gathering spot for fringe performances, and buzzes with places offering a wide and often inventive range of affordable entertainment. **Rock, jazz** and **Latin American** music are well represented in a number of small bars and clubs but the **club scene** is relatively tame: drinks prices are normally fifty percent or so more than what you pay in a bar, but entry prices are low – usually around f10 – and there's rarely any kind of door policy. Most places open around 10pm and close around 4am or slightly later. For more highbrow entertainment, the Concertgebouw assures Amsterdam a high ranking in the **classical music** stakes, and the city has pulled itself up into the big leagues for **dance** and **opera**. The **Uitburo**, or AUB, in the Stadsschouwburg on the corner of Marnixstraat and Leidseplein (daily 10am–6pm, until 9pm on Thurs; ☎020/621 1211), is the best source of information – pick up the free bimonthly *Pop & Jazz Uitljist* – and sells tickets for a f3 fee; tickets can also be bought from VVV. For film and music listings, get hold of a *Week Agenda* from any cinema, or try the alternative fortnightly *Queer Fish*, available in the city centre.

Rock and jazz venues

Akhnaton, Nieuwezijds Kolk 25, city centre (☎020/624 3396). A "Centre for World Culture", specializing in African and Latin American music and dance parties.

Alto, Korte Leidsedwarsstraat 115, near Leidseplein (☎020/626 3249). Legendary jazz bar, with free live music every night 10pm–3am. Big on atmosphere, not space.

Arena, 's-Gravesandestraat 51, near Oosterpark (☎020/694 7444). Multimedia centre featuring live music, cultural events, a bar, coffeeshop and restaurant. Intimate hall features underground bands from around the world. f10–50.

Bimhuis, Oude Schans 73–77 (☎020/623 1361). The city's premier jazz venue. Big name concerts Thurs–Sat, free workshop sessions Mon–Wed.

Casablanca, Zeedijk 26, red-light district (☎020/625 5685). Live jazz every night.

Maloe Melo, Lijnbaansgracht 163, Jordaan (☎020/420 4592). Dark low-ceilinged bar, with a local bluesy act.

Melkweg, Lijnbaansgracht 234a, near Leidseplein (☎020/624 1777). Probably Amsterdam's most famous entertainment venue, with a young hip clientele. Two halls feature a broad range of bands tending towards African music and lesser-knowns. Excellent offbeat disco sessions late on Fri & Sat. Also films, a tearoom selling dope, and a bar and restaurant. Admission f10–50, plus f4.50 membership on door. Closed Mon.

Paradiso, Weteringschans 6–8, near Leidseplein (☎020/626 4521). A converted church featuring semi-big names and up-and-coming bands. Entrance f10–50, plus f4.50 membership on door.

Winston Kingdom, Warmoesstraat 127, red-light district (☎020/623 1380). Small renovated venue with spoken word, jazz-poetry, R&B and punk/noise nights.

Discos and clubs

Dansen bij Jansen, Handboogstraat 11, near Spui. Founded by – and for – students, and very popular; f5 weekends, f2.50 discount during the week with student ID.

Escape, Rembrandtplein 11. Large nightclub packed on weekends, with several floors and top visiting DJs on Sat. Thurs–Sat; f10–20; free for students on Thurs.

iT Amstelstraat 24, near Rembrandtplein. Large disco with popular and glamorous gay nights, but Thurs & Sun are mixed gay/straight and attract a dressed-up, uninhibited crowd.

Mazzo, Rozengracht 114, Jordaan. Perhaps the city's hippest and most laid-back disco, with a choice of music to appeal to all tastes. Nightly; around f10.

The RoXY, Singel 465, near Koningsplein. One of the city's best (and loudest) sound systems – if you can get past the door policy to hear it. On Thurs Holland's top DJ Dimitri is in residence. Around f10.

Soul Kitchen, Amstelstraat 32a, near Rembrandtplein. Relaxed setting for 60s and 70s soul and funk. Fri & Sat only; around f10.

Contemporary music, classical music and opera

Concertgebouw, Concertgebouwplein 2–6 (☎020/671 8345). One of the most dynamic orchestras in the world in one of the finest halls. Free lunchtime concerts Sept–May. f25 and upwards.

Beurs van Berlage, Damrak 213, city centre (☎020/627 0466). The splendid interior of the former stock exchange hosts a wide selection of music from the Dutch Philharmonic and Dutch Chamber Orchestras.

De IJsbreker, Weesperzijde 23 (☎020/668 1805). Large, varied programme of international modern, chamber and experimental music. Admission f15–25. Pleasant canalside café/bar. Tram #3, #6, #7, #10.

Muziektheater, Amstel 3 (☎020/625 5455). Amsterdam's fullest opera programme. Tickets cost f25–115, and sell quickly. Free lunchtime concerts.

Stadsschouwburg, Leidseplein 26 (☎020/624 2311). Somewhat overshadowed by the Muziektheater, but still a significant stage for opera and dance. Tickets f25–50.

Cinema and theatre

Cinemas in Amsterdam rarely show foreign-language films without English subtitles and anything already in English will be subtitled in Dutch. Amsterdam's cinemas excel in Art Deco; try the lavish Tuschinski, Reguliersbreestraat 26, for Hollywood productions and either The Movies, Haarlemmerdijk 161, or Desmet, Plantage Middenlaan 4a, for cult, classic and gay flicks. The Film Museum in Vondelpark shows all kinds of movies from all corners of the world, and has free open-air screenings on summer weekends. The resident English-language **theatre** company, the Stalhouderij, 1e Bloemdwarsstraat 4 (☎020/626 2282), puts on a mixture of twentieth-century British and American plays alongside the classics. Boom Chicago, at Korte Leidsedwarsstraat 12, is a hugely popular rapid-fire comedy troupe, performing nightly in English to crowds of tourists and locals.

Gay Amsterdam

Amsterdam has one of the biggest and best-established **gay scenes** in Europe: attitudes are tolerant and facilities unequalled, with a good selection of bookstores, clubs and bars catering to the needs of gay men – and, to a lesser extent, women. The nationwide gay and lesbian organization, COC, Rozenstraat 14 (☎020/626 3087), can provide on-the-spot **information**, and has a café and popular discos (men Fri, women Sat). For further advice on where to go contact the Gay & Lesbian Switchboard (☎020/623 6565; daily 10am–10pm). There's a good concentration of **bars** around Rembrandtplein, along the Amstel and on Reguliersdwarsstraat. The *Amstel Taveerne*, Amstel 54, is perhaps the best established, at its most vivacious in summer when the guys spill out onto the street by the river; around the corner, *De Steeg*, Halvemaansteeg 10, is a tiny and similarly longtime favourite venue. *April*, Reguliersdwarsstraat 37, is a relaxed afternoon and evening hangout, with newspapers, coffee and cakes as well as booze. *Saarein*, Elandsstraat 119, once the best-known women-only/lesbian café, is now open to both sexes.

Vrolijk, Paleisstraat 135, bills itself as "the largest gay and lesbian **bookstore** on the continent". Xantippe, Prinsengracht 290, has a wide range of books and resources by, for and about women.

Listings

Airlines Aer Lingus, Heiligeweg 14 (☎020/623 8620); Air UK, Schiphol Airport (☎020/601 0633); American Airlines, Schiphol Airport (☎020/446 6175); British Airways, Schiphol Airport (☎020/601 5413); British Midland, Strawinskylaan 721 (☎020/662 2211); KLM, Schiphol Airport (☎020/474 7747); Qantas, Stadhouderskade 6 (☎020/683 8081); Transavia, Schiphol Airport (☎020/604 6555).

Bicycle rental Cheapest from main train stations but try also: Bike City, Bloemgracht 70 (☎020/626 3721); Damstraat, just off Damstraat (☎020/625 5029); or MacBike, Mr Visserpin 2 (☎020/620 0985) and Marnixstraat 220 (☎020/626 6964). All charge around f10 a day plus f200 deposit with ID.

Books Athenaeum, Spui 14–16; Waterstones, Kalverstraat 152; Scheltema Holkema Vermeulen, Koningsplein 20.

Car rental The international companies, which are all close to each other on Overtoom, can be undercut by local operators, such as Diks, van Ostadestraat 278 (☎020/662 3366) and Baas Ouke, van Ostadestraat 366 (☎020/679 4842).

Consulates Australia, Carnegielaan 4, The Hague (☎070/310 8200); Canada, Sophialaan 7, The Hague (☎070/311 1600); Great Britain, Koningslaan 44 (☎020/676 4343); Ireland, Dr Kuyperstraat 9, The Hague (☎070/363 0993); New Zealand, Carnegielaan 10, The Hague (☎070/346 9324); USA, Museumplein 19 (☎020/664 5661).

Exchange GWK, Centraal Station (open 24hr) and Leidseplein corner (daily 8am–11pm). Change Express, Leidsestraat 105, Damrak 17 & 86 and Kalverstraat 150 (all daily until midnight).

Laundry The Clean Brothers, Kerkstraat 56 (daily 7am–9pm; f9 to wash and dry). Alternatives at Oudebrugsteeg 22, Warmoesstraat 30 and Oude Doelenstraat 12.

Left luggage Centraal Station (lockers f4 & f6 for 24hr).

Pharmacy There are no 24hr pharmacies, but every pharmacy has a sign giving the address of the nearest late-opening place.

Police station Headquarters at Elandsgracht 117 (☎020/559 91 11).

Post office Singel 250 (Mon–Fri 9am–6pm, Thurs until 8pm, Sat 10am–1.30pm).

Travel agents NBBS, Rokin 38 and Utrechtsestraat 48, is the Amsterdam branch of the nationwide youth travel organization; central booking on ☎020/620 5071.

Women's contacts The Vrouwenhuis, Nieuwe Herengracht 95 (☎020/625 20 66), is an organizing centre for women's activities; Xantippe, Prinsengracht 290, is a women's bookshop with a wide selection of titles in English.

THE RANDSTAD TOWNS

The string of towns known as the **Randstad**, or "rim town", form the country's most populated region and recall the seventeenth-century heyday of the provinces of North and South Holland, of which they are now a part. Situated amid a typically Dutch landscape of flat fields cut by canals. Much of the area is easily visited by means of day-trips from Amsterdam, but it's more rewarding – and not difficult – to make a proper tour. **Haarlem** is definitely worth an overnight stop. South, the university centre of **Leiden** is a pleasant detour before the refined tranquillity of **The Hague** and the seedy lowlife of **Rotterdam**, while nearby **Delft** and **Gouda** repay visits too, the former with one of the best-preserved centres in the region. To the north, not officially part of the Randstad but still easily visited from Amsterdam, **Alkmaar** is a favourite with day-excursionists to see its rather bogus Friday cheese market.

Haarlem

Just over fifteen minutes from Amsterdam by train, **HAARLEM** is an easily absorbed city of around 150,000 people that sees itself as a cut above its neighbours and makes a good alternative base for exploring the province of North Holland, or even Amsterdam itself. The Frans Hals Museum, in the almshouse where the artist spent his last years, is worth an afternoon in itself, and there are numerous beaches within easy reach, as well as some of the best of the bulbfields.

Haarlem was one of the former Republic's most crucial centres, especially for the arts, and today retains an air of quiet affluence, with all the picturesque qualities of Amsterdam but little of the sleaze. The core of the city is **Grote Markt** and the adjoining Riviervischmarkt, flanked by the gabled, originally fourteenth-century **Stadhuis** and the impressive bulk of the **Grote Kerk of St Bavo** (April–Aug Mon–Sat 10am–4pm, Sept–March 10am–3.30pm; f2.50). Inside, the mighty Christian Müller organ of 1738, with its 5000 pipes and Baroque razzmatazz, is said to have been played by Handel and Mozart, while beneath, Xaverij's lovely group of draped marble figures represents Poetry and Music, offering thanks to the town patron for her generosity. In the choir there's a late fifteenth-century painting traditionally (though dubiously) attributed to Geertgen tot Sint Jans, along with memorials to painters Pieter Saenredam and Frans Hals, both of whom are buried here.

The town's real attraction is the **Frans Hals Museum** at Groot Heiligland 62 (Mon–Sat 11am–5pm, Sun 12–5pm; f10), a five-minute stroll from Grote Markt in the Oudemannhuis almshouse where the aged Hals is supposed to have lived out his last years. It houses a good number of his lifelike seventeenth-century portraits, including (in the west wing) the "Civic Guard" portraits which established his reputation. In the *Officers of the Militia Company of Saint George* (of which Hals was himself a member) he appears in the top left-hand corner, a rare self-portrait. His last, contemplative portraits include the *Governors of the Saint Elizabeth Gasthuis*, painted in 1641. Also on display are works by Gerard David, Jan Mostaert and the Haarlem Mannerists, including Carel van Mander, numerous scenes of Haarlem by Berckheyde and Saenredam, and landscapes by the Ruisdaels.

Look out too for the recently restored and immaculate eighteenth-century **Doll's House**, modelled on an Amsterdam merchant's house and one of only four of its type in the country. Hours of painstaking work were put into producing this tiny piece, at a cost reckoned at a million guilders. Back at the Grote Markt, take a look at the Frans Hals Museum's annexe, **De Hallen** (Mon–Sat 11am–5pm, Sun noon–5pm; f7.50), an old meat market building now filled with touring exhibitions and works by Haarlem-based Kees Verwey, Holland's oldest living painter, whose Impressionistic watercolours are much loved by senior Dutch aficionados.

Just off the eastern side of Grote Markt, the **Teylers Museum**, at Spaarne 16 (Tues–Sat 10am–5pm, Sun noon–5pm; f10), is the oldest museum in Holland, founded back in 1778 by wealthy local philanthropist Pieter Teyler van der Hulst. It should appeal to scientific and artistic tastes alike, containing everything from fossils, bones and crystals to weird, H.G. Wells-type technology and sketches and line drawings by Michelangelo, Raphael, Rembrandt and Claude. Look in on the rooms beyond, which are filled with work by eighteenth- and nineteenth-century Dutch painters, principally Breitner, Israëls, Weissenbruch and Wijbrand Hendriks, who was keeper of the art collection here.

Practicalities

The **train station**, connected to Amsterdam and to Leiden by four trains an hour and to Alkmaar by two an hour, is located on the north side of the city, about ten minutes' walk from the centre; **buses** stop right outside. The **VVV**, attached to the station (Mon–Fri 9.30am–5pm, Sat 10am–2pm; ☎0900/616 1600, f1 per minute), has maps (f4) and can book **private rooms** (③) for a f10 fee, though you'll find more choice in Zandvoort, about twenty minutes away by bus #81 (every 30min from the train station) or by train. The same goes for **hotels**, although Haarlem has a few reasonably priced and central places worth considering such as the *Carillon*, at Grote Markt 27 (☎023/531 0591; ⑤); *Amadeus*, at Grote Markt 10 (☎023/532 4530; ④); and *Joops Innercity Apartments* at Oude Groenmarkt 20 (☎023/532 2008; ④). There's also a **youth hostel** at Jan Gijzenpad 3 (☎023/537 3793; March–Oct; ②); bus #2 from the station (10min). Campers could try the **campsites** among the dunes out at Bloemendaal-aan-zee – *De Lakens* at Zeeweg 60 (☎023/573 2266; April–Oct); *Bloemendaal* at Zeeweg 72 (☎023/573 2178; April–Oct); or *De Branding* at Boulevard Barnaart 30 near Zandvoort (☎023/571 3035; April–Oct). Bus #81 from the train station will take you to all of them. Haarlem's own site, *De Liede*, is at Liewegje 68 (☎023/533 2360) – take bus #80 from Templierstraat.

For **lunches and snacks**, *Café Mephisto*, Grote Markt 29, is open all day and serves Dutch food for f15–25, snacks for much less. *Café 1900*, Barteljorisstraat 10, is also a good place for lunch, serving drinks and snacks in a turn-of-the-century interior. In the evening, there's *Alfonso's* **restaurant** at Oude Groenmarkt 8, which does Tex-Mex meals for around f25; the *Piccolo*, Riviervischmarkt 1, serves pasta and decent pizzas; or try the Indonesian food at *De Lachende Javaen*, on Frankestraat, with *rijsttafels* from f34. *Ze Crack*, at the junction of Lange Veerstraat and Kleine Houtstraat, is a dim, smoky bar with good music and beer by the pint. For a little traditional character, try the **proeflokaal** (a spirit-tasting room turned bar) *In den Uiver*, Riviervischmarkt 13, or, to **surf the Web** try *Hoeksteen's Internet Café* at Lange Herenvest 122.

Alkmaar

An hour from Amsterdam by train, **ALKMAAR** is typical of small-town Holland, its pretty, partly canalized centre surrounded by water and offering an undemanding provincialism which makes a pleasant change after the big city. The town is probably best known for its **cheese market** (mid-April to mid-Sept Fri 10am–noon). Cheese has been sold on the main square here since the 1300s, and although no serious buying goes on now, it's an institution that continues to draw crowds. Be sure to get there early, as by opening time there's already quite a crush.

On the main square, the **Waag** was originally a chapel dedicated to the Holy Ghost, and nowadays houses the **VVV** and the **Kaasmuseum** (April–Oct Mon–Sat 10am–4pm, Fri

9am–4pm; f5), which has displays on the history of cheese, cheese-making equipment and suchlike. Across the square, the **Biermuseum de Boom**, Houttil 1 (April–Oct Tues–Sat 10am–4pm, Sun 1–4pm; f4), in the building of the old De Boom brewery, has exhibits tracing the brewing process from the malting to bottling stage, as well as a top-floor shop in which you can buy a huge range of beers and associated merchandise and a downstairs bar serving some eighty varieties of Dutch ale. The **Stedelijk Museum** (Tues–Fri 10am–5pm, Sat & Sun 1–5pm; f3), on the other side of the town centre in Doelenstraat, displays pictures and artefacts relating to the history of the town, including a *Holy Family* by Honthorst and portraits by Maerten van Heemskerk and Caesar van Everdingen. Close by, at the far end of **Langestraat**, the town's main shopping street, the **St Laurenskerk** (hours variable due to restoration; f1), a Gothic church of the late fifteenth century, is worth looking into for its huge organ, designed by Jacob van Campen and painted by Caesar van Everdingen. In the apse is the tomb of Count Floris V, penultimate in the line of medieval counts of North Holland, who was murdered by nobles in 1296.

Practicalities

Alkmaar's **train station** is fifteen minutes' walk west of the centre of town on Stationsstraat; to get to the centre, turn right outside the station, then left at the traffic lights and follow the road to St Laurenskerk. The VVV is five minutes on from here on Waagplein (Mon 10am–5.30pm, Tues & Wed 9am–5.30pm, Thurs 9am–9pm, Fri 9am–6pm, Sat 9.30am–5pm; ☎072/511 4284) and can arrange **private rooms** (②) for a f3.50 booking fee. *Hotel Stadenland* is about the cheapest and most central **hotel** at Stationsweg 92 (☎072/512 3911; ④). If you're **camping**, there's a site ten minutes' bus ride northwest of the town centre at Bergenweg 20 (☎072/511 6294; May–Sept); take bus #168 or #169 from the station. There are quite a few decent **places to eat**: *Efes*, in the old part of town at Fnidsen 62, is a cosy, wooden-beamed Turkish restaurant with meals from f30; while *Rose's Cantina*, further along at 105, serves Tex-Mex dishes for about f30. There are two main groupings of **bars**: one on Waagplein itself, the other on the nearby canal of Verdronkenoord, by the old Vismarkt. Of the former, *De Kaasbeurs* at Houttil 30 is a lively place during the day but closes in the early evening; while *Café Corridor*, virtually next door, is a lively hangout that plays loud music late into the night. On Verdronkenoord, *De Pilaren* is also noisy, though catering to a slightly older crowd; *Café Stapper*, next door, is a good refuge if the music gets too much.

Leiden

The home of Holland's most prestigious university, **LEIDEN** has an academic air. The students give the town a certain energy, and there's enough here to justify at least a day-trip. Leiden's museums are varied and comprehensive enough to merit a visit in themselves, though the town's real charm lies in the peace and prettiness of its gabled streets and canals.

The Town

Leiden's most appealing quarter is that bordered by Witte Singel and Breestraat, focusing on Rapenburg, a peaceful area of narrow pedestrian streets and canals that is home to perhaps the city's best-known attraction, the **Rijksmuseum Van Oudheden**, Rapenburg 28 (Tues–Fri 10am–5pm, Sat & Sun noon–5pm; f7), the country's principal archeological museum. You can see one of its major exhibits for free in the front courtyard – the first-century AD Temple of Teffeh, a gift from the Egyptian government. Inside the museum are more Egyptian artefacts, along with Classical Greek and Roman sculpture and exhibits chronicling the archeology of the country through prehistoric, Roman and medieval times. Further along Rapenburg, at no. 73, the original home of the university is in part open as a **museum** (Wed–Fri 1–5pm; free), beyond which the **Hortus Botanicus** (Mon–Sat 9am–5pm; April–Sept also Sun 10am–5pm; f5) are among the oldest botanical gardens in Europe, planted in 1587. Across Rapenburg, a network of narrow streets converges on the **Pieterskerk** (daily 1.30–4pm; free), deconsecrated these days but still bearing the tomb of John Robinson, leader of the Pilgrim Fathers, who lived in a house on the site of what is now the **Jan Pesijn Hofje**, at Kloksteeg 21.

East of here, **Breestraat** marks the edge of Leiden's commercial centre, behind which the two rivers converge at the busiest point in town, the site of a vigorous Wednesday and Saturday **market** which sprawls right over the sequence of bridges into the blandly pedestrian **Haarlemmerstraat**, the town's major shopping street. Close by, the **Burcht** (Mon–Sat 10am–11pm, Sun 11am–11pm; free) is a rather ordinary, graffiti-daubed shell of a fort perched on a mound, whose battlements you can clamber up for a view of Leiden's roofs and towers. The nearby **Hooglandsekerk** (mid-May to mid-Sept Mon 1–3.30pm, Tues–Fri 11am–3.30pm, Sat 11am–4pm; free) is a light, lofty church with a central pillar that features an epitaph to Pieter van der Werff, the burgomaster at the time of a 1574 siege by the Spanish, who became a hero by offering his own body as food. His invitation was rejected, but – the story goes – it instilled new determination in the flagging citizens. Across Oude Rijn from here, the **Museum Boerhaave** at Lange Agnietenstraat 10 (Tues–Sat 10am–5pm, Sun noon–5pm; f5) is a brief but absorbing guide to medical developments over the last three centuries, with some gruesome surgical implements, pickled brains and the like. Five minutes' walk away, Leiden's municipal museum, in the old **Cloth Hall**, or Lakenhal, at Oude Singel 28–32 (Tues–Sat 10am–5pm, Sun noon–5pm; f5) has mixed rooms of furniture, tiles, glass and ceramics, and a collection of paintings centred on Lucas van Leyden's *Last Judgment* triptych, plus canvases by Jacob van Swanenburgh, the first teacher of the young Rembrandt, and by Rembrandt himself. Around the corner on Molenwerf, the **Molenmuseum de Valk**, 2e Binnenvestgracht 1 (Tues–Sat 10am–5pm, Sun 1–5pm; f5), is located in a restored grain mill, one of twenty that used to surround Leiden, with living quarters furnished in simple, period style and a slide show recounting the history of windmills in Holland. Between here and the station at Steenstraat 1, the **National Museum of Ethnology** (Rijksmuseum voor Volkenkunde; Tues–Fri 10am–5pm, Sat & Sun noon–5pm; open for exhibitions only during renovations; f10), has extensive sections on Indonesia and the Dutch colonies. Near the station on Darwinweg, Leiden's newest museum, Naturalis, the **Museum of Natural History** (Tues–Sun noon–6pm, daily 10am–6pm during school holidays; f12.50), boasts two dinosaurs, a prehistoric horse and a whole host of exhibits from the animal, vegetable and mineral kingdoms.

Practicalities

Leiden's **train** and **bus stations** are both situated on the northwest edge of town, no more than ten minutes' walk from the centre. The **VVV**, opposite the stations at Stationsweg 20 (Mon–Fri 10am–6.30pm, Sat 10am–2pm; ☎0900/222 2333), has a tourist guide (free) and, for a charge of f4.50, can book **private rooms** for f40 a person. The cheapest central **accommodation** is at *The Rose*, Beestenmarkt 14 (☎071/514 6630; ⑤). Alternatively, for a much better deal try the *Pension Witte Singel* at Singel 80 (☎071/512 4592; ④) about fifteen minutes' walk from the station. You can also get considerably more comfort at the *Pension Van Helvoort*, nearby at Narmstraat 1B (☎071/513 2374; ③), or *Pension Schaefer* ten minutes' walk from the station at Herensingel 1A (☎071/521 8104; ③). If you're **camping**, the closest site is the *Koningshof* (☎071/402 6051) in Rijnsburg, 6km north of Leiden; take bus #40. For lunch, *M'n Broer*, by the Pieterskerk at Kloksteeg 7, has a reasonable Dutch menu, while *Barrera*, on Rapenburg, has good sandwiches. In the **evening**, *De Brasserie*, Lange Mare 38, has Dutch food; *Splinter* is a pleasant, reasonably priced vegetarian restaurant at Noordeinde 30; and the studenty *La Bota*, Herensteeg 9, by the Pieterskerk, has great-value food and beers.

Around Leiden: the Keukenhof Gardens and Aalsmeer

Along with Haarlem to the north, Leiden is the best base for seeing something of the Dutch **bulbfields** which flourish here in spring. The view from the train can be sufficient in itself as the line cuts directly through the main growing areas, the fields divided into stark geometric blocks of pure colour. Should you want to get closer, make a bee-line for LISSE, home to the **Keukenhof Gardens** (late-March to late-May daily 8am–7.30pm; f18), the largest flower gardens in the world. Some six million flowers are on show for their full flowering period, complemented, in case of harsh winters, by 5000 square metres of greenhouses. Special buses (#54) run daily to the Keukenhof from Leiden bus station at seventeen and forty-seven minutes past each hour. You can also see the industry in action in **AALSMEER**, 23km north of Leiden, whose flower auction, held daily in a building approximately the size of 75 football pitches (Mon–Fri 7.30–11am; f7.50), turns over around f2.5 billion worth of plants and flowers a year.

The Hague

With its urbane atmosphere, **THE HAGUE** (Den Haag) is different from any other Dutch city. Since the sixteenth century it's been the Netherlands' political capital and the focus of national institutions, and its older buildings are a rather subdued collection with little of Amsterdam's flamboyance. Diplomats and delegates from multinational businesses ensure that many of the city's hotels and restaurants are firmly in the expense-account category, and the nightlife is similarly packaged. But, away from this mediocrity, The Hague does have cheaper and livelier bars and restaurants, as well as some excellent museums.

Arrival and accommodation

The Hague has two **train stations** – Den Haag HS (Hollands Spoor) and Den Haag CS (Centraal Station), and trains stop at one or the other and sometimes both; the latter is the more convenient, being next to the **VVV** (Mon–Fri 8.30am–5.30pm, Sat 10am–5pm; July & Aug also Sun 11am–3pm; ☎0900/340 3505, 75c per minute). Den Haag HS is about 1km to the south, and frequent rail services connect it to Centraal Station. **Accommodation** in The Hague can be quite expensive. The VVV have a small stock of **private rooms**, or there's a cluster of seedy but reasonably priced **hotels** just outside Den Haag HS station: the cheapest is the *Aristo*, Stationsweg 164–166 (☎070/389 0847; ③), although you get a far better deal 4km away from the centre at the beach resort of Scheveningen, where hotels are more plentiful and a little cheaper, and only a short ride on tram #1, #7 or #9 from Den Haag CS or tram #8 or #11 from Den Haag HS. In Scheveningen, try *Bali*, Badhuisweg 1 (☎070/350 2434; ⑤) or one of the group on the seafront road Zeekant, which include the comfortable *Aquarius*, Zeekant 107 (☎070/354 3543; ⑥). There are three **youth hostels** in the town: the *Scheveningen*, at Gevers Deynootweg 2 (☎070/354 7003; ③); *Marion*, at Havenkade 3a (☎070/350 5050; ③), and the pleasant *HI City Hostel* at Scheepmakerstraat 27 (☎070/315 7878; ④). For **camping**, the best and largest site in the area, *Camping Ockenburgh*, Winjndaelerweg 25 (☎070/325 2364; March–Oct) lies just behind the beach at Kijkduin. Take bus #4 from Den Haag CS or #26 from Den Haag HS.

The City

Right in the centre, the **Binnenhof** is the home of the Dutch parliament. Count William II built a castle here in the thirteenth century, and the settlement that grew up around it became known as the "Count's Domain" – *'s Gravenhage* – the city's official name right up until the 1990s. The present complex is a rather mundane affair, a small lake – the **Hof Vijver** – mirroring the symmetry of the facade; inside there's little to see except the **Ridderzaal**, a slender-turreted structure used for state occasions that can be viewed on regular guided tours from the information office at Binnenhof 8a (Mon–Sat 10am–4pm; f5). Immediately east, the **Royal Picture Gallery Mauritshuis**, Korte Vijverberg 8 (Tues–Sat 10am–5pm, Sun 11am–5pm; f12.50), located in a magnificent seventeenth-century mansion, is of more interest, famous for its extensive range of Flemish and Dutch paintings from the fifteenth to eighteenth century. Early works include paintings by Memling, Rogier van der Weyden and the Antwerp master, Quentin Matsys; there are also a number of Adriaen Brouwer's characteristically ribald canvases, work by Rubens, including a typically grand *Portrait of Isabella Brant*, his first wife, and the intriguing *Adam and Eve in Paradise* – a collaboration between Rubens, who painted the figures, and Jan Brueghel the Elder, who filled in the animals and landscape. In the same room are two examples of the work of Rubens' assistant, Van Dyck.

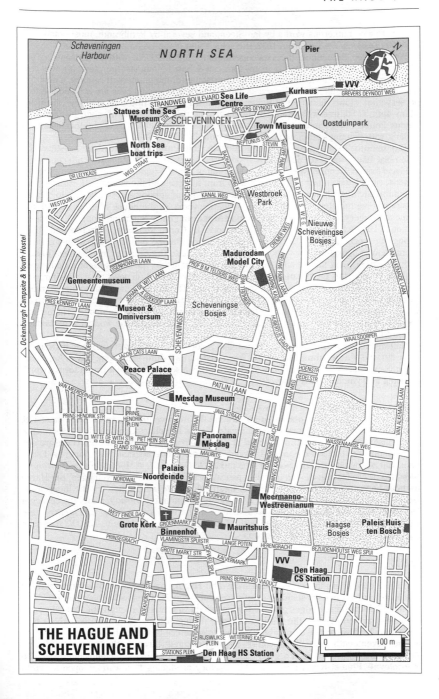

Scheveningen Harbour

NORTH SEA

Pier

VVV
GREVERS DEYNOOT WEG

STRANDWEG BOULEVARD
Sea Life Centre
Kurhaus
Statues of the Sea Museum
GREVERS DEYNOOT WEG
SCHEVENINGEN
Town Museum
Oostduinpark

PRINS WILLEM STR
NEPTUNUS STR
STEVIN
NIEUWE PARK LAAN

North Sea boat trips

DR LELYKADE
WEG STRAAT
BADHUIS HARING KADE

KANAL WEG
Westbroek Park
BADHUIS WEG

WESTDUIN
STATEN LAAN
SCHEVENINGSE

Nieuwe Scheveningse Bosjes

VAN ALKEMADE LAAN

EISENHOWER LAAN

Gemeentemuseum
JOHAN DE WITT LAAN
A BOEKOOP LAAN
PROF B M TELDERS WEG
Madurodam Model City

ORANJE STR
NIEUWE PARK LAAN
HARING KADE

PRES KENNEDY LAAN

Museon & Omniversum
STADHOUDERS LAAN
SCHEVENINGSE
Scheveningse Bosjes
HUBERTUS VIADUCT

JACOB CATS LAAN
WAALSDORPER

Peace Palace
HOENSTR
DEDELSTR

VAN MEERDERVOORT
PATIJN LAAN
MAAM WEG

Mesdag Museum
JAVA STRAAT
VAN ALKEMADE LAAN

PRINS HENDRIK STR
PRINS HENDRIK PLEIN
PAULOWNA STR
ZEE STRAAT
FREDERIK STR
WASSENAARSE WEG

WITTE DE WITH STR
PIET HEIN STR
Panorama Mesdag
ELAND STRAAT
HOGE WAL
MAURITS
KONINGINNE GRACHT

NORDWAL
Palais Noordeinde
NOORD EINDE
PARK STRAAT
VOORHOUT

WEST EINDE DAG
BUITENHOF
Meermanno-Westreenianum

Grote Kerk
GROENMARKT
Mauritshuis
Haagse Bosjes
Paleis Huis ten Bosch

PRINSEGRACHT
Binnenhof
VLAMINGSTR SPUISTR
LANGE POTEN
HERENGRACHT

GROTE MARKT STR
KALVERMARKT
BEZUIDENHOUTSE WEG SPUI

BOEKHORST STR
VVV
Den Haag CS Station

PRINS BERNHARD VIADUCT

△ Ockenburgh Campsite & Youth Hostel

THE HAGUE AND SCHEVENINGEN

STATIONS WEG
RIJSWIJKSE PLEIN
WETERING KADE

STATIONS PLEIN
Den Haag HS Station

0   100 m

There are also numerous works by Jan Steen, and several by Rembrandt, most notably the *Anatomy Lesson of Dr Tulp* from 1632, the artist's first commission in Amsterdam.

West of the Binnenhof, the **Gevangenpoort**, Buitenhof 33, with its Prisoner's Gate Museum (hourly tours: Tues–Fri 10am–4pm; Sat & Sun 1–4pm; last tour 4pm; f6), was originally part of the city fortifications. Used as a prison until the nineteenth century, it now contains an array of guillotine blades, racks and gibbets – and the old cells are in a good state of preservation. Down the street at Buitenhof 35, the **Prince William V Gallery** (Tues–Sun 11am–4pm; f2.50, free with Mauritshuis ticket) has paintings by Rembrandt, Jordaens and Paulus Potter, but it's more interesting as a reconstruction of a typical eighteenth-century gallery, with paintings crammed on the walls from floor to ceiling.

Ten minutes' walk north along Noordeinde, the **Panorama Mesdag**, Zeestraat 65b (Mon–Sat 10am–5pm, Sun noon–5pm; f7.50), was designed in the late nineteenth century by the local painter Hendrik Mesdag. It's a depiction of Scheveningen as it would have appeared in 1881, completed in four months with help from his wife and the young G.H. Breitner, and so naturalistic that it takes a few moments for the skills of lighting and perspective to become apparent. Five minutes away at Laan van Meerdervoort 7f, the house Mesdag bought as a home and gallery today contains the **Mesdag Museum** (Tues–Sun noon–5pm; f5), with a collection of Hague School paintings alongside works by Corot, Rousseau, Delacroix and Millet. Around the corner, framing Carnegieplein, the **Peace Palace** (guided tours: Mon–Fri 10am, 11am, 2pm & 3pm; June–Sept also at 4pm; f5) is home to the Court of International Justice, with tapestries, urns, marble and stained glass on show inside, the donations of various world leaders. North, the **Gemeentemuseum**, Stadhouderslaan 41 (Tues–Sun 11am–5pm; f10; tram #4 from Centraal Station), is the most diverse of The Hague's many museums, with outstanding collections of musical instruments and Islamic ceramics, and an array of modern art which traces the development of Dutch painting through the Romantic, Hague and Expressionist schools to the De Stijl movement – the museum has the world's largest collection of Mondrian's paintings.

Halfway between The Hague and its satellite resort of Scheveningen (reached on tram #1, #7 or #9), the **Madurodam Miniature Town** (daily: April–June 9am–8pm; July & Aug 9am–10pm; Sept–March 9am–5pm; f19.50, children f14) is a scale model of a Dutch town – worth stopping at if you have kids in tow.

Eating and drinking

There are plenty of cheap **places to eat** around the town centre: *Greve*, at Torenstraat 138, north of Grote Kerk, has snacks and full meals; *Pinelli*, Dagelikse Groenmarkt 31, serves pizzas; whilst Indonesian snacks are served at *Eethuis Nirwana*, Prinsestraat 65. There are several options on the streets around Denneweg and Frederikstraat, just north of Lange Voorhout, amongst them the popular vegetarian *De Dageraad*, at Hooikade 4, and *Mevrouw Spoelstra* at Maliestraat 8, which serves pancakes and steaks. In Scheveningen, the Haven harbour has some excellent places to eat fresh fish by the waterside – try the inexpensive *Haven Restaurant* at Treilerdwarsweg 2, or the more upmarket *Ducdalf*, round the corner at Dr Lelykade 5. For **drinking**, two packed studenty bars – *Zwarte Ruiter* and *Jupiter* – face each other across the busy square south of Grote Kerk in The Hague. *The Old Timer*, at Papestraat 23a, is a more peaceful option.

Delft

DELFT, a couple of kilometres inland from The Hague, has considerable charm, with its gabled red-roofed houses standing beside tree-lined canals. The pastel colours of the pavements, brickwork and bridges give the town a faded tranquillity – though one that is increasingly hard to find beneath the tourist onslaught during summer. The town is perhaps best known for **Delftware**, the clunky blue and white ceramics to which the town gave its name in the seventeenth century. If you've already slogged through the vast collection in Amsterdam's Rijksmuseum, it needs no introduction, but for those sufficiently interested, **De Porceleyne Fles** at Rotterdamsweg 196, a factory producing Delftware, is open for visits

(Mon–Sat 9am–5pm, April–Oct also Sun 9.30am–5pm; f5), and the **Huis Lambert van Meerten Museum** at Oude Delft 199 (Tues–Sat 10am–5pm, Sun 1–5pm; f5) has a large collection of Delft and other tiles.

Otherwise **Markt** is the best place to start exploring, with the **Nieuwe Kerk** at one end (April–Oct Mon–Sat 9am–6pm; Nov–March Mon–Fri 11am–4pm, Sat 11am–5pm; f3), under restoration and with a 103-metre tower (closes 30min earlier; f3) giving a wonderful view of the town. The rather uninspiring interior contains the burial vaults of the Dutch royal family. Only the Mausoleum of William the Silent grabs your attention, a hotchpotch of styles concocted by Hendrik de Keyser, architect of the Renaissance **Stadhuis** opposite.

South of here, **Wynhaven**, another old canal, leads to Hippolytusbuurt and the Gothic **Oude Kerk** (closed for restoration until early 2000), arguably the town's finest building. Simple and unbuttressed with an unhealthily leaning tower, it has an intricately carved pulpit dating from 1548, with figures emphasized in false perspective. Opposite the Oude Kerk is the former Convent of Saint Agatha, or **Prinsenhof** (Tues–Sat 10am–5pm, Sun 1–5pm; f5), housing Delft's municipal art collection (a good group of works including paintings by Aertsen and Honthorst), and restored in the style of the late sixteenth century when it served as William the Silent's base in his revolt against the Spanish. It was also the scene of his assassination; the mark of the bullets can still be seen on the walls. Finally, if you have the time, the **Royal Army and Weapon Museum** (Tues–Fri 10am–5pm, Sat & Sun noon–5pm; f6) near the station is worth a visit, with its good display of weaponry, uniforms and military accoutrements from the Spanish wars to the 1950s.

Practicalities

From the **train station**, it's a short walk into town and the **VVV** at Markt 83–85 (April–Sept Mon–Fri 9am–6pm, Sat 9am–5.30pm, Sun 10am–3pm; mid-Oct to March Mon–Fri 9am–5.30pm, Sat 9am–5pm; ☎015/212 6100), which can find you the best **accommodation** deals in the central guest houses. For hotels, try *Les Compagnons* at Markt 61 (☎015/214 0102; ④) or *'t Raedhuys* at Markt 38 (☎015/212 5115; ④). There is also an unofficial **youth hostel**, *Ricardis* (☎015/285 5395; ③), 3km west – catch bus #60 or #62 from the station – and a **campsite**, *De Delftse Hout*, Kortftlaan 5 (☎015/213 0040; bus #64 from station). The cheapest **eating** is available at a number of student mensas (term-time only) such as *De Koornbeurs* near the main square or the Jansbrug, Kornmarkt 50–52. Also try the *Willem Van Orange* centrally located on Markt, for pancakes, *uitsmijters* (ham or cheese with eggs), and light meals for around f10 and three-course menus for around f20. *Locus Publicus*, Brabantse Turfmarkt 67, is a popular local hangout, serving a staggering array of **beers** as well as sandwiches.

Rotterdam

Just beyond Delft lies **ROTTERDAM**, at the heart of a maze of rivers and artificial waterways that forms the seaward outlet of the rivers Rhine and Maas. An important port as far back as the fourteenth century, it was one of the major cities of the Dutch Republic, and today, with the adjoining dockland area of Europoort, is the largest port in the world. The Germans bombed the town centre to pieces in 1940, and rebuilding has produced a sterile assembly of concrete and glass. However, the city has its moments, not least in one of the best and most overlooked galleries in the country, the Boymans-Van Beuningen Museum.

Southeast of the station, the **Lijnbaan** was Europe's first pedestrianized shopping precinct, completed in 1953. Beyond here lies some of the city centre's more fanciful modern architecture, and a seventeenth-century mansion at Korte Hoogstraat 31 housing the **Schielandshuis Museum** (Tues–Fri 10am–5pm, Sat & Sun 11am–5pm; f6), with its displays on the history of Rotterdam. A couple of minutes south, the old city docks are enclosed by the Boompjes, a former sea dyke that's now a major freeway leading southwest to the **Euromast**, on a rather lonely park corner beside the Nieuwe Maas, where the 185-metre-high **Spacetower** (daily April–Sept 10am–7pm, until 10.30pm Tues–Sat in July & Aug, Oct–March 10am–5pm; f15) gives spectacular views. North of here, the **Boymans-Van Beuningen Museum**, Mathenesserlaan 18–20 (Tues–Sat 10am–5pm, Sun 11am–5pm; f7.50, or f10 during exhibitions), is Rotterdam's one great attraction, accessible from Centraal Station by tram #5 or walkable from Eendrachtsplein metro. It's an enormous museum, with a superb collection of work by the Surrealists Dalí, Magritte, Ernst and de Chirico. The Van der Vorm collection on the first floor contains work by Monet, Van Gogh, Picasso, Gauguin, Cézanne and Munch; and a series of small galleries alongside house paintings by most of the significant artists of the Barbizon and Hague Schools. Among the earlier canvases are several by Hieronymus Bosch; Pieter Brueghel the Elder's mysterious *Tower of Babel*; some Jan Steens; Gerrit Dou's *The Quack*; and Rembrandt's intimate *Titus at his Desk*.

If nothing in the city centre can be called exactly picturesque, **Delfshaven** goes some way to make up for it. A good 45-minute walk southwest of Centraal Station – fifteen minutes by tram #6 or #9 – it was from here that the Pilgrims set sail for America in 1620, changing to the more reliable *Mayflower* in Plymouth. Delfshaven was only incorporated into Rotterdam in 1886 and managed to survive World War II virtually intact. It was long a neglected area, but the town council has recognized its tourist potential and has set about conserving and restoring the locality. The **Dubbelde Palmboom Museum**, Voorhaven 12 (Tues–Fri 10am–5pm, Sat & Sun 11am–5pm; f6), once a *jenever* distillery, is now a historical museum with a wide-ranging if unexceptional collection of objects pertaining to life in the Maas delta.

Practicalities

Rotterdam's large centre is bordered by its main rail terminal, **Centraal Station**, which serves as the hub of a useful tram and metro system, though it's a seamy, hostile place late at night. The main **VVV** office is a ten-minute walk away at Coolsingel 67 (Mon–Thurs 9.30am–6pm, Fri 9.30am–9pm, Sat 9.30am–5pm, April–Sept also Sun noon–5pm; ☎0900/403 4065); as well as providing free maps of the tram, bus and underground system and a comprehensive city brochure for f4, it operates an **accommodation** booking service, for which it charges a small fee. It's cheaper to call direct to any of the central, reasonably priced **hotels** 1km southwest of the station, including the *Roxane*, 's-Gravendijkwal 14 (☎010/436 6109; ③; tram #1, #7 or #9), and the more comfortable *Wilgenhof*, Heemraadssingel 92–94 (☎010/425 4892; ⑤; tram #1, #7 or bus #38, #45). Immediately north of the station, the *Bienvenue*, at Spoorsingel 24 (☎010/466 9394; ③), is excellent value. The **youth hostel** is a 25-minute walk from the station at Rochussenstraat 107 (☎010/436 5763; ②; tram #4); the nearest **campsite**, Stadscamping (☎010/415 3440), is north of the station at Kanaalweg 84 – take bus #33.

The cheapest sit-down **meal** in town is served at *Eetcafé Streetlife*, Jonker Franslaan 237; *De Eend*, Mauritsweg 28 (4.30–7.30pm), is also inexpensive. Oude and Nieuwe Binnenweg support a number of good *eetcafés*, including the *Rotown* at Nieuwe Binnenweg 19. *De Consul*, Westersingel 28, serves a variety of dishes at reasonable prices, and vegetarians should try *Eetcafé BlaBla*, Piet Heynstraat 35 in Delfshaven. Grand *Café Dudok*, off Beursplein on Meent, is a good place to **drink**, and *Jazzcafe Dizzy*, 's-Gravendijkwal 127, has regular **live music**. You can access the **Internet** at *CAT@ZINE*, a café on the upper floor of Virgin Megastore on Passage 1.

Gouda

A pretty little place some 25km northeast of Rotterdam, **GOUDA** is almost everything you'd expect of a Dutch country town: a ring of quiet canals encircling ancient buildings and old quays. More surprisingly, its **Markt** is the largest in Holland – a reminder of the town's prominence as a centre of the medieval cloth trade, and later of its success in the manufacture of cheeses and clay pipes. The **cheese market**, held every Thursday morning (9.30am–12.30pm) in June, July and August, is a shadow of its former self – and mercilessly milked by the tour operators – but out of these times the Markt is worth visiting. Slap-bang in the middle, the **Stadhuis** is an elegant Gothic building dating from 1450; on the north side is the **Waag**, a tidy seventeenth-century building decorated with a detailed relief of cheese weighing, with the remains of the old wooden scales inside. The two top floors (April–Oct

Mon–Fri 10am–noon & 2pm–4pm, Sat 11am–3pm; f1) show an only marginally interesting display of cheesy things. To the south, just off the square, the **St Janskerk** (March–Oct Mon–Sat 9am–5pm; Nov–Feb Mon–Sat 10am–4pm; f3.50) was built in the sixteenth century and is famous for its magnificent stained-glass windows, the best executed between 1555 and 1571 when Holland was still Catholic. The post-Reformation windows, dating from 1572 to 1603, are more secular: the *Relief of Leiden*, for example, shows William the Silent retaking the town from the Spanish. By the side of the church, the flamboyant **Lazarus Gate** of 1609 was once part of the town's leper hospital until it was moved to form the back entrance to the Catharina Gasthuis, now the municipal **Stedelijk Museum** (Mon–Sat 10am–5pm, Sun noon–5pm; f5), whose collection incorporates a fine selection of early religious art, notably a large triptych, *Life of Mary*, by Dirk Barendsz, and a characteristically austere *Annunciation* by the Bruges artist Pieter Pourbus. Other highlights include a spacious hall, *Het Ruim*, dominated by two group portraits by Ferdinand Bol, and a selection of Hague and Barbizon School canvases. Gouda's other museum, **De Moriaan** (Mon–Fri 10am–5pm, Sat 10am–12.30pm & 1.30–5.30pm, Sun noon–5pm; free with Stedelijk ticket), in an old merchant's house at Westhaven 29, has a mixed bag of exhibits from clay pipes to ceramics and tiles.

Practicalities

Gouda's **train** and **bus stations** are north of the centre, ten minutes from the VVV, Markt 27 (Mon–Sat 9am–5pm, June–Aug Sun noon–3pm; ☎0182/513666), which offers a limited supply of **private rooms** (③). The most reasonably priced **hotel** is *Het Blauwe Kruis*, near the De Morian Museum at Westhaven 4 (☎0182/512677; ③), otherwise try *H't Trefpunt* further along at no. 46 (☎0182/512879; ④), or *De Keizerskroon* at Keizerstraat 11 (☎0182/528096; ⑤). For **food**, there are literally hundreds of cafés catering to the swarms of tourists who day-trip through Gouda in the high season. You can eat cheaply at *'t Groot Stedelijk*, Markt 44, among other places; *'t Goudse Winkeltje* at Achter de Kerk 9a, has good pancakes, and you can get a decent Indonesian at *Warung Srikandi*, Lange Groenendaal 108. For a **drink**, find your way to the excellent *Eetcafé Vidocq*, Koster Gijzenstraat 8 or check out *Heeren Van Goude* or *Floris 5* on Zeugstraat, which are usually full of young people.

Utrecht

"I groaned with the idea of living all winter in so shocking a place," wrote Boswell in 1763, and **UTRECHT**, surrounded by shopping centres and industrial developments, still promises little as you approach. But the centre, with its distinctive sunken canals – whose brick cellar warehouses have been converted into chic cafés and restaurants – is one of the country's most pleasant.

The focal point is the **Dom Tower**, which, at over 110m, is the highest church tower in the country, soaring to a delicate octagonal lantern added in 1380. A guided tour (Mon–Fri 10am–5pm, Sat & Sun noon–5pm; last entry one hour before closing; f5.50) takes you unnervingly close to the top, from where the gap between the tower and the Gothic **Dom Kerk** is most apparent. Only the eastern part of the great cathedral remains today, the nave having collapsed in 1674. It's worth peering inside though (May–Sept Mon–Fri 10am–5pm, Sat 10am–3.30pm, Sun 2–4pm; Oct–April Mon–Fri 11am–4pm, Sat 10am–3.30pm, Sun 2–4pm; free), to get a sense of the hangar-like space the building once had and to wander through the **Kloostergang**, the fourteenth-century cloisters that link the cathedral to the chapterhouse, now part of the university. South of the church at Nieuwe Gracht 63, the national collection of ecclesiastical art, the **Catharijne Convent Museum** (Tues–Fri 10am–5pm, Sat & Sun 11am–5pm; f7), has a wonderfully exhibited mass of paintings, manuscripts and church ornaments from the ninth century on, including work by Geertgen tot Sint Jans, Rembrandt, Hals and, best of all, a luminously beautiful *Virgin and Child* by Van Cleve. Further along, the **Centraal Museum** at Agnietenstraat 1 (Tues–Sat 10am–5pm, Sun noon–5pm; f6) features a good collection of paintings by sixteenth- and seventeenth-century Utrecht artists, including the vividly individual portraits of Van Scorel's *Jerusalem Brotherhood*.

Practicalities

Train and **bus stations** both lead into the Hoog Catharijne shopping centre. The main VVV office is at Vredenburg 90 (Mon–Fri 9am–6pm, Sat 9am–5pm; ☎0900/414 1414), a five-minute walk away. Of **hotels**, try the *Hotel Ouwi*, FC Donderstraat 12 (☎030/271 6303; ④), a fifteen-minute walk northeast of the centre; or *Parkhotel* at Tolsteegsingel 34 (☎030/251 6712; ③), a similar distance southeast of the station; there's a nice **youth hostel** in an old country manor house at Rhijnauwenselaan 14, Bunnik (☎030/656 1277; ②), 6km out, but linked to the station by bus #40 or #41. The *Strowis Low Budget Hostel* at Boothstraat 8 (☎030/238 0280; ②) is a more central option, a fifteen-minute walk from Centraal Station or a short ride on bus #3, #4, #8 or #11 to the Janskerkhof stop, plus a two-minute walk. The well-equipped **campsite**, *Camping De Berenkuil*, at Ariënslaan 5 (☎030/271 3870) can be reached by a #57 bus from the station. **Restaurants** are mainly situated along Oude Gracht and the Lijnmarkt – the best is the moderately priced *Stadskasteel Oudaen* at no. 99, the oldest house in town, which serves beer from its own steam brewery downstairs. Also try the *Milky*, a good vegetarian restaurant off the canal at Zakkerdragssteeg 22. A really cheap option is to go for a *dagschotel* at *Eetcafé De Baas* at Lijnmarkt 6, and there's *Grand Café Stairway to Heaven* on Mariaplaats 11, with moderately priced meals and regular **live music**. *De Werfking*, at Oude Gracht 123, has good vegetarian food. As for the **bars**, the city's best cluster around the junction of Oude Gracht and the Lijnmarkt; check out the lively *De Witte Ballons* at Lijnmarkt ·10–12, or the *Café Belgie* around the corner at Oude Gracht 196.

BEYOND THE RANDSTAD

Outside the Randstad towns, the Netherlands is relatively unknown territory to tourists. In the north, **Leeuwarden** – a pleasant, if sedate, town with two good museums – is the capital of the maverick province of **Friesland**, whose inhabitants retain their own language. The province of **Groningen** to the east has comparatively few attractions beyond its eponymous capital, a lively cosmopolitan place with a buzzing street- and nightlife and a stunning new museum and art gallery. To the south, the countryside grows steadily more undulating as you head towards Germany. The town of **Arnhem** is famous for its bridge, a key objective in the failed Allied attack of 1944, and a good base for the nearby **Hoge Veluwe National Park**, whose modern art museum is one of the country's best. Further south, in the provinces of North Brabant and Limburg, the landscape slowly fills out, rolling into a rougher countryside of farmland and forests and eventually into the country's only hills, around **Maastricht**, a city whose vibrant, Central European air, is a world away from the clogs and canals of the north.

Leeuwarden

An old market town, **LEEUWARDEN** was the residence of the powerful Frisian Stadholders, who vied with those of Holland for control of the country during the seventeenth century. These days it's a neat and cosy provincial capital, with an air of prosperity and a smug sense of independence. It lacks the concentrated historic charm of many other Dutch towns, but it has a number of grand buildings and two outstanding museums, not to mention an appealingly compact town centre almost entirely surrounded and bisected by water.

The centre of town is **Waagplein**, a narrow open space cut by a canal and flanked by cafés and department stores. The **Waag** itself dates from 1598, but it's been converted into a restaurant and bank. Walking west, **Nieuwestad** is Leeuwarden's main shopping street, from where Kleine Kerkstraat, on the right, leads to the **Oldehoofster Kerkhof** – a large square-cum-car-park near the old city walls – and the precariously leaning **Oldehove**. Something of a symbol for the city, part of a cathedral started in 1529 but never finished because of subsidence, this is a lugubrious mass of disproportion that defies all laws of gravity and geometry; those brave enough to climb it (May–Sept Tues–Sun 2–5pm; f2.50). **Grote Kerkstraat** leads east from here, and at no. 11 you'll pass **Het Princessehof** (Mon–Sat 10am–5pm, Sun 2–5pm; f6.50), a house from 1650 that was once the residence of the Stadholder William Friso and is now a ceramics museum with the world's largest collection of magnificent Dutch tiles. There is also a marvellous collection of Far Eastern ceramics, from original sixteenth-century Chinese porcelain brought over by merchants to later Western imitations. Further along Grote Kerkstraat at no. 212, the house where the World War I spy Mata Hari spent her early years is now the **Frisian Literary Museum** (Mon–Sat 9am–12.30pm & 1.30–5pm; f1). It is a repository for a whole range of Frisian documents, with a permanent display on Frisian Socialist politician and poet P.J. Troelstra and a few derisory exhibits on Mata Hari herself – who is better represented at the Fries Museum (see below). At the far end of Grote Kerkstraat, the unremarkable Gothic **Grote** or **Jacobijner Kerk** (June–Sept Tues–Fri 2–4pm) is another victim of subsidence, tilting towards the south aisle.

South of here on Turfmarkt is the **Fries Museum** (Mon–Sat 11am–6pm, Sun 1–5pm; f7.50), one of the best regional museums in the country, recently revamped with displays that trace the development of Frisian culture from prehistoric times up to the present day. As well as an extensive collection of silverware, there are rooms given over to the gaudy painted furniture of Hindeloopen, and a collection of seventeenth-century Frisian paintings, enlivened by a portrait of Rembrandt's Frisian wife, Saskia, recently found to have been from his studio, rather than by the master himself. The top floor of the new building now houses the Frisian Resistance Museum, a chronological exhibition (all in Dutch) tracing the early days of the Nazi invasion through collaboration and resistance to the Allied liberation.

Practicalities

Leeuwarden's **train** and **bus stations** adjoin each other, five minutes' walk south of the town centre. The **VVV** at the train station (Mon–Fri 9am–5.30pm, Sat 10am–1pm; June–Aug until 4pm on Sat; ☎0900/202 4060) has a short list of **private rooms** (③) and can supply a city centre map detailing all the sights (f2). Two reasonably priced **hotels** in town are the *De Pauw*, near the station at Stationsweg 10 (☎058/212 3651; ③), and the more central *'t Anker*, on the north side of the centre at Eewal 69–73 (☎058/212 5216; ③). For **camping**, Kleine Wielen (☎0511/43 1660) is about 6km out towards Dokkum, nicely sited by a lake – take bus #10, #13 or #51 or #62 from the station. One of the best places to **eat** is *Eetcafé Spinoza* on Eewal, a youthful restaurant with a good range of dishes for around f25. Try also *De Brasserie* at Grote Kerkstraat 7, especially good for lunch; *Pizzeria Sardegna*, Grote Hoogstraat 28, with an extravagant variety of pizzas; or the Mexican food at *Yucatan* on St Jacobsstraat. For **drinking**, the *Fire Palace*, Nieuwestad NZ 49, is a big bar overlooking the canal and doubles as the town's main **disco** at weekends, although there are plenty of bars around Doelesteeg.

Groningen

Nominally a fiefdom of the Bishops of Utrecht from 1040 until 1536, the city of **GRONIN-GEN** was once an important centre of trade, and from 1594 it was capital of the province of the same name. Heavily bombed in World War II, the city is an architectural jumble with few notable sights, but its large, prestigious university gives it a cosmopolitan feel quite unexpected in this part of the country.

The centre of town is **Grote Markt**, a large open space that was badly damaged by wartime bombing and has been reconstructed with little imagination. At one corner is the **Martinikerk** (June–Aug Tues–Sat noon–5pm; f1), a beacon of architectural sanity in the surrounding shambles. Though the oldest parts of the church go back to 1180, most of it is mid-fifteenth-century Gothic. The vault paintings in the nave are beautifully restored, and the lofty choir holds two series of frescoes on the walled-up niches of the clerestory. Adjoining the church is the seventeenth-century tower **Martinitoren** (April–June daily noon–4.30pm; July–Sept 11am–4.30pm, Oct–March Sat & Sun noon–4.30pm; f3). West along A-Kerkhof NZ from Grote Markt, the **Noordelijk Scheepvaart Museum**, Brugstraat 24 (Tues–Sat 10am–5pm, Sun 1–5pm; f6), is one of the most comprehensive maritime museums in the country, with displays on trade with the Indies, the development of peat canals and a series of reconstructed nautical workshops. In the same building, the smaller

Niemeyer Tabaksmuseum is devoted to tobacco smoking from 1600 to the present day. The city's biggest and best museum, the **Groningen Museum** (Tues–Sun 10am–5pm, f10) is housed in spectacular pavilions across from the train station. The west pavilion is given over to travelling exhibitions but also houses the permanent art collection, including Rubens' energetic *Adoration of the Magi* among a small selection of seventeenth-century works, Hague school paintings, and a number of late works by the Expressionists of the Groningen *De Ploeg* group. There is a small collection of ancient amber and bronze jewellery at the other end of the museum – notably miniatures of Minerva and Mercury – and silverware. Above this, diaphanous drapes guide you through vitrines of Far Eastern ceramics and ivory work.

Practicalities

Groningen's **bus** and **train stations** are on the south side of town, fifteen minutes' walk from the VVV at Ged Kattendiep 6 (Mon–Fri 9am–5.30pm, Sat 10am–5pm; ☎0900/202 3050); they will give you a short list of **private rooms** costing f25–35 per person, though few are near the city centre. Otherwise, the cheapest place to stay is in the dorms of *Simplon Jongerenhotel* north of the centre at Boterdiep 73 (☎050/313 5221; ②). Three reasonably priced **hotels** are just south of the Grote Markt: the *Garni Friesland* at Kleine Pelsterstraat 4 (☎050/312 1307; ③); the *Garni Groningen*, Damsterdiep 94 (☎050/313 5435; ④); and the likeable old *Weeva*, Gedempte Zuiderdiep 8 (☎050/312 9919; ⑤), with a decent, reasonably priced restaurant. If you're **camping**, catch bus #4 via Peizerweg from the train station for the ten-minute journey to *Camping Stadspark* (☎050/525 1624; March–Oct).

For the cheapest **food** in town, head for *Roezemoes*, at Gedempte Zuiderdiep 15. Otherwise, the city's best places to eat and drink are concentrated around Poelestraat: *Bistango*, at no.14, is a decent Tex-Mex restaurant with vegetarian specialities, whilst the pizzeria *Costa Smeralda* next door is slightly cheaper; *'t Pakhuis*, around the corner at Peperstraat 8, has good Dutch snacks and a lively bar in an atmospheric building. On the south side of the Grote Markt is a flank of outdoor cafés, best of which are the old-style brown café *Der Witz* at no. 47, the civilized *De Drie Gezusters* at no. 29, with a great old interior, and the *Café Hooghoudt* at no. 42; this last also contains a night café serving food until 4am at weekends. *De Smederij*, over the canal, west of the centre at Tuinstraat 2, is an eetcafé with a great atmosphere, and in the opposite direction at A-Kerkstraat 24, you'll find high-quality, moderately priced vegetarian food in *Brussels Lof*.

Thanks to its large student population, Groningen has lively **nightlife**. For live music try *Muziekcafé* Koekkoek, Peperstraat 4; *Vera*, in the basement at Oosterstraat 44; or *Troubadour*, Peperstraat 19. *De Spieghel* at Peperstraat 11 has live jazz most nights. Good discos include *Index*, Poelestraat 53, and the *Palace*, Gelkingestraat 1, which occasionally hosts live bands.

Arnhem and around

Way south of Groningen in the province of Gelderland, **ARNHEM** was once a wealthy resort, a watering hole to which the merchants of Amsterdam and Rotterdam would flock to idle away their fortunes. This century it's become better known as the place where thousands of British and Polish troops died in the failed Allied airborne operation of September 1944, codenamed "Operation Market Garden", which gutted the greater part of the city. What you see today is inevitably not especially enticing. But Arnhem is a lively town, with plenty going on, and a good centre for seeing the numerous attractions scattered around its forested outskirts.

The best of old Arnhem is the northwest part of the centre, around **Korenmarkt**, a small square which escaped much of the wartime destruction and has one or two good facades. The streets which lead off Korenmarkt are full of restaurants and bars, but otherwise Arnhem deteriorates as you walk southeast towards the **John Frostbrug Bridge** – "The Bridge too Far" – named after the commander of the battalion that defended it for four days. It's just an ordinary bridge, but for Dutch and British alike it remains the symbol and focus of remembrance of the battle. At its north end, the characterless **Markt** is site of the sixteenth-century church of **St Eusabius** (April–Sept Tues–Sat 10am–5pm, Sun noon–5pm; Oct–March Tues–Sat 11am–4.30pm, Sun noon–4pm; free), heavily bombed during World War II and reconstructed in the 1960s, when a new tower was added (same times; f5). To mark the fiftieth anniversary of Operation Market Garden a glassed-in viewing platform was added to the top of the church, from where you can look down on the fifteenth-century **Stadhuis** tucked in behind. In the opposite direction, fifteen-minutes' walk west from the station along Utrechtsestraat, is the **Museum voor Moderne Kunst Arnhem** at Utrechtseweg 87 (Tues–Fri 10am–5pm, Sat & Sun 11am–5pm; f5). It's linked to the **Historisch Museum Het Burgerweehuis**, about ten minutes' walk away at Bovenbeekstraat 21 (same times); collections include numerous archeological finds from the surrounding area, a display of Chinese, Japanese and Delft ceramics, and a modest selection of paintings, with the emphasis on views of the landscape, villages and towns of Gelderland, and canvases by the so-called magic realists.

Arnhem's **train station** is on the edge of the centre, next to the **bus** and **trolley stations**. Always check the destination of buses and trolleys, as several routes share one number. Next door is the **VVV**, Stationsplein 45 (Mon 11am–5.30pm, Tues–Fri 9am–5.30pm, Sat 10am–4pm; ☎0900/202 4075), which operates an **accommodation**-booking service. Among the cheaper choices in the town centre are the *Hotel Pension Parkzicht*, Apeldoornsestraat 16 (☎026/442 0698; ③), ten minutes' walk from the station; *Hotel Rembrandt*, Paterstraat 1 (☎026/442 0153; ③), the second right off Apeldoornsestraat; and the slightly more expensive *Old Dutch* at Stationsplein 8 (☎026/442 0792; ④). Take bus #2 in the direction of Schaarsbergen out from the centre to reach the *Pension Warnsborn*, Schelmseweg 1 (☎026/442 5994; ③). A **youth hostel**, 4km north at Diepenbrocklaan 27 (☎026/442 0114; ②), can be reached by trolley #3 in the direction of Alteveer, and the nearest **campsite** is Camping Warnsborn (☎026/442 3469), 6km northwest of the centre at Bakenbergseweg 257 on bus #31. *Pizzeria Da Leone*, is a good, moderately priced, place to **eat** and there are plenty of cheap options on Jansplein near the post office. For more traditional Dutch fare try the *Old Inn*, Stationsplein 40.

World War II memorials: Oosterbeek

The area around Arnhem is scattered with the graveyards of thousands of soldiers who died during **Operation Market Garden**, not least **OOSTERBEEK**, a prosperous suburb of Arnhem 6km to the west (4 trains hourly), where the **Airborne Cemetery** is a neat, symmetrical tribute to nearly two thousand paratroopers whose bodies were brought here from the surrounding fields. Ten minutes south of the station (or bus #1 from Arnhem), the village proper has spruce **lawns and walls** dotted with details of the battle, and the **Airborne Museum** (Mon–Sat 11am–5pm, Sun noon–5pm; f6), in the former *Hotel Hartenstein* on Utrechtseweg, where the British forces were besieged by the Germans for a week before retreating across the river, their numbers depleted from 10,005 to 2163. With the use of an English commentary, photographs, dioramas and military artefacts, the museum gives an excellent outline of the battle.

The Nederlands Openluchtmuseum

Immediately north of Arnhem, the **Nederlands Openluchtmuseum** (April–Oct daily 10am–5pm; f18; bus #3 towards Alteveer and, during July & Aug special bus #13) is a huge collection of Dutch buildings taken from all over the country. Where possible, buildings have been placed in groups that resemble the traditional villages of the different regions of the Netherlands – from the farmsteads of Friesland to the peat colonies of Drenthe. There are about 120 buildings in all, including examples of farmhouses, bridges and every type of Dutch windmill, and several working craft shops demonstrating traditional skills. Other parts of the museum incorporate one of the most extensive regional costume exhibitions in the country and a modest herb garden. All in all, it's an imaginative attempt to re-create the rural Dutch way of life over the past two centuries, and the museum's own guidebook (around f8) explains everything with academic attention to detail.

The Hoge Veluwe National Park and Rijksmuscum Kröller-Müller

Spreading north from the Openluchtmuseum is the **Hoge Veluwe National Park** (daily: April–Aug 8am–sunset; Sept & Oct 9am–sunset; Nov–March 9am–5.30pm; f7, cars an extra f8.50), an area of heath and woodland that is much the prettiest and most accessible part of the Veluwe district of Gelderland. Formerly the private estate of wealthy local couple Anton and Helene Kröller-Müller, it has three entrances – one near the village of Otterlo on the northwest perimeter, another near Hoenderloo on the northeast edge, and a third to the south at Rijzenburg, near the village of Schaarsbergen, 6km from Arnhem.

There are a number of ways to get to the park by **bus**; easiest is to take the regular museum special from outside Arnhem train station (April–Oct Tues–Sun, bus #12 hourly, f8 return plus f7 park entrance; pay the driver) direct to the **Visitors' Centre** (daily 10am–5pm), which has information on the park and is one of the five places to pick up the white bicycles that are left out for everyone's use at no extra charge – much the best way of getting around. The other sites are outside the Kröller-Müller museum and at the three entrances, so when the bus isn't running, you can either rent a bike at Arnhem station or take bus #107 to the entrance at Otterlo, 4km from the Visitors' Centre.

The main things to see are the **Jachtslot St Hubertus** (April–Oct daily 11am–12.30am & 2–4.30pm; free half-hourly guided tours), 3km north of the Visitors' Centre, an impressive Art Deco hunting lodge built for the Kröller-Müllers by H.P. Berlage in 1920, and the superb **Rijksmuseum Kröller-Müller** (Tues–Sun 10am–5pm; a further f7). One of the country's finest museums, it's a wide cross-section of modern European art from Impressionism to Cubism and beyond, housed in a purpose-built structure by the Belgian architect Van de Velde. There are paintings by Dutch artists such as Mondrian and Charley Toroop and their father Jan, as well as work by Fernand Léger and other Cubist-era artists. But the collection's crowning glory is its array of works by Vincent Van Gogh, housed in a large room around a central courtyard and placed in context by accompanying contemporary pictures. There are early pieces, among them, *Head of a Peasant with a Pipe*, rough unsentimental paintings of labourers from around his parents' home in Brabant; penetrating later self-portraits; examples from the *Sunflowers* series and the joyful *Haystacks in Provence* and *Bridge at Arles*; and later, more sombre creations from his last years, such as *Prisoners Exercising* from 1890. Outside, behind the main building, there's a **Sculpture Park** (April–Oct Tues–Sun 10am–4.30pm; free), spaciously laid out with works by Rodin, Giacometti, Jacob Epstein, Barbara Hepworth – and, most notably, Jean Dubuffet's *Jardin d'Email*.

Maastricht

Situated in a thin finger of land that reaches down between Belgium and Germany, **MAAS-TRICHT**, the capital of the province of Limburg, is one of the most delightful cities in Holland, quite different from the waterland centres of the north and firmly in the heart of Europe. A cosmopolitan place, where three languages and currencies happily coexist, it's also one of the oldest towns in the country. The first settlers here were Roman, when Maastricht became an important stop on the trade route between Cologne and the coast, and the later legacy of Charlemagne – whose capital was at nearby Aachen – is manifest in two of the best Romanesque churches in the Low Countries.

Arrival and accommodation

The centre of Maastricht is on the west bank of the river. You're likely to arrive, however, on the east bank, in the district known as **Wijk**, home to the **train** and **bus stations** and many of the city's hotels. The **airport** is north of the city at Beek, a twenty-minute bus journey; bus #61 runs every thirty minutes to Markt and the train station. The **VVV** is in the centre at Kleine Straat 1, at the end of the main shopping street (May–Oct Mon–Sat 9am–6pm, Sun 11am–3pm; Nov–April Mon–Fri 9am–6pm, Sat 9am–5pm; ☎043/325 2121); it has copies of the what's-on monthly *Maas & Regio* and a tourist guide for f2.50 which includes a decent map and a list of **private rooms** (③). There are several good central **pensions**, including

Chambres d'hotes La Cloche, Bredestraat 41 (☎043/321 2407; ⑤), and *Anno*, just off Klein Gracht at Coxstraat 42 (☎043/325 2305; ③). **Hotels** conveniently located for the station and the city include the two-star *Hotel de Poshoorn*, Stationstraat 47 (☎043/321 7334; ⑤) and the slightly cheaper one-star *Hotel Le Guide* at Number 17a (☎043/321 6176; ④); the *Botel Maastricht* (☎043/321 9023; ④) is moored on the river on Maasboulevard, not far from the Helpoort, and does an excellent breakfast. For **camping**, the large and well-equipped *De Dousberg* site (☎043/343 2171; April–Oct), is a ten-minute ride from the station on bus #55 or #56; the same buses also take you to the **youth hostel** at Dousbergweg 4 (☎043/346 6777; ②), which has access to open-air and indoor swimming pools.

The City

The busiest of Maastricht's many squares is **Markt**, at its most crowded during the Wednesday and Friday morning market. At the centre of the square, the 1664 **Stadhuis** (Mon–Fri 8.30am–12.30pm & 2–5.30pm; free), a typical slice of mid-seventeenth-century Dutch civic grandeur, was designed by Pieter Post. Just west, **Vrijthof** is a grander open space flanked by a line of café terraces on one side and on the other by **St Servaaskerk** (daily 10am–5pm; f4). Only the crypt remains of the original tenth-century church; the rest is mostly of medieval or later construction. On the northern side of the church, the fifteenth-century Gothic cloister leads into the **treasury**, which holds a large collection of liturgical accessories, including a bust reliquary of St Servaas, which is carried through the town in Easter processions.

The second most prominent building on the square, next door, is Maastricht's main Protestant church, the fourteenth-century **St Janskerk** (Easter–Oct Mon–Sat 11am–4pm; free), the baptistry of the church of St Servaas when it was a cathedral and nowadays competing for attention with its high fifteenth-century Gothic tower (f2.50). Inside are some medieval murals, but otherwise climbing the tower is the church's main appeal. Maastricht's other main church, the **Onze Lieve Vrouwe Basiliek**, is a short walk south of Vrijthof, down Bredestraat, in a small shady square crammed with café tables. Founded around 1000, its dark and eerily devotional interior, with a gorgeous galleried choir, is fronted by an unusual fortified west facade. Off the north aisle, the **treasury** (Easter to mid-Sept Mon–Sat 11am–5pm, Sun 1–5pm; f3.50) holds the usual array of ecclesiastical oddments, most notably the tunic of St Lambert, a bishop of Maastricht who was murdered at Liège in 705.

Around the corner from the square, on Plankstraat, the **Museumkelder Derlon** (Sun noon–4pm; free), in the basement of the hotel of the same name, contains a few remnants of Roman Maastricht – the remains of a temple to Jupiter, a well and several layers of pavement, discovered during the building of the present hotel in the mid-1980s. On the other side of the square lies another of Maastricht's most appealing quarters, narrow streets winding out to the fast-flowing River Jeker, which weaves around the various houses and ancient mills and the best surviving part of the city walls, the **Helpoort** of 1229. Continuing south, the **Casemates** in the Waldeck Park (guided tours: July & Aug daily 12.30pm & 2pm; Sept–June Sun only 2pm; f5.75) are further evidence of Maastricht's once impressive fortifications, a system of galleries created through mining between 1575 and 1825 that were used in times of siege for surprise attacks on the enemy. Fifteen minutes' walk further south are more dank passageways, hollowed out of the soft sandstone or *marl* that makes up the flat-topped, 110-metre-high hill of **St Pietersberg**. Of two cave systems, the **Zonneberg** is probably the better, situated on the far side of the hill at Casino Slavante (guided tours in English July & Aug daily 2.15pm; f5.75). There is some evidence of wartime occupation, plus what everyone claims is Napoleon's signature on a graffiti-ridden wall.

Eating and drinking

Eating is never a problem in Maastricht. At the bottom end of the price scale, the street to head for is Koestraat, which runs off Cortenstraat to the south of Onze Lieve Vrouweplein. Here you'll find the excellent and cheap Indonesian *De Branding* at no. 5; the low-cost pizzeria and restaurant *Alexandria* at no. 21; a good-value bakery around the corner; and the slightly upmarket *D'n Blind Genger*, no. 3, with a varied menu and a nice atmosphere. Also nearby, down towards the river on Graanmarkt, *Caribbean Embassy* is an *eetcafé* with reasonably priced Caribbean specialities and cheap snacks, and *Reitz*, Markt 75, is a Maastricht institution serving huge cones of thick Belgian-style frites. The **bars** on the east side of Vrijthof are packed in summer; *In den Ouden Vogelstruys*, on the corner of Platielstraat, is one of the nicest. Away from Vrijthof, *De Bóbbel*, on Wolfstraat just off Onze Lieve Vrouweplein, is a bareboards bar, lively in the early evening; *Falstaff*, on St Amorsplein, down Platielstraat from Vrijthof, is younger and noisier, with good music and a wide range of beers. For **live music** all year round try *D'n Awwestiene* at Kesselskade 43 (Wed–Sun 10pm–5am; f12.50).

travel details

Trains

Amsterdam to: Alkmaar (every 15min; 30min); Arnhem (every 30min; 1hr 10min); Groningen (every 30min; 2hr 20min); Haarlem (every 10min; 15min); The Hague (every 15min; 45min); Leeuwarden (hourly; 2hr 30min); Leiden (every 15min; 35min); Maastricht (hourly; 2hr 30min); Rotterdam (every 30min; 1hr 10min); Schiphol Airport (every 15min; 20min); Utrecht (every 30min; 30min).

Alkmaar to: Haarlem (every 30min; 25min).

Arnhem to: Amsterdam (every 30min; 1hr 10min); Utrecht (7 hourly; 35min).

Groningen to: Amsterdam (every 30min; 2hr 20min); Leeuwarden (every 30min; 50min).

Haarlem to: Alkmaar (every 30min; 25min).

The Hague to: Delft (every 15min; 15min); Gouda (every 20min; 20min); Rotterdam (every 15min; 25min); Utrecht (every 20min; 40min).

Leeuwarden to: Amsterdam (every 30min; 2hr 25min); Groningen (every 30min; 50min).

Leiden to: Amsterdam (every 30min; 35min); The Hague (every 30min; 35min).

Maastricht to: Amsterdam (hourly; 2hr 30min).

Rotterdam to: Gouda (every 20min; 20min); Utrecht (every 20min; 45min).

Utrecht to: Arnhem (every 15min; 30min); Leeuwarden (hourly; 2hr).

CHAPTER 20

NORWAY

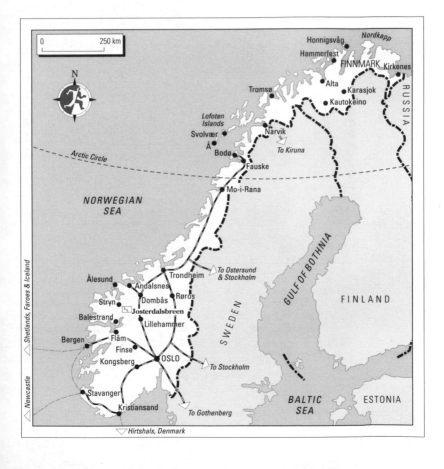

Shetlands, Faroes & Iceland

Newcastle

Introduction

In many ways **Norway** is still a land of unknowns. Quiet for a thousand years since the Vikings stamped their mark on Europe, the country nowadays often seems more than just geographically distant. Beyond Oslo and the famous fjords the rest of the country might as well be blank for all many visitors know – and, in a manner of speaking, large parts of it are. Vast stretches in the north and east are sparsely populated, and it is possible to travel for hours without seeing a soul.

Despite this isolation, Norway has had a pervasive influence. Traditionally its inhabitants were explorers, from the Vikings to more recent figures like Amundsen, Nansen and Heyerdahl, while Norse language and traditions are common to many other isolated fishing communities, not least northwest Scotland and the Shetlands. At home, too, the Norwegian people have striven to escape the charge of national provincialism, touting the disproportionate number of acclaimed artists, writers and musicians (most notably Munch, Ibsen and Grieg) who have made their mark on the wider European scene. It's also a pleasing discovery that the great outdoors – great though it is – harbours some lively historical towns.

Beyond **Oslo**, one of the world's most prettily sited capitals, the major cities of interest are medieval **Trondheim**, **Bergen**, in the heart of the fjords, and hilly, northern **Tromsø**. None is exactly supercharged, but they are likeable, walkable cities worth time for themselves, as well as being on top of startlingly handsome countryside. The perennial draw is the **western fjords** – every bit as scenically stunning as they're cracked up to be. Dip into the region from Bergen or Åndalsnes, both accessible direct by train from Oslo, or take more time and appreciate the subtleties of the innumerable waterside towns and villages. Far to the north of here Norway grows increasingly barren, and what tourist trail there is peters out altogether. The vast lands of **Troms** and **Finnmark** were once the home of outlaws and still boast wild and untamed tracts. There are also the Sami clans and their herds of reindeer, which you'll see on the thin, exposed road up to the North Cape, or **Nordkapp** – the northernmost accessible point of mainland Europe, and the natural end to the long trek north.

Information and maps

Every town has a **tourist office**, usually with a stock of free maps, timetables and other bumph. Many book private rooms and hotel beds, rent out bikes and change money. During the high season – June to August – they normally open daily for long hours while in the shoulder season they mostly adopt shop hours; many close down altogether in winter. The best general **map** of Norway is the *Hallwag International* 1:1,000,000, which comes complete with an index.

Money and banks

Norway has a reputation as one of the most expensive countries in Europe. In terms of consumables – from a cup of coffee to a roll of film – this is true, but certain major necessities – notably transport – are far more reasonably priced. Per day, £25/$40 represents an absolute minimum expenditure, £35–45/$55–70 being a more realistic amount. Norwegian **currency** is the **krone** (kr), one of which is divided into 100 øre. Coins in circulation are 50 øre, 1kr, 5kr and 10kr; notes are for 50kr, 100kr, 200kr, 500kr and 1000kr. Banking hours are Mon–Fri 8am–3.30/4pm, usually open an hour later on Thurs, but closing an hour earlier June–Aug. Some airports, train stations and campsites have **exchange offices** open evenings and weekends, and some tourist offices also change money, though at less favourable rates than the banks and post offices. **ATMs** are common in the larger towns.

Communications

Norwegian communications are excellent, and things are made even easier by the fact that nearly all post and telephone office staff speak good English. **Post office** opening hours are usually Mon–Fri 8am–4pm, Sat 9am–1pm. **Stamps** are available from post offices, kiosks and stationery shops costing 5.5kr for a 20-gram letter or postcard to Europe, 7kr to the rest of the world. Most **telephone** boxes take 1kr, 5kr and 10kr coins, and there is a minimum 2kr charge, but coin-operated phones are gradually giving way to credit- and card-operated public telephones. Widely available, telephone cards come in denominations of 35kr (22 units), 98kr (65 units) and 210kr (150 units). The international access code is ☎00 47, directory enquiries ☎180 for Scandinavian countries and ☎181 otherwise. To make an international collect call dial ☎115.

Getting around

Norway's transport system is comprehensive and reliable. In the winter (especially in the north), services can be cut back severely, but no part of the country is isolated for long. A synopsis of all the main air, train, bus and ferry services is given in the free *Norway Transport and Accommodation* brochure, available in advance from the Norwegian tourist board. This general guide can be supplemented by detailed regional public transport timetables, available at all local tourist offices. Train schedules are detailed in the *NSB Togruter*, free at every station. In addition, Nor-Way Bussekspress co-ordinates long-distance bus services across the country.

■ Trains

Train services are run by Norges Statsbaner (NSB) – Norwegian State Railways. Apart from a few branch lines, NSB work on four main routes. These link Oslo to Stockholm in the east, to Stavanger in the southwest, to Bergen in the west and to Trondheim and on to Fauske and Bodø in the north. The nature of the country makes most of the routes engineering feats of some magnitude and worth a trip in their own right – the tiny Flåm line and sweeping Rauma run to Åndalsnes are exciting examples. **InterRail** and **Eurail** passes are valid, as is the **Scanrail** pass which costs around £130/$215 for five days of travel within fifteen days, £180/$295 for ten days within one month and £200/$320 for 21 consecutive days of unlimited travel. The ScanRail pass is valid for train travel within all of Scandinavia and there is a 25 percent discount for those under 26, 14 percent for seniors (over 60); it also provides free travel or large discounts on many ferry crossings and bus journeys. It is best purchased from travel agents before you go. NSB also have tickets at discounted rates for off-peak travel, pre-booked journeys and weekend excursions; details can be obtained from any major Norwegian train station. Fares are generally reasonable: the popular Oslo-to-Bergen trip, for example, costs about 550kr one-way. Note that most express trains (*Ekspress*) and all overnight trains require advance seat reservation (20kr) whether you have a rail pass or not. In high season it's wise to make one anyway as trains can be packed. Sleepers are reasonably priced, starting at around 100kr for a bed in a three-berth compartment. NSB's website is at *www.nsb.no/persont/*

■ Buses

You'll need to use **buses** principally in the western fjords and the far north, though there are also a series of long-distance **express buses** which connect major towns. **Tickets** aren't too pricey and are usually bought on board, although bus stations sell advance tickets too. Information on specific routes, and timetables, is available from local tourist offices

or from Nor-Way Bussekspress, Karl Johans Gate 2, N–0154 Oslo 1 (☎23.00.24.40; *www.nor-way.no*). Students and InterRail pass holders can get a 50 percent **discount** on bus travel between the two rail termini of Fauske/Bodø and Narvik among several other bus routes. A long-distance bus, the **Nord-Norge Expressen**, runs between Fauske, the northernmost reach of the railway, and Kirkenes, close to the Russian border, a 48-hour journey involving stopovers. The route is operated by several bus companies who combine to run two buses daily all year as far as Narvik, where you usually have to break your journey before embarking on the next two stages – to Alta and then Kirkenes. If you're doing this much bus travel, you should invest in a pass (Nor-way Busspass), which costs 1375kr for seven days and 2200kr for fourteen; you can buy it at major bus stations.

■ Ferries

Travelling by **ferry** is one of the real pleasures of a trip to Norway. Most ferries are on the west coast, and especially among the fjords, though on the main ("E") roads many of them have been replaced by tunnels. Ferry rates are fixed nationally on a sliding scale. The tariff is reasonable, with a fifteen-minute ferry ride costing 15kr for foot passengers, 35kr for a car and driver. Bus fares include the cost of any ferry journey made en route. Drivers should note that almost every ferry operates on a first-come, first-served basis. This presents few problems for most of the year, but in high summer, you should arrive one and a half to two hours before departure to be certain of a space. Some of the busier routes have a control kiosk, where you pay on arrival, but for the most part a sailor comes round to collect fares either on the quayside or on board.

There's also the *Hurtigrute* (literally "rapid route"), a **coastal ferry** service, whose several ships shuttle up and down the Norwegian coast linking Bergen with Kirkenes and stopping off at over thirty ports on the way. **Tickets** for short jumps are quite expensive, certainly compared with the comparable bus fares, and the full eleven-day return cruise (including a cabin and meals) goes for 8000–23,000kr. However, prices are reduced outside May to August, when under-26s can buy a special **coastal pass** (*kystpass*), which costs about 1750kr for 21 days' unlimited travel. Get it on board your first trip or at almost all travel agents at home or in Norway. Although it's a cruise ship you don't need to have a cabin: sleeping in the lounges or on deck is allowed. Plan carefully before buying your ticket, since single tickets only allow one overnight stop. The older ships are the nicest, and tend to have showers you can use on the lower corridors, but they only have room for five or six vehicles so car drivers should use the new ones. Bikes travel free. A 24-hour cafeteria supplies coffee and snacks, and there's a good-value restaurant.

■ Driving

By and large, Norwegian **roads** are excellent, although you'll need to take care on the winding mountain passes and in the enormous tunnels. Venture off the main roads, especially in the north and in the mountains, and you'll need consummate driving skills. In winter, surfaces are often treacherous, many minor roads are closed and for certain parts of the network – like the E6 Arctic Highway – you need to be properly equipped for Arctic conditions. EU **driving licences** are honoured in Norway, but other nationals will need an International Driver's Licence. If you're bringing your own car, you must have vehicle registration papers, adequate insurance, a first aid kit, a warning triangle and a Green Card. Vehicles should be driven on the right, with dipped headlights required at all times; there's a speed limit of 50kph in built-up areas and 90kph on open roads, seatbelts are compulsory for drivers and passengers, and drunken driving is severely punished. If you **break down**, the Norges Automobil-Forbund (NAF) patrols all mountain passes between mid-June and mid-August, and there are emergency telephones along some main roads. NAF's 24hr **emergency number** (for members of AIT-affiliated clubs like the AA and RAC) is ☎81.00.05.05. **Car rental** is expensive: from around 3600kr a week with unlimited mileage.

Accommodation

Inevitably, hotel accommodation is one of the major expenses you will incur on a trip to Norway – but there are budget alternatives, principally private rooms arranged via the tourist office and youth hostels.

■ Youth hostels

Youth hostels provide the accommodation mainstay – there are about ninety in all, spread right across the country. The Norwegian hostelling association, Norske Vandrerhjem, Dronningensgate 26, Oslo (☎23.13.93.00; www.vandrerhjem.no), puts out a free booklet detailing addresses, opening dates and prices. Prices vary greatly – anything from 90kr to 180kr – although the more expensive ones nearly always include a first-rate breakfast. On average, reckon on paying 120kr a night for a bed, 50kr for breakfast and 80–100kr for a hot evening meal. Most hostels have a supply of doubles, often en-suite, for around 300kr. Non-members can use the hostels but pay an extra 25kr a night. Between June and mid-September you should ring ahead to check on space. Most hostels close between 11am and 4pm, and there's normally an 11pm/midnight curfew.

■ Campsites and cabins

Camping is another way of keeping accommodation costs down. There are hundreds of official sites throughout the country, and most are of a high standard; prices are usually around 70kr a tent, plus around 40kr per person. The Norwegian Tourist Board publishes an annual list. Campsites also often have **cabins**, usually four-bedded affairs with kitchen facilities and sometimes a bathroom, for upwards of 150kr. **Camping rough**, as in Sweden, is a tradition enshrined in law. You can camp anywhere in open areas as long as you are at least 150m away from houses or cabins. In all cases a good sleeping bag is essential, since even in summer it can get very cold; in the north a mosquito repellent and sun-protection cream are vital.

■ Hotels, pensions and private rooms

Hotels are generally out of the reckoning for travellers on a budget – the cheapest double room will set you back around 650kr a night. Still, there are bargains to be found, particularly during summer, when most hotels have discounts of between 20 and 40 percent. Remember also that the price of a hotel room always includes breakfast. **Pensions** (*pensjonater*) in the more touristy towns are slightly

---

ACCOMMODATION PRICE CODES

Throughout this guide, accommodation is priced on a scale of ① to ⑨, the number indicating the lowest price per night a single person could expect to pay in that establishment in high season. With hostels this is the nightly rate per person; with hotels, the price is arrived at by dividing the cost of the cheapest double room by two. The prices indicated by the codes are as follows:

① under £5 / $8	④ £15–20 / $24–32	⑦ £30–35 / $48–56
② £5–10 / $8–16	⑤ £20–25 / $32–40	⑧ £35–40 / $56–64
③ £10–15 / $16–24	⑥ £25–30 / $40–48	⑨ £40 / $64 and over

cheaper at about 450kr a double; breakfast is usually extra. Failing that, tourist offices in larger towns can sometimes fix you up with a **private room** in someone's house for around 200-300kr a double, though there's a booking fee (15–25kr) on top and the rooms are mostly way out of the centre.

Food and drink

Norwegian food can, at its best, be excellent: fish is plentiful, and carnivores can have a field day trying meats like reindeer steak or elk. But all this costs money, and those on a tight budget may have problems varying their diet. The same can be said of drinking: buying from the supermarkets and state off-licences, the Vinmonopolet, is often the only way you'll afford a tipple: in a bar, a half litre of beer will cost you around 40kr.

■ Food

Breakfast (*frokost*) – a self-service affair of bread, crackers, cheese, eggs, preserves, cold meat and fish, with unlimited tea and coffee – is usually excellent at youth hostels, and memorable in hotels. Almost everywhere it's included in the price of a room; where it isn't reckon on an extra 60–70kr. **Picnic food** is the best stand-by during the day, although there are a number of **fast food** alternatives. The indigenous Norwegian variety, served up at street stalls (*gatekjøkken*), consists mainly of rubbery hot dogs (*varm pølse*), pizza slices and chicken and chips. A better choice, and often no more expensive, is simply to get a **smørbrød**, a huge open sandwich heaped with a variety of garnishes. You'll see them in **cafés**, or in sandwich bars in larger towns.

Good **coffee** is available everywhere and is often half-price after the first cup. **Tea**, too, is ubiquitous, but the local preference is for lemon tea or a variety of flavoured infusions; if you want milk, ask for it.

The best deals for **sit-down food** are at lunchtime (*lunsj*), when self-service **kafeterias** offer a limited range of daily specials (*dagens rett*) – a fish or meat dish with vegetables or salad, often including a drink, sometimes bread, and occasionally coffee too, that costs around 60–80kr. Most department stores and large supermarkets have surprisingly good *kafeterias*; as do main railway stations. You'll also find them in the larger towns, where they are sometimes called *kaffistovas*. **Restaurants**, serving dinner (*middag*) and classic Norwegian food, are out of the range of many budgets, but the seafood at the best of them is quite superb – main courses average

180–200kr. Again, the best deals are at lunchtime, when many restaurants put out a *koldtbord* (the Norwegian *smörgåsbord*), where, for a fixed price of around 100–150kr, you can get through as much as possible during the three or four hours it's served. There are also a sizeable number of urban **ethnic restaurants**, the most affordable of which are the pizza joints, and **café/bars** where a substantial main course and a couple of small beers will rush you about 200kr.

■ Drink

Norwegian alcohol prices are among the highest in Europe. **Beer** is lager-like and comes in three strengths (classes I, II and III), of which the strongest and most expensive is class III. **Spirits** are also way over the top in price. One local speciality worth trying at least once is *aquavit*, served ice-cold in little glasses and, at 40 percent proof, real headache material. In bars and cafés a half-litre of beer costs about 40kr. Bars tend to close down at around 11pm outside the larger cities, although licensed discos and clubs stay open much later.

Beer is sold in supermarkets and shops all over Norway and is about half the price you'd pay in a bar. Wines and spirits can only be purchased from the state-controlled shops known as Vinmonopolet. There's generally one in each small town, though there are more branches in the cities; opening hours are usually Mon–Wed 10am–4pm, Thurs 10am–3pm, Fri 9am–4pm, Sat 9am–1pm.

Opening hours and holidays

Shop **opening hours** are usually Mon–Wed & Fri 9am–5pm, Thurs 9am–6/7pm, Sat 9am–1/3pm. Newspaper kiosks (*Narvesen*) and takeaway food stalls are open every evening until 10 or 11pm. Most shops and businesses are **closed** on the following days: Jan 1; Maundy Thursday; Good Friday; Easter Sunday & Monday; May 1; Ascension Day (mid-May); May 17; Whit Sunday & Monday; Dec 25 & Dec 26.

Emergencies

Like all the Scandinavian countries, Norway is in general a safe place to travel; the people are friendly and helpful, and petty crime has a relatively low profile. If you have to visit the **police** you'll find them helpful and normally able to speak English. If you have something stolen, be sure to get a police report number – essential for any insurance claim. As for **health problems**, most hotels and tourist offices have lists of local doctors and dentists. You'll pay around 100kr for an appointment and more for treatment, but hospital stays, treatments and consultations are free for EU citizens, providing they're carrying an E111. This does not cover dental treatments or prescription charges. Prescriptions are taken to chemists (*apotek*) which – should they be closed – carry a rota in the window advising of the nearest open shop.

EMERGENCY NUMBERS

Police ☎ 112; Ambulance ☎113; Fire☎110.

OSLO

Despite tourist-office endeavours, **OSLO** retains a low profile among European cities, and even comparisons with other Scandinavian capitals are usually a little less than favourable. Inevitably, though, you'll pass through – the main train routes heading west to the fjords, north to the Arctic, south to the coast and east to Sweden are routed through the city – but take heart: Oslo is definitely worth seeing. The city has some of Europe's best museums, fields a streetlife that surprises most first-time visitors, and helps revive travellers weary of the austere northern wilderness.

Oslo is the oldest of the Scandinavian capital cities, founded, according to the Norse chronicler Snorre Sturlason, around 1048 by Harold Hardråda. Several decimating fires and 600 years later, Oslo upped sticks and shifted west to its present site, abandoning its old name (*Ås*, a Norse word for God, and *lo* meaning field) in favour of Christiania – after the seventeenth-century Danish king Christian IV responsible for the move. The new city prospered and by the time of the break with Denmark (and union with Sweden) in 1814, Christiania – indeed Norway as a whole – was clamouring for independence, something it finally achieved in 1905, though the city didn't revert to its original name for another twenty years. Oslo's centre reflects the era well: wide streets, dignified parks and gardens, solid nineteenth-century buildings and long, consciously classical vistas combine to lend it a self-satisfied, respectable air. Seeing the city takes – and deserves – time. Its half a million inhabitants have room to spare in a city whose vast boundaries encompass huge areas of woods, sand and water, and much of the time you're as likely to be swimming or trail-walking as strolling the city centre.

Arrival and information

International and domestic **trains** use Oslo Sentralstasjon, known as **Oslo S**, at the eastern end of the city centre. The central **bus terminal** (Bussterminalen or **Oslo M**) is handily placed a short walk to the northeast of Oslo S, under the Galleriet Oslo Shopping centre. Oslo M handles most of the bus services within the city as well as those to and from the airport. Long-distance buses arrive and depart here too, but note that some Nor-Way Bussekspress and National Express Eurolines services terminate on the south side of Oslo S. For all bus enquiries, consult the information desk at Oslo M (Mon–Fri 7am–10pm, Sat 8am–5.30pm & Sun 8am–10pm). **Ferries** arrive at either the Vippetangen quays, a twenty-minute walk south of Oslo S, or at Hjortneskaia, some 3km west of the city centre; take bus #56 to the centre – an infrequent service, though it's mostly linked to ferry arrival times – or, failing that, a taxi to Oslo S (150kr). Catamarans (*Hurtigbåt*) from Arendal, on the south coast, dock behind the Rådhus (the town hall). Oslo's gleamingly new **Gardermoen airport**, 45km north of the city, is linked to Oslo S by high-speed train and bus. The former is faster, the latter a tad cheaper.

There's a tourist kiosk inside Oslo S (June–Aug daily 8am–11pm; May & Sept Mon–Sat 8am–11pm; Oct–April Mon–Sat 8am–5pm), but the **main tourist office** is in the Norwegian Information Centre down on the harbourfront at Brynjulf Bulls plass 1 (April, May & Sept Mon–Sat 9am–5pm; June–Aug daily 9am–7pm; Oct–March Mon–Fri 9am–4pm; ☎22.83.00.50; *www.oslopro.no*). Both offices issue a free and detailed guide to the city, provide a monthly free listings booklet *What's On*, give away maps and help you find accommodation. They also sell the useful **Oslo Card**, which gives free admission to most of the museums, discounts in shops and restaurants and unlimited free travel on the transport system, including ferries. Valid for either one, two or three days, it costs 150kr, 220kr and 250kr respectively.

City transport

Most **transport** is operated by AS Oslo Sporveier, whose **Trafikanten information office** is on Jernbanetorget, the pedestrianized square outside Oslo S (Mon–Fri 7am–8pm, Sat 8am–6pm). They have a free useful transit map and a free timetable booklet, *Rutebok for Oslo*, which details every transport schedule in the city. Most **buses** pass through Jernbanetorget; another common stop is outside the National Theatre (Nationaltheatret). Most buses stop running at around midnight, when **night buses** take over on certain routes. The fewer, slower **trams** run on eight lines from east to west, and tend to duplicate the bus routes; major terminals are Jernbanetorget and Nationaltheatret. The underground Tunnelbanen (**T-bane**) has eight lines, all of which converge to share a common slice of track that crosses the city centre from Majorstuen in the west to Tøyen in the east, with Jernbanetorget, Stortinget and Nationaltheatret stations in between. From this central section, four lines run westbound (*Vest*) and four eastbound (*Øst*). Numerous **local ferries** cross the fjord to connect the city with its outlying districts and archipelagos: to Bygdøy and the museums from the piers behind the Rådhus (May–Sept); for the inner Oslofjord islands from Vippetangen quay, behind Akershus Castle (bus #60 from Jernbanetorget).

A flat-fare **ticket** costs 20kr, a 24-hour **travel pass**, 40kr; both are valid on all types of public transport. There is also the Flexikort pass, which entitles the holder to eight journeys for 110kr, as well as passes for longer stays – both are available from Trafikanten. **Taxis** are expensive – around 130kr for up to a ten-minute, 5km ride; to get one ring Oslo Taxi (☎22.38.80.90).

Accommodation

Oslo has the range of hotels you would expect of a capital city, as well as private rooms and youth hostels. To appreciate the full flavour of the city, you're best off staying on or near the western reaches of Karl Johans gate, between the Stortinget and the Nationaltheatret, though the well-heeled area to the north and west of the Royal Palace is enjoyable too. Many of the least expensive lodgings are, however, to be found in the vicinity of Oslo S, and this district – along with the grimy suburbs to the north and east of the station – is best avoided. That said, if money is tight and you're here in July and August, your choice of location may well be very limited as the scramble for **budget beds** becomes acute – or at least tight enough to make it well worth calling ahead to check on space. A positive way to cut the hassle is to use the **accommodation service** provided by the tourist office. Both the office inside Oslo S and at the Norwegian Information Centre, Brynjulf Bulls plass 1, can give you full accommodation lists or make a reservation on your behalf for a nominal fee.

Hostels and private rooms

There are three official IYHF **hostels** in Oslo, each very popular and open to people of any age. Another good budget option are the **private rooms** booked by the tourist office for a cost of about 170kr for a single, 300kr a double; the supply of private rooms rarely dries up and they are something of a bargain, especially as many have self-catering facilities, but they do tend to be out of the city centre, and there's often a minimum two-night stay.

HOSTELS

Oslo Vandrerhjem LBM – Ekeberg, Kongsveien 82 (☎22.74.18.90). Open from June to mid-August, this pocket-sized IYHF hostel is situated 4km east of Oslo S in the suburb of Nordstrand. Take tram #18 or #19 in the direction of Ljabru, get off at the Holtet stop, then it's a 100m walk. ③.

Oslo Vandrerhjem Haraldsheim, Haraldsheimveien 4, Grefsen (☎22.22.29.65). The best of the three IYHF youth hostels, 5km northeast of the centre, and open all year, it has 270 beds, most in rooms for four people. The public areas are comfortable and attractively furnished and the rooms are clean and frugal, over half with their own shower and WC. Advance booking is strongly advised in the summer. Take tram #10 or #11 from Oslo S to the Sinsenkrysset stop, from where it's a ten-minute walk along the signposted footpath that cuts across the field. ③.

Oslo Vandrerhjem Holtekilen, Michelets vei 55, 1320 Stabekk (☎67.51.80.40). Much smaller than Haraldsheim, and only open from the end of May to mid-August, this IYHF hostel is located 10km west of the city centre. From Oslo M, take bus #151 and the hostel is 100m beyond the bus stop. There are kitchen facilities, a restaurant and a laundry. ③.

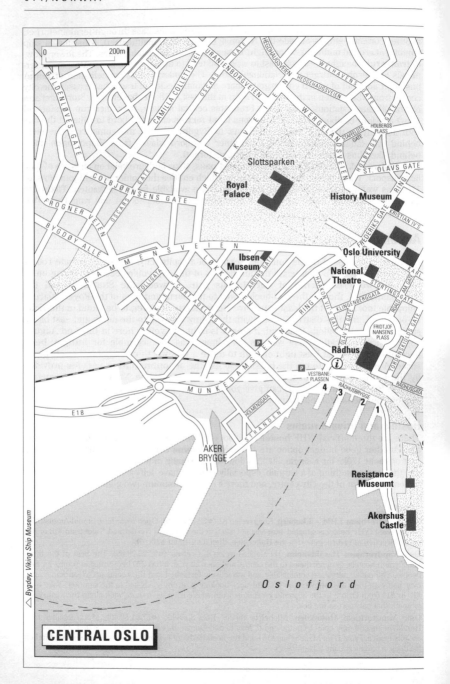

0 200m

Slottsparken

Royal Palace

History Museum

HOLBERGS PLASS

ST. OLAVS GATE

Oslo University

Ibsen Museum

National Theatre

FRIDTJOF NANSENS PLASS

Rådhus

VESTBANE-PLASSEN

4 3 RÅDHUSBRYGGE 2 1

AKER BRYGGE

Resistance Museumt

Akershus Castle

△ *Bygdøy, Viking Ship Museum*

Oslofjord

CENTRAL OSLO

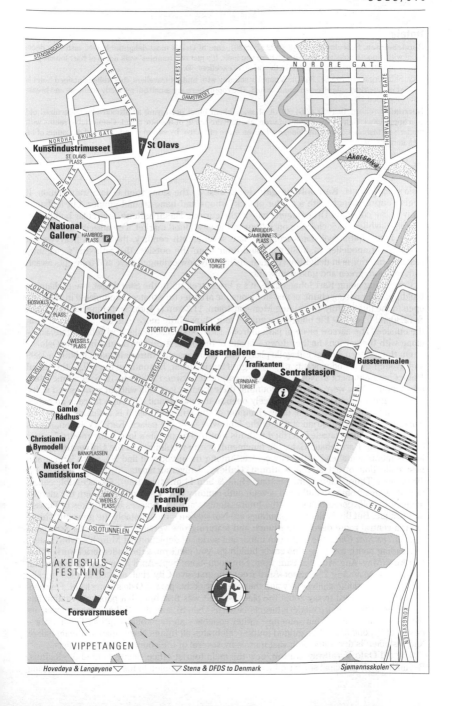

Hotels

Bondeheimen, Rosenkrantz gate 8 (☎22.42.95.30). One of Oslo's most delightful hotels, tastefully decorated with smooth polished pine everywhere you look. It's just two minutes' walk north of Karl Johans gate – and the buffet breakfast, included in the price, is excellent. ⑨.

City, Skippergata 19 (☎22.41.36.10). A popular standby with budget travellers, this well-maintained hotel is located in the grimy side streets around Oslo S. The rooms here are small but perfectly adequate and breakfast is included. ⑦.

Norrøna, Grensen 19 (☎22.42.64.00). A pleasant chain hotel occupying an attractively modernized old apartment block right in the middle of town, about 400m north of the Stortinget. Comfortable rooms with modern furnishings. Excellent value, made even more attractive by summer and weekend discounts of fifteen percent. ⑨.

The City

Oslo's main street, **Karl Johans gate**, leads west up the slope from Oslo S train station. It begins unpromisingly with a clutter of tacky shops and hang-around junkies, but footsteps away at the corner of Dronningens gate is the curious **Basarhallene**, a circular building of two tiers, whose brick cloisters once housed the city's food market. The adjacent **Domkirke** (daily 10am–4pm; free) dates from the late seventeenth century, though its heavyweight tower was remodelled in 1850; plain and dour from the outside, the cathedral's elegantly restored interior is in delightful contrast, its homely, low-ceilinged nave and transepts awash with maroon, green and gold paintwork.

Continuing along Karl Johans gate, it's a brief stroll up to the **Stortinget**, the parliament building, an imposing chunk of neo-Romanesque architecture that was completed in 1866. It's open to the public (July to mid-Aug Mon–Sat 10am, 11.30am & 1pm; Sept–June Sat only 11am & 12.30pm; free), but the obligatory guided tour shows little more than can be gleaned from the outside. The narrow piece of park in front, Eidsvolls plass, flanks Karl Johans gate, and – along with the gardens further down – is one of the busiest centres of summertime Oslo.

On the western side of Eidsvolls plass is the Neoclassical **Nationaltheatret**, built in 1899 and fronted by a stodgy statue of playwright Henrik Ibsen. Beyond, up the hill, is the **Royal Palace,** a monument to Norwegian openness; built between 1825 and 1848, at a time when other monarchies were nervously counting their friends, it stands without railings and walls. The grounds – Slottsparken – are freely open to the public and, although there is no public access to the palace itself, the daily changing of the guard (1.30pm) is a snappy affair, well worth a look. An equestrian statue of the king who built the palace, Karl XIV Johan, stands in front of the main facade inscribed with his motto "The people's love is my reward."

Back along Karl Johans Gate, the nineteenth-century buildings of the **University** fit well in this monumental end of the city centre. Among them you will find Norway's largest and best collection of art at the **National Gallery**, Universitetsgata 13 (Mon, Wed & Fri 10am–6pm, Thurs 10am–8pm, Sat 10am–4pm & Sun 11am–4pm; free). An accessible collection, it ranges from sixteenth- and seventeenth-century religious works, through the gloomy icons of the Novgorod School, to the Impressionists and later pieces by the likes of Picasso and Braque. But the bulk of the paintings are Norwegian – most notably the museum's highlight, a central room devoted to Munch and featuring one version of the famous *Scream* as well as *The Sick Child*, the first of an important series of depictions of Munch's dying sister.

Heading south from the University buildings, you can't miss the sullen brickwork of the **Rådhus** (May–Aug Mon–Sat 9am–5pm, Sun noon–5pm; Sept–April Mon–Sat 9am–4pm, Sun noon–4pm; May–Aug 25kr; Sept–April free), the massive City Hall, opened in 1950 to celebrate the city's 900th anniversary and the most distinctive part of Oslo's waterfront. Few people had a good word to say about the place when it was first built, but popular irritation has moved on to other, more distinctive targets (such as Oslo S), and the Rådhus has worn well, its twin towers a grandiose but somehow rather amiable statement of civic pride. The interior – best seen on one of the free guided tours – celebrates all things Norwegian; the main hall or Rådhushallen is decorated with vast murals by several of the country's leading artists.

The old **Oslo V railway station**, now the main tourist office, stands behind the Rådhus. Beyond, Oslo's principal shipyard has been cleverly remodelled to hold the hi-tech shopping halls of the **Aker Brygge** development. Running east from here, **Rådhusgata** leads to the city's other harbour, the gridiron streets on either side of it a legacy of seventeenth-century Oslo – though sadly it's only the layout that survives. To the south is **Akershus Castle** (May to mid-Sept Mon–Sat 10am–4pm, Sun 12.30–6pm; 20kr, plus free guided tours Mon–Sat 11am, 1pm & 3pm, Sun 1pm & 3pm), the most significant memorial to medieval Oslo and quite separate from the city centre in feel. Built on a rocky knoll overlooking the harbour around 1300, it was modernized in the seventeenth century by Christian IV. A visit to the castle takes in the royal chapel and mausoleum, but it's all rather bland. Rather more diverting is the **Resistance Museum**, beside the castle entrance (daily 10/11am–3/4pm; 20kr), where excellent displays detail the history of the war in Norway, from defeat and occupation through resistance to final victory. Surrounding the castle are the sprawling earth and stone ramparts and bastions of the **Akershus Festning** fortress, dating from the seventeenth century, which were designed to resist artillery bombardments. The part of the fortress adjoining the castle offers fine views over Oslo harbour.

The Bygdøy peninsula

The most enjoyable way to reach the **Bygdøy peninsula**, southwest of the city centre, is by ferry, departing from behind the Rådhus (May–Aug 9am–9pm every 40min; late April & Sept 9am–6pm every 40min, departing and returning to a similar schedule). They have two ports of call on the peninsula, stopping first at Dronningen pier, then at Bygdøynes pier. The two most popular attractions – the Viking Ships and the Norwegian Folk museums – are within easy walking distance of Dronningen pier; the other attractions are a stone's throw from Bygdøynes. If you decide to walk between the two, allow about fifteen minutes: the route is well signposted but dull. The alternative to the ferry is bus #30 (every 15min), which runs all year from Jernbanetorget and the National Theatre to the Viking Ships and Folk museums, and, when the ferry isn't running, to the other three museums as well.

The **Norwegian Folk Museum** on Museumsveien (Jan to mid-May & mid-Sept to Dec daily 11am–3/4pm; mid-May to mid-Sept daily 10am–5/6pm; 50kr) combines indoor collections of furniture, china and silverware with an open-air display of reassembled period farms, houses and other buildings. A few minutes walk away, the **Viking Ship Museum** (daily: April & Oct 11am–4pm; May–Aug 9am–6pm; Sept 11am–5pm; Nov–March 11am–3pm; 30kr) is a large hall specially constructed to house a trio of ninth-century Viking ships, with viewing platforms to enable you to see inside the hulls. The three oak vessels were retrieved from ritual burial mounds in southern Norway towards the end of the last century, each embalmed in a subsoil of clay, which accounts for their excellent state of preservation. The star exhibit is the **Oseberg ship**, thought to be the burial ship of a Viking chieftain's wife. Its ornately carved prow and stern rise high above the hull, where thirty oar-holes indicate the size of the crew. Much of the treasure buried with the boat was retrieved as well, and this is on display at the back of the museum.

Down by Bygdøynes pier, the **Kon-Tiki Museum** (daily: April, May & Sept 10.30am–5pm; June to Aug 9.30am–5.45pm; Oct–March 10.30am–4pm; 30kr) displays the balsawood raft on which Thor Heyerdahl made his now legendary 1947 journey across the Pacific to prove that the first Polynesian settlers could have sailed from pre-Inca Peru. Over the road, the **Fram Museum** (May–Sept daily 9/10am–4.45/6.45pm; Oct–April daily 10/11am–3.45/4.45pm; 25kr) displays the Polar vessel *Fram*, which carried Roald Amundsen to within striking distance of the South Pole in 1911. Complete with most of its original fittings, the interior gives a superb insight into the life and times of these early Arctic explorers. Next door, the **Norwegian Maritime Museum** (Jan to mid-May & Oct–Dec Mon, Wed, Fri, Sat & Sun 10.30am–4pm, Tues & Thurs 10.30am–7pm; mid-May to Sept daily 10am–7pm; 30kr) is a sparkling new building housing a fairly pedestrian collection of maritime artefacts. You'll probably be more taken with the café, a handy vantage point overlooking the bay, beach and city.

The Munch Museum

Also out of the centre but without question a major attraction, the **Munch Museum**, Tøyengata 53 (June to early Sept daily 10am–6pm; mid-Sept to May Tues–Sun 10am–4/6pm;

50kr), is reachable by T-bane: get off at Toyen and it's a signposted five-minute walk. Born in 1863, Edvard Munch is Norway's most famous painter. His lithographs and woodcuts are shown in one half of the gallery, a dark catalogue of swirls and fog, and in the main gallery there are early paintings, along with the great works of the 1890s, considered among Munch's finest achievements. Besides a piercing version of *The Scream*, there's *Dagny Juel*, a portrait of the Berlin socialite, Ducha, with whom both Munch and Strindberg were infatuated, and the chilling *Red Virginia Creeper*, a house being consumed by the plant. Later paintings reflect a renewed interest in nature and physical work, as in the *Workers Returning Home* and the light *Village Street, Kragerø* and *Model by the Wicker Chair*, which reveals a happier, if rather idealized, attitude to his surroundings – also evident in works like *Spring Ploughing*.

Frogner: the Vigeland Sculpture Park

On the other side of the city and reachable on tram #12 from the centre (get off at Vigelandsparken), **Frogner Park** holds one of Oslo's most striking cultural targets in the **Vigeland Sculpture Park**, which commemorates another modern Norwegian artist of world renown, Gustav Vigeland. The open-air sculptures, which Vigeland started in 1924 and was still working on when he died in 1943, are simply fantastic. A long series of life-size figures frowning, fighting and posing lead up to the central fountain, an enormous bowl representing the burden of life, supported by straining, sinewy bronze Goliaths while, underneath, water tumbles out around clusters of playing and standing figures. The twenty-metre obelisk up on the stepped embankment behind, and the grouped granite sculptures around it, comprise the summation of the work, a writhing mass which depicts the cycle of life as Vigeland saw it.

The islands of the inner Oslofjord

The compact archipelago of low-lying, lightly forested islands in the inner Oslofjord is the city's summer playground, and makes going to the beach an unusually viable option for a northern European capital. Jumping on a ferry, attractive enough in the heat of the day, is also one of the more pleasant forms of entertainment during the evenings and, although most of the islets are cluttered with summer homes, the least populated are favourite party venues for the city's preening youth. **Ferries** to the islands leave from Vippetangen quay, beside the grain silo at the foot of Akershusstranda – a twenty-minute walk, or a five-minute ride on bus #60, south from Jernbanetorget.

Conveniently, **Hovedøya** (ferry #92; mid-March to Sept; every 60–90min 7.30am–7pm; Oct to mid-March 3 daily; 10min), the nearest island, is also the most interesting, its rolling hills incorporating both farmland and deciduous woods as well as the overgrown ruins of a twelfth-century Cistercian monastery. There are plenty of footpaths to wander, you can swim from the shingle beaches on the south shore, and there's a seasonal café opposite the monastery ruins. Camping is not permitted, however, as Hovedøya is a protected area – that's why there are no summer homes.

The pick of the other islands is wooded **Langøyene** (ferry #94; June–Aug hourly 10am–6pm; 30min), the most southerly of the archipelago and the one with the best beaches. The H-shaped island has a campsite, *Langøyene Camping* (☎22.11.53.21; June to mid-Aug), and at night the ferries are full of people armed with sleeping bags and bottles, on their way to join swimming parties.

Eating

As befits a capital city, Oslo boasts scores of **eating places**, the sheer variety ensuring there's something to suit almost every budget. Those carefully counting the kroner will find it easy to buy bread, fruit, snacks and sandwiches from stalls, shops and kiosks across the city centre, while fast-food joints offering hamburgers and hot dogs (*pølser*) are legion. Far more interesting are the city's **cafés**. These run the gamut from homely family places to student haunts and ultra-fashionable hangouts, but nearly all of them serve inexpensive lunches and sometimes bargain evening meals too. It's worth noting that quite a few of the cafés detailed below could equally be slotted into our "Bars and pubs" section as the distinction between Oslo's cafés and bars is often very blurred. Regular **restaurants** are more expensive and frequently rather staid, but even here it's possible to find some excellent deals, especially if you stick to pizzas and pastas in one of the growing band of Italian places.

Markets, supermarkets and takeaway snacks

Markets are always good for fruit and vegetables: there's a small one on part of Jernbanetorget, but the main event is on Youngstorget (Mon–Sat 7am–2pm), a brief stroll north of the Domkirke along Torggata. Alternatively, there are a couple of handy fresh fruit and veg stalls in the Basarhallene, beside the Domkirke. The city centre is dotted with supermarkets; Rimi, the biggest name, has an outlet at Akersgata 45, a short walk from the Stortinget. **Takeaway snacks** – burgers, hot dogs, pizza slices, kebabs, felafel, chips, etc – are on sale from kiosks and stalls on virtually every street corner. Burger joints, too, have multiplied in the last few years, with Burger King now claiming several central branches. For healthier snacks, numerous bakeries and cake shops sell a reasonable range of sandwiches.

Cafés and restaurants

Amsterdam, Universitetsgata 11. Done out in the style of a Dutch brown bar, this busy and agreeable café/bar serves an imaginative mixture of international dishes, all at moderate prices. Kitchen closes around 8pm.

Bacchus, in the Basarhallene behind the Domkirke. Cramped café/bar with period decor and a wrought-iron staircase. Classical music during the day, all sorts at night when the seediness of the surrounding area is more noticeable. Great cakes and pastries plus tasty sandwiches.

Celsius, Rådhusgata 19 at Øvre Slotts gate. Hidden behind an unlikely looking eighteenth-century gateway, this laid-back café/bar occupies one of Oslo's older buildings and offers delicious Mediterranean-inspired food at 120kr a dish. It's also a great place for a drink.

Ett Glass, Karl Johans gate 33, entrance round the corner near the bottom of Rosenkrantz gate. Trendy, candlelit café/bar. An imaginative menu focusing on light meals and lunches provides some curious, often mouth-watering delights. Inexpensive.

Kaffistova, Rosenkrantz gate 8. Part of the *Bondeheimen* hotel, this spick and span self-service café serves tasty, traditional Norwegian cooking at very fair prices. There's usually a vegetarian option, too.

Vegeta Vertshus, Munkedamsveien 3b. Near the National Theatre, this unassuming vegetarian restaurant has a help-yourself buffet with fine salads, mixed vegetables, pizza, potatoes and rice.

Drinking

Downtown Oslo has a vibrant **bar** scene, a noisy, boisterous but generally good-tempered affair, at its most frenetic on summer weekends, when the city is crowded with visitors from all over Norway. The busiest and often flashiest bars are concentrated in the side streets near the Rådhus and down along the Aker Brygge, while other popular but less assertively heterosexual bars are clustered around Universitetsgata and on Rosenkrantz gate. Karl Johans gate weighs in with a string of bars too, some of which are staid and stodgy, others – especially those near Oslo S – a fair bit wilder and less conventional.

Many of Oslo's bars stay open until well after midnight, until 3am or 4am in some cases. Drinks are uniformly expensive, and so, if you're after a big night out, it's a good idea to follow Norwegian custom and start with a few warm-up drinks at home.

Bars and pubs

Barbeint, Drammensveien 20. About ten minutes' walk west of the National Theatre. If you're familiar with Scandinavian bands and films then you may recognize a few faces in this jam-packed, fashionable bar. Loud sounds, everything from rap to rock. Daily 8pm–3.30am.

Lipp, Olavs gate 2. Part of the *Continental* hotel, this big and brash bar, all wide windows and wood, is popular with the well-heeled of Oslo. Mon & Sun 3pm–1.30am, Tues–Sat 3pm–2.30am.

Savoy Bar, Universitetsgata 11. With its stained-glass windows and wood-panelled walls, this small, intimate bar is a civilized spot to nurse a beer. Part of the *Savoy* hotel on the corner of Kristian Augusts gate. Daily 5pm–2am.

Sjakk Matt, Haakon VII's gate 5. Informal and very groovy café-bar near the Rådhus. Delicious Mediterranean-style food too, at just 60–70kr a dish.

The Scotsman, Karl Johans gate 17 at Nedre Slotts gate. Many visitors to Oslo seek this bar out – though no one is quite sure why. It's an eccentric kind of place, full of incongruities: the *Angus Steakhouse* restaurant in the basement serves Scottish pizzas and the regular live music acts can be unbelievably bad and/or bizarre, but the place is still packed every night. Outdoor seating on the main drag in summer. Not for the timid. Mon–Sat 11am–2.30am, Sun noon–2.30am.

Nightlife

Tracking down **live music** is straightforward enough, though the domestic rock scene is hardly inspiring – the talent is spread very thin indeed; by comparison, **jazz** fans are well served, with several first-rate nightspots dotted round the city centre. Oslo's busiest **nightclubs** are on and around Karl Johans gate. Entry will set you back in the region of 80kr – though drinks prices are the same as anywhere else. Nothing gets going much before 11pm; closing times are generally around 3–4am. For **entertainment listings** it's always worth checking *Natt & Dag*, a monthly Norwegian-language broadsheet available free from cafés, bars and shops, or the English-language *What's On in Oslo*, a monthly freebie produced by the tourist office.

Nightclubs, rock and jazz venues

Cruise Kafé, Stranden 3, Aker Brygge. This small, modern bar showcases live rock, rock and roll and blues bands, many of whom are American. Open daily till 12.30am, 2.30am at the weekend.

Head On, Rosenkrantz gate 11B. A student favourite with the emphasis on funk and rap. Daily 10pm–3.30am.

Original Nilsen, Rosenkrantz gate 11. Popular bar featuring regular live jazz in the evening. Daily noon–3.30am.

Rockerfeller Music Hall, Torggata 16. Accommodating up to 1500 people, this is one of Oslo's major nightspots, hosting well-known and up-and-coming rock groups with a good side-line in reggae and salsa. Has its own Rock Cinema too.

Smuget, Rosenkrantz gate 22. Large and popular nightclub with bars, a restaurant, a disco and regular live shows by mostly home-grown jazz, rock or blues bands. Daily 8pm–4.30am.

Snorre, Rosenkrantz gate 11. Extremely popular club incorporating a bar, a restaurant and a large dance floor. Smart, youthful scene. Wed–Sat 9am–3.30am.

Listings

Airlines Braathens, at the airport (☎67.58.60.00); British Airways, at the airport (☎80.03.31.42); SAS at *Radisson SAS Scandinavia Hotel*, Holbergs gate 30, and the airport (both ☎81.00.33.00).

Bicycle Rental Vestbanen A/S, metres from the main tourist office at Vestbaneplassen 2. Rental from around 180kr a day, deposit around 1000kr.

Car rental Avis, Munkedamsveien 27 (☎66.77.11.11), and at the airport (☎64.81.06.60); Budget, Sonja Henie plass 4 (☎22.17.10.50), and at the airport (☎80.03.02.10); Europcar, at the airport (☎64.81.05.60).

Embassies Canada, Wergelandveien 7 (☎22.99.53.00); Ireland, Australia and New Zealand, use UK embassy; UK, Thomas Heftyes gate 8 (☎23.13.27.00); USA, Drammensveien 18 (☎22.44.85.50).

Exchange All banks and post offices exchange currency and cash travellers' cheques at comparable rates. Outside of normal banking and post office hours the best bets are the 24hr ATMs or the exchange office at Oslo S (June–Sept daily 7am–10pm; Oct–May Mon–Fri 8am–7.30pm & Sat 10am–5pm). There are also exchange facilities at the airport.

Gay Oslo Not much of a scene as such, but advice is available from and activities and events are organized by LLH, St Olavs plass 2 (Mon–Fri 9am–4pm; ☎22.36.19.48).

Hiking Den Norske Turistforening (DNT), Storgata 3 (Mon–Fri 10am–4pm, Thurs until 6pm, Sat 10am–2pm; ☎22.82.28.00), sells hiking maps and gives general advice and information on route planning – an invaluable first call before a walking trip in Norway. Join here to use their nationwide network of mountain huts; the subscription fee of around 360kr gives a year's membership.

Laundry Mr Clean, Parkveien 6 at Welhavens gate (daily 7am–11pm).

Off-licences Vinmonopolet at Klingenberggaten 4; and Møllergaten 10–12.

Pharmacies Jernbanetorgets Apotek, Jernbanetorget 4b is open round the clock.

Post offices The main office is at Dronningens gate 15 at Prinsens gate (Mon–Fri 8am–6pm, Sat 10am–3pm).

Travel agents Terra Nova, Dronningens gate 26 (☎23.13.93.00); KILROY travels, Nedre Slotts gate 23 (☎23.10.23.00).

SOUTHERN NORWAY

Southern Norway is an immediately appealing region – flatlands and fells fringed by a tempting coastal concentration of islands and long mostly rocky beaches. As such it's the Norwegians' principal domestic holiday choice, though everyone else tends to pass quickly through, which is fair enough if it's a choice between this region and the fjords. However, southern Norway may, of course, be your first view of the country, in which case it's worth spending at least some time at your point of arrival. International ferries put in to the western port of **Stavanger**, the region's major town, and **Kristiansand**, a lively resort. Both are attractive centres in their own right, especially Stavanger with its pretty little old town and sea connections with Bergen to the north.

Stavanger

STAVANGER is something of a survivor. While other Norwegian coastal towns have fallen foul of the precarious fortunes of fishing, Stavanger has grown into one of Norway's most dynamic economic powerhouses. Fish canning and its own merchant fleet brought initial prosperity, which shipbuilding and the oil industry have since sustained. It isn't one of Norway's most alluring cities, but it is a brash, international place, worth a day or so before moving on to the fjords or Oslo.

The old centre, **Gamle Stavanger**, near the international ferry terminal, is of greatest appeal, a pristinely preserved area of wooden warehouses, narrow clapboard houses and cobbled streets that was once home for seamen and visiting merchants. There's a good museum here, the **Canning Museum**, Øvre Strandgate 88 (mid-June to mid-Aug daily 11am–4pm; rest of year Sun 11am–4pm; 30kr), located in a reconstructed sardine-canning factory; it gives a glimpse of the industry that saved Stavanger from decay in the late nineteenth century and smokes its own sardines on the first Sunday of every month and every Tuesday and Thursday from mid-June to mid-August – and very tasty they are too. Beside the harbour, on **Torget**, there's a bustling daily market, while the streets around **Skagen**, on the jut of land forming the eastern side of the harbour, make up the town's shopping area. It's a bright mix of spidery lanes, pedestrianized streets and white-timbered houses covering the area occupied by medieval Stavanger. At the top stands the spiky **Valberg Tower**, a nineteenth-century firewatch, from where there are sweeping views over the city and its industry. The only relic of medieval Stavanger is the twelfth-century **Domkirke** (mid-May to mid-Sept Mon–Sat 10am–6pm, Sun 1–6pm; rest of year Mon–Sat 10am–11.30am & noon–3pm; free), on the fringes of Torget overlooking **Breiavatnet** lake in the middle of the city; its pointed-hat towers signal a Romanesque church altered irredeemably during later renovations.

Practicalities

International ferries arrive a short walk northwest of the main square, the Torget, docking at the Strandkaien quay. **Express boats** from Bergen alight at the terminal at the bottom of Kirkegata, which runs south to the central city lake. The **airport** is 14km south of the city at Sola: a *flybussen* (40kr) runs into Stavanger, dropping you at the **bus and train station** on the south side of Breiavatnet. The **tourist office** is beside the Torget (June–Aug daily 9am–8pm; rest of year Mon–Fri 9am–4/5pm, Sat 9am–2pm). If you decide to **stay**, there's plenty of choice. The cheapest option is the official IYHF-hostel *Mosvangen*, at Henrik Ibsens gate 21 (☎51.87.29.00; ③; mid-May to mid-Sept), a 3km walk from the centre. Amongst several pensions, the *Skagen Gjestehus*, Nedre Holmegate 2 (☎51.89.55.85; ⑤), has frugal but perfectly adequate rooms in an old wooden building on the east side of the harbour. All of the town's hotels have summer deals, including the *Grand*, Klubbgata 3 (☎51.89.58.00; ⑨), an excellent central choice with smart, modern rooms; and the delightful *Skagen Brygge*, Skagenkaien 30 (☎51.85.00.00; ⑨), a tastefully decorated modern place with enjoyable views over the harbourfront.

For **camping**, the campsite next to the hostel (late May to early Sept) has cabins as well as caravan and tent pitches. For **food**, the *Akropolis*, on the Skagen at Sølvberggata 14, dishes up some good medium-priced Greek dishes, and there's superb – and expensive – seafood at *Sjøhuset Skagen*, Skagenkaien 16.

The route to Bergen

If you're a train fanatic or already committed to a rail pass, you need to go back to Oslo to travel on to Bergen. If not, you can get there more directly by bus and/or ferry. For speed, if not economy, the best bet is the **catamaran** (*Hurtigbåt*), which runs all year. This requires advance seat reservations (☎55.23.87.80) and costs around 470kr one way, though students and rail-pass holders qualify for various discounts. The trip takes four hours. The bus trip takes almost twice as long and is only marginally less expensive.

Kristiansand

Founded by and named after King Christian IV, **KRISTIANSAND** is the closest thing to a seaside resort there is in Norway – a bright, energetic place which thrives on its ferry connections with Denmark and its popular beaches. There are also two reminders of its seventeenth-century origins: the quadrant street plan that Christian IV applied to the centre, and the squat **Christiansholm Fortress**, overlooking the colourful marina at the east harbour, which now hosts arts and crafts displays. Several excursions are on offer, the pick being the two-hour cruise along the fretted, islet-studded coastline with the *M/S Maarten* (mid-June to mid-Aug; 100kr), which departs from the quay beside Vestre Strandgate, at the foot of Tollbodgaten. The boat stops at several islands, which have been designated free camping areas, so you can stay overnight and catch the boat back the next day.

Train, **bus** and **ferry** terminals are all close to each other, by Vestre Strand gate, on the edge of the town grid. The **tourist office**, close by at Vestre Strand gate 32 (June–Aug Mon–Fri 8am–8pm, Sat 10am–8pm, Sun noon–8pm; rest of year Mon–Fri 8.30am–3.30pm), can provide a handy map and information on accessible beaches and islands. The rooms at the all-year **youth hostel**, on the edge of the centre at Skansen 8 (☎38.02.83.10; ③), are satisfactory, but the surroundings are a bit grim – the hostel adjoins a mini industrial estate. The **Roligheden campsite** (June–Aug), with a small stretch of beach, is 3km east of the centre on Framnesveien – once across the bridge at the end of Dronningens gate, turn right along Kuholmsveien and then right again at the end of the road and the site is signposted. More up-market is the *Villa Frobusdal*, also on the edge of the central grid at Frobusdalen 2 (☎38.07.05.15; ⑦). This excellent small hotel occupies an attractive old house and the interior is packed with period furnishings and fittings.

BERGEN AND THE FJORDS

The fjords are the most familiar and alluring image of Norway: huge clefts in the landscape which occur along the west coast right up to the Russian border, though the fjord region is usually defined as lying between Stavanger and Ålesund. Wild, rugged and peaceful, these water-filled wedges are visually stunning; indeed, this part of the country elicits inordinate amounts of purple prose from tourist office handouts, and for once it's rarely overstated. Under the circumstances it seems churlish to complain of the thousands of summer visitors who tramp through the villages, quiet and isolated places the other nine months of the year. Though the rolling mountains are roamed by walkers and the fjords cruised by steady flotillas of white ferries, don't be put off: there's been little development and what there is, is seldom intrusive.

Bergen, Norway's second largest city, is a handy springboard for the western fjords, notably the **Flåm Valley** and its inspiring mountain railway, which trundles down to the **Aurlandsfjord**, a tiny arm of the mighty **Sognefjord**, Norway's longest and deepest. North of the Sognefjord, there is the smaller but less stimulating **Nordfjord**, though there's superb compensation in the **Jostedalsbreen** glacier which nudges the fjord from the east. The tiny S-shaped **Geirangerfjord**, further north again, is magnificent too – narrow, sheer and rugged – while the northernmost **Romsdalsfjord** and its many branches and inlets show signs of splintering into the scattered archipelagos which characterize the northern Norwegian coast, reaching pinnacles of isolation in the **Trollstigen** mountain highway nearby.

By **rail**, you can only reach Bergen in the south and Åndalsnes in the north. For everything in between – the Nordfjord, Jostedalsbreen glacier and Sognefjord – you're confined to **buses** and **ferries**, and although they virtually all connect up with each other, it means that there is no set way to approach the fjord region, and routes are really a matter of personal choice. It's a good idea to pick up full bus and ferry **timetables** from the local tourist offices whenever you can; be aware that shorter bus routes are often part of a longer routeing on which the buses and ferries link up. Unlike the car ferries, whose fares are proportional to distance travelled, the impressively speedy **catamaran** (*Hurtigbåt*) services are considered an extension of the train system, and holders of rail passes often qualify for fifty-percent discounts.

Bergen

Though known as one of the rainiest place in rainy Norway, **BERGEN** has a spectacular setting among seven hills and is one of the country's most enjoyable cities. There's plenty to see, from the fine surviving medieval buildings to a series of good museums – the best located in the atmospheric old warehouse quarter, dating from the city's days as the northernmost Hanseatic port. Bergen is also within easy reach of some of Norway's most spectacular scenic attractions, both around the city and further north.

Arrival and accommodation

Bergen is a busy international port and may well be your first stop in Norway. **International ferries** arrive at Skoltegrunnskaien, the quay just beyond Bergenhus fortress, beside the harbour; domestic **ferries** line up on the opposite side of the harbour at the Strandkaiterminalen. The **train** and **bus stations** face Strømgaten, a five-minute walk from the harbour. The **airport**, 20km south of the city, is connected to the bus station by regular *flybussen* (every 20 min; 45kr). The city is also a terminal port for the **coastal steamer** (*Hurtigrute*), which leaves from Frieleneskaien quay behind the university, about 1.5km south of the train station.

The **tourist office** is a few metres from the head of the harbour at Vågsallmenning 1 (June–Aug daily 8.30am–10pm; May & Sept daily 9am–8pm; Oct–April Mon–Sat 9am–4pm). It has free copies of the *Bergen Guide*, an exhaustive consumer's guide to the city, plus plenty of free brochures. They also sell the **Bergen Card**, a 24hr (130kr) or 48hr (200kr) pass which allows free travel on all the city's buses (otherwise a flat-rate fare of 17kr per journey is levied) and free entrance to, or discounts on, most of the city's sights, including sightseeing trips. Another useful link to be aware of is the **ferry** (Mon–Fri 7am–4.15pm; 10kr) across the harbour, from Carl Sundtsgate to the Bryggen.

Budget accommodation is no great problem in Bergen. Of a trio of **hostels**, there's the spartan *Intermission*, Kalfarveien 8 (☎55.31.32.75; ②; mid-June to mid-Aug), a Christian-run private hostel close to the train station; the basic *YMCA Interrail Centre*, Nedre Korskirkealmenning 4 (☎55.31.72.52; ②), a short walk from the stations, close to Bryggen; and the slightly more expensive *Montana Vandrerhjem*, Johan Blyttsveien 30, Landås (☎55.20.80.70; ④), a large and extremely comfortable hostel with views down over Bergen from high on a hillside 5km from the centre. The *Montana* offers en-suite singles and doubles, family rooms and, in the summer, dorm beds; take bus #31 from the bus station and ask the driver to put you off – the hostel is 200m from the bus stop. Alternatively, the tourist office books **private rooms** with a fixed tariff – currently 295kr for a double room (185kr single). They're very popular, so you'll need to get to the tourist office early in summer.

As for **pensions**, *Skansen Pensjonat*, Vetrlidsallmenningen 29 (☎55.31.90.80; ⑤), has a smashing location right in the city centre among old clapboard houses, just up the hill from the funicular station; while the *Crowded House*, is a lively and extremely agreeable hostel-cum-pension a short walk south of the harbour at Håkonsgaten 27 (☎55.23.13.10; ④). Of the **hotels**, the *Rainbow Bryggen Orion*, Bradbenken 3 (☎55.31.80.80; ⑨), is a deservedly popular mid-range hotel with unassuming but perfectly comfortable modern rooms, just steps from the Bergenhus.

The City

Founded in 1070, Bergen was the largest and most important town in medieval Norway, a regular residence of the country's kings and queens, and later a Hanseatic port and religious centre which supported thirty churches and monasteries. Little of that era survives, although the much-modified medieval fortress, the Bergenhus, still commands the entrance to the harbour. The city centre divides into two distinct parts: the wharf area, **Bryggen**, adjacent to the fortress, once the working centre of the Hanseatic merchants and now the oldest part of Bergen; and the **modern centre**, which stretches inland from the head of the harbour and down along the Nordnes peninsula, taking the best of Bergen's museums and shops.

The obvious place to start a visit is the **Torget**, an appealing harbourside plaza that's home to a colourful fish market. From here, it's a short stroll round to the **Bryggen**, the principal historical and cultural target, containing the distinctive wooden gabled trading posts that front the wharf and now house shops, restaurants and bars. Although none of these structures was actually built by the Germans – the originals were destroyed by fire in 1702 – they carefully follow the original building line. Among them, the **Hanseatic Museum** (daily: June–Aug 9am–5pm; Sept–May 11am–2pm; 35kr) is the best preserved of the early eighteenth-century merchants' dwellings, kitted out in late Hanseatic style with the possessions and documents of contemporary families. More than anything else, though, it's the gloomy warren-like layout of the place that impresses, as well as the all-pervading smell of fish. Good though this is, it's the **Bryggens Museum** (May–Aug daily 10am–5pm; Sept–April Mon–Fri 11am–3pm, Sat noon–3pm, Sun noon–4pm; 20kr), just along the harbourfront next to the *SAS Royal Hotel*, which is Bergen's showpiece, displaying all sorts of intriguing artefacts that were retrieved during the detailed archeological excavation of the Bryggen. A series of imaginative exhibitions attempts a complete reassembly of medieval life – from domestic implements, handicrafts and maritime objects through to trading items – contextualized by a set of twelfth-century foundations that were unearthed during the first dig in the 1950s.

A few steps from the museum, Øvregaten has long marked the boundary of the Bryggen. By walking along its length you'll soon reach the terminal for the **Fløibanen**, the quaint funicular railway (every 30min Mon–Fri 7.30am–11pm, Sat 8am–11pm, Sun 9am–11pm; May–Aug till midnight; 35kr return) that runs up to the top of Mount Fløyen, where there are panoramic views over the city.

In the other direction, back along the waterfront, lies the **Bergenhus**, a large, roughly star-shaped, mostly earthen fortification dated to the nineteenth century, but including the remnants of earlier strongholds and now used mostly as a park. Of the two medieval survivors (combined guided tours on the hour: mid-May to Aug daily 10am–4pm; rest of year Mon–Wed & Fri–Sun noon–3pm, Thurs 3–6pm; 15kr), one is the **Håkonshallen**, a dull reconstruction of the Gothic ceremonial hall built for King Håkon in the mid-thirteenth century and, rather better, the adjacent **Rosenkrantztårnet**, a tower whose thirteenth-century winding spiral staircases, medieval rooms, and low rough corridors were enlarged in 1565 by the local lord, who used the place as a fortified residence.

Back in the centre, by the lake, you'll find the **Grieghallen** (Bergen's Festival Hall) on Lars Hilles gate and the **Rasmus Meyer Collection**, nearby on Rasmus Meyers Allé (daily 11am–5pm, but closed Mon from mid-Sept to mid-May; 35kr). The latter holds an extensive collection of Norwegian painting, including many works by **Edvard Munch**.

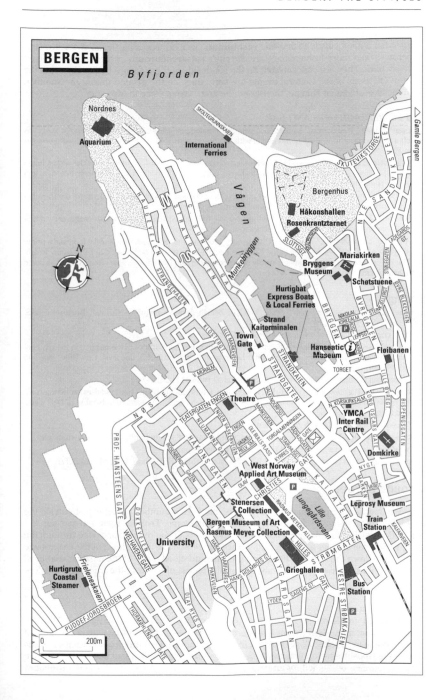

Eating and drinking

Bergen has a good supply of first-rate **restaurants**, with seafood a particular speciality. Less expensive – and more fashionable – are the city's **café/restaurants**, which often double up as lively **bars**. They are concentrated on the south side of the Nordnes peninsula just to the west of Ole Bulls plass. Cultural events are fairly thick on the ground during the summer, with the largest annual shindig, the Bergen Festival, taking place in May.

CAFÉS, RESTAURANTS AND BARS

Bergen Chinese Restaurant, Lodin Lepps gate 2b. Situated just off the Bryggen, this popular spot is as much a café as restaurant, despite the name, with customers sitting on long benches. Tasty main courses from 80kr.

Bryggeloftet & Stuene, Bryggen 11. This restaurant may be slightly stuffy, but it serves the widest range of seafood in town – mouth-watering meals featuring every North Atlantic fish you've ever heard of, and some you probably haven't. Expensive.

Bryggen Tracteursted, Bryggen. Busy bar in one of the old wooden merchants' buildings on the Bryggen – the premises are its main appeal. Occasional live music. Closed Sun.

Café Opera, Engen 24. White wooden building near Ole Bulls plass, bustling with a fashionable crew drinking beer and good coffee. Tasty, filling snacks from as little as 45kr.

Kippers, Kulturhuset USF, Verftsgaten. Ultra groovy café/bar with delicious, inexpensive food and a prime seashore location on the south side of the Nordnes peninsula; its terrace is the place to be in sunny weather. The Kulturhuset occupies an imaginatively recycled old herring factory and, apart from *Kippers*, is home to an arts cinema and a performing arts centre.

Listings

Airlines Braathens, at the airport (☎55.23.55.23); British Airways enquiries through Braathens; SAS, *Radisson SAS Royal Hotel*, Bryggen (☎81.00.33.00).

British consulate Carl Konows gate 34 (☎55.94.47.05).

Car rental Most of the major international car rental companies have offices at the airport. In the city centre, you can find, among others, Budget, Lodin Lepps gate 1 (☎55. 90.26.15); and Avis, Lars Hilles gate 20b (☎55.32.01.30).

Emergencies Casualty (24-hour) at Vestre Strømkai 19 (☎55.32.11.20).

Hiking The DNT-affiliated Bergen Turlag, Tverrgaten 4–6 (Mon–Fri 10am–4pm), advises on hiking trails in the region, sells hiking maps and arranges guided weekend walks. A year's membership of DNT costs around 360kr.

Off licence Vinmonopolet at Nygårdsgaten 6.

Pharmacy Apoteket Nordstjernen, at the bus station (Mon–Sat 8am–midnight, Sun 9.30am–midnight).

Post office Olav Kyrres gate (Mon–Fri 8am–6pm, Sat 9am–3pm).

Travel agents Terra Nova Travel, second floor, Nygaten 3 (Mon–Fri 8.30am–4pm; ☎55.32.23.77).

Around Bergen

There is more to Bergen than the city centre, not least a number of sights just outside the city limits, most notably Edvard Grieg's old lakeside home, **Troldhaugen**. Further out, but still within day-tripping distance, are some of the fjords. If you're not journeying through the fjord region you can get a taste by taking the train to Myrdal, at the head of the remarkable branch line down the valley to **Flåm** and the **Aurlandsfjord** – one of the most popular of all fjord trips. Pick up transport timetables from the tourist office or at the train station before you set out.

Troldhaugen

Troldhaugen (mid-April to Sept daily 9am–6pm; Oct–Nov & Jan to early April Mon–Fri 10am–2pm, Sat noon–4pm except Jan–March, Sun 10am–4pm except Jan; 40kr) was Edvard Grieg's home for the last 22 years of his life. To get there, take a **bus** from Bergen's bus station to the Hopsbroen stop (journey time 15min), turn right, walk about 200m and then take Troldhaugsveien on the left for an easy twenty-minute stroll. A visit begins at the **museum**

where Grieg's life and times are exhaustively chronicled. Close by, the **house** itself is a pleasant and unassuming villa built in 1885, and still much as Grieg left it, with a jumble of photos, manuscripts and period furniture; the obligatory guided tour is quite entertaining. Grieg didn't, in fact, compose much at home, but preferred to walk round to a tiny **hut** he had built just along the shore. The hut has survived, but today it stands beside a modern concert hall, the **Troldsalen**, where there are Grieg recitals from late June through to October: tickets, which include transport, are available from Bergen tourist office. Grieg and his wife – the singer, Nina Hagerup – are buried here, in a curious **tomb** blasted into a rock face overlooking the lake.

The train to Flåm

If you're short on time but want to sample a slice of fjord scenery, make the **train journey** east from Bergen, through Voss, along the main rail line as far as barren Myrdal, from where a branch line plummets 900m down into the **Flåm Valley**. The track took four years to lay and is one of the steepest anywhere in the world. You can make the trip from Bergen on part of the tourist office's "Norway-in-a-Nutshell" ticket, though it's more economical to make your own way via Voss.

FLÅM village, the train's destination, lies alongside meadows and orchards on the **Aurlandsfjord**, a matchstick-thin branch of the Sognefjord. It's a tiny village that can be packed on summer days with tourists who pour off the train, eat lunch and then zoom out by bus and ferry. However, out of season or in the early evening when the day-trippers have all moved on, Flåm can be a wonderfully restful place to spend the night. Hikers can get off the train at Berekvam, the halfway point, and descend from there. If you decide **to stay**, there are a couple of small hotels, the smart *Fretheim* (☎57.63.22.00; ⑨), a couple of hundred metres from the station, and the more homely *Heimly Pensjonat* (☎57.63.23.00; ⑦), a ten-minute walk along the seashore – just follow the signs. Also near to the station is the excellent *Flåm Camping og Vandrerhjem*, a combined campsite and youth hostel offering bike hire and self-catering facilities (☎57.63.21.21; ③; May-Sept). The **tourist office** (May & Sept Mon–Fri 10.30am–6.30pm; June–Aug daily 8.30am–8.30pm; Oct–April Mon–Fri 8am–4pm) at the ferry dock, metres from the train station, has transport timetables and can advise on local hikes.

Incidentally, Myrdal station, where you connect with the branch line to Flåm, is on the main rail line from Bergen to Oslo, an impressive seven-hour cross-country ride, taking in forests, waterfalls, mountains, bleak uplands and plunging valleys. The journey is at its wildest in the vicinity of **FINSE**, which is nothing more than a station and a few isolated buildings, bunkered down against the howling winds that rip across the high plateau in wintertime.

The Sognefjord

Apart from Flåm, you'd do best to explore the **Sognefjord** from the north: it's on that bank that most of its appealing spots lie, and in any case transport connections along the south side are, at best, sketchy. **BALESTRAND** is the prettiest base (express boats from Bergen and Flåm), a tourist destination since the mid-nineteenth century when it was discovered by European travellers in search of cool, clear air and mountain scenery. These days the village is used as a touring centre for the immediate area, though farming remains the villagers' principal livelihood. Buses arrive at the minuscule harbourfront, near which you'll find the **tourist office** (mid-June to mid-Aug Mon–Fri 7.30am–9pm, Sat 7.30am–6.30pm & Sun 8am–5.30pm; rest of year Mon–Fri 9am–3pm). A hundred metres away, in the comfortable *Kringsjå Hotel*, the **youth hostel** (☎57.69.13.03; ③; late June to mid-Aug) provides convenient lodgings, as does the charming *Midtnes Pensjonat* (☎57.69.11.33; ⑤), about 300m from the dock behind the spiky wooden church.

There's not too much to see in Balestrand itself, but several lovely places are within easy striking distance, particularly the delightful village of **FJÆRLAND** which can be reached direct by passenger boat from June through to the middle of September. Formerly one of the most isolated spots on the Sognefjord, Fjærland is now connected to the road system, but it retains its old-fashioned atmosphere and appearance, its handsome clapboard buildings sited at the end of the wildly beautiful Fjærlandsfjord. Alternatively, you can rent a bike at Balestrand tourist office and cycle the 9km round the Sognefjord to **Dragsvik**; from here ferries shuttle across to **VANGSNES**, where Kaiser Wilhelm II, fascinated by Nordic mythology, erected a giant statue of the legendary Viking chief Fridtjof the Bold. Pressing on, it's a further 12km south along the water's edge to the beautiful Hopperstad stave church on the edge of the hamlet of **VIK**. From Balestrand, it's also a straightforward affair to travel by bus to Stryn (see below), on the Nordfjord, the next fjord system to the north.

The Nordfjord and Jostedalsbreen glacier

Comprising several interconnected stretches of water, the **Nordfjord** does not have quite the lustre of its more famous neighbours. But the compensation is the **Jostedalsbreen glacier**, an 800-square-kilometre ice plateau whose lurking presence dominates the whole of the inner Nordfjord region, its 24 arms flowing down into the nearby valleys, giving the local rivers and glacial lakes their distinctive blue-green colouring. In 1991, the glacier was placed within the **Jostedalsbreen Nasjonalpark** in order to co-ordinate its conservation. The main benefit of this for tourists has been to provide guided glacier walks (June to early Sept) on its various arms, ranging from two-hour excursions to all-day, fully equipped hikes. Prices start at around 100kr, with a half-day trip weighing in at about 250kr. A variety of places take bookings for the guided glacier walks – including Stryn tourist office – and these are accepted up until about 6pm the evening beforehand. Equipment is provided, though you'll need good boots, warm clothes, gloves and hat, sunglasses, and food and drink. With your own vehicle, you can get within easy striking distance of the designated starting points for all the glacier walks. By bus it's a little trickier, but it's usually possible with a bit of pre-planning. These starting points are also the places to head for if you just want to get close to the glacier without actually getting on it; two such routes are detailed below.

At the eastern end of the Nordfjord system, **STRYN** is the biggest town in the region and the most obvious target, though its modern centre is far from beguiling. It's also an important transport junction: buses stop beside the fjord, from where it's a five- to ten-minute walk into the town centre, where the **tourist office** (June–Aug daily 9am–6/8pm) takes bookings for guided walks on the Jostedalsbreen. There's inexpensive **accommodation** in Stryn too, most conveniently at the fjordside *Walhalla Gjestgiveri* (☎57.87.10.72; ④), a delightfully unpretentious place among a scattering of old wooden buildings down near the river, about 200m from the tourist office on Perhusvegen. The obvious alternative to Stryn is **LOEN** – just 11km south around the fjord along Hwy 60. The hamlet spreads ribbon-like along the low-lying, grassy foreshore within easy striking distance of an arm of the Jostedalsbreen glacier, and, like Stryn, it's also on the main north–south bus route. It also has the big advantage of being home to one of Norway's more famous **hotels**, the *Alexandra* (☎57.87.50.50; ⑨), a big and flashy modern block tucked in beneath the hills and fringed by carefully manicured gardens, and the slightly less expensive motel-style *Hotel Loenfjord* (☎57.87.57.00; ⑨), across the road, which has comfortable modern rooms. The *Alexandra* has all the **information** you'll need about visiting the nearest glacier nodule, the Kjenndalsbreen, to the southeast of Loen.

The Kjenndalsbreen and the Briksdalsbreen

With your own transport you can follow the single-track road from Loen for 14km up along a beautiful valley with the glacial Loenvaten lake down below. After about 9km, there's a toll post and then the road gets rougher and hairier as it worms its way to the car park and café, from where it's a rocky 3km-walk to the foot of the **Kjenndalsbreen**. The blue and white folds of ice tumble down the rockface here, split by fissures and undermined by a furious foaming river fed by plummeting waterfalls. Guided walks on this part of the glacier traverse the Bødalsbreen nodule, a little to the north of the Kjenndalsbreen. This part of the glacier is popular with visitors, but it's not the target of day-tripping coaches as is the **Briksdalsbreen** nodule further to the south. The fourteen-kilometre-long side road to the

Briksdalsbreen car park begins at **OLDEN**, 7km south of Loen on Hwy 60. From the car park, the footpath leads up the valley for around 3km, passing waterfalls and weaving up the river on the way. Once there it's a simple matter to get close to the ice itself: there's a very flimsy rope barricade and a small warning sign – "be careful!" If you've lacked photo-opportunities thus far, you can rent a pony and trap at the souvenir/café area by the start of the track – costing around 150kr, it's a bit of a swizz when you still have to walk the last bit anyway. Guided glacier walks begin at the café area too.

The Geirangerfjord

The **Geirangerfjord** is one of the region's smallest fjords, but also one of its most breathtaking. A convoluted branch of the Storfjord, it cuts well inland, marked by impressive waterfalls and with a village at either end of its snake-like profile. You can reach the Geirangerfjord by bus or car from the north or south, but you'd do best to approach from the north if you can. From this direction, the journey begins in Åndalsnes from where Highway 63 wriggles over the mountains via the wonderful **Trollstigen Highway**, which climbs through some of the country's highest peaks before sweeping down to the Tafjord. From here, it's a quick ferry ride and dramatic journey along the Ørnevegen, the Eagle's Highway, for a first view of the Geirangerfjord and the village that bears its name glinting in the distance. There is little as stunning anywhere in western Norway, and from June to August it can all be seen on a twice-daily bus following this so-called "Golden Route".

GEIRANGER village enjoys a commanding position at one end of the sixteen-kilometre S-shaped fjord, but it's hopelessly overdeveloped and by far your best bet, especially in high season, is to pass straight through, taking the ferry onto the hamlet of **HELLESYLT**, an hour's ride away through the double bend of the fjord. There's nothing much to the place – it's primarily a stop-off on tourist itineraries – but by nightfall Hellesylt makes for a quiet and peaceful overnight stay. The ferry terminal is a few steps from the turn-of-the-century, wooden *Grand Hotel* (☎70.26.51.00; ⑧), which has a fine fjordside location, a decent restaurant and pleasant rooms in its modern annexe. They also sell fishing licences and rent out boats. The hotel's main competitor is the **youth hostel** (☎70.26.51.28; ④; June–Aug), set on the hillside just above the village – just follow the signs. Alternatively, *Hellesylt Camping* (☎70.26.51.88; summer only) occupies the shadeless field beside the fjord about 300m from the quay. Usefully, Hellesylt is also on the main Bergen/Oslo to Loen, Stryn and Ålesund bus route; buses stop near the jetty.

The Romdalsfjord and around

Travelling north from Oslo by train, the line forks at Dombås – the Dovre line continuing northwards over the fells to Oppdal, and ultimately to Trondheim, the Rauma line beginning a thrilling two-hour roller-coaster rattle west down through the mountains to the **Romdalsfjord**. Apart from the Sognefjord, reached from Bergen, the Romsdalsfjord is the only other Norwegian fjord accessible by train, which explains the number of backpackers wandering its principal town of **ÅNDALSNES**, many people's first – sometimes only – contact with fjord country. Despite a wonderful setting between lofty peaks and looking-glass water, the town is unexciting, but it does make a convenient base for further explorations. The pick of the local routes is the journey south to the Geirangerfjord, over the **Trollstigen Highway** (see above). From June to August, there are two buses a day from Åndalsnes to Geiranger, and three to five buses daily to another tempting destination, Ålesund (see below). Åndalsnes has an outstanding **youth hostel** (☎71.22.13.82; ④; mid-May to mid-Sept), which occupies a group of charming wooden buildings in a rural setting 2km along the E136 towards Ålesund. The hostel also rents out **bikes** and boats. Another very good option is the riverside **campsite**, with cabins and rowboats, a 25-minute walk from the train station – take the first left after the river on the road out to the hostel. The **tourist office** at the train station (late June to late Aug Mon–Sat 10am–7pm, Sun 1–7pm; rest of year Mon–Fri 10am–3pm) has a free and comprehensive guide to local hikes as well as bus, boat and train timetables.

At the end of E136 some 120km west of Åndalsnes, the fishing and ferry port of **ÅLESUND** is immediately and distinctively different from the functional stone and brick of other modern Norwegian town centres. It boasts a conglomeration of proud grey-and-white facades, lavishly decorated and topped with a forest of turrets and pinnacles. In 1904, a disastrous fire left 10,000 people homeless and the town centre destroyed. A hectic reconstruction programme saw almost the entire area rebuilt by 1907 in a style that borrowed heavily from the German Jugendstil movement. Kaiser Wilhelm II, who used to holiday hereabouts, gave assistance, and the architects ended up creating a strange but fetching hybrid of up-to-date foreign influences and folksy local elements, with dragons, faces and fairy-tale turrets. Otherwise, the rest of Ålesund's lively centre, which drapes around its oldest harbour, the **Brosundet**, makes for a pleasant stroll and you can watch the ferries going back and forth to the islands just offshore.

Ålesund **bus station** is situated on the waterfront a few metres south of the Brosundet and across from the **tourist office** in the Rådhus (June–Aug Mon–Fri 8.30am–7pm, Sat 9am–5pm, Sun 11am–5pm; rest of year Mon–Fri 9am–4pm). The pick of the town's **hotels** are the *Comfort Home Hotel Bryggen*, an elegantly converted waterside warehouse at Apotekergata 1 (☎70.12.64.00; ⑨), and the very similar *Brosundet Gjestehus* (☎70.12.10.00; ⑧) next door. There's also a small and central **youth hostel** at Parkgata 14, at the top of Rådstuggata (☎70.11.58.30; ④; May–Sept). For **eating**, the *Sjøbua Fiskerestaurant*, Brunholmgata 1, is an expensive but first-rate seafood restaurant, which comes complete with its own lobster tank. A cheaper option is *Nilles Pizza* at Kirkegata 1. If it's sunny, everyone flocks to the terrace of the *Metz*, a café-restaurant overlooking the Brosundet.

NORTHERN NORWAY

The long, thin counties of **Trøndelag** and **Nordland** mark the transition from rural southern to blustery northern Norway. The main town of Trøndelag, appealing **Trondheim**, is easily accessible from Oslo by train, but north of here feels very far removed from the capital and travelling becomes more of a slog as the distances between places grow ever greater. In **Nordland** things get increasingly wild, though save the scenery there's little of delaying interest and only one sizeable town, industrial **Mo-i-Rana**. Just north of here lies the **Arctic Circle**, beyond which the land becomes ever more spectacular, not least on the offshore chain of the **Lofoten Islands**, whose idyllic fishing villages (and cheap accommodation) richly merit a stop. Back on the mainland, **Narvik** was scene of some of the fiercest fighting by the Allies and Norwegian resistance in World War II and is now a modern port handling vast quantities of iron ore amid some startling rocky surroundings. Further north still, the provinces of **Troms** and **Finnmark** are enticing too, but the travelling can be harder still, the specific attractions well distanced and – when you reach them – subtle in their appeal. It was from **Tromsø**, northern Norway's largest urban centre and a lively university town, that the king and his government proclaimed a "Free Norway" in 1940 before fleeing into exile in Britain. The appeal of Finnmark is less obvious: it was laid waste during World War II, and it's now possible to drive for hours without coming across a building more than fifty years old. Most travellers head straight for **Nordkapp**, from where the Midnight Sun is visible between mid-May and the end of July.

The **train** network reaches as far north as Fauske, **buses** making the link to Narvik, from where a separate rail line runs the few kilometres to the border and then south through Sweden. Further north, approaches are more limited, and access is either by the coastal steamer (*Hurtigrute*) or bus. The *Hurtigrute* takes the best part of two days to circumnavigate the huge fjords between Harstad and Kirkenes; **bus** transport throughout the summer (and some of the winter) is efficient and regular, using the windswept E6 Arctic Highway as far as Kirkenes, branching off to Nordkapp on the way.

Trondheim

TRONDHEIM, an atmospheric city with much of its eighteenth-century centre still intact, has been an important Norwegian power base for centuries, its age-old importance guaranteed by the excellence of its harbour and its position at the head of a wide and fertile valley. The early Norse parliament, or Ting, met here, and the city was a major pilgrimage centre. The city centre sits on a small triangle of land, a pocket-sized area where the main sights – bar the marvellous cathedral – have an amiable low-key quality about them. Trondheim also possesses a clutch of good restaurants and a string of busy bars.

The City

The colossal **Nidaros Domkirke**, Scandinavia's largest medieval building, gloriously restored following the ravages of the Reformation and several fires, remains the focal point of the city centre (May to mid-Sept Mon–Fri 9am–3/6pm, Sat 9am–2pm, Sun 1–4pm; mid-Sept to early April Mon–Fri noon–2.30pm, Sat 11.30am–2pm, Sun 1–3pm; 25kr, tower 5kr). Taking Trondheim's former name (Nidaros means "mouth of the River Nid"), the cathedral is dedicated to King Olav, Norway's first Christian ruler, who was killed at the nearby battle of Stiklestad in 1030. After the battle, Olav's body was spirited away and buried here, his resting place marked by the erection of a chapel, which was altered and enlarged over the years to accommodate the growing bands of pilgrims, achieving cathedral status in 1152. Thereafter, it became the traditional burial place of Norwegian royalty and, since 1814, it has also been the place where Norwegian monarchs are crowned. The stonework of the early Gothic choir is especially fine, with the flying buttresses and pointed arches decorated with all manner of tiny heads and gargoyles. Inside, the gloomy half-light hides much of the lofty decorative work, but it is possible to examine the striking choir screen and font, both the work of the Norwegian sculptor Gustav Vigeland (1869–1943). If possible, visit in the early morning to avoid the tour-bus crowds.

Behind the Domkirke lies the heavily restored archbishop's palace, the **Erkebispegården**, a courtyard complex flanked by stone and brick wings of medieval provenance. The archbishops were kicked out during the Reformation and the palace was subsequently used as the city armoury. Many of the old weapons are now displayed in the west wing, which has been turned into the **Army and Resistance Museum** (June–Aug Mon–Fri 9am–3pm, Sat & Sun 11am–4pm; rest of year Sat & Sun 11am–4pm only; free). Its most interesting section, on the top floor, recalls the German occupation during World War II, dealing honestly with the sensitive issue of collaboration. The east wing houses a lavish **museum** (Mon–Fri 10/11am–3/5pm, Sun noon–4/5pm) displaying a wide selection of medieval sculptures stashed away when the cathedral was partly rebuilt at the end of the nineteenth century. Admission is free on production of a cathedral ticket. A short walk west of the Domkirke, the **Museum of Applied Art**, Munkegata 5 (Tues–Sat 10am–3/4/5pm, Sun noon–4/5pm; plus June–Aug Mon 10am–3/5pm; 30kr), holds a splendid assortment of furniture, tapestries, glassware and silver; it also features a first-rate programme of temporary exhibitions.

Near at hand is **Torvet**, the main city square, a spacious open area anchored by a statue of St Olav, perched on a stone pillar like some medieval Nelson. The broad and pleasant avenues of Trondheim's centre radiate out from here; they date from the late seventeenth century, when they doubled as fire breaks. They were originally flanked by long rows of wooden buildings, now mostly replaced by uninspiring modern structures. One conspicuous survivor is the **Stiftsgården** (June–Aug Mon–Sat 10am–3/5pm, Sun noon–5pm; guided tours every hour on the hour; 35kr), the yellow creation just north of Torvet on Munkegata. Built in 1774–78 as the home of a provincial governor, it's now an official royal residence. A long series of period rooms with fanciful Italianate wall paintings reflect the genteel tastes of the early occupants, and the anecdotal guided tour raises a smile or two.

Practicalities

Trondheim is the first major northbound stop of the Bergen–Kirkenes **coastal steamer** (*Hurtigrute*), which docks behind Sentralstasjon, the **bus and train terminal**. The latter is situated just over the bridge from the town centre, which occupies a small island at the mouth of the River Nid. The **tourist office** is bang in the middle of the town centre, on the main square, the Torvet (mid-May to Aug Mon–Fri 8.30am–6/8pm, Sat & Sun 10am–4/8pm; Sept to mid-May Mon–Fri 9am–4pm). It issues a very useful free city guide, changes money and books **private rooms** for a fixed rate of 350kr for a double plus a 30kr fee. There's a large IYHF **youth hostel** at Weidemannsvei 41 (☎73.87.44.50; ③), twenty minutes' hike east from the centre out over the Bakke bru bridge; bus #63 runs out in that direction. Another inexpensive choice is the *InterRail Centre*, Elgesetergate 1 (☎73.89.95.38; ②; June to late Aug), operated by the university's student society and providing basic bed and breakfast in an unusual round red house with a couple of hundred rooms; it's a twenty-minute walk from Torvet or take bus #41, #42, #48, #49, or #52. More convenient alternatives include *Pensjonat Jarlen*, Kongensgate 40 (☎73.51.32.18; ④), with frugal rooms at bargain prices; the *Rainbow Gildevangen*, Søndregate 22b (☎73.51.01.00; ⑤), a chain **hotel** with comfortable, modern rooms in an imposing old stone building on the north side of Torvet; and the *Rainbow Trondheim*, Kongensgate 15 (☎73.50.50.50; ⑤), a big and popular hotel offering well-maintained modern double rooms at reasonable rates. The city centre is best seen on foot, but if you're staying on the edge of town, take advantage of the brightly coloured **municipal bicycles** that are available from bike racks all over the centre; they are free, but you need 20kr to unlock them – as in a supermarket trolley.

For **eating**, the city's mobile fast-food stalls gather around Sentralstasjon and along Kongensgate, on either side of Torvet. As for cafés and restaurants, the groovy *Ni Muser*, Bispegata 9, footsteps from the cathedral, is a relaxed and fashionable little café serving tasty snacks and meals based on a variety of European cuisines (Tues–Sun 11am–midnight); the *Peking House Restaurant*, Kjøpmannsgata 63, is a competent and reasonably priced Chinese restaurant, specializing in Szechuan dishes; and the *Posepilten*, Prinsens gate 32, is a laid-back café-bar offering tasty, inexpensive snacks and light meals. The town has an active **nightlife**, especially at weekends, when the centre of the action is along Dronningensgate, and adjacent Nordre gate – the *Carl Johan* pub is currently the place to head for. More groovy bars and cafés are clustered around the east end of the old town bridge, the Bybrua, on Bakklandet.

The Arctic Circle, Fauske and Bodø

North of Trondheim, it's a long haul up the coast to the next major places of interest: Bodø, which is the main ferry port for the Lofoten Islands, and the gritty town of Narvik, respectively 740km and 908km away. You can cover most of the ground by train, a rattling good journey with the scenery becoming wilder and bleaker the further north you go; it takes nine hours to reach Fauske, where the railway reaches its northern limit and turns west for the last 65km dash across to Bodø. On the way you cross the **Arctic Circle**, which, considering the amount of effort it takes to get there, is something of an anticlimax. The landscape, uninhabited for the most part, is undeniably bare and bleak, but the gleaming **Arctic Circle Centre** (daily: June–Aug 9am–10pm; May & Sept 10am–6pm) disfigures the scene – a giant lampshade of a building plonked by the E6 highway and stuffed with every sort of tourist bauble imaginable. The train toots its whistle as it passes by, and drivers can, of course, shoot past too – though the temptation to brave the crowds is strong, and even if you resist the Arctic exhibition, you'll probably get snared by either the "Polarsirkelen" certificate, or the specially stamped postcards. Drivers will struggle to complete the journey from Trondheim to Bodø in one day and should consider resting up at the pint-sized, industrial town of **Mo-i-Rana**, just south of the Arctic Circle. The town has a **youth hostel** (☎75.15.09.63; ②; mid-May to Aug) and an excellent **hotel**, the *Meyergården* (☎75.13.40.00; ⑤), an extremely comfortable establishment 200m from the train station.

FAUSKE is, along with Bodø, a departure point of the Nord-Norge ekspressen bus service that complements the trains by carrying passengers as far as Kirkenes, close to the Russian border. You can get tickets from the bus station in Fauske or buy them on the buses, which leave twice daily from outside the train station. There's a fifty-percent discount for InterRail-pass holders on the first step of the route, to Narvik, a gorgeous seven-hour run past fjords and snowy peaks. However, most northbound travellers spend the night in Fauske rather than making a quick change onto the connecting bus, despite the fact that Bodø (see below) is a much more interesting place. From Fauske train station, it's a five- to ten-minute walk down the hill and left at the T-junction to the bus station and adjoining **tourist office** (Mon–Fri 9am–5pm), which helpfully posts the region's ferry timetables in its windows. The E6, running parallel to the fjord, forms the main thoroughfare, Storgata, accommodating the handful of shops that pass for a town centre. It's here, at no. 82, that you'll find the modern *Fauske Hotel* (☎75.64.38.33; ⑨), whose big breakfasts (from 7am; 60kr) are handy for travellers staying at the spartan **youth hostel** (☎75.64.67.06; ②), about 500m west of the hotel – signposted off Storgata. A third option is the *Lundhøgda campsite* (☎75.64.39.66; June–Sept), which overlooks the mountains and the fjord about 3km west of the town centre: head out of town along the E80 towards Bodø and watch for the sign which will take you down a country lane flanked by old timber buildings. The campsite takes caravans, has pitches for tents and offers huts for rental – advance bookings are strongly advised.

An hour west of Fauske, **BODØ** is where the trains terminate. It's also a stop on the coastal steamer route and the main point of departure for the Lofoten Islands. Heavily bombed in World War II, the town is short of sights, but it manages a bright and cheerful air and is home to the **Norwegian Aviation Museum** (mid-June to mid-Aug Mon–Fri 10am–8pm, Sat 10am–5pm, Sun 10am–8pm; rest of year Tues–Fri 10am–4pm, Sat & Sun 11am–5pm; 70kr), whose exhibits include antique planes, a control tower and a flight simulator. The coastal steamer (*Hurtigrute*) and the southern Lofotens ferry (to Moskenes, Værøy and Røst) leave from the docks respectively 700m and 500m northeast of the train station, which is itself just 300m along Sjøgata from the **tourist office**, at Sjøgata 21 (June to late Aug Mon–Fri 9am–8.30pm, Sat 10am–4pm & 6–8pm, Sun noon–4pm & 6–8pm; rest of year Mon–Fri 9am–4pm). The **bus station** is a further 300m along Sjøgata, beside the ponderous *SAS Royal Hotel*. If you're heading further north, note that the same half-price bus deal for rail-pass holders travelling from Fauske to Narvik operates from Bodø, too. Close by the bus station, at the west end of Sjøgata, another dock handles the catamaran (*Hurtigbåt*) services to the Lofotens, notably to Svolvær and Stokmarknes.

Bodø offers plenty of choice in **accommodation**. The tourist office has a small supply of **private rooms** both in the town and its environs, costing 150kr per person, plus a 15kr booking fee (25kr outside town). Alternatively, the no-frills **youth hostel** is next door to the bus station at Sjøgata 55 (☎75.52.11.22; ②). Among several central **hotels**, the pick is the *Comfort Home Hotel Grand*, at Storgata 3 (☎75.54.61.00; ⑧), whose handsome public rooms boast elegant Art Deco flourishes. For **eating**, easily the best bet is the *Pizzakjeller'n*, in the basement of the *SAS Royal Hotel*, where an enormous pizza for two will set you back around 150kr.

The Lofoten Islands

Stretched out in a skeletal curve across the Norwegian Sea, the **Lofoten Islands** are perfect for a simple, uncluttered few days. For somewhere so far north the weather is exceptionally mild, and there's plentiful **accommodation** in *rorbuer* (fishermen's shacks) – usually accommodating two to six people and rented out to tourists during the summer for 400–600kr per night – in addition to five youth hostels and plentiful campsites. The *Hurtigrute* **coastal steamer** calls at two ports, Stamsund and Svolvær, while the southern Lofoten ferry leaves Bodø for Moskenes, Værøy and Røst. There are also passenger **express boats**, which work out slightly cheaper than the coastal steamer, linking both Bodø and Narvik with Svolvær. By **bus** the main long-distance services from the mainland to the Lofotens are from Bodø to Svolvær via Fauske and Narvik.

The islands

The main town on **Austvågøy**, the largest and northernmost island of the group, is **SVOLVÆR**, a rather disappointing place, although it is a hub of island bus routes and you may well arrive here. Pick up island-wide information and bus schedules at the **tourist office**, located beside the main town square (late June to mid-Aug Mon–Fri 9am–10pm, Sat 10am–10pm, Sun 11am–10pm; reduced hours rest of year). One of the most pleasant **places to stay** in Svolvær is the snug, wooden *Svolvær sjøhuscamping* (☎76.07.03.36; ③), by the seashore on Parkgata, five minutes' walk from the square, where the price includes use of a well-equipped kitchen. Alternatively, the central *Hotel Havly* (☎76.07.03.44; ⑨) occupies a plain tower block and has perfectly adequate, en-suite rooms.

Reachable by bus from Svolvær (1–4 daily), **HENNINGSVÆR**, 23km to the southwest, is a much more beguiling village, its cramped and twisting lanes of brightly painted wooden houses lining a postcard-pretty harbour. It's well worth an overnight stay, with the most economical lodgings being the centrally located *Den Siste Viking* (☎76.07.49.11; ②).

However, it's the next large island to the southwest, **Vestvågøy**, which captivates many travellers to the Lofotens. This is due in no small part to the laid-back charm of **STAMSUND**, whose older buildings are strung along its rocky, fretted seashore. This is the first port at which the coastal steamer (*Hurtigrute*) docks on its way north from Bodø, and is much the best place to stay on the island. Getting there by bus from Austvågøy is reasonably easy, too, with several buses making the trip daily, though you do have to change at Leknes, 16km away to the west. In Stamsund, the first place to head for is the exceptionally friendly **youth hostel** (☎76.08.93.34; ②), made up of several *rorbuer* perched over a pint-sized bay, about 1km down the road from the port and 200m from the Leknes bus stop. Fishing around here is first-class: the hostel rents out rowing boats and lines or you can go on an organized trip for just 150kr; afterwards, you can cook your catch on the hostel's wood-burning stoves. For touring the rest of Vestvågøy, the hostel rents out bikes (85kr a day).

By any standard the next two Lofoten islands, **Flakstadøya** and **Moskenesøya**, are extra-ordinarily beautiful. As the Lofotens taper towards their southerly conclusion, rearing peaks crimp a sea-shredded coastline studded with a string of fishing villages. Remarkably, the E10 travels along almost all of this dramatic shoreline, by way of tunnels and bridges, to **MOSKENES**, the ferry port midway between Bodø and the southernmost bird islands of Værøy and Røst. Six kilometres further on the E10 ends at the tersely named Å, one of the Lofoten's most delightful villages, its huddle of old buildings rambling over a foreshore that's wedged in tight between the grey-green mountains and the surging sea. If you want to stay in Å, the same family owns the assortment of smart *rorbuer* (③) that surround the dock, the adjacent **youth hostel** (①), the bar and the only restaurant, where the seafood is very good; accommodation reservations can be made on ☎76.09.11.21.

Local bus #101 runs along the length of the E10 from Leknes to Å twice daily from late June to mid-August, less frequently the rest of the year. Buses do not, however, usually coincide with sailings to and from Moskenes. Consequently, if you're heading from the Moskenes ferry port to Å, you'll either have to walk – it's an easy 6km – or take a taxi.

Narvik

NARVIK was established less than a century ago as an ice-free port to handle the iron ore brought by train from northern Sweden, and the **iron ore docks** are immediately conspicuous upon arrival here, the rust-coloured machinery overwhelming the whole waterfront. There are guided tours around the **dock area** (summer 1 daily; 30kr), interesting if only for the opportunity to spend an hour inside such a hellish mess. Otherwise the town centre lacks appeal, with modern stone and concrete replacing the wooden buildings flattened during the last war. Nonetheless, try and devote an hour or so to the **Krigsminne Museum** (June–Aug Mon–Sat 10am–10pm, Sun 11am–5pm; March to early June & Sept daily 10am–4pm; 30kr), in the main square close to the docks. Run by the Red Cross, it documents the wartime German saturation bombing and bitter sea and air battles for control of the ore supplies, in which hundreds of foreign servicemen died alongside the local population.

The **train station** is at the north end of town and long-distance **buses** pull up outside. From here, it's a five- to ten-minute walk south along the main street to the main square, where the **tourist office** (mid-June to mid-Aug Mon–Fri 9am–7pm, Sat 10am-7pm, Sun noon–7pm; rest of year Mon–Fri 9am–4pm), issues free maps and has a wide range of leaflets on the region's attractions. The best place to stay is the *Briedablikk Gjestehus*, Tore Hundsgate 41 (☎76.94.14.18; ⑤), a well-tended guest house, a short, stiff walk from the tourist office at the top of Kinobakken. The nearest **campsite**, *Narvik camping*, is along the E6 about 1km north of town and has cabins for rent.

On from Narvik

There's a choice of several routes on from Narvik. The **rail link**, cut through the mountains a century ago, runs east and then south into Sweden, reaching Kiruna in three hours. It's a beautiful journey, but **bus** travellers, heading north to Alta, do no worse with a succession of switchback roads, lakeside forests, high peaks and lowlands stretching as far as the eye can see. In summer cut grass dries everywhere, stretched over wooden poles forming long lines on the hillsides like so much washing. Buses also run off the E6 to Tromsø. Note that on buses south from Narvik, to either Fauske or Bodø, InterRail-pass holders get a fifty-percent discount.

Tromsø

TROMSØ was once known, rather preposterously, as the "Paris of the North", and though even the tourist office doesn't make any pretence to such grandiose titles now, the city still likes to think of itself as the capital of northern Norway. Certainly, as a base for this part of the country, it's hard to beat. It's a pleasant, small city, with two cathedrals, a clutch of reasonably interesting museums and an above-average (and affordable) nightlife, patronized by a high-profile student population. In the centre of town, the **Domkirke** (Tues–Sun noon–4pm) reflects the town's nineteenth-century prosperity, the result of its barter trade with Russia. Completed in 1861, it's one of Norway's largest wooden churches, with some imposingly wealthy fixtures in a solemn beige interior. From here, it's a short walk north along the harbourfront to the most diverting of the city's museums, the **Polar Museum** (daily mid-June to Aug 11am–8pm, rest of year 11am–3/6pm; 30kr), whose varied displays include skeletons retrieved from the permafrost of Svalbard and a detailed section on the daring deeds of the polar explorer Roald Amundsen. On the other side of the water, over the spindly Tromsø Bridge, the white and ultramodern **Arctic Cathedral** (May & mid-Aug to mid-Sept daily 4–6pm; June to mid-Aug Mon–Sat 10am–8pm & Sun 1–8pm; 15kr) is spectacularly original, made up of eleven immense triangular concrete sections representing the eleven Apostles left after the betrayal.

Practicalities

The **coastal steamer** (*Hurtigrute*) docks in the centre of town at the foot of Kirkegata; **buses** arrive and leave from the adjacent car park. The **tourist office** is on Storgata, near the Domkirke (June to mid-Aug Mon–Fri 8.30am–6pm, Sat & Sun 10am–5pm; rest of year Mon–Fri 8.30am–4pm), and sells the 24-hour tourist ticket (50kr) valid for unlimited city bus travel. The large and basic **youth hostel**, Gitta Jønsons vei 4 (late June to mid-Aug; ✆77.68.53.19; ③), is located 2km from the quay, a steep twenty-minute walk (bus #24 from outside the Sparebanken on Fr. Langes Gata). The tourist office will book **private rooms** (300kr double; 25kr fee) for you, or try one of two reasonable **pensjonater**: *Skipperhuset Pensjonat*, Storgata 112 (✆77.68.16.60; ④), or *Kongsbakken*, on the hillside directly behind the city centre at Skolegata 24 (✆77 68 22 08; ④). The nearest **campsite**, *Tromsdalen Camping*, lies over the bridge on the mainland, has cabins and is open all year; take bus #36 from outside the Domus store on Stortorget. For **eating**, budget meals are available in the *Sagatun* self-service cafeteria in Richard Withs plass, while the *Vertshuset Skarven*, Strandtorget 1, has a good café-bar downstairs and an excellent, if pricey restaurant above – try the reindeer. The terrace at *Paletten*, Storgata 51, is one of the more appealing and inexpensive places to eat and drink, though drinkers will find that the *Blå Rock Café*, Strandgata 14, puts up some strong competition with its CD jukebox and weekend discos.

Honningsvåg and Nordkapp

Connected to the mainland by an ambitious combination of tunnels and bridges, bleak and treeless Magerøya is Norway's most northerly island. The only settlement of any size here is **HONNINGSVÅG**, a crusty fishing village that strings along the water's edge for a kilometre or two. Apart from the fish, Honningsvåg makes a steady income from accommodating the hundreds of tourists who flood north every summer intent on visiting the country's northernmost point, Nordkapp, just 34km away. Amongst several **hotels**, the least expensive is the *Arctic Hotell Nordkapp*, a workaday chain hotel on the main drag at Storgata 12 (☎78.47.29.66; ⑨). Much cheaper is the **campsite/cabin** complex 8km away on the road to Nordkapp (☎78.47.33.77; ②; mid-May to Sept); reservations are advised. Long-distance buses arrive in the centre of Honningsvåg and there's a limited bus service on to Nordkapp (April to late Oct 1–2 daily; 50min). When the buses aren't running, the only option is a **taxi** (600kr) – assuming, that is, the road is open.

Travellers with the *Hurtigrute* **coastal steamer**, which puts in at Honningsvåg, should note that there's a special coach which gets you to Nordkapp and back within the two-and-a-half-hour stop. If you need to **eat** in Honningsvåg, there are a couple of takeaway kiosks along Storgata and a very good seafood restaurant at the *Rica Bryggen Hotel*.

NORDKAPP itself might be expected to be a bit of a disappointment. It is, after all, only a cliff with an arguable claim to being the northernmost point of Europe. But there is something about this bleak, wind-battered promontory that excites the senses. Originally a Sami sacrificial site, it was named by the English explorer Richard Chancellor in 1553, but it was not until the late nineteenth century that a visit by King Oscar II opened the tourist floodgates. These days the extremely flashy **North Cape Hall** (daily: April to mid-May & Sept 2–5pm; mid-May to June noon–1am; July & Aug 10am–midnight/2am; 175kr) contains a post office (where you can get your letters specially stamped), souvenir shop, wide-screen video show and cafeteria, though it's really only busy when the tour buses arrive – and even then, a few minutes' walk can take you somewhere completely isolated.

travel details

Trains

Åndalsnes to: Dombås (2 daily; 2hr); Oslo (2 daily; 6–8hr).

Dombås to: Trondheim (3 daily; 2hr 30min).

Kristiansand to: Kongsberg (5 daily; 3hr 30min); Oslo (5 daily; 5hr).

Myrdal to: Flåm (June–Sept 11–12 daily; 50min).

Oslo to: Åndalsnes (4 daily; 5hr 50min); Bergen (4–5 daily; 6hr 30min); Kristiansand (3 daily; 5hr); Røros (2 daily; 6hr); Stavanger (3 daily; 8hr); Trondheim (4 daily; 6hr 40min); Voss (4–5 daily; 5hr 15min).

Stavanger to: Kristiansand (3–4 daily; 3hr); Oslo (3 daily; 9hr).

Trondheim to: Bodø (2 daily; 11hr); Dombås (3 daily; 2hr 30min); Fauske (2 daily; 10hr 20min); Mo-i-Rana (2 daily; 7hr 15min); Oslo (3 daily; 6hr 45min); Røros (1–2 daily; 3hr); Stockholm (3 daily; 12hr).

Buses

Ålesund to: Bergen (1 daily except Sat; 11hr); Hellesylt (1–2 daily except Sat; 2hr 40min); Molde (4–6 daily; 2hr 15min); Stryn (1–2 daily except Sat; 4hr); Trondheim (1–2 daily; 8hr 10min).

Alta to: Hammerfest (2–4 daily; 3hr); Honningsvåg (1–2 daily; 5hr); Kautokeino (1 daily; 3hr); Tromsø (1 daily; 7hr).

Åndalsnes to: Ålesund (3–4 daily; 2hr 20min); Geiranger (June–Aug 2 daily; 3–4hr); Molde (3–7 daily; 1hr 30min).

Balestrand to: Sogndal (4–5 daily; 1hr 10min); Stryn (1 daily; 4hr).

Bergen to: Ålesund (1–2 daily; 10hr); Trondheim (1 daily; 15hr); Voss via Norheimsund (3–4 daily; 4hr); Voss (1 daily; 1hr 45min).

Fauske to: Bodø (2 daily; 1hr 10min); Narvik (2 daily; 5hr).

Hammerfest to: Alta (1–2 daily; 3hr); Honningsvåg (1–2 daily; 4hr 20min); Oslo (3 weekly; 29hr).

Kautokeino to: Alta (3 weekly; 1hr 40min); Karasjok (Mon, Wed, Fri & Sun 1 daily; 2hr 15min).

Kongsberg to: Odda (1 daily; 6hr 30min); Oslo (1 daily; 11hr 45min).

Narvik to: Alta (1 daily; 11hr); Tromsø (1–3 daily; 5–6hr).

Oslo to: Bergen (1 daily; 11hr 30min).

Stavanger to: Kristiansand (1–2 daily; 5hr).

Stryn to: Balestrand (1 daily; 4hr); Bergen (2–3 daily; 7hr); Oslo (1 daily; 8hr 30min).

Tromsø to: Alta (1 daily; 7hr); Narvik (1–3 daily; 5hr 30min); Nordkjosbotn (3–5 daily; 1hr 30min).

Trondheim to: Ålesund (1–2 daily; 8hr); Bergen (1 daily; 15hr); Molde (1–2 daily; 6hr); Røros (1–3 daily; 3hr 10min).

Voss to: Odda (1 daily; 2hr 30min); Sogndal (2–4 daily; 3hr–4hr 30min).

Ferries

Arendal to: Oslo (July to mid-Aug 1 daily; 6hr 30min).

Bergen to: Balestrand (2 daily; 4hr); Flåm (1–2 daily; 5hr 30min); Måløy (1–3 daily; 4hr); Stavanger (2–3 daily; 4hr).

Bodø to: Svolvær (1 daily except Sat; 5hr).

Narvik to: Svolvær (1 daily except Sat; 4hr).

Stavanger to: Bergen; (2–3 daily; 4hr 30min).

CHAPTER 21

POLAND

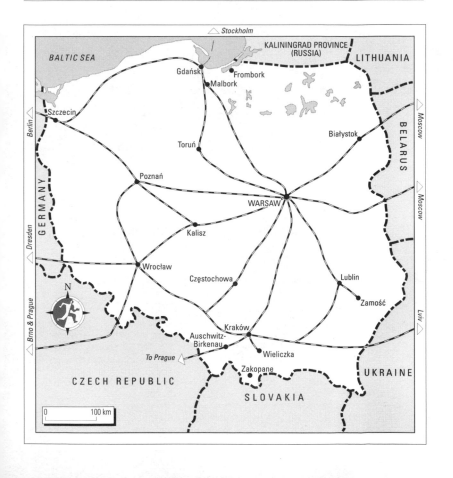

Introduction

Images of **Poland** flooded the world media throughout the 1980s. Strikes and riots at the Lenin Shipyards of Gdańsk were the harbingers of the disintegration of communism in eastern Europe. The decade's end saw the establishment of a government led by the Solidarity trade union, followed by the victory of union leader Lech Wałęsa in Poland's first presidential election since the 1920s – though to many people's surprise, he lost the presidency to "post-communist" Aleksander Kwasniewski in 1995, who remains President with a newly elected right-wing government.

The pattern was familiar enough through the eastern bloc, but the rebirth of democratic Poland was a uniquely Catholic revolution. The **Church** has always been the principal defender of the nation's identity, and its physical presence is inescapable in Baroque buildings, roadside shrines and images of the national icon, the Black Madonna. Encounters with the **people** are at the core of any experience of the country. On trains and buses, in the streets or the village bar, you'll never be stuck for opportunities for contact: Polish hospitality is legendary. Tourism, like every other aspect of the Polish infrastructure, is currently in a state of flux, but it's never been easier to explore the country. Foreigners are no longer subject to currency restrictions and can travel as they please, if not always as smoothly as desired.

Unless you're driving to Poland, you're likely to begin your travels with one of the three major cities. Much of **Warsaw,** the capital, conforms to the stereotype of Eastern European greyness, but its historic centre, extensive parks and vibrant commercial life are diverting enough. **Kraków,** the ancient royal capital, is the real crowd puller, rivalling the Central European elegance of Prague and Vienna. The Hanseatic city of **Gdańsk** offers a dynamic brew of politics and commerce, while nearby **Sopot** features golden beaches. German influences abound in the north and southwest of the country, in Gdańsk itself, in the austere castles and fortified settlements along the River Wisła (Vistula) and in the divided province of Silesia. Yet, to the north of Silesia, quintessentially Polish **Poznań** is revered as the cradle of the nation.

Despite its much-publicized pollution problems, Poland has many regions of unspoilt natural beauty, none more popular than the alpine **Tatras,** the most exhilarating walking terrain in the country.

Information and maps

Poland has no national tourist board, and the provision of information through the independent tourist offices is rather diffuse. The largest of these outfits is **Orbis** (known in some countries as Polorbis), whose offices vary in effectiveness and helpfulness. There are also a number of **independent and municipal tourist agencies,** which are far more acclimatized to the needs of English-speaking travellers. **PTTK,** with offices throughout Poland, has a more direct responsibility for internal tourism. **Almatur** is a student-and-youth travel bureau and tends to have the best English speakers.

The easiest road **map** to follow is Bartholomew's Europmap: Poland (1:800,000), which is especially clear on rail lines. The Orbis Poland: Roadmap (1:750,000) is useful, too, and widely available in Poland. For detailed city maps, try to get hold of the appropriate *plan miasta* available cheaply at local tourist offices, kiosks, street sellers and bookshops. These city maps have tram and bus routes marked on them.

Money and banks

Poland is currently one of the great travel bargains: most of the essentials are still remarkably cheap for anyone with hard currency. The Polish currency is the **złoty** (zł): after a confusing period of transition, the "new" złoty have now completely replaced "old" złoty which are no longer legal tender. One new złoty is equivalent to 10,000 old złoty, so it's easy enough to recognize the old currency (the highest note for new złoty is 200zł and the only note below 200zł in the old currency was a 100zł note with "Proletariat" emblazoned across it). There are about 4zł to the dollar and 6zł to the pound sterling.

There is no longer a significant difference between the **exchange rates** offered by the banks (usually open Mon–Fri 7.30am–5pm, Sat 7.30am–2pm) and those by the omnipresent exchange booths (kantors). Most kantors, however, will not change travellers' cheques. Hotels offer poor exchange rates. Major **credit cards** are accepted by most hotels and restaurants, and you can arrange a cash advance on most cards; an increasing number of shops take plastic, and there are **cashpoint machines** in every city.

Communications

Post offices in Poland are identified by the name Urzed Pocztowy (Poczta for short) or by the acronym PTT. Theoretically, each city's head office has a **poste restante** facility: make sure that anyone addressing mail to you adds "No 1" (denoting the head office) after the city's name. Head office opening hours are usually Mon–Sat 7/8am–8pm; branches usually close at 6pm or earlier. Outbound mail takes a few days; expect airmail delivery within three. Post boxes are red.

A few of Poland's pay phones still accept jetons (tokens) but by far the best way to phone is to buy a phone card. Card phones are increasingly popular and less likely to be out of order. Cards can be purchased from post offices and newsagent kiosks in denominations of 25, 50 and 100 units (6.4zł, 12.8zł & 25zł) and can be used for international calls, but these are expensive.

Getting around

Poland has comprehensive and cheap public transport services, though they can often be overcrowded and excruciatingly slow.

■ Trains

The reasonably efficient Polish State Railways **(PKP)** runs three main types of **trains: express** services (*ekspresowy*), particularly the ones marked IC (intercity) or EC (Eurocity), are the ones to go for if you're travelling long distances, as they stop at the main cities only; seat reservations are compulsory and involve a small supplementary charge. So-called **fast** trains (*pośpieszne*) have far more stops, and reservations are optional. **Normal** services (normalne or osobowe) should be avoided: in rural areas they stop at every haystack. Some two dozen narrow-gauge lines are still in operation, and steam is used on some of these as well as on a few main-line routes.

Even a long cross-country haul will only set you back little more than £15/$20, but it's well worth paying the fifty-percent extra to travel **first-class** or make a **reservation** (miejscówka), as sardine-like conditions are fairly common. Most long journeys are best done overnight; second-class sleepers are a bargain at around £10/$15 per person. Buying tickets in main stations can be a minor hassle though you will rarely have to queue for more than a few minutes. For journeys of over 100km, you can buy tickets at Orbis offices. Tickets for international journeys can be bought at stations (again, there may be a small queue) or at Orbis offices. Rail passes for the whole network are available in Poland for periods of seven, fourteen or twenty-one days or for a whole month, but you'd have to take an awful lot of trains to justify the outlay. However, the Eurotrain Explorer gives you unlimited travel for £20. InterRail passes are valid in Poland, but not Eurail.

■ Buses

Intercity **buses** operated by **PKS**, the national bus company, can be slow and overcrowded; there are few long-haul routes and no overnight journeys. In rural areas, notably the mountain regions, there's greater choice and convenience, and on a rural journey the bus is often considerably faster than the train. Main bus stations are usually alongside the train station. There is a private company called **Polski Express** (☎022/620-0330) which offers slightly pricier intercity journeys in rather more comfortable and quick buses. Seat numbers on most buses are allocated when you buy tickets, though many stations cannot allocate seats for services starting from another town – in such cases you have to buy a ticket from the driver. As with trains, Orbis offices are the best place to go if you want to book on an **international** route.

■ Driving and hitching

Poles are not yet routine car owners and recent inflation has, if anything, cleared roads further. **Renting a car** costs from around £40/$60 a day to £250/$400 a week (unlimited mileage). Many **petrol stations** in cities and on main international routes are open 24 hours a day, others from around 6am to 10pm. In rural areas stations can be a long way apart, so carry a fuel can. **Speed limits** are 60kph in built-up areas, 90kph on country roads, and 130kph on motorways.

Repairs are much less of problem than they used to be. There are authorized dealers for various Western makes of car, and **repair services** of a minor kind are the stock in trade of garages.

Hitchhiking used to be a tradition when there were fewer cars on the road, but today it is not encouraged. The danger of robbery is high, and with public transport so cheap and omnipresent, it's not worth the risk.

Accommodation

Accommodation will almost certainly account for most of your costs in Poland, though there are now plenty of cheap alternatives to the heavily touted **international hotels**. Look out for weekend reductions – special "citybreak" rates in big cities organized by Orbis. Groups can save money by booking triple, quadruple and even dormitory-sized rooms.

■ Hotels

Orbis runs some 55 **international hotels** throughout Poland. A few of these are famous old prewar haunts, but the vast majority are anonymous concrete. They're pricey and often dreary, retaining a musty pre-revolutionary air, but they usually provide bathrooms, satellite TV and breakfast. Average rates are around £40/$65 for a single, £60/$100 for a double, rising to more than £60/$100 per head in Warsaw. In every city there are perfectly **reasonable hotel rooms** for about £10/$15 per person, provided you don't mind using toilets and showers outside the room and paying about 10zł (£2/$3) extra if you opt for breakfast.

■ Hostels

Scattered throughout Poland are some 200 **official youth hostels** (*schroniska młodzieżowe*). Many are only open at the height of summer and are liable to be booked solid, while most of the year-round hostels still conform to the hair-shirt ideals of the movement's founders with lockouts and curfews. Prices are rarely more than £3/$5 a head, though, and many hostels are located close to town centres. For a complete list, contact the Polish Youth Hostel Federation (PTSM) at ul. Chocimska 28, Warsaw (Mon–Fri 8am–3.30pm; ☎022/498-128).

There's a network of **tourist hostels**, often run by PTTK and called either Dom Turysty or Dom Wycieczkowy. Found in both cities and rural locations, these are generally cheaper than any hotel (although the PTTK Dom Turysty in Kraków is expensive and should be avoided), but are often a poor bargain at around £8/$13 for a bed in a small dorm with basic facilities. **Almatur** also organizes summer accommodation in **university hostels**; charges (including breakfast) are around £2/$3 for ISIC card-holding students and £4–6/$7–10 for others (no age limit), depending on whether they wish to share a room. These vacated halls of residence (available from late June to early Sept) are often the best bet in summer, since they are as cheap as youth hostels without the restrictions, and they can be found in any city with a university. A generous number of **refuges** (clearly marked on hiking maps) enable you to make long-distance treks. Accommodation is in basic dormitories, but costs are nominal and you can often get cheap, filling hot meals.

■ Private rooms

It's possible to get a **room in a private house** (kwatery prywatny) almost anywhere in the country. Some are pretty shabby, but it's an ideal way to find out how the Poles themselves live. All major cities have a room-finding service, usually known as the Biuro

Zakwaterowania, and most tourist information offices will also help. Charges are usually £7–8/$11–13 per person, £10/$16 in Warsaw. You'll be given a choice of location and category; it makes sense not to register for too many nights until you know you'll like the place. Some **Orbis offices** also act as agents for householders, but they prefer to get people into their hotels. You're better off asking at the tourist information offices or at offices specifically dealing with private rooms, like Syrena in Warsaw. Many houses in the main holiday areas hang out **signs** saying Noclegi (lodging) or Pokoje (rooms). It's up to you to bargain: £3/$4.50 is the least you can expect to pay. Individuals with rooms to let may approach you at train stations – this can be the way to a bargain but carries all the usual risks of an unofficial deal.

■ Camping

There are some 400 **campsites** throughout the country; for a complete list see the *Campingi w Polsce* map. Apart from main holiday areas, they can be found in most cities: the ones on the outskirts are invariably linked by bus to the centre and often have the benefit of a peaceful location and swimming pool. Most open May–Sept only. Charges usually work out at less than £2/$3 a head, a bit more if you come by car. Many sites have chalets to rent which, though spartan, are good value at around £4/$6 per head. Camping rough, outside of the national parks, is okay if you're discreet.

Food and drink

Poles take their food seriously, providing meals of feast-like proportions for the most casual visitors. The cuisine is a complex mix of influences: Russian, German, Ukrainian, Lithuanian and Jewish traditions have all left their mark.

■ Food

Breakfast might include fried eggs with ham, mild frankfurters, a selection of cold meats and cheese, rolls and jam. A common alternative, however, is to stop at a milk bar or self-service snack bar. Open from early morning till 5 or 6pm, **snack bars** (*samoobsługa*) are soup-kitchen-type places, serving cheap but generally uninspiring food. Milk bars (*bar mleczny*) are similar uninspiring fill-up stations.

Traditional Polish **takeaway stands** usually sell *zapiekanki*, baguette-like pieces of bread topped with melted cheese; a less common but enjoyable version of the same thing comes with fried mushrooms. Hot-dog stalls dole out sub-frankfurter sausages in white rolls; in the tourist resorts are stalls and shops selling chips (*frytki*) with sausage (*kiełbasa*) or chicken (*kurczak*), as well as a growing selection of Western-style takeaway joints. Some of these kiosk-type takeaways offer excellent food, increasingly adding oriental cuisine to their repertoire, plus a plastic table or two in the street for consumption "on the premises".

Many **restaurants** close late, but the older tradition of closing at 9 or 10pm persists in some places so it's advisable to check the opening times before you go in. First on the menu in most places are **soups**, varying from delicate dishes to concoctions that are virtually meals in themselves. Best known is *barszcz*, a spicy beetroot broth that's ideally accompanied by a small pastry. In better restaurants, the **hors d'oeuvres** might include Jewish-style gefilte fish, jellied ham *(szynka w galerecie)*, steak tartare (*stek tatarski*), wild rabbit paté (*pasztet zajeca*), or hard-boiled eggs in mayonnaise, sometimes stuffed with vegetables (*jajka faszerowane*).

The basis of most main courses is fried or grilled **meat** in a thick sauce, such as *kotlet schwabow* (a pork cutlet). Two specialities you'll find everywhere are *bigos* (cabbage stewed with meat) and *pierogi*, dumplings stuffed with meat and mushrooms, or with cottage cheese, onion and spices (*pierogi ruskie*). **Pancakes** (*naleśniki*) often come as a main course, stuffed with cottage cheese (*z serem*). Fried potato pancakes *(placki ziemniaczane)* are particularly good, served in sour cream or spicy paprika sauce.

Cakes, pastries and other sweets are an integral ingredient of most Poles' daily consumption, and the **cake shops** (*cukiernia*) – which you'll find even in small villages – are as good as any in central Europe. *Sernik* (cheesecake) is a national favourite, as are *makowiec* (poppyseed cake), *drożdówka* (a sponge cake, often topped with plums), and *babka piaskowa* (marble cake).

■ Drink

Poles' capacity for alcohol has never been in doubt, and drinking is a national pursuit. All of the cities possess delightful cafés and bars. Hotel bars and "drink bars" are usually best avoided, but whereas a few years ago these were virtually the only source of refreshment there are now countless alternatives in all the cities.

Poles can't compete with their Czech neighbours in the production and consumption of **beer** (*piwo*), but there are a number of fairly drinkable and widely available Polish brands. It's with **vodka** (*wódka*) that Poles really get into their stride. Ideally it is served neat, well chilled, in measures of 25 or 50 grams and knocked back in one go, with a mineral water chaser. Best of the clear vodkas are *żytnia* and *Wyborowa*. Of the flavoured varieties, first on most people's list is *żubrówka*, infused with bison grass.

Opening hours and holidays

Most **shops** open on weekdays from around 10am to 6pm, except food stores which may open as early as 6am and close by mid-afternoon. Many shops close on Saturdays. RUCH kiosks, where you buy newspapers and municipal transport tickets, generally open at about 6am. Increasing numbers of street traders do business well into the evening, and you can find shops in major cities offering late-night opening throughout the week. **Museums** and **historic monuments** almost invariably close one day per week, usually Monday. Entrance tends to cost very little, and is often free on one day of the week. **Public holidays** are: Jan 1; Easter Monday; May 1; May 3; Corpus Christi (variable May/June); Aug 15; Nov 1; Nov 11; Dec 25 & 26.

Emergencies

The biggest potential hassles are hotel room thefts, pickpocketing and car break-ins. Avoid leaving cars unattended overnight in city centres and beware of being mugged in the narrow corridors of trains. The *policja* are responsible for everyday law enforcement.

For serious **health** problems you'll be directed to a **hospital** (*szpital*), where conditions will probably be poor, but some are better than others. Paying for a stay in a private hospital may be forced on you by circumstances, but there are good public hospitals too (usually the teaching hospitals). If you are required to pay for treatment or medication, keep receipts for your insurance claim.

The usual **emergency numbers** (police ☎997, ambulance ☎999, fire ☎998) are of little use if you don't speak Polish. In a medical emergency, ring a **medical centre with English speakers**. The American Medical Centre in Warsaw (☎0-602-24-30-24) provides 24hr emergency availability. It will charge heavily, of course, so use it only in real emergencies.

WARSAW

WARSAW, likely to be most visitors' first experience of Poland, makes an initial impression that is all too often negative. The years of communist rule have left no great aesthetic glories, and there's sometimes a hollowness to the faithful reconstructions of earlier eras. However, as throughout Poland, the pace of social change is tangible and fascinating, as the openings provided by the postcommunist order turn the streets into a continuous marketplace, while the postwar dearth of nightlife and entertainments has become a complaint of the past, as a plethora of new bars, restaurants and clubs establish themselves.

Warsaw became the capital of Poland in 1596, when **King Zygmunt III** moved his court here from Kraków. The city was badly damaged by the Swedes during the invasion of 1655 and was then extensively reconstructed by the **Saxon kings** in the late seventeenth century – the Saxon Gardens (Ogród Saski), right in the centre, date from this period. The **Partitions** abruptly terminated this golden age, as Warsaw was absorbed into Prussia in 1795. Napoleon's arrival in 1806 gave Varsovians brief hopes of liberation, but following the 1815 Congress of Vienna, the city was integrated into the Russian-controlled **Congress Kingdom of Poland**. It was only with the outbreak of World War I that Russian control began to crumble, and with the restoration of Polish independence in 1918, Warsaw reverted to its position as capital. Then, with the outbreak of World War II, came the progressive annihilation of the city. Hitler, infuriated by the **Warsaw Uprising**, ordered the elimination of Warsaw; by the end of the war 850,000 Varsovians – two-thirds of the city's 1939 population – were dead or missing. The task of rebuilding took ten years of ceaseless labour.

Arrival and information

Okęcie international airport is a thirty-minute journey by bus #175 (#611 at night) from central Warsaw – a route well used by pickpockets, so be on your guard. The quicker Airport City bus (8zł) stops at central hotels. **Warszawa Centralna**, the main **train station**, is a ten-minute bus ride from the Old Town (*plan miasta* maps show the numbers of buses and trams that ply this route); there's a 24-hour left-luggage office here, as well as a computerized system for lockers where you can store luggage for up to ten days. Most trains run straight through to Centralna but it's possible that you'll need to change trains at Warszawa Wschodnia (East) station, out in the Praga suburb, or Warszawa Zachodnia (West), in the Ochota district. Centralny Dworzec PKS, the main **bus station**, is across the road from Warszawa Zachodnia.

The wide open expanse of the Wisła river is the most obvious aid to **orientation**. The heart of Warsaw, the **Śródmiescie** district, sits on the left bank; above it is the **Old Town** (Stare Miasto) area, with **plac Zamkowy** a useful central reference, while over on the east bank lies the **Praga** suburb.

There's still no reliable source of general **information**, though the information office in the main station (Mon–Fri 8am–8pm, Sat & Sun 9am–7pm; ☎022/524-5184) can provide plenty of leaflets and books rooms in hotels and hostels. The Informator Turystyczny (IT) point on plac Zamkowy 1/13 (Mon–Fri 9am–6pm, Sat 10am–6pm, Sun 11am–6pm; ☎022/831-0464) is an alternative source of information and bookings, but it is some way from the central station, opposite the Royal Castle. There are **Orbis** information desks in the *Grand Hotel* at ul Kruczna 28 and the *Europejski Hotel* at ul Krakowskie Przedmieście 13, but they provide very little in the way of information and their staff don't speak English. The listings magazine, *Warsaw Insider*, can be bought from information centres and at some hotels and bookstores and costs 6zł.

City transport

Warsaw is too big to get around without using public transport. **Buses** and **trams** are the main forms of transport, and both are still very cheap for foreigners. Regular bus and tram

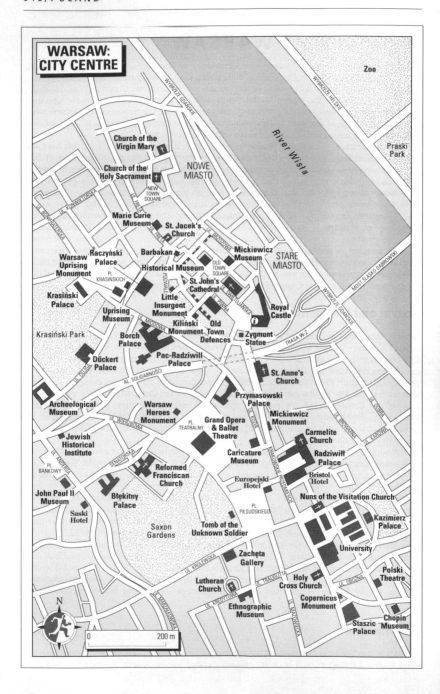

WARSAW: CITY CENTRE

Zoo

Praski Park

River Wisła

Church of the Virgin Mary ✝

NOWE MIASTO

Church of the Holy Sacrament ✝

NEW TOWN SQUARE

Marie Curie Museum

St. Jacek's Church

Raczyński Palace

Barbakan

Mickiewicz Museum

STARE MIASTO

Warsaw Uprising Monument

Historical Museum

OLD TOWN SQUARE

Krasiński Palace

St John's Cathedral ✝

Uprising Museum

Little Insurgent Monument

Royal Castle

Krasiński Park

Borch Palace

Kiliński Monument

Old Town Defences

Zygmunt Statue

ℹ️

Dückert Palace

Pac-Radziwiłł Palace

St. Anne's Church ✝

Archeological Museum

Warsaw Heroes Monument

Przymasowski Palace

Mickiewicz Monument

Jewish Historical Institute

Grand Opera & Ballet Theatre

Carmelite Church ✝

John Paul II Museum

Reformed Franciscan Church

Caricature Museum

Radziwiłł Palace

Europejski Hotel

Bristol Hotel

Błękitny Palace

Nuns of the Visitation Church

Saski Hotel

Saxon Gardens

Tomb of the Unknown Soldier

Kazimierz Palace

University

Zachęta Gallery

Polski Theatre

Lutheran Church

Holy Cross Church ✝

Ethnographic Museum

Copernicus Monument

Staszic Palace

Chopin Museum

N

0   200 m

routes close down about midnight; from 11pm to 5am **night buses** leave every thirty minutes from behind the Palace of Culture. There is also a **metro** underground system running to the centre of town (**Centrum** station), but it has only one line, which doesn't take in many of the sights.

Tickets for both trams and buses are bought from the green shacks marked RUCH (not from drivers), and are currently 2zł each – but prices will certainly go up. For buses or trams you need one ticket per journey by day and three tickets for night buses. You also need a 2zł ticket for bulky luggage. Punch your tickets in the machines on board and every time you change tram – inspectors will fine you 100zł on the spot and 30zł for your luggage if they catch you without a validated ticket. Alternatively you can get day (6zł) or week (20zł) passes from some kiosks; there's an office in Plac Bankowy opposite the *Hotel Saski* where you can buy them. There are now automatic ticket machines in some central locations. Tickets (and costs) for the **metro** are the same as for buses and trams.

For Westerners, **taxis** are reasonable. To avoid being ripped off take the radio taxis, recognizable by the illuminated sign on the roof which has the name of the company, followed by "taxi" and a number (ordinary taxis simply have the word "taxi"). Don't get a taxi from outside the central station – go to the nearby ul Emilii Plater for a radio taxi. Better still, book one; try Sawa Taxi (☎644-4444) or MPT (☎919).

Accommodation

Warsaw has two HI **hostels**, and during July and August the Almatur-run **international student hotels** are another inexpensive possibility, without the problems of lockouts and curfews. The **Almatur** office is at ul Kopernika 23 (Mon–Fri 9am–7pm, Sat 10am–2pm; ☎022/826-3512), and can book you into the student hotels. For **private rooms** go to the Syrena agency at ul Kruczna 17 (Mon–Sat 9am–7pm, Sun 9am–5pm; ☎022/628-7540), about 300m from the Central Station, or two stops on any tram going east. If you arrive after hours you can book a room at the pub next door, *Lokomotyva* (Mon–Fri noon–midnight, Sat & Sun 2pm–midnight), with whom Syrena has a special arrangement. The best bet for help with **hotel bookings** is the Informator Turystyczny at plac Zamkowy 1/13 (Mon–Fri 9am–6pm, Sat 10am–6pm, Sun 11am–6pm; ☎022/831-0464) or the **Orbis** offices in the *Hotel Grand* at ul Kruczna 28 and the *Hotel Europejski* at ul Krakowskie Przedmieście 13.

Hostels

Ul Karolkowa 53a (☎022/632-8829). In the western Wola district – take tram #13, #26 or #34 north of the main station and get off on al Solidarności, near the Wola department store; the better of the two hostels. Reception 5–10pm; curfew 11pm. ②.

Ul Smolna 30 (☎022/827-8952). A five-minute bus ride along al Jerozolimskie from the main station – any bus heading towards Nowy Świat will drop you at the corner of the street. Barrack-like conditions but central location. Reception 4–9pm; curfew 11pm. ②.

Hotels

Bristol, ul Krakowskie Przedmieście 42/4 (☎022/625-2525). The best of the very expensive options, with style as well as opulence. Occasional special offers. ⑨.

Dom Chłopa, pl Powstańców Warszawy 2 (☎022/827-4943). Used by a wider clientele than its name (Farmers' House) suggests. Solid, central and reliable. Has some cheaper rooms without bathrooms. ⑥.

Dom Literatury, ul Krakowskie Przedmieście 87/89 (☎022/635-0404). Cheap and excellent, but not much English spoken. This is basically a few rooms above a pub. Call and try your luck. ③.

Europejski, ul Krakowskie Przedmieście 13 (☎022/826-5051). One of the few Orbis hotels with character. Normally expensive but has special offers at weekends. ⑧.

Harenda, Krakowskie Przedmieście 4/6 (☎022/826-0071). Located just below the university campus. ⑤.

Praski, al. Solidarności 61 (☎022/818-4989). The best choice in town, opposite a park and next to the wonderful *Le Cedre* Lebanese restaurant. In the outer edge of the Praga district of Warsaw over the river, which is not particularly safe, but the tram drops you right outside the hotel. ③.

Saski, pl Bankowy 1 (☎022/620-4611). Well located just off Saski Park, with decent rooms and plenty of character, though the current renovation may push up the price. ③.

Warszawa pl Powstanców Warszawy 9 (☎022/826-9421). The Stalinist architecture may appeal or repel. Enter through columns topped with "Classical" sculptures. ⑤.

Wileński, ul Kłopotowskiego 36 (☎022/818-5317). Across the river from the Royal Castle in the Praga district, a little further on from the *Praski*. Not a very salubrious area, but the prices are very low. ②.

Campsites

Even in Warsaw, **camping** is extremely cheap and popular with Poles and foreigners alike. On the whole, site facilities are reasonable and several offer bungalows (around 20zł per person per night).

Camping Gromada, ul Żwirki i Wigury 32 (☎022/825-4391). Best and most popular of the Warsaw campsites, on the way out to the airport – bus #188 or #175 will get you there. As well as tent space, the site has a number of cheap bungalows (22zł).

Majawa, Boh. Bitwy Warszawskiej 1920r. 15/17 (☎022/233-748). Just south of the bus station – take bus #154. Less crowded than the *Gromada* site, with some bungalows at 70zł, and the usual small extra charges for linen, tents, electricity and car parking.

The City

Wending its way north towards Gdańsk and the Baltic Sea, the **Wisła** (Vistula) river divides Warsaw neatly in half: the main sights are located on the western bank, the eastern consisting predominantly of residential and business districts. Somewhat to the north of the centre, the busy **Old Town** provides the historic focal point. It's worth exploring the backstreets and into the rear courtyards of buildings to appreciate the historical development of the city. Much of Warsaw's history is hidden behind its facades, there are many original nineteenth- and even eighteenth-century buildings intact and free of the postwar plaster that obscures the age of many street-facing frontages.

The Old Town

The title "Old Town" – Stare Miasto – is in some respects a misnomer for the historic nucleus of Warsaw. Forty-five years ago this compact network of streets and alleyways lay in rubble: even the cobbles have been meticulously replaced. **Plac Zamkowy** (Castle Square), on the south side of the Old Town, is the obvious place to start a tour. Here the first thing to catch your eye is the bronze **statue** of Zygmunt III Waza, the king who made Warsaw the capital.

On the east side of the square is the former **Royal Castle** (Zamek Królewski), once home of the royal family and seat of the Polish parliament, now the **Castle Museum** (Tues–Sat 10am–5pm, Sun & Mon 11am–5pm; 14zł, free Sun). Tickets can be bought from around the corner, ul Świćtojańska 2. Though the structure is a replica, many of its furnishings are the originals, scooted into hiding during the first bombing raids. After the Chamber of Deputies, formerly the debating chamber of the parliament, the Grand Staircase leads to the most lavish section of the castle, the **Royal Apartments of King Stanisław August**. Through two smaller rooms you come to the magnificent **Canaletto Room**, with its views of Warsaw by Bernardo Bellotto, nephew of the famous Canaletto – whose name he appropriated to make his pictures sell better. Marvellous in their detail, these cityscapes provided important information for the architects rebuilding the city after the war. Next door is the richly decorated **Royal Chapel**, where an urn contains the heart – sacred to many Poles – of Tadeusz Kościuszko, swashbuckling leader of the 1794 insurrection and hero of the American War of Independence.

On Świćtojańska, north of the castle, stands **St John's Cathedral**, the oldest church in Warsaw, now regaining its old status after the communist era. A few yards away, the Old Town Square – **Rynek Starego Miasta** – is one of the most remarkable bits of postwar reconstruction anywhere in Europe. Flattened during the Warsaw Uprising, its three-storey merchants' houses have been rebuilt to their seventeenth- and eighteenth-century designs, multicoloured facades included. By day the Rynek teems with visitors, who are catered for by buskers, artists, cafés, moneychangers and *dorozki*, the traditional horse-drawn carts that clatter tourists round the Old Town for a sizeable fee. The **Warsaw Historical Museum** (Tues & Thurs noon–6pm, Wed & Fri 10am–3.30pm, Sat & Sun 10.30am–3pm; 6zł, free Sun) takes up a large part of the north side; exhibitions here cover every aspect of Warsaw's life from its beginnings to the present day, with a particularly moving chronicle of everyday resistance to the Nazis. On the east side, the **Mickiewicz Museum** (Mon, Tues & Fri 10am–3pm, Wed & Thurs 11am–6pm, Sun 11am–5pm; 5zł, Thurs free) is a temple to the Romantic national poet.

From the Rynek, ul Nowomiejska leads to the sixteenth-century **Barbakan**, which used to guard the Nowomiejska Gate, the northern entrance to the city. The fortress is part of the old town defences, which run all the way around from plac Zamkowy to the northeastern edge of the district.

The New Town and the Ghetto

Cross the ramparts from the Barbakan and you're into the **New Town** (Nowe Miasto) district, which despite its name dates from the early fifteenth century, but was formally joined to Warsaw only at the end of the eighteenth. **Ulica Freta**, the continuation of Nowomiejska, runs north through the heart of the district to the **Rynek Nowego Miasta**, once the commercial hub of the district, now a soothing change from the bustle of the Old Town. Tucked into the eastern corner is the **Church of the Holy Sacrament**, commissioned by Queen Maria Sobieska in memory of her husband Jan's victory over the Turks at Vienna in 1683; as you might expect, highlight of the sober interior is the Sobieski funeral chapel.

West from the square is the majestic **Krasińskich Palace**, its facade bearing fine sculptures by Andreas Schlüter. Behind the palace are the **gardens**, now a public park, and beyond that the Ghetto area. In 1939 there were an estimated 380,000 Jews living in and around Warsaw – one-third of the total population. By May 1945, around 300 were left, and after the war Jewish Warsaw was replaced by the sprawling housing estates and tree-lined thoroughfares of the **Muranów** and **Mirów** districts, a little to the west of the city centre. However, a few traces of the Jewish presence in Warsaw do remain, and there's a small but increasingly visible Jewish community here. First stop on any itinerary of Jewish Warsaw is the **Nożyk Synagogue** on ul Twarda, the only one of the Ghetto's three synagogues still standing. Built in the early 1900s, it was gutted during the war, and reopened in 1983 after a complete restoration. Marooned in the middle of a drab square to the north of the Ghetto area, the imposing **Ghetto Heroes Monument** – unveiled in 1948 – was made from materials ordered by Hitler for a monument to the Reich's anticipated victory. Further evidence of Jewish Warsaw can be seen in the miraculously untouched street, **Próżna**, its original brickwork dotted with satellite dishes, which is now threatened with renovation (it is best viewed from the Palace of Culture).

Śródmieście

The area stretching from the Old Town down towards Łazienki Park – **Śródmieście** – is the increasingly fast-paced heart of Warsaw. Of all the thoroughfares bisecting central Warsaw from north to south, the most important is the one often known as the Royal Way, which runs almost uninterrupted from plac Zamkowy to the palace of Wilanów. **Krakowskie Przedmieście**, the first part of the Royal Way, is lined with historic buildings.

Even in a city not lacking in Baroque churches, the **Church of the Nuns of the Visitation** stands out, with its columned, statue-topped facade; it's also one of the very few buildings in central Warsaw to have come through World War II unscathed. Its main claim to fame in Polish eyes is that Chopin used to play the church organ here. Most of the rest of Krakowskie Przedmieście is taken up by **Warsaw University**. On the main campus courtyard, the **Library** stands in front of the seventeenth-century **Kazimierz Palace**, once a royal summer residence, while across the street from the gates is the former **Czapski Palace**, now home of the Academy of Fine Arts. Just south is the Baroque **Holy Cross Church** (Kościół Świętego Krzyża), wrecked in a two-week battle during the Warsaw Uprising; photographs of the distinctive figure of Christ left standing among the ruins became poignant emblems of Warsaw's suffering. Another factor increases local affection for this church: on a pillar to the left side of the nave there's an urn containing Chopin's heart.

Biggest among Warsaw's palaces is the early nineteenth-century **Staszic Palace**, now the headquarters of the Polish Academy of Sciences (not open to the public), which virtually blocks the end of Krakowskie Przedmieście. South from the Staszic, the main street becomes **Nowy Świat** (New World), an area first settled in the mid-seventeenth century. Moving down this wide boulevard, the palaces of the aristocracy give way to shops, offices and cafés. West along al Jerozolimskie is the **National Museum** (Tues, Wed & Fri–Sun 10am–6pm, Thurs noon–7pm; 7zł, free Sat), an impressive compendium of art and archeology. The first floor has the ancient art while the European galleries on the upper floors display a wide range of paintings and sculptures – Caravaggio, Bellini, Brueghel and Rodin included. The remarkable display of Polish medieval altarpieces and religious sculpture includes some imaginative and exuberant wooden Madonnas, mainly from the Gdańsk region.

The area below the Saxon Gardens and west of Krakowskie Przedmieście is the busiest commercial zone. **Marszałkowska**, the main road running south from the western tip of the park, is lined with department stores and privately run boutiques and workshops selling everything from jewellery to car spares. Towering over everything is the **Palace of Culture**, a gift from Stalin that the Polish people could hardly refuse. Apart from a vast conference hall, the cavernous interior contains offices, shops, theatres, nightclubs, cinemas, swimming pools, and – the ultimate capitalistic revenge – a casino. Some locals maintain that the best view of Warsaw is from the thirtieth-floor platform – the only viewpoint from which one can't see the palace (daily 9am–6pm; 10zł).

Łazienki Park and Palace

Parks are one of Warsaw's distinctive and most attractive features. South of the commercial district, on the east side of al Ujazdowskie, is one of the best, the **Łazienki Park**. Once a hunting ground, the area was bought by King Stanisław August in the 1760s and turned into an English-style park with formal gardens. A few years later the slender Neoclassical **Łazienki Palace** (Tues–Sun 9.30am–3.30pm; 8zł) was built across the park lake: the best memorial to the country's last and most cultured monarch.

The oak-lined promenades and pathways leading from the park entrance to the palace are a favourite with both Varsovians and tourists. On summer Sunday lunchtimes, concerts and other events take place under the watchful eye of the ponderous **Chopin Monument**, just beyond the entrance. Nazi damage to the rooms themselves was not irreparable, and most of the lavish furnishings, paintings and sculptures survived the war intact, having been hidden during the occupation. The stuccoed **ballroom**, the biggest ground-floor room, is a fine example of Stanisław's classicist predilections, lined with a tasteful collection of busts and classical sculptures. As the adjoining **picture galleries** demonstrate, Stanisław was a discerning art collector. Upstairs are the **king's private apartments**, most of them entirely reconstructed since the war. The nearby **Myśkewicki Palace** (9.30am–3pm; closed Tues; 4zł) is also well worth a visit. The park itself stays open till dusk.

Wilanów

The grandest of Warsaw's palaces, **Wilanów** (Mon & Wed–Sun 9.30am–2.30pm; 9zł, free Mon) makes an easy excursion from the city centre: take bus #122 south from anywhere along the main drag from the Old Town through Krakowskie Przedmieście and Nowy Świat to its terminus. Sometimes called the Polish Versailles, it was the brainchild of King Jan Sobieski, who purchased the existing manor house and estate in 1677 and spent nearly twenty years turning it into his ideal country residence. Among the sixty-odd rooms you'll find styles ranging from the lavish early Baroque of the apartments of Jan Sobieski and John III to the classical grace of the nineteenth-century Potocki museum rooms. Some find the cumulative pomp rather deadening – but if your interest hasn't flagged after the guided tour, there are a couple of other places of interest within the grounds. The gate on the left side beyond the main entrance opens onto the stately **palace gardens** (9.30am till sunset; closed Tues; 2zł), while to the right before you enter is the **Poster Museum** (Tues–Fri 10am–4pm, Sat & Sun 10am–5pm; 4zł), a mishmash of the inspired and the bizarre from an art form which has long had major currency in Poland.

Eating and drinking

Warsaw's **cafés** have long been favoured for get-togethers, clandestine political exchanges, stand-up rows or just passing the time. For basic snacks, **milk bars** (*bar mleczny*), street stalls (those on pl Konstytucji are open into the early hours) and **fast-food** joints provide a good fill for under £3/$5. There are quite a few perfectly good places to eat, and an increasing number of small, well-run private **restaurants** are now appearing. **Bars**, traditionally something of a low spot of Warsaw nightlife, are improving by leaps and bounds.

Cafés

Blikle, Nowy Świat 33. Fashionable café open daily until 11pm.

Brama, ul Marszałkowska 8. Trendy if grungy hangout with good snacks and no smoking policy. Daily till 11pm.

Literacka, Krakowskie Przedmieście 87–9. Good location, with live jazz most evenings; food available. Open 11am–midnight.

Nowy Świat Café, ul Nowy Świat 63. A good place to browse and relax. Fine coffee and English periodicals. Daily till 10pm.

Pożegnanie z Afryką, ul Freta 4/6. Good place for coffee-lovers as there's a variety on offer. Open 11am–9pm.

Snack bars

Mata Hari Nowy Świat 52. Vegetarian kiosk with a courtyard table outside. Tues–Sun 11am–7pm.

Pod Barbakanem, ul Mostowa 29. Deservedly popular New Town milk bar near the Barbakan, where you can sit outside and watch the crowds. Mon–Fri 8am–6pm, Sat & Sun 9am–5pm.

Uniwersytecki, Krakowskie Przedmieście 20. Milk bar much frequented by students; just up from the university gates. Mon–Fri 7am–8pm, Sat & Sun 9am–5pm.

Restaurants

Gessler, Rynek Starego Miasto 21a (☎022/831-1661). Low ceilings and decent Polish cuisine in an Old Town venue that's a favourite with provincial Poles bingeing it for a weekend in the capital. Head down into the labyrinthine cellars underneath rather than the upstairs area. Reasonably priced with meals for £10/$16. Open 1pm–2am.

Klub Aktora al. Ujazdowskie 45 (☎022/628-9366). Good, family-run Polish restaurant with bread baked on the premises. Mon–Sat 10am till last guest.

Le Cedre al Solidarności 61 (☎022/670166). Wonderful Lebanese cuisine next to the *Praski* hotel. 11am–11pm.

Nove Miasto, New Town Square 13/15 (☎022/831-4379). Vegetarian restaurant with a good choice. Also serves fish. Open 10am–midnight.

Qchnia Artystyczna, al Ujazdowskie 6 (☎022/625-7627). Located in a castle near Łazienki Park, with a wonderful view from the terrace. Open noon to midnight. Service is slow so allow time.

Bars

Cotton Club Cafe, al Jana Pawła 52. Open 11am till late. Cafe-bar serving "jazz cocktails". Plans to show jazz films and concerts too.

Irish Pub, ul Miodowa 3. Very popular because of its almost daily live folk music, but pricey if you don't stick to Polish beer.

Lolek ul Rokitnicka 20, in Pole Mokotowskie. One of several watering-holes in the middle of a park bustling with Varsovians on summer nights. Barbecue-type food, beer and live music in and around an overgrown log cabin. One of the few places you can get to on the new metro. Open till dawn.

Między Nami ul Bracka 20. Relaxed gay-friendly café-bar with good salads and an excellent atmosphere. Open Sun–Thurs 10am–10pm, Fri–Sat 10am–midnight.

Nora, ul Krakowskie Przedmieście 20/22. Popular bar; crowded and smoky, but being next to the university it's good for socializing with English-speaking Poles. Open until 10pm (11pm weekends).

Nightlife

The best source of information in English is the monthly *Warsaw Insider*, a city guide with a good map. It is available from some kiosks and hotels or from good bookshops like the

American Bookstore at Koszykowa 55 (inside the Faculty of Architecture building). Regular Warsaw **festivals** include the excellent annual **Jazz Jamboree** in October, the biannual **Warsaw Film Festival**, the **Festival of Contemporary Music** held every September, and the five-yearly **Chopin Piano Competition** – always a launch pad for a major international career – which takes place in 2000.

Clubs, discos and live music

Warsaw's nightlife scene has been feeling the economic pinch in recent years, and appearances by major bands are still a rarity. When big names do turn up, they generally play at the Gwardia Stadium in Praga. The clubs listed below all have something to recommend them in terms of decor, choice of music or atmosphere.

Cul de Sac, ul Foksal 2 (☎022/827-8707). Unsurprisingly located at the end of a street on one side of the courtyard. Leather couches, fussy dress code (no sneakers) and a post-teenage clientele. Wed–Sat till 4am.

Ground Zero, ul Wspólna 62 (☎022/625-4380). Dome-shaped space next to the *Warsaw Tortilla Factory* snack bar. Tends to be crammed with posing mobile-phone carriers, but it looks good. Wed–Sat till 4am.

Harenda, ul Krakowskie Przedmieśccie 4/6. More a ranch than a club. Live music and good atmosphere with room to talk, dance or listen to music. Daily until 3am.

Piekarnia, ul Młocinska 11 (☎022/634979). Has the latest progressive dance music and prides itself on being at the forefront of musical fashion. Thurs–Sun till 4am.

Tam Tam, ul Foksal 18 (☎022/828612). Bar, café and club all in one. Soul on Fridays. Daily till 3am.

Listings

Airlines LOT, al Jerozolimskie 65/79 (☎022/952-953); British Airways, ul Krucza 49 (☎022/628-9431)

Airport information International flights ☎022/650-3943; domestic flights ☎022/650-1750. Within Poland itself you can get information from LOT by simply ringing ☎952 or ☎953.

Bus tickets International tickets from the main bus station (Dworzec PKS) or ring ☎022-9433. Orbis offices also arrange them. The privately run Polski Express at al Jana Pawła (☎022/620-0330) operates a good intercity service.

Car rental Avis, Airport (☎022/650-4872); Hertz, Central Reservation Office (☎022/621-0239); Budget ul 17 Stycznia 32 pav 54 (☎022/868-3336); the *Marriott Hotel* (☎022/630-7280).

Embassies Australia, ul Estońska 3/5 (☎022/617-6081); Britain, al Roź 1 (☎022/628-1001); Canada, ul J. Matejki 1/5 (☎022/629-8051); Ireland, ul Humanska 10 (☎022/849-6633); Netherlands, ul Chocimska 6 (☎022/849-2351); New Zealand, ul Migdalowa 4 (☎022/645-1407); USA, al Ujazdowskie 29 (☎022/628-3041).

Exchange Orbis accept travellers' cheques but banks are the best option. Exchange offices (*Kantors*) change cash without commission, but will not handle travellers' cheques.

Gay Warsaw Much livelier than in the past. Information from Lambda Centre Helpline (Tues, Wed & Fri 6–9pm; ☎022/628-5222). Check out the *Koźla Pub* at ul Koźla 10–12, and the *Paradise* disco at ul Wawelska 5, part of Skra Stadium (Fri–Sat from 10pm). *Mykonos* is a central gay-friendly bar at al Jana Pawła 73, next to the *Hotel Maria*.

Laundry Luxomat, a self-service laundry with a dry-cleaning service, at ul Broniewskiego 89, ul Mangalia 4, ul Staniewicka 2 and a dozen other places; Alba, at ul Chmielna 26 (☎022/827-4510) and other locations.

Medical services The American Medical Centre at ul Wilca 29 (Mon–Fri 8am–6pm, Sat 9am–3pm; ☎022/622-0489) has English-speaking staff.

Pharmacies All-night *apteka* can be found on the top floor of the central railway station, at the Wars Dept. Store on ul Marszałkowska 104/22, at al Solidarności 149 (Pharmacy Beata), and at ul Widok 19 in the central area.

Post offices At ul Świętokrzyska 31/33 (open 24hr) and in the main train station, behind the departures and arrivals board (8am–8pm). Both have a 24-hour telephone and poste restante service: Warsaw 1 for the former, Warsaw 120 for the latter.

Train tickets An alternative to queuing at the station is to book at Orbis offices.

NORTHERN POLAND

Even in a country accustomed to shifts in its borders, northern Poland presents an unusually tortuous historical puzzle. Successively the domain of a Germanic crusading order, of the Hansa merchants and of the Prussians, it's only in the last forty years that the region has really become Polish. **Gdańsk, Sopot** and **Gdynia** – the **Tri-City**, as their conurbation is known – dominate the area from their coastal vantage point. Like Warsaw, historic Gdańsk was obliterated in World War II but now offers some reconstructed quarters, in addition to its contemporary political interest as the birthplace of Solidarity. The most enjoyable excursions from Gdańsk are to the medieval centres of **Malbork** and **Toruń**, or to **Frombork**, chief of many towns in the region associated with the astronomer Nicolaus Copernicus.

Gdańsk

For outsiders, **GDAŃSK** is perhaps the most familiar city in Poland. The home of Lech Wałęsa, the beginning of Solidarity and the former Lenin Shipyards, its images have flashed across a decade of news bulletins. Expectations formed from the newsreels are fulfilled by the industrial landscape, and suggestions of latent discontent, radicalism and future strikes are all tangible, alongside evidence of new wealth and economic renewal. What is more surprising, at least for those with no great knowledge of Polish history, is the cultural complexity of the place. Prewar Gdańsk – or **Danzig** as it then was – was forged by years of Prussian and Hanseatic domination, and the reconstructed city centre looks not unlike Amsterdam.

The City

The **Główne Miasto** (Main Town), the largest of the historic quarters, is the obvious starting point and is within easy walking distance of the train station. Entering it is like walking straight into a Hansa merchants' settlement, but the ancient appearance is deceptive: by May 1945 the fighting between German and Russian forces had reduced the core of Gdańsk to smouldering ruins. As with all the main streets, huge stone gateways guard both entrances to **Ulica Długa**, the main thoroughfare. Start from the sixteenth gate at the top, **Brama Wyżnna**, which provides a brief respite from red brick, and then head in a straight line towards the canal. Topped by a golden statue of King Zygmunt August, which dominates the central skyline, the huge and well-proportioned tower of the **Town Hall** makes a powerful impact. "In all Poland there is no other, so Polish a town hall", observed one local writer, though the Dutch influences on the interior rooms might lead you to disagree. They now house the **Historical Museum** (Tues–Sat 10am–4pm, Sun 11am–4pm; 8zł, free Wed), their lavish decorations almost upstaging the exhibits. Look out for the photographs of Gdańsk before and after the war which give a good indication of the extent of reconstruction.

Past the town hall, the street opens onto the wide expanses of **Długi Targ**, where the **Artus Court** (Dwór Artusa) stands out in a square filled with fine mansions. At the end of the street the archways of the **Green Gate** (Brama Zielona) open directly onto the waterfront. From the bridge over the Motława Canal you get a good view of the granaries on Spichlerze Island and to the left along the old harbour quay, now a tourist hangout and local promenade. Halfway down is the massive and largely original fifteenth-century **Gdańsk Crane**, the biggest in medieval Europe (Tues–Fri 9.30am–4pm, Sat & Sun 10am–4pm; 5zł). A few metres further on is the **Central Maritime Museum** (Centralne Museum Morskie; Tues–Fri 9.30am–4pm, Sat & Sun 10am–4pm), where for 8zł you can buy a "carnet" of tickets entitling you to visit the exhibition of primitive boats and photographs illustrating the life of Polish writer Józef Teodor Konrad Korzeniowski, better known to the world as Joseph Conrad, on one side of the canal, then travel by ferry to the other side and explore an exhibition of Polish naval history and look over the large iron vessel moored nearby, the *Sołdek*.

All the streets back into the town from the waterfront are worth exploring, especially Mariacki, nowadays full of amber-traders, which was used as the setting for the film of

Gunther Grass's *The Tin Drum*. Next up from the Green Gate is **ul Chlebnicka**, which ends at the gigantic **St Mary's Church** (Kościół Mariacki), reputedly the biggest brick church in the world. Inside, the Chapel of 11,000 Virgins has a tortured Gothic crucifix for which the artist apparently nailed his son-in-law to a cross as a model. Ulica Piwna, another street of high terraced houses west of the church entrance, ends at the monumental **Great Arsenal**, now a market, where a right turn takes you past St Nicholas' Church to the ul Podmłyńksa, the main route over the canal into the Old Town.

Dominating the waterside here is the seven-storey **Great Mill** (Wielki Młyn), the biggest mill in medieval Europe – even in the 1930s it was still grinding out 200 tons of flour a day. **St Catherine's Church** (Katarzynka), the former parish church of the Old Town, to the right of the crossway, is one of the nicest in the city. Fourteenth-century – and built in brick like almost all churches in the region – it has a well-preserved and luminous interior. The most interesting part of the district is west along the canal from the mill, centred on the **Old Town Hall** (Ratusz Staromiejski), on the corner of ul Bielanska and Korzenna, with the inevitable Irish pub underneath it. Looming large are the cranes of the famous **Gdańsk shipyards** (Stocznia Gdańska), the crucible of the political struggles of the 1980s. Ironically, the shipyards remain at the leading edge of political developments: the government is attempting to sell them to Western investors. It's worth visiting the gates beside the famous anchor-topped **monument** to the shipyard workers killed during the 1970s riots against price rises, where a range of stone tablets in the wall testify to Solidarity's subsequent long struggle throughout the 1980s.

Stare Przedmieście – the southern part of old Gdańsk – was the limit of the original town, as testified by the ring of seventeenth-century bastions running east from plac Wałowy over the Motława. The main attraction today is the **National Art Museum** (Tues–Sun 10am–3pm; 5zł), at Toruńska 1. There's enough local Gothic art and sculpture here to keep enthusiasts going all day, as well as a varied collection of fabrics, chests, gold and silverware. The museum's most famous possession is Hans Memling's colossal *Last Judgment* (1473), the painter's earliest known work.

One of the best ways to see Gdańsk is from the sea: boat trips to and from neighbouring Gdynia run daily (2pm; 38zł, 28zł to Sopot and back). Many people visit the Tri-City in order to spend time at the sea. The Baltic coast is a great favourite with Poles and foreign tourists alike, and Sopot with its pier, beaches and lively nightlife is an ideal place for a beach holiday. Trains run to and fro between Gdańsk and Sopot every twelve minutes during the day, and the latter has plenty of splendid places to stay, often with views directly onto the sands.

Practicalities

The main **tourist information centre**, a couple of minutes from the train station at ul Heweliusza 27 (Mon–Fri 8am–4pm; ☎058/3014-355), is one of the more helpful in the country – a few minutes' walk beyond the huge high-rise *Hotel Hewelius*. The Almatur **office**, in the centre of town at Długi Targ 11/13 (Mon–Fri 9am–5pm, Sat 10am–2pm; ☎058/301-2931), is also friendly, and employs several English speakers; in summer they'll help you sort out accommodation in student hotels. Tourist Information Gdańsk also runs a very helpful information service from May to October in ul Długa 45 and can arrange rooms (May–Oct Mon–Sat 9am–6pm; ☎058/301-9151). The **hostel** nearest the centre is the one at ul Wałowa 21 (☎058/301-2313; ②), a sizeable red-brick building ten minutes' walk from the main station. Of the cheaper **hotels**, *Jantar*, Długi Targ 19 (☎058/301-9532; ③), has an excellent location in the heart of the Old Town, but a bad reputation for security. Highly recommended are *Dom Harcerza*, ul Za Murami 2/10 (☎058/301-3621; ②), situated above a cinema, and *Dom Aktora* at ul Straganiarska 55/6 (☎058/301-5901; ②), but the pick of the bunch is the lovely *Hotel Wanda* looking over the beach at Sopot, at ul Poniatowski 7 (☎058/550-3037; ③). Orbis has one of its few characterful hotels in Sopot too – the *Grand* at ul PowstancÓw Warszawy 12/14 (☎058/551-0041; ⑥); the high prices are worth it for the Art Nouveau design and proximity to the beach and pier.

The most convenient **campsite** is at ul Jelitkowska 23 (☎058/553-2731; June–Sept), near the beach at Jelitkowo and a short walk from the terminus of trams #2, #6 or #8, or bus #143 from Sopot station.

For **cheap meals**, you should check out the *Bar Neptun* at ul Długa 32/34, one of the city's classic milk bars (closes 8pm). Of the **restaurants**, *Retman*, ul Stagiewna 1, is a fine waterfront fish place (noon–midnight; ☎058/301-9248). In the same league is the *Palowa* café/restaurant underneath the town hall at Długa 47. For cakes and ices try a *cukiernia* (cake shop) such as *Kaliszczak* at Długa 74. The *Jazz Club* at no. 39–40 in the same street opposite the Almatur office is a friendly place for a drink with live music on Fridays and Saturdays (☎058/301-5433). However, the nightlife is livelier in Sopot. The main drag there, ul Bohaterów Monte Cassino, buzzes with life, with a host of good places for a drink and, at the lower end near the pier, a small bungalow called *Kuchnie Wegetariańskie* serving delicious vegetarian snacks till 10pm.

Frombork

A little seaside town 98km east along the Baltic coast from Gdańsk, **FROMBORK** was the home town of Nicolaus Copernicus, the Renaissance astronomer whose ideas overturned the earth-centred model of the universe. Most of the research for his famous *De Revolutionibus* was carried out around this town, and it was here that he died and was buried in 1543. Today it's an out-of-the-way place, almost as peaceful as it must have been in Copernicus' day. The **bus journey** from Gdańsk takes between two and three hours. If there's no direct bus back, take one to Elblàg and change there. The journey can also be managed in roughly the same time by train, once more changing at Elblàg.

The only part of Frombork to escape unscathed from the last war was the **Cathedral Hill**, which you'll find up from the old market square in the centre of town. A compact unit surrounded by high defensive walls, its main element is the Gothic **Cathedral** (Oct–April daily 9.30am–3.30pm, May–Sept 9.30am–4.30pm; 9zł for the whole complex of buildings), with its huge red-tiled and turreted roof. Inside, the lofty expanses of brick rise above a series of lavish altars – the high altar is a copy of the Wawel altarpiece in Kraków. It's kept locked until enough visitors arrive, so ask in the museum and a guide will let you in. To the west of the cathedral, the **Copernicus Tower** is supposed by some to have been the great man's workshop and observatory. Doubting that the local authorities would have let him make use of a part of the town defences, others maintain that he's more likely to have studied at his home, just north of the cathedral complex. The **Radziejowska Tower**, in the southwest corner of the walls, houses an assortment of Copernicus-related astronomical instruments and has an excellent view of the Wiślana lagoon. Further equipment and memorabilia are to be found in the **Copernicus Museum** across the tree-lined cathedral courtyard (Tues–Sun 9am–3.30/4.30pm). Among the exhibits are early editions of Copernicus' astronomical treatises, along with a collection of instruments, pictures and portraits.

For an overnight stay, the budget choice is a decent-quality *PTTK* **hostel** at ul Krasickiego 3, perfectly positioned next to the Cathedral Hill complex (☎055/243-7252; ②), or the more comfortable *Hotel Kopernik* at ul Kościelna 2 (☎055/243-7285; ④). The *PTTK* **campsite** at ul Braniewska 14 (☎055/243-7368; mid-May to mid-Sept) is some way east from the centre on the Braniewo road. Among **places to eat** are the *Restauracja Akcent* at ul Rybacka 4, all garish blue parasols and reflected glass on the outside but pleasant inside (open till 11pm) and the restaurant in the *PTTK* hostel (open 8am–8pm).

Malbork

Following the course of the Wisła south from Gdańsk takes you into the heart of the territory once ruled by the **Teutonic Knights**. From a string of fortresses overlooking the river, this religio-militaristic order controlled the medieval grain trade, and it was under their protection that merchants from the northern Hanseatic League cities established themselves on the Wisła. Their headquarters was at **MALBORK**, where the massive riverside fortress imparts a threatening atmosphere to an otherwise quiet and predominantly modern town. The **train** and **bus stations** are sited next to each other about ten minutes' walk south of the castle; Malbork is on the main Warsaw line, so there are plenty of trains from Gdańsk (30min) as well as a regular bus service.

You approach the **fortress** (Tues–Sun: May–Sept 9am–5pm; Oct–April 9am–2.30pm, 10zł) through the old outer castle, a zone of utility buildings which was never rebuilt after the war. Some parts of the complex are only viewed under supervision, so you may be forced to join a group. Passing over the moat and through the daunting main gate, you come to the **Middle Castle**, built following the Knights' decision to move their headquarters to Malbork in 1309. Spread out around an open courtyard, this part of the complex contains the Grand Master's palace, of which the **Main Refectory** is the highlight; begun in 1330, this huge vaulted chamber shows the growing influence of the Gothic cathedral architecture. Leading off from the **courtyard** are a host of dark, cavernous chambers. The largest ones contain collections of ceramics, glass, sculpture, paintings and, most importantly, a large display of Baltic **amber**, the trade in which formed the backbone of the order's fabulous wealth. From the Middle Castle a passage rises to the smaller courtyard of the **High Castle**, the oldest section of the fortress, harbouring the focus of the Knights' austere monasticism – the vast **Castle Church**.

If you want to **stay** there's a pricey but delightfully positioned hotel in the lower grounds of the castle itself, the *Zamek* (☎055/272-2738; ⑤).

Toruń

Poles are apt to wax lyrical on the glories of their ancient cities, and with **TORUŃ** – the biggest and most important of the Hanseatic trading centres along the Wisła – it is more than justified. Miraculously surviving the recurrent wars afflicting the region, the historic centre is one of the country's most evocative, bringing together a rich assembly of architectural styles. The principal stations are on opposite sides of the Old Town. Toruń Główny, the main **train station**, is south of the river; buses #22 and #27 run to pl Rapackiego, on the western edge of the Old Town. Make sure that you exit the station beyond platform 4 and not by the main hall, where only taxis wait. The two stops to the centre cover quite a distance so it's best to take the bus (every 10min) rather than walk. Buy *bilety* (tickets, 1.15zł) from the kiosk beside the bus stop. From the **bus station** on ul Dabrowskiego it is a short walk south to the centre.

The westerly Old Town area is the most obvious place to start looking around – and as usual it's the mansion-lined **Rynek**, in particular the **Town Hall**, that provides the focal point. Raised in the late fourteenth century on the site of earlier cloth halls and trading stalls, this immensely elegant work is one of the finest Gothic buildings in northern Europe. The **Town Museum** (Tues–Sun 10am–6pm; 3zł), which now occupies much of the building, has a gorgeous collection of the stained glass for which the city was famed and some fine sculptures including the celebrated "Beautiful Madonnas". On the first floor, painting takes over, a small portrait of the most famous burgher, Copernicus, basking in the limelight of a Baroque gallery. The top floor houses an exhibition of modern art. Before leaving the town hall it's also worth climbing the **tower** for a view over the city and the winding course of the Wisła.

West of here, ul Kopernika and its dingy side streets are lined with crumbling Gothic mansions and granaries, evoking a blend of past glory and shabbier contemporary reality. Halfway down Kopernika at no. 15/17 you'll find the **Copernicus Museum** (Tues–Sun 10am–6pm; 3zł), installed in the high brick house where the great man was born and containing a studiously assembled collection of Copernicus artefacts and a half-hourly sound and light show of fifteenth-century Toruń. A planetarium next to the Copernicus University offers further evidence of the influence of the man who, as his statue in the main square says, "stopped the sun and moved the earth".

Following ul Przedzamcze north from the castle brings you onto ul Szeroka, the thoroughfare that links the Old and New Town districts. Although less grand than its mercantile neighbour, the **New Town** still boasts a number of illustrious commercial residences, most of them grouped around the **Rynek Nowomiejski**. The fourteenth-century **St James' Church**, located south of the market area of the Rynek, boasts the largest bell in Poland outside Kraków, the *Tuba Dei*. An unusual feature of this brick basilica is its flying buttresses – a common enough sight in western Europe but rare in Poland. To the north of the square, ul Prosta leads onto Wały Sikorskego, a ring road which more or less marks the line of the old fortifications. Across it there's a small park, in the middle of which stands the former arsenal, now an **Ethnographic Museum** (Mon, Wed & Fri 9am–4pm; Tues, Thurs, Sat & Sun 10am–6pm; 4zł, free Mon) dealing with the customs and crafts of northern Poland, including an outdoor display of wooden buildings. After seeing the sights of the town, you shouldn't miss the opportunity of taking a walk along the river between Toruń's two romantic bridges.

Practicalities

Tourist information is available in Staromejska, in the archway which forms the main western entrance to the Old Town (May–Sept Mon & Sat 9am–4pm, Tues–Fri 9am–6pm, Sun 9am–1pm). You can also book student hotels here. The most attractive budget **hotel** is the *Polonia*, pl Teatralny 5 (☎056/622-3028; ②); *Pod Orłem*, ul Mostowa 17 (☎056/622-6397; ②–④) also has some cheap rooms, but charges a ridiculous 30zł for breakfast – both are within easy walking distance of the Rynek. Orbis's *Hotel Kosmos* at ul Ks.J. Popiełuszki 2 (☎056/622-8900; ⑤) is bright, clean and well located, overlooking the river. The two **youth hostels** are both about 3km from the centre, at ul św Józefa 22/4 to the northwest (☎056/654-4107), and ul Chobrego (at róg Mleczne intersection) to the northeast (☎056/655-8236). The *Tramp* **campsite** at ul Kujawska 14 (☎056/654-7187) is a short walk west of the train station, with bungalows (②) as well as general camping facilities (①).

The town's hotels provide many of the decent places to **eat**, with the *Staropolski* restaurant at ul Żeglarska 10/14 offering a solid Polish menu in a medieval-style banqueting hall. There's a good cheap pizzeria, *Ristorante Italiano*, in vaulted surroundings at Szczytna 4. **Cafés** are in good supply, with terrace places on streets such as ul Szeroka providing an opportunity to pause and enjoy the atmosphere of the Old Town. In the New Town Square, *Pod Modrym Fartuchem* at Rynek Nowomiejski 8, is a good place for coffee and cakes. The best **bar** is the subterranean *Pod Aniołem*, nestling under the town hall near Copernicus' statue in the Rynek, whose speciality is the "Joanna May", a blend of vodka and apple juice. It often becomes a disco later in the evening, staying open till the early hours. In the summer you can sit out among ruins of the Old Town walls in ul Przedzamcze; there is a tremendous bar nestling in the battlements, *Pod Krzywà Wiezà* (Under the Leaning Tower), in the street of that name, open till midnight.

SOUTHERN POLAND

Southern Poland attracts more visitors than any other region in the country, and its attractions are clear enough from just a glance at the map. The **Tatra Mountains**, which form the border with Slovakia, are Poland's grandest and most beautiful, snowcapped for much of the year and markedly alpine in feel. **Kraków** ranks with Prague and Vienna as one of the architectural gems of central Europe, but its significance for Poles goes well beyond the aesthetic, for this was the country's ancient royal capital, and the Catholic Church has often looked to Kraków for guidance – Pope John Paul II was Archbishop of Kraków until his election in 1978. Equally important are Kraków's **Jewish roots**: until World War II, this was one of the great Jewish centres in Europe, a past whose fabric remains clear in the old ghetto area of Kazimierz, and whose culmination is starkly enshrined at the death camps of **Auschwitz-Birkenau**, west of the city. To the north, the major attraction is the pilgrim centre of **Częstochowa**, home of the Black Madonna, the country's principal religious symbol.

Kraków

KRAKÓW was the only major city in the country to come through World War II essentially undamaged, and its assembly of monuments has now been listed by UNESCO as one of the world's twelve most significant historic sites. All the more ironic, then, that the government has had to add a further tag: that of official "ecological disaster area". The communist regime, wishing to break the hold of the university's Catholic, conservative intelligentsia, decided to graft a new working class onto the city by developing on the outskirts one of the largest steel-

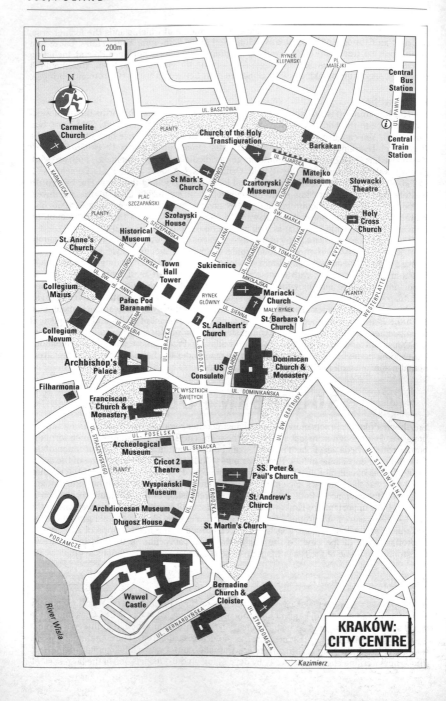

0   200m

N

Carmelite Church

UL. BASZTOWA

PLANTY

RYNEK KLEPARSKI

PL. MATEJKI

Central Bus Station

UL. PAWIA

Central Train Station

Church of the Holy Transfiguration

Barkakan

UL. PIJARSKA

St Mark's Church

UL. SŁAWKOWSKA

Czartoryski Museum

UL. FLORIAŃSKA

Matejko Museum

Słowacki Theatre

PLAC SZCZAPAŃSKI

SW. MARKA

Holy Cross Church

PLANTY

UL. SZCZEPAŃSKA

Szołayski House

UL. SW. JANA

SW. TOMASZA

St. Anne's Church

Historical Museum

UL. SZEWSKA

SW. KVYZA

UL. JAGIELLOŃSKA

Town Hall Tower

Sukiennice

UL. FLORIAŃSKA

WESTERPLATTE

UL. SW. ANNY

MIKOŁAJSKA

Collegium Maius

Pałac Pod Baranami

RYNEK GŁÓWNY

UL. SIENNA

Mariacki Church

PLANTY

MAŁY RYNEK

St. Barbara's Church

UL. WIŚLNA

Collegium Novum

UL. GOŁĘBIA

St. Adalbert's Church

UL. BRACKA

UL. GRODZKA

Archbishop's Palace

US Consulate

UL. SŁAWKOWSKA

Dominican Church & Monastery

Filharmonia

PL WSZYSTKICH ŚWIĘTYCH

UL. DOMINIKAŃSKA

UL. SW. GERTRUDY

UL. STAROWIŚLNA

Franciscan Church & Monastery

UL. POSELSKA

UL. STRASZEWSKIEGO

Archeological Museum

UL. SENACKA

Cricot 2 Theatre

PLANTY

Wyspiański Museum

UL. KANONICZA

UL. GRODZKA

SS. Peter & Paul's Church

Archdiocesan Museum

St. Andrew's Church

Długosz House

St. Martin's Church

PODZAMCZE

River Wisła

Wawel Castle

Bernadine Church & Cloister

UL. BERNARDYŃSKA

UL. STRADOMSKA

KRAKÓW: CITY CENTRE

▽ *Kazimierz*

works in Europe, **Nowa Huta**. Consequently Kraków is faced with intractable economic and environmental problems: how to deal with the acid rain of the steelworks, how to renovate the monuments and how to retain jobs.

Arrival and information

Kraków Główny, the central **train station**, is within walking distance of the city's historic centre; Dworzec PKS, the main **bus station**, is opposite. Kraków is bisected by the **River Wisła**, though virtually everything of interest is concentrated on the north bank; the central area is compact enough to get around on foot – indeed parts are car-free. At the heart of things, enclosed by the **Planty** – a green belt following the course of the old ramparts – is the **Stare Miasto**, the Old Town, with its great central square, the **Rynek Główny**. Just south of the Stare Miasto, looming above the river bank, is **Wawel**, the royal castle hill, beyond which lies the old Jewish quarter of **Kazimierz**.

The main **tourist office** is just down from the station at ul Pawia 8 (Mon–Fri 8am–6pm, Sat 9am–1pm; ☎012/422-6091), offering maps and brochures. Dexter, a private tourist office on the Sukiennice in the Cloth Market (Mon–Fri 8am–6pm, Sat 8.30am–1pm; ☎012/421-7706) is excellent and also makes hotel reservations. Good English and German is spoken in both places. As usual, Orbis have information points in their hotels as well as a central office at Rynek Główny 41 (Mon–Fri 8am–6pm, Sat 8am–1pm; ☎012/422-4035). Just off the main square at ul św Jana 2 is the Centrum Informacji Kulturalnej (Cultural Information Centre; Mon–Fri 10am–7pm, Sat 11am–7pm; ☎012/421-7787), which has listings of cultural events in a special booklet called a *Karnet*, and can advise on how to obtain tickets for these events. Finally, for more local **listings**, *Miesiàc w Krakowie* (This Month in Kraków), available from bookshops and newsagents, is partly in English.

Accommodation

Kraków is turning into one of Europe's prime city destinations – so you should book hotels ahead in summer. If you can't do that, be prepared to try your luck with a **private room**, which run at around 40–50zł for a double, but may well be some way out from the centre; they can be booked at the office at ul Pawia 8 (Mon–Fri 8am–6pm, Sat 9am–1pm; ☎012/422-6091), which also deals with **student hotels**, available from late June to late September when the students are away. For **hotel reservations**, the Dexter office in the Cloth Market is your best bet (☎012/421-7706), since they can obtain discounts. The most popular **campsite**, *Krak Camping*, ul Radzikowskiego 99 (☎012/637-2122), is located in the northwest of the city; get there by buses #173 and #238, or trams #4, #12, #44.

HOSTELS

Express, Ul Wrocławska 91 (☎012/633-8862). Near the centre and the best of the three hostel options. Take tram #3. This is a tourist hostel rather than a youth hostel but is almost as cheap. ②.

Ul Kościuszki 88 (☎012/422-1951). A smaller place, housed in a former convent overlooking the river (trams #1, #2, #6, #21; bus #100). The nicest of the youth hostels but it tends to get booked up early by groups. ①.

Ul Oleandry 4 (☎012/633-8822). The main youth hostel is a huge concrete construction but still manages to get full up in summer. Noisy and with an early curfew, it's definitely a last resort. ①.

HOTELS

Europejski, ul Lubicz 5 (☎012/423-2529). A stone's throw from the train station. ⑤.

Monopol, św Gertrudy 6 (☎012/422-7015). Moderate prices – a good bet. ④

Pollera, ul Szpitalna 30 (☎012/422-1044). Completely revamped under the new management, this place is in a calm, central spot. ⑤.

Polski, ul Pijarska 17 (☎012/422-1144). Very central but a bit expensive. ⑥.

Saski, ul Sławkowska 3 (☎012/421-4222). Central location, great ambience and a wonderful antique lift. ⑤.

Warszawski, ul Pawia 6 (☎012/422-0622). Good location near the train station, but noisy. No private bathrooms. ④.

Wawel Tourist, ul Poselska 22 (☎012/422-0439). Excellent location. Spartan but comfortable, with good rates for groups of up to four sharing a room. ③–④.

The City

The **Rynek Główny** – the core of the Stare Miasto – was the largest square of medieval Europe: a huge expanse of flagstones, ringed by magnificent houses and towering spires. The dominant building on the square is the **Sukiennice**, rebuilt in the Renaissance and one of the most distinctive sights in the country: a vast cloth hall, topped by a sixteenth-century attic dripping with gargoyles. Its commercial traditions are perpetuated by a covered market, which bustles with tourists and street sellers at almost any time of year. The terrace cafés on either side of the hall are classic Kraków haunts, where locals idle away the afternoon over tea and *sernik*. The **Art Gallery** on the upper floor of the Sukiennice (Tues, Wed & Fri–Sun 10am–3.30pm, Thurs noon–6pm; 5zł, free Sun; entrance in the side of the Sukiennice opposite St Mary's Church) is worth a visit for its collection of works by nineteenth-century Polish artists.

To its south is the copper-domed **St Adalbert's** (św Wojchiecha), the oldest building in the square and the first church to be founded in Kraków. The tall **tower** nearby is all that remains of the fourteenth-century town hall; it's worth the climb for an excellent overview of the city. On the east side is one of the finest Gothic structures in the country, the **Mariacki Church** (St Mary's), the taller of its towers topped by an amazing ensemble of spires, elaborated with a crown and helmet. Legend has it that during one of the Tartar raids, the watchman at the top of the tower saw the invaders approaching and took up his trumpet to raise the alarm; his warning was cut short by an arrow through the throat. Every hour on the hour a lone trumpeter plays the sombre *hejnał* melody, halting abruptly at the precise point the watchman was supposed to have been hit. Walking down the nave, you'll have to pick your way past devotees kneeling in front of the fifteenth-century Chapel of Our Lady of Częstochowa, with its copy of the venerated image of the Black Madonna. Focal point of the nave is the huge stone crucifix attributed to Veit Stoss, creator of the majestic high altar at the far east end. Carved between 1477 and 1489, this huge limewood polyptych is one of the finest examples of late Gothic art. The outer sides of the folded polyptych feature reliefs of scenes from the lives of the Holy Family; at noon (Sundays and saints' days excluded) the altar is opened to reveal the inner panel of the *Dormition of the Virgin*, an amazing tableau of life-size figures.

NORTH OF THE RYNEK

Of the three streets leading north off the Rynek, **ul Floriańska** is the busiest and most striking, with fragments of medieval and Renaissance architecture among the myriad shops, cafés and restaurants. **Floriańska Gate**, at the end of the street, marks the edge of the Old Town proper. A square, robust fourteenth-century structure, it's part of a small section of fortifications saved when the old defensive walls were pulled down in the early nineteenth century. The strongest-looking defensive remnant is the **Barbakan**, just beyond Floriańska Gate. A bulbous, spiky fort, added in 1498, it's unusual in being based on Arab defensive architecture, but is currently inaccessible behind ongoing renovation works.

Back through Floriańska Gate, a right turn down the narrow ul Pijarska brings you to the corner of ul św Jana and back down to the main square. On the way, on the left, is the **Czartoryski Palace**, housing Kraków's finest art collection (Tues–Thurs, Sat & Sun 10am–3.30pm, Fri 10am–6pm; 5zł, free Sun). The ancient art section alone contains over a thousand exhibits, from sites in Mesopotamia, Etruria, Greece and Egypt. Another intriguing highlight is the collection of trophies from the Battle of Vienna (1683), which includes sumptuous Turkish carpets, scimitars and other Oriental finery. The picture galleries offer a rich display of art and sculpture ranging from thirteenth- to eighteenth-century works, the most famous being Rembrandt's brooding *Landscape Before a Storm* and Leonardo da Vinci's *Lady with an Ermine*.

THE UNIVERSITY DISTRICT

Head west from the Rynek on any of the three main thoroughfares – ul Szczepańska, ul Szewska or ul św Anny – and you're into the **university area**, whose heart is the Gothic **Collegium Maius** building, at the intersection of ul św Anny with ul Jagiellońska. Through the passageway from the street, you find yourself in a quiet, arcaded **courtyard** with a mar-ble fountain playing in the centre: an ensemble that, during the early 1960s, was stripped of neo-Gothic accretions and restored to something approaching its original form. Now the **University Museum**, the Collegium is open to **guided tours** only (Mon–Fri 11am–2.30pm, Sat 11am–1.30pm; 5zł), for which you need to book places at least a day in advance at ul Jagiellońska 15 (☎012/422-0549). Inside, the ground-floor rooms retain the mathematical and geographical murals once used for teaching; the Alchemy Room, with its skulls and other wizards' accoutrements, was used according to legend by the fabled magician Doctor Faustus. Stairs up from the courtyard bring you to a set of elaborately decorated reception rooms and the Treasury, where the most valued possession is the Jagiellonian globe, con-structed around 1510, and featuring the earliest-known illustration of America.

WAWEL HILL

The traditional route used by Polish monarchs when entering the city took them through the Floriańska Gate, down ul Floriańska to the Rynek, then southwards down ul Grodzka to **Wawel Hill**, where for over five hundred years the country's rulers lived and governed.

The first **Cathedral** (Mon–Sat 9am–3pm Oct–April 9am–5pm May–Sept, Sun/public holi-days 12.15–3pm Oct–April, 5pm May–Sept) was built here around the time King Bolesław the Brave established the Kraków bishopric in 1020, but the present brick-and-sandstone basili-ca is essentially Gothic. All bar four of Poland's forty-five monarchs are buried in the cathe-dral, and their tombs and side chapels are like a directory of the central European architec-ture, art and sculpture of the last six centuries. Beginning from the right of the entrance, the Gothic Holy Cross Chapel (Kaplica Świętokrzyska) is the burial chamber of King Kazimierz IV Jagiełło (1447–92). Third chapel after this is the Baroque mausoleum of the seventeenth-century Waza dynasty, followed by the high spot of the whole cathedral, the opulent Zygmuntowska chapel, whose gilded cupola dominates the courtyard outside. The tomb of King Władysław the Short (1306–33), on the left-hand side of the altar, is the oldest in the cathedral, completed soon after his death; the coronation-robed figure lies on a white sand-stone tomb edged with expressive mourning figures.

An ascent of the **Zygmuntowska Tower** (May–Sept Mon–Sat 9am–5pm, Sun 12.15–5pm; Oct–April Mon–Sat 9am–3pm, Sun 12.15–3pm; 6zł) from the sacristy gives a far-reaching panorama over the city and close-up views of the five medieval bells. The largest, known as Zygmunt, is famed for its deep, sonorous tone, which local legends claim scatters rain clouds and brings out the sun.

The buildings on Wawel Hill are in the midst of a long-term renovation programme; although not too intrusive inside the cathedral, work in the **castle** (Tues & Fri 9.30am–4.30pm, Wed & Thurs 9.30am–3.30pm, Sat 9.30am–3pm, Sun 10am–3pm) is more extensive and the ongoing renovation means that some areas may not be open. The **Royal Treasury and Armoury** (Tues & Fri 9.30am–4.30pm, Wed & Thurs 9.30am–3.30pm, Sat 9.30am–3pm, Sun 10am–3pm; 10zł) is in the northeast corner of the castle (entrance on the ground floor). Much of the treasury's contents had been sold by the time of the Partitions to pay off marriage dowries and debts of state. The vaulted Gothic **Kazimierz Room** contains the finest items from a haphazard display of lesser royal possessions including the burial crown of Zygmunt August, while the prize exhibit in the next-door **Jadwiga and Jagiełło Room** is the solemnly displayed *Szczerbiec*, the thirteenth-century weapon used for centuries in the coronation of Polish monarchs. The **Lost Wawel** exhibition (daily 10am–3pm, closed Tues; 5zł), beneath the old kitchens south of the cathedral, takes you past the excavated remains of the hill's most ancient buildings, including the foundations of the tenth-century **Rotunda of SS Felix and Adauctus**, the oldest-known church in Poland. Return to ground level via the **Dragon's Den** (daily 10am–5pm), a spiral staircase leading to a rocky cavern which is perfect for cooling off in the heat of summer.

KAZIMIERZ

South from Wawel Hill lies the **Kazimierz** district, which in 1495 became the city's Jewish quarter. In tandem with Warsaw, where a **ghetto** was created around the same time,

Kazimierz grew to become one of the main cultural centres of Polish Jewry, but in March 1941 the entire Jewish population of the city was crammed into a tiny ghetto over the river. After waves of deportations to the concentration camps, the ghetto was finally liquidated in March 1943, thus ending seven centuries of Jewish life in Kraków.

The tiny **Remu'h Synagogue** at ul Szeroka 40 (Mon–Fri 9am–4pm; ☎012/422-1274; 5zł), is one of two still functioning in the quarter. Built in 1557 on the site of an earlier wooden synagogue, it was ransacked by the Nazis – tombstones torn up by them have been collaged together to form a high, powerful Wailing Wall just inside the entrance. The grandest of all the Kazimierz synagogues was the **Old Synagogue** on ul Szeroka, completed in 1557 and thus the oldest surviving Jewish religious building in Poland. Since the war it's been carefully restored and turned into a **museum** of the history and culture of Kraków Jewry including a permanent exhibition of traditional art by Polish Jews (Wed, Thurs, Sat & Sun 9am–3.30pm, Fri 11am–6pm; closed first Sat and Sun of the month; 5zł). The museum provides an excellent English-language introduction to the basic beliefs and rituals of Judaism. Another excellent place to visit is the newly-refurbished **Synagoga Izaaka** (Isaac Synagogue) at ul Kupa 18, which has an exhibition of photographs and short silent films illustrating the life of Kazimierz Jews before the war and after the formation of the Jewish ghetto (Mon–Fri 10am–5pm; 5zł).

As the presence of several churches indicates, the western part of Kazimierz was where non-Jews tended to live. Despite its Baroque overlay, the interior of the Gothic **Corpus Christi** church, on the corner of ul Bożego Ciała, retains early features including stained-glass windows installed around 1420. The church looks onto **plac Wolnica**, where the rebuilt town hall now houses the largest **Ethnographic Museum** in the country (Mon 10am–6pm, Wed–Fri 10am–3pm, Sat & Sun 10am–2pm; 3zł, free Sun). The collection focuses on Polish folk traditions, although there's also a selection of artefacts from Siberia, Africa, Latin America and various Slav countries.

Eating and drinking

The *cukiernia* dotted around the city centre provide delicious cakes to most Kraków cafés, and Kraków's tourist status has resulted in one of the best selections of **bars**, **cafés** and **restaurants** in Europe.

CAFÉS, MILK BARS AND SNACKS

Ariel Kawlavnia Artystyczna, ul Szeroka 17. Art café/restaurant in the Jewish quarter with live music. At no. 2 nearby (Noah's Ark) there is also a bookshop, a restaurant and more live music. Both open till 1am.

Chatya Puchatka, pl Mariacki 2. Popular source of crepes during the day. Open 9.30am–8pm.

Chimera, ul św Anny 3 off the main square. A wonderful (largely vegetarian) snack bar-cum-restaurant offering cheap, filling meals in a superb atmosphere. Open 9am–10pm.

Jama Michalika, ul Floriańska 45. Historic artistic café, redolent of old-world *Mitteleuropa*. Open 9am–10pm.

Mata Scena Café-Bar, ul Staszkowska 14. Black-ash Deco in old cellars. Theatre bar open at odd times.

Pasieka, Mały Rynek. A nice place to sit out and enjoy the atmosphere of this attractive square.

Redolfi, Rynek Główny 38 (north side). Splendid Art Nouveau decor, and better than usual coffee.

Różowy Słoń (Pink Elephant), ul Straszewskiego 24, ul Szpitalna 38 and ul Sienna 1. A chain of surrealist café/salad bars, the walls splayed with cartoons. Good for cheap fill-ups. Open till 9pm.

Pożegnanie z Afryką (Out of Africa), ul św Tomasza 21. Open 10am–10pm. Excellent coffee.

RESTAURANTS

Balaton, ul Grodzka 37 (☎012/422-0469). Excellent, very busy Hungarian restaurant. Open 9am–10pm.

Bar Wegetaviański "Vega", ul św Gertrudy 7, next to *Hotel Monopol*. Vegetarian alternative to *Chimera*. Open 10am–9pm.

Cechowa, ul Jagiellońska 11. Handy if you're in the university area, with excellent pancakes and a fast lunchtime service. Open 11am–10pm.

Hawełka, Rynek Główny 34. Popular, central haunt serving *śliwki zawijane w boczku* (plums rolled in bacon) and fortified *młody pitne* wines.

Staropolska, ul Sienna 2 (☎012/422-5821). Deservedly popular Old Town venue with an emphasis on traditional pork and poultry dishes. Booking essential in the evening. Open 11am–11pm.

Wierzynek, Rynek Główny 15 (☎012/422-1035). This stately place is Kraków's most famous restaurant, with specialities like pheasant and lobster, plus vegetarian dishes. For Westerners, prices remain reasonable at around £20/$32 a head. Booking is essential. Open noon–11pm.

BARS

There are always cafés, bars, live music and a lively atmosphere in ul Szeroka, the Kazimierz part of town. A couple of other options are given below.

Pub w Teatrze Buchleina. Open till 4am next to the *Europejski Hotel*. A theatre bar with good atmosphere and vodka.

Pod instytukem, ul Grodzka 49. Cellar-bar beneath the Italian Institute with a dancing area.

Surrestaurant Szuflada, ul Wiślna 5. Bar with food and Surrealist decor – try the table with the zebra. Open noon–1am.

Entertainment

For cultural events consult the English-language *Cracow etc*, or *Miesiàc w Krakówie* (*This Month in Kraków*), which has some English and is clearly laid out. The **Centrun Informacji Kulturalnej** (Central Information Centre), ul św Jana 2 (Mon–Fri 10am–7pm, Sat 11am–7pm; ☎012/421-7787), publishes a useful listings guide (*Karnet*) to cultural events in the city and a helpful *Kraków 2000* guide to cultural events. For **rock** or vaguely alternative events, check posters in the university district. *Pod Jaszczurami* (Under the Lizards), Rynek Główny 7/8, is a **jazz** club with weekend **discos**. There's also live jazz at *U Muniaka* in ul Floriańska 3 (Thurs–Sat). For late-night revelling try *Pub w Teatrze Buchleina* near the *Europejski Hotel*, or, for dancing, *Piwnica pod Ogródkiem* at ul Jagelliońska 6, with a beer garden upstairs and a disco downstairs. Both are open till the early hours.

Listings

Airlines LOT, ul Szpitalna 32 (Mon–Fri 8am–6pm, Sat 9am–2pm; ☎012/422-4215); Swissair, ul Szpitalna 36 (Mon–Fri 8.30am–5.30pm; ☎012/429-1877).

Car rental Europcar, ul Krowaderska 58 (☎012/633-7773); Hertz, *Hotel Cracovia*, al F. Focha 1 (Mon–Sat 8am–6pm; ☎012/637-1120).

Consulates UK ul św Anny 9 (☎012/421-7030); USA, ul Stolarska 9 (☎012/422-1400).

Pharmacies All pharmacies have a list in their window of those currently open 24 hours in the neighbourhood. The Polish word for pharmacy is *Apteka*. If you need medical assistance there is an English-speaking dentist at ul Szkolna 19 (☎012/812-5424) and an English-speaking doctor at ul Niepodległości 2 (☎012/853-7760).

Post office Main office is at ul Wielopole 2 (Mon–Fri 7.30am–8.30pm, Sat 8am–2pm, Sun 9–11am), with 24hr phone services; the one right opposite the station (Mon–Fri 7am–8pm) is also handy.

Taxis Ring ☎919 for English speakers. They are more reliable than cabs hired from the street.

Train tickets Available from the Orbis office at Rynek Główny 41 and the train station.

Oświęcim: Auschwitz-Birkenau

In 1940, **OŚWIĘCIM**, an insignificant town 70km west of Kraków, became the site of the Oświęcim-Brzeżinka concentration camp, better known by its German name of **Auschwitz-Birkenau**. Of the many camps built by the Nazis in Poland and the other occupied countries during World War II, this was the largest and most horrific: something approaching two million people, 85–90 percent of them Jews, died here. If you want all the specifics on the camp, you can pick up a detailed guidebook or join a guided group, often led by former inmates. Children under thirteen are not admitted.

To get to Auschwitz-Birkenau from Kraków, you can take either of the regular bus or train services to Oświęcim station. From there it's a short bus ride to the gates of Auschwitz; there's no bus service to Birkenau, but taxis are available or else it's a 3km walk.

Most of the Auschwitz camp buildings have been preserved as the **Museum of Martyrdom** (daily 8am–3/7pm; ☎033/432-022). The cinema is a sobering starting point: the film was taken by the Soviet troops who liberated the camp in May 1945 – harrowing images of the survivors and the dead confirming what really happened. The bulk of the camp consists of the prison cell blocks, the first section dedicated to "exhibits" found in the camp after liberation. Despite last-minute destruction of many of the storehouses used for the possessions of murdered inmates, there are rooms full of clothes and suitcases, toothbrushes, dentures, glasses, shoes, and a huge mound of women's hair – 154,322 pounds of it. Many of the camp barracks are given over to national memorials, moving testimonies to the sufferings of inmates of the different countries – Poles, Russians, Czechs, Slovaks, Norwegians, Turks, French, Italians. The prison blocks terminate by the gas chambers and the ovens where the bodies were incinerated. The **Birkenau camp** (same hours) is much less visited than Auschwitz, though it was here that the majority of captives lived and died. Killing was the main goal of Birkenau, most of it carried out in the huge gas chambers at the back of the camp, damaged but not destroyed by the fleeing Nazis in 1945. Most of the victims arrived in closed trains – cattle cars mostly – to be driven directly into the gas chambers; railway line, ramp, sidings – they are all still there, just as the Nazis abandoned them.

Częstochowa

Seen from a distance, **Częstochowa**, 100km from Kraków, shows the country at its worst. Its steelworks and textile factories unleash a noxious cocktail of multicoloured fumes, while the city centre is ringed by jerry-built concrete estates. Yet all this is overshadowed by the city's status, courtesy of the monastery of **Jasna Góra** (Bright Mountain), as one of the world's greatest places of pilgrimage. Its **Icon of the Black Madonna** has drawn the faithful here over the past six centuries, and reproductions of it adorn almost every church in the country. On the major Marian festivals – May 3, August 15, August 26, September 8 and December 8 – up to a million pilgrims converge here.

The special position that Jasna Góra and its icon hold in the hearts and minds of the majority of Poles is due to the tenuous position Poland has held on the map of Europe. Each of Poland's non-Catholic enemies – the Swedes, the Russians and the Germans – has laid siege to Jasna Góra, yet failed to destroy it, so adding to the icon's reputation as the guarantor of Poland's very existence.

Częstochowa Główny, the smart, new **train station**, feeds you into a main road with trams. Turn right and after 100m you meet a dead-straight, three-kilometre-long boulevard, aleja Najświętszej Marii Panny (abbreviated as al NMP). This avenue cuts through the heart of Częstochowa, terminating at the foot of Jasna Góra. Inevitably, the **Chapel of the Blessed Virgin** is the focal point of the complex – its walls covered in lockets, jewels and other votive offerings, as well as a pile of crutches and leg braces discarded by the healed. Much of the time, the Black Madonna is invisible behind a screen, each raising and lowering of which is accompanied by a solemn fanfare. Unveiling ceremonies take place daily at 6am, 1pm and 9pm, but even when it's on view you don't get to see very much of the picture itself, as the figures are almost always decked out in jewelled crowns and robes, besides which there are always crowds of pilgrims or sightseers. According to tradition, the Black Madonna was painted by St Luke on a beam from the Holy Family's house in Nazareth, but tests have proved the icon cannot have been executed before the sixth century and is probably Italian in origin. At the southwestern end of the monastery is the **Arsenal** (daily 9am–5pm; voluntary donation), devoted to the military history of the complex. Alongside is the **600th Anniversary Museum** (same times), which tells the monastery's story. Exhibits include offerings from famous Poles, prominent among which is Lech Wałęsa's 1983 Nobel Peace Prize. Garish signs and bankomats in the walls somewhat diminish the religious aura.

A day-trip from Kraków will suffice for most people, but should you want to stay, the best deal for **hotels** are the *Miły* at ul Katedralna 18, by the train station (☎034/324-3391; ②), or *Hotel Ha-Ga* at ul Katedralna 9 (☎034/324-6173; parking facilities; ②). There are **cheap lodgings** just west of the monastery in the *Dom Pielgrzyma* or Pilgrim House (☎034/324-7011; ②), run by nuns, and with parking facilities, and a **campsite** with eighty bungalows for rent as well as general camping facilities can be found at ul Oleńki 10/30 (☎034/324-7495; ①–②).

Zakopane and the Tatras

Ask Poles to define their country's natural attractions and they often come up with the following simple definition: the Lakes, the Sea and the Mountains. "The Mountains" consist of an almost unbroken chain of ridges extending the whole length of the southern border, of which the most spectacular and most revered are the **Tatras** – or *Tatry* as they're known in Polish. Eighty kilometres long, with peaks rising to 2500m, the Polish Tatras are actually a relatively small part of the range, most of which rises across the border in Slovakia. As the estimated 1.5 million annual tourists show, however, the Polish section has enough to keep most people happy: high peaks for the dedicated mountaineers, excellent trails for hikers, cable cars and creature comforts for day-trippers, and ski slopes in winter.

The major resort on the fringes of the mountains is **ZAKOPANE**, a town which has succumbed wholeheartedly to tourism. It's easily reached by train or bus from Kraków, and both **stations** are a ten-minute walk east of the main street, **ul Krupówki**. A bustling pedestrian precinct, this is the focus of the town, given over to a jumble of restaurants, cafés and souvenir shops. Uphill, the street merges into ul Zamoyskiego, which runs on out of town past the fashionable *fin-de-siècle* wooden villas of the outskirts, while in the other direction it follows a rushing stream down towards Gulbałówka hill.

The best place to head for is the well-signposted **tourist information centre**, a sculptured wooden chalet at ul Kościuszki 17 (daily 8am–8pm; ☎018/201-2211). It has maps and English speakers, and can find you rooms but will not make reservations in advance. Orbis at ul Krupówki 22 (Mon–Fri 9am–5pm, Sat 9am–3pm) helps with hotels, train and bus bookings, flights and local trips, while the PTTK office (Mon–Fri 8am–4pm, Sat 8am–2pm; ☎018/201-2429), above the *Snake* disco at ul Krupówki 12 is your best source of information about the Tatra mountains (including, very importantly, precise information on the weather conditions). You can hire an English-speaking guide here for 240–340zł per person, depending on numbers and route, who will supervise challenging hikes involving chains for the steeper parts of the climb. Maps, guidebooks and details on mountain huts can also be obtained here.

For **accommodation** there's an all-year **youth hostel** at ul Nowotarska 45 (☎018/2066-203; ②), but the The *Dom Turysty* at ul Zaruskiego 5 (☎018/206-3281; ②) is a better option for a similar price, being central, attractive and cheap, with a safe car park. Mid-range, central hotels include *Gromada Gazda*, Zaruskiego 2 (☎018/20150-11; ④), and, for a little more but well worth it, the newly restored *Hotel Sabala* at ul Krupówki 11, with superb furnishing in wood (☎018/201-5093; ④–⑤). Central **pensjonat** include *Gladiola*, a somewhat decayed villa at ul Chramcówki 25 (☎018/20686-23; ②), while for splendid views of the Tatras it's worth the bracing walk to *Tatry*, ul Wierchowa 4 (☎018/20660-41; ③), and *Panorama*, ul Wierchowa 6 (☎018/20150-81; ③). The Orbis-run *Hotel Giewont* at ul T. Kościuszki I is expensive, friendly and efficient (☎018/20120-11; ⑤). *Pod Krokwià* **campsite** (☎018/20122-56, ②), located at the end of ul Żeromskiego on the east side of town, has bungalows on offer too, while there is a smaller campsite at ul Za Strugiem 39 (☎018/20145-66; ②), to the west.

If you want a fast **snack** there are plenty of cafés, milk bars, pizzerias and streetside *zapiekanki* merchants to choose from. **Restaurants** are plentiful too, with the *Hotel Sabala*, offering Mediterranean dishes, outside tables and indoor folk music, far outsripping the rest in quality and ambience. Some pleasant timber **pubs** are dotted around the base of the Tatras such as the *Kolibecka* at the top of ul Chałubuskiego on the way to the cable car at Kuźnice – you can even buy a sweater here if you've forgotten the effect of altitude on temperature. For late-night **entertainment** there's always the *Snake* disco at ul Krupówki 12.

The Tatras

Most of the peaks in the **Tatras** are in the 2000–2500m range, but the unimpressive statistics belie their status and their appearance. For these are real mountains, as beautiful as any mountain landscape in northern Europe, the ascents taking you on boulder-strewn paths alongside woods and streams up to the ridges, where grand, windswept peaks rise in the brilliant alpine sunshine. Wildlife thrives here: the whole area was turned into a National Park in the 1950s and supports rare species like lynx, golden eagles and brown bear – which you might even glimpse.

Most foreigners can cross the Slovakia–Poland border with just a passport stamp, and the new political climate means that exploration of the whole Tatra region is possible for the first time since the war. A decent map of the mountains is indispensable. The best is the *Tatrzański Park Narodowy* (1:30,000), which has all the paths accurately marked and colour-coded; the English version, "The Tatra National Park", marks not only hotels for overnight stays but also the distances of each section of pathway in red. The *Polskie Tatry* guidebook (in Polish) is likewise invaluable. **Staying** overnight in the eight PTTK-run huts dotted across the mountains is an experience in itself. **Food** is basic, but pricey for Poles, most of whom bring their own; the huts are an ideal place to meet people, preferably over a bottle of vodka. **Camping** isn't allowed in the National Park area; rock-climbing is, but only with a guide – ask at the PTTK for details. Check there for weather details too. If you run into difficulties, the number for mountain rescue is ☎018/206-3444.

The easiest way up to the peaks is by **cable car** from the hamlet of Kuźnice, a four-kilometre walk or bus journey south from Zakopane. The cable car ends near the summit of **Kasprowy Wierch** (1985m), where weather-beaten signs indicate the border. From here many day-trippers simply walk back down to Kuźnice through the Hala Gąsienicowa. A rather longer alternative is to strike west to the cross-topped summit of **Giewont** (1909m) and head down to Kuźnice; this is fairly easy-going and quite feasible in a day if you start out early.

East of Kasprowy Wierch, the walking gets tougher. From **Świnica** (2300m), a strenuous ninety-minute walk, experienced hikers continue along the **Orla Perć** (Eagles' Path), a challenging, exposed ridge with spectacular views. The *Pięc Stawów* (Five Lakes) **hostel** (②), in the high valley of the same name, provides overnight shelter at the end. From the hostel you can hike back down Dolina Roztoki to **Łysa Polana**, a border crossing point in the valley, and take a bus back to Zakopane. An alternative is to continue a short distance east to the **Morskie Oko Lake** (1399m). Encircled by spectacular sheer cliff faces and alpine forest, this large glacial lake is one of the Tatras' big attractions, most frequently approached on the winding forest road to Łysa Polana. Erosion problems mean that cars and buses now have to park here, the remaining distance being an eleven-kilometre walk. The lakeside *Morskie Oko* **hostel** provides a base for the ascent of **Rysy** (2499m), the highest peak in the Polish Tatras.

Zamość

The old towns and palaces of southeast Poland often have a Latin feel to them, and none more so than **ZAMOŚĆ**, 320km from Kraków. With its superb Renaissance centre, the town was the brainchild of the dynamic sixteenth-century chancellor Jan Zamoyski. Bernardo Morando of Padua, Zamoyski's architect, produced a planned town that was beautifully spacious and practical too: its defensive bastions protected Zamość through the seventeenth-century "Swedish Deluge" that flattened so many other Polish towns. The fortifications lasted until 1866, when the Russians ordered the liquidation of the fortress; parkland now covers much of the battlements. Somehow, the buildings of Zamość managed to get through World War II unscathed, although its people weren't spared: more than 8000 were executed by the Nazis, who also cleared out hundreds of neighbouring villages.

The **Rynek**, or plac Mickiewicza, is ringed by a low arcade and the decorative former homes of the Zamość mercantile bourgeoisie. The geometrically designed **square** is a wide-open space of columned arcades, decorated facades and breezy walkways, dominated from the north side by the **Town Hall**. From the town hall, the vaulted arcade stretching east along ul Ormiańska features several mansions which today house the **Town Museum** (Tues–Sun 9am–4pm; 5zł); the focus is inevitably on the Zamoyskis and family memorabilia. The southern side of the square contains some of the oldest mansions, several designed by Morando himself, including the **Morando Tenement House** at no. 25, where the architect used to live.

Moving **west** of the square, you'll see Morando's towering **Collegiate Church**, a powerful expression of the self-confidence of the Polish Counter-Reformation. West across the main road, ul Academicka, are two buildings that played a key role in the historic life of the town: the **Arsenal**, built by Morando in the 1580s, today houses a small **military museum** (Tues–Sun 10am–3.30pm; 3zł); the massive **Zamoyski Palace** is a shadow of its former self, the original Morando-designed building having undergone substantial modification after the Zamoyskis abandoned it in the early nineteenth century. It is now partly converted into a hotel.

Continuing north along ul Academicka, west of the main street is the **Old Lublin Gate**, oldest of the gates in the fortifications, now covered with neon and used as a "drink bar". If you walk in the parkland further west, you get a good view of the fortifications from the outside. Beyond the impressive-looking former **Zamoyski Academy**, across the street, much of the northern section of the Old Town belongs to the former **Jewish quarter**, centred on ul Zamenhofa and Rynek Solny. As in so many other eastern towns, Jews made up a significant portion of the population of Zamość – some 45 percent on the eve of World War II. The most impressive Jewish monument is the former **Synagogue**, now a public library, a fine early seventeenth-century structure built as part of Zamoyski's original town scheme.

Practicalities

As Zamość is off the main communication lines, there are limited public transport services, with only one overnight train (8hr) and one express bus (6hr) leaving a major city like Kraków every day. Zamość is most easily approached by bus from Lublin (itself more than worth a visit); trains take a very roundabout route. The main **bus station** is over to the east of the town centre – tickets for the 2km ride to the town centre can be purchased from the MZK counter inside the bus station. For details of departures, check at the **tourist office** at Rynek 13, underneath the town hall (Mon–Fri 9am–4pm; ☎084/639-2292). The nearby Orbis office at ul Grodzka 20 deals with advance bus and train tickets. It's worth asking at the tourist office about **private rooms**, especially in summer. For **hotel** accommodation it's a choice between the clean, friendly and newly refurbished *Renesans*, behind the tourist office on ul Grecka 6 (☎084/639-2001; ③), the central but basic *Hotel Marta*, ul Zamenhofa 11 (☎084/639-2639), and splashing out at the new Orbis hotel, the *Zamoyski*, at ul S. Kołłataja 2/4/6, (☎084/639-2886), which was formerly the Zamoyski Palace and Academy.

In the Old Town, the established *Staromiejska* **restaurant**, ul Pereca 12, provides the usual soup-and-pork-chop menu. The *Green Pub* at ul Staszica 2 is good for a cheap, straightforward all-day fill-up, while the café in the *Renesans* serves up standard breakfasts of eggs, cheese and coffee, as well as basic daytime fare. In summer the square is lined with **outdoor cafés** and ice cream stalls. The appropriately named *Café Padua*, Rynek 23, with a wonderful original ceiling, does a respectable coffee. The *Ratuszowa*, strategically placed under the town hall at no. 13 has a quiet ambience: as well as decent cappuccinos and cakes they do meals during the daytime. For **drinking** the *Piwnica Pod Arkadami*, Rynek 25, is a basement beer dive with pool tables, another beery option being the bar round the back of the *Renesans* hotel: both shut at 10pm. *Arkadia*, at no. 9, has a European menu and remains open till midnight. Vegetarians could do worse than the mozzarella and omelettes at *Club Tiffany*, Zamenhofa 10–12. If you want to carry on drinking, try the *Green Pub*, which has a disco at weekends, or the pub in ul Kr. Jadwigi off ul Academicka, clearly visible from the latter, looking like a red-brick ship ploughing through a sea of grass. Culturally the city is gradually on the up. The *Kosz Club*, ul Zamenhofa 3, has a selection of live jazz and blues at the weekends – go round the back to find it.

SILESIA AND WIELKOPOLSKA

In Poland it's known as *Śląsk*, in the Czech Republic as *Sleszko*, in Germany as *Schlesien*: all three countries hold part of the frequently disputed province that's called **Silesia** in English. Since 1945, Poland has held all of it except for a few of the westernmost tracts, a dominance gained as compensation for the Eastern Territories, which were incorporated into the USSR in 1939 as a result of the Nazi–Soviet pact, and never returned. Yet, although postwar Silesia has developed a strongly Polish character, people with family roots in the province are often bilingual and consider their prime loyalty to lie with Silesia rather than Poland. Heavy industry has blighted much of the region, especially in the huge **Katowice** conurbation, the largest unmodernized "black country" left in Europe. Similar problems, albeit on a smaller scale, also affect the province's chief city, **Wrocław**, holding back its potential to become a rival to Kraków, Prague and Budapest as one of central Europe's most enticing cosmopolitan centres. North of Silesia, the region known as **Wielkopolska** formed the core of the original Polish nation, and its chief interest is supplied by the regional capital of **Poznań** – famed within Poland for the 1956 riots that marked the first major revolt against communism.

Wrocław

The special nature of **WROCŁAW** comes from the fact that it contains the soul of two great cities. One of these is the city that has long stood on this spot, Slav by origin but for centuries dominated by Germans and generally known as **Breslau**. The other is Lwów (now L'viv), capital of the Polish Ukraine, which was annexed by the Soviets in 1939. After the war, its displaced population was encouraged to take over the severely depopulated Breslau, which had been confiscated from Germany. The multinational influences which shaped the city are reflected in its architecture: several huge Germanic brick Gothic churches dominate the skyline, intermingled with Flemish-style Renaissance mansions, palaces and chapels of Viennese Baroque, and boldly utilitarian public buildings from the early years of this century, as well as the inevitable concrete boxes filling the gaps left by wartime destruction. The tranquillity of the parks, gardens and riverside walks offer an escape from the urban bustle.

The City

Wrocław's central area is delineated by the River Odra to the north and by the bow-shaped ul Podwale – the latter following the former defensive moat, whose ditch, now bordered by a shady park, still largely survives. At the centre of town is the vast space of the **Rynek**, given over mainly to museums, restaurants, cafés, travel agencies and bookshops. The magnificent **Town Hall** dates largely to the fifteenth century. The famous **west face** and the **south facade** are the real show stoppers, the latter with huge windows, filigree friezes of animals and foliage, and rich statuary. The town hall now serves as the **Historical Museum** (Wed–Fri 10am–4pm, Sat 12noon–6pm, Sun 10am–6pm; 8zł), although it's the largely unaltered interior which constitutes the main attraction: in the resplendent three-aisled Knights' Hall, the keystones of the vault feature character studies of all strata of society.

Of the mansions lining the main sides of the Rynek, those on the south and western sides are the most distinguished and colourful. At no. 6 is the House of the Golden Sun (Pod Złotym Słońcem), home of the **Museum of the Art of Medal Making** (Tues–Sun 10am–5pm; 3zł, free Sun); its shop sells examples of the craft, which must be the classiest souvenirs in town. Just off the northwest corner of the Rynek are two curious Baroque houses known as **Jaś i Małgosia**, linked by a gateway giving access to the close of **St Elizabeth**, the most impressive of Wrocław's churches. Since the mid-fifteenth century, its huge ninety-metre **tower**, which was under construction for 150 years, has been the city's most prominent landmark.

Southwest of the Rynek lies the maze-like former **Jewish quarter**, whose inhabitants fled or were driven from their tenements during the Third Reich. Immediately to the east of the Jewish quarter is a part of the city built in obvious imitation of the chilly classical grandeur of Berlin. Indeed, Carl Gotthard Langhans, designer of the Brandenburg Gate, had a hand in the monumental Royal Palace now housing the **Archeology Museum** (Wed & Fri–Sun 10am–4pm, Thurs 9am–4pm; 4zł, free Sat), a dry survey of the prehistory of the region. Rather more fun is the **Ethnographical Museum** (Tues–Wed & Fri–Sun 10am–4pm, Thurs 9am–4pm; 4zł, free Sat) in the southern wing, a good place to visit if you have kids in tow. Its main draw is a large collection of dolls decked out in what are deemed to be traditional dresses from all around the world. The lofty Gothic brick church of **St Dorothy** stayed in Catholic hands at the Reformation, and its whitewashed interior, littered with gigantic Baroque altars, forms an ornate contrast with other Wrocław churches, which still bear the hallmarks of four centuries of Protestant sobriety. One of the largest synagogues in Poland, the Synagoga pod Białym Bocianem, lies half-hidden through an archway at ul Włodkowica 9. It is at last being refurbished and reopened through combined Polish and German financing, and may be ready by the end of 1999.

Further east, at the northern end of pl Dominikański, are the buildings of the **Dominican monastery**, centred on the thirteenth-century church of St Adalbert (św Wojciecha), which is embellished with fine brickwork and several lavish Gothic and Baroque chapels. A couple of blocks east stands the gargantuan former **Bernardine Monastery**; severely damaged during the war, the church and cloisters have been painstakingly reconstructed to house the **Museum of Architecture** (Tues, Thurs & Fri 10am–3.30pm, Wed & Sat 10am–4pm, Sun 10am–5pm; 2zł, free Wed), a fascinating record of the many historic buildings in the city which were destroyed in the war.

Wrocław's best-loved sight, the **Panorama of the Battle of Racławice** (Tues–Sun: May–Sept 9am–6pm; Oct–April 10am–3.30pm; 15zł), is housed in a specially designed concrete rotunda in the shape of a crown in the park nearby. This painting, 120m long and 15m high, was commissioned in 1894 to celebrate the centenary of the Russian army's defeat by the people's militia of Tadeusz Kościuszko near the village of Racławice, between Kraków and Kielce. Not only is it Poland's most hi-tech tourist attraction, it's also one of the most popular, an icon second only in national affection to the Black Madonna. It is very popular so it is advisable to book in advance (you can book up to a week ahead) although you may have no trouble walking into the next show (every thirty minutes during opening times): make sure you ask to hear the **English-language cassette**, which explains all the details of the painting.

At the opposite end of the park is the ponderously Prussian neo-Renaissance home of the **National Museum** (Tues–Sun 10am–4pm, Thurs 9am–4pm; 6zł), which unites the collections of Breslau and Lwów. One of the most important sections, **medieval stone sculpture**, is housed in the hall around the café. Here you can see the delicately linear carving of *The Dormition of the Virgin* from the portal of St Mary Magdalene. The other major highlight is the poignant early fourteenth-century *Tomb of Henryk the Righteous*, with its group of weeping mourners. On the first floor, the most eye-catching exhibits are the colossal statues of saints from St Mary Magdalene. The foreign paintings in the opposite wing include Cranach's *Eve*, originally part of a scene showing her temptation of Adam which was cut up and repainted as two portraits of a burgher couple in the seventeenth century.

North of the Rynek, the triangular-shaped university quarter, jam-packed with historic buildings, is bounded by two streets: ul Uniwersytecka to the south and ul Grodzka, which follows the Odra. Behind the fourteenth-century church of St Matthew spreads the colossal domed **Ossoliński Library**, built as a hospital at the end of the seventeenth century; one of the city's most impressive buildings, it has frequent exhibitions of items from its vast collection. However, the principal building of this district is the 171-metre-long **Collegium Maximum**, whose main assembly hall or **Aula Leopoldina**, upstairs at pl Uniwersytecki 1 (closed Wed 10am–3.30pm; 5.5zł), is one of the greatest secular interiors of the Baroque age, fusing architecture, painting, sculpture and ornament into one bravura whole.

From the Market Hall, the Piaskowski Bridge leads to the sandbank of **Wyspa Piasek** and the fourteenth-century hall church of **St Mary of the Sands** (Kościół NMP na Piasku), dull on the outside, majestically vaulted and surprisingly light inside. The two elegant little painted bridges of Most Młyński and Most Tumski, which look as though they should belong in an ornamental garden, connect Wyspa Piasek with **Ostrów Tumski**, the city's ecclesiastical heart. Sandbags randomly placed along the banks are a reminder of the 1997 floods which almost engulfed this area.

Ulica Katedralny leads past several Baroque palaces (among which priests, monks and nuns are constantly scuttling) and a wall mural featuring the papal arms marking the papal visit of 1997 to the twin-towered **Cathedral of St John the Baptist**. Three chapels behind the high altar make a visit to the dank and gloomy interior worthwhile (restoration work permitting): St Elizabeth's Chapel, created by followers of Bernini; the Gothic Lady Chapel, with the masterly Renaissance funerary plaque of Bishop Jan Roth; and the Corpus Christi Chapel, a perfectly proportioned and subtly decorated Baroque gem.

Practicalities

The main **train station**, Wrocław Głowny – its facade one of the city's sights, though its interior is seedy – faces the broad boulevard of ul Marsz Józefa Piłsudskiego, about fifteen minutes' walk south of the Rynek; the main **bus station** is at the back of the train station. The ODRA tourist office at ul Piłsudskiego 98 (Mon–Fri 8.30am–4.30pm, Sat 9am–2pm; ☎071/343-0037), on the ground floor of the *Hotel Piast* opposite the station, can arrange **private rooms** at around £10/$16/60zł per person per night. The **main tourist office** in the main square at Rynek 14 (Mon–Fri 9am–5pm, Sat 10am–2pm; ☎071/344-3111) is better for leaflets.

A cluster of rather basic **hotels** can be found near the main train station – nearest of all is the musty *Grand*, ul Piłsudskiego 100 (☎071/343-6071; ③). On the same street is *Piast* at no. 98 (☎071/343-0033; ③) and the more expensive but less dreary and decayed *Europejski* at no. 88 (☎071/343-1071; ④). Closer to the centre is the *Hotel Mirles*, a set of modernized two- and three-bed rooms on the top floor of ul Kazimierza Wielkiego 45 (☎071/344-4384 or 341-0873; ②), while the *Hotel Monopol* at ul H. Modrzejewskiej 2, opposite the opera house, offers faded grandeur at fair prices (☎071/343-7041; ⑤). The most convenient **youth hostel** is 100m from the train station at ul Hugova Kołłataja 20, off ul Piłsudskiego (10am–5pm; lockout and 10pm curfew; ☎071/343-8856; ①), while the better **campsite** is on the east side of town near the Olympic Stadium at al Ignacego Padarewskiego 35 (☎071/348-4651) – trams #9, #12, #17 and #32 run nearby. Information on **summer student hostels** (late June–Sept) is available at Almatur, ul Tadeusza Kościuszki 34 (Mon–Fri 10am–5pm, 6pm July; ☎071/343-4135). These provide a single room for about 60zł and shared rooms for less. Anyone can stay there, though student holders of ISIC cards receive discounts.

Wrocław has a good selection of places to **eat and drink**. The Rynek is bubbling over with outdoor **cafés and restaurants** during the summer, while indoors, the café at Rynek 5, above the *Dwór Polski* restaurant, has a real palm-court atmosphere. There is an excellent **vegetarian restaurant** next to the town hall in the main square called *Vega* (Mon–Fri 8am–7pm, Sat & Sun 9am–5pm). In the university area, try the surreal buildings at the end of ul Kuźnicza. At no. 29a there's a café with beautiful Jugendstil decor, *Pod Kalamburem*, while the tea shop next door offers mystical music and access to the Internet. *Zaczek* opposite at no. 43–45 serves solid canteen-like food till 8pm. The bizarre pub at no. 29b is a good place to rendezvous and sit outside on tiered benches till 10pm in summer, while the *Café Uni* tucked around the corner in pl Uniwersytecki is good in winter (till midnight). The third part of Wrocław to come alive at night is the square Tadeusza Kościuszki. Try *Café Tutti Frutti* at no. 1 which faces the inevitable *McDonald's*, but shuts at 10pm. Bogart fans should seek out the wonderful *Casablanca* café and restaurant at ul Włodkowica 8, which has excellent food and live music, plus a garden area. Dancing options include *Fabryka*, in the centre of the main square at Rynek-Ratusz 11/12, for a daily Eurobop, or *Klub Katakumby*, at ul Grunwaldkza 6 via trams #8, #9 or #17, for the latest sounds.

Poznań

Thanks to its position on the Paris–Berlin–Moscow rail line, and as the one place where all international trains stop between the German border and Warsaw, **POZNAŃ** is many visitors' first taste of Poland. In many ways it's the ideal introduction, as no other city is more closely identified with Polish nationhood. In the ninth century the Polonians founded a castle on an island in the River Warta, and in 968 Mieszko I made this one of the two main centres of his duchy and the seat of its first bishop. The settlement that developed here was given the name Ostrów Tumski (Cathedral Island), which it still retains. Nowadays it's a city of great diversity, its animated centre focused on one of Europe's most attractive squares, and with a dynamic business district to the west, whose trade fair is the most important in the country – it has a distinct influence on accommodation prices.

The City

For seven centuries the grandiose **Stary Rynek** has been the hub of life in Poznań, even if nowadays it has lost its position as the centre of political and economic power. The turreted

Town Hall now houses the **Museum of the History of Poznań** (Mon 9am–4pm, Tues & Fri 9am–3pm, Wed noon–6pm, Sun 10am–3pm; 4zł) though this is less didactic than it sounds; the main reason for entering is to see the building itself. The stunner is the Renaissance **Great Hall** on the first floor, its coffered vault bearing polychrome bas-reliefs which embody the exemplary civic duties and virtues through scenes from the lives of Samson, King David and Hercules. Many a medieval and Renaissance interior lurks behind the Baroque facades of the **gabled houses** lining the outer sides of the Stary Rynek. Particularly fine are those on the eastern side, where no. 45 is the **Museum of Musical Instruments** (Tues 10am–5pm, Wed & Fri–Sat 9am–5pm, Thurs 10am–4pm, Sun 11am–4pm; 3zł, free Fri), the only collection of its kind in Poland.

Just to the west of the Stary Rynek at the end of ul Zamkowa stands a hill with remnants of the inner circle of the medieval walls. This particular section guarded the **Castle**, which was the seat of the rulers of Wielkopolska. Modified down the centuries, it was almost completely destroyed in 1945 but has been partly restored to house the **Museum of Applied Art** (Tues, Wed, Fri & Sat 10am–4pm, Sun 10am–3pm; 3zł, free Fri). This features an enjoyable enough collection from medieval times to the present day, while the Gothic cellars are used for changing displays of individual contemporary artists.

From here it's only a short walk to the vast elongated space of **plac Wolności**, where the **National Museum**, at al Marcinkowskiego 9, houses one of the few important displays of old master paintings in Poland (Tues 10–6pm, Wed & Fri 9am–5pm, Thurs 10am–4pm, Sat 10am–5pm, Sun 11am–4pm; 4zł, free Fri). Dominating the gallery's small but choice Spanish section is the prize exhibit, Zurbarán's *Madonna of the Rosary*, while the extensive display of art from the Low Countries includes a regal *Adoration of the Magi* by Joos van Cleve.

To the south of the Stary Rynek is a complex of former Jesuit buildings, the finest Baroque architecture in the city. The **Parish Church** (Kościół Frany), completed just forty years before the expulsion of the Jesuits in 1773, boasts a magnificently sombre interior of fluted columns, gilded capitals, monumental sculptures, large altarpieces and rich stuccowork

East of the Stary Rynek, the Bolesława Chrobrego bridge crosses to the holy island of **Ostrów Tumski**, a world away in spirit, if not in distance, from the hustle of the city. Only a small portion of the island is built upon, and a few priests and monks comprise its entire population; after 5pm the island is a ghost town. The first building you see is the late Gothic **Psalteria**, characterized by its elaborate stepped gable. Immediately behind is an earlier brick structure, **St Mary's**, while behind that is the **Cathedral of St Peter and Paul**. Most of this cathedral, Poland's oldest, was restored to its Gothic shape after wartime devastation, but a lack of documentary evidence for the eastern chapels meant that their successors had to be retained, as were the Baroque spires and the three lanterns around the ambulatory, which give a vaguely eastern touch. Inside, the **crypt** has been excavated, uncovering foundations of the pre-Romanesque and Romanesque cathedrals which stood on the site, as well as parts of the sarcophagi of the early Polish monarchs, Prince Mieszko I and King Bolesław the Brave. Their current resting place is the luscious Golden Chapel behind the altar, representing the diverse if dubious tastes of the 1830s.

Practicalities

The main **train station**, Poznań Główny, is 2km southwest of the historic quarter; tram #5 runs from the western exit (Dworzec Zachodnia) beyond platform 5 to the city centre. The **bus station** is five minutes' walk to the east along ul Towarowa. The main **tourist information centre** is in the main square at Stary Rynek 59 (☎061/852-6156). The **Eurostop** office at Aleksandra Fredry 7 (Mon–Fri 9am–6pm, Sat 10am–1pm; ☎061/852-0344) incorporates **Almatur** and can therefore arrange accommodation in student hostels (vacated halls of residence) during the summer vacation (late June till mid-September). A monthly guide to what's on in the city containing an English abridgement and a useful map of the city – known as *iks* – is available from tourist information points.

Because of the trade fair, Poznań has plenty of **accommodation**, but hotel prices can double during fairs, which usually take place in June and September. Three **hotels** in the heart of the city are reasonable value: *Rzymski*, al Karola Marcinkowskiego 22, next to the tram stop

Marcinkowskiego (☎061/852-8121; ④–⑤); *Lech*, ul św Marcina 74 (☎061/853-0151; ③–④); and a good moderately priced option perfectly placed next to the main square, the *Dom Turysty Hotel* at Rynek 91 (☎061/852-8893; ③–④).The cheapest central option is the *Royal Hotel* at ul św Martin 71 (☎061/853-7884; ②–③); just follow the "Piccadilly Tube" signs to get there. There is a **youth hostel** 1.5km north of the bus and train stations, at ul Berwiniskiego 2/3 (☎061/866-3680; ①). For renting **private rooms**, the Biuro Zakwaterowania is very near the train station exit at ul Głogowska 16 (Mon–Fri 8am–6pm, Sat 10am–2pm; ☎061/866-5163). Even here, the cost rises from £6 to £10 per head during trade fairs. The nearest **campsite** is *Maltańska*, ul Krancowa (☎061/876-6011), set by a lake 2km east of the centre and reached by trams #6 and #8 (#8 runs from the train station).

In choosing somewhere to **eat and drink**, there are many possibilities in the main square. Two of the best **restaurants** are *Club Elite*, at no. 2, and the wonderfully atmospheric *Stara Ratuszowa* at Stary Rynek 55 (☎061/851-5318), which stays open until 1am. The most interesting food is at the restaurant/gallery/pub *Africana* at ul Zamkowa 3, just off the main square (☎061/853-0819). The mock-African decor may be a bit hard to take, but soup in hollowed-out bread bowls, whisky-soaked shrimps and "jungle juice" cocktails make a change from pork and sauerkraut.

For particularly good value, try one of the Italian **pizzerias** around or just off the main square, such as *Pizzeria di Trevi* at Wodna 7 (noon–11pm), or the salad bar, *Pod Koziołkami* (Under the Goats) at no. 95 of the main square (Stary Rynek). **Vegetarians** can enjoy good food at the *Bar Wegeterianski* at ul Wrocławska 21, off Stary Rynek (Mon–Fri 11am–6pm, Sat 11am–3pm). For coffee, cakes and ice cream try the garish splendours of *Arezzo* at Stary Rynek 49. Best late-night **entertainment** (including live music) can be found in the Irish pub *The Dubliner* in al Niepodległosci at the top of ul św Marcina, behind the grey university buildings, at no. 80–82. This university area is a good place to be in late at night if the heaving crowds around the main square get to be too much.

travel details

Trains

Warsaw to: Częstochowa (9 daily; 2hr 30min–3hr 30min); Gdańsk (14 daily; 3hr 30min–4hr 30min); Gdynia (14 daily; 3hr 30min–4hr 30min); Kraków (14 daily 2hr 30min–4hr 30min); Poznań (16 daily; 2hr 30min–3hr 30min); Toruń (3 daily; 3hr); Wrocław (9 daily; 4hr 30 min–5hr 30min); Zakopane (4 daily; 6–9hr); Zamość (5 daily; 5hr).

Częstochowa to: Kraków (7 daily; 2–4hr); Warsaw (12 daily; 2hr 30min–3hr 30min).

Gdańsk to: Częstochowa (3 daily; 6–8hr); Kraków (6 daily; 6–8hr); Poznań (5 daily; 4hr); Toruń (4 daily; 2hr 30min–3hr 30min); Warsaw (13 daily; 3hr 30min–4hr 30min); Wrocław (5 daily; 6–7hr); Zakopane (1 daily; 12hr).

Kraków to: Częstochowa (7 daily; 2hr); Gdynia (5 daily; 6hr 30 mins–8hr 30min); Poznań (8 daily; 5–7hr); Wrocław (14 daily; 4–5hr 30min); Zakopane (14 daily; 2hr 30min–4hr 30min).

Poznań to: Częstochowa (3 daily; 4hr 30min–6hr); Gdańsk (5 daily; 4hr); Kraków (6 daily; 5hr 30min–6hr); Toruń (5 daily; 2hr–2hr 30min); Warsaw (16 daily; 2hr 30 mins–3hr 30min); Wrocław (20 daily; 2hr); Zakopane (2 daily; 10hr).

Toruń to: Częstochowa (1 daily; 5hr); Gdynia (4 daily; 3–4hr); Kraków (1 daily; 7hr 30min); Poznań (5 daily; 2–3hr); Warsaw (3 daily; 3–4hr); Wrocław (2 daily; 4hr 30min).

Wrocław to: Częstochowa (7 daily; 2hr 30min–3hr); Gdańsk (4 daily; 7hr); Kraków (13 daily; 4hr 30min–5hr); Poznań (19 daily; 2hr); Toruń (2 daily; 4hr 30min); Warsaw (9 daily; 5–7hr); Zakopane (1 daily; 7hr 30min).

Zakopane to: Częstochowa (4 daily; 5–8hr); Gdynia (1 daily; 13hr); Kraków (19 daily; 2hr 30min–4hr); Poznań (2 daily; 10hr 30min); Warsaw (4 daily; 6–9hr); Zamość (1 daily; overnight).

Buses

For intercity routes look out for the more comfortable and faster Polski Express buses, only slightly pricier than the PKP state-run services detailed below:

Kraków to: Zakopane (32 daily; 2hr 15min); Zamość (1 daily).

Warsaw to: Toruń (3 daily); Zakopane (1 daily).

CHAPTER 22

PORTUGAL

Introduction

For so small a country, **Portugal** has tremendous variety both in landscape and in its ways of life and traditions. Along the coast around Lisbon, and on the now well-developed Algarve in the south, there are highly sophisticated resorts, while Lisbon itself has enough diversions to please most city devotees. But in its rural areas this is still a conspicuously underdeveloped country. Tourism is changing many areas, but for anyone wanting to get off the beaten track, there are plenty of opportunities to experience smaller towns and countryside regions that have changed little in the past century.

In terms of population, and of customs, differences between the **north and south** are particularly striking. Above a line more or less corresponding with the course of the River Tagus, the people are of predominantly Celtic and Germanic stock. It was here, at Guimarães, that the "Lusitanian" nation was born, in the wake of the Christian reconquest from the North African Moors. South of the Tagus, where the Moorish and Roman civilizations were most established, people tend to be darker-skinned and maintain more of a "Mediterranean" lifestyle. More recent events are woven into the pattern. The 1974 **revolution** came from the south – an area of vast estates, rich landowners and a dependent workforce – while the conservative backlash of the 1980s came from the north, with its powerful religious authorities and individual smallholders wary of change. More profoundly even than the revolution **emigration** has altered people's attitudes and the appearance of the countryside. After Lisbon, the largest Portuguese community is in Paris, and there are migrant workers spread throughout France and Germany. Returning to Portugal, these emigrants have brought in modern ideas and challenged many traditional rural values.

The greatest of all Portuguese influences, however, is **the sea**. The Portuguese are very conscious of themselves as a seafaring race; mariners like Vasco da Gama led the way in the exploration of Africa and the Americas, and until less than twenty years ago Portugal remained a colonial power. Lisbon's Expo '98 – an aquatic extravaganza which took place 500 years after de Gama set sail for India in June 1498 – reflected this oceanic heritage. The colonies brought African and South American strands to the country's culture: in the distinctive music of *fado*, sentimental songs heard in Lisbon and Coimbra, for example, or in the Moorish-influenced and Manueline architecture that abounds in coastal towns like Belém and Viana do Castelo.

Since Portugal is so compact, it's easy to take in something of each of its elements. Scenically, the most interesting parts of the country are in the north: the **Minho**, green, damp, and often startling in its rural customs; and the sensational gorge and valley of the **Douro**, followed along its course by the railway, off which antiquated branch lines edge into remote **Trás-os-Montes**. For contemporary interest, spend some time in both **Lisbon** and **Porto**, the only two cities of real size. And if it's monuments you're after, the whole centre of the country – above all, **Coimbra** and **Évora** – retains a faded grandeur. The **coast** is virtually continuous beach, and apart from the **Algarve** and a few pockets around Lisbon and Porto, resorts remain low-key and thoroughly Portuguese, with great stretches of deserted sands between them. Perhaps the loveliest are along the northern **Costa Verde**, around Viana do Castelo, or, for isolation, the wild beaches of **southern Alentejo**.

Information and maps

You'll find a tourist office, or **Turismo**, in almost every town of any size. Aside from the help they can give you in finding a room, they often have local maps and leaflets. Their hours are generally Mon–Sat 9am–12.30pm & 2–5.30pm. If you're doing any real exploration, or driving, it's worth investing in a good **road map**. The best are those put out by the Automóvel Clube de Portugal, the Spanish Plaza y Janes, and Michelin #437.

Money and banks

The Portuguese currency is the **escudo** (abbreviated as $ or esc: the $ sign follows the amount of escudos, with divisions after it: ie 100$00 is 100esc). Apart from their slowness, Portuguese **banks** are reasonably efficient, and you'll find at least one in all but the smallest towns. Banking **hours** are Mon–Fri 8.30am–3pm; in Lisbon and in some of the Algarve resorts they may be open in the evening to change money. Some banks are installing ATMs for various currencies and denominations, which are more efficient and only charge a two-percent commission instead of the high rates often levied over the counter. Commission on traveller's cheques is high, so your best bet for cheap exchange is to use a credit- or bank-card at a cashpoint machine, found in most towns.

Communications

Portuguese postal services are reasonably efficient. **Post offices** (*correios*) are normally open Mon–Fri

9am–6pm, some larger ones on Saturday mornings too. To buy **stamps**, stand in line for the counter marked *selos* at the post office, or go anywhere that has the sign of the red horse on a white circle over a green background and the legend *Correio de Portugal – Selos*. For **poste restante** services, look for a counter marked *encomendas*.

International phone calls can be made direct from almost any telephone booth in the country, but in smaller rural towns you'll need a good deal of patience to get a line – making calls at a post office phone section is easier. Phone cards (650esc, 1300esc and 1900esc for 50, 100 and 150 units respectively) are available from post offices and newsagents. There is no cheap-rate period for international calls. The domestic operator number is ☎118; for international assistance – and collect calls – dial ☎098

Getting around

Distances are small in Portugal and you can get almost everywhere easily and efficiently by either train or bus. Although **trains** are usually cheaper, and some lines are highly scenic, it's often quicker to go by **bus** – especially on shorter or less obvious routes.

■ Trains

CP, the Portuguese railway company, operates all trains. About ninety percent are designated *Regional*, stop at most stations en route, and have first- and second-class cars. *Intercidades* are twice as fast and twice as expensive, and you should reserve a seat if using them. The fastest, most luxurious and priciest of all are the *Rápidos* (known as "*Alfa*"), which speed between Lisbon, Coimbra and Porto – sometimes they have only first-class seats. CP sells its own **rail passes** (valid on any train and in first class), but you'd have to do a lot of travelling to make them worthwhile. Both InterRail and Eurail passes are valid, although supplements must be paid to travel on *Intercidades* and *Rápidos* services.

Be aware that stations can be some miles from the town or village they serve, and forget about trains completely on **Friday and Sunday** evenings unless you enjoy playing sardines with the Portuguese army – they're all on the move for weekend leave. Many minor lines have been replaced by buses in the last few years, but might still be marked on maps.

■ Buses

Buses can often be more flexible than trains and fares are usually competitive. The majority of buses

used to be run by the Rodoviaria Nacional (RN), but the company has been broken up and privatized. Most of the former RN services leave from a town's central terminal. On a number of major routes (particularly Lisbon–Algarve) special **express coaches** can knock hours off the standard multiple-stop bus journeys.

■ Driving and hitching

Car rental rates in Portugal are among the lowest in Europe so it's an option worth thinking about – even for just a part of your travels. High-season rates begin at about 35,000esc a week, with low-season discounts knocking up to a quarter off that. However, bear in mind that you'll have to book ahead for a car in the Algarve in summer (which works out cheaper than if you try to rent once you're in Portugal), and that Portugal has one of the highest **accident** rates in Europe, most of them happening on the infamous Lisbon–Porto and Lisbon–Algarve motorways. August is especially lethal, when Portuguese emigrant workers return home.

If you **break down** you can get assistance from the Automóvel Clube de Portugal, which has reciprocal arrangements with most other automobile clubs. In the north, phone their Porto service (☎02/830 1127); in the south, phone Lisbon (☎01/352 2469). Both operate 24 hours a day.

Hitching is variable. It can take hours to get out of Lisbon or Porto because there's nowhere good to stand, but most other towns are very small, their centres within easy reach of the main highways. The Portuguese are a kind, strikingly generous people, and the main difficulty in a predominantly rural country is that they tend not to be driving very far.

Accommodation

In almost any town you should be able to find **accommodation** in a single room for around 2500–3000esc, a double for 3000–4000esc. Even in mid-season you shouldn't have many problems finding a bed, except in Lisbon and the Algarve.

■ Pensions and hotels

The main budget stand-bys are **pensions**, or *pensões* (*pensão* in the singular), which are graded from one to three stars. A three-star *pensão* is usually about the same price as a one-star **hotel**, and sometimes the latter can even be cheaper. Quirks abound in the official municipal grading and pricing systems and you can often pay less in a really luxurious three-star *pensão* than in a one-star pit of a hotel: similarly, some one-star pensions are far nicer than those with two or three.

Additional categories include **pousadas**, run by the state and similar to the Spanish *paradores*. These are expensive, charging at least four-star hotel prices, but they are often converted from old monasteries or castles and can be worth a look, or at least a drink.

■ Hostels

There are twenty-one **youth hostels** (*Pousadas de Juventude*) in Portugal and, unlike in Spain, they do tend to stay open all year. The price for a dormitory bed is around £6/$9 a night, a little extra if you need to rent sheets and blankets. Most have a curfew (usually 11pm or midnight) and all demand a valid HI card.

■ Private rooms

In seaside resorts there are invariably rooms (*quartos* or *dormidas*) to let in **private houses**. These are sometimes advertised, sometimes just hawked by people at the bus and train stations. They're slightly cheaper than pension rooms – especially if you haggle, as is expected in the main resorts. Tourist offices have lists.

■ Camping

Portugal has more than a hundred authorized **campsites**, most of them small, low-key and attractively located, and all of them remarkably inexpensive – it's rare that you'll end up paying more than £3/$5 a person. You can get a fairly complete map list from any Portuguese tourist office, or buy a detailed booklet guide, the Roteiro Campista, from bookshops or large newsstands.

With a little sensitivity you can pitch a tent for a short period almost anywhere in the countryside. The **Algarve** is different – unofficial camping is banned and campsite thefts are a regular occurrence – but over most of the country the locals are extremely honest and you can leave equipment without worrying.

Food and drink

Portuguese food is excellent, cheap and served in quantity. Virtually all cafés, whatever their appearance, will serve you a basic meal, or at least a snack, for under £5/$7.50, and for a little more you have the run of most of the country's restaurants.

■ Food

Often you'll come across a whole range of dishes served at a **café** but they are much more likely to serve just **snacks and basic fare**. Favourites include *prego* (steak sandwich), usually served with a fried egg; *bifoque* (steak, chips, fried egg); *rissóis* (deep-fried meat patties); *pasteis de bacalhau* (codfish cakes); and *sandes* (sandwiches). Sometimes, too, you'll see food displayed on café counters, particularly shellfish – if you see anything that looks appealing, just ask for *uma dose* (a portion). *Uma coisa destas* (one of those) can also be a useful phrase.

Restaurants are required to offer a three-course *ementa turistica*, but since many restaurateurs seem to regard this as an unwarranted piece of governmental interference, it is seldom the most economical way to eat – restaurant servings tend to be so enormous that you can often have a substantial meal by ordering a *meia dose* (half portion), or one portion between two.

Regional differences aren't as great as in Spain, but it's always worth taking stock of the *prato do dia* (dish of the day) and, if you're on the coast, going for fish and seafood. If you've had enough rich food, any restaurant will fix a *salada mista* (a mixed salad), which usually has tomatoes, onions and olives as a base. *Pão integral* (wholemeal bread) is invariably excellent, and available throughout the country, though especially in the north.

Meat – nearly all restaurants have pork, beef, lamb and chicken dishes, and meat is usually of good quality. Pork, particularly *porco á alentejana* (with clams), and smoked hams, are a real feature of

Portuguese cooking. **Soups**, everywhere, are extraordinarily cheap, and the thick vegetable soup often known as *caldo verde*, sometimes boosted with pieces of smoked sausage and black pudding, can be almost a meal in itself.

Cakes – *bolos* or *pastéis* – are often at their best in *casas de chá* (tearooms), though you'll also find them in cafés and in *pastelarias* (cake shops). Among the best are the Sintra cheesecakes (*queijadas de Sintra*), marzipan cakes from the Algarve, and the incredibly sweet egg-based *doces de ovos*.

■ Drink

In addition to food, all **cafés** serve alcohol – and they're much cheaper places to drink than bars, which tend to have slightly more cosmopolitan pretensions and prices. Portuguese **wines** (*tinto* for red, *branco* for white) are dramatically inexpensive and of an amazing quality overall – even the standard *vinho da casa* that you get in the humblest of cafés. The fortified **port** (*vinho do Porto*) and **madeira** (*vinho da Madeira*) wines are by far the best known, and you should certainly aim to sample them both. Among **table wines**, the best of the reds come from the Dão region, a roughly triangular area between Coimbra, Viseu and Guarda. The light, slightly sparkling **vinhos verdes** – "green wines", in age not colour – are produced in the Minho, and are reliable.

Portuguese **brandy** is available in two varieties, Macieiera and Constantino, and like local **gin** is ridiculously cheap; if you're asking for this or any other spirits at a bar always specify you want "*gin nacional*", "*vodka nacional*", etc – it'll save you a fortune.

The most common local **beer** (*cerveja*) in the south is Sagres but there are numerous other varieties – probably the best is Unica Super Bock, more popular in the north. Order *um fino* or *uma imperial* if you want a small glass; *uma caneca* will get you a half-litre.

Coffee (*café*) comes either black, small and espresso-strong (*uma bica*), small and with milk (*um garoto*), or large and with milk but often disgustingly weak (*um galão*). **Tea** (*chá*) is usually plain and is a big drink in Portugal – you'll find elegant *casas de chá* (tearooms) dotted around the country.

Opening hours and holidays

Portugal has held onto the institution of the **siesta**, so most shops and businesses, plus smaller museums and post offices, close for a good lunch-time break – usually from around 12/12.30pm to 2/2.30pm. **Shops** generally open around 9am, close for lunch, then keep going until 7pm. Except in the larger cities, they tend to close for the weekend at Saturday lunchtime. **Museums, churches and monuments** open from around 10am to 6pm; almost all museums and monuments, however, are closed on Mondays, and at Easter when cultural life seems to cease completely.

The main **public holidays** are: Jan 1; April 25; Good Friday; May 1; Corpus Christi (usually early June); June 10; Aug 15; Oct 5; Nov 1; Dec 1; Dec 8; Dec 25.

Emergencies

Portugal is a remarkably crime-free country, though there's the usual petty theft in Lisbon and the larger tourist resorts. Rented cars are always prey to thieves – leave them looking as empty as possible – and campsites in the Algarve are less reliable than elsewhere.

Violations of **drug laws** (possession of marijuana or hash is a criminal offence) carry heavy sentences. Portuguese **police**, though, are relatively easygoing, and don't look for trouble.

For minor health complaints people generally go to a *farmácia* (**pharmacy**), which you'll find in almost any village; in larger towns there's usually one where English is spoken. They are normally open Mon–Fri 9am–1pm & 3–7pm, Sat 9am–1pm. A sign at each one will show the nearest 24hr chemist on duty. Pharmacists are highly trained and can dispense many drugs without a prescription. In the case of serious illness, you can get the address of an English-speaking doctor from a consular office or, with luck, from the local police or tourist office.

EMERGENCY NUMBERS
All emergencies ☎112.

LISBON AND AROUND

There are few more immediately likeable capitals than **Lisbon**. A lively and varied place, it remains in some ways curiously provincial, rooted as much in the 1920s as the 1990s. Wooden trams from before World War I clank up outrageous gradients, past mosaic pavements and Art Nouveau cafés, and the medieval, village-like quarter of Alfama hangs below the city's castle. Modern Lisbon has kept an easy-going, human pace and scale, with little of the underlying violence of most cities and all ports of its size. It also boasts a vibrant, cosmopolitan identity, from large communities of Africans (from Angola, Mozambique and Cape Verde) and Asians (from Macao, Goa and East Timor). In recent years, major infrastructural development has been underway as Lisbon has prepared itself for two landmark celebrations: in 1994 it was European City of Culture, while in summer 1998 the city held the last great Expo of the century.

Art and monuments are relatively thin on the ground, largely as a result of the Great Earthquake of 1755, after which the core of the city was reconstructed on a grid pattern that still endures. But there is one building from Portugal's golden age – the **Mosterio dos Jerónimos** at Belém – that is the equal of any monument in the country. More modern developments include the **Fundação Calouste Gulbenkian** museum complex, with its superb collections of ancient and modern art, and Tómas Taveira's amazing post-modernist shopping centre at **Amoreiras**. The sea is close by, half an hour's journey taking you to the miles of dunes along the **Costa da Caparica**. Slightly further afield lie the lush wooded heights and royal palaces of **Sintra** and the monastery of **Mafra**, one of the most extraordinary buildings in the country.

Arrival and information

From the **airport**, just twenty minutes' drive from the centre, local buses #44 and #45 run from the road outside the airport past the youth hostel to Praça dos Restauradores, Rossío and on to Cais do Sodré Station (for Cascais). It's easier, but more expensive, to take the Aerobus, #91(every 20min 7am–9pm; 450$00), which leaves from right outside the Arrivals Hall and runs to Praça dos Restauradores, Rossío, Praça do Comércio and Cais do Sodré. **Long-distance trains** use the **Santa Apolónia station**, about fifteen minutes' walk from the waterfront Praça do Comércio, or a short ride on buses #9, #39 or #46 to Rossío. **Local trains** from Sintra emerge at the heart of the city in the **Rossío station**, while **trains from the Algarve and south** terminate at **Barreiro**, on the far bank of the river, where you catch a ferry to the **Fluvial** station next to the Praça do Comércio. For **train timetables**, visit the information office on the ground floor of Rossío station (Mon–Sat 9am–7pm) or check out the Web site *www.cp.pt*, which is available in English. The **main bus terminal** is on Avenida Casal Ribeiro (metro Saldanha) and handles most international and domestic departures, including sevices to the Algarve. Other terminals are scattered around the city – check with the tourist office for details, though it's worth knowing that buses from Campo das Cebolas, east of Praça do Comércio, run to the Minho and Algarve, while many southern towns are served by buses from Praça de Espanha (metro Palhavã) and Avda Cinco de Outubro 75 (metro Saldanha).

It could hardly be easier to get your bearings in the **Baixa**, the central city grid. At one end, opening onto the River Tagus, is the broad, arcaded **Praça do Comércio**; at the other stands Praça Dom Pedro IV, or the **Rossío**, merging with the **Praça da Figueira** and **Praça dos Restauradores**. These squares, filled with cafés, occasional street musicians, tourists and streetwise dealers, form the hub of Lisbon's daily activity. At night the focus shifts to the **Bairro Alto**, high above and to the west of the Baixa, and best reached by funicular (Elevador da Glória) or the great street "elevador" (Elevador Santa Justa), built for the city by Raul Mésnier – not, as commonly claimed, by Gustave Eiffel. East of the Baixa, the **Castelo de São Jorge**, a brooding landmark, holds a still taller hill, with the **Alfama** district – the core of the medieval city – sprawled below.

The main **tourist office** is on the western side of Praça dos Restauradores in the Palácio da Foz (Mon–Sat 9am–8pm, Sun 10am–6pm; ☎01/346 33 14); they can supply maps and accommodation lists and book rental cars. There's also a tourist office at the airport (daily

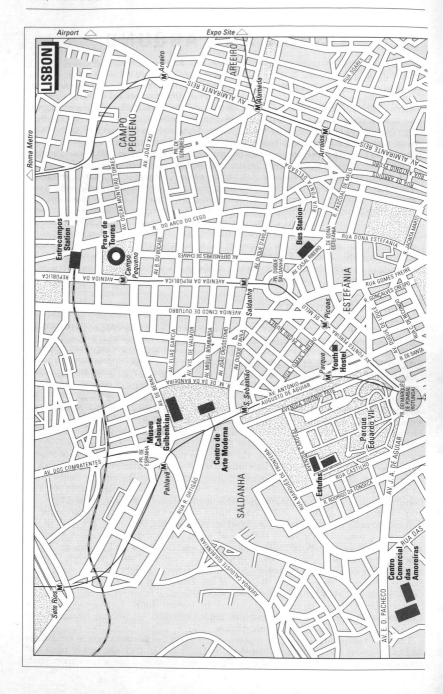

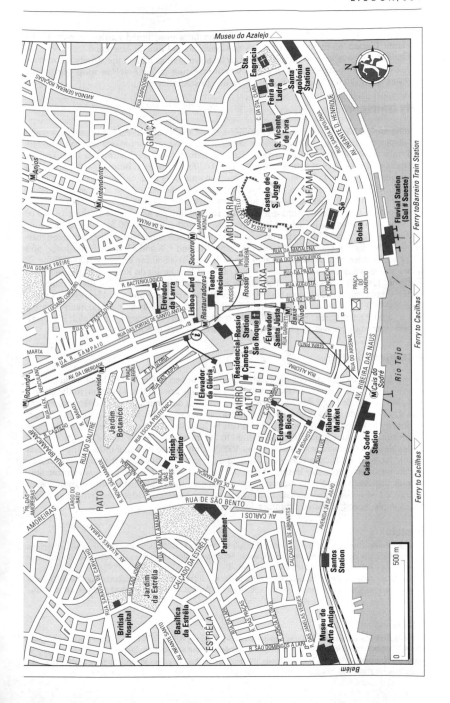

6am–11pm, ☎01/849 36 89), and there will soon be a new, grand tourism centre, **CRIA Turismo Lisboa**, on the corner of Praça do Comércio and Rua do Arsenal.

Finding your way around the old town can be a problem as a lot of the streets are narrow and not marked on most maps. It's well worth investing in the *Falkplan* **map** sold in the newsagent next to the tourist office in Praça dos Restauradores.

City transport

Getting around Lisbon presents few problems. Most places of interest are within easy walking distance – and transport connections are detailed in the text for those that aren't. The bus and tram networks operate from around 6am to midnight and the metro until 1am. **Trams**, the most enjoyable way of getting around, cost 160$00 per journey; **buses** (*carris*) are also a good bet – buy your ticket in advance from a booth (in Praça da Figueira among other places), which is valid for two journeys (160$00); alternatively, there are Passe Turistico bus/metro/elevador **passes**, valid for four days (1680$00) or seven days (2380$00) available from booths. The **metro** covers a few useful routes, though as a visitor to the city you're unlikely to make extensive use of it; tickets are 100$00 each, 800$00 for a block of ten or 260$00 for a day pass. Well worth considering is the **Lisboa Card** which gives unlimited travel on all the city's public transport (except trams #15 and #28 and Elevador Santa Justa) and entry to 25 museums. It costs 1900$00 for 24 hours, 3100$00 for 48 hours, 4000$00 for 72 hours and is available from the Lisboa Card office at Rua Jardin do Regedor 50, opposite the Turismo. Lisbon's **taxis** are excellent value for trips within the city limits. All journeys are metered (starting at 250$00 plus 300$00 for any luggage carried) and should rarely cost more than 500–600$00; they can be found quite easily by day, especially around the main squares, but at night it's a different matter and more costly – if you're leaving a bar or club it's usually best to arrange for one by phone; try Radio Taxis (☎01/815 50 61).

Accommodation

Lisbon has scores of small, cheap **pensions**, often grouped one on top of the other in tall tenement blocks. The most obvious accommodation area is around Rossío station, in the streets and alleys between Praça dos Restauradores and Praça da Figueira – for budget choices, try Rua das Portas de Santo Antão and Rua da Glória. Bairro Alto is the most atmospheric part of the city in which to stay, though rooms can be hard to come by and noisy. At Easter, and in midsummer, room availability is stretched to the limit: many single rooms are "converted" to doubles and prices may start as high as 4000$00. Fortunately, during most of the year you should have little difficulty finding a place, and for maybe a third less than the midsummer prices. For more expensive **hotels**, it can save a lot of walking to use the **reservation service** at the Praça dos Restauradores tourist office or at the airport; there is no commission charge. Most of the pensions listed below are one- or two-star; **addresses**, written as 53-3°, for example, specify the street number followed by the storey.

Hostels

Oeiras Youth Hostel, Catalazete, Estrada Marginal (☎01/443 06 38). Overlooking the beach at Oeiras, 15km outside the city. Take any train from Cais do Sodré and follow signs from Oeiras station. It's small, so phone before setting out. Reception open 6–11pm. ③.

Pousada de Juventude de Lisboa, Rua Andrade Corvo 46 (☎01/353 26 96). Lisbon's main hostel, recently renovated, with good facilities and no curfew. Book in advance. One block south of the Picoas metro stop, or take buses #1, #44 or #45 from Restauradores or Rossío. Dorms ①, doubles ④.

Hotels

Pensão Arco da Bandeira, Rua dos Sapateiros 226-4°, Baixa (☎01/342 34 78). Highly recommended *pensão* with six comfortable rooms with spotless bathrooms, some overlooking Rossío. ③.

Casa de Hóspedes Atalaia, Rua da Atalaia 150-1°, Bairro Alto (☎01/346 44 59). Tolerable at the price, but standards vary and you can find yourself uncomfortably remote from the shared bathrooms. ②.

Residential Camões, Trav. do Poço da Cidade 38-1° (☎01/346 75 10). Brilliant location right in the heart of Bairro Alto, though invest in some earplugs for streetside rooms at weekends. Breakfast included in high season, English spoken. ④.

Pensão Coimbra e Madrid, Praça da Figueira 3-3°, Baixa (☎01/342 17 60). Superb views, though the rooms are noisy. Decent proprietors, shabby though clean furnishings and a TV room, too. ③.

Pensão Dona Maria II, Rua Portas de Santo Antão 9-3°, Baixa (☎01/342 52 68). Large airy rooms (with washbasin) and nice views over Rossío, newly renovated. ③.

Hotel Duas Nações, Rua da Vitória 41, Baixa (☎01/346 07 10). Faded, nineteenth-century hotel. Rooms with bath are more attractive in every way, but cost quite a bit more. ③.

Pensão Duque, Calçada do Duque 53, Bairro Alto (☎01/346 34 44). Near São Roque church, down the steps off the square. Basic rooms but recently redecorated – separate bathrooms. ③.

Residencial Florescente, Rua das Portas de Santo Antão 99, Baixa (☎01/342 66 09). One of the street's best-value establishments, with lots of rooms, some with TV, some without windows, so ask about alternatives. ④.

Pensão Galicia, Rua do Crucifixo 50-4°, Baixa (☎01/342 47 81). Cute little rooms, the best with sunny balconies, and fine Baiza location. ②.

Pensão Globo, Rua do Teixeira 37, Bairro Alto (☎01/346 22 79). Up Trav. da Cara from Elevador da Glória and then right. Rooms are clean, management fine and the location superb. Shared shower and toilet at the top although there are some rooms with shower. ②.

Pensão Lafonense, Rua das Portas de Santo Antão 36-2°, Baixa (01/367 122). With decor that makes you feel as if you're staying at your aged aunt's, this tiny pensão is homely and centrally located. ③.

Pensão Lar do Areeiro, Praça Dr. Francisco de Sá Carneiro 4-1°; metro Areeiro (☎01/849 31 50). Respectable, old-fashioned place. All rooms with bath; those at the back escape the noise of the praça; price includes breakfast. ③.

Pensão Luar, Rua das Gáveas 101-1°, Bairro Alto (☎01/346 09 49). Calm, polished interior whose decently furnished rooms, some with showers, are not too noisy. ③.

Pensão Moderna, Rua dos Correeiros 205-4°, Baixa (☎01/346 08 18). Run-down Baixa *pensão* with big rooms in need of decoration, crammed with old furniture. ③.

Pensão Monumental, Rua da Glória 21, Baixa (☎01/346 98 07). A backpackers' favourite with a mixed bag of rooms in a rambling old building. ③.

Pensão Ninho das Águias, Costa do Castelo 74, Alfama (☎01/886 70 08). On the street looping around the castle, with a lovely garden terrace overlooking the city. Rooms are bright, white and light, management capricious. ④.

Pensão Prata, Rua da Prata 71-3°, Baixa (☎01/346 89 08). Small rooms, some with showers, up three extremely steep flights of stairs in a welcoming, family-run apartment. Book ahead. ③.

Pensão São João de Praça, Rua São João de Praça 97-2°, Alfama (☎01/886 25 91). Clean, quiet and friendly place in a newly painted townhouse just below the cathedral. Front rooms have wrought-iron balconies. During high season half-board is compulsory. ⑥.

Campsites

Costa da Caparica. There are several small and lively campsites on the beaches along here (see "Around Lisbon", below); and at just 30–50min from Lisbon, they make a comfortable alternative to the city site.

Parque Municipal de Campismo (☎01/760 89 38). Main city campsite, in the Parque Florestal Monsanto, about 6km west of the centre. The entrance is on Estrada da Circunvalaço on the park's west side. Take a train from Cais do Sodré to Algés, then bus #50 to the campsite, or bus #43 from Praça da Figueira.

The City

The lower town – the **Baixa** – is very much the heart of the capital, housing many of the country's administrative departments, banks and business offices. Europe's first great example of Neoclassical design and urban planning, it remains an imposing quarter of rod-straight streets, cobbled underfoot and either streaming with traffic or turned over to pedestrians, street performers and pavement artists. Many of the streets in the Baixa grid maintain their crafts and businesses as devised by the autocratic Marquês de Pombal in his post-earthquake reconstruction: Rua da Prata (Silversmiths' Street), Rua dos Sapateiros (Cobblers' Street) and Rua do Ouro (Goldsmiths' Street) are all cases in point. Architecturally, the most interesting places in the Baixa are the squares – the Rossío and Praça do Comércio – and, on the periphery, the lanes leading east to the cathedral and west up towards Bairro Alto. This last area, known as **Chiado**, suffered much damage from a fire that swept across the Baixa in August 1988, but remains the city's most affluent quarter, focused on the fashionable shops and – fortunately spared from the fire – the beautiful old tearooms of the **Rua Garrett**.

The **Rossío** – itself more or less encircled by cafés – is very much a focus for the city, yet its single concession to grandeur is the **Teatro Nacional**, built along the north side in the 1840s. At the waterfront end of the Baixa, the **Praça do Comércio** was intended as the climax to Pombal's design, and has been newly pedestrianized to bring the square back into the hub of city life, but the lack of cafés or shops makes it a little sterile.

A couple of blocks east of the Praça do Comércio is the church of **Conceição Velha**, severely damaged by the earthquake but retaining its flamboyant Manueline doorway, an early example of this style which hints at the brilliance that emerged at Belém. The **Cathedral**, or **Sé** (Mon–Sat 8.30am–6pm), stands very stolidly above. Founded in 1150 to commemorate the city's reconquest from the Moors, it in fact occupies the site of the principal mosque of Moorish Lishbuna. Like so many of the country's cathedrals, it is Romanesque and extraordinarily restrained in both size and decoration. For admission to the thirteenth-century cloisters (Mon–Sat 10am–5pm, Sun 10am–noon) you must buy a ticket (100$00), as you must for the Baroque **sacristy** (40$00) with its small museum of treasures – including the relics of St Vincent, allegedly brought to Lisbon in 1173 in a boat piloted by ravens.

From the Sé, Rua Augusto Rosa winds upward towards the Castelo, past sparse ruins of a Roman theatre and the **Miradouro de Santa Luzia**, where the conquest of Lisbon and the siege of the Castelo de São Jorge are depicted on the walls. At the entrance to the **Castelo** (daily 9am–9pm; free) stands a triumphant statue of Afonso Henriques, conqueror of the Moors. Of the Moorish palace that once stood here only a much-restored shell remains – but the castle as a whole is an enjoyable place to spend a couple of hours, wandering amid the ramparts and towers to look down upon the city. Crammed within the castle's outer walls is the tiny medieval quarter of **Santa Cruz**, once very much a village in itself though now littered with gift shops and restaurants.

The **Alfama** quarter, stumbling from the walls of the Castelo to the banks of the Tagus, is the oldest part of Lisbon. In Arab times this was the grandest part of the city, but with subsequent earthquakes the new Christian nobility moved out, leaving it to the fishing community still here today. It is undergoing some commercialization, thanks to its cobbled lanes and "character", but although the antique shops and restaurants may be moving in, the quarter retains a largely traditional life of its own. The **Feira da Ladra**, Lisbon's rambling and ragged **flea market**, fills the Campo de Santa Clara, at the edge of Alfama, every Tuesday and Saturday. While at the flea market, take a look inside **Santa Engrácia**, the loftiest and most tortuously built church in the city – begun in 1682, its vast dome was finally completed in 1966. Through the tiled cloisters of nearby **São Vicente de Fora** you can visit the old monastic refectory, since 1855 the pantheon of the Bragança dynasty. Here, in more or less complete (though unexciting) sequence, are the bodies of all Portuguese kings from João IV, who restored the monarchy, to Manuel II, who lost it and died in exile in England in 1932.

Mésnier's extraordinary funicular, **Elevador Santa Justa**, just off the top end of Rua do Ouro on Rua de Santa Justa, is the most obvious approach to **Bairro Alto**. Alternatively, there are the two funicular-like trams – the Elevador da Glória from the Praça dos Restauradores (just up from the tourist office) or the Elevador da Bica from Rua de São Paulo/Rua da Moeda. The ruined Gothic arches of the **Convento do Carmo** hang almost directly above the exit of Mésnier's funicular. Once the largest church in the city, this was half-destroyed by the earthquake and is perhaps even more beautiful as a result; sadly it and the small archeological museum are both currently closed. The church of **São Roque**, over towards the Chiado in the Largo Trindade Coelho (Mon–Fri 10am–5pm; free), looks from the outside like the plainest in the city, its bleak Renaissance facade having been further simplified by the earthquake. But hang around in the gloom and the sacristan will come and escort you around, turning on lights to an incredible succession of side chapels, each lavishly embellished. The climax is the Capela de São João Baptista, last on the left. It was ordered from Rome in 1742 by Dom João V to honour his patron saint and was designed using the most costly materials available, including ivory, agate, porphyry and lapis lazuli. Attached is a small museum (Tues–Sun 10am–5pm; free) with more European religious art.

The Parque Eduardo VII and the Gulbenkian Calouste Museum

North of the Praça dos Restauradores are the city's principal gardens, the **Parque Eduardo VII**, most easily approached by metro to Rotunda. Though there are some pleasant cafés here, the park's big attractions are the **Estufas** (daily 9am–4.30/5.30pm; 95$00), huge and wonderful glasshouses filled with tropical plants, flamingo pools, and endless varieties of palms and cacti.

The **Museu Calouste Gulbenkian** (Oct–May Tues–Sun 10am–5pm; June–Sept Tues, Thurs, Fri & Sun 10am–5pm, Wed & Sat 2–7.30pm; 500$00, free Sun), the great museum of Portugal, is ten minutes' walk north of the Parque Eduardo VII – take bus #16, #41 or #46 from the Rossío, or the metro to Palhavã or Praça de Espanha. Established by the Armenian oil magnate Calouste Gulbenkian, the Fundação Calouste Gulbenkian runs this amazing complex – an orchestra, three concert halls and two galleries for temporary exhibitions – as well as financing work in all spheres of Portuguese cultural life, in even the smallest towns. This showpiece museum is divided into two distinct parts – the first devoted to Egyptian, Greco-Roman, Islamic and Oriental arts, the second to European, including paintings from all the major schools. Ghirlandaio's *Portrait of a Young Woman* is followed by outstanding portraits by Rubens and Rembrandt, while Fragonard ushers in an excellent showing of work from France, featuring Corot, Manet and Monet. There's also a stunning room full of the Art Nouveau jewellery by René Lalique. Across the gardens, the separate **Centro de Arte Moderna** (same hours and price as Museu Gulbenkian) has all the big names on the twentieth-century Portuguese scene.

Museu de Arte Antiga

The one other museum that stands up to Gulbenkian standards is the national art collection, the **Museu de Arte Antiga** (Tues 2–6pm, Wed–Sun 10am–6pm; 500$00, free Sun am), situated on the riverfront to the west of the city at Rua das Janelas Verdes 95 (tram #19, bus #40 or #60 from Praça do Comércio). Its core is formed by fifteenth- and sixteenth-century Portuguese works, the acknowledged masterpiece being Nuno Gonçalves' *St Vincent Altarpiece*, a brilliantly marshalled canvas depicting Lisbon's patron receiving homage from all ranks of its citizens. After Gonçalves and his contemporaries, the most interesting works are by Flemish and German artists (Cranach, Bosch – a fabulous *Temptation of St Anthony* – and Dürer), and miscellaneous gems by Raphael, Zurbarán and, rather oddly, Rodin.

Belém and the Monastery of Jerónimos

Even before the Great Earthquake, the **Monastery of Jerónimos** (Mosteiro dos Jerónimos; Tues–Sun 10am–5/6.30pm; 400$00, free Sun am; tram #15 or #17 from Praça do Comércio) at **Belém** was Lisbon's finest monument: since then, it has stood quite without comparison. It was from Belém in 1497 that Vasco da Gama set sail for India, and it was here, too, that he was welcomed home by Dom Manuel "the Fortunate". The monastery was funded by a levy on the fruits of his discovery – a five-percent tax on all spices other than pepper, cinnamon and cloves, whose import had become the sole preserve of the Crown. Begun in 1502, this is the most ambitious achievement of Manueline architecture. The main entrance to the church is a complex, shrine-like hierarchy of figures centred around Henry the Navigator. It's difficult to see the six central columns as anything other than palm trunks, growing into the branches of the delicate rib-vaulting. Vaulted throughout and fantastically embellished, the cloister has a wave-like, rhythmic motion that's complemented by typically Manueline references to ropes, anchors and the sea.

The **Torre de Belém** (Tues–Sun 10am–5pm; 400$00), guarding the entrance to the port around five hundred metres from the monastery, is a multiturreted whimsy built over the last five years of Dom Manuel's reign. Its architect had previously worked on Portuguese fortifications in Morocco, and a Moorish influence is very strong in the delicately arched windows and balconies. The interior is unremarkable except for a "whispering gallery". Back towards the monastery are a number of museums, of which the best is the **Museu de Arte Popular** (Tues–Sun 10am–12.30pm & 2–5pm; 300$00), a province-by-province display of Portugal's still very diverse folk arts, housed in a shed-like building on the waterfront.

Almost adjacent is the vast concrete **Monument to the Discoveries** (Tues–Sun 9.30am–6pm; 320$00), erected in 1960 to commemorate the 500th anniversary of the death of Henry the Navigator; inside, a small exhibition space has changing displays on the city's history, and there are fine views of the Tagus from the top. At the corner of Belém's other main square – Praça Afonso de Abuquerque, a few minutes' walk from the monastery along Rua de Belém – there's the **Museu dos Coches** (Tues–Sun 10am–5.30pm; 450$00, free Sun morning), an interminable line of mainly eighteenth-century royal coaches, the most visited and most tedious tourist attraction in Lisbon. Renovations are being carried out to the roof until Spring/Summer 2000, until which time it has been relocated to the Expo 98 site; take the metro to Oriente.

Eating

Lisbon has some of the best-value **cafés and restaurants** of any European city, serving large portions of food at sensible prices. **Seafood** is widely available – there's an entire central street, Rua das Portas de Santo Antão, as well as a whole enclave of restaurants across the River Tejo at Cacilhas, that specialize in it. Lisbon also has a rich vein of inexpensive **foreign restaurants** featuring food from the former colonies: Brazil, Mozambique, Angola and Goa. There are plenty of restaurants scattered around the Baixa, and there are some good places, too, in all the other areas you're likely to be sightseeing, up in the Alfama and out in Belém. **By night** the obvious place to be is Bairro Alto. Note that many restaurants are **closed on Sundays,** while on Saturday nights in midsummer you may need to book for the more popular places. Assume moderate **prices** at all the places listed below – around 2500$00 per person – unless otherwise stated.

Most bars and cafés serve **snacks** and sandwiches, for listings of these, see the drinking section opposite.

Andorra, Rua das Portas de Santo Antão 82, Baixa. One of the less expensive fish restaurants on this street, with outdoor tables. Closed Sun.

Bota Alta, Trav. da Queimada 37, Bairro Alto. Old tavern restaurant that pulls in the punters for its large portions of traditional Portuguese food. Closed Sat lunch & Sun.

Brasuca, Rua João Pereira da Rosa 7, Bairro Alto (☎01/342 85 42). A lively restaurant, set in an ageing mansion with great Brazilian food. Expensive. Closed Mon.

O Cantinho do Aziz, Rua de São Lourenço 3–5, Alfama. A little hard to find, but well worth the search for its African and Indian food at fairly low prices. Closed Sun.

O Cantinho do Bem Estar, Rua do Norte 46, Bairro Alto. Inexpensive Alentejan restaurant that's as friendly and authentic as you can get. Closed Mon.

Carvoeiro, Rua Vieira Portuense 66–68. One of many inexpensive fish restaurants in this street. Outdoor tables.

Casa Faz Frio, Rua Dom Pedro V 96, Bairro Alto. A beautiful, very traditional restaurant, replete with tiles. Under 2000$00 for a full meal and wine.

Cervejaria da Trindade, Rua Nova da Trindade 20. Wonderful, vaulted beer-hall restaurant. Expensive. Open till 2am.

Hell's Kitchen, Rua da Atalaia 176. Right at the top of the Bairro Alto and well worth finding for a menu of world foods that includes several vegetarian dishes.

Mestré André, Calçadinha de Santo Estevão 4–6, Alfama. A fine neighbourhood tavern, with good grills (*churrasco*). Outdoor seating in summer. Closed Sun.

Rei dos Frangos/Bom Jardim, Trav. de Santo Antão 7–11, Baixa. Excellent for spit-roast chicken – a whole one with fries for about 1000$00.

A Severa, Rua dos Gavéas 57. Good, moderately priced late-night eating option (open till 3.30am). Closed Fri and Sun.

Sinal Vermelha, Rua das Gaveas 89, Bairro Alto (☎01/346 12 52). Popular, trendy city haunt serving recommended Portuguese food. Expensive. Closed Sun.

Solmar, Rua das Portas de Santo Antão 108, Baixa (☎01/342 33 71). A vast showpiece seafood restaurant, with fountain and marine mosaics, and generally deserving of its reputation. Expensive.

Sua Excelência, Rua do Conde 42, Lapa (☎01/60 36 14). Small, intimate restaurant whose marvellously inventive Portuguese cooking is worth the high prices; reservations advised. Closed Wed, Sat & Sun lunch, & all Sept.

Sul, Rua do Norte 13, Bairro Alto. Idiosyncratic restaurant and tapas bar that serves excellent Uruguayan steak dishes – though don't expect them well cooked – and a wine list solely consisting of little-known Portugue vintages. Serves full English brunch on Sundays. Daily 12pm–2am.

Tœnel de Alfama, Rua dos Remedios 132, Alfama. Cheap, substantial meals served in a tiny dining room. Closed Sun.

Yin Yang, Rua dos Correiros 14-1°. Macrobiotic vegetarian lunches (noon–1pm) and light snacks 6–8pm. Closed Sat & Sun.

Drinking and entertainment

Among the city's hundreds of bars and cafés, some of the older **cafés** and *pastelerias* (specializing in cakes) in particular are worth dropping in on at some stage during the day. For night-time drinking, the densest concentration of designer **bars and clubs** is found either in the **Bairro Alto** – traditional centre of Lisbon's nightlife, with its cramped streets sheltering bars, clubs, *fado* houses and restaurants – or on and around **Avenida 24 de Julho**, the avenue running west from Cais do Sodré to the more outlying **Alcântara** district. Take a taxi, or a train to Alcântara Mar station from Cais do Sodré. Tourist brochures tend to suggest that Lisbon entertainment begins and ends with **fado**, the city's traditional "blues" music, offered in thirty or so nightclubs in the Bairro Alto, Alfama and elsewhere. There's no reason – except perhaps ever-rising admission prices, rarely, these days, below 3500$00 – not to sample some *fado*, but don't miss out on other possibilities. Portuguese **jazz** can be good, **rock** can occasionally surprise, and if you check out the posters around Restauradores there's a good chance of catching **African music** from the former colonies. The **techno/house** scene has exploded in the last few years: head for the Bairro Alto and keep ringing doorbells until you find the right vibe. Entertainment listings are available in the *Agenda Cultural*, a free monthly booklet issued by Lisbon city council; in *What's On* and *Lisboa em* available free at the Turismo; or buy the Friday editions of the *Independente* or *Diario de Noticias* newspapers, which both have listings magazines.

Virtually all the city's **cinemas** show original-language films with Portuguese subtitles. Mainstream movies are on show at cinemas around Praça dos Restauradores and Avenida da Liberdade; at the Amoreiras complex (☎01/69 12 75), on Avenida Eng Duarte Pacheco, there are ten screens. The Instituto da Cinemateca Portuguesa, Rua Barata Salgueiro 39 (Avenida metro), is the national film theatre.

Cafes

Antiga Casa dos Pasteis, Rua de Belém 90, Belém. Excellent tiled pastry-shop/café.

Café a Brasileira, Rua Garrett 120. The most famous of Rua Garrett's old-style coffee houses, open until 2am.

Café Nicola, Praça Dom Pedro IV 26. On the west side of Rossío, this grand old place is a good stop for breakfast.

Café Pastelaria Bernard, Rua Garrett 104. Superb cakes and an outdoor terrace on Chiado's most fashionable street.

Café Suiça, Praça Dom Pedro IV 96. Famous for its cakes and pastries, so it can be tough getting an outdoor table here.

Cerca Moura, Largo das Portas do Sol. Nice views up in the Alfama.

Bars and clubs

Alcântara Mar, Rua Cozinha Económica 11, Alcântara. Big house/techno spot. Closed Mon & Tues.

Bar Artis, Rua Diário Notícias 95. Chill to mellow jazz with a good mix of locals and the odd traveller.

Captain Kirk, Rua do Norte121, Bairro Alto. A must for Goa Trance on Wed/Thurs; they know where the big weekend parties are – with Trip-Hop, Break Beat and Rock over the weekend. Daily 10pm–4am. Happy hour before 1am with half-price beer.

Cena de Copos, Rua da Barroca 103–105, Bairro Alto. The place to be if it's after midnight, you're under 25 and you're bursting with energy.

Doca de Santo, Doca de Santo Amaro, under Ponte 25 de Abril. Large palm-fringed club, one of the first and the most popular in this new area.

Fragillux, Avda. Dom Henrique, opposite Santa Apólina Station. Currently very in and very busy. Frantic dance music.

Portas Largas, Rua da Atalaia 105, Bairro Alto. Relaxed partly gay bar with black and white tiles that makes a good place to start the night. Lots of posters and leaflets on where to go next.

Instituto do Vinho do Porto, Rua de São Pedro de Alcântara 45, Bairro Alto. Over 200 types and vintages of port, from 200$00 a glass upwards. It's not as forbidding as it looks. Closed Sun.

Kapital, Avda 24 de Julho 68, opposite Santos station. Full of bright young things paying high prices for drinks.

Kremlin, Escadinhas da Praia 5. One of the city's most fashionable nightspots, this is packed with flash young, raving Lisboetas. Techno still rules. Closed Sun & Mon.

Marquês Rock Club, Largo Marquês do Lavradio, Alfama. Dark rock bar with live music most nights. Thurs–Sat.

Metalúrgica, Avda 24 de Julho 110. Cheaper than usual, dishes out happy pop and soul to a happy, mixed crowd.

Pavilhão Chinês, Rua Dom Pedro V 89, Bairro Alto. A wonderfully decorated bar, completely lined with cabinets of bizarre tableaux of artefacts from around the world. Daily till 2am. Fairly expensive.

Plateau, Escadinhas da Praia 3, Avda 24 de Julho. Gentler admission policy than most, with more of a rock orientation.

República do Alcool, Rua do Diário de Notícias 3, Bairro Alto. Jazz and laid-back dance music in a bar with a heavy gay presence.

A Tasca, Trav. da Quiemada 13–15, Bairro Alto. Cheerful and welcoming tequila bar.

Trumps, Rua da Imprensa Nacional 104b, Rato, north of Bairro Alto. The biggest gay disco in Lisbon with a reasonably relaxed door policy. Closed Mon.

Xeque-Mate, Rua do São Marçal 170. Obnoxiously cruisy bar-disco, although more cosmopolitan in summer.

Web C@fe, Ruo do Diário de Notícias 126, Bairro Alto. A place to come as much to drink and enjoy the friendly, international atmosphere as to use the Internet. Open daily 4pm–2am; Internet 700$00/hr.

Fado

Adega do Machado, Rua do Norte 91, Bairro Alto (☎01/322 46 40). One of the longest-standing Bairro Alto joints. Closed Mon.

Adega do Ribatejo, Rua Diário de Noticias 23, Bairro Alto (☎01/346 83 43). Popular with the locals and has a lower-than-usual minimum charge. Singers include a couple of professionals, the manager and even the cooks.

O Senhor Vinho, Rua do Meio a Lapa 18, Bairro Alto (☎01/397 74 56). Famous Bairro Alto club sporting some of the best singers in Portugal.

A Severa, Rua das Gáveas 55, Bairro Alto (☎01/346 40 06). A city institution: big *fado* names, big prices. Closed Thurs.

Other live music

Coliseu dos Recreios, Rua das Portas de Santo Antão, Baixa (☎01/346 19 97). Main indoor stadium venue for major rock bands.

Hot Clube de Portugal, Praça da Alegria, off Avda da Liberdade. Tiny basement jazz club which hosts local and visiting artists. Closed Mon.

Pê Sujo, Largo de São Martinho 6/7, Alfama (☎01/886 56 29). Drinks here feature lethal Brazilian *caipirinhas*, which regularly results in massive audience participation in table-banging samba sessions. Closed Mon.

Ritz Club, Rua da Glória 55, Baixa (☎01/342 51 40). Lisbon's largest African club, one block west of Avda da Liberdade, with a resident band, plus occasional big-name concerts. Closed Mon.

Listings

Airlines Air France, Avda S de Outubro 206-3° (☎01/356 21 71); Alitalia, Praça de Marquês de Pombal 1-5° (☎01/353 61 41); British Airways, Avda da Liberdade 36-2° (☎01/321 79 00); Iberia, Rua Rosa Araujo 2 (☎01/355 81 51); Swissair, Avda da Liberdade 38-1° (☎01/322 60 00); TAP, Edifício Estação do Oriente, inside the Oriente station building (☎0808/ 205 700).

American Express The local agent is Top Tours, Avda Duque de Loulé 108 (☎01/315 58 77).

Banks Main branches are in the Baixa; Banco Borges & Irmão, Avda da Liberdade 9a, stays open Mon–Fri until 7.30pm. There's a currency exchange office at the airport (open 24hr) and at Santa Apolónia station (daily 8.30am–8.30pm).

Car rental Avis, Avda Praia da Vitória 12c (☎01/356 11 76); Budget, Rua Castilho 167 (☎01/386 05 16); Europcar, Avda António Augusto Aguiar 24 (☎01/353 51 15); Hertz, Rua Castilho 72 (☎01/381 24 30).

Embassies Australian Consulate, Avda da Liberdade 244-4° (☎01/52 33 50); Britain, Rua San Bernado 33 (☎01/392 40 00); Canada, Avda da Liberdade 144-3° (☎01/347 48 92); Ireland, Rua da Imprensa à Estrêla 1-4° (☎01/392 94 40); USA, Avda das Forças Armadas (☎01/727 31 27).

Hospital British Hospital, Rua Saraiva de Carvalho 49 (☎01/395 50 67). For an ambulance call ☎01/301 77 77.

Internet Telepac, inside the Forum Telecom, Avda. Fontes Pereira de Melo 38 (Mon–Fri 9am–7pm; 400$00/hour; metro Picas). *Web C@fe*, Ruo do Diário de Notícias 126, Bairro Alto (see above).

Laundry Lava Neve, Rua de Alegría 37, Bairro Alto; Lavandaria Saus Ana, in the Centro Comercial da Mouraria, Largo Martim Moniz (Mon–Sat 9.30am–8pm).

Police 24-hour office at Rua Capelo 13 (☎01/346 61 41), west of the Baixa near the Teatro São Carlos. Report here if you need to make a claim on your travel insurance.

Post offices The main office is on Praça do Comércio (Mon–Fri 8.30am–6.30pm); more convenient is the office at Praça dos Restauradores 58 (daily 8am–10pm).

Telephones Next to the post office in Praça dos Restauradores; also at no. 65, on the corner of Rossío (daily 8am–11pm).

Travel Agencies Viagen Wasteels, Esação Cams F S Apolónia Gare International (☎01/886 65 77); Abreu, Avda da Liberdade 160 (☎01/347 64 41).

Around Lisbon

The beaches of **Caparica** – which the quirks of the Tagus currents have largely spared from the pollution of Lisbon – and the architectural attractions of **Sintra** and **Mafra** can each be reached on a day-trip from Lisbon; but to do justice to Sintra you'll need to stay overnight.

Costa da Caparica

It takes something over an hour to reach **Costa da Caparica** from the capital, and it's here that most locals come if they want to swim or laze around on the sand. This is a thoroughly Portuguese resort, crammed with restaurants and beach cafés, yet solitude is easy enough to find, thanks to the mini-railway that runs along the 8km of dunes in summer. The most enjoyable approach is to take a **ferry** from the Fluvial station by Praça do Comércio, or from Cais do Sodré, to **Cacilhas**, and then pick up the connecting bus from the dock where the boats come in. Alternatively, you can take the #52 or #53 **bus** direct to Caparica from the main Praça de Espanha terminal (metro Palhavã).

At **CAPARICA** buses either stop at a bus park by the beach, or at the station five minutes back from the sands. From the latter, walk up to the main road, turn right and keep walking until you reach Praça da Liberdade, the main square, where there's a **tourist office** (Mon–Sat 9.30am–1pm & 2.30–6pm, also Sun in summer; ☎01/290 00 71), market, cinema and banks. There aren't very many hotels in Caparica but frankly there's no reason to stay since buses run back to Lisbon/Cacilhas most of the day and night. **Campsites**, which range along the first few kilometres of the beach, are on the whole overcrowded and overpriced, but functional enough. A recommended **restaurant**, among dozens of fish and seafood places along the main Rua dos Pescadores, which leads from the square to the beach, is the *Restaurante Churros* at no. 13.

Sintra

SINTRA'S cool, wooded heights were the summer residence of the kings of Portugal and of the Moorish lords of Lisbon before them. The layout of Sintra – an amalgamation of three villages – can be confusing, but the extraordinary **Palácio Nacional** (tours 10am–1pm & 2–5pm; closed Wed; 400$00,), about twenty minutes' walk from the station, is an obvious landmark. The palace was probably in existence under the Moors, but takes its present form from the rebuilding commissioned by Dom João I and his successor, Dom Manuel in the fourteenth and fifteenth centuries. Its style is a fusion of Gothic and the latter king's Manueline additions. The tours are a pain unless you go early before the groups arrive, but the chapel and its adjoining chamber – its floor worn by the incessant pacing of the half-mad Afonso VI who was confined here for six years by his brother Pedro I – are well worth seeing.

The charms of Sintra lie less in its buildings than in its **walks and paths**; one of the best leads past the church of Santa Maria and up to the ruined ramparts of a **Moorish Castle** (daily 10am–5/7pm; free), from where the views are extraordinary. Beyond the castle, a good ninety-minute walk from town, is the lower entrance to the immense **Pena Park**, at the top end of which rears the fabulous **Palácio de Pena** (Tues–Sun 10am–5/6.30pm; 400$00), a wild 1840s fantasy of domes, towers and a drawbridge that does not draw. The interior has been preserved exactly as left by the royal family on their flight from Portugal in 1910.

After the follies of Pena, a visit to Seteais and Monserrate comes as something of a relief. **Seteais**, just right of the Colares road, fifteen minutes' walk from town, is one of the most elegant palaces in Portugal, completed in the last years of the eighteenth century and entered through a majestic Classical arch; it is now a luxurious hotel and restaurant. Beyond, the road leads past a series of beautiful private estates to **Monserrate** – about an hour's walk. It's difficult to do justice to the beauty of Monserrate, whose vast **gardens** (daily 10am–5/6pm; 200$00), filled with endless varieties of exotic trees and subtropical shrubs and plants, extend as far as the eye can see.

Finding **accommodation** at Sintra in summer can be a problem, though if you arrive early in the day you should end up with something. There are a fair number of **pensions**: best value is probably the *Adelaide*, Rua Guilherme Gomes Fernandes 11 (☎01/923 08 73; ③), midway between the train station and Sintra village; or try *Pensão Económica*, Patio de Olivença 6, handy for the train station (☎01/923 02 20; ②). Alternatively, some well-priced **private rooms** can be booked through the extremely helpful **tourist office** (daily 9am–7/8pm; ☎01/923 11 57) in the centre, just off the central Praça da República. There's a **youth hostel** (☎01/924 12 10; ②) at Santa Eufemia, in the hills above Sintra, 5km from town – take a local bus to São Pedro from outside the train station and walk from there (2km). The nearest **campsites** are well out of town: the most convenient are at the beach-villages of Praia das Maçãs, Praia Grande and Azenhas do Mar, all connected by bus. **Restaurants** are generally poor value, relying heavily on the tour parties. Try *Tulhas* behind the turismo or the two *Adega do Saloio* grillhouses, at the far end of the street. The restaurant in the *Pensão Pielas* on Rua João de Deus 70-72, near the station, does budget menus.

Mafra

Connected by regular buses from Sintra train station and from Lisbon, **MAFRA** is dominated by one building: the vast **Palace-Convent** (10am–1pm & 2–5.30pm; closed Tues) built in emulation of Madrid's Escorial by João V, the wealthiest and most extravagant of all Portuguese monarchs. The convent was initially intended for just thirteen Franciscan friars, but as wealth poured in from Brazil, João amplified it into a massive basilica, two royal wings and monastic quarters for 300 monks and 150 novices. The sheer magnitude is what stands out: there are 5200 doorways, 2500 windows, and two bell towers each containing over 50 bells. Parts of the convent are now used by the military, but one-hour guided tours take you around a sizeable portion. The highlight is the magnificent Rococo library – brilliantly lit and rivalling that of Coimbra in both design and grandeur. The basilica, which can be seen outside the tour, is no less imposing, with the multicoloured marble designs of its floor mirrored in the ceiling decoration.

CENTRAL PORTUGAL

The **Estremadura** region has played a crucial role in each phase of the nation's history – and the monuments are there to prove it. A comparatively small area, it boasts a quite extraordinary concentration of vivid architecture and engaging towns. **Alcobaça**, **Batalha** and **Tomar** – home to the most exciting buildings in Portugal – all lie within ninety minutes' bus ride of one another. With its fertile rolling hills, Estremadura is second in beauty only to Minho, but the adjoining bull-breeding lands of **Ribatejo** (literally "banks-of-the-Tagus") fade into the dull expanses of northwestern Alentejo, and there's no great reason to cross the river unless you're pushing on to Évora or can catch up with one of the region's traditional festivals.

North of Estremadura, life on the fertile plain of the **Beira Litoral** has been conditioned over the centuries by the twin threats of floodwaters from Portugal's highest mountains and silting by the restless Atlantic. The highlight here is **Coimbra**, an ancient university city stacked high on the right bank of the Mondego. Less than half an hour to the north lies the ancient **Forest of Buçaco**, the most exotic of Portugal's landscapes. Further inland the little-explored **Mountain Beiras** region, historically the heart of ancient Lusitânia, where Viriatus the Iberian rebel made his last stand against the Romans. You'll see many signs of this patriotism in the fine old town of **Viseu**, where every other place of refreshment is the *Café Viriate* or the *Restaurante Lusitânia*. At an even higher altitude stands **Guarda**, pretty diminutive for somewhere of such renown, but nonetheless bristling with life, especially on market days.

Óbidos

ÓBIDOS, "The Wedding City", was the traditional bridal gift of the kings of Portugal to their queens, a custom begun in 1282 by Dom Dinis. The town – a couple of hours from Lisbon by train – can hardly have changed in appearance since then: its cobbled streets and whitewashed houses are completely enclosed by medieval walls, and steep staircases wind up to the ramparts, from where you can gaze across a fable-like countryside of windmills and vineyards. The parish church, **Igreja de Santa Maria**, in the central Praça, was chosen for the wedding of the ten-year-old child-king Afonso V and his eight-year-old cousin, Isabel, in 1444. It dates mainly from the Renaissance, though the interior is lined with seventeenth-century blue *azulejos*, or painted tiles, in a homely manner typical of Portuguese churches. The retable in a side chapel on the right-hand side was painted by Josefa de Óbidos, one of the finest Portuguese painters – and one of the few women artists afforded any reputation by art historians. One corner of the triangular fortifications is occupied by a massively towered **Castle** built by Dom Dinis and now converted into a *pousada* (☎062/95 91 05; ⑨).

Other **hotels** in Óbidos also tend to be expensive. Your cheapest option is to consult the list of private houses offering **rooms** which is posted in the **tourist office** (☎062/95 92 31); there are comfortable rooms at Rua Direita 40 (☎062/95 91 88; ②). It's worth staying since, as is so often the case, the town reverts to its own life after the daytime tourists disperse. One of the better budget places to **eat** is the *Café 1 de Dezembro*, next to the church of São Pedro.

Leiria

With regular bus services to the three big sites of northern Estremadura – Alcobaça, Batalha and Fátima – **LEIRIA** makes a handy centre for excursions. The chief sight in Leiria itself is the **Castle** (daily 9am–5.30/6.30pm; 180$00), incorporating an elegant royal palace with a magnificent balcony high above the River Lis. At the heart of the old town, Praça Rodrigues Lobo is surrounded by beautiful buildings and arcades. The **tourist office** (☎044/82 37 73) and **bus station** are on opposite sides of a park overlooking the river in the modern city centre. The **train station** is about 4km out of town, with a connecting bus service. For accommodation, check the **pensions** such as *Pensão Berlinga*, Rua Miguel Bombarda 3D (☎044/ 82 38 46; ④), and restaurants (some offering rooms) around Praça Rodrigues Lobo and on narrow side streets such as Rua Mestre Aviz and Rua Miguel Bombarda. There's also a fancy **youth hostel** with a good atmosphere at Largo Cândido dos Reis 7 (☎044/318 68; ②). As for **restaurants**, try the seafood at *Jardim*, by the tourist office, or real Portuguese cuisine – slightly more expensive, but worth it for the large portions – at *Montecarlo*, Rua Dr Correia Mateus 32–34.

Alcobaça

From the twelfth century until the middle of the nineteenth, the Cistercian **Abbey of Alcobaça** (9am–5/7pm; 400$00) was one of the greatest in the Christian world. Owning vast tracts of farmland, orchards and vineyards, it held jurisdiction over a dozen towns and three seaports until its ultimate dissolution in 1834. The monastery was originally founded by Dom Afonso Henriques in 1147 in celebration of the liberation of Santarém from the Moors, and is a truly vast complex – its main **Church** is the largest in Portugal. The exterior is disappointing, as the Gothic facade has been superseded by unexceptional Baroque additions. Inside, however, all later adornments have been swept away, restoring the narrow soaring aisles to their original vertical simplicity. The only exception to this magnificent Gothic purity is the frothy Manueline doorway to the sacristy, hidden behind the high altar.

The abbey's most precious treasures are the fourteenth-century **tombs of Dom Pedro and Dona Inês de Castro**, each occupying one of the transepts and sculpted with phenomenal wealth of detail to show the story of Pedro's love for Inês de Castro, the daughter of a Galician nobleman. Fearing Spanish influence over the Portuguese throne, Pedro's father, Afonso V, forbade their marriage. The ceremony nevertheless took place in secret, whereupon Afonso sanctioned his daughter-in-law's murder. When Pedro succeeded to the throne in 1357 he exhumed the corpse of his lover, forcing the entire royal circle to acknowledge her as queen by kissing her decomposing hand. The tombs – inscribed with the motto "Até o Fim do Mundo" (Until the End of the World) – have been placed foot to foot so that on the Day of Judgment the lovers may rise and immediately feast their eyes on one another.

The most amazing room in the building is the **kitchen**, with its cellars and gargantuan conical chimney, supported by eight trunk-like iron columns. A stream tapped from the River Alcôa still runs straight through the room: it was used not merely for cooking and washing but also to provide a constant supply of fresh fish. The **Sala dos Reis** (Kings' Room), off the beautiful **Cloisters of Silence**, displays statues of virtually every king of Portugal down to Dom José, who died in 1777. The rest of the abbey, including four cloisters, seven dormitories and endless corridors, is closed to the public.

Alcobaça's **tourist office** (☎062/582 83) is opposite the abbey on Praça 25 de Abril. *Pensão Restaurante Corações Unidos* (☎062/582 142; ③), around the corner at Rua Frei António Brandão 39–45, has decent rooms. The *Quartos Alcôa* (☎062/582 727; ②) off the Praça da República, beside the abbey, is cheaper, but best of all is the *Residençial Mosteiro* (☎062/582 183; ②) on Avda João de Deus 1. There's also a **campsite**, ten minutes north of the bus station along Avda Manuel da Silva Carolino. Good-value places to **eat** include *Frie Bernado*, Rua D Pedro V, a huge place serving huge meals, and *Celeiro dos Frades*, or the monks' barn, atmospherically situated under the arches alongside the abbey.

Batalha

The **Mosteiro de Santa Maria da Vitória**, better known as the **Abbey of Batalha** (Battle Abbey; daily 9am–5/6pm; 400$00, free Sun am), is the finest building in Portugal, classified on UNESCO's World Heritage list, and an enduring symbol of national pride. It was originally founded to commemorate the Battle of Aljubarrota (1385), which sealed Portugal's independence after decades of Spanish intrigue. It is possible to stay in the village around the abbey, but it's best to visit on a trip from Leiria (5 buses daily).

The honey-coloured abbey was transformed by Manueline additions in the late fifteenth and early sixteenth centuries, but the bulk was completed between 1388 and 1434 in a profusely ornate version of French Gothic. Within this flamboyant framework there are also strong elements of the English Perpendicular style, an influence explained by the **Capela do Fundador** (Founder's Chapel), directly to the right upon entering the church: beneath the octagonal lantern rests the tomb of Dom João I and Philippa of Lancaster, their hands clasped in the ultimate expression of harmonious relations between Portugal and England. The four younger sons of João and Philippa are buried along the south wall of the Capela do Fundador in a row of recessed arches. Second from the right is the **Tomb of Prince Henry the**

Navigator, who guided the exploration of Madeira, the Azores and the African coast as far as Sierra Leone. Maritime exploration resumed under João II (1481–95) and accelerated with the accession of Manuel I (1495–1521). The **Claustro Real** (Royal Cloister) dates from this period of burgeoning self-confidence, its intricate stone grilles being added by Diogo de Boitaca, architect of the cloisters at Belém and the prime genius of Manueline art. Off the east side opens the early fifteenth-century **Sala do Capítulo** (Chapter House), remarkable for the unsupported span of its ceiling. The Church authorities were convinced that the whole chamber would come crashing down and only employed as labourers criminals already condemned to death.

The **Capelas Imperfeitas** (Unfinished Chapels) form a separate structure tacked on to the east end of the church and accessible only from outside the main complex. Dom Duarte, eldest son of João and Philippa, commissioned them in 1437 as a royal mausoleum but, as with the cloisters, the original design was transformed beyond all recognition by Dom Manuel's architects. It is unique among examples of Christian architecture in its evocation of the great shrines of Islam and Hinduism: perhaps it was inspired by the tales of Indian monuments that filtered back along the eastern trade routes.

Fátima

FÁTIMA is one of the most important centres of pilgrimage in the Catholic world, a status due to the six **Apparitions of the Virgin Mary**. On May 13, 1917, three peasant children from the village were tending their parents' flock when, in a flash of lightning, they were confronted with "a lady brighter than the sun" sitting in the branches of a tree. The vision returned on the thirteenth day of the next five months, culminating in the so-called Miracle of the Sun on October 13, when a swirling ball of fire cured lifelong illnesses. To commemorate these extraordinary events a vast white **Basílica** and gigantic esplanade have been built, more than capable of holding the crowds of 100,000 who congregate here for the main **pilgrimages** on May 12 & 13 and October 12 & 13. In the church the tombs of two of the children, who died in the European flu epidemic of 1919–20, are the subject of constant attention. Hospices and convents have sprung up in the shadow of the basílica, and inevitably the fame of Fátima has resulted in its commercialization. **Pensions** and **restaurants** abound, but there's little reason to stay except during the big pilgrimages to witness the midnight processions. Regular **bus services** to Fátima from Leiria and Tomar make a day-trip easy.

Tomar

The Convento de Cristo at **TOMAR**, 34km east of Fátima, is an artistic *tour de force* which entwines the main military, religious and imperial strands in the history of Portugal. In addition, Tomar is an attractive town in its own right – especially during the *Festas dos Tabuleiros*, in the first week of July, when the place goes wild. Aim to spend a couple of days here if you can.

Built on a simple grid plan, Tomar's old quarters preserve all their traditional charm – whitewashed, terraced cottages lining narrow cobbled streets. On the central Praça da República stands an elegant seventeenth-century town hall, a ring of houses of the same period and the Manueline church of **São João Baptista**, remarkable for its octagonal belfry and elaborate doorway. Nearby, at Rua Joaquim Jacinto 73, you'll find an excellently preserved fourteenth-century **Synagogue**, now the Museu Luso-Hebraicoa Abraham Zacuta (9.30am–12.30pm & 2–5pm, closed Wed); in 1496 Dom Manuel ordered the expulsion or conversion of all Portuguese Jews, and the synagogue at Tomar was one of the few to survive.

The **Convento de Cristo** (Tues–Sun 9.30am–12.30pm & 2–5pm; 400$00) is set among pleasant gardens with splendid views, about a quarter of an hour's walk uphill from the centre of town. Founded in 1162 by Gualdim Pais, first Master of the Knights Templar, it was the headquarters of the Order. The heart of the complex remains the **Charola**, the temple from which the knights drew their moral conviction. It is a strange place, more suggestive of the occult than of Christianity; like almost every circular church, it is ultimately based on the

Church of the Holy Sepulchre in Jerusalem, for whose protection the Knights Templar were originally founded.

As the Moorish threat receded, the Knights became a challenge to the authority of European monarchs. In Spain this prompted a vicious witch-hunt and many of the Knights sought refuge in Portugal. The highlight of Tomar is the ornamentation of the windows on the main facade of its **Chapter House**, where maritime motifs form a memorial to the sailors who established the Portuguese empire. João III (1521–57) transformed the convent into a thoroughgoing monastic community, adding dormitories, kitchens and no fewer than four cloisters. The adjoining two-tiered **Great Cloisters** comprise one of the purest examples of the Renaissance style in Portugal.

Tomar has a pleasant **campsite** in town and a number of reasonable **pensions**, each with a **restaurant**: *Nun' Álvare* (☎049/31 28 73; ②) and *Tomarense* (☎049/31 29 48; ②) near the bus station; and *Luz* (049/31 23 17; ④) and the very popular *Residencial União* (☎049/32 31 61; ④) in the centre of town at Rua Serpa Pinto.

Coimbra

COIMBRA was Portugal's capital from 1143 to 1255 and it ranks behind only the cities of Lisbon and Porto in historic importance. Its university, founded in 1290 and finally established here in 1537 after a series of moves back and forth to Lisbon, was the only one existing in Portugal until the beginning of this century. For a provincial town it has remarkable riches, and it's an enjoyable place to be, too – lively when the students are in town, sleepy during the holidays. The best time of all to be here is in May, when the students celebrate the end of the academic year in the **Queima das Fitas**, tearing or burning their gowns and faculty ribbons. This is when you're most likely to hear the Coimbra *fado*, distinguished from the Lisbon version by its mournful pace and complex lyrics.

The City

Old Coimbra sits on a hill on the right bank of the River Mondego, with the university crowding its summit. The main buildings of the **Old University**, dating from the sixteenth century, are set around a courtyard dominated by a Baroque clocktower and a statue of João III looking remarkably like Henry VIII. The chapel is covered with *azulejos* – traditional glazed and painted tiles – and intricate decoration, but takes second spot to the **Library** (daily 10am–noon & 2–5pm; 250$00), a Baroque fantasy presented to the faculty by João V in the early eighteenth century.

Below the university a good first stop is the **Museu Machado de Castro** (Tues–Sun 9.30am–12.30pm & 2–5.30pm; 250$00, free Sun am), just down from the unprepossessing **Sé Nova** (New Cathedral). Named after an eighteenth-century sculptor, the museum is housed in the former archbishop's palace, which would be worth visiting in its own right even if it were empty. As it is, it's positively stuffed with sculpture, paintings, furniture and ceramics. The **Sé Velha** (Old Cathedral; daily 10am–12pm & 2–7.30pm, closed Fri–Sun afternoons), halfway down the hill, is one of the most important Romanesque buildings in Portugal, little altered and seemingly unbowed by the years. Solid and square on the outside, it's also stolid and simple within, the decoration confined to a few giant conch shells and some unobtrusive *azulejos*. The Gothic tombs and low-arched **cloister** (100$00) are equally restrained.

Restraint and simplicity certainly aren't the chief qualities of the **Igreja de Santa Cruz** (Mon–Sat 9am–noon & 2–5.45pm; 200$00 for cloister), at the bottom of the hill past the city gates. Although it was founded before the Old Cathedral, nothing remains that has not been substantially remodelled. In the early sixteenth century Coimbra was the site of a major sculptural school; the new tombs for Portugal's first kings, Afonso Henriques and Sancho I, and the elaborately carved pulpit, are among its very finest works. The Manueline theme is at its clearest in the airy arches of the Cloister of Silence, its walls decorated with bas-relief scenes from the life of Christ.

It was in Santa Cruz that Dom Pedro had his court pay homage to the corpse of Inês de Castro, which had lain in the now ruined **Convento de Santa Clara-a-Velha** across the river, alongside the convent's founder, Saint-Queen Isabel. The tombs have long since been moved away, Inês' to Alcobaça and Isabel's to the **Convento de Santa Clara-a-Nova** (Tues–Sun 8.30am–noon & 2–6pm; 100$00 for cloister), higher up the hill. Two features make the climb worthwhile: the silver tomb itself and the vast cloister financed by João V, whose devotion to nuns went beyond the bounds of spiritual comfort. Between the two convents is **Portugal dos Pequeninos** (daily 9am–5.30pm; 800$00), a park full of scale models of many of the country's great buildings, interspersed with "typical" farmhouses and sections on the overseas territories, heavy with the White Man's Burden.

Practicalities

Most mainline **trains** stop at Coimbra B, 3km north of the city, from where there are frequent connecting services to Coimbra A, right at the heart of things. The main **bus station** is on Avenida Fernão de Magalhães, about fifteen minutes' walk from the centre – turn right out of the bus station and head down the main road. The **tourist office** (summer Mon–Fri, 9am–6pm, Sat & Sun 10am–1pm & 2.30–5pm; reduced hours in winter; ☎039/83 30 19) is opposite the bridge in the Largo da Portagem.

Near the station, the sleazy Rua da Sota and its side streets have a few **pensions** that aren't as bad as they look – try the *Pensão Vitória* at Rua da Sota 9 & 19 (☎039/240 49; ③), or the *Residencial Domus* at Rua Adelino Veiga 62 (☎039/285 84; ③). *Pensão Rivoli* (☎039/255 50; ③), nearby at Praça do Comércio 27, has good rooms, some with showers and the best with balconies overlooking the square. Alternatively, there are several options east of the university; beneath the aqueduct, at Rua Castro Matoso 8, *Antunes* (☎039/82 30 48; ④) offers good service. The **youth hostel**, above the park on Rua Henrique Seco 14 (☎039/229 55; ②), is friendly and immaculately run – it's a twenty-minute walk from Coimbra A, or take bus #7, #8, #29, or #46. There's a reasonable all-year **campsite** at the municipal sports complex (☎039/70 14 97); to reach it, take bus #5 from Largo da Portagem.

There are plenty of inexpensive **places to eat** around the centre. For really basic fare, served up with loads of atmosphere, try the little dives tucked into the tiny alleys between the Largo da Portagem, Rua da Sota and Praça do Comércio. *Adega Paço do Conde* on Rua Paço do Conde is a cavernous, locally renowned *churrasqueiria*, whilst *Viela*, at Rua das Azeiteiras 35, serves enormous and reasonably priced portions that can easily be shared between two. Be sure, also, to try one of the traditional **coffee houses** along Rua Ferreira Borges (notably the *Arcadia*) and Rua Visconde da Luz.

The Forest of Buçaco

The **Forest of Buçaco** is the country's most revered woodland, a monastic domain that was later the site of Napoleon's first significant defeat in the Peninsular War. The Benedictines established a hermitage here as early as the sixth century, and the area remained in religious hands right up to the dissolution of the monasteries in 1834. Chiefly thanks to their care, there are over 700 species of trees in the forest, many of them – like the mighty Mexican Cedars – introduced from distant countries. All nonexpress Coimbra–Viseu **buses** take a short detour from Luso through the forest, so you can easily stay over for a few hours on a trip in this direction, or make a day's excursion from Coimbra. Alternatively, you could camp out in the forest or spend a leisurely night in Luso, an easy walk.

Walks are laid out everywhere in Buçaco, but you can wander freely anywhere in the forest, and in many ways it is at its most attractive when it's wildest. One of the two bus stops is by the **Palace Hotel**, built on the site of the monastery as a summer retreat for royalty in the heart of the forest. An enormous imitation Manueline construction, it's dauntingly plush, but anyone can stroll in, have a drink and admire the *azulejos* tiling, which depicts the Battle of Buçaco. The **Via Sacra**, a winding track lined with chapels with terracotta Stations of the Cross, leads from the hotel to the Cruz Alta, a giant cross at the summit. From here there are magnificent panoramas, even if it's not always the haven of peace the monks strove to create. In the opposite direction from the hotel, a small **military museum** (Tues–Sun 9am–5pm; 200$00) near the Portas da Rainha has maps, uniforms and weapons relating to the battle.

Just above it a narrow road climbs to the obelisk memorial, with vistas inland across to the Serra da Estrela; from here the **Porta de Sula** leads back into the forest.

Viseu

From its high plateau, **VISEU** surveys the country around with the air of a feudal overlord, and indeed, this dignified little city is capital of all it can see. Its medieval heart has changed little, though the approach to it is now through the broad avenues of a prosperous provincial centre: parts of the walls survive and it's within their circuit, breached by two doughty gateways, that almost everything of interest lies.

At the city's highest point is the huge **Praça da Sé**, the paved square in front of the cathedral, best approached from the central Rossío through the Porta do Soar. Here, amid a line of granite buildings, stand the white Baroque facade of the **Igreja da Misericórdia** and the **Cathedral**, a weighty twin-towered Romanesque base on which a succession of generations have made their mark. The facade is stern granite, but the interior is a great hall with intricate vaulting, carved to represent twisted and knotted ropes. The cathedral's Renaissance cloister is one of the most graceful in the country; the rooms of its upper level, looking out over the tangled roofs of the oldest part of the town, house the cathedral's treasures, including a twelfth-century Bible. The greatest treasure of Viseu, though, is the adjacent **Museu Grão Vasco** (Tues–Sun 9.30am–12.30pm & 2–5.30pm; 250$00,; closed for restoration until beginning of 2000). Vasco Fernandes – known always as *Grão Vasco*, the Great Vasco – was the key figure in a school of Flemish-influenced painters which flourished here in the first half of the sixteenth century. The centrepiece of the collection is his masterly *St Peter on his Throne*.

The **tourist office** up from the Rossío, just off Avda 25 de Abril (Mon–Fri 9am–12.30pm & 2.30–6pm, Sat & Sun 10am–noon & 3–5.30pm; ☎032/42 09 50), is a good source of information for the region as a whole. **Accommodation** in Viseu is poor, but there are three tolerable places right in the centre: *Pensão Bela Vista*, Rua Alexandre Herculano 510, near the turismo (☎032/42 20 26; ②); *Pensão Rossío Parque*, Praça da República 55 (☎032/42 20 85; ④); and *Residential Duque de Viseu*, Rua das Ameias 22, by the cathedral (☎032/42 12 86; ④). There's a **campsite** (☎032/261 46) in the Parque do Fontelo, about ten minutes' walk east of the centre. Some of the best **food** in the province is to be had at *O Cortiço*, 45 Rua Augusto Hilário, where prices aren't too high but tables can be hard to get. **Moving on** from Viseu, which is a major stopover for routes north, there are regular buses to Lamego via Castro Daire, Guarda, Coimbra, Lisbon and Faro.

Guarda

GUARDA, at over 1000m, is claimed by its inhabitants to be the highest city in Europe – an assertion to be taken with a pinch of salt. It is high enough, though, to be chilly and windswept all year round and to offer superb views. The city was founded in 1197 by Dom Sancho I to guard his borders against both Moors and Spaniards, and though the castle and walls have all but disappeared, its arcaded streets and little squares can be distinctly picturesque.

The **train station** is 3km north of the centre but there is, fortunately, a connecting bus that meets all the major trains; the **bus station** is about four hundred metres southeast of the cathedral, the heart of the old town. Dour and grey, the castellated facade of the **Cathedral** looks like the gateway of a castle, but around the sides the exterior is lightened by flying buttresses, pinnacles and grimacing gargoyles. Inside it's surprisingly lofty, with twisted pillars and vaulting influenced by the Manueline style. The huge carved stone retable is by João de Rouão, a leading figure in the sixteenth-century resurgence of Portuguese sculpture at Coimbra. There are modern and imaginative displays of local archeology, art and sculpture in the **Museu Regional**, a short way east. Of the **Castle**, on a bleak little hill nearby, only the square keep survives, while the **walls** are recalled by just three surviving gates. The cobbled streets of the old town, though, are fascinating in themselves – the tangled area between the **Porta da Estrela** and **Porta do Rei**, north of the cathedral, has changed little in the past four hundred years.

There are two **tourist offices**: a central one on Praça Luis de Canões (Mon–Fri 9am–12.30pm & 2–5.30pm; ☎071/22 22 51), where you can pick up a town map: and a more helpful one next to the modern Câmara Municipal (Tues–Fri 9.30am–noon & 2–6pm, Sat closes 8pm; ☎071/22 18 17). **Places to stay** are fairly easy to come by if not especially cheap: try the attractive *Pensão Moreira*, Rua Mouzinho de Albuquerque 47 (☎071/21 41 31; ③), or cheerful rooms at the *Casa de Sé*, just off Praça Luis de Canões, on Rua Augusto Gil 17 (☎071/21 25 01; ④), off the central square. There is also a new **youth hostel** on Av Alexandre Hercularo (☎071/22 39 38; ②), on the way to Guarda's **campsite**, open all year in a park a short way from the castle; remember, though, that nights can be extremely cold. The **restaurants** between the Porta da Estrela and the church of São Vicente serve basic but good fare.

NORTHERN PORTUGAL

The economic powerhouse of the north is **Porto**, the country's second largest city and most industrious centre. It's an enticingly lively place, made especially attractive by the port-producing suburb of **Vila Nova de Gaia**, whose wines are supplied by the vineyards of the River Douro. The **Douro Valley**, a spectacular rocky gorge as it approaches the sea, is followed by a magnificent **rail route** whose branch lines run along some equally lovely valleys – along the River Tâmega to Amarante, along the Corgo to Vila Real, and along the Tua, from where there are bus connections to **Bragança**, capital of the isolated region of **Trás-os-Montes**. The Portuguese consider the northwest province of the **Minho** to be the most beautiful part of their country, and with its river valleys, wooded hills, trailing vines and wild coastline, the attractions are obvious. A small, thoroughly rural and conservative region, its towns are often outrageously picturesque and full of quiet charm. Monuments and museums are concentrated in **Braga** and **Guimarães**, while between them lie the extensive Celtic ruins of the **Citânia de Briteiros**, the most impressive archeological site in Portugal. **Viana do Castelo**, the main town of the Minho coast, is an enjoyably low-key resort with a wonderful beach.

Porto

Capital of the north, **PORTO** is very different from Lisbon – unpretentious, inward-looking, unashamedly commercial. As the local saying goes: "Coimbra sings; Braga prays; Lisbon shows off; and Porto works." The city's fascination lies very much in the life of the place, with its prosperous business core surrounded by smart suburbs and elegant villas, side by side with a heart of cramped streets and ancient alleys, that has been declared a UNESCO World Heritage Classified Area.

Arrival and information
Most trains will drop you at the distant **Estação de Campanhã**; you should change here for a local train to central **São Bento** – it takes about five minutes and there should never be more than a twenty-minute wait. Certain trains from Minho (Guimarães) and the north coast (Póvoa de Varzim) use the smaller **Estação da Trindade**, from where it's a short walk down Rua da Trindade, past the town hall and into the centre. As a general rule, buses **from the south** come in around Rua Alexandre Herculano, and those **from the north** around the Praça Filipa de Lencastre, or Praça da Trindade.

Just a few yards north of the central São Bento station lies the **Avenida dos Aliados**, Porto's main commercial centre, which culminates at Praça Gen. Humberto Delgado, site of the central post office and the main **tourist office** (Mon–Fri 9am–5.30pm; ☎02/31 27 40).

Accommodation
The **cheapest rooms** in town are on Ruas do Loureiro and Cimo do Vila, around the corner from São Bento. Be warned, though, that this is something of a red-light district. For more salubrious places, your best bet is to head for the areas west or east of Avenida dos Aliados; all the hotels listed below are to the west – with the exception of *Estoril*, which lies to the north.

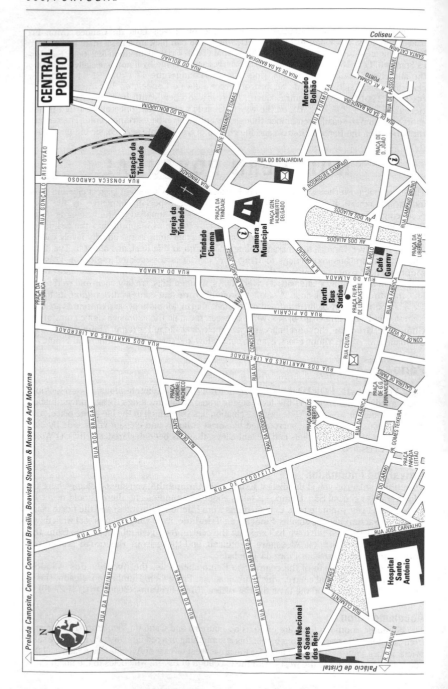

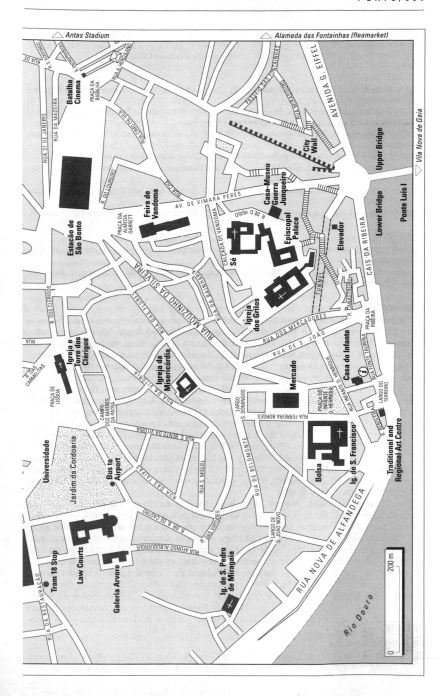

HOSTEL
Pousada de Juventude, Rua Rodrigues Lobo 98 (☎02/606 55 35). Large and clean but lacking in atmosphere. Buses #3, #20 or #52 from Praça da Liberdade – ask for Praça da Galiza. ②.

HOTELS
Pensão Estoril, Rua de Cedofeita 193 (☎02/200 27 51). Wonderful-value, well set-up rooms, with private baths and phones. ③.

Pensão Residencial Duas Nações, Praça Guilherme Gomes Fernandes 59 (☎02/208 16 16). Cheap and dependable, but often full; private bathroom included. ④.

Pensão Pão-de-Açucar, 262 Rua do Almada 262 (☎02/200 24 25). More expensive three-star with private bathrooms. ④.

Pensão Porto Chique, Rua Conde de Vizela 26 (☎02/208 00 69). Reasonable and near São Bento. ③.

Pensão Universal, Auda dos aliados 38 (☎02/200 67 58). Clean and in a perfect position, although it can be noisy. ⑤.

Residencial Paris, Rua da Fábrica 27–29 (☎02/207 31 40). A faded hotel with huge rooms; always popular. Breakfast included. ③.

Residencial Vera Cruz, Rua Ramalho Ortigão 14 (☎02/33 23 96). Smartish and conveniently located. ③.

CAMPSITES
Marisol, Praia da Madalena (☎02/711 59 42). Stunning location on the south side of the river. Bus #57 from São Bento train station.

Prelada (☎02/812 616). The closest of the campsites: take bus #9 from Bolhão (until 9pm), or #56 or #87 from Cordoaria or the airport (until midnight).

The City

The stifled streets of the old town rarely permit any sort of overall view, so it's a good idea to climb the Baroque **Igreja e Torre dos Clérigos** (daily 9am–5.30pm; 500$00) to get your bearings. There are fine views, too, from the courtyard in front of the **Sé** (Mon–Sat 9am–12.30pm & 2.30–5.30pm, Sun for mass only; cloisters 100$00), an austere building standing four-square on its rocky outcrop. Inside it's depressing, even the vaunted silver altarpiece failing to make any impression in the gloom. For a small fee, however, you can escape into the cloisters and climb to the dazzling chapterhouse, with more views over the old quarter.

Around the back, Calçada de Vandoma plunges downwards, lined with the stalls of the **flea market**. Not much goes on at the waterfront since the big ships stopped calling here, but this is definitely the centre for nightlife. To the west, a statue of Porto-born Henry the Navigator faces the pompous Bolsa (Stock Exchange) and the back of **São Francisco** (Mon–Sat 9am–5/6pm; April–Oct also Sun 9am–5pm; 500$00), perhaps the most extraordinary church in Porto. Outside it looks like an ordinary Gothic construction, but the interior has been transformed by an unbelievably ornate attack of eighteenth-century refurbishment. Don't miss the church's small **museum**, which consists largely of artefacts salvaged from the monastery that once stood nearby.

The **Museu Nacional Soares dos Reis** at Rua de Dom Manuel II (Tues–Sun 10am–12.30pm & 2–5.30pm; 400$00), over to the west behind the city hospital, was the first national museum in Portugal. Its collection includes glass, ceramics and a formidable array of eighteenth- and nineteenth-century paintings, as well as the late nineteenth-century sculptures of Soares dos Reis – his *O Desterro* (The Exile) is probably the best-known work in Portugal. Follow the road past the museum, or take any bus from the Cordoaria stop except #6 and #18, and you'll come to the **Jardim do Palácio de Cristal**, a peaceful park dominated by a huge domed pavilion which now serves as an exhibition hall. In summer the park is home to a vast funfair. On the far side, across Rua Entre Quintas, stands the **Solar do Vinho do Porto** (Mon–Fri 10am–11.45pm, Sat 11am–10.45pm), where you can sample one of hundreds of varieties of **port** in air-conditioned splendour – a good prelude to visiting Vila Nova.

VILA NOVA DE GAIA

The suburb of Vila Nova de Gaia is taken over almost entirely by the port trade: the names of the various companies, spelled out in huge white letters across their roofs, dominate even the most distant view. You can walk to Gaia across the **Ponte Dom Luis**: the most direct route to the wine lodges is across the lower level from the Cais da Ribeira, but if you've a head for heights it's an amazing sensation to walk over the upper deck; otherwise, take bus #32, #57 or #91 from São Bento. Almost all the companies offer free **tasting** and tours of their factory. There's little pressure to buy anything – if you do, try the dry white ports, which are expensive and often unobtainable elsewhere.

A more sober visit could be made to the **Casa-Museu de Teixeira Lopes** (Tues–Sat 9am–12.30pm & 2–5.30pm; free), in the south of the suburb – take bus #33, #82, #83, or #84 from Auda Aliados over the top of the bridge. Lopes was Soares dos Reis' principal pupil and at the centre of an artistic set who lived in Gaia at the turn of the century – much of whose work is on show here. With its wonderful sculpture-filled courtyard, it's a good place for a picnic lunch and a couple of hours spent rooting around.

Eating and drinking

Porto's cafés include some elegant rivals to the turn-of-the-century places in Lisbon, while livelier places can be found down on the **waterfronts** on each side of the river – but beware that riverside cafés in Vila Nova de Gaia can be fiendishly expensive. The city's culinary speciality is *Tripas á Modo do Porto* (tripe) and its citizens are affectionately referred to by the rest of the country as *tripeiros*. Don't let this put you off – there's always plenty of choice on the menu, and there are lots of places where you can eat cheaply. At the basic level, there are **workers' cafés** galore, all with wine on tap, and often with a set menu for the day. Prime areas are north and south of the Cordoaria, especially Rua do Almada and Rua de São Bento da Vitória. All are busy in the middle of the day and invariably close around 7.30pm and all of Sunday. The area to head for **at night** is down by the river, around Cais da Ribeira, full of lively bars and clubs, and where numerous cafés and restaurants have been installed under the arches of the first tier of Porto's ranks of dwellings. There are also many good, cheap standbys around Praça da Batalha.

RESTAURANTS

Café Restaurant Miradouro, Cais da Ribeira, on the arches by the entrance to the bridge, a popular local hangout with great salads and cheap meals.

Casa Filha da Mãe Preta, Cais da Ribeira 39. Bustling restaurant with excellent views over the river.

Charrusqueira de Brasil, Campo dos Mártires da Pátria 136, near Torre dos Clerigos. Cheap worker's diner with a lively, friendly atmosphere, and serving ample portions.

Ginjal do Porto, Rua do Bonjardim 724. Bargain local specialities in a no-frills setting.

Montecarlo, Rua Santa Catarina 17-2°. Looks like a 1930s tearoom, has views over the Praça da Batalha and serves good food.

CAFÉS AND BARS

Labirinto, Rua Nossa Senhora da Fátima 334. A "bar-arcade", catering for a wide range of tastes, with exhibitions and live music. Open 9.30pm–3am.

Taberna da Ribeira, Praça da Ribeira. Prime riverside spot with outdoor tables. Open till 2am.

The Douro Line

The valleys of **the Douro** and its tributaries are among the most spectacular landscapes in Portugal, and the Douro Valley itself, a narrow, winding gorge for the majority of its long route east to the Spanish border, is the most beautiful of all. The Douro **rail route**, which joins the river about 60km inland and then sticks to it across the country, is one of those journeys that needs no justification other than the trip itself. At present there are quite regular connections along the line as far as Peso da Régua, though you will most likely find yourself on a single carriage train; beyond Régua, there are less frequent connections to Tua and Pocinho.

Cete, half a dozen stations out of Porto, is just a mile away from the village of **PAÇO DE SOUSA**, a former headquarters of the Benedictines in Portugal and a popular picnic spot for

Porto locals. If you're looking for a bed, it's not much further down the line to Penafiel station, connected by bus to the village itself. Split by main-road traffic, **PENAFIEL** is not that enticing a place, but it has a saving grace in its fabulous local vinho verde wine, served from massive barrels in the **adega** in the central Largo do Padré Américo. *Fado's* restaurant still has barrels but is quite smart – the owner will sing *fado* at weekends if you're lucky; above is the best and cheapest **hotel**, *Casa João da Liza* (✆055/251 58; ②).

At Livração, about an hour from Porto, the Tâmega line cuts off for Amarante in the mountains. Shortly after, the main line finally reaches the Douro and heads upstream until, at Mesão Frio, the valley broadens into the little plain commanded by **PESO DA RÉGUA**, the depot through which port wine must pass on its way from Pinhão – the centre of production – to Porto. The **tourist office** (summer: daily 9am–12.30pm & 2–6pm, winter: Mon–Fri only; ✆054/228 46), 1km from the train station, can inform you about visits to local cellars. Apart from these alcoholic diversions, there's not much to do except wander through the upper village and along the river. If you need to stay, the high-rise *Pensão Império* at Rua José Vasques Osório 8 (✆054/32 23 99; ④) offers good **accommodation**, breakfast and views, and *Pensão Borrajo* on Rua Dos Camilos near the post office is basic but cheap (✆054/233 96; ②). There are plenty of **restaurants** along the main street.

Beyond Peso da Régua begin the terraced slopes where the **port vines** are grown: they look their best in August, with the grapes ripening, and in September when the harvest has begun. The country continues in this vein, craggy and beautiful, with the softer hills of the interior fading dark green into the distance, to Tua (junction for the Tua line) and Pocinho, where buses take over for routes east towards Miranda do Douro. From there it's a straightforward hitch in summer to Zamora in Spain.

Bragança

On a hillock above **BRAGANÇA**, the small and remote capital of Trás-os-Montes in the northeastern tip of Portugal, stands a pristine circle of walls, enclosing a medieval village that rises to a massive keep and castle. Seemingly untouched by the centuries, this extraordinary citadel – along with the fine local museum – is the principal reason for a visit to the town. The twelfth-century council chamber, the **Domus Municipalis**, stands in the heart of the **Citadel**; very few Romanesque civic buildings have survived anywhere in Europe, and no other has this pentagonal form. Next to it is the church of **Santa Maria**, with its eighteenth-century barrel-vaulted, painted ceiling – a feature common to several churches in Bragança. Towering above these two is the **Castle**, which the Portuguese royal family rejected as a residence in favour of their vast estate in the Alentejo. At its side a curious pillory rises from the back of a prehistoric granite pig, or *porca*, thought to have been a fertility idol of a prehistoric cult. Celtic-inspired medieval tombstones rub shoulders with a menagerie of *porcas* in the gardens of **Museu do Abade de Baçal**, between the citadel and cathedral in Rua Abílio Beça (Tues–Fri 10am–5pm, Sat & Sun 10am–6pm; 250$00, free on Sun). Inside, a collection of sacred art and the watercolours of Alberto Souza are the highlights, along with displays of local costumes.

The **tourist office** (✆073/38 12 73) is on an extension of Avda Cidade de Zamora, a couple of hundred metres north of the cathedral. The cheapest **pension** in town is the *Transmontano* at Avda João da Cruz 168 (✆073/33 18 99; ②); you'd be better advised to pay a little more and stay at *Residencial Poças*, Rua Combatentes da G. Guerra 200 (✆073/33 14 28; ②). The nearest **campsite** (✆073/35 15 35: mid-May to Sept) is 6km out of town on the França road; a better option is the plush, private site (✆073/99 371; open all year) 8km down the Vinhais road, with good facilities and a pool. As for **restaurants**, two favourites are *Restaurante Poças*, next to the *Residencial*, serving big wholesome meals, and *Restaurante D Fernando*, Cidadela 147, inside the walled old town, which is surprisingly good value.

Crossing the border

From Bragança the most obvious route into Spain is via Quintanilha (34km), the nearest town to the **San Martin** border post. There are one or two direct buses daily, but any bus to

Miranda do Douro will take you to a crossroads from where you can hitch the 12km to the border. You can stay here above the *Evaristo*, San Martin's only shop, restaurant and **pension**. At 7am there's a bus to Zamora, connected to Madrid by road and rail. In Bragança there's also the possibility of reserving a seat on the Zamora–Valladolid–Madrid **express bus**, which passes through every Monday, Tuesday, Thursday and Friday.

Braga and around

BRAGA, the tourist office pamphlet claims, is Portugal's answer to Rome. This clearly is going over the top – though it illustrates the city's ecclesiastical pretensions. Founded by the Romans in 279 BC, Braga was a bishopric before being occupied by the Moors. It was reconquered early on and by the end of the eleventh century its archbishops were pressing for recognition as "Primate of the Spains", a title they disputed with Toledo over the next six centuries. It is still Portugal's religious capital – the scene of spectacular **Easter celebrations** with torchlit processions and weirdly hooded penitents.

You won't be able to miss the **Archbishop's Palace**, a great fortress-like building, right at the centre of the old town. In medieval times it covered a tenth of the city and today easily accommodates the municipal library and various faculties of the university. Nearby is the Sé, which like the palace encompasses Gothic, Renaissance and Baroque styles. It was founded in 1070 and its south doorway is a survival from this earliest building; its most striking element, however, is the intricate ornamentation of the roofline, executed by João de Castilho, later the architect of Lisbon's Jerónimos Monastery. A guided tour of the interior (8.30am–6/6.30pm; free, museum and Capela dos Reis 300$00) takes you through three Gothic chapels, of which the outstanding specimen is the **Capela dos Reis** (King's Chapel), built to house the tombs of Henry of Burgundy and his wife Teresa, the cathedral's founders and the parents of Afonso Henriques, founder of the kingdom. Beyond the chapels is the cathedral **museum** – one of the richest collections in Portugal, but displayed like a junk shop.

The Art Deco **tourist office** at the corner of Praça da Republica has copies of the local *Correio do Minho*, good for information on most events in the region. Two **hotels** offering excellent value are the *Residencial Inácio Filhos*, Rua Francisco Sanches 42 (☎053/238 49; ③), and the well-located *Grande Residencia Avenida*, Avda da Liberdade 738 (☎053/26 29 55; ③). Braga's well-equipped **youth hostel** is at Rua Santa Margarida 6 (☎053/61 61 63; ②), off Avda Central; the **campsite** (☎053/27 33 55) is a two-kilometre walk along the Guimarães road – but very cheap and right next to the municipal swimming pool. The *Prégão*, on Largo da Praça Velka, at the foot of Rua do Souto, serves good cheap **food** in generous quantities, as does the *Restaurante Moçambicana* at Rua Andrade Corvo 8, one of several excellent cheap restaurants grouped around the Arco da Porta Nova. *Café Astória*, Praça da Republica, is by far the best of the old **coffee houses**, mahogany-panelled and with cut-glass windows; by contrast, *Ciber Braga* on Praça do Municipo is an **Internet** café and the best of the new. *Locomotiva*, beneath the *Hotel Turismo* on Avda da Liberdade, is a popular club, but *Pacha* on Rua Gonçalo Sampaio is definitely the in place to be.

Bom Jesus

BOM JESUS, 3km outside Braga, is one of Portugal's best-known images, as much concept as building, a monumental place of pilgrimage created by Braga's archbishop in the first decades of the eighteenth century. It is a vast ornamental stairway of granite and white plaster cut into a densely wooded mount high above the city. There is no particular reason for its presence, no miracle or vision, yet it remains the object of devoted pilgrimage, penitents often climbing on their knees. **Buses** run from Hospital de S Marcos to the foot of the stairway about every thirty minutes, more frequently at weekends when half the city piles up there to picnic.

If you resist the temptation of the funicular and climb up the stairway, Bom Jesus' simple allegory unfolds. Each landing has a fountain: the first symbolizes the wounds of Christ, the next five the Senses, and the final three represent the Virtues. At each corner are chapels with mouldering wooden, larger-than-life tableaux of the life of Christ, leading to the

Crucifixion at the altar of the church. Beyond are wooded gardens, grottoes and miniature boating pools, and several cheap, lively **restaurants** – filled on Saturdays with a constant stream of wedding parties.

Citânia de Briteiros

Citânias – Celtic hill settlements – lie scattered throughout the Minho. The **Citânia de Briteiros** (daily 9am–6pm; 700$00), midway betwen Braga and Guimarães, is the most spectacular, and is reputed to have been a last stronghold against the Romans. It's an impressive and exciting site, including the foundations of over 150 huts, a couple of which have been rebuilt to give a sense of their scale and design. There's a clear network of paved streets and paths, two circuits of town walls, cisterns, stone guttering and a public fountain. Don't miss the funerary chamber – a fair walk down the hill to the left of the settlement – with its geometrically patterned stone doorway. There are just two daily **buses** direct to Briteiros from Braga. Otherwise you have to **hitch or walk** from Bom Jesus (6km), or from Caldas das Taipas on the Braga–Guimarães bus route (6km).

Guimarães

Birthplace of Afonso Henriques and first capital of medieval Portucale, **GUIMARÃES** remains a lively and atmospheric university town. The town's chief attraction is the **Castelo** (Tues–Sun 10am–12.30pm & 2–5.30pm; free), whose square keep and seven towers are an enduring symbol of the emergent Portuguese nation. Built by Henry of Burgundy, it became the stronghold of his son, Afonso Henriques. From here the reconquest began along with the creation of a kingdom which, within a century of Afonso's death, was to stretch to its present borders. Afonso is said to have been born in the keep, and was probably baptized in the font of the Romanesque chapel of **São Miguel** on the grassy slope below. The third building here, the **Paço dos Duques**, was once the palace of the Dukes of Bragança, but under the Salazar dictatorship was "restored" as an official residence. Looking like a mock-Gothic Victorian folly, it now houses dull collections of portraits, furniture and porcelain.

The other two museums in Guimarães are, in contrast, among the best outside Lisbon. The **Museu Alberto Sampaio**, ten minutes' walk south of the castle (Tues–Sun 10am–12.30pm & 2–5.30pm, July & Aug till 7pm; 200$00, 125$00 for students), is mostly the treasury of the adjoining Colegiada church and the monastery that used to be here. The highlight is a silver-gilt *Triptych of the Nativity*, said to have been found in the King of Castile's tent after the Portuguese victory at Aljubarrota. Like Batalha, the **Colegiada** itself was built in honour of a vow made by João I before that decisive battle. In front of it stands a Gothic canopy-shrine that marks the spot where Wamba, unwillingly elected king of the Visigoths, drove a pole into the ground swearing that he would not reign until it blossomed. Naturally it sprouted immediately. João, feeling this a useful precedent of divine favour, set out to meet the Castilians from this very point.

Finds from various *citânias* are displayed in the **Museu Martins Sarmento** (Tues–Sun 9.30am–noon & 2–5pm; 200$00), housed in the former convent of São Domingo to the south of the bus station. They include a remarkable series of bronze votive offerings, ornately patterned stones and – most spectacularly – the two *Pedras Formosas* and the *Colossus of Pedralva*. The *Pedras* (literally, "stones") are the portals to funerary monuments like that at Briteiros. The colossus is more enigmatic and considerably more ancient, a vast granite hulk with arm raised aloft and an outsized phallus; it shares the bold, powerfully hewn appearance of the stone boars found in Trás-os-Montes and like them may date from pre-Celtic fertility cults.

The finest church in town is **São Francisco**, a short distance east of the tourist office, with its huge eighteenth-century *azulejos*, or decorative tiles, of St Francis preaching to the fishes and its elegant Renaissance cloister and fountain.

Practicalities

Guimarães' **bus station** is fifteen minutes' walk west of town, near the football stadium; the **train station** is to the south. You'll pass one **tourist office** (Mon–Fri 9am–12.30pm &

2–5.30pm; ☎053/41 24 50) as you walk from here to the centre, the other office is in the centre of the old town in Praça de Santiago (same hours; summer also Sat 10am–1pm & 3–5pm, Sun 10am–1pm; ☎053/51 87 90). There is very little cheap **accommodation**. *Casa dos Pombais*, Avda. de Londres, 40 (☎053/41 29 17; ⑤), has beautiful rooms overlooking attractive gardens, or try the less expensive, but spartan *Casa dos Retiros*, Rua Francisco Agra 163 (☎053/51 15 15; ③ including breakfast). The town's **campsite** (☎053/51 59 12) is 6km away at Penha, a pilgrimage mount and chapel; buses leave every thirty minutes between 6am and 10pm (8pm Sun) from Alameda da Resitencia; or take the cable car from the end of Rua de Dr José Sanpaio (11am–6pm; 500$00 return). For **food**, *O Telheiro*, Rua Dom João I 39–41, above *Café Dom João*, serves great dishes in basic but bustling surroundings, and *Oriental* on Largo do Toural has budget, but very good regional specialities. *El Rei*, Praça de Santiago, is worth the moderate rise in price for its location in the heart of the old town.

SOUTHERN PORTUGAL

The huge, sparsely populated plains of the **Alentejo**, to the southeast of Lisbon, are overwhelmingly agricultural, dominated by vast cork plantations well suited to the low rainfall, sweltering heat and poor soil. This impoverished province is divided into vast estates which provide nearly half of the world's cork but only a sparse living for the mass of the agricultural workforce. Visitors to the Alentejo generally head for **Évora**, the province's dominant and most historic city. The plains south of Évora are rather dull, but the Alentejo coastline more than compensates for the lack of urban pleasures and the tedium of the inland landscape.

With its long, sandy beaches and picturesque rocky coves, the southern coastal region of the **Algarve** has attracted more tourist development than the rest of the country put together. The coastline has two different characters. **West of Faro** you'll find the classic postcard images of the province – a series of tiny bays and coves, broken up by weird rocky outcrops and fantastic grottoes, at their most exotic around the resort of **Lagos**. To the **east of Faro** you encounter the first of a series of sandy offshore islets, **the Ilhas**, which front the coastline for some 25 miles. Not only is this the quieter section of the coast but it has the bonus of much warmer water than further west. Throughout the Algarve **accommodation** can be a major problem in summer, with hotels block-booked by package companies and pensions filling up early in the day; private rooms or campsites help fill in the gaps, but if you're unlucky you might find yourself sleeping out for the odd night.

Évora

ÉVORA is one of the most impressive cities in Portugal, its provincial atmosphere the perfect setting for a range of memorable and often intriguing monuments. The Romans were in occupation for four centuries and the Moors, who were here for just as long, have left their stamp in the tangle of narrow alleys which rise steeply among the whitewashed houses. Most of the monuments, however, date from the fourteenth to the sixteenth century, when, with royal encouragement, the city was one of the leading centres of Portuguese art and architecture.

Used as a slaughterhouse until 1870, the **Temple of Diana** in the central square is the best-preserved Roman temple in Portugal, its stark remains consisting of a small platform supporting more than a dozen granite columns with a marble entablature. Directly opposite, the former **Convento dos Lóios**, now converted into a luxuriant *pousada*, has been partly attributed to Francisco de Arruda, architect of the Tower of Belém in Lisbon. To the left of the *pousada* lies the church of the convent, dedicated to **São João Evangelista**. This is the private property of the ducal Cadaval family, who still occupy a wing or two of the adjacent ancestral palace. Wait outside and you should be admitted (for a fee) to see its *azulejos* (decorative tiling), trick paintings and ossuary.

The **Cathedral**, or Sé, was begun in 1186, about twenty years after the reconquest of Évora from the Moors, and the Romanesque solidity of its two huge square towers and battlemented roofline contrasts sharply with the pointed Gothic arches of the porch and central window. The interior is more straightforwardly Gothic, although the choir and high altar were remodelled in the eighteenth century. Adjacent, in the archbishop's palace, is the excellent **Museu de Évora** (Tues–Sun 10am–12.30pm & 2–5pm), housing important collections of fifteenth- and sixteenth-century Flemish and Portuguese paintings assembled from the city's churches and convents. These give a good illustration of the significance of Flemish artists in the development of Portuguese art, and reflect the strong trade links between the two countries.

Perhaps the most memorable sight in Évora is the **Capela dos Ossos** (Chapel of Bones) in the church of **São Francisco**, close to the bus station. A gruesome reminder of mortality, the walls and pillars of this chilling chamber are entirely covered with the bones of more than 5000 monks; an inscription over the door reads, "Nós ossos que aqui estamos, Pelos vossos esperamos" (We bones here are waiting for your bones). Another interesting feature of this church is its large porch, which combines pointed, rounded and horseshoe arches in a manner typical of Manueline architecture. Appropriately enough, the restored **Palácio de Dom Manuel** – the king who gave his name to the style – lies no more than a minute's walk away, in the Jardim Público.

Practicalities

The **Praça do Giraldo**, a short distance west of the Sé, is the centre of Évora's low-key social scene. Here you can find the **tourist office** (summer Mon–Fri 9am–7pm, Sat & Sun 9am–12.30pm & 2–5.30pm; winter daily 9am–12.30pm & 2–5.30pm; ☎066/70 26 71) and a couple of outdoor cafés. All the cheaper **places to stay** are within five minutes' walk, but Évora's tourist appeal pushes prices way over the norm. Cheapest options are *Pesão Os Manuéis*, just west of the square at Rua do Raimundo 35 (☎066/70 28 61; ②); *Pensão Invicta*, Rua Romão Rmalho 37a, overlooking São Francisco (☎066/70 20 47; ②); and *Pensão Giraldo-Anexo* at Rua dos Mercadores 15 (☎066/70 28 33; ③). If you're stuck for a room, the tourist office will sometimes arrange accommodation in private homes. The **campsite** (☎066/70 51 90) is a couple of kilometres out of town on the Alcáçovas road; there's no reliable bus service. **Restaurants** abound in the centre: try *Adega do Alentejano*, 21a Rua Gabriel Vitor do Monte Pereira, or the cheaper *O Portão*, on Rua do Cano alongside the aqueduct.

The Alentejo Coast

The coast south of Lisbon features towns and beaches as inviting as those of the Algarve. Admittedly, it's exposed to the winds and waves of the Atlantic, and the waters are colder, but it's fine for summer swimming and far quieter. Access is straightforward, with local bus services and the twice-daily *Zambujeira Express* from Lisbon, which takes you within easy range of the whole coastline and stops at the beaches of Vila Nova de Milfontes and Zambujeira do Mar.

Five buses a day run from Lisbon to Alcacer do Sal, from where there are reasonable connections south to **SANTIAGO DO CACÉM**, a pleasant little town overlooked by a castle. In turn, there are five buses a day (in summer) from Santiago to **Lagoa de Santo André** and the adjoining **Lagoa de Melides**, with two of the best beaches in the country. Each of these lagoons has its own small summer community entirely devoted to having a good time on the beach. The **campsites** at both places are of a high standard and there are masses of signs offering rooms, chalets and whole houses to let. Beyond the beach-cafés and ice-cream stalls miles and miles of sand stretch all the way to Comporta in the north and Sines in the south. The sea is enticing with high waves and good surf, but take local advice on water conditions, as the undertow can be fierce. If you want to base yourself at Santiago rather than at the beaches, there's no shortage of good **food and accommodation**. The *Restaurante Covas*, by the bus station at Rua Cidade de Setúbal 10 (☎069/226 75; ③), is recommended both for its **rooms** and for its outstanding meals. There are plenty of other places around town advertising rooms, and another great **restaurant** – *Praceta,* at Largo Zeca Afonso (behind the bus station).

On the southern half of the Alentejo coast, **ODEMIRA** is the main inland base. A quiet, unspoiled country town, it has an erratic bus service (8 daily) to the beach at Vila Nova de Milfontes and to Zambujeira do Mar (2 daily). Unless you're camping, you're unlikely to find anywhere to spend the night in these resorts from June to August, so it's not a bad idea to stay in Odemira and take day-trips to the seaside. The town has several restaurants and **pensions**, including *Casa Rita*, Largo do Poço Novo (☎083/225 31; ②), and *Residencial Idálio*, Rua Engl. Arantes Oliveira 28 (☎083/221 56; ②), just to the left when you come out of the bus station. Of the **restaurants**, try *O Tarro*, near the main road junction.

VILA NOVA DE MILFONTES lies on the estuary of the River Mira, whose sandy banks gradually expand and merge into the coastline. This is generally the most crowded and popular resort in the Alentejo, with lines of villas and hotels radiating from the centre of the old village. It's still a pretty place, though, with a handsome little castle and an ancient port, reputed to have harboured Hannibal and his Carthaginians during a storm. Recent development means finding reasonable **rooms** shouldn't be a problem, and there are a couple of large **campsites** to the north of the village: *Parque de Milfontes* (☎083/99 61 04) and the more modest *Campiférias* (☎083/964 09). At **ZAMBUJEIRA DO MAR**, south of Odemira and 7km west of the main road, a large cliff provides a dramatic backdrop to the beach, more than compensating for the winds. There's only a few small pensions, such as the *Mar-e-Sol* (☎083/96 11 71; ⑤), a few *dormidas* and a couple of bars, as well as a reasonable campsite open all year (☎083/611 72), about 1km from the cliffs. Lastly, the resort of **PORTO CÔVO**, although overdeveloped, has plentiful accommodation and beautiful, almost untouched beaches to the south.

Faro

FARO, a sleepy provincial town twenty years ago, now has all the facilities of a modern European city, with an attractive shopping area, some decent restaurants and a "real" Portuguese feel in contrast to many nearby resorts. Excellent **beaches**, too, are within easy reach, and in summer there's quite a nightlife scene, as thousands of travellers pass through on their way to and from the airport, 6km west of the town.

Sacked and burned by the Earl of Essex in 1596, and devastated by the Great Earthquake of 1755, the town has few historic buildings. By far the most curious sight is the Baroque **Igreja do Carmo** (Mon–Fri 10am–1pm & 2.30–5pm, Sat 10am–1pm; 250$00) near the central post office on Largo do Carmo. A door to the right of the altar leads to a macabre **Capela dos Ossos** (Chapel of the Bones), its walls decorated with bones disinterred from the adjacent cemetery. This aside, the most interesting buildings are all in the old, semiwalled quarter on the south side of the harbour, centred around the majestic **Largo da Sé** and entered through the eighteenth-century **Arco da Vila**. The Largo is flanked by the bishop's palace and **Sé** (Mon–Fri 10am–noon & 2.30–5.30pm, Sun for mass only), a miscellany of Gothic, Renaissance and Baroque styles, heavily remodelled after the Great Earthquake. More impressive is the nearby **Museu Arqueológico** (Mon–Fri 9.30am–5pm; 250$00), installed in a fine sixteenth-century convent. The most striking exhibit is a third-century Roman mosaic of Neptune and the four winds, unearthed near Faro train station.

Faro marks a geographical boundary on the Algarve. The whole coastline east from here to Manta Rota, near the Spanish border, is protected by thin stretches of mud flats, fringed in their turn by a chain of long and magnificent sandbanks. The "town beach", **Praia de Faro**, is typical of these sandspit beaches – but atypical in that it's both overcrowded and overdeveloped; bus #16 goes there (hourly 8am–8pm; until 10pm in summer), departing from the stop opposite the bus station.

Practicalities

Taxis from the **airport** to the centre should cost around 1400$00; or take bus #16 (hourly 8am–8/9pm), a twenty-minute journey to town. The bus station is right in the centre, behind the *Hotel Eva*, across from the old town; the train station is a few minutes beyond, up the Avenida da República. There's a **tourist office** at the airport (daily 10am–midnight); the main office is at Rua da Misericordia 8–12 (summer daily 9.30am–7pm; winter Mon–Fri 9.30am–5pm, Sat & Sun 9.30am–12.30pm & 2–5.30pm; ☎089/80 36 04), just beyond the entrance to the old town.

Pensions are concentrated just north of the harbour along Rua Infante D. Henrique and the noisy Rua Conselheiro Bivar, and around Praça Ferreira de Almeida on Rua Vasco da Gama, Rua Filipe Alistão and Rua do Alportel. Among the better places is the increasingly upmarket *Pensão Madalena* (☎089/80 58 06; ④) at Rua C. Bivar 109; *Casa de Hóspedes Adelaide* (☎089/80 23 83; ②), near the bus station at Rua Cruz das Mestras 7–9, is the best budget choice. Also excellent value is the eccentric *Pensão Dandy*, F. Alistão 62 (☎089/82 47 91; ③), and *Pensão São Félipe*, Rua Infante Don Henrique 55a (☎089/82 41 82; ④). The **campsite** (☎089/81 78 76) is at Praia de Faro, and is always packed in summer – phone ahead; take bus #16 from town. There are **restaurants** to meet most budgets: try the *Restaurant Dois Irmãos*, on Largo Terreiro do Bispo, or the *Esplanada-Bar As Parreiras*, Rua Rebelo da Silva 22. The town's **nightlife** centres around Rua do Prior, a cobbled alley full of bars and discos, and Rua Conselheiro Bivar, where *3ʳᵈ Millenium* is one of the best.

Olhão

OLHÃO, 8km east of Faro, is the largest fishing port on the Algarve and an excellent base for visiting the sandbank islands (*ilhas*). **Train** and **bus** stations are near each other off the Avenida da República northeast of town. The **tourist office**, just off Rua do Comércio (summer Mon–Fri 9.30am–7pm, Sat & Sun 9.30am–12.30pm & 2–5.30pm; winter Mon–Fri 9.30am–5.30pm), will provide a town map and advice on rooms. For **accommodation**, try the highly rated *Pensão Bela Vista* (☎089/70 25 38; ③), left out of the tourist office then first left; or the two-star *Pensão Bicuar* at Rua Vasco da Gama 5 (☎089/71 48 16; ③). The nearest **campsite** (☎089/700 1300) is at Marim, 3km east – buses hourly till 7pm from the main station. There are clusters of **restaurants** and **bars** around Rua do Comércio and along the seafront: *Taiti* at Rua Vasco da Gama 24 is reasonably good, as is *Papy's* on Avda 56 de Outubro, past the fish market.

Ferries leave for the **Ilhas of Armona** and **Culatra** from the jetty at the far end of Olhão's municipal gardens, five minutes from the market. The service to **ARMONA** (15min; 180$00 each way) drops you off at a long strip of holiday chalets and huts that stretches right across the island on either side of the main path. This is the only type of **accommodation** available here, and you'll be lucky to get one in summer; phone ahead to book (Orbitur ☎089/71 41 73). On the ocean side, the beach disappears into the distance and a short walk will take you to totally deserted stretches of sand and dune. The beach facing the mainland is smaller and tends to get very crowded in summer, but the water here is always warm and calm, and there is a **campsite** (☎098/71 41 73). Boats to the more distant **Ilha of Culatra** are less frequent (35–45min; 250$00 each way) and call first at unattractive Culatra town, then at **FAROL**, an untidy village of holiday homes edged by beautiful beaches on the ocean side. Note that ferry services are drastically reduced outside July and August.

Tavira

TAVIRA is a clear winner if you are looking for an urban base on the eastern stretch. It's a good-looking little town with superb island beaches in easy reach, yet despite ever-increasing visitors it continues to make its living as a tuna-fishing port. **Buses** pull up at the new terminal by the river, a two-minute walk from the central square, the Praça da República; the **train station** is 1km from the centre of town, straight up the Rua da Liberdade. From May to mid-October, boats cross from Quatro Águas, 2km east of town, to the eastern end of the **Ilha de Tavira**, which stretches west almost as far as Fuzeta, some 14km away. The beach is enormous, backed by dunes, and despite increasing development – a small chalet settlement, watersports, beach umbrellas and half a dozen bar/restaurants facing the sea – it's an enjoyable spot in which to hang out.

There's a **campsite** (☎081/235 05), a minute from the sands, but by far the best place **to** stay in Tavira is the *Residencial Lagoas*, north of the river at Rua Almirante Cândido dos Reis 24 (☎081/32 22 52; ②), with the bonus of the budget eatery, *Bica*, below. Alternatives include the *Pensão do Castelo* (☎081/32 39 42; ②) in the main square, the *Residencial Mirante* at Rua da Liberdade 83 (☎081/32 22 55; ④ with breakfast) just up the main road, and the lovely *Residencial Princesa do Gilão*, across the river on the quayside (☎081/32 51 71; ④), whose front rooms have balconies overlooking the river. If these options fail to produce a bed, the **tourist office** just off the main Praça da República (May–Sept daily 9.30am–7pm; Oct–April Mon–Sat 9am–12.30pm & 2–5pm; ☎081/32 25 11) may be able to find you a **private room**. A succession of **bars and restaurants** line the gardens along the bank of the River Gilão, which flows through the centre of town. Probably the best of the restaurants here is the *Imperial*, which serves some of the finest seafood in the Algarve at fairly reasonable prices. Also good are *Anazu*, Rua Jacques Pessoa 13, a riverfront café, and the *Aquasul Restaurante*, Rua Dr Augusto Da Silva Carvalho 11–13, which serves fresh pizzas and cosmopolitan main dishes. The *Arco*, at Rua Almirante Cândido dos Reis 67, is a friendly, laid-back, gay **bar**.

Portimão and around

PORTIMÃO, the first tolerable place to the west of Faro, is a sprawling port, a major sardine-canning centre and a base for the construction industries spawned by the tourist boom. The best part is the riverfront – a hive of activity with its bars, restaurants and fishing port. The **train station** is inconveniently located at the northern tip of town, with buses running at 45-minute intervals, so you may have to make the twenty-minute walk. Intertown **buses** stop by the waterfront on Largo do Duque. The **tourist office** has just been moved next to the football stadium on Avda. Zeca Afonso (Mon & Fri 9.30am–12.30pm & 2–7pm, Tues–Thurs 9.30am–7pm, Sat & Sun 9.30am–12pm & 2–5.30pm; ☎082/41 91 31); they will help you find a **private room**, or provide a list of **pensions**. Good bets include the *Residencial O Pátio* 3 (☎082/42 42 88; ④ with breakfast), down from the tourist office at Rua Dr João Vitorino Mealha 5, and the spick-and-span *Pensão Arabi* (☎082/260 06; ③) on Praça Manuel Teixeira Gomes. Any of the stalls that line the quayside, underneath the bridge, will charcoal-grill half a dozen huge sardines and serve them up with fries, salad and wine for around 1000$00.

PRAIA DA ROCHA, 3km south of Portimão and served by buses every thirty minutes, was one of the first Algarve tourist developments and has since become one of the most upmarket. The **beach** is among the most beautiful on the entire coast, a wide expanse of sand framed by jagged cliffs and the walls of an old fort (now a restaurant) that once protected the mouth of the River Arade. **Accommodation** is rarely hard to find and cheaper than you might imagine; try *Pensão Oceano* on Avda Tomás Cabreira (☎082/42 43 09; ③), or ask at the **tourist office**, opposite *Hotel Jupiter*, (Mon–Fri 9.30am–7pm, Sat & Sun 9.30am–12.30pm & 2.30–5pm; ☎082/41 91 32), who will readily find you a room.

Silves

Capital of the Moorish kings of the al-Gharb, **SILVES** is still an imposing place and one of the few towns of inland Algarve that merits a detour. The **train station** – an easy approach from Lagos or Faro – lies 2km outside the town; there is a connecting bus, but it's worth walking, allowing the town and its fortress to appear slowly as you emerge from the wooded hills. Under the Moors, Silves was a place of grandeur and industry, described in contemporary accounts as being "of shining brightness" within its triple circuit of walls. In 1189 an army led by Sancho I put an end to this splendour, killing some 6000 Moors in the process. The impressively complete sandstone walls of the Moorish **fortress** (daily 9am–7pm; 250$00) retain their towers and elaborate communication system, but the inside is disappointing: apart from the great vaulted water cisterns that still serve the town, there's nothing left of the old citadel. Just below the fortress is Silves' **Cathedral** (9am–6pm, Sun until 1pm), built on the site of the mosque in the thirteenth century. Flanked by two broad Gothic towers, it has a suitably defiant and military appearance, though the Great Earthquake of 1755 and centuries of impoverished restoration have left their mark inside.

The **tourist office**, in the heart of the town on Rua 25 de Abril (summer daily 9.30am–12.30pm & 2–5.30pm, Mon & Sun closed pm; reduced hours in winter; ☎082/44 22 55), will help you find a **room**. Promising options are the *Residencial Sousa* at Rua Samora Barros 17 (☎082/44 25 02; ③), and *Isabel Maria da Silva* at Rua Cândido dos Reis 36 (☎082/44 26 67; ②), where you share the use of a kitchen and a little outdoor terrace.

Lagos

Once a quiet little town, **LAGOS** now attracts the whole gamut of tourists to its extraordinary beaches. It became a favoured residence of Henry the Navigator, who used Lagos as a base for the new African trade – which explains the formation in 1441 of the town's slave market, held under the arches of the **Customs House** that still stands in the Praça da República near the waterfront. In this same square is the **Church of Santa Maria**, from whose whimsical Manueline windows the youthful Dom Sebastião is said to have roused his troops before the ill-fated Moroccan expedition of 1578 – he was to perish at Alcácer-Quibir with almost the entire Portuguese nobility. He's commemorated in the centre of Lagos by a fantastically dreadful statue. On the waterfront and to the rear of the town are the remains of Lagos' once impregnable fortifications, devastated by the Great Earthquake. One rare and beautiful church which did survive for restoration was the **Igreja de Santo António**; decorated around 1715, its gilt and carved interior is wildly obsessive, every inch filled with a private fantasy of cherubic youths struggling with animals and fish. Next door is the **Municipal Museum** (Tues–Sun 9.30am–12.30pm & 2–5pm; 300$00), a bizarre display ranging from Roman mosaics and folk costumes to misshapen animal foetuses.

The promontory **south** of Lagos is fringed by extravagantly eroded cliff faces that shelter a series of tiny **cove beaches**. All are within easy walking distance of the old town, but the headland is now cut up by campsites, hotels, roads and a multitude of tracks, and the beaches all tend to be overcrowded. Nearest is the **Praia do Pinhão**, down a track just opposite the fire station, and close to the **Praia de Dona Ana** – one of the most photogenic of all Algarve beaches. The path leads all the way to **Praia Camilo** and, right at the point, the **Ponta da Piedade**, where a palm-bedecked lighthouse makes a great vantage point for the sunset.

Practicalities

The **train station** is across the river, fifteen minutes' walk from the centre via the new swing bridge in the marina; the **bus station** is a bit closer in, a block back from the main Avenida dos Descombrimentos. The **tourist office** is inconveniently located about fifteen minutes from the centre on the first main roundabout on the Portimão road (summer daily 9.30am–12.30pm & 2–5.30pm: winter closed Sat pm & Sun; ☎082/76 30 31). They can help find a room for you, but you're better off taking one of the private rooms touted by little old ladies at the bus station. Two of the more convenient and pleasant **pensions** are the *Pensão Caravela* at Rua 25 de Abril 16 (☎082/76 33 61; ④) and the *Residencial Mar Azul*, nearby at no. 13 (☎082/76 91 43; ⑤). There's a **youth hostel** at Rua de Lançarote de Freites 50, off the main Rua Cândido dos Reis (☎082/77 04 50; ③). Lagos has two **campsites**, close to each other on the main Sagres road – the *Campismo da Trindade* (☎082/76 38 93) and the larger and more attractive *Imulagos* (☎082/76 00 31). In season a regular bus service marked "D. Ana/Porto de Mós" connects the bus station with both, and *Imulagos* provides its own free transport from the train station. On foot, follow the main road beyond the fort.

The centre of town is packed with **restaurants**. Some of the better ones are the cheap, good-quality fish and shellfish places by the market, where Rua das Portas de Portugal meets the main avenue. *O Cantinho Algarvio*, Rua Afonso d'Almeida 17, has a wide range of Algarve dishes at good prices; in the same street *Casa do Zé* is popular. For authentic *piri-piri* chicken try the tiny and inexpensive *O Franguinho* at Rua Luís de Azevedo 25. For a more expensive treat, *Dom Sebastião*, on the pedestrianized Rua 25 de Abril, is among the town's finest restaurants, where meals run to around 4000$00. *Mullens* **bar**, Rua Cândido dos Reis 86, serves meals until 10pm, plays jazz and soul on the sound system and stays open until 2am. *Hideaway*, Travessa 1º de Maio 9, just off Praça Luís Camões, is a cosily atmospheric bar, also open till 2am. For contemporary club sounds, *Phoenix*, on Rua 5 de Outobro 11 is open until 4am.

Lagos is the western terminus of the Algarve rail line, so for Sagres take one of the nine daily **buses**. Many of them call at the train station just after the arrival of the trains.

travel details

Trains

Lisbon to: Braga (2 daily; 4hr 40min); Coimbra (13 daily; 2hr–2hr 30min); Évora (1 daily; 3hr); Faro (2 daily; 4hr 30min–6hr); Guarda (5 daily; 6hr); Leiria (6 daily; 2–3hr); Óbidos (change at Cacém; 11 daily; 2hr); Porto (10–13 daily; 3hr 30min–4hr); Sintra (every 15min; 50min); Tavira (4 daily; 6hr); Tomar (hourly; 2hr); Vilar Formoso (for Salamanca and Spain; 1 daily; 6hr 30min).

Coimbra to: Aveiro (hourly; 45min–1hr); Figueira da Foz (17 daily; 1hr–1hr 20min); Lisbon (15–16 daily; 2–3hr); Porto (12 daily; 1hr 20min–2hr).

Figueira da Foz to: Leiria (3–6 daily; 1hr 15min); Lisbon (2 daily; 3hr 10min); Óbidos (6 daily; 2hr 30min).

Guarda to: Coimbra (6 daily; 3hr); Lisbon (5 daily; 6hr); Luso-Buçaco (5 daily; 2hr 30min); Salamanca, Spain (2 daily; 2hr 30min).

Lagos to: Faro (9 daily; 1hr 20min–2hr); Lisbon (5 daily; 5hr); Portimão (13 daily; 20min); Silves (6 daily; 30–40min); Vila Real de Santo António (for Spain; 5 daily; 3–4hr).

Peso da Régua to: Porto (14–15 daily; 2hr 30min); Vila Real (5 daily; 1hr).

Porto to: Aveiro (every 30min; 50min–1hr 30min); Barcelos (11 daily; 1hr 10min–1hr 40min); Braga (13–16 daily; 1hr–1hr 45min); Coimbra (15 daily; 2hr); Guimarães (hourly; 1hr 45min); Lisbon (14–15 daily; 3–4hr); Madrid (2 daily; 12hr); Peso da Régua (4–10 daily; 2hr 30min); Viana do Castelo (9 daily; 1hr 45min–2hr 30min); Vigo (Spain; 3 daily; 4hr 30min).

Buses

Lisbon to: Alcobaça (3 daily; 2hr); Coimbra (8 daily; 2hr 30min); Évora (5 daily; 2hr); Fátima (7 daily; 1hr 45min–2hr 15min); Guarda (1–4 daily; 5–6hr); Leiria (9 daily; 1hr–2hr 10min); Mafra (10 daily; 1hr 30min); Porto (hourly; 3hr 30min); Tomar (2–4 daily; 2hr).

Braga to: Barcelos (every 30min; 50min); Guimarães (every 30min; 45min); Porto (hourly; 1hr 10min); Viana do Castelo (9 daily; 1hr 30min).

Coimbra to: Fátima (5 daily; 1hr–1hr 30min); Guarda (4 daily; 2hr 40min); Lisbon (16 daily; 2hr 20min); Leiria (10 daily; 50min); Luso/Bucaco (2–5 daily; 45min); Porto (7–10 daily; 1hr 30min–2hr 45min); Tomar (2 daily; 2hr); Viseu (2–6 daily; 1hr 20min).

Faro to: Évora (4 daily; 4hr 35min); Olhão (every 15min–1hr 20min); Tavira (hourly; 1hr); Lisbon (5–10 daily; 4hr 30min); Seville (2 daily; 5hr).

Leiria to: Alcobaça (4 daily; 50min); Batalha (5 daily; 15min); Coimbra (10 daily; 1hr 50min); Fátima (9 daily; 25min); Tomar (2 daily; 1hr 10min).

Portimão to: Lagos (hourly; 40min); Silves (6–9 daily; 35min).

Porto to: Braga (hourly; 1hr 10min); Bragança (3 daily; 2hr–3hr 50 min); Coimbra (8 daily; 1hr 30min); Guimarães (12 daily; 2hr); Viana do Castelo (12 daily; 2hr); Vila Real (9 daily; 2hr); Viseu (8 daily; 2hr).

Viseu to: Guarda (2–5 daily; 2hr 15min); Peso da Régua (2–6 daily; 1hr 30min); Porto (2 daily; 5hr).

CHAPTER 23

ROMANIA

Introduction

Travel in **Romania** is as rewarding as it is challenging. The country's mountain scenery and great diversity of wildlife, its various cultures and its people leave few who visit unaffected. However, unless you visit on a package, it is undeniably the hardest country of the former Eastern bloc to cope with. The regime of Nicolae Ceauşescu left Romania on the verge of bankruptcy, and the semireformed economy that has since emerged seems to be characterized by hustle and sharp practice.

Romanians trace their ancestry back to the Romans, and it's not unfair to say that "Latin" traits prevail. The people are generally warm, spontaneous, anarchic, and appreciative of style and life's pleasures. In addition to ethnic Romanians, there are communities from half a dozen other races and cultures: Transylvanian Germans (Saxons) reside around the fortified towns and churches built to guard the mountain passes during the Middle Ages; so do some one and a half million Magyars, many of whom pursue a traditional lifestyle long since vanished in Hungary; and along the coast and in the Danube Delta there's a mixture of Ukrainians, Serbs, Bulgarians, Gypsies, Turks and Tatars.

The capital, **Bucharest** (Bucureşti), would not be a highlight of anyone's European tour, but the recent revolution has given parts of this once-beautiful city a certain voyeuristic appeal. More attractive by far – and easily accessible even on Romania's dilapidated public transport system – is **Transylvania**, a savagely beautiful and historically fascinating region.

Information and maps

Western-style tourist information offices are virtually non-existent in Romania. The national tourist office – the **ONT**, known abroad as ONT-Carpaţi – nowadays concentrates on selling package holidays to the locals rather than helping out foreign visitors. Many private travel agencies have English-speaking staff capable of offering advice – otherwise, you're on your own.

Town **maps** (*plan oraşului*) are hard to come by. In the case of Bucharest, recently published town plans are sporadically available from street vendors, but it's worth getting the Cartographia map before you go. Bear in mind, though, that street names are still changing in postcommunist Romania, so maps may be out of date to some degree.

Money and banks

The **lei** (singular *leu*), Romania's currency, comes in notes of 500, 1000, 5000, 10,000, 50,000 and 100,000 lei, with coins of 100 and 500 lei. Expensive hotels and services might be priced in dollars or Deutschmarks, but you'll be expected to pay for them in lei. The leu has been faring badly against major currencies in recent years, making exchange rates volatile and hard to predict.

Exchanging money in hotels, tourist offices or privately owned exchange bureaux involves less hassle than banks. Don't succumb to the temptation of changing money on the black market: rates are not a lot higher and the characters who operate it are a risky crew, especially in Bucharest and Braşov.

This is a country where cash is king, so take along a stash of **dollars**, preferably in small denominations. However, it's wise to carry a reserve in **travellers' cheques**, chiefly as a safeguard against theft. The only brand of travellers' cheque that guarantees a refund in the event of loss is American Express, whose Romanian agent is near the main ONT office in Bucharest at B-dul Magheru 43. It is generally only possible to cash travellers' cheques at banks, so allow plenty of time for queuing. **Credit cards** are rarely accepted, except when paying at more upmarket restaurants and hotels and for car rental; ATMs (*Bancomats*) can be found in major cities.

Romania's standard of living is abysmal, and although hotel accommodation tends to be overpriced, independent travellers will find **costs** reasonably low outside Bucharest. However, prices are volatile, as are the attitudes of Romanians towards bargaining – some will negotiate for hard currency, others will tell you to take it or leave it.

Communications

Post offices in towns are open Mon–Fri 7am–8.30pm, Sat 8am–noon, and, like the red-painted post boxes, are marked *Poşta*. **Stamps** (*timbru*) and pre-paid envelopes (*plic*) can be bought here.

Local **telephone calls** can be made from blue public call boxes, costing 100 lei for 3 minutes, but it's easier to make long-distance and international calls from a post office or telephone exchange, or from the orange cardphones now appearing in all towns. You can also get through via the international operator (☎971), or by phoning from a good hotel. Using hotel facilities inevitably means a service charge, which can be high, so ask the price beforehand.

Getting around

All forms of public transport in Romania are cheap but slow and fairly primitive. Driving is the only speedy way of getting around, but the roads are in a pretty dire state.

■ Trains

Trains are often the only feasible way of covering distances of over 100km on public transport. Consequently, they're often crowded, so seat **reservations** are advisable. Travelling first class (*clasa întîia*) is one (affordable) way of avoiding the crush. Carriages tend to be dirty and unheated, but many routes are extremely scenic – particularly in Transylvania – and journeys are good occasions to strike up conversation with Romanians. There are a few overpriced *InterCity* trains linking the main cities, but the standard long-distance trains are *Rapids*, while *Accelerats* are slightly cheaper and slower, with more frequent stops. The excruciatingly slow *Personal* trains should be avoided. Some overnight trains have **sleeping cars** (*vagon de dormit*) and **couchettes** (*cušete*), for which a surcharge of about £6/$9 is levied.

Rather than queue at the station, you're better off buying tickets and booking seats at the local **Agenţia CFR** at least 24 hours in advance. Most offices function Mon–Fri 8am–8pm. Return tickets (*bilet dus ši întors*) are rarely issued except for international services. InterRail passes are valid, Eurail are not.

■ Buses

Intercity and rural **bus services** have been restored to a large extent since the revolution, though on many routes there are just one or two services daily. In the countryside, knowing when and where to wait for the day's bus is a local art form, and on Sundays many regions have no public transport at all. In towns, you'll also find **trams and trolleybuses** (*tramvai* and *troleibuz*), which at least stick to their routes.

■ Driving and hitching

Given the state of public transport, it may make sense to travel by **car** – although queues for fuel can be

lengthy, and diesel and lead-free petrol are only available in major cities and on main roads. A national driving **licence** suffices, and if you don't have Green Card **insurance**, a month's cover can be purchased at the border. Foreign motorists belonging to organizations affiliated to the ACR (Romanian Automobile Club) receive free or cut-price technical **assistance**; and you can get motoring information from their head office in Bucharest at Str Tache Ionescu 27 (☎01/650.25.95). For the ACR breakdown services ring ☎12345. Roads are badly maintained, and driving at night can be a hair-raising experience. Major **car rental** companies such as Hertz, AVIS and Europcar now have offices in major cities. Local rates start at around £40/$70 a day with unlimited mileage.

Hitchhiking (*autostop*) is legal on all Romanian roads with the exception of the *Autostradă*, although it takes place there all the same. It's accepted practice to pay for lifts, although this is often waived for foreigners. Advertising some kind of inducement – such as a packet of Kent cigarettes – can dramatically increase your chances of snagging a driver, whom you should then ask: *cît costă pînă la . . .?* (How much to . . .?). Other useful phrases include *Doresc să cobor la . . .* (I want to get off at . . .); *Opriţi la . . .* (Stop at . . .); and *Opriţi aici* (Stop here).

Accommodation

Accommodation is affordable in Romania, but the general standard is low. Beds can be booked through tourist offices, but they'll direct you towards the more expensive options and charge you a hefty fee in the process.

Hotels come graded with one to five stars. The cheapest places (especially those near train stations) can be grubby and depressing – and the upmarket places are invariably infested with hookers and racketeers. In the cheapest hotels, a bed in a double room should cost around £6/$9; a private shower (*cu duš*) adds another £2/$4 or so to the bill. Prices may include breakfast.

The provision of accommodation in **private houses** (*cazare la persoane particulare*) is pretty much in

---

ACCOMMODATION PRICE CODES

Throughout this guide, accommodation is priced on a scale of ① to ⑨, the number indicating the lowest price per night a single person could expect to pay in that establishment in high season. With hostels this is the nightly rate per person; with hotels, the price is arrived at by dividing the cost of the cheapest double room by two. The prices indicated by the codes are as follows:

① under £5 / $8	④ £15–20 / $24–32	⑦ £30–35 / $48–56
② £5–10 / $8–16	⑤ £20–25 / $32–40	⑧ £35–40 / $56–64
③ £10–15 / $16–24	⑥ £25–30 / $40–48	⑨ £40 / $64 and over

its infancy in Romania, with few travel agencies currently offering them on an official basis. Occasionally, you'll be approached by individuals at train stations. It's a reasonable assumption that a private room will be cheaper and more comfortable than a hotel room. The going rate seems to be around £10/$15 per person per night.

In towns with a sizeable student population, rooms in **student residences** (*caminul de studenti*) may be rented out from mid-July to August for a minimal charge – sometimes as little as £1/$2 per night.

There are more than 100 **campsites** across the country, costing around £1/$2.50 for tent space. Some are little more than a field with a tap and a loo, although many offer cabins for about £1.50/$3 a head.

Food and drink

During the Ceauşescu years **food** became a precious commodity in what had been known as the breadbasket of eastern Europe. The situation is now better, but supplies are still unreliable, so be prepared for austerity and carry a reserve of food with you. **Breakfast** (*micul dejun*) is typically a light meal, featuring rolls and butter (*chifle şi unt*) and an *omleta* – or long, unappealing-looking sausages (*patriciani*) – washed down with a large coffee (*cafea mare*) or tea (*ceai*). As for **snacks** – known as *gusteri* – the most common are flaky pastries (*pateuri*) filled with cheese (*cu brânză*) or meat (*cu carne*), often dispensed through hatches in the walls of bakeries; sandwiches (*sandvici* or *tartine*); and a variety of spicy grilled sausages and meatballs such as *mititei* and *chiftele*, which are normally sold by street vendors.

For **sit-down meals** it's best to go upmarket, since the choice of dishes in cheaper restaurants tends to be limited to grilled meats, french fries, burgers and pizzas. The menus of most Romanian restaurants concentrate on grilled meats: *friptura*, *pî rjola* and *cotlet de porc* are all forms of pork chop; while *muşchi de vacă* denotes fillet of beef. Dishes usually arrive with a garnish of french fries, a minimalist side salad, and, occasionally, vegetables. Some restaurants offer a *program* or cabaret – usually involving dancing girls and a couple of singing acts – as a way of justifying a small admission charge.

At smarter **restaurants** there's a fair likelihood of finding traditional Romanian dishes, which can be delicious. The best known of these is *sarmale* – pickled cabbage stuffed with rice, meat and herbs, usually served (or sometimes baked) with sour cream. Stews (*tocane*) and other dishes often feature a scle-

rotic combination of meat and dairy products. "Shepherd's Delight" (*muşchi ciobanesc*) is pork stuffed with ham, covered in cheese and served with mayonnaise, cucumber and herbs; while *muşchi poiana* is beef stuffed with mushrooms, bacon, pepper and paprika, served in a vegetable purée and tomato sauce.

Vegetarians in ordinary restaurants could try asking for *caşcaval pane* (hard cheese fried in breadcrumbs); *ghiveci* (mixed fried veg); *ardei umpluţi* (stuffed peppers) or vegetables and salads. When in doubt, stipulate something *fără carne*, *vă rog* (without meat, please), or enquire *este cu carne?* (does it contain meat?).

Establishments called **cofetărie** serve coffee and cakes, and sometimes beer and ice cream. Coffee, whether *cafea naturală* (finely ground and cooked Turkish fashion), *filtru* (filtered), or *ness* (instant coffee) is usually drunk black and sweet; ask for it *cu lapte* or *fără zahăr* if you prefer it with milk or without sugar. The *cofetărie* is a good place to pick up daytime snacks: *cornuri* are croissants, *chifle* bread rolls, and *prăjituri* sweet buns. Cakes and desserts are sticky and sweet, as throughout the Balkans. Romanians enjoy pancakes (*clătite*) and pies (*plăcintă*) with various fillings; Turkish-influenced *baclava* and *cataif cu frisca*; and the traditional *dulceaţă*, or glass of jam.

Evening **drinking** takes place in outdoor beer gardens (the roughest of which are pretty much all-male preserves), more attractive *cramas* (beer cellars), restaurants (where boozers often outnumber the diners), and in a growing number of western European-style cafés and bars. As an aperitif, or at any other time, people like to drink **ţuică**, a powerful plum brandy taken neat; in rural areas, it is home-made and often twice distilled to yield fearsomely strong *palincă*. Most **beer** (*bere*) is bottled, in the Germanic lager style. Romania's best **wines** are Grasca and *Feteasca Neagră* from the vineyards of Cotnari and Dealul Mare, and the sweet dessert wines of Murfatlar. These can be found in better restaurants; other establishments may just offer you a choice of red and white – usually sold by the bottle rather than the glass. Mineral water (*apă minerală*) and international **soft drinks** like Coke and Pepsi are readily available.

Opening hours and holidays

Like so many things in Romania, opening hours are unreliable. In general **shops** are open Mon–Fri 9am–6pm, with some staying open as late as 8pm and food shops often opening a couple of hours earlier. **Museums** and **castles** are open at similar times (though most are closed on Mondays); **admission charges** are minimal (usually only a few thousand lei) and have therefore not been listed in the text. Most are open on Saturday morning, a few on Sunday morning. **National holidays** are: Jan 1 & 2; Easter Monday; May 1; Dec 1; and Dec 25 & 26.

Emergencies

There's a high incidence of **petty theft** in Romania, although crimes of violence are rare. Beware of pickpockets in Bucharest, and lock the door of your compartment when travelling on overnight trains. If your passport goes missing while in Bucharest, telephone your consulate immediately; anywhere else, contact the **police** (*Poliţia*), who'll issue a temporary visa.

Don't expect the police to do anything more than this though.

In the event of a **health emergency**, dial the number given below or ask someone to contact the local *staţia de salvare* or *prim ajutor* – the casualty (emergency) and first aid stations – which may or may not have ambulances. Don't go to Romania without good health insurance cover, and if you develop any complaint that might require hospital treatment, you should try to get out of the country. If you need medication on a regular basis, take a supply.

EMERGENCY NUMBERS

Police ☎955; Ambulance ☎961.

TRANSYLVANIA AND THE BANAT

The likeliest approach to Romania is by train from adjoining Hungary, from where two main rail routes take you through **Transylvania**. Whether you take the line via Arad, or the less popular one via Cluj, you should disembark before reaching Bucharest to see the best of the country. Thanks to Bram Stoker and Hammer films, Transylvania is famed abroad as the homeland of **Dracula**: a mountainous place where storms lash medieval hamlets, while wolves – or werewolves – howl from the woods. Happily, the fictitious image is accurate, up to a point. The scenery is dramatic, there are spooky Gothic citadels, and one Vlad (born in Sighişoara) did style himself Dracula and earned the grim nickname "The Impaler". But the Dracula image is just one element of Transylvania, whose 99,837 square kilometres take in caves, alpine meadows, dense forests sheltering bears and wild boars, and lowland valleys where buffalo cool off in the rivers.

The population is a jigsaw of Romanians, Magyars, Germans, Gypsies and others, formed over centuries of migration and colonization. The Trianon Treaty of 1920 placed Transylvania within the Romanian state, shifting the balance of power in favour of the Romanian majority, but the character of many towns still reflects past patterns of settlement and domination. **Cluj**, for example, is strongly Hungarian-influenced, but most striking of all are the *Stuhls* – the former seats of Saxon power – with their medieval streets, defensive towers and fortified churches. **Sighişoara**, the most picturesque, could almost be the Saxons' cenotaph: their culture has evaporated here, leaving only their citadels and churches, as it threatens to do in **Braşov** and **Sibiu**, and in the old German settlements roundabout. A similarly complex ethnic mix is found in **the Banat**, to the east of Transylvania proper and the westernmost region of Romania as a whole; the chief town here is **Timişoara**, crucible of the 1989 revolution.

Timişoara

TIMIŞOARA, 50km south of the rail junction at Arad, grew up around a Magyar fortress at the marshy confluence of the Timiş and Bega, and from the fourteenth century onwards functioned as the capital of the Banat. The Turks conquered the town in 1552, and ruled the surrounding terrain from here until 1716. The Habsburgs who ejected them proved relatively benign masters, and during the late nineteenth century the municipality rode a wave of progress, becoming one of the first towns in the world to have horse-drawn trams and to install electric street-lighting. This was also the period when Temeschwar (its German name) acquired many of its current features, including the **Bega Canal**, which cups the southern side of the historic centre and is flanked by a procession of stately **parks**.

Timişoara's fame abroad rests on its crucial role in the overthrow of the Ceauşescu regime. A local Hungarian priest, Lászlo Tökes, took a stand on the rights of his community, and when the police came to turf him out of his house on December 16, 1989, his parishioners barred their way. The five-day battle that ensued ended with the workers at the oil refinery forcing the troops to withdraw by threatening to blow the place sky-high. These events provided crucial inspiration for the people of Bucharest, so that Timişoara now regards itself as the guardian of the revolution – memorials around town mark the places where the democratic martyrs fell, and many streets have been renamed in their honour.

Approaching from the train station along B-dul Republicii, the town's architectural assets don't become evident until one enters the centre, with its carefully planned streets and squares. On Piaţa Huniade, just beyond the plush **Opera House**, you'll find the **Museum of the Banat** (Tues–Sun 10am–5pm) occupying the castle once extended by Iancu de Hunedoara. Warlords and rebels figure prominently in the large historical section, as does the great strike of 1920 in support of the Banat's union with Romania.

The central Piaţa Libertăţii boasts as fine a Baroque **Town Hall** as any municipality could wish for. Two blocks north of here, Piaţa Unirii's **Museum of Fine Arts**, displaying work by minor Italian, German and Flemish masters, is overshadowed by the monumental **Roman Catholic and Serbian Orthodox Cathedrals**. Built between 1736 and 1773, the former is a fine example of Viennese Baroque, designed by Fischer von Erlach; the latter is roughly contemporaneous and almost as impressive. The **Romanian Orthodox Cathedral** is located to the south of here, between the Opera House and the canal; completed in 1946, it blends Neo-Byzantine and Moldavian architectural elements and exhibits a collection of icons (probably Wed–Sun 11am–3pm; ask at the bookstall inside the cathedral) in its basement.

In 1868, the municipality purchased the redundant citadel from the Habsburgs, and demolished all but two sections, the **Bastions**, to the east and west of Piaţa Unirii. Parts of each have been converted into wine bars, whilst to the east another section is occupied by an **Ethnographic Museum** (Tues–Sun 10am–5pm). Varied folk costumes and coloured charts illustrate the region's ethnic diversity effectively, but in an anodyne fashion – for example, there's no mention of the thousands of Serbs deported in 1951 when the Party turned hostile towards Tito's Yugoslavia.

Practicalities
The most reasonable **hotels** are the basic *Banatul*, B-dul Republicii 5 (☎056/19.01.30), just down from the station, which has rooms with shared facilities (①) or ensuite showers (②); and the cleaner, better-equipped *Central*, Str Lenau 6 (☎056/19.00.91; ②). The **campsite**, which has bungalows (①), is on Aleea Pădurea Verde, 4km east of town – take trolleybus #11 from the train station to the Strandul Tineretului terminus.

For **eating**, the restaurant of the *Hotel Continental* on Str. Eminescu is probably the best in town and still eminently affordable, while the *Marele Zid Chinezesc*, Str. V. Alecsandru 3, offers a respectable stab at Chinese cuisine. *Brasserie Opera* on Piaţa Victoriei is a popular venue for daytime **drinking** and also has pizzas and grill-snacks. *Café Colţ*, on the corner of Str V. Lăzar and Str. E. Ungureanu, is the best of the bars.

Cluj

With its cupolas, Baroque outcroppings and weathered *fin-de-siècle* backstreets, downtown **CLUJ** looks like a Hungarian provincial capital – which in a sense it once was. In Hungary, and indeed within Transylvania itself, many people still regret the passing of Kolozsvár (the Hungarian name for the city), fondly recalled as a place that embodied the Magyar *belle époque*. Modern Cluj has scores of factories and over 300,000 inhabitants, but the city has retained something of the languor and raffish undercurrent that characterized it in the olden days – not to mention cultural fixtures like its opera and university. Compared to other large Romanian towns, the restaurants and bars seem livelier, and the shops better stocked.

The Town
Trolleybuses #3, #4 or #9 run from the **train station** to the centre of Cluj, where the pivot of the town is the Piaţa Unirii. The square's centrepiece is the vast **St Michael's Church**, founded in the mid-fourteenth century. Dwarfing the congregation in the bare nave, mighty pillars curve into vaulting like the canopy of a forest. St Michael's Gothic phase of construction ended three years before the death of the Hungarian King, Mátyás Corvinus (1440–90). He and his wife, Beatrix of Naples, had brought the culture of Renaissance Italy to the region, while his formidable "Black Army" kept the Kingdom of Hungary safe from lawlessness and invasion. Outside the church an imposing equestrian statue of the king accepts the homage of four dignitaries, with the crescent banner of the Turks trampled under hoof. Mátyás' birthplace was the small mansion at Str Matei Corvin 6, up a side street leading north off the square. It now houses the Fine Arts faculty of the university, although you can peek inside the courtyard. On the east side of the square, the **Art Museum** (Tues–Sun 10am–6pm) houses the superbly carved sixteenth-century Jimbor altar and paintings by Transylvanian artists. Many of the items were expropriated from Magyar aristocracy, in particular the Bánffy family, whose mansion this building once was.

Just to the north of the main square, at Str Daicovici 2, the **History Museum of Transylvania** (Wed–Sun 10am–4pm) is largely given over to charting the progress from the Neolithic and Bronze ages to the rise of the Dacian civilization, which peaked between the second century BC and the first AD. The Dacii were subdued by Roman legions, and the two races subsequently intermingled to form the ancestors of today's Romanians – or so the official version of Romanian history goes. An alternative theory, promulgated by those who insist on the Hungarian identity of this region, is that the Dacii died out completely, and that the Magyars took possession of a region that had no other legitimate claimants.

West of Piaţa Unirii, at Str Memorandumului 21, Cluj's **Ethnographic Museum** (Tues–Sun 9am–5pm) contains what is probably Romania's finest collection of carpets and folk costumes, demonstrating the country's various styles of weaving, from the dark herringbone patterns of the Padureni region to the bold yellow, black and red stripes of Maramureş – and an even greater variety of clothing and headgear. Three neat wooden churches and other specimens of rural architecture have been assembled at the open-air **Village Museum** (Tues–Sun 9am–4pm) in a park in the northwest part of town, and a visit there will help to put the costumes in perspective.

Practicalities

Cheapest of the **hotels** is *Pax* (☎064/43.29.27; ①), opposite the train station at Piaţa Gǎrii 1, a shabby place that's tolerable for a brief stopover. More comfortable are the hotels around the main square: the *Central-Melody*, Piaţa Unirii 29 (☎064/19.74.65; ②), has crummy but acceptable en-suites; while the *fin-de-siècle Continental*, Str Napoca 1 (☎064/19.54.05) has plusher doubles with en-suite facilities (④) or without (③). There's a **campsite** in the Fǎget hills to the southeast – reached by bus #40A from behind the National Theatre.

Plenty of **eating and drinking** venues are clustered around Piaţa Unirii and the streets leading off it. The *Cofetǎria Silvia* at Str Memorandumului 10 has the best cakes in town, while the *Rex*, in the alleyway behind the *Hotel Melody* at Bolyai Janos 9, has good pizzas. The *Gradina de Varǎ Boema* beer garden at Str Iuliu Maniu 34 features grills, and often a singer in the evenings. Traditional Transylvanian meats and stews can be sampled at *Hubertus*, Str 21 Decembrie 22.

Numerous **bars** are hidden away in the subterranean cellars of central Cluj, many featuring live jazz or rock. *Diesel*, Piaţa Unirii 17, is quite upmarket compared to the more down-to-earth *Club M*, Piaţa Muzeiului, *Music Pub*, Str Horea 5, and *Kings*, next to Matyas Corvinus' birthplace on Str Matei Corvin.

Sibiu

"I rubbed my eyes in amazement", wrote Walter Starkie of **SIBIU** in 1929. "The town where I found myself did not seem to be in Transylvania…the narrow streets and old gabled houses made me think of Nuremberg." Nowadays the illusion is harder to sustain, but Sibiu's older quarters could still serve to illustrate the Brothers Grimm. Some people here speak German and cherish links with faraway Germany, calling Sibiu "Hermannstadt", the name given by the Transylvanian Saxons to this, their chief city. Like Braşov, Sibiu was founded by Germans invited by the Hungarian King Géza II to colonize strategic regions of Transylvania in 1143. Its inhabitants came to dominate trade in Transylvania and Wallachia, forming exclusive guilds under royal charter. The Turks dubbed Sibiu the "Red Town" on account of its red-brick defensive walls with their forty towers, built in the fifteenth century, and the bloodshed in attempting to breach them. Alas for the Saxons, their citadels were no protection against the tide of history, which eroded their influence after the eighteenth century. Within the last decade almost the entire Saxon community has left Romania.

To reach the centre from the main train and bus stations, cross the square and follow Str Gen. Magheru until you hit the Piaţa Mare. Traditionally the hub of public life, it's surrounded by the premises of sixteenth- and seventeenth-century merchants, whose acumen and thrift were proverbial. On its western side stands the **Brukenthal Museum** (Tues–Sun 9am–5pm), one of the finest in Romania. Besides the best of local silverware, pottery and furniture, it has an evocative collection of works by Transylvanian painters. The city's **History Museum** (Tues–Sun 9am–5pm) is housed in the Old City Hall, just to the north, a building well worth a look even if you aren't interested in the contents.

On the north side of Piaţa Mare, the **Councillors' Tower** forms a phalanx with a Catholic church, largely blocking access to the Piaţa Mică (Little Square). Just beyond on Piaţa Huet, the **Evangelical Cathedral** (Mon–Fri 9am–1pm) – a massive hall-church raised during the fourteenth and fifteenth centuries – dominates its neighbours. The crypt contains the tomb of Mihnea the Bad, Dracula's son, who was stabbed to death outside in 1510.

Behind the cathedral, the Passage of Stairs, overshadowed by arches and the medieval citadel wall, descends into the lower town. Just to the east, Str Ocnei runs down through a kind of miniature urban canyon spanned by the elegant wrought-iron **Liars' Bridge** – so called because of the legend that no one can stand on it and tell a lie without the structure collapsing. Further to the east, on the far side of Piaţa Mică another ancient stairway leads down to Str Movilei, pock-marked with medieval windows, doorways and turrets. Down in the rambling lower town is the octagonal-based **Tanners' Tower** on Str Pulberăriei, part of the now-demolished Ocna Gate. Also in the lower town, on Piaţa Cibin, there's a busy market, selling pottery, jewellery and food.

Sibiu's promenade takes place between Piaţa Mare and Piaţa Unirii, along Str N. Bălcescu, where most shops and offices are found. The town's militaristic architecture is exemplified by the ramparts and bastions along the length of Str Cetăţii to the southeast, where three mighty towers were once manned by the carpenters', potters' and crossbow-makers' guilds.

Practicalities

Cheapest of the **hotels** are the privately run *Podul Minciunilor*, Str Azilului 1 (☎069/41.72.59; ①), just beyond the Liars' Bridge, and the *Leu*, Str Moş Ioan Roata 2 (☎069/21.83.92; ①) – although they are no more than converted houses and soon fill up. Alternatives are the uninspiring grey high-rise *Bulevard*, Piaţa Unirii (☎069/21.60.60; ③); and the rather grand *Împăratul Romanilor*, Str Bălcescu 4 (☎069/21.65.00; ③). There's a **campsite** in the Dumbrava forest, 4km south of town; take trolleybus #T1 from the train station.

Places to **eat** are clustered around the Piaţa Mare and Str Bălcescu. *Patiseria Aroma*, Str Bălcescu 1, serves tasty sandwiches and snacks as well as providing a bolt hole for daytime drinkers. The *Bulevard* has a restaurant, but is eclipsed by the sumptuous dining room of the *Hotel Împăratul Romanilor*, where you can enjoy topnotch food and a rowdy floor show for about $8 a head. For **drinking**, the *Sibiule Vechi*, just off Str Bălcescu on Str Papiu Ilarian 3, is an inviting cellar bar which also does traditional Romanian food; while the *Crama Naţional*, Piaţa Mică 21, is more like a student pub.

Sighişoara

A forbidding silhouette of battlements and needle spires looms over **SIGHIŞOARA** as the sun descends behind the hills of the Tîrnave Mare valley, and it seems fitting that this was the birthplace of Vlad Ţepeş – the man known to posterity as Dracula. Sighişoara makes the perfect introduction to Transylvania, especially as the *Dacia, Traianus, Pannonia* and *Alutus* international trains stop here during daylight, enabling travellers to break the long journey between Budapest and Bucharest.

The route from the train and bus stations to the centre passes close to the **Romanian Orthodox Cathedral**, its gleaming white, multifaceted facade a striking contrast to the dark interior, where blue and orange hues dominate the small panels of the iconostasis. Across the Tîrnave Mare river, the **Citadel** dominates the town from a rocky massif whose slopes support a jumble of ancient, leaning houses, their windows sited to cover the steps leading up from Piaţa Hermann Oberth to the main gateway. Above the gateway rises the mighty **Clock Tower** where, at the stroke of midnight, a wooden figure emerges from the belfry to mark the new day. The tower was founded in the fourteenth century when Sighişoara became a free town controlled by craft guilds – each of which had to finance the construction of a bastion and defend it during wartime – and rebuilt after earthquakes and fire in the 1670s. Sighişoara grew rich on the proceeds of trade with Moldavia and Wallachia, as attested by the regalia and strongboxes in the tower's **museum** (Tues–Sun 9am–3.30pm).

In 1431 or thereabouts, the child later known as **Dracula** was born in a two-storey house within the shadow of the clock tower at Str Museului 6. At the time his father – Vlad Dracul – was commander of the mountain passes into Wallachia, but the younger Vlad's privileged childhood ended eight years later, when he and his brother Radu were sent to Anatolia as hostages to the Turks. There Vlad observed the Turks' use of terror, which he would later turn against them, earning the nickname of "The Impaler". Nowadays, Vlad's birthplace is a restaurant, although the **Museum of Armaments** next door (Tues–Sun 10am–3.30pm) has a small Dracula Exhibition. A meagre display of pictures and texts in Romanian shows the local ambivalence towards Sighişoara's most notorious son. The emphasis is on his patriotic anti-Turkish deeds, while his subsequent reputation for cruelty is portrayed as the invention of hostile Saxon propagandists.

Churches are monuments to social identity here, as in many old Transylvanian towns. The Germans raised one opposite the clock tower; its stark, whitewashed interior is hung with colourful carpets, as in the Black Church at Braşov. Their other church, the **Bergkirche** (Church on the Hill), is approached by an impressive covered wooden stairway which ascends steeply from the far end of Str Şcolii. Ivy-grown and massively buttressed, the church has a roomy interior that seems austere despite the blue and canary yellow vaulting. Some lovely stone tombs near the entrance are a harbinger of the German cemetery, a melancholy, weed-choked mass of graves spilling over the hill beside the ruined citadel walls – nine of whose fourteen towers survive.

The **lower town** is less appealing than the Citadel, but there's a nice ambience around the shabby centre – consisting of Piaţa Hermann Oberth and Str 1 Decembrie – where townsfolk gather to consume grilled sausages and watery beer, conversing in Romanian, Magyar and antiquated German.

Private **rooms** (①–②) are available in the old town if you ask around – staff in the souvenir shops near Dracula's birthplace might point you in the direction of a local landlady. The town's main **hotel** is the run-down *Steaua* at Str 1 Decembrie 12 (☎065/77.15.94; ②), but you'll also find two newer private places – the basic but friendly *Chic* (☎069/77.59.01; ①), opposite the train station, and the more comfortable *Poieniţa* (☎065/77.27.39; ③), signposted 3km southeast of the centre in a rustic suburb at Str D. Cantemir 24. There's a rudimentary **campsite**, *Dealul Gării* on the hillside above the train station. There are a few **eating and drinking** venues in town, including the two pizzerias on Piaţa Hermann Oberth – the *Italia* and the *Perla* – and the restaurant and bar in Dracula's birthplace.

Braşov and around

With an eye for trade and invasion routes, the medieval Saxons sited their largest settlements within a day's journey of Transylvania's mountain passes. **BRAŞOV**, which they called Kronstadt, grew prosperous as a result, and for centuries the Saxons constituted an elite whose economic power long outlasted its feudal privileges. The Communist government, wanting to create its "own" skilled working class, brought thousands of Moldavian villagers to Braşov, where they were trained to work in the new factories and given modern housing during the 1960s. As a result, there are two parts to Braşov: the quasi-Gothic bit coiled beneath Mount Tîmpa and Mount Postăvaru, which looks great, and the surrounding sprawl of flats and factories, which doesn't. **Old Braşov** is worth at least a day's sightseeing, and the proximity of "Dracula's Castle" at Bran makes the city a worthy stopoff.

From the train station bus #4 lurches down to the central park beside B-dul Eroilor, which meets the eastern end of the pedestrianized Str Republicii, the hub of Braşov's social life and hosting a constant throng of strollers. At the top of Str Republicii, sturdy buildings line the main square – the Piaţa Sfatului – as if on parade, presenting their shopfronts to the fifteenth-century council house, which has now been relegated to the role of **History Museum** (Tues–Sun 10am–5pm). As can be guessed from the exhibits, Braşov used to be dominated by Saxon guilds, whose main hangout was the Merchants' Hall, built in the "Transylvanian Renaissance" style of the sixteenth century. Within sight of its terrace is the town's most famous landmark, the **Black Church** (Mon–Sat 10am–3.30pm), which stabs upwards like a series of daggers. An endearingly monstrous hall-church that took almost a century to complete (1385–1477), it is so called for its soot-blackened walls, the result of being torched by the Austrian army in 1689. Inside, by contrast, the church is startlingly white, with Oriental carpets hung in splashes of colour along the walls of the nave.

When Turkish expansion became a threat in the fifteenth century, the inhabitants began to fortify Braşov, assigning the defence of each bastion or rampart to a particular guild. A length of fortress wall runs along the foot of Mount Tîmpa, beneath a maze of paths and a **cable car** running up to the summit. Of the original seven bastions the best preserved is that of the weavers, on Str Coşbuc. This complex of wooden galleries and bolt holes now contains the **Museum of the Bîrsa Land Fortifications** (Tues–Sun 10am–4pm). Inside are models, pictures and weaponry recalling the bad old days when the surrounding region was repeatedly attacked by Tatars, Turks and, on a couple of occasions, by Dracula – who impaled hundreds of captives along the heights of St Jacob's Hill to terrorize the townsfolk.

Practicalities

You're more than likely to be offered **private rooms** (①–②) by individuals hanging around the train station. If you don't want to take your chances on these, Exo, at Str Postăvarului 6 (Mon–Sat 11am–8pm, Sun 11am–2pm; ☎068/14.43.91), will do their best to fix you up. Cheapest of the central **hotels** is the *Postăvarul*, just off Str Republicii on Str Politechnicii 2 (☎068/14.43.30; ②). The classier western wing of the *Postăvarul* goes under the name of the *Hotel Coroana* (same telephone number; ④), and offers en-suite rooms with TV. The *Helis*, fifteen minutes' walk from the centre at Str Memorandumului 29, signposted off Str Lungă (☎068/41.02.23; ④), is a cosy suburban **B&B**; take bus #28 from the central park. The *Dîrste* **campsite** is out along the Bucharest road, the best campsite in the country, with permanent hot water – doubtless because of its previous popularity with Securitate campers. To reach it, take a Săcele bus from the Autocamion stop until it turns off the main road which passes the site.

The central Piaţa Sfatului is awash with **eating and drinking** venues. There are a couple of pizzerias on the square, while *Vatra Ardealului*, just off the square on Str Bariţiu 14, has the best pastries and cakes. The flashiest **restaurant** is the *Cinezesc*, Piaţa Sfatului, serving excellent Chinese food, and the *Hotel Coroana* has a good restaurant serving Romanian dishes. Best of the **bars** are Art Café Jazz, just off Str Republicii on Piaţa George Enescu, a pub-like space which sometimes features live music; and the *Britannia Arms*, in a courtyard behind McDonald's at Str Republicii 57, an unpretentious cellar bar patronized by local youth.

Dracula's Castle

The small town of **BRAN**, situated 28km from Braşov and easily reached by bus, lies at the foot of the beautiful Bucegi mountains. What's now billed as **Dracula's Castle** (Tues–Sun 9am–5pm) has only tenuous associations with Vlad the Impaler – it's quite likely that he attacked it in 1460 – but the hyperbole is forgivable as Bran really does look like a vampire count's residence. The castle was built in 1377 to safeguard what used to be the main route into Wallachia until the opening of the Predeal Pass, and it rises in tiers of towers and ramparts from amongst the woods, against a glorious mountain background. A warren of spiral stairs, nooks and secret chambers overhanging the courtyard, the interior is filled with elaborately carved four-poster beds, throne-like chairs and portraits of grim-faced boyars. Despite its medieval aspect, most of the interior dates from a conversion job early this century, the work of a crazed old architect commissioned by British-born Queen Marie of Romania. Marie called Bran a "pugnacious little fortress", but her alterations made it a welcoming abode, at odds with its forbidding exterior. Recent "restoration" has made it even more suburban, with patio windows and buckets of white paint. In the grounds are some old peasant buildings and the **Museum of the Bran Pass** (Tues–Sun 9am–5pm), displaying folk costumes, many of them from Marie's wardrobe. If you want a more authentically medieval experience, jump off the Braşov bus in the nearby village of Râşnov, where the castle on the hilltop at the edge of town has been restored with greater tact than that at Bran.

Buses to Bran leave from opposite the Bartolomeu church, 3km west of central Braşov at the junction of Str Lungă and Calea Făgăraşului (bus #28 from Braşov's central park or bus #10 from the train station). Buses run roughly hourly on the hour, although there's no official stop or timetable information as yet, so be prepared to ask the locals. **Accommodation** in Bran boils down to the rather basic *Castelul Bran* (①) across the road from the castle, the motel (②) on the Braşov road, and private rooms (①–②), found by asking around or by phoning ☎068/23.66.42.

BUCHAREST

BUCHAREST (Bucureşti) is the least ingratiating of Europe's capitals. The weakness of Romania's economy is evident here, with incompetent bureaucrats, unfinished building sites, and cuts in water and power supplies, especially in winter when the temperature can fall to -20°C. Parts of the city, especially the train station, are awash with hustlers, while the lobbies of the fancier hotels are cruised by a range of low-lifes. Foreign visitors who aren't cocooned in a tour group usually find the city bewildering, if not horrendously frustrating.

What charm Bucharest possesses lies in its patchwork of different quarters, green with lime and horse chestnut trees. Much of the old city, however, was demolished on Ceauşescu's orders, to create a Civic Centre worthy of the "capital of the New Socialist Man". His megalomaniacal scheme, which required the demolition of around 9000 houses and some 15 churches is undoubtedly the city's major sight, an extraordinary construction that is one of Europe's most potent political symbols. For the old atmosphere, you now need to wander towards the northern stretches of the Calea Victoriei and between Cişmigiu Gardens and the Gara de Nord, where discreet bourgeois households slowly give ground to the proletarians and the Gypsies, and life retains a village-like slowness and intimacy.

Arrival, information and transport

International **flights** arrive at Otopeni Airport, 16km north of the centre. A taxi from here to the centre shouldn't cost more than $15, otherwise take bus #783 (on the other side of the car park from the arrivals hall), which leaves every thirty minutes for Piaţa Unirii. Almost all **trains** terminate at the ghastly Gara de Nord, a squalid hive with queues for everything. Be careful of pickpockets at the station and in the busier parts of the city, and steer well clear of the black marketeers and self-proclaimed "plain-clothes police". There's a **tourist office** at B-dul Magheru 7 (Mon–Fri 8am–5pm, until 8pm for currency exchange, Sat 8am–3pm & Sun 8am–1pm; ☎01/613.07.59) – useful for changing money, arranging car rental and "programmes", but not much else.

The best way to get around Bucharest is on foot. If you do need to use public transport, your best bet is the **metro system**, which has three lines, of which the most useful are the east–west M1 line and the north–south M2, serving the central squares. It operates from 5am until midnight, with two-journey tickets costing 25 cents, day tickets 35 cents. Public transport above ground is a mess. Chronically overcrowded vehicles seem set to rattle themselves to pieces, and timetables and routes are hard to figure out. **Trolleybuses, buses** and **trams** hit the streets around 5am and fade out by midnight. You should buy tickets from street kiosks (open 5am–8pm) and cancel them on boarding; express buses require special magnetic tickets costing around 15 cents. Always buy enough for a few journeys.

Taxis are easy to find, although private cabs tend not to have meters, so agree on a price beforehand. Short journeys in the centre shouldn't exceed the equivalent of $3–4.

Accommodation

Visitors' options for **accommodation** in Bucharest are pretty dire. The city is well served with crumbling pre-World War II hotels, but the majority of them are run-down and overpriced – although competition prevents rates from becoming too outrageous. Plenty of bud-

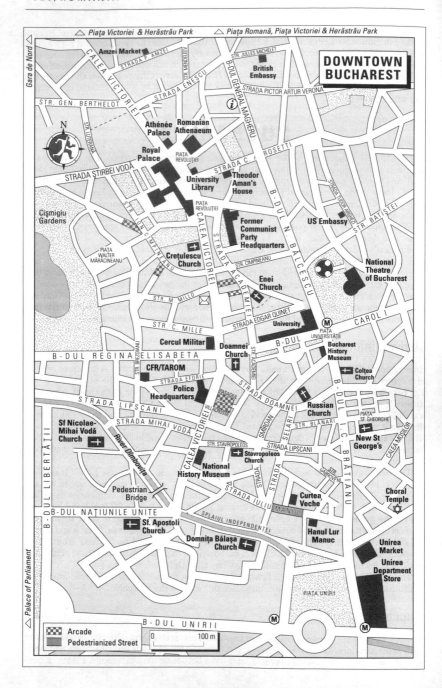

△ *Piaţa Victoriei & Herăstrău Park* △ *Piaţa Romană, Piaţa Victoriei & Herăstrău Park*

DOWNTOWN BUCHAREST

Amzei Market

STRADA P. AMZEI

STR. JULLES MICHELET

British Embassy

STRADA PICTOR ARTUR VERONA

STR. GEN. BERTHELOT

Athénée Palace

Romanian Athenaeum

Royal Palace

PIAŢA REVOLUŢIEI

University Library

Theodor Aman's House

STRADA STIRBEI VODA

PIAŢA REVOLUŢIEI

Cişmigiu Gardens

PIAŢA WALTER MĂRĂCINEANU

Former Communist Party Headquarters

US Embassy

Cretulescu Church

Enei Church

National Theatre of Bucharest

STR. M. MILLO

STR. C. MILLE

STRADA EDGAR QUINET

University

PIAŢA UNIVERSITĂŢII

Cercul Militar

Doamnei Church

Bucharest History Museum

B-DUL REGINA ELISABETA

CFR/TAROM

Coltea Church

STRADA EFORIE

Police Headquarters

STRADA LIPSCANI

STRADA DOAMNEI

Russian Church

STRADA MIHAI VODA

Sf Nicolae-Mihai Vodă Church

River Dîmboviţa

STR. STAVROPOLEOS

Stavropoleos Church

STRADA LIPSCANI

New St George's

National History Museum

Pedestrian Bridge

STRADA IULIU MANIU

Curtea Veche

Choral Temple

B-DUL NAŢIUNILE UNITE

Sf. Apostoli Church

SPLAIUL INDEPENDENTEI

Hanul Lur Manuc

Domniţa Bălaşa Church

Unirea Market

Unirea Department Store

PIAŢA UNIRII

B-DUL UNIRII

Arcade

Pedestrianized Street

0   100 m

get **hotels** are clustered around the Gara de Nord. Although exceptionally grotty by Western standards, they're conveniently sited for getting settled in and away again quickly, and are within striking distance of the parks and leafy suburbs of northern Bucharest. Hotels in the downtown area are by and large more expensive, but offer higher standards in return.

Hostels

Villa Helga, Str Salcimi 2 (π1/610.22.14). Independent youth hostel with communal lounge, cable TV, kitchen, and free use of a washing machine. Bus #79 from the Gara de Nord. ①.

Hotels

Astoria, B-dul D. Golescu 27 (π1/637.73.36). Most comfortable of the hotels near the Gara de Nord, offering clean en-suites with TV. Across the road to the right as you exit the station. ③.

Bulevard, B-dul Regina Elisabeta 21 (π1/315.33.00). A *fin-de-siècle* pile with Louis XIV decor. Comfortable and central. ③.

Bucegi, Str Witing 2 (π1/637.52.25). Immediately on your right as you leave the Gara de Nord. Bucharest at its most basic. ①.

Cerna, B-dul Dinicu Golescu 29 (π1/637.40.87). Across the road from the *Bucegi*. Plain and shabby but acceptable for an overnight stop. ①.

Carpaţi, Str Matei Millo 16 (π1/315.01.40). Recently renovated and comparatively clean and friendly. A couple of blocks away from the main Calea Victoriei. En-suites (④), others (③).

Dâmboviţa, Str Schitu Magureanu 6 (π1/315.62.44). Within a few minutes of both Ceauşescu's palace and the Cişmigiu Gardens. Cramped and old-fashioned. ①.

Hanul lui Manuc, Str Iuliu Maniu 62–64 (π1/313.14.11). A good choice if you want to treat yourself to a classy hotel. Rooms overlook the galleried courtyard of an old inn, situated in the Lipscani quarter – central Bucharest's most picturesque. ④.

Muntenia, Str Academiei 21 (π1/314.60.10). Ageing, but clean, comfortable and central. Rooms with shared facilities (②), en-suites (③), and some triples and quadruples.

Triumf, Şosea Kiseleff 12 (π1/222.31.72). A huge red-brick building in a park-like setting, convenient for the northern suburbs. En-suites with TV. ④.

Campsites

Buftea, a lakeside site with chalets, situated an inconvenient 18km northwest of the city. Take a train (7 daily) from Gara de Nord, or tram #20 or #31 to the Laromet terminus, then bus #460, and walk west.

The City

"A savage hotch-potch" was Ferdinand Lasalle's verdict on Bucharest between the wars, with its boulevards and nightlife, its slums and beggars, its aristocratic mansions and crumbling Orthodox churches. The extremes of wealth and poverty have been mitigated, but otherwise the city has retained many of its old characteristics. Woodlands and a girdle of lakes freshen its northern outskirts, beyond a triumphal arch and a tree-lined avenue extending from Bucharest's main thoroughfare, the Calea Victoriei.

The majority of inner-city sights are within walking distance of **Calea Victoriei** (Street of Victory), a place of vivid contrasts. At its verdant northern end near the Piaţa Victoriei, it has touches of *ancien régime* elegance, but to the south the street becomes an eclectic jumble of apartment blocks, glass and steel facades and cake shops. Fulcrum of the Calea is the large **Piaţa Revoluţiei**, created during the 1930s on Carol II's orders to ensure a field of fire around his new Royal Palace on the western side of the square. The palace now contains the **National Art Museum** (temporary shows only: Wed–Sun 10am–6pm).

North of the palace, the contemporaneous **Athénée Palace Hotel** (now part of the Hilton chain) has always been a hive of intrigue, but was refurbished as a hotel and "intelligence factory" in the 1950s, with bugged rooms, tapped phones and informers everywhere. Opposite the palace stand the **Romanian Athenaeum**, the city's main concert hall, and the **University Library**, torched, allegedly by the Securitate, in the confused fighting of the 1989 revolution, but now rebuilt. The monolithic white building just to the south was the headquarters first of the Communist Party and then of the National Salvation Front, which took over in 1989 and was really the old Communist Party in another guise. It was here that Ceauşescu addressed the populace for the last time on December 21, 1989. Eight minutes into his speech the booing started, and moments later the TV screens went blank, an unambiguous sign that it was all over for Nicolae. He just managed to escape, lifted from the roof in a helicopter so overloaded that a few lackeys were jettisoned to get the thing into the air.

Close by, the battered eighteenth-century **Creţulescu Church** fronts a tangle of streets wending west towards **Cişmigiu Gardens**, Bucharest's oldest park. The gardens originally belonged to a Turkish water inspector, and fittingly contain a serpentine lake upon which small rowing boats glide, rented by couples seeking solitude among the weeping willows. The residential area between Cişmigiu and the Gara de Nord has a real urban-village character, devout women genuflecting as they pass tiny street-corner churches while neighbours gossip outside dimly lit workshops.

Beyond the Creţulescu Church the Calea continues southwards past the police headquarters. Directly opposite is the elegant **Pasajul Villacros** arcade, one of the few remnants of the Bucharest that used to be known as the "Paris of the Balkans". Beyond the junction with B-dul Regina Elisabeta, Bucharest's main east–west boulevard, the Calea crosses Stradă Lipscani, a shabby, shifty marketplace where you can probably buy anything if you know the people to ask. Nearing the river, the **National History Museum** (Tues–Sun 10am–4pm) looms up at no. 1: a downstairs vault holds gold and silverware left by Romania's pre-Christian inhabitants, the Dacians; look out in particular for the fourth-century BC "golden helmet of Coţofeneşti", an ornate piece of headgear decorated with horsemen hunting mythical beasts. Nearby, a vast hall contains life-size copies of the friezes surrounding Trajan's column in Rome – a self-conscious demonstration of Romania's Latin roots.

To the east of here stands the small **Stavropoleos Church**; built in the 1720s, it has gorgeous, almost arabesque, mouldings and patterns decorating its facade, and a columned portico carved with delicate tracery. To the south of the church, a maze of streets and pleasantly decrepit houses surrounds the historical centre of Bucharest, where Vlad the Impaler built a citadel in the fifteenth century. The remains of the **Curtea Veche** (Old Court) are pretty modest: a few rooms, arches and shattered columns, and a cellar containing a **museum** (Tues–Sun 9am–5pm) where the skulls of boyars whom Vlad had decapitated are lovingly displayed.

A few doors along and opposite the Curtea Veche, an austere white building with barred windows conceals Bucharest's most famous hostelry, Manuc's Inn – **Hanul lui Manuc**. Originally a caravanserai founded by a wealthy Armenian, the building contains a restaurant and wine cellar. The inn's southern wall forms one side of the **Piaţa Unirii**, or Square of Union; to its east is a large market where all kinds of Romanians congregate, including the capital's Gypsy flower-sellers and hawkers.

The Centru Civic and Bulevard Brătianu

Between 1984 and 1989 swathes of Bucharest – including thousands of houses and dozens of historic monuments – were demolished to create the **Centru Civic**, intended to comprise scores of tower blocks lining a six-lane, four-kilometre-long Victory of Socialism Boulevard – now called Bulevardul Unirii. At the lower end, a circle of fifty fountains awaits sufficient water pressure, while at the other, Romania's Senate and Chamber of Deputies are to be relocated within the vast **Palace of Parliament**, the third largest building in the world after the Pentagon and the Potala. Having some 1100 rooms, with four subterranean levels and a nuclear bomb-shelter, it's linked to a network of tunnels connecting army bases and ministerial buildings. From the south door you can take a guided tour of the main halls (daily 10am–4pm; $5).

Returning northwards along B-dul Brătianu, you'll see the **Hotel Intercontinental** towering above **Piaţa Universităţii**, a nexus for city life and traffic. This is where the students pitched their post-revolution City of Peace, an encampment broken up by the miners in June 1990. When the miners returned to Bucharest in 1991, this time in protest against the government rather than as its stormtroopers, they camped out here themselves before being rooted out by the police with the same violence they had earlier dispensed.

Just to the east rises the new **National Theatre**, a pet project of Elena Ceauşescu's, resembling an Islamicized reworking of the Colosseum. Further to the west, **Bucharest University** occupies the first block on B-dul Carol I, its forecourt thronged with students and snack stands, while statues of illustrious pedagogues and statesmen gaze blindly at the crowds. The small, bulbous domes of the **Russian Church** appear through a gap in the domed buildings lining the southern side of the boulevard. Faced with yellow brick, Art Nouveau green tiling and pixie-faced nymphs, the church has a small interior, with frescoes so blackened with age and smoke that only the saintly haloes glow like golden horseshoes around Christ.

The northern suburbs

Bulevard Brătianu (subsequently becoming Bulevard Bălcescu, Bulevard Magheru and Bulevard Ipătescu) ultimately unites with Calea Victoriei at Piaţa Victoriei. From here, the tree-lined Şosea Kiseleff heads into one of the more relaxing, leafier parts of the city. Just beyond the Piaţa at Şosea Kiseleff 3 is the **Museum of the Romanian Peasant** (Tues–Sun 10am–6pm), harbouring an imaginatively presented overview of traditional crafts and lifestyles. At the northern end of the Şosea is the **Arc de Triumpf** commemorating Romania's participation on the side of the Allied victors in World War I. Beyond, trees screen the **Village Museum** (Oct–March daily 9am–5pm; Aug–Sept Tues–Sun 9am–8pm, Mon 9am–5pm) adjoining **Lake Herăstrău**, the largest of a dozen lakes which form a continuous line across the northern suburbs. Established in 1936, this fascinating ensemble of nearly three hundred peasant houses and other structures from every region of Romania shows the extreme diversity of folk architecture: oaken houses from Maramureş with their "rope motif" carvings and shingled roofing; gateways carved with suns, moons, the Tree of Life, Adam and Eve, animals and hunting scenes; dug-out homes from Drăghiceni, with vegetables growing on the roof; and windmills from the Danube Delta.

Eating

Hamburger bars and hot-dog stalls are beginning to dominate the **snack food** scene, although you can still find places serving more traditional fast food – grilled meats and pastries – around B-dul Regina Elisabeta and Str Lipscani. The pedestrian concourse adjoining the Piaţa Universităţi metro station contains several stand-up patisseries.

The capital's **restaurants** are pricey but not exorbitant. There's a wider choice of traditional Romanian dishes than elsewhere in the country, and many older establishments have opulent turn-of-the-century interiors. At the height of summer people tend to favour the open-air restaurants in Bucharest's many parks. Most restaurants treat diners to music or cabaret-style entertainment: expect to pay a small cover charge for this.

Berărie Becker Bräu, Calea Rahovei 155. Hearty schnitzel and sausage dishes in beer-hall atmosphere, with ales brewed on the premises. One block south of the Palace of Parliament.

Bistro Atheneu, Str Episcopei 3. Small restaurant opposite the Atheneum, one of the friendliest and cheapest in the city.

Caru cu Bere, Str Stavropoleos 5. Literally the "beer cart", famous for its neo-Gothic interior and grilled sausages.

Casa Capşa, Calea Victoriei 36. One of Bucharest's most elegant and long-established restaurants.

Da Vinci, Str I. Câmpineanu 11. Combined café/patisserie and Italian restaurant popular with a young, fashionable crowd.

Hanul lui Manuc, Str Iuliu Maniu 62. In the historic surroundings of an old coaching inn: a favourite venue for Godfatherish banquets.

Hong Kong, Calea Griviţei 81. Small, pleasant and inexpensive Chinese restaurant, on the way into town from the Gara de Nord.

Pescăruş, Herăstrău Park. Restaurant with fish specialities in the city's northernmost park.

Drinking and nightlife

Although a few pavement cafés emerge with the onset of summer, downtown Bucharest is devoid of the kind of strolling areas where you'll find cafés and bars grouped together. **Drinking** expeditions therefore need to be planned in advance. Many of the nicer places in the centre charge near-Western prices, condemning the majority of Bucharesteans to drink in shabby, suburban dives which serve up sour beer and little else.

In the evenings many of the newer bars feature a DJ or **live music** (jazz, blues or occasionally alternative rock), and can get crowded on gig nights. The free listings magazine *Šapte seri*, which can be picked up from most of the places listed below, gives details of who's playing where.

Most downtown **discos** play eurotechno to an audience of nouveaux riches, footballers and expensive hookers; but at least they stay open until dawn: *Vox Maris*, Piaţa Victoriei, is probably the leading example of the genre.

Cafés and bars

BackStage, Str Gabroveni 14. Relaxed late-night café/bar in a basement just off B-dul Brătianu, with a DJ playing sounds from jungle to alternative rock. Admission charge covers the first drink or two.

Café Indigo, Str Eforie 2. Live jazz at weekends, artsy crowd all week. Just off Calea Victoriei.

The Dubliner, bul Titulescu 18. Best and longest-established of the expat hangouts, north of the centre on the street leading west from Piaţa Victoriei. Serves well-kept beers and hot pies.

Green Hours, Calea Victoriei 120. Tunnel-like subterranean bar which frequently hosts gigs by the best of the local jazz musicians.

The Harp, Piaţa Unirii 1. Irish pub on the southern edge of this vast square, catering for expats and wealthy locals.

Lăptăria lui Enache, On the fourth floor of the National Theatre; access is via the back entrance to the theatre on the *Hotel Intercontinental* side. Roomy bar with bench seating catering to a mixed bag of students and arty types. Occasional live music. On fine evenings, the action moves down to the outdoor terrace on the third floor, which goes under the name of *Motor*.

Terminus Pub, Str G. Enescu 5. Cosy pub-like space on the ground floor, with a more raucous, labyrinthine bar in the basement.

Web Club, bul 1 Mai 12. Upscale but decidedly bohemian bar housed in a turn-of-the century mansion near Piaţa Victoriei. Offers Internet access during the daytime.

Listings

Airlines Aeroflot, Str Biserica Amzei 29 (☎1/615.03.14); Air France, B-dul Bălcescu 35 (☎1/612.00.85); British Airways, B-dul Regina Elisabeta 3 (☎1/303.22.22); Lufthansa, B-dul Magheru 18 (☎1/312.95.59); Swissair, B-dul Magheru 18 (☎1/312.02.38); TAROM, Str Brezoianu 10 (☎1/615.04.99) and Str Buzeşti 68 (☎1/659.41.85).

Car rental ONT at B-dul Magheru 7, or in the de luxe hotels.

Embassies Australia, Str Dr E Racota 16–18 ap.1 (☎1/666.69.23); Britain, Str Jules Michelet 24 (☎1/312.03.03); Canada, Str N Iorga 36 (☎1/650.61.40); USA, Str T Arghezi 7 (☎1/312.40.40).

Hospitals Clinica Batiştei, Str Arghezi 28 (☎1/649.70.30), behind the *Intercontinental*, and Spitalul Clinic Municipal, Splaiul Independenţei 169; both are used to dealing with foreigners. For emergency treatment go to the Spitalul Clinic de Urgenţa (☎1/679.43.10) at Calea Floreasca 8 (metro Ştefan cel Mare). Your embassy can recommend doctors speaking foreign languages.

Post office Main office at Calea Victoriei 37 (Mon–Fri 7.30am–8pm, Sat 7.30am–2pm).

Train tickets Tickets on the day of travel from the train station (note that international tickets are sold from a smaller, unmarked ticket hall which goes under the name of casa bilete speciale). Advance tickets from Agenţie CFR, Str Ion Brezoianu 10 (Mon–Fri 7.30am–7.30pm, Sat 8am–noon) and Calea Griviţei 139 (same hours).

travel details

Trains

Bucharest to: Braşov (16 daily; 2hr 30min–4hr 45min); Cluj (6 daily; 7–11hr); Sibiu (6 daily; 4hr 45min–11hr 30min); Sighişoara (10 daily; 4hr–7hr 30min); Timişoara (4 daily; 7hr –14hr).

Braşov to: Bucharest (16 daily; 2hr 30min–4hr 45min); Cluj (6 daily; 4hr–6hr 30min); Sibiu (9 daily; 2hr–4hr); Sighişoara (19 daily; 1hr 45min–3hr); Timişoara (1 daily; 8hr 40min).

Cluj to: Braşov (6 daily; 4hr–6hr 30min); Bucharest (6 daily; 7hr–11hr 30 min); Sibiu (2 daily; 3hr 30min–4hr); Sighişoara (6 daily; 3–4hr); Timişoara (4 daily; 5hr 30min–6hr 45min).

Sighişoara to: Braşov (19 daily; 1hr 45min–3hr), Cluj (6 daily; 3–4hr).

Timişoara to: Braşov (1 daily; 9hr 15min); Bucharest (4 daily; 7hr–14hr 30min); Cluj (4 daily; 5hr–6hr 30min).

Buses

Braşov to: Bran (8 daily; 45min).

CHAPTER 24

RUSSIA

Introduction

European **Russia** stretches from the borders of the states of Belarus and Ukraine to the Ural mountains, over 1000km east of Moscow; even without the rest of the Russian Federation, it constitutes by far the largest country in Europe. It was also, for many years, one of the hardest to visit. Today, however, Russia is far more accessible, though visas are still obligatory and accommodation has to be booked in advance; it will also be some time before independent travel is at all easy. Consequently, we've weighted this chapter towards Moscow and St Petersburg, the easiest places to visit. For the adventurous, however, travelling to other places is becoming increasingly easy, even without any Russian, and can be booked through various agencies in Russia and abroad.

Moscow and St Petersburg are mutually complementary. **Moscow**, the capital, is hugely enthralling, not a beautiful city by any means, and a somewhat chaotic place. However, Moscow's central core reflects Russia's long and fascinating history at the focus of a vast empire, whether it's in the relics of the communist years, the Kremlin with its palaces and churches of the tsars, or in the massive building projects of the city's dynamic mayor of the last few years, Yuriy Luzhkov, which have radically changed the face of the centre.

By contrast, Russia's second city, **St Petersburg**, is Europe at its most gracious, an attempt by the eighteenth-century Tsar Peter the Great to re-create the best of western European elegance in what was then considered a far-flung outpost. Its position in the delta of the River Neva is unparalleled, full of watery vistas of huge and faded palaces. This is still a transition period for St Petersburg, however, and it has not been repainted and revamped anywhere near as much as Moscow. Though you are extremely unlikely to be bothered by the notorious Russian mafia here, as in any other big city, beware of petty crime.

Information and maps

Russia has no **tourist information offices**. Most travellers use the information desks at the large city hotels, but the best sources of **information** are the English-language newspapers such as the *Moscow Times* (daily) or *St Petersburg Times* (twice weekly), and a number of free quarterly magazines available at leading hotels and kiosks.

Maps of high quality and at very low prices are widely available from kiosks and street vendors, and are often described as "tourist maps", which means they have text in at least one European language – usually English. Those maps most commonly found in the West are produced by Baedeker, Geocenter International and Falk, but these tend to be updated irregularly and do not take account of changing street names, more of which are reverting to their pre-revolutionary names every year.

Money and banks

The official **currency** of Russia is the ruble, each ruble divided into one hundred kopeks: there are 1, 5, 10 and 50 kopek coins, 1, 2 and 5 ruble coins, and notes to the value of 5, 10, 50, 100 and 500 rubles. The currency was devalued on 1 January 1998 as a result of the stabilization of the economy and only notes and coins dated 1997 or after are valid.

Despite the demise of soaring inflation, a financial crisis in August 1998 sent the ruble into freefall for a short period, which severely damaged the banking system. As a result, the **prices** in this chapter are given in US dollars, a fairly stable measure of real costs – but in practice they're charged and paid for in rubles. It is illegal to pay in foreign currency: only taxis and the odd restaurant will take dollars or pounds, usually at a highly disadvantageous rate. The black market offers nothing but risks: always **change money** in an official bank or currency exchange. Most **banks** are open Mon–Sat 9am–6/8pm, or later.

ATMs are now found in plenty, and using your **credit or debit card** to obtain cash from them is a safe way to get money in Russia. Some, however, have a very low cash limit per transaction, which may make your rubles expensive. You can also obtain cash from most banks with a credit card (Visa, Mastercard, Diners and Amex are the most widely accepted). **Travellers' cheques** are time-consuming and expensive to use, and only American Express cheques can be replaced if lost or stolen.

Communications

Communications in Russia have improved greatly in recent years. Most **post offices** are open Mon–Sat 8am–7pm; **stamps** can also be bought in large hotels. All district post offices have **poste restante** (*do vostrébovania*) services, but American Express will hold mail for Amex or travellers' cheque holders for up to two months. Both Moscow and St Petersburg have excellent express-letter post companies such as Post International and Westpost, which despatch mail via Finland or the US for moderate sums.

The few remaining old grey **public phones** (*taksofóny*) take tokens (*zhetony*), which can be purchased at metro stations. For new phones, which are good for local and international calls, you need a **phone card** (available in 25, 50, 100, 200 and 400 units from newspaper kiosks and post offices). Phone booths in airports and major hotels aren't always run by the city phone network, and are much more expensive: $6 per minute to Western Europe, $12 to the US. You can buy cards for these phones on the spot or use your Amex or Visa card. Mobile phone users arriving from abroad are usually linked via the GSM network, which provides the most reliable service offered in Russia. Mobile phones can be hired in Russia, but tend to be prohibitively expensive for anything more than two weeks.

Email and Internet access is offered cheaply via a number of Internet cafes and agencies such as Westpost.

Getting around

With an extensive and relatively efficient network of trains and buses, you'll have few problems **getting around** the most populated parts of Russia.

■ Trains and buses

Buying **tickets** for long-distance or international trains can be complicated. Aside from being unsure which outlet handles bookings for their destination, foreigners are usually charged more for tickets than Russians are. A dozen trains leave Moscow's Leningrad Station within an hour or so of midnight for the 8hr journey to St Petersburg, but only five are fast and comfortable (#2, #4, #6, #10 and #36). These trains are generally safe and reliable.

Most of Moscow's and St Petersburg's outlying sights are accessible by **suburban train** from one of the mainline stations, which have a separate ticket office for suburban trains; fares are extremely cheap, as foreigners pay the same price as Russians. A few sites can be reached by **suburban bus or minibus** from the end of a metro line. Fares are also low, although state-run buses are often packed.

■ Driving and hitching

Traffic in the cities is heavy and many Russian motorists show a reckless disregard for pedestrians and other cars. **Driving**, therefore, requires a fair degree of skill and nerve.

Unless otherwise specified, **speed limits** are 60kph in the city and 80kph on highways. A growing number of **car rental** agencies offer Western models and prefer payment by credit card. Most tend to ask for about $100 a day, after all the hidden charges are taken into account, so you might as well go for a well-known firm. However, it is still impossible to rent a car without a driver.

Most Russians **hitch**, especially after the public transport system closes down, when you'll see people flagging down anything that moves, even ambulances or trucks. If the driver finds the destination acceptable, he'll state a price, which may or may not be negotiable; if you're not happy, wait for another car. Russians will usually pay the ruble equivalent of a dollar or so to ride several kilometres; foreigners are likely to be charged more. Don't get into a vehicle which has more than one person in it, and never accept lifts from anyone who approaches you, particularly outside restaurants and nightclubs: instances of drunken foreigners being robbed in the back of cars have been known. Single women should stick to yellow cabs.

Accommodation

Anyone travelling on a tourist visa to Russia must have **accommodation** arranged before arrival. Most hostels and all hotels can arrange the necessary visa support for you. Business visas – which don't oblige you to prebook lodgings – are fairly easy to obtain, if the business inviting you is registered. As **hotels** in Moscow and St Petersburg are expensive, anyone on a tight budget will almost certainly do better by opting for a **hostel or private accommodation** instead. Forget about campsites, which are miles outside the city, have poor facilities and security, and are often only open over the summer.

ACCOMMODATION PRICE CODES

Throughout this guide, accommodation is priced on a scale of ① to ⑨, the number indicating the lowest price per night a single person could expect to pay in that establishment in high season. With hostels this is the nightly rate per person; with hotels, the price is arrived at by dividing the cost of the cheapest double room by two. The prices indicated by the codes are as follows:

① under £5 / $8	④ £15–20 / $24–32	⑦ £30–35 / $48–56
② £5–10 / $8–16	⑤ £20–25 / $32–40	⑧ £35–40 / $56–64
③ £10–15 / $16–24	⑥ £25–30 / $40–48	⑨ £40 / $64 and over

■ Hotels

Russia's **hotels** range from opulent citadels to seedy pits inhabited by wheeler-dealers, with numerous generally tolerable establishments in between. Two-star hotels mostly consist of 1950s low-rises with matchbox-sized rooms; three-star hotels are typical 1960s and 1970s high-rises, equipped with several restaurants, bars and nightclubs; while four-star hotels tend to date from the 1980s and come closest to matching the standards (and prices) of their Western counterparts. Most still include **breakfast** in the price, but in cheaper places it's wise to check if there's anywhere to eat.

Not all hotels maintain adequate security: whatever class of accommodation you stay in, don't leave valuables in your room, put your money in the hotel safe, stash most other items in a locked suitcase under the bed, and lock the door before going to sleep.

■ Hostels and private accommodation

Hostels are probably the best-value accommodation in Russia. They are much safer than the few hotels that charge similar rates, and can help out with many of the problems that face low-budget travellers. **Reservations** from outside Russia should be made at least three to four weeks in advance, while bookings from within Russia are accepted no more than two weeks in advance. Note that there is no age restriction.

Private accommodation for tourists is slowly catching on, and both Moscow and St Petersburg have agencies where you can just turn up and find a room. Some provide self-contained **apartments**, but most offer **bed and breakfast** in Russian households. The cost varies from $15 to $70 per person per night, depending on the location and whether you opt for B&B or full board.

Food and drink

Moscow and St Petersburg now abound in **cafés and restaurants** offering everything from pizza to Indian, French and Chinese food. Many cater to the new rich or foreign businessmen, but cheap and middle-range establishments are plentiful, serving food with a local flavour. Credit cards are increasingly accepted, particularly in Moscow, though mainly in upmarket and therefore expensive places.

■ Food

Despite the increasing popularity of **fast food** and foreign cuisine, Russians remain loyal to their culinary heritage, above all to **zakuski** – small dishes consumed before a meal, to accompany vodka, as a snack or as a light meal in themselves. Salted herring is a firm favourite, as are gherkins, assorted cold meats and salads. Hard-boiled eggs or pancakes (*bliny*), both served with caviar (*ikra*), are also available.

Most Russians take **breakfast** (*zavtrak*) seriously, tucking into calorific pancakes (*bliny*) or porridge (*kasha*), with curd cheese (*tvorog*) and sour cream (*smetana*). Hotels usually serve a "continental" breakfast, probably just fried egg, bread, butter and jam; ritzier hotels provide a buffet and offer a Western-style brunch on Sundays. The main meal of the day is **lunch** (*obed*), eaten between 1 and 4pm, while **supper** (*uzhin*) traditionally consists of just zakuski and tea. **Restaurants**, on the other hand, make much more of the evening meal, often staying open as late as 1am. **Menus** are usually written in Russian only, but an increasing number of places now offer a version in English. You can always ask what they recommend ("*shto-by vy porekomendovali?*").

After the *zakuski*, the menu continues with a choice of **soup**. Cabbage soup (*shchi*), served with a generous dollop of sour cream, has been the principal Russian dish for the last thousand years. Beetroot soup, or *borshch*, originally from Ukraine, is equally ubiquitous. Soups are often only available at lunchtime, and Russians don't regard even large meaty soups (*kharcho* or *solyanka*) as a main meal. This is no place for vegetarians: **main courses** are overwhelmingly based on meat (*myaso*), usually beef, mutton or pork, sometimes accompanied by a mushroom, sour cream or cheese sauce. Meat also makes its way into *pelmeny*, a Russian version of ravioli. However, Georgian restaurants always have vegetarian dishes such as bean stew. Marinated **fish** is a popular starter (try *selyodka pod shuboy*, herring "in a fur coat" of beetroot, carrot, egg and mayonnaise), while fresh fish – usually salmon, sturgeon or cod – appears as a main course in most self-respecting eateries.

Pastries (*pirozhnoe*) are available from cake shops (*konditerskaya*) and some grocers (*gastronom*). Savoury pies (*pirozhki*) are often sold on the streets from late morning – the best are filled with cabbage, curd cheese or rice; steer clear of the meat ones.

Desserts (*sladkoe*) are not a strong feature of Russian cuisine. Ice cream, fruit, apple pie (*yablochniy pirog*) and jam pancakes (*blinchikiy s varenem*) are restaurant perennials, while in Caucasian restaurants you may get the flaky pastry and honey dessert, *pakhlava*. There are over sixty varieties of **cake** (*tort*); the main ingredients are usually sponge, honey, and a spice like cinnamon or ginger or lots of buttery cream and jam.

■ Drink

Vodka (*vódka*) is the national drink, and the average citizen drinks over a litre of it a week. It is normally served chilled and drunk neat in one gulp, followed by a mouthful of *zakuska*. Local brands have hit back after a brief period of dominance by foreign makes. Highly popular are flavoured vodkas such as Pertsovka (hot pepper vodka), Limonaya (lemon vodka), Okhotnichaya (hunter's vodka, with juniper berries, ginger and cloves) and Zubrovka (bison-grass vodka).

Russians often drink **beer** (*pívo*) in the morning to alleviate a vodka hangover, or merely as a thirst quencher. The numerous local brands (in bottles and on tap) have an excellent fresh taste, with fewer preservatives than imports.

Wine (*vinó*) comes mostly from the vineyards of Moldavia, Georgia and the Crimea. Georgian wines used to be the pick of the bunch, but the quality of their dry wines has declined in recent years – the Moldavian reds and whites are now the best option. However, Georgian semi-sweet wines are still worth tasting – try Kindzmarauli, or Stalin's favourite, Khvanchkara. The Crimea produces mainly fortified wines from Massandra.

Tea (*chay*) is brewed and stewed for hours, and topped up with boiling water from a samovar. Russians drink tea without milk; if you ask for milk it's likely to be condensed or UHT.

Coffee (*kófe*) is readily available and often of reasonable quality. Many places offer espresso, or better still, a Turkish coffee – both served strong and black. Both tea and coffee are often served with sugar already added.

Soft drinks, from the usual market leaders – Pepsi, Coca-Cola and Schweppes – are available. Local **mineral waters**, with and without gas, can be recommended.

Opening hours and holidays

Most **shops** open Mon–Sat 10am–7pm or later; few close for lunch. Sunday opening hours are less predictable, but department stores, bars and restaurants stay open.

Opening hours for **museums** are 10am–5/6pm. You'll find that they are invariably closed at least one day a week and, in addition, one further day in the month will be set aside as a "cleaning day". Opening hours for **churches** are less easy to predict but they tend to be accessible from 8am until the end of the evening service.

Russia's official **national holidays** have been in a state of flux for the past couple of years, since so many were associated with the former Soviet regime. Many of these have now been done away with and replaced by traditional religious holidays. The current public holidays are: Jan 1; Jan 6/7 (Orthodox Christmas); March 8; Good Friday; May 1 and 2; May 9; June 12; Nov 7.

Emergencies

The mafia is less of a hazard in Russia than is **petty crime**, which presents itself mostly as pickpocketing. Sensible precautions include making photocopies of your passport and visa, leaving passports and tickets in the hotel safe, and noting down travellers' cheque and credit card numbers. Do not carry large sums of money around with you and use a money belt if possible.

The **police** (*militia*) can be recognized by their blue-grey uniforms with red lapels and cap bands; some may be armed. If you do have something **stolen**, report it to the *militia*: try the phrase "*Menya obokrali*" ("I have been robbed"). It's unlikely that there'll be anyone who speaks English, and even less likely that your belongings will be retrieved, but you'll need a statement detailing what you've lost for your insurance claim. You're only likely to come across the paramilitary OMON in situations of civil unrest or during raids on nightclubs.

Visitors to Russia are advised to get **booster-shots** for diphtheria, tetanus and polio. If you are on any prescribed medication (particularly insulin), you should bring enough supplies for your stay. For **minor complaints**, it's easiest to go to a high-street pharmacy (*aptéka*). Foreigners tend to rely on **private clinics** with imported drugs and equipment, which charge excessively high rates, so it's a good idea to take out insurance.

EMERGENCY NUMBERS

Police ☎02; Fire ☎01; and Ambulance ☎03.

MOSCOW

MOSCOW is all things to all people. For Westerners, the city may look European, but its unruly spirit seems closer to Central Asia. To Muscovites, however, Moscow is both a "Mother City" and a "big village", a tumultuous community which possesses an underlying collective instinct that shows itself in times of trouble. Home of one in fifteen Russians, it is huge, surreal and apocalyptic. Its beauty and ugliness are inseparable, its sentimentality the obverse of a brutality rooted in centuries of despotism, while private and cultural life in the city are as passionate as business and politics are cynical. Nowhere else reflects the contradictions and ambiguities of the Russian people as Moscow does – nor the stresses of a country undergoing meltdown and renewal.

Moscow's identity has been imbued with a sense of its own destiny since the fourteenth century, when the principality of Muscovy took the lead in the struggle against the Mongol-Tatars who had reduced the Kievan state to ruins. Under Ivan the Great and Ivan the Terrible – the "Gatherers of the Russian Lands" – its realm came to encompass everything from the White Sea to the Caspian, while after the fall of Constantinople to the Turks, Moscow assumed Byzantium's suzerainty over the Orthodox world. Despite the changes wrought by Peter the Great – not least the transfer of the capital to St Petersburg – Moscow kept its mystique and bided its time until the Bolsheviks made it the fountainhead of a new creed.

Since the fall of communism, Muscovites have had to deal with the "Wild Capitalism" that now intoxicates the city, as Mayor Luzhkov puts into effect his Grand Project, consisting of major building programmes which are changing the face of the city more radically than any time since the Stalin era. The construction boom seemed to reach its height with the celebrations of the city's 850th anniversary in 1997, but with major squares and buildings being overhauled at a fantastic rate, the city seems to change every day.

Arrival and information

Arriving by **train** from London, Berlin or Warsaw, you'll end up at **Belarus Station**, about 1km northwest of the Garden Ring, which is served by the Belorusskaya metro. Most trains from the Baltic states arrive at **Riga Station** (Rizhskaya metro line), 2km north of the Garden Ring, while services from Prague and Budapest terminate at **Kiev Station**, south of the Moskva River (Kievskaya metro line). If you're coming from St Petersburg, Finland or Estonia, your train will terminate at **Leningrad Station**. To get into the centre from any of these stations, your safest bet is to take the **metro**, as **taxis** tend to charge whatever they can get away with, which can be quite a hefty sum after the last bus has left.

The main **international airport** is at Sheremetevo-2, 28km northwest of the city centre. To avoid any hassle, or if you know you'll be arriving after dark, the *Travellers Guest House* and most top hotels can arrange for you to be met at the airport. The fee ($40 plus) is similar to what private taxis charge, without any haggling. Taxis leaving from the departures terminal may charge significantly less, as they don't belong to the "taxi mafia" that operates at the arrivals section. The alternative is to get into town by **public transport**, which involves a two-stage journey by bus and metro, and costs the ruble equivalent of $1. This is not feasible after about 10pm. There are two **express buses** into town from outside the arrivals terminal. One runs to Rechnoy Vokzal bus station, near the metro of the same name (every 30min till 8.30pm); the other to the Air Terminal, 600–700m from Aeroport or Dinamo Station, further in on the same metro line (hourly till 10pm).

If you need to pick up leaflets, maps and general **information** on what's going on in and around Moscow, you're best off going to the information desks of the *Intourist Hotel,* Tverskaya ul. 3/5 (☎095/956-8426) or *Metropol Hotel,* Teatralniy pr. 1/4 (☎095/927-6000). The *Travellers Guest House* also functions as an information centre.

City transport

Although central Moscow is best explored **on foot**, the city is so big that you're bound to rely on its famous **metro** system to get around. The metro trains run daily (6am–midnight), with

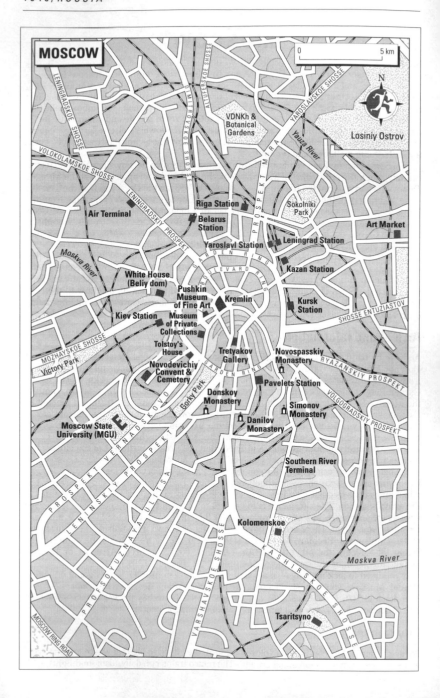

MOSCOW

0   5 km

N

Losiniy Ostrov

VDNKh & Botanical Gardens

Sokolniki Park

Art Market

Riga Station

Air Terminal

Belarus Station

Yaroslavl Station

Leningrad Station

Kazan Station

White House (Beliy dom)

Pushkin Museum of Fine Art

Kremlin

Kursk Station

Kiev Station

Museum of Private Collections

Tolstoy's House

Tretyakov Gallery

Novospasskiy Monastery

Novodevichiy Convent & Cemetery

Pavelets Station

Donskoy Monastery

Simonov Monastery

Danilov Monastery

Moscow State University (MGU)

Southern River Terminal

Kolomenskoe

Moskva River

Tsaritsyno

LENINGRADSKOE SHOSSE

VOLOKOLAMSKOE SHOSSE

Moskva River

LENINGRADSKIY PROSPEKT

ALTUFEVSKOE SHOSSE

DMITROVSKOE SHOSSE

YAROSLAVSKOE SHOSSE

Yauza River

PROSPEKT MIRA

GARDEN RING BOULEVARD RING

SHOSSE ENTUZIASTOV

MOZHAYSKOE SHOSSE

Victory Park

RYAZANSKIY PROSPEKT

GARDEN RING

Gorky Park

VOLGOGRADSKIY PROSPEKT

PROSPEKT VERNADSKOVO

LENINSKIY PROSPEKT

PROFSOYUZNAYA ULITSA

VARSHAVSKOE SHOSSE

KASHIRSKOE SHOSSE

MOSCOW RING ROAD

services every two minutes during peak periods (8–10am & 5–7pm) and every three to five minutes at other times. Passengers buy plastic **tokens** (*zhetony*) to slip into the seemingly barrierless turnstiles, and the cost is minimal, at around 20 cents. Providing you don't leave the metro you can travel any distance, and change lines as many times as you like, using a single token. Stations are marked with a large "M" and have separate doors for incoming and outgoing passengers. All signs and maps are in Russian including "entrance" (*vkhód*), "exit" (*vykhod*) and "passage to another line" (*perekhód*).

As the metro gets you to within fifteen minutes' walk of all the main sights, you're unlikely to need any other forms of public transport, which tend to be less efficient anyway. **Buses, trolleybuses and trams** operate from 5.30am until about 11pm, although the odd trolleybus is occasionally seen at midnight. Buses and trolleybuses run through the centre of the city but there are few trams, except on the outskirts. Bus stops are marked with an "A" (for *avtobus*); trolleybus stops with a Cyrillic "t" resembling a flat-topped "m" (for *trolleybus*) in the centre of town and a small blue sign elsewhere; tram stops (bearing a "T" for *tramvay*) are cream in colour and suspended from the overhead cables above the road. **Tickets** (*talony*) for buses, trolleybuses and trams are available from street vendors, or from the driver of the vehicle, who sells them usually in batches of ten for around $1, though on some buses single tickets can be bought.

The official **taxis** are yellow or grey Volgas, but others can come in all shapes and sizes. Taxi drivers often don't use their meters, so it's best to negotiate the fare before getting in to avoid any unpleasant surprises, especially as foreigners are likely to be charged more than the standard fare. Private cars will also stop if you stick your hand out and can be considerably cheaper when compared to an official taxi with its meter off. They're generally safe but for a woman travelling alone at night they should be avoided.

Accommodation

Independent travellers with a business visa will still find the accommodation situation in Moscow pretty dire. Most of the city's **hotels** are overpriced for what they offer, particularly those in the centre. Areas like Oktyabrskaya ploshchad, Leninksiy prospekt and the Sparrow Hills, located south and southwest of the Kremlin, offer a wider range of cheaper accommodation. If you need help finding somewhere to stay, you can reserve a room and pay for it on the spot at Intourist on Manezhnaya pl., or the hotel reservations desk at Sheremetevo-2 airport – pay for one night only in case you decide to move somewhere else.

A better option if you're on a very tight budget is to try a foreign-run **hostel**, or **private accommodation**, which you can arrange in advance through the *Travellers Guest House* (see below) or the Russian Travel Service, PO Box 311, Fitzwilliam, NH 03447, USA (☎603/585 6534; *jkates@monad.net*).

Hostels

Nasledie Hostel (Heritage Hostel), ul. Kosmonavtov 2 (☎095/975-3501); VDNKh metro. Clean and spartan hostel; entrance to the right of the yellow block with the Avia Biletov sign. ②.

7th Floor, pr. Vernadskovo 88, korpus 1 (☎095/437 99 97); Yugo-Zapadnaya metro (30min ride from the centre). Very small B&B hostel, with efficient and friendly staff. ⑤.

The Travellers Guest House, Bolshaya Pereslavskaya ul. 50 (☎095/971 40 59; *tgh@glasnet.ru*); ten-minute walk from Prospekt Mira metro. Hidden away on the tenth floor, this American-run hostel is pleasant, clean and fairly central, with a laundry, café and bar. It also provides excellent tourist information and advice. ③.

Hotels

Minsk Hotel, Tverskaya ul. 22 (☎095/299 13 49); Mayakovskaya or Pushkinskaya metro. Anonymous 1960s high-rise right in the centre, with a business centre and sauna. ⑤.

Moskva Hotel, Okhotniy ryad 7 (☎095/292 60 70); Okhotniy Ryad or Teatralnaya metro. Sombre Stalinist warren whose west-facing rooms overlook the Kremlin. ⑨.

Pekin, ul. Bolshaya-Sadovaya 5/1 (☎095/209 2442); Mayakovskaya metro. Genuine period charm, plus a Chinese restaurant and a sauna. ⑨.

Rossiya Hotel, ul. Varvarka 6 (☎095/232 60 46); Ploshchad Revolyutsii metro. Gigantic mice-infested labyrinth with 3070 rooms and poor security, but it has a great location just off Red Square and is not too expensive. ⑨.

Tsentralnaya, Tverskaya ul. 10 (☎095/229 8957/747 30 59); Tverskaya, Pushkinskaya and Chekhovskaya metros. Very central characterful hotel, but with a shady clientele. ⑤.

Tsentralniy Dom Turista, Leninskiy pr. 146 (☎095/434 94 67); Yugo-Zapadnaya metro (30min from the centre). Despite its location, this 22-storey building is a good-value place to stay. ⑦.

Universitetskaya, Michurinskiy pr. 8 (☎095/939 97 70); Universitet metro. Large pleasant hotel in the leafy Sparrow Hills. ④.

The City

Discounting a couple of satellite towns beyond the outer ring road, Moscow covers an area of about 900 square kilometres. Yet, despite its size and the inhuman scale of many of its buildings and avenues, the general layout is easily grasped – a series of concentric circles and radial lines, emanating from the Kremlin – and the centre is compact enough to explore on foot.

Red Square and the **Kremlin** are the historic nucleus of the city, a magnificent stage for political drama, signifying a great sweep of history that includes Ivan the Terrible, Peter the Great, Stalin and Gorbachev. Here you'll find Lenin's Mausoleum and St Basil's Cathedral, the famous GUM department store, and the Kremlin itself, whose splendid cathedrals and Armoury museum head the list of attractions. The Kremlin is surrounded by two quarters defined by ring boulevards built over the original ramparts of medieval times, when Moscow's residential areas were divided into the **Beliy Gorod** and the humbler **Zemlyanoy Gorod** – both quarters housing a number of museums and art galleries.

Beyond this historic core Moscow is too sprawling to explore on foot: you'll need to rely on the metro. To the southwest of the Kremlin, **Krasnaya Presnya** describes a swathe which includes the White House (the Russian Parliament building); the Novodevichiy Convent further south across the Moskva River; Victory Park, to the southwest; and the Moscow State University, in the Sparrow Hills. South across the river from the Kremlin, **Zamoskvoreche** is home of the Tretyakov Gallery of Russian art and Gorky Park, while further south are the Donskoy and Danilov monasteries that once stood guard against the Tatars, as well as the romantic ex-royal estate of **Kolomenskoe**. The main reason to venture out to Moscow's northern suburbs is to visit the **VDNKh**, a huge Stalinist exhibition park with amazing statues and pavilions, in the vicinity of Moscow's Botanical Gardens and TV Tower.

Red Square

Every visitor to Moscow is irresistibly drawn to **Red Square**, the historic and spiritual heart of the city, so loaded with associations and drama that it seems to embody all of Russia's triumphs and tragedies. The name Red Square (Krasnaya ploshchad) has nothing to do with communism, but derives from *krasniy*, the old Russian word for "beautiful", which probably came to mean "red" due to people's thirst for bright colour during the long, drab winter months.

The square came into being towards the end of the fifteenth century – after Ivan III ordered the clearance of the wooden houses and traders' stalls that huddled below the eastern wall of the Kremlin – and remained an important political and cultural landmark until Peter the Great moved the capital to St Petersburg in 1712. Only when the Bolsheviks moved the capital back to Moscow in 1918 did the square regain its political significance as the centre for huge parades and demonstrations.

On one side, the Lenin Mausoleum squats beneath the ramparts and towers of the Kremlin, confronted by the long facade of the "State Department Store" (Mon–Sat 8am–9pm, Sun 11am–6pm) – built in 1890–93, and nationalized and renamed **GUM** after the 1917 Revolution – while **St Basil's Cathedral** erupts in a profusion of onion domes and spires at the far end.

In postcommunist Russia, the **Lenin Mausoleum** (Mavzoley V.I. Lenina; Wed, Thurs & Sat 10am–1pm, Sun 10am–2pm) tends to be regarded either as an awkward reminder or a cherished relic of the old days. Most people come to see Lenin's corpse, softly spotlit in a crystal casket, wearing a polka-dot tie and a dark suit-cum-shroud, his body shrunken and waxy, his beard wispy and his fingers discoloured. While leaving Lenin's body *in situ* seems inappropriate (he apparently wished to be buried beside his mother in St Petersburg's Volkov Cemetery), the Mausoleum deserves to be preserved as a stylish piece of architecture and a bizarre, modern counterpart to the pyramids of ancient Egypt. When Boris Yeltsin raised the question of closing the Mausoleum in 1997, communist extremists blew up a monument to Nicholas II on the outskirts of Moscow in protest, and the ultimate fate of both Lenin and the building housing him remains uncertain. For now, the famous goose-stepping guard which used to stand watch over the Mausoleum has been reinstated, mainly for the tourists, but at the more politically correct grave of the Unknown Soldier just off Red Square.

The **Kremlin wall**, behind the Mausoleum – 19m high and 6.5m thick – is topped with swallow-tailed crenellations and defended by eight towers mostly built by Italian architects in the 1490s. Today, it constitutes a kind of Soviet pantheon, which is likely to change should Lenin ever go. Visitors leaving the Mausoleum pass a mass grave of Bolsheviks who perished during the battle for Moscow in 1917, to reach an array of luminaries whose ashes are interred in the wall. These include writer Maxim Gorky and Yuri Gagarin, the first man in space. Beyond lies a select group of Soviet leaders: Chernenko, Andropov, a pompous Brezhnev and a benign-looking Stalin.

No description can do justice to **St Basil's Cathedral** (sobor Vasiliya Blazhennovo; Mon & Wed–Sun 10am–4.30pm; $5), silhouetted against the skyline where Red Square slopes down towards the Moskva River. Commissioned by Ivan the Terrible to celebrate his capture of the Tatar stronghold of Kazan in 1552, its popular title commemorates a "holy fool", St Basil the Blessed, who foretold the fire that swept Moscow in 1547, and was later buried in the Trinity Cathedral that then stood on this site. Despite its apparent disorder, there is an underlying symmetry to the cathedral, which has eight domed chapels symbolizing the eight assaults on Kazan, clustered around a central, lofty tent-roofed spire. In 1588, Tsar Fyodor added a ninth chapel on the northeastern side, to accommodate the remains of St Basil. In modern times, this unique masterpiece was almost destroyed by Stalin, who resented the fact that it prevented his soldiers from leaving Red Square en masse.

At the other end of the square is the **State History Museum** (Istoricheskiy muzey; Mon & Wed–Sun 11am–7pm), with a varied collection of everything from archeological finds to Soviet badges and textiles. On the other side of it is the supreme symbol of Moscow's exchange of communism for capitalism: in place of a vast empty space formerly used for displays of military hardware and demonstrations is Luzhkov's vast underground shopping centre, Okhotniy ryad, buried beneath a mass of fussy and tasteless landscaping.

The Kremlin

Brooding and glittering in the heart of Moscow, the **Kremlin** (10am–5.30pm; closed Thurs; last tickets sold at 4.30pm) thrills and tantalizes whenever you see its towers stabbing the skyline, or its cathedrals and palaces arrayed above the Moskva River. Its name is synonymous with Russia's government, and in modern times assumed connotations of a Mecca for believers, and the seat of the Antichrist for foes of communism.

The founding of the Kremlin is attributed to Prince Yuriy Dolgorukiy, who erected a wooden fort above the confluence of the Moskva and Neglina rivers in about 1147 – although the site may also have been inhabited as long ago as 500 BC. Despite raids by the Mongols and Tatars over the years, the Kremlin, under the building programme of Grand Duke Ivan III (1462–1505), grew to confirm Moscow's stature as the centre of Muscovy. However, as with Red Square, the Kremlin was also largely neglected during the reign of Peter the Great (1682–1725), when he spurned Moscow for St Petersburg – a situation that remained unchanged until 1918, when Lenin moved the seat of government back to Moscow.

One **ticket**, for a dollar or so, admits you to the Kremlin, while separate tickets for about $5 each are required to enter its cathedrals and the Patriarch's Palace. A ticket valid for all sights is available for around $20. While it's possible to see almost everything in one visit, a couple of visits are better if you have the time: one to see the inside and outside of the cathedrals, and another for touring the Armoury Palace, which can only be entered at set times on Kremlin open days. Photography is not permitted inside any of the cathedrals or museums.

Roughly two-thirds of the Kremlin is off-limits to tourists – namely the trio of buildings in the northern half of the citadel, and the wooded Secret Garden sloping down towards the river. The accessible part begins around the corner from the Great Kremlin Palace (closed to the public, except for occasional ballet performances), from where the **Patriarch's Palace** hoves into view. The latter now houses a **Museum of Seventeenth-Century Life and Applied Art** displaying ecclesiastical regalia, period furniture and domestic utensils. The exhibition concludes in the former **Cathedral of the Twelve Apostles**, which forms part of the same structure, also painted flesh-pink. Moving further along, the **Tsar Cannon** (Tsar-pushka), cast by Andrei Chokhov in 1586, is one of the largest cannons ever made and was intended to defend the Saviour Gate – but it has never been fired. Close by looms the earthbound **Tsar Bell** (Tsar-kolokol), the largest bell in the world, cast in 1655.

Beyond the Patriarch's Palace lies **Sobornaya ploshchad** (Cathedral Square), the historic heart of the Kremlin, surrounded by a superb array of buildings that give the square its name. Soaring above the fourteenth-century square, the magnificent white **Ivan the Great Bell Tower** (Kolokolnya Ivana Velikovo) provides a focal point for the entire Kremlin, being the tallest structure within its walls. Opposite stands the oldest and most important of the Kremlin churches, the **Cathedral of the Assumption** (Uspenskiy sobor), which has symbolized Moscow's claim to be the protector of the seat of Russian Orthodoxy ever since the seat of the Church was transferred here from Vladimir in 1326. The cathedral was rebuilt in 1479 by the Bolognese architect Alberti Fioravanti, and its subsequent history reflects its role as Russia's premier church, used throughout tsarist times for coronations and solemn acts of state. Given the cathedral's exalted status, its exterior is remarkably plain, while the interior is spacious, light and echoing, its walls, roof and pillars entirely covered by icons, and frescoes applied onto a gilt undercoating. Tucked away beside the Cathedral of the Assumption is the lowly white **Church of the Deposition of the Robe** (tserkov Rizpolozheniya).

The last of the great churches to be erected on Sobornaya ploshchad, the **Cathedral of the Archangel** (Arkhangelskiy sobor) was built in 1505–08 as the burial place for the rulers of Muscovy. Unlike the vernacular Cathedral of the Assumption, its debt to the Italian Renaissance is obvious: four heavy square pillars take up much of the dimly lit interior, which is covered in frescoes. Around the walls and pillars cluster the tombs of Russia's rulers from Grand Duke Ivan I to Tsar Ivan V. Across from here glints the golden-domed **Cathedral of the Annunciation** (Blagoveshchenskiy sobor), which served as the private church of the grand dukes and tsars. Restored in 1562–64, the cathedral is lofty and narrow, with an interior that seems far more "Russian" than the other Kremlin cathedrals. It also houses some of the finest icons in Russia, with works by Theophanes the Greek and Andrei Rublev.

Situated between the Great Kremlin Palace and the Borovitskiy Gate, the **Armoury Palace** (Oruzheynaya palata; 10am, noon, 2.30 & 4.30pm; sessions last 1hr 45min; $12, $6 for card-carrying students) conceals a staggering array of treasures behind its Russo-Byzantine facade, among them the tsars' coronation robes, carriages, jewellery, dinner services and armour – whose splendour and curiosity value outweigh the trouble and expense involved in seeing them. The exhibits are labelled in Russian only. The palace also houses the **State Diamond Fund** (Almazniy Fond; 20min guided tours; tickets can occasionally be purchased at the Armoury counter for around $20), which contains the most valuable gems in Russia.

The Beliy Gorod

The **Beliy Gorod** or "White Town" is the historic name of the residential district that encircled the Kremlin. This area is known for its main seventeenth-century thoroughfare, **Tverskaya ulitsa**, which owes its present form to a massive reconstruction programme during the mid-1930s, and yet, despite the scale of some of its gargantuan buildings, the variety of older, often charming sidestreets give the avenue a distinctive character. There are countless museums and sights situated in the Beliy Gorod, but probably two of the most important are south of Tverskaya ulitsa, on ulitsa Volkhonka: the Pushkin Museum of Fine Arts and the Museum of Private Collections.

Moscow's **Pushkin Museum of Fine Arts** (muzey Izobrazitelnykh Iskusstv imeni A.S. Pushkina; Tues–Sun 10am–7pm; last tickets sold 6pm; $8), at ul. Volkhonka 12, has a good collection of European painting, from Rembrandt and Poussin to the Impressionists. Not as dauntingly large as St Petersburg's Hermitage Museum, it's still too big to do justice to in a single visit. The display changes slightly due to temporary exhibitions. Most exhibits are captioned in English.

Next door, the new **Museum of Private Collections** (muzey Lichnykh Kollektsiy; Wed–Sun noon–6pm), displays antique and modern art that hasn't been seen in public for decades, if ever. The individual tastes and limited resources of a score of collectors makes for a well-rounded, quirky exhibition flattered by a stylishly refurbished interior. The permanent exhibition begins on the **second floor** with drawings by Salvador Dalí and Matisse, while the **third floor** is more Russian in spirit, with nineteenth-century works by Wanderers such as Ilya Repin. Finally, the **fourth floor** offers a feast of twentieth-century art, including two rooms devoted to Alexander Rodchenko and his wife Varvara Stepanova.

In 1994, Moscow's Mayor Luzhkov took the populist step of announcing the rebuilding of the **Cathedral of Christ the Redeemer** opposite the museums on Volkhonka (display on the building's history: Tues, Thurs, Sat & Sun 10am–6pm, Wed & Fri 11am–7pm). The vast structure, built 1839–83, had been blown up by the Soviet government in 1934 and a swimming pool was built on the site. Financed largely by donations and perceived as a symbol of Moscow's (and Russia's) revival, the rebuilding of the Cathedral is already complete, though work continues on its interior.

The Zemlyanoy Gorod

In medieval times, the white-walled Beliy Gorod was encircled by a humbler **Zemlyanoy Gorod** or "Earth Town". Besides a roll-call of famous residents – Pushkin, Chekhov and Bulgakov – this is one of the best-looking parts of Moscow, with Neoclassical and Art Nouveau mansions on every corner of the backstreets of the **Patriarch's Ponds**. Due south of here, the **Arbat**, which once stood for bohemian Moscow in the way that Carnaby Street represented swinging London, has a vibrant **streetlife** that was unique in Moscow during the 1980s and is still more tourist-friendly than anything else currently on offer.

Admirers of Bulgakov, Chekhov, Lermontov, Gorky, Pushkin or Alexei Tolstoy will find their former homes preserved as museums in and around the pretty, leafy backstreets of the **Patriarch's Ponds** (Patriarshiye prudy), the quarter to the southwest of Tverskaya. The Patriarch's Ponds are, in fact, one large pond which forms the heart of a square surrounded by wrought-iron railings and mature trees and flanked by Art Nouveau mansions on every corner. At Bolshaya Sadovaya ul. 10, a plaque attests that Mikhail Bulgakov lived here from 1921 to 1924; his satirical fantasy *The Master and Margarita* is indelibly associated with this area in particular. To visit, go into the courtyard and look for entrance 6, on the left; the apartment (no. 50) is at the top of the stairs.

On the corner of Sadovaya-Kudrinskaya ulitsa, at no. 6, a pink two-storey dwelling has been preserved as the **Chekhov House-Museum** (Tues–Sun 11am–3pm; closed last day of each month). Here, Anton Chekhov, his parents and his brother lived from 1866 to 1890. The **Gorky House-Museum** (Mon & Thurs 10am–4.30pm; Tues, Wed & Fri noon–6pm; closed last Thurs of each month), on the corner of Povarskaya ulitsa and ulitsa Spiridonovka, is worth seeing purely for its amazing Art Nouveau decor, both inside and out.

Narrow and cobbled, with a tramline down the middle, the **Arbat** was the heart of a bohemian quarter where writers, actors and scientists frequented the same shops and cafés. Today, the Arbat retains some of these characteristics with its array of cafés and antique shops, and more recent fast-food outlets. The area tends to get busier once you get beyond the **Peace Wall** – a cute example of propaganda against Reagan's Star Wars. Portrait artists, buskers, and photographers offering a range of props from Gorby to Mickey Mouse are a few of the sights on offer, while the buildings bloom with bright colours and quirky details. Around the Arbat backstreets, the most notable sight is the **Pushkin Flat-Museum**

(Wed–Sun 11am–6pm; closed last Fri of every month), a sky-blue Empire-style house at no. 53, which enshrines the fleeting domicile of Russia's most beloved writer.

Krasnaya Presnya

Beyond the Garden Ring Road around Zemlyanoy Gorod, Moscow seems an undifferentiated sprawl of blocks and avenues, attesting to its phenomenal growth in Soviet times. West and south of the centre, **Krasnaya Presnya** is a swathe of the city intersected by the loops of the Moskva River, and its sights are easily accessible by metro.

The Krasnaya Presnya district just beyond ploshchad Vosstaniya is chiefly notable for the ex-parliament building known as the **White House** (Beliy dom), a marble-clad hulk known around the world for its starring role in two confrontations in the 1990s: the 1991 putsch against Gorbachev and the 1993 "October Events" when 200 deputies occupied the White House until they were stormed by Yeltsin's troops three weeks later. Since then, the building has been renamed the **House of Government** (Dom Pravitelstva), and its present occupants have taken precautions against future trouble by erecting a concrete-slab fence around the perimeter. Now demonstrations – such as the 1998 three-month camp-out by miners who had not received any pay for over six months – take place regularly on the humped bridge nearby.

Over the river, patriotic ardour reaches a climax at the memorial complex to the Soviet victory in World War II, the sprawling **Victory Park** (Park Pobedy) on the far side of the highway, on Kutuzovskiy prospekt. It's best to come here on Victory Day (May 9) – the only anniversary in Soviet times that was genuinely heartfelt.

Southeast of Victory Park, **Moscow State University** (or MGU, pronounced "em-gay-oo") occupies the largest of the city's Stalin-Gothic skyscrapers which dominates the plateau of the **Sparrow Hills**, overlooking the Moskva River. Besides the university, the attraction is quite simply the panoramic view of Moscow, with Luzhniki stadium and the Novodevichiy Convent in the foreground, the White House and the Kremlin in the middle distance, and six Stalin skyscrapers ranged across the city.

NOVODEVICHIY CONVENT

Where the Moskva River begins its loop around the marshy tongue of Luzhniki, southwest of the Zemlyanoy Gorod, a cluster of shining domes above a fortified rampart proclaims the presence of the **Novodevichiy Convent** (Novodevichiy monastyr; daily 8am–7pm for worship), one of the loveliest monasteries in Moscow. Founded in 1524, Novodevichiy is undeniably rich in historical associations and a coherent architectural ensemble, with the added attraction of Moscow's most venerable cemetery attached to it. A **museum** (Mon & Wed–Sun 10.30am–5.30pm; $5) of icons and manuscripts is found in the grounds, while at the heart of the convent stands the white **Cathedral of the Virgin of Smolensk** (sobor Smolenskoy Bogomateri) resembling the Cathedral of the Assumption in the Kremlin, with a superb interior. To get there take the metro out to Sportivnaya, taking the ulitsa 10-ti Letiya Oktyabrya exit; a ten-minute walk to the end of the road brings you within sight of the convent's towers and ramparts.

Beyond the convent's south wall lies the fascinating **Novodevichiy Cemetery** (Novodovicheskoe kladbishche; daily 10am–6pm), where many famous writers, artists and politicians are buried. During Soviet times, only burial in the Kremlin Wall was more prestigious. The highest concentration of famous dead is in the oldest part of the cemetery, starting with Nikolai Gogol, Anton Chekhov, Konstantin Stanislavsky, Mikhail Bulgakov, Dmitry Shostakovich and the Futurist poet Vladimir Mayakovsky.

Zamoskvoreche

South across the river from the Kremlin is **Zamoskvoreche**, which simply means "Across the Moskva River". This area is clearly defined by geography and history, dating back to medieval times and preserving a host of colourful churches and the mansions of civic-minded merchants.

Founded in 1892 by the financier Pavel Tretyakov, the **Tretyakov** (Tues–Sun 10am–8pm; $9; last ticket sold at 7pm), five minutes' walk from Tretyakovskaya metro, was designed by the Slav Romantic artist Viktor Vasnetsov. By the 1970s, its collection far exceeded its gallery space, which needed renovation anyway, so a new exhibition hall was built on the Krymskiy val, the old gallery closed for renovation, and a modern wing erected alongside it. The result is an airy, modern museum displaying the best collection of Russian art before the Revolution; art from the Soviet era appears at the new "Tretyakovka" annexe on Krymskiy val.

Russian **icons** are housed on the first of the two upper floors. Icons, which originally came to Russia from Byzantium, were valued for their religious and spiritual content rather than artistic merit. Today, pride of place is given to a series of icons by Andrei Rublev, Daniil Cherniy and Dionysius. If you're looking for something a little more "modern", head upstairs where the exhibits are divided into four sections: Portraiture and the Academy, which dominated Russian art until the second half of the nineteenth century; the Wanderers, who used their art to express social criticism; the Slav Romantics and Symbolists; and the avant-garde that exploded onto the Russian scene between 1910 and 1920.

Gorky Park, 3km southwest of the Tretyakov, is famous abroad from Martin Cruz Smith's classic thriller. Inaugurated in 1928, the Soviet Union's first "Park of Culture and Rest" was formed by uniting an exhibition zone near the Krymskiy val with the vast gardens of the Golitsyn Hospital and the Neskuchniy Palace. The park's 300 acres now include funfairs, a large outdoor skating rink and lots of woodland (daily: summer 10am–1am, winter 11am–11pm; $2). The highlights are an American rollercoaster (scary but safe), a retired Soviet space shuttle, and a big wheel, which affords great views over Moscow.

South of Zamoskvoreche

About 2km southeast of Gorky Park, you will come across the massive red-brick walls of the fortified **Donskoy Monastery** (Donskoy monastyr; daily 7am–7pm). In 1591, Tsar Boris Godunov routed the last Crimean Tatar raid on Moscow. The victory was attributed to the mystical powers of the icon of the Don Virgin, and in thanksgiving the Russians erected a church to house the icon and founded a monastery on the spot. The monastery has been restored and runs a publishing house, a workshop for restoring icons and an embroidery and icon-painting school for children. To get there, alight at Shabolovskaya metro and head for Donskaya ulitsa, where you'll find the chunky gateway, surmounted by a three-tiered bell tower. The monastery's two cathedrals are surrounded by a **cemetery** crammed with headstones and monuments.

The **Danilov Monastery** (Danilovskiy monastyr; daily 7am–7pm), founded by Prince Daniil of Moscow in 1282, claims to be the oldest monastery in Moscow. In 1988, it became the seat and official residence of the Russian Orthodox Patriarch and the Holy Synod, although the Patriarch is seldom in residence. To get there, catch the metro to Tulskaya Station and walk 200m along Danilovskiy val. No shorts or bare shoulders are allowed. The **Danilov Cemetery** (Danilovskoe kladbishche; daily 9am–7pm) is overgrown and archaic, but its funerary monuments are fine, owing to the numerous Orthodox metropolitans and nouveaux riches merchants buried here. To get there, alight at the 3-y Verkhniy Mikhailovskiy stop, before the bus turns off Roshchinskiy.

On the steep west bank of the Moskva River, 10km southeast of the Kremlin, **Kolomenskoe** (grounds: daily 9am–7/10pm; museum: Tues–Sun 10.30am–7.30pm) grew from a village founded by refugees from Kolomna during the Mongol invasions of the thirteenth century to become a royal summer retreat. After the Revolution the cemetery was razed and the churches closed; then the village was destroyed by collectivization. Not until 1974 was the area declared a conservation zone, saving 400 hectares of ancient woodland from the factories and apartments that have advanced on all sides.

Though its legendary wooden palace no longer exists, Kolomenskoe still has one of the finest churches in the whole of Russia (services Sunday 8am), and vintage wooden structures such as Peter the Great's cabin, set amid hoary oaks above a great bend in the river. In summer, Muscovites flock here for the fresh air and to sunbathe; in winter, the eerie **Church of the Ascension** rises against a void of snow and mist with nobody around except kids sledging down the slopes. Despite its distance from the centre, getting there is easy: take

Teatralnaya metro, near the Bolshoy Theatre, from where it's only four stops to Kolomenskaya Station, fifteen minutes' walk from the site itself.

The VDNKh – the northern suburbs

The main reason for venturing this far north is the Exhibition of Economic Achievements – or the **VDNKh** ("Vay-den-ha") – a permanent trade-fair-cum-shopping-centre for Russian producers, which reflects the state of the national economy more faithfully than its founders intended. Its genesis was the All-Union Agricultural Exhibition of 1939, a display of the fruits of socialism and a showpiece of Stalinist monumental art. Scores of pavilions trumpeted the achievements of the Soviet republics and the planned economy. Today, imported cars have ousted Soviet products. Shoppers, lured by "Wild Capitalism" (*dikiy kapitalizm*) rather than the Five Year Plan, ignore the gilded fountains and the sows that once attested to the fecundity of Soviet livestock. Shorn of ideological pretensions, it has been renamed the **All Russia Exhibition Centre** (VVTs) – but everyone still calls it VDNKh.

One of the best-ever Soviet monuments is the **Space Obelisk**, consisting of a rocket blasting nearly 100m into the sky on a stylized plume of energy clad in shining titanium. It was unveiled in 1964, three years after Gagarin orbited the earth, an unabashed expression of pride in this unique feat. Off in the other direction, past the main entrance to the VDNKh, stands the famous monument of the **Worker and Collective Farm Girl**. Its colossal twin figures were intended to embody Soviet industrial progress, though in fact they were hand-made.

The VDNKh and its pavilions are open daily (VDNKh Mon–Fri 9am–8pm, Sat, Sun & holidays 9am–9pm). Except for a few pavilions that have become "exclusive" showrooms, free admission is the rule.

Eating and drinking

It's no problem finding good food and drink in Moscow these days. In fact, the problem is choosing where to go. For the homesick there are over twenty American bars and steakhouses alone, plus the same number of American coffee bars. But the wide gap between the top and bottom ends of the market and the relative shortage of places in between means that good, affordable **restaurants** are usually full in the evenings, so reserving in advance is advised. Most have a member of staff with a rudimentary grasp of English, and many offer some kind of entertainment in the evening for which they may levy a surcharge on each guest. Most **cafés** serve food, at much lower prices than full-blown restaurants, and seldom require bookings, making them a boon for budget travellers.

In recent years a large number of small rock **clubs** and **bars** have opened up, offering excellent food at amazingly cheap prices. Ordinary Russians tend to buy alcohol in a shop and drink it at home, but there are more and more Western-style bars springing up all over the place, though few are in the centre of town.

In this list we have weighted the selection towards more traditional Russian eateries – after all, why come to Russia to eat Indian? – and the more long-lasting nightspots, but a full list of literally hundreds of worthy places can be found in the *Moscow Times* supplement, *MT Out*, updated weekly.

Cafés, bars and fast food

Amalteya, Stremyanniy per. 28/1; Serpukhovksya metro. Choose from a vast range of *mezze* in this cheap Turkish café which has a singer in the evenings. Daily 11am–midnight.

American Bar & Grill, 1-ya Tverskaya-Yamskaya 32; Mayakovskaya metro. After a hard night out this is the place to have a health-restoring late supper or early breakfast. Daily noon–5am.

Bubliki & Bagels, ul. Petrovka 24/1; Kuznetskiy Most metro. Cavernous joint which comes alive at night. Daily noon–midnight.

Café Margarita, Malaya Bronnaya ul. 28; Tverskaya/Pushkinskaya metro. Mushrooms are the mainstay of the menu in this tiny café. Daily 1pm–midnight.

Chevignon Internet Café, Stoleshnikov per. 14; Teatralnaya metro. Order enough drinks and the Internet comes free in this loud café. Daily 24hr.

Donna Clara, Malaya Bronnaya ul. 21/13; Mayakovskaya metro. Great views over Patriarch's Ponds, and an atmosphere so relaxed you could stay here all day. Daily 10am–10pm.

Hungry Duck, Kuznetskiy Most metro. An expat favourite, with good food by day and raucous merriment by night. Daily 11am–5am.

Johnny's Fat Boy, Myasnitskaya ul. 22; Turgenevskaya metro. Jukebox, burgers, burritos, pizzas and egg-and-bacon breakfasts. 8am–midnight.

Kot Begemot, Spiridonyevskiy per. 10A; Mayakovskaya metro. Fairly good food in a good location. Daily 10am–11pm.

Patio Pizza, ul. Tverskaya 3; ul. Volkhonka 13a; ul. Tverskaya Yamskaya 2. Branches all over town, offering cheapish wood-oven pizzas and salads. Credit cards accepted. Daily noon–midnight.

Shakespeare, Strastnoy bulvar 10; Chekhovskaya/Pushkinskaya metro. Shepherd's pie, fish 'n' chips and other traditional British grub. Daily 11am–midnight.

Shury-Mury, ul. Petrovka 15/13; Chekhovskaya metro. The name means "hanky-panky" and this is a kitsched-up traditional Russian joint which aims to be a bit classier than other cheap cafés. Daily 11am–11pm.

Traktir Yolki-Palki, Bolshaya Dmitrovka 23/8; Klimentovsky per. 14/1; Novaya Arbatskaya ul. 11; etc. If you want to eat real Russian food at rock-bottom prices, join the queue at one of ten or so branches of this popular eatery.

U Nikitskikh Vorot, Bolshaya Nikitskaya ul. 23/9; Okhotniy Ryad metro. Cheap Georgian food, with a comfortable bar as well as the rather plain restaurant. Daily noon–midnight.

U Pirosmani, Novodevichiy Proyezd 4; Sportivnaya metro. Much-loved and long-established Georgian eatery with a nice view. Daily 1pm–11pm.

Yarilo, Nizhegorodskaya ul. 1a; Taganskaya metro. Takes its name from a pagan sun god, and goes for traditional dishes with an unusual touch. Daily 11am–11pm.

Restaurants

Bochka, ul. 1905 Goda; Ulitsa 1905 Goda metro. The *shashlik* (kebabs) are magnificent and varied in this traditional Russian restaurant. Daily 24hr.

Petrovich Club, Myasnitskaya ul. 24; Chistiye Prudy metro. Russian nouvelle cuisine and 1970s-style decor. Daily 6am–4am.

Raisky Dvor, ul. Spiridonovka 25; Mayakovskaya metro. Russian and European food, and an interior decorated with pictures of animals. Daily noon–6am.

Samovar, Myasnitskaya ul. 13; Turgenevskaya metro. If you want to splash out on the best Russian food available, this is a good place to go – voted "Quintessential Russian Restaurant" in 1999. Expensive. Daily 1pm–11pm.

Nightlife and entertainment

New **nightclubs** and **discos** are opening all the time, but thankfully the days of disco dominance are gone, with plenty of smaller, intimate clubs to offer variety. There's also plenty of **live music** of all genres. Some places are very expensive, others have a strict entrance policy, and some offer comfy sofas and good music in a relaxed atmosphere. In a word, Moscow has it all and, since the ruble's rapid fall in August 1998, at a reasonably affordable price.

Alongside the city's restaurants and clubs, there's a rich **cultural life** in Moscow. Classical music, opera and ballet are strongly represented with a busy schedule of concerts and performances throughout the year, sometimes held in the city's palaces, churches or – in summer – parks and gardens. Even if you don't speak Russian, puppetry and the circus transcend language barriers, while several cinemas show films in their original language. The **American House of Cinema** at the *Radisson-Slavyanskaya Hotel* (☎095/941 87 47) shows films in English and there's a discount for students. At any one time, there are also dozens of **exhibitions** in Moscow's galleries.

Clubs and live music

Bedniye Lyudi, Bolshaya Ordynka ul. 11/6; Tretyakovskaya ul. Live music in a vaulted back room in a space large enough that you can sit at a slight distance and drink in peace. Cheap food too. $3 entry. Daily 5pm–5am.

Jazz Art Club, Begovaya ul. 5. Great jam sessions by Moscow's finest in a former cinema. $3 entry. Fri & Sat 7.30pm–2am.

Krizis Zhanra, Prechistenskiy per. 22/4; Kropotninskaya metro. Ridiculously cheap and mellow bar with a variety of live music. Very popular, so you might be standing. Daily 11am–11pm. Concerts start 8pm.

Propaganda, Bolshoy Zlatoustinskiy per. 7; Kitay-gorod metro. Once the grunge centre of Moscow, this place is moving towards the more sophisticated end of the style world. $2 entry. Thur, Fri & Sat noon–6am, Mon–Wed noon–12:30am.

Svalka, Profsoyuznaya ul. 27/1; Profsoyuznaya metro. This place has taken over from *Propaganda* for grunge, and has much better music. *Svalka* does, after all, mean "rubbish dump". $3 entry. Mon–Sat 6pm–6am.

Territoria, Tverskaya ul.; Okhotniy Ryad metro. Everyone seems to know each other at this fun place, which has excellent DJs and nice squashy sofas. Thurs–Sun 1pm–6am.

Trety put (Third Way), Pyatnitskaya ul. 4; Tretyakovskaya metro. With its ridiculously cheap drinks and weird music, not to mention the chess and videos, this is a cool place to relax. $1 entry. Daily 9pm–2am.

Opera and ballet

The Bolshoy Theatre, Teatralnaya pl. 1 (☎095/292 99 86); Teatralnaya metro. Still has the largest repertoire of any company in the world (22 ballets and 3 operas with balletic scenes). $15–20 for a seat in the fourth- or third-tier balcony (poor views); $20–50 for the second- or first-tier (*beletazh*) balcony; $50–80 for the stalls (*parter*), depending on the row (*ryad*). Performances Tues–Sun at 7pm, and sometimes a noon matinée on Sunday.

Circuses

The New Circus, pr. Vernadskovo 7 (☎095/930 28 15); Universitet metro. Moscow's Circus is one of the finest in the world, but still uses animal acts. Clowns are its forte. Performances Wed–Fri 7pm, Sat & Sun 11.30am, 3pm and 7pm.

Yury Nikulin Circus, Tsvetnoy bul. 13 (☎095/200 06 68); Tsvetnoy Bulvar metro. Performances Mon & Wed–Sun 7pm, also at 11am & 3pm on Sat & Sun.

Listings

Airlines Aeroflot, ul. Koroviy val 7 (☎095/158 80 19); British Airways, Centre for International Trade, Krasnopresnenskaya nab. 12, room #1905 (☎095/258 24 92); Sheremetevo 2 (flight information ☎095/578 9101).

American Express, Sadovaya-Kudrinskaya ul. 21a (Mon–Fri 9am–5pm; ☎095/755 90 00).

Embassies Australia, Kropotkinskiy per. 13 (Mon–Fri 9am–12.30pm & 1.30–5pm; ☎095/956 60 70); Canada, Starokonyushenniy per. 23 (Mon–Fri 8.30am–5pm; ☎095/956 66 66); Great Britain, Sofiyskaya nab. 14 (Mon–Fri 9am–12.30pm & 2–5.30pm; ☎095/956 72 00); Ireland, Grokholskiy per. 5 (Mon–Fri 9.30am–1pm & 2.30–5.30pm; ☎095/975 20 66); New Zealand, Povarskaya ul. 44 (Mon–Fri 9am–5pm; ☎095/956 35 79); USA, Novinskiy bulvar 19/23 (Mon–Fri 9am–5pm; ☎095/252 24 51).

Exchange Sberbank and Promstroybank – branches all over Moscow.

Laundry For laundry try the *Travellers Guest House*, ul. Bolshaya Pereyaslavskaya 50. For dry cleaning try California Cleaners (9am–8pm; ☎095/497 00 05) or Sadovoe koltso (☎095/231 50 68).

Left Luggage Most train stations have lockers and/or a 24hr left-luggage office, but you would be tempting fate to use them.

Pharmacy Stariy Arbat, Arbatskaya ul. 25 (☎095/291 71 05); Multifarma, Tursitskaya ul. 27 (☎095/948 46 01); International Pharmacy, Kozhevnicheskaya ul. (☎095/235 78 53).

Post office Central Telegraph Office at Tverskaya ul. 7, 103009; Intourist Hotel Post Office at Tverskaya ul. 3/5; the Main Post Office (*glávniy póchtamt*) is at Myasnitskaya ul. 26/2, 101000 (Mon–Fri 8am–8pm, Sat & Sun 9am–6pm), near Chistye Prudy metro.

ST PETERSBURG

ST PETERSBURG, Petrograd, Leningrad and now again, St Petersburg – the city's succession of names mirrors Russia's turbulent history. Founded in 1703 as a "window on the West" by Peter the Great, St Petersburg was for two centuries the capital of the tsarist empire, synonymous with excess and magnificence. During World War I the city renounced its German-sounding name and became Petrograd, and as such was the cradle of the revolutions that overthrew tsarism and brought the Bolsheviks to power in 1917. Later, as Leningrad, it epitomized the Soviet Union's heroic sacrifices in the war against fascism, withstanding nine hundred days of Nazi siege. Finally, in 1991 – the year that communism and the USSR collapsed – the change of name, back to St Petersburg, proved deeply symbolic of the country's democratic mood.

St Petersburg's sense of its own identity owes much to its origins and to the interweaving of myth and reality throughout its history. Created by the will of an autocrat, the imperial capital embodied both Peter the Great's rejection of Old Russia – represented by "Asiatic" Moscow, the former capital – and of his embrace of Europe. The city's architecture, administration and social life were all copied or imported.

Today, St Petersburg is a confused city: beautiful yet filthy, both progressive and stagnant, sophisticated and cerebral, industrial and maritime. Grandiose facades conceal warrens of communal apartments where diverse lifestyles flourish behind triple-locked doors, while beggars and nouveaux riches rub shoulders on Nevskiy prospekt. Society is in a state of flux, reeling under the enormous changes of recent years.

Arrival and information

St Petersburg's **international airport**, Pulkovo-2 (☎812/104 34 44), is 17km south of the city centre. From here, there are several ways of getting into the city. A cheap **bus** service (#13) runs every twenty minutes to Moskovskaya ploshchad, where you can change onto the **metro**; purchase your **ticket** (flat fare) from the conductor. You get the bus from the stop nearest to the Arrivals building. **Minibuses** are also a possibility but they're infrequent. There are always plenty of **taxis**, both licensed and unofficial, but, either way, you'll pay over the odds: $12 is more than fair for a ride into the centre, but drivers often open the bidding at $40 or higher.

Information is hard to come by. One godsend for the individual traveller is OST-WEST, 19104, ul. Mayakovskovo 7–27 (☎812/279 70 45), who can do everything from issuing invitations and booking accommodation to buying theatre tickets, advising on restaurants and giving general help and advice should something go wrong. Otherwise, try the city's larger hotels and *St Petersburg: The Official City Guide*, an excellent full-colour freebie updated every couple of months. The Friday edition of *The St Petersburg Times* and the monthly *Pulse* are both free and have good listings and reviews.

City transport

St Petersburg is a big city, which means that sooner or later you're going to want to make use of its cheap and relatively efficient **public transport** system. As well as the fast **metro** network, there is also an overstretched and dilapidated network of **trams**, **buses** and **trolleybuses**, while commercial routes are served by **minibuses**. The **metro** covers most parts of the city that you're likely to visit, with trains running daily from 6am until just after midnight. For general information on tickets and hours of operation for all types of public transport see the "City Transport" section of the Moscow account, most of which also applies to St Petersburg – note, however, that there are conductors on St Petersburg's transport system, and tickets for a single ride only must be purchased from them. Official **taxis** and private taxis are more expensive than private cars, which are likely to stop if you stick out your arm and are generally safe during the day. As a guide, Nevskiy prospekt to the Peter and Paul Fortress is $1.50 to locals, though foreigners are likely to be charged more.

Accommodation

As with Moscow, the **accommodation** situation in St Petersburg is far from ideal, with many establishments charging ridiculously high prices. The buildings themselves range from spartan, low-rise, concrete slabs to deluxe Art Nouveau edifices – some are in prime locations,

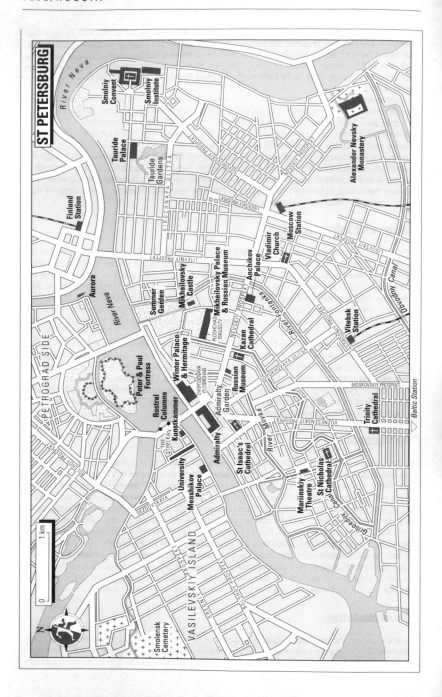

ST PETERSBURG

Smolniy Convent
Smolniy Institute
Tauride Palace
Tauride Gardens
KIROCHNAYA ULITSA
Finland Station
LITEYNIY PROSPEKT
SUVOROVSKIY PROSPEKT
Alexander Nevsky Monastery
LIGOVSKIY PROSPEKT
Moscow Station
Vladimir Church
LIGOVSKIY PROSPEKT
River Neva
Aurora
Summer Garden
Mikhailovsky Castle
Mikhailovsky Palace & Russian Museum
PLOSHCHAD ISKUSSTV
Anchikov Palace
NEVSKIY PROSPEKT
River Fontanka
Obvodniy Canal
Vitebsk Station
ZAGORODNIY PROSPEKT
PETROGRAD SIDE
Peter & Paul Fortress
Winter Palace & Hermitage
DVORTSOVAYA PLOSHCHAD
Admiralty Garden
Kazan Cathedral
Russian Museum
SADOVAYA ULITSA
River Moyka
MOSKOVSKIY PROSPEKT
Baltic Station
Rostral Columns
Kunstkammer
THE STRELKA
Admiralty
St Isaac's Cathedral
VOZNESENSKIY PROSPEKT
Trinity Cathedral
University
Menshikov Palace
SEZDOVSKAYA
BOLSHOY PROSPEKT
Mariinskiy Theatre
St Nicholas Cathedral
Griboedov Canal
1 km
0
N
Smolensk Cemetery
VASILEVSKIY ISLAND
SREDNIY PROSPEKT
BOLSHOY PROSPEKT
River Neva

others in grotty suburbs. If you're looking for a central location, within easy walking distance of the major sights, the choice of **hotels** is extremely limited and prices high. Just a little further out, there are some pleasant and inexpensive options, but **hostels** offer the best alternative, being cheap, reasonably central and with decent facilities; note that there is no age restriction, despite the official title. Excellent accommodation-booking services are offered by OST–WEST, 19104, ul. Mayakovskogo 7–27 (☎812/279 70 45), who can arrange anything from bed and breakfast in a private home to hotel bookings or luxury apartments. St Petersburg Bed & Breakfast (☎812/219 41 16), run by Katya Cherkasova, and HOFA (☎812/275 19 92) can give help in finding bed and breakfast with places suitable for those on a tight budget.

Herzen University Hostel, Kazanskaya ul. 6 (☎812/314 74 72), just behind the Kazan Cathedral off Nevskiy prospekt. Great location; decent facilities, including a solarium and masseur. ③.

Holiday Hostel, ul. Mikhaylova 1, third floor (☎812/542 73 64); Ploshchad Lenina metro. Offers a full range of services, including visa support; some rooms overlook the River Neva. ③.

St Petersburg International Hostel, 3-ya Sovetskaya ul. 28 (☎812/325 8018), Ploshchad Vosstaniya metro. Good facilities and helpful staff. Breakfast is included in the price; separate floors for men and women. In the summer months it's wise to book ahead. ③.

Health Hostel, Prospekt Lunacharskovo 41/1 (☎812/559 9673), Ozerki metro. If you don't mind living amid high-rises, this excellent clean hostel offers everything from visa support to room service to a cyber-café with email access. ③.

Hotels

Matisov Domik, nab. reki Pryazhki 3/1 (☎812/219 54 45). Cosy family hotel near the Mariinskiy, although a bit short on public transport routes. ⑧.

Neva, ul. Chaikovskovo 17 (☎812/278 0500). Chernyshevskaya metro. Clean and old-fashioned, just a hop away from the Summer Garden and the Neva. ④.

Oktyabrskaya, Ligovskiy pr. 10 (☎812/277 63 30). Ploshchad Vosstaniya or Mayakovskaya metro. A gloomy, nineteenth-century warren overlooking Moscow Station; all rooms have satellite TV and bathroom (albeit with dodgy plumbing). ⑤.

Rus, Artillereyskaya ul. 1 (☎812/279 5003). Chernyshevskaya metro. Modern Soviet-style hotel a few minutes' walk from Liteyniy prospekt. ⑤.

The City

Everything in St Petersburg is built on a grand scale, which makes mastering the public transport system a top priority. The city is split by the River Neva and its tributaries, with further sections delineated by the course of the canalized rivers Moyka and Fontanka, all of which conveniently divide St Petersburg into a series of islands, making it fairly easy to get your bearings.

St Petersburg's centre lies on the south bank of the **River Neva**, with the curving River Fontanka marking its southern boundary. The area within the **Fontanka** is riven by a series of wide avenues which fan out from the most obvious landmark on the south bank of the Neva, the Admiralty. Some of the city's greatest sights and monuments – the Winter Palace and the art collections of the Hermitage, the Russian Museum, the Engineers' Castle, the Summer Garden, and the St Isaac and Kazan cathedrals – are located in and around **Nevskiy prospekt**, the main avenue.

Across the River Neva, and connected by Dvortsoviy most (Palace Bridge), is **Vasilevskiy Island**, the largest of the city's islands. In an area known as the **Strelka**, located on the island's eastern tip, are some of St Petersburg's oldest institutions: the Academy of Sciences, the University and the former Stock Exchange, as well as some fascinating museums.

On the north side of the River Neva, opposite the Winter Palace, is the island known as the Petrograd Side, home to the **Peter and Paul Fortress**, whose construction anticipated the foundation of the city itself. As well as its strategic and military purpose, it also housed St Petersburg's first prison and cathedral.

Back on the mainland, east of the River Fontanka, the conventional sights are more dispersed and the distances that much greater. The two most popular destinations in this club-shaped wedge of land, which was largely developed in the latter half of the nineteenth century, are the **Smolniy Complex**, from which the Bolsheviks orchestrated the October Revolution and, further south, the **Alexander Nevsky Monastery**.

Nevskiy prospekt

Nevskiy prospekt has been the backbone of the city for the last two centuries. Built on an epic scale during the reign of Peter the Great, under the direction of the Frenchman Jean-Baptiste Le Blond, it manifests every style of architecture from eighteenth-century Baroque to the *fin-de-siècle* and is home to the city's most important sites.

Set back on the southern side of Nevskiy prospekt is the cream-coloured **Anichkov Palace** – now called the Palace of Youth Creativity; access to the building is limited to concerts and other cultural events. Further west along Nevskiy prospekt, near the Dom Knigi bookshop, the former emporium of the American sewing-machine company, Singer, is **Kazan Cathedral** (Kazanskiy sobor), one of the grandest churches in the city, modelled on St Peter's in the Vatican. The cathedral was built to house the venerated icon, Our Lady of Kazan, reputed to have appeared miraculously overnight in Kazan in 1579, and transferred to St Petersburg by Peter the Great, where it resided until its disappearance in 1904. Now the cathedral has been reconsecrated (services 9am and 6pm daily) and the museum renamed from the Museum of Atheism to the Museum of Religion (Mon, Tues, Thur, Fri 11am–6pm; Sat noon–6pm; Sun 12.30am–6pm). The museum is due to be relocated to Pochtamtskaya ulitsa, when the cathedral will revert to purely religious functions.

The Winter Palace

The **Winter Palace** (Zimniy dvorets), at the westernmost end of Nevskiy prospekt on the Neva embankment, is the finest example of Russian Baroque in St Petersburg, and at the time of its completion was the largest, most opulent palace in the city.

As loaded with history as it is with gilt and stucco, the palace's two-hundred-metre-long facade features a riot of ornamentation in the fifty bays that now face the square. The official residence of every tsar and tsarina since Peter the Great, not to mention the court and 1500 servants, the existing complex is the fourth structure of that name on the embankment. The first two were created for Peter the Great on the site of the present Hermitage Theatre; their remains were discovered during recent restoration and are now open to the public. This final version was completed in 1762, but after a fire in 1837, the palace had to be completely restored.

Along the way, new buildings were also added to the east wing. The first was the long, thin annexe known as the **Small Hermitage** (Maliy Ermitazh), built as a private retreat for Catherine the Great, where she began the art collection that would eventually become one of the world's most impressive. The **Large Hermitage** (Bolshoy Ermitazh), further east, is made up of two separate buildings: the "Old Hermitage", built to house the rapidly expanding imperial collection; and the "New Hermitage", added in the mid-nineteenth century as St Petersburg's first purpose-built public art gallery, but only fully accessible following the October Revolution. By 1922, much of the Winter Palace was given over to the Hermitage art collection.

Beyond stands the **Hermitage Theatre** (Ermitazhniy teatr), built in 1775–84 as a private theatre for Catherine the Great. Nowadays, the theatre is used for conferences and concerts and houses an exhibition documenting the remains of Peter the Great's Winter Palace.

THE HERMITAGE

The **Hermitage** (Ermitazh; Tues–Sat 10.30am–6pm; Sun 10.30am–5pm) is one of the world's great art museums; of awesome size and diversity, it embraces everything from ancient Scythian gold and Kyoto woodcuts to Cubism. It has been calculated that merely to glance at each of the 2.8 million objects it houses would take nine years, and would entail walking a distance of more than 10km. Also of interest is the interior of the Winter Palace itself, with its magnificent state rooms, where the tsars once held court and the Provisional Government was arrested by the Bolsheviks.

The Hermitage closes rooms occasionally, but you should be able to see most of the following highlights: the **Italian art** section with works by Leonardo, Botticelli, Michelangelo, Raphael and Titian; the **Dutch and Flemish art** collection, with the largest gathering of works by Rembrandt outside the Netherlands, as well as paintings by Rubens and Van Dyck; and finally, Flemish landscapes and the most impressive collection of seventeenth- and eighteenth-century **French art** outside France. After the state rooms and the Special Collection, the **third floor** of the Winter Palace is the most universally popular section of the Hermitage, covering modern European art from the nineteenth and twentieth centuries, with a fine spread of Impressionist paintings and works by Matisse and Picasso. Other famous artists whose work is represented here are Rodin, Gauguin, Van Gogh, Henri Rousseau, Delacroix, Cézanne, Pissarro, Monet, Degas and Renoir.

North of Nevskiy prospekt

Before working your way up to the Summer Garden and Palace, there are several points of interest to visit. About 600m north of Nevskiy prospekt, a short distance along the east side of the Moyka, a wide passageway at no. 12 leads to the garden-courtyard of **Pushkin's Apartment** (Mon & Wed–Sun 10.30am–5pm; closed the last Fri of every month). Consisting of eleven rooms, the most evocative is the poet's study, containing a replica of his library of over 4500 books in fourteen languages.

To the east of the apartment stands the multicoloured, onion-domed **Church on Spilled Blood** (Khram "Spasa na krovi"), begun in 1882 to commemorate Tsar Alexander II, who was assassinated on the site the previous year. Designed to resemble St Basil's in Moscow, it is one of St Petersburg's most striking landmarks (Mon–Tues & Thurs–Sun 11am–7pm), quite unlike the rest of the city's architecture. Closed for twenty years, the church was recently fully restored and reopened in 1997.

THE RUSSIAN MUSEUM

East of the Church on Spilled Blood, the **Mikhailovskiy Palace** (Mikhaylovskiy dvorets), now home to the Russian Museum, is one of the largest palaces in the city. Designed by Rossi, its long facade epitomizes the Roman Neoclassical architecture of Alexander I's reign. Little remains of Rossi's original interior, save the main staircase and the austere "White Room". Along with the Tretyakov Gallery in Moscow, the **Russian Museum** (Russkiy muzey; Mon 10am–5pm, Wed–Sun 10am–6pm), on ploshchad Iskusstv, contains the finest collection of Russian art in the world. The museum, which celebrated its hundredth anniversary in 1998, also has three branch palaces with superb displays on selected themes. The **second floor** is devoted to paintings from the fourteenth to nineteenth centuries, including works by Russia's greatest icon-painter, the monk Andrei Rublev (c.1340–c.1430).

The ground floor begins with a demonstration of how Russian art came of age in the late nineteenth century. Works by Ivan Kramskoy (1837–87) and Nikolai Ge (1831–94) are exhibited in the Ivanov rooms, while rooms 33–36 are devoted to Ilya Repin (1844–1930) and Vasiliy Surikov (1846–1916). Traditional Russian folk art is also on display here. A corridor leads to the Benois Wing which, apart from housing temporary exhibitions, presents the movements of the early twentieth century, from Symbolism to Analytical Art. There are also works by Mikhail Vrubel (1856–1910), whose impact on Russian art was comparable to that of Cézanne in the West, the Suprematist Kazimir Malevich (1878–1935), and **agitprop** ("agitational propaganda") posters by revolutionary artists Vladimir Lebedev (1891–1967), Alexander Rodchenko (1891–1956) and the proto-punk poet Mayakovsky (1893–1930). The Benois Wing has its own entrance off Griboyedov Canal, from where you can also gain access to the rest of the museum.

At the turn of this century, the east wing, stables and laundry of the palace were replaced by a Neoclassical annexe built to house the ethnographical collections of the Russian Museum. In 1934, this became an entirely separate **Museum of Ethnography** (Tues–Sun 10am–6pm; closed last Friday of every month), with displays of folk art, costumes, tools, and reconstructed cottage and hut interiors.

THE MIKHAYLOVSKIY CASTLE AND MARSOVO POLE

Moving north from the Museum of Ethnography, up Sadovaya ulitsa, you'll come across the idiosyncratic and heavily fortified **Mikhaylovskiy Castle** (Mikhaylovskiy zamok), begun by Paul I shortly after he assumed the throne in an attempt to allay his fear of being assassinated. To make way for it he had the wooden palace in which he had been born burnt to the ground, and commissioned Vasiliy Bazhenov to design the castle (first known as the Mikhaylovskiy Castle). In an atmosphere of almost pathological fear, Paul moved into the castle in February 1801, but spent only three weeks at the castle before being murdered in his bedroom. Now a branch of the Russian Museum (Mon 10am–5pm, Wed–Sun 10am–6pm), the castle contains displays of portraiture and excellent temporary exhibitions.

Between the River Moyka and the Neva embankment, **Marsovo pole** (Field of Mars) is laid out as a pleasant park, and in the northwestern corner lies the costliest palace yet built in the city, the **Marble Palace** (Mramorniy dvorets; Mon 10am–5pm, Wed–Sun 10am–6pm). Designed by Antonio Rinaldi for Catherine the Great's lover, Count Orlov, the palace is another annexe to the Russian Museum, this time showing works by foreign artists living in Russia in the eighteenth and nineteenth centuries and also modern art displays.

THE SUMMER PALACE

To the east of Marsovo pole is the **Summer Garden** (Letniy sad; daily: summer 8am–10pm; winter 11am–6pm; weekdays free, weekends small admission fee; closed last two weeks of April), the city's most treasured public garden, commissioned by Peter the Great in 1704. The Frenchman, Le Blond, was to design a formal garden in the style of Versailles, with intricate parterres of flowers, shrubs and gravel, a glass conservatory, and numerous marble statues and fountains. However, after the disastrous flood of 1777, which wrecked the garden, Catherine the Great ordered its reconstruction in the less formal, less spectacular English style that survives today. In the northeastern corner of the Summer Garden, Domenico Trezzini began working on a **Summer Palace** (Letniy dvorets; May–Oct 11am–7pm; closed Tues) for Peter the Great in 1710. A modest two-storey building of brick and stucco – one of the first such structures in the city – the new palace was only a small step up from the wooden cottage in which Peter had previously lived on the other side of the river.

Southwest of Nevskiy prospekt

The **Admiralty** (Admiralteystvo), standing at the western end of Nevskiy prospekt, is one of the world's most magnificent expressions of naval triumphalism, extending 407m (1300ft) along the waterfront, from Dvortsovaya ploshchad to ploshchad Dekabristov. The Admiralty was originally founded by Peter the Great in 1704 as a fortified shipyard, with a primitive wooden tower and spire, but as the shipyards moved elsewhere, and the Admiralty became purely administrative in function, a suitable replacement was built in the early 1820s. Today, the key feature of the building is still its central tower (72.5m high), rising from an arched cube and culminating in a slender spire. On any walk along Nevskiy prospekt, you'll inevitably be drawn towards this golden, needle-like spire which asserts the city's European identity – differentiating its skyline from the traditional Russian medley of onion domes.

Largely obscuring the Admiralty, the wooded **Admiralty Garden** (Admiralteyskiy sad) leads towards **ploshchad Dekabristov**, an expanse of fir trees and rose beds – known for the event recalled by its name, "Decembrists' Square". In December 1825, a group of reformist officers marched three thousand soldiers into the square in an attempt to proclaim a constitutional monarchy. This revolt turned from farce to tragedy when Tsar Nicholas I ordered his loyalist troops to attack and crush the rebellion. From here, your eyes are inevitably drawn to Falconet's renowned statue of Peter the Great known as the **Bronze Horseman** (Medny vsadnik), which rears up towards the waterfront, and the newly-weds who come here to be photographed.

Looming majestically above the rooftops, **St Isaac's Cathedral** (Isaakievsky sobor; 11am–7pm; closed Wed; colonnade 11am–5pm), just south of ploshchad Dekabristov, is too massive to grasp at close quarters. Standing in its own square, the cathedral's gilded dome is one of the glories of St Petersburg's skyline, while its opulent interior is equally impressive, decorated with fourteen kinds of marble. The cathedral's height (101.5m) and rooftop statues are best appreciated by climbing the 262 steps up to its dome – the third largest cathedral dome in Europe, with enough gold leaf used to push the total cost of the cathedral to 23,256,000 rubles (six times that of the Winter Palace). After a spell as a Museum of Atheism, the cathedral is now a museum in and of itself.

Few tourists can resist the **St Nicholas Cathedral** (Nikolskiy sobor), to the south of St Isaac's Cathedral and Teatralnaya ploshchad (Theatre Square). Traditionally known as the "Sailors' Church" after the naval officers that once prayed here, the cathedral is a lovely example of eighteenth-century Russian Baroque – painted ice blue with white Corinthian pilasters and aedicules, and crowned by five gilded onion domes. Its low, vaulted interior is festooned with icons, and during services (6pm) the cathedral resounds with the sonorous Orthodox liturgy, chanted and sung amid clouds of incense.

Vasilevskiy Island

Buffeted by storms from the Gulf of Finland, pear-shaped **Vasilevskiy Island** (Vasilevskiy ostrov) cleaves the River Neva into its Bolshaya and Malaya branches. The island forms a strategic wedge whose eastern "spit", or **Strelka**, is as much a part of St Petersburg's waterfront as the Winter Palace or Admiralty, its **Rostral Columns** and **former stock exchange** (now the Naval Museum) reminders that the city's port and commercial centre were once located here.

Originally, Peter envisaged making the island the centre of his capital. Alexander Menshikov, the first governor of St Petersburg, was an early resident – the Menshikov Palace is the oldest building on the island – and Peter compelled other rich landowners and merchants to settle here. By 1726 the island had ten streets and over a thousand inhabitants, but wilderness still predominated, and the hazardous crossings by sailing boat from the mainland destroyed any hope of the island becoming the centre of St Petersburg.

Although you can reach the Strelka by trolleybus (#1, #7 and #10), bus (#7) or express (#47 and #T129) from Nevskiy prospekt, it's better to walk across **Dvortsoviy most** (Palace Bridge), which offers fabulous views of both banks of the Neva. By day, the Strelka steals the show with its Rostral Columns and stock exchange building, an ensemble created at the beginning of the nineteenth century by Thomas de Thomon, who also designed the granite embankments and cobbled ramps leading down to the Neva.

Of great appeal is the **Zoological Museum** (Zoologicheskiy muzey; 11am–5pm; closed Fri), located in the Southern Warehouse on Universitetskaya naberezhnaya, facing Dvortsoviy most. Founded in 1832, the museum has one of the finest collections of its kind in the world, with over one hundred thousand specimens, including a set of stuffed animals that once belonged to Peter the Great. Upstairs, you're confronted by the skeleton of a blue whale, models of polar bears and other arctic life. The most evocative display shows the discovery of a 44,000-year-old mammoth in the permafrost of Yakutia in 1903.

Even more alluring – or repulsive – is the former **Kunstkammer** next door, instantly recognizable by its tower and entered from an alley to the west. Founded by Peter in 1714, its name (meaning "art chamber" in German) dignified his fascination for curiosities and freaks. Peter offered rewards for "human monsters" and unknown birds and animals, with a premium for especially odd ones. Dead specimens had to be preserved in vinegar or vodka (which was reimbursed by the imperial pharmacy), while to attract visitors, each guest received a glass of vodka or a cup of coffee.

Within the Kunstkammer and continuing its work in a contemporary vein is the **Museum of Anthropology and Ethnography** (Muzey Antropologii i Etnografii; 11am–6pm; closed every Thurs & last Wed of every month), displaying everything from Balinese puppets to Inuit kayaks and including some lovely dioramas of native village life. The section upstairs covers Southeast Asia, the Antipodes and Melanesia, while Africa and the Americas are dealt with on the first floor. In the round hall between Africa and the Americas, a selection of Peter's pickled curios still excites wonder and disgust: Siamese twins, a two-faced man and a two-headed calf. Also shown are surgical and dental instruments, and teeth pulled by the tsar himself (a keen amateur dentist).

The chief reason to walk further along the embankment is to visit the **Menshikov Palace** (Menshikovskiy dvorets; Tues–Sun 10.30am–5.30pm), a gabled, yellow-and-white building built in the early eighteenth century which is now a branch of the Hermitage devoted to the life and culture of that time. It was the first residential structure on Vasilevskiy Island and the finest one in the city, surpassing even Peter's Summer Palace. The tsar had no objections, preferring to entertain at the Menshikov Palace, which was furnished to suit his tastes; though not as sumptuous as the later imperial palaces, it sports a fine Petrine-era decor. There are guided tours in Russian every thirty minutes (tours in English, French and German can be booked and paid for in advance, call ☎812/323 11 12); the entrance is below street level, past the main portico.

The Peter and Paul Fortress

Across the Neva from the Winter Palace, on a small island, lies the **Peter and Paul Fortress** (Petropavlovskaya krepost), begun in 1703 and built to secure Russia's hold on the Neva delta. Forced labourers toiled from dawn to dusk to construct the fortress in just seven months. The fortress is permanently open – with no admission charge – but its **cathedral** and **museums** keep regular visiting hours (Mon & Thurs–Sun 11am–6pm; closed every Wed & last Tues of every month) and require tickets. You buy one ticket for the exhibitions, housed in various different buildings and covering the history of the city and Russian life up to 1917.

The **Peter and Paul Cathedral** (Petropavlovskiy sobor) signals defiance from the heart of the fortress. The original wooden church commissioned by Peter on this site was replaced by a stone cathedral, completed by Trezzini in 1733, long after Peter had died. The facade of the cathedral looks Dutch, while the gilded spire was deliberately made higher than the Ivan the Great Bell Tower in the Kremlin – it remained the tallest structure (122m) in the city until the 1960s. Sited around the nave are the tombs of the Romanov monarchs from Peter the Great onwards – excluding Peter II, Ivan VI and Nicholas II. Nicholas and his family, whose bones were discovered in a mine shaft in the Urals in 1989, were finally buried in a chapel by the entrance to the cathedral in July 1998.

The fortress was also used as a prison from 1718, when Peter the Great's son Alexei was tortured to death here. The **Prison Museum**, however, fails to convey its full horror. The accessible cells are stark and gloomy, but far worse ones existed within the ramparts, below the level of the river, where the perpetual damp and cold made tuberculosis inevitable. Prisoners were never allowed to see each other and rarely glimpsed their gaolers. Some were denied visitors and reading material for decades; many went mad and several committed suicide.

The Smolniy Complex

A couple of kilometres to the east of Liteyniy prospekt, which runs due north from Nevskiy prospekt to the Neva, lies the **Smolniy district**, a quiet and slightly remote quarter.

The **Tauride Garden** (Tavricheskiy sad), at the end of Furshtadtskaya ulitsa, backs onto the palace of the same name. The gardens were designed by the English gardener, William Gould, in the eighteenth century but now also boast an antiquated fairground on the western side. On the north side of the park is the **Tauride Palace** (Tavricheskiy dvorets), built by Catherine the Great for her lover, Prince Potemkin, to celebrate his annexation of the Crimea (Tauris) to Russia. Completed in 1789, the palace is one of the city's earliest examples of an austere Neoclassicism, but is sadly closed to the public.

Just east of the Tauride Palace, at the end of Shpalernaya ulitsa, it's impossible to ignore the glorious ice-blue cathedral towering on the eastern horizon, which is the focal point and architectural masterpiece of the **Smolniy Complex**. In the eighteenth century, Empress Elizabeth founded the **Smolniy Convent** (Smolniy monastyr) on the site. Rastrelli's grandiose Rococo plans – including a 140-metre-high bell tower, which would have been the tallest structure in the city – were never completed, and the building was only finished in 1835 by Stasov in a more restrained Neoclassical fashion. The cathedral's austere white interior (10am–5pm; closed Thurs) is disappointingly severe. The first floor now houses temporary exhibitions, as well as concerts. The **Smolniy Institute**, now the Mayor's Office, was built between 1806 and 1808 to house the Institute for Young Noblewomen, but gained its notoriety after the Petrograd Soviet moved here in August 1917 until the city's vulnerability in the Civil War impelled the government to move to Moscow in March 1918. It contains a museum (by appointment only, ☎812/271 9182), which includes Lenin's rooms.

Alexander Nevsky Monastery

Two kilometres south of the Smolniy Complex, at the southeastern end of Nevskiy prospekt, lies the **Alexander Nevsky Monastery** (Aleksandro-Nevskaya lavra). The monastery was founded in 1713 by Peter the Great, and from 1797 it became one of only four in the Russian Empire to be given the title of *lavra*, the highest rank in Orthodox monasticism.

There are two main cemeteries within the monastery: the most famous names reside in the **Tikhvin Cemetery** (Tikhvinskoe kladbishche), the more recent of the two, established in 1823. Among those buried here are Dostoyevsky, Rimsky-Korsakov, Tchaikovsky, Rubinstein and Glinka. Directly opposite is the much smaller **Lazarus Cemetery** (Lazarovskoe kladbishche), established by Peter the Great, and the oldest in the city. There are fewer international celebrities, but it's just as interesting in terms of funereal art. You should be able to locate the tombs of the polymath Lomonosov, and the architects Rossi and Quarenghi. **Tickets** are required for entry into the Tikhvin and Lazarus cemeteries (May–Nov 10am–7pm; Dec–April 10am–4pm; closed Thurs), but not for the monastery or the Trinity Cathedral, which are both open daily from dawn to dusk.

To reach the **monastery** itself, continue along the walled path past Trezzini's **Church of the Annunciation**, the original burial place of Peter III, Catherine the Great's deposed husband (currently closed). Trezzini also drew up an ambitious design for the monastery's **Trinity Cathedral**, but failed to orientate it towards the east, as Orthodox custom required, so the plans were scrapped. The job was left to Ivan Starov, who completed a more modest building in a Neoclassical style which now sits awkwardly with the rest of the complex. The interior, however, is worth exploring, though bear in mind that this is a working church, not simply a museum.

To escape the crowds, head round the back of the cathedral to the **Nicholas Cemetery** (daily: summer 9am–9pm; winter 9am–6pm), an overgrown graveyard where the monastery's scholars and priests are buried, as well as nobles and intellectuals.

Eating and drinking

Numerous small cafés and restaurants have opened in recent years, combining tasty food with moderate prices. Visitors can be sure of decent meals at the top restaurants, and there is also an increasing number of modestly priced, intimate **restaurants** and relaxed **cafés** serving good food and offering a better feel of life in St Petersburg than those aiming to imitate Western stereotypes and prices.

Cafés and bars

Café Ambassador, nab. reki Fontanki 16; 15min walk from Nevskiy Prospekt metro. Decent-sized portions, good selection of salads, and a view of the Mikhaylovskiy Castle thrown in. Daily 1pm–5am.

Carroll's, Nevskiy pr. 35; Gostiniy dvor metro. Fast food – burgers and chips. Daily 9am–11pm.

Green Crest, Vladimirskiy pr. 7; Vladimirskaya/Dostoevskaya metro. Salads, salads and more salads – good healthy eating. Daily 10am–10pm.

Idiot, nab. reki Moyki 82; trolleybus #5 or #22 from Nevskiy prospekt. Relaxed vegetarian bar with books and boardgames. Daily noon–midnight.

Kashtan, nab. reki Fontanki 46; Gostiniy Dvor metro. Tucked away in the yard behind the Foreign Languages Library and the British Council. Serves great soups. Daily noon–10pm.

Krokodil, Galernaya ul. 18l; trolleybus #5 or #22 from Nevskiy prospekt. Café for the in-crowd, with some events and performances. Daily 1pm–11pm or until the last person leaves.

Krunk, Solyanoy per. 14; Chernyshevskaya metro or a 5min walk from Summer Garden. Armenian food and a friendly atmosphere, opposite the Stieglitz Art School. Daily noon–midnight.

Layma, nab. kanala Griboedova 16; Gostiniy Dvor/Nevskiy Prospekt metro. Excellent fast food including steaks and salads, plus beer; great for late, late suppers. Daily 24hr.

La Cucaracha, nab. Reki Fontanki 39; Gostiniy Dvor/Nevskiy Prospekt metro. Mexican waiters, tequila, nachos and a lively atmosphere. Mon–Thurs & Sun noon–1am, Fri & Sat noon–5am.

Minutka, Nevskiy pr. 20; Gostiniy Dvor/Nevskiy Prospekt metro. American-style sandwich and salad bar. Daily 10am–10pm.

Morozhenoe (Frogs' Pool), Nevskiy pr. 24; Gostiniy Dvor/Nevskiy Prospekt metro. Ice cream, snacks and alcohol, with a wondrous Stalinist interior at the back. Daily 10am–11pm.

Russkie bliny, ul. Furmanova 13. Ornate, cosy, very popular and cheap lunchtime spot, off Liteyniy prospekt. Traditional Russian *bliny,* both savoury and sweet. Mon–Fri 11am–6pm.

Sadko's, Mikhalovskaya ul. 1; Nevskiy Prospekt metro. Bistro bar with live music in the evenings. Daily 11–1am.

Scheherezade, Razyezhaya ul. 3; Vladimirskaya/Dostoevskaya metro. Arab-Russian cuisine, with excellent vegetarian food. Daily 11am–11pm.

Staroe Kafe, nab. reki Fontanki 108; Tekhnologicheskiy Institut metro. Tiny, cosy café with traditional Russian food. Daily noon–11pm.

Restaurants

Demyanova Ukha, Kronverkskiy pr. 53 (☎812/232 80 90); Gorkovskaya metro. Serves fish and nothing else; reservations essential. Daily 11am–10pm.

Joy, Nab. Kanala Griboedova 28/1 (☎812/312 1614); Nevskiy Prospekt metro. Inexpensive but tasty food, with views over the Griboedov canal. Daily noon–midnight.

La Strada, Bolshaya Koniushennaya ul. 27 (☎812/312 4700); Nevskiy Prospekt metro. Pizza and pasta in a cunningly converted courtyard. Daily noon–11pm.

1913, Voznesenskiy pr. 13 (☎812/315 51 48); trolleybus #5 or #22 from Nevskiy prospekt. Generous portions of Russian cuisine. Popular with the cultural crowd. Daily noon–11pm.

Pirosmani, Bolshoy pr. 14 (☎812/235 6456); Sportivnaya metro. Heavenly food in this tiny re-creation of a Georgian hill village, complete with a "lake" and tables on "rafts". Daily noon–11pm.

Staraya Derevnya, ul. Savushkina 72 (☎812/239 00 00); trams #2 or #31 from Chernaya Rechka metro. Comfortable interior, with ridiculously cheap, traditional Russian food, plus gypsy and Russian singers Fri–Sun. Daily 1–6pm & 7–10pm.

Nightlife and entertainment

Although St Petersburg has less **nightlife** than most of its Western counterparts, there is lots of potential for a wild night out. Of the permanent **clubs** and **discos**, some are just plain tacky, others have a brash and decadent appeal and feature themed nights, spectacular lights, casinos and raunchy floorshows, while others offer that spartan, underground atmosphere of warehouse clubs. Clubs are occasionally raided by police – if you're there at the time, do as the locals do as the police are unlikely to speak English.

St Petersburg is increasingly attractive to foreign stars, but the chances of you catching anyone famous here are still minimal. For Russians, the city is associated with several home-grown legendary bands and is the most hip place in the country – a sort of Russian Manchester or Seattle.

Clubbing aside, St Petersburg has a wide variety of cultural events such as **classical concerts**, **ballet** and **opera**. For details of what's happening, whatever your preference, check the listings in the free English-language papers – *The St Petersburg Times* (Friday edition) and *Pulse*.

Discos and nightclubs

Club 69, 2-ya Krasnoarmeyskaya ul. 6; Tekhnologicheskiy Institut metro. Wild, gay club with occasional strippers; good restaurant too. Tues–Sun 1pm–6am.

Domenicos, Nevskiy pr. 70; Mayakovskaya metro. The place that brought the Chippendales to Russia. Serves good food. Daily noon–6am.

Griboedov, Voronezhskaya ul. 2a; Ligovskiy Prospekt metro. Coolest of cool dance club in a bomb shelter. Thurs–Sun 5pm–6am.

Hollywood Nites, Nevskiy pr. 46; Nevskiy Prospekt/Gostiniy Dvor metro. Combined disco, casino and restaurant in the centre of town. Occasional big name acts. Tues–Sun 9pm–6am.

Fish Fabrique, Pushkinskaya ul. 10 (entrance from Ligovskiy pr.); Mayakovskogo metro. Café club at the heart of the city's famous artists' colony. Thurs–Sat 5pm–6am.

JFC Jazz Club, Shpalernaya ul. 33; Chernyshevskaya metro. Unstuffy venue with an exciting programme, tucked away in the courtyard. Daily 7–10pm.

Manhattan, Fontanka 90; Pushkinskaya metro. Hip place, with intellectual aspirations and some occasional brilliant jazz improvisation. Daily noon–5am.

Mama, Malaya Monetnaya ul. 3B; Gorkovskaya metro. Fave techno location, with jungle music on Saturdays. Fri & Sat midnight–6am.

Metro, Ligovskiy pr. 174; Ligovskiy Prospekt metro. Middle-class place with a disco and strobe lighting. Daily 10pm–6am.

Moloko, Perekupnoy per. 12; Ploshchad Aleksandra Nevskogo metro. Small basement rock club favoured by students. Fri–Sat 7–11pm.

Money Honey Saloon, Apraksin Dvor 14 (in yard); Gostiniy Dvor/Nevskiy Prospekt metro. Russian rockabilly, cheap beer, always packed; don't forget the leather jacket and quiff. Daily 11am–midnight.

Oktyabrskiy Concert Hall, Ligovskiy pr. 6 (☎812/275 12 75); two blocks north of Ploshchad Vosstaniya metro. Occasional venue for leading Russian rock groups and lesser-known Western bands. Phone or see press for details of what's on.

PORT, per. Antonenko 2; Sennaya Ploshchad metro. Several dance halls and hip exhibitions, and lots of portholes. Just off St Isaac's Square. Daily 3pm–6am.

Opera, ballet and cinema

The Mariinskiy Theatre, Teatralnaya pl. 1 (☎812/114 52 64). Still known as The Kirov in the West. Look out for international ballet stars Faroukh Ruzimatov, Altynai Assymuratova and local girl Ulyana Lopatkina. Foreigners will pay $40 for seats in the stalls but seats are available in the gods for $3. Performances at 6.30pm with Sunday matinees at noon.

English-language **films** can sometimes be seen at Avrora, Nevskiy pr. 60; Barrikada, Nevskiy pr. 15; and Crystal Palace, Nevskiy pr. 72.

Listings

Airlines Aeroflot/Pulkovo Airlines (☎812/315 00 72); British Airways (☎812/329 25 65); Finnair (☎812/325 95 00); Lufthansa (☎812/314 49 79); SAS (☎812/325 3255').

American Express *Grand Hotel Europe*, Mikhaylovskaya ul. 1/7 (Mon–Fri 9am–5pm, Sat 9am–1pm; ☎812/329 60 60).

Embassies Britain, pl. Proletarskoy diktatury 5 (☎812/325 60 36); Canada, Malodetskoselsky pr. 32 (☎812/325 84 48); USA, Furshtadtskaya ul. 15 (☎812/275 17 01).

Emergencies For medical assistance, Clinic Complex, Moskovskiy pr. 22 (Mon–Fri 9am–9pm, Sat 9am–3pm; 24hr emergency service ☎812/316 62 72); American Medical Service, Serpukhovskaya ul. 10 (24hr; ☎812/326 1730), recognized by international insurance companies. For a doctor, Pavlov Medical Institute, ul. Lva Tostovo 6/8 (daily 9am–5pm; ☎812/238 71 85).

Exchange For travellers' cheques and with ATMs for credit-card cash advances: Mostbank, Nevskiy pr. 27; Promstroybank, Mikhaylovskaya ul. 4; *Nevsky Palace Hotel*, Nevskiy pr. 57; *Grand Hotel Europe*, Mikhaylovskaya ul. 1/7. The best cash exchange rate can be found at Nevskiy pr. 78. Bank transfers are available via Western Union in the *Nevsky Palace Hotel*.

Left luggage Most bus and train stations have lockers and/or a 24hr left-luggage office, but you would be tempting fate to use them.

Pharmacy Petropharm, at Nevskiy pr. 22, 24hr (other branches at no. 50, 66 & 83). Homeopathic pharmacies, Nevskiy pr. 50 and Svechnoy per. 7/11.

Post office Pochtamtskaya ul. 9 (Mon–Sat 8am–8pm, Sun 8am–6pm; ☎812/312 83 02), just off St Isaac's Square. Express letter post: Westpost, Nevskiy pr. 86 (Mon–Fri 10am–8pm, Sat noon–6pm; ☎812/275 07 84); Post International, Nevskiy pr. 20 (Mon–Sat 10am–8pm; ☎812/219 44 72).

Telephones The main communications centre is at International Telephone and Telegraph Office, Bolshaya Morskaya ul. 3–5, near the Admiralty Arch (Daily 9am–9pm).

Women's St Petersburg Women's Centre, founded by Olga Lipovskaya, at ul. Stekhanovsteva 13 (☎812/528 18 30).

Around St Petersburg

The chief reason to venture outside St Petersburg is to visit **Peterhof**, one of the most elaborate palaces, 29km west of the city and **Novgorod**, 190km south and the archetypal medieval Russian city. Both are easily accessible by public transport, and so each makes a perfect day-trip.

Peterhof

As the first of the great imperial palatial ensembles to be founded outside St Petersburg, **Peterhof** embodies nearly three hundred years of tsarist self-aggrandizement, and remains most people's first choice among the many summer palaces around the city. As you'd expect from its name (meaning "Peter's Court" in German, and pronounced "Petergof" in Russian), its progenitor was Peter the Great. Flushed with triumph in the Northern War against Sweden, he decided to build a sumptuous palace and town beside the Gulf, although Peterhof's Grand Palace wasn't completed until the reign of Empress Elizabeth (1741–61).

Trains for Peterhof leave daily from Baltic Station (Baltiyskaya metro) every thirty minutes or so (beware, there may be a gap between 10am and noon some days), although in summer one of the best ways of reaching Peterhof is by **hydrofoil**. These depart every ninety minutes (9.30am–5pm) from the Neva embankment outside the Winter Palace, the last return boat leaving Peterhof at 6pm.

The yellow, white and gold **Great Palace** (Bolshoy dvorets; Tues–Sun 10.30am–5pm; closed the last Tues of every month) is far removed from that originally designed for Tsar Peter by Le Blond between 1714 and 1721, but despite later additions, there's a superb cohesion at work, a tribute both to the vision of the palace's creators and the skills of the craftsmen who rebuilt Peterhof from its ashes after World War II. As you arrive by hydrofoil, the palace rises like a golden curtain at the far end of the **Marine Canal** (Morskoy kanal), which flows through Peterhof's Lower Park. From here, you can also see the **Grand Cascade**, which, newly restored, is the pride of Peterhof. With its waterfalls and gilded statues the effect is magnificent, enhancing the splendour of the Great Palace, which sits on the terrace above. The palace entrance is round the back through the formal **Upper Garden**, which rates a brisk tour, although more interesting is the **Lower Park**, nearer to Monplaisir, which deserves a longer ramble; most of its best fountains are either clustered between the Chessboard Hill Cascade and Monplaisir, or ennoble the approaches to the Marly Palace.

Peter the Great's favourite haunt, **Monplaisir** (from the French for "my pleasure"; May–Sept 10.30am–5pm; closed Wed & the last Thurs of every month; Oct–April Sat & Sun 10.30am–4pm) is the major attraction at Peterhof after the Great Palace. It is both homely and extravagant, and was designed by the tsar himself, with the assistance of several architects. The adjacent **Catherine Wing** (Yekaterininskiy Korpus; May–Sept 10.30am–5pm; closed Thurs & the last Fri of every month; Oct–April Sat & Sun 10.30am–4pm) was added to Monplaisir by Empress Elizabeth in the 1740s. Between the Catherine Wing and Monplaisir lies a **garden**, which is centred on the Wheatsheaf Fountain, whose 25 jets of water resemble heads of grain.

Built around the same time as Monplaisir, the **Marly Palace** (May–Sept 10am–5pm; closed every Tues & the last Wed of every month; Oct–April 10.30am–4pm) takes its name and inspiration from the hunting lodge of the French kings at Marly le Rois, which Peter the Great visited during his Grand Tour of Europe. More of a country house than a palace, tickets must be bought at the wooden hut nearby; guided tours last about fifteen minutes.

Finding Peterhof's Great Palace "unbearable", Alexandra Fyodorovna pressed Nicholas I to build a home suited to a cosier, bourgeois lifestyle. The **Cottage Palace** (dvorets Kottedzh; May–Sept 10am–5pm; closed Fri & the last Tues of every month in summer; Oct–Apr Sat & Sun only) is definitely worth the fifteen-minute walk through the overgrown park.

Avoid the palace restaurant: the place **to eat** at Peterhof is the tiny *Trapeza*, just outside the east entrance to the park and palace, which offers traditional Russian food very inexpensively.

Novgorod

Despite its name, **NOVGOROD** – "New Town" – is one of Russia's oldest cities, founded, according to popular belief, by Prince Rurik in 862 AD, and not too difficult to get to from St Petersburg – buses run every two hours from Bus Station #2, nab. Obvodnovo kanala 36 and take three hours to make the journey; excursion buses leave from beside the portico on Nevskiy prospekt 33 (tickets from the kiosk beside Gostiniy Dvor), but the tours are in Russian only. More expensive tours in English are available through hotels. During its most prestigious and wealthy period – from the twelfth to the fifteenth century – Novgorod's republican-minded nobles bestowed a fantastic architectural legacy upon the town, including a Kremlin (a fortified inner city), Russia's oldest cathedral and numerous onion-domed stone churches. However, the foundation of St Petersburg in 1703 was a great blow to Novgorod's commercial prosperity, with the final straw coming in 1851, when the new rail line linked Moscow and St Petersburg and bypassed the town entirely.

The impressive nine-metre-high, red-brick walls of the **Kremlin** date from the fifteenth century, when they formed the inner ring of an entire series of fortifications. As many as eighteen churches and 150 houses were once crammed inside these walls, though much of the Kremlin now consists of open space. The Kremlin's main landmark is **St Sophia's Cathedral** (Sofiyskiy sobor), the city's earliest and the largest by far, representing the peak of princely power in Novgorod and afterwards a symbol of great civic pride. Its five bulbous domes cluster around a slightly raised, golden helmet dome. The cathedral now doubles as a working **church** and **museum** (summer daily noon–1pm & 2.30–5pm; winter closed Mon & Tues). Inside, the well-preserved iconostasis is one of the oldest in Russia and includes works from the eleventh to seventeenth centuries.

The largest building in the Kremlin is an early nineteenth-century mass of administrative offices; nowadays it is home to the **Museum of History, Architecture and Art** (10am–6pm; closed Tues & last Thurs of every month), and contains a fine collection of icons by the colourful Novgorod School, along with paintings, early wood sculpture and numerous other artefacts.

From the river bank on the east side of the Kremlin, there's a great view of the **Commercial Side** (Torgovaya storona), site of Novgorod's medieval market. All that remains now is a long section of the old seventeenth-century arcade. Immediately behind the arcade, where the palace of Yaroslav the Wise once stood, is a grassy area still known as **Yaroslav's Court** (Yaroslavovo dvorishche). Its most important surviving building is the **Cathedral of St Nicholas** (Nikolskiy sobor; 10am–6pm; closed Tues), built in 1113 in a Byzantine style that was a deliberate challenge to St Sophia's.

All that survives of the **Yuryev Monastery** (Yuryev monastyr), founded by Prince Vsevolod in 1117, is the majestic **Cathedral of St George** (Georgievskiy sobor) built by a "Master Peter", renowned as the first truly Russian architect, and is one of the last great churches to be built by the Novgorod princes. Inside, some twelfth-century frescoes survive, but most date from the nineteenth century. The cathedral is currently being restored and the monastery revived – there are already ten monks in residence. In the woods to the west of the Yuryev Monastery is the **Museum of Wooden Architecture** (10am–6pm; closed Wed; Oct–April 10am–4pm), a collection of timber constructions from the surrounding area including two churches and several peasant houses, with some of the buildings dating from the sixteenth century.

If you need somewhere **to stay**, try *Sadko*, Fyodorovskiy ruchey 16 (☎812/754 37; ⑤), a budget hotel on the commercial side. As far as **restaurants** go, the *Detinets*, in the Pokrov Tower of the Kremlin, has a café downstairs and a relaxed restaurant upstairs, which is good for lunch with the occasional bit of live music in the evening; prices are very low (Mon 11am–4pm, Tues–Sun 11am–5pm & 7–11pm). Opposite the west entrance is *Café Charodeika* at ul. Volosova 111, for Italian pizza at reasonable prices.

CHAPTER 25

SLOVAKIA

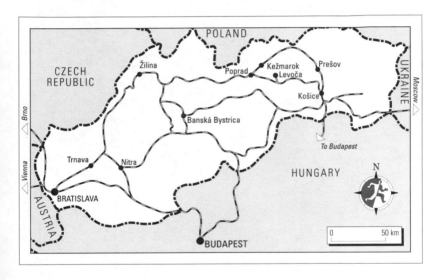

Introduction

The republic of **Slovakia** (Slovensko) – independent since 1993 – consists of the long, narrow strip of land which stretches from the parched plains of the Danube basin up to the peaks of the High Tatras – perhaps Europe's most exhilarating mountain range outside of the Alps. The country's numerous mountains have long formed barriers to industrialization and modernization, preserving and strengthening regional differences in the face of centralizing efforts from Vienna, Budapest, Prague and, now, Bratislava.

Slovak **history** is one of relentless cultural repression by the neighbouring Magyars, yet the Slovaks emerged from a millennium of punishing serfdom inside the kingdom of Hungary with their national identity fairly intact. In 1918, they threw their lot in with their Slav neighbours, the Czechs, forming Czechoslovakia, but after 75 years of playing second fiddle to the Czechs, many Slovaks were ready to go it alone – though it has to be said, many also had major reservations about it, and none were given the chance to decide in a referendum. Political corruption and slow-moving reforms have all put off overseas investors, and consequently the country is much poorer than the Czech Republic.

For the first-time visitor, perhaps the most striking cultural difference from the Czechs is the Slovak attitude to religion. **Catholicism** is much stronger here than in the Czech Republic, and the churches are often full to overflowing on Sundays. The republic also has a much more diverse population with over half a million **Hungarian** speakers in the south as well as thousands of Gypsies and Rusyns in the east. **Bratislava**, the capital, is potentially disappointing, especially for those who arrive expecting a Slovak Prague. Taken on its own terms, however, the city is a rewarding, lively place with a compact old town. **Poprad** provides the transport hub for the **High Tatras**, the tallest of Slovakia's mountains, and is also the starting point for exploring the intriguing medieval towns of the **Spiš region**, east Slovakia's architectural high point. Further east still, **Prešov** is the cultural centre of the Rusyn minority, while **Košice**, Slovakia's second largest city, boasts the easternmost Gothic cathedral in Europe.

Information and maps

The BIS tourist office in Bratislava was specifically set up to give information to foreign visitors, and happily other cities and towns are now beginning to follow suit. Offices are generally open Mon–Fri 9am–noon & 1–5pm, Sat 9am–noon; with longer hours in the height of the summer.

All kinds of **maps** are available in the country. You can buy them, often very cheaply, from bookshops and some hotels – ask for a *plán mesta* (town plan) or *orientačná mapa*. For road maps, the 1:100,000 *Autoatlas* produced by VKÚ is the most detailed, marking all campsites and petrol stations. For **hiking**, the 1:100,000 *turistická mapa* series details the country's complex network of footpaths.

Money and banks

The **currency** in Slovakia is the Slovak crown or *Slovenská koruna* (abbreviated to Sk), which is divided into 100 *halier* (h). Coins come in the denominations 50h, 1Sk, 2Sk, 5Sk and 10Sk; notes as 20Sk, 50Sk, 100Sk, 200Sk, 500Sk and 1000Sk. The Slovak crown is not yet fully convertible, which means it's still technically illegal to import or export more than a small amount of Slovak currency.

Travellers' cheques in US dollars, Deutschmarks or Sterling are undoubtedly the safest way of carrying your money, though it's a good idea to keep at least some hard currency in **cash** for emergencies. **Credit cards** are accepted only in upmarket hotels, restaurants and shops, and you can also get cash on your plastic at some banks and from the many ATMs that have now sprouted up in the towns and cities.

Communications

Most **post offices** (*pošta*) are open Mon–Fri 8am–5pm and Sat 8am–noon – you can also buy stamps from some tobacconists (*tabák*) and street kiosks, though often only for domestic mail. **Poste restante** services are available in major towns, but remember to write *Pošta 1* (the main office), followed by the name of the town.

Cheap local calls can be made from any **phone**, but for international calls it's best to use a card phone, for which you need to buy a telephone card (*telefonná karta*) from a tobacconist or post office. Internet cafés are also beginning to appear in the larger cities.

Getting around

The most pleasant way of travelling around Slovakia is by train – the system is not as extensive as some in the former eastern bloc, but some of the journeys are beautifully scenic. The only time you'll really need buses is in the more remote and mountainous regions of the country.

■ Trains

Slovak Railways, Železnice Slovenskej republiky (ŽSR), run two main types of **trains**: *rýchlik* trains are the faster ones which stop only at major towns, while *osobní* or local trains stop at every station and average about 30km an hour. **Tickets** (*lístok*) for domestic journeys can be bought at the station (*stanica*) before or on the day of departure. Fares are cheap – a second-class single from Bratislava to Košice currently costs around £5/$8. ŽSR run reasonably priced **sleepers** (*ležadlo*) to and from a number of places – make sure you book as far in advance as possible and no later than six hours before departure. InterRail passes are valid; Eurail passes are not.

■ Buses

Trains will take you most places but if you have to change a lot, it might be easier to take one of the regional **buses** (*autobus*) mostly run by the state bus company, Slovenská automobilová doprava (SAD). Bus stations are usually next to the train station, and if there's no separate terminal you'll have to buy your ticket from the driver. It's a good idea to book your ticket in advance if you're travelling at the weekend or early in the morning on one of the main routes.

■ Driving and cycling

Since only around half the population own a vehicle and most of those are only used at the weekend, travelling by **car** in Slovakia is still a relaxing way to travel. **Speed limits** are 130kph on motorways, 100kph on other roads, and 60kph in all cities, towns and villages. To use the country's very small stretches of motorway, you need to buy a 200–400Sk windscreen sticker (*úhrada*) at the border or from a petrol station. There should be **no alcohol** at all in your bloodstream while driving. **Fuel** is currently fairly cheap by European standards, but petrol stations are still not quite as widespread as in Western Europe (though 24-hour ones can be found in the major towns and cities).

Car hire in Slovakia currently starts at around £235/$400 per week. The multinational firms have branches in Bratislava: Hertz are in the *Hotel Fórum* (☎07/5348 155), while Avis are in the *Hotel Danube* (☎07/5340 841). For a cheaper deal you need to contact a local organization like Recar, Svätoplukova 1 (☎07/5266 263), or Adecar, Hybeyova 36 (☎07/285 517).

Accommodation

The **accommodation** situation is much better than it used to be, though it remains the most expensive aspect of travelling in Slovakia. There is no real network of youth hostels, though some are now affiliated to Hostelling International. In Bratislava and the High Tatras, the private-room network makes up for this. However, if you're travelling in July or August and want to save yourself hassle, it's a good idea to arrange accommodation as far in advance as possible.

■ Hotels and private rooms

Hotels are often deliberately priced up for foreigners and consequently relatively expensive (£10/$16 for a double is pretty much the bottom line) compared to other living costs. While the old state hotels are slowly being refurbished, the new hotels and pensions that have opened up, particularly in the more heavily touristed areas, are often a better bet and better value for money. Breakfast is normally included in the newer private ventures, less so at the bigger state hotels. There has been a large increase in the number of **private rooms** available – in fact, these are now your best bet in Bratislava. Elsewhere, just keep your eyes peeled for signs saying *Zimmer Frei*. Prices start at around 200–300Sk per person per night.

■ Hostels and campsites

Bratislava has a few private **youth hostels** which offer varying degrees of discomfort. Elsewhere, the student travel organization, CKM, can give information on cheap **student accommodation** in the big

---

ACCOMMODATION PRICE CODES

Throughout this guide, accommodation is priced on a scale of ① to ⑨, the number indicating the lowest price per night a single person could expect to pay in that establishment in high season. With hostels this is the nightly rate per person; with hotels, the price is arrived at by dividing the cost of the cheapest double room by two. The prices indicated by the codes are as follows:

① under £5 / $8	④ £15–20 / $24–32	⑦ £30–35 / $48–56
② £5–10 / $8–16	⑤ £20–25 / $32–40	⑧ £35–40 / $56–64
③ £10–15 / $16–24	⑥ £25–30 / $40–48	⑨ £40 / $64 and over

university towns during July and August. In the High Tatras, there are also a fair number of **refuges** (*chata*) scattered about the hillsides. Some are little less than hotels and cost around £10/$15 a bed, less for the simpler, more isolated wooden shelters.

Campsites are plentiful all over Slovakia. Many of the sites feature **bungalows** (again, known as *chata*), often available for anything upwards of £5/$8 a bed. A few sites remain open all year round, but most don't open until May at the earliest, closing mid- to late September. Even though prices have been inflated for foreigners, costs are still reasonable.

Food and drink

Slovak food is a strange hybrid, affected both by hundreds of years of Hungarian domination, which has given the Slovaks a penchant for spicier dishes, and by hefty, filling Bohemian fare, which became the national cuisine of the state-sponsored kitchens of Czechoslovakia.

■ Food

The usual mid-morning Slovak snack at the **bufet** (stand-up canteen) is *párek*, perhaps the most ubiquitous **takeaway food** in central Europe, a dubious-looking frankfurter, dipped in mustard and served with a white roll. The Slovak national dish is *bryndzové halušky*, a sort of macaroni cheese, but Hungarian influences are strong here, too. Goulash is very popular, as are *langoše* – deep-fried dough smothered in garlic.

Most menus start with **soup** (*polievka*), one of the country's culinary strong points and mainly served at lunchtimes. **Main courses** are overwhelmingly based on pork or beef, but trout and carp are usually featured somewhere on the menu. Most main courses are served with potatoes (*zemiaky*) – fresh salads or green vegetables are still a rarity in restaurants. With the exception of *palačinky* (pancakes) filled with chocolate or fruit and cream, **desserts**, where they exist at all, will be pretty unexciting.

For a full meal, it's best to go to a **restaurant** (*reštaurácia*) which serves hot meals nonstop from about 11am until 10pm. Lunch (between noon and 2pm) is traditionally the main meal of the day and generally the best time to go to a restaurant as the choice of food is at its widest. Menus and prices are nearly always displayed outside.

Coffee (*káva*) is drunk black – espresso style in the big cities, but sometimes simply hot water poured over real coffee in the smaller towns and villages (described rather hopefully as "Turkish" or *turecká*). The **cake shop** (*cukráres*) is an important

part of the country's social life, particularly on Sunday mornings when it's often the only place that's open in town. Whatever the season, Slovaks love to have their daily fix of **ice cream** (*zmrzlina*), available at *cukráreň* or dispensed from little window kiosks in the sides of buildings.

■ Drink

The vineyards in the south of Slovakia produce some pretty good medium-quality white **wines**, which share characteristics with their Hungarian and Austrian neighbours. The home production of **brandies** is a national pastime, resulting sometimes in almost terminally strong brews. The most famous is *slivovice*, a plum brandy, originally from the border hills between the Czech and Slovak republics, but now available just about everywhere.

After more than seventy years of close association with the Czechs, the Slovaks have also learnt to love draught **beer**, but the *pivnica*, where most heavy drinking goes on, is still less common in Slovakia than in the Czech Republic. Slovaks tend to head instead for restaurants or **wine bars** (*vináreň*), which usually have slightly later opening hours and often double as nightclubs.

Opening hours and holidays

Opening hours for shops in Slovakia are Mon–Fri 9am–5pm, Sat 9am–noon, with some shops and most supermarkets staying open till 6pm or later. Smaller shops close for lunch for an hour or so sometime between noon and 2pm. Most shops are closed on Sunday.

The basic opening hours for **castles** and **monasteries** are Tues–Sun 9am–noon & 1–5pm. In April and October, opening hours are often restricted to weekends and holidays. From the end of October to the beginning of April, most castles are closed. When visiting a sight, always ask for an *anglický text*, an often unintentionally hilarious English resumé. In Bratislava the main **museums** open Tues–Sun 10am–6pm, though there are exceptions. In winter, many museums close half an hour earlier than the times quoted in this guide. Entrance tickets for all sights rarely cost more than £1/$1.67 – hence no prices are quoted in the text.

Public holidays include Jan 1 (Independence Day); Jan 6 (Epiphany); Good Friday; Easter Monday, May 1, July 5 (saints Cyril and Methodius day); Aug 29 (anniversary of the Slovak National Uprising against the Nazis); Sept 1 (Constitution Day), Sept 15 (Our Lady of Sorrows); Nov 1 (All Saints' Day); and Dec 24, 25 & 26.

Emergencies

There are two types of **police** (*polícia*): the state police, who wear the standard khaki uniforms that are a hangover from communist days, and the local municipal or *mestská polícia*, who wear a variety of natty outfits depending on the fashion-consciousness of the local council. For tourists, theft from cars and hotel rooms is the biggest worry – the best way to protect yourself against such disasters is to take out travel insurance. If you are unlucky enough to have something stolen, report it immediately to the nearest police station in order to get a statement detailing what you've lost for your insurance claim. Everyone is obliged to carry some form of ID and you should carry your **passport** with you at all times, though realistically you're extremely unlikely to get stopped unless you're driving.

Minor ailments can be easily dealt with by the **pharmacist** (*lekáreň*), but language is likely to be a major problem. If it's a repeat prescription you want, take any empty bottles or remaining pills along with you. If the chemist can't help, they'll be able to direct you to a **hospital** or *nemocnica*. If you do have to pay for any medication, keep the receipts for claiming on your insurance once you're home.

> ### EMERGENCY NUMBERS
> Police ☎158; Ambulance ☎155; Fire ☎150.

BRATISLAVA

BRATISLAVA has two distinct sides: the old quarter is a manageable and attractive slice of Habsburg Baroque, while the rest of the city has the brash and butchered feel of the average East European metropolis. More buildings have been destroyed here since the war than were bombed out during it, the whole Jewish quarter having been bulldozed to make way for the colossal new suspension bridge. Yet, even though the multicultural atmosphere of the prewar days has gone, there is a certain central European cosmopolitanism here, at the meeting of three nations.

Arrival and information

Bratislava does have an **airport** (letisko Ivánka), but at present there are very few direct flights to or from the rest of Europe, other than the likes of Munich and Prague, plus the odd domestic flight to Košice and Poprad. From the airport take bus #24 to the main train station, or else catch the ASA bus, which runs a shuttle service to and from the ASA office on Stúrova, timed to coincide with the flight schedule. Part of the reason for Bratislava airport's underuse is the proximity of Vienna airport, from which there's a regular bus service that drops passengers at the main bus station in Bratislava (see below).

A short distance north of the city centre is Bratislava's newly spruced-up main **train station** or *hlavná stanica*, where most international or long-distance trains pull in. Once you've arrived, go down to the tram terminus below and, having bought your ticket (10Sk) from one of the machines on the platform, hop on tram #1 into town. Some trains, particularly those heading for destinations within west Slovakia, pass through Bratislava's Nové Mesto station, linked to the centre by tram #6 and to the main train station by hourly train connection. **Buses** usually arrive at the main bus station, or *autobusová stanica*, on Mlynské nivy, fifteen minutes' walk east of the city centre. Trolleybus #210 will take you across town to the main train station; #211 goes past *Hotel Fórum* on Hodžovo námestie. Bratislava's **tourist office**, BIS, is at Klobuanícka 2 (Mon–Fri 8am–5pm, Sat 8am–1pm); it's good for general queries (some English is spoken) and getting hold of a map and the monthly listings magazine, *Kam v Bratislave*; they can also book accommodation.

City transport

The best way to see Bratislava is to walk – in fact it's the only way to see the pedestrianized old town, or staré mesto, where most of the sights are concentrated. However, if you're staying outside the city centre or visiting the suburbs, you'll need to make use of the city's inexpensive and comprehensive **transport system**. Buy your ticket (10Sk) beforehand (from newsagents, kiosks, hotel lobbies or ticket machines), validate it as soon as you get on, and use a fresh ticket each time you change; if you're going to use the system a lot buy a 24-hour pass (*24 hodinový lístok*; 45Sk) from one of the yellow ticket machines, a *tabák*, or from the central transport office on Stúrova. **Night buses** congregate at námestie SNP, every quarter to the hour.

Accommodation

Bratislava's proximity to Vienna, and its capital city status, mean that **hotels** are more expensive than anywhere else in the country. This makes **private rooms** the most popular option for most budget travellers – BIS (see above) can arrange such accommodation for you for a 50Sk fee.

Hostels and camping

Bernolák, Bernolákova 1 (☎07/497 721). The liveliest and cheapest hostel in the city, and only a short tram ride northeast of the centre; tram #7 or #11 from Kamenné námestie. Open July & Aug. ①.

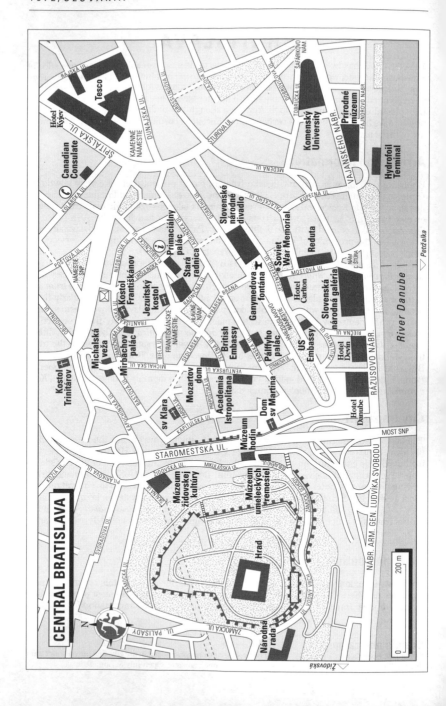

CENTRAL BRATISLAVA

Zlaté piesky (☎07/257 018). Two fairly grim campsites, 8km northeast of the city centre, near the swimming lake of the same name. To get there, take tram #4 from the main train station or tram #4 from Kamenné námestie. Open May–Sept.

Hotels and pensions

Arcus, Moskovská 5 (☎07/555 72 522). Wonderful little pension just east of Americké námestie; take any tram heading up Spitalska from Kamenné námestie. ③.

Astra, Prievozská 14a (☎07/582 381 11). One of the city's cheapest options, just over 2km east of the centre; trolleybus #218 from the main train station, and walking distance from the main bus station. ②.

Chez David, Zámocká 13 (☎07/531 38 24). Swish kosher pension right by the castle and the old Jewish quarter, with a kosher restaurant attached. ⑤.

Clubhotel, Odbojárov 3 (☎07/256 369). Cheap hotel 3km northeast of the centre, but easily reached by tram #2 from the main train station, and by tram #4 or #6 from Kamenné námestie. ②.

Družba, Cheapest hotel in the city, situated on a university campus to the west of town, near the botanical gardens; tram #1 from the train station. ①.

Gremium, Gorkého 11 (☎07/541 31 026). This is the only decent, inexpensive option in the old town, so book ahead if possible. ③.

Rybársky cech, Žižkova 1 (☎07/544 18 334). Pension above excellent fish restaurant on the busy road below the castle. ②.

The City

Trams from the main train station offload their shoppers and sightseers behind the *Hotel Fórum* in Obchodná – literally Shop Street – which descends into Hurbanovo námestie, a busy junction on the northern edge of the old town (staré mesto). Here you'll find the hefty mass of the **Kostol Trinitárov**, one of the city's finest churches, its exuberant trompe l'oeil frescoes creating a magnificent false cupola.

Opposite the church, a footbridge passes under a tower of the city's last remaining double gateway. Below is a small section of what used to be the city moat, now a garden belonging to the Baroque apothecary called *U červeného raka*, on your left between the towers, which now houses a **Pharmaceutical Museum** (Farmaceutická expozícia; Tues–Sun 10am–5pm), displaying everything from seventeenth-century drug grinders to reconstructed period pharmacies. The second and taller of the towers is the **Michalská brána** (Mon & Wed–Sun 10am–5pm), an evocative and impressive entrance to the old town and now a weapons museum; the rooftop view from the top of the tower is superb.

Michalská and Ventúrska, which run into each other, have both been beautifully restored and are lined with some of Bratislava's finest Baroque palaces. There are usually plenty of students milling about amongst the shoppers, as the main university library is on this thoroughfare. The palaces of the Austro-Hungarian aristocracy continue into Panská, starting with the **Pálffy Palace**, today an **art gallery** (Tues–Sun 10am–5pm) housing a patchy collection of Slovak paintings from the nineteenth and twentieth centuries.

A little northeast of here are the adjoining main squares of the old town – **Hlavné námestie** and **Františkánske námestie** – on the east side of which is the **Old Town Hall** or Stará radnica (Tues–Fri 10am–6pm, Sat & Sun 11am–6pm), a lively hotchpotch of Gothic, Renaissance and nineteenth-century styles containing a museum that's worth visiting if only for the medieval torture exhibition in the basement dungeons. The Counter-Reformation, which gripped the parts of Hungary not under Turkish occupation, issues forth from the square's **Jesuit Church**, whose best feature is its richly gilded pulpit. Diagonally opposite is the **Mirbach Palace** (Tues–Sun 10am–5pm), arguably the finest of Bratislava's Rococo buildings, preserving much of its original stucco decor.

Round the back of the Old Town Hall, with the stillness of a provincial Italian piazza during siesta, is the **Primaciálne námestie**, dominated by the Neoclassical **Primate's Palace** (Tues–Sun 10am–5pm), whose pediment frieze is topped by a cast-iron cardinal's hat. The palace's main claim to fame is its Hall of Mirrors, where Napoleon and the Austrian emperor signed the Peace of Pressburg (as Bratislava was then called) in 1805. You can now visit this, and several other rooms hung with portraits of the Habsburgs and seventeenth-century English tapestries, found by chance during the building's renovation.

Despite its proximity to Vienna and Budapest, the city has produced only one composer of note, **Johann Nepomuk Hummel** (1778–1837). The composer's birthplace, a cute apricot-coloured cottage hidden away behind two fashionable shops on Klobuanícka Still, is now a **museum** (Tues–Sun noon–5pm). Beyond, at the top end of Stúrova, is **Kamenné námestie**, overlooked by a giant Tesco supermarket, in front of which the whole city seems to wind up after work, to grab a beer or takeaway from one of the many stand-up stalls, then jabber away the early evening before catching the bus or tram home.

From the Cathedral to the Castle

On the west side of the staré mesto, the most insensitive of Bratislava's postwar developments took place. After the annihilation of the city's Jewish population by the Nazis, the communist authorities tore down virtually the whole of the Jewish quarter in order to build the brutal showpiece bridge, the SNP Bridge or most SNP (see below). The traffic which now tears along Staromestská has seriously undermined the foundations of the Gothic **Cathedral of sv Martin** (Mon–Fri 10–11.45am & 2–4.45pm, Sat 10am–noon & 2–4.45pm, Sun 2–4.45pm), coronation church of the kings and queens of Hungary for over 250 years, whose ill-proportioned steeple is topped by a tiny gilded Hungarian crown.

As you pass under the approach road for the new bridge, you'll notice two old, thin houses standing opposite one another, both of which have been converted into museums. The first is a **Clock Museum** (Múzeum hodin; Mon & Wed–Sun 10am–5pm) with a display of brilliantly kitsch Baroque and Empire clocks; the second the **Museum of Artistic Handicrafts** (Múzeum umeleckých remesiel; times as above), which consists of a few period dining rooms and a lot of fairly ordinary arts and crafts gear. To pay tribute to the large prewar Slovak Jewish population, there is now a **Jewish Museum** (Múzeum židovskej kultúry; Mon–Fri & Sun 11am–5pm) on Židovská, with a display of Judaica and a brief history of Slovak Jews.

The **Castle** or *Hrad* is an unwelcoming giant box built in the fifteenth century by the Emperor Sigismund and burnt down by its own drunken soldiers in 1811. Currently undergoing a dose of much-needed modernization, it houses the half of the uneven collections of the **Slovak National Museum** (Slovenské národné múzeum; Tues–Sun 9am–5pm; 40Sk for all sections) that they couldn't squeeze into the main building on the waterfront. The most interesting section so far is the **Treasures of the Far Past of Slovakia** (10Sk), but most punters will probably get more out of the incredible view from outside the castle gates south across the Danube plain to the Petržalka housing estate, where a third of the city's population lives.

Along the waterfront

Despite the fast dual carriageway of the embankment, it is just about possible to enjoy a stroll along the banks of the (far from blue) **River Danube** – *Dunaj* in Slovak. There's a regular ferry across the river, an alternative to crossing by either of the two bridges. The larger of these is the infamous **Bridge of the Slovak National Uprising** or **most SNP**. Its one support column leans at an alarming angle, topped by a saucer-like penthouse café reminiscent of the *Starship Enterprise*. The view from the café is superlative, though it's pricey by local standards.

While you're in the waterfront district, the **Slovak National Gallery** (Slovenská národná galéria; Tues–Sun 10am–6pm) is worth exploring. There are two entrances: the one on the embankment lets you into the main building, a converted naval barracks, while the one on Stúrovo námestie gives access to the new Esterházy Palace wing – inside, both parts connect on the upper floor. The permanent collection in the main building is an exhaustive rundown of Slovak art from Gothic times to the late nineteenth century, while the Esterházy Palace houses sixteenth- to eighteenth-century paintings of dubious merit. You're better off, instead, heading straight for the fascinating new top-floor display of twentieth-century applied arts, architecture and design.

Further along the quayside, past the rather tatty **Natural History Museum** (Tues–Sun 9am–5pm) and hidden away behind Safárikovo námestie, is Ödön Lechner's sky-blue Art

Nouveau **Little Blue Church** (Modrý kostolík) on Bezruaova, a lost monument to this once-Hungarian city, abandoned in the Slovak capital. It's decorated, inside and out, with the richness of a central European cream cake, and dedicated to Saint Elizabeth, the city's one and only famous saint, born in Bratislava in 1207.

Eating, drinking and nightlife

The choice of places **to eat** in Bratislava has improved enormously over the last few years, as have standards, though you're still unlikely to have the meal of a lifetime here. The most memorable aspect of the whole experience is often the ambience, and exploring the atmospheric streets of the old town by night is all part of the fun. In addition, you can also be fairly sure that, away from the places catering for those on expenses, prices remain uniformly low. **Nightlife** is a little more limited – it's fine for classical music fans, or for a night out at the cinema, but live rock music and clubs are thin on the ground.

Cafés, bars and pubs

Café Mayer, Hlavné námestie 4. A resurrected turn-of-the-century café that tries very hard to emulate its Viennese-style ancestor – very popular with the city's older cake-and-coffee fans.

Dubliners, Sedlárska 6. Every European capital, it seems, has to have an Irish pub, and this, the most popular expat hangout in town, is a no-holds-barred evocation complete with miniature cobbled street.

Gremium, Gorkého 11. Smoky, spacious café downstairs, with pool and more seats up in the balcony. There's a more formal restaurant on the first floor, too.

Korzo, Rybné námestie. Tables outside overlooking the SNP Bridge, or inside with the morning papers – a good place for breakfast.

London Café, Panská 17. Tiny British-Council tearoom that's famous for its quiche and salad, popular with expats and a good place to catch up on the English press. Closed Sat & Sun.

Stará sladovňa, Cintorínska 32. Bratislava's most famous eating and drinking establishment, a bingo hall, amusement arcade and restaurant all rolled into one. Czech beer on tap, and the food isn't at all bad – however, the music is usually oom-pah-pah, and the service often slow.

Restaurants

Arkádia, Zámocké schody. Swish new restaurant serving great Slovak cuisine in an old Renaissance building on the way up to the castle.

Chez David, Zámocká 13. A plush and pricey kosher restaurant. Closed Sat.

Corleone, Palackého 18. Best pizza in the city.

Karmina, Stúrova, junction with Talleran. Stand-up-and-scoff, canteen-style eatery offering no-nonsense Slovak food at low, low prices. Mon–Fri 8am–4pm.

Passage Rybárska brána, off Hviezdoslavovo námestie. A huge complex of eateries from cheap sit-down restaurants to stand-up *bufet* and takeaway stands.

Ravijoma, námestie SNP 8. A huge, popular self-service *bufet* and café upstairs, with fixed seats and formica tables, and not so popular restaurant in the cellar.

Rybársky cech, Žižkova 1. Popular and reliable fish restaurant down by the waterfront motorway below the castle.

U dežmara, Klariská 1. Pleasant hangout by the university library – duck down the passageway off Michalská – with average food.

Theatre, music and cinema

Bratislava's most established **nightlife** is heavily biased towards high culture, with opera and ballet at the Slovak National Theatre (Slovenské národné divadlo or SND) and orchestral concerts at the Reduta, as well as the varied programme put on at the modern Dom odborov complex (tram #4 or #6 from Kamenné námestie). Tickets for the first two are available from the box office behind the SND (look out for the Pokladňa Kasse sign), and for the Dom odborov from a box office inside the building from 3pm. Many theatres close down in July and August. The city hosts a couple of large-scale **festivals**, starting with its own spring music festival in April.

The best alternative venue is the Charlie centrum, Spitálska 4, the entrance is one block east of the *Hotel Kyjev* on Rajská. Inside there's a multiscreen art-house cinema, and a late-night bar/disco in the basement. Another late-night drinking and dancing spot is the student-dominated *Duna*, Radlinského 11, in the basement of the Technical University. *Hysteria*, Odbojárov 9, behind the ice hockey stadium (tram #4 or #6 from Kamenné námestie), is worth the trek for its Tex-Mex food, pool and regular live music.

Listings

Airlines British Airways, Stefankova 22, (☎07/5399 801); ASA, Stúrova 13 (☎07/308 08 944).

Email Kavieren Muzeum, Vajanského Nábr, on the waterfront behind the Prírodné Muzeum. 2Sk per minute.

Embassies Canada, Mišikova 28D (☎07/5361 277); Great Britain, Panská 16 (☎07/544 19 632); South Africa, Janaova 8 (☎07/5311 582); USA, Hviezdoslavovo námestie 4 (☎07/544 30 861).

Pharmacy 24hr emergency service from Mýtná 5.

Police The "foreigners' police" (*cudzinecká polícia*) are at Sasinkova 23.

Post office The main post office is at námestie SNP 35 (Mon–Sat 7am–8pm, Sun 9am–2pm).

Telephone There's a 24hr telephone exchange at Kolárska 12.

THE MOUNTAIN REGIONS

The great virtue of Slovakia is its mountains, particularly the **High Tatras** – which, in their short span, reach alpine heights and have a bleak, stunning beauty. By far the republic's most popular destination, they are, in fact, the least typical of Slovakia's mountains, which are pre-dominantly densely forested, round-topped limestone ranges. In the heart of the mountains is **Banská Bystrica**, one of the many towns in the region originally settled by German miners, and still redolent of those times. Generally, though, the towns in the valley bottoms have been fairly solidly industrialized, and are only good as bases for exploring the surrounding countryside. Railways, where they do exist, make for some of the most scenic train journeys in the country.

Banská Bystrica

Lying at the very heart of Slovakia's mountain ranges, the old German mining town of **BANSKÁ BYSTRICA** (Neusohl) is a useful introduction to the area. Connected to the outlying districts by some of the country's most precipitous railways, it's also a handsome historic town in its own right – once you've made it through the tangled suburbs of the burgeoning cement and logging industry.

Námestie SNP, the old medieval marketplace, is still the centre of life in Banská Bystrica, and has recently been spruced up. The black obelisk of the Soviet war memorial and a revolving fountain, enthusiastically chucking water over a pile of mossy rocks, form the square's centrepiece. One or two of the burgher houses bear closer inspection, particularly the **Venetian House** (Benického dom) at no. 16, with its slender first-floor arcaded loggia. The sgraffitoed building opposite is now an art gallery, just a few doors down from the most imposing building on the square, the honey-coloured Thurzo Palace, decorated like a piece of embroidery and sporting cute oval portholes, and now housing the **town museum** (Mon–Fri 8am–noon & 1–4pm, Sun 9am–noon & 1–4pm) with a small selection of folk art and period furniture.

At the top end of the square, beyond the leaning clock tower, there's an interesting ensemble of buildings which is all that's left of the old castle. The first building in view is the last remaining **barbican** curving snugly round a Baroque tower. Next door, the former **town hall** or *radnica* (Tues–Fri 9am–5pm, Sat & Sun 10am–4pm), a boxy little Renaissance structure, is now the town's main art gallery, which puts on temporary exhibitions from its extensive catalogue of twentieth-century Slovak art. Behind it is the rouge-red church of **Panna Mária**, which dates back to the thirteenth century; the north side chapel contains the town's greatest art treasure, a carved late-Gothic altarpiece by Master Pavol of Levoča.

A short distance southeast of námestie SNP on Kapitulská Ulica, 200m south of the clock tower, is the **SNP Museum** (Tues–Sun: May–Sept 8am–6pm; Oct–April 9am–4pm), looking something like an intergalactic mushroom chopped in half. The museum deals as best it can with the complex issues raised by the Slovak National Uprising (SNP) against the Nazis (and the Slovak puppet regime), which began on August 29, 1944 in Banská Bystrica and which was eventually crushed by the Germans two months later, just a month or so before the town's liberation. Outside on the grass you'll notice a collection of tanks and guns from the uprising amid the bushes and the town's last two surviving medieval bastions.

Banská Bystrica's **bus terminus** and the main **train station** are in the modern part of town, ten minutes' walk east of the centre. A second, smaller train station, Banská Bystrica Mesto, is just a five-minute walk due south of the centre. There's a **tourist office** inside the barbican (Mon–Fri 9am–12.30pm; 1.15–5pm), which can help with **accommodation**. The cheapest options are the *Milvar* (☎088/33279; ①), a five-minute walk to the west of town at Školská 9, and the *Národný Dom* (☎088/723 737; ②). There's a **campsite** 1km west of the main square (open all year), just by the road to Tajov. Filled French sticks can be had from *Copaline Baguette*, at no. 12 on the main square. For a cheap and filling plate of *bryndzové halušky*, head for the *Slovenská pivnica* at Lazovná 18 (closed Sun); for great pizzas try *EVIJO*, on Národná.

The High Tatras

Rising like a giant granite reef above the patchwork Poprad plain, the **High Tatras** are for many people the main reason for venturing this far into Slovakia. Even after all the tourist-board hype, they are still an inspirational sight. A wilderness, however, they are not; all summer, visitors are shoulder to shoulder in the necklace of resorts which sit at the foot of the mountains. But once you're above the tree line, surrounded by bare primeval scree slopes and icy blue tarns, nothing can take away the exhilaration.

The mainline train station for the Tatras is Poprad-Tatry in **Poprad** (the main bus station is next door). From the high-level platform here, cute red tram-like trains trundle across the fields, linking Poprad with the string of resorts and spas nestling at the foot of the Tatras and lying within the **Tatra National Park** or **TANAP**. They're all much of a muchness, a mix of tasteless new hotels and half-timbered lodges from the last century set in eminently civilized spa gardens and pine woods – it's the mountains to which they give access that make them worth visiting. Perhaps the best to head for is **Starý Smokovec**, the central resort.

Poprad

POPRAD is an unprepossessing town, a great swathe of off-white high-rise housing encircling a small old centre – but it's refreshingly free of tour groups and the pretentiousness of higher resorts. In fact, if you can get in at the *Gerlach* on Hviezdoslavovo námestie (☎092/721 945; ①) or the *Hotel Európa* (☎092/721 897; ①), by the train station, they're no bad place to stay. The PIA **information office** (Mon–Fri 8am–6pm, Sat 8am–noon), on the long main square, five minutes' walk south of the train station can book you into **private rooms** in the Tatras. The small vegetable market on the north side of the square is useful for stocking up on provisions, while the stores on the south side include the Christiniana bookshop, which has a good selection of English-language books, and where you might be able to pick up **maps**.

Camping in the High Tatras

Accommodation should be your first priority, since finding a place can be difficult. The cheapest option is **camping**, though all the sites are outside the boundaries of the national park and therefore a long hike from the nearest peaks. The best one is the *Tatracamp pod lesom* (May–Sept) in Dolný Smokovec, with bungalows, hot showers and kitchen facilities. Two camps – *Eurocamp FICC* (all year) and *Športcamp* (May–Sept) – just south of Tatranská Lomnica (get off at Tatranská Lomnica–Eurocamp FICC station) are similarly priced but don't offer kitchen facilities. The cheapest and most basic is the *Jupela* site 1km south of Stará Lesná (May–Sept).

Starý Smokovec – and Tatra hikes

The best base for accommodation in the Tatras is the scattered settlement of **STARÝ SMOKOVEC**, whose nucleus is the stretch of lawn between the half-timbered supermarket and the sandy-yellow *Grand Hotel*. T-Ski (daily 9am–5pm), by the funicular railway behind the *Grand*, is a good source of **information**; they also rent out skis in winter and bikes in summer, and can book accommodation in the region. Climbers and hikers wanting information should go to Horská služba the 24-hour mountain rescue service, close to the train station. The self-service **restaurant** *Central* is the most reasonable place to eat. To book into one of the mountain **refuges** (*chata*), you need to visit Slovakoturist in the neighbouring resort of Horný Smokovec, a couple of minutes' walk to the east.

If the weather's reasonably good, the most straightforward and rewarding climb is to follow the blue-marked path that leads from behind the *Grand Hotel* to the summit of **Slavkovský štít** (2452m), a return journey of nine hours. Alternatively, there's also a narrow-gauge funicular, again starting from behind the *Grand*, which climbs 250m to **HREBIENOK** (45min on foot), one of the lesser ski resorts on the edge of the pine forest. The smart wooden *Bilíkova chata* (☎0969/42 24 39; ②) is a five-minute walk from the top of the funicular. Beyond the *chata*, the path continues through the wood, joining two others, from Tatranská Lesná and Tatranská Lomnica respectively, before passing the gushing waterfalls of the **Studenovodské vodopády**.

Just past the waterfall, a whole variety of trekking possibilities opens up. The right-hand fork takes you up the **Malá Studená dolina** and then zigzags above the tree line to the *Téryho chata*, set in a lunar landscape by the shores of the **Päť Spišských plies**. Following the spectacular trail over the Prieane sedlo to *Zbojnicka chata*, you can return via the Vejká studená dolina – an eight-hour round trip from Hrebienok. Another possibility is to take the left-hand fork to the *Zbojnicka chata*, and continue to Zamruznuté pleso, which sits in the shadow of **Východná Vysoká** (2428m); only a thirty-minute hike from the lake, this dishes out the best view of **Gerlachovský stít** – the highest of the Tatras – that a non-climber can get.

EAST SLOVAKIA

Stretching from the High Tatras east to the Ukrainian border, the landscape of **east Slovakia** is decidedly different from the rest of the country. Ethnically, this is probably the most diverse region in the country, with different groups coexisting even within a single valley. The majority of the country's Romanies live here, mostly on the edge of Slovak villages, in shanty towns of almost medieval squalor. In the ribbon-villages of the north and east, the Rusyn minority struggle to preserve their culture and religion, while along the southern border there are large numbers of Hungarians. After spending time in the rural backwaters, **Košice**, Slovakia's second largest city, can be a welcome though somewhat startling return to city life, containing enough of interest for at least a day's stopover.

The Spiš region

The land that stretches northeast up the Poprad Valley to the Polish border and east along the River Hornád towards Prešov is known as the **Spiš** (Zips) region, for centuries a semi-autonomous province within the Hungarian kingdom. After the devastation of the mid-thirteenth-century Tatar invasions, the Hungarian Crown encouraged Saxon families to repopulate the area. The wealthy settlers built some wonderful Gothic churches, and later enriched almost every town and village with the distinctive touch of the Renaissance. Today, with only a few of its ethnic Germans remaining, the Spiš shares the low living standards of the rest of east Slovakia. But the region's architectural richness offers a glimmer of hope in the growth of tourism.

Kežmarok

Just 14km up the road from Poprad, **KEŽMAROK** (Käsmark) is one of the easiest Spiš towns to visit from the High Tatras. It's an odd place, combining the distinctive traits of a Teutonic town with the dozy feel of an oversized Slovak village. Kežmarok is dominated by the giant, gaudy **Lutheran Church** (May–Oct daily 9am–noon & 2–5pm; Nov–April Tues & Fri 10am–noon), built by Theophil Hansen, the Danish architect responsible for much of late nineteenth-century Vienna, and funded by the town's merchants. It's a seemingly random fusion of styles – Renaissance campanile, Moorish dome, Classical dimensions, all dressed up in grey-green and rouge rendering. Next door is an even more remarkable **wooden Lutheran Church** (times as above), a work of great carpentry that's capable of seating almost 1500 people – you need to get the key from the neighbouring Lutheran Church.

The old town itself is little more than two long leafy streets which fork off from the important-looking central town hall. The town's Catholic church, **sv Kríž**, is tucked away in the tangle of dusty back alleys between the two prongs, once surrounded by its own line of fortifications. It is now protected by a Renaissance belfry whose uppermost battlements burst into sgraffito life in the best Spiš tradition. The **Castle** or zámok (Tues–Sun; entry every hour, 9am–4pm), at the end of the right-hand fork, is impressively fortified and decorated with Renaissance crenellations, but the interior doesn't really justify signing up for the compulsory hour-long guided tour. A better idea is to head for the **town museum** (Tues–Sat 9am–noon & 1–5pm), back along the street at Hradné námestie 55, which contains, among other things, the personal effects of Countess Hedviga Mária Szirmayova-Badányiova.

The **tourist office**, opposite the town hall at Hlavné námestie 46 (Mon–Fri 8.30am–5pm, Sat 9am–2pm), can help with **accommodation**. The best place to stay is the wonderful new *Hotel Club*, on ulica MUDr Alexandra (☎0968/524 051; ③), though the newly opened *Regent Penzion*, 63 Starý Trh, (0968/524258; ②), a good fifteen-minute walk from the train station at the foot of the castle gates, provides some stiff competition. For budget travellers the *Štart* (☎0968/522915; ①), which lies in the woods to the north of the castle, is good value.

Levoča

Twenty-five kilometres east of Poprad across the broad sweep of Spiš countryside, the walled town of **LEVOČA** (Leutschau), set on a slight incline, makes a wonderfully medieval impression. The Euclidian efficiency with which the old town is laid out means you'll inevitably end up at the main square, **námestie Majstra Pavla**. To the north is the square's least distinguished but most important building, the municipal weigh-house; a law of 1321 obliged every merchant passing through the region to hole up at Levoča for fourteen days, pay various taxes and allow the locals first refusal on their goods.

Of the three freestanding buildings on the main square paid for with these riches, it's the Catholic church of **sv Jakub** (June & Sept Mon & Sun 1–5pm, Tues–Sat 8.30am–5pm; July & Aug Mon & Sun 1–6pm, Tues–Sat 9am–6pm; Oct–May Mon & Sun 1–4pm, Tues–Sat 8.30–11.30am) that has the most valuable booty. Every nook and cranny is crammed with religious art, star attraction being the magnificent sixteenth-century wooden altarpiece by Master Pavol of Levoča, which, at 18.6m, is reputedly the tallest of its kind in the world. A small **museum** (Tues–Sun 8–11am & 11.30–4pm) dedicated to Master Pavol stands opposite the church on the eastern side of the square. South of the church is the **town hall** or *radnica* (Tues–Sun 9am–5pm), built in a sturdy Renaissance style. On the first floor, there's a museum on the Spiš region, and some fine examples of Spiš handicrafts on the top floor. The third building in the centre of the square is the oddly squat **Lutheran Church**, built in an uncompromisingly Neoclassical style.

You can get to Levoča by train from Poprad, but you must change at Spišská Nová Ves. The **train** and **bus stations** are southeast of the old town. Outside the annual pilgrimage in early

July, **accommodation** shouldn't be hard to find; the helpful **tourist office** (Mon Fri 10am–noon & 1–4.30pm, Sat & Sun 9am–4.45pm) in the northwest corner of the square can book private rooms. Alternatively, there's the *Penzion pri Košickej bráne* (☎0966/451 2879; ①) and *Arkada* (☎0966/4512 372; ③), both on the main square; the **campsite** (open all year) is a three-kilometre walk north of Levoča. Authentic Slovak pub **food** can be had from *U Janusa*, Klástorská 22, and from *U trí apoštolov*, above a butcher's, on the east side of the main square, while more upmarket fare can be sampled at the *Restaurácia Biela Pani* on the south side. There's also a lunchtime-only veggie restaurant, *Vegeterián*, at Uholná 3 (closed Sat & Sun), northwest of the main square.

Spišský hrad

The road east from Levoča takes you to the edge of Spiš territory, clearly defined by the Branisko ridge which blocks the way to Prešov. Even if you're not going any further east, you should at least take the bus as far as **SPIŠSKÉ PODHRADIE**, for arguably the most spectacular sight in the whole country – the **Spišský hrad** (May–Oct Tues–Sun 9am–6pm). This pile of chalk-white ruins, strung out on a bleak green hill, is irresistibly photogenic and finds its way into almost every tourist hand-out in the country. The ruins themselves don't quite live up to expectations, though the view from the top is pretty good. The *Penzíon Podzámok* at Podzámoková 28 (☎0966/811 755; ②) has superb views up to the castle.

Prešov

Capital of the Slovak Šariš region and cultural centre for the Rusyn minority, **PREŠOV** has a present-day split personality indicative of its long and chequered ethnic history. Over the last few years it has been treated to a wonderful face-lift, and although there's not much of interest beyond its main square, it's a refreshingly youthful and vibrant town, partly due to its university.

The lozenge-shaped main square, **Hlavná ulica**, is flanked by creamy, pastel-coloured, almost edible eighteenth-century facades. At the square's southern tip is the **Greek-Catholic Cathedral**, a wonderful Rococo affair with a fabulously huge iconostasis. Further along, on the same side of the square, is Prešov's **town hall** or *radnica*, from whose unsuitably small balcony Béla Kun's Hungarian Red Army declared the short-lived Slovak Socialist Republic in 1919. Further north along the square, the **town museum**, situated in the dog-tooth-gabled Rákociho dom at no. 86 (Tues–Fri 8am–noon, 12.30–4pm, Sat & Sun 11am–3pm), offers a thorough retelling of the the history of the Šariš region.

Prešov's Catholic and Protestant churches vie with each other at the widest point of the square. The fourteenth-century Catholic church of **sv Mikuláš** has the edge, not least for its modern Moravian stained-glass windows and its sumptuous Baroque altarpiece. Behind sv Mikulás, the much plainer **Lutheran Church**, built in the mid-seventeenth century, bears witness to the strength of religious reformism in the outer reaches of Hungary at a time when the rest of the Habsburgs' lands were suffering the full force of the Counter-Reformation.

Lastly, the town's ornate turn-of-the-century **synagogue** in the northwest corner of the old town – access from Svermova – has been turned into a small **museum of Judaica** (Múzeum Expozícia Judaík; Tues & Wed 11am–4pm, Thurs 3–6pm, Fri 10am–1pm, Sun 1–5pm) with an exhibition on Judaism and Prešov's Jews, 6000 of whom perished in the Holocaust.

The **bus** and **train stations** are situated opposite one another about 1km south of the main square; any of the buses and trolleybuses which stop outside will take you into town. The best budget **accommodation** is to be had at the *Sen*, Vajanského 65 (☎091/733 170; ①), two blocks east of the main square; otherwise there's the *Átrium* (☎091/733 952; ④), west of the main square at Floriánova 4, and the large *Šariš* (☎091/716 351; ③), immediately north of the main square on Sabinovská. The **restaurant** in the *Átrium* is better than average, as is the *Slovenská reštaurácia*, on the main square (closed Sun).

Košice

Slovak towns often never amount to much more than their one long main square, and even KOŠICE, Slovakia's second largest city, is no exception. Rather like Bratislava, Košice was, until relatively recently, a modest little town on the edge of the Hungarian plain. Then, in the 1950s, the communists established a giant steel works on the outskirts of the city. Forty years on, it has a population of over 250,000, a number of worthwhile museums, the best cathedral in the republic, and a lively cosmopolitanism that can be quite reassuring after a week or so in the Slovak back of beyond. Just 21km north of the Hungarian border, Košice also acts as a magnet for the Hungarian community – to whom the city is known as *Kassa* – and the terminally underemployed Romanies of the surrounding region, lending it a diversity and vibrancy absent from small-town Slovakia.

The old town

Almost everything of interest is situated on Košice's long pedestrianized main square, which is called **Hlavná ulica** at its northern and southern extremities, **Hlavné námestie** to the north of the cathedral, and **Námestie slobody**, to the south of the cathedral. Lined with handsome Baroque and Neoclassical palaces, it's dominated by the city's unorthodox Gothic **Cathedral**, its charcoal-coloured stone recently sandblasted back to its original honeyed hue. Begun around 1390, it's an unusual building from the outside, with striped roof tiles and two contorted towers. Inside, Gothic furnishings add an impressive touch to an otherwise plain nave, the main gilded altar depicting scenes from the life of the cathedral's patron, Saint Elizabeth.

On the busy north side of the cathedral, the fourteenth-century **Urbanova veža** (Tues–Sat 9am–5pm, Sun 9am–1pm), which stands on its own set of mini-arcades, has recently been converted into an upmarket café. The public park and fountains beyond are a favourite spot for hanging out and make an appropriately graceful approach to the city's grand Austro-Hungarian **theatre**.

The peculiar **Vojtecha Löfflera Museum** (Tues–Sat 10am–6pm, Sun 1–5pm), on Alžbetina, west off the main square, features the work and private collections of Košice's most prominent communist-sanctioned sculptor. Another unusual attraction is the **Mikluš Prison** (Miklušova väznica; Tues–Sat 9am–5pm, Sun 9am–1pm), east off the square down Univerzitna, whose original dimly lit dungeons and claustrophobic cells graphically transport you into its murky history as the city prison. At the northern tip of the main square, námestie Maratónu mieru is flanked to the east and west by the bulky nineteenth-century **Východoslovenské múzeum** (Tues–Sat 9am–5pm, Sun 10am–1pm). The western building is worth visiting for its basement collection of fifteenth- to seventeenth-century **gold coins** – 2920 in all – minted at Kremnica but stashed away by city burghers and discovered by accident in 1935. Hidden round the back of the museum is a wooden Greek-Catholic Church, brought here from Carpatho-Ruthenia (now in Ukrainian territory).

Practicalities

The **train** and **bus stations** are opposite each other, ten minutes' walk east of the old town. There are two **tourist offices**, one at Hlavná 8 on the main square (Mon–Fri 8am–5pm, Sat & Sun 9am–1pm), which also has an **email** centre (20Sk for 15min), and a second, small kiosk round the corner in the Dargov Mall (Mon–Fri 10am–noon & 1–6pm, Sat 9am–1pm). Both can help with finding **accommodation** including private rooms. The best budget accommodation is provided by the *Hotel Metropole* at Šturova 32, (✆095/6255948; ①), just 100m west of the southern tip of the square. Alternatively, check out the budget *Hotel Kohal* (✆095/316 65 098; ①), by the Ferrocentrum tram stop; catch tram #6 from the southern end of the main square. More upmarket accommodation is provided by the welcoming *Penzión pri radnici*, Bacíkova 18 (✆095/6228 601; ④). The nearest **campsite** (open all year) is 5km south of the city centre and also rents out bungalows; take tram #1 or #4, or bus #22 or #52, from the *Slovan* to the flyover, then get off and walk the remaining 500m west along Alejová, the road to Rožmava.

If you're looking for somewhere to eat, there's *Bakchus*, a popular pub on the west side of the main square; a couple of others worth crawling to are *U dominikánov*, on Mäsiarska, and the lively *Velkopopovická piváreň*, two blocks west of the old town on námestie L. Novomestského; take Postová to the end, turn right up Kuzmányho, then left down Magurská. *Pizza Venezia*, at Mlynská 20 en route from the stations, is a good bet, as is *Ajvega*, Orlia 10, one block east of the main square, a bizarre place doing soya versions of standard Slovak dishes. The *bageteria* on the west side of the square serves healthy, if overpriced snacks. Košice's **nightlife**, such as it is, revolves around the main square and the few streets on either side. The city's Philharmonic Orchestra plays regular **concerts** at the *Dom umenia* on Ždanovova and inside the cathedral itself, and the occasional opera is still performed at the main theatre. Košice has a **Hungarian theatre**, Thália, on Mojmírova, and also boasts Slovakia's one and only **Romany theatre**, Romathan, which puts on a whole range of events from concerts to plays.

travel details

Trains

Bratislava to: Banská Bystrica (2 daily; 4hr); Poprad-Tatry (9 daily; 4–5hr); Prešov (1 daily; 7hr); Košice (9 daily; 5hr–6hr 15min).

Poprad-Tatry to: Starý Smokovec (hourly; 45min); Kežmarok (12 daily; 30min); Prešov (2 daily; 1hr 30min); Košice (12 daily; 1hr 30min).

Buses

Levoča to: Spiyské Podhradie (up to 15 daily; 30min).

Poprad to: Levoča (up to 13 daily; 30–50min); Spiyské Podhradie (up to 12 daily; 30min); Prešov (up to 15 daily; 2hr).

CHAPTER 26

SLOVENIA

Introduction

The northernmost republic of what was once Yugoslavia, **Slovenia** currently appears the most stable, prosperous and welcoming of all Europe's erstwhile communist countries. It was always the richest and most Westernized of the Yugoslav federation, and apart from the Ten-Day War which brought it independence in 1991, it has avoided the strife which has plagued the republics to the south. For centuries, Slovenia was administered by German-speaking overlords and was, until 1918, part of the Austro-Hungarian empire. The Slovenes absorbed the culture of their captors during this period while managing to retain a strong sense of ethnic identity through the Slav-rooted Slovene language, a close relation of Czech, Serbo-Croat and Slovak.

Slovenia's landscape is as varied as it is beautiful: along the Austrian border the **Julian Alps** provide stunning mountain scenery, most accessibly at **Lake Bled** and **Lake Bohinj**; further south, the brittle karst scenery is riddled with spectacular caves like those at **Postojna**. Slovenia's capital, **Ljubljana**, is easily the best of the cities, a vital, youthful place, manageably small and cluttered with Baroque and Habsburg buildings, while the short stretch of Slovenian **coast**, along the northern edge of the Istrian peninsula, is punctuated by a couple of towns that were among the most attractive resorts of the former Yugoslavia – **Piran** and **Portoro** – not to mention the port of **Koper**, with its appealingly ancient centre.

Information and maps

The larger towns and well-touristed places usually have a **tourist information centre** run by the local authority, doling out information and local maps, and usually acting as an agency for private rooms. Elsewhere, travel agencies (Globtour, Alpetour, Generaltourist, Slovenijaturist and Kompas are the biggest-selling chains) can be a useful source of information, although they understandably concentrate on selling you tours and changing your money. English is spoken pretty much everywhere.

There's a good new 1:300,000 **map** of Slovenia published by Freytag & Berndt. Excellent small-scale hiking maps are published by the Slovene Alpine Association (Planinska zveza Slovenije; ☎061/312-553) and are widely available in bookshops in Slovenia.

Money and banks

Slovenia's unit of **currency** is the tolar, which is divided into 100 (virtually worthless) stotini. Coins come in denominations of 50 stotini and 1, 2 and 5 tolars; and there are notes of 10, 20, 50, 100, 200, 500, 1000, 5000 and 10,000 tolars. Prices are usually followed by the initials SIT. The exchange rate is currently approximately 280SIT to £1, and 180SIT to $1.

Banks (*banka*) are generally open Mon–Fri 8.30am–12.30pm & 2–4pm and Sat 8.30am–11pm. Money can also be changed in tourist offices, post offices, travel agencies and exchange bureaux (*menjalnica*), all of which have more flexible hours. Travellers' cheques and credit cards are widely accepted; and you can use credit cards to get cash advances from ATMs and in the bigger banks.

Prices for accommodation and tours are sometimes given in Deutschmarks – although payment is usually made in tolars.

Communications

Most **post offices** (*pošta* or PTT) are open Mon–Fri 8am–6pm and Sat 8am–noon. In big towns and resorts, some offices are open for a few hours on Sunday too. **Stamps** (*znamke*) can also be bought at newsstands.

Public **phone** boxes use cards (*telekartice*), which you can pick up from post offices or newspaper kiosks. When making long-distance and international calls it's usually easier to go to the post office, where you're assigned to a cabin and given the bill afterwards.

Getting around

Traversing Slovenia by any kind of public transport is relatively easy and usually very scenic. Generally speaking, trains provide the fastest means of travelling on the main routes linking the capital with Maribor and Koper, or with Austria and Italy. Everywhere else, buses are far more convenient.

■ Trains and buses

Slovene railways (Slovenske železnice) run a smooth and efficient service. **Trains** (*vlaki*) are divided into *potniški* (slow ones which stop at every halt) and *IC* (intercity trains which are faster and slightly more expensive). Some of the latter, colloquially known as *zeleni vlaki* (green trains), are designated on timetables by the initials ICZV, and are express services on which prior seat reservations (*rezervacije*) are obligatory. Timetable leaflets (*vozni red*) are sometimes available; otherwise you'll have to decipher the boards displayed on station platforms – *odhodi* are departures, *prihodi* arrivals. Both Eurail and InterRail are valid.

Slovenia's **bus** network consists of an array of small local companies, but their services are well co-ordinated. Big towns such as Ljubljana, Maribor and Koper have big bus stations with computerized booking facilities where you can buy your tickets hours (if not days) in advance – recommended if you're travelling between Ljubljana and the coast at the height of summer. Elsewhere, simply pile onto the bus and pay the driver or conductor. You'll be charged extra for cumbersome items of baggage, which must be stored in the hold.

■ Driving and hitching

The road system is both comprehensive and of reasonable quality. Stretches of the main Ljubljana–Koper, Ljubljana–Maribor and Ljubljana–Jesenice routes are classed as motorways (*autoceste*) and large stretches of them have been converted to dual carriageway (tolls are levied on these routes); elsewhere main roads soon get clogged up with summer traffic. **Speed limits** on Slovene roads are 50kph in built-up areas, 80kph on normal roads, 100kph on highways and 130kph on motorways. If you break down, the Slovene Automobile Club (AMZS) has a 24hr emergency service (☎987). **Car rental** charges are about £75/$120 a day for a Renault or Golf-type car with unlimited mileage.

Hitching is pretty common on the main Ljubljana–Maribor, Ljubljana–Koper and Bled–Bohinj routes, although you should be prepared to wait a long time for a lift, and remember that hitching is forbidden on anything classified as a motorway (recognizable by the green road signs). Elsewhere in the country, prospects for hitching are fairly bad.

Accommodation

While tourist **accommodation** is universally clean and good quality, it doesn't come much cheaper than in neighbouring Italy or Austria unless you opt for a private room.

■ Hotels, guesthouses and private rooms

Apart from a couple of turn-of-the-century establishments in Ljubljana, Slovene **hotels** tend to be high-rise concrete affairs providing modern comforts but little atmosphere. They are classified according to the international five-star system, with three-star places (usually offering rooms with en-suite facilities and TV) making up the bulk of the hotel stock. Cheaper two-star places are occasionally available, but anything lower than this is very rare. Expect to pay £30/$48 a double upwards for two-star hotels, £40/$64 a double upwards for three-star. In recent years there's been a growth in the number of family-run **pensions** in rural Slovenia, especially in the alpine regions, offering the same facilities as hotels (and rated according to the same star system), but usually with a cosier atmosphere and a lower price. Outside alpine resorts, however, pensions tend to be well away from town centres and are therefore hard to find unless you have your own transport.

Private rooms (*zasebne sobe*) are available throughout Slovenia, with bookings administered by tourist information centres in places like Ljubljana, or by travel agents like Slovenijatourist or Kompas elsewhere. Private rooms are pretty good value at about £12–18/$19–29 a double, although stays of three nights or under are invariably subject to a thirty percent surcharge. The more expensive private rooms will have en-suite bathrooms, perhaps even a TV. Self-catering **apartments** (*apartmaji*) are also plentiful in the mountains and on the coast, with per-person rates working out the same as, or sometimes cheaper than, private rooms if there are more than two people travelling together.

■ Hostels and campsites

Youth **hostels** are thin on the ground in Slovenia, although there's a modest scattering of student hostels (*dijaški dom*) which open their doors to non-students over the summer and at weekends at other times of year. Beds in all hostels are in short supply,

---

ACCOMMODATION PRICE CODES

Throughout this guide, accommodation is priced on a scale of ① to ⑨, the number indicating the lowest price per night a single person could expect to pay in that establishment in high season. With hostels this is the nightly rate per person; with hotels, the price is arrived at by dividing the cost of the cheapest double room by two. The prices indicated by the codes are as follows:

① under £5 / $8	④ £15–20 / $24–32	⑦ £30–35 / $48–56
② £5–10 / $8–16	⑤ £20–25 / $32–40	⑧ £35–40 / $56–64
③ £10–15 / $16–24	⑥ £25–30 / $40–48	⑨ £40 / $64 and over

and advance booking is advised. Expect to pay about £8–12/$13–19 per person per night.

Campsites are plentiful in the mountains and on the coast and tend to be large-scale, well-organized affairs with plentiful facilities, restaurants and shops. Two people travelling with a tent can expect to pay £8–10/$13–16; add another £2/$3 for a vehicle. Camping rough without permission is punishable by a spot fine.

Serious hikers planning an assault on the peaks of Slovenia's Julian Alps could make use of **mountain huts** (*planinske koče*). The ones on the way up Mount Triglav are little less than hotels; elsewhere they are much more basic. You'll need to book in advance or arrive early. Details can be obtained from the Planinska zveza Slovenije, Dvor'akova 9, Ljubljana (☎061/312-553), or from tourist information centres once you arrive.

Food and drink

Slovene cuisine draws on Austrian, Italian and Balkan influences. There's a native Slovene tradition, too, based on age-old peasant recipes, although this is gradually losing out as restaurants and cafés become increasingly international.

■ Food

Slovenia's well-stocked supermarkets and *delikatesa* are good places to stock up on **sandwich and picnic** ingredients, like local cheese (*sir*) and salami (*salama*). Buy fresh fruit and vegetables (*sadje in zelenjava*) from outdoor markets or roadside stalls, and bread (*kruh*) from a *pekarna* (bakery).

For **breakfast and quick snacks**, *okrepčevalnice* (snack bars) and street kiosks dole out *burek*, a flaky pastry filled with cheese (*sirov burek*) or meat (*burek z mesom*). Sausages (*klobase*) come in various forms, most commonly hot dogs, *hrenovke* (Slovene frankfurters), or *kranjska klobasa* (big spicy sausages of local provenance).

Menus in a Slovene *restavracija* (restaurant) or *gostilna* (inn) are dominated by roast meats (*pečenka*) and schnitzels (*zrezek*), mostly pork (*svinjina*) and veal (*teletina*). The Slovenes are unsqueamish about offal: liver (*jetra*) and grilled or fried brains (*možgani*) are popular standbys in cheaper restaurants. Goulash (*golaž*) is found almost everywhere; *segedin* is goulash with lashings of sauerkraut. Two traditional Slovene dishes are *žlikrofi*, ravioli filled with potato, onion and bacon; and *žganci*, once the staple diet of rural Slovenes, a buckwheat or maize porridge often served with sauerkraut. *Ocvrti sir* (cheese fried in

breadcrumbs) is one of the few dishes that will appease **vegetarians**. On the coast you'll find plenty of fish (*riba*), mussels (*školjke*) and squid (*kalamari*). Italian pasta dishes appear on most restaurant menus, and no Slovene high street is without at least one pizzeria.

Typical **desserts** include several solid central European favourites: strudel, filled with apple or rhubarb; *štruklji*, dumplings with fruit filling; *potica*, a doughy roll filled with nuts and honey; and *prekmurska gibanica*, a delicious local cheesecake.

■ Drink

Daytime drinking takes place in small café/bars, or in a *kavarna*, where a range of cakes, pastries and ice cream is usually on offer. Coffee (*kava*) is usually served black unless specified otherwise – ask for *mleko* (milk) or *smetana* (cream) – and often drunk alongside a glass of mineral water (*mineralna voda*). Tea (*čaj*) is usually served black. Familiar nonalcoholic drinks (*brezalkoholne pijače*) such as Coca-Cola, Pepsi and Sprite are all fairly ubiquitous.

Evening drinking usually goes on in small European-style bars or the more traditional *pivnica* (beer hall) or *vinarna* (wine cellar). Slovene beer (*pivo*) is of the Pilsner type and is usually excellent (*Laško Zlatorog* is regarded as the best), although most breweries also produce *temno pivo* (literally "dark beer"), a Guinness-like stout. The local wine (*vino*) is either *črno* (red) or *belo* (white) and has an international reputation: dry whites like *Lazki rizling* and *Ljutomerčan* are regularly found on Western supermarket shelves; the less common and more refined *Šipon* and *Haložan* are worth seeking out. Best of the reds are the light *Cviček* and the dark, dry *Teran*. Favourite aperitifs include *slivovka* (plum brandy), *vilijemovka* (pear brandy), the fiery *sadjevec*, a brandy made from various fruits, and the gin-like juniper-based *brinovec*.

Opening hours and holidays

Most **shops** open Mon–Fri 9am–7pm and Sat 9am–1pm, although shops outside major centres may take lengthy lunch breaks. **Museum** times differ from place to place, but they're usually closed on Mon.

All shops and banks will be closed on the following **public holidays**: Jan 1 and 2; Feb 8 (Day of Slovene Culture); Easter Monday; April 27 (Resistance Day); May 1 and 2; June 25 (Day of Slovene Statehood); Aug 15 (Assumption); Oct 31 (Reformation Day); Nov 1 (All Saints'); and Dec 25 & 26.

Emergencies

Slovenia's crime rate is low and you're unlikely to have much contact with Slovene **police** (*policija*); if you do, they're generally easy-going and helpful, but unlikely to speak English. As far as health is concerned, citizens of the EU are entitled to free health care. **Pharmacies** (*lekarna*) tend to follow normal shopping hours, and a rota system covers night-time and weekend opening; details are posted in the window of each pharmacy.

EMERGENCY NUMBERS

Police ☎113; Ambulance ☎112; Fire ☎112.

LJUBLJANA AND AROUND

LJUBLJANA curls under its castle-topped hill, an old centre marooned in the shapeless modernity that stretches out across the plain, a vital and self-consciously growing capital. At first glance it seems Austrian, a few strands of Vienna pulled out of place, typically exuberant and refined; but really Ljubljana is Slovenian through and through, with outside influences absorbed and tinkered with over the years. The city's sights are only part of the picture; first and foremost Ljubljana is a place to meet people and to get involved in the nightlife – the buildings just provide the backdrop.

Arrival, information and city transport

Your likely point of arrival (and drop-off point for buses from Brnik airport, 23km north of the city), is the main **train and bus station**, on Trg Osvobodilne Fronte, ten minutes' walk north of the centre. There are branches of the **Tourist Information Office** (TIC) at the train station (daily: June–Sept 8am–9pm; Oct–May 10am–6pm; ☎061/133-9475) and in the old town on Stritarjeva next to the Triple Bridge (Mon–Fri 8am–7pm, Sat 9am–5pm; ☎061/306-1215). Both offices hand out maps and book rooms. Ljubljana's **buses** are cheap, frequent and usually overcrowded. You can pay in cash by depositing notes in a box next to the driver (a single journey currently costs a flat fare of 130SIT) or by using the slightly cheaper tokens (*žeton*; 80SIT) bought in advance from most newspaper kiosks.

Accommodation

The TIC has a limited stock of central **private rooms** (③), and will also book rooms in **student hostels** (open July & Aug only; ②–③). The main venue for these is usually the *Študentsko Naselje* (Student Village) at Cesta 27 Aprila 31 (☎061/223-811; bus #14 or a twenty-minute walk), in a suburb to the west of town. It's important that you check at the TIC first, as venues change regularly. Inexpensive hotels are in short supply, although there's a serviceable **youth hostel**, *Dijaški Dom Tabor*, at Vidovdanska 7 (☎061/316-069; ②; daily in summer, rest of the year weekends only), about 1km southeast of the train station and well signposted.

Five kilometres north of the centre, the **campsite** at Ježica (☎061/168-3913; May–Sept) can be reached by taking bus #8 north along Dunajska Cesta. It's situated in a pleasant recreation area and has a few bungalows (③).

Hotels

Bellevue, Pod Gozdom 12 (☎061/133-4049). Very small, and with few amenities, but occupying an attractive old building above Tivoli Park with a breathtaking view across Ljubljana. ③.

Ilirija, Trg Prekomorskih Brigad 4 (☎061/159-3337). An uninspiring but acceptable modern hotel 2.5km northwest of the city centre off Celovška Cesta. ⑤.

Lipa, Celovška 264 (☎061/159-2850). Comfortable and affordable pension, but not ideally located: it's in a medium-rise building 5km northwest of the centre, beside a busy main road. Buses #1, #15, #16 from the centre. ④.

Pri Mraku, Rimska 4 (☎061/121-9651). Smallish downtown pension, with recently renovated en-suite rooms. ⑤.

Park, Tabor 9 (☎061/133-1306). Cheapest of the central hotels, a slightly shabby medium-rise building a few blocks east of the station. Some rooms with en-suite facilities (④), some without (③).

Turist, Dalmatinova 15 (☎061/132-2343). Bland but comfortable downtown hotel with en-suite rooms and an ideal location. ⑥.

The City

Ljubljana's main point of reference is **Slovenska Cesta**, a busy north–south thoroughfare that slices the city down the middle. Most of the sights are within easy walking distance from

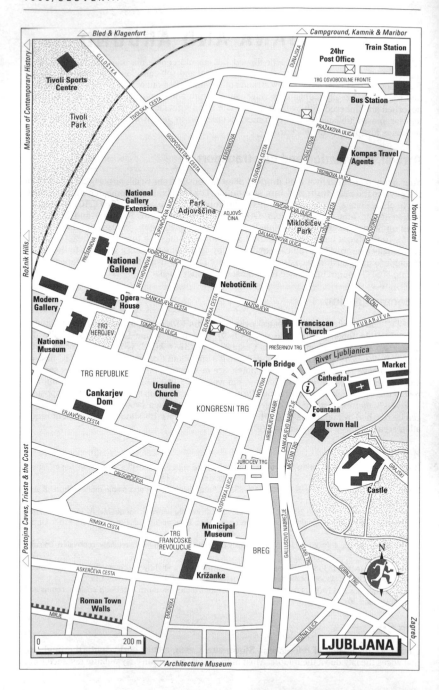

here, with the **Old Town** straddling the River Ljubljanica to the south and east with its castle and cathedral, and the nineteenth-century quarter to the west, where the principal museums and galleries are to be found.

The Old Town

From the bus and train stations, head south down Miklošičeva for ten minutes and you're on **Prešernov Trg**, the hub around which everything in Ljubljana's **Old Town** revolves. Overlooking all, the seventeenth-century **Franciscan Church** (daily 6.45am–12.30pm & 3–8pm) blushes a sandy red above the bustling square and the River Ljubljanica: in its tired-feeling interior the old wall paintings look like faded photographs, and even Francesco Robba's Baroque high altar seems a little weary. Robba, an Italian architect and sculptor, was brought in to remodel the city in its eighteenth-century heyday.

Across the Tromostovje, or Triple Bridge, a **fountain**, also by Robba, symbolizes the meeting of the rivers Sava, Krka and Ljubljanica (he stole the idea from Bernini's fountain in Rome), and the whole stretch down from Prešernov Trg west of the river is decaying Baroque grandeur. East of the river along Gallusovo Nabrežje most of the houses are ramshackle and medieval, occasionally slicked up as clothes shops and stores but mainly high, dark and crumbling – memories of an earlier, less fanciful past.

Opposite Robba's fountain is the **Town Hall** (Magistrat) on Mestni Trg – an undistinguished Baroque building around a courtyard. A little east of here **St Nicholas' Cathedral** (Stolna Cerkev Sv Nikolaja) on Ciril-Metodov Trg is the most sumptuous and overblown of Ljubljana's Baroque statements, all whimsical ostentation and elaborate embellishment, its sheer size inducing hushed reverence as you enter. Designed by Andrea Pozzo (also architect of Dubrovnik's Jesuit Church), this is the best preserved of the city's ecclesiastical buildings. Just to the west of the cathedral buildings you can't fail to miss the **general market** (Mon–Sat) on Vodnikov Trg, a brash free-for-all along the river side, where everyone competes to sell their particular produce.

Opposite the market, Študentska winds up the thickly wooded hillside to the **Castle**, visible from all over town and currently being restored to the glory it had when protecting Ljubljana's defensive position in earlier times – what's left today dates mainly from a sixteenth-century rebuilding. Climb the clock tower (10am–dusk; 300SIT) for a wide and superlative view of the Old Town crowded below, the urban sprawl of high-rises beyond and the Kamniški Alps to the north. The best time to visit is towards sunset, when the haze across the plains burns red and gold, suffusing the town in luxurious light.

Central Ljubljana and beyond

Back on the western side of the river, the broad slash of **Slovenska Cesta** forms the commercial heart of Ljubljana. Dominated by nineteenth- and twentieth-century shops and offices, it's a place to do business rather than sightsee – save perhaps for its only real landmark, **Nebotičnik**: a gaudily painted twelve-storey response to the American Art Deco skyscrapers of the 1930s.

Continuing south along Slovenska Cesta, the park-like expanse of Kongresni Trg slopes away from the early-eighteenth-century **Ursuline Church** (Ursulinska Cerkev), whose looming Baroque coffee-cake exterior is one of the city's most imposing: should you manage to gain entry there's another florid high altar by Robba. Lower down, by the side of the main university building, Vegova Ulica leads southwards from Kongresni Trg towards Trg Francoske Revolucije, passing on the way the chequered pink, green and grey brickwork of the University Library. This was designed in the late 1930s by **Jože Plečnik**, the architect who more than any other determined the appearance of present-day Ljubljana. The whole atmosphere around the River Ljubljanica, including the river banks and several bridges, is the result of rebuilding work by Plečnik. His legacy, in the shape of Neoclassical columns, pillars and miniature brick pyramids scattered all over the city, is impossible to avoid.

One such oddity is the **Illyrian Monument** on Trg Francoske Revolucije, erected in 1930 in belated recognition of Napoléon's short-lived attempt to create a fiefdom of the same name centred on Ljubljana. Virtually next door is the seventeenth-century monastery complex of

Križanke: originally the seat of a thirteenth-century order of Teutonic Knights, its delightful colonnaded courtyard was restored by Plečnik to form a permanent venue for the Ljubljana Summer Festival. Across Gosposka, at no. 15, a seventeenth-century palace contains the **Municipal Museum** (Tues & Thurs 9am–noon & 4–6pm, Sun 9am–noon; 300SIT), a formerly rather dull affair which is currently being transformed into a more visitor-friendly, multimedia experience.

Beyond Trg Francoske Revolucije there's little of importance to see, except for a remaining stretch of the town's **Roman Walls** (again rearranged by Plečnik) on Mirje, and, a little further on, Plečnik's old house – now an **Architectural Museum** (Tues & Thurs 10am–2pm; 600SIT) at Karunova 4, where you can wander around Plečnik's ascetic living quarters.

West of Slovenska: museums and Tivoli Park

West of Slovenska, Cankarjeva heads down towards a neatly ordered corner of town that contains the city's most important **museums**. The **National Museum** (Narodni muzej; Tues–Sun 10am–6pm, Thurs until 8pm; 400SIT) at Trg Herojev 1 contains numerous dim halls of archeological objects, most famous of which is the **Vače Situla**, a locally found Iron Age cauldron decorated with scenes of ritual feasting. The museum's natural history section is notable only for having the one complete mammoth skeleton found in Europe. The **National Gallery** (Tues–Sun 10am–6pm; 500SIT) at Cankarjeva 20 is housed in the former Narodni Dom, built in the 1890s to accommodate Slovene cultural institutions in defiance of the Habsburgs. The gallery is rich in local medieval Gothic work, although most visitors gravitate towards the halls devoted to the Slovene Impressionists Rihard Jakopič, Ivan Grohar, Matija Jama and Matej Sternen. Their movement had considerable importance for the development of the Slovene national consciousness, extolling the virtues of rural Slovene peasantry and elevating them to the status of a subject fit for art. There's more Gothic stuff, as well as high-profile temporary exhibitions, in a new **extension** to the gallery (same times) one block to the north.

Back on the Cankarjeva, the **Modern Gallery** at no. 15 (Tues–Sat 10am–6pm, Sun 10am–1pm; 300SIT) carries on where the National Gallery left off, showing how the Slovene Impressionists developed more experimental styles in the early years of this century. The rest of the collection is pretty uninspiring save for interwar works by the Kralj brothers and paintings from the 1980s by Irwin – a group of artists whose mixing of Slovene folkloric imagery with totalitarian symbols earned them considerable notoriety.

Beyond the art galleries, Cankarjeva leads you past an unobtrusive twentieth-century Serbian Orthodox church to **Tivoli Park**, an expanse of lawns and tree-lined walkways backed by dense woodland. Most of Ljubljana's recreational and sporting facilities can be found in the sports centre at the northern end of the park. A villa above the centre contains the most enjoyable of Ljubljana's museums, the **Museum of Contemporary History** (Tues–Sun 10am–6pm; 600SIT) with dioramas, imaginative lighting, video screens and period music combining to produce an evocative journey through twentieth-century Slovene history.

To the south and west of the park, a succession of pathways winds up into the **Rožnik Hills** – a beautiful, tranquil region of woodland no more than ten minutes from the city centre. There are a number of tracks leading to the not-too-distant summit of Cankarjev Vrh, where you'll find the **Rožnik Inn**, site of a memorial room dedicated to the turn-of-the-century novelist **Ivan Cankar** (summer only 10am–2pm) who died here after one of his customary bouts of heavy drinking. The area comes to life on the night of April 30/May 1, when bonfires are lit near the summit and thousands of locals assemble for a mass outdoor party.

Eating

As befits its sophisticated, cosmopolitan image, Ljubljana is able to boast a tight concentration of **restaurants**, most of which offer excellent value for money. There is a handful of good fish restaurants and many offering traditional Slovene variations, and because of Ljubljana's proximity to Italy, Austria, Hungary and the Adriatic coast, the range is impressive.

Snacks and lunches

For **snacks**, the numerous *burek* kiosks near the station, along with the stands you'll come across throughout town which sell hot dogs and the local *gorenjska* sausages, are the quickest and cheapest choice for on-your-feet eating. You should also try the numerous stalls selling **fish** snacks in the riverside arcade beside the market. The quality of Ljubljana's **delicatessens** makes them a good option for putting together picnics from locally produced cheeses, sausages and hams, washed down with a bottle of decent Slovene wine.

Restaurants

Casa del Papa, Celovška 34a (☎061/134-3158). International food in rooms decorated on an Ernest Hemingway theme (there's a Key West room, a Cuba room and so on). Booking advised.

Čerin, Trubarjeva 57. Chic pizzeria with salad bar and good-value lunchtime menus.

Figovec, Gosposvetska 1. Charmingly old-fashioned downtown restaurant specializing in pony steaks (sic), horsemeat goulash, and a wide range of traditional Slovene standards as well.

Lovec, Trg Mladinskih Delovnih Brigad 1. One of the more characterful places in which to eat medium-priced Slovene standards, five minutes' west of Trg francoske revolucije. Good range of pizzas too.

Meson don Felipe, Streliska 22. Lively tapas bar and restaurant ten minutes east of the cathedral.

Pizza Napoli, Prečna 1. Enormous, reasonably authentic and very cheap pizzas in a lively meeting place.

Pizzeria Foculus, Gregoraiaeva 3. A good range of affordable pizzas in lively surroundings, including several good vegetarian options and a good salad buffet.

Rio, Slovenska 28. Massive beer garden in a cobbled courtyard serving inexpensive grills and stews.

Šestica, Slovenska 38. Traditional place on the main street with elegant vine-trellised interior. Slovene, meat-heavy menu. Closed Sun.

Štajerski Hram, corner of Wolfova and Kongresni Trg. Straightforward Slovene dishes, and some cheap set menus at lunchtimes.

Vinoteka, Dunajska 18. Good for Slovene specialities and fresh fish. Located beneath a circular pavilion in the Ljubljana fair grounds. Excellent wine list. Closed Sun.

Drinking and nightlife

On summer evenings the cafés and bars of Ljubljana's Old Town spill out onto the streets with the hectic atmosphere of a mass open-air bar. A wander up and down the banks of the River Ljubljanica and along Stari Trg and Mestni Trg will yield an interesting locale every fifty yards or so.

Some bars and clubs double up as venues for home-grown rock bands and occasional foreign groups. Otherwise, the bigger acts play in the main hall of the Tivoli sports centre in Tivoli Park. Other gig venues are KUD France Preseren at Karunova 14, the Cankarjev Dom Congress Centre on Trg Republike, or the open-air stage at Križanke, Trg Francoske Revolucije. The free English-language *Ljubljana Life* magazine, available from the tourist office, has excellent – indeed essential – bar and club listings.

Cafés and bars

Čajna hiša pod velbom, Stari Trg 7. Bijou café serving all kinds of tea, alongside excellent sandwiches and cakes.

Club Podhod, Plečnikov podhod (pedestrian subway just off Kongresni Trg). Internet café and meeting place usually open daily 8am–2am for drinking, Mon–Sat 8am–8pm for the computers.

Cutty Sark, courtyard off Wolfova. A lively pub-style venue with a wide range of beers, usually busy at weekends.

Gajo Jazz Club, Beethovnova 8. Refined late-night café with regular live jazz.

Hound Dog, *Hotel Ilirija*, Trg Prekomorskih Brigad. Animated basement bar with regular live (rock) music. A fifteen-minute walk northeast of the centre.

Kratochwill, Kolodvorska 14. Bar with a Czech beer-hall atmosphere which brews its own ale. Try the *mešano pivo* (a mixture of stout and lager).

Maček, corner of Krojačka and Cankarjevo nabrežje. Stylish café with large outdoor terrace. Currently the place to be seen on Ljubljana's riverfront.

Nostalgia, Stari Trg 9. Café with 1950s décor and a wide range of tasty sandwiches.

Orto Bar, Bolgarska 3. Stylish media haunt east of the train station with decor reminiscent of the interior of a submarine. Frequent live-rock evenings.

Patrick's, Prečna. Cosy basement pub with Irish decor and well-kept beers.

Petit Café, Trg Francoske revolucije. Good place for a coffee and croissant as well as for an evening drinking session.

Ragamuffin, Krojaška 4. In an alleyway just behind *Maček* (see above). Small, reggae-orientated café-bar, good for a daytime chill-out or more boisterous evening drink.

Sax Pub, Eiprova. Gaudily decorated youth hangout of many years' standing, occupying a leafy riverside site.

True-bar, Trubarjeva 23. Trendy, youthful hangout with loud hip-hop and techno music.

Clubs and discos

Central, Dalmatinova 15. Mainstream techno and retro club in the centre of town.

Eldorado, Nazorjeva 4. Commercial disco with mainstream techno at weekends and themed retro nights on weekdays.

K4, Kersinikova 4. Mecca of Ljubljana's alternative scene, offering different styles of music on different nights – including at least one gay night (currently Sunday). Good place to check out live bands and alternative happenings.

Metelkova, Metelkova cesta. Old barracks just east of the train station which now functions as an alternative cultural centre. Club nights, gigs and happenings.

Propaganda, Grablovičeva 1. Techno and jungle-orientated bar and club east of the train station, near *Orto Bar* (see "cafés and bars" above).

Classical music, opera and ballet

For a relatively small city, Ljubljana offers a surprisingly rich diet of classical culture. The Cankarjev Dom, Prešernova 10 (ticket office Mon–Fri 10am–2pm & 4.30–8pm, Sat 10am–1pm; ☎061/222-815), is the scene of major orchestral and theatrical events, as well as occasional folk and jazz concerts. Ljubljana's energetic **symphony orchestra**, the Slovenska Filharmonia, performs at Kongresni Trg 9, while the republic's **opera and ballet** companies are housed in the Slovene National Theatre (Slovensko Narodno Gledališče), a sumptuous nineteenth-century Neoclassical building at Zupančičeva 1 (ticket office 11am–1pm and one hour before each performance; ☎061/125-4840). Two big music festivals take place throughout July and August: the Ljubljana **Summer Festival** features orchestral concerts by international artists at Križanke (festival box office 11am–1pm & 6–7pm; ☎061/226-544), while **Summer in Old Ljubljana** concentrates on chamber music in a number of venues scattered throughout the Old Town. **Druga Godba** (again centred on Križanke) is a **world music** festival which attracts big international names in the second week of June. The monthly *Where To? Events* pamphlet, published in English and available from the TIC, has complete listings of concerts and events.

Listings

Airline offices Adria, Gosposvetska 6 (☎061/133-7168); Lufthansa, Gosposvetska 6 (☎061/326-669); Swissair, Hotel Lev, Vošnjakova 1 (☎061/317-647).

Airport information ☎064/222-700.

American Express Trubarjeva 50 (☎061/133-6075).

Books MK, Slovenska 29, has a wide selection of English-language paperbacks. Kod in Kam, Trg francoske revolucije, has a range of maps.

Car rental Avis, Čufarjeva 2 (☎061/132-3395); Kompas Hertz, Miklošičeva 11 (☎061/311-241).

Embassies and consulates Australia, Trg Republike 3 (☎061/125-4252); Britain, Trg Republike 3 (☎061/125-7191); Netherlands, Dunajska 22 (☎061/328-978); USA, Pražakova 4 (☎061/301-427).

Exchange The post office at Trg Osvobodilne Fronte has a desk which is open 24hrs.

Hospital Bohoričeva 4 (☎061/323-060).

Launderette Chemo-express, Wolfova 12 (service washes only; Mon–Fri 7am–6pm).

Library British Council, Cankarjevo nabrežje 27 (Mon–Thurs 9am–8pm, Fri 9am–3pm). English-language newspapers and books.

Pharmacies Lekarna Miklošič, Miklošičeva 24, has a 24hr service.

Police Headquarters at Presernov 18.

Post office Main office at Slovenska 32 (Mon–Fri 7am–8pm, Sat 7am–1pm); 24-hour service for all facilities at Trg Osvobodilne Fronte, next to the train station.

Taxis To book, call ☎9700-9.

Telephones At the main post office.

Travel agents Atlas, Mestni Trg 8; Kompas, Miklošičeva 11; Slovenijaturist, Slovenska 58.

THE REST OF THE COUNTRY

Emphatically not to be missed while you're in Ljubljana is a visit to the **Postojna Caves** – easily managed either as a day-trip or en route south to Slovene Istria, to Croatia or to Italy. A lower-key alternative to the cave stopoff is **Lipica**, where the celebrated white Lipizzaner horses are bred, or **Predjamski Grad**, near Postojna, an atmospherically sombre castle high against a cave entrance in the midst of a dramatic landscape.

Close to the borders with Italy and Croatia, the towns of **Slovene Istria** have long been popular tourist resorts. In recent decades their proximity to northern Europe has proved a tempting target for exploitation, although through all the crowds, concrete and tourist settlements, the region has managed to retain some charm and identity. The basis of this is Italian, coming from the 400 years of Venetian rule that preceded the region's incorporation into the Austro-Hungarian Empire, and eventually into the Yugoslav federation. There's still a fair-sized Italian minority community here although many of the Italian speakers left Istria after World War II, afraid of what might happen once the communists took control. Even so, Slovene Istria remains one of the most Italianate parts of the entire region: there's a steady flow of traffic to and fro across the border, Italian is fairly widely spoken, and road signs are in Italian as well as Slovene. Along the coast, diminutive towns like **Piran**, with their cobbled piazzas, shuttered houses and back alleys laden with laundry, are almost overwhelmingly pretty. **Koper**, too, is worth a look, more port than resort and a good base for exploring northern Istria.

To the northwest of Ljubljana, and within easy reach of the capital, are the **mountain lakes** of **Bled** and **Bohinj**, Slovenia's number-one tourist attraction. The **Soča valley**, on the western side of the Slovene alps, is much less touristed, although small towns like **Kobarid** and **Bovec** are excellent bases from which to indulge in rafting and walking. East of Ljubljana on the main route to Hungary, **Ptuj** is Slovenia's oldest town and one of its most attractive.

Postojna

POSTOJNA is on the main rail route south from Ljubljana, but as the walk to the caves from Postojna train station is further than from the bus stop, most people go by one of the regular buses. Once in the town, signs direct you to the **caves** and their suitably cavernous entrance (tours: April–Oct daily 9am–6/7pm; Nov–March Mon–Fri 9am–3pm, Sat & Sun 9am–4pm; last tour leaves 1hr before closing; 1900SIT); inside a railway whizzes you helter-skelter through 2km of preliminary systems before the guided tour starts. It's little use trying to describe the vast and fantastic jungles of rock formations; the point is to see them for yourself – breathtaking stuff. Postojna's caves are about four million years old and provide a chilly home for *Proteus anguineus*, a weird creature that looks like a cross between a bloated sperm and a prawn. Actually it's a sort of salamander, one of whose odd capabilities is to give birth to live young in temperatures above 16°F (-10°C) and to lay eggs if it's colder. They live their seventy-year lives down here in total darkness and hence are blind – and very confused at being put on display to inquisitive tourists. The temperature underground is a constant 8°F (-16°C), so dress appropriately.

Accommodation in private rooms (②–③) is arranged by Kompas in the town centre at Titov Trg 1a (Mon–Fri 9am–7pm, Sat 9am–1pm; ☎067/24-281). There's a **campsite**, the *Pivka Jama* (☎067/24168), 4km beyond the cave entrance and not served by public transport, which also has four-person apartments and bungalows for about £12/$19 per person. Of the hotels, *Kras*, in the town centre at Tržaska 1 (☎067/24-071; ④), and *Proteus*, 1km south of town at Kosovelova 1 (☎067/24-172; ④), are the most reasonable. There are numerous places to **eat** clustered around the cave entrance.

Predjamski Grad

The other site you're steered to near Postojna is **PREDJAMSKI GRAD** (May–Sept 9am–6pm; Oct–April 10am–4pm; 500SIT), 7km from Postojna and well signposted from the cave. It's walkable if you're in the mood; otherwise it's only accessible with your own transport or on an organized trip. Pushed up high against a cave entrance in the midst of karst landscape, the sixteenth-century castle is damp and melancholy, unimproved by a lacklustre collection of odds and ends from this and an earlier castle that stood nearby. The previous castle was the home of one **Erazem**, a colourful brigand knight of the fifteenth century who spent his days waylaying the merchant caravans that passed through the region. Sheriff of Nottingham to his Robin Hood was the Governor of Trieste, who laid exasperated siege to the castle for over a year. Secure in his defensive position and supplied by a secret passage to the outside world, Erazem taunted the governor by tossing fresh cherries and the occasional roast ox over the wall to show he was far from beaten. Such hubris couldn't go unnoticed, and Erazem finally met with one of the more ignominious deaths on record: blown to bits by a cannonball while sitting on the castle loo. There are guided tours of the cave below the castle (daily May–Sept 11am, 1pm, 3pm & 5pm; 500SIT).

Lipica

After Postojna, Slovenia's most emblematic tourist draw is probably **LIPICA**, 7km west of the drab railway-junction town of Divača near the Italian border. Public transport is meagre: a few buses run from Divača weekday mornings, but you have little time to look around before catching the last bus back. Alternatives include spending a night here in one of the (expensive) hotels, or joining a weekend excursion run by the big high-street travel agents in Ljubljana or Portorož. One-day tours combining Postojna and Lipica currently cost around £35/$56 per person. Lipica gave its name to the **Lipizzaner** horses that are associated with the Spanish Riding School of Vienna. There are three hundred horses here, the results of fastidious breeding that can be dated back to 1580, when the Austrian Archduke Charles established the farm in order to add Spanish and Arab blood to the Lipizzaner strain that was first used by the Romans for chariot races. Though the school is nothing so grand as that at Vienna, tours are given round the **stud farm** (summer 10am–5pm; winter 11am–3pm; 2100SIT), and the horses give the elegant displays for which they're famous (July & Aug daily at 11am; May, June & Sept Tues, Fri & Sun at 3pm; Oct & April Fri & Sun at 3pm). If you've any horse-riding ability, it's also possible to go on rides around the region – a wonderfully relaxing way to explore the area. There are two good, but pricey **hotels** in the stable complex, the *Klub* and *Maestoso* (both ☎067/31580; ⑤).

Koper and around

Arriving on Slovenia's coast, **KOPER**, or Capodistria in Italian, is the first town you reach, a prosperous place sited on what was originally a small island. From the main road it's an unalluring spectacle, dominated by tower blocks, cranes and industrial estates. But within this surge of development, Koper is a rickety old Venetian town, crowded with a dense lattice of narrow streets.

All of Koper's paved alleys lead to **Titov Trg**, the fulcrum of the old city, flanked by a Venetian **Loggia**, dating from 1463 and now a café. At the opposite end is the **Praetor's Palace**, Koper's most enduring symbol, with its battlements, balconies, busts and coats of arms like the stage backdrop for a Renaissance drama. Built originally in the thirteenth century, and added to and adapted 200 years later (the battlements were actually added in 1664 and only ever served a decorative purpose), this was the seat of the mayor and Venetian governor, evidenced by the facade's Lion of St Mark. Also on the square, Koper's **Cathedral** (daily 7am–noon & 3–7pm) is a mixture of architectural styles, its facade blending a Venetian Gothic lower storey with an upper level completed a hundred years later in Renaissance fashion. Dedicated to St Nazarius, patron saint of the town, the interior is large and imposing, and holds a *Madonna and the Saints* by Vittore Carpaccio, hung to the right of the main altar as you face it. Heading downhill from the square along Kidričeva brings you to the **Civic Museum** (Tues–Fri 9am–1pm, Sat 9am–noon; 300SIT) which holds more paintings, including works by Correggio, together with archeological fragments, ancient maps and the like.

Practicalities

Koper's **bus** and **train stations** are located next door to each other, twenty minutes' walk from the town centre, or a short ride on one of the frequent Koper–Piran buses. These drop you just outside the city centre, inside which only residents are allowed to drive. Koper's **tourist office**, on the seafront at Ukmarjev Trg 7 (Mon–Sat 9am–2pm & 5–7pm; Sun 9am–1pm; ☎066/273-791), has plentiful **private rooms** (②), as does nearby Kompas, Pristanička 15–17 (daily 8am–7pm). The best of the more inexpensive **hotels** is the *Žusterna*, on the seafront 2km west of town at Istrska 67 (☎066/284-385; ④), served by Koper–Piran buses or a thirty-minute walk along the seafront path from the centre. There's a **hostel** just east of the old town at Cankarjeva 5, although it's only likely to have room in August and at weekends for the rest of the year. Several **snack bars and restaurants** are clustered around the harbour area: *Skipper*, near the tourist office at Kopalisko Nabrezje 3, has a wide range of seafood; while the next-door *Školjka*, Kopalisko Nabrezje 1, has good pizzas. In the centre of town, *Cantina Istriana Slavček*, Župančičeva 39, has cheap grills and seafood. For **drinking**, *Carpaccio Pub*, near the tourist office at Carpacciov Trg, is an upbeat venue with occasional live music. There are also regular gigs at *MKC*, a youth cultural centre at Gregorčičeva 4. *Ambasada Gavioli*, 5km west of town in Izola, is the coast's best **club**, attracting DJs from all over Europe.

Portorož

Heading west from Koper the road veers right soon after Izola onto a long, tapering peninsula that projects like a lizard's tail north into the Adriatic. **PORTOROŽ** ("Port of Roses") appears almost without warning, a sprawling resort that by the end of the last century was already known for its mild climate and the health-inducing properties of its salty mud baths. Maladied middle-aged Austrians flocked here by the thousand to be smothered with murky balm dredged up from the nearby salt pans. Up went the *Palace Hotel*, in came the opportunists – and so began Portorož, a town entirely devoted to the satisfaction of its visitors. After World War II, the transition from health to package resort wasn't hard to make, and it's now one of the most developed stretches of coast in all Istria, a vibrant strip of hotels and (largely concrete) beaches. Combining Portorož's modernity with the charm of Piran (a short bus ride or forty-minute walk away; see below) is the key to enjoying this brash, consumption-orientated place. There's a **tourist office** on the roundabout that passes for a bus station (Mon–Fri 9am–9pm, Sat & Sun 9am–3pm; ☎066/747-015) offering **rooms** (②), which are also available from either Moana or Rosetour, on the main coastal strip, Obala Maršala Tita, just down from the bus terminal.

Piran

PIRAN, at the very tip of the peninsula 4km from Portorož's bus station, couldn't be more different. There are tourists here too, lots of them, thronging the main square, packing the ranks of restaurants, milling around the souvenir-stacked harbour. But few actually stay (most are in fact from Portorož's hotel complexes), and the town preserves tangible remnants of atmosphere in its sloping web of arched alleys and little Italianate squares.

The centre of town, a couple of hundred metres around the harbour from where the buses stop, is **Tartinijev Trg**, named after the eighteenth-century Italian violinist and composer Giuseppe Tartini, who was born in a house on the square and is remembered by a bronze statue in the centre. It's one of the loveliest squares on this coast, fringed by a mix of Venetian palaces and a portentous Austrian town hall. Just off the square there's a small **Aquarium** (daily 10am–1pm & 2–7pm; 400SIT), with a rather sad set of tanks full of local marine life. Opposite, across the bay of the harbour, the **Maritime Museum** (daily 9am–noon & 4–7pm; 300SIT) pays further homage to Tartini with a copy of his violin and assorted genuine memorabilia, along with an interesting display on Piran's salt industry and a scatter of paintings that includes native ex-votive works by Piran sailors and a ropy portrait of the local authorities by Tintoretto. Follow Ulica IX Korpusa uphill from the square to the barnlike Baroque **Church of Sv Jurij**, which crowns a commanding spot on the far side of Piran's peninsula. The campanile is visible from just about everywhere in the town and may seem familiar – it's a replica of the one in St Mark's Square in Venice. Five minutes' walk further up, the town's formidable sixteenth-century **walls** stagger across the hill, the remaining towers providing excellent views of the town below.

Practicalities

The **tourist office** on Tartinijev Trg (Tues–Sat 10am–5pm, Sun 10am–2pm) is helpful and sells maps. **Rooms** can be booked through Moana, between the bus station and the square at Cankarjevo Nabrežje 7 (Mon–Fri 9am–5pm, Sat 9am–3pm). Cheapest of the **hotels** is *Pension Val*, in the old town at Gregorčičeva 38 (☎066/73773; ③); although the stylish *Tartini*, Tartinijev Trg 15 (☎066/746221; ⑤) is worth the extra money. For **eating**, you'll see several acceptable if unexciting pizzerias between the bus station and Tartinijev Trg. *Mario*, up a flight of steps from Tartinijev Trg, has good value fish and meat dishes in uncomplicated surroundings. Numerous more expensive seafood restaurants line Piran's seafront, of which *Pavel* and *Tri Vdove* are probably the best. *Kavana Galerija Tartini*, on Tartinijev Trg, is the most relaxing place for a daytime or evening **drink**. Liveliest of the **bars** is *Da Noi*, a cellar-like space tucked between restaurants on the seafront.

Bled and Bohinj

Northwest of Ljubljana, towards Austria and at the eastern end of the Julian Alps, are the **mountain lakes** of **Bled** and **Bohinj**, Slovenia's number one tourist attraction. While Bled, surrounded by Olympian mountains and oozing charm, lives up to expectations it's also chock-full with tourists, which can't help but temper its delights. Bohinj, in contrast, is less visited, more beautiful and much cheaper – and, should you want to explore the imposing and exhilarating mountains around Mt Triglav, at 2864m Slovenia's highest peak, this is the place to go. For anyone interested in serious **hiking**, good maps are essential: your best bets are the 1:50,000 *Triglav National Park*, the 1:25,000 *Mount Triglav*, and the 1:25,000 *Bled and environs* – all published by the Slovene alpine association. Pick them up in Ljubljana bookshops or from the tourist offices in Bled and Ribčev Laz.

Buses are the easiest way to reach both Bled and Bohinj (hourly from Ljubljana; 1hr 15min to Bled, 2hr to Bohinj). **Rail** access to the region is either via the main northbound line from Ljubljana, which calls at Bled-Lesce 3km southeast of Bled itself (and linked to Bled by a regular bus), or a branch line which leaves the main Ljubljana–Villach route at Jesenice and crosses the mountains towards Italy and the coast, calling at Bled-Jezero and Bohinjska Bistrica on the way. The trip from Jesenice, chugging steadily through the mountains and karst, is as impressive as you'd imagine. Train buffs should note that a **steam train**, the museum train or muzejni vlak, is laid on in summer months, at considerable additional expense.

Bled

There's no denying that the lake resort of **BLED** has all the right ingredients to make up a memorable visit – a placid mirror lake with a romantic island, a fairy-tale castle high on a bluff, leafy lakeside lanes and a backdrop of snow-tipped mountains. As such it's worth a day of anyone's time, and one advantage of the tourist trade is that everything is efficiently packaged. In summer the lake, fed by warm water springs that take the water temperature up to 76°F, forms the setting for a whole host of water sports – major rowing contests are held here throughout summer – and in winter the surface becomes a giant skating rink.

Paths uphill from Bled's bus station run up to **Bled Castle** (daily 8am–8pm; 400SIT) – now a pricey restaurant with a fine view and a very ordinary museum, its only surprise a small sixteenth-century chapel.

During the day a constant relay of stretched gondolas leaves from below the *Park Hotel* or the bathing resort below the castle, ferrying tourists back and forth to Bled's picturesque **island** (1200SIT return). With an early start (and by renting your own rowing boat or canoe from the same places as the gondolas) you can beat them to it. Crowning the island, the Baroque-decorated **Church of Sv Marika Božja** is the last in a line of churches on a spot that's long held religious significance for the people around the lake: under the present building are remains of early graves and, below the north chapel, a pre-Roman temple. In summer months it's feasible to swim from the western end of the lake to the island, but remember to bring some light clothes in a watertight bag if you want to get into the church. During winter, under the snug muffle of alpine snow, you can walk or skate across. The main attraction in the outlying hills is the **Vintgar Gorge** (mid-May to September daily 9am–6pm; SIT400), 5km north of town, an impressive defile accessed by a wooden walkway. To get there, head northwest out of Bled on the Vintgar road (just up from the bus station), turning right on the outskirts of town towards the villages of Gmajna and Zasip. Head uphill through Zasip to the hilltop chapel of Sv Katarina (where you can savour an excellent view back towards the lake), before picking up a path through the forest to the gorge entrance.

The helpful **tourist office** near the lakefront at Cesta Svobode 15 (Mon–Sat 8am–5pm, Sun noon–4pm; ☎064/741-122) hands out maps and brochures, although **private rooms** are available through Kompas, in the shopping centre at Ljubljanska 4 (Mon–Sat 8am–7pm, Sun 8am–noon & 4–7pm), or Globtour further up Ljubljanska at no. 7 (Mon–Fri 8am–3pm, Sat 8am–noon). There's a **youth hostel** (☎064/745-251; ②) just above the bus station at Grajska 17, and a couple of reasonable **pensions** – the smallish *Pletna* at Cesta Svobode 37 (☎064/77-584; ③) and the *Alp*, 2km west of town along the lakeside road at Cankarjeva 20a (☎064/741-614; ④). The nearest **campsite**, *Zaka* (☎064/741-117) is beautifully placed, sheltered at the western end of the lake amid the pines and with its own stretch of beach; catch a bus towards Bohinj and ask to be set down near the access road.

One downside of the all-embracing tourist industry around here is that there are few cheap places to eat – the best places to look are in the hillside area between Bled's bus station and castle. *Gostilna Pri Planincu*, Grajska 8, offers solid Slovene home cooking, while *Pizzeria Portobello* on Rikljeva is probably the best of the Italian places. For a treat, the highly regarded *Okarina*, Rikljeva 9, offers traditional Slovene meals for around 5000–6000SIT per person.

Lake Bohinj

It's 30km from Bled to Lake Bohinj and buses run hourly through the **Sava Bohinjka Valley** – dense, verdant and often laden with mist and low cloud. In appearance and character **Lake Bohinj** is utterly different from Bled: the lake crooks a narrow finger under the wild mountains, woods slope gently down to the water, enclosing it in secretive tranquillity, and a lazy stillness hangs over all – in comparison to Bled it feels almost uninhabited.

BOHINJSKA BISTRICA, 4km before Lake Bohinj on the Bled–Bohinj bus route, has little except a few rooms. **RIBČEV LAZ** (often referred to as Jezero on bus timetables, after the name of a local hotel) at the eastern end of the lake, is where most facilities are based, including the **tourist office** (July & Aug daily 7am–8pm; rest of year Mon–Sat 8am–6pm, Sun 9–3pm; ☎064/746-010), which offers rooms (②) and apartments around Ribčev Laz and in the idyllic village of **STARA FUŽINA** 1km north. The main attraction in Ribčev Laz is the **Church of Sv Janez** (July & Aug daily 9am–noon & 3–6pm), a solid-looking structure whose nave and frescoes date back to the fourteenth century. Beyond the church, a road leads to Stara Fužina, a traditional Slovene alpine village filled with the timber hay-drying barns (*kozolci*) which are particular to the region. There's a **museum of highland pasture life** (Planšarski muzej; Tues–Sun: summer 11am–9pm; winter 10am–noon & 4–6pm; 200SIT) housed in a former dairy in the centre of the village. The key to the museum is kept in the *Okrepčevalnica Planšar* immediately opposite, a snack bar selling local cheeses (including *mohant*, a sharp cream cheese made by only a few local households). **Walking trails** lead round both sides of the lake, or northwards onto the eastern shoulders of the Triglav range. One route leads north from Stara Fužina into the Voje valley, passing through the dramatic **Mostrica Canyon**, a popular local beauty spot.

Five kilometres from Ribčev Laz at the western end of the lake is the hamlet of **UKANC**, although the area is more popularly referred to as Zlatorog, after the local hotel. There are several **private rooms** (②) and apartments here, which you can book through the tourist office in Ribčev Laz. The **campsite** (☎064/723-482), just east of the bus stop, occupies an idyllic lakeside position.

An easy walk back east takes you to the **cable car** (žičnica; daily 7.30am–6pm, every 30min; closed Nov; 1200SIT return) at the foot of **Mt Vogel** (1540m). If the Alps look dramatic from the lakeside, from Vogel's summit they're breathtaking. As the cable car briskly climbs the 1000-metre drop, the panorama is gradually revealed, with Mount Triglav forming the crest of a line of pale red mountains, more like a clenched claw than the three-headed god after which it's named.

An hour's walk north from Zlatorog are the photogenic **Savica Waterfalls** (Slap Savice; mid–April to Oct 9am–5pm; 400SIT). The falls themselves mark the start of one of the most popular hiking routes up Mount Triglav, which zig-zags up the mountain wall to the north before bearing northwest into the **Valley of the Seven Lakes** – an area strewn with eerie boulders and hardy firs – before continuing to the summit of Triglav itself. Although steep in parts, it's not a hike of great technical difficulty, although good maps and careful planning are required. The Seven Lakes can be treated as a day-long hiking expedition from Bohinj, but the assault on Triglav itself requires at least one night in a mountain hut. The tourist office in Ribčev Laz will supply details and book you a place, although huts on Triglav are only open from late June to late September – the upper stretches of the mountain shouldn't be tackled outside these times.

Finally, if you're around Bohinj in September, the return of the cattle from the higher alpine pastures is celebrated in the mass booze-up called the **Kravji Bal** or "Cow Dance" (held on the second or third weekend of the month in Ukanc).

The Soča valley

On the other, less-touristed side of the mountains from Bohinj, the river Soča cuts through the western spur of the Julian Alps, running parallel with Slovenia's border with Italy. During World War I, the Soča (Isonzo in Italian) marked the front line between the Italian and Austro-Hungarian armies, and three years of bitter warfare on the surrounding peaks rivalled the Western Front in terms of futile offensives and wasted lives. Memorial chapels and abandoned fortifications abound, located incongruously amidst awesome alpine scenery. However there's more to the Soča valley than military history: it's also a major centre for activity-based tourism, with the foaming river itself providing the ideal venue for **rafting** and **kayaking** throughout the spring and summer. Main tourist centres are **Kobarid** and **Bovec**, both small towns with a range of **walking** possibilities right on the doorstep. The 1:50,000 *Posočje* **map** covers trails in the region: pick it up in Ljubljana if you can, as not all local shops have it.

Although both places are served by three daily buses from Ljubljana, transport connections with the rest of Slovenia are patchy. Approaching the Soča valley from the Bled-Bohinj area involves catching one of five daily trains from Bled-Jezero or Bohinjska Bistrica to **Most na Soči**, where buses run onwards up the valley. Getting here from the coast entails catching buses working the Koper-Sežana-Nova Gorica-Tolmin-Kobarid route (minimum journey time of 4hr depending on connections), although you might have to change at each stage of the journey.

Kobarid

It was at the little alpine town of **KOBARID** (Italian Caporetto) that German and Austrian troops finally broke through Italian lines in 1917, almost knocking Italy out of the war in the process. Ernest Hemingway, then a volunteer ambulance driver on the Italian side, took part in the chaotic retreat that followed – an experience which resurfaced in his novel *A Farewell to Arms*. A processional way leads up from Kobarid's main square to a monumental, three-tiered **Italian War Memorial** (Italijanska Kostnica) officially opened by Benito Mussolini in 1938, and a fitting place from which to enjoy views of the surrounding Alps and ponder Kobarid's violent past. Back in town, the **Kobarid museum** at Gregorčičeva 10 (Kobariški muzej; summer daily 8am–7pm; winter Mon–Fri 10am–5pm, Sat & Sun 9am–6pm; 500SIT), presents a thoughtful and balanced record of the war with a gripping collection of photographs. Continue past the museum, head downhill and take the Drežnica road across the river Soča to pick up trails to the **Kozjak waterfall** (Slap Kozjak; 50min), less impressive for its height than for the cavern-like space which it has carved out of the surrounding rock. Numerous paths branch off from here into the wooded hills, passing trench systems dug by the Italians during the war. The *Kobarid Historical Walk* brochure, available from the museum, maps out a few potential itineraries.

Kobarid's **tourist office** is housed in the museum (same times; ☎065/85055), and has a limited number of **private rooms** (②) in Kobarid and surrounding villages. The chic rooms at the *Hvala* **hotel** on the main square (☎065/191-930; ⑤) are remarkably good value for the level of comfort on offer. There's also a **campsite**, the *Koren* (☎065/85312), about 500m out of town on the way towards the Kozjak waterfall. As for **eating**, there's nowhere cheap in town save for *Pizzeria pri Vitku*, hidden away in a residential district (take the road south out of town and follow the signs). The *Topli Val*, attached to the *Hotel Hvala*, is one of the best restaurants in the country and specializes in fish (including Soča trout); and with meals costing from around £20/$32 per person it's well worth a splash-out.

Details of local firms offering **rafting** trips can be picked up from the tourist office or the reception area of the *Hotel Hvala*. One of the biggest is Alpin Action in Trnovo ob Soči, 6km north of town (☎065/85022). Expect to pay £20/$32 to £30/$48 per trip.

Bovec

Twenty-five kilometres up the valley from Kobarid, the village of **BOVEC** straggles between imperious mountain ridges. A useful base for the Soča valley, it has more in the way of accommodation than Kobarid because of its status as a winter ski resort. It's also the location of most of the rafting and adventure sport companies, and is the departure point for any number of alpine walks. The quickest route up into the mountains is provided by the **gondola** (Gondolna žičnica; daily July, Aug & Dec–March; 2000SIT return) at the southern entrance to the village, which ascends to the pasture-cloaked Mt Kanin over to the west. Private **rooms** (②) and apartments are available from either *Gotour*, in a courtyard just off the main street at Trg 50 (☎065/86220), or *Avrigo*, uphill from the main street towards the church at Trg golobarskih žrtev 14 (☎065/86123). The nearest **campsite** is *Polovnik*, Ledina 8 (☎065/86069); follow the road north out of the village and it's signed to the right after 500m. There are plenty of places to **eat** and **drink** on and around the main square, although the atmosphere in all of them ranges from the boisterous to the deathly depending on how many tourists are in town. *Sovdat*, Trg 24, is a homely and unpretentious place with a good range of mid-priced Slovene standards. Soča Rafting, next door to *Avrigo* on Trg golobarskih žrtev (☎065/196-200), is the biggest of many companies grouped around the main square offering **rafting** trips (with prices working out much the same as in Kobarid; see above). It also organizes kayaking and canyoning and rents out mountain bikes.

Ptuj and around

One hundred and twenty kilometres northeast of Ljubljana, **PTUJ** is the oldest town in Slovenia and about the most attractive as well, rising up from the Drava Valley in a flutter of red roofs and topped by a friendly looking castle. But the best thing is its streets, with scaled-down mansions standing shoulder to shoulder on scaled-down boulevards, medieval fantasies crumbling next to Baroque extravagances. Out of the windows hang plants and the locals; watching the world go by is a major occupation here.

Ptuj is on the main rail line from Ljubljana to Budapest (the Venice–Ljubljana–Budapest express passes through here once a day in both directions), and can also be reached by bus from Slovenia's second-largest city **Maribor**, which is on the Ljubljana-Vienna line. On arriving at Maribor, turn left outside the train station and head downhill – the bus station is on the other side of the crossroads.

The Town

Ptuj's main street, Prešernova Cesta, snakes along the base of the castle-topped hill. At its eastern end is the **Priory Church of St George** (open mornings only), a building of twelfth-century origin that holds a statue of its patron unconcernedly killing a rather homely dragon. Nearby, its rather unambitious **tower** started life in the sixteenth century as a bell tower, became city watchtower in the seventeenth century and was retired in the eighteenth, when it was given an onion bulb spire for decoration. Roman tombstones have been embedded in its lower reaches, but a more noticeable leftover of Roman times is the **tablet** that stands below like an oversize tooth, actually a funeral monument to a Roman mayor. It's just possible to make out its carvings of Orpheus entertaining assembled fauna.

From here Prešernova Cesta leads to the **Archeological Museum** (April–Dec Mon–Fri 10am–3pm, Sat & Sun 10am–4pm; 300SIT) housed in what was once a Dominican monastery, a mustardy building gutted in the eighteenth century and now hung with spidery decoration, and worth a look for the carvings and statuary around its likeably dishevelled cloisters.

A path opposite the monastery winds up to the **Castle** (guided tours mid-April to Nov daily 9am–5pm; 450SIT). There's been a castle of sorts here for as long as there's been a town, since Ptuj was the only bridging point across the Drava for miles around, holding the defences against the tribes of the north. An agglomeration of styles from the fourteenth to the eighteenth centuries, the castle was home to a succession of noble families who made it rich in the town. Most prominent were the Herbersteins, Austro–Slovene aristocrats who made their fortune in the Habsburg Empire's sixteenth- and seventeenth-century wars against the Turks. Their portraits hang on the walls of the castle's **museum**, a collection mixed in theme and quality, containing period rooms with original tapestries and wallpaper on the first floor.

At Shrovetide (late Feb/early March) Ptuj is venue to one of the oldest and most unusual customs in Slovenia. The *Kurenti* **processions** are a sort of fertility rite and celebration of the dead confused together: participants wear sinister masks of sheepskin and feathers with a coloured beak for a nose and white beads for teeth, and possibly represent ancestral spirits. So dressed, the *Kurenti* move in hopping procession from house to house, scaring off evil spirits with the din from the cowbells tied to their costumes. At the head of the procession is the Devil, wrapped in a net to symbolize his capture: behind the *Kurenti*, the *Orači* ("the ploughers") pull a small wooden plough, scattering sand around to represent the sowing of seed, and housewives smash clay pots at their feet in the hope that this will bring health and luck to their households.

Practicalities

Ptuj's **train station** is 500m northeast of the centre on Osojnikova Cesta, the **bus station** 100m nearer town on the same road. From both points, walk down Osojnikova to its junction with ul. Heroja Lacka: a right turn here lands you straight in the centre. The **tourist office** in the clocktower outside the church (Mon–Sat 8am–5pm, Sun 10am–3pm; ☎062/779-601) has **private rooms** in local farmhouses (③), although you'll probably need your own transport to reach any of them. There are two moderately priced **hotels**, the central *Mitra*, Prešernova 6 (☎062/779-822; ④); and the *Poetovio*, near the bus station at Trstenjakova 13 (☎062/779-820; ④). The well-regimented *Terme Ptuj* **campsite**, Pot v Toplice 9 (☎062/771-721), lies among fields 2km east of town.

For **eating**, *Slonček*, Prešernova 19, is a convenient pizzeria in the centre of town, while *Bambusov Gozd*, down by the riverfront on Dravska, serves Chinese food in lively surroundings. *Ribič*, also on Dravska, is an excellent but expensive fish restaurant with a riverside terrace. If you can't stretch to that, *Stari Ribič*, set back from the river at Vosnjakova 11, also specializes in fish and is slightly cheaper. *Café Bo* and *Café Orfei* on Prešernova are both good places to enjoy an evening **drink**.

travel details

Trains

Bohinjska Bistrica to: Most na Soai (5 daily; 45min).

Ljubljana to: Divača (hourly; 1hr 20min); Koper (3 daily; 2hr 30min); Maribor (10 daily; 2hr 20min–3hr 20min); Postojna (hourly; 1hr); Ptuj (3 daily; 2hr 30min).

Buses

Ljubljana to: Bled (hourly; 1hr 15min); Bohinj (hourly; 2hr); Bovec (3 daily; 4hr 45min); Divača (8 daily; 1hr 30min); Kobarid (3 daily; 4hr); Koper (8 daily; 2hr); Maribor (6 daily; 3hr 45min); Piran (8 daily; 2hr 40min); Postojna (8 daily; 1hr); Ptuj (3 daily; 4hr).

Kobarid to: Bovec (5 daily; 40min); Ljubljana (3 daily; 4hr); Nova Gorica (3 daily; 1hr 15min).

Koper to: Bled (1 daily; 3hr 30min); Piran (every 20min; 40min); Portorož (every 20min; 30min); Trieste (Mon–Sat hourly; 1hr).

Maribor to: Ptuj (every 30min; 40min).

CHAPTER 27

SPAIN

Introduction

Spain might appear from the tourist brochures to be no more than a clichéd whirl of bullfights and crowded beaches, castles and Moorish palaces. Travel for any length of time, however, and the sheer variety of this huge country, which in the north can look like Ireland and in the south like Morocco, cannot fail to impress. The separate kingdoms which made up the original Spanish nation remain very much in evidence, in a diversity of language, culture and artistic traditions.

The sheer pace of change in the wake of the forty-year dictatorship of Franco is one of the country's most stimulating aspects. Early in the 1990s, Spain enjoyed the fastest economic growth in Europe (now slowed by an acute slump); for the first time in centuries, there is a feeling of political stability. Spanish culture has been allowed off the leash, and virtually every aspect of life has been radically transformed. 1992, Spaniards believe, was the year which restored them to their rightful place among Europe's leading nations: Barcelona hosted the Olympics, Seville the World Fair, and Madrid was official "Cultural Capital of Europe", all 500 years after Columbus discovered America.

In the **cities** there is always something happening – in clubs, on the streets, in fashion, in politics – and even in the most out-of-the-way places there's nightlife, music and entertainment, not to mention the more traditional fiestas. In the **countryside** you can still find villages which have been decaying steadily since Columbus set sail: rural areas are more and more depopulated as the young head for the cities. Yet for the visitor the landscape retains its fascination; even local variations can be so extreme that a journey of just a few hours can take you through scenes of total contrast. Spain is as mountainous a nation as any in Europe and the sierras have always formed formidable barriers to centralization.

It's almost impossible to summarize Spain as a single country. **Catalunya** is vibrant and go-ahead; **Galicia** rural and underdeveloped; the **Basque** country fighting postindustrial depression with spectacular new civic initiatives; **Castile** and the south still, somehow, quintessentially "Spanish". There are definite highlights to Spanish travel: the three great cities of **Barcelona, Madrid** and **Sevilla**; the Moorish monuments of **Andalucía** and the Christian ones of **Old Castile**; beach-life in **Ibiza** or on the more deserted sands around **Cádiz** and in the north; and, for some of the best trekking in Europe, the **Pyrenees** and the Asturian **Picos de Europa**.

Information and maps

The **Spanish National Tourist Office** (Informació or Iniciativo de turismo) has a branch in virtually every major town, giving away a variable array of maps, accommodation lists and leaflets – in the busiest towns they often run out. Offices are often supplemented by provincial or municipal **Turismo** bureaux, which also vary enormously in quality – the Basque and Catalan ones are superb, while Andalusian offices can be very poor. Both types of office are usually open Mon–Fri 9am–1pm & 4–7pm, Sat 9am–1pm.

Among the best **road maps** are those published by Editorial Almax, which also produces reliable indexed street plans of the main cities. Good alternatives are the 1:800,000 map produced by RV (Reise-und Verkehrsverlag, Stuttgart) and packaged in Spain by Plaza & Janes, and the less detailed offerings from Michelin, Firestone or Rand McNally. Serious **trekkers** should look for topographical maps issued by two government agencies: the IGN (Instituto Geográfico Nacional) and the SGE (Servicio Geográfico del Ejército), although in the northern mountain areas, Editorial Alpina is more practical.

Money and banks

The Spanish **peseta** circulates in coins of 1, 5, 10, 25, 50, 100, 200 and 500ptas, and notes of 1000 (green), 2000 (red), 5000 (brown) and 10,000 (blue) ptas. **Banks** and *cajas de ahorro* (equivalent to a building society or savings and loan) have branches in all but the smallest towns. The Banco Central has generally the lowest rate of commission on exchange, but if you've got American Express travellers' cheques, Central Hispano charges no commission at all. **Hours** are Mon–Fri 9am–2pm in summer, plus Sat 9am–1pm in winter. Outside these times it's usually possible to change cash at larger hotels (generally bad rates, but low commission) or with travel agents in the cities and big resorts. In tourist areas you'll also find **casas de cambio**, with more convenient hours, though their rates vary a lot. ATMs are widespread throughout Spain and accept both credit cards and ordinary bank cards with the Cirrus symbol. They are more convenient to use than travellers' cheques, and can be just as cheap, with withdrawal fees of around two percent.

Spain has embraced the euro with enthusiasm: shops and banks now give values in euros as well as pesetas. Notes and coins for the euro will come into circulation at the beginning of 2002, with the peseta continuing to exist alongside the new currency for another six months.

Communications

You can have your letters sent **poste restante** to any Spanish post office: they should be addressed to "Lista de Correos" followed by the name of the town and province. **American Express** in Madrid and Barcelona will hold mail for a month for cardholders. **Post offices** (Correos) are open Mon–Fri 8am–2pm & Sat 9am–noon, though big branches in large cities have longer hours. Queues can be long, but stamps are also sold at tobacconists (Tabacos).

Since 1998 all Spanish regional prefixes have become an integral part of **telephone numbers**. For example, in Madrid the first two digits of all phone numbers are 91 and it is necessary to dial these digits even when calling from within the city. However, on business cards and other publicity these preliminary digits may not appear and people do not always include them when giving out a number.

You can make **international phone calls** direct from almost any phone box, and from booths in *locutorios* or Telefónica offices, where you pay afterwards. Phone boxes take 5-, 25- or 100-peseta pieces – for international calls, make sure you have a good stock of 100-peseta pieces; phones in Spain are very expensive. Most phone boxes accept coins and 1000/2000-peseta telecards (available from tobacconists). The **operator** number is ☎1003 for domestic calls, ☎025 for international information. The international access code is ☎00.

Getting around

Most of Spain is well covered by both bus and rail networks and for journeys between major towns there's often little to choose between the two in cost or speed. On shorter or minor routes buses tend to be quicker and will normally take you closer to your destination. Car rental is worth considering, with costs among the lowest in Europe if you book in advance from home.

■ Trains

RENFE, the Spanish rail company, operates a horrendously complicated variety of **train** services. It is divided into three sections, each with a colour-scheme. *Cercanías* (red) are local trains in and around the major cities. *Regionales* (orange) are equivalent to buses in speed and cost, and run between cities – *regional exprés* and *delta* trains can cover longer distances. *Largo recorrido* express trains (some variation on grey) have a bewildering number of names. In ascending order of speed and luxury, they are known as *Diurno*, *Intercity (IC)*, *Estrella (*)*, *Talgo*, *Talgo*

P(endular), *Talgo 200 (T200)*, and *Trenhotel*. Anything above *Intercity* can cost upwards of twice as much as standard second class. There is also a growing number of private super-high-speed trains from Madrid, such as *AVE* to Sevilla and *EuroMed* to Alicante. These are white, look like aeroplanes, and for those who can afford it have cut travelling times drastically. Budget travellers, however, may need to switch between *regional* trains to find an alternative route, and rail staff can be reluctant to work these out for you.

A good way to avoid the queues is to buy tickets at travel agents which display the RENFE sign – they have a sophisticated computer system which can also make seat reservations (500ptas), obligatory on *largo recorrido* trains; the cost is the same as at the station. Most larger towns also have a RENFE office in the centre.

InterRail and Eurail **passes** are valid on all RENFE trains and also on EuroMed but supplements are charged on the fastest trains. The Tarjeta Turística, which can only be purchased by non-residents, is valid for three to ten days' unlimited rail travel; a second-class pass costs $154 for three days, $218 for five days; and $378 for ten days. The only pass available within Spain itself is the **RENFE Tarjeta Explorerail** (under 30s with ISIC card), accepted on all trains except some high-speed services; second-class passes are available for seven days (19,000ptas), fifteen days (23,000ptas) or thirty days (30,000ptas).

■ Buses

Unless you're travelling on a rail pass, **buses** will probably meet most of your transport needs; many smaller villages are accessible only by bus, almost always leaving from the capital of their province. Service varies in quality, but the buses are reliable and comfortable enough, with prices pretty standard at around 850ptas per 100km. Many towns still have no main station, and buses may leave from a variety of places. All public transport, and the bus service especially, is drastically reduced on **Sundays and holidays** – it's best to avoid travelling to out-of-the-way places on these days.

■ Driving and hitching

You obviously have much more freedom if you have your **own car**. Major roads are generally good, and traffic, while a little hectic in the cities, is usually well behaved. Speed limits are 60kph in built-up areas, 120kph on highways and 90–100kph on other roads. The national **breakdown service**, Ayuda en Carretera, is run by the Guardia Civil. Roadside phones on major routes are connected to the local police station, who will arrange assistance. On minor routes, contact the nearest police station via the operator.

You'll find a choice of **car rental** firms in all major towns, with the biggest ones represented at the airports and in town centres. These all charge about the same, upwards of £150/$240 a week, but you can usually get a deal from local operators (Atesa is the main Spanish company). If you know in advance that you'll need a car, it's still a lot cheaper to arrange it before you arrive.

Hitching in Spain is not a reliable means of long-distance travel. The road down the east coast is notoriously difficult, and trying to get out of either Madrid or Barcelona can prove a nightmare; thumbing on back roads, though, can be surprisingly productive. The Basque country and the north in general often prove quite easy, whereas Andalucía involves long, hot waits. From the big cities you're best off taking a bus out to a smaller place on the relevant road.

Accommodation

Simple, reasonably priced rooms are widely available in Spain, and in almost any town you'll be able to get a double for around 2000–3000ptas, a single for 1200–2500ptas. Only in major resorts and a handful of tourist cities need you pay more. In Spain, unlike most countries, you don't seem to pay extra for a central location, though you do tend to get a comparatively bad deal if you're travelling on your own as there are few single rooms. It's always worth bargaining over room prices, and although they're officially regulated this doesn't necessarily mean much. In high season you're unlikely to have much luck, but at quiet times you may get quite a discount. For groups, most places have rooms with three or four beds at not a great deal more than the double room price.

■ Hotel-type accommodation

The one thing all travellers need to master is the elaborate variety of types and places to stay.

Cheapest of all, but increasingly rare, are **fondas** (identifiable by a square blue sign with a white F on it), closely followed by **casas de huéspedes** (CH on a similar sign), **pensiones** (P) and, less commonly, **hospedajes**. Distinctions between all of these are rather blurred, but in general you might find food served at both *fondas* and *pensiones* (some of which may offer rooms only on a meals-inclusive basis). *Casas de huéspedes* – literally "guest houses" – were traditionally for longer stays, and to some extent they still are.

Slightly more expensive than all these, but far more common are **hostales** (marked Hs) and **hostal-residencias** (HsR). These are categorized from one to three stars, but prices vary enormously according to location. Most *hostales* offer good functional rooms, usually with private shower, and, for doubles at least, they can be excellent value. The *residencia* designation means that no meals other than perhaps breakfast are served.

Moving up the scale you finally reach **hoteles** (H), again star-graded by the authorities. One-star hotels cost no more than three-star *hostales* – sometimes they're actually cheaper – but at three stars you pay a lot more, at four or five you're in the luxury class with prices to match. Near the top end of this scale there are also state-run **paradores**: beautiful places, often converted from castles, monasteries and other minor Spanish monuments.

Tourist offices always have lists of places to stay, but often miss the cheaper deals. You can also buy the *Guía de Hoteles* (1300ptas), which includes some *hostales*.

■ Private rooms and hostels

Outside all of these categories you will sometimes see **camas** (beds) and **habitaciones** (rooms) advertised in private houses or above bars, often with the phrase "*camas y comidas*" (beds and meals) – these can be the cheapest of all options. **Youth hostels** (*Albergues Juveniles*), on the other hand, are rarely very practical, except in northern Spain where it can be difficult for solo travellers to find any other bed in

---

ACCOMMODATION PRICE CODES

Throughout this guide, accommodation is priced on a scale of ① to ⑨, the number indicating the lowest price per night a single person could expect to pay in that establishment in high season. With hostels this is the nightly rate per person; with hotels, the price is arrived at by dividing the cost of the cheapest double room by two. The prices indicated by the codes are as follows:

① under £5 / $8
② £5–10 / $8–16
③ £10–15 / $16–24
④ £15–20 / $24–32
⑤ £20–25 / $32–40
⑥ £25–30 / $40–48
⑦ £30–35 / $48–56
⑧ £35–40 / $56–64
⑨ £40 / $64 and over

summer. Few stay open all year, and in towns they are often inconveniently located. They tend to have curfews, are often block-reserved by school groups, and demand production of an HI card (though this is generally available on the spot). At between 1000 and 2000ptas a person, you can easily pay more than for sharing a cheap double room in a *fonda* or *casa de huéspedes*. It is sometimes possible to stay at Spanish **monasteries**, which may let empty cells for around 450ptas a person, but if you want to be sure of a reception it's best to approach the local Turismo first, and phone ahead. In northern Spain, the Basque Country's *agroturismo* and Navarra's *casa rural* programmes offer excellent cheap accommodation in rural areas, usually in beautifully preserved and well-maintained private houses. Full lists are available from the relevant tourist offices. Other parts of the country, including Andalucía, have recently launched similar initiatives.

■ Camping

There are over 350 authorized **campsites** in Spain, mostly on the coast. They usually work out at about 450ptas per person plus the same again for a tent and a similar amount for each car or caravan. If you plan to camp extensively pick up the free *Mapa de Campings* from the National Tourist Board or the more complete *Guía de Campings* (1000ptas). **Camping rough** is legal, but in practice you can't camp on tourist beaches – though you can nearby, and with some sensitivity you can pitch a tent almost anywhere in the countryside except in national parks, where you usually have to stick to official sites.

Food and Drink

There are two ways to eat in Spain: you can go to a *restaurante* or *comedor* (dining room) and have a full meal, or you can have a succession of *tapas* (small snacks) or *raciones* (larger ones) at one or more bars.

■ Food

For **breakfast** you're probably best off in a bar or café, though some *hostales* and *fondas* will serve the "continental" basics. Traditionally, it's *churros con chocolate* – long tubular doughnuts with thick drinking chocolate – but most places also serve *tostadas* (toasted bread) with oil (*con aceite*) or butter and jam (*con mantequilla y mermelada*), or more substantial egg dishes. Cold *tortilla* (omelette) also makes an excellent breakfast. **Coffee and pastries** (*bollería*) or doughnuts are available at most cafés, too, though for a wider selection of cakes you should head for one of the many excellent *pastelerías* or *confiterías*.

One of the advantages of eating in **bars** is being able to experiment. **Tapas** are small portions, three or four small chunks of fish or meat, or a dollop of salad, which traditionally used to be served up free with a drink. These days you have to pay for anything more than a few olives, but a single helping rarely costs more than 200-400ptas. In the Basque Country and Navarra bars often have on offer a mouth-watering selection of *pinchos* – meat, fish or just about anything else on a cocktail stick – on the bar. **Raciones** are simply bigger plates of the same for 400-900ptas, and can be enough in themselves for a light meal. If you're pushed for money, or just hungry, you can order most *tapas/raciones* fare as **bocadillos** (sandwiches in French bread). *Tascas, bodegas, cervecerías* and *tabernas* are all types of bar where you'll find *tapas* and *raciones*. Most have separate prices depending on whether you eat at the bar or at a table (up to fifty percent more expensive – more if you sit out on a terrace).

For main meals, **comedores** are the places to seek out if your main criteria are price and quantity, although they're increasingly hard to find as the tradition is on the way out. Sometimes they're attached to a bar, *pensión* or *fonda*, but as often as not they're virtually unmarked. Since they're essentially workers' cafés they tend to serve more substantial meals at lunchtime and may be closed altogether in the evening. When you can find one you'll pay around 750-1300ptas for a *menú del día* or *cubierto*, a three-course meal (usually) with wine.

Replacing *comedores* are **cafeterías**. These can be good value, especially the self-service places, but their emphasis is more northern European, and their light snack-meals tend to be dull. Food often comes as a *plato combinado* – literally a combined plate – something like egg and fries or calamares and salad, often with bread and a drink included. This usually costs 500-900ptas. *Cafeterías* often serve a set meal (*menú del día*) as well. You may prefer to get your *plato combinado* at a bar, which in small towns with no *comedores*, may be the only way to eat inexpensively.

Moving up the scale there are **restaurantes** (graded by one to five forks) and **marisquerías**, the latter serving exclusively fish and seafood. Cheaper *restaurantes* are often not much different in price to *comedores*. A fixed-price *cubierto*, *menú del día* or *menú de la casa* (all of which mean the same) is often the best value here: two or three courses plus wine and bread for 750-1500ptas. IVA (a value added tax) may be charged separately at seven percent. Above two forks, however, prices can escalate rapidly. In all but the cheapest places it is usual to leave a tip: ten percent is quite sufficient.

Fish and seafood form the basis of a vast variety of *tapas* and are fresh and excellent even hundreds of miles from the sea; though it's not cheap, you really should make the most of what's on offer. Fish stews (*zarzuelas*) and rice-based paellas (which also contain meat, usually rabbit or chicken) are often memorable. **Meat** is most often grilled and served with a few fried potatoes and salad, or cured and served as a starter or in sandwiches. *Jamón Serrano*, the Spanish version of Parma ham, is superb. **Vegetarians** have a fairly hard time of it in Spain, although an increasing number of vegetarian restaurants are springing up in the larger cities. Even in the smallest bar there's always something to eat, but you may get weary of eggs and omelettes (*tortilla francesa* is a plain omelette, *con champiñones* with mushrooms).

■ Drink

Wine, either *tinto* (red), *blanco* (white) or *rosado/clarete* (rosé), is the invariable accompaniment to every meal and is extremely cheap. The most common bottled variety is Valdepeñas, from New Castile; Rioja, from the area around Logroño, is better but more expensive. Other good wines include Penedes and Bach from Catalunya, Ribera del Duero from Castile and Mendizabal, a wonderful, light Rioja rosé.

The classic Andalusian wine is **sherry** – *Vino de Jerez*. This is served chilled and, like everything Spanish, comes in a perplexing variety of forms: *fino* or *Jerez seco* (dry sherry), *amontillado* (medium), or *oloroso* or *Jerez dulce* (sweet). **Cerveza**, lager-type beer, is generally pretty good, though more expensive than wine. Local brands, such as Cruz Campo in Sevilla or Alhambra in Granada, are often better than the national ones. Equally refreshing, though often deceptively strong, is **sangría**, a wine-and-fruit punch which you'll come across at fiestas and in tourist bars. **Sidra**, a dry farmhouse cider, is most typical in the Basque Country and Asturias.

In mid-afternoon – or even at breakfast – many Spaniards take a *copa* of **liqueur** with their coffee, or else tip the liqueur or brandy into the coffee, calling the concoction *carajillo*. The best are *anís* (like Pernod) or *coñac*, excellent local brandy with a distinct vanilla flavour. Most **spirits** are ordered by brand name, since there are generally cheaper Spanish equivalents for standard imports. Specify *nacional* to avoid getting an expensive foreign brand.

Coffee – served in cafés, *heladerías* (ice-cream parlours) and bars – is invariably espresso, slightly bitter and served black, unless you specify *cortado* (with a drop of milk) or *con leche* (a more generous dollop). **Tea** is also available at most bars, although Spaniards usually drink it black. If you want milk, ask

afterwards: ordering *té con leche* might well get you a glass of milk with a teabag floating on top.

Opening hours and holidays

Almost everything in Spain – shops, museums, churches, tourist offices – closes for a **siesta** of at least two hours in the hottest part of the day. There's a lot of variation, and certain **shops** now stay open all day, but basic summer working hours are Mon–Sat 9.30am–1.30pm & 5–8pm. **Museums**, with few exceptions, take a break between 1 and 4pm, and are closed Sunday afternoon and all day Monday. The really important **churches**, including most cathedrals, operate similarly; others open only for worship in the early morning and/or the evening.

There are twelve national **holidays** and scores of local ones. The national ones are: Jan 1; Jan 6; Maundy Thursday, Good Friday; Easter Sunday; May 1; Aug 15; Oct 12; Nov 1; Dec 6; Dec 8; Dec 25. Certain *Comunidades* (regions) also observe Easter Monday; Corpus Christi (early or mid-June); June 24; and July 25.

Emergencies

Though their role has been cut back since the days when they operated as Franco's right hand, the **Guardia Civil** (green uniforms and patent-leather hats or green kepis) are the most officious of Spain's police, and the ones to avoid. If you do need the police, you should always go instead to the more sympathetic **Policía Nacional, Policía Municipal**, or **Patrulla Rural** in outlying areas.

A common source of trouble is **petty theft**, which has risen to almost epidemic proportions in cities like Sevilla and Barcelona. If you take normal precautions and don't wave money around, you've little to worry about, though fiestas seem to be a particularly dangerous time. Should you be arrested on any charge, you have the right to contact your consulate, and they are required to assist you to some degree if you have your passport stolen or lose your money.

For minor **health** complaints it's easiest to go to a *farmacia*, which you'll find in almost any town. In more serious cases you can get the address of an English-speaking doctor from the nearest relevant consulate, or from a *farmacia*, the local police or Turismo.

EMERGENCY NUMBERS

All emergencies ☎112.

MADRID

MADRID became Spain's capital simply through its geographical position at the centre of Iberia. When Philip II moved the seat of government here in 1561 his aim was to create a symbol of the unification and centralization of the country. The city has few natural advantages – it is 300km from the sea on a 650-metre-high plateau, freezing in winter, burning in summer – and only the determination of successive rulers to promote a strong central capital ensured its success. Today, it is a vast, predominantly modern city, with a population of some five million and growing. Pretty it isn't, but the streets at the heart of the city are a pleasant surprise, with odd pockets of medieval buildings and narrow atmospheric alleys. There may be few sights of great architectural interest, but the monarchs did acquire outstanding picture collections, which formed the basis of the **Prado** museum. This has long ensured Madrid a place on the European art tour, and the more so since the 1990s arrival of the **Reina Sofía** and **Thyssen-Bornemisza** galleries, state-of-the-art homes to fabulous arrays of modern Spanish painting (including Picasso's *Guernica*) and European and American masters.

Galleries and sights aside, though, the capital has enough going for it in its own city life and style to ensure a diverting stay. As you get to grips with the place you soon realize that it's the inhabitants – the Madrileños – that are the capital's key attraction: hanging out in the traditional cafés and *chocolaterías* or the summer *terrazas*, packing the lanes of the Sunday Rastro flea market, or playing hard and very, very late in a thousand bars, clubs, discos and *tascas*. Whatever Barcelona or San Sebastián might claim, the Madrid scene, immortalized in the movies of Pedro Almodóvar, remains the most vibrant and fun in the country.

Arrival and information

Barajas airport is 16km out of town but connected with the centre by bus (every 15min (5.17am–1.51am; 380ptas). The journey takes about half an hour and the terminal is in the underground car park in the Plaza Colón. Taxis from the airport take four people and cost about 2300ptas unless you get caught in rush-hour traffic. A new metro station that will connect the airport with the city centre should have opened by the time this book goes to print.

Trains from the north and from Portugal arrive at the **Estación de Chamartín**, rather isolated in the north of the city. A metro line connects it with the centre and a suburban train line runs to the much more central **Estación de Atocha** – for travel to and from the south, east, west, and Andalucía. Many local trains, or *cercanías*, use the **Estación de Príncipe Pío**, also known as Estación del Norte, near the central Plaza de España. **Bus terminals** are scattered throughout the city, but the largest – used by all international services – is the **Estación Sur** (metro Méndez Álvaro) on c/Méndez Álvaro, south of Atocha station.

Tourist offices can be found at: the Mercado Puerta de Toledo, Stand 3134 (Mon–Fri 9am–7pm, Sat 9.30am–1.30pm; ☎91 364 18 76); c/Duque de Medinaceli 2 near the Prado (Mon–Fri 9am–7pm, Sat 9am–1pm; ☎91 429 49 51); the airport (Mon–Fri 8am–8pm, Sat 9am–1pm; ☎91 305 86 56); and in Chamartín station (Mon–Fri 9am–8pm, Sat 8am–1pm; ☎91 315 99 76). There's also a busy municipal tourist office at Plaza Mayor 3 (Mon–Sat 10am–8pm, Sun 10am–3pm; ☎91 588 16 36). All supply free leaflets and maps of Madrid and – if you're lucky – other Spanish cities. The best and most detailed city map is, in fact, the bus map, also free.

For details of **what's on**, check out the weekly *Guía del Ocio* or the listings in the daily *El Pais* or *El Mundo* newspapers (both have entertainments supplements on Fri). The free tourist office handout, *En Madrid*, is also quite useful but best of all is the excellent free monthly *In Madrid*, also available at tourist offices and in many bars.

City transport

By far the easiest way of getting around Madrid is by **metro**, and the system serves most places you're likely to want to get to. It runs from 6am until 1.30am with a flat fare of 130ptas, or 670ptas for the metrobus ten-ride ticket, valid for both bus and metro. You can get a free colour map of the system at any station. The urban **bus network** is more comprehensive but also more complicated. There's a transport information stand in the Plaza de Cibeles, whose advice you should trust before that of any handout. Buses run from 6am to 11.30pm, but there are also several nightbus lines around the central area (every 30min midnight–3am, hourly 3–6am, from Plaza de Cibeles and Puerta del Sol). At night, though, it's much safer to take a **taxi** – a white car with a diagonal red stripe on the side. There are thousands of them and they're surprisingly cheap.

Accommodation

An **accommodation service**, Brújula, has offices at the airport bus station (daily 8am–10pm; ☎91 575 96 80), Atocha (daily 8am–10pm; ☎91 539 11 73) and Chamartín (daily 7.30am–11pm; ☎91 315 78 94) train stations. The service covers the whole of Spain and costs from 300ptas. You shouldn't really need it, however; once you start to look there's an astonishing amount of cheap accommodation available in the old town.

Much of the cheapest accommodation is to be found in the area immediately **around the Estación de Atocha**, though the places closest to the station are rather grim and at night the area can feel somewhat threatening. Better to head up c/Atocha towards the centre, where you'll find better pickings in the streets surrounding the trendy **Plaza Santa Ana**. Prices rise as you get up towards the Plaza Mayor and Puerta del Sol (metro Sol), but even here there are affordable options. Other promising areas are along the **Gran Vía**, where the huge old buildings hide a vast array of hotels and *hostales* at all prices, and north of here up **c/Fuencarral** towards Malasaña.

Hostels

Hostel Richard Schirmann, in the Casa del Campo (☎91 463 56 99). Way out in the park west of the centre, but friendly, comfortable, clean and cheap, with an enjoyably noisy bar. Metro El Lago or bus #33; you can call and they'll pick you up at the metro station, roughly 1km away – you certainly shouldn't walk there alone after dark. ②.

Hostel Santa Cruz de Marcenado, c/Santa Cruz de Marcenado 28 (☎91 547 45 32). North of the Plaza de España near the Palacio Liria; reasonably pleasant, modern and quiet. Curfew 1.30am. Often full, so arrive early morning if possible. Metro Argüelles. ②.

Hotels

Hostal Aguilar, Carrera San Jerónimo 32 (☎91 429 36 61). Just one in a building packed with possibilities. ③.

Hostal Alcázar Regis, Gran Vía 61 (☎91 547 93 17). Near the Plaza de España, deservedly popular and often full. Others in the same building. ③.

Hostal Alonso, c/Espoz y Mina 17 (☎91 531 56 79). Very cheap, if a little shabby; family-run, excellent situation. ②.

Hostal Armesto, c/San Agustín 6 (☎91 429 09 40). Small very pleasant hostal, well positioned for the Santa Ana area and the art galleries. ③.

Hostal Cruz Sol, Plaza Santa Cruz 6 (☎91 532 71 97). Slightly run-down, but in great, quiet position at other side of Plaza Mayor. Some very cheap doubles. ②.

Hostal Lisboa, c/Ventura de la Vega 17 (☎91 429 98 94). Good 3-star hostal, central but not too hectic. ③.

Casa de Huéspedes Marcelino, c/Cruz 27. Cheap, central, pleasant and friendly. ②.

Pensión Mollo, c/Atocha 104 (☎91 528 71 76). Close to the station on the way up the hill; no lift and on the fourth floor, so not convenient if you're heavily laden. ②.

Hostal Plaza D'Ort, Plaza del Angel 13 (☎91 429 90 41). Well-equipped hostal with some self-catering apartments, making it a good option for groups. ③.

Hostal Regional, c/del Príncipe 18 (☎91 522 33 73). Comfortable place in elegant old building off Plaza Santa Ana; several others share the same building. ②.

Hostal Ribadavia, c/Fuencarral 25 (☎91 531 10 58). Clean, friendly place, with others in the same building. ②.

Hostal Riosol, c/Mayor 5 (☎91 532 31 42). Just off Puerta del Sol towards Plaza Mayor. A few cheaper rooms without bath. ③.

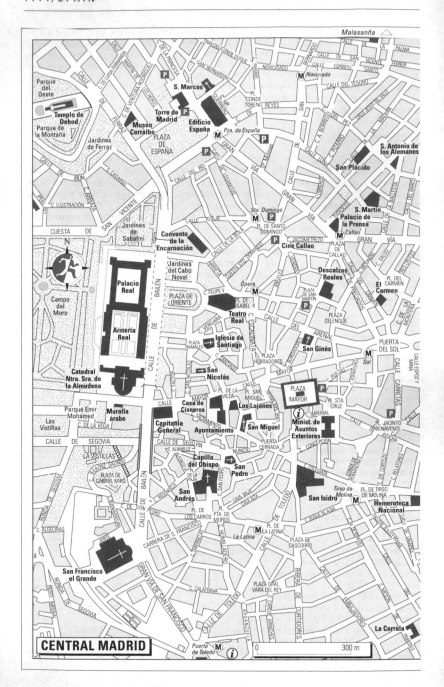

CENTRAL MADRID

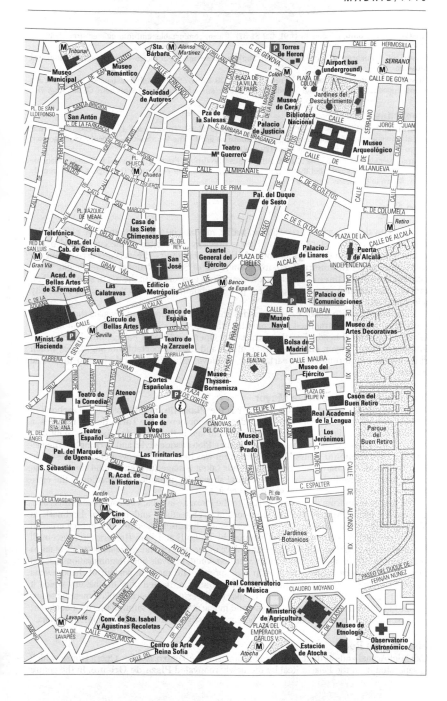

Hostal San Antonio, c/León 13 (☎91 429 51 37). Clean, comfortable, and in a quieter street between Atocha and Santa Ana. ②.

Hostal Sil, c/Fuencarral 95 (☎91 448 89 72). Slightly quieter area near metro Tribunal and the Municipal Museum. ③.

Hostal Sud-Americana, Paseo del Prado 12 (☎91 429 25 64). Surprisingly reasonable considering it's almost opposite the Prado; though standards vary, there are some excellent rooms here. Closed Aug. ③.

Campsites

Madrid, on the N1 Burgos road at kilometre 11 (☎91 302 28 35). Theoretically a second-class site, hence slightly cheaper than *Osuna*, but facilities are almost as good – there's a swimming pool and it's quieter. Metro Plaza de Castilla followed by bus #129 or #151.

Osuna, Avenida de Logroño (☎91 741 05 10), out near the airport. Friendly, with good facilities, reasonable prices and plenty of shade, but the ground is rock-hard and, being so close to the airport, it's extremely noisy. Metro to Canillejas, then bus #105.

The City

The **Puerta del Sol**, with its crowds and traffic, may not be the most attractive place in the city but it's a suitable starting point. This is officially the centre of the capital and of the nation: a stone slab in the pavement outside the main building – the casa de correos – on the south side marks **Kilometre Zero**, from where six of Spain's National Routes begin, while beneath the streets, three of the city's ten metro lines converge. On the north side, at the bottom of c/del Carmen, is a statue of a bear pawing a bush; this is both the emblem of the city and a favourite meeting place.

Immediately **north** of Sol, c/de Preciados and c/del Carmen head towards the Gran Vía; both have been pedestrianized and constitute the most popular **shopping** area in Madrid. **West**, c/del Arenal heads directly towards the Opera and Royal Palace, but there's more interest along c/Mayor, one of Madrid's oldest and most important thoroughfares, which runs southwest, through the heart of the medieval city, also to end close to the Royal Palace.

Plaza de la Villa and Plaza Mayor

About two-thirds of the way along c/Mayor is the **Plaza de la Villa**, almost a casebook of Spanish architectural development. The oldest survivor here is the **Torre de los Lujanes**, a fifteenth-century building in Mudéjar style; next in age is the **Casa de Cisneros**, built by a nephew of Cardinal Cisneros in sixteenth-century Plateresque style; and to complete the picture the **Ayuntamiento** (tours Mon at 5pm; free) was begun in the seventeenth century, but later remodelled in Baroque mode. Baroque is taken a stage further, around the corner in c/San Justo, where the church of **San Miguel** shows the unbridled imagination of the eighteenth-century Italian architects who designed it.

Walking straight from the Puerta del Sol to the Plaza de la Villa, you could easily miss altogether the **Plaza Mayor**, the most important architectural and historical landmark in Madrid. This almost perfectly preserved, extremely beautiful, seventeenth-century arcaded square, set back from the street, was planned by Philip II and Juan Herrera (architect of El Escorial; see p.1127) as the public meeting place of the new capital: *autos-da-fé* (trials of faith) were held by the Inquisition here, kings were crowned, festivals and demonstrations passed through, bulls were fought, and gossip was spread. The more important of these events would be watched by royalty from the **Casa Panadería**, named after the bakery which it replaced. Along with its popular cafés, the plaza still performs several public functions today. In summer it becomes an outdoor theatre and music stage; in the autumn there's a book fair; and just before Christmas it becomes a bazaar for festive decorations and religious regalia.

The Palacio Real

Calle del Arenal ends at the Plaza Isabel II opposite the **Teatro Real** or Opera House, which is separated from the Palacio Real by the newly renovated **Plaza de Oriente**. In the centre of the square is a superb statue of Felipe IV on horseback; it was based on designs by Velázquez, and Galileo is said to have helped with the calculations to make it balance.

The chief attraction of this otherwise rather barren area, however, is the **Palacio Real** or Royal Palace (Mon–Sat 9/9.30am–5/6pm, Sun 9am–2/3pm; 850ptas/950 ptas guided, free Wed for EU citizens). Built after the earlier Muslim Alcazar burned down on Christmas Day 1734, this was the principal royal residence until Alfonso XIII went into exile in 1931. The present royal family inhabits a more modest residence on the western outskirts of the city, using the Palacio Real only on state occasions. The building scores high on statistics: it claims more rooms than any other European palace; a **library** with one of the biggest collections of books, manuscripts, maps and musical scores in the world; an **armoury** with an unrivalled collection of weapons dating back to the fifteenth century; and an original **pharmacy**, a curious mixture of alchemist's den and early laboratory, its walls lined with jars labelled for various remedies.

It is no longer compulsory to follow a guided tour, so you can take your own time to contemplate the extraordinary opulence of the place: acres of Flemish and Spanish tapestries, endless Rococo decoration, bejewelled clocks and pompous portraits of the monarchs. In the **Sala del Trono** (Throne Room) there's a magnificent frescoed ceiling by Tiepolo representing the glory of Spain – an extraordinary achievement for an artist by then in his seventies.

Facing the Palacio Real, to the south, across the shadeless Plaza Armeria, is Madrid's brand new **Cathedral** (daily 10am–1.30pm & 6–8pm). This was planned centuries ago and worked upon for decades but only opened for business in 1993 with an inauguration by Pope John Paul II. Its Neoclassical bulk is as undistinguished inside as out, though the boutique-like Opus Dei chapel has, at least, novelty value.

The Gran Vía

North from the palace, c/Bailén runs into the **Plaza de España**, home to a couple of ageing skyscrapers, for long the city's tallest. These look over an elaborate monument to Cervantes in the middle of the square, which in turn overlooks the bewildered bronze figures of Don Quixote and Sancho Panza. The square, however, is not a place to linger – the area is popular with junkies – and it's best to head off smartly along the **Gran Vía**, the capital's major thoroughfare, which effectively divides the old city to the south from the newer parts. Permanently crowded with shoppers and sightseers, this Gran Vía is appropriately named, with splendidly quirky Art Nouveau and Art Deco facades fronting its banks, offices and apartments, and huge hand-painted posters on the cinemas. At its far end, by the magnificent cylindrical **Edificio Metropolis**, the street joins with c/Alcalá on the approach to Plaza de la Cibeles. Just across the junction is the majestic old **Círculo de las Bellas Artes**, a contemporary art exhibition space with a rather formal-looking but very trendy bar (entry charge of 100ptas for non-members during exhibitions).

On an entirely different plane, the **Monasterio de las Descalzas Reales** (Tues–Thurs & Sat 10.30am–12.45pm & 4–5.45pm, Fri 10.30am–12.45pm, Sun 11am–1.45pm; 650ptas), one of the hidden treasures of the city, lies just south of the Gran Vía on the Plaza de las Descalzas. This convent was founded by Juana de Austria, daughter of Carlos V, sister of Philip II and, at nineteen, already the widow of Prince Don Juan of Portugal. In her wake came a succession of titled ladies (the name means the Convent of the Barefoot Royals) who brought fame and, above all, fortune. The place is unbelievably rich and also quite beautiful, the tranquillity within its thick walls making an extraordinary contrast to the frenzied commercialism all around. A whistle-stop guided tour takes you through the cloisters and up a ridiculously fancy stairway to a series of chambers packed with art and treasures of every kind.

Santa Ana and Huertas

Although there are few sights here, the area east of the Puerta del Sol, a rough triangle bordered to the east by the Paseo del Prado, on the north by c/Alcalá, and along the south by c/Atocha, is likely to claim more of your time than any conventional tourist attraction, due to its superb concentration of bars and restaurants. This area developed in the nineteenth century and has a strong literary past: there are streets named after **Cervantes** and **Lope de Vega** (where one lived and the other died), the *Atheneum* club is here, as is the *Círculo de las Bellas Artes* (see "The Gran Vía", above) and the *Teatro Español*. The *Cortes,* Spain's parliament, also sits here.

The **Paseo del Prado** is part of one of the city's great avenues, running from Atocha station (opposite which is the Centro Reina Sofía), past the Prado and Thyssen galleries, to the **Plaza de la Cibeles,** named after a fountain and statue of the goddess Cibeles awash in a sea of traffic in the middle. Dominating this square is Madrid's fabulously ornate central post office, the **Palacio de Comunicaciones** – a much more convincing cathedral than the real one by the Palacio Real. To the north of Cibeles, the *paseo* continues, with name-changes first to **Recoletos** and then **Castellana,** past the major shopping and business areas. In summer, the centre of Paseo de Castellana becomes an almost continuous line of *terrazas,* or pavement café/bars, where Madrid's sleepless society comes to talk, drink and be seen from midnight to dawn.

The Prado

The **Museo del Prado** (Tues–Sat 9am–7pm, Sun 9am–2pm; 500ptas, free Sat after 2.30pm and Sun; admission can be gained with the little advertised "Paseo del Arte" voucher, which includes entrance to all three of the great art museums, costs 1275ptas, and is valid for a year) has been one of Europe's key art galleries ever since it was opened to the public in 1819. It houses the finest works collected by Spanish royalty – for the most part avid, discerning, and wealthy buyers – as well as standout items from other Spanish sources: over three thousand paintings in all, including the world's finest collections of Goya, Velázquez and Bosch. Although all the major works are still on display, ongoing restoration work means that many paintings are being temporarily rehung elsewhere in the gallery, so pick up a leaflet at the entrance to find any changes to the plan described here.

Even in a full day you couldn't hope to do justice to everything in the Prado, and it's much more enjoyable to make short visits with a clear idea of what you want to see. Perhaps the best approach to the museum is through the Puerta de Goya, the side entrance on c/Felipe IV. In the first rooms on the ground floor are early Spanish paintings, mostly religious subjects, then in a series of rooms to your left the early **Flemish masters** are displayed. The great triptychs of **Hieronymus Bosch** – the early *Hay Wain,* the middle-period *Garden of Earthly Delights* and the late *Adoration of the Magi* – are familiar from countless reproductions but infinitely more chilling in the original, and there's much more of his work here, along with that of **Pieter Brueghel the Elder,** Rogier van der Weyden, Memling, Bouts, Gerard David and Massys. The few German paintings are dominated by four Dürers.

The long, central downstairs gallery houses the **early Spanish collection,** and a dazzling array of portraits and religious paintings by the Cretan-born **El Greco,** among them his mystic and hallucinatory *Crucifixion* and *Adoration of the Shepherds.* Beyond this is the beginning of the Prado's Italian treasures: the superb **Titian** portraits of Charles V and Philip II, as well as works by Tintoretto, Bassano, Caravaggio and Veronese. Upstairs are Goya's unmissable **Black Paintings** – best seen after visiting the rest of his work on the top floor – and, to the left of the Puerta de Goya entrance, the Italian paintings include a series of panels by **Botticelli** illustrating a story from the *Decameron.* The museum's collection of over 160 works of **later Flemish and Dutch art** has been imaginatively rehoused in a new suite of twelve rooms off the main gallery on the first floor. Rubens is extensively represented – by the beautifully restored *Three Graces* among others – as are Van Dyck and Jan Brueghel.

Continuing on the first floor you come to the great Spanish painters, where the outstanding presence is **Velázquez** – among the collection are intimate portraits of the family of Felipe IV, most famously his masterpiece *Las Meninas.* Adjacent are important works by Zurbarán and Murillo.

The top floor of the building is devoted almost entirely to **Francisco de Goya,** whose many portraits of his patron, Charles IV, are remarkable for their lack of any attempt at flattery while those of Queen María Luisa, whom he despised, are downright ugly. He was an enormously versatile artist: contrast the voluptuous *Majas* with the horrors depicted in *The Second of May* and *The Third of May*, on-the-spot portrayals of the rebellion against Napoleon and the subsequent reprisals.

South of the Prado is the **Casón del Buen Retiro**, which used to house Picasso's *Guernica* (now in the Reina Sofía) but is now devoted to nineteenth-century Spanish art. It is currently closed for major restoration work.

The Thyssen-Bornemisza collection

The **Colleción Thyssen-Bornemisza** (Tues–Sun 10am–7pm; 700ptas) occupies the old Palacio de Villahermosa, diagonally opposite the Prado, at the end of the Carrera de San Jerónimo. This prestigious site played a large part in Spain's acquisition – for a knock-down $300,000,000 in June 1993 – of what was perhaps the world's greatest private art trove. The seven-hundred-odd paintings accumulated by father-and-son Swiss steel magnates contain examples of every major period and movement: **medieval to seventeenth century** on the top floor, **Rococo and Neoclassicism to Fauves and Expressionists** on the first floor, and **Surrealists, Pop Art and the Avant Garde** on ground level. How the Thyssens got hold of classic works by everyone from Duccio and Holbein, through El Greco and Caravaggio, to Schiele and Rothko, takes your breath away. Surprises include a strong showing of nineteenth-century Americans, some very early and very late van Goghs, and side-by-side hanging of parallel Cubist studies by Picasso, Braque and Mondrian. The museum has a handy **bar and cafeteria** in the basement and allows re-entry, so long as you get your hand stamped at the exit desk.

Centro de Arte Reina Sofía

Luckily, the **Centro de Arte Reina Sofía** (Wed–Sat & Mon 10am–9pm, Sun 10am–2.30pm; 500ptas, free Sat after 2.30pm and Sun), facing Atocha station at the end of Paseo del Prado, keeps different opening hours and days from its neighbours. For this permanent collection of modern Spanish art, and leading exhibition space, is another essential stop on the Madrid art scene. The museum, a massive former convent and hospital, is a kind of Madrid response to the Pompidou Centre in Paris. Transparent lifts shuttle visitors up the outside of the building, whose levels feature a cinema, excellent art book and design shops, a print, music and photographic library, restaurant, bar and café, as well as the exhibition halls (top floor) and the collection of twentieth-century art (second floor).

It is for **Picasso's Guernica** that most visitors come to the Reina Sofía, and rightly so. Superbly displayed, along with its preliminary studies, this icon of twentieth-century Spanish art and politics – a response to the fascist bombing of the Basque town of Guernica in the Spanish Civil War – carries a shock that defies all familiarity. The painting is in Room 7, midway around, after strong rooms on **Cubism** and the **Paris School**. The post-Guernica halls are devoted to Dalí and Miró, while the final rooms, entitled **"Proposals"**, contain an evolving display of contemporary art, both Spanish and foreign.

Retiro and other parks

When you get tired of sightseeing, Madrid's many parks provide great places to escape for a few hours. The most central and most popular is the **Parque del Buen Retiro** behind the Prado, a delightful mix of formal gardens and wider spaces. Originally the grounds of a royal retreat (*retiro* in Spanish), it has been public property for more than a hundred years; the palace itself burned down in the eighteenth century. In its 330 acres you can jog, row a boat, picnic, have your fortune told, and above all promenade – on Sunday half of Madrid turns out for the *paseo*, after the Rastro market. Travelling art exhibitions are frequently housed in the beautiful **Palacio de Velázquez** and the nearby **Palacio de Cristal** (times and prices vary according to exhibition). The nearby **Jardines Botanicos** (daily 10am–sunset; 200ptas; metro Atocha), whose entrance faces the southern end of the Prado, are also delightful.

The Rastro

The area south of the Plaza Mayor and c/Atocha has traditionally been a tough, working-class district. In many places the old houses survive, huddled together in narrow streets, but the character of **La Latina** and **Lavapiés** is beginning to change as their inhabitants, and the districts themselves, become younger and more fashionable. Part of the reason for this rise in status must be the **Rastro** (metro La Latina), which is as much part of Madrid's weekend ritual as a mass or a *paseo*. This gargantuan, thriving, thieving shambles of a street **market** sprawls south from metro La Latina to the Ronda de Toledo, especially along c/Ribera de Curtidores. Through it, crowds flood between 10am and 3pm every Sunday and to a modest degree on Fridays and Saturdays too. Don't expect to find fabulous bargains; the serious antique trade has mostly moved off the streets and into the shops. It's definitely worth a visit, though, if only to see the locals out in their thousands and to drop into traditional bars for tapas. Keep a tight grip on your bags, pockets, cameras and jewellery.

North of Gran Vía: Chueca, Malasaña and beyond

The chief reason to explore the quarters **north of Gran Vía** is for restaurants and nightlife. Although the late-late-nightclubs and discos are scattered around the city, and some even a few kilometres out from the centre, it is in **Chueca** and **Malasaña** that you'll find by far the heaviest concentration of bars and clubs downtown. Heading up in this direction by day, you might stop off at the **Museo Municipal**, c/Fuencarral 78 (Tues–Fri 9.30am–8pm, Sat & Sun 10am–2pm; 300ptas; metro Tribunal). Better known for its superb Churrigueresque facade than its contents, this eighteenth-century building houses exhibits tracing the development of Madrid from prehistoric times, with some fascinating scale models of the city as it used to be.

Malasaña, centred on the Plaza Dos de Mayo, was the focus of the *movida Madrileña*, the "happening scene" of the late 1970s and early 1980s after the death of Franco. Then it was the mecca of the young: bars appeared behind every doorway, drugs were sold openly in the streets, and there was an extraordinary atmosphere of new-found freedom. To some extent it still is like this, but the shops and restaurants now reflect increasingly upmarket tastes. **Chueca**, at least in the centre around the Plaza Chueca, is much less respectable, but here, as you walk east towards the expensive shopping areas around the Paseo Recoletos, are some of the city's most enticing streets. Offbeat restaurants, small private art galleries, and odd corner shops are to be found here in abundance and c/Almirante has some of the city's most expensive designer clothes shops too.

Salamanca, across the Paseo Recoletos from Chueca, is full of fashionable apartments and expensive shops. A stroll up **c/Serrano** will take you past many of these and past a trio of museums and galleries. At no. 13 is the dusty and chaotic **Museo Arqueológico** (Tues–Sat 9.30am–8.30pm, Sun 9.30am–2.30pm; 500ptas, free Sat pm & Sun; metro Colón), which contains the celebrated Celto-Iberian bust known as *La Dama de Elche*, the slightly later *Dama de Baza*, and a wonderfully rich hoard of Visigothic treasures found at Toledo. In the gardens you can visit a replica of the Altamira Caves complete with convincing copies of their prehistoric wall paintings. At no. 60 is the Fundación La Caixa, a superb exhibition space maintained by the Barcelona savings bank. And finally, at no. 122, is the **Museo Lazaro Galdiano** (Tues–Sun 10am–2pm; 500ptas, Sat free; metro Rubén Darío), the pick of Madrid's smaller museums. This originally private collection, donated to the state by José Galdiano, spreads over the four floors of his former home, its jumble of art works including paintings by Bosch, Rembrandt, Velázquez, El Greco and Goya.

Not far to the west of here, across the Paseo de la Castellana, is one of the hidden treasures of Madrid, the **Museo Sorolla**, c/General Martínez Campos 37 (Tues–Sat 10am–3pm, July & Aug closes 2.30pm; Sun 10am–2pm; 400ptas, free Sun; metro Rubén Darío/Iglesia). This is a large collection of work by the painter Joaquín Sorolla (1863–1923), displayed in his old home and studio. The ground floor has been kept largely intact, re-creating the atmosphere of the artist's living and working areas, while upstairs is a gallery displaying a variety of his striking impressionistic work.

Eating and drinking

Madrid is a superb place to eat and, above all, drink: there can be few places in the world which rival the area around **Puerta del Sol** in either quantity or variety of outlets, from bars with spectacular seafood displays to old-time canteens offering modest-priced *menús del día*, from haute Spanish (or French, or Moroccan) cuisine to drinkers' dive bars and traditional *chocolate con churros* cafés. And the feasts continue in all directions, especially towards **Plaza Santa Ana** and along **c/de las Huertas** to Atocha, but also south in the neighbourhood haunts of La Latina and Lavapiés, and north in the grungier district **Malasaña**.

In summer, all areas of the city spring forth *terrazas* – pavement café/bars – where coffees are taken by day and drinks pretty much all night. The prime area is **Paseo Castellana**, where many of the top discos encamp (and charge accordingly). Smaller scenes are in Plaza de Chueca, Paseo Rosales del Pintor along the Parque del Oeste, and the more modest and relaxed **Las Vistillas**, on the south side of the viaduct on c/Bailén, due south of the royal palace.

Tapas bars

El Abuelo, c/Nuñez de Arce 5, Huertas. Excellent selection of tapas and *raciones*. Another branch on c/de la Victoria is a stand-up bar serving just 4 delicious prawn dishes.

Casa Alberto, c/de las Huertas 18. One of the most traditional Huertas bars: very friendly, lots of tables and huge portions. Also a restaurant at the back.

Almendro 13, c/del Almendro 13. Fashionable wooden panelled bar that serves great *fino* and innovative tapas.

El Anciano Rey de los Vinos, c/Bailén. Wine and sherry in the traditional manner straight from the barrel.

Las Bravas, c/Espoz y Mina, Huertas. One of many straightforward tapas bars here – stand at the bar to sample the tortillas and *patatas bravas*.

El Chiky, c/Coloreros 3. Atmospheric bastion of fine tapas, grilled meats and paella right by Plaza Mayor.

Café Comercial, Glorieta de Bilbao. Traditional café and meeting place to linger over coffee, *coñac* and cakes.

Café Gijón, Paseo de Recoletos 21 north of Plaza de Cibeles. Traditional nineteenth-century café, tremendously atmospheric. Lunchtime menu and summer terrace.

La Mallorquina, c/Mayor, right on Puerta del Sol. Good for breakfast or snacks – try one of their *napolitanas* (filled croissants).

Mejillonera El Pasaje, Pasaje Matheu, off c/Vitoria, near Sol. One of many places filling the narrow street with outdoor tables – this specializes in mussels served in every way conceivable.

Museo del Jamón, Carrera San Jerónimo 6, Puerta del Sol end. Extraordinary place where hundreds of hams hang from the ceiling, and you can sample the different (expensive) varieties over a glass or two; also has full meals and the best breakfast deal in town for 260ptas. Branches at c/Atocha and c/Postas.

Café de Oriente, Plaza de Oriente. Rich kids' haunt with expensive food, but a lovely old café with a small summer *terraza* looking over to the Palacio Real.

Casa Rúa, c/Ciudad Rodrigo 3, just off Plaza Mayor. Stand-up seafood tapas bar, popular with a young crowd.

Viña P, Plaza de Santa Ana 3. Friendly bar, decked out in bullfighting mementos, and serving a great range of tapas.

Mainly-for-drinking bars

Cervecería Alemána, Plaza Santa Ana. One of Hemingway's favourite haunts and consequently full of Americans; good traditional atmosphere none the less.

Bodega Ángel Sierra, Plaza Chueca. Great old bar, just the place for an aperitif.

La Fidula, c/Huertas 57. The *grande dame* of the dozens on this street: here you can sip *fino* to the accompaniment of classical tunes performed from the tiny stage.

Los Gabrieles, c/Echegaray 17. One of the most spectacular tiled bars in Madrid, with fabulous nineteenth-century drinking scenes on the glazed ceramic tileworks (or *azulejos*), including a great version of Velázquez's *Los Borrachos* (the drunkards).

La Luna, Amor de Diós, off Huertas. A perennially popular dive.

La Venencia, c/Echegaray 7. Marvellous old wooden bar, serving only sherry and the most basic of tapas – cheese and pressed tuna. A must.

Star's Dance Café, c/Marqués de Valdeiglesias 5. Hip, happening gay/mixed bar with funky basement grooves at weekends.

Viva Madrid, c/Manuel Gonzales. More splendid tiles and a great atmosphere.

Restaurants

Artemisa, c/Ventura de la Vega 4. Decent low-priced vegetarian restaurant.

Casa Alberto, c/Huertas 18. Small traditional *taberna* where you can eat at the bar or a small dining room at the back.

Casa Ciriaco, c/Mayor 84. Good, traditional restaurant, not too expensive for the area.

La Casevola, c/Echegaray 5, Huertas. Reasonably priced Asturian food and tapas.

Casa Eduardo, Cava San Miguel, next to the market behind Plaza Mayor. Outdoor tables, Galician specialties and very cheap set menu.

Creperie Ma Bretagne, c/San Vicente Ferrer. Tiny place with good pancakes, open until after midnight.

El Estragón, Plaza de la Paja 10. Good vegetarian tapas and an economical *menú del día*.

Fernández, c/Palma 6. Simple, inexpensive restaurant, always packed with locals and adventurous low-budget travellers.

El Gambón, c/Barbieri 1, Chueca. Excellent African food: more expensive than many of its basic neighbours, but worth it.

El Granero de Lavapiés, c/Argumosa 10, near metro Lavapiés. Macrobiotic and vegetarian fare. Open Mon–Fri 1–4pm only.

Gula Gula, c/Infante 5 & Gran Vía 1. Extremely popular and very funky restaurants with unbeatable vegetarian salad bar.

Casa Mingo, Paseo de la Florida next to chapel of San Antonio de la Florida. Asturian place where you eat roast chicken washed down with cider. Good value and great fun, especially on Sunday afternoons.

Sabatini, c/Bailén 15, opposite Jardines Sabatini. Outdoor tables looking towards the Palacio Real in summer; the food's significantly less expensive than you might expect.

La Trucha, c/Manuel Fernández y González, between Echegaray and c/del Principe, Huertas. Not the cheapest, but excellent meals in very Madrileño atmosphere.

Viuda de Vacas, c/ Cava Alta 23. Good value no-frills Castilian restaurant in an area packed with great bars.

Nightlife

The **bars, clubs and discos** of **Malasaña**, or down south in **Lavapiés**, and **Huertas** around Plaza Santa Ana, could easily occupy your whole stay in Madrid, with the most serious clubs starting around 1am and staying open until well beyond dawn. The names and styles change constantly but even where a place has closed down a new alternative usually opens up at the same address. To supplement our listings, check out the English-language magazine *En Madrid*, or the quarterly *Madrid Concept* for *terrazas* (open-air terrace bars), *bares de noche* (nightclubs), *discotecas* and *actuaciones* (where you'll often find live music).

   Music concerts – classical, flamenco, salsa, jazz and rock – are advertised on posters around Sol and are also listed in the *Guia del Ocio* and in the newspaper, *El Pais*. In July and especially in August there's not too much happening inside, but the city council sponsors a "Veranos de la Villa" programme in some attractive outside venues.

   If you find that you've somehow stayed out all night and feel in need of early morning sustenance, a final station on the clubbers' circuit is to take *chocolate con churros* at the *Chocolatería San Gines* (Tues–Sun 10am–7pm) on c/de Coloreros, just off c/Mayor.

Discos, music bars and clubs

Discos and music bars can be found all over the city. Of the big **nightclubs**, *Pacha*, c/Barcelo 11, is the eternal survivor – it's exceptionally cool during the week, less so at weekends when the out-of-towners take over. Other good clubs include *El Sol* on c/Jardines 3 (metro Gran

Vía) for house, soul and acid jazz, plus live music; *Torero* on c/de la Cruz 26 for house/Latino (near Huertas, metro Sevilla); *Kathmandu*, c/Señores de Luzón 3 (metro Sol), for funk and acid jazz; *La Vía Lactea*, c/Velarde 18 (Malasaña, metro Tribunal) for indie and grunge; *Soma* c/Leganitas 25 (metro Plaza España) for goa trance; and *Morocco*, c/Marqués de Leganes 7 (metro Santo Domingo).

For diving in and out of clubs, however, as Madrileños like to do, **Malasaña** holds most promise. **Chueca** is more exclusively (but not entirely) **gay** these days – c/Pelayo is a good point to start from, with the quarter's most eclectic bar, *Torito*, at no. 4 and several gay bars, including *New Leather* at no. 42 and *LL* at no. 11. Be aware that Chueca is also a big drug-dealing centre, especially around the central Plaza de Chueca. Over in **Malasaña**, there are drugs, too, mainly around Plaza Dos de Mayo, while the music in the clubs is more on a grunge trip. A key street to start off explorations is c/San Vicente Ferrer, where *Maravillas* at no. 35 sometimes has live music. *La Habana* at Atocha no. 107 has a great mix of salsa and reggae. For more of a chance to talk, try *Café Manuela* or *Estar*, both in c/San Vicente Ferrer, or three pubs in the Plaza Dos de Mayo: *El Arco–Café Mahon*, *El Sol de Mayo* and *Pepe Botella*.

Finally, the **Lavapiés** area, south of Sol, is an emerging bar and club locale: popular spots are *Medea*, the city's premier lesbian disco (closed Mon) at c/de la Cabeza 33; and *Barbieri* (closed Mon), a disco/pub on Avenida María 45.

Live music

The music scene in Madrid sets the pattern for the rest of the country, and the best **rock bands** either come from Madrid or make their name here. For young local groups try *Al Laboratorio*, c/ Colón 14. Bigger rock concerts are usually held in one of the football stadiums or at *La Riviera* on Paseo Bajo Virgen del Puerto. A good array of **jazz bars** includes the topnotch *Café Central*, Plaza del Ángel 10, near Sol, *Clamores* in c/Albuquerque 14, and *Café Populart* at c/de las Huertas 22. **South American** music is on offer at various venues, especially during summer festivals; the best year-round club is the *Café del Mercado* in the Mercado Puerta de Toledo, which puts on live salsa more or less every night. **Flamenco** can also be heard at its best in the summer festivals, especially at the *noches de flamenco* in the beautiful courtyard of the old barracks on c/de Conde Duque. Promising year-round venues include *Caracol*, c/Bernardino Obregón 18; *Café de Chinitas*, c/Torija 7; *La Solea*, Cava Baja 27; *Casa Patas*, Cañizares 10; and Wednesdays at *Suristán*, which is the place to head for modern flamenco.

Film and theatre

Cinemas can be found all over the central area, with the biggest on Gran Vía. The Spanish routinely dub foreign movies, but a few cinemas specialize in original-language screenings. These include the Alphaville, Renoir and Lumière at c/Martín de los Heros 14 and 12, near Plaza de España, the California at c/Andrés Mellado 53 (metro Moncloa) and the six-screen Multicinés Ideal at c/Doctor Cortezo 6, near Sol. A programme of classic films is shown at the very pleasant Filmoteca at c/Santa Isabel 3, which in summer has an outdoor *cine-terraza*.

Classical Spanish **theatre** performances can be seen at the Teatro Español, Plaza Santa Ana, and more modern works in the Centro Cultural de la Villa, Plaza de Colón, and in the beautiful Círculo de Bellas Artes, Marqués de Casa Riera 2. Cultural events in English are held from time to time at the **British Institute**, c/Almagro 5, metro Alonso Martínez, which can also be a useful point for contacts.

Listings

Airlines Almost all have their offices along the Gran Vía, on c/de la Princesa, its continuation beyond the Plaza de España, or in the Torre de Madrid on the Plaza. Exceptions are Iberia, c/Goya 29 (☎91 587 8 100), and British Airways, c/Serrano 60 5° (☎91 305 42 12 or 91 205 43 17).

American Express Plaza de las Cortes 2 (Mon–Fri 9am–5.30pm, Sat 9am–noon; ☎91 322 55 00, helpline ☎91 572 03 03).

Books There's a good stock of English titles at Booksellers S.A., c/José Abascal 48 (metro Iglesias or Ríos Rosas) and a huge selection at the Casa del Libro on Gran Vía 29.

Bullfights Madrid's Plaza de Toros – Las Ventas – hosts some of the year's most prestigious events, especially during the May/June San Isidro festivities. Tickets are available at the box office (except for big events).

Car rental Atesa, Infanta Mercedes 90 (☎91 571 19 31); Budget, c/Alcantara 59 (☎91 402 14 80); Europcar, Estación de Atocha (☎91 555 99 30); Hertz, Estación de Atocha (☎91 468 13 18); Auto Chamartín, Estación de Chamartín (☎91 733 33 79).

Embassies Australia, Santa Engracia 120 (☎91 441 93 00); Britain, Fernando el Santo 16 (☎91 319 02 00); Canada, Nuñez de Balboa 35 (☎91 431 43 00); Ireland, Paseo de la Castellana (☎91 577 89 31); New Zealand, Plaza de la Lealtad 2 (☎91 523 02 26); USA, c/Serrano 75 (☎91 587 22 00).

Exchange Round the clock at the airport. Branches of El Corte Inglés department store all have exchange offices with long hours and highly competitive rates and commissions. Banco Central for American Express travellers' cheques.

Football Real Madrid play at the Estadio Bernabéu in the north of the city; bus #150 stops outside. Atlético play at Vicente Calderón, nearest metro is Pirámides. Tickets available at the grounds a few days before the match.

Hospitals El Clínico, Plaza de Cristo Rey (☎91 330 37 47); Ciudad Sanitaria La Paz, Avenida Castillana #261. For an ambulance, call ☎061 or 092.

Laundry c/Barco 26 (metro Gran Vía); c/Donoso Cortés 17 (metro Quevedo); c/Hermosilla 121 (metro Goya); c/Palma 2 (metro Tribunal).

Left luggage At Estación Sur de Autobuses, c/Méndez Álvaro; Auto-Res; Continental Auto stations; and the airport bus terminal beneath Plaza Colón. Lockers at Atocha and Chamartín stations.

Post office Palacio de Comunicaciones in the Plaza de las Cibeles (Mon–Fri 8.30am–9.30pm, Sat 9.30am–9.30pm, Sun 8.30am–2pm) for stamps, telegrams, poste restante and registered delivery.

Telephones Telefónica, Gran Vía 30 (daily 9am–11.30pm).

Travel agencies Viajes TIVE, c/Fernando el Católico 88 (metro Moncloa; ☎91 543 02 08), for discount air fares, rail passes and bus tickets; Viajes Zeppelin, Plaza Santo Domingo 2 (metro Santo Domingo; ☎ 91 542 51 54), is a helpful company offering excellent deals on flights and holidays.

AROUND MADRID

Circling the capital are some of Spain's most fascinating cities, all making an easy day-trip from Madrid, but also lying on the main routes out. From **Toledo** you can turn south to Andalucía or strike west towards Extremadura. To the northwest the roads lead past **El Escorial**, from where a bus runs to Franco's tomb at El Valle de los Caídos, and through the dramatic scenery of the **Sierra de Guadarrama**, with Madrid's weekend ski resorts, to Ávila and Segovia. From **Ávila** it's just a short way on to Salamanca, or there are beautiful routes down through the **Sierra de Gredos** into Extremadura. From **Segovia** the routes north to Valladolid, Burgos and beyond await. To the east there's less of interest, but Alcalá de Henares and Guadalajara can both offer a worthwhile break in the journey into Aragón and Catalunya.

Toledo

Capital of medieval Spain until 1560, **TOLEDO** remains the seat of the Catholic primate and a city redolent of past glories. Set in a landscape of abrasive desolation, Toledo sits on a rocky mound isolated on three sides by a looping gorge of the Río Tajo (Tagus). Every available inch of this outcrop has been built on: houses, synagogues, churches and mosques are heaped upon one another in a haphazard spiral which the cobbled lanes infiltrate as best they can. Despite the extraordinary number of day-trippers, and the intense summer heat, Toledo is one of the most extravagant of Spanish experiences. The sightseeing crowds are in any case easy enough to avoid; simply slip into the backstreets or stay the night, for by 6pm the buses will have all gone home.

Arrival and accommodation

Toledo's **train station** is some way out on the Paseo de la Rosa, a beautiful twenty-minute walk or a bus ride (#5 or #6) to the heart of town. The **bus station** is on Avenida de Castilla la Mancha in the modern, lower part of the city; buses run frequently to the central Plaza Zocódover. The main **tourist office** (July & Aug: Mon–Sat 9am–7pm, Sun 9am–3pm; Sept–June Mon–Fri 9am–6pm; ☎925 22 08 43), outside the walls opposite the Puerta de Bisagra, has full lists of places to stay, maps, and an information board outside; there's also a useful central office in the Plaza Ayuntamiento (Mon–Fri 9am–2pm & 4–6pm).

If your first concern is **accommodation**, head directly for the old town. In summer rooms can be very hard to find, so it's worth arriving early; you may be picked up by a guide who'll earn commission for taking you to a particular place – but should at least know where there's space. Among the more central cheap establishments are *Pensión Lumbreras*, Juan Labrador 7 (☎925 22 15 71; ②), *Pension Segovia*, Recoletos 2 (☎925 21 11 24; ②); *Pensión Virgen de la Estrella*, Real del Arrabal 18 (☎925 25 31 34; ②), on the main road uphill from the Puerta de Bisagra; and the *Hostal las Armas* on the corner of Plaza Zocódover at c/Armas 7 (☎925 22 16 68; ②). Moving up a notch, you could try the comfortable new *Hostal Madrid*, c/Marqués de Mendigorría 7 (☎925 22 11 14; ③), or the *Hostal Nuevo Labrador* at Juan Labrador 10 (☎925 22 26 20; ③). The **youth hostel** is on the outskirts of town in a wing of the Castillo San Servando (☎925 22 45 54; ②). The nearest **campsite**, *El Circo Romano* (☎925 22 04 42), is a ten-minute walk from the Puerta de Bisagra on the road to Puebla de Montalbán and enjoys great views of the city. Sometimes there are also rooms available in the **university** – ask at the Oficina de Información Juvenil in c/Trinidad, by the cathedral.

The City

Right at the heart of the city sits the **Cathedral**. A robust Gothic construction which took over 250 years (1227–1493) to complete, its rich internal decoration includes masterpieces of the Gothic, Renaissance and Baroque periods. The exterior is best appreciated from outside the city, from where the hundred-metre spire and the weighty buttressing can be seen to advantage. The main entrance is at present through the **Puerta Llana** on the southern side of the main body of the cathedral, opposite the ticket office (Mon–Sat 10.30am–1pm & 3.30–6/7pm, Sun 10.30am–1.30pm; plus Sun 4–6pm in summer; 500ptas). At the heart of the church, blocking the nave, is the Choir, or **Coro** (closed Sun morning), with two tiers of magnificently carved wooden stalls. Directly opposite stands the gargantuan altarpiece of the **Capilla Mayor**, one of the triumphs of Gothic art, overflowing with intricate detail; it contains a synopsis of the entire New Testament, culminating in a Calvary at the summit. Directly behind the main altar is perhaps the most extraordinary piece of fantasy in the cathedral, the **Transparente**. Wonderfully Baroque, with marble cherubs sitting on fluffy marble clouds, it's especially magnificent when the sun reaches through the hole punched in the roof specifically for that purpose. Over twenty chapels are dotted around the walls, all of them of interest. In the **Capilla Mozárabe** mass is still celebrated daily according to the ancient Visigothic rites; if you want to look inside, get there at 9.30am, when the mass is celebrated. You should also see the Capilla de San Juan, housing the riches of the cathedral **Treasury**; the **Sacristía**, with the cathedral's finest paintings, including works by El Greco, Velázquez and Goya; and the **New Museums** (closed Mon), with more work from El Greco, who was born in Crete but settled in Toledo in about 1577.

Toledo is physically dominated by the bluff, imposing **Alcázar** (Tues–Sun 9.30am–2.30pm; 200ptas), to the east of the cathedral. There has probably always been a **fortress** in this commanding location, though it has been burned and bombarded so often that almost nothing is original. The most recent destruction was in 1936, during one of the most symbolic episodes of the Civil War, when some six hundred barricaded Nationalists held out for over two months against everything the Republicans could throw at them, until finally relieved by one of Franco's armies. Franco's regime completely rebuilt the fortress as a monument to the glorification of its defenders.

An excellent collection of El Grecos can be seen to the north of here in the **Hospital de Santa Cruz** (Mon 10am–2pm & 4–6.30pm, Tues–Sat 10am–6.30pm, Sun 10am–2pm; 200ptas, free Sat afternoon and Sunday morning), a superlative Renaissance building which also boasts outstanding works by Goya and Ribera, a huge collection of ancient carpets and faded tapestries, sculpture and a small archeological collection. The **Museo de Arte Visigótico** (Tues–Sat 10am–2pm & 4–6.30pm, Sun 10am–2pm; 100ptas), in the Mudéjar church of **San Román** – a short way northwest of the cathedral – is also well worth a visit. The Visigothic jewellery and other artefacts are perhaps outshone by the building – a delightful combination of Moorish and Christian elements.

The masterpiece of El Greco, *The Burial of the Count of Orgaz*, is housed in an annexe to the nearby church of **Santo Tomé** (daily 10am–5.45/6.45pm; 200ptas). From Santo Tomé the c/de San Juan de Dios leads down to the old Jewish quarter and to the **Casa del Greco** (Tues–Sat 10am–2pm & 4–6pm, Sun 10am–2pm; 400ptas; free Sat afternoon and Sun morning), which wasn't where the artist actually lived, but is a construction of a typical Toledan home of the period. Almost next door, on c/Reyes Católicos, is the synagogue of **El Tránsito**, built along Moorish lines by Samuel Levi in 1366. Nowadays it houses a small **Sephardic Museum** (Tues–Sat 10am–2pm & 4–6pm, Sun 10am–2pm; 400ptas, free Sat afternoon and Sun morning), tracing the distinct traditions and development of Jewish culture in Spain. The only other surviving synagogue, **Santa María la Blanca** (10am–2pm & 3.30–6/7pm; 200ptas), is a short way down the same street. Like El Tránsito, which it predates by over a century, it has been both church and synagogue, though it looks more like a mosque.

Continuing down c/Reyes Católicos, you come to the superb church of **San Juan de los Reyes** (daily 10am–1.45pm & 3.30–5.45/6.45pm; 200ptas), with its magnificent double-storey cloister. If you leave the city here by the **Puerta de Cambrón** you can follow the Paseo de Recaredo, which runs alongside a stretch of Moorish walls towards the **Hospital de Tavera** (10am–1.30pm & 3.30–6pm; 500ptas), a Renaissance palace with beautiful twin patios, housing a number of fine paintings. Heading back to town, you can pass through the main city gate, the **Nueva Puerta de Bisagra**, marooned in a constant swirl of traffic. The main road bears to the left, but on foot you can climb towards the centre of town by a series of stepped alleyways, past the intriguing Mudéjar church of **Santiago del Arrabal** and the tiny mosque of **Santo Cristo de la Luz**. Built in the tenth century on the foundations of a Visigothic church, this is one of the oldest Moorish monuments surviving in Spain. Only the nave, however, with its nine different cupolas, is the original Arab construction.

Eating and drinking

Food is relatively expensive in Toledo, but at least it's easy to find. *La Bisagra*, c/Arrabal 14, just uphill from the Puerta Bisagra, and *Arrabal*, opposite, are touristy but reasonably priced; similar tourist places surround the Plaza Magdalena, southwest of Zocódover, and the surrounding alleys. One of the best here is *Bar Ludeña* at Plaza Magdalena 10, with a cheap set menu and the local meat speciality, *carcamusa*. Northeast from Zocódover, c/Santa Fe has several outdoor cafés popular with young people in the evenings, including *Yogui's*. Less obvious places, all with good-value lunchtime menus, include: the well-hidden *Posada del Estudiante*, c/de San Pedro 2 behind the cathedral; *Restaurante Palacios*, c/Alfonso X El Sabio 3; *Bar Mesón El Greco* on c/de Bodegones 10; *Bar La Ria*, a fish restaurant and *sidreria* also on c/de Bodegones; and *Cafétéria Nano* and *Almanar* on c/Santo Tomé. At night there's not a whole lot of action, but there are a couple of late **bars** worth a look along c/de la Sillería and c/de los Alfileritos: try *La Abadía* which caters for an older crowd. *Broadway Jazz Club* on Plaza Marrón and the popular *Black & Blue* just off c/Santa Fe usually offer **live music**. There are **discos** in the eerie underground centre beneath the Paseo del Miradero, but they're not up to much.

El Escorial and El Valle de Los Caídos

Northwest of Madrid extends the line of mountains formed by the Sierra de Guadarrama and the Sierra de Gredos, snowcapped and forbidding even in summer. Beyond them lie Ávila and Segovia, but on the near side, in the foothills of the Guadarrama, is **SAN LORENZO DEL ESCORIAL** and the bleak monastery of **El Escorial** (Real Monasterio del Escorial; Tues–Sun 10am–5/6pm; 850ptas, Wed free for EU citizens). Enormous and overbearing, its severe grandeur can be impressive, but all too often it's just depressing. Planned by Philip II as a monastery and mausoleum, it was the centre of his web of letters, a place from which he boasted he could "rule the world with two inches of paper". Later, less ascetic monarchs enlarged and richly decorated the palace quarters, but Philip's simple rooms, with the chair that supported his gouty leg and the deathbed from which he could look down into the church where mass was constantly celebrated, remain the most fascinating.

Visits used to be deeply regulated, with guided tours to each section, but recently they've become more relaxed and you can use your ticket to enter, in whatever sequence you like, the basilica, sacristy, chapter houses, library and royal apartments. The outlying **Casita del Príncipe** (aka de Abajo) and **Casita del Infante** (aka de Arriba) charge separate admission. To avoid the worst of the crowds don't come on a Wednesday, and try visiting just before lunch, or pick that time for the royal apartments, which are the focus of all the bus tours. A good starting place is the **west gateway**, facing the mountains, and through the traditional main entrance. It leads into the **Patio de los Reyes**, where to the left is a school, to the right the monastery, both of them still in use, and straight ahead the **church**. In here, notice above all the flat vault of the *coro* above your head as you enter, apparently entirely without support, and the white marble Christ carved by Benvenuto Cellini. This is one of the few things permanently illuminated in the cold, dark interior, but put some money in the slot to light up the main altarpiece and the whole aspect of the church is brightened.

Back outside and around to the left are the **Sacristía** and the **Salas Capitulares** (Chapterhouses) which contain many of the monastery's religious treasures, including paintings by Titian, Velázquez and Ribera. Beside the sacristy a staircase leads down to the **Panteón de los Reyes**, the final resting place of virtually all Spanish monarchs since Charles V. Just above the entry is the *Pudrería*, a separate room in which the bodies rot for twenty years or so before the cleaned-up skeletons are moved. Their many children are laid in the **Panteón de los Infantes**. Nearby are the **Library**, with probably the most valuable collection of books in Spain, and the so-called **New Museums**, where much of the Escorial's art collection – works by Bosch, Gerard David, Dürer, Titian, Zurbarán and many others – is kept in an elegant suite of rooms.

Finally, there's the **Palace** itself, with its apartments crammed full of treasures – don't miss the spartan quarters inhabited by Philip II. Afterwards, you can wander at will in some of the courtyards and in the **Jardín de los Frailes** on the south side (open lunchtime only).

Nine kilometres north of El Escorial is **El Valle de los Caídos** (Tues–Sun: April–Sept 9.30am–7pm; Oct–March 10am–6pm; 650ptas; free Wed for EU citizens) – The Valley of the Fallen. This is an equally megalomaniacal yet far more chilling monument: an underground basilica hewn under Franco's orders, allegedly as a monument to the Civil War dead of both sides, though in reality it's a memorial to the Generalísimo and his regime. The dictator himself lies buried behind the high altar, while the only other named tomb is that of his guru, the Falangist leader José Antonio Primo de Rivera, who was shot dead by Republicans at the beginning of the war. The "other side" is present only in the fact that the complex was built by the Republican army's survivors – political prisoners on quarrying duty. Above the complex is a vast **cross**, reputedly the largest in the world, and visible for miles around. From the entrance to the basilica a shaky **funicular** (Tues–Sun April–Sept 11am–1.30pm & 4–6.30pm; Oct–March 11am–1.30pm & 3–5.30pm; 350ptas) ascends to its base, offering superlative views over the Sierra de Guadarrama and of the giant, grotesque figures propping up the cross.

Practicalities

There are up to 27 **trains** a day from Madrid to El Escorial, though **buses** (every 30–60min) are faster, slightly cheaper and take you right to the monastery. If you arrive by train get immediately on the local bus which shuttles up to the centre of town; it leaves promptly and it's a long uphill walk if you miss it. From El Escorial the local bus run by Herranz makes the

day-trip to El Valle de los Caídos (Tues–Sun; departs 3.15pm returns 5.30pm) – buy your ticket at the *Bar Manises*, opposite the post office.

Though often visited on a day-trip, El Escorial does offer **accommodation** which is useful if you're making a trip to El Valle de los Caídos; cheap *hostales* include *Pensión El Retiro*, c/Aulencia 24 (☎91 890 14 62; ②) and *Hostal Vasco*, Plaza Santiago (☎91 890 16 19; ②). There's also a **campsite** 2km out on the road to Ávila and a **youth hostel** (☎91 890 36 40; ②), usually crowded with school groups, in Finca de la Herrería.

Eating is expensive everywhere, but try the bar just inside the gate. Further up the hill on c/Reina Victoria, near the bus and train arrival point from Madrid, there are a few affordable restaurants. *Restaurante Cubero* on c/Don Juan Delegraz has cheap set menus. The **tourist office** (summer Mon–Sat 11am–6pm, Sun 10am–3pm; winter Mon–Fri 10am–2pm & 3–5pm, Sat & Sun 10am–3pm; ☎91 890 15 54) is at c/Floridablanca 10.

Ávila

Two things distinguish **ÁVILA**: its medieval walls and St Teresa, who was born here and whose spirit still dominates the city. It's the **walls** (daily 10am–6pm; 200ptas; access from steps just inside Puerta del Alcázar) which first impress, especially if you approach the city with the evening sun highlighting their golden tone and the details of the 88 towers around the ramparts. Modern life takes place almost exclusively in the new developments outside the fortifications, but restoration is slowly bringing life back to the old town.

The legacy of **Santa Teresa**, who was born here to a noble family in 1515, is expressed in the many convents and churches with which she was associated. By the age of seven she was already deeply religious, running away with her brother to be martyred by the Moors. The spot where they were recaptured and brought back, **Los Cuatro Postes**, 1.5km along the Salamanca road, is a fine vantage point from which to admire the walls. She went on to reform the Carmelite order, found many convents of her own and become one of the most important figures of the Counter-Reformation. Perhaps the most interesting of the monuments associated with the saint is the **Convento de San José** (daily 9.30/10am–1/1.30pm & 3/4–6/7pm; 150ptas), the first one she founded, in 1562. Its **museum** contains relics and memorabilia including assorted personal possessions and the coffin in which she once slept. The **Convento de Santa Teresa** (daily 9.30am–1.30pm & 3.30–7.30pm; free), built over the saint's birthplace, is less interesting, although the reliquary beside the gift shop contains not only her rosary beads, but one of the fingers she used to count them with. The third major point of pilgrimage is the **Convento de la Encarnación** (daily 9.30am–1pm & 3.30/4–6/7pm; 150ptas), where she spent 27 years as a nun. The rooms are labelled with the various things the saint did in each of them, and everything she touched and looked at or could have used is on display.

The most beautiful churches in Ávila – the cathedral, San Vicente and the convent of Santo Tomás – are less directly associated with its most famous resident. The **Cathedral** (daily 10am–1pm & 3.30–5/6pm; 250ptas) was started in the twelfth century but has never been finished: the earliest parts were as much fortress as church, and the apse forms an integral part of the city walls. Inside, the succeeding changes of style are immediately apparent: the old parts are Romanesque in design and made of a strange red-and-white mottled stone, but then there's an abrupt break and the rest of the main structure is pure white and Gothic. The basilica of **San Vicente** (daily 10am–1.30pm & 4–6.30pm; 200ptas) displays a similar mixture of styles: its twelfth-century doorways and the portico which protects them are magnificent examples of Romanesque art, while the church itself shows the influence of later trends. St Vincent was martyred on this site, and his tomb depicts a series of gruesome deaths.

El Real Monasterio de Santo Tomás (cloisters daily 10/11am–1pm & 4–7/8pm; 100ptas; museum daily 11am–12.45pm & 4–6pm; 200ptas) is a Dominican monastery founded in 1482, but greatly expanded over the following decade by Ferdinand and Isabella, whose summer palace it became. On every surface is carved the yoke-and-arrows motif of the *Reyes Católicos*, surrounded by pomegranates, symbol of the newly conquered kingdom of Granada. Inside are three exceptional cloisters, the largest of which contains an **oriental col-**

lection, an incongruous display accumulated by the monks over centuries of missionary work in the Orient. In the **Church** is the elaborate tomb of Prince Juan, Ferdinand and Isabella's only son, whose early death opened the way for Charles V's succession. Notorious inquisitor Torquemada is buried in the sacristy. Santo Tomás is quite a walk (downhill) from the south part of town – you can get back up by the #1 bus, whose circular route takes in much of the old city.

Practicalities

Up to seventeen **trains** make the journey each day from Madrid via El Escorial to Ávila, with onward connections to Salamanca and Valladolid. The **train station** is at the bottom of Avda José Antonio, to the east below the new part of town. **Buses** to and from Madrid and Segovia use a terminal on the Avda de Madrid. The **tourist office** (daily 9/10am–2pm & 4/5–7pm; ☎920 21 13 87) is in the Plaza de la Catedral, directly opposite the cathedral entrance.

Cheap **rooms** are easy enough to come by, though many of them are around the train station or at the end of Avda José Antonio, which is neither the most central nor the most pleasant place to be based. Nearer the centre, *Hostel Santa Ana*, c/Alfonso de Montalvo 2 (☎920 22 00 63; ③), is a good-value place near the church of the same name. Within the walls, places are likely to be more expensive, but the *Hostal Continental* at Plaza de la Catedral 4 (☎920 21 15 02; ②) and *Hostal el Rastro* at Plaza del Rastro 1 (☎920 21 12 18; ③) are pleasant and not too exorbitant. *Hostal Bellas*, c/Caballeros 19 (☎920 21 29 10; ②), is excellent value, especially out of season. There's a **youth hostel** in Avda de Juventud (☎920 22 17 16; ②), out past the Convento de Santo Tomás, but it's very small, has a strict 11pm curfew, and is only open from July to mid-August.

For cheap **meals** you're best off in the heart of the old town around the unfinished Plaza de la Victoria or, again, down by the train station. Two places off this plaza are *Cafeteria Baviera*, c/Vallespin 10, for a cheap set menu, and the *Bar El Rincón*, Plaza Zurraquín 4, for a more expensive but generous three-course deal. The *Cafeteria Maspalomas*, opposite the bus station, offers cheap, simple food. Other places are *Mesón del Rastro*, Plaza del Rastro 1, with a good, reasonably priced restaurant, and *La Posada de la Fruta*, Plaza de Pedro Dávila 8, with an attractive, sunny courtyard to drink in. There are excellent **bars** in c/García Villareal at the western edge of the old town.

Segovia

For such a small city, **SEGOVIA** has a remarkable number of outstanding architectural monuments. Most celebrated are the Roman aqueduct, the cathedral and the fairy-tale Alcázar, but the less obvious attractions – the cluster of ancient churches and the many mansions found in the lanes of the old town, all in a warm, honey-coloured stone – are what really make it worth visiting. In winter, at over 1000m, it can be very cold here.

The **Cathedral** (daily 9am–6/7pm) was the last major Gothic building in Spain, probably the last anywhere. Accordingly it takes that style to its logical extreme, with pinnacles and flying buttresses tacked on at every conceivable point. Though impressive for its size alone, the interior is surprisingly bare, and spoiled by a great green marble *coro* at its very centre. The treasures are almost all confined to the **museum** which opens off the cloisters (300ptas).

Down beside the cathedral, c/de Daoiz leads past a line of souvenir shops to the church of San Andrés and onto a small park in front of the **Alcázar** (daily 10am–6/7pm; 400ptas). It's an extraordinary fantasy of a castle which, with its narrow towers and many turrets, looks like something out of Disneyland. And indeed it is a sham – originally built in the fourteenth and fifteenth centuries but almost completely destroyed by a fire in 1862, it was rebuilt as a deliberately hyperbolic parody of the original. Still, it should be visited, if only for the magnificent panoramas from the tower.

The **Aqueduct**, over 800m long and at its highest point towering some 30m above the Plaza de Azoguejo, stands up without a drop of mortar or cement. No one knows exactly when it was built, but it was probably around the end of the first century AD under the Emperor Trajan. If you climb the stairs beside the aqueduct you can get a view looking down over it from a surviving fragment of the city walls; though frankly it's more impressive from a distance.

Segovia is an excellent city for walking, with some fine views and beautiful churches to be enjoyed just outside the boundaries. Perhaps the most interesting of all the ancient churches here is **Vera Cruz** (Tues–Sun 10.30am–1.30pm & 3.30–6.30/7pm; 200ptas), a remarkable twelve-sided building in the valley facing the Alcázar. It was built by the Knights Templar in the early thirteenth century on the pattern of the church of the Holy Sepulchre in Jerusalem, and once housed part of the True Cross. Inside, the nave is circular, its heart occupied by a strange two-storeyed chamber – again twelve-sided – in which the knights, as part of their initiation, stood vigil over the cross. Climb the tower for a highly photogenic vista of the city. While you're over here you could also visit the prodigiously walled **Convento de los Carmelitas** (daily 10am–1.30pm & 4–6.30/8.30pm; closed Tues morning; free), with the gaudy mausoleum of its founder-saint and the rather damp, ramshackle **Monasterio del Parral** (Mon–Sat 10am–12.30pm & 4–6.30pm, Sun 10–11.30am & 4–6.30pm; free).

Practicalities

You can get here by **train** or **bus** from Madrid; there are onward connections by bus to Ávila and Valladolid, and by train to Valladolid. The **train station** is some distance out of town; take any bus (every 15min) marked Puente Hierro/Estacion Renfe to the central Plaza Mayor. Surprisingly, this main square, right by the cathedral and surrounded by pricey cafés, is the place to start looking for somewhere to stay. There are two cheap **fondas** – *Cubo* (☎921 46 09 17; ①) and *Aragón* (☎921 46 09 14; ②) – on different floors of the same building at Plaza Mayor 4; *Hostal Juan Bravo*, on c/Juan Bravo 12 (☎921 46 34 13; ②) has lots of big comfortable rooms, while there are other cheap possibilities in the streets behind the plaza or near the aqueduct. The **youth hostel** (☎921 42 00 27; ②) is on Paseo Conde de Sepulveda near the train station; there's a **campsite**, *Camping Acueducto* (April–Sept), a couple of kilometres out on the road to La Granja.

The **tourist office** (Mon–Fri 10am–2pm & 5–8pm, Sat 10am–2pm, Sun 10am–2pm; ☎921 46 03 34) is also in the Plaza Mayor. The Calle de la Infanta Isabella, which opens off the plaza beside the tourist office, is packed with noisy **bars** and cheap **places to eat**. Segovia's culinary speciality is roast suckling pig (*cochinillo asado*) and you'll see the little pink creatures hanging in the windows of restaurants. But it's very expensive unless you're in a large group, and to many tastes overrated. *Mesón del Campesino* is one of the best in c/Infanta Isabella 14, with decent value *menús. Casa Duque*, at Cervantes 12 on the way down to the aqueduct, is much more expensive but well worth it, with excellent paella. Other recommended places include *José María* at c/Cronista Lecea 11, *Santa Bárbara* at c/Ezequiel Gonzáles 32, *Narízotas* in Plaza de San Martin, and the *Cocina de San Millán* at c/San Millán 3.

EXTREMADURA

The harsh environment of **Extremadura**, west of Madrid, was the cradle of the conquistadores, men who opened up a new world for the Spanish Empire. Remote before and forgotten since, Extremadura enjoyed a brief golden age when the heroes returned with their gold to live in a flourish of splendour. **Trujillo**, the birthplace of Pizarro, and **Cáceres** both preserve entire towns built with conquistador wealth, the streets crowded with the ornate mansions of returning empire builders, and there is also **Mérida**, the most completely preserved Roman city in Spain.

Trujillo

TRUJILLO, about thirty minutes by bus from Cáceres, is the first place you're likely to want to stop on the main road from Madrid to Extremadura and Portugal. At its heart – on a rise dominating the surrounding plains – is a walled town virtually untouched since the sixteenth century, redolent above all of the exploits of the conquerors of the Americas; Francisco

Pizarro was born here, as were many of his tiny band who defeated the Incas with such extraordinary cruelty.

From the bus station work your way uphill through the narrow streets to the huge Plaza Mayor, where a statue of the town's most famous son bars the way to the monuments on the hill behind. In the southwest corner is the **Palacio de la Conquista** (closed for lengthy restoration), perhaps the grandest of Trujillo's mansions, and just one of many built by the Pizarro clan. Diagonally opposite is the bulky church of **San Martín** with the tomb, among others, of the Orellana family; Francisco de Orellana was the first explorer of the Amazon. From here you can begin to climb into the walled town – where much restoration work is going on as people move into and do up the old houses – and towards the Moorish castle at its highest point.

From the plaza, c/de Ballesteros leads up to the walls, past the domed **Torre Del Alfiler** with its coats of arms and storks' nests, and through the gateway known as the Arco de Santiago. Here, to the left, is **Santa María Mayor** (daily 10.30am–2pm & 4.30–7/8pm; 100ptas), the most interesting of the town's many churches. Of the many remaining mansions, or *solares*, the **Palacio de Orellana-Pizarro** nowadays houses the local school. The castle itself is now virtually in open countryside; for the last hundred metres of the climb you see nothing but the occasional broken-down remnant of a wall clambered over by sheep and dogs. The fortress, its original Moorish towers much reinforced by later defenders, has recently been restored. Below the castle, the **Casa Museo Pizarro** commemorates the conquistador's life and exploits in Peru, but is a dull, overpriced affair (daily 11am–2pm & 4–7pm; 250ptas).

Plaza Mayor is the site of the **tourist office** (Tues–Fri 9.30am–2pm & 4/5–6.30/7.30pm, Sat & Sun 9.45am–2pm; ☎927 32 26 77) and a couple of **hostales**. *La Cadena* at no. 8 (☎927 32 14 63; ③) and *Hostal Nuria* at no. 17 (☎927 32 09 07; ③) offer a degree of luxury, while *Pensión Boni*, c/Domingo de Ramos 11, off the northeast corner (☎927 32 16 04; ③), is a clean, well-run budget choice. There are plenty of places to **eat** in the Plaza Mayor: perhaps the best is *La Troya*, with its huge *menús*; the *Pizarro* is a rather more fancy restaurant, or there are excellent tapas at the *Bar Las Cigüeñas* and *Bar Pillete*, around the corner.

Cáceres

CÁCERES is in many ways remarkably like Trujillo: its centre is an almost perfectly preserved medieval town adorned with mansions built on the proceeds of American exploration, and every available tower and spire crowned by a clutch of storks' nests. Cáceres has perhaps been over-restored, and it can be very commercial – on the other hand it's a much larger and livelier place, a rapidly growing provincial capital which is also home to the University of Extremadura.

Even with a map you'll probably get lost among the winding alleys of the old town, so as a preliminary orientation try standing in the Plaza Mayor opposite the tourist office. To your left is the **Torre del Bujaco** – whose foundations date back to Roman times – with a chapel next to it and steps leading up to the low **Arco de la Estrella**, piercing the walls. To the right is the **Torre del Horno**, one of the best-preserved Moorish mud-brick structures surviving in Spain. A staircase leads up to another gateway, and beyond this is the most intact stretch of the ancient walls with several more of the original towers. Though basically Moorish in construction, the walls have been added to, altered and built against ever since. Around the other side of the old town, one Roman gateway, the **Arco del Cristo**, can still be seen.

Inside the walls, almost every building is magnificent – look out in particular for the family crests adorning many of the mansions. Through the Estrella gate, the **Casa de Toledo-Montezuma** with its domed tower is immediately to the left. To this house a follower of Cortés brought back one of the New World's more exotic prizes – a daughter of the Aztec emperor as his bride. Directly ahead is the **Plaza Santa María** with an impressive group of buildings around a refreshingly unencumbered Gothic church. The church of **San Mateo**, on the site of the ancient mosque at the town's highest point, is another Gothic structure with several attractive chapels. In the Casa de las Valetas, on Plaza San Mateo, is the **Museo**

Provincial (Tues–Sat 9.30am–2.30pm, Sun 10.15am–2.30pm; 200ptas; free for EU citizens), worth visiting as much for the chance to see inside one of the finer mansions as for its well-displayed local collection. Its highlight is the cistern of the original Moorish Alcázar with fine rooms of excellent horseshoe arches. The same ticket admits you to the **Fine Arts** section in the Casa de los Caballos behind it, where the work is all religious in inspiration; the same building also has two floors dedicated to contemporary art and sculpture, with work by Miró and Picasso as well as younger, up-and-coming artists.

Practicalities

The **train station** and the new **bus station** face each other across the Carretera Sevilla, some way out; buses run from here (every 15min) to a square in the new part of town near the centre, with signs leading on towards the Plaza Mayor and the **tourist office** (Mon–Fri 9am–2pm & 4/5–6.30/7.30pm, Sat & Sun 9.45am–2pm; ☎927 24 63 47). The best **places to stay** are all in its immediate vicinity – try the basic, but clean, convenient and friendly, *Pensión Carretero* at no. 22 (☎927 24 74 82; ②). If you have no luck round here, try the good-value *Hostal Princesa*, c/Camino Llano 34 (☎927 22 70 00; ②), down the hill out of the gate and to the left. Right on Plaza Mayor, the cheapest **meals** are served at *El Puchero*, though the food is nothing special; the slightly more expensive *El Pato Blanco* is probably worth the extra. *El Figón*, in Plaza San Juan just off c/Pintores, is another step up in class. Calle de Pizarro, just outside the walls on the west side of the old town, is a good place for **bars**, or try *Lancelot*, off Cuesta del Marqués in the old town, run by an Englishman and classy but fun.

Mérida

Former capital of the Roman province of Lusitania, **MÉRIDA** contains one of the most remarkable assemblages of Roman monuments to be found anywhere – scattered in the midst of the modern city are remains of everything from engineering works to domestic villas. With the aid of a map and a little imagination, it's not hard to reconstruct the Roman city within the not especially attractive modern town. A single ticket, costing 750ptas, gains access to all the main sites (open daily 9.30am–1.45pm & 4/5–6.15/7.15pm) except the museum.

Start your tour by the magnificent **Puente Romano**, the Roman bridge across the islet-strewn Guadiana – sixty arches long, though seven in the middle were replaced in the fifteenth century. It is defended by an enormous, plain **Alcazaba**, built by the Moors to replace a Roman construction. The interior is a rather barren archeological site, though you can descend into the impressive cistern. Nearby is the sixteenth-century **Plaza de España**, the heart of the modern town, while on c/Romero Leal Sagasta east of here is the so-called **Templo de Diana**, currently the object of an overzealous restoration project. In the other direction you'll find the **Arco Trajano**, an unadorned triumphal arch 15m high and 9m across.

By far the most important site, however, is that containing the **Teatro Romano** and **Anfiteatro**. The theatre, a present to the city from Agrippa around 15 BC, is one of the best preserved anywhere, and one of the most beautiful monuments of the entire Roman world. The stage is in a particularly good state of repair, while many of the seats have been rebuilt to offer more comfort to the audiences of the annual July season of classical plays. The adjacent amphitheatre is a slightly later and much plainer construction which in its day could accommodate as many as fifteen thousand people – almost half the current population of Mérida.

Just across from these buildings is the vast, red-brick bulk of the **Museo Nacional de Arte Romano** (Tues–Sat & 10am–2pm & 4/5–6/7pm, Sun 10am–2pm; 400ptas, free Sat pm and Sun am), a magnificent new museum which does full justice to its high-class collection, including portrait statues of Augustus, Tiberius and Drusus, and some glorious mosaics. One of two Roman villas in Mérida, the **Casa Romana Anfiteatro** (same hours as all the main sights; 300ptas) lies immediately below the museum. The other, the **Mitreo**, is situated in the shadow of the Plaza de Toros. Both have good mosaics – especially the Casa Romana. The remaining monuments are further out, near the rail lines. A feat of imagination is required to re-create the **circus** in one's mind, as almost nothing of the masonry is left. The **Acueducto de los Milagros** is more satisfying, with a good portion surviving in the midst of vegetable gardens. Its tall arches of granite with brick courses brought water to the city in its earliest days from the reservoir at Proserpina, 5km away.

Practicalities

Mérida is a lively place for its size, and the whole area between the train station and the Plaza de España is full of **bars and cheap restaurants**. There are good-value four-course deals at the *Restaurante Naya*, Cardero 7, close to the station, and better food for slightly more money at the *Restaurante Briz*, Félix Valverde Lillo 5, just off the plaza. Budget **accommodation**, on the other hand, is not plentiful. Best bet is the popular *Pensión El Arco*, c/Cervantes, 16 (☎924 31 83 21; ②), near the Arco Trajaro. Otherwise the following are good value: *Hostal Nueva España*, Avda Extremadura 6 (☎924 31 33 56; ③); *Hostal Salud*, c/Vespasiano 41 (☎924 31 22 59; ③); or *Hostal Bueno*, c/Calvario 9 (☎924 30 29 77; ③). There's a **campsite** not far out of town on the highway, or a much more attractive site at Proserpina (May–Sept), some 5km north, where you can swim in the reservoir. The **tourist office** is at the entrance to the Roman theatre site (Mon–Fri 9am–2pm & 4/5–6.30/7.30pm, Sat & Sun 9.30am–2pm; ☎924/ 31 53 53) on Paseo José Saenz de Burnaga.

ANDALUCÍA

Above all else – and there is plenty – it is the great Moorish monuments that vie for your attention in **Andalucía**. The Moors, a mixed race of Berbers and Arabs who crossed into Spain from North Africa, occupied *al-Andalus* for over seven centuries. Their first forces landed at Tarifa in 711 AD and within a decade they had conquered virtually the whole of Spain; their last kingdom, Granada, fell to the Christian Reconquest in 1492. Between these dates they developed the most sophisticated civilization of the Middle Ages, centred in turn on the three major cities of **Córdoba, Sevilla** and **Granada**. Each one preserves extraordinarily brilliant and beautiful monuments, of which the most perfect is Granada's **Alhambra palace**.

On **the coast** it's easy to despair. Extending to either side of **Málaga** is the **Costa del Sol**, Europe's most developed resort area, with its beaches hidden behind a remorseless curtain of concrete hotels and apartment complexes. However, there is life beyond the Costa del Sol, especially the beaches of the Costa de la Luz towards Cádiz on the Atlantic coast, and those around Almería in the southeast corner of Spain.

Inland, and in the cities away from the tourist gaze, this is still an undeveloped, often extremely poor part of the country. For all its poverty, however, Andalucía is also Spain at its most exuberant: the home of flamenco and the bullfight, and the traditional images of exotic Spain. These are best absorbed at one of the hundreds of annual **ferias** and **romerías**. The best of them include the giant April Fair in Sevilla, the pilgrimage to El Rocío near Huelva in late May, and the Easter celebrations at Málaga and Sevilla.

Córdoba

CÓRDOBA is a minor provincial capital, prosperous in a modest sort of way. Once, however, it was the largest city of Roman Spain, and for three centuries it formed the heart of the great medieval caliphate of the Moors. For visitors, it's attraction comes down to a single building, the **Mezquita** – the grandest and most beautiful mosque ever constructed by the Moors. This stands right in the centre of the city, surrounded by the labyrinthine Jewish and Moorish quarters, and is a building of extraordinary mystical and aesthetic power. The Mezquita apart, Córdoba itself is an engaging atmospheric city, easily explored and with some excellent budget accommodation.

Arrival and accommodation

Close to the **train station**, the broad Avda del Gran Capitán leads down to the old quarters and the Mezquita. **Bus terminals** are numerous and scattered. The main company, Alsina Graells, is at Avda de Medina Azahara 29, two or three blocks to the west of the Paseo de la Victoria gardens; they run services to and from Sevilla, Granada and Málaga. Apart from the Málaga service, the buses will be quicker, unless you can afford the surcharge for the fast train to Sevilla.

The **tourist office** at the Palacio de Congresos y Exposiciones in c/Torrijos alongside the Mezquita (Mon–Fri 9.30am–7/8pm, Sat 10am–7/8pm, Sun 10am–2pm; ☎957 47 12 35) has free maps to help you negotiate the narrow, wandering streets of the Judería. Watch out for the tiled street signs: elegant as they are, they look exactly the same as the plaques on bars and houses. The best **places to stay** are concentrated in the narrow maze of streets north-east of the Mezquita. Corregidor Luis de la Cerda, parallel to the river, has a good selection of *hostales*, many with beautiful tiled courtyards and greenery: cheapest is the *Trinidad* at no. 58 (☎957 48 79 05; ②). Calle Rey Heredía also has some good places including *Pension Rey Heredía* at no. 26 (☎957 47 41 82; ②). Less savoury, but likely to have room, are the cheap, run-down *fondas* in the wonderfully ramshackle **Plaza de la Corredera**: *Hostal Plaza Corredera* (☎957 48 45 70; ②), at the corner of the plaza and c/Rodríguez Marin, is clean and friendly, with great views over the plaza from some rooms. There's a new **youth hostel** with double rooms in the Plaza Judá Leví (☎957 29 01 66; ②) and a **campsite** – *Campamento Municipal* – 2km north on the road to Villaviciosa, take the #10 bus.

The City

Córdoba's domination of Moorish Spain began thirty years after the conquest, in 756, when the city was placed under **Abd ar-Rahman I**, who established control over all but the north of Spain. It was he who commenced the building of the Great Mosque – **La Mezquita**, in Spanish – which was enlarged by **Abd ar-Rahman II** (822–52). In the tenth century **Abd ar-Rahman III** (912–67) re-established order after a period of internal strife and settled Córdoba firmly at the head of a caliphate that took in much of Spain and North Africa. His son **al-Hakam II** virtually doubled the mosque's extent, demolishing the south wall to add fourteen extra rows of columns, and employing Byzantine craftsmen to construct a new *mihrab* (prayer niche); this remains complete and is perhaps the most beautiful example of all Moorish religious architecture. The final enlargement, under the chamberlain-usurper **al-Mansur** (977–1002), involved adding seven rows of columns to the whole east side. This spoiled the symmetry of the mosque, depriving the *mihrab* of its central position, but it meant there was a bay for every day of the year.

The **Mezquita** (daily 10am–5.30/7.30pm; 800ptas, free Sun mornings for worship) is approached through the **Patio de los Naranjos**, a classic Islamic court which preserves both its orange trees and the fountains for ritual purification before prayer. Originally all nineteen naves of the mosque were open to this court, so that the rows of interior columns appeared as an extension of the trees. Inside, nearly a thousand twin-layered red and white pillars combine to mesmeric effect, the harmony culminating only at the foot of the exquisite **Mihrab**, aligned to Mecca and the focus for prayer.

Originally the whole design of the mosque would have directed worshippers naturally towards the *mihrab*. Today, though, you almost stumble upon it, for in the centre of the mosque squats a vulgar Renaissance **choir**. To the left of the choir stands an earlier and happier Christian addition – the Mudéjar **Capilla de Villaviciosa**, built by Moorish craftsmen in 1371. Beside it are the dome and pillars of the earlier *mihrab*, constructed under Abd ar-Rahman II.

After the Mezquita, the rest of Córdoba can only be anticlimactic, though there are plenty of pleasant strolls to be had. The **river** with its great **Arab waterwheels** and its **bridge** built on Roman foundations comprises perhaps the most attractive area. Down behind the **Episcopal Palace** you can visit the **Alcázar de los Reyes** (Mon–Sat 10am–2pm & 4.30/5–6.30/7pm, Sun 9.30am–3pm; 300ptas, free Fri), a fortified palace built by Ferdinand and Isabella and later occupied by the Inquisition: the gardens are more enjoyable than the interior.

North of the Mezquita lies the **Judería**, Córdoba's old Jewish quarter, a fascinating network of lanes that are more atmospheric and less commercialized than Sevilla's. Near the heart of the quarter, at c/Maimonides 18, is a tiny **synagogue** (Mon–Sat 10.30am–1pm & 3.30–5.30pm, Sun 10am–1.30pm; 50ptas; free to EU citizens), one of only three in Spain that survived the Jewish expulsion of 1492 – the other two are in Toledo. Nearby is a rather bogus **Zoco** – an Arab *souk* turned into a crafts arcade – and, adjoining this, the small but fabulously kitschy **Museo Municipal Taurino** (Tues–Sat 10am–2pm & 5/6–7/8pm, Sun 9.30am–3pm; 450ptas, free Fri).

East of the Judería, the **Museo Arqueológico** (Tues 3–8pm, Wed–Sat 9am–8pm, Sun 9am–3pm; 250ptas, EU citizens free) occupies a small Renaissance mansion in which Roman foundations were discovered during conversion: these have been incorporated into an imaginative and enjoyable display. A couple of blocks below, back towards the river, you'll come upon the **Plaza del Potro**, a fine old square named after the colt (*potro*) which adorns its fountain. This, as local guides proudly point out, is mentioned in *Don Quixote*, and indeed Cervantes himself is reputed to have stayed at the inn opposite, the **Mesón del Potro**. On the other side of the square is the **Museo de Bellas Artes** (Tues 3–8pm, Wed–Sat 9am–8pm, Sun 9am–3pm; 250ptas, free to EU citizens) with paintings by Ribera, Valdés Leal and Zurbarán.

Eating and drinking

Bars and **restaurants** are on the whole reasonably priced – you need only to avoid the touristy places round the Mezquita. Loads of alternatives can be found not too far away in the Judería and in the old quarters off to the east, above the Paseo de la Ribera: one of the best (and most expensive) in the former is *El Churrasco* at c/Romero 16; more reasonable is *El Extremeño* at Plaza Agrupacíon de Cofradias, just north of the Mesquita. *Taberna Salinas*, c/Tundidores 3 off the Plaza Corredera, is also excellent.

For **drinking** and tapas, try *Sociedad Plateros* at c/Deanes 5. The local barrelled **wine** is mainly *Montilla* or *Moriles* – both are magnificent, vaguely resembling mellow, dry sherries. Near the synagogue, *Bodega Guzmán* on c/Judíos 7 is loaded with Andalusian atmosphere. **Flamenco** performances take place at *La Buleria*, c/Pedro López 3, from 10pm every night; there's no entrance fee, but food and drink are expensive to compensate.

Sevilla

SEVILLA is the great city of the Spanish south, intensely hot in summer and with an abiding reputation for theatricality and intensity. It has three important monuments – the **Giralda tower**, the **Cathedral** and the **Alcázar** – and an illustrious history, but it's the living self of this city of Carmen, Don Juan and Figaro that remains the great attraction. It is expressed on a phenomenally grand scale at the city's two great festivals – the **Semana Santa**, during the week before Easter, and the **April Feria**, which lasts a week at the end of the month. Sevilla is also Spain's second most important centre for **bullfighting**, after Madrid.

The birthplace of **Felipe González**, Sevilla benefited considerably from his term as Prime Minister – above all through gaining the **Expo 92** world fair, with all the attendant benefits for the infrastructure. None the less it remains poor: petty crime is a big problem, especially in the form of bag-snatching and breaking into cars. The fairgrounds for Expo 92 are at **La Isla de la Cartuja**, northwest of the centre across the river, where Columbus' remains are said to have rested before finally being moved to the Dominican Republic. Bus #5 goes from Avda Sanjurjo to La Puerto Triana.

Arrival and information

The new **train station**, Santa Justa, is a fair way out of the centre on Avda Kansas City, which is also the airport road; bus #70 connects it to the El Prado de San Sebastian bus station. There is an hourly bus service (6.15am–10.30pm; 750ptas) connecting the **airport** to the town. The **main bus station** is at the Plaza de Armas beside the river by the Puente del Cachorro, but buses for destinations within Andalucía leave from the more central terminal at Plaza de San Sebastián. Bus #C4 connects the two terminals. The **tourist office** is at Avda de la Constitución 21 (Mon–Sat 9am–7pm, Sun 10am–2pm; ☎95 422 14 04).

Accommodation

The most attractive **area to stay** in town is undoubtedly the maze-like **Barrio Santa Cruz**, near the cathedral, although this is generally reflected in the prices you have to pay. Rooms are relatively expensive everywhere, in fact, and almost impossible to find during the big festivals. If you can't find anything in the Barrio, try on its periphery or slightly further out beyond the Plaza Nueva, over towards the river and the new bus station on Plaza de Armas.

HOSTELS AND HOTELS

Albergue Juvenil Sevilla, c/Isaac Peral 2 (☎95 461 31 50). Refurbished youth hostel some way out in the university district but can be crowded; take bus #34 from Puerta de Jerez or Plaza Nueva. ②.

Hostal Buen Dormir, c/Farnesio 8 (☎95 421 74 92). Friendly place in a street with several possibilities; check the room. ③.

Hostal Bienvenido, c/Archeros 14 (☎95 441 36 55). Another fairly small place; small rooms but nice roof terrace, with several other likely places nearby. ②.

Hostal Capitol, Zaragoza 66 (☎95 421 24 41). Just off Plaza Nueva – a range of rooms and prices, so look first. ⑤.

Hostal Goya, c/Mateos Gago 31 (☎95 421 11 70). Good value, with a range of rooms, in another street with several choices. ③.

Hostal Lis, c/Escarpín 10 (☎95 421 30 88). A good bet just north of Plaza de la Encarnación. ②.

Hostal Monreal, c/Rodrigo Caro 8 (☎95 421 41 66). Plenty of rooms in this very central, newly converted town house. ③.

Hostal Santa María, c/Hernando Colón 19; (☎95 422 85 05). Small place on a noisy street, but in the Giralda's shadow. Price doubles in high season. ③–⑤.

Hotel Simón, c/García de Vinuesa 19 (☎95 422 66 60). Well-restored mansion with excellent position across from the cathedral. Can be a bargain out of season. ③.

Pensión Alcázar, c/Deán Miranda 12 (☎95 422 84 57). Tiny place in a tiny street beside the Alcázar, good value if they have space. ③.

Pensión Pérez Montilla, Plaza Curtidores 13 (☎95 442 18 54). Many facilities, including air-conditioning. ④.

CAMPSITES

Camping Sevilla (☎95 451 43 79). Right by the airport. Relatively cheap place with a pool. A site bus shuttles in and out daily except Sun, or bus #70 will drop you at a petrol station 1km away.

Club de Campo (☎95 472 02 50). About 12km out in Dos Hermanas, a pleasant shady site with a pool. Half-hourly buses from the bus station.

The City

Sevilla was one of the earliest **Moorish conquests** (in 712) and, as part of the Caliphate of Córdoba, became the second city of al-Andalus. When the Caliphate broke up in the early eleventh century it was the most powerful of the independent states to emerge, and under the Almohad dynasty became the capital of the last real Moorish empire in Spain from 1170 until 1212. The Almohads rebuilt the Alcázar, enlarged the principal **mosque** and erected a new and brilliant minaret – the **Giralda** – topped with four copper spheres that could be seen from miles round. This minaret was used by the Moors both for calling the faithful to prayer and as an observatory, and was so venerated that they wanted to destroy it before the Christian conquest of the city. Instead the Giralda became the bell tower of the Christian **Cathedral**, and continues to dominate the skyline. You can ascend to the bell chamber for a remarkable view of the city and of the Gothic details of the cathedral's buttresses and statuary. But most impressive of all is the tower's inner construction, a series of 35 gentle ramps wide enough to allow two mounted guards to pass.

Originally the mosque was reconsecrated as the cathedral. But in 1402 the cathedral chapter dreamt up plans for a new monument to Christian glory: "a building on so magnificent a scale that posterity will believe we were mad". From the old structure only the Giralda

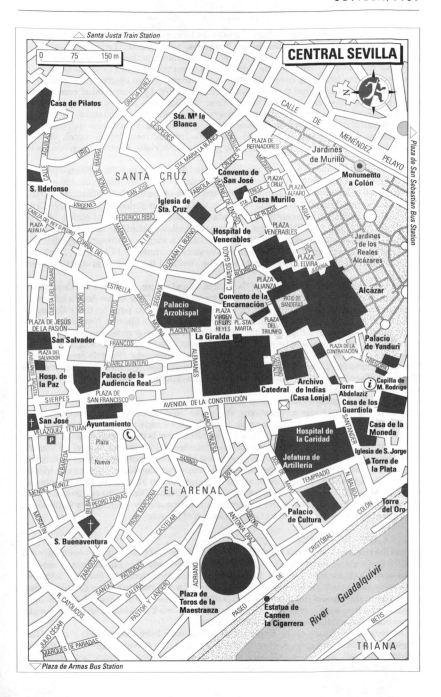

Santa Justa Train Station

0   75   150 m

CENTRAL SEVILLA

N

Plaza de San Sebastian Bus Station

CALLE DE MENÉNDEZ PELAYO

Casa de Pilatos

GRACIA PÉREZ
CÉSPEDES
AGUILAS
LIRIO
CALLE
CONDE DE IBARRA
STA MARIA LA BLANCA
DONCELLAS
CRUCES

Sta. Mª la Blanca

PLAZA DE REFINADORES

Jardines de Murillo

SANTA CRUZ

S. Ildefonso

VÍRGENES
CABEZA DEL REY D.PEDRO
PLAZA ALFALFA
CORRAL DEL
SAN JOSÉ
FABIOLA
FEDERICO RIBIO
MÁRMOLES
A.T.R.E.
GUZMÁN EL BUENO

Convento de San José

PLAZA S.CRUZ
PLAZA ALFARO
STA TERESA
DE RUEDA

Casa Murillo

Iglesia de Sta. Cruz

XIMÉNEZ DE ENCISO

Hospital de Venerables

PLAZA VENERABLES

Monumento a Colón

Jardines de los Reales Alcázares

AGUA

PLAZA D. ELVIRA
JUDERÍA

ESTRELLA
CUESTA DEL ROSARIO
SAN ISIDORO
PAJARITOS
ARGOTE DE MOLINA
SEGOVIA
C. MATEOS GAGO
RODRIGO

PLAZA ALIANZA

Convento de la Encarnación

PATIO DE BANDERAS

Alcázar

PLAZA DE JESÚS DE LA PASIÓN

Palacio Arzobispal

PLAZA VIRGEN DE LOS REYES
PL. STA MARTA

PLAZA DEL TRIUNFO

La Giralda

PLACENTINES

San Salvador

PLAZA DEL SALVADOR
FRANCOS
ÁLVAREZ QUINTERO
ALEMANES

PLAZA DE LA CONTRATACIÓN

S. GREGORIO

Palacio de Yanduri

JOVELLANOS
SAGASTA

Hosp. de la Paz

Palacio de la Audiencia Real

SIERPES

PLAZA DE SAN FRANCISCO

Catedral

Archivo de Indias (Casa Lonja)

Torre Abdelaziz

i **Capilla de M. Rodrigo**

Casa de los Guardiola

San José

VELÁZQUEZ   TETUÁN

Ayuntamiento

P
ALBAREDA
MÉNDEZ NÚÑEZ
MORATÍN

Plaza Nueva

AVENIDA DE LA CONSTITUCIÓN

GARCÍA L'INVESA

HARINAS

Hospital de la Caridad

SANTANDER

Casa de la Moneda

Iglesia de S. Jorge

Jefatura de Artillería

Torre de la Plata

BILBAO
PEDRO PARIAS
PADRE MARCHENA
CASTELAR

S. Buenaventura

ZARAGOZA
SANTAS
PATRONAS
GALERA
R. CATÓLICOS
PASTOR Y LANDERO
JULIO CÉSAR
MARQUÉS DE PARADAS

ARFE
DOS DE MAYO
TEMPRADO

EL ARENAL

ANTONIA DÍAZ

ADRIANO

Plaza de Toros de la Maestranza

PASEO

COLÓN

Torre del Oro

Palacio de Cultura

CRISTÓBAL

DE

River Guadalquivir

BETIS

Estatua de Carmen la Cigarrera

TRIANA

Plaza de Armas Bus Station

(Mon–Sat 10.30am–5pm, Sun 2–6pm; 700ptas including entrance to cathedral) and the Moorish entrance court, the **Patio de los Naranjos**, were spared. The cathedral was completed in just over a century and is the largest Gothic church in the world by cubic capacity. The nave rises to 42m, and even the side chapels seem tall enough to contain an ordinary church while the total area covers 11,520 square metres. In the centre of the church, an impressive choir opens onto the Capilla Mayor, dominated by a vast Gothic **retable** composed of 45 carved scenes from the life of Christ. The lifetime's work of a single craftsman, Pierre Dancart, this is the supreme masterpiece of the cathedral – the largest altarpiece in the world and one of the finest examples of Gothic woodcarving. You can also visit the domed Renaissance **Capilla Real**, built on the site of the original royal burial chapel, the **Sala Capitular**, with paintings by Murillo, and the grandiose **Sacristía Mayor**, which houses the treasury.

Rulers of Sevilla have occupied the site of the **Alcázar** (Tues–Sat 9.30am–5pm, Sun 9.30am–1.30pm; 600ptas) from the time of the Romans. Under the Almohads, the complex was turned into an enormous citadel, forming the heart of the town's fortifications. Parts of the walls survive, but the palace was rebuilt in the Christian period by **Pedro the Cruel** (1350–69), employing workmen from Granada and utilizing fragments of earlier Moorish buildings. His works, some of the best surviving examples of **Mudéjar architecture**, form the nucleus of the Alcázar today. Later additions include a wing in which early expeditions to the Americas were planned, and the huge Renaissance apartments of Charles V. Don't miss the beautiful and rambling **Alcázar gardens**, the confused but enticing product of several eras.

Just ten minutes' walk to the east of the cathedral and centre, the **Plaza de España** and adjoining **María Luisa Park**, laid out in 1929 for an abortive "Fair of the Americas", are an ideal place to spend the middle part of the day. En route you pass by the **Fábrica de Tabacos**, the old tobacco factory that was the setting for Bizet's *Carmen*. Nowadays it's part of the university. Towards the end of the María Luisa Park, the grandest surviving pavilions from the fair (which was scuppered by the Wall Street Crash) have been adapted as museums. The furthest contains the city's **archeology** collections (Tues 3–8pm, Wed–Sat 9am–8pm, Sun 9am–2.30pm; 250ptas, free to EU citizens), and opposite is the **Popular Arts Museum** (Tues 3–8pm, Wed–Sat 9am–8pm, Sun 9am–2.30pm; 250ptas, free to EU citizens), with interesting displays relating to the April *feria*.

Down by the **Guadalquivir** the main landmark is the twelve-sided **Torre del Oro**, built in 1220 as part of the Alcázar fortifications. The tower later stored the gold brought back to Sevilla from the Americas – hence its name. It now houses a small **naval museum** (Tues–Fri 10am–2pm, Sat & Sun 11am–2pm; 100ptas). One block away is the **Hospital de la Caridad** (Mon–Sat 9am–1.30pm & 3.30–6.30pm; 400ptas) founded in 1676 by Don Miguel de Manara, the inspiration for Byron's Don Juan, who repented his youthful excesses and set up this hospital for the relief of the dying and destitute. There are some magnificent paintings by Murillo and Valdés Leal inside. There's more art further along at the **Museo de Bellas Artes** on Plaza del Museo (Tues 3–8pm, Wed–Sat 9am–8pm, Sun 9am–2.30pm; 250ptas, free to EU citizens), housed in a beautiful former convent. Outstanding are the paintings by Zurbarán of Carthusian monks at supper and El Greco's portrait of his son.

TRIANA AND LA CARTUJA

Across the river lies the **Triana** barrio that was once home to the city's gypsy community and is still a lively and atmospheric place. At Triana's northern edge lies **La Cartuja** (Tues–Sun 11am–8pm; 300ptas, free Tues for EU citizens), a fourteenth-century former Carthusian monastery expensively restored as part of the Expo 92 world fair. Part of the complex is now given over to the **Museo del Arte Contemporáneo** (Tues–Sat 10am–8pm, Sun 10am–3pm; 300ptas, free Tues for EU citizens), which, in addition to work by *andaluz* artists, frequently stages important exhibitions by international artists.

The remnants of much of the **Expo 92** site itself have been incorporated into the **Isla Mágica** (May–Sept and most weekends in March, April, Oct & Nov 11am–11pm; 3400ptas, half-day 2300ptas), an amusement park based on sixteenth-century Spain, with water and rollercoaster rides, shows and period street animations.

Eating, drinking and nightlife

Sevilla is a tremendously atmospheric place, and the city is packed with lively bars. Remember, though, that it can also be expensive, particularly in the Barrio Santa Cruz. If you want to **eat** well and cheaply you'll generally have to steer clear of the sights, but there are exceptions: c/Sta María La Blanca has numerous cheap restaurants – notably the *Alta Mira* – as does c/Mateus Gago opposite La Giralda – try the *Alcazaba* or *Bar-Pizzeria El Artesano*. Other promising central areas are down towards the bullring and north of here towards the Plaza del Duque de la Victoria, where you'll find cheap *comidas* at places on c/Marqués de Paradas, c/Canalejas and particularly c/San Eloy, where the *El Patio San Eloy* is particularly good. *Zucchero* is a pleasant vegetarian restaurant on c/Golfo near Plaza Alfalfa.

For straight drinking and occasional tapas you can be much less selective. There are **bars** all over town – a high concentration of them with barrelled sherries from nearby Jerez and Sanlúcar (the locals drink the cold, dry *fino* with their tapas, especially shrimp). In the centre of **Santa Cruz** one of the liveliest places is *Las Teresas* in c/Ximénez de Enciso (expensive tapas), but perhaps the best tapas bar in the city, with just about every imaginable snack, is the *Bar Modesto* at c/Cano y Cuento 5, up at the north corner of the quarter by Avda Menéndez Pelayo. *Bar Giralda* at c/Mateus Gago is also excellent, as is the *Bodega Santa Cuiz* on c/Rodrigo Caro just off Mateus Gago. The Alfalfa area just north of the cathedral is a lively, young area with loud **music** in many of the bars: *El Lamentable*, a gay bar; *Bar Nao* and *Sopa de Ganso* in c/Pérez Galdos; and *Empinado* in c/Alcaicería near Plaza Alfalfa are all worth a look. The other main area for nightlife, popular with the large foreign student population, is just across the river on c/Betis.

Flamenco – or more accurately *Sevillanas* – music and dance are offered at dozens of places in the city, some of them extremely tacky and expensive. Unless you've heard otherwise, avoid the fixed "shows", or *tablaos*, and stick to bars – an excellent bar which often has spontaneous *Sevillanas* is *La Carbonería* at c/Levías 18, tricky to find but slightly to the northeast of the Iglesia de Santa Cruz.

Listings

American Express In the *Hotel Inglaterra* on Plaza Nueva 7 (☎95 421 16 17).

Car rental Most agents are along the Avda de la Constitución, although one of the cheapest operators, Atesa, is on c/Almirante Lobo 2 (☎95 451 47 35).

Consulates Australia, Federico Rubio 14 (☎95 422 02 40); Britain, Plaza Nueva 88 (☎95 422 88 75); Canada, Avda de la Constitución 30, 2° (☎95 422 94 13); USA, Paseo de las Delicias 7 (☎95 423 18 83).

Hospital English-speaking doctors are available at the Hospital Universitario, Avda Dr. Fedriani, 3 (☎95 455 74 00).

Police Plaza de la Gavidia (☎95 422 88 40).

Post Office Avda de la Constitución 32, by the cathedral; poste restante stays open Mon–Fri 8.30am–8.30pm, Sat 9.30am–2pm.

Telephones Through an archway on c/Sierpes 11, near Plaza Duque de la Victoria (Mon–Sat 10am–2pm & 5–9pm, Sun 10am –2pm).

Train tickets RENFE office at c/Zaragoza 29, off Plaza Nueva (☎95 422 26 93).

Cádiz and around

CÁDIZ is among the oldest settlements in Spain, founded about 1100 BC by the Phoenicians and one of the country's principal ports ever since. Its greatest period, however, was the eighteenth century, when it enjoyed a virtual monopoly on the Spanish-American trade in gold and silver. Inner Cádiz, built on a peninsula-island, remains much as it must have looked in those days, with its grand open squares, sailors' alleyways and high, turreted houses. Crumbling from the effect of the sea air on its soft limestone, it has a tremendous atmosphere – slightly seedy, definitely in decline, but still full of mystique.

Arriving by **train** you'll find yourself on the periphery of the old town, close to the Plaza de San Juan de Dios, busiest of the many squares. By **bus** you'll be a few blocks further north, along the water. With its blind alleys, cafés and backstreets, Cádiz is fascinating to wander around: to understand the city's layout, climb the **Torre Tavira** (daily 10am–6/8pm; 500ptas), tallest of the 160 lookout towers in the city, with an excellent camera obscura. Some specific sites to check out are the **Museo de Cádiz** at Plaza de Mina 5 (Tues 2.30pm–8pm, Wed–Sat 9am–8pm, Sun 9am–2pm; 250ptas, free for EU citizens), just across from the **tourist office** (Mon–Fri 9am–2pm & 5–8pm; ☎956 24 10 01), and the cathedrals. The huge **Catedral Nueva** (Tues–Sat 10am–noon) is an unusually successful blend of High Baroque and Neoclassical, decorated entirely in stone and with perfect proportions, while the "Old" Cathedral, **Santa Cruz**, is worth a look mainly for an interior studded with coin-in-the-slot votive candles. The oval, eighteenth-century chapel of **Santa Cueva** (Mon–Fri 10am–1pm; 50ptas; temporarily closed for renovation) has three frescoes by Goya.

Plaza de San Juan de Dios, protruding across the neck of the peninsula from the port, has several cafés and cheap **restaurants**. *La Caleta*, whose interior is built like the bow of a ship, is particularly good. There's plenty of budget **accommodation** in the dense network of alleyways around the square: *hostales*, *fondas* and straightforward dosshouses. *El Isleña*, on Plaza San Juan de Dios 12 (☎956 28 70 64; ②), is a reasonable place to stay, though in general the more salubrious places are to be found a couple of blocks away, on or just off c/Marquez de Cádiz. The best bet is *Pension Fontani,* c/Flamenco, 5 (☎956 28 27 04; ②), but *Hostal España*, c/Marquez de Cádiz 9 (☎956 28 55 00; ②) is also good. There is a smart new **youth hostel** on c/Diego Arias, 1 (☎956 22 19 39; ②).

Jerez de la Frontera

JEREZ DE LA FRONTERA, inland towards Sevilla, is the home and heartland of sherry and also, less known but equally important, of Spanish brandy. It seems a tempting place to stop, arrayed as it is round the scores of wine *bodegas*. But you're unlikely to want to make more than a quick visit (and tasting) between buses; the town itself is hardly distinctive unless you happen to arrive during one of the two big **festivals** – the May Horse Fair, or the celebration of the vintage towards the end of September.

The **tours of the sherry and brandy processes**, however, can be interesting, if not intoxicating, and provided you don't arrive in August, when most of the industry closes down (check with the tourist office to see which *bodegas* stay open), there are a great many firms and *bodegas* to choose from. Many of the firms were founded by British Catholic refugees who even now form a kind of Anglo-Andalusian aristocracy. One *bodega* that does stay open all summer is also one of the most central: next to the large ruins of the Moorish alcazar (daily 10am–6/8pm; 200ptas) on Manuel Maria González is **González Byass** (10am–2pm & 4.30–6.30pm; tours in English on the hour; Mon–Fri 450ptas; Sat & Sun 550ptas).

Most of the other *bodegas* are on the outskirts of town; pick up a plan of them from the **tourist office** (Mon–Fri 9am–2pm & 4/5–7/8pm, Sat 10am–2pm & 5–7pm; ☎956 33 11 50) at Alameda Cristina 7. The **train** and **bus stations** are more or less next door to each other, eight blocks east of the González *bodega* and the central Plaza de los Reyes Católicos. For **accommodation**, head for c/Higueras, off c/Medina (left out of the bus station and 3 blocks along) or c/Morenos, off the parallel c/Arcos: cheaper options include *Las Palomas* (☎956 34 37 73; ②) on Higueras, or the excellent *Hostal Sanvi*, c/Morenos 10 (☎956 34 56 24; ②–③).

Algeciras

The main reason to visit **ALGECIRAS**, along the coast from Cádiz, is for the **ferry to Morocco** – and the number of people passing through guarantees plenty of rooms. If you have trouble finding space, pick up a plan and check out the list in the **tourist office** on c/Juan de la Cierva (☎956 60 09 11), towards the river and rail line from the port. The port/harbour area also has plenty of **places to eat** – among them, down by the tourist office and invariably crowded, the very good-value *Casa Alfonso*.

There are hourly **crossings to Tangier** (1hr 30min) and to the Spanish *presidio* of **Ceuta** (1hr 30min) from 7am to 9.30pm each day. **Tickets** are available at scores of travel agents all along the waterside and on most approach roads. Wait till Tangier – or if you're going via Ceuta, Tetouan – before buying any Moroccan currency. Local **buses** connect La Línea – the frontier town for Gibraltar – and Algeciras (every 30min), and there are equally regular direct services between Algeciras and Gibraltar.

Gibraltar

The interest of **GIBRALTAR** is essentially its novelty: the genuine appeal of the strange, looming physical presence of its rock, and the increasingly dubious one of its preservation as one of Britain's last colonies. It's a curious place to visit, not least to witness the bizarre process of its opening to mass tourism from the Costa del Sol – although recent disputes with the Spanish over fishing rights have led to renewed tensions and consequent delays at the frontier. Mass tourism threatens to destroy Gibraltar's highly individual society – a polyglot mix of shady expats, Moroccans, Jews, Maltese and Andalusians – making it much more British, after the fashion of the expatriate communities and huge resorts of the Costa. Beware that the **currency** used here is the Gibraltar pound (the same value as the British pound, but different notes and coins); if you pay in pesetas, you generally pay about five per cent more.

Town and rock have a necessarily simple layout. **Main Street** (La Calle Real) runs for most of the town's length a couple of blocks back from the port; from the frontier it's a short bus ride or about a fifteen-minute walk. From near the end of Main Street, however, you can hop on a **cable car** (Mon–Sat 9.30am–6pm; £4.90 return, including Apes' Den and St Michael's Cave) which will carry you up to the summit of Gibraltar – **The Top of the Rock** (daily 9.30am–7pm; £5) as it's logically known – via **Apes' Den** halfway up; or take a tour minibus (most of which leave around lunchtime) to The Top. This is a fairly reliable viewing point to see the tailless monkeys and hear the guides explain their legend. From The Top you can look over to the Rif Mountains and down to the town and nearby beaches. From the Apes' Den it's an easy walk south along Queens Road to **St Michael's Cave**, an immense natural cavern which led ancient people to believe the rock was hollow and gave rise to its old name of *Mons Calpe* (Hollow Mountain).

Although you can be lazy and take the cable car both ways, you might instead walk up via Willis Rd to visit the **Tower of Homage**. Dating from the fourteenth century, this is the most visible survival from the old **Moorish Castle**. Further up you'll find the **Upper Galleries**, blasted out of the rock during the Great Siege of 1779–82 in order to point guns down at the Spanish lines. To walk down, take the **Mediterranean Steps** – a very steep descent most of the way down the east side, turning the southern corner of the Rock. You'll pass through the Jews' Gate and into Engineer Rd. From here, return to town through the Alameda Gardens and the **Trafalgar Cemetery**. This grand tour takes a half to a full day and shows you almost all there is to see: all sites on it are open Monday to Saturday from 10am to 5pm in summer.

Practicalities

The main **information office** (Mon–Fri 9am–5.30pm, Sat & Sun 10am–4pm; ☎9567/749 82) is on the Piazza, and there are also tourist offices at the airport and the Gibraltar Museum. If you have a car, don't attempt to bring it to Gibraltar – the queues at the border are nearly always atrocious, and parking is a nightmare.

Shortage of space also means that **accommodation** is at a premium. The only remotely cheap beds are at the tiny *Seruya's Guest House*, 92 Irish Town (☎9567/732 20; ③) or the *Toc H Hostel* at 36a Line Wall Rd (☎9567/734 31; ②), both invariably full and the latter irredeemably seedy. Not cheap, but certainly not seedy, is the brand new *Cannon Hotel*, 9 Cannon Lane, off Main St (☎9567/517 11; ④). Currently there's a reduced rate for young travellers (with full English breakfast) at the *Queen's Hotel* on Boyd St, next to the cable car (☎9567/740 00; ②), but you'd better ring ahead to check. **Camping** is strictly forbidden, but there is a new and central **youth hostel**, *Emile*, at Montagu Bastion on Linewall Rd (☎9567/511 06; ②, breakfast included). **Food and drink** are fairly expensive by Spanish standards, though pub snacks or fish and chips are reliable standbys. Main St is crowded with touristy places, among which *Mr Smith's Fish and Chip Shop*, opposite the Convent, is worth a try. Elsewhere, try the *Penny Farthing* on King St, *Happy Eater* in Cornwall's Lane,

Corks Wine Bar in Irish Town, the *Market Café* in the public market, or *Splendid Bar* in George's Lane. **Pubs** all tend to mimic traditional English styles (and prices), the difference being that they are open all day and often into the wee hours. Places on Main St tend to be rowdy at night – full of squaddies and visiting sailors.

A functional attraction of Gibraltar is its role as a **port for Morocco**. There are ferries to Tangier on Monday, Wednesday and Friday at 6.30pm (1hr; £30 return), with cheaper day-return tickets available on Monday and Wednesday. Tickets are sold in scores of travel agent shops around Gibraltar.

The Costa del Sol

Perhaps the outstanding feature of the **Costa del Sol** is its ease of access. Hundreds of charter flights arrive here every week, and it's often possible to get an absurdly cheap ticket from London. **Málaga airport** is positioned midway between Málaga, the main city on the coast, and Torremolinos, its most grotesque resort. You can get to either town, cheaply and easily, by taking the electric rail line (every 30min) along the coast between Málaga and Fuengirola. Granada, Córdoba and Sevilla are all within easy reach of Málaga; so too are Ronda and the "White Towns". In some ways then, this coast's enormous popularity is not surprising: what is surprising is that the **beaches** are generally grit-grey rather than golden and the sea is none too clean.

Málaga

MÁLAGA is the second city of the south, after Sevilla, and also one of the poorest. Yet though the clusters of high-rises look pretty grim as you approach, it can be a surprisingly attractive place. Around the old fishing villages of El Palo and Pedregalejo, now absorbed into the suburbs, are a series of small beaches and an avenue, or *paseo*, lined with some of the best fish and seafood cafés in the province. And overlooking the town and port are the Moorish citadels of the **Alcazaba** (Mon & Wed–Sun 9.30am–6pm; free) and **Gibralfaro** (daily 9.30am–7pm, free), just fifteen minutes' walk from the train or bus stations, and visible from most central points. The palace near the top of the hill was the residence of the Arab Emirs of Málaga, who briefly ruled an independent kingdom from here, though the archeological museum and castle are both currently closed for renovation.

These monuments aside, Málaga's greatest claim to fame is undoubtedly its **fried fish**, acknowledged as the best in Spain. It's served everywhere, especially around the Alameda, or you can take bus #11 (from the Paseo del Parque) out to **Pedregalejo**, where the seafront **paseo** begins. Almost any of the cafés and restaurants here will serve terrific fish, though you'll have to watch the price. There are plenty of reasonably priced **rooms** if you want to stay in Málaga, above all in the grid of streets north of the Alameda. You're likely to get an offer of somewhere to stay as soon as you arrive – if not, a couple to try are the *Hostal La Palma*, c/Martínez 7 (☎95 222 67 72; ②), and the *Pension Rossa*, c/Martinez 10 (☎95 221 27 16; ③). The closest **campsite** is at Torremolinos on Ctra. National (☎95 238 26 02).

Bus #3 connects the centre to the main **train and bus stations**, which are very close to each other; the main **tourist office** (Mon–Fri 9am–7pm, Sat & Sun 9am–2pm; ☎95 221 34 45) is at Pasaje de Chinitas 4, off c/Marqués de Larios (Mon–Fri 9am–6pm, Sat 10am–2pm), with a branch at the bus station. Arriving at the **airport**, catch the electric train to Renfe Station for trains and the bus station, or continue another stop to Guadalmedina for the city centre.

Along the coast

It's estimated that three hundred thousand foreigners live on the **Costa del Sol**, the richest and fastest-growing resort area in the Mediterranean. Approached in the right kind of spirit it's possible to have fun in **TORREMOLINOS**, a resort so over-the-top it's magnificent, and with furious competition keeping prices down. The concrete is a little less in evidence at **Carihuela**, 15 minutes' walk west of Torremolinos Station, where *Hostal Pedro*, Pareo Maritimo La Carihuela 67 (☎95 238 54 79; ②), is the best place, or try the more expensive *Prudencio* (③) next door. A good time costs more in chic **MARBELLA**, where

HAMISH BROWN

The walls, Essaouira, Morocco

FRANCESCA YORKE

FRENS HARINGHANDEL

AMSTERDAM

Amsterdam, Netherlands

GREG EVANS

1953

The Old Town square, Warsaw, Poland

Fjords, West Coast, Norway

Landscape & haystacks, Poland

Cais da Ribeira, Porto, Portugal

Domes of St Basil's Cathedral, Moscow, Russia

Masquers at a festival in Portugal

Local architecture, Stockholm, Sweden

Mosaic lizard, Parc Güell, Barcelona, Spain

Sevilla house front, Spain

House in Transylvania, Romania   Iztuzu Beach, Dalyan, Turkey

Brunnersee, Switzerland

there are bars and nightclubs galore alongside a surprisingly well-preserved old village and some wonderfully conspicuous consumption. But if you've come to Spain to be in Spain, put on the shades and stay on the bus at least until you reach **ESTEPONA** – it may be somewhat drab, but at least it's restrained, and there's space to breathe. The long dark-pebbled beach has been enlivened a little by a promenade studded with flowers and palms, and, away from the seafront, the old town is very pretty, with cobbled alleyways and two delightful plazas. There's a **campsite** here, and a number of **hostales**, such as the *Hostal Vista al Mar*, c/Real 154 (☎95 280 32 47; ②), which has an excellent fish restaurant/bar just round the corner.

Ronda

Andalucía is dotted with small, brilliantly whitewashed settlements known as the **Pueblos Blancos** or "White Towns", most often straggling up hillsides towards a castle or towered church. The most spectacular lie in a roughly triangular area between Málaga, Algeciras and Sevilla, at whose centre is the startling town of **RONDA**, connected by a marvellous rail line to Algeciras. Built on an isolated ridge of the sierra, and ringed by dark, angular mountains, Ronda is split in half by a gaping river gorge that drops sheer for 130m. Still more spectacular, the gorge is spanned by a stupendous eighteenth-century arched **bridge**, while tall whitewashed houses lean from its precipitous edges. The town itself is fascinating to wander around and has sacrificed surprisingly little of its character to the flow of day-trippers from the Costa.

Crossing the eighteenth-century **Puente Nuevo** from the Plaza de España takes you from the modern **Mercadillo** quarter to the old Moorish town, the **Ciudad**, centred around the church of **Santa María la Mayor**, originally the mosque. Turning off the main street to the left takes you steeply down to the old bridges – the **Puente Viejo** of 1616 and the Moorish single-span **Puente Arabe**. Nearby, on the southeast bank of the river, are the distinctive **Baños Árabes** (Tues 3–5.30pm, Wed–Sat 10am–2pm & 3–5.30pm, Sun 10am–2pm; free). Crossing the old bridge takes you back to the modern town via the **Jardin de la Mina**, which ascends the gorge in a series of stepped terraces with superb views of the river, new bridge and remarkable stairway of the **Casa del Rey Moro** (daily 10am–7pm; 700ptas), an early eighteenth-century mansion built on Moorish foundations whose 365 steps were cut by Christian slaves in the fourteenth century and were intended to guarantee a water supply in times of siege. Near the centre of the Ciudad stands the splendid Renaissance **Palacio del Marqués de Salvatierra** (Mon–Wed & Fri–Sat 11am–2pm & 4–6/7pm, Thurs & Sun am only; 300ptas), and behind the church, the **Casa de Mondragón** (Mon–Fri 10am–6/7pm, Sat & Sun 10am–3pm; 250ptas), probably the palace of the Moorish kings and now home to the **Museo Municipal**. A good path descends to the river from here. The principal gate of the town, through which the Christian conquerors passed, stands at the entrance to the suburb of San Francisco, beside the ruins of the **Alcázar**, destroyed by the French in 1809. Back in Mercadillo quarter is the **bullring** (daily 10am–7pm; 400ptas including museum) – one of the most prestigious in Spain – and the beautiful clifftop *paseo*, facing the open valley and the dramatic mountains of the Serrenía de Ronda.

Practicalities

The **tourist office** is on Plaza de España (Mon–Fri 9am–7pm, Sat & Sun 10am–2pm; ☎95 287 12 72). All the **places to stay** are in the Mercadillo quarter. Cheap and very close to the bridge near the Plaza de España is the *Hostal Virgen del Rocío* on c/Nueva (☎95 287 74 25; ③). Various options can be found going up c/Lorenzo Borrego, off the Plaza del Socorro, including the cheap *Hostal Ronda Sol* (☎95 287 44 97; ②) at c/Cristo 11; and the *Hostal Virgen de los Reyes* (☎95 287 11 40; ③). There are three **campsites** at the ends of town; the best is *El Sur* (☎95 287 59 39), 2km down the Algeciras road.

As for **eating**, most of the bargain options are grouped round the far end of the Plaza del Socorro: as you leave it on c/Almendra, *La Rosalejo* is excellent, and *El Brillante* on c/Sevilla is cheap. Drinks on the terrace of the *Parador* on Plaza de España are not too costly.

Granada

If you see only one town in Spain it should be **GRANADA**. For here, extraordinarily well preserved and in a tremendous natural setting, stands the **Alhambra** – the spectacular and serene climax of Moorish art in Spain. Granada was established as an independent kingdom in 1238 by **Ibn Ahmar**, a prince of the Arab Nasrid tribe which had been driven south from Zaragoza. By a series of shrewd manoeuvres, the Moors of Granada maintained their autonomy for two and a half centuries, but by 1490 only the city itself remained in Muslim hands. **Boabdil**, the last Moorish king, appealed in vain for help from his fellow Muslims in Morocco, Egypt and Turkey, and in the following year Ferdinand and Isabella marched on Granada with an army said to total 150,000 troops. For seven months, through the winter of 1491, they laid siege to the city. On January 2, 1492, Boabdil surrendered: the Christian Reconquest of Spain was complete.

Arrival and information

Virtually everything of interest in Granada – including the hills of **Alhambra** (to the east) and **Sacromonte** (to the north) – is within easy walking distance of the centre. The only times you'll need a bus are when arriving and leaving, since bus and train stations are both some way out. The **train station** is a kilometre or so out on the Avda de Andaluces, and is connected to the centre by buses #11 and #4. The **main bus station** – the *Alsina Graells* terminal on the Carretera de Jaén – is a bit further out, take the #3 bus into town. If you **fly** in, there's a bus (Mon–Sat 9.15am–7.20pm; 425ptas) connecting the airport with Plaza Isabel la Católica, by the cathedral. Details and timetables of all buses, trains, and much else besides, are posted on the walls of the **tourist office** on c/Mariana Prieda off c/Reyes Católicas (Mon–Sat 9am–7pm, Sun 10am–2pm; ☎958 22 59 90). There is another regional branch in Plaza Mariana Pineda (☎958 22 66 88).

Accommodation

The **Gran Vía** is Granada's main street, cutting through the middle of town. It forms a "T" at its end with **c/Reyes Católicos**, which runs east to the **Plaza Nueva** and west to the **Puerta Real**, the city's two main squares. Finding a **place to stay** in this area is easy except at the very height of season (Semana Santa is impossible). You may well be greeted by touts at the train or bus stations, and on the whole it seems safe to take their offers, though check the address. Otherwise, try the streets to either side of the Gran Vía, at the back of the Plaza Nueva, around the Puerta Real and Plaza del Carmen (particularly c/de Navas), the Plaza de la Trinidad in the university area, or along the Cuesta de Gomérez, which leads up from the Plaza Nueva towards the Alhambra.

HOTELS AND HOSTELS

Hotel América, Real de la Alhambra 53 (☎958 22 74 71). Simple 1-star hotel, in the Alhambra grounds: you pay for the location, but it's worth it. Booking is essential. ⑤–⑥.

Pensión Atenas, Gran Vía de Colón 38 (☎958 27 87 50). Large place, so worth a try, though rooms vary in quality. ③.

Hostal Britz, Cuesta de Gomérez 1 (☎958 22 36 52). Noisy, but otherwise very comfortable and well placed. Some rooms with bath. ②.

Hostal Europa, c/Fabrica Vieja 16 (☎958 27 87 44). Friendly, cheap and small, just west of the cathedral. ②.

Casa de Huéspedes González, c/Buensuceso 51 (☎958 26 03 51), between Plaza de Trinidad and Plaza de Gracia west of the cathedral. Perfectly good rooms, very good value. ②.

Hostal Lisboa, Plaza del Carmen 27 (☎958 22 14 13). Noisy at the front, but clean and comfortable. ③.

Hostal Navarro-Ramos, Cuesta de Gomérez 21 (☎958 25 05 55). Small rooms, small balconies, bargain prices but showers are extra. ②.

Pensión Olimpia, Alvaro de Bazán 6, off Gran Vía de Colón, opposite Banco de Jeréz (☎958 27 82 38). Central, good-value place, nice people. ②.

Hotel La Perla, c/Reyes Católicos 2 (☎958 22 34 15). Simple hotel right in the centre, near the cathedral. ②.

Hostal Terminus, Avda de Andaluces 10, on the right outside the train station (☎958 20 14 23). Absolutely no frills, but cheap and good if you arrive by train late at night. ②.
Youth Hostel, Avda Ramón y Cajal 2 (☎958 27 26 38). Handy for the train station (from RENFE, turn left onto c/ del Halcón, then first left across the railway line), with lots of facilities including a pool, but institutional and unfriendly. ②.

CAMPSITES

Camping Reina Isabal, Carretera Granada. Near the town of Zubia.
Camping Sierra Nevada, Avda de Madrid 107. The closest site to the centre and probably the best too; easily reached on bus #3. March–Oct.

The City

There are three distinct groups of buildings on the **Alhambra** hill: the **Palacios Reales** (Royal Palace), the palace gardens of the **Generalife**, and the **Alcazaba**. The last was all that existed when Ibn Ahmar made Granada his capital, but from its reddish walls the hilltop had already taken its name: *al-Hamra* in Arabic means literally "the red". Ibn Ahmar rebuilt the Alcazaba and added to it the huge circuit of walls and towers. Within the walls he began a palace, which he supplied with running water by diverting the River Darro; water is an integral part of the Alhambra and this engineering feat was Ibn Ahmar's greatest contribution. The palace was essentially the product of his fourteenth-century successors, particularly Mohammed V. After their conquest of the city, Ferdinand and Isabella lived for a while in the Alhambra. They restored some rooms and converted the mosque but left the palace structure unaltered. As at Córdoba and Sevilla, it was their grandson Charles V who wreaked the most destruction: he demolished a whole wing to build yet another grandiose Renaissance palace. This and the Alhambra itself were simply ignored by his successors and by the eighteenth century the Royal Palace was in use as a prison. In 1812 it was taken and occupied by Napoleon's forces, who looted and damaged whole sections of the palace, and on their retreat from the city tried (but fortunately failed) to blow up the entire complex.

The standard approach to the **Alhambra** (summer Mon–Sat 8.30am–8pm, Sun 9am–6pm, also Tues, Thurs & Sat 10pm–midnight; winter Mon–Sun 9am–5.45pm & Sat 8–10pm; 1000 ptas) is along the Cuesta de Gomérez, the road that climbs uphill from the Plaza Nueva. After a few hundred metres you reach the **Puerta de las Granadas**, a massive Renaissance gateway erected by Charles V. Here two paths diverge to either side of the road: the one on the right leads towards the ticket office and a group of fortified towers, the **Torres Bermejas**, which may date from as early as the eighth century. The left-hand path leads through the woods to the main entrance, the magnificent tower gateway known as the **Puerta de la Justicia**. Buy your ticket early (or at the *Banco BBV* in Plaza Isabel la Católica between 9am and 2pm for 125ptas extra) to avoid huge queues or a long wait – during busy periods tickets can specify an entry time much later in the day; between 4 and 8pm, after most tours have left, is generally quieter.

Ideally you should start your visit with the earliest, most ruined, part of the fortress – the **Alcazaba**. At the summit of the Alcazaba is the **Torre de la Vela**, named after a huge bell on its turret, from where there's a fine overview of the whole area. It's in the **Casa Real**, however, that the real wonders start: the first being that the place itself has survived, since it was built from wood, brick and adobe, and was designed not to last but to be renewed and redecorated by succeeding rulers. Its buildings show a brilliant use of light and space but they are principally a vehicle for ornamental stucco decoration, in rhythmic repetitions of supreme beauty. Arabic inscriptions feature prominently: some are poetic eulogies of the buildings and rulers, but most are taken from the Koran.

The palace is in three parts, each arrayed round an interior court and with a specific function. The sultans used the **Mexuar**, the first series of rooms, for business and judicial purposes, and this is as far as most people would have penetrated. In the **Serallo**, beyond, they received embassies and distinguished guests: here the royal throne room, known as the **Hall of the Ambassadors**, the largest room of the palace. The last section, the **Harem**, formed their private living quarters and would have been entered by no one but their family

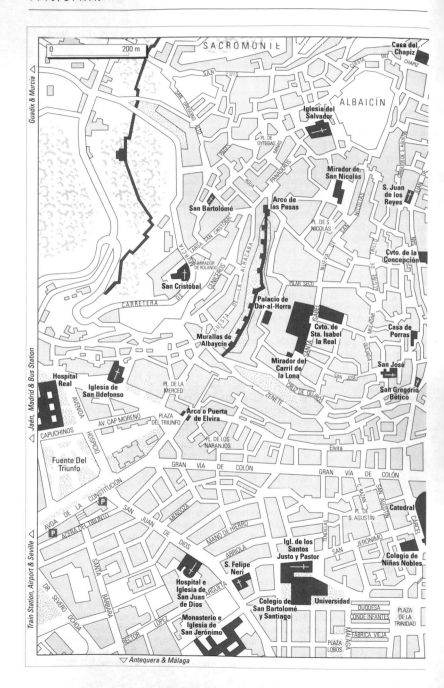

SACROMONTE

ALBAICÍN

Casa del Chapiz

Iglesia del Salvador

Mirador de San Nicolás

S. Juan de los Reyes

San Bartolomé

Arco de las Pesas

Cvto. de la Concepción

San Cristóbal

Palacio de Dar-al-Horra

Murallas de Albaycín

Cvto. de Sta. Isabel la Real

Casa de Porras

Mirador del Carril de la Lona

San José

San Gregorio Bético

Hospital Real

Iglesia de San Ildefonso

PL. DE LA MERCED

Arco o Puerta de Elvira

Fuente Del Triunfo

PLAZA DEL TRIUNFO

PL. DE LOS NARANJOS

GRAN VÍA DE COLÓN

GRAN VÍA DE COLÓN

Elvira

Catedral

Igl. de los Santos Justo y Pastor

S. Felipe Neri

Colegio de Niñas Nobles

Hospital e Iglesia de San Juan de Dios

Colegio de San Bartolomé y Santiago

Universidad

Monasterio e Iglesia de San Jerónimo

DUQUESA
CONDE INFANTES
FÁBRICA VIEJA
PLAZA DE LA TRINIDAD

PLAZA LOBOS

⊲ Guadix & Murcia

⊲ Jaén, Madrid & Bus Station

⊲ Train Station, Airport & Seville

▽ Antequera & Málaga

0   200 m

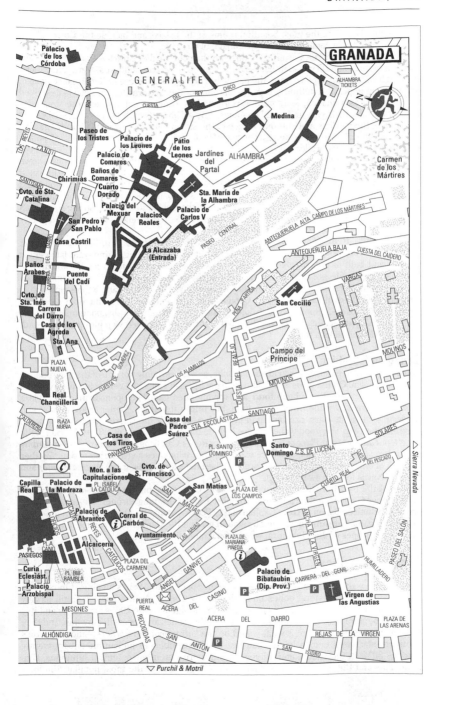

GRANADA

Palacio de los Córdoba

GENERALIFE

Medina

ALHAMBRA TICKETS

Paseo de los Tristes
Palacio de los Leones
Pátio de los Leones
Jardines del Partal
ALHAMBRA

Carmen de los Mártires

Palacio de Comares
Baños de Comares
Chirimías
Cuarto Dorado
Cvto. de Sta. Catalina
Palacio del Mexuar
Palacios Reales
Palacio de Carlos V
Sta. María de la Alhambra

San Pedro y San Pablo
Casa Castril

La Alcazaba (Entrada)

PASEO CENTRAL

ANTEQUERUELA ALTA
CAMPO DE LOS MÁRTIRES

ANTEQUERUELA BAJA
CUESTA DEL CAIDERO

Baños Árabes
Puente del Cadí
Cvto. de Sta. Inés
Carrera del Darro
Casa de los Ágreda
Sta. Ana

VARGAS

San Cecilio

BELÉN

PLAZA NUEVA

Real Chancillería

Campo del Príncipe

MOLINOS

LOS ALAMILLOS

MOLINOS

PLAZA NUEVA

SANTIAGO

SOLARES

CUESTA DE GOMEREZ

Casa del Padre Suárez
STA. ESCOLÁSTICA

Casa de los Tiros
PAVANERAS

PL. SANTO DOMINGO

Santo Domingo
P.S. DE LUCENA

DEL PESCADO

Mon. a las Capitulaciones
PL. ISABEL LA CATÓLICA

Cvto. de S. Francisco

San Matías

PLAZA DE LOS CAMPOS

CUARTO REAL

Capilla Real
Palacio de la Madraza

Palacio de Abrantes
Corral de Carbón

Ayuntamiento

PLAZA DE MARIANA PINEDA

Alcaicería

PL. CANO
PL. PASIEGOS

Curia Eclesiást.
Palacio Arzobispal

PL. BIB-RAMBLA

PLAZA DEL CARMEN

Palacio de Bibataubín (Dip. Prov.)
CARRERA DEL GENIL

HUMILLADERO

PASEO DEL SALÓN

Virgen de las Angustias

MESONES

PUERTA REAL
ACERA DEL CASINO

ALHÓNDIGA

ACERA DEL DARRO

PLAZA DE LAS ARENAS

REJAS DE LA VIRGEN

SAN ANTÓN

SAN ISIDRO

△ Sierra Nevada

▽ *Purchil & Motril*

or servants. These are the most beautiful rooms of the palace, and include the **Court of the Lions**, which has become the archetypal image of Granada.

The usual exit from the Casa Real is through the courtyard of **Charles V's palace** – now housing a museum (Tues–Sat 9am–2.30pm; free) – where bullfights were once held. Although wilfully out of place here, the palace is a distinguished piece of Renaissance design, stamping an imperialist authority over the gardens of the **Generalife**. Paradise is described in the Koran as a shaded, leafy garden refreshed by running water where the "fortunate ones" may take their rest under tall canopies. It is an image which perfectly describes the Generalife, the gardens and summer palace of the sultans. Its name means literally "garden of the architect" and the grounds consist of a luxuriantly imaginative series of patios, enclosed gardens and walkways.

From just below the entrance to the Generalife the **Cuesta del Rey Chico** winds down towards the River Darro and the old Arab quarter of the Albaicín. Here the little-visited **Baños Árabes** (Tues–Sat 10am–2pm; free) at 31 Corredera del Darro are marvellous, and the plaza in front of the church of **San Nicolás** offers probably the best view of the Alhambra in town. To the southwest of the Albaicín, opposite the Capilla Real, is the strangely painted **Palacio de Madraza**, a fourteenth-century Islamic college that retains part of its old prayer hall, including a magnificently decorated *mihrab*.

The **Capilla Real** (Mon–Sat 10.30am–1/1.30pm & 3.30/4–6.30/7pm, Sun 11am–1pm & 3.30/4–6.30/7pm; 300ptas, free Sun) is itself an impressive building, flamboyant late Gothic in style and built in the first decades of Christian rule as a mausoleum for Ferdinand and Isabella. Their tombs are as simple as could be imagined, but above them is a fabulously elaborate monument erected by their grandson Charles V. For all its stark Renaissance bulk, Granada's **Cathedral**, adjoining the Capilla Real and entered from the door beside it (Mon–Sat 10.30am–1.30pm & 3.30–6.30pm, Sun 3.30–6.30pm), is a disappointment. It was begun in 1521, just as the chapel was finished, but left uncompleted well into the eighteenth century, and still lacks a tower.

Eating and drinking

You don't come to Granada for food and nightlife, and it's certainly not one of the gastronomic centres of Spain. On the other hand, like so many Spanish cities, the centre has plenty of animated bars serving good, cheap **food** and staying open late. The open-air places on Plaza Nueva are great to while away some time, but pricey if you eat. Better value dining, and numerous late-night bars, can be found in "Little Morocco", the warren of streets between here and the Gran Vía: good-value choices include the *Nueva Bodega* at c/Cetti Merién 3, the excellent *Gargantua* at Placeta Sillería 7 (near c/Reyes Católicos), and *Cafetería-Restaurante La Riviera* at c/Cetti Merién 5, whose *menú económico* includes a vegetarian option. Another nucleus of cheap eateries is the area around Plaza del Carmen (near the *Ayuntamiento*) and along c/Navas leading away from it.

One of the best **bars** in the centre is *Bodegas Castañeda*, on the corner of c/Elvira and c/Almireceros opposite the cathedral. The best area for drinking through the early hours is around the university, on c/Gran Capitán and c/Pedro Antonio de Alarcón. In term time, students also gather in **pubs** near the bus station around the Campo del Príncipe, a square on the eastern slopes of the Alhambra, where you'll often find great tapas.

Almería province

The **province of Almería** is a strange corner of Spain. Inland it has an almost lunar landscape of desert, sandstone cones and dried-up riverbeds. On the coast it's still largely unspoiled; lack of water and roads frustrated development in the 1960s and 1970s and it is only now beginning to take off. A number of good beaches are accessible by bus, and they are worth considering during what would be the "off-season" elsewhere, since Almería's summers start well before Easter and last into November. In midsummer it frequently touches 38°C in the shade, and all year round there's an intense, almost luminous, sunlight. This and the weird scenery have made Almería one of the most popular film locations in Europe – much of *Lawrence of Arabia* was shot here, along with scores of the so-called spaghetti westerns.

Almería city

ALMERÍA itself is a pleasant modern city, spread at the foot of a stark grey mountain at whose summit is a tremendous **Alcazaba** (summer daily 10am–2pm & 5.30–8.30pm; winter 9am–1.30pm & 3.30–6.30pm; 250ptas, free to EU citizens). From here there's a superb view of the coast, of Almería's cave quarter – the *Barrio de la Chanca* on a low hill to the left – and of the city's strange fortified **Cathedral** (Mon–Fri 10am–5pm, Sat 10am–1pm, Sun for mass only; 300ptas). There's little else to do in town, and your time is probably best devoted to strolling between the cafés, bars and *terrazas* on the main Paseo de Almería, which runs from the central Puerta de Purchena down towards the harbour, and taking day-trips out to the beach. The city's own **beach**, southeast of the centre beyond the rail lines, is long but dismal.

Best for **accommodation** is the area between the bus and train stations and the centre. Possibilities include *Pensión Alcazaba*, c/Antonio Vico 1 (☎950 23 44 22; ②), off c/Granada, or *Hostal Maribel*, Avda Lorca 153 (☎950 23 51 73; ③); the nearest **campsite** is on the coast at La Garrofa, 5km west, reached by buses to Aguadulce and Roquetas de Mar (where there's another, giant site). The **tourist office** (Mon–Fri 9am–7pm, Sat & Sun 10am–2pm; ☎950 27 43 55) is towards the train station, on c/Hermanos Muchado 4, at the south end of the Avda Federico García Lorca.

The beaches

Almería's best **beaches** lie on its eastern coast, on the strip between Carboneras and La Garrucha, centred on the town of Mojácar. This is some way up the coast and to get there you'll have to travel through some of Almería's distinctive desert scenery. There are two possible routes: via Níjar to Carboneras, or via Tabernas and Sorbas to Mojácar. **MOJÁCAR** – Almería's chief resort – lies a couple of kilometres back from the sea, a striking town of white cubist houses wrapped round a harsh outcrop of rock. There's plenty of development here, and prices can seem inflated, but it's still pleasant. There's a handful of small **hostales** in town, but you're probably best off down at the beach where there's a cheap **campsite**, lots of fine beach bars, rooms to let and several hostales on Paseo Mediterraneo – try the *Bahia* (☎950 47 80 10; ③) or the *Puntazo* (☎950 47 82 29; ④, breakfast included), for which it's often necessary to book ahead. The **beach** itself is excellent and the water warm and brilliantly clear.

OLD CASTILE

The foundations of modern Spain were laid in the kingdom of **Castile**. A land of frontier fortresses – the *castillos* from which it takes its name – it became the most powerful and centralizing force of the Reconquest, extending its domination through military gains and marriage alliances. The monarchs of this triumphant and expansionist age were enthusiastic patrons of the arts, endowing their cities with superlative monuments above which, quite literally, tower the great Gothic cathedrals of **Salamanca**, **León** and **Burgos**. The most impressive of the castles are at **Coca**, **Gormaz** and **Berlanga de Duero**, and there's also a wealth of Romanesque churches spread along the **Pilgrim Route to Santiago** which cuts across the top of the province.

Over the past decades these and the other historic cities of Old Castile have grown to dominate the region more than ever. Although its soil is fertile, the harsh extremes of land and climate don't encourage rural settlement, and the vast central plateau is given over almost entirely to grain. The sporadic and depopulated villages are rarely of interest – travel consists of getting quickly from one grand town to the next.

Salamanca

SALAMANCA is probably the most graceful city in Spain. For four centuries it was the seat of one of the most prestigious universities in the world, and it has kept the unmistakable atmosphere of a seat of learning. It's still a small place, untouched by the piles of suburban concrete which blight so many of its contemporaries, and given a gorgeous harmony by the golden sandstone from which almost the entire city seems to be constructed. The architectural hoard is endless: two cathedrals, one Gothic, the other Romanesque, vie for attention with Renaissance palaces; the Plaza Mayor is the finest in Spain; and the surviving university buildings are tremendous.

Two great architectural styles were developed, and see their finest expression, in Salamanca. **Churrigueresque**, a particularly florid form of Baroque, takes its name from José Churriguera (1665–1723), the dominant member of a prodigiously creative family. **Plateresque** came earlier, a decorative technique of shallow relief and intricate detail named for its alleged resemblance to the art of the silversmith (*platero*).

The City

If on arrival you'd like to get a picture-perfect overall view of Salamanca, go to the extreme south of the city and cross its oldest surviving monument, the much-restored **Puente Romano** (Roman Bridge), some 400m long and itself worth seeing. Otherwise make for the grand **Plaza Mayor**, its bare central expanse completely enclosed by one continuous four-storey building decorated with iron balconies and medallion portraits. Nowhere is the Churrigueras' inspired variation of Baroque so refined as here, where the restrained elegance of the designs is heightened by the changing strength and angle of the sun. From the south side, Rua Mayor leads to the vast Baroque church of **La Clerecía**, seat of the Pontifical University (open for visits only half an hour before mass, which takes place Mon–Sat 1.15 & 7.30pm, Sun 12.30pm), and the celebrated **Casa de las Conchas**, or House of Shells (Mon–Fri 9am–9pm, Sat 9am–2pm & 4–7pm, Sun 11am–2pm & 4–7pm; free) so called because its facades are decorated with rows of carved scallop shells, symbol of the pilgrimage to Santiago.

From the Casa de las Conchas, c/Libreros leads to the **Patio de las Escuelas** and the Renaissance entrance to the **University** (Mon–Sat 9.30am–1.30pm & 4–7pm, Sun 10am–1pm; 300ptas). The ultimate achievement of Plateresque art, this reflects the tremendous reputation of Salamanca in the early sixteenth century, when it was one of Europe's greatest universities. Today it's socially prestigious, academically no great shakes. It does, however, run a highly successful summer language school – nowhere in Spain will you see so many young Americans.

As a further declaration of Salamanca's prestige, and in a glorious last-minute assertion of Gothic, the **Catedral Nueva** (daily: summer 9am–2pm & 4–8pm; winter 10am–1pm & 4–6pm; free) was begun in 1512. It was built within a few yards of the university and acted as a buttress for the Old Cathedral which was in danger of collapsing. The main Gothic-Plateresque facade is contemporary with that of the university and equally dazzling in its wealth of ornamental detail. Alberto Churriguera and his brother Joaquín both worked here – the former on the choirstalls, the latter on the dome. Entry to the **Catedral Vieja** (same times; 300ptas) is through the first chapel on the right. Tiny by comparison and stylistically entirely different, its most striking feature is the massive fifteenth-century retable. In the chapterhouse there's a small **museum** with a fine collection of works by Fernando Gallego, Salamanca's most famous painter.

Another faultless example of Plateresque art, the **Convento de San Esteban** (daily 9am–1pm & 4–6pm; 200ptas) is a short walk down c/del Tostado from the Plaza de Anaya at the side of the Catedral Nueva. Its golden facade is divided into three horizontal sections and covered in a veritable tapestry of sculpture, while the east end of the church is occupied by a huge Baroque retable by José Churriguera himself. The monastery's cloisters, through which you enter, are magnificent too, but the most beautiful cloisters in the city stand across the road in the **Convento de las Dueñas** (daily 10.30am–1pm & 4.30–5.30/7pm; 200ptas). Built on an irregular pentagonal plan in the Renaissance-Plateresque style, it has upper-storey capitals wildly carved with human heads and skulls. You should also see the **Convento de Santa Clara** (Mon–Fri 9.30am–1.40pm & 4–6.40pm, Sat & Sun 9am–2.40pm; 200ptas), outwardly plain but with interior features in virtually every important Spanish style.

Most of the remaining interest lies in the western part of the city. If you follow c/de la Compañía from the Casa de las Conchas, you pass the Plaza San Benito, which has some fine houses, and come to the Plaza Agustinas. Buildings to look out for here include the large sixteenth-century **Palacio de Monterrey**, the seventeenth-century Augustinian monastery of **La Purísima** (Fri & Sat noon–1pm & 5–7pm; free), opposite, and another interesting convent, **Convento Las Ursulas** (daily 11am–1pm & 4.30–6pm; 100ptas), behind the Palacio. Facing the east wall of its church is the impressive facade of the **Casa de las Muertes**, and following c/de Fonseca leads to the magnificent Plateresque palace known as the **Colegio de los Irlandeses**.

Practicalities

The **bus and train stations** are on opposite sides of the city, each about fifteen minutes' walk from the centre. There's a **tourist office** at the edge of Plaza Mayor (daily 9.30am–noon & 4.30–6.30pm), or the main office at Casa de las Conchas (Mon–Fri 9am–2pm & 5–7pm, Sat & Sun 10am–2pm & 4–7pm; ☎923 26 85 71). Prices for **accommodation** are reasonable, but it can be hard to find in high season – especially at fiesta time in September. Touts tend to be out in force at the RENFE station during the summer. On the way into town from here, there are a few choices around Plaza de España – try the *Hostal Internacional*, Avda de Mirat 15 (☎923 26 27 99; ②). Otherwise, the Plaza Mayor is the most obvious place to head for – in the small streets surrounding it you'll find scores of small *fondas* and *hostales*, most of a high standard: *Pensión Lisboa*, on one of the best streets, c/Meléndez 1 (☎923 21 43 33; ②), is particularly good. The cheapest option of all is a room in a *casa particular*, available outside university terms. There are a couple of **campsites** nearby, the best at Santa Marta, about 5km out but served by regular local buses.

The **cafés** in Plaza Mayor are nearly twice the usual price but worth every peseta. Close by in Plaza del Mercado (by the **market**, itself a good source of provisions), there's a row of lively tapas bars, while the university area has loads of good-value **bars and restaurants** catering to student budgets. Good-value food places include *Rio Tormes*, Plaza Corrillo 20, *Mandala*, near the university entrance on c/de Serranos 9, and *El Bardo*, c/Compañía 8, which sells vegetarian food and alcohol. **Late-night bars** abound in the Gran Vía area; among the most popular are *El Corrillo*, in c/Melendez, for jazz, and *El Callejón* at c/España 68, for folk. *El Savor*, c/San Justo 28, has good Latin music, while *El Moderno* at c/España 65 has an excellent DJ in between sets of live music. The most popular **clubs** include *El Cum Laude*, off Plaza Mayor; *Camelot*, on c/Bordadores; and *El Puerto de Chus*, on Plaza de San Julian.

Zamora

Leaving Salamanca to the north, you can be in **ZAMORA** within an hour by rail or road. The quietest of the great historic cities of the heartland, with a population of sixty thousand, it was known in medieval times as *la bien cercada* (the closed one) on account of its strong fortifications: one siege here lasted seven months. Its old quarters, medieval in appearance, are spread out along the sloping banks of the Río Duero (known as the Douro once it crosses into Portugal) and there are a dozen **Romanesque churches** within ten minutes' walk of the centre. Apart from the **cathedral** with its superlative collection of tapestries (Tues–Sat 11am–2pm & 4/5–6/8pm, Sun 11am–2pm; 300ptas), no single church stands out above the others, but their unassumingly beautiful architecture is the city's most distinctive feature.

There's a **tourist office** at c/Santa Clara 20 (Mon–Fri 9am–2pm & 5–7pm, Sat & Sun 10am–2pm & 5–8pm; ☎980 53 18 45), and plenty of **places to stay**. Among the best are the *Hostal La Reina*, c/la Reina 1 (☎980 53 39 39; ②), and the *Pensión Balborraz*, c/Balborraz 25 (☎980 51 55 19; ②), both close to the Plaza Mayor.

Burgos

BURGOS has always been a military town. For some five centuries of the Middle Ages the city was the capital of Old Castile: in the eleventh century it was the home of El Cid; in the thirteenth century of Fernando III, who began the city's famous Gothic cathedral – one of the greatest in all Spain, it seems somehow to share the forceful solemnity and severity of Burgos' history. More recently Burgos was a Francoite stronghold – his temporary capital during the Civil War and strongly loyal to the end, with an abiding reputation for conservatism.

The City

Orientation in Burgos could not be simpler, since wherever you are the **Cathedral's** (daily 9.30am–1pm & 4–7pm) profile of spires and pinnacles makes its presence felt. The church is so large and varied that it's hard to appreciate as a whole, but it's magnificent from almost any angle. It is currently being restored, however, so some wings are obscured by scaffolding. Inside, you're immediately struck by the size and number of side chapels, the greatest of which, the Capilla del Condestable, is almost a cathedral in itself. The most curious, though, is the Capilla del Santo Cristo (first right) which contains the *Cristo de Burgos*, a cloyingly realistic image of Christ endowed with real human hair and nails and covered with the withered hide of a water buffalo, still popularly believed to be human skin. To get into some of these smaller chapels you'll have to buy a treasury ticket (400ptas), which also admits you to the cloisters, the diocesan museum inside them, and the choir at the heart of the cathedral, which affords the best view into the dome.

Overlooking the plaza in front of the cathedral stands the fifteenth-century church of **San Nicolás**. Unassuming from the outside, it has an altarpiece within by Francisco de Colonia, which is as rich as anything in the city. At the side of San Nicolás, c/Pozo Seco ascends to the early Gothic church of **San Esteban**, now the **Museo del Retablo** (summer Tues–Sat 10.30am–2pm & 4.30–7pm, Sun 10.30am–2pm; winter Sat 10.30am–2pm & 4.30–7pm, Sun 10.30am–2pm; 200ptas) which houses a fine collection of icons and altarpieces. Beyond San Esteban lies the ruined castle with a fine view of the city and the surrounding countryside.

On the outskirts are two monasteries. The closer is the Cistercian **Monasterio de las Huelgas** (summer Tues–Sat 10.30am–1.15pm & 3.30–5.45pm, Sun 10.30am–2.15pm; winter Tues–Sat 11am–1.15pm & 4–5.15pm, Sun 10.30am–2.15pm; 650ptas includes guided tour, Wed free) on the "new side" of the river, about twenty minutes' walk from the city centre: cross the bridge, turn right and follow the signs along the riverbank. Founded in 1187, the convent grew to extraordinary wealth and power, and is remarkable for its wealth of Mudéjar craftsmanship. Priceless embroidery, jewellery and weaponry of regal splendour are exhibited in a small museum, but the highlight is the Mudéjar-Gothic cloister.

Practicalities

The **bus station** is south of the Puente de Santa María at c/ Miranda 4; the **train station** a short walk away at the bottom of Avda Conde Guadalhorce. The main **tourist office** (summer Mon–Fri 9am–2pm & 5–7pm, Sat & Sun 10am–2pm & 4.30–7.30pm; ☎947 20 31 25) is at Plaza de Alonso Martínez 7, around the side of the cathedral and up c/Lain Calvo.

For **rooms**, the best areas to try are around the tourist office and c/San Juan, or near the bus station: *Pensión Peña*, c/La Puebla 18 (☎947 20 63 23; ②) is near the former; next to the latter is the more expensive, but delightful *Pensión Ansa*, c/Miranda 9-1 (☎947 20 47 67; ②). *Pensión Manjón*, c/Conde Jordana 1–7 (☎947 20 86 89; ②), is a clean and comfortable option near to the river. There's a **youth hostel** (☎947 22 03 62; July–Sept; ②) about 2km out of town on c/Avda. de General Vigón, and a good **campsite**, *Fuentes Blancas* (☎947 48 60 16; April–Sept), 45 minutes' walk out on the Cartuja road, or a bus ride (every 40min in summer) from the Cid statue. There are several tapas **bars** and a swarm of **nightclubs** around c/Huerto del Rey behind the cathedral: *Mesón Astorga* and *Mesón El Cardenal* are both good. More formal **restaurants** include the *Rincón de España* between the river and the cathedral, and the cheapish *Don Diego*, immediately behind the cathedral on c/Porcelos.

León

The stained glass in the cathedral of **LEÓN** and the Romanesque wall paintings in its Royal Pantheon are reason enough for many people to visit the city, but León is also – unusually for this part of the country – as attractive and enjoyable in its modern quarters as it is in those areas that remain from its heyday. In 914, as the Reconquest edged its way south from Asturias, the Christian capital moved to León. Despite being sacked by al-Mansur in 996, the new capital and its territories grew rapidly: in 1035 the county of Castile matured into a fully fledged kingdom, and for the next two centuries León and Castile jointly spearheaded the war against the Moors until by the thirteenth century Castile had come to dominate her mother kingdom.

León's **Cathedral** (daily 8.30am–1.30pm & 4–7pm) dates from the final years of greatness. It is said to be a miracle that it's still standing: it has the largest proportion of window to stone of any Gothic cathedral. The stained-glass **windows**, a stunning kaleidoscope of light, present one of the most magical and harmonious spectacles in Spain and the colours used – reds, golds and yellows – could only be Spanish. The glass screen added to the choir this century to give a clear view up to the altar enhances the sensation of light with its bewildering refractions. Outside, the west facade, dominated by a massive rose window, is also magnificent.

The other great attraction is the church of **San Isidoro** and the Royal Pantheon of the early kings of León and Castile. Ferdinand I, who united the two kingdoms in 1037, commissioned the complex as a shrine for the bones of St Isidore and a mausoleum for himself and his successors. The bones of the patron saint lie in a reliquary on the high altar: the **Pantéon** (Mon–Sat 9am–1.30pm & 4–7pm, Sun 9am–2pm; 400ptas), a pair of small crypt-like chambers, is in front of the west facade. One of the earliest Romanesque buildings in Spain (1054–63), it was decorated towards the end of the twelfth century with some of the most imaginative and impressive paintings of Romanesque art. They are extraordinarily well preserved and their biblical and everyday themes are perfectly adapted to the architecture of the vaults. Eleven kings and twelve queens were laid to rest here, but the chapel was desecrated during the Peninsular War and their tombs command little attention in such a marvellous setting.

Also worth seeing is the opulent **Monasterio de San Marcos**, built in 1168 for the Knights of Santiago, one of several chivalric orders founded in the twelfth century to protect pilgrims on their way to Santiago and lead the Reconquest. In the sixteenth century the monastery was rebuilt as a palatial headquarters for the order, its massive facade lavishly embellished with Plateresque designs. Fittingly, it has been converted into a *parador*, where the guests enjoy the luxury of a magnificent church of their own – though it can be visited by non-patrons too. This is the **Iglesia San Marcos**, whose sacristy (Tues–Sat 10am–2pm & 4.30/5–8/8.30pm, Sun 10am–2pm; 200ptas) houses a small **museum** of beautiful and priceless exhibits, grouped in a room separated from the lobby of the hotel by a thick pane of glass.

Practicalities

The **train and bus stations** are both just south of the river; the train station at the end of Avenida de Palencia, the bridge across into town, and the bus station on Paseo Ingeniero Saenz de Miera – from here, turn left onto Paseo Ingeniero Miera to reach the bridge. From the roundabout, just across the river at Glorieta Guzmán El Bueno, you can see straight down the Avenida de Ordoño II and across the Plaza de Santo Domingo to the cathedral. Directly opposite the cathedral's west facade stands the friendly main **tourist office** (Mon–Fri 9am–2pm & 5–7pm, Sat & Sun 10am–2pm & 5–8pm; ☎987 23 70 82).

There are plenty of places **to stay**, particularly on the main roads leading off the Glorieta – Avda de Roma and Avda Ordoño II: try the *Pensión Oviedo*, Avda de Roma 26 (☎987 22 22 36; ②); the *Hostal Central*, Avda Ordoño II 27-3° (☎987 25 18 06; ②); or the *Pensión Suarez*, right next to the cathedral on c/Ancha 7-2° (☎987 25 42 88; ②). There's a **youth hostel** with a pool at c/de la Corredera 4 (☎987 20 22 01; ①; July & Aug); follow Avda de Independencia from Plaza de Santo Domingo. The city **campsite** (☎987 68 02 33) is 5km out on the Valladolid road.

For sheer enjoyment, the best time of year to be in León is for the **fiesta** of St Peter in the last week of June. The rest of the year, the liveliest **bars and restaurants** tend to be those in the small square of San Martín, behind Plaza Mayor, and the dark narrow streets which surround it. You'll find good food at the *Restaurante Fornos*, c/Cid 8, *Mesón Leones Racimo de Oro*, Caño Badillo 2 (closed Tues), and *La Bodeguita*, on Plaza Mayor behind the city hall.

THE NORTH COAST

Spain's **Atlantic coast** is very different from the popular image of the country, with a rocky, indented coastline full of cove beaches and fjord-like *rías*. It's an immensely beautiful region – mountainous, green and thickly forested. It rains often, and much of the time the country-side is shrouded in a fine mist. But the summers, if you don't mind the occasional shower, are a glorious escape from the unrelenting heat of the south.

In the east, butting against France, is **Euskadi** – the **Basque country** – which, despite some of the heaviest industrialization on the peninsula, remains remarkably unspoiled – neat and quiet inland, rugged and enclosed along the coast, with easy, efficient transport everywhere. **San Sebastián** is the big draw on the coast, a major resort with superb but crowded beaches, but there are any number of lesser-known, equally attractive coastal vil-lages all the way to **Bilbao** and beyond. Note that the Basque **language**, which bears almost no relation to Spanish, is very widespread (we've given the alternative Basque names where popularly used) and the most obvious sign of Spain's strongest separatist movement.

To the west lies **Cantabria**, centred on the port of **Santander**, with more good beaches and superb trekking in the mountains of the **Picos de Europa**. The mountains extend into **Asturias**, the one part of Spain never to be conquered by the Moors. It remains today an idio-syncratic principality standing slightly apart from the rest of the nation. Its high, remote val-leys are mining country, providing the raw materials for the heavy industry of the three cities: **Gijón**, **Avilés** and **Oviedo**.

In the far west, **Galicia** looks like Ireland, and there are further parallels in its climate, cul-ture and – despite its fertile appearance – its history of famine and poverty. While right-wing Galicia may not share the radical traditions of the Basque country or of industrial Asturias it does treasure its independence, and Gallego is still spoken by around 85 percent of the pop-ulation – again, we've given Gallego place names in parentheses. For travellers, the obvious highlight is **Santiago de Compostela**, the greatest goal for pilgrims in medieval Europe.

Once you leave the Basque country, communications in this region are generally slow. If you're not in a great hurry, you may want to make use of the independent **FEVE rail line** (rail passes are not valid). The rail line begins at Bilbao and follows the coast, with an inland branch to Oviedo, all the way to El Ferrol in Galicia. Despite recent major repairs and upgrad-ing, it is still a slow, but terrific journey, skirting beaches, crossing rivers and snaking through a succession of limestone gorges.

Irún

You're likely to approach the north coast through **IRÚN**, a major border-crossing from France. Like most border towns, its chief concern is how to make a quick buck from pass-ing travellers, and the main point in its favour is the ease with which you can leave: there are trains to Hendaye in France and to San Sebastián throughout the day, and regular long-distance and international connections. For one night, though, it's not a bad place to stay; prices are much lower than in France, and San Sebastián is no place to arrive late at night without a reservation. The train station is surrounded by small **hostales**, none of them expensive, and **bodegas and restaurants** specializing in surprisingly good "typi-cal" Spanish food. *Bar Pensión los Fronterizos* (☎943 61 92 05; ②) along c/Estación, lead-ing from the main station, has some of the cheapest rooms; for more comfort go to the nearby *Hostal Irún*, c/Zubiaurre 5 (☎943 61 16 37; ②), or *Lizaso*, c/Aduana 5 (☎943 61 16 00; ②).

San Sebastián

The undisputed queen of the Basque resorts, **SAN SEBASTIÁN** (Donostia), just half an hour down the coast from Irún, is a picturesque – though expensive – town with excellent beaches. Along with Santander, it has always been the most fashionable place to escape the heat of the southern summers, and in July and August it's always packed. Though it tries hard to be chic, San Sebastián is still too much of a family resort to compete with the south of France. Set around the deep, still bay of La Concha and enclosed by rolling low hills, it's beautifully situated; the old town sits on the eastern promontory, its back to the wooded slopes of Monte Urgull, while newer development has spread inland along the banks of the River Urumea and around the edge of the bay to the foot of Monte Igüeldo.

The **old quarter** is the centre of interest – cramped and noisy streets where crowds congregrate in the evenings to wander among the small bars and shops or sample the shellfish from the traders down by the fishing harbour. Prices tend to reflect the popularity of the area, especially in the waterside restaurants, but it's no hardship to survive on the delicious tapas which are laid out in all but the fanciest bars – check the prices first, as it's quite easy to run up a sizeable bill; around 120ptas per *pincho* is now the norm. Here too are the town's chief sights: the gaudy Baroque facade of the church of **Santa María**, and the more elegantly restrained sixteenth-century **San Vicente**. The centre of the old part is the Plaza de la Constitución, known locally as "La Consti"; the numbers on the balconies of the buildings around the square refer to the days when it was used as a bullring. Just behind San Vicente, the excellent **Museo de San Telmo** (Tues–Sat 10.30am–1.30pm & 4–8pm, Sun 10.30am–2pm; free) is a fascinating jumble of Basque folklore, funerary relics and assorted art works. At the end of the harbour is the expensive **Aquarium** (daily 10am–8pm; 1100ptas, children 550ptas), now with an undersea viewing tunnel. If you get hooked, there is a **diving** shop a few doors down, Scuba Du (☎943 42 24 26), which rents equipment and runs courses. Behind this, **Monte Urgull** is crisscrossed by winding footpaths (buses may run in summer – ask at the tourist office on c/Reina Regente). From the mammoth figure of Christ on its summit there are great views out to sea and back across the bay to the town. Still better views across the bay can be had from the top of **Monte Igüeldo**: take the bus or walk around the bay to its base, from where a funicular (daily: July–Sept 10am–10pm; Oct–March 11am–6pm; April–June 11am–8pm, closed Wed; 190ptas) will carry you to the summit.

There are three **beaches** in San Sebastián: the Playa de la Concha, Ondaretta and the Playa de la Zurriola. **La Concha** is the most central and the most celebrated, a wide crescent of yellow sand stretching round the bay from the town. Despite the almost impenetrable mass of flesh here during most of the summer, this is the best of the beaches. Out in La Concha bay is a small island, **Isla de Santa Clara**, which makes a good spot for picnics; a boat leaves from the port every thirty minutes in the summer from 10am to 8pm. **Ondaretta**, considered the best beach for swimming and never quite as packed as La Concha, is a continuation of the same strand beyond the rocky outcrop which supports the **Palacio Miramar**, once a summer home of Spain's royal family. The atmosphere here is rather more staid – it's known as *La Diplomática* for the number of Madrid's "best" families who vacation here. Though it's far less crowded, don't bother with the **Playa de Zurriola**, otherwise aptly named the Playa de Gros. Outside the shelter of the bay it's very exposed, and it's the repository for all the filth that comes floating down the river.

Practicalities

Most **buses** use the terminal at Plaza Pío XII, twenty minutes' walk inland along the river, the rest go from the Plaza de Guipúzcoa. The main-line **train station** is across the River Urumea on the Paseo de Francia, although local lines to Hendaye and Bilbao have their terminus on c/Easo (rail passes not valid). The **tourist office**, on c/Reina Regente beside the Puente Kursaal in the old town (summer Mon–Sat 8am–8pm, Sun 10am–1pm; winter Mon–Sat 9am–2pm & 3.30–7pm, Sun 10am–1pm; ☎943 48 11 66), is very helpful in finding a place to stay and providing accommodation, although for a greater selection of pamphlets, there is a useful Basque Government **tourist office** at Paseo de los Fuieros 1, just off Avda de la Libertad (Mon–Sat 9am–1pm & 3.30–6.30pm, Sun 9.30am–1.30pm, closed Sat afternoon and Sun mornings in winter).

Accommodation, though plentiful, is not cheap and can be very hard to come by in season. In the old town, look around La Consti and c/San Jerónimo; in the central district there's better value around the cathedral, especially Calles Easo, San Martin and San Bartolomé; or on the other side of the river try behind the Plaza de Cataluña, where you'll also find excellent tapas bars. Places to try in the old part include *Pensión San Jeromino*, c/San Jeromino 25-2° (☎943 28 64 34 or 943 28 16 89; ②); *Pension Amaiur*, c/31 de Agosto 44-2° (☎943 42 96 54; ②); and *Pensión Aussie*, c/San Jeromino 23-2° (☎943 42 08 30; ③). Around the cathedral, try the *Hostal Easo*, c/San Bartolomé 24 (☎943 45 39 12; ③); *Pensión La Perla*, c/Loyola 10 (☎943 42 81 23; ③); *Hostal Comercio*, c/Urdaneta 24 (☎943 46 44 14; ③); *Pensión San Martin*, c/San Martin 10-1° (☎943 42 87 14; ③); or *Eder II*, Alameda del Boulevard 16 (☎943 42 64 49; ④). San Sebastián's **campsite** (☎943 21 45 02) is excellent, but it's a long way from the centre on the landward side of Monte Igüeldo, reached by bus #16 from the Alameda del Boulevard. The **youth hostel** (☎943 31 02 68; ②), known as "La Sirena", is located on Paseo de Igüeldo, just a few minutes' walk back from the end of Ondarreta Beach.

If you're in the mood for some spectacularly expensive **food**, San Sebastián has some of the best restaurants in the country. Less exalted cuisine is easy enough to find, though nowhere is very cheap: if you want a meal rather than tapas, try the fixed menu at places near the cathedral such as *Bodegón Ardandegi*, c/Reyes Católicos 7; *La Barranquesa*, c/Larramendi 21; *Bar Etxadi*, c/Reyes Católicos 9; or, in the old quarter, *Morgan Jatetxea* on c/Narrika Kalea. Alternatively, order some well-priced *raciones* at either *Gaztelu*, c/31 de Agosto 22, or *Bar Beti-Ja*, both on c/Narrika, in the old town.

In the evenings you'll find no shortage of action, with **clubs** and **bars** wherever the tourists congregate. The fanciest are along the promenade by the beach, Paseo de la Concha; the cheaper places are mostly in the old town where people normally start the evening off – later everyone heads to the area along c/Reyes Católicos behind the cathedral or c/San Bartolomé for the young crowd. For late nights, head for *Etxekalte* at 11 c/de Mar, overlooking the port and beach, where a funky clientele groove to choice jazz, urban soul and even some trip-hop (free entry). Throughout the summer, too, there are constant **festivals**, many involving Basque sports including the annual rowing races between the villages along the coast. The *International Jazz Festival*, at different locations throughout the town in the third week of July, invariably attracts top performers as well as hordes of people on their way home from the fiesta in Pamplona.

Bilbao

Despite a terrible legacy of all things industrial, **BILBAO** (Bilbo) seems determined to face the new millennium with confidence and plenty of civic swagger. A state-of-the-art metro (designed by Sir Norman Foster) is up and running; the awesome new Guggenheim Museum is already a major draw; a unified transport terminus is planned and there are various bids to further develop the riverfront with University buildings and public parks connected by footpaths, dramatic bridges and a tramway. Bilbao is beginning to pull itself out of a post-industrial limbo. Fumes still belch from gargantuan factories, the Río Nervión still froths and foams with waste and pollution; but the gleaming new buildings and parks are steadily reclaiming the city. Despite these changes, Bilbao remains a city with an unmistakable feel, with incredibly friendly citizens and some of the best cafés, restaurants and bars in Euskadi.

The **Casco Viejo**, the old quarter on the east bank of the river, is still a main point of interest for the beautiful **Teatro Arriaga**, the elegantly arcaded **Plaza Nueva**, the Gothic **Catedral de Santiago** (currently closed) and an interesting **Basque Museum** in Plaza Miguel Unamuno (Tues–Sat 10.30am–1.30pm & 4–7pm, Sun 10.30am–1.30pm; 300ptas).

It is along the Río Nervíon that a whole number of exciting new buildings have appeared. A good route through leads from the Casco Viejo down the river past the imposing Zubizuri bridge to the billowing curves of the **Guggenheim Museum** (Tues–Sun 10am–8pm; 800ptas/400ptas concessions), and on to the Palacio de Congress y de la Musica. Inside, the Guggenheim is divided into two parts: the permanent collection is housed in more traditional (rectangular) galleries, and descends in chronological order from the Picassos and Surrealists on the third floor to the Pop and contemporary artists at ground level; temporary exhibitions and individual artists' collections are displayed in the huge sculptured spaces nearer the river. Further along the river from the Guggenheim, on the edge of the Parque de Doña Casilda de Hurriza, is the **Museo de Bellas Artes** (Tues–Sat 10am–1.30pm & 4–7.30pm, Sun 10am–2pm; 400ptas, Wed free), which houses works by Goya and El Greco and has played host to some acclaimed temporary exhibitions.

Football fans shouldn't miss the chance to venture a little further east to one of the shrines of Spanish football, **El Estadio San Mamés**. Known as "La Catedral", it is home to Athletic Bilbao and is famed for its atmosphere and discerning spectators. Tickets for home matches are available at the stadium (☎94 424 08 77).

Practicalities

The **tourist office** (Mon–Fri 9am–2pm & 4–7.30pm, Sat 9am–2pm, Sun 10am–2pm; ☎94 479 57 60) is just north of the Teatro Arriaga on Paseo del Arenal; there's another branch just outside the Guggenheim (Tues–Fri 11am–2pm & 4–6pm, Sat 11am–2pm & 5–7pm). The best **places to stay** are almost all in the Casco Viejo – especially along and around the streets leading off c/Bidebarrieta, which leads from Plaza Arriaga to the cathedral. Prices have risen substantially since the opening of the Guggenheim, but good possibilities are the *Hostal Gurea*, c/Bidebarrieta 14 (☎94 416 32 99; ②); *Hostal La Estrella*, c/María Muñoz 6, off Plaza Miguel Unamuno (☎94 416 40 66; ③); the *Hostal Arana*, c/Bidebarrieta 2 (☎94 415 64 11; ③); the superb *Pensión Ladero* c/Lotería 1 (☎94 415 09 32; ②); and *Hostal Roquefer*, c/Lotería 2 (☎94 415 07 55; ③). For a medium range hotel, the *Hotel Arriaga*, c/Ribera 3 (☎ 94 479 00 01; ④) is a friendly and convenient option next to the Teatro.

Eating and drinking are also best in the Casco Viejo, although there are few regular restaurants – this is one of those cities where the most enjoyable way to eat is to move from bar to bar, snacking on tapas: Plaza Nueva has numerous options. For breakfast try the excellent *Café Boulevard* on Paseo del Arenal, and for a mid-afternoon coffee you can't beat the Arabic style *Café Iruña* across the river at c/Jardines de Albia 5. Bilbao can be very lively indeed at **night** – and totally wild during the August **fiesta**, "La Semana Grande", which usually begins on the first Saturday after August 15, with scores of open-air bars, live music and impromptu dancing in an incredible atmosphere. Try especially around c/Licenciado Poza and c/Ledesma.

Santander and around

Long a favourite summer resort of Madrileños, **SANTANDER** has a French feel – an elegant, reserved resort in a similar vein to San Sebastián. Some people find it a clean, restful base for a short stay; for others it is dull and snobbish. On a brief visit, the balance is tipped in its favour by its excellent (and no longer polluted) beaches, and the sheer style of its setting. The narrow **Bahía de Santander** is dramatic, with the city and port on one side in clear view of open countryside and high mountains on the other; a great first view of Spain if you're arriving on the **ferry** from Plymouth.

Santander was severely damaged by fire in 1941, and what's left of the city divides into two parts: the **town and port**, which are still quite a tangle, having been reconstructed on the old grid around the cathedral; and the beach suburb of **El Sardinero**, a twenty-minute walk (or bus #1 or #2, amongst others) from the centre, more if you follow the coast around the wooded headland of **La Magdalena**. There are few real sights to distract you: the **Cathedral**, with its Gothic crypt, is of passing interest; the pick of the museums is the **Museo Provincial de Prehistoria**, c/Casimiro Sainz (Tues–Sat 9/10am–1pm & 4–7pm, Sun 11am–2pm; free), where finds from the province's numerous prehistorically inhabited caves are exhibited. The chief pleasures lie on the **beaches**. The first of these, **Playa de la**

Magdalena, begins on the near side of the headland. The beautiful yellow strand, sheltered by cliffs and flanked by a summer windsurfing school, is deservedly popular, as is **El Sardinero** itself. If you find both beaches too crowded for your taste, there are long stretches of dunes across the bay at **Somo** (which has windsurfing boards for rent and a summer campsite) and **Pedreña**; to get to them, jump on a lancha, the cheap taxi-ferry which leaves every fifteen minutes from the central dock.

Practicalities

The RENFE and FEVE **train stations** are side by side, just off the waterside; the **bus station** is directly across the Plaza Porticada. There are two **tourist offices**: the best is in the Jardines de la Pereda (summer daily 9am–2pm & 4–9pm; winter Mon–Fri 9.30am–1.30pm & 4–7pm, Sat 10am–1pm; ☎942 36 20 54); the other is in the ferry terminal (Mon–Fri 9am–1pm & 4–7pm). Good places to start looking for **rooms** are c/de Rodríguez in front of the station – *San Miguel* at no. 9 (☎942 22 03 63; ③) – and c/de Hernán Cortés near the main square – *La Corza* at no. 25 (☎942 21 29 50; ③) are recommended. There are some very popular cheapish places by the beach, on the Avda de los Castros at Sardinero, including the *Botín* on c/Isabel Segundo 1 (☎942 21 00 94; ②), and a **campsite** (☎942 39 15 70) a short walk further down the coast on Cabo Mayor. **Food** options are plentiful along c/San Simón and c/Río de la Pila, above Plaza de Velarde, as well as around the main square and station. If you're after seafood, wander down to the fishing port, to the east of the ferry port and stations. There's no shortage of places along the c/Marqués de la Ensanada here, but check prices before ordering.

Oviedo and around

The principal reason for visiting **OVIEDO** is to see three small churches. They are perhaps the most remarkable in Spain, built in a unique style during the first half of the ninth century, a period of almost total isolation for the tiny Asturian kingdom, which was then the only part of Spain under Christian rule. Oviedo, the modern capital of Asturias, became the centre of this outpost in 810. Here King Alfonso II built a chapel, the Cámara Santa, to house the holy relics rescued from Toledo when it fell to the Moors. Remodelled in the twelfth century, this now forms the inner sanctuary of the **Cathedral** (Mon–Fri 10am–1pm & 4–6/7pm, Sat 10am–1pm & 4–6pm; 200ptas, 400ptas including museum, free Thurs), a fine Gothic structure at the heart of the modern city. Around the cathedral, enclosed by scattered sections of the medieval town walls, is what remains of **old Oviedo**: a compact, attractive quarter in what is a fairly bleak industrial city. Some of the **palaces** – not least the archbishop's, opposite the cathedral – are worth a look, though none are open to visitors. Of interest, too, is the **Archeological Museum**, immediately behind the cathedral in the former convent of San Vicente (Tues–Sat 10am–1.30pm & 4–6pm, Sun 11am–1pm; free), which displays various pieces of sculpture from the "Asturian-Visigoth" churches.

The nearest of these churches, **Santullano**, lies ten minutes' walk to the northeast along c/de Gijón, right next to a busy main road. Built around 830, it's considerably larger and more spacious than the other Asturian churches, with an unusual "secret chamber" built into the outer wall. It is kept locked but the keys are available at the priest's house to the left; there are original frescoes inside, executed in similar style to Roman villas. The most impressive of the churches is **Santa María del Naranco** (summer Mon–Sat 9.30am–1pm & 3–7pm, Sun 9.30am–7pm, winter Tues–Sat 10am–1pm & 3–5pm, Mon & Sun 10am–1pm; 250ptas, free Mon), majestically located on a wooded slope 3km above the city. It's a 45-minute walk from the centre along a beautiful marked route, or thirty minutes from the station. This perfectly harmonious little building was designed not as a church but as a royal palace or hunting lodge: the present structure was just the main hall. A couple of hundred metres beyond Santa María is the palace chapel, **San Miguel de Lillo** (same hours and prices as Santa María), built with soft golden sandstone and red tiles. This is generally assumed to be by the same architect as Santa María, though its design, the Byzantine cross-in-square, is quite different.

Practicalities

Central Oviedo is easy enough to find your way around, but transport can be confusing. Most **buses** use the underground station in the Plaza General Primo de Rivera, but it's worth checking departures with the **tourist office** (Mon–Fri 9.30am–1.30pm & 4.30–6.30pm, Sat 9am–2pm; winter closed Sat; ☎98 521 33 85) in the cathedral square, or at the municipal branch on the corner of Campo de San Francisco (same hours, also open Sun 11am–2pm). For trains, there are two FEVE **stations** in addition to the regular RENFE one serving León. The FEVE Asturias, next to the RENFE, is for the line to Santander; the so-called FEVE Basque, oddly enough, serves stations west to El Ferrol. They're fifteen minutes apart, so don't try to make too tight a connection.

Accommodation is plentiful, with many **hostales** on c/de Uría alongside San Francisco park, including *Hostal Arcos*, c/Magdalena 3 (☎98 521 47 73; ②). Other promising areas are c/Jovellanos north of the cathedral – the *Pomar* (☎98 521 98 40; ②) is friendly – and c/9 de Mayo or c/de Caveda near the main train stations. For **food**, try any number of good restaurants at c/Gascona. And lastly, whether you stay or not, don't leave without ordering at least one glass of Asturian *sidra* (cider) – if only for bewilderment's sake. Onlookers will show you the correct drinking protocol, and if the cloudy nectar is to your taste there is a new **cider museum** in Nava on the road to Santander (summer Tues–Sat noon–2pm & 4–8pm, Sun noon–2pm & 6–9pm; winter Tues–Fri 11am–2pm & 4–7pm, Sat 11am–3pm, Sun 11am–2pm; 400ptas).

Santiago de Compostela

SANTIAGO DE COMPOSTELA, built in a warm golden granite, is one of the most beautiful of all Spanish cities. The medieval city has been declared a national monument in its entirety, and remains a remarkably integrated whole, all the better for being almost completely pedestrianized. The **pilgrimage** to Santiago captured the imagination of medieval Christian Europe on an unprecedented scale. At the height of its popularity, in the eleventh and twelfth centuries, the city was receiving over half a million pilgrims each year. People of all classes came to visit the supposed shrine of St James the Apostle (Santiago to the Spanish), making this the third-holiest site in Christendom, after Jerusalem and Rome. The atmosphere of the place is much as it must have been in the days of the pilgrims, though tourists are now as likely to be attracted by art and history as by religion. But it's by no means a dead city – Santiago is the seat of Galicia's regional government and there's a large student population too. It's also a manageable size – you can wander fifteen minutes out of town and reach wide open countryside.

The City

All roads to Santiago lead to the **Cathedral** (daily 7.30am–9pm), whose sheer grandeur you first appreciate upon venturing into the vast expanse of the Plaza de Obradoiro. Directly ahead stands a fantastic Baroque pyramid of granite, flanked by immense bell towers and everywhere adorned with statues of St James in his familiar pilgrim guise with staff, broad hat and scallop-shell badge. This **Obradoiro facade** was built in the mid-eighteenth century by an obscure Santiago-born architect, Fernando Casas y Novoa, and no other work of Spanish Baroque can compare with it.

The main body of the cathedral is Romanesque, rebuilt in the eleventh and twelfth centuries after a devastating raid by the Moors. The building's highlight is the **Pórtico de Gloria**, the original west front, which now stands inside the cathedral behind the Obradoiro. This was both the culmination of all Romanesque sculpture and a precursor of the new Gothic realism, with a host of wonderfully carved figures. St James sits on the central column, beneath Christ and just above eye level; the pilgrims would give thanks at journey's end by praying with the fingers of one hand pressed into the roots of the *Tree of Jesse* below the saint. So many millions have performed this act of supplication that five deep and shiny holes have been worn into the solid marble. On the other side of the pillar, kneeling at the foot, is the sculptor himself, Maestro Mateo. Pilgrims would touch the statue's head with their fore-heads to absorb his wisdom.

The spiritual climax of the pilgrimage was the approach to the **High Altar**. This remains a peculiar experience: you climb steps behind the altar, embrace the Most Sacred Image of Santiago, kiss his bejewelled cape, and are handed, by way of certification, a document in Latin called a *Compostela*. The altar is a riotous creation of eighteenth-century Churrigueresque, but the statue has stood there for seven centuries and the procedure is quite unchanged. You'll notice an elaborate pulley system in front of the altar. This is for moving the immense incense-burner which, operated by eight priests, is swung in a vast ceiling-to-ceiling arc across the transept. It is stunning to watch, but takes place only during certain services such as Friday and Saturday mass at noon – check with the tourist office.

You can visit the treasury, cloisters, archeological museum and the beautiful crypt (summer Mon–Sat 10am–1.30pm & 4–7.30pm, Sun 10am–1.30pm; winter 11am–1pm & 4–6pm, Sun 10am–1.30pm; 500ptas). The late Gothic **cloisters** in particular are well worth seeing: from the plain, mosque-like courtyard you get a wonderful view of the riotous mixture of the exterior, crawling with pagodas, domes, obelisks, battlements, scallop shells and cornu-copias.

The north side of the cathedral is occupied by the **Palace of Archbishop Gelmírez** (Easter–Sept only Mon–Sat 10am–1.30pm & 4.30–7.30pm; 200ptas). Gelmirez was one of the seminal figures in Santiago's development: he rebuilt the cathedral in the twelfth century, raised the see to an archbishopric, and most importantly made the place extremely rich. In his palace, suitably luxuriant, are a vaulted kitchen and some fine Romanesque chambers.

Further afield, the main interest lies in the multifarious monasteries and convents. The enormous Benedictine **San Martín** stands close to the cathedral, the vast altarpiece in its church depicting its patron riding alongside St James. Nearby is **San Francisco**, reputedly founded by the saint himself during his pilgrimage to Santiago. In the north of the city are Baroque **Santa Clara**, with a unique curving facade, and a little beyond it, **Santo Domingo**. This last is perhaps the most interesting of the buildings, featuring a magnificent seventeenth-century triple stairway, each spiral leading to different storeys of a single tower, and a fascinating museum of Gallego crafts and traditions, the **Museo do Pobo Gallego** (Mon–Sat 10am–1pm & 4–7pm; free).

Practicalities

Arriving at the **bus station** you are 1km or so north of the town centre; bus #10 will take you in to the Plaza de Galicia at the southern edge of the old city. The **train station** is a walkable distance south of this plaza along c/del Horreo. The **tourist office** is at Rúa do Vilar 43 (Mon–Fri 10am–2pm & 4–7pm, Sat 11am–2pm & 5–7pm, Sun 11am–2pm; ☎981 58 40 81), and can provide complete lists of accommodation and facilities.

You should have no difficulty finding an inexpensive **room** in Santiago, though note that *pensiones* here are often called *hospedajes*. The biggest concentration of places is on the three parallel streets leading down from the cathedral: Rua Nueva, Rua do Vilar and c/del Franco. *Hospedaje Santa Cruz*, Rua do Vilar 42 (☎981 58 23 62; ②), has very friendly English speaking owners; *Hostal Residencia La Estela*, Avda Rajoy 1 (☎981 58 27 96; ③), just off Plaza Obradoiro, has rooms overlooking the front of the cathedral; and *Hostal Barbantes*, c/del Franco 3 (☎981 58 10 77; ②) has a lively bar and restaurant. Another very cheap place is *Hospedaje Vitoriano* on Plaza Mazarelos 7 (☎981 58 51 85; ①) – the indomitable owner also has dozens of other rooms scattered around town. The **campsite**, *Camping As Cancelas*, just outside Santiago (☎981 58 02 66), is excellent.

Thanks, perhaps, to the students, there are plenty of cheap **places to eat** here, along with excellent **bars**; it's also the best place in Galicia to hear local Breton-style **music**, played on *gaitas* (bagpipes). An excellent student haunt is the *Casa Manolo* at Rua Traviesa 27, while c/del Franco is full of bars with reliable tapas such as *El Bombero* and *Tacita de Juan*. *Bodegón de Xulio* here is a really good seafood restaurant. Livelier places to drink include *Bar Ourense* and *O'Barril* on c/del Franco, *O Gato Negro* on c/Raiña, and *O'Galo d'Ouro*, in a cellar on the Cuesta Conga.

THE PYRENEES

With the singular exception of **Pamplona** at the time of its bull-running fiesta, the area around the Spanish Pyrenees is little visited – most people who come here at all travel straight through. In doing so they miss out on some of the most wonderful scenery in Spain, and some of the country's most attractive trekking. You'll also be struck by the slower pace of life, especially in **Navarra** (in the west, a partly Basque region) and **Aragón** (in the centre) – the **Catalan** Pyrenees, along with **Andorra**, are more developed. There are few cities here – Pamplona itself and **Zaragoza**, with its fine Moorish architecture, are the only large centres – but there are plenty of attractive small towns and of course the mountains themselves, with several beautiful **national parks** as a focus for exploration.

Pamplona

PAMPLONA (Iruña) has been the capital of Navarra since the ninth century, and long before that was a powerful fortress town defending the northern approaches to Spain. Even now it has something of the appearance of a garrison city, with its hefty walls and elaborate pentagonal citadel. There's plenty to look at – the elaborately restored **Cathedral** with its magnificent cloister and interesting **Museo Diocesano** (summer Mon–Sat 10am–2pm & 4–7pm, Sun 10am–2pm; Winter Mon–Sat 10.30am–1.30pm & 4–6pm, closed Sat afternoon and Sun except services; 500ptas), the colossal **city walls** and **citadel**, the display of regional archeology, history and art in the **Museo de Navarra** (Tues–Sat 10am–2pm & 5–7pm, Thurs until 9pm, Sun 11am–2pm; 300ptas, free Sat afternoon & Sun), and much more – but ninety percent of visitors come here for just one thing: the thrilling week of the **Fiesta of San Fermín**. From midday on July 6 until midnight on July 14 the city gives itself up to riotous nonstop celebration.

The centre of the festivities is the **encierro**, or running of the bulls – in which the animals decisively have the upper hand. Six bulls are released each morning at eight to run from their corral near the Plaza San Domingo to the bullring. In front, around and occasionally under them run the hundreds of locals and tourists who are foolish or drunk enough to test their daring against the horns. It was Hemingway's *The Sun Also Rises* that really put "Los San Fermines" on the map, and the area in front of the Plaza de Toros has been renamed Plaza Hemingway by a grateful council. To watch the *encierro* it's essential to arrive early – crowds have already formed an hour before it starts. The best **vantage points** are near the starting point or on the wall leading to the bullring. The event divides into two parts: there's the actual running of the bulls; and then after the bulls have been through the streets, bullocks with padded horns are let loose on the crowd in the bullring. If you watch the actual running, you won't be able to get into the bullring, so go on two separate mornings to see both. **Bullfights** take place daily at 6.30pm, with the bulls that ran that morning; tickets are expensive (2000–12,500ptas from the Plaza del Toros one day before the show) and are fiendishly difficult to get hold of. At the end of the week (midnight on July 14) there's a mournful candlelit procession, the **Pobre De Mi**, at which the festivities are officially wound up for another year.

Practicalities

The **train station** is a long way from the old part of town, but bus #9 runs every twenty minutes to the end of Paseo de Sarasate, a few minutes' walk from the central Plaza del Castillo – there is a RENFE ticket office at c/Estella 8. The **bus station** is more central, on c/Conde Oliveto in front of the citadel, while the **tourist office** (summer Mon–Sat 10am–2pm & 4–7pm, Sun 10am–2pm; winter Mon–Fri 10am–2pm & 4–7pm, Sat & Sun 10am–2pm; ☎948 22 07 41) is found at c/Duque de Ahumada 3, just off Plaza del Castillo. During San Fermín, there is also an information bus on Plaza del Castillo, and the main office is open from 10am–5pm.

You'll find a cluster of cheap **hostales** on noisy c/San Nicolás and its continuation c/San Gregorio, off Plaza del Castillo. Rooms are in short supply during summer, and at fiesta time you've virtually no chance of a place on spec. Prices are fairly similar, but good ones to try include *Hostal Otano*, c/San Nicolás 5 (☎948 225095; ②); *Pensión Casa García*, c/San Gregorio 12 (☎948 223893; ②); and *Hostal Beaván*, c/San Nicolás 25 (☎948 223428; ③). Most raise their prices during the fiesta. Otherwise, try nearer the cathedral – *Santa Cecilia*, c/Navarrería 17 (☎948 222230; ②) is good. There's a **campsite**, *Ezcaba* (☎948 33 16 65), 7km out of town on the road to France; again it fills several days before the fiesta. The bus service to the campsite is poor, but it's easy to hitch or get a lift on a tour bus.

The best **bars** are on and around c/San Nicolás but there's also a number of grungy late-night dives on Calderia S. Augustin on the other side of the square. For cheap **food** try the streets around c/Major, in particular *Bar la Cepa*, *Bar Poliki* and *Restaurante Lanzale* on c/San Lorenzo and *Bar la Campana* on c/de la Campana, all of which offer a combination of *bocadillos* and good, cheap *menús*. *Café Roch* on c/de las Comedias is great for tapas or, to get away from the crowds, go to the elegant *Meson del Caballo Blanco* on c/Redin up above the ramparts behind the cathedral – you can order cheap *raciones* upstairs. The elegant *Café Iruña*, on Plaza del Castillo, is the place to sit over a leisurely coffee as you take in the action.

Zaragoza

ZARAGOZA is the capital of Aragón, and easily its largest and liveliest city, with over half the province's one million people and the majority of its industry. There are some excellent bars and restaurants tucked in among its remarkable monuments, and it's also a handy transport centre, with good connections into the Pyrenees and east towards Barcelona. If you're in town during Semana Santa – the week before easter – you can watch some spectacular processions.

The most imposing of the city's churches, majestically fronting the River Ebro, is the **Basilica de Nuestra Señora del Pilar** (daily 6am–8pm, earlier in winter), one of Zaragoza's two cathedrals. It takes its name from the column which the Virgin is said to have brought from Jerusalem during her lifetime to found the first Marian chapel in Christendom. Topped by a diminutive image of the Virgin, the pillar forms the centrepiece in the Holy Chapel and is the focal point for pilgrims, who line up to kiss an exposed section encased in a silver sheath. The cathedral also has a couple of small museums, a few minor dome frescoes by Goya, and a curious display of two unexploded bombs dropped on the cathedral during the Civil War, but stylistically the building itself is something of an outsized Baroque shed. In terms of beauty it can't compare with the nearby Gothic-Mudéjar old cathedral, **La Seo** (Tues–Sun 10am–2pm & 4–8pm), at the far end of the pigeon-thronged Plaza del Pilar.

The highlight of Zaragoza, which you should see even if you plan to do no more than change trains or buses here, is the city's only surviving legacy from Moorish times. From the tenth to the eleventh century Zaragoza was the centre of an independent dynasty, the Beni Kasim. Their palace, the newly restored **Aljafería** (Tues–Wed & Fri–Sat 10am–2pm & 4/4.30–6.30/8pm, Sun 10am–2pm, closed Fri morning; 300ptas), was built in the heyday of their rule in the mid-eleventh century, and thus predates the Alhambra in Granada as well as Sevilla's Alcázar. Much was added after the Reconquest, when the palace was adapted and used by the kings of Aragón. From the original design the foremost relic is a tiny and beautiful **mosque** adjacent to the ticket office. Further on is an intricately decorated court, the Patio de Santa Isabella. Crossing from here, the Grand Staircase (added in 1492) leads to a succession of mainly fourteenth-century rooms, remarkable chiefly for their carved ceilings. There are guided tours on the half hour (included in the entry fee).

If you're interested in chasing the Moorish influence further, four **Mudéjar towers** survive in Zaragoza, perhaps the finest of which is the square tower of the church of **Santa María Magdalena**.

Practicalities

Points of arrival in Zaragoza are rather scattered. From the **train station** (*Estación Portillo*), walk down the short c/General Mayandia, turn right onto Paseo María Agustín and take bus #22 to Plaza España – or walk it in about 25 minutes. There are various **bus terminals**; most long-distance services leave from the Agreda terminal at Paseo María Agustín 7 (right from the train station), although destinations for León and the north coast leave from the Plaza del Portillo, just north of the train station. For closer destinations (such as Pamplona or Jaca) check with one of the city's two **tourist offices**. The Aragonese regional office is in the Torreón de la Zuda (usually Mon–Sat 10am–2.30pm & 5–7.30pm, Sun 10am–2pm, but times do vary), part of the city fortifications overlooking the river, but the more useful city office is in the Plaza del Pilar (summer daily 10am–8pm; winter Mon–Sat 9.30am–1.30pm & 4.30–7.30pm, Sun 10am–2pm; ☎976 20 12 00). In summer there is an information point at the train station.

There are **rooms** – and some cheap **restaurants** – close to the train station, along c/Madre Sacramento, parallel to Paseo María Agustín. *Fonda Miramar*, c/Capitán Casado 17 (☎976 28 10 94; ②) is better than most. However, there's more atmosphere, better accommodation possibilities and most of the city's nightlife crowded into an area known as **El Tubo**, between c/de Alfonso I and c/Don Jaime I, close to the Plaza del Pilar. There are upwards of a dozen cheap *fondas* and *pensiones* here, rarely full: try particularly along c/Estébares. Other recommended lodgings include *Hostal Cumbre*, Avda de Cataluña 24 (☎976 29 11 48; ③), *Hostal Estrella*, Avda de Clave 27 (☎976 28 30 61; ②), and *Hotel Las Torres*, Plaza del Pilar 11 (☎976 39 42 50; ④), right next to the tourist office where all rooms have baths. You can also **camp** at the large, barren *Camping Casablanca* (April to mid-Oct), on Paseo del Canal, 2km west of the city. Take bus #36 or #24 from the train station or Plaza de España.

Jaca and around

Heading towards the Pyrenees from Zaragoza, **JACA** is the northernmost town of any size in Aragón and an obvious staging post. It's also a place of considerable interest – an early capital of the kingdom of Aragón that lay astride one of the main medieval pilgrim routes to Santiago. Accordingly, a magnificent **Cathedral** (daily 9am–1.30pm & 4–8pm), the first in Spain to be built in the Romanesque style, dominates the centre of town from its position at the north edge of the old quarter. It remains impressive despite much internal remodelling over the centuries, and there's a powerful added attraction in its **Museo Diocesano** (summer daily 10am–2pm & 4–8pm; winter Tues–Sun 11am–1.30pm & 4–6.30pm; 300ptas), which should not be missed. The dark cloisters are home to a beautiful collection of twelfth- to fifteenth-century frescoes, gathered from village churches in the area and from higher up in the Pyrenees.

Although barely 800m up, Jaca ranks as a Pyrenean resort, becoming crowded in August; even at other times of the year, accommodation prices tend to be pushed up by the ski and cross-border trade. But Jaca is foremost an army town, with a mass of conscripts attending the local mountain warfare academy. The military connection is nothing new: the **Ciudadela**, a sixteenth-century fort built to the stellar ground plan in vogue at the time, still offers good views of surrounding peaks. You can visit the interior (daily 11am–noon/12.30pm & 4/5–5/6.30pm; 300ptas including guided tour), but it's hardly worth it, as the outside, with slumbering deer in the dry moat, is by far the most interesting part.

Arriving in Jaca by **train**, you'll find yourself more than a kilometre's walk out of town; move quickly and take the city bus which connects with most trains. Returning, the bus leaves twenty minutes before train departures from the small square at the end of c/Mayor, just down from the Ciudadela. The more central **bus station** is on Avda Jacetania, 200m northwest of the cathedral. The **tourist office** (Mon–Fri 9am–1.30/2pm & 4.30–7/8pm, summer Sat 10am–1.30pm & 5–9pm, Sun 10am–1.30pm) – worth a browse for its noticeboards offering all sorts of sport- and mountaineering-related services – is on Avda Regimiento Galicia, just downhill from the bus stop and Ciudadela.

All of Jaca's budget **accommodation** can be found on the northeast edge of the old town, with two good, quiet choices being *Hotel Alpina*, c/Mayor 57 (☎974 44 81 48; ③), and *Hostal Paris* by the cathedral, Plaza de San Pedro 5 (☎974 36 10 20; ②). There's also a **youth hostel** (☎974 36 05 36; ①) on Avda Perimetral, next to the ice rink at the southern end of town, and two **campsites** – the closer but more basic *Victoria* (☎974 36 03 23) is 1km west of town on the Pamplona road, the wooded *Peña Oroel* (☎974 36 02 15) is 3km down the Sabiñanigo road. Good-value **eating** is found in the same part of the old district: carnivores will appreciate *La Fragua* at c/Gil Berges 4 (closed Wed), while *La Cabaña* at c/del Pez 10 and *La Abuela Primera* at c/de la Población 3 both offer cheap but filling set menus.

The Aragonese Pyrenees

If you're not a keen trekker or skier, then the foothill villages of **ANSÓ** and **HECHO** (often spelt without the 'h') set in their beautiful namesake valleys are perhaps your best single target in the **Aragonese Pyrenees**: they're noted for their distinctive, imposing architecture, and accessible by a 6.30pm bus (Mon–Sat) from Jaca, returning 6am from Ansó, 6.45am from Hecho. Hecho, to the east, is more visited and inevitably more expensive for **accommodation and food**: try *Casa Blasquico*, Plaza de la Fuente (☎974 37 50 07; ④), and the *comedor* at the *Fonda Lo Foratón* respectively. There's also a delightful campsite, *Valle de Hecho* (☎974 37 53 61). In the westerly valley, less frequented Ansó offers several reasonable places to **stay** and **eat**, including the *Posada Veral,* in the heart of town at c/Cocorro 6 (☎974 37 01 19; ②), and *Hostal Aisa* (☎974 37 00 09; ③) on Plaza Domingo Miral.

As a worthwhile target for a winter visit to alpine Aragón the adjacent ski resorts of **ASTÚN-CANDANCHU**, north of Jaca, are easily reached by bus. *Hostales* are uniformly pricey; if your budget is limited and/or you're primarily interested in nordic skiing, than either of the two year-round *albergues*, the highly considered *El Aguila* (☎974 37 32 91; ②) or *Valle de Aragón* (☎974 37 32 22; ③) should suit you nicely. Between Jaca and the slopes lies **CANFRANC**, the final stop on the rail line up from Zaragoza since the French discontinued the onward section of track in a fit of pique over the success of the Spanish ski resorts. There are trains from Jaca (2 daily), or use the same buses as for Candanchu (5–6 daily). The small village is rather forlorn now, and you wouldn't come especially to see it, but you can **stay** at *Hotel Ara* at Plaza del Ayuntamiento 2 (☎974 37 30 28; ②), and **eat** at *Casa Flores* at the other end of c/Fernando Católico.

For a summertime walking visit, there's no better taster for the Aragonese Pyrenees than the **Parque Nacional de Ordesa**, centred on a vast, trough-like valley flanked by imposingly striated limestone palisades. On Monday to Saturday a 10.15am bus from Jaca serves Sabiñanigo, from where there's a **bus** at 11am (plus an evening service at 6.30pm in high season) to Torla, the best base for the park; the return bus leaves Torla at 3.30pm. Approaching Sabiñanigo by bus or train from Zaragoza, you'll need departures before 8.30am and 7.15am respectively to make the connection.

TORLA itself, formerly a sleepy, stone-built village, has, since the 1980s, been overwhelmed in its role as gateway to the park; the older corners though are still visually attractive. Don't hope for a **room** or refuge bed from late July to late August, however, without reserving well in advance – even the two **campsites**, *San Antón* (☎974 48 60 63) and *Valle de Bujaruelo* (☎974 48 63 48), 2km and 3km north, can often fill up. At other times of the year you can usually find space at the central *Hotel Ballarín*, c/Capuvita 11, (☎974 48 61 55; ③); *Hotel Villa de Torla*, Plaza Nueva 1 (☎974 48 61 56; ③); or the thirty-bunk *Refugio Lucien Briet* (☎974 48 62 21; ①). Both the *Fonda* and the *Bar Brecha*, which manages the *albergue*, serve good-value **meals**.

Vehicle entrance to the **park** itself lies 5km by road beyond Torla, but trekkers should opt instead for the lovely hour-and-a-half trail-walk on the far side of the river, well marked as part of the Pyrenean GR (long-distance path) system and once actually in Ordesa. Further **treks** can be as gentle or as strenuous as you like, the most popular outing being the all-day trip to the **Circo de Soaso** waterfalls.

Several valleys east of Torla and Ordesa and cradled between the two highest summits in the Pyrenees, **BENASQUE** serves as another favourite jump-off point for mountain rambles. There is a twice-daily bus service from Jaca at 8am and 3pm (change at Barbastro), and a marginally better chance of finding a **bed** during high season. *Fonda Barrabes*, c/Mayor 5 (☎974 55 16 54; ②), is the budget standby; try also the unmarked *Hostal Valero* (③), managed by the pricier *Hotel Aneto* next door on c/Anciles (☎974 55 10 61; ④). Best **meals**, strangely, are above the *Disco Ñaka* near the church, venerable focus of the very attractive backstreets.

CATALUNYA

With its own language, culture and, to a degree, government, **Catalunya** (Cataluña in Castilian Spanish, traditionally Catalonia in English) has a unique identity. **Barcelona**, the capital, is very much the main event. One of the most vibrant and exciting cities in Europe, it is one of those places where you stay far longer than planned. Inland, the monastery of **Montserrat**, Catalunya's main "sight," is perched on one of the most unusual rock formations in Spain, and there are provincial cities too – **Tarragona, Girona** and **Lleida** – of considerable charm and historic interest. Sadly, large tracts of the coastline are a disaster, with much of the **Costa Brava** in particular a turgid sprawl of concrete. There are parts of the northernmost stretch, from **Cadaqués** to **Port Bou** on the French border, which have managed to retain some attraction but on the whole if it's beaches you're after you'd do better to keep going south – or take a ferry from Barcelona for the Balearics. As for the **Catalan Pyrenees**, they are more developed than their western neighbours, but access to the mountains is easier. Since the use of the Catalan language is so widespread, we've used Catalan spellings, with Castilian equivalents in parentheses.

Barcelona

BARCELONA, the self-confident and progressive capital of Catalunya, is a tremendous place to be. Though it boasts outstanding Gothic and Art Nouveau buildings, and some great museums – most notably those dedicated to Picasso, Miró and Catalan art – it is above all a place where there's enjoyment simply in walking the streets, stopping in at bars and cafés, soaking up the atmosphere. A thriving port and the most prosperous commercial centre in Spain, it has a sophistication and cultural dynamism way ahead of the rest of the country. In part this reflects the city's proximity to France, whose influence is apparent in the elegant boulevards and imaginative cooking. But Barcelona has also evolved an individual and eclectic cultural identity, most perfectly and eccentrically expressed in the architecture of Antoni Gaudí. The planning for the 1992 Olympics led to a new wave of civic pride, culminating in gleaming, renovated monuments and some spectacular modern buildings too. There are, however, darker sides to this prosperity and confidence: there is a great deal of poverty and a considerable drug problem, which means that the **petty crime** rate is high. It's not unusual for tourists to feel threatened in the seedier areas flanking the Ramblas. It's wise to take a few precautions: leave passports and tickets locked up in your hotel, don't be too conspicuous with expensive cameras and, if attacked, don't offer any resistance.

Arrival and information

The **airport**, 12km southwest of the city, is linked by a train service (every 30min 6am–10.30pm; Mon–Sat 305ptas, Sun 350ptas) to the main **Estació de Sants**, from where you can take the metro to the city centre (line #3 to Liceu for the Ramblas). Many trains from the airport also run on to **Plaça de Catalunya**, a more direct way of reaching the Barri Gòtic. Alternatively, there's the efficient **Airbus** (every 15min 5.30/6am–11pm; 475ptas), which departs from outside the terminals on a circular route and runs into the centre via Plaça Espanya, Gran Vía and Plaça de Catalunya. A **taxi** will cost around 1750ptas to Estació de Sants, 2000ptas to somewhere more central.

Estacío de Sants is the city's main **train station**, for national and some international arrivals. The **Estació de França** (or Estació Terminal), next to the Parc de la Ciutadella, is the terminal for long-distance Spanish and European express and intercity trains. Leaving França you can take the metro (line #4) from nearby Barceloneta, or simply walk into the Barri Gòtic, up Vía Laietana and into c/Jaume. The main **bus terminal** is the **Estació del Nord** (three blocks north of the Parc de la Ciutadella; metro Arc de Triomf). If, by chance, you don't arrive here, you'll be dropped at a central point within easy reach of a metro station. Arriving by **ferry** from the Balearics, you'll dock at the Estació Marítima at the bottom of the Ramblas on Moll de Barcelona.

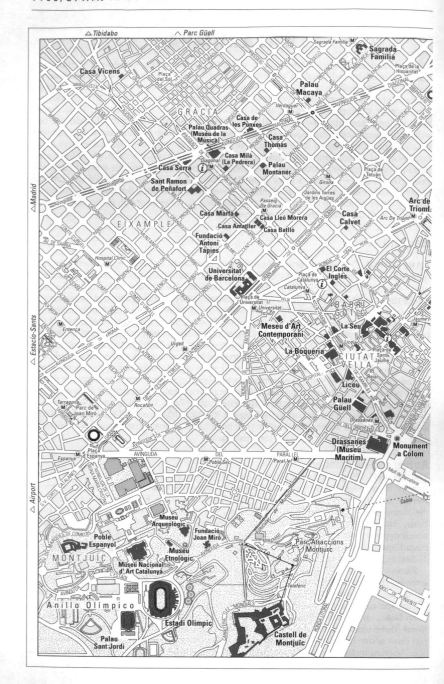

△ *Tibidabo* ∧ *Parc Güell*

Casa Vicens

Palau
Macaya

Sagrada Família M
Sagrada
Família
Plaça de la
Hispanitat

GRACIA

Palau Quadras
(Museu de la
Música)

Casa de
les Punxes

Verdaguer M

Casa
Thomas

Casa Serra

Casa Milà
(La Pedrera)

Diagonal M

Palau
Montaner

Sant Ramon
de Peñafort

Girona

Jardins Torres
de les Aigües

Plaça de
Tetuán

Arc de
Triomf

EIXAMPLE

Casa Marfà

Passeig
De Gracia

Casa Lleó Morera

Casa
Calvet

Arc De Triomf

AV. DE SARRIA

Casa Amatller

Casa Batlló

Fundació
Antoni
Tàpies

Hospital Clínic M

△ Madrid

Universitat
de Barcelona

Plaça de
Catalunya

El Corte
Inglés

Plaça de
l'Universitat

Catalunya

Entença M

M Universitat

BARRI
GOTIC

Jaume I

Meseu d'Art
Contemporani

La Seu

Urgell

Liceu M

△ Estació-Sants

La Boqueria

CIUTAT
VELLA

Pl.
Reial

Plaça de
Sants
Jaume

Rocafort M

Liceu

Tarragona M
Parc de
Joan Miró

Palau
Güell

Drassanes M

Plaça
d'Espanya

AVINGUDA

DEL

PARAL·LEL

AV. DEL DRASSANES

Espanya

Paral·lel M

Drassanes
(Museu
Marítim)

Monument
a Colom

△ Airport

Poble Sec M

Moll de Barcelona

Cable

Museu
Arqueològic

Fundació
Joan Miró

MIRAMAR

Parc Atraccions
Montjuïc

Poble
Espanyol

Museu
Etnològic

MONTJUIC

Museu Nacional
d' Art Catalunya

Telefèric

Anillo Olímpico

MOLL DE PONIENTE

Estadi Olímpic

Palau
Sant Jordi

Castell de
Montjuïc

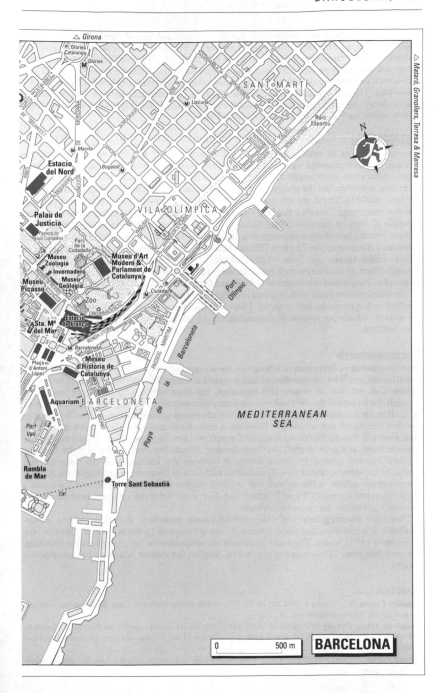

The **tourist offices** in Barcelona are very well organized: any of them will give you free, large-scale **maps** of the city and transport networks. The best office is beneath the Plaça de Catalunya (daily 9am–9pm; ☎906 30 12 82 or 93 423 18 00). Other offices are at the airport (Mon–Sat 9.30am–8pm, Sun 9.30am–3pm); Estació de Sants (Mon–Fri 8am–8pm, Sat & Sun 8am–2pm); and Passeig de Gràcia 107 for information on Catalunya (Mon–Fri 9am–7pm, Sat 9am–2pm). There's also a 24-hour, English-speaking **information service** (call ☎010) and you could try the municipal office, at Plaça de Sant Jaume 1 (Mon–Fri 8.30am–6pm; ☎903 402 70 00), which isn't so tourist-orientated but will help.

City transport

The quickest way of getting around is by the modern and efficient **metro**; stations are marked by a red diamond sign. The metro starts at 5am (6am on Sun) and shuts down at 11pm – just when most people in Barcelona are thinking of going out. It's extended to 2am on Friday, Saturday, and the evening before a holiday, and to midnight on Sunday. **Bus** routes (5/7am–10.30/11.30pm) are far more complicated, but every bus stop displays a comprehensive route map. There's a flat **fare** on both metro and buses of 145ptas; if you're staying a couple of days or more it's better to buy a ticket strip or **tarja** from metro station ticket offices, which gives you ten journeys at a discounted price. The T1 costs 795ptas and covers buses and the metro; the T2 costs 790ptas and only covers the metro. A limited number of yellow **night buses** run from 10.30/11.30pm to 3.30/4.30am, most starting or passing through Plaça de Catalunya; they cost a little more than daytime services. Cards valid for all forms of city transport are available at 1900ptas for three days and 2400 ptas for five days.

Black and yellow **taxis** (with a green roof-light lit when available for rent) are inexpensive, plentiful and very useful late at night. There's a minimum charge of 285ptas, and after that it's around 100ptas per kilometre, depending on the time of day. Most journeys will cost less than 1000ptas.

Accommodation

Accommodation in Barcelona is among the most expensive in Spain and unless you stay in a youth hostel, you'll be hard-pushed to find a room for under 3000ptas for a double. The tourist offices dish out lists of **hotels** and **hostales**, but these are hardly necessary as a walk through the streets of the old town reveals heavy concentrations of places to stay and it's easy to stroll around comparing rooms. Most of the **cheapest accommodation** is to be found in the side streets off and around the Ramblas, a convenient and atmospheric area in which to base yourself. The further down towards the port you get, the less salubrious and noisier the surroundings: as a general rule, anything above c/Escudellers tends to be all right. Perhaps the best hunting ground for cheap rooms is between the Ramblas and the Plaça de Sant Jaume, in the area bordered by c/Escudellers and c/de la Boqueria near Plaça Reial. A **hotel reservations office** at the airport and at Sants station (daily 8am–10pm) will book you a place on arrival (there's a fee of 100ptas), but they won't book the very cheapest places and you won't get to see the room beforehand.

There are several official and not-so-official **youth hostels** in Barcelona, where accommodation is in multi-bedded dorm rooms. Prices are around 1500ptas each in a private hostel, more in an HI hostel. There are hundreds of **campsites** on the coast in either direction, but none less than 11km from the city; we've detailed the easiest to access, out towards the airport.

HOSTELS

Pensión Colom 3, c/Colom 3 (☎93 318 06 31). The better hostel choice in Plaça Reial: central, with single and double rooms available too. ③.

Hostal de Joves, Passeig de Pujades 29 (☎93 300 31 04). An HI hostel right by the Parc de la Ciutadella and handy for the Nord bus terminal and Estació de França. Open 7–10am and 3pm–midnight. Breakfast included. ②.

Alberg Palau, c/Palau 6 (☎93 412 50 80). Central, friendly and secure. Curfew 3am. Breakfast included. ②.

Albergue Pere Tarres, c/Numancia 149 (☎93 410 23 09). Near Sants station (metro Maria Cristina). Open 8.30am–11am & 3pm–11pm. Breakfast included. ②.
Albergue Mare de Déu de Montserrat, Passeig Mare de Déu del Coll 41–51, metro Vallcarca (☎93 210 51 51). An HI hostel a long way out of the city. Open 7–10am & 2pm–midnight. ②.

HOTELS
Residencia Australia, Ronda Universitat 11 (☎93 317 41 77). Just off Plaça Catalunya and very popular; reserve in advance. ③.
Hostal Canaletes, Ramblas 133 (☎93 301 56 60). Near Plaça de Catalunya (and at the top of a building containing other *pensiones*); fair rooms, though hot and noisy in summer. ②.
Hostal Levante, Baixada Sant Miquel 2 (☎93 317 95 65). Just off the Plaça de Sant Miquel, behind the Ajuntament, this quiet, friendly place has decent, plain rooms in a well-kept building. ②.
Hostal Mont Thabor, Ramblas 86 (☎93 317 66 66). At the heart of the Ramblas. ③.
Hotel Oriente, Ramblas 45 (☎93 302 25 58). Stylish 3-star hotel on the Ramblas; attractive turn-of-the-century decor and modern rooms with bath are worth the splurge. ⑥.
Hostal Opera, c/de Sant Pau 20 (☎93 318 82 01). Close enough to the Ramblas to make you overlook the rather unkempt rooms. Cheaper rooms without shower too. ③.
Hostal Rembrandt, c/Portaferrissa 23 (☎93 318 10 11). Spotless rooms with shower and balcony, cheaper rooms without. ③.
Hostal Residencia Europa, c/de la Boqueria 18 (☎93 318 76 20). Some rooms have a balcony overlooking the street; cheaper rooms without bath available too. ③.
Hostal Windsor, Rambla de Catalunya 84, metro Pg. de Gràcia (☎93 215 11 98). Small *hostal* on the Eixample's nicest avenue with well-kept and reasonably priced doubles. ④.

CAMPSITES
Cala-Gogo, El Prat de Llobregat (☎93 379 46 00). Open mid-March to mid-Oct, bus from Plaça d'Espanya or 30min on foot.
Masnou, Canetra N-11 (☎93 555 15 03). About 200m from Masnou station, take the train from Sants or Plaça de Catalunya.

The City
Scattered as Barcelona's main sights may be, the greatest concentration of interest is around the **old town** (*La Ciutat Vella*). These cramped streets above the harbour are easily manageable, and far more enjoyable, on foot. Start, as everyone else does, with the Ramblas.

AROUND THE RAMBLAS
It is a telling comment on Barcelona's character that one can recommend a single street (or strictly streets) – **the Ramblas** – as a highlight. The heart of Barcelona's life and self-image, the Ramblas are littered with cafés, shops, restaurants and newspaper stands, a focal point for locals as much as for tourists. Heading down from the Plaça de Catalunya, you gradually leave the opulent facades of the banks and department stores for a seedier area towards the port where the Ramblas cut right through the heart of the notorious red-light district, with side streets at the harbour end packed with dimly lit clubs, bars and sex shops. It's much less threatening than it once was, however: the Olympic clean-up and the transformation of the Port Vell area has meant new hip bars and clubs now rub shoulders with sleazy old ones.

On your way down there are plenty of interesting buildings, some of them open for visits: don't miss the glorious **La Boqueria**, the city's main food market (Mon–Sat 8am–8pm), a splendid gallery of sights and smells with several excellent snack bars and a restaurant at the back selling market-fresh dishes. Almost adjacent is the shell of the **Liceu**, Barcelona's celebrated opera house that went up in smoke in January 1994 and is now being rebuilt, scheduled to reopen in October 1999. More or less opposite is the famous *Café de l'Ópera*, an opulent high society meeting place – though not as expensive as you might imagine. A few minutes' walk north of here is the stunning new **Museu d'Art Contemporani** (Mon & Wed–Fri 11am–7.30pm, Sat 10am–10pm, Sun 10am–3pm; 750ptas, 350 ptas on Wed) with exciting, evolving displays by international and national artists. Exhibitions focus upon photography, film and video.

A little way down from the Liceu, hidden behind an archway just off the Ramblas and easy to miss, lies the elegant nineteenth-century **Plaça Reial**. Decorated with tall palm trees and iron lamps (by the young Gaudí), it's the haunt of punks, bikers, Catalan eccentrics, the odd drunk and hundreds of alfresco diners and drinkers.

Gaudí's magnificent **Palau Güell** (Mon–Fri 10am–1pm & 4–6.30pm; 300ptas) stands just off the Ramblas, towards the bottom, at c/Nou de la Rambla 3. Much of Gaudí's early career was spent constructing elaborate follies for wealthy patrons, the most important of whom was Don Eusebio Güell, a shipowner and industrialist. In 1885 he commissioned this mansion, an essential stop, where Gaudí's feel for different materials and textures is astounding. Wrought-iron supports blend magnificently with granite, marble, ceramics, woodwork and stained and etched glass. Don't miss the roof.

Right at the harbour end of the Ramblas, Columbus stands pointing out to sea from the top of a tall, grandiose column, the **Monument a Colom** (summer daily 9am–8.30pm; winter Mon–Fri 10am–1.30pm & 3.30–6.30/7.30pm, Sat & Sun 10am–6.30/7.30pm; 250ptas). Risk the elevator to his head (it fell down in 1976) for a fine view of the city. Opposite, to the west side of the Ramblas, are the Drassanes, medieval shipyards originating from the thirteenth century. The impressive stone-vaulted buildings are home to a fine **Museu Marítim** (Tues–Sat 10am–7pm; 400ptas), whose star exhibit is a sixteenth-century Royal Gallery.

THE BARRI GÒTIC

A remarkable concentration of beautiful medieval Gothic buildings, just a couple of blocks off the Ramblas, the **Barri Gòtic** forms the very heart of the old city. What you see now dates principally from the fourteenth and fifteenth centuries, when Catalunya reached the height of its commercial prosperity. The quarter is centred on the **Plaça de Sant Jaume**, on one side of which stands the restored town hall, the **Ajuntament**, open on weekend mornings only (10am–2pm; call ☎93 402 73 52 to arrange a visit). Across the square rises the **Palau de la Generalitat**, home of the Catalan government (only open April 23; massive queues); restored during the sixteenth century in Renaissance style, it has a beautiful cloister on the first floor with superb coffered ceilings. Just behind the square, the **La Seu**, Barcelona's cathedral (daily 8am–1.30pm & 4–7.30pm, weekends opens at 5pm) is one of the great Gothic buildings of Spain. Modern lighting shows off the soaring airiness of the interior superbly. Outside, the magnificent **cloisters** (8.45am–1.15pm & 4–7pm) look over a lush tropical garden with soaring palm trees and white geese, and open into, among other things, the small **cathedral museum** (Tues–Sat 10am–2pm & 5–8pm, Sun 11am–2pm; 200ptas). Nearby, next to the Palau Episcopal and at various points in and near Vía Laietana, you can see some of the city's remaining **Roman walls**.

The cathedral and its associated buildings aside, the most concentrated batch of historic monuments in the Barri Gòtic is the grouping around the nearby **Plaça del Rei**. Barcelona's finest Roman remains were uncovered beneath the **Palau Reial** (the former Palace of the Counts of Barcelona) which now houses the **Museu d'Història de la Ciutat** (summer Tues–Sat 10am–8pm, Sun 10am–2pm; winter Tues–Sat 10am–2pm & 4–8pm; 500ptas, free first Sat of month). Underground, both Roman and Visigothic remains have been preserved where they were discovered during works in the 1930s. The museum also gives access to the beautiful fourteenth-century **Capella Reial de Santa Àgata** with its tall single nave and unusual stained glass, and to an extension of the royal palace known as the **Saló de Tinell**, a fine spacious example of fourteenth-century secular Gothic architecture. It was on the steps leading from the Saló de Tinell into the Plaça del Rei that Ferdinand and Isabella stood to receive Columbus on his return from America. The **Museu Marès** (Tues–Sat 10am–5pm, Sun 10am–2pm; 300ptas, Wed 150ptas, free first Sun of month) occupies another wing of the palace, behind the *plaça*. The bulk of the museum consists of religious sculpture, including a vast number of wooden crucifixes from the twelfth to the fifteenth centuries. The upper floors house the **Museu Sentimental** of local sculptor Federico Marès, an incredible jumble gathered during fifty years of travel. Don't miss it.

For a quick respite from the city centre, nip into the greenery and relative peace of **Parc de la Ciutadella**, which is within easy walking distance of the Barri Gòtic. Its attractions include a lake, Gaudí's monumental fountain and the city zoo (daily: summer 9.30am–7.30pm;

winter 10am–5pm; 1500ptas), and you'll also find the meeting place of the Catalan parliament and the **Museu d'Art Modern** (Tues–Sat 10am–7pm, Sun 10am–2.30pm; 500ptas), whose collection ranges from the eighteenth century to the 1980s.

PICASSO AND THE CARRER DE MONTCADA

Heading east from the palace, you'll cross Vía Laietana and reach the Carrer de Montcada, crowded with beautifully restored old buildings. One of these houses the **Museu Picasso** (Tues–Sat 10am–8pm, Sun 10am–3pm; 600ptas, free first Sun of month; costs more for visiting exhibitions), one of the most important collections of Picasso's work in the world and the only one of any significance in his native country. Continue down the street and you'll come out opposite the great basilica of **Santa María del Mar** (Mon–Sat 9am–1.30pm & 4.30–8pm, Sun 9am–2pm & 5–8.30pm except during mass), built on what was the seashore in the fourteenth century. Its soaring lines were the symbol of Catalan supremacy in Mediterranean commerce and it is still much dearer to the heart of the average local than the cathedral. The stained glass is especially beautiful.

PORT VELL AND VILLA OLYMPICA

The whole **Port Vell** area has been revitalized, notably with the construction of the harbourside *passeig* and the vast new Maremagnum complex reached from near the Monument a Colom via a dramatic wooden walkway. The city planners' desire to refocus attention on the sea has provided an upmarket shopping mall, an excellent aquarium, a cinema, an IMAX theatre and a multitude of bars and restaurants all grouped together in the old harbour area with fine views back to the old city, the marina and Montjuic.

Looping back towards the city towards Plaça d'Antoni López is the new **Museo d'Historia de Catalunya** (Tues–Thurs 10am–7pm, Fri & Sat 10am–8pm, Sun 10am–2.30pm; 500ptas), housed in the Palau de Mar, a historic old dock building. There are great views from the restaurant terrace. The museum is on the fringe of the **Barceloneta district**, home to Barcelona's cleaned up beaches. *Telefericos* (cable cars) run from here to Montjuic via Port Vell (summer 10.30am–8pm, winter noon–5.30pm; 1200ptas return). Walk 1km east along the beach and you'll find Port Olímpic with its myriad bars and restaurants. At night the tables are stacked up, dance floors emerge and the area hosts one of the city's most vibrant dance scenes. Dozens of bars pump out a pulsating mix of salsa, house and techno to an uptown clientele.

ANTONI GAUDÍ AND THE SAGRADA FAMÍLIA

Besides modern art, Barcelona offers – above all through the work of **Antoni Gaudí** (1852–1926) – some of the most fantastic and exciting modern architecture to be found anywhere in the world. Without doubt his most famous creation is the incomplete **Temple Expiatiori de la Sagrada Família** (daily 9am–6/8pm; 800ptas, lift to top of the pinnacles 200ptas; metro Sagrada Família), a good way northeast of the Plaça de Catalunya. Amid great controversy, work to complete the cathedral has begun, turning the interior into a giant building site, but it's fascinating to watch Gaudí's last known plans being slowly realized. The size alone is startling, with eight spires rising to over 100m. For Gaudí these were metaphors for the Twelve Apostles; he planned to build four more above the main facade and to add a 180-metre tower topped with a gallery over the transept, itself to be surrounded by four smaller towers symbolizing the Evangelists. Take the lift, or climb up one of the towers, and you can enjoy a dizzy view down over the whole complex and clamber still further round the walls and into the towers.

Inside the Temple a small **Gaudí museum** traces the career of the architect and the history of the building. The tourist offices also issue a handy leaflet describing all his works, with a map of their locations. Above all, check out the **Parc Güell** (daily 10am–6/9pm; free), his most ambitious project apart from the Sagrada Família. This almost hallucinatory experience, with giant decorative lizards and a vast Hall of Columns, contains another small **museum** (daily 10am–6/8pm; 300ptas) with some of the furniture Gaudí designed. To get there, take the metro to Lesseps or bus #24 from the Plaça de Catalunya to Travesera de Dalt, from where it's a half-kilometre walk to the main gates on c/d'Olot.

MONTJUÏC

The hill of **Montjuïc** has far more varied attractions – five museums, an amusement park, the "Spanish Village", the Olympic arena and a castle with grand views of the city. The most obvious way to approach is to take a bus or metro to the Plaça d'Espanya and walk from there up the imposing Avda de la Reina María Cristina, past the 1929 International Fair buildings and the rows of fountains. If you'd rather start with the castle, take the **funicular railway** (every 10min: summer daily; winter weekends only; 375ptas return) which runs from Parallel metro station to the start of the cable car (summer only), which in turn leads to the amusement park and castle. And lastly there are **buses**: #61 from Plaça d'Espanya to the amusement park, or a bus from the *plaça* to the Poble Espanyol, or #55 from Plaça de Catalunya to Passieg Sta. Maradona, just above the archeological museum.

If you tackle the stiff climb from the Plaça d'Espanya you'll arrive at the **Palau Nacional**, centrepiece of Barcelona's 1929 International Fair and now home to one of Spain's great museums, the **Museu Nacional d'Art de Catalunya** (Tues–Sat 10am–7pm, Thurs until 9pm & Sun 10am–2.30pm; 800ptas), with its two enormous main collections. The Gothic collection is fascinating, but it's the Romanesque section that is the more remarkable, perhaps the best collection of its kind in the world: 35 rooms of eleventh- and twelfth-century frescoes, meticulously removed from a series of small Pyrenean churches and beautifully displayed.

Barcelona's important **Museu Arqueològic** (Tues–Sat 9.30am–7pm, Sun 10am–2.30pm; 500ptas, free Sun) stands to the east of the Palau Nacional, lower down the hill. Nearby is the **Fundació Joan Miró** (Tues–Sat 10/11am–7/8pm, Thurs until 9.30pm, Sun 10.30am–2.30pm; 800ptas), the most adventurous of Barcelona's art museums, devoted to one of the greatest Catalan artists. A beautiful white building houses a permanent collection of paintings, graphics, tapestries and sculptures donated by Miró himself and covering the period from 1914 to 1978.

A short walk over to the other side of the Palau Nacional will bring you to the **Poble Espanyol** or "Spanish Village" (Tues–Thurs 9am–2am, Fri & Sat 9am–4am, Sun 9am–midnight; 950ptas, free Wed & Thurs & Sun after 8pm), consisting of replicas of famous or characteristic buildings from all over Spain, and with a lively club scene at night. Prices, especially for products of the "genuine Spanish workshops" (and in the bars), are exorbitant. Just down the road, the reconstruction of the **Mies van der Rohe Pavilion** (daily 10am–6/8pm; 300ptas) is a far greater treat.

From the Poble Espanyol, the main road climbs around the hill to what was the principal **Olympic arena**, passing some dazzling new buildings – the Picornell swimming pools and the Japanese-designed Palau Sant Jordi. These are overshadowed only by the Olympic Stadium itself, the **Estadi Olimpic** (May–Oct 10am–6pm; free), built originally for the 1929 Exhibition and completely refitted by Catalan architects to accommodate the 1992 opening and closing ceremonies. The new Olympic museum, the **Galeria Olímpica**, on Passeig Olimpic (summer Tues–Sat 10am–2pm & 4–7/8pm, Sun 10am–2pm; winter Tues–Fri 10am–1pm & 4–6pm, Sat & Sun 10am–2pm; 475ptas), is a hands-on affair covering the staging of the Games in the city. Far above this complex of museums and sports arenas, and offering magnificent views across the city, stands the eighteenth-century **Castell de Montjuïc**, built on seventeenth-century ruins.

TIBIDABO

If the views from the Castell de Montjuïc are good, those from the top of **Mount Tibidabo** – which forms the northwestern boundary of the city – are legendary. On one of those mythical clear days you can see across to Montserrat and the Pyrenees, and out to sea even as far as Mallorca. The name is taken from the Temptations of Christ in the wilderness, when Satan led him to a high place and offered him everything that could be seen: *Haec omnia tibi dabo si cadens adoraberis me* (All these things will I give thee, if thou wilt fall down and worship me). At the summit there's a wonderfully old-fashioned **Parc d'Atraccions** (unlimited funfair rides 2400ptas, cheaper limited tickets available), and all around there are pleasant walks through the woods. To get there, take the Ferrocarriles Catalanes rail line from Plaça de Catalunya to Avda Tibidabo; from there the Tramvia Blau (tram) connects with the funicular rail line to the top (7.15am–9.45pm; 400ptas return).

MONESTIR DE PEDRALBES

On the outskirts of the city, about fifteen minutes' walk from the metro at Palau Reial is the Gothic **Monestir de Pedralbes** (Tues–Sun 10am–2pm; 300ptas, free first Sun of month, joint ticket with Collecció Thyssen-Bornemisza 700ptas; #22 bus from Passeig de Gràcia). The monastery gives a vivid impression of monastic life, but perhaps more engaging is the superb collection of fourteenth- to eighteenth-century religious paintings here that form part of the Thyssen-Bornemisza art collection, the remainder of which is displayed in Madrid.

Eating, drinking and nightlife

There's a huge variety of **food** available in Barcelona and even low-budget travellers can do well for themselves. Be aware that a lot of places close on Sundays and throughout August, and that the *menú del día* is rarely available in the evening. If you want to buy picnic material the covered **market** (Mercat Sant Josep/La Boqueria) off the Ramblas is the place to go. A couple of **supermarkets** to know about are Centro Comercial Simago, Ramblas 113 (food department in the basement); and Drugstore, Passeig de Gràcia 71, which is open all night.

Amusing yourself in Barcelona is unlikely to be a problem. There are hundreds of excellent **bars** and **cafés** in the city centre to start your evening, including the lively tapas places in the Barri Gòtic. Around the Museu Picasso is a particularly good area: the Passeig del Born, the square at the end of c/Montcada behind Santa María del Mar, is crowded with popular bars. Gràcia, north of the centre, is the most studenty area in Barcelona and ideal for low-key, lateish drinking, especially on the numerous little squares around the main Plaça del Sol, itself bordered by café terraces. Barcelona's **nightlife** is some of Europe's most exciting. It keeps going all night too, the music bars closing at 3am, the discos at 4 to 5am, and (for the seriously dissipated) some clubs opening between 5am and 9am on weekends. Among the more expensive, trendier places, *bars modernos* are still in fashion, hi-tech theme palaces concentrated mainly in the Eixample, or in the rich kids' stamping ground bordered by c/Ganduxer, Avda Diagonal and Vía Augusta, west of Gràcia. Drinks are expensive, the music echoes the often elaborate decorations, and the "in" places change rapidly, with new ones starting up all the time. Currently, the waterfront Port Olímpic area seems to be in favour, although weekdays out of summer are dead. **Clubbing** can be more expensive still; in the most exclusive places even a beer is going to cost you roughly ten times what it costs in the bar next door.

For **listings** of almost anything you could want in the way of entertainment and culture, buy a copy of the weekly *Guía del Ocio* (125ptas) from any newsstand. There's a thriving **gay scene** in Barcelona: *SexTienda*, at c/Rauric 11 (very near Plaça Reial), supplies free maps of gay Barcelona with a list of bars, clubs and contacts.

TAPAS BARS

Bar Celta, c/de la Mercè 16, Barri Gòtic. Galician tapas specialities, including excellent fried calamares, and heady Galician wine. Very popular. Open until 1am.

La Soccarena, c/de la Mercè 21. Asturian cider bar serving goat's cheese, cured meats and excellent Asturian cider – which the waiter pours into glasses from over the back of his head to aereate the cider.

Les Tepes, Plaça Regomis 4, Barri Gòtic. Superb Anglo-Hispanic-owned bar with well-priced food and always a character to talk to.

El Xampanyet, c/de Montcada 22, Barri Gòtic. Terrific blue-tiled champagne bar with fine seafood tapas, cava by the glass and local *sidra*. Closed Mon, Sun night & Aug.

RESTAURANTS

Amaya, Rambla Santa Mónica 20–24. Busy, smoke-filled tapas bar on one side, mid-range (around 3000ptas) restaurant on the other, the Amaya serves Basque specialities.

Bar-Restaurant Candanchu, Plaça Rius i Taulet 9, Gràcia; metro Fontana. Sit outside and enjoy a sandwich or tortilla, or go for the 925ptas *menú del día*. Closed Tues.

El Cangrejo Loco, Moll del Gregal 29, Port Olímpic. As its name suggests, "The Crazy Crab", serves Mediterranean/seafood cuisine (around 3000ptas) with lively, lateish (1am) drinking.

Los Caracoles, c/Escudellers 14, Barri Gòtic. Barcelona landmark restaurant whose name means "snails", the house speciality, along with spit-roast chicken on display in the street outside. Around 3500ptas if you include both as part of a big meal; call in during the day to reserve a table.

Les Corts Catalanes, Gran Vía 603 (corner Rambla de Catalunya), Eixample; metro Catalunya. Vegetarian restaurant that doubles as a health food store. A 950ptas *menú del día* (Mon–Fri lunch only), otherwise 2000–2500ptas a head to fill up on Catalan dishes, pizzas and salads.

El Convent, c/Jerusalem 3, Barri Xines. Long-standing favourite restaurant, with an extensive Catalan menu. You can eat well for around 2500ptas. Closed Sun.

España, c/Sant Pau 9–11, Barri Xines. Eat fine food in *modernista* splendour in a building designed by Domenèch i Montaner. The *menú del día* is good value, but not available at night when a full meal costs upwards of 3000ptas a head.

La Fonda, c/Escudellas, 10 Barri Gòtic. Central location, good Spanish cooking for less than 1500ptas, delightful colonial surroundings plus a lively atmosphere. Very popular, with no booking, so arrive to queue at least half an hour before 9pm opening.

El Gallo Kiriko, c/Avinyo 19, Barri Gòtic. Filling, reasonable Pakistani curries plus Pakistani TV in what looks like a bathroom – for as little as 500ptas.

Gardu-a, c/Morera 17–19, Barri Xines. At the back of the Sant Josep market, this offers one of the city's best paellas and good, fresh market produce. Lunch menu for 1100ptas; dinner more like 2500ptas. Closed Sun.

El Jardin, in El Mercadillo off Portaferrisa. Eclectic, healthy food in a delightful garden setting.

Perú, Passeig de Bourbó 10, Barceloneta. Barcelona's best seafood is served in Barceloneta. This is one of the few there that has a *menú del día*, good value at around 1500ptas depending on when you eat.

Pitarra, c/d'Avinyó 56, Barri Gòtic. A Catalan cookery in operation since 1890, lined with paintings and serving good, reasonably priced food. Closed Sun.

Pollo Rico, c/Sant Pau 31, Barri Xines. Spit-roasted chicken, fries and a glass of cava for under 700ptas make this one of the area's most popular budget spots. Closed Wed.

Self Naturista, c/Santa Ana 15, Barri Gòtic. Popular self-service vegetarian restaurant with functional feel, queues, a 910ptas fixed menu and dishes that change daily. Open Mon–Sat until 10pm.

Set Portes (Las Siete Puertas), Passeig d'Isabel II 14, Barri Gòtic (☎93 319 30 33). Wood-panelled classic whose decor has barely changed in 150 years. Elegant but not exclusive, though you'll need to book ahead. The seafood is excellent, particularly the dark paella. From 4000ptas a head.

CAFÉS AND BARS

Ambos Mundos, Plaça Reial 10, Barri Gòtic. Touristy choice in the plaça, but a good vantage point for taking in some of the stranger local characters. Closed Tues.

Berimbau, Passeig del Born 17, Barri Gòtic. Cool bar with Brazilian sounds and cocktails.

Café de l'Òpera, Ramblas 74. Elegant turn-of-the-century café/bar with fine coffee and a range of cakes and snacks. Open daily until 2am.

Café del Sol, Plaça del Sol 29, Gràcia. Trendy hangout, just one of several similar places in this square.

Horchatería Fillol, Plaça de la Universitat 5, Eixample. *Horchata* as well as enormous milk shakes and other delights. Breakfast of coffee and croissant for 220ptas.

Jugolandia, Moll de Mestral 6, Port Olimpic. Great tropical fruit juices and a perfect setting overlooking the Olympic marina.

El Paraigua, Plaça Sant Miquel, Barri Gòtic. Expensive café/bar, with a chic Art Nouveau interior. Closed Sun.

Téxtil Café, c/Montcada, 12. In the atmospheric medieval courtyard of the textile museum, with braziers in winter, although fairly pricey drinks keep out the art students.

Els Quatre Gats, c/Montsió 5, Barri Gòtic. *Modernista*-designed, haunt of Picasso and his contemporaries, still an interesting and arty place for a drink. Closed Sun lunch.

DESIGNER BARS AND CLUBS

Apolo, c/Nou de la Rambla 113, Barri Xines. Trip-hop and techno for a gay/straight crowd, old town location; from 11pm until 6am.

La Fira, c/Provença 171, Eixample, metro Provença. A museum-bar with seats in turn-of-the-century fairground rides, plus a bar under a circus awning. Open until 4.30am, Sun until 1am.

KGB, c/Alegre de Dalt 55, Gràcia. Pop sounds becoming hardcore later. Open until 8am.

Mirablau, Plaza Doctor Andreu. Cocktail bar and popular disco in dramatic location at the foot of the cable car to Mt Tibidabo, with fantastic views. Open until 5am.

Moog, Arc del Teatre 3, Barri Xines. Techno temple. Regular appearances from top UK and Euro DJs. Best on Sun, open 11pm–3am.

Nick Havanna, c/Rosselló 208, Eixample, metro Diagonal. One of the most futuristic bars in town, enormous, yet packed to the gills at weekends. Open 8pm–4am.

Otto Zutz, c/Lincoln 15, Gràcia. A 3-storey warehouse converted into a nocturnal shop window of everything that's for sale or rent in Barcelona. With the right rags and face you're in for free. The club starts at 2am; it's a bar before that.

Paradís, c/Paradís 4. Reggae, African and Latin sounds in the Barri Gòtic.

Torres de Avila, Avda Marqués de Comillas 25, Poble Espanyol, Montjuïc. The city's newest and most fantastic bar yet – see it to believe it. Attracts an international crowd. Open 9pm–4am.

Universal Bar, c/Mariano Cubí 184, Gràcia, metro Fontana. Postmodern bar, long one of the trendiest. Open until 3am.

Up & Down, c/Numancia 179. More chic than trendy, but very much in vogue after refit. Open from midnight.

Yabba Dabba Club, c/Avenir 63, Gràcia. Haunt of the spiky-haired crowd, with Gothic decor including candelabras and a sculpted torso protruding from the wall. Open until 3am, closed Sun.

Listings

Airlines Air France, Pg. de Gràcia 56 (☎93 214 7900); British Airways, Pg. de Gràcia 85 (☎93 215 69 00); Iberia, Disputació 258 (☎93/240 05 00); TWA, Crusell Cent, 360 (☎93/215 84 86).

American Express c/Rosellon 269, off Pg. de Gràcia 101 (Mon–Fri 9.30–6pm, Sat 10am–noon; ☎93 217 00 70; 24hr helpline ☎900 99 44 26).

Books In English Itaca, Rambla de Catalunya 81, Salas, c/Jaume-I 5; The Book Store, c/la Granja 13; and from newspaper stands down the Ramblas.

Buses The main bus station is the Estació del Nord on Avda Vilanova for departures throughout Catalunya, Spain and beyond. On long-distance routes, book at least a day in advance if possible. The tourist offices or travel agencies can assist with timetables.

Car rental Most rental agencies are represented at the airport. In town, contact Atesa, c/Balmes 141 (☎93 478 58 02); Avis, c/Casanovas 209 (☎93 209 95 33); Hertz, c/Tuset 10 (☎93 217 32 48); Ital-Budget, Traversera de Gràcia 71 (☎93 201 21 99).

Consulates Australia, Gran Vía Carles III 98 (☎93 330 94 96); Britain, Avda Diagonal 477 (☎93 419 90 44); Canada, Pg de Gràcia 77 (☎93 215 07 04); Ireland, Gran Vía Carles III 94 (☎93 491 50 21); New Zealand, Trav. de Grácia 64 (☎93 209 03 99); USA, Passeig de la Reina Elisenda 23 (☎93 280 22 27).

Exchange Most banks are located in Plaça de Catalunya and Pg. de Gràcia. Money can also be changed at the airport (daily 7.30am–10.45pm); Estacío de Sants (daily 8am–10pm, Sun closes 9pm); Víajes Marsans, Ramblas 134 (Mon–Fri 9am–1.30pm & 4–7.30pm); and at *Casas de Cambio* throughout the centre.

Ferries Tickets for Balearic ferries from Transmediterránea, at the Estacío Maritima (☎93 443 25 32). Book in advance July & Aug.

Hospitals Hospital de la Creu Roja, c/Dos de Maig 301 (☎93 433 1551); Hospital Clinic I Provincial, c/Villaroel 170 (☎93 454 60 00). For emergency doctors or ambulance dial ☎061.

Left luggage Lockers at Sants station (6.30am–11pm; 200/600ptas a day); Estacío Maritima (9am–1pm & 4–11pm; 300/500ptas); Estacío França (6am–11.30pm; 400/600ptas); Estacío del Nord (24hr; 600ptas); and Airport (24hr; 600ptas).

Police Turism Attention, Las Ramblas 43 (summer 7am–2am; winter 7am–midnight; ☎93 301 90 60).

Post office Correus, Plaça Antoni Lòpez at the bottom of Vía Laietana (Mon–Fri 8am–9pm, Sat 8am–2pm & Sun 9am–1pm); poste restante at Window 17 (Mon–Fri 9am–9pm, Sat 9am–2pm).

Telephones Telefónica at Sants station (daily 8am–10.30pm, Sun opens 9am; also has a fax machine), and at Las Ramblas 88 Local 46 (daily 10am–11pm).

Travel agencies TIVE at Gran Vía 1, between the Rambla and Plaça de la Universitat; other general travel firms can be found around the Gran Vía, Pg. de Gràcia, Vía Laietana and the Ramblas.

Montserrat

The extraordinary mountain of **Montserrat**, with its weirdly shaped crags of rock, its monastery and its ruined hermitage caves, stands just 40km northwest of Barcelona, off the road to Lleida, and is an ideal natural sanctuary from the city heat in summer. This sawtoothed outcrop is one of the most spectacular of all Spain's natural sights, and legends hang easily upon it. Saint Peter is said to have deposited a carving of the Virgin by St Luke in one of the mountain caves, fifty years after the birth of Christ; another tale claims this as the spot where Parsifal discovered the Holy Grail. Inevitably it's no longer remote, but the place itself is still magical and you can avoid the crowds by striking out along well-marked paths to deserted hermitages. Another option is to stay the night, since the crowds disperse by early evening.

It is the **Black Virgin** (La Moreneta), the icon supposedly hidden by St Peter, which is responsible for the monastery's existence: over 150 churches were dedicated to her in Italy alone, as were the first chapels of Mexico, Chile and Peru – even a Caribbean island bears her name. According to the story it was lost after being hidden during the Moorish invasion and reappeared here in 880: in the first of its miracles, it could not be moved. The chapel built to house it was the predecessor of the present monastic structures, about three-quarters of the way up the mountain.

The **monastery** itself is of no particular architectural interest, except in its monstrous bulk. Only the sixteenth-century **Basilica** is open to the public, where you can catch the boys' choir singing the famous "Salve Regina" (daily 1pm). La Moreneta, blackened by the smoke of countless candles, stands above the high altar, reached from behind, up a stairway. Near the entrance to the basilica is a **museum** (older section open Tues–Sun 10.30am–2pm; newer section open daily 3–6pm; 500ptas) containing paintings by Caravaggio and El Greco. The **walks** around the woods and mountainside of Montserrat are a greater attraction, with tracks to caves and hermitages in every direction. You can also take funicular rail lines to the hermitages of **Sant Joan** and **Sant Jeronimo**, near the summit of the mountain at 1300m.

Practicalities

The most thrilling approach is by train and cable car, about an hour and a half from Barcelona. The Ferrocarriles Catalanes **trains** leave from beneath the Plaça de Espanya (9.10am–3.10pm every 1–2hr), connecting at Montserrat Aeri with a cable car for an exhilarating ride. Combined tickets, bought at Plaça d'Espanya, cost 2500ptas. There are also **tour buses** from Barcelona, leaving at 9am from Sants bus station and returning 5pm – tickets (4000ptas, including breakfast, lunch and museum entrance) are available from any travel agent.

There's a **campsite** up by the funicular rail lines and a **hotel** which should be booked in advance: the *Hostal-Residencia El Monasterio* (☎93 835 02 01; ⑤). The **bar** in the square outside the monastery gates serves sandwiches, and there are a couple of high-priced **restaurants** and gift shops too.

The Catalan Pyrenees

The Catalan Pyrenees, every bit as spectacular as their Aragonese neighbours, have been exploited for far longer. While this has resulted in numerous less-than-aesthetic ski resorts and hydroelectric projects, it also means good public transport to the villages and a well-developed tourism infrastructure. In the less frequented corners, such as the westerly **Parc Nacional**, the scenery is the equal of any in Europe, while even the touristy train ride up to **Núria** to the east rarely fails to impress. The principality of **Andorra**, between these two attractions, has considerably less going for it, though **La Seu d'Urgell**, on the approach from the south, is a bit more worthwhile.

The Parc Nacional and around

After Ordesa, the most popular target of trekkers in the Pyrenees is the **Parc Nacional de Sant Maurici and Aigües Tortes**, covering nearly 200 square kilometres of forest, lakes and cirques, presided over by 3000-metre snow-capped peaks. For the less adventurous, there are lower-altitude track walks through fine scenery and visits to several villages around the park. Initial access is from Pobla de Segur, reached by 7.15am bus or morning train from Barcelona, or by the 4.30pm bus from Lleida (weekdays only). The other access town is Pont de Suert – buses leave from Lleida daily at 9am & 5pm.

The two main "base" villages are Boí and Espot, west and east of the park boundaries respectively, with Capdella to the south a less busy alternative; all are set in their own gorgeous valleys. BOÍ is 21km from Pont de Suert on the main road up to the Viella tunnel, served by daily bus from Pobla at 11.15am via Pont de Suert. In the town itself, the tiny old quarter is dwarfed by modern construction, and tourism facilities are expensive. Exceptions include a few nameless *habitaciones* (③) for **accommodation** in the old quarter, or try *Hostal Peregort* (☎973 69 60 06; ③); *Casa Higinio*, 200m up the road to Taüll, is a good place to eat. If you draw a blank here, the more handsome neighbouring village of **TAÜLL**, uphill and east, has a single pension, *La Coma*, c/Únic (☎973 69 60 25; ②), several possibilities in its *cases de pagès* (rural home-stays; ②) and an attractive **campsite** (☎973 69 61 74). Although further from the park entrance, Taüll also boasts the Romanesque **Church of Sant Climent**, one of several in the area. **ESPOT** lies only 7km off the main road between Pobla and the overrated Vall d'Aran (see opposite), but there's no bus service, and failing a lift, you'll face a steep two-hour climb. Once there, the place is appealing enough, with *Hotel Roya* (☎973 63 50 40; ③) providing the least expensive **accommodation**. One of the three local **campsites**, *Solan* (☎973 62 40 68) also has a few cheap rooms to let. **Restaurants** are generally expensive, but best of these is *L'Isard*. **CAPDELLA** is served by a single afternoon bus at 5.15pm from Pobla (weekdays only), and boasts two **hostales**, both of which provide **meals**: *Leo* (☎973 66 31 57; ②) and *Montseny* (☎973 66 30 79; ③).

Within the park itself, camping is forbidden and accommodation is limited to four **mountain refuges** (②), but there are as many more in nearly as impressive alpine areas just outside the park boundaries. Trails or cross-country routes are, not surprisingly, well marked, and you rarely have to walk more than four hours between the huts.

North of the park, the long, narrow **Vall d'Aran** was once a sort of Pyrenean Shangri-La, where summer hay-reapers picturesquely wielded scythes against a backdrop of stone-built villages with pointy-steepled churches, but the giant Baqueira-Beret ski complex, phalanxes of holiday condos and swarms of French trippers have put paid to that. It's now easily the most expensive corner of Catalunya outside of Barcelona, and only worth passing through on your way to or from Aigües Tortes.

Near the top of the valley, **SALARDÚ** will be your most likely target, the meeting point of two walking routes serving the national park. There are several reasonable places to **stay**, among which the *Pension Villa Maladeta*, Pl. Major (☎973 64 60 04; ③) and the *Pension Montaña* c/Major (☎973 64 41 08; ②) can be singled out. **VIELLA**, 9km west and much lower, is the capital of the region and cross point for the two bus routes from Pobla: one (summer only) via Baqueira-Beret and Salardú, the other (11.50am) through the namesake tunnel. It's not a particularly memorable town, but if you're forced by the bus schedules to **stay**, try the *Pension Busquets*, c/Major 9 (☎973 64 02 38; ②), and the *Pension Puig* north of the main drag at c/Camí Reiau 6 (☎973 64 00 31; ②).

Andorra and La Seu

As recently as 1960, **ANDORRA** was virtually cut off from the rest of the world, a semi-autonomous principality conceived late in the thirteenth century to resolve a quarrel between the counts of Foix in France and the bishops of La Seu. There are still no planes or trains, but any quaintness has been banished by Andorra's current role as a drive-in, duty-free supermarket: the main highway through the tiny country is clogged with French and Spanish tourists after the cheap electronic and sports gear, the (not especially) cheap booze in the restaurants and a tankful of discounted petrol. Andorra has no currency of its own, so both francs and pesetas are accepted. The capital, **ANDORRA LA VELLA**, must once have been an attractive town, but it's now a seething mass of cars, touristy restaurants (6-language menus a speciality) and shopfronts. For travellers, the bazaar ethic makes this a foolproof spot to cheaply replace lost or worn-out trekking or skiing items – otherwise you're best off moving on. Fortunately, not all of Andorra is like this, and with the good local bus service it's easy to escape to the resort-villages of Arsinal, Ordino and El Serrat, all close to trailheads for summer trekking.

The twice-daily bus from Barcelona to Andorra (6am & 3pm; 5hr; continues to France) stops in **LA SEU D'URGELL**, 18km south, from where there is also a more frequent local service to Andorra. Named after its imposing twelfth-century cathedral, La Seu is a fairly sleepy place. The **Cathedral** itself, at the end of c/Major, has been restored over the years but retains some graceful interior decoration and an exceptional cloister with droll column capitals; the **Cloister**, along with the adjacent **Museu Diocesano**, has controlled admission (Oct–May Mon–Fri noon–1pm, Sat & Sun 11am–1pm; June–Sept Mon–Sat 10am–1pm & 4–7pm, Sun 10am–1pm). The **tourist office** (summer Mon–Fri 9am–9pm, Sat & Sun 10am–2pm & 4–8pm; winter Mon–Sat 10am–2 & 4–7pm, Sun 10am–2pm) is on Plaça dels Oms near the **Town Hall** and there is another branch at the Parc del Segre complex (Mon–Sat 9am–2pm & 3–7pm, Sun 10am–2pm). The **bus station** is on Avda Joan Garriga Masso, just north of the old quarter. This offers a rather limited number of inexpensive places to **stay**: closest to the terminal are *Hotel Avenida* at Avda Pau Clavis 24 (☎973 35 01 04; ③) and *Habitaciones Europa* at Avda del Valira 5 (☎973 35 18 56; ②). **Eating** is best at *Cal Pacho*, c/del Font.

Núria and beyond

For a beautiful but easy way to see the Pyrenees, look no further than the *Ferrocarril Cremallera* (**rack-and-pinion rail line**) up to the cirque and shrine at **NÚRIA**. After a leisurely start from Ribes de Freser (see below), the tiny two-carriage train lurches up into the mountains, following a river between great crags. Occasionally it stops, the track only inches away from a terrifying drop, a sheer rock face soaring way above you. Once through a final tunnel, the train emerges alongside a small lake (dry in summer), at the other side of which is the one giant building that constitutes Núria. A severe stone structure, it combines church, café, hotel and ski centre all in one; behind it is an official **campsite**.

The *Hotel Vall de Núria* (☎972 73 20 00; ⑥, including breakfast) is expensive in summer, but the price halves in winter; there are also several dorm-style **refuges** around, though they are often full of Spanish groups, in which case you'll have to use the campsite or the **youth hostel** *Pic de l'Aliga* (☎972 73 20 48; ③) at the end of the cable car. You'll need good equipment, even in summer, since it gets cold at night. As for **food**, you can buy hot snacks or breakfast at the *Bar Finestrelles*; there's a self-service place for midday or evening meals; and the hotel dining room is another modestly priced possibility.

Moving on, the privately owned Núria train (4 hourly; 2075ptas return; rail passes not valid) runs all year, from Ribes-Enllaç, via the towns of Ribes de Freser and Queralbs, where there are also places to stay. Trains from Barcelona connect with the Cremallera train at Ribes-Enllaç (Barcelona–Núria return summer/weekends 3225ptas, off-peak 2950ptas). Main-line trains continue to Puigcerdà, right on the **French frontier**, astride the only surviving rail link over the Pyrenees to France. Four trains a day currently leave for La Tour de Carol, 3km over the border, but if you miss them it's easy enough to walk a slightly shorter distance east to Bourg-Madame, the actual border town. **PUIGCERDÀ** is a lot cheaper than anywhere in France, should schedules compel an **overnight stay**: try the *Hostal La Muntanya*, c/Coronel Molera 1 (☎972 88 02 02; ③), or *Pensión Sala*, c/Alfons Primero 17 (☎972 88 01 04; ④). **Restaurant** prices are slightly inflated by the cross-border trade, but good bets include *La Cantonada*, c/Major 46 (beyond the bell tower) and *Bar-Restaurant Kennedy*, c/Espanya 33.

The Costa Brava

The **Costa Brava** (Rugged Coast), stretching from **Blanes** to the French border, with its wooded coves, high cliffs, pretty beaches and deep blue water, was once the most beautiful part of the Spanish coast. Today, although the natural beauty cannot be entirely disguised, it's an almost total disaster, with a density of concrete tourist developments greater even than the Costa del Sol. The southern part, including the monstrous resort of **Lloret de Mar**, is the worst: further up the main road runs inland and coastal development is relatively low-key. Added attractions here are the ancient Greek site of **Empuries**, and Dalí's birthplace **Figueres**.

Buses in the region are almost all operated by the *SARFA* company, with an office in every town. Although they are reasonably efficient in the summer months, it can be frustrating either trying to get to some of the smaller coastal villages or simply attempting to stick to the coast. A car or bike solves all your problems; otherwise it's worth considering using Figueres or Girona as a base for lateral trips to the coast – both are big bus termini. There is also an expensive private **boat service** (*Cruceros*) which runs in the summer from Lloret de Mar to Palamos, calling chiefly at Blanes, Lloret, Tossa, Sant Feliu and Platja d'Aro. It's worth taking at least once, since the rugged coastline makes for an extremely beautiful ride.

Tossa de Mar

Leaving Barcelona, there's really nowhere to tempt you to stop before **TOSSA DE MAR**. Out of season it's a really attractive place to spend some time, and even in high summer, arriving at Tossa by boat is one of the Costa Brava's highlights, the medieval walls and turrets pale and shimmering on the hill above the modern town. The walls themselves still surround an **old quarter**, all cobbled streets and flower boxes, offering terrific views over beach and bay, and there are a couple of good beaches. If you're going to stay, pick up a free map and accommodation lists from the **tourist office** (winter Mon–Fri 10am–1pm & 4–7pm, Sat 10am–1pm; summer Mon–Sat 9am–9pm, Sun 10am–1pm; ☎972 34 01 08), in the same building as the **bus station**, and then head straight down the road in front of you and turn right at the roundabout for "downtown" and beaches. There is cheapish **accommodation** to be had in the maze of tiny streets around the church and below the old city walls – try *Pensión Moré*, c/Sant Elmo 9 (☎972 34 03 39; ②) – and there are a couple of **campsites** within half an hour's walk of the centre. **Eating and drinking** is not cheap in Tossa – this is package-tourist land – but there are some good deals around, as well as endless "Full English Breakfast" bargains.

Palafrugell and Empuries

Tossa is something of an aberration. The coast immediately to the north is thoroughly spoiled, with another immense concentration of cement in the area around La Platja d'Aro. **PALAFRUGELL**, an old town at its liveliest during the morning market, is little to get excited about either, but it has been overlooked by most tourists and hence remains pleasant even if there's little to see. It's also a convenient and relatively cheap place to base yourself if you're aiming for the delightful coastline a few kilometres away: pine-covered slopes and some quiet little coves with scintillatingly turquoise waters. The *Pensión Familiar*, c/Sant Sebastian 23 (☎972 30 00 43; ②), just off the central square, is the cheapest **accommodation** in Palafrugell, very clean and attached to an excellent *bar/comedor*. Such is the popularity of the nearby **beaches** that in summer a virtual shuttle service runs from the **bus station** to Calella and then on to Llafranc every thirty minutes. You might as well get off at Calella – a beautiful fishing port with tiny, crowded beaches – since Llafranc is only a twenty-minute walk away and you can get a return bus from there. Other, less frequent services run to the even lovelier Tamariu (a 90min walk from Calella, with a campsite) and to Begur.

From Palafrugell you're within striking distance of **EMPURIES**, one of the most interesting archeological sites in Spain. It started life in 550 BC as Greek *Emporion* (literally "Trading Station") and for three centuries conducted a vigorous trade throughout the Mediterranean. Later a splendid Roman city with an amphitheatre, fine villas and a broad marketplace grew up above the old Greek town. The Romans were replaced in turn by the Visigoths, who built several basilicas and made it the seat of a bishopric. The **site** (daily 10am–6/8pm; 400ptas) lies behind a sandy bay about 2km north of L'Escala. The remains of the original Greek colony occupy the lower ground, where remains of temples, the town gate, agora and several streets can easily be made out, along with a mass of house foundations (some with mosaics) and the ruins of the Visigoth basilicas. A small **museum** stands above with audiovisuals, and beyond it stretches the vast but only partly excavated Roman town.

There are buses to **L'ESCALA** from Palafrugell (2–3 daily) and Figueres (5 daily), arriving and leaving from the *SARFA* company's office just down the road from the combined tourist office/post office at the top of town. L'Escala usually has **rooms** available but it's an expensive and unattractive place, where you're still a fair walk from the ruins and the good beaches. You could instead **camp** out on the beaches and in the woods around the archeological site, where there's little development apart from the one-star *Ampurias* (June–Sept only, ☎972 77 02 07; ④) and a few villas. Alternatively there's a **youth hostel**, *L'Escala*, c/Les Coves 41 (☎972 77 12 00; ②), with **camping**, right on the beach by the ruins; though this is often full.

Figueres

The northernmost resorts of the Costa Brava are reached via **FIGUERES**, a provincial Catalan town with a lively Rambla and plenty of cheap food and accommodation. The place would pass almost unnoticed, however, were it not for the most visited museum in Spain after the Prado: the **Museu Dalí** (July–Sept daily 9am–7.15pm; 1200ptas; Oct–June Tues–Sun 10.30am–6pm; 1000ptas). Dalí was born in Figueres and, on January 23, 1989, died there; his embalmed body now lies in a glass case inside the museum. Installed by the artist in a building as surreal as the exhibits, the Museu Dalí is a treat, appealing to everyone's innate love of fantasy, absurdity and participation.

To make your way into the middle of town, simply follow the "Museu Dalí" signs from the **train station**. For a comfortable **room** try the *Pensión Bartis*, c/Méndez Núñez 2 (☎972 50 14 73; ②). There's a good all-year **youth hostel** (☎972 50 12 13; ②) at c/Anicet de Pages 2, off the Plaça del Sol; the town **campsite**, *Pous* (☎972 67 54 96), is on the way to the castle. There's a gaggle of cheap tourist **restaurants** in the narrow streets around the Dalí museum and, although a little more expensive, some nice pavement cafés lining the Rambla. The **tourist office** (summer Mon–Sat 8.30am–9pm; winter Mon–Fri 8.30am–3pm) is in front of the post office building by the Plaça del Sol, and dishes out timetables for all onward transport.

Girona

The ancient walled town of **GIRONA** stands on a fortress-like hill, high above the Riu Onyar. It's a fine place, full of interest and oddly devoid of tourists considering that the town's airport serves most of the Costa Brava's resorts. Much of the pleasure of being in Girona is simply wandering around. The streets are narrow and medieval, the churches are cool and fascinating, while above the river high rows of houses lean precipitously on the banks. A combined 800ptas ticket from the tourist office gives entry to all of the following sights.

Centrepoint of the old town is the **Cathedral** (daily 10am–6pm), a mighty Gothic building approached by a magnificent seventeenth-century flight of Baroque steps. Inside it is equally awesome, just one tremendous single-naved vault with a span of 22m, the largest in the world. This emphasis on width and height is a feature of Catalan Gothic with its "hall churches", of which, unsurprisingly, Girona's is the perfect example. Buy a ticket to visit the superb cloisters, the sacristy and the **Museu Capitular** (Tues–Sat 10am–2pm & 4–6pm, Sun 10am–2pm; 400ptas), with an excellent small collection of religious art. If you find the collection interesting, the **Museu d'Art** (Tues–Sat 10am–6/7pm, Sun 10am–2pm; 300ptas) contains further examples; it's housed alongside in the Episcopal Palace.

The well-preserved **Banys Arabs** (summer Mon–Sat 10am–7pm, Sun 10am–2pm; winter Tues–Sat 10am–2pm; 200ptas, free Sun), built by Moorish craftsmen in the thirteenth century, long after the Moors' occupation of Girona had ended, are also well worth a look, as is the surviving portion of the **Jewish quarter**, *El Call*. This was centred on c/de la Força, off which a steep alley leads up to the **Centre Bonastruc Ça Porta** (Mon–Fri 10am–6/8pm, Sun 10am–2pm; 200ptas), a little complex of rooms, staircases and adjoining buildings restored in an attempt to give expression to the cultural and social life of Catalunya's Jews in medieval times.

Practicalities

If you're using **Girona airport**, 13km from the city centre, bear in mind that there's no bus service from the town and a taxi will be pretty expensive; most charters coming from England are linked directly by bus with the Costa Brava. The large **bus station** (behind the **train station**) is well connected with most of Catalunya. From here it's a ten-minute walk up to the river and the Pont de Pedra, just over which is the **tourist office**, on the left at

Rambla de Llibertat 1 (Mon–Fri 8am–8pm, Sat 8am–2pm & 4–8pm, Sun 9am–2pm; ☎972 22 65 75). There's a second information office at the train station (July & Aug only Mon–Fri 9am–2pm).

There's plenty of cheap **accommodation** in Girona, with all the best places to stay found in the old town. The *Pension Vlladomat*, c/Ciutadans 5 (☎972 20 31 76; ③), is centrally located and good value; the *Bellmirall* is also near the cathedral, at c/Bellmirall 3 (☎972 20 40 09; ④). For cheaper rooms, the *Fonda Barnet*, c/Santa Clara 16 (☎972 20 00 03; ②), just to the left before you cross the Pont de Pedra, is not up to the same standard but has some rooms overlooking the river. There's a new **youth hostel**, very central at c/dels Ciutadans 9, off Plaça del Vi (☎972 21 80 03; ②).

There are several good, reasonably priced **restaurants** on c/de la Força, near the cathedral, best value being the *Bar-Restaurant Los Jara* at no. 4. *L'Arcada*, underneath the arches at Rambla de Llibertat 38, is a nice bar/restaurant with a pleasant old-time interior and good breakfast fixings. There are also some good *menús* to be had at the terraces on Plaça Independencia.

VALENCIA AND THE EAST COAST

The area known as the **Levante** (the East) is a bizarre mixture of ancient and modern, of beauty and beastliness. The rich *huerta* of **Valencia** is said to be the most fertile slab of land in Europe, crowded with orange, lemon and peach groves, and with rice fields still irrigated by systems devised by the Moors. Yet **Murcia**, to the south, could hardly provide a more severe contrast, with some of the driest land in Europe, some of it virtually a desert. Despite a few fine beaches, much of the region's **coast** – with the exception of the coastline from Jávea to Altea – is marred by the southbound highway, the industrial development which has sprouted all around it, and of course the heavy overdevelopment of villas and vacation homes.

Valencia

VALENCIA, the third largest city in Spain, may not approach the vitality of Barcelona or the cultural variety of Madrid, but it does at least have a lively night scene, and its clothes and furniture designers are renowned throughout Spain. As a whole the city is sprawling and confused, marred by unthinking modernization, but there are some exquisite corners away from the crowds, a few really fine buildings and a couple of excellent museums. Probably the most attractive features are the relaxed pavement café scene around the Plaza San Jaime and the colourful markets – Central Market, Mercado Colon and Ruzafa Market. The most interesting area for wandering is undoubtedly the mazelike **Barrio del Carmen**, the oldest part of town, roughly between c/de Caballeros and the Río Turia around the Puerta de Serranos. Among Valencia's renowned **fiestas** is *Las Fallasde San José* (March 12–19) when dozens of giant wooden caricatures are displayed and then ceremoniously burned amidst a riot of fireworks that explode on the final night of the festival.

Arrival and information

Valencia's **train station** is reasonably central: Avda Marqués de Sotelo leads from opposite the entrance towards the main Plaza del Ayuntamiento, beyond which lie the old parts of the city. The **bus station** is further out, at Avda Menéndez Pidal 13, on the far bank of the dried-up river from the centre. From here it's easier to take a local bus (#8) into the centre; allow fifteen minutes if you decide to walk. The **Balearic ferry terminal** is connected to a terminus by the Ayuntamiento by bus #19.

The **Plaza del Ayuntamiento** is home to the **post office** as well as the municipal **tourist office** (Mon–Fri 8.30am–2.15pm & 4.15–6.15pm, Sat 9.15am–12.45pm). The regional tourist office is in c/de la Paz (Mon–Fri 10am–2pm & 4–7pm, Sat 10am–2pm), and there's a third inside the train station (Mon–Fri 9am–6.30pm).

Accommodation

Most of the cheaper **places to stay** are very near the train station, in c/Bailén and c/Pelayo, which run parallel to the tracks off c/Játiva. This area, however, is pretty sleazy; you may feel more comfortable spending more in the centre, or much further out near the beach. Budget accommodation can be found at the basic *Hostal Residencial Don Pelayo*, c/Pelayo 7 (☎96 352 11 35; ②); the *Pensión Paris*, c/Salvia 12 (☎96 352 67 66; ②); the excellently sited and very popular *El Rincón*, c/Carda 11, near Plaza del Mercado (☎96 391 60 83; ②); and the nearby *Hospedería del Pilar*, Plaza del Mercad 19 (☎96 391 66 00; ②). More upmarket, the *Hotel Alkázar*, c/Mosén Femades 11 (☎96 352 95 75; ③), is a dependable and well-cared-for town-centre establishment, near the post office, while the *Hotel La Pepica*, Paseo de Neptuno 2, near the beach (☎96 371 41 11; ③), offers good-value rooms with bath, and an excellent restaurant. There are two **youth hostels**, the less attractive halfway to the port on Avda del Puerto 69 (☎96 361 74 59; July & Aug; midnight curfew; ②); the newer one is behind the sports centre on Plaza Hombres del Mar 28 (☎96 355 33 08; ②; no curfew, but silence after 11pm as it's used by early-rising fishermen). The most convenient **campsite** is the all-year *El Salér*, on a good beach, 10km south of the city; a regular bus goes there from the Gran Vía Germanicas on the corner with c/Sueca (hourly 7am–9pm, every 30min 9.30am–7.30pm). The same bus goes to the *El Palmar* site (July & Aug), 16km out, by La Albufera.

The City

The distinctive feature of Valencian architecture is its wealth of elaborate Baroque facades – you'll see them on almost every old building in town, but none so extraordinary or rich as the **Palacio del Marqués de Dos Aguas**, a short walk north of the train station. Hipólito Rovira, who designed its amazing alabaster doorway, died insane in 1740, which should come as no surprise to anyone who's seen it. Inside is the **Museo Nacional de Cerámica** (Mon–Sat 10am–2pm & 4–8pm, Sun 10am–2pm; free) with a vast collection of ceramics from all over Spain. In the same decorative vein is the church of **San Juan de la Cruz** next door. Nearby, in the Plaza Patriarca, is the Neoclassical former university – with its beautiful cloisters and a series of classical concerts in July – and the beautiful Renaissance **Colegio del Patriarca**, whose small **art museum** (daily 11am–1.30pm;100ptas) includes excellent works by El Greco, Morales and Ribalta.

It's not far from here, up c/de la Paz, to the **Plaza Zaragoza** and Valencia's **Cathedral**. The plaza is dominated by two octagonal towers, the florid spire of the church of Santa Catalina and the **Miguelete**, the unfinished bell-tower of the cathedral. You can make the long climb up to its roof (daily 10am–1pm & 4.30–7/8pm; 200ptas) for a fantastic view over the city with its many blue-domed churches. The cathedral's most attractive feature is the lantern above the crossing, its windows glazed with sheets of alabaster; there's also a **museum** (Tues–Sun 10am–8pm; 500ptas) whose exhibits include a gold and agate cup (the Santo Cáliz) said to be the one used by Christ at the Last Supper – the Holy Grail itself.

A side exit leads from the cathedral to the **Plaza de la Virgen**, where you'll find the Archbishop's Palace and the tiny chapel of **Nuestra Señora de los Desamparados**. Here, thousands of candles constantly burn in front of the image of the Virgin, patron of Valencia. Five minutes' walk away, is the enormous **Mercado Central**, a huge iron and glass structure housing one of the biggest markets in Europe, replete with amazing local fruit, fish and vegetables; it closes around 2pm every day. Other museums worth visiting include **IVAM**, the modern art museum on c/Guillém de Castro 118 (Tues–Sun 10/11am–7/8pm; 350ptas), and the **Museo de Bellas Artes** on c/San Pío V (Tues–Sat 10am–2.15pm & 4–5.30pm, Sun 10am–2.15pm; free).

Also worth a look are the town's defences, including the fourteenth-century **Torres de Serranos**, an impressive gateway defending the entrance to the town across the Río Turia. The river itself, diverted after serious flooding in 1956, which damaged much of the old part of the city, is no more than a trickle now, and a huge park has been landscaped in the riverbed; the park has been grassed and planted, and includes a sports stadium, football pitches and even a huge Gulliver to climb on. Near here stands the **Palau de la Música**, a futuristic glass-structure venue for concerts, and the site of the **City of Arts and Sciences**, an ambitious project for an Expo-style group of pavilions including more concert halls, a science museum, and a giant Oceanographic theme park. Currently, only the futuristic-looking Hemisféric is completed, containing a planetarium, laser display and inevitable IMAX theatre (daily 10am–11.30pm; 1000ptas). Ask at the tourist office for further information as work is ongoing, although due to be completed by the end of 1999.

Eating, drinking and nightlife

Food in the **restaurants** in Valencia can be poor, especially considering that this is the home of paella. Decent mid-range possibilities include *Bar Ancoa,* Plaza San Lorenzo at c/Novellos, which does cheap *platos*; *El Generalife* nearby behind the cathedral on Plaza de la Virgen, where the superb fixed menu costs 1300ptas; *La Utielana*, Plaza Picadero de los Aguas, with good roast lamb and *cocido*, though you may have to wait for a table; and *Bar Odín*, Avda Antic Regne de Valencia, for good tapas and pizzas. For bistros and cheap restaurants the best general area is the Barrio del Carmen around c/Caballeros. A traditional place to go for *mejillones* (mussels) is the *Bar Pilar* on the corner of c/Moro Zeit, on Plaza del Espart off c/Caballeros. A good vegetarian option is *La Lluna*, San Ramón 23. For paella, go to either Malvarossa's *La Pepica* on Paseo Neptuno, or – best of all – go out of town on the El Saler bus down the south-coast road to the villages of El Palmar or El Perellonet.

If you don't know where to go, Valencia can seem dead at night: the action is widely dispersed, with many locations across the Turia. To get back late at night you'll have to walk or take a taxi. In summer everyone is in the **bars** lining the polluted Malvarrosa Beach, including *Genaro* and *Tropical*, large bar/discos on c/Eugenio Vines (the beach road). To get there, take bus #1, #2 from the bus station or #19 – the last from Plaza del Ayuntamiento. Back in town, the youngest and loudest bars are on c/Bailén and c/Pelayo beside the train station. The best of the **nightlife**, though, is around the central Barrio del Carmen (c/Caballeros and c/Quart); *Fox Congo* and *Johnny Mardcas* on c/Caballeros 35 and 39 are fashionable late-night bars. Another area is above the Gran Vía de Fernando el Católico, along c/Juan Llorens and c/Calixto, where the *Café Carioca* and *Café La Havana*, at c/Juan Llorens 52 and 41, are currently in favour. The new university area, around Avda Blasco Ibáñez, is also popular: try the *Metro*; *El Asesino* or *Hipódromo* for Salsa, or the bars on Plaza Xuquer, just off Blasco Ibáñez. A more upmarket zone is the Plaza Cánovas del Castillo and the side streets off it, full of *pubs* (music bars) where people go to see and be seen. Most **gay bars**, like *Dakota* or *Viktor's*, are around or in the c/Quart. Many of the **discos** are in the university area – they include *Woody* at Menéndez y Pelayo 25 and the perennially popular *Warthol*, Blasco Ibáñez 111. For more hard-core club music, the area around the train station is best – *Gon* on c/Cadiz has a young, local crowd. For more details about **what's on**, buy one of the two weekly listings guides, *Qué y Dónde* and *Turia*.

Listings

Airlines Iberia and Aviaco, c/de la Paz 14 (☎96 351 97 37); British Airways, c/Moratin 14 (☎96 351 22 84).

Airport Manises, 12km away; airbus to and from bus station every 30min; enquiries ☎96 159 85 15.

Balearic ferries Information and tickets from Transmediterránea, Avda Manuel Soto 15 (☎96 367 07 59), or from any of the half-dozen travel agents on Plaza del Ayuntamiento.

Car rental Cheapest is probably Cuñat Car Hire, c/Burriana 51 (☎96 374 85 61). Otherwise, there's Avis at c/Isabel la Católica 17 (☎96 351 07 34); Hertz at c/Segorbe 7 (☎96 341 50 36); and Atesa at Avda del Cid 64 (☎96 379 91 08).

Consulates USA, c/Paz 6 (☎96 351 69 73); UK Honorary Consul (☎96 352 07 10).

Exchange Main branches of most banks are around the Plaza del Ayuntamiento or along c/Játiva 24. Outside banking hours, try: Caja de Ahorros, c/Játiva 14, to the left as you come out of the train station; or Nuevo Centro, near the bus station (both Mon–Sat 9am–8pm). The División Internacional, at Banco de Valencia, c/Colon 20, currently charges the lowest commission.

Hospitals General hospital on Avda Cid, at the Tres Cruces junction (☎96 386 29 00).

Left luggage Self-store lockers at RENFE; 24hr access.

Police Headquarters at Gran Vía Ramón y Cajal 40 (☎96 352 34 43).

Post office Plaza del Ayuntamiento 24 (Mon–Sat 9am–9pm & Sun am).
Telephones Pasaje Rex 7, off Avda M. de Sotelo (Mon–Fri 9am–2.30pm & 4–8.30pm, Sat 9am–2pm).
Taxis ☎96 370 33 33.

The Costa Blanca

South of Valencia stretches the **Costa Blanca**, a long strip of country with, between Gandía and Benidorm, some of the best beaches on this coast. Much of it, though, suffers from the worst excesses of package tourism and in the summer it's hard to get a room anywhere – in August virtually impossible. Campers have it somewhat easier – there are hundreds of camp-sites – but driving can be a nightmare unless you stick to the dull highway. **Gandía** is the first of the big resorts, and one of the best bets for a room, since the quiet and provincial old town lies a few kilometres inland. Oliva, 8km south, is a much lower-key development. Again the village is set back from the coast and although the main road charges through its centre, it's relatively unspoiled and there's a number of *hostales* and *fondas*.

DENIA is a far bigger place, a sizeable town even without its summer visitors, and less appealing. You might though be tempted to take the daily **boat to Palma, Mallorca** or **Ibiza**. A rattling narrow-gauge rail line (FEVE) runs hourly down the coast from Alicante. Beneath the wooded capes beyond, bypassed by the main road, stretch probably the most beautiful beaches on this coastline, centred on Javea – but you'll need a car to get to any of them, and even if you have a vehicle there's barely a cheap room to be found.

Back on the main road again, **ALTEA** is set on a small hill overlooking this whole stretch of coastline. Restrained tourist development is centred on the seafront, and being so close to Benidorm it does receive some overspill. In character, however, it's a world apart. The old village up the hill is picturesquely attractive with its white houses, blue-domed church and pro-fuse blossoms.

Beyond Altea there's nothing between you and the crowded beaches at **BENIDORM**. If you want hordes of British and Scandinavian sunseekers, scores of "English" pubs, at least seventy discos and bacon and eggs for breakfast, this is the place to come. The beach – nearly 6km of it, regularly topped up with imported Moroccan sand – is undeniably impressive, backed by a Manhattan skyline. Surprisingly, except in August, you can usu-ally find a room in Benidorm, though it takes a lot of walking. The cheaper places are all near the centre and away from the sea, but out of season many of the giant hotels and apartment buildings slash their prices dramatically. Check with the **tourist office** (Mon–Sat 10am–2pm & 4/5–7/9pm; ☎96 585 32 24), at the bottom of Avda Martínez Alejos, near the old village.

Alicante

Locals describe **ALICANTE** as *la millor terra del mond* and while that's a gross exaggeration it is at least a living city, thoroughly Spanish, and a definite relief after some of the places you may have been passing through. There are good beaches nearby, too, a lively nightlife in sea-son and plenty of cheap places to stay and to eat. Wide esplanades such as the Rambla de Méndez Núñez and Avda Alfonso Sabio give the town an elegant air, and around the Plaza de Luceros and along the seafront *paseo* you can relax in style at terrace cafés – paying a bit extra for the palm tree setting, of course. The most interesting area is around the Ayuntamiento, where, among the bustle of small-scale commerce, you'll see plenty of evi-dence of Alicante's large Algerian community – the links with Algeria have always been strong, and boats depart from here for Oran twice a week.

The rambling **Castillo de Santa Bárbara** on the bare rock behind the town beach is Alicante's only real "sight" – with a tremendous view from the top. It's best approached from the seaward side where a lift shaft has been cut straight up through the hill to get you to the top; the lift is directly opposite Meeting Point 5 on the other side of the road from Playa Postiguet. For the best local **beaches** head for San Juan de Alicante, 6km out, reached either by half-hourly bus from the Plaza del Mar or the FEVE rail line. Still better, take a trip to the

island of Tabarca to the south – boats leave from Puerto on the Explanada de España daily in summer, weather permitting.

Practicalities

The main **train station** is on Avda Salamanca, but trains on the private FEVE line to Benidorm and Denia leave from the small station at the far end of the Playa del Postiguet. The **bus station** for local and international services is in c/Portugal. Tickets and information for the Denia or Valencia services are available from any travel agent in the harbour area. The **airport**, 12km west, is connected to the bus station by bus #C6 which stops in town along the way. The very helpful **tourist office** is on Explanada de España (Mon–Sat 10am–7/8pm; ☎96 520 02 43). There are also information desks at the bus station (closed weekends) and at the airport.

Except in August you should have little problem finding a **room**, with the bulk of the possibilities concentrated at the lower end of the old town, above the Explanada de España and around the Plaza Gabriel – especially on c/San Fernando, c/San Francisco, c/Jorge Juan and c/Castaño. Places to try include the beautiful *Les Monges*, c/Las Monjas 2 (☎96 521 50 46; ②), the *Mexico* at c/General Primo de Rivera 10 (☎96 520 93 07; ②), which has a kitchen, and the no-frills *La Milagrosa*, c/Villavieja 8 (☎96 521 69 18; ②). There are cheaper places on c/San Francisco, but they are all pretty seedy and probably not advisable for lone women. There's a **youth hostel**, 2km west of the centre on Avda Orihuela 59 (☎96 511 30 44; ①), and several **campsites**; one in the Albufereta to the north, connected by FEVE and bus #D, and one at La Marina, south of town in woods on a good beach.

Cheap **restaurants** are clustered around the Ayuntamiento, including a couple of places where you can eat couscous on c/Miquel Saler. Over on the other side of town c/San Francisco, leading off a square near the bottom end of the Rambla, has a group of cheap restaurants with seats outside. For tapas try the *Taberna Castellana* on c/Loaces, on the other side of Avda Dr Gadea. For **bars** and the best **nightlife**, head into the Barrio Santa Cruz, whose narrow streets lie roughly between the cathedral, Plaza Carmen and Plaza San Cristóbal. At night *El Barrio*, as it's called, is avoided by many of the locals, but it's really not too rough, and there are so many bars here that you can easily steer clear of the questionable places. For **dancing**, try *Bugati* on c/San Fernando or the new Puerto area, where *Maskarón* is one of a number of bars/clubs.

THE BALEARIC ISLANDS

The four chief **Balearic islands** – Ibiza, Formentera, Mallorca and Menorca – maintain a character distinct from the mainland and from each other. **Ibiza**, firmly established among Europe's trendiest resorts, has an intense, outrageous streetlife and a floating summer population that seems to include every club-going Spaniard from Sevilla to Barcelona. It can be fun, if this sounds like your idea of island activity, and above all if you're gay – Ibiza is a very tolerant place. **Formentera**, small and a little desolate, is something of a beach-annexe to Ibiza, though it struggles to present its own alternative image of reclusive artists and "in the know" tourists. **Mallorca**, the largest and best-known Balearic, also battles with its image, popularly reckoned as little more than sun, booze and beach parties. In reality you'll find all the clichés, most of them crammed into the mega-resorts of the Bay of Palma, but there's certainly much else besides: mountains, lively fishing ports, some beautiful coves and the Balearics' one real city, **Palma**. Mallorca is in fact the one island in the group you might come to other than for beaches and nightlife, with scope to explore, walk and travel about. And last, to the east, there is windswept **Menorca** – more conservative in its development, more modest in its clientele and, after the others, a little dull.

Ferries from mainland Spain (and Marseille) are severely overpriced considering the distances involved; likewise, monopolies keep rates high for inter-island ferries, and for journeys like Ibiza–Mallorca or even Mallorca–Menorca it can be cheaper to fly. The catch here is that in mid-season flights are often booked out: the solution is to get up before dawn, head for the airport and get yourself on a waiting list for the first flight.

Expense and overdemand can be crippling in other areas too. As "holiday islands", each with a buoyant international tourist trade, the Balearics charge considerably above mainland prices for **rooms** – which from mid-June to mid-September are in very short supply. If you go at these times, and you're not into camping, it's sensible to try to fix up some kind of reservation in advance. Something you may want to do, and which will alleviate accommodation problems to some extent, is to rent transport: **cars** (also in short supply in season) can be driven off and slept in, and a **moped** will get you and a sleeping bag to some tempting and acceptable spots.

Ibiza

IBIZA (Eivissa) is an island of excess. Beautiful and indented with scores of barely accessible cove beaches, it's nevertheless the islanders and their visitors who make it special. However outrageous you may want to be (and outrageousness is the norm), the locals have seen it all before. By day thousands of Nivea-smeared tourists spread themselves across the nudist beaches, preparing for the nightly flounce through bars and clubs. For years it was *the* European hippie escape, but nowadays is as popular with modern youth and sociable gays as with its 1960s denizens, who keep coming back.

Ibiza Town

In physical, as well as atmospheric terms, **IBIZA TOWN** is the most attractive place on the island. Most people stay in rented apartments or small *pensiones* which means fewer hotels to ruin the skyline and no package incursions. Approach by sea and you'll get the full frontal effect of the old town's walls rising like a natural extension of the rocky cliffs which protect the port. Within the walls, the ancient quarter is topped by a sturdy **Cathedral**, whose illuminated clock shines out across the harbour throughout the night.

The capital is a simple enough place to find your way around. From the **ferry terminal**, the old streets of the **Sa Peña** quarter lead straight ahead towards the walls of the ancient city – **D'Alt Vila**. A waterside walk will take you from here – past bars and restaurants which at night give front-row viewing for the fashion display – round to the harbour wall from where the entire bay can be surveyed. Continue past the port and you'll be in the new town, below the old to the west. If you fly in you'll arrive at the **airport** about 6km out; there's a regular bus from here between 7.30am and 10.30pm, or you can take a taxi for around 1400ptas. In the airport there's an efficient **tourist office** (May–Sept daily 10am–midnight) which can provide maps and lists of accommodation as well as details on vehicle rental.

The principal **tourist office** on the harbourfront on Passeig des Moll (June–Sept Mon–Fri 9.30am–1.30pm & 5–7pm, Sat 10.30am–1pm; Oct–May Mon–Fri 9.30am–1.30pm; ☎971 30 19 00) can offer more extensive lists of **hotels and hostales** for the whole island, as well as details of apartments for stays of a week or more – not cheap, but abundant and usually pleasant. Most of the cheaper hotels are in the area around the tourist office. Even if you stay a kilometre or so east of town in Talamanca, or on the other side of the port in Figueretas, you're not that far removed from the action. A couple of starter possibilities are *Hostal Sol y Brisa*, Avda Bartolomeu Vicente Ramón 15 (☎971 31 08 18; ③), near the port in the street parallel to Vara de Rey, which has many others; *Hostal Las Nieves*, c/Juan de Austria 18 (☎971 31 58 22; ②), in the street below Vicente Ramón; and there's a choice of rooms at *Hostal La Marina*, in front of the ferry at the port (☎971 31 01 72; ②), next to other options.

Daylight hours are usually spent on the **beaches** at Las Salinas/Es Cabellet (both a short bus ride away) or the nearer but not as nice Figueretas. At night, before the discos open their doors, the shops stay open until 11pm to provide entertaining window-shopping on the way to supper. Most of the cheaper **places to eat** are in the Sa Peña quarter. One of the best bets is smoky *C'an Costa* at c/Cruz 19; along the road on the corner, *La Victoria*, c/Rimbau 1, is another popular and long-established eatery. Down by the waterside, or up in the walled town, you'll be paying a lot more; *Sam's Hamburger Bar* by the port is popular among the less adventurous (and passing US marines), while *San Juan*, c/Montgri 8, is cheap but surly.

The bulk of the **bars** in which to begin your night out are in the area around the port and c/D'Enmig. There are a few **gay bars** here too (*Bobby's, Teatro, JJ's* and *Movie*), but the most crowded ones are found up by the city walls – *Incognito's* and *Angelo's* are neighbours nestling by the Portal de las Tablas. As for **discos**, even if you haven't heard of *Pacha* or the gay *Amnesia*, you'll certainly be made aware of them during your wanderings round the port in the evening. Each – and many of their younger rivals – employs teams of PR artistes to drum up business; competition is fierce. None of them really get going much before midnight, and the dancing goes on until dawn.

Around the island

Nowhere else can compare with the capital, certainly not the second city, San Antonio Abad, which is a highly avoidable package-resort nightmare. **SANTA EULALIA**, the only other real town, retains a certain charm in its hilltop church looking down over the sprawling old town and modern seafront, while close by the persistent can find a number of relatively empty beaches. The same holds true for most of the rest of the coast – plenty of golden sands but a good deal of effort required to reach them. The one major exception is the northern bay of **Portinatx**, connected by a relatively major road and, despite hotel development, with a number of clean, not overly populated beaches. **Inland** there's little of anything – a few villages and holiday homes that are exceedingly pretty to drive through but offer little if you stop.

There is a good **bus service** between Ibiza town, San Antonio Abad, Santa Eulalia, Portinatx and a few of the larger beaches, but hiring a vehicle will widen your options no end. It should prove particularly useful on Ibiza for finding accommodation – as difficult here as on any of the other islands and even more expensive. You may well be reduced to one of the five **campsites**. Only one of these – *Cala Llonga* (☎971 33 21 18) on the road to Playa d'en Bossa – is at all near the capital; the tourist office can provide details of the others.

Formentera

Just three nautical miles south of Ibiza, **FORMENTERA** (population 4000) is the smallest of the inhabited Balearics and is thoroughly barren, the few crops having to be protected, as on Menorca, against the lashing of winter winds. Most of the island is covered in rosemary, growing wild everywhere, and crawling with thousands of brilliant green lizards. Its income is derived from tourism (especially German and British), taking advantage of some of Spain's longest, whitest and least-crowded beaches. The shortage of fresh water, fortunately, continues to keep away the crowds and for the most part visitors are seeking escape with little in the way of sophistication. It is, however, becoming more popular, and is certainly not the paradise it once was.

The crossing from Ibiza is short, but strong currents ensure that it's slow – between thirty minutes to an hour – and rough. Fares are about 2200ptas (3800ptas on the hydrofoil) and there are usually rival sailings to choose from: check the return times before deciding. Boats dock at the tiny but functional harbour of **LA SABINA**, where the two waterside streets are lined with places offering cars, mopeds or bicycles for rent, interspersed with the odd bar and café. This is the place to get yourself mobile, but if possible phone ahead, certainly if you want a car – try Moto Rent La Sabina (☎971 32 22 75), Moto Rent Pujol (☎971 32 24 88) or Autos Formentera (☎971 32 21 56). Check with the **tourist office** by the harbour if you need help with this, or with island accommodation (see below). The capital, **SAN FRANCISCO JAVIER**, is just a couple of kilometres away, easily reached on foot or by local bus or taxi. As well as the whitewashed fortified church – now stripped of its defensive cannon – this metropolis has several restaurants and cafés, at least three banks, four bars, a hotel, supermarkets, a pharmacist, a doctor and a *Telefónica* for international calls. An open-air market adds a touch of interest.

Formentera's main road continues from San Francisco to the island's easternmost point at La Mola. Along it, or just off it, are concentrated almost all of the island's habitation and most of the beaches. The next largest town, **SAN FERNANDO** – with a bar, a church and a *hostal* or two – serves the beach of Es Pujols where the package-tour industry, such as it is, is concentrated. Despite relative crowding, it's a beautiful coast with clear water and pure white sand dunes backed by low pines. **Playa Mitjorn**, on the south side of this narrow stretch of the island, is an enormous stretch of sand broken only by the occasional bar or hotel. Formentera's strict regulations on new building mean that this area will remain relatively undeveloped: rather soulless, but definitely the place to head for total isolation, and the main area for nude sunbathing.

Practicalities

Most people treat Formentera as a day-trip from Ibiza, and if you want to be one of the few who **stay** you may have difficulty finding anywhere not given over entirely to agency reservations. Among the better deals are *Hostal La Sabina* (☎971 32 22 79; ③ with breakfast), just outside La Sabina; *Casa Rafal* in San Francisco Javier (☎971 32 22 05; ③ with breakfast); *Hostal Pepe* (☎971 32 80 33; ②) in San Fernando; *Hostal Bar Los Rosales* (☎971 32 81 23; ⑤) and *Tahiti* (☎971 32 81 22; ③ with breakfast) on Playa Pujols; and *Hostal Sol y Mar* (☎971 32 81 80; ⑤) on Playa Mitjorn. Although there's no official **campsite**, finding a secluded spot should not prove too difficult. There's a basic bus service from La Sabina but journeys rarely keep to timetables, and they connect only the towns, leaving you long, hot walks to the beaches. **Taxis** are cheap with ranks at La Sabina, San Francisco and Es Pujols.

There aren't many cheap places to eat on the island. All the *hostales* mentioned above serve **food** – particularly good value at *Casa Rafal* – or you can get your own supplies from the market and supermarket in San Francisco. Es Pujols has the most restaurants; generally speaking, though, **beach bars** serve better food.

Mallorca

MALLORCA, perhaps more than anywhere in Spain, has a split identity. So much so, in fact, that there's a long-standing joke here about a fifth Balearic island, *Majorca*, a popular sort of place that pulls in an estimated three million tourists a year. There are sections of coast where high-rise hotels and shopping centres are continuous, wedged beside and upon one another and broken only by a dual carriageway down to more of the same. But the spread of development, even after 25 years, is surprisingly limited: "Majorca" occupies only the Bay of Palma, a forty-kilometre strip flanking the island capital. Beyond, to the north and east, things are very different. Not only are there good cove beaches, but there's a really startling variety and physical beauty to the land itself, which makes the island many people's favourite in the group.

Palma

You may arrive by boat from Menorca at Puerto de Alcúdia in the north of the island, but the odds are you'll find yourself in **PALMA DE MALLORCA**, the capital and the only real "city" in the Balearics. Palma is in some ways like a mainland Spanish city – lively, solid and industrious – though it is immediately set apart by its insular, Mediterranean aura. The port is by far the largest in the Balearics, the evening *paseo* the most ingrained, and, in the evenings at least, you feel the city has only passing relevance to the tourist enclaves around its bay. Arriving by sea, it is also beautiful and impressive, with the grand limestone bulk of the cathedral towering above the old town and the remnants of medieval walls.

The **ferry port** is some 3.5km west of Palma, connected to the centre by the buses #1, #3 and #21; Palma **airport**, 7km east of the city, is served by bus #17 (every 20min) to the Plaza de España. Finding your way around is fairly straightforward once you're in the centre. Around the **Cathedral** is the **Portela quarter**, "Old" Palma, a cluster of alleyways and lanes that become more spacious and ordered as you move towards the zigzag of avenues built beside or in place of the city walls. Cutting up from the sea, beside the cathedral, is **Paseo Borne**, garden promenade as well as boulevard, and way up the hill to the northeast lies the **Plaza Mayor**, target for most of the day-tripping tourists.

There are hundreds of *pensiones* and hotels, and your first move in the summer should be to pick up the official lists of these from the **tourist office** at Plaça de la Reina 2 (daily 9am–2.30pm & 3–8pm; ☎971 71 22 16). They can also supply various maps, bus schedules and leaflets, and, if you can afford full hotel prices, will try to book you a **room**. Best initial areas to look for yourself are around the Paseo Majorca, on c/Apuntadores or c/San Felio running west from Paseo Borne (cheaper), and on c/San Jaime at the top of the Paseo Borne (mid-range). Specific recommendations are probably futile in summer, but some to try are *Hostal Borne*, c/San Jaime 3 (☎971 71 29 42; ⑤) with breakfast), very popular, with a court-yard café; *Hostal Ritzi*, c/Apuntadores 6 (☎971 71 46 10; ②); and *Hostal Valencia*, c/Santa Ramón y Cajal 21 (☎971 73 31 47; ③), between the waterfront and the Plaza Gomilla and perhaps the best value. There's also a **youth hostel** at c/Costa Brava 13 in El Arenal (☎971 26 08 92; ②), but it's well out of town and invariably booked en masse by school groups; take bus #15 from Plaza de España.

Eating in Palma can be cheaper than anywhere else in the Balearics. Some of the least expensive places are on or near c/Apuntadores at the lower end of Paseo Borne – *La Zamorana* is a good choice here. Elsewhere, there are varied *bocadillos* at *Diplomatic* on Palau Reial and at the friendly *Es Parlament* in c/Conquistador 11. If you want really low-price tapas try *Meriendas Neska*, c/de la Riera opposite the Teatro Principal. Surprisingly, the restaurants aimed at tourists along Avda Antoni Mauri, at the bottom of Paseo Borne, often have extremely good-value *menús* too: try the *Iska*, or the *Cafetería El Rey* on Avda Rey Jaime III, more or less opposite the tourist office. Good fish dishes can be found at the *Caballito de Mar* on Paseo Sagrada 5 and at the *Mediterraneo 1930* on Paseo Maritimo 33.

Most **nightlife** takes place at Terreno along the hotel mile of Avda Joan Miró. This is not very promising, and can be ludicrously expensive, but there's a fair selection of **discos** – both straight and gay – amid the souvenir shops and hamburger bars. Many of these are free to get in, though they make up for it behind the bar.

Around the island

When you feel you've exhausted the city's possibilities move across to Sóller/Deyá, Puerto Pollensa, Puerto de Alcúdia or one of the small resorts around Porto Cristo on the southeast coast. **Accommodation** is reasonable at each of these towns, though in July or August it'll be almost impossible to find. **Camping** is an alternative but not particularly provided for – there's only one "official" campsite (at Platja Brava) and a scattering of private ones regis-tered with the Palma tourist office. You can survive by discreet use of a tent at many of the island's best beaches: pick a spot near a hotel and, again discreetly, make use of the outside showers they generally provide for guests.

Mallorca's **bus service** is reasonably good and there are even a couple of **train lines** – one, a beautiful ride up through the mountains from Palma to Sóller, is an attraction in itself. Transport of your own, though, is a strong advantage – the Palma tourist office can again advise on rental.

Menorca

Second largest of the Balearics, **MENORCA** is littered with stone reminders of its prehistoric past: rock mounds known as *talayots*, megalithic *taulas* (huge stones topped with another to form a T, around 4m high) and *navetas*, stone slab constructions shaped like an inverted loaf tin. These, and the incessant wind, are the island's most characteristic features. There's not much in the way of excitement, but if you're looking for peace and for some beautiful, rela-tively isolated beaches, Menorca is probably your best Balearic bet.

The island is boomerang shaped, stretching from Mahón in the east to the smaller, pretty port of Ciudadela in the west. **Bus routes** are limited, adhering mostly to the main central road between these two, occasionally branching off to the major coastal towns. You'll need your own vehicle to get to any of the more attractive beaches. There are one or two points to remember, though. To reach any of the emptier sands you'll probably have to drive down a track fit only for four-wheel drive – and the wind, which can be very helpful when it's blowing behind you, is distinctly uncomfortable if you're trying to ride into it on a moped. Bear in mind too that petrol stations are widely scattered. After 10pm and on Sundays and fiestas only a few pumps are open; take note of the rota posted outside and keep a full tank.

Accommodation is at a premium, with little of anything outside the bigger coastal towns. Once you find something reasonable, stay there. There's just one fairly pricey **campsite**, at Cala Santa Galdana on the coast south of Ferrerías.

Mahón

If you arrive by ferry from Barcelona or Palma you'll sail into the vast natural harbour of **MAHÓN** (Maó), the island capital. (The airport, 5km out, is served only by taxi.) It's a respectable, almost dull little town: the people are restrained and polite, and the architecture is a strange hybrid of classical Georgian bay-windowed town houses and tall, gloomy Spanish apartment buildings shading the narrow streets. Four adjacent squares form a hub close to the docks. The **Plaza España** is reached by a twisting flight of steps from the pier and offers great views right across the port and bay; there's a fish market here in the early mornings. Immediately behind is the **Plaza Carmen**, with a simple Carmelite church whose cloisters have been adapted to house a small museum. Wander on from here up c/Virgen del Carmen and take any of the streets to the left to reach one of the oldest and most atmospheric parts of town, overlooking the port from on high. In the other direction from Plaza España lie the **Plaza de la Conquista**, with the town's main church, and the Plaza de la Constitución.

Mahón's main square is actually the **Plaza Explanada**, some way above all these along c/Hanover and c/Dr Orfila. The main **tourist office** (Mon–Fri 9am–8pm, Sat 9.30am–1pm; ☎971 36 37 90) is here and it's also home to a bunch of overfed pigeons and a military barracks. Otherwise the only excitement is on Sunday, when crowds converge on its bars and ice cream parlours, and street entertainers play to the strolling multitudes. The **port area** is considerably more interesting, and you can walk the entire length of the quayside from the *Xoriguer* gin distillery (free samples in the shop) to the suburb of Villacarlos, passing through Cala Figuera and Castelfons – a relaxed stroll past any number of small restaurants and bars.

Mahón is the best bet for **accommodation** on the island, and those possibilities that exist are all fairly central. The best place to start looking is around Plaza Reial: try the American/Scottish-owned *Hostal Orsi* at 19 c/Infanta (☎971 36 47 51; ③) or *Hostal La Isla* at c/Santa Catalina 4 (☎971 36 64 92; ③). Mahón has a place in culinary history as the birthplace of mayonnaise (*mahonesa*), and you should have no problem finding somewhere to **eat**. In the Plaza Bastión there are two friendly bar/restaurants serving basic fare at reasonable prices. *Alfabrega*, just below here at c/San Jerónimo 31, is also very reasonably priced, as is the basic place known simply as *Comidas Económicas* at c/Rosario 27. Other than these, the majority of restaurants are down by the port, where expensive French cuisine, local tapas, good seafood and the standard steak and french fries are all available.

travel details

Trains

Madrid to: Algeciras (1 daily; 11hr); Alicante (7 daily; 4hr); Almería (1–2 daily; 6hr 45min); Avila (17 daily; 2hr); Barcelona (10 daily; 7–8hr); Bilbao (2 daily; 6–8hr); Burgos (7 daily; 3–4hr); Cáceres (5 daily; 4–4hr 30min); Cádiz (2 daily; 5–7hr); Córdoba (15 daily; 1hr 40min–3hr); Girona (2 daily; 8hr 30min–10hr 30min); Granada (2 daily; 6–9hr); Jaca (1 daily; 7hr); Lisbon (1 daily; 10hr); León (8 daily; 4–6hr); Málaga (11 daily; 4hr 30min–6hr 50min); Mérida (6 daily; 4–7hr); Oviedo (4 daily; 6hr); Pamplona (2 daily; 5–6hr); Paris (1 daily; 12hr

30min); Salamanca (4 daily; 3hr 30min); San Sebastián (4 daily; 6–8hr 30min); Santander (3 daily; 5hr 30min–9hr); Santiago (2 daily; 8hr 30min); Segovia (9 daily; 2hr); Sevilla (19 daily; 2hr 30min–3hr 30min); Valencia (8 daily; 4hr); Vigo (2 daily; 8–11hr); Zaragoza (12 daily; 3–4hr).

Algeciras to: Córdoba (5 daily; 4–5hr); Granada (4 daily; 4hr); Málaga (3 daily; 3–4hr); Ronda (3 daily; 1hr); Sevilla (3 daily; 5hr).

Barcelona to: Bilbao (2 daily; 9–10hr 30min); Figueres (hourly; 1hr 30min–2hr); Geneva (3 daily; 9–12hr); Girona (hourly; 1hr 30min); Lleida (15 daily;

2hr 30min); Milan (1 daily; 12hr); Paris (7 daily; 12–15hr); Puigcerdà (6 daily; 3hr); Valencia (7 daily; 3–4 hr); Zaragoza (15 daily; 3hr 30min–6hr).

Bilbao to: Barcelona (3 daily; 9hr–10hr 30min); Madrid (2 daily; 6–9hr); San Sebastián (every 30min; 2hr 30min); Santander (4 daily; 2hr).

Burgos to: Bilbao (5 daily; 3–4hr); Irún (10 daily; 3hr 30min–4hr); Madrid (7 daily; 3–4hr); San Sebastián (7 daily; 3–4hr).

Córdoba to: Madrid (22 daily; 1hr 40min–3hr); Málaga (12 daily; 2–3hr); Sevilla (22 daily; 1hr–1hr 30min).

Granada to: Alicante (2 daily; 8hr–11hr 30min); Madrid (4 daily; 6–9hr); Ronda (3 daily; 3hr); Valencia (2 daily; 8hr 30min).

León to: Avila (2 daily; 2hr 30min); Barcelona (4 daily; 9hr 30min–10hr 30min); Burgos (6 daily; 2–3hr); Madrid (8 daily; 4–6hr); Oviedo (6 daily; 2hr–2hr 30min); Salamanca (6 daily; 3–5hr); Santiago (2 daily; 5hr 30min–7hr).

Málaga to: Córdoba (10 daily; 2hr 30min–3hr 30min); Granada (4 daily; 3hr); Madrid (6 daily; 4–6hr); Ronda (3 daily; 2hr); Sevilla (2 daily; 3hr).

Salamanca to: Ávila (3 daily; 2hr 30min); Burgos (2hr 30min–4hr); Madrid (4 daily; 3hr); Valladolid (10 daily; 1hr 30min–2hr).

San Sebastián to: Bilbao (9 daily; 2hr 30min–3hr); Burgos (8 daily; 3–4hr); Madrid (6 daily; 6–9hr); Pamplona (4 daily; 2hr); Salamanca (2 daily; 8hr); Valencia (1 daily; 12hr); Zaragoza (3 daily; 4hr).

Santiago to: La Coruña (15 daily; 1hr); León (2 daily; 7hr); Madrid (2 daily; 8–9hr); Pontevedra (13 daily; 1hr 15min); Vigo (18 daily; 1hr 30min–2hr).

Sevilla to: Cádiz (14 daily; 1hr 30min–2hr); Córdoba (14 daily; 1–2hr); Madrid (12 daily; 2hr 30min–3hr 30min).

Valencia to: Alicante (7 daily; 2hr); Barcelona (8 daily; 4–5hr); Madrid (9 daily; 4hr); Zaragoza (3 daily; 5hr).

Zaragoza to: Barcelona (9–11 daily; 3hr 30min–4hr 30min); Canfranc (2 daily; 3hr 30min); Huesca (3 daily; 1hr 15min); Jaca (3 daily; 3hr); Lleida (11 daily; 2hr); Madrid (11 daily; 3hr 30min–4hr 30min).

Buses

Madrid to: Alicante (6 daily; 6hr); Almería (5 daily; 7hr); Ávila (4 daily; 1hr 45min); Barcelona (15 daily; 7hr 30min); Bilbao (11 daily; 4hr 30min); Burgos (11 daily; 3hr); Cáceres (10 daily; 4hr); Cádiz (6 daily; 8hr); Córdoba (6 daily; 4hr 30min); Granada (13 daily; 5hr); Lagós, (1 daily; 12 hr); León (11 daily; 4hr); Lisbon (3 daily; 8hr); Málaga (7 daily; 6hr); Mérida (10 daily; 4hr 30min); Oviedo (11 daily; 5hr);

Pamplona (5 daily; 5hr); Salamanca (14 daily; 2hr 30min–3hr); San Sebastián (8 daily; 6hr 30min); Santander (7 daily; 6hr); Santiago (2 daily; 9hr); Sevilla (11 daily; 6hr); Toledo (every 30min; 1hr); Trujillo (10 daily; 4–5hr); Valencia (13 daily; 4–5hr); Zamora (9 daily; 3hr 30min); Zaragoza (14 daily; 4hr).

Alicante to: Almería (2 daily; 7hr); Barcelona (7 daily; 8hr); Granada (3 daily; 9hr); Madrid (3 daily; 6hr); Málaga (6 daily; 9hr); Valencia (hourly; 2hr 30min–3hr 30min).

Barcelona to: Alicante (5 daily; 8hr); Andorra (3 daily; 5hr); Girona (5–9 daily; 1hr 30min); Madrid (8 daily; 8hr); Seu d'Urgell (4 daily; 5hr); Tarragona (hourly; 1hr 30min); Valencia (6–8 daily; 4hr 30min); the Vall d'Aran (1 daily; 6hr 30min); Zaragoza (8 daily; 4–5hr).

Burgos to: Bilbao (12 daily; 2hr); León (2 daily; 2hr 30min); Madrid (11 daily; 3hr 30min); Santander (5 daily; 3hr).

Córdoba to: Granada (7 daily; 3hr); Madrid (4 daily; 7hr); Malaga (5 daily; 3hr–3hr 30min); Sevilla (10 daily–2hr 30min).

Figueres to: Barcelona (4–6 daily; 2hr 15min); Cadaqués (3–5 daily; 1hr 15min); L'Escala (6 daily; 45min); Girona (4–6 daily; 1hr); Palafrugell (4 daily; 1hr 30min).

Granada to: Alicante (3 daily; 5hr); Almería (4–6 daily; 2–3hr); Cádiz (2 daily; 6hr); Córdoba (7 daily; 3hr); Madrid (6–9 daily; 6hr); Sevilla (7–9 daily; 4hr 30min); Valencia (3 daily; 7hr).

León to: Madrid (7 daily; 4hr 30min); Oviedo (7 daily; 1hr 30min); Santander (1 daily; 5hr); Valladolid (4 daily; 4hr 30min).

Málaga to: Algeciras (10 daily; 3hr); Córdoba (5 daily; 3hr); Granada (14 daily; 2hr); Osuna (2 daily; 3hr); Ronda (6 daily; 3hr); Sevilla (11 daily; 3hr); Torremolinos (every 30min; 30min).

Oviedo to: León (8 daily; 1hr 30min–2hr); Madrid (7 daily; 5hr).

Salamanca to: Ávila (4 daily; 1hr 30min); León (4–6 daily; 3hr); Madrid (14 daily; 2hr 30min–3hr); Mérida (3 daily; 4hr); Santander (1 daily; 5hr 30min); Sevilla (5 daily; 7hr); Zamora (10–15 daily; 1hr).

San Sebastián to: Bilbao (1–2 hourly; 2hr); Burgos (5 daily; 3hr); Pamplona (13 daily; 2hr)

Santander to: Bilbao (12 daily; 2hr 30min); Burgos (4 daily; 4hr); Madrid (6 daily; 6hr); Oviedo (4 daily; 3hr 30min); Pamplona (2 daily; 3hr).

Santiago to: Bilbao (3 daily; 9hr); Madrid (3 daily; 9hr); Porto (Portugal; 2 daily; 5hr); Vigo (15 daily; 2hr 30min).

Sevilla to: Cádiz (10 daily; 2hr); Córdoba (10 daily; 2hr 30min); Granada (9 daily; 3hr 30min–4hr 30min); Lagós, (1 daily; 9hr); Madrid (5 daily; 8hr).

Valencia to: Alicante (9 daily; 3hr); Barcelona (8–10 daily; 4hr 30min); Cuenca (4 daily; 3hr 30min); Madrid (13 daily; 4–5hr); Sevilla (2 daily; 12hr).

Zaragoza to: Barcelona (8 daily; 4hr); Huesca (9 daily; 1hr); Lleida (5 daily; 3hr); Madrid (12–15 daily; 3hr); Pamplona (6 daily; 2hr).

Ferries

Barcelona to: Ibiza (4–6 weekly; 9hr 30min); Mahón (2–6 weekly; 9hr); Palma (1–2 daily; 8hr 30min).

Bilbao: Portsmouth, Britain (2 weekly; 24hr).

Ibiza to: Formentera (6–9 daily; 1hr); Palma (1–3 weekly; 6hr 30min); Valencia (6 weekly; 7hr).

Palma to: Ibiza (1–2 weekly; 6hr 30min); Mahón (1 weekly; 6hr 30min).

Santander to: Plymouth, Britain (2 weekly; 24hr).

Valencia to: Ibiza (1–6 weekly; 7hr); Palma (6 weekly; 8–9hr).

CHAPTER 28

SWEDEN

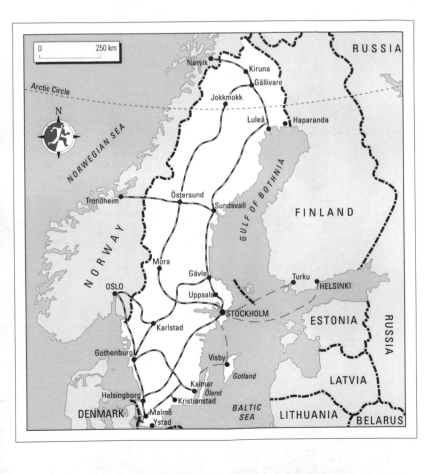

Introduction

Sweden is a large, remote and contented country whose sense of space is perhaps its best feature. Away from the relatively densely populated south, travelling without seeing a soul is not uncommon. The **south and southwest** of the country are flat holiday lands, long-disputed Danish territory and harbouring a host of historic ports – **Gothenburg**, **Helsingborg** and **Malmö**. Off the **southeast** coast, the Baltic islands of **Öland** and **Gotland** are the country's most hyped resorts, and with good reason, supporting a lazy beach-life to match that of the best southern European spots but without the hotel blocks and crowds.

Stockholm, the capital, is of course the country's supreme attraction, a bundle of islands which houses monumental architecture, fine museums and the country's most active culture and nightlife. The two university towns, **Uppsala** and **Lund**, demand a visit too, while, moving northwards, **Gävle**, **Gällivare** and **Kiruna**, still further north, all make justified demands on your time. This area, **central and northern** Sweden, is the country of tourist brochures: great swathes of forest, inexhaustible lakes – around 96,000 – and some of the best wilderness hiking in Europe. Two train routes link it with the south. The eastern run, close to the **Bothnian coast**, passes old wood-built towns and planned new ones, and ferry ports for connections to Finland. In the centre, the trains of the **Inlandsbanan** strike off through lakelands and mountains, clearing reindeer off the track as they go. The routes meet in Sweden's **far north** – home of the *Same*, the oldest indigenous Scandinavian people.

Information and maps

Most towns in Sweden have a **tourist office**, giving out maps, timetables and other bumph, and sometimes booking private rooms, renting bikes and changing money. Some also sell discount cards during the summer which give reductions on local travel, museum entry and other freebies. They're normally open daily in high season, shorter hours during the rest of the summer, and infrequently in winter. The best general **map** of Sweden is the *Hallwag* one.

Money and banks

Swedish **currency** is the *krona* (plural *kronor*), made up of 100 *öre*. It comes in coins of 50öre, 1kr, 5kr and 10kr; and notes of 20kr, 50kr, 100kr, 500kr, 1000kr and 10,000kr. You can change money in **banks** all over

Sweden, which are open Mon–Fri 9.30am–3pm, Thurs also 4–5.30pm. Outside normal banking hours you can change money in exchange offices at airports and ferry terminals, and in post offices (look for the *"Växel"* sign), as well as at Forex exchange offices, which usually offer the best rates – expect to pay a minimum 20kr commission or 15kr per travellers' cheque. Bankomat machines give cash advances and accept most credit cards – check with your bank before you go.

Communications

Post and phones in Sweden are good, and as most people speak at least some English you won't go far wrong in the post or telephone office. **Post offices** open Mon–Fri 9am–6pm, Sat 10am–1pm. You can buy stamps at post offices, and at most newspaper kiosks, tobacconists and hotels.

For international **telephone calls** you can dial direct from public phones. These take 1kr and 5kr coins (minimum charge 2kr), but card phones (*Telefonkort*) are more common; cards are available from newsagents and kiosks. It is also possible to use credit cards in many payphones, marked with the "CCC" sign. All operators speak English (domestic directory enquiries ☎07975; international ☎07977). The international access code is ☎009. To make a collect call to Britain, phone ☎020 795 144.

Getting around

Sweden's internal transport system is quick and efficient and runs through all weathers. Services are often reduced in the winter (especially on northern bus routes), but it's unlikely you'll ever get stranded. In summer, when everyone is on holiday, trains and buses are packed: on long journeys it's a good idea to make reservations. All train, bus and ferry schedules are contained within the giant **Rikstidtabellen** (80kr), or pick up specific route information from train station offices on the computerized information boards.

■ Trains

Swedish State Railways (**SJ** – Statens Järnvägar) have an extensive network, running right into the north of the country above the Arctic Circle and on into Norway. **Tickets** are expensive but happily it's almost never necessary to pay the full rate. Buying a *Reslust* card (150kr, valid for two people for one calendar year) entitles you to a 25-percent discount or 50 percent off red departures (*Röd avgång* on the timetables). It can be used at any time, but you must book and pay for your ticket at least seven days in advance. InterRail and Eurail passes are valid, as is the **ScanRail pass**, which costs £126/$202 (or £94/$150 if you are under 25) for five days' travel in fifteen, £171/$274 (£128/$205) for ten days' travel in a month, or £198/$317 (£149/$238) for 21 consecutive days. This gives you unlimited travel in the four main Scandinavian countries, plus large discounts on many ferry crossings and bus journeys.

To ensure a seat, you might want to make a **reservation**; on some trains – indicated by an "R" or "IC" in the timetable – this costs 30kr; on the high-speed X2000 trains there's a reservation fee of 125kr, payable even if you have a pass. One booklet worth picking up is the quarterly *SJ Tågtider* **timetable** from any train station, an accurate and comprehensive list of the most useful train services in the country, except for those of the Inlandsbanan up to northern Sweden (InterRail valid) and the Pågatågen private rail line in the south (InterRail valid). The Inlandsbanan is only open during the summer and the *Relust* card is not valid.

Buses

Complementing the rail system are **long-distance buses** (*Expressbussar*), operated by Swebus and Svenska Buss between large towns and to and from Stockholm. Services tend to be cheaper and slower than the equivalent train ride. In the north, buses are more frequent since they're used to carry mail to isolated regions. Several companies operate daily services, and fares are broadly similar. You can pick up a comprehensive **timetable** at any Expressbuss terminal, which will normally be adjacent to the train station.

Ferries

Unlike Norway and Finland, there are few domestic **ferry** services in Sweden. The various archipelagos on the southeast coast are served by small ferries, the most comprehensive network being within the Stockholm archipelago, for which you can buy an island-hopping boat pass. The other major link is between the Baltic island of **Gotland** and the mainland at Nynäshamn and Oskarshamn, very popular routes in summer for which you should really book ahead.

Driving and hitching

Driving presents few problems since roads are good and generally reliable. The only real dangers are the reindeer and elk which wander onto roads in the north. To drive, you need a full licence and the vehicle registration document. Speed limits are 110kph on motorways, 90kph and 70kph on other roads, 50kph in built-up areas. It's compulsory to use dipped headlights during daylight hours. Swedish drink-driving laws are among the toughest in Europe and random breath-tests the norm. For **emergency assistance** on the road call ☎020/241000.

Car rental is uniformly expensive, though most hire companies have special weekend tourist rates – from around 500kr. Otherwise, expect to pay upwards of 3000kr a week, with unlimited mileage. Lead-free petrol is widely available at around 8kr per litre. Most petrol stations are self-service, and lots of them have automatic pumps where you fill up using 100kr notes.

Despite the amount of holiday traffic and the number of young Swedes with cars, **hitching** is rarely worth the effort as lifts are so few and far between. Shorter hops are a little easier to find, especially when travelling along the coasts and in the north. If you do try it though, always use a sign.

Accommodation

Finding somewhere cheap to sleep is not the hassle that might be expected in what is an otherwise expensive country, provided you're prepared to do some advance planning. There's an excellent network of youth hostels and campsites, while in the cities private rooms and bed and breakfast places are a common alternative to hotels.

ACCOMMODATION PRICE CODES

Throughout this guide, accommodation is priced on a scale of ① to ⑨, the number indicating the lowest price per night a single person could expect to pay in that establishment in high season. With hostels this is the nightly rate per person; with hotels, the price is arrived at by dividing the cost of the cheapest double room by two. The prices indicated by the codes are as follows:

① under £5 / $8
② £5–10 / $8–16
③ £10–15 / $16–24
④ £15–20 / $24–32
⑤ £20–25 / $32–40
⑥ £25–30 / $40–48
⑦ £30–35 / $48–56
⑧ £35–40 / $56–64
⑨ £40 / $64 and over

■ Hotels and private rooms

Hotels come cheaper than you'd think, especially in Stockholm and the bigger cities during the summer, when many Swedes are out of the country. The rest of the year, rooms at weekends are much cheaper than midweek: on average, for a room with TV and bathroom you can expect to pay from 500kr a double. Nearly all hotels include breakfast in the price, which can be a useful bonus. **Package deals** operating in Malmö, Stockholm and Gothenburg get you a hotel bed for one night, breakfast and the relevant city discount card from around 350–400kr per person. These schemes are generally valid from mid-June to mid-August and at weekends throughout the year. Further details are available in the free booklet *Hotels in Sweden*, available from the National Tourist Board and larger tourist offices, which also lists every hotel in the country. A further option is a **private room**, booked through tourist offices for 90–140kr per person, with access to showers and sometimes a kitchen.

■ Hostels

The biggest choice lies with the country's huge chain of **youth hostels**, operated by the Svenska Turistföreningen (STF), PO Box 25, 10120, Stockholm (☎08/4632100; *www.stfturist.se*). There are 280 hostels in the country, usually with single and double rooms too. Virtually all have well-equipped self-catering kitchens and serve a buffet breakfast. Prices are low (100–150kr); non-HI/YHA members pay an extra 40kr a night. The STF publish a comprehensive handbook for 95kr, available from hostels, tourist offices and large bookshops. Always ring ahead in the summer, and bear in mind that hostels usually close between 10am and 5pm, with curfews around midnight.

■ Campsites and cabins

Practically every town or village has at least one **campsite**, generally of a high standard. Pitching a tent costs around 100kr for two people sharing in July and August, 50kr during the rest of the year, though all costs are considerably higher near the big cities. Most sites are open June to September, some throughout the year, and most are approved and classified by the Swedish Tourist Board; a comprehensive listings book, *Camping Sverige*, is available at larger sites and most Swedish bookshops. The Swedish National Tourist Board also puts out a short free list. Note that at most sites you'll need a camping card (49kr from your first stop) and that camping gas is tricky to get hold of in Sweden. Many campsites also boast **cabins**, usually decked out with bunk beds,

kitchen and equipment but not sheets. They're an excellent alternative to camping for a group or couple; cabins go for around 250–350kr for a four-bedded affair. It's wise to ring ahead to secure one. It's also possible to **camp rough** throughout the country, without asking permission, provided you stay a reasonable distance away from other dwellings.

Food and drink

Eating and drinking is going to take up a large slice of your daily budget in Sweden, though you'll always get good value for money. At its best, Swedish food is excellent, largely meat, fish and potato based, but varied and generally tasty and filling. Specialities include the northern Swedish delicacies – reindeer and elk meat, and wild berries – and herring in many different guises. On a budget, fuel up on breakfast and lunch, both of which offer good-value options.

■ Food

Breakfast (*frukost*) is invariably a help-yourself buffet served in most youth hostels and some restaurants for around 50kr, free in hotels, consisting of juice, cereals, bread, boiled eggs, jams, salami, tea and coffee on even the most limited tables. Something to watch out for is the jug of *filmjölk* next to the ordinary milk, a thicker, sour milk for pouring on cereals. **Coffee** in Sweden is always good, often free after the first cup. **Tea** is weak as a rule but costs around the same – 10–15kr. For **snacks** and lighter meals the choice expands. A *Gatukök* (street kitchen) or *Korvstånd* (hot-dog stall) will serve a selection of hot dogs, burgers, chips and the like for around 30kr. **Burger bars** are spreading like wildfire and a hefty burger and chips meal will set you back a shade over 50kr: the local *Clockburger* is cheaper than *McDonald's* and *Burger King*, but all are generally the source of the cheapest coffee in town. If you can afford a little extra, it's far better to hit the coffee shops (*konditori*), which always display a range of freshly baked pastries and cakes. They're not particularly cheap (coffee and cake for 20–35kr) but are generally good, also serving *smörgåsar*, open **sandwiches** piled high with an elaborate variety of toppings for 30–40kr a time. For the cheapest eating, it's hard to beat the **supermarkets** and **markets**. National chains to watch for are Åhléns and Domus.

Eating in a **restaurant** is cheapest at lunchtime, when most places offer something called the *Dagens Rätt* at 50–60kr, often the only affordable way to sample real Swedish cooking. Served between 11am and 2pm, it consists of a main dish with bread and salad, sometimes a drink, and coffee. Other cheapish places for lunch are **cafeterias**, usually self-service with cheaper snacks and hot meals; large department stores and train stations are good places to look. More expensive but good for a blowout are restaurants and hotels that put out the *Smörgåsbord* at lunchtime for 150–200kr, where you help yourself to unlimited portions of herring, hot and cold meats, eggs, potatoes, salad, cheese and fruit. A variation on the buffet theme is the *Sillbricka*, a specialist buffet for around the same price where the dishes are all based on cured and marinated herring.

If you don't eat the set lunch, meals in restaurants, especially at **dinner** (*middag*), can be very expensive: 150–200kr for a three-course affair, plus 30–50kr for a beer and at least 100kr for a bottle of house plonk. Pizzerias and Chinese restaurants offer better value. Large pizzas cost 40–50kr, usually with free salad and bread, and the price is generally the same at lunch and dinner. Chinese restaurants nearly always offer a set lunch for around 50kr, though they're pricier in the evening. Also widespread are Middle Eastern kebab takeaways and cafés, where you'll get something fairly substantial in pitta bread for around 30kr.

■ Drink

Drinking is notoriously pricey. The cheapest choice is probably **beer**, which costs 30–40kr for 400ml of lager-type drink – a *storstark*. Unless you specify, it will be *starköl*, the strongest Class III beer, or the slightly weaker *mellanöl*; *folköl* is the Class II and cheaper and weaker brew; cheapest (around half the price) is *lättöl*, a Class I concoction that is virtually nonalcoholic. Classes I and II are available in supermarkets; Class III is only on sale in state-licensed liquor stores, where it's around a third of the price you'll pay in a bar. *Pripps* and *Spendrups* are the two main brands. A glass of **wine** in a bar or restaurant costs around 30–40kr. For experimental drinking, **aquavit** is a good bet, served ice-cold in tiny shots and washed down with beer. There are various different "flavours", too, with spices and herbs added.

You'll find **bars** in all towns and cities and most villages, though they're not the focus of the social scene. In Stockholm and the larger cities the move is towards brasserie-type places; elsewhere there are more down-to-earth drinking dens, where the clientele is normally male and drunk. Wherever you drink, you'll find that things close down around 11pm or midnight, though not in Gothenburg and Stockholm, where you can keep drinking into the small hours. The *Systembolaget* (state off-licence) is a deliberately unattractive place to buy booze, and apart from strong beer (12kr for a third-litre) the only bargain is the imported wine at 50kr a bottle. The shops are open Mon–Fri 9am–6pm, the minimum age for being served is 20, and you may need to show ID.

Opening hours and holidays

Shops are open Mon–Fri 9am–6pm, Sat 9am–1/4pm. Some larger department stores stay open until 8/10pm, and open Sun noon–4pm. Banks, offices and shops close on the following days and may close early on the preceding day: Jan 1; Jan 6; Good Friday; Easter Sunday & Monday; May 1; Ascension (around mid-May); Whit Sunday & Monday; Midsummer's Eve & Day; All Saint's Day (the Sat between Oct 31 and Nov 6); Dec 24, 25, 26 & 31.

Emergencies

You're unlikely to encounter too many problems with **crime** in Sweden, and thus will have little need to contact the police. If you do, you'll find them courteous and generally able to speak English. In case of **health problems**, there is no GP system and you should instead go direct to a hospital with your passport, where for 140kr you'll receive treatment and if you have to stay in hospital it will cost you an additional 80kr per day. If you need medicine, take your prescription to a **pharmacist** – *Apotek* in Swedish – which will be open shop hours, although Stockholm has a 24-hour pharmacy. Larger towns operate a rota system of late opening, with the address of the nearest late-opener posted on the door of each pharmacy.

EMERGENCY NUMBERS

All emergencies ☎ 112.

STOCKHOLM AND AROUND

STOCKHOLM comes lauded as Sweden's most beautiful city, and apart from a couple of sticky modern developments and a tangled road junction or two, it lives up to it – it's delightful, not least as a contrast to the apparently endless lakes and forests of the rest of the country. It's also a remarkably disparate capital, one whose tracts of water and range of monumental buildings give it an ageing, lived-in feel and an atmosphere quite at odds with its status as Sweden's most contemporary, forward-looking city.

Built on fourteen small islands, Stockholm was a natural site for the fortifications, erected by one Birger Jarl in 1255, that grew into the current city. In the sixteenth century, the city fell to King Gustav Vasa, a century later becoming the centre of the Swedish trading empire that covered present-day Scandinavia. Following the waning of Swedish power it entered something of a quiet period, only rising to prominence again last century when industrialization sowed the seeds of the Swedish economic miracle.

Arrival and information

By **train**, you arrive at **Central Station**, a cavernous structure on Vasagatan in Norrmalm. All branches of the Tunnelbana, Stockholm's underground system, meet at T-Centralen, the station directly below Central Station. **Cityterminalen**, adjacent, handles all the **bus** services, both domestic and international, including the airport bus. Viking Line **ferries** arrive at **Tegelvikshamnen** in Södermalm, in the south of the city, a thirty-minute walk from the modern centre, or connected by bus to Slussen and then by Tunnelbana to T-Centralen. Birka Cruises services dock in Södermalm, too, just up the quayside at Stadsgården. The Silja Line terminal is in the northeastern reaches of the city, a short walk from Gärdet or Ropsten, from where you can take the Tunnelbana. **Arlanda airport** is 45km north of Stockholm; buses run every fifteen minutes to Cityterminalen (6.30am–11pm; journey time 35–40min; 60kr). The direct rail link to Arlanda is scheduled to open in September 1999, connecting the airport with Central Station in just twenty minutes.

You should be able to pick up a map of the city at most points of arrival, but it's worth making your way to one of the **tourist centres**, which hand out fistfuls of free information and sell decent maps for 15kr. The **main office** (Mon–Fri 8/9am–6pm, Sat & Sun 9am–3/5pm; ☎08/789 24 90; *www.stoinfo.se*) is on Hamngatan in Norrmalm, on the ground floor of *Sverigehuset*, and sells the invaluable **Stockholm Card** (199kr for 24hr, 398kr for 48hr, 498kr for 72hr), which gives unlimited travel on city transport (except on direct buses to the airport or on the connecting night bus to the Nynäshamn ferry terminal), free museum entry, and discounts on boat trips and tours. The office also rents out the digital pocket guide, *Citikey*, for 69kr per day, and stocks free copies of *Stockholm This Week* listing forthcoming events. For **Internet** use, choose from *Internet Café* on the third floor of *Pub* department store, 63 Drottningatan; *Café Access*, Kulturhuset, Sergels torg; *Internet aswellas Coffee*, Tegnergatan 33; and *NK IT-Center*, Hamngatan 18-20.

City transport

The best way to explore Stockholm's initially confusing centre is to **walk** – it takes about 25 minutes to cross central Stockholm on foot – but to reach the more distant sights you'll have to use some form of **transport**. Storstockholms Lokaltrafik (SL) operates a comprehensive system of buses and trains (underground and local) reaching well out of the city centre. The **SL-Center** information office (Mon–Fri 6am–11.15pm, Sat & Sun 7am–11.15pm), inside T-Centralen station at Sergels Torg, doles out timetables and sells a useful transport map (35kr). Quickest of the transport systems is the **Tunnelbana** (T-bana) underground, based on three main lines. **Buses** can be less direct due to the nature of Stockholm's islands and central pedestrianization. **Ferries** also link some of the central islands: Djurgården is connected with Nybroplan in Norrmalm in summer, and Skeppsbron in Gamla Stan (all year).

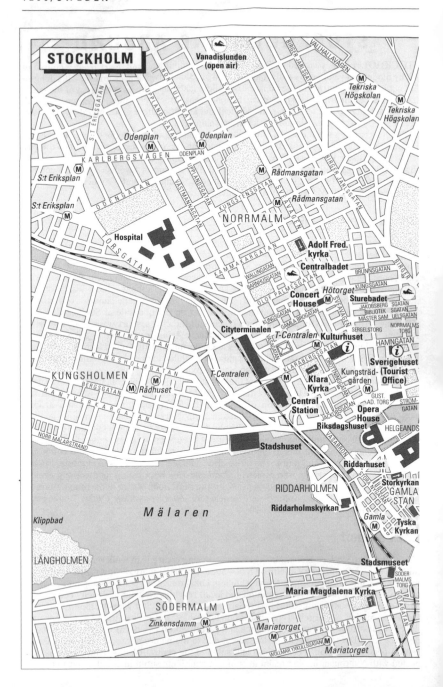

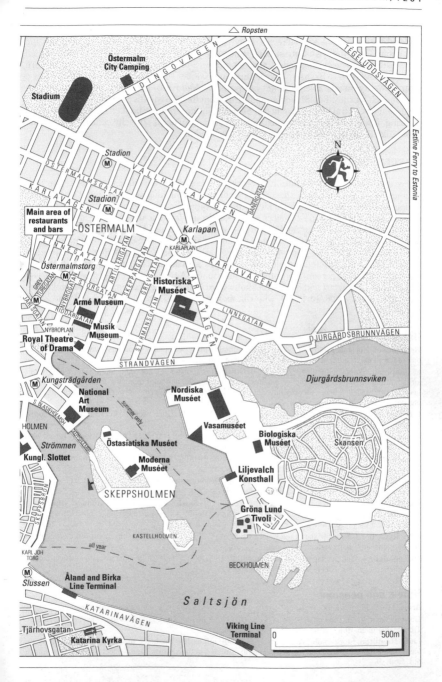

Ferry trips cost 15kr one way, while land transport costs 13kr within one zone, 6.50kr for each additional zone – so you're normally better off investing in a **pass**. Apart from the Stockholm Card, there's a **tourist card** valid for 24 hours (60kr) or 72 hours (120kr), which gives unlimited travel on public transport within Stockholm county. The three-day card includes admission to Skansen, Gröna Lund and Kaknäs Tower. Alternatively, you can buy a strip of twenty transferable SL **ticket coupons** (*Rabbat Kuponger*, 95kr), using two per person for each journey. Buy SL tickets and cards from the tourist office and SL offices inside T-Centralen or Central Station. **Taxis** can be hailed in the street, or booked on ☎08/15 00 00. If you ring, it will cost 25kr for the taxi to get to you; a trip across the city centre costs around 100–120kr (5–10 percent less for women at weekends).

Accommodation

There's plenty of **accommodation** in Stockholm, especially for budget travellers, but don't turn up late in summer and expect to get a cheap bed. Booking your first night's accommodation in advance is always a good idea, either through the Sverigehuset tourist centre or by phoning direct. The cheapest choices, on the whole, are found to the north of Cityterminalen, in the streets to the west of Adolf Fredriks Kyrka. There's also **Hotellcentralen**, a booking service on the lower level of Central Station (daily: May & Sept 8am–7pm; June–Aug 7am–9pm; Oct–April 9am–6pm; ☎08/789 24 25), which charges a fee of 40kr per room, 15kr for a youth hostel. Hotellcentralen also brokers special deals, including the Stockholm Package (398kr per person), available mid-June to mid-Aug at weekends, which gets you a hotel room, breakfast and a free Stockholm Card. For **private rooms**, contact Hotelltjänst, Vasagatan 15–17 (☎08/10 44 67), who can fix you up with a double room for around 225kr per person.

Hostels

Brygghuset, Norrtullsgatan 12 (☎08/31 24 24). Situated near Odenplan T-bana this converted brewery is one of the more tranquil in Stockholm. Open June to mid-Sept. ②.

af Chapman, Skeppsholmen (☎08/463 22 66). Official hostel on a ship moored at Skeppsholmen. Without a reservation, the chances of a space in summer are negligible, although queueing from around 7am has been known to yield a bed. Full of facilities, it is now linked to the HI's growing worldwide computer booking system. ③.

City Backpackers, Barnhusgatan 16, Norrmalm (☎08/20 69 20). Curfewless hostel with four-bed rooms. Ten minutes' walk from Central Station. ③.

Columbus Hotell & Vandrarhem, Tjärhovsgatan 11, Södermalm (☎08/644 17 17). A friendly hostel with cheap beds, housed in a former brewery. T-bana Medborgarplatsen. ⑤.

Gustav af Klint, Stadsgårdskajen 153, Södermalm (☎08/640 40 77). Singles, doubles and four-bedded cabins in this floating hotel-hostel, which tends to be very noisy. ⑤.

Hantverkshuset, Skeppsholmen (☎08/86 20 51). Dead-central official hostel, at the foot of the *af Chapman*'s gangplank and better for speculative arrivals. ②.

Långholmen, Kronohäktet, Långholmen (☎08/668 05 10). Stockholm's newest and grandest official hostel, in an old prison on Långholmen island, with ordinary doubles in summer as well as hostel beds. Some rooms have TVs, phones and showers. T-bana to Hornstull and follow the signs. ⑤.

M/S Rygerfjord, Söder Mälarstrand-Kaj 12 (☎08/84 08 30). Homely hostel-ship moored on Södermalm close to Slussen T-bana station. ③.

Zinkensdamm, Zinkens väg 20, Södermalm (☎08/616 81 00). T-bana Zinkensdamm. Huge official hostel with kitchen facilities. Nicely situated by the water. ③.

Hotels and pensions

Anno 1647, Mariagränd 3 (☎08/442 16 80). Near Slussen, a handy location for the old town. ⑨.

Gustav Vasa, Västmannagatan 61 (☎08/34 38 01). Not a bad location, in the northern part of Norrmalm. T-bana Odenplan. ⑨.

Lady Hamilton, Storkyrkobrinken 5 (☎08/23 46 80) and its brother hotel, the **Lord Nelson**, nearby on Vasterlanggatan 22 (☎08/23 23 90), are beautifully situated in the old town, and perfect if you want to splash out. Both ⑨.

Stockholm, Norrmalmstorg 1 (☎08/440 57 60) Very central, situated in the top floor of an office block with fantastic views over the water. T-bana Östermalmstorg or KungstrádgÜrden. ⑨.

Tre smü rum, Högbergsgatan 81 (☎08/641 23 71). T-bana Mariatorget. Six bright modern rooms in the heart of Söder. ④.

Campsites

Ängby. (☎08/37 04 20). West of the city on Lake Mälaren and near the beach. T-bana line #18 or #19 to Ängbyplan, then a 300m walk. Open all year.

Bredäng. (☎08/97 70 71). 10km southwest of the centre and also by Lake Mälaren. Pricey place with a youth hostel and restaurant on site. T-bana line #13 and #15 to Bredäng then a 700m walk. Open April–Oct.

Flaten. (☎08/773 01 00). One-star place 15km southeast of city in a rural setting near a lake. Bus #401 from Slussen. Open May–Sept.

Klubbensborg. (☎08/646 12 55). In a peaceful location on a small peninsula on Lake Mälaren, with a youth hostel, café and bakery on site. T-bana line #13 and #18 to Mälarhojden and then a ten-minute walk. Open June–Sept.

Solvalla City Camping, Sundbybergkopplet (☎08/627 03 80). 8km from the city on a gravel site. Take T-bana to Rissne.

The City

The **Stadhuset**, (which you can only visit on a guided tour: June–Aug 10am, 11am, noon & 2pm; Sept–May 10am & noon; 30kr) at the water's edge near Central Station, and particularly its gently-tapering red-brick **tower** (May–Sept daily 10am–4.30pm), 347-feet-high, give the best fix on the city's layout. The building itself, a flagship of the National Romantic movement in the 1910s and 1920s, draws heavily on Swedish materials and themes, exemplified in the cavernous Blue Room, where the Nobel prize-givings are held, and the Golden Room, where a precis of Swedish history covers the walls in a gilt mosaic.

Gamla Stan

Three islands make up **Gamla Stan** or **Old Stockholm** – Riddarholmen, Staden and Helgeandsholmen – a clutter of seventeenth- and eighteenth-century Renaissance buildings, hairline medieval alleys and tall, dark houses whose intricate doorways still bear the arms of the wealthy merchants who once dwelled within. On Helgeandsholmen, the **Riksdagshuset** is the Swedish parliament building, which can be visited on free guided tours starting from the glassed-in rear (June–Aug Mon–Fri 12.30pm & 2pm). Being Sweden rather than Westminster, the members' seating is arranged in nonadversarial rows by constituency, not by party. In front of the Riksdagshuset, accessible by a set of steps leading down from Norrbro, the **Medeltidsmuseum** (July & Aug Tues–Thurs 11am–6pm, Fri–Mon 11am–4pm; 40kr) is the best city-related historical collection in Stockholm. Ruins of medieval tunnels and walls were discovered during excavations under the parliament building, and they've been incorporated into a walk-through underground exhibition. There are reconstructed houses, models and pictures, boats and street scenes.

Over a second set of bridges is the most distinctive monumental building in Stockholm, the **Kungliga Slottet** (Royal Palace), a beautiful Renaissance successor to the original castle of Stockholm. Finished in 1760, it's a striking achievement, outside sombre, inside a magnificent Baroque and Rococo swirl. The **Apartments** (May–Aug daily 10am–4pm; rest of year Tues–Sun noon–3pm; 50kr) form a relentlessly linear collection of furniture and tapestries; the **Treasury** (May–Aug daily 10am–4pm; rest of year Tues–Sun 12–3pm; 50kr) has ranks of jewel-studded crowns, the oldest that of Karl X (1650). Also worth catching is **Livrustkammaren**, the Royal Armoury, (May–Aug daily 10am–4pm; rest of year Tues–Sun 11am–4pm; 60kr), less to do with weapons than with ceremony – suits of armour, costumes and horse-drawn coaches from the sixteenth century onwards, most notably the stuffed horse and mud-spattered garments of King Gustav II Adolf, who died in the Battle of Lützen in 1632. For those with the energy, the **Gustav III's Antikmuseum** (May–Aug daily 10am–4pm; rest of year Tues–Sun noon–3pm; 50kr) con-

tains parts of the older castle, its ruins underneath the present building and an extensive collection of antique sculptures.

Beyond the palace lies Gamla Stan proper, where the streets suddenly narrow and darken. The first major building is the **Storkyrkan**, a rectangular brick church consecrated in 1306, that is technically Stockholm's cathedral – the monarchs of Sweden are married and crowned here. The Baroque interior is marvellous, with an animated fifteenth-century sculpture of *St George and the Dragon*, and – perhaps more impressive – the royal pews, more like golden billowing thrones, and a monumental black and silver altarpiece. **Stortorget**, Gamla Stan's main square, is handsomely proportioned and crowded with eighteenth-century buildings. The surrounding narrow streets house a succession of arts and craft shops, restaurants and discreet fast-food outlets, clogged by summer buskers and evening strollers. Just off Västerlånggatan, on Tyska Brinken, the **Tyska kyrkan**, or "German Church" (Sat & Sun noon–4pm), which belonged to Stockholm's medieval German merchants, is a copper-topped red-brick church that was also richly fashioned in the Baroque period.

Keep right on as far as the handsome Baroque **Riddarhuset** (Mon–Fri 11.30am–12.30pm; 40kr), in whose Great Hall the Swedish aristocracy met during the seventeenth-century Parliament of the Four Estates. Their coats of arms – around 2500 of them – are splattered across the walls. Take a look downstairs, too, in the Chancery, which stocks heraldic bone china by the shelf-load and racks of fancy signet rings. From here it's a matter of seconds across the bridge onto **Riddarholmen** ("Island of the Knights"), and to **Riddarholms Kyrkan** (May–Aug daily 10am–4pm; Sept Sat & Sun noon–3pm; closed Oct–April; 20kr), originally a Franciscan monastery and long the burial place of Swedish royalty. You'll find the unfortunate Gustav II Adolf in the green marble sarcophagus.

Skeppsholmen

Off Gamla Stan's eastern reaches, but not connected by bridge, the island of **Skeppsholmen** is home to an eclectic clutch of museums. Among them is the **Moderna Muséet** (Tues–Thurs 11am–10pm, Fri–Sun 11am–6pm; 60kr), which houses one of the best collections of modern art in Europe, with work by many of the twentieth century's greatest artists: from Matisse, Picasso, Dalí and Man Ray to Francis Bacon, Warhol and Lichtenstein. A steep climb up the nearby hill, to the northern tip of the island, leads to the **Östasiatiska Muséet** (Tues noon–8pm; Wed–Sun noon–5pm; 40kr), whose Eastern antiquities display incredible craftsmanship – fifth-century Chinese tomb figures, delicate jade amulets, an awesome assembly of sixth-century Buddhas, Indian watercolours and gleaming bronze Krishnas.

By the bridge to the island is the waterfront **National Art Museum** (Tues & Thurs 11am–8pm, Wed & Fri–Sun 11am–5pm; 60kr), another impressive collection of applied art – beds slept in by kings, cabinets used by queens, plates eaten off by nobles, alongside Art Nouveau coffeepots and vases and examples of Swedish furniture design. Upstairs there is a plethora of European sculpture, mesmerizing sixteenth- and seventeenth-century Russian Orthodox icons, and, among a quality selection of paintings, Rembrandt's *Conspiracy of Claudius Civilis*, one of his largest works; there are also minor works by other, later masters, notably Renoir. The gallery explores the development of the Swedish "oppositionists", who were inspired by the French Impressionists; the works of Carl Frederick Hill and Ernst Josephson's *Portrait of a Journalist* are particularly striking.

Norrmalm and Östermalm

Modern Stockholm lies immediately to the north of Gamla Stan. It's split into two distinct sections: the central **Norrmalm** and the classier, residential streets of **Östermalm** to the east – though there's not much apart from a couple of specialist museums to draw you here. On the waterfront, at the foot of Norrbro, is **Gustav Adolfs Torg**, more a traffic island than a square, with the eighteenth-century **Opera House** its proudest and most notable building. It was at a masked ball here in 1792 that King Gustav III was shot by one Captain Ankarström; you'll find Gustav's ball costume, as well as the assassin's pistols and mask, displayed in the palace armoury in Gamla Stan. Gustav's statue marks the centre of the square, where, apart from the views, the only affordable entertainment is to rent a fishing rod and try and land a

fish in the **Strömmen**, which flows through the centre of the city – a right Stockholmers have enjoyed since the seventeenth century.

Just off the square, at Fredsgatan 2, the **Medelhavsmuseet** is devoted to Mediterranean and Near Eastern antiquities (Tues 11am–8pm, Wed–Fri 11am–4pm, Sat & Sun noon–5pm; 50kr), with an enormous display showing just about every aspect of Egyptian life up to the Christian era. The huge Cypriot collections – the largest outside the island itself – depict life through a period spanning 6000 years. North of here Klarabergsgatan leads to the **Klara Kyrka** (Mon–Fri 10am–6pm, Sat 10am–7pm, Sun 8.30am–6pm), typical of Stockholm's hidden churches, hemmed in on all sides and with a light and flowery eighteenth-century painted interior and an impressive golden pulpit. Back towards the water, Norrmalm's eastern boundary is marked by **Kungsträdgården**, the most fashionable and central of the city's numerous parks – once a royal kitchen garden and now Stockholm's main meeting place, especially in summer when there's almost always something going on.

On the opposite side of Norrmalm in Östermalm is the **Historiska Muséet** (Tues–Sun 11am–5pm; open late on Thurs in winter; 60kr). Ground-floor highlights include a Stone Age household and a mass of Viking weapons, coins and boats, while upstairs there's a worthy collection of medieval church art and architecture, evocatively housed in massive vaulted rooms, including some rare reassembled bits of stave churches uncovered on the Baltic island of Gotland. To get there, take the T-bana to Karlaplan.

Djurgården

Djurgården is Stockholm's nearest large expanse of park. A royal hunting ground throughout the sixteenth to eighteenth centuries, it is actually two distinct park areas separated by the water of Djurgårdsbrunnsviken, which freezes over in winter to provide some central skating. You could walk to the park from Central Station, but it's quite a hike: take the bus instead – #44 from Karlaplan or #47 from Nybroplan – or in summer, the ferry from Nybroplan, or year round from Slussen on Skeppsbron.

From the northeast of the park are excellent views from 155-metre-high **Kaknäs TV tower** (daily: May–Aug 9am–10pm; winter 10am–9pm; 25kr), Scandinavia's tallest building. South over Djurgårdsbron are numerous museums. Palatial **Nordiska Museet** (Tues–Sun 10am–9pm; 60kr) is a good attempt to represent Swedish cultural history in an accessible fashion, with a particularly good *Same* section. On the ground floor of the cathedral-like interior is Carl Milles' statue of Gustav Vasa, the sixteenth-century king who drove out the Danes. Close by, the **Vasa Muséet** (daily: mid-June to mid-Aug 9.30am–7pm; rest of year 10am–5pm and until 8pm on Wed; 60kr) is an essential stop, displaying the *Vasa* warship which sank in Stockholm harbour after just twenty minutes of its maiden voyage in 1628. Preserved in mud for over 333 years, the ship was raised along with 12,000 objects in 1961, and now forms the centrepiece of a startling, purpose-built hall on the water's edge. Walkways bring you nose to nose with the cannon hatches and restored decorative relief, exhibition halls display the retrieved bits and pieces, while films and videos explain the social and political life of the period – all with excellent English notes.

Södermalm and Långholmen

It's worth venturing beyond Slussen's traffic interchange for the heights of **Södermalm's** crags, an area largely neglected by most visitors to the city. The perched buildings are vaguely forbidding, but get beyond the speeding main roads skirting the island and a lively and surprisingly green area unfolds – one that's still, at heart, emphatically working-class. By bus, take the #48 or #53 from Tegelbacken, or use the T-bana and get off at either Slussen or Medborgarplatsen (on Götagatan). Walking, you reach the island over a double bridge from Gamla Stan, to the south of which is the rewarding **Stadsmuseet** (Tues–Sun 11am–5pm, Thurs until 9pm in summer and 7pm in winter; 40kr), hidden in a basement courtyard, which houses a set of collections relating to the city's history as a sea port and industrial centre. Nearby, take a look at the **Katarina kyrka**, rebuilt in Renaissance style in the eighteenth century. On this site the victims of the so-called "Stockholm Blood Bath" were buried in 1520,

the betrayed nobility of Sweden who had opposed King Christian II's Danish invasion and were burned as heretics outside the city walls.

Whether you stop in Södermalm or not, the buses and T-bana trains come this way for the island of **Långholmen**, just off its western side. There's a popular **beach** here, which gets packed in the summer, a chance to swim and plenty of shady walks through the island's trees, as well as the city's best **youth hostel**. You don't have to come through Södermalm to reach Långholmen – though if you do, get off the T-bana at Hornstull and follow the signs.

Eating and drinking

For **self-catering**, the *Hötorgshallen* in Hötorget is a cheap and varied indoor market, awash with small cafés and ethnic snacks. The three main areas for decent eating, day or night, are Norrmalm, Gamla Stan and Södermalm. It's most expensive to eat in the old town, but **set lunch** deals make even that affordable. Drinking in **bars** is expensive, though less so in Stockholm, where there's healthy competition, than elsewhere in Sweden. Wherever there's live music you'll pay a cover charge of 30–50kr, as well as 10kr to leave your coat at the cloakroom. There's a fairly fine line between cafés, restaurants and bars in Stockholm, many offering music and entertainment in the evening and food during the day.

Cafés and restaurants

Café Art, Västerlånggatan 60–62, Gamla Stan. A fifteenth-century cellar-café with sandwiches, good coffee and cakes and art for sale.

Café Norr, Central Station. Good substantial food at reasonable prices, with salad and seafood snacks from 50kr.

Collage, Smålandsgatan 2. All-you-can-eat buffet for 35kr plus a disco until late. Cheap drinks until 10pm.

Hard Rock Café, Sveavägen 75, Norrmalm. Loud rock music, hefty burger meals from around 70kr and the obligatory queue.

Hermans, Stora Nygatan 11. Non-earthy vegetarian place; 50kr lunches and 60kr dinners until 7.30pm.

Kaffegillet, Trångsund 4, Gamla Stan. Fourteenth-century cellar-restaurant with traditional Swedish food. Lunches around the 50kr mark.

Lasse i Parken, Högalidsgatan 56, Södermalm. Daytime café housed in an eighteenth-century house with a pleasant garden. T-bana Hornstull.

Lilla Budapest, Götgatan 27, Södermalm. A good stop for weighty Hungarian lunches, and with a bar whose drinks are a few crowns cheaper than most other places.

Lotus, Katrina Bangatan 21, is the hangout of the alternative crowd and always has an intellectual buzz.

Markurells, Vasagatan 26, Norrmalm. Popular and cheap, mainly Swedish menu; lunch 50kr.

Operakällaren, Gustav Adolfs Torg, Norrmalm. Pricey restaurant but with a fabulous daily *smörgåsbord* for 250kr per person. Lunch in the attached *Café Opera* is 100kr.

Ritorno, opposite Vasparken on Odengatten. Serves high quality coffee and cakes in a bohemian atmosphere. Ideal place to spend an afternoon trying to work out which of your fellow customers are celebrities.

Samborombon, Stora Nygatan 28, Gamla Stan. Argentinian restaurant serving steaks with excellent homemade sauce, as well as South American wines.

Slingerbulten, Stora Nygatan 24, Gamla Stan. Traditional Swedish food – good lunches from 55kr.

Soldaten Svejk, Östgötagatan 35, Södermalm. Lively Czech-run joint, popular with students. Cheap (40kr) evening meals Mon & Tues.

Teatercaféet, Stadsteater, Sergels Torg, Norrmalm. Set lunch for 45–50kr Mon–Fri, always including a vegetarian dish, and a reasonably priced à la carte menu.

Bars, brasseries and pubs

Brasserie Vau de Ville, Hamngatan 17, Kungsträdgården, Norrmalm. Popular brasserie with snacks and drinks, as well as a regular menu.

Fenix, Götgatan 40, Södermalm. Trendy and lively American-style bar. Good selection of beers and cheapish food.

Gråmunken, Västerlånggatan 18, Gamla Stan. Cosy café with live jazz several nights a week.

Halfway Inn, Wollmar Yxkullsgatan, opposite T-bana Mariatorget, Södermalm. Best of several English-style pubs on Södermalm with decent bar lunches.

Hannas Krog, Skånegatan 80. A restaurant with a basement bar that's been the living room of Nineties Swedish pop music. *Hannas Deli* opposite is more relaxed and has bar 'K' in the basement.

Kristina, Västerlånggatan 68, Gamla Stan. Café by day (with a 50kr lunch); happy hour 4–8pm when beer is only 30kr, and live jazz after 8pm.

Mushrooms, Nybroplan 6. Always full to bursting with loud happy beer-drinkers. A youthful venue.

O'Learys, Götgatan 11, Södermalm. A good bar restaurant for watching sport on the widescreen TV.

Sloppy's, Hamngatan, 2. A popular bar and nightclub open until 5am; serves food from around 39kr.

Söders Hjärta, Bellmansgatan 22, Södermalm. Swanky restaurant with a less intimidating and friendly bar on the mezzanine floor.

Nightlife

There's plenty to keep you occupied at night in Stockholm but the drawback, again, is the price. As well as the weekend, Wednesday night is an active time, with usually plenty going on and queues at the more popular places. At specifically **live-music venues** you'll pay 60–100kr entrance. For up-to-date **what's on information**, check *På Stan*, the Friday supplement of the *Dagens Nyheter* newspaper, or the latest issue of *Stockholm This Week*, free from the tourist centre. Popular venues in the summer are Kungsträdgården and Skansen, where there's always something going on.

Live music

Engelen, Kornhamnstorg 59, Gamla Stan. Jazz, rock and blues nightly until 3am.

Fasching, Kungsgatan. Stockholm's premier jazz venue, with local acts and big names.

Kaos, Stora Nygatan 21, Gamla Stan. Good live music from 9pm nightly; rock bands on Fridays and Saturdays in the cellar and reasonable late-night food.

Stampen, Stora Nygatan 5, Gamla Stan. Long-established and rowdy jazz club.

Tre Backar, Tegnérgatan 12–14, Norrmalm; T-bana Rådmansgatan. Good, cheap pub with a live cellar venue. Music every night; open until midnight (closed Sun).

Discos and clubs

Daily's Bar & Nattklub, Kungsträdgården, Norrmalm. There are two discos inside this café/restaurant, both doing good business. A fairly young crowd.

Gossip, Sveavägen 36. T-bana Hötorget. On two floors with lots of dark corners.

La Isla, Fridhemsplan. Latin platters into the small hours, as well as salsa dancing. Underground in the Fridhemsplan T-bana station complex.

Snaps, Medborgarplatsen. Cosy bar with a dancefloor in the basement. Always popular and fills up quickly.

Gay Stockholm

There is a far smaller gay scene in Stockholm than in Copenhagen, and being openly gay in the smaller towns and rural areas of Sweden can stimulate discrimination and hassle. The city's gay baths and saunas have now been closed down, but there are some provisions for gays, and a central point of contact: *Stockholm Gay Centre*, at Sveavägen 57 (T-bana Rådmansgatan; ☎08/736 02 12), which has a café and bookshop, counselling and meeting facilities. As the scene in Stockholm is mobile, keep up with the latest happenings by checking the widely available *QX* paper.

Gays are welcome at *Pensionat Oden*, Odengatan 38 (☎08/612 43 49; ⑨). For bars, try *Hjärtet Dam*, Polhemsgatan, 23, *Junkyard Bar*, Birkagatan 10 and *Piccolino*, Kungstradgarden, a café in Gustav Adolfs Torg, which is the place to see and be seen.

Listings

Airlines British Airways, Hamngatan 11 (☎08/679 78 00); Delta, Kungsgatan 18 (☎08/796 96 00); Finnair, Box 1762 (☎020/78 11 00); KLM, Arlanda Airport (☎08/593 624 30); Lufthansa, Norrmalmstorg 1 (☎08/611

22 88); SAS, Stureplan 8 (☎020/72 75 55 international, ☎ 020/72 70 00 domestic); Air New Zealand, Kungsbron 1G (☎08/21 91 80); Qantas, Kungsgatan 64 (☎08/24 25 02); United, Kungsgatan 3 (☎08/678 15 70).

American Express Birger Jarlsgatan 1 (Mon–Fri 9am–5pm, Sat 10am–1pm; ☎08/679 78 80).

Car rental Avis, Sveavägen 61 (☎08/34 99 10); Budget, Sveavägen 115 (☎08/33 43 83); Europcar/InterRent, Arlanda airport (☎08/593 609 40).

Doctor Medical Care Information, ☎08/411 71 77.

Embassies Australia, Sergels Torg 12 (☎08/613 29 00); Britain, Skarpögatan 6–8 (☎08/671 90 00); Canada, Tegelbakken 4 (☎08/453 30 00); Ireland, Östermalmsgatan 97 (☎08/661 80 05); Netherlands, Götgatan 16a (☎08/24 71 80); USA, Strandvägen 101 (☎08/783 53 00).

Exchange At Arlanda airport (daily 7am–10pm); Forex offices at Central Station (daily 7am–9pm), Cityterminalen (Mon–Fri 8am–9pm, Sat 8am–4pm) and Sverigehuset (daily 8am–6pm).

Ferries Tickets for Finland from Silja Line, Kungsgatan 2 at Stureplan (☎08/22 21 40); Viking Line, Central Station (☎08/452 40 00); Birka Cruises, Södermalmstorg 2 (☎08/714 55 20).

Left luggage On the lower level at Central Station (daily 7am–11.30pm; 40kr); there are safe lockers, too, all over Central Station (25kr, 20kr or 15kr).

Pharmacy 24hr service from C.W. Scheele, Klarabergsgatan 64 (☎08/454 81 30).

Police Stations are in Central Station and Brunkebergs torg 1–5. For the 24hr station, go to Bryggargatan 19 or Torkel Knutsonsgatan 20 (☎08/40 10 00).

Post office Vasagatan 28–34 (Mon–Fri 8am–6.30pm, Sat 10am–2pm). Also in Central Station (Mon–Fri 7am–10pm, Sat 10am–7pm).

Travel agency Kilroy Travels, Kungsgatan 4 (☎08/23 45 15).

Millesgarden and Drottningholm

Just a short way to the northeast of the city centre, on the mainly residential island of **Lindingö**, the **Millesgarden** (summer daily 10am–5pm; winter Tues–Sun noon–4pm; 50kr) is the outdoor sculpture garden of Carl Milles (1875–1955), one of Sweden's greatest sculptors. Arranged on a number of garden terraces carved from the steep cliffs, this is one of the most enticing visual attractions within easy reach of central Stockholm – to get there, take the T-bana to Ropsten and then go on by train one stop to Torvikstorg. Milles' animated, classical figures perch precariously on pillars, overlooking the distant harbour, while the sculptor's former home contains his staggeringly rich collection of Greek and Roman antiquities.

Try also to visit the harmonious royal palace of **Drottningholm** (May daily 11am–4.30pm; June–Aug daily 10am–4.30pm; Sept daily noon–3.30pm; 40kr), beautifully located on the shores of leafy Lovön island, 11km west of the centre. It's a lovely fifty-minute boat trip there (70kr return); ferries leave every thirty minutes from Stadshusbron to coincide with the opening times. You could also take the T-bana to Brommaplan and then bus #301–323 from there – a less thrilling ride, but free with the Stockholm Card. Modelled in a thoroughly French style, Drottningholm is perhaps the greatest achievement of the architects Tessin – father and son – and was begun in 1662 on the orders of King Karl X's widow, Eleonora. Good English notes are available to help you sort out the riot of Rococo decoration. Though it's an expensive extra, try not to miss the **Court Theatre** (tours May–Aug daily 11am–4.30pm; Sept daily noon–3.30pm; April & Oct daily 1–3.30pm; 40kr) in the grounds, which dates from 1766. The original backdrops and stage machinery are still in place, complete with a display of the eighteenth-century special effects – wind and thunder machines, trapdoors and simulated lightning. If you've time to spare, the extensive palace grounds also yield the **Chinese Pavilion** (May–Aug 11am–4.30pm; Sept noon–3.30pm; April & Oct daily 1–3.30pm; 40kr), a sort of eighteenth-century royal summer house.

Uppsala and around

An hour north of Stockholm, **UPPSALA** is regarded as the historical and religious centre of the country. It's a tranquil daytime alternative to the capital, with a delightful river-cut centre, not to mention an active student-geared nightlife. Centre of the medieval town, a ten-minute

walk from the train station, is the great **Domkyrkan** (daily 8am–6pm; free), Scandinavia's largest cathedral. The echoing interior remains impressive, particularly the French Gothic ambulatory, sided by tiny chapels, one of which contains a lively set of fourteenth-century wall paintings that tell the legend of St Erik, Sweden's patron saint, while another contains his relics. Poke around and you'll also find the tombs of Reformation rebel Gustav Vasa and his son Johan III, and that of the great botanist Linnaeus, who lived in Uppsala.

Opposite the cathedral is the **Gustavianum** (summer daily 11am–4pm, Thurs till 9pm; winter closed Mon & Tues; 40kr) built in 1625 as part of the university, and much touted for its tidily preserved anatomical theatre. The same building houses a couple of small collections of Egyptian, Classical and Nordic antiquities and the **Uppsala University Museum** which contains the glorious Augsberg Art Cabinet, an ebony treasure chest presented to Gustav II Adolf. The current **University** building (Mon–Fri 8am–4pm) is the imposing nineteenth-century Renaissance edifice over the way, among whose alumni are Anders Celsius, inventor of the temperature scale. No one will mind if you stroll in for a quick look at the extensive collection of portraits and the imposing central hall. A little way beyond is the **Carolina Rediviva** (mid-June to mid-Aug Mon–Fri 9am–8pm, Sat 10am–6pm, Sun 11am–4pm; rest of year closed Sun), one of Scandinavia's largest libraries, with a collection of rare letters and other paraphernalia, including a beautiful sixth-century Silver Bible and Mozart's manuscript for *The Magic Flute*. The **Castle** (summer daily 11am–4pm, also Wed 7–9pm; 35kr) has recently been made open to the public– a 1702 fire that destroyed three-quarters of the city did away with all but one side and two towers of this opulent palace. Now you can wander around the excavations and peruse the waxworks in authentic costumes. There are also guided tours in English (mid-June to mid-August daily noon & 2pm; 35kr) of the opulent **State Appartments**.

Practicalities

Uppsala's **train** and **bus stations** are adjacent to each other, not far from the **tourist office** (Mon–Fri 10am–6pm, Sat 10am–3pm; July also Sun noon–4pm; ☎018/27 48 00), Fyris Torg 8, which hands out an English guide to the town with a map inside. The beautifully sited official **hostel** is 6km south at Sunnerstavägen 24 (☎018/32 42 20; open all year; ③) – take bus #14 from Dragarbrunnsgatan.

A central **hotel** is *Basic*, Kungsgaten 27 (☎018/480 50 00; ⑤) with simple, bright and clean rooms. For **camping**, there's a site 7km out by Lake Mälaren at Graneberg, which also has two- to four-berth cabins for 250kr a night; take bus #14 from Dragarbrunnsgatan. For **snacks**, try the *Alma* café in the basement of the university building, though it's difficult to beat lunch at *Sten Sture & Co.*, a large wooden house immediately below the castle off Nedre Slottsgatan, with a good range of meat-based dishes during the day and live bands in the evening. Similar and equally popular is the *Café Katalin* on Svartbäcksgatan, with sporadic jazz nights; *Ofvandahls Konditori* on Sysslomansgatan is a stylish nineteenth-century café with a "salon" atmosphere. Many **restaurants**, such as the vegetarian *Max & Marie* on Drottninggaten, offer special discounts on production of a valid student card. The summer brings a glut of open-air cafés around town, the most popular on the river: *Åkanten* below St Erik's Torg is among the best.

Gamla Uppsala

Five kilometres north of town three huge **barrows**, royal burial mounds dating back to the sixth century, mark the original site of Uppsala, **GAMLA UPPSALA** – reached on bus #24 (every 30min Mon–Sat) or #25 (every 30min Sat afternoon & Sun) from Dragarbrunnsgatan. This was a pagan settlement and a place of ancient sacrificial rites: every ninth year a festival demanded the death of nine men, hanged from a nearby tree until their corpses rotted. The pagan temple where this took place is marked by the Christian **Gamla Uppsala Kyrka** (daily 9am–4/6pm), built when the Swedish kings first took baptism in the new faith. Look in for the faded wall paintings and the tomb of Celsius. There's little else to Gamla Uppsala, which is perhaps the reason the site remains so atmospheric.

SOUTHERN SWEDEN

The **south** of Sweden is a nest of coastal provinces, extensive lake and forest regions and gracefully ageing cities. Much of the area, especially the southwest coast, is the target of Swedish holidaymakers, chock-full of campsites, beaches and cycle tracks if rather thin on specific sights. But there is real historical interest in the cities that line the coast, grandest of which is **Gothenburg**, Sweden's second city and, beyond its gargantuan shipyards, worth more time than the traditional post-ferry exodus allows.

South of here, **Helsingborg**, a stone's throw from Denmark, and **Malmö**, still solidly sixteenth century at its centre, are both worth at least a stop-off, and **Lund**, a medieval cathedral and university town, is an obvious and enjoyable point between the two. To the east, Renaissance **Kristianstad** is a less obvious target than the south coast resorts, but repays a stop on the southern routes to and from Stockholm, as does **Kalmar**, a historic fortress town further north towards the capital. Close by, the island of **Gotland** has long been a domestic tourist haven for its climate, beaches and medieval Hanseatic capital, **Visby**, and is easy and inexpensive to reach by ferry from the Småland port of Västervik, as well as from Nynäshamn, south of Stockholm.

Gothenburg

Arriving in **GOTHENBURG** by ship provides an abrupt, if misleading, introduction to Scandinavia's largest port. Ferry arrivals from Harwich are shuttled in alongside the dock-strewn river, a ride offering glimpses of colossal industrial concentration. Coming from Denmark, the images are less fleeting as the ship or catamaran pulls up right in the centre of the port and shipyards. Although the occasional rusting and abandoned dry dock bears witness to the effects of the recession in the shipping industry, it's difficult to remain unimpressed by the sheer bulk of the surviving and working hardware. And beyond the shipyards Gothenburg is the prettiest of Sweden's cities, with traffic-free streets and broad avenues split and ringed by a canal system of simple elegance.

Arrival and information

You're likely to arrive in Gothenburg by **ferry**. Scandinavian Seaways ferries from England dock well out of the centre at Skandiahamn. A special bus waits outside to fill up and then shuttles into the city, to Nils Ericsonsplatsen – tickets 40kr, valid one hour; for departures, catch the bus from Nils Ericsonsplatsen 90 minutes before the ship leaves. Other arrival points string out along the docks. Stena Line ferries from Frederikshavn in Denmark dock within twenty minutes' walk of the centre; their direct competition, Sea Catamarans, a further ten minutes out; and the Kiel ferries another ten (3km from the centre in all). Bus #86 runs past all three to the centre, as does tram #3, which continues on to the Nordengården **youth hostel**. **Trains** arrive at Central Station on Drottningtorget. **Buses** from all destinations use Nils Ericsonsplatsen bus terminal behind Central Station. The **airport** is 25km east of the city, linked with the centre by buses running every fifteen minutes (35min; 45kr).

Gothenburg has two **tourist offices**: a kiosk in Nordstan, the shopping centre next to Central Station (Mon–Fri 9.30am–6pm, Sat 9.30am–3pm), and a **main office** on the canal front at Kungsportsplatsen 2 (June–Aug daily 9am–6/8pm; rest of year Mon–Fri 9am–5/6pm, Sat 10am–2pm; *www.gbg-co.se*). Both have free maps and a room-booking service (60kr fee for private rooms, 30kr for hotel rooms). They also sell the **Gothenburg Card**, giving unlimited bus and tram travel, free or half-price museum entry and other concessions, including a free boat trip to Elfsborgs fortress and free entry to the Lisebergs amusement park (mid-April to Sept). The card is valid for 24 hours and costs 75kr.

Gothenburg is perhaps the most immediately attractive Swedish city around which to **walk**, though you may well use the **public transport** system of trams and buses. Each city journey costs 16kr for adults, though it's cheaper to buy a 10-trip ticket card for 100kr. Fare dodging now incurs an instant 600kr fine, and ticket inspectors are on the increase. Just get on and punch "2" for city rides and "BYTE" if you are continuing on another bus or tram. Tid Punkten offices or Pressbyrån shops also sell a **24-hour pass** for 40kr. **Taxi** rides (☎031/65 00 00) within the city centre cost around 70kr, and there are twenty-percent discounts for women travelling at night, but check with the driver first.

Accommodation

Of the **hostels**, the most central and best appointed is the excellent *Slottskogens*, Vegagatan 21 (☎031/42 65 20; open all year; ②) two minutes' walk from Linnégatan – take train #1 or #2 to Olivedahlsgatan. The newly renovated *Masthuggsterrassens*, Masthuggstorget (☎031/42 48 20; ②; open all year) is also fairly central and served by trams #3, #4 and #9. If you want something a little more peaceful try *Kvibergs*, Kvibergsvägen 5 (☎031/43 50 55; ②; open all year), housed in an old barracks building and close to Gothenburg's largest weekend fleamarket. Take tram #6 or #7 to Kviberg. If it's vital to stay right in the middle of things, take advantage of the tourist office's special **hotel deal**, called the Gothenburg package (from 390kr per person), which gets you a room in a central hotel, with breakfast and a free Gothenburg Card. The package operates every weekend, and daily from June to August. If this is beyond your budget, the tourist office can book **private rooms** for 150kr a head (plus 60kr fee). Alternatively, try the *Allén* hotel, Parkgatan 10 (☎031/10 14 50; ⑥), near the Heden bus terminal; the *Maria Erikssons Pensionat*, Chalmersgatan 27a (☎031/20 70 30; ④); or the *City Hotel*, Lorensbergsgatan 6 (☎031/708 40 00; ④), located on a street parallel to Avenyn. All these drop a category or two at weekends. Much more expensive is the more interesting *Hotel II*, Maskingatan 11 (☎031/779 11 11; ⑨) at the harbour.

The all-year *Kärralunds* campsite (140kr per pitch) is 4km out (tram #5 to Welandergatan) and has four-bed cabins for 400kr and an attached **hostel** (☎031/84 02 00; ②). For beaches, the two campsites at Askim, 12km out, are better – notably *Askim Strand* (☎031/28 62 61; early May to late-Aug), which has cabins (②). Catch the Blå Express (5am–midnight every 15min; 25min) from the bus terminal.

The City

King Gustav II Adolf, looking for western trade, founded Gothenburg in the early seventeenth century as a response to the high tolls charged by the Danes for using the narrow sound between the two countries. As a Calvinist and businessman, Gustav much admired Dutch merchants, inviting them to trade and live in Gothenburg, and it's their influence that shaped the city, parts of which have an oddly Dutch feel. The area defined by the central canal represents what's left of old Gothenburg, centring on **Gustav Adolfs Torg**, a windswept square flanked by the nineteenth-century **Börshuset** (Exchange Building), and the fine **Rådhus**, originally built in 1672. Around the corner, the **Kronhuset**, off Kronhusgatan, is a typical seventeenth-century Dutch construction, built in 1643, and looks like the backdrop to a Vermeer. The cobbled courtyard outside is flanked by the mid-eighteenth-century **Kronhusbodarna** (Mon–Fri 11am–4pm, Sat 11am–2pm), now togged up as period craft shops selling sweets and souvenirs.

The **Stadsmuseum**, Norra Hamngatan 12 (May–Sept daily 11am–4pm; Oct–April closed Mon; 40kr), housed in the eighteenth-century headquarters of the East India Company, has recently been restored and now incorporates a rich collection of archeological, cultural and industrial exhibits. Close by, the **Maritima Centrum** (March–Nov daily 10am–4/6pm; July till 9pm, 50kr) allows you to clamber aboard a destroyer and submarine moored at the quayside. It is worth coming down here just to look at the shipyards beyond, like a rusting Meccano set put into sharp perspective by the new technology industries. Another draw is the **Opera House** (daily noon–6pm; ☎031/13 13 00; tickets from 50kr), a graceful and imaginative ship-like structure.

Crossing the canal from Kungsportsplatsen and running all the way up to Götaplatsen, Kungsportsavenyn is Gothenburg's showiest thoroughfare. Known simply as **Avenyn**, this wide strip was once flanked by private houses fronted by gardens and is now lined with pavement restaurants and brasseries. About halfway down, the excellent **Röhsska Museum of Arts and Crafts** at Vasagatan 37–39 (May–Aug Mon–Fri noon–4pm, Sat & Sun noon–5pm;

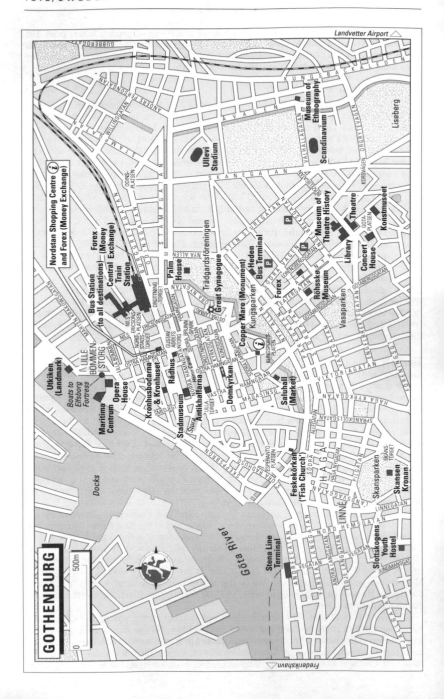

Landvetter Airport △

Fredrikshavn ▽

GOTHENBURG

0   500m

N

Göta River

Docks

Boats to Elfsborg Fortress

Utkiken (Landmark)

Maritima Centrum

Opera House

Kronhusbodarna & Kronhuset

Stadsmuseum

Rådhus

Stora Antikhallarna

Domkyrkan

Feskekörkan ('Fish Church')

Stena Line Terminal

Slottskogens Youth Hostel

Skansen Kronan

Skansparken

HAGA

LINNÉ

Saluhall (Market)

Copper Mare (Monument)

Kungsparken

Great Synagogue

Trädgårdsföreningen

Palm House

Central Train Station

Bus Station to all destinations

Forex (Money Exchange)

Nordstan Shopping Centre and Forex (Money Exchange)

Heden Bus Terminal

Forex

Röhsske Museum

Vasaparken

Library

Museum of Theatre History

Theatre

Concert House

Konstmuseet

Museum of Ethnography

Scandinavium

Ullevi Stadium

Liseberg

Sept–April Tues noon–9pm, Wed–Fri noon–4pm, Sat & Sun noon–5pm; 25kr), celebrates Swedish design through the ages, among other things. At the top end, **Götaplatsen** is the modern cultural centre of Gothenburg, home to a concert hall, theatre and **Art Museum** (summer Mon–Fri 11am–4pm, Sat & Sun 11am–5pm; winter closed Mon; 35kr), whose enormous collections include a good selection of Impressionist paintings, Pop Art and – most impressively – superb Swedish work. Just a few minutes' walk to the west from Engelbreksgatan or Vasagatan, the old working-class district of **Haga** is now the trendiest area of gentrified chic, while **Linnégatan**, a few steps further, is fast rivalling Avenyn as the place to eat, drink and stroll, while retaining a far more authentic character. Five minutes' walk beyond here, on the edge of the centre, is **Liseberg**, an amusement park (mid-April–Sept every weekend, May–late Aug daily; 40kr) with some high-profile rides and acres of gardens, restaurants and fast food. In the opposite direction, great views of the harbour and around can be had from the excursion boats that run from Lilla Bommen to the **Nya Elfsborg Fortress** (early May to mid-Aug daily 9.30am–3pm; 70kr, including guided tour of fortress), a seventeenth-century island defence guarding the harbour entrance, whose surviving buildings have been turned into a museum and café.

Eating and drinking

There's no shortage of places to **eat** in Gothenburg, and the city's range of ethnic restaurants is particularly good, reflecting its trading past. For **picnic food**, the Stora Saluhallen, the indoor market in Kungstorget (Mon–Thur 9am–6pm, Fri 8am–6.30pm, Sat 8am–3pm), is tempting beyond words, and houses the two cheapest snack bars in town. Many of the most stylish and glitzy places to **eat** flank Avenyn; less obvious but more interesting and usually cheaper areas to ferret around are the streets clustered on Haga Nygatan and further west off Linnégatan. For **sit-down food**, the student canteen, *Kåren*, Götabergsgatan 17, has the cheapest deal in town, with set lunches for 30kr, though if you can do without meat you can't beat the vegetarian and vegan meals for 55–65kr at *Solrosen*, Kaponjärgatan 4a, which turns into a lively drinking venue at night. *Krakow*, Karlgustavsgatan 28, a central, cheap Polish eatery, with good Polish nosh and booze, challenges the reasonably priced Czech food at *Gyllene Prag*, Sveagatan 25, for the students' attentions. *Hemma Hos*, Haga Nygatan 12, serves some of the best lunches along this street for 59kr, or you could settle for huge open sandwiches at *Fröken Olssens Kafe*, Östra Latmgatan 14, which serves just as well as a stop for cake and great coffee, though it's quite expensive. For a decent coffee and information on budget and alternative Gothenburg head for the Dutch-run *Café Krasnapolsky* on Storgatan – as well as an info-wall, hitching centre and radical bookshop it also has a "rainy day" cinema showing an eclectic range of films. Also worth a try are the 24-hour student cafés on Engelbreksgatan and Vasagatan; they do superb light meals and have a real buzz – particularly *Café Engelen* on Engelbreksgatan and *Café Java* on Vasagatan.

There's an excellent choice of places to **drink**, some staying open well into the small hours. Avenyn is the focal point of much of night-time Gothenburg; *Junggrens Café* at no. 37 is a Gothenburg institution and the only reasonably priced place on the avenue. At the junction of Avenyn and Kristinelundsgatan, *Tvåkanten* is an amiable coffee bar with seats outside in the summer. *C Van*, Linnegatan 23, is an excellent watering hole with cheap drinks, a small restaurant and occasional live music. There's more live music at the *Auld Dubliner* on Ostra Hamngatan, which claims to have been established in 1870 and serves *Guinness* and whiskey. *Nefertiti* Hvitfeldtsplatsen 6, is one of the best places to see live jazz and world **music**.

Listings

Car rental Avis, at Central Station (☎031/80 57 80); Europcar, Stampgatan 22D (☎031/80 53 90); Hertz, Spannmalsgatan 16 (☎031/80 37 30).

Exchange Forex exchange office inside Central Station (daily 8am–9pm).

Pharmacy Apoteket Vasen, Götagatan 10, in the Nordstan shopping centre, is open 24hr (☎031/80 44 10).

Police Ernst Fontells Plats (☎031/700 20 00)

Post office Main office in Nordstan (Mon–Fri 9am–7pm, Sat 10am–3pm, Sun noon–3pm).

Travel agent Kilroy Travels, Berzeliigatan 5 (☎031/20 08 60). Stena Line and Sea Catamaran both have offices in Nordstan, and the Scandinavian Seaways building is opposite the main tourist office.

Helsingborg

At **HELSINGBORG** only a narrow sound separates Sweden from Denmark; indeed, Helsingborg was Danish for most of the Middle Ages, with a castle controlling the southern regions of what is now Sweden. The town's enormously important strategic position meant that it bore the brunt of repeated attacks and rebellions, the Swedes conquering the town on six separate occasions, only to lose it back to the Danes each time. Finally, in 1710, a terrible battle saw off the Danes for the last time, and the battered town lay dormant for almost two hundred years, depopulated and abandoned. Only in the nineteenth century, when the harbour was expanded and the railway constructed, did Helsingborg find new prosperity, though today the town finds it hard to persuade people to stay for longer than it takes to make their train connections.

The **waterfront** is the obvious place to begin explorations, though admittedly beyond the busy harbours there's not much to see. Up from Hamntorget and the harbours, the massive, neo-Gothic **Rådhus** marks the bottom of **Stortorget**, the long thin square sloping up to the lower battlements of what's left of Helsingborg's castle, the **kärnan** or keep (daily: June–Aug 10am–7pm; April & May 9am–4pm; Sept–March 10am–2pm; 15kr), a fourteenth-century brick tower, only survivor from the original fortress. The views from the top are worth the entrance fee although you don't miss much from the lower (free) battlements. Off Stortorget, **Norra Storgatan** contains Helsingborg's oldest buildings, attractive seventeenth- and eighteenth-century merchants' houses with quiet courtyards.

Apart from the Sundbussern passenger ferry to Helsingør, which pulls up across an arm of the docks, all **ferries**, **trains** and **buses** arrive at Knutpunkten, the harbourside **central terminal** and home to the **tourist office** (June–Aug Mon–Fri 9am–8pm, Sat & Sun 9am–5pm; Sept–May Mon–Fri 9am–6pm, Sat 10am–2pm; ☎042/12 03 10), which has free city maps and books **private rooms** at 125kr per person (plus 70kr fee). Otherwise, the cheapest of the central **hotels** is *Linnea*, Prästgatan 4 (☎042/21 46 60; ⑤), which drops prices in summer and at weekends. The *Villa Thalassa* **youth hostel** (☎042/21 03 84; ③; bus #7, or #44 after 7pm) is 4km north along Drottninggatan. For **camping**, try the waterfront site at Kustgatan Råå, 5km southeast; bus #1A or #1B from outside the Rådhus.

You shouldn't have any difficulty finding somewhere to eat. Lovely daytime **cafés** include the classic *Fahlmans* on Stortorget and the trendier *Café Mmmums*, on Södra Storgatan 3 behind St Maria Church, for salads with style. There's a vegetarian buffet lunch for 52kr at the café inside Åhlens department store on Kuhlagatan. The cheapest **restaurant** is the unglamorous *Graffitti* at Knutpunkten.

There are several happening **clubs**, including Sweden's biggest jazz club, *Jazz Klubben*, Nedre Lngvinkelsgatan 22 (Wed–Sat), and the noisy, popular *Tivoli* club, Hamntorget 11, where you can get down to the very latest sounds for a 60kr entrance.

Lund

Just forty minutes south of Helsingborg and fifteen minutes from Malmö, **LUND** is the most obvious target for a trip, a beautiful university town with a quiet medieval centre and some of the best nightlife of the region. Its weather-beaten **Domkyrkan** (Mon–Fri 8am–6pm, Sat 9.30am–5pm, Sun 9.30am–6pm), consecrated in 1145, is considered by many to be Scandinavia's finest medieval building. Its plain interior culminates in a delicate, semicircular apse with a gleaming fifteenth-century altarpiece and a mosaic of Christ surrounded by angels – although what draws most attention is a fourteenth-century astronomical clock, revealing an ecclesiastical Punch and Judy show daily at noon and 3pm. Below the apse is a crypt, supported by vividly sculpted pillars and littered with elaborately carved tombstones.

Outside the cathedral, **Kyrkogatan**, lined with staunch, solid, nineteenth-century civic buildings, leads into the main square, **Stortorget**, off which **Kattesund** is home to a glassed-in set of excavated medieval walls. Adjacent is the **Drottens Kyrkoruin** (Tues–Fri & Sun noon–4pm, Sat 10am–2pm; 10kr), the remains of a medieval church in the basement of another modern building, but the real interest is in the powerful atmosphere of the old streets behind the Domkyrkan. **Kiliansgatan**, directly behind the cathedral's apse, is a delightful cobbled street, whose fine houses sport tiny courtyards and gardens. In this web of streets, **Kulturen** (May–Sept daily 11am–5pm, Thurs till 9pm; Oct–April Tues–Sun noon–4pm; 40kr) is a mixture of indoor and open-air collections of southern Swedish art, silverware, ceramics, musical instruments, etc. Finish off your meanderings with a visit to the **Botaniska Trädgård** (daily 6am–8pm) just beyond, an extensive botanical garden with some shaded pathways.

Trains arrive on the western edge of town, an easy walk from the centre. The **tourist office** is opposite the Domkyrkan and is well signposted from the train station (June–Aug Mon–Fri 10am–6pm, Sat & Sun 10am–2pm; rest of year Mon–Fri 10am–5pm). Lund makes an appealing alternative stopover to Malmö or Helsingborg by virtue of private rooms which the tourist office can book for 175kr plus a 50kr booking fee. Its unusual **youth hostel**, *Tåget*, Vävaregatan 22 (☎046/14 28 20; ②), packs you into three-tiered sleeping compartments of six 1940s carriages parked on a branch line behind the train station; turn right and follow the signs. *Hotel Överliggaren*, Bytaregatan 14 (☎046/15 72 30; ⑤) is a central **hotel**. There are plenty of cheap places to **eat**. *Cafe Ariman*, attached to the Nordic Law Department on Kungsgatan, is a deliberately shabby, left-wing coffee house with good food, and *Conditori Lundagård* on Kykogatan is the classic student café. *Fellini*, opposite the train station, is a popular Italian eatery, and *Gloria's*, Sankt Petri Kyrkogata, is hugely popular for drinking, and has live music (Fri & Sat) by local bands. *Tegnesterass*, next to the student union, serves really fine food at student prices. For **vegetarian** eats, head for *Govindas* at Bredgatan 28.

Malmö

The third largest city in Sweden, **MALMÖ**, won back for Sweden from Denmark by Karl X in the seventeenth century, was a handsome city then and now, with a cobbled medieval core that has a lived-in, workaday feel worlds apart from the museum-piece quality of most other Swedish town centres. If you're planning to come from Copenhagen by catamaran, a quick and easy crossing, Malmö will be your first sight of Sweden – and it's not a bad introduction at all.

If local predictions are realized, however, the new **Øresund Link**, due to open in May 2000, may well render travel by catamaran and ferry almost defunct. The part-tunnel, part-bridge between Copenhagen and Malmö should encourage locals to commute and make Copenhagen airport a viable point of entry for visitors to southern Sweden. The project involved building an 4km-long artificial island at the point where the link changes from a tunnel into a bridge, which can justifiably claim to be the world's longest cable-stayed bridge to carry trains and cars (albeit with a steep toll). InteRail and ScanRail passes should be valid.

Arrival and accommodation

Central Station is where **trains** arrive, including the private Pågatåg services (to and from Helsingborg, Lund and Ystad; rail passes valid). The train station also has showers and beds (6am–11pm; 15kr per hour). The main **bus terminal** is outside Central Station, in Centralplan, though buses from Stockholm, Helsingborg and Gothenburg arrive at Slussplan, east of Central Station, at the end of Norra Vallgatan. **Ferries and catamarans** from Copenhagen dock at various terminals along Skeppsbron. Prices vary from 29kr to 90kr one way, depending on the time of year and company so it's best to shop around; Pilen is usually the cheapest at 30kr one way (Mon–Thurs noon–2pm). The **ferry** from Dragör to Limhamn, just south of Copenhagen (50kr one way), drops you at the southwestern edge of town – bus #82 runs up nearby Strandgatan to Central Station.

The **tourist office** is inside the station (June–Aug Mon–Fri 9am–7pm, Sat & Sun 10am–3pm; Sept–May Mon–Fri 9am–5pm, Sat 10am–2pm; ☎040/30 01 50). This stocks the handy *Malmö This Month* and sells the Malmö Card, which gives free museum entry, plus discounts on public transport and crossings to Copenhagen; it costs 125kr for 24 hours and is also available for 48 hours (150kr) and 72 hours (175kr). The tourist office also sells a good-value round-trip ticket (149kr), valid for two days for the train to Lund and Helsingborg, the crossing to Helsingør, travel on to Copenhagen (museum discounts in Copenhagen and Malmö) and then return by catamaran to Malmö. There may also be good-value deals involving the Øresund Link. For **Internet** use, head for *Surfer's Paradise*, Amira Isgatan 14, *Cyber Space*, Engelbrektsgatan 13A, or of course the library.

Malmö is one of the easier places in the south to find good, cheap **accommodation**. The tourist office sells the useful Malmö Package, providing a double room in a central **hotel**, breakfast and Malmö Card, for 375kr per person. Of the many hotels within the scheme, one comfortable option is the *Good Morning Hotel*, Citadellvägen 4 (☎040/23 96 05; ⑨), which is far more pleasant than its drab Fifties office-block facade would suggest. For a stunning hotel with well-reduced summer prices, try the small but pleasant *Hotel Tunneln*, Adelgatan 4 (☎ 040/10 16 20; ⑦). By far the better of the two **youth hostels** is *City Youth Hostel*, Västergatan 9 (☎ 040/97 56 51; June–Aug; ②;). If it's full, try *STF Vandrarhem*, Backvägen 18 (☎040/822 20; Feb–Nov; ②), 5km out – take bus # 21A from Centralplan. The nearest **campsite** is *Sibbarps Camping* (☎040/34 26 50) on Strandgatan; bus #82 from Centralplan.

The City

Few places in Sweden are more enjoyable – or more conducive to a leisurely stroll – than Malmö, with its canals, parks, and largely pedestrianized streets and squares. Most of the medieval centre was taken apart in the early sixteenth century to make way for **Stortorget**, a vast market square. It's as impressive today as it must have been when it first appeared, flanked on one side by the **Rådhus**, built in 1546 and popping with statuary and spiky accoutrements; there are tours of the well-preserved interior. **Södergatan**, Malmö's main pedestrianized shopping street, runs south from here towards the canal. Behind the Rådhus sits the **St Petri Kyrka** (Mon–Fri 8am–6pm, Sat 10am–6pm, Sun 10am–6pm), a fine Gothic church with an impressively decorative pulpit and a four-tiered altarpiece. **Lilla Torget** is everyone's favourite part of the city, a late sixteenth-century spin-off from an overcrowded Stortorget, usually full and doing a roaring trade from jewellery stalls and summer buskers. The southern side of the square is formed by a row of mid-nineteenth-century brick and timber warehouses, unremarkable given the other preserved buildings around, except that they contain the **Form Design Centre** (Tues–Fri 11am–5pm, Sat 10am–4pm; free), a kind of yuppies' *Habitat* museum. The shops around here sell books, antiques and gifts, though the best place to drop into is the nearby **Saluhallen**, an excellent indoor market. Further west still lie the **Kungsparken** and the **Malmöhus** (daily 10am/noon–4pm; 40kr), a low fortified castle defended by a wide moat, two circular keeps and grassy ramparts, raised by Danish King Christian III in 1536. For a time a prison (Bothwell, third husband of Mary, Queen of Scots, was the most notable inmate), the castle and its outbuildings now constitute a series of exhibitions including Malmö's main **museum**, and collections covering areas including natural history, science, maritime history, military life and city-related art, unfortunately with no information in English. There's a café inside, too, and the grounds, peppered with small lakes and an old windmill, are good for a stroll.

Eating, drinking and nightlife

The Saluhalle on Landbygatan by Lilla Torget stocks a marvellous array of picnic supplies. For **lunch**, *Årstiderna*, on Stortorget, dishes up a good range of Swedish foods in a sixteenth-century cellar (quite pricey). *Bageri Café* at Saluhall (Mon–Fri 8am–6pm, Sat 10am–4pm) is excellent for filled baguettes and healthfoods while *La Empanada*, Själbodgatan 10, is a canteen-style Mexican restaurant serving generous portions of tasty food. *Spot* restaurant, Stora Nygatan 33, is chic Italian and very good for cheese, fish and meat. For **drinking**, Lilla Torget swarms with bustling venues through the evening. *Gustav Adolf*, Gustav Adolfs Torg, is popular at weekends. The best place for occasional live music is *Matssons Musikpub*, Göran Olsgatan 1, behind the Rådhus. A twenty-minute walk south from the docks is Möllevångens Torget, where *Nyhavn* is one of the more appealing of the bar/pubs that litter the south city immigrant quarter.

Ystad

An hour by train from Malmö, **YSTAD** sits at the end of a coasting ride through rolling farmland. The train station is by the docks, a murky area that gives no hint of the cosy little town to come. In the nineteenth century, its inhabitants made a mint from smuggling, a profitable occupation in the days of Napoleon's Continental Blockade. Quite apart from coming to see the crumbling medieval market town, you might well be leaving Sweden from here: ferries depart for the Danish island of Bornholm and for Poland.

The narrow, cobbled streets wind up to **Stortorget**, a well-proportioned square, at the back of which sits the grand **Sta Maria Kyrka**, a church which has been added to continually since its original foundation in the fourteenth century. The red-brick interior displays heavy, decorative tablets lining the aisle walls and enclosed wooden pews – the end-pieces sculpted with flowers and emblems. The green box-pews at either side of the entrance were reserved for women who hadn't yet been received back into the church after childbirth. From the church, take a walk down **Lilla Västergatan**, the main street in Ystad in the seventeenth and eighteenth centuries, with neat pastel-coloured houses. Walk back through Stortorget and it's not far down to the old **Greyfriars Monastery** and museum (kloster; Mon–Fri noon–5pm, Sat & Sun noon–4pm; 10kr), a thirteenth-century survival in a pleasant setting which contains the usual local cultural and historical collections.

From the **train station**, cross the tracks to St Knuts Torg, where you'll find the **tourist office** (early June to mid-Aug Mon–Fri 9am–7pm, Sat 10am–7pm, Sun 11am–6pm; rest of year Mon–Fri 9am–5pm; ☎0411/776 81). The square is also where **buses** from Lund, Malmö and Kristianstad will drop you. There are several **hotels** in town, the most charming being *Anno 1793 Sekelgården Hotel*, Stora Västergatan 9 (☎0411/739 00; ⑨). The **youth hostel** (☎0411/665 66; ②) has one branch inside the central station and another 2km away at Sandskogen, where there's also a **campsite**, open May to mid-September, with cabins for rent – take bus #572 or #573. *Brasseriet*, Österportstorg, is a good place to **eat** well fairly cheaply, or try the popular *Lotta's* (Mon–Sat 5–11pm) in central Stortorget.

Kristianstad

Located about 95km northeast of Mälmo, **KRISTIANSTAD** is the creation of Denmark's seventeenth-century builder-king Christian IV. The earliest and most evocative example of his architectural preoccupations, its central squares and broad gridded streets flank a wide river. The town's most striking building is directly opposite the train station, the **Trefaldighetskyrkan** (daily 9am–5pm) – a symbol of all that was glorious about Christian's Renaissance ideas. A forest of pews fills the cool white church from back to front, their high sides and carved gargoyles obstructing a clear view of altar and pulpit. Kristianstad also attracts interest among movie enthusiasts, since Sweden's first films were made here between 1909 and 1911; they flicker to life at the **Film Museum** in a former studio at Östra Strandgatan 53 (Tues–Fri & Sun 1–4pm; free). But above all, perhaps, Kristianstad is a pleasant place to hang around and do nothing in particular.

The **tourist office** on Stora Torg (June–Aug Mon–Fri 9am–7pm, Sat 9am–3pm, Sun 2–6pm; Sept–May Mon–Fri 10am–5pm) is down Nya Boulevarden, right from the station, then second left. The **campsite**, *Charlottsborg Camping* (☎044/210767), is 3km west and also has a small **hostel** (②); to get there, take bus #22 or #23 or bus #17 on Friday and Saturday nights, to VÄ from Busstorget, near Lilla Torget.

Kalmar

Bright **KALMAR** had much to do with Sweden's medieval development. It was the scene of the first meeting of the *Riksdag* called by failing king Magnus Eriksson in the mid-fourteenth century, and played host to the formation of the Kalmar Union, the 1397 agreement uniting Sweden, Norway and Denmark – a history manifest in the surviving **Kalmar Slott** (April–Sept 10am–4/6pm; Oct–March 11am–4pm; 60kr), beautifully set on a tiny island a few minutes' walk away from the bus and train stations. Defended by a range of steep embankments and gun emplacements, the fourteenth-century buildings survived eleven sieges virtually unscathed, a record not respected by King Johan III who rebuilt the structure in the late sixteenth century. The castle is now a storybook confection, with turrets, ramparts, moat and drawbridge. The spruce interior repays a long dawdle; highlights include the intricately panelled Lozenge Hall and a dark dungeon.

If the castle seems to defend nothing in particular it's because the town was shifted to Kvarnholmen, an island to the north, in the mid-seventeenth century following a fire. This is modern Kalmar, a graceful, straightforward grid settlement which centres on the Baroque **Domkyrkan** (daily 10am–6pm) on Stortorget. Time is best spent wandering the streets around **Lilla Torget**: there's not a great deal left – some seventeenth-century buildings and city walls – but what remains is authentic and atmospheric enough. The one place really worth making a beeline for is the **Kronan Exhibition**, the main attraction of the **Länsmuseum**, Skeppsbrogatan (mid-June to mid-Aug daily 10am–6pm, Sun noon–4pm; rest of year Tues–Fri 10am–4pm, Sat & Sun noon–4pm; 40kr). The *Kronan* was one of the three biggest ships in the world – twice the size of the *Vasa* – when it went down after an explosion in the gunpowder magazine in 1676, lying undisturbed until 1980. There's an inventive walk-through reconstruction of the gun decks and admiral's cabin, as well as a swag of gold coins, clothing, sculpture, jewellery and weapons – in fact, a complete picture of seventeenth-century maritime life and a remarkable insight into a society at the height of its political powers.

The **tourist office** at Larmgatan 6 (mid-June to Aug daily 9am–7/9pm; rest of year Mon–Fri 9am–5pm), a spit away from the **train station** and **bus terminal**, doles out a decent map of Kalmar and arranges **private rooms** from around 250kr a double. Or stay at the **youth hostel** at Rappegatan 1c (☎0480/129 28; ③), 1500m away on Ängo, the next island north. The *Sjöfartsklubben* on Skeppsbrogatan (a seaman's mission but open to all) has doubles for 250kr and cheaper dorm accommodation, while there's a **campsite** on Stensö island, 3km from the centre, with a few cheap cabins. For **food**, most places centre around Larmtorget, where you can get a tasty and filling lunch for around 50kr. For an atmospheric café, try the elegant *Kullzenska Caféet*, upstairs at Kaggensgatan 26. The *Lodbroks* café and pub at Norra Långgatan 20 (4pm–1am) has occasional live jazz and blues **evenings**.

Gotland

The rumours about good times on **Gotland** are rife. You'll hear that the short summer season really motors like nowhere else in Sweden, and it's hot and fun. Largely, these rumours are true: the island has a youthful feel as young, mobile Stockholmers desert the capital for a boisterous summer on its beaches. But it's not all just brochure fodder. The island was an important trading post during Viking times, and later a powerbase of the Hanseatic League. The capital Visby became one of the great cities of medieval Europe, and no other part of Scandinavia has such a concentration of unspoilt medieval country churches.

Numerous **ferries** to Gotland, operated by Destination Gotland, run from Nynäshamn and Oskarshamn, but are packed in summer, so try to plan ahead. In Stockholm, Gotland City at Kungsgatan 57 (☎08/406 15 00) can provide plenty of information and sell advance tickets. One-way **fares** cost 140kr and 185kr at the weekends during the summer. Students are entitled to a 35-percent discount and under-26s may find flying a competitive option, with one-way fares from around 300kr standby.

Visby

Undoubtedly the finest approach to **VISBY** is by ship, seeing the old trading centre as it should be seen. The magnificent three-kilometre city **wall** was built around the end of the thirteenth century to isolate the city's foreign traders from the islanders. The old Hanseatic **harbour** at Almedalen is now a public park and nothing is much more than a few minutes' walk from here. Close by, pretty **Packhusplan**, the oldest square in the city, is bisected by curving Strandgatan which runs south to the fragmentary ruins of **Visborg Castle**, overlooking the harbour. Built in the fifteenth century by Erik of Pomerania, it was blown up by the Danes in the seventeenth.

In the opposite direction, Strandgatan runs towards the sea and the lush **Botanical Gardens**, just beyond which is the **Jungfrutornet** (Maiden's Tower) where a local goldsmith's daughter was walled up alive, reputedly for betraying the city to the Danes. Strandgatan is the best place to view the merchants' houses looming over the narrow streets, and is also home to the **Gotlands Fornsal Museum** at no. 14 (mid-May to Aug daily 10am–6pm; rest of year Tues–Sun noon–4pm; 40kr), which, along with the usual Viking and medieval relics, claims the largest collection of painted windows in Scandinavia. The museum also tells the tale of the slaughter of thousands of Swedes by the Danes in 1361 – an event remembered by **Valdemar's Cross**, a few hundred metres east of Söderport, where excavations earlier this century revealed a mass grave. The strikingly towered **Domkyrkan**, a short walk west of the museum (daily 8am–5pm), was built between 1190 and 1225, just before the great age of Gothic church building on the island. Used both as warehouse and treasury, it's been heavily restored and about the only original fixture left is the thirteenth-century sandstone font.

Ferries serving Visby dock just outside the city walls; turn left and keep walking for the centre, where the **tourist office** (June–Aug Mon–Fri 7am–7pm, Sat & Sun 10am–4pm; Sept & May Mon–Fri 8am–5pm, Sat & Sun 8am–6pm; Oct–April Mon–Fri 10am–3pm; ☎0498/20 17 00) is in Burmeister House on Donnersplats and sells the excellent *Turistkarta Gotland* (25kr) describing all points of interest. Alternatively, a short way to the right along the harbour front leads to *Gotlandsresor*, at Färjeledon 3, which has a room-booking service. For getting around the island it's best to rent a **bike** and there are plenty of places to do this, all charging about 60kr a day. The tourist office can book **private rooms** in town from 150kr a head and advise on the latest location of the itinerant **youth hostel**, currently at Hus 55, Gamla A7 Omradet (☎0498/49 12 20; ②). For a cheapish **hotel**, *Donnersplats Hotel,* Donnersplats 6 (☎0498/21 49 45; ⑨) has apartments for around 900kr for three people. *Gotlands Ice Hockey Federation Youth Hostel* (☎0498/24 82 02) charges 400kr in total for a four-bed room, but is 3km from the centre; ask the bus driver to drop you at Isall (Ice-hall). Gotland is a great place for **camping**; *Nordenstrands* is the closest site, 1km outside the city walls and open from May to September – follow the cycle path that runs through the Botanical Gardens along the seafront. For **eating**, Adelsgatan is lined with cafés and snack bars and has a couple of cheap kebab takeaways. Best place for sit-down **drinking** is the hugely popular bar/restaurant *Muntkälleren*, Lilla Torggränd, though queues can be long.

The rest of the island

There is a real charm to the rest of Gotland: rolling green countryside, forest-lined roads, fine beaches and small fishing villages. Everywhere, churches – many of them built in the unique Baltic Gothic style – dominate the rural skyline. The north is especially picturesque. Try **BUNGE**, with its bright fourteenth-century fortified church and **open-air museum** (daily mid-May to Aug 10am–4/6pm; 40kr), then take the Farosund ferry (every 30min; journey time 3min; free) to the island of Fårö, ringed with popular beaches and some of the island's finest limestone stacks. **SLITE**, just to the south, has a sandy beach and a campsite. There's another coastal campsite, open June to August, at Aminne, further south, and, a few kilometres away at **DAHLEM** perhaps the best example of a church in the Gotland Gothic style. Its chancel and nave date from the mid-thirteenth century, and the interior detail – like the decorative woodcarvings on the fourteenth-century choirstalls – is delicate and precise. For **beaches**, head for the east coast around **LJUGARN**, about the closest thing to a resort in Gotland, with a small **youth hostel** (☎0498/49 31 84; ②; May–Aug). At **KATTHAM-MARSVIK**, to the north, there's another lengthy beach with jetties.

CENTRAL AND NORTHERN SWEDEN

In many ways, the long wedge of land that comprises **central and northern Sweden** – from the northern shores of Lake Vänern to the Norwegian border – encompasses all that is most popular and typical of the country. Rural and underpopulated, this is Sweden as seen in the brochures – lakes, holiday cottages, forests and reindeer. Essentially the region divides into two. On the eastern side, Sweden's coast forms one edge of the **Gulf of Bothnia**. With its jumble of erstwhile fishing towns and squeaky-clean contemporary urban planning, this corridor of land is quite unlike the rest of the country – worth stopping off in if you're travelling north or have just arrived from Finland by ferry. Though the weather isn't as reliable as further south, you're at least guaranteed clean beaches, crystal-clear waters and fine hiking. To the west, folklorish **Dalarna** county is the most intensely picturesque region, with sweeping green countryside and inhabitants who maintain a cultural heritage (echoed in contemporary handicrafts and traditions) that goes back to the Middle Ages. This is *the* place to spend midsummer, particularly Midsummer's Night when the whole region erupts in a frenzy of celebration. The **Inlandsbanan**, the great Inland Railway, cuts right through this area from Lake Siljan through the shimmering, modern lakeside town of **Östersund** to **Gällivare** above the Arctic Circle. An enthralling 1300-kilometre, two-day ride, it ranks with the best European train journeys.

Gävle

It's only two hours north by train from Stockholm to **GÄVLE**, principal city of the county of Gästrikland and communications hub for the west and north. Gävle's charter was granted in 1446, but the town was almost completely redesigned after a fire in 1869. Its large squares, broad avenues and proud monumental buildings, centring on the roomy **Stortorget**, reflect its late nineteenth-century success as an export centre for timber and metal. The place to head for is the one surviving part of the old town, **Gamla Gefle**, an area of wooden cottages and narrow cobbled streets on the other side of the river. **Länsmuséet Gävleborg**, on the riverfront at Södra Strandgatan 20 (Tues, Thurs & Fri 10am–4pm, Wed 10am–9pm, Sat & Sun 1–5pm; 25kr, free for students), has work by many Swedish artists from 1600 to the present including local naive painter Johan Erik Olson. The **Joe Hill-Gården** at Nedre Bergsgatan 28 (June–Aug daily 10am–3pm; free) is the birthplace museum of US labour organizer Joe Hill. Born Johan Emanuel Hägglund in 1879, he emigrated in 1902, rallying comrades to the International Workers of the World with his songs and speeches until he was framed for murder and executed in 1915. The most piquant items are Hill's last testament and the telegram announcing his execution.

The **train** and **bus stations** are at the east end of the city, only a few minutes from the centre or Gamle Gefle. The **tourist office** is opposite the train station at Drottninggatan 39 (June–Aug daily 9am–6pm; rest of year Mon–Fri 9am–4pm), with maps and information about furnished **apartments** in central Gävle, from 250kr a night per person. The **youth hostel** is well placed in the old town at Södra Rådmansgatan 1 (☎026/62 17 45; ②), or you can try for a summer price at the central **hotels** like the *Aveny*, Södra Kungsgatan 31 (☎026/61 55 90; ⑦). As a rule, places round Nygatan and Stortorget are good for basic daily **lunch**: for a change, *Bali Garden*, Nygatan 37, is Indonesian, while the *Roma* next door does takeaway pizzas from 45kr.

Sundsvall

Known as the "Stone City", **SUNDSVALL** is immediately and obviously different. Once home to a rapidly expanding nineteenth-century sawmill industry, the whole city burned down in 1888 and a new centre built completely of stone emerged within ten years. The result is a living document of turn-of-the-century urban architecture, designed by architects who were engaged in rebuilding Stockholm's residential areas at the same time. This was achieved at a price, however: the workers who built 573 residential buildings in four years became the victims of their own success, and were shifted from their old homes in the centre and moved to a poorly serviced suburb.

The materials are limestone and brick, the style simple and the size often overwhelming. The **Esplanaden**, a wide central avenue, cuts the grid in two, itself crossed by **Storgatan**, the widest street. The area around **Stortorget** is still the roomy commercial centre that was envisaged. Behind the mock-Baroque exterior of the **Sundsvall Museum** (Mon–Thurs

10am–7pm, Fri 10am–6pm, Sat & Sun 11am–4pm; free), four late nineteenth-century ware-houses have been developed into a cultural complex called Kulturmagasinet (Culture Warehouse) devoted to art exhibits and city history. The **Gustav Adolfs Kyrkan** (daily 11am–2/4pm) – a soaring red-brick structure whose interior looks like a large Lego set – marks one end of the new town. To get the best perspective on the city's plan, climb to the heights of **Gaffelbyn** and the **Norra Bergets Hantyerks Och Friluttsmuseum** (summer Mon–Fri 9am–5pm, Sat & Sun 11am–3pm; winter closed Sun; free), an open-air crafts muse-um down Storgatan and over the main bridge.

From the **train station** the centre is five minutes' walk away, with the **tourist office** in the main Stortorget (mid-June to mid-Aug, Mon–Fri 10am–6pm, Sat 10am–3pm; rest of year Mon–Fri 10am–5pm). The **bus station** is at the bottom of Esplanaden. The **youth hostel** (☎060/61 21 19 from 4 to 6pm; ②) is a cheap and grotty camping and cabin affair at Norra Berget, and you might prefer the **private rooms** from 125kr per person plus a 60kr booking fee; otherwise *Svea Hotel*, Rådhusgatan 11 (☎060/61 16 05; ④), has doubles. For **eating**, Storgatan is lined with restaurants, most offering daily lunch menus, or *Spezia*, Sjögatan 6, has bargain pizzas for around 45kr.

Dalarna

It's fruitless to dwell too much on the agreed beauty of **Dalarna**. It holds a special, misty-eyed place in the Swedish heart and should certainly be seen, though not to the exclusion of points further north. And despite its charms, you may soon tire of the prominent folksy image: one small lakeside town looks pretty much like another, as do the ubiquitous handi-crafts and souvenirs. Dalarna actually spreads further north and west than most brochures ever acknowledge. They, like most tourists, prefer to concentrate on the area immediately surrounding Lake Siljan – which on the whole isn't a bad idea. Most of the towns are con-nected by rail, and there are ferries across the lake at Mora and Leksand; you also don't need to worry unduly about accommodation, of which there is plenty. North of Orsa, the county becomes more mountainous and less populous.

Lake Siljan is what draws many tourists to Sweden, its gentle surroundings, traditions and local handicrafts weaving a subtle spell. There's a lush feel to much of the region, the vegetation enriched by the lake, which adds a pleasing dimension to what are, essentially, small, low-profile towns and villages. If you've only got time to see part of the lake, **MORA** is as good a place as any, and a starting point for the *Inlandsbanan* rail route (see overleaf). At the northwestern corner of Lake Siljan, the little town is more or less a showcase for the work of Anders Zorn, the Swedish painter who lived in Mora and whose work is exhibited in the **Zorn Museum**, Vasagatan 36 (mid-May to mid-Sept Mon–Sat 9–5pm, Sun 11am–5pm; 25kr), along with his small but well-chosen personal collection. Zorn's oils reflect a passion for Dalarna's pastoral lifestyle, but it's his earlier watercolours of southern Europe and North Africa that really stand out. It's also possible to see his former home and studio, **Zorngården** (frequent guided tours in English; 30kr). The **tourist office** (early June to mid-Aug Mon–Fri 9am–8pm, Sat 10am–8pm, Sun 11am–8pm; rest of year Mon–Fri 9am–5pm, Sat 10am–1pm) is down on the quayside, and the **youth hostel** at Fredsgatan 6 (☎0250/381 96; ②).

At **RÄTTVIK**, on the eastern bulge of the lake, there's an introductory spread of museums and craft exhibitions, the **Gammelgård** (mid-June to mid-Aug Mon–Sat 11am–5pm, Sun noon–5pm), 2km from town, with reconstructed buildings, period furniture and traditional costumes. The **tourist office** is at the train station (mid-June to mid-Aug Mon–Fri 9am–8pm, Sat 10am–8pm, Sun 11am–8pm; rest of year Mon–Fri 9am–5pm, Sat noon–4pm). The **youth hostel** is in Knektplatsen, a few hundred metres away at the end of Järnvägsgatan (☎0248/105 66; ②); and there's a **campsite** (☎0248/116 91) on the lakeside.

LEKSAND is perhaps the most popular and traditional of the Dalarna villages and cer-tainly worth making the effort to reach at midsummer, when the festivals recall age-old may-pole dances, the celebrations culminating in the **church boat races**, an aquatic procession of decorated longboats which the locals once rowed to church every Sunday. The **tourist**

office in Norsgatan has bikes for rent, as does the **youth hostel** (☎0247/152 50; ②), 2km south of the centre at Parkgården.

Nearby **FALUN** was prosperous in the seventeenth and eighteenth centuries due to its **copper mines** (May–Aug daily 10am–4.30pm; Sept to mid-Nov, March & April Sat & Sun 12.30–4.30pm; 60kr). Two-thirds of the world's copper ore was mined here, and Falun acquired buildings and a proud layout in line with its status as Sweden's second largest town. An unnerving element of eighteenth-century mining was the omnipresence of copper vitriol fumes, a strong preservative. One case records the body of a young man found in the mines in 1719, who died 49 years previously in an accident; his corpse was so well preserved that his erstwhile fiancée, by then an old woman, recognized him immediately. Falun's **tourist office** is in the main square (June–Aug Mon–Sat 9am–7pm, Sun 11am–5pm; rest of year Mon–Fri 9am–5pm, Sat 9am–1pm), and there's a **youth hostel** (☎023/105 60; ②; bus #701) 4km away at Haraldsbro. The **campsite** is at the National Ski Stadium at Lugnet.

The Inlandsbanan

The Inlandsbanan (Inland Railway), linking central Sweden with Gällivare 1300km further north, is the most charismatic of Scandinavian rail routes, the trip everyone wants to make. Long under threat of closure, the line has now been privatized and looks like surviving for the moment, but only operates between early June and late August. InterRail pass holders get a fifty-percent discount off the full fare which, travelling second class from Mora–Östersund ranges from 175kr depending on the time of year. Cunning timetabling on the single daily service allows unlimited breaks in your journey but enforces a stop at Östersund whichever way you travel. For up-to-date information on the line, contact the Inlandståget, Kyrkgatan 56, Östersund (Mon–Fri 8am–6pm; ☎063/10 15 90).

Mora to Östersund

The Inlandsbanan begins in **Mora** (see p.1221), making its first stop at **ORSA**, fifteen minutes up the line, where the nearby **Grönklitt bear park** (mid-May to mid-Sept daily 10am–3/5pm; 60kr) provides the best chance to see the bears that roam the wild countryside. The **youth hostel** at the park (☎0250/462 00; ②) has fine facilities.

Several hours north of here, the line's halfway point is marked by **ÖSTERSUND**, the largest town until Kiruna in the far north. It's a welcoming place, and its **Storsjön** – or Great Lake – gives it a holiday atmosphere unusual this far north. You can make a tour of the lake on a **steamboat cruise** (June to early Aug; 55–100kr). Otherwise, the main thing to do in town is to visit **Jamtli** (daily 11am–5pm; 80kr, 50kr in winter), an impressive open-air museum fifteen minutes' walk north along Rådhusgatan, full of volunteers milling around in traditional country costume. They live here throughout the summer and everyone is encouraged to join in – baking, tree felling, grass cutting. For kids it's ideal, and you'd have to be pretty hard-bitten not to enjoy the enthusiastic atmosphere. On the way in, the **Länsmuseum** (late June to mid-Aug daily 11am–5pm; rest of year Tues 11am–9pm, Wed–Sun 11am–5pm; 50kr) shows off the county collections, a rambling houseful of local exhibits that includes monster-catching gear from the last century. Back in the centre, the town slopes steeply down to the water, and it's tiring work strolling the pedestrianized streets that run around Stortorget. Apart from the **Stadmuseum** (late June to early Aug daily noon–4pm; rest of year for special exhibitions only; free), a crowded 200 years of history in a house the size of a shoebox, there's not a vast amount in the way of sights. The **harbour** is a better bet, from where you can take the bridge over the lake to **Frösön** island, site of the original Viking settlement here.

The **tourist office** is at Rådhusgatan 44 (June to mid-Aug Mon–Sat 9am–9pm, Sun 9am–7pm; mid-Aug to May Mon–Fri 9am–5pm; ☎063/14 40 01) and sells the Storsjökortet (June to mid-Aug; 110kr), giving free public transport and access to the town's sights, and half price on the steamboat cruise for nine days. For a central **hotel**, try either *City Hotellet*, Artillerigatan 4 (☎063/10 84 15; ④), or *Hotell Linden*, close to the train station at Storgatan 64 (☎063/51 73 35; ⑥). The STF **youth hostel** in Östersund (☎063/10 23 43; ②) is a ten-minute walk from the train station at Södra Gröngatan 34 in the town centre. More atmospheric is the **hostel** at Jamtli (☎063/10 59 84; ②; take bus #2 to the end of the line) – although slightly more expensive, staying there saves on entrance fees to the museum. **Campers** can stay at either *Östersunds Camping*, 2km down Rådhusgatan, or on Frösön island at *Frösö camping* (early June to early Aug; bus #3 or #4 from the centre). For **food**, try the young and trendy *Brunkullans* restaurant at Postgränd 5, or the daily specials at the Australian *Captain Cook*, Hamngatan 9 – very popular for **drinking** too.

Storuman, Sorsele, Arvidsjaur and the Arctic Circle

If you are travelling on the Inlandsbanan, you may well spend the night at **STORUMAN**, five hours north of Östersund and ten hours from Gällivare. You can pick up mountain hiking details from the **tourist office** at the train station or just sleep in one of the private rooms or at the **youth hostel** another 400m to the left of the station (☎0951/777 00; ②; mid-June to mid-Aug). **SORSELE** is the next major stop on the Inlandsbanan, a pint-sized town that became a cause célèbre among conservationists in Sweden, pushing the government to abandon its plans to regulate the flow of the River Vindel here by building a hydroelectric station. It remains wild, untouched and seething with rapids, with a **campsite** on the river bank, open all year. There's also a **youth hostel** (☎0952/100 48; ②), a small place open from mid-June to early August. **ARVIDSJAUR** contains Sweden's oldest surviving *Same* village, dating from the late eighteenth century, a huddle of houses that was once the centre of a great winter market. They were not meant to be permanent homes, but rather a meeting place during festivals, and the last weekend in August is still taken up by a great celebratory shindig. There's a cosy private **youth hostel** at Västra Skolgatan 9 (☎0960/124 13; ②), and for cabins *Camp Gielas* lies beside one of the lakes 1km south of the station. A couple of hours north of Arvidsjaur the Inlandsbanan finally crosses the **Arctic Circle**, signalled by a bout of whistle-blowing as the train pulls up. Painted white rocks curve away over the hilly ground, a crude but popular representation of the Circle.

Jokkmokk

In the midst of remote, densely forested, marshy country, **JOKKMOKK** is a welcome oasis. Once a wintertime *Same* quarters, the town is today a renowned handicraft centre, with a *Same* high school keeping the language and culture alive. The **Ájtte Museum** (mid-June to end-Aug Mon–Fri 9am–6pm, Sat & Sun 11am–6pm; rest of year Mon–Fri 9am–4pm, Sat & Sun noon–4pm; 40kr) on Kyrkegatan is the place to see some of the intricate work. Have a glance, too, at the so-called **Lapp Kyrka**, in which corpses were interned in wall vaults during winter, waiting for the thaw when the *Same* could go out and dig graves – the temperatures in this part of Sweden plunge below -35°C in winter. The great **winter market** still survives, now nearly 400 years old, held on the first Thursday, Friday and Saturday of each February, when 30,000 people gather in town. It's the best time to be in Jokkmokk, and staying means booking accommodation a good six months in advance. A smaller, less traditional autumn fair at the end of August is an easier though poorer option. The **tourist office** is at Stortorget 4 (mid-June to mid-Aug daily 9am–7pm; during Winter Market Thurs–Sun 8am–6pm; rest of year Mon–Fri 8.30am–4pm). In summer there should be no problem getting a place at the **youth hostel** (☎0971/559 77; ②); just follow the signs from the station. The **campsite** is open all year, 3km east on route 97.

Gällivare

GÄLLIVARE is one of Europe's most important sources of iron ore, while Europe's largest open-cast copper mine sears the landscape 20km to the south, its gargantuan bucket-shovels and dump trucks just dots 250m down. The tourist office ferries trips to the **iron-ore mines** (mid-June to mid-Aug Mon–Fri 10am–2pm; 160kr) and **copper mine** (June–Aug Mon–Fri 2pm; 140kr). Astounding statistics – 300 tons of high explosives are used for each blast – pepper the tour, which also takes in Kåkstan, a rebuilt shantytown on the site of the original iron-ore mine; and you stop long enough to sample local delicacies like reindeer, salmon and lingonberry juice, all for 65kr at *Café Endast för Nyktra*. There's not much to Gällivare itself. Little remains of the seventeenth-century *Same* village, and the river and surrounding mountains are really the nicest feature of the town. You can walk up to **Björnfällän**, a four-kilo-metre hike on a well-marked path, and the views are magnificent. Buses make the journey (140kr return) to the summit 3km north beyond Björnfällan to see the Midnight Sun daily between mid-June and mid-July. Buses leave from the train station at 11pm, returning at 1am.

The **tourist office** is at Storgatan 16 (mid-June to mid-Aug daily 9am–8pm; rest of year Mon–Fri 9am–4pm). Its long summer hours are aimed at late Inlandsbanan arrivals, and the office has a café downstairs and a museum upstairs dealing with *Same* history. The **youth hostel** (☎0970/143 80; ②) is behind the train station, and offers accommodation in small cabins. There's also a small **private hostel**, *Lapphärbärget* (☎0970/125 34; ②), next to the Lappkyrkan by the river, and a **hotel**, the *Dundret*, Per Högströmsgatan 1 (☎0970/550 40; mid-May to mid-Sept; ③), close to the station. The **campsite** is by the river; for **snacks** or an evening coffee and cakes by the river, make for the *Strand Kaféet* near the campsite, beside some relocated vernacular buildings and a few captive reindeer.

Kiruna

KIRUNA was the hub of the battle for control of the iron-ore supply during World War II, and suffered considerably. The **mines** still dominate the town, ugly, brooding reminders of Kiruna's prosperity, and despite the new central buildings and parks, the town retains something of a frontier feel. *Kiruna Guidetur*, Vänortsgatan 4, around the corner from the tourist office, runs guided tours (June–Aug daily 10am, noon, 2pm & 4pm; 85kr); a bus takes visitors underground and stops off at a "tourist" mine, part of a leviathan structure containing service stations, restaurants, trains and crushing mills.

The other sights in town are also wedded to the all-important metal in one way or another. The tower of the **Rådhus** (summer daily 9am–6pm; winter Mon–Fri 9am–5pm) is obvious even from the train station, a strident metal pillar harbouring an intricate latticework, clock face and sundry bells which chime raucously at noon. Inside, there's a tolerable art collection, *Same* handicraft displays and a small tourist information stall. A few minutes up the road, the **Kiruna kyrka** (daily 11am–5pm; July till 10pm; free) is built in the style of a *Same* hut, a massive creation of oak beams and rafters the size of a small aircraft hangar. LKAB, the iron-ore company that paid for its construction, was also responsible for **Hjalmar Lundbohmsgården** (June–Aug daily 10am–8pm; rest of year Mon–Fri 10am–4pm; free), a country house once used by the managing director of the company and "founder" of Kiruna. Displays inside mostly consist of turn-of-the-century photographs featuring the man himself and assorted *Same* in their winter gear. The **Kiruna Samegård** at Brytaregatan 14 (mid-June to Sept daily 8am–6pm; 20kr) is the most rewarding exhibition of *Same* culture in town, with a good art display and a general store where visiting *Same* buy basic handicraft materials – antler bone, reindeer skin and rope sold by the metre.

The **tourist office** (mid-June to end-Aug Mon–Fri 9am–8pm, Sat & Sun 9am–6pm; rest of year Mon–Fri 9am–4pm) is in the *Folkets Hus*, Lars Janssongatan 17. The **youth hostel**, Skyttegatan 16 (☎0980/171 95; mid-June to Aug; ②) is a well-signposted twenty-minute walk across town. Similar accommodation is also on offer for a touch more at *Yellow House*, Hantverkaregatan 25 (☎0980/137 50; ②), the continuation of Vänortsgatan. The **campsite**, a twenty-minute walk from the centre on Campingvägen, has expensive cabins.

travel details

Trains

Stockholm to: Gällivare (2 daily; 16hr 30min); Gävle (hourly; 2hr); Gothenburg (17 daily; 3hr 10min–4hr 30min); Helsingborg (8 daily; 6hr 30min); Kalmar, change at Alvesta (8 daily, 3 Sun; 6hr); Kiruna (2 daily; 17hr); Kristianstad (7 daily; 6hr); Lund (6 daily; 4hr 40min); Malmö (6 daily; 4hr 50min); Mora (7 daily; 5hr); Narvik (2 daily; 20hr); Östersund (4 daily; 6hr); Sundsvall (6 daily; 5hr); Uppsala (2–4 hourly; 50min).

Gällivare to: Kiruna (3 daily, 1hr); Narvik (2 daily; 4hr 40min).

Gothenburg to: Copenhagen (5–8 daily; 5hr); Helsingborg (6–9 daily; 2hr 40min); Kalmar (3–5 daily;

4hr 40min); Lund (6–9 daily; 3hr 30min); Malmö (6–9 daily; 3hr 45min); Oslo (4 daily; 4hr 40min).

Malmö to: Helsingborg (at least hourly; 1hr); Lund (at least hourly; 15min); Ystad (Mon–Fri hourly, Sat & Sun 4–6 daily; 1hr).

Sundsvall to: Gävle (8 daily; 2hr 30min); Östersund (6 daily; 4hr 15min).

Uppsala to: Gävle (hourly; 1hr); Mora (7 daily; 4hr 15min).

Buses

Stockholm to: Gävle (3 Fri, 1 Sat, 4 Sun; 1hr 30min); Gothenburg (4 Fri, 3 Sun; 9hr 20min); Helsingborg (1 Fri, 1 Sun; 9hr); Kalmar (2–5 daily; 6hr 30min); Malmö (1 Fri, 1 Sun; 10hr); Oskarshamn (2–5 daily; 4hr 30min); Oslo (1 Fri, 1 Sun; 9hr); Sundsvall (3 Fri, 1 Sat, 4 Sun; 6hr); Uppsala (3 Fri, 1 Sat, 4 Sun; 1hr).

Gothenburg to: Gävle (1–2 daily; 10hr); Kalmar (1 Fri, 1 Sun; 6hr 30min); Kristianstad (1 Fri, 1 Sun; 5hr); Malmö (3 Fri, 3 Sun; 4hr 40min); Oslo (3–4 daily; 4hr 50min); Uppsala (1 Fri, 1 Sun; 8hr).

Ferries

Nynäshamn to: Visby (mid-June to mid-Aug 2 daily; 5hr).

Oskarshamn to: Visby (mid-June to mid-Aug 2 daily; 4hr).

International ferries

Stockholm to: Helsinki (Helsingsfors), Finland (2 daily; 15hr); Tallinn (1 every 2 days; 15hr); Turku (Åbo), Finland (4 daily; 13hr).

Gothenburg to: Frederikshavn (6–8 daily; 3hr 15min); Harwich (April–Oct 4 weekly; 24hr); Newcastle (mid-June to mid-Aug 1 weekly; 24hr); Kiel (1 daily; 14hr).

Malmö to: Travemünde (June–Aug 2 daily; 8–10hr).

CHAPTER 29

SWITZERLAND

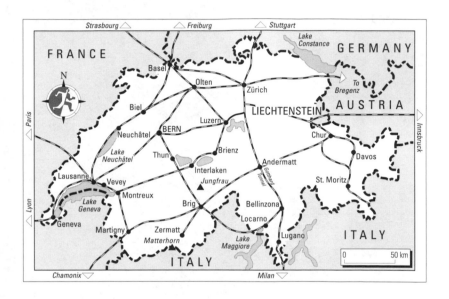

Introduction

The renowned Swiss obsessiveness with cleanliness, punctuality and hard work, coupled with a strong sense of public duty and rock-solid community respect, makes **Switzerland** one of the least problematic of countries in which to travel. Sights are stupendous, transport links are excellent, the tourist infrastructure is highly developed, and the Swiss themselves are unfailingly courteous. Most of them speak some English and at least one of the official Swiss languages – German, French, Italian, or, in the southeast, Romansh. It's unfortunate that the standard of living – Europe's highest – can make travel nastily expensive.

But although this quadrilingual confederation of 26 partly autonomous cantons is regarded by many as an island of stability in a turbulent Europe, Switzerland spent the first five hundred years of its existence rent by conflict, and fought a civil war as recently as 1847. The Swiss Confederation dates back to 1291, when the peasantry of central Switzerland formed an alliance to defend themselves against the Habsburgs. By the early 1500s, the Confederation had grown into a military superpower feared throughout Europe. It was only with the Reformation that the Swiss began to earn their reputation for neutrality. This served them well during the boom years after World War II; only now, with Switzerland lying outside the dynamics of European integration set in motion by the EU, is it beginning to look a little complacent. Recent exposés of Swiss banks' collusion with the Nazis has tainted the country's image, and the Swiss tourist industry is keen to reassure and attract visitors.

As for **where to go**, the country's breathtaking concentration of mountainous scenery has drawn travellers since the beginning of the nineteenth century, and these days it's not always easy to avoid the crowds. The advantage is that the country is so small you can cross it by train in as little as four hours, and you can see a fair bit from one central base. Of the northern German-speaking cities, **Zürich** provides a wealth of sightseeing and nightlife possibilities as well as a base for venturing south towards the Alps. **Basel** and **Bern** – the capital – are quieter, but each has an attractive historic core, while **Luzern** is in an appealing setting close to lakes and mountains. The most visited **alpine** area is the central **Bernese Oberland**, which has the highest concentration of picturesque peaks and mountainside villages, although the loftiest Alps are those of **Valais** in the south, where the small but crowded resort of **Zermatt** provides access to the country's most distinctive mountain, the Toblerone-peaked **Matterhorn**. The isolated mountain valleys of **Graubünden**, in the eastern corner of the country,

provide the setting for resorts like **St Moritz** and **Davos**. In the west, the cities lining the northern shore of **Lake Geneva** – notably **Geneva** itself, and **Lausanne** – make up the heart of Francophone Switzerland. South of the Alps, sunny Italian-speaking **Ticino** can seem a world apart from the rest of the country, particularly the palm-fringed lakeside resorts of **Lugano** and **Locarno**, with their Mediterranean, riviera atmosphere.

Information and maps

Almost all towns have a **tourist office** (*Verkehrsverein* or *Tourismus*; *Office du Tourisme*). Outside large cities, opening hours generally allow for a long lunch and can be limited in the off-season or at weekends. Most staff speak English and are scrupulously helpful, briefed to attract budget travellers as well as more well-heeled visitors. Phone Anglophone (☎157 50 14) for information in English. Tourist offices always have **maps**, but otherwise the Freytag & Berndt 1:460,000 and Bartholomew 1:300,000 cover the country. The Office fédérale de topographie/ Bundesamt für Landestopographie produces a series of more detailed 1:100,000 regional maps as well as 1:50,000 and 1:25,000 walkers' maps.

Money and banks

Prices in Switzerland are in Swiss francs (*Schweizer Franken*, *francs suisses* or *franchi svizzeri*; Sfr). Each franc is divided into 100 *Rappen* (Rp), also known as *centimes* or *centisimi* (c). There are coins of 5c, 10c, 20c, 50c, Sfr1, Sfr2 and Sfr5, and notes of Sfr10, Sfr20, Sfr50, Sfr100, Sfr200 and Sfr1000. Train stations are the best places for **changing** money; almost all have a change counter that's open long hours. You can also change money at banks, which are usually open Mon–Fri 8.30am–4.30pm; some outside major cities close between noon and 2pm. Some city and tourist resort banks open Sat 9am–4pm, although times vary. Post offices give a similar exchange rate to banks. **ATMs** are everywhere.

Communications

Post offices tend to open Mon–Fri 7.30am–noon & 1.30–6.30pm, Sat 8–11am, although watch out for regional variations and restricted hours in smaller branches. It costs Sfr1.10 to send a postcard to Europe, Sfr1.80 worldwide. A few **public phones** still accept coins, but the majority take only phonecards (*taxcards*), available from post offices, newsagents and vending machines in Sfr5, Sfr10,

Sfr20 and Sfr50 denominations. Card-phones also accept credit cards. The absurdly expensive international operator is on ☎1141; instead, phone direct by dialling ☎00 followed by the country and area codes. Cheap rates operate after 10pm. For the domestic operator call ☎111.

Getting around

The efficiency of the massively comprehensive Swiss **public transport** system remains one of the wonders of the modern world. Services depart on the dot, and rail timetables are well integrated with those of the postbus system, which operates on routes not covered by rail, including the more remote villages and valleys.

■ Trains and buses

Travelling through Switzerland by **train** is invariably comfortable, hassle-free and extremely scenic, with many mountain routes an attraction in their own right. The main state-run network, SBB-CFF-FFS (Schweizerische Bundesbahnen, Chemins de Fer Fédéraux, Ferrovie Federali Svizzere), covers much of the country, but many routes, especially alpine lines, are operated by the privately owned rail companies which pioneered them. One-way fares work out at roughly Sfr30 per 100km. The **Swiss Pass**, obtainable from Swiss tourist offices at home or main stations in Switzerland, allows free unlimited travel on all state and most private railways, as well as on all boats and most postbuses and city tram-and-bus networks. Where travel is not free, such as on cable-cars and mountain railways, discounts apply. A four-day second-class Swiss Pass costs £90 (Sfr216), an eight-day costs £112 (Sfr270). Fifteen- and thirty-day passes are also available. Other options include the **Swiss Flexi-pass** (£90 or Sfr216), which gives three days' travel in fifteen with the same privileges as the Swiss Pass; and the **Half-Fare Travel Card** (£38 or Sfr90), which gives fifty percent off all trains, buses, boats and most city trams for a month. If you plan to concentrate on one region, check out the welter of **regional passes**, usually giving five days' free travel in fifteen, often with discounts on travel in the other ten days.

The national **timetable**, covering all rail, bus, boat and cable-car services, costs Sfr16, though most main stations have a copy to consult. The national enquiry number is ☎157 22 22, but ask ticket-office staff how to get from any station to any other and they'll print out an itinerary for you showing exact connection times.

In mountain areas, the preferred method of transport is bus. These are usually yellow PTT-run **postbuses**, which invariably depart from train station forecourts. Transport-pass holders must pay a Sfr5–10 supplement on fast buses.

■ Boats

All of Switzerland's bigger lakes are crossed by **ferry services** of one sort or another, but most run only during the summer season (April–Oct) and are primarily pleasure-orientated, duplicating routes which can be covered more cheaply and quickly by rail. Only on lakes such as at Luzern or Lugano, where hilly shoreline terrain makes other forms of transport difficult, do ferries run throughout the year (albeit with limited services in winter), used by locals as much as visitors.

Driving, hitching and cycling

Switzerland's **road network** is as comprehensive and well planned as you'd expect, and although the mountainous terrain can make for some circuitous routes there is, of course, the compensation of impressively scenic – if sometimes hair-raising – mountain drives. **Speed limits** are 50kph in built-up areas, 80kph on main roads and 120kph on motorways. To drive on motorways (signed in green) you must pay Sfr40 for a *vignette* or tax disc, which is valid for a year and available from Swiss tourist offices abroad, at every border-post and at petrol stations around the country. It's easy, though, to stick to main roads (signed in blue), which are fast and free. The Touring Club Suisse operates a 24-hour break-down service on ☎140. **Car rental** costs upwards of Sfr60/day for a small car, plus about Sfr1 per kilometre, or about Sfr750/week with unlimited mileage and occasional offers. Most firms require the driver to be over 21.

Hitching is feasible on the main routes linking the cities of the north and east, or on a through-trip to the south, but the really scenic bits of Switzerland are so widely scattered, and the terrain so awkward, that it's usually difficult to get a direct ride. The risks attached to hitching are the same as in any country, particularly to women travelling alone.

Given the nature of the landscape, **cycling** is not the easiest way of exploring the country, but the scenery often more than compensates for the extra effort required. It's a popular Swiss pursuit, especially along valley floors and around lakes; there are nine national long-distance cycle routes, and city bike-lanes abound. Tourist offices can give you a map showing routes. Virtually all train stations have hundreds of new city- and mountain-bikes for **rent** from Sfr25/day. Zürich, Geneva and Bern even have free bike-rental year-round. You can avoid difficult mountain stretches by taking your bike on regional trains for Sfr7.

Accommodation

Accommodation in Switzerland is expensive, but nearly always excellent. Tourist offices can generally book rooms for free in their area, and outside office hours they normally have a display-board on the street with details of the region's hotels, often with a courtesy phone. In many cases you'll find these boards at train stations. You should always ask for a **guest card** (*Gästekarte, carte de visiteurs*) when you check-in: these can give substantial discounts on local attractions and transport (including into the mountains).

■ Hotels and private rooms

Just about every Swiss settlement above hamlet-size offers a choice of **hotels**, where accommodation is of a uniformly high standard, though not cheap. Double rooms with shared shower and toilet start at about Sfr85; only hostels offer cheaper doubles, and a more usual hotel average is Sfr115. En-suite rooms cost from Sfr135 or so. There are occasionally less expensive **private rooms**, but they aren't as widespread as in other parts of Europe and are confined mainly to rural and alpine resort areas (look for signs offering *Zimmer frei, Chambres à louer* or *Affitasi camere*). Most tourist offices tend not to help with private-room bookings, although they may dole out lists of addresses and phone numbers; an additional snag is that many private rooms are only let for a week at a time (Sat to Sat).

■ Hostels and campsites

If you're travelling on a budget, you'll need to rely a great deal on **youth hostels** (*Jugendherbergen, Auberges de Jeunesse, Alberghi per la Gioventù*), though they can get very full between June and September, when you should book in advance. Official HI hostels are of a high standard and feature a good proportion of double rooms as well as small dorms. Prices depend on the category of hostel, and range from Sfr19 to Sfr40; the average is Sfr25 for a dorm bed including breakfast and bedding. Non-HI members pay

Sfr5 extra. Annual membership costs Sfr25 or is automatic after six nights of paying the supplement. Note that under-25s are given priority and that there's usually a three-night maximum stay during summer in the towns. Meals, where available, are around Sfr10. For more details contact Schaffhauserstrasse 14, CH-8042 Zürich. Many new hostels have opened in the last few years to supplement the official ones, and there's now a rival group known as Swiss Backpackers, whose lively hostels are less institutional, are often in prime locations in the centres of town and cities, and are priced to compete. Their informative *Swiss Backpacker Newspaper* is available from PO Box 530, CH-8027 Zürich. Comparatively priced Naturfreunde hotels are an alternative to youth hostels.

The typical Swiss **campsite** is similarly clean and well equipped, although the higher the altitude the more limited the opening times; many close altogether outside the summer season (May–Sept). Prices tend to be around Sfr8 per person plus Sfr8–12 per pitch and per vehicle. Many sites require an international camping carnet. Camping outside official sites is against the law. For those hiking in the mountains there's a network of Swiss Alpine Club **huts**, for which you will pay around Sfr30 per night.

Food and drink

Food and drink can inflict another fairly massive hole in your budget. Prices are more expensive across the board than in the rest of Europe, although by combining a judicious choice of eateries with forays into picnicking and self-catering you can get by on a tight budget without too much compromise on nutrition.

■ Food

You'll have no trouble finding places to **snack** on the universal standbys of burgers, pizza slices and kebabs. In German areas you'll also find plentiful street vendors serving sausages (*Bratwürste* is the most popular), while French Switzerland rejoices in a wide range of delicious patisserie goodies. The few important native **dishes** are mostly simple and substantial peas-

---

ACCOMMODATION PRICE CODES

Throughout this guide, accommodation is priced on a scale of ① to ⑨, the number indicating the lowest price per night a single person could expect to pay in that establishment in high season. With hostels this is the nightly rate per person; with hotels, the price is arrived at by dividing the cost of the cheapest double room by two. The prices indicated by the codes are as follows:

① under £5 / $8	④ £15–20 / $24–32	⑦ £30–35 / $48–56
② £5–10 / $8–16	⑤ £20–25 / $32–40	⑧ £35–40 / $56–64
③ £10–15 / $16–24	⑥ £25–30 / $40–48	⑨ £40 / $64 and over

ant fare. In French Switzerland, cheese is the thing, headed by *fondue*, a pot of fragrant bubbling cheese and wine into which you dip cubes of bread or potato, and *raclette*, where the melted cheese is spread on a plate, with similarly starchy scoopers. Both are extremely tasty and filling. A staple in German Switzerland is *Rösti*, grated potatoes which are fried or baked, the resulting golden-brown hash often topped with cheese, chopped ham or an egg – each establishment has its own variant. Another native dish found in German-speaking areas is *Berner Platte* or *Bernerteller*, a pile of half-a-dozen hot meats with sauerkraut. Ticino revels in the northern Italian favourites of risotto and polenta. Swiss lakes and mountain streams abound with excellent trout.

The line between a **café**, a bar and a **restaurant** is blurred: just about anywhere that's open during the day will also do food, although generally only at set times (mostly noon–2pm & 6–10pm), with only snacks available in between. The key to avoiding expense is to make lunch your main meal, and always to plump for the *plat du jour* or *Tagesmenu*, often substantial, quality nosh –whether in a café or a proper restaurant – for Sfr15 or less. The same meal in the evening (or choosing *à la carte* anytime) can cost double, although beerhalls in the German cities often serve hearty inexpensive evening meals, and simple pizza or pasta dinners will fill your stomach for Sfr18. Budget travellers should head for the often surprisingly good **self-service** restaurants attached to chain department-stores in town-centres nationwide, with pick-and-choose meals at Sfr10–13; Manora is usually best, followed by Migros, EPA, and Coop. At the other end of the scale, formal restaurants are universally pricey, although inexpensive staples are common, and gourmet lunches might still be only Sfr25. Watch out for *sinalco*, or *alkohol-frei* restaurants, as well as the noticeably tiny number of establishments with smoking restrictions.

■ Drink

Cafés are open from breakfast till about midnight–3am and often sell alcohol too; **bars** and pubs tend to open their doors for late-afternoon and evening business only. Daytime places for tea and cakes are dubbed **tearooms**. Other than pubs, drinking venues vary according to region. Cosy *Bierstuben* – replete with wood-beams and Swiss kitsch – are regular features of the urban scene in German-speaking Switzerland, while in the Francophone cities pavement cafés are more common. Table service is ubiquitous, except at the English or Irish pubs gracing most towns. Local **beers** vary between regions, and are invariably excellent, costing Sfr3.50–4 for a third-litre. **Wine** can be costly: a bottle will set you back

at least Sfr14, but restaurants always offer "open" wines, sold by the decilitre (small glass Sfr3.50–5). Premier Swiss wines are the Valais whites (Fendant) and reds (Dôle). Also look out for *Kirsch* (cherry brandy) produced in Zug, near Luzern, and excellent Ticinese *grappa*. You can cut alcohol costs by buying from supermarkets, where a litre of beer or table wine starts from as little as Sfr3.

Opening hours and holidays

Shop **opening hours** are customarily Mon–Fri 9am–noon & 2–6.30pm, Sat 8.30am–noon, although it's becoming more common in the cities to ignore the lunch break and stay open on Saturday until 4pm; the flipside is that many places take Monday morning off. Most shops now have one day of late-opening, often Thursday until 9pm; those in the subterranean malls at train stations stay open daily, and close later. Most stations also have 24-hour vending machines dispensing loaves of bread, cheese and cartons of milk. Museums and attractions might be open on Sundays, but are almost invariably closed on Mondays.

Almost everything is closed on the following **public holidays**: Jan 1; Good Friday; Easter Monday; Ascension Day; Whit Monday; Dec 25 & 26. In addition, some shops and banks close for all or part of Swiss National Day (Aug 1) and on certain cantonal holidays.

Emergencies

Compared to most Europeans, the Swiss are law-abiding to a fault, rendering even the minimal **police** presence superfluous. That said, urban Switzerland does have a serious drug problem, sometimes all too evident in Zürich and Bern, though, curiously, drug laws are enforced less rigorously in the German areas than in the French. Many Swiss cities can seem eerily quiet after about 9pm, but the streets are safe enough. Regarding **health problems**, all hospitals have some kind of 24-hour service, although you will have to either pay or show your insurance policy. The E111 is not valid in Switzerland; you must have private cover. Every district has a rota system whereby one local **pharmacy** (*Apotheke, pharmacie, farmacia*) stays open outside normal shopping hours. Each pharmacy will have a sign in the window telling you where the nearest open one is; local newspapers also have details.

EMERGENCY NUMBERS

Police ☎117; Ambulance ☎144; Fire ☎118.

LAKE GENEVA

The northern shore of **Lake Geneva** – *Lac Léman* in French, *Genfersee* in German – forms the economic and cultural focus of French-speaking Switzerland, *la Suisse romande*. The ambience here is thoroughly Gallic: historical animosity between Calvinist Geneva and Catholic France has nowadays given way to a yearning on the part of most urban Francophone Swiss to abandon their bumpkin compatriots in the east and embrace the EU. The short train-ride from the Swiss-German cities of the *Mittelland* crosses more than just a linguistic boundary – it seems to span a whole continent of attitude.

Romandie's main city, **Geneva**, at the lake's southwestern tip, was once a haven for free-thinkers from all over Europe; now it's a city of diplomats and big business. Halfway around the lake, **Lausanne** is full of young people, an energetic, funky town acclaimed as the skate-boarding capital of Europe. Further east, the lakeshore is lined with vineyards and opulent villas – **Montreux** is particularly chic – although you can still taste the unspoilt paradise which drew Byron and the Romantic poets (Mary Shelley wrote *Frankenstein* here). Mont Blanc, overlooking Geneva, is visible from the city on a clear day, while Montreux has breath-taking views across the water towards the French Alps. Taking one of the boat-trips which criss-cross the lake will help bring home the full grandeur of the setting.

Geneva

The Puritanism of **GENEVA** (*Genève* in French, *Genf* in German) is inextricably linked with the city's struggle for independence. Long ruled by the Dukes of Savoy, who regarded the local bishopric as their private property, sixteenth-century Genevans saw the Reformation in neighbouring Switzerland as a useful aid in their struggle to rid themselves of Savoyard influence. By the time the city's independence was won in 1602, its religious zeal had painted it as the "Protestant Rome". What continues to be known today as the "Republic and Canton of Geneva" remained outside the Swiss Confederation until 1815 (the Catholic cantons opposed its entry), and acquired a reputation for joylessness which it still struggles to shake off.

Arrival and accommodation

From Geneva's **airport**, 6km north of the town, trains run every fifteen minutes to the main **train station**, Gare Cornavin, at the head of Rue du Mont-Blanc; you can also take bus #10, which drops you in the heart of the city. Through-trains go from the airport direct to towns around Switzerland. Cornavin is also a mainline terminus of the French SNCF network (you'll go through passport control before entering the station proper), but local French trains from Annecy/Chamonix terminate at Gare des Eaux-Vives on the other side of town (tram #12 or #16 into the centre). The international **bus station** is on Place Dorcière. Branches of the **tourist office** are at 3 Rue du Mont-Blanc (Mon–Sat 9am–6pm), and in Cornavin station (slightly longer hours), with stacks of material in English, including the useful *Genève Agenda*, the weekly listings magazine. There are dozens of **tours** offered around the city, including self-guided tours by Walkman (Sfr10), guided walks (mostly June–Oct; Sfr12), and boat trips (lake cruises from Sfr11; down-river journey Sfr22).

Geneva's essential sights are best explored on foot, but for longer journeys local **trams** and **buses** are quick and efficient. A three-stop ticket costs Sfr1.50, while a zone pass, covering the whole city, is Sfr2.20 for one hour or Sfr5 for one day. Geneva has plenty of budget **accommodation** – ask at the tourist office about multi-night cut-price deals. Their brochure *Young People* lists 24 **hostels**, six of them women-only, including the popular *Home St Pierre*, 4 Cour St Pierre beside the cathedral (☎022/310 37 07; ③). The youth hostel, 30 Rue Rothschild (☎022/732 62 60; ②) is bustling and well maintained, as is the backpackers' *Forget Me Not*, 8 Rue Vignier, Plainpalais (☎022/320 93 55; ②). *Centre Masaryk*, 11 Avenue de la Paix (☎022/733 07 72; ③) and *Cité Universitaire*, 46 Avenue Miremont (☎022/839 22 22; ②) have dorms and cut-price rooms. Of cheaper **hotels**, *De la Cloche*, 6 Rue de la Cloche (☎022/732 94 81; ⑤) and *St Victor*, 1 Rue François-LeFort (☎022/346 17 18; ⑤) are quiet and character-

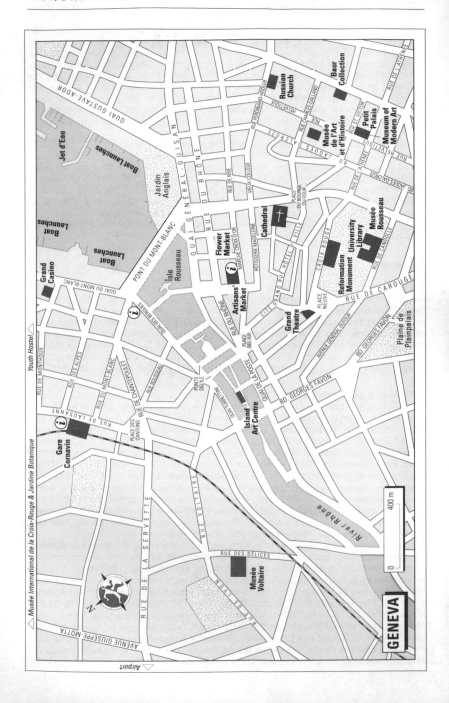

GENEVA

△ Airport

△ Musée International de la Croix-Rouge & Jardine Botanique

Youth Hostel ▷

Jet d'Eau

Boat Launches

Boat Launches

Boat Launches

Grand Casino

QUAI GUSTAVE-ADOR

QUAI DU MONT-BLANC

PONT DU MONT-BLANC

Jardin Anglais

Isle Rousseau

QUAI GÉNÉRAL-GUISAN

QUAI DU RHÔNE

QUAIS DES BERGUES

RUE DE RIVE

RUE DE MONTHOUX

RUE DES ALPES

RUE DU MONT-BLANC

RUE DE CHANTEPOULET

RUE ROUSSEAU

PLACE DES CANTONS

PONTS DE L'ILE

QUAI TURRETTINI

QUAI DE LA POSTE

Russian Church

Baur Collection

RUE DE L'ATHÉNÉE

HELVETIQUE

RUE FERDINAND-HODLER

RUE CHARLES-GALLAND

RUE JACQUES-DALCROZE

Musée de l'Art et d'Histoire

Petit Palais

Museum of Modern Art

RUE VICTOR

BD. JACQUES-DALCROZE

RUE HELVETIQUE

RUE DE L'ATHÉNÉE

VIEUX COLLÈGE

RUE DE LA CROIX D'OR

ROTISSERIE MADELEINE

MARCHÉ CROIX D'OR

RUE GRAND RUE HÔTEL DE VILLE

PLACE DU BOURG DU FOUR

CITÉ

Flower Market

Artisans' Market

RUE DU RHÔNE

RUE DE LA MADELEINE

PLACE BEL-AIR

Cathedral

Musée Rousseau

CROIX ROUGE

Reformation Monument

University Library

RUE DE CANDOLLE

RUE DE CAROUGE

PLACE NEUVE

Grand Theatre

BD. GEORGES FAVON

AVENUE GÉNÉRAL-DUFOUR

BD. GEORGES FAVON

Plaine de Plainpalais

Island Art Centre

Gare Cornavin

RUE DE LAUSANNE

RUE DE LA SERVETTE

AVENUE GIUSEPPE-MOTTA

RUE DE LA SERVETTE

RUE VOLTAIRE

RUE DES DÉLICES

Musée Voltaire

River Rhône

PONT TOUR

N

0   400 m

ful; *Du Lac*, 15 Rue des Eaux-Vives (☎022/735 45 80; ⑤) is good value; and *Luserna*, 12 Avenue de Luserna (☎022/345 46 76; ⑥) has great service. Choicest **campsite** –14km north-east, just before the French frontier – is *Camping d'Hermance* (☎022/751 14 83; April–Sept; bus #E), with free lake access.

The City

Genevans orientate their city around the Rhône, which flows from the lake west into France. The **Rive Gauche**, on the south bank, takes in a grid of waterfront streets which comprise the main shopping and business districts and the adjacent high ground of the Old Town. Behind the grand hotels lining the northern **Rive Droite** waterfront is the main station and the cosmopolitan Les Pâquis district, filled with cheap restaurants and sex-shops. Further north are the offices of the dozens of international organizations headquartered in Geneva.

On the Rive Gauche, the ornamental flowerbeds of the **Jardin Anglais** are renowned for the **Horloge Fleurie** or floral clock, beyond which erupts the 140-metre-high plume of Geneva's trademark **Jet d'Eau**. Immediately beside Pont du Mont-Blanc, **Île de Rousseau** bears a seated statue of the Genevan philosopher. Three blocks down river, **Pont de l'Île** has a thirteenth-century tower dominating another island in the Rhône, from where Rue de la Monnaie leads up to the main thoroughfare of the Old Town, the cobbled, steeply ascending **Grande Rue**. Here, among the secondhand bookshops and galleries, you'll spot the seven-teenth-century **Hôtel de Ville** and the arcaded **armoury**, backed by a lovely terrace with the longest wooden bench in the world (126m). A few steps north is **Maison Tavel**, 6 Rue Puits-St-Pierre (Tues–Sun 10am–5pm; free), an old patrician house containing the town museum and an impressive model of Geneva circa 1850. A block away is the late-Romanesque **cathedral** (June–Sept Mon–Sat 9am–7pm, Sun 11am–7pm; Oct–May Mon–Sat 10am–noon & 2–5pm, Sun 11am–12.30pm & 1.30–5pm), with an incongruous eighteenth-century portal and a plain, soaring interior. The frescoes of the internal Chapelle des Maccabées, with their intri-cate floral patterns and lute-strumming angels, are modern versions of the faded fifteenth-century originals now in Geneva's main museum. The north tower (Sfr3), which closes thir-ty minutes before the cathedral, has superb views. Round the corner is **Place du Bourg-de-Four**, a picturesque split-level square perched on the hillside, with alleys winding down to the university park and its austere **Wall of the Reformation** (1909–17). The park gates open onto **Place Neuve**, framed by the Grand-Théâtre and the porticoed **Rath Museum** (Tues & Thurs–Sun 10am–5pm, Wed noon–9pm; from Sfr5), hosting a changing programme of high-profile art exhibitions.

A few metres east of the Old Town is the gigantic **Musée d'Art et d'Histoire**, 2 Rue Charles Galland (Tues–Sun 10am–5pm; free). Upstairs is a graceful *Venus and Adonis* sculp-ture and two powerful Rodins. The collection is crowned by Konrad Witz's famous altar-piece, made for the cathedral in 1444, showing Christ and the fishermen transposed onto Lake Geneva. Other highlights are by local artist Félix Vallotton; Cézanne, Renoir and Modigliani; and some striking blue Swiss landscapes by Bern-born symbolist Ferdinand Hodler. The basement holds the massive archeological collection, including Egyptian mum-mies and Greek and Roman statuary. Nearby is the astonishing **Collections Baur**, 8 Rue Munier-Romilly (Tues–Sun 2–6pm; Sfr5), the country's premier collection of East Asian art, featuring luminescent yellow Yongzhang ceramics and spectacular porcelain and jade.

Twenty minutes south by tram (#12) is the late-Baroque suburb of **Carouge**, originally a separate town beyond the city walls built by the King of Sardinia in the eighteenth century. Its dinky Italianate houses and leafy lanes are now largely occupied by fashion designers and small galleries, and the area's reputation as an outpost of hedonism beyond Geneva's juris-diction lives on in its numerous cafés and music bars. Carouge hosts a colourful **market** on Wednesdays and Saturdays; the flea market at Plainpalais, near Geneva's Old Town, is also worth a browse.

North of the Botanic Gardens, on Avenue de la Paix, is the thought-provoking **International Museum of the Red Cross** (Mon & Wed–Sun 10am–5pm; Sfr10; bus #8 or #F to Appia), which documents the origins, growth, and achievements of the organization without resorting to self-congratulation. Carefully chosen audiovisual material combines with quietly dramatic exhibits – such as the seven million file-cards recording family details of World War I POWs – to leave a powerful impression.

Eating, drinking and nightlife

Central Geneva has plenty of cafés and bars offering lunchtime *plats du jour*, as well as inexpensive evening food. The tourist office provides a list of cheap eateries. The smoky upstairs bar in the L'Usine squat, Place des Volontaires, a young people's cultural centre, offers **food** for Sfr10; *Le Zofage*, 6 Rue des Voisins, is a university cafeteria open to non-students; and *Manora*, 4 Rue de Cornavin, is a high-quality self-service restaurant with plentiful vegetarian selections and meals from Sfr12. *Café Gallay*, 42 Boulevard St Georges, is a friendly neighbourhood café-bar; *Al-Amir*, 12 Rue des Alpes, does excellent Lebanese kebabs and falafel (from Sfr7); budget veggies are equally well served at *Hang-Zhou*, 19 Rue de la Coulouvrenière (Chinese) and *Jeck's*, 14 Rue de Neuchâtel (Thai) – both offer Sfr15 lunches. *Au Petit Chalet*, 6 Rue Chaponnière, is least pretentious for Swiss cuisine; *Vesuvio*, 7 Rue Cherbuliez, for Italian. As for **drinking**, Place du Bourg-de-Four's pavement cafés are packed during the day. In the Old Town, *Flanagan's*, 4 Rue de Cheval Blanc, is an Irish pub with live music (Thurs–Sat). *Le Chat Noir*, 13 Rue Vautier, Carouge, is a bar and cellar venue dedicated to live performance, nightly until 4am; close by are the traditional *Café des Amis*, 23 Rue Ancienne, and boisterous *La Marchand de Sable*, 4 Rue Vautier. Sleek, postmodern *Le 2e Bureau*, 9 Rue du Stand, thumps with deep beats, and the nearby *Café Mozart* waterfront wine-bar, 4 Quai des Forces Motrices, hosts some live jazz. Tiny, kitschy *La Bretelle*, 15 Rue des Etuves, features great drag cabaret.

Listings

Books Elm Books, 5 Rue Versonnex, for new; Bookworm, 5 Rue Sismondi, for secondhand. L'Inédite, 15 Rue St-Joseph in Carouge, is a women's bookshop.

Consulates Australia, 56 Rue Moillebeau (☎022/918 29 00); Canada, 1 Chemin du Pré-de-la-Bichette (☎022/919 92 00); New Zealand, 28a Chemin du Petit-Saconnex (☎022/734 95 30); UK, 37 Rue de Vermont (☎022/918 24 00); USA, 29 Route de Pré-Bois (☎022/798 16 15).

Email and Internet *Café Video ROM* (Mon–Thurs 11am–8.30pm, Fri & Sat 11am–10pm, Sun 1–8.30pm; Sfr5/hr) is under the station.

Hospital Hôpital Cantonal, 24 Rue Micheli-du-Crest (☎022/372 33 11).

Laundry Lavseul, 29 Rue de Monthoux (daily 7am–midnight).

Post office 18 Rue du Mont-Blanc (Mon–Fri 7.30am–6pm, Sat 8–11am).

Lausanne

Geneva's neighbour **LAUSANNE** is interesting, attractive, worldly, and well aware of how to have a good time. Tiered above the lake on a succession of south-facing terraces, with the Old Town at the top, the train station and commercial districts in the middle, and the one-time fishing village of **Ouchy**, now prime territory for waterfront café-lounging and strolling, at the bottom, it has incredibly steep hills which may do your legs in after a while. If so, copy the locals and catch a bus into the Joret forests above the city, and then blade or **skateboard** your way down to Ouchy, 400m below: aficionados have been clocked doing 90kmh through the streets this way, and when the sun shines, every public space hisses with the spinning of tiny wheels. Intrepid Lausannois have even been known to ski down to Ouchy after days of heavy snow. Switzerland's biggest university aids the youthful spirit, and a wealth of international-student programmes feeds an unusually diverse, multi-ethnic makeup. Offered the chance to host the Winter Olympics a few years back, the locals dismayed the municipality and the International Olympic Committee (headquartered in the city) by voting the idea down, and then choosing to host the Roller and Skateboarding World Championships instead.

To get to the central **Place St François** from the train station, either walk up the steep Rue du Petit-Chêne, or take the metro to Flon; from the metro platforms, elevators shuttle you up to the level of the giant **Grand Pont**, surfing between Place Bel-Air on the left and St

François on the right. Glitzy **Rue de Bourg** entices shoppers uphill from St François; beside it, Rue St-François drops down into the valley and up the other side to the cobbled **Place de la Palud**, an ancient, fountained square flanked by the arcades of the Renaissance town hall. From here the medieval **Escaliers du Marché** lead up to the **Cathedral**, a fine Romanesque-Gothic jumble, its clean lines only peripherally adorned with memorials and fifteenth-century frescoes. The **tower** (Mon–Sat 8.30–11.30am & 1.30–4.30/5.30pm, Sun 2–4.30/5.30pm; Sfr2) gives fabulous views over the town and lake. Opposite, in the former bishop's palace, is the **Musée Historique** (Tues–Sun 11am–6pm, Thurs until 8pm; Sfr4, students free), which houses a model of old Lausanne – invaluable for grasping the topography – with a superb accompanying English explanation. Further up, behind the cathedral, you'll find the fourteenth-century **château**, now occupied by cantonal government offices. Lausanne suffered from many medieval fires, and is the last city in Europe to keep alive the tradition of the nightwatch: every night, on the hour (10pm–2am), a sonorous-voiced civil servant calls out from the cathedral tower "C'est le guet; il a sonné l'heure" ("This is the nightwatch; the hour has struck"), assuring the lovers and assorted drunks below that all is well.

West of the cathedral hill is **Place de la Riponne**, an arid expanse of concrete dominated by the splendidly ostentatious **Palais de Rumine**, housing the university library and various museums. Save your francs for the outstanding **Collection de l'Art Brut**, 11 Avenue des Bergières (Tues–Sun 11am–1pm & 2–6pm; Sfr6), ten minutes' walk northwest of Riponne on Avenue Vinet, or bus #2 or #3 to Jomini. This unique gallery is filled with the work of "outsider" artists – ordinary people who discovered their talents late in life, the mentally ill, long-term prisoners, lone obsessives, and so on. Relating the potted biographies of each artist (often heart-rendingly sad) to the work they produced (often passionate and brilliant) is sobering, but the art also stands alone for its quality. On the other hand, Lausanne's flagship **Olympic Museum**, 1 Quai d'Ouchy (May–Sept daily 9am–7pm; Oct–April Tues–Sun 10am–6pm; Sfr14) is a vacuous and expensive place, trumpeting the Olympic ideal by means of snippets of archive footage, stirring music and Carl Lewis's old running shoes.

Practicalities

There are **tourist offices** in the train station (daily 9am–7pm), and beside Ouchy metro station (daily: April–Sept 9am–9pm; Oct–March 9am–6pm). City **transport** costs Sfr2.20 (one hour) or Sfr6.50 (24hr). A two-day Lausanne Card (Sfr15) gives free transport and discounts around town. Best low-cost accommodation is offered by the modern and well-run **youth hostel** complex, *Jeunotel*, 36 Chemin du Bois-de-Vaux (☎021/626 02 22; ③), with four-bed dorms; take bus #2 (to Bourdonnette) from St François or Ouchy as far as Bois de Vaux. Of the **hotels**, *Pension Old Inn*, 11 Avenue de la Gare (☎021/323 62 21; ④) is friendly and pleasant; *Astoria*, 17 Avenue Dapples (☎021/616 51 55; ④) rather depressing. *Hotel du Raisin*, 19 Place de la Palud (☎021/312 27 56; ⑤), and *du Marché*, 42 Rue Pré-du-Marché (☎021/647 99 00; ⑦) are better placed, but booking is essential. The most useful **campsite** is lakeside *Vidy* (May–Sept; ☎021/624 20 31), close to *Jeunotel*.

The self-service *Manora* **restaurant**, 17 Place St-François, has a wide range of excellent cheap food; just down from it, *Ma Jong* does freshly wok-fried meals for Sfr14; the atmospheric *Café de l'Évêché*, below the cathedral at 4 Rue Curtat, is also affordable, fondue sharing the menu with horse steaks. *Café Romand*, Place St-François (under *Pizza Hut*) is a heartwarming place for beer, coffee or Swiss gutliners; *Laxmi*, 5 Escaliers du Marché, has excellent Indian/veggie food; and *Au Couscous*, 2 Rue Enning, does Arabic/veggie. *Le Bleu Lézard*, 10 Rue Enning, is a chic and lively café-bar, while *Le Bossette*, way up above Place du Nord, is calmer and cosier. You can check **email** for free at the library inside Palais de Rumine. **Bars** and **nightlife** abound. The first place to look is Le Flon, a low-lying warehouse district bounded by Bel-Air, Grand Pont and the metro. Hereabouts you'll find genteel *Lecaféthéâtre*, featuring live *chansons*; the infamous *MAD* (*Moulin à Danse*), a dance club with adjoining theatre, galleries and alternative-style café; and *Le D* and *Le Loft*, both equally happening clubs. Otherwise, around Place du Tunnel are funky *Au Château*, serving flavourful home-brewed beers; *VO Le Jazz Café*; and *Kerrigan's*, a hilltop Irish pub on Rue de la Barre. *The Captain Cook*, 2 Rue Enning, shows English football on TV. Ouchy's waterfront hosts regular free music events all summer, and people come down here to do a spot of café sun-bathing, or blade-cruise (rent from 6 Place de la Navigation; afternoons only). Lausanne's big party is the **Festival de la Cité** held in early July, featuring impromptu music in the streets. Nearby Nyon's prestigious **Paleo Rock Festival** in late July draws 200,000 people.

Vevey and Montreux

The stretch of Lake Geneva coastline east from Lausanne to Montreux is known as the **Lavaux**. Lush, floral waterside promenades flanked by wide expanses of vines and vistas across to the French Alps make this a beautiful area to spend a restful day or two.

The small-town atmosphere of **VEVEY**, a vine-growing and market centre just east of Lausanne, may prove a welcome change from the more cosmopolitan hubs on either side. The town's charm centres on the huge lakeside **Grande Place**, a few minutes' walk south-east of the station – known also as **Place du Marché** and packed with market stalls at week-ends – and the narrow streets which lead off into the old town to the east. The **Musée Jenisch** on Rue de la Gare (Tues–Sun 10.30am–noon & 2–5.30pm; Nov–Feb afternoon only; Sfr6) features graphics by Le Corbusier; and a **Town Museum**, 2 Rue du Château (same times) is devoted to Vevey's mammoth Wine-Growers' Festival, held roughly five times a century. Uphill from the big green building west of the centre (Nestlé's world HQ) is **CORSIER**, location of the grave of Charlie Chaplin, who moved here in the 1950s to escape from McCarthyite America. There's a picturesque statue of "The Tramp" on the lakeside just east of Place du Marché.

Bus #1 regularly plies the coast road from Vevey east to Montreux and Chillon, but it's a good idea to walk the lakeside promenade at least as far as Vevey's sister town of **LA TOUR DE PEILZ**, a colourful port beside a whitewashed thirteenth-century chateau which now hosts the excellent hands-on **Swiss Toy Museum** (Tues–Sun 2–6pm; Sfr6).

MONTREUX itself is a snooty place, full of money and not particularly exciting, but it enjoys spectacular views of the Dents-du-Midi peaks opposite, and deserves a stop if only to relish the panorama. The whole town is protected from chill northerlies by a wall of mountains and so basks in its own micro-climate: the lakeside palm-trees grow naturally. The zigzagging streets and hillside terraces of the old quarter above the train station provide marginally more interest than the thronging honky-tonk of Rue de Casino below, although you should make time for the touching statue of one-time resident Freddie Mercury silently serenading the swans. A modest **Museum of Old Montreux**, 40 Rue de la Gare (daily April–Oct 10am–noon & 2–5pm; Sfr6) illustrates the town's history, especially the impact of tourism.

The climax of a journey around Lake Geneva is the stunning thirteenth-century **Château de Chillon** (daily: April–Sept 9am–7pm; Oct–March 9.30/10am–5/6pm; last entry one hour before closing; Sfr7), perhaps the best-preserved medieval castle in Europe. Whether you opt for the 45-minute shoreline walk east from Montreux, bus #1 from Vevey or Montreux, a bike, or best of all a boat (year-round), your first glimpse of the castle is unforgettable – an elegant, turreted pile jutting out into the water, framed by trees and craggy mountains. At the gate you'll get a follow-the-numbers pamphlet, which plunges you into the dungeons where the Dukes of Savoy imprisoned François Bonivard, a Genevan priest, from 1530 to 1536 (he was manacled to the fifth pillar along). Lord Byron, after a sailing trip here with Shelley in 1816, was so affected by the story that he wrote *The Prisoner of Chillon* next day in his Ouchy hotel-room. Byron's signature, scratched on the dungeon's third pillar, probably isn't genuine, but has been absorbed into the legend nonetheless. As you look out onto the lake, it's sobering to realize how sheer the rock is that Chillon's built on: just below the castle walls yawns 165m of cold water, enough to swallow St Paul's Cathedral without a trace. The real glory of the castle lies in the rooms upstairs, gloriously grand knights' halls, secret twisting passages between lavish bed-chambers, gothic windows with dreamy views and a frescoed chapel.

Practicalities

You can pick up identical information from **tourist offices** in Vevey, on Grande Place (July–Sept Mon–Sat 8.30am–7pm, Sun 10am–7pm; Sept–June Mon–Fri 8.30am–noon &

1.30–6pm, Sat 8.30am–noon); and Montreux, below the station in a lakefront hut, 5 Rue du Théâtre (April–Sept Mon–Sat 9am–6pm, Sun 9am–noon; Oct–March Mon–Fri 9am–6pm, Sat 9am–noon). The excellent brochure *On The Trail of Hemingway* pinpoints a welter of sites in the area with famous-name associations. The cheapest **hostel** is the pristine "Swiss Backpackers" *Riviera Lodge*, 5 Grande Place in Vevey (☎021/923 80 40; ②). An HI hostel is east of Montreux, 8 Passage de l'Auberge, Territet (☎021/963 49 34; ③); take bus #1 to L'Endine. The best budget **hotels** are in Vevey: *Des Négociants*, 27 Rue du Conseil (☎021/922 70 11; ⑤) or *Hostellerie de Genève*, 11 Place du Marché (☎021/921 45 77; ⑦) in the centre; or rustic *De La Place*, 5 Place du Temple in Corsier (bus #11; ☎021/921 12 87; ⑤). In Montreux, aim for *Pension Wilhelm*, 13 Rue du Marché (☎021/963 14 31; ④) or *Hotel Elite*, 25 Avenue du Casino (☎021/966 03 03; ④). You can **camp** east of Vevey at lakeside *La Maladaire* (☎021/944 31 37).

Vevey has a self-service *Manora* **restaurant** in the St Antoine mall outside the station, and plenty of pavement cafés in the centre; *Close-Up*, 8 Rue du Lac, is peaceful and jazzy, while the fare at *Hôtel Des Négociants* is particularly good. Montreux has plenty of eateries near the station on Avenue des Alpes, including some with lakeview terraces. For a few francs more, you can indulge in Arabic specialities at Montreux's oriental-fantasy *Palais Hoggar*, 14 Quai du Casino; meals start from Sfr25, or you could just savour the views over a Moroccan mint tea. Montreux's star-studded **Jazz Festival** featuring world-famous artists from REM to B.B. King takes place in early July. Tickets (Sfr40–100) are available from the tourist office, or check the Web site at *www.montreuxjazz.com* well in advance; otherwise, just join the street-parties and free entertainment all over town.

Beyond Montreux

From Montreux, the main line from Lausanne heads south and then east along the Rhône Valley below Canton Valais' high mountains to **Brig** and the region's best-known giant, the **Matterhorn**. From Montreux, hourly local trains (InterRail and Eurail fifty-percent discount) wind their laborious way northeast to the hill stations of **Glion** and **Caux**, and, after another half-hour, to the vantage point of **LES ROCHERS DE NAYE**. Hourly trains also climb from Montreux to **Les Avants** – with a number of beautiful walks – and **Montbovon**, access point for the gorgeous countryside around picturesque **GRUYÈRES**. An hour east of Montbovon is the exclusive alpine resort of **GSTAAD**, on the route towards Interlaken.

THE NORTHERN CITIES

Northern Switzerland, much of it known as the *Schweizer Mittelland* – the populated countryside between the high Alps to the south and the Jura ridges to the north – is the site of most agricultural, commercial and industrial activity. It's a region of gentle hills, lakes and some high peaks, though ones by no means as grandiose as the heights further south. There's a wealth of cultural and historical interest in the German-speaking cities of **Zürich**, **Basel**, **Luzern** and the federal capital, **Bern**. Wherever you base yourself, the mountains are never more than a couple of hours away by train.

Zürich

Not so long ago, **ZÜRICH** was famed for being the cleanest, most icily calm city in Europe. Apocryphal stories abound from the 1970s of tourists embarking on efforts to find a cigarette butt discarded on the streets ... and drawing a blank every time. This is no longer the case, however. If you are tiring of Switzerland's picture-perfect country towns, visiting Zürich will be a welcome relief – you can walk on crowded, multi-ethnic streets, get a drink after midnight and feel a lived-in urban buzz. This most beautiful of Swiss cities, astride a river and turned towards a crystal-clear lake and distant snowy peaks, will have plenty to keep you occupied. The steep cobbled alleys of the Old Town are perfect for exploratory wanderings, and with the most engaging café culture in German-speaking Switzerland and a wealth of nightlife, you could easily spend days here. To do so, however, you'll have to marry up the appeal of the place with its expense, prohibitive even by Swiss standards.

Arrival and accommodation

Trains run from Zürich's **airport**, 11km northeast, to the giant **Hauptbahnhof** (HB) in the city centre (every 15min); through-trains also go from the airport direct to resorts and cities around Switzerland. The **tourist office**, on the station concourse under the blue angel (Mon–Fri 8.30am–7/8.30pm, Sat & Sun 8.30/9am–6.30pm), has maps, books rooms for free, and offers plenty of tours including guided walks (Sfr18) and river and lake cruises (from Sfr13).

You can cover most sights on foot, but the **public transport** system is easy to use. **Tickets** are purchased in advance from machines – all cover transport on trams, buses, some boats and local trains (not to/from the airport); choose between the green button (Sfr7.20; 24hr validity); blue button (Sfr3.60; 1hr); or yellow button (Sfr2.10; short one-way hops). The most important hubs are Bahnhofplatz, and Central, a small square just across the Bahnhofbrücke on the east side of the Limmat. The "Zürich Night Card" (Sfr20) gives free city transport on three consecutive nights from 5pm until the last (ordinary) bus, tram or train, plus discounts around town.

Accommodation costs can be frightful, but there's plenty of choice and a good chance you'll find something in your price range. **Hostels** pack the Niederdorf district, on the east bank of the river, including *Marthahaus Hostel*, Zähringerstrasse 36 (☎01/251 45 50; ④), and the excellent *City Backpacker/Hotel Biber*, Niederdorfstrasse 5 (☎01/251 90 15; ③). Zürich's institutional HI *Jugendherberge*, Mutschellenstrasse 114 (☎01/482 35 44; ③), is way south; take tram #6 or #7 to Morgental, then it's a five-minute walk. Church-run *Foyer Hottingen*, Hottingerstrasse 13 (☎01/261 93 15; ④) is for women only. Many of Niederdorf's budget **hotels** are overpriced, but not all. Laid-back *Otter*, Oberdorfstrasse 7 (☎01/251 22 07; ⑤) is comfy and colourful; *Splendid*, Rosengasse 5 (☎01/252 58 50; ④) and *Villette*, Kruggasse 4 (☎01/251 23 35; ⑤) are plain; *Leonhard*, Limmatquai 136 (☎01/251 30 80; ⑦) worth the extra. *Rothaus*, Sihlhallenstrasse 1 (☎01/241 24 51; ④) is on the hip Langstrasse; its clean, spacious rooms are a bargain, if you can overlook the neighbourhood's red-light tendencies. **Campers** should head for lakeside *Seebucht*, Seestrasse 559 (☎01/482 16 12; May–Oct); bus #161 or #165 from Bürkliplatz to Stadtgrenze.

The City

Zürich straddles the River Limmat at its outflow from the Zürichsee, with the narrow pedestrian-only streets of the medieval town, the **Niederdorf**, on the east bank of the river. The west bank is the site of most business and commercial activity, as well as being the city's main shopping area, although there's a sprinkling of sights here too. On the lake itself, shoreline promenades extend from central Zürich along both banks, leading past a sequence of *Strandbäder* (pay beaches) which are packed on summer days.

NIEDERDORF

From Central, the Niederdorf district stretches south along the riverside, tranquil during the day and bustling after dark. The waterfront is lined with fine Baroque *Zunfthäuser* (guildhalls), arcaded lower storeys fronting the quayside, their extravagantly decorated dining-rooms now mostly restaurants. The narrow pedestrianized **Niederdorfstrasse**, initially tacky, offers plenty of opportunities to explore atmospheric cobbled side-alleys and secluded courtyards: Spiegelgasse 14 was Lenin's digs in 1917 (pre-Revolution), and a pub at Spiegelgasse 1 – long since renovated – housed the original *Cabaret Voltaire*, birthplace of the Dada art movement. Just south is the twin-towered **Grossmünster** (Mon–Sat 9/10am–4/6pm), where Huldrych Zwingli, father of Swiss Protestantism, began preaching in 1519. Its exterior is largely fifteenth-century, while the towers were topped with distinctive octagonal domes three hundred years later. The interior is austere but for the intensely coloured choir windows by Alberto Giacometti and the Romanesque crypt which contains a fifteenth-century statue of Charlemagne, popularly associated with the foundation of the

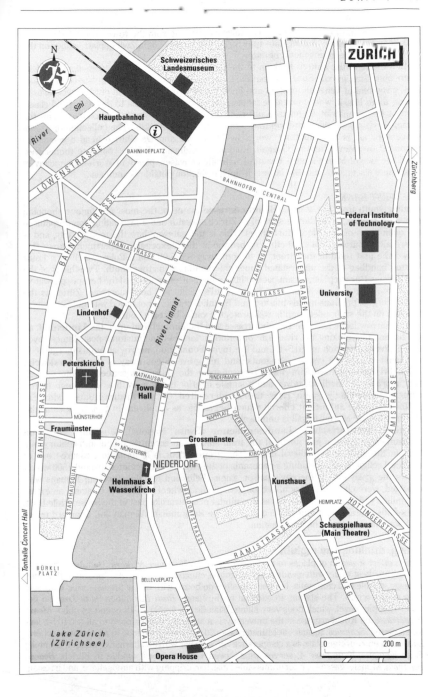

church in the ninth century. Great city views can be had from the **tower** (March–Oct daily 1.30–5pm; Nov–Feb Sat & Sun 1.30–4pm; Sfr2). As you leave onto Zwingliplatz, a door on the right gives into the atmospheric **cloister**.

Alleys behind the church lead up to the **Kunsthaus** (Tues–Thurs 10am–9pm, Fri–Sun 10am–5pm; Sfr6, free on Sun), Switzerland's best gallery. Some fascinating late-Gothic paintings, a roomful of Venetian masters and fine Flemish work are fleshed out by Swiss artists, among them Füssli, whose macabre fantasies form a stark contrast to the restrained classicism of his compatriot Angelika Kauffmann (both of whom worked in London), and the deranged visions of nineteenth-century Symbolist Arnold Böcklin. The collection of twentieth-century art is also stunning: works by Miró, Dalí and De Chirico head a wonderful Surrealist overview; Picasso, Chagall, Klee and Kandinsky all have rooms to themselves; there are two of Monet's most beautiful waterlily canvases, plenty of Warhols, an array of Giacometti's sculpture, and the largest Munch collection outside Scandinavia.

THE WEST BANK

Leading south from the station, **Bahnhofstrasse** is one of the most prestigious shopping streets in Europe, an enduring symbol of Zürich's wealth and a fascinating counterpoint to the quaintness of the Niederdorf alleys. This is the gateway into the modern city, and is where all of Zürich strolls, whether to browse at the inexpensive department stores that crowd the first third of the street, or to sign away Sfr25,000 on a Rolex watch or a Louis Vuitton handbag at the understated super-chic boutiques further south. Two-thirds of the way down is **Paradeplatz**, a tram-packed little square offering some of the best people-watching in the city, and where most of Switzerland's banks are headquartered. Zürich is the world's largest precious-metals market, and Bahnhofstrasse, if not paved with gold, is at least founded on the stuff, piled high in well-protected vaults beneath your feet.

The narrow lanes between Bahnhofstrasse and the Limmat lead up to the **Lindenhof**, an old bastion overlooking the river, site of a Roman fortress and customs post. James Joyce wrote *Ulysses* in Zürich in 1915–19, and the Joyce Foundation, nearby at Augustinergasse 9, can point you to his various hangouts, and his grave. Steps away is the **Peterskirche** (Mon–Fri 8am–6pm, Sat 8am–4pm), renowned for the enormous sixteenth-century clock face adorning its medieval tower and a simple interior that's more like a ballroom than a church. Immediately south rises the slender-spired Gothic **Fraumünster** (Mon–Sat 9/10am–4/6pm), an ancient church which began life as a convent in 853; its spectacular stained glass by Marc Chagall is unmissable.

The **Schweizerisches Landesmuseum** (Swiss National Museum; Tues–Sun 10.30am–5pm; free) is just north of the train station, an eccentric nineteenth-century pile built in the style of a medieval castle. The ground floor is a veritable treasure-trove of medieval religious art, including a panorama of the city of Zürich painted around 1500 which shows the grisly end of the city's patron saints, Felix and Regula, Christian Romans who deserted, were chased to Zürich, decapitated, put on a wheel and boiled. Upstairs, an extensive military history section serves as a reminder of the warlike past of the Swiss, while Dark Ages finds reveal something of the culture of the Burgundian, Aleman and Lombard tribes who were later to form the Swiss nation.

Eating, drinking and nightlife

Zürich offers a wealth of places to **eat cheaply**, with self-service *Manora*, Bahnhofstrasse 75, offering the best value, with a wide range of simple, cheap food. Niederdorf groans with falafel, sausage, noodle and chip-stalls, but you can often do better with one of the beerhalls' daily specials (about Sfr12). The station, in addition to the handy *Rösti Bar*, hides *Suan Long* on the lower shopping-level, which does very filling Asian dishes for Sfr12–15 (stand-up only). *Mensa Polyterrasse*, on Künstlergasse at the university, is a student cafeteria open to all (Sfr10.50, less for students). *Schlauch*, upstairs at Münstergasse 20, serves health food in a quiet atmosphere; *Zähringer*, on Zähringerplatz, is a co-operative-run café-bar with an alternative-minded clientele; *Pinte Vaudoise*, Kruggasse 4, serves what's been voted the best fondue in Zürich; *Bodega Española*, Münstergasse 15, is an unmissable tapas bar, dripping with atmosphere, and a restaurant serving delectable *paella*; *Hiltl*, Sihlstrasse 28, is a top-quality buffet vegetarian, with cheaper prices for take-away. Frothy *Café Schober*, Napfgasse 4, could bring out the little old lady in anyone – don't leave Zürich without sampling their hot chocolate. Of Niederdorf's innumerable **bars**, *Pigalle*, Marktgasse 14, is a popular hangout; *Wüste*, Oberdorfstrasse 7, is mellow and comfortable; *Babalu*, Schmidgasse 6, chic and black-lit. Lenin once watched the world go by from the *Odeon*, Limmatquai 2; and legend has it that if you can swing up and wriggle your way through the gap between beam and ceiling at the *Oepfelchammer*, Rindermarkt 12, then your beers are on the house. *Rheinfelder Bierhalle*, Niederdorfstrasse 76, is choice of the hearty beerhalls. On the west bank, *James Joyce*, Pelikanstrasse 8, comprises an original nineteenth-century Dublin bar interior, transported here piece-by-piece, while *Nelson*, Beatengasse 11, and *Noble Dubliner*, Talstrasse 82, are English-style pubs. *Barfüsser*, Spitalgasse 14, is Europe's longest-running gay bar, and *Venus*, Badenerstrasse 219, is women-only.

Supplementing its lively **music** venues, Zürich's **club** scene has sky-rocketed recently, and you'll find dancefloors heaving. The industrial quarter northwest of Langstrasse is where the best underground clubs hide themselves; check flyers in Zap Records, Zähringerstrasse 47. *Rote Fabrik*, Seestrasse 395, is a subcultural former-squat venue with live bands and big-name DJs (as well as excellent cheap food); *Abart*, Manessestrasse 170, has good live music; *Casa Bar*, Münstergasse 20, and *Moods*, Sihlamtstrasse 5, focus on jazz; *Dynamo*, Wasserwerkstrasse 21, hosts alternative, punkish bands and dance nights; *Labyrinth*, Pfingstweidstrasse 70, plays house (mixed gay/straight); and *Oxa*, Andreasstrasse 70, is famous for its after-hours techno parties (Sat & Sun 5–11am). Early August sees the Street Parade, a hedonistic weekend of street-dancing second only to Berlin's Love Parade held the week beforehand. Complete **listings** are in *ZüriTipp*, Friday supplement to *Tages Anzeiger* newspaper. The fortnightly tourist booklet *Zürich News* is also handy.

Listings

Books Stäheli, Bahnhofstrasse 70; Travel Bookshop, Rindermarkt 20.

Email and Internet *Stars Bistro* in the station (Sfr5/20min); *Café Urania*, Uraniastrasse 9, costs the same but you can pay by the minute.

Hospital Permanence Medical Centre, Bahnhofplatz 15 (24-hour casualty; ☎01/215 44 44). Dial ☎01/269 69 69 for a doctor or dentist.

Laundry Mühlegasse 11, Niederdorf.

Pharmacy Bellevue, Theaterstrasse 14 (daily 24hr).

Post office Kasernenstrasse, beside the station (Mon–Fri 6.30am–10.30pm, Sat 6.30am–8pm, Sun 11am–10.30pm).

Basel

With both a gigantic river-port – Switzerland's only outlet to the sea – and the research head-quarters of several pharmaceutical multinationals, **BASEL** (*Bâle* in French), nurtures a reputation as Switzerland's wealthiest city. Its medieval past is endowed with some of the greatest minds of European history, including Erasmus, Zwingli, and later Nietzsche and Hesse, and its long-standing patronage of the arts has resulted in a panoply of first-rate museums and galleries, which are well worth visiting, as is its historic centre. However, it's almost as if Baslers lost the plot when it came to defining their city for today. You might expect the city, situated on the Rhine exactly where Switzerland, Germany and France touch noses, to hum with pan-European energy, but most people seem to favour the option of discreet wealth-generation, saving money shopping in France and having a better time partying in Germany. The only fly in the ointment is recent journalistic inquiries indicating that Basel spent the 1930s and '40s quietly laundering the Nazis' ill-gotten gains. Evidence of such murky banking practice was received with shock, anger and disbelief, and has yet to be fully accepted.

The City

Basel's old town lies to the north of the main **train station**. It revolves around hectic Barfüsserplatz, where the city's cultural pre-eminence in the fifteenth and sixteenth centuries is amply demonstrated in the **Historical Museum** (Mon & Wed–Sun 10am–5pm; Sfr5, free on first Sun of month), housed in the bare-footed Franciscans' splendid Barfüsserkirche; don't miss the sumptuous medieval tapestries, hidden behind protective blinds. Shop-lined Gerbergasse and Freiestrasse run north to Marktplatz, boasting the elaborate scarlet **Rathaus** facade; the central section is sixteenth-century, while the tower and side-annexe are both late-nineteenth-century. Quiet old lanes climb steeply west towards the former city walls; up here are the Gothic **Peterskirche** (Tues–Sun 9/10am–5pm) on Petersgraben, whose plain exterior harbours late-medieval frescoes; and the **Spalentor**, most elaborate of the surviving city gates.

From Barfüsserplatz, Steinenberg climbs past the **Kunsthalle** (Tues–Sun 11am–5pm, Wed until 8.30pm; Sfr9), with contemporary art exhibitions, to the **Antikenmuseum**, St Alban-Graben 5 (Tues–Sun 10am–5pm; Sfr5, free on first Sun of month), displaying superb Greek and Etruscan pottery. Nearby is the absorbing **Kunstmuseum**, St Alban-Graben 16 (Tues–Sun 10am–5pm; Sfr7, also gives entry to Museum of Contemporary Art; free on first Sun of month). Its dazzling array of twentieth-century art, including paintings by Léger, Chagall, Munch, Braque and the Impressionists, is surpassed by a medieval collection featuring roomfuls of works by the prolific Holbein family. Down to the river, then right, is the **Museum of Contemporary Art**, St Alban-Rheinweg 60 (Tues–Sun 11am–5pm; joint admission with Kunstmuseum), with installations by Frank Stella and Joseph Beuys sharing space with recent German painting. On the north bank, in Solitude Park, is the beautifully designed **Museum Jean Tinguely** (Wed–Sun 11am–7pm; Sfr7), dedicated to one of Switzerland's best-loved artists. Tinguely's Monty-Pythonesque moving mechanical sculptures made of scrap are quite unique, and though most are imbued with an irreverent sense of humour, some, such as the *Mengele-Dance of Death*, are darkly apocalyptic. A Tinguely fountain spits and burbles outside the Kunsthalle.

Sixteenth-century Rittergasse leads from the Kunstmuseum to the impressive red sandstone **Münster** (Easter–Oct Mon–Fri 10am–5pm, Sat 10am–4pm, Sun 1–5pm; Oct–Easter Mon–Sat 11am–4pm, Sun 2–4pm). Medieval stone carving above the main portal shows the cathedral's founder, Emperor Heinrich II, holding a model of the church; beside him is a Foolish Virgin. Inside, in the north aisle, is the tomb of the Renaissance humanist Erasmus, who lived in Basel from 1521 until his death in 1536. The ninth-century remains of an earlier cathedral can be seen in the crypt, and the adjoining cloisters are memorably atmospheric. Tranquil alleys run north to the **Mittlere Brücke**, for many centuries the only bridge across the Rhine. The working-class quarter across the river, known as Kleinbasel, was traditionally the object of scorn for the cosmopolitan city-centre merchants: their **Lällekönig** statue faces down the bridge, still sticking out its tongue at the Kleinbaslers.

Basel's single unmissable gallery is **Fondation Beyeler** (daily 10am–6pm, Wed until 8pm; Sfr8; tram #6 to Riehen Dorf from Barfüsserplatz), sympathetically designed by Renzo Piano, architect of Paris's Pompidou Centre. A small but exceptionally high-quality collection features some of the best works by Picasso, Giacometti, Rothko, Rodin, Bacon, Miró and others. Sink into a huge white sofa opposite a giant Monet, where piped Debussy (daily at 1pm) fuels dreamy contemplation of the waterlilies.

Practicalities

Stay overnight in Basel and you're automatically entitled to a Mobility Card giving **free city transport**, even from before your hotel check-in (so you can take a tram to your hotel with a clear conscience). Basel has two **train stations** straddling three countries. Basel SBB is the main one, most of it in Switzerland, although the section known as Bâle SNCF is in French territory (passport control). Trams #1 and #8 shuttle to Barfüsserplatz. Fast trains from Germany terminate at Basel SBB, but local Freiburg trains stop short at Basel Badischer Bahnhof (Basel Bad. for short), in a German enclave within Kleinbasel (passport control); tram #6 runs to Barfüsserplatz.

There's a **tourist office** at SBB station (June–Sept Mon–Fri 8.30am–7pm, Sat 8.30am–12.30pm & 1.30–6pm, Sun 10am–2pm; Oct–May Mon–Fri 8.30am–6/7pm, Sat 8.30am–12.30pm; reservations Sfr10), and a larger one in the centre at Schifflände 5

(Mon–Fri 8.30am–6pm, Sat 10am–4pm; reset vations Sfr5). Basel thrives on conference business, so accommodation prices drop at weekends. The cheapest place is the pleasant riverside **youth hostel** at St Alban-Kirchrain 10 (☎061/272 05 72; ③). Hotels include *Stadthof*, in the old town at Gerbergasse 84 (☎061/261 87 11; ⑤), and the friendlier *Klingental* at Klingental 20 in Kleinbasel (☎061/681 62 48; ⑤); *Rochat*, Petersgraben 23 (☎061/261 81 40; ⑥), and characterful *Au Violon*, Im Lohnhof 4 (☎061/269 87 11; ⑦) are much more pleasant. You can **camp** at *Waldhort*, Heideweg 16, Reinach (☎061/711 64 29).

Plenty of cafés and *Bierstuben* around Marktplatz and Barfüsserplatz offer cheap **food**; *Mr Wong*, Steinenvorstadt 3, piles your dish high for Sfr12; *Zum Roten Engel*, Andreasplatz, is a pleasant vegetarian café; *Pfalz*, Münsterberg 11, has fresh juices and a salad buffet; arty literati meet at the leafy Kunsthalle terrace-café; tranquil *Zum Isaak*, Münsterplatz, knows its Darjeeling from its Lapsang-souchong. Kleinbasel offers more conviviality for less money: friendly *Parterre*, Klybeckstrasse 1, has excellent food, as does adjacent *Kaserne* (with shady outdoor tables); *Hirscheneck*, Lindenberg 23, has menus for under Sfr15; *El Platanero*, Webergasse 21, offers *chorizo picante*, fried bananas and loud salsa. These places often serve for **drinking** too: *Hirscheneck* rubs shoulders with the excellent *Fischerstube* beerhall, Rheingasse 45. *Grenzwert*, Rheingasse 3, is spotlit and jazzy, while the convivial bar at *Kaserne* mutates on Tuesdays into Basel's premier gay/lesbian meeting-point. *Atlantis*, Klosterberg 13, also features regular music and dance. Basel's **carnival** is famous, the parades beginning at 4am on the Monday after Mardi Gras and lasting for 72 more-or-less-continuous hours.

Luzern

An hour south of Basel and Zürich, and boasting invigorating mountain views, lake cruises and a picturesque old quarter, **LUZERN** (*Lucerne* to Francophones) has long been one of Europe's most heavily touristed towns, these days hosting five million admirers a year. The River Reuss splits the town, flowing rapidly out of the northwestern end of the oddly shaped **Vierwaldstättersee** ("Lake of the Four Forest Cantons" or plain Lake Luzern) at the geographical and spiritual heart of Switzerland. In the Middle Ages, the communities dotted around the lake guarded the northern approaches to the Gotthard Pass, the main route between northern and southern Europe. When Habsburg overlords tried to encroach on their privileges, the communities formed an alliance in 1291 at the lakeside **Rütli Meadow** which was to prove the beginning of the Swiss Confederation. Luzern, as the principal market town for the region, was drawn into the bond shortly after.

Evidence of Luzern's medieval prosperity is manifest in the frescoed facades of its Old Town and the two surviving covered wooden bridges spanning the river, both formerly part of the city's fortifications (and so with higher side-walls facing away from the town) and both boasting unique triangular paintings fixed to their roof-beams. In 1993, fire almost destroyed the fourteenth-century **Kapellbrücke**, a dog-leg angled around the mid-river **Wasserturm**; it was reconstructed with facsimiles of the roof-paintings (although a few charred originals remain) – check out no. 31's William Tell. The **Spreuerbrücke** downstream is also worth a look for its macabre "Dance of Death" paintings. The north bank is home to a compact cluster of medieval houses, with Mühlenplatz, Weinmarkt, Hirschenplatz and Kornmarkt forming an ensemble of cobbled, fountained squares ringed by colourful facades. Next to the Renaissance town hall on Kornmarkt is **Am Rhyn-Haus**, Furrengasse 21 (daily: April–Oct 10am–6pm; Nov–March 11am–1pm & 2–4pm; Sfr6), containing a small Picasso collection supplemented by hundreds of intimate photographs of the artist's later years. A few minutes west along riverside St Karliquai brings you to the **Nölliturm**, a fortified gate marking the southwestern extent of a lengthy stretch of the surviving fourteenth-century town walls. Pass through the gate and head right up the hill to gain access to the **battlements** (Easter–Sept daily 8am–7pm) and their impressive views. Northeast of the Old Town, off Löwenplatz, is the moving **Lion Memorial**, a dying beast hewn out of a cliff-face to commemorate the 700 Swiss mercenaries killed by French revolutionaries in 1792 for defending Louis XVI. Adjacent is the **Gletschergarten**, Denkmalstrasse 4 (daily 9/10am–5/6pm; Nov–Feb closed Mon;

Sfr8), a set of geological pot-holes demonstrating Luzern's prehistoric subglacial existence, far outweighed in fascination by a nightmarish Mirror Maze.

A big reason to visit Luzern is the **Verkehrshaus**, 2km east of the centre at Lidostrasse 5 (daily: April–Oct 9am–6pm; Nov–March 10am–5pm; Sfr18, discounts with rail passes) – take bus #6 or #8 from the station, or take the pleasant lakeside walk. The museum, inadequately translated as the "Transport Museum", is a vast complex that could keep you amused all day: packed with railway locomotives (including a walk-through account of the digging of the Gotthard tunnel dramatized with slides and soundtrack), aeroplanes, cable-cars and other monuments to Swiss engineering skill, it also includes Switzerland's only **IMAX cinema** (an additional Sfr14), loads of hands-on technology including videophones and fully equipped TV and radio studios, various original space capsules and, as an incongruous highlight, a wonderful museum to Swiss artist **Hans Erni**.

Practicalities

Luzern's **train station** is on the south bank, where the lake narrows into the river, metres from the Kapellbrücke. There's a **tourist office** 50m west at Frankenstrasse 1 (April–Oct Mon–Fri 8.30am–6pm, Sat 9am–5pm, Sun 9am–1pm; Nov–March Mon–Fri 8.30am–noon & 2–6pm, Sat 9am–1pm). The **youth hostel** is northwest of town by Lake Rotsee, Sedelstrasse 12 (bus #18 to Jugendherberge; ☎041/420 88 00; ③). Friendly *Backpackers*, Alpenquai 42 (bus #6/7/8 to Weinbergli, then cut left; ☎041/360 04 20; ③) and central *Tourist Hotel*, St Karliquai 12 (☎041/410 24 74; ④) also have dorms. Of the **hotels**, *Schlüssel*, Franziskanerplatz 12 (☎041/210 10 61; ⑤) is most characterful, while atmospheric *Des Alpes*, Rathausquai 5 (☎041/410 58 25; ⑧) has a picturesque waterfront setting and good restaurant; *Mr Pickwick* next door (☎041/410 59 27; ④) is in spartan contrast. The *Löwengraben*, Löwengraben 18 (☎041/417 12 12; ⑤) was Luzern's prison from 1862 to 1998 – now you can bed down in the comfortably refurbished cells. *Camping Lido*, Lidostrasse 8 (☎041/370 21 46), also has some non-reservable dorm beds.

Eating and **drinking** venues crowd the waterfront and the Old Town squares. *EPA* on Mühlenplatz is the top self-service choice, but shabby *Bahnhof Buffet*, on the top floor of the station, charges budget prices for gourmet menus prepared by the Michelin-recommended *Au Premier* adjacent. *Hofgarten*, Stadthofstrasse 14, has excellent veggie food; relaxed and inexpensive *Parterre*, Mythenstrasse 7, offers Internet access. Top **bars** include the buzzing *Jazz Kantine*, Grabenstrasse 8, with DJs and live bands downstairs; *Wärchhof*, Werkhofstrasse 11, with Sfr5 meals, free Internet, music galore and women-only nights (Mon); chic *Löwengraben*, Löwengraben 18; and frenetic *Schüür*, Tribschenstrasse 1, with excellent music and cheap weekday lunches. Luzern's infamously raucous six-day **carnival**, ending on Mardi Gras night, is the biggest and best in Switzerland, knocking Basel's stand-and-watch parades into a cocked hat.

Lake Luzern

You shouldn't leave Luzern without taking a trip on the **lake**, Switzerland's most beautiful and dramatic by far, the thickly wooded slopes rising sheer from the water, bays and peninsulas giving constantly changing views. Of the lakeside towns, **VITZNAU** is the base-station of the oldest rack-railway in the world, serving **Mount Rigi**; and **KEHRSITEN** has a funicular up to **Bürgenstock**, from where a twenty-minute clifftop walk brings you to Europe's fastest outdoor elevator, swishing you in seconds to the **Hammetschwand** summit. These have limited road and rail access, but **FLÜELEN** is on a main train line: taking a boat there and catching a train back to Luzern (4hr total), or on to Zürich (5hr) or Lugano (6hr), is highly recommended. A ten-minute trainride south of Luzern is **HERGISWIL**, home to the excellent **Glasi Hergiswil** (Mon–Fri 9am–noon & 1.30–5.30pm, Sat 9am–noon; free), a rejuvenated nineteenth-century lakeside glassworks. The on-site museum – actually an engaging and highly inventive audio-visual walk-through history of glass-making (in English) – delivers you to a gallery above the blazing-hot factory floor to watch a team of glass-blowers at work.

Bern

Of all Swiss cities, **BERN** is most immediately charming. Founded in 1191 by powerful local family the Zähringens, it began life as a fortress town peopled by knights. The growth of the Swiss Confederation in subsequent centuries owed much to the conquests of the warlike Bernese. Crammed onto a steep-sided peninsula in a crook of the fast-flowing River Aare, the city's quiet, cobbled lanes, lined with sandstone arcaded buildings, have changed barely at all in over five hundred years. The hills all around, and the steep banks of the river, are still liberally wooded. It's sometimes hard to remember that this dinky museum-piece of just 130,000 is the nation's capital, home of the Swiss parliament and wielder of final federal authority.

The City

Bern's old centre – designated a UN World Heritage Site (in company with the Pyramids and Taj Mahal) for the preservation of its medieval street-plan – is best explored from the focal east–west **Spitalgasse**. This becomes Marktgasse, Kramgasse, and then Gerechtigkeitsgasse, and is lined with seventeenth- and eighteenth-century houses, fountains and arcaded shops. Some 200m east of the station, the street crosses **Bärenplatz**, site of much outdoor daytime drinking and a vibrant Saturday morning market, to the right of which is the **Bundeshaus** or Federal Parliament Building, a domed neo-Renaissance edifice. Beyond Bärenplatz, Marktgasse continues under the oft-rebuilt **Käfigturm** (prisoners' tower), which marked the western entrance to the thirteenth-century town. Further along is an eleventh-century town gate, later converted into the **Zytglogge** – a clocktower adorned with brightly coloured figures which judder into movement four minutes before each hour. To the left, in Kornhausplatz, is the most famous of Bern's many ornate fountains, the **Kindlifresserbrunnen**, depicting an ogre munching a struggling child head-first.

Further along the main street, the **Albert Einstein House**, Kramgasse 49 (Feb–Nov Tues–Fri 1–5pm, Sat noon–4pm; Sfr2), preserves the study occupied by the famous physicist for two productive years from 1903. Münstergasse, one block south, leads to the fifteenth-century Gothic **Münster** (Easter–Oct Tues–Sat 10am–5pm, Sun 11am–5pm; Nov–Easter Tues–Fri 10am–noon & 2–4pm, Sat until 5pm, Sun 11am–2pm), noted for the magnificently gilded high-relief *Last Judgment* above the main entrance. Its 254-stepped **tower** (closes 30min earlier; Sfr3), the tallest in Switzerland, offers marvellous views of the city and distant mountains. At the eastern end of the centre, the Nydeggbrücke crosses the river to the **Bärengraben** (daily: May–Sept 8am–6pm, Oct–April 9am–4pm), Bern's famed bear-pits, which have housed generations of morose shaggies since the early sixteenth century. Legend has it that the town's founder Berchtold V of Zähringen named Bern after killing one of the beasts during a hunt, and the bear has remained a symbol of the town ever since.

Bern's magical **Kunstmuseum**, Hodlerstrasse 8–12 (Tues 10am–9pm, Wed–Sun 10am–5pm; Sfr8) spans everything from Fra Angelico to Matisse, Kandinsky, Braque and Picasso. Whole rooms are devoted to Paul Klee, who was born in Bern and who returned here from Germany after the rise of Nazism. Adjacent is the tiny **Frauen-Kunstforum** on Hodlerstrasse 16 (Tues 10am–9pm, Wed–Sat 10am–5pm; free), showing contemporary art by Swiss women. Many museums are grouped around Helvetiaplatz, south of the Aare. The **Swiss Alpine Museum** at no. 4 (May–Oct Mon 2–5pm, Tues–Sun 10am–5pm; Oct–May closed noon–2pm; Sfr5) houses detailed displays probing mountain culture. You could spend hours exploring the seven-floored **Bernisches Historisches Museum** across the square (Tues–Sun 10am–5pm; Sfr5, free on Sat) – check out the "Dance of Death" sequence in the basement, and their fine late-medieval Flemish tapestries and weaponry.

Practicalities

Bern's main **train station** is at the western end of the old centre; cross Bahnhofplatz and turn left into Spitalgasse. The **tourist office** is in the station (June–Sept daily 9am–8.30pm; Oct–May Mon–Sat 9am–6.30pm, Sun 10am–5pm). The **youth hostel**, Weihergasse 4 (☎031/311 63 16; ③), is below the Bundeshaus, and there are dorms at *Landhaus*,

Altenbergstrasse 4 (☎031/331 41 66; ③). Other options include the excellent *Marthahaus*, Wyttenbachstrasse 22a (bus #20 to Gewerbeschule; ☎031/332 41 35; ⑨); *National*, Hirschengraben 24 (☎031/381 19 88; ⑥); and *Glocke*, Rathausgasse 75 (☎031/311 37 71; ⑥). The best **campsite** is *Eichholz*, Strandweg 49 (☎031/961 26 02; April–Sept), a fifteen-minute tram ride (#9) towards Wabern. For **eating**, *Manora*, just off Bahnhofplatz, has filling cheap food, and the popular *Reithalle*, a dilapidated squat-cum-arts centre beside the tracks northeast of the station, offers a Sfr5 meal daily along with its cheap beer and liberal dope-smoking policy. Cosy *Brasserie Lorraine*, Quartiergasse 17, has excellent food and a top Sunday brunch; *Café Bubenberg Vegi*, Bubenbergplatz 8 upstairs, quality veggie menus for Sfr15; *Anker*, Kornhausplatz 16, is a locals' pub serving fondue and Rösti; and the old Toblerone factory at Länggassstrasse 49a (bus #12), now absorbed by the university, has a lively student café at the back. There's no shortage of good **café-bars**; those ringing Bärenplatz give excellent people-watching opportunities. *Café des Pyrénées*, Kornhausplatz, is a jovial hangout for artists, alcoholics and others with loud voices, or you can try *Drei Eidgenossen*, Rathausgasse 69; traditional *Klötzlikeller*, Gerechtigkeitsgasse 62; *Kornhauskeller*, Kornhausplatz (currently under renovation); or homely *Zum Blauen Engel*, Seidenweg 9b.

Listings are in *Berner Woche*, Thursday supplement to *Der Bund* newspaper, free from many cinemas; the free fortnightly *Bern aktuell* has information and some listings. The *Reithalle* and *Dampfzentrale*, Marzilistrasse 47, are the two premier venues for **live music** and dance; *Wasserwerk*, Wasserwerkgasse 5, is a big techno joint; *U1*, Junkerngasse 1, is a subterranean DJ-bar; and *ISC*, Neubrückstrasse 10, is a student gig venue. There's a carnival in mid-February, a major jazz festival in May and a huge open-air rock festival in July.

Listings

Books Stauffacher, Neuengasse 25, is one of Switzerland's best bookstores.

Email and Internet Jäggi Books, Loeb department store basement, opposite the station (20min free).

Embassies Australia, Alpenstrasse 29 (☎031/351 01 43); Canada, Kirchenfeldstrasse 88 (☎031/352 63 81); Ireland, Kirchenfeldstrasse 68 (☎031/352 14 41); UK, Thunstrasse 50 (☎031/352 50 21); USA, Jubiläumstrasse 93 (☎031/357 70 11). New Zealanders should contact their UN mission in Geneva.

Hospital Inselspital University Hospital, Freiburgstrasse (☎031/632 21 11). Call ☎031/311 22 11 if you need a doctor or dentist.

Post office Schanzenstrasse, behind the station (Mon–Fri 7.30am–6.30pm, Sat 7.30–11am).

ALPINE SWITZERLAND

South of Bern and Luzern lies the grand Alpine heart of Switzerland, a massively impressive region of classic Swiss scenery – high peaks, sheer valleys and cool lakes – that makes for great hiking and gentle walking, not to mention world-class winter sports. The **Bernese Oberland** is the most accessible and touristed area, but beyond this first great wall of peaks is another even more daunting range in Canton Valais, in which the **Matterhorn**, marking the Italian border, is star attraction. The wild summits and remote valleys of **Graubünden**, in the southeastern corner of Switzerland, can provide a welcome escape into areas of great natural beauty that are less reliant on tourist income to survive.

The Bernese Oberland

Most spectacular of the Alpine regions, the **Bernese Oberland** is best known for a grand triple-peaked ridge – the Eiger, Mönch and Jungfrau (Ogre, Monk and Virgin), cresting 4000m. Most beautiful of the surrounding countryside is the **Lauterbrunnen valley**, with the resorts of **Wengen** and **Mürren** perched on plateaus above providing excellent winter skiing and summer hiking, as does **Grindelwald**, in its own valley slightly east. **Interlaken** is the main transport hub for the region, but the sheer volume of tourist traffic passing through the town can make it a less-than-restful place to stay; you may prefer lakeside **Thun**, halfway from Bern, or one of the mountain villages themselves. Tourist offices control the

Oberland's thousands of **chalets and private rooms** – most of which close in the quiet "between-seasons" of April–May and October–November – and can also provide details of the region's numerous **mountain huts** (generally open June–Sept), which exist to offer hikers a bed and simple comforts in the wilds of nature.

Thun

Set astride the River Aare on the lake which bears its name, **THUN**, with its picturesque castle and quaint medieval centre, is well worth a visit, if only for the views of the Eiger, Mönch and Jungfrau and, closer at hand, the giant pyramidal Niesen and flat-topped Stockhorn. After World War II, the authorities decided that in the event of a future invasion, the whole of Switzerland south of Thun was to be abandoned, and the entire population was to assemble here for dispersal into mountain retreats. As a result, Switzerland's largest hospital, pristine and fully equipped, was built inside the Niesen (though so far it has never been used), and there's also a big army base outside town. Across the river from the station, Thun's Old Town, which was disastrously flooded in May 1999, is renowned for the arcading of the main street, split-level **Obere Hauptgasse**, and **Rathausplatz** at its northwestern end. Steps lead up to the fairytale **castle**, built in 1190 and occupied by the Bernese in 1386, which now contains a **museum** (daily: April–Oct 9/10am–5/6pm; Feb & March 1–4pm; Sfr5) with the usual period furniture and militaria. At the lakeshore but on the station side of the river is Schadau Park, home to a lavish nineteenth-century folly and, beside it, the **Wocher Panorama** (May–Oct Tues–Sun 10am–5/6pm), which depicts the daily life of Thun circa 1810.

The **train station** is five minutes southwest of the centre, with a **tourist office** adjacent (July & Aug Mon–Fri 9am–7pm, Sat 9am–4pm; Sept–June Mon–Fri 9am–noon & 1–6pm, Sat 9am–noon). Turn right outside the station for the spotless *Herberge zur Schadau* **hostel** (☎033/222 52 22; ③). Of cheaper **hotels**, *Metzgern* (☎033/222 21 41; ⑤) is most atmospheric; or you could plump for a bunk in a metal tubular module at *Swisstube* (☎033/336 40 67; ③), part of the *Younotent* lakeside **campsite** at Gwatt, a 3km bus-ride southwest. The **restaurants** around Scheibenstrasse are varied and competitively priced, and there are pavement cafés on the central shopping street, Bälliz. Scheibenstrasse has numerous **bars** and *Mokka*, Allmendstrasse 14, is a surprisingly exciting club and venue. For those with time, travelling on to Interlaken by boat provides a pleasant means of taking a leisurely look at the small towns along the Thunersee, most notably tranquil **SPIEZ**, also a major rail junction for the Brig/Zermatt and Montreux lines.

Interlaken

INTERLAKEN isn't much more than its long main street, **Höheweg**, with a train station at each end. It has little to amuse the trippers passing through on their way to the mountains, save for the cafés and hotel bars lining Höheweg and some great **views** towards the Jungfrau massif, perfectly framed between two hills and best savoured from Höhematte, a central grassy rectangle of parkland. The town lies on a neck of land between two of Switzerland's cleanest **lakes**: the best way to arrive is by boat.

Interlaken Ost is the terminus of mainline trains and the departure point for branch lines into the mountains; boats also dock here from Brienz, on the Luzern rail line. Trains from the Bern direction pass first through **Interlaken West** (docking-point for Thunersee boats), and this station is nearer to the main branch of the **tourist office** at Höheweg 37 (Mon–Fri 8am–noon & 2–6pm, also June–Sept Sat 8am–5pm, Oct–May Sat 8am–noon; July & Aug also Sun 5–7pm). Beware that accommodation fills up very quickly at the frantic height of summer and winter high-seasons. Interlaken's **youth hostel** is 2km east (bus #1) in Böningen, at Aareweg 21 (☎033/822 43 53; ③); better is the excellent *Balmer's Herberge*, fifteen minutes south of town at Hauptstrasse 23, Matten (☎033/822 19 61; ②), filled with North American backpackers. There are quieter hostels in town: *Alp Lodge*, Marktgasse 59 (☎033/822 47 48; ③), *Happy Inn*, Rosenstrasse 17 (☎033/822 32 25; ②), and the quality *Backpackers Villa Sonnenhof*, Alpenstrasse 16 (☎033/826 71 71; ③). The nearest **campsite** is *Sackgut* (☎033/822 44 34; May–Oct) behind Ost station. *Beyeler* at Bernastrasse 37 (☎033/822 90 30; ④) is a comfortable family-run **hotel**. For budget **food**, visit *Migros* restaurant opposite West station; *PizPaz* on Centralstrasse for pasta, pizza and fish dishes at Sfr16 upwards; or *El Azteca*, Jungfraustrasse 30, offering Mexican set-meals from Sfr13. *Café Runft* opposite West station is a tearoom, snackerie and **bar** open until 3am; *Positiv Einfach*, Centralstrasse 11, is a small music bar; and *Balmer's* has cheap beer. *Weltraum*, Rosenstrasse 5, offers **Internet** access.

The Jungfraujoch railway

Switzerland's most popular (and expensive) mountain railway trundles through lush countryside south from Interlaken before coiling spectacularly up across mountain pastures, breaking the treeline and tunnelling clean through the Eiger to emerge at the **JUNGFRAU-JOCH**, an icy, windswept col just beneath the Jungfrau summit with the awesome Aletsch glacier, largest in the Alps, for company. The top station, inevitably, is a tourist circus of ice sculptures, husky sleigh rides, glacier walks, a short ski run, restaurants and a post office, all 3454m above sea-level and invariably overflowing with tour-groups – but nonetheless, on a clear day, worth the expense to reach. Panoramic views from the Sphinx Terrace (3571m) to Germany's Black Forest in one direction and across a gleaming wasteland to the Italian Alps in the other are heart-thumping.

There are two **routes** to the top. Trains head southwest from Interlaken Ost along the valley floor to Lauterbrunnen, from where you pick up the mountain line which climbs through Wengen; trains also head southeast from Interlaken Ost to Grindelwald, where you change for the climb, arriving from the other direction. All trains terminate at Kleine Scheidegg, where you must change for the final pull to Jungfraujoch; the popular practice is to go up one way and down the other. The adult round-trip **fare** from Interlaken is a budget-crunching Sfr159; InterRail and EuroDomino aren't valid, but Eurail knocks 25 percent off. Even the five-day Jungfraubahnen Pass (Sfr133; Sfr85 with a Half-Fare Card), which buys extensive free travel, and the broader seven-day Bernese Oberland Pass (Sfr165/132), both pointlessly stop short at Kleine Scheidegg, requiring you to shell out an extra Sfr50 to reach the summit. The Swiss Pass is valid up to Wengen and Grindelwald; above them, you must pay 75 percent. There's also a discounted **Good Morning ticket** (Sfr120; Eurail Sfr105; Swiss Pass Sfr94), for those travelling up on the first train of the day (6.35am from Interlaken; arrival 9am), and leaving the summit by noon (Nov–April: first or second train plus later departure permitted). **Walking** some sections of the journey, up or down, is perfectly feasible in summer, and can save a lot of money. Excellent transport networks and vista-rich footpaths linking all the villages means that with judicious use of a hiking map and timetable you can see and do a great deal in a day and still get back to Interlaken, or even Bern or Zürich, by nightfall. Check the pictures from the summit, broadcast live on Interlaken cable-TV, for an idea of the weather conditions.

The Lauterbrunnen valley

The village of **LAUTERBRUNNEN** lies at the bottom of an immense U-shaped valley, famous for the many waterfalls cascading down its sides, including the **Staubbachfälle**, the highest in Switzerland at nearly 300m, which tumble just beyond the village. There's a **tourist office** (Mon–Fri 8am–noon & 2–6pm; July & Aug also Sat & Sun 8am–3pm) 200m up from the train station. Among cheaper **hotels** are *Horner* (☎033/855 16 73; ⑤), beyond the tourist office; and *Bahnhof* (☎033/855 17 23; ⑤), beside the station. Just over the river, *Matratzenlager Stocki* (☎033/855 17 54; Jan–Oct; ①) has good dorms in a converted farmhouse. There are two **campsites**, *Jungfrau* (☎033/856 20 10) and the quieter *Schützenbach* (☎033/855 12 68), both with dorms and rooms (②). Three kilometres up the valley are the **Trümmelbachfälle** (daily: July & Aug 8am–6pm; Sept–June 9am–5pm; Sfr10), a series of impressively thunderous waterfalls – the runoff from the high mountains – which have carved corkscrew channels through the valley walls; to get there it's a scenic thirty-minute walk or the hourly postbus. The same bus continues to **STECHELBERG** at the end of the road, where you'll find a *Naturfreundehaus* (☎033/855 12 02; ②). A cable-car from Stechelberg leaps the valley's west wall to reach the quiet village of **GIMMELWALD**, with the popular self-catering *Mountain Hostel* (no reservations; ①), then rises further to car-free

MÜRREN, a holiday village which has managed to retain its endearing desert-island atmosphere (in the off-season at least), also accessible from Lauterbrunnen station via a funicular and spectacular cliff-edge train, well worth taking. From Mürren, the valley floor is 800m straight down, and the panorama of peaks filling the sky is dazzling. The sports centre houses the **tourist office** (Mon–Fri 9am–noon & 1–6.30pm, Thurs until 8.30pm; July–Sept & Dec–April also Sat & Sun 1–5.30pm). For **accommodation**, *Belmont* (☎033/855 35 35; ③) is outside the train station, at the other end of the village from the cable-car. Mürren has good skiing in winter, great hiking in summer, and a breathtaking cable-car ride up to the **SCHILTHORN** (2970m), where you can enjoy exceptional panoramic views and sip cocktails in the revolving *Piz Gloria* summit restaurant, featured in the James Bond film *On Her Majesty's Secret Service* – the trip's less expensive than the Jungfraujoch, and also less of a merry-go-round, but just as memorable. For extra thrills, contact Adventure World (☎033/826 77 11) to bungee 180m out of the cable-car (May–Oct; Sfr240).

On the other side of the valley, trains bound for Kleine Scheidegg grind up from Lauterbrunnen to **WENGEN**, another gorgeous, car-free paradise perched on a shelf of tranquil southwest-facing meadow, which stays lively with skiers well into April. Once the snows have receded, it sits amidst ideal hiking country. The village is overlooked by the Jungfrau and, with such a lofty outlook, enjoys unrivalled valley sunsets. There's a **tourist office** (Mon–Fri 8am–noon & 2–6pm, Sat 8.30–11.30am; July–Sept & Dec–April also Sat & Sun 4–6pm) on the main street, just up from the train station. Several **hotels** offer dorm beds: best is Christian-run *Bergheim* (☎033/855 27 55; ③), part of *Hotel Jungfraublick*. The popular *Hot Chili Peppers Café* (☎033/855 50 20; ③) has dorms and rooms, while smoke-free *Edelweiss* (☎033/855 23 88; ⑥) overlooks the valley. Every January, Wengen hosts World Cup downhill and slalom ski-races on the Lauberhorn, which are great to watch (Sfr20), but can book the village, and the valley, out.

Grindelwald

There's a wider range of accommodation in **GRINDELWALD**, nestling under the craggy trio of the Wetterhorn, Mättenberg and Eiger. Numerous trails around **Pfingstegg** and especially **First** – both at the end of gondola lines from Grindelwald – provide excellent hiking, and the icy caverns of the Oberer Gletscher are a ninety-minute walk, plus 890 stairs, away (May–Oct daily 9am–6pm; Sfr5). The **tourist office** (July & Aug Mon–Fri 8am–7pm, Sat 8am–5pm, Sun 9–11am & 3–5pm; Sept–June Mon–Fri 8am–noon & 2–6pm, Sat 8am–noon & 2–5pm) is near the station, with info on accompanied paragliding (Sfr150), alongside the Oberland's main **Bergsteigerzentrum** (Mountaineering Centre; ☎033/853 52 00), offering easy guided ascents (Sfr75 to the 2928-metre Schwarzhorn), canyon jumps (Sfr95), glacier abseils (Sfr44), and more. A bus from opposite *Hotel Bernerhof*, or a steep fifteen-minute walk, will get you to Terrassenweg, a quiet lane running above the village, where there's an excellent **youth hostel** (☎033/853 10 09; ③) and a *Naturfreundehaus* (☎033/853 13 33; ②). *Mountain Hostel* (☎033/853 39 00; ③) is on the valley floor, beside Grindelwald-Grund station. The nearby **Grosse Scheidegg** pass is closed to private cars, but you can cross it by postbus; **MEIRINGEN** on the other side has trains to Interlaken and Luzern.

Kleine Scheidegg

KLEINE SCHEIDEGG – four buildings huddled below the Eiger's sheer north face – throngs with daytime crowds switching trains for the Jungfraujoch, but sees virtually nobody staying overnight, although the "Good Morning" return to Jungfraujoch from here is a moderate Sfr58 (first train 8am). The station has comfortable dorms and rooms (☎033/855 11 51; ③), and is the trailhead for a wealth of high-country walks (mostly June–Sept). Hikes down to Wengen (roughly 2hr) or Grindelwald (roughly 4hr), or up the "back" of the Lauberhorn (1hr), are easy. The picturesque route to **Männlichen**, perched on a ridge, is particularly lovely (1hr 30min). The Männlichen–Wengen cable-car suffered avalanche-damage in 1999; instead, take the amazing half-hour gondola ride the other direction to Grindelwald-Grund.

Zermatt and the Matterhorn

The shark's-tooth **Matterhorn** (4478m) is the most famous, if not the highest, of Switzerland's peaks, and climbing it is a serious business. But the land all around is perfect walking country, with numerous trails stemming from the bustling village of **Zermatt**, reached via the main rail junction at **Brig**. Trains from Lake Geneva cruise up the Rhône Valley through Sion to Brig; those from Bern use the Lötschberg Tunnel at Kandersteg to cut south under the Jungfrau range. From Zürich and the east, you'll either approach via the Lötschberg or you could opt for the mountain-top Furka–Oberalp line via Andermatt (Eurail and InterRail not valid; closed in winter); this comprises the central section of the St Moritz–Zermatt "Glacier Express" which takes in some of Switzerland's finest scenery in a day-long journey by panoramic train. Just as stunning is the lusher scenery on the slow Centovalli line from Locarno via Domodossola in Italy (passport needed), arriving at Brig through the Simplon Tunnel. All these, apart from the Glacier Express, necessitate changing – either at Brig, where the Zermatt train (Eurail not valid, InterRail half price) departs from Bahnhofplatz outside the main station, or at Visp nearby.

An hour south of Visp, car-free **ZERMATT** is a mountaineer's and hiker's paradise. Its main street throngs with fiacres and electric minibuses, linking the train station at the northern end to the cable-car terminus at the south. The **Alpine Museum** (summer daily 10am–noon & 4–6pm; winter Sun–Fri 4.30–6.30pm; Sfr3), commemorates the tragic first ascent of the Matterhorn, led by Edward Whymper in 1865: on the way down, one of his party slipped, sending himself and three others to their deaths. They, and many more Matterhorn hopefuls, are commemorated in the town's burgeoning cemetery. Opposite the train station, the *Gornergrat-Bahn* (Eurail not valid, InterRail half price, Swiss Pass 25-percent reduction) departs roughly every half-hour all day, giving spectacular Matterhorn views (sit on the right) all the way up to the **Gornergrat**, a vantage point with a magnificent panorama of the Valaisian Alps and Monte Rosa massif: Switzerland's highest peak, the Dufourspitze (4634m), is 10km southeast. At the south end of Zermatt village a cable-car heads up to the **Schwarzsee**, the most popular point from which to view the Matterhorn, and, when the snow clears, the trailhead for a hairy two-hour walk to the **Hörnlihütte**, right below the mountain at 3260m. All the area's cable-cars – to Trockener Steg, Klein Matterhorn and more – offer hikes and spectacular views.

Practicalities

There's a list of **hotels** and a courtesy phone in the station; otherwise consult the overworked **tourist office** nearby (June–Sept & Dec–April Mon–Fri 8.30am–noon & 2–7pm, Sat 8.30am–7pm, Sun 9.30am–noon & 4–7pm; rest of year Mon–Fri 8.30am–noon & 1.30–6pm, Sat 8.30am–noon). The **mountain guides** office (July–Sept Mon–Fri 8.30am–noon & 4–7pm, Sat 4–7pm, Sun 10am–noon & 4–7pm; Jan–May daily 5–7pm; ☎027/967 34 56) provides information and organizes tours and climbs. The excellent **youth hostel** is on the east side of the village (closed May & Nov; ☎027/967 23 20; ④), near the *Matterhorn Hostel* (☎027/966 27 37; ③). *Camping Zermatt* (☎027/967 54 14; June–Sept) is below the station on the road back down the valley; *Camping Alpbühel* (☎027/967 36 35) is 5km away at Täsch, where drivers must park. Of the many **hotels**, *Bahnhof* (☎028/967 24 06; ③; dorms ②) is basic and popular, as is central *Weisshorn* (☎027/967 11 12; ⑤). *Bellavista* (☎027/966 28 10; ⑦), above town, has great Matterhorn views. **Mountain hotels and huts** at Gornergrat, Schwarzsee and Hörnlihütte bring you closer to the elements. Aside from the rock-bottom *Big Shop* diner near the church, hotel food is good value; the *Weisshorn* and *Café du Port* next door have the best local ambience.

Graubünden

Switzerland's largest canton is known as *Graubünden* in German, *Grisons* in French (though it has no French-speaking communities), *Grigioni* in Italian and *Grischun* in Romansh, a variant of Latin unique to the area. If you stick to the tourist centres, you'll see and hear only

Swiss-German, but if you venture into the countryside you'll find signs to the *staziun* pointing along *Via principala*, or hear people greeting each other with "Allegra!" in what sounds like Italian with a Swiss-German accent but is in fact one of the five dialects of Romansh, first language of some 70,000 people. Graubünden extends south of the Alps – to within spitting distance of Bellinzona (see below) – and so also incorporates a substantial Italian-speaking minority. Its name, translating as "The Grey Leagues", stems from a 1471 pact of commoners which overthrew the rule of the region's bishop-princes. Since that time, Bündners have been free, and they relish the fact more than most other Swiss: it took until 1803 for them to assent to join the Confederation, and even today the canton votes unequivocally against joining the EU. Its landscape of deep, isolated valleys and thick pine forests makes it the wildest and loneliest part of Switzerland, despite the presence of renowned mountain resorts such as **St Moritz** and **Davos**. The cantonal capital **Chur** is on a fast train link from Zürich.

Chur

Sitting in a deep valley carved by the Rhine, **CHUR** has been a powerful ecclesiastical centre since the earliest times, and is dominated by its **cathedral**, occupying high ground just east of the town centre. Inside there are fragments of frescoes, a fifteenth-century altarpiece depicting Christ stumbling under the weight of the cross, surrounded with scenes from the life of St Catherine, and, below the choir, four carved stone figures of the Apostles dating from around 1200. The **treasury**, too, is worth a look (daily 10am–noon & 2–4pm) for its set of ancient reliquaries and statuary. The cathedral is surrounded by the eighteenth-century buildings of the **Hof**, the Bishop's palace. Steps descend to the **Rätisches Museum** (Tues–Sun 10am–noon & 2–5pm; Sfr5), largely devoted to folk costumes and domestic utensils from the Graubünden region. A picturesque town centre nestles below, a succession of fountained squares bisected by the main north–south thoroughfare, **Poststrasse**, which leads past the arcaded courtyard of the fifteenth-century town hall. On Postplatz at Poststrasse's northern end, Chur's **Kunstmuseum** (Tues–Sun 10am–noon & 2–5pm, Thurs until 8pm; Sfr7) features paintings by Graubünden artists Angelika Kauffmann, Giovanni Giacometti, and his son Alberto.

Chur's **train** and huge **postbus station** is five minutes northwest of the centre at the head of Bahnhofstrasse, which links to Postplatz. In this landscape, buses are often better than trains: the fastest way to Ticino, for instance, is by postbus via the scenic San Bernardino route. As well as maps, the **tourist office**, Grabenstrasse 5, east of Postplatz (Mon 1.30–6pm, Tues–Fri 8.30am–noon & 1.30–6pm, Sat 9am–noon) has pamphlets explaining the red and green footprints painted on Chur's pavements, which show the routes of self-guided walking tours. The cheapest **hotels** are *Rosenhügel*, Malixerstrasse 32 (☎081/252 23 38; ③) and *Franziskaner*, Kupfergasse 18 (☎081/252 12 61; ④). *Camping Au* is at Felsenaustrasse 61 (☎081/284 22 83). With the canton's only matriculation college, Chur has loads of pre-university students packing the dozens of bars around the Obertor: *Street Café*, Grabenstrasse 47, is most popular, but *Rock Me*, Goldgasse 3, tends to play better music.

Davos

Twinned with Aspen, Colorado, **DAVOS** isn't so much a resort as a full-blown town, way up at 1560m. Its two halves, Davos-Platz and Davos-Dorf, are strung along a four-kilometre ribbon of low-key development: Platz is where most hotels and amenities are; Dorf is where locals take refuge; and between the two the giant Kongresszentrum, where world leaders meet every January to discuss global cashflow. Davos, however, is most famous for the freshness of its air and for its excellent snow cover, and has recently gained new life (and hipness) with the seal of approval of Switzerland's snowboarding cognoscenti. In summer hotel prices plummet, but the town can be very restful and is surrounded by beautiful countryside for walking in. Sole attraction in town, 2km east of Platz along the main street, Promenade, is the **Kirchner Museum** (Christmas–Easter & July–Sept Tues–Sun 10am–noon & 2–6pm; rest of year Tues–Sun 2–6pm; Sfr8), a vibrant collection by the German Expressionist painter Ernst Ludwig Kirchner, who emigrated to Davos, was tagged "degenerate" by the Nazis, and committed suicide in 1938. There are many routes up the slopes on both sides of the valley to launch skiing or hiking trips; one of the best, the **Parsennbahn** funicular, heads from the Dorf end of Promenade up the **Weissfluh**, the mountain which dominates the resort and whose snowfields provide some of Switzerland's best ski-runs. It terminates at the **Weissfluhjoch**, a col below the summit, from where a cable-car runs to the top; the invigorating walk down takes a couple of hours. There are almost limitless possibilities for easier walks, especially in the meadows and woods around the small Davosersee lake, a short distance beyond Dorf.

A **branch line**, operated by the local Rhätische Bahn, runs from Landquart (15km north of Chur) to Davos, and on to Filisur on the St Moritz line; trains stop at both Davos-Dorf and Davos-Platz. Postbuses run direct from Chur. There are **tourist offices** opposite Dorf station and at Promenade 67 in Platz (both June–Oct Mon–Fri 8.30am–6pm, Sat 8.30am–4/5pm; Dec–March also Sun 10am–noon; April, May & Nov Sat closes 12.30pm). Most **hotels** and facilities are closed in the off-seasons, from mid-April until June and mid-October until mid-December. Cheapest in Platz are *Soliva*, Symondstrasse 7 (☎081/416 57 27; ④) and *Albana*, Talstrasse 18 (☎081/413 58 41; ⑤); and in Dorf *Montana*, Bahnhofstrasse 2 (☎081/413 34 08; ②) and *Bristol*, Promenade 121 (☎081/416 30 33; ④) – codes refer to summer prices, which can double in winter. A Guest Card gives free unlimited use of Davos's excellent public transport, covering buses and trains between Platz and Dorf, and along 15km of the valley floor; this makes it easy to reach the youth hostel (☎081/416 14 84; ②; closed May & Nov; bus #6 or #11), overlooking Davosersee. The riverside *Färich* **campsite** (☎081/416 10 43) is ten minutes' walk from Dorf towards the Flüelapass.

St Moritz

Plopped down amidst the quiet villages of the wild and touchingly gorgeous Engadine Valley that runs for 100km along the south side of the Alps, brassy **ST MORITZ** is the prime winter retreat of the international jet set, who over the years have created a mini-Manhattan of Vuitton and Armani in this stunningly romantic setting of forest, lake and mountains; when the tourist office trumpets St Moritz's "champagne climate", they don't necessarily mean the sparkling sunshine (although there's plenty of that as well). The town spans two villages, St Moritz-Bad on the Lej da San Murezzan (Lake St Moritz in Romansh), and St Moritz-Dorf on the hillside above. This time it's Dorf that's the swishy one, and Bad – site of a Roman spa – that's more affordable. Via dal Bagn runs down the hill from Dorf to Bad, passing on the way the **Engadiner Museum** (June–Oct Mon–Fri 9.30am–noon & 2–5pm, Sun 10am–noon; Sfr5), housed in a solid stone building that's one of the few surviving pieces of vernacular architecture in the town. Immediately above, a curious domed affair holds the excellent **Giovanni Segantini Museum** (June–Oct & Dec–April Tues–Sun 10am–noon & 3–6pm; Sfr7), displaying the mystically beautiful work of this largely self-taught Symbolist, acclaimed as the definitive painter of Alpine life.

Rhätische-Bahn trains from Chur and postbuses from Lugano stop at St Moritz's **train station** below Dorf, from where Via Serlas winds up to a central square and the **tourist office**, Via Maistra 12 (July–Aug & Dec–April Mon–Sat 9am–6pm; Christmas–March also Sun 4–6pm; rest of year Mon–Fri 9am–noon & 2–6pm, Sat 9am–noon). The **youth hostel**, Via Surpunt 60 (☎081/833 39 69; ④), is twenty minutes' walk around the lake (or bus-stop Sonne), close to the **campsite** (☎081/833 40 90) just beyond Bad. For **hotels**, *Bellaval* (☎081/833 32 45; ⑤) beside Dorf station, and *Sonne* (☎081/833 03 63; ⑤) in Bad have affordable **restaurants**, as does Via dal Bagn. For a **drink**, try *Bobby's Pub*, Via dal Bagn 52, or *Garage Pit Stop*, Via Maistra 33, which has live music and a disco.

St Moritz boasts legendary bob and toboggan courses, including the death-defying **Cresta Run** (five rides Sfr450), and the famous five-kilometre **Preda–Bergün toboggan run**. Wooden sleds can be rented to make the winter run from Preda station (Sfr10), and the specially modified road run takes you down through the scenic Albula valley to Bergün, where RhB trains will cart you back to the beginning (Sfr29 for a day ticket). Trains run late, so you can sled the illuminated route by night.

TICINO

The Italian-speaking canton of **Ticino** (*Tessin* in German and French) occupies the balmy, lake-laced southern foothills of the Alps. It's radically different from the rest of the country in almost every way: culture, food, architecture, attitude and driving style owe more to Milan than Zürich, and the famously sunny skies even draw in fog-bound Milanese for a breath of air. The Swiss have controlled the area since the early 1500s, when they moved to secure the southern approaches of the St Gotthard Pass against the Dukes of Milan; despite some ups and downs since then, the Ticinesi – appearances notwithstanding – remain resolutely and contentedly Swiss. However, although a local dialect exists, almost everyone prefers to speak Italian, thus making it almost impossible for an outsider to tell the locals apart from the 36,000 Italian *frontalieri* who cross into Ticino daily to work for salaries well below the Swiss average. It's a cruel irony that Ticino suffers Switzerland's highest unemployment rates, even while its service industries thrive – staffed by Italians and paid for by thousands of Swiss-German tourists and second-home-owners.

The main attractions are the lakeside resorts of **Locarno** and **Lugano**, where mountain scenery merges with the subtropical flora encouraged by the warm climate. The area is also known for its old churches, many containing medieval frescoes and most featuring huge external murals of St Christopher, patron saint of travellers. Unless you approach Ticino from Italy, there's only one train line in – through the 16km **Gotthard Tunnel**, the world's longest. The track's contortions on the northern approach climb are famous: trains pass Wassen's onion-domed church three times, first far above you, then on a level, and finally far below, before entering blackness at Göschenen and emerging (often into broad sunshine) at Airolo for the descent to Ticino's capital, **Bellinzona**.

Bellinzona

Guarding the southern approaches to the San Gottardo and San Bernardino passes, **BELLINZONA** is the junction-point through which most traffic flows without stopping, but it's worth spending some quiet time here before the bustle of the lakes. High on the town's central rock, and accessible by lift from behind Piazza del Sole, is **Castelgrande** (Tues–Sun 9am–midnight), most impressive of Bellinzona's three medieval castles. Steps wind down from here to the elegant Renaissance buildings of **Piazza Collegiata**, dominated by a lavish church and surrounded by atmospheric old-town alleys – Piazza Nosetto is just south, as is peaceful Piazza Indipendenza. On the eastern side of the square, a path rises to **Castello di Montebello** (Tues–Sun 8am–6pm), with great views, from where a stiff 45-minute climb further up will bring you to **Castello di Sasso Corbaro** (April–Oct Tues–Sun 8am–6pm), with a particularly welcome vine-shaded restaurant and a spectacular rampart panorama. All three castles house missable historical and/or archeological museums (combi ticket Sfr8, student discount). South of Indipendenza, **Villa dei Cedri**, Piazza San Biagio, houses the town's art collection (Tues–Sun 10am–noon & 2–5pm; Sfr8), focusing on nineteenth- and twentieth-century Swiss and Italian art. The frescoed church of **San Biagio** adjacent is undergoing renovation, as is the church of **Santa Maria delle Grazie** across the tracks – this was severely damaged by fire after a nativity scene caught alight on New Year's Eve 1996, but attempts are being made to restore its enormous sixteenth-century *Crucifixion*.

Bellinzona's **train station** is ten minutes north of the centre. The **tourist office** (Mon–Fri 8am–6.30pm; also April–Sept Sat 9am–5pm, Oct–March Sat 9am–noon), under the arcades just off Piazza Nosetto, has lots of material and will give you some excellent walking suggestions. The riverside *Molinazzo* **campsite** (May–Oct; ☎091/829 11 18) is well north of town. Best of the few budget **hotels** are *Garni Moderno*, Viale Stazione 17b (☎091/825 13 76; ④) and *Metropoli*, Via Lodovico il Moro 5 (☎091/825 11 79; ④). Cheap food can be had at *Inova*, Ticino's version of *Manora*, in the Innovazione store on Viale Stazione. Castelgrande houses the *Grotto San Michele* (a *grotto* is a Ticinese tavern for local wine and cheap home-cooking), where you can eat on the panoramic terrace for Sfr14–20. Pavement **café-bars** abound, especially around Via Codeborgo, where you'll see (or hear) *Amadeus*, a popular music bar on Vicolo Torre.

Locarno

Mainline trains speed south to Lugano and Milan, while a branch line heads west to Lake Maggiore and its principal Swiss resort, **LOCARNO**, overrun with the rich and wannabe-famous on summer weekends yet still managing to retain its Mediterranean, shades-and-*gelati* cool. The focus of town is **Piazza Grande**, a busy arcaded square just off the lakefront. The palm-fringed promenade runs south to the **Bosco Isolino** park, five minutes away, but most interest lies in the narrow streets of the old town, ranged on gently rising ground behind Piazza Grande: wandering through the alleys with an ice-cream is the best way to blend in with local life. From the west end of the piazza, lanes run up to Via Citadella and the richly Baroque **Chiesa Nuova**, with a sumptuously stuccoed ceiling featuring fleshy cherubs. Via Borghese, one street further up, brings you to the huge and rather sombre church of **San Antonio**, next to which is **Casa Rusca** (Tues–Sun 10am–noon & 2–5pm; Sfr5), an art museum focusing on modern Swiss artists such as Jean Arp. Alleys lead south downhill to the tall fourteenth-century church of **San Francesco**, with faded Baroque frescoes, and further down to the thirteenth-century **Castello Visconteo**, housing an archeological museum (April–Oct Tues–Sun 10am–noon & 2–5pm; Sfr5), especially strong on beautiful Roman glass. East of the station is the austere twelfth-century Romanesque basilica of **San Vittore**, with an earlier crypt and medieval fresco-fragments. Most striking of all, though, is the church of **Madonna del Sasso** (daily 8am–6pm), an impressive ochre vision floating above the town founded in 1480 by one of the brothers from San Francesco. The walk up (or down) through a wooded ravine and past decaying shrines, is glorious; or take the funicular from just west of the station to Ticino's greatest photo opportunity, looking down on the church and lake. From the top, the cable-car further up to Cardada, where there are more walking routes, should be back in operation by 2000. East of Locarno is **Valle Verzasca**, where deathwish freaks can re-enact the opening scene of another James Bond film, *Goldeneye*, by bungeeing a world-record 220m off the **Verzasca Dam** (☎01/950 33 88; April–Oct; Sfr260).

Practicalities

Locarno's **train station** is steps from both Piazza Grande and **Lake Maggiore**, which extends way south into Italy; summer boats run to nearby Swiss lakeside resorts such as Ascona, and on to Italian ones such as Stresa. The **tourist office** (March–Oct Mon–Fri 9am–6pm, Sat 10am–4pm, Sun 10am–2pm; Oct–March Mon–Fri 9am–12.30pm & 2–6pm) is in the Casino complex on Largo Zorzi. Both the modern **youth hostel** *Ostello Palagiovani*, Via Varenna 18 (☎091/756 15 00; ③) – bus #31 or #36 (direction Centovalli) to Cinque Vie – and central *Città Vecchia*, Via Torretta 13 (March–Oct; ☎091/751 45 54; ③) have dorms and rooms; *Ostello Giaciglio*, Via Rusca 7 (☎091/751 30 64; ③) has dorms only. A small step up are *Reginetta*, Via alla Motta 8 (March–Oct; ☎091/752 35 53; ④); *Cittadella*, Via Cittadella 18 (☎091/751 58 85; ⑤); and characterful *Vecchia Locarno*, Via Motta 10 (☎091/751 65 02; ⑥). The pricey *Delta* **campsite** (☎091/751 60 81) is fifteen minutes south along the lakeshore. There's a self-service *Inova* beside the station and Piazza Grande is full of cafés and pizzerias buzzing from morning until after midnight, although **eating** and **drinking** is more atmospheric in the old town alleys. *Cittadella* (see above) serves affordable pizzas downstairs, and pricier fish dishes upstairs; friendly *Bar del Pozzo* is on Piazza Sant'Antonio; *Cantina Canetti* off Piazza Grande has live accordion on weekend nights; *Simba*, Lungolago 3a, is a popular DJ bar. The excellent **Locarno International Film Festival**, held in early August, is stealing a march on Cannes for movie-quality and star-appeal; catch nightly offerings on the huge open-air screen in Piazza Grande.

The Centovalli railway

Locarno is the eastern terminus of the wonderful **Centovalli railway**. Dinky trains depart from beneath the station for the impressive Centovalli – so named for its "hundred" valleys –

most of the time sidewinding above ravine-like depths (sit on the left). On the way, tiny **VER-SCIO** houses *Teatro Dimitri*, a highly acclaimed international mime school staging regular budget performances in summer, while **INTRAGNA**'s graceful 70m bridge was the scene for Switzerland's first bungee attempt, still a choice spot for leaping. After the border (passport needed), trains roll through rustic villages and ease down into bustling **DOMODOSSOLA** – in Italy, but considered a terminus of the Swiss network. Connections from here run west to Brig and Bern, and south to Milan. Locarno's **Lago Maggiore Express** ticket combines the Centovalli line with a Domodossola–Stresa connection, plus a boat back to Locarno (Sfr42; 9hr).

Lugano

With its compact cluster of Italianate piazzas and extensive tree-lined promenades, **LUGANO** is the most alluring of Ticino's lake resorts, less touristic than Locarno but with, if anything, double the chic. Centre of town is **Piazza di Riforma**, a huge café-lined square perfect for eyeballing passers-by over a cappuccino. **Lake Lugano** is metres away, as are the characterful steep lanes of the old town: through the maze northwest of Riforma, Via Cattedrale dog-legs up to **Cattedrale San Lorenzo**, characterized by a fine Renaissance portal, fragments of interior frescoes, and spectacular views from its terrace. Also from Riforma, Via Nassa – rivalling Zürich's Bahnhofstrasse for big-name designer glitz – heads southwest to the medieval church of **Santa Maria degli Angioli**, containing a stunning wall-sized fresco of the Crucifixion. A little further south is the **Museo d'Arte Moderna**, Riva Caccia 5 (Tues–Sun 9am–7pm; Sfr10), with high-quality temporary shows; and a little further still is the modestly named district of **PARADISO**, from where a funicular rises to **San Salvatore**, a rugged rock pinnacle offering fine views of the lake and surrounding countryside. East from Riforma, you'll find the **Museo Cantonale d'Arte**, Via Canova 10 (Tues 2–6pm, Wed–Sun 10am–6pm; Sfr10), which has work by Klee and Renoir amongst local depictions of peasant life. In the attractive Parco Civico, five minutes' east, Villa Ciani, with some sumptuously decorated ceilings, houses the **Museo Civici di Belle Arti** (Tues–Sun 10am–noon & 2–6pm; Sfr5), showing works by Cranach, Giovanni Serodine and Henri Rousseau. If you continue east along the shore (or take bus #1), you'll come to the gates of **Villa Favorita** (Easter–Oct Fri–Sun 10am–5pm; Sfr10), home to part of the Thyssen-Bornemisza art collection, the world's second-greatest in private hands (after the Queen's). After the Old Masters were shipped to Madrid in 1992, what's left are excellent nineteenth- and twentieth-century European and American works, many of them by relative unknowns but all the more eye-opening for that. The villa can only be approached via a long cypress-lined path through lavishly beautiful waterside gardens, a dreamy wander almost worth the entrance fee by itself. Seriously wealthy **CASTAGNOLA** covers the slopes of **Monte Brè** behind, while a funicular rises from the adjacent district of **CASSARATE** to the summit, with bracing walks and views; alternatively you could continue a stroll east on the Sentiero di Gandria around to the picturesque frontier village of **GANDRIA**, rising straight from the water. On the opposite shore is the tiny Italian enclave of **CAMPIONE**, lacking lire or passport controls but benefiting from liberal Italian gaming law: its massive casino is where Lugano's many high-rollers dally. The best of the lake, though, is behind San Salvatore on the Ceresio peninsula, accessed by boats or postbuses. Here you'll find tiny **MONTAGNOLA**, where Hermann Hesse lived for 43 years; his first house, Casa Camuzzi, is now a small museum (March–Oct Tues–Sun 10am–12.30pm & 2–6.30pm; Nov–Feb Sat & Sun same times; Sfr5), with an excellent 45-minute English film on Hesse's life in Ticino. Jewel of the lake, however, is **MORCOTE** on the gorgeous southern tip of the peninsula. Tranquil stepped lanes lead up to its photogenic church of **Santa Maria del Sasso**, with striking interior frescoes and a grand vista. Several walks explore the lush woodlands, including a trail back to San Salvatore (2hr 30min).

Practicalities

Lugano's **train station** overlooks the town from the west, linked to the centre by funicular or by steps down to Via Cattedrale. If you're going on to Milan, ask for a free city-transport pass with your train ticket. Lugano's **tourist office** is in the Palazzo Civico, between Riforma and the lake (April–Oct Mon–Fri 9am–6.30pm, Sat 9am–12.30pm & 1.30–5pm, Sun 10am–2pm; Nov–March Mon–Fri 9am–12.30pm & 1.30–5.30pm). One of Switzerland's best and cheapest **youth hostels** (complete with swimming pool), is at Via Cantonale 13, Savosa (April–Oct; ☎091/966 27 28; ②) – bus #5 to Crocifisso from the stop 200m left out of the train station. *Montarina*, Via Montarina 1 (☎091/966 72 72; ③), behind the station, also has dorms. Good-value cheaper **hotels** include *Pestalozzi*, Piazza Indipendenza 9 (☎091/921 46 46; ⑤) and central *Zurigo*, Corso Pestalozzi 13 (☎091/923 43 43; ⑤). Agno, a short train ride west, has several lakeside **campsites**, including *Molinazzo* (☎091/605 17 57). Lugano is blessed with both espresso bars as it should be, such as *La Cafferia Cattedrale*, Via Cattedrale 6, and reasonably priced **eateries** on all the central piazzas: Piazza Cioccaro, the lower terminus of the funicular, is home to a big *Inova* and *Sayonara* (for pasta not sushi), while the smaller pizza-pasta *Commercio* is a couple of blocks north on Via Ariosto. The Riforma cafés, especially *Olimpia*, do surprisingly good inexpensive food, while *La Tinèra*, off Via dei Gorini, behind Riforma, has tasty Ticinese chicken stews and *Hotel Pestalozzi* (see above) has a good vegetarian restaurant. *City-Disc*, Piazza Dante, offers **Internet**. Although the many bars and cafés around Riforma are packed with evening **drinkers**, hip Luganese tuck themselves away elsewhere: off Via Vegezzi, east of the post office, pumping *La Salsita* doubles as cool drinking den and Mexican eatery, while in the unlikely warren of the Quartiere Maghetti nearby is *Etnic*, with superb inexpensive Mediterranean-style food, beer, cocktails and a cosy local atmosphere.

travel details

Trains

Basel to: Bern (hourly; 1hr); Geneva (hourly; 2hr 50min); Interlaken West & Ost (hourly; 2hr 10min); Lausanne (hourly; 2hr 30min); Lugano (hourly; 3hr 50min); Luzern (hourly; 1hr 5min); Zürich (every 30min; 1hr).

Bellinzona to: Locarno (every 30min; 20min); Lugano (every 30min; 25min); Luzern (hourly; 2hr 35min); Zürich (hourly; 2hr 45min).

Bern to: Basel (hourly; 1hr); Brig (hourly; 1hr 40min); Geneva (every 30min; 1hr 45min); Interlaken West & Ost (hourly; 45min); Lausanne (every 30min; 1hr 10min); Luzern (every 2hr; 1hr 20min); Thun (twice hourly; 20min); Zürich (every 30min; 1hr 10min).

Brig to: Bern (hourly; 1hr 40min); Lausanne (twice hourly; 1hr 45min); Zermatt (hourly; 1hr 20min).

Chur to: Davos (hourly; 1hr 35min – change at Landquart in summer); St Moritz (hourly; 2hr); Zürich (hourly; 1hr 35min).

Davos to: Chur via Landquart (hourly; 1hr 35min); St Moritz via Filisur (hourly; 1hr 35min).

Geneva to: Basel (hourly; 2hr 50min); Bern (hourly; 1hr 45min); Brig (twice hourly; 2hr 20min); Lausanne (3 hourly; 35min); Montreux (hourly; 1hr 5min); Vevey (hourly; 1hr); Zürich (every 30min; 3hr).

Grindelwald to: Interlaken Ost (hourly; 20min); Kleine Scheidegg (every 30min; 35min).

Interlaken Ost to: Bern (hourly; 50min); Grindelwald (hourly; 40min); Lauterbrunnen (hourly; 20min); Luzern (hourly; 1hr 55min); Thun (hourly; 30min); Zürich (hourly; 2hr 15min).

Interlaken West to: Bern (hourly; 45min); Thun (hourly; 25min); Zürich (hourly; 2hr 10min).

Kleine Scheidegg to: Grindelwald (every 30min; 35min); Jungfraujoch (every 30min; 50min); Lauterbrunnen (every 30min; 1hr); Wengen (every 30min; 30min).

Lausanne to: Basel (hourly; 2hr 30min); Bern (every 30min; 1hr 10min); Brig (every 30min; 1hr 40min); Geneva (3 hourly; 35min); Montreux (every 20min; 25min); Vevey (every 20min; 15min); Zürich (every 30min; 2hr 30min).

Lauterbrunnen to: Interlaken Ost (hourly; 20min); Kleine Scheidegg (every 20min; 45min); Wengen (every 20min; 15min).

Locarno to: Bellinzona (every 30min; 20min); Domodossola, Italy (hourly; 1hr 45min).

Lugano to: Bellinzona (twice hourly; 30min); Luzern (hourly; 2hr 50min); Milan, Italy (hourly; 1hr 30min); Zürich (hourly; 3hr 10min).

Luzern to: Basel (hourly; 1hr 15min); Bern (every 2hr; 1hr 20min); Brienz (hourly; 1hr 35min); Interlaken Ost (hourly; 1hr 55min); Lugano (hourly; 2hr 50min); Zürich (every 30min; 45min).

Montreux to: Brig (twice hourly; 1hr 20min); Geneva (twice hourly; 1hr 20min); Interlaken (every 2hr; 3hr –

change at Zweisimmen & Spiez); Lausanne (every 20min; 25min); Vevey (3 hourly; 10min).

St Moritz to: Chur (hourly; 2hr).

Thun to: Bern (twice hourly; 20min); Interlaken West & Ost (hourly; 25min).

Vevey to: Brig (twice hourly; 1hr 30min); Geneva (twice hourly; 1hr 10min); Lausanne (every 20min; 15min); Montreux (3 hourly; 10min).

Wengen to: Kleine Scheidegg (every 30min; 30min); Lauterbrunnen (every 20min; 15min).

Zürich to: Basel (every 30min; 1hr); Bern (every 30min; 1hr 10min); Chur (hourly; 1hr 35min); Geneva (every 30min; 3hr); Interlaken Ost (hourly; 2hr 15min); Lausanne (every 30min; 2hr 30min); Lugano (hourly; 3hr 10min); Luzern (hourly; 50min).

Buses

Bellinzona to: Chur (every 2hr; 2hr 15min).

Lugano to: St Moritz (twice daily; 4hr).

Boats

(May–Sept summary; very few boats run in winter)

Geneva to: Lausanne (3 daily; 3hr 30min); Montreux (3 daily; 5hr); Vevey (3 daily; 4hr 30min).

Interlaken Ost to: Brienz (hourly; 1hr 20min).

Interlaken West to: Thun (hourly; 2hr).

Lausanne to: Evian, France (hourly; 40min); Geneva (3 daily; 3hr 30min); Montreux (5 daily; 1hr 30min); Vevey (5 daily; 1hr).

Luzern to: Flüelen (8 daily; 2hr 50min); Kehrsiten (hourly; 35min); Vitznau (hourly; 1hr).

CHAPTER 30

TURKEY

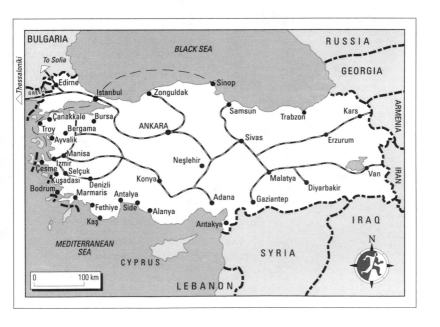

Introduction

Turkey is a country with a multiple identity, poised uneasily between East and West. The country is now keen to be accepted on equal terms by the West – it has aspirations to EU membership and is the only NATO ally in the Middle East region. But it is by no stretch of the imagination a Western nation, and the contradictions persist: mosques coexist with churches and remnants of the Roman Empire crumble alongside ancient Hittite sites. Politically, modern Turkey was a bold experiment, founded on the remaining Anatolian kernel of the Ottoman Empire and almost entirely the creation of a single man, Kemal Atatürk. An explicitly secular republic, though one in which almost all of the inhabitants are at least nominally Muslim, it's a vast country and incorporates large disparities in levels of development. But it's an immensely rewarding place to travel, not least because of the people, whose reputation for friendliness and hospitality is richly deserved.

Western Turkey is the most visited and economically developed part of the country. **İstanbul**, straddling the Black and Marmara seas, is touted as Turkish mystique par excellence, and understandably so: it would take months even to scratch the surface of the old imperial capital, still the cultural and commercial centre of the country. Flanking it on opposite sides of the **Sea of Marmara** are the two prior seats of the Ottoman Empire, **Bursa** and **Edirne**, and, just beyond, the **Dardanelles**, with their World War I battlefields. Moving south, the **Aegean Coast** comes to the fore in the olive-swathed country around **Bergama** and **Ayvalık**. Beyond the functional city of **İzmir** are ancient sites, notably **Ephesus**, that have been a magnet for travellers since the eighteenth century; these days this is Turkey at its most developed, with large numbers of visitors drawn to resorts like **Çeşme**, **Bodrum** and **Marmaris**, beyond which the Mediterranean Coast begins. There are remnants of the Lycians at **Xanthos**, and more resorts in **Kaş** and **Fethiye**, along the aptly named "Turquoise Coast".

Further along, **Antalya** is Turkey's fastest-growing city, a sprawling place that is the best starting point on the stretch of shoreline that reaches as far as the Syrian border, with extensive sands and archaeological sites – most notably at **Perge** and **Aspendos** – until castle-topped **Alanya**, where the tourist numbers begin to diminish. It's worth heading inland from here for the spectacular attractions of **Cappadocia**, with its famous rock churches, subterranean cities and tufa-pinnacle landscapes, and the Selçuk architecture and dervish associations of **Konya**. Further north, towards İstanbul, **Ankara**, Turkey's capital, is a planned city whose contrived Western feel gives some indication of the priorities of the modern Turkish Republic.

Information and maps

Most Turkish towns of any size will have a Turizm Danivma Bürosu or **tourist office**, although outside the larger cities and resorts there's often very little actual information available and no guarantee that anyone will speak English. Tourist offices are generally open Mon–Fri 8.30am–12.30pm & 1.30–5.30pm, with extended evening and weekend hours in big resorts and cities and during the peak summer periods.

The best available **maps** – though still rife with errors – are the Geo Centre/RV ones, *Turkey, West* and *Turkey, East*, widely on sale at major resorts. City tourist offices normally stock reasonable **street plans**. If you're spending much time in İstanbul, the *A–Z Atlas of İstanbul* published by Asya is a worthwhile investment. Otherwise Hallwag or Falk do a good central street map.

Money and banks

Turkish currency is the **lira**, abbreviated as TL. Coins come in denominations of 5000, 10,000 (written on the coin as "10 bin"), 25,000 ("25 bin") 50,000 ("50 bin") and 100,000 ("100 bin"). Notes come as 50,000, 100,000, 250,000, 500,000, 1,000,000 and 5,000,000. Some bank notes, particularly the 100,000 and 5,000,000, look very similar, so be careful about which size bank note you are giving as it is an old trick to swap them around at a naive visitors expense. **Rates** for foreign currency are always better inside Turkey, and because of the TL's constant devaluation you should only change money as you need it, every few days. Many pensions and hotels, particularly in the popular destinations, will quote prices in US$ as well as TL and you can pay in both.

Banks are open Mon–Fri 8.30am–noon & 1.30–5pm, and most charge a commission of about $2.50 for travellers' cheques. However, it is worth shopping around as some banks try to charge outrageous amounts for commission. Between April and October many coastal resorts between Çanakkale and Alanya have weekend and evening hours at specific *nöbetçi* banks; a list is posted in the window or door of each branch. You can also use the **exchange booths** run by banks in coastal resorts, airports and ferry docks, where service is usually quicker and commissions nonexistent. The cashpoint machines of the Yapi Kreoi and a few other banks will accept Visa, plus Cirrus system cards, provided you know your PIN. The **post office**, particularly in a sizeable town, is also often able to change currency and cheques, both travellers' and Euro, for one percent commission. Remember to count what you have just changed as the millions of Turkish lira you will receive can seem bewildering at first.

Communications

The Turkish **postal and telephone service** is run by the **PTT**. In larger towns and resorts the phone division of the main PTT is open 24 hours, with mail accepted from 8am until 7pm. Elsewhere, expect both facilities to be open Mon–Sat 8am–10pm & Sun 9am–7pm. Post boxes are clearly labelled with categories of destination – "yurtdışı" means overseas.

The PTT is the best place to make **phone calls**. For local calls, you can buy jetons; for trunk or overseas calls, **phone cards** (available in denominations of 30, 60 and 100 units) or **metered booths** are better value. Direct-dial long-distance calls can also be made at any phone box labelled Şehirlerarası (intercity) or Milletlerarası (International). For Turkish **trunk calls**, dial 0 (wait for a change in tone), and then the city code plus the subscriber number. To make an **international call**, dial 00, then the country/area codes and the local number. The **operator** numbers are ☎118 for local directory assistance, ☎131 for long-distance and ☎115 for the English-speaking international operator.

Getting around

Public transport is fairly comprehensive in Turkey. Where a destination is not on the skeletal train network, private bus companies more than compensate, and are reasonably cheap and efficient. Short stretches are best covered by dolmuş – either shared taxis in towns or minibuses linking rural villages.

■ Trains

Turkey's **train network**, run by the TCDD or Turkish State Railways, is far from exhaustive, and is best used to span the distances between the three largest cities and the main provincial centres. Trains often follow ludicrously tortuous routes and take up to twice as long as buses, although west of Ankara the best services, denoted mavı tren or ekspresi, almost match long-distance buses in speed and frequency.

Reservations for most journeys can be made in İzmir, İstanbul or Ankara, though are only really necessary for the major routes. Basic prices are about the same per kilometre as the buses; students with an ISIC card get a ten-percent discount. InterRail passes are valid, Eurail are not.

■ Buses and dolmuşes

Long-distance bus is the best way of getting around. There is no national bus company; most routes are covered by several firms, all of whom have ticket booths at the otogars (bus stations) from which they operate and (more conveniently) at offices in the town centre. Most bus companies, particularly the better ones, will run a minibus transfer service to and from their city or town centre offices to the otogar. This can be extremely useful if the bus station is a distance out of town. Check when buying your ticket. It is a good idea to try and check the route taken as some make very long detours and have extended breaks which can almost double the journey time on long routes. There's also no such thing as a comprehensive timetable, although individual companies often provide their own. Even these seem redundant at all except the very best companies and you may be told that journey times are shorter in order to entice you onto a particular service. Outside the main tourist season, generally October to April, the better bus companies may stop running altogether along routes that normally service a large amount of visitors. You may have to make do with a network of slower and more uncomfortable local minibus services that are only a couple of steps up from a dolmuş. Stations are full of touts waiting to take you to the company of their choice, though it may not have the promptest departure, or the best service. **Fares** vary only slightly between the best and scruffiest companies – as a broad example, on the better buses, expect to pay about $3 per 100km. It's worth the bit extra in comfort, service and safety to travel with the top names such as Ulusoy, Pamukkale, Kamil Koç and Varan, though the latter covers few routes.

For short hops you're most likely to use a **dolmuş**, a car or minibus that runs along a set route, picking passengers up along the way. On busy urban routes it's better to take the dolmuş from the start of its run; sometimes the destination will be posted on a sign at the kerbside, though generally you'll have to ask, or look at the dolmuş windscreens themselves. Otherwise, to stop a dolmuş, hail it like a taxi. It's always difficult to know how much to pay if you're only going part-way, but **fares** are in any case very low; traditionally passengers make up change between themselves and pass the total up to the driver. This system is less haphazard than it sounds.

■ Driving, hitching and taxis

Given the excellent bus services, you don't need to **drive** in Turkey, but it can make it possible to see more of the country more quickly. Roads are usually adequate, although often dangerously narrow. You drive on the right, and give priority to the right, even on roundabouts. Speed limits are 50kph in towns, 90kph on main roads and highways. Foreigners are rarely stopped by the police at the frequent checkpoints, but if you are you will be required to produce your driving licence and proof of ownership of the car (or car rental papers). You may also be stopped and given an on-the-spot fine for not wearing a seatbelt or for speeding. Of late, highway police have become less polite – if things get tense, it's best to demonstrate (or feign) ignorance of any Turkish. A full driving licence is valid and Green Card insurance carries an expensive extra supplement to become valid in Turkey. The Turkish motoring organization, TTOK, have a **breakdown service** (☎0212/280 4449), free to members of most foreign motoring organizations. **Car rental** is expensive, with rates from $500 a week with unlimited mileage. Local chains tend to charge twenty to thirty percent less than the multinationals and competition is pushing prices down, so shop around, particularly in the most popular destinations.

Hitching is a viable option where public transport is scarce or unavailable, and lifts tend to be frequent and friendly. You may be expected to share a glass of tea with the driver on reaching your destination. It is polite to offer a little money, though it will almost always be refused.

If you are travelling in a small group of three to four people, it can be an easier, more comfortable and much quicker, though more expensive, option to negotiate a price with a taxi. This is a very good idea if you want to string a couple of sites together in a day and may work out cheaper than the collective bus or *dolmuş* fares you would pay.

■ Ferries

Nearly all of Turkey's **ferries** are run by the Türkiye Denizcilik Fuletmesi (Turkish Maritime Lines or TML), who operate everything from shuttle city services and inter-island lines to international services. All overnight services are enormously popular, and reservations must be made in advance through authorized TML agents. There are five classes of cabin on long-haul ferries; it's also possible to reserve a *pulman koltuk* or reclining chair, but if you leave bookings to the last minute you won't even get one of these. No one will mind if you sleep up on deck but you do need a confirmed seat booking to be allowed on the boat in the first place. Fares are reasonable – for example, about $50 in a third-class double cabin from İstanbul to İzmir – and students up to age 28 (inclusive) enjoy a fifty-percent discount with ISIC. Cars cost almost as much again as a passenger berth.

■ Planes

Turkey's internal air network is now fairly comprehensive, but full-fare prices are roughly five times that of ground transport. Still, the country's size means that you may want to use air services at least once to make the most of a short, non-package visit. Besides the state-run THY and its subsidiary THT, there are private lines like İstanbul Hava Yollari and Sultan Air who often have advantageous rates undercutting THY – though the latter offers a healthy student discount.

Accommodation

Finding a bed for the night is generally no problem in Turkey, except in high season at the busier coastal resorts and larger towns. Prices, while still cheap by northern European standards, are no longer rock-bottom.

■ Hotels and pensions

Turkish **hotels** are officially graded by the tourism ministry on a scale of one to five stars; there is also a lower tier of unstarred establishments, licensed by municipalities. Most one-star places cost $15–25 a double in season, with breakfast sometimes included.

ACCOMMODATION PRICE CODES

Throughout this guide, accommodation is priced on a scale of ① to ⑨, the number indicating the lowest price per night a single person could expect to pay in that establishment in high season. With hostels this is the nightly rate per person; with hotels, the price is arrived at by dividing the cost of the cheapest double room by two. The prices indicated by the codes are as follows:

① under £5 / $8	④ £15–20 / $24–32	⑦ £30–35 / $48–56
② £5–10 / $8–16	⑤ £20–25 / $32–40	⑧ £35–40 / $56–64
③ £10–15 / $16–24	⑥ £25–30 / $40–48	⑨ £40 / $64 and over

Unrated hotels can be as good as the lower end of the one-star class, though on average expect spartan rooms with possibly a washbasin and shower, and a squat toilet down the hall, for $4–8 a head. Often the most pleasant places to stay are **pensions** (*pansiyons*), small guesthouses which proliferate wherever you find large numbers of holidaymakers. If there are vacancies in season, touts in the coastal resorts and other tourist targets descend on every incoming bus, *dolmuş* or boat; at other times, look for signs saying *Boş oda var* (rooms free). Rooms tend to be sparse but clean, though pensions in general are friendlier than hotels. Expect to pay $15–25 for a double with en-suite bath, $10–20 without. Many pensions and some small hotels close at some point during the low season (Nov–April) in the resort destinations. It would be wise to call either the establishments themselves or the local tourist office first to check what is open if you are planning to travel during this time. Also within the low season, prices drop to almost half the summer rate at some places as the owners are eager to earn a bit of out-of-season cash.

■ Campsites and hostels

Wherever *pansiyons* are found, there will also be **campsites**, often run by the same people. Charges per head run from a couple of dollars for the most basic places to $10 in a well-appointed site at a major resort in season, plus $3–4 per tent. You may also be charged for your vehicle – anything from $5 to $20. Campsites often rent out tents or provide chalet accommodation, for which you'll pay $10–20. Camping rough is not illegal, but hardly anybody does it except when trekking in the mountains.

There are few hostels outside İstanbul, and most – called *yurts* – are poky dormitories aimed at local students on summer holiday. Spurred on by private enterprise and affiliated to Hostelling International, a fledgling Interyouth Hostel network is starting to take shape, with hostels in İstanbul, Marmaris and Çanakkale.

Food and drink

At its finest, Turkish food is some of the best in the world, and prices won't break your budget. Unadventurous travellers are prone to get stuck in a kebab rut, but in fact all but the strictest vegetarians should find enough variety.

■ Food

The usual Turkish **breakfast** (*kahvaltı*) served at hotels and *pansiyons* is invariably a pile of bread slices accompanied by a pat of margarine, cheese, jam and a couple of olives. Only the tea is likely to be available in quantity, and you're often better off using street stands or snack joints. Many workers start the morning with a *börek*, a rich, flaky, layered pastry containing bits of mince or cheese, sold at a tiny *büfe* (stall/café) or from street carts. Others content themselves with a simple *simit* (bread rings speckled with sesame seeds), or a bowl of *çorba* (soup) with lemon.

Later in the day, vendors hawk *lahmacun*, small "pizzas" with meat-based toppings, and, in coastal cities, *midye tava* (deep-fried mussels). Not to be confused with *lahmacun* is *pide*, Turkish pizza – flat bread with various toppings, served in a *pideci* or *pide salonu*. Another snack speciality is *mantı* – meat-filled ravioli drenched in yoghurt and oil.

For more substantial food, a *lokanta* is a **restaurant**, a *çorbacı* is a soup kitchen, and a *kebabcı* specializes in kebabs. Most budget-priced restaurants are alcohol-free; any place marked *içkili* (licensed) is likely to be more expensive. A useful exception is a *meyhane* (tavern), a smoky dive where eating is considered secondary to drinking, though these can be fairly rough.

Prices vary widely according to the type of establishment: from $3 a head at a simple soup kitchen up to $10–20 at the flashier resort restaurants. Many places don't have **menus**; you'll need to ascertain the prices of most main courses beforehand. A good thing to try is **mezes**, or appetizers, usually a bewildering array of dishes that, along with dessert, are really the core of Turkish cuisine. Ones you'll find everywhere are *imam bayıldı* (cold baked aubergine with onion and tomato) and *dolma* (any stuffed vegetable). **Main courses** include a number of **vegetable** standbys, though they're often prepared with lamb- or chicken-based stock. Full-on **meat** dishes include several variations on the kebab, for example *İskender* kebab, *köfte* (meatballs), *şiş* (stewed meat chunks) and *çöp* (bits of lamb or offal). **Fish and seafood** are good, if usually pricey, and sold by weight more often than by item. Budget mainstays include freshly grilled *sardalya* (sardines), *palamut* (tuna), *iskumru* (mackerel), *küpes* (bogue) and *kefal* (grey mullet).

Finally, those with a sweet tooth will find every imaginable concoction at the *pastane* (sweet-shop): best are the honey-soaked **baklava**, and a variety of **milk puddings**, most commonly *sütlaç* (rice pudding) – one dessert that's consistently available in ordinary restaurants. Other **sweets** include *aşure*, a sort of rosewater jelly laced with pulses, raisins and nuts, and, the best-known Turkish sweet, *lokum* or "Turkish Delight" – solidified sugar and pectin, flavoured with rosewater and sometimes pistachios and sprinkled with powdered sugar.

■ Drink

Tea (*çay*) is the Turkish national drink, served in tiny tulip-shaped glasses, with sugar on the side but no milk. **Coffee** (*kahve*) is not as common, although instant coffee is increasingly popular. **Fruit juice** (*meyva suyu*) can be excellent if it's pulp in a bottle, available in unusual flavours. The good stuff is so thick you might want to cut it with *memba suyu* (spring water), found at the tableside in most restaurants, or fizzy *maden suyu* (mineral water). *Meşrubat* is the generic term for all carbonated **soft drinks** such as Coca Cola, Fanta and the like – available pretty much everywhere now. You'll also come across *ayran*, watered-down yoghurt.

Despite inroads made by Islamic fundamentalists, **alcoholic drinks** (*içkiler*) are available virtually without restriction in resorts, though you may have some thirsty moments in interior towns. **Beer** (*bira*), sold principally in bottles, comes in two main brands, Efes Pilsen and Tuborg. Turkish **wine** (*şarap*), can be very good; names to watch for include *Kavaklıdere*, *Doluca*, and *Kavalleros*. The Turkish national aperitif is **rakı**, not unlike Greek *ouzo* but rougher and stronger. It's usually drunk with ice, topped up with water.

Opening hours and holidays

Ordinary **shops** are open from around 9am until 7pm or 8pm, depending on the owner. **Museums** are generally open from 8am or 8.30am until 5pm or 6pm, closed on Monday and often at lunchtime (usually 12.30–1.30pm). **Archeological sites** have variable opening hours, but are generally open daily from just after sunrise until just before sunset. **Mosques** frequented by tourists are kept open all the time; others open only for *namaz*, or Muslim prayer, five times a day. It's a courtesy for women to cover their heads before entering a mosque, and for both men and women to cover their legs – shorts are considered offensive. Shoes should always be removed.

Emergencies

With the exception of recent passport-related crimes (see box on p.1263), you're unlikely to encounter any trouble in Turkey. Violent street crime is uncommon,

theft is rare and the authorities usually treat tourists with courtesy. Keep your wits about you and an eye on your belongings and you shouldn't have any problems. **Civilian police** come in a variety of subdivisions: the green-uniformed *Polis* are the everyday security force in the towns and cities; there's the *Trafik Polis*, recognizable by their white caps; the *Belediye Zabitası*, navy-clad market police, patrol the markets and bazaars; and, in rural areas, you'll find the *Jandarma*, a division of the regular army.

> In recent years it has become apparent that there is a thriving trade in **stolen British passports** in Turkey, and it would appear that British citizens of Asian extraction are particularly at risk of being robbed – several have even gone missing, and at least one murder is known to have occurred. We would advise any such visitors to exercise caution, particularly in Istanbul, and particularly if travelling alone.

For **minor health complaints** head for the nearest *eczane* or pharmacist, where you'll be able to obtain cheap remedies for ailments like diarrhoea, sunburn and flu, though you may find it difficult to find exact equivalents to any home prescriptions. Night-duty pharmacists are known as **nöbet(ci)**; a list of the current rota is posted in every chemist's front window. For more **serious ailments**, your consulate or the tourist office may be able to provide you with the address of an English-speaking doctor. Otherwise it's best to go direct to a **hospital** (*klinik*) – either public (*Devlet Hastane* or *SSK Hastanesi*), or private (*Özel Hastane*). The latter are far preferable in terms of cleanliness and standard of care, and since all foreigners must pay for medical attention, you may as well get the best available.

EMERGENCY NUMBERS

Police ☎155; Fire ☎110; Ambulance ☎112. These all cost one small jeton.

İSTANBUL

Arriving in **İSTANBUL** can come as a shock. You may still be in Europe, but a walk down any backstreet will be enough to convince you that you have entered a completely different environment. Traders with handcarts, stevedores carrying burdens twice their size, limbless beggars and shoeshine boys all frequent the streets around the city centre. Men monopolize public bars and teahouses, while many women cover their heads, their gaze downcast. In summer, dust tracks take the place of pavements, giving way in winter to a slurry of mud. Where there are pavements, they are punctuated at intervals with unmarked pits large enough to swallow you without trace. And this is before you even begin to cross any bridges into Asia.

Yet İstanbul is the only city in the world to have played capital to consecutive Christian and Islamic empires, and retains features of both, often in congested proximity. **Byzantium**, as the city was formerly known, was an important centre of commerce, but only gained real power in the fourth century AD, when Constantine chose it as the new capital of the **Roman Empire**. Later Constantinople became increasingly disassociated from Rome, adopting the Greek language and Christianity and becoming, in effect, the capital of an independent empire. In 1203 the city was sacked by the Crusaders, and by the time the Byzantines, led by Michael VIII Palaeologus, regained control in 1261, many of the major buildings had fallen into disrepair and the empire itself had greatly diminished in size. As the Byzantines declined, the **Ottoman Empire** prospered, and in 1453 the city was captured by Mehmet the Conqueror, who shortly after began to rebuild the city. In the following century, the victory was reinforced by the great military achievements of Selim the Grim, and by the reign of Süleyman the Magnificent, whose conquests helped fund the greatest of all Ottoman architects, Mimar Sinan.

By the nineteenth century, however, the glory days of Ottoman domination were firmly over. Defeat in World War I was followed by the **War of Independence**, after which Atatürk created a new capital in Ankara – although İstanbul retained its importance as a centre of trade and commerce. In **recent years**, the population of the city has risen to some ten million, almost a fifth of the country's total, and is still on the increase, the effects of which have added to the cacophony and congestion.

Arrival and information

İstanbul's **airport**, 24km southwest of the city, splits between two terminals, international and domestic, 500m apart and connected by bus. The same buses run into the city at Şişhane, near Taksim Square ($3) via Aksaray from where trams are available for Sultanahmet (40¢). Taxis taking the direct route along the seafront (Sahil Yolu) cost $12–15 – but make sure they use the meter. A new international air terminal, next to the existing one, is due to be completed by the year 2000 along with an express metro link to the city centre, which should ease things considerably. There are two **train stations**, one for trains from other parts of Europe, at **Sirkeci**, the other, **Haydarpaşa**, for trains from Asian Turkey. From Sirkeci station it's a short tram ride to Sultanahmet or Lâleli. **Ferries** cross the Bosphorus from Haydarpaza station to Karaköy, from where buses run across to Sultanahmet. İstanbul's new **otogar** (bus station) at Esenler, around 15km northwest of the centre, is connected by **metro** (actually an express tramway) with Aksaray, where you can change to the Eminönü-bound tram line which passes through Sultanahmet and Sirkeci. The better bus companies run courtesy minibuses to various points of the city including Taksim, although it might be quicker to take the metro if you're going towards Sultanahmet. Most buses now arrive here, including European and Asian services, although some connect with Harem in Asia. If your journey terminates at Harem, there are *dolmuşes* every few minutes to Kadıköy. The most central **tourist office** is in Sultanahmet near the Hippodrome on Divanyolu Caddesi (daily 9am–5pm; ☎212/518 1802); they're not very helpful but might be able to spare a map.

City transport

The city's **public transport system** is undergoing rapid modernization, with plans to extend the efficient single-line metro into a network that will eventually include the airport. Single journey tickets cost 40¢ and are bought from a counter (*gişe*) at the entrance to every station. **Buses**, sadly, don't publish or advertise any route maps. There are two kinds of buses, the private (orange) buses, and municipally run **belediye** buses. You need to buy **tickets** in advance from bus station ticket offices, newspaper stands or fast-food booths, or from touts who sell at slightly inflated prices around some bus terminals. Tickets are sold in blocks of ten for around 40¢ each. On certain buses, identified with the sign "iki bilet geçerlidir", you need two tickets; buses for which only one ticket is required have a sign saying "tam bilet geçerlidir". Tickets should be deposited next to the driver on boarding, although on orange buses you can usually pay the driver in cash. There are two **tram lines** on the European side, one running from Eminönü through Sultanahmet to Topkapı and outlying suburbs; the other runs the length of Asytikal Caddesi from Beyoğlu to Taksim using turn-of-the-century trams with the conductor dressed appropriately. Tickets (40¢) are bought from a booth before you enter the platform. There is a **municipal train network**, consisting of two lines, one on each side of the Bosphorus, but it's hardly comprehensive. Tickets, which cost the same as for buses, are bought on the platform and should be retained until leaving. There are also **dolmuşes** or shared taxis – usually cars rather than the minibuses you'll see in other parts of Turkey. They have their point of departure and destination displayed somewhere about the windscreen and you can board and alight where you want en route – flag them down as you would a taxi. Many useful routes are covered by the **passenger boats** up and down the waterways and between Europe and Asia; you need a small jeton (40¢), available from the dockside kiosks.

Accommodation

Finding **somewhere to stay** in İstanbul is rarely a problem, but it's best to phone ahead to avoid a lot of trudging from one full *pansiyon* to the next; in mid-season anything up to a week's advance booking wouldn't go amiss. Some of the city's nicest small hotels and *pansiyons* are situated in **Sultanahmet**, right at the heart of İstanbul, particularly around Yerebatan Caddesi and in the less prominent but equally atmospheric backstreets between the Sultanahmet mosque and the sea. However, prices can be high in this area and it's worth shopping around for a good deal; most hotels include breakfast in the price and some offer air-con and cable TV. Failing that, there's another concentration of hotels about a mile up Ordu Caddesi, in the areas of **Aksaray** and **Lâleli**. One word of warning – Lâleli has fallen into disrepute as a red-light district infamous for its "Natashas" (Eastern European prostitutes) and, although lively, some of the hotels are swamped by Russians who come to the city on shopping sprees. **Taksim** is also a convenient base from which to sightsee, and comes into its own at night, when it becomes the centre of cultural and culinary activity.

Sultanahmet

Alp Guesthouse, Adliye Sok 4, Sultanahmet (☎212/517 9570). Very friendly with clean and pleasant, if slightly pricey, rooms, and a roof terrace. ⑥.

Antique, Küçük Ayasofya Cad, Oğul Sok 17 (☎212/516 4936). Comfortable hotel in a quiet neighbourhood. Ask for the rooms at the top with excellent sea views. ④.

Buhara, Küçük Ayasofya Cad, Yegen Sok 11 (☎212/517 3427). Pleasant hotel with outstanding views from its rooftop terrace. ④.

Cem, Kutlügien Sok 30, Sultanahmet (☎212/516 5041). Friendly, popular and clean, near the Blue Mosque. Dorms ①, doubles ③.

Ema, Yerebatan Cad, Salkim Söğüt Sok 18 (☎212/511 7166). Clean and quiet double rooms with showers. Prices can be bargained down for longer stays. ③.

Hanedan, Akbiyik Cad, Adliye Sok 3 (☎212/516 4869). A budget alternative with dorms and rooms – basic, but with good views from the rooftop café. ③.

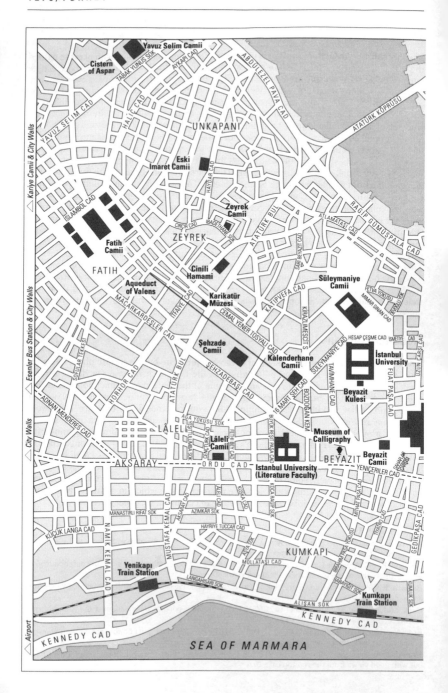

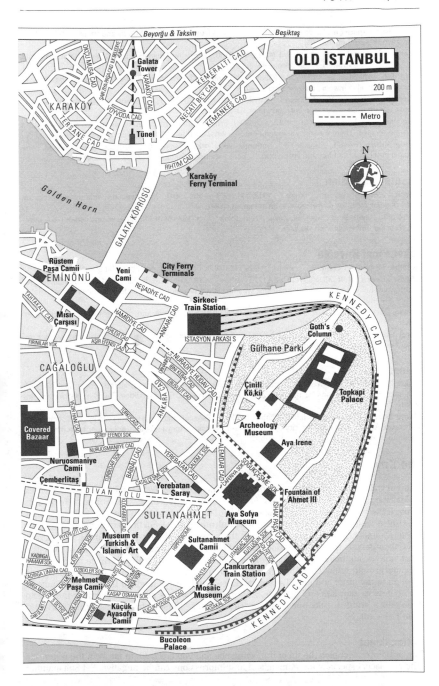

OLD İSTANBUL

0   200 m

------- Metro

N

Beyorğu & Taksim

Beşiktaş

Galata Tower

KARAKÖY

Tünel

Golden Horn

Karaköy Ferry Terminal

Rüstem Paşa Camii

EMİNÖNÜ

Yeni Cami

City Ferry Terminals

Mısır Çarşısı

Sirkeci Train Station

İSTASYON ARKASI S

Goth's Column

Gülhane Parki

CAĞALOĞLU

Çinili Kö,kü

Topkapi Palace

Archeology Museum

Nuruosmaniye Camii

Covered Bazaar

Aya Irene

Çemberlitaş

DIVAN YOLU

Yerebatan Saray

SULTANAHMET

Fountain of Ahmet III

Aya Sofya Museum

Museum of Turkish & Islamic Art

Sultanahmet Camii

Cankurtaran Train Station

Mehmet Paşa Camii

Mosaic Museum

Küçük Ayasofya Camii

Bucoleon Palace

KENNEDY CAD

Hotel Best Hipodrom, Üçler Sok 9 (☎212/516 0902). Convenient, clean rooms and friendly staff, but the prices are creeping up. ④.

Interyouth Hostel, Caferiye Sok 6/1 (☎212/513 6150). Large, well-managed hostel next to Aya Sofya with good amenities, dormitories and rooms. ①–②.

Optimist, Atmeydanı 68 (☎212/516 2398). Basic hotel with lovely views of Sultanahmet. Book well in advance. They also have a *pansiyon* behind. ③.

Orient International Youth Hostel, Akbıyık Cad 13 (☎212/517 9493). Basic hostel with clean dorms and rooms. Also has a bar and free entertainment. ①–②.

Side Pansiyon, Utangaç Sok 20 (☎212/517 6590). Friendly staff, with clean rooms and excellent sea views from the terrace. There's also an adjoining hotel in what used to be a tea garden. Hotel ⑦, *pansiyon* ④.

Valide Sultan Konağı, Izakpaza Cad, Kutluqun Sok 1 (☎212/638 0600). Charming, well-positioned, comfortable hotel with roof bar and restaurant. A more expensive though luxurious option. ⑨.

Aksaray and Lâleli

Burak, Fethi Bey Cad, Ağa Yokuzu 1 (☎212/511 8679 or 522 7904). Quite ordinary with signs in Russian, and a popular café/bar downstairs on an animated street. ③.

Hotel Kul, Büyük Reşit Paşa Cad, Zeynep Kamil Sok 27 (☎212/526 0127). Basic rooms which have showers, near the univerzite tram stop. ③.

Taksim and Beyoğlu

Alibaba, Meşrutiyet Cad 119, Tepebazi (☎212/144 0781). Plain and simple, but a bit scruffy. ②.

Büyük Londra Oteli, Meşrutiyet Cad 117, Tepebazi (☎212/249 1025). Italian-built in the mid-nineteenth century and full of character, with spacious, well-furnished rooms – the splendour is just about affordable for the odd night. ⑧.

Dünya, Meşrutiyet Cad 79, Tepebaşi (☎212/144 0940). Run-down and peeling but clean and quite cheap. ②.

Hotel Gezi, Mete Cad 42 (☎212/251 7430). Well run and quite classy with Bosphorus views from the restaurant and some of the rooms. ⑧.

Campsites

Ataköy Tatil Köyü, Rauf Orbay Cad, Ataköy (☎212/559 6000). Ten minutes from the airport (taxi $5), with an attractive setting on the Marmara Sea, 16km from city centre. Good facilities. Take bus #81 for Taksim Square.

Florya Tourist Camping, Yeşilköy Halkalı Cad, Florya. Pleasant and leafy, well served by public transport, and cheap. About 25km from the city by #73 bus from Taksim, Florya–Topkapı *dolmuş*, or train from either Eminönü or Ataköy.

The City

İstanbul is divided in two by the **Bosphorus**, which runs between the Black Sea and the Sea of Marmara, dividing Europe from Asia. At right angles to it, the **Golden Horn** cuts through the city centre, on the European side of the Bosphorus. To the west is the old imperial centre which stretches from the **Sultanahmet** district northwest to the Süleymaniye mosque complex, the covered bazaar and the remains of the city walls. To the east, across the Galata Bridge, the old Levantine areas of **Galata** and **Pera** are home to one of the city's most famous landmarks, the Galata tower. Not far from here is the entrance to the **Tünel**, an underground funicular railway, running up to the start of Astiklâl Caddesi, which runs through to the large and ugly **Taksim Square**, the heart of modern İstanbul and home to much of its restaurants and nightlife. Any number of **buses** cross the Horn via the Galata and Atatürk bridges. Take ones marked "Beyoğlu" or "Taksim" from Aksaray, or "Karaköy" from Eminönü.

Sultanahmet

The old centre occupies the tip of the peninsula, and you are seldom far from the water. It's a hustly place, especially for women, and first impressions can be negative. Yet Sultanahmet is home to the main sightseeing attractions: the church of **Aya Sofya**, the **Topkapı Palace** and the **Blue Mosque**, and many people spend all their time here.

AYA SOFYA

Perhaps the single most compelling sight in Sultanahmet is the former church of **Aya Sofya**, the massive domed church commissioned in the sixth century by the Emperor Justinian. It was converted to a mosque in 1453, after which the minarets were added. In 1934 it became a **museum** (9am–4pm; closed Mon, Tues–Sun 9am–4pm; $3). For centuries this was the largest enclosed space in the world, and the interior – filled with shafts of light from the high windows around the dome – is still profoundly impressive.

The building is presently filled with scaffolding in preparation for a massive **renovation** programme, but this does little to mar the effects of its decoration and, in fact, helps bring home the scale of the place. Inside there are a few features left over from its time as a mosque – a *mihrab*, a *mimber* and the enormous wooden plaques which bear sacred names of God, the Prophet Mohammed and the first four caliphs – but the most interesting elements are the Byzantine ones. Between the four great piers that hold up the dome, columns of green marble support the galleries; the smaller columns above are a deep red. The balconies, pediments and capitals are of white marble, the latter a riot of interlacing leaf carvings, many bearing the monograms of Justinian and his wife Theodora. Upstairs in the western gallery a large circle of green Thessalian marble marks the position of the throne of the empress.

There are also remains of abstract and figurative **mosaics**. One, beyond a pair of false marble doors in the south gallery, depicts Christ, the Virgin and St John the Baptist; another, on the east wall of the gallery, shows Christ flanked by an emperor and empress – believed to be Constantine IX Monomachus and the Empress Zoë. One of the most beautiful of all the mosaics can be seen downstairs in the Vestibule of Warriors; dated to the last quarter of the tenth century, it shows Virgin and Child flanked by the emperors Justinian, offering a model of the church, and Constantine, offering a model of the city.

THE TOPKAPI PALACE

Immediately to the north of Aya Sofya, the **Topkapı Palace** (summer daily 9am–4.30pm; winter closed Tues; $4) is the other unmissable sight in this part of town, the centre of the Ottoman Empire for nearly four centuries until the removal of the retinue to Dolmabahçe in 1853. Built between 1459 and 1465, it consists of a collection of buildings arranged around a series of courtyards. The first courtyard, as service area of the palace, was always open to the general public and is today home to the ticket office. The second courtyard is the site of the **Divan**, although this is currently closed to the public and all you can do is peer through the windows at the Council Chamber and the couch which gave the institution its name. The **Divan tower**, visible from many vantage points all over the city, was rebuilt in 1825 by Mahmut II. Next door is the **Inner Treasury**, a six-domed hall that holds an exhibition of arms and armour. Across the courtyard are the **palace kitchens**, with their magnificent rows of chimneys, the furthest of which have been restored complete with a fascinating array of utensils, while others house a collection of some of the finest porcelain in the world – an ever-changing display continually replenished from the Topkapı collection.

Around the corner, you have to pay extra for a guided tour of the **Harem** (hourly 9am–4pm; $2.50), but it's worth it, as more rooms are gradually being opened to the public. The harem consists of over four hundred rooms; the only men that were allowed to enter were the black eunuchs and the imperial guardsmen, who were only employed at certain hours and even then were blinkered. Tours take in a good part of the complex, including the the **Hünkar Sofası** (Imperial Hall), where the sultan entertained his visitors, and the bedchamber of Murat III – a masterwork of the architect Sinan – covered in sixteenth-century İznik tiles and kitted out with a marble fountain and bronze fireplace.

Back in the main body of the palace, in the third courtyard, the **throne room**, mainly dating from the reign of Selim I, was where the sultan awaited the outcome of sessions of the Divan in order to give his assent or otherwise to their proposals. On the southwest side of the court are the rooms of the **Palace School**, where boys recruited from Christian families were converted to Islam and educated to become members of the janissary corps. Nearby, the **Pavilion of the Conqueror** houses the Topkapı treasury, filled with excesses like the Topkapı Dagger, decorated with three enormous emeralds, and the Spoonmaker's Diamond, the fifth largest diamond in the world. Across the courtyard from the treasury, the **Pavilion of the Holy Mantle** houses the holy relics brought home by Selim the Grim after his conquest of Egypt in 1517, including a footprint, hair and a tooth of the Prophet Mohammed as well as his mantle and standard. Next door, the former **Hall of the Treasury** holds a selection from Topkapı's collection of paintings and miniatures, the earliest dating from the reign of Süleyman the Magnificent. Beyond, the fourth courtyard consists of gardens graced with pavilions where sultans would take their pleasure. The **Mecidiye Köşkü** – the last building to be erected at Topkapı – commands the best view of any of the Topkapı pavilions and has been opened as a terrace café.

Just north of Topkapı, **Gülhane Parki**, once the gardens of the palace, is the location of the **Archeological Museum** (Tues–Sun 9am–4pm; $3). Well-lit and attractive displays with comprehensive explanatory audiovisual effects enhance exhibits of spectacular jewellery uncovered at Troy. The entrance to the Archeological Museum also provides access to the graceful **Çinili Köşk**, the oldest secular building in İstanbul, constructed in 1472 as a kind of grandstand from which the sultan could watch sporting activities and now a **Museum of Ceramics** (Tues, Thurs & Sat 9.30am–5pm; $3). Close by, the **Museum of the Ancient Orient** (Wed, Fri & Sun 9.30am–5pm; $3) contains a small but dazzling collection of Anatolian, Egyptian and Mesopotamian artefacts.

AROUND THE HIPPODROME

South of Aya Sofya, the arena of the **Hippodrome**, originally constructed by Septimus Severus in 200 AD, is now the site of a narrow and rather unprepossessing municipal park. At its southern end is the **Egyptian Obelisk**, originally 60m tall, but only the upper third survived shipment from Egypt in the fourth century. Though commissioned to commemorate the campaigns of Thutmos III in Egypt during the sixteenth century BC, the scenes on its base record its erection in Constantinople under the direction of Theodosius I. Nearby, the **Serpentine Column** comes from the Temple of Apollo at Delphi and was brought here by Constantine.

The **Sultanahmet Camii**, or **Blue Mosque**, on the Hippodrome's southeast side, is undeniably impressive, and its six minarets are instantly recognizable – though inside it's rather clumsy, its four "elephant foot" pillars obscuring parts of the building and tending to dwarf the modest dome they support. The main attraction is the tiles which give the mosque its name, over twenty thousand of them, still with the clear, bright colours of late sixteenth-century İznik ware, including flower and tree panels as well as more abstract designs. Outside the precinct wall is the **tomb of Sultan Ahmet** (9.30am–4.30pm; closed Tues), where the sultan is buried along with his wife and three of his sons; like the mosque, it's tiled with seventeenth-century İznik tiles.

On the other side of the Hippodrome, the former palace of Abrahim Paza, completed in 1524 for the grand vizier of Süleyman the Magnificent, is a fitting home for the **Museum of Turkish and Islamic Art** (Tues–Sun 9am–4pm; $3), a well-planned museum containing what is probably the best-exhibited collection of Islamic artefacts in the world, with examples of Selçuk, Mameluke and Ottoman Turkish art. Abrahim Paza's magnificent audience hall is devoted to a collection of Turkish carpets; on the ground floor, in rooms off the central courtyard, is an exhibition of the folk art of the Yörük tribes of Anatolia.

North of here, along Yerebatan Caddesi, the intriguing **Yerebatan Saray** or "Sunken Palace" (daily: summer 9am–5.30pm; winter 9am–4.30pm; $3) is one of several underground cisterns which riddle the foundations of the city, but the only one to have been extensively excavated. Probably built by Constantine and enlarged by Justinian, the cistern supplied water to the Great Palace of the Byzantine emperors. Raised pathways allow you to walk through the cistern's forest of columns, and gaze upon the monumental Medusa heads which support two of them. In the opposite direction from Sultan Ahmet, the **Mosaic Museum** (Tues–Sun 9am–4pm; $1.50), on Torun Sokak behind the Blue Mosque, displays some magnificent scenes of domestic life and animals in their natural habitats, which once decorated the floors of the Great Palace. This vast complex covered an enormous area from the Hippodrome down to the sea walls, where you can still see the great marble-framed windows of the **Bucoleon**, a pavilion looking out on to what was once the emperors' private harbour.

Beyazit and Eminönü

West of Sultanahmet, continue along the run-down and busy **Divan Yolu** to the **Column of Constantine (Cemberlitaş)**, erected in 330 AD to mark the city's dedication as capital of the Roman Empire. Off the main street to the right lies the district of **BEYAZIT**, centring on the **covered bazaar**, and, beyond it, the university. In a pleasant area of shady courtyards behind the university stands one of the finest of all the Ottoman mosque complexes, the **Süleymaniye Camii**.

THE COVERED BAZAAR

A huge web of passageways housing over four thousand shops, the **Kapali Çarzi**, the covered bazaar (Mon–Sat 9am–6pm) has long since spilled out of the **covered area**, sprawling into the streets which lead down to the Golden Horn. It's a wonderful if manic place to wander through, and there are several good carpet shops around the fountain at the intersection of Keseciler and Takkeciler Caddesis, as well as cheaper, rather scruffier places on Halıcılar Çarvısı Caddesi. When you need a break, the *Şark Kahvesi*, on Yağlıkçilar Sokak almost opposite Zenneciler Sokak, is a good place to drink strong tea while gloating over hard-won booty. West of the bazaar, peek into the **Beyazit Camii**, completed in 1506 and the oldest surviving imperial mosque in the city, with a beautiful, sombre courtyard full of richly coloured marble. The interior of the mosque is a perfect square of exactly the same proportions as the courtyard, its plan basically a simplified version of Aya Sofya, with highly crafted sixteenth-century fittings.

THE SÜLEYMANIYE CAMII

Built in the 1550s by Mimar Sinan in honour of his most illustrious patron, Süleyman the Magnificent, the **Süleymaniye Camii** is arguably his greatest achievement. The dome of the light and spacious mosque collapsed during the earthquake of 1766, and in the nineteenth century further damage was done by the Fossati brothers, whose attempt at Ottoman Baroque redecoration jars with the simplicity of the building. But the original stained glass of Abrahim the Mad remains, above a simply graceful marble *mimber*, along with a few İznik tiles – a first cautious use of tiling by Sinan. Outside, the **cemetery** (Wed–Sun 9.30am–4.30pm) holds the tombs of Süleyman the Magnificent and of Roxelana, his powerful wife. Süleyman's tomb is particularly impressive, with doors inlaid with ebony and ivory, silver and jade and a peristyle supported by four antique columns leading through to the huge turban of the sultan. The rest of the complex is made up of the famous **Süleymaniye library**, established by Süleyman in an effort to bring together collections of books scattered throughout the city, and the **Tomb of Mimar Sinan**, a simple tomb except for a magnificent carved turban, a measure of the architect's high rank.

EMINÖNÜ

The area sloping down to the river behind the bazaar is known as **Eminönü**, adjacent to which lies **Sirkeci**, home to the main **train station** and ferry docks. Close by, on the waterfront, is the last of İstanbul's imperial mosques to be built in the Classical era, **Yeni Cami**. A large, grey edifice, it's one of the least impressive of the city centre's mosques, partly owing to the heavy layer of soot from the nearby ferry port which covers its walls and windows. Next door, the **Mısır Carşısı** or Egyptian Bazaar, also known as the **Spice Bazaar**, is a good place to buy anything from saffron to aphrodisiacs. A short walk west, the **Rüstem Paşa Cami** is one of the most attractive of İstanbul's smaller mosques, built for Süleyman the Magnificent's grand vizier, Rüstem Paza. Designed by Sinan on a particularly awkward site, above a tangle of streets that seem to offer no room for such a building, it is barely detectable as you wander about in the streets below. But it's a successful, dramatic structure, with tiles that are among the most profuse in Turkey, from the finest period of İznik tile production.

On the waterfront, the most prominent landmark is the **Galata Bridge**, an ugly modern two-tier structure which provides access to Galata (and 1.5km beyond, Taksim) on the opposite side of the Golden Horn.

West to the city walls

West of Beyazit, İstanbul becomes tattier and more intimate, almost like a collection of villages intersected by major roads. These areas contain some of the city's most compelling sites, including the magnificent Byzantine mosaics and frescoes in the **Kariye Camii** and the great **Land Walls** that barred the peninsula to attackers for 800 years, and there are several other sites worth visiting on the way.

On the far side of the **Aqueduct of Valens** – part of a fourth-century water system that remained in use right up to the end of the nineteenth century – is **Şehzade Camii**, "The Mosque of the Sultan's Son" (closed for restoration at time of writing). Commissioned in 1543 on the death of Zehzade Mehmet, the 21-year-old heir of Süleyman the Magnificent, it was the first major building of Mimar Sinan. Across Atatürk Bulvarı, the aqueduct continues into **ZEYREK**, an attractively tatty area notable for its steep, cobbled streets and ramshackle wooden houses. At the top of the hill stands **Zeyrek Camii**, the twelfth-century Byzantine monastery church of Christ Pantocrator, which served as a mausoleum for the Comneni dynasty. Now a mosque, it is open only at prayer times, though you may persuade the imam to show you round. Beyond Zeyrek, **Fatih** ("the Conqueror") is a fundamentalist area, where even the language is different, full of Arabic words long discarded elsewhere in Turkey. In the centre of the district, the **Fatih Camii** on Aslambol Caddesi was begun in 1463 just ten years after the conquest of Constantinople, although much of it was rebuilt after an eighteenth-century earthquake.

Twenty minutes' walk north of here, **Yavuz Selim Camii**, on Yavuz Selim Caddesi, holds a commanding position over the surrounding suburbs. It was begun in the reign of Selim the Grim, after whom it is named, and the bleak exterior seems a fitting memorial to a man with such a reputation for cruelty. Once inside, though, it's one of the most attractive of all the imperial mosques: a simple, restrained building, its long pendentives alternating with tall arches to support the great shallow dome. The **Tomb of Selim the Grim** (closed for restoration at the time of writing), next door, has lost its original decoration inside, but retains two beautiful tiled panels on either side of the door.

KARIYE CAMII

About 25 minutes' walk northwest of the Selim mosque is one of the city's most compelling sights, **Kariye Camii** (9.30am–4pm; closed Wed; free). It can also be reached by taking the metro to Topkapı, and walking north beside the city walls as far as the Edirnekapa gate, from where it's signposted. This is the former church of St Saviour in Chora, built in the early twelfth century on the site of a building which predated the walls, hence the name – "in chora" meaning "in the country". The building contains a series of superbly preserved fourteenth-century frescoes and mosaics that are among the most evocative of all the city's Byzantine treasures. Most prominent of the mosaics are those in the narthex, the largest of which are a Christ Pantocrator and another showing the builder of the church, Metochites, offering a model of the building to a seated Christ. The frescoes in the burial chapel are equally eloquent, the most spectacular being the Resurrection, a dramatic representation of Christ trampling the gates of Hell underfoot and forcibly dragging Adam and Eve from their tombs.

THE WALLS

Six kilometres long in total, İstanbul's **Land Walls** are among the most fascinating Byzantine remains in Turkey. Raised by the Emperor Theodosius II, they are the result of a hasty rebuilding to repel Attila the Hun's forces in 447 AD; an ancient edict was brought into effect whereby all citizens, regardless of rank, were required to help in the labour, and sixteen thousand men finished the project in just two months. They originally consisted of an inner wall, 5m thick and 12m high, plus an outer wall of 2m by 8m, and a twenty-metre-wide moat. Most of the outer wall and its 96 towers are still standing, and their construction can be examined in detail if you are dressed to clamber in the dirt and brick dust. Nowadays the remains provide shelter for many of İstanbul's homeless, and there are gypsy encampments in the localities of Topkapı and Edirnekapı; you'll probably be left to your own devices but do pay attention to your personal security here. If travelling alone it may be wise to pair up with someone. Plenty of buses run from Eminönü and Sultanahmet, including the #80 to Yedikule, #84 to Topkapı and #86 to Edirnekapı, although the best way of reaching the walls is probably to take the metro from Aksaray to the Topkapı gate.

At the extreme southern end, **Yedikule** is an attractive quarter, home to a concentration of Greek-influenced houses and Orthodox churches, as well as a few reasonable restaurants and cafés where you can stop before setting off on your exploration of the walls. The most impressive sections of wall here have been designated the **Yedikule Museum** (9.30am–4pm; closed Wed; $2), off Yedikule Caddesi. The **Golden Gate**, flanked by two marble towers, was constructed on this site by Theodosius I in 390, before the walls themselves. It was bricked up in the declining years of the empire, but the shape of the three arches is still visible on both sides of the wall. It takes a degree of imagination, however, to invest the structure with the glamour and dignity it once possessed. The other five towers of the Yedikule fortifications were added by Mehmet the Conqueror, and with their twelve-metre-high curtain walls form an enclave which can be seen today, including two prison towers covered with inscriptions carved into the walls by prisoners.

Across the Golden Horn

Across the Galata Bridge from the old centre, the settlement at **Galata** is as ancient as the city itself. In the fifth century the area already had city walls, and towards the end of the century Tiberius is said to have built a fortress on this side of the Horn, to facilitate the closure of the water to enemy shipping. Later the area became the main stronghold of the Genoese, and during the early centuries of Ottoman rule it became established as the city's European quarter, home to Jewish, Moorish, Greek and Armenian refugees and a popular haunt of visiting merchants, seamen and dignitaries. As Galata became crowded, the Europeans gradually spread into the district above Galata, **Beyoğlu**. By the nineteenth and early twentieth centuries, the area had become fashionable for its music halls, taverns, cinemas and restaurants, and it was only after the exodus of the Greek population from İstanbul in the 1920s that Galata and Pera began to lose their cosmopolitan flavour. The area has been cleaned up of late, although there's plenty remaining of the district's seamier side, brothels and "adult" cinemas existing alongside bars, *meyhanes* and restaurants.

GALATA

The **Galata Tower** (daily 9am–6.30pm; $2), built in 1348, is the area's most obvious landmark, and one of the first places to head for on a sightseeing tour, since its viewing galleries, reached by means of a modern lift, offer the best panoramas of the city. Up towards Taksim from here, an unassuming doorway leads to the courtyard of the **Galata Mevlevihane** (9am–4pm; closed Tues; $1.50), a former monastery and ceremonial hall of the "Whirling Dervishes" and now a museum of the Mevlevi sect, which was banned by Atatürk along with other Sufi organizations because of its political affiliations. Exhibits include instruments and dervish costumes, and the building itself has been beautifully restored to late eighteenth-century splendour. Continuing to the bottom of **İstiklâl Caddesi**, Beyoğlu's main boulevard, which was once known as the Grande Rue de Pera, is now a pedestrian precinct, with a tram line running along its 1200-metre length to **Taksim Square** – an undeniably impressive open space, if only for its size. The **Military Museum** (Wed–Sun 9am–4pm; $1.50), about 1500m north along Cumhuriyet Caddesi, is worth visiting mainly for the traditional Mehter band who play Ottoman music outside every afternoon that it's open, although its assortment of Ottoman armour and weaponry, along with various campaign memorabilia including the tent used by campaigning sultans, may appeal to military buffs.

THE DOLMABAHÇE AND YILDIZ PALACES

Beyond Taksim, along the European shore of the Bosphorus, the most obvious place to head for is **Beşiktaş** (best reached direct by ferry from Eminönü; bus #30b and frequent *dolmuşes* run there from Taksim), where the **Dolmabahçe Palace** (Tues, Wed & Fri–Sun 9am–3.30pm; guided tours only; $9) is the largest and most sumptuous of all the palaces on the river, built in the mid-nineteenth century to replace Topkapı as the imperial residence of the Ottoman sultans. To the contemporary eye it's not so much magnificent as a grossly excessive display of ostentatious wealth, suggesting that good taste suffered along with the fortunes of the Ottoman Empire. But it retains an Oriental feel in the organization of its rooms, divided into *selâmlık* and harem by the enormous throne room – where the ceremonies were watched by women of the harem through grilles. The four-tonne chandelier in the throne room, one of the largest ever made, was a present from Queen Victoria. In the east wing of the palace, the former apartments of the heir to the throne now house a **Museum of Fine Arts** (Wed–Sun 9am–4pm; $2.50), with paintings from the late nineteenth and early twentieth centuries that give an intriguing insight into the lifestyle and attitudes of the late Ottoman Turks.

Back towards the ferry landing, the **Maritime Museum** (Mon, Tues & Fri–Sun 9am–noon & 1–5pm; 75c) is one of the city's most interesting, with a collection divided between two buildings, one facing the water housing seagoing craft, and the other, on Cezayir Caddesi, devoted to the maritime history of the Ottoman Empire and the Turkish Republic. A short walk from the main square is the **Yıldız Parkı** (daily 9am–sunset), a vast wooded area dotted with lakes and gardens that was the centre of the Ottoman Empire for thirty years during the reign of Abdül Hamid. The buildings in and around the park constitute **Yıldız Palace** (Tues–Sun 9.30am–4pm; $3), a collection of structures in the old Ottoman style, and a total contrast to Dolmabahçe. Most of the pavilions date from the reign of Abdül Aziz, but it was Abdül Hamid – a reforming sultan whose downfall was brought about by his intense paranoia – who transformed Yıldız into a small city and power base. The most important surviving building is **Şale Köşkü** (9.30am–4pm; closed Thurs; $4), which resembles a Swiss chalet and was built for the first visit of Kaiser Wilhelm II in 1889.

Eating

The historical centre around Sultanahmet is increasingly well-served by decent **restaurants**, although there's always been a higher concentration of eateries around Taksim and Galata. The Balık Pazar, behind the Çiçek Pasajı off İstiklâl Caddesi in Beyoğlu, is a great area for **seafood cafés**. Once a flower market, Çiçek Pasajı also now houses several good cafés and is popular for lunch. If you're just after a **snack**, you can find it almost anywhere. Snack options vary from the excellent fish sandwiches served off boats by fishermen in Kadıköy, Karaköy and Eminönü, to the piles of sheep's innards – *kokoreç* – sold from booths in less salubrious areas.

Ahtapot, Köyiçi Kilise Meydanı 50, Beşiktaş. Small, friendly fish restaurant near the market that's less pricey than establishments right on the Bosphorus.

Aksu Ocakbaşi, Aksaray Cad, Azımkar Sok 5, Lâleli. Well-prepared, interesting food which isn't too expensive, and the service is friendly.

Altın Sofrası, Süleymaniye Cad 33. A good bet for lunch on a visit to Süleymaniye; certainly better than any of the touristy restaurants that face the mosque.

Borsa Lokantasi, Astiklâl Cad 87; Yalıkövkuvkü Ivhanı 60/62, Eminönü. Excellent restaurants, part of a chain, serving perhaps the best Turkish meat dishes in the country.

Bursa Kebapci, Sakizağaci Cad, İstikal Cad. Simple çorba and kebab place near Taksim, good for a quick nosh.

Çatı, İstiklâl Cad, A. Apaydın Sok 20, Baro Han, floor 7, Beyoğlu (☎212/251 0000). Well established among İstanbul's intelligentsia but unknown to tourists, this attractive restaurant deserves its reputation for good food – you can eat for around $10 a head. Live entertainment is usually jazz. Book a window seat for good views of the city lights. Open Mon–Sat.

Cennet, Divan Yolu Cad. Anatolian cuisine, live traditional music and cushions on the floor. Reasonably priced if you don't over-tip the musicians.

Demgâh, Nevizade Sok 15, Balik Pasar, Beyoqlu. One of the best pavement-cafés for *meze* and fish in this street full of good eateries, which has now replaced the Çiçek Pasajı in popularity.

Doy Doy, Zifa Hamama Sok 13, off Küçükayosofya Cad at the Hippodrome end. Simple, cheap and basic kebabs.

Hacı Abdullah, Sakızaqacı Cad 19, Beyoğlu. Excellent place, well known among locals as a cheap alternative to the flashier places nearby. No alcohol.

Hasır I, Muallim Naci Cad, just past Ortakoy. Very popular Turkish *meyhane*. Excellent food, and lots of vegetarian options. Order a minimal selection from the menu as the best food will periodically be brought around on a large tray.

Havuzlu Lokantası, Gani Çelebi Sok 3, Kapalı Çarzı. Probably the best eating establishment in the bazaar.

Konyali, Ankara Cad 233, Sirkeci. Excellent pastry shop frequented by the quarter's business people, who eat their breakfast standing at the counter. Also operates a decent self-service restaurant around the back in Mimar Kemalettin Cad.

Mercan, Sahne Sok, Balik Pazar, Beyoqlu. Basic fish and beer place popular with locals, in the heart of the fish market.

Nature and Peace, Büyükparmakkapi Cad 21, Astikal Cad. Vegetarian place three blocks away from Taksim, offering lentil *köfte* and other veggie favourites.

Rumeli Café, Ticarethane Sok 8, Divan Yolu Cad. Chic establishment serving breakfasts and light meals such as omelettes and salads.

Subaşı, Kılıçlar Sok 48/2. A spit-and-sawdust place near the bazaar. Excellent lunchtime food, far better than anything else in the area. Go early as it gets packed.

Türkistan Aşevi, Tavukhane Sokaqı 36. Behind the Blue Mosque, a conventional Ottoman house specializing in central Asian cuisine with a good set menu. You'll be asked to take off your shoes.

Vitamin, Divan Yolu Cad 16. Despite becoming increasingly popular with travellers, you'll find plenty of locals and a wide and reasonably priced menu here.

Yesil Ev, Kabasakal Cad 5. An old Ottoman mansion tastefully refurbished as an upmarket hotel with a striking green exterior. Hides a pleasant garden restaurant – expect to pay around $15.

Nightlife

Traditional İstanbul **nightlife** centres around restaurants and *gazinos* – clubs where *meze* are served, accompanied by singers and Oriental dancers. However, new Western-style bars and clubs are gaining in popularity – they're often no more than pastiches, but sometimes have the charm of a good location or attract an interesting clientele. Locations tend to centre around Taksim and its nearby suburbs, and along the Bosphorus, particularly the district of Ortaköy, just beyond Bezaktaz.

Bars

Adi, Ancili Çavuz Sok 8/1, Sultanahmet. Nice decor, friendly atmosphere and good music. Usually open until 3am.

Hangi Rock Bar, İmam Adnan Sok, İstiklal Cad. Raucous music bar just west of Taksim Square.

Hayal Kahvesi, Büyükparmakkapi Sok 19, Astikal Cad. Upmarket café/bar with live jazz and blues.

North Shields Bar, Çalikuzu Sok, Barbaros Bul, Levent. Expat hangout with a range of British and European beers, about 4km beyond Bezaktaz.

Tribunal, Muammer Karaca Çikmazi, Astiklal Cad, Beyoğlu. Basement bar in a medieval French courthouse. Live Greek rembeika and gypsy music.

Underground, Ticaret Hane Sok. Lively basement bar off Divan Yolu Cad.

Clubs and discos

Andon, Siraselviler Cad 89, Taksim. Different bars on three floors plus a snug in the basement.

Club Coppa Cabana, Büyük Parmak Sok, Astiklal Cad. Not the most happening club in town but a decent choice for a cheap night out.

Çubukulu 29, Pazabahçe Yolu 24, Çubukulu. Large outdoor club right on the water, partly lit by flaming torches. The music is mambo and soul, the crowd is all ages and very energetic.

Gitanes, Tel Sok, off Büyükparmakkapi Sok, Taksim. Packed lively rendezvous for a grungy student crowd.

Memo's, Salhane Sok 10/2, Ortaköy. Classy joint with beautiful Bosphorus views and discos after 11pm. Hard to get in unless they like the look of you.

Roxy, Aslanyataqi Sok 113, Siraselviler Cad, Taksim. DJs and occasional live bands in a pricey, yuppy-orientated bar-disco.

Şamdansa, Turkbostan Sok 22, Yeniköy, Landscaped gardens and sculpture provides a backdrop for the best sounds in the city.

Listings

Airlines Aeroflot, Mete Cad 30, Taksim (☎212/243 4725); British Airways, Cumhuriyet Cad 10 (☎212/234 1300); Olympic Airways, Cumhuriyet Cad 171a (☎212/246 5081); THY Turkish Airlines, Cumhuriyet Cad 199–201, Harbiye (☎212/225 0556).

Banks The Garanti Bankası in Sultanahmet stays open through lunchtime, and the Azbaak at the airport is open 24hr. To change money you'll get a better rate at the Tahtakale or the streets below the bazaar than in the banks; for cash you'll get a better deal at the Döviz offices throughout the city (open daily and evenings).

Books The following have English books: Librarie de Pera, Galip Dele Cad 22; Tünel and Pandora, Büyükparmakkapi, Sok 3, Astiklal Cad. Sahaflar Çarzisi, the market on the Beyazit side of the covered bazaar, has lines of bookshops and is well worth a visit.

Bosphorus Ferry journeys up the Bosphorus are regarded by many as one of the city's highlights. There are special sightseeing boats throughout the year from Eminönü – $6 for the 2-hour journey to Anadolu Kavaqı. Otherwise the normal ferries are reasonably frequent, and if you get stranded (the last one from Anadolu Kavaqı in summer is at 5pm) you can always resort to a bus or *dolmuş*.

Buses Pamukkale (☎212/658 2222), Varan (☎212/658 0277), Ulusoy (☎212/658 3000) and Kâmil Koç (☎212/658 2010) are the better bus companies.

Car rental Airtour, Perpa Ticaret Centre 1671, 11th Floor (☎212/210 1990); Globcar, Zehit Muhtar Cad 17/2, Taksim (☎212/237 4479); Europcar, Topcu Cad 4721, Taksim (☎212/254 7788); Hertz, Cumhuriyet Cad 295, Harbiye (☎212/233 7101) and Atatürk airport (☎212/663 0807).

Consulates Australia, Tepecik Yolu 58, Etiler (☎212/257 7050); Britain, Mezrutiyet Cad 34, Tepebazı, Beyoğlu (☎212/252 6436); Canada, Buyukdere Cad 107/3 Begun Han, Gayrettepe (☎212/272 5174); Ireland, Cumhuriyet Cad 26a, Elmadaq (☎212/246 6025); Netherlands, Astiklâl Cad 393, Galatasaray, Beyoğlu (☎212/251 5030); USA, Mezrutiyet Cad 104–108, Tepebazı, Beyoğlu (☎212/251 3602).

Hospitals The city's best hospitals are the foreign-funded establishments: the American Admiral Bristol Hospital, Güzelbahçe Sok 20, Nizantazı (☎212/231 4050), or International Hospital, İstanbul Cad 82, Yezilköy (☎212/663 3000).

Laundry Active, Dr Eminpasa Sok 14, off Divan Yolu; the Hobby, Caferiya Sok 6/1, Sultanahmet (9am–8pm).

Left luggage Left-luggage offices (*Emanet*) can be found in both Sirkeci and Haydarpaza train stations.

Police The tourist police are at Yerebatan Cad, Sultanahmet (☎212/527 4503). Zabita offices are found all over, including one at the far end of the Hippodrome from Sultanahmet.

Post office The main post office is on Yeni Posthane Cad in Sirkeci (daily 9am–5.30pm; 8am–8pm for stamps).

Train stations Haydarpaza (☎216/336 0475) and Sirkeci (☎212/527 0051).

Travel agents For plane and bus tickets try Marco Polo, Divan Yolu Cad 54/11, Sultanahmet (☎212/519 2804), or Imperial, Divan Yolu Cad 30, Sultanahmet (☎212/513 9430).

Turkish baths The most central, and most frequented by tourists, are the four-hundred-year-old Çemberlitaz Hamam, on Divanyolu, and Cağaoğlu Hamam, Hilali Ahmed Cad 34 (daily 7am–10pm men, 8am–8pm women). Expect to pay between $10 and $30. *Hamam*s are much cheaper in smaller towns.

AROUND THE SEA OF MARMARA

Despite their proximity to İstanbul, the shores and hinterland of the Sea of Marmara are relatively neglected by foreign travellers. This is not altogether surprising: here Turkey is at its most Balkan, and, at first glance, least exotic. But it may well be your first view of the country and it is not entirely without charm or interest. The border town of **Edirne**, at the end of the Roman and Byzantine Via Egnatia, later the medieval route to the Ottoman parts of Europe, is home to some superb early Ottoman architecture, and the early Ottoman centre of **Bursa**, which you may pass through on your way to the Aegean coast, has one of the country's most exquisite city centres. Many visitors, also, justifiably stop off at the extensive World War I battlefields and cemeteries of the **Gelibolu peninsula** (Gallipoli), either using the north Marmara port of **Gelibolu** as a base, or, more commonly, **Çanakkale** – a town which is also a good centre for seeing the ruins of ancient Troy a little further south.

Edirne

More than just a border town, **EDIRNE** makes an impressive and easily digestible introduction to Turkey. It is a lively and attractive city, its life in part derived from day-tripping foreigners and a sizeable student population, and it boasts a clutch of elegant, early Ottoman monuments. Best of these, crowning the town hillock and reason itself for a detour, is the architect Sinan's supreme achievement, the **Selimiye Camii**, a testament to the time when it was the Ottoman capital and, later, a favourite haunt of the sultans.

You can see the main sights of Edirne on foot, but they're widely scattered and you'll need a full day. The best starting point is the **Eski Camii** bang in the centre, the oldest mosque in town and a boxy structure begun in 1403 that's a more elaborate version of Bursa's Ulu Camii. The interior is now rather a mess as a gaudy late-Ottoman paint job threatens to overshadow the giant calligraphy for which the mosque is famous. Just across the way, the **Bedesten** was Edirne's first covered market, though the tatty plastic goods it touts are no match for the building. Nearby, the **Semiz Ali Paşa Çarşısı** is the other main bazaar, begun by Sinan in 1568 at the behest of Semiz Ali, one of the most able of the Ottoman grand viziers. A short way north of here, the name of the **Üç Şerefeli Camii**, dating from 1447, means "three-balconied", derived from the presence of three galleries for the muezzin on the tallest of the four idiosyncratic minarets, which you can sometimes climb. A little way west, the masterly **Selimiye Camii** was designed by the eighty-year-old Sinan in 1569 at the command of Selim II. Its four slender **minarets** also have three balconies, and at 71m are the second tallest in the world after those in Mecca, although it's the interior which is most impressive, the dome planned to surpass that of Aya Sofya in İstanbul – which, at 31.5m in diameter, it manages by a few centimetres. Next door, the **Museum of Turkish and Islamic Arts** (Tues–Sun 9am–noon & 1–5pm; $1.50) houses assorted wooden, ceramic and martial knick-knacks from the province, plus a portrait gallery of grease-wrestling champions – a speciality of Edirne. The main **Archeological Museum** (Tues–Sun 8.30am–noon & 1–5.30pm; $1.50), just east of the mosque, contains a predictable assortment of Greco-Roman fragments, and an ethnographic section that focuses on carpet-weaving and other local crafts. Ten minutes further on, along Mimar Sinan Caddesi, the **Muradiye Camii** was built as a sanctuary for Mevlevi dervishes by the pious Murat II in 1435, its interior distinguished by some of the best İznik tiles outside Bursa.

Practicalities

From elsewhere in Turkey, you'll most likely arrive at Edirne's **bus station**, around 2km southeast of the centre, from where red city buses or *dolmuşes* whisk you to the centre of town. The **train station** is 1km further out in the same direction. There are two **tourist offices**, both on Talat Paza Cad: the main one about 500m west towards the Gazi Mihal bridge at no. 76a, and an annexe up near Hürriyet Meydanı, by the traffic signals (daily 8am–5.30/6.30pm).

Edirne has few genuinely **budget hotels**, and those that exist are either substandard or booked solid by truck drivers. The tourist office usually points backpackers to nearby Maarif Cad, where the *Otel Anil*'s (①) deceptive exterior at no. 8 fronts a grim dosshouse; the *Konak* (①) next door is little better. The *Aksaray*, Alipaza Ortakapı Cad 8 (☎284/212 6035; ①), is cleaner and more salubrious, but there are better options further south, along and across Saraçlar Cad: *Otel Açıkgöz*, Tüfekçiler Çarşısı, Sümerbank Arkası 74 (☎284/213 1944; ①), is probably the best deal, although it's worth paying the extra for the relative comfort of *Şaban Açıkgöz*, Cilingirler Cad 9 (☎0284/213 0313; ④), where rooms have en-suite facilities and TV, or the *Rüstem Paşa Kervanseray*, just off the main Hurriyet Meydani on Iki Kapili Han Cad (☎0284/212 6119; ④), which has rooms surrounding a quiet courtyard. **Campsites** are liberally sprinkled around Edirne, though strongly orientated towards caravanners. Try *Fifi Mocamp*, 8km along the road to İstanbul, or *BP Kervansaray*, near the bus station.

Restaurants are plentiful and cheap in Edirne, but not particularly inspiring. For snack lunches, look out for the tiny *ciğerci* booths serving the city speciality, deep-fried liver. Otherwise, some of the eateries on Saraçlar Cad aren't bad – the *Kerevan* is a busy, fast-food-style joint offering *pide*, *lahmacun* and doner kebabs, while the *Urfa-Gaziantep Kepapcisi* at no. 22 has good-value kebab fare and an upstairs dining room where female travellers will feel at home. Next to *Selimiye Camii*, *Vatan*, Kriyik Cad is a popular local haunt with a wider choice of steam-tray food. For **drinking**, the unlicensed *Café Tunca* on Hurriyet Meydani is a relaxing daytime venue, while *Zogo Pastanesi*, Saraçlar Cad 41 is the best place for sweets. The bar of the *Rustem Paşa Kervansaray* is good for a relaxing and not too pricey night-time drink.

Crossing the borders

The closest crossing into **Greece** from Edirne is 7km away at Pazarkule, separated from the Greek frontier post at Kastaniés by a kilometre-wide no-man's-land. Opening times, though, are only Monday to Friday from 9am to noon, and 9am to 11am at weekends. Red **city buses** run from Edirne to Karaqac, the nearest village, every twenty minutes, as do **dolmuşes** from behind the town hall. The alternative is to take a **taxi** ($9) all the way from Edirne to Pazarkule, and from there a Greek taxi to the Kastaniés post – $5 per car for the one-kilometre gap. On the Greek side three daily trains, and about as many buses, make the three-hour run down to Alexandhroúpoli, the first major Greek city, between 8am and 1pm, with a couple more later in the day.

The **Bulgarian** border is less problematic. The vast complex at Kapikule, 18km northwest of Edirne, straddles the busy E5/100 expressway and is open around the clock. Although international trains stop at Edirne en route to Bulgaria, it's impossible to buy a ticket here, so it's best to travel to Kapikule by other means and arrange onward transport from there. The frontier can be reached by *dolmuş* from Edirne (every 20min 6.30am–9pm, from behind the Eski Camii). You can walk across the border, pick up a taxi to Svilengrad train station ($10; no public transport), from where there are five trains a day to Plovdiv.

The Gelibolu peninsula

Though endowed with some fine scenery and beaches, the slender **Gelibolu peninsula**, which forms the northwest side of the **Dardanelles**, is mainly known for its grim military history. In April 1915 it was the site of a plan (devised by Winston Churchill) to land Allied troops, many of them Australian and New Zealand units, with a view to their linking up to neutralize the Turkish shore batteries controlling the Dardanelles. It was a harebrained scheme and failed miserably, with massive casualties. The fate of the Australian and New Zealand forces was particularly horrific; they were dug in here for around six months, and suffered a carnage which engendered a bitterness and suspicion of the big Western powers that endures to this day.

The battlefields, cemeteries and beaches

The **World War I battlefields** and **Allied cemeteries** scattered along the Gelibolu peninsula are by turns moving and numbing in the sheer multiplicity of graves, memorials and obelisks. It's difficult to imagine the bare desolation of 1915 in the lush landscape of much of the area, but the final 20km have been designated a **national park**, and some effort has been made by the Turkish authorities to signpost road junctions and sites. The open-air sites have no admission fees or restricted hours, but since there's little public transport through the area you should take a **tour** unless you have your own vehicle. The first stop on most tours is the **Kabatepe Orientation Centre and Museum** ($1.50), 6km along, beyond which are the **Beach**, **Shrapnel Valley** and **Shell Green** cemeteries, followed by **Anzac Cove** and **Arıburnu**, site of the bungled ANZAC landing and ringed by more graves. Looking inland, you'll see the murderous badlands that gave the defenders such an advantage. Beyond Arıburnu, a left fork leads towards the beaches and salt lake at **Cape Suvla**, today renamed Kemikli Burnu; most tourists bear right for Büyük Anafartalar village and **Çonkbayırı hill**, where there's a massive New Zealand memorial and a Turkish memorial describing Atatürk's words and deeds. The spot where the Turkish leader's pocket watch stopped a fragment of shrapnel is highlighted, as is the grave of a Turkish soldier discovered in 1990 when the trenches were reconstructed. Working your way back down towards the visitors' centre, you pass **The Nek, Walker's Ridge** and **Quinn's Post**, where the trenches of the opposing forces lay within a few metres of each other – the modern road corresponds to no-man's-land. From here the single, perilous supply line ran down-valley to the present location of **Beach Cemetery**.

Practicalities

The peninsula's principal town, **Gelibolu** – an inviting place with a colourful fishing harbour ringed by cafés and restaurants – is a good base from which to visit the battle sites. The **ferry jetty** is right at the inner harbour entrance; the **bus terminal** is on the opposite side next to the old tower. There's a good range of **accommodation**. At one corner of the port on Liman Caddesi is the *Anzac Pension* at no. 2 (☎286/566 3596; ①); roughly opposite and owned by the same people is the *Hotel Yılmaz* at no. 6 (☎286/566 1256; ②). Out by the lighthouse you'll find the *Motel Anzac* (☎286/566 3591; ②). Between the lighthouse and an army camp is a serviceable beach, with a campsite. You can join morning and afternoon **tours** of the World War I sites for about $30 per person – ask in the hotels for details, but it is cheaper to take a tour from Çanakkale. For **eating out**, the *Imren Restaurant* on the waterfront is cheap, licensed and does excellent local sardines.

Çanakkale

Though celebrated for its setting on the **Dardanelles**, **ÇANAKKALE** has little to detain you. However, it is the best base for visiting the Gallipoli sites and the sparse ruins of Troy. Among things to see in the town, the **Çimenlik Park** (daily, though sometimes closed for military exercises, 9am–10pm), southwest of the bazaar, is home to a replica of the minelayer *Nusrat*, which stymied the Allied fleet by re-mining zones at night that the French and British had swept clean by day – it is festooned inside with rather forgettable newspaper clippings of the era. The **Naval Museum** nearby (daily 8.30am–noon & 1–5pm; 35¢) is more worthwhile, featuring photos – parts of Gelibolu in ruins after Allied shelling, Atatürk's funeral – and military paraphernalia, including Atatürk's pocket watch which stopped a shell fragment at Gelibolu and saved his life. Two kilometres south of the centre of town, the **Archeological Museum** (Tues–Sun 8.30am–noon & 1–5pm; $1.50) is accessible by any *dolmuş* along Atatürk Caddesi labelled "Kepez" or "Güzelyalı" and has exhibits from all over the area, including exquisite gold jewellery from nearby tombs.

Practicalities

Everything you'd want to see or do in Çanakkale, except for the Archeological Museum, is within walking distance of the **ferry docks**, close to the start of the main Demircioğlu Caddesi. The nearby **tourist office** (summer daily 8am–8pm; winter daily 9am–5.30pm) is worth a stop if only for their free map of the Gallipoli battlefields. Arriving by bus, the bus station is out on Atatürk Caddesi, the local name for the coastal İzmir–Bursa highway, a fifteen-minute walk from the waterfront. If you arrive on the bus from İstanbul, get off at the ferry rather than going to the bus station. If you're seeing the **Gallipoli battlefields** from here, the principal **tour operators** are Hassle Free, Cumhuriyet Meydani 61 (☎286/217 0156), who also pick up from various pensions in Sultanahmet, İstanbul, and the nearby Troy Anzac at Yali Cad 2 (☎286/217 5849), both of which have English-speaking guides. Expect to pay around $15–20 a head.

Except for a crowded couple of weeks during mid-August when the Çanakkale/Troy Festival is being staged, or on Anzac Day (April 25) when the town is inundated with Antipodeans, you'll have little trouble finding a room. The friendliest of the budget **hotel** options is *Anzac House*, Cumhuriyet Meydani 61 (☎0286/213 5969; ①), with small but neat rooms. The dilapidated, eccentric *Kervansaray* round the corner at Fetvahane Sok 13 (☎0286/217 8192; ①) is a quiet place in an old mansion. The *Avrupa Pansiyon*, Matbaa Sok 8 (☎0286/217 4084; ①), tucked in between Fetvahane Sokaqi and the quay is spartan, but able to offer cleanish doubles with baths. Clean and airy, the *Yellow Rose*, Yeni Sok 5 (☎0286/217 3343; ③), in the street behind *Kervansaray*, is a good option with a garden, friendly proprietor, and some en-suite rooms. The *Hotel Anzac*, Saat Kulesi Meydani 8 (☎0286/217 7777; ④) is a more modern and upmarket hotel with en-suite facilities. The nearest **camping** site is at Güzelyali, 12km to the south, accessible by minibus. Of the quayside **restaurants** south of the ferry jetty, the *Entellektüel* has the widest range of *meze* and fish, but is not cheap. The *Şehir Lokantası*, at the southern end of the esplanade, is a good place to sample the local fish. Inland, the food is more modest and cheaper. Best and friendliest of the bunch in the bazaar is the *Yilmaz Restaurant*, one street back from the water. *Trakya*, on the main square, offers cheap kebabs, while the nearby *Taş Firin* on Cumhuriyet Cad does a brisk trade in *lahmacun* and *pide*-style fast food. For **drinking**, the *TNT* on Saat Kule Meydani is a popular bar with both travellers and locals.

Troy

Although by no means the most spectacular archeological site in Turkey, **TROY** (Truva), thanks to Homer's *Iliad*, is probably the most celebrated. The ruins of the ancient city, just west of the main road around 20km south of Çanakkale, consist of some fortification remains and a few vague piles of stone with the catch-all label "Defensive Wall" – and a lot of visitors come away disappointed. But if you lower your expectations and use your imagination, you may be impressed.

Troy was generally thought to have existed in legend only until 1871 when a German businessman, Heinrich Schliemann, excavated the site. Schliemann's work actually caused a certain amount of damage, and he removed many of his discoveries to Germany without Turkish permission. But his digging uncovered nine layers of remains, representing distinct and consecutive city developments spanning four millennia. The oldest, Troy I, dates back to about 3600 BC and was followed by four similar settlements. Troy VI is known to have been destroyed by an earthquake in about 1275 BC, while Troy VII shows signs of having been destroyed by fire about a quarter of a century later, around the time historians generally estimate the Trojan War to have taken place. Troy VIII, which thrived from 700 to 300 BC, was a Greek city, while the final layer of development, Troy IX, was built between 300 BC and 300 AD, during the heyday of the Roman Empire.

The **site** (daily: summer 8am–8pm; winter 8am–5pm; $3) is signalled by the ticket office opposite the bus drop-off point, from where a road leads to a giant wooden horse. Just beyond is the ruined city itself, a craggy outcrop overlooking the plain, which stretches about 8km to the sea. It's a bleak sight, and leaves you in no doubt as to the thinness of Troy's remains, but as you stand on what's left of the ramparts and look out across the plain, it's not too difficult to imagine a besieging army, legendary or otherwise, camped out below. Walking around the site, the **walls** of Troy VI are the most obvious feature, curving around in a crescent from the entrance; there are also more definite and visible remains from Troys VIII–IX, including a council chamber and a small theatre a little way north.

Practicalities

Çanakkale is the most sensible base for seeing Troy, since its bus station is connected to the site by fairly frequent *dolmuşes* in summer. Anatour and Troy Anzac back in Çanakkale both offer guided tours for around $12–15 a head. Failing that, you can **stay** in the nearby village of **Tevfikıye**, in the none-too-luxurious *Yarol Pension* (①), or closer near the gates at the slightly more up-market *Hisarlik* (③). The *dolmuş* to the site drops you off here in front of a cluster of shops and relatively humble **eateries**.

Bursa

Draped along the leafy lower slopes of Uludağ, which towers more than 2000m above, **BURSA** – first capital of the Ottoman Empire and the burial place of several sultans – does more justice to its setting than any other Turkish city besides İstanbul. Gathered here are some of the finest early Ottoman monuments in the Balkans, in a city centre that's one of the most appealing in Turkey. Although sometimes touted as a day out from İstanbul, it really deserves at least an overnight stay.

The City

Flanked by the busy Atatürk Cad, the compact **Koza Parkı**, with its fountains, benches, crowds and cafés, is the real heart of Bursa. On the far side looms the **Ulu Cami**, built between 1396 and 1399 by Yıldırım Beyazit I, from the proceeds of booty won from the Crusaders at Nicopolis on the Danube. Before the battle Yıldırım had vowed to construct twenty mosques if victorious. The present building of twenty domes was his rather free interpretation of this promise. The interior is dominated by a huge *şadırvan* pool (for ritual ablutions) in the centre, whose skylight was once open to the elements, and an intricate walnut *mimber* (pulpit) pieced together, it's claimed, without nails or glue. Close by is Bursa's **covered market**, the **Bedesten**, given over to the sale of jewellery and precious metals, and the **Koza Hanı**, flanking the park, still entirely occupied by silk and brocade merchants. Across the river to the east, the **Yeşil Cami** is easily the most spectacular of Bursa's imperial mosques – though never completed, as you can see from the entrance. The hundreds of tiles inside give the mosque its name ("Green Mosque"). Tucked above the foyer, and usually closed to visits, the imperial loge is the most extravagantly decorated chamber of all, the work attributed to a certain Al-Majnun, which translates most accurately as "intoxicated on hashish". The nearby hexagonal **Yeşil Türbe** (daily 8am–noon & 1–7pm; free) contains the sarcophagus of Çelebi Mehmet I and assorted offspring, though otherwise the immediate environs of the mosque are twee in the extreme, busy with tourists and souvenir shops. The *medrese*, the largest surviving dependency of the mosque, now houses Bursa's **Museum of Turkish and Islamic Art** (Tues–Sun 8am–noon & 1–5pm; $1) – not a bad ethnographic collection, with İznik ware, Çanakkale ceramics, glass items and a mock-up of an Ottoman circumcision chamber.

In the opposite direction from the centre of town, the **Hisar** (meaning "citadel") district was Bursa's original nucleus, though it nowadays retains just a few clusters of dilapidated Ottoman housing along its warren of narrow lanes, and a few stretches of rampart, given over to ribbons of park and tea gardens. The best-preserved dwellings are a little way west in medieval **Muradiye**, where the **Muradiye Külliyesi** mosque and *medrese* complex was begun in 1424 by Murat II, the last imperial foundation in Bursa – although it's most famous for its tombs, set in lovingly tended gardens. Best of these are that of Zehzade Ahmet and his brother Zehinzah, both murdered in 1513 by their cousin Selim the Grim to preclude any succession disputes, covered with İznik tiles and contrasting sharply with the adjacent austerity of Murat II's tomb, where Roman columns inside and a wooden awning are the only superfluities: in accordance with his wishes, both the coffin and the dome were originally open to the sky "so that the rain of heaven might wash my face like any pauper's".

From Muradiye it's a short walk down to Çekirge Caddesi and the southeast gate of the **Kültür Parkı**, where there's a popular tea garden, a small boating lake and three pricey restaurants. At the far end there's also an **Archeological Museum** (Tues–Sun 8am–noon & 1–5pm; $1), whose exhibits include metal jewellery from all over Anatolia, a collection of Roman glass items, and Byzantine and Roman bronzes. Just beyond the Kültür Parkı, the **Yeni Kaplıca** (daily 9am–11pm; $3), accessible by a steep driveway, are the closest of Bursa's baths, a faded reminder of the days when the town was patronized as a spa.

Practicalities

Bursa's new **bus terminal** is 5km north of the centre on the main road to İstanbul – bus #90 connects with the old *otogar*, 1km from the city centre at the bottom of Fevzi Cakmak Cad. A ten-minute walk or short *dolmuş* ride will bring you to the bazaar area, just beyond which is the Atatürk Cad and Koza Parki. Bursa's **tourist office** (Mon–Fri 8.30am–6pm) is in a subterranean mall at one corner of the Koza Parkı, well signposted on the north side of Atatürk Cad. Most of the numerous **hotels** ringing the bus station are pretty grim, although *Hotel Kardeş* (☎224/272 1770; ④), on the corner of Fevzi Çakmak and Kibris Zehitler, and *Belkis*,

Celal Baya Cad 168 (☎0224/254 8322; ②), are reasonably quiet and comfy. In the centre, at Ressam Zefik Bursah Cad 30, *Hotel Bilgiç* (☎224/220 3190; ③), is clean and friendly, while the *Hotel İpekçi*, Çanilar Cad 38 (☎0224/221 1935; ③) in the Bazaar area northwest of Koza Parka, has bright and spacious rooms. A step up-market, *Çeşmeli*, Heykel Gümüzçeken Cad 6 (☎224/224 1512; ④), is quiet and central.

There's a fair amount of **culinary variety** to be had in Bursa, with a host of small restaurants scattered throughout the bazaar. *Konyali Lokantasi*, in the central courtyard of Koza Hani is one of the better lunchtime *pide* and kebab joints. *Adanur Hacibey*, off Koza Parki at Unlu Cad, Yilmaz Izhani Girizi, is one of the best-value places to sample the local speciality, *İskender kebap*. *Hacibey İskender*, Tazkapi Sok 4, Atatürk Cad, serves up similar fare, although you pay for the attractive olde-world Ottoman ambience. The *Canlı Balık*, Yeni Balık Pazarı 14, in the fish market, is a licensed and cheap fish restaurant; *Çiçek İzgara*, Belediye Cad 15, is more elegant but still reasonable. In the evening, head for Kuruçezme Mh. Sakarya Caddesi at the foot of the citadel, where you'll find a street of lively fish restaurants. *Arap Sükrü* at no. 6 is reasonably priced and not quite as male-dominated as some of the others. For **drinking**, the *Tino Bar*, at the end of Atatürk Cad, by the Setbazı Bridge, has an outdoor terrace, while Sakarya Cad harbours a string of pub-like drinking venues.

THE AEGEAN COAST

The **Aegean coast** is Turkey's most visited region. But it is also, in many ways, the most enticing destination for visitors, home to some of the best of its classical antiquities and the most appealing resorts. The north shore sees the fewest visitors: a quiet, rocky region, not over-endowed with fine beaches and with a much shorter summer season, but reasonably rich in Hellenistic remains. **Ayvalık**, the north's longest-established resort, makes an excellent place to stop for a few days, with good beaches and easy access to **Bergama** a little inland, with its unmissable ruins. Further south, **İzmir** is for most travellers an obstacle on the way to more compelling destinations. But you may arrive here, and, on closer examination, the city is not without charm and serves as a base for day-trips to adjacent sights and beaches. The territory to the south is home to the best concentration of classical, Hellenistic and Roman ruins, notably **Ephesus**, usually first on everyone's list of dutiful pilgrimages, and the remains at **Aphrodisias** and **Hierapolis**, inland – although the latter is more often visited for the pools and rock formations of adjacent **Pamukkale**. The **coast** itself is better down here, too, and although the larger resorts – **Çesme**, **Kuşadası**, **Marmaris** and **Bodrum** – are beginning to be lost to the developers, Bodrum and Çesme still have a certain amount of charm.

Ayvalık and around

AYVALIK, a couple of kilometres west of the main coast road, is a small fishing port that also makes a living from olive-oil production and tourism. However, the latter is reasonably low-key and the town makes a nice base for beach-lounging and ruin-spotting at Bergama, 70km southeast. Refounded during the 1400s on ancient ruins, Ayvalık has suffered two serious earthquakes this century, though the most devastating effect on the town occurred when its mainly Greek inhabitants were kicked out during the exchange of populations that followed the Greek-Turkish war of 1920–22. There's not a great deal to see, though its tangle of central streets, lined with terraces of sumptuous Greek houses and clattering with speeding horsecarts, is worth a wander, and there are some decent beaches in the surrounding area.

About 6km south, **SARIMSAKLI** (literally "Garlic Beach") is a resort development accessible by *dolmuş* or municipal bus. Across the bay from Ayvalık, the island of **CUNDA** is also a good day-trip destination, with a couple of stretches of beach on its west and north edges and some excellent harbour fish restaurants. The best way to get here in summer is by boat, though at other times you'll have to rely on the roughly hourly bus service from Atatürk Square or a taxi across the causeway connecting the island to the mainland. **Accommodation** possibilities on the island include the *Artur Motel* (☎266/327 1014; ②), on the square and the *İlker Pansiyon* (no sign out; ☎266/327 1034; ①). There's also the *Günay Motel* (☎266/327 1048; ②). The main **campsite**, *Ortunç Camping*, about 4km southwest of town, also has a restaurant and some rooms. The *Günay's* restaurant is reckoned about the best, though you've several more to choose from on the quay itself.

Practicalities

Ayvalık is a fairly small town, with a centre concentrated around a small square 1500m south of the main **bus station**. Buses from the south will drop you off near the centre on Atatürk Cad while buses from the north tend not to make the detour to Ayvalık – it's best to change at Edremit, 45km away, onto a minibus which terminates near the PTT. At the time of writing, a brand new bus station was being built just outside of town in order to alleviate high season pollution, but it may not be ready for some time. Changing money is not a problem, with various banks and exchange offices on the main street along the sea front, though if you want to change money out of season, many of the banks refuse to offer exchange facilities or else charge excessive commissions on travellers cheques.

The **tourist office** (summer Mon–Fri 8am–noon & 1–6pm, Sat 9am–noon & 2–6pm; winter Mon–Fri 8am–noon & 1–5pm; ☎266/312 2122) is ten to fifteen minutes' walk south of the town centre on the main coast road. There's a wealth of **pensions** in Ayvalık's old houses, the best is the laid-back and spotless *Taksiyarhis* (☎266/312 1494; ①), behind the Taksiyarhis church, a couple of blocks inland from the seafront. Try also: *Chez Beliz*, Fethiye Mahallesi, Marezal Çakmak Cad 28 (☎266/312 4897; ③; May–Sept), deeper into the old town and well signposted from the seafront; and *Bonjour*, Marezal Çakmak Cad, Bezinci Sok 6 (☎266/313 8085; ③; May–Sept), which has rooms in an old mansion. **Eating** and **drinking** possibilities include *Dayim*, on Atatürk Cad, with well-priced local fare and friendly service; *Kardeşler Pide Salonu*, opposite the PTT on Anönü Cad, with a good choice of kebabs; and *Öz Canli Balık* on the seafront, specializing in fish and *mezes*. The *Circus Bar*, on Gümrük Sok, is one of the better drinking dens.

Tickets to the Greek island of **Lésvos** are sold at Jale Tour, Gümrük Cad 41/A (☎266/312 2740) or Yeni İstanbul Tur (☎266/312 6123). Ferries run three times a week from June to September with a chance of a boat making the trip in May if there are enough passengers. Bear in mind, though, that you may only be allowed to travel on the afternoon Greek boat if you arrived on it. Fares are $50 single, $65 open return.

Bergama

Frequently touted as a day-trip from Ayvalık, **BERGAMA** is the site of the Hellenistic – and later Roman – city of Pergamon, ruled for several centuries by a powerful local dynasty. Excavations were completed here in 1886, but unfortunately much of what was found has since been carted off to Germany. However, the acropolis of Eumenes II remains a major attraction, and there are a host of lesser sights and an old quarter of chaotic charm to detain you for a day or so.

The old town lies at the foot of the acropolis, about ten minutes' walk from the bus station. Its foremost attraction is the **Kızıl Avlu** or "Red Basilica" (daily 9am–5/7pm; $3), a huge edifice on the river not far from the acropolis, originally built as a temple to the Egyptian god Osiris and converted to a basilica by the early Christians, when it was one of the Seven Churches of Asia Minor addressed by St John in the book of Revelation – though sadly it's now a crumbling ruin with a mosque in one of its towers. The area around the basilica is a jumble of ramshackle buildings, carpet and antique shops, mosques and maze-like streets. South of here along the main street is the **Archeological Museum** (Tues–Sun 8.30am–5.30pm; $2), which has a large collection of locally unearthed booty, including a statue of Hadrian from the Asclepion (see overleaf), and various busts of figures like Zeus and Socrates. There's also a model of the Zeus altar, complete with the Berlin-resident reliefs.

Bergama has a particularly good **hamam** at Bankalar Cad 32. Ancient employees, who're stronger than they look, will give you the full Turkish bath treatment for $9.

The ruins

The **Acropolis** (daily 9am–5/7pm; $3), the ancient city of the kings of Pergamon, is set on top of a rocky bluff towering over modern Bergama, accessible by taxi from the bus station (they'll ferry you around all Bergama's ruins for about $12; expect to pay $6 for a straight trip from the centre to the acropolis) or on foot – a fair walk up a path from the old town, but quite manageable if it's not too hot. There are also plans to run a minibus service to the ruins so check for this development. The first main attraction up here is the huge horseshoe-shaped **Altar of Zeus**, built during the reign of Eumenes II to commemorate his father's victory over the Gauls, and formerly decorated with reliefs depicting the battle between the giants and the gods. Even today its former splendour is apparent, though it has been much diminished by the removal of the reliefs to Berlin.

North of the Zeus altar lie the sparse remains of a **Temple of Athena**, above which loom the restored columns of the **Temple of Trajan**, where the deified Roman emperor and his successor Hadrian were revered in the imperial era. From the Temple of Athena a narrow staircase leads down to the **theatre**, the most spectacular part of the ruined acropolis, capable of seating ten thousand spectators, and a **Temple of Dionysus**, just off-stage to the northwest.

Bergama's other significant archeological site is the **Asclepion** (daily: summer 9am–7pm; winter 9am–5pm; $3), a Greco-Roman medical centre which can be reached on foot from the road beginning at the Kursunlu Cami in the modern town. Much of what can be seen today was built during the first- and second-century heyday of the centre, when its function was similar to that of the nineteenth-century spa. The main features are a **Propylon** or monumental entrance gate, built during the third century AD, and a circular **Temple of Asclepios**, dating from 150 AD and modelled on the Pantheon in Rome. At the western end of the northern colonnade is a **theatre** with a seating capacity of 3500, while at the centre of the open area a **sacred fountain** still gushes mildly radioactive drinking water, near to which an underground passage leads to the two-storey circular **Temple of Telesphorus**.

Practicalities

Bergama is due to have a new **bus station** by 2000, which will take you straight into town. The very helpful **tourist office** is on the main drag between the *otogar* and the centre; ignore the misleading signposts. In an attempt to attract more backpackers, prices in all pensions have been fixed at about $7, which normally includes breakfast. Many **hotels** tend to be in the old town, although there are a few reasonable possibilities near the main bus station. Some 400m from the *otogar*, *Manolya*, Tanpinar Sok 5 (☎232/633 4488; ①), is well appointed and good value. In the old town, *Athena*, Barbaros Mahalli, Amam Çıkmazi 5 (☎232/633 3420; ①), has elegant rooms in a nineteenth-century mansion, while the *Pergamon Pansiyon*, Bankalar Cad 3 (☎232/633 2395; ①), occupies another atmospheric old house, but is in a noisy location above a busy restaurant. A good option is the *Bobligen*, Zafer Mah, Cad 2 (☎232/633 2153; ①), a clean and professionally run venture on the way to the Asclepion. For **food**, the restaurant in the courtyard of the *Pergamon Pansiyon* has some reasonable home cooking and *Saelam 3*, on the main street at Hükümet Meydanı 29, has an excellent range of traditional Turkish food and a shady courtyard.

İzmir

Turkey's third city and its second port after İstanbul, **İZMİR** – ancient Smyrna – is home to nearly three million people. It is blessed with a mild climate and an enviable position, straddling the head of a fifty-kilometre-long gulf fed by several streams and flanked by mountains on all sides. But despite an illustrious history, most of the city is relentlessly modern, and even enthusiasts will concede that a couple of days here are plenty.

İzmir was the Ottoman Empire's window to the west, but after World War I Greece was given an indefinite mandate over İzmir and its hinterland. This lasted until the entry into Smyrna of the Turkish army on September 9, 1922, and three days of murder and plunder in which seventy percent of the city burned to the ground. The modern city has been built pretty much from scratch, its central boulevards wide and tree-lined, and is nowadays booming; yet it is also home to some of the more persistent street hustlers in Turkey, a consequence of the disparity between the chi-chi waterfront and the grim shantytowns, further aggravated by the large numbers of foreign servicemen around due to the city's role as headquarters of NATO Southeast.

Arrival and accommodation

Ferries anchor at the **Alsancak terminal**, 2km north of the centre; take a taxi into town (for around $2), or walk 250m south and pick up a #2 blue and white bus from the nearby suburban train station. Most **trains** pull in at **Basmane station**, 1km from the seafront at the eastern end of Fevzipaşa Bulvari. If you **fly**, use the frequent shuttle train from the **airport** to Alsancak train station (for the #2 bus). The brand new **bus station**, reminiscent of the Cloud City in Star Wars, is about 8km out on the east side of the city, from where you can take either a bus #60 or #64 or a taxi for about $7 to Konak on the seafront, an important transport hub. If travelling to and from destinations on the Çeşme peninsula, buses depart from the Uckuyular bus station about 5km west along the sea front from Konak. Bus #169 links Konak to this bus station. There's a **tourist office** in the airport arrivals hall and another near the seafront, next door to the *Efes Hotel* at Akdeniz Mah. 1344 Sok 2 (summer: daily 9am–5pm; winter: Mon–Sat 8am–5pm). The modern city is somewhat confusing to negotiate but most points of interest are close together and the most enjoyable way of exploring is on foot. If you're using **public transport**, you must buy tickets in advance (40¢) from white kiosks near most stops, and then cancel them on board.

The main areas for budget **hotels** are immediately west of Basmane train station in Çankaya, a recently pedestrianized area north of Fevzipaza Bulvari, and Akinci, south of the boulevard. In Akinci, the *Saray*, Anafartalar Cad 635 (☎232/483 6946; ①), has heated rooms with shared facilities; while the rooms at the *Imperial*, 1296 Sok 54 (☎232/484 9771; ③), have en-suite facilities. In Çankaya, *Oba*, at 1369 Sok 27 (☎232/483 5474; ②) is worth trying, as is the *Güzel İzmir*, 1368 Sok 8 (☎232/483 5069; ②), which has small rooms with en-suite bathrooms.

The City

İzmir cannot really be said to have a single centre, although **Konak**, the busy park, bus terminal and shopping centre on the waterfront, is the spot where visitors spend most time. It's marked by the ornate **Saat Kulesi** (clock tower), the city's official symbol, and the **Konak Camii**, distinguished by its facade of enamelled tiles. Southwest of here, the **Archeological Museum** (Tues–Sun 8.30am–5pm; $3) features an excellent collection of finds from all over İzmir province and beyond, including the showcased bronze statuette of a runner and a large Roman mosaic, as well as a graceful Hellenistic statuette of Eros clenching a veil in his teeth. The **Ethnographic Museum** (Tues–Sun 8.30am–5pm; $1.50), opposite the Archeological Museum, is a more enjoyable and certainly more interesting collection, with reconstructions of local mansions and the first Ottoman pharmacy in the area, a nuptial chamber, a sitting room and circumcision recovery suite, along with vast quantities of household utensils and Ottoman weaponry.

Immediately east of Konak, İzmir's **bazaar** warrants a stroll. Anafartalar Caddesi, the main drag, is lined with clothing, jewellery and shoe shops; Fevzipaşa Bulvari and the alleys just south are strong on leather garments, for which the city is famous. Still further east, across Gaziosmanpaşa Bulvari, the **Agora** (daily 8.30am–5.30pm; $1.50) is the most accessible of İzmir's ancient sites, and the most visited, dating back to the early second century BC, although what you see now are the remains of the later reconstruction, financed during the reign of the Roman emperor, Marcus Aurelius. Above this, the **Kadifekale** (Velvet Castle) is perhaps the one sight in the city you shouldn't miss. The less energetic can take a red and white city bus #33 from Konak, but the best introduction to the citadel is to walk up from the agora, the route threading through a once-elegant district of narrow streets and dilapidated pre-1922 houses. The irregularly shaped fortress dates from Byzantine and Ottoman times, and gives great views over the city from its pine-shaded tea garden.

Eating and drinking

For a city of İzmir's size, **restaurants** are fairly thin on the ground. The obvious clutch of eateries within sight of Basmane station are undistinguished, and as so often in Turkey there's a far better choice in the bazaar area, although unfortunately most of them close up early evening. The *Aksüt*, 873 Sok 113, does excellent dairy products and breakfast pastries. The *Halikarnass Balık Lokantası*, overlooking the fountain at the junction of 870, 871 and 873 Sokaks, is a simple unlicensed fish restaurant; the *Şükran Lokantası*, Anafartlar Cad 61, is relatively expensive but has an elegant courtyard and serves alcohol until late. The *Öz Ezo Gelin*, on the corner of 848 Sok and Anafartalar Cad, serves soups, kebabs and puddings, though no alcohol, in an elegant dining room. For pudding or ice cream only, try *Bolulu Hasan Usta*, 853 Sok 13/B, which does the best in town. *Ömür*, Anafartalar Cad 794, is cheap and friendly, serving ready-prepared dishes but no alcohol. Heading north across Fevzipaza into Alsancak district, you're entering posher territory, but even here there are some affordable options: the *Altınkapı*, 1444 Sok 14/A, is good for grills and has outdoor seating. *Kemal'ın Yeri*, 1453 Sok 20/A, is famous for its seafood, but it's a pricey upmarket place. The north end of Alsancakis is also the trendy **nightlife** quarter; a stroll along the various inland alleys will turn up possibilities, which tend to change frequently.

Listings

Airlines British Airways, Zair Ezref Bul 3, Suite 304 (☎232/441 3829); THY, Büyük Efes Hoteli, Gaziosmanpaşa Bul 1 (☎232/484 1220).

Car rental Avis, Zair Ezref Bul 18/D (☎232/441 4417); Merve, Gaziosmanpas Bul. Yeni Asir İşh (☎232/484 4466).

Consulates Britain, Mahmut Esat Bozkurt Cad 49 (☎232/463 5151); Netherlands, Cumhuriyet Meydanı Bulvar Apt. (☎232/463 4963).

Exchange The PTT on Cumhuriyet Meydanı offers 24-hour exchange; also numerous, reputable *döviz* (exchange houses) in Çankaya.

Ferries Tickets and information on international and domestic services from the Turkish Maritime Lines facilities at the Alsancak dock (☎232/421 1484).

Hospitals Most central is the state-run Atatürk Devlet Hastanesi in Yesalyurt (☎232/4343), though the private Özel Sawlik Hastanesi at 1399 Sok in Alsancak may be preferable.

Left luggage On the left side of Basmane station as you face it (daily 7am–7.30pm) and at the bus station (7am–midnight; $1 per piece).

Post office There's a 24hr office, with phones, on Cumhuriyet Bulvari.

Çeşme and around

An attractive town of old Greek houses wrapped around a Genoese castle, **ÇEŞME** is the most relaxed of the southern Aegean resorts, an agreeable stopover on the way to Híos in Greece. The town's two main streets are **İnkilap Caddesi**, the main bazaar thoroughfare, and Çarşı Caddesi, its continuation, which saunters south along the waterfront. Çeşme's **sights** are, however, soon exhausted. You're free to clamber about every perilous inch of the waterfront **Castle** (daily 8.30am–noon & 1–5.30pm), and a **Museum** (Tues–Sun 8.30am–noon &1–5.30pm) of finds from the nearby site of Erythrae. You can purchase a joint ticket for both for $3 from the entrance to the castle. The **Kervansaray**, a few paces south, dates from the reign of Süleyman the Magnificent and is now a luxury hotel.

Coming by **ferry** from Híos (Chios in Turkish), you arrive at the small jetty in front of the castle. Arriving by **bus** from İzmir you'll probably arrive at the *otogar* 1km south, although some services meet the top of İnkilap Cad. **Dolmuşes** to Dalyan leave from the roundabout at the northeast of İnkilap Cad; those to other nearby attractions depart from next to the

tourist office at the harbour (winter Mon–Fri 8.30am–5.30pm, Sat 9am–5pm; summer daily 8.30am–5pm). During the summer months there are many options for accommodation, with a clutch of pensions on the right-hand side of the castle as it faces the sea. The *Tarhan Pansiyon* (☎232/712 6599; ①), behind the *kervansaray*, offers a few run-down rooms with bath, while the efficient *Avrupali* (☎232/712 7039; ②) has a picturesque garden and well-appointed rooms including suites with kitchenettes. *Özge* (☎232/712 7021; ③) is immaculately kept and comfortable but, if full or too expensive, try *Nergis* (☎232/712 6639; ②) next door, which is almost as good. A bit further along and away from the harbour past the local **hamam** is the friendly, clean and basic *Aras Apartments* (☎232/712 7375; ②), which offers rooms with balconies in and out of season. Down in the flatlands the *Alim Pansiyon*, Müftü Sok 3 (☎232/712 8319; ②), offers en-suite bath and breakfast. Among Çeşme's better **restaurants** are the waterfront *Rıhtım* and *Muhsin*, both past the PTT – the latter is more reasonable – while *Körfez*, on the marina, is possibly the most elegant, serving up excellent charcoal-grilled fish, but at a price. Inland, the *Özen Pide Salonu*, just off İnkilap Cad behind the former Greek church, offers kebab and *pide* regulars. *Rumeli Pastanesi* at no. 44 İnkilap, serves some of the best ice cream on the Aegean, and specializes in desserts and jams made from the sap of gum trees. Sakarya, also on İnkilap Caddesi, is a popular local restaurant and therefore cheaper.

For **ferry tickets to Híos**, contact the Ertürk agency (☎232/712 6768) in front of the tourist office, or Karavan (☎232/712 7230), next door. Ferries go once weekly in winter (Thurs) and increase to twice weekly in May and October (Tues & Thurs). There are four sailings a week in June and September (Tues, Thurs, Sat & Sun) and five in July and August (Tues & Thurs–Sun), with most departures at about 9am and some at 4pm. Current rates are $30 single, $40 open return for a foot passenger and $70–90 extra for a car. No taxes are applicable from Çeşme but they will be levied, at roughly $20, from Híos (Chios).

The closest beach to Çeşme is at **BOYALIK**, 1500m east of town, but the sand is painfully exposed to cold winds and washed-up rubbish, like most beaches on this side of the peninsula. Far better to bypass it in favour of **ILICA**, 4km further on, where there's an excellent long beach but mostly package accommodation. Due to hot thermal springs, the water here is relatively warm and nearby Sifne's mud baths remain a therapeutic attraction throughout the year.

Kuşadası

KUŞADASI is Turkey's most bloated resort, a brash coastal playground which extends along several kilometres of seafront. In just three decades its population has swelled from about 6000 to around 50,000, though how many of these are year-round inhabitants is debatable. The town is many people's introduction to the country: efficient ferry services link it with the Greek islands of Sámos and Míkonos, plus the resort is an obligatory port of call for Aegean cruise ships, which disgorge vast numbers in summer, who delight the local souvenir merchants after a visit to the ruins of Ephesus just inland.

Liman Caddesi runs from the ferry port up to **Atatürk Bulvarı**, the main harbour esplanade, from which pedestrianized **Barbaros Hayrettin Bulvarı** ascends the hill. To the left of here, the **Kale** district, huddled inside the town walls, is the old and most appealing part of town, with a namesake mosque and some fine traditional houses. If you want to swim, Kuşadası's most famous **beach**, the **Kadınlar Denizi** (Ladies' Beach), around 3km southwest of town, is a popular strand, usually too crowded for its own good in season. **Güvercin Island**, closer to the centre, is mostly landscaped terraces, dotted with tea gardens and snack bars, but the swimming is rocky. For the closest decent sand, head 500m further south to the small beach north of **Yılancı Burnu**, or to **Tusan** beach, 7km north of town; all Kuşadası–Selçuk *dolmuşes* pass by, as well as more frequent ones labelled "Zehir Açi". Much the best beach in the area, though, is **Pamucak**, at the mouth of the Küçük Menderes River 15km north, an exposed, four-kilometre-long stretch of sand that is as yet little developed. There are regular *dolmuşes* from both Kuşadası and Selçuk in season.

Practicalities

Ferries arrive at Liman Cad, right by the **tourist office** (May–Oct daily 8am–7pm; Nov–April Mon–Fri 8am–noon & 1.30–5.30pm; ☎256/614 1103), which has exhaustive lists of accommodation. The combined **dolmuş** and long-distance **bus station**, where you'll be left if coming from the south, around 2km out, is past the end of Kahramanlar Cad on the ring road to Söke, while the *dolmuş* stop is closer to the centre on Adnam Menderes Bulvarı.

There are plenty of **places to stay**. The best area to look is just south of the core of the town, uphill from Barbaros Hayrettin Bulvarı, particularly the upper reaches of Arslanlar Cad and Bezirgan Sok. *Stella*, Bezirgan Sok 44 (☎256/614 1632; ⑥; April–Sept), has comfortable en-suite rooms with an on-site swimming pool. *Sammy's Pension*, aka *Rose*, Aslanlar Cad Aydinlik Sok 7 (☎256/614 2588; ①; April–Sept), is firmly on the ANZAC network and is a lively and friendly place with an assortment of rooms and dorms and, when full, there is always the roof. *Kalyon*, Kibris Cad 7 (☎256/614 3346; ②), is friendly, and has en-suite rooms with balconies. Next door is the *Ozhan*, Kibris Cad 5 (☎256/614 2932; ②), which has basic rooms. For **campers**, the *Turyat* out at Tusan beach is well appointed but expensive. The *Önder* and *Yat*, both behind the yacht marina, are marginally cheaper, well kept and popular.

The *Önder* has a decent restaurant – perhaps the best in town – but with that honourable exception, value for money is not the order of the day as far as **food** goes in Kuşadası. *Konyali*, Saglik Cad 40, is a basic kebab place much patronized by the locals and open 24 hours a day. *Öz Urfa*, in the Kale district on Cephane Sok, offers excellent-value *lahmacun* and *pide*; while the *Avlu*, also on Cephane Sok, has a wide range of kebab and steam-tray food and a cosy outdoor courtyard. If you want to eat by the water without emptying your entire wallet, you might try the *Ada Restaurant-Plaj-Café*, on Güvercin Adası. For a **drink**, there's *Bebop*, Cephane Sok 20 in the Kale, or *She*, corner of Bahar and Sakarya Sokaks and half a dozen more along Kizla Sok close by. Rather more down-market and livelier are the dozen-plus "Irish" and "English" pubs along an inland alley officially renamed Barlar Sok (Pub Lane).

The agent for most of the **ferries to Samos** is Diana on Kibris Cad (☎256/614 4900). The morning Turkish boat is handled by Azim, Liman Cad Yayla Pasajı (☎256/614 1553). In winter there is only one crossing for a chartered group, though there may be space on board for extra passengers, while from the beginning of April to the end of October there is a daily crossing. Fares are $30 single, $35 day return and $55 open return. Add $70–130 if you want to take a car. The once-weekly Minoan Lines ferry to Greece and Italy is handled by Karavan, Kıbrıs Cad 2/1 (☎256/614 1279).

Selçuk and around

SELÇUK has been catapulted into the limelight of first-division tourism by its proximity to the ruins of Ephesus, and a number of other attractions within the city limits or just outside. The flavour of tourism here, though, is different from that at nearby Kuşadası, its inland location and ecclesiastical connections making it a haven for a disparate mix of backpackers and Bible-Belters from every corner of the globe. Furthermore the beaches in and around Kuşadası are easily accessible with a short dolmuş ride.

The **hill of Ayasoluk** (daily 8am–5/6pm; $2.50) is the first point you should head for, the traditional burial place of Saint John the Evangelist, who died here around 100 AD. Justinian built a basilica here that was one of the largest Byzantine churches in existence – various colonnades and walls have been re-erected, giving a hint of the building's magnificence. The tomb of the evangelist is marked by a slab at the former site of the altar; beside the nave is the baptistry, where religious tourists pose in the act of dunking as friends' cameras click. The **Castle**, 200m past the church, is closed but is virtually empty inside anyway. You're allowed to make a full circuit on the ramparts – worth it for the views. Just behind the tourist office, the **Archeological Museum** (daily 8am–noon & 1–4.30/6pm; $4) has galleries of finds from Ephesus, including the famous Artemis room, with two renditions of the goddess studded with multiple testicles (not breasts, as is commonly believed) and tiny figurines of real and mythical beasts, honouring her role as mistress of animals. Beyond the museum,

600m along the road toward Ephesus, are the scanty remains of the **Artemision** or sanctuary of Artemis, a massive Hellenistic structure that was considered one of the Seven Wonders of the Ancient World, though this is hard to believe today. Within sight of here, the fourteenth-century **İsa Bey Camii** is the most distinguished of various Selçuk monuments.

At the base of the castle hill, a **pedestrian precinct** leads east to the **train station**. Following the main highway a bit further south brings you to the **bus** and **dolmuş terminal**, opposite which the **tourist office** (daily May–Sept 8.30am–6.30pm) has exhaustive lists of accommodation. Some of the better pensions and hotels will organize a free lift from the bus station if you call them when you arrive. **Hotel** touts have become particularly aggressive in Selçuk; just ignore them, and head for the grid of residential streets behind the tourist office and the museum where the best of the pensions are situated. The *Barım*, Turgut Reis Sok 34 (☎232/892 6923; ②), an eccentric rambling old house, is reasonable, and the large *Australian New Zealand*, Ataturk Mah 1064 Sok 7 (☎232/892 6050; ②), run by a family of returned Turkish-Australians, is good value, with great facilities, free lifts from the bus station and to and Ephesus, full-board rates and vegetarian food, with a carpet shop attached. A new addition is the central *Outback Pension*, Atatürk Mah 1045 Sok 34 (232/892 2452; ②), which has a terrace bar and provides free lifts to and from Ephesus. The *Otel Ürkmez*, Namık Kemal Cad 20 (☎232/892 6312; ②), near the *hamam*, is run by the very likeable and helpful multilingual Oşkan brothers, who offer a free pick-up from the *otogar*. Their establishment has en-suite facilities throughout, a roof terrace and rooms with balconies. Ask for the rooms at the top which afford excellent views across the surrounding landscape and the storks that nest on the nearby ruined aqueduct. Selçuk's **campsite**, *Garden*, lies just beyond the *Isa Bey Camii* and is well rated; alternatively, there's the *Blue Moon/Develi*, 9km west at Pamucak Beach, served by Selçuk-Kuşadası *dolmuşes*. The *Australian New Zealand* pension is also due to open a campsite with a pool by 2000, about 2km south of the town near the top entrance to the Ephesus site; contact the pension for details. Best of the **restaurants** are in the pedestrianized grid of streets in the centre of town. *Köfteci Turhan*, Cengiz Topal Cad, and *Ephesus*, Namik Kemal Cad, are worth a try. The **hamam**, next to the main police station, is also worth a visit, providing a comparatively gentler introduction to the delights of a good Turkish scrub and massage. Expect to pay about $9 for the full treatment plus a small tip for the masseur.

Efes (Ephesus)

With the exception of Pompeii and some inaccessible Libyan ruins, **EPHESUS** is the largest and best-preserved ancient city around the Mediterranean, and is justifiably one of the most visited attractions in Turkey. Originally situated close to a temple devoted to the goddess Artemis, its location by a fine harbour was the secret of its success in ancient times, eventually making it the wealthy capital of Roman Asia, ornamented with magnificent public buildings by a succession of emperors. Later, after Christianity took root, St John the Evangelist arrived here, and St Paul spent the years 51 to 53 AD in the city. During the Byzantine era the city went into decline, owing to the abandoning of Artemis-worship, Arab raids, and (worst of all) the final closing off of the harbour, leading the population to siphon off to the nearby hill crowned by the tomb and church of St John, future nucleus of the town of Selçuk.

Approaching the **site** (daily: summer 8.30am–6.30pm; winter 8.30am–4.30pm; $6) from Kuşadası, get the *dolmuş* to drop you at the *Tusan Motel* junction, 1km from the gate. From Selçuk it's a three-kilometre walk. In the centre of the site, the **Arcadian Way** (partially closed) is a forlorn echo of the era when it was lined with hundreds of shops and illuminated at night – although its neglect is refreshing when compared to the nearby **theatre**, recently and brutally restored to give more seating for the various summer festivals. It is, however, worth the climb to the top for the views over the surrounding countryside. From the theatre, the **Marble Street** heads south, passing the main **agora**, currently closed for excavations, and a **Temple of Serapis** where the city's Egyptian merchants would have worshipped. About halfway along is an alleged signpost (a footprint, a female head and a heart etched into the rock) for a **brothel**, at the junction with the Street of the Curetes, the other main street. Inside are some fine floor mosaics denoting the four seasons.

Across the intersection looms the **Library of Celsus**, erected by the consul Gaius Julius Aquila between 110 and 135 AD as a memorial to his father Celsus Polemaeanus, entombed under the west wall. The elegant, two-storey facade was fitted with niches for statues of the four personified intellectual virtues, today filled with plaster copies (the originals are in Vienna). Just uphill from here, a **Byzantine fountain** looks across the Street of the Curetes to the **public latrines**, a favourite with visitors owing to the graphic obviousness of their function. Continuing along the same side of the street, you'll come to the so-called **Temple of Hadrian**, actually donated in 118 AD by a wealthy citizen in honour of Hadrian, Artemis and the city in general. Behind sprawl the **Baths of Scholastica**, so named after a fifth-century Byzantine woman whose headless statue adorns the entrance and who restored the complex, which was actually four hundred years older. On the far side of the street from the Hadrian shrine lies a huge pattern **mosaic**, which once fronted a series of shops. Nearby, a sign points to the **terrace houses** (admission only by application to the Selçuk Museum) which give a good idea of everyday life during imperial and early Byzantine times, with well-preserved mosaics and murals. Further up Curetes, you pass the **Temple of Domitian**, the lower floor of which houses a marginally interesting **Museum of Inscriptions** (summer daily 8am–5pm; free), on the way to the large, overgrown upper agora, fringed by a colonnade to the north, and a restored *odeion* and *prytaneum* or civic office.

Bodrum and its peninsula

In the eyes of its devotees, **BODRUM** – ancient Halicarnassos – with its whitewashed square houses and subtropical gardens, is the most attractive and most versatile Turkish resort, a quality outfit in comparison to its upstart Aegean rivals. And it is a pleasant town in most senses, despite having no real beach – although development has proceeded apace over the last couple of decades, spreading beyond the town boundaries into the until recently little-disturbed peninsula. The centrepiece of Bodrum is the **Castle of St Peter** (Tues–Sun 8am–noon & 1–5pm; $5), built by the Knights of St John over a Selçuk fortress between 1437 and 1522. The castle was subsequently neglected until the nineteenth century, when the chapel was converted to a mosque and a *hamam* installed, though the place was not properly refurbished until the 1960s, when it was turned into a museum. Inside, there are bits of ancient masonry incorporated into the walls, coats of arms, and a chapel housing a local Bronze Age and Mycenaean collection. The various towers house a **Museum of Underwater Archeology** which includes coin and jewellery rooms, Classical and Hellenistic statuary and Byzantine relics retrieved from two wrecks, alongside a diorama explaining salvage techniques. The **Carian princess hall** (Tues–Fri 10am–noon & 2–4pm; an extra $2.50) displays the skeleton and sarcophagus of a fourth-century BC Carian noblewoman unearthed in 1989. There is also the **Glass Wreck Hall** (Tues–Fri 10–11am & 2–4pm; an extra $2.50) containing the wreck and cargo of an ancient Byzantine ship, which sunk at Serce near Marmaris. Immediately north of the castle lies the **bazaar**, most of which is pedestrianized along the main thoroughfares of Kale Caddesi and Dr Alim Bey Caddesi and given over to souvenir stores and the like.

From here, stroll up Türkkuyusu Caddesi and turn left to the town's other main sight, the **Mausoleum** (daily 8.30am–noon & 1–5pm; $2.50). This is the burial place of Mausolus, who ruled Halicarnassos in the fourth century BC, greatly increasing its power and wealth. His tomb, completed by Artemisia II, his sister and wife, came to be regarded as one of the Seven Wonders of the Ancient World, and was the origin of the word "mausoleum". Decorated with friezes, it stood nearly 60m high – though its present condition is disappointing, with little left besides the precinct wall, assorted column fragments and some subterranean vaults. By way of contrast, the ancient **amphitheatre**, just above the main highway to the north, has been almost overzealously restored and is used during the September festival. Begun by Mausolus, it was modified in the Roman era and originally seated thirteen thousand, though it has a present capacity of about half that.

Practicalities

Ferries dock at the jetty west of the castle, quite close to the **tourist office** on İskele Meydanı (summer Mon–Fri 8.30am–5.30pm, Sat & Sun 8.30am–5.30pm; winter Mon–Fri

8am–noon & 1–5pm). The bus station is 500m up Cevat Şakir Cad, which divides the town roughly in two. Some of the best accommodation is southeast of the **bus station** in Kumbahçe. *Emiko*, Atatürk Cad, Uslu Sok 11 (☎252/316 5560; ②), has a pleasant courtyard, a friendly Japanese owner and quiet, en-suite rooms. The *Durak*, Rasthane Sok 8 (☎252/316 1564; ③) has clean, tidy en-suite rooms, some with balconies, as does *Uğur*, Rasthane Sok 13 (☎252/316 2106; ②), just across the road. West of the bus station, the recently renovated *Melis*, Türkkuyusu Cad 50 (☎252/316 1487; ③), has en-suite rooms and attractive courtyards. *Alias* behind Neyzen Tevfik Cad (☎252/316 3146; ③; May–Oct), is set in an attractive courtyard and has a pool. There are three small **campsites** on Gelence Sokaqı, west of Türkkuyusu Cad.

You don't come to Bodrum to ease your budget, and **eating out** is no exception. Best of the budget places is *Sakalli Köfteci* in the bazaar area. A little further east, *Mayalle* on 3 Sok and *Çorba Manti* (open 24hr) on Dr Alim Bey Cad offer solid Turkish fare and are popular with the locals. At the western end of town opposite the yacht harbour, *Gemibaşi* on the corner of Firkayten Sok and Neyzen Tevfik, and *Amphora*, Neyzen Tevfik 164, are good for a no-nonsense meat meal. The *Sünger* pizza restaurant at Neyzen Tevfik 218 is lively and inexpensive. Most places to have a drink are along Dr Alim Bey Cad, although "in" places change from one season to the next: *Bebek* has endured longer than most and *Stone House* is well worth trying. There are also a number of good bars along Neyzen Tevfik Cad.

Ferry tickets to Kos are best booked through the two main agents, next to each other at the ferry dock: Bodrum Express Lines (☎252/316 1087) handles Kos hydrofoils ($20 single; $30 day return; $54 open return), whereas Bodrum Ferryboat Association (☎252/316 0882) handles ferries to Kos ($20 single; $26 day return; $36 open return) as well as domestic services to Marmaris and Datça.

Around the peninsula

Dolmuşes from Bodrum's main bus station provide access to some good nearby beaches. Roughly 3km west of Bodrum, the rapidly growing **GÜMBET** is the closest resort to Bodrum, and the 600-metre, tamarisk-lined gritty beach is usually jam-packed. **BITEZ**, the next cove west and reached by a different side road, is a little more upmarket, but the beach is negligible. Better to continue along the south peninsular trunk road to **ORTAKENT**, an inland village, from where a road winds down several kilometres to the longest **beach** on the peninsula, its two-kilometre extent fringed by a clutter of shops, campsites and hotels, most of which will be packed with Turkish holidaymakers.

Marmaris

MARMARIS rivals Kuşadası as the largest and most developed Aegean resort, its huge marina and proximity to Dalaman airport meaning that tourists pour in more or less nonstop during the warmer months. According to legend, the place was named when Süleyman the Magnificent, not finding the castle here to his liking, was heard to mutter "*Mimarı as*" (Hang the architect), later corrupted to "Marmaris" – a command which should perhaps still apply to the designers of the seemingly endless high-rises. Ulusal Egemenlik Bulvarı cuts Marmaris in half, and the maze of narrow streets east of it is home to most things of interest to the average tourist, though little is left of the sleepy fishing village that Marmaris was a mere two decades ago. The bazaar has been ruthlessly commercialized, and only the **Kaleiçi** district, the warren of streets at the base of the tiny castle, offers a pleasant wander. The **castle museum** (Tues–Sun 8am–noon & 1–5.30pm; $1) has a worthwhile archeology and ethnography collection.

A new **bus station** has recently opened about 1.5km south of the town centre, from where you can pick up a *dolmuş* to take you to the town centre, or a taxi, which should cost about $3. Many of the bus companies also offer a free transfer minibus to their offices in the centre. Arriving by **ferry**, the dock abuts İskele Meydanı, on one side of which stands the very helpful **tourist office** (summer daily 8.30am–7.30pm; winter Mon–Fri 8.30am–noon & 1.30–5.30pm), which dispenses town plans and **accommodation** details. The development of package tourism has ensured that hotels here are expensive and welcoming *pansiyons* few and far between. Furthermore, hotel touts have become particularly vociferous in Marmaris, promising all kinds of luxury to gullible newcomers. It is best to politely and firmly refuse their advances and if you are struggling to find a decent place the tourist office is tuned in to the needs of backpackers. The cheapest option is the *Interyouth Hostel 1* at Tepe Mahallesi 42, Sok 45, in the bazaar close to the Atatürk statue (☎252/412 3687; ①), with around 180 beds in single, double and dormitory rooms, a lively rooftop café, and facilities including Internet access and a competitively priced travel service. There is another hostel in town called *Interyouth 2* just past the hospital, though it is nothing to do with the one in the bazaar and offers nothing like the same facilities. Also in the bazaar is the *Kordon Pansiyon*, 53 Sok 25 (☎252/412 4762; ④), which is central and clean, though basic. A better budget pension is the *Yaprak*, west of the centre towards Uzunyali beach at Atatürk Cad 4/A (☎252/412 3001; ③), a well-maintained place offering en-suite rooms. For something a touch classier and right by the Marina, try the *Marina Motel* (☎252/412 6598; ④), which has clean en-suite rooms and a breakfast terrace.

Getting a decent **meal** at a reasonable price is a challenge. However there is a fabulous restaurant, *Kırçiçeği* on Kübilay Alpagün Cad, behind the bazaar, which offers excellent traditional Turkish food at reasonable prices. Among the several options in the bazaar area close to the PTT, *Sofra*, *Marmaris* and *Liman* are all acceptable for a cheap feed and are frequented by the locals. To the west, Uzunyali harbours various pizza joints and a reasonable Turkish restaurant, *Turhan*, at Uzunyali 26. Not surprisingly, most of Marmaris' drinking happens on the Netsel Marina, where pubs such as *Scorpio* and *Pineapple* cater to the yachting crowd. If that doesn't appeal, the nearby Haca Mustafa Sokaqi (dubbed "Bar Street") contains a wealth of other drinking venues.

Authorized agents for the **crossings to Rhodes** include Yeşil Marmaris, Barbaros Cad 11 (☎252/412 2290), and Engin Turizm, Kordon Cad 10 (☎252/412 1082). In the winter, there is one crossing a week to Rhodes, depending on the weather, but from the middle of April to the start of October there are daily crossings. Expect to pay $47 return for the **hydrofoil** and $38 return for the **ferry**. Both prices include tax. In summer there are bargains to be had on these crossings and it may be wise to approach the tourist office first to find out where they can be had.

Datça

Though too manicured these days, **DATÇA**, 30km west of Marmaris, is still many times calmer than Bodrum or Marmaris. It's essentially the shore annexe of inland Reşadiye village, but under the ministrations of visiting yachtspeople and package operators has outgrown its parent. Carpet shops are big news here, with prices still relatively low. The town is principally a single high street meandering between two sheltered bays separated by a hillock and then a narrow isthmus. As far as things to do go, it's really a matter of picking your swimming and sunbathing spot. The **east beach**, part sand, part cement quay with cafés, is quieter but the cleanliness is suspect. The **west beach**, mixed pebble and sand, is acceptable and becomes better the further you get from the yachts. The nearest good beaches are at **Özil** (15km), **Aktur** (30km) and **Perili Köşk** (15km) on the road to Marmaris.

Datça's new **otogar** is located around 1.5km from the centre connected by service bus or *dolmuş*. Bodrum-bound **ferries**, operated by the Bodrum Ferryboat Service, run from Körmen Limanı, 9km north, connected by a short bus ride, with tickets available from Kavya Tours or Varan. The **tourist office** is on the main road near the PTT (summer daily 8.30am–6.30pm, closed on some Sundays; winter Mon–Fri 8am–noon & 1–5pm). A good **place to stay** is the hillock separating the two bays, where the *Huzur* (☎252/712 3052; ③) is the most modern, with *Tunç* (☎252/712 3036; ③) near the centre of town offering clean, pleasant en-suite rooms. Also near the centre and the beach is *Mandalına* (☎252/712 4995; ③), a brand new establishment with comfortable en-suite rooms. For **food**, the *Defne Pide Salonu* on the main drag, or inland sidewalk eateries like *Korsan*, *Valentino* and *Kemal*, are all reasonably affordable. The west harbour is the place to look for music **bars** and pubs.

Aphrodisias

Situated on a high plateau around 100km inland, **APHRODISIAS** is one of the more isolated of Turkey's major archeological sites. It was one of the earliest occupied centres in Anatolia, but remained for many centuries only a shrine, and never really grew into a town until the second century BC, when it became a major cultural centre. It was renowned in particular for its school of sculpture, benefiting from nearby quarries of high-grade marble, examples of which adorned every corner of the empire.

A loop path around the **site** (daily 8am–5.30pm; $3.50) passes all of the major monuments, beginning with the virtually intact **theatre**, founded in the first century BC but extensively modified by the Romans three centuries later. Further on you pass the **double agora**, two squares ringed by Ionic and Corinthian stoas, and the fine **baths of Hadrian**, well preserved right down to the floor tiles and the odd mosaic. North of the baths, several columns sprout from a multi-roomed structure commonly known as the **bishop's palace**, east of which is the appealing Roman **odeon**, with nine rows of seats. Perhaps the most impressive feature of the site is, however, the 30,000-seat **stadium**, a little way north, one of the largest and best preserved in Anatolia. The **museum** (daily 8am–5.30pm; $2.50) consists almost entirely of sculpture recovered from the ruins, including statuary related to the cult of Aphrodite, a joyous satyr carrying the child Dionysus in his arms, and a quasi-satirical portrait of Flavius Palmatus, Byzantine governor of Asia.

Aphrodisias is situated 13km east of Karacasu, the nearest sizeable town, which is connected by frequent **dolmuş** to **NAZİLLİ**, 50km away. If you're staying in Pamukkale, it's tempting to try and devise a loop back to Denizli through Tavas, but you must get to Tavas in time for the last *dolmuş* back to Denizli, and thence to Pamukkale, which is difficult. Whatever happens, try to avoid getting stranded at Aphrodisias or Karacasu. If you are going to get stuck, you're better off doing so at **GEYRE**, site of *Chez Mestan*, campsite/pension (①), 600m from Aphrodisias on the main highway.

Denizli, Pamukkale and Hierapolis

Devastated by earthquakes in 1710 and 1899, **DENİZLİ**, 50km east of Nazıllı, is a gritty agricultural town of just under two hundred thousand inhabitants. It has little appeal itself, but you may well pass through, especially if you're heading on to Pamukkale, to which there are regular buses and *dolmuşes*. If you decide **to stay** in Denizli, try the *Denizli Pension*, 1993 Sok 14 (☎258/261 8738; ①), which has friendly staff, a free pick-up from the bus station and free lifts to Pamukkale.

The rock formations of **PAMUKKALE**, 10km or so north – literally "Cotton Castle" – are perhaps the most visited attraction in this part of Turkey, a series of white terraces saturated with dissolved calcium bicarbonate, bubbling up from the feet of the Çal Dağı Mountains beyond. As the water surges over the edge of the plateau and cools, carbon dioxide is given off and calcium carbonate precipitated as hard chalk or travertine. The spring emerges in what once was the exact middle of the ancient city of **Hierapolis**, the ruins of which would merit a stop even if they weren't coupled with the natural phenomenon. Sadly, however, the Pamukkale travertine has gradually turned from white to yellow and even to brown in some places and is thought to be drying up. Thirsty **hotels**, which have been thrown up to accommodate ever-growing numbers of visitors, have been blamed by the government which has decided to take drastic action. Many of the shops and hotels around the site are being demolished and, though this is ultimately good news for Pamukkale, it means finding somewhere to stay is getting harder.

Most travellers still stay in **PAMUKKALE KÖYÜ**, above which the **travertine terraces** are deservedly the first item on their agenda, although the pools are very shallow – original water levels are depleted by the diversion of water to pools of nearby hotels. Nearly all of the terraced pools have been closed and tourists are no longer allowed to walk on the terraces at all. In the very long term this should return the terraces to their natural state and some visitors are already speaking of marked improvements on a couple of years ago.

All Visitors should bear in mind the fragility of this natural phenomenon when coming to Pamukkale.

If you want to take a bath in the springs, *Pamukkale Motel* (☎258/272 2024) up on the plateau encloses the **sacred pool** of the ancients, with mineral water bubbling from its bottom at 35°C (daily 9am–6pm; $4).

The **archeological zone** of Hierapolis lies west of Pamukkale Köyü, via a narrow road winding up past the *Turism Motel*. Its main features include a **temple of Apollo** and the adjacent **Plutonium** – the latter a cavern emitting a toxic gas, probably a mixture of sulphur compounds and carbon dioxide, capable of killing man and beast alike. There's also a restored **Roman theatre**, just east of here, dating from the second century AD and in exceptionally good shape, with most of the stage buildings and their elaborate reliefs intact. Arguably the most interesting part of the city, though, is the colonnaded street which once extended for almost 1km from a gate 400m southeast of the sacred pool, terminating in monumental portals a few paces outside the walls – only the most northerly of which, a triple arch flanked by towers and dedicated to the Emperor Domitian in 84 AD, still stands. Just south of the arch is the elaborate tomb of Flavius Zeuxis – the first of more than a thousand tombs constituting the **necropolis**, the largest in Asia Minor, extending for nearly 2km along the road. There's also a **museum** (daily 9am–noon & 1.30–5pm), housed in the restored, second-century AD baths, whose disappointing collection consists of statuary, sarcophagi, masonry fragments and smaller knick-knacks recovered during excavations.

Practicalities

With over forty pensions, there's no shortage of **accommodation** in Pamukkale Köyü, and touts at the bus stand can be particularly aggressive. One of the best and friendliest is the *Kervansaray* (☎258/272 2209; ③), with central heating, free minibus pickup at the Denizli or Pamukkale bus station and a good rooftop restaurant. If they're full, you'll be pointed a few metres further out of town to the *Aspava* (☎258/272 2094; ①). Southwest of here, the *Koray* (☎258/272 2222; ③) also has free minibus transfer from the bus station and en-suite rooms, a garden and a good buffet breakfast. *Arkadaş* (☎258/272 2183; ①) near the centre of the village may not have a swimming pool but compensates with a leafy courtyard. **Eating out**, the situation is dire, with only a handful of tourist restaurants; if you're staying at a *pansiyon* which offers an evening meal, it's probably best to stay put. The exceptions are the *Kervansaray* and the pricey *Pammukkale Motel* poolside restaurant.

THE MEDITERRANEAN COAST

The first stretch of Turkey's **Mediterranean Coast**, dominated by the Arkdağ and Bey mountain ranges of the Taurus chain and known as the "Turquoise Coast", is perhaps its most popular, famed for its pine-studded shore, minor ruins and beautiful scenery. Most of this is connected by Highway 400, which winds precipitously above the sea from Marmaris to Antalya. In the west of the region, **Dalyan** is renowned for its beach – a breeding ground of loggerhead turtles – as well as being a characterful small resort. West, **Fethiye**, along with the nearby lagoon of **Ölüdeniz**, is a full-blown regional centre, and gives good access to some of the pick of the region's Lycian ruins, the best of which – **Xanthos** and **Patara** – are close to one of the coast's nicest beaches. The region's second major resort, **Kaş**, smaller than Fethiye but no less popular, is a good base for scenery which becomes increasingly spectacular until you reach the site of **Olympos**, close to another fine beach. Further along, past the port and major city of **Antalya**, the landscape becomes less dramatic but is home to yet more impressive ruins, notably those of the old Pamphylian cities of **Perge** and **Aspendos**. **Side**, too, has its share of antiquities, although it's better known as a tourist resort, as is the former pirate refuge of **Alanya**, set on a spectacular headland topped by a stunning Selçuk citadel. Beyond here you're entering the relatively undiscovered reaches of eastern Turkey.

Dalyan

DALYAN, 7km off Highway 400, is one of the calmer resorts along this stretch of coast, and a good base for surrounding attractions. Life here centres on the Dalyan River, which flows past the village – the one drawback in the summer months is mosquitoes, especially along the riverbank, for which the area has been notorious since antiquity. Go armed with a good repellent, and buy an *esemymat*, a machine that plugs into the electricity supply to dispatch mosquitoes, from any good chemist in Turkey. **Pension** prices are fixed by the municipality, but tend to be a bit high: all doubles without baths ②, with bath ③. There are a string of pleasant places on the riverbank, one of the nicest being *Midas Pansiyon* (☎252/284 2195; ③), at the far end, or the smaller *Lindos* (☎252/284 2005; ②), next door, which is cheaper with a couple of cabin rooms right on the water; other good options are *Aktaş Pansiyon* (☎252/284 2042; ③), or its friendly neighbour, *Miletos Pansiyon* (☎252/284 2532; ③). **Restaurants** in Dalyan are fairly undistinguished, though the best are the central *Çiçek*, with a varied menu and a garden setting, and the seafront *Sürmen*, offering fish specialities – although neither is cheap.

İstuzu Beach, a twelve-kilometre drive south, and accessible by *dolmuş*, is the breeding ground of the loggerhead turtle, which means entry is banned at night between May and October. During the day the beach is open to the public, and is a good place to swim and sunbathe, although you should be careful of disturbing the turtle eggs and nests, which are easily disrupted.

Fethiye and around

FETHIYE is well situated for access to some of the region's ancient sites, many of which date from the time when this was the independent kingdom of Lycia. And although the region's best beaches, around the Ölüdeniz Lagoon, are now much too crowded for comfort, Fethiye still has qualities which set it above many other Mediterranean resorts. It's a real market town, soon perhaps to be capital of a newly designated province; there are other nearby attractions and beaches besides Ölüdeniz; and, unlike Kaş, which is confined by its sheer rock backdrop, Fethiye has been able to spread to accommodate the increase in tourist traffic.

Fethiye occupies the location of the Lycian city of **Telmessos**, the remains of which, in the shape of a number of Lycian rock tombs, cover the hillside above the bus station. Most notable is the **Amyntas Tomb**, carved in close imitation of the facade of a temple. There's not all that much else to see in Fethiye, although you can visit the remains of the medieval **fortress**, on the hillside behind the harbour area of town. In the centre of town, off Atatürk Caddesi, Fethiye's **museum** (Tues–Sun 8.30am–5.30/7.30pm; $1.50) is badly labelled and very small, but some of the exhibits help to enhance the nearby archeological sights. The most interesting piece is the stela found at the Letoön, dating from 358 BC, which was important in translating the Lycian language.

One of the most dramatic sights in the area is the ghost village of **KAYA KÖYÜ** (Levissi), 7km out of town, served by *dolmuşes* from behind the PTT. The village was abandoned in 1923, when its Anatolian Greek population were relocated, along with more than a million others, to a country which had never been their homeland, and whose language many of them couldn't speak. All you see now is a hillside covered with more than two thousand ruined cottages and an attractive **basilica**, to the right of the main path 200m up the hill from the road, one of three churches here – but the general state of neglect only serves to highlight the plight of the former inhabitants. There are plans to make an international "peace and friendship" conference centre here, but ordinary travellers must still stay at a couple of *pansiyons* at the edge of Kaya. You can walk from Kaya Köyü to **Ölüdeniz** – about two hours, through the village, over the hill and down to the lagoon – although it is also served by frequent **dolmuşes** from Fethiye. The warm waters of the lagoon make for pleasant swimming if you don't mind paying the small entrance fee, although the crowds can reach saturation level in high season – in which case the nearby, more prosaic beaches of Belceğiz and Kidrak are better bets.

Practicalities

Fethiye's new **bus station** is about 2km east of the centre; *dolmuşes* to Ölüdeniz, Çalış beach and Kaya village arrive and leave from the old *otogar*, east of the central market. The **tourist office** is near the harbour at İskele Meydanı 1 (daily: summer 8.30am–7.30pm; winter 8am–5pm). There are two main concentrations of **hotels** – in the downtown area and in the suburb of Karagözler overlooking the marina to the west. *Dolmuşes* to Karagözler run direct from the bus station. Downtown, try the *Ülgen Pansiyon* (☎252/614 3491; ②), up the stairs beyond Paspatir Cad. Southeast of the centre and handiest for the bus station, *Sinderella*, Merdivenli Geçit 3 (☎252/614 6363; ②), has quiet en-suite rooms and friendly English-speaking staff. In the quieter Karagözler, the *Savaşci* (☎252/614 4108; ②) is well situated high above the marina with a great terrace, while the *Pinara*, Fevzi Çakmak Cad 39 (☎252/614 2151; ②), is slightly noisier but has friendly staff. Just behind it and before you reach the *Savaşci* is *Ideal* (☎252/614 1981; ③), which is friendly and has a great terrace though the rooms are a bit small and overpriced. If you travel further along the road that skirts the marina you will come to the *Sonnen Panorama* (☎252/614 305; ④) which has efficient, clean rooms with en-suite facilities and air-con. For **camping**, one of the best sites is the *Ölüdeniz*, which has its own beach and restaurant; it's just past the official entrance to Ölüdeniz Lagoon on the left.

Some of the best **food** in Fethiye can be had at *Paşa Kebap* on Çarşi Cad; while *Şedir*, Tütün Sok 3, is a good grill house much favoured by the locals, as is the excellent *Bırlık Lokantasi* on Ataturk Cad just opposite the PTT. Here traditional Turkish food is offered at reasonable prices along with homemade ice cream during the warmest months. Several outdoor cafés along the seafront provide ample **drinking** opportunities, and there are also a couple of bars on the hillside above the tourist office: the garish *Yasmin* specializes in live Turkish music, while the neighbouring *Spartacus* is a smaller, rock-orientated bar.

Around Fethiye: the Lycian sites

East of Fethiye lies the heartland of ancient Lycia, home to a number of archeological sites, all within easy reach of Fethiye. The closest is the **LETOÖN**, accessible by taking a *dolmuş* from Fethiye to Kumluova, the site lying 4km off the main highway. The Letoön was the official sanctuary of the Lycian Federation, and the extensive **ruins** ($1.50 admission when warden present) to be seen today bear witness to its importance. The low ruins of three **temples** occupy the centre of the site, the westernmost of which bears a dedication to Leto. The central temple, dating from the fourth century, is identified by a dedication to Artemis, while the easternmost temple has a floor mosaic of a lyre, bow and quiver, suggesting a dedication to Artemis and Apollo, who were apparently the region's most revered deities. Beyond the temple, to the southwest, is a **nymphaeum**, with statue niches, though it's now permanently flooded. There is also a large, well-preserved **theatre** on the right, entered through a vaulted passage.

On the other side of the valley, the remains of the hilltop city of **XANTHOS** are perhaps the most fascinating of the Lycian sites, though sadly the most important relic discovered at the site, the fourth-century Nereid Monument, is now in the British Museum. However, there is still enough to see here to reward a lengthy visit. Buses between Fethiye and Patara drop you off in Kanak, from where it's a ten-minute walk up to the ruins ($1.50 admission when attended). West of the car park are the acropolis and agora and a Roman theatre, beside which are two Lycian tombs – the so-called **Harpy Tomb**, a cement cast of the original decorated with pairs of bird-woman figures carrying children in their arms, and a Lycian-type **sarcophagus** standing on a pillar tomb, thought to date from the third century BC. Northeast of the agora looms a structure known popularly as the Xanthian obelisk – in fact the remains of a pillar tomb covered on all four sides by the longest-known Lycian inscription, running to 250 lines and including twelve lines of Greek inscription. The nearby Roman theatre is pretty complete, only missing the upper seats which were incorporated into the Byzantine city wall.

PATARA, a little way south and reachable by regular *dolmuş* from Fethiye and Kaş in season (otherwise, Fethiye–Kaş buses will drop you 4km north of the site) was the principal port of Lycia, famed for its oracle of Apollo and as the birthplace of St Nicholas, the Western Santa Claus. Two kilometres from the modern village of Gelemiş, the site (daily: summer

7.30am–7pm; winter 8am–5.30pm; $3.50) is marked by a triple-arched Roman gateway, which is reasonably intact if a little overgrown. The site itself has some well-preserved **baths** and a small **temple** lodged in a course of boundary wall. To the south, close to the beach, is a **theatre**, the cavea of which is now half full of sand – although the stage building is partly intact.

Nowadays Patara is best known for its white sand beach, served by *dolmuş* from Gelemiş. It can get a bit crowded in season, but the walk along the dunes towards the river mouth, 7km northwest, turns up more than enough solitary spots. If you are planning to visit Patara or Gelemiş out of season it's best to call ahead as most facilities close down for winter.

For **accommodation** the best budget option is the well-run *Flower Pansiyon* (☎242/843 5164; ②) at the entrance to the village, which has excellent en-suite rooms with balconies and air-con. They will also pick you up from the main road for free, and from Dalaman Airport for petrol money. Just behind this is the reasonable *Rose Pension* (☎242/843 5165; ②), with basic, clean, en-suite rooms with balconies. They also offer a free pick-up from the main road and petrol money pick-up from the airport. Another choice is the Otlu brothers' long-running *Golden Pansiyon* (☎242/843 5162; ③) at the crossroads, which has been joined by their posher, and well-positioned *Patara View Point Hotel* (☎242/843 5184; ④) on the ridge east of the main crossroads. Another good option in the centre of the village is the *St Nicolas Pansiyon* (☎232/843 5024; ③). While accommodation is plentiful in summer, it can fill up quickly so reservations may be required at the better places. Make sure too that your lodgings have some form of mosquito nets and bring repellent. **Eating** possibilities aren't scintillating, though the *Golden Pansiyon*'s diner often has trout. *Dardanos* is blatantly touristy, and the two cafés down at the beach feature *manti* or Turkish ravioli.

Kaş and around

KAŞ, 41km further east from Patara, is beautifully situated, nestled in a curving bay against a backdrop of vertical, 500-metre-high cliffs. However, what was a quaint fishing village as recently as 1983 has grown to become a tourist metropolis. There's no beach to speak of in Kaş itself, but there's plenty to see in the countryside around, and the town does get lively at night. It's also the site of ancient **Antiphellos**, the ruins of which litter the streets of the modern town, as well as covering the peninsula to the west. Most interesting of these is the **lion tomb**, a towering structure that had two burial chambers, at the top of Uzun Çarşi. Half a kilometre from the main square, along Hastane Caddesi, a small, almost complete Hellenistic **theatre** looks out to sea; on a nearby hilltop stands a unique rock-cut **Doric tomb**, also almost completely intact. The closest decent beach near Kaş is **Kaputaş**, 10km west on the way to Kalkan, a small stretch of pebbles and sand which understandably gets crowded.

The **bus station** is a five-minute walk from the waterfront on the Elmali road – just head downhill. The **tourist office** is at Cumhuriyet Meydanı 5 (summer daily 8am–7pm; winter Mon–Fri 8am–5pm; ☎242/836 1238). They have lists of **hotel** and **pension** prices, but, really, you're strictly on your own. *Golden Pension* (☎242/836 1736; ②), just up from the harbour, is probably the cheapest option, with basic rooms and shared bathrooms, although quieter options can be found west of the centre along Hastane Cad. *Yalı*, Hastane Cad 11 (☎242/836 1132; ③), has en-suite rooms and sea views, as does the *Andiflı* next door (☎242/836 1042; ③). Further along, the *Gülşen*, Hastane Cad 23 (☎242/836 1171; ③), has rooms and a few sea-facing balconies as does the *Karakedi Korsan Hotel* up the hill to the north at Yeni Cami Sok 7 (☎242/836 1887; ④) features a roof terrace overlooking the amphitheatre. There are two **campsites** close to Kaş. The tidy *Olympos* site is just about 1km from the centre on the Kalkan road. *Kaş Camping* is on the west side of town, a kilometre out on Kastane Caddesi, and has its own seaside diving platform, restaurant and bar.

The unlicensed *Mevlana*, Elmali Cad, is probably the cheapest of the **restaurants**, offering simple kebab dishes. Otherwise, the *Ota*, opposite the main post office, serves good Turkish home cooking, though at a price. *Chez Evy*, in the backstreets east of the waterfront at Terzi Sok 2, serves up an enticing blend of Turkish and French cuisine. The bar at *Evy*'s is the best place to start an evening's **drinking**. *Mavi/Blue* on the harbour front is louder and there's a string of other bars, many with live music, along the coast road east of the harbour.

East of Kaş: Demre, Myra and Andriake

A winding 45-minute drive beyond Kaş lies the river delta town of **DEMRE** (officially Kale), a rather scruffy citrus- and tomato-growing town, too far away from the coast to be worthy of the "seaside" tag and afforded more attention by tour parties than it can really deal with. However, it is worth visiting for its **Church of St Nicholas** (Tues–Sun 8am–5.30/7pm; $3), in the centre of town on Müze Caddesi, highly evocative of the life and times of its patron saint – even if the saint's **sarcophagus**, left of the entrance, is not considered the real one (which lies under the floor), and its atmosphere is diminished by an outsized protective cover. The remains of the ancient Lycian city of **Myra** (daily 8am–7pm; $3), 2km north of the centre, make up one of the most beautiful Lycian sites, consisting mainly of a large theatre and some of the best examples of house-style rock tombs to be seen in Lycia. And the site of the ancient city's port, **Andriake**, now known as Çayağzı, 2km west of Demre, is also worth a visit, and is close to a minimally developed sandy **beach**. The substantial remains of the so-called **Hadrian's granary** are the most prominent feature of the site, built between 119 and 139 AD by the Emperor Hadrian and consisting of eight rooms constructed of well-fitting blocks, the outer walls still standing to their original height on the far bank of the stream running parallel to the road to the beach. Above the main gate are busts of Hadrian and a woman who is thought to be the Empress Sabina.

It's best to treat Demre as a day out from Kaş, as decent **pensions** here are few and far between. Best is the *Kent* (☎242/871 2042; ③), north of the centre on the road to Myra. The closest **campsite** is the *Ocakbaşi*, at Andriake.

Olympos

Around 50km east of Demre, fifteen minutes' walk from the hamlet of Çıralı, is another Lycian city, **OLYMPOS**, an idyllic site ($1.50 admission when gates are staffed), located on a beautiful sandy bay and the banks of a river which nearly dries up in summer. On the south bank is part of a quay wall and a warehouse; to the east on the same side lie the walls of a Byzantine church; while further back, in the undergrowth, there is a theatre, most of whose seats have gone. On the north side of the river are more striking ruins, namely a well-preserved marble door frame, and, at its foot, a statue base with an inscription to Marcus Aurelius. Beyond is a Byzantine *hamam* with mosaic floors, and a Byzantine canal which would have carried water to the heart of the city.

About an hour's well-marked stroll above the citrus groves of nearby Çıralı flickers **Chimaera**, a series of eternal flames issuing from cracks in the bare rock which can be extinguished but will always re-ignite. It's not known what causes the phenomenon; a survey by oil prospectors in 1967 detected traces of methane in the gas but otherwise its make-up is unique to this spot. What is known, however, is that the fire has been burning since antiquity, and inspired the Lycians to worship the god Hephaestos (the Roman Vulcan) here. The mountain was also associated with a fire-breathing monster, also known as the Chimaera, with a lion's head, a goat's rear and a snake for a tail.

There is one daily minibus from Çıralı to Antalya and back; otherwise, catch any Kaş–Antalya bus and hitch the 8km down the most northerly or closest to Kemer of three side-turnings from the main highway – it's a fair walk in the heat. More than a dozen fairly basic **pensions** (①) hide in the citrus groves behind the beach; *Flora* on the approach to the beach is basic but pleasant (☎242/871 7201; ②) and the nearby *Bariş Pansiyon* (☎242/825 7080; ③), just behind the beach, has en-suite rooms. Rough **camping** on the beach is frowned on now that an official campsite, *Green Point*, has begun operating. Beach **restaurants** are simple and short-lived, owing to battles with the forest service (the area is officially a National Park); most durable seem to be *Olympos Yavuz* and the *Star*. Several establishments outside the Olympos site itself offer tree-house-style accommodation; *Kadir* (②) and *Bayram* (②) being the most popular. You'll be a bit cut off here, but there is, at least, minibus transport to the main road.

Antalya and around

Turkey's fastest growing city, **ANTALYA** is also the one metropolis besides İstanbul that's simultaneously a major tourist destination. Blessed with an ideal climate and a stunning setting, Antalya has seen the annual tourist influx grow to almost match its permanent population, which now stands at just under half a million. Despite the appearance of its grim concrete sprawl, it's an agreeable place, although the main area of interest for visitors is confined to the relatively tiny old quarter; it also makes a good base for visiting the nearby ancient sites of Perge and Aspendos.

Arrival and accommodation

The central **bus station** is 8km north of town, although regular *dolmuşes* run from here to a terminal at the top of Kazım Özalp Cad, still universally referred to by its old name of Sarampol, which runs for just under a kilometre down to the Saat Kulesi on the fringe of the old town. A **taxi** from the *otogar* to the old town will cost around $7. About 5km west of the centre is the **ferry dock**, also connected by *dolmuş*. Antalya's **airport** is around 10km northeast of the city centre; THY buses make the fifteen-minute trip into town and city centre-bound *dolmuşes* pass nearby. The main **tourist office**, beside THY on Cumhuriyet Cad (Mon–Fri 8am–5pm, Sat & Sun 9am–5pm, sometimes closed Sat & Sun in winter), provides only very basic information but supplies free city maps.

Most travellers **stay** in the atmospheric old town, called Kaleiçi, where almost every other building is a *pansiyon*, although there's also a nucleus of hotels between the bus station and the bazaar. The *Sabah Pansiyon*, Hesapçı Sok 60/A (☎242/247 5345; ②), is clean and well run with air-con in all rooms and its patron is friendly and speaks good English; book ahead in summer as it soon fills up. At the far end near the Hadarlak Kulesi, *Hadrianus*, Zeytin Sok 4/A (☎242/244 0030; ③) is in an ageing building with a wonderful garden, but the rooms are airless, and it is a touch overpriced. There are unparalleled rooftop views from *Keskin*, Hadarlak Sok 35 (☎242/241 2865; ③), and *Senem*, Zeytingeçidi Sok 9 (☎242/247 1752; ③), which has a family atmosphere, modern rooms and sea views. *Bacchus*, Zeytin Sok 6 (☎242/241 6941; ③), is a good choice, with an excellent roof terrace and clean en-suite rooms. The basic *Adler Pansiyon*, Barbaros Mahalle Civelek Sok 16 (☎242/321 7818; ②), is one of the least expensive of the old town pensions, but it has character. The *Antique Pansiyon*, Tuzcular Mah, Paza Cami Sok 28 (☎242/242 4615; ③), is a very atmospheric original old Anatolian building and the best of the bunch, with an owner who speaks perfect English. *Bambus* **camping**, 3km south of town on the Lara road, is expensive but has its own rocky cove for swimming.

The City

The intersection of Cumhuriyet Caddesi and Sarampol is the most obvious place to begin a tour of Antalya, dominated by the **Yivli Minare** or "Fluted Minaret", erected in the thirteenth century and today something of a symbol of the city. Downhill from here is the **old harbour**, recently restored and site of the evening promenade for half of Antalya. North is the disappointing bazaar, while south, beyond the Saat Kalesi, lies **Kaleiçi** or the old town, currently succumbing to tweeness as every house is redone as a carpet shop, café or pension. On the far side, on Atatürk Caddesi, the triple-arched **Hadrian's Gate** recalls a visit by the emperor in 130 AD, while Hesapçı Sokak leads south past the **Kesik Minare** (Broken Minaret) to a number of tea gardens and the **Hıdırlık Kulesi**, of indisputable Roman vintage but ambiguous function – it could have been a lighthouse, bastion or tomb. The one thing you shouldn't miss while in Antalya is the **Archeological Museum** (Tues–Sun 8am–5/6pm; $4), one of the top five archeological collections in the country; it's on the western edge of town at the far end of Kenan Evren Bulvarı, reachable by any *dolmuş* marked KonyaaltaİLiman. Highlights include an array of Bronze Age urn burials from near Elmalı, and finds from an unusually southerly Phrygian tumulus. There's also second-century statuary from Perge, an adjoining sarcophagus wing with an almost undamaged coffer depicting the life of Hercules, a number of mosaics and a reliquary containing some purported bones of St Nicholas – not to mention an ethnography section with ceramics, household implements, weapons and embroidery and a small but well-thought-out children's section.

Antalya's **beaches** don't rate much consideration. **Konyaaltı**, 3km west of Kalekapısı, is divided into paying sections and free zones but all are shadeless, pebbly and polluted. **Lara**, 10km distant in the opposite direction and reached by *dolmuşes* running along Atatürk Caddesi, has fine sand but is accessible only for a fee. A new tram service connects Lara beach to the archeological museum. Prices and times were not fixed at time of writing, but there should be at least an hourly service with a single journey costing roughly 40¢.

Eating, drinking and nightlife

Many *pansiyons* have their own restaurant in Kaleiçi, and you may prefer to eat in rather than attempt to explore the limited and overpriced options. For elegant dining, *Antique Pansiyon*'s evening menu is particularly good. Otherwise, a couple of suggestions are *Parlak*, just off Sarampol Cad, a licensed place that mainly serves delicious grilled chicken – something of a local speciality – and *Ünal Restaurant*, on Imaret Sok, Kalekapısı 8. Cumhuriyet Cad is the location of a number of **cafés and restaurants** with terraces offering excellent views of the harbour – good for leisurely breakfasts. Southwest of the junction of Cumhuriyet Cad and Atatürk Bulvarı, is the covered pedestrian precinct, Eski Sebzeciler Açi Sokak, which has recently been modernized and lost some of its atmosphere, but still has a small number of restaurants serving the local speciality *tandir kebap* – mutton roast in a clay pot. The *Gaziantep* eatery, at the edge of the bazaar through the *pasaj* at Asmet Paza Cad 3, is excellent. Two other recommended restaurants on the same street are *Nasreddin Hoca Sofrasi* and *Kafkas Etli Pide*. To all intents and purposes **nightlife** is down at the harbour, where the *Café İskele*, its tables grouped around a fountain, is pleasant and not overpriced. *Club 29*, nearby, is expensive, but offers disco, terrace, pool and restaurant. *CC*, also on the harbour, often has live music, but the most popular place is the *Olympos* disco, next door to *Falez Hotel* near the archeological museum. Be warned, however, that some of these nightspots do not allow entry to unmarried men.

East of Antalya: Perge and Aspendos

East of Antalya lies an area known in ancient times as Pamphylia, a remote region that was home to four great cities – Perge, Sillyon, Aspendos and Side. The closest to Antalya is **PERGE**, about 15km east, reachable by taking a *dolmuş* to the village of Aksu on the main eastbound road, from where it's a fifteen-minute walk to the site (daily 8am–5/6pm; $4). Perge was founded around 1000 BC and is an enticing spot nowadays, the ruins expansive and impressive. Just beyond the site entrance, the **theatre** was originally constructed by the Greeks but substantially altered by the Romans in the second century AD; built into the side of a hill, it could accommodate 14,000 people on 42 seating levels. Northeast of here is Perge's massive horseshoe-shaped **stadium**, the largest in Asia Minor and excellently preserved. East of the stadium is the city proper, marked by a cluster of souvenir and soft drinks stands. Just in front of the outer gates is the **tomb of Plancia Magna**, a benefactress of the city, whose name appears later on a number of inscriptions. Inside is a **Byzantine basilica**, beyond which lies the fourth-century AD **agora**; southwest are some **Roman baths**, a couple of whose pools have been exposed. At the northwest corner of the agora is Perge's **Hellenistic Gate**, with its two mighty circular towers, the only building to have survived from the period. Behind, there's a 300-metre-long colonnaded street, with a water channel running down the middle and shells of shops on either side.

The next best Pamphylian site is **ASPENDOS** (daily 8am–5/6pm; $4), off the main road close to the villages of Serik and Belkis and accessible from Antalya by regular *dolmuş* during summer. The principal feature is the well-preserved **theatre**, built in the second century AD to a Roman design, with an elaborate stage behind which the scenery could be lowered. The stage, auditorium and arcade above are all intact, and what you see today is pretty much what the spectators saw during the theatre's heyday – a state of preservation due in part to Atatürk, who after a visit declared that it should be preserved and used for performances rather than as a museum. Later, the theatre was used as a Selçuk *kervanseray*, and restoration work from that period – plasterwork decorated with red zigzags – is visible over the stage.

Side

About 25km east of Aspendos, **SIDE**, a ruined Hellenistic port and one-time trysting place of Antony and Cleopatra, was perhaps the foremost of the Pamphylian cities, and the ruins of the ancient port survive. Over the last few years or so, however, Side has changed almost unrecognizably due to indiscriminate tourist development. If it's sun, sand and surf you're after, you may want to spend some time here – the beaches are superb. If you're more interested in the ruins, try and visit out of season.

Fortunately, even the inroads of mass tourism have been unable to smother the grandeur of ancient Side's buildings and monuments. The **city walls** are particularly well preserved, with a number of towers still in place, and the **agora** is today fringed with the stumps of many remaining columns. Opposite the agora is the site of the former **Roman baths**, now restored to house a **museum** (Tues–Sun 8am–noon & 1.30–5/6pm; $4) with a cross-section of locally unearthed objects – mainly Roman statuary, reliefs and sarcophagi. South of here, a still-intact monumental gateway serves as an entrance to the modern resort and to Side's 20,000-seat **theatre** (officially closed for renovation, though it's relatively easy to climb in), the largest in Pamphylia, and supported by arched vaults rather than built into a hillside, unlike those at Perge and Aspendos. At the back of the theatre, reached via the agora, is a row of ancient **toilets**, complete with niches for statues facing the cubicles.

Side has some fine sandy **beaches**. To the **west** the beach stretches for about 10km, lined by hotels and beach clubs, though the crowds can be heavy during high season. To the **east** the sands are emptier and stretch all the way to Alanya, though there's less in the way of facilities. Side's new *otogar* is around 1km from the central waterfront, close to the monumental gateway, although most **buses** working the main Antalya–Alanya route don't stop here, dropping passengers off at the turn-off 3km to the north, from where *dolmuşes* run into town. Travelling on from Side, it's best to get a *dolmuş* to the town of Manavgat, 10km east, where the local bus station has good connections with the rest of the south coast.

The **tourist office** (summer daily 8am–6pm; winter Mon–Fri 9am–5pm) is on the main road into town just before the first city gate and around 300m before the *otogar*. **Accommodation** possibilities are endless, although Side is thronging with north European package tourists from mid-March onwards and *pansiyon* prices are relatively steep. The best hunting ground is in the warren of alleys east of the main street. *Morning Star* (☎242/753 1389; ③) is friendly and has en-suite rooms, first-floor ones with balconies, but it charges by the room so may be a bit pricey if travelling on your own; *Evin* (☎242/753 1074; ③) has clean, bright rooms near the agora; *Yıldız Pansiyon* (☎242/753 1045; ③) is an uninspiring but acceptable alternative, as is *Dilek Pansiyon* (☎242/753 4024; ③). For **camping**, there are a number of sites along the western beach, beginning about 500m from the theatre. There's no shortage of places to **eat and drink**: try the *Toros Restaurant* near the harbour, where you can sample reasonably priced fish dishes on the terrace, or the *Aphrodite*, which has excellent swordfish. A good cheapie is the *Bademalti* on the main drag. The *Apollonik*, just west of the temple of Apollo, is an atmospheric bar. Further east, *Stones Bar* and *Barracuda* are louder and offer fine views out onto the Mediterranean.

Alanya

Until a little over ten years ago, **ALANYA** was a sleepy coastal town with no more than a handful of flyblown hotels. Now it's one of the Mediterranean coast's major resorts, a booming place but one that has fortunately managed to hold on to much of its character and is much less crowded than Side, even in midsummer.

Most of old Alanya lies on the great rocky promontory that juts out into the sea, dominating the modern town, the bulk of which is occupied by the **castle** – an hour's winding climb or a short ride on an hourly bus from the tourist office. At the end of the road is the **İç Kale**, or inner fortress (daily 8am–8pm; $3), built in 1226, pretty much intact, with the shell of a Byzantine **church**, decorated with fading frescoes, in the centre. In the northwestern corner of the fortress, a platform gives fine views of the western beaches and the mountains, though it originally served as a springboard from which prisoners were thrown to their deaths on the rocks below. On the opposite side of the promontory, the **Kızılkule** – "Red Tower"– is a 35-metre-high defensive tower that today houses a pedestrian **Ethnographic Museum** (Tues–Sun 8am–noon & 1.30–5pm; $2), and has a roof terrace that overlooks the town's eastern harbour. Back down at sea level, apart from the hotels and restaurants, modern Alanya has little to offer. On the western side of the promontory, the **Alanya Museum** (Tues–Sun 8am–noon & 1.30–5.30pm; $2) is filled with local archeological finds and ethnological ephemera, though the best thing about it is the garden, a former Ottoman graveyard. Nearby, the **Damlataş** or "Cave of Dripping Stones" (daily 10am–sunset; $1.50), is a stalactite- and stalagmite-filled cavern with a moist, warm atmosphere said to benefit asthma sufferers. It's accessible from behind the *Damlataş Restaurant*.

Alanya's **beaches**, though not particularly clean, are at least extensive, stretching 3km west and 8km east. Finer sand and fewer crowds can be found 23km away on the Side road at **Incekum** (meaning "fine sand"), still a beautiful spot despite recent bouts of hotel building.

Practicalities

Alanya's **bus station** is a twenty-minute walk from the centre, but if you come in by local bus from Side or Manavgat you'll probably arrive at the *dolmuş* terminal, five minutes north of the centre. The **tourist office** is at Çarşı Mahallesi, Kalearkası (summer daily 8am–6.30pm; winter Mon–Fri 9am–5.30pm), opposite the town museum. As in Side, **accommodation** soon fills up and prices can be high, although there's a concentration of *pansiyons* in the grid of streets between the bus station and the seafront. *Oba*, Meteorologi Sok 8 (☎242/513 2675; ③), is a good budget choice, as is *Kuşad*, a couple of blocks east on Zilinevter Sok (☎242/513 2854; ③). Nearer the centre, behind Dalmataş Cad, *Pension Best*, Alaaddinoğlu Sok 28 (☎242/511 0171; ④), has immaculately clean rooms and apartments and a very helpful host. Two other central alternatives are *Hotel Günaydin*, Kültür Cad 26 (☎242/513 1943; ③), and *Otel Eser*, Bostancipinari Cad 10 (☎242/512 4828; ③). There are a couple of **campsites** west of Alanya on the Side road: the *Alanya-Motorcamp*, about 25km out just before a large hotel complex, newly built and with a restaurant and shops, and the *BP-Kervansaray Motorcamp*, a little closer, where you get roughly the same deal. For **food**, the small streets running between Gazipaşa Cad and Hükümet Cad have lots of cheap *pide* and kebab places. Immediately north of here, *Burak*, Müftüler Cad, Kalgadam Sok 7, and *Buhara* and *Gülistan* on Kuyular Önü Sok offer excellent steam-tray and grilled food at very reasonable prices. For seafood, try the invariably pricey restaurants on the seafront.

CENTRAL TURKEY

When the first Turkish nomads arrived in Anatolia during the tenth and eleventh centuries, the landscape must have been strongly reminiscent of their Central Asian homeland. The terrain that so pleased the tent-dwelling herdsmen of a thousand years ago, however, has few attractions for modern visitors: monotonous, rolling vistas of stone-strewn grassland, dotted with rocky outcrops, hospitable only to sheep. In winter it can be numbingly cold here, while summer temperatures can rise to unbearable levels.

It seems appropriate that the heart of original Turkish settlement should be home to the political and social centre of modern Turkey, **Ankara**, a modern European-style capital, symbol of Atatürk's dream of a secular Turkish republic. The south central part of the country draws more visitors, not least for **Cappadocia** in the far east of the region, where water and wind have created a land of fantastic forms from the soft tufa rock, including forests of cones, table mountains and canyon-like valleys, all further hewn by civilizations that have found the area sympathetic to their needs. Further south still, **Konya** is best known as the birthplace of the Sufi Muslim sect and is a good place to stop over between Cappadocia and the coast.

Ankara

Modern **ANKARA** is really two cities, a double identity that is due to the breakneck pace at which it has developed since being declared capital of the Turkish Republic in 1923. Until then Ankara – known as Angora – had been a small provincial city, known chiefly for the production of soft goat's wool. This city still exists, in and around the old citadel that was the site of the original settlement. The other Ankara is the modern metropolis that has grown up around a carefully planned attempt to create a seat of government worthy of a modern, Western-looking state. It's worth visiting just to see how successful this has been, although there's not much else to the place, and its museums and handful of other sights need only detain you for a day or two at most.

Arrival and information

Ankara's Esenboğa **airport** is 33km north of town and buses into the centre ($3) tend to depart about thirty minutes after flights land; a taxi will set you back about $17. Ankara's imposing new **otogar** lies around 8km to the southeast. Some bus companies run service minibuses to the centre, otherwise take the **Ankaray** rapid transit system (no single tickets; a five-journey ticket costs S1.50), which will take you to Kızılay, in the heart of modern Ankara. To catch a *dolmuş* from the *otogar* to Ulus, where most of the budget hotels are found, follow the signs to the Ankaray station and ascend to street level. Otherwise you can change from the Ankaray to Ankara's other underground railway system, the metro, at Kızılay and take this to Ulus. The main **train station** is at the corner of Talat Paşa Cad and Cumhuriyet Bulvari. Frequent buses run from here to Kızılay and Ulus.

Getting around the city is no problem, with plenty of **buses** running the length of the main Atatürk Bulvarı. Bus tickets are bought in advance from kiosks next to the main bus stops. If you plan to use the bus a lot it would be a good idea to stock up on tickets when you can as in some areas of the city there are no kiosks. Ankara has two linked underground train systems: the metro runs from Kızılay northbound through Ulus and the Ankaray cuts east to west with an interchange at Kızılay. Tickets, each with five journeys, are interchangable between the two systems. There is a **tourist office** at Gazi Mustafa Kemal Bulvarı 121, just outside the Maltepe Ankaray station (summer Mon–Fri 9am–6.30pm, Sat & Sun 10am–5pm; winter Mon–Fri 9am–5pm).

Accommodation

Most of the cheaper **hotels** are in the streets east of Atatürk Bulvarı between Ulus and Opera Meydanı; north of Ulus, on and around Çankırı Cad, are a few more upmarket places. There are also clusters along Gazi Mustafa Kemal Bulvarı in Maltepe and on Atatürk Bulvarı south of Kızılay, with prices increasing as you move south.

Buhara, Sanayi Cad 13, Ulus (☎312/310 7999). One of the better choices in Ulus. ③.

Devran, Opera Meydanı, Ulus (☎312/311 0485). Small but clean rooms with en-suite facilities. ②.

Hisar, Hisarparkı Cad 6, Ulus (☎312/311 9889). Washbasins only, but the rooms are clean and presentable. ①.

Mithat, İtfaiye Meydanı, Tavus Sok 2, Ulus (☎312/311 5410). Reasonable single and double rooms with bathrooms. ③.

Olimpiyat, Rüzgarlı Eşdost Sok 1, Ulus (☎312/324 3088). Good rooms at a reasonable price. ②.

Güleryüz, Sanayi Cad 37, Ulus (☎312/310 4910). A little bit further up the price and comfort scale. ③.

Ergen, Karanfil Sok 48, Kızılay (☎312/417 5906). Not a budget choice but very comfortable, with TV, air-con and all rooms en-suite. ④.

The City

Finding your way around Ankara is fairly easy. The city is bisected north–south by **Atatürk Bulvarı**, and everything you need is in easy reach of this broad and busy street. At the northern end, **Ulus Meydanı** (known simply as Ulus), a large square and an important traffic intersection marked by a huge equestrian Atatürk statue, is the best jumping-off point for the old part of the city, a village of narrow cobbled streets and ramshackle wooden houses cen-

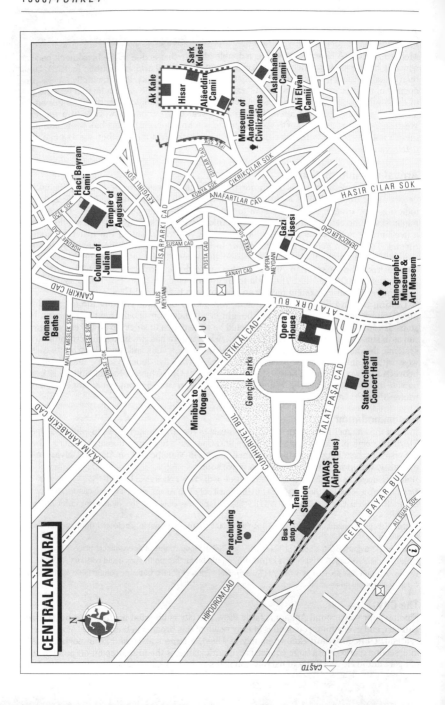

CENTRAL ANKARA

Ak Kale
Hisar
Sark Kulesi
Aläeddin Camii
Aslanhane Camii
Ahi Elvan Camii
Museum of Anatolian Civilizations
Haci Bayram Camii
Temple of Augustus
Column of Julian
Gazi Lisesi
Ethnographic Museum & Art Museum
Roman Baths
Opera House
State Orchestra Concert Hall
Minibus to Otogar
Genclik Parki
HAVAŞ (Airport Bus)
Train Station
Parachuting Tower
Bus stop

İPEK SOK
KEVGİRLİ SOK
KONYA SOK
CIKRIKCILAR SOK
ANAFARTLAR CAD
ESKİCİLAR CAD
HASIR CILAR SOK
ÇİÇEK SOK
HOKUME CAD
HISARPARKI CAD
SUSAM CAD
POSTA CAD
SANAYI CAD
ŞERKES SOK
OPERA MEYDANI
DENİZCİLER CAD
ATATÜRK BUL
ÇANKIRI CAD
ULUS MEYDANI
U L U S
İSTİKLAL CAD
CUMHURİYET BUL
TALAT PAŞA CAD
MALİYE MESLEK SOK
NEŞE SOK
SINASI SOK
KAZIM KARABEKİR CAD
CELAL BAYAR BUL
ALTISOY SOK
HIPODROM CAD

N

CASTD

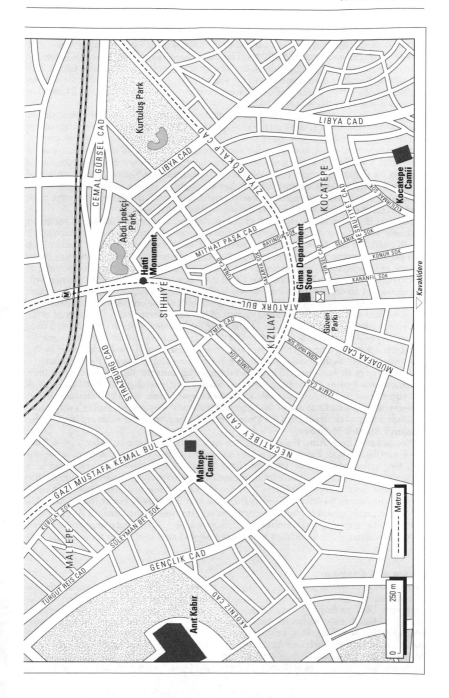

tring on the **Hisar**, Ankara's old fortress and citadel. It was the Gauls who built the first fortifications on this site, but most of what can be seen today dates from Byzantine times, with substantial Selçuk and Ottoman additions. There are tremendous views of the rest of the city from inside, as well as an unexceptional twelfth-century mosque, the **Alâeddin Camii**. The **Aslanhane Camii**, in the bazaar area to the south, is more impressive, built by the Selçuks during the thirteenth century, with a carved wooden ceiling supported by 24 wooden columns and a distinctive blue-tiled *mihrab*.

Follow Kadife Sokak from here towards the modern city and you come to the **Museum of Anatolian Civilizations** (Tues–Sun 8.30am–5pm; $5), which boasts an incomparable collection of archeological objects housed in a restored Ottoman *bedesten* or covered market. Hittite carving and relief work form the most compelling section of the museum, mostly taken from Carchemish, a city which occupied a site near the present Syrian border. There are also Neolithic finds from Çatal Höyük, 52km southeast of Konya, the site of one of Anatolia's oldest settlements; early Bronze Age stag figures, pottery and vessels unearthed at Kültepe, near Kayseri; examples of Urartian metalwork; and Phrygian finds from the royal tombs at Gordion, many of which have a distinctly Hellenistic feel.

North of Ulus Meydanı is what's left of Roman Ankara, namely the **Column of Julian** on Hükümet Meydanı, erected in honour of a visit to Ankara by Julian the Apostate, who reigned briefly from 361 AD. Close by, the **Hacıbayram Camii** was erected on the ruins of the **Temple of Augustus and Rome**, built by the Phrygians during the second century BC in honour of Cybele. Today the remains of the temple wall on the square next to the mosque are about all that's left. The Hacıbayram Camii itself was built in 1400 by Hacı Bayram Veli, the founder of an order of dervishes, whose tomb in front is a popular place of pilgrimage. South down Atatürk Bulvarı, the **Gençlik Parkı** was built on the orders of Atatürk to provide a recreational spot for the hard-toiling citizens of his model metropolis; it features an artificial lake, funfair, cafés and an **Opera House** near the entrance – Atatürk developed a taste for opera while serving in Sofia in 1905. Further down Atatürk Bulvarı, the **Ethnography Museum** (closed at time of writing for restoration) boasts rooms used as an office by the great man, as well as the usual collection of folk costumes and Ottoman art and artefacts.

Across the main west–east rail line lies **Sıhhıye Meydanı** and the real heart of modern Ankara, which focuses on the large square of **Kızılay**, the main transport hub of the city. A few streets east rise the four minarets of the **Kocatepe Camii**, a modern mosque built in Ottoman-style that ranks as one of the biggest in the world. Beyond lies Turkey's parliament building, a strip of embassies and the **Presidential Palace**, whose grounds are home to the **Çankaya Atatürk Museum**.

Northeast of here, **Anıt Kabir** is the site of Atatürk's mausoleum (Mon 1.30–4/5pm, Tues–Sun 9am–4/5pm; bus #265 from Ulus and near Tandoğan Ankaray station), at the end of a long colonnaded avenue lined by Hittite lions. A twentieth-century reworking of a Hellenistic temple, it's almost bare inside except for the 40,000-kilogram sarcophagus and the guards who keep an eye on visitors to make sure they evince an appropriate degree of respect. Outside, on the left of the courtyard, is the **sarcophagus of İsmet İnönü**, Atatürk's friend and prime minister, who succeeded him as president of the republic. At the southeastern end of the courtyard is a **museum** (Sun only 1.30–4.30pm) containing various pieces of Atatürk memorabilia, including a number of Lincoln limousines which served as his official transport.

Eating and drinking

Standard *pide* and kebab places can be found on just about every street in Ankara and there's an abundance of good sweet and cake shops, though really good **restaurants** are surprisingly rare. Ulus, particularly along Çankırı Cad, is a good place to look for cheap lunchtime venues, although most night-time eating and drinking takes place in the modern centre around Kızılay where a grid of streets comprising Sakarya, Selanik and Bayindir Soks harbours a range of possibilities, or further south in the well-heeled district of Kavakladere.

Akman Boza ve Pasta Salonu, Atatürk Bulvarı 3, Ulus. In a shopping plaza just south of the Atatürk statue, serving light meals, pastries and boza, a refreshing millet-based drink. A good place for breakfast.

Altin Şiş, Karanfil Sok 17, Kızılay. A reasonably priced kebab place which does good puddings.

Ankara Sofrasi, Hoşdere Cad 76, Çankaya. Traditional Turkish dishes including excellent *manti*. A little off the beaten track but worth the effort.

Boyacizâde Konaği, Berrak Sok 7–9 (☎312/310 2525). One of several old-citadel restaurants in restored houses. Though aimed at tourists, it's very pleasant and a meal here won't break the bank. Booking essential.

Dadaşlar, Denizciler Cad. Good value kebab and grill joint just below the citadel, with outdoor garden seating.

Hacı Mehmet Özlek, Sanayi Cad 7, Ulus. A pleasant, friendly place with a decently priced menu. Ask to be seated upstairs.

Hünkar kebap, Selanik Sok 16, Kızılay. Excellent place to savour İskender kebab dishes.

Kebabıstan, Karanfil Sok/Yüksel Cad, Kızılay. Plush kebab restaurant, offering all kinds of kebab including excellent mushroom şiş.

Körfez Lokantası, Bayındır Sok 24. Arguably the best restaurant in town, always packed, and serving good-sized portions of excellent, moderately priced Turkish food.

Kebab 49, Necatibey Cad, Kızılay & Buklum Sok, Tunalı Cad. Cheap, reliable and decent *pide*, kebab and various other Turkish staples.

Osmanbey Sofrasee, Kediseven Sok 4, Ulus. Extensive menu and decent prices.

Sam & Ba, Selanik Cad 6, Kızılay. Great *pide* and friendly staff at the heart of the Kızılay restaurant quarter.

Uğrak Piknik and Uğrak Lokantası, Çankırı Cad, Ulus. A cafeteria with fixed meals for about $2.50 along with a proper restaurant.

Bars and cafés

There are some possibilities in the more affluent parts of town towards the southern end of Atatürk Bulvarı. A good starting point would also be Sakarya Cad in Kızılay where there are a number of decent watering holes in the neighbouring streets.

Alesta, Bayındır Sok, Kızılay. Small and friendly bar with live music from local cover bands.

Café Seven, Reşit Galip Cad 57/A, Gaziosmanpaşa. A café/bar student hangout with live music in the evening. Snack food available.

Eylül Bar, Noktali Sok, behind the *Sheraton*. A pleasant garden café.

Sherlock Holmes, Güvenlik Cad 97, off Atatürk Cad. A very fashionable and expensive bar and eatery.

Nightlife

Cinema Foreign language films are usually shown in the original with Turkish subtitles. Most cinemas show mainsteam releases with regularly changing programmes. Try the six-screen Metropol, Selanik Cad 76, Kızılay.

Discos *Graffiti* and *Complex*, both on Farabi Sok, Çankaya.

Opera The Opera House at Opera Meydanı is great value. Admission is usually less than $5 for lively and well-attended performances of works like *Madame Butterfly* and *La Bohème*.

Listings

Airlines British Airways, Atatürk Bul 237/29 (☎312/467 5557); THY, Atatürk Bul 154 (☎312/428 0200).

Buses Most bus companies have offices on Gazi Mustafa Kemal Bulvarı, Ziya Gökalp Cad, Azmir Cad and Menekze Sok, where you can buy tickets in advance.

Car rental Avis, Tunus Cad 68/2, Kavaklıdere (☎312/467 2313); Budget, airport & Tunus Cad (☎312/425 8081); Europcar, Küçük Esat Cad 25/C, Bakanlıkar (☎312/418 3430).

Embassies Australia, Nenehatun Cad 83, Gaziosmanpaşa (☎312/446 1180); Canada, Nenehatun Cad 75, Gaziosmanpaşa (☎312/436 1275); Great Britain, Zehit Ersan Cad 46/A, Çankaya (☎312/468 6230); Netherlands, Uq/ur Mumcu Cad 16, Gaziosmanpaşa (☎312/446 0470); USA, Atatürk Bulvarı 110, Kavaklıdere (☎312/468 6110).

Exchange Outside banking hours use the main PTT, open 24hr.

Hamams Karacabey Hamami, Talatpaza Bulvarı 101 (men 6.30am–11pm & women 8am–7pm; prices start from around $5), dates back to 1441 AD; Küçüksat Hamam, Küçükesat Cad 81/A (daily 7am–10pm, Tues women only 7am–6pm).

Hospital The Hacettepe Hastanesi, just west of Hasırcılar Sok in Sihhiye, normally has an English-speaking doctor available.

Left luggage At the bus station and at the train station. Both charge $2 per piece.

PTT Main PTT is the Merkez Postahane, on Atatürk Bulvarı Kizilay just up from the Opera House in Ulus. Poste restante is at PTT, Ezref Bitlis Cad.

Cappadocia

A land created by the complex interaction of natural and human forces over vast spans of time, **Cappadocia**, around 150km southeast of Ankara, is initially a disturbing place, the great expanses of bizarrely eroded volcanic rock giving an impression of barrenness. It's in fact an exceedingly fertile region, and one whose weird formations of soft, dusty rock have been adapted over millennia by many varying cultures, from Hittites to later Christians hiding away from Arab marauders. There are more than a thousand rock-churches in Cappadocia, dating from the earliest days of Christianity to the thirteenth century, and some caves are still inhabited; the fields are still fertilized with guano collected in rock-cut pigeon houses; and pottery is still made from the clay of the Kızılırmak River. It's a popular area with tourists, and getting more so, but the crowds are largely confined to a few areas.

The **best-known sites** are located within the triangle delimited by the roads connecting Nevşehir, Avanos and Ürgüp. Within this region is the greater part of the valleys of fairy chimneys, the rock-cut churches of the **Göreme** open-air museum, with their amazing selection of frescoes, and the **Zelve** monastery, a complex of troglodyte dwellings and churches hewn out of the rock. **Nevşehir** itself isn't much of a town, but it's an important travel centre, and while **Ürgüp** makes perhaps a more attractive base from which to tour the surrounding valleys, it isn't as well served by public transport. Outside the triangle to the south are the underground cities of **Derinkuyu** and **Kaymaklı**, fascinating warrens attesting to the ingenuity of the ancient inhabitants.

Nevşehir

Though said to be Turkey's richest town, **NEVŞEHİR**, at the very heart of Cappadocia, can hardly be accused of an ostentatious wealth. However, it is a useful base for the region. Frequent bus services all over Cappadocia run from here, and in some cases it's necessary to make a wide detour to the city in order to travel between two neighbouring towns.

The Ottoman castle stands at the heart of the old city, southwest of the modern centre, and is a good landmark. The new city below is divided by two main streets, **Atatürk Bulvarı**, on which are situated most of the hotels and restaurants, and **Lale Caddesi**, turning into Gülzehir Caddesi to the north, where you'll find the main *dolmuş* station. The remains of the citadel are no big deal in themselves but the views are good. On the side of the hill, the eighteenth-century **Damat İbrahim Paşa Camii** is set in a large precinct made all the more impressive by the surrounding cramped streets, and has a cool, dark interior further enhanced by small decorative details. Opposite, the **Damat İbrahim Paşa Hamamı** (7.30am–9pm; Sat women only, other days men only; $4) is also in good working order and well run. The **Nevşehir Museum**, on Yeni Kayseri Caddesi (Tues–Sun 8am–noon & 1.30–5pm, Mon 1.30–5pm; $1.50), is well worth the twenty-minute walk from the tourist office, with a collection that includes three terracotta sarcophagi dating from the third to fourth century AD, finds from the Phrygian and Byzantine periods, and Turkish carpets, kilims and looms.

There is only one **tourist office**, on Atatürk Bulvarı, on the right as you head downhill towards Ürgüp (summer daily 8am–5pm; winter Mon–Fri 8am–5pm), which will arm you with a hotel price list and a map. There is also an information office at the bus station which is run by a private tour company. Local *dolmuşes* and those for the underground cities leave from the bus station. Several companies run **organized tours** of the area; try Agami on Lale Cad (☎384/212 7854), or Rock City, next to the *Hotel Orsan*, Atatürk Bulvarı (☎384/212 0603). **Pensions** in Nevşehır are neither as cheap nor as good as elsewhere in Cappadocia. *Hotel Şems* (☎384/213 3597; ③) on Atatürk Bulvarı above the *Aspava Restaurant*, is comfortable and friendly. A step up, *Orsan*, Atatürk bul (☎384/213 5427; ④), is comfortable and has a swimming pool. Also just opposite the *Orsan* is *Hotel Seven* (☎384/213 4979; ③), which provides a cheaper option. The nicest of the **campsites** in the region, the *Koru Mocamp*, is signposted off to the right as you turn from Nevşehir into Üçhisar. For **food**, the *Aspava Restaurant*, Atatürk Bulvarı 29, serves well-prepared dishes, and the *Lâle*, Gazhane Sok, has a good choice of *meze* and kebabs. The *Park*, in gardens just off Atatürk Bulvarı, is more pricey.

Derinkuyu and Kaymaklı

Among the most extraordinary phenomena of the Cappadocia region are the remains of a number of underground settlements, some of them large enough to have accommodated up to thirty thousand people. The cities are thought to date back to Hittite times, though the complexes were later enlarged by Christian communities who created missionary schools, churches and wine cellars. A total of forty such settlements, from villages to vast cities, have been discovered, but only a few are open to the public.

The most thoroughly excavated is in the village of **DERİNKUYU** (daily 8am–5/6pm; $3), 29km from Nevşehir and accessible by *dolmuş*. The city is well lit and the original ventilation system still functions remarkably well, but some of the passages are small and cramped. The size of this rock-cut warren is difficult to comprehend even on a thorough exploration, since only part of what has been excavated is open, and even this is thought to comprise only a quarter of the original city. The area consists of a total of eight floors reaching to a depth of 55m. What you'll see includes – on the first two floors – stables, wine presses and a dining hall or school room with two long, rock-cut tables; living quarters, churches, armouries and tunnels on the third and fourth floors; and a crucifix-shaped church, a meeting hall, a dungeon and a grave on the lower levels.

Nine kilometres north of Derinkuyu on the Nevşehir–Niğde highway you'll have passed **KAYMAKLI** (March–Sept 8am–6pm; Oct–Feb 8am–5pm; $3). Smaller and consequently less popular than Derinkuyu, only five of its underground levels have been excavated to date. The layout is very similar, networks of streets with small living spaces leading off into underground plazas with various functions, the more obvious of which are stables, smoke-blackened kitchens, storage spaces and wine presses.

Göreme and around

The small town of **GÖREME** is of central importance to Cappadocian tourism, principally because it is the best known of the few remaining Cappadocian villages whose rock-cut houses and fairy chimneys are still inhabited. However, in the last few years these ancient living quarters have slowly been destroyed by development and tourism, which has led to a "Save Göreme" campaign to try to get the government to act in order to preserve the unique geology that has provided homes to the indigenous population for hundreds of years. It is still possible to get away from what is now essentially a holiday village, though, and the tufa landscapes are just a short stroll away. Göreme also makes a good base from which to explore the nearby attractions and sites. When approaching Göreme from elsewhere in Turkey, bear in mind that only two bus companies – Göreme and Nevtour – actually travel here direct. Other firms may sell you a ticket to Göreme, but will merely drop you off in Nevşehir, where you'll have to continue your journey by local bus or *dolmuş* (the last of which leaves Nevşehir at about 8pm in summer, 6pm in winter).

There are two **churches** in the hills above, the **Durmuş Kadir Kilisesi**, clearly visible across the vineyard next to a cave-house with rock-cut steps, and the double-domed **Karşıbucak Yusuf Koç Kilisesi**, which houses frescoes in very good condition. About 2km outside the village, the **Göreme Open-Air Museum** (daily 8am–5/6pm; $6), up a steep hill on the road to Ürgüp, is the best known and most visited of all the monastic settlements in the Cappadocia region, the site of over thirty churches, mainly dating from the ninth to the end of the eleventh century and containing some of the best of all the frescoes in Cappadocia. Most are barely discernible from the outside, apart from a few small holes serving as windows or air shafts. But inside, the churches re-create many of the features of Byzantine buildings, with domes, barrel-vaulted ceilings and cross plans supported by mock pillars, capitals and pendentives. The best-preserved church is the **Tokalı Kilise**, "the Church with the

Buckle", located away from the others on the opposite side of the road about 50m back towards the village. It's two churches, in fact, both frescoed, an **Old Church**, dating from the second decade of the tenth century, and a **New Church**, whose frescoes represent some of the finest examples of tenth-century Byzantine art. The best known of the churches in the main complex are the three columned churches, the **Elmalı Kilise** (Church of the Apple), the **Karanlık Kilise** (Dark Church; $9 extra admission) whose frescoes have recently been restored, and the **Çarıklı Kilise** (Church of the Sandals) – eleventh-century churches heavily influenced by Byzantine forms and painted with superb skill. Look, too, at the church of **St Barbara**, named after the depiction of the saint on the north wall, although most famous for the strange insect figure – the significance of which can only be guessed at.

ZELVE

The deserted **monastery complex** in the three valleys of **ZELVE** (daily 8am–5/6pm; $3.50), a few kilometres north of Göreme off the Avanos–Çavuşin road, is one of the most fascinating remnants of Cappadocia's troglodyte past. The churches here date back to before the ninth century, but the valley was inhabited by Turkish Muslims, who hacked their dwellings out of the tufa rock face, until about thirty years ago. On the left-hand side of the first valley, about halfway up, are the remains of a small Ottoman mosque, the prayer hall and *mihrab* of which are partly hewn from the rock, and a large number of chapels and medieval oratories are scattered up and down the valleys, many of them decorated with carved crosses. A thorough exploration really requires a torch and old clothes: some of the rooms are entered by means of precarious steps, others by swinging up through holes in the floors, and, on occasion, massive leaps to a lower floor – good fun if you're reasonably energetic and have a head for heights.

PRACTICALITIES

The offices of Göreme's private tour operators are plastered with signs offering "information" – make sure you head for the establishment marked "official information" (only open in summer) in the bus station, where there's a noticeboard displaying **pensions** and prices. The cheapest option is probably the *Tuna Caves* (no telephone; ②) which has cave rooms/dorms and a pleasant terrace, while the *Blue Moon*, just east of the *otogar* (☎384/271 2248; ③), features immaculate rooms with en-suite facilities. Among the best places are the *Paradise* (☎384/271 2248; ③), which has constant hot water, some cave rooms and a cave bar, the *Peri Pansiyon* (☎384/271 2136; ③), unique and pretty with its high-rise chimneys – both towards the Open-Air Museum – and *L'Elysee Pension* (☎384/271 2244; ③) which has clean simple rooms. If you want a bit of luxury try the brand new *Göreme House* (☎384/271 2060; ④), just up a dirt track behind the mosque, which has excellent en-suite rooms, central heating and a fantastic terrace. This place can be a real bargain in winter and some rooms even have jacuzzis. There are several **campsites** on the fringes of Göreme. The best are *Panorama*, 1km out on the Üçhisar road, and *Dilek*, on the Ürgüp road near the *Peri Pansiyon*, which is more sheltered and has a nice little restaurant. Both have swimming pools. There are a number of tour operators, bike, moped and car rental agencies at the bus station.

There is also plenty of accommodation in **Ürgüp**, a pretty old town (with its own cave dwellings) 5km east of Göreme. In some ways, this can make a more sophisticated alternative to Göreme as it has managed to accommodate tourism much better and still allows access to the more traditional aspects of Turkish life. The informative **tourist office** (summer daily 8.30am–7pm; winter Mon–Fri 8.30am–5.30pm) on the main shopping street, Kayseri Cad, maintains an up-to-date price list of **hotels and pensions**. They also keep information on where current bargains may be had in terms of tours. Looking for accommodation is straightforward and there are several decent places on the road to Nevşehir: the *Cappadoce Hotel* (☎384/341 4714; ②), is basic and occupies an old Greek monastery; the *Hitit*, İstiklâl Cad 46 (☎384/341 4481; ④) is another old house with attractive courtyard and pleasant en-suite rooms; the *Sun Pansiyon*, behind the *hamam* on Astiklâl Cad (☎384/341 4493; ③), has a few cave rooms; and the *Yildiz Hotel*, just past the police station on the Kayseri road (☎384/341 4610; ②), has basic spacious en-suite rooms. There are numerous tour operators in Ürgüp; try Magic Valley, on Kayseri Cad 5 (☎384/341 6203).

Eating in Göreme can prove expensive as almost everything caters only for tourists. If you want to eat well try the *Hotel Ataman*, which probably harbours the best **restaurant**, serving everything from local specialities to French soufflés. The *Ottoman House* is another place to sample traditional cuisine. Among the handful of the over-priced restaurants on the main road, the *Sultan* serves vegetarian food and pasta while the *Sedef* is more lively. Ürgüp's best restaurant is the *Sömine* in the central square, Cumhuriyet Meydanı (above the taxi rank on Suat Hayrı Ürgüplu Cad), serving well-prepared Turkish specialities. Another excellent and very affordable choice is the *Cappadocia*, Kongre Salonu Yanı, which belies its scruffy appearance and serves quality Turkish home cooking. On Cumhuriyet Meydanı, *Kardeşler 2* offers an excellent vegetarian *güveç*. Cheaper options include the *Kardeşler Pide Salonu*, Dumlupınar Cad 13, which serves good *pide*, and the neighbouring *Kent*, which serves excellent *saç kavurma*.

Konya

The home of Celalledin Rumi or the **Mevlâna** ("Our Master"), the mystic who founded the Mevlevi or "Whirling Dervish" sect, and the centre of Sufic mystical practice and teaching, **KONYA** is a place of pilgrimage for the entire Muslim world. It was also something of a capital during the Selçuk era, many of the buildings from which are still standing, along with examples of their highly distinctive crafts and applied arts which are on display in Konya's museums. As a result, although initially not a very appealing city of over half a million people, it's well worth a stop for a night at least, especially if you're making your way down to the coast from Cappadocia. In recent years, Konya has developed a reputation as a hot-bed of fundamentalism, though this now appears to be on the decline.

The City

The **Mevlâna Müzesi** (Mon 10am–5/6.30pm, Tues–Sun 9am–5/6.30pm; $3) is among Turkey's more rewarding sights, housed in the first lodge (*tekke*) of the Mevlevi dervish sect, at the eastern end of Mevlâna Bulvarı, and easily recognizable by its distinctive fluted turquoise dome. The *tekke* served as a place of teaching, meditation and ceremonial dance from shortly after Rumi's death in 1273 until 1925, when Atatürk banned all Sufic orders. The main building of the museum holds the **mausoleum** containing the tombs of the Mevlâna, his father and other notables. You should leave your shoes at the door and shuffle along in a queue of pilgrims; women must cover their heads, and if you're wearing shorts you'll be given a skirt-like affair to cover your legs, regardless of gender. It is permitted to take photographs of the mausoleum, but remember to be respectful and that for some of the people it is an extremely holy and venerated site. In the adjoining room, the original **semahane** (or ceremonial hall) exhibits include some of the musical instruments of the first dervishes, the original illuminated *Mathnawi* – the poetical work of the Mevlâna – and silk and woollen carpets, including one 500-year-old silk carpet from Selçuk Persia that is supposedly the finest ever woven. The latticed gallery above was for women spectators, a modification introduced by the followers of the Mevlâna after his death. In the adjoining room, a casket containing hairs from the beard of the Prophet Mohammed is displayed alongside illuminated medieval Korans.

At the opposite end of Mevlâna Caddesi (later Alâeddin Caddesi, once west of Aziziye Caddesi) from the Mevlâna Müzesi, the **Alâeddin Parkı** is a nice place to stroll. This is the site of the original Selçuk acropolis and the source of finds dating back to 7000 BC, most of which are now in the museum in Ankara. At the foot of the hill to the north are the scant remains of a Selçuk palace, although you'd do better to head straight for the imposing **Alâeddin mosque**, begun in 1130 and completed in 1221, with an odd facade graced with bits of masonry from an earlier construction. Recently restored, the interior has distinctly Selçuk features like a network of wooden beams, and the remains of eight Selçuk sultans are enshrined in the courtyard. The nearby **Karatay Medrese** on Alâeddin Bulvarı (daily 8am–noon & 1–5/6pm; $1.50) is another important Selçuk monument, built in 1251 and combining elements such as Arabic striped stonework and Greek Corinthian columns with a structure which is distinctly Selçuk, its tall doorway surmounted by a pointed stalactite arch. Inside, the symmetrical design of the dome of stars forms a perfect backdrop for the Selçuk **ceramics** on display, which are covered with striking images of birds, animals and even angels. Behind its fine Selçuk portal the **İnce Minare Medrese** (daily 8am–noon & 1–5/6pm; $1.50), below the park on Alâeddin Bulvarı, is also now a museum, featuring stone and woodcarving, with exhibits from the palace on the present site of the Alâeddin Parkı. The other museum worthy of note is the **Museum of Archeology** (Tues–Sun 8am–noon & 1–5/6pm; $1) in the south of the city, containing the only pre-Selçuk remains in the city, including a few Hittite artefacts and three well-preserved Roman sarcophagi from Pamphylia.

Practicalities

Konya's **bus station** is over 2km out on Ankara Cad – take the *Konak–Otogar dolmuş* into town or take the tram to Alâeddin Park; the **train station** is around the same distance out from the centre at the far end of İstasyon Cad, connected to the centre by bus #71 every thirty minutes. The **tourist office** is at Mevlâna Cad 21 (Mon–Fri 8.30am–12 & 1–5pm). Konya's better **hotels** are on or just north of Mevlâna Cad. The recently renovated *Otel Tur*, Esarizade Sok 13 (☎332/351 9825; ③), is quiet, comfortable and friendly; the *Yeni Köşk*, Kadılar Sok 28 (☎332/352 0671; ③), has clean rooms with en-suite facilities and is probably the best of the cheapish options; and the *Otel Çeşme* at Akifpaşa Sok 35, off İstanbul Cad (☎322/351 2426; ③), has rooms with baths which can be bargained down except in December during the annual Mevlâna festival when many hotels fill up. It's worth also keeping in mind the reasonable *Bella Hotel*, Aziziye Cad 19 (☎322/351 4070; ③). As for **eating**, the *Şifa Lokantası*, Mevlâna Cad 29, is popular and very reasonably priced. Just opposite at Mevlâna Cad 53 is the similar *Altınşiş*, which has excellent Adana kebabs and wonderful bread. The *Tilsum Restaurant*, west of the centre on Meram Cad, serves excellent kebabs but closes early. The *Hanedan* on Mevlâna Cad 44 has kebabs, *pide* and steam-tray dishes.

travel details

Trains

Ankara to: İzmir (2 daily; 14hr).

İstanbul to: Ankara (5 daily; 8hr); Edirne (1 daily; 6hr 30min); Denizli (1 daily; 14hr 30min); İzmir (2 daily; 11hr); Konya (3 daily; 14hr).

İzmir to: Selçuk (3 daily; 2hr).

Buses and dolmuşes

Ankara to: Antalya (12 daily; 10hr); Bodrum (10 daily; 12hr); Bursa (hourly; 7hr); İstanbul (every 30min; 6hr); İzmir (hourly; 9hr); Konya (14 daily; 3hr 30min); Nevşehir (12 daily; 4hr 30min).

Antalya to: Alanya (hourly; 2hr); Antakya (1 daily; 12hr); Denizli (6 daily; 5hr 30min); Fethiye, by inland route (3 daily; 4hr); İzmir (6 daily; 9hr 30min); Kav (7 daily; 4hr 30min); Konya (6 daily; 6hr 30min); Side (3 an hour; 1hr 15min).

Ayvalık to: Bergama (8 daily; 1hr); Bursa (10 daily; 4hr 30min); Çanakkale (hourly; 3hr); İzmir (hourly; 2hr 30min).

Bergama to: Ayvalık (8 daily; 1hr); İzmir (12 daily; 2hr).

Bodrum to: Ankara (several daily; 13hr); Fethiye (6 daily; 4hr 30min); Marmaris (8 daily; 3hr 15min).

Bursa to: Çanakkale (hourly; 6hr); Ankara (hourly; 7hr); İstanbul (hourly; 5hr); İzmir (15 daily; 7hr).

Çanakkale to: Ayvalak (hourly; 3hr); Bursa (16 daily; 6hr); İzmir (hourly; 5hr 30min).

Datça to: Ankara (3 daily; 15hr); Marmaris (13 daily; 2hr 15min).

Denizli to: Antalya (8 daily; 5hr 30min); Bodrum (2–3 daily; 4hr 30min); Konya (several daily; 7hr 15min); Marmaris (6 daily; 4hr).

Edirne to: Çanakkale (2 daily; 4hr 30min); İstanbul (hourly; 3hr).

Fethiye to: Ankara (2 daily; 12hr); Antalya (8 daily; 4hr); Bodrum (6 daily; 5hr); Denizli (5 daily; 4hr); İzmir (every 30min; 7hr); Kav (15 daily; 2hr 30min); Marmaris (10 daily; 3hr); Patara (10 daily; 1hr 30min).

Kuşadası to: Bodrum (3 daily; 3hr); Pamukkale (12 daily; 3hr 30min).

İstanbul to: Alanya (hourly; 14hr); Ankara (every 30min; 6hr); Antalya (4 daily; 12hr); Ayvalık (4 daily;

9hr); Bodrum (4 daily; 12hr); Bursa (hourly; 5hr); Çanakkale (hourly; 5hr 30min); Datça (1 daily; 17hr); Denizli (hourly; 15hr); Fethiye (hourly; 15hr); İzmir (hourly; 10hr); Göreme (5 daily; 12hr 30min); Kuşadası (3 daily; 11hr); Marmaris (4 daily; 13hr); Nevşehır (3 daily; 12hr); Side (1 daily; 13hr); Ürgüp (5 daily; 12hr 30min); Konya (7 daily; 11hr).

İzmir to: Ankara (8 daily; 9hr); Antalya (8 daily; 8hr 30min); Ayvalık (every 30min; 2hr 30min); Bergama (hourly; 2hr); Bodrum (hourly; 4hr); Bursa (6 daily; 7hr); Çanakkale (4 daily; 5hr 30min); Çeşme (every 15–20min; 1hr 30min); Datça (hourly; 7hr); Denizli (hourly; 4hr); Fethiye (12–18 daily; 7hr); Kuşadası (every 30min; 1hr 40min); Marmaris (hourly; 5hr); Selçuk (every 20min; 1hr 20min).

Kaş to: Antalya (6 daily; 5hr); Bodrum (3 daily; 7hr); Fethiye (8 daily; 2hr 30min); Marmaris (4 daily; 4hr

30min); Pamukkale (2 daily; 10hr); Patara (10 daily; 1hr).

Marmaris to: Ankara (14 daily; 13hr); Bodrum (8 daily; 3hr 15min); Dalaman (hourly; 1hr 30min); Denizli (6 daily; 4hr); Fethiye (10 daily; 3hr).

Nevşehır to: Antalya (1 daily; 11hr); İzmir (1 daily; 12hr); Konya (4 daily; 3hr); Marmaris (1 daily; 14hr).

Selçuk to: Bodrum (hourly; 3hr); İzmir (hourly; 1hr); Kuşadası (every 30min; 40min).

Domestic ferries

Çanakkale to: Eceabat (hourly; 20min).

Datça to: Bodrum (April–Oct 2 daily; 2hr).

Gelibolu to: Lapseki (15 daily; 20min).

İzmir to: İstanbul (1 weekly; 19hr).

Kilitbahir to: Çanakkale (hourly; 10min).

INDEX

Stay in touch with us!

ROUGH*NEWS* is Rough Guides' free newsletter. In four issues a year we give you news, travel issues, music reviews, readers' letters and the latest dispatches from authors on the road.

I would like to receive ROUGH*NEWS*: please put me on your free mailing list.

NAME . . . .

ADDRESS . . . .

Please clip or photocopy and send to: Rough Guides, 62–70 Shorts Gardens, London WC2H 9AB, England or Rough Guides, 375 Hudson Street, New York, NY 10014, USA.

ROUGH GUIDES: Travel

AVAILABLE AT ALL GOOD BOOKSHOPS

ROUGH GUIDES: Mini Guides, Travel Specials and Phrasebooks

MINI GUIDES
Antigua
Bangkok
Barbados
Big Island of
  Hawaii
Boston
Brussels
Budapest

Dublin
Edinburgh
Florence
Honolulu
Jerusalem
Lisbon
London
  Restaurants
Madrid
Maui
Melbourne
New Orleans
Seattle
St Lucia

Sydney
Tokyo
Toronto

TRAVEL SPECIALS
First-Time Asia
First-Time
  Europe
Women Travel

PHRASEBOOKS
Czech
Dutch

Egyptian Arabic
European
French
German
Greek
Hindi & Urdu
Hungarian
Indonesian
Italian
Japanese

Mandarin
  Chinese
Mexican
  Spanish
Polish
Portuguese
Russian
Spanish
Swahili
Thai
Turkish
Vietnamese

the perfect getaway vehicle

low-price holiday car rental.

rent a car from holiday autos and you'll give yourself real freedom to explore your holiday destination. with great-value, fully-inclusive rates in over 4,000 locations worldwide, wherever you're escaping to, we're there to make sure you get excellent prices and superb service.

what's more, you can book now with complete confidence. our £5 undercut* ensures that you are guaranteed the best value for money in holiday destinations right around the globe.

drive away with a great deal, call holiday autos now on **0990 300 400** and quote ref RG.

holiday autos miles ahead

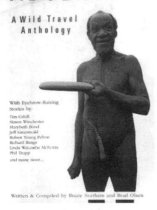

Under 30s' Travel Cover

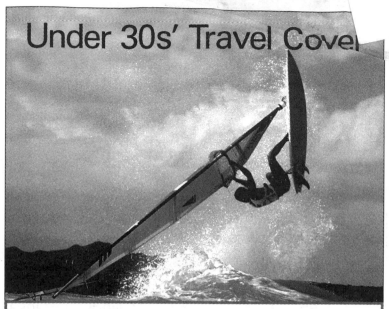

Your only worry is where to land next

Ready to take off round the world? Before you go, make sure you're fully equipped with Under 30s' Travel Cover.

It's got everything you need, like up to £10 million medical emergency cover. You're also covered if you lose your tickets, or need to return home during your trip.

You're even covered if you cut it short to re-sit exams or take up a job offer. And we can cover you for exploits like wind surfing and jet skiing too. So if you're heading off for between 3 and 13 months, call the number below for instant cover. Then the rest of your trip should be plain sailing.

0800 277 377